Tolley Corporation Tax 2007–08

by
Mary Hyland CA CTA (Fellow)
Kevin Walton BA (Hons)

LexisNexis®
Tolley

Members of the LexisNexis Group worldwide

United Kingdom	LexisNexis Butterworths, a Division of Reed Elsevier (UK) Ltd, Halsbury House, 35 Chancery Lane, LONDON, WC2A 1EL, and London House, 20–22 East London Street, EDINBURGH EH7 4BQ
Argentina	LexisNexis Argentina, BUENOS AIRES
Australia	LexisNexis Butterworths, CHATSWOOD, New South Wales
Austria	LexisNexis Verlag ARD Orac GmbH & Co KG, VIENNA
Benelux	LexisNexis Benelux, AMSTERDAM
Canada	LexisNexis Canada, MARKHAM, Ontario
Chile	LexisNexis Chile Ltda, SANTIAGO
China	LexisNexis China, Beijing and Shanghai
France	LexisNexis SA, Paris
Germany	LexisNexis Deutschland, Gmbh, MUNSTER
Hong Kong	LexisNexis Hong Kong, HONG KONG
India	LexisNexis India, NEW DELHI
Italy	Giuffrè Editore, MILAN
Japan	LexisNexis Japan, TOKYO
Malaysia	Malayan Law Journal Sdn Bhd, KUALA LUMPUR
Mexico	LexisNexis Mexico, Mexico
New Zealand	LexisNexis NZ Ltd, WELLINGTON
Poland	Wydawnictwo Prawnicze LexisNexis Sp, WARSAW
Singapore	LexisNexis Singapore, SINGAPORE
South Africa	LexisNexis Butterworths, DURBAN
USA	LexisNexis, DAYTON, Ohio

Published by LexisNexis Butterworths

A CIP Catalogue record for this book is available from the British Library.
ISBN 9 780754 532736

Typeset by Kerrypress Ltd, Luton, Bedfordshire

Printed in the United Kingdom by Polestar Wheatons Ltd

Visit LexisNexis Butterworths at www.lexisnexis.co.uk

About This Book

Corporation tax commenced in 1964 as the tax to be levied on the income, profits and gains of companies. Much of the law and practice relating to income tax and capital gains continued to apply to companies but a separate body of legislation was superimposed and has been added to during the subsequent years. It is the legislation and practice currently applying to companies which is contained in this work together with some additional information of interest to users.

From the mid-1990s the move has been towards a separate computational regime for corporation tax, with special rules on, for example, interest, intangible assets, property income and research and development. The law relating to the taxation of 'trading income' was consolidated in the Income Tax (Trading and Other Income) Act 2005 (ITTOIA 2005) as part of the Tax Law Rewrite programme with effect for income tax purposes for 2005/06 and subsequent years and, for corporation tax purposes where relevant, for accounting periods ending after 5 April 2005. However, for corporation tax purposes, income continues to be computed under the various schedules as if they were still part of income tax law, and not under ITTOIA 2005. Accordingly, it can no longer be assumed that the coverage in Tolley's Income Tax of any particular type of trading receipt or deduction etc. applies equally for corporation tax purposes and so all such matters are now dealt within this work.

This 43rd edition contains all the current provisions relevant to corporation tax, including those of the Finance Act 2007, HMRC Statements of Practice and Extra-Statutory Concessions, other HMRC statements and information, case law and further important information up to 1 July 2007. Summaries of the corporation tax provisions of the 2007 Finance Act are included at Chapter 71.

The enactments relating to income tax and corporation tax (other than on chargeable gains) were consolidated in the Income and Corporation Taxes Act 1988, those relating to chargeable gains in the Taxation of Chargeable Gains Act 1992, and those relating to capital allowances in the Capital Allowances Act 1990, the latter also being rewritten as the Capital Allowances Act 2001. The enactments relating to employment, pension and social security income have similarly been rewritten as the Income Tax (Employment and Pensions) Act 2003. The enactments relating to trading income for income tax purposes have been rewritten as noted above in the Income Tax (Trading and Other Income) Act 2005. All other income tax matters have been rewritten in the Income Tax Act 2007. A summary of the approach adopted to consolidated and rewritten statutory references is given overleaf.

HMRC's Inspector's Manual has been withdrawn, but, as the replacement material has still to be published, the existing references have been retained and will be replaced when the new material is available

Comments and suggestions for improvements are always welcomed.

Contents

Bibliography Etc.

Financial Years run from 1 April. The 'financial year 2007' means the year from 1 April 2007 to 31 March 2008.

Years of Assessment run from 6 April. Thus '2007/08' or 'the year 2007/08' means the year from 6 April 2007 to 5 April 2008.

HMRC explanatory publications may be obtained from the local HMRC offices (except where otherwise stated, see list in Chapter 33) and are free. Most HMRC publications are available on the Internet (at www.hmrc.gov.uk).

HMRC Statements of Practice (see Chapter 35) are published on HMRC's website (at www.hmrc.gov.uk).

Tolley's Income Tax 2007/08 is a comprehensive, detailed guide to income tax with relevant statute and case law etc. up to 1 July 2007 and including the Finance Act 2007.

Tolley's Corporation Tax 2007/08 is a comprehensive and detailed guide to corporation tax with relevant statute and case law etc. up to 1 July 2007, including the provisions of the Finance Act 2007.

Tolley's Capital Gains Tax 2007/08 is a comprehensive, detailed guide to capital gains tax with relevant statute and case law etc. up to 1 July 2007, including the Finance Act 2007.

Tolley's Inheritance Tax 2007/08 is a detailed guide to the inheritance tax provisions with relevant statute, case law forms and case studies up to 1 July 2007, including the Finance Act 2007.

Tolley's Value Added Tax 2007/08 is a comprehensive guide to value added tax, covering legislation, HMRC notices and leaflets and all other relevant information. It is published in two editions, up to 31 January 2007 and up to 1 July 2007 including the Finance Act 2007.

Tolley's Tax Cases 2007 contains over 2,800 summaries of cases up to 1 January 2007 relevant to current legislation. Arranged alphabetically by subject, it includes sections on Close Companies and Corporation Tax.

Tolley's Tax Computations 2007/08 contains copious worked examples covering income tax, corporation tax, capital gains tax, inheritance tax and value added tax.

Tolley's Practical Tax is an eight-page fortnightly, containing news, articles and other items of practical use to all involved with UK tax.

Abbreviations and References

ABBREVIATIONS

ACT	=	Advance Corporation Tax.
APRT	=	Advance Petroleum Revenue Tax.
APRTA 1986	=	Advance Petroleum Revenue Tax Act 1986.
art	=	Article.
CAA	=	Capital Allowances Act.
CA	=	Court of Appeal.
CCA	=	Court of Criminal Appeal.
CCAB	=	Consultative Committee of Accountancy Bodies.
Ch D	=	Chancery Division.
CES	=	Court of Exchequer (Scotland).
Cf.	=	compare.
CFC	=	Controlled Foreign Company.
CGT	=	Capital Gains Tax.
CGTA 1979	=	Capital Gains Tax Act 1979.
CIR	=	Commissioners of Inland Revenue ('the Board').
CJEC	=	Court of Justice of the European Communities.
CRCA	=	Commissioners for Revenue and Customs Act.
CT	=	Corporation Tax.
CTT	=	Capital Transfer Tax.
CTTA 1984	=	Capital Transfer Act 1984.
EC	=	European Communities.
ECJ	=	European Court of Justice.
EEC	=	European Economic Community.
EU	=	European Union.
Ex D	=	Exchequer Division.
FA	=	Finance Act.
FII	=	Franked Investment Income.
FY	=	Financial Year.
HC(I)	=	High Court (Ireland).
HL	=	House of Lords.
HMRC	=	Her Majesty's Revenue and Customs
ICAEW	=	Institute of Chartered Accountants in England and Wales.
ICTA	=	Income and Corporation Taxes Act.
IHTA 1984	=	Inheritance Tax Act 1984.
IR	=	Inland Revenue.
ITA	=	Income Tax Act 2007
ITEPA 2003	=	Income Tax (Earnings and Pensions) Act 2003.
ITTOIA 2005	=	Income Tax (Trading and Other Income) Act 2005
KB	=	King's Bench Division.
NI	=	Northern Ireland.
OTA	=	Oil Taxation Act.
PC	=	Privy Council.
PDA	=	Probate, Divorce and Admiralty Division (now Family Division).
POCA 2002		Proceeds of Crime Act 2002
QB	=	Queen's Bench Division.
RI	=	Republic of Ireland (Eire).
s	=	Section.
SCS	=	Scottish Court of Session.
Sch	=	Schedule.
SI	=	Statutory Instrument.

SP	=	Revenue Statement of Practice.
Sp C	=	Special Commissioners.
SR&O	=	Statutory Rules and Orders.
TCGA 1992	=	Taxation of Chargeable Gains Act 1992.
TMA 1970	=	Taxes Management Act 1970.
VAT	=	Value Added Tax.
VATA 1994	=	Value Added Tax Act 1994.

REFERENCES

(*denotes a series accredited for citation in court).

All E R	=	*All England Law Reports, (Butterworths, Halsbury House, 35 Chancery Lane, London WC2A 1EL).
AC or App Cas	=	*Law Reports, Appeal Cases, (Incorporated Council of Law Reporting for England and Wales, 3 Stone Buildings, Lincoln's Inn, London WC2A 3XN).
Ch	=	*Law Reports, Chancery Division.
Ex D	=	*Law Reports, Exchequer Division (see also below).
IR	=	*Irish Reports, (Law Reporting Council, Law Library, Four Courts, Dublin).
LR Ex	=	*Law Reports, Exchequer Division.
SSCD	=	Simon's Tax Cases Special Commissioners' Decisions, (Butterworths as above).
STC	=	*Simon's Tax Cases, (Butterworths as above).
STI	=	Simon's Tax Intelligence, (Butterworths as above).
TC	=	*Official Reports of Tax Cases, (H.M. Stationery Office, PO Box 276, London, SW8 5DT.
WLR	=	*Weekly Law Reports, (Incorporated Council of Law Reporting, as above).

The first number in the citation refers to the volume, and the second to the page, so that [1999] 1 All ER 15 means that the report is to be found on page fifteen of the first volume of the All England Law Reports for 1999. Where no volume number is given, only one volume was produced in that year. Some series have continuous volume numbers.

Where legal decisions are very recent and in the lower courts, it must be remembered that they may be reversed on appeal. But references to the official Tax Cases (TC) and to the Appeal Cases (AC) may generally be taken as final.

In English cases, Scottish and Northern Irish decisions (unless there is a difference of law between the countries) are generally followed but are not binding, and Republic of Ireland Decisions are considered (and vice versa).

Acts of Parliament, Command Papers, 'Hansard' Parliamentary Reports and Statutory Instruments (SI) are obtainable from The Stationery Office Ltd (TSO), (London bookshop at 123 Kingsway, WC2B 6PQ; mail orders to P.O. Box 29, Norwich NR3 1GN; telephone orders to 0870 600 5522; web order helpline 0870 242 2345, email support@tso.co.uk). **Hansard** references are to daily issues and do not always correspond to the columns in the bound editions. **N.B.** Statements in the House, while useful as indicating the intention of enactments, have no legal authority and the Courts may interpret the wording of an Act differently, although they may in limited circumstances be prepared to consider evidence of parliamentary intent.

1 Introduction and Rates of Tax

Cross reference. See 49 NON-CORPORATE DISTRIBUTIONS RATE, 63 SMALL COMPANIES—REDUCED RATES.

Simon's Direct Tax Service Part D2.

1.1 GENERAL

Since 1 April 1964, companies have been liable to corporation tax on their 'profits' (i.e. income and chargeable gains).

A company making qualifying DISTRIBUTIONS (23) had, before 6 April 1999, to pay ADVANCE CORPORATION TAX (see 3 ADVANCE CORPORATION TAX – SHADOW ACT). Such tax (ACT) was then set off against the company's 'mainstream' corporation tax liability on its income for the ACCOUNTING PERIODS (2) in which the distributions were made. The ACT paid was generally treated as a tax credit in the hands of the recipient of the distributions. Such distributions received by a company were called FRANKED INVESTMENT INCOME (29) and the credit is generally available for set-off against its own liability to ACT. This is known as the 'imputation system'. See, however, 3.1 ADVANCE CORPORATION TAX – SHADOW ACT as regards the abolition of ACT from 6 April 1999.

Tax law rewrite. Tax law is being rewritten over a number of years in more simple language in order to make the legislation clearer. The project has so far issued *CAA 2001*, *ITEPA 2003*, *ITTOIA 2005* and *ITA* (*Income Tax Act*) *2007*, which received Royal Assent on 22 March 2007 and came into force on 6 April 2007. Draft clauses on the rewrite of corporation tax have been published for public consultation – see Paper CC/SC (06) 06, the first set of draft clauses in Bill 5, on ITTOIA related provisions and Paper CC/SC (06) 07 on trading and property income and partnerships. The draft legislation is available on the HMRC website (at www.hmrc.gov.uk/rewrite/index.htm#1).

The new Management Act project has been postponed meantime.

Corporation Tax Reform. The Government published on 5 August 2002 a consultation document 'Reform of corporation tax' seeking views on three potential areas for reform of the corporate tax system:

(*a*) the tax treatment of capital assets not covered by earlier reforms;

(*b*) rationalisation of the way in which the schedular system taxes various types of income; and

(*c*) the differences in the tax treatment of trading and investment companies.

Following further consultation (see the technical note, 'Corporation tax reform: the next steps', published as part of the Pre-Budget Report on 10 December 2003), the following legislation was introduced in *Finance Act 2004* to have effect from 1 April 2004:

(i) reform of the rules on transfer pricing and thin capitalisation (see 67 TRANSFER PRICING) extending the scope of transfer pricing to UK transactions, repealing the thin capitalisation rules and including them within the transfer pricing legislation; and

(ii) the extension of tax relief for the expenses of managing investments to companies with an investment business whether or not they qualify as investment companies (see 42 INVESTMENT COMPANIES AND INVESTMENT BUSINESS).

Further legislation was introduced in *Finance Act 2006* to reform the taxation of leased plant and machinery with effect from, broadly, 1 April 2006 to give entitlement to capital allowances to the lessee rather than to the lessor and to remove the difference in the tax rules between loan finance and leasing finance (see 10.34 CAPITAL ALLOWANCES). (See the technical note, 'Corporation Tax Reform' published as part of the Pre-Budget Report on 2 December 2004.) Further amendments have been made to leasing transactions in *FA 2007, s 31, Sch 6*.

The reforms set out below have been considered. In the Pre-Budget Report of December 2005, the Government stated that, following discussion with business, it 'has no current plans to take forward proposals on partial schedular reform or the taxation of capital assets' but 'continues to consider the scope for modernising capital allowances' (paragraphs 5.97–5.99). Changes to the balancing allowance regime for industrial buildings allowance and agricultural business allowance have been introduced in *FA 2007, s 36* (see http://www.hmrc.gov.uk/budget2007/bn07.htm), and further changes were announced in the Budget 2007, to take effect from April 2008.

Schedular reform. The proposals for schedular reform provide for a single set of computational rules within an expanded Schedule D Case I to include income and expenses from all commercial activities for the whole of a company's 'operating business', allowing for the pooling of trades with letting business and certain items falling within Schedule D Case VI. The 'operating business' would exclude capital gains and losses, non-trading loan relationship credits and debits, dividends and management expenses. There would also be a single set of loss relief rules, resulting in a more generous treatment for losses (and, as a consequence, further provisions to prevent avoidance). It is also proposed that the current tax treatment of charges be abolished and that items treated as charges are dealt with like other expenses.

Capital assets. There are proposals to allow assets qualifying for capital allowances to be removed from the capital gains regime. Gains would be taxed as income through the mechanism of the capital allowance pool which would deal with all qualifying expenditure and proceeds and which would allow for a form of deferral relief. A similar approach is being considered for buildings allowances (industrial, agricultural and hotels) and it is proposed that 'integrated facilities' of a building (such as air conditioning, lifts, etc.) are treated as part of the building rather than as plant. Land may also be brought into such pools, but for the purpose only of bringing profits and losses within the income regime. The technical note also suggests options for simplifying the treatment for cars costing more than £12,000.

Trading and investment companies. Consideration will continue to be given to the case for extending the substantial shareholding exemption to disposals by companies not within the definition of a trading company, or a trading group.

The documents noted above are available on HMRC's website.

1.2 THE CHARGE TO TAX

Any company which is resident in the UK is chargeable to corporation tax in respect of all its 'profits' *wherever arising*. A non-resident company which carries on a trade in the UK through a permanent establishment (see 60.5 RESIDENCE — for accounting periods beginning before 1 January 2003, through a branch or agency) is liable to corporation tax on the income and gains of the permanent establishment (or branch or agency). [*ICTA 1988, ss 6(1), 8(1), 11; TCGA 1992, ss 10(3), 10B*]. See 21 CONTROLLED FOREIGN COMPANIES for treatment of interests in certain non-resident companies.

Members of a group of companies are each dealt with independently, but there are a number of special provisions relating to the taxation of such members. Similar rules apply to the members of a consortium. See 32 GROUPS OF COMPANIES.

'*Profits*' are defined as income and chargeable gains. [*ICTA 1988, s 6(4)(a)*]. See 55 PROFIT COMPUTATIONS and 11 CAPITAL GAINS.

Corporation tax is charged on the profits of '*financial years*', which run from 1 April, e.g. the 'financial year 2006' means the year from 1 April 2006 to 31 March 2007. [*ICTA 1988, ss 6(1), 834(1)*].

The profits of a company are calculated (and assessments are made) by reference to its ACCOUNTING PERIODS (2) and are then, when necessary, apportioned on a time basis between the financial years in which the accounting period falls, according to the number of days falling in each year. [*ICTA 1988, ss 8(3), 72*].

'*Company*' for corporation tax purposes means 'any body corporate or unincorporated association' (including an authorised unit trust as defined in *ICTA 1988, s 468(6)*). It does not include a partnership, a local authority or a local authority association. [*ICTA 1988, s 832(1)(2)*]. See *Conservative and Unionist Central Office v Burrell CA 1981, 55 TC 671* (in which the Conservative Party was held not to be an unincorporated association) and *Blackpool Marton Rotary Club v Martin Ch D 1988, 62 TC 686* (Rotary Club an unincorporated association and not a partnership). For the treatment of income arising to certain unit trusts for the benefit of individuals, see 43.8 INVESTMENT FUNDS.

Anything to be done by a company under the *Taxes Acts* must be done by the 'proper officer of the company' (usually the company secretary, except where a liquidator or (in relation to companies entering administration on or after 15 September 2003 when the *Enterprise Act 2002, s 248* came into force) an administrator has been appointed) or by any person having express, implied or apparent authority to act on its behalf (again, unless a liquidator or administrator has been appointed). [*TMA 1970, s 108(1)(3); FA 1993, Sch 14 para 7; FA 2003, Sch 41 paras 2, 5(1)*]. See also 53.6 PAYMENT OF TAX.

Reduced rates of corporation tax apply to 'small' companies. These are defined by reference to their profits in an accounting period. See 63 SMALL COMPANIES—REDUCED RATES.

1.3 RATES OF TAX

(*a*) Corporation tax on income

The **full** and **small companies' rates** and **starting rate** of corporation tax for each financial year are as set out in the following table.

	Full rate	Small companies rate	Starting rate
Financial year 2007	30%	20%	—
Financial year 2006	30%	19%	—
Financial years 2002 to 2005	30%	19%	0%
Financial years 2000 and 2001	30%	20%	10%
Financial year 1999	30%	20%	—
Financial year 1998	31%	21%	—
Financial year 1997	31%	21%	—
Financial year 1996	33%	24%	—
Financial years 1991 to 1995	33%	25%	—
Financial year 1990	34%	25%	—
Financial years 1988 and 1989	35%	25%	—
Financial year 1987	35%	27%	—
Financial year 1986	35%	29%	—

For financial year 2008, the full rate is set at 28%. For 2008 and 2009 the Government has announced that the small companies' rate will be 21% and 22% respectively. However, the rates on 'ring fence profits' (see 63.1 SMALL COMPANIES—REDUCED RATES) remain at 30% for the full rate and will remain at 19% for the small companies' rate throughout.

[*FA 1986, s 18; FA 1987, ss 21, 22(1); FA 1988, ss 26, 27(1); FA 1989, ss 34, 35; FA 1990, ss 19, 20; FA 1991, ss 23(1), 24, 25; F(No 2)A 1992, ss 21, 22; FA 1993, ss 53, 54; FA 1994, ss 85, 86; FA 1995, ss 37, 38; FA 1996, ss 77, 78; F(No 2)A 1997, s 18;*

FA 1998, ss 28, 29; FA 1999, ss 27, 29; FA 2000, ss 35, 36; FA 2001, ss 54–56; FA 2002, ss 30–32; FA 2003, ss 133–135; FA 2004, ss 25–27; FA 2005, ss 10–12; FA 2006, ss 24–26; FA 2007 ss 2, 3].

See 63 SMALL COMPANIES—REDUCED RATES for profit limits for the starting rate or small companies rate to apply and for marginal relief limits.

The starting rate of corporation tax (together with the non-corporate distribution rate (see below)) is abolished for the financial year 2006 onwards.

(*b*) Corporation tax on chargeable gains

For accounting periods beginning **after 16 March 1987**, the whole of the chargeable gains (less allowable losses) is included in the profits chargeable to corporation tax. [*TCGA 1992, s 8*]. The rate of corporation tax applicable will either be the full rate as in (*a*) above or the starting or small companies rate (with marginal relief as appropriate). See 63 SMALL COMPANIES—REDUCED RATES.

For accounting periods beginning before 17 March 1987 and ending after 16 March 1987, there are transitional provisions whereby, broadly, the accounting period is split into two notional accounting periods. The first period is deemed to end immediately before 17 March 1987 and is treated as below for accounting periods ending before 17 March 1987. The second period is deemed to commence on 17 March 1987 and is treated as above for accounting periods beginning after 16 March 1987. [*FA 1972, s 93(2)(3); F(No 2)A 1987, s 74(1)(3)(4)(6), Sch 5 paras 1, 2*].

For accounting periods ending before 17 March 1987, corporation tax on chargeable gains is levied at the full rate of corporation tax, but those gains are reduced for tax purposes by such fractions as Parliament may from time to time determine giving an effective rate of tax of 30% in most cases. The fractions determined are as follows.

Financial year 1983	2/5	[*FA 1984, s 18*].
Financial year 1984	1/3	[*FA 1984, s 18*].
Financial year 1985	1/4	[*FA 1984, s 18*].
Financial year 1986	1/7	[*FA 1984, s 18*].

Where an accounting period straddles financial years in which different fractions apply, the chargeable gains for that period are apportioned and reduced accordingly. [*FA 1972, s 93*].

(*c*) **Corporation tax on distributions to non-corporates**

With effect for distributions made **after 31 March 2004 and before 1 April 2006,** a special rate, the '*non-corporate distribution rate*', applies where a company, which has an underlying rate of corporation tax of less than that rate (19% for the financial years 2004 and 2005), makes (or is treated as making) one or more '*non-corporate distributions*' in any accounting period. [*ICTA 1988, s 13AB, Sch A2; FA 2004, s 28, Sch 3; FA 2005, s 13; FA 2006, s 26*]. See 49 NON-CORPORATE DISTRIBUTION RATE for further details.

(*d*) **Advance corporation tax**

ACT was **abolished** after 5 April 1999 (see 3.1 ADVANCE CORPORATION TAX – SHADOW ACT).

Any ACT payable in respect of a distribution made *before 6 April 1999* in a financial year in which the rate was changed was calculated at the rate fixed for the preceding financial year. [*ICTA 1988, s 246(6)*]. The rate was therefore effectively fixed from 6 April to 5 April (a 'year of assessment') notwithstanding the reference to a 'financial year'.

Date of dividend etc.	*Rate of ACT*	
1 April 1979 — 31 March 1986	3/7ths	(i.e. 30% of dividend etc. plus ACT)
1 April 1986 — 31 March 1987	29/71sts	(i.e. 29% of dividend etc. plus ACT)
1 April 1987 — 31 March 1988	27/73rds	(i.e. 27% of dividend etc. plus ACT)
1 April 1988 — 31 March 1993	1/3rd	(i.e. 25% of dividend etc. plus ACT)
1 April 1993 — 31 March 1994	9/31sts	(i.e. 22.5% of dividend etc. plus ACT)
1 April 1994 — 5 April 1999	**1/4th**	(i.e. 20% of dividend etc. plus ACT)

[*F(No 2)A 1979, s 5; FA 1980, s 20; FA 1981, s 21; FA 1982, s 22; FA 1983, s 12; FA 1984, s 19; FA 1985, s 35; FA 1986, s 17(1); FA 1987, s 20(1); FA 1988, s 23; FA 1989, s 30; FA 1990, s 17; FA 1991, s 21; FA 1992, s 10(1); FA 1993, s 78(1)*].

2 Accounting Periods

Simon's Direct Tax Service D2.107.

2.1 APPORTIONMENT

Assessments to corporation tax are made on the basis of accounting periods but, for calculating the corporation tax payable thereon, the profit of each accounting period is, if necessary, apportioned, on a time basis, between the financial years (see 1.2 INTRODUCTION) which overlap the accounting period. Corporation tax is then charged on each proportion so computed at the rate fixed for the financial year concerned. [*ICTA 1988, s 8(3)*].

2.2 *Example*

For the year ended 30 June 2007, the following information is relevant to A Ltd, a company with no associated companies.

	£
Trading income	200,600
Property income	25,000
Income from not-trading loan relationships	30,000

The small companies' rate of corporation tax for the financial year 2006 is 19% and the rate for the financial year 2007 is 20%.

The corporation tax computation of A Ltd for the 12-month accounting period ended on 30.6.07 is as follows.

		£	
Schedule D, Case I		200,600	
Schedule A		25,000	
Schedule D, Case III		30,000	
		255,600	
Total profits apportioned			
1.7.06 — 31.3.07	9/12 ×	£255,600	£191,700
1.4.07 — 30.6.07	3/12 ×	£255,600	£63,900
Tax chargeable			
19% × £191,700			36,423
20% × £63,900			12,780
Total tax charge			£49,203

2.3 ESTABLISHING ACCOUNTING PERIODS

Commencement of accounting period. An accounting period of a company **begins** whenever

(*a*) 'the company, not then being within the charge to corporation tax, comes within it, whether by the company becoming resident in the UK or acquiring a source of income, or otherwise', or (*b*) a previous 'accounting period of the company ends without the company then ceasing to be within the charge to corporation tax'. [*ICTA 1988, s 12(2)*].

A company resident in the UK, if not otherwise within the charge to corporation tax, is treated as coming within the charge when it commences business. [*ICTA 1988, s 12(4)*]. If a chargeable gain or allowable loss accrues to a company not otherwise in an accounting period, an accounting period then begins and the gain or loss accrues in that period. [*ICTA 1988, s 12(6)*]. As regards whether a company is 'within the charge to corporation tax' in the absence of income or gains, see *Walker v Centaur Clothes Group Ltd HL 2000, 72 TC 379*.

2.4 **End of accounting period.** An accounting period of a company **ends** on the first occurrence of any of the following

(*a*) the expiration of twelve months from the beginning of the accounting period;

(*b*) an accounting date of the company or, if there is a period for which the company does not make up accounts, the end of that period;

(*c*) the company's beginning or ceasing to trade or to be, in respect of the trade or (if more than one) of all the trades carried on by it, within the charge to corporation tax;

(*d*) the company's beginning or ceasing to be resident in the UK;

(*da*) (in relation to companies entering administration on or after 15 September 2003 when the *Enterprise Act 2002, s 248* came into force) the company's ceasing to be in administration under *Insolvency Act 1986, Sch B1* (or any corresponding event otherwise than under that *Act*);

(*e*) the company's ceasing to be within the charge to corporation tax. [*ICTA 1988, s 12(3); FA 2003, Sch 41 paras 1, 5(1)*].

Where *more than one trade* is carried on and accounting dates differ, the company determines which date is to prevail under (*b*). HMRC may, however, select such different one of those dates as appears to them appropriate where they are of the opinion, on reasonable grounds, that the date selected by the company is inappropriate. [*ICTA 1988, s 12(5)(5A)*].

2.5 **Commencement or end of accounting period uncertain.** Where the beginning or end of an accounting period is uncertain, HMRC may choose such period (not exceeding twelve months) as appears appropriate and, on further facts coming to their knowledge, HMRC may revise that period, but the company has rights of appeal. [*ICTA 1988, s 12(8)*]. See *R v Ward, R v Special Commr (ex p Stipplechoice Ltd) (No 3) QB 1988, 61 TC 391*, where determination of an appeal was quashed because the company did not receive notification that the inspector intended to seek confirmation of the assessment under appeal after revision of the terminal date. The validity of extended time limit assessments made by virtue of the predecessor to *section 12(8)*, and subsequently varied by the inspector, was challenged in *Kelsall v Stipplechoice Ltd CA 1995, 67 TC 349*. It was held that the question of whether there was doubt as to the beginning or end of an accounting period at the time the assessment was made (so that the dates could subsequently be revised by the inspector) is to be determined subjectively by reference to the state of mind of the inspector at that time. This reversed the decision in the High Court, where it was also held that no further leave of the General or Special Commissioners was required for the revision of an extended time limit assessment made by virtue of *section 12(8)* where the original leave to assess was given on the footing that it would be open to the company to contend for a different accounting date on appeal. The Court of Appeal expressed no view on this aspect of the decision.

2.6 **Accounts in excess of twelve months.** Where accounts are made up for a period in excess of twelve months, apportionments of profits or gains to different periods are, except where otherwise provided, made on a time basis [*ICTA 1988, s 834(4)*], and in the case of profits or gains chargeable under Schedule D, Case I, II or VI it is specifically provided that apportionment is to be made on the basis of the number of days falling in each period. [*ICTA 1988, s 72*]. Where, however, a more satisfactory basis of arriving at the profit of each accounting period is available, the inspector may apply that basis instead (*Marshall Hus & Partners Ltd v Bolton Ch D 1980, 55 TC 539*). Other Schedule D income is apportioned on an arising basis in accordance with income tax law and practice as if accounting periods were years of assessment [*ICTA 1988, s 9(1)*], except that income from an overseas property business (see 56 PROPERTY INCOME) chargeable under Schedule D, Case V is computed as if it were a Schedule A business (so that Schedule D, Case I principles apply). [*ICTA 1988, s 70A(5)*]. The Schedule D, Case III charge in respect of a non-trading credit on loan relationships is calculated by reference to accounting periods (see 46.3, 46.5 LOAN RELATIONSHIPS). Chargeable gains are apportioned on an arising basis. [*TCGA 1992, s 8(1)*]. Charges are included in the period in which they are paid. [*ICTA 1988, s 338*].

2.7 **Accounts made up to varying dates.** Where accounts are made up to slightly varying dates (e.g. the last Saturday in a specified month), provided the variation is not more than four days from a mean date, HMRC will (if the taxpayer agrees in writing) normally accept treatment of each period of account as if it were a twelve month accounting period ending on the mean date. (HMRC Company Taxation Manual, CTM 01560).

See HMRC Extra-Statutory Concession, C12 for concessional yearly accounting periods where a retail co-operative society prepares half-yearly or quarterly accounts.

2.8 *Example*

B Ltd prepares accounts for 16 months ending on 31 March 2008. The following information is relevant.

	£
Profit for 16 months	800,000
Schedule D, Case III income (not in respect of loan relationships) received on 1 March and 1 September each year	50,000
Capital gain (after indexation) arising on 1.6.07	100,000
Tax written down value of plant pool at 1.12.06	40,000
Plant purchased 1.2.07	200,000
Plant purchased 1.2.08	246,000
Proceeds of plant sold 31.12.07 (less than cost)	4,000

B Ltd will be chargeable to corporation tax as follows.

	Accounting period 12 months to 30.11.07	Accounting period 4 months to 31.3.08
	£	£
Adjusted profits (apportioned 12:4)	600,000	200,000
Capital allowances (see note)	(90,000)	(135,167)
Schedule D, Case I	510,000	64,833
Schedule D, Case III	100,000	50,000
Chargeable gain	100,000	—
Chargeable profits	710,000	114,833

Note

Capital allowances are calculated as follows.

12 months to 30.11.07

	FYAs	Pool	Allowances
	£	£	£
WDV b/f		40,000	
Additions	200,000		
FYA at 40%	(80,000)		80,000
	120,000		
WDA at 25%		(10,000)	10,000
Transfer to pool	(120,000)	120,000	
Total allowances			£90,000
WDV c/f		£150,000	

4 months to 31.3.08

	FYAs	Pool	Allowances
	£	£	£
WDV b/f		150,000	
Additions	246,000		
FYA at 50%	(123,000)		123,000
	123,000		
Disposals		(4,000)	
		146,000	
WDA at 25% × 4/12		(12,167)	12,167
Transfer to pool	(123,000)	123,000	
Total allowances			£135,167
WDV c/f		£256,833	

It is assumed that the conditions for the 40% and 50% first-year allowances for the additions on 1.2.07 and 1.2.08 respectively are met. Writing-down allowances, but not first-year allowances, are a proportionately reduced percentage of 25% if the accounting period is only part of a year. [*CAA 2001, s 56(3); CAA 1990, s 24(2)*].

2.9 **Liquidations etc.** For accounting periods in relation to *liquidations* and *administrations* and other insolvency aspects, see 45.6 LIQUIDATION ETC.

2.10 **Sale of lessors.** See also 5.17 ANTI-AVOIDANCE in relation to an accounting period ending and a new one starting on the change of ownership of a company leasing plant or machinery. [*ICTA 1988, s 12(9); FA 2006, Sch 10 para 43*].

3 Advance Corporation Tax—Shadow ACT

Cross-references. See also 29 FRANKED INVESTMENT INCOME, 32.2–32.4 and 32.5 GROUPS OF COMPANIES.

Simon's Direct Tax Service See **D1.321** *et seq.*

The headings in this chapter are as follows.

3.1 **ACT PRE-6 APRIL 1999**

Where a UK-resident company resident in the UK made a qualifying distribution (including the payment of a dividend — see 23 DISTRIBUTIONS) before 6 April 1999, it became liable to pay advance corporation tax (ACT) [*ICTA 1988, s 14(1); FA 1998, Sch 3 para 8*] (subject to relief for FRANKED INVESTMENT INCOME (29) received — see 3.3 below). The ACT could then be offset against the company's liability to 'mainstream' corporation tax on its profits for that accounting period subject to a maximum set-off.

Intra-group dividends were exempt if an election was made as described under 32.2 GROUPS OF COMPANIES.

ACT was abolished from 6 April 1999 [*FA 1998, s 31*], subject to a continuing 'shadow' system for relief of '*surplus ACT*' (ACT which could not be set-off against 'mainstream' corporation tax) prior to that date (see 3.2 *et seq.* below). For the provisions for computing ACT arising before this date and its offset against the liability to 'mainstream' corporation tax, see Tolley's Corporation Tax 2005–06 or earlier editions.

Distributions to non-resident companies. In the combined cases of *Metallgesellschaft and Others Ltd v CIR* and *Hoechst AG v CIR, [2001] STC 452*, it was held that the requirement that both parties to a group income election under *ICTA 1988, s 247* (for the payment of dividends prior to the abolition of ACT on 6 April 1999, see 32.3 GROUPS OF COMPANIES) be UK-resident contravened EC law. Following this, it was held in *Pirelli Cable Holding NV and Others v CIR, HL [2006] STC 548* (unanimously reversing the Court of Appeal's decision) that, had such a group income election been made (had it been available), the non-UK resident parent would not have been entitled to tax credits available under double tax agreements (see 24.3 DOUBLE TAX RELIEF) in respect of the distributions made by the UK-resident subsidiary. Thus, such tax credits could be taken into account in calculating any compensation in a claim for restitution of ACT. See also 32.3 GROUPS OF COMPANIES in relation to cases regarding compensation.

Distributions from non-resident companies. See 29.4 FRANKED INVESTMENT INCOME in relation to claims that the UK's system of advance corporation tax, as in force from 1973 to 1999, contravened what is now Article 43 of the EC Treaty.

3.2 **SHADOW ACT**

Following the abolition of ACT for distributions made after 5 April 1999, a system of 'shadow ACT' was introduced to enable surplus ACT (see 3.5 below) as at that date to be relieved broadly in accordance with companies' expectations prior to abolition. The system, introduced by the *Corporation Tax* (*Treatment of Surplus Advance Corporation Tax*) *Regulations 1999* (*SI 1999 No 358*), under the enabling provisions of *FA 1998, s 32*, operates broadly as set out at 3.3 *et seq.* below. An accounting period straddling 5 April 1999 is treated as two separate accounting periods, ending on and commencing immediately after that date, with profits being time-apportioned between those accounting periods.

[*SI 1999 No 358, reg 3*].

3.3 **Computation of Shadow ACT.** Shadow ACT is computed for the accounting period on a similar basis and at the same rate as applied before 6 April 1999. For the financial year 1999 onwards, shadow ACT is treated as having been paid at the rate of 25% of the amount or value of the 'relevant distributions' (i.e. 20% of the dividend etc. plus the shadow ACT).

'*Relevant distributions*'. The distributions in respect of which the shadow ACT computation is made include all distributions made on or after 6 April 1999 within *ICTA 1988, Pt VI* (see 23.1-23.6 DISTRIBUTIONS), including both qualifying and non-qualifying distributions (see 23.17 DISTRIBUTIONS), and also certain deemed distributions arising in respect of benefits provided to participators in close companies (see 23.19 DISTRIBUTIONS), but *excluding* manufactured dividends within *ICTA 1988, Sch 23A* (as amended by *ITA 2007 Sch 1 para 238*) (see 5.9 ANTI-AVOIDANCE) and most intra-group distributions.

[*SI 1999 No 358, regs 3, 11*].

3.4 **Reduction for franked investment income.** Where FRANKED INVESTMENT INCOME (29) ('FII') is received in an accounting period, or surplus FII is brought forward (including a surplus arising before 6 April 1999), shadow ACT is *not* treated as having been paid in that period except to the extent that '*franked distributions*' (i.e. distributions plus the shadow ACT thereon) exceed the sum of nine-eighths of the FII received and the amount of any surplus FII brought forward.

'*Franked investment income*' ('FII') is the sum of the amount or value of dividends and other qualifying distributions (see 23.7 DISTRIBUTIONS) received by a UK resident company from another UK resident company and such proportion of each distribution as corresponds to the 'tax credit fraction' in force when the distribution is made. From 6 April 1999, the tax credit fraction is one-ninth of the amount or value of the relevant distribution (i.e. 10% of the dividend etc. plus the tax credit). Thus, a dividend of £360 amounts to FII in the hands of a UK recipient company of £400.

Dividends or interest, or (from 6 April 2005) alternative finance return or profit share return under ALTERNATIVE FINANCE ARRANGEMENTS (4), received from BUILDING SOCIETIES (9), are **not** included in the definition of franked distributions or FII. [*ICTA 1988, s 476(3), s 477A(3)(b); FA 2005, Sch 2 para 5*]. The definition of FII is, however, subject to a number of restrictions in relation to replacement of interest income by income consisting of distributions, arrangements to pass on the value of FII, distributions received by dealers and intra-group distributions.

[*ICTA 1988, ss 231(1), 238(1), 832(1); F(No 2)A 1997, s 30; FA 1998, Sch 3 paras 11, 39; ITTOIA 2005, Sch 1 paras 113, 337; SI 1999 No 358, regs 3, 7-10*].

3.5 **Utilisation of shadow ACT and surplus ACT.** Shadow ACT which is treated as having been paid by a company in respect of any relevant distribution made by it in an accounting period is set against its liability to corporation tax on any profits charged to corporation tax for that accounting period, but no actual corporation tax relief is given for such amounts of shadow ACT. The capacity for offset against corporation tax available (see below) is allocated first to the shadow ACT so computed. Any balance of the offset capacity available for an accounting period is then allocated to surplus ACT brought forward at 6 April 1999, for which actual corporation tax relief is then given.

The *maximum* set-off is the amount of shadow ACT that would have been payable in respect of a franked distribution equal to the profits and made at the end of the accounting period (i.e. 20% of profits chargeable to corporation tax).

Surplus shadow ACT. If the shadow ACT exceeds the offset capacity for the period, it is treated as 'surplus shadow ACT', to be carried back and treated as shadow ACT in respect of distributions made in accounting periods beginning in the previous six years (but not before 6 April 1999), with any unused balance being carried forward to the next accounting period. Surplus shadow ACT is, however, not carried back so as to displace actual surplus ACT relieved in an earlier period except in the period beginning 24 months before the *end* of the accounting period in which the surplus shadow ACT arose and ending the day before the commencement of that period.

[*SI 1999 No 358, regs 3, 12, 14, 15*].

For cases turning on whether there was an accounting period in relation to surplus ACT, see *Walker v Centaur Clothes Group Ltd HL 2000, 72 TC 379* and *Aproline Ltd v Littlejohn (Sp C 36), [1995] SSCD 201*.

3.6 **Withdrawal from shadow ACT system.** A company may opt out of the shadow ACT system by notifying HMRC that it will not seek, or will cease to seek, recovery of unrelieved surplus ACT. Where such notice was given in the accounting period beginning on 6 April 1999 (as in 3.2 above) and related to that period, the company was thereby excluded from the shadow ACT arrangements from the start. Where it is given in any accounting period and indicates that the company wishes that accounting period to be the last for which it will seek recovery of unrelieved surplus ACT (the 'final accounting period'), then no further recovery will be possible after that period. In those circumstances, and also in relation to the accounting period in which all surplus ACT is exhausted, the shadow ACT computation continues to be made for (normally) the following accounting period, with any surplus shadow ACT arising in that period being carried back to displace surplus ACT relieved as under 3.5 above in the final accounting period (and in that case the accounting period from which the surplus shadow ACT is carried back becomes the final accounting period, i.e. the last period for which surplus ACT relief may be obtained). (These displacement provisions are more complex where accounting periods are not of twelve months' duration.) The latter prevents excessive relief being obtained by the restriction of dividends, and consequent ability to reclaim unrelieved surplus ACT, in the final period within the arrangements, followed by the payment of exceptional dividends in (normally) the following accounting period. There are special rules in relation to determination of the final accounting period for these purposes in the case of groups of companies (see generally 3.7 below).

[*SI 1999 No 358, regs 4, 5*].

3.7 **Intra-group allocation of shadow ACT.** Special rules determine when and how shadow ACT generated within a group of companies is to be allocated, and the allocation of group surplus shadow ACT. Broadly, no company in a group gets relief for surplus ACT until all group shadow ACT has been offset.

Where a group member generates shadow ACT in excess of its maximum capacity to utilise it in the period in which it is generated, the excess is to be allocated by the parent company to another or other group member(s), but not so as to displace their own shadow ACT or to exceed their maximum capacity for using shadow ACT in the same period.

Where the total group shadow ACT exceeds the group capacity to use it, the balance remaining after the allocation to other group companies is to remain in the company in which it arose and to be carried forward.

Where the total group shadow ACT does not exceed the group capacity, the parent company determines which other group members are to receive the allocation and the amounts to be allocated to them, in accordance with their capacity to use that amount. HMRC may allocate the excess in accordance with the regulations where the company fails to do so, but such allocation can subsequently be overridden by an allocation made by the parent company.

There are also provisions dealing with a company joining or leaving a group, or being a member of more than one group. 'Group' for these purposes is broadly a company and its 51% subsidiaries, but is specially defined to take into account certain special rights.

[*SI 1999 No 358, regs 6, 13*].

3.8 **Changes in ownership of a company.** The provisions of *ICTA 1988, ss 245-245B* relating to changes in ownership of companies under the pre-April 1999 rules were imported, with appropriate modifications, into the shadow ACT rules.

Major change in business. If a 'major change in the nature or conduct of a trade or business' takes place within three years of (or at the same time as) a change in ownership of a company (see 47.13 LOSSES), a new accounting period is deemed to commence at the time of the change in ownership. This applies for the purposes of setting off unrelieved surplus ACT against the company's liability to corporation tax on any profits charged to corporation tax for an accounting period ending after the change of ownership. For this purpose the profits of the company charged to corporation tax for the accounting period is to be apportioned to the revised accounting periods on a time basis.

In this case, unrelieved surplus ACT may not be carried forward from the accounting period ending with the change in ownership (such surplus ACT accordingly being lost). The prohibition on the carry forward of unrelieved surplus ACT also applies to ACT which had been surrendered to the company (see 32.5 GROUPS OF COMPANIES).

'*Major change in the nature or conduct of a trade or business*' includes

(*a*) a major change in the type of property dealt in or services or facilities provided;

(*b*) a major change in customers, outlets or markets;

(*c*) the company's ceasing to be a 'trading company' and becoming an 'investment company' (or vice versa);

(*d*) where the company is an investment company, a major change in the nature of its investments.

The change may be the result of a gradual process which began outside the relevant period. See 47.13 LOSSES for HMRC practice as regards what constitutes a major change in the nature or conduct of a trade or business.

'*Trading company*' means a company the business of which consists wholly or mainly of the carrying on of a trade or trades.

'*Investment company*' means a company (other than a 'holding company'), the business of which consists wholly or mainly of making investments whence the principal part of its income is derived.

'*Holding company*' means a company the business of which consists wholly or mainly in the holding of shares or securities of companies which are its 90% subsidiaries and which are trading companies.

Revival of business. Similar consequences ensue if, once the scale of the activities in its trade or business has become small or negligible, there is a change in the ownership of the company before any considerable revival of that trade or business.

Surrendered ACT. Where there is a change in the ownership of a company (see 47.13 LOSSES) to which ACT had been surrendered (see 32.5 GROUPS OF COMPANIES) in respect of a distribution made before the change, and in the period from three years before to three years after the change there is 'a major change in the nature or conduct of a trade or business' (see above) of the surrendering company, any unrelieved surplus ACT which had been so surrendered may not be carried forward to an accounting period ending after the change (the accounting period in which the change occurred being treated as two separate accounting periods, up to and after the change, for this purpose).

Assets acquired after change. Where there is a change in the ownership of a company (see 47.13 LOSSES) which carries forward unrelieved surplus ACT of an accounting period beginning before the change to an accounting period ending after the change, and

(i) after the change the company acquires an asset from a fellow group member under the no gain, no loss provisions of *TCGA 1992, s 171* (see 12.2 CAPITAL GAINS—GROUPS), and

(ii) within three years of the change in ownership, a chargeable gain accrues to the company on its disposal of that asset (or of an asset deriving its value in whole or part from that asset),

the ACT set-off limit (in 3.5 above) for the period in which the chargeable gain arises is reduced by an amount equal to 20% of the gain.

Application of losses provisions. The provisions in *ICTA 1988, s 768*(*8*)(9), and the rules in *ICTA 1988, s 769* are applied as if the benefit of losses were a reference to the benefit of unrelieved surplus ACT. For *sections 768* and *769*, see 47.13 LOSSES.

[*SI 1999 No 358, regs 16–18*].

In the case of *CIR v Aberdeen Milk Co Ltd CS, 73 TC 563*, surplus ACT arising to a successor company on privatisation could not be carried back to the period before the transfer.

3.9 **Other provisions.** *Controlled foreign companies.* The profits against which unrelieved surplus ACT may be set include amounts chargeable on the company in respect of CONTROLLED FOREIGN COMPANIES (21) (see *SI 1999 No 358, regs 3*(*3*)*, 20*).

Foreign tax credit relief. Where relief is available for a foreign tax credit, the income or gain subject to the foreign tax is excluded from profits for the purpose of determining the maximum shadow ACT set-off and the foreign tax credit is deducted from the corporation tax liability. Shadow ACT can be set against the corporation tax liability relating to the foreign income or gain limited to the maximum ACT credit that would have applied had the foreign income or gain been the only income or gain for the accounting period or, if lower, the corporation tax liablity as reduced by the foreign tax credit (see *SI 1999 No 358, reg 12*(*4*)(*5*)).

Recovery of surplus ACT wrongly set off. Any necessary assessment may be made to recover tax which ought to have been paid (including interest thereon) as a result of an excessive set-off of ACT, and to restore the tax position of those concerned (see *SI 1999 No 358, reg 19*).

Life insurance companies. There are also special provisions relating to life assurance companies (*SI 1999 No 358, reg 22* as amended by *SI 2003 No 1861*).

Simon's Direct Tax Service. See D1.311 *et seq.*, **D1.804.**

3.10 **Examples**

(A) Utilisation of surplus ACT

H Ltd, a company with no associated companies, has chargeable profits for the year ending 31 December 2007 of £1,600,000. During the year it pays a dividend of £500,000. At 1 January 2007, it has surplus ACT brought forward of £300,000.

H Ltd may obtain relief in the year ended 31.12.07 for surplus ACT as follows.

	£
Maximum ACT limit (£1,600,000 @ 20%)	320,000
Less Shadow ACT (£500,000 × 20/80)	125,000
ACT set-off	£195,000

Corporation tax for the y/e 31.12.07 is payable as follows.

	£
Corporation tax payable (£1,600,000 @ 30%)	480,000
Less ACT	195,000
Tax payable	£295,000

Surplus ACT memorandum

	£
ACT brought forward at 1.1.07	300,000
Less Used y/e 31.12.07	195,000
ACT carried forward at 31.12.07	£105,000

(B) Shadow ACT and tax credits

J Ltd (which has no associated companies) pays a dividend of £1,000 on 30 June 2007 and receives a dividend of £800 on the same date.

J Ltd will have made a franked distribution as follows.

	£
Distribution	1,000
Shadow ACT (@ 20/80)	250
Franked distribution	£1,250

J Ltd will have received franked investment income

	£
Distribution	800
Tax credit (@ 10/90)	89
Franked investment income	889
Amount available to set against franked distribution: (FII × 9/8)	1,000
Shadow ACT treated as paid: ((1,250–1,000) × 20%)	50

(C) Allocation of shadow ACT among group members

A Ltd owns 51% of the share capital of both B Ltd and C Ltd. The following information is relevant.

Year ended 31.3.07	A Ltd	B Ltd	C Ltd
	£	£	£
(Loss)/Profits	(10,000)	80,000	110,000
Dividends paid (to companies other than to group companies)	80,000	70,000	16,000
Shadow ACT thereon	20,000	17,500	4,000
Year ended 31.3.08			
Profits	70,000	90,000	120,000
Dividends paid (to companies other than to group companies)	60,000	80,000	40,000
Shadow ACT thereon	15,000	20,000	10,000

3.10 Advance Corporation Tax—Shadow ACT

C Ltd has surplus ACT brought forward of £5,200 at 1 April 2006, not having been able to utilise it in prior years.

Year ended 31.3.07		A Ltd		B Ltd		C Ltd
	£	£	£	£	£	£
CT on profits at 19%		—		15,200		20,900
ACT capacity	—		15,200		20,900	
Shadow ACT	20,000		17,500		4,000	
Surplus shadow ACT	20,000		2,300		—	
Spare ACT capacity	—		—		16,900	
Allocation by parent company	(16,900)		—		(16,900)	
Set-off of surplus ACT					—	—
Surplus shadow ACT c/fwd	3,100		2,300		—	
Surplus ACT c/fwd	—		—		5,200	
Corporation tax liability		—		15,200		20,900

Year ended 31.3.08		A Ltd		B Ltd		C Ltd
	£	£	£	£	£	£
CT on profits at 20%		14,000		18,000		24,000
ACT capacity	14,000		18,000		24,000	
Shadow ACT in year	15,000		20,000		10,000	
Shadow ACT b/fwd	3,100		2,300		—	
Surplus shadow ACT	4,100		4,300		—	
Spare ACT capacity	—		—		14,000	
Allocation by parent company	(4,100)		(4,300)		(8,400)	
Set-off of surplus ACT					5,600	(5,600)
Surplus ACT c/fwd	—		—		—	
Corporation tax liability		14,000		18,000		18,400

4 Alternative Finance Arrangements

Cross references. See 9 BUILDING SOCIETIES, 37.3 INCOME TAX IN RELATION TO A COMPANY, 43.6 INVESTMENT FUNDS, 46 LOAN RELATIONSHIPS, 61.24 RETURNS.

Simons Direct Tax Service. See A1.6.

4.1 INTRODUCTION

The provisions set out below provide for the taxation of finance arrangements (known as '*alternative finance arrangements*') entered into on or after 6 April 2005 that do not involve the receipt or payment of interest. It is intended to provide a tax regime for financial products that are economically equivalent to conventional banking products but which, instead of interest, involve arrangements of the kind described in 4.2–4.6 below.

The legislation seeks to ensure that such products are taxed no more or less favourably than equivalent products involving interest. Such products are usually aimed at individuals who wish to adhere to Shari'a law, which prohibits the receipt or payment of interest. Prior to *FA 2005*, the tax treatment of such products was in some areas uncertain and in others could produce anomalous results. For example, finance arrangements based on asset sale and purchase might have fallen within the CGT rules, but this in turn could have depended on the nature of the asset; and returns from profit-share arrangements could have been treated as distributions. The return from such products ('alternative finance return' in the case of the first and 'profit share return' in the second case) is instead taxed as though it were interest.

The legislation is not restricted to Shari'a-compliant products but applies to any finance arrangement that falls within its terms. It does not change the nature of the financial arrangements, nor does it deem interest to arise where there is none. Instead, it brings certain types of finance arrangements, and the returns from those arrangements, within the pre-existing tax regime for receipts and payments of interest.

The Treasury have power by statutory instrument to designate arrangements further to those in 4.2–4.5 below as alternative finance arrangements. Such arrangements must equate in substance to a loan, deposit or other transaction that does not involve the payment of interest but achieves a similar effect.

The provisions at 4.2–4.5 below are subject to the financial arrangements being entered into on an arm's length basis (see 4.7 below).

[*FA 2005, ss 47, 49, 53, 54, 56; FA 2006, s 98*].

It has been announced by the Treasury that legislation will be introduced in *Finance Bill 2007* to facilitate the UK issuance and trading of Sukuk, the Islamic equivalent of securitisations.

4.2 ALTERNATIVE FINANCE RETURN — PURCHASE AND RE-SALE

These provisions apply to arrangements entered into after 5 April 2005 between two persons (at least one of whom must be a financial institution) where one person buys an asset and sells it, either immediately or once the conditions below are met, to the other person for a deferred (or partly deferred) consideration which is greater than the purchase price, the difference (the '*effective return*') equating, in substance, to the return on an investment of money at interest. The conditions are that the person buying the asset must be a 'financial institution' (see below) and the asset is purchased for the purpose of a sale under an alternative finance arrangement.

Where the whole of the sale price is paid on one day, the effective return is taken to be equal to the alternative finance return included within the sale price. Where the sale price is to be paid by instalments, each instalment is to be taken to include alternative finance return equal to an amount of interest that would have been included in the instalment if:

(i) the effective return were interest payable on a loan equal to the purchase price of the asset;

(ii) the instalment were a part repayment of the principal with interest; and

(iii) the loan were made on arm's length terms and accounted for under generally accepted accounting practice.

In either case, the arrangements are treated for corporation tax purposes as a loan relationship to which the company is a party. (See 46 LOAN RELATIONSHIPS.) The amount of the purchase price is treated as if it were a loan made to the company from the other party (or by the company to the other party as the case may be) and the alternative finance return is treated as if it were interest payable under the loan relationship. The effective return is ignored in determining the consideration for the purchase or sale of the asset for tax or capital gains purposes (this not overriding any tax or capital gains provisions which provide for the consideration to be other than the actual consideration).

A '*financial institution*' for these purposes is:

- a bank (within *ICTA 1988, s 840A*) or a wholly-owned subsidiary of a bank;
- a building society (within the meaning of the *Building Societies Act 1986*) or a wholly-owned subsidiary of a building society;
- a person authorised by a licence under the *Consumer Credit Act 1974, Pt 3* to carry on consumer credit business or consumer hire business within the meaning of that Act; or
- a person authorised in a non-UK jurisdiction to receive deposits or other repayable funds from the public and to grant credits for its own account.

[*FA 2005, ss 46–48, 50*(*1*)*, 53, 56*(*1*)*, 57; FA 2006, s 96*(*1*)(*2*)].

Non-residents. Where a non-resident company is party to an alternative finance arrangement, the company is not treated as having a UK permanent establishment by virtue of anything done in relation to the arrangement. [*FA 2003, s 148*(*5A*)*; FA 2005, s 48*(*2*)]. Equally, where a UK-resident person is a party to or acts for a non-resident person who is party to, an alternative finance arrangement, that person is not regarded as the UK representative of the non-resident in relation to the arrangement. [*FA 1995, s 127*(*1*)(*cc*)*; FA 2005, s 48*(*3*)]. (See 60.5 RESIDENCE).

4.3 ALTERNATIVE FINANCE RETURN — DIMINISHING SHARED OWNERSHIP

These provisions apply to arrangements entered into on or after 1 April 2006 under which a financial institution (see 4.2 above) acquires a beneficial interest in an asset and another person ('the eventual owner'):

(*a*) also acquires a beneficial interest in the asset;

(*b*) is to make a series of payments to the financial institution amounting in total to the amount paid to acquire its beneficial interest;

(*c*) is to acquire (in stages or otherwise) the financial institution's beneficial interest as a result of those payments;

(*d*) is to make additional payments to the financial institution (whether under a lease or otherwise);

(*e*) has the exclusive right to occupy or otherwise use the asset; and (*f*) is exclusively entitled to any income, profit or gain arising from or attributable to the asset, including, in particular, any increase in its value.

It is immaterial whether or not the financial institution acquires its beneficial interest from the eventual owner (for example, in a case where there is an initial conveyance of real property to the eventual owner followed by a sub-sale from the eventual owner to the financial institution), whether the eventual owner (or another person other than the financial institution) also has an interest in the asset and whether or not the financial institution has a legal interest in the asset.

The condition in (*e*) above does not preclude the eventual owner granting an interest or right in the asset to someone else, e.g. he may sub-let the asset; but the person to whom the interest or right is granted cannot be the financial institution, a person controlled by the financial institution or a person controlled by a person who also controls the financial institution, and the grant must not be required by the financial institution or by arrangements to which the financial institution is a party. The condition in (*f*) above does not prevent the financial institution from having to bear any loss (or a share of any loss) resulting from a decrease in the asset's value (and the total payments in (*b*) above may be reduced to reflect any such loss).

Payments made by the eventual owner under these arrangements are treated as alternative finance return, except in so far as they are the payments within (*b*) above or they constitute arrangement fees or legal or other costs or expenses which the eventual owner is required to pay under the arrangements.

If the financial institution is within the charge to corporation tax, the alternative finance return is treated as if it were interest receivable under a loan relationship and the consideration paid by the financial institution for its interest is treated as a loan made to (or by) the company by (or to) the other party to the arrangements. The alternative finance return is excluded in determining the consideration given for the purchase or sale of the asset for CGT or other tax purposes.

Arrangements within these provisions are not to be treated as a partnership for tax purposes.

[*FA 2005, ss 46, 47A, 50, 53; FA 2006, s 96(1)(3)(4)(6)(8)*].

An example of an arrangement that the above is intended to cover is the Shari'a compliant finance product known as diminishing musharaka. 'Musharaka' denotes a partnership or joint venture, and covers a wide spectrum, including arrangements identical to a normal partnership under which the partners share income or profits from a business or other asset. The above conditions are intended to exclude such arrangements (which are taxed in the same way as a conventional partnership — see 52 PARTNERSHIPS) from the scope of these provisions. (Treasury Explanatory Notes to Finance Bill 2006).

Capital allowances. In HMRC Brief 26/07, HMRC state that where diminishing share ownership ('DSO') arrangements are entered into to acquire assets which would qualify for capital allowances, then the buyer or lessee is entitled to claim capital allowances on capital payments for those assets when they are brought into use.

Capital gains. In HMRC Brief 26/07, HMRC state that, subject to there being any unusual conditions in the DSO arrangements, the buyer will be treated as acquiring the asset in full when unconditional contracts are entered into to acquire a beneficial interest. Taper relief and indexation allowance are computed accordingly.

4.4 PROFIT SHARE RETURN — DEPOSIT

The provisions below apply in relation to arrangements entered into after 5 April 2005, but where they have been entered into before 6 April 2005 and the profit share return is payable on or after that date, then for the purposes of the loan relationships regime, the loan treated as made by or to the company is treated as made on 6 April 2005 of an amount equal to the notional carrying value of the asset or liability representing the existing profit share arrangements. The notional carrying value in this case is the amount which would have been the carrying value of the asset or liability in the company accounts (prepared in accordance with generally accepted accounting practice) if a period of account had ended immediately before 6 April 2005.

The provisions apply to arrangements under which a person deposits money with a financial institution (see 4.2 above), which is used by that institution, together with other money deposited, with a view to profit from which payments are made or credited to the depositor in proportion to the amount deposited, which equate in substance to the return on an investment of money at interest.

The arrangements are treated for corporation tax purposes as a loan relationship to which the company is a party. (See 46 LOAN RELATIONSHIPS.) The amount of the deposit is treated as if it were a loan made by the company to the financial institution (or by the financial institution to the company as the case may be) and the profit share return is treated as if it were interest payable under the loan relationship. The profit share return is not to be treated as a distribution under *ICTA 1988, s 209(2)(e)(iii)*. Nor are payments made on or after 6 April 2005 under profit share arrangements existing before that date to be treated as such.

[*FA 2005, ss 46, 49, 50(2), 54(1), 56; FA 2006, s 95(1)(2)*].

4.5 **PROFIT SHARE RETURN — AGENCY.**

The provisions below apply in relation to arrangements entered into on or after 1 April 2006, but where they have been entered into before 1 April 2006 and the profit share return is payable on or after that date, then for the purposes of the loan relationships regime, the loan treated as made by or to the company is treated as made on 1 April 2006 of an amount equal to the notional carrying value of the asset or liability representing the existing profit share arrangements. The notional carrying value in this case is the amount which would have been the carrying value of the asset or liability in the company accounts (prepared in accordance with generally accepted accounting practice) if a period of account had ended immediately before 6 April 2005. [*FA 2005, s 56(1)(2)(4)(5); FA 2006, s 95(11)*].

The provisions apply to arrangements under which:

- a person ('the principal') appoints a financial institution (see 4.2 above) as his agent;
- the agent uses money provided by the principal with a view to producing profits;
- the principal is entitled to those profits to a specified extent;
- the agent is entitled to any profits in excess of those to which the principal is entitled (and may also be entitled to be paid a fee by the principal); and
- the payment to the principal of his entitlement to profits equates, in substance, to the return on an investment of money at interest.

Amounts paid or credited in satisfaction of the principal's profit entitlement as above are profit share return, with tax consequences as in 4.4 above. The principal is not treated for tax purposes as entitled to any of the profits to which the agent is entitled.

[*FA 2005, ss 46, 49A; FA 2006, s 95(1)(3)*].

An example of an arrangement that the above is intended to cover is the Shari'a compliant finance product known as wakala (Treasury Explanatory Notes to Finance Bill 2006).

Non-residents. Where a non-resident company is party to such arrangements as above, the company is not treated as having a UK permanent establishment by virtue of anything done in relation to the arrangements. Where a non-UK resident is a party to any such arrangements, neither the other party to those arrangements nor any person acting for the non-resident in relation to the arrangements is regarded as the UK representative of the non-resident in relation to alternative finance return. (See 60.5 RESIDENCE). [*FA 1995, s 127(1)(cb); FA 2003, s 148(5B); FA 2006, s 95(9)(10)*].

4.6 ALTERNATIVE FINANCE INVESTMENT BOND

The following provisions apply to companies from 1 April 2007, both for taxation of income and capital gains. 'Additional payments' under arrangements falling within the definition of alternative finance investment bond are alternative finance returns.

The arrangements covered involve the bondholder paying a sum of money (the '*capital*') to a bond issuer, where the assets or class of assets to be invested to generate income or gains, and the period of the arrangement, are specified. The bond issuer undertakes to sell the assets at the end of the term, or any that are still in his possession at that time, repay the capital either during the term or at its end, in one or more amounts and make other payments ('*additional payments*') to the bondholder at one or more times during, or at the end of the bond term. The other conditions are:

(*a*) the additional payments represent a reasonable commercial return on a loan of the capital;

(*b*) the bond issuer undertakes to manage the assets to produce income to repay the capital at the end of the term and make additional payments;

(*c*) the bondholder is entitled to transfer his rights to another person;

(*d*) the arrangements are listed on a recognised stock exchange;

(*e*) the arrangements are wholly or partly treated as a financial instrument of the bond issuer under international accounting standards.

Flexibility is allowed for in the terms of the 'arrangements', for example the bond issuer may acquire the assets before or after the arrangements are in place, the arrangements may include provision for them to be terminated before the end of the term and the termination payment may be reduced should the value of the bond assets fall or the income on them be reduced. For further examples of possible terms of the arrangements see *FA 2005, s 48A(2)*.

The effect is that the bondholder is not treated as having the legal or beneficial interest in the bond assets, and any profits or gains arising on them is the income of the **bond issuer** not the bondholder. However, redemption or additional payments to the bondholder by the bond issuer are treated for tax purposes as made by him in a fiduciary capacity. The bondholder is not entitled to tax relief on capital expenditure on the bond assets. Such arrangements may qualify as employment-related securities. The bond issuer is not a securitisation company by reason only that it participates in such an alternative finance investment bond. The effective return is ignored for capital gains purposes.

An additional payment or any part of a redemption payment is not treated as a distribution.

[*FA 2005, ss 48A, 48B, 51A, 54(2); FA 2007, s 53*].

4.7 ARRANGEMENTS NOT AT ARM'S LENGTH

The arrangements at 4.2–4.6 above are not treated as alternative finance arrangements if:

- they are not entered into at arm's length;
- the transfer pricing rules under *ICTA 1988, Sch 28AA para 1(2)* require the alternative finance or profit share return (or amount representing it) to be recomputed on an arm's length basis; and
- the party receiving the return is not subject to income or corporation tax, or a corresponding tax under a foreign jurisdiction, on the return.

In this case, the person paying the return is not entitled to any deduction in respect of the return in computing profits or gains for income tax or corporation tax purposes or to any deduction against total income or profits. Nor can the prohibited deduction be surrendered by way of group relief.

[*FA 2005, s 52; FA 2006, ss 95(5), 96(5); FA 2007, s 53(6)*].

4.8 **DEDUCTION OF INCOME TAX AT SOURCE**

Alternative finance arrangements where there are profit share returns or alternative finance returns (see 4.3–4.6 above and 42.4 INVESTMENT COMPANIES AND INVESTMENT BUSINESS) are to be treated as deposits on which interest is payable for the purposes of deduction of income tax at source by deposit takers and building societies.

[*FA 2005, Sch 2; ITA 2007, Sch 1 para 602*].

5 Anti-Avoidance

Cross references. See 10.38(C) CAPITAL ALLOWANCES for 'control' and 'main benefit' transactions, 11.17–11.21 CAPITAL GAINS for value-shifting provisions, 11.4–11.6 CAPITAL GAINS and 12.18, 12.22 CAPITAL GAINS—GROUPS for avoidance utilising losses, pre-entry losses and pre-entry gains, 16.18 CLOSE COMPANIES in respect of close investment holding companies, 21 CONTROLLED FOREIGN COMPANIES in relation to the apportionment of profits of controlled foreign companies in 'low tax' jurisdictions, 32.27, 32.32, 32.35 GROUPS OF COMPANIES in respect of dual resident investing companies and exempt distributions, 46.24 LOAN RELATIONSHIPS in relation to loan relationships for unallowable purposes, 47.10, 47.14, 47.15 LOSSES in respect of company reconstructions, farming and market gardening and leasing, 49 NON-CORPORATION DISTRIBUTION RATE for the tax treatment of dividends paid to non-corporate members, 51.9 OIL COMPANIES in relation to transfer pricing, 52.7 PARTNERSHIPS in relation to the realisation of capital from a partnership in a non-taxable form, and 67 TRANSFER PRICING.

Other sources. See Tolley's Anti-Avoidance Provisions.

5.1 The **anti-avoidance legislation** contained in *ICTA 1988, ss 125* (5.20), *127A* (5.23), *231B* (5.21), *399* (5.22), *703–709* (5.2), *729–739* (5.3 to 5.7 and 5.9), *774A–774G* (5.13), *741–746, 775–786* (5.14 to 5.18), *Sch 5AA* (5.23), *FA 2004, ss 306–319* and associated regulations (5.26) and *TCGA 1992, ss 137, 138* can apply to both companies and individuals. See also Tolley's Capital Gains Tax (under Anti-Avoidance).

For the **general approach of the Courts** to transactions entered into solely to avoid or reduce tax liability, leading cases are *Duke of Westminster v CIR HL 1935, 19 TC 490; W T Ramsay Ltd v CIR, Eilbeck v Rawling HL 1981, 54 TC 101; CIR v Burmah Oil Co Ltd HL 1981, 54 TC 200; Furniss v Dawson (and related appeals) HL 1984, 55 TC 324; Countess Fitzwilliam v CIR HL, [1993] STC 502;* and *CIR v McGuckian HL 1997, 69 TC 1*. See also *Cairns v MacDiarmid CA 1983, 56 TC 556; Ingram v CIR Ch D, [1985] STC 835; Craven v White, CIR v Bowater Property Developments Ltd,* and *Baylis v Gregory HL 1988, 62 TC 1*, heard together in the HL; *Shepherd v Lyntress Ltd Ch D 1989, 62 TC 495; Moodie v CIR and Sinnett HL 1993, 65 TC 610; Hatton v CIR Ch D, [1992] STC 140; Ensign Tankers (Leasing) Ltd v Stokes HL 1992, 64 TC 617; Pigott v Staines Investment Co Ltd Ch D 1995, 68 TC 342;MacNiven v Westmoreland Investments Ltd HL 2001, 73 TC 1; Barclays Mercantile Business Finance Ltd v Mawson [2005] STC 1* and *CIR v Scottish Provident Institution HL [2005] STC 15*.

The classical interpretation of the constraints upon the Courts in deciding cases involving tax avoidance schemes is summed up in Lord Tomlin's statement in the *Duke of Westminster* case that '... every man is entitled if he can to order his affairs so that the tax attaching ... is less than it otherwise would be.' The case concerned annual payments made under covenant by a taxpayer to his domestic employees, which were in substance, but not in form, remuneration. The judgment was thus concerned with the tax consequences of a single transaction, but in *Ramsay*, and subsequently in *Furniss v Dawson*, the Courts have set bounds to the ambit within which this principle can be applied in relation to modern sophisticated and increasingly artificial arrangements to avoid tax. *Ramsay* concerned a complex 'circular' avoidance scheme at the end of which the financial position of the parties was little changed, but it was claimed that a large capital gains tax loss had been created. It was held that where a preconceived series of transactions is entered into to avoid tax, and with the clear intention to proceed through all stages to completion once set in motion, the *Duke of Westminster* principle does not compel a consideration of the individual transactions and of the fiscal consequences of such transactions taken in isolation.

The House of Lords' opinions in *Furniss v Dawson* are of outstanding importance, and establish, inter alia, that the *Ramsay* principle is not confined to 'circular' devices, and that if a series of transactions is 'preordained', a particular transaction within the series, accepted as genuine, may nevertheless be ignored if it was entered into solely for fiscal reasons and without any commercial purpose other than tax avoidance, even if the series of transactions as a whole has a legitimate commercial purpose.

In *Craven v White* the House of Lords indicated that for the *Ramsay* principle to apply all the transactions in a series have to be preordained with such a degree of certainty that, at the time of the earlier transactions, there is no practical likelihood that the transactions would not take place. It is not sufficient that the ultimate transaction is simply of a kind that was envisaged at the time of the earlier transactions. However, the decision in this case was distinguished in the *Scottish Provident Institution* case where the HL held that 'it would destroy the value of the *Ramsay* principle' if the composite effect of transactions 'had to be disregarded simply because the parties had deliberately included a commercially irrelevant contingency, creating an acceptable risk that the scheme might not work as planned' and that 'the composite effect of such a scheme should be considered as it was intended to operate and without regard to the possibility that, contrary to the intention and expectations of the parties, it might not work as planned.'

The inheritance tax case *Fitzwilliam v CIR* appears to further restrict the application of the *Ramsay* principle, in that the HL found for the taxpayer in a case in which all their Lordships agreed that, once the scheme was embarked upon, there was no real possibility that the later transactions would not be proceeded with. There is, however, some suggestion that a decisive factor was that the first step in the transactions took place before the rest of the scheme had been formulated. Again, in the case of *MacNiven v Westmoreland Investments Ltd* it was held that the *Ramsay* principle did not apply where a company loaned money to a subsidiary to enable it to pay up outstanding interest and thus crystallise tax losses. The interest had been paid within the meaning of the legislation and the manner in which the payment was funded was irrelevant.

Simon's Direct Tax Service. See A1.314–A1.317.

The headings in this chapter are as follows.

5.26	Disclosure of tax avoidance schemes. [*FA 2004, ss 306–309*].	5.27	Tax arbitrage. [*F(No 2)A 2005, ss 24–31, Sch 3*].

5.2 **TRANSACTIONS IN SECURITIES**

Where, in consequence of transaction(s) in securities (including interests in companies not limited by shares, and such transaction(s) coupled with liquidation of a company), *combined with* any of the relevant circumstances mentioned below, a person is able to obtain a corporation tax advantage, HMRC may make adjustments counteracting that advantage (having first given notice of their intention to do so), unless the person concerned is able to show that the transactions were made (1) for *bona fide* commercial reasons or in the ordinary course of investment management, and (2) without corporation tax advantages being their main object, or one of their main objects. [*ICTA 1988, s 703*]. For 'transactions in securities' see *CIR v Joiner HL 1975, 50 TC 449* (in which a variation of rights prior to a liquidation was held to be such a transaction) and *CIR v Laird Group plc HL, [2003] STC 1349* (in which the payment of a dividend representing previously undistributed profits was held not to be). For '*bona fide* commercial reasons' see *Laird Group* in the *Ch D ([2001] STC 689*) and *CIR v Brebner HL 1967, 43 TC 705, Clark v CIR Ch D 1978, 52 TC 482* and *Marwood Homes Ltd v CIR Tribunal 1998, [1999] SSCD 44*. In *Lewis (as a trustee of the Redrow Staff Pension Scheme) v CIR (Sp C 218), [1999] SSCD 349*, a distribution by way of purchase of its own shares by a company from the trustees of its pension scheme, pursuant to legislation requiring the trustees to reduce their holding, was held to be a transaction carried out by the trustees both for *bona fide* commercial reasons and in the ordinary course of investment management.

The relevant circumstances are those where a person:

A in connection with (i) the distribution, transfer or realisation of a company's profits, income, reserves or other assets, or (ii) a sale or purchase of securities followed by the purchase or sale of the same or other securities, *receives an abnormal amount* (see definition below) *by way of dividend* (or other qualifying distribution, see *ICTA 1988, s 14(2)*) which is taken into account for purposes of:

(*a*) tax exemption; or

(*b*) setting-off losses against profits or income; or

(*c*) group relief (see *ICTA 1988, s 402*); or

(*d*) payments within *ICTA 1988, s 348* (*ITA 2007, ss 899, 901 with effect from 6 April 2007*) or *s 349(1)*; or

(*e*) setting against income of interest paid; or

(*f*) the application of franked investment income in relation to 'shadow ACT' computations (see 3.4 ADVANCE CORPORATION TAX – SHADOW ACT); or

B in connection with A(i) and (ii) above, *becomes entitled to a deduction from profits because of a decrease in value of securities* held, formerly held, or sold which arises from payment of a dividend thereon or from any other dealing with a company's assets (or where another company obtains the benefit of such a deduction by way of group relief); or

C in consequence of a transaction whereby (see *CIR v Garvin HL 1981, 55 TC 24* and *Bird v CIR HL 1988, 61 TC 238*, and contrast *Emery v CIR Ch D 1980, 54 TC 607*) another person has received or subsequently receives an abnormal amount (see definition below) by way of dividend, or has become, or subsequently becomes, entitled to a deduction, as in B above, *receives a consideration not taxable as income* (apart from the present provisions) representing the value of a company's trading stock, future receipts, or assets which are, or would otherwise have been, available for distribution (see *CIR v Brown CA 1971, 47 TC 217*) as dividend, and which, in the case of a company incorporated abroad, do not represent a return of capital to subscribers; or

D in connection with the distribution of the profits, income, reserves or other assets of a company (including any body corporate) under the control of *five or fewer persons*, or whose shares are not listed and dealt in on the Stock Exchange (but excluding in either case any company under control of one or more companies to which D does not apply), *receives a consideration not taxable as income* as in C above; or

E in connection with (i) the transfer of the assets of a company to which D above applies, to another such company, or (ii) a transaction in securities in which two or more such companies are concerned, receives, in the form of *share capital or securities* of such a company, any non-taxable consideration representing the value of distributable assets of such a company. (Adjustments under this heading may be made immediately if the consideration consists of securities or redeemable share capital, but in the case of non-redeemable share capital *not unless*, and until, *that capital is repaid* (including repayments in liquidation).)

As regards D above, there are provisions effective from 29 April 1996 for the additional exclusion of companies whose shares are dealt in on the Unlisted Securities Market, until the closure of that Market.

[*ICTA 1988, s 704; FA 1996, s 175; FA 1998, Sch 3 para 33; SI 1999 No 358, reg 23*].

C, D and E above are in practice unlikely to apply unless the company in question has (or has recently had) distributable reserves. (HMRC Inspector's Manual, IM 4516–4518).

For **other cases** under C and D above, see *CIR v Cleary HL 1967, 44 TC 399; Anysz v CIR Ch D 1977, 53 TC 601; Williams v CIR HL 1980, 54 TC 257; CIR v Wiggins Ch D 1978, 53 TC 639*. In determining 'under the control' in D, the relevant date is the date of the dividend (*CIR v Garvin* above).

An abnormal amount by way of dividend etc. is one which substantially exceeds either:

(*a*) a normal return on the consideration provided for the shares, with market value at time of acquisition used if less than consideration or if no consideration provided, and, in determining 'normal return', regard will be had to length of time the shares were held and other distributions received in respect of them; or

(*b*) the proportion of the dividend arising during ownership (where the dividend is at a fixed rate and the recipient sells, disposes of, or acquires an option to sell, the securities within six months of purchase). [*ICTA 1988, s 709(4)–(6)*].

'Dividend' includes interest and any other qualifying distribution. The amount of a qualifying distribution includes the related tax credit for these purposes (*CIR v Universities Superannuation Scheme Ltd Ch D 1996, 70 TC 193*). In the case of a purchase by a company of its own shares treated as a distribution under *ICTA 1988, s 209(2)(b)* (see 20.3 DISTRIBUTIONS), it was held that the return was not abnormal (*CIR v Sema Group Pension Scheme Trustees CA, [2003] STC 95*).

Tax advantage means any relief or repayment (or increases thereof) or avoidance or reduction of a charge or assessment to tax, whether effected by receipts accruing as non-taxable or by deductions from profits or gains. For distributions made on or after 8 October 1996, it is made clear that this includes a tax credit, or (before 6 April 1999) the payment of an amount in respect of a tax credit. [*ICTA 1988, s 709(1)(2A); FA 1997, s 73; F(No 2)A 1997, Sch 4 para 19*].

For 'tax advantage' see *CIR v Cleary HL 1967, 44 TC 399* (tax advantage obtained where taxpayers' company purchased shares from them) and contrast *CIR v Kleinwort, Benson Ltd Ch D 1968, 45 TC 369* (no tax advantage where merchant bank purchased debentures with interest in arrear shortly before redemption). The decision in *Sheppard and another (Trustees of the Woodland Trust) v CIR (No 2) Ch D 1993, 65 TC 724* that no tax advantage could arise where relief was obtained by virtue of charitable exemption was doubted in *CIR v Universities Superannuation Scheme Ltd Ch D 1996, 70 TC 193*, in which the opposite conclusion was reached. Prior to the hearing of the latter case, HMRC had, in any event, indicated that they would continue to proceed under *ICTA 1988, s 703* on the footing that tax-exempt bodies obtain a tax advantage whenever they receive abnormal dividends, since they considered that there would have been good grounds for challenging the earlier decision had it not been for a defect in the assessment under appeal. This continues to be the HMRC approach. (Revenue Tax Bulletin August 1993 p 90, April 1998 p 537, October 1998 pp 590–592). For the quantum of the tax advantage, see *Bird v CIR HL 1988, 61 TC 238*. On the question of whether a tax advantage was a 'main object' of a transaction, see *Marwood Homes Ltd v CIR (Sp C 106), [1997] SSCD 37*. See also *Laird Group plc v CIR Ch D, [2001] STC 689*.

Procedure.

(i) HMRC must notify person (or personal representatives if deceased [*ICTA 1988, s 703*(*11*)]) that they have reason to believe *section 703* may apply to him in respect of transaction(s) specified in notification. [*ICTA 1988, s 703*(*9*)]. See *Balen v CIR CA 1978, 52 TC 406*. No assessment may be made later than six years after the chargeable period to which the tax advantage relates. [*ICTA 1988, s 703*(*12*)].

(ii) Person notified may make, within 30 days, statutory declaration that in his opinion *section 703* does not apply and state supporting facts and circumstances. [*ICTA 1988, s 703*(*9*)]. For acceptance of late statutory declarations, see Revenue Tax Bulletin April 1999 p 656.

(iii) HMRC must then either take no further action or send declaration together with certificate that they see reason to take further action (and any counter-statement they wish to submit) to tribunal (appointed by Lord Chancellor) which will decide either (*a*) there is no *prima facie* case for proceeding further (against this the Crown cannot appeal) or (*b*) there is such a case. [*ICTA 1988, s 703*(*10*)]. The taxpayer is not entitled to see HMRC's counter-statement nor to be heard by the tribunal (*Wiseman v Borneman HL 1969, 45 TC 540*). See also *Howard v Borneman HL 1975, 50 TC 322* and *Balen v CIR CA 1978, 52 TC 406*.

(iv) If tribunal decides there is a case, or *if no statutory declaration is made by taxpayer*, HMRC will make adjustments to counteract the specified tax advantages and notify the taxpayer. [*ICTA 1988, s 703*(*3*)].

(v) Taxpayer may, within 30 days, appeal to Special Commissioners against adjustments. After appeal has been heard and determined either side may, by notice within 30 days to the Special Commissioners, require the appeal to be re-heard by the tribunal, with usual rights of further appeal by case stated in the High Court. As regards re-hearing applications, see *Marwood Homes Ltd v CIR, [1998] SSCD 53* (for the tribunal decision in which see *[1999] SSCD 44*). [*ICTA 1988, ss 705–705B; SI 1994 No 1813; FA 1998, Sch 3 para 34*].

(vi) HMRC have power to require of any person information (within 28 days of written notice) relevant to transaction(s) which it appears to HMRC may give rise to a liability on that person under these provisions. [*ICTA 1988, s 708*]. For the way in which HMRC should exercise these powers, see *R v CIR (ex p Preston) HL 1985, 59 TC 1*.

(vii) The application of these provisions is outside self-assessment, so that returns should be made without having regard to a possible charge (although taxpayers may wish to draw the inspector's attention to any correspondence with the Business Tax Clearance Team (see below) in connection with any particular transaction). Enquiries into the possible application of these provisions will accordingly be carried out independently of any enquiry into the self-assessment return (Revenue Tax Bulletin April 2000 pp 742, 743).

Distributions, etc. Income tax payable by a person under D or E above is limited to that which would arise in respect of a qualifying distribution of an amount equal to the consideration referred to in D or E above (as appropriate) received on the same day as that consideration. [*ICTA 1988, s 703(3A); FA 1998, Sch 3 para 32(2)(4)*].

Interest on tax. Corporation tax charged in accordance with a notice under *ICTA 1988, s 703(3)* is payable under *TMA 1970, s 59D* and carries interest from nine months after the end of the accounting period. [*TMA 1970, s 87A*]. Under HMRC practice, such assessments carried interest only from 30 days after the assessment was actually made and such practice may continue to be applied for periods up to 25 August 2006. (See HMRC Tax Bulletin, August 2006 p 1304.)

Clearance. Taxpayer may take the initiative by submitting to HMRC particulars of any transaction effected or contemplated; HMRC may, within 30 days of receipt, call for further information (to be supplied within 30 days). Subject to this, they must notify their decision within 30 days of receipt of the particulars or further information, and if they are satisfied that no liability arises the matter is concluded as regards that transaction by itself, provided that all facts and material particulars have been fully and accurately disclosed. [*ICTA 1988, s 707*]. HMRC is not obliged to give reasons for refusal of clearance but where the applicant has given full reasons for his transactions the main grounds for refusing clearance will be indicated. A refusal to give clearance indicates that counteraction would be taken if the transaction were completed. (HMRC Statement of Practice, SP 3/80).

Applications for clearance should be directed to the Clearance and Counteraction Team, First Floor, 22 Kingsway, London WC2B 6NR for the attention of Mohini Sawhney (or, if market-sensitive information is included, Eric Gardner). Applications may be faxed to 020–7438 4409 or emailed to reconstructions@hmrc.gsi.gov.uk (in both cases after telephoning Eric Gardner (on 020–7438 6585) if market-sensitive information is included). A hard copy need not then be sent. Only a single application need be made as above for clearances under any one or more of: *ICTA 1988, s 707* (as above), *ICTA 1988, s 215* (demergers), *ICTA 1988, s 225* (purchase of own shares), *TCGA 1992, s 138(1)* (share exchanges), *TCGA 1992, s 139(5)* (reconstructions involving the transfer of a business), *TCGA 1992, s 140B* (transfer of a UK trade between EU member states), *TCGA 1992, s 140D* (transfer of a non-UK trade between EU member states) and *FA 2002, Sch 29 para 88* (various clearances under the corporation tax intangible assets regime).

Revenue 'Working Together' Bulletin August 2001 pp 8, 9 contain a checklist of the items of information whose omission from clearance applications most commonly causes delay in the processing of applications.

Simon's Direct Tax Service. See **A7.101** *et seq*.

5.3 TRANSFERS OF RIGHTS TO RECEIVE INCOME FROM SECURITIES

Income assessable on seller. Where the owner of securities sells or transfers the right to the interest, dividends, annuities etc. therefrom *but not to the securities themselves*, such interest etc. is treated for income or corporation tax purposes as income of that owner (or, where the owner is not the beneficial owner, of the beneficiary entitled to the income) for the chargeable period in which the right to receive the interest was sold. (In relation to sales or transfers before 2 December 2004, the income treated as that of the owner or beneficiary cannot be treated as the income of any other person.) If the interest etc. on the securities is of such character that it may be paid gross, an assessment to income tax is made on the owner unless the owner shows that the proceeds of any sale etc. have otherwise been taxed.

Credit is given in the assessment for any tax which the income is shown to have already borne. If income tax would have been chargeable on relevant foreign income on the remittance basis on the interest etc., the assessment is correspondingly limited to the amounts remitted. HMRC have power to obtain information.

For company accounting periods beginning after 30 September 2002, *section 730* does not have effect for the purposes of the loan relationships legislation (see 46 LOAN RELATIONSHIPS).

In relation to sales or transfers **on or after 2 December 2004**, as a consequence of the introduction of separate legislation on corporate strips (see Tolley's Income Tax under Savings and Investment Income) and on transfers of rights to receive annuities and other annual payments (see 5.4 below), the above provisions no longer apply to interest and annuities but are instead restricted to sales or transfers of distributions (usually dividends) payable on company shares. The order of priority of charge is reversed, so that if the proceeds of sale or transfer are otherwise chargeable to tax there is no charge under these provisions.

In relation to subsequent sales or other realisations, **on or after 20 January 2006**, by the purchaser of a right to receive the distribution, the proceeds of the sale or realisation are treated as the income of the purchaser or person on whose behalf the right is otherwise realised. (HMRC will contest any losses claimed in transactions entered into before 20 January 2006. See Explanatory Notes to Finance (No 2) Bill 2006.)

[*ICTA 1988, s 730; FA 1996, Sch 7 para 23; FA 2002, Sch 25 para 51; ITTOIA 2005, Sch 1 para 300; F(No 2)A 2005, Sch 7 para 2; FA 2006, Sch 6 para 2*].

Simon's Direct Tax Service. See **A7.4**.

5.4 TRANSFERS OF RIGHTS TO RECEIVE ANNUAL PAYMENTS

If, on or after **16 March 2005**, a person sells or transfers the right to receive an annual payment and the consideration for the sale etc. would not otherwise be chargeable to tax, the seller or transferor is liable to corporation tax under Schedule D Case III, for the accounting period in which the sale etc. occurs, on an amount equal to the market value of the right to receive the annual payment. However, this does not apply in the case of a life annuity or pension annuity (both as defined) or (before 6 April 2007) an annual payment to which *ICTA 1988, s 347A* applies (annual payments that are not charges on income) or, for income tax purposes from 6 April 2005, an annual payment in respect of which, by virtue of *ITTOIA 2005, s 727* (annual payments made by individuals and arising in the UK), no liability to income tax arises under *ITTOIA 2005, Pt 5* (miscellaneous income).

These provisions also apply in relation to parts of annual payments as they apply in relation to the whole of an annual payment. The transfer of *all* the rights under an agreement to receive annual payments is also within the scope of the provisions.

Previously, there were provisions to counter the tax advantage of selling or transferring certain annuities, but those provisions do not apply in relation to any such sale or transfer on or after 2 December 2004 — see 5.3 above.

[*ICTA 1988, s 775A; F(No 2)A 2005, Sch 7 para 4*].

5.5 REPOS – NEW REGIME

A new regime for repos, introduced by *FA 2007*, will apply from a date to be determined by statutory instrument (after the consultation process is complete). The intention is that a transaction involving the sale and repurchase of securities, which is economically equivalent to a loan secured by those securities, is treated as a loan for corporation tax purposes (except to the extent of charging corporation tax on capital gains on quasi-repos).

5.5 Anti-Avoidance

For the purpose of this legislation, repos are analysed into debtor repos, debtor quasi-repos, creditor repos and creditor quasi-repos.

Debtor repos. A borrower company (or a partnership of which it is a member) has a debtor repo if all the following conditions are met:

(*a*) under an arrangement, it receives an advance (in the form of money or an asset);

(*b*) under generally accepted accounting practice ('GAAP') it is obliged to bring a financial liability into its accounts;

(*c*) under the arrangement, it sells securities to the lender at any time;

(*d*) there is a right or obligation on it to buy back the same or similar securities at any later time;

(*e*) under GAAP this repurchase would eliminate the liability in its accounts.

Where (*c*) (*d*) or (*e*) above are not satisfied, the repo legislation may still apply if the repo falls within the definition of a debtor quasi-repo.

For a quasi-repo to exist, conditions (*a*) and (*b*) above must apply, in addition to the following:

(i) under any arrangements or any other arrangements, the borrower company or any other person sells any securities at any time;

(ii) under those arrangements either:

- the borrower company is obliged to or has a right to buy any securities at any time, or
- there is such a right or obligation on any other person and provision is made under the arrangements for the borrower company to provide money or an asset to the other person to purchase the securities; and the arrangements make other relevant provision;

(iii) under generally accepted accounting practice ('GAAP') the financial liability in the accounts of the borrower company would be removed by the purchase of securities, receipt of an asset or the discharge of a liability in (ii) above.

In (ii) above 'other relevant provision' is made if provision is made under the arrangements for the borrower company to discharge a liability of another person to it to enable them to purchase a security.

A company which has a debtor repo or debtor quasi-repo or has liability which is discharged under a relevant arrangement, in respect a repo transaction where condition (ii) above is satisfied, is treated for the purposes of corporation tax on the transaction as if it still held the securities, provided that this treatment is in accordance with the company's accounts, prepared using GAAP. Any manufactured payments representing income on the securities paid to the borrower company will not be taxable on it. Instead, it will be taxed on the interest or dividends actually arising on the securities. Special rules apply where overseas securities form the subject of the repo at outset.

Under the loan relationship rules (see 46 LOAN RELATIONSHIPS), where the borrower company has a debtor repo or debtor quasi-repo, the advance under the repo is to be treated as a money debt of the borrower company or partnership (of which a company is a member) due to the person who originally bought the securities. Any amount paid in respect of the arrangements, which is treated under GAAP as a finance charge is treated for corporation tax purposes as interest paid at the earlier of the date the repurchase takes place or it becomes apparent that there will be no repurchase.

The disposal and repurchase are ignored for capital gains purposes. When it becomes apparent that the repurchase will not take place or the liability no longer appears in the borrower company's balance sheet (other than because of repurchase of the securities) ('the accounting condition'), the borrower company is treated for corporation tax on capital gains as disposing of the securities at market value on that date. However, where a chargeable gain has been triggered under *FA 2007, Sch 13 para 6(3)* in respect of the original sale of securities and the borrower subsequently repurchases the security, the repurchase is ignored for the purpose of corporation tax on a capital gain.

Creditor repos. 'Creditor repos' look at the repo transaction from the point of view of the lender i.e. the party purchasing the securities forming the subject of the repo. A creditor repo arises where:

I under the arrangement, the borrowing company receives from the lender money or other assets ('the advance');

II under GAAP the lender's accounts show a financial asset in respect of the advance;

III under the arrangement the borrower sells securities at any time to the lender;

IV under the arrangement, there is a right or obligation on the lender to sell the securities at any later time;

V under GAAP the subsequent sale would cancel the financial asset in the lender's accounts.

A *creditor quasi-repo* exists where I and II above are satisfied and, in addition:

(A) under that or any other arrangement a person sells securities to any person;

(B) the lender is obliged or has a right under the arrangements to sell any securities at any time or there is such a right or obligation on any other person and the arrangements make other relevant provision;

(C) under GAAP, the financial asset in the accounts of the lender company is removed by the sale of securities, receipt of an asset or the discharge of a liability under the arrangements.

The term '*lender*' includes a partnership of which the lender is a partner.

'*Other relevant provision*' is made by an arrangement where it makes provision for:

- receipt of any asset from the lender under that arrangement to enable the other person to make a subsequent sale; or
- the discharge of any liability to the lender (by set off or otherwise) under that arrangement to so enable the other person.

Where a lender company has a creditor repo or a creditor quasi-repo, it is treated as not holding the securities for corporation tax purposes, unless under GAAP it is recognised in the lender's profit and loss account, statement of recognised gains and losses, statement of changes in equity or any other statement relating to the profit and loss account. Therefore there may be no corporation tax on income arising on the securities, and no corporation tax relief on any manufactured payment.

For corporation tax purposes, the holder of a creditor or creditor quasi-repo is treated as if he had made a loan to the borrower and the advance as a money debt under the loan relationships rules. Any return on the loan accounted for under GAAP is to be treated as if it were interest received at the earlier of when the repurchase takes place or it becomes clear that the repurchase will not take place.

No chargeable gain will arise on the securities sold under a creditor repo, unless it becomes clear that the securities will not be sold or 'the accounting condition' is not met. This occurs if the holder's accounts, as prepared under GAAP, do not show the amount advanced under the repo as a financial asset.

Extensive powers to implement the new regime by statutory instrument are provided for.

5.6 Anti-Avoidance

Anti-avoidance. Where there is no creditor repo or creditor quasi-repo, but under an arrangement a person receives an advance, in money or assets, from a company or a partnership with a company as a member, under 'the applicable accounting assumption' there would be a creditor repo or creditor quasi-repo taking V above into account, the arrangement is intended to provide a return which equates to interest on an investment and the purpose or one of the main purposes is the realisation of a tax advantage, the company is treated as having a creditor repo and quasi-interest is treated as received. '*The applicable accounting assumption*' is that, under GAAP, the accounts of the company or partnership for the period in which an advance is made, show the advance as an asset.

Where, under a creditor repo, the lender is required to make a payment to the borrower representing income on the securities forming the subject of the repo, it is treated as making manufactured payments on the dates of payment and income tax is deductible from the payments by the lender [*ITA 2007, ss 918–926*]. There is a similar provision for debtor repos. Where there is a charge on a manufactured payment, any actual payment made is treated as not made for the purposes of deduction of income tax at source.

Definitions. For the purpose of the new repo regime:

'A*rrangement*' includes any legally binding, or non-enforceable agreement or understanding and an arrangement is in force from the date of sale of the securities until the earlier of the date of the relevant repurchase and when it becomes apparent that repurchase will not take place.

Reference to receiving an asset includes deriving any value or benefit from an asset, whether directly or indirectly.

Where a person is acting as nominee in a purchase or sale of securities, or in an option or with regard to an obligation to buy securities, then the purchase of the rights is treated as that of the person for whom he is acting.

Where accounts are not drawn up in accordance with GAAP, for the purposes of taxing repo transactions it is assumed that they were so drawn up.

An arrangement is in force from the date of original sale of the securities until the earlier of the date the relevant repurchase occurs and when it becomes apparent that the repurchase will not take place.

[*FA 2007, Sch 13*].

5.6 REPOS – OLD REGIME

This regime will cease to apply from the date the new repo regime (see 5.5 above) takes effect. (The date is to be determined by statutory instrument.)

Subject to the exception mentioned below, where a person (the 'original owner') has transferred securities to another person (the 'interim holder') under an agreement to sell them entered into on or after 1 May 1995 and before a date to be determined by statutory instrument, and the original owner or a CONNECTED PERSON (19) is required to buy them back under, or in consequence of the exercise of an option (whether a put or a call option) acquired under, the same or a 'related' agreement at a different price, the difference between the sale and repurchase price is treated for income and corporation tax purposes as a payment of interest which:

(*a*) where the repurchase price is greater than the sale price, is made by the repurchaser on a deemed loan from the interim holder of an amount equal to the sale price; and

(*b*) otherwise is made by the interim holder on a deemed loan from the repurchaser of an amount equal to the repurchase price.

In either case, the deemed interest is treated for income and corporation tax purposes as becoming due when the repurchase price becomes due and, accordingly, as paid when that price is paid. For income and corporation tax purposes (other than those of the current provisions and *ICTA 1988, ss 737A, 737C* — see 5.9 below), and for the purposes of *TCGA 1992* (unless *TCGA 1992, s 263A*, see below, applies), the repurchase price is treated as reduced by the amount of the deemed interest where (*a*) above applies or as increased by that amount where (*b*) above applies. For the purposes of *ICTA 1988, s 209(2)(d)* (interest treated as a distribution, see 23.4 DISTRIBUTIONS) any deemed interest payment under (*a*) above is deemed to be interest in respect of securities issued by the repurchaser and held by the interim holder; for 2003/04 and earlier years, this also applied for the purposes of *ICTA 1988, s 209(2)(da)* (now repealed).

The repurchase price, in a case where *ICTA 1988, s 737A* (see 5.9 below) applies (or would apply were it in force in relation to the securities in question) is that price which is or would be applicable by virtue of *ICTA 1988, s 737C(3)(b), (9)* or *(11)(c)*. For agreements made after 8 April 2003, in cases involving the exercise of an option (whether a put or a call option), the sale price must be adjusted for any consideration given for the option (except where such consideration is brought into account under the derivative contracts provisions for companies (see 28 FINANCIAL INSTRUMENTS AND DERIVATIVE CONTRACTS).

For corporation tax purposes, deemed interest under these provisions is treated as payable under a loan relationship, in respect of which the debits and credits to be brought into account are trading or non-trading according to the extent to which the repurchase is in the course of activities forming an integral part of the company's trade. Any foreign exchange gain or loss arising on the original sale price over the period of the sale and repurchase agreement is to be similarly treated under the loan relationship rules; *ICTA 1988, s 730BB*, which applies to agreements made after 8 April 2003, is designed to provide clarity of treatment for such gains and losses. See 46 LOAN RELATIONSHIPS.

For purposes other than corporation tax, HMRC generally accept that the deemed interest is short interest, except where it is clear that the transaction was entered into as a substitute for long term finance, and in particular where it is clear finance was arranged in this way specifically to avoid deduction of tax at source. (Revenue Tax Bulletin December 1995 p 266).

The exception referred to above disapplies these provisions (unless regulations under *ICTA 1988, s 737E*; see 5.9 below, otherwise provide) if the agreement(s) in question are non-arm's length agreements, or if all the benefits and risks arising from fluctuations in the market value of the securities accrue to, or fall on, the interim holder.

The Treasury has power to make regulations providing for an amount of deemed interest under these provisions to fall within the exemptions for pension business of insurance companies, for exempt approved pension schemes or superannuation funds or certain other such schemes, or for funds held for personal pension schemes or retirement annuity contracts. See *SI 1995 No 3036* (as amended).

See also *SI 1998 No 3177, regs 16, 17* (as amended) as regards securities which, prior to their repurchase, are converted from currencies of States which have adopted the euro into euros.

[*ICTA 1988, ss 730A, 730BB*); *FA 2002, Sch 25 para 52; FA 2003, Sch 38 paras 5, 10–12, 16, 20, 21(2)(3); FA 2004, Sch 10 para 78, Sch 42 Pt 2(2)*].

Where the above provisions apply (or would apply were the sale and repurchase price different), the acquisition and disposal by the interim holder, and (except where the repurchaser is or may be different from the original owner) the disposal and acquisition (as repurchaser) by the original owner, are disregarded for capital gains tax purposes. This does not, however, apply:

(A) where the repurchase price falls to be computed by reference to provisions of *ICTA 1988, s 737C* (see 5.9 below) which are not in force in relation to the securities when the repurchase price becomes due; or

(B) if the agreement(s) in question are non-arm's length agreements, or if all the benefits or risks arising from fluctuations in the market value of the securities accrue to, or fall on, the interim holder; or

(C) in relation to any disposal or acquisition of qualifying corporate bonds (see Tolley's Capital Gains Tax under Qualifying Corporate Bonds) where the securities disposed of by the original owner, or those acquired by him or another person as repurchaser, are not such bonds.

See also *SI 1998 No 3177, regs 14–18* (as amended) as regards conversions of securities from currencies of States which have adopted the euro into euros.

[*TCGA 1992, s 263A; FA 2007, Sch 14 paras 4, 5, 7, 8, 12*].

Interpretation. For the above purposes, the following apply.

(i) Agreements are 'related' if entered into in pursuance of the same arrangement.

(ii) References to buying back securities include buying back similar securities, and 'repurchase' is construed accordingly. Securities are 'similar' if they give entitlement to the same rights against the same persons as to capital, interest and dividends, and to the same enforcement remedies. Where securities are converted from the currency of a State which has adopted the euro into euros (a '*euroconversion*'), the new securities are treated as 'similar' (see *SI 1998 No 3177, regs 3, 14*).

(iii) 'Securities' had the same meaning as in *ICTA 1988, s 737A* (see 5.9 below).

[*ICTA 1988, s 730B; FA 2007, Sch 14 para 7*].

The Treasury has broad powers to make regulations providing for the above provisions to apply with modifications (including exceptions and omissions) in relation to cases involving any arrangement for the sale and repurchase of securities where the obligation to repurchase is not performed, or the repurchase option not exercised, or where provision is made by or under any agreement:

(*a*) for different or additional securities to be treated as, or included with, securities which, for the purposes of the repurchase, are to represent securities transferred in pursuance of the original sale; or

(*b*) for any securities to be treated as not included with securities which, for repurchase purposes, are to represent securities transferred in pursuance of the original sale; or

(*c*) for the sale or repurchase price to be determined or varied wholly or partly by reference to fluctuations, in the period from the making of the agreement for the original sale, in the value of securities transferred in pursuance of that sale, or in the value of securities treated as representing those securities, or for any person to be required, where there are such fluctuations, to make any payment in the course of that period and before the repurchase price becomes due.

Regulations may also make such modifications in relation to cases where corresponding arrangements are made by an agreement, or by related agreements, in relation to securities which are to be redeemed in the period after their sale, those arrangements being such that the vendor (or a person connected with him), instead of being required to repurchase the securities or acquiring an option to do so, is granted rights in respect of the benefits that will accrue from their redemption. They may also provide for modifications in relation to cases involving any arrangement for the sale and repurchase of securities in relation to which there is an agreement which would not have been entered into by persons dealing at arm's length.

[*ICTA 1988, s 737E; FA 2003, Sch 38 paras 8, 13, 21(2); FA 2007, Sch 14, para 8*].

Although of wider general application, these provisions were introduced as part of a package of measures designed to facilitate an open market in the sale and repurchase of gilt-edged securities ('gilt repos'). See also 5.9 below, 37.8 INCOME TAX IN RELATION TO A COMPANY. For a brief overview of the changes made by *FA 2003* to the tax provisions on sale and repurchase agreements, see Revenue Tax Bulletin August 2003 pp 1052, 1053.

Simon's Direct Tax Service. See **A7.13**.

5.7 INCOME RECEIVED ON SECURITIES HELD FOR ONE MONTH OR LESS

The following provisions apply to income received on securities held for one month or less, or held for more than one month but not more than six months *and either* purchase or sale was not at current market price *or* agreement regarding sale was made at, or before, purchase (see *ICTA 1988, s 731(3)*). [*ICTA 1988, ss 731–735; FA 2007, Sch 14 para 6*].

Effects as regards various classes of recipient are as in (*a*) to (*d*) below.

In ascertaining whether the securities are held for more than one or six months, sale under prior option is regarded as a sale at option date [*ICTA 1988, s 731(4)*], and a sale of 'similar securities' is taken into account. [*ICTA 1988, s 731(5)(10)*]. A purchase or sale effected as a direct result of the exercise of a 'qualifying option' (broadly, a traded or financial option within *TCGA 1992, s 144(8)*) is treated as being at current market price (and so excluded from these provisions) if the first buyer acquired, or became subject to, the option on arm's length terms. [*ICTA 1988, s 731(4A)–(4C)*]. The '*appropriate amount*' is the pre-acquisition portion of the dividend, interest etc. calculated from last 'ex-div' day. [*ICTA 1988, s 735(3)*]. See *ICTA 1988, s 735(4)* if there is no last 'ex-div' day. In the case of (*a*) below, the portion taken is of net interest after deduction of tax and the amounts of actual dividends. In the case of (*b*), (*c*) and (*d*) below, it is the gross amount of interest and the amounts of dividends plus related tax credits. In all cases, special rules apply in relation to foreign income dividends within *ICTA 1988, Pt VI, Ch VA* (prior to their abolition after 5 April 1999). [*ICTA 1988, s 731(9)-(9B), s 735(1)(2); F(No 2)A 1997, Sch 6 para 14*].

These provisions do not apply where the purchaser is required by the purchase agreement to make to the vendor, before his re-sale of the securities, a payment representative of the interest, or where the purchaser is treated by *ICTA 1988, s 737A(5)* (see 5.9 below) as being required to make a payment representative of a dividend on them. [*ICTA 1988, s 731(2A)*].

Where there is a 'repo agreement' in relation to any securities, neither their purchase or repurchase, nor their sale or sale back, is taken into account under these provisions. The securities purchased by the original owner from the person to whom securities were sold under the agreement (the '*interim holder*') are instead treated under these provisions as the same securities, and as purchased at the same time, as his original holding This does not, however, apply if the agreement(s) under which the arrangements are made are on non-arm's length terms, or if the interim holder bears any of the benefits or risks of market value fluctuations before the securities are repurchased. There is a '*repo agreement*' if the original owner sells the securities in pursuance of an agreement, and under the same or a related agreement either:

- is required to buy back the securities, either as a result of a straightforward obligation or the interim holder's exercise of an option; or
- acquires an option to buy them back which he subsequently exercises; or
- is entitled to receive from the interim holder an amount equal to any redemption proceeds.

See *ICTA 1988, s 730B* (under 5.6 above) for 'related agreements', 'securities' and the extended meaning of 'buying back' securities. From a date to be determined by statutory instrument, the references to 'related agreements' and the extended meaning of 'buying back' securities is in *ICTA 1988, s 731(2F),(2G); FA 2007, Sch 14 para 6.*

[*ICTA 1988, s 731(2B)–(2F); FA 2003, Sch 38 paras 6, 21(2); FA 2007, Sch 14 para 6*].

(*a*) **Share dealers.** The net 'appropriate amount' of the interest etc. is treated for all tax purposes as a reduction of the purchase price. This treatment does not apply if the interest falls to be taken into account in computing the first buyer's Schedule D, Case I or II profits (see 66.74 TRADING INCOME). It also does not apply to overseas securities if *ICTA 1988, s 732(4)* is complied with. [*ICTA 1988, s 732*].

See *ICTA 1988, s 731(7)(8)* regarding change in ownership, or commencement, of trade.

HMRC may make regulations by statutory instrument, effective from a day to be appointed therein, imposing conditions for the exclusion of market makers to apply, and making appropriate provision in regard to recognised investment exchanges other than the Stock Exchange. [*ICTA 1988, s 738(1)*].

(*b*) **Person entitled to exemption from tax.** Exemption does not extend to the gross 'appropriate amount' of the interest etc. and any annual payment out of the interest etc. is treated as not paid out of taxed income. [*ICTA 1988, s 733*].

(*c*) **Traders other than share dealers** (whether company or not). The gross 'appropriate amount' of the interest etc. and tax thereon is ignored in calculating loss repayment claim under *ICTA 1988, s 380* or *s 381* (see Tolley's Income Tax under Losses). [*ICTA 1988, s 734(1)*].

(*d*) **Companies other than share dealers**. The gross 'appropriate amount' and tax thereon is ignored for tax purposes except that net equivalent is treated as capital distribution in calculation of chargeable gain. [*ICTA 1988, s 734(2)*].

'Securities' are defined to exclude those within the accrued income scheme (see Tolley's Income Tax under Accrued Income Scheme). [*ICTA 1988, s 731(9)*].

Simon's Direct Tax Service. See A7.3.

5.8 **'DIVIDEND STRIPPING'**

The 'dividend stripping' provisions of *ICTA 1988, s 736* apply where a **share dealing company holds shares or securities amounting to 10% of all the shares etc. of that class** issued by a company resident in the UK and, as a result of one or more distributions made in respect of that holding, the value at any accounting date (but see below) of any share or security comprised therein is materially reduced below its value at the time when it was acquired. So much of that reduction as is attributable to the distribution or distributions (the '*relevant reduction*'), is treated as a trading receipt of the dealing company when the holding is realised (or appropriated so that it is no longer dealing stock). Until such realisation or appropriation, the relevant reduction is treated as an addition to the value of the holding for valuation purposes.

Where only part of the holding is realised or appropriated, a proportionate part of the relevant reduction is brought into account as a trading receipt.

A reduction in value immediately before realisation or appropriation (as well as at an accounting date) is within this section.

Securities, shares, etc. having different entitlements or obligations are treated as being of different classes, and a company's holdings of different classes are treated as separate holdings. Subject to this, however, a company has a 10% holding in a particular class if the aggregate of its own holdings and those of persons connected with it (see 19 CONNECTED PERSONS) amounts to 10%.

A company is a *dealing company* in relation to a holding if a profit on its sale would be taken into account in computing the company's trading profits.

Where *section 736* applies in relation to a distribution to which *ICTA 1988, s 732* (reduction in price of shares purchased by dealers) also applies, any reduction, under that section, in the purchase price of the shares is to be adjusted 'as seems appropriate to HMRC'.

[*ICTA 1988, s 736*].

Simon's Direct Tax Service. See A7.1201.

5.9 'MANUFACTURED' DIVIDENDS OR INTEREST

The provisions of *ICTA 1988, s 736A, Sch 23A* have effect in relation to certain cases (see (*a*)–(*c*) below) where, under a contract or other arrangement for the transfer of shares or securities, a person is required to pay to the other party an amount representing a dividend or payment of interest thereon.

Where these provisions apply, the intention is that both payer and recipient of the amount in question should be in the same position, for tax purposes, as if the payment had in fact been a dividend or payment of interest. See *Schedule 23A paras 2–6* for the detailed mechanism by which this is achieved in each case. See also Tolley's Income Tax under Anti-Avoidance for the application of the manufactured dividends provisions to individuals and trusts.

The circumstances in which these provisions apply are as follows.

(*a*) *Manufactured dividends on UK equities.* This applies where one of the parties to a transfer of UK equities is required to pay the other an amount (a '*manufactured dividend*') representative of a dividend thereon. Special provisions apply in relation to foreign income dividends within *ICTA 1988, Pt VI, Ch VA* (until their abolition after 5 April 1999).

(*b*) *Manufactured interest on UK securities.* This applies where one of the parties to a transfer of UK securities is required to pay the other an amount ('*manufactured interest*') representative of a periodical payment of interest thereon. (See 46.42 LOAN RELATIONSHIPS for the corporation tax treatment of manufactured interest.)

(*c*) *Manufactured overseas dividends.* This applies where one of the parties to a transfer of overseas securities (including, before 1 April 2001, quoted Eurobonds held in a recognised clearing system, see Tolley's Income Tax under Deduction of Tax at Source) is required to pay the other an amount (a '*manufactured overseas dividend*') representative of an overseas dividend thereon.

As regards (*c*) above, HMRC was able before 1 November 2003 to arrange for manufactured overseas dividends to be paid without deduction of tax in certain cases where a double taxation agreement is in force with the territory in which the recipient of the dividend (not being UK resident) is resident. See *SI 1993 No 1957* (as amended and revoked with effect from 1 November 2003). From 1 November 2003, the general requirement for the payer to deduct and account for tax in relation to payments of manufactured overseas dividends to non-UK recipients is removed by *SI 2003 No 2582*.

There are provisions to counteract any artificial allocation of a payment between the manufactured dividend or interest and any associated stock lending fee.

There are also provisions which deny tax relief for manufactured payments made by a company in pursuance of any arrangements that have an unallowable purpose, to the extent the relief is attributable (on a just and reasonable basis) to the unallowable purpose. Arrangements have an unallowable purpose where the purposes for which the company is a party to them include a purpose which is not among the business or other commercial purposes of the company. This provision applies to manufactured payments made by companies after 1 July 2004 except where the arrangements (or part of the arrangements) were entered into or acted upon before that date. In that case the provisions apply to manufactured payments made on or after 22 July 2004 to the extent that the income or gains arise or accrue (on a just and reasonable apportionment) after 1 July 2004 and are chargeable to corporation tax. HMRC have published a guidance note (available on their website) on this provision and on how it will be applied (see Revenue Tax Bulletin August 2004 p 1132).

The Treasury may make 'dividend manufacturing regulations' for the purposes of these provisions which may, *inter alia*, extend the circumstances in which (*a*)-(*c*) above may apply. See *SI 1993 No 2004* (as amended) and *SI 1996 No 1826* (as amended).

[*ICTA 1988, s 736A, Sch 23A; F(No 2)A 1997, Sch 6 para 17; FA 2000, Sch 40 Pt II(17); FA 2004, s 137; SI 2004 No 2310, Article 37*].

The Treasury has power to make regulations providing for any manufactured payment within *Schedule 23A* to be treated as falling within the exemptions for pension business of insurance companies, for exempt approved pension schemes or superannuation funds or certain other such schemes, or for funds held for personal pension schemes or retirement annuity contracts. [*ICTA 1988, s 737D*]. See *SI 1995 No 3036* (as amended) as regards payments.

Stock lending arrangements. Special rules apply to stock lending arrangements. Where, under such an arrangement, interest (including dividends) on stock transferred is paid to a person other than the lender, with no provision for the lender to receive a payment representative of that interest, *Schedule 23A* (and regulations thereunder) apply as if the borrower were required to make, and did make, such a payment on the date the interest it represents is paid. For deemed payments made after 2 October 2000, the borrower is not entitled to any deduction in computing profits or gains for income or corporation tax purposes or against total income or (as the case may be) total profits, and (in the case of a company) no amount for which a deduction is so prohibited may be surrendered by way of group relief. [*ICTA 1988, s 736B; FA 2001, s 84; SI 1997 Nos 992, 993* (*as amended*)].

See generally HMRC Inspector's Manual IM 4345 *et seq.* Guidance notes to help people in the financial markets to comply with the tax rules on manufactured payments are available on HMRC's website.

Deemed interest on cash collateral. Where a borrower is treated under the above provisions as paying an amount representative of interest on any securities ('*the relevant securities*') and also an amount ('*cash collateral*') is payable (under any arrangement) to the lender to secure the discharge of the requirement to transfer the relevant securities back to the lender, the borrower is treated as receiving an amount of interest payable in respect of the cash collateral. This applies to stock-lending arrangements **made on or after 5 December 2005** which are designed to produce a return to the borrower which equates in substance to a return on an investment of money at interest and where the main purpose, or one of the main purposes, of the arrangement is the avoidance of tax. Where an arrangement was entered into before 5 December 2005, the interest will be treated as received on any cash collateral computed from the date there is any substitution of securities under that arrangement. The interest is treated as payable on a money debt and taxable under *FA 1996, s 100* of the loan relationship rules, the credit to be brought into account using an amortised cost basis of accounting (see 46.46 LOAN RELATIONSHIPS). (The measure effectively applies where a company swaps taxable interest on cash for income on the relevant securities such as dividends, the income being either not taxed or less highly taxed.)

The interest is to be computed at a commercial rate of interest and treated as if it is received on the date of the transfer back of the relevant securities and payable in respect of the period beginning with the date on which they were transferred to the borrower and ending with the return date. It is reduced by any interest which the borrower actually receives in respect of the collateral for the period. Where the stock-lending arrangement is made after 21 March 2006, it is payable on the amount of the cash collateral at the return date but if the amount of collateral varies at any time on or before the return date, it is taken as payable on the highest amount. Reference to the transfer of securities back has the same meaning as under *TCGA 1992, s 263B* (as amended by *FA 2007, Sch 14 para 12*) and if it becomes apparent that the borrower will not transfer any securities back, the borrower is treated as transferring them back on the date it becomes so apparent.

[*ICTA 1988, s 736C; FA 2006, Sch 6 para 3*].

Quasi-stock lending arrangements and quasi-cash collateral. Where an arrangement, made after 21 March 2006, is not a stock-lending arrangement it is treated as if it were a stock-lending arrangement if, under the arrangement (a '*quasi-stock lending arrangement*'), a lender transfers securities to a borrower and a requirement is imposed on the borrower or other person to transfer any or all of the securities, or other property, back to the lender or other person. In relation to arrangements made after 21 March 2006, cash collateral (see above) under either stock-lending or quasi-stock lending arrangements includes '*quasi-cash collateral*' which is any money payable or any property transferable to or for the benefit of the lender under such an arrangement, or a person connected with that lender (see 19 CONNECTED PERSONS) , for the purpose of securing the discharge of the requirement to transfer any or all of the securities or other property back to the lender or other person. The amount of quasi-cash collateral relating to property other than money is determined by reference to its market value.

Where a quasi-stock lending arrangement involving cash collateral (see above) is designed to provide a tax advantage for a person other than the borrower, that other person is treated as the person receiving the deemed interest in respect of the cash collateral. In any quasi-stock lending arrangement involving cash collateral, the references in *ICTA 1988, s 736C* (above) are widened such that a cash collateral payable to or for the benefit of a lender includes it being payable to a person connected with the lender, a return designed to benefit a borrower includes a return designed to benefit any other person and a transfer back of any or all securities or other property by the borrower to the lender includes such transfers by any person to the lender or any other person.

[*ICTA 1988, s 736D; FA 2006, Sch 6 para 4*].

Sale and repurchase of securities. From a date to be determined by statutory instrument (when the new regime for repos is introduced – see 5.5 above) the following provisions will be repealed.

ICTA 1988, Sch 23A above and the dividend manufacturing regulations thereunder apply where a person (the 'transferor') agrees to sell any 'securities', and under the same agreement (or under another agreement under the same arrangement) he (or a person connected with him (within *ICTA 1988, s 839*)) is required to buy back the same or 'similar' securities (whether as a result of a straightforward obligation or the exercise of a put option), or acquires an option (which he subsequently exercises) to buy them back, and either of the following two sets of conditions is fulfilled. The first set of conditions is that:

(*a*) as a result of the transaction, a dividend on the securities is receivable by a person other than the transferor;

(*b*) the agreement(s) do not contain a requirement for an amount representative of the dividend to be paid to the transferor on or before the date the repurchase price becomes due; and

(*c*) it is reasonable to assume that the repurchase price took into account the fact that the dividend was receivable by a person other than the transferor.

The second set of conditions (relevant only to agreements made after 8 April 2003) is that:

(*a*) a dividend which becomes payable in respect of the securities is receivable otherwise than by the transferor;

(*b*) the transferor (or a person connected with him) is required to make a payment representative of the dividend;

(*c*) there is no requirement for a person to pay to the transferor an amount representative of the dividend on or before the date the repurchase price becomes due; and

(*d*) it is reasonable to assume that, in arriving at the repurchase price, account was taken of these circumstances.

The provisions apply (subject to below) as if the person from whom the securities are repurchased (or from whom the transferor has the right to repurchase them) were required under the arrangements for transfer of the securities to pay the transferor an amount representative of the dividend mentioned in (*a*) above, and a payment were accordingly made by that person to the transferor on the date the repurchase price of the securities becomes due. For the corporation tax treatment of such deemed payments, see 46.42 LOAN RELATIONSHIPS.

In relation to agreements made after 26 June 2006 to sell securities, where the borrower is not the person to whom the transferor agreed to sell the securities, the borrower is not entitled to any deduction in computing profits or gains for income or corporation tax purposes or against total income or total profits, and no amount for which a deduction is so prohibited may be surrendered by way of group relief. This provision is intended to reverse the effect of the decision by the High Court (confirming the Special Commissioners' decision) in *Bank of Ireland Britain Holdings Ltd v HMRC Ch D [2007] EWHC 941 (Ch)*. The case involved a repo agreement between an Irish bank, its UK subsidiary and a Cayman Islands company in which a deemed interest payment from the Cayman Islands company to the Irish bank was treated as arising under *ICTA 1988, s 730A*(*2*) (which was non-taxable in the UK) and a corresponding deemed dividend payment by the UK company to the Irish bank was treated as arising under *ICTA 1988, s 737A*(*5*) which was tax deductible.

'*Securities*' means UK equities and securities and overseas securities (as under *ICTA 1988, Sch 23A para 1*(*1*)), and securities are '*similar*' if they carry the same entitlement as to capital and interest (or dividends) and the same enforcement remedies. Where securities are converted from the currency of a State which has adopted the euro into euros (a '*euroconversion*'), the new securities are treated as 'similar' (see *SI 1998 No 3177, regs 3, 14*). References in *ICTA 1988, s 737A* to dividends are, in the case of UK securities, to periodical payments of interest, and in the case of overseas securities, to overseas dividends (as under *ICTA 1988, Sch 23A para 1*(*1*)).

There are special provisions (in *ICTA 1988, s 737C*) for determining the amount of the deemed manufactured dividend or interest for these purposes, and for a corresponding adjustment to be made for tax purposes to the repurchase price of the securities.

Special provisions apply to dividends that represent payments of distributions of the tax-exempt profits of a REIT or principal company of a REIT group (see 44.11 INVESTMENT TRUSTS).

See also *SI 1998 No 3177, reg 17* as regards securities which, prior to their repurchase, are converted from currencies of States which have adopted the euro into euros.

[*ICTA 1988, ss 737A, 737B, 737C*); *FA 2003, Sch 38 paras 1–3, 7, 17, 21*(*1*)(*2*); *FA 2006, s 139*(*5*), *Sch 6 para 5; FA 2007, Sch 14*].

See *SI 1995 No 3220* as regards such modification in cases where securities are redeemed rather than being repurchased, and where other securities are substituted for those originally transferred.

See also 5.7 above and, as regards application of accrued income scheme to such securities, Tolley's Income Tax under Accrued Income Scheme.

Simon's Direct Tax Service. See A7.8.

5.10 **TREASURY CONSENTS — TRANSFER ETC. OF SECURITIES TO NON-RESIDENTS**

Consent must be obtained from the Treasury for a body corporate resident in the UK (*a*) to cause or permit a non-resident body corporate over which it has 'control' to create or issue any share or debenture; or

(*b*) to transfer, or cause or permit to be transferred, to any person any share or debenture of a non-resident body corporate over which it has 'control' (or a beneficial interest in such share or debenture), if the resident body has an interest in such share or debenture. [*ICTA 1988, s 765*(*1*)(*c*)(*d*)].

'*Control*' is the power to secure that the affairs of a body corporate are conducted in accordance with the wishes of the resident body, whether by shareholding, voting power or powers given by Articles of Association etc., and whether directly or through another body corporate. If the non-resident body would be a partnership if resident in the UK, the resident body has control if it is entitled to more than half of the income or assets of the non-resident body. [*ICTA 1988, ss 767*(*5*), *840*].

Exemptions apply as follows.

(i) The giving by a non-resident body corporate to its bankers of any security for moneys due or to become due from one to the other by reason of a transaction entered into between them in the normal course of the latter's business as bankers (see (*a*) above). [*ICTA 1988, s 765*(*2*)].

(ii) The giving by a non-resident body corporate to an 'insurance company' of any security for moneys due or to become due from one to the other by reason of a transaction entered into between them in the ordinary course of the latter's business by way of investment of its 'funds' (see (*a*) above). [*ICTA 1988, s 765*(*3*)].

For this purpose '*insurance company*' means a body corporate lawfully carrying on business as an insurer, and '*funds*' means the funds held by it in connection with that business. [*ICTA 1988, s 767*(*5*)].

(iii) The transfer of shares to qualify a person to act as a director (exempted from (*b*) above). [*ICTA 1988, s 765*(*1*)(*d*)].

(iv) Neither (*a*) nor (*b*) above applies to a transaction which is a movement of capital within *Directive No 88/361/EEC, Article 1* (which includes such movements within the European Economic Area). Where but for this exemption a transaction would be unlawful (in particular, where it is not within the general consents), the UK resident company must:

(A) within six months of the transaction give to HMRC such information relating to the transaction or to persons connected with it as HMRC may by regulation require (see *SI 1990 No 1671*); and

(B) give to HMRC such further particulars as HMRC may by notice require, within 60 days.

The address for such notification is Mary Sharp, Peter Steeds or Des Hanna (for s 765) or David Price (for s 765A), CT & VAT (International CT), 100 Parliament Street, London SW1A 2BQ.

Penalties of up to £3,000 (and £600 per day for continued failure) may be imposed under *TMA 1970, s 98* for failure to comply with the above requirements. [*ICTA 1988, s 765A; SI 1990 No 1671*].

HMRC Statement of Practice, SP 2/92 (as revised) sets out the views of the Treasury and HMRC where there may be doubt as to whether a transaction is a movement of capital to which *Article 1* relates, and gives guidance on the procedure for making a report as required under (A) above. See also HMRC Company Taxation Manual, CTM 34490.

Granting of consent. The Treasury may give a general consent or confine it to specified transactions of, or relating to, a specified body corporate ('special' consent). Conditions may be imposed in either case and a general consent may be revoked. The consent 'shall be published in such a way as to give any person entitled to the benefit of it an adequate opportunity of getting to know of it, unless in the opinion of the Treasury publication is not necessary for that purpose'. [*ICTA 1988, s 765*(*4*)].

The Treasury is also empowered to give general consents (and see HMRC Company Taxation Manual, CTM 34490 as regards the application in practice of their requirements). See also CTM 34470 for the definitions of 'resident group', 'overseas group' and 'territorial group' in the General Consents. Notes for guidance on applications for Special Treasury Consent may be obtained from the same address. Applications should be sent to CT & VAT (International CT) 100 Parliament Street, London SW1A 2BQ.

Penalties. Any person who knowingly and actively participates in an offence under this section is liable to imprisonment for two years or to a fine of £10,000 or to both. If the offender is a body corporate, the maximum fine is £10,000 or three times the amount of tax attributable to the income, profits or gains (including chargeable gains) arising in the three years immediately preceding the commission of the offence, whichever is the greater. [*ICTA 1988, s 766*(*1*)(*3*)].

Proceedings under this section may not be instituted in England or Wales without the consent of the Attorney-General, or in Northern Ireland without the consent of the Attorney-General for Northern Ireland. In any proceedings against a director (or purported director) of the resident body corporate, he is assumed to be a party to any act of that body, unless he proves that it was done without his consent or connivance, and to have known that such an act would result in an offence under this section, unless he proves the contrary. [*ICTA 1988, s 766*(*2*)(*4*)].

See 54 PENALTIES.

Company becoming non-resident. See 60.7, 60.8 RESIDENCE.

Simon's Direct Tax Service. See D4.130 *et seq.*, **D4.140.**

5.11 **TRANSFER PRICING**

ICTA 1988, Sch 28AA imposes a charge to eliminate a tax advantage gained where transactions are not carried out at arm's length prices. The scope of the transfer pricing rules were extended by *FA 2004, ss 30–37, Sch 5*, with effect for accounting periods beginning on or after 1 April 2004, to include domestic transactions between UK parties. At the same time, the thin capitalisation rules under *ICTA 1988, s 209*(*2*)(*da*)(*8A*)–(*8F*) (see 23.5 DISTRIBUTIONS) were repealed and subsumed within the transfer pricing regime. See 67 TRANSFER PRICING.

5.12 **TRANSACTIONS OF CERTAIN DEALING AND NON-DEALING COMPANIES**

This section applies if a company dealing in securities, land or buildings is entitled to a deduction in computing its profits for a payment made to, or for depreciation of a right against, an associated company which does not deal in shares etc. Where the amount of the payment or depreciation is not brought into account in computing the profits or gains of the non-dealing company, the non-dealing company is charged to corporation tax under Schedule D, Case VI. If the non-dealing company carries on a trade, the amount may be charged as part of its normal trading income, if the company so elects. If it carries on a number of trades, the amount may be allotted to whichever trade the non-dealing company chooses.

A payment made in respect of abortive expenditure of a non-dealing company carrying on (or formed to carry on) a trade is excluded.

The amount is deemed to have been received on the last day of the dealing company's accounting period.

HMRC have powers to require information of any person who may have incurred liability under this section.

[*ICTA 1988, s 774; ITTOIA 2005, Sch 1 para 310*].

Simon's Direct Tax Service. See **D2.527**.

5.13 FACTORING OF INCOME RECEIPTS ETC.

The provisions described below are intended to counter, from **6 June 2006**, the situation in which a person enters into financing arrangements that equate in substance to his taking out a loan but which are structured in such a way as to effectively give him tax relief for repayment of principal as well as for finance charges.

Say, for example, a borrower (B) has the opportunity to take out a loan of £50,000, under which B would repay the loan to the lender (L) over five years together with total interest of £5,000. Tax relief might be available for the £5,000 interest but not for the repayment of the £50,000 principal. As an alternative, B transfers to L for £50,000 an asset that is fully expected to produce income of £55,000 over the next five years, at the end of which the asset will be transferred back to B for nothing. L receives £55,000 for an outlay of £50,000. B then claims that the transfer of the asset to L either gives rise only to a chargeable gain (which may be relatively small due to high base cost and available reliefs) or is not taxable at all, and that he is not chargeable on the income of £55,000 which is received not by him but by L. B effectively obtains tax relief on £55,000 (less any CGT payable).

Sometimes, instead of the borrower forgoing income, the arrangements generate a tax deduction for the borrower. Say B grants a long lease of freehold property to L for a premium of £50,000. L then grants a five-year sub-lease back to B at a rent of £11,000 per year. The arrangements will provide for the benefits of ownership to revert to B at the end of the five years. Again, L receives £55,000 for an outlay of £50,000. B obtains tax relief for rent payments of £55,000. For transactions entered into before 6 June 2006, this type of scheme may have been countered by the rent factoring legislation at *ICTA 1988, ss 43A–43G* (see 56.14 PROPERTY INCOME) (repealed by *FA 2006, Sch 6 para 1* as a consequence of the introduction of the wider provisions described below).

Changes have been introduced in *FA 2007* to tackle variants of the above arrangements.

With effect for disposals on or after 6 March 2007 (whenever the arrangements were entered into) the legislation is amended to bring within it re-financing arrangements where an existing loan agreement is replaced by a structured financing arrangement and arrangements where the asset transferred does not produce an income flow immediately. However, where the arrangements were entered into prior to 6 March 2007, only amounts arising on or after that date are liable under these provisions.

Commencement and transitional. Except where otherwise indicated, the following provisions apply in relation to any arrangements whenever made. However, in relation to any arrangements made before 6 June 2006, any amount otherwise falling to be brought into account as a result of these provisions in determining taxable income is to be brought into account only if the amount arises on or after that date. In relation to the second type of arrangement described above, the following provisions do not apply in relation to a pre-6 June 2006 arrangement in so far as the (now repealed) rent factoring legislation (at 56.14 PROPERTY INCOME) applies to that arrangement.

Arrangements involving disposals of assets. The anti-avoidance provisions apply only where there is a '*structured finance arrangement*'. Other than in relation to arrangements involving partnership changes (for which see below), such an arrangement exists in relation to a person (the borrower) where:

- under the arrangement the borrower receives from another person (the lender) any money or other asset (the advance) in any period;
- in accordance with generally accepted accounting practice (GAAP) the accounts of the borrower for that period record a financial liability in respect of the advance;
- the borrower (or a person connected with the borrower) disposes of an asset (the security) under the arrangement to or for the benefit of the lender (or a person connected with the lender);
- the lender (or a person connected with the lender) is entitled under the arrangement to payments in respect of the security; and
- in accordance with GAAP those payments reduce the amount of the financial liability recorded in the borrower's accounts.

For the purposes of the second bullet point above, for transactions on or after 19 July 2007, it has to be assumed that the period of account in which the advance is received ended immediately after the receipt of the advance.

For these purposes, *ICTA 1988, s 839* (see 19 CONNECTED PERSONS) applies to determine whether persons are connected, except that the lender cannot be regarded as a person connected with the borrower and *vice versa*. If the borrower is a partnership (of which a company is a member), references above to accounts are to the accounts of any member of the partnership as well as the partnership itself. References to accounts also include consolidated group accounts of a group of which the borrower is a member. 'Arrangement' is widely defined for the purposes of these provisions to include any agreement or understanding (whether or not legally enforceable). 'Payments' is also widely defined to include any obtaining of value or benefit. Where it is not the case, these provisions apply as if the accounts in question had been prepared in accordance with GAAP.

If an arrangement is a structured finance arrangement in relation to the borrower, then:

(*a*) if, as a result of the arrangement, an amount of otherwise chargeable income would escape tax in the hands of the borrower (or a person connected with the borrower), it does not escape tax;

(*b*) if, as a result of the arrangement any amount, which would otherwise fall to be taken into account in computing income of the borrower (or a person connected with the borrower) for tax purposes, is not so brought into account, that amount shall be so brought into account; and

(*c*) if, as a result of the arrangement, the borrower (or a person connected with the borrower) becomes entitled to a deduction in computing any taxable income, or a deduction against total income, there shall be no so entitlement.

If the borrower is a partnership (of which a company is a member), the above have effect by reference to any member of the partnership. In all cases, if the borrower is a company within the charge to corporation tax and the advance is treated as a money debt owed by the company under the loan relationship rules, the arrangement is to be treated as a loan relationship of the company (as a debtor relationship) and any amount which, in accordance with GAAP, is recorded in the accounts as a finance charge in respect of the advance is to be treated as interest payable under that relationship. The intended effect is to place the borrower in the same position for tax purposes as if he had taken out a loan instead of entering into the structured finance arrangement. (If the borrower is a partnership, it is the partnership itself that is deemed to be paying interest, even if the finance charge appears in the accounts of a member.) The time at which this notional interest is to be treated as having been paid depends on the timing of the payments made to the lender in respect of the security; each such payment is treated as if it were part repayment of principal and part interest.

See also below under Exceptions.

Arrangements involving partnership changes. More complex types of arrangement might be involved where the borrower (B) is a partnership. For example, B might transfer an income-producing asset to a partnership of which it is a member. The lender (L) then joins the partnership for a capital contribution of £50,000 in return for the right to receive partnership profits of £55,000 over the next five years but no profits beyond that period. B claims not to be taxable on the £55,000 of partnership profits diverted to L. In another scenario, an established partnership may already hold an income-producing asset and the above steps then follow without the need for the initial transfer of an asset by B. In this case, the members of the partnership whose profits are thereby reduced claim not to be taxable on the partnership profits diverted to L.

There are similar anti-avoidance provisions to catch this type of arrangement. See *ICTA 1988, ss 774C, 774D*. These provisions rely on an alternative definition of 'structured finance arrangement', tailored to the type of arrangement at which they are aimed. If, as a result, an arrangement is a structured finance arrangement in relation to the borrower partnership, the partnership change is treated for tax purposes as if it had not occurred. For this purpose, the 'partnership change' might be the admission of the lender as a partner or a change in profit-sharing ratios affecting the lender's share. The provisions are widely drawn so as also to catch changes made indirectly and/or involving a person connected with the lender. Again, as above, there is provision for a finance charge to be treated as if it were interest paid on a loan.

See also below under Exceptions.

Exceptions. The above provisions are disapplied if the whole of the advance under the structured finance arrangement falls to be brought into account in determining the taxable income of a 'relevant person'. (However, the effect of the legislation relating to the rent factoring of leases of plant or machinery at 5.16 below, where relevant, is to be ignored for this purpose.) This includes a case where the advance falls to be brought into account as a disposal receipt, or in otherwise computing a balancing charge, for capital allowances purposes, but not if any such balancing charge would fall to be restricted under the capital allowances legislation. In respect of amounts brought into account before 6 March 2007 under arrangements made before that date, a '*relevant person*' was a person otherwise affected by the provisions. On or after 6 March 2007, a '*relevant person*' means the borrower under the arrangements or a person connected with the borrower or, if the borrower is a partnership, another partner.

The provisions are also disapplied if the whole of the advance under the structured finance arrangement is a debtor relationship of the borrower under the loan relationship rules or would be if the borrower were a company within the charge to corporation tax. A debtor relationship in this case does not include a relationship to which *FA 1996, s 100* applies (see 46.46 LOAN RELATIONSHIPS). Where the structured finance arrangement rules would not apply but the lender is directly or indirectly in receipt of any payment in respect of the asset disposed of by the borrower and the amount is set against the borrower's liability in his accounts, this amount is treated as the borrower's income.

There are also exclusions in cases where pre-existing statutory provisions specified in *ICTA 1988, s 774E* do in any case result in the arrangement being taxed as intended. These include, for example, certain repo and stock lending arrangements (see 5.6 above and 46.25 LOAN RELATIONSHIPS), ALTERNATIVE FINANCE ARRANGEMENTS (4) and certain sale and finance leaseback transactions. The Treasury have power to specify further exclusions by statutory instrument, and any such exclusions may be given retrospective effect.

Miscellaneous. The lease premium rules at *ICTA 1988, s 34* (see 56.8 PROPERTY INCOME) are disapplied where the grant of the lease constitutes the disposal of an asset for the purposes of these provisions.

In any case where, in relation to arrangements made before 6 June 2006, a person is treated as being a party to a loan relationship as a result of these provisions, a period of account is to be treated for loan relationship purposes as beginning on that date. For those purposes, the loan relationship is to be treated as being entered into for a consideration equal to the 'notional carrying value' of the liability representing the relationship. The '*notional carrying value*' for this purpose is the amount that would have been the carrying value (as defined in *FA 1996, Sch 9 para 19A*) in the accounts if a period of account had ended immediately before 6 June 2006. (See 46.7 LOAN RELATIONSHIPS.) In any case where, in relation to arrangements made before 6 March 2007, a person is treated as a party to a loan relationship as a result of the *FA 2007, Sch 5* amendments, a period of account is to be treated for loan relationship purposes as beginning on that date and the consideration for the transactions is the notional carrying value of the liability.

See *TCGA 2002, s 263E* as regards the CGT consequences of structured finance arrangements.

[*ICTA 1988, ss 774A–774G; FA 2006, Sch 6 para 6; FA 2007 Sch 5 paras 3–8*].

5.14 TRANSACTIONS IN LAND

The following provisions apply to all persons, whether UK residents or not, if all or any part of the land in question is in the UK. [*ICTA 1988, s 776(14)*].

Where:

(*a*) land (or any property deriving its value from land) is acquired with the sole or main object of realising a gain from disposing of it; or

(*b*) land is held as trading stock; or

(*c*) land is developed with the sole or main object of realising a gain from disposing of it when developed,

any capital gain from disposal of the land or any part of it (i.e. any amount not otherwise falling to be included in any computation of income for tax purposes [*ICTA 1988, s 777(13)*]) which is realised (for himself or for any other person) by the person acquiring, holding or developing it (or by any connected person, as defined by *ICTA 1988, s 839* (see 19 CONNECTED PERSONS), or a person party to, or concerned in, any arrangement or scheme to realise the gain indirectly or by a series of transactions) is, subject as below, treated for all tax purposes as income of the person realising the gain (or the person who transmitted to him, directly or indirectly, the opportunity of making that gain [*ICTA 1988, s 776(8)*]). The gain is assessable to corporation tax under Schedule D, Case VI, for the chargeable period in which the gain is realised. [*ICTA 1988, s 776(1)–(3A); ITTOIA 2005, Sch 1 para 312(2)(3)*]. See *Yuill v Wilson HL 1980, 52 TC 674* and its sequel *Yuill v Fletcher CA 1984, 58 TC 145; Winterton v Edwards Ch D 1979, 52 TC 655*; and *Sugarwhite v Budd CA 1988, 60 TC 679. Bona fide* transactions, not entered into with tax avoidance in view, may be caught by the legislation—see *Page v Lowther and Another CA 1983, 57 TC 199.*

'*Land*' includes buildings, and any estate or interest in land or buildings. [*ICTA 1988, s 776(13)(a)*].

'*Property deriving its value from land*' includes any shareholding in a company, partnership interest, or interest in settled property, deriving its value, directly or indirectly, from land, and any option, consent or embargo affecting the disposition of land. [*ICTA 1988, s 776(13)(b)*]. See, however, 'Exemptions' below.

Land is '*disposed of*' for the above purposes if, by any one or more transactions or by any arrangement or scheme (whether concerning the land or any property deriving its value therefrom), the property in, or control over, the land is effectively disposed of. [*ICTA 1988, s 776(4)*]. Any number of transactions may be treated as a single arrangement or scheme if they have, or there is evidence of, a common purpose. [*ICTA 1988, s 776(5)(b)*]. See also under 'General' below.

For the date of the capital gain where instalments are involved, see *Yuill v Fletcher CA 1984, 58 TC 145.*

Exemptions

(i) An individual's gain made from the *sale etc., of his residence* exempted from capital gains tax under *TCGA 1992, s 222* or which would be so exempt but for *TCGA 1992, s 224(3)* (acquired for purpose of making a gain). [*ICTA 1988, s 776(9)*].

(ii) A gain on the sale of *shares in a company holding land as trading stock* (or a company owning, directly or indirectly, 90% of the ordinary share capital of such a company) *provided that* the company disposes of the land by normal trade and makes all possible profit from it, and the share sale is not part of an arrangement or scheme to realise a land gain indirectly. [*ICTA 1988, s 776(10)* and see *Chilcott v CIR Ch D 1981, 55 TC 446*].

(iii) (If the liability arises solely under (*c*) above.) Any part of the gain fairly attributable to a period *before the intention was made* to develop the land. [*ICTA 1988, s 776(7); ITTOIA 2005, Sch 1 para 312(5)*].

Gains are to be computed 'as is just and reasonable in the circumstances', allowance being given only for expenses attributable to the land disposed of, and the following may be taken into account.

(A) If a leasehold interest is disposed of out of a freehold, the Sch D, Case I treatment in such a case of a company dealing in land (see 66.70 TRADING INCOME).

(B) Any adjustments under *ICTA 1988, s 99(2)(3)* for tax on lease premiums.

[*ICTA 1988, s 776(6); ITTOIA 2005, Sch 1 para 312(4)*].

Where the computation of a gain in respect of the development of land (as under (*c*) above) is made on the footing that the land or property was appropriated as trading stock, that land etc., is also to be treated for purposes of capital gains tax (under *TCGA 1992, s 161*) as having been transferred to stock. [*ICTA 1988, s 777(11)*].

Where, under *ICTA 1988, s 775* or *s 776*, tax is assessed on, and paid by, a person other than the one who actually realised the gain, the person paying the tax may recover it from the other party (for which purpose HMRC will, on request, supply a certificate of income in respect of which tax has been paid). [*ICTA 1988, s 777(8)*].

Clearance. The person who made or would make the gain may (if he considers that (*a*) or (*c*) above may apply), submit to his Inspector of Taxes particulars of any completed or proposed transactions. If he does so the inspector must, within 30 days of receiving those particulars, notify the taxpayer whether or not he is satisfied that liability under this section does not arise. If the inspector is so satisfied no assessment can thereafter be made on that gain, provided that all material facts and considerations have been fully and accurately disclosed. [*ICTA 1988, s 776(11)*].

General. See *ICTA 1988, s 777(2)(3)* for provisions to prevent avoidance by the use of indirect means to transfer any property or right, or enhance or diminish its value, e.g., by sales at less, or more, than full consideration, assigning share capital or rights in a company or partnership or an interest in settled property, disposal on the winding-up of any company, partnership or trust etc. For ascertaining whether, and to what extent, the value of any property or right is derived from any other property or right, value may be traced through any number of companies, partnerships and trusts, at each stage attributing property held by the company, partnership or trust to its shareholders etc., 'in such manner as is appropriate to the circumstances'. [*ICTA 1988, s 777(5)*]. Where the person liable is non-resident, HMRC may direct that any part of an amount taxable under these provisions on that person be paid under deduction of tax as if made other than out of taxable income. [*ICTA 1988, s 777(9); ITTOIA 2005, Sch 1 para 313(2)*].

For the above purposes HMRC may require, under penalty, any person to supply them with any particulars thought necessary, including particulars of:

(I) transactions etc., in which he acts, or acted, on behalf of others; and

(II) transactions etc., which in the opinion of HMRC should be investigated; and

(III) what part, if any, he has taken, or is taking, in specified transactions etc. (Under this heading a *solicitor* who has merely acted as professional adviser is not compelled to do more than state that he acted and give his client's name and address.) [*ICTA 1988, s 778*].

The transactions of which particulars are required need not be identified transactions (*Essex v CIR CA 1980, 53 TC 720*).

Simon's Direct Tax Service. See **B3.636** *et seq.*

5.15 **LAND SOLD AND LEASED BACK**

Tax deductions for rent limited to commercial rent. Where land (or any interest or estate in land) is transferred from one person to another (by sale, lease, surrender or forfeiture of lease etc.) and:

(*a*) under a lease of the land, or any part of it, granted then or subsequently by the transferee to the transferor; or

(*b*) as a result of a transaction or transactions affecting the land or interest,

the transferor, or any person associated with him, becomes liable to pay any lease rent (including any premium treated as rent — see 56.8, 56.14 PROPERTY INCOME), or rent charge on, or connected with, the land which would be allowable as a deduction:

(i) in computing trading profits; or

(ii) in computing profits or losses under Case VI; or

(iii) as a management expense under *ICTA 1988, s 75* or expenses of insurance companies under *ICTA 1988, s 76*; or

(iv) against employment income, under *ITEPA 2003, s 336*; or

(v) in computing profits from woodlands; or

(vi) in computing the profits of a UK property business under Schedule A,

the allowance for tax purposes in respect of that rent or other payment (apart from any portion which properly relates to services, tenant's rates, or the use of assets other than land) is limited to the commercial rent of the land to which it relates for the period for which the payment is made. In the case of a lease, '*commercial rent*' means the open-market rent, at the time the actual lease was created, under a lease whose duration and repair terms are the same as under the actual lease but stipulating a rent payable at uniform intervals at a uniform rate, or progressively increasing proportionately to any increases provided by the actual lease. For other transactions, it is the open market rent which would be payable under a tenant's repairing lease (as defined by *ICTA 1988, s 779(12)*) for the period over which payments are to be made, or 200 years if they are for a longer period or are perpetual. [*ICTA 1988, s 779(1)–(4), (10)(12); ITTOIA 2005, Sch 1 para 314*].

Any part of a payment which is disallowed under the above provisions may be carried forward as an addition to the next subsequent payment, and so on. All payments for the same period are amalgamated, including apportioned parts of periods which overlap. A payment for a period falling, wholly or partly, beyond one year from the date of payment is treated as being for the year commencing with the date on which it is paid. [*ICTA 1988, s 779(5)–(9)*].

'Associated persons'

A. Spouse or (from 5 December 2005) civil partner, their relatives and spouses or civil partners;

B. the trustee of a settlement and the settlor or any person associated with him;

C. a person and any body, or bodies of persons (including partnerships) which he, or any persons associated with him, or he and any persons associated with him, controls (as under *ICTA 1988, s 840*, see 19 CONNECTED PERSONS and note that, in the case of a partnership, control means the right to more than a half share in assets or income);

D. any bodies of persons associated with the same person under C above;

E. joint owners of the land etc. the subject of disposal, including their associates;

F. the transferor and any other transferor acting in concert, or reciprocally, with him, and their associates;

G. any two or more companies participating in the reconstruction, or amalgamation, of a company or companies.

[*ICTA 1988, s 779(11), s 783(10); ITTOIA 2005, Sch 1 para 318; SI 2005 No 3229, reg 98*].

Proportion of capital sum received taxed as income in certain circumstances. As regards arrangements as in *ICTA 1988, s 779* (see above), made after 21 June 1971, where the lease when sold has no more than 50 years still to run and the period for which the premises are leased back is 15 years or less, the increased rent payable, so far as it does not exceed a commercial rent (see above), is allowable as a deduction from profits, but of the consideration received by the lessee for giving up the original lease (or undertaking to pay an increased rent) a proportion equivalent to one-fifteenth of that consideration multiplied by the number of years by which the term of the lease-back falls short of 16 years will be treated as income chargeable to corporation tax under Schedule D, Case VI, not capital. Appropriate adjustment to be made where the lease-back is of part only of the property previously leased. For the above purposes the term of the new lease is deemed to end on any date whereafter the rent payable is reduced, or, if the lessor or lessee has power to determine the lease or the lessee has power to vary its terms, on the earliest date on which the lease can be so determined or varied. [*ICTA 1988, s 780; ITTOIA 2005, Sch 1 para 315*].

Rent factoring. See 5.16 below with regard to a lease of land that includes plant and machinery that are fixtures.

Simon's Direct Tax Service. See **B3.647, B3.648.**

5.16 LEASES OF ASSETS OTHER THAN LAND

Capital sum received by person who pays lease rentals is taxable — to the extent of tax allowances on such lease rentals. Where any payment under a lease, created after 14 April 1964, of any asset not falling under *ICTA 1988, s 779* (see 5.15 above) or *s 782* (see below), is allowable as a deduction:

(i) in computing trading profits; or

(ii) in computing profits or losses under Schedule D, Case VI; or

(iii) as a management expense or expenses of an insurance company under *ICTA 1988, ss 75, 76*; or

(iv) against employment income under *ITEPA 2003, s 336*; or

(v) in computing profits from woodlands,

then if at any time the person making the payment has obtained, or obtains, a capital sum (whether money, or money's worth, but not so far as it falls to be taken into account as a receipt in computing profits or is taxable under Case VI) in respect of the lessee's interest in the lease (including by surrender to the lessor, assignment, subleasing, or receipt under insurance — and see *ICTA 1988, s 783*), or any person associated with the payer has obtained a capital sum for an interest in the asset, the recipient of that capital sum is chargeable to corporation tax under Case VI, for the accounting period in which the capital sum was obtained, on a figure equal to the amount of the payment under the lease which is allowable for tax purposes as above (or the effectively allowable part of it, where the whole or part of the period in which the payment would normally be allowed is not a basis period for assessment), subject to the overriding limitation that the amount(s) so charged shall not exceed the capital sum received (or, where the lease is a hire-purchase agreement, that sum less the recipient's capital expenditure on the asset — see *ICTA 1988, s 784*).

Apportionments are made in the case of recipients who are partners or persons with a joint interest in the asset. 'Associated persons' are as listed in A to E of 5.15 (relating to *ICTA 1988, s 779*) above. Assessments to give effect to the above provisions may be made up to five years after 31 January following the tax year in which the allowable payment was made or, for corporation tax purposes, six years after the end of the accounting period in which it was made.

[*ICTA 1988, ss 781(8), 783(10), 785; FA 1996, s 135, Sch 21 para 21; ITTOIA 2005, Sch 1 paras 316, 318, 319*].

Previously owned for trade etc. by taxpayer — deductions for lease rentals are limited to commercial rent. Any payment under a lease, created after 14 April 1964, of any asset (other than land or an interest in land) which at any time prior to the lease was used for the purpose of the lessee's trade (or any other trade carried on by him) and was then owned by the person carrying on the trade in which it was used is limited, in computing profits or losses of the lessee's trade, to the commercial rent of the asset for the period covered by the payment, i.e. a rent representing a reasonable return, by uniform instalments at uniform intervals over the remainder of the asset's anticipated normal working life (as under *ICTA 1988, s 782(6)*), on its market value at the time the lease was created. *ICTA 1988, s 782(3)–(5)* contains similar provisions (disallowed payments carried forward etc.) to *ICTA 1988, s 780(4)–(6)* — see 5.15 above. These provisions do not apply to payments due on or after 1 April 2006 under a long funding lease (within 10.34 CAPITAL ALLOWANCES). [*ICTA 1988, s 782; ITTOIA 2005, Sch 1 para 317; FA 2006, Sch 9 para 3*].

Leasing partnerships — restriction on use of losses. Where a plant or machinery leasing business (as defined in 5.17 below), within the charge to corporation tax, is carried on by a company in partnership, certain losses derived from capital allowances are restricted as set out below. This provision has effect in relation to any business carried on by a company in partnership in any accounting period ending on or after 5 December 2005. In relation to accounting periods straddling that date, the provision applies only if the company starts to carry on the business in partnership, or a 'relevant change' in the company's interest in the business occurs, on or after that date. A '*relevant change*' in the company's interest in the business is a change to a basis of profit sharing which is not 'allowable'. The interest of a company in the leasing business during the partnership's accounting period is determined on an '*allowable*' basis if (for the purposes of *ICTA 1988, s 114(2)* – see 52.2 PARTNERSHIPS) the company's share in the profits (excluding chargeable gains) or loss of the leasing business and its share in any 'relevant capital allowances' for that period are both determined by reference to the same, single percentage. '*Relevant capital allowances*' are capital allowances in respect of expenditure incurred on the provision of plant or machinery wholly or partly for the purposes of the leasing business.

Where the company's interest in the leasing business during the accounting period of the partnership is not determined on an allowable basis, any loss incurred in its 'notional business' in its accounting period comprising (wholly or partly) the partnership accounting period, is restricted to the extent that it derives from any relevant capital allowances. For this purpose, the loss is calculated on the basis that any relevant capital allowances are the final amounts to be deducted. The company's '*notional business*' is the business treated as carried on alone by that company and from which its share in the profits or loss of the partnership business is treated as deriving under *ICTA 1988, s 114(2)* (see 52.2 PARTNERSHIPS).The restricted part of the loss can only be set off against income of the company's notional business deriving from a lease of plant or machinery which was entered into before the end of the accounting period in which the loss of the notional business was incurred.

[*ICTA 1988, ss 785ZA, 785ZB; FA 2006, s 83*].

Rent factoring of leases of plant and machinery — consideration for transfer of right to receive rental income treated as income. Where a person enters into arrangements **after 1 July 2004** to transfer a right to receive some or all of his rentals from a lease of plant and machinery to which he is entitled and which would have been brought into account as his income for income or corporation tax purposes, the consideration for the transfer is to be treated as such income to the extent it would have been so treated (had the right not been transferred) and does not otherwise fall to be treated for tax purposes as his income or a capital allowances disposal receipt. The consideration so treated as income for tax purposes is taxable as rentals receivable under the lease in the period of account in which it is receivable. The transfer of a right to receive rental income includes any arrangements which result in the rentals no longer being brought into account as the transferor's taxable income. Transfers of rights to receive rental income also includes transfers made by partners even if the partnership is a legal person or body corporate. This provision does not apply in so far as the structured finance arrangements provisions in 5.13 above (rent factoring of income receipts etc.) apply in relation to the above arrangements as a result of the transfer of the right to receive some or all of the rentals from a lease of plant or machinery. [*ICTA 1988, s 785A, FA 2004, s 135; FA 2006, Sch 6 para 7*].

See also HMRC guidance on 'Plant or Machinery Rent Factoring' (available on their website) on the interaction of *ICTA 1988, s 785A* with *ss 43A–43G* (rent factoring – see 56.14 PROPERTY INCOME), *s 343* (company reconstruction without change of ownership) and *CAA 2001, ss 266, 267* (successions).

Simon's Direct Tax Service. See **A4.106A, B3.661** *et seq* and **B3.664.**

5.17 SALE OF LESSORS

The following provisions apply where a company, which carries on a business of leasing plant or machinery on its own or in partnership, changes ownership, or changes its interest in a business carried on in partnership, after 4 December 2005. See Explanatory notes to Finance Bill 2006 (and the HMRC Technical Note published on 31 March 2006) for background information on these provisions which ensure that on a change of ownership, or interest in a partnership, a charge is borne by the original owner and an equal and opposite relief is granted to the new owner. The charge applies in respect of long-leases where in the early years of a lease the capital allowances available to the lessor are greater than the rental income from the lease, giving rise to losses, the charge broadly equating to the tax benefit of such losses. This prevents the lessor making use of such losses, for example, by way of group relief, where the profits arising in the later years of the lease (when the rental income is greater than the capital allowances) are sheltered on the sale of the lessor company to a group with tax losses. The charge thus counters the losses available to the original owner and the corresponding relief counters the profits passed on to the new owner.

Leasing business carried on by a company alone. Where there is a 'qualifying change of ownership' of a company within the charge to corporation tax, which carries on a 'business of leasing plant or machinery' otherwise than in partnership, the accounting period of the company ends on the day of the change (the '*relevant day*') and a new accounting period begins on the following day. The company is treated as receiving a taxable business receipt in the accounting period ending on the relevant day and as incurring a deductible business expense equal to that amount in the new accounting period. Any loss derived from such expense (to be calculated on the basis that the expense is the final amount to be deducted) cannot be carried back under *ICTA 1988, s 393A(1)(b)* as a trading loss for offset against profits of earlier accounting periods.

A '*qualifying change of ownership*' is a 'relevant change in the relationship' between a company and its 'principal company' (with an exception for certain intra-group reorganisations). A company is a '*principal company*' of another company if that other company is its 'qualifying 75% subsidiary' (broadly as defined for group relief purposes) and it is not itself a qualifying 75% subsidiary of a third company. There is a '*relevant change in the relationship*' between a company and its principal company on any day that the company ceases to be a qualifying 75% subsidiary of that principal company. The same applies in the case of a chain of companies where the principal company is at the top of the chain, the '*relevant change*' occurring whenever any of the links in the 75% chain are broken. In the case of consortium relationships, a company (company B) is the principal company of another company if it is itself not a qualifying 75% subsidiary of any company and if that other company is owned by a consortium, or is a 'qualifying 90% subsidiary' (broadly as defined for group relief purposes) of a company owned by a consortium, of which company B is a member. If company B is a qualifying 75% subsidiary of another company, company A, company A would become the principal company provided it is not itself a qualifying 75% subsidiary of another company. In this case, there is a '*relevant change in the relationship*' between a company and its principal company on any day if there is a fall in the 'relevant fraction' or if company B ceases to be a qualifying 75% subsidiary of company A or if there is a similar break in the link in the case of a chain. The '*relevant fraction*' in the case of a consortium relationship is the lowest of the percentage of the ordinary shares held by the principal company, its entitlement to profits available for distribution and the assets available for distribution to it on a winding up.

A company carries on a '*business of leasing plant or machinery*' for this purpose if either at least half of the 'accounting value' of the plant or machinery owned by the company relates to 'qualifying leased plant or machinery', or at least half of the company's income over the twelve-month period before the relevant day, derives from 'qualifying leased plant or machinery'. The '*accounting value*' of the plant or machinery is broadly the amounts recorded in the balance sheet of the lessor company at the start of the relevant day together with the value of any plant or machinery transferred to the lessor company on that day by 'associated companies' (as defined). '*Qualifying leased plant or machinery*' is broadly leased plant or machinery on which the lessor company can claim capital allowances. In determining the company's income over the twelve-month period before the relevant day, any necessary apportionment is to be made on a time basis or, where this leads to an unjust result, on a just and reasonable basis. The proportion of income that derives from qualifying plant or machinery is to be determined on a just and reasonable basis.

The basic amount of the taxable receipt (which is not to be less than nil and is subject to adjustment as below) is calculated by the formula PM – TWDV which is broadly the net book value of the plant or machinery less its tax written down value for capital allowances purposes, defined in more detail as follows.

PM is the net book value (or carrying amount) of the plant or machinery and the net investment in respect of finance leases of the plant or machinery shown in the balance sheet of the lessor company ('*the relevant company*') at the start of the relevant day together with such amounts in the balance sheets of any associated company from which any plant or machinery is transferred to the relevant company on that day. This is on the assumption that the balance sheet is drawn up at the start of the relevant day in accordance with generally accepted accounting practice and that where assets have been acquired from connected parties, the plant or machinery had been acquired at its market value on the relevant day (where that day falls after 21 March 2006). Plant or machinery for this purpose is any plant or machinery (whether or not subject to a lease) apart from assets treated as owned by other persons under *CAA 2001, s 67* (hire-purchase and similar contracts) and those on which the company has incurred expenditure which is not qualifying expenditure for capital allowances purposes by virtue of *CAA 2001, s 34A* (expenditure for long funding leasing). Where any of the plant or machinery is a fixture in land the amount of the net book value (or carrying amount) in respect of the fixture is determined on a just and reasonable basis. Where any of the plant or machinery, together with any other land or asset, is subject to a finance lease, the amount of the net investment in respect of the finance lease of that plant or machinery is determined on a just and reasonable basis.

TWDV is the total amount of unrelieved qualifying expenditure on plant or machinery in all single asset, class pools and main pool brought forward under the capital allowances provisions at the start of the new accounting period following the relevant day. The amount excludes any expenditure on the acquisition of plant or machinery on the relevant day other than acquisitions from associated companies.

An adjustment is made to the basic amount as calculated above to reflect the degree to which the economic control of the lessor company has changed. The adjustment is made where a company ceases to be a 75% subsidiary of another company and becomes instead owned by a consortium (or a 90% subsidiary of a company owned by a consortium) of which that other company is a member. The taxable receipt is limited to the 'appropriate percentage' of the basic amount, the '*appropriate percentage*' being the difference between 100% and the relevant fraction (as defined above) at the end of the relevant day. Where the change in relationship arises from a change in a consortium relationship the '*appropriate percentage*' is the decrease in the relevant fraction at the end of the relevant day from that at the start of the relevant day. If the relevant fraction at the start of the relevant day is lower than that at the end, the taxable amount is limited to that lower relevant fraction of the basic amount.

If a company (other than one in partnership) comes within the charge to corporation tax on any day as a result of migration into the UK and there is a qualifying change of ownership on that day in relation to that company, any plant or machinery owned by that company immediately before that day is ignored in determining the taxable amount

Leasing business carried on by a company in partnership. Where on any day ('the relevant day') there is a 'qualifying change' in the interest of a company ('the partner company') in a 'business of leasing plant or machinery' carried on in partnership with other persons, the partner company is treated as receiving a taxable receipt in relation to its 'notional business' and any other corporate partner is treated as incurring a deductible expense in relation to its notional business. The companies in question must be within the charge to corporation tax and the respective amounts are brought into account in the accounting periods in which they are treated as received or incurred. A company's '*notional business*' is the business treated as carried on alone by that company and from which its share in the profits or loss of the partnership business is treated as deriving under *ICTA 1988, s 114(2)* (see 52.2 PARTNERSHIPS).

There is a '*qualifying change*' in a company's interest in a business if there is a fall on any day of its percentage share in the profits or loss of the business (which may include a nil share whether or not as a result of the dissolution of the partnership). The percentage share for this purpose is to be determined on a just and reasonable basis and with regard, in particular, to the allocation of profits under *ICTA 1988, s 114(2)* (see 52.2 PARTNERSHIPS) and the allocation of any capital allowances and charges. 'Profits' and 'loss' for this purpose do not include chargeable gains or allowable losses. The definition of a '*business of leasing plant or machinery*' is the same as that above for a leasing business carried on by a company alone as modified for the context of a partnership.

The basic amount of the taxable receipt (which is not to be less than nil and is subject to adjustment as below) is calculated by the formula as above of PM – TWDV as follows.

PM has the meaning given above but references to the relevant company are to be read as references to the partnership and references to an associated company are to be read as references to a '*qualifying company*' which includes:

(*a*) the partner company or a company which is an associated company of the partner company on the relevant day;

(*b*) any other partner company in relation to which, or in relation to whose interest in the business, there is a qualifying change of ownership on the relevant day; and

(*c*) a company which is an associated company on the relevant day of any partner company mentioned in (*b*) above.

TWDV is the total amount of unrelieved qualifying expenditure on plant or machinery in all single asset, class pools and main pool brought forward under the capital allowances provisions at the start of the new chargeable period following the relevant day. The amount excludes any expenditure on the acquisition of plant or machinery on the relevant day other than acquisitions from qualifying companies.

An adjustment is made to the basic amount of income as calculated above to reflect the change in a company's percentage share in the profits or loss of the business ('*relevant percentage share*'). The taxable receipt is limited to the 'appropriate percentage' of the basic amount, the *appropriate percentage* in this case being the decrease in the company's relevant percentage share (as defined above) at the end of the relevant day from that at the start of the relevant day.

An adjustment is also made to the expense treated as incurred by another company where the percentage of that company's share in the profits or loss of a business has increased as a result of a change in the partner company's interest in the business. Such increase can be from a nil share (whether as a result of it becoming a partner or otherwise). In this case, the expense is limited to the 'appropriate percentage' of the amount of the income. The '*appropriate percentage*' in this case is the proportion of the other company's percentage share in the profits or loss of the business immediately after the change that is wholly attributable to the change.

Change in ownership of a corporate partner. Where there is a qualifying change of ownership of a company within the charge to corporation tax, which carries on a business of leasing plant or machinery in partnership with other persons, the accounting period of the company ends on the day of the change (the '*relevant day*') and a new accounting period begins on the following day. The company is treated as receiving a taxable receipt of its notional business in the accounting period ending on the relevant day and as incurring a deductible business expense equal to that amount in the new accounting period. Any loss derived from such expense (to be calculated on the basis that the expense is the final amount to be deducted) cannot be carried back under *ICTA 1988, s 393A(1)(b)* as a trading loss for offset against profits of earlier accounting periods.

The amount of the income is calculated by first applying the formula above (PM – TWDV) to give the basic amount as though the company were the 'partner company' in the definition of that formula and making any adjustment to reflect the degree to which the economic control of the company has changed as set out above under 'Leasing business carried on by a company alone'. The taxable income is then limited to an 'appropriate percentage' of this adjusted, basic amount to reflect the corporate partner's interest in the partnership business. The 'appropriate percentage' is the company's percentage share in the profits or loss of the business on the relevant day or, if there is a qualifying change in the company's interest in the business on that day, its percentage share in the profits or loss of the business at the end of that day.

Relief for expense in subsequent accounting period. A special provision applies where a company, including a corporate partner, is treated under the above provisions as incurring an expense in a new accounting period and the company also makes a loss in that accounting period. To the extent that the loss derives from the expense, the loss being calculated on the basis that the expense is the final amount to be deducted, it is to be treated as an expense. So much of that loss (or part of the loss) that is treated as an expense, and would be carried forward if it wasn't so treated, is deductible from the profits of the business for the 'subsequent accounting period'. The '*subsequent accounting period*' is one which starts within the period of twelve months from the relevant day and does not start as a result of a change of ownership.

Anti-avoidance. Where a company enters into any 'arrangements' (as defined), the main purpose or one of the main purposes of which is to secure that it is treated as incurring an expense under these provisions, any loss it incurs deriving from the expense can only be carried forward and set off against 'relevant leasing income'. '*Relevant leasing income*' is income deriving from any plant or machinery lease which was entered into before the day on which the company is treated as incurring the expense and which is not an excluded lease of background plant or machinery for a building. The loss is to be calculated on the basis that the expense is the final amount to be deducted.

The following provisions apply where, on any qualifying change in ownership of a company on or after 22 November 2006 or a change in its qualifying interest in a business on or after that date, a question arises (see below) as to whether or not these provisions apply, reference must be made, in determining that question, to any entries in or which would appear in the balance sheet of any company in respect of plant and machinery, whether (apart from the effect of these provisions) the amount representing plant and machinery would increase or decrease, such change would arise in any way from any arrangements (see below) and the main purpose or one of the main purposes is the obtaining of a 'relevant tax advantage'.

A '*relevant tax advantage*' arises if, other than under these provisions:

(*a*) any company would not be treated, alone or in partnership, as carrying on a business of leasing of plant or machinery;

(*b*) any income any company is treated as receiving under these provisions is reduced; or

(*c*) any expense any company is treated as incurring under these provisions is increased.

A question arises as to whether or not these provisions apply if there is doubt as to whether any company is carrying on a business of leasing plant or machinery (alone or in partnership) or as to the amount of income or expense any company is treated as receiving under *FA 2006, Sch 10*).

'*Arrangements*' includes any agreement, understanding, scheme, transaction or series of transactions, whether or not legally enforceable and whether the person intended to receive the tax advantage is a party to them.

FA 2006, Sch 10 para 38B is introduced for any qualifying change of ownership occurring on or after 22 November 2006, where any qualifying change in a company's interest in a business happens on or after that date. It applies if a company owns any plant or machinery at any time on any day ('*the relevant day*'), *Sch 10* may apply, depending on what, if anything, is shown in the company's balance sheet for plant and machinery and either:

A no amount would appear in the company's balance sheet for plant and machinery; or

B the amount which would appear is less than the figure which would appear were the company to have no liabilities of any kind (including share capital) in its balance sheet on the relevant day.

[*FA 2006, Sch 10 para 38B; FA 2007, Sch 6*].

Disposal of leased asset. If, on the relevant day, the company or the partnership of which the company is a member disposes of any relevant plant or machinery subject to a lease while retaining a right to part of the income stream from the lease under *CAA 2001, s 228K* (see 10.38(L) CAPITAL ALLOWANCES), the above provisions do not apply in relation to that disposal. In relation to disposals made on or after 2 June 2006, the above provisions do not apply in so far as the taxable receipt and deductible expense arises by reference to the relevant leased plant or machinery disposed of which is subject to the charge under *CAA 2001, s 228K*.

[*FA 2006, s 82, Sch 10*].

Reconstructions of companies with leasing trades. An anti-avoidance measure has been introduced, with effect for cessations on or after 22 November 2006, to counter the use of reconstructions of companies with leasing trades to avoid tax. It applies only where the trade is part of a 'business of leasing plant or machinery' as above which the predecessor or the successor carries on on the day of cessation. Provided the business is carried on other than in partnership, the parties are not treated as the successor and predecessor.

Where the parties are carrying on the leasing trade in partnership and cessation occurs on or after 21 March 2007, the predecessor has to stop trading on the date of transfer for *s 343(2)* to apply.

The effect of these provisions is that *s 343(2)* does not apply unless the companies share the same principal company or companies for the purposes of *FA 2006, Sch 10*.

If *s 343(2)* does not apply to a transfer, for capital allowances purposes there is deemed to be a disposal by the predecessor of the leasing assets at market value and an acquisition by the successor at that value on the date of cessation of the trade. 'Market value' is to be determined on the assumption that there is a disposal by the absolute owner and that the asset has no leases or other encumbrances over it. [*FA 2006, Sch 10 para 41(8); FA 2007, Sch 6 para 2*].

[*ICTA 1988, s 343A*; *FA 2007, Sch 6 para 1*].

5.18 LOAN TRANSACTIONS

Where, with reference to lending money or giving credit (or varying the terms of a loan or credit):

- (i) a transaction provides for the payment of an *annuity or other annual payment* (other than interest) — that payment is treated as if it were of annual interest. [*ICTA 1988, s 786(3)(3A); ITTOIA 2005, Sch 1 para 320(2)(3)*];
- (ii) any person *assigns, surrenders, waives or forgoes* income on property (without a sale or transfer of the property) — that person is chargeable to corporation tax under Schedule D, Case VI, on a sum equal to the income assigned, surrendered, waived etc. This does not apply where the person is chargeable to tax on that amount of income by virtue of the structured finance arrangements provisions in 5.13 above (rent factoring of income etc.). [*ICTA 1988, s 786(5); ITTOIA 2005, Sch 1 para 320(4); FA 2006, Sch 6 para 8*];
- (iii) if credit is given for the purchase price of property and during the subsistence of the debt, the purchaser's rights to income from the property are suspended or restricted — he is treated for the purpose of (ii) above as if he had made a surrender of that income. [*ICTA 1988, s 786(6)*].

Transactions with CONNECTED PERSONS (19) are included.

Simon's Direct Tax Service. See **E1.524**.

5.19 RELIEF BY CREDIT UNDER DOUBLE TAX AGREEMENT

Wide-ranging anti-avoidance provisions have been introduced which apply to certain schemes or arrangements in relation to relief by way of credit under a double tax agreement (SEE 24.5 DOUBLE TAX RELIEF), the main purpose or one of the main purposes of which is the avoidance of tax. The legislation applies in relation to any credit for foreign tax which is connected either with a payment of foreign tax on or after **16 March 2005** or with income received on or after that date from which foreign tax has been deducted (or treated as deducted) at source. An earlier commencement date of 10 February 2005 applies to the extent that the scheme or arrangement is within (iv) below. For payments of foreign tax on or after 6 December 2006, income received on or after that date or any act or omission on or after that date, 'foreign tax' includes UK tax treated as foreign tax by *ICTA 1988, s 801*.

These provisions, together known as the 'DTR anti-avoidance provisions' apply to any action (or failure of such action) taking place under a scheme or arrangement on or after 6 December 2006.

HMRC may issue a notice (a '*section 804ZA notice*') to a company requiring that it make adjustments to or amend the company tax return to nullify the effects of any scheme or arrangement where they have reasonable grounds to believe that, in relation to any income or gains taken into account in determining the tax liability for a chargeable period:

— relief by way of credit against UK tax is available under a double tax agreement for the foreign tax suffered on the income or gain;

— there is a scheme or arrangement, which is a 'prescribed scheme or arrangement', the main purpose, or one of the main purposes, of which is to provide for an amount of foreign tax to be taken into account; and

— the aggregate amount of credit relief which can be or has been claimed for the foreign tax by the company, and by any connected persons in a corresponding chargeable period (where the chargeable periods in question have at least one day in common), is at least £100,000 (see para 29 of HMRC's draft guidance referred to below).

A section 804ZA notice will not be issued in the simple case of a company holding foreign shareholdings within an investment portfolio where the dividends are taxed as investment income (with credit for foreign tax deducted but no entitlement to underlying tax credit). Nor will a notice be issued in the case where a company holds intellectual property acquired or established in the course of its trade and tax is deducted from royalty income (but this exemption will not apply if intellectual property is created specifically for the purpose of creating an avoidance scheme or arrangement). These let-outs will not apply if income is received by a company for the purpose of benefiting from the let-out, for example if income is deliberately diverted to a non-trading company from a connected company in order to fall within the portfolio investment clearance. (See paras 27, 30 and 31 of HMRC's draft guidance).

There is no formal clearance procedure but HMRC will be prepared to give advice concerning actual or proposed transactions and, where appropriate, will confirm that no section 804ZA notice will be issued in respect of the disclosed transactions (see paras 23 to 25 of their draft guidance).

A scheme or arrangement is a '*prescribed scheme or arrangement*' if any one or more of the following applies to it.

(i) A scheme enables foreign tax which is properly attributable to one source of income or gain to be paid in respect of a different source of income or gain.

(ii) It enables any scheme participant to claim credit for a payment of foreign tax that increases the total amount of foreign tax paid by all the scheme participants by less than the amount which that person can claim (for example, because the payment made by the claimant is matched by a tax saving for another scheme participant).

(iii) It involves a scheme participant making a claim or election etc. or omitting to make a claim or election etc. which in either case has the effect of increasing the credit for foreign tax available to any scheme participant. References here to claims and elections or suchlike are to claims etc. made under the law of any territory or under the terms of a double tax agreement.

(iv) It has the effect of reducing a scheme participant's total UK tax liability on income and chargeable gains to less than it would have been in the absence of the transactions made under the scheme. This will be the case, for example, where the credit for foreign tax on the scheme income covers not only the UK tax on that income but at least some of the UK tax on other income, thereby reducing total liability.

(v) Under the scheme, a tax deductible payment is made by a person, in return for which that person or a connected party (within the meaning of *ICTA 1988, s 839*) receives consideration which is taxable in a foreign territory (and thus on which credit relief can be obtained in respect of the foreign tax).

Where one of the main purposes of the scheme is to obtain relief for underlying tax in respect of a dividend paid by a foreign company, the above schemes are treated as prescribed schemes of the foreign company if they would be treated as such if the company were UK resident (without assuming its activities are carried on in a different place).

See *ICTA 1988, s 804ZA* for the form of notice. Where a company tax return is made within 90 days after the issue of a section 804ZA notice, the notice may be disregarded when making the return, as long as the return is then amended in accordance with the notice before the end of that 90-day period.

Once a return has been made, HMRC may only issue a section 804ZA notice if a notice of enquiry has been issued in respect of the return, but an enquiry may be opened for just that purpose. If a section 804ZA notice is then issued, the company must then amend the return accordingly within the 90 days beginning with the date of issue of the notice.

Failure to make or amend a return in accordance with a section 804ZA notice results in the return becoming an incorrect return (so that penalties potentially apply). An enquiry cannot be closed until either the amendment is made or the 90-day period for making it expires. Disputes between Revenue and taxpayer are settled under the normal self-assessment enquiry procedures and with the normal rights of appeal (see paras 15 to 17 of HMRC draft guidance referred to below).

Where an enquiry into a return has been completed, a section 804ZA notice can only be issued where HMRC could not have been reasonably expected to realise that a notice was required on the basis of the information supplied before the enquiry was completed, or, had requests for information by HMRC in the course of the enquiry been complied with, it is reasonable to suppose that they would have issued a notice at that time. Once a section 804ZA notice is issued in such circumstances, a related 'discovery' assessment cannot be made until either the necessary amendment is made to the tax return or the 90-day period for making it expires. The conditions at 7.2(*a*) and (*b*) ASSESSMENTS for making a discovery assessment are disapplied (being replaced by the above conditions for issuing the notice).[*ICTA 1988, ss 804ZA–804ZC, Sch 28AB; FA 2005, ss 87, 88, Sch 5; FA 2007 s 35*].

See generally HMRC's draft guidance on 'Double Taxation Relief: Anti Avoidance' issued on 6 May 2005 (at www.hmrc.gov.uk/budget2005/dtraa.pdf).

5.20 ANNUAL PAYMENTS FOR DIVIDENDS OR NON-TAXABLE CONSIDERATION

Any payment (whenever the liability to make it was incurred, but subject to exceptions as below) which is not interest but is an annuity or other annual payment charged with tax under Schedule D, Case III and made for a consideration which is *not wholly* included in the income for tax purposes of the person making the annual payment, shall be paid without deduction of tax and not allowed as a deduction from corporation tax. Nor could such payments made before 16 March 2005 be allowed as a charge on income (after which time they are not treated as a charge on income, see 55.4 PROFIT COMPUTATIONS). With effect for annual payments made on or after 2 December 2004 (irrespective of when the contract or other arrangement is made), these provisions also apply if the payment is made in consideration for the receipt or the right to receive a dividend. Certain admission rights in return for annual payments to charities are disregarded for this purpose (see 14.12(*c*) CHARITIES).

Exceptions to the above provisions are:

(i) certain payments relating to settlements (see Tolley's Income Tax under Settlements (Settlor Retaining an Interest);

(ii) any payments to an individual for surrendering, assigning or releasing an interest in settled property to a person having a subsequent interest;

(iii) payments of any annuity granted in the ordinary course of a business of granting annuities; or

(iv) payments of any annuity charged on an interest in settled property and granted before 30 March 1977 by an individual to a company whose business was wholly or mainly in acquiring such interests or which was carrying on life assurance business in the UK.

For Scotland, reference to settled property refers to property held in trust. For position prior to these provisions see *CIR v Plummer HL 1979, 54 TC 1*, and *Moodie v CIR and Sinnett HL 1993, 65 TC 610*, in which the decision in *Plummer* on similar facts was reversed on *Ramsay* principles (see 5.1 above).

[*ICTA 1988, s 125; FA 2005, s 91(2)(3)(7); ITTOIA 2005, Sch 1 para 107; F(No 2)A 2005, s 38(3)(7)(13), Sch 11 Pt 2(7); ITA 2007 Sch 1 para 125*].

Simon's Direct Tax Service. See **D2.210, E1.502, B5.309**.

5.21 **ARRANGEMENTS TO PASS ON VALUE OF DIVIDEND TAX CREDIT**

Special provisions apply where:

(*a*) a person ('A') is entitled to a tax credit in respect of a qualifying distribution,

(*b*) arrangements (as widely defined) subsist such that another person ('B') obtains, whether directly or indirectly, a payment representing any of the value of the tax credit;

(*c*) the arrangements (whether or not made directly between A and B) were entered into for an 'unallowable purpose'; and

(*d*) had B been entitled to and received the distribution when it was made, he would not have been entitled to payment of the tax credit and, if a company, could not have used the income consisting of the distribution to frank a distribution made in the same accounting period (after using any actual franked investment income).

They apply equally where an amount representing any of the value of the tax credit is applied at the direction of, or otherwise in favour of, some other person, as if that other person had obtained a payment representing that value.

Where these provisions apply:

(i) no claim may be made for payment of the tax credit or for set-off against tax on other income;

(ii) the income consisting of the distribution is not regarded as franked investment income; and

(iii) no transitional charity relief payment (see 14.5 CHARITIES) may be claimed.

This does not, however, apply to the extent that the tax advantage otherwise obtained under the arrangements is cancelled or reduced by any other provision. 'Tax advantage' for this purpose is as under *ICTA 1988, s 709* (see 5.2 above), but also includes the obtaining of a payment representing any of the value of a tax credit where, had the person obtaining the payment been entitled to and received the distribution when it was made, that person would not have been entitled to payment of the tax credit and, if a company, could not have used the income consisting of the distribution to frank a distribution made in the same accounting period (after using any actual franked investment income).

Arrangements are entered into for an '*unallowable purpose*' if any person is a party to the arrangements for purposes which include a purpose other than a business or commercial purpose (which includes the efficient management of investments). The purpose of obtaining a tax advantage for any person is not a business or commercial purpose unless it is not a main purpose of entering into the arrangements.

[*ICTA 1988, s 231B; F(No 2)A 1997, s 28; ITTOIA 2005, Sch 1 para 116*].

5.22 DEALINGS IN COMMODITY FUTURES

Withdrawal of loss relief. For accounting periods beginning on or after 1 October 2002, if, apart from *ICTA 1988, s 128* and *TCGA 1992, s 143(1)*, gains arising in the course of dealing in financial futures or qualifying options would constitute profits or gains chargeable to corporation tax under Schedule D, Case V or VI other than as profits of a trade, any loss arising in the course of that dealing is not allowable against profits or gains so chargeable. For earlier periods, for both income tax and corporation tax purposes, similar provisions applied, but with the exclusion of losses arising from transactions to which *ICTA 1988, Sch 5AA* applied (see 5.23 below).

If a company carries on the trade of dealing in commodity futures in partnership, and a scheme has been effected or arrangements have been made whereby the sole or main benefit that might be expected to accrue to the company from its partnership interest is the making of a loss to be set off against general income under *ICTA 1988, s 393(2)* or *s 393A(1)* (see 47.2 and 47.6 LOSSES), such relief is denied. Any relief already given is recouped by an assessment under Schedule D, Case VI.

[*ICTA 1988, s 399; FA 2002, Sch 27 para 4; ITTOIA 2005, Sch 1 para 171*].

Simon's Direct Tax Service. See D2.408.

5.23 FUTURES AND OPTIONS — TRANSACTIONS WITH GUARANTEED RETURNS

The following provisions **cease to apply for the purposes of corporation tax for accounting periods beginning after 30 September 2002**, being replaced thereafter by specific provisions (to similar effect) in *FA 2002, Sch 26 para 6* and *FA 1996, s 93A* (see 28.8(i) and (ii) and 28.11(E) FINANCIAL INSTRUMENTS AND DERIVATIVE CONTRACTS and 46.39 LOAN RELATIONSHIPS).

The special provisions described below apply to a 'disposal of futures or options' if it is one of two or more 'related' transactions, and it is reasonable to assume that a main purpose of the transactions, taken together, is or was to produce a 'guaranteed return', either from the disposal itself or together with another such disposal or disposals. The likely effect of the transactions, and/or the circumstances in which they, or any of them, is or are entered into, are taken into account for this purpose. For accounting periods ending after 25 July 2001, the provisions also apply to a transaction if it is one of the disposals of futures or options to which *FA 1996, s 93A* (inserted by *FA 2002, s 76*) refers (see 46.39 LOAN RELATIONSHIPS).

A disposal is a '*disposal of futures or options*' if it consists in a disposal of one or more 'futures' or 'options' or of any combination thereof. A '*future*' is any outstanding rights and obligations under a commodity or financial futures contract, and an '*option*' is one listed on a recognised stock or futures exchange or otherwise relating to currency, shares, stock, securities, an interest rate or rights under a commodity or financial futures contract. The existence or timing of a disposal is determined in accordance with *TCGA 1992, ss 143(5)(6), 144, 144A* (see Tolley's Capital Gains Tax under Disposal) and other relevant provisions of that *Act*, modified as necessary for this purpose, on the assumption that all futures are assets. However, a disposal consisting in the grant of an option, which precedes at least one 'related' transaction (or 'associated' transaction within *FA 1995, s 93A*) which is a disposal other than the grant of an option, is deemed for these purposes to be made at the time of (or of the first) such subsequent disposal (except in so far as the provisions of *TCGA 1992* referred to above require the grant of an option and the transaction entered into to fulfil obligations under the option to be treated as a single transaction, and determine the time at which that single transaction is treated as entered into).

Transactions are '*related*' or '*associated*' for these purposes if they are entered into in pursuance of a scheme or arrangements (including understandings of any kind, whether or not legally enforceable). This may include transactions with different parties, or with parties different from the parties to the scheme or arrangements. It also includes any case in which it would be reasonable to assume, from the likely effect of the transactions and/or the circumstances in which they, or any of them, is or are entered into, that neither or none of them would have been entered into independently of the other(s).

A '*guaranteed return*' is produced wherever risks from fluctuations in the subject matter to which the futures or options (or their value) are referable are so eliminated or reduced as to produce a return equating, in substance, to interest and not significantly attributable (otherwise than incidentally) to any such fluctuations. This includes any case where a main reason for the choice of subject matter is that it appears that there is no (or only an insignificant) risk that it will fluctuate. The return from one or more disposals is for these purposes that represented by the total net profits or gains (or all but an insignificant part of those profits or gains), aggregating where appropriate profits or gains of persons who are 'associated' (as specially defined) in relation to the disposals.

Profits or gains realised from a transaction to which these provisions apply (whether capital or not) are treated as income of the person by whom they are realised, chargeable under Schedule D, Case VI for the chargeable period in which the disposal takes place. There are exclusions for profits or gains within the financial instruments provisions of *FA 1994, Pt IV, Ch II* (see 28.29 et seq. FINANCIAL INSTRUMENTS AND DERIVATIVE CONTRACTS) or arising to an authorised unit trust within *ICTA 1988, s 468* (see 43.5 INVESTMENT FUNDS), and for so much of any profits or gains as is chargeable under Case I or Case V of Schedule D on the person to whom they arise. A loss sustained is similarly a Case VI loss within *ICTA 1988, s 392* or *s 396* for the chargeable period of the disposal. The profits or gains (or losses) are not otherwise brought into account for tax purposes (other than as receipts for a Case I computation for life insurance companies under *FA 1989, s 83*).

The charge is extended to cases where there are related (or associated) transactions one of which is or would be the creation or acquisition of a future or option, and another of which is or would be the running of the future to delivery or the exercise of the option, and the latter transaction is not treated under the current provisions as a disposal of a future or option. (Transactions are related or associated for this purpose if they would be but for *TCGA 1992, s 144(2)* or *(3)*, which in certain cases treat the grant or exercise of an option and the transaction in fulfilment of the obligations under the option as a single transaction, see Tolley's Capital Gains Tax under Disposal.) The current provisions then apply to the parties to the future or option as if there was a disposal of the future or option under the arrangements for the related or associated transactions immediately before the future runs to delivery or, as the case may be, the option is exercised. The disposal is treated, in the case of a person whose rights and entitlements under the future or option have a market value at that time, as at that value, or in the case of any other person as made for nil consideration with costs equivalent to those required at arm's length to obtain release of his obligations and liabilities under the future or option. There are special provisions preventing double charge or relief under the current provisions and capital gains tax (or corporation tax on chargeable gains), for which see *ICTA 1988, Sch 5AA para 4A(5)-(10)*.

Insurance companies. For the purposes of *ICTA 1988, s 432A,* income and losses under these provisions are generally treated as gains or losses accruing on the disposal of an asset.

Recovery of assets under Proceeds of Crime Act 2002, Pt 5. Where the transfer of futures or options is a *Pt 5* transfer under *Proceeds of Crime Act 2002* and no compensating payment is made to the transferor, it is not treated as a disposal for the purposes of these provisions. [*Proceeds of Crime Act 2002, Sch 10 paras 8, 10; ITTOIA 2005, Sch 1 para 583*].

[*ICTA 1988, s 127A, Sch 5AA; FA 1998, s 99; FA 2002, ss 78, 141, Sch 27 paras 14, 25, Sch 40 Pt 3(13); ITTOIA 2005, Sch 1 para 109*].

Simon's Direct Tax Service. See B7.204A, D2.1919.

5.24 COMPANIES IN PARTNERSHIP

Where a company realises capital from a partnership on or after 17 March 2004 such that the capital realised exceeds the company's contribution to the partnership and that excess results wholly or partly from an arrangement under which the partnership profits were not fully allocated to the company in accordance with its capital share, the company is chargeable to tax under Schedule D Case VI on the lower of:

(*a*) the excess of the realised capital over contributions; and

(*b*) the amount by which the company's due share of allocated profits exceed the amount allocated to it where those profits would have otherwise been chargeable to corporation tax.

See 52.7 PARTNERSHIPS. [*FA 2004, ss 131–133*].

5.25 CHANGE IN OWNERSHIP OF A COMPANY

There are a number of anti-avoidance provisions relating to the change in ownership of a company which are dealt with as indicated below.

3.8	advance corporation tax – shadow act [*SI 1999 No 358, regs 16–18*].
5.17	Sale of lessors
11.9	CAPITAL GAINS (reconstructions and amalgamations) [*TCGA 1992, ss 101, 101B*].
12.8, 12.20, 12.22, 12.32–12.40	CAPITAL GAINS—GROUPS (pre-entry losses, pre-entry gains and group transactions) [*TCGA 1992, ss 176–179*].
32.12	GROUPS OF COMPANIES [*ICTA 1988, ss 403A–403C, 409, 410*].
42.8	INVESTMENT COMPANIES AND INVESTMENT BUSINESS [*ICTA 1988, ss 768B, 768C, Sch 28A*].
47.13	LOSSES (restrictions on losses carried forward) [*ICTA 1988, ss 768–769*].
53.5	payment of tax (change in ownership of company) [*ICTA 1988, ss 767A, 767B*].

5.26 DISCLOSURE OF TAX AVOIDANCE SCHEMES

With effect on and after **1 August 2004**, *FA 2004* imposes obligations, as outlined below, on promoters of certain tax avoidance schemes, and in some cases on persons entering into transactions under such schemes, to disclose those schemes to HMRC. The primary legislation in *FA 2004, ss 306–319* provides the framework for these disclosure rules but the detailed provisions are mostly contained in regulations. Originally, the provisions required disclosure only of schemes connected with employment or involving financial products, but with effect, broadly, from 1 August 2006, the provisions are extended to cover the whole of income tax, capital gains tax and corporation tax. From that date, the disclosure requirements are triggered where arrangements feature one of seven hallmarks.

Disclosure can be made online via HMRC's Anti-Avoidance Group website (www.hmrc.gov.uk) or alternatively forms for making disclosures can be downloaded from the same location.

Arrangements requiring disclosure. '*Notifiable arrangements*' requiring disclosure under the provisions are 'arrangements' which:

- fall within any description prescribed by Treasury regulations (see below);
- enable, or might be expected to enable, any person to obtain an 'advantage' in relation to any tax (which may include capital gains tax and corporation tax) that is so prescribed in relation to arrangements of that description; and
- are such that the main benefit, or one of the main benefits, that might be expected to arise from the arrangements is the obtaining of that advantage.

The provisions also require disclosure of '*notifiable proposals*', i.e. proposals for arrangements which would be notifiable arrangements if entered into, whether the proposal relates to a particular person or to any person who may seek to take advantage of it.

For these purposes, '*arrangements*' include any scheme, transaction or series of transactions. An '*advantage*', in relation to any tax, means:

- relief or increased relief from, or repayment or increased repayment of, that tax;
- the avoidance or reduction of a charge or assessment to that tax;
- the avoidance of a possible assessment to that tax;
- the deferral of any payment of tax;
- the advancement of any repayment of tax; or
- the avoidance of any obligation to deduct or account for any tax.

[*FA 2004, ss 306, 318*(*1*)].

Enforcement. *FA 2007, s 108* gives HMRC powers to deal with situations where they have grounds for believing that a disclosure should have been made, but either none has been made or that made is thought to be incomplete. They give HMRC the right to apply to the Special Commissioners for an order to treat a scheme or arrangements as notifiable where there is doubt as to whether or not they are so notifiable. The Special Commissioners must be satisfied that the application is reasonable and that all reasonable steps have been taken by HMRC to determine whether the scheme or arrangements are notifiable. Although *FA 2004, s 306A*(*5*) sets out three factors which might make HMRC suspect a scheme is notifiable, these are not exclusive.

Prior to requesting an order, HMRC may issue a written notice to a suspected promoter asking if in his opinion the scheme or arrangements are notifiable by him and, if not, his reasoning in arriving at this decision, by reference to the DOTAS legislation. Once the promoter's reply has been received, HMRC have the right to apply to the Special Commissioners for an order requiring him to produce further information or documents.

The above orders must be complied with within 'the prescribed period' from the date the orders are issued. The period will be set out in a statutory order.

Although these provisions come into force on **19 July 2007**, they may apply to events occurring before that date.

[*FA 2004, ss 306A, 308A, 313A, 313B, 314A, 317A; FA 2007 s 108*].

Prescribed arrangements — August 2006 onwards. With effect as indicated below, any arrangements which fall within any of the descriptions (or '*hallmarks*') listed below are prescribed by the Treasury for the purposes of these provisions. The taxes covered are income tax, capital gains tax and corporation tax. These provisions apply with effect from 1 August 2006 but do not apply to notifiable proposals where the relevant date (see below) is before that date nor to notifiable arrangements, in relation to which the disclosure requirement falls on:

- a promoter, where the promoter first becomes aware of any transaction forming part of the arrangements before that date; or
- a person other than a promoter, where any transaction forming part of the arrangements is entered into before that date.

The hallmarks are as follows.

(1) *Confidentiality in cases involving a promoter.* Arrangements fall within this hallmark if it might be reasonably expected that a promoter would wish the way in which the arrangements secure a tax advantage to be kept confidential from any other promoter at any time in the period beginning with the date of the first transaction forming part of the arrangements and ending with the date by which the user of the arrangements must notify HMRC of the reference number (see below). Arrangements also fall within this hallmark if either:

  - the promoter would, but for these provisions, wish to keep the way in which the arrangements secure a tax advantage confidential from HMRC for some or all of that period and a reason for doing so is to facilitate repeated or continued use of the element of the arrangements which secure the advantage or of substantially the same element; or
  - where there is no promoter by virtue only of legal professional privilege ((C) below) or the promoter is not UK resident, the user of the arrangements wishes to keep confidential from HMRC the way that the arrangements secure a tax advantage for some or all of that period.

(2) *Confidentiality in cases not involving a promoter.* Arrangements fall within this hallmark if there is no promoter and:

  - the intended user of the arrangements is a business (as defined) which is not a '*small or medium-sized enterprise*' (broadly, a micro, small or medium-sized enterprise as defined in the Commission Recommendation of 6 May 2003);
  - the user wishes the way in which the arrangements secure a tax advantage to be kept confidential from HMRC for some or all of the period beginning with the date on which he enters into the first transaction forming part of the arrangements and ending with the latest date by which he must notify HMRC of the reference number; and
  - a reason for doing so is to facilitate repeated or continued use of the element of the arrangements which secure the advantage or of substantially the same element.

(3) *Premium fee.* Arrangements fall within this hallmark if they are such that it might reasonably be expected that a promoter or a person connected with a promoter of arrangements that are the same as, or substantially similar to, the arrangements in question, would, but for these provisions, be able to obtain a 'premium fee' from a person experienced in receiving services of the type being provided. Arrangements where there is no promoter or where the tax advantage is intended to be obtained by an individual or business which is a small or medium-sized enterprise are excluded. A '*premium fee*' for this purpose is one chargeable by virtue of any element of the

arrangements from which the tax advantage is expected to arise and which is to a significant extent attributable to, or to any extent contingent on the obtaining of, that advantage.

(4) *Off market terms.* Arrangements fall within this hallmark if:

- the tax advantage expected from the arrangements arises, to more than an incidental degree, from the inclusion of one or more 'financial products';
- a promoter or person connected with the promoter becomes party to one or more of those products; and
- the price of the product or products differs significantly from that which might reasonably be expected to apply in the open market.

For this purpose, the following are '*financial products*':

(*a*) loans (excluding finance leases);

(*b*) derivative contracts under *FA 2002, Sch 26*, including contracts otherwise excluded by virtue of their underlying subject matter (see 28 FINANCIAL INSTRUMENTS AND DERIVATIVE CONTRACTS);

(c) contracts which would be within (*b*) above if they were contracts of a company;

(*d*) agreements for the sale and repurchase of securities as described in *ICTA 1988, s 730A*(*1*) (see 5.6 above);

(*e*) stock lending arrangements within *TCGA 1992, s 263B*(*1*) (see Tolley's Capital Gains Tax under Shares and Securities);

(*f*) shares; and

(*g*) any contract (other than the above) whether on its own or in combination with other contracts (including any of the above) which in accordance with UK generally accepted accounting practice is in substance and so treated as a loan or the advancing or depositing of money in whatever form (excluding finance leases).

Financial products held within an ISA are excluded.

(5) *Standardised tax products.* Arrangements fall within this hallmark if they are 'tax products' which are made available by a promoter for implementation by more than one person. A 'product' is a '*tax product*' for this purpose if it would be reasonable for an informed observer who had studied the arrangements to conclude that their main purpose was to enable a client to obtain a tax advantage. Arrangements are a '*product*' if:

- they have substantially standardised documentation to enable implementation of the arrangements by the client and the form of that documentation is determined by the promoter and not tailored to any material extent to the client;
- the client must enter into a specific transaction or series of transactions; and that transaction or series of transactions are substantially standardised in form.

Arrangements which are the same, or substantially the same, as arrangements first made available for implementation before 1 August 2006 are excluded, as are arrangements consisting solely of one more plant or machinery leases (see (7) below), an Enterprise Investment Scheme (See Tolley's Income Tax under Enterprise Investment Scheme) or ISA, arrangements using the CORPORATE VENTURING SCHEME (22) or VENTURE CAPITAL TRUSTS (69), arrangements qualifying for COMMUNITY INVESTMENT TAX RELIEF (17), specified approved employee share schemes, certain pension schemes and schemes to which *ITTOIA 2005, s 731* (periodical payments of personal injury damages) applies.

(6) *Loss schemes.* Arrangements are within this hallmark if the promoter expects more than one individual to implement them or to implement arrangements which are substantially the same and an informed observer, having studied them, could reasonably conclude that the main benefit of the arrangements for some or all of the participants would be the provision of losses which they would be expected to use to reduce their liability to income tax or capital gains tax.

(7) *Leasing arrangements.* Arrangements falling within this hallmark include a high value plant or machinery lease which is not a short-term lease where one of three additional conditions are met as set out below.

A '*plant or machinery lease*' for this purpose is:

- any agreement or arrangement which, in accordance with generally accepted accounting practice, falls (or would fall) to be treated as a lease under which the lessor grants to the lessee the right to use the plant or machinery for a period;
- any other agreement or arrangement to the extent that, in accordance with generally accepted accounting practice, it conveys or falls (or would fall) to be regarded as conveying the right to use the plant or machinery; or
- a finance lease under *CAA 2001, s 221(1)(c)* where the plant or machinery is the subject of a sale and finance leaseback as defined under that section.

The lease is a '*high value*' lease if the lower of the cost to the lessor, or the market value, of either:

- any one asset forming part of the plant or machinery leased or to be leased under the arrangements is at least £10 million; or
- the aggregate of all the assets forming part of the plant or machinery leased or to be leased under the arrangements is at least £25 million.

The lease is a '*short-term lease*' if it has a term not exceeding two years. It will not be a short-term lease if the lessee can extend the term beyond two years by the exercise of an option or by some other arrangement entered into at the inception of the lease. Nor will it be a short-term lease if arrangements are entered into, at or about the time of the inception of the lease, for the assets to be leased to one or more other persons under one or more other leases and the aggregate of the terms of the lease to the lessee and to such other persons as are connected with the lessee exceed two years.

The three additional additions, one of which must also be met, are as follows.

- Condition 1 is that the arrangements are designed such that one or more of the leases comprised in the arrangements are, or would be, entered into by one party who has the right to claim capital allowances on expenditure incurred on the plant or machinery and by another party (ignoring guarantors) who is not, or would not be, chargeable to corporation tax (whether or not there are other parties to the lease who satisfy neither of those conditions).
- Condition 2 is that the arrangements are designed to remove the whole or greater part of any risk of a loss which would otherwise fall directly or

indirectly upon the lessor if the payments due under the lease are not made in accordance with its terms and the risk is so removed by the provision of money or a money debt (as defined in *ITEPA 2003, s 702(6)*).

- Condition 3 is that the arrangements are designed to consist of, or include, a sale and finance leaseback arrangement (within *CAA 2001, s 221*) or a lease and finance leaseback (within *CAA 2001, s 228F(5)*). This does not apply where assets leased, or to be leased, under sale and finance leaseback arrangements are, or will be, unused and not second-hand at the time when the assets are acquired or created and where the interval between the acquisition or creation of the assets and their sale under the arrangements is not more than four months.

  Condition 3 does not apply if the plant or machinery is, or the promoter expects it to become, a fixture (as defined by *CAA 2001, s 173(1)*) which is leased with relevant land (as defined by *CAA 2001, s 173(2)*) unless it is used for storage or production (as defined). It will, however, apply if the qualifying expenditure incurred on that fixture amounts or will amount to more than 50% of the aggregate value of assets subject to the lease and the rent payable under the lease is directly or indirectly dependent on the availability of capital allowances on expenditure on any plant or machinery comprised in the lease. In determining the value of the assets subject to the lease, the value of the land is the market value of the lessor's interest and the value of plant or machinery is to be determined in the same manner as for a 'high value' lease above.

For the purpose only of determining whether arrangements are prescribed by (1)–(3) or (7) above, the provision that persons are not to be treated as promoters by virtue of legal professional privilege ((C) below) is disregarded.

[*SI 2006 No 1543*].

See also HMRC's guidance published on their website on 16 June 2006.

Prescribed arrangements — pre-August 2006. Prior to the introduction of the hallmark system above, there were two types of arrangements prescribed by the Treasury. They were arrangements connected with employment (for details of which see Tolley's Income Tax), and arrangements related to financial products. The taxes covered were income tax, capital gains tax and corporation tax.

The arrangements in relation to financial products which had to be disclosed were those where the tax advantage was expected to derive to a significant degree from the inclusion of any financial products (defined as above).

Disclosure of arrangements relating to financial products was not required where:

- they (or similar arrangements) were not reasonably expected to generate premium fees for their promotion; and
- the tax advantage expected to be obtained did not arise from any element of the arrangements which the promoter might reasonably have expected to be kept confidential from other promoters.

Disclosure was also not required where:

- the only financial products involved in the arrangements were assets held within an ISA or a PEP; or
- the promoter (or person connected with the promoter) became a party to the financial product which did not differ significantly from that which might reasonably be expected to be offered in the open market.

[*SI 2004 No 1863, Sch paras 6–8; SI 2004 No 2429; SI 2006 No 1543, reg 18*].

For examples of transactions which would and would not fall within these provisions, see HMRC's guidance material published on their website (www.hmrc.gov.uk) on 29 July 2004.

Disclosure by promoter. A 'promoter' must provide HMRC with specified information on any 'notifiable proposal' within a prescribed period of five business days after the 'relevant date'. The '*relevant date*' is the date on which he makes the proposal available for implementation by any person or, if earlier, the date he first becomes aware of any transaction forming part of arrangements implementing the proposal or by 30 September 2004 if later. The time limit for disclosure is extended where the promoter reasonably expects to make a clearance application (see below) to HMRC under certain specified provisions.

There is a separate requirement for a 'promoter' to provide HMRC with specified information relating to notifiable arrangements and to do so within a prescribed period of five business days after the date on which he first becomes aware of any transaction forming part of those arrangements, or by 30 September 2004 if later; but this does not apply if the arrangements implement a proposal which has been notified as above.

The disclosure under these provisions must provide sufficient information as might be reasonably expected to enable a Revenue officer to comprehend the manner in which the proposal or arrangements are intended to operate, including the details specified in *SI 2004 No 1864, reg 3*.

Where two or more persons are promoters in relation to the same proposal or arrangements, notification by one promoter discharges the obligations of the others. If a promoter has discharged his obligations in relation to a proposal or arrangements, he is not required to notify proposals or arrangements which are substantially the same as those already notified (whether or not they relate to the same parties).

Transitional provisions. The above obligations do not apply in the case of any notifiable proposal for which the relevant date (as above) fell before 18 March 2004, or in the case of any notifiable arrangements which implement such a proposal or any notifiable arrangements which include a transaction entered into before that date. In the case of notifiable proposals or arrangements relating to financial products, the requirements do not apply if the relevant date or, as appropriate, the date on which the promoter first becomes aware of any transaction forming part of the arrangements, falls before 22 June 2004. The time limit for disclosure of all notifiable proposals or arrangements is extended to 31 October 2004 where the relevant date or, as appropriate, the date on which the promoter first becomes aware of any transaction forming part of the arrangements, falls before 1 August 2004.

Meaning of promoter. A person is a '*promoter*' in relation to a notifiable proposal if, in the course of a 'relevant business', he is to any extent responsible for the design of the proposed arrangements or he makes the notifiable proposal available for implementation by others. A person is a '*promoter*' in relation to notifiable arrangements if, by virtue of his having made the proposal available for implementation, he is a promoter in relation to a notifiable proposal which is implemented by those arrangements or if, in the course of a 'relevant business', he is to any extent responsible for the design of the arrangements or the organisation or management of the arrangements.

The regulations (*SI 2004 No 1865*, as amended by *SI 2004 No 2613*) exclude from the definition of promoter:

(A) a company providing taxation services to another company in the same 51% group;

(B) employees of employers who are promoters of or enter into transactions forming part of proposed arrangements;

(C) a person who is not required to provide the prescribed information by virtue of legal professional privilege (see below under Legal professional privilege);

(D) persons not responsible for the design of any element of the proposals or arrangements giving rise to the expected tax advantage;

(E) persons who are to any extent responsible for the design of the proposals or arrangements but who do not provide tax advice in relation to them in a professional capacity;

(F) persons not responsible for the design of all the elements of the proposals or arrangements giving rise to the expected tax advantage, who could not reasonably be expected to have sufficient information so as to know whether the proposals or arrangements fall within these provisions or sufficient information to be able to comply with the duties of a promoter;

(G) a person not connected with a promoter in relation to the arrangements or arrangements which are substantially the same as those arrangements.

A '*relevant business*' is any trade, profession or business which involves the provision to other persons of taxation services or is carried on by a bank or a securities house. Where companies form a 51% group, anything done by one group company for the purposes of another company's relevant business is brought within the above disclosure requirements.

[*FA 2004, ss 307, 308, 319(3); SI 2004 No 1864, regs 1, 3(1)(2), 4(1)–(3), 5, 6; SI 2004 No 1865; SI 2004 No 2613*].

Disclosure by person dealing with non-UK promoter. A person who enters into any transaction forming part of notifiable arrangements in relation to which there is a non-UK resident promoter (and no UK resident promoter) must himself provide HMRC with specified information (similar to that which a promoter must provide) relating to those arrangements. He must do so within a prescribed period of five business days after entering into the transaction or by 30 September 2004 if later. This obligation is discharged if a promoter makes disclosure of the notifiable proposal for the arrangements in question.

This provision does not apply in relation to any notifiable arrangements which include transactions entered into before 23 April 2004. In the case of notifiable arrangements relating to financial products, the provision does not apply if the date on which any transaction forming part of the arrangements is entered into falls before 22 June 2004. The time limit for disclosure of all notifiable arrangements is extended to 31 October 2004 where the date on which any transaction forming part of the arrangements is entered into falls before 1 August 2004.

[*FA 2004, ss 309, 319(4); SI 2004 No 1864, regs 1, 3(3), 4(4)(7), 6*].

Disclosure by parties to notifiable arrangements not involving a promoter. A person who enters into any transaction forming part of notifiable arrangements in respect of which neither he nor any other person in the UK has an obligation as above must himself provide HMRC with specified information (similar to that which a promoter must provide) relating to those arrangements. Such disclosure must normally be made within 30 days beginning with the day after the day in which he enters into the first transaction forming part of the arrangements. However, where a person is not to be treated as a promoter in relation to notifiable arrangements by virtue of legal professional privilege (see below under Legal professional privilege), the disclosure must be made within five business days after entering into the transaction (subject to the transitional commencement provisions below). Before 1 August 2006, a disclosure under these provisions could, unless the five-day time limit applied, be made at any time after the date of the first transaction and before the person was first required to notify HMRC of the reference number for the arrangements (see below).

This does not apply in relation to any notifiable arrangements which include a transaction entered into before 23 April 2004. In the case of notifiable arrangements relating to financial products, the provision does not apply if the date on which any transaction forming part of the arrangements is entered into falls before 22 June 2004. The time limit for disclosure of all notifiable arrangements is extended to 31 October 2004 where the date on which any transaction forming part of the arrangements is entered into falls before 1 August 2004.

[*FA 2004, ss 310, 319(4); SI 2004 No 1864, regs 1, 3(4), 4(5)(5A), 6; SI 2004 No 2613, reg 2; SI 2006 No 1544, reg 4*].

Reference numbers allocated to arrangements. Where a person has made a disclosure as above, HMRC may allocate a reference number to the arrangements in question and must notify the number to that person within 30 days after the disclosure. (The allocation of a reference number does not in itself indicate that HMRC consider the scheme will result in the successful avoidance of tax.) A promoter who is providing services to a client in connection with notifiable arrangements must pass on to the client the reference number for those arrangements or for arrangements which are substantially the same as those arrangements. He must do so within 30 days after the date he first becomes aware of any transaction forming part of the arrangements or, if later, the date on which the reference number is notified to him by HMRC.

A company which is a party to any notifiable arrangements giving rise to a corporation tax or capital gains tax advantage must quote the allocated reference number in its company tax return for the accounting period in which the company is notified of the number (or, if earlier, the accounting period in which the tax advantage is expected to arise) and in all subsequent returns until the advantage ceases to apply to the company. The company must also quote the accounting period in which, or the date on which, the advantage is expected to arise. Comparable provisions apply for income tax. For arrangements under which a tax advantage is expected to arise by reason of a person's employment, the obligation falls on the employer to quote the reference number etc. on a return in such form as HMRC may specify. Where the arrangements are connected with employment under the pre-August 2006 regulations (see above), the employer must quote the reference number etc. in the annual return on form P35 for the appropriate tax year. Persons not required to file a tax return or, as the case may be, a P35 return, must instead provide HMRC with specified information no later than what would have been the filing date for such a return.

[*FA 2004, ss 311–313; SI 2004 No 1864, reg 8; SI 2006 No 1544, reg 6*].

Legal professional privilege. These provisions do not require the disclosure of privileged information, i.e. information with respect to which a claim to legal professional privilege (or Scottish equivalent) could be maintained in legal proceedings. [*FA 2004, s 314*]. Where a person is not to be treated as a promoter for this reason, the party to the notifiable arrangements or notifiable proposals (the taxpayer making use of the scheme) must make the appropriate disclosure.

Penalties. The maximum penalty for failure to comply with any of the disclosure obligations above is £5,000 (such penalty to be determined by the Special Commissioners). In the case of continuing failure after such a penalty is imposed, there is a daily penalty of up to £600 per day. Penalties of the same level apply if a promoter fails in his duty to notify a reference number to a client.

A party to notifiable arrangements who fails to give the reference number as required (for example, by including it in his tax return) is liable to a penalty of £100 for each scheme (i.e. each set of notifiable arrangements) to which the failure relates. A second such failure within a period of 36 months gives rise to a penalty of £500 per scheme. A third or subsequent failure within 36 months gives rise to a penalty of £1,000 per scheme. The pre-existing penalty regime for incorrect tax returns is, however, disapplied in relation to any such failure.

Statutory clearances. Special provisions apply where a promoter reasonably expects to make a clearance application on behalf of a client relating to:

- distributions and payments (*ICTA 1988, s 215* – see 32.39);

- purchase of own shares (*ICTA 1988, s 225* – see 57.6);
- the transfer of long-term insurance business (*ICTA 1988, s 444A*);
- transactions in securities (*ICTA 1988, s 707* – see 5.2 above); or
- share exchanges (*TCGA 1992, ss 138, 139, 140B, 140D* – see Tolley's Capital Gains under Anti-Avoidance).

If the promoter:

(i) reasonably expects to make such an application; and

(ii) must also disclose a notifiable proposal for which the relevant date is the date on which he makes the proposal available for implementation by any other person,

then the prescribed period for making the disclosure is the period beginning with the day after that relevant date and ending on the date on which the transaction first occurs in pursuance of the arrangements. But if the promoter ceases to hold a reasonable expectation of making the clearance application, the prescribed period ends five business days after he ceases to hold it.

[*SI 2004 No 1864, reg 5*].

Simon's Direct Tax Service. See **A3.19**.

5.27 **TAX ARBITRAGE**

F(No 2)A 2005 introduced anti-avoidance provisions to prevent the exploitation by companies of differences between or within national tax codes using hybrid entities or instruments (known as tax arbitrage). The provisions operate by reducing or disallowing deductions or by bringing receipts into charge, but apply only where HMRC issue a notice to the company. Separate provisions apply in relation to deductions cases and receipts cases. See below for the commencement rules.

The following apply for the purposes of the provisions. A '*scheme*' is any scheme, arrangements or understanding of any kind, whether or not legally enforceable, involving a single transaction or two or more transactions. The circumstances in which any two or more transactions are to be taken as forming part of a series of transactions or a scheme include any case in which it would be reasonable to assume that one or more of them would not have been entered into independently of the others or if entered into independently would not have taken the same form or have been on the same terms. It is immaterial in determining whether any transactions form part of a series of transactions that the parties to any of the transactions are different from the parties to another of the transactions. A scheme achieves a '*UK tax advantage*' for a person if in consequence of the scheme that person is in a position to obtain, or has obtained:

- a relief (including a tax credit) or increased relief from,
- a repayment or increased repayment of, or
- the avoidance or reduction of a charge to

income tax or corporation tax. In particular, avoidance or reduction of a charge to tax may be effected by receipts accruing in such a way that the recipient does not pay or bear tax on them or by a deduction in computing profits or gains. [*F(No 2)A 2005, s 30*].

Deductions cases. Subject to the commencement rules below, the following provisions apply to a company which is resident in the UK, or a non-resident company which is within the charge to corporation tax, if the following conditions are satisfied in relation to a transaction to which the company is a party.

(*a*) The transaction forms part of a scheme which is a 'qualifying scheme' (see below).

(*b*) The scheme is such that for corporation tax purposes the company is in a position to claim, or has claimed, an amount by way of deduction in respect of the transaction or is in a position to set off, or has set off, against profits in an accounting period an amount relating to the transaction.

(*c*) The main purpose, or one of the main purposes, of the scheme is to achieve a UK tax advantage for the company.

(*d*) The amount of the UK tax advantage is more than a minimal amount.

If the Commissioners for HMRC consider, on reasonable grounds, that the above conditions are or may be satisfied they may give the company a notice specifying the transaction involved, the accounting period in respect of which condition (*b*) above is or may be satisfied and informing the company that as a consequence the provisions apply. The Commissioners may issue such a notice to a company in respect of two or more transactions.

If a company receives a notice and conditions (*a*)–(*d*) above are in fact satisfied at the time it is given, the company must compute (or recompute) its income or chargeable gains for corporation tax purposes or its liability to corporation tax for the specified accounting period and any subsequent accounting period in accordance with the following two rules.

The first rule is that no deduction is allowable in respect of the transaction specified in the notice to the extent that an amount in relation to the expense in question may be otherwise deducted or allowed in computing the income, profits or losses of any person for the purposes of any tax (including foreign tax (within the meaning of *ICTA 1988, s 403D*) but excluding petroleum revenue tax and tax chargeable under *ICTA 1988, s 501A(1)* in respect of ring fence trades), or would be so deductible or allowable but for a rule (whether a UK or non-UK tax provision) that has the same effect as this provision.

The second rule applies where a transaction or series of transactions forming part of the scheme involves a payment which creates a deduction or allowance for tax purposes (including foreign tax purposes) for the payer or another party to the scheme but the payee is not liable to tax on the receipt or has its tax liability reduced as a result of the scheme. For this purpose, the circumstances in which a payee is treated as having its liability to tax reduced as a result of the scheme include where it can set-off against its income an expense or relief arising out of the scheme. A payee is not treated as not liable to tax on the receipt if it is not liable to tax on any income or gains under the tax law of any territory or if it is not liable to tax on the receipt because of a statutory exemption which exempts it from tax in respect of income or gains without providing that those income or gains are to be treated as those of another person.

Where the second rule applies, the aggregate of the amounts allowable as a deduction in computing profits for corporation tax purposes arising from the transaction specified in the notice and any other transactions forming part of the scheme and to which the company is party must be reduced. If the payee is not liable to tax on the receipt (as above), the aggregate is reduced to nil. If the payee is liable to tax on part of the receipt or its liability to tax is reduced as above, the aggregate is reduced proportionately to correspond to the payee's liability (treating the amount by which the payee's liability is reduced as an amount on which the payee is not liable to tax).

Instead of applying the above two rules, the company may choose to incorporate in its tax return for the specified accounting period any adjustments that are necessary to counteract the effects of the scheme that are referable to the purpose mentioned in (*c*) above. The adjustments to be made are to treat all or part of a deduction as not being allowable, or all or part of an amount which may be set off against profits as not falling to be set off. If the adjustments fully counteract the effects of the scheme the company is treated as having complied with the provisions. Clearance can be sought as to the amount of the necessary adjustment (see under '*Clearance*' below).

See below for further provisions governing the effects of a notice under the above provisions.

The above provisions apply for accounting periods of a company beginning on or after 16 March 2005. Accounting periods straddling that date are treated for this purpose as consisting of two accounting periods, the first ending on 15 March 2005, and the second beginning on 16 March 2005. The provisions do not, however, apply in the case of a transaction to which a company is party on 16 March 2005 if the company is not on that date connected (within *ICTA 1988, s 839*) with any other person who is on that date a party to, or concerned in, the scheme, and the scheme ceases to exist before 31 August 2005.

[*F(No 2)A 2005, ss 24, 25, 31(1)–(3)(5)*].

Qualifying scheme. A scheme is a '*qualifying scheme*' for the purposes of the above provisions if it is one of the following types.

(1) A scheme in which a party to a transaction forming part of the scheme is a 'hybrid entity'. For this purpose, an entity is a '*hybrid entity*' if under the tax law of any territory it is regarded as a person but its profits or gains are, for the purposes of a '*relevant tax*' (i.e. income tax, corporation tax or similar non-UK tax) under the law of any territory, treated as the profits of gains of a different person or persons. An entity is not so treated by reason only of its profits or gains being subject to a non-UK tax rule similar to that in *ICTA 1988, s 747(3)* (imputation of profits of CONTROLLED FOREIGN COMPANIES (21)).

(2) A scheme where one of the parties to the scheme is party to an instrument of which, under the law of a particular territory, a 'relevant characteristic' may be altered on the election of any party to the instrument. A characteristic of an instrument is a '*relevant characteristic*' if, under the law of a particular territory, altering it has the effect of determining whether or not, for that territory's tax purposes, the instrument is taken into account as giving rise to income or capital. For this purpose, an instrument is taken into account as giving rise to capital if a gain on disposal would be a chargeable gain, or would be if the person making the disposal were UK-resident.

(3) A scheme which includes the issuing by a company of shares subject to conversion or the amendment of rights attaching to shares issued by a company such that the shares become shares subject to conversion. Shares of a company are subject to conversion for this purpose if the rights attaching to them include provision by virtue of which a holder is entitled, on the occurrence of an event, to acquire securities (within the meaning of 23.13 DISTRIBUTIONS) in that or another company by conversion or exchange and the occurrence of that event is within the reasonable expectation of the company either at the time when the shares are issued or at the time the rights attaching to the shares are amended.

(4) A scheme which includes the issuing by a company of securities subject to conversion or the amendment of rights attaching to securities issued by a company such that the securities become securities subject to conversion. Securities of a company are subject to conversion for this purpose if the rights attaching to them include provision by virtue of which a holder is entitled, on the occurrence of an event, to acquire shares in that or another company by conversion or exchange and the occurrence of that event is within the reasonable expectation of the company either at the time when the securities are issued or at the time the rights attaching to the securities are amended.

(5) A scheme which includes a 'debt instrument' issued by a company that is treated as equity in the company under generally accepted accounting practice (within *FA 2004, s 50*). A '*debt instrument*' for this purpose is an instrument issued by a company that represents a loan relationship (see 46.2 LOAN RELATIONSHIPS), or would do if the company were UK-resident.

(6) A scheme which includes the issue by a company to a connected person (within *ICTA 1988, s 839*) of shares other than shares which, on their issue, are ordinary shares that are fully paid-up, which confer a 'qualifying beneficial entitlement' at all times in the accounting period in which they are issued and in respect of which there is no arrangement or understanding at the time of issue under which the rights attaching to the shares may be amended. A share in a company confers a '*qualifying beneficial entitlement*' if it confers a beneficial entitlement to the same proportion of any profits available for distribution to equity holders of the company, and of any assets available for distribution to equity holders on a winding-up, as the proportion of the issued share capital represented by that share. *ICTA 1988, Sch 18* (equity holders and profits or assets available for distribution — see 32.8, 32.9 GROUPS OF COMPANIES) applies for this purpose as it applies for the purposes of group relief.

(7) A scheme which includes a transaction or series of transactions under which a person transfers rights to receive a payment under a 'relevant security' to one or more other persons or otherwise secures that one or more other persons are similarly benefited (i.e. that they receive a payment which would, but for the transaction or series of transactions, have arisen to the transferor), and:

- the transferor and at least one of the persons to whom a transfer of rights is made, or similar benefit is secured, are connected (within *ICTA 1988, s 839*); and
- following the transfer of rights or securing of the similar benefit, two or more persons either hold rights to receive a payment under the security or enjoy a similar benefit, and the rights held and benefits enjoyed by such of those persons as are connected have, taken together, a market value equal to or greater than the market value of any other such rights and benefits, taken together.

For this purpose, a '*relevant security*' is a security or any agreement under which a person receives an annuity or other annual payment (whether payable annually or at shorter or longer intervals) for a term which is not contingent on the duration of a human life or lives.

[*F(No 2)A 2005, Sch 3*].

Receipts cases. The provisions below apply to a company resident in the UK if the following conditions are satisfied.

(i) A scheme makes or imposes provision (the '*actual provision*') as between the company and another person (the '*paying party*') by means of a transaction or series of transactions.

(ii) The actual provision includes the making by the paying party, by means of a transaction or series of transactions, of a 'qualifying payment'. For this purpose, a '*qualifying payment*' is a contribution to the capital of the company made on or after 16 March 2005.

(iii) As regards the qualifying payment made by the paying party, there is an amount that is available for deduction for UK tax purposes or that may be deducted or otherwise allowable under the tax law of a territory outside the UK. (Such an amount is, however, disregarded for this purpose if or to the extent that it is set for tax purposes against any income arising to the paying party from the transaction or transactions forming part of the scheme.) This condition is not treated as satisfied if the paying party is a dealer (as defined) who incurs losses in the ordinary course of his business in respect of the transaction or transactions and the amount by reference to which this condition would otherwise be satisfied is an amount in respect of those losses.

(iv) At least part of the qualifying payment is not:

(A) income or gains arising to the company in the accounting period in which the qualifying payment was made; or

(B) income arising to any other company resident in the UK in a 'corresponding' accounting period (i.e. an accounting period with at least one day in common with the accounting period in (A) above); or

(C) taken into account in determining the loan relationship credits or debits to be brought into account by a company as respects a share in another company under *FA 1996, ss 91A, 91B* (shares treated as loan relationships — see 46.35 LOAN RELATIONSHIPS).

(v) On entering into the scheme the company and the paying party expected that a benefit would arise as a result of (iv) above being satisfied (whether by reference to all or part of the qualifying payment).

If the Commissioners for HMRC consider, on reasonable grounds, that the above conditions are or may be satisfied they may give the company a notice specifying the qualifying payment involved, the accounting period in which the payment is made and informing the company that as a consequence the following provisions apply.

If a company receives a notice and conditions (i)–(v) above are in fact satisfied at the time it is given, the company must compute (or recompute) its income or chargeable gains for corporation tax purposes or its liability to corporation tax for the specified accounting period as if the part of the qualifying payment by reference to which (iii) and (iv) above are satisfied were an amount of income arising to the company in that period and chargeable under Schedule D, Case VI. If (iii) and (iv) above are satisfied in relation to the whole of the qualifying payment, the whole of the payment is so chargeable.

See below for further provisions governing the effects of a notice under the above provisions.

[*F(No 2)A 2005, ss 26, 27, 31(4)(5)*].

Effects of a notice. If a notice under either of the above provisions is given before the company has made its return for the specified accounting period then, if the return is made in the period of 90 days beginning with the day on which the notice is given, it may disregard the notice, and at any time before the end of the 90 days the company may amend the return in order to comply with the notice.

If no notice has been given before the company's return has been made, a notice may only be given if the company has been given a notice of enquiry (see 61.10 RETURNS) in respect of the return. After an enquiry has been completed, a notice may only be given if:

- at the time the enquiry was completed the Commissioners for HMRC could not have reasonably been expected, on the basis of the information made available (within *FA 1998, Sch 18 para 44(2)(3)* — see 7.2(*b*) ASSESSMENTS) to them or an officer of Revenue and Customs before that time, to have been aware that the circumstances were such that a notice could have been given; and
- the company was requested to provide information during the enquiry and, if it had been so provided, the Commissioners could reasonably have been expected to give the company a notice.

If the notice is given after the company has made its return, it may amend the return to comply with the notice within 90 days beginning with the day on which the notice is given. If the notice is given after an enquiry into the return has started, a closure notice (see 61.14 RETURNS) may not be issued until the end of the period of 90 days beginning with the issue of the notice or, if earlier, an amendment is made to the return complying with the notice. If the notice is given after the completion of an enquiry, a discovery assessment (see 7.2 ASSESSMENTS) in relation to the income or chargeable gain to which it relates may not be made until the end of the period of 90 days beginning with the issue of the notice or, if earlier, an amendment is made to the return complying with the notice.

Where a notice is issued and no amendment is made to the return for the purpose of complying with it, the above provisions do not prevent a return becoming incorrect if such an amendment should have been made.

[*F(No 2)A 2005, s 28*].

Clearance. Requests can be made to HMRC for advice about the legislation, including whether it will apply to a planned series of transactions that may constitute a scheme and, where possible, they will advise whether any notice will be issued in respect of the disclosed transactions. They will not give a clearance where the company seeking the clearance has not provided all the relevant information necessary for them to decide whether the legislation is applicable. Clearance applications and questions regarding the clearance procedures should be made to Andrew Hoar, HMRC (International CT), 100 Parliament Street, London, SW1A 2BQ (Email: Andrew.hoar@hmrc.gsi.gov.uk, Tel: 020 7147 2719). The International unit will aim to respond within 28 days provided all relevant information is included but if a request is made for a clearance decision to be given by a specific date, HMRC will try to meet that request. Certain information is required in all cases but the information required depends to some extent on the nature and characteristics of each case. HMRC will consider itself bound by a clearance given in accordance with the required procedure. (See Annex C of HMRC's guidance notes on 'Avoidance through Arbitrage' available on the HMRC website (at www.hmrc.gov.uk/international/arbitrage-guidance.pdf).

HMRC guidance. See generally HMRC guidance 'Avoidance involving Tax Arbitrage' including a series of worked examples available on the HMRC website (at www.hmrc.gov.uk/international/arbitrage.htm).

6 Appeals

Cross references. See 5 ASSESSMENTS, 14.10 CHARITIES, 15.6 CLAIMS for appeals in connection with claims not made in the company tax return, 30.4 FRAUDULENT OR NEGLIGENT CONDUCT for investigatory powers of HMRC, 33.2 HMRC: ADMINISTRATION as regards Appeal Commissioners, 53.4 PAYMENT OF TAX for payment of tax in relation to appeals and 54.12 PENALTIES.

Simon's Direct Tax Service A3.5, A3.7.

The Department for Constitutional Affairs has produced a leaflet: 'Tax Appeals: A Guide to Appealing against Decisions of the Inland Revenue on Tax and Other Matters', which replaces Inland Revenue leaflet IR 37 from July 2004. The leaflet should be available from HMRC offices and enquiry centres.

The headings in this chapter are as follows.

6.1 INTRODUCTION

For accounting periods ending **on or after 1 July 1999**, a company self-assesses its own tax liability and HMRC may then commence an enquiry following which the company may amend the return (see 61.15 RETURNS), failing which HMRC may amend the return. HMRC is also empowered to make determinations in the absence of a return and also discovery assessments or determinations (see 7.2 ASSESSMENTS, 61.18 RETURNS).

Notice of appeal. Notice of appeal against an HMRC amendment to a corporation tax return following an enquiry, or against an assessment which is not a self-assessment, must be given, within 30 days after the notification of the amendment, or assessment, to the HMRC officer who issued it. It must specify the grounds of appeal, although on the hearing of the appeal the Commissioners may consider new grounds if they are satisfied that their omission was not wilful or unreasonable. [*FA 1998, Sch 18 paras 34, 48, 92*].

Appeals heard by General or Special Commissioners. An appeal against:

(*a*) an amendment by HMRC of a self-assessment during an enquiry to prevent a loss of tax, or of a company tax return on completion of the enquiry where the company fails to amend the return within 30 days; or

(*b*) a determination, where a return incorrectly states an amount affecting a tax liability of another period or another company, of the amount which ought to have been stated in the return; or (*c*) an assessment other than a self-assessment,

is to the Special Commissioners if the appeal is against a decision of the Commissioners of HMRC, otherwise to the General Commissioners. However, if, during an enquiry into a return, a question relating to the subject matter of the appeal has been referred to the Special Commissioners (see 61.13 RETURNS), or would have been so referred but for being withdrawn, an appeal within (*a*) or (*b*) above lies to the Special Commissioners (subject to any contrary direction by the Special Commissioners). Otherwise, subject to *TMA 1970, ss 44–59*, an appeal is to the General Commissioners unless the company elects for it to be heard by the Special Commissioners (see 6.3 below). HMRC may, however, refer any such election to the General Commissioners, who must direct that the election be disregarded unless satisfied that the company has arguments to present or evidence to adduce on the merits of the appeal.

[*FA 1998, Sch 18 paras 93, 94; FA 2001, Sch 29 para 13; SI 1998 No 3173*].

An appeal against a corporation tax assessment relates to the total profits chargeable, and sources of profit not specified in the assessment may be taken into account in determining the appeal. An estimated assessment was raised on a company showing chargeable profits consisting of building society interest and dividends less charges. The Commissioners' decision on appeal, to increase the assessment to an amount comprising agreed figures for Schedule A income and capital gains less management expenses and charges, was upheld (*Owton Fens Properties Ltd v Redden Ch D 1984, 58 TC 218*).

See 25.4 EUROPEAN COMMUNITY LEGISLATION regarding the application of the corporation tax provisions where a company ceases to be UK-resident in the course of the formation of an SE or where an SE becomes non-UK resident.

Simon's Direct Tax Service. See D2.837.

6.2 LATE APPEALS

The normal time limit for giving notice of appeal is as stated in 6.1 above. A late appeal may be accepted by HMRC if satisfied that there was a reasonable excuse for the delay. If not accepted, HMRC must refer the application to the Commissioners (normally the General Commissioners) for their decision. [*TMA 1970, s 49*]. In the event of refusal to accept a late appeal, the decision is not subject to appeal by way of stated case (*R v Special Commrs (ex p Magill) QB (NI) 1979, 53 TC 135*, but is subject to judicial review (see *R v Hastings and Bexhill General Commrs and CIR (ex p Goodacre) QB 1994, 67 TC 126*, in which a refusal was quashed and the matter remitted to a different body of Commissioners). In *R (oao Browallia Cal Ltd) v General Commissioners of Income Tax QB 2003, [2004] STC 296*, it was held that the Appeal Commissioners have a wider discretion than HMRC in considering a late appeal. The court held that the Commissioners in that case had misunderstood their powers and that the lack of any reasonable excuse was 'potentially relevant' but was 'not conclusive'.

6.3 ELECTION TO BRING APPEAL BEFORE SPECIAL COMMISSIONERS

As stated at 6.1 above (with the exceptions there stated), and subject to 6.4 below, an appeal is normally brought to the General Commissioners. However, an appellant may elect to bring an appeal before the Special Commissioners instead. The election must be made either with the notice of appeal or by separate notice given within the time limit for giving the notice of appeal.

The election is, however, disregarded if the appellant and HMRC so agree in writing before the appeal is determined. Alternatively, HMRC may refer the election to the General Commissioners (after notifying the appellant). The General Commissioners must then direct that the election be disregarded unless satisfied that the appellant has arguments to present or evidence to adduce on the merits of the appeal. Such a direction may be revoked at any time before determination of the appeal if that condition is subsequently satisfied. The decision to give or revoke a direction is final.

[*TMA 1970, s 46(1); FA 1998, Sch 18 para 94*].

Appeals to the General Commissioners may, if the parties so apply and the Commissioners consent, be transferred to the Special Commissioners (and vice versa) despite the expiry of the time limit for election above or the making of such an election. [*TMA 1970, s 44(3)*].

6.4 **JURISDICTION OF APPEAL COMMISSIONERS**

Certain questions which may be in dispute on appeal (but not necessarily the entire appeal) must be determined by the Special Commissioners. The questions concerned involve the application of provisions on:

- an appeal against an amendment of a company tax return by HMRC during an enquiry to prevent the loss of tax (see 61.12 RETURNS);
- an appeal against an amendment of a company tax return by HMRC after an enquiry (see 61.15 RETURNS);
- an appeal against an assessment which is not a self-assessment;
- an appeal against a conclusion stated or amendment made by a closure notice relating to a claim or election made otherwise than in a return, or an appeal against a decision contained in such a notice disallowing all or part of such a claim or election (see 15.6 CLAIMS).

They also include any question as to the value for the purposes of capital gains tax or corporation tax on chargeable gains of any unquoted shares or securities in a UK resident company (any question for those purposes as to the value of any land or lease of land being determined by the relevant Lands Tribunal). They also include any question as to the application of:

- corporation tax chargeable on profits apportioned in respect of controlled foreign companies (see 21.7 CONTROLLED FOREIGN COMPANIES);
- the interest of a company in the residue of a deceased person's estate; and
- the provisions for liability in relation to territorial sea and designated areas (see 60.10 RESIDENCE).

[*TMA 1970, ss 46B, 46D; FA 2001, s 88, Sch 29 paras 27, 29; ITEPA 2003, Sch 6 para 129; ITTOIA 2005, Sch 1 para 373*].

Where, on an appeal, the question in dispute concerns a claim made (in a tax return) to the Commissioners of HMRC or made under any one or more specified provisions, the question must be determined by the Special Commissioners. The specified provisions cover double tax relief, exemptions for certain friendly societies, trade unions and employers' associations, and reliefs in respect of royalties, copyright payments etc. This applies in relation to appeals against conclusions and amendments following an enquiry into a return and appeals against certain Revenue amendments to returns and self-assessments to prevent loss of tax. [*TMA 1970, s 46C; FA 2001, s 71(4), s 88, Sch 24 para 2, Sch 29 para 28; ITTOIA 2005, Sch 1 para 374*]. Comparable provisions apply under *TMA 1970, Sch 1A* (see 15.6 CLAIMS) as regards claims not included in returns.

Appeals to the General Commissioners for which election for transfer to the Special Commissioners could be made may, if the parties so apply and the Commissioners consent, be transferred to the Special Commissioners (and *vice versa*) despite the expiry of the time limit for election as above or the making of such an election. [*TMA 1970, s 44(3)*]. In addition, the General Commissioners may arrange that an appeal brought before them be transferred to the Special Commissioners, with the Special Commissioners' consent, if, after considering any representations made to them by the parties to the appeal, the

General Commissioners consider that, because of the complexity of, or likely time required to hear, the appeal, it should be so transferred. [*TMA 1970, s 44(3A)*].

The Special Commissioners go on circuit to the chief provincial towns, but appeals to them may generally by arrangement be heard in London, which is usually more convenient if it is intended to engage counsel.

Rules for assigning procedures to General Commissioners. For proceedings relating to:

- corporation tax under self-assessment;
- income tax where a UK resident company is a party; or
- tax assessable under *ICTA 1988, ss 419, 420* in respect of close company loans,

either the corporate taxpayer or an officer of HMRC (whichever commences the proceedings) may elect by notice to the other in writing for the proceedings to be heard in the division in which is situated either the corporate taxpayer's place of residence, head office or principle place of business or the division in which, at the time the election is made, the trade or business is carried on. An officer may make the election if the taxpayer fails to exercise his right to do so when giving notice of appeal or otherwise commencing proceedings or at such later time as HMRC allow. The taxpayer's election is irrevocable.

Notwithstanding the above, HMRC may direct that specified proceedings be brought before the General Commissioners for a specified division. An officer of HMRC must serve on the taxpayer written notice stating the effect of the direction, and the taxpayer may object in writing within 30 days of the notice being served, in which case the direction has no effect. HMRC may also give directions for determining the appropriate division where there is no place of residence or business as described above, or where that place would otherwise be outside the UK; procedure is as above except that the taxpayer has no right of objection.

The parties to proceedings may supersede the above rules by coming to an agreement that the proceedings be brought before the General Commissioners for a division specified therein. The rules are also subject to specified provisions in relation to which two or more parties other than HMRC are involved (which have their own rules), to regulations under *TMA 1970, s 46A* (see above), to provisions relating to the valuation of trading stock and work in progress (*ICTA 1988, s 102(1)*), to provisions relating to the apportionment of profits in company reconstructions where there is no change of ownership (*ICTA 1988, s 343(10)*), apportionments in the case of certain leased assets (*ICTA 1988, s 783(10)*) and questions relating to apportionment in respect of capital allowances (*CAA 2001, s 563*).

[*TMA 1970, s 44(1)(2), Sch 3; ITEPA 2003, Sch 6 para 142; ITTOIA 2005, Sch 1 para 383*].

Comparable rules under earlier legislation were held to be directory and not mandatory (*CIR v Adams CA 1971, 48 TC 67; Murphy v Elders Ch D 1973, 49 TC 135*). A determination of the General Commissioners cannot be invalidated for want of jurisdiction if there was no objection to jurisdiction before the determination. [*TMA 1970, s 44(4)*]. See also *R v Kingston & Elmbridge Commrs QB 1972, 48 TC 75; R v St Pancras Commrs QB 1973, 50 TC 365; Parikh v Birmingham North Commrs CA, [1976] STC 365*.

Simon's Direct Tax Service. See E1.839.

6.5 SETTLEMENT OF APPEALS BY AGREEMENT

Where agreement, written or otherwise, has been reached at any time between HMRC and the appellant or agent on his behalf on any appeal to General or Special Commissioners, against any assessment or decision under appeal, the assessment or decision as upheld, varied, discharged or cancelled by that agreement, is treated as if it had been determined on appeal, provided that:

(*a*) the taxpayer may withdraw from the agreement by giving written notice within 30 days of making it; and

(*b*) oral agreements are of no effect unless confirmed in writing by either side (the date of such confirmation then being the effective date of the agreement).

[*TMA 1970, s 54*].

The agreement must specify the figure for assessment or a precise formula for ascertaining it (*Delbourgo v Field CA 1978, 52 TC 225*). The inspector has no power unilaterally to 'vacate' an assessment (*Baylis v Gregory CA, [1987] STC 297*). An agreement only covers the assessments which are the subject of the appeal, and does not bind HMRC for subsequent years, e.g. where relievable amounts are purported to be carried forward from the year in question (*MacNiven v Westmoreland Investments Ltd HL 2001, 73 TC 1*). For the extent to which further assessments or error or mistake relief claims are permissible if an appeal has been determined by agreement, see 7.2 ASSESSMENTS.

The issue of an amended notice of assessment by the inspector does not of itself constitute an offer for the purposes of an agreement under *TMA 1970, s 54*, nor can a lack of response by the taxpayer constitute acceptance of an offer (*Schuldenfrei v Hilton CA 1999, 72 TC 167*). For the general requirements for an agreement, see *Cash & Carry v Inspector (Sp C 148), [1998] SSCD 46*.

An agreement under *TMA 1970, s 54* does not prevent an assessment being revised to correct an error, where the effect of the error was that the common intention of the parties was not recorded by the agreement (*R v HMIT(ex p Bass Holdings Ltd) QB 1992, 65 TC 495*). An agreement based on a mutual mistake of fact was thereby vitiated, so that the taxpayer could proceed with his appeal (*Fox v Rothwell (Sp C 50), [1995] SSCD 336*).

A taxpayer cannot withdraw an appeal made to Commissioners (see 6.1 above) but if, having appealed, the taxpayer or agent acting in that appeal, gives the inspector oral or written notice of his desire not to proceed, then, unless the inspector gives written notice of objection within 30 days thereof, the appeal is treated as if settled by agreement, as above, at the date of the taxpayer's notification. [*TMA 1970, s 54(4)*].

See also *Tod v South Essex Motors (Basildon) Ltd Ch D 1987, 60 TC 598*, for a case concerning the agreement of capital losses under *TMA 1970, s 54* based on an erroneous view of the law. See also HMRC Capital Gains Manual CG 40234. (For accounting periods ending on or after 1 July 1999 to which self-assessment applies, capital losses are subject to a formal notification procedure, see 11.3 CAPITAL GAINS.)

6.6 NOTIFICATION OF HEARING

Appeal meetings must be notified to the appellant and the inspector (or other HMRC party). In practice, the inspector normally gives details of appeals ready for hearing to the Clerk to the Commissioners, who, after consulting the inspector and, in important appeals, the taxpayer or his agent as appropriate, makes the necessary arrangements, notifies the inspector and issues notices of the hearing to the appellant. In some Divisions he may, by arrangement, also notify the appellant's agent. See also 6.9, 6 16 below.

6.7 APPEAL COMMISSIONERS — INTRODUCTION

The Lord Chancellor has wide regulatory powers in relation to the practice and procedure to be followed in connection with appeals, including the power to make different provision for different cases and different circumstances. Regulations may also provide for the transfer of appeals between the General and Special Commissioners or between General Commissioners for different divisions, and for varying the number of General or Special Commissioners required or permitted to hear appeals. [*TMA 1970, ss 46A, 56B–56D*]. With effect from 1 September 1994, regulations [*SI 1994 No 1812*] were introduced governing the jurisdiction of the General Commissioners and the procedure for proceedings before them (see 6.8–6.13 below). At the same time, similar regulations [*SI 1994 No 1811*] were introduced in relation to the Special Commissioners (see 6.14–6.17 below).

Useful independent information on the role and stance of the General Commissioners is published on the National Association of Tax Commissioners website (www.natax.org.uk). The Department for Constitutional Affairs publishes a leaflet containing guidance on taking appeals to the Commissioners. The leaflet, 'Tax Appeals: A guide to appealing against decisions of HMRC on tax and other matters', can be obtained from HMRC.

Simon's Direct Tax Service. See A3.5.

6.8 **GENERAL COMMISSIONERS**

Constitution of tribunal. Two or more, but not more than five, General Commissioners for a division may hear any proceedings. [*SI 1994 No 1812, reg 2*]. They will themselves decide which one of them will preside at the hearing. Where possible at least three will sit, and, with the consent of all the parties, proceedings may be continued by any one or more of them. [*SI 1994 No 1812, reg 11*]. For the effect of personal business connection between a Commissioner and a party to proceedings, see *R v Holyhead Commrs (ex p Roberts) QB 1982, 56 TC 127.*

The Clerk to the Commissioners, who is frequently a local solicitor, normally attends the meeting to take minutes and to advise them as required, but a meeting without the Clerk would not be invalid (*Venn v Franks CA 1958, 38 TC 175*).

6.9 **Preparation for hearing.** *Listing and notice of hearing.* Except in relation to proceedings under *TMA 1970, s 100C* (see 54.12 PENALTIES), any party to the proceedings may serve notice on the Clerk to the Commissioners that he wishes a date for the hearing to be fixed, on receipt of which the Clerk must send notice to each party of the place, date and time of the hearing. Unless the parties otherwise agree, or the Commissioners otherwise direct, the date must not be earlier than 28 days after the date of the Clerk's notice. [*SI 1994 No 1812, reg 3*].

Witnesses. A General Commissioner, on the application of any party to the proceedings, may issue a witness summons (in Scotland, a witness citation) requiring any person in the UK either to attend the hearing of those proceedings to give evidence or to produce any relevant document in his possession, custody or power. The party applying for issue of the summons is responsible for its service (for which see *reg 4(3)*), and attendance may not be required within seven days of service unless the witness informs the Clerk that he accepts shorter notice. That party must also agree to meet the witness's reasonable travelling expenses. The witness may apply, by notice served on the Clerk, for the Commissioner to set aside the summons (in whole or part), on which application the party on whose application the summons was issued is entitled to be heard.

Except in Scotland, a witness so summoned to give evidence may only be cross-examined by the party on whose application the summons was issued if the Commissioners decide that the witness is a hostile witness and give leave.

A witness cannot be compelled to give evidence or produce documents which he could not be compelled to give or produce in an action in a court of law. An auditor or tax adviser (within *TMA 1970, s 20B(10)*) cannot be compelled to produce any document which he would not be obliged to deliver or make available by notice under *TMA 1970, s 20(3)* or *(8A)* (having regard to *TMA 1970, s 20B(9)–(13)*), and copies of, or of parts of, documents may similarly be produced in certain cases (see 30.4 FRAUDULENT OR NEGLIGENT CONDUCT).

In the event of failure by a witness to attend in obedience to the summons, or refusal to be sworn or to affirm, or refusal to answer any lawful question or to produce a document he is required to produce by the summons, the Commissioners may summarily determine a penalty not exceeding £1,000, to be treated as tax charged by an assessment and due and payable.

[*SI 1994 No 1812, reg 4*].

Joint hearings. The Commissioners have powers to direct that two or more proceedings, in one or more divisions, with common issues be heard at the same time or consecutively within one division, either of their own motion or on an application by any of the parties to any of those proceedings. All the parties must be notified, and are entitled to be heard before such a direction is given. On the giving of a direction, the Clerk must send notice of its date and terms to all parties. [*SI 1994 No 1812, reg 6*]. The Commissioners have an inherent power to deal with two or more appeals simultaneously where the appellants' affairs are so intermingled as to be incapable of separation, and where they are satisfied that it would result in no injustice to either party (*Johnson v Walden; King v Walden CA 1995, 68 TC 387*).

Postponements and adjournments. The Commissioners may postpone or adjourn the hearing of any proceedings, the Clerk being responsible for notifying all parties of the place, date and time of the postponed or adjourned hearing (unless announced before an adjournment in the presence of all parties). Where a hearing is adjourned for the obtaining of further information or evidence, the Commissioners may direct the parties regarding the disclosure of such information or evidence prior to resumption. [*SI 1994 No 1812, reg 8*]. In *Packe v Johnson Ch D 1991, 63 TC 507*, a determination was quashed because of the Commissioners' refusal to consider all relevant information in deciding to refuse an adjournment at a second hearing.

Other matters in preparation for hearing. There are also regulations dealing with the agreement of documents [*reg 5*], the joinder of additional parties to the proceedings [*reg 7*] and the admission of expert evidence [*reg 9*].

6.10 **Hearing and determination of proceedings.** Where proceedings are commenced after 30 December 2002, the hearing is in public. The Commissioners may, however, direct (dependent on certain criteria, e.g. national security, interests of justice, protection of private life etc., and subject to all parties having opportunity to make representations) that all or part of a hearing be in private, such direction to be made of their own volition or on the application (by written notice to the Clerk) of any or all of the parties. In such circumstances, they may also direct that *information* about the proceedings should not be made public. Certain persons with official responsibilities may be present at *any* hearing, and may remain present during, but not take part in, the Commissioners' deliberations. With the consent of the parties, the Commissioners may permit any other person to attend an otherwise private hearing. They may exclude a person from all or part of any hearing on grounds of disruptive or potentially disruptive conduct. Before 31 December 2002, hearings were in private, though with similar provision as above as to the presence of others. [*SI 1994 No 1812, reg 13; SI 2002 No 2976, regs 1, 10*].

Preliminary points will be considered prior to the hearing of the substantive appeal only in cases where the facts are complicated and the legal issue is short and easily decided (*Investment Trust v CIR (Sp C 173), [1998] SSCD 287*).

Power to obtain information. The Commissioners may, at any time before final determination of the proceedings, serve on any party to the proceedings (other than HMRC) notice (a 'precept') requiring that party, within a specified time:

(*a*) to deliver such particulars as may be required to determine any issue of the proceedings; and

(*b*) to make available for inspection by the Commissioners or by an HMRC officer such specified or described books, accounts etc. in his possession or power as may, in their opinion, contain information relevant to the proceedings.

The Commissioners may summarily determine a penalty (to be treated as tax charged in an assessment and due and payable) of up to £300 for failure to comply with such a notice, plus up to £60 per day for continuing failure after such a penalty is determined. Any

HMRC officer (and the Commissioners in the case of (*b*)) may, at all reasonable times, take copies of, or extracts from, any such particulars, books etc. [*SI 1994 No 1812, reg 10*].

Representation at hearing. A party to the proceedings may be represented by any person, except that the Commissioners may, if satisfied that there are good and sufficient reasons for doing so, refuse to permit a party to be represented by a particular person, not being a legally qualified person or a person who is currently (see *Cassell v Crutchfield (No 1) Ch D 1995, 69 TC 253*) a member of an incorporated society of accountants. In practice, most bodies of Commissioners permit the taxpayer to be represented by any person who they are satisfied is competent to present the appellant's case. HMRC may be represented by a barrister, advocate, solicitor or any HMRC officer. [*SI 1994 No 1812, reg 12*]. The HMRC representative is normally an inspector. The secretary or 'other proper officer' represents a company (the liquidator if in liquidation or (where the company enters administration on or after 15 September 2003) the administrator if in administration). [*TMA 1970, s 108; FA 2003, s 196, Sch 41 para 2; SI 2003 No 2093*].

Failure to attend hearing. Where a party fails to attend or be represented at a hearing of which he has been duly notified, the Commissioners may postpone or adjourn a hearing or (unless satisfied that there is good and sufficient reason for such failure, and after considering any written or other representations) hear and determine the proceedings. [*SI 1994 No 1812, reg 14*]. Determinations in the absence of the taxpayer or his agent have been upheld where notice of the meeting was received by the appellant (*R v Tavistock Commrs (ex p Adams) (No 1) QB 1969, 46 TC 154*; *R v Special Commr (ex p Moschi) CA, [1981] STC 465* and see *Fletcher & Fletcher v Harvey CA 1990, 63 TC 539*), but Commissioners were held to have acted unreasonably in refusing to re-open proceedings when the taxpayer's agent was temporarily absent when the appeal was called (*R & D McKerron Ltd v CIR CS 1979, 52 TC 28*). Where the taxpayer was absent through illness, a determination was quashed because the Commissioners, in refusing an adjournment, had failed to consider whether injustice would thereby arise to the taxpayer (*R v Sevenoaks Commrs (ex p Thorne) QB 1989, 62 TC 341* and see *Rose v Humbles CA 1971, 48 TC 103*). See also *R v O'Brien (ex p Lissner) QB, [1984] STI 710* where the determination was quashed when the appellant had been informed by the inspector that the hearing was to be adjourned.

Procedure and evidence at hearing. The Commissioners have wide discretion as to the manner in which the proceedings are conducted, and should seek to avoid inappropriate formality. They may require any witness to give evidence on oath or affirmation, and may admit evidence which would be inadmissible in a court of law (and see *Taylor v Cox (Sp C 163), [1998] SSCD 179* for the acceptance of computer-generated documents in evidence). Evidence may be given orally or, if they so direct, by affidavit or statement recorded in a document (and they may, on their own motion or on the application of any party, at any stage require the personal attendance as a witness of the maker of such a statement or affidavit or the person who recorded the statement). They may take account of the nature and source of any evidence, and the manner in which it is given, in assessing its truth and weight. The parties may be heard in any order, but are entitled to give evidence, to call witnesses, to question witnesses (including other parties who give evidence), and to address the Commissioners both on the evidence and on the subject matter of the proceedings. [*SI 1994 No 1812, reg 15*]. A party to the proceedings cannot insist on being examined on oath (*R v Special Commrs (in re Fletcher) CA 1894, 3 TC 289*). False evidence under oath would be perjury under criminal law (*R v Hood Barrs CA, [1943] 1 All ER 665*). A taxpayer was held to be bound by an affidavit he had made in other proceedings (*Wicker v Fraser Ch D 1982, 55 TC 641*). A remission to Commissioners to hear evidence directed at the credit of a witness was refused in *Potts v CIR Ch D 1982, 56 TC 25*. Rules of the Supreme Court under which evidence can be obtained from a witness abroad cannot be used in proceedings before the Commissioners (*Leiserach v CIR CA 1963, 42 TC 1*). As to hearsay evidence under the *Civil Evidence Act 1968*, see *Forth Investments Ltd v CIR Ch D 1976, 50 TC 617* and *Khan v Edwards Ch D 1977, 53 TC 597*.

The inspector is entitled to ask the Commissioners to exercise their powers to increase an assessment, and to adduce evidence in support of his application (*Glaxo Group Ltd and others v CIR CA 1996, 68 TC 166*).

The Commissioners are under no obligation to adjourn an appeal for the production of further evidence (*Hamilton v CIR CS 1930, 16 TC 28*; *Noble v Wilkinson Ch D 1958, 38 TC 135*), and were held not to have erred in law in determining assessments in the absence abroad of the taxpayer (*Hawkins v Fuller Ch D 1982, 56 TC 49*).

The taxpayer has no general right to conduct his appeal in writing without attending the hearing (*Banin v Mackinlay CA 1984, 58 TC 398*), although written pleadings may, at the Commissioners' discretion, be taken into account (*Caldicott v Varty Ch D 1976, 51 TC 403*).

In reaching their decision, the Commissioners may not take into account matters appropriate for application for judicial review (*Aspin v Estill CA 1987, 60 TC 549*). They do not generally have the power to review on appeal the exercise of a discretion conferred on HMRC by statute (see *Slater v Richardson & Bottoms Ltd Ch D 1979, 53 TC 155*; *Kelsall v Investment Chartwork Ltd Ch D 1993, 65 TC 750*), although in certain cases such power of review is itself statutory; see e.g. *SI 1993 No 743, reg 10(4)*, which in effect reversed the decision in *Richardson & Bottoms Ltd* above.

For the extent to which Commissioners may use their local knowledge, see *Forest Side Properties (Chingford) Ltd v Pearce CA 1961, 39 TC 665*.

Onus of proof. The onus is on the appellant to displace an assessment (but see 30.2 FRAUDULENT OR NEGLIGENT CONDUCT for onus on Crown to prove fraud or wilful default to support extended time limit assessments). See *Brady v Group Lotus Car Companies plc CA 1987, 60 TC 359* where the onus of proof remained with the taxpayer where the amount of normal time limit assessment indicated contention of fraud. The general principle emerges in appeals against estimated assessments in 'delay cases', which, before self-assessment, made up the bulk of appeals heard by the General Commissioners. For examples of cases in which the Commissioners have confirmed estimated assessments in the absence of evidence that they were excessive, see *T Haythornthwaite & Sons Ltd v Kelly CA 1927, 11 TC 657*; *Stoneleigh Products Ltd v Dodd CA 1948, 30 TC 1*; *Rosette Franks (King St) Ltd v Dick Ch D 1955, 36 TC 100*; *Pierson v Belcher Ch D 1959, 38 TC 387*. In a number of cases, the courts have supported the Commissioners' action in rejecting unsatisfactory accounts (e.g. *Cain v Schofield Ch D 1953, 34 TC 362*; *Moll v CIR CS 1955, 36 TC 384*; *Cutmore v Leach Ch D 1981, 55 TC 602*; *Coy v Kime Ch D 1986, 59 TC 447*) or calling for certified accounts (e.g. *Stephenson v Waller KB 1927, 13 TC 318*; *Hunt & Co v Joly KB 1928, 14 TC 165*; *Wall v Cooper CA 1929, 14 TC 552*). In *Anderson v CIR CS 1933, 18 TC 320*, the case was remitted where there was no evidence to support the figure arrived at by the Commissioners (which was between the accounts figure and the estimated figure assessed), but contrast *Bookey v Edwards Ch D 1981, 55 TC 486*. The Commissioners are entitled to look at each year separately, accepting the appellant's figures for some years but not all (*Donnelly v Platten CA(NI) 1980, [1981] STC 504*). Similarly, the onus is on the taxpayer to substantiate his claims to relief (see *Eke v Knight CA 1977, 51 TC 121*; *Talib v Waterson Ch D, [1980] STC 563*).

For the standard of proof required in evidence, see *Les Croupiers Casino Club v Pattinson CA 1987, 60 TC 196*.

6.11 **The Commissioners' decision.** The HMRC representative must not be present while the Commissioners are deliberating their decision unless the other party or parties (or their representative(s)) are also present (*R v Brixton Commrs KB 1912, 6 TC 195*). The Commissioners' determination was quashed where the Clerk had discussed the case with Revenue representatives between hearing and announcement of determination (*R v Wokingham Commrs (ex p Heron) QB 1984, [1984] STI 710*).

If, on an appeal, it appears to the Commissioners:

(*a*) that the appellant is overcharged or undercharged by a self-assessment; or

(*b*) that the appellant is overcharged or undercharged by an assessment other than a self-assessment,

they must reduce or increase the assessment or amounts accordingly, but otherwise the assessment or statement stands good. The Commissioners are given the power to vary the extent to which a claim or election included in a tax return is disallowed following an enquiry. (Separate rules apply to claims and elections made outside returns, for which see 15.6 CLAIMS.) In a case within (*b*) above, the Commissioners can normally only reduce or increase the amount assessed, and this determines the appeal; they are not obliged to determine the revised tax payable. These provisions apply as from, broadly, 11 May 2001, though comparable provisions applied previously, the changes being in consequence of the revised procedures for completion of an enquiry (see 61.14 RETURNS). [*TMA 1970, s 50(6)–(9); FA 2001, s 88, Sch 29 para 30*].

Any decision is by a majority of the Commissioners hearing the proceedings, with the presiding Commissioner having a casting vote where necessary. The final determination may be announced orally at the end of the hearing or may be reserved. In either case, the Clerk to the Commissioners must send to each party a notice (including details of the procedure for appeals from the General Commissioners) setting out the determination, and unless the determination was given at the hearing, the date of such notice is the date of the determination. [*SI 1994 No 1812, reg 16*]. Where the Clerk announced the decision wrongly, it was held that the correct decision stood good (*R v Morleston & Litchurch Commrs KB 1951, 32 TC 335*) (and see 6.13 below under Irregularities).

Where Commissioners determined appeals in principle and held a further hearing to adjust assessments, their action in refusing to admit further evidence for the taxpayer at the later hearing was upheld (*R v St Marylebone Commrs (ex p Hay) CA 1983, 57 TC 59*). They are entitled, however, to alter their decision in principle at a later hearing (*Larner v Warrington Ch D 1985, 58 TC 557*). See also *Gibson v Stroud Commrs Ch D 1989, 61 TC 645*.

A decision of the Commissioners is not legally binding on them or any other Commissioners in any other proceedings, even on appeal by the same taxpayer against a similar assessment for another year (*CIR v Sneath CA 1932, 17 TC 149* and cf. *Edwards v 'Old Bushmills' Distillery HL 1926, 10 TC 285; Abdul Caffoor Trustees PC 1961, 40 ATC 93*).

Review of the Commissioners' final determination. A decision of the Commissioners is generally final and conclusive [*TMA 1970, s 46(2)*], but the Commissioners may review and set aside or vary their final determination on the application of any party or of their own motion where they are satisfied that either:

- it was wrongly made as a result of administrative error; or
- a party entitled to be heard failed to appear or be represented for good and sufficient reason; or
- relevant information had been supplied to the Clerk or to the appropriate inspector or other HMRC officer prior to the hearing but was not received by the Commissioners until after the hearing.

A written application for such a review must be made to the Commissioners not later than 14 days after the date of the notice of the determination (or by such later time as the Commissioners may allow), stating the grounds in full. Where the Commissioners propose of their own motion to review a determination, they must serve notice on the parties not later than 14 days after the date of the notice of the determination.

The parties are entitled to be heard on any such review or proposed review. If practicable, the review is to be determined by the Commissioners who decided the case, and if they set aside the determination, they may substitute a different determination or order a rehearing before the same or different Commissioners. A decision to vary or substitute a final determination is to be notified in the same way as the original determination (see above).

[*SI 1994 No 1812, reg 17*].

See 6.24 below as regards application for judicial review where the Commissioners have acted unfairly or improperly.

6.12 **Special procedures.** *Proceedings relating to tax on chargeable gains.* Where material, the market value of an asset or the apportionment of an amount or value is, if so required by any party, to be recorded in the final determination. They may be proved in any proceedings relating to tax on chargeable gains by a certificate signed by the Clerk to the Commissioners (in certain cases the clerk or registrar of another tribunal), or by the inspector where the appeal was settled by agreement, stating the material particulars. [*SI 1994 No 1812, reg 18*].

Reference to other tribunals. Certain questions relating to the value of land or of a lease of land must be referred to the appropriate Lands Tribunal, and questions in relation to unquoted shares and to certain specified claims must be referred to the Special Commissioners (see *TMA 1970, ss 46B, 46C, 46D* at 6.4 above). The instant proceedings are to be determined without awaiting the outcome of such referral. [*SI 1994 No 1812, reg 19*].

6.13 **Miscellaneous.** *Irregularities.* Any irregularity resulting from failure to comply with regulations or with any Commissioners' direction given before a final determination is reached, shall not, of itself, render the proceedings void, and before reaching that determination the Commissioners may, and if they consider that any person has been prejudiced by the irregularity must, give such direction as they think just to cure or waive any irregularity which comes to their attention. Clerical errors in any document recording a direction or decision of the Commissioners may be corrected by any of the Commissioners concerned (or by the Clerk if all the Commissioners have died or ceased to be Commissioners) by certificate under his hand. [*SI 1994 No 1812, reg 24*].

Notices must be in writing unless the Commissioners authorise them to be given orally. [*SI 1994 No 1812, reg 25*].

Service of any notice or document (other than a witness summons, see 6.9 above) may be by post, by (legible) facsimile transmission etc. or by delivery at the proper address. [*SI 1994 No 1812, reg 26(1)*]. The persons and addresses to whom and which a document may be sent or delivered are set out in *reg 26(2)(3)*, and the provisions for substituted or waived service in certain cases in *reg 27*.

Penalties. Any appeal against summary penalties determined pursuant to regulations under 6.7 above lies to the High Court (in Scotland, the Court of Session). [*TMA 1970, s 53(1)*].

Guidance notes on Appeals to the General Commissioners (TAXGUIDE 4/00) were published in June 2000 by the Tax Faculty of the ICAEW. The National Association of Tax Commissioners also publish on their website (www.natax.org.uk) useful notes for appellants on what they may expect of General Commissioners.

Protection of General Commissioners. From 1 April 2001 (except in Scotland), the following apply. There is no right of action against a General Commissioner in respect of any act or omission of his in the execution of his duty, except with respect to matters outside his jurisdiction and then only if it is proved that he acted in bad faith. [*TMA 1970, s 2(9)(10); Access to Justice Act 1999, s 101; SI 2001 No 916*]. With limited exceptions, such as if his having acted in bad faith is proved, a General Commissioner cannot be ordered by a court to pay *costs* in respect of any act or omission of his in the execution of his duty. The court may, however, order the Lord Chancellor to make such payment instead, subject to such exceptions and procedures (for determining costs) as are provided for by regulations. [*TMA 1970, s 2A; Access to Justice Act 1999, s 102; SI 2001 Nos 916, 1304*]. There are provisions for the Lord Chancellor to indemnify a General Commissioner or his clerk from certain sums incurred, i.e. costs, damages etc., in connection with proceedings in respect of any act or omission of his in the execution of his duty, again unless it is proved that he acted in bad faith. [*TMA 1970, s 3A; Access to Justice Act 1999, s 103; SI 2001 No 916*].

6.14 **SPECIAL COMMISSIONERS**

Except where otherwise stated or required by context, the provisions applicable to the General Commissioners in 6.8–6.13 above) apply equally to the Special Commissioners, with the variations and additions in 6.15–6.17 below.

6.15 **Constitution of tribunal.** Any one, two or three of the Special Commissioners may hear any proceedings. If two or three Commissioners are sitting, the Presiding Special Commissioner, or, if he is not sitting, the Commissioner nominated by him, shall preside at the hearing. With the consent of all parties, proceedings may be continued by any one or two of the Commissioners unless the Presiding Special Commissioner otherwise directs. [*SI 1994 No 1811, regs 2, 13*].

6.16 **Preparation for hearing.** *Listing and notice of hearing.* Before notifying the parties of the place, date and time of a hearing, the Clerk to the Commissioners must satisfy himself that the Special Commissioners have jurisdiction over the proceedings and that he has sufficient particulars for determination. The Presiding Special Commissioner may direct that such notifications are not to be sent. [*SI 1994 No 1811, reg 3*].

General power to give directions. The Commissioner(s) have wide direction-giving powers, on the application of any of the parties to proceedings or of their own motion. Applications by the parties (otherwise than during the hearing) must be in writing to the Clerk, and if not made with the consent of all the parties, must be served by the Clerk on any affected party, who may object. [*SI 1994 No 1811, reg 4*].

Witnesses. The maximum penalty which the Commissioner(s) may summarily determine for failure to attend or refusal to be sworn or affirm, to answer any lawful question or to produce documents as required is £10,000. [*SI 1994 No 1811, regs 5, 24(2)*].

Preliminary hearing. Where it appears to a Special Commissioner that any proceedings would be facilitated by holding a preliminary hearing, he may, on the application of a party or of his own motion, give directions for such a hearing to be held. The Clerk to the Special Commissioners must give to all the parties 14 days' notice (or such shorter time as the parties agree or the Commissioner sees fit to impose) of the time and place of the hearing. On a preliminary hearing, the Commissioner has wide direction-giving powers, and may, if the parties so agree, determine the proceedings without any further hearing. [*SI 1994 No 1811, reg 9*]. See 6.17 below as regards powers of Commissioner to obtain information on preliminary hearing of any proceedings.

6.17 **Hearing and determination of proceedings.** Hearings before the Special Commissioner(s) are normally in public. Where proceedings are commenced after 30 December 2002, rules equivalent to those for the General Commissioners in 6.10 above apply as regards private hearings in certain cases and the right to attend. Broadly similar rules applied before 31 December 2002, although an explicit direction for a hearing to be in private was required only where the application was made by HMRC. [*SI 1994 No 1811, reg 15; SI 2002 No 2976, regs 1, 6*].

Power to obtain information. The powers of General Commissioners to obtain information apply to both a preliminary hearing before a Special Commissioner and to the hearing of the proceedings, except that the specific penalty provisions for failure to comply with a notice do not apply (although the general penalty for failure to comply with Commissioner's direction, see below, *does* apply). [*SI 1994 No 1811, regs 10, 24(1)*].

The Commissioners' decision. The recording of the Commissioner(s)' decision must contain a statement of the facts found and the reasons for the determination. After reserving the final determination, the Commissioner(s) may give a written decision in principle on one or more of the issues arising, and adjourn the making of the final determination until after that decision has been issued and any further questions arising from it have been agreed by the parties or decided by the Commissioner(s) after hearing the parties. A decision in principle must contain a statement of the facts and the reasons for the decision, and these need not be repeated in the document recording the final determination. [*SI 1994 No 1811, reg 18*].

Review of the Commissioners' decision in principle may proceed in the same way as a review of a final determination. [*SI 1994 No 1811, reg 19*].

Publication of decisions in principle or final determinations. The Presiding Special Commissioner may arrange for the publication of such reports of decisions in principle and final determinations as he considers appropriate. If the proceedings (or any part) were held in private, he must ensure that the report is in a form which, so far as possible, prevents the identification of any person whose affairs are dealt with. [*SI 1994 No 1811, reg 20*].

An application for non-publication of a decision on the grounds of inadequate anonymity, or for publication of a short summary only, was refused by the Presiding Special Commissioner in *Y Co Ltd v CIR (Sp C 69), [1996] SSCD 147*. The policy on anonymisation was quoted as: 'In cases where anonymisation is required, the Presiding Special Commissioner will seek to achieve this in co-operation with the parties. If a decision or determination cannot be anonymised to the complete satisfaction of the party requiring it, the Presiding Special Commissioner's policy is to report it in as anonymised a form as he, in consultation with the Special Commissioner[s] deciding the case, considers to be appropriate. To this there is one exception, which is that no report will be published where the decision cannot be effectively anonymised and to report it would defeat the ends of justice, e.g. where particulars of a secret process would otherwise have to be disclosed or in cases where minors were involved. The Presiding Special Commissioner will consider cases falling outside this exception on their merits.'

A substantial number of cases is now reported, and these are referred to in the text of this publication where relevant. The Special Commissioners expect to have their attention drawn in appropriate cases to any of their previous published decisions which is relevant, unless superseded by a higher court decision. HMRC considers that, whilst not creating any binding legal precedent, these decisions may be relevant in other cases, particularly if not appealed against, but that it would be inappropriate to enter into any discussion of a case which is, or may be, the subject of appeal to the High Court etc. (Revenue Tax Bulletin October 1995 pp 258, 259).

Orders for costs. The Commissioner(s) may make an order awarding costs (in Scotland expenses) of, or incidental to, the hearing of any proceedings against any party who has, in their opinion, acted wholly unreasonably in connection with the hearing, but not without giving that party the opportunity of making representations against the award. The award may be of all or part of the costs of the other party or parties, such costs to be taxed in the county court (in Scotland the sheriff court) if not agreed. In Northern Ireland, the Commissioners may determine the costs. [*SI 1994 No 1811, reg 21*]. For this purpose an act 'in connection with the hearing' includes any action taken once the appeal has been consigned by one or both parties to the Special Commissioners (*Carter v Hunt 1999 (Sp C 220), [2000] SSCD 17*). Failure by the taxpayer to attend or be represented at the hearing without giving prior notification may be a contributory factor in an award of costs, as may a failure to comply with a Commissioners' direction (*Phillips v Burrows 1998 (Sp C 229, 229A), [2000] SSCD 107, 112*).

For cases in which costs/expenses were awarded against HMRC, see *Scott and another (trading as Farthings Steak House) v McDonald (Sp C 91), [1996] SSCD 381*, *Robertson v CIR (No 2) (Sp C 313), [2002] SSCD 242* and *Carvill v Frost (Sp C 447), [2005] SSCD 208*.

In *McEwan v O'Donoghue (No 2) (Sp C 488), [2005] SSCD 681* the appellant was denied costs even though it was held that the Revenue had behaved wholly unreasonably, because the result of the appeal was that each party succeeded in roughly equal amounts. In *Salt v Young (Sp C 205), [1999] SSCD 249*, the Revenue were refused costs on the grounds that although the taxpayer had, on an objective test, behaved unreasonably, he had not been *wholly* unreasonable, and his unreasonableness was connected with the hearing only to a very minor extent. Only in 'a very rare case' would the court interfere with the Commissioners' decision as regards costs (see *Gamble v Rowe Ch D 1998, 71 TC 190* in which a refusal of costs was upheld). For the basis for assessment of costs see *Carvill v Frost (No 2) (Sp C 468), [2005] SSCD 422.*

Dismissal of appeal without full hearing. An appeal may be dismissed without a full hearing if there is no longer any live issue between the parties and it would not be in the public interest to proceed (*Self-assessed v Inspector of Taxes (No 2) 1999 (Sp C 224), [2000] SSCD 47*).

Penalty for failure to comply with Commissioner(s)' direction. The Commissioner(s) may summarily determine a penalty of up to £10,000 for any such failure, to be treated as if it were tax charged in an assessment and due and payable. [*SI 1994 No 1811, reg 24(1)(3)*].

6.18 APPEALS TO THE HIGH COURT — INTRODUCTION

Prior to the determination of an appeal by the Commissioners, the court may be prepared to consider an application seeking a determination as to whether HMRC may make use of certain 'tax-altering' provisions in relation to the assessments under appeal (*Balen v CIR Ch D 1976, 52 TC 406*; *Beecham Group plc v CIR Ch D 1992, 65 TC 219*). In general, 'there is an absolute exclusion of the High Court's jurisdiction only when the proceedings seek relief which is more or less co-extensive with adjudicating on an existing open assessment ... the more closely the High Court proceedings approximate to that in their substantial effect, the more ready the High Court will be, as a matter of discretion, to decline jurisdiction' (*Glaxo Group Ltd and others v CIR Ch D 1995, 68 TC 166*).

In *Autologic Holdings plc and others v HMRC (Re Claimants under Loss Relief Group Litigation Order) [2005] STC 1357*, the House of Lords held that claims direct to the High Court side-stepping the prescribed statutory procedure, whereby the issues of disputed tax law should be resolved on appeals to the Commissioners, were a misuse of the court's process. (See 32.6 GROUPS OF COMPANIES with regard to the Loss Relief Group Litigation Order in which a number of large companies applied to the Ch D for a declaration that certain provisions of UK legislation, which denied group relief to UK companies in certain circumstances, contravened Article 43 of the EC Treaty, and the standard OECD Double Taxation Convention.)

Simon's Direct Tax Service. See A3.7.

6.19 APPEAL FROM THE GENERAL COMMISSIONERS

Case stated procedure. Within 30 days of the date of final determination of an appeal (or of the variation or substitution of such a determination, see 6.11 above) any party dissatisfied with the determination as being erroneous in point of law (for which see e.g. *Billows v Robinson CA 1991, 64 TC 17*) may serve notice on the Clerk requiring the Commissioners to state and sign a case for the opinion of the High Court (in Scotland the Court of Session, in Northern Ireland the Court of Appeal (NI)), setting forth the facts and final determination of the Commissioners. See *Grainger v Singer KB 1927, 11 TC 704* as regards receipt of the case. The 30-day time limit for requesting a case does not apply to the payment of the fee (*Anson v Hill CA 1968, 47 ATC 143*). The Commissioners may serve notice on the person who required the stated case requiring him, within a specified period of not less than 28 days, to identify the question of law on which he requires the case to be stated. They may refuse to state a case until such notice is complied with, or if they are not satisfied that a question of law is involved, or if the requisite fee (see below) has not been paid. A requirement for a case to be stated becomes invalid if the determination to which it relates is set aside or varied. The case stated procedure does not apply to a final determination by the General Commissioners of an appeal in which a question has been referred to another tribunal (the Lands Tribunal or the Special Commissioners — see *TMA 1970, ss 46B, 46C, 46D* at 6.4 above) and all appeal rights have been exhausted. [*SI 1994 No 1812, regs 20, 23*].

A fee of £25 is payable to the Clerk by the person requiring the case before he is entitled to have it stated. [*TMA 1970, s 56(3); SI 1994 No 1813*]. A single case may have effect as regards each of a number of appeals heard together (*Getty Oil Co v Steele and related appeals Ch D 1990, 63 TC 376*).

Although the case stated procedure envisages the determination of the proceedings before the Commissioners, where an appeal has been decided in principle but there may be considerable delay in reaching figures for the formal determination, the court will accept a case stated in principle (see e.g. *Rank Xerox Ltd v Lane HL 1979, 53 TC 185*).

The case stated procedure is not open to a successful party to an appeal (*Sharpey-Schafer v Venn Ch D 1955, 34 ATC 141*), but where another party requires a case, the successful party may invite the Commissioners to include in the case an additional question relating to another ground on which the Commissioners had found against it (*Gordon v CIR CS 1991, 64 TC 173*).

6.20 **Consideration of draft case.** Within 56 days of receipt of a notice requiring a stated case (or of the Commissioners being satisfied as to the question of law involved), the Clerk must send a draft of the case to all the parties. Written representations thereon may be made to the Clerk by any party within 56 days after the draft case is sent out, with copies to all the other parties, and within a further 28 days further representations may similarly be made in response. Any party to whom copies of representations are not sent may apply to the Clerk for a copy. The validity of a case after it has been stated and signed (see 6.21 below), and of any subsequent proceedings, is not affected by a failure to meet these time limits or by a failure to send copies of representations to all parties. [*SI 1994 No 1812, reg 21*].

An application for the taxpayer's name to be withheld was refused (*In re H Ch D 1964, 42 TC 14*) as was an application for the deletion of a passage possibly damaging the taxpayer (*Treharne v Guinness Exports Ltd Ch D 1967, 44 TC 161*). An application for judicial review on the ground that the case did not cover all matters in dispute was refused in *R v Special Commrs (ex p Napier) CA 1988, 61 TC 206*. In *Danquah v CIR Ch D 1990, 63 TC 526*, an application for the statement of a further case was refused where the case did not set out all the questions raised by the taxpayer in the originating motion by which he had sought an order directing the Commissioners to state a case. The proper course was for the taxpayer to apply for remission of the case for amendment under *TMA 1970, s 56(7)*. See also *Consolidated Goldfields plc v CIR Ch D 1990, 63 TC 333* (dealt with further at 6.22 below) in which a request to remit a case to the Commissioners for further findings of fact was refused.

6.21 **Preparation and submission of final case.** As soon as may be after the final date for representations (see 6.20 above and see *McKinney v Hagans Caravans (Manufacturing) Ltd CA (NI) 1997, 69 TC 526*), the Commissioners, after taking into account any representations, must state and sign the case. In the event of the death of a Commissioner, or of his ceasing to be a Commissioner, the case is to be signed by the remaining Commissioner(s) or, if there are none, by the Clerk. The case is then sent by the Clerk to the person who required it to be stated, and the other parties notified accordingly.

In England, Wales and Scotland, the party requiring the case must transmit it to the High Court (in Scotland, the Court of Session) within 30 days of receiving it, and at or before the time he does so must notify each of the other parties that the case has been stated on his application and send them a copy of the case. The fact that the same case may have been transmitted timeously by another party, where there are cross-appeals, does not relieve the appellant of the requirement to transmit the case timeously if his appeal is to be heard (*Petch v Gurney CA 1994, 66 TC 743*). The case must be *received* by the High Court (or

Court of Session) within the 30-day time limit (*New World Medical Ltd v Cormack Ch D, [2002] STC 1245*). It is mandatory (*Valleybright Ltd (in liquidation) v Richardson Ch D 1984, 58 TC 290*; *Petch v Gurney CA 1994, 66 TC 743*), and may run from the date the case is received by the taxpayer's authorised agent (*Brassington v Guthrie Ch D 1991, 64 TC 435*) (these latter three cases having been determined under the similar earlier provisions of *TMA 1970, s 56(4)*). The notification (and copy) to the other parties is required only to give 'adequate notice' of the appeal and not to be 'too long delayed' (*Hughes v Viner Ch D 1985, 58 TC 437*). In Northern Ireland, slightly different rules apply (and see *CIR v McGuckian CA (NI) 1999, 72 TC 343*).

[*SI 1994 No 1812, regs 22, 23*].

6.22 **The hearing.** The High Court (or Court of Session or Court of Appeal (NI)) hears and determines any question(s) of law arising on the case, and may reverse, affirm or amend the determination of the Commissioners, or may remit the matter to the Commissioners with the opinion of the Court thereon, or may make such other order as to the court seems fit. The court may also cause the case to be sent back for amendment (see further below). An appeal from the decision of the High Court lies (in England and Wales) to the Court of Appeal and thence (with leave) to the House of Lords. In certain cases, 'leap-frog' appeals direct from the High Court to the House of Lords may be permitted under *Administration of Justice Act 1969, s 12* (see e.g. *Fitzleet Estates Ltd v Cherry HL 1977, 51 TC 708*). In the case of an appeal against a decision on an appeal against an assessment, tax must be paid in accordance with the Commissioners' decision. Following the decision on appeal, any tax overpaid is refunded with such interest as the court may allow, and any amount under-charged is due and payable 30 days after the inspector issues a notice of the amount due. [*TMA 1970, s 56(6)–(9)*].

Once set down for hearing, a case cannot be declared a nullity (*Way v Underdown CA 1974, 49 TC 215*) or struck out under *Order 18, Rule 19 of the Rules of the Supreme Court* (*Petch v Gurney CA 1994, 66 TC 473*), but the appellant may withdraw (*Hood Barrs v CIR (No 3) CA 1960, 39 TC 209*, but see *Bradshaw v Blunden (No 2) Ch D 1960, 39 TC 73*). Where the appellant was the inspector and the taxpayer did not wish to proceed, the court refused to make an order on terms agreed between the parties (*Slaney v Kean Ch D 1969, 45 TC 415*).

The court may, however, return a case for amendment. [*TMA 1970, s 56(7)*]. In *Consolidated Goldfields plc v CIR Ch D 1990, 63 TC 333*, the taxpayer company's request that the High Court remit a case to the Commissioners for further findings of fact was refused. Although the remedy was properly sought, it would only be granted if it could be shown that the desired findings were (*a*) material to some tenable argument, (*b*) reasonably open on the evidence adduced, and (*c*) not inconsistent with the findings already made. However, in *Fitzpatrick v CIR CS 1990, [1991] STC 34*, a case was remitted where the facts found proved or admitted, and the contentions of the parties, were not clearly set out, despite the taxpayer's request for various amendments and insertions to the case, and in *Whittles v Uniholdings Ltd (No 1) Ch D, [1993] STC 671*, remission was appropriate in view of the widely differing interpretations which the parties sought to place on the Commissioners' decision (and the case was remitted a second time (see *[1993] STC 767*) to resolve misunderstandings as to the nature of a concession made by the Crown at the original hearing and apparent inconsistencies in the Commissioners' findings of fact). If a case is remitted, the taxpayer has the right to attend any further hearing by the Commissioners (*Lack v Doggett CA 1970, 46 TC 497*) but the Commissioners may not, in the absence of special circumstances, admit further evidence (*Archer-Shee v Baker CA 1928, 15 TC 1*; *Watson v Samson Bros Ch D 1959, 38 TC 346*; *Bradshaw v Blunden (No 2) Ch D 1960, 39 TC 73*), but see *Brady v Group Lotus Car Companies plc CA 1987, 60 TC 359* where the Court directed the Commissioners to admit further evidence where new facts had come to light suggesting the taxpayers had deliberately misled the Commissioners. Errors of fact in the case may be amended by agreement of the parties prior to hearing of the case (*Moore v Austin Ch D 1985, 59 TC 110*). See *Jeffries v Stevens Ch D 1982, 56 TC 134* as regards delay between statement of case and motion for remission.

A new question of law may be raised in the courts on giving due notice to the other parties (*Muir v CIR CA 1966, 43 TC 367*) but the courts will neither admit evidence not in the stated case (*Watson v Samson Bros Ch D 1959, 38 TC 346*; *Cannon Industries Ltd v Edwards Ch D 1965, 42 TC 625*; *Frowd v Whalley Ch D 1965, 42 TC 599*, and see *R v Great Yarmouth Commrs (ex p Amis) QB 1960, 39 TC 143*) nor consider contentions of which evidence in support was not produced before the Commissioners (*Denekamp v Pearce Ch D 1998, 71 TC 213*).

Following the decision in *Pepper v Hart HL 1992, 65 TC 421*, the courts are prepared to consider the parliamentary history of legislation, or the official reports of debates in Hansard, where all of the following conditions are met:

- legislation is ambiguous or obscure, or leads to an absurdity;
- the material relied upon consists of one or more statements by a Minister or other promoter of the Bill together if necessary with such other parliamentary material as is necessary to understand such statements and their effect;
- the statements relied upon are clear.

Any party intending to refer to an extract from Hansard in support of any argument must, unless otherwise directed, serve copies of the extract and a brief summary of the argument intended to be based upon the extract upon all parties and the court not less than five clear working days before the first day of the hearing (Supreme Court Practice Note, 20 December 1994) (1995 STI 98).

Many court decisions turn on whether the Commissioners' decision was one of fact supported by the evidence, and hence final. The courts will not disturb a finding of fact if there was reasonable evidence for it, notwithstanding that the evidence might support a different conclusion of fact. The leading case is *Edwards v Bairstow & Harrison HL 1955, 36 TC 207*, in which the issue was whether there had been an adventure in the nature of trade. The Commissioners' decision was reversed on the ground that the *only* reasonable conclusion from the evidence was that there had been such an adventure. For a discussion of the application of this principle, see *Milnes v J Beam Group Ltd Ch D 1975, 50 TC 675*.

A court decision is a binding precedent for itself or an inferior court except that the House of Lords, while treating its former decisions as normally binding, may depart from a previous decision should it appear right to do so. For this see *Fitzleet Estates Ltd v Cherry HL 1977, 51 TC 708*. Scottish decisions are not binding on the High Court but are normally followed. Decisions of the Privy Council and of the Irish Courts turning on comparable legislation are treated with respect. A court decision does not affect other assessments already final and conclusive (see 7.5 ASSESSMENTS) but may be followed, if relevant, in the determination of any open appeals against assessments and in assessments made subsequently irrespective of the years of assessment or taxpayers concerned (*Re Waring decd Ch D, [1948] 1 All ER 257*; *Gwyther v Boslymon Quarries Ltd KB 1950, 29 ATC 1*; *Bolands Ltd v CIR SC(I) 1925, 4 ATC 526*). Further, a court decision does not estop the Crown from proceeding on a different basis for other years (*Hood Barrs v CIR (No 3) CA 1960, 39 TC 209*). A general change of practice consequent on a court decision may affect error or mistake relief (see 15.9 CLAIMS).

For joinder of CIR in non-tax disputes, see *In re Vandervell's Trusts HL 1970, 46 TC 341*.

6.23 APPEAL FROM THE SPECIAL COMMISSIONERS

In the case of an appeal to the Special Commissioners, if the appellant or HMRC is dissatisfied in point of law with a decision (whether in principle or on final determination) or with a decision varying or substituting such a decision, appeal may (except in certain Lands Tribunal cases) be made to the High Court. Under *Order 55* of the Supreme Court Practice, the appeal must be lodged in the High Court within 28 days from the date on which notice of the decision is given. Further appeal may be made to the Court of Appeal and thence (with leave) to the House of Lords. A 'leap-frog' appeal to the Court of Appeal may be made if all the parties agree, the Commissioners certify that a point of law is involved relating wholly or mainly to the construction of an enactment which was fully argued and considered before them, and the leave of the Court of Appeal has been obtained. In Scotland appeals are to the Court of Session, in Northern Ireland to the Court of Appeal (NI), and thence in either case to the House of Lords. When a decision against which an appeal has been made is set aside or varied under *SI 1994 No 1811, reg 19* (see 6.17 above), the appeal is treated as withdrawn.

In the case of an appeal against a decision on an appeal against an assessment, tax must be paid in accordance with the Commissioners' decision. Following the decision on appeal, any tax overpaid is refunded with such interest as the court may allow, and any amount undercharged is due and payable 30 days after the inspector issues a notice of the amount due.

[*TMA 1970, ss 56A, 58; ITTOIA 2005, Sch 1 para 375*].

For case law applicable equally to appeals from the Special Commissioners, see 6.22 above in relation to appeals from the General Commissioners.

6.24 JUDICIAL REVIEW

A taxpayer who is dissatisfied with the exercise of administrative powers may in certain circumstances (e.g. where HMRC has exceeded or abused its powers or acted contrary to the rules of natural justice, or where the Appeal Commissioners have acted unfairly or improperly) seek a remedy in one of the prerogative orders of mandamus, prohibition and certiorari. This is now done by way of application for judicial review under *Supreme Court Act 1981, s 31* and *Order 53* of the *Rules of the Supreme Court.*

The issue on an application for leave to apply for judicial review is whether there is an arguable case (*R v CIR (ex p Howmet Corporation and another) QB, [1994] STC 413*). The procedure is generally used where no other, adequate, remedy, such as a right of appeal, is available. See *R v Special Commrs (ex p Stipplechoice Ltd) (No 1) CA 1985, 59 TC 396, R v HMIT (ex p Kissane and Another) QB, [1986] STC 152, R v Sevenoaks Commrs (ex p Thorne) QB 1989, 62 TC 341, R v Hastings and Bexhill General Commrs and CIR (ex p Goodacre) QB 1994, 67 TC 126* and *R v CIR (ex p Ulster Bank Ltd) CA 1997, 69 TC 211.*

There is a very long line of cases in which the courts have consistently refused applications where a matter should have been pursued through the ordinary channels as described above. See, for example, *R v Special Commrs (ex p Morey) CA 1972, 49 TC 71*; *R v Special Commrs (ex p Emery) QB 1980, 53 TC 555*; *R v Walton General Commrs (ex p Wilson) CA, [1983] STC 464*; *R v Special Commrs (ex p Esslemont) CA, 1984 STI 312*; *R v Brentford Commrs (ex p Chan) QB 1985, 57 TC 651*; *R v CIR (ex p Caglar) QB 1995, 67 TC 335.* See also, however, *R v HMIT and Others (ex p Lansing Bagnall Ltd) CA 1986, 61 TC 112* for a successful application where the inspector issued a notice under a discretionary power on the footing that there was a mandatory obligation to do so, and *R v Ward, R v Special Commr (ex p Stipplechoice Ltd) (No 3) QB 1988, 61 TC 391*, where insufficient notice was given of revision of an accounting period under *ICTA 1988, s 12(8)* prior to appeal hearing.

In *R v CIR (ex p J Rothschild Holdings) CA 1987, 61 TC 178*, the Revenue were required to produce internal documents of a general character relating to their practice in applying a statutory provision, but in *R v CIR (ex p Taylor) CA 1988, 62 TC 562* discovery of internal Revenue correspondence was refused as there was no material indication that it had any bearing on the question of whether the decision taken by the inspector could be challenged. In *R v CIR (ex p Unilever plc) CA 1996, 68 TC 205*, an application for judicial review for a Revenue decision to refuse a late loss relief claim was successful. The Revenue's refusal was 'so unreasonable as to be, in public law terms, irrational' in view of an administrative procedure established with the company over many years of raising assessments on estimates of net taxable profits, adjusted when the final accounts became available without regard to the loss claim time limit. A confirmation by the local inspector that capital allowances were available in relation to an enterprise zone property trust scheme was not binding where the promoters were aware that clearance applications were required to be made to a specialist department, and failed to disclose that the scheme involved 'artificial provisions' (*R v CIR (ex p Matrix-Securities Ltd) HL 1994, 66 TC 587*). As regards informal advice by the Revenue generally, they were not bound by anything less than a clear, unambiguous and unqualified representation (*R v CIR (ex p MFK Underwriting Agencies Ltd) QB 1989, 62 TC 607*), and in *R v CIR (ex p Bishopp and another) QB, [1999] STC 531*, an application for judicial review of informal advice given by the Revenue in relation to a proposed transaction was refused. See, generally, 33.4 HMRC: ADMINISTRATION. See also *R v CIR (ex p Camacq Corporation) CA 1989, 62 TC 651*, where a Revenue decision to revoke its authorisation to pay a dividend gross was upheld, *R v CIR (ex p S G Warburg & Co Ltd) QB 1994, 68 TC 300*, where a decision not to apply a published practice was upheld, and *R (oao Bamber) v HMRC QB 2005, 2006 STI 46*, where a Revenue decision to resile from a written agreement was upheld as being in the public interest.

The underlying facts in *Carvill v CIR (No 3) Ch D, [2002] STC 1167* were that in two separate appeals relating to different tax years, income from an identical source had been held liable to tax for some years (the earlier years) but not others. An appeal against the Revenue's refusal to refund tax, and interest on tax, paid for the earlier years was rejected; the assessments for those years were valid assessments which the Special Commissioner in question had had jurisdiction to determine, and the taxpayer the right to challenge, and those assessments had not been set aside. An application for judicial review on the grounds that the Revenue's refusal to repay was unfair was dismissed (*Carvill (R oao) v CIR QB 2003, 75 TC 477*).

See 30.4 FRAUDULENT OR NEGLIGENT CONDUCT as regards challenges to the validity of notices under *TMA 1970, s 20*.

The first step is to obtain leave to apply for judicial review from the High Court. Application for leave is made ex parte to a single judge who will usually determine the application without a hearing. The court will not grant leave unless the applicant has a sufficient interest in the matter to which the application relates. See *CIR v National Federation of Self-Employed and Small Businesses Ltd HL 1981, 55 TC 133* for what is meant by 'sufficient interest' and for discussion of availability of judicial review generally.

Time limit. Applications must be made **within three months** of the date when the grounds for application arose. The court has discretion to extend this time limit where there is good reason, subject to conditions, but is generally very reluctant to do so. Grant of leave for review does not amount to a ruling that application is made in good time (*R v Tavistock Commrs (ex p Worth) QB 1985, 59 TC 116*).

6.25 COSTS

Costs may be awarded by the courts in the usual way. In suitable cases, e.g. 'test cases', HMRC may undertake to pay the taxpayer's costs. There is no provision for the award of costs of appearing before the General Commissioners. See 6.17 above as regards award of costs of Special Commissioners' hearings against parties acting 'wholly unreasonably'. Costs awarded by the courts may include expenses connected with the drafting of the case stated (*Manchester Corporation v Sugden CA 1903, 4 TC 595*). Costs of a discontinued application for judicial review were refused where the Revenue were not informed of the application (*R v CIR (ex p Opman International UK) QB 1985, 59 TC 352*). Law costs of appeals are not allowable for tax purposes generally (*Allen v Farquharson KB 1932, 17 TC 59*; *Smith's Potato Estates Ltd v Bolland HL 1948, 30 TC 267*; *Rushden Heel Co v Keene HL 1948, 30 TC 298*; *Spofforth & Prince v Golder KB 1945, 26 TC 310*).

7 Assessments

Cross references. See 6 APPEALS; 15.7 CLAIMS; 21.7 CONTROLLED FOREIGN COMPANIES; 30 FRAUDULENT OR NEGLIGENT CONDUCT; 52.2 PARTNERSHIPS; 55.9 PROFIT COMPUTATIONS with regard to European Economic Interest Groupings; 60.5 RESIDENCE; and 61.18 RETURNS for determination of tax liability where no return is delivered.

Simon's Direct Tax Service D2.7, D2.8.

7.1 ASSESSMENTS

Notwithstanding the introduction of SELF-ASSESSMENT (62) for accounting periods ending on or after 1 July 1999, HMRC retain the power to make assessments where necessary, most notably 'discovery' assessments (see 7.2 below). Corporation tax assessments on companies are made for accounting periods.

An assessment is made by an officer of Revenue and Customs (or, before 18 April 2005, by an officer of the Board) by the giving of a notice of assessment. The notice must be served on the person assessed (normally by post) and must state its date of issue and the time limit for giving notice of appeal (6.1 APPEALS). Where any statutory provision gives the Commissioners for HMRC (or, before 18 April 2005, the Board of Inland Revenue) the power to make an assessment, the assessment is nevertheless to be made by an officer in like manner as above. [*TMA 1970, s 30A(1)–(3)(5); FA 1998, Sch 18 para 47(1); ITTOIA 2005, Sch 1 para 370; CRCA 2005, ss 5, 7, Sch 4 para 68*].

An assessment must include a statement of the tax actually payable (*Hallamshire Industrial Finance Trust Ltd v CIR Ch D 1978, 53 TC 631*). An assessment defective in form or containing errors may be validated by *TMA 1970, s 114(1)*, or in some cases the court may choose to use its powers under *TMA 1970, s 56(6)* (see 6.22 APPEALS) to alter an assessment on appeal (*Pickles v Foulsham HL 1925, 9 TC 261*; *Bath & West Counties Property Trust Ltd v Thomas Ch D 1977, 52 TC 20*). However, *section 114(1)* does *not* extend to integral fundamental parts of the assessment such as an error in the year of assessment for which it is made (*Baylis v Gregory HL 1988, 62 TC 1*).

A taxpayer may authorise HMRC (on form 64–8) to automatically provide his agent with a copy of any assessment made on him. If an assessment is not dealt with promptly, interest (or additional interest) may arise on unpaid tax, and any appeal may be out of time.

An officer's power of assessment is not limited to persons (or sources of income) within the area of his tax office (*R v Tavistock Commrs (ex p Adams) (No 2) CA 1971, 48 TC 56*).

See 7.6 below for the normal time limits within which an assessment may be made. For extended time limits in cases of fraudulent or negligent conduct, see 30.3 FRAUDULENT OR NEGLIGENT CONDUCT.

See 61.18 RETURNS for HMRC's power to make a determination of the tax liability in a case where a company tax return has been issued but not filed. Tax is payable as if the determination were a self-assessment, with no right of appeal, and the determination can only be displaced by the filing of a return and the making of a self-assessment based thereon.

See 25.4 EUROPEAN COMMUNITY LEGISLATION regarding the application of the corporation tax provisions where a company ceases to be UK-resident in the course of the formation of an SE or where an SE becomes non-UK resident.

7.2 DISCOVERY

If HMRC discover that an amount which ought to have been assessed to tax has not been assessed, or that an assessment has become insufficient, or that relief has been given which is, or has become, excessive, they may make a 'discovery assessment' in the amount (or further amount) which, in their opinion, should be charged in order to make good the loss of tax. Similarly, if they discover that a return for an accounting period incorrectly states an amount that affects, or may affect, the tax payable for another accounting period or by another company, they may make a 'discovery determination' of the amount which, in their opinion, ought to have been stated in the return. Notice of a discovery assessment or determination must be served on the company, stating the date of issue and the time limit for any appeal, and the assessment or determination may be altered after the notice has been served only under express provisions.

A discovery assessment will thus be appropriate where, for example, a discovery leads to an additional tax liability on the company for the period. A discovery determination would be appropriate where there is a discovery that losses carried forward or surrendered as group relief have been overstated. If such a determination reduces losses, etc. available for another period or to another company, and the time allowed for the required amendment has expired, a discovery assessment would be appropriate. (HMRC Company Taxation Manual, CTM 95520 and CTM 95530).

In practice, where a return has been filed and the time limit for opening an enquiry has not expired (nor an enquiry already been closed), HMRC normally deal with matters by opening an enquiry rather than by issuing a discovery assessment or determination. (HMRC Company Taxation Manual, CTM 95520). For the limited circumstances in which a discovery assessment may be made even though the deadline for opening an enquiry has not passed, see HMRC Enquiry Manual, EM 3255 and Revenue Tax Bulletin August 2001 pp 875, 876.

Subject to the exceptions below, a discovery assessment for an accounting period for which the company has delivered a return, or a discovery determination, may only be made in the following circumstances:

(*a*) where the discovery arose from a situation attributable to FRAUDULENT OR NEGLIGENT CONDUCT (30) on the part of the company, a person acting on behalf of the company, or a partner of the company at the relevant time; or

(*b*) where, at the time HMRC ceased to be entitled to give notice of enquiry into the return (see 61.10 RETURNS) or completed their enquiries into the return, they could not reasonably have been expected, on the basis of the information made available to them before that time, to be aware of the situation giving rise to the discovery. Information is for this purpose regarded as made available to HMRC if it is contained:

   (i) in the company's returns (or accompanying documentation) for the period or the two immediately preceding accounting periods; or

   (ii) in a claim (or accompanying documentation) made by the company as regards the period; or

   (iii) in any documents, accounts or information produced to, or provided for, HMRC for the purposes of an enquiry into a return (as in (i)) or claim (as in (ii)),

   or if it is information the existence and relevance of which are notified in writing to HMRC by the company (or a person acting on its behalf) or could reasonably be expected to be inferred by HMRC from information falling within (i)–(iii) above.

As regards (*b*) above, there is an onus on the company to draw attention to any important information relevant to a tax liability, particularly if there is some doubt as to the interpretation which could be placed on that information. Information made available by the company's agent on its behalf is made available by the company, but where information is made available by, or on behalf of, someone other than the company, e.g. in the return of another group company, a discovery assessment or determination on the company is not precluded. (HMRC Company Taxation Manual, CTM 95550).

The above restrictions do not apply where a discovery assessment or determination gives effect to a discovery determination duly made in relation to another company's return. Nor do they apply in relation to any income or gains in respect of which a notice under *ICTA 1988, s 804ZA* (schemes and arrangements designed to increase double taxation relief — see 5.19 ANTI-AVOIDANCE), *TCGA 1992, s 184G* or *s 184H* (avoidance utilising losses — see 11.4 CAPITAL GAINS) or *F(No 2)A 2005, s 24* or *s 26* (tax arbitrage — see 5.27 ANTI-AVOIDANCE) has been given after enquiries have been completed into the return.

A discovery assessment or determination may in any event not be made if the discovery arose from a situation attributable to a mistake in the return as to the basis on which the company's liability ought to have been computed, and the return was in fact made on the basis of, or in accordance with, the practice generally prevailing at the time the return was made.

Any objection to a discovery assessment or determination on the grounds that the above conditions have not been complied with can only be made on an appeal against the assessment or determination.

See HMRC Statement of Practice SP 1/06 on 'Self-Assessment: Finality and Discovery' which clarifies how much information a taxpayer needs to provide in the tax return to remove the possibility of a discovery assessment. The Statement is intended to provide more certainty for both individuals and companies following the decision in the case of *Langham v Veltema CA 2004, 76 TC 259* where it was held that a discovery assessment could be made once the enquiry window was closed even though the Revenue was made aware of the possibility that a property valuation might have been insufficient. The Statement provides three examples of where the taxpayer can rely on information in the tax return to provide against protection from a later discovery assessment provided the information is reasonable and true.

- In a valuation case, the information should state that a valuation has been used, by whom it has been carried out, that it was carried out by a named independent and suitably qualified valuer and, if that was the case, the appropriate basis of the valuation.
- In the case of an exceptional item in the accounts, for example concerning repairs, the information should state that a programme of work has been carried out, what it included, the total cost allocated to revenue and capital and the particular basis of allocation.
- In a case where the taxpayer adopts a different view of the law from that published as HMRC's view, the tax return should indicate that a different view had been adopted by providing comments to the effect that HMRC guidance has not been followed or that no adjustment has been made to take account of it.

The Statement stresses that only the minimum information necessary to make disclosure of an insufficiency should be submitted. 'Information will not be treated as being made available where the total amount supplied is so extensive that an officer "could not have been reasonably expected to be aware" of the significance of particular information and the officer's attention has not been drawn to it by the taxpayer or taxpayer's representative.' It further states that the *Veltema* judgement does not require the provision of enough information to quantify the effect on the assessment.

[*FA 1998, Sch 18 paras 41-45; FA 2005, s 88(4)(5); F(No 2)A 2005, s 29(2); FA 2006, s 71(3)*].

Simon's Direct Tax Service. See D2.836, D2.837.

7.3 **Over-repayments.** The discovery assessment provisions at 7.2 above apply also to an amount paid to a company by way of repayment of tax (or payment of tax credit),

INTEREST ON OVERPAID TAX (40), 'land remediation tax credit' (see 55.8 PROFIT COMPUTATIONS), research and development tax credits (see 59 RESEARCH AND DEVELOPMENT) or film tax credits (see 66.52 TRADING INCOME), to the extent that it ought not to have been paid, unless it is recoverable under *ICTA 1988, s 826(8A)* (interest recoverable as if it were INTEREST ON UNPAID TAX (41)). Any such assessment is under Schedule D, Case VI, and INTEREST ON UNPAID TAX (41) runs from the date when the payment being recovered was made. For these purposes amounts allowed by way of set-off are treated as paid, and an intended repayment which exceeds the tax paid is nonetheless treated as a repayment. In the case of an assessment to recover tax repaid in respect of an accounting period (or interest thereon), income tax repaid in respect of a payment received in an accounting period (or interest thereon), or land remediation or research and development tax credits paid for an accounting period, the assessment is treated as being for that accounting period.

Except in cases of fraud or negligence (for which see 7.6 below), the time limit for a discovery assessment by virtue of these provisions is (where relevant) extended to the later of the end of the accounting period following that in which the amount assessed was paid and the expiry of three months from the day on which HMRC complete an enquiry into a relevant company tax return (see 61.14 RETURNS).

[*FA 1998, Sch 18 paras 52, 53; FA 2001, Sch 23 para 5; FA 2002, Sch 14 para 3; FA 2006, Sch 5 para 28*].

7.4 DOUBLE ASSESSMENT

If HMRC are satisfied, on a written claim by a company, that it has been assessed (including self-assessment) more than once for the same cause and for the same accounting period, they must take the necessary steps to eliminate the double charge. An appeal against their decision on a claim may be brought before the Commissioners having jurisdiction to hear an appeal relating to the assessment (or the later of the assessments) to which the claim relates. [*FA 1998, Sch 18 para 50*].

7.5 FINALITY OF ASSESSMENTS

An assessment cannot be altered after the notice has been served except in accordance with the express provisions of the *Taxes Acts* (for example where the taxpayer appeals — see 6 APPEALS). [*FA 1998, Sch 18 paras 47(2), 49*]. Where over-assessment results from an *error or mistake* in a return, see 15.9 CLAIMS.

Where an amount required to be included in a company tax return may affect tax payable for another accounting period or by another company, and that amount can no longer be altered (for which see *FA 1998, Sch 18 para 88(3)-(5)*), it is taken as conclusively determined in relation to the other period or company (without affecting HMRC's power to make assessments). [*FA 1998, Sch 18 para 88*].

7.6 TIME LIMITS

Subject to any specific provision allowing a longer period, assessments and discovery determinations must be made within six years after the end of the accounting period to which they relate, increased to 21 years where fraud or negligence is involved. Any objection to an assessment or determination as out of time can only be made on an appeal against the assessment or determination. [*FA 1998, Sch 18 paras 46, 49*].

7.7 APPEALS

An appeal may be brought against any discovery assessment or determination by written notice to HMRC within 30 days after issue of the notice of the assessment or determination. [*FA 1998, Sch 18 paras 48, 49*].

8 Banks

Cross-reference. 24.15 DOUBLE TAX RELIEF.

Simon's Direct Tax Service D4.11.

8.1 **BANKING BUSINESSES**

Banking businesses are assessable on their profits under normal taxation provisions with interest on advances to customers included under Schedule D, Case I. The profits continue to be taxable under Schedule D, Case I where, for accounting periods beginning on or after 1 January 2005, changes in the fair value of securities (held for the purpose of carrying on a banking or insurance business or a business consisting of dealing in securities) are accounted for in reserves (either in the statement of recognised gains and losses or statement of changes in equity). For the Schedule D, Case VI charge on certain net receipts arising during compulsory liquidation, see *F(No 2)A 1992, Sch 12* (as amended).

See *Pattison v Marine Midland Ltd HL 1983, 57 TC 219*, 26.2 EXCHANGE GAINS AND LOSSES, as regards matching of foreign currency assets and liabilities, and that chapter generally as regards special legislation.

In general, the term 'bank' is defined by reference to the carrying on of a *bona fide* banking business, but for certain purposes it is specially defined as:

(*a*) the Bank of England;

(*b*) a person who has permission under *Financial Services and Markets Act 2000, Pt 4* to accept deposits (excluding building and friendly societies, credit unions and insurance companies);

(*c*) an EEA firm within *Financial Services and Markets Act 2000, Sch 3 para 5*(*b*) which has permission under *para 15* of that *Schedule* (as a result of qualifying for authorisation under *para 12*(*1*)) to accept deposits;

(*d*) an international organisation of which the UK is a member and which is designated as a bank for the particular purpose by Treasury order (e.g. the European Investment Bank, see *SI 1996 No 1179*); or

(*e*) on or after 6 April 2007, the European Investment Bank.

(Before 1 December 2001, (*b*) and (*c*) above were replaced by the following:

(*b*) an institution authorised under the *Banking Act 1987*;

(*c*) a European authorised institution (within the *Banking Co-ordination* (*Second Council Directive*) *Regulations 1992*) in relation to the establishment of a branch of which the requirements of *Sch 2 para 1* of those regulations have been complied with.)

See 8.2 below, 14.9(F), 14.9(3) CHARITIES, 23.17 DISTRIBUTIONS, 37.3(*b*) INCOME TAX IN RELATION TO A COMPANY, 61.24, 61.26 RETURNS.

[*ICTA 1988, ss 472A, 840A; FA 1996, Sch 37 para 1(1); SI 2001 No 3629, Article 46; SI 2002 No 1409; FA 2004, s 54; FA 2005, Sch 4 para 50; ITA 2007, Sch 1 para 226*].

8.2 The normal rules for deduction of tax from payments of **yearly interest** (see 37.3(*b*) INCOME TAX IN RELATION TO A COMPANY) do not apply, for advances made on or after 29 April 1996, to interest payable on an advance from a bank (within *ICTA 1988, s 840A*, see 8.1 above) where the person beneficially entitled to the interest is within the charge to corporation tax in respect of it, or to interest paid by such a bank in the ordinary course of its business. Previously, the exclusion applied to yearly interest payable in the UK on an advance from a bank carrying on a *bona fide* banking business in the UK or paid by such a bank in the ordinary course of such a business. There are transitional provisions preserving relief as regards interest payable or paid on or after 29 April 1996 on an advance made before that day. [*ITA 2007 ss 878, 899; ICTA 1988, s 349(3)(a)(b)(3AA)(3AB)); FA 1996, Sch 37 Pt II*]. For what constitutes a *bona fide* banking business, see *Hafton Properties Ltd v McHugh Ch D 1986, 59 TC 420*, and as regards whether interest is 'payable in the UK', see *Mistletoe Ltd v Flood (Sp C 351), [2003] SSCD 66*. See below as regards payments 'in the ordinary course' of business. The bank may be required by an inspector to make a return of interest paid. [*TMA 1970, s 17; FA 1990, s 92*]. See 61.24 RETURNS.

Payments by individuals to certain banks of 'relevant loan interest' are, however, paid under deduction of tax [*ICTA 1988, s 369*] (see 37.6 INCOME TAX IN RELATION TO A COMPANY), and see 8.9 below as regards payment of 'relevant interest' by banks.

Interest paid by a bank is accepted by HMRC as being paid 'in the ordinary course of its business' unless either (i) the characteristics of the transaction giving rise to the interest are primarily attributable to an intention to avoid UK tax, or (ii) the borrowing relates to the capital structure of the bank (and this includes borrowings conforming to any of the definitions of tier 1, tier 2 or (tier 3 capital, whether or not they count towards such capital). Banks not recognised as such by HMRC before 29 April 1996 continue to have to deduct tax in certain cases. (HMRC Statement of Practice, SP 4/96,).

8.3 **Overseas debts.** There is a concessional relief for certain receipts and debts the proceeds of which cannot be remitted to the UK but which form part of profits within Case I or Case II of Schedule D (see 66.83 TRADING INCOME). This concession applies to unremittable interest accrued on a loan made in the normal course of trade by a bank or other financial institution. It does not apply to the principal, or to a loan made in a currency other than the local currency of the country imposing currency restrictions where the interest is paid in the local currency and is available to be re-lent in that currency. (HMRC Extra-Statutory Concession, B38).

8.4 Where a banking business is carried on in the UK **by a person not resident** or not ordinarily resident in the UK, the provisions of *ICTA 1988, ss 474, 475* apply. See 60.9 RESIDENCE.

8.5 **Non-resident central banks** as specified by Order in Council are exempt from tax on interest, public annuities and dividends paid out of UK public revenue (but may be taxable thereon if carrying on business in the UK) and also on chargeable gains. [*ICTA 1988, s 516*]. Profits, income and chargeable gains of the issue departments of the Reserve Bank of **India** and the State Bank of **Pakistan** are exempt. [*ICTA 1988, s 517; TCGA 1992, s 271(8)*].

8.6 For accounting periods beginning before 1 April 2004, **savings banks** are treated as investment companies, such distinction being no longer necessary for accounting periods beginning on or after that date by virtue of the extension of the relief for management expenses to include all companies with investment business. (See 42 INVESTMENT COMPANIES AND INVESTMENT BUSINESS.) [*ICTA 1988, s 130; FA 2004, s 38*].

8.7 For security given in certain circumstances by a non-resident company to its bankers, see 5.10(i) ANTI-AVOIDANCE.

8.8 Contributions to the Deposit Protection Fund are deductible as expenses in computing trading profits, and any repayment of such contribution is treated as a trading receipt. [*Banking Act 1979, s 33*].

8.9 DEDUCTION OF TAX FROM INTEREST

Any 'deposit-taker' paying or crediting interest on a 'relevant deposit' must deduct therefrom a sum representing income tax thereon (at the lower rate for the year of assessment in which the payment is made), unless the conditions for gross payment contained in *The Income Tax (Deposit-takers) (Interest Payments) Regulations 1990 (SI 1990 No 2232)* (see below) are met. *ITA 2007, ss 449, 899, 901* (formerly *ICTA 1988, s 349*) do not apply to such payments.

ALTERNATIVE FINANCE ARRANGEMENTS (4) are treated as if they were deposits and alternative finance return or profit share return payable under those arrangements as if they were interest. This applies to alternative finance arrangements entered into on or after 6 April 2005 subject to commencement rules for arrangements entered into before that date where a profit share return is payable on or after that date.

The deposit-taker must treat all deposits as relevant deposits unless satisfied to the contrary, but if so satisfied may treat a deposit as not being a relevant deposit until he comes into possession of information reasonably indicative that the deposit is, or may be, a relevant deposit.

For these purposes '*deposit-taker*' means the Bank of England, persons authorised under the *Banking Act 1987* (or municipal bank within that *Act*) or the *Financial Services and Markets Act 2000*, the Post Office (until its dissolution), any local authority and any other deposit-taker prescribed by Treasury order. A 'European deposit-taker' (see *SI 1992 No 3234 as amended*) is included, as is any financial instruments dealer authorised under the *Financial Services and Markets Act 2000* (see *SI 2002 No 1968*).

A '*relevant deposit*' (subject to the exclusions below) is a deposit where either:

(*a*) the person beneficially entitled to any interest is an individual (or the persons so entitled are all individuals), or is a Scottish partnership all the partners of which are individuals; or

(*b*) the person entitled to the interest receives it as the personal representative of a deceased individual (but note particularly the ordinary residence requirement at (xii) below); or

(*c*) the interest arises to the trustees of a discretionary or accumulation trust (as under *ICTA 1988, s 686*, see Tolley's Income Tax under Settlements).

This does not apply to deposits made before 6 April 1995 unless the deposit-taker has, since that date but before the making of the payment, been notified by HMRC or the trustees that the interest is income of such a trust (and HMRC have wide information powers in relation to such notices). The form of notification by the trustees is laid down by *SI 1995 No 1370*, under which payments may continue to be made gross for up to 30 days after receipt of notice (whether by the trustees or by HMRC) where deduction within that period has not become reasonably practicable. Notification may be cancelled by HMRC where appropriate. There are transitional provisions treating the source as ceasing where a payment on a deposit made before 6 April 1996 is brought within the scheme before 6 April 1998.

Deposits are not relevant deposits (so interest is paid gross) if they are:

(i) (for corporation tax purposes) deposits in respect of which a certificate of deposit (as defined in *ICTA 1988, s 56(5)*) has been issued for £50,000 or more (or foreign equivalent at the time the deposit is made) and which are repayable within five years;

(ii) (for income tax purposes from 2005–06) deposits in respect of which uncertificated eligible debt security units being a certificate or units (as defined in *ITTOIA 2005, s 552(2)*) have been issued for £50,000 or more (or foreign equivalent at the time the deposit is made) and which are repayable within five years;

(iii) non-transferable deposits of £50,000 or more (or foreign equivalent at the time the deposit is made) repayable at the end of a specified period of not more than five years;

(iv) (for corporation tax purposes) a '*qualifying deposit right*', i.e. a right to receive an amount in pursuance of a deposit of money under an arrangement within *ICTA*

1988, s 56A) under which no certificate of deposit has been issued, although the person entitled to the right could call for the issue of such a certificate, which otherwise meets the conditions in (i) above;

(v) (for income tax purposes from 2005–06) a '*qualifying deposit right*', i.e. a right to receive an amount in pursuance of an uncertificated right within *ITTOIA 2005, s 552(1)(c)*, under which no uncertificated eligible security units have been issued, although the person entitled to the right could call for the issue of such units, which otherwise meets the conditions in (ii) above;

(vi) debentures (as defined in *Companies Act 1985, s 744*);

(vii) loans made by a deposit-taker in the ordinary course of his business;

(viii) debts on securities listed on a recognised stock exchange;

(ix) deposits in a '*general client account deposit*', i.e. a client account, other than an account for specific clients, if the depositor is required by law to make payments representing interest to any of the clients whose money it contains;

(x) Lloyd's underwriters' premiums trust funds;

(xi) (before 1 December 2001) deposits by Stock Exchange money brokers (recognised by the Bank of England) in the course of business as such a broker;

(xii) deposits held at non-UK branches of UK resident deposit-takers;

(xiii) deposits with non-UK resident deposit-takers held other than in UK branches; and

(xiv) deposits in respect of which the 'appropriate person' has declared in writing (or, from 6 April 2001, by electronic means) to the deposit-taker that:

(1) where (*a*) above applies, the individual (or all of the individuals) concerned is (are), at the time of the declaration, not ordinarily resident in the UK; or

(2) where (*b*) above applies, the deceased, at the time of his death, was not ordinarily resident in the UK; or

(3) where (*c*) above applies, at the time of the declaration the trustees are not UK resident and do not have any reasonable grounds for believing that any of the beneficiaries (as defined for this purpose) is a UK ordinarily resident individual or a UK resident company.

The '*appropriate person*' is any person beneficially entitled to the interest, or entitled to receive it in his capacity as a personal representative or trustee, or to whom it is payable. The declaration must be in such form, and contain such information, as is required by HMRC, and must include an undertaking to notify the deposit-taker should any individual concerned become ordinarily resident in the UK, or the trustees or any company concerned become resident in the UK, or any UK ordinarily resident individual or UK-resident company become a beneficiary of the trust to which the declaration relates. HMRC have powers to review all declarations received by a deposit-taker. For payments before 6 April 2001, a certificate by the deposit-taker is required in cases where a declaration of non-ordinary residence does not include the depositor's permanent address, but from that date the address must be included in any such declaration. Declarations in similar terms made to a building society which converts to company status (see 9.6 BUILDING SOCIETIES) are, by concession, treated as having been made to the successor company. (HMRC Extra-Statutory Concession, A69).

The deposit-taker has to treat all deposits as relevant deposits unless satisfied to the contrary, but if so satisfied can treat a deposit as not being a relevant deposit until he comes into possession of information reasonably indicative that the deposit is, or might be, a relevant deposit.

The Treasury and HMRC are given wide powers to alter the legislation by statutory instrument, in particular in relation to the declaration required at (xiv) above.

In the case of depositors who make the appropriate declaration for their deposit to be excluded from being a relevant deposit (see (xiv) above) to a deposit-taker other than a bank, the normal deduction rules under *ITA 2007, s 449* (formerly *ICTA 1988, s 349(2)*) are disapplied by *ITA 2007, s 449* (formerly *section 349(3)(h)* (introduced by *FA 1993, s 59*)) as they are disapplied in the case of banks by *section 349(3)(a)*.

The collection procedure of *ITA 2007, s 946–960* (formerly *ICTA 1988, Sch 16*) (see 37.5 INCOME TAX IN RELATION TO A COMPANY) applies, *mutatis mutandis*, to such payments whether or not the deposit-taker is UK-resident. In outline, returns are required at quarterly intervals, and tax is due without assessment within 14 days of the date for making the return. Income tax suffered by deduction in a return period may be set against liability of the period under these provisions.

HMRC have wide regulatory powers for giving effect to these provisions.

HMRC Savings, Pensions, Share Schemes may be contacted for technical advice in relation to the tax deduction scheme on 0151–472 6156.

Gross payment may be made on relevant deposits where the person beneficially entitled to the interest is UK ordinarily resident and has supplied the appropriate certificate to the deposit-taker to the effect that he is unlikely to be liable to income tax for the year of assessment in which the payment is made or credited (taking into account for this purpose all interest arising in the year of assessment concerned which would, in the absence of such a certificate, be received under deduction of tax). The certificate must be in prescribed form and must contain the name, permanent address, date of birth and (where applicable) national insurance number of the person beneficially entitled to the interest, and the name (and if necessary branch) of the deposit-taker and account number. It must also contain an undertaking to notify the deposit-taker if the person beneficially entitled to the payment becomes liable to income tax for the year in which the payment is made or credited. HMRC Explanatory Leaflet IR 110 outlines the conditions for certification (which are described in detail below) and contains the appropriate Form R85(1990) on which application may be made (and of which further copies may be obtained from banks, building societies, post offices and tax offices). From 6 April 2001, provision is made for certification by electronic means.

Such a certificate may only be given by:

(i) a depositor aged 16 or over at the beginning of the year of assessment in which the payment is made or credited, or who attains age 16 during that year, who is beneficially entitled to the payment; or

(ii) the parent or guardian of a person beneficially entitled to the payment who is under 16 at the beginning of that year; or

(iii) a person authorised by power of attorney to administer the financial affairs of the person beneficially entitled to the payment; or

(iv) the parent, guardian, spouse, civil partner (see below), son or daughter of a mentally handicapped person, or any person appointed by a court to manage the affairs of a mentally handicapped person; or

(v) a person appointed by the Secretary of State to receive benefits on behalf of a person who is for the time being unable to act.

A certificate may not be given where the payment is treated as income of a parent of the person beneficially entitled to the payment, or where HMRC has issued a notice in relation to the account concerned requiring deduction of tax (see below).

The certificate must be supplied before the end of the year of assessment in which the payment is made or credited, or, in the case of a certificate given by a person who will attain 16 years of age during a year of assessment, before the end of that year.

A person who gives such a certificate fraudulently or negligently, or fails to comply with any undertaking contained in the certificate, is liable under *TMA 1970, s 99A* (introduced by *FA 1991, s 82*) to a penalty up to £3,000.

Tax deducted from payments in a year prior to receipt of a certificate relating to that year may be refunded, and a like amount recovered by the deposit-taker from HMRC, provided that a certificate of deduction of tax has not been furnished to the depositor prior to receipt of the gross payment certificate.

The fact that payments are made gross does not mean that the interest is thereby exempted from the charge to tax.

In HMRC's Guidance Notes for Deposit Takers (Tax Deduction Scheme for Interest) (November 2003), their position as regards incorrect certification for gross payment is explained. Paragraph 3.12 explains that where Revenue auditors are not satisfied that certificates are valid (because they contain other than trivial errors or omissions, which are described in Appendix 2 of the notes), they will seek recovery of lower-rate tax that should have been deducted (and interest and penalties — paragraphs 9.24 and 9.25) Paragraph 3.52 explains that such registrations will be cancelled.

With regard to (iv) above, references to spouses were generally extended by the *Tax and Civil Partnership Regulations 2005* (*SI 2005 No 3229*) to cover civil partners from 5 December 2005.

A certificate ceases to be valid:

(*a*) where the deposit-taker is notified (as above) that the person beneficially entitled to the payment is liable to income tax for the year in which the payment is made;

(*b*) where it was given by a parent or guardian, at the end of the year of assessment in which the person beneficially entitled to the payment attains 16 years of age;

(*c*) where it was given by a person who attained 16 years of age during the year of assessment in which a payment was made or credited, but who was not the holder of the account to which the certificate relates, and that person fails to become the holder before the first payment is made or credited after the end of that year of assessment;

(*d*) where the deposit-taker is notified that the person by or on whose behalf the certificate was given has died; and

(*e*) where HMRC, having reason to believe that a person beneficially entitled to a payment of interest has become liable to income tax, give notice requiring the deposit-taker to deduct tax from payments of interest made, more than 30 days after the issue of the notice (or from earlier payments, if practicable), to or for the benefit of that person on a specified account held by or on behalf of that person.

A notice under (*e*) above must be copied to the person to whom it refers, and a further certificate in respect of the account referred to in the notice may not be given by or on behalf of that person (unless the notice is subsequently cancelled, see below).

A notice under (*e*) above may be cancelled (and the deposit-taker and person referred to in the notice so informed) if HMRC are satisfied that the person referred to in the notice was not at the date of the notice, and has not since become, liable to income tax, or is no longer so liable.

Certificates of non-liability given to a building society which converts to company status (see 9.6 BUILDING SOCIETIES) are, by concession, treated as having been given to the successor company. (HMRC Extra-Statutory Concession, A69).

Tax position of recipient company. The tax deduction scheme described above does not apply to interest on deposits by companies. Such payments by banks are made gross, although payments by other deposit-takers may fall to be made under deduction of tax under *ICTA 1988, s 349(2)*.

Joint accounts. The position as regards certification by each of joint holders of an account is considered separately. Payments are apportioned equally to each joint holder, and tax deducted in respect of that part of a payment to which certification does not apply. The deposit-taker may, however, deduct tax from the whole of payments in respect of joint accounts where certification does not apply to all the joint holders, after giving notice to HMRC of its intention to do so (which notice the deposit-taker may subsequently cancel).

Information. HMRC may by notice require any deposit-taker (within not less than 14 days) to furnish them with such information (including books, records etc.) as they require, in particular

(I) for verification of payments made without deduction of tax and of the validity of certification for gross payment, and

(II) for verification of the amount of tax deducted from payments of interest (but this does not include copies of books, records etc. from which the depositor can be ascertained).

Copies of the deposit-taker's books, records etc. must be made available when required by HMRC. Certificates for gross payment must be retained for at least two years after they expire.

Subject to *FA 1989, s 182(5)*, information obtained under these provisions may not be used other than for the purposes of the provisions or for the ascertainment of the tax liability of the deposit-taker or of the person beneficially entitled to interest paid without deduction of tax to whom the information relates.

HMRC may also make regulations providing for the exclusion from its information powers of accounts held by non-UK ordinary residents.

For HMRC audit powers and further information powers, see *SI 1992 Nos 12, 15* as amended.

HMRC's Code of Practice No 4 sets out their standards for the carrying out of inspections of tax deduction schemes operated by financial intermediaries.

[*ITA 2007 s 451; ICTA 1988, ss 480A–482A*); *FA 2000, ss 111(3)(6), 145(10)(11); ITTOIA 2005, Sch 1 paras 185–187; FA 2005, s 56, Sch 2 para 6; ITA 2007 Sch 1 para 602; SI 1990 No 2232; SI 1992 Nos 12–15, 3234; FA 1995, s 86; SI 1995 No 1370; SI 2001 Nos 405, 406; SI 2001 No 3629, Article 39; SI 2002 No 1968*].

Simon's Direct Tax Service. See D4.1111 *et seq.*

9 Building Societies

Simon's Direct Tax Service D4.7.

9.1 **PAYMENT OF INTEREST**

Building societies deduct savings rate tax from interest payments unless a certificate is supplied to the effect that the recipient is unlikely to be liable to income tax for the year. [*ICTA 1988, s 477A*]. Regulations provide for the detailed implementation of the scheme (see *The Income Tax (Building Societies) (Dividends and Interest) Regulations 1990* (*SI 1990 No 2231*)).

With effect for payments made or credited on or after 6 April 2005, *ICTA 1988, s 477A* applies to alternative finance return and profit share return as it applies to interest in respect of a deposit or loan.

This applies to ALTERNATIVE FINANCE ARRANGEMENTS (4) entered into on or after 6 April 2005 subject to commencement rules for arrangements entered into before that date where a profit share return is payable on or after that date. [*FA 2005, s 56, Sch 2 para 5; ITA 2007 Sch 1 para 602 SI 2005 No 3474*].

9.2 **DEFINITION**

For these purposes, a building society is one within the meaning of the Building Societies Act 1986. [*ICTA 1988, s 832(1); Building Societies Act 1986, s 120, Sch 18*].

9.3 **TAX LIABILITY OF A BUILDING SOCIETY ITSELF**

(*a*) A building society deducts savings rate income tax from certain payments to investors, others being made gross (see 9.4 below). Liability for interest and dividends or, (from 6 April 2005) alternative finance return or profit share return under ALTERNATIVE FINANCE ARRANGEMENTS (4), is treated as arising under a loan relationship, and so relievable under the LOAN RELATIONSHIPS (46) provisions. Interest under 'SAYE savings arrangements' within *ITTOIA 2005, s 702* and as defined by *ITTOIA 2005, s 703* (or before 2005/06 terminal bonuses under contractual savings schemes *ICTA 1988, s 326*) are treated in the same way as dividends, and dividends and interest are not treated as distributions of the society or as FRANKED INVESTMENT INCOME (29) of any UK-resident company. [*ICTA 1988, s 477A(3)–(4); FA 1991, s 52, Sch 11; FA 2002, Sch 25 para 47; FA 2005, s 56, Sch 2 para 5; ITTOIA 2005, Sch 1 para 184; ITA 2007 Sch 1 para 602*].

The collection procedure of *ICTA 1988, Sch 16* (see 37.5 INCOME TAX IN RELATION TO A COMPANY) applies in the normal way in relation to the income tax deducted by the building society from payments to investors (whether under regulations under *section 477A* or, in the case of 'marketable securities' (see 9.4 below), under *ITA 2007 s 889* (formerly *ICTA 1988, s 349(3A)*)), except that returns are required for each complete payment quarter (i.e. a quarter ending on the last day of February, May, August and November in an accounting period, and for each part of an accounting period which is not a complete payment quarter. [*SI 1990 No 2231; FA 1991, Sch 11 para 3*]. Relief under *ITA 2007 ss 946–960* (formerly *ICTA 1988, Sch 16 para 5*) (see 37.5 INCOME TAX IN RELATION TO A COMPANY) for tax borne by deduction may not be claimed more than once in respect of the same deduction. [*FA 1991, Sch 11 para 4*].

These provisions apply also to annuities and other annual payments from which income tax is deductible under (*ITA 2007 s 901* (formerly *ICTA 1988, s 349(1)*)). [*SI 1991 No 512*].

(*b*) See 9.7 below as regards costs of issue of permanent interest bearing shares.

(*c*) For the purpose of corporation tax on chargeable gains, assets disposed of by one society to another on an amalgamation or transfer of engagements are treated as disposed of for a consideration of such amount as would secure that no gain or loss accrues on the disposal. [*TCGA 1992, s 215*].

Simon's Direct Tax Service. See **D4.731** *et seq.*

9.4 **INTEREST AND DIVIDENDS PAID TO INVESTORS**

Tax position of recipient company. Interest and dividends paid or credited by building societies to companies (including all bodies corporate and unincorporated associations other than partnerships and local authority associations) in respect of shares in, deposits with or loans to the society are paid without deduction of tax by virtue of the regulations contained in *SI 1990 No 2231* (as amended). *SI 2005 No 3474* extends this to payments (on or after 5 April 2005) of alternative finance return or profit share return in relation to certain ALTERNATIVE FINANCE ARRANGEMENTS (4). Such interest etc. is chargeable under Schedule D, Case III.

IR Savings, Pensions, Share Schemes may be contacted for technical advice in relation to the tax deduction scheme on 0151–472 6156.

Marketable securities. Dividends or interest paid in respect of shares or securities (other than 'qualifying certificates of deposit' or a 'qualifying deposit right') listed, or capable of being listed, on a recognised stock exchange when the dividend, etc. became payable are not within the regulations under *section 477A* referred to above, but are subject to deduction of tax under *ITA 2007 s 901* (formerly *ICTA 1988, s 349*) unless the securities are within the 'quoted Eurobonds' exemption (see 37.3(*b*) INCOME TAX IN RELATION TO A COMPANY). 'Permanent interest bearing shares' (see 9.7 below) issued by a society are within these provisions. With effect for payments on or after 6 April 2005, references to dividends or interest paid subject to deduction of tax under *ICTA 1988, s 349* include references to alternative finance return or profit share return (see 4 ALTERNATIVE FINANCE ARRANGEMENTS). This applies to alternative finance arrangements entered into on or after 6 April 2005 subject to commencement rules for arrangements entered into before that date where a profit share return is payable on or after that date.

A '*qualifying certificate of deposit*' is a certificate of deposit for £50,000 or more, exclusive of interest, (or foreign equivalent at the time of the deposit) repayable within five years. A '*qualifying deposit right*' is a right to receive an amount in pursuance of a deposit of money under an arrangement under which no certificate of deposit has been issued, although the person entitled to the right could call for the issue of such a certificate, which otherwise meets the same conditions as a qualifying certificate of deposit.

[*ITA 2007, s 901, Sch 1 para 602; ICTA 1988, s 349(3A)(3B)(4)), s 477A(1A); FA 2000, s 111(4)(6); SI 2001 No 404; FA 2005, s 56, Sch 2 para 3*].

Information powers apply broadly as under 8.9 BANKS. [*SI 1992 No 10*].

Code of Practice. HMRC's Code of Practice (No 4) sets out their standards for the carrying out of inspections of tax deduction schemes operated by financial intermediaries.

See also 37.5 INCOME TAX IN RELATION TO A COMPANY.

For the tax position of recipient individuals etc., see Tolley's Income Tax under Building Societies.

Simon's Direct Tax Service. See **D4.727** *et seq.*

9.5 **INTEREST PAID BY BORROWERS**

Payments of 'relevant loan interest' by certain borrowers are made under deduction of tax. See 37.6 INCOME TAX IN RELATION TO A COMPANY.

9.6 TRANSFER OF BUSINESS TO COMPANY

FA 1988, s 145, Sch 12 introduced various provisions, as below, where there is a transfer of the whole of a building society's business to a successor company in accordance with the *Building Societies Act 1986* and *The Building Societies (Transfer of Business) Regulations 1988* (*SI 1988 No 1153*).

Capital allowances. For capital allowance purposes, the society's trade is not treated as ceasing and the successor company is not treated as commencing a new trade. Allowances are computed on a continuing basis. [*FA 1988, Sch 12 para 3*].

Capital gains: assets transferred. If the society and the successor company are not members of the same group of companies (within *TCGA 1992, s 170*, see 12.1 CAPITAL GAINS—GROUPS) at the time of transfer of the business, then

(*a*) they are treated for capital gains purposes as if any transfer of an asset was made at such an amount as would produce neither a gain nor a loss to the society, and

(*b*) if the transfer of the business causes a company to cease to belong to the same group as the society, the notional sale and reacquisition under *TCGA 1992, s 179* (see 12.32 CAPITAL GAINS—GROUPS) does not apply.

If the society and the successor company cease to belong to the same group at some time after the transfer of the business, *TCGA 1992, s 179* similarly does not apply to any asset acquired from the society or another group member either

(i) by the successor company on or before the transfer, or

(ii) by any other company which, at the time of the transfer, is a member of the same group.

If a company which is a member of the same group as the society at the time of the transfer ceases to be a member of that group, and becomes a member of the same group as the successor company, and subsequently leaves the latter group, *TCGA 1992, s 179* applies on the latter event to any 'relevant asset' acquired by it otherwise than from the successor company as if the acquisition had been from the successor company. This does not, however, apply where the company which acquired the asset and the company from which it was acquired cease simultaneously to be members of the successor company's group but continue to be members of the same group as one another, and one of those companies is a 75% subsidiary of the other. '*Relevant asset*' means an asset acquired by the company from the society, or from another company which belongs to the same group at the time of the transfer, when the company, the society and (if applicable) the other company were members of the same group.

For the residence requirement as regards groups of companies, see 12.1 CAPITAL GAINS—GROUPS. [*TCGA 1992, s 216*].

Intangible assets. Provisions equivalent to those relating to capital gains in *TCGA 1992, s 216* (above) apply similarly to treat the transfer of chargeable intangible assets as tax-neutral. [*FA 2002, Sch 29 para 90*].

Shares and rights to shares in successor company. If, in connection with a transfer, members of a society are given rights to acquire free shares in a successor company, or to acquire such shares in priority to other subscribers, or at a discount, any such right is treated for capital gains tax purposes as an option (within *TCGA 1992, s 144*) granted for no consideration and having no value at the time of grant. Otherwise, shares issued to members by the successor company, or disposed of to members by the society, are regarded as acquired for any new consideration given and as having at the time of acquisition a value equal to such new consideration (if any). Where shares are so issued or disposed of to trustees on terms providing for their transfer to members for no new consideration, and they constitute settled property in the trustees' hands, then (*a*) they are regarded as acquired by the trustees for no consideration,

(*b*) a member's interest in the settled property is regarded as acquired for no consideration and as having no value at the time of acquisition,

(*c*) on the member's becoming absolutely entitled to any of the settled property, or where such entitlement would arise but for the member's being an infant or otherwise under disability, the shares are treated as disposed of and re-acquired by the trustees at no gain/no loss, and

(*d*) on the member's disposing of his interest in the settled property, any gain is a chargeable gain (notwithstanding *TCGA 1992, s 76*(*1*)).

Any gain on the disposal by the society of shares in the successor company in connection with the transfer is not a chargeable gain. [*TCGA 1992, s 217*].

The conferral of any benefit as above on a member of a society in connection with a transfer, or any payment in lieu of such a benefit, or any distribution in pursuance of *Building Societies Act 1986, s 100*(*2*)(*b*), is not regarded as either the making of a distribution (see 23 DISTRIBUTIONS) or the payment of a dividend by the society (see 9.4 above). [*FA 1988, Sch 12 para 6*].

SAYE savings arrangements. The disregarding for income tax and capital gains tax purposes of certain sums payable under SAYE schemes within *ITTOIA 2005, s 702* (or before 2005/06 *ICTA 1988, s 326*) continues to apply to payments after the transfer under a scheme which was within that *section* in relation to the society immediately before the transfer, notwithstanding that it ceased to be so by reason of the transfer. [*FA 1988, Sch 12 para 7; ITTOIA 2005, Sch 1 para 404*].

Stamp duty. Transfers under *Building Societies Act 1986, s 97*(*6*)(*7*) are exempt from stamp duty. [*FA 1988, Sch 12 para 8*].

Declarations, etc. given to a society prior to incorporation. Declarations made as to the ordinary residence of depositors, and certificates of non-liability given to societies, in order that interest may be paid gross are treated as having been made or given to the successor company (see 8.9 BANKS). (HMRC Extra-Statutory Concession, A69).

Costs of conversion. In *Halifax plc v Davidson (Sp C 239), [2000] SSCD 251*, (and associated cases), costs incurred by a building society on conversion to a public limited company were disallowed as capital expenditure to the extent that they related to payment of statutory cash bonuses to non-voting members of the society, but otherwise allowed.

Simon's Direct Tax Service. See D4.771–D4.773.

9.7 PERMANENT INTEREST BEARING SHARES

Since 1991, under the *Building Societies* (*Designated Capital Resources*) (*Permanent Interest Bearing Shares*) *Order 1991* (*SI 1991 No 702*), made under *Building Societies Act 1986*, building societies have been able to issue a type of perpetual share known as a 'permanent interest bearing share' ('PIBS'). *FA 1991, s 51, Sch 10* introduced taxation provisions in relation to 'qualifying shares'. A share in a building society is a '*qualifying share*' if it is either a PIBS or a similar freely transferable security of a description specified for the purpose in Treasury regulations. Following changes to the building society legislation, including the repeal of *SI 1991 No 702*, provision was made for the definition of 'PIBS' in those regulations to be retained for tax purposes (subject to minor modifications) by the *Capital Gains Tax* (*Definition of Permanent Interest Bearing Share*) *Regulations 1999* (*SI 1999 No 1953*). It is now contained in the General Prudential Sourcebook made by the Financial Services Authority under the *Financial Services and Markets Act 2000 SI 2006 No 3291* (formerly Prudential Sourcebook (Building Societies)).

For accounting periods beginning before 1 October 2002, PIBS do not constitute loan relationships (see 46.2 LOAN RELATIONSHIPS), although interest arising on them is within the loan relationship rules (see 46.46 LOAN RELATIONSHIPS).

Capital gains exemption. Other than in relation to relief for losses on loans to traders under *TCGA 1992, s 254* (which is repealed in relation to loans made on or after 17 March 1998), building society shares which are qualifying shares expressed in sterling (and which are not convertible into, or redeemable in, a currency other than sterling) are *for purposes other than those of corporation tax* (and subject to *TCGA 1992, s 117(2)*) 'qualifying corporate bonds' within *TCGA 1992, s 117*, and hence exempt from capital gains tax. As regards corporate holders, however, they are *not* qualifying corporate bonds and hence chargeable gains (or allowable losses) arise on disposal in the normal way. [*TCGA 1992, s 117(A1)(4)–(6)(11)–(13)*].

Accrued income scheme. 'Securities' for the purposes of *ITA 2007 ss 616–677* (formerly *ICTA 1988, ss 711–728*) (accrued income scheme) includes building society shares which are qualifying shares. [*ICTA 1988, s 710(2A)*].

Incidental costs of issue. A deduction is allowed, in computing the trading income of a building society for corporation tax purposes, for the incidental costs of obtaining finance by the issue of qualifying shares, provided that the amount of any dividend or interest on the shares is an allowable deduction. However, a deduction is not allowed to the extent that such costs are brought into account as debits under the LOAN RELATIONSHIPS (46) rules in accounting periods beginning on or after 1 October 2002. The incidental costs allowed are expenditure (including abortive expenditure) on fees, commissions, advertising, printing and other incidental matters (but not stamp duty) wholly and exclusively for the purpose of obtaining the finance or of providing security for it or repaying it. Costs in consequence of, or for protection against, exchange rate losses, or of repayment of the shares so far as attributable to their issue at a discount or repayment at a premium, are excluded. [*ICTA 1988, s 477B; FA 2002, Sch 25 para 48*].

Preferential rights of acquisition. Where a building society confers on members or former members priority rights to acquire shares in the society which are qualifying shares, the rights are regarded, for capital gains tax purposes, as options acquired for no consideration and having no value when acquired. [*TCGA 1992, s 149*].

Simon's Direct Tax Service. See **D4.705.**

10 Capital Allowances

Simon's Direct Tax Service Part B2.

Cross-reference. See 14.13 CHARITIES for gifts of plant or machinery to charities; 55.8 PROFIT COMPUTATIONS for relief for capital expenditure on contaminated land remediation.

Other sources. See Tolley's Capital Allowances.

Headings in this chapter are as follows.

10.1 INTRODUCTION

The law relating to capital allowances was consolidated in *Capital Allowances Act 2001* (*CAA 2001*) as part of the Tax Law Rewrite programme. *CAA 2001* also made some (relatively minor) changes to pre-existing law and, subject to the election below, has effect for corporation tax purposes as respects capital allowances (and balancing charges) falling to be made for accounting periods ending after 31 March 2001. [*CAA 2001, s 579*]. Where a change in the law effected by *CAA 2001* alters the tax consequences for a 'relevant chargeable period' of a transaction or event occurring before the 'relevant date', the person affected may elect for that change not to have effect as regards that chargeable period. With the exception noted in 10.2(v) below (and also applied in 10.2(vi) below), a '*relevant chargeable period*' is a chargeable period (see below) ending on or straddling the relevant date. The '*relevant date*' for corporation tax purposes is 1 April 2001. Where the same transaction or event so affects more than one person, an election by one is of no effect unless all elect. For corporation tax purposes, an election must be made within two years after the end of the relevant chargeable period. [*CAA 2001, s 577(1), Sch 3 para 8*].

Capital allowances (balancing charges) are a deduction from (addition to) the profits etc. of trades and other qualifying activities in arriving at the taxable amount for the chargeable period to which they relate. The amount of depreciation charged in the accounts of a business is not so allowed. For a full list of qualifying activities in relation to which plant and machinery allowances are available, see 10.24 below. Certain allowances are given only in relation to trades, some only in relation to particular kinds of trade, and some additionally given against particular sources of non-trading income — details are given in the relevant section of the chapter (see list of headings below). For corporation tax purposes, a '*chargeable period*' is an accounting period. [*CAA 2001, s 6(1); CAA 1990, s 161(2)*].

Capital allowances are granted in respect of certain types of expenditure detailed in 10.3–10.52 below. Allowances are given only if a claim is made. For capital allowances for investment companies or, for accounting periods beginning on or after 1 April 2004, companies with an investment business, see 42.5 INVESTMENT COMPANIES AND INVESTMENT BUSINESS.

10.2 MATTERS OF GENERAL APPLICATION

(i) **Claims.** A capital allowance claim under self-assessment must be included in the company tax return (or amended return) (see 61.3, 61.6 RETURNS) for the accounting period for which the claim is made. It must specify the amount claimed, which must be expressed in figures at the time the claim is made. It must be made (and may be amended or withdrawn) at any time up to the latest of:

(*a*) the first anniversary of the filing date for the company tax return;

(*b*) 30 days after closure of any enquiry into that return (unless the enquiry, being otherwise out of time, was limited, as referred to in 61.12 RETURNS, to matters to which a previous amendment making or withdrawing a capital allowance claim relates, or which are affected by the amendment);

(*c*) 30 days after notice of any amendment of that return by HMRC following such an enquiry; and

(*d*) 30 days after determination of any appeal against an amendment within (iii),

or at a later time if HMRC allow it (for which see 47.2 LOSSES).

These time limits override the normal time limits for amendment of a company tax return. Amendments or withdrawals of claims must be made by amending the return.

If the effect of a claim is to reduce the available capital allowances for another accounting period for which a return has already been made, the company has 30 days to make the necessary amendments of that return. If it fails to do so, HMRC may, by written notice and subject to a right of appeal within 30 days of the issue of the notice, amend the return to correct the position (notwithstanding any time limit otherwise applicable).

[*FA 1998, Sch 18 Pt IX*].

For claims for **accounting periods ending before 1 July 1999**, i.e. before the introduction of self-assessment, see the 2005–06 edition of Tolley's Corporation Tax.

(ii) **Capital expenditure.** References in the capital allowances legislation to the incurring of capital expenditure and the paying of capital sums exclude any sums allowed as deductions in computing the payer's profits or earnings and sums payable under deduction of tax. Corresponding rules apply as regards the receipt of such sums. [*CAA 2001, s 4, Sch 3 para 9; CAA 1990, s 159(1)(1A); ITEPA 2003, Sch 6 para 247; ITTOIA 2005, Sch 1 para 525*].

(iii) **Time expenditure incurred.** Capital expenditure (other than that constituted by an 'additional VAT liability' — see (viii) below) is generally treated, for capital allowances purposes, as incurred as soon as there is an unconditional obligation to pay it, even if all or part of it is not required to be paid until some later date. However, expenditure is treated as incurred on a later date in the following circumstances.

- Where any part of the expenditure is not required to be paid until a date more than four months after the date determined as above, it is treated as incurred on that later date.
- Where an obligation to pay becomes unconditional earlier than in accordance with normal commercial usage, with the sole or main benefit likely to be the bringing forward of the chargeable period in which the expenditure would otherwise be treated as incurred, it is instead treated as incurred on the date on or before which it is required to be paid.

Where, as a result of an event such as the issuing of a certificate, an obligation to pay becomes unconditional within one month after the end of a chargeable period, but at or before the end of that chargeable period the asset concerned has become the property of, or is otherwise attributed under the contract to, the person having the obligation, the expenditure is treated as incurred immediately before the end of that chargeable period.

The above provisions do not override any specific rule under which expenditure is treated as incurred later than the relevant time given above.

[*CAA 2001, s 5; CAA 1990, s 159(2)–(8)*].

Simon's Direct Tax Service. See **B2.104**.

(iv) **Exclusion of double allowances.** Where an allowance is made under one of the following codes of allowances, it cannot be made under another of those codes in respect of that expenditure or the provision of any asset to which that expenditure related:

- agricultural buildings allowances (10.3 below);
- allowances for expenditure on business premises renovation (10.5 below);
- allowances for expenditure on dredging (10.6 below);
- allowances for dwelling-houses let on assured tenancies (10.8 below);
- allowances for expenditure on flat conversion (10.9 below);
- industrial buildings allowances (10.10–10.22 below);
- allowances for mineral extraction (10.39–10.49 below);
- research and development (formerly scientific research) allowances (10.52 below).

Similarly, no allowance under any of the above codes can be made in respect of any expenditure that has been allocated to a plant and machinery pool (see 10.28 below), and on which a plant or machinery allowance (or balancing charge) has consequently been given (or made), or any related asset (as above); and expenditure which has attracted an allowance under any of the above codes (and any related asset) cannot be allocated to a plant and machinery pool.

Additional rules apply under *CAA 2001, s 9* to prevent double allowances in relation to plant or machinery treated as fixtures (as at 10.33 below).

[*CAA 2001, ss 7–10, Sch 3 para 10; CAA 1990, s 147*].

Where an item of expenditure qualifies for more than one type of capital allowance, it is the taxpayer's choice as to which to claim, but he cannot alter his choice in later years. (HMRC Capital Allowances Manual CA 16000).

Simon's Direct Tax Service. See **B2.114**.

(v) **Expenditure met by another's contributions.** Subject to the exceptions below, a person is not regarded as incurring expenditure for capital allowances purposes (other than for dredging — see below) to the extent that it is met, or will be met, directly or indirectly by another person or by a '*public body*', i.e. the Crown or any government or public or local authority (whether in the UK or elsewhere). For the scope of 'public authority', see *McKinney v Hagans Caravans (Manufacturing) Ltd CA(NI) 1997, 69 TC 526*. There is an exception where the expenditure is met by a Regional Development Grant or Northern Ireland equivalent (for which see *SI 1995 No 611, SI 1997 No 660, SI 1999 No 719, SI 2001 No 810* and predecessor orders). (Note that applications for Regional Development Grants were not accepted after 31 March 1988, but Northern Ireland equivalents do continue.) Expenditure met by insurance or other compensation money due in respect of a destroyed, demolished or defunct asset is not excluded from allowances (though this exception did not apply for the purpose of research and development (formerly scientific research) allowances before *CAA 2001* had effect).

As regards allowances for dredging (see 10.6 below), the above is replaced by a rule to the effect that a person is not regarded as incurring expenditure for the purposes of a trade or future trade to the extent that it is met, or will be met, directly or indirectly by a public body or by capital sums contributed by another person for purposes other than those of the fore-mentioned trade.

The main rule above (but not the rule for dredging) is disapplied, and allowances are thus available, if the contributor is not a public body and can obtain neither a capital allowance on contributions by virtue of (vii) below nor a deduction against profits of a trade, profession or vocation. Where *CAA 2001* has effect (see 10.1 above), and for the purposes of plant and machinery allowances only, this is extended to cover profits of any qualifying activity within 10.24(iii)–(vi) below. In relation to this particular change in law, the '*relevant chargeable period*' for the purposes of the election in 10.1 above (to defer the application of *CAA 2001*) is the earliest chargeable period for which the tax consequences of the transaction or event are altered — this exception to the rule recognises that a contribution might be made before the relevant date in 10.1 above to expenditure incurred in a chargeable period beginning after that date.

[*CAA 2001, ss 532–536, Sch 2 para 19, Sch 3 paras 106–108; CAA 1990, ss 134(8), 153; ICTA 1988, s 91(9), s 532(1); ITTOIA 2005, Sch 1 para 570*].

Repaid grants. Where a grant which has been deducted from expenditure qualifying for capital allowances (as above) is later repaid (in whole or part), the repayment will, by concession, be treated as expenditure qualifying for capital allowances. Where allowances were restricted in respect of a contribution from a person (other than a public body) who himself obtained either a capital allowance under (vii) below or a trading deduction for his contribution (as above), this treatment is dependent upon the repayment falling to be taxed on the recipient through a balancing charge or as a trading receipt. (HMRC Extra-Statutory Concession B49 as revised).

Simon's Direct Tax Service. See **B2.111**.

(vi) **Contribution allowances.** Contributors towards another person's capital expenditure on an asset may receive allowances ('*contribution allowances*') where the contribution is for the purposes of a trade or 'relevant activity' carried on (or to be carried on) by the contributor, and where the expenditure would otherwise have entitled the other person (assuming him not to be a public body) to agricultural buildings, industrial buildings, plant and machinery or mineral extraction allowances. Contribution allowances are not available where the contributor and the other person are CONNECTED PERSONS (19). A '*relevant activity*' is a profession or vocation or, where *CAA 2001* has effect and for the purposes of plant and machinery allowances only, an activity within 10.24(iii)–(vi) below; the same comments apply as in (vi) above as regards this particular change in the law.

Contribution allowances are such as would have been made if the contribution had been expended on the provision for the contributor's trade etc. of a similar asset and as if the asset were at all material times used for the purposes of the contributor's trade etc. (so that balancing adjustments do not apply to such contributions). As regards plant and machinery, the contributor's deemed expenditure can only be allocated to a single asset pool (see 10.28 below). On a transfer of the trade etc., or part thereof, the allowances (or part) are subsequently made to the transferee.

In relation to agricultural buildings and industrial buildings allowances, the conditions are satisfied if the contribution is made for the purposes of a trade etc. carried on by a tenant of land in which the contributor has an interest. Entitlement to writing-down allowances passes to any person becoming entitled to the interest held by the contributor at the time of the contribution.

[*CAA 2001, ss 537–542, Sch 3 paras 109, 110; CAA 1990, ss 154, 155; FA 2001, s 67, Sch 19 Pt II paras 3, 4; FA 2005, s 92, Sch 6 para 5*].

Capital contributions towards expenditure on dredging are treated as expenditure incurred by the contributor on that dredging. [*CAA 2001, s 543; CAA 1990, s 134(8)*].

Simon's Direct Tax Service. See **B2.112**.

(vii) **VAT capital goods scheme.** Under the VAT capital goods scheme, the input tax originally claimed on the acquisition of certain capital assets is subject to amendment within a specified period of adjustment in accordance with any increase or decrease in the extent to which the asset is used in making taxable, as opposed to exempt, supplies for VAT purposes. The items covered by the scheme are limited to land and buildings (or parts of buildings) worth at least £250,000 and computers (and items of computer equipment) worth at least £50,000. See Tolley's Value Added Tax under Capital Goods Scheme for a full description.

Special capital allowances provisions apply where a VAT adjustment is made under the capital goods scheme. These affect allowances for industrial buildings, plant and machinery, business premises renovation and research and development (formerly scientific research), and the provisions specific to each are described in the appropriate sections of this chapter. General definitions and provisions are described below.

'*Additional VAT liability*' and '*additional VAT rebate*' mean, respectively:

- an amount which a person becomes liable to pay; or
- an amount which he becomes entitled to deduct,

by way of adjustment under the VAT capital goods scheme in respect of input tax. Generally (but see below), such a liability or rebate is treated as incurred or made on the last day of the period:

- which is one of the periods making up the applicable VAT period of adjustment under the VAT capital goods scheme; and
- in which occurred the increase or decrease in use giving rise to the liability or rebate.

However, for the purpose of determining the chargeable period (see 10.1 above) in which it accrues, an additional VAT liability or rebate is treated as accruing on whichever is the relevant day below.

- Where the liability or rebate is accounted for in a VAT return, the last day of the period covered by that return.
- If, before the making of a VAT return, Customs assess the liability or rebate, the day on which the assessment is made.
- If the trade (or other qualifying activity — see 10.24 below) is permanently discontinued before the liability or rebate has been accounted for in a VAT return and before the making of an assessment, the last day of the chargeable period in which the cessation occurs.

Where an allowance or charge falls to be determined by reference to a proportion only of the expenditure incurred or a proportion only of what that allowance or charge would otherwise have been, a related additional VAT liability or rebate is similarly apportioned.

[*CAA 2001, ss 546–551; CAA 1990, s 159A; FA 2005, s 92, Sch 6 para 6*].

Simon's Direct Tax Service. See **B2.103, B2.104**.

(viii) **Composite sales** may be apportioned by Appeal Commissioners regardless of any separate prices attributed in the sale agreement. [*CAA 2001, ss 562–564; CAA 1990, ss 150, 151*]. See *Fitton v Gilders & Heaton Ch D 1955, 36 TC 233*, and *Wood v Provan CA 1968, 44 TC 701*.

(ix) **Finance leasing.** There are restrictions in *FA 1997, Sch 12* (see 66.54 TRADING INCOME) on capital allowances where certain finance leasing arrangements are involved. These are disapplied from, broadly, 1 April 2006 in relation to long funding leases. See also 10.28, 10.34, 10.38(A)(C) below.

(x) **Recovery of assets under *Proceeds of Crime Act 2002, Pt 5*.** *Proceeds of Crime Act 2002, Pt 5 Ch 2* provides for the recovery, in civil proceedings before the High Court (or, in Scotland, the Court of Session), of property which is, or represents, property obtained through 'unlawful conduct' (as defined in the *Act*). If the Court is satisfied that any property is recoverable under the provisions, it will make a '*recovery order*', vesting the property in an appointed trustee for civil recovery. Alternatively, the Court may make an order under *section 276* of the *Act* staying (or, in Scotland, sisting) proceedings on terms agreed by the parties. The vesting of property in a trustee for civil recovery or any other person, either under a recovery order or in pursuance of a *section 276* order, is known as a *Pt 5* transfer. A '*compensating payment*' may in some cases be made to the person who held the property immediately before the transfer. If the order provides for the creation of any interest in favour of that person, he is treated as receiving (in addition to any other compensating payment) a compensating payment equal to the value of the interest. [*Proceeds of Crime Act 2002, ss 240(1), 266(1)(2), 276, 316(1), 448, Sch 10 para 2*].

Where the property in question is plant or machinery, the relevant interest in an industrial building or in a flat (within 10.9 below), or an asset representing qualifying expenditure on research and development (within 10.52 below), there are provisions to ensure that the *Pt 5* transfer has a tax-neutral effect, unless a compensating payment is made to the transferor in which case its amount and/or value must be brought into account as a disposal value or, as the case may be, as proceeds from a balancing event. [*Proceeds of Crime Act 2002, Sch 10 paras 12–29*].

(xi) **Avoidance affecting proceeds of balancing event.** An anti-avoidance rule has been introduced to prevent a balancing allowance being created or increased by means of any tax avoidance scheme that depresses an asset's market value and thus the amount to be brought into account on a balancing event (e.g. a sale) or as a disposal value. The rule denies entitlement to a balancing allowance, though the unrelieved balance of expenditure immediately after the event must be computed as if the allowance had been made. The rule applies to allowances for industrial buildings, agricultural buildings, business premises renovation, flat conversion, dwelling-houses let on assured tenancies and mineral extraction (but not, for example, to plant and machinery allowances). It applies in relation to any event occurring after 26 November 2002 that would otherwise occasion a balancing allowance, except where it occurs in pursuance of a contract entered into on or before that date and is not consequent upon the exercise after that date of any option or right. [*CAA 2001, s 570A; FA 2003, s 164; FA 2005, s 92, Sch 6 para 9*].

Simon's Direct Tax Service. See **B2.244**.

10.3 AGRICULTURAL BUILDINGS AND WORKS

Agricultural buildings allowances are to be phased out. The first stage is the removal of balancing allowances and charges on balancing events (see below).

The current code of capital allowances for agricultural buildings and works (as described below) applies to expenditure incurred **on or after 1 April 1986 (1 April 1987** where it was incurred under a contract entered into before 14 March 1984). [*CAA 2001, Sch 3 para 82; CAA 1990, s 123*].

Qualifying buildings etc. Writing-down, and previously (in certain cases) initial, allowances (see below) are given in respect of capital expenditure incurred for the purposes of 'husbandry' on the construction of buildings (such as farmhouses (but see (*b*) below), farm buildings or cottages), fences or other works. [*CAA 2001, s 361(1)(2); CAA 1990, ss 123, 124(1), 124A*]. 'Capital expenditure on construction' includes preliminary demolition costs (unless already taken into account for industrial buildings allowance purposes, see 10.15 below), expenditure on reconstruction, alteration or improvement and architect's fees, and 'other works' includes e.g. drainage and sewage works, water and electricity installations, walls, shelter belts of trees, silos, farm roads, land reclamation and hedge demolition. (HMRC Capital Allowances Manual CA 40100, 40200). Cottages occupied by retired farm workers and buildings constructed to provide welfare facilities for employees may qualify for allowances, as may farm shops to the extent that they sell produce of the farm. (HMRC Capital Allowances Manual CA 40100). '*Husbandry*' includes any method of intensive rearing of livestock or fish on a commercial basis for the production of food for human consumption, and also 'short rotation coppice' (i.e. a perennial crop of tree species planted at high density, the stems of which are harvested above ground level at intervals of less than ten years). [*CAA 2001, s 362; CAA 1990, s 133(1); FA 1995, s 154(1)(3); ITTOIA 2005, Sch 1 para 481*].

Market gardening, whether of plants or flowers or for the production of food, is treated in the same way as farming for allowance purposes, and a house which is the centre of such operations is treated as a farmhouse (see (*b*) below). (This commentary is not included in the current HMRC Capital Allowances Manual but was previously at CA 4509 and is presumed still to be of application.)

Qualifying expenditure. Allowances are available where a person who has a 'freehold' or 'leasehold' interest in land in the UK occupied wholly or mainly for the purposes of husbandry incurs capital expenditure on qualifying buildings etc. (as set out above) for the purposes of husbandry on that land. The building etc. on which the expenditure is incurred does not have to be on the land in question, e.g. a farmworker's cottage in a nearby village might qualify (this commentary, although not included in the current HMRC Capital Allowances Manual having previously been at CA 4504 and being presumed still to be of application). A '*freehold*' interest in land is the fee simple estate in the land or an agreement to acquire that interest (or Scottish equivalent), and a '*leasehold*' interest is the interest of a tenant in property subject to a lease (including an agreement for a lease if the lease term has begun and any tenancy, but excluding a mortgage). The expenditure is '*qualifying expenditure*' except that:

(*a*) expenditure on the acquisition of the land or rights over the land is excluded;

(*b*) a maximum of one-third of expenditure on the construction of a farmhouse may qualify (reduced as is just and reasonable where the accommodation and amenities are disproportionate to the nature and extent of the farm). For the meaning of 'farmhouse', see *Lindsay v CIR CS 1953, 34 TC 289, CIR v Whiteford & Sons CS 1962, 40 TC 379, Korner v CIR HL 1969, 45 TC 287*, and HMRC Capital Allowances Manual CA 40100 (including the circumstances in which it may be accepted that a farm has two farmhouses); and

(*c*) only a just and reasonable proportion of expenditure on assets (other than the farmhouse) only partly used for the purposes of husbandry on the land in question may qualify.

[*CAA 2001, ss 361*(*1*)(*2*)*, 363, 369, 393, Sch 3 para 81; CAA 1990, ss 123, 124*(*1*)(*2*)*, 124A*(*4*)*, 125*(*1*)*, 133*(*1*)(*6*)].

As regards *buildings etc. bought unused*, similar provisions apply as in the case of industrial buildings (see 10.12 below), modified to take account of the restrictions and exclusions referred to above. [*CAA 2001, ss 370, 374; CAA 1990, ss 127, 127A, 133*(*7*)*; FA 1993, Sch 12 paras 5, 6*].

Where a person is entitled to different 'relevant interests' (see below) in different parts of the land, the expenditure is apportioned on a just and reasonable basis, and these provisions apply separately to the expenditure apportioned to each part. (This is now provided for by *CAA 2001, s 371*, but HMRC consider that the requirement for apportionment was implicit in the provisions applying before *CAA 2001* came into effect (see 10.1 above). See Note 49 in Annex 2 to the Explanatory Notes to the 2001 Capital Allowances Bill.)

Initial allowances. An initial allowance was available to a person incurring qualifying expenditure under a contract entered into in the twelve-month period **1 November 1992 to 31 October 1993 inclusive**, or for the purpose of securing compliance with obligations incurred under a contract entered into during that period, but not for expenditure incurred under a contract entered into for the purpose of securing compliance with obligations under a contract entered into before 1 November 1992. The qualifying building must have come to be used for the purposes of husbandry before 1 January 1995, and, if this condition was not satisfied or if the building first came to be used for purposes other than husbandry, any initial allowance given will have been withdrawn. The initial allowance was **20%** of the expenditure incurred, and was given for the chargeable period related to the incurring of the expenditure. Either a smaller initial allowance could be claimed or the initial allowance not claimed at all; for accounting periods ending before 1 October 1993, a company could disclaim the initial allowance in whole or in part by giving written notice to the inspector within two years after the end of the accounting period concerned. [*CAA 1990, s 124A*(*1*)*–*(*3*)*,* (*5*)*–*(*7*)*; FA 1993, Sch 12 para 3*].

Writing-down allowances are made to the person who for the time being has the '*relevant interest*' in relation to the qualifying expenditure, i.e. (except as follows) the interest in the land in question to which the person incurring the expenditure was entitled when the expenditure was incurred. If there is more than one such interest and one was reversionary on all the others, that one is the relevant interest. The creation of a lease to which the relevant interest is subject is disregarded for these purposes. Where an interest in land has been conveyed or assigned by way of security subject to a right of redemption, it will still be treated as belonging to the person with the right of redemption. [*CAA 2001, ss 361(3), 364-366; CAA 1990, ss 123(1), 125(1)-(4), 126(4), 133(4)*].

When a leasehold relevant interest is surrendered or reverts, the interest into which it merges becomes the relevant interest, unless a new lease takes effect on the extinguishment. Otherwise, on a leasehold relevant interest coming to an end, if a new lease is granted to the former lessee, the lessee is treated as continuing to have the same relevant interest. (Under *CAA 2001* this applies equally where the new lease is of only part of the land subject to the old lease. This makes statutory the approach previously adopted in practice, see Change 42 listed in Annex 1 to the Explanatory Notes to the 2001 Capital Allowances Bill.) If the new lease is granted to a person other than the former lessee, the relevant interest is treated as acquired by the new lessee if he makes a payment to the former lessee for the assets representing the expenditure in question. In any other case, the interest of the landlord under the former lease is treated as becoming the relevant interest. [*CAA 2001, ss 367, 368; CAA 1990, ss 125(4), 126(4)(5)*].

A person is entitled to an allowance for any chargeable period (see 10.1 above) at any time during which he is entitled to the relevant interest. Allowances are given at the rate of **4% p.a.** of the qualifying expenditure (or such lesser amount as may be claimed) during a period of 25 years beginning on the first day of the chargeable period (of the person incurring the expenditure) during which the expenditure was incurred, so as to give aggregate allowances (including any initial allowance) up to the amount of that expenditure. If the buildings etc. in fact come to be first used other than for the purposes of husbandry, no writing-down allowance can be made in respect of the related expenditure and any allowance previously given is withdrawn. A writing-down allowance could be given for the same chargeable period as an initial allowance under *CAA 1990, s 124A* (see above) in respect of the same expenditure, but only if the building etc. came to be used for the purposes of husbandry before the end of that chargeable period. [*CAA 2001, ss 372-374; CAA 1990, s 123, s 124(2), s 124B; FA 1993, Sch 12 para 3*]. If the conditions are met when the expenditure is incurred and the first use is for the purposes of husbandry, allowances continue throughout the writing-down period without regard to any change of use of the building in later years. (HMRC Capital Allowances Manual CA 41100).

Transfer of relevant interest. Where a person entitled to allowances in respect of capital expenditure as above ceases to own the relevant interest in the land (or part of the land) giving rise to that entitlement, and another person acquires that interest, the right to the writing-down allowances (or appropriate part) is transferred to the new owner of the interest (proportionate allowances being given where the transfer falls during a chargeable period (see 10.1 above) of either the former or the new owner). See below as regards allowances where the transfer is a 'balancing event'. [*CAA 2001, s 375; CAA 1990, s 126(1)–(3); FA 1993, Sch 12 para 4(1)(2)*]. If, by virtue of a transfer of the relevant interest, the total allowances which were or could have been claimed (disregarding any anti-avoidance etc. restrictions on balancing allowances) during the writing-down period would otherwise be less than the amount of the expenditure, then the difference is made up in the chargeable period in which the writing-down period ends. [*CAA 2001, s 379; CAA 1990, s 126(6)*].

Balancing events. A '*balancing event*' occurs when the relevant interest in land (or part) is acquired by another person (see above) or when the building etc. (or part) on construction of which the expenditure was incurred is demolished, destroyed, or otherwise ceases altogether to be used. A balancing event will not give rise to a balancing adjustment where the event takes place on or after 21 March 2007, except where the event occurs before 1 April 2011 under a relevant pre-commencement contract. Such a contract must be:

(i) made in writing before 21 March 2007;

(ii) unconditional or its conditions have been satisfied before that date;

(iii) final before 21 March 2007 – i.e. no terms had to be agreed on or after that date; and

(iv) not significantly varied on or after that date.

When there is a 'post-commencement balancing event', the amount on which the purchaser may claim writing down allowances is the balance of unrelieved expenditure immediately before that event (i.e. the seller's written down value). A '*post-commencement balancing event*' is a sale or other event which would have given rise to a balancing adjustment under legislation in force before 21 March 2007.

Prior to 21 March 2007, there was a balancing event giving rise to a balancing adjustment *provided that* a written election to that effect was made. (Before the enactment of *CAA 2001* (see 10.1 above), the words 'ceases to exist as such' rather than 'ceases altogether to be used' were employed. See Change 44 listed in Annex 1 to the Explanatory Notes to the 2001 Capital Allowances Bill.) The election must be made no later than two years after the end of the chargeable period in which the balancing event occurs. The election must be made jointly in the case of acquisition of the relevant interest, but otherwise by the former owner only. An election may not be made by a person outside the charge to income tax or corporation tax, nor if the sole or main benefit of an acquisition was the obtaining of an allowance or greater allowance (but ignoring *CAA 2001, ss 568, 573* (previously *CAA 1990, s 157*), see below). [*CAA 2001, ss 381, 382; CAA 1990, s 129; FA 2007, s 35(4)–(7)*].

Where a balancing event occurs in a chargeable period for which an allowance would otherwise have been available, no such allowance is made, but a balancing adjustment arises for that period on or to the person entitled to the relevant interest immediately before the balancing event. If the residue of expenditure immediately before the balancing event (i.e. after deducting any allowances previously given and adding any balancing charges previously made) exceeds any sale, compensation etc. receipts, a balancing allowance equal to that excess is made (subject to the anti-avoidance rule at 10.2(xi) above). If any sale, compensation etc. receipts exceed that residue, a balancing charge is made equal to the excess (but limited to the allowances previously given to the person on whom the charge arises). [*CAA 2001, ss 377, 380, 383-388, Sch 3 para 80; CAA 1990, s 128*].

Where a balancing event occurs on the transfer of the relevant interest, the writing-down allowances available to the new owner consist of the residue of expenditure (see above) immediately before the balancing event, plus any balancing charge or less any balancing allowance consequent on that event, spread over the period from the balancing event to the end of the original 25-year writing-down period. For this purpose, any balancing allowance which (on that or any previous balancing event) has been reduced or denied under *CAA 2001, s 389* or *CAA 1990, s 130* (see below) is treated as having been made in full. [*CAA 2001, ss 376, 378; CAA 1990, ss 129(3), 130(3)*].

Making of allowances and charges. Initial allowances, writing-down allowances and balancing adjustments for a chargeable period are given effect by treating allowances as expenses, and charges as receipts, of the trade. If no trade is carried on in that chargeable period, then allowances and charges are treated as expenses and receipts of a Schedule A business (see 56.1 PROPERTY INCOME) or, where the taxpayer is not, in fact, carrying on such a business, of a notional Schedule A business. [*CAA 2001, ss 391, 392; CAA 1990, s 132; ITTOIA 2005, Sch 1 para 558*]. See also 10.2(i)(ii)(xi) above.

There are **connected person** and **anti-avoidance provisions** in respect of certain balancing events, similar to those applicable to industrial buildings allowances (see 10.22(i) below). [*CAA 2001, ss 389, 390, 567, 568, 570(1), 573; CAA 1990, ss 130, 133(8)(9), 157, 158(5); ITTOIA 2005, Sch 1 para 557*].

Simon's Direct Tax Service. See **B2.5**.

10.4 *Examples*

(A) Giles Ltd, a farming company, prepares accounts annually to 31 December and has incurred the following expenditure

10.4 Capital Allowances

		£
12.1.01	Extension to farm store	4,000
3.6.02	Construction of cattle court	15,000
26.4.03	Erection of barn	10,000
15.10.06	Replacement barn for that acquired on 26.4.03 which was destroyed by fire in September 2006.	20,000
	The insurance proceeds totalled £5,200	

The agricultural buildings allowances are as follows.

Date of expenditure	Cost	Residue brought forward	Allowances WDA 4%	Residue carried forward
	£	£	£	£
Accounting period ending 31.12.01				
12.1.01	4,000		160	3,840
Accounting period ending 31.12.02				
12.1.01	4,000	3,840	160	3,680
3.6.02	15,000		600	14,400
	£19,000	£3,840	£760	£18,080
Accounting period ending 31.12.03				
12.1.01	4,000	3,680	160	3,520
3.6.02	15,000	14,400	600	13,800
26.4.03	10,000		400	9,600
	£29,000	£18,080	£1,160	£26,920
Accounting period ending 31.12.04				
12.1.01	4,000	3,520	160	3,360
3.6.02	15,000	13,800	600	13,200
26.4.03	10,000	9,600	400	9,200
	£29,000	£26,920	£1,160	£25,760

Date of expenditure	Cost	Residue brought forward	Allowances WDA 4%	Residue carried forward
Accounting period ending 31.12.05				
12.1.01	4,000	3,360	160	3,200
3.6.02	15,000	13,200	600	12,600
26.4.03	10,000	9,200	400	8,800
	£29,000	£25,760	£1,160	£24,600

Accounting period ending 31.12.06

(*i*) *No election for a balancing adjustment*

Date of expenditure	Cost	Residue brought forward	Allowances WDA 4%	Residue carried forward
12.1.01	4,000	3,200	160	3,040
3.6.02	15,000	12,600	600	12,000
26.4.03	10,000	8,800	400	8,400
15.10.06	20,000		800	19,200
	£49,000	£24,600	£1,960	£42,640

(*ii*) *Election for a balancing adjustment*

Date of expenditure	Cost	Residue brought forward	Allowances WDA 4%	Residue carried forward
12.1.01	4,000	3,200	160	3,040
3.6.02	15,000	12,600	600	12,000
15.10.06	20,000		800	19,200
	£39,000	£15,800	£1,560	£34,240

	£	
Proceeds	5,200	
Written-down value	8,800	
Balancing allowance		£3,600

(B) Had the disposal taken place in the accounting period ending 31.12.07, the position would have been as shown at (i) above – Giles Ltd would not have had the option to make an election.

10.5 BUSINESS PREMISES RENOVATION

For expenditure incurred on or after 11 April 2007 and subject to the conditions below, 100% capital allowances (known as business premises renovation allowances) are available for qualifying expenditure (see below) incurred by companies (and individuals), whether as landlords or tenants, on the conversion or renovation of vacant business premises in any of the disadvantaged areas of the UK designated as 'Enterprise Areas' for the purpose of bringing those premises back into business use. The premises must have been unused for at least one year before the date the work begins. The scheme is expected to run for five years from date of commencement, but is capable of being extended. [*CAA 2001, ss 360A–360Z4; FA 2005, s 92, Sch 6 para 1; SI 2007, No 949*].

Business premises renovation allowances are available to the person who incurred the qualifying expenditure and has the 'relevant interest' in the 'qualifying building'. [*CAA 2001, s 360A(2)*]. The '*relevant interest*' in relation to qualifying expenditure is determined in similar manner, with appropriate modifications, as for industrial buildings allowances (see 10.14 below), except that for the present purposes it cannot be transferred by the grant of a lease. In its simplest form, the relevant interest is the interest in the qualifying building to which the person incurring the expenditure was entitled when it was incurred. [*CAA 2001, ss 360E, 360F*]. As regards termination of leases, provisions similar to those of *CAA 2001, s 359* apply (see 10.14 below). [*CAA 2001, s 360Z3*]. '*Lease*' is defined (as are related expressions) accordingly, and in particular includes an agreement for a lease whose term has begun and a tenancy. [*CAA 2001, s 360Z4*].

Qualifying expenditure means capital expenditure incurred before the 'expiry date' on, or in connection with:

- the conversion of a 'qualifying building' into 'qualifying business premises';
- the renovation of a 'qualifying building' if it is, or will be, 'qualifying business premises'; or
- repairs to a 'qualifying building' (or to a building of which the 'qualifying building' forms part), to the extent that they are incidental to either of the above (and for this purpose repairs are treated as capital expenditure if disallowable in computing the taxable profits of a property business or of a trade, profession or vocation),

other than expenditure incurred on, or in connection with:

- the acquisition of, or of rights in or over, land;
- the extension of a qualifying building (except to the extent necessary to provide access to 'qualifying business premises');
- the development of adjoining or adjacent land; or
- the provision of plant and machinery, unless it is, or it becomes, a fixture as in 10.33 below.

The '*expiry date*' is the fifth anniversary of the day appointed for these provisions to come into force, but may be a later date if the Treasury so decide and prescribe by regulations.

[*CAA 2001, s 360B(1)–(4)*].

A '*qualifying building*' is any building or structure (or part of a building or structure) which:

(*a*) is situated in an area which, on the date the conversion or renovation work begins, is a 'disadvantaged area';

(*b*) was unused for at least one year before the date the work begins;

(*c*) was last in use for the purposes of a trade, profession or vocation or as an office or offices;

(*d*) was not last in use as a dwelling or part of a dwelling; and

(*e*) (in the case of part of a building or structure) had not last been occupied and used in common with another part of the building or structure which was last in use as a dwelling or which does not meet itself the one-year rule in (*b*) above.

A '*disadvantaged area*' is an area specified as a development area by the *Assisted Areas Order 2007* or Northern Ireland. Any such regulations may designate an area for a limited time only. The areas targeted by the legislation are the 1,997 (at time of writing) most deprived areas of the UK, originally announced in the 2002 Pre-Budget Report and often known as 'Enterprise Areas' (Treasury Explanatory Notes to the 2005 Finance (No 2) Bill). If a building or structure is situated partly in a designated area and partly outside it, expenditure is to be apportioned on a just and reasonable basis in determining how much of it is qualifying expenditure.

[*CAA 2001, s 360C(1)–(6); SI 2007 No 945*].

For any premises (i.e. a building or structure or part thereof) to be '*qualifying business premises*':

- they must be a qualifying building as above;
- they must be used, or available and suitable for letting for use, for '*qualifying purposes*', i.e. the purposes of a trade, profession or vocation or as an office or offices; and
- they must not be used, or available for use, as a dwelling or part of a dwelling.

Once premises are qualifying business premises, they do not cease be so by reason only of *temporary* unsuitability for use, or for letting, for qualifying purposes.

[*CAA 2001, s 360D(1)–(3)*].

However, if the person entitled to claim is carrying on a relevant trade or the premises are wholly or partly used for such a trade, the buildings do not qualify for business premises renovation allowances. A relevant trade for this purpose is a trade in any of the following sectors: fisheries and aquaculture, shipbuilding, coal, steel, synthetic fibres, the primary production of certain agricultural products, and the manufacture or marketing of products which imitate or substitute for milk and milk products. [*SI 2007 No 945*].

The above definitions of qualifying expenditure, qualifying building and qualifying business premises may be amended by Treasury regulations. [*CAA 2001, s 360B(5), s 360C(7), s 360D(4)*].

Initial allowances. The initial allowance is **100%** of the qualifying expenditure, may be claimed in whole or in part, and is made for the chargeable period (see 10.1 above) in which the expenditure is incurred. The initial allowance is not available if the qualifying building is not qualifying business premises at the 'relevant time'; any initial allowance already made is withdrawn in such circumstances, and is also withdrawn if the person to whom the allowance was made has sold the relevant interest before the 'relevant time'. The '*relevant time*' is the time the premises are first used by the person with the relevant interest or, if not so used, are first suitable for letting for qualifying purposes. [*CAA 2001, ss 360G, 360H*].

Writing-down allowances (WDAs) are available where the expenditure has not been wholly relieved by an initial allowance. The annual WDA is **25%** of the qualifying expenditure, on a straight line basis, proportionately reduced or increased if the chargeable period is less or more than a year, and may be claimed in whole or in part. The WDA cannot exceed the residue, i.e. the unrelieved balance, of the qualifying expenditure. The person who incurred the expenditure is entitled to a WDA for a chargeable period if *at the end of that period*:

- the person is entitled to the relevant interest (see above) in the qualifying building;
- the person has not granted, out of the relevant interest, a long lease (exceeding 50 years) of the qualifying building for a capital sum; and
- the qualifying building is qualifying business premises.

There is nothing to prevent a WDA being given in the same chargeable period as an initial allowance for the same expenditure.

[*CAA 2001, ss 360I–360K, 360Q, 360R*].

Effect of grants on entitlement to allowances. No initial allowance or WDA is available to the extent that the qualifying expenditure is taken into account for the purposes of a relevant grant or a relevant payment made towards that expenditure; any allowance already made is withdrawn to the appropriate extent. To the extent (if any) that a relevant grant or payment is repaid by the grantee, it is treated as having never been made. Any assessments, or adjustments of assessments, necessary to give effect to these rules are not out of time if made within three years after the chargeable period in which the grant or payment was made or, as the case may be, repaid. A grant or payment is '*relevant*' if it is a State aid notified to, and approved by, the European Commission or any other grant or subsidy nominated by Treasury order for these purposes. [*CAA 2001, s 360L*].

Balancing allowances and charges. If a 'balancing event' occurs, a balancing adjustment, i.e. a balancing allowance or balancing charge, is made to or on the person who incurred the qualifying expenditure and for the chargeable period in which the event occurs. If more than one balancing event occurs, a balancing adjustment is made only on the first of them. **No balancing adjustment** is made in respect of a balancing event occurring **more than seven years** after the time the premises were first used, or suitable for letting, for qualifying purposes. Any of the following is a '*balancing event*':

(i) the sale of the relevant interest (see above) in the qualifying building;

(ii) the grant, out of the relevant interest, of a long lease (exceeding 50 years) of the qualifying building for a capital sum;

(iii) (where the relevant interest is a lease) the coming to an end of the lease otherwise than on the person entitled to it acquiring the reversionary interest;

(iv) the death of the person who incurred the qualifying expenditure;

(v) the demolition or destruction of the qualifying building;

(vi) the qualifying building's otherwise ceasing to be qualifying business premises.

The proceeds of a balancing event depend upon the nature of the event and are as follows.

(1) On a sale of the relevant interest, the net sale proceeds receivable by the person who incurred the qualifying expenditure.

(2) On the grant of a long lease, the capital sum involved or, if greater, the premium that would have been paid in an arm's length transaction.

(3) In an event within (iii) above, where the persons entitled to, respectively, the lease and the superior interest are CONNECTED PERSONS (19), the market value of the relevant interest in the qualifying building at the time of the event.

(4) On death, the residue (see below) of qualifying expenditure.

(5) On demolition or destruction, the net amount received for the remains by the person who incurred the qualifying expenditure, plus any insurance or capital compensation received by him.

(6) On the qualifying building's otherwise ceasing to be qualifying business premises, the market value of the relevant interest in the qualifying building at the time of the event.

If the residue, i.e. the unrelieved balance, of qualifying expenditure immediately before the event exceeds the proceeds of the event (including nil proceeds), a balancing allowance arises, equal to the excess. (This is subject to the anti-avoidance rule at 10.2(xi) above.) If the proceeds exceed the residue (including a nil residue), a balancing charge arises, normally equal to the excess but limited to the total initial allowances and WDAs previously given to the person concerned in respect of the expenditure.

[*CAA 2001, ss 360M–360P*].

Note that, by virtue of *CAA 2001, s 572*, a surrender for valuable consideration of a leasehold interest is treated as a sale (for equivalent proceeds), and thus falls within (1) above (if not caught by (3) above).

Any proceeds of sale of the relevant interest or other proceeds of a balancing event are, if attributable to both, apportioned on a just and reasonable basis between assets representing qualifying expenditure and other assets, and only the first part taken into account as above. [*CAA 2001, s 360Z2*].

Demolition costs. Where a qualifying building is demolished, the net cost (after crediting any money received for remains) of demolition borne by the person who incurred the expenditure is added to the residue of qualifying expenditure immediately before the demolition, and is thus taken into account in computing the balancing adjustment; no amount included in gross demolition costs can then be included for any capital allowances purposes as expenditure on replacement property. [*CAA 2001, s 360S*].

Making of allowances and charges. If the person entitled to allowances or liable to charges under these provisions carries on a trade or occupies the qualifying building for the purposes of a trade, profession or vocation, the allowances/charges are treated as expenses/receipts of the trade, profession or vocation.

If the company's interest in the qualifying building is an asset of a Schedule A business (see 56.1 PROPERTY INCOME) carried on by it at any time in the accounting period (see 10.1 above) in question, allowances/charges under these provisions are treated as expenses/receipts of that business. If the above is not the case but the company's interest in the building is nevertheless subject to a lease or a licence, it is deemed to be carrying on a Schedule A business anyway, and allowances/charges given effect accordingly. [*CAA 2001, ss 360Z, 360Z1*].

Additional VAT liabilities and rebates. See 10.2(vii) above as regards these generally. The initial allowance above is also available in respect of any additional VAT liability incurred at a time when the qualifying building is, or is about to be, qualifying business premises; the allowance is made for the chargeable period in which the liability accrues. For the purposes of WDAs, the residue of qualifying expenditure is treated as increased by the amount of an additional VAT liability at the time it accrues. The making of an additional VAT rebate is a balancing event, but it does not give rise to a balancing allowance and gives rise to a balancing charge only if it exceeds the residue (including a nil residue) of qualifying expenditure at the time the rebate accrues; otherwise the residue is treated as reduced by the amount of the rebate at the time it accrues. [*CAA 2001, ss 360T–360Y*].

Connected persons and other anti-avoidance provisions. The provisions at 10.22(i) below for industrial buildings allowances apply equally to business premises renovation allowances, *except* that the election to treat a sale etc. as being at tax written-down value is *not* available in the instant case. [*CAA 2001, ss 567-570, 573, 575(1), 577(4); FA 2005, s 92, Sch 6 paras 7, 8, 10*].

10.6 DREDGING

Writing-down, balancing and, previously, initial allowances may be claimed for capital expenditure on **dredging** incurred for the purposes of a *qualifying trade* (provided that neither industrial buildings allowances (see 10.10 below) nor plant and machinery allowances (see 10.24 below) are available in respect of the same expenditure).

'*Dredging*' must be done in the interests of navigation, and either

(i) the qualifying trade must consist of the maintenance or improvement of navigation of a harbour, estuary or waterway, or

(ii) the dredging must be for the benefit of vessels coming to, leaving or using docks or other premises used in the qualifying trade.

It includes removal, by any means, of any part of, or projections from, any sea or inland water bed (whether then above water or not), and the widening of any inland waterway.

A '*qualifying trade*' is one either within (i) above or within the industrial buildings allowance definitions at 10.11(*a*)-(*c*) below. Expenditure only partly for a qualifying trade is apportioned as may be just and reasonable, and for this purpose, where part only of a trade qualifies, the qualifying and non-qualifying parts are treated as separate trades.

[*CAA 2001, ss 484, 485; CAA 1990, s 134(1)(6), s 135(1)(3)*].

Initial allowances were given for the accounting period in which the expenditure was incurred at the following rates.

From 6 April 1956 — 10%
From 15 April 1958 — 15% (5% where certain investment allowances were payable between 8 April 1959 and 16 January 1966).

[*CAA 1968, s 67(1)(a)(8), Sch 1*].

Initial allowances were **abolished** for expenditure incurred **after 31 March 1986,** unless incurred before 1 April 1987 under a contract entered into before 14 March 1984 by the person incurring the expenditure. [*FA 1985, s 61*].

Writing-down allowances are given to the person for the time being carrying on the trade during a writing-down period of 25 years (50 years for expenditure incurred before 6 November 1962) beginning with the first day of the chargeable period in which the expenditure was incurred, subject to an overall restriction on allowances (initial and writing-down) of the amount of the expenditure. No allowance is given for a chargeable period in which a balancing allowance arises (see below). The rates of allowance, fixed by the date expenditure was incurred, are as follows (although a lesser amount may be claimed).

Before 6 November 1962 — 2% p.a.
From 6 November 1962 — 4% p.a.

[*CAA 2001, ss 487, 489, Sch 3 para 103; CAA 1990, s 134(1), s 135(2), s 146; FA 1994, s 211(2), s 213(9), Sch 26 Pt V(24)*].

Expenditure incurred for a trade before it is carried on attracts allowances as if it were incurred on the first day on which the trade was carried on. Similarly, expenditure incurred in connection with a dock etc. with a view to occupying it for the purposes of a qualifying trade other than one within (i) above attracts allowances as if it were incurred when the dock etc. is first so occupied. [*CAA 2001, s 486*]. Slightly different rules applied before *CAA 2001* came into effect (see 10.1 above and Change 57 listed in Annex 1 to the Explanatory Notes to the 2001 Capital Allowances Bill). [*CAA 1990, ss 134(7), 135(2)*].

A balancing allowance is given for the chargeable period of *permanent discontinuance* of the trade, equal to expenditure incurred less initial and writing-down allowances given, to the person last carrying on the trade. The allowance includes expenditure incurred before 6 April 1956, but in relation to such expenditure, all possible allowances (other than initial allowances) are deemed to have been given in respect of 1955/56 and earlier years as if the provisions introduced by *FA 1956* had always been in force.

Permanent discontinuance includes sale of the business (unless it is a sale between CONNECTED PERSONS (19), or without change of control, or one the sole or main benefit of which appears to be a capital allowance advantage), but not deemed discontinuance under *ICTA 1988, s 337(1)*.

[*CAA 2001, s 488, Sch 3 para 104; CAA 1990, s 134(2)-(4); ITTOIA 2005, Sch 1 para 568*].

Contributions to expenditure. See 10.2(v)(vi) above.

Simon's Direct Tax Service. See **B2.8**.

10.7 *Example*

D Ltd operates an estuary maintenance business preparing accounts to 30 June. Expenditure qualifying for dredging allowances is incurred as follows.

	£
Year ended 30.6.06	4,000
Year ended 30.6.07	5,000

On 2 January 2008, D Ltd sells the business to an unconnected third party.

The allowances available are

Date of expenditure	Cost	Residue brought forward	Allowances WDA 4%	Residue carried forward
	£	£	£	£
Accounting period ended 30.6.06				
2006	4,000	—	160	£3,840
Accounting period ended 30.6.07				
2006	4,000	3,840	160	3,680
2007	5,000	—	200	4,800
			£360	£8,480
Six months ending 2.1.08				
Balancing allowance			£8,480	

10.8 **DWELLING-HOUSES LET ON ASSURED TENANCIES**

Legislation was introduced by *FA 1982* to give capital allowances on capital expenditure incurred by an '*approved body*' (i.e. a body specified by the Secretary of State under *Housing Act 1980, s 56(4)*), on the construction of buildings consisting of, or including, dwelling-houses let on assured and certain other tenancies, after 9 March 1982 and before 1 April 1992. [*CAA 2001, ss 490(1), 491, 492; CAA 1990, ss 84, 96(3)*]. The provisions were substantially modified following repeal of the relevant sections of the *Housing Act 1980* by the *Housing Act 1988*.

A dwelling-house is a '*qualifying dwelling-house*' when it is let on a tenancy being an assured tenancy within *Housing Act 1980, s 56* (or, not being an assured shorthold tenancy, within *Housing Act 1988*) and continues to qualify at any time when:

(i) it is subject to a regulated tenancy or a housing association tenancy (as defined in the *Rent Act 1977*); and

(ii) the landlord under the tenancy either is or has been an approved body.

[*CAA 2001, s 490(2)-(5); CAA 1990, s 86(1)(2)(4), s 97(1)*].

A dwelling-house does not qualify:

(*a*) unless the landlord is a company (applicable to expenditure contracted and incurred after 4 May 1983, or where a person other than a company becomes entitled to the 'relevant interest' after that date) and either is entitled to the relevant interest in the dwelling-house or is the person who incurred the capital expenditure on the construction of the building containing it; or

(*b*) if the landlord is a housing association approved under *ICTA 1988, s 488* (co-operative housing association) or is a self-build society under the *Housing Associations Act 1985*; or

(*c*) if the landlord and tenant, or a company of which the tenant is a director, are CONNECTED PERSONS (19); or

(*d*) if the landlord is a close company and the tenant is a participator, or associate of a participator, in that company; or

(*e*) if the tenancy is part of a reciprocal arrangement between the landlords or owners of different dwelling-houses designed to counter the restrictions in (*c*) or (*d*) above.

[*CAA 2001, ss 504, 505; CAA 1990, s 86*].

Capital expenditure attributable to a dwelling-house is limited to £60,000 if it is in Greater London and £40,000 elsewhere, and is:

(A) where the building consists of a single qualifying dwelling-house, the whole of the expenditure on its construction;

(B) where the dwelling-house forms part of a building, (i) the proportion of capital expenditure attributable to that dwelling-house, and (ii) such proportion of the capital expenditure on any common parts of the building as is just and reasonable, but not exceeding one-tenth of the amount in (i).

[*CAA 2001, s 511; CAA 1990, s 96(1)(2)*].

The acquisition of, or of rights in or over, any land is not included in expenditure incurred on the cost of construction of a building for these purposes. Any capital expenditure incurred on repairs is treated as if incurred on the construction for the first time of that part of the building. [*CAA 2001, s 493; CAA 1990, ss 93(1), 97(2)*].

Buildings bought unused. The provisions in *CAA 2001, ss 502, 503* or *CAA 1990, s 91* are similar to those for industrial buildings in *CAA 2001, ss 295, 296* or *CAA 1990, s 10*, for which see 10.12, 10.13 below.

Expenditure met by another's contributions. See 10.2(v) above.

Initial allowances were, and **writing-down allowances** are, given in a similar manner, at similar rates and under similar conditions as for industrial buildings, for which see 10.13, 10.14 below. [*CAA 2001, ss 507-510, 519; CAA 1990, ss 85, 87(7)(8); FA 1994, s 213(7), Sch 26 Pt V(24)*].

References to 'temporary disuse' [*CAA 2001, s 506(2); CAA 1990, s 89(2)*], 'residue of expenditure' [*CAA 2001, ss 512, 523-528; CAA 1990, s 90*], and 'relevant interest' [*CAA 2001, ss 495-498, 500; CAA 1990, s 95*] should be taken as they apply for industrial buildings allowances, but it should be noted that the creation of a subsidiary interest (e.g. leasehold out of freehold) does not transfer the relevant interest.

Balancing allowances and charges are made in a similar manner and under similar conditions as for industrial buildings in *CAA 2001, s 314 et seq.* or *CAA 1990, s 4* (see 10.15 below). [*CAA 2001, s 513 et seq.; CAA 1990, ss 87, 88; FA 1994, Sch 26 Pt V(24)*].

Where *cessation of qualifying use occurs* otherwise than by sale or transfer of the relevant interest, that interest is treated as having been sold at the time of cessation at the open market price. [*CAA 2001, s 506(1); CAA 1990, s 89(1)*].

Making of allowances and charges. Allowances and charges are made in a similar way as they apply to lessors and licensors of industrial buildings, for which see 10.17 below. [*CAA 2001, s 529; CAA 1990, ss 92, 140–145; FA 1998, s 38, Sch 5 para 58; ITTOIA 2005, Sch 1 para 569*].

Holding over by lessee etc. Where the relevant interest in relation to the capital expenditure incurred on the construction of a building is an interest under a lease, the following provisions apply. The lease will be treated as continuing where (i) with the consent of the lessor, a lessee remains in possession of any building after his lease ends and without a new lease being granted, (ii) where a lease ends and a new lease is granted to the same lessee under an option available in the first lease, and (iii) where a lease ends and another lease is granted to a different lessee who pays a sum to the first lessee (i.e. the transaction is treated as an assignment). However, where a lease ends and the lessor pays any sum to the lessee in respect of the building, the transaction is treated as if the lease had come to an end by reason of its surrender in consideration of the payment. [*CAA 2001, s 499; CAA 1990, s 94*].

Connected persons and other anti-avoidance provisions. The provisions of *CAA 2001, ss 567-570* (and forerunners) apply to certain sales as they apply to sales of industrial buildings (see 10.22 below) but an election is only available if both the seller and the buyer are, at the time of the sale (or were at any earlier time), approved bodies. Any transfer of relevant interest which is not a sale will be treated as a sale other than at market price under these provisions but there is no balancing allowance or charge if the dwelling-house is treated as having been sold for a sum equal to the residue of expenditure before the sale. [*CAA 2001, ss 569(5), 570(4), 573; CAA 1990, ss 87(5), 88(4), 158(3)*]. See also the anti-avoidance rule at 10.2(xi) above.

Simon's Direct Tax Service. See **B2.9**.

10.9 FLAT CONVERSION

For expenditure incurred **on or after 11 May 2001**, subject to the conditions below, 100% capital allowances (known as flat conversion allowances) are available for qualifying expenditure (see below) on converting former residential space above shops and other commercial premises in the UK into flats for letting or on renovating such flats. [*CAA 2001, ss 393A–393W; FA 2001, s 67, Sch 19 Pt I*]. The allowances are available only in computing the profits of a Schedule A business (see 56.1 PROPERTY INCOME).

Flat conversion allowances are available to a company (or a person) which incurred the qualifying expenditure and has the 'relevant interest' in the flat. [*CAA 2001, s 393A(2)*]. The '*relevant interest*' in relation to qualifying expenditure is determined in similar manner, with appropriate modifications, as for industrial buildings allowances (see 10.14 below), except that for the present purposes it cannot be transferred by the grant of a lease. In its simplest form, the relevant interest is the interest in the flat to which the person incurring the expenditure was entitled when it was incurred. [*CAA 2001, ss 393F, 393G*]. As regards termination of leases, provisions similar to those of *CAA 2001, s 359* apply (see 10.14 below). [*CAA 2001, s 393V*]. '*Lease*' is defined (as are related expressions) accordingly, and in particular includes an agreement for a lease whose term has begun and a tenancy. [*CAA 2001, s 393W*].

For these purposes, a '*flat*' is a separate set of premises (covering one or more floors) forming part of a building and divided horizontally from another part. [*CAA 2001, s 393A(3)*]. See below for 'qualifying flat'.

Qualifying expenditure means capital expenditure incurred on, or in connection with:

- the conversion of part of a 'qualifying building' into a 'qualifying flat';
- the renovation of a flat in a 'qualifying building' if the flat is, or will be, a 'qualifying flat'; or

- repairs to a 'qualifying building', to the extent that they are incidental to either of the above (and for this purpose repairs are treated as capital expenditure if disallowable in computing the profits of a UK property business),

other than expenditure incurred on, or in connection with:

- the acquisition of, or of rights in or over, land;
- the extension of a qualifying building (except to the extent necessary to provide access to a 'qualifying flat');
- the development of adjoining or adjacent land; or
- furnishings or chattels.

The part of the building being converted, or the flat being renovated, must have been unused, or used only for storage, throughout the 12 months immediately preceding the commencement of the work.

[*CAA 2001, s 393B(1)–(4); ITTOIA 2005, Sch 1 para 559*].

For a building to be a '*qualifying building*':

- all or most of its ground floor must be 'authorised for business use';
- its construction must have been completed before 1 January 1980 (disregarding any extension completed on or after that date but before 1 January 2001);
- it must have no more than four storeys above ground floor (disregarding an attic storey, unless used, or previously used, as a dwelling or part of a dwelling); and
- at time of construction, all such storeys must have been primarily for residential use.

[*CAA 2001, s 393C(1)(3)(4)*].

'*Authorised for business use*' is defined by reference to specified uses designated in the relevant ratings rules for England and Wales, Scotland and NI. [*CAA 2001, s 393C(2)*]. Included are retail shops, food and drink outlets, premises offering financial and professional services, other offices, medical and dental practices, and premises used for research and development and industrial processes which can be carried out in residential areas (Revenue Budget Notes REV BN 15, 7 March 2001).

For a flat to be a '*qualifying flat*':

(*a*) it must be in a qualifying building;

(*b*) it must be suitable for letting as a dwelling (disregarding any temporary unsuitability where previously suitable);

(*c*) it must be held for short-term letting, i.e. on leases of five years or less;

(*d*) it must be accessible by some means other than via the ground floor business area;

(*e*) it must have no more than four rooms (disregarding kitchens and bathrooms of whatever area, and closets, cloakrooms and hallways of no more than five square metres in each case);

(*f*) it must not be a 'high value flat';

(*g*) it must not be (or have been) created or renovated as part of a scheme involving the creation etc. of one or more 'high value flats'; and

(*h*) it must not be let to a person connected (within *ICTA 1988, s 839* — see 19 CONNECTED PERSONS) with the person who incurred the conversion or renovation expenditure.

[*CAA 2001, s 393D(1)–(4)*].

A flat is a '*high value flat*' if the 'notional rent' exceeds the relevant limit below.

No. of rooms (as in (e) above)	*Greater London*	*Outside Greater London*
1 or 2	£350 per week	£150 per week
3	£425 per week	£225 per week
4	£480 per week	£300 per week

The '*notional rent*' is the rent that could reasonably have been expected, at the time expenditure on the conversion etc. work is first incurred, if the work had been completed and the flat was then let furnished, on a shorthold tenancy (not applicable in NI), other than to a CONNECTED PERSON (19), and otherwise than for any additional payment, such as a premium.

[*CAA 2001, s 393E(1)–(5)(7)*].

The above definitions of qualifying expenditure, qualifying building and qualifying flat and the above notional rent limits may be amended by Treasury regulations. [*CAA 2001, s 393B(5), s 393C(5), s 393D(5), s 393E(6)*].

Initial allowances. The initial allowance is **100%** of the qualifying expenditure, may be claimed in whole or in part, and is made for the chargeable period (see 10.1 above) in which the expenditure is incurred. The initial allowance is not available if the flat is not a qualifying flat at the time it is first suitable for letting as a dwelling or if the person who incurred the expenditure sells the relevant interest (see above) before that time; any initial allowance already made is withdrawn in such circumstances. [*CAA 2001, ss 393H, 393I*].

Writing-down allowances (WDAs) are available where the expenditure has not been wholly relieved by an initial allowance. The annual WDA is **25%** of the qualifying expenditure, on a straight line basis, proportionately reduced or increased if the chargeable period is less or more than a year, and may be claimed in whole or in part. The WDA cannot exceed the residue, i.e. the unrelieved balance, of the qualifying expenditure. The person who incurred the expenditure is entitled to a WDA for a chargeable period if *at the end of that period*:

- he is entitled to the relevant interest (see above) in the flat;
- he has not granted, out of the relevant interest, a long lease (exceeding 50 years) of the flat for a capital sum; and
- the flat is a qualifying flat.

There is nothing to prevent a WDA being given in the same chargeable period as an initial allowance for the same expenditure.

[*CAA 2001, ss 393J–393L, 393Q, 393R*].

Balancing allowances and charges. If a 'balancing event' occurs, a balancing adjustment, i.e. a balancing allowance or balancing charge, is made to or on the person who incurred the qualifying expenditure and for the chargeable period in which the event occurs. If more than one balancing event occurs, a balancing adjustment is made only on the first of them. **No balancing adjustment** is made in respect of a balancing event occurring **more than seven years** after the time the flat was first suitable for letting as a dwelling. Any of the following is a '*balancing event*':

(i) the sale of the relevant interest (see above) in the flat;

(ii) the grant, out of the relevant interest, of a long lease (exceeding 50 years) of the flat for a capital sum;

(iii) (where the relevant interest is a lease) the coming to an end of the lease otherwise than on the person entitled to it acquiring the reversionary interest;

(iv) the death of the person who incurred the qualifying expenditure;

(v) the demolition or destruction of the flat;

(vi) the flat's otherwise ceasing to be a qualifying flat.

The proceeds of a balancing event depend upon the nature of the event and are as follows.

(1) On a sale of the relevant interest, the net sale proceeds receivable by the person who incurred the qualifying expenditure.

(2) On the grant of a long lease, the capital sum involved or, if greater, the premium that would have been paid in an arm's length transaction.

(3) In an event within (iii) above, where the persons entitled to, respectively, the lease and the superior interest are CONNECTED PERSONS (19), the market value of the relevant interest in the flat at the time of the event.

(4) On death, the residue (see below) of qualifying expenditure.

(5) On demolition or destruction, the net amount received for the remains by the person who incurred the qualifying expenditure, plus any insurance or capital compensation received by him.

(6) On the flat's otherwise ceasing to be a qualifying flat, the market value of the relevant interest in the flat at the time of the event.

If the residue, i.e. the unrelieved balance, of qualifying expenditure immediately before the event exceeds the proceeds of the event (including nil proceeds), a balancing allowance arises, equal to the excess. (This is subject to the anti-avoidance rule at 10.2(xi) above.) If the proceeds exceed the residue (including a nil residue), a balancing charge arises, normally equal to the excess but limited to the total initial and writing-down allowances previously given to the person concerned in respect of the expenditure.

[*CAA 2001, ss 393M–393P*].

Note that, by virtue of *CAA 2001, s 572*, a surrender for valuable consideration of a leasehold interest is treated as a sale (for equivalent proceeds), and thus falls within (1) above (if not caught by (3) above).

Any proceeds of sale of the relevant interest or other proceeds of a balancing event are, if attributable to both, apportioned on a just and reasonable basis between assets representing qualifying expenditure and other assets, and only the first part taken into account as above. [*CAA 2001, s 393U*].

Demolition costs. Where a qualifying flat is demolished, the net cost (after crediting any money received for remains) of demolition borne by the person who incurred the expenditure is added to the residue of qualifying expenditure immediately before the demolition, and is thus taken into account in computing the balancing adjustment; no amount included in gross demolition costs can then attract capital allowances of any kind. [*CAA 2001, s 393S*].

Making of allowances and charges. If the company is within the charge to corporation in respect of the allowance and it's interest in the flat is an asset of a Schedule A business (see 56.1 PROPERTY INCOME) carried on by it at any time in the chargeable period (see 10.1 above) in question, allowances/charges under these provisions are treated as expenses/receipts of that business. If the above is not the case, the company is deemed to be carrying on a Schedule A business anyway, and allowances/charges given effect accordingly. [*CAA 2001, s 393T; ITTOIA 2005, Sch 1 para 560*].

Connected persons and other anti-avoidance provisions. The provisions at 10.22(i) below for industrial buildings allowances apply equally to flat conversion allowances, *except* that the election to treat a sale etc. as being at tax written-down value is *not* available in the instant case. [*CAA 2001, ss 567-570, 573, 575(1), 577(4); FA 2001, s 67, Sch 19 Pt II paras 5–7*].

HMRC guidance. See generally HMRC leaflet IR 2007 'Capital Allowances for Flats over Shops' or the notes on the HMRC website at www.hmrc.gov.uk/specialist/flatsovershops.htm

Simon's Direct Tax Service. See **B2.10.**

10.10 INDUSTRIAL BUILDINGS

Industrial buildings allowances are to be phased out. The first stage is the removal of balancing allowances and charges on balancing events (see 10.15 below).

Allowances are given in respect of certain capital expenditure (see 10.12 below) on industrial buildings (see 10.11 below), and are available to traders and to lessors and licensors of industrial buildings for use by traders. The main elements of the scheme of allowances are dealt with as follows

10.11	Qualifying buildings	10.17	Making of allowances and charges
10.12	Qualifying expenditure	10.18	Hotels
10.13	Initial allowances	10.19	Enterprise zones
10.14	Writing-down allowances	10.20	— examples
10.15	Balancing allowances and charges	10.21	Small workshops
10.16	— examples	10.22	General matters

Simon's Direct Tax Service. See **B2.2.**

10.11 **Qualifying buildings.** An 'industrial building' is a building or structure, or part of a building or structure, in use either

(*a*) for the purposes of a trade, or part of a trade (see (A) below), consisting of:

(i) the manufacture or processing of goods or materials; or

(ii) after 9 March 1982, the maintaining or repairing of goods or materials (but not goods etc. employed by the person carrying out the repair or maintenance in any trade or undertaking unless that trade etc. itself qualifies the building as an industrial building); or

(iii) the storage of (*a*) raw materials for manufacture, (*b*) goods to be processed, (*c*) goods manufactured or processed but not yet delivered to any purchaser, or (*d*) goods on arrival in the UK from a place outside the UK; or

(iv) the working of mines, oil wells etc. or foreign plantations; or

(v) agricultural operations on land not occupied by the trader; or

(vi) catching fish or shellfish; or

(*b*) for the purposes of:

(i) a transport, dock, inland navigation, water, sewerage, electricity, hydraulic power, bridge or tunnel undertaking; or

(ii) in relation to any chargeable or basis period ending after 5 April 1991, a toll road undertaking or, for expenditure incurred after 5 April 1995, a 'highway undertaking' (see below); or

(*c*) for the welfare of workers employed in a trade or undertaking within (*a*) or (*b*) above; or

(*d*) as a sports pavilion for the welfare of workers employed in any trade; or

(*e*) as a qualifying hotel (see 10.18 below).

As regards (*a*) above, following the decision in *Bestway (Holdings) Ltd v Luff Ch D 1998, 70 TC 512*, the Revenue changed their view in two respects.

(A) Previously they had considered that, provided it was self-contained, anything done in the course of a trade was part of a trade for this purpose. Their revised view is that, whilst the activities in question do not need to be self-contained, they must be a significant, separate and identifiable part of the trade carried on. (HMRC Capital Allowances Manual CA 32300).

(B) They previously considered the main test under (*a*)(iii) above to be whether the further conditions as to use of the goods or materials stored were satisfied. They have now adopted the Court's preliminary test that the determining factor in deciding whether a building is used for storage is the purpose for which the goods or materials are kept or held — it is used for storage only if the purpose of keeping them there is their storage as an end in itself and not some other purpose. (HMRC Capital Allowances Manual CA 32224).

This change of view is most likely to be significant in wholesale trades where it has previously been accepted that there was a qualifying part trade of storage of goods or materials to be used in the manufacture of other goods or materials or subjected to a process. For allowances to continue to be available, the storage must be conducted as a purpose and end in itself, not just as a necessary and transitory incident of the conduct of the wholesale business. Where claims have previously been accepted under the earlier view, the revised view should be applied to claims for chargeable periods ending after 31 December 1999. (See HMRC Capital Allowances Manual CA 32224).

As regards (*b*) above, *CAA 2001* omits the previous reference to 'a trade carried on in a mill, factory or other similar premises'. This is because case law indicates that all trades within the earlier provision are subsumed within (*a*)(i) above (see Note 45 in Annex 2 to the Explanatory Notes to the 2001 Capital Allowances Bill).

A building the whole of which is in use partly for qualifying and partly for non-qualifying purposes may qualify for allowances in full provided that the qualifying use is at least 10% of the total use. (HMRC Capital Allowances Manual CA 32315). See also *Saxone Lilley & Skinner (Holdings) Ltd* below.

Excluded from the definition of 'industrial building' are buildings or structures in use as, or as part of, dwelling-houses, retail shops, showrooms, offices or hotels (but see 10.18 below as regards expenditure on hotels after 11 April 1978), or for purposes ancillary thereto. See HMRC Capital Allowances Manual at CA 32312 for what is an 'office' for these purposes, and at CA 32313 for purposes 'ancillary' to those of a retail shop. In *Girobank plc v Clarke CA 1998, 70 TC 387*, a bank document and data processing centre was held not to be an office. In *Sarsfield v Dixons Group plc CA 1998, 71 TC 121*, a warehouse used by a group distribution company for receiving, storing and delivering goods purchased by the group for sale from its shops was held to be used for purposes ancillary to those of the group's retail shops.

Where only part of a building or structure, representing 25% (10% for expenditure incurred before 16 March 1983 or deemed so incurred under *CAA 1990, s 10*(*1*)(*2*), see 10.12 below) or less of the total cost, falls within these exclusions, the whole building or structure continues to qualify. Note that when alterations, extensions etc. or changes in use result in the 25% limit being exceeded, no amendment is made to allowances for chargeable (or basis) periods before that of the change, and allowances continue to be available in respect of that part of the building or structure not excluded. Similarly, where the 25% condition commences to be met, allowances are available for the whole of the building or structure only for the chargeable (or basis) period of the change and subsequent periods.

Buildings or structures constructed for occupation by, or welfare of, employees in mines, oil wells etc. or foreign plantations, and likely to have little or no value on the ending of the working of the mine etc. or of the foreign concession, also qualify.

Buildings or structures *outside the UK* can only qualify if the trade for which they are in use is assessable in accordance with the rules that apply for calculating trading profits for income tax purposes or that apply to Schedule D, Case I for corporation tax purposes. A building or structure used by more than one licensee of the same person only qualifies if each of the licensees uses the building or structure, or his part of it, for the purposes of a trade as above under licences granted after 9 March 1982.

[*CAA 2001, ss 271(1)(2), 274–278, 280, 282, 283, Sch 3 paras 57, 59, 74; CAA 1990, ss 14, 18; FA 1991, s 60(4)(10); FA 1993, s 113(6); FA 1995, ss 99(5), 101; ITTOIA 2005, Sch 1 para 552*].

A '*highway undertaking*' (see (*b*)(ii) above) means so much of any undertaking relating to the design, building, financing and operation of roads as is carried on for the purposes of, or in connection with, the exploitation of 'highway concessions'. A '*highway concession*', in relation to a road, means any right, in respect of public use of the road, to receive sums from the State, or, in the case of a toll road, the right to charge tolls. [*CAA 2001, ss 274(1), 341(4)(5); CAA 1990, s 21(5AA); FA 1995, s 99(7); FA 2001, s 69, Sch 21 para 6*].

As regards (*c*) above, this is regarded by HMRC as including canteens, day nurseries, garages, hard tennis courts, hostels and indoor sports halls. It does not, however, include buildings or structures excluded as above from being 'industrial buildings' (e.g. a grocery shop with extended hours for the convenience of workers, or holiday accommodation). Also as regards (*c*) above, the workers for whose welfare a building or structure is provided must be workers engaged directly in the productive, manufacturing or processing side of the business, rather than office staff or management, although the whole of a building or structure provided for staff generally may qualify provided use by production workers is not negligible. Similarly, use by outsiders as well as workers does not exclude the building or structure from relief. (HMRC Capital Allowances Manual CA 32320).

For cases in which industrial buildings allowances were **refused** see *Dale v Johnson Bros KB(NI) 1951, 32 TC 487* (warehouse — contrast the non-tax case *Crusabridge Investments Ltd v Casings International Ltd Ch D 1979, 54 TC 246*); *CIR v National Coal Board HL 1957, 37 TC 264* (colliery houses capable of alternative use); *Bourne v Norwich Crematorium Ch D 1967, 44 TC 164* (furnace chamber etc.); *Abbott Laboratories Ltd v Carmody Ch D 1968, 44 TC 569* (separate administrative block); *Buckingham v Securitas Properties Ltd Ch D 1979, 53 TC 292* (building used for wage packeting); *Vibroplant Ltd v Holland CA 1981, 54 TC 658* (depots of plant hire contractor, but now see (*a*)(ii) above); *Copol Clothing Co Ltd v Hindmarch CA 1983, 57 TC 575* (inland storage of goods imported in containers); *Carr v Sayer Ch D 1992, 65 TC 15* (quarantine kennels, claimed under (*a*)(iii)(*d*) above); *Girobank plc v Clarke CA 1998, 70 TC 387* (bank document and data processing centre); *Bestway (Holdings) Ltd v Luff Ch D 1998, 70 TC 512* (cash-and-carry wholesale warehouse); and *Sarsfield v Dixons Group plc CA 1998, 71 TC 121* (warehouse used by retail group distribution company for receiving, storing and delivering goods).

For cases where allowances were **granted**, see *CIR v Lambhill Ironworks Ltd CS 1950, 31 TC 393* (drawing office); *Kilmarnock Equitable Co-operative Society Ltd v CIR CS 1966, 42 TC 675* (coal packing not ancillary to retail shop); *Saxone Lilley & Skinner (Holdings) Ltd v CIR HL 1967, 44 TC 122* (warehouse for shoes both bought and manufactured); *Maco Door & Window Hardware (UK) Ltd v HMRC CA [2007] All ER(D) 183(Jun)* (building used for part of trade consisting of storage).

Temporary disuse. A building or structure which falls temporarily out of use after a period in which it qualified as an 'industrial building' is treated as continuing to so qualify during disuse. [*CAA 2001, s 285; CAA 1990, s 15*]. All disuse other than that preceding demolition or dereliction is in practice regarded as temporary.

Simon's Direct Tax Service. See **B2.203** *et seq.*

10.12 **Qualifying expenditure.** Qualifying expenditure is the cost of construction of the building or structure including the cost of preparing, cutting, tunnelling or levelling land, but excluding expenditure on the land itself or on rights therein. [*CAA 2001, ss 272(1), 294; CAA 1990, ss 1(1), 3(1), 21(1)*]. A just and reasonable apportionment is required to exclude unallowable expenditure (and see *Bostock v Totham Ch D 1997, 69 TC 356* as regards the basis of such apportionment). [*CAA 2001, s 356; CAA 1990, s 21(3)*]. Anything with four walls and a roof is a building for these purposes, provided that it is of a reasonably substantial size. Anything smaller may be a structure. A structure is something which has been artificially erected or constructed, and which is distinct from the surrounding earth, e.g. roads, paved car parks or tennis courts, tunnels, culverts, bridges, walls and fences. (HMRC Capital Allowances Manual CA 31110, 31120). The fees of professionals involved in the design and construction of a building or structure (e.g. architects, quantity surveyors and engineers) are also included. (HMRC Capital Allowances Manual CA 31400). Expenditure on repairs which is, exceptionally, disallowable as capital expenditure in computing profits is treated as the cost of constructing that part of the building or structure [*CAA 2001, s 272(2)(3); CAA 1990, s 12*], and the cost of preparing etc. land as a site for the installation of plant or machinery is, if no relief would otherwise be available under industrial buildings or plant and machinery allowances, treated as attracting allowances as if the plant or machinery were a building or structure. [*CAA 2001, s 273; CAA 1990, s 13*]. Where, for the purpose of erecting a new building or structure on the same site, costs are incurred in demolishing an existing building or structure, and the costs cannot be taken into account in calculating a balancing adjustment (see 10.15 below) on the demolished building or structure (e.g. because more than 25 (or 50) years has elapsed since it was first used), the demolition costs may be treated as expenditure on construction of the new building or structure. (HMRC Capital Allowances Manual CA 31400).

Roads on an industrial trading estate most of the buildings on which are industrial buildings will themselves be treated as industrial buildings. [*CAA 2001, s 284; CAA 1990, s 18(8)*].

See 10.25 below for certain expenditure on existing buildings or structures treated as being on plant or machinery.

The following are considered by HMRC to be excluded from being qualifying expenditure: expenditure on obtaining planning permission (although if a builder's costs are inclusive of such expenditure, no apportionment will be made); capitalised interest; public enquiry costs; land drainage and reclamation and landscaping; and legal expenses. (HMRC Capital Allowances Manual CA 31400).

Abortive expenditure. Expenditure (including professional fees) incurred on the construction of a building or structure which never becomes an industrial building (e.g. because it is never completed) cannot be qualifying expenditure. (HMRC Capital Allowances Manual CA 31410).

Buildings bought unused. If the 'relevant interest' (see 10.14 below) in a building or structure is sold before it is used, the purchaser (the last purchaser if more than one before the building or structure is used) is treated as having incurred on its construction, at the time the purchase price becomes payable, the lesser of the actual cost of construction and the net purchase price of the interest (excluding any part attributable to the land, see HMRC Capital Allowances Manual CA 31305). Where the original expenditure was incurred by a builder as part of the builder's trade of constructing such buildings or structures with a view to sale, the purchaser's deemed construction cost is the net purchase price paid by the purcaher or, if there have been previous sales unused, the lesser of the net purchase price paid by the purchaser and the net price paid to the builder on the first sale. (Note that this latter provision does not apply for agricultural buildings allowances purposes, for which the provisions are otherwise similar.) [*CAA 2001, ss 294-296, 299, 300; CAA 1990, s 10(1)–(3)*]. Except where the purchase price is specially defined by virtue of an election under *CAA 2001, s 290* or *CAA 1990, s 11* (see 10.14 below), the net purchase price of the interest includes acquisition costs, i.e. legal fees, surveyors' fees and stamp duty. (HMRC Capital Allowances Manual CA 33520).

The initial allowance under *CAA 1990, s 2A* (see 10.13 below) could be claimed by the purchaser (or last purchaser) of an unused building or structure regardless of the date of sale providing some or all the actual construction expenditure fell within those provisions, i.e. it was incurred in, broadly, the year ending 31 October 1993. It could also be claimed where the actual construction expenditure was incurred by a builder (as above) *at any time* before 1 November 1993, the sale occurred between 1 November 1992 and 31 October 1993 inclusive and the vendor had been entitled to the relevant interest since before 1 November 1992. Such construction expenditure was deemed for these purposes to fall within *section 2A*. In both circumstances, it remained a condition that the building or structure came to be used before 1 January 1995 (see 10.13 below). Where only part of the actual construction expenditure was within *section 2A*, the purchaser's deemed construction cost was computed as above and then divided into a *section 2A* element qualifying for the initial allowance and a residual element qualifying only for writing-down allowances. The *section 2A* element was the proportion of the deemed expenditure that corresponded to the proportion of actual construction expenditure that was within *section 2A*. [*CAA 2001, Sch 3 para 77; CAA 1990, s 10(3A), s 10C(1)–(10); FA 1993, s 113(3)(4)*].

Appropriation from trading stock. A building or structure appropriated by a builder from trading stock to capital account (with a corresponding market value credit to profit and loss) and let as an industrial building, is eligible for writing-down allowances based on the construction cost (rather than on the transfer value). Initial allowances were not available in these circumstances. (This commentary is not included in the current HMRC Capital Allowances Manual but was previously at CA 1212 and is presumed still to be of application.)

Arrangements having an artificial effect on pricing. Where certain 'arrangements' have been entered into relating to, or with respect to, any interest in or right over a building or structure, special rules apply for determining any amount which is to be taken to be:

(*a*) for the purposes of the provisions relating to buildings bought unused or, after use, from the original builder or, in certain cases, within two years after first use (see above and 10.19 below), the sum paid on the sale of the relevant interest, and

(*b*) for the purposes of allowances and charges generally (see above and 10.13–10.19 below), the amount of any proceeds from a subsequent balancing event where a person is deemed under any of the provisions referred to in (*a*) above to have incurred expenditure on the construction of the building or structure of an amount equal to the price paid on a sale of the relevant interest.

Where these provisions apply, the amount falling to be determined is reduced to the extent that the sale price or the amount of the sale etc. moneys is more than it would have been if the arrangements had not contained the provision in (iii) below.

The '*arrangements*' in question are those:

(i) entered into at or before the 'specified time';

(ii) having the effect at that time of enhancing the value of the relevant interest in the building or structure; and

(iii) containing any provision having an artificial effect on pricing,

and as regards (iii) above, arrangements are treated as containing such a provision to the extent that they go beyond what, at the time they were entered into, it was reasonable to regard as required by the prevailing market conditions in similar arm's length transactions. For examples of the sort of arrangements considered by HMRC to be most likely to be used, see HMRC Capital Allowances Manual CA 39620.

The '*specified time*' is the time of the fixing of the sale price:

(A) in relation to the determination of an amount within (*a*) above, for the sale in question; and

(B) in relation to the determination of an amount within (*b*) above, for the sale by reference to which the amount of the deemed expenditure fell to be determined.

These provisions do not apply if the sale price referred to became payable before 29 November 1994 (6 April 1995 where the price was fixed under a contract entered into before 29 November 1994).

[*CAA 2001, ss 357, 564(3), Sch 3 para 78; CAA 1990, s 10D; FA 1995, s 100*].

Simon's Direct Tax Service. See **B2.222** *et seq.*

10.13 **Initial allowances.** In general, initial allowances were **abolished** for expenditure incurred after 31 March 1986, or after 31 March 1987 in the case of expenditure incurred after 13 March 1984 under a contract entered into before 14 March 1984 by the person incurring the expenditure. [*FA 1984, Sch 12 para 1*]. However, they continue at a rate of 100% for certain expenditure in enterprise zones (see 10.19 below), and were temporarily reinstated at a rate of 20% for general expenditure incurred in, broadly, the year ended 31 October 1993 (see below). They also continue to be available at the appropriate rate in respect of any additional VAT liability (see 10.2(vii) above) in respect of such expenditure. [*CAA 2001, ss 305, 306, 346, Sch 3 paras 75-77; CAA 1990, ss 1(1), 2A; FA 1991, Sch 14 para 2*].

Initial allowances were temporarily reintroduced in respect of qualifying expenditure (see 10.12 above) incurred under a contract entered into in the twelve-month period **1 November 1992 to 31 October 1993 inclusive** or for the purpose of securing compliance with obligations incurred under a contract entered into during that period, but not for expenditure incurred under a contract entered into for the purpose of securing compliance with obligations under a contract entered into before 1 November 1992. The qualifying building or structure must have come to be used before 1 January 1995, and if this condition was not satisfied, any initial allowance given will have been withdrawn. The initial allowance was **20%** of the expenditure incurred. These provisions did not apply where initial allowances would otherwise have been available as above. They do apply to qualifying hotels (see 10.18 below), and also in respect of any 'additional VAT liability' (see 10.2(vii) above) incurred in respect of expenditure falling within these provisions. [*CAA 2001, Sch 3 paras 75-77; CAA 1990, s 2A; FA 1993, s 113(1)*].

The general conditions for the grant of initial allowances apply to the temporary allowances as above and (subject to the special provisions described in 10.19 below) to the 100% enterprise zone allowances generally in the same way as they applied to the pre-1984 allowances. The allowances are available to a person incurring qualifying expenditure (see 10.12 above) on a building etc. which is to be in use as an 'industrial building' (see 10.11 above) for a trade carried on by that person or by his lessee or, for licences granted after 9 March 1982, by his licensee. [*CAA 2001, s 305, Sch 3 para 64; CAA 1990, s 1(1)(4)*]. See also 10.12 above as regards buildings or structures bought unused. An initial allowance is given for the chargeable period in which the expenditure is incurred. [*CAA 2001, s 306(3); CAA 1990, s 1(1)*]. Expenditure for the purposes of a trade incurred by a person about to carry it on is treated as if incurred on the day the trade is actually commenced, but this applies only for the purpose of determining the chargeable period for which the allowance may be made (and not, for example, to determine the availability or otherwise of an initial allowance under *CAA 1990, s 2A* — see above). [*CAA 2001, s 306(4); CAA 1990, s 1(10)*]. See also 10.2(iii) above generally as to the time at which expenditure is treated as being incurred.

Expenditure taken into account for the purposes of certain grants or payments specified by the Treasury for the purpose are excluded from initial allowances. [*CAA 2001, s 308, Sch 3 para 65; CAA 1990, s 1(7)-(9)*]. See also 10.2(v) above.

Initial allowances may be claimed in whole or part. [*CAA 2001, s 306(2); CAA 1990, s 1(5); FA 1990, Sch 17 para 2*]. They are withdrawn if, when the building or structure comes to be used, it is not an 'industrial building', or (in relation to the vendor) if it is sold before being used. [*CAA 2001, s 307; CAA 1990, s 1(6)*].

Earlier rates of initial allowance were as follows.

After 5 April 1944	— 10%	
After 5 April 1952	— Nil	
After 14 April 1953	— 10%	
After 6 April 1954	— Nil	
After 17 February 1956	— 10%	
After 14 April 1958	— 15%	
After 7 April 1959	— 5%	
After 16 January 1966	— 15%	
After 5 April 1970	— 30%	(40% if building or structure in development or intermediate area or N. Ireland)
After 21 March 1972	— 40%	
After 12 November 1974	— 50%	(20% on hotels and 100% in enterprise zones and on certain small workshops, from later dates, see 10.18, 10.19 and 10.21 below)
After 10 March 1981	— 75%	(— as above —)
After 13 March 1984	— 50%	(— as above, omitting reference to workshops from 27 March 1985 —)
After 31 March 1985 to 31 March 1986	— 25%	(— as above —)

Simon's Direct Tax Service. See **B2.232** *et seq.*

10.14 **Writing-down allowances.** These are available where a qualifying building or structure (see 10.11 above) is in use as such (or in temporary disuse following such use, see 10.11 above) at the end of a chargeable period. They are available to the person entitled to an interest which is the 'relevant interest' in the building or structure at the end of that period. A writing-down allowance can be given for the same chargeable period as an initial allowance (see 10.13 above) in respect of the same expenditure.

For expenditure incurred between 6 April 1946 and 5 November 1962 inclusive, the rate of allowance is 2% p.a.

For expenditure incurred **after 5 November 1962,** the rate of allowance is **4% p.a.** (but see 10.19, 10.21 below as regards 25% annual allowances in certain cases) or such smaller amount as may be claimed.

The allowances are calculated on the qualifying expenditure (see 10.12 above) incurred, and continue until the 'residue of expenditure' is nil. The annual writing-down allowance is available in full where the expenditure is incurred during the chargeable period, but is proportionately reduced where the chargeable period is less than twelve months (or, for income tax purposes, increased if the chargeable period exceeds twelve months). [*CAA 2001, ss 309, 310, 312, Sch 3 para 66; CAA 1990, s 3(1)(2)(4); FA 1994, s 213(2), Sch 26 Pt V(24)*].

Where an 'additional VAT liability' (see 10.2(vii) above) is incurred in respect of any qualifying expenditure, the amount of the liability qualifies for writing-down allowances as if it were additional capital expenditure incurred on the construction in question; the 'residue of expenditure' is increased by that amount at the time the liability accrues. For chargeable periods ending after the time the liability accrues, writing-down allowances are given of the proportion of the residue of expenditure immediately after that time which the length of the chargeable period bears to the length of the period from the date of the incurring of the liability to the 25th anniversary of the first use of the building or structure for any purpose. Similar provisions apply where an 'additional VAT rebate' (see 10.2(vii) above) is made, the residue being reduced by the amount thereof (but see 10.15 below where the rebate exceeds the residue). [*CAA 2001, ss 311, 347, 349–351; CAA 1990, s 3(2A)–(2C), s 8(12A); FA 1991, Sch 14 paras 3, 5(2); FA 1994, Sch 26 Pt V(24)*].

If the 'relevant interest' in a building or structure is sold, and the sale is a balancing event (see 10.15 below), subsequent writing-down allowances are given to the purchaser and are calculated on the 'residue of expenditure' immediately after the sale, spread over the period from the date of sale to the 25th anniversary of the first use of the building or structure for any purpose (50th anniversary for expenditure incurred before 6 November 1962). [*CAA 2001, s 311, Sch 3 para 67; CAA 1990, s 3(3); FA 1994, Sch 26 Pt V(24)*].

For a sale *before 18 December 1980* (or pursuant to a contract made before that date) at a time when the building or structure was not in use as an 'industrial building', so that no balancing adjustment arose (see 10.15 below), writing-down allowances to the purchaser (for subsequent chargeable (or basis) periods at the end of which the building or structure has reverted to use as an 'industrial building') continue at the rate after the most recent sale while in use as an 'industrial building' or, if there has been no such sale, the full 4% (or 2%) rate. [*CAA 1968, s 2; FA 1981, s 74*].

'*Residue of expenditure*' is original capital expenditure:

- *minus* all industrial buildings and research and development (or scientific research) allowances (see 10.52 below) granted, including balancing allowances; and
- *minus* 'notional writing-down allowances' for periods, following first use of the building or structure for any purpose, at the end of which the building or structure was not in use as an 'industrial building'; and
- *plus* any balancing charges made; and
- *plus* or *minus* any 'additional VAT liability' or 'additional VAT rebate' (see 10.2(vii) above) incurred or made in respect of that expenditure.

Where the Crown is entitled to the relevant interest for a period immediately before a sale etc., allowances and charges which could have been made if the building or structure had been in use by a non-corporate trader entitled to that interest for that period are taken into account for this purpose. For sales etc. after 28 July 1988, this treatment applies also to prior entitlement by any person not within the charge to income tax or corporation tax.

Where a balancing charge arises on the excess of allowances given over adjusted net cost following a sale after non-qualifying use (see 10.15 below), the residue after the sale is restricted to the net sale proceeds.

[*CAA 2001, ss 313, 332–339, 348, Sch 3 paras 72, 73; CAA 1990, s 3(2A)(b), s 8; FA 1991, Sch 14 paras 3(1), 5; FA 1994, s 213(3), Sch 26 Pt V(24)*].

'*Notional allowances*' are calculated on the original qualifying expenditure or, if the building etc. has subsequently been sold in circumstances giving rise to a balancing adjustment (see 10.15 below), at the appropriate rate following that sale. [*CAA 2001, s 336(3)(4); CAA 1990, s 8(7)*].

'*Relevant interest*' is, in relation to any expenditure incurred on the construction of the building or structure, the interest (freehold or leasehold) in that building or structure to which the person who incurred the expenditure was entitled when he incurred it. If there is more than one such interest, and one was reversionary on all the others, the reversionary interest is the relevant interest. The creation of a subordinate interest (e.g. leasehold out of freehold) does not generally transfer the relevant interest (but see below). An interest arising on or as a result of completion of construction is treated as having been held when the expenditure was incurred. If a leasehold relevant interest is extinguished by surrender, or by the person entitled to it acquiring the interest reversionary on it, the interest into which it merges becomes the relevant interest. A highway concession (see 10.11 above) is not generally an interest in a road, but is treated as the relevant interest where the person who incurred expenditure on construction of the road was not then entitled to an interest in the road but was entitled to the highway concession in respect of it. [*CAA 2001, ss 286–289, 342; CAA 1990, ss 20, 21(2); FA 1991, s 60(5); FA 1995, s 99(6)*].

However, where a lease of more than 50 years is granted out of a 'relevant interest' the lessor and the lessee may jointly elect for allowances to apply to the leasehold interest. The grant of the lease is then regarded as a sale to the lessee, the capital sum as the purchase price, and the lessee's interest as replacing all the lessor's relevant interest. The election is not available if lessor and lessee are CONNECTED PERSONS (19) (unless the lessor controls the lessee and has statutory functions) or if the sole or main benefit which may be expected to accrue to the lessor is a balancing allowance (see 10.15 below). The election must be in writing to the inspector within two years after the date on which the lease takes effect. [*CAA 2001, ss 290, 291; CAA 1990, s 11*].

Requisitioned land. Allowances may be available for buildings on land requisitioned by the Crown. See *CAA 2001, s 358; CAA 1990, s 16(1)-(3)*.

Termination of leases. (i) Where a lease ends and the lessee, with the lessor's consent, remains in possession without a new lease being granted, the lease is treated as continuing. (ii) A new lease granted on the termination of an old lease on exercise of an option available under the old lease is treated as a continuation of the old lease. (iii) If on termination of a lease the lessor pays any sum to the lessee in respect of a building comprised in the lease, the lease is treated as surrendered in consideration of the payment. (iv) If, on the termination of a lease, a lessee who is granted a new lease makes a payment to the lessee under the old lease, the two leases are treated as the same lease, the old lessee having assigned it to the new lessee for payment. [*CAA 2001, s 359; CAA 1990, s 16(4)-(7)*].

Buildings bought after use. Where a person carrying on a trade, consisting wholly or partly of the construction of buildings or structures with a view to their sale, incurs expenditure on such a construction and after the building or structure has been used, he sells the relevant interest in the course of the trade, the purchaser is entitled to allowances as if the original expenditure had been capital expenditure and all appropriate writing-down allowances and balancing allowances or charges (see 10.15 below) had been made to or on the vendor. Normally, the effect will be that the purchaser obtains allowances on the lesser of the net purchase price and the cost of construction. This provision applies in any case where the purchase price becomes payable after 26 July 1989. [*CAA 2001, s 297, Sch 3 para 60; CAA 1990, s 10(4)(5)*]. Previously, a similar rule operated by extra-statutory concession. (HMRC Extra Statutory Concession B20).

Simon's Direct Tax Service. See B2.234 *et seq.*

10.15 **Balancing allowances and charges.** Where a balancing event takes place on or after 21 March 2007 (a post-commencement relevant event) and neither:

(i) involves qualifying enterprise zone expenditure; nor

(ii) arises from a relevant pre-commencement contract,

no balancing allowance or charge will arise and the purchaser will be entitled to capital allowances on the vendor's balance of unrelieved expenditure.

A post-commencement balancing event includes a 'relevant event' (as defined in *ICTA 1988 s 311*) taking place on or after 21 March 2007, but does not include an event occurring on or after 21 March 2007 and before 1 April 2011 under a relevant pre-commencement contract. Such a contract must be:

(*a*) made in writing before 21 March 2007;

(*b*) unconditional or its conditions have been satisfied before that date;

(*c*) final before 21 March 2007 – i.e. no terms had to be agreed on or after that date; and

(*d*) not significantly varied on or after that date.

[*FA 2007 s 35*].

For events up to and including 20 March 2007, a balancing allowance or charge could arise to or on the person entitled to the 'relevant interest' (see 10.14 above) in a building or structure when it is sold, destroyed or permanently put out of use, or when the relevant interest is lost on termination of a lease or foreign concession, or when a highway concession (see 10.11 above) is brought to or comes to an end (see also below), *provided that* that event occurs within 25 years (50 years for expenditure incurred before 6 November 1962) of the building or structure's first being used. On a sale etc. **after 17 December 1980** (unless pursuant to a contract made on or before that date) of a building or structure which has been an industrial building (or used for research and development, see 10.52 below) throughout the 'relevant period', the balancing adjustment is calculated as follows.

If the 'residue of expenditure' (see 10.14 above) immediately before the sale etc. exceeds the proceeds of any sale, insurance, salvage or compensation, the difference is allowed as a balancing allowance (subject to the anti-avoidance rule at 10.2(xi) above); if it is less, the difference is the subject of a balancing charge.

Where the building or structure has at any time in the 'relevant period' been neither an 'industrial building' nor in use for research and development (or scientific research), a balancing charge will be made to recover all allowances given where the proceeds of sale, insurance, salvage or compensation equal or exceed the 'starting expenditure'. Where those proceeds are nil or less than the 'starting expenditure', a balancing allowance will be given (or a balancing charge made) on the excess of the 'adjusted net cost' of the building or structure over the allowances given (or *vice versa*).

For this purpose, the allowances given include all industrial buildings, research and development (or scientific research), and mills, factories or exceptional depreciation allowances, and any balancing charge raised may not exceed the total of such allowances, less any balancing charges previously made.

'*Relevant period*' means the period beginning at the time when the building or structure was first used for any purpose and ending with the event giving rise to the balancing adjustment, unless there have been previous sales, when the relevant period begins on the day following the last sale.

'*Starting expenditure*' means the expenditure incurred on the construction of the building or structure (less any balancing charge made in respect of an 'additional VAT rebate' — see below) or, in the case of a second-hand building or structure, the residue of expenditure (see 10.14 above) at the beginning of the relevant period, together (in either case) with the net cost of demolition (see below) if appropriate.

'*Adjusted net cost*' means the amount by which starting expenditure exceeds the proceeds, reduced in the proportion that the period of qualifying use bears to the relevant period.

[*CAA 2001, ss 314(1)-(4), 315, 316, 318-324, 343, 350(5), Sch 3 paras 68-70; CAA 1990, s 4; FA 1991, Sch 14 para 4(4)(5); FA 1995, s 99(3)*].

Successive sales etc. during non-use as industrial building. Where there are two or more sales etc. in a period during which a building or structure is not an 'industrial building', a balancing adjustment arises only on the first such sale etc. [*CAA 2001, s 314(5); CAA 1990, s 4(2); FA 1991, Sch 14 para 4(2)*].

Additional VAT rebate. Where an 'additional VAT rebate' (see 10.2(vii) above) is made in respect of qualifying expenditure, and this exceeds the residue of expenditure (see 10.14 above), a balancing charge, equal to the excess, will be made. [*CAA 2001, s 350; CAA 1990, s 4(1)(e)(2A); FA 1991, Sch 14 para 4(1)(3)*].

In the case of a *highway concession* (see above), no balancing adjustment arises (and writing-down allowances continue) where, on the coming to an end of the concession, the period for which it was granted is extended, i.e. the person entitled to it is granted a renewal of the concession in respect of the whole or part of a road, or the person or a CONNECTED PERSON (19) is granted a new concession in respect of the same road (or part of it or a road of which it is part). Where the extension relates to part only of a road, a 'just and reasonable' apportionment is made to determine the expenditure in respect of which a balancing adjustment arises. [*CAA 2001, s 344; CAA 1990, s 4(2AA)(2AB); FA 1995, s 99(4)*].

Buildings for miners etc. Special provisions apply to certain balancing allowances arising in the chargeable period in which a trade consisting of or including the working of a source of mineral deposits ceases, but which cannot be given effect because of an insufficiency of profits. Where the allowances are in respect of buildings occupied by, or for the welfare of, persons employed at or in connection with the working of the source, and they arise because of the source ceasing to be worked or the coming to an end of a foreign concession, the allowances may (subject to restrictions) be carried back to earlier chargeable periods. [*CAA 2001, s 355; CAA 1990, s 17*].

On a sale etc. **before 18 December 1980** (or pursuant to a contract made before that date), a balancing adjustment arose only when the building or structure was in use as an 'industrial building' at the time of the sale etc. Any balancing adjustment which did arise was calculated as follows. If the 'residue of expenditure' (see 10.14 above) immediately before the sale etc. exceeded the proceeds of any sale, insurance, salvage or compensation, the difference was allowed as a balancing allowance; if it was less, the difference was the subject of a balancing charge, subject to two restrictions:

(*a*) the charge may not exceed the total of industrial buildings, scientific research, and mills, factories or exceptional depreciation allowances given; and

(*b*) where during any part of the 'relevant period' (see below) the building or structure has not attracted writing-down or scientific research allowances, the charge is reduced to the proportion which the parts of the 'relevant period' which were included in basis periods for which such allowances were given bears to the whole of the 'relevant period'. For this purpose the '*relevant period*' is the period from first use of the building or structure to date of the sale etc. or, if that date is not the last day of a basis period, the most recent day before the sale etc. which was the last day of a basis period.

A restriction similar to that in (*b*) above could be placed on balancing allowances on election by the vendor. [*CAA 1968, s 3 as originally enacted*].

Demolition. The net cost (after crediting sales of materials and scrap) of demolition borne by the person on whom a balancing adjustment arises is added to 'residue of expenditure' (see 10.14 above) for balancing allowance and balancing charge calculations (and those costs are then not taken into account for capital allowance purposes except in the case of dwelling-houses let on assured tenancies, see 10.8 above). [*CAA 2001, s 340; CAA 1990, s 8(12)*]. Where this is not possible (e.g. because more than 25 (or 50) years has elapsed since the building or structure was first used), and if the holder of the relevant interest demolishes the building or structure for the purpose of erecting a new building or structure on the same site, the demolition costs may be treated as expenditure by the holder on construction of the new building or structure. (HMRC Capital Allowances Manual CA 31400).

See also 10.22(i) below as regards certain transactions between connected persons and other anti-avoidance provisions.

Simon's Direct Tax Service. See **B2.237** *et seq.*

10.16 *Examples*

Writing-down allowances and balancing adjustments

(A) Prior to commencing business on 1 June 1996, P Ltd incurred the following expenditure.

	£
10.1.96 Plot of land	50,000
20.2.96 Clearing and levelling site	20,000
20.4.96 Construction of factory	500,000
	£570,000

The factory was brought into use for a qualifying purpose on commencement of trade, and remained in such use until 1 May 2006, when it was sold to Y Ltd for £550,000, being £480,000 for the factory and £70,000 for the land. P Ltd drew up accounts annually to 31 May. Y Ltd draws up accounts to 30 April, having commenced trading on 1 May 2006, and uses the factory for a qualifying purpose.

The allowances available to P Ltd are as follows.

Accounting period ended				Residue of expenditure £
31 May 1997		Qualifying expenditure		520,000
		Writing-down allowance	4% of £520,000	(20,800)
				499,200
31 May 1998		Writing-down allowance for 8 years	4% of £520,000 × 8	(166,400)
	1999			
	2000			
	2001			
	2002			
	2003			
	2004			
	2005			
				332,800
31 May 2006		Sale proceeds		(480,000)
		Balancing charge		£147,200

The allowances available to Y Ltd are as follows.

Date of first use	1.6.96
Date of purchase by Y Ltd	1.5.06
Number of years remaining	15 years 1 month
Residue of expenditure	£480,000

Y Ltd is therefore entitled to writing-down allowances of £31,824 p.a. until total allowances reach £480,000. The first writing-down allowance will be given for the accounting period 1.5.06 to 30.4.07.

Note

(*a*) No allowances are due on the cost of the land (see 10.12 above).

Non-qualifying purposes and balancing adjustments

A Ltd prepares accounts annually to 31 March. The company incurred £40,000 of capital expenditure in 1986 (and before 31 March 1986) on the construction of a building which was brought into use as an industrial building on 1 April 1987. After three years of use for a qualifying industrial purpose, it was used for three years, from 1 April 1990 to 31 March 1993, for non-qualifying purposes after which the original qualifying activity was resumed until the building was destroyed by fire.

The fire occurred on 1 October 2006 with an insurance recovery of (i) £50,000 (ii) £35,000. The company's industrial buildings allowance position for the accounting period ended 31 March 2007 will be as follows.

Year ended 31 March 2007: Balancing charge

(i) *Proceeds exceed cost*		
Actual allowances given	note (*a*)	£35,600
Balancing charge		£35,600

		£
(ii) *Proceeds less than cost*		
Net cost (£40,000 – £35,000)		5,000
Reduction 3y/19 yrs 6m	note (*b*)	(769)
Adjusted net cost		4,231
Allowances given	note (*a*)	35,600
Excess		£31,369
Balancing charge		£31,369

Notes

(*a*) Allowances given in previous years are:

	£
Initial allowance £40,000 × 25%	10,000
Writing-down allowances £40,000 × 4% × 16	25,600
	£35,600

Writing-down allowances would not have been given for the three years to 31 March 1993 as the building was not an industrial building at the end of each of those years (see 10.14 above).

(*b*) In example (ii), the net cost is reduced by the proportion which the period of non-qualifying use bears to the total period from first use to date of balancing event (see 10.15 above).

(B) Had the fire taken place on 1 March 2008, there would have been no balancing allowance or charge.

10.17 **Making of allowances and charges.** For traders, allowances and charges are given effect in calculating profits. This applies equally to professions and vocations. [*CAA 2001, s 352; CAA 1990, ss 9(2), 140(2); FA 1994, s 211*]. A highway undertaking (see 10.11 above) is treated as a trade. [*CAA 2001, s 341(1); CAA 1990, ss 21(5A), 140(6)*].

Allowances to, and charges on, traders are treated as trading expenses and receipts [*CAA 2001, s 352(1); CAA 1990, s 140; FA 1994, s 211*] and are calculated by reference to events in accounting periods (see 10.1 above).

Temporarily unused buildings. Where an allowance or charge falls to be made in a period during which a building or structure is temporarily out of use but deemed still to be an industrial building (see 10.11 above) and, since it was last used as such, the trade in question has ceased (or, where the relevant interest was subject to a lease, or the building or structure used under licence, the lease or licence has come to an end), such allowances and charges are dealt with in the same way as those falling to be made to or on lessors (see below). Where a balancing charge falls to be made on any person following such a period of temporary disuse, and the most recent use was as an industrial building for the purposes of a trade carried on by that person which has since ceased, the same deductions can be made from the charge as can be made under *ICTA 1988, s 105* from a post-cessation receipt (without prejudice to the deduction of any amounts allowable against the balancing charge under other provisions). [*CAA 2001, s 354; CAA 1990, s 15(2)(2A)(3), s 15ZA, s 15A; ITTOIA 2005, Sch 1 para 556*].

Lessors (and licensors) of industrial buildings may claim allowances for an accounting period. Allowances and balancing charges are treated as expenses and receipts of a Schedule A business (see 56.1 PROPERTY INCOME) or, if the lease or licence is an asset of an overseas property business (see 56.17 PROPERTY INCOME), of that business. Where it is not an asset of any property business, allowances and charges are treated as expenses and receipts of a notional Schedule A business. [*CAA 2001, s 353; CAA 1990, ss 9, 141, 161(2A); ITTOIA 2005, Sch 1 para 555*].

Simon's Direct Tax Service. See **B2.241** *et seq.*

10.18 **Hotels.** Expenditure incurred after 11 April 1978 and before 1 April 1986, or before 1 April 1987 under a contract entered into before 14 March 1984 by the person incurring the expenditure, on construction or extension of a 'qualifying hotel' attracted an initial allowance of 20% and writing-down allowances of 4% p.a.. The 20% initial allowance under *CAA 1990, s 2A* for expenditure incurred in, broadly, the year ending 31 October 1993 (see 10.13 above) applied equally to 'qualifying hotels'. For subsequent expenditure, 'qualifying hotels' attract writing-down allowances as industrial buildings in the normal way (see 10.14 above). Certain expenditure on fire safety and thermal insulation may be treated as on plant and machinery, see 10.25 below.

A '*qualifying hotel*' must have accommodation in building(s) of a permanent nature and be open for at least four months during April–October, and whilst open during those months: (i) must have at least ten letting bedrooms, i.e. private bedrooms for letting to the public generally and not normally in same occupation for more than a month; (ii) must offer sleeping accommodation consisting wholly or mainly of letting bedrooms; and (iii) its services must normally include providing breakfast and evening meals, making beds and cleaning rooms. The provision of breakfast and dinner must be offered as a normal event in the carrying on of the hotel business and must not be exceptional or available only on request. (HMRC Statement of Practice 9/87). Buildings provided (and in use) for the welfare of employees are regarded as part of a qualifying hotel. Accommodation which, when the hotel is open during April-October, is normally used as a dwelling by an individual carrying on (including in partnership) the hotel (or by a member of his family or household) is excluded (unless the proportion of the total cost attributable to excluded accommodation is less than 25% (10% before 16 March 1983), in which case the whole of the expenditure qualifies).

The meeting of the above conditions at any time during a chargeable period is determined by reference to their being met during a twelve-month period as follows. If the hotel was in use for the trade throughout the twelve months ending with the last day of the chargeable period, it is that twelve-month period. If the hotel was first used for the purposes of the trade after the beginning of such a period (or the ten-bedroom requirement commenced to be met after the beginning of such a period), it is the twelve months from commencement (or from the requirement being first met). The conditions are not met at any time in a chargeable period after the hotel has ceased altogether to be used. An hotel in temporary disuse (see 10.11 above) ceases to qualify two years after the end of the chargeable period in which it fell out of use. An hotel outside the UK may qualify provided that the profits etc. are assessable in accordance with the rules that apply to Schedule D, Case I for corporation tax purposes (or for calculating trading profits for income tax purposes).

A balancing event will not give rise to a balancing adjustment where the event takes place on or after 21 March 2007, except where the event occurs before 1 April 2011 under a relevant pre-commencement contract or the expenditure relates to a structure in an enterprise zone. A pre-commencement contract must be:

(i) made in writing before 21 March 2007;

(ii) unconditional or its conditions have been satisfied before that date;

(iii) final before 21 March 2007 – i.e. no terms had to be agreed on or after that date; and

(iv) not significantly varied on or after that date.

Where there is a 'post-commencement balancing event' (see 10.15 above), the amount on which the purchaser can claim writing down allowances is the balance of unrelieved expenditure immediately before that event.

Prior to 21 March 2007, balancing adjustments arose on a balancing event falling within *CAA 2001, s 315* or *CAA 1990, s 4* (see 10.15 above) (whether or not the hotel is at the time a 'qualifying hotel') or, if the hotel ceases to qualify and there is no such balancing event within two years of the end of the chargeable period in which it ceases to qualify, at the end of that two years, when the hotel is treated as having been sold at market value. The latter 'two-year' rule does not apply to qualifying hotels in enterprise zones (see 10.19 below).

[*CAA 2001, ss 271(1)(b), 279, 282, 283, 285, 317, Sch 3 para 58; CAA 1990, ss 7, 19; ITTOIA 2005, Sch 1 para 552; FA 2007, s 35*].

Simon's Direct Tax Service. See B2.252 *et seq.*

10.19 **Enterprise zones.** An 'enterprise zone' is an area designated as such by the Secretary of State (or by Scottish Ministers, the National Assembly for Wales or, for Northern Ireland, the Department of the Environment). [*CAA 2001, s 298(3); CAA 1990, s 21(4); FA 2001, s 69, Sch 21 para 5*]. Areas designated are as follows.

Zones whose ten-year life expires after 31 March 2006

Tyne Riverside (North Tyneside) (No 2) (from 26 August 1996, *SI 1996 No 1981*)
Tyne Riverside (North Tyneside and South Tyneside) (from 21 October 1996, *SI 1996 No 2435*)

Zones whose ten-year life expired before 1 April 2006

Allerdale, see Workington (Allerdale)
Arbroath, see Tayside (Arbroath)
Ashfield, see East Midlands (No 7)
Barnsley, see Dearne Valley
Bassetlaw, see East Midlands (No 4)
Belfast (from 21 October 1981, *SR 1981 No 309*)

Clydebank (from 3 August 1981, *SI 1981 No 975*)
Corby (from 22 June 1981, *SI 1981 No 764*)
Dearne Valley (Nos 1 to 6) (from 3 November 1995, *SI 1995 No 2624*)
Delyn (from 21 July 1983, *SI 1983 No 896*)
Derbyshire (NE), see East Midlands (Nos 1 to 3)
Doncaster, see Dearne Valley
Dudley (Round Oak) (from 3 October 1984, *SI 1984 No 1403*)
Dudley (not Round Oak) (from 10 July 1981, *SI 1981 No 852*)
Dundee, see Tayside (Dundee)
Easington, see East Durham
East Durham (Nos 1 to 6) (from 29 November 1995, *SI 1995 No 2812*)
East Midlands (Nos 1 to 3) (from 3 November 1995, *SI 1995 No 2625*)
East Midlands (No 4) (from 16 November 1995, *SI 1995 No 2738*)
East Midlands (No 7) (from 21 November 1995, *SI 1995 No 2758*)
Flixborough, see Glanford (Flixborough)
Gateshead (from 25 August 1981, *SI 1981 No 1070*)
Glanford (Flixborough) (from 13 April 1984, *SI 1984 No 347*)
Glasgow (from 18 August 1981, *SI 1981 No 1069*)
Hartlepool (from 23 October 1981, *SI 1981 No 1378*)
Holmewood, see East Midlands (Nos 1 to 3)
Inverclyde (from 3 March 1989, *SI 1989 No 145*)
Invergordon (from 7 October 1983, *SI 1983 No 1359*)
Isle of Dogs (from 26 April 1982, *SI 1982 No 462*)
Kent (NW) (zones 1 to 5 only) (from 31 October 1983, *SI 1983 No 1452*)
Kent (NW) (zones 6 and 7 only) (from 10 October 1986, *SI 1986 No 1557*)
Lanarkshire (Hamilton) (from 1 February 1993, *SI 1993 No 23*)
Lanarkshire (Monklands) (from 1 February 1993, *SI 1993 No 25*)
Lanarkshire (Motherwell) (from 1 February 1993, *SI 1993 No 24*)
Lancashire (NE) (from 7 December 1983, *SI 1983 No 1639*)
Liverpool (Speke) (from 25 August 1981, *SI 1981 No 1072*)
London, see Isle of Dogs
Londonderry (from 13 September 1983, *SR 1983 No 226*)
Lower Swansea Valley (from 11 June 1981, *SI 1981 No 757*)
Lower Swansea Valley (No 2) (from 6 March 1985, *SI 1985 No 137*)
Middlesbrough (Britannia) (from 8 November 1983, *SI 1983 No 1473*)
Milford Haven Waterway (North Shore) (from 24 April 1984, *SI 1984 No 443*)
Milford Haven Waterway (South Shore) (from 24 April 1984, *SI 1984 No 444*)
Newcastle (from 25 August 1981, *SI 1981 No 1071*)
Rotherham (from 16 August 1983, *SI 1983 No 1007*), and see Dearne Valley
Salford Docks (from 12 August 1981, *SI 1981 No 1024*)
Scunthorpe (Normanby Ridge and Queensway) (from 23 September 1983, *SI 1983 No 1304*)
Speke, see Liverpool (Speke)
Sunderland (Castletown and Doxford Park) (from 27 April 1990, *SI 1990 No 794*)
Sunderland (Hylton Riverside and Southwick) (from 27 April 1990, *SI 1990 No 795*)
Swansea, see Lower Swansea Valley and Lower Swansea Valley (No 2)
Tayside (Arbroath) (from 9 January 1984, *SI 1983 No 1816*)
Tayside (Dundee) (from 9 January 1984, *SI 1983 No 1817*)
Telford (from 13 January 1984, *SI 1983 No 1852*)
Trafford Park (from 12 August 1981, *SI 1981 No 1025*)
Tyne Riverside (North Tyneside) (No 1) (from 19 February 1996, *SI 1996 No 106*)
Wakefield (Dale Lane and Kingsley) (from 23 September 1983, *SI 1983 No 1305*)
Wakefield (Langthwaite Grange) (from 31 July 1981, *SI 1981 No 950*)
Wellingborough (from 26 July 1983, *SI 1983 No 907*)
Workington (Allerdale) (from 4 October 1983, *SI 1983 No 1331*)

Advantageous provisions apply to expenditure on the construction of an industrial building, which for this purpose includes a 'qualifying hotel' or a 'commercial building or structure', which is incurred (or contract entered into) within ten years of the inclusion of the site in an enterprise zone. Expenditure incurred more than 20 years after a site was first included in an enterprise zone does not attract enterprise zone allowances, regardless of when the contract for the expenditure was entered into. [*CAA 2001, ss 271(1)(b), 298; CAA 1990, ss 1(1)(2), 17A; F(No 2)A 1992, Sch 13 para 10*].

'*Qualifying hotel*' has the same meaning as in 10.18 above. (Note that any hotel not qualifying under this heading will qualify as a commercial building.)

'*Commercial building or structure*' means a building or structure which is used for the purposes of a trade, profession or vocation or as an office for any purpose, but does not include any building in use as, or as part of, a dwelling house. [*CAA 2001, s 281; CAA 1990, s 21(5)*].

The allowances given are as follows.

An initial allowance of 100% is given but the full amount need not be claimed. If any part of the initial allowance is not claimed, then **writing-down allowances at 25% p.a.** of cost on the straight line basis will apply to the unclaimed balance. [*CAA 2001, s 306(1)(2), s 310(1)(a); CAA 1990, ss 1, 6; FA 1990, Sch 17 para 2*].

For the general provisions relating to industrial buildings allowances, see 10.11 *et seq.* above. As regards enterprise zone allowances, the following special rules apply.

(i) *Date expenditure incurred. CAA 2001, s 306(4)* (or *CAA 1990, s 1(10)*)(pre-trading expenditure treated as incurred on first day of trading, see 10.13 above) do not apply in determining whether expenditure attracts enterprise zone allowances (i.e. whether it is incurred at a time when the building or structure is in an enterprise zone).

As regards buildings or structures bought unused, where the purchase price becomes payable after 15 December 1991, the normal rules under *CAA 2001, ss 294–296* (or *CAA 1990, s 10*) apply (see 10.12 above), except that:

(*a*) where some or all of the actual construction expenditure is incurred (or incurred under a contract entered into) within ten years of the inclusion of the site in an enterprise zone, a corresponding proportion of the purchaser's deemed expenditure is treated as giving rise to entitlement to enterprise zone allowances, notwithstanding that it may be deemed to have been incurred outside that ten-year period;

(*b*) where (*a*) does not apply, the purchaser's deemed expenditure is treated as not giving rise to entitlement to enterprise zone allowances, notwithstanding that it may be deemed to have been incurred during the ten-year period.

Where some of the actual construction expenditure fell within (*a*) above and some or all of the balance could qualify for a 20% initial allowance by virtue of the provisions in 10.12 above, the above provisions and those in 10.12 above interacted. The purchaser could thus obtain a 100% enterprise zone initial allowance on part of his deemed expenditure and the 20% initial allowance on another part or, where appropriate, on the balance.

[*CAA 2001, ss 300, 302, Sch 3 para 61; CAA 1990, ss 10A, 10C(11); F(No 2)A 1992, Sch 13 paras 2–7, para 14; FA 1993, s 113(4)*].

(ii) *Buildings purchased within two years of first use*. Where some or all of the construction expenditure on a building or structure first used after 15 December 1991 is incurred (or incurred under a contract entered into) within ten years of the inclusion of the site in an enterprise zone, and the 'relevant interest' (see 10.14 above) is sold during the two years (but see below) following the first use of the building or structure (whether or not there have been any sales while the building or structure was unused), then on that sale (or the first such sale) the normal balancing allowance or charge rules apply to the vendor (see 10.15 above), but the purchaser is deemed to have incurred expenditure on purchase of a building or structure bought unused (see 10.12 and (i) above). A proportion of the deemed expenditure corresponding to the proportion of the actual construction expenditure which was incurred within ten years of the inclusion of the site in the enterprise zone is treated as giving rise to entitlement to enterprise zone allowances, notwithstanding that it may be deemed to have been incurred outside the ten-year period. The balance of the deemed expenditure does not attract enterprise zone allowances. If the purchase is directly from a person who constructed the building or structure in the course of a trade of constructing such buildings or structures for sale, the part of the purchaser's deemed expenditure which does *not* attract enterprise zone allowances is calculated by reference to the actual expenditure of the vendor if that is less than the price actually paid by the purchaser. [*CAA 2001, ss 301, 303, 304, Sch 3 para 62; CAA 1990, s 10B; F(No 2)A 1992, Sch 13 paras 8, 9, 15*]. The two-year period is extended to 31 August 1994 where it would otherwise end within the period beginning 13 January 1994 and ending 31 August 1994, and the relevant interest was sold within that period and outside the two-year period. [*CAA 2001, Sch 3 para 63; FA 1994, s 121*].

(iii) *Plant and machinery* forming an integral part of a building or structure was not subject to the restriction of first-year allowances to lessors under *CAA 1990, s 22(4)* (see 10.35 below) (and see now below). [*CAA 1990, s 22(5)*].

(iv) *Balancing charge on realisation of capital value.* Where capital expenditure on construction of a building or structure in an enterprise zone has been incurred (or is deemed to have been incurred) under a contract entered into after 12 January 1994 (or which becomes unconditional after 25 February 1994), and 'capital value' is received in respect of the building or structure, a balancing charge (but not a balancing allowance) may arise. This applies generally where the payment is made (or an agreement to make it made) seven years or less after the date of the agreement relating to the expenditure (or the date on which that agreement became unconditional). Where, however, there are certain guaranteed exit arrangements, it applies throughout the normal balancing adjustment period (i.e. 25 years from first use, see 10.15 above).

'*Capital value*' is realised when a sum is paid which is attributable to an interest in land to which the relevant interest in the building or structure in question is or will be subject, e.g. where a lease is granted out of the relevant interest, unless *CAA 2001, s 290* (or *CAA 1990, s 11*)(see 10.14 above) applies to the grant of that interest. There are detailed provisions as to the form and amount of the capital value, and as to its attribution to the grant of the interest. See HMRC Capital Allowances Manual CA 37730 *et seq.*

[*CAA 2001, ss 327-331, Sch 3 para 71; CAA 1990, s 4(1)(dd)(9A), s 4A; FA 1994, s 120; ITTOIA 2005, Sch 1 para 554*].

(v) *Partially completed buildings.* For HMRC interpretation of the allowances available where a partially completed building or structure is acquired in an enterprise zone, see Revenue Tax Bulletin June 1998 p 553.

(vi) It should be noted that where a building or structure in an enterprise zone is sold and the purchaser is *not* treated as having incurred expenditure on its construction, the residue of expenditure (if any) is allowed over the balance of the period of 25 years from first use of the building etc., and not at the 25% writing-down rate (see HMRC Capital Allowances Manual CA 37375).

An 'additional VAT liability' (see 10.2(vii) above) incurred in respect of qualifying expenditure, within ten years of the inclusion of the site in the enterprise zone, is itself qualifying expenditure for the chargeable period in which the liability accrues. [*CAA 2001, s 346; CAA 1990, s 1(1A); FA 1991, Sch 14 para 1*]. Where a 100% initial allowance was not claimed on the expenditure to which the additional VAT liability relates, a 100% allowance may nevertheless generally be claimed for the additional VAT liability. If less than the full 100% allowance is claimed for the additional VAT liability, writing-down allowances for the whole of the expenditure on the building or structure in question will be recomputed as under 10.14 above, resulting in a substantial reduction in the rate of annual allowance.

For balancing adjustments after non-qualifying use, see 10.15 above. For transfers between connected persons etc., see 10.22(i) below.

For the special treatment for tax purposes of investors in enterprise zone property schemes, see *SI 1988 No 267* and *SI 1992 No 571* (and see HMRC Inspector's Manual IM 4213 *et seq.*).

Plant or machinery. Expenditure on plant or machinery, or on thermal insulation treated as plant or machinery under 10.25(ii) below, which is to be an integral part of an industrial or commercial building in an enterprise zone may be treated as part of the expenditure on construction of the building or structure, and so attract the 100% initial allowance. A claim for expenditure on plant or machinery to be so treated does not prevent a subsequent purchaser of the building or structure from claiming plant and machinery allowances on that expenditure and industrial buildings allowances on the fabric of the building. (This commentary is not included in the current HMRC Capital Allowances Manual, but was previously at CA 1060 and is presumed still to be of application.)

Simon's Direct Tax Service. See **B2.262** *et seq.*

10.20 *Examples*

(i)

In 2004, J, a builder, incurred expenditure of £400,000 on the construction of a building in a designated enterprise zone. The whole of the expenditure was incurred (or contracted for) within ten years of the site's first being included in the zone. In January 2005, he sold the building unused to K Ltd for £600,000 (excluding land). In February 2005, K Ltd let the building to a trader who immediately brought it into use as a supermarket. K Ltd claims a reduced initial allowance of £50,000. In March 2007, it sells the building to L Ltd for £750,000 (excluding land). K Ltd draws up accounts to 31 March each year.

K Ltd's allowances are as follows.

Accounting period ended		£	Residue of expenditure £
31 March 2005	Qualifying expenditure		600,000
	Initial allowance (maximum 100%)	50,000	
	Writing-down allowance 25% of £600,000	150,000	
	Total IBA due	200,000	(200,000)
31 March 2006	Writing-down allowance	150,000	(150,000)
			250,000
31 March 2007	Writing-down allowance	—	—
	Sale proceeds		(750,000)
			£500,000
	Balancing charge (restricted to allowances given)		£350,000

Notes

(*a*) K Ltd's qualifying expenditure would normally be the lesser of cost of construction and the net price paid by it for the building. However, on purchase from a builder, whose profit on sale is taxable as a trading profit, the qualifying expenditure is equal to the net price paid for the relevant interest (excluding the land). See 10.12, 10.19(i) above.

(*b*) K Ltd's allowances and balancing charges are treated as expenses and receipts of a Schedule A business. See 10.17 above. K Ltd could have claimed a 100% initial allowance in the year ended 31 March 2005.

(*c*) Providing the building continues to be used for a qualifying purpose, L Ltd can claim writing-down allowances over the remainder of the 25-year writing-down period. Its qualifying expenditure is restricted to £600,000, i.e. the residue of expenditure (£250,000) plus the balancing charge on K Ltd. See 10.14 above.

(*d*) In this example, the first sale after the building was first used took place just over two years after the date of first use. If the sale had taken place within two years after first use, the balancing charge on K Ltd would have been computed in the same manner, but L Ltd could have claimed an initial allowance and 25% writing-down allowances as if it had bought the building unused. L Ltd's qualifying expenditure would again have been restricted to £600,000, being the lesser of the price paid by it for the relevant interest in the building and that paid on the original purchase by K Ltd from the builder. See 10.19(ii) above.

(ii)

The facts are as in (i) above, except that, of the £400,000 construction expenditure actually incurred, only £360,000 is incurred (or contracted for) within ten years of the site's first being included in an enterprise zone, and the first sale occurred after the expiry of that ten-year period.

K Ltd's qualifying expenditure of £600,000 (arrived at as in (i) above) is divided into an enterprise zone element and a non-enterprise zone element.

The enterprise zone element is

$$£600,000 \times \frac{360,000}{400,000} = £540,000$$

The non-enterprise zone element is £600,000 – £540,000 = £60,000

The non-enterprise zone element does not qualify for enterprise zone allowances. See 10.19(i) above. (It could have qualified for normal IBAs if the building had been an industrial building.)

K Ltd's allowances are as follows.

Accounting period ended		£	Residue of expenditure £
31 March 2005	Qualifying expenditure (enterprise zone element)		540,000
	Initial allowance (maximum 100%)	50,000	
	Writing-down allowance (25% of £540,000)	135,000	
		185,000	(185,000)
31 March 2006	Writing-down allowance	135,000	(135,000)
			220,000
31 March 2007	Writing-down allowance	—	—
	Sale proceeds £750,000 × $\frac{540,000}{600,000}$		(675,000)
			£455,000
	Balancing charge (restricted to allowances given)		£320,000

L Ltd's qualifying expenditure is £540,000, i.e. the residue of £220,000 plus the balancing charge of £320,000 on K Ltd.

Note

(*a*) The apportionment of sale proceeds in the year ended 31 March 2007 is considered to be 'just and reasonable'.

10.21 **Small and very small workshops.** Expenditure incurred after 26 March 1980 and before 27 March 1985 on the construction of an industrial building (or permanently separated part of a larger building or structure, intended and suitable for separate occupation, but common facilities are excepted) of, before 27 March 1983, 2,500 square feet or less, and, after 26 March 1983 and before 27 March 1985, 1,250 square feet or less of gross internal floor space (including ancillary works) qualified for an initial allowance of 100% with similar rights to reduce or disclaim this and receive writing-down allowances of 25% as described in 10.19 above. Similarly the provisions stated at (i), (ii) in 10.19 above applied also to small workshops. [*FA 1980, s 75, Sch 13 Pt I; FA 1982, s 73*]. (HMRC Statement of Practice 6/80; obsolete). For balancing adjustments after non-qualifying use, see 10.15 above. For transfers between connected persons etc., see 10.22(i) below.

See HMRC Statement of Practice 4/80 for the application of these provisions where individual units in a larger development did not exceed 2,500 square feet.

The limit of 1,250 square feet could be exceeded in certain cases where existing buildings were converted into separate units. [*FA 1983, s 31*].

10.22 **General Matters.** The following general matters apply.

(i) *Connected persons and other anti-avoidance provisions.* Special provisions apply to sales of industrial buildings where

(*a*) the sale results in no change of control, or

(*b*) the sole or main benefit apparently arising is the obtaining of an industrial buildings allowance.

Paragraph (*a*) also covers sales between CONNECTED PERSONS (19), and (*b*) includes cases where the anticipated benefit is a reduction in a charge or the *increase* of an allowance. Normally, where these provisions apply, market value is substituted for purchase price (if different), and this also applies to transfers other than by way of sale. However, provided that (*b*) above does not apply, for sales within (*a*) above and other transfers the parties may elect for the substitution of the residue of expenditure (see 10.14 above) if this is lower than market value, and for any subsequent balancing charge on the buyer to be calculated by reference to allowances etc. of both buyer and seller. Such an election is *not* available if the circumstances are such that an allowance or charge which otherwise would or might fall, in consequence of the sale, to be made to or on *any* of the parties to the sale cannot fall to be made. The election must be made within two years after the sale. The election also covers qualifying hotels and commercial buildings etc. in enterprise zones. [*CAA 2001, ss 567-570, 573, 575(1), 577(4); CAA 1990, ss 21(6)(7), 157, 158; FA 1993, s 117(2)(4)(5); FA 1994, s 119(1)*].

Balancing allowances (see 10.15 above) are restricted on sales after 13 June 1972 where the relevant interest (see 10.14 above) in an industrial building is sold subject to a subordinate interest (e.g. in a sale and lease-back) and either

(1) the seller, the purchaser of the interest, and the grantee of the subordinate interest (or any two of them) are CONNECTED PERSONS (19), or

(2) the sole or main benefit appears to be the obtaining of an industrial buildings allowance.

In such cases the net sale proceeds are increased, in determining any balancing allowance, by

(A) where less than a commercial rent is payable under the subordinate interest, the difference between actual sale proceeds and market value had a commercial rent been payable, and

(B) the amount of any premium receivable for the grant of the subordinate interest and not chargeable under *ICTA 1988, s 34*,

but not by more than is required to eliminate any balancing allowance. Special provisions apply if the terms of the subordinate interest are varied before the sale. The residue of expenditure (see 10.14 above) following the sale is, however, calculated as if the balancing allowance had been made without the application of these provisions.

[*CAA 2001, ss 325, 326; CAA 1990, s 5; ITTOIA 2005, Sch 1 para 553*].

(ii) *Double allowances.* See 10.2(iv) above.

(iii) *Partnerships*, including partnerships of which companies are members, are entitled to industrial buildings allowances in respect of qualifying expenditure (see 10.12 above) on industrial buildings (see 10.11 above).

Following a change in the persons carrying on the trade etc., other than one resulting in the activity being treated for tax purposes as permanently discontinued, unexhausted allowances are carried forward, and subsequent balancing adjustments (see 10.15 above) made as if the new partnership etc. had carried on the trade etc. before the change. [*CAA 2001, ss 557, 558; CAA 1990, s 152(3); FA 2001, s 69, Sch 21 para 4(2); ITTOIA 2005, Sch 1 para 571*]. See also (iv) below as regards allowances on successions to trades.

(iv) *Successions.* Following a change in the persons carrying on the trade etc., such that the activity is treated for tax purposes as permanently discontinued, any asset transferred, without being sold, to the new owner for continuing use in the trade is treated as sold at market value on the date of change, although no initial allowance is available to the new owner. [*CAA 2001, ss 557, 559; CAA 1990, s 152(1)(2); ITTOIA 2005, Sch 1 para 572*].

For transfers under *ICTA 1988, s 343* (company reconstructions without a change in ownership) see 47.10 LOSSES. For transfers between companies in different EU member states *under CAA 2001, s 560*, see 11.11 CAPITAL GAINS, and between such companies on the formation of an SE by merger under *CAA 2001, s 561A*, see 11.13 CAPITAL GAINS.

10.23 'KNOW-HOW'

Expenditure incurred after 31 March 1986. Subject to what is said below regarding the INTANGIBLE ASSETS (39) regime, expenditure on acquiring 'know-how' (so far as not otherwise deductible for corporation tax purposes) gives rise to writing-down and balancing allowances (and balancing charges) where the company acquiring it either:

(i) is then carrying on a trade for use in which it is acquired; or

(ii) subsequently commences such a trade (in which case the expenditure is treated as incurred on commencement); or

(iii) acquires it with a trade (or part) in which it was used, and either the parties to the acquisition make the appropriate joint election under *ICTA 1988, s 531(3)(a)* or *ITTOIA 2005, s 194* (election for disposal of know-how on disposal of trade not to be treated as disposal of goodwill), or corporation tax equivalent, or the trade was carried on wholly outside the UK before the acquisition.

The same expenditure may not be taken into account in relation to more than one trade.

Expenditure is, however, *excluded* where the buyer and seller are bodies of persons (which includes partnerships) under common control.

[*CAA 2001, ss 452(1), 454, 455; ICTA 1988, ss 530(1)(7), 531(7); ITTOIA 2005, Sch 1 paras 207, 562, 563*].

Allowances are not available where know-how falls within the regime for intangible assets. See in particular the commencement and transitional rules for that regime at 39.37 INTANGIBLE ASSETS.

'*Know-how*' means any industrial information and techniques of assistance in (*a*) manufacturing or processing goods or materials, (*b*) working, or searching etc. for, mineral deposits, or (*c*) agricultural, forestry or fishing operations. [*CAA 2001, s 452(2)(3); ICTA 1988, s 533(7)*]. For expenditure on offshore divers' training courses treated as on know-how, see HMRC Capital Allowances Manual CA 74000.

All qualifying expenditure of a trade is pooled, and:

(1) if the 'available qualifying expenditure' exceeds the 'total disposal value', a writing-down allowance is available of **25%** of the excess, proportionately reduced or increased where the period is less or more than one year, or if the trade has been carried on for part only of a chargeable period (and subject to any lesser amount being

claimed), *except that* if the chargeable period is that of permanent discontinuance of the trade, a balancing allowance of **100%** of the excess is available;

(2) if the 'total disposal value' exceeds the 'available qualifying expenditure', a balancing charge arises of **100%** of the excess.

'*Available qualifying expenditure*' in a pool for a chargeable period consists of qualifying expenditure allocated to the pool for that period and any unrelieved qualifying expenditure brought forward in the pool from the previous chargeable period (usually referred to as the written-down value brought forward). In allocating qualifying expenditure to the pool, rules identical to those for patent rights at 10.50(i) and (ii) below must be observed.

The '*total disposal value*' is the aggregate of any disposal values to be brought into account for the period, i.e. the net sale proceeds (being capital sums) from any disposal of know-how on which qualifying expenditure was incurred (but excluding any sale the consideration for which is treated as a payment for goodwill under *ICTA 1988, s 531(2)* or *ITTOIA 2005, s 194(2)*. (The restriction to capital sale proceeds is introduced by *CAA 2001* (see 10.1 above) — see Change 55 in Annex 1 to the 2001 Capital Allowances Bill.)

The allowances and charges are given effect as deductions or receipts of the relevant trade.

[*CAA 2001, ss 456-463; ICTA 1988,s 530(2)-(5)(8); ITTOIA 2005, Sch 1 para 564*].

For receipts arising from sales of know-how, see also 66.62 TRADING INCOME.

Expenditure incurred before 1 April 1986. A *writing-down allowance* of one-sixth per annum of the expenditure incurred was available during the six years beginning with the chargeable period in whose

basis period the expenditure was incurred. A *balancing allowance* was given of the expenditure unallowed on the trade ceasing during that six years. [*ICTA 1988, s 530(6)-(8) prior to repeal*]. There were no provisions for a balancing charge.

Simon's Direct Tax Service. See B2.615 *et seq.*

10.24 **PLANT AND MACHINERY**

Proposed reforms. From 2008/09 the rate of writing-down allowances for plant and machinery in the general pool will be reduced from 25% to 20%, and the rate of writing-down allowances for long life assets will be increased from 6% to 10%.

The Government will consult on further changes, effective from 2008/09, to set the rate of writing-down allowances on certain fixtures at 10%, to introduce a payable tax credit for losses resulting from capital expenditure on 'green technologies' and to replace first-year allowances for small and medium-sized businesses from 2008/09 with an annual investment allowance of £50,000.

None of the proposed changes to capital allowances will apply to North Sea oil and gas ring fence activities.

Qualifying expenditure and activities. Allowances are available in respect of 'qualifying expenditure' incurred by a person carrying on a trade or other 'qualifying activity'. Subject to 10.25, 10.26 below and to other specific exclusions, expenditure is '*qualifying expenditure*' if it is 'capital expenditure' (see 10.2(ii) above) incurred on the provision of plant or machinery wholly or partly for the purposes of the qualifying activity carried on by that person, and as a result of which that person owns the plant or machinery (for which see the paragraph on 'Ownership' in 10.27 below). [*CAA 2001, s 11; CAA 1990, ss 22(1), 24(1)*]. See 10.30(C) below as regards partial use for other purposes. Provided these tests are met (but subject to specific restrictions — see, for example, 10.38(C) below), it is irrelevant whether or not the object of the person incurring the expenditure was, or included, the obtaining of capital allowances (see the CA judgment in *Barclays Mercantile Business Finance Ltd v Mawson HL 2004, [2005] STC 1*, a case involving complex 'finance leasing' arrangements). Expenditure incurred for the purposes of, and prior to the commencement of, a qualifying activity is treated as incurred on the first day on which the activity is carried on. [*CAA 2001, s 12; CAA 1990, s 83(2)*].

Any of the following is a '*qualifying activity*':

- (i) a trade, profession or vocation;
- (ii) an employment or office;
- (iii) a Schedule A business or overseas property business (see 56 PROPERTY INCOME);
- (iv) a furnished holiday lettings business (see 56.5 PROPERTY INCOME);
- (v) any of the concerns listed in *ICTA 1988, s 55(2)* (mines, quarries and sundry other undertakings) (not applicable before *CAA 2001* had effect, see 10.1 above, unless the concern qualified as a trade);
- (vi) managing the investments of a company with investment business (previously, broadly before 1 April 2004, the managing of an investment company) (see 42 INVESTMENT COMPANIES AND INVESTMENT BUSINESS);
- (vii) special leasing, i.e. the hiring out of plant or machinery otherwise than in the course of another qualifying activity (see 10.37 below);

but, for chargeable periods ending after 20 March 2000 (and other than for the purposes of 10.35 and 10.38(C) below), to the extent only that the profits therefrom are within the charge to UK tax (or would be if there *were* any profits).

[*CAA 2001, ss 15–18, 19(1), 20; CAA 1990, ss 27–29, 61(1), 83(2A), 161(2A); FA 1998, Sch 5 para 61; FA 2000, s 75(1)(6); ITEPA 2003, Sch 6 para 248; SI 2004 No 2310, Sch paras 52, 53; ITTOIA 2005, Sch 1 paras 526–529*].

As regards (iii) and (vii) above, expenditure in providing plant or machinery for use in a dwelling-house (or flat — see HMRC Capital Allowances Manual CA 20020, 20040) is not qualifying expenditure. Expenditure on plant and machinery partly for such use is apportioned as is just and reasonable. [*CAA 2001, s 35; CAA 1990, ss 28A(3)(4), 61(2); ITTOIA 2005, Sch 1 para 533*].

With minor exceptions, expenditure on plant or machinery used for providing business entertainment is excluded [*CAA 2001, s 269, Sch 2 para 51; ICTA 1988, s 577(1)(c)*]

Expenditure incurred on the provision of plant or machinery for long funding leasing is excluded from being qualifying expenditure (see 10.34 below). See 10.33 below as regards fixtures which become part of land or buildings.

Whether plant or machinery is acquired new or second-hand is generally irrelevant (but see 10.38(C) below as regards certain sales between connected persons etc.). A *share* in plant or machinery can qualify for allowances [*CAA 2001, s 270; CAA 1990, s 83(4)*].

Any still unrelieved expenditure incurred before 27 October 1970, and not brought within the then current rules by *FA 1976, s 39*, is outside the scheme of allowances described in this chapter. [*CAA 2001, Sch 3 para 55; CAA 1990, s 82(1)*]. A different scheme applies, for detailed coverage of which see the 1981/82 and earlier editions.

Simon's Direct Tax Service. See **B2.3**.

The main elements of the scheme of allowances are dealt with as follows.

10.25	Eligible expenditure	10.28	Pooling, writing-down allowances and balancing adjustments
10.26	Restrictions on eligible expenditure	10.29	Disposal events and values
10.27	First-year allowances	10.30	Exclusions from the main pool of qualifying expenditure (including certain

10.25 **Eligible expenditure.** The capital expenditure eligible for allowances includes that on alteration of existing buildings incidental to the installation of plant or machinery for the purposes of a trade or other qualifying activity [*CAA 2001, s 25; CAA 1990, s 66*] and on demolition of plant or machinery which it replaces [*CAA 2001, s 26(1)(2); CAA 1990, s 62(1)(a)(2)*]. Costs of moving plant from one site to another and re-erecting it, so far as not deductible in computing profits, qualify for allowances (HMRC Capital Allowances Manual CA 21190). Capital expenditure on animals and other living creatures kept for the purposes of farming or any other trade, or on shares in such animals etc., is excluded. [*CAA 2001, s 38; CAA 1990, s 82(2); ITTOIA 2005, Sch 1 para 534*].

Meaning of plant or machinery: leading cases. Plant and *machinery* are not statutorily defined. *Machinery* is accordingly given its ordinary meaning, but *plant* has been considered in many cases. It includes apparatus kept for permanent employment in the trade etc., but a line is drawn between that which performs a function in the business operations (which may be plant) and that which provides the place or setting in which these operations are performed (which is not). See *Cole Bros Ltd v Phillips HL 1982, 55 TC 188* (electric wiring and fittings in department store held not to be plant) and *St. John's School v Ward CA 1974, 49 TC 524* (prefabricated school buildings held not to be plant) and contrast *CIR v Barclay, Curle & Co Ltd HL 1969, 45 TC 221* (dry docks, including cost of excavation, held to be plant) and *CIR v Scottish & Newcastle Breweries Ltd HL 1982, 55 TC 252* (lighting and decor of licensed premises held to be plant). If an item used for carrying on a business does not form part of the premises and is not stock-in-trade, then it is plant (*Wimpy International Ltd v Warland CA 1988, 61 TC 51*).

Permanent employment demands some degree of durability, see *Hinton v Maden & Ireland Ltd HL 1959, 38 TC 391* (shoe manufacturer's knives and lasts, average life three years, held to be plant). In practice, a life of two years or more is sufficient, and this applies equally as regards animals functioning as apparatus with which a trade is carried on (see HMRC Capital Allowances Manual CA 21100, 21220).

Held to rank as plant. Movable office partitions (*Jarrold v John Good & Sons Ltd CA 1962, 40 TC 681*); mezzanine platforms installed in a warehouse (but not ancillary lighting) (*Hunt v Henry Quick Ltd Ch D 1992, 65 TC 108*); swimming pools for use on caravan site (*Cooke v Beach Station Caravans Ltd Ch D 1974, 49 TC 514*); grain silos (*Schofield v R & H Hall Ltd CA(NI) 1974, 49 TC 538*); barrister's books (*Munby v Furlong CA 1977, 50 TC 491*); Building Society window screens (*Leeds Permanent Building Society v Proctor Ch D 1982, 56 TC 293*); light fittings (*Wimpy International Ltd v Warland CA 1988, 61 TC 51*); synthetic grass football pitch (*CIR v Anchor International Ltd CS, 2004 STC 411*).

Film production and acquisition expenditure incurred by a person carrying on a trade is treated for tax purposes as revenue expenditure. In relation to certified films (broadly, British or European films), an election may be made to disapply this rule (and effectively to treat the expenditure as capital expenditure on plant) where the master version is expected to realise its value over a period of two years or more. See *Ensign Tankers (Leasing) Ltd v Stokes HL 1992, 64 TC 617* for relief to investor in film production partnership.

Held not to be plant. Stallions (*Earl of Derby v Aylmer KB 1915, 6 TC 665*); wallpaper pattern books (*Rose & Co Ltd v Campbell Ch D 1967, 44 TC 500*); canopy over petrol-filling station (*Dixon v Fitch's Garage Ltd Ch D 1975, 50 TC 509*); ship used as floating restaurant (*Benson v Yard Arm Club Ltd CA 1979, 53 TC 67*); false ceilings (*Hampton v Fortes Autogrill Ltd Ch D 1979, 53 TC 691*); a football stand (*Brown v Burnley Football Co Ltd Ch D 1980, 53 TC 357*); an inflatable tennis court cover (*Thomas v Reynolds Ch D 1987, 59 TC 502*); shop fronts, wall and floor coverings, suspended floors, ceilings and stairs etc. (*Wimpy International Ltd v Warland, Associated Restaurants Ltd v Warland CA 1988, 61 TC 51*); permanent quarantine kennels (allowances having been granted for movable kennels) (*Carr v Sayer Ch D 1992, 65 TC 15*); lighting ancillary to mezzanine platform installation qualifying as plant (*Hunt v Henry Quick Ltd Ch D 1992, 65 TC 108*); a planteria (a form of glasshouse, see also below) (*Gray v Seymours Garden Centre (Horticulture) CA 1995, 67 TC 401*); access site and wash hall containing car wash equipment (*Attwood v Anduff Car Wash Ltd CA 1997, 69 TC 575*); housing for underground electricity sub-station (*Bradley v London Electricity plc Ch D 1996, 70 TC 155*); golf putting greens (*Family Golf Centres Ltd v Thorne (Sp C 150), [1998] SSCD 106*); an all-weather horse racing track (*Lingfield Park 1991 Ltd v Shove CA, 2004 76 TC 363*).

In *McVeigh v Arthur Sanderson & Sons Ltd Ch D 1968, 45 TC 273*, held that cost of blocks etc. of a wallpaper manufacturer (admitted to be plant) should include something for the designs but the designs, following *Daphne v Shaw KB 1926, 11 TC 256*, were not plant. (*Daphne v Shaw* has since been overruled by *Munby v Furlong* above.)

Interest etc. on money borrowed to finance purchases of plant and charged to capital, held not eligible for capital allowances (*Ben-Odeco Ltd v Powlson HL 1978, 52 TC 459* and cf *Van Arkadie v Sterling Coated Materials Ltd Ch D 1982, 56 TC 479*). It is understood that the Revenue consider this exclusion to apply also to architects' fees and preliminary expenses on plant included in building works (Tolley's Practical Tax 1983 p 28, and see also ICAEW TAXline March 1993, para 40).

Lighting. The extent to which lighting and lighting systems may qualify as plant, i.e. as part of the business apparatus as opposed to the setting, is discussed on the HMRC website at www.hmrc.gov.uk/capital_allowances/eca-guidance.htm#lightingappendix. An office lighting system incorporating anti-glare lighting throughout to enable effective use of personal computers may be plant, for example.

Cable television. The cost of provision and installation of ducting in connection with construction of cable television networks is regarded as expenditure on plant or machinery (Revenue Press Release 15 March 1984).

Glasshouses are likely to be accepted as plant only where, during construction, sophisticated environmental control systems are permanently installed, incorporating e.g. a computer system controlling heating, temperature and humidity control, automatic ventilation systems and automatic thermal or shade screens (Revenue Tax Bulletins November 1992 p 46, June 1998 p 552). See, for example, *Gray v Seymours Garden Centre (Horticulture) CA, 67 TC 401*, where a 'planteria' was held to be premises. See also 10.26 below and, as regards whether glasshouses are 'long-life assets', 10.30(G) below.

See generally HMRC Capital Allowances Manual CA 21000 *et seq.*

Certain expenditure on buildings, as below, is treated for capital allowance purposes as being on plant and machinery (unless tax relief could otherwise be obtained). On any disposal, the disposal value (see 10.29 below) in respect of expenditure within (i)–(iii) below is taken as nil [*CAA 2001, s 63(5); CAA 1990, ss 67(1), 69(1), 70(1)*].

(i) *Fire safety expenditure* incurred in a trade or other qualifying activity in taking steps specified in a notice under *Fire Precautions Act 1971, s 5(4)* (or which might have been so specified but were in fact specified in a document from the fire authority on application for a fire certificate under that *Act*) and similarly for expenditure incurred in order to avoid restriction of use of premises by a prohibition notice under *section 10* of that *Act*. [*CAA 2001, ss 27, 29; CAA 1990, s 69*]. Applies to Northern Ireland by concession (HMRCExtra Statutory Concession B16 as revised). Applies by Order to hotels and boarding houses (*SI 1972 No 238*) and to premises of factories, offices, shops and railways with minimum of 10 employees (*SI 1976 No 2009*). *Lessors of such premises* may claim allowances on contributions (see 10.2(vi) above) towards tenants' qualifying expenditure or own similar direct expenditure (HMRC Extra Statutory Concession B16 as revised).

(ii) Expenditure on *thermal insulation of existing industrial building* by a person occupying the building for the purposes of a trade carried on by him or letting the building in the course of a UK property business or overseas property business.

[*CAA 2001, ss 27, 28; ICTA 1988, s 32(1B)(1C); CAA 1990, s 67; FA 1998, s 38, Sch 5 para 56; FA 2001, s 69, Sch 21 para 1; ITTOIA 2005, Sch 1 para 531*].

(iii) *Sports ground expenditure* incurred by a person carrying on a trade or other qualifying activity to comply with a safety certificate issued or to be issued under the *Safety of Sports Grounds Act 1975* or certified by local authority as falling within requirements if such certificates had been (or could have been) applied for. Also, expenditure incurred by a trade in respect of a 'regulated stand' (as defined by the *Fire Safety and Safety of Places of Sport Act 1987*) to comply with a safety certificate (as defined by that *Act*) issued for the stand or to take steps specified by the local authority as being necessary under the terms, or proposed terms, of such a safety certificate issued, or to be issued, by it. [*CAA 2001, ss 27, 30–32; CAA 1990, s 70*]. See also 10.2(v)(vi) above as regards certain contributions to expenditure.

(iv) *Hotels and restaurants.* HMRC regard as eligible for capital allowances expenditure on *apparatus* to provide electric light or power, hot water, central heating, ventilation or air conditioning, alarm and sprinkler systems. Also on cost of hot water pipes, baths, wash basins etc. Also expenditure on alterations to *existing* buildings which is incidental to the installation of plant and machinery. (CCAB Statement, 9 August 1977.) See now *Cole Bros Ltd v Phillips HL 1982, 55 TC 188* and *CIR v Scottish & Newcastle Breweries Ltd HL 1982, 55 TC 252.*

See 10.26 below for provisions restricting allowances for certain expenditure on buildings and structures.

Where it appears that any sums, not otherwise taxable, are to be payable, directly or indirectly, to the owner of plant or machinery in respect of, or to take account of, the *whole* of the **depreciation** of that plant or machinery, the expenditure incurred in providing that plant or machinery for the purposes of the qualifying activity is not qualifying expenditure. [*CAA 2001, s 37; CAA 1990, s 80(1)*]. As regards subsidies towards *partial* depreciation, see 10.38(J) below.

Computer software. Subject to the application of the INTANGIBLE ASSETS (39) regime, where capital expenditure is incurred after 9 March 1992 on the acquisition of computer software for the purposes of a trade or other qualifying activity, the software, if it would not otherwise be plant, is treated as such for capital allowances purposes. Similarly, where capital expenditure is incurred after that date in acquiring for such purposes a right to use or otherwise deal with computer software, both the right and the software are treated as plant provided for the purposes of the qualifying activity and (so long as entitlement to the right continues) as belonging to the person incurring the expenditure.

Where, after 9 March 1992, a right is granted to another person to use or deal with the whole or part of software or rights which are treated as plant, and the consideration for the grant consists of (or would if it were in money consist of) a capital sum, a disposal value (see 10.29 below) has to be brought into account (unless the software or rights have previously begun to be used wholly or partly for purposes other than those of the qualifying activity, or the activity for which they were used has been permanently discontinued). The amount of the disposal value to be brought into account is the net consideration in money received for the grant, plus any insurance moneys or other capital compensation received in respect of the software by reason of any event affecting that consideration. However, market value is substituted where the consideration for the grant was not, or not wholly, in money, or where:

- no consideration, or money consideration less than market value, was given for the grant;
- there is no charge under *ITEPA 2003* (i.e. on employment, pension or social security income); and
- the grantee cannot obtain plant and machinery or research and development (formerly scientific research) allowances for his expenditure or is a dual resident investing company connected with the grantor.

Where a disposal value falls to be calculated in relation to software or rights, then for the purpose of determining whether it is to be limited by reference to the capital expenditure incurred (see 10.29 below), that disposal value is increased by any disposal value previously falling to be brought into account as above in respect of the same person and the same plant.

[*CAA 2001, ss 71–73, Sch 3 para 18; CAA 1990, s 24(6A), s 26(1)(ea)(eb)(ec)(2AA), s 67A; F(No 2)A 1992, s 68; ITEPA 2003, Sch 6 para 251*].

See also 39.3 INTANGIBLE ASSETS for the extent to which computer software may be included in that regime (and hence excluded from the above provisions).

Enterprise zones. Expenditure on plant or machinery which is to be an integral part of an industrial or commercial building in an enterprise zone may qualify for 100% industrial buildings allowance. See 10.19 above.

Simon's Direct Tax Service. See **B2.305** *et seq.*

10.26 **Restrictions on eligible expenditure.** For expenditure incurred after 29 November 1993 (subject to transitional provisions, see below), legislation was introduced by *FA 1994, s 117* (see now *CAA 2001, ss 21–24*) to exclude certain expenditure from the definition of plant and machinery for capital allowances purposes. Assets which have been held to be plant under specific court decisions continue to qualify for plant and machinery allowances, and assets not covered by the *FA 1994* provisions remain subject to prevailing case law on plant. (Revenue Press Release 17 December 1993).

Transitional provisions. Expenditure was not affected by the above-mentioned provisions where it was incurred before 6 April 1996 in pursuance of a contract entered into either before 30 November 1993 or for the purposes of securing compliance with obligations under a contract entered into before that date. [*FA 1994, s 117(2)*].

General exceptions. Expenditure falling within any of *CAA 2001, ss 28–33, 71* and *F(No 2)A 1992, s 40D* or earlier equivalents (relating to thermal insulation, fire safety, safety of sports grounds, security assets, computer software, and films and sound recordings — see 10.25 above) is not affected by the provisions described below. [*CAA 2001, s 23(1)(2); CAA 1990, Sch AA1 para 4; FA 1994, s 117(1); ITTOIA 2005, Sch 1 para 530*].

Expenditure on buildings which does not qualify for allowances. Expenditure on the construction or acquisition of a building will not qualify for plant and machinery allowances where it is incurred after 29 November 1993 (subject to the above transitional provisions and general exceptions and to the specific exceptions listed at (1)–(33) below). For these purposes the expression 'building' includes:

- any assets incorporated in the building;
- any assets which, although not incorporated in the building (because they are movable or for some other reason), are nevertheless of a kind which are normally incorporated into buildings; and

- any of the following:
  - (i) walls, floors, ceilings, doors, gates, shutters, windows and stairs;
  - (ii) mains services, and systems, of water, electricity and gas;
  - (iii) waste disposal systems;
  - (iv) sewerage and drainage systems;
  - (v) shafts or other structures in which lifts, hoists, escalators and moving walkways are installed; and
  - (vi) fire safety systems.

[*CAA 2001, s 21; CAA 1990, Sch AA1 para 1*(*1*)(*2*)(*4*), *para 5*(*1*)*; FA 1994, s 117*(*1*)].

Expenditure on structures which does not qualify for allowances. 'Structure' means a fixed structure of any kind, other than a building. A structure is 'any substantial man-made asset' (see Revenue Press Release 17 December 1993).

Expenditure on the construction or acquisition of a structure or any other asset listed immediately below, or on any works involving the alteration of land, will not qualify for plant and machinery allowances where it is incurred after 29 November 1993 (subject to the above transitional provisions and general exceptions and to the specific exceptions listed at (1)–(33) below).

- A tunnel, bridge, viaduct, aqueduct, embankment or cutting.
- A way, hard standing (such as a pavement), road, railway, tramway, a park for vehicles or containers, or an airstrip or runway.
- An inland navigation, including a canal or basin or a navigable river.
- A dam, reservoir or barrage (including any sluices, gates, generators and other equipment associated with it).
- A dock, harbour, wharf, pier, marina or jetty, or any other structure in or at which vessels may be kept or merchandise or passengers may be shipped or unshipped.
- A dike, sea wall, weir or drainage ditch.
- Any structure not included above, except
  - (i) a structure (other than a building) within the definition of an 'industrial building' (see 10.11 above),
  - (ii) a structure in use for the purposes of a gas undertaking, or
  - (iii) a structure in use for the purposes of a trade consisting in the provision of telecommunications, television or radio services,

  and see *CIR v Anchor International Ltd CS 2004, [2005] STC 411*, in which a synthetic football pitch was held not to be within this exclusion.

[*CAA 2001, s 22, Sch 3 para 13; CAA 1990, Sch AA1 para 2*(*1*)(*2*)(*4*), *para 5*(*1*)*; FA 1994, s 117*(*1*)].

Specific exceptions. The above exclusions do not affect the question as to whether expenditure on any of the items listed in (1)–(33) below qualifies for plant and machinery allowances. Note that items (1)–(16) below do not include any asset whose principal purpose is to insulate or enclose the interior of a building or to provide an interior wall, floor or ceiling which (in each case) is intended to remain permanently in place.

(1) Any machinery (including devices for providing motive power) not within any other item in this list.

(2) Electrical systems (including lighting systems) and cold water, gas and sewerage systems provided mainly to meet the particular requirements of the qualifying activity, or provided mainly to serve particular plant or machinery used for the purposes thereof.

(3) Space or water heating systems; powered systems of ventilation, air cooling or air purification; and any ceiling or floor comprised in such systems.

(4) Manufacturing or processing equipment; storage equipment, including cold rooms; display equipment; and counters, checkouts and similar equipment.

(5) Cookers, washing machines, dishwashers, refrigerators and similar equipment; washbasins, sinks, baths, showers, sanitary ware and similar equipment; and furniture and furnishings.

(6) Lifts, hoists, escalators and moving walkways.

(7) Sound insulation provided mainly to meet the particular requirements of the qualifying activity.

(8) Computer, telecommunication and surveillance systems (including their wiring or other links).

(9) Refrigeration or cooling equipment.

(10) Fire alarm systems; sprinkler and other equipment for extinguishing or containing fires.

(11) Burglar alarm systems.

(12) Strong rooms in bank or building society premises; safes.

(13) Partition walls, where movable and intended to be moved in the course of the qualifying activity.

(14) Decorative assets provided for the enjoyment of the public in hotel, restaurant or similar trades.

(15) Advertising hoardings; signs, displays and similar assets.

(16) Swimming pools (including diving boards, slides and structures on which such boards or slides are mounted).

(17) Any glasshouse constructed so that the required environment (namely, air, heat, light, irrigation and temperature) for the growing of plants is provided automatically by means of devices forming an integral part of its structure; see also below.

(18) Cold stores.

(19) Caravans provided mainly for holiday lettings. (Under *CAA 2001, s 23(5)*, 'caravan' includes, in relation to a holiday caravan site, anything treated as such for the purposes of the *Caravan Sites and Control of Development Act 1960* (or Northern Ireland equivalent). Before *CAA 2001* had effect (see 10.1 above) the definition in *section 29(1)* of the fore-mentioned 1960 Act was adopted by concession, see HMRC Extra-Statutory Concession B50.)

(20) Buildings provided for testing aircraft engines run within the building.

(21) Movable buildings intended to be moved in the course of the qualifying activity.

(22) The alteration of land for the purpose only of installing plant or machinery.

(23) The provision of dry docks.

(24) The provision of any jetty or similar structure provided mainly to carry plant or machinery.

(25) The provision of pipelines, or underground ducts or tunnels with a primary purpose of carrying utility conduits.

(26) The provision of towers provided to support floodlights.

(27) The provision of any reservoir incorporated into a water treatment works or any service reservoir of treated water for supply within any housing estate or other particular locality.

(28) The provision of silos provided for temporary storage; or storage tanks.

(29) The provision of slurry pits or silage clamps.

(30) The provision of fish tanks or fish ponds.

(31) The provision of rails, sleepers and ballast for a railway or tramway.

(32) The provision of structures and other assets for providing the setting for any ride at an amusement park or exhibition.

(33) The provision of fixed zoo cages.

Before *CAA 2001* had effect (see 10.1 above), these rules operated slightly more restrictively in that the exceptions at (18)–(21) above applied only in relation to buildings, and certain of the other exceptions applied only in relation to structures (see the 2000/01 and earlier editions).

As regards expenditure on *glasshouses* (item 17 above), see 10.25 above for HMRC approach to allowances for such expenditure, and 10.30(G) below as regards whether glasshouses are 'long-life assets'.

[*CAA 2001, s 23(3)–(5); CAA 1990, Sch AA1 para 1(3)(4), para 2(3)(4), para 5(1)(2)); FA 1994, s 117*].

Interests in land. Expenditure on the provision of plant or machinery does not include expenditure incurred after 29 November 1993 (subject to the above transitional provisions) on the acquisition of an interest in land, but this restriction does not apply to any asset which is so installed or otherwise fixed in or to any description of land as to become, in law, part of that land. 'Land' does not include buildings or other structures but is otherwise as defined in *Interpretation Act 1978, Sch 1*. 'Interest in land' for these purposes has the same meaning as in *CAA 2001, s 175* (allowances for fixtures — see 10.33 below). [*CAA 2001, s 24; CAA 1990, Sch AA1 paras 3, 5; FA 1994, s 117(1)*].

Simon's Direct Tax Service. See B2.308.

10.27 **First-year allowances.** A person is entitled to a first-year allowance (FYA) for a chargeable period (see 10.2(i) above) in respect of any 'first-year qualifying expenditure' which he incurs in that period on plant and machinery which he owns (see below under *Ownership*) at some time during that period. He may claim the allowance in respect of the whole or a part of the first-year qualifying expenditure. In determining for these purposes the time at which expenditure is incurred, *CAA 2001, s 12* (pre-commencement expenditure — see 10.24 above) is disregarded. Otherwise, see 10.2(iii) above as regards the date on which expenditure is treated as having been incurred.

Subject to the exclusions below, qualifying expenditure (as in 10.24 above) is '*first-year qualifying expenditure*' if it is incurred:

(*a*) **after 1 July 1997** by a **'small or medium-sized enterprise'**, in which case the maximum FYA is as follows:

(i) except where (ii) below applies, **40%** (of the amount of the expenditure) for expenditure incurred **after 1 July 1998** (but long-life assets are excluded);

(ii) in the case of a **'small enterprise'** only (as distinct from a 'small or medium-sized enterprise') **50%** for expenditure incurred in the 24 months beginning 1 April 2006 and previously in the twelve months beginning 1 April 2004 (but long-life assets remain excluded); and

(iii) **50%** for expenditure incurred **before 2 July 1998** (**12%** in the case of long-life assets — see 10.30(G) below); or

(*b*) **after 31 March 2000 and before 1 April 2004** by a **'small enterprise'** (as distinct from a 'small or medium-sized enterprise') on **'information and communications technology'**, in which case the maximum FYA is **100%**; or

(*c*) **after 11 May 1998 and before 12 May 2002** by a **'small or medium-sized enterprise'** on the provision of plant and machinery for use primarily in **Northern Ireland**, in which case the maximum FYA is **100%**; or

(*d*) **after 31 March 2001** by any person on **'energy-saving plant or machinery'** which is unused and not second-hand, in which case the maximum FYA is **100%** (available for income tax periods of account ending after 5 April 2001); or

(*e*) **after 16 April 2002 and before 1 April 2008** by any person on cars first registered after 16 April 2002 which are either **'electrically-propelled'** or have **'low carbon dioxide emissions'**, and which are unused and not second-hand, in which case the maximum FYA is **100%**; or

(*f*) **after 16 April 2002 and before 1 April 2008** by any person on plant or machinery, unused and not second-hand, installed at a **'gas refuelling station'** for use solely for or in connection with refuelling vehicles with natural gas or hydrogen fuel, in which case the maximum FYA is **100%**; or

(*g*) **after 16 April 2002** by a company on plant or machinery for use wholly for the purposes of a **'ring fence trade'** within *ICTA 1988, s 501A* (petroleum extraction activities), in which case the maximum FYA is **100%** (reduced to **24%** where the plant etc. is a long-life asset, see 10.30(G) below); (the relief is, however, withdrawn where the plant etc. is used for less than five years in such a trade, see *CAA 2001, s 45G; FA 2002, Sch 21 para 4*); or

(*h*) **after 31 March 2003** by any person on **'environmentally beneficial plant or machinery'**, unused and not second-hand, in which case the maximum FYA is **100%** (but long-life asset expenditure, see 10.30(G) below, does not qualify).

Exclusions. FYAs are not available under *any* of (*a*)–(*h*) above in the circumstances listed below (and note also the exclusion of long-life assets from (*a*)(i) and (*a*)(ii) above and from (*h*) above).

(i) The expenditure is incurred in the chargeable period in which the qualifying activity is permanently discontinued.

(ii) The expenditure is incurred on the provision of a '*car*', defined for these purposes (by *CAA 2001, s 81*) as a mechanically propelled road vehicle which is neither (1) of a construction primarily suited for the conveyance of goods or burden of any description nor (2) of a type not commonly used as a private vehicle and unsuitable for such use; a 'car' thus includes a motor cycle.

As regards (2), see employee benefits case of *Gurney v Richards Ch D 1989, 62 TC 287* (fire brigade car equipped with flashing light held within excluded class), decided on similarly worded legislation. See also *Bourne v Auto School of Motoring Ch D 1964, 42 TC 217* (driving school cars) and *Roberts v Granada TV Rental Ltd Ch D 1970, 46 TC 295* (mini-vans etc.).

This exclusion does *not* apply as regards (*e*) above, in relation to which the above definition of 'car' applies but with the specific inclusion of any mechanically-propelled road vehicle of a type commonly used as a hackney carriage, and the specific exclusion of motorcycles.

(iii) The expenditure is on a ship or railway asset of a kind excluded from being a long-life asset (see 10.30(G)(iii)(iv) below).

(iv) The plant or machinery would be a long-life asset but for the transitional provisions of *CAA 2001, Sch 3 para 20* (see 10.30(G) below).

(v) The expenditure is on plant or machinery for leasing (whether or not in the course of a trade). For this purpose, 'leasing' expressly includes the letting of a ship on charter or of any other asset on hire. This exclusion does *not* apply as regards expenditure incurred after 16 April 2002 and before 1 April 2006 within (*d*), (*e*) or (*f*) above or expenditure before 1 April 2006 within (*h*) above. The exclusion continues not to apply as regards expenditure incurred on or after 1 April 2006 within (*d*), (*e*) or (*h*) above, but, in the case of (*d*) and (*h*), only if the plant or machinery is leased under an 'excluded lease of background plant or machinery for a building' (see 10.34(1)(B) below). To summarise, expenditure on or after 1 April 2006 on plant or machinery for leasing does not qualify for FYAs unless it is within (*e*) above or is on background plant or machinery and within (*d*) or (*h*) above.

Expenditure by a company on plant and machinery to be used by its subsidiary in return for an annual charge fell within the exclusion (*M F Freeman (Plant) Ltd v Jowett (Sp C 376), [2003] SSCD 423*).

In an article published initially on their website and subsequently in their Tax Bulletin, HMRC announced a change of view concerning the supply by a business of plant or machinery with an operator. Where the equipment is to be operated solely by the operator thus provided, HMRC now accept that this is the provision of a service and not merely plant hire. FYAs are not excluded in such a case. Previously, this applied only where overall supervision and control rested with the operator and not, as is usual, with the hirer; the change of view cannot be used to reopen closed periods. They also now accept that the provision of building access services by the scaffolding industry (but not simply the supply of scaffolding poles etc. for use by others) is the provision of a service. (Revenue Internet Statement 2 June 2003; HMRC Capital Allowances Manual CA 23115).

(vi) The provision of the plant or machinery is connected with a change in the nature or conduct of a trade or business carried on by a person other than the person incurring the expenditure on its provision, and the obtaining of an FYA was the main benefit, or one of the main benefits, which could reasonably be expected to arise from the making of the change.

(vii) The provision of the plant of machinery is by way of gift (see 10.38(D) below).

(viii) The plant or machinery was previously used by the owner for purposes other than those of the qualifying activity (see 10.38(E) below), which includes the purposes of long funding leasing (see 10.34 below).

(ix) The plant or machinery is acquired by means of a transaction with a connected person (within *ICTA 1988, s 839* — see 19 CONNECTED PERSONS), or a sale and leaseback (or sale and finance leaseback) transaction, or a transaction the sole or main benefit of which would be the obtaining of a plant and machinery allowance (see *CAA 2001, ss 217, 223, 232; CAA 1990, ss 75, 76(1), 76A(1); F(No 2)A 1997, s 46(2)(3)* and note the definition of 'finance lease' at 10.38(C) below).

Also excluded from (*b*) above (expenditure on information and communications technology) is expenditure incurred after 25 March 2003 on software (including software rights) if the person incurring the expenditure does so with a view to granting to another person a right to use or otherwise deal with any of the software in question. This is intended to exclude the *sub-licensing* of software rights; *leasing* activities were already excluded by virtue of (v) above.

Also excluded from (*c*) above (expenditure for Northern Ireland purposes) is expenditure on long-life assets (see 10.30(G) below), on aircraft or hovercraft or on goods vehicles for use in a trade consisting primarily of the conveyance of goods, and unauthorised expenditure on plant or machinery for use primarily in agriculture, fishing or fish farming or in any transportation, storage, preparation, processing or packaging activities carried out in bringing any agricultural produce, fish or fish product to market. Expenditure is unauthorised for this purpose unless it is authorised by the Department of Agriculture and Rural Development in Northern Ireland, and provision is made for the necessary exchange of information between HMRC and that Department. Expenditure is also excluded where, when it is incurred, the person incurring it intends the plant or machinery to be used partly outside Northern Ireland, and there are arrangements (of which the transaction under which the expenditure is incurred forms part) from which the main benefit, or one of the main benefits, which could reasonably be expected is the obtaining of an FYA (or greater FYA) in respect of so much of the expenditure as is attributable (on a just and reasonable basis) to the intended use outside NI. There are also provisions for the withdrawal of FYAs if, within two years of the expenditure being incurred (five years where the expenditure concerned exceeds £3.5 million), and at a time when the plant or machinery belongs to the person who incurred it (or a connected person), the primary use to which it is put is a use outside Northern Ireland, or it is held for use otherwise than primarily in NI. Any person whose return is rendered incorrect by such a change of use must (subject to penalty) amend the return within three months of becoming aware that it has become incorrect.

Definitions. '*Small or medium-sized enterprise*' is defined for the purposes of (*a*) and (*c*) above by reference to the *Companies Act 1985, s 247* (or Northern Ireland equivalent) definition of 'small or medium-sized company'. Broadly, the requirement is that two of the following three conditions are fulfilled: that the turnover not exceed £22.8 million; that the assets not exceed £11.4 million; and that there be not more than 250 employees. (For accounting periods ended before 30 January 2004, the two monetary thresholds were £11.2 million and £5.6 million respectively — there is provision to prevent the benefit of the increased limits being brought forward by a change of accounting date — see HMRC Press Release 30 January 2004 and *SI 2004 No 16*.) If an enterprise which previously qualified fails to satisfy this requirement over two consecutive financial years, it will cease to qualify with effect from the second of those years, and an enterprise which did not previously qualify but which satisfies the requirement over two consecutive financial years will qualify with effect from the second of those years. In the case of a company which is a member of a group of companies, the requirements apply to the group as a whole. For expenditure incurred after 11 May 1998 (but not for the purposes of the allowances available for expenditure incurred before 2 July 1998, or for the purposes of those available for expenditure incurred thereafter where the contract was entered into before 12 May 1998), the group which has to be considered in this context includes any international group of which the company is a member.

'*Small enterprise*' is similarly defined for the purposes of (*a*)(ii) and (*b*) above, but by reference to the *Companies Act 1985* definition of 'small company', i.e. where two of the following three conditions are fulfilled: that the turnover does not exceed £5.6 million; that the assets are not more than £2.8 million; and that there be not more than 50 employees. (For accounting periods ended before 30 January 2004, the two monetary thresholds were £2.8 million and £1.4 million respectively — there is provision to prevent the benefit of the increased limits being brought forward by a change of accounting date — see Revenue Press Release 30 January 2004 and *SI 2004 No 16*.)

'*Information and communications technology*' is divided for the purposes of (*b*) above into three classes: computers and associated equipment (but excluding computerised control or management systems or other systems that are part of a larger system whose principal function is not processing or storing information); other qualifying equipment (i.e. WAP and third generation mobile telephones and data network reception and transmission devices for use with television sets, and similar devices capable of receiving and transmitting information from and to data networks); and software (i.e. the right to use or otherwise deal with software for the purposes of equipment within the first two classes). The class of 'other qualifying equipment' may be further defined or added to by Treasury order.

'*Energy-saving plant or machinery*', for the purposes of (*d*) above, is plant or machinery which, either at the time the expenditure is incurred or at the time the contract for its provision is entered into, is of a description specified by Treasury order *and* meets the energy-saving criteria specified by Treasury order for plant or machinery of that description. Expenditure incurred, or incurred under a contract entered into, after 31 March 2001 but before 16 July 2001 (the date of making of the first Treasury order) qualifies if it would have done so had that order already been made when the expenditure was incurred. A Treasury order may identify qualifying plant or machinery by reference to lists of technology or products issued by the relevant Secretary of State; the first order refers to the Energy Technology Product List (ETPL) initially published on 1 April 2001 (and available at www.eca.gov.uk). An order may also provide that, in specified cases, no FYA is to be given under (*d*) above unless a '*relevant certificate of energy efficiency*' is in force, i.e. a certificate issued by the Secretary of State, the Scottish Ministers, the Welsh Assembly or the relevant Northern Ireland department, or by persons authorised by them, to the effect that a particular item, or an item constructed to a particular design, meets the relevant energy-saving criteria. The first order so specifies certain combined heat and power equipment. With effect after 4 August 2003, component based fixed systems falling within the technology class 'automatic monitoring and targeting equipment' (see below) were also specified. If a certificate is revoked, it is treated as having never been in issue, with the result that FYAs under (*d*) above will not have been available. Subject to penalty under *TMA 1970, s 98* for non-compliance, a person who has consequently made an incorrect tax return must give notice to HMRC, specifying the amendment required to the return, within three months of his becoming aware of the problem. Technology classes initially included in the ETPL, subject to the appropriate criteria, certification or product approval, were boilers, combined heat and power, lighting, motors and drives, pipework insulation, refrigeration and thermal screens. The following classes have since been added:

- (with effect after 4 August 2002) heat pumps for space heating, radiant and warm air heaters, compressed air equipment and solar thermal systems;
- (with effect after 4 August 2003) automatic monitoring and targeting equipment; and
- (with effect after 25 August 2004) air-to-air energy recovery equipment, compact heat exchangers and heating, ventilation and air conditioning zone controls.

With effect after 21 September 2005 the qualifying criteria for some of the qualifying technologies were updated and clarified, including heat pumps, certain types of boilers, refrigeration controls and single speed motors. Claim values have also been added for air-to-air energy recovery equipment, heating, ventilation and air condition controls, and warm air and radiant heating. With effect from 7 September 2006, thermal screens and electronic drain traps are removed from the list.

If one or more components of an item of plant and machinery qualify under these provisions, but the whole item does not, normal apportionment rules are disapplied, and instead the first-year qualifying expenditure under (*d*) above is limited to the amount (or aggregate amount) specified in the ETPL for that component (or those components); where relevant, each *instalment* of expenditure falls to be apportioned in the same way as the whole. See generally the detailed guidance Notes on the HMRC website (at www.hmrc.gov.uk/capital_allowances/eca-guidance.htm).

For the purposes of (*e*) above, a car has '*low carbon dioxide emissions*' if it is first registered on the basis of an EC certificate of conformity, or a UK approval certificate, which specifies a carbon dioxide emissions figure of 120g/km or less (a combined figure not exceeding that limit where more than one figure is specified). In the case of a bi-fuel car (whether petrol/road fuel gas or diesel/road fuel gas), the limit applies by reference to the lowest figure specified by the certificate (the lowest combined figure where more than one figure is specified for each fuel). The 120g/km limit is variable by Treasury order. A car is '*electrically-propelled*' if is propelled solely by electrical power derived from an external source or from a storage battery not connected to any source of power when the car is in motion. See also HMRC Capital Allowances Manual CA 23153.

For the purposes of (*f*) above, a '*gas refuelling station*' is any premises (or part) where mechanically-propelled road vehicles are refuelled with natural gas or hydrogen fuel. Plant or machinery installed for use solely for or in connection with such refuelling includes any storage tank for such fuels, any compressor, pump, control or meter used in the refuelling and any equipment for dispensing such fuels to vehicles' fuel tanks.

'*Environmentally beneficial plant or machinery*', for the purposes of (*h*) above, is plant or machinery which, either at the time the expenditure is incurred or at the time the contract for its provision is entered into, is of a description specified by Treasury order *and* meets the environmental criteria specified by Treasury order for plant or machinery of that description. A Treasury order may identify qualifying plant or machinery by reference to technology lists or product lists issued by the relevant Secretary of State. The intention is to promote the use of technologies, or products, designed to remedy or prevent damage to the physical environment or natural resources (Revenue Press Release BN 26, 9 April 2003); the first order refers to the Water Technology Product List (WTPL) initially published in April 2003 (and available at www.eca-water.gov.uk). Expenditure incurred, or incurred under a contract entered into, after 31 March 2003 but before 11 August 2003 (the date of making of the first Treasury order) qualifies if it would have done so had that order already been made when the expenditure was incurred or the contract entered into.

An order may provide that, in specified cases, no FYA is to be given under (*h*) above unless a '*relevant certificate of environmental benefit*' is in force, i.e. a certificate issued by the Secretary of State, the Scottish Ministers, the Welsh Assembly or the relevant Northern Ireland department, or by persons authorised by them, to the effect that a particular item, or an item constructed to a particular design, meets the relevant environmental criteria (though the first order makes no such provision). If a certificate is revoked, it is treated as having never been in issue, with the result that FYAs under (*h*) above will not have been available. Subject to penalty under *TMA 1970, s 98* for non-compliance, a person who has consequently made an incorrect tax return must give notice to HMRC, specifying the amendment required to the return, within three months of his becoming aware of the problem.

Technology classes initially included in the WTPL, subject to the appropriate criteria or product approval, are water meters, flow controllers, leakage detection equipment, low flush toilets and efficient taps. Since then, the following items have been added:

- (with effect after 25 August 2004) rainwater harvesting equipment;
- (with effect from 22 September 2005) membrane filtration systems for wastewater treatment, cleaning in place equipment and efficient showers;
- (with effect from 7 September 2006) efficient washing machines and small scale slurry and sludge dewatering equipment.

If one or more components of an item of plant and machinery qualify under these provisions, but the whole item does not, normal apportionment rules are disapplied, and instead the first-year qualifying expenditure under (*h*) above is limited to the amount (or aggregate amount) specified in the WTPL for that component (or those components); where relevant, each *instalment* of expenditure falls to be apportioned in the same way as the whole.

[*CAA 2001, ss 39–52, Sch 3 paras 14, 48–50; CAA 1990, s 22(1)(1AA)(3C)–(3H)(6B)–(7)(10), ss 22A, 22AA, 22B, 22C, 50(2); FA 1990, Sch 17 para 3; F(No 2)A 1997, s 42; FA 1998, ss 83–85; FA 1999, s 78; FA 2000, ss 70–72; FA 2001, s 65, Sch 17, Sch 33 Pt II(4); FA 2002, ss 59, 61–63, Sch 19 paras 2–5, Sch 20, Sch 21 Pt 1; FA 2003, ss 165–167, Sch 30; FA 2004, s 142; FA 2006, s 30; FA 2007, s 36; SI 1999 No 2119; SI 2001 No 2541; SI 2002 No 1818; SI 2003 No 1744; SI 2003 No 2076; SI 2004 No 2093; SI 2004 No 2094; SI 2005 No 2423; SI 2005 No 2424; SI 2006 No 2233; SI 2006 No 2235*].

In general, where expenditure has qualified for an FYA (including a universal FYA — see below), any 'additional VAT liability' (see 10.2(vii) above), incurred in respect of that expenditure at a time when the plant or machinery in question is provided for the purposes of the qualifying activity, also qualifies — at the same rate and for the chargeable period in which the liability accrues. Where *CAA 2001* has effect (see 10.1 above), it is made clear that an additional VAT liability incurred at a time when the plant or machinery is used for overseas leasing other than protected leasing (see 10.35 below) does not qualify for an FYA, and nor does such a liability qualify if incurred at a time when an FYA given on the original expenditure has fallen to be withdrawn under the Northern Ireland provisions above. However, there is nothing in *CAA 2001* to prevent an FYA in respect of an additional VAT liability from being available in the chargeable period in which the qualifying activity is permanently discontinued, notwithstanding exclusion (i) above, where the liability (but not the original expenditure) is incurred in that period; on a strict interpretation, this was not previously the case. [*CAA 2001, ss 236, 237, Sch 3 paras 46–50; CAA 1990, s 22(1A)(1B); FA 1991, Sch 14 para 6*].

Partial use for non-trade etc. purposes results in FYAs being scaled down as is just and reasonable. [*CAA 2001, s 205; CAA 1990, s 79;*]. See 10.30(C) below as regards writing-down allowances in such cases.

See 10.38(J) below for the scaling down of FYAs where it appears that a *partial depreciation subsidy* will be payable.

See 10.38(G) below for the denial of FYAs on plant and machinery treated as changing hands by virtue of certain partnership changes and other *successions*.

Ownership. Before *CAA 2001* had effect (see 10.1 above), the question of whether a person *owns* plant and machinery at some time in the chargeable period in which the expenditure is incurred was expressed in terms of whether it *belonged* to him at some time during the chargeable period related to the incurring of the expenditure. [*CAA 1990, s 22(1)*]. 'Belongs' has its ordinary meaning and normally entails a right of disposition over the thing possessed. See also *Bolton v International Drilling Co Ltd Ch D 1982, 56 TC 449, Ensign Tankers (Leasing) Ltd v Stokes HL 1992, 64 TC 617, Melluish v BMI (No 3) Ltd HL 1995, 68 TC 1* and *BMBF (No 24) Ltd v CIR Ch D, [2002] STC 1450*. Following the decision in *Stokes v Costain Property Investments Ltd CA 1984, 57 TC 688*, specific provisions were introduced to determine entitlement to allowances for plant or machinery which are fixtures (see 10.33 below). See 10.38(A) below as regards plant and machinery acquired on hire-purchase, and 10.38(K) below as regards certain expenditure incurred by a lessee under the terms of a lease. For ownership of certain assets transferred under oil production sharing contracts to the government or representative of the production territory, see *CAA 2001, s 171* (formerly *CAA 1990, s 64A* introduced by *FA 2000, s 81*). The change in terminology in *CAA 2001* is not intended to be a change in the law.

Universal FYAs (*no longer available*). FYAs were previously available universally (as opposed to being specifically targeted as above) at the following rates.

After 26 October 1970	— 60%	*After* 13 March 1984	— 75%
After 19 July 1971	— 80%	*After* 31 March 1985	— 50%
After 21 March 1972	— 100%		

Universal FYAs were subject to the same general conditions being satisfied as to ownership of the plant or machinery and the expenditure being qualifying expenditure (see 10.24

above). Claims could be made for all or part of the allowances available. They were generally **abolished** for expenditure **after 31 March 1986**, although they continued at the 100% rate for expenditure incurred before 1 April 1987 in certain cases involving pre-14 March 1984 contracts.

As a temporary measure, universal FYAs were reinstated at a rate of **40%** in respect of expenditure incurred **after 31 October 1992 and before 1 November 1993**, disregarding the effect of *CAA 1990, s 83(2)* (pre-commencement expenditure — see 10.24 above), and in respect of any 'additional VAT liability' (see 10.2(vii) above) incurred (at whatever time) in relation to such expenditure.

Exclusions similar to those for targeted FYAs in (i) and (ix) above applied for universal FYAs. In addition, the following did not qualify for universal FYAs.

(A) Cars, defined as in (ii) above, except where provided wholly or mainly for a trade of hire to, or carriage of, members of the public (i.e. not where hiring etc. is limited to a certain class of customers, such as business connections or group companies), but see also below.

(B) Certain assets used for leasing (see 10.35 below).

[*CAA 2001, Sch 3 paras 46, 47(1)–(3); CAA 1990, s 22(1)(3B)(4)(a)(b); FA 1993, s 115*]

The exception in (A) above for hire etc. cars applies only if the vehicle was either not normally on hire etc. to the same person (or a person connected with him, see 19 CONNECTED PERSONS) for a period of 30 or more consecutive days or for 90 or more days in any 12-month period; or was provided to a person who himself satisfied those conditions in using it wholly or mainly for a trade of hire etc. to members of the public (e.g. a taxi driver). These restrictions do not, however, apply to vehicles supplied for the use of persons receiving a social security mobility allowance, disability living allowance or war pensioners' mobility supplement and certain other like payments. [*CAA 1990, ss 22(4)(b), 36; SI 1991 No 2874*].

As regards partial use for non-trade purposes, partial depreciation subsidies, and successions, the same comments apply as for targeted FYAs above.

Ships (*postponement of FYAs*). Where a ship qualifies for an FYA (and note the exclusion at (iii) above), the person entitled may, by written notice, *postpone* all or part of the allowance. The amount to be postponed must be specified in the notice. Where an FYA is claimed in respect of part only of the qualifying expenditure, the above applies in respect of the FYA claimed. The notice must be given no later than two years following the end of the chargeable period for which the allowance is due. Available qualifying expenditure for writing-down allowances (see 10.28 below) is computed as if the postponed FYA had, in fact, been made. Postponed FYAs may be claimed over one or more subsequent chargeable periods. [*CAA 2001, s 130(1)(3)–(6), s 131(1)(2)(4)(7); CAA 1990, s 30; FA 1990, Sch 17 para 7; FA 1993, Sch 13 para 3; FA 1996, s 135, Sch 21 para 27*]. See 10.30(B) below for postponement of writing-down allowances and deferment of balancing charges.

Simon's Direct Tax Service. See **B2.320** *et seq.*

10.28 **Pooling, writing-down allowances and balancing adjustments.** Qualifying expenditure (as in 10.24 above) is *pooled* for the purpose of determining entitlement to writing-down allowances and balancing allowances and liability to balancing charges. In addition to the *main pool* for each qualifying activity, there may be a *single asset pool* and/or a *class pool*, and qualifying expenditure falling to be allocated to either of the latter (see 10.30, 10.35, 10.38(J) below) cannot be allocated to the main pool.

For each pool of qualifying expenditure, a **writing-down allowance (WDA)** is available for each chargeable period (see 10.1 above) other than the 'final chargeable period' and is equal to a maximum of **25%** of the amount (if any) by which 'available qualifying expenditure' exceeds the total of any disposal values (see 10.29 below) falling to be brought into account. See 10.30(G) below (long-life assets) and 10.35(*a*)(*b*) below (overseas leasing) for exceptions to the 25% rate. The WDA is proportionately reduced if the chargeable period is less than a year (or, for income tax purposes, increased if the chargeable period is more than a year), or if the qualifying activity has been carried on for part only of the chargeable period. A claim for a WDA may require it to be reduced to a specified amount. For the 'final chargeable period', a **balancing allowance** is available, equal to the excess (if any) of (1) 'available qualifying expenditure' over (2) total disposal values. If, for *any* chargeable period, (2) exceeds (1), there arises a liability to a **balancing charge**, equal to that excess.

The '*final chargeable period*', as regards the main pool, is the chargeable period in which the trade or other qualifying activity is permanently discontinued. As regards a single asset pool, it is normally the first chargeable period in which a disposal event (see 10.29 below) occurs. As regards class pools, see 10.30(G) (long-life assets) and 10.35(*a*) (overseas leasing) below.

'*Available qualifying expenditure*' in a pool for a chargeable period consists of qualifying expenditure allocated to the pool for that period and any unrelieved qualifying expenditure brought forward in the pool from the previous chargeable period (usually referred to as the written-down value brought forward). There are rules requiring an allocation to a pool in specific circumstances, for example where an item falls to be transferred from one type of pool to another, and prohibiting the allocation of certain excluded expenditure. These are listed in *CAA 2001, s 57(2)(3)* and are covered elsewhere in this chapter where appropriate. See 10.38(C) below as regards restrictions under connected persons and other anti-avoidance provisions.

In allocating qualifying expenditure to the appropriate pool, the following rules must be observed (and see below for interaction with first-year allowances).

(*a*) Qualifying expenditure can be allocated to a pool for a chargeable period only to the extent that it has not been included in available qualifying expenditure for an earlier chargeable period. (Before *CAA 2001* had effect, see 10.1 above, there was some doubt as to whether qualifying expenditure could be allocated to a pool for a chargeable period later than that in which it was incurred, except where a first-year allowance had been given in the immediately preceding period (though this seems to have been accepted in practice). For chargeable periods covered by *CAA 2001*, this doubt is removed and, in addition, there is now nothing to prohibit the allocation of *part only* of a particular amount of qualifying expenditure for a particular chargeable period.)

(*b*) Qualifying expenditure cannot be allocated to a pool for a chargeable period earlier than that in which it is incurred.

(*c*) Qualifying expenditure can be allocated to a pool for a chargeable period only if the person concerned *owns* the plant or machinery at some time in that period. (Before *CAA 2001* had effect, see 10.1 above, this was expressed in terms of the item *belonging* to that person, but no change in the law is intended; see 10.27 above and 10.33 below for meaning of 'belongs'. See 10.38(K) below as regards certain expenditure by a lessee.)

Where an 'additional VAT liability' (see 10.2(vii) above) is incurred in respect of qualifying expenditure, at a time when the plant or machinery in question is provided for the purposes of the qualifying activity, it is itself expenditure on that plant or machinery and may be taken into account in determining available qualifying expenditure for the chargeable period in which it accrues.

The net cost of demolition of plant and machinery demolished during a chargeable period, and not replaced, is allocated to the appropriate pool for that chargeable period.

Interaction with first-year allowances. If a first-year allowance (FYA) (see 10.27 above) is made in respect of an amount of first-year qualifying expenditure, none of that amount can be allocated to a pool for the chargeable period in which the expenditure is incurred, and only the balance (after deducting the FYA) can be allocated to a pool for a subsequent chargeable period.

However, expenditure which qualifies for an FYA for a chargeable period is not excluded from being allocated to a pool for that period if either (1) the FYA is not claimed or (2) it is claimed in respect of part only of the expenditure (in which case the remaining part can be so allocated). Before *CAA 2001* had effect (see 10.1 above), an election was required to allocate the expenditure to the pool if (1) applied. The election had to be made no later than two years following the end of the chargeable period. For chargeable periods covered by *CAA 2001*, no such election is required.

If an FYA is made in respect of an amount of qualifying expenditure, at least some of the balance (after deducting the FYA) must be allocated to a pool for a chargeable period no later than that in which a disposal event (see 10.29 below) occurs in relation to the item in question. It will usually be beneficial to choose to allocate the whole balance. A nil balance (following a 100% FYA) is deemed to be so allocated. Such allocation is necessary to enable a disposal value to be properly brought into account. Before *CAA 2001* had effect (see 10.1 above), a similar rule applied but only if a disposal value fell to be brought into account for the chargeable period related to the incurring of the expenditure; the change in law is a consequence of the removal of doubt referred to in (*a*) above.

[*CAA 2001, s 26(3)–(5), ss 53–59, 65, 235; CAA 1990, s 24(1)–(5), s 25(1)–(5)(9), s 41(1)(c), s 62(1)(b)(2); FA 1990, Sch 17 paras 5, 6; FA 1991, Sch 14 para 7; FA 1994, s 118(6), s 213(4)FA 1996, s 135, Sch 21 para 26; FA 2000, ss 73, 74; FA 2001, Sch 20 para 5(2)*].

See *Example* (*C*) at 10.31 below.

Finance and certain operating lessors. If a leasing company incurs capital expenditure on or after 1 April 2006, on the provision of plant or machinery under a 'finance lease' (see 10.38(C) below), or under a 'qualifying operating lease' (see below) a restriction applies where the company is a member of a group and has a different accounting date from the principal company in that group. Only a proportion of the capital expenditure during the chargeable period may be brought in as available qualifying expenditure for that period. The proportion is the same as the proportion of the chargeable period which falls after the time the expenditure was incurred, so that, e.g. only one-quarter is brought in where expenditure is incurred three months before the end of a twelve-month period. This does not apply where a disposal value (see 10.29 below) is brought in in respect of the plant or machinery in the same period. The balance of the expenditure may be brought in in the following chargeable period or periods. A '*qualifying operating lease*' is one that is not a finance lease but is a 'funding lease' (see 10.34(2) below) with a term of between four and five years. The capital gains tax provisions (under *TCGA 1992, s 170(3)*) apply to determine whether a company is a member of a group, and which company is its principal company, with modifications in the case where a subsidiary company does not have ordinary share capital.

For expenditure incurred after 1 July 1997 (or in the following twelve months under a contract entered into on or before that date) and **before 1 April 2006**, the above restriction applies only in the case of finance leases and is not restricted to companies.

[*CAA 2001, s 220, Sch 3 para 44; CAA 1990, s 25(5A)-(5C); F(No 2)A 1997, s 44; FA 2006, Sch 9 para 15*].

See HMRC Capital Allowances Manual CA 28600 for a general article on how these and associated capital allowance restrictions are intended to operate. In particular the following apply in relation to the instant provisions.

- As a transitional measure, up to the end of 2001, lessors may agree with the local inspector to adopt a mean expenditure date for weekly or monthly batches of small items, or some other form of simplified calculation giving broadly the correct result.

Thereafter, any basis adopted must ensure that no more than the correct amount is included in qualifying expenditure, e.g. by using the end rather than the mean date for batched items.

- Where the limit on allowances for cars costing over £12,000 applies (see 10.30(A) below), it operates after the restriction under these provisions.
- Where the plant or machinery is a fixture let under an equipment lease and does not belong to the lessor at any time during the chargeable period in which the expenditure is incurred, because the lessee has not commenced trading (see 10.33(*b*) below), no allowances are due for that period. The restriction thus does not apply, and the expenditure is brought in in full in the period in which the fixture first belongs to the lessor (i.e. in which the lessee starts to trade). If the lessee starts to trade during the period in which the expenditure is incurred, the expenditure is apportioned from the date the expenditure is incurred, and not from the date the lessee starts to trade.

See also 10.38(A)(C) below, 66.54 TRADING INCOME as regards finance lease allowance restrictions. See 10.34 below as regards long funding leases.

Simon's Direct Tax Service. See B2.331, B2.332 *et seq.*

10.29 **Disposal events and values.** Where a person has incurred qualifying expenditure (see 10.24 above) on plant or machinery, a **disposal value** must be brought into account for a chargeable period (see 10.1 above) in which any one of the following **disposal events** occurs (but normally only in relation to the first such event to occur in respect of that plant or machinery).

(i) The person ceases to own the plant or machinery.

(ii) The person loses possession of it, and it is reasonable to assume the loss is permanent.

(iii) It has been in use for 'mineral exploration and access' (see 10.40(*a*) below) and the person abandons it at the site where it was so in use.

(iv) It ceases to exist as such (by reason of its destruction, dismantling or otherwise).

(v) It begins to be used wholly or partly for purposes other than those of the qualifying activity.

(va) It begins to be leased under a long funding lease (see 10.34 below under Lessors).

(vi) The qualifying activity is permanently discontinued.

The amount to be brought into account depends upon the nature of the event.

(*a*) On a sale (other than one within (*b*) below), it is the net sale proceeds plus any insurance or capital compensation received (by the person concerned) by reason of any event affecting the sale price obtainable.

(*b*) On a sale at less than market value, it is market value, unless

  (i) the buyer (not being a dual resident investing company connected with the seller) can claim plant or machinery or research and development (formerly scientific research) allowances for his expenditure, or

  (ii) the sale gives rise to a charge to tax under *ITEPA 2003* (i.e. on employment, pension or social security income),

  in which case (*a*) above applies.

(*c*) On demolition or destruction, it is the net amount received for the remains, plus any insurance or capital compensation received.

(*d*) On permanent loss (otherwise than within (*c*) above), or, where *CAA 2001* has effect (see 10.1 above), on abandonment as in (iii) above, it is any insurance or capital compensation received.

(*da*) On commencement of a long funding lease, it is as stated in 10.34 below under Lessors.

(*e*) On permanent discontinuance of the qualifying activity preceding an event in (*a*)–(*d*) above, it is whatever value would otherwise have applied on the occurrence of that event.

(*f*) On a gift giving rise to a charge to tax on the recipient under *ITEPA 2003* (i.e. on employment, pension or social security income), it is nil. (Before *CAA 2001* had effect, see 10.1 above, a similar result was achieved slightly differently in that no disposal value was required to be brought into account in such circumstances). See also HMRC Capital Allowances Manual CA 23250.

(*g*) On any other event, it is market value at the time of the event.

However, the disposal value is in all cases limited to the qualifying expenditure incurred on the plant or machinery by the person in question. In addition, where *CAA 2001* has effect (see 10.1 above), there is no requirement to bring a disposal value into account if none of the qualifying expenditure in question has been taken into account in determining the person's available qualifying expenditure (see 10.28 above) for any chargeable period up to and including that in which the disposal occurs. As regards both these rules, see also 10.38(C)(i) below as regards certain transactions between connected persons.

Additional VAT rebates. Where an 'additional VAT rebate' (see 10.2(vii) above) is made in respect of an item of qualifying expenditure, a disposal value of an equivalent amount must be brought into account (on its own or as an addition to any other disposal value brought into account for that item) for the chargeable period in which the rebate accrues. Any disposal value brought into account for a subsequent chargeable period is limited to the original qualifying expenditure less all additional VAT rebates accrued in all chargeable periods up to (but not including) that chargeable period. If the disposal value is itself the result of an additional VAT rebate, it is limited to the original qualifying expenditure less *any* disposal values brought into account as a result of earlier events. (Before *CAA 2001* had effect, see 10.1 above, reference here to earlier events did not include the making of additional VAT rebates.)

[*CAA 2001, ss 60, 61, 62(1), s 63(1), s 64(1)(5), ss 238, 239; CAA 1990, s 24(6)(7)(8), s 26; FA 1991, Sch 14 paras 7(2), 8; FA 1994, Sch 26 Pt V(24); ITEPA 2003, Sch 6 paras 249, 250; FA 2006, Sch 8 para 5*].

The rules at (*b*)(ii) and (*f*) above where there is a charge to tax under *ITEPA 2003* (previously under Schedule E) are understood to apply where there would be such a charge but for the exemptions relating to compensation for loss of employment (Tolley's Practical Tax 1984 p 114).

See 10.38(C)(ii) below for certain anti-avoidance rules. See 10.34 below under Lessees for a further disposal event in the case of long funding leasing, and for the appropriate disposal value.

Simon's Direct Tax Service. See **B2.334**.

10.30 **Exclusions from the main pool. Items excluded from the main pool of qualifying expenditure** are as follows.

(A) **Cars costing over £12,000** acquired for purposes of a trade or other qualifying activity. For this purpose, 'car' is as defined at 10.27(ii) above, but with the exclusion of hire etc. cars as at 10.27(A) above and cars qualifying for first-year allowances under 10.27(*e*) above. Qualifying expenditure (see 10.24 above) on a car costing over £12,000 can only be allocated to a *single asset pool* (see 10.28 above). Writing-down allowances (WDAs) are limited to a maximum of **£3,000** per chargeable period (proportionately reduced or increased for chargeable periods of less or more than a year).

Separate rules apply to reduce the maximum WDA in cases involving contributions towards capital expenditure (as in 10.2(v)(vi) above) and partial depreciation subsidies (as in 10.38(J) below). If the car begins to be used *partly* for purposes other than those of the qualifying activity, the single asset pool continues and no disposal value is brought into account. For a chargeable period in which such part use exists, the WDA and any balancing allowance or charge is reduced to such amount as is just and reasonable (though the full amount is deducted in arriving at any unrelieved qualifying expenditure carried forward).

For expenditure incurred before 11 March 1992 or under a contract entered into before that date, these provisions apply to cars costing over *£8,000* and by reference to a maximum WDA of *£2,000*.

[*CAA 2001, ss 74–78, 81, 82, Sch 3 para 19; CAA 1990, s 34(1)–(3)(5), s 35(1), s 36; F(No 2)A 1992, s 71; FA 1994, s 213(5)(6); FA 2002, Sch 19 para 6; SI 1991 No 2874*].

See 10.38(C)(ii) below for special rule determining the disposal value of a car within these provisions on a sale etc. to which the anti-avoidance provisions there mentioned apply. See 66.23 TRADING INCOME as regards expenditure on *hiring* a car whose retail price when new exceeded £12,000 (previously £8,000).

See Simon's Direct Tax Service B2.342.

Cars costing £12,000 or less. Cars costing £12,000 or less previously had to be included in a class pool (see 10.28 above). This requirement is abolished, for chargeable periods ending after 31 March 2000 (subject to election to defer this for one year), and qualifying expenditure on such cars may now be allocated to the main pool (unless excluded for other reasons, e.g. partial use for non-trade etc. purposes — see (C) below). For expenditure incurred before 11 March 1992 or under a contract entered into before that date, these provisions applied to cars costing £8,000 or less. See 10.35(*a*) below.

(B) Ships. Qualifying expenditure (see 10.24 above) on the provision of a ship for the purposes of a trade or other qualifying activity can only be allocated to a *single asset pool* (see 10.28 above), known as a *single ship pool*. This does not apply if:

- an election is made to exclude such treatment (see below); or
- the qualifying activity is one of special leasing (see 10.37 below); or
- the ship is otherwise provided for leasing (which expressly includes letting on charter), *unless* it is not used for 'overseas leasing' (other than 'protected leasing') at any time in the 'designated period' *and* it appears that it will be used only for a 'qualifying purpose' in that period (see 10.35 below for meaning of expressions used here).

When a disposal event occurs in relation to a single ship pool, the available qualifying expenditure (see 10.28 above) in that pool for the chargeable period in question is transferred to the '*appropriate non-ship pool*' (i.e. the pool to which the expenditure would originally have been allocated in the absence of the single ship pool rules), and the single ship pool is brought to an end with no balancing allowance or charge. The disposal value is brought into account in the pool now containing the qualifying expenditure. In addition to the circumstances at 10.29 above, a disposal event occurs if a ship is provided for leasing or letting on charter and begins to be used otherwise than for a 'qualifying purpose' at some time in the first four years of the 'designated period' (see 10.35 below as regards expressions used).

If the ship ceases to be used by the person who incurred the qualifying expenditure, without his having brought it into use for the purposes of the qualifying activity, then, in addition to any adjustments required as above, any writing-down allowances (WDAs) previously made (or postponed — see below) are withdrawn, and the amount withdrawn is allocated to the 'appropriate non-ship pool' (see above) for the chargeable period in question.

A person who has incurred qualifying expenditure on a ship may elect, for any chargeable period, to disapply the single ship pool provisions in respect of:

- all or part of any qualifying expenditure that would otherwise be allocated to a single ship pool in that period; or
- all or part of the available qualifying expenditure (see 10.28 above) already in a single ship pool,

with the result that the amount in question is allocated to the 'appropriate non-ship pool' (see above). The election must be made no later than two years after the end of the chargeable period in question.

Postponement of WDAs. A person entitled to a WDA for a chargeable period in respect of a single ship pool may, by written notice, postpone all or part of it to a later period. The amount to be postponed must be specified in the notice. Where a reduced WDA is claimed, all or part of the reduced amount may be postponed. The time limits for giving notice are the same as for the election referred to immediately above. Available qualifying expenditure (see 10.28 below) is computed as if the postponed WDA had, in fact, been made. Postponed WDAs may be claimed over one or more subsequent chargeable periods. See 10.27 above for postponement of first-year allowances.

[*CAA 2001, ss 127–129, s 130(2)(7), s 131(1)(3)–(7), ss 132, 133, 157(1); CAA 1990, ss 31–33, 40(4); FA 1990, Sch 17 para 8; FA 1993, s 116(1)(4); FA 1996, s 135, Sch 21 paras 28, 29; FA 1998, Sch 5 para 52*].

Deferment of balancing charges on qualifying ships. Balancing charges on ships may be deferred and set against subsequent expenditure on ships for a maximum of six years from the date of disposal. A claim for deferment of the whole or part of a balancing charge may be made by the shipowner where a disposal event within 10.29(i)–(iv) above occurs after 20 April 1994 in relation to a 'qualifying ship' (the old ship). A '*qualifying ship*' is, broadly, a ship of a sea-going kind of 100 gross registered tons or more, excluding offshore installations (as now defined by *ICTA 1988, s 837C* — for earlier definition, see *CAA 2001, s 153 as originally enacted*) and ships of a kind used or chartered primarily for sport or recreation (but passenger ships and cruise liners are not so excluded). The provisions also apply to ships of less than 100 tons in cases where the old ship is totally lost or is damaged beyond worthwhile repair. A ship brought into use in the trade on or after 20 July 1994 must within three months of first use (unless disposed of during those three months) be registered in the UK, the Channel Islands, Isle of Man, a colony (as to which see Revenue Tax Bulletin June 1998 p 553 and HMRC Capital Allowances Manual CA 25230), a European Union State or a European Economic Area State and must continue to be so until at least three years from first use or, if earlier, until disposed of to an unconnected person. It is a further condition that no amount in respect of the old ship has been allocated to an overseas leasing pool (see 10.35 below), a 'partial use' single asset pool (see (C) below), a 'partial depreciation subsidy' single asset pool (see 10.38(J) below) or a pool for a qualifying activity consisting of special leasing (see 10.37 below).

The balancing charge on the old ship is in effect calculated as if allowances had been granted, and the charge arises, in a single ship pool, with appropriate assumptions where that is not, in fact, the case (see *CAA 2001, s 139*, or for earlier chargeable periods *CAA 1990, s 33B*).

Deferment is achieved by allocating the amount deferred to the 'appropriate non-ship pool' (see above) for the chargeable period in question, so that it is effectively set against the disposal value brought into account in that pool (see above) as a result of the disposal event concerned. The *maximum deferment* is the *lowest* of (i) the amount treated as brought into account in respect of the old ship under *CAA 2001, s 139* (see above), (ii) the amount to be expended on new shipping (see below), so far as not already set against an earlier balancing charge, in the six years starting with the date of disposal of the old ship, (iii) the amount which, in the absence of a deferment claim, would have been the total balancing charge for the chargeable period in question in the appropriate non-ship pool, and (iv) the amount needed to reduce the profit of the trade or other qualifying activity to nil (disregarding losses brought forward), no deferment being possible if no such profit has been made. If the amount actually expended within (ii) above turns out to be less than the amount deferred, the amount of the deficiency is reinstated as a balancing charge for the chargeable period to which the claim relates. (Before *CAA 2001* had effect (see 10.1 above), the amount calculated at (iii) above could also include balancing charges in certain other pools and may therefore have been a larger amount.)

Where an amount is expended on new shipping within the six-year period allowed and is attributed by the shipowner, by notice to HMRC, to any part of an amount deferred, an amount equal to the amount so matched is brought into account as a disposal value, for the chargeable period in which the expenditure is incurred, in the single ship pool to which the expenditure is allocated, thus reducing the amount on which allowances may be claimed on the new ship. No amount of expenditure can be attributed to a deferment if there is earlier expenditure on new shipping within the said six-year period which has not been attributed to that or earlier deferments. An attribution may be varied by the trader by notice to the inspector within a specified time (see *CAA 2001, s 142*, or for earlier chargeable periods *CAA 1990, s 33F(4)* and *FA 1995, s 98(6)(b)*).

For the purposes of these provisions, an amount is expended on new shipping if it is qualifying expenditure, incurred by the claimant wholly and exclusively for the purposes of a qualifying activity, on a ship (the new ship) which will be a qualifying ship (see above) for at least three years from first use or, if earlier, until disposed of to an unconnected person. Expenditure is treated as incurred by the claimant if it is incurred by a successor following a partnership change or company reconstruction in consequence of which the qualifying activity was not treated as discontinued. Expenditure incurred on a ship which has belonged to either the shipowner or a connected person within the previous six years or which is incurred mainly for tax avoidance reasons does not qualify. The expenditure must be allocated to a single ship pool. If an election is made to disapply the single ship pool provisions, the expenditure is deemed never to have been expenditure on new shipping (but must nevertheless be treated as such in matching expenditure with deferments, so that the election prevents further matching of amounts already deferred). Expenditure does not qualify if the overseas leasing provisions at 10.35 below come to apply to the new ship.

For corporation tax purposes, the claim for deferment must be made within two years after the end of the chargeable period of deferment. Where a claim for deferment is found to be erroneous as a result of subsequent circumstances, the shipowner must, within three months after the end of the chargeable period in which those circumstances first arise, notify HMRC accordingly (failure to do so incurring a penalty under *TMA 1970, s 98*); consequential assessments may be made within twelve months after notice is given, notwithstanding normal time limits.

[*CAA 2001, ss 134–158, Sch 3 para 24; CAA 1990, ss 33A–33F; FA 1995, ss 94–98; FA 1996, Sch 35; FA 2004, Sch 27 paras 9, 11; ITTOIA 2005, Sch 1 paras 542–544; SI 1996 No 1323; SI 1997 No 133*].

See Simon's Direct Tax Service B2.350–B2.353.

(C) Plant and machinery partly used for non-trade etc. purposes. Qualifying expenditure (see 10.24 above) incurred partly for the purposes of the trade or other qualifying activity and partly for other purposes can only be allocated to a *single asset pool* (see 10.28 above). (See 10.27 above as regards first-year allowances.) Where in other cases plant or machinery *begins to be used* partly for other purposes, such that a disposal value falls to be brought into account (see 10.29(v) above) in a pool, an amount equal to the disposal value is allocated to a single asset pool for the chargeable period in question (but see (A) above as regards cars costing over £12,000). In respect of a single asset pool under these provisions, writing-down allowances and balancing allowances and charges are reduced to such amount as is just and reasonable (though the full amount is deducted in arriving at any unrelieved qualifying expenditure carried forward).

Where, after 20 March 2000, circumstances change such that the proportion of use for purposes other than those of the qualifying activity increases during a chargeable period, and the market value of the plant or machinery at the end of the period exceeds the available qualifying expenditure (see 10.28 above) in the pool for that period by more than £1 million, then if no disposal value would otherwise fall to be brought into account for the period, a disposal value must be brought into account (equal to market value — see 10.29(*g*) above) and, in the next or a subsequent chargeable period, an equivalent amount may be allocated to a new single asset pool as if it were qualifying expenditure newly incurred.

[*CAA 2001, ss 206–208, Sch 3 para 42; CAA 1990, ss 79, 79A; FA 1990, Sch 17 para 14; FA 2000, s 75(2)(6)*].

See also *Kempster v McKenzie Ch D 1952, 33 TC 193* and *G H Chambers (Northiam Farms) Ltd v Watmough Ch D 1956, 36 TC 711* and HMRC Capital Allowances Manual CA 23530, 27100 as regards further adjustment for any element of personal choice.

See Simon's Direct Tax Service B2.359.

(D) Plant and machinery in respect of which a **partial depreciation subsidy** is received (see 10.38(J) below).

(E) Plant and machinery used for overseas leasing (see 10.35 below).

(F) Short-life assets. A person who has incurred qualifying expenditure (see 10.24 above) on an item of plant or machinery may elect for it to be treated as a short-life asset, provided it is not an excluded item (see list below). There is no requirement as to the expected useful life of the item, but short-life asset treatment will be of no practical benefit where the item remains in use for five years or more. The election is irrevocable and must be made no later than two years after the end of the chargeable period in which the expenditure (or earliest expenditure) is incurred.

In general, HMRC will require sufficient information in support of an election to minimise the possibility of any difference of view at a later date (e.g. on a disposal) about what was and was not covered by the election, and to ensure that it does not incorporate any excluded items (see list below). Where separate identification of short-life assets acquired in a chargeable period is either impossible or impracticable, e.g. similar small or relatively inexpensive items held in very large numbers, perhaps in different locations, then the information required in support of the election may be provided by reference to batches of acquisitions. (HMRC Statement of Practice 1/86).

Each of the following items of plant or machinery is excluded from being a short-life asset.

(i) A car, defined as at 10.27(ii) above with the exception of cars hired out to persons receiving certain disability allowances or mobility supplements. (Before *CAA 2001* had effect, see 10.1 above, it would appear that this exclusion was narrower in that *all* hire etc. cars within 10.27(A) above were excepted from it).

(ii) A ship.

(iii) An item which is the subject of special leasing (see 10.37 below).

(iv) An item acquired partly for the purposes of a trade or other qualifying activity and partly for other purposes.

(v) An item which is the subject of a partial depreciation subsidy (see 10.38(J) below).

(vi) An item received by way of gift or whose previous use by the person concerned did not attract capital allowances (see 10.38(D)(E) below and, as regards long funding leasing, 10.34 below).

(vii) An item the expenditure on which is within the long-life asset provisions (see (G) below).

(viii) An item provided for leasing, unless it will be used within the 'designated period' for a 'qualifying purpose' (see 10.35 below as regards these expressions), and with the exception in any case of cars hired out to persons receiving certain disability allowances or mobility supplements.

(ix) An item leased overseas such that it attracts only a 10% writing-down allowance (see 10.35(*a*) below).

(x) An item leased to two or more persons jointly such that *CAA 2001, s 116* applies (see 10.35(*f*) below).

(xi) An item qualifying for a universal first-year allowance (see 10.27 above) other than the reinstated allowance for expenditure in the twelve months to 31 October 1993. (An item qualifying for one of the targeted first-year allowances at 10.27(*a*)–(*h*) above is *not* automatically excluded from short-life asset treatment.)

Qualifying expenditure in respect of a short-life asset can only be allocated to a *single asset pool* (see 10.28 above), known as a *short-life asset pool*. If no disposal event within 10.29(i)–(vi) above occurs in any of the chargeable periods ending on or before the fourth anniversary (referred to below as the '*four-year cut-off date*') of the end of the chargeable period in which the expenditure is incurred (or the first such period in which any of it was incurred), the short-life asset pool is brought to an end on the four-year cut-off date but with no balancing allowance or charge and no denial of a writing-down allowance for the final period. The item ceases to be a short-life asset and the available qualifying expenditure in the pool is allocated to the main pool for the first chargeable period ending *after* the four-year cut-off date.

The following applies where short-life asset treatment has been claimed on the basis that the item has been provided for leasing, but will be used within the 'designated period' for a 'qualifying purpose' (so is not excluded by (viii) above). (See 10.35 below as regards expressions used here.) If, at any time in a chargeable period ending on or before the four-year cut-off date (as above), the item begins to be used otherwise than for such a purpose, and that time falls within the first four years of the 'designated period', the short-life asset pool is brought to an end at that time but with no balancing allowance or charge and no denial of a writing-down allowance for the final period. The item ceases to be a short-life asset and the available qualifying expenditure in the pool is allocated, for the chargeable period in which that time falls, to the main pool (or, where appropriate and prior to its abolition, to the separate class pool for cars — see (A1) above and 10.35(*a*) below).

If at any time before the four-year cut-off date (as above), a short-life asset is disposed of to a connected person (within *ICTA 1988, s 839* — see 19 CONNECTED PERSONS), short-life asset treatment continues in the connected person's hands (though the original four-year cut-off date remains unchanged). If both parties so elect (within two years after the end of the chargeable period in which the disposal occurs), the disposal is treated as being at a price equal to the available qualifying expenditure (see 10.28 above) then in the short-life asset pool, and certain anti-avoidance provisions on transactions between connected persons are disapplied. If no election is made, the anti-avoidance provisions at 10.38(C) below apply in full, and the exception at 10.29(*b*)(i) above is disapplied (so that market value can be substituted for a lesser sale price even where the buyer is entitled to capital allowances).

If a disposal event occurs in respect of a short-life asset pool such that the pool ends and a balancing *allowance* arises (see 10.28 above), and an 'additional VAT liability' (see 10.2(vii) above) is subsequently incurred in respect of the item concerned, a further balancing allowance of that amount is given for the chargeable period in which the additional VAT liability accrues.

HMRC accept that it may not be practicable for individual pools to be maintained for every short-life asset, especially where they are held in very large numbers. Statement of Practice 1/86 sets out examples of acceptable bases of computation where the inspector is satisfied that the actual life in the business of a distinct class of assets with broadly similar average lives, before being sold or scrapped, is likely to be less than five years.

[*CAA 2001, ss 83–89, 240; CAA 1990, ss 37, 38, 40(4); FA 1991, Sch 14 para 9; F(No 2)A 1992, s 68(7); FA 1993, s 116(1)(4), Sch 13 para 4; FA 1996, s 135, Sch 21 para 30; FA 1997, Sch 14 para 3; ITEPA 2003, Sch 6 para 252*].

See *Example (A)* at 10.31 below.

See Simon's Direct Tax Service B2.343.

(G) Long-life assets. There are special provisions for chargeable periods ending on or after 26 November 1996 relating to certain 'long-life asset expenditure'. These do not apply to expenditure incurred before 26 November 1996, or to expenditure incurred before 1 January 2001 under a contract entered into before 26 November 1996 (except that the later start date does not apply to any increased expenditure resulting from a variation of the contract on or after 26 November 1996). '*Long-life asset expenditure*' is qualifying expenditure (as in 10.24 above) incurred on the provision of a 'long-life asset' for the purposes of a qualifying activity (but see below for exclusions by reference to a monetary limit).

Subject to below, a '*long-life asset*' is plant or machinery which it is reasonable to expect will have a useful economic life of at least 25 years (or where such was a reasonable expectation when the plant or machinery was new, i.e. unused and not second-hand). For these purposes, the useful economic life of plant or machinery is the period from first use (by any person) until it ceases to be, or to be likely to be, used by anyone as a fixed asset of a business. Where part only of capital expenditure on an item of plant or machinery falls within these provisions, that part and the remainder are treated as expenditure on separate items, any necessary apportionments being made on a just and reasonable basis. As an introduction to a detailed discussion of what constitutes a long-life asset (including twelve examples), HMRC have stated that they 'will generally accept the accounting treatment as determining whether an asset is long-life provided it is not clearly unreasonable'. (See HMRC Capital Allowances Manual CA 23700–23780). For whether glasshouses (for which see generally 10.25 and 10.26(17) above) are long-life assets, see HMRC Capital Allowances Manual CA 23785. For aircraft, see HMRC Capital Allowances Manual CA 23781, CA 23782 .

The following *cannot* be long-life assets.

(i) Fixtures (see 10.33 below) in, or plant or machinery provided for use in, a building used wholly or mainly as a dwelling-house, showroom, hotel, office or retail shop or similar retail premises, or for purposes ancillary to such use.

(ii) Cars, as defined at 10.27(ii) above.

(iii) (In relation to expenditure incurred before 1 January 2011) ships of a seagoing kind, other than offshore installations (as now defined by *ICTA 1988, s 837C* — for earlier definition, see *CAA 2001, s 94 as originally enacted*), and not of a kind used or chartered primarily for sport or recreation (which expression does not encompass passenger ships or cruise liners).

(iv) (In relation to expenditure incurred before 1 January 2011) 'railway assets' used only for a 'railway business' (as defined).

Long-life asset expenditure which is incurred wholly and exclusively for the purposes of a qualifying activity, and which does not require allocation under other rules to a single asset pool, can only be allocated to a *class pool* (see 10.28 above), known as the *long-life asset pool*. The final chargeable period (see 10.28 above) of a long-life asset pool is that in which the qualifying activity is permanently discontinued.

Writing-down allowances for a chargeable period in respect of long-life asset expenditure (whether in the long-life asset pool or a single asset pool) are restricted to **6%** (instead of the normal 25% or, where the overseas leasing rules in 10.35(*a*) below apply, 10%), proportionately reduced or increased if the chargeable period is less or more than a year, or if the qualifying activity has been carried on for part only of the chargeable period. A claim for a writing-down allowance may require it to be reduced to a specified amount. Where plant and machinery allowances have been claimed for long-life asset expenditure, any earlier or later expenditure on the same asset for which allowances are subsequently claimed, unless excluded by (i)–(iv) above, is treated as also being long-life asset expenditure if it would not otherwise be so. This over-rides the exclusion of expenditure within the monetary limit referred to below.

Where a disposal value less than the 'notional written-down value' would otherwise fall to be brought into account in respect of long-life asset expenditure which has attracted restricted allowances as above, an adjustment may be required. Where the event giving rise to the disposal value is part of a scheme or arrangement a main object of which is the obtaining of a tax advantage under these provisions, the 'notional written-down value' is substituted for the disposal value. The '*notional written-down value*' is qualifying expenditure on the item in question less maximum allowances to date, computed on the assumptions that the expenditure was not excluded from being long-life asset expenditure by the operation of the monetary limit below and that all allowances have been made in full.

Monetary limit. Expenditure is not long-life asset expenditure if it is expenditure to which the monetary limit (see below) applies and it is incurred in a chargeable period for which that limit is not exceeded. The limit applies to expenditure incurred by an individual who devotes substantially the whole of his time in that chargeable period to the carrying on of the qualifying activity for the purposes of which the expenditure was incurred. In the case of a partnership of individuals, at least half the partners must satisfy the requirement as to devotion of time, but a company falls outside that requirement. In any case, the monetary limit does not apply to the following types of expenditure:

- expenditure on a share in plant or machinery; or
- a contribution treated as plant or machinery expenditure under *CAA 2001, s 538* (see 10.2(vi) above); or
- expenditure on plant or machinery for leasing (whether or not in the course of a trade).

The monetary limit is £100,000, proportionately reduced or increased for chargeable periods of less or more than a year and, as regards companies, divided by one plus the number of associated companies (as under *ICTA 1988, s 13* — see 63 SMALL COMPANIES — REDUCED RATES). For the purpose of applying the monetary limit, all expenditure under a contract is treated as incurred in the first chargeable period in which any expenditure under the contract is incurred.

Transitional rule for second-hand assets. A second-hand asset is excluded from the long-life asset provisions if

- the previous owner properly claimed plant and machinery allowances for expenditure on its provision,
- his expenditure did not fall to be treated as long-life asset expenditure, and
- his expenditure would have fallen to be so treated if the long-life asset rules (apart from this transitional rule) had always been law.

A provisional claim to 25% writing-down allowances may be made by a purchaser on this basis, before the vendor has made the appropriate return, provided that reasonable steps have been taken to establish that entitlement will arise, and that the appropriate revisions will be made, and assessments accepted, if entitlement does not in the event arise (HMRC Capital Allowances Manual CA 23700–23780).

[*CAA 2001, ss 56(5), 65(1), 90–104, Sch 3 para 20; CAA 1990, ss 38A–38H, 83(1); FA 1997, Sch 14; FA 2004, Sch 27 paras 8, 11*].

For an article explaining how HMRC interpret and operate these provisions, see Revenue Tax Bulletin August 1997 pp 445–450. For their application to modern equipment used in the printing industry, see HMRC Capital Allowances Manual CA 23790.

See *Example* (*B*) at 10.31 below.

See Simon's Direct Tax Service B2.344.

10.31 *Examples*

(*A*) *Short-life assets*

A Ltd is a small business. It prepares trading accounts to 30 September each year, and buys and sells machines, for use in the trade, as follows.

	Cost	Date of acquisition	Disposal proceeds	Date of disposal
Machine X	£40,000	30.4.02	£13,000	1.12.02
Machine Y	£25,000	1.9.02	£4,000	1.12.05

A Ltd elects under what is now *CAA 2001, s 83* for both machines to be treated as short-life assets. The main pool of qualifying expenditure brought forward at the beginning of the accounting period 1.10.01–30.9.02 is £80,000.

A Ltd's capital allowances are as follows.

	Main Pool	Short-life asset pools		Total Allowances
		Machine X	Machine Y	
	£	£	£	£
Accounting period 1.10.01–30.9.02				
WDV b/f	80,000			
Additions		40,000	25,000	
FYA 40%		(16,000)	(10,000)	26,000
WDA 25%	(20,000)	—	—	20,000
	60,000	24,000	15,000	£46,000
Accounting period 1.10.02-30.9.03				
WDA 25%	(15,000)	(6,000)	(3,750)	£24,750
	45,000	18,000	11,250	

Accounting period 1.10.03-30.9.04				
Disposal		(13,000)		
Balancing allowance		£5,000		5,000
WDA 25%	(11,250)		(2,813)	14,063
				£19,063
	33,750		8,437	
Accounting period 1.10.04–30.9.05				
WDA 25%	(8,437)		(2,109)	£10,546
	25,313		6,328	
Accounting period 1.10.05–30.9.06				
WDA 25%	(6,328)		(1,582)	£7,910
	18,985		4,746	
Accounting period 1.10.06–30.9.07				
Transfer to pool	4,746		(4,746)	
	23,731		—	
Disposal	(4,000)			
	19,731			
WDA 25%	(4,933)			£4,933
WDV c/f	£14,798			

Note

The fourth anniversary of the end of the chargeable period in which the expenditure is incurred is 30.9.06 (the four-year cut-off date). The balance of expenditure on Machine Y is thus transferred to the pool in the accounting period 1.10.06–30.9.07, this being the first chargeable period ending after the four-year cut-off date.

(*B*) *Long-life assets*

B Ltd prepares trading accounts to 31 December. In the year to 31 December 2005, the company has built new factory premises for use in its trade, which include a building mainly in use as offices (on which 20% of the cost of the premises is expended). Industrial buildings allowances are available on the construction expenditure. The main plant and machinery pool written-down value at 1 January 2005 is £800,000, and the disposal value to be brought into account in respect of plant and machinery in B Ltd's previous premises is £720,000. Machines installed in the new factory cost £920,000. No first-year allowances are available.

B Ltd also claims, for the year to 31 December 2005, plant and machinery allowances for expenditure of £520,000 incurred on fixtures integral to the new premises, which are agreed to have an expected life in excess of 25 years. Of this expenditure, it is agreed £120,000 should be apportioned to the offices.

On 1 May 2006 B Ltd incurs additional expenditure on upgrading the fixtures of £19,000, none of it relating to office fixtures.

On 1 October 2007 B Ltd moves to new premises, disposing of the old premises for a consideration including £425,000 relating to the integral fixtures (of which £95,000 relates to the office fixtures) and £510,000 relating to other plant and machinery.

Plant and machinery in the new premises costs £960,000, none of which relates to integral fixtures (which are included in the industrial buildings allowances claim for the new premises).

The plant and machinery allowances computations for relevant periods are as follows.

	Main Pool	Long-life asset pool	Total allowances
	£	£	
Accounting period ending 31.12.05			
WDV b/f	800,000	—	
Additions (see note (*a*))	1,040,000	400,000	
Disposals	(720,000)	—	
	1,120,000	400,000	
WDA	280,000	24,000	£304,000
WDV c/f	840,000	376,000	
Accounting period ending 31.12.06			
Additions (see note (*b*))	—	19,000	
	840,000	395,000	
WDA	210,000	23,700	£233,700
WDV c/f	630,000	371,300	
Accounting period ending 31.12.07			
Additions	960,000	—	
Disposals	(605,000)	(330,000)	
	985,000	41,300	
WDA (see note (*c*))	246,250	2,478	£248,728
WDV c/f	£738,750	£38,822	

Notes

(*a*) Expenditure on fixtures provided for use in offices is excluded from being long-life asset expenditure (regardless of whether the office building itself attracts industrial buildings allowances because it represents not more than 25% of the overall cost of premises otherwise qualifying).

(*b*) Additional expenditure on existing long-life assets is within the provisions even if within the annual monetary limit.

(*c*) The long-life asset pool comes to an end only on permanent discontinuance of the trade and not before. Allowances therefore continue to be given at 6% p.a. on the residue of expenditure on long-life assets despite their having been disposed of.

(C) *Pooling, writing-down allowances, cars, acquisitions from connected persons and balancing adjustments*

A Ltd is in business as a building and demolition contractor. Its business qualifies as a small business for the purposes of first-year allowances. The company makes up accounts to 31 March. The accounts for the year to 31 March 2008 reveal the following additions and disposals.

	£
Additions	
Plant	
Dumper Truck	5,000
Excavator	32,000
Bulldozer	20,000
	£57,000
Fittings	
Office furniture	£2,000
Motor Vehicles	
Land Rover	6,000
Van	5,000
Car 2	12,200
	£23,200

Disposals	Cost	Proceeds
	£	£
Excavator	32,000	30,000
Digger loader	15,000	4,000
Car 1	14,200	4,200
Fittings	3,500	500

The dumper truck was bought second-hand from Q Ltd, a company connected with A Ltd, but had not been used in a trade or other qualifying activity. The truck had originally cost Q Ltd £6,000, but its market value at sale was only £2,000.

The excavator was sold without having been brought into use.

The bulldozer was purchased from P Ltd, another connected company and had originally cost P Ltd £25,000. It had been used for the purposes of a qualifying activity, and the price paid by A Ltd was less than the market value.

The written-down values at 31 March 2007 of the main plant and machinery pool and Car 1 are £7,500 and £3,900 respectively.

The plant and machinery allowances for the accounting period ending on 31 March 2008 are:

	Expenditure qualifying for FYAs 50%	Main Pool 25%	Expensive car pools: Car 1	Expensive car pools: Car 2	Total allow-ances
	£	£	£	£	£
WDV b/f		7,500	3,900		
Additions					
Excavator (note (*a*))	32,000				
Dumper truck (notes (*b*)(*c*))		2,000			
Bulldozer (notes (*b*)(*d*))		20,000			
Furniture	2,000				
Land Rover and van	11,000				
Cars				12,200	
	45,000				
FYA (50%)	(22,500)				22.500
Transfer to pool (£32,000 less 50% (note (*a*))	(16,000)	16,000			
	6,500				
Disposals					
Excavator		(30,000)			
Digger		(4,000)			
Fittings		(500)			
Car 1			(4,200)		
		11,000	(£300)	12,200	
WDA (25%)		(2,750)			2.750
WDA (restricted)				(3,000)	3.000
Transfer to pool	(£6,500)	6,500			
WDV c/f		£14,750		£9,200	
Total allowances					£28,250
Balancing charge					(£300)

Notes

(*a*) First-year allowances (10.27 above) and writing-down allowances (10.28 above) are available even though an item of plant or machinery is disposed of without being brought into use, always provided that the expenditure is qualifying expenditure (see 10.24 above). See 10.28 above as regards the requirement, where a first-year allowance has been given, to allocate the expenditure to a pool for a chargeable period no later than that in which a disposal event occurs.

(*b*) No first-year allowance is available in respect of an item of plant or machinery purchased from a connected person. See 10.27(ix) above.

(*c*) Qualifying expenditure on the dumper truck is restricted to the lowest of

(i) market value;

(ii) capital expenditure incurred by the vendor (or, if lower, by a person connected with him);

(iii) capital expenditure incurred by the purchaser.

See 10.38(C) below.

(*d*) Qualifying expenditure on the bulldozer is the lesser of A's actual expenditure and the disposal value brought into account in the vendor's computations (see 10.38(C) below). (The vendor's disposal value would have been market value but for the fact that the purchaser is himself entitled to claim capital allowances on the acquisition (see 10.29(*b*)(i) above).) A's qualifying expenditure is thus equal to his actual expenditure.

(*e*) Car 2, by virtue of its costing over £12,000, is allocated to a single asset pool (see 10.30(A) above), and the same applied to Car 1.

(*f*) The writing-down allowance on Car 2 is restricted to £3,000 before adjustment for private use (see 10.30(A) above).

10.32 **Making of allowances and charges.** Where the qualifying activity is within 10.24(i) or (iii)–(v) above, plant and machinery allowances are treated as expenses of, and balancing charges are treated as receipts of, the trade, profession, vocation, Schedule A business, overseas property business, furnished holiday lettings business or *ICTA 1988, s 55(2)* concern. [*CAA 2001, ss 247–252, 262; CAA 1990, ss 27(1), 28A(1), 29(1), 73(1), 140(2)(4), 144(2), 161(5); FA 1994, s 211; FA 1997, Sch 15 paras 3, 4; FA 1998, Sch 5 para 61; ITEPA 2003, Sch 6 para 253; ITTOIA 2005, Sch 1 paras 546, 547*].

Allowances and charges are computed for corporation tax purposes by reference to events in accounting periods (see 10.1 above). [*CAA 2001, ss 2(1), 6(1); CAA 1990, ss 140(1), 144(1), 161(2); FA 1994, ss 211, 212(2)*].

See 10.37 below as regards a qualifying activity of special leasing (as in 10.24(vii) above).

See 10.2(i)(ii) above as regards the *claiming* of capital allowances.

Simon's Direct Tax Service. See B2.380 *et seq.*

10.33 **Fixtures.** For expenditure incurred after 11 July 1984 (but excluding, for chargeable periods ending after 23 July 1996, expenditure under a contract entered into on or before that date, or pursuant to an obligation in a lease, or agreement for a lease, entered into on or before that date), there are special provisions to determine entitlement to allowances on fixtures, i.e. plant or machinery which, by law, becomes part of the building or land on which it is installed or otherwise fixed, including any boiler or water-filled radiator installed as part of a space or water heating system. A dispute may arise as to whether fixtures have, in law, become part of a building or land. Where two or more persons' tax liabilities are affected by the outcome of such a dispute, the question is determined for tax purposes by the Special Commissioners, before whom all those persons are entitled to appear and be heard or to make written representations. [*CAA 2001, s 172(1)(2), s 173, s 204(1)–(3); CAA 1990, s 51(1)-(2A)(7); FA 1997, Sch 16 para 2(5)(6); FA 2000, s 78*].

In *J C Decaux (UK) Ltd v Francis (Sp C 84), [1996] SSCD 281*, automatic public conveniences and other street furniture such as bus shelters were held to be fixtures forming part of the land (and see (*a*) below).

These provisions determine ownership for capital allowances purposes of plant or machinery that is (or becomes) a fixture and determine entitlement to allowances in each of the various circumstances described at (*a*)–(*f*) below. See 10.34 below for the disapplication of these provisions in cases involving long funding leases of plant or machinery that is (or becomes) a fixture. Before *CAA 2001* had effect (see 10.1 above), the provisions also denied allowances to any person other than the person to whom plant or machinery was thereby treated as belonging. The provisions do not affect the entitlement of a contributor towards capital expenditure (see 10.2(vi) above). [*CAA 2001, s 172(1)(2)(5); CAA 1990, s 51(1)(8)*]. See after (*f*) below for provisions determining cessation of ownership (and consequent disposal values), acquisition of ownership in certain cases and restrictions of qualifying expenditure where allowances previously claimed.

Although the rules apply strictly on an asset-by-asset basis, the HMRC accept that in practice they may be applied to groups of assets provided that this does not distort the tax computation (HMRC Capital Allowances Manual CA 26100).

For the purposes of the fixtures provisions, an '*interest in land*' means:

(i) the fee simple estate in the land;

(ii) in Scotland, in the case of feudal property prior to abolition of feudal tenure, the estate or interest of the proprietor of the *dominium utile*, and in any other case, the interest of the owner;

(iii) a lease (defined for these provisions in relation to land as any leasehold estate in (or, in Scotland, lease of) the land (whether a head-lease, sub-lease or under-lease) or any agreement to acquire such an estate (or lease));

(iv) an easement or servitude;

(v) a licence to occupy land,

and any agreement to acquire an interest as in (i)–(iv) above. Where an interest is conveyed or assigned by way of security subject to a right of redemption, the interest is treated as continuing to belong to the person having the redemption right. [*CAA 2001, ss 174(4), 175, Sch 3 para 29; CAA 1990, s 51(3)(4)*]. As regards (v) above, for the HMRC view of when a licence to occupy land exists for these purposes, see HMRC Capital Allowances Manual CA 26100).

See generally HMRC Capital Allowances Manual CA 26000 *et seq.*

(*a*) *Expenditure incurred by holder of interest in land.* Where a person having an interest in land incurs capital expenditure on plant or machinery which becomes a fixture in relation to that land, for the purposes of a trade or other qualifying activity, then, subject to the election in (*b*) or (*f*) below, the fixture is treated as belonging to that person. If there are two or more such persons, with different interests, the only interest to be taken into account for this purpose is:

  (i) an easement or servitude, or any agreement to acquire same;

  (ii) if (i) does not apply to any of those interests, a licence to occupy the land;

(iii) if neither (i) nor (ii) applies to any of those interests, that interest which is not directly or indirectly in reversion on any other of those interests in the land (in Scotland, that of whichever of those persons has, or last had, the right of use of the land).

[*CAA 2001, s 176; CAA 1990, s 52; FA 2001, s 66, Sch 18 para 3*].

In *J C Decaux (UK) Ltd v Francis (Sp C 84), [1996] SSCD 281*, suppliers to local authorities of automatic public conveniences and other street furniture such as bus shelters, which were held to be fixtures forming part of the land, were held not to have an interest in the land.

(*b*) *Expenditure incurred by equipment lessor.* An 'equipment lease' exists where:

- a person incurs capital expenditure on an item of plant or machinery for leasing;
- an agreement is entered into for the lease, directly or indirectly from that person (the '*equipment lessor*'), of the item to another person (the '*equipment lessee*');
- the item becomes a fixture; and
- the item is not leased as part of the land in relation to which it is a fixture.

Such an agreement, or a lease entered into under such an agreement, is an '*equipment lease*'. Provided that:

(i) under the equipment lease, the plant or machinery is leased for the purposes of a trade or other qualifying activity carried on (or to be carried on in future) by the equipment lessee;

(ii) it is not for use in a dwelling-house;

(iii) the equipment lessee is within the charge to UK tax on profits from the qualifying activity for use in which the equipment is leased (but see below for supersession of this requirement);

(iv) the equipment lessor and equipment lessee are not CONNECTED PERSONS (19);

(v) if the expenditure on the fixture had been incurred by the equipment lessee, he would have been entitled to allowances under (*a*) above,

the equipment lessor and equipment lessee may jointly elect for the fixture to be treated, from the time the expenditure is incurred by the equipment lessor (or, if later, from the commencement of the lessee's qualifying activity), as owned by the lessor and not the lessee.

Where the following conditions are met, (i), (iii) and (v) above do not have to be satisfied (and the potentially later start date of the election is not relevant):

(1) the plant or machinery becomes a fixture by being fixed to land which is neither a building nor part of a building;

(2) the lessee has an interest in that land when he takes possession of the plant or machinery under the equipment lease;

(3) under the terms of the equipment lease the lessor is entitled, at the end of the lease period, to sever the plant or machinery from the land to which it is then fixed, whereupon it will be owned by the lessor;

(4) the nature of the plant or machinery and the way it is fixed to the land are such that its use does not, to any material extent, prevent its being used, after severance, for the same purposes on different premises; and

(5) the equipment lease is such as falls under generally accepted accounting practice to be treated in the accounts of the equipment lessor as an operating lease.

For chargeable periods ending after 20 March 2000, the requirement at (iii) above is repealed, having been superseded by the general exclusion of non-UK taxable activities in 10.24 above. The general exclusion applies even where (1)–(5) above are met.

In relation to agreements entered into before 19 March 1997, the election is not available where the lessee's trade was not being carried on at the time of the agreement, and the waiver of certain requirements (as above) where conditions (1)–(5) above are satisfied does not apply. For expenditure incurred by the equipment lessor before 24 July 1996, conditions (ii) and (iii) above do not apply, and (v) above is replaced by a requirement that, if the expenditure had been incurred by the equipment lessee, the equipment would, under (*a*) above, have been treated as belonging to him (for which see *Melluish v BMI (No 3) Ltd HL 1995, 68 TC 1*).

The election must be made within two years after the end of the equipment lessor's chargeable period in which the expenditure is incurred.

Where expenditure is incurred on or after 28 July 2000 and before 1 January 2008 on plant or machinery consisting of a boiler, heat exchanger, radiator or heating control installed in a building as part of a space or water heating system, and the equipment lease is approved under the Affordable Warmth programme by the Secretary of State (or the responsible Scottish, Welsh or Northern Ireland body), these provisions have effect without (i)–(iii) and (v) above having to be satisfied. If the approval is withdrawn, it is treated as never having had effect. The taxpayer must notify the inspector, within three months of his becoming aware that a return of his has become incorrect by reason of the withdrawal of approval, of the amendments to the return required in consequence of the withdrawal, subject to penalties for failure.

[*CAA 2001, s 174(1)–(3), ss 177–180, 203, Sch 3 paras 30–33; CAA 1990, s 53; FA 1996, s 135, Sch 21 para 31; FA 1997, Sch 16 para 3; FA 2000, s 75(5)(6), s 79; FA 2002, Sch 40 Pt 3(16)*].

See (*f*) below as regards expenditure incurred by an energy services provider.

(*c*) *Expenditure included in consideration for acquisition of existing interest in land.* Where a person acquires a pre-existing interest in land to which a fixture is attached, for a consideration in part treated for capital allowance purposes as being expenditure on provision of the fixture, the fixture is treated as belonging to the person acquiring the interest. This applies equally where the fixture in question was previously let under an 'equipment lease' (see (*b*) above) and, in connection with the acquisition, the purchaser pays a capital sum to discharge the equipment lessee's obligations under that lease. For corporation tax accounting periods ending after 31 March 2001, it also applies where the fixture was provided under an energy services agreement (see (*f*) below) and, in connection with the acquisition, the purchaser pays a capital sum to discharge the client's obligations under that agreement.

Where the purchaser acquired the interest before 24 July 1996, the above applied with the additional condition that either no person had previously been entitled to allowances on the fixture, or any person previously so entitled has been or is required to bring in a disposal value (other than by virtue of an 'additional VAT rebate' — see 10.2(vii) above) in respect of the fixture.

[*CAA 2001, s 181(1)(4), s 182(1), 182A(1), Sch 3 paras 34, 35; CAA 1990, s 54; FA 1991, Sch 14 para 10; FA 1997, Sch 16 paras 2, 4, 5; FA 2001, s 66, Sch 18 paras 5, 6*].

Where the above provisions would otherwise apply, they are treated as not applying (and as never having applied) where the following conditions are met.

(A) Before *CAA 2001* had effect (see 10.1 above):

(i) an interest in any land in which the whole or part of the land to which the fixture is attached is held by any person immediately after the time of the above acquisition (where that time is after 23 July 1996);

(ii) that interest is not the one acquired by the purchaser;

(iii) the person in (i) above is treated as the owner of the fixture (other than under *CAA 1990, s 154* (contributions to expenditure — see 10.2(vi) above)) immediately before the time referred to in (i) above, in consequence of having incurred expenditure on its provision; and

(iv) that person is entitled to, and claims, an allowance in respect of that expenditure.

(B) Where *CAA 2001* has effect (see 10.1 above):

(i) a person is treated as the owner of the fixture (other than under *CAA 2001, s 538* (contributions to expenditure — see 10.2(vi) above)) immediately before the time of the above acquisition, in consequence of having incurred expenditure on its provision; and

(ii) that person is entitled to, and claims, an allowance in respect of that expenditure.

Where any person becomes aware that a return of his has become incorrect because of the operation of this provision, the necessary amendments to the return must be notified to HMRC within three months of the taxpayer becoming so aware, subject to penalties for failure.

[*CAA 2001, s 181(2)(3), s 182(2)(3), s 182A(2)(3), s 203; CAA 1990, ss 51(6A), 56A; FA 1997, Sch 16 para 2(4)(7), paras 4, 9; FA 2001, ss 66, 69, Sch 18 paras 6, 11, Sch 21 para 2(1)-(3)*].

(*d*) *Expenditure incurred by incoming lessee: election to transfer lessor's entitlement to allowances.* Where a person with an interest in land to which a fixture is attached grants a lease and that person would (or if chargeable to tax would) be entitled, for the chargeable period in which the lease is granted, to capital allowances in respect of the fixture, and the consideration given by the lessee falls, in whole or in part, to be treated for plant and machinery allowances purposes as expenditure on the provision of the fixture, an election is available to the lessor and lessee. They may jointly elect (by notice to HMRC within two years after the date on which the lease takes effect) that, from the grant of the lease, the fixture is treated as belonging to the lessee and not to the lessor. No such election is available if lessor and lessee are CONNECTED PERSONS (19), or (where the lease was granted before 24 July 1996) if it appears that the sole or main benefit to the lessor from the grant of the lease and the election would be enhanced capital allowances or a reduced balancing charge; see now the anti-avoidance provision at *CAA 2001, s 197* below. The instant provisions apply to the entering into of an agreement for a lease as they apply to a grant of a lease. [*CAA 2001, ss 174(4), 183, Sch 3 para 36; CAA 1990, s 55*].

(*e*) *Expenditure incurred by incoming lessee: lessor not entitled to allowances.* Where:

- a person with an interest in land to which a fixture is attached grants a lease;

- the provisions at (*d*) above do not apply, because the lessor is not entitled to capital allowances in respect of the fixture;
- before the lease is granted, the fixture has not been used for the purposes of a trade or other qualifying activity by the lessor or a person connected with the lessor (see 19 CONNECTED PERSONS); and
- the consideration given by the lessee includes a capital sum falling, in whole or in part, to be treated for plant and machinery allowances purposes as expenditure on the provision of the fixture,

the fixture is treated as belonging to the lessee from the time the lease is granted.

Where the lease was granted before 24 July 1996, these provisions applied with the additional condition that at the time of grant no person had previously become entitled to an allowance in respect of any capital expenditure incurred on the provision of the fixture. Where the lease is granted on or after that date, rules similar to those of *CAA 2001, s 181(2)(3), s 182(2)(3), s 182A(2)(3), s 203* at (*c*) above apply instead (by reference to the time of grant).

[*CAA 2001, s 184, Sch 3 para 37; CAA 1990, ss 52, 56; FA 1997, Sch 16 paras 3, 4, 6; FA 2001, s 69, Sch 21 para 2(4)*].

(*f*) *Expenditure incurred by energy services provider.* An '*energy services agreement*' is an agreement entered into by an 'energy services provider' and his client that provides, with a view to the saving or more efficient use of energy, for:

- the design of plant or machinery or of systems incorporating it;
- the obtaining and installation of the plant or machinery; and
- its operation and maintenance,

and under which any payment by the client in respect of the operation of the plant or machinery is wholly or partly linked to the energy savings or increased energy efficiency. An '*energy services provider*' is a person carrying on a qualifying activity consisting wholly or mainly in providing energy management services. [*CAA 2001, s 175A; FA 2001, s 66, Sch 18 para 2*].

For corporation tax accounting periods ending after 31 March 2001, where:

- an energy services agreement is entered into;
- the energy services provider incurs capital expenditure after 31 March 2001 under the agreement on an item of plant or machinery;
- the item becomes a fixture;
- at the time the item becomes a fixture, the client has an interest in the land in relation to which it is a fixture but the provider does not;
- the item is neither leased nor used in a dwelling-house;
- the operation of the item is carried out wholly or substantially by the provider or a person connected with him; and
- provider and client are not CONNECTED PERSONS (19),

the energy services provider and the client may jointly elect for the fixture to be treated, from the time the expenditure is incurred, as owned by the former and not the latter. This opens the way for the energy services provider to claim 100% first-year allowances where his expenditure is within 10.27(*d*) above. The election must be made no later than two years after the end of the accounting period in which the expenditure is incurred. If the client would not have been entitled to allowances under (*a*) above if he had incurred the expenditure himself, the election is available only if the item belongs to the technology class 'Combined Heat and Power' in the Energy Technology Criteria List (see 10.27 above), as specified by Treasury order *SI 2001 No 2541*, or to any other class of plant or machinery specified for this purpose by Treasury order; the intention is that, in such specified cases, allowances to the provider are not to be denied only because the client is a non-taxpayer. [*CAA 2001, s 180A; FA 2001, s 66, Sch 18 para 4*]. See also HMRC Capital Allowances Manual CA 23150.

Cessation of ownership

(A) If a person is treated as owning a fixture under *CAA 2001, s 176* (see (*a*) above) *s 181, 182* or *182A* (see (*c*) above), *s 183* (see (*d*) above) or *s 184* (see (*e*) above), that person is treated as ceasing to be the owner if and on ceasing to have the 'qualifying interest'. The '*qualifying interest*' is the interest in the land in question, except that where (*d*) or (*e*) above apply it is the lease there referred to. There are rules (see *CAA 2001, s 189*) for identifying the qualifying interest in special cases.

(B) Where, under (*d*) above, the lessee begins to be treated as owning the fixture, the lessor is treated as ceasing to own it at that time.

(C) Where a fixture is permanently severed from the building or land, such that it is no longer owned by the person treated as owning it, that person is treated as ceasing to own it at the time of severance.

(D) Where an equipment lessor is treated as owning a fixture (see (*b*) above) and either the lessor assigns the rights under the equipment lease or the financial obligations of the equipment lessee (or the assignee etc.) are discharged, the equipment lessor is treated as ceasing to own the fixture at that time (or the earliest of those times).

(E) Where an energy services provider is treated as owning a fixture (see (*f*) above) and either the provider assigns the rights under the energy services agreement or the financial obligations of the client (or the assignee etc.) are discharged, the energy services provider is treated as ceasing to own the fixture at that time (or the earliest of those times).

[*CAA 2001, ss 188–192A; CAA 1990, s 57(2)–(5)(7), s 58(1)(5); FA 2001, s 66, Sch 18 paras 7, 8*].

The *disposal value* to be brought into account in relation to a fixture depends upon the nature of the event.

(1) On cessation of ownership under (A) above due to a sale of the qualifying interest (other than where (2) below applies), and subject to the election below, it is that part of the sale price that falls (or would, if there were an entitlement, fall) to be treated for plant and machinery allowances purposes as expenditure by the purchaser on the provision of the fixture.

(2) On cessation of ownership under (A) above due to a sale of the qualifying interest at less than market value (unless the buyer (not being a dual resident investing company connected with the seller) can claim plant or machinery or research and development (formerly scientific research) allowances for his expenditure, in which case (1) above applies), it is the amount that, if that interest were sold at market value (determined without regard to the disposal event itself) at that time, would be treated for plant and machinery allowances purposes as expenditure by the purchaser on provision of the fixture.

(3) On cessation of ownership under (A) above where neither (1) or (2) above applies but the qualifying interest continues (or would do so but for being merged with another interest), it is an amount determined as in (2) above.

(4) On cessation of ownership under (A) above due to the expiry of the qualifying interest, it is any capital sum received by reference to the fixture, or otherwise nil.

(5) On cessation of ownership under (B) above, and subject to the election below, it is that part of the capital sum given by the lessee for the lease as qualifies for plant and machinery allowances as the lessee's expenditure on the fixture.

(6) On cessation of ownership under (C) above, it is market value at time of severance.

(7) On cessation of ownership under (D) above, it is the consideration for the assignment or, as the case may be, the capital sum, if any, paid to discharge the equipment lessee's financial obligations.

(8) On cessation of ownership under (E) above, it is the consideration for the assignment or, as the case may be, the capital sum, if any, paid to discharge the client's financial obligations.

(9) On permanent discontinuance of the trade or other qualifying activity followed by the sale of the qualifying interest, it is an amount determined as in (1) above.

(10) On permanent discontinuance of the qualifying activity followed by demolition or destruction of the fixture, it is the net amount received for the remains, plus any insurance or capital compensation received.

(11) On permanent discontinuance of the qualifying activity followed by permanent loss (other than as in (10) above) of the fixture, it is any insurance or capital compensation received.

(12) On the fixture's beginning to be used wholly or partly for purposes other than those of the qualifying activity, it is that part of the sale price that would fall to be treated for plant and machinery allowances purposes as expenditure by the purchaser on the provision of the fixture if the qualifying interest were sold at market value.

If, before 24 July 1996, a person is treated as ceasing to own a fixture by virtue of (A), (B) or (C) above, and another person incurs expenditure on the fixture, allowances are not available on so much (if any) of that expenditure as exceeds the former owner's disposal value.

[*CAA 2001, s 196, Sch 3 para 41; CAA 1990, s 26(1)(f), s 57(1), s 58(2)(4)(5), s 59; FA 2001, s 66, Sch 18 para 10*].

Where the event concerned occurs after 23 July 1996, fixtures are treated as disposed of at their 'notional written-down value' (if greater than would otherwise be the case) where the disposal event is part of a scheme or arrangement having tax avoidance (whether by increased allowances or reduced charges) as a main object. The '*notional written-down value*' is qualifying expenditure on the item in question less maximum allowances to date, computed on the assumption that all allowances have been made in full. [*CAA 2001, s 197; CAA 1990, s 59A; FA 1997, Sch 16 para 5*].

A special election is available where the disposal value of fixtures falls to be determined under (1) or (5) above at a time on or after 19 March 1996. Subject as below and to *CAA 2001, ss 186, 187* (see below) and *s 197* (above), the seller and purchaser (or, where (5) above applies, the lessor and lessee under (*d*) above) may jointly elect to fix the amount so determined at a figure not exceeding either the capital expenditure treated as incurred on the fixtures by the seller (or lessor) former owner or the actual sale price (or capital sum). The remainder (if any) of the sale price (or capital sum) is attributed to the other property included in the sale. The notice of election must be given within two years after the interest is acquired (or the lease granted), and is irrevocable. A copy must also accompany the return of the persons making the election. The notice must contain prescribed information and must quantify the amount fixed by the election, although if subsequent circumstances reduce the maximum below that fixed, the election is treated as being for that reduced maximum amount. There are provisions for the determination of questions relating to such elections by Appeal Commissioners. Where a person has made a tax return and becomes aware that it has become incorrect because of such an election (or because of subsequent circumstances affecting the election), the necessary amendments to the return must be notified to HMRC within three months of his becoming so aware, subject to penalties for failure. [*CAA 2001, ss 198–201, 203, 204(4)–(6); CAA 1990, s 51(6A), ss 59B, 59C; FA 1997, Sch 16 para 2(4)(7), paras 6, 9; FA 1999, Sch 11 para 6*]. In practice, HMRC normally accept an election covering a group of fixtures, or all the fixtures in a single property, but not one covering fixtures in different properties (e.g. where a portfolio of properties is sold) (HMRC Capital Allowances Manual CA 28600).

Acquisition of ownership in certain cases. If, on the termination of a lease, the outgoing lessee is treated under (A) above as ceasing to own a fixture, the lessor is thereafter treated as the owner. This applies in relation to a licence as it does in relation to a lease. [*CAA 2001, s 193; CAA 1990, s 57(6)*].

The following apply where an election is made under (*b*) above (election to treat fixture as owned by equipment lessor), and either:

- the equipment lessor assigns his rights under the equipment lease; or
- the equipment lessee's financial obligations under the lease (or those of his assignee etc.) are discharged (on the payment of a capital sum).

If the former applies, then, from the time of the assignment, the fixture is treated as belonging to the assignee for capital allowance purposes, and the consideration for the assignment treated as consideration given by him on provision of the fixture. If the assignee makes any further assignment, he is treated under this provision as if he were the original lessor.

If the latter applies, the capital sum is treated as consideration for the fixture, and the fixture is treated from the time of the payment as belonging to the equipment lessee (or to any other person in whom his obligations under the lease have become vested).

[*CAA 2000, ss 194, 195; CAA 1990, s 58(2)–(5)*].

The same applies, with appropriate modifications, where the election in question was under (*f*) above (election to treat fixture as owned by energy services provider). [*CAA 2001, ss 195A, 195B; FA 2001, s 66, Sch 18 para 9*].

Restriction of qualifying expenditure where allowance previously claimed. Where:

(i) a fixture is treated under these provisions as belonging to any person (the current owner) in consequence of his incurring capital expenditure on its provision;

(ii) the plant or machinery is treated (other than under *CAA 2001, s 538* — contributions to expenditure, see 10.2(vi) above) as having belonged at a 'relevant earlier time' to a person (who may be the same as the person within (i) above) in consequence of his incurring expenditure other than that within (i) above; and that person, having claimed a plant and machinery allowance for that expenditure, must bring a disposal value into account *by reason of an event occurring after 23 July 1996*,

so much (if any) of the expenditure referred to in (i) above as exceeds the 'maximum allowable amount' is left out of account in determining the current owner's qualifying expenditure or, as the case may be, is taken to be expenditure which should never have been so taken into account.

A '*relevant earlier time*' is any time before the earliest time when the plant or machinery is treated as belonging to the current owner in consequence of the expenditure referred to in (i) above. The relevant earlier time does not, however, include any time before an earlier sale of the plant or machinery other than as a fixture and other than between CONNECTED PERSONS (19).

The '*maximum allowable amount*' is the sum of the disposal value referred to in (ii) above and so much (if any) of the expenditure referred to in (i) above as is deemed under *CAA 2001, s 25* (installation costs, see 10.25 above) to be on provision of the plant or machinery. Where (ii) above is satisfied in relation to more than one disposal event, only the most recent event is taken into account for this purpose.

Where a person has made a return and becomes aware that it has become incorrect because of the operation of this provision, the necessary amendments to the return must be notified to HMRC within three months of his becoming so aware, subject to penalties for failure.

[*CAA 2001, ss 185, 203, Sch 3 para 38; CAA 1990, ss 51(6A), 56B; FA 1997, Sch 16 para 2(4)(7), paras 4, 9*].

Where:

(I) a person has claimed industrial buildings allowances for expenditure partly on the provision of plant or machinery, and transfers the relevant interest in the building concerned; and

(II) the transferee, or any other person to whom the plant or machinery is subsequently treated under these provisions as belonging, claims plant and machinery allowances for expenditure incurred thereon *at a time after 23 July 1996* when it is a fixture in the building,

the qualifying expenditure in respect of which the claim in (II) above is made is restricted to the '*relevant amount*', i.e. the proportion of the consideration for the transfer referred to in (I) above attributable to the fixture. It is assumed for this purpose that the transfer was a sale for an amount equal to the residue of expenditure (see 10.14 above) immediately after the transfer.

A similar restriction applies where research and development (formerly scientific research) allowances have previously been claimed.

[*CAA 2001, ss 186, 187, Sch 3 paras 39, 40; CAA 1990, ss 56C, 56D; FA 1997, Sch 16 para 4; FA 2000, Sch 19 para 8*].

Simon's Direct Tax Service. See **B2.355** *et seq.*

Finance leasing. See 66.54 TRADING INCOME as regards restrictions on capital allowances where certain finance leasing arrangements are involved. See also 10.28 above, 10.34 and 10.38(A)(C) below.

10.34 **Long funding leasing.** The rules on leasing of plant and machinery are reformed by *FA 2006, s 81, Sch 8* as set out below with effect from, broadly, **1 April 2006** (and see below under Commencement/transitional provisions). For 'long funding leases', the new regime grants entitlement to capital allowances to the lessee rather than to the lessor as previously. There are corresponding changes to the tax treatment of lease rentals, to ensure that the lessor is no longer taxed on, and the lessee does not obtain a deduction for, the capital element of rentals (see 66.64 TRADING INCOME). The new regime applies only to leases which are essentially financing transactions, known as '*funding leases*', comprising mainly finance leases but also some operating leases. Leases of less than five years' duration are excluded from the regime, as are pre-1 April 2006 leases (subject to transitional rules). There are transitional rules to enable leases finalised on or after 1 April 2006 to remain within the pre-existing regime in appropriate circumstances. The coverage below is divided into sections on lessees, relevant definitions, lessors, fixtures, miscellaneous and commencement/transitional provisions.

Lessees. Where a person carrying on a qualifying activity (see 10.24 above) incurs expenditure (whether or not capital expenditure) on the provision of plant or machinery for the purposes of that activity under a 'long funding lease' (see (1) below), the plant or machinery is treated as owned by him at all times whilst he is the lessee. He is then treated as having incurred *capital expenditure* on the provision of the plant or machinery, of an amount determined as below depending on whether the lease is a 'long funding operating lease' (see (3) below) or a 'long-funding finance lease' (see (4) below), at the 'commencement' (see *CAA 2001, s 70YI(1)*) of the term of the lease. (The combined effect is to treat that capital expenditure as qualifying expenditure (as in 10.24 above) of the lessee for the purposes of plant and machinery capital allowances and, where appropriate, as first-year qualifying expenditure (as in 10.27 above) for the purposes of first-year allowances.)

If the lease is a 'long funding operating lease' (see (3) below), the capital expenditure is equal to the market value of the plant or machinery as at the commencement of the term of the lease or, if later, the date on which the plant or machinery is first brought into use for the purposes of the qualifying activity.

If the lease is a 'long funding finance lease' (see (4) below), then, subject to the possible addition and restriction described below, the capital expenditure is equal to the present value, as at the commencement of the term of the lease or, if later, the date on which the plant or machinery is first brought into use for the purposes of the qualifying activity, of the 'minimum lease payments' (see (5) below). Present value is computed as it would be if accounts were prepared in accordance with generally accepted accounting practice (GAAP) on the date on which that value is first recognised in the lessee's books or other financial records. If the lessee paid rentals under the lease before its term commenced, the capital expenditure also includes the amount of any such rentals for which tax relief is otherwise unavailable (and would still have been unavailable even if the plant or machinery had been used pre-commencement). If a main purpose of entering into the lease (or arrangements that include the lease) was to obtain capital allowances on an amount materially greater than the market value of the leased asset at the commencement of the term of the lease, the capital expenditure is restricted to that market value.

If the *lessor* under the long funding finance lease subsequently incurs additional expenditure such that the lease rentals increase, the *lessee* is treated as incurring further capital expenditure on the plant or machinery. The further expenditure is equal to the increase (if any) in the present value of the minimum lease payments and is treated as incurred on the date it is first recognised in the lessee's books or other financial records.

As regards long funding finance leases, the same principles apply whether the lease is accounted for as a lease or as a loan.

Disposal events and values. The termination of a long funding lease is a disposal event, and a **disposal value** (see 10.29 above) must be brought into account by the lessee for the chargeable period in which that event occurs, computed as follows.

If the lease is a 'long funding operating lease', the disposal value is equal to the sum of elements A and B where:

- element A is the excess (if any) of the original amount of capital expenditure (computed as above) over the total *reductions* falling to be made under *ICTA 1988, s 502K* (see 66.64 TRADING INCOME under Lessees) (and its income tax equivalent) for periods of account in which the person concerned was the lessee; and
- element B is the total of any amounts payable to the lessee that are calculated by reference to 'termination value' (as defined by *CAA 2001, s 70YH*), e.g. lease rental refunds.

If the lease is a 'long funding finance lease', the disposal value is equal to the sum of Elements C and D less any amount payable by the lessee to the lessor in consequence of the termination, where:

- element C is the total of any amounts payable to the lessee that are calculated by reference to 'termination value' (as defined by *CAA 2001, s 70YH*), e.g. lease rental refunds; and

- element D is, if the lease terminates short of its full term, the present value, immediately before the termination, of the excess of the original amount of the 'minimum lease payments' (see (5) below), over what would have been the amount of the minimum lease payments had the lease had been designed to expire when it did.

If the termination would also give rise to a disposal event within 10.29 above in the case of the lessee, that disposal event is ignored.

[*CAA 2001, ss 70A–70E; FA 2006, Sch 8 para 6*].

Definitions. The following definitions apply for these purposes.

(1) A '*long funding lease*' is a 'funding lease' (as in (2) below) that is not a 'short lease' (see (A) below), is not an 'excluded lease of background plant or machinery for a building' (see (B) below) and is not excluded under the *de minimis* provision at (C) below for plant or machinery leased with land. Where, at the 'commencement' (see *CAA 2001, s 70YI(1)*) of the term of a plant or machinery lease (as widely defined by *CAA 2001, s 70K*), the plant or machinery is not being used for the purposes of a qualifying activity, but subsequently is so used, the lease is a long funding lease if it would otherwise have been a long funding lease at its 'inception' (see *CAA 2001, s 70YI(1)*); this covers, for example, the situation where either the lessor or the lessee is originally non-UK resident and subsequently becomes UK resident. However, the treatment of a lease as a long funding lease as regards the *lessee* is always subject to the following two conditions.

- The lessee must treat the lease as a long funding lease in his first tax return (and thus his first accounts) the profits declared by which are affected by the question of whether or not the lease is a long funding lease. That tax return cannot be altered in this respect by a subsequent error or mistake claim.

- A lease is not a long funding lease as regards the lessee if either the lessor or any superior lessor under a chain of leases (as defined) is entitled, at the commencement of the term of the lease, to any capital allowance (not necessarily a plant or machinery allowance) in respect of the leased plant or machinery. This also applies if such entitlement would have arisen but for *CAA 2001, s 70V* (see below under Miscellaneous: Tax avoidance involving international leasing). It also applies if the entitlement arose at an earlier time but no requirement has yet arisen to bring into account a disposal value as described below under Lessors. These conditions are applied on the assumption that the lessor in question is within the charge to UK tax, even if that is not, in fact, the case. However, where the inception of the lease is before 28 June 2006 and the lessor remains entitled to capital allowances by virtue only of the exception under (2)(iii) below the lease is still regarded as a long funding lease as regards the lessee.

Certain leases held by tonnage tax companies are not to be treated as being long funding leases (see 55.16 PROFIT COMPUTATIONS).

[CAA 2001, ss 70G, 70H, 70Q; FA 2006, Sch 8 para 7].

The above-mentioned exclusions from long funding lease treatment are defined in (A)–(C) below.

(A) A '*short lease*' is defined as a lease whose term is five years or less or, if three conditions are met, a lease whose term is more than five years but no more than seven. (The 'term' of a lease is defined by *CAA 2001, s 70YF*.) The first two conditions are that (i) the lease falls to be treated under GAAP as a finance lease and (ii) the residual value of the plant or machinery implied in the terms of the lease must not be more than 5% of its market value at commencement of the lease term. The third condition compares the lease rentals due in each year of the lease term (ignoring any variations resulting from changes in published interest rates); the total rentals due in Year 1 must not be more than 10% less than those due in Year 2, and the total rentals due in any of Years 3 to 7 must not be more than 10% greater than those due in Year 2. There is an anti-avoidance rule at *s 70I(9)* (effective for leases entered into on or after 7 April 2006) aimed at preventing arrangements between CONNECTED PERSONS (19) being used to create artificially short leases. [*CAA 2001, ss 70I, 70YI(4); FA 2006, Sch 8 para 7*].

(B) An '*excluded lease of background plant or machinery for a building*' occurs where 'background plant or machinery' is affixed to (or otherwise installed in or on) land that consists of (or includes) a building and is leased with that land under a 'mixed lease' (as defined by *CAA 2001, s 70L* — broadly a lease of plant or machinery plus other assets — see also below under Miscellaneous: Mixed leases). '*Background plant or machinery*' is plant or machinery of such description as might reasonably be expected to be installed in various buildings and whose sole or main purpose is to contribute to the functioning of the building or its site as an environment in which activities can be carried on. The Treasury has supplemented this definition in SI 2007/303.

The following are examples of plant and machinery that may fall within the definition of background plant and machinery in the building:

(i) heating and air conditioning installations;

(ii) ceilings which are part of an air conditioning system;

(iii) hot water installations;

(iv) electrical installations that provide power to a building, such as high and low voltage switchgear, all sub-mains distribution systems and standby generators;

(v) mechanisms, including automatic control systems, for opening and closing doors, windows and vents;

(vi) escalators and passenger lifts;

(vii) window cleaning installations;

(viii) fittings such as fitted cupboards, blinds, curtains and associated mechanical equipment;

(ix) demountable partitions;

(x) protective installations, such as lightning protection, sprinkler and other equipment for containing fires, fire alarm systems and fire escapes; and

(xi) building management systems.

However, the above is subject to the list of plant or machinery *not* deemed to be background plant or machinery if it is used as follows:

(i) for storing, moving or displaying goods to be sold in the course of a wholesale or retail trade;

(ii) manufacturing goods or materials;

(iii) processing goods or materials;

(iv) storing goods or materials for manufacture or storing manufactured or imported goods pending delivery subject to any item being deemed to be background plant and machinery, as below.

The following are deemed to be background plant or machinery:

(i) lighting installations including all fixed light fittings and emergency lighting systems;

(ii) telephone, audio-visual and data installations incidental to the occupation of the building;

(iii) computer networking facilities incidental to the occupation of the building;

(iv) sanitary appliances and other bathroom fittings including hand driers, counters, partitions, mirrors, shower and locker facilities;

(v) kitchen and catering facilities for producing and storing food and drink for the occupants of the building;

(vi) fixed seating;

(vii) signs;

(viii) public address systems; and

(ix) intruder alarm systems and other security equipment including surveillance equipment.

[*SI 2007 No 303*].

There are anti-avoidance provisions to prevent this exclusion from applying if a main purpose of the mixed lease (or of transactions of which it is part) is to entitle the lessor to capital allowances on the background plant or machinery or if the rentals vary according to the value of allowances available to the lessor. [*CAA 2001, ss 70R–70T; FA 2006, Sch 8 para 7*].

(C) The *de minimis* provision referred to above applies in a case in which relatively small amounts of plant and machinery are leased with land and the exclusion at (B) above would have applied but for the plant or machinery not being 'background plant or machinery'. The lease is excluded from long funding lease treatment if, at commencement of its term, the aggregate market value of all such plant or machinery does not exceed 10% of the aggregate market value of any 'background plant or machinery' leased with the land *and* does not exceed 5% of the market value of the land (including buildings and fixtures and assuming an absolute interest). [*CAA 2001, s 70U; FA 2006, Sch 8 para 7*].

(2) A '*funding lease*' is a plant or machinery lease (as widely defined by *CAA 2001, s 70K*) which meets the 'finance lease test', the 'lease payments test' or the 'useful economic life test' (see bullets below) (or meets more than one of these tests) and does not fall within either of the exceptions below.

- A lease meets the '*finance lease test*' as regards any person if it is one that, under GAAP, falls (or would fall) to be treated in that person's accounts as either a finance lease or a loan. A lease also meets the finance lease test as regards *the lessor* if it is one that, under GAAP, falls (or would fall) to be so treated in the accounts of a person connected with him (within 19 CONNECTED PERSONS). The Treasury has power to vary the finance lease test by statutory instrument.
- A lease meets the '*lease payments test*' if the present value of the 'minimum lease payments' (see (5) below) is not less than 80% of the 'fair value' of the

leased plant or machinery. Present value is calculated using the interest rate implicit in the lease (applying normal commercial criteria including GAAP or, in default, the temporal discount rate contained in *FA 2005, s 70* or amending regulations). '*Fair value*' means market value less any grants receivable towards the purchase or use of the plant or machinery.

- A lease meets the '*useful economic life test*' if the term of the lease exceeds 65% of the remaining useful economic life (see *CAA 2001, s 70YI(1)*) of the leased plant or machinery. (The 'term' of a lease is defined by *CAA 2001, s 70YF*.)

Exceptions

(i) A contract within 10.38(A) below (hire-purchase contracts etc.) is not a funding lease.

(ii) A lease is not a funding lease if, before the 'commencement' (see *CAA 2001, s 70YI(1)*) of its term, the lessor has leased the same plant or machinery under one or more other plant or machinery leases, none of which were funding leases, and the aggregate term of those other leases exceeds 65% of the remaining useful economic life of the plant or machinery at the commencement of the earliest lease (for this purpose only, any person who was a lessor under a pre-1 April 2006 lease is treated as the same person as the lessor under the first post-1 April 2006 lease).

(iii) A lease is not a funding lease as regards the lessor if, before 1 April 2006, the plant or machinery had, for a period or periods totalling at least ten years, been the subject of one or more leases and the lessor was also the lessor of the plant or machinery on the last day before 1 April 2006 on which it was leased.

[CAA 2001, ss 70J, 70N–70P, 70YI(4), 70YJ; FA 2006, Sch 8 para 7].

(3) A '*long funding operating lease*' is any long funding lease that is not a long-funding finance lease within (4) below. [*CAA 2001, s 70YI(1); FA 2006, Sch 8 para 7*].

(4) A '*long funding finance lease*' is a long funding lease that meets the *finance lease test* at (2) above (disregarding the connected persons rule). [*CAA 2001, s 70YI(1); FA 2006, Sch 8 para 7*].

(5) The '*minimum lease payments*' are the minimum payments under the lease over the term of the lease (including any initial payment). In the case of the lessee, they also include so much of any 'residual amount' as is guaranteed by him or a person connected with him. In the case of the lessor, they also include so much of any 'residual amount' as is guaranteed by the lessee or a person who is not connected with the lessor. Any payment representing charges for services or representing 'taxes' to be paid by the lessor must be excluded from 'minimum payments' for the purposes of this definition. ('*Taxes*' means UK or foreign taxes or duties, but not income tax, corporation tax or foreign equivalents.) '*Residual amount*' means so much of the 'fair value' (see the 'lease payments test' in (2) above) of the plant or machinery subject to the lease as cannot reasonably be expected to be recovered by the lessor from the payments under the lease. [*CAA 2001, s 70YE; FA 2006, Sch 8 para 7*]. This definition of 'minimum lease payments' is based on GAAP (Treasury Explanatory Notes to Finance Bill 2006).

(6) For the purposes of these provisions, the *market value* of any plant or machinery at any time is to be determined on the assumption of a disposal by an absolute owner free from all leases and other encumbrances. [*CAA 2001, s 70YI(2); FA 2006, Sch 8 para 7*].

Lessors. Expenditure incurred on the provision of plant or machinery for leasing under a long funding lease is not qualifying expenditure for the purposes of plant and machinery capital allowances. [*CAA 2001, s 34A; FA 2006, Sch 8 para 3*].

Where expenditure on plant or machinery is already included in qualifying expenditure and the plant or machinery begins to be leased under a long funding lease, a disposal event then occurs and a disposal value must be brought into account as follows.

- If the lease is a 'long funding operating lease' (see (3) above), the disposal value is the market value of the plant or machinery at commencement of the lease.
- If the lease is a 'long funding finance lease' (see (4) above), the disposal value is the amount that would fall to be recognised as the lessor's net investment in the lease if accounts were prepared in accordance with GAAP on the date on which the lessor's net investment in the lease is first recognised in the lessor's books or other financial records.

[*CAA 2001, s 61(1)(ee), (2); FA 2006, Sch 8 para 5*]. (See 10.29 above as regards disposal events and disposal values generally.)

Where the owner of plant or machinery has been leasing it under a long funding lease and ceases to do so but continues to use it for the purposes of a qualifying activity (see 10.24 above), writing-down allowances are available to him as if he had, on the day after the cessation, incurred capital expenditure on the acquisition of that plant or machinery and as if he owned it as a result of that notional capital expenditure. The plant or machinery is thereafter treated as if it were not the same plant or machinery that existed previously. The amount of the notional capital expenditure is equal to the 'termination amount' in relation to the long funding lease under which the plant or machinery was last leased. First-year allowances are not, however, available on the notional capital expenditure, and nor can it qualify for short-life asset treatment as in 10.30(F) above. [*CAA 2001, ss 13A, 46(2), 84; FA 2006, Sch 8 paras 2, 4, 8*].

The *termination amount*' is determined as follows.

- If that lease terminated as a result of a disposal event or if a disposal event is triggered by the termination, the termination amount is the disposal value that would have fallen to be brought into account by the lessor on the fictional assumptions that he had been entitled to capital allowances on the plant or machinery and had claimed his full entitlement. 'Disposal event' is itself to be construed in accordance with those assumptions. See generally 10.29 above as regards disposal events and disposal values.
- If the above does not apply and the lease is a 'long funding operating lease' (see (3) above), the termination amount is the market value of the plant or machinery immediately after the termination.
- If the above does not apply and the lease is a 'long funding finance lease' (see (4) above), the termination amount is the value at which, immediately after the termination, the plant or machinery is recognised in the lessor's books or other financial records.

[*CAA 2001, s 70YG; FA 2006, Sch 8 para 7*].

Note that where plant or machinery either begins or ceases to be leased under a long funding lease, there is also, by virtue of *TCGA 1992, s 25A*, a deemed disposal and reacquisition, at similar values as above, for CGT purposes. See Tolley's Capital Gains Tax under Assets.

Fixtures. The fixtures rules at 10.33 above do not apply to determine either ownership or entitlement to allowances of either the lessee or the lessor, where plant or machinery that is (or becomes) a fixture is the subject of a long funding lease. If the lessee under the long funding lease himself leases out all or any of the plant or machinery under a lease that is not a long funding lease, the provisions at 10.33 are similarly disapplied as regards both the lessor and the lessee under that sub-lease. (Thus, the allowances (for expenditure on fixtures) available to any such lessors and lessees are to be determined under the rules applicable to long funding leases, rather than the rules applicable to fixtures.) [*CAA 2001, ss 172(2A), 172A; FA 2006, Sch 8 para 9*].

Miscellaneous. *Mixed leases.* There is provision for a situation where plant or machinery is leased with other types of asset (whether plant or machinery or not). In such case, different leases are deemed to exist so that the above rules (and those at 66.64 TRADING INCOME) can be applied to each such notional lease ((known as a '*derived lease*') (see, for example, (1)(B) above). [*CAA 2001, ss 70L, 70M; FA 2006, Sch 8 para 7*].

Transfers, assignments etc. Where a *lessor* of plant or machinery transfers it to a new lessor (other than by granting him a lease), it is treated for the purposes of these provisions (as regards lessors) as the termination of the existing lease and the creation of a new lease commencing at the date of transfer (which may or may not be the case in reality). Provided there is effectively no change to the term of the original lease or to the payments due under it, then, as regards the new lessor, the new lease retains the classification of the original lease (i.e. as a long funding lease or as a lease other than a long funding lease, as the case may be) and, as regards the lessee, the old and new leases are treated as a single continuing lease. [*CAA 2001, s 70W; FA 2006, Sch 8 para 7*].

The above also applies, with the appropriate modifications, where a *lessee* of plant or machinery transfers it to a new lessee. [*CAA 2001, s 70X; FA 2006, Sch 8 para 7*].

Extension of the term of a lease. Where the term of a *long funding operating lease* (see (3) above) is extended as a result of one or more specified events (involving variations to the provisions of the lease, the granting or exercise of options etc.), a new lease is deemed to begin. [*CAA 2001, s 70YB; FA 2006, Sch 8 para 7*].

Where the term of a lease that is *not* a long funding lease is extended as a result of one or more specified events (as above), it is necessary to consider whether or not it thereby becomes a long funding lease. If, were it to be assumed that the lease has then terminated and a new lease commenced, the new lease would be a long funding lease, that assumption is made, and the 'new' lease is a long funding lease as regards the lessor, If not, the term of the lease is taken to be the term as extended. [*CAA 2001, s 70YC; FA 2006, Sch 8 para 7*].

Tax avoidance involving international leasing. There are anti-avoidance rules aimed at arrangements such that a non-UK resident leases plant and machinery to a UK resident who then leases it back to a non-UK resident (other than under a long funding lease) in order to obtain the benefit of UK capital allowances. The rules deem the leasing by the UK resident to be long funding leasing, so that capital allowances are not available to him. They apply where the provision of the asset by the non-UK resident is itself long funding leasing as regards the UK resident or is under a contract within 10.38(A) below (hire-purchase contracts etc.), such that the UK resident would otherwise be entitled to capital allowances. They are not aimed at normal commercial arrangements (see also Treasury Explanatory Notes to Finance Bill 2006). [*CAA 2001, s 70V; FA 2006, Sch 8 para 7*].

Sale and leaseback/lease and leaseback arrangements. Where an existing long funding lessor transfers (e.g. by selling or leasing) the plant or machinery that is the subject of the existing lease to another person and leases the plant or machinery back from that other person, the leaseback is a long funding lease as regards both of them. Similar treatment is applied where the leaseback is via a series of leases. [*CAA 2001, s 70Y; FA 2006, Sch 8 para 7*].

Change in the accountancy classification of a long funding lease. There are rules to cater for changes in generally accepted accounting practice (GAAP) such that an operating lease falls to be reclassified as a finance lease for accounting purposes or *vice versa*. [*CAA 2001, s 70YA; FA 2006, Sch 8 para 7*].

Increase in proportion of residual amount guaranteed. The following applies as regards the lessor if, in the case of a lease other than a long funding lease and as a result of arrangements, there is an increase in the proportion of the residual amount that is guaranteed by the lessee (or by a person not connected with the lessor) (as to which see (5) above) and the lease would have been a long funding lease if those arrangements had been made before its 'inception' (see *CAA 2001, s 70YI(1)*). The lease is treated as terminated, and a new lease treated as commenced, as at the time of the arrangement (or the latest arrangement if more than one). [*CAA 2001, s 70YD; FA 2006, Sch 8 para 7*].

Commencement/transitional provisions. The long funding leasing rules above (and those at 66.64 TRADING INCOME) apply in respect of a lease where one of the conditions at (*a*) and (*b*) below is met. However, regardless of these conditions, a lease 'finalised' (see below) before 21 July 2005 cannot be a long funding lease but this let-out is itself disapplied if the lessor does not come within the charge to UK tax until after 17 May 2006.

(*a*) Condition 1 is that the lease is not an 'excepted lease' and that it is 'finalised' on or after 1 April 2006 or the 'commencement' (see *CAA 2001, s 70YI(1)*) of its term is on or after that date.

(*b*) Condition 2 applies if the commencement of the term of the lease was before 1 April 2006 but the plant or machinery is not brought into use by the person concerned for the purposes of a qualifying activity (see 10.24 above) until on or after that date. (This covers, for example, the situation where the person concerned becomes UK resident on or after that date, such that his activity becomes a qualifying activity. The person concerned may be the lessor or the lessee depending on from whose point of view one is applying the provisions.)

The Treasury has made regulations (*SI 2007 No 304*) enabling a *lessor* to elect for a lease to be treated, as regards him only, as a long funding lease if it would not otherwise be such a lease. The election applies to all of the lessor's eligible leases and 'qualifying incidental leases'. The election must be made, in the case of an individual or partnership, within the period commencing with the end of the year of assessment to which the election relates and ending a year after 31 January next following that year of assessment. For corporation tax, the election must be made in the period between the end of the accounting period to which the election relates and ending two years later.

Where an election is made, it applies to all eligible leases and qualifying incidental leases finalised on or after the later of 1 April 2006 and the beginning of the year of assessment or accounting period to which the election applies, and the leases are treated as if they had been long funding leases since they were finalised.

A lease is eligible if:

- it is a lease of plant or machinery;
- it is not otherwise a long funding lease;
- it is finalised on or after 1 April 2006;
- it is for 12 months or more;
- the plant etc. was unused and not second hand at the start of the lease;
- the plant or machinery was leased previously, the last lease was a long funding lease and a valid election under *CAA 2001 s 227* was made before the lessor made a return for the period covering the commencement of the lease or replaces similar plant or machinery;
- the subject of the lease is not a car (*CAA 2001 s 81*);
- the asset leased is not valued at more than £10m at the start of the lease;
- the plant is not background plant or machinery (*CAA 2001 s 70R*) or does not have a low percentage value (*CAA 2001 s 70U*); and

- any assignment of the lease was made within four months of the commencement of its term and no other lessor must have claimed capital allowances in respect of the plant or machinery.

A qualifying incidental lease is one of plant and machinery where the lease is wholly incidental to an eligible lease, and would itself be an eligible lease under the above criteria, except that the condition that the lease be for a year or more need not be satisfied.

[*SI 2007 No 304*]

For these purposes, a lease is '*finalised*' when there is a written contract for it between lessor and lessee, the contract is unconditional (or any conditions have already been met) and there are no terms still to be agreed.

For the purposes of (*a*) above, a lease is an '*excepted lease*' if it meets *all* the following conditions.

(i) Condition 1 is that before 21 July 2005 there was written evidence of an agreement or common understanding (the '*pre-existing heads of agreement*') between (or effectively between) the lessor and lessee as to the 'principal terms of the lease' (as defined).

(ii) Condition 2 is that the leased plant or machinery was 'under construction' (as defined) before 1 April 2006.

(iii) Condition 3 is that the lease is 'finalised' (see above) before 1 April 2007 (but see below).

(iv) Condition 4 is the commencement of the term of the lease is before 1 April 2007 (but see below).

(v) Condition 5 is that the lessee is the person(s) identified as such in the 'pre-existing heads of agreement' (within (i) above).

(vi) Condition 6 is that the principal terms of the lease are not materially different from those in the 'pre-existing heads of agreement' (within (i) above).

The date in (iii) and (iv) above is deferred to 1 April 2009 if construction of the asset proceeds continuously from 1 April 2006 (and at the normal pace for an asset of its type) and the lease commences as soon as is practicable after construction is substantially complete. There is provision to treat this condition as satisfied if it is failed only by reason of unforeseen events beyond the control of the parties (including the main constructor).

There are rules (see *FA 2006, Sch 8 paras 20, 25*) as to how these transitional provisions are to be applied in a case where the 'pre-existing heads of agreement' (see (i) above) relates to two or more assets.

If a person incurs expenditure before 19 July 2006 for leasing under a long funding lease which does not meet all the conditions in (i)–(vi) above but in respect of which there was a 'pre-existing heads of agreement' before 21 July 2005 (as in (i) above), such expenditure (the '*old expenditure*') is treated as separate from any expenditure incurred on or after date (the '*new expenditure*'). *FA 2006, Sch 8 para 22* provides rules, for this purpose only, as to the time at which an amount of expenditure is treated as being incurred. The old and new expenditure are treated as if incurred on separate assets leased under separate leases; the notional lease relating to the old expenditure is then deemed to be an excepted lease. The lease rentals are apportioned between the two notional leases in just and reasonable manner. These splitting provisions apply in determining the income tax or corporation tax liability of anyone who is at any time the lessor or the lessee under the actual lease.

Mixed leases. Where a lease is a mixed lease (see above under Miscellaneous), it is first necessary to consider whether the mixed lease is itself an 'excepted lease' for the purposes of these transitional provisions. If it is not, one can then consider separately, in the case of each derived lease, whether that lease is an 'excepted lease'.

Transfers. There is provision to ensure that a lease that is outside the long funding leasing regime (by virtue of the commencement/transitional provisions) remains outside that regime if it is transferred from one lessor to another or from one lessee to another. For this to have effect, there must be no effective change to the term of the lease or to the payments due under it, and the lessor or lessee (as the case may be) must be within the charge to UK tax immediately before the transfer.

[*FA 2006, Sch 8 paras 15–27*].

10.35 **Overseas leasing.** For the purposes of the provisions described below, plant or machinery is used for overseas leasing if it is leased to a person who:

(1) is not resident in the UK; and

(2) does not use the plant or machinery exclusively for earning profits chargeable to UK tax (which includes profits from exploration or exploitation activities carried on in the UK or its territorial sea).

However, in determining whether plant or machinery is used for overseas leasing, no account is to be taken of any lease finalised on or after **1 April 2006** (as to which see 10.34 above under Commencement/transitional provisions).

For the purpose of (2) above, profits chargeable to UK tax do not include profits in respect of which the trader etc. is entitled to tax relief under a double taxation agreement. This does not apply in the case of leases entered into before 16 March 1993 for which, in addition, the use of the plant or machinery does not have to be *exclusively* for the purposes stated.

[*CAA 2001, s 105(2)–(4), Sch 3 para 21; CAA 1990, ss 42(1), 50(3A); FA 1993, s 116(2)–(4); FA 2006, Sch 9 para 13*].

For the purposes of the provisions described below, a 'lease' includes a sub-lease, with 'lessor' and 'lessee' being construed accordingly, and 'leasing' is regarded as including the letting of any asset on hire or of a ship or aircraft on charter (and see *Barclays Mercantile Industrial Finance Ltd v Melluish Ch D 1990, 63 TC 95* at (*d*) below). [*CAA 2001, s 105(1); CAA 1990, s 50(1)(2)*].

The provisions apply in relation to 'new expenditure'. '*New expenditure*' means expenditure incurred after 31 March 1986 on plant and machinery other than certain cars costing £12,000 or less (see (*a*) below), provided that it is not 'old expenditure'. '*Old expenditure*' means, broadly, expenditure incurred before 1 April 1986, although certain post-31 March 1986 expenditure was included in the term under transitional provisions, as was post-31 March 1986 expenditure qualifying for a universal (as opposed to targeted) first-year allowance (see 10.27 above) other than the temporarily reinstated 40% allowance for expenditure in the twelve months to 31 October 1993.

[*CAA 1990, s 50(3); FA 1993, Sch 13 para 11(1); F(No 2)A 1997, s 42(6); FA 1998, s 85(4); FA 2000, s 71(2)*].

Where there is a chain of leases, HMRC now consider that the provisions apply where any lessee in the chain falls within (1) and (2) above. The original HMRC view was that only the end lessee need be considered, and HMRC will act in accordance with that original view for leasing arrangements entered into before 19 April 1999, or within three months after that date where the principal terms had been agreed in writing before that date (e.g. in an agreed term-sheet or accepted offer letter) and had not materially altered in the intervening period. (HMRC Capital Allowances Manual CA 24010).

The HMRC continued to be of the opinion that in determining whether or not overseas leasing is 'protected leasing' (see (*a*) and (*e*) below), it was necessary to consider only the end lease in a chain. HMRC now take the view that every lease in the chain must be considered; if the leasing under any of the leases is not 'protected leasing', the overseas leasing restrictions apply to the whole chain. HMRC will apply their earlier view to leasing arrangements entered into before 3 February 2005, or within three months after that date where the principal terms were agreed in writing before that date and did not materially alter in the intervening period. (HMRC Internet Statement 3 February 2005).

The provisions referred to above are as follows.

(*a*) *Separate pooling and restriction of writing-down allowances.* Separate pooling provisions apply to qualifying expenditure (see 10.24 above) if it is incurred on the provision of plant or machinery for leasing and if that plant or machinery is at any time in the 'designated period' (see (*c*) below) used for overseas leasing other than 'protected leasing' (see (*e*) below). They do not apply to long-life asset expenditure (see 10.30(G) above) or to expenditure which can only be allocated to a single asset pool (see 10.28 above). Qualifying expenditure meeting the above conditions can only be allocated to a *class pool* (see 10.28 above), known as the *overseas leasing pool.* The final chargeable period (see 10.28 above) of the overseas leasing pool is the chargeable period at the end of which circumstances are such that no further disposal values (see 10.29 above) could fall to be brought into account.

Writing-down allowances on qualifying expenditure meeting the above conditions are restricted to **10% p.a.** (instead of the normal 25% p.a.).The restriction applies whether such expenditure falls to be allocated to the overseas leasing pool or to a single asset pool (including, where *CAA 2001* has effect, see 10.1 above, a pool for partial non-business use as in 10.30(C) above). The 10% rate does not, however, displace the 6% rate applicable to long-life asset expenditure (see 10.30(G) above). The 10% allowance is proportionately reduced or increased if the chargeable period is less or more than a year, or if the qualifying activity has been carried on for part only of the chargeable period. A claim for a writing-down allowance may require it to be reduced to a specified amount.

[*CAA 2001, ss 56(5), 65(4), 107, 109; CAA 1990, s 41(1)–(4)(6), s 42(2); FA 1990, Sch 17 para 9; FA 1997, Sch 14 paras 4, 5; FA 2000, s 74(1)*].

When plant or machinery in the overseas leasing pool is disposed of to a CONNECTED PERSON (19) (otherwise than on a change in the members of a partnership or a company reconstruction in circumstances such that, in each case, the qualifying activity is treated as continuing) the disposal value to be brought into account (see generally 10.29 above) is its market value or, if lower, its original cost, and the person acquiring it may claim allowances on the same value. [*CAA 2001, s 108; CAA 1990, s 41(5); ITTOIA 2005, Sch 1 para 537*].

Cars costing £12,000 or less (£8,000 for expenditure incurred before 11 March 1992 or under a contract entered into before that date), and which are not leased so as to be otherwise within these provisions, previously had to be included in a similar class pool, but *not* the same pool as that used for overseas leasing. This car pool also included certain 'old expenditure' (see above) on plant or machinery provided for leasing. The separate pooling requirement is, however, abolished for periods of account ending after 5 April 2000, except that an election may be made to treat the abolition as deferred by one year in any particular case. Any unrelieved qualifying expenditure brought forward from the immediately preceding chargeable period in the separate pool is included in the main pool of qualifying expenditure for the chargeable period for which abolition has effect. [*CAA 1990, s 41(1)(b)(c)(4); FA 2000, s 74*].

(*b*) *Prohibition of allowances.* No writing-down or balancing allowances are available in respect of qualifying expenditure meeting the conditions in (*a*) above if the plant or machinery is used other than for a 'qualifying purpose' (see (*d*) below) *and*:

(i) there is more than one year between consecutive payments due under the lease; or

(ii) any payments other than periodical payments are due under the lease or under any collateral agreement; or

(iii) any payment expressed monthly under the lease or any collateral agreement is not the same as any other such payment, but disregarding variations due to changes in rates of tax, capital allowances, interest which is linked with rates applicable to inter-bank loans or changes in premiums for insurances of any kind by a person not connected with the lessor or lessee; or

(iv) either the lease is for a period exceeding 13 years or there is any provision for its extension or renewal or for the grant of a new lease such that the leasing period could exceed 13 years; or

(v) at any time, the lessor or CONNECTED PERSON (19) could be entitled to receive from the lessee or any other person a payment (not insurance money) of an amount determined before expiry of the lease and referable to the value of the plant or machinery at or after that expiry (whether or not the payment relates to a disposal of the plant or machinery).

See Revenue and Customs Brief 40/07: in certain circumstances, for leases entered into before 1 April 2006, where the plant is used for overseas leasing and the European Economic Area country gives the leasee a relief similar to capital allowances, a restricted capital allowance will be given (at 10%) but *CAA 2001, s 110* will not be applied to deny capital allowances. Where the EEA country does not give an allowance allied to capital allowances, a 25% writing-down allowance will be given.

[*CAA 2001, s 110; CAA 1990, s 42*(*3*)].

Where allowances (including any first-year allowance) have been made (and not fully withdrawn under the excess relief provisions in (*g*) below) but by reason of any event in the 'designated period' (see (*c*) below) the expenditure is brought within the above provisions, the net allowances are clawed back by means of a balancing charge. For this purpose only, the allowances made are determined as if the item of plant or machinery in question were the only item, i.e. as if it had not been pooled. A disposal value equal to the balance of the expenditure is also brought into account so as to effectively remove the item from the pool. Where the item was acquired from a CONNECTED PERSON (19), or as a part of a series of transactions with connected persons, allowances made to those persons are also taken into account in computing the balancing charge, with any actual consideration on a connected persons transaction being ignored and with the amount of such allowances being adjusted 'in a just and reasonable manner' where balancing allowances/charges have already been made in respect of the item in question. This does not apply in the case of transactions between connected persons which are treated as not involving a cessation of the quality activity, i.e. where there is a change in the members of a partnership but there is at least one continuing partner or where the activity is treated as continuing by virtue of *ICTA 1988, s 114*(*1*) (partnership changes involving companies) or *ICTA 1988, s 343*(*2*) (company reconstructions without change of ownership). [*CAA 2001, ss 114, 115; CAA 1990, s 42*(*4*)–(*9*); *FA 1993, Sch 13 para 6; FA 1998, s 85*(*4*); *FA 2000, s 71*(*2*); *ITTOIA 2005, Sch 1 para 539*].

(*c*) '*Designated period*'. For the purposes of these provisions, the '*designated period*' is the period of ten years after the item of plant or machinery in question is first brought into use by the person who incurred the expenditure. It is, however, brought to an end at any time within that ten-year period at which that person ceases to own the item, disregarding any disposal to a CONNECTED PERSON (19) or on a change in members of a partnership where there is at least one continuing partner or which is disregarded under *ICTA 1988, s 114*(*1*) (partnership changes involving companies). For leases entered into before 16 March 1993, the ten-year period was reduced to one of four years if the plant or machinery was used for a 'qualifying purpose' (see (*d*) below); for later leases, this continues to apply only for the purposes of the provisions for separate pooling of ships (see 10.30(B) above) and short-life assets (see 10.30(F) above). [*CAA 2001, 106; CAA 1990, s 40(4)(5); FA 1993, s 116(1); ITTOIA 2005, Sch 1 para 536*].

(*d*) '*Qualifying purpose*'. Plant or machinery on which a person (the buyer) has incurred expenditure is used for a '*qualifying purpose*' at any time if, at that time:

(i) the lessee uses it for the purposes of a qualifying activity without leasing it; and had the lessee bought the plant or machinery himself at that time, his expenditure would have fallen to be wholly or partly included in his available qualifying expenditure (see 10.28 above) for a chargeable period; or

(ii) the buyer uses it for 'short-term leasing' (see (*e*) below); or

(iii) the lessee uses it for 'short-term leasing' and is either UK resident or so uses it in the course of a qualifying activity carried on in the UK; or

(iv) the buyer uses it for the purposes of a qualifying activity without leasing it.

For the purposes of (ii) and (iv) above, where the plant or machinery is disposed of to a connected person, or on a change in the members of a partnership where there is at least one continuing partner or which falls to be disregarded under *ICTA 1988, s 114(1)* (partnerships involving companies), the new owner is treated as the 'buyer'.

[*CAA 2001, ss 122, 125; CAA 1990, s 39(1)–(5)(10); FA 1993, Sch 13 para 5(1); ITTOIA 2005, Sch 1 paras 540, 541*].

As regards the reference to 'leasing' in (i) above, the word is to be construed in accordance with the narrow test applicable to leases of land, so that distribution agreements entered into by film lessee companies were not leases for these purposes but arrangements entered into in the ordinary course of their businesses (*Barclays Mercantile Industrial Finance Ltd v Melluish Ch D 1990, 63 TC 95*).

Ships, aircraft and transport containers. Without prejudice to (i)–(iv) above, a ship is also used for a '*qualifying purpose*' at any time when it is let on charter in the course of a trade of operating ships if the lessor is resident, or carries on the trade, in the UK and is responsible as principal (or appoints another person to be responsible as principle) for navigating and managing the ship and for defraying substantially all its expenses except those directly incidental to a particular voyage or charter period. The same applies with necessary modifications in relation to aircraft. However, neither ship nor aircraft chartering qualifies if the main object, or one of them, of the chartering (or of a series of transactions of which the chartering was one) was the obtaining by any person of an unrestricted writing-down allowance (or a universal first-year allowance for expenditure in the twelve months to 31 October 1993 — see 10.27 above). A transport container is also used for a '*qualifying purpose*' at any time when it is leased in the course of a trade carried on in the UK or by a UK resident if either the trade is one of operating ships or aircraft and the container is at other times used by the trader in connection with such operation, or the container is leased under a succession of leases to different persons who, or most of whom, are not connected with each other. [*CAA 2001, ss 123, 124, Sch 3 para 23; CAA 1990, s 39(6)–(9); FA 1993, Sch 13 para 5(2)*].

(*e*) '*Protected leasing*' means 'short-term leasing' (see below) or, in the case of a ship, aircraft or transport container, its use for a qualifying purpose (see (*d*) above). [*CAA 2001, s 105(5); CAA 1990, ss 42(1), 50(3)*].

'*Short-term leasing*' means leasing an item of plant or machinery in such a manner

(i) that (A) the number of consecutive days for which it is leased to the same person will normally be less than 30 and (B) the total number of days to the same person in any period of 12 months will normally be less than 90; or

(ii) that (A) the number of consecutive days for which it is leased to the same person will not normally exceed 365 and (B) the aggregate of the periods for which it is leased to lessees not falling within (*d*)(i) above in any period of 4 consecutive years within the 'designated period' (see (*c*) above) will not exceed 2 years.

For the above purposes, persons who are connected with each other (see 19 CONNECTED PERSONS) are to be treated as the same person. Where plant or machinery is leased from a group of items of similar description and not separately identifiable, all the items in the group may be treated as used for short-term leasing if substantially the whole of the items in the group are so used.

[*CAA 2001, s 121; CAA 1990, s 40(1)–(3)*].

(*f*) *Joint lessees.* The following applies where an item of plant or machinery is leased (otherwise than by 'protected leasing'—see (*e*) above) to two or more persons jointly, and at least one of the joint lessees is a person within (1) and (2) above (definition of overseas leasing). An unrestricted writing-down allowance is due if the lessees use the item for the purposes of a qualifying activity or activities (but not for leasing) but only to the extent that it appears that the profits therefrom throughout the 'designated period' (see (*c*) above), or the period of the lease if shorter, will be chargeable to UK income tax or corporation tax. The part of the expenditure so qualifying for unrestricted allowances is treated as if it were expenditure on a separate item of plant or machinery (outside the overseas leasing pool) with the remaining part treated as expenditure within the overseas leasing provisions, with such apportionments as are necessary.

Excess relief is recoverable under (*g*) below if at any time in the designated period while the item is so leased, no lessee uses it for the purposes of a qualifying activity the profits of which are chargeable to UK tax as above (referred to below as '*eligible use*') or if, at the end of the designated period, it appears that the actual extent of eligible use was less than anticipated. In the latter case the amount of excess relief recoverable is in proportion to the reduction in eligible use and any disposal value subsequently brought into account is apportioned to the extent of the eligible use as determined at the end of the designated period.

The above provisions (including the clawback of excess relief) apply in respect of the temporarily reinstated 40% universal first-year allowance for expenditure incurred in the twelve months to 31 October 1993 as they apply in respect of writing-down allowances.

[*CAA 2001, ss 116, 117, Sch 3 para 22; CAA 1990, s 43(1)–(3), 44; FA 1993 Sch 13 paras 7, 8; FA 1997, Sch 14 para 6*].

(*g*) *Recovery of excess relief.* Where expenditure has qualified for a normal 25% writing-down allowance (or for a first-year allowance) and the plant or machinery is used for overseas leasing (other than 'protected leasing'— see (*e*) above) at any time in the 'designated period' (see (*c*) above), any 'excess relief' is recovered. This is achieved by means of a balancing charge of an amount equal to the excess relief, to be made on the person who owns the item when it is first so used, for the chargeable period in which it is first so used. The item is removed from its existing pool by means of a disposal value equal to the item's written-down value for capital allowances purposes at the end of that period. The '*excess relief*' is the excess, if any, of the allowances made, up to and including the chargeable period in question, over the maximum allowances that could have been made if the expenditure had been within (*a*) or (*b*) above from the outset. The allowances made are determined for this purpose as if the item in question were the only item, i.e. as if it had not been pooled with any other item of plant or machinery. The sum of the excess relief and the disposal value is then allocated to the appropriate pool (usually the overseas leasing pool) for the following chargeable period.

Where the person on whom the balancing charge falls to be made acquired the item in question from a CONNECTED PERSON (19), or as part of a series of transactions with connected persons, the allowances taken into account in computing the excess relief include the allowances made to such person(s), any consideration passing between them for the item being ignored. The amount of excess relief is adjusted 'in a just and reasonable manner' where balancing allowances/charges have been made on any of the transactions. However, these modifications do not apply in the case of transactions between connected persons which are treated as not involving a cessation of the quality activity, i.e. where there is a change in the members of a partnership but there is at least one continuing partner or where the activity is treated as continuing by virtue of *ICTA 1988, s 114(1)* (partnership changes involving companies) or *ICTA 1988, s 343(2)* (company reconstructions without change of ownership).

In the case of a ship, any allowance previously postponed (see 10.27, 10.30(B) above) cannot be made for any chargeable period in or after that in which the ship is first used for overseas leasing (other than protected leasing) within the designated period. The total of any such allowances is instead allocated to the appropriate pool for the following chargeable period as if it were itself qualifying expenditure.

[*CAA 2001, ss 111–113; CAA 1990, s 46; FA 1990, Sch 17 para 10; FA 1993, Sch 13 para 9; FA 1997, Sch 14 para 7; F(No 2)A 1997, s 42(6); FA 1998, s 85(5); FA 2000, s 71(3); ITTOIA 2005, Sch 1 para 538*].

(*h*) *Information* must be provided to HMRC, by the then owner, where expenditure on plant or machinery has qualified for a normal 25% writing-down allowance (or for a first-year allowance) and the item is subsequently used for overseas leasing (other than 'protected leasing'— see (*e*) above) at any time in the 'designated period' (see (*c*) above). Information must also be provided to HMRC, by the lessor, where plant or machinery is leased to joint lessees as described in (*f*) above and, in addition, if circumstances occur such that excess relief is recoverable. In all cases, the time limit for providing the information is three months after the end of the chargeable period in which the item is first so used (or the said circumstances occur), extended to 30 days after the informant came to know that the item was being so used (if the informant could not reasonably have been expected to know earlier).

Where expenditure has not yet qualified for a normal 25% writing-down allowance or a first-year allowance or for either and the item is used for overseas leasing which is protected leasing, a claim for a first-year allowance or writing-down allowance thereon must be accompanied by a certificate describing the protected leasing.

[*CAA 2001, ss 118–120, 126; CAA 1990, ss 44(2), 48, 50(3); FA 1990, Sch 17 para 12; FA 1993, Sch 13 para 10; FA 1997, Sch 14 para 8; F(No 2)A 1997, s 42(6); FA 1998, s 85(5); FA 2000, s 71(3)*].

Restriction of first-year allowances. The targeted first-year allowances at 10.27(*a*)–(*h*) above are *not* generally available in respect of expenditure on plant or machinery for leasing (see 10.27(v) above for details and exceptions). Such expenditure is not automatically precluded from qualifying for the temporarily reinstated 40% universal first-year allowance for expenditure incurred in the twelve months to 31 October 1993 (see 10.27 above), but *is* so precluded if:

(I) it appears that the expenditure would fall within (*a*) or (*b*) above such that writing-down allowances would be restricted or prohibited (but see below re joint lessees); or

(II) the expenditure is incurred after 13 April 1993, the person to whom the plant or machinery is to be, or is, leased (or a person connected with that person) used the plant or machinery for any purpose at any time before its provision for leasing, *and* the plant or machinery does not fall into any of the following qualifying categories:

- plant or machinery which it appears will be used only for a 'qualifying purpose' (see (*d*) above) in the 'designated period' (see (*c*) above);
- plant or machinery which is to be an integral part of a building qualifying for enterprise zone allowances (see 10.19 above);
- plant or machinery fixed to a building or land of which the person incurring the expenditure is the lessor, where a transfer of the lessor's interest in the building etc. would operate to transfer the lessor's interest in the plant or machinery; and
- cars hired out to persons receiving certain disability allowances or mobility supplements.

Preclusion under (I) above does not apply to the extent that it appears that the plant or machinery will be leased to joint lessees as described at (*f*) above, such that (*a*) and (*b*) above are disapplied in respect of all or part of the expenditure. See (*f*) above for the potential clawback of the allowance in specified circumstances.

[*CAA 2001, Sch 3 para 47(4)–(8); CAA 1990, s 22(4)(c)(5)(6)(6A)(11), s 43(4); FA 1993, s 115(3), Sch 13 para 7; SI 1991 No 2874*].

Simon's Direct Tax Service. See **B2.345** *et seq.*

10.36 *Examples*

Separate pooling

L Ltd has a leasing business preparing accounts annually to 31 May. In the year to 31 May 2006, its expenditure included the following.

		£
(i)	Machine 1, leased to M Ltd, a UK-resident company for the purposes of its trade	20,000
(ii)	Machine 2, leased to N, a UK-resident individual, for private use	8,000
(iii)	Machine 3, leased to P, a non-UK resident, for his overseas trade	16,000
(iv)	Fixtures and fittings for use in L Ltd's business	2,000
(v)	Car used by L Ltd for business	6,000

At 1 June 2005, there is a written-down value of £40,000 brought forward in L Ltd's main plant and machinery pool.

The leasing in (iii) above is not 'protected leasing' (see 10.35(*e*) above), but neither does it fall within 10.35(*b*) above (prohibition of allowances). All leases were finalised before 1 April 2006. None of the expenditure qualifies for first-year allowances.

L Ltd's plant and machinery allowances for the year ended 31 May 2006, assuming no capital expenditure other than as listed above, are as follows.

	Main Pool	Overseas leasing pool	Total allowances
	£	£	£
WDV b/f	40,000		
Additions	36,000	16,000	
WDA 25%	(19,000)		19,000
WDA 10%		(1,600)	1,600
WDV c/f	£57,000	£14,400	
Total allowances			£20,600

Notes

(*a*) Machines 1 and 2 go into the main plant and machinery pool, as do the fixtures and fittings and the car. Machine 3 goes into an overseas leasing pool under 10.35(*a*) above.

(*b*) The writing-down allowance for Machine 3 is restricted to 10%.

Recovery of excess relief

M Ltd, which has a 30 September accounting date, incurred expenditure of £16,000 in October 2003 on a machine leased to Q Ltd, a company trading in the UK. In December 2005, Q Ltd terminated the lease and M Ltd then leased the machine, with effect from January 2006, to P Ltd, a company resident in Panama, for the purposes of its trade there. The leasing was not 'protected leasing' (see 10.35(*e*) above).

A balancing charge arises in the accounting period to 30.9.06 as follows.

Actual allowances

	£	Total allowances £
Expenditure (y/e 30.9.04)	16,000	
WDA 25% for y/e 30.9.04	4,000	4,000
	12,000	
WDA 25% for y/e 30.9.05	3,000	3,000
	9,000	
WDA 25% for y/e 30.9.06	2,250	2,250
Balance of expenditure	£6,750	
Total allowances claimed		£9,250

Notional allowances

	£	Total allowances £
Expenditure (y/e 30.9.04)	16,000	
WDA 10% for y/e 30.9.04 note (*a*)	1,600	1,600
	14,400	
WDA 10% for y/e 30.9.05	1,440	1,440
	12,960	
WDA 10% for y/e 30.9.06	1,296	1,296
	£11,664	
Notional allowances		£4,336
Balancing charge, equal to the excess of actual allowances over notional allowances, for y/e 30.9.06		£4,914

M Ltd will then be deemed to have incurred qualifying expenditure of £11,664 (equal to the balance of expenditure plus the balancing charge) for the year ended 30.9.07, i.e. the chargeable period following that in which the change of use arose, and will then be entitled to writing-down allowances of 10% for that and subsequent chargeable periods. The expenditure will constitute, or form part of, an overseas leasing pool under 10.35(*a*) above.

Notes

(*a*) Notional writing-down allowances are restricted to 10% notwithstanding the fact that the machine was used for a qualifying purpose up to December 2005. It is used for overseas leasing (other than protected leasing) at some time in the 'designated period' (see 10.35(*a*) above).

(*b*) In practice, the machine would originally have been included in the main plant and machinery pool. For the purpose of calculating the balancing charge, it is assumed to have been the only item of plant and machinery qualifying for writing-down allowances. For the year ended 30 September 2006, a disposal value equal to the residue of expenditure (£6,750) must be brought into account in the main pool, so as to effectively remove the item from that pool.

(*c*) If the expenditure had qualified for a first-year allowance, this also enters into the calculation of excess relief and is thus effectively clawed back.

10.37 **Special leasing.** '*Special leasing*' is the hiring out of plant or machinery otherwise than in the course of a trade or other qualifying activity. It is itself a qualifying activity for the purpose of claiming plant and machinery allowances. However, plant or machinery provided for use in a dwelling-house or flat is excluded from being qualifying expenditure. See 10.24 above.

Where a person hires out more than one item of plant and machinery, that person has a *separate qualifying activity* in relation to each item. A qualifying activity of special leasing begins when the plant or machinery is first hired out. It is permanently discontinued if the lessor permanently ceases to hire it out. (Before *CAA 2001* had effect, see 10.1 above, the legislation was ambiguous as to whether a balancing allowance, see 10.28 above, could arise in this situation, but it is clear that it can arise under *CAA 2001*.) [*CAA 2001, s 19(2)–(4); CAA 1990, s 61(1)*].

Manner of making allowances and charges for special leasing. For *corporation tax*, a plant and machinery allowance is given effect by deduction from the company's income for the accounting period in question from qualifying activities of special leasing. If, however, the plant or machinery was not used for the whole (or for a part) of the accounting period for the purposes of a qualifying activity carried on by the *lessee*, the allowance (or a proportionate part) can only be set against the lessor's income from that particular qualifying activity of special leasing.

Any excess of allowances over the income for an accounting period against which they may be set may be:

(*a*) carried forward against such income in succeeding accounting periods; or

(*b*) deducted from profits generally.

A claim for relief under (*b*) above may, if the allowances exceed the profit of the accounting period, require the excess to be relieved (as far as possible) against the profits of an immediately preceding period of equal length. Relief under (*b*) above is only available where the lessee does not use the assets concerned for the purposes of a trade, and group relief is similarly restricted in such circumstances (see 32.10 GROUPS OF COMPANIES). A claim must be made within two years of the end of the accounting period in which the excess allowances arose.

A balancing charge is taxed as income from special leasing and is included in the income against which an allowance may be set as above.

Special leasing: partnerships. The above provisions in relation to allowances and charges do not apply in the case of a company:

(i) which carries on, in partnership with other persons in a chargeable period of the partnership, a 'business of leasing plant or machinery' (as defined in 5.17 ANTI-AVOIDANCE); and

(ii) which is entitled to such special leasing allowances in any chargeable period comprising (wholly or partly) the partnership accounting period,

where the company's interest in the leasing business during the partnership's chargeable period is not determined on an 'allowable' basis. A company's interest in the leasing business is determined on an '*allowable*' basis if (for the purposes of *ICTA 1988, s 114(2)* – see 52.2 PARTNERSHIPS) the company's share in the profits (excluding chargeable gains) or loss of the leasing business and its share in any 'relevant capital allowances' for that period are both determined by reference to the same, single percentage. '*Relevant capital allowances*' are capital allowances in respect of expenditure incurred on the provision of plant or machinery wholly or partly for the purposes of the leasing business.

This provision has effect in relation to any business carried on by a company in partnership in any accounting period ending on or after 5 December 2005. In relation to accounting periods straddling that date, the provision applies only if the company starts to carry on the business in partnership, or a 'relevant change' in the company's interest in the business occurs, on or after that date. A '*relevant change*' in the company's interest in the business is a change to a basis of profit sharing which is not allowable.

Where the company's share in profits for a chargeable period is not the same as its share of capital allowances for that period there are restrictions on how it may set off excess capital allowances, as follows: excess capital allowances from special leasing may not be set against profits of the current or any previous accounting period within the carry back period (ie a period the same length as the current accounting period, ending when that period starts). Where an accounting period is partly within the carry back period the excess allowances may be set off proportionately. See HMRC Capital Allowances Manual CA 29450.

[*CAA 2001, s 3(4), ss 258–260, 261A; CAA 1990, ss 61(5)(7), 73, 83(1), 141, 145(2)–(4); ITTOIA 2005, Sch 1 para 548; FA 2006, s 83*].

Simon's Direct Tax Service. See **B2.385.**

10.38 **Miscellaneous.** The following also apply for the purposes of capital allowances on plant and machinery.

(A) Hire-purchase and similar contracts. The following applies where a person incurs capital expenditure, on the provision of plant or machinery for the purposes of a trade or other qualifying activity, under a contract providing that that person shall or may become the owner of it on performance of the contract. One example of such a contract is a hire-purchase agreement. That person is treated for the purposes of plant and machinery allowances as the sole owner of the plant or machinery for as long as that person is entitled to the benefit of the contract. When the plant or machinery is brought into use for the purposes of the qualifying activity, the full outstanding capital cost (i.e. excluding the hire or interest element) attracts capital allowances immediately. Any such capital payments made before it is brought into use attract allowances as they fall due.

As regards any such contract finalised on or after 1 April 2006 (as to which see 10.34 above under Commencement/transitional provisions) that, in accordance with generally accepted accounting practice (GAAP), falls to be treated as a lease (or would so fall if the person prepared accounts), the person mentioned above is treated as owning the plant or machinery only if the contract falls (or would fall) under GAAP to be treated by that person as a *finance lease*. At any time at which, by virtue only of the preceding rule, the lessee is *not* treated as owning the plant or machinery, no-one else is treated as owning it either; so, in these circumstances, neither lessee nor lessor are entitled to capital allowances. (According to the Treasury Explanatory Notes to Finance Bill 2006, the treatment of ordinary hire-purchase contracts, with a nominal option fee payable to acquire the plant or machinery at the end of the lease, remains unaltered as such contracts will fall to be accounted for as finance leases.)

Also as regards contracts finalised on or after 1 April 2006, these provisions are extended so as to apply where the plant or machinery is used for the purposes of any overseas activity that would be a qualifying activity within 10.24 above if the person carrying it on were UK resident.

Also as regards contracts finalised on or after 1 April 2006, any two or more agreements (or undertakings) are treated for these purposes as a single contract if, when taken together, they have the effect that the person concerned will (or may) become the owner of the plant or machinery on performance of the 'contract'.

If the person mentioned above is treated as owning the plant or machinery but the contract is not completed so that he does not, in fact, become the owner of the plant or machinery, he is treated as ceasing to own it on ceasing to be entitled to the benefit of the contract. The resulting disposal value (see 10.29 above) depends on whether the plant or machinery has been brought into use for the purposes of the qualifying activity. If it has, the disposal value is:

(i) the total of any capital sums received by way of consideration, compensation, damages or insurance in respect of the person's rights under the contract or the plant or machinery itself; plus

(ii) the capital element of all instalments treated as paid (see above) but not, in fact, paid.

This is subject to the over-riding rule that the disposal value cannot exceed the qualifying expenditure brought into account (see 10.29 above).

If the plant or machinery has not been so brought into use, then where *CAA 2001* has effect (see 10.1 above), the disposal value is the total in (i) above (but see below as regards assignments). Previously, no specific rule was provided in such a case, so disposal value was equal to market value by virtue of 10.29(*g*) above.

[*CAA 2001, ss 67, 68, Sch 3 para 15; CAA 1990, s 60; FA 2006, Sch 9 para 12*].

See 66.23 TRADING INCOME as regards hire-purchase agreements relating to cars whose retail price when new exceeded £12,000.

The above rules do not apply to expenditure incurred on 'fixtures' within *CAA 2001, ss 172–204* (see 10.33 above), and if (at a time on or after 28 July 2000) plant or machinery which has been treated under the above rules as owned by a person becomes such a fixture, that person is treated as ceasing to own it at that time (unless it is treated as belonging to that person under *sections 172–204*). [*CAA 2001, s 69, Sch 3 para 16; CAA 1990, s 60A; FA 2000, s 80*].

With effect for chargeable periods ending on or after 2 July 1997, the above rules similarly do not apply (except in relation to deemed ownership of the asset concerned) to expenditure incurred after 1 July 1997 (unless it is incurred before 1 July 1998 under a contract entered into on or before 1 July 1997) if the person mentioned above acquires the plant or machinery for leasing under a 'finance lease' (as defined in (C) below, and note the exclusion of long funding leases from that definition from, broadly, 1 April 2006). [*CAA 2001, s 229(3), Sch 3 para 44; CAA 1990, s 60(2A); F(No 2)A 1997, s 45*]. See HMRC Tax Bulletin June 1998 pp 539–544 for a general article on how these and associated capital allowance restrictions are intended to operate. In particular it is noted that the commencement rules for the fore-mentioned restriction apply before the rule above for bringing in capital costs before they are actually incurred, so that where the asset is brought into use by the lessor in a chargeable period ending on or after 2 July 1997, only expenditure actually incurred before that date (or before 2 July 1998 under an existing contract) can be brought into account at that time. See also 10.28 above, (C) below and 66.54 TRADING INCOME as regards finance lease allowance restrictions. See 10.34 above as regards long funding leasing.

If the person entitled to the benefit of a hire-purchase or similar contract assigns that benefit before the plant or machinery is brought into use, and the assignee's allowances fall to be restricted under the anti-avoidance provisions at (C)(ii) below, both the disposal value and the expenditure against which it is set are increased by the capital expenditure he would have incurred if he had wholly performed the contract. The same applies in finance lease cases. This is to protect the assignee against an undue repression of qualifying expenditure by reference to the assignor's disposal value (see (C)(ii) below). [*CAA 2001, s 229*]. Before *CAA 2001* had effect (see 10.1 above), a similar rule as to acceleration of expenditure operated under *CAA 1990, s 25(6)*, though in more limited circumstances.

For a further anti-avoidance rule, see 10.34 above under Miscellaneous: Tax avoidance involving international leasing.

Simon's Direct Tax Service. See **B2.340**.

(B) Abortive expenditure. The rules at (A) above for hire-purchase and similar contracts can equally be applied to expenditure under other contracts which proves to be abortive. A disposal value falls to be brought into account as in (A) above when the contract fails to be completed. Thus, for example, plant and machinery allowances can be obtained in respect of a non-refundable deposit paid on an item of plant or machinery which is never actually supplied, notwithstanding the fact that the item is never owned by the person incurring the expenditure.

(C) Connected persons and other anti-avoidance measures. See 19 CONNECTED PERSONS for the definition of that term for these purposes.

(i) For disposals of plant or machinery acquired as a result of transaction(s) between connected persons, the limit on the disposal value (see 10.29 above) is to the greatest amount of qualifying expenditure incurred on it by any of the participants in the transaction(s) (after deducting any 'additional VAT rebates' made — see 10.2(vii) above).

The normal absence of any requirement to bring a disposal value into account if none of the qualifying expenditure in question has been taken into account in determining available qualifying expenditure (see 10.29 above) does not apply if the person concerned acquired the plant or machinery as a result of such transaction(s) as are mentioned above *and* any earlier participant was required to bring a disposal value into account. Instead, the current participant's qualifying expenditure is deemed to be allocated (if this is not actually the case), for the chargeable period in which the current disposal event occurs, to whichever pool is appropriate, thus requiring the bringing into account of a disposal value (which is then subject to the above-mentioned limit).

[*CAA 2001, s 62(2)–(4), s 64(2)–(5), s 239(5)(6); CAA 1990, s 26(3)(4); FA 1991, Sch 14 para 8(3)*].

(ii) Where plant or machinery is purchased from a connected person, or in a 'sale and leaseback transaction', or in transaction(s) from which the sole or main benefit appears to be the obtaining of a plant and machinery allowance, no first-year allowances (where otherwise relevant) are available (see 10.27(ix) above), and, in determining the buyer's qualifying expenditure, there is disregarded any excess of his expenditure (including any 'additional VAT liability' incurred in respect thereof — see 10.2(vii) above) over the disposal value to be brought into account by the seller. Where no such disposal value is to be brought into account (e.g. where the seller is non-UK resident), the buyer's qualifying expenditure (if otherwise greater) is restricted to the lesser of:

(*a*) market value at time of sale; and

(*b*) the capital expenditure, if any, incurred by the seller or any person connected with him,

with modifications to allow for 'additional VAT liabilities' and 'rebates' — see 10.2(vii) above.

For these purposes, a sale is a '*sale and leaseback transaction*' if the plant or machinery:

(A) continues to be used for the purposes of a 'qualifying activity' carried on by the seller; or

(B) is used at some time after the sale for the purposes of a 'qualifying activity' carried on by the seller (or by a connected person other than the buyer) without having been used in the meantime for the purposes of any other 'qualifying activity' except that of leasing the plant or machinery.

For the purposes of these provisions, a '*qualifying activity*' is any activity within 10.24(i)–(vii) above regardless of whether or not profits therefrom are within the charge to UK tax.

These restrictions do not apply to the supply of unused plant or machinery in the ordinary course of the seller's business. Also, for chargeable periods ending before 12 May 1998, where the plant or machinery had not before the sale been used in a qualifying activity carried on by the seller or any person connected with the seller, first-year allowances (where otherwise relevant) were available, on the lesser of (*a*) and (*b*) above (if less than actual expenditure).

The above provisions apply to contracts for future delivery, hire-purchase etc. contracts, and hire-purchase etc. contract assignments as they apply to direct sales.

[*CAA 2001, s 213(1)(2), ss 214–218, 230–233, 241, 242; CAA 1990, ss 75, 76*].

The 'sole or main benefit' restriction referred to above does not generally apply to straightforward finance leasing transactions (*Barclays Mercantile Industrial Finance Ltd v Melluish Ch D 1990, 63 TC 95*). However, with effect for expenditure incurred on or after 2 July 1997 (unless incurred before 2 July 1998 under a pre-2 July 1997 contract), the above rules are extended to further restrict allowances in the case of 'sale and finance leasebacks'. A '*sale and finance leaseback*' is a transaction which either:

- meets one of the conditions at (A) and (B) above; or
- in which the plant or machinery is used at some time after the sale etc. for the purposes of a non-qualifying activity carried on by the seller (or by a connected person other than the buyer) without having been used in the meantime for the purposes of a 'qualifying activity' (defined as above) except that of leasing the plant or machinery,

where the availability of the plant or machinery for the use in question is a direct or indirect consequence of its having been leased under a 'finance lease'.

Where an item of plant or machinery is the subject of a sale and finance leaseback, the buyer's qualifying expenditure (*and* in this case the seller's disposal value, if any) is further limited to the item's notional written-down value, computed on the assumption that all available allowances have been made in full. There are also restrictions on the qualifying expenditure of any future owner of the item. Where the finance lessor has substantially divested himself of any risk that the lessee will default, the lessor's expenditure does not qualify for plant and machinery allowances at all (and this applies regardless of any election as below). Modifications to these rules allow for any 'additional VAT liabilities' and 'rebates' — see 10.2(vii) above.

A '*finance lease*' is any arrangements for plant or machinery to be leased or made available such that the arrangements (or arrangements in which they are comprised) would fall, in accordance with generally accepted accounting practice (see 55.1 PROFIT COMPUTATIONS), to be treated in the accounts of one or more of those companies as a finance lease or as a loan. However, with effect, broadly, from 1 April 2006 (but see 10.34 above under Commencement/transitional provisions), any arrangements which are a long funding lease (as in 10.34) as regards the lessor are not within the definition of 'finance lease' for these purposes (and for the purposes of (iv) below).

With effect from 28 July 2000, in the case of sale and leaseback (and sale and finance leaseback) transactions within the above provisions, a joint (irrevocable) election may be made by the seller (or assignor) and the lessor (within two years of the sale etc.) provided that:

- the seller (or assignor) incurred capital expenditure on acquiring the plant or machinery unused (and not second-hand) and not under a transaction itself within the above provisions;
- the sale etc. takes place not more than four months after the plant or machinery is first brought into use for any purpose; and
- the seller (or assignor) has not claimed capital allowances for the expenditure or included it in a pool of qualifying expenditure.

The effect of the election is that no allowances are made to the seller (or assignor) in respect of the expenditure, and that allowances which are accordingly available to the lessor are given by reference to the lesser of his expenditure and the amount in (*b*) above, i.e. disregarding the current market value at the time of the sale etc. (and, in the case of sale and finance leasebacks, the item's notional written-down value).

[*CAA 2001, ss 219, 221–228, 243–245, Sch 3 paras 45, 51; CAA 1990, ss 76(7), 76A, 76B, 82A; FA 2000, s 77; FA 2001, s 69, Sch 21 para 3; FA 2002, Sch 40 Pt 3(16); FA 2005, s 80, Sch 4 para 33; FA 2006, Sch 9 para 14*].

(iii) Where a disposal value is required to be brought into account in respect of a car costing over £12,000 (previously £8,000) (see 10.30(A) above) on a sale (or on the performance of a contract) within any of the provisions in (ii) above, the disposal value is equal to the lesser of market value at the time of the event and the capital expenditure incurred (or treated as incurred) on it by the person disposing of it. The new owner is treated as having incurred capital expenditure on the car of the same amount. [*CAA 2001, s 79; CAA 1990, s 34(4)*].

(iv) In a case where an item of plant or machinery is the subject of a sale and finance leaseback (as defined in (ii) above) and the seller's disposal value falls to be restricted as in (ii) above, further anti-avoidance provisions apply in relation to periods ending after 16 March 2004 (but subject to the transitional provisions below) so as to limit the amount of lease rentals deductible in computing the lessee's income or profits. The amount deductible is limited to the aggregate of the finance charges shown in the accounts and the depreciation that would have been charged if the value of the item at the beginning of the leaseback had been taken for this purpose to be equal to the restricted disposal value.

In the accounting period in which the leaseback terminates:

- the above restriction on deductible lease rentals does not apply to any refund of lease rentals;
- the aforementioned aggregate is increased by a proportion of the net book value of the item immediately before the termination, such proportion to be computed in accordance with a formula in *CAA 2001, s 228B(4)*;
- (other than where a pre-17 March 2004 leaseback terminates before that date) the lessee's income/profits from the qualifying activity for the purposes of which the leased item was used immediately before the termination are increased by a proportion of the original consideration on the sale less the restricted disposal value, such proportion to be computed in accordance with a formula in *CAA 2001, s 228C(3)*.

The above rules do not apply to a lessee who became the lessee by means of an assignment of the lease.

For the above purposes and those below, a '*termination*' of a leaseback includes an assignment of the lessee's interest, the making of any other arrangements under which a person other than the lessee becomes liable to make payments under the leaseback and any variation as a result of which the leaseback ceases to be a finance lease.

In any case in which the above restriction on the lessee's deductible lease rentals potentially applies (or would do so if he had not obtained his interest by way of assignment), the following apply in computing the income/profits of the *lessor* for an accounting period. Amounts receivable by the lessor under the leaseback are included as income without netting off any amounts due by the lessor to the lessee. However, amounts receivable are not included as income to the extent that they exceed the aggregate of the gross earnings under the leaseback as shown in the lessor's accounts (effectively the finance charge element of the lease rentals) and a proportion of the restricted disposal value, such proportion to be computed in accordance with a formula in *CAA 2001, s 228D(4)*. These rules do not apply if the lessee became the lessee by means of an assignment of the lease made before 17 March 2004.

Where the leaseback terminates and the lessor disposes of the plant or machinery in circumstances such that the resulting disposal value is limited under the general rule in 10.29 above (disposal value of plant or machinery to be limited to qualifying expenditure incurred on its acquisition) or by that rule as modified under (i) above, then, in computing the lessor's income/profits for the accounting period in which termination occurs, any amount refunded to the lessee is deductible only to the extent that it does not exceed the limited disposal value. This does not apply in the case of a pre-17 March 2004 leaseback terminating before that date.

Special provision is made for cases in which accounts are not drawn up in accordance with generally accepted accounting practice (GAAP). Additionally, the above rules are adapted, in so far as they relate to the lessee, in a case where the leaseback does not fall under GAAP to be treated in the lessee's accounts as a finance lease but does fall to be so treated in the accounts of a person connected with the lessee. If the leaseback falls to be so treated in the accounts of neither the lessee nor a person connected with him, those rules are disapplied. In that case, however, where the term of the leaseback begins after 17 May 2004, the lessee's income/profits for the accounting period during which it begins are increased by the sale consideration less the restricted disposal value.

Where plant or machinery, whilst continuing to be the subject of a sale and finance leaseback, is leased to the original owner, or a person connected with him, under an operating lease (meaning, for this purpose, a lease that does not fall under GAAP to be treated in the lessee's accounts as a finance lease) commencing after 17 May 2004, the following apply. In computing the income/profits of the lessee (i.e. the lessee under the operating lease), the deduction for operating lease rentals is restricted to the 'relevant amount'. In computing the income/profits of the lessor (i.e. the lessor under the operating lease), amounts receivable by the lessor under the operating lease are included as income without netting off any amounts due by the lessor to the lessee. However, amounts receivable are not included as income to the extent that they exceed the 'relevant amount'. In each case, the '*relevant amount*' is the maximum amount of finance lease rentals deductible in computing the finance lessee's income/profits (see above). In applying these rules, such apportionments are to be made as are just and reasonable where only some of the plant or machinery subject to the sale and finance leaseback is also subject to the operating lease.

Lease and finance leasebacks. The above rules also apply, again in relation to periods ending after 16 March 2004 (subject to the transitional provisions below), to a 'lease and finance leaseback' but with appropriate modifications; in particular, depreciation is disregarded in computing the finance lessee's lease rentals and the above limitation on the finance lessor's income/profits applies by reference only to the gross earnings under the leaseback. A '*lease and finance leaseback*' occurs if a person leases plant or machinery to another in circumstances such that, had it been a sale, the transaction would have been a sale and finance leaseback as defined in (ii) above (except that the availability of the plant or machinery for the use in question must in this case be a *direct* consequence of its having been leased under a finance lease). For this purpose, a person is regarded as leasing an item of plant or machinery to another person only if he grants that other person rights over the item for consideration and is not required to bring all of that consideration into account under the plant and machinery capital allowances code; there is a let-out where the last condition is met only because a joint election under *CAA 2001, s 199* was made by lessor and lessee before 18 May 2004 in relation to a fixture (see 10.33 above under Cessation of ownership).

Transitional provisions. In relation to any leasebacks whose term commenced before 17 March 2004, transitional rules seek to preserve the pre-existing treatment of lease rentals payable before that date or in respect of any period ending before that date and a time proportion of lease rentals payable for periods straddling that date. For the effect on the lease rental deductions due to the lessee, see *FA 2004, Sch 23 paras 2, 3*; for the equivalent rules affecting computation of the lessor's income/profits, see *FA 2004, Sch 23 paras 7, 8*.

The increase in the lessee's income/profits for the accounting period in which the leaseback terminates is capped, in accordance with a formula in *FA 2004, Sch 23 para 5*, if a pre-17 March 2004 leaseback terminates early, i.e. other than by expiry of its term.

The increase in the lessee's income/profits for the accounting period in which the leaseback terminates is abated if a pre-17 March 2004 leaseback terminates early, the lessee reacquires ownership of the plant or machinery and the lessee's capital expenditure on reacquisition is itself restricted under (ii) above. If the restriction equals or exceeds the increase in profits/income, the increase is cancelled; in other cases, the increase is reduced by the restriction. However, the increase is reinstated in modified form if a disposal event (see 10.29 above) occurs in relation to the whole or part of the plant or machinery within six years after the leaseback terminates. See *FA 2004, Sch 23 para 6*.

Where a pre-17 March 2004 lease and finance leaseback terminates and the finance lessee then disposes of the plant or machinery, there is provision for his chargeable gain to be reduced for capital gains tax purposes. See *FA 2004, Sch 23 para 10*.

See Tolley's Capital Allowances for more detail on these transitional provisions.

[*CAA 2001, ss 228A–228J; FA 2004, s 134, Sch 23*].

Simon's Direct Tax Service. See **B2.365, B2.366, B2.368, B2.369**.

See HMRC Capital Allowances Manual CA 28600 for a general article on how these and associated capital allowance restrictions are intended to operate. In particular the article considers sale and leaseback by novation or new contract, or on defeased terms, and assets with long build times. See also 10.28 above, (A) above and 66.54 TRADING INCOME as regards finance lease allowance restrictions .See 10.34 above as regards long funding leasing.

See (G) below as regards succession to a trade or other qualifying activity carried on by a 'connected person'.

(D) Where plant or machinery received by way of gift is brought into use for the purposes of a trade or other qualifying activity carried on by the donee, the donee is entitled to writing-down allowances as if he had purchased it from the donor at the time it is brought into use and at its market value at that time. Where the gift was brought into use between 1 November 1992 and 31 October 1993 inclusive, the donee's deemed expenditure qualified for the temporarily reinstated 40% first-year allowance (see 10.27 above), but such deemed expenditure cannot qualify for any of the targeted first-year allowances introduced subsequently. [*CAA 2001, ss 14, 213(3), Sch 3 paras 12, 43; CAA 1990, s 81; FA 1993, Sch 13 para 12(1)*]. See Simon's Direct Tax Service B2.303.

(E) Previous use outside trade etc. Where a person brings into use, for the purposes of the trade or other qualifying activity, plant or machinery which that person previously owned for purposes not providing entitlement to plant and machinery allowances in respect of that activity, writing-down allowances are calculated as if the trader etc. had, at the time of bringing it into use, incurred expenditure on its acquisition equal to its market value at that time. Actual cost, if less, is substituted for market value where the plant or machinery is brought into trade etc. use after 20 March 2000. The actual cost for this purpose is reduced to the extent that it would have been reduced under the anti-avoidance provisions of *CAA 2001, s 218* or *s 224* or earlier equivalents (see (C) above) had it been expenditure on plant or machinery for use in the qualifying activity.

Where the plant or machinery was brought into use between 1 November 1992 and 31 October 1993 inclusive, the deemed expenditure qualified for the temporarily reinstated 40% first-year allowance (see 10.27 above); such first-year allowances were not, however, available where plant or machinery was transferred from one qualifying activity to another carried on by the same person and was brought into use in the second activity after 13 April 1993. Expenditure deemed to be incurred under these provisions does not qualify for any of the targeted first-year allowances introduced subsequently.

[*CAA 2001, s 13, Sch 3 para 11; CAA 1990, s 81; FA 1993, Sch 13 para 12; FA 2000, s 75(3)(6)*].

See also 10.34 above as regards an asset ceasing to be used for long funding leasing but being retained by the lessor for use in a qualifying activity.

Simon's Direct Tax Service. See **B2.303**.

(F) **Partnerships** are entitled to allowances in respect of an item of plant or machinery used for the trade or other qualifying activity carried on by the partnership, and owned by one or more partners without being partnership property. Any transfer of the item between partners, whilst it continues to be so used, does not require a disposal value to be brought into account. These provisions do not apply if such an item is *let* by one or more partners to the partnership or otherwise made available to it in consideration of a tax-deductible payment. [*CAA 2001, s 264; CAA 1990, s 65*].

Following a change in the persons carrying on a trade or other qualifying activity, other than one resulting in the activity being treated as permanently discontinued, allowances are subsequently given and balancing charges subsequently made as if the new partnership etc. had carried on the activity before the change. For this purpose, a '*qualifying activity*' does not include an office or employment but otherwise includes any of the activities at 10.24(i)–(vii) above regardless of whether or not the profits therefrom are within the charge to UK tax. [*CAA 2001, s 263; CAA 1990, s 78(3)(4); FA 2001, s 69, Sch 21 para 4(1); ITTOIA 2005, Sch 1 para 549*]. See (G) below as regards partnerships treated as discontinued and successions to trades generally.

Simon's Direct Tax Service. See **B2.390**.

(G) **Successions.** Following a change in the persons carrying on a trade or other qualifying activity, such that the activity is treated as permanently discontinued, any plant or machinery transferred, without being sold, to the new owner for continuing use in the qualifying activity is treated as sold at market value on the date of change, although no first-year allowance (where otherwise applicable) is available to the new owner. For this purpose, a '*qualifying activity*' does not include an office or employment but otherwise includes any of the activities at 10.24(i)–(vii) above regardless of whether or not the profits therefrom are within the charge to UK tax. These provisions apply equally to plant or machinery not in use but provided and available for use for the purposes of the qualifying activity. Where *CAA 2001* has effect (see 10.1 above), they apply only to plant and machinery actually owned by the predecessor. [*CAA 2001, s 265; CAA 1990, s 78(1)(5) ; ITTOIA 2005, Sch 1 para 550*].

Where a person succeeds to a trade or other qualifying activity carried on by a person 'connected' with that person, each is within the charge to UK tax on the profits, and the successor is not a dual resident investing company, they may jointly elect, within two years after the date of change, for plant or machinery to be treated as transferred at a price giving rise to neither a balancing allowance nor a balancing charge. This applies to plant or machinery which immediately before and after the succession is owned by the person concerned and either in use, or (where *CAA 2001* has effect — see 10.1 above) provided and available for use, for the purposes of the qualifying activity, and regardless of any actual sale by the predecessor to the successor. Allowances and charges are subsequently made as if everything done to or by the predecessor had been done to or by the successor. Where *CAA 2001* has effect, it is expressly provided that the deemed sale takes place when the succession takes place.

For this purpose, persons are '*connected*' if

(*a*) they are CONNECTED PERSONS (19) within *ICTA 1988, s 839*, or (*b*) one of them is a partnership in which the other has the right to a share of assets or income, or both are partnerships in both of which some other person has the right to such a share, or

(*c*) one of them is a body corporate over which the other has control (within *CAA 2001, s 574*), or both are bodies corporate, or one a body corporate and one a partnership, over both of which some other person has control.

An election in relation to a succession occurring after 26 July 1989 precludes the application of *CAA 2001, s 104* (disposal value of long-life assets in avoidance cases — see 10.30(G) above), *CAA 2001, s 265* (see above) and the similar provisions in *CAA 2001, s 108* (see 10.35(*a*) above), and their forerunners. First-year allowances would appear to be precluded by 10.27(ix) above.

These provisions did not apply in this form to successions occurring before 29 July 1988.

In relation to successions occurring after 4 December 2005, the above election does not have effect in relation to qualifying leased plant or machinery where the transferee succeeds to a trade carried on by the transferor which is a 'business of leasing plant or machinery' as defined in 5.17 ANTI-AVOIDANCE.

For transfers under *ICTA 1988, s 343* (company reconstructions without a change in ownership) see 47.10 LOSSES. For transfers between companies in different EU member states *under CAA 2001, s 560*, see 11.11 CAPITAL GAINS, and between such companies on the formation of an SE by merger under *CAA 2001, s 561A*, see 11.13 CAPITAL GAINS.

[*CAA 2001, ss 266–267A, Sch 3 para 52; CAA 1990, s 77; FA 1997, Sch 14 para 9; FA 2006, s 85*].

Simon's Direct Tax Service. See **B2.390**.

(H) A renewals basis is generally available as an alternative to capital allowances. A deduction is allowed in computing profits of the cost of a replacement item less the proceeds of sale (or scrap value) of the item replaced. Where, however, the replacement item is an improvement on that replaced, the deduction is restricted to the cost of replacing like with like. See *Caledonian Railway Co v Banks CES 1880, 1 TC 487; Eastmans Ltd v Shaw HL 1928, 14 TC 218*; *Hyam v CIR CS 1929, 14 TC 479.*

Cost of renewals of trade implements, utensils etc. are allowed as a deduction under *ICTA 1988, s 74(1)(d)*, but cf. *Hinton v Maden & Ireland Ltd HL 1959, 38 TC 391* and also see *Peter Merchant Ltd v Stedeford CA 1948, 30 TC 496* (provision for future renewals not allowable). Replacement of parts is allowed under general principles so far as identity of plant or machinery is retained. For further details of 'renewals basis' and change from renewals basis to normal capital allowances and *vice versa*, see HMRC Extra-Statutory Concession B1 as revised and HMRC Business Income Manual BIM 46935, 46950, 46955.

Simon's Direct Tax Service. See **B2.312**.

A **valuation basis** is a variation of renewals basis in which a class of assets, for example spare parts for plant and machinery, are dealt with in a similar way to trading stock, involving opening and closing valuations. For further detail, and for change from capital allowances to valuation basis, see HMRC Business Income Manual BIM 46940, 46960.

(J) Partial depreciation subsidies, i.e. sums, not otherwise taxable on the recipient, are payable to him, directly or indirectly, by any other person in respect of, or to take account of, *part* of the depreciation of plant or machinery resulting from its use in the recipient's trade or other qualifying activity.

Where it appears that a partial depreciation subsidy will be payable, a first-year allowance (where available — see 10.27 above) can nevertheless be given, but must be scaled down as is just and reasonable (though the full amount is deducted in arriving at the balance of expenditure available for writing-down allowances).

Qualifying expenditure (see 10.24 above) which has been the subject of a partial depreciation subsidy can only be allocated to a *single asset pool* (see 10.28 above). Where qualifying expenditure has otherwise been allocated to a pool and a partial depreciation subsidy is received for the first time in respect of it, it must be transferred to a single asset pool. This is achieved by bringing in a disposal value (equal to market value — see 10.29(*g*) above) in the original pool for the chargeable period in which the subsidy is paid and allocating an equivalent amount to the single asset pool. Writing-down allowances and balancing allowances and charges in respect of the single asset pool are reduced to such amounts as are just and reasonable (though the full amount is deducted in arriving at any unrelieved qualifying expenditure carried forward).

[*CAA 2001, ss 209–212; CAA 1990, s 80(2)–(7); FA 1990, Sch 17 para 15*].

See 10.25 above as regards subsidies towards the whole of such depreciation. See 10.2(v)(vi) above as regards contributions by others towards *expenditure* qualifying for plant and machinery and other capital allowances.

Simon's Direct Tax Service. See B2.360.

(K) **A lessee required to provide plant or machinery** under the terms of the lease (including any tenancy), and using it for the purposes of a trade or other qualifying activity, is treated as if he owned it (for as long as it is used for those purposes), but is not required to bring in a disposal value (see 10.29 above) on termination of the lease. If:

- the plant or machinery continues to be so used until termination of the lease;
- the lessor holds the lease in the course of a qualifying activity; and
- on or after termination, a disposal event occurs at a time when the lessor owns the plant or machinery,

the *lessor* is required to bring in a disposal value, for the chargeable period in which the disposal event occurs, in the pool to which the expenditure would have been allocated if incurred by the lessor. These rules do not, however, apply where the plant or machinery becomes, by law, part of the building in which it is installed or attached (see 10.33 above) under a lease entered into after 11 July 1984 unless pursuant to an agreement made on or before that date. [*CAA 2001, s 70, Sch 3 para 17; CAA 1990, s 61(4)(8)*].

(L) **Disposal of leased asset where income retained.** Where, after 4 December 2005, a lessor sells or disposes of plant or machinery which is subject to a lease but remains entitled immediately after the disposal to some or all the rental income payable after that date in respect of the lease, the disposal value to be brought into account by the lessor is determined as follows. Where the disposal consideration exceeds the limit imposed in 10.29 above (broadly, the original cost) the disposal value is to equal the consideration received and that limit does not apply. In any other case, but subject to that limit, the disposal value is to equal the sum of the consideration received plus the 'net present value' of the rentals payable (after 4 December 2005) to which the lessor remains entitled immediately after the disposal. In so far as any such future rentals receivable by the lessor are brought into account in determining the disposal value, the amount of the rentals equal to their value so brought into account is to be excluded in calculating the lessor's leasing business income for corporation tax purposes (any necessary apportionment to be made on a just and reasonable basis).

The '*net present value*' of the rentals is the amount as determined under *CA 2001, s 228L* using a discount rate of 3.5% (which can be varied by regulation). If any land or asset other than plant or machinery is subject to the lease, the net present value of the rentals relating to the plant or machinery is to be determined using a just and reasonable basis.

Any rentals receivable by the lessor before 22 March 2006 are to be excluded in calculating the lessor's leasing business income for corporation tax purposes.

This provision applies to a lessor which carries on a '*business of leasing plant or machinery*' as defined in 5.17 ANTI-AVOIDANCE and the disposal of plant or machinery for this purpose is that on whose provision expenditure is incurred wholly or partly for the purposes of the business. A '*lease*' in this case includes an underlease, sublease, tenancy or licence or an agreement for any of those things.

[*CAA 2001, ss 228K–228M; FA 2006, s 84*].

10.39 **MINERAL EXTRACTION**

Mineral extraction allowances are available in respect of qualifying expenditure (see 10.40 below) incurred by a person carrying on a 'mineral extraction trade'. A '*mineral extraction trade*' is a trade consisting of or including the working of a source of '*mineral deposits*', i.e. such deposits of a wasting nature including any natural deposits or geothermal energy capable of being lifted or extracted from the earth. A '*source of mineral deposits*' includes a mine, an oil well and a source of geothermal energy. [*CAA 2001, s 394; CAA 1990, s 98(1), s 121(1)(2), s 161(2)*]. A *share* in an asset may qualify for mineral extraction allowances. [*CAA 2001, s 435; CAA 1990, s 121(5)*].

The main elements of the code of mineral extraction allowances are dealt with as follows.

Simon's Direct Tax Service. See **B2.4**.

10.40 **Qualifying expenditure and first-year qualifying expenditure.** '*Qualifying expenditure*' means capital expenditure, incurred for the purposes of a mineral extraction trade, on:

(*a*) '*mineral exploration and access*' (i.e. searching for or discovering and testing the mineral deposits of any source, or winning access to any such deposits);

(*b*) acquisition of a '*mineral asset*' (i.e. any mineral deposits or land comprising mineral deposits, or any interest in or right over such deposits or land) (subject to the limitations in 10.41 below);

(*c*) construction of works, in connection with the working of a source of mineral deposits, which are likely to become of little or no value when the source ceases to be worked;

(*d*) construction of works which are likely to become valueless when a foreign concession under which a source of mineral deposits is worked comes to an end.

Included in (*a*) above is abortive expenditure (including appeal costs) on seeking planning permission for the undertaking of mineral exploration and access or the working of mineral deposits. Expenditure on the acquisition of, or of rights over, mineral deposits or the site of a source of mineral deposits falls into (*b*) rather than (*a*) above.

However, the following are *not* qualifying expenditure:

- expenditure on the provision of plant or machinery (except certain pre-trading expenditure — see below), and see 10.47 below;
- expenditure on acquisition of, or of rights in or over, the *site* of any works in (*c*) or (*d*) above;

- expenditure on works constructed wholly or mainly for processing the raw products, unless the process is designed to prepare the raw products for use as such;
- (subject to *CAA 2001, s 415* — see below) expenditure on buildings and structures for occupation by, or welfare of, workers;
- expenditure on a building constructed *entirely* for use as an office;
- expenditure on the office part of a building or structure constructed *partly* for use as an office, where such expenditure exceeds 10% of the capital expenditure on construction of the whole building.

[*CAA 2001, ss 395–399, 400(1), 403(1)(2), 414; CAA 1990, ss 105, 121(1)*].

Qualifying expenditure also includes capital contributions, for the purposes of a mineral extraction trade carried on outside the UK, to the cost of accommodation buildings, and certain related utility buildings and welfare works, for employees engaged in working a source, provided that the buildings or works are likely to be of little or no value when the source ceases to be worked, that the expenditure does not result in the acquisition of an asset, and that relief is not due under any other tax provision. [*CAA 2001, s 415; CAA 1990, s 108*]. Net expenditure incurred on the restoration of the site of a source of mineral deposits (or land used in connection with working such a source) within three years after the cessation of the trade is also qualifying expenditure, treated as incurred on the last day of trading, unless relieved elsewhere. [*CAA 2001, s 416; CAA 1990, s 109*].

Pre-trading expenditure for the purposes of a mineral extraction trade is treated as incurred on the first day of trading. This applies equally to pre-trading expenditure on mineral exploration and access, but in determining whether such expenditure is qualifying expenditure within (*a*) above, the following limitations apply.

(i) In the case of pre-trading expenditure on plant or machinery which is used at a source but is sold, demolished, destroyed or abandoned before commencement of the mineral extraction trade, qualifying expenditure is limited to net expenditure after taking account of sale proceeds, insurance money or capital compensation.

(ii) In the case of pre-trading exploration expenditure other than on plant or machinery, qualifying expenditure is limited to net expenditure after taking into account any reasonably attributable capital sums received before the first day of trading.

In either case, if mineral exploration and access is not continuing at the source on the first day of trading, qualifying expenditure is further limited to net expenditure incurred in the six years ending on that day.

[*CAA 2001, s 400(2)–(5), 401, 402, 434; CAA 1990, ss 105(2), 106, 107, 120*].

Qualifying expenditure (as above) incurred by a company **after 16 April 2002** is '*first-year qualifying expenditure*' if it is incurred wholly for the purposes of a 'ring fence trade' within *ICTA 1988, s 501A* (petroleum extraction activities, see 51 OIL COMPANIES), subject to the exclusion of expenditure on:

(A) acquisition of mineral assets (see (*b*) above); and

(B) acquisition of an asset representing expenditure incurred by a connected company (within *ICTA 1988, s 839*, see 19 CONNECTED PERSONS), including any results obtained from any search, exploration or enquiry on which mineral exploitation and access expenditure was incurred.

For this purpose, *CAA 2001, ss 400(4), 434* (see above), which treat certain expenditure as having been incurred on the first day of trading, do not apply.

[*CAA 2001, ss 416A–416C; FA 2002, Sch 21 para 9*].

Simon's Direct Tax Service. See B2.406 *et seq.*

10.41 **Limitations on qualifying expenditure.** Qualifying expenditure within 10.40(*b*) above (acquisition of mineral asset) is limited in the following circumstances.

If the mineral asset is an interest in land, an amount equal to the 'undeveloped market value' of the interest is excluded. '*Undeveloped market value*' is the market value of the interest at the time of acquisition ignoring the mineral deposits and assuming that development of the land (other than that already lawfully begun or for which planning permission has already been granted) is, and will remain, unlawful. Where the undeveloped market value includes the value of buildings or structures which, at any time after acquisition, permanently cease to be used, their value at acquisition (exclusive of land and after deducting any net capital allowances received in respect of them) is treated as qualifying expenditure incurred at the time of cessation of use. These provisions operate by reference to the actual time of acquisition, regardless of any different time given by the pre-trading expenditure provisions at 10.40 above. They do not apply where an election is made under *CAA 2001, s 569* or its forerunner (election to treat connected persons transactions as made at written-down value). [*CAA 2001, ss 403(3), 404, 405, Sch 3 para 84; CAA 1990, s 110*].

Where a deduction has been allowed under *ICTA 1988, s* 87 (or, for income tax purposes from 2005/06, under *ITTOIA 2005, ss 60–67*) in respect of a premium under a lease (see 66.71 TRADING INCOME), the qualifying expenditure allowable in respect of the acquisition of the interest in land to which the premium relates is correspondingly reduced. [*CAA 2001, s 406; CAA 1990, s 111; ITTOIA 2005, Sch 1 para 561*].

Simon's Direct Tax Service. See **B2.410**.

10.42 **Second-hand assets.** Where:

(*a*) an asset is acquired from another person; and

(*b*) either that person or any previous owner incurred expenditure on it in connection with a mineral extraction trade,

the buyer's qualifying expenditure is restricted to the seller's qualifying expenditure on the asset less net allowances given to him. If an oil licence (or an interest therein) is acquired, the buyer's qualifying expenditure is limited to the amount of the original licence fee paid (or such part of it as it is just and reasonable to attribute to the interest). However, these restrictions do not affect amounts *treated* under rules below as qualifying expenditure on mineral exploration and access. In relation to a mineral asset situated in the UK, the restrictions do not apply to an acquisition under a pre-16 July 1985 contract, and the reference above to previous owners excludes any person who has not been the owner at any time after 31 March 1986.

Where:

(i) the purchased asset above is a mineral asset; and

(ii) part of its value is properly attributable to expenditure on mineral exploration and access incurred as in (*b*) above,

so much if any of the buyer's expenditure as it is just and reasonable to attribute to the part of the value in (ii) above (not exceeding the amount of original expenditure to which it is attributable) is treated as qualifying expenditure on mineral exploration and access, with the remainder treated as expenditure on acquisition of a mineral asset. In relation to an asset situated in the UK, this rule does not apply to an acquisition under a pre-16 July 1985 contract, and the reference to previous owners excludes any person who has not been the owner at any time after 31 March 1986. In relation to claims made after 25 November 1996, expenditure deducted by a previous owner in computing taxable profits is excluded for these purposes from the original expenditure.

Where:

- capital expenditure is incurred in acquiring assets for a mineral extraction trade from a person (the seller) who did *not* carry on a mineral extraction trade; and
- the assets represent expenditure on mineral exploration and access incurred by the seller,

the buyer's qualifying expenditure is limited to the amount of the seller's expenditure. Assets include any results obtained from any search, exploration or inquiry on which the expenditure was incurred. This restriction does not apply if the asset is an interest in an oil licence acquired by the buyer after 12 September 1995; in this case, so much if any of the buyer's expenditure as it is just and reasonable to attribute to the part of the value of the licence attributable to the seller's expenditure (but limited to the amount of that expenditure) is treated as qualifying expenditure on mineral exploration and access, with the cost of the oil licence being reduced by the buyer's expenditure so attributable (without limitation).

Where a mineral asset is transferred between companies under common control, and no election is made under *CAA 2001, s 569* or its forerunner (election to treat connected persons transactions as made at written-down value), the buyer's expenditure is limited to that of the seller. However, this does not affect amounts *treated* under rules above as qualifying expenditure on mineral exploration and access. Where the asset is an interest in land, the limitations at 10.41 above generally apply as if the buyer acquired the interest when the seller acquired it (or, in the case of a sequence of such transactions, when the first seller acquired it).

[*CAA 2001, ss 407–413, Sch 3 paras 85–87; CAA 1990, ss 113–118; FA 1997, s 66*].

Simon's Direct Tax Service. See **B2.411** *et seq.*

10.43 **First-year and writing-down allowances and balancing adjustments.** For each item of first-year qualifying expenditure (see 10.40 above), a **first-year allowance (FYA)** of up to **100%** is available for the chargeable period in which the expenditure is incurred. No FYA is available, however, to the extent that a transaction is attributable to any scheme, agreement or understanding, whether or not legally enforceable, a main purpose of which is the obtaining of a first-year allowance which would not otherwise have been available (or of a greater allowance than would otherwise have been available).

For each item of qualifying expenditure (see 10.40 above), a **writing-down allowance (WDA)** is available for each chargeable period (see 10.1 above) and is equal to a set percentage (as below) of the amount (if any) by which 'unrelieved qualifying expenditure' exceeds the total of any disposal values falling to be brought into account as in 10.44 below. The WDA is proportionately reduced or increased if the chargeable period is less or more than a year, or if the mineral extraction trade has been carried on for part only of the chargeable period.

In the circumstances listed at 10.45 below, a **balancing allowance** is available, instead of a WDA, equal to the excess (if any) of (1) 'unrelieved qualifying expenditure' over (2) total disposal values. (This is subject to the anti-avoidance rule at 10.2(xi) above.) If, for any chargeable period, (2) exceeds (1), there arises a liability to a **balancing charge**, normally equal to that excess but limited to net allowances previously given (including, where a balancing charge arises in respect of first-year qualifying expenditure incurred in the period, any FYA given on that expenditure). A claim for a WDA *or* a balancing allowance may require it to be reduced to a specified amount.

Rates of WDA are as follows:

Acquisition of a mineral asset (see 10.40(*b*) above)	**10% p.a.**
Other qualifying expenditure	**25% p.a.**

'*Unrelieved qualifying expenditure*' means qualifying expenditure (other than first-year qualifying expenditure) incurred in the chargeable period and the tax written-down value brought forward (i.e. net of allowances and any disposal values) of qualifying expenditure (including first-year qualifying expenditure) incurred in a previous chargeable period. If a disposal receipt falls to be brought into account in the case of first-year qualifying expenditure for the chargeable period in which it was incurred, any balance of that expenditure after deducting any FYA given in respect of it is treated as unrelieved qualifying expenditure *but only* for the purpose of determining whether there is a balancing allowance or charge for that period and, if so, the amount of such an allowance or charge.

[*CAA 2001, ss 416D–419; CAA 1990, ss 98, 100; FA 1994, s 213(8); FA 2002, Sch 21 paras 11–13*].

The net demolition costs (i.e. the excess, if any, of demolition costs over money received for remains) of an asset representing qualifying expenditure is added to that expenditure in determining the amount of any balancing allowance or charge for the chargeable period of demolition, and is not then treated as expenditure incurred on any replacement asset. [*CAA 2001, s 433; CAA 1990, s 103*].

There is no provision for pooling expenditure (cf. plant and machinery at 10.28 above). In practice, HMRC do not object to the grouping together of assets for computational convenience, provided individual sources are kept separate and assets attracting different rates of WDA are not grouped with each other. However, where a disposal value falls to be brought into account or a balancing allowance arises, it will sometimes be necessary to reconstruct separate computations for individual items of expenditure previously grouped. (HMRC Capital Allowances Manual CA 50410).

Simon's Direct Tax Service. See **B2.419** *et seq.*

10.44 **Disposal events and values.** A disposal value must be brought into account (by deduction from unrelieved qualifying expenditure — see 10.43 above), for the chargeable period in which the event occurs, on the occurrence of any of the following events.

(i) An asset representing qualifying expenditure (see 10.40 above) is disposed of or permanently ceases to be used for the purposes of a mineral extraction trade (whether because of cessation of trade or otherwise).

(ii) A mineral asset begins to be used (by the trader or another person) in a way which constitutes development which is neither 'existing permitted development' nor development for the purposes of a mineral extraction trade. Development is '*existing permitted development*' if, at the time of acquisition, it had already lawfully begun or the appropriate planning permission had already been granted.

(iii) In a case not within (i) or (ii) above, a capital sum is received which, in whole or in part, it is reasonable to attribute to qualifying expenditure.

The amount to be brought into account depends upon the nature of the event.

(*a*) On an event within (i) or (ii) above, it is an amount determined in accordance with the list at 10.29(*a*)–(*g*) above (disregarding (*f*), the reference to abandonment at (*d*) and the text immediately following the list). However, if the asset is an interest in land, the amount so ascertained is then restricted by excluding the '*undeveloped market value*', determined as in 10.41 above but by reference to the time of disposal.

(*b*) On an event within (iii) above, it is so much of the capital sum as is reasonably attributable to the qualifying expenditure.

[*CAA 2001, ss 420–425; CAA 1990, ss 99, 112; ITEPA 2003, Sch 6 para 254*].

In relation to sales at other than market value, the connected person and other anti-avoidance provisions, and election potential, of *CAA 2001 ss 567–570* (and forerunners) apply with appropriate modifications for mineral extraction allowances as they do for industrial buildings allowances (see 10.22(i) above).

Simon's Direct Tax Service. See B2.420.

10.45 **Balancing allowances.** A person is entitled to a balancing allowance (instead of a writing-down allowance) for a chargeable period if:

- the chargeable period is that in which the first day of trading falls, and either the qualifying expenditure is pre-trading expenditure on plant or machinery within 10.40(i) above or it is pre-trading exploration expenditure within 10.40(ii) above where mineral exploration and access is not continuing at the source on the first day of trading; or
- the qualifying expenditure was on mineral exploration and access, and in that chargeable period that person gives up the exploration, search or inquiry to which the expenditure related, without subsequently carrying on a mineral extraction trade consisting of or including the working of related mineral deposits; or
- in that chargeable period that person permanently ceases to work particular mineral deposits and the qualifying expenditure was on mineral exploration and access relating solely to those deposits or on the acquisition of a mineral asset consisting of those deposits or part of them; but where two or more mineral assets are comprised in, or derive from, a single asset, the above applies only when *all* the relevant mineral deposits cease to be worked; or
- the qualifying expenditure falls within *CAA 2001, s 415* (capital contributions to certain buildings or works for benefit of employees abroad — see 10.40 above), and in that chargeable period, the buildings or works permanently cease to be used for the purposes of or in connection with the mineral extraction trade; or
- the qualifying expenditure was on the provision of any assets, and in that chargeable period, any of those assets is disposed of or otherwise permanently ceases to be used for purposes of the trade; or
- the qualifying expenditure is represented by assets, and in that chargeable period those assets are permanently lost or cease to exist (due to destruction, dismantling or otherwise) or begin to be used wholly or partly for purposes other than those of the mineral extraction trade; or
- the mineral extraction trade is permanently discontinued in that chargeable period.

[*CAA 2001, ss 426–431; CAA 1990, s 101*].

Simon's Direct Tax Service. See B2.421.

10.46 **Making of allowances and charges.** Mineral extraction allowances (or balancing charges) are given (or made) as trading expenses (or trading receipts) in calculating the profits of the mineral extraction trade. [*CAA 2001, s 432; CAA 1990, ss 104, 140, 144; FA 1994, s 211*].

Simon's Direct Tax Service. See B2.423.

10.47 **Plant and machinery allowances.** Plant and machinery is normally excluded from relief under the current provisions, but certain pre-trading expenditure may qualify (see 10.40 above). The normal plant and machinery rules (see 10.24 *et seq.* above) apply to plant and machinery provided for mineral exploration and access in connection with a mineral extraction trade. [*CAA 2001, ss 159, 160; CAA 1990, s 83(1)(6)*]. Where such expenditure (limited to capital expenditure where *CAA 2001* has effect — see 10.1 above) is incurred prior to the date of commencement of a mineral extraction trade and the plant or machinery is still owned at that date, it is treated as if sold immediately before that date and re-acquired on that date. The capital expenditure on re-acquisition is deemed to be equal to the actual expenditure previously incurred. [*CAA 2001, s 161, Sch 3 para 25; CAA 1990, s 63*].

10.48 *Example*

X Ltd operates a mining business with two mineral sources, G and S. Accounts are prepared to 30 September. On 31 December 2006 the mineral deposits and mineworks at G are sold at market value to Z Ltd for £80,000 and £175,000 respectively. A new source, P, is purchased on 30 April 2007 for £170,000 (including land with an undeveloped market value of £70,000) and the following expenditure is incurred before the end of the accounting period ended 30 September 2007.

	£
Plant and machinery	40,000
Construction of administration office	25,000
Construction of mining works which are likely to have little value when mining ceases	50,000
Staff hostel	35,000
Winning access to the deposits	150,000
	£300,000

During the year to 30 September 2007, X Ltd also incurred expenditure of £20,000 in seeking planning permission to mine a further plot of land, Source Q. Permission was refused.

Residue of expenditure brought forward		£
(based on accounts to 30 September 2006)		
Mineral exploration and access	– Source G	170,000
	– Source S	200,000
Mineral assets	– Source G	95,250
	– Source S	72,000

The mineral extraction allowances due for the year ending 30 September 2007 are as follows.

	£	£
Source G		
Mineral exploration and access		
WDV b/f	170,000	
Proceeds	175,000	
Balancing charge	£5,000	(5,000)

	£	£
Mineral assets		
WDV b/f	95,250	
Proceeds	80,000	
Balancing allowance	£15,250	15,250
Source S		
Mineral exploration and access		
WDV b/f	200,000	
WDA 25%	(50,000)	50,000
WDV c/f	£150,000	
Mineral assets		
WDV b/f	72,000	
WDA 10%	(7,200)	7,200
WDV c/f	£64,800	
Source P		
Mineral exploration and access		
Expenditure	150,000	
WDA 25%	(37,500)	37,500
WDV c/f	£112,500	
Mineral assets		
Expenditure note (*c*)	100,000	
WDA 10%	(10,000)	10,000
WDV c/f	£90,000	
Mining works		
Expenditure	50,000	
WDA 25%	(12,500)	12,500
WDV c/f	£37,500	
Source Q		
Mineral exploration and access		
Expenditure note (*b*)	20,000	
WDA 25%	(5,000)	5,000
WDV c/f	£15,000	
Total allowances (net of charges)		£132,450

Notes

(*a*) Allowances are not due on either the office or staff hostel although the hostel may qualify for industrial buildings allowances (see 10.11 above). The plant and machinery qualify for plant and machinery allowances (see 10.24 above) rather than for mineral extraction allowances (see 10.47 above).

(*b*) Abortive expenditure on seeking planning permission is qualifying expenditure as if it were expenditure on mineral exploration and access (see 10.40 above).

(*c*) The undeveloped market value of land is excluded from qualifying expenditure (see 10.41 above).

10.49 **Transition to current code of allowances.** The current code of allowances, as described at 10.39–10.46 above was introduced for expenditure incurred after 31 March 1986 (though a trader could elect to continue to apply the old code to certain expenditure incurred in the twelve months to 31 March 1987). Any unrelieved balance of expenditure at 1 April 1986 (or 1 April 1987 where applicable) under the old code was treated for the purposes of the current code as expenditure incurred on that day for the purposes for which the original expenditure was actually incurred. If expenditure had been fully relieved under the old code but the assets remained in use, the current code applies as if the expenditure had been incurred on 1 April 1986 and had been fully relieved under the current code (thus enabling balancing charges to accrue subsequently).

Expenditure on mineral exploration and access, or on acquisition of mineral assets, or on construction of certain works, which did not qualify for allowances under the old code because either the trade, or output from the source, had not commenced, or for some other reason, was treated as incurred on 1 April 1986 and relieved as appropriate under the new code.

Special rules apply where the old code expenditure on a mineral asset included the acquisition of an interest in land. The undeveloped market value of that interest was not excluded from the relievable expenditure where some relief had already been given under the old code, but nor is such value excluded under 10.44(*a*) above from any disposal value to be brought into account.

In making balancing charges where old code expenditure has been brought under the new code, allowances given under the old code will be taken into account together with those given under the new code.

[*CAA 2001, Sch 3 para 88; CAA 1990, s 119*].

Simon's Direct Tax Service. See **B2.455**.

10.50 PATENT RIGHTS

Subject to the application of the regime for INTANGIBLE ASSETS (39), allowances are available, and balancing charges made, in respect of 'qualifying expenditure' on the purchase of patent rights, i.e. the right to do or authorise the doing of anything which would, but for that right, be a patent infringement. The obtaining of a right to acquire future patent rights and the acquisition of a licence in respect of a patent are each treated for these purposes as a purchase of patent rights.

Allowances are not available where the intangible assets regime applies to the patent rights. See in particular the commencement and transitional provisions for that regime at 39.37 INTANGIBLE ASSETS.

'*Qualifying expenditure*' may be either

- '*qualifying trade expenditure*', i.e. capital expenditure incurred by a person on purchase of patent rights for the purposes of a trade carried on by him and within the charge to UK tax; or

- '*qualifying non-trade expenditure*', i.e. capital expenditure incurred by a person on purchase of patent rights if the above does not apply but any income receivable by him in respect of the rights would be liable to tax.

Expenditure incurred by a person for the purposes of a trade he is about to carry on is treated as if incurred on the first day of trading, unless all the rights in question have been sold before then. The same expenditure cannot be qualifying trade expenditure in relation to more than one trade.

The grant of a licence in respect of a patent is treated as a sale of part of patent rights. The grant by a person entitled to patent rights of an exclusive licence, i.e. a licence to exercise the rights to the exclusion of the grantor and all others for the remainder of their term, is, however, treated as a sale of the whole of those rights.

[*CAA 2001, ss 464–469; ICTA 1988, ss 520(1)–(3), 533(1)–(3)(5)(6)*].

Qualifying expenditure incurred after 31 March 1986 is pooled for the purpose of determining entitlement to writing-down allowances and balancing allowances and liability to balancing charges. A separate pool applies for each separate trade and for all qualifying non-trade expenditure.

For each pool of qualifying expenditure, a **writing-down allowance (WDA)** is available for each chargeable period (see 10.1 above) other than the 'final chargeable period' and is equal to a maximum of **25%** of the amount (if any) by which 'available qualifying expenditure' exceeds the total of any disposal values falling to be brought into account. The WDA is proportionately reduced or increased if the chargeable period is less or more than a year, or if (where relevant) the trade has been carried on for part only of the chargeable period. A claim for a WDA may require it to be reduced to a specified amount. For the 'final chargeable period', a **balancing allowance** is available, equal to the excess (if any) of (1) 'available qualifying expenditure' over (2) total disposal values. If, for *any* chargeable period, (2) exceeds (1), there arises a liability to a **balancing charge**, equal to that excess.

The '*final chargeable period*', as regards a pool of qualifying trade expenditure, is the chargeable period in which the trade is permanently discontinued. As regards a pool of non-qualifying trade expenditure, it is the chargeable period in which the last of the patent rights in question either comes to an end (without any such rights being revived) or, where *CAA 2001* has effect (see 10.1 above), is wholly disposed of.

'*Available qualifying expenditure*' in a pool for a chargeable period consists of qualifying expenditure allocated to the pool for that period and any unrelieved qualifying expenditure brought forward in the pool from the previous chargeable period (usually referred to as the written-down value brought forward).

In allocating qualifying expenditure to a pool, the following must be observed.

(i) Qualifying expenditure can be allocated to a pool for a chargeable period only to the extent that it has not been included in available qualifying expenditure for an earlier chargeable period. (Before *CAA 2001* had effect, see 10.1 above, there was some doubt as to whether qualifying expenditure could be allocated to a pool for a chargeable period later than that in which it was incurred. For chargeable periods covered by *CAA 2001*, this doubt is removed and, in addition, there is now nothing to prohibit the allocation of *part only* of a particular amount of qualifying expenditure for a particular chargeable period.)

(ii) Qualifying expenditure cannot be allocated to a pool for a chargeable period earlier than that in which it is incurred.

(iii) Qualifying expenditure cannot be allocated to a pool for a chargeable period if in any earlier period the rights in question have come to an end (without any of them being revived) or have been wholly disposed of.

[*CAA 2001, ss 470–475; ICTA 1988, s 520(2)(4)–(6), s 521(1), s 528(1); FA 1994, s 214(4)*].

A *disposal value* falls to be brought into account for a chargeable period in which a person sells the whole or part of any patent rights on the purchase of which he has incurred qualifying expenditure. The disposal value is equal to the net sale proceeds (limited to *capital* sums where *CAA 2001* has effect — see 10.1 above), except that:

(1) it cannot exceed the qualifying expenditure incurred on purchase of the rights in question; and

(2) where the rights were acquired as a result of a transaction between CONNECTED PERSONS (19) (or a series of such transactions), (1) above shall have effect as if it referred to the greatest capital expenditure incurred on the purchase of those rights by any of those connected persons.

[*CAA 2001, ss 476, 477; ICTA 1988, s 521(2)–(4); FA 1994, Sch 26 Pt V(24)*].

Connected persons and anti-avoidance. Where a person incurs capital expenditure after 26 July 1989 on the purchase of rights either from a connected person (see 19 CONNECTED PERSONS), or so that it appears that the sole or main benefit from the sale and any other transactions would have been the obtaining of an allowance under these provisions, the amount of that expenditure taken into account as qualifying expenditure may not exceed an amount determined as follows:

(*a*) where a disposal value (see above) falls to be brought into account, an amount equal to that value;

(*b*) where no disposal value falls to be brought into account, but the seller receives a capital sum chargeable under Schedule D, Case VI or *ITTOIA 2005, s 587* (see 55.11 PROFIT COMPUTATIONS), an amount equal to that sum;

(*c*) in any other case, an amount equal to the smallest of:

- market value of the rights;
- the amount of capital expenditure, if any, incurred by the seller on acquiring the rights;
- the amount of capital expenditure, if any, incurred by any person connected with the seller on acquiring the rights.

[*CAA 2001, s 481, Sch 3 para 102; ICTA 1988, s 521(5)–(7); FA 1989, Sch 13 para 27; ITTOIA 2005, Sch 1 para 566*]. Previously, the restriction was by reference to the disposal value only. See also (2) above.

Making of allowances and charges. An allowance (or balancing charge) in respect of qualifying *trade* expenditure is given effect as a trading expense (or trading receipt). [*CAA 2001, s 478; CAA 1990, ss 140, 144; ICTA 1988, s 528(1); FA 1994, s 211*].

An allowance in respect of qualifying *non-trade* expenditure is set against the company's 'income from patents' for the same accounting period, with any excess being carried forward without time limit against such income for subsequent accounting periods. A balancing charge is treated as income from patents. For these purposes, '*income from patents*' embraces royalties and similar sums, balancing charges under these provisions, and receipts from the sale of patent rights taxable under *ICTA 1988, s 524* or *s 525*. [*CAA 2001, ss 479, 480, 483; ICTA 1988, s 528(2)–(4), s 533(1); ITTOIA 2005, Sch 1 paras 205, 209, 565, 567*].

For expenditure incurred before 1 April 1986, a different set of rules applied, for which see the 2004/05 and earlier editions of Tolley's Income Tax.

Trading partnerships and successions are treated in the same way as for industrial buildings allowances (see 10.22(iii)(iv)).

Simon's Direct Tax Service. See **B2.601–B2.609.**

10.51 *Example*

P Ltd, who prepares accounts to 31 December, acquires two new patent rights for trading purposes.

	Date	Term	Cost
Patent 1	19.4.06	15 years	£4,500
Patent 2	5.10.07	5 years	£8,000

On 1.12.06 P Ltd sold part of the rights under patent 1 for £2,000.

The allowances for each patent are

	Pool	WDA
Y/e 31.12.06		
	£	£
Expenditure (patent 1)	4,500	
WDA 25%	(1,125)	£1,125
	3,375	
Y/e 31.12.07		
Expenditure (patent 2)	8,000	
Disposal proceeds (patent 1)	(2,000)	
	9,375	
WDA 25%	(2,344)	£2,344
WDV c/f	£7,031	

10.52 **RESEARCH AND DEVELOPMENT (FORMERLY SCIENTIFIC RESEARCH)**

'Qualifying expenditure' incurred by a trader on 'research and development' (R & D) attracts an allowance equal to **100%** of the expenditure. A claim for an allowance may require it to be reduced to a specified amount (but the part of the allowance thus forgone cannot be claimed for a later chargeable period). References below to R & D, except in the definition thereof, also embrace scientific research.

'*Qualifying expenditure*' is capital expenditure incurred by a trader on R & D related to the trade and undertaken directly or on his behalf (i.e. by an agent or other person in a similar contractual relationship, see *Gaspet Ltd v Elliss CA 1987, 60 TC 91*). It includes such expenditure incurred before commencement of the trade (pre-commencement expenditure). Expenditure potentially leading to or facilitating an extension of the trade is related to that trade, as is expenditure of a medical nature specially related to the welfare of workers in the trade. A just and reasonable apportionment may be made of capital expenditure only partly qualifying.

Expenditure on the acquisition of, or of rights in or over, land cannot be qualifying expenditure, except in so far as, on a just and reasonable apportionment, such expenditure is referable to a building or structure already constructed on the land, or to plant or machinery which forms part of such a building or structure, and otherwise qualifies as R & D expenditure.

Expenditure on R & D includes all expenditure incurred for carrying out (or providing facilities for carrying out) R & D. Expenditure on the acquisition of rights in, or arising out of, R & D is, however, excluded. Also excluded is expenditure on provision of a *dwelling*, except where not more than 25% of the expenditure (disregarding any 'additional VAT liability' or 'rebate' — see 10.2(vii) above) on a building consisting partly of a dwelling and otherwise used for R &D is attributable (on a just and reasonable apportionment) to the dwelling, in which case the dwelling can be ignored and the whole of the building treated as used for R & D.

An 'additional VAT liability' (see 10.2(vii) above) incurred in respect of qualifying expenditure is itself qualifying expenditure, provided the same person still owns the asset in question and it has not been demolished or destroyed.

Making of allowances. The allowance is given as a trading expense of the chargeable period (see 10.1 above) in which the expenditure is incurred (or, in the case of pre-commencement expenditure, the chargeable period in which the trade commences). An allowance in respect of an additional VAT liability is similarly given, but by reference to the time the *liability* is incurred.

[*CAA 2001, ss 437(1), 438–441, 447, 450, Sch 3 paras 89, 90; CAA 1990, ss 137, 139(1)(2), 140(1)(2)(5); FA 1991, Sch 14 para 12; FA 1994, ss 211, 213(10); FA 2000, Sch 19 para 8, Sch 40 Pt II(7)*].

'*Research and development*' is, from 6 April 2007, as defined by *ITA 2007 s 1006* and, before that date, as defined by *ICTA 1988, s 837A* and supporting regulations (see 59.1 RESEARCH AND DEVELOPMENT EXPENDITURE), but also includes oil and gas exploration and appraisal (within *ICTA 1988, s 837B*). [*CAA 2001, s 437(2); CAA 1990, s 139(1)*].

For accounting periods ended before 1 April 2000, the term 'scientific research' was used rather than 'research and development'. '*Scientific research*' is defined as activities in the fields of natural or applied science for the extension of knowledge. [*CAA 1990, s 139(1)*]. Any question of whether, and to what extent, any activities constitute scientific research, or any asset is used for scientific research, is ultimately referred to the Secretary of State for a final decision. [*CAA 1990, s 139(3)*]. For a case in which allowances were refused on the grounds that the research was not related to the trade of publishing *inter alia* the findings of the research, see *Salt v Golding (Sp C 81), [1996] SSCD 269.*

For special provisions relating to oil licences, see *CAA 2001, ss 552–556, Sch 3 para 91.*

Disposal events and balancing charges. Where *CAA 2001* has effect (see 10.1 above), if a disposal value (see below) falls to be brought into account for the same chargeable period as that for which the related allowance falls to be given, the allowance is given on the excess (if any) of the expenditure over the disposal value; this previously operated slightly differently, but with a similar result, in that the allowance was given on the full expenditure and a balancing charge brought in as below.

If a disposal value falls to be brought into account for the chargeable period after that for which the related allowance is given, liability to a balancing charge arises for that later chargeable period. Effect is given to the charge by treating it as a trading receipt. The charge is equal to disposal value (or, where a reduced allowance was claimed, the excess, if any, of disposal value over unrelieved expenditure), except that it cannot exceed the allowance given (less any earlier balancing charges arising from 'additional VAT rebates' — see below).

A disposal value falls to be brought into account for a chargeable period in which a disposal event occurs, or, if such an event occurs later, for the chargeable period in which the trade is permanently discontinued. If, exceptionally, a disposal event occurs *before* the chargeable period for which the related allowance falls to be given, it is brought into account for the later chargeable period; before *CAA 2001* had effect (see 10.1 above), the resulting net allowance was given for the chargeable period *in which the disposal event occurred.*

Either of the following is a disposal event (unless it gives rise to a balancing charge under the rules for industrial buildings or plant and machinery allowances).

(*a*) The trader ceases to own the asset representing the qualifying expenditure;

(*b*) An asset representing the qualifying expenditure is demolished or destroyed before the trader ceases to own it.

On the sale of an asset, the seller is treated for these purposes as ceasing to own it at the earlier of the time of completion and the time when possession is given.

The amount of the disposal value depends on the nature of the disposal event, as follows.

- If the event is a sale of the asset at not less than market value, it is the *net* sale proceeds; (before *CAA 2001* had effect, see 10.1 above, it was the sale proceeds).

- If the event is the demolition or destruction of the asset, it is the net amount received for the remains, plus any insurance or *capital* compensation received (but see below as regards demolition costs); (before *CAA 2001* had effect, *any* compensation received had to be taken into account).

- In any other event, it is the market value of the asset at the time of the event.

An 'additional VAT rebate' (see 10.2(vii) above) made in respect of qualifying expenditure, before the asset in question ceases to belong to the trader or has been demolished or destroyed, must be brought into account as a disposal value (or as an addition to a disposal value otherwise arising) for the chargeable period in which the rebate accrues or, if later, the chargeable period in which the trade commences.

[*CAA 2001, ss 441(1), 442–444, 448, 449–451; CAA 1990, s 138(1)–(4)(6)(7)(8), s 139(4); FA 1991, Sch 14 para 13; FA 2000, Sch 19 para 8*].

Demolition costs. On demolition of an asset (within (*b*) above), the disposal value is reduced (or extinguished) by any demolition costs incurred by the trader. If the demolition costs exceed the disposal value, then, provided the asset had not begun to be used for non-qualifying purposes, the excess is itself treated as qualifying R & D expenditure, incurred at time of demolition (or, if earlier and where relevant, immediately before cessation of the trade). The demolition costs cannot be treated for any capital allowances purposes as expenditure on any replacement asset.

[*CAA 2001, s 445; CAA 1990, ss 138(5), 139(5)*].

Connected persons and other anti-avoidance provisions apply to substitute market value for sale consideration on certain 'sole or main benefit' transactions, sales without change of control and sales between connected persons. For most sales, the election referred to at 10.22(i) above is available, with the result that an asset representing expenditure for which an R & D allowance has been made as above will be treated as transferred for nil consideration. [*CAA 2001, ss 567–570; CAA 1990, ss 157, 158; FA 1993, s 117(3)–(5); FA 1994, s 119(1)*].

For R & D expenditure of an HMRC nature, see 66.73 TRADING INCOME. For enhanced tax reliefs, see 59 RESEARCH AND DEVELOPMENT EXPENDITURE.

Simon's Direct Tax Service. See B2.7.

10.53 *Example*

C Ltd is in business manufacturing and selling cosmetics, and prepares accounts annually to 30 June. For the purposes of this trade, the company built a new laboratory adjacent to its existing premises, incurring the following expenditure.

		£
April 2005	Laboratory building	50,000
June 2005	Technical equipment	3,000
March 2006	Technical equipment	4,000
July 2006	Plant	2,500
August 2007	Extension to existing premises comprising 50% further laboratory area and 50% sales offices.	30,000

In September 2006 a small fire destroyed an item of equipment originally costing £2,000 in June 2005; insurance recoveries totalled £3,000. In March 2007, the plant costing £2,500 in July 2006 was sold for £1,800.

The allowances due are as follows.

		£
Y/e 30.6.05		
Laboratory building		50,000
Technical equipment		3,000
		£53,000
Y/e 30.6.06		
Technical equipment		4,000
		£4,000
Y/e 30.6.07		
Net allowance on plant sold	(note (*a*))	£700
Balancing charge on equipment destroyed	(note (*b*))	(£2,000)
Y/e 30.6.08		
Extension (qualifying R & D expenditure only)		£15,000

Notes

(*a*) As the plant is sold in the accounting period in which the expenditure is incurred, the disposal value of £1,800 is set against the expenditure of £2,500, resulting in a net allowance of £700.

(*b*) The destruction of the equipment in the year to 30 June 2007 results in a balancing charge limited to the allowance given. The charge accrues in the accounting period in which the event occurs.

11 Capital Gains

Cross-reference. See also 12 CAPITAL GAINS—GROUPS, 13 CAPITAL GAINS—SUBSTANTIAL SHAREHOLDINGS, 26.29 EXCHANGE GAINS AND LOSSES, 27 EXEMPT ORGANISATIONS, 46.35 LOAN RELATIONSHIPS.

Simon's Direct Tax Service C3.1.

Other sources. See Tolley's Capital Gains Tax.

The headings in this chapter are as follows.

11.1 LIABILITY OF COMPANIES TO CORPORATION TAX ON THEIR CAPITAL GAINS

Companies resident in the UK are liable to corporation tax on their chargeable gains (i.e. capital gains chargeable to tax). These gains are included in their profits subject to corporation tax as described in 11.2 below. [*ICTA 1988, s 6(3)*]. This applies equally to non-resident companies in respect of assets of a UK permanent establishment (see 60.5 RESIDENCE — for accounting periods beginning before 1 January 2003, assets of a UK branch or agency). [*TCGA 1992, ss 10(3), 10B; FA 2003, s 149(4)(6)*].

Companies accordingly do not pay 'capital gains tax' as such but their chargeable gains less allowable losses are computed *in accordance with the provisions relating to capital gains tax* (for which see Tolley's Capital Gains Tax) **except**

(i) computations are made by reference to accounting periods instead of years of assessment [*TCGA 1992, s 8(3)*],

(ii) provisions in the legislation confined solely to individuals do not apply to companies [*TCGA 1992, s 8(4)(5)*],

(iii) the indexation allowance rules applied (subject to transitional provisions) to disposals after 31 March 1982, and not 5 April 1982 as for individuals, and the *FA 1985* rules operated similarly after 31 March 1985 instead of 5 April 1985 [*FA 1982, s 86(1)(a); FA 1985, s 68, Sch 19*],

(iv) special provisions apply after 31 March 1996 to gilts, loan stock etc. acquired by companies (see 46 LOAN RELATIONSHIPS),

(v) taper relief, applicable to individuals, trustees etc. after 5 April 1998, does not apply to companies, for which, however, indexation is not frozen at its April 1998 level [*FA 1998, ss 121, 122*],

(vi) identification rules for shares and securities acquired after 5 April 1998 are different for companies [*FA 1998, ss 123, 124*],

(vii) gains and losses on INTANGIBLE ASSETS (39) created or acquired by companies after 31 March 2002 are taxed as income rather than under the chargeable gains regime, and

(viii) as further indicated below.

See *TCGA 1992, ss 284A, 284B* for anti-avoidance legislation bringing into charge certain gains deferred under extra-statutory concessions.

European single currency (*the 'euro'*). Under *FA 1998, s 163*, the Treasury has power to make regulations to implement tax changes needed as a result of the introduction of the single currency. See *SI 1998 No 3177* as amended, in particular *regs 36–39*.

Substantial shareholdings exemption. For the exemption of substantial shareholdings of companies, see 13 CAPITAL GAINS—SUBSTANTIAL SHAREHOLDINGS.

11.2 RATE OF CORPORATION TAX IN RESPECT OF CAPITAL GAINS

The whole of the chargeable gains (less allowable losses under 11.3 below) of a company is included in the profits chargeable to corporation tax. The rate of corporation tax applicable will either be the full rate as in 1.3 INTRODUCTION AND RATES OF TAX or the starting rate or small companies rate (see SMALL COMPANIES—REDUCED RATES (63)) (with marginal relief as appropriate) but the rate so determined applies to both income and chargeable gains included in the chargeable profits. If the company's accounting period straddles different financial years, chargeable profits are apportioned on a time basis between the years. [*ICTA 1988, ss 8(3), 13, 13AA*].

For a summary of the provisions applicable for accounting periods ending before 17 March 1987, or straddling that date, see 1.3(*b*) INTRODUCTION AND RATES OF TAX.

See 9 BUILDING SOCIETIES and 43 INVESTMENT FUNDS for special provisions in relation to these organisations.

11.3 CAPITAL LOSSES

The amount of chargeable gains assessable for an accounting period is the total chargeable gains accruing to the company in that period less allowable losses in that period and allowable losses brought forward from any previous period. The resulting net figure is treated as in 11.2 above. Allowable losses include short-term losses accruing under Schedule D, Case VII for years before 1971/72 which remain unrelieved. [*TCGA 1992, s 8(1), Sch 11 para 12*]. This is the only instance where losses incurred before 6 April 1965 can be carried forward.

For corporation tax on chargeable gains purposes an allowable loss does not include:

(*a*) any loss which, if it had been a gain, would have been exempt from corporation tax in the hands of the company; or

(*b*) any loss accruing on a disposal on or after 5 December 2005 directly or indirectly in consequence of, or otherwise in connection with, any 'arrangements' the main purpose of which, or one of the main purposes of which, is to secure a 'tax advantage'.

For the purposes of (*b*) above, it does not matter whether the loss accrues at a time when there are no chargeable gains against which it could be set or whether the tax advantage would be secured for the company incurring the loss or for another company. '*Arrangements*' include any agreement, understanding, scheme, transaction or series of transactions, whether or not legally enforceable. '*Tax advantage*' means relief or increased relief from, or repayment or increased repayment of, corporation tax or the avoidance or reduction of a charge or assessment to corporation tax or the avoidance of a possible assessment to corporation tax.

[*TCGA 1992, ss 8(2), 16A, 184D; FA 2006, ss 69, 70(2); FA 2007, s 27*].

HMRC consider that interdependence of transactions or of the terms on which transactions take place is a strong indicator (although not a necessary condition) of the existence of an arrangement. In their view, if, on the facts, any participant in arrangements is found to have a main purpose of achieving a tax advantage, that is sufficient to demonstrate that one of the main purposes of the arrangements is the securing of a tax advantage. HMRC is likely to examine carefully any relevant case in which a normal commercial objective is lacking, or where commercial objectives are not being sought in a genuine and straightforward manner. Where there is more than one way of achieving a commercial objective and a course of action is chosen on commercial grounds, any incidental tax advantage is not relevant. However, where the tax advantage was material to the choice, the anti-avoidance legislation may be in point, but HMRC have indicated that this is unlikely to be the case unless there is evidence of additional, complex or costly steps included solely for tax reasons. (HMRC Guidance 'Avoidance through the creation and use of capital losses by companies', 27 July 2006).

Allowable capital losses *cannot* normally be offset against trading profits or other income (but see 47.19 LOSSES). However, trading losses can be offset against chargeable gains within the same accounting period and, if unexhausted, against chargeable gains arising in earlier periods (47.2, 47.6 LOSSES). Management expenses of a company with investment business (for accounting periods beginning before 1 April 2004, an investment company) may be offset against chargeable gains within the same or a succeeding accounting period (42 INVESTMENT COMPANIES AND INVESTMENT BUSINESS). [*ICTA 1988, s 75(9)* (*previously ICTA 1988, s 75(3)*); *FA 2004, s 38(1)*].

Capital losses are generally computed in the same way as capital gains. A capital loss is not an allowable loss unless it is claimed in a quantified amount. The time limit for such claims is six years after the end of the accounting period in which the loss was incurred. Where unused losses are brought forward and set against chargeable gains in a later accounting period, losses incurred after the start of self-assessment are used before earlier ones. [*TCGA 1992, s 16; FA 1995, s 113; F(No 2)A 2005, Sch 4 para 7*].

Anti-avoidance. There are a number of anti-avoidance provisions relating specifically to corporate capital losses. In particular, *FA 2006* introduced three targeted provisions attacking arrangements entered into which have as a main purpose the obtaining of a tax advantage. For details of the provisions, see (*b*) above, 11.4–11.6 below (avoidance utilising losses) and 12.7 CAPITAL GAINS—GROUPS (gain buying and loss buying). See also 12.8–12.21 CAPITAL GAINS—GROUPS for the restriction, where the provisions at 12.5–12.7 CAPITAL GAINS—GROUPS do not apply, on the set-off of pre-entry losses where a company joins a group, and see 12.22–12.27 CAPITAL GAINS—GROUPS for the restriction (now repealed) on the set-off of losses against pre-entry gains where a company joins a group.

11.4 AVOIDANCE UTILISING LOSSES

As part of a general initiative countering various avoidance schemes (see 11.3 above) provisions were introduced by *FA 2006* to ensure that capital losses cannot be used against income profits. The provisions apply to disposals on or after 5 December 2005. [*FA 2006, s 71(4)*]. HMRC have indicated that the provisions are intended to affect only companies that deliberately and knowingly enter into arrangements to avoid tax (HMRC Guidance 'Avoidance through the creation and use of capital losses by companies', 27 July 2006).

Two strategies to utilise capital losses are targeted by the provisions. The first is to turn an income receipt into capital (see 11.5 below). The second is to generate a deduction from income as part of arrangements to crystallise a capital gain (see 11.6 below). The effect is to restrict the use of capital losses. In both cases, the provisions apply only where HMRC issue a notice to the company concerned (see below).

Both sets of provisions require that there be 'arrangements', the main purpose, or one of the main purposes, of which is to secure a 'tax advantage' (although each contains a qualification of the definition of tax advantage given below — see 11.5 and 11.6 below). [*TCGA 1992, s 184G(2)(5), 184H(2)(4); FA 2006, s 71(1)*].

'*Arrangements*' for this purpose include any agreement, understanding, scheme, transaction or series of transactions, whether or not legally enforceable. A '*tax advantage*' means obtaining or increasing relief from, or repayment of, corporation tax, the avoidance or reduction of a corporation tax charge or assessment or the avoidance of a possible assessment to corporation tax. [*TCGA 1992, s 184D, 184G(10), 184H(10); FA 2006, ss 70(2), 71(1)*].

For HMRC's view on the application of the terms 'arrangements', 'tax advantage' and 'main purpose', see 11.3 above and HMRC Guidance 'Avoidance through the creation and use of capital losses by companies', 27 July 2006, available on their website (www.hmrc.go-v.uk).

HMRC notices. As noted above, the application of the provisions is contingent upon the issue of a notice to the company by HMRC. Such a notice may be issued if HMRC have reasonable grounds for considering that the statutory conditions triggering the legislation are present. It must specify the arrangements in question, the accounting period (or periods) involved and the effect of the anti-avoidance provisions.

If the company has not yet made a return for the accounting period it may, if it makes a return within the 90-day period beginning with the day on which the notice is given, make the return disregarding the notice and make any necessary amendment later within the same 90-day period.

If the company has already made a return for the accounting period, HMRC may only issue a notice if a notice of enquiry (see 61.10 RETURNS) has been given in respect of that return. The company may amend its return in light of the notice at any time within the 90-day period beginning with the day on which the notice is given. A closure notice in respect of the enquiry may not be issued before the earlier of the company amending its return or the end of the 90-day period.

If enquiries into the return have been completed, HMRC's power to issue a notice is subject to two requirements, both of which must be met. The first is that at the time enquiries were completed HMRC could not, on the basis of information made available to them (within *FA 1998, Sch 18 para 44(2)(3)* — see 7.2 ASSESSMENTS) before that time, reasonably have been aware of circumstances indicating that a notice could have been issued. The second is that a request for information was made during the enquiry which, if duly complied with, would have resulted in a reasonable expectation that HMRC would issue a notice. If a notice is issued in these circumstances no discovery assessment may be made before the earlier of the company amending its return or the end of the 90-day period beginning with the day on which the notice is given. However, the normal restrictions on making discovery assessments in *FA 1998, Sch 18 paras 43, 44* do not apply (see 7.2 ASSESSMENTS).

On receiving a notice containing HMRC's view of the position, it is up to the company to decide if it needs to amend its self-assessment. If it fails to make an amendment which ought to have been made its return will be incorrect (with all the resulting implications for penalties, etc.).

[*TCGA 1992, ss 184G(6)(8)(9), 184H(6)(8)(9), 184I; FA 2006, s 71(1)*].

Clearances. HMRC operate an informal clearance procedure and will give advice on actual or proposed transactions. Applications for clearance procedure should be sent to

HM Revenue & Customs, Clearance & Counteraction Team, Anti Avoidance Group Intelligence, First floor, 22 Kingsway, London WC2B 6NR. HMRC will aim to give a response within 30 days of receipt of a clearance application. A clearance will state the terms on which it has been given and HMRC will regard itself bound by a clearance provided that all relevant facts are accurately given and (where the clearance is sought in advance) the transaction is executed in accordance with the proposals set out in the clearance application. Where a clearance cannot be given HMRC will state the reasons, but taxpayers are not bound by their decision. For details of the information required by HMRC in clearance applications see HMRC Guidance 'Avoidance through the creation and use of capital losses by companies', 27 July 2006, available on their website (www.hmrc.gov.uk).

11.5 **Schemes converting income into capital.** HMRC may issue a notice (see 11.4 above) invoking anti-avoidance measures where it has reasonable grounds for considering that the following four conditions are, or may be, satisfied:

- any receipt arises to a company (the '*relevant company*') on the disposal of an asset and that receipt arises directly or indirectly in consequence of, or otherwise in connection with, any arrangements (see 11.4 above);
- a chargeable gain (the '*relevant gain*') accrues to the relevant company on the disposal and that company has allowable losses available;
- but for the arrangements an amount would have been taken into account wholly or partly instead of the capital receipt as income of the relevant company (or as the income of a company in the same capital gains tax group (see 12.1 CAPITAL GAINS—GROUPS) at any time in the period beginning with the time at which the arrangements were made and ending when the matters, other than the tax advantage, intended to be secured by the arrangements are secured); and
- the main purpose, or one of the main purposes, of the arrangements was the obtaining of a tax advantage (see 11.4 above) involving the deduction of the capital losses from the relevant gain.

If all these conditions are satisfied when the HMRC notice is given, the relevant company may not deduct any loss from the relevant gain.

[*TCGA 1992, s 184G*(*1*)–(*5*)(*7*)(*10*)*; FA 2006, s 71*(*1*)].

11.6 **Schemes securing deductions.** HMRC may issue a notice (see 11.4 above) invoking anti-avoidance measures where it has reasonable grounds for considering that the following four conditions are, or may be, satisfied:

- a chargeable gain (the '*relevant gain*') accrues to a company (the '*relevant company*') directly or indirectly in consequence of, or otherwise in connection with, any arrangements (see 11.4 above) and that company has capital losses available;
- the relevant company, or a company connected with it, incurs expenditure in connection with the arrangements which is deductible in calculating total profits but not in calculating chargeable gains;
- the main purpose, or one of the main purposes, of the arrangements was the obtaining of a tax advantage (see 11.4 above) involving both the deduction of the expenditure in calculating total profits and the deduction of losses from the relevant gain; and
- the arrangements are not 'excluded arrangements' (see below).

It does not matter whether the tax advantage is secured for the relevant company or any other company.

'*Excluded arrangements*' are certain arm's length sale and leaseback transactions involving land within *ICTA 1988, s 779*(*1*)(*2*) (see 5.15 ANTI-AVOIDANCE) where there is no connection between the lessor and the lessee.

If all the above conditions are satisfied when the HMRC notice is given, the relevant company may not deduct any loss from the relevant gain.

[*TCGA 1992, s 184H(1)–(5)(7)(10)(11); FA 2006, s 71(1)*].

11.7 LIQUIDATION

The vesting of a company's assets in a liquidator is disregarded. All the acts of the liquidator in relation to such assets are treated as acts of the company. [*TCGA 1992, s 8(6)*].

See also 45 LIQUIDATION ETC.

11.8 RECOVERY FROM SHAREHOLDERS

Where a person connected with a UK resident company (see 19 CONNECTED PERSONS) receives, or becomes entitled to receive, in respect of shares in that company, a *capital distribution* which is not a reduction of capital but which constitutes, or is derived from, a disposal of assets from which a chargeable gain accrues to the company, and the company does not pay, within a specified time (see below), the corporation tax due from it for the accounting period in which the gain accrues, the recipient of the distribution may, by assessment within two years of the due date, be required to pay so much of that corporation tax as relates to chargeable gains but not exceeding the lesser of:

(i) a part of that tax, at the rate in force when the gain accrued, proportionate to his share of the total distribution made by the company; and

(ii) the value of the distribution he received or became entitled to receive.

The person then has a right of recovery against the company, including any interest charged on him under *TMA 1970, s 87A* (see 41.1 INTEREST ON UNPAID TAX).

The time specified (as above) is the date the tax became payable by the company or, if later, the date the assessment was made on the company.

[*TCGA 1992, s 189*].

See also 53.5 PAYMENT OF TAX as regards recovery of tax from third parties generally.

Simon's Direct Tax Service. See D2.302.

11.9 RECONSTRUCTIONS INVOLVING TRANSFER OF BUSINESS

Subject to the following, where a 'scheme of reconstruction' involves the transfer of a company's business to another company for no consideration (other than the assumption of liabilities of the business), capital assets (not used as trading stock by either company) are regarded as being transferred at a 'no gain, no loss' price, and the acquiring company takes over the disposing company's acquisition date. In relation to shares or debentures issued on or after 17 April 2002, '*scheme of reconstruction*' is a scheme of merger, division or other restructuring meeting both of conditions (*a*) and (*b*) below and either condition (*c*) or condition (*d*) below. In relation to shares or debentures issued before that date, the legislation referred instead to a '*scheme of reconstruction or amalgamation*', defined as a scheme for the reconstruction of any company or companies or the amalgamation of any two or more companies (for which see HMRC Capital Gains Manual, CG 52730–52733).

(*a*) *Issue of ordinary share capital.* The scheme must involve the issue of 'ordinary share capital' of a company or companies (the 'successor company' or 'successor companies') to holders of ordinary share capital of another company or companies (the 'original company' or 'original companies') or, if the original company or any of the original companies has more than one class of ordinary shares, to holders of one or more classes of ordinary share capital of any such company. The scheme must not involve the issue of ordinary share capital of the successor company or companies to anyone else. '*Ordinary share capital*' of a company is all the issued share capital of the company other than capital the holders of which have a right to a dividend at a fixed rate but no other right to share in company profits, and also includes interests possessed by members in a company which has no share capital, and rights in unit trust schemes which are treated as shares under *TCGA 1992, s 99(1)(b)*.

(*b*) *Equal entitlement to new shares.* The entitlement of any person to acquire ordinary share capital of the successor company or companies by virtue of holding ordinary share capital (or any class of such capital) of the original company or companies which is involved in the scheme (as in (*a*) above) must be the same as that of any other person holding such shares (or shares of that class). (See the example in HMRC's Capital Gains Manual at CG 52707b.)

Where a reorganisation (within *TCGA 1992, s 126*) of the share capital of the original company, or of any of the original companies, is carried out for the purposes of the scheme, (*a*) and (*b*) above apply in relation to the position after the reorganisation. An issue of shares in or debentures of the successor company, or any of the successor companies, after the latest date on which any ordinary share capital of the successor company, or of any of them, is issued in consideration of the transfer of any business (or part) under the scheme, or in pursuance of the compromise or arrangement referred to in (*d*) below, is disregarded for the purposes of (*a*) and (*b*) above.

As referred to above, both (*a*) and (*b*) above and either (*c*) or (*d*) below must be satisfied.

(*c*) *Continuity of business.* The effect of the restructuring must be either:

(i) if there is one original company, that the business or substantially the whole of the business carried on by the original company is carried on by a successor company (which must not be the original company) or successor companies (which may include the original company); or

(ii) if there is more than one original company, that all or part of the business(es) carried on by one or more of the original companies is carried on by a different company, and the whole or substantially the whole of the business(es) carried on by the original companies are carried on by the successor company (which may be one of the original companies) or successor companies (which may be the same as or include the original companies).

The requirement in (i) and (ii) above that the whole or substantially the whole of a business or businesses be carried on by two or more companies is satisfied where the activities of those companies taken together embrace the whole or substantially the whole of the business or businesses concerned. See HMRC Capital Gains Manual, CG 52709 as regards the meaning of 'business' for these purposes.

A business carried on by a company under the control (within *ICTA 1988, s 840*) of another company is for these purpose treated as carried on by both the controlling and the controlled company.

The holding and management of assets retained by the original company (or by one of the original companies) for the purpose of making a capital distribution (within *TCGA 1992, s 122*) in respect of shares in the company is disregarded for these purposes.

(*d*) *Compromise or arrangement with members.* The scheme must be carried out in pursuance of a compromise or arrangement under *Companies Act 1985, s 425* (or NI or foreign equivalent), and no part of the business of the original company, or any of the original companies, must be transferred under the scheme to any other person.

The application of these provisions is conditional on:

(A) either the transferee company being UK resident at the time of acquisition or the assets being 'chargeable assets' in relation to that company immediately after that time; and

(B) either the transferor company being UK resident at that time or the assets being 'chargeable assets' in relation to that company immediately before that time.

For these purposes, an asset is a '*chargeable asset*' in relation to a company at a particular time if, on a disposal by the company at that time, any gain would be a chargeable gain and within the charge to corporation tax by virtue of *TCGA 1992, s 10* or *s 10B* (non-UK resident company trading through UK permanent establishment or branch or agency, see 60.5, 60.6 RESIDENCE).

[*TCGA 1992, s 139(1)(1A)(2)(9), Sch 5AA; FA 2002, Sch 9 paras 3, 5(7), Sch 40 Pt 3(2); FA 2003, Sch 27 para 2(3)*].

For practical illustrations of 'schemes of reconstruction', see HMRC Capital Gains Manual, CG 52720–52729.

Under the law as it applied for shares or debentures issued before 17 April 2002, the second company should, strictly, carry on substantially the same business and have substantially the same members as the first, but in practice the identity of shareholdings is not insisted upon where the scheme is for *bona fide* commercial reasons or where there is segregation of trades or businesses into identifiable parts which are capable of being carried on in their own right. This applies equally to a demerger within *ICTA 1988, ss 213–218* (see 32.31 GROUPS OF COMPANIES) involving the transfer of shares in a 75% subsidiary to a newly formed company. (HMRC Statement of Practice, SP 5/85). For shares or debentures issued on or after 17 April 2002, the statutory definition of 'scheme of reconstruction' (above) incorporates this practice. Under the old definition, *TCGA 1992, s 139* could be used on its own to transfer a business (see the example in HMRC's Capital Gains Manual at CG 52833), but this is no longer possible; under the revised definition, there must be a scheme of reconstruction that meets the conditions of *TCGA 1992, Sch 5AA* and includes an issue of shares under *TCGA 1992, s 136*.

Anti-avoidance, disapplication of relief and advance clearance. *TCGA 1992, s 139* does not apply unless the scheme is for *bona fide* commercial reasons and not to avoid corporation tax, capital gains tax or income tax, or where HMRC, on written application by the acquiring company, has notified its satisfaction with the scheme before the transfer is made. Applications for such clearance should be addressed to Mohini Sawhney, Clearance and Counteraction Team, Anti-Avoidance Group Intelligence, First Floor, 22 Kingsway, London WC2B 6NR (or, if market-sensitive information is included, to Eric Gardner, Team Leader, at that address). Applications may be faxed to 020–7438 4409 or emailed to reconstructions@hmrc.gov.uk (after advising Eric Gardner (on 020–7438 6585) if market-sensitive information is included). Application may be made in a single letter to the same address for clearance under *TCGA 1992, s 139* and under any one or more of *ICTA 1988, s 215* (demergers, see 32.39 GROUPS OF COMPANIES), *ICTA 1988, s 225* (see 57.6 PURCHASE BY A COMPANY OF ITS OWN SHARES), *ICTA 1988, s 707* (transactions in securities, see 5.2 ANTI-AVOIDANCE), *TCGA 1992, s 138(1)* (share exchanges, see Tolley's Capital Gains Tax under Anti-Avoidance), *TCGA 1992, s 140B* (transfer of a UK trade between EU member states, see 11.11 below), *TCGA 1992, s 140D* (transfer of non-UK trade between EU member states, see 11.12 below) and *FA 2002, Sch 29 para 88* (see 39.27 INTANGIBLE ASSETS). The application should give full details of the transactions and of all the companies directly involved, their tax districts and references. Copies of accounts for the last two years for which accounts have been prepared should accompany the application. HMRC may, within 30 days of receipt, call for further particulars (to be supplied within 30 days, or longer if HMRC allows; if the information is not supplied, the application lapses). Subject to this, HMRC must notify its decision within a further 30 days. If not so notified, or if dissatisfied with the decision, the applicant may within a further 30 days require HMRC to refer the application to the Special Commissioners for their decision. All material facts and considerations must be disclosed, otherwise any decision is void. If any tax arising on the transfer is not paid by the disposing company within six months of a specified date, then, within two years of that date, the tax may be assessed on any person who:

(*a*) holds all or any of the assets to which the tax relates; and

(*b*) is either the acquiring company or any other group member to which the assets have been subsequently transferred.

The date specified (as above) is the date the tax became payable by the company or, if later, the date the assessment was made on the company.

The tax charge will be proportionate to the assets held and the paying company has the right of recovery against the original disposing company of the tax charged and any interest thereon under *TMA 1970, s 87A* (see 41.1 INTEREST ON UNPAID TAX). Where the disposing company has been wound up, any tax due from it may be recovered from the acquiring company. [*TCGA 1992, s 139(5)–(8)*].

The provisions of *TCGA 1992, s 139* do not apply to the transfer of the whole or part of a company's business to a unit trust scheme (where it is either within *TCGA 1992, s 100(2)* or an authorised unit trust, see 43.3 INVESTMENT FUNDS), to an investment trust (see 44.1 INVESTMENT TRUSTS) or to a venture capital trust (see 69.2 VENTURE CAPITAL TRUSTS). [*TCGA 1992, s 139(4); FA 1998, s 134(1)(4)*].

Where *section 139* has applied in relation to a transfer to a company which was not then an investment trust but which subsequently becomes one for an accounting period, then any assets of the business transferred which are still owned by the company at the beginning of that accounting period are deemed to have been sold and immediately reacquired by the transferee company, immediately after the transfer, at their market value at that time. The resulting chargeable gain or allowable loss is deemed to accrue to the transferee company immediately before the end of the accounting period preceding that in which the company becomes an investment trust. Notwithstanding normal time limits, a corporation tax assessment in respect of any resulting liability can be made within six years after the end of the accounting period in which the company becomes an investment trust.

Similar provisions apply where, after a transfer to which *section 139* applied,the transferee company becomes a venture capital trust (within *ICTA 1988, s 842AA*, see 69.2 VENTURE CAPITAL TRUSTS). They apply by reference to the time at which HMRC's approval for the purposes of *section 842AA* comes into effect, and the resulting gain or loss is deemed to accrue immediately before that time rather than at the time of the deemed disposal. In a case in which HMRC's approval has effect as from the beginning of an accounting period, any consequential corporation tax assessment can be made, notwithstanding normal time limits, within six years after the end of that accounting period. These provisions do not apply if those above relating to investment trusts have already applied (in relation to the same transfer of assets) and *vice versa*.

[*TCGA 1992, ss 101, 101B*].

See 11.23 below as regards disapplication of *section 139* in relation to certain dual resident companies.

Simon's Direct Tax Service. See D2.303.

11.10 TRANSFER OF ASSETS TO NON-RESIDENT COMPANY

Where a UK resident company carrying on a trade outside the UK through a permanent establishment (see 60.5 RESIDENCE — previously a branch or agency) transfers the whole or part of that trade together with its assets, or its assets other than cash, to a company not resident in the UK in exchange, wholly or partly, for shares (or shares and loan stock) in that company, so that thereafter it holds one-quarter or more of the transferee company's ordinary share capital, and the chargeable gains on the transfer exceed the allowable losses, the proportion of the resulting net chargeable gains relating to the shares (in proportion that the market value of the shares at the time of the transfer bears to the market value of the whole consideration received) may be claimed by the transferor company as being deferred and not treated as arising until the happening of one of the following events:

(i) the *transferor company disposes* of all or any of the shares received. The appropriate proportion of the deferred gain (in so far as not already charged under this specific provision or under (ii) below) is then added to the consideration received on the disposal. The '*appropriate proportion*' is the proportion which the market value of the shares disposed of bears to the market value of the shares held immediately before the disposal. However, deferred gains relating to events occurring before 1 April 1982 are disregarded for this purpose;

(ii) the *transferee company disposes*, within six years of the transfer, of the whole or part of the assets on which chargeable gains were deferred. The gain chargeable (in so far as it has not already been charged under this provision or under (i) above) is the proportion which the deferred gain on the assets disposed of bears to the total deferred gains on assets held immediately before the disposal.

The following disposals are disregarded.

- For the purposes of (i) above, intra-group transfers within *TCGA 1992, s 171* (see 12.1 onwards CAPITAL GAINS—GROUPS). A charge will arise when a subsequent owner makes a disposal outside the group.
- For the purposes of (i) above, transfers to an SE in the process of forming it in circumstances in which *TCGA 1992, s 140E* applies (see 11.13 below). In relation to a subsequent disposal of the shares or disposal by the transferee company of assets within (ii) above, the SE is treated as if it were the transferor company.
- For the purposes of (ii) above, intra-group transfers which would be within *TCGA 1992, s 171* if for those purposes a group included (without qualification) non-UK resident companies. A charge will arise when a subsequent owner makes a disposal outside the group.

No claim may be made under these provisions as regards a transfer in relation to which a claim is made under *TCGA 1992, s 140C* (see 11.12 below).

[*TCGA 1992, s 140, Sch 4 para 4; F(No 2)A 2005, s 64(2)*].

For the interaction between (i) above and the substantial shareholdings exemption, see 13.22 CAPITAL GAINS—SUBSTANTIAL SHAREHOLDINGS.

Simon's Direct Tax Service. See **D2.305.**

11.11 TRANSFER OF UK TRADE BETWEEN COMPANIES IN DIFFERENT EU MEMBER STATES

A special relief may be claimed where a 'qualifying company' resident in one EU member state transfers the whole or part of a trade carried on by it in the UK to a 'qualifying company' resident in another member state in exchange for shares or debentures (for issues effected before 1 April 2005, securities (including shares)) in the latter company, provided that certain conditions (see below) are met. On such a claim, any assets included in the transfer are treated for the purposes of corporation tax on chargeable gains as transferred for a no gain/no loss consideration, and *TCGA 1992, s 25(3)* (deemed disposal by non-resident on ceasing to trade in the UK through a permanent establishment (or branch or agency), see Tolley's Capital Gains Tax under Overseas Matters) does not apply to the assets by reason of the transfer.

A '*qualifying company*' is a body incorporated under the law of a member state.

A company is regarded for the above purposes as resident in a member state under the laws of which it is chargeable to tax because it is regarded as so resident (unless it is regarded under a double tax relief arrangement entered into by the member state as resident in a territory not within any of the member states).

The conditions referred to above are:

(*a*)

(i) if the transferee company is non-UK resident immediately after the transfer, any chargeable gain accruing to it on a disposal of the assets included in the transfer would form part of its corporation tax profits under *TCGA 1992, s 10(3)* or *s 10B* (see 60.5, 60.6 RESIDENCE); or

(ii) if it is UK resident at that time, none of the assets included in the transfer is exempt from UK tax on disposal under double tax relief arrangements; and

(*b*) the transfer is effected for *bona fide* commercial reasons and not as part of a scheme or arrangement a main purpose of which is avoidance of income tax, corporation tax or capital gains tax.

Advance clearance in relation to (*b*) above may be obtained from HMRC on the application of the companies, subject to the same conditions and appeal procedures as apply to clearances under *TCGA 1992, s 138* (see Tolley's Capital Gains Tax under Anti-Avoidance). Applications for clearance should be addressed to Mohini Sawhney, Clearance and Counteraction Team, First Floor, 22 Kingsway, London WC2B 6NR (or, if market-sensitive information is included, to Eric Gardner at that address). Applications may be faxed to 020–7438 4409 or emailed to reconstructions@gtnet.gov.uk (after advising Eric Gardner (on 020–7438 6585) if market-sensitive information is included). Application may be made in a single letter to the same address for clearance under *TCGA 1992, s 140B* and under any one or more of *ICTA 1988, s 215* (demergers, see 32.39 GROUPS OF COMPANIES), *ICTA 1988, s 225* (see 57.6 PURCHASE BY A COMPANY OF ITS OWN SHARES), *ICTA 1988, s 707* (transactions in securities, see 5.2 ANTI-AVOIDANCE), *TCGA 1992, s 138(1)* (share exchanges, see Tolley's Capital Gains Tax under Anti-Avoidance), *TCGA 1992, s 139(5)* (reconstructions involving the transfer of a business, see 11.9 above), *TCGA 1992, s 140D* (transfer of non-UK trade between EU member states, see 11.12 below) and *FA 2002, Sch 29 para 88* (see 39.27 INTANGIBLE ASSETS).

[*TCGA 1992, ss 140A, 140B; F(No 2)A 1992, s 44; F(No 2)A 2005, s 59(3)(7)*].

Capital allowances. Where the above provisions apply (and, if immediately after the transfer the transferee company is non-UK resident, where at that time it carries on in the UK through a permanent establishment (or branch or agency) a trade consisting of or including the trade (or part) transferred), (with appropriate appeals procedures). *ICTA 1988, s 343(2)* (see 47.10 LOSSES) does not apply where a claim is made under these provisions. [*CAA 2001, s 561; CAA 1990, s 152B; F(No 2)A 1992, s 67*].

Simon's Direct Tax Service. See D2.304A.

11.12 TRANSFER OF NON-UK TRADE BETWEEN COMPANIES IN DIFFERENT EU MEMBER STATES

Where:

(*a*) a 'qualifying company' resident in the UK transfers to a 'qualifying company' resident in another member state the whole or part of a trade carried on by the UK company immediately before the transfer through a permanent establishment (see 60.5 RESIDENCE — previously through a branch or agency) in a member state other than the UK;

(*b*) the transfer includes all the UK company assets used in that trade or part (with the possible exception of cash);

(*c*) the transfer is wholly or partly in exchange for shares or debentures (for issues effected before 1 April 2005, securities (including shares)) in the non-UK company;

(*d*) the aggregate of the chargeable gains accruing to the UK company on the transfer exceeds the aggregate of the allowable losses so accruing; and (*e*) the transfer is effected for *bona fide* commercial reasons and not as part of a scheme or arrangement a main purpose of which is avoidance of income tax, corporation tax or capital gains tax,

the UK company may claim that the transfer be treated as giving rise to a single chargeable gain of the excess at (*d*) above. No claim may, however, be made where a claim is made under *TCGA 1992, s 140*, see 11.10 above, in relation to the same transfer.

A '*qualifying company*' is a body incorporated under the law of a member state.

For the purposes of (*a*) above, a company is not regarded as resident in the UK if it is regarded under any double tax relief arrangements to which the UK is a party as resident in a territory not within any of the member states. A company is regarded as resident in another member state under the laws of which it is chargeable to tax because it is regarded as so resident (unless it is regarded under a double tax relief arrangement entered into by the member state as resident in a territory not within any of the member states).

Advance clearance in relation to (*e*) above may be obtained from HMRC on the application of the UK company, subject to the same conditions and appeal procedures as apply to clearances under *TCGA 1992, s 138* (see Tolley's Capital Gains Tax under Anti-Avoidance). Applications for clearance should be addressed to Mohini Sawhney, Clearance and Counteraction Team, First Floor, 22 Kingsway, London WC2B 6NR (or, if market-sensitive information is included, to Eric Gardner at that address). Applications may be faxed to 020–7438 4409 or emailed to reconstructions@hmrc.gsi.gov.uk (after advising Eric Gardner (on 020–7438 6585) if market-sensitive information is included). Application may be made in a single letter to the same address for clearance under *TCGA 1992, s 140D* and under any one or more of *ICTA 1988, s 215* (demergers, see 32.39 GROUPS OF COMPANIES), *ICTA 1988, s 225* (see 57.6 PURCHASE BY A COMPANY OF ITS OWN SHARES), *ICTA 1988, s 707* (transactions in securities, see 5.2 ANTI-AVOIDANCE), *TCGA 1992, s 138(1)* (share exchanges, see Tolley's Capital Gains Tax under Anti-Avoidance), *TCGA 1992, s 139(5)* (reconstructions involving the transfer of a business, see 11.9 above), *TCGA 1992, s 140B* (transfer of a UK trade between EU member states, see 11.11 above) and *FA 2002, Sch 29 para 88* (see 39.27 INTANGIBLE ASSETS).

ICTA 1988, s 442(3) is ignored in arriving at the chargeable gains and allowable losses accruing on the transfer.

[*TCGA 1992, ss 140C, 140D; F(No 2)A 1992, s 45; F(No 2)A 2005, s 59(4)(7)*].

Double tax relief. Where the above provisions apply, and the gains accruing to the UK company on the transfer would, but for the Mergers Directive, have been chargeable to tax in the other member state, the amount of tax (as calculated on the required basis) is treated for double tax relief purposes as tax paid in that other member state. The onus is on the company to calculate the amount of notional foreign tax in support of a relief claim (see HMRC Capital Gains Manual, CG 45734).

These provisions also apply where the provisions at 11.13 below dealing with mergers not leaving assets within the UK tax charge apply.

[*ICTA 1988, s 815A; F(No 2)A 2005, s 59(1)*].

Merger Directive. The EC Mergers Directive (*90/434/EEC*), which took effect from 1 January 1992, applies to transactions set out at (*a*) to (*c*) above, broadly the transfer of assets of a UK company's permanent establishment in one member state to a company resident in another member state in exchange for shares in that company. The above provisions give effect to the Directive. Where the Directive applies, the host country of the permanent establishment is not permitted to tax any capital gain arising on the transfer except where the State of the transferring company applies a worldwide system of taxation. In that case, the State of the transferring company may tax any profits or capital gains of the permanent establishment resulting from a merger, division or transfer of assets (as defined in the Directive) provided it gives relief for the tax which would, but for the provisions of the Directive, have been charged on those profits or capital gains in the host country of the permanent establishment as if that tax had been actually charged and paid.

On 17 February 2005, the European Commission adopted a modified version of a proposal (COM(2003) 613) amending the Mergers Directive to cover all companies subject to tax within the European Union regardless of their legal form (including the new European Company – see 11.13 below and 25.5 EUROPEAN COMMUNITY LEGISLATION), transfers of all registered offices between member states, the tax deferral regime on the conversion of a foreign branch into a subsidiary and the valuation of securities and assets exchanged in cross-border mergers and divisions. Information on the Mergers Directive is available on the Taxation and Customs part of the Europa Internet site (www.europa.eu) (see in particular the European Commission Press Releases IP/03/1418 of 20 October 2003, IP/05/193 of 17 February 2005 and IP/04/1446 of 7 December 2004).

FA 2007, s 110 gives HMRC the power to issue regulations, by statutory instrument, where it is necessary to amend the existing UK taxation law in order for the UK to comply with the Mergers Directive.

Simon's Direct Tax Service. See D2.304B.

11.13 TRANSFER OF ASSETS ON FORMATION OF EUROPEAN COMPANY

The European Company Statute provides for the formation of a European Company or *Societas Europaea* ('SE') and applies to all member states with effect from 8 October 2004 (see 25.4 EUROPEAN COMMUNITY LEGISLATION). The *Statute* permits the formation of new SEs and also allows for the 'transformation' of existing companies into SEs and for the merger between two (or more) companies in different member States into an SE. Special UK tax provisions are required to deal with the formation of SEs by cross-border merger and those relating to capital gains are described below. The provisions are intended to be broadly tax-neutral. (Revenue Technical Note, 'Implementation of the European Company Statute', January 2005).

The provisions apply where an SE is formed on or after 1 April 2005 by the merger of two or more companies in accordance with *Council Regulation (EC) No 2157/2001, Arts 2(1), 17(2)* and each merging company is resident in a member state but not all of them are resident in the same member state.

A company is resident in a member state for this purpose if it is within a charge to tax under the law of the State as being resident for that purpose and it is not regarded, for the purposes of any DOUBLE TAX RELIEF (24) arrangements to which the State is a party, as resident in a territory not within a member state.

Treatment of securities issued on merger. If it does not constitute or form part of a scheme of reconstruction within the meaning of *TCGA 1992, s 136* (see Tolley's Capital Gains Tax under Shares and Securities), the merger is nevertheless treated as if it were a scheme of reconstruction for the purposes of that section. This means that the shares in or debentures of the SE issued on its formation to persons in exchange for (and in proportion to) their holdings of shares in or debentures of any of the old companies are treated as the same assets for *TCGA 1992* purposes as those old holdings.

Merger leaving assets within charge to UK tax. If *TCGA 1992, s 139* (reconstruction involving transfer of business — see 11.9 above) does not apply to the merger, any 'qualifying transferred assets' are treated for chargeable gains purposes as acquired by the SE for a consideration resulting in neither gain nor loss for the transferor (the tax thus being deferred until the SE realises the gain).

For this purpose, an asset transferred to the SE as part of the merger process is a '*qualifying transferred asset*' if:

- either the transferor was resident in the UK at the time of the transfer or any gain accruing on disposal of the asset immediately before that time would have been a chargeable gain forming part of the transferor's chargeable profits by virtue of *TCGA 1992, s 10B* (trade carried on via UK permanent establishment — see 11.1 above); and

- either the SE is resident in the UK on formation or any gain accruing to it on disposal of the asset immediately after the transfer would have been a chargeable gain forming part of its chargeable profits by virtue of *TCGA 1992, s 10B*.

Merger not leaving assets within charge to UK tax. If:

- in the course of the merger a company resident in the UK (company A) transfers to a company resident in another member state all the assets and liabilities relating to a business carried on by company A in a member state other than the UK through a permanent establishment; and
- the aggregate chargeable gains accruing to company A on the transfer exceed the aggregate allowable losses,

the allowable losses are treated as set off against the chargeable gains and the transfer is treated as giving rise to a single chargeable gain equal to the excess. Where this provision applies, the double tax relief provisions in 11.12 above are also to apply.

Anti-avoidance. The above provisions do not apply if the formation of the SE is not effected for *bona fide* commercial reasons or if it forms part of a scheme or arrangements of which the main purpose, or one of the main purposes, is avoiding liability to UK tax. The advance clearance provisions of *TCGA 1992, s 138* (see Tolley's Capital Gains Tax under Anti-Avoidance) apply, with any necessary modifications, for the purpose of these provisions.

[*TCGA 1992, ss 140E–140G; F(No 2)A 2005, s 51*].

Capital allowances. Where there is a merger leaving assets within the charge to UK tax to which the above provisions apply (or would apply but for *TCGA 1992, s 139* applying), the SE takes over the capital allowance position of the transferor company in relation to any 'qualifying assets' transferred as part of the merger on or after 1 April 2005, so that no allowances or charges arise from the transfer. Any necessary apportionments are made in a reasonable manner. *ICTA 1988, s 343(2)* (see 47.10 LOSSES) does not apply where this provision applies. An asset is a '*qualifying asset*' if it is transferred to the SE as part of the merger, either the transferor is resident in the UK at the time of transfer or the asset is an asset of the transferor's UK permanent establishment, and either the SE is resident in the UK on formation or the asset is an asset of the SE's UK permanent establishment on formation. [*CAA 2001, s 561A; F(No 2)A 2005, s 56*].

Held-over gains. Provision is made for continuity of group membership on the formation of an SE by merger for the purposes of certain hold-over reliefs. See 11.10 above and 12.32 CAPITAL GAINS—GROUPS. See also Tolley's Capital Gains Tax under Qualifying Corporate Bonds and Rollover Relief. [*F(No 2)A 2005, s 64*].

11.14 INTEREST CHARGED TO CAPITAL

In relation to interest referable to an accounting period ending before 1 April 1996, before the introduction of the LOAN RELATIONSHIPS (46) provisions, interest on money borrowed by a company for the construction of any building, structure or works, and referable to a period before disposal, could be added to the expenditure allowable as a deduction under *TCGA 1992, s 38* in computing the gain on the disposal by the company of the building etc. This was subject to the proviso that the expenditure on the construction itself was allowable, and that the interest was neither allowable as a deduction in computing any profits or gains for corporation tax purposes (nor would have been so but for an insufficiency of profits or gains) nor a charge on income (see 55.4 PROFIT COMPUTATIONS). [*TCGA 1992, s 40; FA 2002, Sch 25 para 60*].

11.15 GOVERNMENT SECURITIES ETC. AND QUALIFYING CORPORATE BONDS

See the general taxation provisions relating to LOAN RELATIONSHIPS (46).

11.16 SHARES — ACQUISITIONS AND DISPOSALS WITHIN SHORT PERIOD

The ordinary rules (see Tolley's Capital Gains Tax) for matching disposals with 'acquisitions' are modified for disposals before 5 December 2005 by a company of shares (including securities) if:

(*a*) the company acquired shares ('*available shares*') of the same class within one month before or after the disposal where the disposal was through a stock exchange or Automated Real-Time Investments Exchange Ltd, or otherwise within six months before or after the disposal; and

(*b*) the number of that class of shares held by the company during the period prescribed under (*a*) before the disposal was not less than 2% of the number issued.

Where the company making the disposal ('company X') is a member of a group and the period prescribed under (*a*) above begins on or after 1 April 2000, the following apply.

(i) Where shares of the same class are held by another group member, and at any time in that prescribed period before the disposal either:

(A) the other group member is UK resident; or

(B) the shares are 'chargeable shares' in relation to that other group member,

those shares are treated for the purposes of (*b*) above as held by company X.

(ii) Where shares of the same class are acquired by another group member, and either (i)(A) or (i)(B) applies at the time of acquisition, those shares are treated for the purposes of (*a*) above as acquired by company X.

(iii) Where shares of the same class are acquired by company X from a company which was a member of the group throughout that prescribed period before and after the disposal, and either (i)(A) or (i)(B) applies throughout that part of that period during which the other group member held the shares, those shares are disregarded for the purposes of (*a*) above.

Shares are '*chargeable shares*' in relation to a company at a particular time if, on a disposal by the company at that time, any gain would be a chargeable gain and within the charge to corporation tax by virtue of *TCGA 1992, s 10* or *s 10B* (non-UK resident company trading through UK permanent establishment or branch or agency, see 60.5, 60.6 RESIDENCE). Membership of a group is determined as in 12.1 CAPITAL GAINS—GROUPS.

Where the company making the disposal is a member of a group and the period prescribed under (*a*) above begins before 1 April 2000, similar provisions apply but taking into account the fact that under 12.1 CAPITAL GAINS—GROUPS, as it applied before the change in the residence requirement, a group is restricted to UK-resident companies.

Disposals are matched with available shares before other shares and with available shares acquired by the disposing company before those acquired by a fellow group member, and then with acquisitions before the disposal (latest ones first) rather than after (when earliest ones are taken first).

Where disposals are identified with acquisitions of another group member, the cost to that member will be allowed to the disposing company plus the usual incidental costs of disposal. Shares identified with a disposal are precluded from further identification with a later disposal.

'*Acquisitions*' above do not include shares acquired as trading stock or from another group member.

The above identification rules have priority over those generally applicable (see Tolley's Capital Gains Tax under Shares and Securities—Identification Rules) and, additionally, shares acquired and disposed of on the same day are matched under *TCGA 1992, ss 105, 105A.*

[*TCGA 1992, ss 106, 108(8); FA 2000, Sch 29 para 18; FA 2003, Sch 27 para 2(3); FA 2006, s 72(1)(3), Sch 26 Pt 3(10)*].

The above provisions are repealed with effect for disposals on or after 5 December 2005. They are considered to be unnecessary following the introduction of the provision at 11.3(*b*) above which denies relief for losses arising from arrangements intended to secure a tax advantage and therefore provides an alternative mechanism to prevent loss creation using bed and breakfasting of shares. (Treasury Explanatory Notes to the Finance (No 2) Bill 2006).

Insurance companies. Special provision is made in relation to insurance company holdings of '*section 440A securities*', i.e. shares, or securities of a company, and any other assets of a nature to be dealt in without identifying the particular assets disposed of or acquired. This applies to disposals on or after 23 December 2002, except that it applies to such disposals made before 1 January 2003 only if the allowable losses referable to the company's life assurance business which would have accrued on those disposals would (but for these provisions) have been at least £10 million. Where:

(1) within a period of ten days, an insurance company disposes of a number of *section 440A* securities and (whether before or after the disposal) the company acquires a number of such securities;

(2) the securities disposed of decrease, and those acquired increase, the size of the same separate holding within *section 440A*, being a holding either of assets referable to basic life assurance and general annuity business or a holding of assets included in the long-term insurance fund and not within any other separate holding; and

(3) an allowable loss would otherwise accrue on the disposal,

the securities disposed of are identified with those acquired. All same-day acquisitions or disposals are treated as a single acquisition or disposal and the acquisition matched, as far as possible, with the disposal. Subject to this, disposals are matched with pre-disposal acquisitions (latest ones first) before post-disposal acquisitions (when earliest ones are taken first), and acquisitions are matched with pre-acquisition before post-acquisition disposals. The identification of securities acquired with securities disposed of precludes their identification with a later disposal.

The above provisions do *not* apply to securities which are *TCGA 1992, s 212* assets within the meaning of *TCGA 1992, s 214(1)* (rights under authorised unit trusts and interests in offshore funds), or to securities deemed to be disposed of and immediately reacquired by *ICTA 1988, s 440, Sch 19AA para 3* (assets becoming or ceasing to be assets of overseas life assurance fund), or to certain transfers of assets between linked funds made with a view to adjusting the values of fund assets to match liabilities.

[*TCGA 1992, s 210B; FA 2003, Sch 33 para 15*].

Simon's Direct Tax Service. See **D2.327.**

11.17 VALUE-SHIFTING

For the provisions of general application to individuals, etc. as well as companies, see Tolley's Capital Gains Tax under Anti-Avoidance. *FA 1989, ss 135–137* introduced various extensions to the scope of *CGTA 1979, s 26* which apply to companies disposing of assets, and these, now contained in *TCGA 1992, ss 30–34*, are described below.

Following the introduction by *FA 2002, s 84, Sch 29* of a special regime for taxation of INTANGIBLE ASSETS (39), taking assets chargeable under that regime out of chargeable gains taxation, the appropriate modifications are applied to *TCGA 1992, ss 30–33* to ensure that those provisions continue to apply to such assets. [*TCGA 1992, s 33A; FA 2002, Sch 30 para 6*].

TCGA 1992, s 30 applies to the disposal of an asset if a scheme has been effected or arrangements made (whether before or after the disposal) whereby the value of the asset, or of a 'relevant asset', has been materially reduced and a 'tax-free benefit' is conferred at any time on:

(*a*) the person making the disposal or a person connected with him (see 19 CONNECTED PERSONS); or

(*b*) any other person unless tax avoidance was not a main purpose of the scheme or arrangements.

Where the disposal of the asset precedes its acquisition, references to a reduction include references to an increase.

The consideration for the disposal in the capital gains computation is increased by a just and reasonable amount having regard to the scheme or arrangements and the 'tax-free benefit'. Where the consideration for the disposal of one asset has been so increased and the 'tax-free benefit' was an increase in the value of another asset, the consideration for the first subsequent disposal of that other asset is reduced by a just and reasonable amount. (There is no provision for the acquirer's cost to be correspondingly adjusted.)

These provisions do not apply to, *inter alia*, disposals between companies in a group (see 12.1 CAPITAL GAINS—GROUPS). [*TCGA 1992, s 30(1)(4)–(7)(9)*].

An asset ('the second asset') is a '*relevant asset*' if:

(1) the disposal of an asset (here called 'the first asset') is made by a company ('the disposing company');

(2) the first asset comprises shares in, or securities (within *TCGA 1992, s 132*) of, a company; and

(3) the second asset is owned at the time of disposal of the first asset by a company 'associated' (see 11.19 below) with the disposing company.

A reduction in value of a relevant asset is not taken into account except in a case where:

(A) during the period from the reduction in value to the time immediately before the disposal of the first asset there is no disposal of it other than one within *TCGA 1992, s 171(1)* (see 12.2 CAPITAL GAINS—GROUPS);

(B) no disposal of that asset is treated as occurring during that period under *TCGA 1992, s 179* (see 12.32 CAPITAL GAINS—GROUPS); and

(C) if the reduction had not occurred, but any consideration given for the relevant asset and any other material circumstances (including any consideration given before the disposal for the first asset disposed of) were unchanged, the value of the first asset would have been materially greater at the time of its disposal.

[*TCGA 1992, s 30(2)*].

A '*tax-free benefit*' arises to a person if he becomes entitled to money or money's worth, or his interest in the value of any asset is increased, or he is wholly or partly relieved of any liability to which he is subject, *and* none of the foregoing benefits, when conferred, is otherwise liable to income tax, capital gains tax or corporation tax. [*TCGA 1992, s 30(3)*].

It is understood that HMRC do not regard ordinary group relief transactions (e.g. the purchase of group relief) as falling within *TCGA 1992, s 30*.

Where a disposal within *TCGA 1992, s 30* forms the basis of a claim for relief under *ICTA 1988, ss 573, 574* (see 47.19 LOSSES), *section 30* applies if *any* benefit is conferred, whether tax-free or not. [*ICTA 1988, s 576(2)*].

See HMRC Capital Gains Manual, 46800 *et seq.*

Simon's Direct Tax Service. See D2.669.

11.18 **Certain disposals of shares by companies.** The following provisions apply where a disposal within 11.17 above ('the *section 30* disposal') is of shares ('the principal asset') which are owned by a company ('the first company') in another company ('the second company'). [*TCGA 1992, s 30(8)*].

Distributions within a group followed by a disposal of shares. If a reduction in the value of an asset is attributable to the payment of a dividend by the second company while the two companies are 'associated' (see 11.19 below), it is not treated as a reduction for the purposes of 11.17 above except to the extent (if any) that the dividend is attributable (see below) to 'chargeable profits' of the second company; and, in such a case, the tax-free benefit is ascertained without regard to any part of the dividend that is not attributable to such profits.

'*Chargeable profits*' are:

(*a*) the 'distributable profits' of a company, to the extent that they arise from a 'transaction caught by this *section*'; and

(*b*) the 'distributable profits' of a company, to the extent that they represent so much of a distribution received from another company as was attributable to chargeable profits of that company (including ones similarly representing a distribution).

'*Distributable profits*' are such profits computed on a commercial basis as, after allowance for any provision properly made for tax, the company is empowered, assuming sufficient funds, to distribute to persons entitled to participate in its profits. So far as possible, in ascertaining distributable profits, losses and other amounts to be set against profits must be set against profits other than ones which could be chargeable profits.

Profits arising on a '*transaction caught by this section*' are profits of a company ('company X') where the following three conditions are met but the three exceptions to them (see below) do not apply.

(1) The transaction is:

   (i) a no gain/no loss disposal by company X to another group company within *TCGA 1992, s 171(1)* (see 12.2 CAPITAL GAINS—GROUPS); or

   (ii) an exchange, or deemed exchange, of shares in or debentures of a company held by company X for shares in or debentures of another company which, immediately after the transaction, is 'associated' (see 11.19 below) with company X, being a transaction treated by virtue of *TCGA 1992, s 135* or *s 136* as a reorganisation of share capital; or

   (iii) a revaluation of an asset in the accounting records of company X.

(2) No disposal of the 'asset with enhanced value':

   (i) occurs, other than one within *TCGA 1992, s 171(1)*, during the period beginning with the transaction within (1) above and ending immediately before the *section 30* disposal; or

   (ii) is treated as having occurred during that period by virtue of *TCGA 1992, s 179* (see 12.32 CAPITAL GAINS—GROUPS).

(3) Immediately after the *section 30* disposal the asset with enhanced value is owned by a person other than the disposing company or a company 'associated' with it (see 11.19 below).

'*Asset with enhanced value*' is defined as follows, according to which transaction within (1)(i), (1)(ii) or (1)(iii) above occurs, respectively: the asset acquired from company X; the shares or debentures acquired by company X as a result of the exchange; and the revalued asset.

The three exceptions to the foregoing three conditions are as follows.

(A) At the time of the transaction within (1) above, company X carries on a trade, and a profit on a disposal of the asset with enhanced value would form part of the trading profits.

(B) By reason of the nature of the asset with enhanced value, there could be no chargeable gain or allowable loss on its disposal.

(C) Immediately before the *section 30* disposal, the company owning the asset with enhanced value carries on a trade, and a profit on disposal would form part of the trading profits.

Attribution of profits to a distribution is made by determining the total distributable profits and chargeable profits which remain at the time of distribution, after allowing for all earlier distributions and distributions to be made then or subsequently in respect of other classes of shares, etc., and so far as possible attributing distributable profits other than chargeable profits.

Chargeable profits are treated as arising to shareholders etc. proportionately to their holdings of shares etc.

[*TCGA 1992, s 31; FA 2002, Sch 9 para 5(2)*].

See generally HMRC Capital Gains Manual, CG 46805–CG 46834.

Asset-holding company leaving the group. The following provisions apply wherever profits of a company would be profits on a transaction caught by *TCGA 1992, s 31* (see above) but for the fact that condition (3) above is not satisfied. In those circumstances, the profits are treated as arising on a transaction caught by *section 31* (with the result that *TCGA 1992, s 30* (see 11.17 above) has effect) if, at any time during the period of six years beginning with the date of the *section 30* disposal, either:

(*aa*) an event occurs which consists of the 'asset-holding company' ceasing to be a member of the 'disposal group' (otherwise than by virtue of the principal company of the group becoming a member of another group, i.e. the group being taken over); or

(*bb*) the 'asset-holding company' ceases to be a member of the 'disposal group' by virtue only of the principal company of the group becoming a member of another group *and* an event occurs as a result of which either:

 (i) there is no member of the 'disposal group' of which the 'asset-holding company' is a 75% subsidiary; or

 (ii) there is no member of the 'disposal group' of which the 'asset-holding company' is an effective 51% subsidiary (see 12.1 CAPITAL GAINS—GROUPS).

These provisions do not, however, apply (and there is thus no double charge), if, during that six-year period but prior to the occurrence of an event within (*aa*) or (*bb*) above, a disposal of the asset with enhanced value has been treated as having occurred by virtue of *TCGA 1992, s 179* (company leaving a group after acquiring an asset intra-group, see 12.32 CAPITAL GAINS—GROUPS).

The '*asset-holding company*' at any time is the company holding the asset with enhanced value at that time. The '*disposal group*' is the group of which the company which made the *section 30* disposal was a member at the time of that disposal (or a group regarded as being the same as that group under *TCGA 1992, s 170(10)*, see 12.1 CAPITAL GAINS—GROUPS).

Where *TCGA 1992, s 30* has effect as above, the consideration for the *section 30* disposal is not adjusted, but a chargeable gain is treated as accruing to the 'chargeable company' immediately before the event within (*aa*) or (*bb*) above. The '*chargeable company*' is normally the company which made the disposal. If, however, that company is, immediately before the event within (*aa*) or (*bb*) above, no longer a member of the disposal group, the chargeable company is any member of the group immediately before the event which is so designated for the purpose by HMRC by notice served on the company. The amount of the imputed gain is the shortfall between the allowable loss or chargeable gain which accrued on the *section 30* disposal and the allowable loss or chargeable gain which would have accrued on that disposal if the consideration had been treated as increased as in 11.17 above.

If an allowable loss arose on the *section 30* disposal and has not been otherwise utilised, it may be set against the imputed gain arising as above, notwithstanding the connected persons rule in *TCGA 1992, s 18(3)*.

[*TCGA 1992, s 31A*].

Disposals within a group followed by a disposal of shares. A reduction in the value of an asset is not treated as a reduction for the purposes of 11.17 above if it is attributable to the disposal of any asset ('the underlying asset') by the second company while the two companies are 'associated' (see 11.19 below), and the disposal is within *TCGA 1992, s 171(1)*, unless:

(I) the actual consideration for the disposal of the underlying asset is less than both its market value and its 'cost';

(II) the disposal is not effected for *bona fide* commercial reasons and forms part of a scheme or arrangements of which a main purpose is the avoidance of a corporation tax liability; and

(III) the first company is not treated as disposing of an interest in the principal asset by virtue of a distribution in a dissolution or winding-up of the second company.

For the purpose of (I) above, the '*cost*' of an asset is the aggregate of any capital expenditure incurred by the company in acquiring or providing it, or in respect of it while owned after its acquisition.

In the case of a part disposal of an underlying asset:

(AA) the market value in (I) above is the market value of the asset acquired by the transferee; and

(BB) the amounts attributed to the cost of the underlying asset are reduced to the '*appropriate proportion*' thereof; i.e.

- (i) the proportion of capital expenditure properly attributed in the company's accounting records to the asset acquired by the transferee; or
- (ii) if (i) does not apply, such proportion as is just and reasonable.

[*TCGA 1992, s 32*].

11.19 **Interpretation.** The following interpretational provisions apply.

As regards any asset ('the original asset'), the provisions in (1)–(5) below apply in relation to the enactments mentioned in (*a*) and (*b*) below.

(*a*) The enactments concerning relevant assets in *TCGA 1992, s 30(2)*: namely, in 11.17 above, (1)–(3) and (A)–(C).

(*b*) The enactments concerning distributions within a group followed by a disposal of shares in *TCGA 1992, s 31(7)–(9)*: namely, in 11.18 above, the second and third conditions ((2) and (3)) and the three exceptions ((A)–(C)) to the three conditions.

The provisions in (1)–(5) below also apply in connection with *TCGA 1992, s 31A* (see 11.18 above) for the purpose of determining any question in relation to the asset with enhanced value.

(1) In (A) and (B) in 11.17 above and in condition (2) in 11.18 above, references to the disposal of an asset do not include a part disposal. The same applies as regards the reference in relation to 11.18(*aa*) and (*bb*) above to a disposal occurring by virtue of *TCGA 1992, s 179*.

(2) For the purposes of the enactments referred to in (*a*) and (*b*) above, references to an asset are to the original asset, except that if subsequently one or more assets are treated under (4) or (5) below as the same as the original asset:

   (i) if there has been no disposal falling within (A) or (B) in 11.17 above or (2) in 11.18 above, the references are to the asset(s) so treated; and

   (ii) in any other case, the references are to the asset(s) representing that part of the value of the original asset remaining after allowing for earlier disposals within the relevant provision.

   For the above purposes a disposal includes a part disposal which would have been within (A) or (B) in 11.17 above or (2) in 11.18 above if it had not been excluded by (1) above.

   For the purposes of *TCGA 1992, s 31A* at 11.18 above, the following apply where one or more assets is treated under (4) or (5) below as the same as the asset with enhanced value.

   (I) If, in the period beginning with the transaction in 11.18(1) above and ending immediately before the event in 11.18(*aa*) or (*bb*) above, there is no disposal of the asset with enhanced value to any person other than on a no gain/no loss intra-group disposal within *TCGA 1992, s 171(1)* (see 12.2 CAPITAL GAINS—GROUPS), and no disposal of that asset is treated as having occurred by virtue of *TCGA 1992, s 179* (see 12.32 CAPITAL GAINS—GROUPS), then references to the asset with enhanced value are to the asset(s) treated under (4) or (5) below as the same as that asset.

   (II) In any other case, references to the asset with enhanced value are to the asset(s) representing that part of the value of the asset with enhanced value remaining after allowing for disposals of either kind referred to in (I) above.

(3) If, by virtue of (2) above, a reference to an asset is treated as a reference to two or more assets:

   (i) the assets are treated as a single asset;

   (ii) a disposal of any of them is a part disposal; and

   (iii) the reference to the second asset in (3) in 11.17 above, to the asset in condition (3) in 11.18 above and to the asset in the definition of 'asset-holding company' in 11.18 above is in each case a reference to all or any of those two or more assets.

(4) If there is a part disposal of an asset, that asset and the asset acquired by the transferee are treated as the same.

(5) Where:

(i) the value of an asset is derived from another asset owned by the same or an 'associated' company (see below); and

(ii) assets have been merged or divided or have changed their nature, or rights or interests in or over assets have been created or extinguished.

the two assets are treated as the same.

Where a reduction in the value of a relevant asset is to be taken into account under *TCGA 1992, s 30(2)* (see (1)–(3) and (A)–(C) in 11.17 above) and at the time of the disposal of the first asset in 11.17(1) by the disposing company:

(A) references to the relevant asset are treated under (1)–(5) above as references to two or more assets treated as a single asset; and

(B) one or more, but not all, of those assets is owned by a company 'associated' (see below) with the disposing company,

the amount of the reduction in the value of the relevant asset to be taken into account is reduced to such an amount as is just and reasonable.

For the purposes of the provisions in TCGA 1992, s 31 concerning distributions within a group followed by a disposal of shares (see 11.18 above), the reduction in value of the principal asset (see 11.18 above) is to be reduced to such amount as is just and reasonable if:

(*aa*) a dividend paid by the second company is attributable to that company's chargeable profits; and

(*bb*) the criterion in (2), (3) or (C) in 11.18 above is satisfied by reference to an asset, or assets treated as a single asset, treated under (2)(ii) above as the same as the asset with enhanced value.

Where *TCGA 1992, s 31A* (see 11.18 above) treats profits as arising on a transaction caught by *TCGA 1992, s 31* (see 11.18 above) and either condition (2) or condition (*aa*) or (*bb*) in 11.18 above is satisfied by reference to an asset (or assets treated as a single asset) treated by virtue of (2)(II) above as the same as the asset with enhanced value, the reduction in value of the principal asset (see 11.18 above) is to be reduced to such amount as is just and reasonable.

The definitions relating to groups of companies in TCGA 1992, s 170(2)–(11) apply as in 12.1 CAPITAL GAINS—GROUPS; and companies are '*associated*' if they are members of the same group.

[*TCGA 1992, s 33*].

11.20 **Transactions treated as a reorganisation of share capital.** If the following conditions apply, a 'disposing company' is treated as receiving the amount specified in (*b*) below on a part disposal within *TCGA 1992, s 128(3)* of the 'original holding'.

(*a*) But for the rules whereby shares, etc. held after a reorganisation, reconstruction, etc. are treated as the same as those held beforehand, *TCGA 1992, s 30* in 11.17 above would apply on an exchange by a company (the 'disposing company') of shares, etc. in another company (the 'original holding') for shares, etc. in a further company which immediately afterwards is not in the same group (as defined in *TCGA 1992, s 170(2)–(11)*, see 12.1 CAPITAL GAINS—GROUPS) as the disposing company.

(*b*) If *TCGA 1992, s 30* had applied, any allowable loss or chargeable gain on the disposal would have been calculated as if the consideration had been increased by an amount.

Similarly if, but for the rules referred to in (*a*) above, *section 30* would have applied by virtue of *TCGA 1992, s 31A* (see 11.18 above) on an exchange of the kind referred to in (*a*) above, *section 31A* is applied (with appropriate modification) as if the said rules did not apply. In the computation of the shortfall under that *section*, an allowable loss is in this case regarded as a chargeable gain of nil.

These provisions are interpreted as if *TCGA 1992, s 136* had effect generally for the capital gains tax legislation.

[*TCGA 1992, s 34*].

11.21 CLOSE COMPANY TRANSFERRING ASSET AT UNDERVALUE

Where, after 5 April 1965 (31 March 1982 where, on the ultimate disposal after 5 April 1988, market value at that date is substituted for cost), a close company transfers an asset to any person otherwise than at arm's length for a consideration less than market value, the difference is apportioned among the issued shares of the company so as to reduce the deductible cost in the capital gains tax computation on disposal of those shares; but this does not apply to transfers within a group. [*TCGA 1992, s 125*]. By concession, *section 125* is not applied where the transferee is a participator (or associate) and the transfer is treated as an income distribution under *ICTA 1988, s 209(2)(b)* or *(4)* (see 23.2, 23.7 DISTRIBUTIONS) or as a capital distribution under *TCGA 1992, s 122* (see Tolley's Capital Gains Tax under Shares and Securities), or where the transferee is an employee and is assessed as employment income on the excess of the market value of the asset over any amount paid for it. (HMRC Extra-Statutory Concession, D51).

Where the transfer is to a trust for the benefit of the employees of the transferring company, the difference that is apportioned is limited (where it would otherwise be greater) to any excess of allowable expenditure over the transfer consideration. [*TCGA 1992, s 239*].

Simon's Direct Tax Service. See **D2.318.**

11.22 COMPANIES IN PARTNERSHIP

A charge to corporation applies under *FA 2004, s 131* where a company realises capital from a partnership on or after 17 March 2004 by disposing of all or part of it's partnership interest on or after that date in connection with certain anti-avoidance schemes which shelter taxable profits within a partnership structure. The provisions ensure that any amounts subject to the change under *section 131* are taken into account in computing gains under the chargeable gains legislation so as to avoid double taxation and it specifically sets out the amounts which will fall within *TCGA 1992*. See 52.7 PARTNERSHIPS.

[*FA 2004, s 131, 133*].

11.23 DUAL RESIDENT COMPANIES

Special provisions applied **before 30 November 1993** to '*dual-resident companies*', i.e. companies resident both in the UK and, under any double taxation relief arrangements, in a territory outside the UK. From that date, they are replaced by *FA 1994, s 249*, which has effect to treat companies otherwise regarded as UK-resident as non-resident where they are so treated under such arrangements. See 60.1 RESIDENCE.

11.24 PRIVATISATION

British Telecommunications plc ('British Telecom') is treated for all purposes of corporation tax as being the same person as British Telecommunications, to whose business it succeeded on privatisation, except that it is not regarded as a nationalised undertaking within *TCGA 1992, s 170(12)*. [*Telecommunications Act 1984, s 72*]. Similar provisions apply in relation to the successor companies to the British Airways Board and the National Freight Corporation [*ICTA 1988, s 513*], the British Airports Authority [*British Airports Act 1986, s 77*], the British Gas Corporation [*Gas Act 1986, s 60*], the British Steel Corporation [*British Steel Act 1988, s 11*], the General Practice Finance Corporation [*Health and Medicines Act 1988, s 6*], statutory port undertakings [*Ports Act 1991, s 35*], the National Research Development Council and National Enterprise Board [*British Technology Group Act 1991, s 12*], milk marketing boards [*Agriculture Act 1993, Sch 2 Pt I; FA*

1996, s 203], Northern Ireland Airports Ltd [*FA 1994, s 253, Sch 25*] and the Atomic Energy Authority [*Atomic Energy Authority Act 1995, Sch 3*]. See also *Water Act 1989, s 95, Electricity Act 1989, s 90, Sch 11, Environmental Protection Act 1990, ss 6–9, Coal Industry Act 1994, Sch 4, Broadcasting Act 1996, Sch 7, Transport Act 2000, Sch 26* and *Scottish Water (Transfer of Functions, etc.)(Tax Provisions) Order 2002* (*SI 2002 No 653*), and, as regards the *Railways Act 1993, FA 1994, s 252, Sch 24*.

Surplus ACT arising to the successor company on privatisation may not be carried back to a period before the transfer (*CIR v Aberdeen Milk Co Ltd CS, 73 TC 563*).

11.25 INDEXATION ALLOWANCE

The basic indexation provisions applicable to individuals up to 5 April 1998 continue to apply to companies. For companies, however, they applied initially to disposals after 31 March 1982 instead of 5 April 1982, and the revised rules introduced by *FA 1985* applied to disposals after 31 March 1985 instead of 5 April 1985. The rules introduced by *FA 1988* apply only to disposals after 5 April 1988. See Tolley's Capital Gains Tax for full details.

12 Capital Gains—Groups

Cross-reference. See also 13 CAPITAL GAINS—SUBSTANTIAL SHAREHOLDINGS, 26.29 EXCHANGE GAINS AND LOSSES, 27 EXEMPT ORGANISATIONS, 46.35 LOAN RELATIONSHIPS.

Simon's Direct Tax Service C3.1.

Other sources. See Tolley's Capital Gains Tax.

The headings in this chapter are as follows.

12.1 GROUPS OF COMPANIES

The following definitions apply for the purposes of this chapter.

Definition of company. '*Company*' means one within the meaning of the *Companies Act 1985* or the corresponding enactment in Northern Ireland or which is constituted under any other Act, Royal Charter, or letters patent or under the law of a country outside the UK. It also includes a registered INDUSTRIAL AND PROVIDENT SOCIETY (38), a building society (see 9.2 BUILDING SOCIETIES) and (from 17 March 1998) an incorporated friendly society (see 31.2 FRIENDLY SOCIETIES).

Residence. From (broadly) April 2000, any company, whatever its country of residence, can be a member of a group (previously a company had to be UK-resident), and can be taken into account in establishing the existence of a group, for the purposes of corporation tax on chargeable gains. See 32.6 GROUPS OF COMPANIES for the corresponding group relief provisions. For transitional measures which ensure continuity of treatment as regards a pre-existing group of companies, see (iii) below.

[*TCGA 1992, s 170(2)(a)(9); FA 2000, s 102, Sch 29 paras 1, 46(1)-(3)*].

Definition of group. A '*group*' comprises:

(*a*) a company ('*the principal company of the group*'); and

(*b*) that company's '75 per cent subsidiaries' (i.e. where not less than 75% of the 'ordinary share capital' is beneficially owned directly or indirectly by the principal company), and those subsidiaries' 75 per cent subsidiaries (and so on), except that any 75 per cent subsidiary which is not 'an effective 51 per cent subsidiary' of the principal company is excluded. Beneficial ownership is not affected by the existence of an option which may require disposal of shares at a future date (see *J Sainsbury plc v O'Connor CA 1991, 64 TC 208*).

This definition is subject to the following rules.

(i) A company ('the subsidiary') which is a 75 per cent subsidiary of another company cannot be a principal company of a group, unless:

(A) because of the exclusion in (*b*) above, the two companies are not in the same group;

(B) the requirements of the definition of a group in (*a*) and (*b*) are otherwise satisfied; and

(C) no further company could, under this provision, be the principal company of a group of which the subsidiary would be a member.

(ii) If a company would otherwise belong to more than one group (the principal company of each of which is below called the '*head of a group*'), it belongs only to the group which can first be determined under the following tests.

(I) The group to which it would belong if the exclusion of a company which is not an 'effective 51 per cent subsidiary' in (*b*) above were applied without the inclusion of any amount to which the head of a group:

(*a*) is entitled of any profits available for distribution to equity holders of a head of another group; or

(*b*) would be entitled of any assets of a head of another group available for distribution to its equity holders on a winding-up.

(II) The group the head of which is entitled to a greater percentage than any other head of a group of its profits available for distribution to equity holders.

(III) The group the head of which would be entitled to a greater percentage than any other head of a group of its assets available for distribution to equity holders on a winding-up.

(IV) The group the head of which owns (as in *ICTA 1988, s 838(1)(a)*) directly or indirectly more of its ordinary share capital than any other head of a group.

(iii) *Transitional.* If a group is reconstituted purely because of the amendment made by *FA 2000* to the residence requirement (see above), such that the principal company of the 'old' group is not the principal company of the 'new' group, a subsidiary which is not an 'effective 51 per cent subsidiary' of the 'new' principal company remains part of the group for so long as it remains such a subsidiary of the 'old' principal company.

A company ('the subsidiary') is '*an effective 51 per cent subsidiary*' of another company ('the parent') at any time if and only if:

(A) the parent is entitled to more than 50 per cent of any profits available for distribution to equity holders of the subsidiary; and

(B) the parent would be entitled to more than 50 per cent of any assets available for distribution to the equity holders on a winding-up.

ICTA 1988, Sch 18 (group relief: equity holders and profits or assets available for distribution, see 32.8, 32.9 GROUPS OF COMPANIES) applies with minor modification for (ii) and (A) and (B) above. One modification to *Schedule 18* for these purposes disapplies the requirement that certain arrangements for changes in profit or asset shares are assumed to take place in applying the 50% test. The anti-avoidance measures of *paras 5B–5E* of *Schedule 18* (introduced by *F(No 2)A 1992, Sch 6*, see 32.9 GROUPS OF COMPANIES, with effect from 15 November 1991) do not apply for these purposes.

[*TCGA 1992, s 170(2)–(8); ICTA 1988, s 838; FA 2000, Sch 29 para 46(4)–(6)*].

A group remains the same group so long as the same company remains the principal company of the group, and if at any time the principal company of a group becomes a member of another group, the first group and the other group are regarded as the same, and the question whether or not a company has ceased to be a member of a group is determined accordingly. [*TCGA 1992, s 170(10)*].

Where the principal company of a group:

- becomes an SE (see 11.13 CAPITAL GAINS) on or after 1 April 2005 by reason of being the acquiring company in the formation of an SE by merger by acquisition (in accordance with *Council Regulations (EC) No 2157/2001, Arts 2(1), 17(2) and 29(1)*);
- becomes a subsidiary of a holding SE (formed on or after 1 April 2005 in accordance with *Art 2(2)*); or
- is transformed on or after 1 April 2005 into an SE (in accordance with *Art 2(4)*),

the group and any group of which the SE is a member on formation are regarded as the same, and the question whether or not a company has ceased to be a member of a group is determined accordingly. [*TCGA 1992, s 170(10A); F(No 2)A 2005, s 62*].

The passing of a resolution, or the making of an order, or any other act for the winding-up of a member of a group is not treated as an occasion on which any company ceases to be a member of the group. [*TCGA 1992, s 170(11)*].

General. '*Ordinary share capital*' means all issued share capital of a company except that carrying a fixed rate of dividend only. [*ICTA 1988, s 832(1)*]. Any share capital of a registered industrial and provident society is treated as ordinary share capital. 'Issued share capital' does not include founder members' deposits in a company limited by guarantee (*South Shore Mutual Insurance Co Ltd v Blair (Sp C 215), [1999] SSCD 296*).

As regards nationalised industries, etc. see *TCGA 1992, s 170(12)–(14)* as amended.

Where it is assumed, for any purpose, that a group member has acquired or sold an asset, it is also assumed that it was not a sale to, or acquisition from, a group member. [*TCGA 1992, s 171(1) as originally enacted; TCGA 1992, s 171(6) as introduced by FA 2000, Sch 29 para 2(5)*].

With effect for disposals on or after 1 April 2006, it is specifically provided that an open-ended investment company (see 43 INVESTMENT FUNDS) cannot be the principal company of a group [*TCGA 1992, s 170(4A)* treated as inserted by *SI 2006 No 964, reg 107*] or a member of a group (see HMRC Capital Gains Manual, CG 45173).

Simon's Direct Tax Service. See D2.650 *et seq.*

12.2 DISPOSALS AT 'NO GAIN, NO LOSS' PRICE – EXCEPTIONS

Disposals of capital assets by one member of a group to another are treated as if made at a 'no gain, no loss' price except for:

(i) *assumed* (as opposed to actual) transfers;

(ii) a disposal of a *debt* due from a group member effected by satisfying it (or part of it);

(iii) a disposal on redemption of *redeemable shares*;

(iv) a disposal of an interest in shares in consideration of a *capital distribution*;

(v) the receipt of *compensation* for destruction etc. of assets (in that the disposal is treated as being to the insurer or other person who ultimately bears the burden of furnishing the compensation);

(vi) a disposal by or to an investment trust (and see 12.37 below);

(vii) a disposal to a 'dual resident investing company' (see 32.27 GROUPS OF COMPANIES);

(viia) a disposal by or to a real estate investment trust (see 65.4 UNIT TRUSTS ETC.);

(viib) a disposal by one member of a group to another in fulfilment of its obligations under an option granted to that other member at a time when the two companies were not members of the same group; this applies where the option is exercised on or after 6 March 2007 (even if the option is granted before that date);

(viii) a disposal by or to an incorporated friendly society entitled to tax exemptions under *ICTA 1988, s 461B* (see 31.2 ET SEQ. FRIENDLY SOCIETIES);

(ix) a disposal by or to a venture capital trust (and see 12.38 below);

(x) a disposal on or after 16 March 2005 where *FA 1996, s 91A* (certain shares subject to outstanding third party obligations — see 46.35 LOAN RELATIONSHIPS) does not apply to the asset in relation to the company making the disposal ('the vendor') immediately before the disposal but does apply in relation to the acquiring company ('the buyer') immediately after its acquisition, or where that section applies in relation to the vendor immediately before the disposal but not to the buyer immediately afterwards.

The conditions for intra-group transfers of assets to be treated as no gain, no loss disposals are:

(*a*) that either the transferor company is UK resident at the time of disposal or the asset is a 'chargeable asset' in relation to that company immediately before that time, and

(*b*) that either the transferee company is UK resident at that time or the asset is a 'chargeable asset' in relation to that company immediately after that time.

For these purposes, an asset is a '*chargeable asset*' in relation to a company at a particular time if, on a disposal by the company at that time, any gain would be a chargeable gain and within the charge to corporation tax by virtue of *TCGA 1992, s 10* or *s 10B* (non-UK resident company trading through UK permanent establishment or branch or agency, see 60.5, 60.6 RESIDENCE).

[*TCGA 1992, s 171; FA 2002, Sch 9 para 5(10); FA 2003, Sch 27 para 2(3); F(No 2)A 2005, Sch 7 para 9; FA 2007, Sch 5 para 10*].

As regards (iv), the assets acquired in the capital distribution are nevertheless treated as transferred at a 'no gain, no loss' price (see *Innocent v Whaddon Estates Ltd Ch D 1981, 55 TC 476*). Where an exchange of securities for those in another company is, under *TCGA 1992, ss 127, 135*, not treated as involving a disposal of the original shares or the acquisition of a new holding, it is not treated as a 'no gain, no loss' transfer as above. [*TCGA 1992, s 171(3)*]. Where the consideration given for shares consists of qualifying corporate bonds, see Revenue Tax Bulletin December 1996 p 372 for an analysis of the consequences.

Where a disposal is to be dealt with on a 'no gain, no loss' basis, indexation allowance will be taken into account (see Tolley's Capital Gains Tax under Indexation).

HMRC have indicated that they will not seek to apply the '*Ramsay* principle' (see 5.1 ANTI-AVOIDANCE) where straightforward transfers of assets between members of the same group enable asset sales to be routed through group members with allowable capital losses. Where the effect of a series of transactions is to transfer the benefit of capital losses from one group to another, the *Ramsay* principle may be applicable, depending on the relationship between the amounts of the loss involved, the period for which the company with the loss has been within the group and on the circumstances in which the losses have arisen. (ICAEW Guidance Note TR 588, 25 September 1985).

Simon's Direct Tax Service. See D2.652.

12.3 **DISPOSAL OUTSIDE GROUP TREATED AS PRECEDED BY INTRA-GROUP TRANSFER**

Where two companies ('X' and 'Y') are members of a group, and X disposes of an asset to a person outside the group (the 'actual disposal'), X and Y may jointly elect to the effect that, for the purposes of corporation tax on chargeable gains:

(*a*) the asset (or a specified part of it) is deemed to have been transferred by X to Y immediately before the actual disposal;

(*b*) that transfer is deemed to be a no gain, no loss disposal within *TCGA 1992, s 171* (see 12.1 above);

(*c*) the actual disposal (or the part of it to which the election relates) is deemed to have been made by Y; and

(*d*) X's actual incidental disposal costs are deemed to be such costs to Y of making the deemed disposal.

The election must be made in writing to an officer of HMRC within two years after the end of the accounting period of X in which the actual disposal was made. It can only be made if an actual transfer of the asset (or part) from X to Y would have been a no gain, no loss disposal within *section 171* (although, in relation to disposals on or after 23 December 2002, this does not apply where Y is an insurance company and *section 171* is precluded from applying by *ICTA 1988, s 440(3)*, the asset (or part) involved then being treated for these purposes as not being part of Y's long-term insurance fund).

Any payment agreed between X and Y in connection with the election is ignored in computing profits or losses for corporation tax purposes, and is not regarded as a distribution or (for payments before 16 March 2005) a charge on income (see 55.4 PROFIT COMPUTATIONS), provided that it does not exceed the amount of the chargeable gain or allowable loss treated, as a result of the disposal, as accruing to Y.

For disposals on or after 16 March 2005, where Y is not resident in the UK but is carrying on a trade in the UK through a permanent establishment there, the asset deemed to be transferred by X to Y is treated for the purposes of these provisions as having been acquired by Y for use by or for the purposes of the permanent establishment (so that, if the asset is situated in the UK, the deemed transfer is a no gain/no loss disposal and the deemed disposal by Y is a deemed disposal of a chargeable asset). This treatment is not taken to affect the question of whether the asset or part is situated in the UK.

This provision is intended to facilitate the bringing together of chargeable gains and allowable losses within one group company.

[*TCGA 1992, s 171A; FA 2001, s 77; FA 2003, Sch 33 para 17; F(No 2)A 2005, s 36, Sch 11 Pt 2(7)*].

Simon's Direct Tax Service. See D2.652A.

12.4 **INTRA-GROUP TRANSFERS INVOLVING TRADING STOCK**

Where a company ('company A') acquires an asset as trading stock of a trade from another member of the group ('company B'), and the asset did not form part of the trading stock of a trade carried on by company B, company A is treated for the purposes of *TCGA 1992, s 161* or *Sch 7AC para 36* (see 13.23 CAPITAL GAINS—SUBSTANTIAL SHAREHOLDINGS) as acquiring the asset otherwise than as trading stock and immediately appropriating it as trading stock. The effect is that, subject to an election being made under *section 161(3)*, a chargeable gain or allowable loss accrues to company A based on the difference between market value and the no gain, no loss transfer value (see 12.2 above).

Where a company ('company C') disposes of an asset forming part of the trading stock of a trade to another member of the group ('company D'), and the asset is acquired by company D otherwise than as trading stock of a trade carried on by it, company C is treated for the purposes of *TCGA 1992, s 161* or *Sch 7AC para 36* (see 13.23 CAPITAL GAINS—SUBSTANTIAL SHAREHOLDINGS) as appropriating the asset immediately before the disposal for a purpose other than use as trading stock. The effect is that company C is deemed to have acquired the asset at that time at the amount brought into the accounts of the trade for tax purposes on the deemed appropriation.

Although a non-UK resident company can be a member of a group (see 12.1 above), references above to a trade do not include a trade carried on by a non-UK resident company unless it is carried on in the UK through a permanent establishment (see 60.5 RESIDENCE — previously a branch or agency).

[*TCGA 1992, s 173*].

Acquisition 'as trading stock' implies a commercial justification for the acquisition, see *Coates v Arndale Properties Ltd HL 1984, 59 TC 516, Reed v Nova Securities Ltd HL 1985, 59 TC 516, N Ltd v Inspector of Taxes (Sp C 90), [1996] SSCD 346* and *Property Dealing Company v Inspector of Taxes (Sp C 360), [2003] SSCD 233.*

Simon's Direct Tax Service. See **D2.656**.

12.5 **BUYING GAINS OR LOSSES**

Background. Over the years, governments have introduced three sets of anti-avoidance provisions designed to prevent groups of companies buying and selling companies in order to make use of capital losses suffered by another company or group.

The first set of provisions, introduced in 1993 and described at 12.8–12.21 below, applies to prevent 'loss buying' where a group of companies with unrealised gains would acquire a company with realised or unrealised losses. The assets in question would then be transferred to the new group company at no gain/no loss as in 12.2 above, and the gain would then realised by that company, thus enabling the losses to be utilised against the gain. The provisions operate by restricting the deduction of losses accruing to a company before the time it becomes a member of a group or which accrue on assets held by it at such a time.

These provisions were supplemented in 1998 by provisions, described at 12.22–12.27 below, countering 'gain buying', where a group of companies with unrealised capital losses would acquire a company with a realised gain. The assets in question would then be transferred to the new group company, and the losses then realised by that company in the same accounting period as it realised the gain, thus enabling the losses to be utilised against the gain. Under the 1998 provisions the losses that can be set against a gain realised before a company joins a group are restricted to those that arose before it joined the group and those that arise after it joins the group on assets which that company held at the time of its joining the group.

The last set of provisions was introduced in *FA 2006* as part of a package of anti-avoidance provisions relating to capital losses of companies (see 11.3 and 11.4 CAPITAL GAINS). The provisions restrict the use of losses in both loss buying and gain buying situations where there is a change of ownership of a company as a result of arrangements with a tax avoidance purpose and are described below. The provisions apply in priority to the original loss buying provisions and replace the original gain buying provisions, which are repealed (with effect as indicated at 12.22 below). The provisions are wide in scope and can apply in certain cases where there is no group of companies involved (see (*c*) below).The stated intention of the provisions is to ensure that relief for a company's capital losses should only be available against its own capital gains or those of companies that were under the same economic ownership both when the capital loss was realised and when the loss is used to reduce other gains. (Treasury Explanatory Notes to the Finance Bill 2006). Some companies were using the limited set off allowed under the *FA 2006* provisions to sell a company with a capital gain or loss, along with its subsidiaries, the shares in which were pre-change assets. *FA 2007 s 32* counteracts such arrangements by amending *TCGA 1992* (see 12.6 below).

12.6 **Tax avoidance schemes.** Subject to the commencement provisions below, the provisions described below to restrict loss buying and gain buying apply where:

(A) there is a 'qualifying change of ownership' of a company (the '*relevant company*'); and

(B) the change occurs directly or indirectly in consequence of, or otherwise in connection with, any 'arrangements' the main purpose, or one of the main purposes, of which is to secure a 'tax advantage'.

For this purpose, there is a '*qualifying change of ownership*' of a company if any of the following occur.

(*a*) The company joins a group of companies. Whether a company is a member of a group is determined as in 12.1 above except that nothing in *TCGA 1992, s 170*(*10*) or (*10A*) is treated as preventing all the companies of one group from being regarded as joining another group when the principal company of the first group becomes a member of the other group at any time unless:

(i) the same persons own the 'shares' of the principal company of the first group immediately before that time and the shares of the principal company of the other group immediately after that time;

(ii) the principal company of the other group was not the principal company of any group immediately before that time; and

(iii) immediately after that time the principal company of the other group had assets consisting entirely (or almost entirely) of shares of the principal company of the first group.

References above to '*shares*' of a company are to the shares comprised in the company's issued share capital.

(*b*) The company ceases to be a member of a group.

(*c*) The company becomes subject to different control, i.e. one or more of the following occur:

(i) a person who did not previously have control (within *ICTA 1988, s 416*) of the company (whether alone or together with one or more others) comes to have control;

(ii) a person who previously had control of the company alone comes to have control of the company together with one or more others; or

(iii) a person ceases to have control of the company (whether the person had control alone or together with one or more others).

A company is not, however, treated as becoming subject to different control where it joins a group of companies in circumstances in which (*a*)(i)–(iii) above apply or where, although there is a change in the direct ownership of the company, it continues to be a 75% subsidiary of the same company.

'*Arrangements*' include any agreement, understanding, scheme, transaction or series of transactions, whether or not legally enforceable. '*Tax advantage*' means relief or increased relief from, or repayment or increased repayment of, corporation tax or the avoidance or reduction of a charge or assessment to corporation tax or the avoidance of a possible assessment to corporation tax.

[*TCGA 1992, ss 184A*(*1*)(*4*), *184B*(*1*)(*4*), *184C, 184D, 288*(*1*); *FA 2006, s 70*(*2*)].

For HMRC's views on the application of the terms 'arrangements', 'tax advantage' and 'main purpose', see 11.4 CAPITAL GAINS and HMRC Capital Gains Manual CG 47024–47029. For HMRC's views generally, see HMRC Capital Gains Manual CG 47020–47338.

Loss buying. The loss buying provisions apply where conditions (A) and (B) above are met and the tax advantage under the arrangements involves the deduction from any chargeable gains of a loss (a '*qualifying loss*') accruing to the relevant company on a disposal of a 'pre-change asset' (see below). In these circumstances, the qualifying loss is not deductible from a company's chargeable gains except where the gains arise on the disposal before 21 March 2007 of a pre-change asset. It is immaterial whether the loss accrues before, after or at the time of the qualifying change of ownership, whether the loss accrues at a time when there are no gains from which it could be deducted, whether the tax advantage also involves something other than the deduction of a qualifying loss or whether the advantage would be secured for the company to which the loss accrues or any other company. [*TCGA 1992, s 184A(1)(2)(5); FA 2006, s 70(2); FA 2007, s 32(2),(7)*].

Gain buying. The gain buying provisions apply where conditions (A) and (B) above are met and the tax advantage under the arrangements involves the deduction of a loss from a gain (a '*qualifying gain*') accruing to the relevant company or any other company on a disposal before 21 March 2007 of a pre-change asset. In these circumstances, only a loss arising on a disposal of a pre-change asset can be deducted from a qualifying gain. It is immaterial whether the gain accrues before, after or at the time of the qualifying change of ownership, whether the gain accrues at a time when there are no losses which could be deducted from it, whether the tax advantage also involves something other than the deduction of a loss from a qualifying gain or whether the advantage would be secured for the company to which the gain accrues or any other company. [*TCGA 1992, s 184B(1)(2)(5); FA 2006, s 70(2); FA 2007, s 32(3)(8)*].

For HMRC examples of the operation of the provisions, see HMRC Guidance 'Avoidance through the creation and use of capital losses by companies', 27 July 2006, available on their website (www.hmrc.gov.uk).

Commencement. The above provisions apply for the purpose of determining the chargeable gains to be included in a company's total profits for accounting periods ending on or after 5 December 2005. Transitional rules apply, however, where the change does occur before that date and:

- the change occurs because the relevant company ceases to be a member of a group (whether or not it also occurs for any other reason);
- the principal company of the group continues to have control of the relevant company;
- (for disposals before 21 March 2007) the principal company does not, at or after the time of the change, join another group other than in circumstances in which (*a*)(i)–(iii) above apply;
- for disposals on or after 9 May 2007, there is no qualifying change of ownership of the principal company of the group directly or indirectly in consequence of, or in connection with, any arrangements with a main purpose of securing a tax advantage involving the deduction of a qualifying loss from a chargeable gain; and
- a qualifying loss or, for disposals before 21 March 2007, qualifying gain accrues to the relevant company or any other company on a pre-5 December 2005 disposal.

For disposals on or after 21 March 2007, where the transitional rules apply, the gain buying provisions have effect:

- so that a loss arising on a disposal of a pre-change asset can be deducted from a qualifying gain; and
- as if any asset held before the time of the change of ownership by any company meeting the following conditions were a pre-change asset. The conditions are that the company must have been a member of the relevant company's group immediately before the time of the change of ownership and that the company must, throughout the period beginning with that time and ending immediately after the asset's disposal, have remained under the control of the company which was the principal company of that group at that time.

For disposals before 21 March 2007, the provisions apply to the qualifying loss or gain as if any asset held before the time of the change of ownership by any company which was a member of the relevant company's group immediately before that time were a pre-change asset.

[*FA 2006, s 70(6)–(11); FA 2007, s 32(5),(6),(9)*].

12.7 **Pre-change assets.** For the purposes of the above provisions, a '*pre-change asset*' is an asset held by the relevant company before the qualifying change of ownership occurs.

An asset ceases to be a pre-change asset on disposal by a company other than the relevant company if, after the qualifying change of ownership, it has been disposed of otherwise than by an intra-group no gain/no loss transfer within 12.2 above. If the company making the latter disposal retains an interest in or over the asset, that interest continues to be a pre-change asset.

If the relevant company or any other company holds an asset ('*the new asset*') at or after the time of the qualifying change of ownership, the value of which derives in whole or in part from a pre-change asset, the new asset is also treated as a pre-change asset provided that the company concerned did not acquire the asset as a result of a transfer other than an intra-group no gain/no loss transfer. For this purpose, the cases in which the value of an asset is derived from another asset include any case where assets have been merged or divided or have changed their nature and where rights or interests in or over assets have been created or extinguished.

Where a pre-change asset is the 'old asset' for the purposes of *TCGA 1992, s 116*, (reorganisation of share capital involving qualifying corporate bonds (see Tolley's Capital Gains Tax)) the 'new asset' under that section is also a pre-change asset. Where a pre-change asset is the 'original shares' for the purposes of *TCGA 1992, ss 127–131* (reorganisation of share capital — see Tolley's Capital Gains Tax under Shares and securities), the 'new holding' under those provisions is also a pre-change asset.

Where one of the deferral provisions listed below applies to defer a gain on the disposal of a pre-change asset, so much of any gain or loss accruing on a subsequent occasion as accrues in consequence of the application of the deferral provision is treated as a gain or loss on the disposal of a pre-change asset. The provisions are:

- *TCGA 1992, s 139* (reconstruction involving transfer of business — see 11.9 CAPITAL GAINS);
- *TCGA 1992, s 140* (transfer of assets to non-resident company — see 11.10 CAPITAL GAINS);
- *TCGA 1992, s 140A* (transfer of UK trade between companies in different EC member states — see 11.11 CAPITAL GAINS);
- *TCGA 1992, s 140E* (formation of SE by merger leaving assets within UK tax charge — see 11.13 CAPITAL GAINS);
- *TCGA 1992, ss 152, 153* (rollover relief on the replacement of business assets — see 12.29 below); and
- *TCGA 1992, s 187* (postponement of charge on deemed disposal on company ceasing to be UK resident — see 60.7 RESIDENCE).

If a pre-change asset is transferred by the relevant company to another company directly or indirectly in consequence of, or in connection with the arrangements in (A) above, and any of *TCGA 1992, ss 139, 140A* or *140E* apply to the transfer, the asset is a pre-change asset in the hands of the transferee company. The above provisions for determining when an asset ceases to be a pre-change asset then apply as if the transferee company were the relevant company.

Pooled assets. Special identification rules apply where a pre-change asset (whether held by the relevant company or, as a consequence of an intra-group no gain/no loss transfer, by another company) consists of a 'section 104 holding' or '1982 holding' (see Tolley's Capital Gains Tax under Shares and securities — identification rules) of shares, securities or other assets dealt in without identifying the particular asset disposed of or acquired. Such a holding (a '*pre-change pooled asset*') cannot be added to as a result of any disposal or acquisition taking place after the qualifying change of ownership. Any shares etc. that would otherwise be added to the pre-change pooled asset instead form or are added to a separate section 104 holding (the '*other pooled asset*').

Shares etc. of the same class as those comprised in the other pooled asset which are disposed of at or after the time of the qualifying change of ownership are identified:

- first with shares etc. forming part of the other pooled asset;
- next with shares etc. forming part of the pre-change pooled asset; and
- finally, in accordance with the normal identification rules (see Tolley's Capital Gains Tax under Shares and securities — identification rules).

These identification rules apply even if some or all of the assets disposed of are separately identified by the disposal or by a transfer or delivery giving effect to it. Shares etc. disposed of by a company in one capacity are not identified with shares etc. which are held, or which can only be disposed of, in some other capacity. Shares or securities of a company are not treated as being of the same class unless they are so treated by the practice of a recognised stock exchange or would be if dealt with on such an exchange.

[*TCGA 1992, ss 184A(3), 184B(3), 184E, 184F; FA 2006, s 70(2)*].

12.8 PRE-ENTRY LOSSES—THE 1993 RULES

General outline and commencement. Where the loss buying provisions at 12.6 above do not apply, *TCGA 1992, Sch 7A* restricts losses accruing to a company before the time it becomes a member of a group of companies and losses accruing on assets held by any company at such a time. The restriction is described in detail at 12.9–12.21 below.

The restrictions apply for the calculation of the amount to be included in respect of chargeable gains in a company's total profits for any accounting period ending after 15 March 1993. However, the restrictions apply only in relation to the deduction from chargeable gains accruing after 15 March 1993 of amounts in respect of, or of amounts carried forward in respect of:

(*a*) 'pre-entry losses' accruing, before it became a member of a UK capital gains group, to a company whose membership of that group began or begins after 31 March 1987; and

(*b*) losses accruing on the disposal of any assets so far as it is by reference to such a company that the assets fall to be treated as being or having been 'pre-entry assets' or assets incorporating a part referable to pre-entry assets.

The restriction does not apply where the loss buying provisions at 12.6 above apply.

[*TCGA 1992, s 177A, Sch 7A; FA 1993, s 88, Sch 8; FA 2006, s 70(3)*].

The restriction is widely drawn, and whilst its stated principal intention is to prevent the fiscal effectiveness of an acquisition of a 'capital loss' company (i.e. a company that has a *realised* allowable loss as its only commercial feature) it may also impinge on an acquisition of a company solely for commercial reasons where it becomes a member of a group whilst holding an asset which is later disposed of (whether by the company itself, or by another group member to whom the asset has been transferred) outside the group at a loss. Further restrictions are imposed by *FA 1994, s 94* in relation to the deduction of a loss from a chargeable gain where either the gain or the loss accrues after 10 March 1994. See 12.1 above as regards the definition of a group of companies for the purposes of these provisions.

See HMRC Capital Gains Manual CG 47500 *et seq.*

Simon's Direct Tax Service. See D2.670 *et seq.*

12.9 **Application and construction of TCGA 1992, Sch 7A.** *Schedule 7A* has effect, in the case of a company which is or has been a member of a group of companies (within *TCGA 1992, s 170*, see 12.1 above, and referred to as '*the relevant group*'), in relation to any 'pre-entry losses'. A '*pre-entry loss*', in relation to a company, means any allowable loss that accrued to it at a time before it became a member of the relevant group or the 'pre-entry proportion' (see 12.10–12.13 below) of any allowable loss accruing to it on the disposal of any 'pre-entry asset'. [*TCGA 1992, Sch 7A para 1*(*1*)(*2*)].

A '*pre-entry asset*', in relation to any disposal, means any asset that was held, at the time immediately before the 'relevant event' occurred in relation to it, by any company (whether or not the one which makes the disposal) which is or has at any time been a member of the relevant group.

The '*relevant event*' occurs in relation to a company when it becomes a member of the relevant group provided that either the company is UK resident at that time or the asset is then a 'chargeable asset' in relation to it. If the company is an SE (see 11.13 CAPITAL GAINS) resident in the UK and the asset was transferred to the SE as part of the process of its formation on or after 1 April 2005 by the merger by acquisition of two or more companies in accordance with *Council Regulation* (*EC*) *No 2157/2001, Arts 2*(*1*) and *17*(*2*), the relevant event occurs when the asset becomes a chargeable asset in relation to the SE or, if at the time of the formation of the SE the asset was a chargeable asset in relation to a company which ceased to exist as part of the process of the formation of the SE, when the asset became a chargeable asset in relation to that company. In any other case a relevant event subsequently occurs when the company becomes UK resident or the asset become a chargeable asset in relation to it (whichever is the earlier).

For these purposes, an asset is a '*chargeable asset*' in relation to a company at a particular time if, on a disposal by that company at that time, any gain would be a chargeable gain and would be within the charge to corporation tax by virtue of *TCGA 1992, s 10* or *s 10B* (non-UK resident company trading in the UK through a permanent establishment (previously a branch or agency) — see 11.1 CAPITAL GAINS) or, if the company is an SE formed on or after 1 April 2005, by virtue of the asset having been transferred to the SE on its formation.

[*TCGA 1992, Sch 7A para 1*(*3*)(*3A*)*; FA 2000, Sch 29 para 7*(*2*)(*3*)(*6*)-(*9*)*; FA 2003, Sch 27 para 2*(*3*)*; F*(*No 2*)*A 2005, s 65*(*2*)(*3*)(*6*)].

Subject to 12.11 below, an asset is not, however, a pre-entry asset if the company which held the asset at the time the relevant event occurred in relation to it is not the company which makes the disposal and since that time the asset has been disposed of otherwise than on the no gain, no loss basis of *TCGA 1992, s 171* (see 12.2 above), except where the company making the disposal retains an interest in or over the asset (when the interest is treated as a pre-entry asset). [*TCGA 1992, Sch 7A para 1*(*4*)*; FA 2000, Sch 29 para 7*(*4*)(*6*)-(*8*)].

Subject to 12.11 below, an asset ('*the second asset*'), which derives its value wholly or partly from another asset ('*the first asset*') acquired or held by a company at any time, is treated as the same asset if it is held subsequently by the same company, or by any company which is or has been a member of the same group of companies as that company (e.g. a freehold derived from a leasehold where the lessee acquires the reversion). Where this treatment applies, whether under this provision or otherwise (e.g. under *TCGA 1992, s 43*, for which see Tolley's Capital Gains Tax), the second asset is treated as a pre-entry asset in relation to a company if the first asset would have been. [*TCGA 1992, Sch 7A para 1*(*8*)].

In relation to a pre-entry asset, references in *Schedule 7A* to '*the relevant time*' are references to the time when the relevant event occurred in relation to the company by reference to which that asset is a pre-entry asset. Where a relevant event has occurred in relation to a company more than once, an asset is a pre-entry asset in relation to that company if it would be a pre-entry asset in relation to that company in respect of any of those occasions, but in these circumstances any reference to the time when a relevant event occurred in relation to the company is a reference to the last such occasion. [*TCGA 1992, Sch 7A para 1*(*5*)*; FA 2000, Sch 29 para 7*(*5*)-(*8*)].

Subject to so much of *para 9*(*6*) (see 12.17 below) as requires groups of companies to be treated as separate groups for the purposes of *TCGA 1992, Sch 7A para 9*, if:

(*a*) the principal company of a group (the '*first group*') has at any time become a member of another group (the '*second group*') so that the two groups are treated as the same under *TCGA 1992, s 170*(*10*) or (*10A*) (see 12.1 above); and

(*b*) the second group, together (in pursuance of *TCGA 1992, s 170*(*10*) or (*10A*)) with the first group, is the relevant group,

then except where the circumstances are as in *TCGA 1992, Sch 7A para 1*(*7*) (below), the members of the first group are treated for the purposes of *Schedule 7A* as having become members of the relevant group at that time, and not (by virtue of *TCGA 1992, s 170*(*10*) or (*10A*)) at the times when they became members of the first group. [*TCGA 1992, Sch 7A para 1*(*6*)*; F*(*No 2*)*A 2005, s 65*(*4*)]. See *Limitgood Ltd and another v HMRC SpC 612*.

The circumstances mentioned in *para 1*(*6*) are where:

(1) the persons who immediately before the time when the principal company of the first group became a member of the second group owned the shares comprised in the issued share capital of the principal company of the first group are the same as the persons who, immediately after that time, owned the shares comprised in the issued share capital of the principal company of the relevant group; and

(2) the company which is the principal company of the relevant group immediately after that time:

   (i) was not the principal company of any group immediately before that time; and

   (ii) immediately after that time had assets consisting entirely, or almost entirely, of shares comprised in the issued share capital of the principal company of the first group.

[*TCGA 1992, Sch 7A para 1*(*7*)].

Where an allowable loss accrues to a company under *TCGA 1992, s 116*(*10*)(*b*) (crystallisation of gain or loss on shares exchanged on reorganisation, etc. for qualifying corporate bonds, see Tolley's Capital Gains Tax and 12.15 below), that loss is deemed to accrue at the time of the reorganisation etc. for the purposes of deciding whether a loss accrues before a company becomes a member of the relevant group. [*TCGA 1992, Sch 7A para 1*(*9*)]. Likewise, the annual deemed disposals of unit trust etc. holdings of a life assurance company's long-term insurance fund under *TCGA 1992, s 212* are deemed to occur for this purpose without regard to the 'spreading' provisions of *TCGA 1992, s 213*. [*TCGA 1992, Sch 7A para 1*(*10*)].

12.10 **Pre-entry proportion of losses on pre-entry assets.** Subject to 12.11–12.13 below, the '*pre-entry proportion*' of an allowable loss accruing on the disposal of a pre-entry asset is the allowable loss that would accrue on that disposal if that loss were the sum of the amounts determined, for every item of '*relevant allowable expenditure*' (i.e. expenditure within *TCGA 1992, s 38*(*1*)(*a*) or (*b*)), according to the following formula:

$$A \times \frac{B}{C} \times \frac{D}{E}$$

where

A is the total amount of the allowable loss;

B is the sum of the amount of the item of relevant allowable expenditure concerned and, for disposals before 30 November 1993, the '*indexed rise*' in that item (as in *TCGA 1992, s 54* (see Tolley's Capital Gains Tax) but ignoring the effect of *TCGA 1992, s 110* where the above formula is applied for the purposes of 12.11 below);

C is the sum of the total amount of all such expenditure and, for disposals before 30 November 1993, the indexed rises in each of the items comprised in that expenditure;

D is the length of the period beginning with 'the relevant pre-entry date' and ending with the relevant time or, if that date is after that time, nil (i.e. there is no pre-entry proportion if the relevant time precedes the relevant pre-entry date); and

E is the length of the period beginning with the relevant pre-entry date and ending with the day of disposal.

[*TCGA 1992, Sch 7A para 2(1)(2)(9); FA 1994, s 93(8)(a)*].

'*The relevant pre-entry date*', in relation to any item referred to above, is the later of 1 April 1982 and the date the asset was acquired or provided or, as the case may be, improvement expenditure became due and payable (such date being subject to the assumptions of *TCGA 1992, Sch 7A para 2(4)(5)* (below) and additionally, in relation to the deduction of a loss from a chargeable gain where either the gain or the loss accrues after 10 March 1994, to those of *para 2(6A)(6B)*). [*TCGA 1992, Sch 7A para 2(3); FA 1994, s 94(1)(2)(4)*].

Where any 'original shares' are treated as the same asset as a 'new holding' (within *TCGA 1992, s 127*), the above formula and (where applicable) the provisions in 12.11 below are applied (except, for disposals before 30 November 1993, in relation to the calculation of any indexed rise):

(*a*) as if any item referred to above consisting in consideration given for the acquisition of the new holding had been incurred at the time the original shares were acquired; and

(*b*) where there is more than one such time, as if that item were incurred at those different times in the same proportions as the consideration for the acquisition of the original shares.

[*TCGA 1992, Sch 7A para 2(4); FA 1994, s 93(8)(b)*].

Without prejudice to (*a*) and (*b*) above, the formula is applied to any asset which:

(i) was held by a company at the time when it became a member of the relevant group; and

(ii) is treated as having been acquired by that company on *any* no gain/no loss corresponding disposal,

as if the company and every person who acquired that asset or 'the equivalent asset' at a 'material time' had been the same person and, accordingly, as if the asset had been acquired by the company when it or the equivalent asset was acquired by the first of those persons to have acquired it at a material time, and the time at which any expenditure had been incurred were to be determined accordingly. [*TCGA 1992, Sch 7A para 2(5)*].

A '*material time*' is any time before an acquisition of an asset in circumstances as in (ii) above and is, or is after, the last occasion before the occasion on which any person acquired that asset or the equivalent asset otherwise than on an acquisition which is within (ii) above, or is an acquisition by virtue of which any asset is treated as the equivalent asset; and the formula is applied in relation to any asset within (i) and (ii) above without regard to *TCGA 1992, s 56(2)* (consideration on no gain/no loss disposal deemed to include indexation allowance). [*TCGA 1992, Sch 7A para 2(6)*].

In relation to the deduction of a loss from a chargeable gain where either the gain or the loss accrues after 10 March 1994, and notwithstanding anything in *TCGA 1992, s 56(2)* (see above), where in the case of the disposal of any pre-entry asset any company has, between the relevant time and the time of the disposal, acquired that asset or 'the equivalent asset', and the acquisition was either an acquisition in pursuance of a no gain/no loss disposal under *TCGA 1992, s 171* (see 12.2 above) or an acquisition by virtue of which an asset is treated as 'the equivalent asset', the items of relevant allowable expenditure in the above formula, and the times they are treated as having been incurred, are determined on the assumption that the company by reference to which the asset in question is a pre-entry asset, and the company which acquired the asset or the equivalent asset as above (and every other company which has made such an acquisition), were the same person and, accordingly, that the pre-entry asset had been acquired by the company disposing of it at the time when it or the equivalent asset would have been treated as acquired by the company by reference to which the asset is a pre-entry asset. [*TCGA 1992, Sch 7A para 2(6A)(6B); FA 1994, s 94(1)(2)(4)*].

In relation to the deduction of a loss from a chargeable gain where either the gain or the loss accrues after 10 March 1994, for the purposes of the provisions in *TCGA 1992, Sch 7A para 2(5)(6)(6A)(6B)* (above), '*the equivalent asset*', in relation to another asset acquired or disposed of by any company, is any asset which falls in relation to that company to be treated (whether under *TCGA 1992, Sch 7A para 1(8)* (see 12.9 above) or otherwise) as the same as the other asset or which would fall to be so treated after applying, as respects other assets, the assumptions for which those provisions provide. In relation to the deduction of a loss from a chargeable gain where both the gain and the loss accrue before 11 March 1994, for the purposes of the provisions in *para 2(5)(6)* (above), '*the equivalent asset*', in relation to the acquisition of any asset by any company, is any asset which (whether under *para 1(8)* or otherwise) would be treated in relation to that company as the same as the asset in question. [*TCGA 1992, Sch 7A para 2(7); FA 1994, s 94(1)(2)(4)*].

The above provisions and (where applicable) those in 12.11 below have effect where a loss accrues to a company under *TCGA 1992, s 116(10)(b)* (crystallisation of gain or loss on shares exchanged on reorganisation, etc. for qualifying corporate bonds; see 12.9 above), and the shares are treated under 12.11 below as including pre-entry assets, as if the disposal on which the loss accrues were the disposal of the shares assumed to be made by *section 116(10)(a)* at the time of reorganisation etc. [*TCGA 1992, Sch 7A para 2(8)*].

In relation to disposals on or after 30 November 1993, where, by virtue of *TCGA 1992, s 55(8)*, the allowable loss (or part) accruing on the disposal of a pre-entry asset is attributable to an amount of rolled-up indexation, the total relevant allowable expenditure is treated for the purposes of *TCGA 1992, Sch 7A para 2* as increased by that rolled-up amount, each item of expenditure being treated as increased by the attributable proportion of the total. [*TCGA 1992, Sch 7A para 2(8A); FA 1994, s 93(8)(c)*].

Also in relation to disposals on or after 30 November 1993, where *TCGA 1992, s 56(3)* applies to reduce the total allowable expenditure on the disposal of a pre-entry asset on which an allowable loss accrues, the amount of each item of relevant allowable expenditure is treated for the purposes of *para 2* as reduced by so much of that reduction as is attributable to it. [*TCGA 1992, Sch 7A para 2(8B); FA 1994, s 93(8)(c)*].

12.11 **Disposals of pooled assets.** Subject to 12.12 and 12.13 below, the provisions below apply where any assets acquired by any company fall to be treated with other assets as indistinguishable parts of the same asset ('*a pooled asset*') and the whole or part of that asset is referable to pre-entry assets.

For the purposes of *Schedule 7A*, where a pooled asset has at any time contained a pre-entry asset, the pooled asset is treated, until on the assumptions below all the pre-entry assets included in the asset have been disposed of, as incorporating a part which is referable to pre-entry assets, the size of that part being determined as below. [*TCGA 1992, Sch 7A para 3*(*1*)(*2*)].

Where there is a disposal of any part of a pooled asset and the proportion of the asset which is disposed of does not exceed the proportion of that asset which is represented by any part of it which is not, at the time of disposal, referable to pre-entry assets, that disposal is treated for the purposes of *Schedule 7A* as confined to assets which are not pre-entry assets. Consequently, no part of any loss accruing on that disposal is treated as a pre-entry loss (except where *para 4*(*2*), see 12.12 below, applies), and the part of the pooled asset which after the disposal is treated as referable to pre-entry assets is correspondingly increased (without prejudice to the effect of any subsequent acquisition of assets to be added to the pool in determining whether, and to what extent, any part of the pooled asset is to be treated as referable to pre-entry assets). [*TCGA 1992, Sch 7A para 3*(*3*)(*11*)].

Where such a disposal does give rise to such an excess, the disposal is treated for the purposes of *Schedule 7A* as relating to pre-entry assets only so far as required for the purposes of the excess. Consequently:

(*a*) any loss accruing on that disposal is treated for the purposes of *Schedule 7A* as an allowable loss on a pre-entry asset;

(*b*) the pre-entry proportion of that loss is deemed (except where *para 4*(*3*), see 12.12 below, applies) to be the amount (in so far as it does not exceed the amount of the loss actually accruing) which would have been the pre-entry proportion under 12.10 above of any loss accruing on the disposal of the excess if the excess were a separate asset, and

(*c*) the pooled asset is treated after the disposal as referable entirely to pre-entry assets (without prejudice to the effect of any subsequent acquisition of assets to be added to the pool in determining whether, and to what extent, any part of the pooled asset is to be treated as referable to pre-entry assets).

[*TCGA 1992, Sch 7A para 3*(*4*)(*11*)].

Where there is a disposal of the whole or part of a pooled asset at a time when the asset is referable entirely to pre-entry assets, (*a*) and (*b*) above apply to the disposal of the asset or the part as they apply in relation to the assumed disposal of the excess mentioned in the preamble to (*a*) and (*b*) but, where the whole of an asset only part of which is referable to pre-entry assets is disposed of, the reference in (*b*) above to the excess is taken as a reference to that part. [*TCGA 1992, Sch 7A para 3*(*5*)].

In applying (*b*) above, for the purposes of determining what would have been the pre-entry proportion of any loss accruing on the disposal of any assets as the separate asset mentioned in (*b*) above, it is assumed that none of the assets treated as comprised in that separate asset has ever been comprised in a pooled asset with any assets other than those which are taken to constitute that separate asset. [*TCGA 1992, Sch 7A para 3*(*6*)].

Assets comprised in any asset which is treated as separate are identified on the following assumptions:

(i) that assets are disposed of in the order of the relevant pre-entry dates in relation to the acquisition consideration as under 12.10 above;

(ii) subject to (i), that assets with earlier relevant times are disposed of before those with later ones;

(iii) that disposals made when a company was not a member of the relevant group are made in accordance with *para 3*(*1*)–(*6*) and (i) and (ii) above, as they have effect in relation to the group of companies of which the company was a member at the time of disposal or, as the case may be, of which it had most recently been a member before that time; and

(iv) subject to (i)–(iii) above, that a company disposes of assets in the order in which it acquired them.

[*TCGA 1992, Sch 7A para 3(7)*].

Where there is more than one relevant pre-entry date in relation to the consideration for any acquisition, the date in (i) above is the earlier or earliest of those dates if any such date relating to an option to acquire the asset is disregarded. [*TCGA 1992, Sch 7A para 3(8)*].

Where a second asset falls to be treated as acquired at the same time as a first asset which was acquired earlier (whether under *para 1(8)*, see 12.9 above, or otherwise), and the second asset is either comprised in a pooled asset partly referable to pre-entry assets, or is or includes an asset which is to be treated as so comprised, (i)–(iv) above apply not only in relation to the second asset as if it were the first asset but also, in the first place, for identifying the asset which is to be treated as the first asset under the above provisions. [*TCGA 1992, Sch 7A para 3(10)*].

Where the formula in 12.10 above is applied to an asset treated as above as a separate asset, the amount or value of the asset's acquisition or disposal consideration and any related incidental costs are determined, not under *TCGA 1992, s 129* or s *130*, but by apportioning the consideration or costs relating both to that asset and to other assets acquired or disposed of at the same time according to the proportion that is borne by that asset to all the assets to which the consideration or costs related. [*TCGA 1992, Sch 7A para 3(9)*].

12.12 **'Anti-flooding'.** The rules below to prevent pre-entry losses on pooled assets being treated as post-entry losses (*'anti-flooding'*) apply if:

(*a*) there is a disposal of any part of a pooled asset which under 12.11 above is treated as including a part referable to pre-entry assets;

(*b*) the assets disposed of are or include assets (*'the post-entry element of the disposal'*) which for the purposes of 12.11 above are treated as having been included in the part of the pooled asset which is not referable to pre-entry assets;

(*c*) an allowable loss (*'the actual loss'*) accrues on the disposal; and

(*d*) the amount which in computing the allowable loss is allowed as a deduction of relevant allowable expenditure (*'the expenditure actually allowed'*) exceeds such expenditure attributable to the post-entry element of the disposal.

[*TCGA 1992, Sch 7A para 4(1)*].

Subject to *para 4(6)* below, where the post-entry element of the disposal comprises all of the assets disposed of, the actual loss is treated for the purposes of *Schedule 7A* as a loss accruing on the disposal of a pre-entry asset; and the pre-entry proportion of that loss is treated as being the amount (in so far as it does not exceed the amount of the actual loss) of the excess referred to in (*d*) above. [*TCGA 1992, Sch 7A para 4(2)*].

Also subject to *para 4(6)* below, where the actual loss is treated under 12.11 above as a loss accruing on the disposal of a pre-entry asset, and the expenditure actually allowed exceeds the actual cost of the assets to which the disposal is treated as relating, the pre-entry proportion of the loss is treated as being the amount which (in so far as it does not exceed the amount of the actual loss) is equal to the sum of that excess and what would, apart from these provisions and those in 12.13 below, be the pre-entry proportion of the loss accruing on the disposal.

For this purpose, the actual cost of the assets to which the disposal is treated as relating is taken to be the sum of:

(i) the relevant allowable expenditure attributable to the post-entry element of the disposal; and

(ii) the amount which, in computing the pre-entry proportion of the loss under *para 3(4)(b)* and *para 3(6)*, for which see 12.11 above, would be treated for the purposes of C in the formula in 12.8 above as the total amount allowable as a deduction of relevant allowable expenditure in respect of such of the assets disposed of as are treated as having been incorporated in the part of the pooled asset referable to pre-entry assets.

[*TCGA 1992, Sch 7A para 4(3)(4)*].

Without prejudice to *para 4(6)* below, where *para 4(2)* or *(3)* above applies for the purpose of determining the pre-entry proportion of any loss, no election can be made under 12.13 below for the purpose of enabling a different amount to be taken as the pre-entry proportion of that loss. [*TCGA 1992, Sch 7A para 4(5)*].

Where:

(A) the pre-entry proportion of the loss accruing to any company on the disposal of any part of a pooled asset falls to be determined under *para 4(2)* or *(3)* above;

(B) the amount determined thereunder exceeds the amount determined under *para 4(7)* below ('the alternative pre-entry loss'); and

(C) the company makes an election for the purpose,

the pre-entry proportion of the loss determined as specified in (A) above is reduced to the amount of the alternative pre-entry loss. [*TCGA 1992, Sch 7A para 4(6)*]. For this purpose '*the alternative pre-entry loss*' is whatever, apart from these provisions, would have been the pre-entry proportion of the loss on the disposal in question, if the identification of the assets disposed of for the purposes of *Schedule 7A* were to be made disregarding the part of the pooled asset which was not referable to pre-entry assets, except to the extent (if any) by which the part referable to pre-entry assets fell short of what was disposed of. [*TCGA 1992, Sch 7A para 4(7)*].

An election for the purposes of (C) above with respect to any loss must be made by the company incurring the loss by notice to the inspector given within the period of two years beginning with the end of the accounting period of that company in which the disposal giving rise to the loss is made, or within such longer period as HMRC may by notice allow. The provisions in 12.13 below may be taken into account under *para 4(7)* in determining the amount of the alternative pre-entry loss as if an election had been made under 12.13, but only if the election under (C) above contains an election corresponding to the election that, apart from this provision, might have been made under 12.13 below. [*TCGA 1992, Sch 7A para 4(8)*].

For the purposes of the above, the relevant allowable expenditure attributable to the post-entry element of the disposal is the amount which, in computing any allowable loss accruing on a disposal of that element as a separate asset, would have been allowed as a deduction of relevant allowable expenditure if none of the assets comprised in that element had ever been comprised in a pooled asset with any assets other than those which are taken to constitute that separate asset for the purposes of this provision. [*TCGA 1992, Sch 7A para 4(9)*]. To identify the assets which are to be treated for this purpose as comprised in the post-entry element of the disposal, a company is taken to dispose of assets in the order in which it acquired them. [*TCGA 1992, Sch 7A para 4(10)*].

TCGA 1992, Sch 7A para 3(9), for which see 12.11 above, is applied as suitably modified for the purposes of *para 4(9)* above, as is *para 3(10)*, for which see 12.11 above, for the purposes of this provision in relation to *para 4(10)* above. [*TCGA 1992, Sch 7A para 4(11)*].

In the above provisions, references to an amount allowed as a deduction of relevant allowable expenditure are references to the amount falling to be so allowed in accordance with *TCGA 1992, 38(1)(a)* and *(b)* and (so far as applicable) *s 42*, together (for disposals before 30 November 1993) with the indexed rises in the items comprised in that expenditure or, as the case may be, in the appropriate portions of those items. Nothing in the above provisions affects the operation of the rules contained in 12.11 above for determining, for any purposes other than those of *para 4(7)* above, how much of any pooled asset at any time consists of a part which is referable to pre-entry assets. [*TCGA 1992, Sch 7A para 4(12)–(14); FA 1994, s 93(9)*].

12.13 **Alternative calculation by reference to market value.** Subject to *TCGA 1992, Sch 7A para 4(5)*, see 12.12 above, and the following provisions, if an otherwise allowable loss accrues on the disposal by any company of any pre-entry asset, and that company makes an election accordingly, the pre-entry proportion of that loss (instead of being the amount determined under the preceding provisions of *Schedule 7A*) is to be whichever is the smaller of:

(*a*) the amount of any loss which would have accrued if that asset had been disposed of at the relevant time at its market value at that time; and

(*b*) the amount of the otherwise allowable loss accruing on the actual disposal of that asset.

[*TCGA 1992, Sch 7A para 5(1)(2)*].

In relation to disposals on or after 30 November 1993, in determining the amount of any notional loss under (*a*) above, it is assumed that the prohibition on indexation allowance enhancing an allowable loss under *FA 1994, s 93* has effect for disposals on or after the day on which the relevant time falls. [*TCGA 1992, Sch 7A para 5(2A); FA 1994, s 93(10)*].

Where no loss would have accrued on the deemed disposal assumed in (*a*) above, the loss accruing on the disposal mentioned in (*b*) above is deemed not to have a pre-entry proportion. [*TCGA 1992, Sch 7A para 5(3)*]. The election mentioned above must be made by the company incurring the loss by notice to the inspector given within the period of two years beginning with the end of its accounting period in which the disposal giving rise to the loss is made, or within such longer period as HMRC may by notice allow. [*TCGA 1992, Sch 7A para 5(8)*].

The provisions in *para 5(5)* below apply where an election is made in relation to any loss accruing on the disposal ('*the real disposal*') of the whole or any part of a pooled asset, and the case is one in which (but for the election) the provisions in 12.11 above would apply for determining the pre-entry proportion of a loss accruing on the real disposal. [*TCGA 1992, Sch 7A para 5(4)*]. In these circumstances, these provisions have effect as if the amount specified in (*a*) above were to be calculated:

(i) on the basis that the disposal which is assumed to have taken place was a disposal of all the assets falling within (*aa*)–(*cc*) below; and

(ii) by apportioning any loss that would have accrued on that disposal between:

  (A) such of the assets falling within (*aa*)–(*cc*) below as are assets to which the real disposal is treated as relating; and

  (B) the remainder of the assets so falling,

  according to the proportions of any pooled asset whose disposal is assumed which would have been, respectively, represented by assets mentioned in (A) above and by assets mentioned in (B) above.

Where assets falling within (*aa*)–(*cc*) below have different relevant times there is assumed to have been a different disposal at each of those times. [*TCGA 1992, Sch 7A para 5(5)*].

Assets fall to be included within (A) and (B) above if:

(*aa*) immediately before the time which is the relevant time in relation to those assets, they were comprised in a pooled asset which consisted of or included assets which fall to be treated for the purposes of 12.11 above as:

(i) comprised in the part of the pooled asset referable to pre-entry assets; and

(ii) disposed of on the real disposal;

(*bb*) they were also comprised in such a pooled asset immediately after that time; and

(*cc*) the pooled asset in which they were so comprised immediately after that time was held by a member of the relevant group.

[*TCGA 1992, Sch 7A para 5*(*6*)].

Where:

(AA) an election is made under *para 4*(*6*), see 12.12 above, requiring the determination by reference to these provisions of the alternative pre-entry loss accruing on the disposal of any assets comprised in a pooled asset; and

(BB) under that election any amount of the loss that would have accrued on an assumed disposal is apportioned in accordance with (i) and (ii) above to assets ('*the relevant assets*') which:

(I) are treated for the purposes of that determination as assets to which the disposal related; but

(II) otherwise continue after the disposal to be treated as incorporated in the part of that pooled asset which is referable to pre-entry assets,

then, on any further application of these provisions for the purpose of determining the pre-entry proportion of the loss accruing on a subsequent disposal of assets comprised in that pooled asset, that amount (without being apportioned elsewhere) is deducted from so much of the loss accruing on the same assumed disposal as, apart from the deduction, would be apportioned to the relevant assets on that further application of these provisions. [*TCGA 1992, Sch 7A para 5*(*7*)].

12.14 **Restrictions on the deduction of pre-entry losses.** In the calculation of the amount to be included in respect of chargeable gains in any company's total profits for any accounting period:

(*a*) if in that period there is any chargeable gain from which the whole or any part of any pre-entry loss accruing in that period is deductible in accordance with the provisions in 12.15 below, the loss or, as the case may be, that part of it is deducted from that gain;

(*b*) if, after all the deductions in (*a*) above have been made, there is in that period any chargeable gain from which the whole or any part of any pre-entry loss carried forward from a previous accounting period is deductible in accordance with the provisions in 12.15 below, the loss or, as the case may be, that part of it is deducted from that gain;

(*c*) the total chargeable gains (if any) remaining after all the deductions in (*a*) or (*b*) above is subject to deductions in accordance with *TCGA 1992, s 8*(*1*) (chargeable gains less allowable losses of company to be included in chargeable profits) in respect of any allowable losses that are not pre-entry losses; and

(*d*) any pre-entry loss which has not been the subject of a deduction under (*a*) or (*b*) above (as well as any other losses falling to be carried forward under *section 8*(*1*)) are carried forward to the following accounting period of that company.

[*TCGA 1992, Sch 7A para 6*(*1*)].

Subject to (*a*)–(*d*) above, any question as to which or what part of any pre-entry loss has been deducted from any particular chargeable gain is decided:

(i) where it falls to be decided in respect of the setting of losses against gains in any accounting period ending before 16 March 1993 as if:

   (A) pre-entry losses accruing in any such period had been set against chargeable gains before any other allowable losses accruing in that period were set against those gains;

   (B) pre-entry losses carried forward to any such period had been set against chargeable gains before any other allowable losses carried forward to that period were set against those gains; and

   (C) subject to (A) and (B) above, the pre-entry losses carried forward to any accounting period ending after 15 March 1993 were identified with such losses as may be determined in accordance with such elections as may be made by the company to which they accrued;

   and

(ii) in any other case, in accordance with such elections as may be made by the company to which the loss accrued,

and any question as to which or what part of any pre-entry loss has been carried forward from one accounting period to another shall be decided accordingly. [*TCGA 1992, Sch 7A para 6*(*2*)].

An election under (i)(C) above must be made by the company by notice to the inspector within two years of the end of its accounting period which was current on 16 March 1993. An election under (ii) above must similarly be made within two years of the end of the company's accounting period in which the gain in question accrued. [*TCGA 1992, Sch 7A para 6*(*3*)].

For the purposes of *Schedule 7A*, where any matter falls to be determined under these provisions by reference to an election, but no election is made, it shall be assumed, so far as consistent with any elections that have been made, that losses are set against gains in the order in which the losses accrued; and that the gains against which they are set are also determined according to the order in which they accrued with losses being set against earlier gains before they are set against later ones. [*TCGA 1992, Sch 7A para 6*(*4*)].

12.15 **Gains from which pre-entry losses are to be deductible.** A pre-entry loss that accrued to a company before it became a member of the relevant group is deductible from a chargeable gain accruing to that company if the gain is one accruing:

(*a*) on a disposal made by that company before the date on which it became a member of the relevant group ('*the entry date*');

(*b*) on the disposal of an asset which was held by that company immediately before the entry date; or

(*c*) on the disposal of any asset which:

   (i) was acquired by that company on or after the entry date from a person who was not a member of the relevant group at the time of the acquisition; and

   (ii) since its acquisition from that person has not been used or held for any purposes other than those of a trade which was being carried on by that company at the time immediately before the entry date and which continued to be carried on by that company until the disposal.

[*TCGA 1992, Sch 7A para 7*(*1*)].

The pre-entry proportion of an allowable loss accruing to any company on the disposal of a pre-entry asset is deductible from a chargeable gain accruing to that company if:

(A) the gain is one accruing on a disposal made, before the date on which it became a member of the relevant group, by that company and that company is the one (*'the initial company'*) by reference to which the asset on the disposal of which the loss accrues is a pre-entry asset;

(B) the pre-entry asset and the asset on the disposal of which the gain accrues were each held by the same company at a time immediately before it became a member of the relevant group; or

(C) the gain is one accruing on the disposal of an asset which:

  (i) was acquired by the initial company (whether before or after it became a member of the relevant group) from a person who, at the time of the acquisition, was not a member of that group; and

  (ii) since its acquisition from that person has not been used or held for any purposes other than those of a trade which was being carried on, immediately before it became a member of the relevant group, by the initial company and which continued to be carried on by the initial company until the disposal.

[*TCGA 1992, Sch 7A para 7*(*2*)].

Where two or more companies become members of the relevant group at the same time and those companies were all members of the same group of companies immediately before they became members of the relevant group, then, without prejudice to the provisions in 12.17 below:

(*aa*) an asset is treated for the purposes of (*b*) above as held, immediately before it became a member of the relevant group, by the company to which the pre-entry loss in question accrued if that company is one of those companies and the asset was in fact so held by another of those companies;

(*bb*) two or more assets are treated for the purposes of (B) above as assets held by the same company immediately before it became a member of the relevant group wherever they would be so treated if all those companies were treated as a single company; and

(*cc*) the acquisition of an asset is treated for the purposes of (*c*) and (C) above as an acquisition by the company to which the pre-entry loss in question accrued if that company is one of those companies and the asset was in fact acquired (whether before or after they became members of the relevant group) by another of those companies.

[*TCGA 1992, Sch 7A para 7*(*3*)].

TCGA 1992, Sch 7A para 1(*4*) (see 12.9 above) is applied as suitably modified for determining, for the purposes of the above provisions, whether an asset on the disposal of which a chargeable gain accrues was held at the time when a company became a member of the relevant group. [*TCGA 1992, Sch 7A para 7*(*4*)].

Subject to *para 7*(*6*) (below), where a gain accrues on a disposal of the whole or any part of:

(1) any asset treated as a single asset but comprising assets only some of which were held at the time mentioned in (*b*) or (B) above; or

(2) an asset which is treated as held at that time by virtue of a provision requiring an asset which was not held at that time to be treated as the same as an asset which was so held (see 12.9 above),

a pre-entry loss is deductible under (*b*) or (B) above from the amount of that gain to the extent only of such proportion of that gain as is attributable to assets held at that time or, as the case may be, represents the gain that would have accrued on the asset so held. [*TCGA 1992, Sch 7A para 7*(*5*)].

Where:

(AA) a chargeable gain accrues under *TCGA 1992, s 116*(*10*) on the disposal of a qualifying corporate bond which has been exchanged for shares etc. (see Tolley's Capital Gains Tax under Qualifying Corporate Bonds and 12.9 above);

(BB) that bond was not held as required by (*b*) or (B) above at the time mentioned respectively in (*b*) or (B); and

(CC) the whole or any part of the asset which is the 'old asset' for the purposes of *TCGA 1992, s 116* was so held,

the question as to whether that gain is one accruing on the disposal of an asset the whole or any part of which was held by a particular company at that time is determined for the purposes of *para 7* as if the bond were deemed to have been so held to the same extent as the old asset. [*TCGA 1992, Sch 7A para 7*(*6*)].

12.16 **Change of a company's nature.** If:

(*a*) within any period of three years, a company becomes a member of a group of companies and there is (either earlier or later in that period, or at the same time) a major change in the nature or conduct of a trade carried on by that company; or

(*b*) at any time after the scale of the activities in a trade carried on by a company has become small or negligible, and before any considerable revival of the trade, that company becomes a member of a group of companies,

the trade carried on before that change, or which has become small or negligible, is disregarded for the purposes of 12.15(*c*) and (C) above in relation to any time before the company became a member of the group in question.

A '*major change in the conduct of a trade*' includes a reference to a major change in services or facilities provided in the trade or a major change in customers of the trade or a change in the nature of investments held. Regard will also be had to appropriate changes in other factors such as the location of the company's business premises, the identity of the company's suppliers, management or staff, the company's methods of manufacture, or the company's pricing or purchasing policies to the extent that these factors indicate that a major change has occurred. Efficiency changes and technological advancements would not in themselves indicate that a major change in the nature or conduct of a trade has occurred. HMRC will compare any two points in three years which include the date of change of ownership of the company. This applies even if the change is the result of a gradual process which began outside the period of three years mentioned in (*a*) above. They take note of both qualitative and quantitative issues, as discussed in the cases of *Willis v Peeters Picture Frames Ltd CA(NI) 1982, 56 TC 436* and *Purchase v Tesco Stores Ltd Ch D 1984, 58 TC 46* respectively. (HMRC Statement of Practice, SP 10/91). See also 47.13 LOSSES.

Where the operation of the above provisions depends on circumstances or events at a time after the company becomes a member of any group of companies (but not more than three years after), an assessment to give effect to the provisions may be made within six years from that time or the latest such time. [*TCGA 1992, Sch 7A para 8*].

The above provisions are similar to those in *ICTA 1988, s 768* regarding the disallowance of trading losses on a change in ownership of a company. See 47.13 LOSSES for coverage of these provisions.

12.17 **Identification of the 'relevant group'.** The provisions below apply where there is more than one group of companies which would be the relevant group in relation to any company.

Where any loss has accrued on the disposal by any company of any asset, *Schedule 7A* does not apply by reference to any group of companies in relation to any loss accruing on that disposal unless:

(*a*) that group is a group in relation to which that loss is a pre-entry loss because it is an allowable loss that accrued to that company at a time before it became a member of the group or, if there is more than one such group, the one of which that company most recently became a member;

(*b*) that group, in a case where there is no group falling within (*a*) above, is either:

 (i) the group of which that company is a member at the time of the disposal; or

 (ii) if it is not a member of a group of companies at that time, the group of which that company was last a member before that time;

(*c*) that group, in a case where there is a group falling within (*a*) above or, in relation to the deduction of a loss from a chargeable gain where either the gain or the loss accrues after 10 March 1994, (*b*) above, is a group of which that company was a member at any time in the accounting period of that company in which it became a member of the group falling within (*a*);

(*d*) that group is a group the principal company (see 12.1 above) of which is or has been, or has been under the control (within *ICTA 1988, s 416*) of:

 (i) the company by which the disposal is made; or

 (ii) another company which is or has been a member of a group by reference to which *Schedule 7A* applies in relation to the loss in question under (*a*), (*b*) or (*c*) above; or

(*e*) that group is a group of which either:

 (i) the principal company of a group by reference to which *Schedule 7A* applies; or

 (ii) a company which has had that principal company under its control,

is or has been a member.

In the case of a loss accruing on the disposal of any asset where, under (*a*)–(*e*) above, there are two or more groups ('*connected groups*') by reference to which *Schedule 7A* applies, the further provisions in *para 9(3)*–*(5)* below apply. [*TCGA 1992, Sch 7A para 9(1)(2); FA 1994, s 94(1)(3)(4)*].

Schedule 7A is applied separately in relation to each of the connected groups (so far as they are not groups in relation to which the loss is a pre-entry loss because it is a loss that accrued to a company at a time before it became a member of the group) for the purpose of determining whether the loss on the disposal of any asset is a loss on the disposal of a pre-entry asset, and calculating the pre-entry proportion of that loss. [*TCGA 1992, Sch 7A para 9(3)*].

Subject to *para 9(5)* below, the provisions in 12.14 above have effect:

(A) as if the pre-entry proportion of any loss accruing on the disposal of an asset which is a pre-entry asset in the case of more than one of the connected groups were the largest pre-entry proportion of that loss as calculated under *para 9(3)* above; and

(B) so that, where the loss accruing on the disposal of any asset is a pre-entry loss because it is an allowable loss that accrued to a company at a time before it became a member of a group in the case of any of the connected groups, the pre-entry loss for the purposes of 12.14 above is that loss, and not any amount which is the pre-entry proportion of that loss in relation to any of the other groups.

[*TCGA 1992, Sch 7A para 9(4)*].

Where, on the separate application of *Schedule 7A* in the case of each of the groups by reference to which *Schedule 7A* applies, there is, in the case of the disposal of any asset, a pre-entry loss by reference to each of two or more of the connected groups, no amount in respect of the loss accruing on the disposal is to be deductible under 12.15 above from any chargeable gain if any of the connected groups is a group in the case of which, on separate applications of the provisions in 12.15 above in relation to each group, the amount deductible from that gain in respect of that loss is nil. [*TCGA 1992, Sch 7A para 9(5)*].

Notwithstanding that the principal company of one group ('*the first group*') has become a member of another ('*the second group*'), those two groups are not treated for the purposes of the above provisions as the same group by virtue of *TCGA 1992, s 170(10)* or *(10A)* (see 12.1 above) if the principal company of the first group was under the control, immediately before it became a member of the second group, of a company which at that time was already a member of the second group. In addition, in relation to accounting periods ending after 16 March 1998, again where the principal company of the first group has become a member of the second group, the two groups are not for those purposes treated, in relation to any company that is (or has become) a member of the second group, as the same group if the time at which that company became a member of the first group falls in the same accounting period as that in which the principal company of the first group became a member of the second group. [*TCGA 1992, Sch 7A para 9(6); FA 1998, s 138; F(No 2)A 2005, s 65(5)*]. For an example, see HMRC Capital Gains Manual, CG 47944.

Where, in the case of the disposal of any asset:

(*aa*) two or more groups which but for *para 9(6)* above would be treated as the same group are treated as separate groups because of the treatment therein; and

(*bb*) one of those groups is a group of which either:

(i) the principle company of a group by reference to which *Schedule 7A* applies by virtue of (*a*), (*b*) or (*c*) above in relation to any loss accruing on the disposal; or

(ii) a company which has had that principal company under its control,

is or has been a member,

the above provisions have effect as if that principal company had been a member of each of the groups mentioned in (*aa*) above.

[*TCGA 1992, Sch 7A para 9(7)*].

12.18 **Appropriations to stock in trade.** Where, but for an election under *TCGA 1992, s 161(3)*, there would be deemed to have been a disposal at any time by any company of any asset, the amount by which the market value of the asset may be treated as increased in pursuance of that election does not include the amount of any pre-entry loss that would have accrued on that disposal; and *Schedule 7A* has effect as if the pre-entry loss of the last mentioned amount had accrued to that company at that time. [*TCGA 1992, Sch 7A para 10*].

12.19 **Continuity provisions.** The provisions below apply where provision has been made by or under any enactment ('*the transfer legislation*') for the transfer of property, rights and liabilities to any person from:

(*a*) a body established by or under any enactment (as defined) for the purpose, in the exercise or statutory functions (as defined), of carrying on any undertaking or industrial or other activity in the public sector or of exercising any other statutory functions;

(*b*) a subsidiary of such a body; or

(*c*) a company wholly owned by the Crown (as defined).

A loss is not a pre-entry loss for the purposes of *Schedule 7A* in relation to any company to whom a transfer has been made by or under the transfer legislation if that loss:

(i) accrued to the person from whom the transfer has been made; and

(ii) falls to be treated, in accordance with any enactment made in relation to transfers by or under that legislation, as a loss accruing to that company.

For the purposes of *Schedule 7A*, where a company became a member of the relevant group by virtue of the transfer by or under the transfer legislation of any shares in or other securities of that company or any other company;

(A) a loss that accrued to that company before it so became a member of that group is not a pre-entry loss in relation to that group; and

(B) no asset held by that company when it so became a member of that group shall by virtue of that fact be a pre-entry asset.

[*TCGA 1992, Sch 7A para 11*].

12.20 **Companies changing groups on certain transfers of shares.** For the purposes of *Schedule 7A*, and without prejudice to the provisions in 12.19 above, where:

(*a*) a company which is a member of a group of companies becomes at any time a member of another group of companies as the result of a disposal of shares in or other securities of that company or any other company; and

(*b*) that disposal is one of the no gain/no loss disposals mentioned in *TCGA 1992, s 35(3)(d)* (assets held on 31 March 1982, see Tolley's Capital Gains Tax),

Schedule 7A has effect in relation to the losses that accrued to that company before that time and the assets held by that company at that time as if any time when it was a member of the first group were included in the period during which it is treated as having been a member of the second group.

[*TCGA 1992, Sch 7A para 12*].

12.21 *Example*

C Ltd has a 100% subsidiary, D Ltd. D Ltd acquired a 100% subsidiary, E Ltd, on 1 April 2002 and a 75% subsidiary, F Ltd, on 1 April 2004. All the companies prepare their accounts to 31 March. The following information is relevant (neither E Ltd nor F Ltd having realised any gains or losses except as stated).

(i) At 1 April 2002, E Ltd had unrelieved capital losses of £120,000 and its assets included a freehold property which it had acquired on 1 July 1998 for £700,000 and on which it had incurred enhancement expenditure of £100,000 on 1 October 1999. The property was valued at £700,000 at 1 April 2002. During the year ended 31 March 2006, E Ltd realised chargeable gains of £30,000 on assets held at 1 April 2002 and it also realised an allowable loss of £10,000 on an asset purchased on 31 May 2002. On 1 October 2006, the company sold the above-mentioned freehold property for £550,000.

(ii) F Ltd had no capital losses brought forward at 1 April 2004. At that date, it held 100,000 ordinary shares in XYZ plc, a quoted company. It had acquired 60,000 of these on 1 May

1998 for £100,000 and 40,000 on 1 June 2002 for £70,000. The shares had an indexed pool value of £186,790 at 1 April 2004, and their market value at that date was £110,000. On 1 November 2004, F Ltd acquired a further 50,000 XYZ ordinary shares for £30,000 and on 31 August 2006 it sold 120,000 such shares for £60,000.

F Ltd also made two disposals other than of XYZ shares during the year to 31 March 2007, realising chargeable gains on each. The first disposal, on which the gain was £55,000, was of an asset acquired by transfer from C Ltd (at no gain/no loss by virtue of *TCGA 1992, s 171*). The second, on which the gain was £35,000, was acquired from outside the group in December 2004 and used since that time in F Ltd's trade, which has continued unchanged since 31 March 2004.

The provisions restricting set-off of pre-entry losses have the following effects.

(i) E Ltd

For the year to 31.3.07, E Ltd can elect (before 1 April 20098) for the whole of the £30,000 gain to be regarded as covered by pre-entry losses. The £100,000 losses carried forward at 31.3.06 then comprise pre-entry losses of £90,000 and other losses of £10,000. In the absence of an election, losses are set against gains on a first in/first out basis for these purposes, so the same result would accrue in this case. See 12.14 above.

The £90,000 pre-entry losses are carried forward and may be set only against gains on other assets held by E Ltd immediately before 1.4.02 or gains on assets acquired by it on or after that date from outside the group and not used or held for any purposes other than those of the trade carried on by E Ltd immediately before that date and which continued to be carried on by it up to the date of disposal. See 12.15 above.

The overall loss on the disposal of the freehold property is as follows.

	£	£
Proceeds (1.10.06)		550,000
Cost (1.7.98)	700,000	
Enhancement expenditure (1.10.99)	100,000	800,000
Allowable loss		£250,000

The pre-entry proportion of the allowable loss is calculated as follows.

	£
$£250,000 \times \dfrac{700,000}{800,000} \times \dfrac{3y\ 9m\ (1.7.98-1.4.02)}{8y\ 3m\ (1.7.98-1.10.06)} =$	99,432
$£250,000 \times \dfrac{100,000}{800,000} \times \dfrac{2y\ 6m\ (1.10.99-1.4.02)}{7y\ 0m\ (1.10.99-1.10.06)} =$	11,161
Pre-entry proportion	£110,593
Balance of allowable loss	£139,407

See 12.10 above.

E Ltd may elect (before 1 April 2009) to use an alternative method of computing the pre-entry proportion of the allowable loss, as follows.

	£	£
Market value (1.4.01)		700,000
Cost (1.7.98)	700,000	
Enhancement expenditure (1.10.99)	100,000	800,000
Pre-entry proportion of allowable loss		£100,000
Balance of allowable loss (£250,000 – £100,000)		£150,000

See 12.13 above.

The whole of the loss of £250,000 is available for carry-forward but the pre-entry proportion of the allowable loss (£100,000 on the assumption that the election referred to above is made) can be set only against the same types of gain against which the pre-entry losses of £90,000 can be set (see above).

(*ii*) *F Ltd*

Allowable loss on XYZ plc ordinary shares

	Number of shares	Qualifying expenditure £	Indexed pool £
Acquisition 1.5.98	60,000	100,000	
Acquisition 1.6.02	40,000	70,000	
At 1.4.04	100,000	170,000	187,380
Indexed rise to 1.11.04: £187,380 × 0.018			3,373
Acquisition 1.11.04	50,000	30,000	30,000
	150,000	200,000	220,753
Indexed rise to 31.8.06: £220,753 × say 0.070			15,453
			236,206
Disposal 31.8.06	(120,000)	(160,000)	(188,965)
Pool carried forward	30,000	£40,000	£47,241

	£
Proceeds 31.8.06	60,000
Cost	160,000
Allowable loss	£100,000

Indexation allowance would be £28,965 (£188,965 – £160,000), but indexation allowance cannot increase an allowable loss.

Pre-entry proportion of allowable loss

Stage 1 (*see* 12.11 *above*)

The proportion of the pool disposed of (120,000 shares) exceeds the proportion *not* referable to pre-entry assets (50,000 shares). The excess of 70,000 shares is regarded as a separate asset made up as follows.

		Cost
		£
60,000 shares acquired 1.5.98		100,000
10,000 shares acquired 1.6.02	(£70,000 × ¼)	17,500
		£117,500

	£
Proceeds of 70,000 shares £60,000 × 7/12	35,000
Cost as above	117,500
Notional allowable loss on pre-entry assets	£82,500

The pre-entry proportion of the allowable loss is calculated as follows.

£

$$£82,500 \times \frac{100,000}{117,500} \times \frac{5y\ 11m\ (1.5.98 - 1.4.04)}{8y\ 4m\ (1.5.98 - 31.8.06)} = 49,851$$

$$£82,500 \times \frac{17,500}{117,500} \times \frac{1y\ 10m\ (1.6.02 - 1.4.04)}{4y\ 3m\ (1.6.02 - 31.8.06)} = 5,300$$

	£
Pre-entry proportion of allowable loss (subject to below)	£55,151

Stage 2 (*see* 12.12 *above*)

		£
The amount deductible in computing the allowable loss is	(I)	150,000
The amount deductible which is attributable to the post-entry element of the disposal (50,000 shares acquired on 1.11.04) is	(II)	30,000

As (I) exceeds (II), an adjustment is required to the figure calculated at *Stage 1* above, as follows.

	£	£
Expenditure actually allowed		160,000
Deduct Actual cost of assets disposed of:		
pre-entry element (see *Stage 1* above)	117,500	
post-entry element (see (II) above)	30,000	147,500
Excess		£12,500

The excess is added to the pre-entry proportion as calculated at *Stage 1* above. The pre-entry proportion of the allowable loss is thus

£55,151 + £12,500 = £67,651

(Because an adjustment is required under *Stage 2*, the election for the alternative method (see 12.13 above) is *not* available. If the election *had been* available, the calculation would have been as follows.

	£
Market value of 100,000 shares held at 1.4.04	110,000
Unindexed pool value at 1.4.04	170,000
Notional loss on 100,000 shares	£60,000

As only 70,000 of the 100,000 shares held at 1.4.04 are regarded as included in the disposal on 31.8.06 (see *Stage 1* above), the pre-entry proportion of the allowable loss would have been £60,000 × 7/10 = £42,000.)

Stage 3 (*see* 12.12 *above*)

As the adjustment at *Stage 2* applies, F Ltd may elect (before 1 April 2009) that the pre-entry proportion of the loss calculated at *Stage 2* (£67,651) be reduced to the amount of the 'alternative pre-entry loss', if lower. In calculating the alternative pre-entry loss, *Stage 1* is recomputed as if the disposal was primarily of pre-entry assets, as follows.

	Cost £
60,000 shares acquired 1.5.98	100,000
40,000 shares acquired 1.6.02	70,000
	£170,000

	£
Proceeds of 100,000 shares £60,000 × 10/12	50,000
Cost as above	170,000
Notional allowable loss on pre-entry assets	£120,000

The pre-entry proportion of the allowable loss is calculated as follows.

		£
$£120,000 \times \frac{100,000}{170,000} \times \frac{5y\ 11m\ (1.5.98 - 1.4.04)}{8y\ 4m\ (1.5.98 - 31.8.06)}$	=	50,118
$£120,000 \times \frac{70,000}{170,000} \times \frac{1y\ 10m\ (1.6.02 - 1.4.04)}{4y\ 3m\ (1.6.02 - 31.8.06)}$	=	21,315
Alternative pre-entry loss (subject to below)		£71,433

The alternative loss is higher than the pre-entry proportion of the allowable loss calculated at *Stage 2* (£67,651), so, subject to *Stage 4* (below), the election would not be made.

Stage 4 (*see* 12.12, 12.13 *above*)

In making an election under *Stage 3*, F Ltd may specify that the alternative method (see 12.13 above) be used, as follows.

	£
Market value of 100,000 shares held at 1.4.04	110,000
Unindexed pool value at 1.4.04	170,000
Notional loss on 100,000 shares	£60,000

As all the 100,000 shares held at 1.4.04 are regarded as included in the disposal on 31.8.06 (see *Stage 3*), the alternative pre-entry loss is £60,000. It is therefore beneficial for F Ltd to make the election mentioned at *Stage 3*, imputing an election as under 12.13 above.

The pre-entry proportion of the allowable loss is then reduced from £67,651 (*Stage 2*) to	£60,000
Balance of allowable loss is £100,000 – £60,000 =	£40,000

Utilisation of losses (*see* 12.14, 12.15 *above*)

The pre-entry loss may be set against the gain of £35,000. It may not be set against the gain of £55,000. The balance of the allowable loss can be set against the gain of £55,000. F Ltd's chargeable gains for the year ended 31.3.07 are therefore as follows.

	£	£
Total gains		90,000
Deduct Pre-entry losses	35,000	
Other allowable losses	40,000	75,000
Chargeable gains		£15,000
Losses carried forward (all pre-entry losses) £(60,000 – 35,000)		£25,000

12.22 **PRE-ENTRY GAINS—THE 1998 RULES**

The provisions of *TCGA 1992, s 177B, Sch 7AA* (added by *FA 1998, s 137, Sch 24*), as described at 12.23–12.27 below, were introduced to prevent 'gain buying'. The provisions are **repealed** with effect from the time that the provisions at 12.6 above, which prevent gain buying where there is a tax avoidance motive, take effect.

Under those provisions, the losses that a company (the '*relevant company*') may set against capital gains which arose before it joined a group of companies, or before it was transferred from one group to another are restricted. The only losses which are allowed against such earlier gains are those arising in the company before it joined the new group and those arising after that time on assets it held when it entered the new group. The provisions have effect in relation to accounting periods ending after 16 March 1998 where a company joins a group after that date and cease to have effect from the time that the provisions at 12.6 above take effect (see 12.6 above under Commencement). [*TCGA 1992, s 177B, Sch 7AA; FA 1998, s 137, Sch 24; FA 2006, s 70(4)(6)–(11), Sch 26 Pt 3(10)*].

Whilst the stated intention of these provisions is to prevent tax avoidance by groups of companies using 'gain buying' in order to set losses against gains which have arisen on assets held in different economic ownership, they may also impinge on an acquisition of a company solely for commercial reasons where it becomes a group member whilst holding an asset which is later disposed of (whether by the company itself or by another group member to whom the asset has been transferred) outside the group at a gain.

Insurance companies. A chargeable gain or allowable loss treated as accruing at the end of an accounting period under *TCGA 1992, s 213(1)c*) or *s 214A(2)(b)* is for these purposes treated as having accrued before the time (or the earliest time) at which the relevant company joined a group of companies. [*TCGA 1992, Sch 7AA para 7; FA 1998, s 137, Sch 24*].

Simon's Direct Tax Service. See D2.685 *et seq.*

12.23 **Company joining a group of companies.** For the purposes of *Schedule 7AA*, a company joins a group of companies when, at any time on or after 17 March 1998, it becomes a member of any group of which it was not a member immediately before becoming a member. When the 'principal company' (see 12.1 above) of one group becomes a member of another group, all the other members of the first group are for these purposes treated as joining the other group. [*TCGA 1992, Sch 7AA para 1(3)(4); FA 1998, s 137, Sch 24*]. See 12.1 above as regards determining for the purposes of these provisions whether a company is a member of a group. [*FA 2000, Sch 29 para 8*].

12.24 **Pre-entry gains.** A '*pre-entry gain*' is a chargeable gain accruing to a relevant company in an accounting period (the '*gain period*') in which the company joins a group of companies but after the gain has accrued to it. The chargeable gains to be included in the relevant company's total profits for that period (notwithstanding anything in *TCGA 1992, Sch 7A* (pre-entry losses, see 12.8 *et seq.* above)) are the sum of the 'adjusted amounts' of the pre-entry gains of the period and other net chargeable gains (disregarding certain losses applied in reducing pre-entry gains, see below).

The '*adjusted amount*' of a pre-entry gain for a gain period is the amount of that gain after deducting 'qualifying losses' of the period (so far as not set against other pre-entry gains), but excluding 'pre-entry losses' unless deductible from the gain under *TCGA 1992, Sch 7A para 7* (see 12.15 above) and certain losses on disposals to CONNECTED PERSONS (19). Losses so set against pre-entry gains are not available for carry-forward.

The following are '*qualifying losses*' of a period:

(*a*) a loss brought forward to that period;

(*b*) a loss of the gain period which accrued before or at the same time as the pre-entry gain;

(*c*) a loss of the gain period which accrued after the pre-entry gain but before the relevant company joined any group; and

(*d*) a loss of the gain period which accrued after the pre-entry gain and at the same time as or after the relevant company joined any group provided that immediately before the time when it joined the group the asset on which the loss arose was held either by the company itself or by another company which was a member of the same group and which joined the new group at the same time.

As regards (*d*) above, see 12.25, 12.26 below in relation to certain assets acquired at different times but treated as the same asset.

[*TCGA 1992, Sch 7AA paras 1(2), 2-4; FA 1998, s 137, Sch 24*].

12.25 **Pooled assets.** Where an allowable loss arises on a disposal of 'securities' (as widely defined) which are pooled for capital gains purposes, special rules apply to determine the extent to which the securities were held at a time when the relevant company (or a member of its group) joined a new group (the '*entry time*') (see 12.24 above). The rules apply in respect of any such disposal made in the gain period and at or after the '*relevant entry time*' (i.e. the entry time or, if there is more than one such time in the gain period, the earliest entry time).

Actual losses on the disposals referred to above are matched with the 'notional net pre-entry loss' in the order in which the actual losses accrued. The actual aggregate loss is regarded as a loss on disposal of securities held at the entry time to the extent that there is (or, in the case of a second or subsequent entry time, that there remains) an amount with which it can be so matched.

For the purposes of determining the '*notional net pre-entry loss*', securities acquired at or after the relevant entry time ('*post-entry securities*') are not added to the pool existing immediately before the relevant entry time, which thus continues to consist only of securities acquired (and not disposed of) before that time ('*pre-entry securities*'). Disposals within these provisions (see above) are matched with the pool of pre-entry securities in preference to post-entry securities. Gains and losses on those disposals matched with pre-entry securities are computed and aggregated. If the net result of that aggregation is a loss, the amount of that loss is the notional net pre-entry loss. If the net result is a gain, there is no notional net pre-entry loss. For an example, see HMRC Capital Gains Manual, CG 48214.

For the purposes of determining whether securities are pre-entry or post-entry securities, *TCGA 1992, s 127* (reorganisation of share capital) is to be disregarded in as much as it would treat a new holding as having been acquired at the same time as an original holding.

There are provisions to ensure that securities held by the relevant company or by any 'associated company' at the relevant entry time are taken to be pre-entry securities if, since the relevant entry time but prior to the disposal in question, they have been disposed of by way of intra-group disposal. An '*associated company*' is one which was a member of the same group as the relevant company immediately before the relevant entry time and which joined the new group, along with the relevant company, at that time.

[*TCGA 1992, Sch 7AA para 5; FA 1998, s 137, Sch 24*].

12.26 **Assets acquired at different times.** Special rules apply to the following.

(*a*) An asset which is treated as a single asset but comprises assets only some of which were held at the 'entry time' (see 12.25 above) by the relevant company or an 'associated company' (see 12.25 above).

(*b*) An asset which is treated as held at the entry time by the relevant company (or by another company which was a member of the same group immediately before the entry time and which joined the new group at the same time) by virtue of any provision which treats an asset not held at that time as one which was so held.

An apportionment is necessary if an asset within (*a*) or (*b*) above (other than a pooled asset as in 12.25 above) is disposed of (or part disposed of) by the relevant company (at a loss) in the gain period (see 12.23 above) and at or after the entry time.

The proportion of the allowable loss treated as relating to a pre-entry asset (which is thus a qualifying loss, see 12.24 above) is made up of:

(i) the proportion of the loss which, on a just and reasonable apportionment, is properly attributable to assets in fact held at the entry time; and

(ii) such proportion of the loss not within (i) above as represents the loss that would have accrued if the asset disposed of had been the asset in fact held at that time.

[*TCGA 1992, Sch 7AA para 6; FA 1998, s 137, Sch 24*].

12.27 *Example*

G Ltd has a 100% subsidiary, H Ltd. On 1 May 2005, G Ltd acquired from A Ltd all the shares in its two wholly-owned subsidiaries, B Ltd and C Ltd. Before that date, on 1 March 2005, C Ltd had sold an asset realising a gain of £120,000. All companies make up accounts to the year ending 31 December.

On 1 June 2005, B Ltd transferred machinery to C Ltd for its net book value of £150,000, and, on the same date, H Ltd transferred a freehold property and a leasehold property to C Ltd for their net book values of £400,000 and £350,000 respectively. All these assets were transferred intra-group under *TCGA 1992, s 171*, so that neither a chargeable gain nor an allowable loss arises.

On 10 June 2005 C Ltd sold the freehold property realising a loss of £95,000.

On 12 July 2005 C Ltd sold the leasehold property realising a gain of £75,000.

On 1 September 2005 C Ltd sold the machinery realising a loss of £65,000.

The provisions restricting set-off the losses against pre-entry gains have the following effects.

Only qualifying losses may be set against pre-entry gains. The loss on the disposal of the machinery of £65,000 is a qualifying loss because the asset on which it is incurred was owned at the entry date by a company in the same group (the A Ltd group) as C Ltd. The loss of £95,000 is not a qualifying loss as it does not satisfy any of the conditions for a qualifying loss:

(*a*) it is not a pre-entry loss brought forward by C Ltd;

(*b*) it is not a pre-entry loss accruing to C Ltd in the gain period prior to the entry date of 1 May 2005 (either before, at the same time or after the gain accrued); and (*c*) it is not a loss occurring after 1 May 2005 but on an asset held by C Ltd or B Ltd at the entry date.

The adjusted amount of the pre-entry gain is as follows.

Pre-entry gain £120,000 less qualifying loss £65,000 = £55,000

The chargeable gain to be included in C Ltd's profits is calculated as follows.

	£	£	£
Adjusted pre-entry gains			55,000
Total gains (£120,000 + £75,000)		195,000	
Less: pre-entry gain		(120,000)	
		75,000	
Total losses (£95,000 + £65,000)	160,000		
Less: loss allowed in adjusted pre-entry gain	(65,000)	(95,000)	nil
Chargeable gain			£55,000
Loss carried forward		£20,000	

Without the pre-entry gains provisions, the net gain assessable would have been £35,000 (£195,000 – £160,000) with no losses to carry forward.

12.28 DISPOSAL OR ACQUISITION OUTSIDE A GROUP

(*a*) Where there is a disposal of an asset acquired in circumstances in which *TCGA 1992, s 140A* (see 11.11 CAPITAL GAINS) applied or *TCGA 1992, s 171* applied, or would have applied but for certain exceptions (see 12.2 above and the exceptions at 12.2 (ii)–(iv)(vi)–(x)), allowable losses are restricted by reference to capital allowances (see *TCGA 1992, s 41* and Tolley's Capital Gains Tax under Disposal) in relation to capital allowances made to the person from whom it was acquired (so far as not taken into account in relation to a disposal by that person) and so on as respects previous such acquisitions. This does not affect the 'no gain, no loss' consideration for which the asset is deemed under the above-mentioned provisions to have been acquired. [*TCGA 1992, ss 41(8), 174(1)-(3); FA 2000, Sch 29 para 12*].

Where a company which is or has been a group member disposes of an asset which it acquired from another group member as a result of a no gain, no loss disposal within *TCGA 1992, s 171(1)* (see 12.2 above), the provisions relating to the valuation of assets held on 6 April 1965 apply as if all group members were one person (see Tolley's Capital Gains Tax under Assets held on 6 April 1965). As regards acquisitions before 1 April 2000, this provision was dependent on the asset having been acquired at a time when both parties to the transaction were members of a group, regardless of whether or not the transfer was within 12.2 above, except that it did not apply if the transfer was within 12.2(vi) (transfer by or to an investment trust). See 12.1 above) with regard to determining whether a company is a member of a group for these purposes. [*TCGA 1992, s 174(4)(5); FA 2000, Sch 29 para 13*].

See **Simon's Direct Tax Service** D2.657.

(*b*) Where a company disposes of an asset acquired after 5 April 1988 from a fellow group member, and the no gain/no loss provisions of *TCGA 1992, s 171* (see 12.2 above) applied on the acquisition, an election under *TCGA 1992, s 35(5)* (see 12.30 below and Tolley's Capital Gains Tax under Assets held at 31 March 1982) by the transferee company does not apply on the subsequent disposal, but such an election made by the transferor company applies on that subsequent disposal whether or not the transferee company has made such an election. Where, however, the acquisition by the transferor company was also within *section 171* and took place after 5 April 1988, an election by the transferor company does not have effect on the ultimate disposal, but an election made by the last company by which the asset was acquired after 5 April 1988 otherwise than within *section 171* (or, if there is no such company, by the company which held the asset on 5 April 1988) does have effect on the ultimate disposal. [*TCGA 1992, Sch 3 para 2*].

See Simon's Direct Tax Service D2.660.

12.29 **ROLLOVER RELIEF**

Rollover relief on the *replacement of business assets* is granted under *TCGA 1992, ss 152–158* (see Tolley's Capital Gains Tax under Rollover Relief) and in relation to groups:

(i) all the trades carried on by group members are treated as a single trade (except as regards intra-group transfers);

(ii) *TCGA 1992, s 154* (special rules for depreciating assets) applies as if all group members were the same person.

A disposal by a company when it is a member of a group, and an acquisition by another company when it is a member of the same group, are treated as made by the same person. Claims to relief must be made by both companies concerned. It is not necessary for the companies making the disposal and acquisition to be members of the group throughout the period between the transactions, as long as each is a member at the time of its own transaction.

Where a non-trading group member disposes of or acquires assets used only for the trades within (i) above, relief is given as if it were carrying on a trade.

The relief is not available in respect of consideration applied in the acquisition of new assets by a 'dual resident investing company' (see 32.27 GROUPS OF COMPANIES). See also 11.23 CAPITAL GAINS as regards other dual resident companies.

Relief is also denied where the acquisition of the new asset is one to which any of the no gain/no loss provisions in *TCGA 1992, s 35(3)(d)* (see Tolley's Capital Gains Tax under Assets held on 31 March 1982) applies.

In determining whether a company is a member of a group for the these purposes with regard to either the acquisition or the disposal (or both) , see 12.1 above. However, the reference above to 'trade' does not include a trade carried on by a non-UK resident company otherwise than through a permanent establishment in the UK (see 60.5 RESIDENCE — for accounting periods beginning before 1 January 2003, a branch or agency). Where either the acquisition or the disposal (but not both) was before 1 April 2000, this applies also to that acquisition or disposal.

Where the disposal or the acquisition, or both, occur on or after 1 April 2000 and are made by different group companies,

(i) either the company making the disposal must be UK resident at the time of the disposal or the assets must be 'chargeable assets' (see 12.2 above) in relation to that company immediately before that time; and

(ii) either the company making the acquisition must be UK resident at the time of the acquisition or the assets must be chargeable assets in relation to that company immediately after that time.

Compulsory acquisitions of land. For the purposes of the rollover relief under *TCGA 1992, s 247* (see Tolley's Capital Gains Tax under Land), a disposal by a company when it is a member of a group, and an acquisition by another company when it is a member of the same group, are treated as made by the same person, provided that relief is claimed by both companies. Relief is, however, denied where the acquisition of the new land is one to which any of the no gain/no loss provisions in *TCGA 1992, s 35(3)(d)* (see Tolley's Capital Gains Tax under Assets held on 31 March 1982) applies.

[*TCGA 1992, ss 175, 247(5A); FA 1995, s 48(1)(3)(4); FA 2000, Sch 29 para 10; FA 2003, Sch 27 para 2(3)*].

Where (i) above applies in a case where one member of a group makes the disposal and a second the acquisition, it may happen that the disposal takes place after the first company has ceased to trade, or the acquisition takes place before the second company commences trading. Relief will then be restricted in respect of the period during which the assets disposed of were not used for business purposes, and will be conditional on the replacement assets not being used or leased for any purpose prior to the second company's commencing trading, and being taken into use for the purposes of the trade on its commencement. (HMRC Statement of Practice, SP 8/81).

For the *interaction of rollover relief with the exemption for substantial shareholdings*, see 13.24 CAPITAL GAINS—SUBSTANTIAL SHAREHOLDINGS. For the *transitory interaction with relief on reinvestment in fixed intangible assets*, see *FA 2002, Sch 29 para 132* (as amended by *F(No 2)A 2005, s 41(4)(1)*).

Simon's Direct Tax Service. See **D2.658**.

12.30 ASSETS HELD ON 31 MARCH 1982

See Tolley's Capital Gains Tax under Assets held on 31 March 1982 for details of these provisions generally, and in particular for the election under *TCGA 1992, s 35(5)* for all disposals by a person after 5 April 1988 of assets held on 31 March 1982 to be subject to the general re-basing rule of *TCGA 1992, s 35(1)(2)*. This election is subject to the following special provisions in relation to groups of companies.

Election by principal company. No group member other than the 'principal company' of a group (for which see *TCGA 1992, s 170* as in 12.1 above) may make an election under *TCGA 1992, s 35(5)* unless the company did not become a group member until after the 'relevant time'. An election by the principal company does, however, have effect as an election by any other company which is a group member at the 'relevant time', except that this does not apply to a company which, in some period after 5 April 1988 and before the 'relevant time', makes a disposal, at a time when it is not a group member, of an asset held on 31 March 1982, and does not itself make the election within the prescribed time limit. The time limit for the making of the election by the principal company is two years (or such longer time as HMRC may allow) from the end of the accounting period in which occurs the first disposal after 5 April 1988 of an asset held on 31 March 1982 by a company which is a group member (other than an 'outgoing company' in relation to the group) or which is an 'incoming company' in relation to the group. See, however, HMRC Statement of Practice, SP 4/92 as regards certain disposals which are ignored for this purpose. See HMRC Capital Gains Manual, CG 46374 for the circumstances in which a late election may be accepted.

An election by the principal company of a group continues to apply to a company leaving the group after the 'relevant time', unless it is an 'outgoing company' in relation to the group and the principal company election is made after it ceases to be a group member.

The '*relevant time*' is the earliest of:

(i) the first time when a group member (other than an 'outgoing company' in relation to the group) makes a disposal after 5 April 1988 of an asset held on 31 March 1982;

(ii) the time immediately after the first occasion on which an 'incoming company' in relation to the group becomes a group member; and

(iii) the time when the principal company makes the election.

An '*outgoing company*', in relation to a group, is a company which ceases to be a group member before the end of the period during which an election could be made which would apply to it, and at a time when no such election has been made.

An '*incoming company*', in relation to a group, is a company which makes its first disposal after 5 April 1988 of an asset held on 31 March 1982 at a time when it is not a group member, and which becomes a group member before the expiry of the time limit for making an election which would apply to it without that election having been made.

In relation to a determination as to whether a company is a member, or the principal member, of a group, see 12.1 above.

[*TCGA 1992, s 35*(*5*), *Sch 3 paras 8, 9; FA 2000, Sch 29 para 38*].

Valuation. Companies and groups with sufficiently large property portfolios may ask HMRC to agree a professional 31 March 1982 valuation of the portfolio (or a clearly distinguishable part thereof meeting the minimum size requirement). See Revenue Tax Bulletins December 2000 pp 813, 814, April 2001 p 838, February 2002 pp 917–919, October 2003 pp 1064–1065.

Simon's Direct Tax Service. See **D2.660.**

12.31 COLLECTION OF UNPAID TAX FROM GROUP MEMBERS AND DIRECTORS

Where a chargeable gain accrues to a company (the 'taxpayer company') and either:

(i) that company is UK resident at the time the gain accrues; or

(ii) the gain is within the charge to corporation tax by virtue of *TCGA 1992, s 10*(*3*) or *s 10B* (non-UK resident company trading in the UK through a permanent establishment or branch or agency, see 60.5, 60.6 RESIDENCE),

the following rules apply where all or part of the corporation tax assessed on the taxpayer company for the accounting period in which the gain accrues remains unpaid six months after it became payable.

HMRC may serve on any of the following persons a notice requiring that person to pay, within 30 days, the unpaid tax or, if less, an amount equal to corporation tax on the chargeable gain at the rate in force when the gain accrued:

(*a*) if the taxpayer company was a member of a 'group' at the time when the gain accrued, the 'principal company' of the 'group' at that time and any other company which was, at any time in the twelve months before the gain accrued, a member of the same 'group' and owned the asset disposed of, or any part of it, or where that asset is an interest or right in or over another asset, owned either asset or any part of either asset;

(*b*) if the gain forms part of the chargeable profits of the taxpayer company for corporation tax purposes by virtue of *TCGA 1992, s 10*(*3*) (see (ii) above), any person who is, or during the twelve months before the gain accrued was, a 'controlling director' of the taxpayer company or of a company which has, or within that twelve-month period had, 'control' over the taxpayer company.

For the purpose of (*a*) above, '*group*' and '*principal company*' are as defined as in 12.1 above but as if references there to 75 per cent subsidiaries were to 51 per cent subsidiaries. In determining whether a company is a member of a group at any time in the twelve-month period referred to in (*a*) and (*b*) above, see 12.1 above. As regards (*b*) above, '*control*' is as under *ICTA 1988, s 416* (see 16.2 CLOSE COMPANIES), and a '*controlling director*' is a 'director' (within the extended meaning under the employment income benefits legislation and *ICTA 1988, s 417*(*5*)(*6*)) with such control.

The notice must state the amount of tax assessed, the original due date and the amount required from the person on whom it is served. It has effect, as regards collection, interest and appeals, as if it were a notice of assessment on that person. The notice must be served within three years beginning with the date on which the liability of the taxpayer company for the accounting period in question was finally determined (including a determination under *FA 1998, Sch 18 para 36* or *37* in the absence of a full return, see 61.18 RETURNS). In the case of a self-assessed liability, including one superseding a determination, the date of determination of the liability is taken as the last date on which notice of an enquiry into the return may be given (see 61.10 RETURNS), or, if such notice is given, 30 days after the action which concludes the enquiry process. In the case of a discovery assessment (see 7.2 ASSESSMENTS), it is the due and payable date or (if there is an appeal against the assessment) the date the appeal is finally determined.

A person paying an amount under these provisions may recover it from the taxpayer company, but such an amount is not deductible for any tax purpose.

[*TCGA 1992, s 190; FA 2000, Sch 29 para 9; FA 2003, Sch 27 para 2(3)*].

See also 60.5, 60.6 RESIDENCE as regards tax unpaid by non-resident companies.

Simon's Direct Tax Service. See **D2.659.**

12.32 DEGROUPING CHARGE

Where a company ceasing to be a member of a group owns a capital asset which has been transferred to it by another group member within the preceding six years, that company is treated as if, immediately after its acquisition of the asset, it had sold, and immediately reacquired, the asset at its then market value. There will thus be a liability on the market value less the sum of the 'no gain, no loss' transfer price and any indexation allowance due under 12.2 above or, conversely, an allowable loss. Any chargeable gain or allowable loss arising is treated as accruing immediately after the beginning of the company's accounting period in which (or at the end of which) the company ceases to be a member of the group, or (if later) the time when the company actually acquires the asset from a fellow group member. See 12.34–12.36 below for certain relieving provisions.

The companies involved in the asset transfer do not both have to be members of the group at the time of transfer for this degrouping charge to apply. It is sufficient that the transferee company leaves the group of which the transferor company was a member at the time of transfer, though in practice a charge can only arise if the transfer was other than at market value and in particular if it was at no gain/no loss. (HMRC Capital Gains Manual CG 45411).

In relation to assets acquired by intra-group transfer on or after 1 April 2000, the degrouping charge can apply only if the asset is within the charge to UK corporation tax both before and after the transfer, the precise conditions being similar to those for intra-group transfers at 12.2 above. Where the transfer occurred before 1 April 2000 and the degrouping charge would otherwise arise on or after that date, there can be no such charge where the transferee company leaves the group whilst remaining in a wider worldwide group of which it became a member by virtue of the relaxationin the residence rules from 1 April 2000 (see 12.1 above). The fact that the company may not be an effective 51% subsidiary of the principal company of the worldwide group does not prevent it being a member of that group *for so long as* it remains an effective 51% subsidiary of the company which, prior to the change in the residence requirement, was the principal company of the narrower group. See for example HMRC Capital Gains Manual, CG 45406, CG 45407.

[*TCGA 1992, s 179(1)(1A)(3)(4); FA 2000, Sch 29 para 4(2)(6), para 47; FA 2001, s 79; FA 2002, Sch 8 para 2; FA 2003, Sch 27 para 2(3)*].

The time limit for electing for 6 April 1965 value (normally two years from the end of the accounting period in which the disposal took place) is concessionally extended. (HMRC Statement of Practice, D21).

These provisions do not apply if, before the chargeable company leaves the group (or leaves a second group, see below), it has already been deemed to have sold and reacquired the asset in question at the time mentioned above by virtue of its having since become an investment trust or a venture capital trust (see, respectively, 12.37 and 12.38 below). [*TCGA 1992, s 179(2C)(2D); FA 1998, s 133(2)(3), s 135(3)(5)*].

ICTA 1988, ss 403A, 403B (limits on group relief by reference to overlapping periods, see 32.12 GROUPS OF COMPANIES) have effect subject to the above. [*TCGA 1992, s 179(4)*].

The provisions also apply to a company leaving a group which acquired an asset as described above where it or an 'associated company' also leaving the group at the same time owns (otherwise than as trading stock):

(i) the asset; or

(ii) property to which a gain on the disposal of the original asset has been carried forward under rollover relief; or

(iii) an asset the value of which is wholly or partly derived from the original asset.

[*TCGA 1992, s 179(3)(10)(b)(c)*].

The provisions do not apply in relation to transfers of assets between associated companies leaving the group at the same time. [*TCGA 1992, s 179(2)*]. This does not exclude cases where the association ceases at the time the companies leave the group (*Dunlop International AG v Pardoe CA 1999, 72 TC 71*). Where, however, the company which acquired the asset subsequently leaves another group which has a 'connection' with the first, the provisions apply as if it was the second group of which both companies were members at the time of the acquisition. There is a '*connection*' between the two groups if, when the company leaves the second group, the 'principal company' (see 12.1 above) of that group is under the 'control' of the principal company of the first group (or, if the first group no longer exists, of the principal company at the time the company left the first group), or of certain other companies exercising higher levels of 'control' or where common control of the two groups is exercised by any person or persons (which includes natural persons as well as companies). '*Control*' in this context is as under *ICTA 1988, s 416* (see 16.2 CLOSE COMPANIES) but disregarding control by banks deriving from loan capital or debt issued or incurred in the normal course of the banking business. [*TCGA 1992, s 179(2A)(2B)(9A); FA 2000, Sch 29 para 4(3)(4)(6)*].

The above provisions also do not apply where a company ceases to be a member of a group in consequence of another group member ceasing to exist. [*TCGA 1992, s 179(1); F(No 2)A 1992, s 25*]. HMRC take the view that this 'liquidation let out' only applies to the case of a parent company ceasing to be a member of a group on the occasion of its only subsidiary ceasing to exist on dissolution (or all its subsidiaries ceasing to exist simultaneously on dissolution). (HMRC Capital Gains Manual, CG 45441–45445).

In relation to events at any time, HMRC has confirmed it does not apply the deemed sale and reacquisition where the company receiving the asset ceases to be a group member as a result of its only subsidiary leaving the group except where the parent company emigrated before 1 April 2000, thereby causing the group to break up. (HMRC Capital Gains Manual, CG 45450).

Where, as part of a process of merger to form an SE in circumstances in which *TCGA 1992, s 140E* applies (formation of SE by merger: assets left within UK tax charge — see 11.13 CAPITAL GAINS), a company which is a member of a group ceases to exist and as a consequence assets, or shares in one or more companies which were also members of the group, are transferred to the SE, the company which has ceased to exist and any company whose shares have been transferred to the SE are, for the purposes of these provisions, not treated as having left the group. The SE and the company which ceased to exist are treated as the same entity and, if the SE is itself a member of a group on its formation, any company which was a member of the first group and became a member of the SE's group as a result of the SE's formation is treated as if the two groups were the same. [*TCGA 1992, s 179(1B)(1C); F(No 2)A 2005, s 64(4)*].

If:

(*a*) a company ceases to be a member of a group only through the principal company becoming a member of another group (e.g. see 12.1 above); and

(*b*) under the provisions described above, it would be treated as selling an asset at any time,

the following provisions apply.

(A) The company in question is not treated as selling the asset at that time.

(B) If:

(i) within six years of that time the company in question ceases at any time ('*the relevant time*') to satisfy the following conditions, namely that it is:

(*aa*) a 75 per cent subsidiary of one or more members of the other group mentioned in (*a*) above; and

(*bb*) an 'effective 51 per cent subsidiary' (as defined in 12.1 above) of one or more of those members; and

(ii) at the relevant time the company in question or a company in the same group, owns (otherwise than as trading stock) the asset, or property to which a chargeable gain has been rolled over from the asset,

the company in question is treated as if, immediately after acquiring the asset, it had sold and reacquired it at its market value at the time of acquisition.

(C) Any gain or loss on the deemed sale is treated as arising at the relevant time.

[*TCGA 1992, s 179(5)–(8)*].

Companies are '*associated*' if they would form a group by themselves. [*TCGA 1992, s 179(10)(a)*].

If, under any of the foregoing provisions, a deemed sale arises, and on an actual sale at market value at that time any loss or gain would, under the value shifting provisions of *TCGA 1992, s 30* (see 11.17 CAPITAL GAINS), have been calculated as if the consideration were increased by an amount, the market value at the time of the deemed sale is treated as having been greater by that amount. [*TCGA 1992, s 179(9)*].

In relation to gains accruing before 1 April 2000, if the tax is not paid within six months of a specified date, then, within two years of that date, it may be assessed on (*a*) the principal company of the group or (*b*) a company which owned the asset on that date or when the chargeable company left the group. There is then a right of recovery of the tax and of any interest thereon under *TMA 1970, s 87A* (see 41.1 INTEREST ON UNPAID TAX) from the chargeable company. The date specified as above is the date the tax became payable by the company or, if later, the date the assessment was made on the chargeable company. For gains accruing on or after 1 April 2000, see the general recovery provisions at 12.31 above. [*TCGA 1992, s 179(11)(12); FA 2000, Sch 29 para 4(5)(7)*].

Certain mergers are exempt from this provision if the merger was carried out for '*bona fide* commercial reasons' and that the avoidance of liability to tax was not a main purpose of the merger. [*TCGA 1992, s 181; FA 2000, Sch 29 para 28*].

See 9.6 BUILDING SOCIETIES as regards application of these provisions where a building society's business is transferred to a company.

Simon's Direct Tax Service. See **D2.661, D2.662**.

12.33 *Example*

A Ltd had the following transactions.

1.3.80	Purchased a freehold property £100,000.
31.3.82	Market value £250,000.
1.12.00	Sold the freehold to B Ltd (a wholly-owned subsidiary) for £250,000 (market value £620,000).
31.7.06	Sold its interest in B Ltd (at which time B Ltd continued to own the freehold property).

Both companies prepare accounts to 30 April.

Relevant values of the RPI are: March 1982: 79.44, December 2000: 172.2.

(i) A Ltd's disposal of the property to B Ltd is to be treated as one on which, after taking account of the indexation allowance, neither gain nor loss arises.

Indexation factor:

$$\frac{172.2 - 79.44}{79.44} = 1.168$$

	£
Cost to A Ltd	100,000
Indexation allowance £250,000 × 1.168 (see note (*a*))	292,000
Deemed cost to B Ltd	£392,000

(ii) Following the sale of A Ltd's shares in B Ltd on 31.7.06 (i.e. within six years after the transaction in (i) above), B Ltd will have a deemed disposal as follows.

Deemed disposal on 1.12.00

	£	£	£
Market value at 1.12.00		620,000	620,000
Cost (as above)	392,000		
Less indexation to date	292,000		
		100,000	
Market value at 31.3.82			250,000
Unindexed gain		520,000	370,000
Indexation allowance	£250,000 × 1.168		
		292,000	292,000
Indexed gain		£228,000	£78,000
Chargeable gain subject to CT			£78,000
B Ltd's new base cost for future gains			£620,000

Although the deemed disposal occurs on 1 December 2000, i.e. immediately after B Ltd's acquisition, the gain is treated as accruing on 1 May 2006, i.e. the beginning of the accounting period in which B Ltd left the group, being later than the date of the deemed disposal. The gain thus forms part of B Ltd's profits for the year ended 30 April 2007.

Notes

(*a*) The indexation allowance on the no gain/no loss transfer is calculated by reference to the market value at 31 March 1982 as this is higher than the original cost. [*TCGA 1992, s 55*(*1*)(*2*)].

(*b*) For re-basing purposes, B Ltd is deemed to have held the asset at 31 March 1982. [*TCGA 1992, Sch 3 para 1*]. *TCGA 1992, s 55*(*5*)(*6*) apply in the computation of B Ltd's chargeable gain.

12.34 **Transfer of degrouping charge to another company in the group.** Where, **after 31 March 2002**, a company (company A) ceases to be a member of a group such that the provisions of *TCGA 1992, s 179* in 12.32 above apply, the company may jointly elect with another company (company C) for the resultant gain or loss to be treated as accruing to company C instead of company A. Where the degrouping charge arises under *TCGA 1992, s 179*(*5*)–(*8*), the election is available only where the 'relevant time' (see 12.32(B)(i) above) falls after 31 March 2002.

Except where the degrouping charge arises under *TCGA 1992, s 179*(*5*)–(*8*), the two parties to the election must be members of the same group at the 'time of accrual': for this purpose the '*time of accrual*' is the time at which the gain or loss is treated as accruing and not, if earlier, the time at which the deemed sale and reacquisition in 12.32 above is treated as occurring. Where the charge arises under *TCGA 1992, s 179*(*5*)–(*8*), company C must be a member of the second group referred to at 12.32(*a*) above at the 'time of accrual': for this purpose the '*time of accrual*' is the latest time at which company A satisfies the conditions at 12.32(B)(i) above.

In either case, the following further conditions must all be met at the relevant time of accrual.

(*a*) Company C must either be UK-resident or own assets that are chargeable assets in relation to it. For this purpose, an asset is a chargeable asset in relation to a company at a particular time if, on a disposal by that company at that time, any gain would be a chargeable gain and would be within the charge to corporation tax by virtue of *TCGA 1992, s 10*(*3*) or *s 10B* (non-UK resident company trading in the UK through a permanent establishment or branch or agency — see 60.5, 60.6 RESIDENCE).

(*b*) Company C cannot be an investment trust (within *ICTA 1988, s 842* see 44.1 INVESTMENT TRUSTS), a venture capital trust (within *ICTA 1988, s 842AA*, see 69.2 VENTURE CAPITAL TRUSTS) or a dual resident investing company (within *ICTA 1988, s 404*, see 32.28 GROUPS OF COMPANIES).

(*c*) Neither company A nor company C can be a qualifying friendly society (as at 12.2(viii) above).

On the making of a joint election by company A and company C, the chargeable gain or allowable loss on the deemed sale under *TCGA 1992, s 179*, or such part of that gain or loss as is specified in the election, is treated as accruing not to company A but to company C. The election must be made by notice in writing to HMRC within two years after the end of the accounting period of company A in which the time of accrual fell. More than one election may be made, with more than one other company, within the time limit, each specifying part of the gain or loss (but the sum of the parts cannot exceed the whole).

If company C is a non-UK resident company, the gain or loss is treated as accruing in respect of a chargeable asset held by it and thus remains within the charge to corporation tax. Any payment made by company A to company C, or *vice versa*, in connection with the election is not to be taken into account in computing profits or losses of either company or treated as a distribution or (for payments made before 16 March 2005) a charge on income (see 55.4 PROFIT COMPUTATIONS), provided it does not exceed the chargeable gain or allowable loss thereby treated as accruing to company C.

[*TCGA 1992, s 179A; FA 2002, s 42(1)(4); F(No 2)A 2005, Sch 4 para 8; Sch 11 Pt 2(7)*].

The above provisions can be applied in combination with those at 12.35 below.

12.35 **Rollover of degrouping charge into new business assets.** Where, **after 31 March 2002**, a company ceases to be a member of a group such that a gain arises under *TCGA 1992, s 179* (see 12.32 above) on a deemed sale and reacquisition of an asset, and the asset is a qualifying asset for rollover relief purposes (see 12.29 above), the company may claim such relief if it acquires a new qualifying asset. The normal rollover relief rules apply in the modified form described below. Where the degrouping charge arises under *TCGA 1992, s 179(5)–(8)*, rollover relief is available only where the 'relevant time' (see 12.32(B)(i) above) falls after 31 March 2002. [*TCGA 1992, s 179B(1)(2); FA 2002, s 43(1)(2)(4)*].

Interaction with TCGA 1992, s 179A. These provisions can be applied in combination with those at 12.34 above. Thus, where a joint election has been made under *TCGA 1992, s 179A* by company A and company C at 12.34 above to allocate the whole of the degrouping charge to company C, and that company acquires a new qualifying asset and takes it into use for the purpose of its trade, a rollover relief claim can by made by company C (but cannot be made by company A). In these circumstances, references below to company A should be read as references to company C where appropriate. Where the *section 179A* election covers only part of the gain, rollover relief is potentially available to each company, in relation to its proportion of the gain, as if the deemed sale under *TCGA 1992, s 179* had been of two separate assets. [*TCGA 1992, s 179B(3)–(6); FA 2002, s 43(1)*].

The relief. Relief under *TCGA 1992, s 152* (see 12.29 above) is available to the company leaving the group (company A), where all of the following conditions are satisfied.

(*a*) Company A is deemed under 12.32 above to have sold and immediately reacquired an asset ('*the old asset*'), and the company from which the asset was transferred (company B) was carrying on a trade at the time of transfer.

(*b*) Throughout its ownership by company B, the asset was used, and used only, for the purposes of that trade.

(*c*) A gain (as opposed to a loss) accrues to company A on the deemed sale.

(*d*) An amount equivalent to the deemed sale proceeds is applied by company A in acquiring other assets or an interest in other assets ('*the new assets*') within the time limit below (but see below as regards partial relief).

(*e*) On acquisition, the new assets are taken into use, and used only, for the purposes of a trade carried on by company A.

(*f*) Both the old and new assets are within the classes of assets listed in *TCGA 1992, s 155* (see under *Qualifying assets* below).

On a claim by company A to that effect, the deemed sale proceeds (if otherwise of a greater amount) are reduced by the amount necessary to secure that neither a gain nor a loss accrues on the deemed sale. The consideration given by company A for the new assets is treated as reduced by the same amount. This does not affect the treatment for the purposes of *TCGA 1992* of the other party to the transaction involving the new assets. There is no reduction in the amount for which company A is deemed to have reacquired the old asset.

The acquisition of the new assets must take place **within one year before, or three years after**, the 'time of accrual' (though HMRC have discretion to extend the specified period in either direction). It is sufficient if an unconditional contract for acquisition is entered into within the specified period, but adjustments can be made to the tax position, without time limit, if the contract is not completed.

The '*time of accrual*' is the time at which the gain on the deemed sale is treated as accruing under 12.32 above (and not, if earlier, the time at which the deemed sale is treated as taking place). Where the degrouping charge arises under *TCGA 1992, s 179(5)–(8)*, the time of accrual is the latest time that company A satisfies the conditions at 12.32(B)(i) above.

The other provisions of *TCGA 1992, s 152* apply as suitably modified. This applies equally to the provisions of *section 152(6)(7)(9)(11)* (partial non-trade use); in particular, references there to the 'period of ownership', in so far as they relate to the old asset, are to be taken as references to the period during which that asset was owned by company B.

[*TCGA 1992, ss 152, 179B, Sch 7AB paras 1, 2; FA 2002, s 43, Sch 7*].

Partial relief. Where the above conditions are satisfied except that the amount applied by company A in acquiring the new assets is less than the deemed sale proceeds, the provisions of *TCGA 1992, s 153* (see Tolley's Capital Gains Tax under Rollover Relief) apply with similar modifications as above. The part of the deemed proceeds not so applied must be less than the amount of the gain on the deemed sale; the relief then operates by reducing the gain to the amount of the said part and treating the consideration given for the new assets as reduced by the same amount. [*TCGA 1992, ss 153, 179B, Sch 7AB paras 1, 3*].

Claims for relief. By virtue of *TMA 1970, s 43* and HMRC Capital Gains Manual CG 60600, the time allowed for making a claim under *TCGA 1992, s 152* or *s 153* above is six years after the later of:

(i) the end of the accounting period of company A in which falls the 'time of accrual' (as defined above); and

(ii) the end of the accounting period of company A in which the new assets are acquired.

It is considered that (i) above applies by reference to an accounting period of company A even if it is company C (see above) that claims the relief.

The procedure in *TCGA 1992, s 153A* for making *provisional claims* (see Tolley's Capital Gains Tax under Rollover Relief) applies as suitably modified. The 'relevant day' for the purpose of such claims is the fourth anniversary of the last day of the accounting period of company A (not of company C, see above, even if it is that company that provisionally claims the relief), in which falls the 'time of accrual' (as defined above). [*TCGA 1992, ss 153, 179B, Sch 7AB paras 1, 4*].

Qualifying assets. The classes of assets qualifying for the relief are as listed in *TCGA 1992, s 155* (see Tolley's Capital Gains Tax under Rollover Relief). Note that certain of the classes listed are of no relevance to companies where the post-31 March 2002 intangible assets regime has effect (see 39 INTANGIBLE ASSETS). As regards Class 1, Head A (land, buildings etc.), the trade there referred to is, in relation to the old asset, the trade carried on by company B and, in relation to the new asset, the trade carried on by company A. [*TCGA 1992, ss 155, 179B, Sch 7AB paras 1, 5*].

Qualifying activities. The provisions of *TCGA 1992, s 158* (see Tolley's Capital Gains Tax under Rollover Relief) have effect to the extent that these are relevant to companies.

New assets acquired by another group member. The provisions of *TCGA 1992, s 175* (see Tolley's Capital Gains Tax under Rollover Relief) are adapted to make the above relief available where company A is a member of a group at the time of accrual (as defined above), the acquisition of the new assets is made by another member of that group (judged at the time of acquisition) and the claim is made by both companies. The conditions to be met are that:

(A) *either* company A is UK-resident at the time of accrual *or* the old asset (or, where relevant, the replacement property referred to in 12.32 above) is a chargeable asset in relation to that company immediately before that time; and

(B) *either* the acquiring company is UK-resident at the time of acquisition *or* the new assets are chargeable assets in relation to that company immediately after that time.

The relief is also available where:

(1) company B was not carrying on a trade when it transferred the old asset to company A but was a member of a group at that time; and

(2) immediately before that time, the old asset was used, and used only, for the purposes of the trade treated by *TCGA 1992, s 179(1)* as a single trade carried on by all the trading members of the group.

The relief can similarly be claimed where the acquiring company is a non-trading company but the new assets are taken into use, and used only, for the purposes mentioned in (2) above. In no case is relief available where the acquisition of new assets results from a no gain/no loss disposal, e.g. where the assets are acquired from another group member.

[*TCGA 1992, ss 175, 179B, Sch 7AB paras 1, 7; FA 2003, Sch 27 para 2(3)*].

Wasting assets. The depreciating asset provisions of *TCGA 1992, s 154* (see Tolley's Capital Gains Tax under Rollover Relief) apply equally in relation to the relief described above.

Overseas matters. Under a modified version of *TCGA 1992, s 159* (see Tolley's Capital Gains Tax under Overseas Matters), the above rollover relief is not available if the old asset (or, where relevant, the replacement property referred to in 12.32 above) is a chargeable asset in relation to company A at the time of accrual (as defined above) unless the new assets are chargeable assets in relation to company A immediately after they are acquired. This does not, however, apply where company A acquires the new assets after the time of accrual and is UK resident immediately after acquiring them (unless it is then dual resident and the assets are prescribed assets). The exclusion of rollover relief where a company becomes non-UK resident between the time of accrual and the acquisition of the new assets also applies in suitably adapted form. [*TCGA 1992, ss 159, 179B, 185, Sch 7AB paras 1, 6, 8; FA 2003, Sch 27 para 2(3)*].

12.36 **Exemption for substantial shareholdings.** Where a company ceases to be a member of a group and is deemed under *TCGA 1992, s 179* to have sold and immediately reacquired at market value an asset transferred to it by another group member, then normally the time of the deemed sale is immediately after the transfer (see 12.32 above). However, where:

(*a*) a company ceases to be a member of a group at any time (the '*time of degrouping*') after 31 March 2002; and

(*b*) a degrouping charge (as in 12.32 above) arises in relation to an asset; and

(*c*) a gain on a disposal of that asset (by the company then owning it) immediately before the time of degrouping would have been exempt under the provisions at 13 CAPITAL GAINS—SUBSTANTIAL SHAREHOLDINGS,

the deemed sale and reacquisition is instead treated as taking place immediately before the time of degrouping.

A comparable rule applies where the degrouping charge arises under *TCGA 1992, s 179(5)–(8)* and the 'relevant time' (see 12.32(B)(i) above) falls after 31 March 2002. In this case, the rule applies by reference to the 'relevant time' rather than the 'time of degrouping'.

[*TCGA 1992, Sch 7AC para 38; FA 2002, s 44(2)(4), Sch 8 para 1*].

12.37 COMPANY BECOMING AN INVESTMENT TRUST AFTER ACQUIRING ASSET INTRA-GROUP

Similar treatment as in 12.32 above (company leaving group) applies where a company (the '*acquiring company*') becomes an investment trust (within *ICTA 1988, s 842*, see 44.1 INVESTMENT TRUSTS) for an accounting period beginning after 16 March 1998 and, within six years before the commencement of that period, it had acquired an asset from another company in its group, the corresponding disposal having been treated by virtue of

TCGA 1992, s 171 (intra-group transfers, see 12.2 above) as a no gain/no loss disposal. The provisions apply where, at the beginning of the accounting period in which it became an investment trust, the acquiring company owns, otherwise than as trading stock, either the asset itself or replacement property (i.e. property into which a chargeable gain on disposal of the asset has been rolled over, see 12.29 below). An asset acquired is deemed for these purposes to be the same as an asset owned subsequently if the value of the latter asset is derived, wholly or partly, from the original asset (in particular where the original was a leasehold and the lessee has acquired the freehold reversion). The provisions do not apply if the acquiring company was an investment trust at the time of the corresponding disposal (in which case the no gain/no loss treatment would not have applied, see 12.2(vi) above) nor if it has been an investment trust for any intervening accounting period.

The acquiring company is treated as if, immediately after the corresponding disposal, it had sold and immediately reacquired the asset at its market value at that time. The resulting chargeable gain or allowable loss is treated as accruing immediately before the end of the acquiring company's accounting period which immediately preceded that in which it became an investment trust. Notwithstanding normal time limits, any consequential corporation tax assessment may be made at any time within six years after the end of the accounting period in which the company became an investment trust. These provisions are disapplied if, prior to the company becoming an investment trust, the above treatment has already applied to the asset by virtue either of 12.32 above or 12.38 below (company becoming a venture capital trust).

[*TCGA 1992, s 101A; FA 1998, s 133(1)(3)*].

Simon's Direct Tax Service. See **D2.653**.

12.38 COMPANY BECOMING A VENTURE CAPITAL TRUST AFTER ACQUIRING ASSET INTRA-GROUP

The same treatment as in 12.37 above (company becoming an investment trust) applies where the acquiring company was granted approval as a venture capital trust (VCT) (within *ICTA 1988, s 842AA*, see 69.2 VENTURE CAPITAL TRUSTS) with effect from a time after 16 March 1998, and within six years before that time it had acquired an asset intra-group by means of a no gain/no loss disposal under *TCGA 1992, s 171* (see 12.2 above). The provisions apply where, at the time the approval became effective, the acquiring company owned, otherwise than as trading stock, either the asset itself (with the same rules as in 12.37 above as to derivation of assets) or replacement property (as in 12.37 above). The provisions do not apply if the acquiring company was a VCT at the time of the intra-group disposal (in which case the no gain/no loss treatment would have applied only if that disposal occurred before 17 March 1998, see 12.2(vii) above) nor if it has been a VCT at any time in the intervening period. Nor do they apply if, prior to the company becoming a VCT, the said treatment has already applied to the asset by virtue either of 12.37 above or 12.32 above (company leaving group).

The chargeable gain or allowable loss resulting from the deemed disposal at market value immediately after the intra-group transfer is treated as accruing to the acquiring company immediately before the time approval as a VCT became effective. Notwithstanding normal time limits, any consequential corporation tax assessment may, in a case in which HMRC's approval has effect as from the beginning of an accounting period, be made at any time within six years after the end of that accounting period.

[*TCGA 1992, s 101C; FA 1998, s 135(2)(5)*].

Simon's Direct Tax Service. See **D2.655**.

12.39 DEPRECIATORY TRANSACTIONS

Where two or more group companies are parties to a disposal of assets at other than market value, and such a disposal **materially reduces the value of the shares or securities of**

one of those companies (a '*depreciatory transaction*'), any loss arising on the ultimate disposal of those shares by a member or former member of the group (having been a member when the transaction took place) is to be allowable only so far as is 'just and reasonable'. This applies where the earlier disposal is after 6 April 1965 (or after 31 March 1982 where, on the ultimate disposal after 5 April 1988, market value at that date is substituted for cost). Account may be taken of any other transaction which may have:

(i) enhanced the value of the assets of the company the shares in which are being disposed of; *and*

(ii) depreciated the value of the assets of any other member of the group.

The restriction is applied to the allowable loss after indexation, rather than to the unindexed loss before indexation (*Tesco plc v Crimmin Ch D 1997, 69 TC 510*), and in arriving at the amount by which it was 'just and reasonable' to reduce the allowable loss, indexation should be applied to the value of the depreciatory transaction(s) from the date(s) of the transaction(s) to the date of the ultimate disposal (*Whitehall Electric Investments Ltd v Owen (Sp C 312), [2002] SSCD 229*). See, however, 11.25 CAPITAL GAINS as regards prohibition on indexation allowance creating or enhancing a loss.

Where such a reduction is made, any chargeable gain accruing on the disposal within six years of the transaction of the shares etc. in any other party thereto is to be reduced as is 'just and reasonable' (but not so as to exceed the reduction in the allowable loss). Regard may also be had to the effect of the depreciatory transaction on the value of the shares at the date of disposal.

A 'depreciatory transaction' also includes any other transaction where:

(*a*) the company, the shares or securities in which are the subject of the ultimate disposal, or any 75% subsidiary of that company, was party to that transaction; and

(*b*) the parties to the transaction were, or included, two or more companies which, when the transaction occurred, were in the same group.

A transaction is not depreciatory to the extent that it is a payment which is brought into account in computing a chargeable gain or allowable loss of the company making the ultimate disposal. Cancellation within *Companies Act 1985, s 135* of shares or securities of one group member which are owned by another is deemed to be a depreciatory transaction unless it falls within this exemption.

Claims under *TCGA 1992, s 24(2)* that shares or securities have become of negligible value also come within this section.

References to the disposal of assets include appropriation by one member of a group of the goodwill of another.

'*Securities*' includes loan stock or similar securities, whether secured or unsecured.

'*Group of companies*' includes non-resident companies (before, on and after 1 April 2000, see 12.1 above).

[*TCGA 1992, s 176; FA 2000, Sch 29 para 24*].

As regards distributions out of post-acquisition profits, see HMRC Capital Gains Manual, CG 46580 *et seq.*

Simon's Direct Tax Service. See D2.665.

12.40 **Restriction of capital losses because of depreciatory transactions.** The restriction on capital losses because of 'depreciatory transactions' (see 12.39 above) also applies where a 'first company' has a holding in a 'second company' which amounts (with or without the addition of holdings by CONNECTED PERSONS (19)) to 10% of all the holdings of the same class in the second company (and the first company is not a dealing company in relation to the holding) and a distribution is, or has been, made in respect of the holding which materially reduces the value of the holding. Distributions brought into account in computing a chargeable gain or allowable loss accruing to the ultimate disponor are ignored. [*TCGA 1992, s 177; FA 2000, Sch 29 para 25*].

Simon's Direct Tax Service. See **D2.667**.

13 Capital Gains—Substantial Shareholdings

Simons Direct Tax Service. See **D2.15**

The headings in this chapter are as follows.

13.1 **INTRODUCTION**

As detailed in this chapter, a gain on a disposal by a company of shares **after 31 March 2002** is exempt (and a loss is not allowable) where, throughout a continuous twelve-month period beginning not more than two years before the disposal, the company (the '*investing company*') held a 'substantial shareholding' (broadly, at least a **10%** interest) in the company (the '*investee company*') whose shares are the subject of the disposal. The exemption extends to assets 'related to shares' (as in 13.5 below). The investing company must be a trading company or a member of a trading group and the investee company must be a trading company or the holding company of a trading group (or subgroup). Shares held by members of a worldwide group are aggregated in determining whether a company holds a substantial shareholding. [*TCGA 1992, s 192A, Sch 7AC; FA 2002, s 44(1)–(3), Sch 8 para 1*].

See generally HMRC Capital Gains Manual, CG 53000–53240.

13.2 **Definition of company and group.** For the purposes of these provisions, a '*company*' is as defined at 12.1 CAPITAL GAINS—GROUPS. A '*group of companies*' is also as defined at 12.1 but as if each reference there to '75%' were a reference to '51%'. Thus, subject to the detailed rules there, a '*group*' comprises a company and its 'effective 51% subsidiaries' (within *ICTA 1988, s 838*), and may include non-UK resident companies. A '*holding company*' of a group is the principal company of the group (within the meaning given in 12.1). A '*subgroup*' is a number of companies that *would* form a group were it not for the fact that one of them (the '*holding company*' of the subgroup) is itself a 51% subsidiary. [*TCGA 1992, Sch 7AC para 26; FA 2002, Sch 8 para 1*].

13.3 **Application of exemptions.** The exemptions described in this chapter are of no application to a disposal the gain (or loss) on which would, by virtue of some other enactment, not be a chargeable gain (or an allowable loss). Neither do they apply to a disposal which, by virtue of any chargeable gains enactment, is a 'no gain/no loss' disposal, or to a deemed market value disposal and reacquisition of an asset transferred by an insurance company from one category of business to another. [*TCGA 1992, Sch 7AC para 6(1); FA 2002, Sch 8 para 1*].

13.4 **THE EXEMPTIONS**

Exemption for shares. A gain accruing to a company (the '*investing company*') on a disposal of shares (or an 'interest in shares' — see 13.27 below) in another company (the '*investee company*') is not a chargeable gain if:

(*a*) the investing company held a 'substantial shareholding' (see 13.9 below) in the investee company throughout any continuous period of twelve months beginning not more than two years prior to the disposal (see 13.10 below);

(*b*) the investing company meets the requirements at 13.11 below; and

(*c*) the requirements at 13.13 below are met in relation to the investee company.

See also the anti-avoidance rule at 13.8 below.

[*TCGA 1992, Sch 7AC paras 1, 7, 28; FA 2002, Sch 8 para 1*].

By virtue of *TCGA 1992, s 16(2)* (see 11.3 CAPITAL GAINS), a loss on a disposal is not an allowable loss if a gain on that disposal would not have been a chargeable gain.

The nature of the condition at (*a*) above is such that part disposals out of a once-substantial shareholding can continue to attract the exemption for up to a year after the shareholding has ceased to be substantial.

The exemption is available even where the shares disposed of are not the shares that meet the substantial shareholding requirement at (*a*) above. If (*a*) above is met in relation to ordinary shares (and (*b*) and (*c*) are also met), a disposal of a holding of, say, fixed-rate preference shares in the investee company will qualify for the exemption, irrespective of the size and duration of that holding. (HMRC Capital Gains Manual, CG 53155).

The exemption is automatic and does not require the making of a claim.

13.5 **Exemption for assets related to shares.** A gain accruing to a company (company A) on a disposal of an asset 'related to shares' in another company (company B) is not a chargeable gain (and a loss is not an allowable loss) if:

(i) at the time of the disposal, company A holds shares (or an 'interest in shares' — see 13.27 below) in company B; and

(ii) any gain on a disposal at that time of those shares (or that interest) would be exempt under 13.4 above (disregarding 13.3 above).

This exemption also applies where:

(*a*) the shares etc. are held not by company A itself but by another member of a group of companies (see 13.2 above) of which company A is a member; and

(*b*) any gain on a disposal at that time of those shares etc., on the assumption that they were held by company A, would be exempt under 13.4 above (disregarding 13.3 above).

Where assets of a company are vested in a liquidator, the above applies as if they were vested in the company and as if the acts of the liquidator were the acts of the company (disposals by the company to the liquidator, and *vice versa*, being disregarded).

See also the anti-avoidance rule at 13.8 below.

[*TCGA 1992, Sch 7AC paras 2, 6(2); FA 2002, Sch 8 para 1*].

The exemption is automatic and does not require the making of a claim.

For this purpose, an asset is '*related to shares*' in a company if it is:

(1) an option to acquire or dispose of shares (or an 'interest in shares' — see 13.27 below) in that company; or

(2) (broadly) a security that is convertible or exchangeable into shares (or an interest in shares) in that company, or into an option within (1) above, or into another security within this definition; or

(3) an option to acquire or dispose of a security within (2) above (or an interest in any such security); or

(4) an interest in, or option over, any option or security within (1)–(3) above; or

(5) an interest in, or option over, any interest or option within (4) above (or an interest in, or option over, any interest or option within this sub-paragraph).

As regards (2) above, a convertible or exchangeable security is not an asset related to shares if, when the conversion etc. rights were granted, there was no more than a negligible likelihood that they would be exercised to any significant extent. It is therefore not possible to bring a security within the scope of the exemption by attaching some spurious or extremely remote rights to convertibility in the event of some unlikely occurrence. (HMRC Capital Gains Manual, CG 53010).

Certain securities, options etc. are outside the scope of corporation tax on chargeable gains, and thus outside the exemptions in this chapter, due to their falling within the special LOAN RELATIONSHIPS (46) or FINANCIAL INSTRUMENTS AND DERIVATIVE CONTRACTS (28) rules. (HMRC Capital Gains Manual, CG 53010).

An '*interest*' in a security or option has a similar meaning to an 'interest in shares' at 13.27 below.

[*TCGA 1992, Sch 7AC para 30; FA 2002, Sch 8 para 1*].

13.6 **Exemption where main conditions previously met.** A further possibility of exemption is provided, as detailed below, where the exemption at 13.4 or 13.5 above, whichever is relevant, does not apply because some of the conditions were not satisfied at the time of the disposal even though they *had been* satisfied at a time in the two years immediately preceding the disposal.

A gain accruing to a company (company A) on a disposal of shares (or an interest in shares — see 13.27 below), or an asset 'related to shares' (see 13.5 above), in another company (company B) is not a chargeable gain (and a loss is not an allowable loss) if the conditions at 13.4 or 13.5 above, whichever is relevant, are not fully met (with the result that a chargeable gain or allowable loss would otherwise arise on the disposal) but *all* of the following conditions *are* met.

(*a*) At the time of disposal, company A had held a 'substantial shareholding' (see 13.9 below) in company B throughout any continuous period of twelve months beginning not more than two years prior to the disposal (see also 13.10 below).

(*b*) At the time of disposal, either company A is UK-resident or any chargeable gain accruing to it on the disposal would form part of its corporation tax profits by virtue of *TCGA 1992, s 10(3)* or *s 10B* (trade carried on through UK permanent establishment or branch or agency — see 60.5, 60.6 RESIDENCE).

(*c*) There was a time within the two years ending with the disposal (the '*relevant period*') when a gain on a hypothetical disposal by:

 (i) company A; or

 (ii) a company that at any time in the relevant period was a member of the same group (see 13.2 above) as company A,

being a disposal of shares (or an interest in shares) in company B that the disposing company then held, would have been exempt under 13.4 above (disregarding 13.3 above, and see also below).

(*d*) If, at the time of disposal, the requirements at 13.13 below as to the investee company are not met in relation to company B, there was a time within the relevant period (as defined at (*c*) above) when company B was controlled by:

(i) company A; or

(ii) company A together with any persons connected with it (within *TCGA 1992, s 286* — see 19.8 CONNECTED PERSONS); or

(iii) a company that at any time in the relevant period was a member of the same group (see 13.2 above) as company A; or

(iv) any such company together with persons connected with it.

'Control' is to be construed in accordance with *ICTA 1988, s 416* (see 16.2 CLOSE COMPANIES).

If the exemption at 13.4 or 13.5 above is not available for the sole reason that the investing company fails to meet the requirement at 13.11(*b*) below (as to its status immediately after the time of the disposal), this further possibility of exemption is available only if the failure is due to the actual or imminent winding-up or dissolution of the investing company (provided that, in a case where this is imminent, it actually takes place as soon as is reasonably practicable in the circumstances).

For the purpose only of determining the 'relevant period' for the purposes of (*c*) or (*d*) above, the time of disposal is taken as the time the contract is made, notwithstanding that the contract may be conditional. In determining whether the gain on the hypothetical disposal in (*c*) above would have attracted the exemption at 13.4 above, the requirements at 13.11(*b*) below and 13.13(*b*) below as to the status of the investing and investee companies immediately after the time of disposal are taken to be satisfied.

See also the anti-avoidance rule at 13.8 below.

[*TCGA 1992, s 288(1), Sch 7AC para 3(1)–(4)(7)(8), para 6(2); FA 2002, Sch 8 para 1; F(No 2)A 2005, Sch 4 para 9*].

Thus, for example, where the investee company ceases to trade on being put into liquidation, so that it can no longer meet the requirements at 13.13 below, disposals by the investing company (including capital distributions) can continue to attract the exemption for a further two years.

It should be noted, however, that the above exemption also contains an anti-avoidance element in that if, for example, the investee company's trade is transferred elsewhere (within a group, for instance) and the conditions above are all met, a loss on a disposal by the investing company within the two years following the transfer will not be an allowable loss.

A further anti-avoidance measure applies as follows to prevent the exemption from applying where value has been transferred into the investee company within the said two-year period. Where the above exemption would otherwise apply but

(1) immediately before the disposal by company A, company B holds an asset, and

(2) the allowable expenditure attributable to that asset has been reduced by a claim for gifts hold-over relief under *TCGA 1992, s 165* (see Tolley's Capital Gains Tax under Hold-Over Reliefs) on an earlier disposal of the asset within the relevant period (as defined above),

a gain on the disposal by company A does not attract the exemption *but* a loss on the disposal is not an allowable loss. (Where assets of company B are vested in a liquidator, (1) above applies as if they were vested in the company.)

[*TCGA 1992, Sch 7AC para 3(5)(6); FA 2002, Sch 8 para 1*].

The exemption is automatic and does not require the making of a claim.

13.7 *Example*

Swallow Ltd acquired 1,500 shares in Summer Ltd in April 1992. Swallow Ltd holds no other investments in any company, has been a trading company throughout its existence, and is not a member of a group. Summer Ltd has 10,000 issued shares and has been a trading company since itsformation. Swallow Ltd makes the following disposals of Summer Ltd shares.

31 May 2006	600 shares
30 April 2007	400 shares
30 June 2007	500 shares

The effect of the disposals for the purpose of corporation tax on chargeable gains is as follows.

31 May 2006 disposal

Swallow Ltd held at least 10% of the ordinary share capital of Summer Ltd throughout the two years prior to the disposal. The disposal is therefore part of a substantial shareholding and no chargeable gain or allowable loss arises on the disposal.

30 April 2007 disposal

Although Swallow did not hold at least 10% of the shares in Summer Ltd immediately before the disposal (the minimum holding being only 900 of 10,000 shares), there is a twelve-month period beginning within two years prior to the disposal throughout which it did hold at least 10%. The period is 1 June 2005 to 31 May 2006. Accordingly, the substantial shareholding exemption applies and no chargeable gain or allowable loss arises on the disposal.

30 June 2007 disposal

Swallow Ltd holds only 5% of the share capital of Summer Ltd immediately before the disposal. In the period from 1 July 2005 to 30 June 2007, the company held at least 10% of Summer Ltd's shares only from 1 July 2005 to 31 May 2006. This is not a continuous twelve-month period beginning two years prior to the disposal, and therefore the substantial shareholding exemption will not apply. A gain on the disposal of 500 shares will be a chargeable gain, and a loss an allowable loss.

13.8 **ANTI-AVOIDANCE**

None of the exemptions in 13.4–13.6 above are available where:

(*a*) an 'untaxed' gain accrues to an investing company (Company A) on a disposal of shares (or an interest in shares, see 13.27 below), or an asset related to shares (see 13.5 above), in another company (Company B);

(*b*) before the accrual of that gain, either:

   (i) Company A acquired control of Company B, or the same person(s) acquired control of both companies; or

   (ii) there was a 'significant change of trading activities affecting Company B' at a time when it was controlled by Company A or when both companies were controlled by the same person(s); and

(*c*) these circumstances occur in pursuance of arrangements (including any scheme, agreement or understanding, whether or not legally enforceable) from which the sole or main benefit that could be expected is that the gain would be exempt under any of 13.4–13.6 above.

For the above purposes:

(A) a gain is '*untaxed*' if it (or all but an insubstantial part of it) represents profits that have not been brought into account (in the UK or elsewhere) for the purposes of tax on profits for a period ending on or before the date of the disposal. Profits in respect of which an amount is apportioned to a UK resident company under the CONTROLLED FOREIGN COMPANIES (21) rules are brought into account for this purpose 'Profits' means income or gains (whether or not realised);

(B) 'control' is to be construed in accordance with *ICTA 1988, s 416* (see 16 2 CLOSE COMPANIES); and

(C) there is a 'significant change of trading activities affecting Company B' if:

   (i) there is a 'major change in the nature or conduct of a trade' carried on by Company B or a '51% subsidiary' (within *ICTA 1988, s 838*) of Company B; or

   (ii) there is a major change in the scale of the activities of a trade carried on by Company B or a 51% subsidiary; or

   (iii) Company B or a 51% subsidiary begins to carry on a trade.

By virtue of *ICTA 1988, s 768*, a '*major change in the nature or conduct of a trade*' includes a major change in the type of property dealt in or services or facilities provided, or in customers, outlets or markets. See 47.13 LOSSES.

[*TCGA 1992, s 288(1), Sch 7AC para 5; FA 2002, Sch 8 para 1*].

HMRC expect cases where this anti-avoidance rule is in point to be unusual and infrequent. It is a question of fact as to whether a gain wholly (or wholly but for an insubstantial part — interpreted by HMRC as 20% or less) represents untaxed profits; this involves looking at how the consideration obtained for the disposal by Company A is derived from assets held directly or indirectly by Company B. Profits are not 'untaxed' if they are simply covered by a specific relief or if they represent dividends which are themselves paid out of taxed profits. If a gain represents both taxed and untaxed profits, it should be taken as first representing taxed profits, with only any remaining balance representing untaxed profits. (HMRC Statement of Practice SP 5/02). HMRC have published on their website some practical illustrations of when the anti-avoidance rule will or may apply and when it will not (at www.hmrc.gov.uk/cgt/anti_avoid_examples.htm).

13.9 'SUBSTANTIAL SHAREHOLDING' REQUIREMENT

Meaning of substantial shareholding. For the purposes of these provisions, a company holds a '*substantial shareholding*' in another company if it holds shares (or 'interests in shares' — see 13.27 below) in that company by virtue of which:

(*a*) it holds **at least 10%** of the company's ordinary share capital;

(*b*) it is beneficially entitled to at least 10% of the profits available for distribution to equity holders of the company; and

(*c*) it would be beneficially entitled on a winding-up to at least 10% of the assets of the company available for distribution to equity holders.

ICTA 1988, Sch 18 applies, with suitable modifications, to define an 'equity holder' and to determine the profits or assets available for distribution (see 32.8, 32.9 GROUPS OF COMPANIES).

[*TCGA 1992, Sch 7AC para 8; FA 2002, Sch 8 para 1*].

For the purposes of deciding whether the 'substantial shareholding' test is satisfied, holdings of shares (and interests in shares) by members of the same group of companies (which may be a worldwide group — see 13.2 above) are aggregated. [*TCGA 1992, Sch 7AC para 9(1); FA 2002, Sch 8 para 1*].

Where assets of the investing company, or of a member of the same group as the investing company, are vested in a liquidator, they are treated for the purposes of the substantial shareholding requirement (and those of 13.16, 13.17 below) as if they were vested in the company and as if the acts of the liquidator were the acts of the company (disposals by the company to the liquidator, and *vice versa*, being disregarded). [*TCGA 1992, Sch 7AC para 16; FA 2002, Sch 8 para 1*].

Insurance companies. Special rules apply in relation to assets of long-term insurance funds where the investing company is an insurance company, or in certain cases a 51% subsidiary of an insurance company, or a member of the same group as an insurance company. [*TCGA 1992, Sch 7AC paras 9(2), 17; FA 2002, Sch 8 para 1*].

13.10 **Holding period.** As stated at 13.4(*a*) above, the investing company must have held a substantial shareholding in the investee company throughout a continuous period of twelve months beginning not more than two years prior to the disposal. Shares are treated as having been held for such a period if, for example, they were acquired at any time on 15 June 2002 and sold at any time on 14 June 2003; they do not have to be held on the anniversary of the acquisition. (HMRC Capital Gains Manual, CG 53008). The following special rules apply.

No gain/no loss transfers. Where the investing company acquired any shares from another company by means of a 'no gain/no loss' transfer, i.e. under any chargeable gains enactment that states that a disposal is to be treated as made for such consideration that no gain or loss accrues, the period during which it is treated as holding those shares is extended to include the period during which the previous owner held them. The period is further extended back through any series of no gain/no loss transfers by which the shares arrived in the hands of the present owner. The present owner is treated as having had the same entitlements, to shares and to any rights enjoyed by virtue of holding shares, as the company or companies by which they were held at any earlier time in the extended period. These include any entitlements etc. arising from the aggregation rule for groups of companies in 13.9 above. These rules also cover 'interests in shares' (see 13.27 below), and the extension also covers any period during which the asset held by any of the previous companies concerned in the no gain/no loss series consisted of shares (or an interest in shares) from which the current shares (or interest) are 'derived'.

For the above purposes, any transfer which, by virtue of *TCGA 1992, s 171(3)*, is not treated as a no gain/no loss transfer (intra-group share exchanges, see 12.2 CAPITAL GAINS—GROUPS), and which would otherwise have been so, is treated as if it had been a no gain/no loss transfer.

Shares (or interests in shares) are '*derived*' from other shares (or interests) only where:

(*a*) a company becomes co-owner of shares previously owned by it alone, or *vice versa*;

(*b*) a company's interest in shares as co-owner changes (but co-ownership continues);

(*c*) a shareholding is treated by virtue of *TCGA 1992, s 127* (including its application by virtue of another enactment) as the same asset as another shareholding; or

(*d*) there is a sequence of two or more of the above occurrences.

[*TCGA 1992, Sch 7AC para 10; FA 2002, Sch 8 para 1*].

Deemed disposals and reacquisitions. Where, under any corporation tax enactment, shares have been deemed to be disposed of and immediately reacquired by a company, the company is regarded as not having held the shares during any part of the holding period falling before the deemed disposal and reacquisition. This rule extends to 'interests in shares' (see 13.27 below) and to shares (or interests) from which the current shares (or interest) are 'derived' (as above). [*TCGA 1992, Sch 7AC para 11; FA 2002, Sch 8 para 1*].

Sale and repurchase agreements (*repos*). Where the company that holds shares transfers them under a repo (as defined), such that, by virtue of *FA 2007, Sch 13 para 6* or *TCGA 1992, s 263A* (see Tolley's Capital Gains Tax under Shares and Securities), the disposal falls to be disregarded, it is similarly disregarded for the purposes of the provisions in this chapter. Thus, during the period covered by the repo, the ownership of the shares, and the entitlement to any rights attached to them, rests with the original owner and not the interim holder. If, at any time during that period, the original owner, or a member of the same group (see 13.2 above) as the original owner, becomes the *actual* holder of any of the shares transferred (or any shares directly or indirectly representing them), this rule ceases to have effect at that time in relation to the shares concerned. [*TCGA 1992, Sch 7AC para 12; FA 2002, Sch 8 para 1; FA 2003, Sch 38 para 9; FA 2007 Sch 14 para 13*]

Stock lending arrangements. Rules identical to those above for repos apply where shares are transferred under a stock lending arrangement (as defined), such that, by virtue of *TCGA 1992, s 263B(2)* (see Tolley's Capital Gains Tax under Shares and Securities), the disposal falls to be disregarded. [*TCGA 1992, Sch 7AC para 13; FA 2002, Sch 8 para 1*].

13.11 REQUIREMENTS TO BE MET BY INVESTING COMPANY

The requirements to be met by the investing company for the purposes of the exemption at 13.4 above are that:

(*a*) it must have been a sole 'trading company' (see 13.12 below) or a member of a 'qualifying group' (see below) throughout the period:

- (i) beginning with the start of the latest twelve-month period (within the two years prior to disposal) for which the substantial shareholding requirement (see 13.4(*a*) above) was met; and
- (ii) ending with the time of the disposal; and

(*b*) it must be a sole 'trading company' or a member of a 'qualifying group' immediately after the time of the disposal.

A '*qualifying group*' is a 'trading group' (see 13.12 below) or a group that would be a trading group if the activities of any group member not established for profit were disregarded to the extent that they are carried on otherwise than for profit. In determining whether a company is established for profit, any object or power which is merely incidental to the company's main objects is to be ignored.

The requirement at (*a*) above is met if the company was a sole trading company for part of the said period and a member of a qualifying group for the rest of it.

Where the disposal is made under a contract and, by virtue of *TCGA 1992, s 28* (see Tolley's Capital Gains Tax under Disposal), the time of disposal for tax purposes precedes the conveyance or transfer of the asset disposed of, the requirements at both (*a*) and (*b*) above must be met by reference to the time of conveyance or transfer as well the time of the disposal.

The requirement at (*a*) above is treated as met if, at the time of the disposal (and, where relevant, the time of the conveyance or transfer):

(1) the investing company is a member of a group (as in 13.2 above); and

(2) the requirement is not met by that company but would have been met by another group member if, immediately before the disposal, the subject matter of the disposal had been transferred to that member under the no gain/no loss provisions of *TCGA 1992, s 171* (see 12.2 CAPITAL GAINS—GROUPS) and that member had then made the disposal.

[*TCGA 1992, Sch 7AC para 18; FA 2002, Sch 8 para 1*].

13.12 **Trading company and trading group.** For the purposes of this chapter, a '*trading company*' is a company whose activities do not include to a 'substantial' extent activities other than 'trading activities'. A '*trading group*' is a group (as in 13.2 above), one or more of whose members carry on 'trading activities' and the activities of whose members, taken together, do not include to a 'substantial' extent activities other than 'trading activities'. '*Substantial*' in this connection is taken by HMRC to mean 'more than 20%'. (HMRC Capital Gains Manual, CG 53116).

In relation to a single company, '*trading activities*' means 'activities' carried on by the company:

(*a*) in the course of, or for the purposes of, a 'trade' being carried on by it; or

(*b*) for the purposes of a 'trade' that it is preparing to carry on; or

(*c*) with a view to its acquiring or starting to carry on a trade; or

(*d*) with a view to its acquiring a 'significant interest' in the share capital of another company that is itself a trading company or the 'holding company' (as in 13.2 above) of a trading group or 'trading subgroup' (see 13.14 below) and that is not already a member of the same group as the acquiring company.

'*Activities*' is interpreted by HMRC to mean what a company does, so that the expression in itself includes engaging in trading activities, making and holding investments, planning, holding meetings and so on. (HMRC Capital Gains Manual, CG 53113).

'*Trade*' means any trade, profession or vocation (within the meaning of the *Income Tax Acts*) conducted on a commercial basis with a view to profit. It also comprises the commercial letting of furnished holiday accommodation (see 56.2(C) PROPERTY INCOME). Activities qualify under (*c*) or (*d*) above only if the acquisition is made, or the trade commenced, as soon as is reasonably practicable in the circumstances. A company acquires a '*significant interest*' (see (*d*) above) if it acquires sufficient ordinary share capital in the other company to make that company its '51% subsidiary' within *ICTA 1988, s 838*, or to give the acquiring company a 'qualifying shareholding' in a 'joint venture company' (see 13.18 below) without making the two companies members of the same group.

In relation to a group, '*trading activities*' means activities carried on by a member of the group, being activities that would fall within (*a*)–(*d*) above if these were interpreted by reference not only to that member but also to any other member of the group. The activities of group members are regarded as a single business, so that intra-group activities are disregarded. A group member acquires a '*significant interest*' (see (*d*) above) if it acquires sufficient ordinary share capital in the other company to make that company a member of the same group as the acquiring company, or to give the acquiring company a 'qualifying shareholding' in a 'joint venture company'.

[*TCGA 1992, Sch 7AC paras 20, 21, 26(4), 27; FA 2002, Sch 8 paras 1, 3*].

Many of the expressions used above are considered further in the HMRC Capital Gains Manual, CG 53110 to CG 53119. A company could, prior to 19 July 2006, ask its tax district to give a view on its status for the above purposes under Code of Practice 10, but any opinion expressed is subject to revision to the extent that it relates to a time for which the full facts are not yet available. (HMRC Capital Gains Manual, CG 53120 and HMRC Tax Bulletin August 2006 p 1308).

See 13.18 below as regards the treatment of holdings in joint venture companies.

13.13 **REQUIREMENTS RELATING TO INVESTEE COMPANY**

The requirements to be met in relation to the investee company for the purposes of the exemption at 13.4 above are that:

(*a*) it must have been a 'qualifying company' (see below) throughout the period:

(i) beginning with the start of the latest twelve-month period (within the two years prior to disposal) for which the substantial shareholding requirement (see 13.4(*a*) above) was met; and

(ii) ending with the time of the disposal; and

(*b*) it must be a 'qualifying company' immediately after the time of the disposal.

A '*qualifying company*' is a 'trading company' (see 13.12 above) or the 'holding company' (as in 13.2 above) of a 'trading group' (see 13.12 above) or 'trading subgroup' (see 13.14 below).

Where the disposal is made under a contract and, by virtue of *TCGA 1992, s 28* (see Tolley's Capital Gains Tax under Disposal), the time of disposal for tax purposes precedes the conveyance or transfer of the asset disposed of, the requirements at both (*a*) and (*b*) above must be met by reference to the time of the conveyance or transfer as well as the time of the disposal.

[*TCGA 1992, Sch 7AC para 19; FA 2002, Sch 8 para 1*].

13.14 For the purposes of this chapter, a '*trading subgroup*' is a 'subgroup' (as in 13.2 above), one or more of whose members carries on 'trading activities' and the activities of whose members, taken together, do not include to a 'substantial' extent (see 13.12 above) activities other than 'trading activities'. '*Trading activities*' are defined in relation to a subgroup as they are in relation to a group (for which see 13.12 above), with the appropriate modifications. [*TCGA 1992, Sch 7AC para 22; FA 2002, Sch 8 para 1*].

See 13.18 below as regards the treatment of holdings in joint venture companies.

13.15 SHARE REORGANISATIONS ETC.

Treatment of certain events as disposals. Without the special rules below, the exemptions at 13.4–13.6 above would be of no relevance to any of the following events (in relation to shares held by the investing company in the investee company).

(*a*) A reorganisation of share capital, company take-over/reconstruction or conversion of securities which, by virtue of *TCGA 1992, s 127*, does not constitute a disposal (see Tolley's Capital Gains Tax under Shares and Securities), the 'new holding' standing in the shoes of the original shares.

(*b*) An event which would have been within (*a*) above but for the fact that the 'new asset' consists of a qualifying corporate bond and which, by virtue of *TCGA 1992, s 116(10)* (see Tolley's Capital Gains Tax under Qualifying Corporate Bonds), is not treated as a disposal.

(*c*) A tax-exempt distribution on a demerger which, by virtue of *TCGA 1992, s 192* (see 32.34 GROUPS OF COMPANIES), does not constitute a capital distribution.

To the extent that a gain would thereby be exempt (or a loss non-allowable) under 13.4–13.6 above, the enactment mentioned in (*a*), (*b*) or (*c*) above, whichever is relevant, is disapplied, so that an event in (*a*) or (*b*) is treated as a disposal, a distribution in (*c*) is treated as a capital distribution and the new shares or securities are normally treated as acquired at market value. This disapplication does not, however, have effect if the result would be a withdrawal or reduction (under *FA 2000, Sch 15 para 46*) of investment relief under the CORPORATE VENTURING SCHEME (22.11). Where it does have effect, the provisions at 22.24 CORPORATE VENTURING SCHEME, where relevant, are modified accordingly.

[*TCGA 1992, Sch 7AC para 4; FA 2002, Sch 8 paras 1, 5*].

13.16 **Effect of earlier company reconstruction etc.** The following applies where:

(*a*) shares held by the investing company in the investee company were acquired as a result of either:

(i) an exchange of securities within *TCGA 1992, s 135*; or

(ii) a scheme of reconstruction within *TCGA 1992, s 136*; and

(*b*) *TCGA 1992, s 127* applied, such that the event was not treated as a disposal and the 'new holding' stood in the shoes of the original shares; and

(*c*) *TCGA 1992, s 127* did not fall to be disapplied by 13.15 above (because, for example, the conditions for the exemptions at 13.4–13.6 above were not satisfied or the event took place before 1 April 2002).

The question of whether, at any time *before* the event in (*a*)(i) or (ii) above, the substantial shareholding requirement at 13.9 above was met, or the requirements relating to the investee company at 13.13 above were met, is determined by reference to the shares held by the investing company at that time. This rule can apply more than once, i.e. where there has been more than one event within (*a*)(i) or (ii) above, and it can apply in combination with the rule at 13.17 below where there have been one or more transfers within that paragraph as well as one or more events within (*a*)(i) or (ii) above.

[*TCGA 1992, Sch 7AC paras 14, 25; FA 2002, Sch 8 para 1*].

13.17 **Effect of earlier demerger.** The following applies where:

(*a*) shares held by the investing company in the investee company were acquired as a result of a transfer by a parent company of shares in its subsidiary; and

(*b*) the demerger provisions of *TCGA 1992, s 192* (see 32.34 GROUPS OF COMPANIES) applied, such that the transfer was not treated as a capital distribution and the transferred shares in the subsidiary fell to be treated as received as a result of a reorganisation of share capital and thus (by virtue of *TCGA 1992, s 127*) as standing in the shoes of the shares previously held in the parent company.

The question of whether, at any time *before* the transfer, the substantial shareholding requirement at 13.9 above was met, or the requirements relating to the investee company at 13.13 above were met, is determined by reference to the shares held by the investing company at that time. This rule can apply more than once, i.e. where there has been more than one such transfer, and it can apply in combination with the rule at 13.16 above where there have been one or more events within that paragraph as well as one or more transfers within this paragraph.

[*TCGA 1992, Sch 7AC paras 15, 25; FA 2002, Sch 8 para 1*].

13.18 TREATMENT OF HOLDINGS IN JOINT VENTURE COMPANIES (JVCS)

For the following purposes, a company is a '*joint venture company*' ('JVC') if (and only if):

(i) it is a 'trading company' (see 13.12 above) or the 'holding company' (as in 13.2 above) of a 'trading group' (see 13.12 above) or 'trading subgroup' (see 13.14 below); and

(ii) there are five or fewer persons who between them hold **75% or more** of its ordinary share capital (within *ICTA 1988, s 832(1)*, see 12.1 CAPITAL GAINS—GROUPS) (counting members of a group of companies, as in 13.2 above, as if they were a single company).

The following provisions apply only where a company has a 'qualifying shareholding' in a JVC. A company has a '*qualifying shareholding*' in a JVC if (and only if):

(*a*) it is a sole company (i.e. not a member of a group) and it holds shares, or an 'interest in shares' (see 13.27 below), in the JVC by virtue of which it holds **10% or more** of the JVC's ordinary share capital; or (*b*) it is a member of a group, the group members between them hold 10% or more of the ordinary share capital of the JVC and the company itself holds part of that ordinary share capital.

Where the above conditions are satisfied, definitions of 'trading company', 'trading group' and 'trading subgroup' have effect with the modifications in (1)–(3) below. Where the JVC is itself a 'holding company' (as in 13.2 above), the references in (1), (2) and (3) below to its activities are to the activities (other than intra-group activities) of the JVC and its '51% subsidiaries' (within *ICTA 1988, s 838*. Each reference below to a holding of shares in a JVC includes securities of the JVC or an interest in shares in, or securities of, the JVC.

(1) In determining whether a company with a qualifying shareholding in a JVC is a 'trading company' (see 13.12 above), its holding of shares in the JVC is disregarded. It is treated as carrying on a share of the JVC's activities proportionate to its percentage shareholding in the JVC. This does not apply if the company and the JVC are members of the same group of companies.

(2) In determining whether a group, of which a company with a qualifying shareholding in a JVC is a member or is the holding company, is a 'trading group' (see 13.12 above), there is disregarded any holding of shares in the JVC by any member of the group which has a qualifying shareholding in the JVC. Each such member is treated as carrying on a share of the JVC's activities proportionate to its percentage shareholding in the JVC. This does not apply if the JVC is itself a member of the group.

(3) In determining whether a company with a qualifying shareholding in a JVC is the holding company of a 'trading subgroup' (see 13.14 above), there is disregarded any holding of shares in the JVC by the company and by any of its 51% subsidiaries which itself has a qualifying shareholding in the JVC. The company and each such subsidiary is treated as carrying on a share of the JVC's activities proportionate to its percentage shareholding in the JVC. This does not apply if the JVC is a member of the same group as the company.

[*TCGA 1992, Sch 7AC paras 23, 24, 26(4); FA 2002, Sch 8 para 1*].

13.19 CONSEQUENTIAL RULES

Degrouping charge. See 12.36 CAPITAL GAINS—GROUPS for interaction between the exemptions in this chapter and the charge where a company ceases to be a member of a 75% group of companies and has had an asset transferred to it by another group member within the preceding six years.

13.20 **Negligible value claims.** Where:

(*a*) a company makes a negligible value claim under *TCGA 1992, s 24(2)* (see Tolley's Capital Gains Tax under Losses) in respect of an asset; and

(*b*) by virtue of the provisions in this chapter, a loss on a disposal of that asset at the time of the claim would not be an allowable loss,

the consequent deemed disposal and reacquisition is regarded as taking place at the time of the claim and cannot be backdated to an earlier time. Thus, in these circumstances, a negligible value claim cannot result in an allowable loss. [*TCGA 1992, Sch 7AC para 33; FA 2002, Sch 8 para 1*].

13.21 **Reorganisation involving qualifying corporate bond.** Where, on a reorganisation of share capital, the 'new asset' consists of a qualifying corporate bond (see Tolley's Capital Gains Tax under Qualifying Corporate Bonds), the exemptions in this chapter do not apply to or affect the chargeable gain or allowable loss deemed to accrue under *TCGA 1992, s 116(10)(b)* on a subsequent disposal of the whole or part of the new asset. This does not apply if the 'reorganisation' was, in fact, a deemed disposal and reacquisition within *FA*

1996, s 92(7) (asset ceasing to be a 'convertible security' but continuing to be a creditor relationship of the company — see 46.37 LOAN RELATIONSHIPS). [*TCGA 1992, Sch 7AC para 34; FA 2002, Sch 8 para 1*].

Note that the above is of no application where the reorganisation has itself been treated as an exempt disposal by virtue of 13.15 above.

13.22 **UK resident company transferring assets to overseas company.** Where in specified circumstances a UK resident company transfers its non-UK trade to a non-UK resident company in exchange (or part exchange) for securities, the whole (or part) of any resulting gain may be deferred under *TCGA 1992, s 140* (see 11.10 CAPITAL GAINS). If, subsequently,

(*a*) the UK resident company disposes of any securities received in exchange for the transfer, such that all or part of the deferred gain would normally become chargeable; but

(*b*) by virtue of the provisions in this chapter, any gain on the disposal would not be a chargeable gain,

the provisions at 11.10(i) CAPITAL GAINS are disapplied. Instead, the deferred gain, or the 'appropriate proportion' of it (as there defined), is treated as a gain accruing to the company at the time of the disposal in (*a*) above and as being a gain which is outside the exemptions in this chapter. Any gain on the disposal of the securities themselves may still attract the exemptions in this chapter (and, equally, any loss may be non-allowable). [*TCGA 1992, Sch 7AC para 35; FA 2002, Sch 8 para 1*].

13.23 **Appropriation of asset to trading stock.** Where an asset acquired by a company otherwise than as trading stock is appropriated by the company for the purposes of its trade as trading stock (whether on the commencement of the trade or otherwise) and, if the company had then sold the asset for its market value, a chargeable gain or allowable loss would have accrued to the company but for the exemption under the current provisions, the company is treated for chargeable gains purposes as if it had thereby disposed of the asset for its market value. *TCGA 1992, s 173* applies for this purpose as it does for the purposes of *TCGA 1992, s 161* (see 12.4 CAPITAL GAINS—GROUPS). [*TCGA 1992, Sch 7AC para 36; FA 2002, Sch 8 para 1*].

13.24 **Held-over gains on gifts of business assets.** Where:

(*a*) a company disposes of an asset;

(*b*) the allowable expenditure attributable to that asset would have been greater were it not for a claim for gifts hold-over relief under *TCGA 1992, s 165* (see Tolley's Capital Gains Tax under Hold-Over Reliefs) having been made in respect of an earlier disposal; and

(*c*) by virtue of the provisions in this chapter, any gain on the disposal in (*a*) above would not be a chargeable gain,

the amount of the held-over gain is treated as a gain accruing to the company at the time of the disposal in (*a*) above and as being a gain which is outside the exemptions in this chapter. If the disposal in (*a*) above is a part disposal, only an appropriate proportion of the held-over gain becomes chargeable on that occasion. [*TCGA 1992, Sch 7AC para 37; FA 2002, Sch 8 para 1*].

13.25 **FOREX matching regulations.** No gain or loss is treated as arising under *SI 1994 No 3227* (matching of foreign exchange differences — see 26.15 EXCHANGE GAINS AND LOSSES) on a disposal on which any gain would be exempt under the provisions in this chapter. [*TCGA 1992, Sch 7AC para 39; FA 2002, Sch 8 para 1*].

13.26 MISCELLANEOUS

The question of whether an asset is a chargeable asset for the purposes of corporation tax on chargeable gains generally is to be determined without regard to the availability, or potential availability, of the exemptions covered in this chapter, and references elsewhere to 'chargeable assets' should be read accordingly. Similarly, the definition of 'chargeable shares' at 11.16 CAPITAL GAINS is to be read without regard to the exemptions in this chapter. [*TCGA 1992, Sch 7AC para 32; FA 2002, Sch 8 para 1*].

13.27 For the purposes of this chapter, an '*interest in shares*' is an interest as a co-owner of shares (whether they be owned jointly or in common and whether the interests of the co-owners are equal or disparate). [*TCGA 1992, Sch 7AC para 29; FA 2002, Sch 8 para 1*].

13.28 From 1 June 2007, the Code of Practice ('COP') facility to obtain clearance for transactions will be reinstated (having been discontinued for transactions on or after 19 July 2006) The applications will be handled by specialist teams in the Large Business Office ('LBO'). Where a company's affairs are not dealt with by an LBO, they should send the application to their usual HMRC officer in the first instance. Those companies whose affairs are dealt with by an LBO should send the application to the officer who deals with their affairs. Applications should be marked on the envelope and the covering letter with 'compliance – Code of Practice 10 application – substantial shareholding exemption'. See HMRC Brief 41/2007 1 June 2007.

14 Charities

(See also Detailed Guidance at www.hmrc.gov.uk/charities/chapter_1.htm and HMRC Pamphlets IR 64 'Giving to Charity by Businesses', IR 178, 'Giving shares and securities to Charity', IR 2001, 'Trading by Charities', and CWL 4, 'Fund Raising Events: Exemption for Charities and other Qualifying Bodies'. See also 'A guide to tax incentives for corporate giving', published jointly by the Treasury and Home Office (and available at www.hmrc.gov.uk/charities/guide_tax_incentives.pdf).

Cross-references. See also 27 EXEMPT ORGANISATIONS and 66.56 TRADING INCOME.

Simon's Direct Tax Service C4.5.

Other sources. See Tolley's Charities Manual.

The headings in this chapter are as follows.

14.1 CHARITY AND CHARITABLE PURPOSES

'Charity' means any body of persons or trust resident in the UK and established for charitable purposes only. [*ICTA 1988, s 506*(*1*)]. See *Dreyfus Foundation Inc v CIR HL 1955, 36 TC 126* as to requirement for UK residence. Charities which are registered under *Charities Act 1993* are eligible for relief (see 14.2 below), and must submit periodic accounts as required by the Charity Commissioners. Relief, however, is not conditional on registration.

'Charitable purposes' comprise the relief of poverty, the advancement of education and of religion, and other purposes 'beneficial to the community' (per Lord MacNaghten in *Special Commrs v Pemsel HL 1891, 3 TC 53*). There is an overriding requirement of 'public benefit' (which is not satisfied if the beneficiaries are confined to a company's workforce and/or their dependants (*Oppenheim v Tobacco Securities Trust Co Ltd HL, [1951] AC 297*)) unless the trust is for the relief of poverty (*Dingle v Turner HL, [1972] AC 601*). For examples of purposes held to be charitable, see Tolley's Income Tax under Charities.

Under *Recreational Charities Act 1958, s 1*, the provision, in the interests of social welfare, of facilities for recreation or other leisure time occupation is deemed to be charitable (subject to the 'public benefit' criterion).

By concession, where land given for educational and certain other charitable purposes ceases to be used for such purposes and, under the *Reverter of Sites Act 1987*, is held by the trustees on a trust for sale for the benefit of the revertee, then unless the revertee is known to be a charity, there is a deemed disposal and reacquisition for capital gains purposes, which may give rise to a chargeable gain. Any income arising from the property will be liable to income tax, and a chargeable gain may also arise on a subsequent sale of the land. By concession, where the revertee is subsequently identified as a charity or disclaims all entitlement to the property (or where certain orders are made by the Charity Commissioners or the Secretary of State), provided that charitable status is re-established within six years of the date on which the land ceased to be held on the original charitable trust, any capital gains tax paid as above in the interim period will be discharged or repaid (with repayment supplement where appropriate) as will any income tax (provided that the income charged was used for charitable purposes). Partial relief will be given where the above conditions are only satisfied in respect of part of the property concerned. A request by the trustees for postponement of the tax payable will be accepted by HMRC where the revertee has not been identified and this concession may apply. (HMRC Extra-Statutory Concession, D47).

In respect of covenanted donations by companies, the Trustees of the National Heritage Memorial Fund are treated as established for charitable purposes only. [*ICTA 1988, s 339(9)*].

As regards the time at which charitable purposes arise, see *Guild and Others (as Trustees of the William Muir (Bond 9) Ltd Employees' Share Scheme) v CIR CS 1993, 66 TC 1* (trustees of share scheme required to repay loans out of proceeds of distribution and to apply balance to charitable purposes; held not to apply proceeds of distribution for charitable purposes).

Charitable Trusts (Validation) Act 1954 validates as charitable a trust set up before 1953, notwithstanding that it embraced non-charitable purposes, if its income and property were applied for charitable purposes only. All non-charitable powers are removed by the Act.

See, however, 14.9 below as regards restrictions on relief.

HMRC Charities provides guidance on the HMRC website (at www.hmrc.gov.uk/charities) and may be contacted at local call rates on 08453 020203.

Simon's Direct Tax Service. See **C4.505**.

14.2 SPECIFIC EXEMPTIONS AND RELIEFS FROM TAX

Apart from the exemptions at 14.3–14.8 below, charities are subject to tax on investment and rental income and gains and on profits from trades carried on in order to raise funds. The Schedule D exemptions at 14.3, 14.4 and 14.6 below are not general exemptions and hence do not extend to trades not falling within 14.6 below or to Case VI income generally (cf. *Grove v Young Men's Christian Association KB 1903, 4 TC 613* and *Rotunda Hospital, Dublin v Coman HL 1920, 7 TC 517*).

The exemptions are subject to the restrictions at 14.9 below.

Claims can be made, generally within six years of the end of the accounting period to which they relate, to HMRC Charities, St John's House, Merton Road, Bootle, Merseyside L69 9BB (tel: 08450 020203 (option 3)). [*ICTA 1988, s 505(1)*]. HMRC have powers to require the production of books, documents etc. relevant to any claim for exemption under *ICTA 1988, s 505(1), s 507* or *s 508* (see 27.3, 27.8, 27.11, 27.12, 27.17 EXEMPT ORGANISATIONS) leading to the repayment of income tax or the payment of tax credits. [*F(No 2)A 1992, s 28*]. Further guidance is available on the HMRC website (www.hmrc.gov.uk/charities).

Simon's Direct Tax Service. See **C4.517** *et seq.*

14.3 **Rents.** Profits or gains in respect of rents or other receipts from an estate, interest or right in or over any land (whether in the UK or elsewhere) vested in any person for charitable purposes, and otherwise chargeable to corporation tax under Schedule A or Schedule D (or to income tax under *ITTOIA 2005, Pt 2* (trading income) or *Pt 3* (property income)), are exempt to the extent they are applied to charitable purposes only. [*ICTA 1988, s 505(1)(a); FA 1996, s 146(2)(5); ITTOIA 2005, Sch 1 para 198(2)*].

14.4 **Interest, distributions, etc.** Income of a charitable company, or applicable for charitable purposes under an Act of Parliament, charter, decree, deed of trust or will, is exempt so far as applied to charitable purposes and consisting of:

- (for corporation tax) **Schedule D, Case III**; or
- (for income tax) income within *ITTOIA 2005, Pt 4 Ch 2* (interest), *Ch 7* (purchased life annuity payments), *Ch 8* (profits from deeply discounted securities) or *Ch 10*

(distributions from unauthorised unit trusts), annual payments within *ITTOIA 2005, s 579* (royalties etc. from intellectual property) and *ITTOIA 2005, Pt 5 Ch 4* (non-trading income from telecommunications rights) or *Ch 7* (annual payments not otherwise charged); or

- (for corporation tax) overseas income equivalent to Schedule D, Case III income but chargeable under Schedule D, Case V); or
- dividends from UK resident companies; or
- distributions from non-UK resident companies.

From 1 April 2002 exemption for corporation tax also applies to tax under **Schedule D, Case VI** in respect of non-trading gains of companies on intangible fixed assets under *FA 2002, Sch 29* (see 39.6 INTANGIBLE ASSETS).

Where under a will, a business was bequeathed to trustees to carry it on and pay the net profits to a charity, the amounts so paid were held to be annual payments (*R v Special Commrs (ex p Shaftesbury Homes) CA 1922, 8 TC 367*). In *Lawrence v CIR KB 1940, 23 TC 333* copyright royalties were held to be annual payments.

Income of trustees arising from public revenue dividends, and which is applicable towards repairs of any cathedral, college, church, chapel etc., being income otherwise chargeable to corporation tax under Schedule D (or to income tax under *ITTOIA 2005, Pt 4 Ch 2* (interest)), is also exempt so far as applied to those purposes only.

[*ICTA 1988, s 505(1)(c)(d),(1AA); FA 1996, s 146(3)(5), Sch 7 para 19; FA 2002, Sch 30 para 3 ITTOIA 2005, Sch 1 para 198(2)(3)*].

14.5 **Dividend tax credits.** From 6 April 1999, the tax credit attached to a qualifying distribution, of 10% of the gross amount of the distribution, i.e. one-ninth of the actual amount of the distribution, ceased to be repayable to exempt bodies, including charities. [*F(No 2)A 1997, s 30; ITTOIA 2005, Sch 1 para 496*].

As a transitional relief for charities, and for other bodies similarly treated under *ICTA 1988, s 507* or *s 508* (see 27.3, 27.8, 27.11, 27.12, 27.17 EXEMPT ORGANISATIONS), a compensatory payment may be claimed by the charity etc. in respect of qualifying distributions received from UK companies between 6 April 1999 and 5 April 2004 inclusive, provided that the charity is entitled to exemption from tax in respect of the distribution. The payment is treated for the purposes of *ICTA 1988, s 252* (see 23.7 DISTRIBUTIONS) as if it were a payment of tax credit.

The claim must be made within two years after the end of the chargeable period in which the distribution is made. Where (and to the extent that) the claim is accepted, the charity etc. will be entitled to be paid by HMRC, out of money provided by Parliament, a proportion of the amount or value of the distribution as follows:

(*a*) 21% for a distribution made in 1999/2000;

(*b*) 17% for a distribution made in 2000/01;

(*c*) 13% for a distribution made in 2001/02;

(*d*) 8% for a distribution made in 2002/03;

(*e*) 4% for a distribution made in 2003/04.

Any entitlement to a payment under these provisions is subject to a power of HMRC to determine, whether before or after the payment is made, and having regard to *ICTA 1988, s 703* (anti-avoidance provisions, see 5.2 ANTI-AVOIDANCE), that the charity etc. is to be treated as not entitled to the payment or to a part of it. An appeal may be made against any such decision by written notice to HMRC within 30 days of receipt of written notification of the decision, the appeal being to the Special Commissioners. For the purposes of *section 703 et seq.*, the payment is treated as repayment of tax. *F(No 2)A 1997, Sch 5* similarly removes or restricts the right to payments under these provisions where anti-avoidance provisions in *ICTA 1988, ss 235–237* (distributions of exempt funds, bonus issues) would have applied before 6 April 1999 to deny repayment of tax credits.

[*F(No 2)A 1997, s 35, Sch 5*].

Claims for payments under the transitional relief arrangements should be made on form R68 (introduced from April 1999), accompanied by Schedule R68(TCTR).

14.6 **Trading profits.** Profits of trades carried on (in the UK or elsewhere) by, and applied solely for the purposes of, charities, being profits otherwise chargeable to corporation tax under Schedule D (or to income tax under *ITTOIA 2005, Pt 2* (trading income)) are exempted if either:

(*a*) the trade is exercised in the course of carrying out a primary purpose of the charity; or

(*b*) the work is mainly carried on by its beneficiaries.

For accounting periods beginning on or after 22 March 2006, where the trade is exercised partly in the course of carrying out a primary purpose of the charity and partly otherwise, each part is treated as a separate trade. Similarly, where the work is carried out partly but not mainly by beneficiaries, the part carried on by the beneficiaries and the other part are treated as separate trades. Expenses and receipts are to be reasonably apportioned between the separate trades.

[*ICTA 1988, s 505(1)(e)(1B); FA 1996, s 146(4)(5) ; ITTOIA 2005, Sch 1 para 198(2); FA 2006, s 56*].

See also the specific exemptions at (i)–(iv) below.

For trades held to fall within the exemption, see *Glasgow Musical Festival Assn CS 1926, 11 TC 154*; *Royal Choral Society v CIR CA 1943, 25 TC 263* and *Dean Leigh Temperance Canteen Trustees v CIR Ch D 1958, 38 TC 315*. For regular trading within Schedule D, Case I see *British Legion, Peterhead Branch v CIR CS 1953, 35 TC 509*. (In practice, HMRC may in such cases allow a reasonable deduction for services etc. provided free.) For annual shows of agricultural societies, see 27.1 EXEMPT ORGANISATIONS.

Detailed guidance notes are available from HMRC Charities (see 14.1 above for details), which includes guidance on 'Trading by Charities' (at www.hmrc.gov.uk/charities/trading-by-charities.htm#7) giving advice on the tax treatment of particular types of trade commonly carried on by charities. It includes guidance as to the type of fund-raising activities originally covered by extra-statutory concession C4 (see (ii) below) and the conditions the activities must satisfy, the kind of profits covered by the concession and the consequences if an event is not covered by it. Advice can also be given on the Charities helpline, 08453 020203.

(i) **Exemption for small trades.** A tax exemption applies, on a claim made to HMRC, to profits and other income which is chargeable to corporation tax under Schedule D, Case I or Case VI (or to income tax as trading income (subject to below) under any of the provisions listed in *ICTA 1988, s 836B* (miscellaneous income)) and is not otherwise exempted from tax, provided the income is applied solely for the purposes of the charity and either:

(*a*) the gross income (potentially within this exemption and before deducting expenses) for the chargeable period, i.e. the tax year or company accounting period, does not exceed the 'requisite limit'; or

(*b*) the charity had, at the beginning of the chargeable period, a reasonable expectation that its gross income (as above) would not exceed that limit.

The '*requisite limit*' is the greater of:

(1) £5,000; and

(2) the lesser of £50,000 and 25% of the charity's total incoming resources for the chargeable period.

Both the above monetary limits are proportionately reduced for chargeable periods of less than twelve months.

The extension of the exemption to Schedule D, Case VI (and to miscellaneous) income is intended to cover miscellaneous fund-raising activities not within Case I (or treated as trading). Certain specified tax charges under Case VI (listed in *ICTA 1988, s 836B*) are excluded from the exemption (see *FA 2000, s 46(2)(2A)*).

[*FA 2000, s 46; ITTOIA 2005, Sch 1 para 514*].

HMRC's guidance is that they will consider any evidence to satisfy the reasonable expectation test in (*b*) above. Such evidence may include minutes of meetings at which the expectations were discussed, copies of cash-flow forecasts and business plans prepared for these meetings and copies of the previous year's accounts.

(ii) **Small-scale fund-raising events.** Profits from events such as bazaars, jumble sales, gymkhanas, carnivals etc., arranged by voluntary organisations or charities, held for, and promoted as being held for, the purpose of raising funds for charity, are not taxed if:

(*a*) the organisation or charity is not regularly carrying on these trading activities;

(*b*) it is not competing with other traders; and

(*c*) the profits are transferred to charities or otherwise applied for charitable purposes.

The exemption covers up to 15 of each type of event in any one location in any financial year of the charity etc. and includes events accessed electronically. Small events, e.g. jumble sales or coffee mornings, do not count toward the limit to the extent that the gross takings therefrom do not exceed £1,000 in any week. The limit of 15 is increased or reduced proportionately for financial years of more or less than 12 months.

The exemption corresponds with the VAT exemption for fund-raising events, for which see the corresponding chapter of Tolley's Value Added Tax. Any event meeting the criteria for the VAT exemption will automatically qualify for the income tax exemption if the condition at (*c*) above is satisfied.

(HMRC Extra-Statutory Concession, C4).

(iii) **Lotteries.** Lottery profits applied solely to the charity's purposes, being profits otherwise chargeable to corporation tax under Schedule D (or to income tax under *ITTOIA 2005, Pt 2* (trading income) or *Pt 5* (miscellaneous income)), are exempt, provided that the lottery is promoted and conducted in accordance with *Lotteries and Amusements Act 1976, s 3* or *s 5* (or NI equivalent). [*ICTA 1988, s 505(1)(f); FA 1995, s 138; ITTOIA 2005, Sch 1 para 198(2)*].

(iv) **Underwriting commissions** are taxable, whether chargeable as trading income or Case VI (although see (i) above for exemption for small trades).

14.7 **Capital Gains.** Charities are exempt from capital gains tax on gains applicable, and applied, for charitable purposes. Where property held on charitable trusts ceases to be subject to those trusts without actually having been disposed of, the trustees are nevertheless deemed to have disposed of, and immediately reacquired, the property at its market value at that time, and the notional gain arising is liable to tax. Furthermore, in so far as that property represents, directly or indirectly, gains which have accrued to the trustees from disposals made during the currency of the charity, tax is chargeable as if the exemption had never applied. Tax on such gains may be assessed within three years after the year of assessment or accounting period in which the cessation occurs. [*TCGA 1992, s 256*].

The exemption also applies to capital payments made to UK charities as beneficiaries of an offshore settlement, in respect of which a chargeable gain would be treated as accruing to it under *TCGA 1992, s 87*. The exemption applies only to the extent that the payment is applicable and is applied for charitable purposes. (Revenue Tax Bulletin Issue 36, August 1998 pp 573, 574).

See also *TCGA 1992, s 257* as regards gifts to charities treated as made for a 'no gain, no loss' consideration.

14.8 **Miscellaneous.** Charities are exempt from tax on offshore income gains if applicable and applied for charitable purposes (see 50 OFFSHORE FUNDS). [*ICTA 1988, s 761(6)*].

Charitable unit trust schemes are excluded from the normal income tax treatment of unauthorised unit trusts, and are thus able to pass on their income to participating charities without deducting tax. [*SI 1988 No 267; SI 1994 No 1479*].

Employee secondment. For deduction under Schedule D, Case I etc. for employees seconded by companies to charities, see 66.56 TRADING INCOME.

14.9 **Restrictions on exemptions.** For chargeable periods beginning on or after 22 March 2006, if a charity incurs (or is treated as incurring) 'non-charitable expenditure' (see below under that heading) in a chargeable period, relief for 'relievable income and gains' is restricted to the amount by which they exceed the non-charitable expenditure. If a charity's non-charitable expenditure exceeds its 'total income and gains', the excess is treated as non-charitable expenditure of the previous period for this purpose. Excess non-charitable expenditure may arise in a chargeable period wholly or partly as result of the carry back in which case the excess is to be carried back to the previous period and so on, but only to chargeable periods ending not more than six years before the end of the period in which the expenditure was actually incurred. Any necessary adjustments are to be made accordingly by assessment or otherwise.

Where a charity's relievable income and gains are so restricted (whether by carry back or otherwise), the charity may specify (by notice to HMRC) which items of income or gains are to be disallowed. If such a notice is required by HMRC and the charity fails to comply within 30 days from the date the requirement is imposed, HMRC will determine which items to disallow.

'*Relievable income and gains*' means broadly income and gains eligible for relief for exemption under 14.2 et seq. above. '*Total income and gains*' means the aggregate of relievable income and gains, other income and gains which are chargeable to tax and donations, legacies and other similar receipts which are not chargeable to tax.

Where the carry back of excess non-charitable expenditure causes an amount to be treated as non-charitable expenditure of a chargeable period beginning before 22 March 2006, the disallowance in respect of that period is not to exceed the amount which would have been disallowed under the rules (below) operating for chargeable periods beginning before that date.

[*ICTA 1988, s 505(3)–(7); FA 2006, s 55(1)(5)*].

For chargeable periods beginning before 22 March 2006, a restriction of the exemptions in 14.2 *et seq.* above applies in any chargeable period in which a charity:

(*a*) has 'relevant income and gains' of £10,000 or more (but see below) which exceed the amount of its 'qualifying expenditure'; and

(*b*) incurs, or is treated as incurring, 'non-qualifying expenditure'.

Where (*a*) and (*b*) above apply, exemption under *ICTA 1988, s 505*(*1*) and *TCGA 1992, s 256* is not available for so much of the excess at (*a*) as does not exceed the 'non-qualifying expenditure' incurred in that period. Where the exemption is not so available, the charity may, by notice in writing, specify which items of its 'relevant income and gains' are wholly or partly to be attributed to the amount concerned. If, within 30 days of a request to do so, the charity does not give such notice, HMRC determines the attribution.

The £10,000 *de minimis* limit in (*a*) above is proportionately reduced where a chargeable period is less than twelve months, and does not apply where two or more charities acting in concert are engaged in transactions aimed at tax avoidance and where HMRC, by notice in writing, so direct. An appeal, as against a decision on a claim, may be made against such a notice.

'*Relevant income and gains*' means the aggregate of:

(i) income which, apart from *section 505*(*1*), would not be exempt from tax, together with any income which is taxable notwithstanding *section 505*(*1*); and

(ii) gains which, apart from *TCGA 1992, s 256*, would be chargeable gains, together with any gains which are chargeable gains notwithstanding *section 256*.

[*ICTA 1988, s 505*(*3*)*–*(*8*) *as originally enacted; FA 2006, s 55*].

Charitable and non-charitable expenditure. For chargeable periods beginning on or after 22 March 2006, the terms 'charitable expenditure' and non-charitable expenditure' replace the terms 'qualifying expenditure' and non-qualifying expenditure'. The meanings are the same and, except as otherwise noted, the provisions below relate to chargeable periods beginning before and to those beginning on or after that date.

'*Non-charitable expenditure*' is expenditure other than 'charitable expenditure'. If the charity invests any funds in an investment which is not a 'qualifying investment', or makes a loan (not as an investment) which is not a 'qualifying loan', the amount invested or lent is treated as non-charitable expenditure. Where the investment or loan is realised or repaid in whole or in part in the chargeable period in which it was made, any further investment or lending of the sum realised or repaid in that period is, to the extent that it does not exceed the sum originally invested or lent, ignored in arriving at non-charitable expenditure of the period.

For chargeable periods beginning before 22 March 2006, where the aggregate of the qualifying and non-qualifying expenditure incurred in a chargeable period (the '*primary period*') exceeds the relevant income and gains of that period, so much of the excess as does not exceed the non-qualifying expenditure constitutes '*unapplied non-qualifying expenditure*'. Except to the extent (if any) that it represents the expenditure of 'non-taxable sums' received in the primary period, the unapplied non-qualifying expenditure may be treated as non-qualifying expenditure of a chargeable period ending not more than six years before the end of the primary period. '*Non-taxable sums*' are donations, legacies and other sums of a similar nature which, apart from *ICTA 1988, s 505*(*1*) and *TCGA 1992, s 256*, are not within the charge to tax. Where an amount of unapplied non-qualifying expenditure (the '*excess expenditure*') falls to be treated as non-qualifying expenditure of earlier periods, it is attributed only to those periods in which, apart from the attribution in question but taking account of any previous attribution, the relevant income and gains exceed the aggregate of the qualifying and non-qualifying expenditure in that period; and such attribution is not to be greater than the excess. Attributions are made to later periods in priority to earlier periods. Any excess expenditure which cannot be attributed to an earlier period is ignored altogether for attribution purposes. Adjustments by way of further assessments, etc. are made in consequence of an attribution to an earlier period.

'*Charitable expenditure*' is expenditure incurred exclusively for charitable purposes. A payment made (or to be made) to a body situated outside the UK is not qualifying expenditure unless the charity concerned has taken all reasonable steps to ensure that the payment will be applied for charitable purposes. Expenditure incurred in a particular period may be treated as incurred in another period if it is properly chargeable against income of that other period and is referable to commitments (contractual or otherwise) entered into before or during that other period.

'*Qualifying investments*' are the following.

(A) Investments within *Trustee Investments Act 1961, Pts I, II* (*para 13* (*mortgages, etc.*) *excepted*) *and III*.

(B) Investments in a common investment fund established under *Charities Act 1960, s 22* (or NI equivalent) or *Charities Act 1993, s 24*, or a common deposit fund established under *Charities Act 1960, s 22A* or *Charities Act 1993, s 25*, or similar funds under other enactments.

(C) Any interest in land other than a mortgage, etc.

(D) Shares or securities of a company listed on a recognised stock exchange (within *ICTA 1988, s 841; FA 2007, Sch 26; ITA 2007, s 1005*) or dealt in on the Unlisted Securities Market.

(E) Units in unit trusts (as defined).

(F) Deposits with a recognised bank or licensed institution (but see below) in respect of which interest is payable at a commercial rate, but excluding a deposit made as part of an arrangement whereby the bank, etc. makes a loan to a third party.

(FA) Uncertificated eligible debt security units within *ITTOIA 2005, s 552*(*2*).

(G) Certificates of deposit within *ICTA 1988, s 56*(*5*) for corporation tax purposes (or *ITTOIA 2005, s 552*(*2*) for income tax purposes).

(H) Loans or other investments as to which HMRC are satisfied, on a claim, that the loans or other investments are made for the benefit of the charity and not for the avoidance of tax (whether by the charity or by a third party). Loans secured by mortgage, etc. over land are eligible.

Deposits within (F) above (and money placed within (3) below) on or after 29 April 1996 must be with a bank within *ICTA 1988, s 840A* (see 8.1 BANKS) rather than with a recognised bank or licensed institution.

For accounting periods beginning on or after 1 April 2006, shares in an open-ended investment company are also treated as qualifying investments by *ICTA 1988, Sch 20 para 6A* (treated as inserted by *SI 2006 No 964, reg 94*(*7*)).

'*Qualifying loans*'. A loan which is not made by way of investment is a qualifying loan if it is one of the following.

(1) A loan made to another charity for charitable purposes only.

(2) A loan to a beneficiary of the charity which is made in the course of carrying out the purposes of the charity.

(3) Money placed on a current account with a recognised bank or licensed institution (as in (F) above) otherwise than under arrangements as in (F) above.

(4) A loan, not within (1) to (3) above, as to which HMRC are satisfied, on a claim, that the loan is made for the benefit of the charity and not for the avoidance of tax (whether by the charity or by a third party).

[*ICTA 1988, s 506, Sch 20; ITTOIA 2005, Sch 1 para 347; FA 2006, s 55*(*2*)(*3*), *Sch 26 Pt 3*(*5*)].

Payments between charities. Any payment received by one charity from another, other than in return for full consideration, which would otherwise not be chargeable to tax (and which is not of a description within any of the relieving provisions of *ICTA 1988, s 505*, see 14.2 *et seq.* above), is chargeable to tax under Schedule D, Case III or to income tax under *ITTOIA 2005, Pt 5 Ch 7* (annual payments not otherwise charged), but is eligible for relief under *section 505(1)(c)* (see 14.4 above) as if it were an annual payment. [*ICTA 1988, s 505(2); ITTOIA 2005, Sch 1 para 198(4)*].

Simon's Direct Tax Service. See C4.527.

14.10 **Transactions with substantial donors.** Payments made by a charity in the course of, or for the purposes of, the transactions in (*a*) to (*e*) below between a charity and its 'substantial donors' are treated as non-charitable expenditure (see 14.9 above). This applies to transactions occurring on or after 22 March 2006 but not those entered into in pursuance of a contract made before that date (unless in pursuance of a variation on or after that date).

The transactions are:

(*a*) the sale or letting of property by (or to) a charity to (or by) a substantial donor;

(*b*) an exchange of property between a charity and a substantial donor;

(*c*) the provision of services by (or to) a charity to (or by) a substantial donor;

(*d*) the provision of 'financial assistance' by (or to) a charity to (or by) a substantial donor; and

(*e*) investment by a charity in the business of the donor.

As regards (*d*) above, '*financial assistance*' includes the provision of a loan, guarantee or indemnity or entering into ALTERNATIVE FINANCE ARRANGEMENTS (4).

If the terms of the transaction are less beneficial to the charity than would be expected if made at arm's length, the charity will be treated as incurring non-charitable expenditure at such time (or times) as determined by HMRC and equal to an amount determined by HMRC as the cost to the charity of the difference in terms. In this case, an amount will be deducted from the amount so determined equal to any payment by the charity treated as above as non-charitable expenditure in respect of the same transaction.

A payment of remuneration to a substantial donor will also be treated as non-charitable expenditure unless it is for remuneration for services as a trustee (duly approved by the Charity Commission, a court or other body with regulatory responsibility under UK legislation). Where the payment is other than a monetary payment, this provision applies to the cash equivalent of the payment, calculated in accordance with the benefit in kind rules (see Tolley's Income Tax under Employment Income).

The above provisions apply where a transaction is entered into in a chargeable period with a donor who is a substantial donor in respect of that period, even if the donor does not fall within the definition of a 'substantial donor' until after the transaction is entered into.

A '*substantial donor*' is a person who provides the charity with 'relievable' gifts of at least £25,000 in a twelve-month period, or at least £100,000 in a six-year period (including non-monetary gifts of that value), in which the chargeable period wholly or partly falls (such amounts and time periods being variable by Treasury order). If by virtue of the above a person falls within the definition of a substantial donor, that person continues to be a substantial donor to the charity for the following five chargeable periods. A person may satisfy the definition of substantial donor by reference to gifts made at any time (whether before, on or after 22 March 2006). A gift is 'relievable' if it falls within the provisions set out in 14.11, 14.13 or 14.14 below or the provisions for individual gift aid (*FA 1990, s 25*), gifts of chargeable assets (*TCGA 1992, s 257*), gifts of trading stock from individual traders (*ITTOIA 2005, s 108*), payroll giving (*ITEPA 2003, ss 713–715*) or gifts from settlor-interested trusts (*ITTOIA 2005, ss 628, 630*). A company wholly owned by a charity will not be treated as a substantial donor in relation to that charity or any charities which own it.

Charities which are connected (in matters relating to the structure, administration or control of a charity) are treated as a single charity. (Accordingly, relievable gifts made to those charities by a donor will be aggregated for the purpose of the substantial donor test.)

Appeals. An appeal against an assessment to tax under the above provisions can be reviewed by the Special Commissioners.

Exceptions. The above provisions do not apply:

(i) where a substantial donor sells or lets property, or provides services, to a charity which HMRC determine to be on arm's length terms in the course of a business and not as part of an arrangement to avoid tax;

(ii) to the provision of services to a substantial donor if HMRC determines that they are provided on arm's length terms in the course of the actual carrying out of a primary purpose of the charity;

(iii) to the provision of financial assistance to a charity by a substantial donor if HMRC determines that it is provided on arm's length terms and not as part of an arrangement to avoid tax;

(iv) to an investment by a charity in the business of a substantial donor where the investment takes the form of the purchase of shares or securities listed on a recognised stock exchange; or

(v) to disposals at an undervalue of gifts to charity under *TCGA 1992, s 257(2)* or *ICTA 1988, s 587B* (see 14.14 below).

Payments by a charity, or benefits arising to a substantial donor from a transaction, are disregarded to the extent they relate to a gift aid payment and do not exceed the permitted limits under *ICTA 1988, s 339* (see 14.11 below) or *FA 1990, s 25* (donations by individuals, see Tolley's Income Tax under Charities).

References above to substantial donors or other persons include persons connected with them (see 19 CONNECTED PERSONS). A registered social landlord or housing association will not be treated as a substantial donor in relation to a charity with which it is connected.

[*ICTA 1988, ss 506A–506C, FA 2006, s 54*].

14.11 GIFT AID DONATIONS BY COMPANIES

A company may claim relief as a charge on income (see 55.4 PROFIT COMPUTATIONS) for a 'qualifying donation' to a charity, provided that the company is not itself a charity. The provisions for relief of payments under deeds of covenant (see 14.12 below) are now subsumed within these provisions. See further below for the exclusion of certain payments by CLOSE COMPANIES (16).

A '*qualifying donation*' is a single payment of a sum of money made by the company to a charity, excluding

(*a*) a payment which is to be regarded as a distribution (see 23 DISTRIBUTIONS) under any provisions of the *Taxes Acts* other than *ICTA 1988, s 209(4)* (transfer of assets or liabilities by a company to its members at undervalue, see 23.8 DISTRIBUTIONS); and

(*b*) a payment deductible in computing profits for corporation tax purposes (see 66.56 TRADING INCOME).

The payment is treated as an annual payment in the hands of the recipient.

As regards (*a*) above, with effect for payments made on or after 1 April 2006, a payment (other than a dividend) made by a company which is wholly owned by a charity is not to be regarded as a distribution. For payments made before 1 April 2006, the legislation was worded so as to allow gift aid treatment only where the company was wholly owned by a single charity. *FA 2006* extends the gift aid treatment to payments made by companies wholly owned by one or more charities.

In the case of *Noved Investment Co v HMRC (2006) Sp C 521*, the Special Commissioners held that *ICTA 1988, s 209(4)* was not restricted to bilateral transactions and that transfers of assets or liabilities by a company to its members at an undervalue can include cash. Accordingly, such cash transfers were qualifying donations. This is in contradiction of HMRC's view (announced in the course of this case) that such transfers do not include cash, having changed their view from that previously adopted that such assets could include cash (see HMRC Statement of 3 November 2005 available at www.hmrc.gov.uk/practitioners/distributions-legislation.htm).

'*Charity*' for this purpose has the same meaning as in *ICTA 1988, s 506* and includes the British Museum, the British Museum (Natural History), the National Heritage Memorial Fund, the Historic Buildings and Monuments Commission for England, and any scientific research association within *ICTA 1988, s 508*. (Foreign charities are currently excluded from *ICTA 1988, s 506* by virtue of *ICTA 1988, s 506(3)* and the European Commission has sent a formal request to the UK under Article 226 of the EC Treaty to end what it considers to be discrimination of foreign charities which is contrary to the EC Treaty (see IP/06/964, 10 July 2006).)

A payment by a company (or, for payments made before 1 April 2006, a payment made only by a close company, see 16 CLOSE COMPANIES) is not a qualifying donation if:

(i) it is made subject to a condition as to repayment; or

(ii) the company or a connected person (see 19 CONNECTED PERSONS), or a person connected with such a person, receives a benefit in consequence of the gift, and either:

    (A) the aggregate value of the benefits received in relation to the gift exceeds:

        (1) 25% of a donation of up to £100;

        (2) £25 where the donation is more than £100 but not more than £1,000; or

        (3) from 6 April 2007, 5% (prior to 6 April 2007 2½%) of a donation of more than £1,000; or

    (B) the aggregate of the value of the benefits received in relation to the gift and the value of any other benefits received in relation to qualifying donations made by the company to the charity earlier in the accounting period exceeds £500 (from 6 April 2007) or £250 (prior to 6 April 2007); or

(iii) it is conditional on, associated with, or part of an arrangement involving the acquisition of property by the charity from the company or a connected person (see 19 CONNECTED PERSONS), otherwise than by way of a gift.

Where a benefit:

(1) consists of the right to receive benefits at intervals over a period of less than twelve months;

(2) relates to a period of less than twelve months; or

(3) is one of a series of benefits received at intervals in consequence of making a series of gifts at intervals of less than twelve months,

the value of the benefit and the amount of the gift are 'annualised' for the purposes of (ii) above. Where a one-off benefit is received in consequence of making a gift which is one of a series of gifts made at intervals of less than twelve months, the amount of the gift is likewise 'annualised' for the purposes of (ii)(A) above (but not in this case the value of the benefit). For these purposes a gift or benefit is '*annualised*' by multiplying the amount or value by 365 and dividing the result by the number of days in the period of less than twelve months or the average number of days in the intervals of less than twelve months as appropriate.

For the purpose of calculating the donor benefits, where an accounting period straddles 1 April 2000, the accounting period is treated as two separate accounting periods, the first ending on 31 March 2000 and the second beginning on 1 April 2000.

Acknowledgement of a donor in the charity's literature does not amount to a benefit *provided that* it does not take the form of an advertisement for the donor's business (see para 3.27 of the HMRC guide referred to below).

Charity trading subsidiaries. Where a qualifying donation is made by a company that is wholly owned by a charity, the company can claim that the donation, or any part of it, is to be treated as made in an earlier accounting period falling wholly or partly within the nine months prior to the date of the donation. A claim to have the payment treated as paid in an earlier accounting period must be made within two years from the end of the accounting period in which the payment is made, or such longer period as HMRC may allow. A company is treated as wholly owned by a charity if all its ordinary share capital is directly or indirectly owned by one or more charities, or if it is limited by guarantee and every person beneficially entitled to participate in its divisible profits, or to share in the net assets available for distribution in a winding-up, is or must be a charity or a company wholly owned by a charity.

[*ICTA 1988, s 339; FA 2000, s 40; FA 2006, ss 57, 58; ITA 2007 Sch 1 para 125; FA 2007, s 60(2)*].

For a similar relief for donations by individuals, see Tolley's Income Tax under Charities. See generally the detailed guide to Gift Aid on the HMRC website at www.hmrc.gov.uk/charities/guidance-notes/chapter3/index.htm.

For donations made before 1 April 2000, see 14.12 below and the 2005–06 and earlier editions of Tolley's Corporation Tax.

Simon's Direct Tax Service. See **D2.231**.

14.12 COVENANTED PAYMENTS

The separate tax relief for payments to a charity made under deed of covenant is **withdrawn** for payments made by companies **on or after 1 April 2000**. Payments on or after that date are relieved under the Gift Aid scheme (see 14.11 above). [*FA 2000, s 41*]. By concession, charitable companies which, before 1 April 2000, made payments under deed of covenant to another charity are treated as eligible for relief as if the withdrawal of relief did not come into effect until 1 April 2001. (Revenue Press Release 10 November 2000).

For payments made before 1 April 2000, see the 2005–06 and earlier editions of Tolley's Corporation Tax.

14.13 GIFTS IN KIND TO CHARITIES

Relief is available to companies carrying on a trade or profession which give certain articles to charities within *ICTA 1988, s 506* (see 14.1 above) or to bodies treated as such under *ICTA 1988, s 507(1)* (see 27.3, 27.8, 27.11, 27.17 EXEMPT ORGANISATIONS). The gift must consist of either:

(*a*) articles manufactured, or of a type sold, in the course of the donor's trade; or

(*b*) machinery or plant used in the donor's trade or profession.

Where the donor is eligible for relief, no amount is required to be brought into account for corporation tax purposes in respect of the donated article either as a trading receipt or (for capital allowance purposes) as a disposal value. However, if the donor or any connected person (see 19 CONNECTED PERSONS) receives any benefit in any way attributable to the gift, the donor is chargeable on an amount equal to the value of that benefit, for the chargeable period in which it is received, under either Schedule D, Case I or II or, if the company is not chargeable to tax under either of those Cases for that period, under Schedule D, Case VI.

[*ICTA 1988, s 83A; CAA 2001, s 63(2), Sch 2 para 16; ITTOIA 2005, Sch 1 paras 57, 535(2)*].

For extension of these reliefs to gifts to community amateur sports clubs under *FA 2002, Sch 18*, see 70.8 VOLUNTARY ASSOCIATIONS.

Foreign charities are currently excluded from *ICTA 1988, s 506* by virtue of *ICTA 1988, s 506(3)* and the European Commission has sent a formal request to the UK under Article 226 of the EC Treaty to end what it considers to be discrimination of foreign charities which is contrary to the EC Treaty (see IP/06/964, 10 July 2006).

14.14 GIFTS OF SHARES, SECURITIES AND REAL PROPERTY

Relief is available to companies other than charities which dispose of the whole of the beneficial interest in the '*qualifying investments*' listed below, otherwise than by way of a bargain at arm's length, to charities within *ICTA 1988, s 506* (see 14.1 above) or to bodies treated as such under *ICTA 1988, s 507(1)*:

(*a*) shares and securities listed or dealt in on a recognised stock exchange or on or after 6 April 2007 dealt in on any designated market in the UK;

(*b*) units in authorised unit trusts (see 43.3 INVESTMENT FUNDS);

(*c*) shares in open-ended investment companies (see 43.2 INVESTMENT FUNDS);

(*d*) interests in offshore funds (see 50 OFFSHORE FUNDS); and

(*e*) from 1 April 2002, a 'qualifying interest in land'.

The donor can claim relief for the 'relevant amount' as a charge on income for the accounting period in which the disposal is made. Where relief is claimed under *ICTA 1988, s 587B*, no relief can be claimed under *ICTA 1988, s 83A* (see 14.13 above) or any other provision for the same disposal. For disposals to a charity after **1 July 2004** (otherwise than in performance of a contract entered into on or before that date and not varied after that date), the '*relevant amount*' is the value of the 'net benefit to the charity' either at the time the disposal is made or immediately after that time (whichever gives the lower value), or (where the disposal is at an undervalue) the excess (if any) of that value over any consideration given for the disposal. The '*net benefit to the charity*' is normally the market value of the investment. Where, however, the charity is, or becomes, subject to a 'related obligation' to *any* person (whether or not the donor or a connected person), it is the market value of the investment reduced by the aggregate 'related liabilities' of the charity. An obligation is a '*related obligation*' if it is reasonable to suppose that the disposal would not have been made in its absence or if it relates to, or is framed by reference to, or is conditional upon the charity receiving, the investment in question or a related investment (as widely defined); 'obligation' is itself widely defined so as to include any scheme, arrangement or understanding (whether or not legally enforceable) and any series of obligations. A charity's '*related liabilities*' are its liabilities under the related obligation (or under each of them). Contingent obligations are taken into account if the contingency actually occurs.

Previously, the '*relevant amount*' was the market value of the investment at the time of the disposal, or (where the disposal was at an undervalue) the excess of that value over any consideration given for the disposal.

The market value of the investment is determined as for capital gains tax purposes. In computing the amount deductible, any consideration receivable at a future time, contingently or otherwise, is brought fully into account as it is for capital gains tax purposes (see Tolley's Capital Gains Tax under Disposal).

The amount deductible is reduced by the value of any benefits received by the donor company or any connected person (see 19 CONNECTED PERSONS). The amount deductible is increased by any incidental costs of disposal (construed as for capital gains tax purposes) incurred by the person making it. Where consideration is received for the disposal, this increase is limited to the excess, if any, of the deemed consideration for capital gains tax purposes (disposal deemed to be at no gain/no loss) over the actual consideration. The cost of the asset to the charity for capital gains tax purposes is reduced by the amount deductible as above, or, if it is less than that amount, is reduced to nil.

A '*qualifying interest in land*' is a freehold interest (or a leasehold interest which is a term of years absolute) in UK land (but not an agreement to acquire freehold land or for a lease). The following two circumstances are additionally brought within the relief.

(i) Where there is a disposal of the beneficial interest in a qualifying interest in land, and there is also a disposal to the charity of any easement, servitude, right or privilege so far as benefiting that land, relief is also available for the latter disposal.

(ii) Where a person with a freehold or leasehold interest in UK land grants to a charity a lease, for (except in Scotland) a term of years absolute, of the whole or part of that land, this is regarded as a disposal for which the relief is available.

In the application of the above in Scotland:

(1) references to a freehold interest in land are to the interest of the owner;

(2) references to a leasehold interest in land which is a term of years absolute are to a tenant's right over or interest in a property subject to a lease; and

(3) references to an agreement for a lease do not include missives of let that constitute an actual lease.

The following supplementary provisions apply to disposals of qualifying interests in land.

(A) Where two or more persons are entitled jointly or in common to a qualifying interest in land, the relief applies only if each person disposes of the whole of his beneficial interest in the land to the charity. Relief is then allowed to each of those persons, being apportioned between or amongst them as they may agree.

(B) The relief is dependent on the receipt by the person disposing of the interest of a certificate given by or on behalf of the charity specifying the description of the interest concerned and the date of the disposal, and stating that the charity has acquired the interest.

(C) If a 'disqualifying event' occurs at any time in the period from the date of the disposal to the sixth anniversary of the end of the accounting period of the disposal, the person (or each of the persons) making the disposal is treated as never having been entitled to the relief in respect of the disposal (and HMRC has the necessary assessment, etc. powers). A '*disqualifying event*' occurs if the person (or any one of the persons) who made the disposal, or any connected person within *ICTA 1988, s 839* (see 19 CONNECTED PERSONS), either becomes entitled to an interest or right in relation to all or part of the land to which the disposal relates, or becomes party to an arrangement under which he, or a person connected with him, enjoys some right in relation to all or part of that land, otherwise than for full consideration in money or money's worth. This does *not* apply if the person became so entitled as a result of a disposition of property on death, whether by will, by intestacy or otherwise.

General matters. The above relief is in addition to existing capital gains tax relief (see Tolley's Capital Gains Tax). Where the asset is subsequently disposed of by the charity, its base cost for capital gains tax purposes as determined by *TCGA 1992, s 257(2)(a)* (disposal at no gain, no loss), is to be reduced by the relevant amount, or, if less than the relevant amount, to nil.

Special provisions apply to companies carrying on a life assurance business.

[*ICTA 1988, ss 587B, 587C; FA 2002, s 97; FA 2004, ss 139, 145, Sch 26 para 10; ITTOIA 2005, Sch 1 para 249*].

See also HMRC Pamphlet IR 178.

Foreign charities are currently excluded from *ICTA 1988, s 506* by virtue of *ICTA 1988, s 506(3)* and the European Commission has sent a formal request to the UK under Article 226 of the EC Treaty to end what it considers to be discrimination of foreign charities which is contrary to the EC Treaty (see IP/06/964, 10 July 2006).

[*ICTA 1988, s 587BA; ITA 2007, Sch 1 para 138; FA 2007, Sch 26 para 7*].

14.15 GIFTS OF MEDICAL SUPPLIES AND EQUIPMENT

With effect **from 1 April 2002**, where a company makes a gift from trading stock, for humanitarian purposes, of medical supplies or equipment for human use, no amount is required to be brought into account for tax purposes in respect of the donated items as a trading receipt. Transportation, delivery or distribution costs incurred by the company in making the gift are deductible in arriving at the trading profits for the accounting period in which they were incurred.

The receipt of any benefit by the company, or by any connected person within *ICTA 1988, s 839* (see 19 CONNECTED PERSONS), which is in any way attributable to a gift (or to ancillary costs) for which relief has been given as above results in a charge to corporation tax on the company under Schedule D, Case I or Case VI, as appropriate, on the amount of the benefit, for the accounting period in which it is received.

The Treasury may by order exclude from the relief medical supplies or equipment of any specified description.

No claim form or entry on the CT600 tax return is required for operation of the relief. For this and for the 'humanitarian purposes' requirement, and the broad scope of 'medical supplies or equipment', see the article on the operation of the scheme in the Revenue Tax Bulletin October 2002, pp 975–977.

[*FA 2002, s 55*].

14.16 CHARITIES AND REITS

Charitable companies exempt from tax on property, trading or savings income are exempt on REIT distributions, provided that the shares are beneficially owned by the charitable company and the income is applied for charitable purposes only.

[*ICTA 1988, s 505(1)(aa); FA 2007, Sch 17 para 17*].

15 Claims

Cross references. See 10.2(i) CAPITAL ALLOWANCES; 11.3 CAPITAL LOSSES for requirement to notify losss; 22.4 CORPORATE VENTURING SCHEME; 24.5 DOUBLE TAX RELIEF; 59.4, 59.13 and 59.21 RESEARCH AND DEVELOPMENT.

Simon's Direct Tax Service A3.605, D2.841 *et seq.*

15.1 CLAIMS AND ELECTIONS

All claims must be expressed in figures at the time the claim is made, and (subject to any provision prescribing a different time limit) must be made within six years from the end of the accounting period to which they relate. Claims and elections may be amended by the making of a supplementary claim or election within the time allowed for the original claim or election. [*FA 1998, Sch 18 paras 54–56*].

Subject to any express provision to the contrary:

(*a*) claims and elections affecting only one accounting period, and which are made after notice has been given requiring the delivery of a company tax return for that period, must be made in the return, or by amendment of the return, if they can be so made. A claim, etc. made after the return has been delivered is treated as an amendment of the return (as under 61.8 RETURNS). Group relief and capital allowance claims (see further below) and claims to research and development tax credits (see 59 RESEARCH AND DEVELOPMENT) can *only* be made by inclusion in a tax return;

(*b*) claims, etc. which affect an accounting period or periods other than that in which the event or occasion giving rise to the claim, etc. occurs are treated as amending the return for that period (or for the period affected), as under 61.8 RETURNS, where that return has already been delivered and can be so amended;

(*c*) otherwise, *TMA 1970, Sch 1A* (as amended by *FA 1998, Sch 19 para 42*) provides the procedure for claims etc. (see 15.6 below).

(*a*)–(*c*) above do not, however, affect the time limit or any other condition for making a claim or election.

A joint claim or election may be made in a return. The written claim etc. signed by the appropriate person(s) need be delivered with only one of the returns to which it applies, the return(s) of the other party or parties being required to reveal its existence and be prepared in accordance with it. (Revenue Guide to Self-Assessment, para 7.6.6).

[*FA 1998, Sch 18 paras 10(2), 57–60; FA 2002, Sch 14 para 2*].

Certain claims not required to be made in a company tax return may not be made before the return for the period to which the claim relates is delivered. This applies to claims for payment of tax credits, where still available (see 29.2 FRANKED INVESTMENT INCOME), excluding claims by companies entitled to certain corporation tax exemptions unless *ICTA 1988, Sch 19AB* applies, to certain claims for income tax repayments, and to claims for relief under *FA 2000, Sch 15 Pt V* (CORPORATE VENTURING SCHEME (22)). [*FA 1998, Sch 18 para 9*].

Consequential claims. For consequential claims, elections etc. arising out of HMRC assessments or amendments to self-assessments, see 15.5 below.

Simon's Direct Tax Service. See **D2.841** *et seq.*

15.2 **Group relief.** A claim to group relief must be included in the company tax return (or amended return) for the accounting period for which the claim is made. It must specify the quantum of the amount claimed and the surrendering company. For accounting periods ending on or after 1 April 2000, it must also state whether any of the following:

(1) the claimant company;

(2) the surrendering company; or

(3) any other company by reference to which either those companies are members of the same group or the conditions for consortium relief are satisfied,

was not UK resident in either or both of the surrendering company's accounting period to which the surrender relates or the corresponding accounting period of the claimant company.

The claim must be made (and may be withdrawn) at any time up to the latest of:

(i) the first anniversary of the filing date for the company tax return;

(ii) 30 days after closure of any enquiry into that return (unless the enquiry, being otherwise out of time, was limited, as referred to in 61.12 RETURNS, to matters to which a previous amendment making or withdrawing a group relief claim relates, or which are affected by the amendment);

(iii) 30 days after notice of any amendment of that return by HMRC following such an enquiry; and

(iv) 30 days after determination of any appeal against an amendment within (iii),

or at a later time if HMRC allow it (for which see 47.2 LOSSES).

These time limits override the normal time limits for amendment of a company tax return. Withdrawals of claims must be made by amending the return, and a claim can only be amended by withdrawal and replacement by another claim.

A claim may be made after the surrendering company has left the group (*A W Chapman Ltd v Hennessey Ch D 1981, 55 TC 516*).

A claim may be made for less than the full amount available for surrender at the time of the claim, but is ineffective if it is for more than that amount. The amount available for surrender at any time is the total amount available under *ICTA 1988, s 403* (see 32.10 GROUPS OF COMPANIES) on the basis of the surrendering company's tax return, disregarding any amendment whose effect is deferred pending completion of an enquiry (see 61.12 RETURNS), *less* all amounts for which notices of consent (see below) have been given and not withdrawn. Withdrawals are given effect before any claims made on the same day. Where claims are made on the same day for an aggregate amount in excess of the amount available for surrender, HMRC determines which of the claims is to be ineffective to prevent an excess arising. In practice, they will treat as ineffective the claim(s) in the lowest amount(s) consistent with achieving this objective (see HMRC Company Taxation Manual, CTM 97070).

Claims may be made by more than one company in respect of the same surrendering company accounting period.

A claim requires the written consent of the surrendering company (and a consortium claim also that of each member of the consortium), which must be given to the officer of HMRC to whom the company makes its tax returns at, or before, the time the claim is made, and a copy of which must accompany the claim. The consent notice must give the names and tax district references of the surrendering company and the company to which relief is being surrendered, the amount of the relief, and the surrendering company accounting period to which the surrender relates. It may not be amended, but may be withdrawn (by notice to the officer to whom the consent was notified) and replaced within the normal time limits (as above). Notice of withdrawal must be accompanied by the written consent of the claimant company, unless the withdrawal is the result of a reduction in the amount available for surrender (for which see below), and the claimant company must, so far as it may do so, amend its return accordingly.

See, however, below as regards simplified claim and surrender procedures.

Where the surrendering company has already made its return for the period to which the surrender relates, it must, at the same time as giving its consent, amend its return to reflect that consent. Where the consent relates to a trading loss for which relief has already been obtained by carry-forward, the surrendering company must (notwithstanding any time limits otherwise applicable) amend its return(s) for the subsequent period(s) in which relief was given for the loss to reflect the consent (relief for such periods being treated as given for carry-forward losses of earlier accounting periods before later ones).

Where there is a reduction in the total amount available for surrender (as above) below the amount for which consent to surrender has already been given, the company must, within 30 days, withdraw its consent (and may issue new notices of consent) so as bring the total of amounts for which consent is given within the total amount available. Copies of the withdrawal notices and any new consents must be sent to the companies affected and to HMRC. If the company fails to take such corrective action, HMRC may by written notice to the company give directions as to which consents are to be treated as reduced or eliminated to the extent necessary to achieve that objective (subject to appeal in writing by the company within 30 days of the notice to the officer by whom it was given), and must copy the notice to any claimant company affected by those directions. A claimant company notified of any withdrawal or new consent or HMRC direction must, so far as it may do so, amend its return for the period in question accordingly.

Where a claimant company becomes liable to tax in consequence of receiving a notice of withdrawal or new consent or HMRC direction (as above), and any of the tax is unpaid six months after the company's 'time limit for claims' (see below), HMRC may, up to two years after that time limit, make an assessment in the name of the claimant company on any other company which has obtained group relief as a result of the surrender. The amount of the assessment is limited to the lesser of the amount of the unpaid tax and the amount of tax the other company saves by virtue of the surrender. The other company may recover the tax (and any interest thereon) from the claimant company. The company's 'time limit for claims' for this purpose is the latest of the dates in (i)–(iv) above on which the company could make or withdraw a group relief claim for the accounting period for which the claim in question was made.

An assessment may be made to recover group relief which in the opinion of HMRC is, or has become, excessive. This is without prejudice to the making of a discovery assessment (see 7.2 ASSESSMENTS) or to the making of adjustments by way of discharge or repayment of tax. As regards notices of assessment, time limits and appeals, the same conditions apply as in relation to discovery assessments. Where a claimant company fails, or is unable, to amend its return following receipt of a notice of withdrawal or new consent or HMRC direction (as above), an assessment may be made (if otherwise out of time) up to one year after the date of the notice (the date of the new notice if a new notice of consent follows a withdrawal notice).

Simplified group relief procedures. Under *The Corporation Tax (Simplified Arrangements for Group Relief) Regulations 1999 (SI 1999 No 2975)*(as amended), a group of companies all, or substantially all, of whose tax returns are made to the same tax office, may enter into special arrangements enabling an authorised company within the group to act for the group in relation to group relief claims. The authorised company may then, in a form provided or authorised by HMRC, provide a written statement containing the information necessary for the amendment of company tax returns of the companies covered by the arrangements for the purpose of making or withdrawing group relief claims and surrenders. Group companies remain liable for any incorrect claim or return arising from the authorised company's statement. Consortium companies which can claim or surrender group relief may be included in the arrangements (and the authorised company may be a consortium company). For the detailed requirements as to the making of an application by an authorised company, and the consequences of entering into such arrangements, see *SI 1999 No 2975* (as amended).

Overseas losses of non-resident companies. The above provisions apply to claims (from 1 April 2006) in respect of overseas losses of non-resident companies (see 32.6(*b*) and 32.16 GROUPS OF COMPANIES) with the following modifications. References to the relief being surrendered is to the EEA amount. References to the surrendering company's accounting period are to its deemed accounting period under 32.16(iii) GROUPS OF COMPANIES. Notice of consent of the surrendering company is to be given by the claimant company to the officer of HMRC to whom that company makes its returns and the requirement for the notice to contain details of tax district reference does not apply. Notice of withdrawal of consent is to be given by the claimant company and not the surrendering company. A notice of withdrawal and any new notice of consent under *FA 1998, Sch 18 para 75* (reduction in amount available for surrender) is to be sent to an officer of HMRC by the claimant rather than the surrendering company and any notice containing directions by an officer of HMRC is to be given to the claimant company. The claimant company rather than the surrendering company can appeal against such directions and the rest of *Sch 18* is to be similarly read with appropriate modifications.

Where a notice to produce documents is given to the claimant company for the purposes of an enquiry, the notice may require the claimant company to explain why the EEA amount meets the conditions for it to be treated as a qualifying loss and to provide details of the recalculation required (see 32.16 GROUPS OF COMPANIES). The claimant company may also be required to explain why the EEA amount is not prevented from being surrendered by virtue of the unallowable losses provision in 32.17 GROUPS OF COMPANIES.

[*ICTA 1988, s 402(5); FA 1998, Sch 18 paras 10(2), 66–77A; FA 2006, Sch 1 para 8*].

See HMRC Company Taxation Manual, CTM 97600 *et seq.*

15.3 **Capital allowances.** A capital allowance claim under self-assessment must be included in the company tax return (or amended return) for the accounting period for which the claim is made. It must specify the quantum of the amount claimed. It must be made (and may be amended or withdrawn) at any time up to the latest of:

(A) the first anniversary of the filing date for the company tax return;

(B) 30 days after closure of any enquiry into that return (unless the enquiry, being otherwise out of time, was limited, as referred to in 61.12 RETURNS, to matters to which a previous amendment making or withdrawing a capital allowance claim relates, or which are affected by the amendment);

(C) 30 days after notice of any amendment of that return by HMRC following such an enquiry; and

(D) 30 days after determination of any appeal against an amendment within (iii),

or at a later time if HMRC allow it (for which see 47.2 LOSSES).

These time limits override the normal time limits for amendment of a company tax return. Amendments or withdrawals of claims must be made by amending the return.

If the effect of a claim is to reduce the available capital allowances for another accounting period for which a return has already been made, the company has 30 days to make the necessary amendments of that return. If it fails to do so, HMRC may, by written notice and subject to a right of appeal within 30 days of the issue of the notice, amend the return to correct the position (notwithstanding any time limit otherwise applicable).

[*FA 1998, Sch 18 paras 10(2), 78–83; CAA 2001, Sch 2 para 103*].

15.4 **Other claims.** For claims for payment of research and development tax credits, see 59 RESEARCH AND DEVELOPMENT. For claims for payment of film tax credits see 66.52 TRADING INCOME.

For consequential claims, elections etc. arising out of HMRC assessments or amendments to self-assessments (which may generally be made within one year from the end of the accounting period in which the assessment was made or the enquiry into the relevant return closed), or where an assessment is made in a case involving fraud or negligence, see 15.5 below.

15.5 CONSEQUENTIAL CLAIMS

Where:

(*a*) a company tax return is amended by HMRC under *FA 1998, Sch 18 para 34(2)(b)* (i.e. an amendment, following closure of an enquiry, to a return other than the return which was the subject of the enquiry) so that the tax payable is increased (see 61.15 RETURNS); or

(*b*) a discovery assessment (see 7.2 ASSESSMENTS) is made; or

(*c*) an assessment to recover excessive group relief (see 15.2 above) is made,

the following provisions apply to allow certain claims, elections, applications and notices to be made or given, or revoked or varied. Where an assessment is made in a case involving fraudulent or negligent conduct (see 7.2 ASSESSMENTS), the more restricted relief described below applies instead.

A claim, etc. relating to the accounting period in respect of which the amendment or assessment was made, or made or given by reference to an event occurring in that period, and the making etc. of which has or could have the effect of reducing a 'relevant liability' of the company, may be made or given at any time within one year from the end of the '*relevant accounting period*', i.e. that in which the closure notice was issued or the assessment made. Similarly, if previously made or given, it may be varied or (unless irrevocable) revoked in the same manner as it was made or given, and by or with the consent of the same person(s) who made it, gave it or consented to it (or their personal representatives). A '*relevant liability*' is the increased liability arising from the amendment or assessment, or any other liability of the company for the accounting period to which the amendment or assessment relates or any subsequent accounting period ending not later than one year after the end of the relevant accounting period.

If the effect of a consequential claim, etc. as above would be to alter the tax liability of another person, the written consent of that person (or their personal representative) to the claim, etc. is required. If the effect is to increase that person's liability, neither the above provisions nor *TMA 1970, s 43A* (the corresponding income and capital gains tax provisions) apply in relation to any amendment or assessment made because of the increased liability.

Where one or more claims etc. as above are made in consequence of an amendment or assessment, the combined tax liability of the company and any other persons affected cannot be reduced by an amount which exceeds the additional tax liability resulting from that amendment or assessment. Where this limitation involves more than one period or more than one person, the limited amount available is apportioned between the periods or persons concerned. The manner in which the apportionment is to be made is specified by HMRC by written notice to the person(s) concerned, who may, however, within 30 days from the date of the notice (where more than one person is concerned, the last notice), give (or jointly give) written notice substituting a different manner of apportionment.

The claims appeals provisions are appropriately modified in relation to revocations or variations of claims under the above provisions.

Where an assessment is made in a case involving *fraudulent or negligent conduct*, the above provisions for consequential claims are disapplied. Instead, if the company so requires, effect is given, in determining the tax charged by the assessment, to any relief or allowance to which the company would have been entitled for the accounting period on a claim or application made within the normal time limits. The claims or applications must be made either before the assessment is made or within the time provided for an appeal against the assessment (see HMRC Company Taxation Manual, CTM 90665).

[*FA 1998, Sch 18 paras 61–65*].

Simon's Direct Tax Service. See D2.844.

15.6 CLAIMS ETC. NOT INCLUDED IN RETURNS

Subject to any specific provision requiring a claim or election to be made to HMRC, a claim or election made otherwise than in a return must be made to an officer of HMRC. The claim etc. must include a declaration by the claimant that all particulars are correctly stated to the best of his information or belief. No claim requiring a tax repayment can be made unless the claimant has documentary proof that the tax has been paid or deducted. The claim must be made in a form determined by HMRC and may require, *inter alia*, a statement of the amount of tax to be discharged or repaid and (except as below) supporting information and documentation. In practice, HMRC do not generally determine the particular form in which a claim must be made. In the case of a claim by or on behalf of a person who is not resident in the UK, HMRC may require a statement or declaration in support of the claim to be made by affidavit.

A person who may wish to make a claim must keep all such records as may be requisite for the purpose and must preserve them until such time as HMRC may no longer enquire into the claim or such enquiries are treated as completed. There is a maximum penalty of £3,000 for non-compliance in relation to any claim *actually made*. Similar provisions and exceptions apply as in 61.9 RETURNS as to the preservation of the information contained in documents and other records instead of originals and the exception from penalty for non-compliance in relation to dividend vouchers, interest certificates etc.

A claimant may, at any time within twelve months of making a claim, amend the claim by notice to an officer of HMRC. An officer of HMRC may similarly, at any time within nine months of the claim being made, amend the claim to correct any obvious errors or mistakes (including errors of principle and arithmetical mistakes). No such amendments may, however, be made while the claim is under enquiry (see below). HMRC have powers to enquire into a claim etc. (or amendment thereof) similar to those relating to company tax returns (see 61.10 RETURNS). Notice of intention to enquire must be given by the first anniversary of the end of the accounting period to which the claim relates or, if later, by the quarter day (meaning 31 January, 30 April etc.) next following the first anniversary of the date of claim etc. In the event of such an enquiry, they have powers to call for documents, etc. similar to those relating to enquiries into company tax returns (see 61.11 RETURNS). Where an enquiry is in progress, an officer of HMRC may give provisional effect to the claim etc. (or amendment thereof) to such extent as he thinks fit.

For enquiries commencing on or after (or in progress on) 11 May 2001, the enquiry is complete when HMRC's officer issues a closure notice informing the claimant of his conclusions. If the claim is for discharge or repayment of tax, the notice must either state that, in the officer's opinion, no amendment of the claim is required or amend the claim so as to make good or eliminate any deficiency or excess which in the officer's opinion has arisen (the latter only applying, in the case of an enquiry into an amendment of a claim, so far as the deficiency or excess is attributable to that amendment). In the case of any other claim, the notice must either allow the claim or disallow it wholly or to the extent the officer considers appropriate. The claimant may apply to the Commissioners for a direction to issue a closure notice in the same way as applies to enquiries into returns (see 61.14 RETURNS). For earlier enquiries, the provisions for amendment of claims on completion of an enquiry were similar to those which apply to amendment of a company's return on completion of an enquiry (see 61.15 RETURNS).

HMRC must give effect to such an amendment, by assessment if necessary, within 30 days after issue of the closure notice (or, before 11 May 2001, of the amendment being made).

An appeal may be made against an amendment by HMRC to a claim following an enquiry, written notice of appeal to be given normally within 30 days after the amendment is made (extended to three months where questions of residence are involved). If an amendment is varied on appeal, HMRC have a further 30 days to give effect to the variation. Where a claim etc. does not give rise to a discharge or repayment of tax (for example, a claim to carry forward trading losses), there are provisions as to disallowance of such claims on completion of the enquiry, with appeal procedures similar to those above.

Appeals against amendments to claims are normally made to the General Commissioners. Where the claim was made to HMRC under certain specified provisions, appeal is to the Special Commissioners, and this also applies (unless the Special Commissioners otherwise direct) where a question has been referred to them during an enquiry into a return (whether or not the referral was withdrawn). In other cases, there are special rules enabling the taxpayer to elect to bring the appeal before the Special Commissioners, but this election may be disregarded in certain circumstances. If the taxpayer also has an appeal pending concerning an assessment and the appeals relate to the same income, both appeals must be to the same body of Commissioners.

Where these provisions apply to a claim, etc. which results in an increase in the tax payable, all necessary adjustments, by way of assessment or otherwise, may be made so as to give effect to it.

[*TMA 1970, s 42(11), Sch 1A; FA 1998, Sch 18 para 60(3); FA 2001, Sch 29 paras 10, 12, 13, 34*].

Simon's Direct Tax Service. See **D2.842**.

15.7 TIME LIMITS

Unless otherwise specified, claims for relief from corporation tax must be made within six years of the end of the accounting period to which they relate. [*FA 1998, Sch 18 para 55*]. See 65 TIME LIMITS and Tolley's Income Tax under Time Limits—Fixed Dates and Time Limits—Miscellaneous. See also 15.10 below with respect to recovery of tax paid under mistake of law.

15.8 APPEALS IN RESPECT OF CLAIMS

Appeals have to be made in writing within 30 days of the issue of a notice of amendment to a self-assessment or of a notice of an assessment which is not a self-assessment. See 7.2 ASSESSMENTS, 61.15 RETURNS, 6.1 APPEALS. As regards claims etc. to which *TMA 1970, Sch 1A* applies (see below), appeals against amendments to claims etc. must be made within 30 days of the amendment being made, extended to three months where the appeal relates to certain residence etc. claims or to pension funds for overseas employees. [*TMA 1970, Sch 1A para 9*]. *TMA 1970, Sch 1A* (as amended) deals with all aspects of claims not within *FA 1998, Sch 18 paras 57, 58* (mainly those not included in the company tax return (or amended return), see 15.1 above). [*FA 1998, Sch 18 para 59*]. *TMA 1970, ss 46B–46D* (as amended) have effect as respects the Tribunal to which an appeal under that *Schedule* lies.

15.9 ERROR OR MISTAKE RELIEF

Where a company believes it has paid too much tax under an assessment (or self-assessment) by reason of some error or mistake in a return, it may claim relief by written notice to HMRC not more than six years after the end of the accounting period to which the return relates. After enquiring into the matter, and having regard to all the relevant circumstances, HMRC will then give by repayment such relief as is just and reasonable. In determining the claim they will, in particular, consider whether the granting of relief would result in amounts being excluded from the charge to tax, taking into consideration accounting periods of the company other than that to which the claim relates. No relief may, however, be given in respect of a mistake as to the basis on which the liability ought to have been computed where the return was made on the basis, or in accordance with the practice, generally prevailing at the time. Nor may relief be given where the mistake was in a claim or election included in the return.

An appeal against a decision of HMRC on a claim lies to the Special Commissioners, who determine the claim in accordance with the same principles as apply to HMRC's decision. An appeal to the High Court against a decision of the Special Commissioners can only be made on a point of law in connection with the computation of profits (including amounts chargeable under *ICTA 1988, s 419* (loans to participators, see 16.9 *et seq.* CLOSE COMPANIES) and *ICTA 1988, s 747* (CONTROLLED FOREIGN COMPANIES (21)). [*FA 1998, Sch 18 para 51*]. A claim to error or mistake relief may still be made in relation to an amendment to a self-assessment notwithstanding an agreement with the inspector preceding that amendment (*Wall v CIR (Sp C 303), [2002] SSCD 122*).

See also 15.10 below for recovery of tax paid under mistake of law.

Simon's Direct Tax Service. See A3.1001, D2.846.

15.10 CLAIM FOR RESTITUTION OF TAX PAID UNDER MISTAKE OF LAW

It was held in *Woolwich Equitable Building Society v CIR* (see 40.7 INTEREST ON OVERPAID TAX) that tax paid pursuant to an *ultra vires* demand was recoverable as of right at common law and without need to invoke mistake of law by the taxpayer.

It was further held, *inter alia*, in *Deutsche Morgan Grenfell Group plc v CIR and A-G Ch D, [2003] STC 1017* that the common law remedy of restitution of payment made under a mistake of law applies to payments of tax as it does to other payments. In *CIR v Deutsche Morgan Grenfell Group plc, CA [2005] STC 329*, the CA, reversing the High Court decision, held that the general rules on mistake of law, applicable in private transactions, do not apply to claims for overpayment of taxes and that, a remedy in such cases was only available under the principle established in the *Woolwich* case (see above) or under the statutory regime (in this case under *TMA 1970, s 33* – see 15.9 CLAIMS). It was held by the House of Lords in *Deutsche Morgan Grenfell Group plc v CIR* HL that English law recognised a restitution claim for tax paid under a mistake of law and that the limitation period (under the *Limitation Act 1980*) ran from the date the mistake at law was discovered, which, in Deutsche Morgan's case, was the date of the ECJ decision which made it clear that a mistake in law had occurred (8 March 2001). The decision was in favour of the taxpayer. House of Lords (and cross appeal), HL [2006] UKHL 49. This confirmed the ruling by the High Court, following which provisions were introduced by *FA 2004, s 320* to prevent the *Limitation Act 1980, s 32(1)(c)* from applying in actions for restitution brought after 7 September 2003.

PBR 2006 re-emphasised the Government's intention to restrict the limitation period for recovery of direct tax paid under a mistake of law to six years. This provision will have retrospective effect for actions brought before 8 September 2003 and not decided by a final judgment by 6 December 2006. See http://www.hmrc.gov.uk/pbr2006/six-year-limit-statement.pdf

By virtue of the *Limitation Act 1980, s 32(1)(c)* (or in Northern Ireland *Article 71(1)(c)* of the *Limitation (Northern Ireland) Order 1989* (*SI 1989 No 1339*)), the six-year period of limitation in the case of mistake of law does not begin to run until the claimant discovers the mistake (or could with reasonable diligence have discovered it). However, under provisions introduced by *FA 2004, s 320*, this does not apply in relation to a mistake of law relating to taxes administered by HMRC where the action for restitution is brought after 7 September 2003. The effect is that court actions for restitution based on mistake of law must generally be brought within six years of the tax having been paid.

New claims arising from existing actions for a different payment, period, transaction or other matter is not treated as part of the original action (by virtue of *Limitation Act 1980, s 35(5)(a)* (or in Northern Ireland *Article 73(4)(a)* of the *Limitation (Northern Ireland)*

Order 1989) where the new claim is made after 19 November 2003. An action is deemed to be discontinued on 22 July 2004 (and any payment made by HMRC in relation to the action may be recovered with due interest) where:

(*a*) an action is brought before 22 July 2004 and after 7 September 2003 and a defence of limitation would have been available had the above provisions been in force; or

(*b*) a claim in relation to an existing action is made before 22 July 2004 but after 19 November 2003 but would not have been allowed had the above provisions been in force.

These provisions do not apply to claims made before 20 November 2003 that would be treated as actions brought before 8 September 2003. A claim is treated as made before 20 November 2003 where HMRC have consented in writing before that date to the making of the claim or, where the consent of the Commissioners has been sought or an application has been made to the courts for permission to make the claim, the consent or application has not been refused immediately before that date.

Similar provisions apply to proceedings commenced in the courts after 7 September 2003 to disapply the *Prescription and Limitation* (*Scotland*) *Act 1973, s 6*(*4*)(*a*)(*ii*) in relation to an obligation based on redress of unjust enrichment arising from an error of law relating to a Revenue taxation matter in Scotland. The effect in this case is that court actions for restitution based on mistake of law must generally be brought within five years of the tax having been paid.

[*FA 2004, ss 320, 321*].

FA 2007, s 107 extends the existing treatment of claims for restitution of tax paid under mistake of law to apply to past transactions as well as future transactions. It provides that the *Limitation Act 1980, s 32*(*1*)(*c*) does not apply to an action for restitution of direct tax due to a mistake of law brought before 8 September 2003, whether the action relates solely to a claim for restitution or otherwise. However, this rule does not apply to actions on which judgment on the application of the *Limitation Act 1980, s 32*(*1*)(*c*) had been given by the House of Lords in favour of the taxpayer (or another party in a group litigation order) before 6 December 2006.

Where a court has decided in favour of a taxpayer on or after 6 December 2006 but before **19 July 2007** and tax has been repaid, the judgment is reversed so far as restitution is concerned and the amount received is repayable with interest.

[*FA 2007, s 107*].

16 Close Companies

Simon's Direct Tax Service Part D3.

The headings in this chapter are as follows.

16.1 CLOSE COMPANY — DEFINITION

A company is close if:

(*a*) it is under the 'control' of five or fewer 'participators' [*ICTA 1988, s 414*(*1*)]; or

(*b*) it is under the control of participators who are 'directors' [*ICTA 1988, s 414*(*1*)]; or

(*c*) five or fewer participators, or participators who are directors, together possess or are entitled to acquire such rights as would, in the event of a winding-up, entitle them to receive the greater part of the assets available for distribution among participators (assuming assets distributed to company participators are similarly distributed on). The test is applied with and without taking rights as a loan creditor into account. Participators in and directors of companies entitled to receive assets in such a notional winding-up are treated as participators in or directors of the company under consideration, but company participators are disregarded (except as above) unless acting in a fiduciary or representative capacity. [*ICTA 1988, s 414*(*2*)–(*2D*)].

For exceptions, see 16.6 below.

Simon's Direct Tax Service. See D3.102–D3.112, D3.121.

16.2 **'Control'** means the ability to exercise, or to acquire, control, whether direct or indirect, over the company's affairs. It includes the possession of, or right to acquire:

(i) the greater part of the share capital or issued share capital; or

(ii) the greater part of the voting power; or

(iii) so much of the issued share capital as would give the right to receive the greater part of the company's income, were all that income distributed; or

(iv) rights to the greater part of the company's assets in a distribution on a winding-up or in any other circumstances. [*ICTA 1988, s 416*(*2*)].

Future rights and rights of nominees are included. [*ICTA 1988, s 416*(*4*)(*5*)]. The first-mentioned holder of shares in joint ownership is treated as able alone to exercise the rights attaching thereto. (*Harton Coal Co Ltd Ch D 1960, 39 TC 174*).

Two or more persons have control of a company if their aggregated rights satisfy the above conditions. [*ICTA 1988, s 416*(*3*)]. There may be attributed to any person the rights and powers of any 'associate' or associates of his, or of any company or companies controlled by him (with or without his associates), together with those of any nominee of such company or associate. However the rights and powers of associates' associates and of companies controlled only by associates, are disregarded. [*ICTA 1988, s 416*(*6*)]. See 16.5 below. For circumstances in which HMRC are bound so to attribute such rights and powers, see *R v CIR (ex p Newfields Developments Ltd) HL 2001, 73 TC 532.*

See also 63.7 SMALL COMPANIES—REDUCED RATES.

16.3 **'Participator'** means a person having a share or interest in the capital or income of the company and includes:

(i) any person possessing, or entitled to acquire, share capital or voting rights;

(ii) any 'loan creditor' (see below);

(iii) any person possessing, or entitled to acquire, a right to receive, or to participate in, distributions or any amount payable by the company (in cash or in kind) to loan creditors (see below) by way of premium on redemption ('distribution' is not to be given the extended meaning explained in 23.19 DISTRIBUTIONS); and

(iv) any person entitled to ensure that present or future income or assets of the company will be applied directly or indirectly for his benefit.

Future rights are included. [*ICTA 1988, s 417(1)*].

A '*loan creditor*' is a person to whom money is owed by the company in respect of:

(A) any money borrowed by the company; or

(B) any capital asset acquired by the company; or

(C) any right to receive income created in the company's favour; or

(D) any redeemable loan capital issued by the company; or

(E) any debt the value of which (to the company) at the time the debt was incurred (including any premium thereon) substantially exceeded the consideration therefor.

[*ICTA 1988, s 417(7)*].

The definition includes persons other than the actual creditor who have a beneficial interest in the debt or loan capital. [*ICTA 1988, s 417(8)*].

A person carrying on a banking business is not deemed to be a loan creditor in respect of any loan capital issued or debt incurred by the company for money lent by him to the company in the ordinary course of that business. [*ICTA 1988, s 417(9)*]. As to what constitutes a *bona fide* banking business, see *Hafton Properties Ltd v McHugh Ch D 1986, 59 TC 420.*

Similarly, a recognised money broker is not treated as a participator in a stock-jobbing company solely by reason of short-term loans or advances arising in the ordinary course of their respective trades. (HMRC Extra-Statutory Concession, C8).

16.4 **'Director'** includes any person:

(i) who occupies the position of director (by whatever name called); or

(ii) in accordance with whose directions or instructions the directors are accustomed to act (although it is thought that HMRC will not seek to bring professional advisers, acting purely in their capacity as such, within this head); or

(iii) who is a manager of the company (or otherwise concerned in the management of the company's trade or business) and who is the beneficial owner of, or able directly or indirectly to control, at least 20% of the ordinary share capital (i.e. all issued share capital other than that entitled only to a fixed rate of dividend) of the company. For this purpose, the holdings and powers of his associates may be attributed to him. For the meaning of 'associates', see 16.5 below.

[*ICTA 1988, s 417(5)(6)*].

16.5 An '**associate**' of a person who is a participator is:

(i) any relative of that person, i.e. that person's spouse or (from 5 December 2005) civil partner , parent or remoter forebear, child or remoter issue, or brother or sister;

(ii) any partner of that person;

(iii) the trustee(s) of any settlement of which that person, or any relative of his (living or dead), is or was a settlor, (see 19.7 CONNECTED PERSONS for the definitions of 'settlement' and of 'settlor');

(iv) where that person is interested in any shares or obligations of the company which are subject to a trust or which are part of the estate of a deceased person, the trustee(s) or personal representatives concerned and, if the participator is a company, any other company interested in those shares or obligations.

[*ICTA 1988, s 417(3)(4); ITTOIA 2005, Sch 1 para 173; SI 2005 No 3229, reg 72*].

Trustees are interested in shares comprised in the settlement (*J Bibby & Sons Ltd v CIR HL 1945, 29 TC 167*). Holders of units in a unit trust are not 'associates' merely by reason of their common membership of the unit trust. (CCAB Memorandum, June 1968).

'*Wife*' does not include 'widow', see *Vestey's Executors v CIR HL 1949, 31 TC 1*. Note that the definition of 'associate' (unlike that of 'connected person' in *ICTA 1988, s 839*) does not include the spouse or (from 5 December 2005) civil partner of a relative. See 19 CONNECTED PERSONS.

16.6 **EXCEPTIONS**

The following are not close companies:

(*a*) a **non-resident** company (see 60 RESIDENCE);

(*b*) a registered **industrial and provident society** (see 38 INDUSTRIAL AND PROVIDENT SOCIETIES);

(*c*) a **building society** or similar entity (see 9.2 BUILDING SOCIETIES);

(*d*) a company **controlled by the Crown** or by persons acting on behalf of the Crown and independently of any other person (provided that it could not also be treated as under the control of five or fewer persons acting independently of the Crown);

(*e*) a company **controlled by another company which is not close** (other than by reason of non-residence) or by more than one such company, provided that such a non-close company is one of the necessary five or fewer participators without which the original company could not be treated as close;

(*f*) a company which can only be close by **taking as a participator,** entitled to receive assets on a winding-up (see 16.1 and 16.2(iv) above), **a loan creditor which is a non-close company** (other than by reason of non-residence);

(*g*) certain companies with **listed shares** (see further below).

[*ICTA 1988, s 414(1)(4)–(6), s 415; FA 1989, s 104(3)*].

The conditions for exception under (*g*) above are as follows.

(A) Shares or stock (exclusive of shares etc. entitled to a fixed rate of dividend, whether also participating in profits or not) must, within the twelve months before the date at which the company's status is to be determined, have been dealt in on, and listed in the official list of, a 'recognised stock exchange'.

(B) Such shares carrying at least 35% of the total 'voting power' in the company must be 'beneficially held' by 'the public'.

(C) The voting power (including that attributable to shares etc. entitled to a fixed rate of dividend) possessed by 'principal members' of the company must not exceed 85% of the total voting power in the company. [*ICTA 1988, s 415(1)(2); FA 1996, Sch 38 para 6*].

From 6 April 2007, a '*recognised stock exchange*' means:

(*a*) any market of a recognised investment exchange designated by HMRC; and

(*b*) any market outside the UK which is designated by HMRC.

[*ICTA 1988, s 841; ITA 2007, s 1009; FA 2007, s 109, Sch 26 para 1*].

HMRC issued a guidance note on 29 March 2007 on the treatment of AIM shares and the designation of recognised investment exchanges as recognised stock exchanges. See SWTI Issue 14, 13 April 2007.

Prior to **19 July 2007**, '*recognised stock exchange*' meant The Stock Exchange (or such other recognised investment exchange as may be prescribed by HMRC for this purpose) and any non-UK stock exchange designated by HMRC. [*ICTA 1988, s 841*]. See HMRC Company Taxation Manual, CTM 60310. The position may be affected by a double taxation agreement (see 24 DOUBLE TAX RELIEF).

'*Voting power*' includes the power exercisable by any associate or associates of the shareholder, or of any company or companies controlled by him (with or without his associates), together with that of any nominee of his or of such company or associate. [*ICTA 1988, ss 415(7), 416(5)(6)*]. See also 16.2 above.

Shares '*beneficially held*' by a person include those allotted unconditionally to, or acquired unconditionally by, him but not yet registered in his name. [*ICTA 1988, s 416(1)*].

'*The public*' for this purpose does not include:

(i) a director of the company (see 16.4 above);

(ii) an associate of such director (see 16.5 above);

(iii) any company controlled by such director or associate, or by two or more directors and/or associates;

(iv) a company associated with the quoted company (i.e. where one company controls the other or both are under common control [*ICTA 1988, s 416(1)*]) either at the time the question arises for determination or within the preceding twelve months (as to the interpretation of 'associated company', see HMRC Statement of Practice, C4 and 63.7 SMALL COMPANIES—REDUCED RATES);

(v) any fund wholly or mainly for the benefit of the directors or employees, present or past, of the company or of any company within (iii) or (iv) above, or their dependants;

(vi) a 'principal member' of the company (but see below);

(vii) the nominees of (i)–(vi) above.

[*ICTA 1988, s 415(3)–(5)*].

(vi) above does not exclude from '*the public*' a 'principal member' which is a non-close company (other than by reason of non-residence) or is an exempt approved occupational pension scheme. [*ICTA 1988, s 415(4)(a)(b)*].

A '*principal member*' of a company is a person possessing more than five per cent of the voting power of that company or, where there are more than five such persons, one of the five persons possessing the greatest percentages. Where there are equal percentage holdings (so that the greatest percentages are held by more than five persons), a principal member is any one of that number (provided he holds more than five per cent). [*ICTA 1988, s 415(6)*].

Example

A holds 10% of the voting power of X Ltd. B and C hold 8% each, D and E hold 7% each and F holds 6%. No other member holds more than 5%. A, B, C, D and E each hold more than 5% and are principal members of the company, as they are the five persons holding the greatest percentages. F is not a principal member, as he does not meet the latter requirement. If, with the facts as above, G acquires a 10% holding, he will also become a principal member of the company. Since D and E have equal shareholdings, both will remain principal members, making six in total.

Simon's Direct Tax Service. See D3.113, D3.114.

16.7 *Example*

A plc is a quoted company whose ordinary share capital is owned as follows.

		%
B	a director	10
C	wife of B	5
D	father of B	4
E		17
F	business partner of E	2
G	a director	10
H		8
I Ltd	a non–close company	30
J		7
100	other shareholders	7
		100

It can be shown that A plc is a close company by considering the following three steps.

(i) Is A plc controlled by five or fewer participators or by its directors?

		%	%
I Ltd			30
B	own shares	10	
	C's shares	5	
	D's shares	4	
			19
E	own shares	17	
	F's shares	2	
			19
			68

As A plc is controlled by three participators, the initial conclusion is that the company is close.

(ii) Is A plc a quoted company, with at least 35% of the voting power owned by the public?

	%
I Ltd	30
J	7
100 other shareholders	7
	44

As at least 35% of the share capital is owned by the public it appears that A plc is exempt from close company status, subject to step (iii).

(iii) Is more than 85% of the voting power in A plc owned by its principal members?

	%
I Ltd	30
B	19
E	19
G	10
H	8
	86

Although J owns more than 5% of the share capital, he is not a principal member because five other persons each hold more than J's 7% and so themselves constitute the principal members.

Because the principal members own more than 85% of the share capital A plc is a close company.

16.8 APPORTIONMENT OF UNDISTRIBUTED INCOME ETC.

These provisions are repealed in relation to accounting periods beginning **after 31 March 1989.** Previously, the excess of a close company's 'relevant income' over its distributions (or in certain cases the whole 'relevant income') was liable to apportionment amongst its participators, subject to a number of exceptions and relieving measures. For detailed coverage, see Tolley's Corporation Tax 1996/97 or earlier. [*ICTA 1988, ss 423–430, Sch 19; FA 1989, s 103, Sch 17 Pt V*].

16.9 LOANS TO PARTICIPATORS

Where a close company, otherwise than in the ordinary course of a business carried on by it which includes the lending of money, makes any loan or advances any money to an individual who is a 'participator' in the company or is an 'associate of a participator', an amount equal to 25% of the amount of the loan or advance is assessed on and recoverable from the company as if it were corporation tax chargeable for the accounting period in which the loan, etc. was made. Such an amount is due from the company without assessment. [*ICTA 1988, s 419(1); FA 1998, Sch 3 para 24*]. HMRC do not accept that separate accounts with the same participator may be aggregated or 'netted off' for these purposes. (HMRC Company Taxation Manual, CTM 61550).

For a case in which a loan by an investment company to its chairman was held not to have been made in the ordinary course of its business, so that *section 419* applied, see *Brennan v Deanby Investment Co Ltd CA(NI) 2001, 73 TC 455.*

'*Participator*' and '*associate of a participator*' are as defined in 16.3 and 16.5 above, save that a participator in a company which controls the lending company is specifically included. [*ICTA 1988, s 419(1)(7)*].

These provisions also apply to a loan etc. made to a company receiving it in a fiduciary or representative capacity (or, in relation to a loan etc. made in an accounting period ending before 31 March 1996, to a non-resident company) as if the company was an individual. [*ICTA 1988, s 419(6); FA 1996, s 173(4)(6)*]. Such a company must also be a participator or an associate of a participator.

For the exclusion from these provisions of loans to Scottish partnerships or to partnerships of which the lending company is itself a member, see HMRC Company Taxation Manual, CTM 61515.

The inspector has appropriate information powers. [*FA 1989, Sch 12 Pt I; ITTOIA 2005, Sch 1 para 412*].

See further ICAEW Technical Release TAX 11/93, 'Tax implications of certain payments to directors' (25 June 1993) for guidance as to application of these provisions in practice.

Simon's Direct Tax Service. See D3.401.

16.10 **Loans or advances** which are within these provisions include:

(*a*) a debt incurred to the close company (unless for goods or services supplied by it in the ordinary course of its trade or business and on credit no longer than normally allowed to customers, with a maximum of six months);

(*b*) the assignment to the close company of a debt due to a third party;

(*c*) a loan or advance not otherwise within *section 419(1)* where, under arrangements made by any person otherwise than in the ordinary course of a business carried on by him, some person other than the close company making the loan etc. makes a payment or transfers property to, or releases or satisfies (in whole or in part) a liability of, an individual who is a participator, or the associate of a participator, in the lending company. '*Individual*' here includes fiduciary, representative and non-resident companies as mentioned in 16.9 above. Loans etc. which would be included for tax purposes in the total income of the participator or associate are excluded;

(*d*) loans etc. by a company controlled by the close company and not otherwise within *section 419(1)* (but see below);

(*e*) loans etc. not within *section 419(1)* made by a company of which a close company subsequently acquires control (such loans being treated as made at the date of acquisition of control) (but see below).

[*ICTA 1988, s 419(2)(5)(6), s 420(1), s 422*].

As regards (*a*) above, in *Andrew Grant Services Ltd v Watton and cross-appeal Ch D 1999, 71 TC 333*, the company supplied services to a partnership in which it was a limited partner, and of which its controlling director was the general partner, under an agreement for reimbursement of the amounts charged in the company's accounts (plus a mark up), but with no formal or implied agreement as to the time payment would be made. It was held that the debt was incurred for the purposes of *section 419* when the debtor became legally committed to expenditure in relation to the services supplied to the partnership.

The provisions in (*d*) and (*e*) above apply equally where two or more close companies control, or acquire control of, the lending company. The loan is apportioned between them in proportion to the nature and amount of their respective interests in the lending company. *Sections 419* and *422* are to be interpreted in relation to the company which actually made the loan. These provisions *do not apply* if it is shown that there is no arrangement (otherwise than in the ordinary course of business) connecting the making of the loan with:

(i) the acquisition of control; or

(ii) the making of any payment or the transfer of any property (whether directly or indirectly) by the close company to the lending company; or

(iii) the releasing or satisfying by the close company (in whole or in part) of any liability of the lending company.

[*ICTA 1988, s 422*].

The misappropriation of the company's money by a participator may give rise to a debt within (*a*) above. (*Stephens v Pittas Ltd Ch D 1983, 56 TC 722*).

16.11 **Excluded loans.** Loans etc. are excluded from *section 419* if they are made to a director or employee of a close company (or of its associated company) *and*:

(*a*) the total loans outstanding from the close company and any associated company to the borrower (or, for loans made before 6 April 1990, to the wife or husband of the borrower) made *after* 30 March 1971, together with any such loans made *before* 31 March 1971 for the purpose of purchasing an only or main residence, do not exceed £15,000 (and the total of pre-31 March 1971 'housing' loans outstanding does not exceed £10,000); *and*

(*b*) the borrower works full-time for the close company or any of its associated companies; *and*

(*c*) the borrower does not have a 'material interest' in the close company or any of its associated companies.

[*ICTA 1988, s 420(2)*; *FA 1988, Sch 3 para 16*].

A company is an '*associated company*' if it controls, or is under the control of, the close company or both are under common control. [*ICTA 1988, s 416(1)*].

'*Director*' is as defined in 16.4 above. [*ICTA 1988, s 417(5)*].

'*Wife*' does not include a widow, see *Vestey's Exors v CIR HL 1949, 31 TC 1.*

A director or employee is generally treated as working *full-time* if his hours are at least three-quarters of the company's normal working hours subject, it is understood, to a minimum of 28 hours per week.

A person has a '*material interest*' in a company if he (alone or with associates) or any associate (see 16.5 above) of his:

(i) is the beneficial owner of, or otherwise able directly or indirectly to control, more than five per cent of the ordinary share capital of the company; or

(ii) in the case of a close company, is entitled to more than five per cent of the company's assets available for distribution to participators. [*ICTA 1988, ss 168(11), 420(2); FA 1989, Sch 12 para 8; ITEPA 2003, s 68*].

If the borrower acquires such a material interest whilst any part of a post-30 March 1971 loan remains outstanding, the company is to be regarded as making to him at that time a loan equal to the amount outstanding. [*ICTA 1988, s 420(2)*].

16.12 **Procedure.** Assessments under *section 419* are subject to the general administrative provisions relating to corporation tax, except as below. If the loan, etc. is repaid or (after 5 April 1999) released or written off, the tax is repaid or discharged (or, under self-assessment, set off in the company tax return), with proportional treatment if only part of the loan is repaid, released or written off. For a loan etc. made in an accounting period ending after 30 March 1996, where the repayment, release or writing off of the loan etc. (or part) occurs after the tax under these provisions has become due and payable, the repayment or discharge of that tax is not made before nine months after the end of the accounting period in which the loan, etc. was repaid, released or written off. A claim for repayment must be made within six years of the end of the financial year in which the loan is repaid, released or written off. If, however, the tax was paid late, and a charge to INTEREST ON UNPAID TAX (41) incurred, the interest is not refunded. [*ICTA 1988, s 419(4)-(4B); TMA 1970, s 109(1)(4); FA 1996, s 173(3)(6); FA 1998, Sch 3 para 24, Sch 19 para 47(3)(4)*].

In *Earlspring Properties Ltd v Guest CA 1995, 67 TC 259*, it was held that a failure to notify liability under *section 419* constituted neglect and gave rise to a liability to interest under *TMA 1970, s 88* and to penalties. See also *Joint v Bracken Developments Ltd Ch D 1994, 66 TC 560*. See below and generally 30 FRAUDULENT OR NEGLIGENT CONDUCT.

Tax under *section 419* is due and payable nine months after the end of the accounting period, and INTEREST ON UNPAID TAX (41) arises accordingly. If the loan, etc. is repaid, released or written off, interest ceases from the date of the repayment, etc. [*ICTA 1988, s 419(3); TMA 1970, s 109(3)(3A); FA 1996, s 173(2)(6); FA 1998, Sch 3 para 6*]. Payslips will not be issued routinely in advance of assessment, and companies paying in advance of assessment should do so under cover of a letter identifying the liability and the accounting period to which it relates. Interest charges will not be raised, or demand notes for tax or interest issued, until the liability has been assessed. (Revenue Tax Bulletin August 1993 p 85).

16.13 **Loans written off or released.** Where a loan or advance charged under *section 419* is wholly or partly written-off or released, the amount so written off or released is treated as the income of the borrower, grossed up at the dividend (or before 2005/06, the Schedule F) ordinary rate of income tax (currently 10%). The notional dividend ordinary rate tax is not repayable, and there is no liability to pay it. However, tax at the dividend upper rate, currently 32.5%, may be payable on the gross amount of the notional income (broadly to the extent that the total income exceeds the basic rate income tax limit). The grossed-up amount of the income is treated as not brought into charge to income tax for the purposes of *ITA 2007, ss 449, 901* (formerly *ICTA 1988, ss 348, 349(1)*) (so that it may not be used to cover charges). [*ICTA 1988, s 421(1); ITTOIA 2005, Sch 1 para 174*]. Where, under the terms of a deed, a company accepted the replacement of the participator by a third party as its debtor, this amounted to the release of the debt (*Collins v Addies; Greenfield v Bains CA 1992, 65 TC 190*).

See 16.12 above as regards repayment to the company where a loan etc. is released or written off after 5 April 1999. See also Tolley's Income Tax.

Where the borrower is both a participator in and an employee of the lending company, and the waiver of a loan is subject to charge under *ICTA 1988, s 421*, it is understood that HMRC would not seek to treat the amount written off or released as a distribution under *ICTA 1988, s 209* or *s 410* (see 23 DISTRIBUTIONS) or to raise an assessment under the beneficial loan provisions of *ITEPA 2003, s 188* (previously *ICTA 1988, s 160(2)*) (see Tolley's Income Tax under Employment Income).

16.14 *Example*

T is a participator in V Ltd, a close company. V Ltd loaned T £100,000 on 10 May 2005. On 2 March 2006, T repays £73,000 and on 11 February 2007, V Ltd agrees to waive the balance of the loan. V Ltd has a year end of 31 March and is not a large company for instalment payment purposes.

The effect of these transactions is as follows.

V Ltd

On 1.1.07	The company becomes liable to pay corporation tax of (£100,000 – £73,000 =) £27,000 × 25%	£6,750
On 31.12.07	The company is due a repayment of £27,000 × 25%	£6,750

T		
On 11.2.07	T's 2006/07 taxable income is increased by £27,000 × 10/9	£30,000
	and he is credited with dividend ordinary rate tax paid of £30,000 at 10%	£3,000
	If T pays tax at the higher rate, the deemed income will be subject to tax at the dividend upper rate of 32.5% on £30,000	9,750
	Less: tax credit (as above)	3,000
	T's tax liability	£6,750

16.15 **ADDITIONAL ITEMS TREATED AS DISTRIBUTIONS**

As regards certain benefits provided by close companies to participators and/or directors, which are classed as distributions, see 23.8, 23.10, 23.18 DISTRIBUTIONS. See also 23.15(*g*)(*i*) DISTRIBUTIONS for items *not* treated as distributions.

16.16 **CLOSE COMPANY TRANSFERRING ASSET AT UNDERVALUE**

See 11.21 CAPITAL GAINS.

16.17 **DEMERGERS**

For treatment of certain 'chargeable payments' made following an 'exempt distribution', see 32.35 GROUPS OF COMPANIES.

16.18 **CLOSE INVESTMENT-HOLDING COMPANIES**

The SMALL COMPANIES—REDUCED RATES (63) provisions do not apply to a company for any accounting period at the end of which the company is a 'close investment-holding company'.

A close company is a '*close investment-holding company*' for an accounting period unless throughout the period it exists wholly or mainly for one or more of the following purposes.

(*a*) The carrying on of trade(s) on a commercial basis.

(*b*) The making of investments in land, or estates or interests in land, let, or intended to be let, other than to CONNECTED PERSONS (19) of the company or to certain individuals related to such connected persons.

(*c*) The holding of shares in and securities of, or making loans to, a company or companies which, or each of which, is either:

(i) a 'qualifying company'; or

(ii) a company under its 'control', or under the 'control' of the same company as it, which itself exists wholly or mainly for the purpose of holding shares in or securities of, or making loans to, one or more 'qualifying companies'.

(*d*) The co-ordination of the administration of two or more 'qualifying companies'.

(*e*) The purposes of trade(s) carried on on a commercial basis by one or more 'qualifying companies', or by a company which has 'control' of the company in question.

(*f*) The making, by one or more 'qualifying companies' or by a parent company, of investments within (*b*) above.

A '*qualifying company*' in relation to the company in question is a company which is under its 'control', or under the 'control' of the same company as it, and which exists wholly or mainly for either or both of the purposes in (*a*) or (*b*) above.

'*Control*' for all these purposes is as under *ICTA 1988, s 416* (see 16.2 above).

A company is not treated as failing to comply with the above conditions in the accounting period beginning at the commencement of its winding-up (see 45.6 LIQUIDATION ETC.) if it complied with them in the immediately preceding period. If, however, there is an interval between cessation of trading and commencement of winding-up, this will obviate the relief but HMRC will review the position where a company has not been able to avoid a short gap and would suffer significantly if not given the protection of *section 13A (4)* (see HMRC Company Taxation Manual, CTM 60780).

[*ICTA 1988, ss 13(1)(a), 13AA(8)(b),13A; FA 2006, s 26(3), Sch 27 Pt 3(1)*].

The inspector has appropriate information powers. [*FA 1989, Sch 12 Pt I; ITTOIA 2005, Sch 1 para 412*].

Simon's Direct Tax Service. See D3.2.

17 Community Investment Tax Relief

Simon's Direct Tax Service E3.8.

The headings in this chapter are as follows.

17.1 INTRODUCTION

The Community Investment Tax Credit scheme provides tax relief to individuals and companies investing in Community Development Finance Institutions ('CDFIs') which have been accredited by the Government under the rules of the scheme. The intention is that CDFIs will use investors' funds to finance small businesses and social enterprises in disadvantaged communities. The relief takes the form of a reduction in the investor's income tax or corporation tax liability. The quantum of the relief is a maximum of 25% of the amount invested (which may be by way of loan or by subscription), spread over five years, but relief cannot in any year exceed the amount needed to reduce the investor's tax liability to nil. The relief is available for investments made on or after 17 April 2002. Claims for relief may be made after 22 January 2003. A CDFI which is accredited at any time before 6 April 2003 is to have its accreditation backdated to 17 April 2002. (Treasury Explanatory Notes to Finance Bill 2002). [*FA 2002, s 57, Sch 16; SI 2003 No 88*].

No exemption is provided for chargeable gains on disposals of investments in CDFIs.

For the conditions for accreditation of CDFIs, and for the application of these provisions to individual investors, see *SI 2003 No 96*, HMRC Community Investment Tax Relief Manual, CITM 2010–2130 and Tolley's Income Tax under Community Investment Tax Relief.

The European Commission has determined that the scheme is outside the scope of, or compatible with, EU state aid rules.

References in this chapter to the '*investment date*' are to the day on which the investment in the CDFI is made, and references to the '*five-year investment period*' are to the five years beginning with that day. [*FA 2002, Sch 16 para 3*]. The investment term need not, however, be limited to five years.

Guidance is available in HMRC Community Investment Tax Relief Manual and on HMRC's website.

17.2 ELIGIBILITY FOR RELIEF

A company which makes an investment in a body is eligible for community investment tax relief in respect of that investment if:

(*a*) the body is accredited as a CDFI at the time the investment is made;

(*b*) the investment is a 'qualifying investment' (see 17.6 below); and (*c*) the general conditions at 17.10 below are satisfied.

[*FA 2002, Sch 16 para 1*].

For these purposes, a company makes an investment in a body when:

(i) it makes a loan (whether secured or unsecured) to the body (otherwise than by providing overdraft facilities or acquiring securities), or

(ii) an 'issue of securities or shares' (as defined) of or in the body, for which it has subscribed, is made to the company.

Where a loan agreement authorises the body to draw down amounts of the loan over a period of time, the loan is treated for the purposes of (i) above as made when the first amount is drawn down.

[*FA 2002, Sch 16 paras 2, 46*].

17.3 **FORM OF CORPORATION TAX RELIEF**

Where a company which is eligible for relief makes a claim for relief for any one of the 'relevant accounting periods', its corporation tax liability for that period falls to be reduced by the lesser of:

(*a*) 5% of the 'invested amount' (see 17.4 below) in respect of the investment in question; and

(*b*) an amount sufficient to reduce that liability to nil.

The reduction in corporation tax liability is made after any reduction in respect of investment relief under the CORPORATE VENTURING SCHEME (22) but before any double tax relief.

The '*relevant accounting periods*' are the accounting period in which the investment date falls, and each of the accounting periods in which the subsequent four anniversaries of that date fall.

Claims. The company is entitled to make a claim for a relevant accounting period if it appears to the company that the conditions for the relief are for the time being satisfied. The company *must* also have received a tax relief certificate from the CDFI. No claim can be made before the end of the accounting period to which it relates. Otherwise, by default, the general time limit for making claims applies. See 17.5 below for specific circumstances in which no claim for relief can be made.

[*FA 1998, Sch 18 para 8(1); FA 2002, Sch 16 para 20, Sch 17 para 5*].

17.4 **Meaning of the 'invested amount'.** For the purposes of 17.3 above, in respect of a **loan**, the '*invested amount*' is as follows.

(*a*) In the accounting period in which the investment date falls, it is the 'average capital balance' (see below) for the first year of the five-year investment period (see 17.1 above).

(*b*) In each subsequent accounting period (subject to (*c*) below), it is the average capital balance for the one year beginning with the anniversary of the investment date falling in that tax year.

(*c*) For any accounting period after that in which the first anniversary of the investment date falls, it is initially determined as in (*b*) above but is restricted to, if less, the average capital balance for the six-month period beginning eighteen months after the investment date.

For the purposes of (*a*)–(*c*) above, the '*average capital balance*' of a loan for any period of time is the mean of the daily balances of capital outstanding during that period.

In respect of **securities or shares**, the '*invested amount*' for any accounting period is the amount subscribed for them (not necessarily in that accounting period).

[*FA 2002, Sch 16 para 21*].

See 17.11 below as regards receipt of value which may lead to restriction of the invested amount.

17.5 **Circumstances in which no claim for relief can be made.** In the circumstances listed below, no claim for community investment tax relief can be made.

Loans: disposals and excessive repayments/receipts of value. No claim can be made for an accounting period in respect of a loan if:

(*a*) the investor disposes of all or any part of the loan (disregarding any repayment of the loan) before the 'qualifying date' relating to that period; or

(*b*) at any time after the investment is made but before that 'qualifying date', the amount of the capital outstanding on the loan is reduced to nil; or

(*c*) before that 'qualifying date', cumulative loan repayments (or receipts of value treated as repayments) trigger the withdrawal of relief provisions (see 17.11 below).

The '*qualifying date*' relating to an accounting period is the anniversary of the investment date next occurring after the end of that period.

[*FA 2002, Sch 16 para 22*].

Securities or shares: disposals and excessive receipts of value. No claim can be made for an accounting period in respect of any securities or shares other than those held by the investor (as sole beneficial owner) continuously (see 17.15 below) throughout the period beginning when the investment is made and ending immediately before the 'qualifying date' (as in (*a*) above) relating to that period. In addition, no claim can be made for an accounting period if, before the 'qualifying date' (as above) relating to that period, cumulative receipts of value trigger the withdrawal of relief provisions (see 17.11 below). [*FA 2002, Sch 16 para 23*].

Loss of accreditation by the CDFI. Where the CDFI ceases to be accredited as such during the first year of the five-year investment period, no claim for relief can be made. Where accreditation is lost at any later time within the five-year investment period, no claim can be made for the accounting period in which falls the most recent anniversary of the investment date preceding (or coinciding with) the date the accreditation is lost, or for any subsequent accounting period. (There is no withdrawal of relief for any earlier accounting period). [*FA 2002, Sch 16 para 24*].

Accreditation of the investor. Provisions similar to those applying on loss of CDFI accreditation (as above) apply if the investor becomes accredited as a CDFI within the five-year investment period. [*FA 2002, Sch 16 para 25*]. This does not apply to individual investors.

17.6 QUALIFYING INVESTMENTS

An investment is a '*qualifying investment*' in a CDFI (and thus meets condition (*b*) at 17.2 above) if:

(*a*) the investment consists of a loan, securities or shares satisfying the conditions at 17.7 or, as the case may be, 17.8 below;

(*b*) the investor receives from the CDFI a valid tax relief certificate (see 17.14 below); and

(*c*) the conditions at 17.9 below (pre-arranged protection against risks) are met.

[*FA 2002, Sch 16 para 8*].

17.7 **Conditions to be satisfied in relation to loans.** There are three such conditions.

(1) Either the CDFI receives from the investor, on the investment date, the full amount of the loan or, in the case of a loan made under a drawdown facility, the loan agreement provides for the CDFI to receive the full amount of the loan within 18 months after the investment date.

(2) The loan must not carry any present or future right to be converted into, or exchanged for, a loan, securities, shares or other rights, any of which are redeemable within the five-year investment period.

(3) The loan must not be made on terms that allow any person to require:

(*a*) repayment within years 1 and 2 (of the five-year investment period) of any of the loan capital advanced during those two years; or

(*b*) repayment within year 3 of more than 25% of the balance of loan capital outstanding at the end of year 2; or

(*c*) repayment before the end of year 4 of more than 50% of the balance of loan capital outstanding at the end of year 2; or

(*d*) repayment before the end of year 5 of more than 75% of that balance.

Any of the above percentages may be altered by Treasury order, but only in relation to loans made on or after a date specified in the order. For the above purposes, there is disregarded any requirement to repay that may arise as a consequence of certain standard commercial default provisions in the loan agreement.

[*FA 2002, Sch 16 para 9*].

17.8 **Conditions to be satisfied in relation to securities or shares.** There are two such conditions.

(1) The securities or shares must be subscribed for wholly in cash and fully paid for (in the case of shares, fully paid up and with no undertaking for any further payment in connection with the acquisition) on the investment date.

(2) The second is that they must not carry:

(*a*) any present or future right to be redeemed within the five-year investment period; or

(*b*) any present or future right to be converted into, or exchanged for, a loan, securities, shares or other rights, any of which are redeemable within the five-year investment period.

[*FA 2002, Sch 16 paras 10, 11*].

17.9 **Pre-arranged protection against risks.** Any arrangements (as very broadly defined) under which the investment in the CDFI is made (or arrangements preceding the investment but relating to it) must not include arrangements a main purpose of which is to provide (by means of any insurance, indemnity, guarantee or otherwise) complete or partial protection for the investor against the normal risks attaching to the investment. Arrangements are, however, allowed if they do no more than provide the kind of commercial protection, e.g. the use of property as security for a loan, that might be expected if the investment were made by a bank. [*FA 2002, Sch 16 para 13*].

17.10 GENERAL CONDITIONS FOR ELIGIBILITY

No control of CDFI by investor. The investor must not control the CDFI at any time in the five-year investment period. 'Control' is construed in accordance with *ICTA 1988, s 840* where the CDFI is a body corporate, with similar rules applying in other cases, with any potential future rights and powers of the investor, and any rights and powers held or exercisable by another on his behalf, taken into account. References to 'the investor' include any person connected with it (within *ICTA 1988, s 839* — see 19 CONNECTED PERSONS).

Beneficial ownership. The investor must be the sole beneficial owner of the investment when it is made (which in the case of a loan means sole beneficial entitlement to repayment).

Investor not to be accredited. The investor must not itself be accredited as a CDFI as at the investment date. See 17.5 above as regards denial of relief where an investor company subsequently becomes a CDFI.

No acquisition of share in partnership. Where the CDFI is a partnership, the investment must not consist of or include any capital contributed by the investor on becoming a member of the partnership. This includes the provision of loan capital treated as partners' capital in the partnership accounts.

No tax avoidance purpose. The investment must not be made as part of a scheme or arrangement a main purpose of which is the avoidance of tax.

[*FA 2002, Sch 16 paras 14–18, 51(3)*].

17.11 WITHDRAWAL OR REDUCTION OF RELIEF

Community investment tax relief may fall to be withdrawn or reduced on a disposal of the investment, on repayment of an investment consisting of a loan, or if value is received in respect of the investment. [*FA 2002, Sch 16 paras 27–39*]. For the detailed provisions (which apply equally to individual investors), see Tolley's Income Tax under Community Investment Tax Relief.

Where relief given falls to be withdrawn or reduced, and also where it is found not to have been due in the first place, the withdrawal etc. is achieved by means of an assessment to corporation tax under Schedule D, Case VI for the accounting period for which the relief was obtained. [*FA 2002, Sch 16 para 27(4)*].

17.12 COMPANY RESTRUCTURING

For the attribution of relief to any loan, securities or shares for these purposes, see *FA 2002, Sch 16 para 26*.

Reorganisations of share capital. The following apply where the CDFI is a company and the investment consists of shares or, in the case of 17.13 below, shares or securities.

Rights issues etc. Where:

(*a*) a reorganisation (within *TCGA 1992, s 126*) involves an allotment of shares or debentures in respect of, and in proportion to, an existing holding of shares of the same class in the CDFI held by the investor in a single capacity;

(*b*) community investment tax relief is attributable to the shares in the existing holding or to the allotted shares; and

(*c*) if the relief is attributable to the shares in the existing holding, those shares have been held continuously (see 17.15 below) by the investor since they were issued,

the share reorganisation rules of *TCGA 1992, ss 127–130* are disapplied. The effect is that the allotted shares are treated as a separate holding acquired at the time of the reorganisation. This does not, however, apply in the case of bonus shares where these are issued in respect of shares comprised in the existing holding and are of the same class and carry the same rights as those shares. (For *TCGA 1992, ss 126–130*, see Tolley's Capital Gains Tax under Shares and Securities.)

Reorganisation involving issue of QCB. If, in a case otherwise within *TCGA 1992, s 116(10)* (see Tolley's Capital Gains Tax under Qualifying Corporate Bonds):

(i) the old asset consists of shares to which community investment tax relief is attributable and which have been held continuously (see 17.15 below) by the investor since they were issued; and

(ii) the new asset consists of a qualifying corporate bond,

the usual treatment is disapplied. The effect is that the investor is deemed to have disposed of the shares at the time of the reorganisation, and the resulting chargeable gain or allowable loss crystallises *at that time*.

[*FA 2002, Sch 16 paras 26, 40, 51(2)*].

17.13 **Company reconstructions.** *TCGA 1992, s 135* (exchange of securities for those in another company) and *s 136* (schemes of reconstruction involving issue of securities), which normally equate the new holding with the original shares, are disapplied in the following circumstances:

(*a*) an investor holds shares in or debentures of a company (company A);

(*b*) community investment tax relief is attributable to those shares;

(*c*) those shares have been held continuously (see 17.15 below) by the investor since they were issued; and

(*d*) there is a reconstruction whereby another company issues shares or debentures in exchange for, or in respect of, company A shares or debentures.

The result is that the transaction is treated, both for the purposes of this chapter and for the purposes of taxing chargeable gains, as a disposal of the original securities or shares (and an acquisition of a new holding). (For *TCGA 1992, ss 135, 136*, see Tolley's Capital Gains Tax under Shares and Securities.)

[*FA 2002, Sch 16 paras 26, 41, 48(2)*].

17.14 TAX RELIEF CERTIFICATES

Before an investment in a CDFI can qualify for tax relief, the CDFI must issue to the investor a tax relief certificate (see 17.3, 17.6(*b*) above) in a specified form. In relation to an accreditation period, a CDFI may issue tax relief certificates in respect of investments made in it within that period of an aggregate value of up to £20 million in the case of a 'wholesale CDFI' (i.e. one whose objective is to finance other, generally smaller, CDFIs) or £10 million in the case of a 'retail CDFI' (i.e. one whose objective is to invest directly in enterprises. The Treasury may substitute other figures by order but not so as to reduce them for periods beginning before the order takes effect. Any tax relief certificate issued wholly or partly in contravention of these limits is invalid (and thus the investment in question does not satisfy 17.6(*b*) above and does not attract tax relief). A CDFI is liable to a penalty of up to £3,000 for the issue of a tax relief certificate made fraudulently or negligently. [*FA 2002, Sch 16 paras 4(6)(7), 12*].

17.15 MISCELLANEOUS

Circumstances in which investment not held 'continuously'. An investor is not treated for the purposes of this chapter as having held an investment (or a part of an investment) continuously throughout a period if:

(*a*) under any provision of *TCGA 1992*, the investment (or part) has been deemed to be disposed of and immediately reacquired by the investor at any time in that period; or

(*b*) there has been at any time in that period a transaction treated, by virtue of 17.13 above (company reconstructions etc.), as a disposal by the investor.

[*FA 2002, Sch 16 para 49*].

17.16 **Nominees and bare trustees.** For the purposes of this chapter, actions of a person's nominee or bare trustee in relation to loans, shares or securities are treated as actions of that person. [*FA 2002, Sch 16 para 44*].

17.17 **Information to be provided by investor.** Certain events giving rise to withdrawal or reduction of investment relief must be notified to HMRC by a company investor within twelve months after the end of its accounting period in which the event occurs. If the requirement arises from the receipt of value by a connected person, each of the above deadlines is extended to, if later, the end of the period of 60 days beginning when the investor gains knowledge of the event. The penalty provisions of *TMA 1970, s 98* apply in the event of non-compliance. [*FA 2002, s 57, Sch 16 para 42, Sch 17 para* [illegible]].

17.18 **Disclosure.** There are provisions for the exchange of information between the Secretary of State and HMRC in so far as this is necessary to enable them both to discharge their functions appertaining to community investment tax relief. Information thus obtained cannot be further disclosed except for the purposes of legal proceedings arising out of those functions. [*FA 2002, Sch 16 para 43*].

18 Compensation, Damages etc.

Simons Direct Tax Service. See **C1.325** *et seq*, **A1.210** *et seq*.

18.1 For capital sums received as compensation for damage or injury to, or the destruction or depreciation of, assets, see Tolley's Capital Gains Tax under Disposal. For compensation for loss of office, etc., see Tolley's Income Tax under Compensation for Loss of Employment. Other types of compensation received or paid are dealt with below.

18.2 COMPENSATION FOR COMPULSORY ACQUISITION

Following *Stoke-on-Trent City Council v Wood Mitchell & Co Ltd CA 1978, [1979] STC 197*, any element of compensation, paid by an authority possessing compulsory purchase powers for the acquisition of property used for a trade or profession, representing temporary loss of profits, will be treated as a trading receipt. Compensation for losses on trading stock and to reimburse revenue expenditure, such as removal expenses and interest, will be similarly treated. (HMRC Statement of Practice, SP 8/79).

18.3 CANCELLATION OR VARIATION OF TRADING AGREEMENTS

Compensation etc. received on the cancellation or variation of contracts which, if completed, would have given rise to trading receipts, is normally also treated as a trading receipt of the accounting period in which the cancellation or variation took place. See *Short Bros Ltd v CIR CA 1927, 12 TC 955* (cancellation of shipbuilding contract); *Northfleet Coal & Ballast Co Ltd KB 1927, 12 TC 1102* (cancellation of contract for minerals extraction); *J Robinson & Sons v CIR KB 1929, 12 TC 1241* and *Creed v H & M Levinson Ltd Ch D 1981, 54 TC 477* (cancellation of contract for sale of goods); *Greyhound Racing Association (Liverpool) Ltd v Cooper KB 1936, 20 TC 373* (surrender of hiring agreement); *Bush, Beach & Gent Ltd v Road KB 1939, 22 TC 519* (cancellation of merchanting franchise); *Shove v Dura Manufacturing Co Ltd KB 1941, 23 TC 779* (cancellation of commission agreement); *Shadbolt v Salmon Estate (Kingsbury) Ltd KB 1943, 25 TC 52* (withdrawal of building rights); *Sommerfelds Ltd v Freeman Ch D 1966, 44 TC 43* (breach of contract for sale of goods — rights assigned). For further cases on this point, see Tolley's Tax Cases. See also 18.6 below.

18.4 TERMINATION OF AGENCIES

Compensation received on the termination of agencies is a trading receipt (unless the agency, by reason of its relative size, etc., is part of the 'whole structure of the recipient's profit-making apparatus', see 18.7 below). See *Kelsall Parsons & Co v CIR CS 1938, 21 TC 608* (manufacturers' agency); *Fleming v Bellow Machine Co Ltd Ch D 1965, 42 TC 308* (distributors' sub-agency); *Anglo-French Exploration Co Ltd v Clayson CA 1956, 36 TC 545* and *Blackburn v Close Bros Ltd Ch D 1960, 39 TC 164* (provision of agency, managerial and secretarial services). In all these cases, compensation was held to be a trading receipt, but compare *Ellis v Lucas Ch D 1966, 43 TC 276* where a certified accountant, who was auditor to a number of companies and carried out related accountancy work, was paid compensation on his agreeing to relinquish his post as auditor. In the absence of a finding by the Commissioners that the auditorship did not constitute an asset of the taxpayer's profession, except in so far as it included general accountancy work, so much of the payment as did not relate to general accountancy work was compensation for loss of office and therefore within the charge to tax as employment income (although exempt under what is now *ITEPA 2003, Pt 6 Ch 3*) (see Tolley's Income Tax under Compensation for Loss of Employment and Damages) and only the balance constituted a trading receipt. For further cases on this point, see Tolley's Tax Cases. See also 18.5 below.

For payments received on termination of building society agencies, see HMRC Capital Gains Tax Manual, CG 13050 *et seq*.

18.5 **EX GRATIA PAYMENTS**

In *Walker v Carnaby, Harrower, Barham & Pykett Ch D 1969, 46 TC 561*, a sum equivalent to the audit fee was paid to a firm of accountants as a solatium on their agreeing not to seek re-election as auditors to a group of companies. It was held that, but for being voluntary, the payment would have been taken into account as part of the firm's profits, but that 'ordinary commercial principles' did not require the bringing into account of a voluntary payment not made as consideration for past services, but in recognition of such services or by way of consolation for the termination of a contract. Voluntary payments were also held not to be assessable under Schedule D in *Brander & Cruickshank HL 1970, 46 TC 574* (loss of company secretaryships by firm of advocates); *Chibbett v Joseph Robinson & Sons KB 1924, 9 TC 48* (loss of office as ship-managers on liquidation); *Simpson v John Reynolds & Co (Insurances) Ltd CA 1975, 49 TC 693* (loss of client by insurance brokers) and *Murray v Goodhews CA 1977, 52 TC 86* (termination of caterers' tenancies). However, ex gratia payments to an estate agent who, contrary to local custom, had not been given an agency which he expected were held to be assessable as additional remuneration for work already carried out (*McGowan v Brown & Cousins Ch D 1977, 52 TC 8*), and a non-contractual payment to a diamond broker by a fellow-broker, as compensation for transfer of a client's business after substantial work had been done on the client's behalf but before any corresponding benefit had been gained from purchases by the client, was held to be a trading receipt (*Rolfe v Nagel CA 1981, 55 TC 585*). See also *Falkirk Ice Rink Ltd CS 1975, 51 TC 42* where the payment related to future services, and for further cases on this point, see Tolley's Tax Cases.

18.6 **OTHER RECEIPTS ASSESSABLE AS INCOME**

Damages awarded to producers for breach of a sole licence to perform a play were held assessable in *Vaughan v Parnell & Zeitlin Ltd KB 1940, 23 TC 505* as was statutory compensation for the restriction of development rights (*Johnson v W S Try Ltd CA 1946, 27 TC 167*). Retrospective compensation for requisitioned trading stock was held to be a trading receipt of the year of requisition in *Newcastle Breweries Ltd HL 1927, 12 TC 927*, as were compensation to a shipping company for delay in the overhaul of a ship (*Burmah Steam Ship Co v CIR CS 1930, 16 TC 67*) and to a jetty owner for loss of use (*London & Thames Haven Oil Wharves Ltd v Attwooll CA 1966, 43 TC 491*). For further cases on this point, see Tolley's Tax Cases. See also 18.7 below.

18.7 **COMPENSATION RELATING TO CAPITAL ASSETS**

An agreed sum received on the termination of 'pooling agreements' between two companies was held to be a capital receipt on the ground that the agreements '*related to the whole structure of the appellants' profit-making apparatus*' in *Van Den Berghs v Clark HL 1935, 19 TC 390*. This was followed in *Barr, Crombie & Co Ltd v CIR CS 1945, 26 TC 406* (terminating ship-managers' agreement) and *Sabine v Lookers Ltd CA 1958, 38 TC 120* (variation of car distributor's agreement). See also *British-Borneo Petroleum Syndicate Ltd v Cropper Ch D 1968, 45 TC 201* (cancellation of royalty agreement).

Compensation paid to a company making fireclay goods for refraining from working a fireclay bed was held to be capital in *Glenboig Union Fireclay Co Ltd v CIR HL 1922, 12 TC 427* but cf. *Waterloo Main Colliery Co Ltd v CIR (No 1) KB 1947, 29 TC 235* where compensation for the requisition of part of a mining area was held to be a trading receipt. Reimbursement for restoration expenditure on a ship which had deteriorated whilst requisitioned was held to be a capital receipt in *Francis West CS 1950, 31 TC 402*, but compensation for loss of use of a requisitioned ship was assessable as a trading receipt in *Ensign Shipping Co Ltd v CIR CA 1928, 12 TC 1169*. For further relevant cases, see Tolley's Tax Cases. See also 18.6 above.

18.8 **PAYMENT OF COMPENSATION**

(*a*) **Deductible as revenue expenditure.** A substantial payment by a principal for the cancellation of an expensive agency agreement was held deductible in *Anglo-Persian*

Oil Co Ltd v Dale CA 1931, 16 TC 253, on the grounds that it was made not only to commute revenue expenditure but also to rationalise the principal's working arrangements. The decision was applied in *Croydon Hotel & Leisure Co Ltd v Bowen (Sp C 101), [1996] SSCD 466*, in which a payment for the termination of a hotel management agreement was held to be allowable. Contrast *Mallett v Staveley Coal & Iron Co Ltd CA 1928, 13 TC 772* where a payment to surrender certain onerous mining leases was held to secure an advantage for the enduring benefit of the trade and therefore to be capital expenditure. For other items held to be revenue expenditure, see *Commr of Taxes v Nchanga Consolidated Copper Mines Ltd PC 1964, [1964] AC 948* and *United Steel Companies (below)*, *Mitchell v B W Noble Ltd CA 1927, 11 TC 372* (payment to get rid of director) and *O'Keeffe v Southport Printers Ltd Ch D 1984, 58 TC 88* (payments on cessation in lieu of notice). See also *G Scammell & Nephew v Rowles CA 1939, 22 TC 479.*

(*b*) **Capital expenditure.** A payment by the operator of a single ship for cancelling an order for a second was held to be on capital account (*'Countess Warwick' Steamship Co Ltd v Ogg KB 1924, 8 TC 652*) as were payments by a steel company to secure the closure of railways steelworks (*United Steel Companies Ltd v Cullington (No 1) CA 1939, 23 TC 71*, which also involved payments by sub-contractors on revenue account); for cessation of mining to prevent subsidence (*Bradbury v The United Glass Bottle Manufacturers Ltd CA 1959, 38 TC 369*); for the cancellation of an electricity agreement on the closure of a quarry (*William Sharp & Son CS 1959, 38 TC 341*) and as compensation on the termination of tied tenancies by a brewery company (*Watneys London Ltd v Pike Ch D 1982, 57 TC 372*).

(*c*) **Other expenditure not deductible.** Damages paid by a brewery to a hotel guest injured by a falling chimney were held to have been incurred as a property owner and not as a trader (*Strong & Co of Romsey Ltd v Woodifield HL 1906, 5 TC 215*). Penalties for the breach of war-time regulations (and associated costs) were disallowed in *Alexander von Glehn & Co Ltd CA 1920, 12 TC 232* and damages for breach of American anti-trust law (but **not** the associated legal expenses) in *Cattermole v Borax & Chemicals Ltd KB 1949, 31 TC 202*. See also *Fairrie v Hall KB 1947, 28 TC 200* (damages for libel) and *Knight v Parry Ch D 1972, 48 TC 580* (damages for breach of contract of employment).

(*d*) **Date of payment.** Where damages awarded by a court against a solicitor were later compounded, the compounded amount (accepted as allowable) was held to be an expense of the year in which the court award was made (*Simpson v Jones Ch D 1968, 44 TC 599*). See also *Hugh T Barrie Ltd CA (NI) 1928, 12 TC 1223.*

For further relevant cases, see Tolley's Tax Cases.

19 Connected Persons

Note. This chapter sets out the definition of 'connected persons' under the general provision of *ICTA 1988, s 839*, to which reference is made throughout the Taxes Acts. It should be noted that a modified definition may be applied in relation to any specific legislation, to which reference is made as appropriate in the text describing that legislation. *ICTA 1988, s 839* was modified by the the *Tax and Civil Partnership Regulations 2005* to cover civil partners from 5 December 2005. [*SI 2005 No 3229, reg 100*].

Simon's Direct Tax Service C2.110.

19.1 **DEFINITIONS**

An individual is connected with his spouse or (from 5 December 2005) civil partner, any 'relative' (see 19.7 below) of himself or of his spouse or civil partner, and with the spouse or civil partner of any such relative. It appears that a widow or widower is no longer a spouse (*Vestey's Exors and Vestey v CIR HL 1949, 31 TC 1*). Spouses divorced by decree nisi remain connected persons until the divorce is made absolute (*Aspden v Hildesley Ch D 1981, 55 TC 609*).

19.2 **A trustee of a 'settlement'**, in his capacity as such, is connected with:

(*a*) the 'settlor' (if an individual) (see 19.7 below); and

(*b*) any person connected with the settlor (if within (*a*)); and

(*c*) a 'body corporate connected with the settlement' (see 19.7 below).

19.3 **Partners** are connected with each other and with each other's spouses (see 19.1 above) and relatives (see 19.7 below) except in connection with acquisitions and disposals of partnership assets made 'pursuant to *bona fide* commercial arrangements'.

19.4 **A 'company'** (see 19.7 below) **is connected with another company if:**

(*a*) the same person 'controls' both; or

(*b*) one is controlled by a person who has control of the other in conjunction with persons connected with him; or

(*c*) a person controls one company and persons connected with him control the other; or

(*d*) the same group of persons controls both; or

(*e*) the companies are controlled by separate groups which can be regarded as the same by interchanging connected persons.

19.5 **A company is connected with a person who** (either alone or with persons connected with him) has control of it. It is understood that HMRC will accept that a **partnership and a company under common control** are connected (see Tolley's Practical Tax 1981 p 142) in relation to the treatment for capital allowances of assets transferred on a succession.

19.6 **Persons acting together to secure or exercise control of a company** are treated in relation to that company as connected with each other and with any other person acting on the direction of any of them to secure or exercise such control. For the meaning of 'acting together to secure or exercise control', see *Steele v EVC International NV (formerly European Vinyls Corp (Holdings) BV) CA 1996, 69 TC 88*. Control may be 'exercised' passively. (See *Floor v Davis HL 1979, 52 TC 609*).

19.7 '*Company*' includes any body corporate, unincorporated association or unit trust scheme. It does not include a partnership.

'*Control*' is as defined in *ICTA 1988, s 416* (see 16.2 CLOSE COMPANIES).

'*Relative*' means brother, sister, ancestor or lineal descendant.

'*Settlement*' includes any disposition, trust, covenant, agreement, arrangement or transfer of assets (but not a charitable loan arrangement). [*ITTOIA 2005, s 620, Sch 1 para 273; ICTA 1988, s 660G(1)*].

'*A body corporate connected with the settlement*' is a close company (or one which would be close if resident in the UK) the participators in which include the trustees of the settlement, or a company of which such a close company etc. has control (as defined by *ICTA 1988, s 840*). [*ITTOIA 2005, s 637(8), Sch 1 para 276; ICTA 1988, ss 682A(2), 839(3A)*].

'*Settlor*' is any person by whom the settlement was made or who has directly or indirectly (or by a reciprocal arrangement) provided, or undertaken to provide, funds for the settlement. [*ITTOIA 2005, s 620, Sch 1 para 273; ICTA 1988, s 660G(1)(2)*].

19.8 The same definitions are applied for the purposes of corporation tax on chargeable gains by *TCGA 1992, s 286*.

19.9 **VARIATIONS**

Specific variations are made in the rules given above for the particular purposes of *TCGA 1992, s 177* (see 12.40 CAPITAL GAINS—GROUPS) and *ICTA 1988, s 736* (see 5.8 ANTI-AVOIDANCE). For the purposes of these sections, persons acting together to secure or exercise control of, or to acquire a holding in, a company are connected with each other and with any other person acting on the direction of any of them to secure or exercise such control or to acquire such a holding.

20 Construction Industry Scheme

See also HMRC Publications IR 14/15(CIS), IR 40(CIS), IR 116(CIS), IR 117(CIS), IR 148, and IR 180(CIS). HMRC guidance is provided in the HMRC Construction Industry Scheme Manual and on their website under 'CIS: Construction Industry Scheme' (at www.hmrc.gov.uk/cis). See also HMRC publication CIS 340 and HMRC guidance on the new construction industry scheme (at www.hmrc.gov.uk/new-cis).

Simon's Direct Tax Service E5.5.

The headings in this chapter are as follows.

20.1 SCHEME APPLICABLE FROM APRIL 2007

A revised construction industry scheme was introduced from 6 April 2007. The framework of the new scheme is provided for in *FA 2004*, but much of the detail is contained in regulations (see *The Income Tax (Construction Industry Scheme) Regulations 2005 (SI 2005 No 2045)*). HMRC are given wide powers to make regulations governing the scheme as they consider necessary or expedient. [*FA 2004, ss 73, 76, 77(1), Sch 12 para 9; ITA 2007, Sch 1 para 461*].

Change was felt to be necessary to reduce the administrative burden that the system of registration cards and tax certificates imposed on the industry; to improve the level of compliance within the industry; and to encourage the correct identification of employment status (see Treasury Notes to the Finance Bill 2004). Accordingly, features of the new scheme include:

- a verification service to enable contractors to check whether sub-contractors are registered for gross or net payment (see 20.9 below); and
- periodic returns by contractors to replace the voucher system (see 20.9 below).

In other respects the new scheme is very similar to the previous scheme (see 20.11 below onwards) and many existing provisions on payment and recovery of sums deducted are preserved. However, it should be noted that the new scheme will operate under a new legislative framework and regulations, and there are differences from the current scheme throughout.

For various transitional measures on the introduction of the new scheme, see 20.10 below.

Outline of the revised scheme. Where a 'contractor' makes a 'contract payment' to a 'sub-contractor' under a 'construction contract', and that sub-contractor is either registered under the scheme for payment under deduction (as opposed to being registered for gross payment), or is not registered at all, the contractor must make a deduction from the payment. The amount deducted must then be paid over to HMRC. The deduction is greater if the sub-contractor is unregistered. It is up to the contractor to verify with

HMRC the registration status of a sub-contractor. The contractor must make periodic returns to HMRC concerning contract payments, as well as providing information about such payments to the sub-contractor.

For HMRC guidance see Explanatory Booklet CIS340 Construction Industry Scheme — Guide for contractors and sub-contractors. Links to this and other HMRC guidance on the new scheme are provided by HMRC on their website (at www.hmrc.gov.uk/new-cis/new_guidance.htm). HMRC sent paper copies of CIS 350 'New CIS – An Introduction to the Changes', to all registered contractors in January 2006 to explain the fundamentals of the new scheme and help them prepare for the changes. Copies of leaflet CIS 340, various Factsheets and letters were also sent to registered contractors and sub-contractors in March 2006. These publications are available on the HMRC website (at www.hmrc.gov.uk/new-cis/mailshots.htm).

20.2 **Definitions.** The scheme is concerned with payments under a '*construction contract*', being a contract relating to 'construction operations' and involving a 'sub-contractor' and a 'contractor'. A contract of employment is specifically excluded from the definition of a construction contract. [*FA 2004, s 57(2)*]. For a discussion of the indicators of employment status, see Tolley's Income Tax under Employment Income.

Construction operations. The following operations are '*construction operations*':

(*a*) construction, alteration, repair, extension, demolition or dismantling of buildings or structures, including offshore installations and temporary structures;

(*b*) construction, alteration, repair, extension or demolition of works forming part of the land, and this specifically includes walls, roadworks, power-lines, electronic communications apparatus, aircraft runways, docks and harbours, railways, inland waterways, pipe-lines, reservoirs, water-mains, wells, sewers, industrial plant and installations for purposes of land drainage, coast protection or defence;

(*c*) installation of heating, lighting, air-conditioning, ventilation, power supply, drainage, sanitation, water supply or fire protection;

(*d*) internal cleaning if carried out during construction, alteration, repair, extension or restoration; and

(*e*) painting or decorating (internal and external).

Operations which are an integral part of operations in the above list are also included; for instance, site clearance, earth-moving, excavation, tunnelling and boring, laying of foundations, erection of scaffolding, site restoration, landscaping and the provision of roadways and other access works.

Specifically excluded from the definition of construction operations are:

(i) operations outside the UK and its territorial sea;

(ii) drilling for, or extraction of, oil or natural gas, and extraction of minerals;

(iii) manufacture of building or engineering components or equipment and delivery of these to site;

(iv) manufacture of components for heating, ventilation etc. systems and delivery to site;

(v) the work of architects, surveyors and consultants;

(vi) making, installing or repairing artistic works;

(vii) signwriting and erecting, installing or repairing signboards and advertisements;

(viii) installation of seating, blinds and shutters;

(ix) installation of security systems and public address systems.

The Treasury may, by order, amend the definition of construction operations.

[*FA 2004, s 74*].

Sub-contractor. A person is a 'sub-contractor' if the contract imposes on him a duty to:

(A) carry out construction operations; or

(B) furnish his own labour or the labour of others in carrying out construction operations; or

(C) arrange for the labour of others to be furnished in carrying out construction operations.

Alternatively, a person may be a sub-contractor if, under the construction contract, he is answerable to the contractor for construction operations carried out by others who are working for him (whether under a contract or other arrangements).

[*FA 2004, s 58*].

Contractor. A '*contractor*' in relation to a construction contract is a body or person falling within one of the following categories.

(1) Persons who are automatically classed as contractors. These are:

- (*a*) any person carrying on a business which includes construction operations; and
- (*b*) the Secretary of State if the contract is made by him under the *Housing Associations Act 1985, s 89.*

(2) Persons carrying on a business at any time which exceeds a set level of expenditure on construction operations. That level is:

- (*a*) £1,000,000 per year on average over the period of three years ending at the same time as the last period of account; or
- (*b*) where the business was not being carried on at the beginning of that three-year period, total expenditure in the truncated period exceeds £3,000,000.

Once defined as a contractor under this category, the person is deemed to continue to be a contractor until HMRC are satisfied that expenditure on construction operations has been less than £1,000,000 for each of three successive years beginning in or after the period of account in which contractor status was acquired. For the purposes of all these limits, where a trade is transferred from one company to another and *ICTA 1988, s 343* (no change of ownership) applies, the transferor's expenditure will be treated as the transferee's, with apportionment by HMRC (subject to appeal) when only part of the trade is transferred.

(3) Bodies or persons specified in the following list, provided their average annual expenditure on construction operations in any three-year period ending on 31 March exceeds £1,000,000. Contractor status ceases to apply if, subsequently, there are three successive years (ending on 31 March) in which expenditure was less than £1,000,000. The bodies or persons specified are:

- (*a*) any public office or department of the Crown (including any Northern Ireland department and any part of the Scottish Administration);
- (*b*) the Corporate Officer of the House of Lords, the Corporate Officer of the House of Commons, and the Scottish Parliamentary Corporate Body;
- (*c*) any local authority;
- (*d*) any development corporation or new town commission;

(*e*) the Commission for the New Towns;

(*f*) the Housing Corporation, a housing association, a housing trust, Scottish Homes, and the Northern Ireland Housing Executive;

(*g*) any NHS trust; and

(*h*) any HSS trust.

The definition includes a person who is himself a sub-contractor under another construction contract relating to any or all of the same construction operations, e.g. a gang-leader.

[*FA 2004, ss 57(2), 59*].

Contract payments. 'Contract payments' are payments under a construction contract from the contractor to:

- a sub-contractor;
- a nominee of the sub-contractor or the contractor; or
- a nominee of a person who is a sub-contractor under another construction contract relating to the construction operations.

Where the contractor makes a payment to a third party which discharges his obligation to pay a person within the above list, that payment is deemed to have been made directly to that person.

The following payments are not, however, contract payments.

(I) Payments to agency workers (i.e. earnings under *ITEPA 2003, Pt 2 Ch 7*).

(II) Payments where the recipient is registered for gross payment (see 20.4 below) when the payment is made (but see below for certain qualifications in the case of nominees and partnerships).

(III) Payments excepted by regulations. These comprise:

- small payments, i.e. payments made by contractors within 20.2 1(*b*), 2 or 3 above and approved for this purpose, in a case where the total payments under the construction contract (excluding direct cost of materials) do not, or are not likely to, exceed £1,000;
- payments made by a contractor within 20.2 1(*a*) above, and approved for this purpose, to a body or person for work carried out on land owned by that body or person or on agricultural property (as defined) of which that body or person is a tenant, in a case where the total payments under the construction contract (excluding direct cost of materials) do not, or are not likely to, exceed £1,000;
- reverse premiums (within the meaning of *FA 1999, Sch 6* — see 66.71 TRADING INCOME — as modified for this purpose);
- payments by local authority maintained schools under devolved budgets;
- payments made by contractors within 20.2 (2) above in respect of construction operations relating to property used (as defined) in their own or another group company's business;
- payments made by public bodies within 20.2 1(*b*) or (3) above under a private finance transaction (as defined); and
- payments made by any body of persons or trust established for charitable purposes only.

The qualifications to the exception at (II) above are as follows:

(*aa*) where the recipient is a nominee, then the nominee, the person who nominated him and the person for whose labour the payment is made (employee's labour in the case of a company) must all be registered for gross payment when the payment is made;

(*bb*) where the recipient is registered for gross payment as a partner in a firm, the exception only applies to payments under contracts where the firm is a sub-contractor or, where the firm has been nominated to receive payments, the person who nominated the firm is a sub-contractor. Note that, in such a case, the person nominating the firm must also be registered for gross payment;

(*cc*) where the recipient is registered for gross payment other than as a partner in a firm but is or becomes a partner in a firm, the exception does not apply to payments under contracts where the firm is a sub-contractor or, where the firm has been nominated to receive payments, the person who nominated the firm is a sub-contractor.

[*FA 2004, s 60; SI 2005 No 2045, regs 18–24*].

20.3 **Payments from which tax must be deducted.** On making a contract payment the contractor must make a deduction on account of tax. This is calculated by first excluding the cost of materials and then applying the 'relevant percentage', which has been set in *SI 2007/0046* as 20% for sub-contractors registered for payment under deduction and 30% for sub-contractors not so registered. Thus the percentage varies in accordance with the registration status of the person for whose labour (or, in the case of companies, whose employees' labour) the payment is made.

The amount deducted from a contract payment by the contractor must be paid to HMRC and is treated for tax purposes as not diminishing the amount of that payment.

Where the sub-contractor is not a company, the amounts deducted are treated as income tax paid in respect of the profits of the trade, with any excess being treated as Class 4 National Insurance contributions.

Where the sub-contractor is a company, the treatment of the amounts deducted is to be governed by regulations. The order of set-off is first against 'relevant liabilities', whether arising before or after the deduction in question, then against corporation tax, with any excess to be repaid. For this purpose, '*relevant liabilities*' are payments due under the contractor's obligations as employer or contractor (e.g. PAYE, Class 1 National Insurance contributions, deductions under the CIS).

HMRC have extensive powers to make regulations governing the treatment of sums deducted.

[*FA 2004, ss 61, 62*].

20.4 **Registration.** In order to be registered, an applicant must provide sufficient documents, records and information to establish, to the satisfaction of HMRC, his identity and address. If, in addition, the requirements for gross payment are met (see below) then the applicant will be registered for gross payment. Otherwise, the applicant will be registered for payment under deduction. See below for appeal provisions.

There is a penalty of up to £3,000 for knowingly or recklessly making a statement, or supplying a document, for the purpose of becoming registered which is false in a material particular.

[*FA 2004, ss 63, 72*].

Registration for gross payment. The requirements for registration for gross payment vary, depending upon whether the applicant is:

(*a*) an individual (see 20.5 below);

(*b*) a company (see 20.6 below); or

(*c*) an individual or company applying as a partner in a firm (see 20.7 below).

Provisions in respect of the documents, records and information to be provided to HMRC in support of an application for registration are set out in *SI 2005 No 2045*. The regulations also provide for appeals against a notice of cancellation of, or a refusal to grant, registration. The Treasury is specifically empowered to alter, by order, the conditions relating to registration for gross payment.

[*FA 2004, s 64, Sch 11 para 13; SI 2005 No 2045, regs 25, 26*].

Cancellation of registration. Failure to comply with the requirements of the construction industry scheme may result in the cancellation of a person's registration.

In the case of registration for gross payment, the conditions relating to cancellation may be divided into two by reference to the gravity of the offence. Lesser offences are as follows.

(i) At the time in question, HMRC would refuse a hypothetical application for gross payment registration.

(ii) The person has made an incorrect return or provided incorrect information under any construction industry scheme provision (whether as contractor or sub-contractor).

(iii) There is any failure to comply with any such provision (whether as contractor or sub-contractor).

If it appears to HMRC that any of these apply, a determination may be made cancelling a person's registration with effect from 90 days after the date of notice of cancellation (see below). However, the effective date may be delayed by an appeal (see below) to the latest of:

- the abandonment of the appeal;
- determination of the appeal by the Commissioners; or
- determination of the appeal by the High Court.

If gross payment registration is cancelled because of the above type of offence, the person will then be registered for payment under deduction.

More serious offences are:

(A) becoming registered for gross payment on the basis of false information;

(B) making a fraudulently incorrect return, or fraudulently providing incorrect information under any construction industry scheme provision (whether as contractor or sub-contractor); or

(C) knowingly failing to comply with any such provision (whether as contractor or sub-contractor).

HMRC must have reasonable grounds to suspect such an offence, and if so they may make a determination cancelling registration with immediate effect. HMRC then has discretion whether to register the person for payment under deduction.

On any cancellation, HMRC must, without delay, give a notice stating the reasons for the cancellation. The person whose registration is cancelled may not re-apply for gross payment registration for at least a year after the cancellation takes effect.

[*FA 2004, ss 66, 67(5); SI 2005 No 2045, reg 26*].

In the case of registration for payment under deduction, the conditions relating to cancellation (and appeal against such a decision) are governed by regulations. [*FA 2004, s 68; SI 2005 No 2045, reg 25*].

Appeals. An appeal may be made against the cancellation or refusal of a registration for gross payment by giving notice to HMRC within 30 days of the decision. The notice must state the reasons why the decision is believed to be unjustified. Appeal is to the General Commissioners or, by election, to the Special Commissioners. The Commissioners may review any relevant decision made in relation to registration. In the case of registration for payment under deduction, the conditions relating to refusal (and appeal against such a decision) are governed by regulations. [*FA 2004, ss 67, 68; SI 2005 No 2045, reg 25*].

20.5 **Registration for gross payment — individuals.** The conditions to be satisfied by individuals comprise three tests: a business test, a turnover test, and a compliance test.

The business test. The business carried on by the individual must be carried on in the UK. It must include either carrying out construction operations, or furnishing labour for construction operations, or arranging for the furnishing of labour. It must, to a substantial extent, be carried on using an account with a bank. The evidence required to satisfy HMRC that these conditions are met (prescribed by *SI 2005 No 2045, reg 27*) includes the business address, invoices, contracts or purchase orders and payment details for the construction work, the business's books and accounts and details of the business bank acount, including bank statements.

The turnover test. The individual must satisfy HMRC that the likely receipt of 'relevant payments' in the year following the application is not less than the relevant turnover threshold which, in the case of individuals, is £30,000. '*Relevant payments*' for this purpose are payments under contracts relating to 'construction operations' (see 20.2 above) or contracts relating to the work of individuals in the carrying out of construction operations. Payments representing the cost of materials are excluded.

The evidence required to satisfy the turnover test (prescribed by *SI 2005 No 2045, reg 29*) comprises:

(*a*) evidence of the turnover during the twelve months prior to the application (the '*qualifying period*') (this is the net turnover excluding VAT and cost of materials, see HMRC factsheet CIS343);

(*b*) evidence of relevant payments which may include bank statements and paid cheques;

(c) evidence that total relevant payments received in the twelve months prior to the application equalled or exceeded the relevant turnover threshold (£30,000); or, for the purposes of cancellation of registration for gross payment (under *FA 2004, s 66*), evidence that the relevant payments in the qualifying period equalled or exceeded the relevant turnover threshold,or the average amount of relevant payments received in the three years prior to the application equalled or exceeded the relevant turnover threshold;

(*d*) documentary evidence that construction operations were carried out during the qualifying period.

A business that does not meet the turnover test can be treated as if it did if:

(i) the business does not consist mainly of construction operations;

(ii) overall turnover in the year prior to making the application exceeds the relevant turnover threshold; and

(iii) any relevant payments likely to be received in the year following the application will relate to construction operations which are an ancillary part of the business.

This is designed to cover the situation where overall turnover exceeds the threshold but relevant payments derive from an ancillary part of the business and are less than the threshold.

The compliance test. In the twelve months prior to the application (the '*qualifying period*') the individual must have complied with all tax obligations (i.e. imposed by the *Tax Acts*, *TMA 1970* or regulations thereunder (see *SI 2005 No 2045, reg 32*), including the construction industry scheme itself) and there must be reason to expect that the applicant will continue to comply with tax obligations and requests for documents, etc. after the end of that period. The applicant must have supplied to HMRC, during the qualifying period, all requested information and accounts concerning the applicant's business. These requirements also apply to any company controlled (within *ICTA 1988,s 416(2)–(6)*) by the applicant, in respect of periods falling within the qualifying period. Compliance for this purpose must be within any required time limits or at the required time.

The above compliance requirements are relaxed in two respects, as follows:

(A) HMRC are of the opinion that the applicant or company had a reasonable excuse for the failure and that the failure has been remedied without unreasonable delay after the excuse ceased to apply; or

(B) the obligation or request is of a kind prescribed in column 2 of Table 3 in *SI 2005 No 2045, reg 32*. This provision is intended to replace the previous 'minor and technical failings' rule (see 20.14 below).

HMRC will require evidence (as prescribed in *SI 2005 No 2045, regs 33–36*) that an applicant was not subject to any compliance obligations because of absence abroad, unemployment, or being in full-time education. In the case of absence abroad, the applicant must also show evidence of compliance with comparable obligations under the tax laws of the country of residence.

The applicant must have paid any National Insurance contributions as they fell due. This is not subject to the 'reasonable excuse' defence.

Finally, there must be reason to expect that the applicant will continue to comply with compliance obligations and requests for documents etc., and continue to pay his national insurance contributions, after the qualifying period.

[*FA 2004, s 64, Sch 11 paras 1–4, 14; SI 2005 No 2045, regs 27–29, 31–37*].

20.6 **Registration for gross payment — partners.** An individual applying for registration for gross payment as a partner in a firm must first meet the compliance test laid down for individuals (see 20.5 above). A company applying for such registration must first meet all the tests for companies (see 20.7 below) as appropriate. In addition, the firm itself must meet the following business, turnover and compliance tests.

The business test. The firm's business must be carried on in the UK. It must include either the carrying out of construction operations, or the furnishing of, or arranging for the furnishing of, labour for construction operations. It must, to a substantial extent, be carried on using an account with a bank. The evidence required to satisfy HMRC that these conditions are satisfied is as prescribed for individuals by *SI 2005 No 2045*, see **17.12** above.

The turnover test. The partners must satisfy HMRC that the likely receipt of relevant payments (see 20.5 above) in the year following the application is not less than the smaller of:

(*a*) the relevant turnover threshold which, in the case of partnerships, is £200,000; and

(*b*) the 'multiple turnover threshold'.

The '*multiple turnover threshold*' is obtained by adding together:

(i) the number of individuals in the partnership multiplied by the threshold for individuals (£30,000, see 20.5 above); and

(ii) in respect of each company (if any) in the partnership, the threshold that would obtain were the company to be applying in its own behalf (see 20.7 below).

Where the number of partners in (i) above has fluctuated over the twelve-month period prior to the application, the number is taken to be the maximum number of partners at any one time in that period. In calculating the figure in (ii) above, it is necessary to ignore companies whose only shareholders are other companies which are limited by shares and registered for gross payment.

The evidence required to satisfy the turnover test (prescribed by *SI 2005 No 2045, reg 29*) includes the evidence as prescribed for individuals in 20.5 above by reference to the above turnover threshold for partnerships. In the case of a new business carried on by the firm where there is no evidence as prescribed in (*a*), (*c*) or (*d*) in 20.5 above, the following evidence can be given instead, but only in relation to one application for registration for gross payment:

(A) evidence of relevant payments which may include bank statements and paid cheques;

(B) evidence of turnover of partners during the qualifying period;

(C) evidence of construction contracts entered into by the firm including payment schedules where the aggregate value of contracts exceeds £200,000 and payments have been made of at least £30,000.

A firm that does not meet this test may be treated as if it did (as in the case of individuals — see 20.5 above).

The compliance test. Each of the partners at the time of the application must, during the qualifying period (see 20.5 above), have complied with all tax obligations in relation to any income tax or corporation tax charge which was computed by reference to the firm's business. Over the same period, the applicant must have supplied all requested information and accounts concerning the firm's business or his share of that business. Compliance must be within any required time limits or at the required time. Similar provisions as for individuals at 20.5(A), (B) above apply to treat a person as not having failed a compliance obligation in certain circumstances.

There must be reason to expect that, following the qualifying period, each of the persons who are from time to time partners in the firm will continue the record of compliance.

[*FA 2004, s 64, Sch 11 paras 5–8, 14; SI 2005 No 2045, regs 27–37*].

20.7 **Registration for gross payment — companies.** In order to register for gross payment, a company must pass the business, turnover and compliance tests described below. However, HMRC may, in addition to these tests, make a direction applying the conditions relating to individuals (see 20.5 above) to the directors of the company. If the company is a close company, this is extended to include the beneficial owners of shares in the company. Rather than apply all the conditions to all of the directors or shareholders, the direction may specify which conditions are to apply, and to which directors or shareholders.

In particular, HMRC may make such a direction where there has been a change in control (within *ICTA 1988, s 840*) of a company that either is, or is applying to be, registered for gross payment. HMRC are empowered to make regulations requiring the submission of information concerning changes in control of such companies.

The business test. The company's business must be carried on in the UK. It must include either the carrying out of construction operations, or furnishing of, or arranging for the furnishing of labour for construction operations. It must, to a substantial extent, be carried on using an account with a bank. The evidence required to satisfy HMRC that these conditions are satisfied is prescribed for individuals by *SI 2005 No 2045* in **17.12** above.

The turnover test. A company may pass this test by:

(*a*) satisfying HMRC that its only shareholders are companies limited by shares and registered for gross payment; or

(*b*) providing HMRC with evidence that relevant payments (see 20.5 above) received in the year following the application are likely to equal or exceed a set threshold.

The set threshold is the smaller of:

(i) the relevant turnover threshold which, in the case of companies, is £200,000; and

(ii) the individual threshold (£30,000, see 20.5 above) multiplied by the number of 'relevant persons'. A '*relevant person*' is a director (within *ITEPA 2003, s 67*) or, for close companies, a director or a beneficial owner of shares. Where the number of relevant persons has fluctuated over the twelve-month period prior to the application, the number is taken to be the maximum number of such relevant persons at any one time in that period.

The evidence required to satisfy the turnover test (prescribed by *SI 2005 No 2045, reg 29*) includes the evidence as prescribed for individuals in 20.5 above but by reference to the above set threshold for companies. In the case of a new business carried on by the company where there is no evidence as prescribed in (*a*), (*c*) or (*d*) in 20.5 above, the following evidence may be given instead, but only in relation to one application for registration for gross payment:

(A) evidence of relevant payments which may include bank statements and paid cheques;

(B) evidence of turnover of relevant persons during the qualifying period;

(C) evidence of construction contracts entered into by the company including payment schedules where the aggregate value of contracts exceeds £200,000 and payments have been made of at least £30,000;

(D) where the business was acquired from another person, firm or company, similar evidence as above in relation to the transferor.

A company that does not meet this test may be treated as if it did (as in the case of individuals — see 20.5 above).

The compliance test. The provisions relating to companies mirror those relating to individuals (see 20.5 above). However, in addition to this a company must have complied with certain *Companies Act 1985* (or the Northern Ireland equivalent) obligations during the qualifying period. Those obligations are under:

- *sections 226*, *241* and *242* (contents, laying and delivery of annual accounts);
- *section 288*(*2*) (return of directors and secretary and notification of changes therein);
- *sections 363–365* (annual returns);
- *sections 691* and *692* (registration of constitutional documents and list of directors and secretary of overseas company, notification of changes to these);
- *section 693* (overseas company to state name and country of incorporation);
- *section 699* (obligations of companies incorporated in Channel Islands of Isle of Man);
- *Pt 23 Ch 2* (accounts of overseas company).

[*FA 2004 s 64 and Sch 11 paras 9–12, 14; SI 2005 No 2045, regs 27–37*].

20.8 **Charities.** Charities which are deemed contractors under the existing scheme, should not be registered as contractors under the new scheme – to continue to represent themselves as contractors will be illegal. [*SI 2006/2045 para 24*]. HMRC charities is reviewing all charities which are deemed contractors with a view to de-registering them.

However, charities which are sub-contractors continue to have an obligation under the new scheme. Similarly, subsidiary companies of charities, which are not registered charities in their own right, should remain or become registered under the new CIS scheme.

20.9 **Procedures and administration.** Detailed procedures and administrative arrangements for the operation of the scheme applying from April 2007 are contained in *The Income Tax (Construction Industry Scheme) Regulations 2005 (SI 2005 No 2045)* and *The Income Tax (Construction Industry Scheme) (Amendment) Regulations 2007.* [*SI 2007 No 672*]. There are detailed provisions governing verification of contractors, returns by contractors, payments and recovery of amounts deducted, electronic communications and methods of payment, and HMRC powers to inspect records. Further regulations may be made by statutory instrument. [*FA 2004, ss 69–71, 73; ITA 2007 Sch 1 para 461*]. For general guidance see HMRC publication CIS340, 'Guide for Contractors and Subcontractors' (for the new scheme).

Multiple contractors. A contractor may elect to be treated as different contractors for each of any specified group of sub-contractors. The election must be made (or revoked) by notice to an officer of HMRC before the beginning of the tax year for which it is to have effect. There are special provisions which apply where a contractor acquires the business of another contractor. [*SI 2005 No 2045, reg 3*].

Verification of status of sub-contractors. Anyone making contract payments must verify with HMRC the registration status of the recipient. Verification is not necessary if the recipient has been included in the contractor's returns (see below) in the current or previous two tax years. Where the contractor is a company the return could include one made by another company in the same group and, where a multiple contractors election has been made (see above), the return may include one from a different specified group of sub-contractors. Where this condition is met and the business is transferred as a going concern, no further verification is required by the transferee provided the contractor has notified HMRC of the transfer. HMRC must notify a contractor if a person registered for gross payment becomes registered for payment under deduction, or vice versa, or if a registered person has ceased to be so registered. Once a person has been verified as being registered (whether for gross payment or payment under deduction) the contractor is entitled to assume that the person has not subsequently ceased to be so registered. [*SI 2005 No 2045, reg 6*]. The new verification system effectively replaces the requirement under the pre-2007 scheme for the sub-contractor to present documents which the contractor must inspect, and thus reduces some of the bureaucratic burden.

Monthly returns by contractors. There are detailed provisions for monthly returns by contractors of payments made to sub-contractors. A contractor must make monthly returns to HMRC within 14 days after the end of every tax month and written information must also be provided to sub-contractors who are registered for payment under deduction or who are not registered. Where a return has been made, or should have been made, and no contract payments are made in the tax month following that return, the contractor must make a nil return for that month unless the contractor has notified HMRC that no further contract payments are to be made within the following six months. The returns are subject to the penalty provisions in *TMA 1970, s 98* (see 54.9 PENALTIES). [*SI 2005 No 2045, reg 4*]. The new system of monthly returns replaces the pre-2007 requirement for vouchers and end of year returns and also provides for the option of electronic submission to reduce the administrative burden of reporting.

Scheme representative. A contractor company may appoint another company in the same group ('a scheme representative') to act on its behalf in relation to the requirement to make a return or other such requirements under the regulations. [*SI 2005 No 2045, reg 5*].

Collection and recovery of sums deducted. The arrangements for accounting for tax deductions and for interest on unpaid and overpaid tax broadly follow those for PAYE (see Tolley's Income Tax under Pay as You Earn and HMRC publication CIS340). There are detailed provisions governing methods of payment and electronic communications. [*FA 2004, s 71; ITTOIA 2005, Sch 1 para* 630*; SI 2005 No 2045, regs 7–17, 44–49, 58; SI 2007, No 672*].

20.10 **Commencement and transitional provisions.** The new scheme is to be introduced in relation to payments made on or after 6 April 2007. [*FA 2004, s 77(1)*]. There are transitional provisions covering existing paperwork and existing commercial relationships.

Pre-existing certificates and registration cards. Where a sub-contractor's tax certificate (see 20.14 above) is in force immediately before the appointed day, the sub-contractor is to be treated as if he had been registered for gross payment on the appointed day. Similarly, where a registration card (see 20.13 below) is in force immediately before the appointed day, the sub-contractor is to be treated as having been registered for payment under deduction on the appointed day. [*FA 2004, s 77(2)(3)*].

Existing relationships. A contractor will not have to verify the status of a particular sub-contractor if:

(*a*) he has already paid that sub-contractor under a construction contract before the appointed day;

(*b*) the last such payment was within either the same tax year as the first payment under the new scheme or the preceding two tax years;

(*c*) at the time of the last payment a tax certificate or registration card was in force; and

(*d*) at the time of the first payment under the new scheme the contractor has no reason to believe that the sub-contractor did not benefit from automatic registration on the appointed day under the rules described above, and is still unregistered.

Where these conditions apply, the contractor may continue to assume the sub-contractor is registered unless HMRC notify him of a change in status.

[*FA 2004, s 77(4)–(6)*].

20.11 SCHEME APPLICABLE FROM 1 AUGUST 1999 TO 31 MARCH 2007

With effect for payments made on or after 1 August 1999, the scheme for deduction of tax from payments to construction sub-contractors who do not have a tax certificate entitling them to gross payment, and the arrangements and conditions for the issue of such certificates, are substantially revised. The revised scheme is described at 20.12 *et seq.* below. It is intended that, under the revised scheme, most sub-contractors will *not* hold tax certificates, but will hold registration cards (see 20.13 below) and receive payments after deduction on account of tax. The main changes from the scheme as it applied before 1 August 1999 are as follows.

(*a*) The 23% deduction is replaced by a deduction of a percentage determined by the Treasury by order, which may not exceed the basic rate (and is set at 18% from 6 April 2000).

(*b*) A minimum anticipated annual turnover (prescribed by regulation and, in the case of firms or companies, broadly geared to the number of individuals who are partners or directors) is a precondition for the issue of a tax certificate.

(*c*) The limited certificates for school leavers and where a bank guarantee is in force are withdrawn.

(*d*) A general exemption from deduction is provided where conditions to be prescribed are met in relation to a payment under any contract and to the person making the payment.

(*e*) All public offices and departments of the Crown, and such statutory bodies as are designated in regulations, are normally to be treated as contractors for the purposes of the deduction scheme. However, for these and the other public bodies treated as contractors, an exemption based on the average annual construction expenditure test already used for businesses is introduced. Government departments treated as contractors will be subject to the same obligations, sanctions and HMRC powers of enforcement as other contractors.

(*f*) The average annual expenditure on construction operations which renders the person incurring the expenditure a contractor for the purposes of the deduction scheme is increased from £250,000 to £1,000,000.

(*g*) The conditions for a tax certificate for an individual partner in a firm are generally aligned with those for sole traders, in so far as they relate to the circumstances of the individual. The individual conditions relating to the length of time the business has been carried on are removed.

(*h*) The fine (maximum £5,000) on summary conviction for certain fraudulent attempts to obtain or misuse a tax certificate is replaced by a penalty up to £3,000.

Exemption certificates covering periods beginning before and ending after 31 July 1999 cease to have effect after that date.

Registration cards. As referred to above, in conjunction with the revised deduction scheme, a mandatory registration card system is introduced for sub-contractors not holding a tax certificate. See 20.12, 20.13 below. In outline, the registration card system is as follows.

(i) The card carries the sub-contractor's name and photograph, the tax reference and the national insurance number.

(ii) Contractors are required to check cards before making payments under deduction.

(iii) The cards are available on request to anyone working, or intending to work, in the construction industry.

(iv) A penalty of up to £3,000 applies for failure by a contractor to take the necessary steps to require the production of registration cards and to check their validity, or to make accurate returns in relation to registration card payments (unless there were reasonable grounds for accepting the validity of a card and all reasonable steps were taken to ensure the correctness of the return).

Transitional arrangements. For the period 1 August 1999 to 5 September 1999, arrangements were made for the issue by tax offices of temporary Tax Payment Cards (forms CIS65) which enabled contractors to make payments under deduction of tax in certain cases where the sub-contractor had not applied for a registration card or certificate in time for the scheme commencement or, exceptionally, had applied for but not received it. Additionally, up to 5 November 1999, contractors were able to accept registration card, temporary tax payment card or certificate details where the document was photocopied onto the sub-contractor's original headed paper, and where contractors still believed they would be unable to pay their workers and/or complete the appropriate vouchers, they could apply for a dispensation. Payments after 5 November 1999 can only be made where the full new scheme conditions are complied with. (Revenue Press Releases 7 July 1999, 15 July 1999).

20.12 **Payments from which tax must be deducted.** Where a 'contractor' carrying on a business which includes 'construction operations' makes any payment (except as below) to, or to the nominee of, a 'sub-contractor' under a contract relating to 'construction operations' in the UK or on offshore installations within UK territorial waters, then, unless the recipient meets the conditions for gross payment (see 20.14 below), the payer must deduct, and pay over to HMRC, a specified percentage of so much of the payment (excluding any VAT and CITB levy) as does not represent the cost of materials. Before making any such payment, the contractor must ensure that the sub-contractor produces a valid registration card (see 20.13 below), and must satisfy himself that the person producing it is the person to whom it was issued (or an authorised user of a company card, being a director or secretary of the company), unless he has done so on a previous occasion and has no reason to doubt that it remains valid for the person who produced it. Possession of a registration card by a sub-contractor does not, however, relieve the contractor of the responsibility to establish whether the sub-contractor is employed or self-employed (see 20.17 below). A penalty not exceeding £3,000 may apply for failure by a contractor to carry out these checks. These provisions do not apply to: payments under a contract of employment; payments chargeable as employment income under *ITEPA 2003, ss 44–47* (previously *ICTA 1988, s 134*) (workers supplied by agencies — see Tolley's Income Tax under Employment Income); or payments excluded by regulations (including certain payments under contracts of value £1,000 or less). The percentage deduction rate is determined by the Treasury by order, and may not exceed the basic rate of income tax. [*ICTA 1988, s 559(1)–(4A), s 560(1), s 561(1), s 566(2B), s 567(1)(b); FA 1995, s 139, Sch 27 para 1; FA 1996, s 178(1); FA 1998, s 55(2)(3); SI 1993 No 743, reg 7F; SI 1998 No 2622, reg 8; SI 2000 No 922*].

The specified rate of deduction is reduced from 23% to 18% with effect from 6 April 2000. [*SI 2000 No 921*].

It is understood that the 'cost of materials' which may be excluded in determining the amount subject to deduction may include a reasonable commercial charge for plant supplied by the sub-contractor for the period of the contract. Where a sub-contractor does not supply evidence of the cost to him of materials, the contractor should make a fair estimate of the actual cost.

A '*sub-contractor*' is a party to a contract relating to 'construction operations' who is under a duty to carry out, or to furnish his own, or others', labour in the carrying out of, such operations, or is otherwise answerable to the contractor for the carrying out of such operations by others.

A '*contractor*' is:

(*a*) any person carrying on a business which includes 'construction operations';

(*b*) any person carrying on a business at any time if his average annual expenditure on construction operations in the three years up to the end of his last period of account exceeded £1,000,000 or, where the business was not being carried on at the beginning of that three-year period, if his total expenditure on such operations up to the end of that last period of account exceeded £3,000,000. A person who is a contractor under this provision will continue within that definition until he satisfies HMRC that his expenditure on construction operations has been below £1,000,000 in each of three successive years beginning in or after that period of account. For the purposes of these expenditure limits, where a trade is transferred from one company to another and *ICTA 1988, s 343* (no change of ownership) applies, the transferor's expenditure will be treated as the transferee's, with apportionment by HMRC (subject to appeal) when only part of the trade is transferred; and

(*c*) any public office or department of the Crown; any local authority; any development corporation or new town commission; the Commission for the New Towns; the Housing Corporation; the Secretary of State for Wales (in relation to a contract made under *Housing Associations Act 1985, s 89*); any housing association or trust; Scottish Homes; the Northern Ireland Housing Executive; any NHS trust (or NI equivalent); the Corporate Officers of the Houses of Parliament; and the Scottish Parliamentary Corporate Body. Apart from the Secretary of State for Wales, such offices, departments and bodies are, however, defined as contractors only at a time when their average annual expenditure on 'construction operations' in the three-year period to 31 March immediately preceding that time exceeded £1,000,000, but once so included they continue to be so until expenditure on 'construction operations' has been below £1,000,000 in each of three successive years after the end of the three-year period.

The definition includes a person who is himself a sub-contractor in relation to construction operations, e.g. a gang-leader.

[*ICTA 1988, ss 559(1), 560(2)–(5); FA 1998, Sch 8 para 2(2)–(4); Government of Wales Act 1998, Sch 16 para 58; SI 1993 No 743, reg 3A, Sch A1; SI 1998 No 2622, regs 4, 37; SI 1999 No 2159, reg 9; SI 2000 No 1880*].

Where payments by any of the bodies, etc. which are contractors by virtue of (*b*) or (*c*) above are made under a contract in respect of which the total contract payments (excluding materials) do not exceed (and are not likely to exceed) £1,000, and the body, etc. is approved by the inspector for the purpose, the payments are excluded from the application of these provisions. [*SI 1993 No 743, reg 20B; SI 1998 No 2622, reg 13*].

Private householders having work done on their own premises are *not* contractors for these purposes.

'*Construction operations*' are widely defined to cover installing heating, lighting, drainage, etc. systems, internal cleaning of buildings in the course of their construction, alteration or repair, and internal or external painting, as well as constructing, altering, repairing or demolishing buildings, walls, roadworks, etc., but to *exclude* drilling for oil or gas, mining operations, the professional work of architects, surveyors, etc., the installation, etc. of sculptures, murals, and other artistic works, signwriting, advertisements, seating, blinds, shutters, security and public address systems, computer or telecommunications wiring through pre-existing ducts and the manufacture of components for heating, lighting, drainage, etc. systems. The Treasury may add to these categories by order made by statutory instrument. [*ICTA 1988, s 567*]. Carpet fitting is outside the scope of the scheme. (HMRC Statement of Practice, SP 12/81). For detailed guidance on the scope of 'construction operations', see HMRC Construction Industry Scheme Manual, CIS 1315 *et seq.*

A signed *tax payment voucher* (form CIS25) must be given by the contractor to the sub-contractor within 14 days of the end of a tax month in respect of all payments made under deduction of tax as above during the month. The contractor must also within 14 days of the end of each tax month either send the top copies of all forms CIS25 to the HMRC (where three-part forms CIS25(I) or (M) have been used) or transmit specified particulars to them electronically (where single-part forms CIS25(E) have been used). [*SI 1993 No 743, reg 7; SI 1998 No 2622, reg 7*].

See generally HMRC Pamphlet IR 164(CIS) 'Advice to sub-contractors going onto deduction'. For application of the scheme to non-residents, see IR 180(CIS).

20.13 **Registration cards.** Registration cards (see 20.11 above) are issued, renewed or replaced by an inspector or other person nominated by HMRC. An inspector may require their surrender or cancel them. They must be produced for inspection, or surrendered, when required by any authorised officer of HMRC. A refusal to issue or replace a registration card, or its cancellation, is subject to the normal right of appeal, although it is expected that cards will be available on request to anyone intending to commence work, or working, within the construction industry. They need only complete a form, supply a photograph and attend an identity check.

Cards (form CIS4(P)) other than temporary cards carry the sub-contractor's name, photograph and signature, the national insurance number (or, exceptionally, a 'system identifier'), and a distinctive reference number assigned to the card. They may also include a name under which the business is carried on. They have no expiry date. In the case of a partner in a firm, they must include the name of the firm for which the partner is acting. Company cards issued to a director or secretary of the company authorised to use the card must similarly include the name of the company for whom the director or secretary is acting. If a business name is included on a partner's or company card, it must be the same for all partners or directors and secretaries. Temporary registration cards (form CIS4(T)), which carry a date of expiry instead of the national insurance number, may be issued with a maximum validity of twelve months or, where the issuer deems it appropriate, 36 months (before 20 September 2002, the maximum validity was three months).

[*ICTA 1988, s 566(2A); SI 1993 No 743, regs 7A–7E, Sch 1; SI 1998 No 2622, regs 8, 38; SI 2002 No 2225, regs 3–5*].

See 20.17 below as regards penalties relating to registration card failures.

20.14 **Sub-contractors' tax certificates.** Where a tax certificate (form CIS5 or CIS6) has been issued to a sub-contractor and is in force when a payment is made, and the various regulatory requirements as regards production and validation, etc. of the certificate (see below) are complied with, the deduction requirements under 20.12 above do not apply. Possession of a tax certificate by a sub-contractor does not, however, relieve the contractor of the responsibility to establish whether the sub-contractor is employed or self-employed (see 20.17 below). Certificates form CIS5 and (from 1 May 2001) CIS5 (Partner), which do not have to be produced to contractors (see alternative verification procedure described below) and which obviate the requirement to supply gross payment vouchers to contractors (see below), may only be issued when the inspector considers that a form CIS6 certificate would be inappropriate in all the circumstances. HMRC have indicated that a CIS5 certificate will only be issued to a company which either:

(*a*) is a plc or a subsidiary of a plc; or

(*b*) has a turnover of at least £1 million (£3 million before December 2000), or has taken over and will continue an established concern with such a turnover which was previously owned by a director or directors of the company and which met certain other conditions as to previous compliance; or

(*c*) is a subsidiary or associate of an established company holding a CIS5 (or predecessor 714C) certificate (and which would still qualify for a CIS 5 certificate); or

(*d*) shows that operating with a CIS6 certificate would cause substantial difficulties.

As regards (*b*) above, following the reduction in the required turnover, a company already qualifying for a CIS6 certificate with a turnover of £1 million or more in its last set of accounts or tax return can apply for a CIS5 certificate. If it presently holds a CIS6 certificate with at least six months remaining, it may make a written request, and a CIS5 certificate issued in these circumstances will bear the same expiry date as the CIS6 certificate (which must be surrendered). If a CIS6 certificate with less than six months remaining is held, or the company does not currently hold a certificate, formal application for a CIS5 certificate must be made in the normal way. (Revenue Tax Bulletin December 2000 p 815).

As regards (*d*) above, evidence would have to be produced either of:

- an administrative need, i.e. that using CIS6 certificates would involve either a high volume of vouchers – normally 300 or more per year but 150 or more per year may suffice in certain cases; or
- an excessive amount of time spent travelling specifically to present a certificate – at least 200 hours over a three-year period or 100 hours in any one of those years; or
- of a commercial need, i.e. where the applicant's trade is largely based on, or potentially involves, work for contractors who give work only to CIS5 certificate holders. (Revenue Tax Bulletin April 1999 pp 635, 636).

For more detailed guidance on the issue of CIS5 certificates, see HMRC Construction Industry Scheme Manual.

From 1 May 2001, a CIS5 (Partner) certificate may be issued, but only to a single partner in a particular firm, in his capacity as such, at any one time. The conditions for issue, and the alternative verification procedure, are similar to those applicable to CIS5 certificates.

Verification. Before a gross payment can be made, and subject to the alternative verification procedure described below for CIS5 certificate holders, the sub-contractor must produce the certificate to the contractor, who must satisfy himself by inspecting the certificate that the sub-contractor is the user of the certificate (or authorised to produce it on behalf of a company which is the user). Where the user receives the payment as a nominee, the person nominating the user must also produce his certificate for validation. Further inspections of the certificate are not required for so long as the contractor has no reason to doubt that it is still valid.

There is an alternative verification procedure where the user of a CIS5 certificate (not being a nominee) has notified the inspector of particulars of the company bank account into which payments, which must be under a written contract between the company and the contractor, are to be made. The user may produce to the contractor a 'certification document' signed by the secretary or a director of the company, and providing that the contractor has no reason to doubt that the information shown on the document is correct (and the payment date falls within the period of validity of the certificate referred to in the document), he may make payments gross. The certification document must certify that the company is the user of a valid company tax certificate form CIS5. It must specify the name, address (of the registered office) and registration number of the user, the distinctive number, expiry date (and, if any, commencement date) of the certificate, and details of the nominated bank account. It may also include the user's business name. To allay any doubt concerning the certification document, the contractor may, within 14 days of receipt of the document, apply to the inspector for confirmation that a valid certificate has been issued to the company and that the information on the certification document agrees with the inspector's records.

See above as regards certificates CIS5 (Partner).

[*SI 1993 No 743, regs 33, 34; SI 1998 No 2622, reg 25; SI 2001 No 1531*].

Payments. Payments to a holder of certificate form CIS5 should only be made by cheque or credit transfer, and *never* by cash.

Completion of vouchers. A sub-contractor with a certificate form CIS6 must, within 14 days after the end of each income tax month, give two signed copies of a gross payment voucher (form CIS24) containing specified particulars to the contractor in respect of all contract payments received gross in the month (or, if the contractor so requests, for each such payment). The contractor must complete the form with his distinctive reference number and deliver the appropriate copy to the sub-contractor. Where vouchers are not supplied, or are incorrectly completed, by the sub-contractor, and further payments are due, the contractor should reconsider the validity of the certificate. Duplicates should be requested of vouchers claimed to have been lost in the post. If a proper voucher is not supplied despite the contractor taking reasonable steps to obtain one, he should report the matter to HMRC.

Where a sub-contractor has a certificate form CIS5, the contractor must complete a construction gross payment voucher (form CIS23(M) or CIS23(I)) containing specified particulars in respect of all gross payments in any income tax month (or transmit the specified particulars to HMRC electronically). Within 14 days after the end of each income tax month the contractor must forward to HMRC all forms CIS24, CIS23(M) or CIS23(I) given to or obtained or completed by him in the month. [*SI 1993 No 743, regs 35, 37A, 38, 39; SI 1998 No 2622, regs 26, 29–31*].

Issue of a certificate. Application for a tax certificate is made on form CIS2 or CIS3 as appropriate, and at least one month should be allowed for the application to be approved. Ten working days should be allowed after notification of approval for issue of the certificate.

For a tax certificate to be issued, HMRC must be satisfied that the sub-contractor is carrying on a business in the UK consisting of or including the carrying out of construction operations (see 20.12 above), or the furnishing (or arranging for the furnishing) of labour for such operations, with proper premises, equipment, stock and other facilities. There must be a bank account through which the business is substantially conducted and proper records must be kept, and the applicant must also satisfy the 'turnover test' described at 20.15 below. Certificates are normally valid for either three years or one year, depending on the basis on which the turnover test is satisfied (see 20.15 below), although the initial issue of certificates under the new scheme will adjust the three-year period by up to six months to achieve an even rate of expiry of certificates. Certificates issued to partners in a firm or to a company at different times will have a common expiry date. HMRC has wide powers to cancel certificates and require their surrender (also see 20.17 below).

An *individual applicant* (whether or not a partner in a firm) must have complied timeously with all tax and national insurance obligations (including supplying accounts and other information relating to any business of the applicant to the inspector on request) in respect of periods ending within the three years preceding the date of application (the '*qualifying period*'). There must also be reason to expect that future such obligations will be complied with, and provided that this expectation is not rendered open to doubt, 'minor and technical failings' in relation to past obligations may be disregarded at HMRC's discretion (but see *T & C Hill (Haulage) v Gleig (Sp C 227), [2000] SSCD 64* for a case in which refusal of a certificate was upheld on the grounds of late submission of returns and payment of tax liabilities after the due date, and *Vicky Construction Ltd* (referred to below)). See HMRC Pamphlet IR 40(CIS), Appendix 2 for HMRC interpretation of 'minor and technical failings' (but see *Cormack v CBL Cable Contractors (referred to* below)). Where the applicant claims not to have been subject to an obligation for these purposes, he must satisfy HMRC of that fact by evidence prescribed by regulation, and where he claims to have been non-resident, he must also satisfy HMRC by such evidence that any comparable foreign obligations have been met (see *SI 1993 No 743, regs 22-23B; SI 1998 No 2622, regs 15-17*). Any company of which the individual had control (within *ICTA 1988, s 416(2)-(6)*) during the qualifying period must also satisfy those conditions in respect of any accounting period ending within the qualifying period at a time when the applicant had such control.

A *company applicant* (whether or not a partner in a firm) must have a similarly satisfactory record of past and prospective compliance with all its taxation and National Insurance and certain Companies Act obligations. In *HMRC v Facilities and Maintenance Engineering Ltd [2006] STC 1887*, the High Court held that if a company failed to comply with its obligations in the last three years, and the failures were too serious to rank as merely minor or technical, the necessary conditions were not satisfied and HMRC had no power to issue a certificate even if they were convinced that the company would comply in the future. In *Gorge Fabrications Ltd v Wilson (Sp C 214), [1999] SSCD 293*, the Special Commissioner upheld an inspector's refusal of a certificate to a company which had, within the three-year period in question, entered into a voluntary arrangement with its creditors resulting in 75% of its outstanding corporation tax liabilities (amounting to £2,927) remaining unpaid (its PAYE/NIC liabilities of over £30,000 having been treated as preferential and met in full). The inspector's refusal to renew a certificate because of a record of late payment of PAYE tax was similarly upheld in the High Court, a claim that the lateness was of a 'minor and technical nature' being rejected and the refusal being held not to give rise to any breach of the *European Convention on Human Rights (Shaw v Vicky Construction Ltd Ch D 2002, 75 TC 26*). See also *Arnold (Insp of Taxes) v G-Con Ltd CA [2006] STC 1516* in which it was considered that the question of whether the failings were minor and technical was not affected by compliance in respect of other tax matters and that the absence of a prior warning was irrelevant. In *Cormack v CBL Cable Contractors Ltd Ch D [2005] EWHC 1294*, the High Court, in dismissing HMRC's appeal in respect of its refusal to renew a company's CIS certificate, held that the words 'minor and technical' were not primarily or exclusively concerned with size and frequency. HMRC's appeal was similarly dismissed in *Templeton v Transform Shop Office and Bar Fitters Ltd Ch D (2005) 77 TC 229* in which the Commissioners' conclusions were upheld that non-compliance, although persistent, could be regarded as minor and technical having regard to the regularity of late payments and HMRC's acquiescence over the whole period of the non-compliance. In *Hudson Contract Services Ltd v HMRC [2007] All ER(D) 273 (Jan)* the High Court upheld the Commissioners' decision that the company's activities were within the construction industry scheme, but found that the company's failures were not 'minor and technical'.

HMRC may also, in certain cases where there is a limited history of construction operations, or where there has been a change of control, issue a direction under *ICTA 1988, s 561(6)* that the directors (and, if the company is close, the beneficial shareholders) must satisfy any or all of the conditions imposed on individual applicants (see above). Where the introduction of a new shareholder into a close private company results in a change of control, the company must notify the inspector of the new shareholder within 30 days (see *SI 1993 No 743, reg 42*).

Each of the *partners in a firm* (applying as such), in addition to meeting the requirements for individual or company applicants (as above), as appropriate, must also satisfy the requirements as to the meeting of tax obligations (and requests by the inspector) in relation to the firm's business.

[*ICTA 1988, ss 561, 562, 564, 565; SI 1993 No 743, regs 25, 26; SI 1998 No 2622, regs 19, 20; SI 1999 No 2156*].

Changes in a business. Where an individual or firm incorporates, or a partnership becomes a sole trader, the new business will require a new certificate. However, if the business is essentially the same, the new business may apply immediately on the basis of the three-year test (applied in the light of the particular circumstances of the case), rather than having to wait six months to apply on the basis of the six-month test. Changes in the number of partners in a firm or directors/shareholders in a company, without any change in the business, do not require the turnover test to be re-applied before the certificate falls to be renewed, unless the inspector suspects manipulation of the threshold provisions. New partners/directors can apply for additional certificates. (HMRC Pamphlet IR 40(CIS) p 6).

Simon's Direct Tax Service. See **E5.510**, *et seq*, **E5.550**, **E5.566**.

20.15 **Turnover test.** *Individuals* (*other than in relation to applications as partners in firms*). The turnover test requires the applicant to satisfy HMRC that, during the period of validity of the certificate, the aggregate annual amount of 'relevant payments' received is likely to be not less than the 'individual turnover threshold' of £30,000. (It should, however, be noted that HMRC Pamphlet IR 40(CIS) states: 'If you are using the six-month test, you should show the actual amount you received in the period. Where you are using a three-year test on the basis of accounts, we would not expect you to adjust figures for gross construction turnover and materials for debtors or creditors to arrive at the net "payments received" in the three years. Just use the figures earned, as shown in your accounts.'.) '*Relevant payments*' are all payments, net of the cost of materials, under contracts relating to, or to the work of individuals participating in the carrying out of, construction operations (see 20.12 above), whether or not within the scheme (i.e. including work for private householders, etc.).

To satisfy HMRC, either a six-month test or a three-year test must be satisfied (and depending on which test is satisfied, the certificate will generally be valid for one year or three years (subject to variation on the initial issue, see 20.14 above) respectively). The six-month test is not available where the applicant has been a sub-contractor for a continuous period of four years up to the date of application and three successive one-year certificates have been issued to him.

The six-month test requires the production of evidence (i.e. tax payment vouchers and gross payment vouchers and documentary evidence of relevant payments and of the direct cost of materials) that relevant payments (i.e. turnover) during a consecutive period of up to six tax months in the year preceding the date of application amounted to at least 70% of the individual turnover threshold (i.e. currently £21,000).

The three-year test requires the production of such evidence that relevant payments (i.e. turnover) in a consecutive period of three years in the four years preceding the date of application averaged at least 90% of the average of the individual turnover thresholds for those three years (i.e. currently £27,000) and were at least equal to that threshold in two of the three years. Accounts will also generally be required.

Companies. The turnover test requires a company applicant to satisfy HMRC that either:

(i) the annual receipts test is satisfied; or

(ii) all the company's shareholders are themselves companies limited by shares with current valid certificates.

The annual receipts test requires that, during the period of validity of the certificate, the aggregate annual amount of 'relevant payments' (as above) received is likely to be not less than the smaller of:

(*a*) the individual turnover threshold (currently £30,000), as above, multiplied by the number of 'relevant persons' in relation to the company; and

(*b*) a specified amount (currently £200,000).

A person is a '*relevant person*' in relation to a company if he is a director of the company or (where the company is a close company) a beneficial owner of shares in the company. To satisfy HMRC as regards (*a*) above, the six-month or three-year tests described above in relation to individual applicants are applied, but by reference to the '*multiple company turnover threshold*', i.e. (subject to special rules where a business is transferred by an individual or firm to a company as a going concern) the individual turnover threshold multiplied by the number of relevant persons. For the six-month test, the number of relevant persons is the maximum number at any time in the six-month (or shorter) period concerned. For the three-year test it is the maximum number at any time in the relevant year, except that for applications before 1 August 2001, by concession, the maximum number at any point during the last six months of the three-year period could be substituted for each of the three years if this assisted the sub-contractor to meet the test. (HMRC Extra-Statutory Concession, B52). As regards (*b*) above (the '*alternative company turnover threshold*'), the three-year test is applied, but by reference to the £200,000 annual limit.

Individuals applying as partners in firms. The turnover test requires the partners in the firm to satisfy HMRC that, during the period of validity of the certificate, the aggregate annual amount of 'relevant payments' (as above) received is likely to be not less than the smaller of:

(A) the sum of the individual turnover threshold (as above) multiplied by the number of individual partners and, for each corporate partner (other than a company within (ii) above), the turnover threshold which would have applied if the company had itself applied for a certificate (as above); and

(B) a specified amount (currently £200,000).

To satisfy HMRC as regards (A) above, the six-month or three-year tests described above in relation to individual applicants are applied, but by reference to the '*multiple partnership turnover threshold*', i.e. the individual turnover threshold multiplied by the sum of the number of individual partners and the number of relevant persons which would have been taken into account under (*a*) above in relation to company partners. For the six-month test, the number of partners is the maximum number at any time in the six-month (or shorter) period concerned. For the three-year test, it is the maximum number at any time in the relevant year, except that for applications before 1 August 2001, by concession, the maximum number at any point during the last six months of the three-year period could be substituted for each of the three years if this assisted the sub-contractor to meet the test.

(HMRC Extra-Statutory Concession, B52). As regards (B) above (the '*alternative partnership turnover threshold*'), the three-year test is applied, but by reference to the £200,000 annual limit.

[*ICTA 1988, ss 562(2A)(2B), 564(2A)-(2C), 565(2A)-(2D); FA 1998, Sch 8 paras 3-5; FA 1999, s 53; SI 1993 No 743, regs 21A-21E; SI 1998 No 2622, reg 14; SI 1999 No 2159, regs 4-6*].

See generally Revenue Tax Bulletin December 1998 pp 615–617 and, as regards how the test is applied where the applicant's business changes (e.g. where a partnership becomes a sole trader or *vice versa* or a sole trader or partnership becomes a company, or where sole traders or partnerships merge to form a new partnership), June 1999 pp 667, 668.

Simon's Direct Tax Service. See **E5.513** *et seq.*

20.16 **Renewal of certificates.** Applications for renewal of a certificate may be made at any time within six months before the date of expiry. The conditions are exactly the same as for the initial issue. [*SI 1993 No 743, reg 27*].

20.17 **Administration.** Detailed administrative arrangements for the operation of the scheme are contained in *The Income Tax (Sub-contractors in the Construction Industry) Regulations 1993* (*SI 1993 No 743*) as amended by the (*Amendment*) *Regulations 1998* (*SI 1998 No 2622*), *1999* (*SI 1999 No 825*), *2000* (*SI 2000 No 2742*), *2002* (*SI 2002 No 2225*) and *2003* (*SI 2003 No 536*). The arrangements for accounting for deductions and for interest on unpaid or overpaid tax (see *SI 1993 No 743, regs 8-19; SI 1998 No 2622, regs 9, 10; SI 1999 No 825, reg 2; SI 2000 No 1151; SI 2003 No 536, regs 4–6; FA 2003, s 147(1)*) broadly follow those for PAYE (see Tolley's Income Tax under Pay As You Earn), and there are detailed provisions governing the form and use of sub-contractor's tax certificates (see *SI 1993 No 743, reg 24, Sch 1; SI 1998 No 2622, regs 18, 38; SI 1999 No 2159, reg 10; SI 2002 No 2225, reg 6*) and the requirements for contractors' end of year returns of all payments to sub-contractors (see *SI 1993 No 743, reg 40A; SI 1998 No 2622, reg 33*). See also below under *Failure to deduct and under-deduction*. HMRC have powers to inspect records of contractors and sub-contractors (see *SI 1993 No 743, regs 41, 41A; SI 1998 No 2622, reg 34; SI 1999 No 2159, reg 8; SI 2003 No 536, reg 7*). Further regulations may be made by statutory instrument. [*ICTA 1988, s 566; FA 1998, Sch 8 para 6*]. See HMRC Pamphlet IR 109 as regards negotiation of settlements. HMRC Code of Practice (No 3, available from local tax offices) sets out their standards for the way in which inspections of contractors' records are conducted and the rights and responsibilities of taxpayers.

Contractors are able to submit some of the vouchers information using electronic data interchange ('EDI'). [*SI 1993 No 743, reg 7(4)(b), reg 37A(2)(b), reg 40A(9)(b), reg 44A, reg 44B; SI 1998 No 2622, regs 7(4)(5), 29, 33, 35; SI 2003 No 536, reg 8*]. For an outline of how EDI may be used, see Revenue Press Release 1 September 1998.

Multiple contractors. There are provisions allowing a contractor to elect to be treated as a different contractor for each of any specified groups of sub-contractors. [*SI 1993 No 743, reg 4*].

Appeals. There is a right of appeal (to the Commissioners, within 30 days) against the refusal or cancellation of a sub-contractor's tax certificate, and the Commissioners have the jurisdiction to review the exercise of any discretionary powers by HMRC. [*ICTA 1988, s 561(9)*]. See also below under *Failure to deduct and under-deduction* and *Assessment*.

Cancellation. A certificate may at any time be cancelled by HMRC, and its surrender demanded, if it was issued on false information, or has been misused by the holder, or if the holder no longer meets the requirements for the issue of a certificate or if, in the case of a company, there has been a change of control (within *ICTA 1988, s 840*) and the information required concerning that change has not been furnished. [*ICTA 1988, s 561(8)*].

Employment status. Where a worker in the construction industry is recategorised as an employee, HMRC adopt a practical approach to the year of change. The liability for the year is calculated as if there was a cessation of trade, but with no prior year adjustments, and a commencement of employment on the date of the change. Trading profits of the year of cessation are generally taken either as those actually arising in the year or as the appropriate proportion of the profits from the end of the previous year's basis period to cessation, but any basis giving a reasonable result may be accepted. A due proportion of a full year's capital allowances is given for the final year, with no disposal value being brought in. See Taxation Vol 138, No 3596 p 643, 6 March 1997 for this and other aspects.

Possession of a registration card (see 20.4 above) or tax certificate (see 20.3 above) by a sub-contractor does not relieve the contractor of the responsibility to establish whether the sub-contractor is employed or self-employed. A telephone helpline (0345–335588) is available for contractors and workers needing general assistance in determining whether workers are employed or self-employed.

See generally HMRC Pamphlets IR 56 and IR 148 and Revenue Tax Bulletin April 1997 pp 405–413.

Penalties. For fraudulent attempts to obtain or misuse a certificate, penalties of up to £3,000 may be exacted. [*ICTA 1988, s 561(10)(11)*]. A maximum penalty of £3,000 similarly applies for failure to comply with obligations in relation to registration cards (see 20.2 above). [*ICTA 1988, s 566(2B)-(2F)*]. Penalties under *TMA 1970, s 98A* apply in cases of failure to make required end-of-year returns. [*SI 1993 No 743, reg 40A(16); SI 1998 No 2622, reg 33*].

Deduction of tax. If exemption is not obtained, but a registration card is produced, the sub-contractor will receive payments under deduction of tax as under 20.2 above, and will receive from the contractor(s) form(s) CIS25 vouching the tax deducted (see 20.2 above). He will be treated for tax purposes as having received the full amount, the tax deducted and vouched on forms CIS25 being treated as a payment in respect of his income or corporation tax liability on the profits of the trade in the year of assessment or accounting period in which the deduction was made. In the case of an individual, any excess is treated as a payment on account of his Class 4 contributions under the Social Security Acts, any further excess being repaid. In the case of a company, regulations will require the offset of amounts deducted from payments on or after 6 April 2002 against liabilities as an employer or contractor for the current year of assessment. Any further excess may then be treated as corporation tax paid in respect of profits of the trade before repayment is made. (Deductions cannot be applied against future corporation tax liabilities (HMRC Construction Industry Scheme Manual, CIS 7317).) Previously, the only offset for deductions suffered by companies was against tax paid in respect of profits of the trade. [*ICTA 1988, ss 559(4)-(5A), 559A; FA 1998, Sch 8 para 2(1); FA 2002, s 40, Sch 40 Pt 3(1)*].

To the extent that any liability for a year of assessment is met by tax deducted in that year, no interest charge will arise in e.g. a case of failure to notify liability. For the set-off of any corporation tax repayment due under these provisions against liabilities of certain intermediaries, see Tolley's Income Tax under Personal Service Companies Etc.

Provisional repayments to individuals (or partners in firms) of tax vouched on forms CIS25 may, on application to the inspector, be made before the end of the tax year to which they relate. They may not be made after the end of the tax year. All earlier year income tax and Class 4 national insurance liabilities of the business must have been paid, and repayment is restricted to the excess of the deductions over the sum of the liability to income tax and Class 4 national insurance for the year on profits or gains of the business and on any income arising during the year up to the date of application from which tax has not been deducted (in either case whether or not yet due and payable) and any other sums due and payable from the applicant, including sums he has himself deducted as a contractor. A claim, accompanied by all the forms CIS25 relevant to the claim, is required on form CIS40 (obtainable from local tax offices), or form CIS41 in the case of a partner. In the case of a claim by a partner, the form must be signed by all individual partners and by the secretary or a director of all corporate partners. [*SI 1993 No 743, reg 20A; SI 1998 No 2622, reg 12*].

Failure to deduct and under-deduction. If the contractor fails to deduct the tax, he is nevertheless liable for the tax which should have been deducted (see *Ladkarn Ltd v McIntosh Ch D 1982, 56 TC 616*). However, where the Collector is satisfied that the contractor took reasonable care, and that the failure was due to an error made in good faith or to a genuine belief that the payment was not subject to deduction, the Collector may waive the liability. An appeal may be made (within 30 days) against a decision not so to waive liability. Liability in respect of such failure may also be waived at the contractor's request where the inspector is satisfied that the sub-contractor to whom the payment was made either was not chargeable to tax thereon or has made the appropriate return and paid the tax and any Class 4 contributions. [*SI 1993 No 743, reg 10*].

See HMRC Pamphlet IR 109 as regards negotiation of settlements.

Assessment. If the inspector considers it necessary to do so in all the circumstances, he may raise an assessment on the contractor in any amount which, to the best of his judgement, the contractor is liable to pay under the scheme regulations. The assessment is treated in the same way as an income tax assessment for assessment, appeal and recovery purposes. Tax is due and payable 14 days after the date of the assessment. [*SI 1993 No 743, reg 14*]. As regards interest on tax unpaid or overpaid on such assessments, similar provisions apply as for PAYE (see Tolley's Income Tax under Pay As You Earn). [*SI 1993 No 743, regs 16–18*].

21 Controlled Foreign Companies

Cross-reference. See also 24.12 DOUBLE TAXATION RELIEF, 26 EXCHANGE GAINS AND LOSSES.

Simon's Direct Tax Service D4.12 *et seq.*

The headings in this chapter are as follows.

21.1 INTRODUCTION

The provisions described in this chapter apply in relation to an accounting period (see 21.8 below) of a company which was, in that accounting period, a 'controlled foreign company' (a 'CFC') (see 21.2 below). [*ICTA 1988, ss 747(1)(2), 751(4)*]. A charge (see 21.8 below) may then arise on certain companies having an 'interest' (see 21.7 below) in the CFC. For limitations on direction-making powers and clearances, see 21.12 below.

Under SELF-ASSESSMENT (62) UK companies are required to include details of significant interests in CFCs in their tax returns and to self-assess any CFC tax due. [*FA 1998, s 113, Sch 17*]. Guidance notes are provided in HMRC International Manual, INTM 200000 *et seq.* These are referred to below where HMRC interpretation or practice is explained in the guidance. Guidance on particular cases may be sought (provided that it is not with a view to facilitating tax avoidance) from HMRC, Revenue Policy International, 100 Parliament Street, London SW1A 2BQ. Clearances may be sought from the same source (see HMRC International Manual, INTM 214120–214150). See generally INTM 214000 *et seq.* as regards completion of the self-assessment return.

Compatibility with EC law. The High Court granted an application for a CFC and EU Dividend Group Litigation Order on 30 July 2003, to manage claims which seek to challenge the UK CFC provisions, and provisions which make dividends received by UK companies from non-UK resident companies subject to corporation tax, on the basis they are contrary to EC law. In the case of *Cadbury Schweppes plc and Cadbury Schweppes Overseas Ltd v CIR, [2004] SSCD 342 (Sp C 415)*, the question was referred to the European Court of Justice as to whether the application of the CFC legislation to Cadbury Schweppes Irish financing subsidiaries constitutes a breach of the freedom of establishment under *Article 43* of the EC Treaty, of the freedom to provide services under *Article 49* and of the freedom of movement of capital and payments under *Article 56*. The ECJ ruled in *Cadbury Schweppes plc and another v CIR [2006] STC 1908 (CJEC Case C-196/04)* on 12 September 2006 that the UK CFCs legislation constitutes a restriction on the freedom of movement in the case where companies could be objectively judged to be established in a host member state and carrying on genuine economic activities there. Subject to the existing exceptions (as set out in 21.12 *et seq.* below), the legislation should apply only to 'wholly artificial' arrangements entered into to escape the national tax normally payable. The fact that a CFC's activities could equally well have been carried out in the parent's member state does not imply wholly artificial arrangements. The ECJ has said that it was up to the UK courts to decide whether the motive test (see 21.12 below) can be interpreted as limiting the CFC legislation to wholly artificial arrangements intended to circumvent national tax law (in which case it would be compatible with EC law), or whether the motive exception does not apply if the CFC had been incorporated with the central intention of reducing UK tax even if there was no artificial arrangement in place (in which case, the legislation would not comply with EC law and would have to be changed). The ECJ decision does not include a time limit on the making of claims. (See also the European Commission press release of 14 September 2006 and Tax Journal 25 September 2006 p 7.)

As a result of the decision of the ECJ in the *Cadbury Schweppes* case (*[2006] STC 1908 (CJEC Case C-196/04)*) the CFC rules have been amended with effect from 6 December 2006 (see 21.6, 21.7, 21.15). In addition, the publicly quoted condition is withdrawn.

For CFCs resident in the EC or in certain EEA states there is an additional condition. Such concerns must have sufficient staff, with the appropriate skills, working for the CFC in the state in which the company is resident, to be able to undertake all, or substantially all, of that company's business. If they are not employees of the CFC, they must work in the CFC's state of residence, have decision making powers and work separately for the CFC, not as part of a job for another employer.

HMRC's view is that profits from capital, or intellectual property or from intra-group transactions will not normally qualify as 'genuine economic activity'.

The draft legislation can be found at: http://www.hmrc.gov.uk/pbr2006/controlled-foreign-companies.pdf.

In the case of *HMRC v Vodafone 2, CA [2006] STC 1530*, the Court of Appeal unanimously upheld the Special Commissioners' decision that Vodafone need not provide documents or information relating to its subsidiary in Luxembourg (to prove it was entitled to exemption from the CFC regulations by reason of the motive test (see 21.12 below)), and that the case could be referred to the ECJ to determine whether the CFC legislation was compatible with Articles 43EC and 56EC of the EC Treaty.

21.2 CONTROLLED FOREIGN COMPANY

A company which is:

(*a*) resident outside the UK (see 60.2 RESIDENCE);

(*b*) 'controlled' by persons resident in the UK; and

(*c*) subject to a 'lower level of taxation' (see 21.4 below) in the territory in which it is 'resident' (see 21.3 below),

is a '*controlled foreign company*'. [*ICTA 1988, s 747*(*1*)(*2*)].

Any company which is resident both in the UK and, under double taxation relief arrangements, in a territory outside the UK is treated by *FA 1994, s 249* as resident outside the UK and as not resident in the UK (see 60.1 RESIDENCE). However, from 1 April 2002, in determining for any purposes of the CFC provisions *other than* (*a*) above whether a company is a person resident in the UK, *section 249* is disregarded (thus, a UK resident company deemed to be non-resident by virtue of a double tax treaty, remains subject to the CFC provisions). The CFC rules do not apply to any company that, by virtue of *section 249*, was treated immediately before 1 April 2002 as resident outside the UK, and not UK-resident, and which has not subsequently ceased to be so treated unless either of the following events occurs in relation to the non-resident company at any time after 21 March 2006:

(i) the non-resident company, which immediately before 22 March 2006 does not own (directly or indirectly) any subsidiary companies, acquires (directly or indirectly) a UK-resident subsidiary company; or

(ii) the non-resident company, which immediately before 22 March 2006 owns (directly or indirectly) any subsidiary companies, acquires (directly or indirectly) a UK-resident subsidiary company as a consequence of, or in connection with, which there is a major change in the nature, conduct or scale of the activities of either the non-resident company or the group of companies of which the non-resident company is a member.

[*ICTA 1988, s 747(1B); FA 2002, s 90; FA 2006, s 78*].

'Control'. '*Control*' of a company is defined for these purposes as the power of a person to secure that the affairs of the company are conducted in accordance with his wishes, either by means of shareholding or voting power in or in relation to the company or any other company, or by virtue of any powers conferred by the articles of association or other document regulating the company or any other company. Two or more persons together having such power are taken as controlling the company. In determining whether a person or persons have such control, a wide range of rights and powers is attributed to them, in so far as not already so attributed (see *ICTA 1988, s 755D(5)-(11)*). These include future rights and powers and rights and powers of certain connected and other persons. [*ICTA 1988, s 755D*]. Where a company would not otherwise be treated as controlled by UK-resident persons, it is so treated if there are two persons, one of whom is UK resident, who together control the company, and a '40% test' is satisfied in relation to each of them. This requires that each of them has interests, rights and powers representing at least 40% of the holdings, rights and powers in respect of which they fall to be taken as together controlling the company (after a similar attribution of rights and powers as applies in determining that control), and that in the case of the non-UK resident such holdings etc. do **not** exceed 55%. [*ICTA 1988, ss 747(1A), 755D(3)-(11)*].

The advice of HMRC International Division may be sought (see 21.1 above) where there is doubt as to whether an overseas entity is a company.

Simon's Direct Tax Service. See D4.1202 *et seq.*

21.3 **'Residence'**. For the purposes of these provisions, a company is regarded, in any accounting period in which it is resident outside the UK (see 60.2 RESIDENCE), as '*resident*' in the territory in which, throughout that period, it is liable to tax by reason of domicile, residence or place of management. 'Territory' includes jurisdictions which do not have full independent status, such as the Channel Islands, but not individual states of a federal state (e.g. in the USA), and 'tax' in this context means a tax similar in nature to UK income tax or corporation tax, and not e.g. turnover or payroll taxes or flat-rate levies. (For these and for the interpretation of 'domicile, residence or place of management', see HMRC International Manual, INTM 202050).

If there are two or more such territories and no election or designation is made (see below), the company is regarded as resident in only one of them, namely:

(i) the company's place of effective management (for which see HMRC International Manual, INTM 202050) throughout the period or, if two or more territories would still be the territory of residence under this definition, the one from those territories in which the greater amount of the company's assets is situated at the end of the period, determined by reference to their market value at that time;

(ii) if (i) does not apply, the territory in which the greater amount of the company's assets is situated at the end of the period (determined as in (i));

(iii) if (i) and (ii) do not apply to determine a single territory of residence, the territory which may be specified in an election (for which see below) or if no timeous election is made, HMRC may designate in which of those territories the CFC is to be regarded as resident on a just and reasonable basis.

Election or designation. As regards (iii) above, subject to the continuing application of an earlier election as described below, the election may be made, by any one or more persons who together have a 'majority assessable interest' in the CFC in the accounting period, specifying in which of those territories the CFC is to be regarded as resident for these purposes. One or more persons have such a '*majority assessable interest*' in a CFC in an accounting period if it is likely that, were an apportionment of chargeable profits to be made for the period, more than 50% of the aggregate amounts so chargeable would be chargeable on him or on them together. For this purpose an application under *ICTA 1988, s 751A* is disregarded (see 21.6). Where such an election or HMRC designation has effect for an accounting period, the CFC continues to be regarded as resident in the same territory for subsequent accounting periods up to (but not including) the next one in which the territories in which the CFC is liable to tax by reason of domicile, residence or place of management are different. An election under this provision, which is irrevocable, must be made to HMRC within twelve months after the end of the CFC accounting period in relation to which it is made, must be signed by the persons making it, and must state, as regards each of those persons, the percentage of chargeable profits and creditable tax (if any) of the CFC for that period which would be likely to be apportioned to them in the event of an apportionment being made. A designation by HMRC as above is irrevocable, and must be notified to every UK-resident company which it appears to HMRC would be chargeable under these provisions were an apportionment of chargeable profits of the accounting period in question to be made.

[*ICTA 1988, ss 749, 749A; FA 2007, Sch 15 para 2*].

See generally HMRC International Manual, INTM 202050.

21.4 **Territories with a 'lower level of taxation'.** A company regarded as resident in a particular territory outside the UK (see 21.3 above) is considered to be subject to a '*lower level of taxation*' (see 21.2 above) for an accounting period if the tax paid under the law of that territory in respect of profits (other than capital profits) from that period (the 'local tax') is less than three-quarters of the 'corresponding UK tax' on those profits.

The '*corresponding UK tax*' on the profits of an accounting period is the corporation tax (at the small companies rate where appropriate) which would be chargeable, on the assumptions set out in *ICTA 1988, Sch 24* (see 21.10 below), on the CFC's 'chargeable profits' (see 21.10 below) for that period.

For this purpose:

(*a*) it is assumed that an apportionment of chargeable profits falls to be made under these provisions (see 21.7 below);

(*b*) (for periods on or after 6 December 2006) any application under *ICTA 1988, s 751A* is to be disregarded (see 21.6 below);

(*c*) double taxation relief in respect of the local tax is disregarded; and

(*d*) a deduction is made from the corporation tax calculated as above in respect of

- any amount which would be set off under *ICTA 1988, s 7(2)* (sums received under deduction of income tax, see 37.6 INCOME TAX IN RELATION TO A COMPANY) on the assumptions set out in *ICTA 1988, Sch 24* (see 21.10 below); and
- any income or corporation tax actually charged in respect of the chargeable profits,

provided that such amounts have not been, and do not fall to be, repaid to the company.

Tax paid in third countries is relieved against both local tax and corresponding UK tax, according to the rules applicable in each jurisdiction (see HMRC International Manual, INTM 202030).

For accounting periods of non-UK resident companies beginning on or after 2 December 2004, subject to the anti-avoidance provision below, in determining the amount of local tax paid by those companies for the above purposes, a reduction in the amount of the local tax is to be made:

(i) by discounting any income or expenditure which has been brought into account by the overseas company in computing its profits for local tax purposes which would not be so brought into account in computing profits chargeable to UK tax under these provisions (see 21.10 below); and

(ii) to the extent of any tax which has been paid by the company but which has been repaid, or paid by way of tax credit, directly or indirectly to a person other than the company.

Where the overseas company's accounting period would have ended on or after 2 December 2004 but is amended on or after that date so as to end before that date, it will be deemed to have ended on 1 December 2004.

[*ICTA 1988, s 750(1)–(4); FA 1993, s 119; F(No 2)A 2005, s 44; FA 2007, Sch 15 para 4*].

See generally HMRC International Manual, INTM 202030.

See 21.12 below as regards countries in which a company will be excluded from charge under these provisions.

Designer rate regimes. Where a company would be treated under the above rules as subject to a lower level of taxation in a territory in an accounting period but for the local tax not being less than three-quarters of the corresponding UK tax, but that local tax is determined under 'designer rate tax provisions', the company is treated as being subject to a lower level of taxation in that territory in that period. '*Designer rate tax provisions*' are provisions which appear to HMRC to be designed to enable companies to exercise significant control over the amount of tax they pay, and which are specified in regulations (which may make different provision for different cases or with respect to different territories, and may contain supplementary, incidental, consequential or transitional provisions). The first such regulations (see below) may take effect for accounting periods beginning up to 15 months before the date the regulations are made. [*ICTA 1988, s 750A*].

The regulations apply to the following.

- Guernsey — bodies with international tax status;
- Jersey — international business companies;
- Isle of Man — international companies; and
- Gibraltar — income tax qualifying companies.

[*SI 2000 No 3158*].

Further regimes may in future be added to this list.

Simon's Direct Tax Service. See D4.1205, D4.1205A.

21.5 **Example** CC Co, an unquoted company, is incorporated and resident in Blueland and carries on business there as a wholesaler. It obtains the majority of its goods from associated companies although 10% is obtained from local suppliers. The goods are exported to UK customers — the major one of which is ADE Co Ltd. CC Co has a share capital of 1,000 ordinary shares which are owned as follows:

SS Co Ltd (non-UK resident company)	50
ADE Co Ltd (UK incorporated and resident company)	150
John James (UK domiciled and resident individual)	300
Mrs James (wife of John James)	300
Caroline James (daughter of Mr & Mrs James) living in France	200
	1,000

The shareholders of SS Co Ltd are all non-UK residents. The shareholders of ADE Co Ltd are Mr & Mrs Andrew James (parents of John James).

The following figures (converted into sterling) have been obtained for CC Co for the year to 30 April 2007.

	£
Profit before tax	7,000,000
Depreciation	1,000,000
Dividend proposed for year	500,000
Blueland tax paid on profits of year	1,200,000
Market value of plant and machinery at 1.5.06	2,500,000
Additions to plant and machinery in year	1,800,000
Original cost of industrial buildings (acquired prior to 1.5.06)	1,500,000

There were no disposals of fixed assets during the year.

The company is not a CFC with respect to any earlier accounting period.

CC is a controlled foreign company because:

(i) it is resident outside the UK;

(ii) it is controlled by persons resident in the UK, as follows:

	UK residents Ordinary shares	Non-UK residents Ordinary shares
ADE Co Ltd	150	
John James	300	
Mrs James	300	
SS Co Ltd		50
Caroline James		200
	750	250
Percentage holding	75%	25%

(iii) it is subject to a lower level of taxation in the country where it is resident, as follows:

Notional UK chargeable profits

Year ended 30 April 2007	£
Profit before tax	7,000,000
Add Depreciation	1,000,000
	8,000,000
Capital allowances (see note below)	1,135,000
	£6,865,000
£6,865,000 @ 30%	£2,059,500
75% thereof	£1,544,625
Overseas tax paid	£1,200,000

The overseas tax paid is less than three-quarters of the 'corresponding UK tax' so the company is regarded as being subject to a lower level of taxation.

Note

Capital allowances:

Plant and machinery	Pool	Allowances
	£	£
Market value at 1.5.06	2,500,000	
Additions	1,800,000	
	4,300,000	
WDA (25%)	(1,075,000)	1,075,000
WDV c/f	£3,225,000	
Industrial buildings allowance		
Original cost of building = £1,500,000		
WDA £1,500,000 at 4%		60,000
Total allowances		£1,135,000

It is assumed that the company is not small or medium-sized for the purposes of plant and machinery first-year allowances.

21.6 **Activities of EEA businesses.** For accounting periods beginning on or after 6 December, 2006 (subject to transitional provisions for accounting periods straddling that date, where the following conditions are satisfied):

(*a*) a controlled foreign company is liable to apportionment in an accounting period;

(*b*) the company has had a business establishment in an 'EEA territory' throughout that period;

(*c*) it has employees working for it in the 'EEA territory' throughout the period; and

(*d*) a UK resident company has a 'relevant interest' (see 21.8 below) in it in the period,

the UK resident may apply to HMRC (in a form laid down by HMRC and attaching any relevant information and documentation) for a reduction in the CFC's chargeable profits for that period. If the application is granted, the CFC's chargeable profits for that period will be reduced by the amount specified in the application and its creditable tax will be reduced on a just and reasonable basis. The reductions are made for the purposes only of determining the sum chargeable on the UK company. HMRC may only grant the application if they are satisfied that the specified amount does not exceed the economic value arising to the CFC, persons who have an interest in it and other group companies directly from 'qualifying work'. This is work done by individuals directed by the CFC to perform duties on its behalf in a particular EEA territory in which the CFC had a business throughout the accounting period in question.

The application must be made on or before the filing date of the company's corporation return for the accounting period to which it relates. It may be amended or withdrawn at any time before HMRC accept it. If an application is accepted after the company has filed its corporation tax return for the period, it has 30 days (commencing with the date of acceptance) within which to amend the return.

Where an application is refused, the taxpayer company has a right of appeal to the Special Commissioners: an appeal must be made to HMRC in writing within 30 days of the refusal. If the Special Commissioners find that the amount applied for is the correct amount, they must direct HMRC to accept the application; if the amount in respect of which the application should have been made differs from those specified in the application, they must direct HMRC to accept the application for that amount and in other cases the appeal must be dismissed.

An '*EEA territory*' at any time is a territory which is an EEA state at that time, other than the UK.

[*ICTA 1988, ss 751A, 751B*; *FA 2007, Sch 15 paras 5, 6, 10*].

21.7 COMPANIES CHARGEABLE IN RESPECT OF CFC

Where these provisions apply in respect of an accounting period of a CFC (see 21.1 above), the 'chargeable profits' (see 21.10 below) and 'creditable tax' (see 21.11 below) are apportioned amongst all the persons (whether UK resident or not) having an 'interest' (see below) in the CFC at any time in the accounting period. Any UK resident company to which those sums are apportioned is then chargeable on a sum as if it were corporation tax (see 21.8 below). [*ICTA 1988, s 747(3)(4)*].

The following have an '*interest*' in a CFC:

(*a*) any person possessing, or entitled to acquire, share capital or voting rights in the CFC;

(*b*) any person possessing, or entitled to acquire, a right to receive or participate in distributions of the CFC ('distribution' not being limited by reference to UK resident companies, see 23 DISTRIBUTIONS) or (except as below) any amounts payable (in cash or kind) by the CFC to loan creditors (as defined in *ICTA 1988, s 417*, see 16.3 CLOSE COMPANIES) by way of premium on redemption;

(*c*) any person entitled to secure (other than on a default of the CFC or any other person, which has not occurred, under an agreement) that income or assets, present or future, of the CFC will be applied directly or indirectly for his benefit; and

(*d*) any other person who, with or without others, has control (see 21.2(*b*) above) of the CFC.

In (*a*), (*b*) and (*c*), the entitlement to do anything includes present entitlement to do it at a future date and future entitlement. [*ICTA 1988, s 749*(*5*)–(*7*)]. See HMRC International Manual, INTM 210040–210070.

Where an apportionment is made to a UK resident company which has made a successful application under *ICTA 1988, s 751A*, its apportionment is to be governed by that section. Where that company has associates or persons connected with it, it is assumed that they all had made successful applications under *s 751A*.

[*ICTA 1988, s 747*(*3A*), (*5A*); *FA 2007 Sch 15*(*1*)].

A person or persons having an interest in a company which has an interest in a CFC are treated themselves as having a corresponding interest in the CFC. Joint interests (other than in a fiduciary or representative capacity) are treated as being in equal shares. [*ICTA 1988, s 749B*].

Any determination by HMRC of the amounts of chargeable profits and creditable tax for a CFC accounting period which fall to be apportioned under these provisions requires the sanction of HMRC. There is, however, an exception, in relation to a notice of closure of an enquiry into a company tax return or a discovery assessment, where those amounts are the subject of an agreement with HMRC (for the requirements for which see *ICTA 1988, s 754B*(*6*)-(*9*)). Where a determination thus requiring the sanction of HMRC is made for the purpose of giving a closure notice or making a discovery assessment, and the notice of the closure or discovery assessment is given without the determination, so far as taken into account in the notice or assessment, having been approved by HMRC, or without notification of such approval having been served at or before the time the notice was given, the closure notice or discovery assessment is deemed to have been given or made as if the determination had not been taken into account. Notification of HMRC's approval must be in writing, and must state that HMRC have given approval on the basis that stated amounts of chargeable profits and creditable tax (which may be nil) fall to be apportioned under these provisions for the accounting period in question. The approval must apply specifically to the case in question and the amount determined, but may otherwise be given (either before or after the making of the determination) in any such form or manner as HMRC may determine. An appeal relating to a determination approved by HMRC may not question HMRC's approval except to the extent that the grounds for questioning the approval are the same as the grounds for questioning the determination itself. [*ICTA 1988, s 754B*]. See generally HMRC International Manual, INTM 214060–214090 as regards HMRC enquiries into CFC returns.

Simon's Direct Tax Service. See D4.1207–D4.1218.

21.8 BASIS OF CHARGE

Where a part of a CFC's 'chargeable profits' (see 21.10 below) is apportioned (as below) to a UK resident company (see 21.7 above), a sum equal to corporation tax at the 'appropriate rate' on those profits, less the part of the CFC's 'creditable tax' (see 21.11 below) (if any) so apportioned, is chargeable on the company as if it were corporation tax. No charge arises, however, unless at least 25% of the CFC's 'chargeable profits' for the period in question is apportioned either to the UK resident company or to persons 'connected' (see 19 CONNECTED PERSONS) or 'associated' (as defined in *ICTA 1988, s 783*(*10*)) with it.

The '*appropriate rate*' is the full corporation tax rate (or average rate) applicable to the accounting period in which ends the CFC's 'accounting period' (see below) whose 'chargeable profits' are the subject of the apportionment. [*ICTA 1988, s 747*(*4*)(*5*)].

Apportionment. An apportionment of chargeable profits and creditable tax for an accounting period is to be made as follows. Where:

(A) the persons with 'relevant interests' in the CFC at any time in the period have those interests by virtue only of direct or indirect holdings of ordinary shares in the CFC;

(B) each of those persons is either UK-resident throughout the period or not UK-resident at any time in the period; and

(C) no company has an 'intermediate interest' in the CFC at any time in the period other than by virtue of a direct or indirect holding of ordinary shares in the CFC,

the apportionment is made amongst the persons within (A) above in direct proportion to the percentage holding of the CFC's issued ordinary shares which their relevant interests represent (see below). Otherwise, the apportionment is made on a just and reasonable basis amongst the persons who have a 'relevant interest' in the CFC at any time in the period (and see 21.17 below for HMRC's right to determine a basis different from that selected by the company in certain cases).

An '*accounting period*' of a CFC begins whenever:

(*a*) the company comes under the control (see 21.2(*b*) above) of persons resident in the UK; or

(*b*) the CFC, not having previously been subject to an apportionment under these provisions (see 21.7 above), commences business; or

(*c*) an accounting period ends without the CFC ceasing either to carry on business or to have any source of income at all,

and ends when:

(i) it ceases to be under the control (as above) of persons resident in the UK; or

(ii) it becomes, or ceases to be, liable to tax by reason of domicile, residence or place of management in a territory; or

(iii) it ceases to have any source of income at all.

In addition, the normal rules of *ICTA 1988, s 12(3)(5)(7)* relating to the end of accounting periods, and to the winding-up, of UK resident companies (see 2.4 ACCOUNTING PERIODS and 45.6 LIQUIDATION ETC.) apply, with the omission of the provisions relating to a company's coming or ceasing to be within the charge to corporation tax. Also, where it appears to HMRC that the beginning or end of an accounting period is uncertain, they may specify an appropriate period not exceeding twelve months as an accounting period, and the period specified may subsequently be amended in the light of further facts.

[*ICTA 1988, s 751(1)–(5)*]. See also 26.31 EXCHANGE GAINS AND LOSSES.

A UK-resident company with a direct interest in a CFC has a '*relevant interest*' in the CFC by virtue of that interest. This applies similarly to an indirect interest in the CFC unless it arises by virtue of a direct or indirect interest in another UK-resident company. A '*related person*' (i.e. a person, other than a UK-resident company, who is connected or associated (as above) with a UK-resident company which has a relevant interest in the CFC) with a direct or indirect interest in a CFC has a '*relevant interest*' in the CFC by virtue of that interest except:

(I) to the extent that a UK-resident company has the whole or any part of the same interest indirectly (by virtue of a direct or indirect interest in the related person), and itself has a relevant interest in the CFC by virtue of that indirect interest; and

(II) in the case of an indirect interest, if it is held by virtue of a direct or indirect interest in a UK-resident company or another related person.

A direct interest in a CFC which does not give rise to a relevant interest under the above rules is nonetheless a '*relevant interest*' except to the extent that another person has the whole or a part of the same interest indirectly and itself has a relevant interest in the CFC by virtue of that indirect interest.

No '*relevant interest*' arises in a CFC except as above. The percentage of the issued ordinary shares of a CFC which a relevant interest (by virtue of a holding of those shares) represents for an accounting period is determined under *ICTA 1988, s 752B*, broadly by taking successive proportions in the case of indirect holdings and by averaging where holdings vary over the period.

See *ICTA 1988, s 752C* as regards nominee or bare trustee holdings and other holdings in a fiduciary or representative capacity, and as regards interpretation generally.

[*ICTA 1988, ss 752-752C*].

See generally HMRC International Manual, INTM 210000 *et seq.*

Simon's Direct Tax Service. See D4.1250–D4.1252.

21.9 *Example*

Following the example at 21.5 above, CC Co's notional UK chargeable profits and creditable tax are apportioned among the persons who had an interest in the company during its accounting period.

Shareholder	% shareholding	Attributable profits	Creditable tax
		£	£
SS Co Ltd	5	343,250	60,000
ADE Co Ltd	15	1,029,750	180,000
John James	30	2,059,500	360,000
Mrs James	30	2,059,500	360,000
Caroline James	20	1,373,000	240,000
	100%	£6,865,000	£1,200,000

ADE Co Ltd is the only UK resident company to which chargeable profits and creditable tax are apportioned. ADE Co Ltd is chargeable to corporation tax on a sum equal to the profits of CC Co which are apportioned to it, and this corporation tax charge is then reduced by the apportioned amount of creditable tax. The corporation tax rate applicable is the rate (or average rate) applicable to ADE Co Ltd's own profits for the accounting period in which CC Co's accounting period ends. ADE Co Ltd has a 30 April year end.

ADE Co Ltd

Year to 30 April 2007

Tax computations — before apportionment

	£
Schedule D, Case I	8,000,000
Losses brought forward	—
	8,000,000
Schedule D, Case III	50,000
Schedule D, Case V	1,250,000
Chargeable gains	250,000
	£9,550,000
	£
UK tax at 30%	2,865,000
DTR on Schedule D, Case V income	(412,500)
Mainstream CT liability	£2,452,500

Tax computations — after apportionment

	£
Schedule D, Case I	8,000,000
Losses brought forward	—
	8,000,000
Schedule D, Case III	50,000
Schedule D, Case V	1,250,000
Chargeable gains	250,000
CFC apportionment	1,029,750
	£10,579,750
	£
UK tax at 30%	3,173,925
DTR on Schedule D, Case V income	(412,500)
CFC creditable tax	(180,000)
Mainstream CT liability	£2,581,425
Additional tax	£128,925

21.10 **'Chargeable profits'.** 'Chargeable profits' of a CFC for an accounting period are the total profits (but excluding chargeable gains), as defined for corporation tax purposes, on which, on the assumptions set out in *ICTA 1988, Sch 24* (see below) and after allowing for any available deductions from those profits, it would be chargeable to corporation tax for the period. The *Schedule 24* assumptions do not, however, affect the corporation tax liability of any non-UK resident company in respect of any trade carried on in the UK through a permanent establishment (see 60.5 RESIDENCE — previously a branch or agency). [*ICTA 1988, s 747, Sch 24 para 1*(*5*)].

Where (under (ii) below) a company is deemed to become, or cease to be, resident during a period of account, profits will generally be time-apportioned, but if the true profit of the period of deemed residence can be established by reference to transactions, etc. of that period at reasonable cost, then it should be used instead (see HMRC International Manual, INTM 209030).

Except as otherwise provided in *Schedule 24*, it is assumed that, for the purpose of calculating chargeable profits or corresponding UK tax under that *Schedule* for any accounting period, such a calculation has been made for all previous accounting periods which did not precede the first such period for which an apportionment has been made under these provisions (see 21.7 above), or is treated as having been made (see (i) below). [*ICTA 1988, Sch 24 para 2*(*2*)].

Double tax treaty exemptions which may have applied to income of the CFC are of no application in relation to the computation of chargeable profits (*Bricom Holdings Ltd v CIR CA 1997, 70 TC 272*).

For the treatment in determining chargeable profits of debits and credits in respect of intangible fixed assets, see 39.35 INTANGIBLE ASSETS.

The assumptions set out in *Schedule 24* are as follows.

(i) For the purpose of determining the chargeable profits of an accounting period at a time when no apportionment has been made under these provisions (see 21.7 above) for that or any earlier accounting period, it is assumed, for the purposes of any provision of *Schedule 24* which refers to the first accounting period for which an apportionment has been made, that an apportionment has been made for that period. Similarly where an apportionment has not been made for that or any earlier accounting period and where it has not been established that that or any earlier accounting period is an 'ADP exempt period', that accounting period is treated, for the purposes of any provision of *Schedule 24*, as one for which an apportionment has been made or which is an ADP exempt period. An '*ADP exempt period*' is an accounting period beginning after 27 November 1995 in respect of which the company pursued an acceptable distribution policy (see 21.13 below).

(ii) The CFC is UK resident with effect from the beginning of the first accounting period in respect of which an apportionment has been made under these provisions or which is an ADP exempt period (as above), and remains UK resident until it ceases to be controlled by UK residents. This assumption does not, however, require any assumption to be made of a change in the place(s) at which the CFC's activities are carried on.

(iii) The CFC is not a close company (see 16 CLOSE COMPANIES).

(iv) The CFC has made all relevant claims and elections so as to obtain maximum relief, subject, for accounting periods in respect of which an apportionment has been made under these provisions or which are ADP exempt periods (as above), to a right of the UK resident company which has (or such companies which together have) a 'majority interest' in the CFC, by notice to HMRC, to modify or cancel such claims or elections. See HMRC International Manual, INTM 209110 as regards form of notice of disclaimer. Such notice must be given within 20 months of the end of the accounting period (for periods prior to the commencement of self-assessment (see 21.1 above), within the normal time limit for making appeals under these provisions (see 21.17 below) for an accounting period for which a direction is given, or within 20 months of the end of the accounting period if it is an ADP exempt period). In either case, HMRC may allow a longer period (and see HMRC International Manual, INTM 209130). '*Majority interest*' for this purpose is by reference to chargeable profits of the CFC (for the period, or first period, for which the relief in question is available) apportioned to a company or companies as a proportion of such profits apportioned to *all* UK resident companies and giving rise to any liability on such companies (see 21.8 above) (in the case of an ADP exempt period, on the assumption that an apportionment has been made for the period). As regards disclaimers and variations, see HMRC International Manual, INTM 209100.

(v) The CFC is not a member of a group or consortium (see 32 GROUPS OF COMPANIES). Notwithstanding this assumption, where there is in fact a surrender by the CFC by way of group relief (see 32.6 GROUPS OF COMPANIES), the CFC's chargeable profits are to be increased to the extent of the relief surrendered and allowed.

(vi) (For payments made on or before 11 May 2001) the conditions for an election by the CFC under *ICTA 1988, s 247* (group income, see 32.2 GROUPS OF COMPANIES) are not fulfilled.

(vii) Except in so far as the CFC may carry on a trade in the UK through a permanent establishment (see 60.5 RESIDENCE — previously a branch or agency), it can never be the 'successor' to another company within *ICTA 1988, s 343* (company reconstructions, see 47.10 LOSSES).

(viii) Where trading losses have been incurred by the CFC in an accounting period during which it was non-UK resident (and which is not an ADP exempt period for which it is assumed to be UK resident under (ii) above) and which ended less than six years before the start of the first accounting period for which an apportionment has been made under these provisions, the UK resident company or companies having a majority interest (see (iv) above) in the CFC may claim to have chargeable profits of the CFC computed for any such period as is specified in the claim (and for subsequent accounting periods) on the assumption that an apportionment has been made in respect of the period specified in the claim. The claim must be made in writing to HMRC within 20 months after the end of the first accounting period for which an apportionment has been made.

(ix) Writing-down allowances and balancing adjustments are given or charged as if machinery or plant on which expenditure was incurred before the 'starting period' (i.e. the first accounting period for which an apportionment has been made under these provisions or which is an ADP exempt period) was not brought into use for trade purposes before the starting period, and is thus brought in at market value at the beginning of that period.

Where the chargeable profits for an accounting period are to be computed and expressed in a currency other than sterling (see below), any amount relevant to the computation of capital allowances for the period which was arrived at in relation to accounting periods before the first one beginning on or after 23 March 1995 is converted into the relevant foreign currency at the London closing rate on the first day of the period. The amounts referred to in *ICTA 1988, ss 578A, 578B* and *CAA 2001, ss 74-76* (previously *CAA 1990, ss 34, 35*) (relating to expensive motor cars) and *CAA 2001, s 511* (previously *CAA 1990, s 96*) (relating to dwelling-houses) are, for such a period, converted into the relevant foreign currency at the London closing rate for the day the expenditure in question was incurred.

It is not possible to disclaim or postpone plant and machinery allowances under (iv) above for periods for which an apportionment under these provisions has not been made and which are not ADP exempt periods, since the right to disclaim applies only to such periods. Capital allowances other than plant and machinery allowances are given according to the normal rules (see HMRC International Manual, INTM 209140).

(x) Relief for unremittable overseas income is extended to include inability to remit to the territory of residence, and notice of desire for such relief may be given by the UK resident company or companies having a majority interest in the CFC (see (iv) above).

(xi) Where, for accounting periods beginning before 1 October 2002, the chargeable profits for an accounting period are computed and expressed in a currency other than sterling (see below), the EXCHANGE GAINS AND LOSSES (26) provisions are revised to apply by reference to that currency rather than by conversion to sterling (for which see in particular 26.8, 26.18, 26.21, 26.23, 26.24 EXCHANGE GAINS AND LOSSES). Exchange gains and losses of accrual periods constituting or falling within accounting periods before the 'first relevant accounting period' (see below) are disregarded as regards later accounting periods. These provisions are **repealed** for accounting periods beginning **on or after 1 October 2002** following their assimilation within the rules for LOAN RELATIONSHIPS (46) and FINANCIAL INSTRUMENTS AND DERIVATIVE CONTRACTS (26).

(xii) For accounting periods beginning before 1 April 2004 and to which self-assessment applies (see 21.1 above), the application of the transfer pricing provisions (see 67 TRANSFER PRICING) to the computation of CFC chargeable profits is modified (see *ICTA 1988, Sch 24 para 20*). Broadly, a compensatory adjustment is made to CFC profits where, as a result of transactions between the CFC and a UK company, the latter's profits have been increased under the transfer pricing rules. Also, subject to certain conditions, those rules (and the related provision at *ICTA 1988, s 209(2)(da)*, see 23.5 DISTRIBUTIONS) do not apply to transactions between CFCs.

[*ICTA 1988, Sch 24; CAA 2001, Sch 2 para 66; FA 2001, Sch 33 Pt II(10); FA 2002, Sch 40 Pt 3(10); FA 2004, s 37(2), Sch 5 para 4; ITTOIA 2005, Sch 1 para 349*].

Computation of chargeable profits in a currency other than sterling. Where, for accounting periods beginning before 16 March 2005, a company's chargeable profits fall to be determined for the 'first relevant accounting period' of the company or any subsequent accounting period, then notwithstanding any other rule (statutory or otherwise), they are computed and expressed for any such period in the currency used in the accounts for the 'first relevant accounting period'. Where, as a result of the adoption of the euro by a State, the currency used for the 'first relevant accounting period' is to be replaced by the euro, there is provision for the euro to be substituted (although the local currency may continue to be used for accounting periods during any part of which it continues to be a legal sub-unit of the euro). The '*first relevant accounting period*' is the first accounting period for which an apportionment has been made, or for which it can reasonably be assumed that an apportionment would have been made but for its pursuing an 'acceptable distribution policy' (see 21.13 below).

Similarly, where a company's chargeable profits fall to be determined for any accounting period falling before its first relevant accounting period, they are computed and expressed for any such period in the currency used in the accounts for the accounting period concerned.

In either case, the 'accounts' concerned are those the company is required to keep by the law of the country or territory under whose law it is incorporated or formed, or if it is not required under that law to keep accounts, those which most closely correspond to those required under UK law.

The chargeable profits computed and expressed in a currency other than sterling (as above) for an accounting period are converted into sterling by reference to the London closing rate for the last day of the accounting period for the purposes of:

(1) determining the apportioned amount thereof under *ICTA 1988, s 747(4)* (see 21.7 above);

(2) the exception under *ICTA 1988, s 748(1)(d)* (see 21.12(iv) below); and

(3) the calculation of corresponding UK tax under *ICTA 1988, s 750(2)(3)* (see 21.4 above).

This provision is repealed for accounting periods beginning on or after 16 March 2005 following the introduction of the corporation tax currency provisions for periods of account beginning on or after 1 January 2005 (see 26.35–26.37 EXCHANGE GAINS AND LOSSES).

[*ICTA 1988, s 747(4A)(4B), s 747A, s 748(4)(5), s 750(5)–(8); SI 1998 No 3177, reg 40; FA 2005, s 80, Sch 4 para 24*].

See generally HMRC International Manual, INTM 209060.

Simon's Direct Tax Service. See **D4.1210** *et seq.*

21.11 **'Creditable tax'.** 'Creditable tax' of a CFC's accounting period is the aggregate of:

(i) the double taxation relief, in respect of tax on income brought into account in determining chargeable profits of the period (see 21.10 above), which would be available on the assumptions set out in *ICTA 1988, Sch 24* (see 21.10 above and 24.2 DOUBLE TAX RELIEF) and assuming the company to be liable to corporation tax on those chargeable profits;

(ii) the set-off available under *ICTA 1988, s 7(2)* (sums received under deduction of income tax, see 37.6 INCOME TAX IN RELATION TO A COMPANY) against those chargeable profits on the assumptions in (i) above; and

(iii) the amount of any income or corporation tax actually charged in respect of those chargeable profits, less any such tax which has been or falls to be repaid to the CFC.

[*ICTA 1988, s 751(6)*].

Tax spared in the overseas territory, and for which provision is made in the relevant double tax agreement, may be included in creditable tax up to the limit specified in the agreement. Foreign taxes are converted into sterling for these purposes at the exchange rate prevailing at the time the taxes become payable. (See HMRC International Manual, INTM 209220).

See **Simon's Direct Tax Service D4.1218**.

21.12 EXCEPTIONS

Subject to the territorial exclusions described below, a CFC is excepted from an apportionment under these provisions (see 21.7 above) for an accounting period if:

(i) it pursues an 'acceptable distribution policy' (see 21.13 below) in respect of the period; or

(ii) throughout the period it is engaged in 'exempt activities' (see 21.15 below); or

(iii) for accounting periods of CFCs beginning on or before 5 December 2006, it meets the 'public quotation' condition (*FA 2007, Sch 15 para 8(1)*. See 21.16 below), or

(iv) its chargeable profits for the period do not exceed £50,000 or pro rata for periods of less than twelve months; or

(v) it is, as respects the period, resident (within the meaning of regulations made for these purposes) in a territory specified in those regulations, and meets such conditions with respect to its income or gains, and any other conditions, as may be specified in those regulations (see below); or

(vi) in that period:

(*a*) in so far as any transaction(s) reflected in the profits of the period achieved a 'reduction in UK tax', either it was minimal or that reduction was not a main purpose of the CFC, or of any person having an interest (see 21.7 above) in it in that period, in carrying out the transaction(s); and

(*b*) it was not a main reason for the CFC's existence to achieve a 'reduction in UK tax' by a 'diversion of profits' from the UK.

This is known as the 'motive test'. For a case in which a captive insurance company was held to have failed the test in (*b*) (although passing that in (*a*)), see *Association of British Travel Agents Ltd v CIR (Sp C 359), [2003] SSCD 194.*

[*ICTA 1988, s 748*(*1*)(*3*), *Sch 25 para 18*].

Exclusions to exceptions. None of the above exceptions applies, however, for an accounting period beginning **on or after 24 July 2002** where either:

(I) the CFC is incorporated in a territory specified for the purpose as respects that accounting period in Treasury regulations; or

(II) it is at any time in that accounting period liable to tax in such a territory by reason of domicile, residence or place of management; or

(III) at any time in that accounting period it carries on business through a permanent establishment (see 60.5 RESIDENCE — previously a branch or agency) in such a territory (unless the business it carried on in that period through permanent establishments (or branches or agencies) in such territories, taken as a whole, is only a minimal part of the whole of the business it carried on in that period).

The Treasury regulations prescribing such territories may make different provision for different cases or with respect to different territories, and may contain such incidental, supplemental, consequential or transitional provision as the Treasury may think fit. [*ICTA 1988, s 748A; FA 2002, s 89*].

Clearances. HMRC will be prepared to confirm, on the facts provided, whether the CFC meets any of the exemption tests and will thus not be subject to these provisions. It should in most cases be possible for HMRC to give an advance ruling covering a number of years, provided that all the relevant facts have been accurately disclosed and there is no change in the nature and conduct of the CFC's business. Details of how to make a clearance application and guidance on the information which will be required can be obtained from CT & VAT (International CT), 100 Parliament Square, London SW1A 2BQ. (See HMRC International Manual, INTM 214120–214150 for clearance procedures).

Excluded countries. As regards (v) above, see *The Controlled Foreign Companies* (*Excluded Countries*) *Regulations 1998* (*SI 1998 No 3081* as amended). These exclude territories specified in *Schedule 2* to the Regulations (for accounting periods in which self-assessment applies) where:

- in the case of a company resident in a territory specified in *Part I* of the Schedule, the company satisfies the income and gains requirement set out in the Regulations; and
- in the case of a company resident in a territory specified in *Part II* of the Schedule, the company satisfies the income and gains requirement and is not entitled to any tax benefit, or does not fall within any condition, specified in Part II of the Schedule in relation to the territory concerned.

The income and gains requirement is that the 'non-local source income' (as defined) does not exceed the greater of £50,000 (on an annual basis) and 10% of its 'commercially quantified income' (as defined). See generally HMRC International Manual, INTM 203000 *et seq.*

The regulations were amended by *SI 2002 No 2406* to remove the Republic of Ireland from the list of excluded countries. Regulations *SI 2005 No 185* make further amendments to the above regulations to counter avoidance with effect for accounting periods of non-UK resident companies beginning on or after 3 December 2004 by making changes to the tests for residence and control, by restricting certain income from connected persons from inclusion in 'commercially quantified income' and by including certain income from connected persons in 'non-local source income'. Regulations *SI 2005 No 186* introduce an additional requirement that controlled foreign companies, with effect for accounting periods beginning on or after 31 March 2005, should not be involved in a scheme or arrangement one of the main purposes of which is the reduction of UK tax.

[*SI 1998 No 3081*; *SI 2002 No 2406*; *SI 2005 No 185*; *SI 2005 No 186*].

Motive test. For HMRC's view of the 'motive test' in (vi) above, see (A)–(I) below. As regards that test, a transaction (or two or more transactions taken together) achieves a '*reduction in UK tax*' if, had it not been effected, any person would have been liable for, or for more, UK tax, or would have been entitled to a smaller (or no) relief from or repayment of UK tax. For these purposes, UK tax means income, corporation and capital gains taxes. There is a reduction in UK tax by a '*diversion of profits*' from the UK in an accounting period resulting from a CFC's existence if it is reasonable to suppose that (1) and (2) below would have applied had it not been for the CFC's existence (or for the existence of a company resident outside the UK, 'connected' (see 19 CONNECTED PERSONS) or 'associated' (as defined in *ICTA 1988, s 783(10)*) with the CFC, which fulfils or could fulfil, directly or indirectly, substantially the same function as the CFC in relation to any UK resident company or companies):

(1) the whole or substantial part of the CFC's receipts in the period would have been received by a UK resident individual or company, or by such a company it is reasonable to suppose would have been established in those circumstances; and

(2) that company or individual (or any other person resident in the UK) would have been liable for (or for more) UK tax or entitled to a lesser (or no) relief from or repayment of UK tax.

[*ICTA 1988, Sch 25 paras 16, 17, 19*].

HMRC have provided guidance on the application of the 'motive test' at (vi) above in their International Manual, INTM 200000 *et seq.* The following points are of particular interest.

(A) The motive test is entirely separate from the tests at (i) to (v) above, and failure to satisfy those other tests will not prejudice consideration of the motive test, except that where there is a marginal and isolated failure to satisfy those other tests this is regarded as an indication that the CFC is not being used to reduce tax liabilities (HMRC International Manual, INTM 208170, HMRC International Manual, INTM 208180).

(B) In determining what the tax position would have been had a transaction not been carried out, hypothetical transactions which might have taken place instead are not taken into account (HMRC International Manual, INTM 208060).

(C) Tax consequences remote from the transaction are not regarded as resulting from it (e.g. a fee received for giving tax planning advice to an unconnected UK resident would not lead to failure of the motive test merely because that person achieved a tax reduction by acting on that advice) (HMRC International Manual, INTM 208060).

(D) A reduction in tax which is substantial in absolute terms will not be regarded as 'minimal' merely because it represents a relatively small proportion of the total liability of the company concerned (HMRC International Manual, INTM 208070).

(E) The motives of a CFC's customers have no relevance to the motive test (HMRC International Manual, INTM 208080).

(F) As regards (1) above, it would be rare for this not to apply, as it is unlikely that a group would allow the diversion of receipts within the group to an outsider, and any claim that the law of the territory in which the CFC is resident would prevent a UK company from acquiring the CFC's receipts 'would have to be looked at very carefully' (HMRC International Manual, INTM 208140).

(G) The transfer of the activities of an overseas branch to a non-resident subsidiary will often be made for predominantly commercial reasons, e.g. as a necessary preliminary to expanding the overseas business or attracting local capital, and in such cases the motive test will often be satisfied as tax considerations will normally be only a subsidiary reason for the transfer. HMRC will, however, wish to consider in depth the reasons for incorporation (HMRC International Manual, INTM 208200).

(H) HMRC will, on receipt of a satisfactory clearance application (see above), accept that the motive test is satisfied in the case of newly-acquired overseas subsidiaries up to the end of the first full twelve-month accounting period following acquisition. This applies only to CFCs not previously under UK control and whose main business remained unchanged throughout the period in question (HMRC International Manual, INTM 208210).

(I) The UK holder of an interest in a CFC may also be treated as having a creditor relationship with the CFC (see 46.2 LOAN RELATIONSHIPS). Where this is so and the increase in value under the loan relationships provisions reflects the chargeable profits arising for an accounting period, the motive test is accepted as applying for that period. This is because the reduction in UK tax is fully compensated for by the tax charge on the UK parent, indicating that the achievement of that reduction is not a main reason for the CFC's existence (HMRC International Manual, INTM 208270).

For the circumstances in which holding companies (and in particular 'brass plate' holding companies) may satisfy the motive test, see HMRC International Manual, INTM 208220–208250.

A number of examples of different aspects of the motive test are included at HMRC International Manual, INTM 208280–208350.

See 21.1 above under 'Compatibility with EC law' with regard to the ECJ judgment in the case of *Cadbury Schweppes plc v CIR and Cadbury Schweppes Overseas Ltd v CIR (CJEC Case C-196/04)* in which the ECJ has said that it was up to the UK courts to decide whether the motive test can be interpreted as limiting the CFC legislation to wholly artificial arrangements intended to circumvent national tax law (in which case it would be compatible with EC law), or whether the motive exception does not apply if the CFC had been incorporated with the central intention of reducing UK tax even if there was no artificial arrangement in place (in which case, the legislation would not comply with EC law and would have to be changed).

Simon's Direct Tax Service. See D4.1208–D4.1209C.

21.13 **'Acceptable distribution policy'.** As regards 21.12(i) above, a CFC pursues an '*acceptable distribution policy*' in respect of an accounting period if, and only if, the amount of all dividends paid for the accounting period during, or within 18 months of the end of, that period, other than out of specified profits, which is paid to UK residents is not less than 90% of the CFC's 'net chargeable profits' for that period. (The 18-month limit may be extended, exceptionally, at HMRC's discretion and an extension is normally agreed where, following an enquiry, amendments are made to profits such that further distributions would be required to meet the test — see HMRC International Manual, INTM 204030.) A dividend which is not paid for the period(s) the profits of which are, in relation to the dividend, 'relevant profits' for the purposes of *ICTA 1988, s 799* (see 24.10 DOUBLE TAX RELIEF) is treated as so paid, and where a dividend is paid for a period which is not an accounting period but which falls wholly within an accounting period, it is treated as paid for that accounting period. A dividend paid for a period falling within two or more accounting periods is apportioned and treated as separate dividends paid for each accounting period.

A dividend paid by a CFC is disregarded for these purposes to the extent that the relevant profits in relation to the dividend (see *ICTA 1988, s 799(3)(4)*) derive from dividends or other distributions paid to the CFC at any time to which *ICTA 1988, s 208* (UK company distributions, see 23.16 DISTRIBUTIONS) applied, or would have applied had the CFC then been UK-resident. A dividend paid by a CFC *to* a company is also disregarded for these purposes unless it is taken into account in computing the recipient company's income for corporation tax and, in relation to a dividend paid after 6 March 2001 for an accounting period ending after that date, it is not so chargeable under Case I of Schedule D (or, in the case of certain insurance companies, under Case VI but on profits computed as under Case I) or, if so chargeable, the payment is not involved in a UK tax avoidance scheme (as specially defined, see *ICTA 1988, Sch 25 para 2B*).

Where the CFC accounts are drawn up in a foreign currency, they do not have to be translated into sterling for these purposes. A dividend equalling 90% of the appropriate foreign currency profits will meet the test. (See HMRC International Manual, INTM 204140.)

'*Net chargeable profits*' of an accounting period are the chargeable profits for that period (see 21.10 above) less the amount of any creditable tax (see 21.11 above) which would arise for the period were an apportionment to be made (see 21.7 above) if the restriction of *ICTA 1988, s 797* did not apply to limit relief to the attributable corporation tax (see 24.5 DOUBLE TAX RELIEF). Where the CFC pays a dividend out of specified profits representing dividends received, directly or indirectly, from another CFC, so much of those profits as is equal to the dividend paid out of them is left out of account in determining chargeable profits.

The gross amount of the dividend (i.e. the amount before deduction of any tax withheld on payment to the UK recipient) is taken into account for the purposes of the acceptable distribution test (see HMRC International Manual, INTM 204150).

The above 90% test is applied by reference to a part only of the net chargeable profits where, throughout the accounting period, the CFC has either:

(*a*) only one class of shares in issue; or

(*b*) only two classes of shares in issue, being either fixed rate preference shares (as defined in *ICTA 1988, Sch 18 para 1*, see 32.8 GROUPS OF COMPANIES) carrying no voting rights (or only carrying such a right, contingent upon non-payment of a dividend on the shares, which has not become exerciseable prior to payment of a dividend for the period in question) (the 'non-voting shares') or shares carrying the right to vote at general meetings (the 'voting shares');

and

(i) at the end of the period, some of the issued shares are held by persons resident outside the UK; and

(ii) no person has an interest in the CFC (see 21.7 above) other than one derived from issued shares.

Where (*a*) above applies, the fraction of net chargeable profits considered is that fraction of the issued shares at the end of the period which gives rise to interests in the CFC at that time by persons resident in the UK. If such persons hold both immediate and indirect interests in the CFC, and the immediate interests do not reflect the proportion of issued shares by virtue of which they have those interests (e.g. where they hold shares in a company having a direct or indirect interest in the CFC), the number of shares held by them is treated for this purpose as reduced to such number as is appropriate having regard to the immediate interests held by persons resident in the UK and any intermediate shareholdings between those interests and the shares in the CFC. Where (*b*) above applies, the amount of net chargeable profits considered is:

$$\frac{P \times Q}{R} + \frac{(X - P) \times Y}{Z}$$

where:

P is the amount of dividends (as above) paid in respect of non-voting shares;

Q is the number of non-voting shares by virtue of which UK residents have interests in the CFC at the end of the period;

R is the number of non-voting shares in issue at that time;

X is the net chargeable profits for the period;

Y is the number of voting shares by virtue of which UK residents have interests in the CFC at the end of the period; and

Z is the number of voting shares in issue at that time.

The number of shares under Q and Y may be reduced in the same way as where (*a*) above applies (see above) where UK resident persons hold both immediate and indirect interests in the CFC.

See HMRC International Manual, INTM 204080–204130.

Dividends taken into account. Where the main condition detailed below is satisfied in relation to a particular accounting period (the '*relevant accounting period*'), dividends to be taken into account, in addition to those paid for that period, are any paid (other than out of specified profits) for the immediately preceding accounting period and (if the condition is satisfied for that period) for the accounting period before that and so on. There is an additional condition in each case, that the dividend is not an '*excluded dividend*', i.e. it is not paid, in whole or part, out of total profits from which are derived the chargeable profits for an '*excluded period*', i.e. a period in respect of which an apportionment under these provisions falls to be made. The main condition in relation to any such accounting period is that either there were no 'relevant profits' for the period or:

(A) a dividend or dividends is (are) paid for the period to UK residents;

(B) the amount or aggregate amount of such dividends is not less than the relevant profits for the period (or, where only a part of the net chargeable profits is taken into account, a corresponding part of those relevant profits); and

(C) any dividends to be taken into account are paid not later than the time by which dividends paid for the relevant accounting period are required to be paid.

'*Relevant profits*' are the profits which would be the relevant profits for the purposes of *ICTA 1988, s 799* (see 24.10 DOUBLE TAX RELIEF) if a dividend were actually paid for the period. See also HMRC International Manual, INTM 204070 for the calculation of relevant profits.

Where no apportionment could be made under these provisions for an earlier period because the company pursued an acceptable distribution policy for that period, dividends are excluded from treatment as above to the extent that they are required to be taken into account for that purpose.

A dividend paid by a CFC to a non-UK resident company is regarded as paid to a UK resident and as meeting the requirements as regards chargeability in the UK (see above) to the extent that it is represented by a subsequent dividend paid to that UK resident by that other company (or by a 'related' company) out of profits derived, directly or indirectly, from the whole or part of the initial dividend paid by the CFC. The subsequent dividend must be taken into account in computing the recipient company's income for corporation tax and, in relation to a dividend paid after 6 March 2001 for an accounting period ending after that date, must not be chargeable under Case I of Schedule D (or, in the case of certain insurance companies, under Case VI but on profits computed as under Case I) or, if so chargeable, the payment must not be involved in a UK tax avoidance scheme (as specially defined, see *ICTA 1988, Sch 25 para 4A*). A company is '*related*' to another if at least 10% of its voting power is 'controlled' (see 21.2(*b*) above) by that other company or its parent company, or where there is a chain of such relationships, and, in relation to dividends paid after 6 March 2001 for an accounting period ending after that date, neither company is UK-resident.

[ICTA 1988, s 748(1)(a)(2), Sch 25 Pt I; FA 2001, s 82].

See generally HMRC International Manual, INTM 204000 *et seq.*

Returns where not established if acceptable distribution policy applies. Where a UK-resident company has an interest in a CFC at any time during an accounting period of the CFC, and at the time when the company delivers its company tax return it is not established whether or not the CFC has pursued an acceptable distribution policy in relation to that period, then:

(i) if the company considers that the CFC is likely to do so, it must make the return on the basis that it does so;

(ii) otherwise, it must make the return on the basis that it does not do so.

HMRC do not object to a company erring on the side of caution by acting as under (ii) above even though it thinks it likely that an acceptable distribution policy will be pursued (see HMRC International Manual, INTM 214050).

If (i) above applies but in the event the CFC does not do so, or if (ii) above applies but in the event the CFC does do so, the company must amend the return accordingly. Any such amendment must be made within 30 days after the end of the period allowed for establishing an acceptable distribution policy in relation to the CFC accounting period, i.e. the period ending 18 months after the end of the accounting period or at such later time as HMRC allows for payment of a dividend (see above). Otherwise, the normal return amendment provisions apply. If it has not been established by the end of the period allowed that the CFC pursued an acceptable distribution policy in relation to an accounting period, it is for these purposes assumed that it did not do so. Failure to make a timeous amendment where (i) above applies but the CFC did not in the event pursue an acceptable distribution policy in relation to the period renders the company liable to a penalty not exceeding the amount of tax understated. [*ICTA 1988, s 754A*].

Simon's Direct Tax Service. See **D4.1220** *et seq.*

See 24.12 DOUBLE TAX RELIEF for the separate streaming for double tax credit relief purposes and for restriction of underlying tax relief in respect of certain dividends paid in pursuit of an acceptable distribution policy.

21.14 *Example*

DEF Co Ltd, a UK incorporated and resident company with two associated companies, holds 35% of the shares of LNB Co, an unquoted non-trading controlled foreign company resident in Pinkland, where tax is levied at only 10%.

LNB Co has chargeable profits (see 21.10 above) for the year ended 31 March 2007 of £500,000. No withholding tax is applicable in Pinkland.

The following information is available in respect of DEF.

Year to 31 March	2006	2007
	£	£
Schedule D, Case I profit	600,000	780,000
Schedule D, Case III income	10,000	10,000
Chargeable gains	90,000	—
Schedule D, Case V income (gross) (tax suffered £30,000)	100,000	—

LNB Co

Calculation of profits apportioned to DEF Co Ltd and dividend required to avoid apportionment.

	£
Chargeable profits for the year ended 31 March 2007	500,000
Deduct Creditable tax	50,000
Net chargeable profits	£450,000
Amount of distribution required to avoid apportionment 90% × £450,000	£405,000

	Apportionment of profit	Dividend
DEF share	£	£
35% × £500,000: 35% × £405,000	175,000	141,750
Creditable/underlying tax	17,500	15,750
		157,500

DEF Co Ltd

With apportionment

Year to 31 March	2006	2007
	£	£
Schedule D, Case I	600,000	780,000
Schedule D, Case III	10,000	10,000
Chargeable gains	90,000	—
Schedule D, Case V income	100,000	—
CFC apportionment	175,000	—
	£975,000	£790,000

UK tax thereon at 30%		292,500	237,000
Less			
DTR on Case V income	(30,000)		
CFC creditable tax	(17,500)	(47,500)	
Mainstream tax payable		£245,000	£237,000

If dividend paid in y/e 31.3.2008

Year to 31 March	2006	2007
	£	£
Schedule D, Case I	600,000	780,000
Schedule D, Case III	10,000	10,000
Chargeable gains	90,000	—
Schedule D, Case V income	100,000	157,500
	£800,000	£947,500
UK tax thereon at 30%	240,000	284,250
Less DTR	(30,000)	(15,750)
Mainstream tax payable	£210,000	£268,500
Tax saving (cost)	£35,000	£(31,500)

DEF Co Ltd will make a net tax saving of £3,500 in tax if LBN Co pays the required dividend for the year ended 31 March 2007 by 31 March 2008.

21.15 **'Exempt activities'**. As regards 21.12(ii) above, a CFC is engaged in '*exempt activities*' in an accounting period if, and only if, throughout that accounting period, it has a 'business establishment' in the territory in which it is 'resident' (see below), its business affairs in that territory are 'effectively managed' there, and either (1), (2), (3) or (4) below is satisfied.

(1)

(*a*) At no time in the accounting period does the company's main business (for which see HMRC International Manual, INTM 205060) consist of either investment business (see INTM 205070), including the holding of intellectual property (see *ICTA 1988, Sch 25 para 9*) or of dealing in goods (i.e. buying and selling goods in unchanged form, see INTM 205080) for delivery to or from the UK or to or from connected or associated persons (see 21.12 above) which are not actually delivered to the territory in which it is resident, and

(*b*) in the case of a company mainly engaged in the period in wholesale, distributive or financial or (for accounting periods beginning after 20 March 2000, service) business (as exemplified in *ICTA 1988, Sch 25 para 11(1)*), less than 50% of its gross trading receipts from that business (net of the cost of any description of property or rights, sale proceeds of which are included therein) is derived, directly or indirectly, from connected or associated persons (see 21.12 above) or persons with an 'interest' in the company. For accounting periods beginning on or after 27 November 2002, this is extended to other persons being companies either UK-resident or carrying on business through a UK permanent establishment (see 60.5 RESIDENCE — previously through a UK branch or agency), by reference only to receipts derived from that permanent establishment, or individuals habitually resident in the UK (although this extension does *not* apply to certain CFCs engaged in insurance business, see *ICTA 1988, Sch 25 paras 6(2B), 11A, 11B*). Guidance on the extended provision is included in HMRC International Manual, INTM 205090. A person has an '*interest*' for this purpose if, on an apportionment under these provisions, at least 25% of the CFC's chargeable profits of the period would be apportioned to that person. For accounting periods beginning after 20 March 2000, where a company is a CFC only by virtue of joint control by two persons within *ICTA 1988, s 747(1A)* (see 21.2 above), the connected or associated persons to be considered also include persons connected or associated with either of those two persons. Special provisions apply as regards application of the requirement to banking or similar concerns and to insurance business of any kind (see *ICTA 1988, Sch 25 para 11(3)–(9)* and INTM 205100, 205110.

(2) The company is a 'local holding company', i.e. a 'holding company' 90% of whose gross income in the accounting period is derived directly from companies it controls (see 21.2(*b*) above) and which, throughout that period, are resident in the territory in which the holding company is 'resident' (see below) and are not themselves holding companies or 'superior holding companies' but either are engaged in exempt activities or are 'exempt trading companies'. In addition, the income must, (for accounting periods beginning after 20 March 2000) be received by the 'holding company' in its territory of residence.

(3) The company is a 'holding company' other than a local holding company (see (2) above) 90% of whose gross income during the accounting period is derived directly from companies it controls (see 21.2(*b*) above) and which are themselves throughout the period either local holding companies or not themselves 'holding companies' or 'superior holding companies' but either engaged in exempt activities or 'exempt trading companies'. In addition, (for accounting periods beginning after 20 March 2000) either 90% of the gross income of the 'holding company' must consist of 'qualifying dividends', or the company from which the 'holding company' directly derives 90% of its gross income must, throughout the accounting period in question, be resident in the territory in which the 'holding company' is resident and in which it must receive that income. A '*qualifying dividend*' is any dividend other than one for which the paying company is entitled to a deduction against its profits for tax purposes under the law of the territory in which it is resident.

(4) The company is a 'superior holding company' 90% of whose gross income during the accounting period represents 'qualifying exempt activity income of its subsidiaries' and is derived directly from companies it controls (see 21.2(*b*) above) and each of which, throughout that accounting period, either:

(*a*) not itself being a 'superior holding company', is otherwise either engaged in exempt activities or an 'exempt trading company'; or

(*b*) is itself a 'superior holding company' 90% of whose gross income during the accounting period represents 'qualifying exempt activity income of its subsidiaries' and is derived directly from companies which it controls (see 21.2(*b*) above) and which themselves fall within this subparagraph or within (*a*) above.

In addition, (for accounting periods beginning after 20 March 2000) either 90% of the gross income of the 'superior holding company' (under either leg of the test) must consist of 'qualifying dividends' (as in (3) above), or the company from which the 'superior holding company' directly derives 90% of its gross income must, throughout the accounting period in question, be resident in the territory in which the 'superior holding company' is resident and in which it must receive that income.

In (2), (3) and (4) above, a 'holding company' or 'superior holding company' is treated as controlling any trading company in which it holds the maximum amount of ordinary share capital permitted under the law of the territory in which that trading company is resident, and from whose laws it derives its status as a company. A trading company for this purpose includes (for accounting periods beginning after 20 March 2000) any trading company which is a CFC under the 40% joint control test (see 21.2 above) where the non-UK resident joint owner also controls the 'holding company' or 'superior holding company'. For the 90% of gross income test, see *ICTA 1988, Sch 25 para 12(4)–(6)* and INTM 205170–205200. See INTM 205160 for the circumstances in which a holding company may be deemed to pass the motive test where its subsidiaries carry on broadly commercial activities along the lines of the exempt activities test, or where it controls a holding company which is not a local holding company.

As regards (4) above, see *ICTA 1988, Sch 25 para 12A(3)(4)* as regards the profits out of which dividends are regarded as paid, and see also INTM 205190.

A '*business establishment*' means 'premises' from which the company's business in the territory in which it is 'resident' (see below) is wholly or mainly carried on, and which are, or are intended to be, occupied and used with a reasonable degree of permanence. HMRC's interpretation of this requirement is set out at INTM 205030. An office building, or even a single office, shared by a number of companies can be the 'business establishment' of each company. The requirement that the premises be 'occupied and used with a reasonable degree of permanence' depends on the nature of the company's business. Thus a holding company's business might need only occasional attendance of its staff at the premises, and the use of an office on such occasions would suffice, provided that it was retained by the company for its use for a considerable period of time. Continuous occupation of the office during normal working hours would not be required. The occasional hiring of, say, a hotel room for meetings would not qualify as having a 'business establishment'.

Again, a company (e.g. a bank) purporting to do business with the general public would be expected to have an office, shop, etc. actually occupied by its staff for at least a substantial part of each working day.

'*Premises*' includes an office, shop, factory or other building (or part); a mine, oil well, gas well or quarry or other place of extraction of natural resources; or a building, construction or installation site where the project has a duration of at least twelve months. A company whose business in the territory of residence is carried on from a number of sites in the territory will be treated as having a business establishment there even if no one site can be identified as the main place of business in the territory (see INTM 205030).

'*Resident*' in this context is as defined in 21.3 above. However, a non-UK resident company which, for the accounting period in question, is not liable to tax in any territory by reason of domicile, residence or place of management, but whose affairs are 'effectively managed' in a territory outside the UK in which companies are not liable to tax by reason of domicile, residence or place of management, is treated for this purpose as resident in the latter territory or, if there is more than one, in such a territory as is notified to HMRC for this purpose by the UK resident company or companies having a majority interest in the CFC (see 21.10(iv) above). Where, however, the territory in which it is 'effectively managed' is either the Hong Kong or the Macao Special Administrative Region of the People's Republic of China, and it is liable to tax for the period in that Region, it is instead treated as resident in that Region.

The requirement that the CFC's business affairs be '*effectively managed*' in the territory of residence is not regarded as satisfied unless the number of employees in the territory is adequate to deal with the volume of the company's business, and unless any services provided for persons resident outside the territory (other than through a permanent establishment (or branch or agency) liable to UK tax on its profits or gains, or for arm's length consideration through any other person so liable) are not in fact performed in the UK (or are merely incidental to services performed outside the UK). Employees in the territory include persons engaged in the company's business but paid by a person connected (see 19 CONNECTED PERSONS) with, and resident in the same territory as, the CFC, provided that they are engaged in the CFC's business (wholly or mainly so engaged in the case of a company other than a 'holding company' or 'superior holding company'). The requirement as to the number of employees does not mean that every person involved in the company's business must be located in the territory of residence, but the staff employed there must be sufficient, in numbers and in qualifications and experience, to supervise and control profit-making activities of the company (see INTM 205040). For accounting periods beginning on or after 6 December 2006, the 'effectively managed' condition will not be fulfilled unless there are sufficient employees of that company in the company's country of residence who have the skills and authority to conduct all, or substantially all, of the company's business. Where an accounting period straddles 6 December 2006, the accounting period is treated as if it were two periods, one comprising the period ending on 5 December and the other runnning on and after 6 December 2006. Profits and creditable tax are apportioned on a just and reasonable basis.

A '*holding company*' is a company whose business consists wholly or mainly in holding shares or securities in companies which are either its 90% subsidiaries and local holding companies (see (2) above) or its 51% subsidiaries and trading companies or companies in which it holds the maximum permitted amount of ordinary share capital (see below); or a company which would satisfy that condition if so much of its business were disregarded as consists in holding property or rights wholly or mainly for use by fellow resident companies controlled by it (see 21.2(*b*) above). However, in determining whether a company is a local holding company for this purpose, the reference in the definition of holding company to companies which are 90% subsidiaries and local holding companies is omitted. Determination of 51% or 90% subsidiary status is by reference to direct ownership, of more than 50% or not less than 90% respectively, of ordinary share capital.

For the purposes of (2) and (3) above, income of a holding company is treated as *not* being derived directly from a company it controls where:

(*a*) the controlled company from which it derives the income is not itself a holding company or 'superior holding company' but either is engaged in exempt activities or is an 'exempt trading company'; and

(*b*) the income was, or could have been, paid out of any non-trading income (i.e. income which would not be chargeable on a UK resident company under Schedule D, Case I on normal corporation tax principles) of the controlled company derived, directly or indirectly, from a third company connected or associated with it (see 21.12 above).

For the purpose of (2), (3) and (4) above, in the case of a holding company or 'superior holding company' part of whose business consists of activities other than holding shares, securities, property or rights, gross income of an accounting period is determined by:

(i) leaving out of account any part derived from any activity which, of itself, would satisfy (1) above; and

(ii) to the extent that the company's receipts from any other activities included proceeds of sale of any description of property or rights, deducting the cost of the property or rights (up to the amount of the receipts therefrom), and making no other deduction in respect of that activity.

A '*superior holding company*' is a company whose business consists wholly or mainly in holding shares or securities in holding companies or local holding companies or other superior holding companies, or which would satisfy that condition if so much of its business were disregarded as consists in holding property or rights wholly or mainly for use by fellow resident companies controlled by it (see 21.2(*b*) above).

A company is an '*exempt trading company*' throughout a period if it is a trading company throughout each of its accounting periods falling wholly or partly within the period, and in each of those accounting periods:

(A) it is not subject to a lower level of taxation (see 21.4 above) in the territory in which it is resident;

(B) it is within 21.12(v) above; and

(C) it satisfies the conditions in 21.12(vi) above,

and income of a company during a period represents '*qualifying exempt activity income of its subsidiaries*' if it is derived directly or indirectly from companies which it controls (see 21.2(*b*) above) and which, throughout that period, fall within (4)(*a*) above, but which are not holding companies other than local holding companies.

On or after 6 December 2006, companies resident in an EEA territory are liable under the CFC legislation in the same way as companies resident elsewhere.

[*ICTA 1988, s 748(1)(b), Sch 25 Pt II; FA 2003, ss 200, 201, Sch 42; FA 2007, Sch 15 para 7, 10*].

See generally HMRC International Manual, INTM 205000 *et seq.*

Simon's Direct Tax Service. See **D4.1230** *et seq.*

21.16 The 'public quotation condition'. For accounting periods commencing on or after 6 December 2006, the public quotation condition does not apply. Where an accounting period straddles 6 December 2006, the period is apportioned into two periods for CFC purposes.

The 'public quotation condition' is met by a CFC in an accounting period if:

(i) shares or stock (other than that entitled to a fixed rate of dividend, whether also participating in profits or not) have, within the twelve months to the end of the accounting period, been dealt in on, and listed in the official list of, a recognised stock exchange (i.e. one designated as such by HMRC, see HMRC International Manual, INTM 206010–206050) in its territory of residence; and

(ii) such shares, etc. carrying at least 35% of the total voting power in the company have been 'beneficially held by the public' throughout the accounting period, and have been acquired unconditionally by the public; and

(iii) the voting power possessed by 'principal members' of the company (including that attributed to shares entitled to a fixed rate of dividend) has not at any time in the accounting period exceeded 85% of the total voting power in the company.

Shares etc. are '*beneficially held by the public*' if held by any person other than a person connected or associated with the CFC (see 21.8 above) or a 'principal member' of the company.

A '*principal member*' of a company is a person possessing more than 5% of the voting power in the company or, where there are more than five such persons, those five persons holding the highest percentages. Where more than one person possesses a percentage which would, if held by only one person, be the fifth largest percentage holding, each of those persons is a principal member in addition to the four persons possessing higher percentage holdings.

Any person's holding of shares for these purposes includes all nominee holdings for him, and a person's voting power includes that of his associates (see 16.5 CLOSE COMPANIES), of any company which he controls (see 21.2(*b*) above) with or without his associates, and of any nominees for him, his associates or such companies. Voting power of associates' associates and of companies controlled only by associates is disregarded.

[*ICTA 1988, Sch 25 paras 13–15; FA 2007 Sch 15 paras 8, 10*].

See generally HMRC International Manual, INTM 206000 *et seq.*

Simon's Direct Tax Service. See **D4.1240**.

21.17 ASSESSMENT, RECOVERY AND POSTPONEMENT OF TAX

The normal corporation tax provisions apply to the charge to tax of a sum under these provisions as under 21.8 above, including those relating to company tax returns, to the assessment, collection and receipt of corporation tax, and to appeals, administration, penalties, interest and priority in insolvency. The provisions of *TMA 1970* thus apply as if references to corporation tax referred also to amounts charged under these provisions, and as if references to company profits referred also to chargeable profits apportioned to a company under these provisions. A sum chargeable under these provisions is chargeable for the accounting period in which ends the CFC accounting period whose chargeable profits were apportioned.

Just and reasonable apportionments. Where an apportionment of chargeable profits for an accounting period of a CFC falls to be made on a just and reasonable basis (see 21.8 above), and a company uses a particular basis in its tax return, HMRC may determine that a different basis is to be used, and require the company to provide such documents and information as are reasonably required for this purpose. A basis so determined is then treated as if it were the only basis permissible. A determination may be questioned (in an appeal against an amendment to the company's tax return) only on the ground that the basis determined is not just and reasonable.

Appeals against amendments to company tax returns (or against discovery assessments or determinations) relating to charges under these provisions are to the Special Commissioners. Where their determination of a particular question is likely to affect the liability of more than one person under these provisions in relation to the CFC concerned, every such person is entitled to appear and be heard by the Special Commissioners, or to make written representations to them, and their determination of that question is treated as separate from any other determination on the appeal and as if each of those persons were a party to the appeal on that question.

The *reliefs* which may be claimed against a liability under these provisions are as follows:

(*a*) *Trading losses, etc.* Where a company is regarded as liable to corporation tax in respect of chargeable profits apportioned to it (as above), it may claim to set against its liability a sum equal to corporation tax, at the rate (or average rate) applicable to profits of the accounting period, on all or part of a loss. (which is then treated as having been set off against profits of the company). Such a loss may be a trading loss, Schedule A loss, charge on income, management expense, excess capital allowance, group relief claim or non-trading loan relationship deficit.

(*b*) *Surplus ACT.* Surplus ACT (from accounting periods beginning before 6 April 1999) (see 3.2 ET SEQ. ADVANCE CORPORATION TAX—SHADOW ACT) of an accounting period for which a company is regarded as liable to corporation tax in respect of chargeable profits apportioned to it (as above) may, on a claim, be set against that liability (so far as it is not relieved, and could not be relieved, under (*a*) above), and is then treated as having been set against a corporation tax liability of the period. The maximum set-off allowed is the amount of shadow ACT on a distribution made at the end of the accounting period, where the amount of the distribution plus the shadow

ACT in respect of it is equal to the apportioned chargeable profits in respect of which the company is chargeable for the period less any deduction under (*a*) above. [*SI 1999 No 358, reg 20*].

(*c*) *Dividends from the CFC.* The total of assessments on UK resident companies under these provisions in respect of a CFC's chargeable profits (the '*gross attributed tax*') is treated as underlying tax for double taxation relief purposes (see 24.10 DOUBLE TAX RELIEF) where a dividend is paid by the CFC wholly or partly out of profits from which those chargeable profits derive. The gross attributed tax is *not*, however, treated as increasing the amount of the dividend income in determining liability on that income.

Special recovery powers. Where the same interest in a CFC is held directly by one person and indirectly by another, and the company to be treated as holding the interest is defined by 21.8(1) to (3) above, special recovery powers apply to any overdue tax chargeable on that company. HMRC may serve notice of liability to that overdue tax on another UK resident company (the '*responsible company*') which holds or has held, directly or indirectly, the same interest in the CFC as the chargeable company. Interest both up to the date of the notice and thereafter is then payable by the responsible company. If tax and interest is not paid by the responsible company within three months of the date of HMRC's notice, it may be recovered from either the responsible company or the company originally chargeable.

[*ICTA 1988, s 754, Sch 26*].

HMRC guidance. See generally HMRC International Manual, INTM 214000 *et seq.*

Simon's Direct Tax Service. See **D4.1250** *et seq.*

21.18 **MISCELLANEOUS**

Corporation tax on chargeable gains on disposal of shares: relief may be claimed where:

(i) an apportionment is made under these provisions (see 21.7 above) in respect of a CFC's accounting period;

(ii) a UK resident company (the '*claimant company*') disposes of shares, acquired before the end of that accounting period, in either the CFC or another company whose shares give rise to the claimant company's interest in the CFC (see 21.7 above); and

(iii) chargeable profits (see 21.8 above) of the CFC are apportioned to the claimant company, and a sum accordingly becomes chargeable on it as if it were corporation tax (see 21.7 above).

Where a claim is made, in the computation of the chargeable gain accruing on the disposal in (ii) above, a deduction is allowed of the sum chargeable to tax as in (iii) above, reduced to the proportion thereof that the average market value, in the period for which the apportionment was made, of the interest in the CFC in respect of which the charge as in (iii) above arose bears to the average market value in that period of the shares disposed of. A sum chargeable to tax as at (iii) above may only be relieved once in this way.

Relief may, however, be restricted where, before the disposal, a dividend is paid by the CFC out of profits from which the chargeable profits in (iii) above derived. If either:

(*a*) the effect of the payment of the dividend is to reduce the value of the shares disposed of as in (ii) above; or

(*b*) the claimant company obtains relief as under 21.17(*c*) above in respect of a dividend paid on the shares disposed of as in (ii) above, by reference to sums including that referred to in (iii) above, then relief is denied in respect of so much of the sum chargeable to tax as corresponds to the part of the chargeable profits in (iii) above corresponds to the profits which the dividend represents.

Claims for relief must be made within three months of the later of the end of the accounting period in which the disposal occurs and the date the charge to tax in (iii) above becomes final and conclusive.

Identification of shares disposed of for this purpose is with those acquired earlier before those acquired later.

[*ICTA 1988, Sch 26 para 3*].

See Simon's Direct Tax Service D4.1263.

See generally HMRC International Manual, INTM 211120.

See 21.17(*c*) above as regards restriction of dividend relief following relief under this provision.

ICTA 1988, s 739 (transfer of assets abroad). Where a sum forming part of a CFC's chargeable profits (see 21.10 above) would otherwise be deemed income of an individual under *section 739* (see Tolley's Income Tax under Anti-Avoidance) that deemed income is reduced by the proportion of those chargeable profits which gives rise to a liability to tax on UK resident companies by virtue of an apportionment under these provisions (see 21.8 above). [*ICTA 1988, s 747(4)(b)*].

Insurance companies. For the treatment of chargeable profits and creditable tax apportioned to companies carrying on life assurance business, see *ICTA 1988, s 755A*. Broadly, they are treated as if they represented a dividend paid by the CFC. See also *ICTA 1988, s 755B*, which extends certain time limits in respect of any amendment of or enquiry into an insurance company's tax return which has regard to accounts of a CFC prepared on a non-annual basis, and *ICTA 1988, s 755C*, which provides regulation-making powers relating to cases where a CFC carrying on general insurance business prepares accounts on a non-annual basis (and see *SI 1999 No 1408* which *inter alia* introduces a new *ICTA 1988, s 754AA* dealing with returns where it is not established whether a non-resident company carrying on such business is a CFC).

See generally HMRC International Manual, INTM 213000 *et seq.*

22 Corporate Venturing Scheme

See also HMRC Pamphlet IR 2000 'The Corporate Venturing Scheme'.

Simon's Direct Tax D2.13.

The headings in this chapter are as follows.

22.1 INTRODUCTION

For shares issued on or after 1 April 2000 but before 1 April 2010, a scheme is introduced whereby most trading companies are able to obtain corporation tax relief at 20% ('*investment relief*') on corporate venturing investments, i.e. acquisitions (by cash subscription) of minority shareholdings in 'small higher risk' trading companies. In addition, investing companies are able to postpone chargeable gains ('*deferral relief*') on disposals of corporate venturing investments where they reinvest in other shares attracting investment relief. Also, an allowable capital loss on the disposal of a corporate venturing investment, computed net of investment relief, can be relieved against *income* of the accounting period in which the loss arises and accounting periods ending in the previous 12 months (but may alternatively be relieved against chargeable gains in the normal way). [*FA 2000, s 63(1)(4), Sch 15 para 1*].

Investee companies are limited to those with gross assets not exceeding £15 million immediately before the investment and £16 million immediately afterwards. Such companies must exist for the purpose of carrying on trading activities other than the kind of 'lower risk' activity excluded under the Enterprise Investment Scheme (see Tolley's Income Tax) or the provisions for VENTURE CAPITAL TRUSTS (69). Potential investee companies may request advance clearance from HMRC. The maximum investment qualifying for relief is 30% of the issued ordinary share capital of the investee company, and no minimum investment is stipulated. It is a further condition that at least 20% of the ordinary share capital of the investee company be held by individuals (other than directors and employees of the investing company). To qualify for the relief, the investing company must retain the shares acquired for at least three years. Investing companies carrying on financial trades (e.g. banking, share dealing etc.) are not eligible.

See generally HMRC Venture Capital Schemes Manual, VCM 10000–17320, VCM 50000 *et seq.*

22.2 INVESTMENT RELIEF

Eligibility. An investing company is eligible for investment relief (see 22.3 below) in respect of an amount subscribed by it for shares in an investee company (the '*issuing company*') if:

(*a*) the shares (the '*relevant shares*') are issued to the investing company;

(*b*) the investing company is a 'qualifying investing company' (see 22.5 below);

(*c*) the issuing company is a 'qualifying issuing company' (see 22.6 below) in relation to the relevant shares; and

(*d*) the general requirements at 22.8 below are met.

For advance clearance as regards (*c*) and (*d*) above, see 22.9 below.

Qualification period. In these provisions, the '*qualification period*' is normally the three-year period beginning with the date of issue of the relevant shares. If, however, the money raised by the issue is employed wholly or mainly for the purposes of a qualifying trade (or trades) (see 22.7 below) which, on the date of issue, was not being carried on by the issuing company or a qualifying 90% subsidiary (or, for shares before 17 March 2004, a qualifying subsidiary (see 22.6 below)), the qualification period begins on the date of issue and ends immediately before the third anniversary of the date of commencement of the trade (or the latest such date where there is more than one such trade). In determining when the trade begins for this purpose in relation to shares issued on or after 17 March 2004, the carrying on of any trade by a subsidiary before it became a qualifying 90% subsidiary is to be disregarded.

[*FA 2000, Sch 15 paras 2, 3, 102(8); FA 2004, s 95, Sch 20 paras 3, 13, 15*].

22.3 **Form of relief.** Where an investing company is eligible for investment relief (see 22.2 above) in respect of amounts subscribed by it for shares, its corporation tax liability for the accounting period in which the shares are issued is reduced, on a claim (see 22.4 below), by the lesser of:

(*a*) 20% of the amount (or aggregate amount) subscribed; and

(*b*) the amount which reduces the liability to nil.

The reduction in corporation tax liability is made before any deduction for COMMUNITY INVESTMENT TAX RELIEF (17) or DOUBLE TAX RELIEF (24).

[*FA 2000, Sch 15 para 39, Sch 16 para 5(1)(2); FA 2002, Sch 17 para 5*].

Investment relief is said to be 'attributable to shares' if relief as above has been obtained in respect of those shares and has not been withdrawn — see 22.10 below. Where for any one accounting period relief has been obtained by reason of more than one issue of shares, the relief is attributed to those issues in proportion to the amounts subscribed. Relief attributable to any one issue of shares is attributed *pro rata* to each share in that issue, and any reduction of relief (see 22.10 below) is similarly apportioned between the shares in question. For these purposes, any bonus shares, issued in respect of the original shares and being shares in the same company, of the same class and carrying the same rights, are treated as if comprised in the original issue, and relief is apportioned to them accordingly. This applies only if the original shares have been held continuously since issue (as in 22.20(*a*) below), and, where it does apply, the bonus shares are themselves treated as having been held continuously since the time of the original issue. [*FA 2000, Sch 15 para 45*].

22.4 **Claims for relief.** No deadline is specified for making a claim, so the general six-year time limit applies as in 15.7 CLAIMS. A claim for relief cannot be made in respect of any investment until the 'funded trade' has been carried on by no person other than the issuing company or a qualifying 90% subsidiary (for shares issued before 17 March 2004, simply by the issuing company or a subsidiary) for at least four months and the investing company has received from the issuing company a 'compliance certificate' (see below). In determining whether the 'funded trade' has been carried on for four months, the time spent *preparing* to carry on the trade and, in relation to shares issued on or after 17 March 2004, where the funded trade is carried on by a partnership or joint venture, the other partners or parties to the joint venture, are to be disregarded.

No postponement of tax pending appeal (see 53.4 PAYMENT OF TAX) can be made on the grounds of eligibility for investment relief until a claim for that relief can be and has been made. The '*funded trade*' is the trade or trades by reference to which the requirement at 22.8 below as to 'use of money raised' is met (or, where applicable, the notional trade of research and development therein mentioned). A claim *can* be made if the funded trade is carried on as above for less than four months by reason of the winding-up or dissolution of any company (or, for shares issued before 17 March 2004, the issuing company or subsidiary concerned) or its going into administration or receivership (both as defined), provided that this is for commercial reasons and not part of tax avoidance arrangements.

A '*compliance certificate*' is a certificate issued, with the authority of HMRC and in such form as they may direct, by the issuing company in respect of the relevant shares and confirming that, from the issuing company's point of view, the requirements for investment relief are for the time being met in relation to the shares. To obtain authority for the issue of a certificate, the issuing company must provide HMRC with a 'compliance statement' in respect of the issue of shares which includes the relevant shares. Where notice of an event giving rise to withdrawal etc. is given to HMRC by or in relation to the issuing company (see 22.10 below), any authority already given is invalid unless renewed.

A '*compliance statement*' is a statement, in respect of an issue of shares, to the effect that, from the issuing company's point of view, the requirements for investment relief are for the time being met in relation to the shares and have been met at all times since the shares were issued. The statement must be in required form and must contain any additional information HMRC reasonably require, a declaration that it is correct to the best of the company's knowledge and belief, and such other declarations as HMRC reasonably require. A compliance statement cannot be made until such time as the funded trade has been carried on for at least four months (or such shorter time as is specified above). It *must* be made within two years after the end of the accounting period in which the shares were issued or, if later, two years after the minimum period of trading condition is satisfied.

The issuing company may give notice of appeal, within 30 days, against a refusal by HMRC to authorise a compliance certificate (as if that refusal were the disallowance of a claim other than for discharge or repayment of tax — see 15.8 CLAIMS).

The issuing company is liable to a penalty of up to £3,000 for issuing a compliance certificate which is made fraudulently or negligently or without HMRC authority, or for making a compliance statement fraudulently or negligently.

[*FA 2000, Sch 15 paras 40–44, 102(4); FA 2004, Sch 20 paras 12, 15*].

22.5 QUALIFYING INVESTING COMPANY

The investing company is a '*qualifying investing company*' (see 22.2(*b*) above) in relation to the relevant shares if it meets all the requirements below as to absence of material interest, reciprocal arrangements, control and tax avoidance, the nature of its activities, and the relevant shares being a chargeable asset. [*FA 2000, Sch 15 para 4*].

No material interest requirement. At no time in the qualification period (see 22.2 above) must the investing company have a material interest in the issuing company. For this purpose, a person has a material interest in a company if he (alone or together with any person connected with him (within *ICTA 1988, s 839*, see 19 CONNECTED PERSONS)) directly or indirectly possesses, or is entitled (or will in future be entitled) to acquire (at present or at a future date), more than **30%** of:

(*a*) the 'ordinary share capital' of; or

(*b*) the voting power in,

the company or any 51% subsidiary. In applying the test, there must be attributed to a person any rights or powers of any associate of his (as defined by *FA 2000, Sch 15 para 99*). For these purposes, a company's '*ordinary share capital*' comprises:

(i) all of its issued share capital other than 'relevant preference shares'; and

(ii) all of its loan capital (as widely defined but excluding a bank overdraft or an ordinary business debt) that carries a right to convert into, or to acquire, shares which would fall within (i) above.

'*Relevant preference shares*' are, broadly, non-voting, non-convertible shares issued for new consideration and carrying no right to dividends other than dividends which:

(A) are of a fixed amount or at a rate which is fixed or which varies according to a standard published interest rate, a tax rate, a retail price index or an official share price index; and

(B) which are not dependent on the company's business results or asset values and do not represent more than a reasonable commercial return on the investment.

[*FA 2000, Sch 15 paras 5, 7, 9, 102(3)*].

No reciprocal arrangements requirement. The investing company's subscription for the relevant shares must not be part of any arrangements which provide for any other person to subscribe for shares in a 'related company'. A '*related company*' is a company in which the investing company, or any other person who is party to the arrangements, has a 'material interest' (as defined immediately above). Arrangements are disregarded to the extent that they provide for the issuing company to subscribe for shares in any qualifying subsidiary (see 22.6 below). [*FA 2000, Sch 15 para 6*].

No control requirement. At no time in the qualification period (see 22.2 above) must the investing company 'control' the issuing company. '*Control*' is determined in accordance with *ICTA 1988, s 416(2)–(6)* (see 16.2 CLOSE COMPANIES) as modified for this purpose. [*FA 2000, Sch 15 para 8*].

No tax avoidance requirement. The relevant shares must be subscribed for by the investing company for commercial reasons and not as part of a tax avoidance scheme or arrangement. [*FA 2000, Sch 15 para 14*].

Non-financial activities requirement. Throughout the qualification period (see 22.2 above), the investing company:

(*a*) if a '*single company*' (i.e. a company which is not a parent company or a 51% subsidiary), must exist wholly for the purpose of carrying on one or more 'non-financial trades'; and

(*b*) if a '*group company*' (i.e. a parent company and any of its subsidiaries), must be part of a 'non-financial trading group' and must either exist wholly for the purpose of carrying on one or more 'non-financial trades' or businesses other than trades or be the parent company of the group.

In determining the purpose for which a company exists, purposes having no significant effect (other than in relation to incidental matters) on the extent of the company's activities are disregarded. Purposes for which a company exists are also disregarded to the extent that they consist of:

(i) (as regards a single company) the holding and managing of property used by the company for one or more 'non-financial trades' carried on by it;

(ii) (as regards a group company) any activities within (I) or (II) below; or

(iii) (as regards any company) holding shares to which investment relief is attributable (see 22.3 above) unless the holding of such shares is a substantial part of the company's business.

A trade is a '*non-financial trade*' if:

(A) it is conducted on a commercial basis and with a view to profit; and

(B) it does not consist, wholly or as to a substantial part, in the carrying on of 'financial activities'.

'*Financial activities*' include for this purpose:

(1) banking, or money-lending, carried on by a bank, building society or other person;

(2) debt factoring, finance-leasing or hire-purchase financing;

(3) insurance;

(4) dealing in shares, securities, currency, debts or other assets of a financial nature; and

(5) dealing in commodity or financial futures or options.

A group is a '*non-financial trading group*' unless the business of the group (treating the activities of the group companies, taken together, as a single business) consists, wholly or as to a substantial part, in the carrying on of trades other than non-financial trades (as above) and/or businesses other than trades. Activities of a group company are disregarded to the extent that they consist of:

(I) holding shares in or securities of, or making loans to, another group company;

(II) holding and managing property used by a group company for the purposes of one or more non-financial trades carried on by a group company; or

(III) holding shares to which investment relief is attributable (see 22.3 above), unless the holding of such shares is a substantial part of the company's business.

Amendments to the non-financial activities requirement may be made in the future by Treasury Order.

[*FA 2000, Sch 15 paras 10–12, 101, 102*(*1*)].

Requirement as to shares being a chargeable asset. The relevant shares must be a 'chargeable asset' of the investing company immediately after they are issued to it. For this purpose, an asset is a '*chargeable asset*' at a particular time if, on a disposal at that time, a gain would be a chargeable gain. [*FA 2000, Sch 15 para 13*].

22.6 QUALIFYING ISSUING COMPANY

The issuing company is a '*qualifying issuing company*' (see 22.2(*c*) above) in relation to the relevant shares if it meets all the requirements below as to unquoted status, independence, individual-owners, partnerships and joint ventures, qualifying subsidiaries, property managing subsidiaries, gross assets, trading activities and, on or after **19 July 2007** or later, number of employees. [*FA 2000, Sch 15 para 15; FA 2004, Sch 20 para 3*].

Unquoted status requirement. At the time of issue of the relevant shares, none of the issuing company's shares, debentures or other securities must be listed on a recognised stock exchange or a 'designated' exchange outside the UK or be dealt in outside the UK by 'designated' means, and there must be no arrangements in existence for such a listing or such dealing. This applies whether or not the company is UK-resident. '*Designated*' means designated by order of HMRC for the purposes of *ICTA 1988, s 312*(*1B*) (enterprise investment schemes, see Tolley's Income Tax). The company does not fail to meet the requirement simply because a designation order is made, or a stock exchange obtains recognition, after the time of issue of the shares.

If, at the time of issue of the relevant shares, arrangements are in existence for the issuing company to become a wholly-owned subsidiary of a new holding company by means of a share exchange within 22.24 below, there must be no arrangements made for any of the new company's shares, debentures or other securities to be listed or dealt in as above.

[*FA 2000, Sch 15 para 16*].

Independence requirement. At no time in the qualification period (see 22.2 above) must the issuing company be a 51% subsidiary of another company or otherwise under the control (within *ICTA 1988, s 840*) of another company or of another company and persons connected with it (within *ICTA 1988, s 839*, see 19 CONNECTED PERSONS). No arrangements must exist at any time during the qualification period whereby the company could become such a subsidiary or fall under such control (whether during that period or otherwise). Arrangements with a view to a company reconstruction within 22.24 below are disregarded for this purpose. [*FA 2000, Sch 15 paras 17, 102(3)*].

Individual-owners requirement. Throughout the qualification period (see 22.2 above), at least **20%** of the issued ordinary share capital of the issuing company must be beneficially owned by one or more 'independent individuals'. An '*independent individual*' is one who is not, at any time during the qualification period when he holds ordinary shares in the issuing company, a director or employee of the investing company or of any company connected with it (within *ICTA 1988, s 839*, see 19 CONNECTED PERSONS), or a relative (i.e. spouse or (from 5 December 2005) civil partner, forebear or issue) of such a director or employee. Where an independent individual owned shares immediately prior to his death, they are treated for these purposes as continuing to be owned by an independent individual until they cease to form part of the deceased's estate. [*FA 2000, Sch 15 paras 18, 102(3); SI 2005 No 3229, reg 132*].

Partnerships and joint ventures requirement. At no time in the qualification period (see 22.2 above) must the issuing company or any qualifying subsidiary (see below) be a member of a partnership or a party to a joint venture where:

(*a*) a trade by reference to which the trading activities requirement (see below) is met by the issuing company is being carried on, or is to be carried on, by the partners in partnership or, as the case may be, by the company or a qualifying subsidiary (see below) as a party to the joint venture;

(*b*) the other partners or parties to the joint venture include at least one other company; and

(*c*) the same person(s) is/are the beneficial owner(s) of more than 75% of the issued share capital or the ordinary share capital of both the issuing company and at least one of the other partners/parties.

For these purposes, there must be attributed to any person any share capital held by an associate of his (within *FA 2000, Sch 15 para 99*).

[*FA 2000, Sch 15 para 19*].

Qualifying subsidiaries requirement. At no time in the qualification period (see 22.2 above) must the issuing company have a 'subsidiary' other than a 'qualifying subsidiary'. For this purpose, a '*subsidiary*' of a company is any company which it controls (within *ICTA 1988, s 416(2)–(6)*, see 16.2 CLOSE COMPANIES), with or without the aid of CONNECTED PERSONS (19). A subsidiary is a '*qualifying subsidiary*' of another company (the '*relevant company*') if the following conditions are met:

(i) *in relation to shares issued on or after 17 March 2004,* the subsidiary is a 51% subsidiary (within *ICTA 1988, s 838*) of the relevant company;

(ii) *in relation to shares issued before 17 March 2004,* the relevant company, or another of its subsidiaries, possesses at least 75% of the issued share capital of, and the voting power in, the subsidiary, and is beneficially entitled to at least 75% of the assets available for distribution to shareholders on a winding-up etc. and of the profits available for distribution to shareholders; and

(iii) in either (i) or (ii) above, no other person has control (within *ICTA 1988, s 840*) of the subsidiary; and no arrangements exist whereby any of these conditions could cease to be satisfied (though see also below).

The fact that a subsidiary or another company is wound up or otherwise dissolved or goes into administration or receivership (both as defined) does not mean the subsidiary ceases to be a qualifying subsidiary, provided that the winding-up etc., and anything done as a consequence of administration or receivership, is for genuine commercial reasons and not part of a tax avoidance scheme or arrangements. Similarly, the fact that arrangements may exist to dispose of the entire interest held in the subsidiary does not prevent the subsidiary from being a qualifying subsidiary of the relevant company if the disposal is to be for commercial reasons and is not to be part of a tax avoidance scheme or arrangements.

[*FA 2000, Sch 15 paras 20, 21, 102(3)(4); FA 2004, s 95, Sch 20 paras 4, 5, 15, Sch 42 Pt 2(12)*].

Property managing subsidiaries requirement. In relation to shares issued after 16 March 2004, the issuing company must not have, at any time in the qualification period, a 'property managing subsidiary' other than one which is its 'qualifying 90% subsidiary'. For this purpose, a '*property managing subsidiary*' is a qualifying subsidiary (see above) whose business consists wholly or mainly in the holding or managing of land or any property deriving its value from land (and the terms 'land' and 'property deriving its value from land' have the same meaning as in *ICTA 1988, s 776*, see 5.14 ANTI-AVOIDANCE). [*FA 2000, Sch 15 para 21A; FA 2004, Sch 20 paras 6, 15*].

Qualifying 90% subsidiary. A subsidiary is a '*qualifying 90% subsidiary*' of the issuing company if the following conditions are met.

(1) The issuing company possesses at least 90% of the issued share capital of, and the voting power in, the subsidiary, and is beneficially entitled to at least 90% of the assets available for distribution to shareholders on a winding-up etc. and of the profits available for distribution to shareholders;

(2) No other person has control (within *ICTA 1988, s 840*) of the subsidiary; and

(3) No arrangements exist whereby (1) or (2) could cease to be satisfied (though see also below).

The fact that a subsidiary or another company is wound up or otherwise dissolved or goes into administration or receivership (both as defined) does not mean the subsidiary ceases to be a qualifying 90% subsidiary of the issuing company, provided that the winding-up etc., and anything done as a consequence of administration or receivership, is for genuine commercial reasons and not part of a tax avoidance scheme or arrangements. Similarly, the fact that arrangements may exist to dispose of the entire interest held in the subsidiary does not prevent the subsidiary from being a qualifying 90% subsidiary of the issuing company if the disposal is to be for commercial reasons and is not to be part of a tax avoidance scheme or arrangements.

On or after 6 April 2007, a company (company A) is also a qualifying 90% subsidiary of the issuing company if:

- company A would be a qualifying 90% subsidiary of another company (company B) if company B were the issuing company, and company B is a 'qualifying 100% subsidiary' of the issuing company; or
- company A is a qualifying 100% subsidiary of company B and company B is a qualifying 90% subsidiary of the issuing company.

No account is taken for this purpose of any control the issuing company may have of company A. The definition of a qualifying 90% subsidary is used to define a 'qualifying 100% subsidiary', replacing the references in that definition to 'at least 90%' with references to '100%'.

[*FA 2000, Sch 15 para 23(10)(11); FA 2004, Sch 20 paras 7(d), 15; FA 2007, Sch 16 para 14*].

Gross assets requirement. The value of the company's gross assets must not exceed £7 million immediately before the issue of the relevant shares or £8 million immediately afterwards. As regards shares issued before 6 April 2006, these limits were £15 million and £16 million respectively. The latter limits continue to apply in relation to shares issued on or after 6 April 2006 to persons who subscribed for them before 22 March 2006. If the company is the parent company of a group, those limits apply by reference to the aggregate value of the gross assets of the group (disregarding certain assets held by any member of the group which correspond to liabilities of another member). The limits may be amended in the future by Treasury Order. [*FA 2000, Sch 15 paras 22, 101; FA 2006, Sch 14 para 3*].

The general approach of HMRC is that the value of a company's gross assets is the sum of the value of all the balance sheet assets. Where accounts are actually drawn up to a date immediately before or after the issue, the balance sheet values are taken provided that they reflect usual accounting standards and the company's normal accounting practice, consistently applied. Where accounts are not drawn up to such a date, such values will be taken from the most recent balance sheet, updated as precisely as practicable on the basis of all the relevant information available to the company. Values so arrived at may need to be reviewed in the light of information contained in the accounts for the period in which the issue was made, and, if they were not available at the time of the issue, those for the preceding period, when they become available. The company's assets immediately before the issue do not include any advance payment received in respect of the issue. Where shares are issued partly paid, the right to the balance is an asset, and, notwithstanding the above, will be taken into account in valuing the assets immediately after the issue regardless of whether it is stated in the balance sheet. (HMRC Statement of Practice, SP 2/00).

Trading activities requirement. Throughout the qualification period (see 22.2 above), the issuing company must meet the trading activities requirement, which is as follows. If the company is a single company (i.e. neither the parent company of a group nor a subsidiary), it must exist wholly for the purpose of carrying on one or more 'qualifying trades' (see 22.7 below) and must actually be carrying on such a trade or preparing to do so. Purposes having no significant effect (other than in relation to incidental matters) on the extent of the company's activities are disregarded. For the ascertainment of the purposes for which a company exists, see HMRC Venture Capital Schemes Manual, VCM 15070, VCM 50140.

If the company is a parent company, the business of the group (treating the activities of the group companies, taken together, as a single business) must not consist wholly or as to a substantial part (i.e. broadly 20%, but see HMRC Venture Capital Schemes Manual, VCM 17040, VCM 50140) in any 'non-qualifying activities', and at least one company in the group (which, in relation to shares issued after 16 March 2004, must be either the issuing company or a qualifying 90% subsidiary (see above) of the issuing company) must satisfy the above trading activity requirement for a single company. '*Non-qualifying activities*' means 'excluded activities' (as in 22.7 below, and with similar exceptions in relation to the letting of ships and the receiving of royalties or licence fees) and non-trading activities.

Where the trading activities requirement would otherwise be met by reason of the company *preparing* to carry on a qualifying trade, the requirement is treated as not having been met at any time if that trade does not commence within two years after the issue of the relevant shares. In determining when the trade begins for this purpose in relation to shares issued on or after 17 March 2004, the carrying on of any trade by a subsidiary before it became a qualifying 90% subsidiary is to be disregarded.

Purposes for which a company exists are disregarded to the extent that they consist of:

(A) (as regards a single company) the holding and managing of property used by the company for one or more qualifying trades carried on by it;

(B) (as regards a group company) any activities within (1), (2) or (4) below; or

(C) (as regards any company) holding shares to which investment relief is attributable (see 22.3 above), unless the holding of such shares is a substantial part of the company's business.

For the purposes of determining the business of a group, activities of a group company are disregarded to the extent that they consist of:

(1) holding shares in or securities of, or making loans to, another group company;

(2) holding and managing property used by a group company for the purposes of one or more qualifying trades carried on by a group company;

(3) holding shares to which investment relief is attributable (see 22.3 above), unless the holding of such shares is a substantial part of the company's business; or

(4) incidental activities of a company which meets the above trading activities requirement for a single company.

A company does not cease to meet the trading activities requirement purely by reason of it or a qualifying subsidiary (see above) being wound up or otherwise dissolved, provided that the winding-up or dissolution is for commercial reasons and not part of a tax avoidance scheme or arrangements. A similar let-out applies in relation to a company or its qualifying subsidiary going into administration or receivership (both as defined) and to anything done as a consequence thereof.

Amendments to the trading activities requirement (including the provisions at 22.7 below) may be made in the future by Treasury Order.

[*FA 2000, Sch 15 paras 23, 24, 101, 102(1)(4)(8); FA 2004, Sch 20 paras 7, 8, 13, 15, Sch 27 para 6(2), Sch 42 Pt 2(12)*].

The corporation tax liability of a qualifying issuing company, and the monitoring of the company during the qualifying period, will be dealt with by the Small Company Enterprise Centre, Ty Glas, Llanishen, Cardiff CF14 5ZG (tel. 029–2032 7400; fax 029–2032 7398; e-mail enterprise.centre@ir.gsi.gov.uk).

Number of employees requirement. When the shares are issued and the company is not part of a group, it must have a full-time equivalent of less than 50 employees. Where the company is the parent company of a group, the total full-time equivalent employees of it and all its subsidiaries must be less then 50 when the shares are issued. For this purpose, directors are included as employees but those on maternity or paternity leave or students on vocational training are not included. Full-time equivalents are to be calculated by adding to the number of full-time employees a just and reasonable fraction for each part-time employee.

[*FA 2000 Sch 15 para 22A; FA 2007 Sch 16 para1*].

22.7 **Qualifying trades.** A trade is a '*qualifying trade*' if it is conducted on a commercial basis with a view to the realisation of profits and it does not, at any time in period B (as defined) consist to a substantial extent in the carrying on of 'excluded activities'. '*Period B*' for these purposes is broadly the period beginning with the date of issue of the shares and ending three years after that date. For these purposes, 'trade' (except in relation to the trade mentioned in (*m*) below) does not include a venture in the nature of trade. '*Excluded activities*' are:

(*a*) dealing in land, commodities or futures, or in shares, securities or other financial instruments; or

(*b*) dealing in goods otherwise than in an ordinary trade of wholesale or retail distribution (see below); or

(*c*) banking, insurance or any other financial activities; or

(*d*) (before 7 March 2001) oil extraction activities (but without prejudice to relief in respect of oil exploration above) for which the activities would otherwise qualify); or

(*e*) leasing or letting or receiving royalties or licence fees; or (*f*) providing legal or accountancy services; or

(*g*) 'property development';

(*h*) farming or market gardening;

(*j*) holding, managing or occupying woodlands, any other forestry activities or timber production;

(*k*) operating or managing hotels or comparable establishments (i.e. guest houses, hostels and other establishments whose main purpose is to offer overnight accommodation with or without catering) or property used as such;

(*l*) operating or managing nursing homes or residential care homes (both as defined) or property used as such;

(*m*) providing services or facilities for any trade, profession or vocation concerned in (*a*) to (*l*) and carried on by another person (other than a parent company), where one person has a 'controlling interest' in both trades.

As regards (*f*) above, the provision of the services of accountancy personnel is the provision of accountancy services (*Castleton Management Services Ltd v Kirkwood (Sp C 276), [2001] SSCD 95*).

Exclusions (*k*) and (*l*) apply only if the person carrying on the activity in question has an estate or interest (e.g. a lease) in the property concerned or occupies that property.

HMRC regard as 'substantial' for the above purposes a part of a trade which consists of 20% or more of total activities, judged by any reasonable measure (normally turnover or capital employed). (HMRC Venture Capital Schemes Manual VCM 17040). As regards (*a*) above, dealing in land includes cases where steps are taken, before selling the land, to make it more attractive to a purchaser; such steps might include the refurbishment of existing buildings. (HMRC Venture Capital Schemes Manual VCM 17050).

As regards (*b*) above, a trade of wholesale distribution is a trade consisting of the offer of goods for sale either to persons for resale (or processing and resale) (which resale must be to members of the general public for their use or consumption) by them. A trade of retail distribution is a trade in which goods are offered or exposed for sale and sold to members of the general public for their use or consumption. A trade is not an ordinary wholesale or retail trade if it consists to a substantial extent of dealing in goods collected or held as an investment (or of that and any other activity within (*a*)–(*m*) above), and a substantial proportion of such goods is held for a significantly longer period than would reasonably be expected for a vendor trying to dispose of them at market value. Whether such trades are 'ordinary' is to be judged having regard to the following features, those under (A) supporting the categorisation as 'ordinary', those under (B) being indicative to the contrary.

(A)

(i) The breaking of bulk.

(ii) The purchase and sale of goods in different markets.

(iii) The employment of staff and incurring of trade expenses other than the cost of goods or of remuneration of persons connected (within *ICTA 2007, s 839*) with a company carrying on such a trade.

(B)

(i) The purchase or sale of goods from or to persons connected (within *ICTA 1988, s 839*) with the trader.

(ii) The matching of purchases with sales.

(iii) The holding of goods for longer than would normally be expected.

(iv) The carrying on of the trade at a place not commonly used for wholesale or retail trading.

(v) The absence of physical possession of the goods by the trader.

As regards the application of (*e*) above in relation to shares issued after 5 April 2000, a trade is not excluded from being a qualifying trade solely because at some time in period B it consists to a substantial extent in the receiving of royalties or licence fees substantially attributable (in terms of value) to the exploitation of 'relevant intangible assets'.

A '*relevant intangible asset*' is an 'intangible asset' the whole or greater part of which (by value) has been created by the issuing company or by a company which was a qualifying subsidiary (as defined) of the issuing company throughout the period during which it created the whole or greater part (by value) of the asset. For this purpose only, '*issuing company*' includes a company all of whose shares were acquired by the issuing company at a time when the only shares issued in the issuing company were subscriber shares and the consideration for the acquisition consisted wholly in the issue of shares in the issuing company. Before 6 April 2007, the whole or greater part of the asset had to be created by the company carrying on the trade or by a company which throughout the creation of the asset was the 'holding company' of that company or a qualifying subsidiary of that holding company. In relation to shares issued before 6 April 2007, an activity is not treated as an excluded activity if it would otherwise have become such an activity on or after that date by reason only of the change in this definition.

A '*holding company*' is for these purposes a company with one or more 51% subsidiaries which is not itself a 51% subsidiary. Where the asset is 'intellectual property', it is treated as created by a company only if the right to exploit it vests in that company (alone or with others). The term '*intellectual property*' incorporates patents, trade marks, copyrights, design rights etc. and foreign equivalents. An '*intangible asset*' is an asset falling to be treated as such under generally accepted accounting practice, including all intellectual property and also industrial information and techniques (see HMRC Venture Capital Schemes Manual VCM 17310).

As regards the application of (*e*) above in relation to shares issued before 6 April 2000, a company engaged throughout period B in the production of original master films, tapes or discs is not excluded from the scheme by reason only of its receipt by way of trade of royalties or licence fees, provided that all royalties and licence fees received by it in the relevant period are in respect of films etc. produced by it in that period or in respect of by-products arising therefrom. The company may also be engaged in the distribution of films produced by it in period B. Similarly, royalties and licence fees attributable to research and development which a company carrying on a trade has engaged in throughout the period B do not prevent the trade being a qualifying trade.

Also as regards (*e*) above, a trade will not be excluded by reason only of its consisting of letting ships, other than offshore installations (previously oil rigs) or pleasure craft (as defined), on charter, provided that

(i) the company beneficially owns all the ships it so lets,

(ii) every ship beneficially owned by the company is UK-registered,

(iii) throughout period B, the company is solely responsible for arranging the marketing of the services of its ships, and

(iv) in relation to every letting on charter, certain conditions as to length and terms of charter, and the arm's length character of the transaction, are fulfilled, and if any of (i)–(iv) above is not fulfilled in relation to certain lettings, the trade is not thereby excluded if those lettings and any other excluded activities taken together do not amount to a substantial part of the trade.

For HMRC's views on the scope of the exclusions in relation to (*e*) above, see Revenue Tax Bulletin August 2001 pp 877, 878.

'*Property development*' in (*g*) above means the development of land by a company, which has (or has had at any time) an 'interest in the land' (as defined), with the sole or main object of realising a gain from the disposal of an interest in the developed land.

As regards (*m*) above, a person has a '*controlling interest*' in a trade etc. carried on by a company if:

- he controls (within *ICTA 1988, s 416*) the company; or
- if the company is close and he or an 'associate' is a director of the company and the owner of, or able to control, more than 30% of its ordinary share capital; or
- if at least half of its ordinary share capital is directly or indirectly owned by him.

In any other case a controlling interest is obtained by such a person being entitled to at least half of the assets used for, or income arising from, the trade etc. In either case, the rights and powers of a person's 'associates' are attributed to him. An '*associate*' of any person is any 'relative' (i.e. spouse, civil partner, ancestor or linear descendant) of that person, the trustee(s) of any settlement in relation to which that person or any relative (living or dead) is or was a settler and, where that person has an interest in any shares or obligations of a company which are subject to any trust or are part of a deceased estate, the trustee(s) of the settlement or the personal representatives of the deceased and, if that person is a company, any other company which has an interest in those shares or obligations. For this purpose, 'settlor' is defined as in *ICTA 2007, ss 685A–D*.

[*ICTA 1988, ss 297, 298, 312; FA 2000, Sch 17 para 13; FA 2001, Sch 15 paras 5, 40; FA 2004, Sch 27 para 4; FA 2007, Sch 16 paras 11(1)(7), 13, 14*].

The Treasury may, by statutory instrument, amend any of the above provisions. [*ICTA 1988, s 298(4)*].

22.8 **GENERAL REQUIREMENTS**

For investment relief to be available in respect of the relevant shares (see 22.2 above), the following requirements (see 22.2(*d*) above) must be met as to the shares, the use of money raised by the issue, the absence of pre-arranged exits, the absence of a tax avoidance motive and the maximum amount raised annually through risk capital schemes. [*FA 2000, Sch 15 para 34*].

The shares. The relevant shares must be ordinary, fully paid up, shares and must be subscribed for wholly in cash. Shares are not fully paid up for this purpose if there is any undertaking to pay cash to the issuing company at a future date or, in relation to shares issued on or after 17 March 2004, to any person at a future date in respect of the shares (i.e. the whole of the subscription price must actually have been paid at the time of issue, see HMRC Venture Capital Schemes Manual, VCM 50020). At no time in the qualification period (see 22.2 above) must the shares carry any present or future preferential right to dividends or to assets on a winding-up, or any present or future right to be redeemed. [*FA 2000, Sch 15 para 35; FA 2004, Sch 20 paras 10, 15*].

Use of money raised. At least 80% of the money raised by the 'relevant issue of shares' must be employed wholly (disregarding any insignificant amount) for the purposes of a 'relevant trade' not later than:

(*a*) the end of the 12 months beginning with the date of issue; or (*b*) if later, the end of the 12 months beginning when the issuing company or a subsidiary begins to carry on the relevant trade,

and *all* the money so raised must be so employed within 12 months after the end of whichever of those 12-month periods applies. These rules apply to shares issued on or after 7 March 2001, and to those issued before that date but after 31 March 2000 to which the relief was attributable immediately before 7 March 2001. Previously, *all* the money had to be so employed before the end of the 12-month period in (*a*) or (*b*) above (whichever applies). In determining when the trade begins for this purpose in relation to shares issued on or after 17 March 2004, the carrying on of any trade by a subsidiary before it became a qualifying 90% subsidiary is to be disregarded.

For these purposes, employing money for the purposes of *preparing* to carry on a trade (other than a notional trade of research and development — see 22.7 above) is equivalent to employing it for the purposes of a trade. Money whose retention can reasonably be regarded as necessary or advisable for financing current trade requirements is regarded as employed for trade purposes (see HMRC Venture Capital Schemes Manual, VCM 12080, VCM 50030).

The '*relevant issue of shares*' means the issue of shares which includes the relevant shares. A '*relevant trade*' is a trade by reference to which the issuing company meets the trading activities requirement in 22.6 above. Where the trade by reference to which the trading activities requirement is met is a notional trade of research and development (see 22.7 above), the term 'relevant trade' also refers to any qualifying trade which is derived or benefits from that notional trade and is carried on by the issuing company or a qualifying 90% subsidiary (or, in relation to shares issued before 17 March 2004, a qualifying subsidiary, see 22.6 above); in this case, the 80% requirement referred to above does not apply, and all the money raised by the issue must be employed for the purposes of that trade before the third anniversary of the date of issue of the shares, notwithstanding that a later date may be given by virtue of (*b*) above.

[*FA 2000, Sch 15 paras 36, 102*(*8*)*; FA 2001, Sch 16 para 5; FA 2004, Sch 20 paras 11, 13, 15*].

No pre-arranged exits. The arrangements (as very broadly defined) under which the relevant shares are issued to the investing company (including arrangements preceding the issue but relating to it and, in certain cases, arrangements made on or after the issue and within the qualification period) must not:

(i) provide for the eventual disposal by the investing company of the relevant shares or other shares or securities of the issuing company;

(ii) provide for the eventual cessation of a trade of the issuing company or a person connected with it;

(iii) provide for the eventual disposal of all, or a substantial part of, the assets of the issuing company or of a person connected with it; or

(iv) provide (by means of any insurance, indemnity, guarantee or otherwise) partial or complete protection for investors against the normal risks attaching to the investment (but excluding commercial arrangements which merely protect the issuing company and/or its subsidiaries against normal business risks).

Arrangements with a view to a company reconstruction within 22.24 below are excluded from (i) above. Arrangements applicable only on an unanticipated winding-up of the issuing company for commercial reasons are excluded from (ii) and (iii) above.

[*FA 2000, Sch 15 paras 37, 102*(*1*)].

No tax avoidance motive. The relevant shares must be issued for commercial reasons and not as part of a tax avoidance scheme or arrangement. [*FA 2000, Sch 15 para 38*].

For the year up to the date of the current issue, the amount of 'relevant investments' made in the issuing company (or in any company which is a subsidiary at any time in the year) must not exceed £2 million. A '*relevant investment*' in a company is one which is made by a VCT or under a corporate venturing or EIS arrangement. VCT investments made before 6 April 2007 or from 'protected money' are not included. '*Protected money*' is money raised by an issue of shares or securities of the VCT before 6 April 2007, or money derived from the investment of such money.

[*FA 2000 Sch 15 para 35A; FA 2007 Sch 16 paras 4, 8*].

22.9 **ADVANCE CLEARANCE**

A *potential* qualifying issuing company (see 22.6 above) may apply to HMRC for an advance clearance notice in respect of an issue of shares. An application must contain particulars, declarations and undertakings as required and must disclose all material facts and circumstances. An advance clearance notice states that, on the basis of the particulars etc. provided by the applicant, HMRC are satisfied that, at the time the shares are issued, the requirements of 22.6–22.8 above will be met (or, in the case of a requirement that can only be met in the future, will for the time being be met).

Applications for clearance should be sent to Small Company Enterprise Centre, Centre for Research and Intelligence (CRI), Ty Glas, Llanishen, Cardiff CF14 5ZG. For guidance on HMRC requirements as to content of applications for advance clearance, the information and documents needed and the undertakings required, see HMRC Statement of Practice, SP 1/00. Where subscribers to the same issue of shares are expected to include individuals who may wish to claim relief under the Enterprise Investment Scheme (see Tolley's Income Tax under Enterprise Investment Scheme), any request for informal clearance under that scheme should accompany the application under the Corporate Venturing Scheme.

Within 30 days after receiving an application (or within 30 days after an 'information notice' is complied with), HMRC must either issue an information notice (or further information notice), issue an advance clearance notice, or refuse the application. An '*information notice*' is a notice requiring further particulars to be provided within such time, not being less than 30 days, as is stated therein. If the applicant fails to comply timeously with an information notice, HMRC need not proceed further with the application. If the shares in question are issued before the advance clearance notice is given or the application refused, then again HMRC need not proceed further.

Within 30 days after a refusal of an application, or a failure to give a decision, the applicant can require HMRC to transmit the application, together with any information notices given and further particulars provided, to the Special Commissioners, whose approval, if given, has effect as if it were an advance clearance notice given by HMRC.

An advance clearance notice is rendered void if it transpires that any particulars provided did not fully and accurately disclose all facts and circumstances material for the decision, or if the applicant or any subsidiary (including any new subsidiary) fails to act in accordance with any declaration or undertaking given as part of the application.

[*FA 2000, Sch 15 paras 89–92*].

22.10 **WITHDRAWAL OR REDUCTION OF INVESTMENT RELIEF**

Investment relief falls to be withdrawn or reduced on a disposal of the relevant shares (see 22.11 below), if value is received in respect of the shares (see 22.12–22.15 below), or on the grant of certain options relating to the shares (see 22.16 below).

Where investment relief given falls to be withdrawn or reduced, and also where it is found not to have been due, the withdrawal etc. is achieved by means of an assessment under Schedule D, Case VI for the accounting period of the investing company *in which the relief was given.* For relief to be withdrawn on the grounds that the issuing company is not a qualifying issuing company (see 22.6 above), or that the general requirements at 22.8 above are not met, or by virtue of value received by the investing company (see 22.12 below) or other persons (see 22.15 below), certain statutory notice procedures must be followed. The investing company may give notice of appeal, within 30 days, against an HMRC notice pending withdrawal of relief on such grounds (as if the giving of that notice were the disallowance of a claim other than for discharge or repayment of tax — see 15.8 CLAIMS).

HMRC cannot make an assessment to withdraw (or reduce) investment relief, or give statutory notice pending withdrawal of relief on the above-mentioned grounds, more than six years after the end of whichever is the later of the following accounting periods:

(*a*) the accounting period in which falls the deadline for employing money raised by the issue of the shares (see 22.8 above); and

(*b*) the accounting period in which occurs the event giving rise to withdrawal (or reduction) of relief.

The above is subject to the extended time limit for assessments in cases of fraud or negligence (see 7.6 ASSESSMENTS).

In most cases, interest on overdue tax runs from the date of the event giving rise to withdrawal (or reduction) of relief, if this is later than the normal due date, or the latest such date, for payment of corporation tax for the accounting period for which the assessment is made (see 53.2 PAYMENT OF TAX).

[*FA 2000, Sch 15 paras 60–63*].

Information. Certain events giving rise to withdrawal or reduction of investment relief must be notified to HMRC, generally within 60 days, by the investing company or the issuing company (or any person connected with the issuing company and having knowledge of the matter), as the case may be. HMRC have power to require information from such persons where they have reason to believe that such notice should have been given or from a person whom they believe to have given or received value which would have triggered a requirement to give such notice but for the amount of value being insignificant (see 22.12 below). The penalty provisions of *TMA 1970, s 98* apply in the event of non-compliance with these information provisions. [*FA 2000, Sch 15 paras 64–66, Sch 16 para 1*].

22.11 **Disposal.** Where, during the qualification period (see 22.2 above), the investing company disposes of any shares to which relief is attributable (see 22.3 above) and which it has held continuously since their issue (see 22.20(*a*) below), relief is withdrawn or reduced as set out below. See 22.10 above re consequences of withdrawal etc.

If the disposal is either:

(*a*) by way of bargain at arm's length for full consideration; or

(*b*) by way of a distribution on a dissolution or winding-up of the issuing company; or

(*c*) a disposal within *TCGA 1992, s 24(1)* (entire loss, destruction etc. of asset); or

(*d*) a deemed disposal under *TCGA 1992, s 24(2)* (assets of negligible value),

the relief attributable to the shares disposed of is withdrawn, or is reduced by 20% of the disposal consideration (if such reduction would not amount to full withdrawal). If the relief initially obtained was less than 20% of the amount subscribed for those shares (i.e. because the company's corporation tax liability was insufficient to fully absorb the available relief), the reduction is correspondingly restricted.

In the case of any other disposal, for example a transaction not at arm's length, the relief attributable to the shares disposed of is withdrawn.

[*FA 2000, Sch 15 para 46*].

For the above purposes, shares are regarded as being disposed of if they are so regarded for the purposes of corporation tax on chargeable gains, and see also 22.23 below (certain company reconstructions and amalgamations treated as disposals). [*FA 2000, Sch 15 para 96*]. In the case of a part disposal, see 22.17 below for the rules for identifying shares disposed of.

22.12 **Value received by investing company.** Subject to 22.14 below (replacement value), where during the 'period of restriction' the investing company 'receives value' (see 22.13 below), other than an 'amount of insignificant value', from the issuing company, investment relief attributable to the relevant shares is withdrawn, or is reduced by 20% of the amount of value received (if such reduction would not amount to full withdrawal). If the relief initially obtained was less than 20% of the amount subscribed for those shares (i.e. because the company's corporation tax liability was insufficient to fully absorb the available relief), the reduction is correspondingly restricted. These provisions apply equally to receipts of value by and from persons connected (within *ICTA 1988, s 839*, see 19 CONNECTED PERSONS), at any time in the period of restriction, with the investing company or, as the case may be, the issuing company. See 22.13 below for the meaning of 'value received' and the determination of the amount of value received. See 22.10 above re consequences of withdrawal etc.

The '*period of restriction*' in relation to the relevant shares is the period beginning one year before their issue and ending at the end of the qualification period in 22.2 above.

Where two or more issues of shares have been made by the same issuing company to the same investing company, in relation to each of which investment relief is claimed, and value is received during a period of restriction relating to more than one such issue, the value received is apportioned between them by reference to the amounts subscribed for each of those issues.

An '*amount of insignificant value*' is an amount of value which:

(*a*) does not exceed £1,000; or

(*b*) is insignificant in relation to the amount subscribed by the investing company for the relevant shares.

If at any time in the period beginning one year before the date of issue of the relevant shares and ending with the date of issue, there are in existence arrangements (as very broadly defined) providing for the investing company to receive, or become entitled to receive, any value from the issuing company at any time in the period of restriction (see above), no amount of value received by the investing company is treated as an amount of insignificant value.

There are provisions to aggregate a receipt of value, whether insignificant or not, with amounts of insignificant value received previously, and treating that aggregate, if it is not itself an amount of insignificant value, as an amount of value received at the time of the latest actual receipt.

Where relief is withdrawn or reduced by reason of a disposal (see 22.11 above), the investing company is not treated as receiving value from the issuing company in respect of the disposal.

[*FA 2000, Sch 15 paras 47, 48, 51–53, 102(1)*].

22.13 *Meaning of, and amount of, value received.* The investing company '*receives value*' from the issuing company if the latter (and see 22.12 above re connected persons):

(*a*) repays, redeems or repurchases any part of the investing company's holding of the issuing company's share capital or securities, or makes any payment to the investing company in respect of the cancellation of any of the issuing company's share capital or any security;

(*b*) repays, in pursuance of any arrangements for or in connection with the acquisition of the relevant shares, any debt owed to the investing company other than one incurred by the issuing company on or after the date of issue of the shares and otherwise than in consideration of the extinguishment of a debt incurred before that date;

(*c*) makes any payment to the investing company in respect of the cancellation of any debt owed to it;

(*d*) releases or waives any liability of the investing company to the issuing company (which it is deemed to have done if discharge of the liability is twelve months or more overdue) or discharges, or undertakes to discharge, any liability of the investing company to a third person;

(*e*) makes a loan or advance to the investing company which has not been repaid in full before the issue of the relevant shares; for this purpose a loan includes any debt incurred, other than an ordinary trade debt (as defined), and any debt due to a third person which is assigned to the issuing company;

(*f*) provides a benefit or facility for the directors or employees of the investing company or any of their associates (as defined), except in circumstances such that, if a *payment* had been made of equal value, it would have been a 'qualifying payment';

(*g*) disposes of an asset to the investing company for no consideration or for consideration less than market value (as defined), or acquires an asset from the investing company for consideration exceeding market value; or

(*h*) makes a payment to the investing company other than a 'qualifying payment'.

References above to a debt or liability do not include one which would be discharged by making a 'qualifying payment'. References to a payment or disposal include one made indirectly to, or to the order of, or for the benefit of, the person in question.

Each of the following is a '*qualifying payment*':

(i) a reasonable (in relation to their market value) payment for any goods, services or facilities provided by the investing company in the course of trade or otherwise;

(ii) the payment of interest at no more than a reasonable commercial rate on money lent;

(iii) the payment of a dividend or other distribution which represents no more than a normal return on investment;

(iv) a payment to acquire an asset at no more than its market value;

(v) a payment not exceeding a reasonable and commercial rent for property occupied; and

(vi) a payment discharging an ordinary trade debt.

The *amount of value received* is:

(A) in a case within (*a*), (*b*) or (*c*) above, the amount received or, if greater, the market value of the shares, securities or debt in question;

(B) in a case within (*d*) above, the amount of the liability;

(C) in a case within (*e*) above, the amount of the loan etc. less any amount repaid before the issue of the relevant shares;

(D) in a case within (*f*) above, the cost (net of any consideration given for it by the recipient or his associate) of providing the benefit etc.;

(E) in a case within (*g*) above, the difference between market value and the consideration received (if any); and

(F) in a case within (*h*) above, the amount of the payment.

[*FA 2000, Sch 15 paras 49, 50, 99, 102(5)*].

22.14 *Replacement value.* The provisions at 22.12 above are disapplied if the person from whom the value was received (the '*original supplier*') receives, by way of a 'qualifying receipt' and whether before or after the original receipt of value, at least equivalent replacement value from the original recipient. From 7 March 2001, any reduction in the value originally received by virtue of its having been received during a period of restriction relating to more than one issue is disregarded for this purpose. Thus in any case where there is a receipt of value at a time which falls in two or more periods of restriction relating to investments made in the issuing company, investment relief will be withdrawn in respect of all those investments unless restitution is made of the whole amount of the value received. A receipt is a '*qualifying receipt*' if it arises by reason of:

(*a*) a payment by the original recipient to the original supplier other than an 'excepted payment' (before 7 March 2001, such a payment other than a qualifying payment as in 22.13 above or a payment for any shares or securities in any company in circumstances not within (*c*) below);

(*b*) (where the original receipt of value falls within 22.13(*d*) above) an event having the effect of reversing the original event; or

(*c*) the acquisition of an asset by the original recipient from the original supplier for consideration exceeding market value (as defined), or the disposal of an asset by the original recipient to the original supplier for no consideration or for consideration less than market value. (Before 7 March 2001, this applied only where the original receipt of value fell within 22.13(*g*) above.)

An '*excepted payment*' is:

(I) a reasonable (in relation to their market value) payment for any goods, services or facilities provided (in the course of trade or otherwise) by the original supplier;

(II) a payment of interest at no more than a reasonable commercial rate on money lent to the original recipient;

(III) a payment not exceeding a reasonable and commercial rent for property occupied by the original recipient;

(IV) a payment within 22.13(iii), (iv) or (vi) above; or

(V) a payment for any shares or securities in any company in circumstances not within (*c*) above.

References in (I)-(III) above to the original supplier or recipient include a reference to any person who at any time in the period of restriction is an 'associate' of his (within *FA 2000, Sch 15 para 99*) or, in the case of an original supplier, is 'connected' with him (within *ICTA 1988, s 839*).

The amount of replacement value is:

(i) in a case within (*a*) above, the amount of the payment;

(ii) in a case within (*b*) above, the same as the amount of the original value; and

(iii) in a case within (*c*) above, the difference between market value and the consideration received (if any).

The receipt of replacement value is disregarded if:

(A) it occurs before the start of the period of restriction (see 22.12 above);

(B) there was an unreasonable delay in its occurrence; or

(C) it occurs more than 60 days after the relief falling to be withdrawn (or reduced) has been determined on appeal.

It is also disregarded if it has previously been set against a receipt of value for these purposes.

Where:

(1) the receipt of replacement value is a qualifying receipt (as above),;and

(2) the event giving rise to the receipt is (or includes) a subscription for shares by the investing company or a person connected (within *ICTA 1988, s 839*, see 19 CONNECTED PERSONS) with it at any time in the period of restriction,

the subscriber is not eligible for investment relief, enterprise investment scheme income tax relief (see Tolley's Income Tax) or enterprise investment scheme capital gains deferral relief (see Tolley's Capital Gains Tax) in relation to those shares or any other shares in the same issue.

[*FA 2000, Sch 15 paras 54, 55, 102(3)(5); FA 2001, Sch 16 paras 6, 7*].

22.15 **Value received by other persons.** Investment relief is withdrawn (or reduced) in certain cases of value received by persons other than the investing company (see 22.10 above re consequences of withdrawal etc.). This applies where, during the period of restriction (as in 22.12 above), the issuing company or a 'subsidiary':

(*a*) repays, redeems or repurchases any part of its share capital from a member (other than the investing company) unless the member thereby suffers a withdrawal or reduction of any investment relief, enterprise investment scheme income tax relief (see Tolley's Income Tax) or enterprise investment scheme capital gains deferral relief (see Tolley's Capital Gains Tax) attributable to his shares (or, from 7 March 2001, is only prevented from suffering such a withdrawal or reduction under the 'insignificant value' rules); or

(*b*) makes any payment to any such member in respect of the cancellation or extinguishment of any of the share capital of the issuing company or subsidiary.

The investment relief attributable to the relevant shares held by the investing company is withdrawn, or is reduced by 20% of the amount received by the member (if such reduction would not amount to full withdrawal). If the relief initially obtained was less than 20% of the amount subscribed for those shares (i.e. because the company's corporation tax liability was insufficient to fully absorb the available relief), the reduction is correspondingly restricted. The amount received is also apportioned between investing companies (by reference to amounts subscribed) where the receipt of value causes a withdrawal or reduction of more than one such company's investment relief. Where the receipt of value falls into overlapping periods of restriction in relation to more than one issue of shares which includes shares to which investment relief is attributable, the value received is similarly apportioned between issues.

If the amount received by the member in question is insignificant in relation to the remaining share capital (from 7 March 2001, the remaining issued share capital) of the issuing company or, as the case may be, subsidiary, it is disregarded. In applying this test, the market value, immediately before the event concerned, of the shares to which the event relates is substituted for the amount received if this would give a greater amount. The assumption is made that the shares in question are cancelled at the time of the event. This let-out does not apply if at any time in the period beginning one year before the date of issue of the relevant shares and ending with the date of issue, there are in existence arrangements (as very broadly defined) providing for a payment within these provisions to be made, or entitlement to such a payment to come into being, at any time in the period of restriction.

For the above purposes, a '*subsidiary*' is a company which is a 51% subsidiary of the issuing company at any time in the period of restriction, whether or not at the time of receipt of value.

The above provisions do not apply to the redemption, within twelve months of issue, of any share capital of nominal value equal to the authorised minimum issued to comply with *Companies Act 1985, s 117* (or NI equivalent).

[*FA 2000, Sch 15 paras 56–58, 102(1); FA 2001, Sch 16 paras 8, 9*].

22.16 **Put options and call options.** Where there is granted during the qualification period (see 22.2 above):

(*a*) an option, the exercise of which would bind the grantor to purchase any of the relevant shares from the investing company; or

(*b*) an option, the exercise of which would bind the grantor, in this case the investing company, to sell any of the relevant shares,

investment relief attributable (see 22.3 above) to those of the relevant shares which would (on given assumptions) be treated as disposed of on exercise of the option is withdrawn. See 22.10 above re consequences of withdrawal.

[*FA 2000, Sch 15 para 59*].

22.17 **IDENTIFICATION RULES**

The rules below apply, for the purpose of identifying shares disposed of, where a company makes a part disposal of a holding of shares of the same class in the same company, and the holding includes shares to which investment relief is attributable (see 22.3 above) and which have been held continuously (see 22.20(*a*) below) since the time of issue. The rules apply for the purposes of the corporate venturing scheme and for the purposes of corporation tax on chargeable gains generally. As regards the latter, the normal rules (see Tolley's Capital Gains Tax under Shares and Securities) are disapplied.

Where shares comprised in the holding have been acquired on different days, a disposal is identified with acquisitions on a first in/first out basis. In matching the shares disposed of with shares acquired on a particular day, shares to which investment relief is attributable and which have been held continuously are treated as being disposed of *after* any other shares acquired on that day.

If, on a reorganisation of share capital (e.g. a scrip issue), a new holding falls, by virtue of *TCGA 1992, s 127*, to be equated with the original shares (see Tolley's Capital Gains Tax under Shares and Securities, and see also 22.22 below), shares comprised in the new holding are deemed for the above purposes to have been acquired when the original shares were acquired.

[*FA 2000, Sch 15 para 93; FA 2002, Sch 9 para 6(4); FA 2006, s 72(2)(e)*].

22.18 **CHARGEABLE GAINS AND ALLOWABLE LOSSES**

A gain on the disposal at any time by the investing company of shares to which investment relief is attributable (see 22.3 above) is a chargeable gain, though see 22.21 below as regards possibility of deferral relief. A loss on such a disposal is an allowable loss — see 22.19 below as to the computation of the loss and 22.20 below as regards possibility of setting the loss against income rather than gains. For the rules for identifying disposals with acquisitions, see 22.17 above.

22.19 **Computation of allowable loss.** If a loss would otherwise accrue on a disposal by the investing company of shares to which investment relief is attributable, and the investment relief does not fall to be withdrawn (as opposed to reduced) as a result of the disposal (see 22.10 above), the company's acquisition cost for the purposes of corporation tax on chargeable gains is reduced by the amount of investment relief attributable to the shares immediately after the disposal, but not so as to convert the loss into a chargeable gain. This applies only if the condition at 22.20(*a*) below (shares held continuously) is met from issue to disposal. [*FA 2000, Sch 15 para 94*].

22.20 **Set-off of allowable loss against income.** Subject to all the conditions at (*a*)–(*c*) below being satisfied and a claim being made, an allowable loss, on a disposal by the investing company of shares to which investment relief is attributable (see 22.3 above), may be set against *income* (as an alternative to setting it against chargeable gains in the normal way — see 11.3 CAPITAL GAINS). The loss is as computed after applying the reduction at 22.19 above. The conditions are as follows.

(*a*) The shares must have been held continuously by the company from time of issue to time of disposal. If, during any period:

(i) the company was deemed under any provision of *TCGA 1992* to have disposed of and immediately reacquired the shares; or

(ii) following a scheme of reconstruction or amalgamation within *TCGA 1992, s 136* (or which would have been within that *section* but for the provisions of *TCGA 1992, s 137(1)*, which excludes schemes effected other than for *bona fide* commercial reasons or for tax avoidance), the company was deemed by virtue of 22.23 below to have made a disposal of shares which it retained under the scheme,

it is not treated for the purposes of the corporate venturing scheme provisions as having held the shares continuously throughout that period.

(*b*) The investment relief must not fall to be withdrawn in full as a result of the disposal.

(*c*) The disposal must be either:

(i) by way of bargain at arm's length for full consideration; or

(ii) by way of a distribution on a dissolution or winding-up of the issuing company; or

(iii) a disposal within *TCGA 1992, s 24(1)* (entire loss, destruction etc. of asset); or

(iv) a deemed disposal under *TCGA 1992, s 24(2)* (assets of negligible value).

The set-off is against income of the accounting period in which the loss is incurred. As regards any unrelieved balance, the claim may be extended to income of accounting periods ending within the 12 months immediately preceding the accounting period in which the loss is incurred. Income of an accounting period beginning before, and ending within, that 12 months is apportioned on a time basis so as to exclude income thereby deemed to have accrued prior to that 12-month period. The income of each accounting period included in the claim is treated as reduced by the loss, or by so much of it as cannot be relieved in a later accounting period. Where claims are made to relieve two or more losses, they are relieved in the order in which they were incurred. Relief is given before any relief claimed under *ICTA 1988, s 573* (loss incurred by investment company on disposal of unlisted shares — see 47.19 LOSSES) and before any deduction for charges on income or other amounts which may be deducted from or set against or treated as reducing profits of any description. Once relief has been obtained under these provisions for an amount of loss, that amount cannot be relieved under *section 573(2)* or against chargeable gains.

Claims must be made within two years after the end of the accounting period in which the loss is incurred.

Where a claim is made under these provisions, *TCGA 1992, s 30* (value shifting to give tax-free benefit, see 11.17 CAPITAL GAINS) has effect in relation to the disposal if *any* benefit is conferred, whether tax-free or not. No loss relief against income is available if the disposal is the result of a scheme of reconstruction effected for tax avoidance rather than commercial reasons.

[*FA 2000, Sch 15 paras 67–72, 97; FA 2002, Sch 9 para 6(2)*].

22.21 **Deferral relief** is available where a chargeable gain would otherwise accrue to the investing company:

(*a*) on a disposal of shares to which investment relief was attributable (see 22.3 above) immediately before the disposal and which satisfy the condition at 22.20(*a*) above (shares held continuously) from issue to disposal; or

(*b*) on the occurrence of a chargeable event under these provisions (see below),

and the company makes a 'qualifying investment'. A '*qualifying investment*' is a subscription for shares ('*qualifying shares*') on which investment relief is obtained under the corporate venturing scheme, other than shares issued by a 'prohibited company'. The qualifying shares must be issued to the investing company within the one year immediately preceding or the three years immediately following the time the chargeable gain in question accrues. If the qualifying shares are issued *before* the gain accrues, they must have been held continuously (see 22.20(*a*) above) by the investing company from issue until the time the gain accrues, and investment relief must still be attributable to them. A '*prohibited company*' means either:

(i) the company whose shares are disposed of (as in (*a*) above) or, or as the case may be, in relation to whose shares the chargeable event occurred (as in (*b*) above); or

(ii) a company which, when the gain accrues or when the qualifying shares are issued, is a member of the same group as the company in (i) above.

Deferral relief is said to be 'attributable to shares' if expenditure on those shares has been used to defer the whole or part of a chargeable gain and no chargeable event has occurred resulting in the deferred gain being brought back into charge.

The following themselves become qualifying shares:

(A) any bonus shares, issued in respect of the qualifying shares and being shares in the same company, of the same class and carrying the same rights;

(B) any shares issued on a company reconstruction within 22.24 below in exchange for qualifying shares.

Postponement of the original gain. On a claim by the investing company, the whole or part of the chargeable gain can be deferred. The amount to be deferred is the lower of:

(I) the amount of the gain (or the amount remaining in charge after any previous deferral relief claim);

(II) the amount subscribed for the qualifying shares (to the extent that it has not been used in previous deferral relief claims); and

(III) the amount specified by the company in the claim.

No time limit is specified for making a claim, so the general six-year time limit applies as in 15.7 CLAIMS.

Deferred gain becoming chargeable. The deferred gain will become chargeable on the occurrence of, *and at the time of*, one of the following chargeable events:

(1) a disposal of qualifying shares by the investing company; or

(2) any other event giving rise to a withdrawal of, or reduction in, the investment relief attributable to qualifying shares (see 22.10 above).

If the qualifying investment is made before the gain accrues, there is disregarded for the purposes of (2) above any reduction made by reason of an event occurring before the gain accrues.

The chargeable gain accruing to the investing company at the time of the chargeable event is equal to so much of the deferred gain as is attributable to the shares in relation to which the chargeable event occurs. For these purposes, a proportionate part of the net deferred gain (i.e. the deferred gain less any amount brought into charge on an earlier chargeable event, e.g. a part disposal) is attributed to each of the qualifying shares held immediately before the chargeable event. Thus, a part disposal of qualifying shares brings into charge a proportionate part of the deferred gain.

Provision is made to ensure that a previously deferred gain accruing as above is brought into charge under *TCGA 1992, s 10B* (see 60.5 RESIDENCE — previously under *TCGA 1992, s 10*, see 60.6 RESIDENCE) in the case of a non-UK resident company carrying on a trade or vocation through a UK branch or agency.

[*FA 2000, Sch 15 paras 73–79; FA 2003, Sch 27 para 8*].

22.22 COMPANY RESTRUCTURING

Reorganisations of share capital. The following applies where a company holds shares in another company, being shares of the same class, held in the same capacity and forming part of the ordinary share capital of that other company, and there is a reorganisation within the meaning of *TCGA 1992, s 126*. If the shares fall within two or more of the categories below, *TCGA 1992, s 127*, or, where appropriate, *TCGA 1992, s 116*, applies separately to each category. (This is subject to the disapplication of those provisions in the circumstances set out below.) The categories are:

(*a*) shares to which deferral relief is attributable (see 22.21 above);

(*b*) shares to which investment relief, but not deferral relief, is attributable (see 22.3 above) and which have been held continuously (see 22.20(*a*) above) by the company since they were issued; and

(*c*) shares in neither of the categories above.

[*FA 2000, Sch 15 para 80*].

Rights issues etc. Where:

(i) a reorganisation (within *TCGA 1992, s 126*) involves an allotment of shares or debentures in respect of and in proportion to an existing holding;

(ii) investment relief is attributable (see 22.3 above) to the shares in the existing holding or to the allotted shares; and

(iii) if investment relief is attributable to the shares in the existing holding, those shares have been held continuously (see 22.20(*a*) above) by the company since they were issued,

the share reorganisation rules of *TCGA 1992, ss 127–130* are disapplied. The effect is that the allotted shares are treated as a separate holding acquired at the time of the reorganisation. This does not apply in the case of bonus shares where these are issued in respect of shares comprised in the existing holding and are of the same class and carry the same rights as those shares.

If, in a case otherwise within *TCGA 1992, s 116(10)* (see Tolley's Capital Gains Tax under Qualifying Corporate Bonds):

(A) the old asset consists of shares to which investment relief is attributable and which have been held continuously (see 22.20(*a*) above) by the company since they were issued; and

(B) the new asset consists of a qualifying corporate bond,

the usual treatment is disapplied. The effect is that the investing company is deemed to have disposed of the shares at the time of the relevant transaction, and the resulting chargeable gain or allowable loss crystallises *at that time*.

[*FA 2000, Sch 15 para 81*].

22.23 **Company reconstructions and amalgamations.** Subject to 22.24 below, *TCGA 1992, s 135* and *s 136*, which equate the new holding with the original shares, are disapplied in the following circumstances:

(a) a company holds shares in another company (Company A);

(*b*) investment relief is attributable (see 22.3 above) to those shares;

(*c*) those shares have been held continuously (see 22.20(*a*) above) by the investing company since they were issued; and

(*d*) there is a reconstruction or amalgamation whereby a third company issues shares or debentures in exchange for, or in respect of, Company A shares or debentures.

The result is that the transaction is treated, both for the purposes of the corporate venturing scheme provisions and for the purposes of corporation tax on chargeable gains generally, as a disposal of the original shares (and an acquisition of a new holding).

[*FA 2000, Sch 15 paras 82, 96*].

22.24 **Issuing company becoming wholly-owned subsidiary of new holding company.** Notwithstanding 22.23 above, *TCGA 1992, s 135* is not disapplied (and there is thus no disposal and acquisition) where, by means entirely of an exchange of shares, all the shares in one company (the '*old shares*') are acquired by another company, and the conditions below are satisfied. Following such a share exchange, the shares thereby issued by the acquiring company (the '*new shares*') stand in place of the old shares, so that:

(i) any investment relief or deferral relief attributable to the old shares (see, respectively, 22.3, 22.21 above) is attributed to the new shares for which they were exchanged;

(ii) the new shares are treated as having been issued at the time the old shares were issued and as having been held continuously (see 22.20(*a*) above) by the investing company since that time (provided the old shares had been so held);

(iii) generally speaking, anything done, or required to be done, by or in relation to the acquired company is treated as having been done etc. by or in relation to the acquiring company; and

(iv) certain of the requirements of 22.5, 22.6 above which were met to any extent in relation to the old shares are deemed to be met to the same extent in relation to the new shares.

The conditions to be satisfied are as follows.

(*a*) The consideration for the old shares consists entirely of the issue of the new shares.

(*b*) New shares are issued only at a time when the issued shares in the acquiring company consist entirely of subscriber shares (and any new shares already issued in consideration of old shares).

(*c*) The consideration for new shares of each description consists entirely of old shares of the 'corresponding description'.

(*d*) New shares of each description are issued to holders of old shares of the 'corresponding description' in respect of, and in proportion to, their holdings.

(*e*) Before any exchange of shares takes place, HMRC have given an 'approval notification'.

For the purposes of (*c*) and (*d*) above, old and new shares are of a '*corresponding description*' if, assuming they were shares in the same company, they would be of the same class and carry the same rights. All references above to 'shares' (other than to 'subscriber shares') include references to 'securities'. An '*approval notification*' (see (*e*) above) is given by

HMRC, on an application by either company involved, if they are satisfied that the share exchange will be effected for commercial reasons and does not form part of a scheme or arrangements to avoid liability to corporation tax or capital gains tax.

The provisions of *FA 2000, Sch 15 para 80* (see 22.22 above) are applied to a reconstruction within the above provisions where a company's holding of 'old shares' falls within more than one of the categories there mentioned.

[*FA 2000, Sch 15 paras 83–87*].

For interaction between these provisions and the exemptions relating to substantial company shareholdings, see 13.15 CAPITAL GAINS—SUBSTANTIAL SHAREHOLDINGS.

23 Distributions

Cross-references. See 9.6 BUILDING SOCIETIES, 32 GROUPS OF COMPANIES, 46.35 LOAN RELATIONSHIPS, 49 NON-CORPORATE DISTRIBUTION RATE and 57 PURCHASE BY A COMPANY OF ITS OWN SHARES.

Simon's Direct Tax Service D1.1.

The headings in this chapter are as follows.

23.1 SCOPE OF DISTRIBUTIONS

The term 'distribution' is widely defined in *ICTA 1988, ss 209-211*. Subject to the exceptions listed at 23.15 below, it includes any of the items listed below as follows. See also the additional items at 23.18, 23.19 below.

(a) Dividends (including capital dividends). [*ICTA 1988, s 209(2)(a)*].

(b) Any distribution in respect of shares (see 23.2 below).

(c) Issue of redeemable share capital or any security (see 23.3 below).

(d) Interest or other distribution exceeding a reasonable commercial return (see 23.4 and 23.7 below).

(e) Thin capitalisation — interest or other distribution paid by 75% subsidiary (see 23.5 and 23.7 below).

(f) Interest in respect of certain securities (see 23.6 and 23.7 below).

The following definitions are provided at 23.11 to 23.14.

23.11 'new consideration'

23.12 'shares'

23.13 'security'

23.14 'in respect of' shares'

See also HMRC Tax Bulletin Issue 76, April 2005 p 1199 for HMRC's view that, in the majority of cases, where goodwill is transferred by a sole trader (or partnership) to a company on the incorporation of a business, before the company has commenced trading, at a value higher than its market value, the excess is to be treated as a distribution for the purposes of *ICTA 1988,s 209(2)(b)* (see 23.2 below) or *209(4)* (see 23.8 below). If it is clear that there was no intention to transfer the goodwill at excess value and that reasonable efforts were made to carry out the transfer at market value by using a professional valuation, the distribution can be 'unwound'. Where the transfer takes place on or after 1 April 2004, the distribution is to be taken into account in computing the corporation tax liability at the NCD rate (see 49 NON-CORPORATE DISTRIBUTION RATE).

Simon's Direct Tax Service. See **D1.102, D1.103**.

23.2 **Distribution in respect of shares.** A distribution includes any distribution (whether in cash or otherwise) in respect of shares in the company the cost of which is borne by the company, except in so far as:

(i) it represents a repayment of share capital (but see 23.10 below); or

(ii) it is equal to any 'new consideration' (see 23.11 below) received by the company for the distribution.

[*ICTA 1988, s 209(2)(b), s 254(9)*].

However, a transfer of assets (other than cash) or of liabilities made between companies resident in the UK is not to be treated as a distribution provided that neither company is the '51% subsidiary' of a non-resident company and that the companies are not under the control of the same person or persons either at the time of, or as a result of, the transfer. [*ICTA 1988, s 209(6)*].

A company is a '*51% subsidiary*' if more than 50% of its ordinary share capital is owned directly or indirectly by another. [*ICTA 1988, s 838(1)(a)*].

See also, however, 23.8 below and 57 PURCHASE BY A COMPANY OF ITS OWN SHARES.

23.3 **Issue of redeemable share capital or any security.** A distribution includes the issue in respect of shares or securities in the company of redeemable share capital or any security (in so far as it is not referable to 'new consideration', see 23.11 below). [*ICTA 1988, s 209(2)(c)*]. The value of any redeemable share capital (or security) is the amount of the share capital (or principal) together with any premium payable on redemption (or maturity), or in a winding-up, or in any other circumstances. [*ICTA 1988, s 209(8)*]. The paying-up of issued share capital by the company also falls under this head. [*ICTA 1988, s 254(10)*]. See also 23.17 below.

23.4 **Interest or other distribution exceeding a reasonable commercial return.** A distribution includes any interest or other distribution in respect of securities (except any part representing principal), the cost of which is borne by the company, to the extent that it exceeds a reasonable commercial return for the use of the principal secured. [*ICTA 1988, s 209(2)(d)*]. See also 23.7 below.

With effect for interest etc. paid **after 16 April 2002**, where a security is issued by a company for new consideration (see 20.12 below) in excess of the amount of the principal secured by the security, the amount of the principal so secured is treated for this purpose as increased to the amount of the new consideration, subject to the further provisions below. [*ICTA 1988, s 209(3AA); FA 2002, s 102(1)*].

Link to shares of company or associated company (i.e. where one company 'controls' the other or both are under common control). *Section 209(3AA)* does not apply where the security is one which to a significant extent reflects dividends or other distributions in respect of, or fluctuations in the value of, shares in one or more companies each of which is either the issuing company or an associated company. There is, however, an exception (so that *section 209(3AA) does* apply) if the security is issued in the ordinary course of its business by a bank (within *ICTA 1988, s 840A*, see 8.1 BANKS) or 'securities house' (as defined) and the link to shares is by reason only that the security reflects fluctuations in an index whose underlying subject matter is shares in other companies as well as the issuing company (or associated companies), those other companies' shares representing a significant proportion of the underlying market value. '*Control*' for this purpose is the power of any person to secure that the affairs of the company are conducted in accordance with his wishes, whether by means of shareholding or voting power in or in relation to any company or by virtue of any powers conferred by the articles of association or other regulatory document of any company. Shares held by a company (and voting or other powers arising from such shares) are left out of account for this purpose if a profit on sale of the shares would be treated as a trading receipt of the company's trade and the shares are not assets of an insurance company's long-term insurance fund (within *ICTA 1988, s 431(2)*).

Hedging arrangements. *Section 209(3AA)* also does not apply (and *section 209(2)(d)* has effect as if it never had applied) at any time at which there are (or have at any earlier time after 16 April 2002 been) 'hedging arrangements' (as defined) relating to some or all of the issuing company's liabilities under the security. There is, however, an exception (so that *section 209(3AA) does* apply) where the following four conditions are met at that time *and* at all earlier times after 16 April 2002 when there have been such hedging arrangements.

(i) The hedging arrangements must not constitute, include or form part of any scheme or arrangement a main purpose of which is avoidance of tax, stamp duty or stamp duty land tax.

(ii) They must be such that where, at any time, a corporation tax deduction falls to be made by the issuing company in respect of the security, then at that time (or within a reasonable time before or after it) any offsetting amounts under the arrangements arise to the issuing company or to a fellow group member (see 32.7 GROUPS OF COMPANIES).

(iii) The whole of every offsetting amount under (ii) above must be brought into charge to corporation tax by a company (or together by companies) within (ii) above.

(iv) Any corporation tax deduction for expenses of establishing or administering the arrangements must be reasonable in proportion to the amounts required to be brought into charge under (iii) above.

[*ICTA 1988, ss 209A, 209B; FA 2002, s 102(2); FA 2003, Sch 18 para 3(2)*].

23.5 **Interest or other distribution paid by 75% subsidiary — thin capitalisation.** For accounting periods beginning before 1 April 2004, a distribution includes any interest or other distribution (except any part representing principal or within 23.4 above), the cost of which is borne by the company, in respect of securities held by a company of which the issuing company is a '75% subsidiary' (or where both companies are 75% subsidiaries of a third company), to the extent that it would not have fallen to be paid if there had been no formal or informal relationship, arrangements or other connection between the companies (other than the securities themselves). The determination of whether such a relationship, etc. exists must take account of all factors, including whether, in the absence of the relationship, etc., the loan would have been made at all, or in a different amount, or at a different rate of interest or on other agreed terms. The taxpayer is required either to show that no relationship, etc. exists or to show the amount of interest which would have been paid in the absence of the relationship, etc. Where there is a relationship, etc., and it is not part of the lending company's business to make loans generally, the latter is disregarded. However, in determining:

(i) the appropriate level or extent of the issuing company's overall indebtedness;

(ii) whether it might be expected that the issuing company and a particular person would have become parties to a transaction involving the issue of a security by the issuing company or the making of a loan, or a loan of a particular amount, to that company; and

(iii) the rate of interest and other terms that might be expected to be applicable in any particular case to such a transaction,

no account is to be taken of (or of any inference capable of being drawn from) any other formal or informal relationship, etc. between the issuing company and any other person, unless that person has no 'relevant connection' with the issuing company, or is a member of the same 'UK grouping'. A person has a '*relevant connection*' with the issuing company if they are CONNECTED PERSONS (19) within *ICTA 1988, s 839* or if that person is an 'effective 51% subsidiary' of the issuing company or the issuing company is such a subsidiary of that person. '*UK grouping*' is defined by reference to 'effective 51% subsidiary' relationships. '*Effective 51% subsidiary*' is as under *TCGA 1992, s 170(7)* (see 12.1 CAPITAL GAINS—GROUPS) but applied as if the question of whether the effective 51% subsidiaries of a company (the '*putative holding company*') resident in the UK and not dual resident (see 32.27 GROUPS OF COMPANIES) include either the issuing company or a company of which the issuing company is an effective 51% subsidiary were to be determined without regard to any beneficial entitlement of the putative holding company to any profits or assets of any company resident outside the UK.

This does *not*, however, apply to any interest, etc. paid to a charity (including any of the bodies treated as charities, see 27.3, 27.8, 27.11, 27.17 EXEMPT ORGANISATIONS). See also 23.6 below as regards certain other exceptions from distribution treatment.

For accounting periods **beginning on or after 1 April 2004**, these provisions are repealed and the thin capitalisation rules are subsumed within the transfer pricing rules. An excessive payment of interest is no longer re-characterised as a distribution under the new rules. See specifically 67.4, 67.8 and 67.9 TRANSFER PRICING and 67 TRANSFER PRICING generally for other rules applying in relation to thin capitalisation. Where an accounting period of a company straddles 1 April 2004, it is treated, for the purposes of calculating the company's profits and losses, as two separate accounting periods, the first ending on 31 March 2004 and the second, to which the new rules apply, beginning on 1 April 2004.

[*ICTA 1988, ss 209(2)(da)(8A)–(8F), 212(4); FA 2004, ss 34(1), 37*].

See Revenue Tax Bulletin June 1995 pp 218–220 for the Revenue's approach to the question of what would have happened in the absence of a relationship, etc. as above, and for a detailed discussion of the relevance of debt/equity and income cover ratios. In particular, it is stressed that the provisions are capable of applying to treat the whole of the interest on a loan as a distribution even though a loan on identical terms could have been obtained from a third party (the instance being quoted of a company replacing a fixed interest third party loan with a loan at a higher (though currently commercial) rate of interest for the same remaining term from a related company). Advances from companies in Austria, Barbados, the Faroe Islands, Fiji, Germany, Israel, Japan, Kenya, Luxembourg, South Africa, the Sudan and Zambia are identified as those most likely to be affected by the new provisions. Guidance may be obtained from HMRC International Division 5/2, Melbourne House, Aldwych, London WC2B 4LL, to whom correspondents should identify the parties concerned and supply as much information as possible about the existing financial structures and/or proposals. See also Revenue Tax Bulletin June 1998 pp 554–556 for the Revenue response to various questions put to them by representative bodies on the application of *section 209(2)(da)*.

See also 23.7 below.

Companies resident in EU member states. In the case of *Lankhorst-Hohorst GmbH v Finanzamt Steinfurt CJEC (Case C-324/00), [2003] STC 607*, the European Court of Justice held that a German tax provision requiring certain payments of interest on debts due to parent companies to be recharacterised as 'covert distributions of profits', and which differentiated between resident and non-resident parent companies, contravened European law. Following this case, the High Court granted an application for a 'Thin Cap' Group Litigation Order (encompassing *ICTA 1988, ss 209, 212, Sch 28AA*) to manage claims that the thin capitalisation ('Thin Cap') provisions are contrary to EC law. Judgment was given in the case by CJEC on 13 March 2007. The case concerned UK companies' claims to deduct interest paid on advances from non-UK resident parents. CJEC found that it was unlawful to restrict relief for such interest in a situation where resident companies would obtain relief, unless the 'legislation provides for a consideration of objective and verifiable elements which make it possible to identify the existence of a purely artificial arrangement, entered into for tax reasons alone, to be established'. The taxpayer must be given a reasonable opportunity to produce evidence of commerciality. If, on this test, the interest falls to be treated as a distribution, there will be apportionment of the payment between what is commercial (and justifiable) and what is not. Only the latter will be treated as a distribution. This judgment applies where all parties are resident in member states: if, for example, the ultimate parent of the borrower and lender is resident outside EC, it will not apply, see *Test Claimants in the 'Thin Cap' Group Litigation v CIR, CJEC C/524/04 13 March 2007 unreported.*

23.6 **Interest in respect of certain securities.** A distribution includes any interest or other distribution not representing principal or within 23.4 (or for accounting periods beginning before 1 April 2004, 23.5 above), the cost of which is borne by the company, in respect of:

(i) bonus securities issued under 23.3 above in respect of shares (for issues after 5 April 1965) or securities (for issues after 5 April 1972) of the company; or

(ii) securities convertible directly or indirectly into shares in the company which are neither listed on a recognised stock exchange nor issued on terms reasonably comparable to those on which securities so listed were issued; or

(iii) securities issued after 5 April 1972 carrying a right to receive shares in, or securities of, the company (being neither quoted nor issued on comparable terms, see (ii) above); or

(iv) securities the interest on which varies with the results of the company's business. This does not apply by reason only of the terms of a security providing for the interest to be reduced if the results improve or increased if they deteriorate (commonly known as 'ratchet loans'); or

(v) securities carrying rights such that it is 'necessary or advantageous' for the holder, disposer, or acquirer of those securities to hold, dispose of, or acquire, a proportionate holding of shares. Such securities are '*connected with*' the shares; or

(vi) 'equity notes' held by a company which either is '*associated with*' the issuing company (i.e. one is a '75% subsidiary' of the other or both are such subsidiaries of a third company) or is a '*funded company*' (i.e. there are arrangements involving the company being put in funds (directly or indirectly) by the issuing company or by a company associated with the issuing company).

Where an accounting period of a company straddles 1 April 2004, it is treated, for the purposes of calculating the company's profits and losses, as two separate accounting periods, the first ending on 31 March 2004 and the second, to which the new rules apply, beginning on 1 April 2004.

[*ICTA 1988, ss 209(2)(e)(10)(11), 254(2); FA 2004, ss 34(1), 37*].

A company is a '*75% subsidiary*' if not less than 75% of its ordinary share capital is owned directly or indirectly by another. [*ICTA 1988, s 838*].

Interest within (i)–(vi) (or, for accounting periods beginning before 1 April 2004, 23.5) above on securities issued by a company to another company within the charge to corporation tax is *not* treated as a distribution *provided that* the recipient company is neither exempt from tax in respect of the interest, etc. (other than under the general corporation tax exemption of UK company distributions) nor (where 23.5 above applies) otherwise outside the matters in respect of which that company is within the charge to corporation tax, *unless* the securities are within (iv) above and:

(*a*) the principal does not exceed £100,000;

(*b*) the principal and interest must be repaid within five years of the principal being paid to the borrower; and (*c*) the obligation was entered into before 9 March 1982, or was entered into before 1 July 1982 pursuant to negotiations in progress on 9 March 1982, the borrower having before that date applied for the loan and supplied any documents required in support of his application.

Where the repayment period of either principal or interest is extended after 8 March 1982 (but is still within (*b*) above), (i)–(vi) above and 23.5 above do not apply to any interest etc. paid after the repayment period in force at that date.

[*ICTA 1988, s 212*].

As regards (vi) above, a security is an '*equity note*' if, as regards the whole or any part of the principal, any of the following apply:

(1) under the terms of issue, either there is no particular redemption date, or the latest (or only) redemption date falls more than 50 years after the date of issue; or

(2) under the terms of issue, redemption is to occur more than 50 years after the date of issue if a particular event occurs, and (judged at the time of issue) that event is certain or likely to occur; or

(3) the issuing company can secure that there is no particular redemption date or that the redemption date falls more than 50 years after the date of issue.

[*ICTA 1988, s 209(9)*].

HMRC have confirmed that ownership of shares in the company holding the security will not of itself be treated as bringing the issuing company within (3) above, and that a demand loan is not regarded as an equity note. The word 'arrangements' in relation to the definition of a funded company implies a purposive connection, and would not for example apply were a bank group to loan money to a company which, as a separate matter, happened to acquire equity notes issued by the group. (Law Society Press Release 15 February 1993; ICAEW Technical Release TAX 5/93, 17 February 1993).

See generally Revenue Tax Bulletin May 1993 p 68 as regards the definition of an equity note.

See also 23.7 below.

23.7 *'Principle'*.

As regards 23.4 and 23.6 above (and, for accounting periods beginning before 1 April 2004, 23.5 above):

(i) no amount is regarded as representing principal secured by a security in so far as it exceeds 'new consideration' (see 23.11 below) received by the company for its issue; and

(ii) where a security is issued at a premium consisting of 'new consideration', references to the principal represented by a distribution are taken as referring to the aggregate of the principal and the premium represented by the distribution (and a similar rule applies as regards 23.4 above in relation to the reasonable commercial return for the use of principal represented by a distribution). This does *not* have effect as regards 23.4 above where (as referred to in 23.4 above) *ICTA 1988, s 209(3AA)* applies (and is not disapplied by *ICTA 1988, ss 209A, 209B*).

Where an accounting period of a company straddles 1 April 2004, it is treated, for the purposes of calculating the company's profits and losses, as two separate accounting periods, the first ending on 31 March 2004 and the second, to which the new rules apply, beginning on 1 April 2004.

[*ICTA 1988, s 209(3)(3A); FA 2004, ss 34(1), 37*].

23.8 **Transfer of assets or liabilities between company and members.** The transfer of assets or liabilities between a company and its members is treated as a distribution in so far as the market value of any benefit received by a member exceeds that of any 'new consideration' (see 23.11 below) given by him. Such a transfer is not, however, to be treated as a distribution if it is made between companies resident in the UK and *either*:

(i) the transferor company is a 51% subsidiary (see below) of the transferee company; *or*

(ii) both are 51% subsidiaries of a company resident in the UK.

[*ICTA 1988, s 209(4)(5)*].

In the case of *Noved Investment Co v HMRC (2006) Sp C 521*, the Special Commissioners held that transfers of assets or liabilities by a company to its members at an undervalue under *ICTA 1988, s 209(4)* can include cash. Distributions are excluded from being treated as qualifying charitable donations under *ICTA 1988, s 339(1)(a)* apart from such transfers (see 14.11(a) CHARITIES) and therefore, the decision in this case allows such cash transfers to be treated as qualifying donations. The decision in this case contradicts HMRC's view in a change to their previously adopted view (announced in the course of this case) that such transfers do not include cash. (HMRC Internet Notice 3 November 2005).

In determining whether a company is a 51% subsidiary of another, that other's holding (whether direct or indirect) of shares in a non-resident company or of shares any profit on the sale of which would be a trading receipt, are disregarded. [*ICTA 1988, s 209(7)*].

Transfers of assets (other than cash) or of liabilities are excluded if they fall within *section 209(6)*, see 23.2 above, where '51% subsidiary' is defined without the restriction on shareholdings to which regard is to be had.

For the 'unwinding' of distributions inadvertently caught by *section 209(4)*, see HMRC Corporation Tax Manual, CT 1529a.

23.9 **Repayment of share capital followed by a bonus issue.** Where a company repays share capital (and see 23.10 below), or has done so at any time after 6 April 1965, and at the same time or later issues any share capital as paid up (otherwise than by the receipt of 'new consideration', see 23.11 below), the amount so paid up is treated as a distribution. Such a distribution is treated as made in respect of the bonus shares and is limited to the total amount of share capital repaid less any amount previously treated as a distribution under this provision. [*ICTA 1988, s 210(1)*]. Where the bonus share capital is issued after 5 April 1973, this provision only applies if the issue is made within ten years of the repayment or is of redeemable share capital. [*ICTA 1988, s 210(3)*]. The original rules apply unaltered, however, if the company is under the control of not more than five persons or is unquoted (disregarding debentures and preference shares), unless it is under the control of a company (or companies) which is (or are) neither controlled by five or fewer persons nor unquoted. [*ICTA 1988, ss 210(3), 704D*]. 'Control' is as defined in 16.2 CLOSE COMPANIES.

Example

In 1997 X Ltd, a close company, redeemed £50,000-worth of variable-rate preference shares. In 2000 it made a bonus issue of one ordinary share of £1 for every ten held, which amounted to £20,000. In 2002 it made a further bonus issue of ordinary shares on a 1:11 basis, which also amounted to £20,000. X Ltd is treated as having made a distribution of £20,000 in each of the financial years 2000 and 2002. If X Ltd makes a similar bonus issue of 1:12 in 2006, the amount treated as a distribution (assuming that there has been no further repayment of share capital) will be limited to £10,000, being the balance of the £50,000 repaid in 1997.

These provisions do not apply to the repayment of fully-paid 'preference shares' which

(i) existed as such on 6 April 1965, or

(ii) were issued as such after 6 April 1965 wholly for 'new consideration not derived from ordinary shares'

and in either case remained fully-paid preference shares until the date of repayment. [*ICTA 1988, s 210(2)*].

'*Preference shares*' are defined for this purpose as shares carrying the right to a dividend at a fixed percentage of the nominal value only and such other rights in respect of dividends and capital as are comparable with those general for fixed-dividend shares listed in the Official List of the Stock Exchange. Thus variable-rate preference shares (as in the example above) are outside this definition.

'*New consideration not derived from ordinary shares*' means 'new consideration' (see 23.11 below) except in so far as it consists of

(*a*) the surrender, transfer or cancellation of 'ordinary shares' in the company or any other company, or

(*b*) the variation of rights in such shares, or

(*c*) consideration derived from a repayment made in respect of such shares.

'*Ordinary shares*' are all shares except preference shares as defined above.

[*ICTA 1988, s 210(4); FA 1996, Sch 38 para 7*].

23.10 **Repayment of share capital.** Where a company issues (or has issued at any time after 6 April 1965) any 'share capital' as paid up (the amount so paid up not constituting 'new consideration' (see 23.11 below) or a qualifying distribution), any subsequent distribution in respect of that share capital is not treated as a repayment of share capital (so that the exclusion from distribution treatment in 23.2(i) does not apply), except in so far as the repayment exceeds the amount so paid up. (The excess is generally a distribution as under 23.2 above.) [*ICTA 1988, s 211(1)(3)*].

'Share capital' for this purpose includes:

(*a*) all the shares of the same class;

(*b*) shares issued in respect of any shares under (*a*) above;

(*c*) shares exchanged for any shares under (*a*) above (whether directly or indirectly);

(*d*) shares into which any shares under (*a*) above have directly or indirectly been converted. [*ICTA 1988, s 211(4)*].

Where shares have been issued at a premium representing new consideration, the premium (less any amount that has been applied in paying up share capital) is treated as part of the share capital in determining whether any repayment is to be treated as a distribution. [*ICTA 1988, s 211(5)(6)*]. Subject to this, premiums paid on the redemption of share capital are not to be treated as repayments of share capital. [*ICTA 1988, s 211(7)*].

A distribution is outside *section 211(1)* if it is made:

(i) more than ten years after an issue of shares within that subsection; and

(ii) otherwise than in respect of redeemable share capital; and

(iii) by a company which is neither under the control of five or fewer persons nor unquoted (disregarding debentures and preference shares), or which is controlled by a company (or companies) which is or are neither controlled by five or fewer persons nor unquoted.

[*ICTA 1988, ss 211(2), 704D*].

23.11 **'New consideration'.** '*New consideration*' means consideration provided otherwise than out of the assets of the company (i.e. where the cost does not fall on the company).

Amounts retained by the company by way of capitalising a distribution do not constitute new consideration, but a premium paid on the issue of shares which is later applied in paying up further share capital may be treated as new consideration (except in so far as it has been taken into account to enable a distribution to be treated as a repayment of share capital (see 23.10 above)). [*ICTA 1988, s 254(1)(5)*].

Consideration derived from the value of any share capital or security of, or from voting or other rights in, a company is new consideration only if it represents:

(i) money or value received from the company as a qualifying distribution (see 23.16 below); or

(ii) money received from the company which, for the purposes of *Part VI* of *ICTA 1988*, constitute a repayment of share capital (see 23.10 above) or of the principal of the security; or

(iii) the giving up of the right to the share capital or security on its cancellation, extinguishment or acquisition by the company.

But in so far as any amount under (ii) or (iii) exceeds any payment made to the company for the issue of the share capital or security or, in the case of share capital which constituted a qualifying distribution (see 23.17 below), exceeds the nominal value of that share capital, it is not to be treated as new consideration. [*ICTA 1988, s 254(6)(7)*].

23.12 **'Shares'.** '*Shares*' includes stock and any other interest of a member in a company. [*ICTA 1988, s 254(1)*].

23.13 **'Security'.** '*Security*' includes securities not creating or evidencing a charge on assets. Interest paid, or other consideration given, by a company for money advanced without the issue of a security is nevertheless treated as if paid or given in respect of a security issued for that advance by the company. Where securities are issued at a discount, and are not listed on a recognised stock exchange, the principal secured is to be taken as not exceeding the issue price, unless the terms of issue are reasonably comparable with those of securities so listed. [*ICTA 1988, s 254(1)(11); FA 1996, Sch 38 para 6*].

23.14 **'In respect of shares'.** A thing is to be regarded as done '*in respect of*' shares or securities if it is done to the holder or former holder thereof (as such), or in pursuance of a right granted or offer made in respect of a share. Anything so done by reference to shareholdings at a particular time is regarded as done to the then holder or his personal representatives. [*ICTA 1988, s 254(12)*]. If reciprocal arrangements are entered into among companies to make distributions to each other's members, the acts of one may be attributed to another. [*ICTA 1988, s 254(8)*].

23.15 ITEMS NOT TREATED AS DISTRIBUTIONS

(*a*) Distributions made in respect of share capital on LIQUIDATION ETC. (45) [*ICTA 1988, s 209(1)*], or (in most circumstances) on *dissolution under Companies Act 1985, s 652 or s 652A*. (HMRC Extra-Statutory Concession, C16).

(*b*) Small distributions to members on *dissolution of an unincorporated association* which is of a social or recreational nature and has not carried on a trade or investment business. (HMRC Extra-Statutory Concession, C15).

(*c*) Payments for *group relief* (or for the *surrender of ACT* on dividends paid prior to 6 April 1999) (see 32.5, 32.20 GROUPS OF COMPANIES) [*ICTA 1988, ss 240(8), 402(6); FA 1998, Sch 3 para 13*], except in so far as they exceed the amount surrendered.

(*d*) *Share or loan interest* paid by registered INDUSTRIAL AND PROVIDENT SOCIETIES (38) or certain co-operative associations. [*ICTA 1988, s 486(1)(8)(9)*].

(*e*) *Dividends or bonuses* deductible in computing the income of REGISTERED INDUSTRIAL AND PROVIDENT SOCIETIES (38) or MUTUAL COMPANIES (48). [*ICTA 1988, s 486(10)–(12)*].

(*f*) *Dividends or interest* payable in respect of shares in, deposits with, or loans to, BUILDING SOCIETIES (9). [*ICTA 1988, s 476(3)(c), s 477A(3)(b); FA 1990, Sch 5 para 4*].

(*g*) *Stock dividends* (see Tolley's Income Tax under Savings and Investment Income). [*ICTA 1988, s 230; ITTOIA 2005, Sch 1 para 112*].

(*h*) *Interest on securities* not within 23.4–23.6 above.

(*i*) Money provided by a close company for the *purchase of its shares by trustees of its profit sharing scheme*. (CCAB Memorandum TR 308, June 1978).

(*j*) Certain *purchases by a company of its own shares* (see PURCHASE BY A COMPANY OF ITS OWN SHARES (57)). [*ICTA 1988, ss 219–229*].

(*k*) Profit share return under ALTERNATIVE FINANCE ARRANGEMENTS (4) with effect for payments on or after 6 April 2005. [*FA 2005, s 54*].

(*l*) Additional payments and any part of a redemption payment under alternative finance arrangements within *FA 2005, s 48A* (alternative finance investment bonds) (See 4.6 ALTERNATIVE FINANCE ARRANGEMENTS) with effect from 1 April 2007.

HMRC will give 'sympathetic consideration' to cases where a terminal payment is made by a continuing company to an arm's length director or employee, where the sum is both reasonable in amount (having regard to past services and length of service), and an admissible deduction for corporation tax purposes. (CCAB Memorandum TR 127, 19 February 1974).

A bonus issue of *non-redeemable share capital* does not constitute a distribution unless it follows a repayment of share capital (see 23.10 above).

23.16 EFFECT OF DISTRIBUTION

A distribution is not chargeable to corporation tax in the hands of the recipient company, nor taken into account in computing the income of the paying company for corporation tax purposes. [*ICTA 1988, s 208*]. But see 23.17 below. See also 49 NON-CORPORATE DISTRIBUTION RATE for the effect on the corporation tax rate of distributions made to non-corporate members.

Where the special rules in *ICTA 1988, ss 219–229* do *not* apply on the occasion of a PURCHASE BY A COMPANY OF ITS OWN SHARES (57), so that the purchase is treated as a distribution, and the shareholder is itself a company, the distribution is included in the consideration which, for the purposes of corporation tax on chargeable gains, the shareholder company is treated as receiving for disposal of the shares. This treatment was confirmed in *Strand Options & Futures Ltd v Vojak CA 2004, 76 TC 220*, where it was held that *section 208* exempted the consideration from the Schedule F charge on the dividends but not on the distribution element of the chargeable gain.

23.17 TAX CREDITS

Where a UK-resident company makes a 'qualifying distribution' on or after 6 April 1999 to a another UK-resident company, the recipient of such a distribution is entitled to a 10% tax credit, equivalent to one-ninth of the dividend. The distribution, together with the tax credit, is FRANKED INVESTMENT INCOME (29) in the hands of a UK-resident recipient company. [*ICTA 1988, ss 231, 832(1)*]. A company resident in the UK was, until 6 April 1999, liable to advance corporation tax in respect of its qualifying distributions (but not its non-qualifying distributions) made before 6 April 1999, the recipient being entitled to a tax credit. [*ICTA 1988, ss 14(1), 238(1); FA 1998, Sch 3 para 8*].

'*Qualifying distributions*' are any distributions other than:

(*a*) bonus redeemable share capital and bonus securities within *ICTA 1988, s 209(2)(c)* (see 23.3 above) which are not distributions within *ICTA 1988, s 210* (see 23.8 above); and

(*b*) share capital or securities which the distributing company has directly or indirectly received from the issuing company as a distribution under (*a*) above.

[*ICTA 1988, s 14(2)*].

Returns of non-qualifying distributions must be made under *ICTA 1988, s 234(5)–(9)*. See 61.22 RETURNS.

Any company making a payment of dividend or interest to any person must, within a reasonable period, send a written statement giving details of the payment to that person or, if the payment is made direct to a bank (within *ICTA 1988, s 840A*, see 8.1 BANKS) or building society, either to the bank or building society or to the account holder. Nominee recipients are similarly obliged to provide a statement when passing on the payment. The statement must include:

(i) in the case of interest (not being a qualifying distribution or part), the gross amount, the rate and amount of income tax deducted from the gross amount, the net amount actually paid and the date of payment;

(ii) in the case of a dividend or interest which is a qualifying distribution or part, the amount paid, the date of payment and the related tax credit.

HMRC have powers by regulation to provide alternative rules for compliance. [*ICTA 1988, s 234A*].

For dividends payable to non-residents, see 24.13 DOUBLE TAX RELIEF.

Simon's Direct Tax Service. See D1.411, B11.303.

23.18 **CLOSE COMPANIES — ADDITIONAL DISTRIBUTIONS**

Certain payments made and benefits given to participators and their associates by close companies are treated as distributions, see 23.19 below. Unless otherwise stated, terms have the same meaning as in 16.1–16.5 CLOSE COMPANIES. The exceptions listed in 23.15 above apply. [*ICTA 1988, s 418*].

23.19 **Benefits to participators and their associates.** Where a close company incurs expense in, or in connection with, the provision for any 'participator' (or an associate of his) of living or other accommodation, entertainment, domestic or other services, or of other benefits or facilities of whatever nature, so much of that expense as is not made good by the participator is treated as a distribution. [*ICTA 1988, s 418(2)(8)*]. The distribution treatment does not apply to benefits provided to a participator who is an employee to whom the earnings and benefit code under *ITEPA 2003, Pt 3* applies in the case of: the provision of benefits given, on that person's death or retirement, to the spouse, children or dependants; the provision of living accommodation (under *ITEPA 2003, ss 97–113*) and the benefits under *ITEPA 2003, ss 114–215* (cars and vans, loans, etc) and *s 223* (payments of director's tax) ignoring the exclusion for lower paid employees in *s 216*. (For accounting periods ending before 6 April 2003, before the consequential amendments made by *ITEPA 2003*, the distribution treatment did not apply to amounts already treated as a benefit to a director or to an employee with emoluments at a rate of £8,500 p.a. or more for income tax purposes nor to the provision of living accommodation taxable as a benefit on any employee, or the provision of retirement pensions, terminal payments etc. The change in the wording of the legislation broadly reflects HMRC practice (see HMRC Company Taxation Manual CT6610).) [*ICTA 1988, s 418(1)–(3); ITEPA 2003, Sch 6 para 55*].

'*Participator*' includes a participator in a company which controls the company providing the benefit. [*ICTA 1988, s 418*(*8*)].

Reciprocal arrangements whereby each of a number of companies makes a payment etc. to a participator in another are included. [*ICTA 1988, s 418*(*7*)].

The measure of the distribution is the cash equivalent of the benefit or expense as defined in the employment benefits legislation (see Tolley's Income Tax under Employment Income) less any amount made good to the company. [*ICTA 1988, s 418*(*4*)].

These provisions do not apply where the company and the participator are resident in the UK and:

(*a*) one is a '51% subsidiary' of the other or both are 51% subsidiaries of a third company so resident; and

(*b*) the benefit arises on or in connection with the transfer of assets or liabilities between the company and the participator. [*ICTA 1988, s 418*(*5*)].

'*51% subsidiary*' is as defined in 23.7 above. [*ICTA 1988, s 418*(*6*)].

Simon's Direct Tax Service. See D3.117.

23.20 *Example*

R is a participator in S Ltd, a close company, but he is neither a director nor an employee earning £8,500 a year or more. For the whole of 2007/08, S Ltd provided R with a new car of which the 'price' for tax purposes (i.e. under *ITEPA 2003, ss 122–124*) was £23,200, and which had a carbon dioxide emissions figure of 235 g/km. R was required to, and did, pay S Ltd £500 a year for the use of the car. The cost of providing the car, charged in S Ltd's accounts for its year ended 31 March 2008, was £5,000.

Deemed distribution

If the benefit of the car had been assessable as employment income, the cash equivalent would have been:

	£
£23,200 @ 34%	7,888
Less contribution	500
	£7,388

S Ltd is treated as making a distribution of £7,388 to R.

Income of R for 2007/08 £7,388 × 100/90	£8,209
Tax credit for R for 2007/08 £8,209 @ 10%	£821

The income is dividend income and thus taxable at 10% (satisfied by the tax credit) except to the extent that it falls within R's higher rate band, in which case it would be taxable at the dividend upper rate of 32.5%.

S Ltd's taxable profits

In computing S Ltd's profits chargeable to corporation tax, the actual expenditure charged (£5,000) must be added back.

23.21 **MUTUAL AND NON-TRADING COMPANIES**

Payments made to members of:

(*a*) MUTUAL COMPANIES (48) (other than those carrying on life assurance business); or

(*b*) companies which were not formed to carry on, and which have never carried on, a trade or the business of holding investments,

are within the above provisions only if made out of income chargeable to corporation tax or out of FRANKED INVESTMENT INCOME (29). [*ICTA 1988, s 490*].

23.22 **FRIENDLY SOCIETIES**

Payments made by certain FRIENDLY SOCIETIES (31) are qualifying distributions. [*ICTA 1988, s 461*(*3*)].

23.23 **DISCRETIONARY PAYMENTS FROM TRUSTS**

Where on or after 2 July 1997, trustees of a settlement make a discretionary distribution to a company, other than a charity ((within *ICTA 1988 s 506*(*1*)) or a body treated as a charity (under *ICTA 1988 ss 507, 508*) the payment is disregarded for corporation tax purposes, and no credit is given, or repayment made, of the tax deducted at the rate applicable to trusts. In the case of non-UK resident companies, this applies to so much (if any) of the payment as is comprised in the company's profits for corporation tax purposes.

[ICTA 1988, ss 687, 687A; F(No 2)A 1997 s 27].

24 Double Tax Relief

Cross-references. See 5.11, 5.19 ANTI-AVOIDANCE; 11.23 CAPITAL GAINS; 21 CONTROLLED FOREIGN COMPANIES; 32.27 GROUPS OF COMPANIES; 60 RESIDENCE.

Simon's Direct Tax Service. See Part **F1–F7**.

Other sources. See Tolley's Double Taxation Relief.

The headings in this chapter are as follows.

24.1 **INTRODUCTION**

Where the same income is liable to be taxed in both the UK and another country, relief may be available:

(*a*) under the specific terms of a double tax agreement between the UK and that other country — see 24.3 below [*ICTA 1988, s 788*];

(*b*) under special arrangements with Ireland — see Tolley's Income Tax under Double Tax Relief; or

(*c*) under the unilateral double tax relief provisions contained in UK tax legislation — see 24.2 below. [*ICTA 1988, s 790*].

See also HMRC Pamphlet IR 6.

As announced in the Budget 2007, the Treasury has issued a discussion document entitled 'Taxation of the foreign profits of companies' in June 2007. This is available at the HMRC website, under 'What's new' – 21 June 2007.

24.2 **UNILATERAL RELIEF**

Taxes, other than those for which credit is available under the bilateral double tax agreements in 24.3 below, payable under the law of any territory outside the and computed by reference to income or gain *arising in that territory* are allowed (to the extent defined below) as a credit against UK income tax or corporation tax paid on that income or gain by UK residents. Relief is only available against UK tax chargeable under the same Schedule and Case as that under which the foreign income on which the foreign tax was borne is chargeable (*George Wimpey International Ltd v Rolfe Ch D 1989, 62 TC 597*). Where appropriate an apportionment must be made to determine what part of income may be regarded as 'arising in' the overseas territory, and in making that apportionment it is the principles of UK tax law which are to be applied (see *Yates v GCA International Ltd and cross-appeal Ch D 1991, 64 TC 37* and HMRC Statement of Practice, SP 7/91, 16 July 1991). The machinery and limits (with modifications as below) are substantially the same as those under which the bilateral agreements operate and the credit given is, basically, such as would be allowable were a double taxation agreement in force with the territory concerned. [*ICTA 1988, s 790(1)–(4), s 794*].

Unilateral relief is not allowed where credit could be claimed under a double tax agreement under 24.3 below, or in cases or circumstances in which such an agreement made on or after that date specifically prohibits relief. [*ICTA 1988, s 793A(2)(3)*].

Unilateral relief under *ICTA 1988, s 790* is available on dividends received from overseas companies:

(*a*) for overseas tax directly charged on the dividend which would not have been charged if the dividend had not been paid; and

(*b*) for tax in respect of the overseas company's profits paid under the law of the country in which it is resident where

(i) the dividend is paid by a company resident overseas to a company resident in the UK, or to a company resident outside the UK but forming part of the profits of a UK permanent establishment (see 60.5 RESIDENCE — previously a UK branch or agency) of the company, and

(ii) the recipient company (or a company of which it is a 'subsidiary') controls at least 10% of the voting power in the overseas company

(but see also 24.9 below).

In (*b*)(i) above, in the case of a company resident outside the UK but forming part of the profits of a UK permanent establishment, relief is limited to the amount which could be claimed in the same circumstances by a UK-resident company. (For insurance companies see *ICTA 1988, ss 804A–804F*.)

'*Subsidiary*' means a company of which 50% or more of the voting power is controlled, directly or indirectly, by the other.

[*ICTA 1988, s 790(4)–(6A), s 794(2)(bb), ss 800–802; FA 2001, Sch 27 paras 3, 7*].

For the scope of 'dividends', see *Memec plc v CIR CA 1998, 71 TC 77* (in which receipts under a silent partnership agreement were held not to attract relief). See also HMRC Tax Bulletin June 2006 p 1295 for an article on the classification of foreign entities for UK tax purposes and for a list of overseas business entities on whose classification for UK tax purposes HMRC has been asked to express a view.

To be eligible for relief, the taxes must be charged on income and correspond to income tax or corporation tax in the UK but, subject to this, provincial, state and municipal taxes are included. [*ICTA 1988, s 790(12)*]. See *Yates v GCA International Ltd and cross-appeal Ch D 1991, 64 TC 37* where a tax imposed on gross receipts less a fixed 10% deduction was held to correspond to UK income tax or corporation tax. Following that decision, HMRC amended their practice. (HMRC Statement of Practice, SP 7/91, as revised). For claims made on or after 13 February 1991, and earlier claims unsettled at that date, foreign taxes will be examined to determine whether, in their own legislative context, they serve the same function as UK income and corporation taxes in relation to business profits, and are thus eligible for unilateral relief. As regards those overseas taxes which HMRC consider admissible (or inadmissible) for relief, these are listed by country in HMRC Double Taxation Relief Manual, DT 2100 *et seq.* and DT 17350 *et seq.* See also HMRC Business Income Manual, BIM 45905. Current information may be obtained from the HMRC website (www.hmrc.gov.uk/international).

Simon's Direct Tax Service. See F1.123

24.3 RELIEF BY AGREEMENT

A list is given in 24.14 below of the bilateral agreements made by the UK which are currently operative. Subject to the following general provisions, the extent of such relief depends on the terms of the relevant double tax agreement, which should be carefully studied.

Arrangements under such an agreement may provide for:

(i) relief from income or corporation tax in respect of income or chargeable gains;

(ii) charging UK income to non-UK residents;

(iii) determining income to be attributed to non-UK residents or their agencies, etc., or to UK residents who have special relationships with non-UK residents;

(iv) granting non-UK residents the right to set-off or repayment of the tax credit in respect of distributions made to them by UK resident companies; or

(v) exchange of information concerning taxes covered by the agreement, particularly in relation to the prevention of fiscal evasion.

[*ICTA 1988, s 788(3); ITTOIA 2005, Sch 1 para 321; FA 2006, ss 173–175* (*previously ICTA 1988, s 788(2) as amended by FA 2003, s 198*)].

As regards (i) above, it was held, in the case of *NEC Semi-Conductors v CIR (and related appeals) (re Class 3 ACT Group Litigation Order), CA [2006] STC 606*, that the phrase 'corporation tax in respect of income or chargeable gains' in *ICTA 1988, s 788(3)(a)* did not include ACT. Thus, the restriction of the group income election to UK-resident companies was not contrary to the non-discrimination article of double tax convention concerned (between UK and Japan).

As regards (iv) above, the general abolition of the repayment of tax credits after 5 April 1999 does not affect the entitlement of a non-UK resident to payment in respect of a tax credit under such arrangements (although it should be noted that in practice, with the reduction after that date to one-ninth in the rate of tax credit, such repayments will be very limited). [*F(No 2)A 1997, s 30(9)(10); ITTOIA 2005, Sch 1 para 496*]. Similarly, the tax credit payment restrictions applicable to pension funds in relation to distributions made after 1 July 1997 do not apply to non-residents' entitlements under such arrangements. [*ICTA 1988, s 231A(6)(b); F(No 2)A 1997, s 19(2), Sch 8 Pt II(9)*].

Also as regards (iv) above, in the combined cases of *Metallgesellschaft and Others Ltd v CIR,* and *Hoechst AG v CIR, [2001] STC 452*, it was held that the requirement that both parties to a group income election under *ICTA 1988, s 247* (for the payment of dividends prior to the abolition of ACT on 6 April 1999) be UK-resident, contravened EC law. Following this, it was held in *Pirelli Cable Holding NV and Others v CIR, HL [2006] STC 548* (unanimously reversing the Court of Appeal's decision) that, had such a group income election been made (had it been available), the non-UK resident parent would not have been entitled to tax credits in respect of the distributions made by the UK-resident subsidiary. *The* CJEC, in *Test Claimants in Class IV of the ACT Group Litigation (Pirelli UK plc, Essilor Ltd, Sony UK Ltd and BMW (GB) Ltd) v CIR, CJEC Case C-374/04*); 12 December 2006. The ECJ held that EC Treaty Articles 43 and 56 did not preclude a member state from granting a tax credit to a company resident within it on dividends received from other resident companies, although no such credit was available on dividends from companies resident in other member states. Where the two states have a double taxation agreement in force between them and a third state does not, granting of a tax credit on a dividend paid by a company in the first state to one in the second state, but not to one in the third state, is not precluded. In the case of *UBS AG v HMRC CA [2007] STC 588,* it was held by the Court of Appeal that it was not discriminatory to deny the UK branch of a Swiss bank the benefit of a claim under *ICTA 1988, s 243* (for accounting periods beginning before 2 July 1997, set off of surplus franked investment income against trading losses brought forward) in respect of entitlement to repayment of tax credits under *ICTA 1988, s 788(3)(d.*

As regards the concept of 'permanent establishment' on which taxation rights are based under most treaties, HMRC take the view that a website, or a server on which e-commerce is conducted through a website, is not of itself a permanent establishment. (See HMRC International Manual, INTM 266100 and 60.5 RESIDENCE).

For the circumstances in which HMRC will certify that a company is UK resident for the purposes of double tax agreements, see Revenue Tax Bulletin December 2002 pp 989–991.

For the scope of 'dividends' attracting treaty relief, see *Memec plc v CIR CA 1998, 71 TC 77* (in which receipts under a silent partnership agreement were held not to attract relief), and see also Revenue Tax Bulletin February 1999 p 627 for an article on the classification of foreign entities for UK tax purposes. See also Revenue Tax Bulletin December 2000 pp 809–812 for a list of overseas business entities on whose classification for UK tax purposes HMRC has been asked to express a view.

In *R v CIR (ex p Commerzbank AG) QB 1991, 68 TC 252*, interest on unpaid tax was held not to fall within the scope of double tax agreements, but on a reference to the European Court of Justice (see *68 TC 264*), the Court upheld the view that, in the case of EC member states, such discrimination against non-UK resident companies was prevented by the relevant Articles of the Treaty of Rome. For claims to such interest following that judgment, see 40.4 INTEREST ON OVERPAID TAX. See HMRC Double Taxation Relief Manual, DT 1950 *et seq.* for HMRC's approach to non-discrimination claims generally.

See, however, HMRC Statement of Practice, SP 2/95 for HMRC's view of the restricted operation of non-discrimination clauses in double tax treaties.

Mutual agreement procedure. Double tax agreements normally contain a 'mutual agreement procedure' provision enabling a taxpayer who considers that the action of a tax authority has resulted, or will result, in taxation not in accordance with the agreement to present his case to the competent authority in his state of residence. The UK competent authority is HMRC, and the address to which all relevant facts and contentions should be sent is Revenue Policy International, 100 Parliament Street, London SW1A 2BQ. For the presentation of such cases, and for giving effect to solutions and agreements reached under such procedures, see *ICTA 1988, s 815AA*. Details of the procedures can be found in the HMRC Double Taxation Relief Manual.

Simon's Direct Tax Service. See **F1.124** *et seq.*

24.4 **SPECIFIC MATTERS**

Relief by deduction. An election can be made not to claim relief by way of credit (see 24.5 below), for example where there is no or insufficient UK tax payable on the foreign income against which the foreign tax can be credited. Where such an election is made or where a credit for foreign tax is not taken under treaty or unilateral relief, or is not otherwise allowable in respect of foreign income (see also 24.5 below under Relief for disallowed credit), any foreign tax paid on that income is generally deductible from that income for purposes of UK assessment. This does not apply to underlying tax excluded from a claim for relief under *ICTA 1988, s 799(1B)* (to prevent the application of the 'mixer' cap in certain cases – see 24.11 below). Where foreign tax for which such a deduction has been given is subsequently adjusted, the UK tax charge may be revised within six years from date of the foreign tax adjustment. Where, by reason of the adjustment, relief has become excessive, written notice of that fact must be given to HMRC within one year of the date of the adjustment subject to a penalty for failure to comply not exceeding the amount of the additional UK tax payable. [*ICTA 1988, ss 805, 811*].

Foreign tax levied by reference to the value of assets employed to produce income chargeable to UK tax may, in practice, be allowed as a business expense under normal Schedule D, Case I rules. (HMRC International Tax Handbook, ITH 602).

Simon's Direct Tax Service. See **F1.128**.

Prevention of double relief. Credit may not be given for foreign tax for which relief is available in the territory in which it would otherwise be payable, either under double tax arrangements or under the law of that territory in consequence of any such arrangements.

It is also made clear that unilateral relief will not be allowed where credit could be claimed under a double tax agreement, or in cases or circumstances in which such an agreement made after 20 March 2000 specifically prohibits relief. [*ICTA 1988, s 793A*].

Simon's Direct Tax Service. See **F1.123, F2.110**.

Tax sparing relief. Under *ICTA 1988, s 788(5)* it may be provided in a double tax agreement that any tax which would have been payable in a foreign country but for a relief under the law of that territory given with a view to promoting industrial, commercial, scientific, educational or other development therein is nevertheless treated for purposes of credit against UK tax as if it had been paid. (It is not available for unilateral relief or where relief is given by way of deduction from dividend income.) See, for example, HMRC Double Taxation Relief Manual at DT 12758 in the case of Malaysia and at DT 16911 in the case of Singapore.

Matching credit for tax spared below immediate overseas subsidiary. Where:

(*a*) an amount of tax would, but for a relief, have been payable by a company ('company A'), in respect of any of its profits, under the law of its territory of residence;

(*b*) company A pays a dividend out of those profits to another company ('company B') resident in the same territory;

(*c*) company B, out of profits consisting of or including all or part of that dividend, pays a dividend to a UK-resident company ('company C'); and

(*d*) had company B been UK resident, it would have been entitled under a double tax agreement with its actual territory of residence to relief for the spared tax,

then the spared tax is taken into account for the purposes of unilateral relief for underlying tax as if it had been payable and paid. If these conditions are not fulfilled, unilateral relief is not available for spared tax in respect of any dividend paid by a non-UK resident company to a UK-resident company, notwithstanding any double tax agreement with the territory concerned providing any relief for spared tax. Without prejudice to the above specific relief, treaty relief for underlying tax which is spared below the level of the immediate non-resident subsidiary is denied unless it is specifically provided for in a double tax agreement. [*ICTA 1988, s 788(5), s 790(10A)-(10C)*].

Simon's Direct Tax Service. See **F2.121, F2.210**.

Acquisitions and disposals of loan relationships. Special provision is made for the relief of foreign tax relating to accrued interest in relation to which a non-trading credit (or, if the Treasury so provides by order, a trading credit) is brought into account (see 46.3 LOAN RELATIONSHIPS), and for foreign tax to be disregarded where it is attributable to interest accruing under a loan relationship (see 46.2 LOAN RELATIONSHIPS) at a time when the company concerned was not a party to the relationship (unless it ceased to be a party under certain repo or stock-lending arrangements).

Foreign tax attributable to 'relevant payments' within *FA 2002, Sch 27 para 12* (or, for accounting periods beginning before 1 October 2002, to 'qualifying payments' within *FA 1994, s 153(a)* or (*b*), see 28.33(*a*)(*b*) FINANCIAL INSTRUMENTS AND DERIVATIVE CONTRACTS) are to be disregarded where it is attributable to a time when the company was not a party to the derivative contract (or, for accounting periods beginning before 1 October 2002, to the interest rate or currency contract) concerned.

Where shares are treated as loan relationships in relation to shares held by a company on or after 16 March 2005 (see 46.35 LOAN RELATIONSHIPS), the above provisions have effect for share distributions as they would for interest under a loan relationship. The foreign tax is disregarded where it is attributable to the distribution accruing in respect of shares at a time when the company does not hold the shares (unless it ceased to hold the shares under certain repo or stock-lending arrangements)

[*ICTA 1988, s 807A; FA 2002, Sch 27 para 12; F(No 2)A 2005, Sch 7 para 5; FA 2007, Sch 14 para 10*].

Simon's Direct Tax Service. See **F2.126**.

Special relationships: interest. Agreements under *section 788* making provision in relation to interest may also have a provision dealing with cases where, owing to a special relationship, the amount of interest paid exceeds the amount which would have been paid in the absence of that relationship, and requiring the interest provision to be applied only to that lower amount. Any such special relationship provision has to be construed:

(*a*) as requiring account to be taken of all factors, including whether, in the absence of the relationship, the loan would have been made at all, or would have been in a different amount, or a different rate of interest and other terms would have been agreed. This does not apply, however, where the special relationship provision expressly requires regard to be had to the debt on which the interest is paid in determining the excess interest, and accordingly expressly limits the factors to be taken into account, and in the case of a loan by one company to another, the fact that it is not part of the lending company's business to make loans generally is disregarded; and

(*b*) as requiring the taxpayer either to show that no special relationship exists or to show the amount of interest which would have been paid in the absence of that relationship.

[*ICTA 1988, s 808A*].

With regard to (*a*) above, see HMRC International Manual, INTM 501010 for a further discussion of the tax considerations of intra-group funding, the special relationship provision and transfer pricing.

Simon's Direct Tax Service. See **F1.221**.

Special relationships: royalties. Agreements may make similar provision in relation to royalties. Where royalties are payable on or after 28 July 2000, any special relationship provision, unless it expressly requires regard to be had to the use, right or information for which royalties are paid in determining the excess royalties, has to be construed as requiring account to be taken of all factors. These include:

(A) in the absence of the relationship, whether the royalty agreement would have been made at all, or the rate or amount of royalties and other terms which would have been agreed; and

(B) if the asset in respect of which the royalties are paid (or any asset which it represents or from which it is derived) had previously been in the beneficial ownership of:

  (i) the person liable to pay the royalties;

  (ii) a person who has at any time carried on a business which, when the royalties fall due, is carried on in whole or part by the person liable to pay the royalties; or

  (iii) a person who is or has been an 'associate', as specially defined, of a person within (i) or (ii),

the amounts paid under the transaction(s) which resulted in the asset falling into its present beneficial ownership, the amounts which would have been so paid in the absence of the special relationship, and the question as to whether the transaction(s) would have taken place at all in the absence of that relationship.

The taxpayer must also show either that no special relationship exists, or the amount of royalties which would have been paid in the absence of the relationship, and if he cannot show that (B) above does not apply, he must show that the transaction(s) mentioned therein would have taken place in the absence of a special relationship, and the amounts which would then have been paid under those transaction(s).

[*ICTA 1988, s 808B*].

Simon's Direct Tax Service. See **F1.222.**

Royalties and 'know-how' payments. Notwithstanding that credit for overseas tax is ordinarily given only against income which arises (or is deemed to arise) in the overseas territory concerned, HMRC treatment as regards this class of income is as follows.

Income payments made by an overseas resident to a UK trader for the use, in that overseas territory, of any *copyright, patent, design, secret process or formula, trade mark etc.*, may be treated, for credit purposes (whether under double tax agreements or by way of unilateral relief) as income arising outside the UK — *except* so far as they represent consideration for services (other than merely incidental) rendered in the UK by the recipient to the payer (HMRC Extra Statutory Concession B8).

For the treatment of sales of 'know-how' etc., see 66.62 TRADING INCOME and 55.11 PROFIT COMPUTATIONS.

24.5 RELIEF BY WAY OF CREDIT

Relief is to be allowed by way of credit against attributable corporation tax (i.e. UK tax otherwise chargeable) on any income or chargeable gain ('the relevant income or gain') up to the amount of that tax (see below in relation to trade receipts). The foreign tax on the overseas income can only be set against the corresponding UK tax in respect of the same income (see 24.7 below). [*ICTA 1988, s 797(1)(2)*]. This applies both to unilateral relief [*ICTA 1988, s 790(1)–(3)*] and to relief by agreement, though it is confined in the latter case to those UK taxes which are covered by the agreement. [*ICTA 1988, s 793*]. Relief is only available against UK tax chargeable under the same Schedule and Case as that under which the foreign income on which the foreign tax was borne is chargeable (*George Wimpey International Ltd v Rolfe Ch D 1989, 62 TC 597*).

Both reliefs apply to corporation tax on chargeable gains as they do to income. [*ICTA 1988, ss 788(1), 790(1)*]. Relief for overseas tax paid is available against UK tax on chargeable gains provided that both liabilities relate to the same source, i.e. notwithstanding that they may arise at different times or be charged on different persons. (HMRC International Manual, INTM 161040 and HMRC Statement of Practice, SP 6/88).

Relief under an agreement is limited to that which would be allowed if all reasonable steps had been taken, including all relevant claims, elections, etc., under the law of the territory concerned or under double tax arrangements with that territory, to minimise the foreign tax payable. [*ICTA 1988, s 795A*].

As regards what HMRC considers taxpayers can and cannot reasonably be expected to do, the former is likely to include appeals against excessive assessments, claims for reliefs generally known to be available, and selection of any option which produces a lower tax liability, and the latter is likely to include claims to reliefs whose availability is uncertain, and where disproportionate expenditure would be required to pursue a claim, substituting carry-forward claims for carry-back claims and *vice versa*, and attempting to exercise influence the taxpayer does not have on the underlying tax paid by a subsidiary. See the brief note on HMRC's website (www.hmrc.gov.uk/international/dtr26.htm).

Trade income. The following restriction applies in relation to a credit for foreign tax in connection either with a payment of foreign tax on or after 16 March 2005 or with income received on or after that date in respect of which foreign tax has been deducted at source. This is subject to a transitional rule in relation to dividends paid before 1 January 2006, whereby the restriction cannot reduce the allowable credit for the foreign tax to less than 50% of the amount of that tax (unless the foreign tax is paid as part of a scheme or arrangement designed or entered into in order to benefit from the relaxation).

The meaning of 'relevant income or gain' under *ICTA 1988, 797(1)* (see above) is amended in relation to 'trade income' to refer only to so much of the income arising or gains accruing out of transactions in connection with which the foreign tax arises. For this purpose, '*trade income*' includes income or profits chargeable under Schedule D Cases I, II or V (see 66 TRADING INCOME) or of a property business (see 56.3 PROPERTY INCOME) or post-cessation receipts chargeable to corporation tax under Schedule D Case VI (see 66.3 TRADING INCOME) and any other case where the rules applicable to Schedule D Case I are used to calculate profits (but this does not apply to income of an insurance company to which *ICTA 1988, s 804C* applies).

In determining the corporation tax attributable to any income or gain, account is to be taken of deductions or expenses etc. that would be allowable and are directly attributable to the income and also a reasonable proportion of expenses etc. that are only partly attributable, e.g. overheads. Connected company (within *ICTA 1988, s 839*) expenses are also to be taken into account in so far as they are reasonably attributable to the income or gain.

Special cases. Where a foreign tax payment is made in connection with an asset which is in a 'hedging relationship' (as defined) with a derivative contract, the reference to 'relevant income or gain' for these purposes is extended to include the income arising out of the assets and the derivative contract taken together (but only so as to include the income or loss from the derivative contract as is reasonably attributable to the hedging relationship).

Where royalties from different non-UK jurisdictions are paid in respect of the same asset, the royalty income in a year of assessment in respect of that asset is to be treated as arising from a single transaction and the foreign tax credits in respect of such income are to be aggregated.

Where a person ('A) carrying on a trade enters into a scheme or arrangement with another person ('B') in order to circumvent the above provisions in relation to A, any income received in pursuance of the scheme or arrangement is to be treated as trade income of B.

Where there is a series or group of transactions, arrangements or assets (a 'portfolio') and a number of tax credits arise in respect of that portfolio, the income or gains arising from the portfolio or part of the portfolio may be aggregated and apportioned in a fair and reasonable manner. This is provided it is not reasonably practicable to prepare separate computations for each transaction etc. or separate computations would not, when compared with an aggregate computation, make a material difference to the amount of allowable credit for foreign tax.

[*ICTA 1988, ss 798A, 798B; FA 2005, s 86(1)(3)–(5)*].

See HMRC draft guidance 'Double Taxation Relief: Trade Receipts' issued on 6 May 2005 (available on their website at www.hmrc.gov.uk/budget2005/dtrtr.pdf).

See also 24.15 below in relation to banks and other financial traders regarding the case of *Legal & General Assurance Society Ltd v HMRC, Ch D [2006] STC 1763* (which preceded the above changes made by *FA 2005*).

Relief for disallowed credit. Where an amount of credit for foreign tax is disallowed because of the application of *ICTA 1988, s 797* above, relief may be available instead as a deduction in computing taxable profits. This has effect in relation to a credit for foreign tax in connection with either a payment of foreign tax on or after 16 March 2005 or with income received on or after that date in respect of which foreign tax has deducted at source, and has effect notwithstanding the general rule *in ICTA 1988, s 795(2)* that relief may be by credit or deduction but not a mixture of the two. The amount that can be deducted is the lower of the disallowed credit and the amount of any loss, *after* deducting foreign tax, that is attributable to the income in respect of which the foreign tax was paid; if there is no such loss, no deduction is available. [*ICTA 1988, s 798C; FA 2005, s 86(1)(3)(4)*]. See HMRC's draft guidance (available at www.hmrc.gov.uk/budget2005/dtrtr.pdf).

Anti-avoidance. See 5.19 for wide-ranging anti-avoidance provisions introduced by *FA 2005* applying to schemes or arrangements the main purpose or one of the main purposes of which is to obtain credit relief for foreign tax. This legislation was extended in *FA 2007*. [*ICTA 1988, ss 804ZA–804ZC, Sch 28AB; FA 2005, s 87, Sch 5; FA 2007 s 35*].

Simon's Direct Tax Service. See **F2.111** *et seq.*

Claims. Relief must be claimed within six years after the end of the accounting period for which the income or gains are chargeable or, if later, within one year after the end of the accounting period in which the foreign tax is paid. Where the amount of foreign tax payable is adjusted subsequent to a claim for relief, with the result that the tax credit becomes excessive, the taxpayer must give written notice to HMRC of this fact within one year of the date on which the adjustment is made, subject to a penalty for failure to comply which may not exceed the excess relief. Certain cases where the adjustment is taken into account under regulations relating to Lloyd's underwriters are excluded from this requirement. For this, and for HMRC view of what constitutes an 'adjustment', see HMRC International Manual, INTM 162120. [*ICTA 1988, s 806*]

Simon's Direct Tax Service. See **F1.134**.

24.6 **Utilisation of unrelieved foreign tax.** The provisions in 24.5 above apply, in the case of profits from an 'overseas permanent establishment' (for accounting periods beginning before 1 January 2003, a foreign branch or agency), to 'unrelieved foreign tax' (but not so as to permit carry back to an accounting period ending before 1 April 2000). '*Unrelieved foreign tax*' on any income is the excess of the amount of the credit for foreign tax which would (disregarding the limitation to corporation tax on that income) be available under any double tax arrangements against corporation tax in respect of the income over the amount which is actually so allowed. (There are no comparable provisions for unilateral relief (see 24.2 above).)

An '*overseas permanent establishment*' for this purpose is a 'permanent establishment' through which a company carries on a trade in a territory outside the UK, and '*permanent establishment*' has the meaning given by any double tax agreement with that territory or, in the absence of such a definition, the meaning given by *FA 2003, s 148* (see 60.5 RESIDENCE).

Where an amount of unrelieved foreign tax arises in respect of any UK-resident company 'qualifying income', the unrelieved foreign tax may, on a claim, be treated as if it were paid in respect of, and computed by reference to, income of the same description and from the same source in either:

(*a*) the next accounting period (and successive accounting periods), whether or not there is any income from that source in that accounting period; or

(*b*) such one or more preceding accounting periods, beginning not more than three years before that in which the unrelieved foreign tax arises, as results from applying the rules described below,

or partly in one way and partly in the other. The rules referred to in (*b*) above require that the unrelieved foreign tax must be so treated that:

(1) credit for it (or for any remaining balance) is allowed against corporation tax in respect of income of a later period before an earlier one; and

(2) before allowing credit for it against corporation tax in respect of any income of an accounting period, credit for foreign tax must be allowed first for foreign tax in respect of the income of that period (other than unrelieved foreign tax of another period), and then for unrelieved foreign tax arising in an earlier accounting period before a later one.

Where unrelieved foreign tax of an accounting period is treated as paid in respect of income of another accounting period, no further application of these provisions may be made in relation to that tax.

'*Qualifying income*' of a permanent establishment (or branch or agency) is those of its profits which are chargeable under Schedule D, Case I (or certain other such profits e.g. of life insurance companies). If a particular permanent establishment (or branch or agency) ceases in an accounting period, unrelieved foreign tax relating to it may not be carried forward from that period. If the company subsequently in the same period has a permanent establishment (or branch or agency) in the same territory, it is treated as a new and different source. However, two or more overseas permanent establishments (or branches or agencies) in the same territory which are taxed as one under the law of that territory are treated for the purposes of these provisions as a single permanent establishment (or branch or agency).

Claims to relief under (*a*) or (*b*) above must be made within six years of the end of the accounting period in which the unrelieved foreign tax arose (or, if later, within one year of the end of the accounting period in which the foreign tax in question is paid) and must specify the amounts to be dealt with under each of (*a*) and (*b*) above.

[*ICTA 1988, ss 806L, 806M; FA 2000, Sch 30 para 23; FA 2003, Sch 27 para 1*(*3*)].

There are similar provisions relating to underlying tax relief on dividend income (see 24.10 below). See *ICTA 1988, ss 806D–806G*.

Simon's Direct Tax Service. See F2.116.

24.7 **Allocation of charges.** In arriving at corporation tax attributable to the relevant income or gain for a relevant accounting period, the following is to be taken into account.

(i) Charges on income, expenses of management, expenses of insurance companies or other amounts which can be deducted from or set against or treated as reducing profits of more than one description may be allocated as the company thinks fit. [*ICTA 1988, s 797*(*3*)*; SI 2004 No 2310, Article 34*]. Charges so allocated may not, however, exceed the income against which they are set (*Commercial Union Assurance Co plc v Shaw CA 1999, 72 TC 101*).

(ii) Where a non-trading credit is brought into account as regards a loan relationship (see 46.3 LOAN RELATIONSHIPS), special provision is made for the attribution of corporation tax to such credits for the purposes of relief of any foreign tax on the item. A similar provision applies from 1 April 2002 in relation to non-trading credits on intangible fixed assets (see 39.6 INTANGIBLE ASSETS). [*ICTA 1988, ss 797A, 797B; FA 1998, s 82*(*2*)*; FA 2002, Sch 25 para 55, Sch 30 para 5*(*4*)]. Where, as regards loan relationships, this does not apply, and there is a non-trading deficit (see 46.3 LOAN RELATIONSHIPS) on the company's loan relationships, the deficit is allocated for foreign tax relief purposes in the same way as relief is claimed or is available under *FA 1996, s 83*. [*ICTA 1988, s 797*(*3A*)(*3B*)*; FA 1998, s 82*(*2*)*; FA 2002, Sch 25 para 54*].

(iii) (For accounting periods beginning on or after 1 January 2003) *ICTA 1988, s 11AA* (profits attributable to permanent establishments, see 60.5 RESIDENCE), and regulations thereunder, apply (with the necessary modifications) for these purposes. [*ICTA 1988, s 797*(*2A*)*; FA 2003, s 154*].

Simon's Direct Tax Service. See F2.112.

Example

The following information about A Ltd (which owns 20% of the voting power of B Ltd, a non-resident company) for the year ended 31 March 2008 is relevant.

	£
UK income	1,200,000
UK chargeable gains	300,000
Overseas income (tax rate 40%) from B Ltd (gross)	300,000
Charges paid (qualifying charitable donations)	150,000

A Ltd may allocate charges as it wishes in order to obtain maximum double tax relief. The following calculation shows how this is best done.

	UK income and gains	Overseas income	Total
	£	£	£
Income and gains	1,500,000	300,000	1,800,000
Deduct Charges	15,000	—	15,000
	£1,485,000	£300,000	£1,785,000
CT at 30%	445,500	90,000	535,500
Deduct Double tax relief	—	(90,000)	(90,000)
CT liability	£445,500	—	£445,500

If charges were set off against overseas income first, the following tax would be payable.

	UK income and gains	Overseas income	Total
	£	£	£
Income and gains	1,500,000	300,000	1,800,000
Deduct Charges	—	15,000	15,000
	£1,500,000	£285,000	£1,785,000
CT at 30%	450,000	85,500	535,500
Deduct Double tax relief	—	(85,500)	(85,500)
CT liability	£450,000	—	£450,000

This gives a maximum double tax relief of £85,500. Compared with the recommended allocation, £4,500 of double tax relief (£90,000 – £85,500) is lost, representing an increase in the corporation tax liability of £4,500 (£450,000 – £445,500).

24.8 **Shadow ACT.** Where relief is available for a foreign tax credit, the income or gain subject to the foreign tax is excluded from profits for the purpose of determining the maximum set-off of shadow ACT and surplus ACT (from accounting periods beginning before 6 April 1999, see 3.2 *et seq.* ADVANCE CORPORATION TAX—SHADOW ACT) and the foreign tax credit is deducted from the corporation tax liability. Shadow ACT can be set against the corporation tax liability relating to the foreign income or gain limited to the maximum ACT credit that would have applied had the foreign income or gain been the only income or gain for the accounting period or, if lower, the corporation tax liablity as reduced by the foreign tax credit (see *SI 1999 No 358, reg 12(4)(5)*).

24.9 UNDERLYING TAX

Underlying tax attributable to dividends. Where a dividend is paid to a UK resident company or to a non-resident company but forming part of the profits of a UK permanent establishment (see 60.5 RESIDENCE — previously a UK branch or agency) by a 'related company' in the circumstances set out in 24.2(*b*) above, relief is given for the following taxes payable by the overseas company in respect of its profits:

(*a*) any UK income or corporation tax; and

(*b*) any tax imposed by the law of any other territory,

being underlying tax, which is any tax not chargeable directly on, or by deduction from, the dividend.

Where the overseas company has received a dividend from a third company similarly related to the overseas company, relief may similarly be claimed (subject to certain restrictions on the taxes to be taken into account) for underlying tax payable by the third company, to the extent that it would have been taken into account had it been paid direct to a UK-resident company entitled to relief. Dividends payable through a chain of related companies may similarly be relieved. While relief is given only for underlying tax (and not withholding tax), it is given for withholding tax arising on dividends paid between foreign companies in a chain, which is treated as part of the underlying tax charge, under (*b*) above, in the recipient companies.

For this purpose, the 'related company' criteria in 24.2(*b*) above (where companies are treated as related where one company, or a company of which it is a subsidiary, controls at least 10% of the voting power in the other company) are amended where the dividend is paid on or after 1 January 2005 (for the purpose of implementing the amended Parent/Subsidiary Directive (see 24.13 below)). The companies in this case are also related where one company, or a company of which it is a subsidiary, controls at least 10% of the ordinary share capital of the other company.

See, however, 24.11 below as regards a general restriction on the amount of relief applicable where dividends are paid through so-called 'mixer' companies. See also 24.12 below as regards a restriction on the relief applicable where the overseas company is a controlled foreign company which is exempt from apportionment by virtue of an acceptable distribution policy.

In relation to claims for credit relief made on or after 31 March 2001 (where the dividend concerned was paid after that date) and to dividends paid before 2 December 2004, where the company paying the dividend up to the overseas company is UK-resident, any amount by which the underlying tax is restricted by virtue of the application of the mixer cap formula (see 24.11 below) to the dividend is allowed as an additional credit.

[*ICTA 1988, s 801; FA 2001, Sch 27 paras 3, 7; FA 2005, s 91(4)–(6)(8), Sch 11 Pt 9; F(No 2)A 2005, s 43*].

Simon's Direct Tax Service. See **F2.203**, **F2.229**.

Restriction of relief. Where an 'avoidance scheme' is involved, and underlying tax relating to a dividend includes an amount in respect of tax payable (by reference to the profits which bear that tax) at a rate in excess of the full corporation tax rate in force at the time the dividend was paid, relief is restricted as if tax had been payable at the corporation tax rate. An '*avoidance scheme*' for this purpose is a scheme or arrangement of any kind, a main purpose of which is to claim relief for an amount of underlying tax, and the parties to which include the company claiming the relief (or a related company or a connected person within *ICTA 1988, s 839*) and a person not under the control (as specially defined) of that company at any time before anything is done in relation to the scheme etc. [*ICTA 1988, s 801A; FA 2000, Sch 30 para 4(10)-(12)(14)*]. For an indication of Revenue practice as to the circumstances in which *section 801A* may be applied, see Revenue Tax Bulletin June 1997 p 441. Note that for dividends paid to the UK after 30 March 2001 this provision is largely redundant due to the introduction of the 'mixer' cap rules (see 24.11 below).

Example — ICTA 1988, s 801A

T Ltd, a UK-resident company liable to corporation tax at the full 30% rate for the year ended 31 March 2008, receives a dividend on 1 January 2008 of £18,500 (tax withheld £925) from X inc, a non-UK resident company in which it holds 20% of the voting power. It claims relief for underlying tax of £6,500 as follows.

£1,500 tax at 10% on profits of £15,000 out of which £13,500 dividend paid.

£5,000 tax at 50% on profits of Y pty (a subsidiary of X inc) from whom dividend received out of which £5,000 dividend paid.

T Ltd computes relief as follows.

		£	£
Gross dividend received			18,500
plus underlying tax			6,500
			£25,000
Tax thereon at 30%			7,500
less	underlying tax	6,500	
	tax withheld	925	7,425
Corporation tax payable			£75

It transpires, however, that the dividend from Y pty was bought in as part of a tax avoidance scheme, so that the provisions of *ICTA 1988, s 801A* apply. The computation is therefore revised as follows.

		£	£
Gross dividend received			18,500
plus underlying tax (see below)			3,643
			£22,143
Tax thereon at 30%			6,643
less	underlying tax	3,643	
	tax withheld	925	4,568
Corporation tax payable			£2,075

Underlying tax

The relief for underlying tax in respect of the dividend from Y pty is recalculated as if the tax rate on the underlying profits had been the corporation tax rate of 30% applicable at the time of receipt of the dividend from X inc by T Ltd.

£5,000 × 100/70 = £7,143 on which 30% tax is £2,143.

The total underlying tax is thus (£2,143 + £1,500 =) £3,643.

Simon's Direct Tax Service. See **F2.214.**

Foreign mergers. In relation to dividends received by a UK-resident company from an overseas company, relief for underlying tax also includes cases where profits of an overseas company ('company A'), which have borne foreign tax, become profits of another overseas company ('company B') other than by payment of a dividend (e.g. following a merger), and company B then pays a dividend to another company out of those profits. For the purposes of underlying tax relief, company B is treated as having paid the tax paid by company A in respect of those of its profits which have become profits of company B. However, the amount of relief accordingly available to a UK-resident company is limited to that which would have been available had the profits been transferred from company A to company B by way of dividend. [*ICTA 1988, s 801B*].

Simon's Direct Tax Service. See **F2.228.**

Group treated as a single entity. There are provisions enabling two or more overseas companies which are taxed as a single entity in the country or territory in which they are resident to be treated as a single company for underlying tax relief purposes in relation to the payment of a dividend to another company by any one of the overseas companies. [*ICTA 1988, s 803A*]. For this and for HMRC response to various questions on other aspects of the application of *section 803A* (with several examples), see Revenue Tax Bulletin August 2001 pp 870–874, now superseded by HMRC International Manual, INTM 164150. For the implications of their application in various countries, see Revenue Tax Bulletins February 2002 pp 911–913, February 2003 p 1007 and October 2003 pp 1063–1064.

With effect for dividends paid on or after 16 March 2005, the single company treatment does not apply to a controlled foreign company to which exemption applies under the 'acceptable distribution policy' test (see 21.13 CONTROLLED FOREIGN COMPANIES). [*ICTA 1988, s 803A(1A); FA 2005, s 90*].

Simon's Direct Tax Service. See **F2.226.**

24.10 **Calculation of underlying tax relief.** The underlying tax is calculated in accordance with *ICTA 1988, s 799*, by reference to the paying company's 'relevant profits'. It is so much of:

(*a*) the tax attributable to the proportion of the 'relevant profits' represented by the dividend;

(*b*) as does not exceed (for claims made *on or after 31 March 2001*) the formula of M% × (D+U), this being the corporation tax rate in force at the time the dividend is paid (M) applied to the sum of the dividend (D) and the underlying tax (U). The formula has come to be known as the 'mixer cap' formula (see 24.11 below).

With effect for dividends paid *on or after 16 March 2005*, no relief for underlying tax is given if a deduction is allowed in a foreign jurisdiction in respect of an amount determined by reference to the dividend.

The meaning of '*relevant profits*' was considered, in the case of *Bowater Paper Corporation Ltd v Murgatroyd HL 1969, 46 TC 37*, to be the profits available for distribution as shown by the accounts and not as computed for foreign tax purposes. This is added to any tax chargeable directly on, or deducted from, the dividend, and the total is deducted from the UK tax as under 24.5 above. '*Relevant profits*' are specifically defined in *ICTA 1988, s 799(5)-(7)* (as amended by *FA 2005, s 80, Sch 4 para 7*) as profits of any period shown as available for distribution in the accounts of the company paying the dividend. The 'accounts' in this case are those drawn up in accordance with the law of the country or territory in which the distributing company is incorporated or formed, with no provision for reserves, bad debts, impairment losses or contingencies except as required under that law.

The '*relevant profits represented by the divided*' are the profits of the specified period covered by the dividend or, if not paid for a specified period, the profits of the last period of account made up to the date before the dividend became payable. Where the total dividend exceeds the profits available for distribution of that period, the relevant profits are the profits of that period plus so much of the profits remaining available for distribution of preceding periods equal to the excess, taking the most recent preceding period before the next most recent preceding period and so on. In relation to dividends paid before 31 March 2001, the company paying the dividend could specify that it was paid out of '*specified*' profits, e.g. out of a dividend received from another company or out of trading profits of a particular period (*ICTA 1988, s 799(3)(b)* prior to its repeal). If no particular profits or period were specified, then, as above, the dividend was taken to be paid out of the profits of the last accounting period to have ended before the dividend became payable.

[*ICTA 1988, s 799*].

Where the paying company has *accumulated losses*, HMRC consider that the 'relevant profits' for this purpose are the undistributed profits of the most recent period available at the time of payment. Computations in line with a previous practice will, however, continue to be accepted for dividends paid between 31 March 2000 and 31 December 2001 inclusive. (HMRC Statement of Practice SP 3/01; Revenue Press Release 27 November 2001 and Annex D to Technical Note 'An Exemption for Substantial Shareholdings').

Rates of underlying tax are calculated by HMRC, Revenue Policy International (Underlying Tax Group), PO Box 46, Fitz Roy House, Nottingham NG2 1BD (tel. 0115–974 2033) in accordance with the following formula.

$$\frac{\text{actual tax paid} \times 100}{\text{actual tax paid} + \text{relevant profit}}$$

This formula automatically takes into account any deferred taxation charged plus under- and over-provisions for tax in previous years. (CCAB Memorandum 19 October 1979).

Example

A Ltd, a company resident in the UK, receives a dividend of £1,000 gross from B Ltd, an overseas company in which it controls 10% of the voting power. Overseas tax of £100 is deducted. The underlying tax rate for the dividend is agreed at 18%.

			£
Gross dividend			1,000.00
Underlying tax @ 18%			219.51
Underlying assessable income			£1,219.51
Corporation tax thereon @ say 30%			365.85
Overseas tax suffered:	Direct tax	100.00	
	Underlying tax	219.51	
Tax credit relief due			319.51
Corporation tax payable			£46.34

If the corporation tax liability were at 19% (£231.71), the relief would be restricted to this amount.

The underlying tax for which relief is given is limited in certain cases to the amount of the tax actually paid by the overseas company on the particular profits out of which the dividend is paid. This applies in particular to dividends declared by and from a company resident in Belize, the Gambia, Malaysia, Malta or Singapore (where relief is given under an agreement) or Guernsey or Jersey (where the relief is unilateral), each of which operates a 'company tax deducted' system whereby tax is deducted from the dividend at the standard corporate rate and accounted for to the tax authorities, but subject to subsequent adjustment. In so far as that tax is refunded or found not to be due, double tax relief is denied. (SP 12/93, 27 July 1993).

Credit for underlying tax along a chain of shareholdings is concessionally given to:

(i) portfolio shareholders (where relief is given under the relevant double tax agreement for underlying tax); or

(ii) resident insurance companies carrying on part of their business through an overseas branch or agency; or

(iii) resident companies controlling at least ten per cent of the voting power of an overseas company carrying on insurance business. Credit under this last head is subject to apportionment.

(HMRC Extra-Statutory Concession, C1).

General guidance on computing an underlying rate and information about underlying tax in overseas countries, is available from HMRC International, address as above. See also HMRC International Manual, INTM 164100 *et seq.* and INTM 164400 *et seq.* For calculation of relief for tax in overseas countries, see HMRC Double Taxation Manual, DT 2140 onwards (for example, for the calculation of relief for Californian corporate franchise tax, see DT 19855).

For underlying tax generally see *Barnes v Hely-Hutchinson HL 1939, 22 TC 655*; *Canadian Eagle Oil Co Ltd v R HL 1945, 27 TC 205*; *Brooke Bond & Co Ltd v Butter Ch D 1962, 40 TC 342.*

Split rate taxes. Where foreign tax on profits is dependent on how much of the profits is distributed, HMRC consider that the underlying tax in relation to a dividend should reflect the rate of tax on distributed profits rather than the average rate. For dividends paid between 31 March 2000 and 31 December 2001 inclusive, however, HMRC will in practice accept computations on either basis. (SP 3/01, 27 November 2001 and Annex D to Technical Note 'An Exemption for Substantial Shareholdings').

Simon's Direct Tax Service. See F2.202 *et seq.*, **F2.206, F2.209**.

24.11 MIXING AND ONSHORE POOLING

Restriction of relief — 'mixer' companies. Provisions which effectively eliminate the tax advantage of routing overseas dividends through 'mixer' companies in favourable foreign jurisdictions (such as the Netherlands) apply to claims for credit relief made on or after 31 March 2001, unless the dividend concerned was paid to the UK-resident company before that date. (For the purposes of such claims made on or after that date, however, all payments of dividends to the 'mixer' company or at more remote levels are deemed to have been subject to the new provisions.) In relation to such claims, the relievable underlying tax in respect of any dividend paid up through an overseas subsidiary (including a lower-tier subsidiary) is restricted by the formula of M% × (D+U), the restriction being to the corporation tax rate in force at the time the dividend was paid (M), applied to the sum of the dividend (D) and the underlying tax (U) to be taken into account (apart from these provisions). The claim for relief may, however, be so framed as to exclude any specified amounts of underlying tax from being taken into account for this purpose (which may prevent the application of the cap in certain cases and so allow for onshore pooling – see below).

The 'mixer cap' restriction does not, however, apply where the overseas companies paying and receiving the dividend are 'related' (in the circumstances described at 24.2(*b*) above). Neither does it apply where the companies are both resident in the same overseas territory (subject to Treasury regulations which may prescribe cases where this exclusion will not apply, for which see *SI 2001 No 1156* which prevents certain dual-resident companies resident in the same overseas territory from obtaining the benefit of mixing).

[*ICTA 1988, s 799(1)(b)(1A)(1B), s 801; FA 2000, Sch 30 paras 8, 11; FA 2001, Sch 27 para 2*].

Examples

(*A*) *Simple mixer company*

UK plc wholly owns Dutch Holding BV which in turn wholly owns Low Tax Co which pays tax at 10% and High Tax Co which pays tax at 40%. Both subsidiaries make pre-tax profits of £100 and make full distributions to the UK via Dutch Holding BV which does not pay any tax on the dividends. Low Tax Co is a trading company which is exempt from the CFC rules otherwise than through pursuing an acceptable distribution policy. All three subsidiaries are resident in different countries. The tax position for UK plc is as follows.

	£
Net dividend (69 + 90)	150
Underlying tax (10 + 40)	50
Schedule D Case V	200
Corporation tax @ 30%	60
Double tax relief (Low Tax Co £10 and High Tax Co £30 as restricted by the mixer cap)	(40)
UK tax liability	20
Unused tax credits	10

Note that for dividends paid to the UK before 31 March 2001, full relief would have been available for the foreign tax of £50 as the restriction would have applied only to the mixed dividend paid by Dutch Holding BV.

(*B*) *Simple mixer company with withholding tax*

The position is as in (A) above but the dividend paid by High Tax Co to Dutch Holding BV suffers withholding tax of £9.

Dividend from:	Low Tax Co	High Tax Co	Dutch Holding BV	
	£	£	£	£
Net dividend	90	60	141	
Underlying tax	10	40	50	
Withholding tax (see note below)			9	
Schedule D Case V	100	100		200
Corporation tax @ 30%	30	30		60
Double tax relief (as restricted)	(10)	(30)		(49)
UK tax liability				11
Unused tax credits				10

Note that under *ICTA 1988, s 801(1)(b)*, credit relief is given for any tax paid by an overseas company under the law of any other territory. Thus the withholding tax of £9 paid by Dutch Holding BV (via deduction at source) is treated as underlying tax in respect of its own profits (see 24.9 above).

(*C*) *Chain of subsidiaries – high into low tax mixing*

UK plc wholly owns Low Tax Co which pays tax at 20% and which in turn wholly owns High Tax Co which pays tax at 40%. Both subsidiaries (which are resident in different countries) make pre-tax profits of £100 and make full distributions. Low Tax Co is a trading company which is exempt from the CFC rules otherwise than through pursuing an acceptable distribution policy. The dividend from High Tax Co is exempt from tax in the hands of Low Tax Co. The tax position for UK plc is as follows.

	£
Net dividend	140
Underlying tax	60
Schedule D Case V	200
Corporation tax @ 30%	60
Double tax relief (Low Tax Co £20 and High Tax Co £30 as restricted by the mixer cap)	(50)
UK tax liability	10
Unused tax credits	10

(D) Chain of subsidiaries – low into high tax mixing

UK plc wholly owns High Tax Co which pays tax at 40% and which in turn wholly owns Low Tax Co which pays tax at 20%. Both subsidiaries (which are resident in different countries) make pre-tax profits of £100 and make full distributions. Low Tax Co is a trading company which is exempt from the CFC rules otherwise than through pursuing an acceptable distribution policy. The dividend from Low Tax Co is exempt from tax in the hands of High Tax Co. The tax position for UK plc is as follows.

	£
Net dividend	140
Underlying tax	60
Schedule D Case V	200
Corporation tax @ 30%	60
Double tax relief (see below)	(60)
UK tax liability	—

The mixer cap restriction does not apply to the dividend paid by Low Tax Co to High Tax Co because the tax paid of £20 is lower than £30 which is 30% of the sum of the dividend (£80) and the underlying tax (£20). Equally, the mixer cap restriction does not apply to the dividend paid by High Tax Co to UK plc because the total tax paid of £60 (£20 + £40) is no higher than 30% of the sum of the dividend of £140 (£80 + £60) and the underlying tax of £60 (£20 + £40).

See HMRC International Manual at INTM164220 and 164230 for a summary (with example) of these provisions. See also below for provisions which permit a degree of 'onshore pooling' of dividend income against the tax on which relief at a rate of up to 45% may be obtained for underlying tax so capped in certain cases.

Simon's Direct Tax Service. See **F2.211, F2.216–F2.218**.

Onshore pooling and utilisation of eligible unrelieved foreign tax. In relation, broadly, to dividends paid on or after 31 March 2001, relief for underlying tax on dividends paid up through overseas subsidiaries is generally restricted to corporation tax, at the full rate in force when the dividend is paid, on the gross amount of the dividend (the 'cap' aimed at avoidance through the use of so-called 'mixer' companies, see above). However, a partial relief from this capping restriction is provided by the concurrent introduction of a system of 'onshore pooling' of certain foreign dividends, against the tax on which may be set the excess tax over the cap, allowing relief up to a maximum of 45% in total. Relief may similarly be obtained up to the same overall 45% limit for unrelieved withholding and underlying tax on dividends received directly from overseas subsidiaries.

The scheme provides for the set-off of '*eligible unrelieved foreign tax*' against the UK tax arising on '*qualifying foreign dividends*'.

Eligible unrelieved foreign tax (EUFT) is the excess, subject to the 45% maximum limit, of:

(i) the credit for the foreign tax, excluding any underlying tax which has been restricted by the 30% cap, of a foreign dividend over the UK tax charged on the dividend (this being referred to as 'Case A' EUFT); and

(ii) the underlying tax of a foreign dividend which has been restricted by the mixer cap (this being referred to as 'Case B' EUFT).

Qualifying foreign dividends (QFDs) are foreign dividends other than:

- dividends paid by controlled foreign companies to satisfy the acceptable distribution policy test (see below), or dividends representing such dividends; and
- dividends for which relief is itself restricted (and so gives rise to EUFT – referred to as '*tainted dividends*'). Under *ICTA 1988, s 799(1B)*, a claim for relief can exclude a specific amount of underlying tax from being taken into account so as to prevent a dividend from becoming 'tainted'.

Other exclusions, both from pooling and from the categories of dividend on which unrelieved tax may be treated as eligible for relief under these provisions, are dividends treated (or which could be treated) as trading income under *ICTA 1988, s 393* (see 47.4 LOSSES), dividends the underlying tax on which is subject to restriction under *ICTA 1988, s 801A* (see 24.9 above) or *ICTA 1988, s 803* (see 24.15 below), and dividends treated under *ICTA 1988, s 811* as reduced by foreign tax paid for which no credit is allowable (see 24.4 above).

Relief for EUFT. For the purpose of giving relief, the following totals are aggregated (for any accounting period) and are treated as a single dividend or a single item of tax, as the case may be:

(*a*) 'related QFDs';

(*b*) 'unrelated QFDs';

(*c*) underlying tax on related QFDs; and

(*d*) withholding tax on both related and unrelated QFDs.

A '*related QFD*' is any QFD paid to a UK resident company by a foreign company which, at the time the dividend is paid, is related to the UK company (under the circumstances set out in 24.2(b) above). An '*unrelated QFD*' is a QFD paid by any other foreign company.

Credit relief is then given:

- firstly, for the aggregate underlying tax on related QFDs ((*c*) above) against the UK tax arising on the single related QFD ((*a*) above) (which must be grossed up for the underlying tax); and
- secondly, for the aggregate withholding tax ((*d*) above) against the UK tax arising on the single related QFD ((*a*) above) or against that arising on the single unrelated QFD ((*b*) above) or partly against both.

Any remaining UK tax arising on the QFDs (under (*c*) and (*d*) above) may then be reduced or eliminated by any EUFT, which is aggregated into:

(1) relievable underlying tax which can be set off against UK tax arising on the single related QFD ((*a*) above); and then

(2) relievable withholding tax which may be set off against UK tax arising on the single related QFD ((*a*) above) or the single unrelated QFD ((*b*) above) or partly against both.

Utilisation of EUFT. Provision is made for relief to be given in the same accounting period or in accounting periods beginning not more than three years before that in which the relievable tax arises, or to be carried forward, broadly in the same way as applies in relation to foreign tax on income other than dividend income (see 24.6 above). Repayment supplement is restricted where relief is carried back to an earlier accounting period, in the same way as applies in relation to the carry back of losses, loan relationship deficits, etc. (see 40.1 INTEREST ON OVERPAID TAX). Regulations allow the surrender of foreign tax relievable as above between members of GROUPS OF COMPANIES (32).

[*ICTA 1988, ss 806A–806J, 826(7BB)(7BC); FA 2000, Sch 30 paras 21, 29; FA 2001, Sch 27 paras 4, 5; SI 2001 Nos 1163, 3873; SI 2003 No 1829*].

UK permanent establishments. These provisions are applied to UK permanent establishments (or branches or agencies) of non-UK residents as they are to UK resident companies. [*ICTA 1988, s 806K; FA 2000, Sch 30 para 22*].

Controlled foreign company dividends. See 24.12 below as regards separate streaming and the restriction on relief for underlying tax where the overseas company is a controlled foreign company which is exempt from apportionment by virtue of an acceptable distribution policy.

Examples

(*E*) *Pooling*

UK plc has two wholly owned foreign subsidiaries, High Tax Co which pays tax at 40% and Low Tax Co which pays tax at 10%. Both subsidiaries (which are resident in different countries) make pre-tax profits of £100 and make full distributions to the UK. Low Tax Co is a trading company which is exempt from the CFC rules otherwise than through pursuing an acceptable distribution policy.

High Tax Co suffers underlying tax of £40 and withholding tax of £3, which is restricted by the mixer cap, giving rise to Case B EUFT of £10 and Case A EUFT of £3. Low Tax Co suffers underlying tax of £10, leaving a UK tax liability of £20. This can be relieved by the EUFT of £13 leaving a net liability of £7.

	High Tax Co	Low Tax Co	Pool
	£	£	£
Net dividend	60	90	150
Underlying tax	40	10	50
Schedule D Case V	100	100	200
Corporation tax @ 30%	30	30	60
Double tax relief (High Tax Co £30 restricted – mixer cap)	(30)	(10)	(40)
UK tax liability	—	20	20
Case B EUFT	10		(10)
Case A EUFT	3		(3)
Net liability			7

Had High Tax Co been subject to tax at 50%, the Case B EUFT would have been restricted to £15 (maximum relievable tax at 45% (£45) less the underlying tax as restricted by the mixer cap at 30% (£30)), leaving £5 of foreign tax which could not be used, and a net UK tax liability of £2.

(F) 'Tainted' dividends

UK plc wholly owns Dutch Holding BV which in turn wholly owns High Tax Co A which pays tax at 40% and Low Tax Co which pays tax at 10%. UK plc also wholly owns High Tax Co B which pays tax at 50%. All the subsidiaries make pre-tax profits of £100 and make full distributions (High Tax Co A and Low Tax Co via Dutch Holding BV). Low Tax Co is a trading company which is exempt from the CFC rules otherwise than through pursuing an acceptable distribution policy. All three subsidiaries are resident in different countries.

High Tax Co A suffers underlying tax of £40 which is restricted by the 30% mixer cap giving rise to Case B EUFT of £10. The dividend paid up to UK plc is a blend of this capped dividend and the 10% taxed dividend from Low Tax Co. Since EUFT has arisen on it, the dividend is not a QFD and so does not qualify for onshore pooling. UK tax of £20 arises (after relief for the underlying tax) on the Low Tax Co element of the blended dividend but the Case B EUFT of £10 cannot be relieved against it and can only be carried back or carried forward (assuming there is no other UK tax liability on low taxed dividends against which it could be relieved).

High Tax Co B suffers underlying tax of £50 which is restricted by the 30% mixer cap giving rise to Case B EUFT of £15 (limited by the 45% cap). Since the blended dividend from Dutch Holding BV is not a QFD and cannot be pooled, the EUFT can only be carried back or carried forward, leaving a net UK tax liability of £20.

	Dutch Hold-ing BV	High Tax Co B	Total
	£	£	£
Net dividend	150	50	200
Underlying tax	50	50	100
Schedule D Case V	200	100	300
Corporation tax @ 30%	60	30	90
Double tax relief (restricted by mixer cap)	(40)	(30)	(70)
UK tax liability	20	—	20
Unused Case B EUFT	10	15	

(G) Excluding underlying tax from a claim to avoid 'tainting'

The above situation in (F) could be mitigated by limiting the claim to High Tax Co A's underlying tax to 30%. In this case, the blended dividend from Dutch Holding BV would be a QFD and qualify for onshore pooling. The UK tax of £20 could be relieved by the Case B EUFT of £15 suffered by High Tax Co B, leaving a net UK tax liability of £5. The Case B EUFT of £10 arising on the dividend from High Tax Co A would be lost.

	Dutch Holding BV	High Tax Co B	Pool
	£	£	£
Net dividend	150	50	200
Underlying tax	50	50	100
Schedule D Case V	200	100	300
Corporation tax @ 30%	60	30	90
Double tax relief (as per limited claim)	(40)	(30)	(70)
UK tax liability	20	—	20
Case B EUFT (restricted to 45%)	—	15	(15)
Net UK tax liability			5

See HMRC International Manual at INTM164210–164340 for summaries of the provisions for onshore pooling and relief for eligible unrelieved foreign tax ('EUFT'), and of the CFC dividend provisions, together with a number of examples.

Simon's Direct Tax Service. See **F2.123, F2.218–F2.225**.

24.12 CONTROLLED FOREIGN COMPANY DIVIDENDS

Separate streaming of dividend. Where a controlled foreign company ('CFC') is exempt from a profit apportionment under *ICTA 1988, s 747* solely by virtue of the payment of a dividend or dividends satisfying the 'acceptable distribution policy' test (see 21.13 CONTROLLED FOREIGN COMPANIES), and any dividend by virtue of which that test is met (an 'ADP dividend') is a dividend paid by the CFC to another non-UK resident company and subsequently paid on to a UK resident, there are provisions for the separate streaming of the dividend for all credit relief purposes, thus in effect preventing the avoidance of tax on dividends paid in order to gain exemption from CFC apportionment. (See HMRC International Manual, INTM 204010 *et seq.*) These provisions have effect as above, broadly for dividends paid on or after 31 March 2001. [*ICTA 1988, s 801C; FA 2000, Sch 30 para 13*].

Restriction of relief for underlying tax. Where a dividend is paid on or after 2 December 2004 by an overseas company which is a CFC which is exempt from a profit apportionment under *ICTA 1988, s 747* solely by virtue of the payment of a dividend or dividends satisfying the ADP test (as above), and the dividend in question is an ADP dividend, anti-avoidance provisions apply to prevent the ADP dividend from attracting double tax relief in excess of that which would have been due in respect of an apportionment had the CFC not paid a dividend. A modified version of the 'mixer cap' formula (see 24.11 above) applies to restrict relief for underlying tax on dividends paid to the CFC by related companies (whether or not they are resident in the same overseas territory as the CFC). In this case, the relievable underlying tax in respect of any dividend paid up to the CFC is restricted by the formula of X × (D÷(1–X)) where X is the corporation tax rate in force at the time the dividend was paid (expressed as a decimal fraction) and D is the amount of the dividend. The effect is that credit relief in relation to dividends paid to the CFC is restricted to the amount of the current rate of corporation tax applied to the gross dividend, or the actual foreign tax paid if lower. [*ICTA 1988, s 801; FA 2005, s 89*].

See generally HMRC's draft guidance on 'Double Taxation Relief: Underlying Tax' (at www.hmrc.gov.uk/budget2005/dtrutc.pdf).

24.13 **DIVIDENDS, INTEREST, ETC. PAID TO NON-RESIDENTS**

Dividends. Before the abolition of ACT on 6 April 1999, HMRC could make arrangements with a UK resident company whereby it could pay to a non-resident shareholder that part of the tax credit relating to a dividend to which he was entitled under the terms of a double tax agreement (see 24.3 above). Such payment by the company discharged a corresponding amount of its liability to ACT. Under most agreements, half of the tax credit attached to a dividend, less a deduction by reference to a percentage of the sum of the dividend and the tax credit (see below), could be paid to the non-resident or set off against UK liabilities.

See *Steele v EVC International NV (formerly European Vinyls Corp (Holdings) BV) CA 1996, 69 TC 88* for refusal of tax credit in the case of certain 'connected' companies. See also *Océ Van Der Grinten NV v CIR ECJ Case C-58/01 [2003] STC 1248* where a challenge to the deduction from the payment of the half tax credit was dismissed by the European Court of Justice. See also 24.3 above for cases in connection with the various ACT group litigation orders in which it was found that UK legislation contravened EC law and regarding the restitution of ACT.

Where a treaty provides for an overseas recipient of distributions from a UK resident company to receive a tax credit determined by reference to the credit a UK resident individual would receive, subject to a deduction calculated by reference to the sum of the distribution and the tax credit paid, the deduction is to be calculated without any allowance for the deduction itself. [*FA 1989, s 115*].

Where set-off or repayment of a sum in respect of a tax credit would be available under an agreement, it may nevertheless be denied where the non-resident recipient is, or is an 'associated company' of, a company with a 'qualifying presence' in a 'unitary state'. A company has such a '*qualifying presence*' if it is a member of a 'group' 7½% of whose property, payroll or sales in the territory of which the state is a part are in that state. The Treasury may instead provide by order either that a company has a qualifying presence in a 'unitary state' if it is liable to tax on income or profits in that state, or alternatively that it has such a presence if its principal place of business is in that state, including the place(s) where central management and control and immediate day-to-day management are exercised. A '*unitary state*' is broadly a state, etc. which reserves the right to tax companies with sources of income within the state by taking into account the company's activities outside the territory of which the state is a part. The Treasury has powers to prescribe states, etc. as unitary states. A fine may be imposed where a tax credit is repaid despite its being within these provisions, and there are provisions for claiming tax credits following remedial legislation effective before 1 January 1987 in the unitary state, and to prevent avoidance by the payment of interest or the allowing of a discount in substitution for a distribution. Other terms are specifically defined in *ICTA 1988, s 812(5)*. These provisions, if applied, will take effect for distributions on or after a date to be appointed by the Treasury by statutory instrument, although implementation has now been indefinitely deferred, see Revenue Press Release 15 September 1993. [*ICTA 1988, ss 812–815; FA 1998, Sch 3 para 37; ITTOIA 2005, Sch 1 para 326*].

The European 'Parent-Subsidiary' Directive 90/435/EEC, which came into force on 1 January 1992, applies where the parent company holds a specified minimum of the capital of a company in another member state (or, by bilateral agreement, a specified minimum of the voting rights). The *Directive* provides that dividends paid to such a parent company are to be exempt from withholding tax in the country of the paying company, that the country of the parent company is equally not to charge withholding tax on the dividend received, and that the recipient country must either exempt the dividend from corporation tax or give credit for the proportion of the subsidiary's corporation tax relating to the dividend. Where the *Directive* applies and gives more favourable treatment than the dividends article in a double taxation agreement, the *Directive* is to take precedence over the agreement. The *Directive* applied (before 1 January 2005) where the parent company held a minimum of 25% of the capital of a company in another member. It was amended by *Directive 2003/123/EC*, which came into force on 2 February 2004 to be implemented with effect from 1 January 2005. The amended *Directive* gradually reduces the minimum capital holding to 20% from 1 January 2005, 15% from 1 January 2007 and 10% from 1 January 2009. A member state can instead, by means of a bilateral agreement, substitute a voting power test such as the 10% test used by the UK (see 24.2 above). The *Directive* is extended to cover all companies subject to tax within the European Union regardless of their legal form (including the new European Company – see 25.4 EUROPEAN COMMUNITY LEGISLATION), and the amendments extend double taxation relief by making a tax credit available for underlying tax paid by second-tier and lower-tier subsidiaries.

Interest etc. Where payments required or authorised to be made under deduction of UK income tax are made to non-UK residents, the payer may be authorised by HMRC, International — Centre for Non-Residents, by a notice under *SI 1970 No 488*, to make payments without deduction of tax, or under deduction of tax at a specified or maximum rate (but see below under European member states and also 37.4 INCOME TAX IN RELATION TO A COMPANY). Payments may normally only be so made once the notice has been given by HMRC following application by the overseas recipient, and there may be a substantial delay in HMRC being in a position to issue a notice in response to such an application. Accordingly, a Provisional Treaty Relief scheme provides for two types of loan, the one-to-one company loan (provided that there is no common shareholding or ownership) and the syndicated loan, where there is a syndicate manager. This allows the UK borrower to apply for immediate authority to make payments incorporating the treaty relief, pending a decision by HMRC on the issue of a formal notice. It is a condition of the scheme that the recipient's application for relief (certified by the overseas tax authority) is received by HMRC within three months of the provisional authority, and if that condition is not met, or the relief is found not to be due, HMRC will look to the payer for the tax that should have been deducted (and any interest thereon). In the case of a syndicated loan, a composite application for relief (which does not need overseas tax authority certification) must be made by the syndicate manager within three months of the provisional authority.

Application for provisional relief is made on form PTR PAY 1 (in the case of one-to-one loans) or forms PTR SM 1 or PTR SM 1A (in the case of syndicated loans), which may be obtained from HMRC's website (www.hmrc.gov.uk/cnr/dtt_inter.htm) or from HMRC, International — Centre for Non-Residents, Fitz Roy House, PO Box 46, Nottingham NG2 1BD (tel. 0115–974 1940). Explanatory 'Guidelines' may be obtained from the same address. For a summary of the scheme, see Revenue Tax Bulletin June 1999 pp 668–670.

European member states. With effect for payments made **on or after 1 January 2004**, FA 2004 implements the European *Directive 2003/49/EC* adopted by the EU on 3 June 2003 whereby certain payments of interest and royalties between associated companies of different EU member states are exempt from income tax. See 37.4 INCOME TAX IN RELATION TO A COMPANY. [*FA 2004, ss 97–106; ITTOIA 2005, ss 757–767, Sch 1 paras 631–639*].

There is a limited discretion available to UK companies or permanent UK establishments of EU companies, which believe that a royalty payment is exempt from deduction of tax at source. Payment may be made gross to an EU company. However, tax will be due if payment is made gross but it subsequently appears that exemption was not available. [*ITA 2007, s 758, Sch 1 paras 576, 577*]

Beneficial ownership. One of the most important conditions for treaty relief is that the recipient must be the 'beneficial owner' of the interest or dividend, etc. In determining whether the recipient of dividends, interest or royalties is the 'beneficial owner', HMRC will, as far as UK double taxation conventions are concerned, interpret 'beneficial ownership' using the 'international fiscal meaning'. In the case of *Indofood International Finance Ltd v JP Morgan Chase Bank NA [2006] EWCA Civ 158*, the Court of Appeal supported the view (in the OECD Model Convention on Income and on Capital) that, under an 'international fiscal meaning', beneficial ownership is to be determined by reference to a test which requires that the recipient 'enjoy the full privilege to directly benefit from the income'. It added that where recipients are bound in commercial and practical terms to pass on the income, they will not be the beneficial owner of the income and so not entitled to treaty relief. See HMRC guidance provided in their Internet Statement of 9 October 2006 (at www.hmrc.gov.uk/news/indofood.pdf) which follows the *Indofood* case and which discusses their practice in relation to existing treaty clearances.

Simon's Direct Tax Service. See F1.302-F1.304.

24.14 AGREEMENTS IN FORCE

Agreements with the following countries came into force from the date specified in each agreement and remain so until further notice. *SI* dates and numbers are given in round brackets. For the agreement relating to the Republic of Ireland, see Tolley's Income Tax. For details of agreements, see Simon's Direct Tax Service Part F4.

Antigua and Barbuda (1947/2865, 1968/1096); **Argentina** (1997/1777); **Australia** (1968/305, 1980/707, 2003/3199)(new treaty applies from 1 April 2004 (UK) and from 1 July 2004 (Australia)); **Austria** (1970/1947, 1979/117, 1994/768); **Azerbaijan** (1995/762);

Bangladesh (1980/708); **Barbados** (1970/952, 1973/2096); **Belarus** (1986/224 – see note below); **Belgium** (1987/2053); **Belize** (1947/2866, 1968/573, 1973/2097); **Bolivia** (1995/2707); **Bosnia-Hercegovina** (1981/1815 – see note below); **Botswana** (1978/183, 2006/1925) (new treaty applies from 1 April 2007 with respect to corporation tax, from 6 April 2007 with respect to income tax and capital gains tax (UK) and 1 July 2007 (Botswana)); **Brunei** (1950/1977, 1968/306, 1973/2098); **Bulgaria** (1987/2054); **Burma** (see Myanmar);

Canada (1980/709, 1980/1528, 1985/1996, 2003/2619) (new protocol to take effect from 1 April 2005 (UK) and 1 January 2005 (Canada)), (1980/780, 1987/2071, 1996/1782 revoked from 1 January 2001 – see 2000/3330); **Chile** (2003/3200) (from 1 April 2005 (UK) and 1 January 2005 (Chile)); **China** (1984/1826, 1996/3164) (see also note below); **Croatia** (1981/1815 – note below); **Cyprus** (1975/425, 1980/1529); **Czech Republic** (1991/2876 – see note below);

Denmark (1980/1960, 1991/2877, 1996/3165);

Egypt (1980/1091); **Estonia** (1994/3207);

Falkland Islands (1997/2985); **Fiji** (1976/1342); **Finland** (1970/153, 1980/710, 1985/1997, 1991/2878, 1996/3166); **France** (1968/1869, 1973/1328, 1987/466, 1987/2055);

Gambia (1980/1963); **Georgia** (2004/3325) (from 1 April 2006 (new treaty applies from 6 April 2006 with respect to income tax and capital gains tax) (UK) and 1 January 2006 (Georgia)) (see also note below); **Germany** (1967/25, 1971/874); **Ghana** (1993/1800); **Greece** (1954/142); **Grenada** (1949/361, 1968/1867); **Guernsey** (1952/1215, 1994/3209); **Guyana** (1992/3207);

Hungary (1978/1056);

Iceland (1991/2879); **India** (1993/1801); **Indonesia** (1994/769); **Ireland** (Republic of) (1976/2151, 1976/2152, 1995/764, 1998/3151); **Isle of Man** (1955/1205, 1991/2880, 1994/3208); **Israel** (1963/616, 1971/391); **Italy** (1990/2590); **Ivory Coast** (1987/169);

Jamaica (1973/1329); **Japan** (1970/1948, 1980/1530, 2006/1924) (new treaty applies from 1 January 2007 with respect to taxes withheld at source, from 1 April 2007 with respect to corporation tax, from 6 April 2007 with respect to income tax and capital gains tax (UK) and 1 January 2007 (Japan)); **Jersey** (1952/1216, 1994/3210); **Jordan** (2001/3924) (from 1 April 2003 (UK) and 1 January 2003 (Jordan));

Kazakhstan (1994/3211, 1998/2567); **Kenya** (1977/1299); **Kiribati and Tuvalu** (1950/750, 1968/309, 1974/1271); **Korea (South)** (1996/3168); **Kuwait** (1999/2036) (from 1 April 2001 (UK) and 1 January 2001 (Kuwait)); **Kyrgyzstan** (see note below);

Latvia (1996/3167); **Lesotho** (1997/2986) from 1 April 1998; **Lithuania** (2001/3925, 2002/2847) (from 1 April 2002 (UK) and 1 January 2002 (Lithuania) (subject to protocol)) (and see note below); **Luxembourg** (1968/1100, 1980/567, 1984/364);

Macedonia (1981/1815 – note below); **Malawi** (1956/619, 1964/1401, 1968/1101, 1979/302); **Malaysia** (1997/2987); **Malta** (1995/763); **Mauritius** (1981/1121, 1987/467, 2003/2620); **Mexico** (1994/3212); **Moldova** (see note below); **Mongolia** (1996/2598); **Montserrat** (1947/2869, 1968/576); **Morocco** (1991/2881); **Myanmar** (1952/751);

Namibia (1962/2352, 1967/1490); **Netherlands** (1980/1961, 1990/2152) (1967/1063 revoked from 1 January 2001 – see 2000/3330); **New Zealand** (1984/365, 2004/1274) (new protocol applies from 1 April 2005 (4 November 2003 with respect to capital gains and exchange of information) and from 1 January 2005 (New Zealand)); **Nigeria** (1987/2057); **Norway** (1985/1998, 2000/3247)(new treaty applies from 1 April 2001 (UK) and 1 January 2001 (Norway));

Oman (1998/2568);

Pakistan (1987/2058); **Papua New Guinea** (1991/2882); **Philippines** (1978/184); **Poland** (2006/3323); **Portugal** (1969/599);

Romania (1977/57); **Russian Federation** (1994/3213);

St. Christopher (St. Kitts) and Nevis (1947/2872); **Serbia and Montenegro** (1981/1815 – see note below); **Sierra Leone** (1947/2873, 1968/1104); **Singapore** (1997/2988); **Slovak Republic** (1991/2876 – see note below); **Slovenia** (1981/1815 – see note below); **Solomon Islands** (1950/748, 1968/574, 1974/1270); **South Africa** (1969/864, 2002/3138) (new treaty applies from 1 April 2003 (UK) and 1 January 2003 (South Africa)); **Spain** (1976/1919, 1995/765); **Sri Lanka** (1980/713); **Sudan** (1977/1719); **Swaziland** (1969/380); **Sweden** (1984/366) (1961/619 revoked from 1 January 2001 – see 2000/3330); **Switzerland** (1978/1408, 1982/714, 1994/3215);

Taiwan (2002/3137) from 1 April 2003 (UK) and 1 January 2003 (Taiwan); **Tajikistan** (1986/224 – see note below); **Thailand** (1981/1546); **Trinidad and Tobago** (1983/1903); **Tunisia** (1984/133); **Turkey** (1988/932); **Turkmenistan** (1986/224 – see note below);

Uganda (1993/1802); **Ukraine** (1993/1803); **USA** (1980/568; 2002/2848) (from 1 April 2003 (UK) (1 May 2003 with respect to taxes withheld at source) and 1 January 2004 (US) — 1946/1331, 1955/499, 1961/985, 1980/779, 1994/1418, 1996/1781 all revoked from 1 January 2001 (see 2000/3330) and see note below); **USSR** (see note below); **Uzbekistan** (1994/770);

Venezuela (1996/2599); **Vietnam** (1994/3216);

Yugoslavia (see note below);

Zambia (1972/1721, 1981/1816); **Zimbabwe** (1982/1842).

Shipping & Air Transport only — Algeria (Air Transport only) (1984/362), Argentina (but see now above), Belarus (but see now above), Brazil (1968/572), Cameroon (Air Transport only) (1982/1841), China (Air Transport only) (1981/1119), Ethiopia (Air

Transport only) (1977/1297), Hong Kong (Air Transport only) (1998/2566), Hong Kong (Shipping only) (2000/3248) from 1 April 2002, Iran (Air Transport only) (1960/2419), Jordan (1979/300), Kuwait (Air Transport only) (1984/1825), Lebanon (1964/278), Russia (but see now above), Saudi Arabia (Air Transport only) (1994/767), Venezuela (but see now above), USSR (but see now above), Ukraine (but see now above), Uzbekistan (but see now above), Zaire (1977/1298).

Notes.

China. The Convention published as *SI 1984 No 1826* does not apply to the Hong Kong or Macao Special Administrative Regions. (Revenue Tax Bulletin October 1996 p 357). See above as regards Hong Kong Air Transport and Shipping agreements.

Czechoslovakia. The Convention published as *SI 1991 No 2876* is treated as remaining in force between the UK and, respectively, the Czech Republic and the Slovak Republic. (HMRC Statement of Practice, SP 5/93).

USA. For an article setting out the understanding of HMRC on how certain of the provisions of the new USA treaty will be interpreted and applied, see Revenue Tax Bulletin Special Edition April 2003.

USSR. Following the dissolution of the USSR, new agreements have come into force with Azerbaijan, Estonia, Kazakhstan, Latvia, Lithuania (subject to protocol), the Russian Federation, Ukraine and Uzbekistan (see above). *SI 1986 No 224* (the former USSR agreement) is treated as continuing to apply to Belarus, Tajikistan and Turkmenistan (in the case of Belarus until the coming into force of *SI 1995 No 2706*). It was similarly so treated by the UK until 31 March 2002 in the case of Armenia, Georgia, Kyrgyzstan, Lithuania and Moldova (none of which considered itself bound by that convention) but as ceasing so to apply after that date (although new treaties are in force with Lithuania (subject to protocol) and with Georgia). (HMRC Statement of Practice, SP 4/01, as revised).

Yugoslavia. The Convention published as *SI 1981 No 1815* is treated as remaining in force between the UK and, respectively, Bosnia-Herzegovina, Croatia, Macedonia, Serbia and Montenegro and Slovenia. Negotiations for a new double taxation convention are taking place with Croatia, Serbia and Montenegro and Slovenia. A new agreement was signed with Macedonia on 8 November 2006, but it has not yet entered into force. (HMRC Statement of Practice 3/2004 (superseding SP 6/93), Revenue Press Release, 29 September 2004).

24.15 BANKS AND OTHER FINANCIAL TRADERS

Restriction of credit relief: post FA 2005. Special provisions restrict the amount of double taxation relief which can be claimed by banks or other financial concerns involved in overseas lending. .With effect for payments of foreign tax on or after16 March 2005, or income received on or after that date in respect of which foreign tax has been deducted at source, see 24.5 above for the restrictions which apply to credit relief for foreign tax in connection with trade income. Provisions also restrict underlying tax which a UK bank (or a company connected with the bank) can claim on dividends received from a foreign related company. The restriction applies where the underlying tax is (or includes) foreign tax on interest or dividends earned or received by the foreign related company (or by a third, fourth or successive company); and where the restrictions set out in 24.5 above in relation to trade income would have applied to that company if it were UK resident. The credit for underlying tax is not to exceed the UK corporation tax, at the rate in force at the time when the foreign tax was chargeable, on the amount of interest or dividends less the company's 'relevant expenditure' which is properly attributable to the earning of the interest or dividends.

[*ICTA 1988, ss 798–798C, 803*; *FA 2005, s 86*].

See *Legal & General Assurance Society Ltd v HMRC, Ch D [2006] STC 1763* (which preceded the changes made by *FA 2005*), where the High Court confirmed (in dismissing HMRC's appeal) that the legislation did not require the identification of the UK profit which corresponded exactly with the foreign taxable income for the purpose of determining the credit available for foreign tax paid.

See HMRC's draft guidance 'Double Taxation Relief: Trade Receipts' issued on 6 May 2005 (available on their website at www.hmrc.gov.uk/budget2005/dtrtr.pdf).

Restriction of credit relief: pre FA 2005. Before the above modifications, the position is, broadly, that the amount of double taxation relief available is restricted by reducing the amount of any interest or dividends by 'financial expenditure' (such as interest, discounts, etc. as defined) and by restricting the foreign tax on interest or withholding tax on dividends to 15 per cent of the gross amount before any adjustment to that amount for tax spared. Where the foreign tax includes spared tax, the foreign interest or dividends are treated as increased by the amount of spared tax up to a limit of 15%, this being the maximum credit which can be obtained. Similar provisions limit underlying tax which a UK bank (or a company connected with the bank) can claim on dividends received from a foreign related company. The restriction applies where the underlying tax is (or includes) foreign tax on interest or dividends earned or received by the foreign related company (or by a third, fourth or successive company); and where the above restrictions would have applied to that company if it were UK resident. The credit for underlying tax is not to exceed the UK corporation tax, at the rate in force at the time when the foreign tax was chargeable, on the amount of interest or dividends less the company's 'relevant expenditure' (the 'financial expenditure' as above if the company were UK resident) which is properly attributable to the earning of the interest or dividends.

[*ICTA 1988, ss 798–798B, 803* (as originally enacted)*; FA 2002, Sch 23 para 20, Sch 27 para 11; SI 1999 No 3330*].

See Revenue Tax Bulletin April 1996 p 306.

Foreign residents. Non-UK resident persons (whether companies or individuals) trading in the UK through permanent establishments (or branches or agencies) may claim tax credit relief for tax withheld by a third country from interest on a loan to a resident of that country. [*ICTA 1988, s 794(2)(bb); FA 2001, Sch 27 para 7*].

See *CIR v Commerzbank AG; CIR v Banco Do Brasil SA Ch D 1990, 63 TC 218* for a case on interest exemption under the UK/USA Agreement.

See also 47.25 LOSSES.

Simon's Direct Tax Service. See F3.101 *et seq.*

24.16 OIL COMPANIES

There are special provisions relating to oil fields which straddle international boundaries. [*FA 1980, s 107*].

25 European Community Legislation

25.1 **EC STATEMENTS**

Statements of the European Council and European Commission are graded under the *EC Treaty* as follows.

(*a*) **Regulations** are binding in their entirety and have general effect in all member states. They are directly applicable in the legal systems of member states and do not have to be implemented by national legislation.

(*b*) **Directives** are binding as to result and their general effect is specific to named member states. The form and methods of compliance are left to individual member states, which are normally given a specific period in which to implement the necessary legislation.

(*c*) **Decisions** are binding in their entirety and are specific to a member state, commercial enterprise or private individual. They take effect on notification to the addressee.

(*d*) **Recommendations and opinions** are not binding and are directed to specific subjects on which the Council's or Commission's advice has been sought.

25.2 **EC JURISDICTION**

European Community law is effective in the UK by virtue of *European Communities Act 1972, s 2*, and the European Court of Justice has held that 'wherever the provisions of a Directive appear ... to be unconditional and sufficiently precise, those provisions may ... be relied upon as against any national provision which is incompatible with the Directive in so far as the provisions define rights which individuals are able to assert against the State' (*Becker v Finanzamt Munster-Innenstadt [1982] 1 CMLR 499*). Judgments in the European Court of Justice also have supremacy over domestic decisions, even if the proceedings commenced in another member state.

25.3 **APPLICABLE REGULATIONS AND DIRECTIVES**

In contrast to the extensive application of EU legislation in the VAT sphere, direct taxes are currently subject to only the following specific measures.

(*a*) *Council Regulation 2137/85* (25 July 1985) concerning European Economic Interest Groupings.

(*b*) *Directive 90/434/EEC* (23 July 1990) concerning deferral of tax on income and gains on mergers, divisions, transfers of assets and exchanges of shares between companies of different member states (as amended by *Directive 2005/19/EC*, 17 February 2005 concerning the transfer of registered offices of European companies between member states).

(*c*) *Directive 90/435/EEC* (23 July 1990) as amended by *Directive 2003/123/EC* (2 February 2004) concerning distributions of profits to parent companies.

(*d*) *Directive 2003/48/EC* (3 June 2003) concerning the taxation of savings income.

(*e*) *Directive 2003/49/EC* (3 June 2003) concerning interest and royalty payments.

See also 25.4 below on the European Company.

As regards (*a*), see the related UK legislation at 55.9 PROFIT COMPUTATIONS, and as regards (*b*), 11.11, 11.12 CAPITAL GAINS. As regards (*c*), see 24.13 DOUBLE TAX RELIEF. As regards (*d*), see 61.24 RETURNS and as regards (*e*), see 37.3 INCOME TAX IN RELATION TO A COMPANY.

For a case on the application of *Directive 90/434/EEC*, see *Leur-Bloem v Inspecteur der Belastingdienst/Ondernemingen Amsterdam 2 (Case C-28/95) ECJ, [1997] STC 1205.*

In addition to the above, *Convention 90/436/EEC* (23 July 1990), concerning arbitration in double taxation disputes, came into force on 1 January 1995. See 5.11 ANTI-AVOIDANCE.

25.4 THE EUROPEAN COMPANY

The European Public Limited-Liability Company Regulations 2004 (*SI 2004 No 2326*) give effect to the*The European Company Statute Regulation* (*Council Regulation (EC) No 2157/2001*) *and Directive 2001/86/EC*, which was adopted on 8 October 2001 (see European Commission Press Release IP/01/1376), and applies to all member states with effect from 8 October 2004. It creates the legal framework for a new corporate entity, the European Company or 'Societas Europaea' (SE), to facilitate cross-border activities within the European Union including cross-border mergers. The new form of company, which is entirely voluntary and available to commercial bodies which operate in more than one member state, is a European public limited-liability company registered in one of the member states, with a minimum share capital of 120,000 euros. The company can be formed in a number of ways as set out in the Regulations (broadly formation by merger, formation of a holding SE or a subsidiary SE, or by conversion of a public limited company into an SE). (See DTI Press Release 13 September 2004.)

F(No 2)A 2005, ss 51–65 included provisions dealing with the tax consequences of the formation of an SE by merger of two or more companies resident in different member states (a company being treated as resident in a member state if it is within a charge to tax under the law of the State as a resident and is not treated under a double tax treaty as resident outside the EC). The provisions cover the deferral of tax charges on the formation of the SE that would otherwise arise in respect of:

- capital gains and capital allowances (see 11.13 CAPITAL GAINS);
- intangible assets (see 39.24 INTANGIBLE ASSETS);
- loan relationships (see 46.23 LOAN RELATIONSHIPS); and
- derivative contracts (see 28.20 FINANCIAL INSTRUMENTS AND DERIVATIVE CONTRACTS).

Anti-avoidance provisions ensure that the rules apply only to the formation of an SE by merger effected for *bona fide* commercial reasons and which is not part of a scheme or arrangements of which the main purpose (or one of the main purposes) is avoiding a liability to tax. There are provisions for obtaining advance clearance from HMRC that the transactions satisfy the anti-avoidance provision. The provisions have effect in relation to the formation of SEs occurring on or after 1 April 2005.

Residence. For the residence for tax purposes of an SE transferring its registered office to the UK, see 60.1 RESIDENCE.

Continuity on ceasing to be UK resident. If at any time a company ceases to be resident in the UK in the course of the formation of an SE by merger (whether or not the company continues to exist following the merger), *FA 1998, Sch 18* (company RETURNS (61), ASSESSMENTS (7), APPEALS (6), etc.) applies after that time in relation to liabilities accruing and other matters arising before that time as if the company were still UK-resident and, if the company has ceased to exist, as if the SE were the company.

Where an SE transfers its registered office outside the UK and ceases to be UK-resident, *FA 1998, Sch 18* applies after that time in relation to liabilities accruing and other matters arising before that time as if the SE were still UK-resident.

[*F(No 2)A 2005, s 61*].

25.5 HOME STATE TAXATION FOR SMES

The European Commission has adopted a Communication proposing that EC member states allow small and medium-sized enterprises (SMEs) to compute their taxable corporate profits according to the tax rules of the home state of their parent company or head office ('Home State Taxation'). The different national tax rates would then apply to the share of profits allocated to each member state according to an agreed allocation mechanism. The system, which would apply to SMEs which establish subsidiaries or permanent establishments in another member state, would be voluntary for member states and would initially run as a pilot scheme for five years. Member states agreeing to introduce the scheme could do so through bilateral or multilateral agreements, protocols supplementing existing double taxation treaties or multilateral conventions or by concluding new multilateral conventions.

An SME would be defined in accordance with the general EC definition in *Commission Recommendation 2003/361/EC* familiar in all member states, that is, a company with less than 250 employees and having a turnover not exceeding €50 million and/or a balance sheet total not exceeding €43 million. The Commission suggests that member states may restrict the application of the scheme to small enterprises (companies with less than 50 employees and having a turnover not exceeding €10 million and/or a balance sheet total not exceeding €10 million).

The '*home state*' of a participating SME-group is defined as the country of tax residence of the lead company. In the case of doubt or dual residence, it would be the country in which the place of effective management (or central management and control) of the lead company is located and where this company is subject to corporation tax before entering the pilot scheme. Where this rule does not resolve the issue, the tax administrations of the member states in which the group is active must agree on the home state in order for the company to take part in the pilot scheme.

The Commission suggests a simple formula be used for apportioning the tax base between participating member states. It recommends using the respective share in a combination of the total payroll and overall turnover.

Qualifying enterprises could join the scheme at any time during the five-year period and thus participate for shorter periods. However, once a company joins the scheme, the Commission considers it should remain in the scheme until its pre-determined end. If it is made possible for the enterprise to leave the scheme early, the tax years under the scheme would be re-assessed with retroactive application of the normal tax rules. Companies in certain sectors subject to specific corporation tax rules, such as shipping, financial services, oil and gas trade and exploration and agricultural services, can be excluded from the scheme. The scheme would apply to corporation taxes only but member states could apply national or local profit-related surcharges on the member state's share of corporation tax. Non-profit related local or regional taxes could also be levied under the rules of the member states involved.

The pilot scheme will include rules for exceptional cases and anti-avoidance provisions.

See European Commission Press Release IP/06/11 of 10 January 2006 (SWTI 2006 p 171).

26 Exchange Gains and Losses

Simon's Direct Tax Service. See **B3.17, D2.9, D2.18, D2.19**.

Cross references. See 28 FINANCIAL INSTRUMENTS DERIVATIVE CONTRACTS AND SECURITISATION and 46 LOAN RELATIONSHIPS.

The headings in this chapter are as follows.

26.1 INTRODUCTION

For accounting periods beginning on or after 23 March 1995 and before 1 October 2002, the provisions of *FA 1993, ss 125–169, Schs 15–18*, as set out in 26.5 to 26.32 below, apply to the determination, and charge or relief, of exchange gains and losses of companies (other than certain charitable companies, investment trusts and deemed companies in relation to authorised unit trusts, see 26.6 below).

With effect for accounting periods beginning **on or after 1 October 2002**, these provisions have been **repealed** by *FA 2002, s 79, Sch 23* and assimilated into the rules applying for LOAN RELATIONSHIPS (46) and FINANCIAL INSTRUMENTS AND DERIVATIVE CONTRACTS (28) (see 26.5 below). In tandem with these changes, the corporation tax currency provisions set out in 26.33 to 26.42 below have been extended and simplified.

For accounting periods beginning before 23 March 1995 (and for companies to which the provisions do not apply), the position continues to be as described at 26.2 *et seq.* below (which also applies to taxpayers other than companies).

Notwithstanding the above, for accounting period beginning on or after 1 January 2000, the provisions relating to foreign currency accounting as described at 26.39–26.42 below continue to apply as revised by *FA 2004, Sch 10 para 77*, described at 26.35–26.38. The legislation is changed by *FA 2004, s 52, Sch 10* (as amended) for the revised UK financial reporting standard for foreign currencies (FRS 23 – the pre-FA 2004 provisions having been based on SSAP 20) which is based on the international accounting standard (IAS) 21, the adoption of which is mandatory for listed companies and optional for other companies for accounting periods beginning on or after 1 January 2005 (mandatory for unlisted companies using fair value measures for accounting periods beginning on or after 1 January 2006). The new provisions thus have effect for periods of account beginning on or after 1 January 2005 and are referred to in this chapter as the 'post-2004 basis of computation'. [*FA 2004, s 52, Sch 10 para 77; FA 2005, Sch 4 para 50*].

26.2 **GENERAL CASE LAW AND PRACTICE**

Under general case law, exchange differences are taken into account in computing trading profits if they relate to the circulating capital of the business but not otherwise. In *Overseas Containers (Finance) Ltd v Stoker CA 1989, 61 TC 473*, exchange losses arising on loans transferred to a finance subsidiary set up to convert the losses to trading account were held not to arise from trading transactions.

In *Davies v The Shell Co of China Ltd CA 1951, 32 TC 133*, a petrol marketing company operating in China required agents to deposit Chinese dollars with it, repayable on the ending of the agency. Exchange profits it made on repaying the deposits were held to be capital. In *Firestone Tyre & Rubber Co Ltd v Evans Ch D 1976, 51 TC 615*, a company repaid in 1965 a dollar balance due to its US parent, the greater part of the balance representing advances in 1922–1931 to finance the company when it started. The Commissioners' finding that 90% of the substantial resultant exchange loss was capital, and not allowable, was upheld. A profit by an agent on advances to the principal to finance purchases by the agent on behalf of the principal was held to be a trading receipt (*Landes Bros v Simpson KB 1934, 19 TC 62*), as was a profit by a tobacco company on dollars accumulated to finance its future purchases (*Imperial Tobacco Co Ltd v Kelly CA 1943, 25 TC 292*). See also *McKinlay v H T Jenkins & Son Ltd KB 1926, 10 TC 372*; *Ward v Anglo-American Oil Ltd KB 1934, 19 TC 94*; *Beauchamp v F W Woolworth plc HL 1989, 61 TC 542*; and contrast *Radio Pictures Ltd v CIR CA 1938, 22 TC 106*. Where a bank operated in foreign currencies and aimed at, and generally succeeded in, matching its monetary assets and liabilities in each currency, it was held that there could be no profit or loss from matched transactions where there were no relevant currency conversions (*Pattison v Marine Midland Ltd HL 1983, 57 TC 219*). In *Whittles v Uniholdings Ltd (No 3) CA 1996, 68 TC 528*, it was held that a dollar loan and a simultaneous forward contract with the same bank for dollars sufficient to repay the loan had to be treated, for tax purposes, as separate transactions, each giving rise to its own consequences. In *Finance Ltd v Inspector of Taxes [2005] SSCD 407 (Sp C 466)*, it was held that the foreign exchange legislation in *FA 1993, ss 125–170* applied to funding bonds issued in respect of interest obligations and that *ICTA 1988, s 582* did not prevent the application of that legislation.

Simon's Direct Tax Service. See B3.1706, B3.1707.

26.3 **Revenue practice.** Following the decision in the *Marine Midland* case (see 26.2 above), HMRC issued a Statement of Practice (HMRC Statement of Practice, SP 1/87) setting out their views on the general treatment of exchange differences for tax purposes. These are summarised at 26.4 below. Following the introduction of the *FA 1993* provisions described at 26.5 *et seq.* below, which applied to 'qualifying companies' for accounting periods beginning after 22 March 1995, SP 1/87 continued to apply to non-qualifying companies and to individuals and partnerships. For accounting periods beginning on or after 1 October 2002, the *FA 1993* provisions are repealed (see 26.5 below), and exchange gains and losses of *all* companies within the charge to corporation tax are brought within the LOAN RELATIONSHIPS (46) or FINANCIAL INSTRUMENTS AND DERIVATIVE CONTRACTS (28) rules. Statement of Practice SP 1/87 accordingly ceases to apply to companies within the charge to corporation tax, and is replaced by Statement of Practice SP

2/02, 30 September 2002, which continues to apply to other persons carrying on a trade (see Tolley's Income Tax under Trading Income).

Simon's Direct Tax Service. See **B3.1708**.

26.4 **Statement of Practice SP 1/87.** Where currency assets are matched by currency liabilities in a particular currency, so that a translation adjustment on one would be cancelled out by a translation adjustment on the other, no adjustment is required for tax purposes.

Where currency assets are not matched, or are incompletely matched, with currency liabilities in a particular currency, the adjustment required to the net exchange difference debited or credited in the profit and loss account is determined along the following lines.

(i) The aggregate exchange differences, positive and negative, on capital assets and liabilities in the profit and loss account figure are ascertained;

(ii) if there are no differences as at (i), no adjustment is required;

(iii) if the net exchange difference as at (i) is a loss, and the net exchange difference in the profit and loss account is also a loss, the smaller of the two losses is the amount disallowed for tax purposes;

(iv) if the net exchange difference as at (i) is a profit, and the net exchange difference in the profit and loss account is also a profit, the smaller of the two profits is allowed as a deduction for tax purposes;

(v) if the net exchange difference as at (i) is a loss, and the net exchange difference in the profit and loss account is a profit, or vice versa, no adjustment is required for tax purposes.

Where net exchange differences are taken to reserve rather than to the profit and loss account, the nature of the assets and liabilities will need to be considered to determine whether or not a tax adjustment is required, applying the principles as above.

In considering whether a trader is matched in a particular foreign currency, *forward exchange contracts* and *currency futures* entered into for hedging purposes may be taken into account, provided the hedging is reflected in the accounts on a consistent basis from year to year and in accordance with accepted accountancy practice. *Currency swap agreements* are treated as converting the liability in the original currency into a liability in the swap currency for the duration of the swap. Hedging through *currency options* does not result in any matching.

The Statement of Practice also indicates that the accounts treatment of financial assets of financial concerns held on the 'realisation' basis (i.e. where profits for tax purposes are assessable only on their disposal) will be acceptable for tax purposes where the profits or losses on realisation are in effect recognised for accounts purposes net of exchange differences.

Where an *overseas trade*, or an *overseas branch* of a trade, is carried on primarily in a non-sterling economic environment, HMRC will accept computations based on:

(*a*) local currency accounts, with the adjusted profit (before capital allowances) translated into sterling at either average or closing rate; or

(*b*) the sterling equivalent of local currency accounts, translated using the 'net investment/closing rate' method (see Statement of Standard Accounting Practice SSAP 20 paras 25, 46); or

(*c*) sterling accounts produced by the 'temporal' method (see SSAP 20 paras 4–12),

provided the same method is applied consistently from year to year. The principles outlined in the Statement of Practice should be applied in considering any adjustment necessary in respect of exchange differences in the foreign currency accounts.

Where *roundabout loan arrangements* are employed in unmatched or partly matched situations, HMRC consider that, applying the *Ramsay* principle (see 5.1 ANTI-AVOIDANCE), such arrangements may fall to be treated for tax purposes by reference to their composite effect, depending on the facts of the particular case.

Groups of companies and non-trading companies. The principles outlined in the Statement of Practice apply only to individual trading companies and are inapplicable to a group of companies as a whole, or in a way which recognises 'matching' between assets and liabilities of different companies in a group. The Statement of Practice has no application to non-trading companies.

It will generally be for the trader to justify the adoption of any basis other than that outlined above in the particular circumstances of his case.

(**Note.** A new Statement of Practice (SP 2/02, 30 September 2002) replaces SP 1/87 following the changes referred to at 26.3 above. It does not, however, apply to companies within the charge to corporation tax. The changes from SP 1/87 reflect in the main changes in accounting practice. The main differences are as follows.

- Gains and losses taken to reserve are now not recognised for tax purposes even if they are not capital items.
- In the case of financial assets held on the realisation basis but revalued for accounting purposes to reflect exchange rate fluctuations, the accounts treatment *must* be followed.
- In the case of overseas trades, or overseas branches of trades, computations must be based on the sterling equivalents, translated using the 'net investment/closing rate' method (as in (*b*) above, neither (*a*) nor (*c*) now being acceptable).
- The reference to 'roundabout loan arrangements' is now omitted.)

26.5 FA 1993 PROVISIONS FOR QUALIFYING COMPANIES

For accounting periods beginning **on or after 1 October 2002**, the *FA 1993* provisions for qualifying companies, as set out in this paragraph and in 26.6 to 26.32 below, are repealed (subject to savings and transitional regulations) by *FA 2002, s 79, Sch 23* and assimilated into the rules applying for LOAN RELATIONSHIPS (46) and FINANCIAL INSTRUMENTS AND DERIVATIVE CONTRACTS (28). The relevant sections of this legislation are accordingly reproduced within those rules subject to modifications as follows.

(i) The 'matching rules' (26.15) have been replaced in their entirety.

(ii) The arm's length test (26.17) is now redundant, as *ICTA 1988, Sch 28AA* will apply to any non-arm's length element.

(iii) Deferral of unrealised gains (26.18) is no longer available, subject to transitional rules (see also 26.32).

(iv) The rules for irrecoverable debts (26.20) have been aligned with those for loan relationships.

(v) Relief for excess gains and losses (26.23) is no longer available.

The Treasury has the power to make regulations to meet the circumstances of particular cases to incorporate savings of regulations made under *FA 1993*, and of transitional provisions which still apply (see 26.32 below), and to bring amounts into account in accounting periods beginning on or after 1 October 2002, either as debits or credits within the LOAN RELATIONSHIPS (46) rules or as chargeable gains or losses within *TCGA 1992*. [*FA 2002, s 81*]. See *SI 2002 No 1969*.

Transitional rules prevent forestalling by bringing an accounting period to an end prematurely to gain a tax advantage by avoiding the effect of the new rules (see 26.32 below).

For accounting periods beginning before 1 October 2002, the main elements of the provisions in *FA 1993, ss 60, 92–96, 125–170, Schs 15–18*, which are described in detail in 26.6 to 26.32 below, are as follows.

(*a*) Exchange gains and losses in respect of qualifying assets and liabilities and forward currency contracts are recognised as they accrue between set translation times.

(*b*) Trading exchange gains and losses are treated as trading items. net non-trading exchange gains are assessed under Schedule D, Case VI, and there are special provisions for the relief of net non-trading exchange losses.

(*c*) Certain unrealised exchange gains on long-term capital items may be deferred.

(*d*) Exchange differences are generally calculated in sterling, although trading profits or losses (excluding capital allowances) may in certain circumstances be calculated in non-sterling currencies.

(*e*) Regulations may provide for the matching of borrowings with certain non-qualifying assets.

(*f*) Capital gains tax will cease to apply to qualifying assets.

(*g*) Anti-avoidance provisions are designed to prevent abuse of these provisions.

There are a number of exclusions from the operation of the provisions, and special rules in relation to insurance companies.

For the commencement of these provisions, see 26.32 below.

HMRC published an Explanatory Statement on Exchange Gains and Losses and Financial Instruments, containing guidance on these provisions and those relating to FINANCIAL INSTRUMENTS AND DERIVATIVE CONTRACTS (28), to which reference is made in the text as appropriate. Section 2.1 of the Explanatory Statement indicates that the *FA 1993* rules mirror normal accountancy practice, so that it should not generally be necessary to compute exchange gains and losses separately for each individual transaction. Section 2.5 indicates that the new rules do not apply to non-resident companies unless they carry on a trade in the UK (subject to special rules concerning CONTROLLED FOREIGN COMPANIES (21) (see 26.15(A), 26.31 below)).

Simon's Direct Tax Service. See **D2.9** *et seq*, **D2.18, D2.19**.

26.6 **'Qualifying company'.** A company is a '*qualifying company*' unless it is:

(*a*) the trustees of a unit trust scheme (who may by virtue of *ICTA 1988, s 468(1)* be treated as a company, see 43.5 INVESTMENT FUNDS), for any accounting period as respects which it is an authorised unit trust; or

(*b*) a company for any accounting period for which it is approved for the purposes of *ICTA 1988, s 842* (investment trusts, see 44.1 INVESTMENT TRUSTS).

[*FA 1993, s 152*].

Simon's Direct Tax Service. See **D2.905**.

26.7 **Accrual of gains and losses.** Where a qualifying company:

(i) holds a 'qualifying asset' or owes a 'qualifying liability'; or

(ii) enters into a 'currency contract'; or

(iii) holds an asset or owes a liability consisting of a right to settlement or a duty to settle under a 'qualifying debt',

an 'initial exchange gain' or 'initial exchange loss' falls to be calculated in the circumstances described at 26.8–26.10 below respectively, and to be treated as described at 26.10 *et seq.* below. [*FA 1993, ss 125–127*].

A company holds an asset at any time when it is entitled to it (see 26.26 below) and owes a liability at any time when it is subject to it (see 26.27 below). [*FA 1993, ss 154*(*14*), *155*(*13*)].

Simon's Direct Tax Service. See D2.918.

26.8 *Accrual on qualifying assets and liabilities.*

Where a qualifying company holds a 'qualifying asset' or owes a 'qualifying liability', an '*exchange difference*' arises for an 'accrual period' as regards the asset or liability where there is a difference between the 'local currency equivalent' of the 'basic valuation' of the asset or liability at the 'translation times' which begin and end the accrual period. If the exchange difference represents an increase over the accrual period in the case of an asset, or a decrease in the case of a liability, an '*initial exchange gain*' equal to the difference accrues to the company for the period as regards the asset or liability. If it represents a decrease in the case of an asset or an increase in the case of a liability, an '*initial exchange loss*' similarly accrues. [*FA 1993, s 125*].

The following are '*qualifying assets*' as regards a qualifying company.

(*a*) A right to settlement under a 'qualifying debt' (whether or not it is a debt on a security).

(*b*) A unit of currency.

(*c*) A share (in any company) held in 'qualifying circumstances'.

Excluded from (*a*), however, are a right under a 'currency contract' (see 26.9 below), and where the company having a right to settlement under a 'qualifying debt' holds an asset representing the debt which is either a convertible security within *FA 1996, s 92* (see 46.37 LOAN RELATIONSHIPS) or represents a loan relationship linked to the value of chargeable assets within *FA 1996, s 93* (see 46.39 LOAN RELATIONSHIPS). [*FA 1993, s 153*(*1*)(*3*)(*4*)].

A duty to settle under a 'qualifying debt' (whether or not it is a debt on a security) is a '*qualifying liability*' as regards a qualifying company, provided that it is not a duty under a currency contract.

A provision made by a qualifying company in respect of a duty to which it may become subject and which would be within the above definition is also a '*qualifying liability*', provided that the duty to settle would be owed for trade purposes, and the provision falls to be taken into account (apart from these provisions) in computing corporation tax profits or losses of the trade.

The following are also '*qualifying liabilities*':

(A) a duty to transfer a right to settlement under a 'qualifying debt' which is a debt on a security, where the duty subsists under a contract and the company is not entitled to the right, provided that the right would be a qualifying asset if the company were entitled to it; and

(B) a duty to transfer a share or shares, where the duty subsists under a contract and the company is not entitled to the share(s), provided that the share (or each of the shares) would be a qualifying asset if the company were entitled to it.

[*FA 1993, s 153*(*2*)(*5*)–(*9*)].

A '*qualifying debt*' is a debt falling to be settled by the payment of money (an ecu being regarded as money), or by the transfer of a right to settlement under another debt falling to be settled by the payment of money. [*FA 1993, s 153*(*10*)].

For these purposes, interest accrued in respect of a debt is not treated as part of the debt. [*FA 1993, s 153*(*12*)].

'*Qualifying circumstances*', in relation to an asset consisting of a share or a right to settlement, are circumstances where:

(I) the qualifying company carries on a trade;

(II) a transfer of the asset would fall to be taken into account (apart from these provisions) in computing corporation tax profits or losses of the trade; and

(III) if the asset were held at the end of an accounting period, the valuation to be shown in the accounts for that time would fall to be found by taking the 'local currency equivalent' at that time of the valuation put on the asset by the company (whether at that time or earlier) expressed in the nominal currency of the asset (the 'local currency' concerned being that of the trade for the accounting period).

[*FA 1993, s 153*(*11*)].

As regards a qualifying asset or liability or a currency contract (see 26.9 below), an '*accrual period*' is a period which begins with a 'translation time' (other than the last), and ends with the next 'translation time', as regards the asset, liability or contract. [*FA 1993, s 158*(*4*)].

A '*translation time*' as regards as asset, liability or contract is any one of the following.

(*aa*) The time immediately after the company becomes entitled to the asset, subject to the liability, or entitled to rights and subject to duties under the contract.

(*bb*) The time immediately before the company ceases to be entitled to the asset, subject to the liability, or entitled to rights and subject to duties under the contract.

(*cc*) Any time when an accounting period of the company ends, provided that it is later than the time in (*aa*) and earlier than the time in (*bb*).

[*FA 1993, s 158*(*1*)–(*3*)].

The '*local currency equivalent*' of a valuation of an asset or liability, or of an amount, is that valuation or amount expressed in terms of the 'local currency' (sometimes known as 'translation'). The 'local currency' is generally sterling, but see 26.24 below. [*FA 1993, ss 163*(*1*), *164*(*5*)].

The '*basic valuation*' of an asset or liability is generally such valuation as the company puts on it with regard to the time immediately after the company becomes entitled or subject to it or, if different, that which it would put on it with regard to that time under generally accepted accounting practice (see 55.2 PROFIT COMPUTATIONS). Where that valuation would otherwise be in a currency other than the 'nominal currency', it is converted to the nominal currency equivalent by reference to the London closing exchange rate for the day.

As regards a liability falling within (A) or (B) above, the '*basic valuation*' is the consideration for the company becoming subject to the liability (including the open market value, at the time when the company becomes subject to the liability, of any non-pecuniary consideration). Where the consideration is part pecuniary, the non-pecuniary part is expressed in the same currency as the part which is pecuniary. Where, however, the basic valuation would accordingly be in a currency other than the nominal currency, it is converted to the nominal currency, calculated by reference to the London closing exchange rate for the day on which the company becomes subject to the liability.

Where a company becomes entitled to a right of settlement under a qualifying debt on a security on any transfer by virtue of which it becomes a party to a loan relationship, and that transfer is with accrued interest, the basic valuation of that right is the consideration for its becoming entitled to that right less the accrued interest transferred.

[*FA 1993, s 159*(*1*)–(*5*)].

As regards a qualifying asset consisting of a right to settlement under a qualifying debt, or a qualifying liability other than one within (A) above, the '*nominal currency*' is the 'settlement currency' of the debt. As regards a qualifying asset consisting of a unit of currency, the '*nominal currency*' is the currency concerned. As regards a qualifying asset consisting of a share held in qualifying circumstances or a qualifying liability within (A) above, the '*nominal currency*' is the currency in which the share is (or shares are) denominated. [*FA 1993, s 160*]. The '*settlement currency*' of a debt is the currency in which ultimate settlement of the debt falls (or would fall) to be made, except that where the amount of that currency falls (or would fall) to be determined by reference to the value at any time of an asset consisting of or denominated in another currency, the '*settlement currency*' is that other currency. Where the settlement currency cannot be determined under these provisions, it is the currency that can reasonably be regarded as the most appropriate having regard to these provisions and deeming the state of affairs at settlement to be the same as the state of affairs immediately after the company becomes entitled or subject to the asset or liability in question. For these purposes the ecu is regarded as a currency. [*FA 1993, s 161*].

Simon's Direct Tax Service. See **D2.906, D2.907, D2.915** *et seq.*

26.9 *Accrual on currency contracts.*

Where a qualifying company enters into a 'currency contract', there is an '*exchange difference*' for an accrual period (see 26.8 above) as regards the contract where, as regards either of the currencies involved, there is a difference between the local currency equivalent (see 26.8 above) of the amount of the currency at the translation times (see 26.8 above) which begin and end the accrual period.

A '*currency contract*' is a contract under which a company becomes entitled to a right, and subject to a duty, to receive payment at a specified time of a specified amount of a currency (the '*first currency*'), and simultaneously to pay in exchange a specified amount of another currency (the '*second currency*'). It is immaterial whether those rights and duties may be exercised and discharged by the making or receiving of a net payment of an amount representing any difference in value between the payments at the specified time, and a contract requiring a payment of such an amount at a specified time is treated as a currency contract. Where, as a result of the adoption of the euro by a State, the conversion of the amounts of one or both of the currencies in a currency contract results in the contract being rescinded and replaced by a new contract which, but for the adoption of the euro, would have been a currency contract, the new contract is in effect treated as if it were the original currency contract. [*SI 1998 No 3177, reg 10*].

In relation to the first currency, if the exchange difference represents an increase over the accrual period, an '*initial exchange gain*' equal to the difference accrues to the company for the period as regards the contract. If it represents a decrease, an '*initial exchange loss*' similarly accrues. In relation to the second currency, a decease gives rise to an '*initial exchange gain*', an increase to an '*initial exchange loss*'.

[*FA 1993, s 126*].

For general guidance on the treatment of currency contracts, see section 7 of the Explanatory Statement referred to at 26.5 above, and Annexes 1 and 2 thereto.

A company becomes entitled to a right, and subject to a duty, under a contract when it enters into the contract. It holds a currency contract at a particular time if it is then entitled to rights and subject to duties under the contract, regardless of when the rights and duties fall to be exercised and performed. [*FA 1993, s 157*].

Simon's Direct Tax Service. See **D2.925** *et seq.*

26.10 *Accrual on debts whose amounts vary.*

Where a qualifying company holds an asset consisting of a right to settlement under a qualifying debt (see 26.8 above) or owes a liability consisting of a duty to settle under such a debt, and the nominal amount of the debt outstanding varies during an accrual period,

26.8 above does not apply. Instead, two amounts (the 'first amount' and the 'second amount') are determined, and the difference between those amounts represents either an '*initial exchange gain*' or an '*initial exchange loss*' for the accrual period.

For these purposes, where an amount in respect of any discount or premium relating to a debt accrues at any time under the LOAN RELATIONSHIPS (46) provisions (or would do so were an accruals basis of accounting used), then there is deemed to be a variation at that time in the nominal amount of the debt outstanding. The variation is an increase by the amount accruing (or which would accrue) in the case of a discount, a decrease by that amount in the case of a premium.

Where the company holds a right to settlement under the debt, and the second amount exceeds the first, an '*initial exchange gain*' accrues to the company in respect of the right. Where the first amount exceeds the second, an '*initial exchange loss*' accrues. Where the company has a duty to settle under the debt, the second amount exceeding the first gives rise to an '*initial exchange loss*', the first exceeding the second to an '*initial exchange gain*'. In all cases, a negative first amount is less than the second amount.

The '*first amount*' is the net amount of the local currency equivalents of:

(*a*) the nominal amount of the debt outstanding at the translation time which begins the accrual period; and

(*b*) any increases or decreases in that nominal amount during the accrual period at the times they occur.

The '*second amount*' is the local currency equivalent of the nominal amount of the debt outstanding at the translation time which ends the accrual period.

The nominal amount of a debt outstanding at any time is the outstanding amount at that time expressed in terms of the settlement currency of the debt (see 26.8 above). Where a payment or repayment is made at any time in a currency other than the settlement currency of the debt, and it falls to be decided whether there is in consequence an increase or decrease in the nominal amount of the debt outstanding, the amount of the payment or repayment is taken to be its equivalent expressed in terms of the settlement currency of the debt (any translation being by reference to the London closing exchange rate for the day in which the time concerned falls).

Where there is a difference between the 'basic valuation' of the asset or liability and the nominal amount of the debt outstanding at the translation time with which the accrual period begins:

(i) in arriving at the first amount, the nominal amount taken into account at the beginning of the accrual period is replaced by the basic valuation, and decreases in the nominal amount are replaced by proportionate decreases of the basic valuation; and

(ii) in arriving at the second amount, the nominal amount taken into account at the end of the accrual period is replaced by the basic valuation, increased by any increases in the nominal amount during the accrual period and decreased by any proportionate decreases taken into account under (i) above.

[*FA 1993, ss 127, 162*].

For '*basic valuation*', see 26.8 above. However, where this provision and either *FA 1993, s 125* (see 26.8 above) or this provision apply respectively to two consecutive accrual periods as regards an asset or liability, then the basic valuation of the asset or liability as regards the later period is taken to be either:

(A) the nominal amount of the debt outstanding immediately before the beginning of the later period; or

(B) if this provision, modified as above where the basic valuation differs from the initial nominal amount of the debt, applies as regards the earlier period, the second amount as determined under (ii) above.

The same basic valuation applies as regards subsequent accrual periods, subject to any further application of this provision.

[*FA 1993, s 159(10)–(12)*].

Simon's Direct Tax Service. See D2.919.

26.11 **Trading gains and losses.** Where an initial exchange gain accrues to a qualifying company for an accrual period (see 26.8–26.10 above) as regards an asset, liability or contract which, at any time in the period, was held or owed for the purposes of a trade (or part of a trade), the gain (or that part justly and reasonably attributed to the trade (or part)) is an '*exchange gain*' of the trade (or part) for the period. The amount of the exchange gain is treated as a receipt of the trade (or part) for the accounting period in which the accrual period falls (or with which it coincides). An initial exchange loss may similarly give rise to a loss in the trade (or part).

For these purposes, a part of a trade is any part which is treated as a separate business for the purposes of *FA 1993, s 93* (use of non-sterling currency for corporation tax purposes, see 26.40 below) for the accounting period which constitutes or contains the accrual period in question.

It is irrelevant whether the asset, contract or liability is held or owed on capital or revenue account, and the general prohibitions on trading deductions under *ICTA 1988, s 74* do not prevent the deduction of an exchange loss.

Where an exchange gain or loss of a trade (or part) would otherwise accrue as regards a liability consisting of a duty to settle under a qualifying debt (see 26.8 above), but a charge is allowed under *ICTA 1988, s 338* (see 55.4 PROFIT COMPUTATIONS) in respect of the debt, the exchange gain or loss is treated as not accruing. A charge is for this purpose treated as allowed if it would be allowed if the duty were settled by payment out of the company's chargeable profits, or if the company's profits were sufficient, or both.

Where a qualifying company accounting period begins on or after its 'commencement day' (see 26.32 below), and a gain or loss attributable to currency fluctuations (whether or not realised) accrues to the company as regards a qualifying asset or a qualifying liability or a currency contract otherwise than by virtue of these provisions, the gain or loss is not taken into account in calculating the company's trading profits or losses for corporation tax purposes for the period.

[*FA 1993, s 128*].

An exchange gain or loss under *FA 1993, s 128* may be taken into account as an adjustment under *FA 1994, s 162* (see 28.39 FINANCIAL INSTRUMENTS AND DERIVATIVE CONTRACTS).

Simon's Direct Tax Service. See D2.940.

26.12 *Example*

Tinman plc, a UK trading company, prepares its annual accounts to 31 March. On 4 December 2001 it sells goods to a customer in the land of Oz for Oz$540,000. The customer pays Oz$140,000 on account on 1 February 2002, and the balance of Oz$400,000 remains outstanding on 31 March 2002. The exchange rates on the relevant dates are as follows.

4 December 2001	£1 = Oz$3
1 February 2002	£1 = Oz$2.9
31 March 2002	£1 = Oz$2.75

The account can be summarised over the accrual period (4 December 2001 to 31 March 2002) as follows.

Date	*Amount (Oz$)*	*Exchange rate (Oz$/£)*	*(Decrease)*	*£ equivalent*
4 December 2001	540,000	3.0	—	180,000
1 February 2002	400,000	2.9	(140,000)	(48,276)
31 March 2002	400,000	2.75	—	145,455

The exchange gain is calculated as follows.

	£	£
Sterling equivalent 31 March 2002		145,455
Less sterling equivalent 4 December 2001	180,000	
adjusted for decrease	(48,276)	131,724
Exchange gain		£13,731

The exchange gain falls to be included in Tinman plc's profits chargeable to corporation tax for the year ended 31 March 2002.

26.13 **Non-trading gains and losses.** Where an initial exchange gain accrues to a qualifying company for an accrual period (see 26.8–26.10 above) as regards an asset, liability or contract, any part of the gain which is not an exchange gain of a trade (or part) (see 26.11 above) is a '*non-trading exchange gain*' for the period. An initial exchange loss may similarly give rise to a '*non-trading exchange loss*'.

However, a non-trading exchange gain or loss is treated as not accruing (if it would otherwise do so) where the asset or liability concerned consists of a right to settlement, or duty to settle, under a qualifying debt, and:

(*a*) in the case of a right to settlement, the right is a right to receive income and not interest falling to be brought into account under the LOAN RELATIONSHIPS (46) provisions;

(*b*) in the case of a duty to settle, a charge is allowed under *ICTA 1988, s 338* in respect of the debt (or would be so allowed were the duty settled by payment out of the company's chargeable profits, or were the company's profits sufficient).

The amount of the non-trading exchange gain or loss is treated as a receipt or loss in respect of the asset, liability or contract in the accounting period in which the accrual period falls (or with which it coincides), and the provisions at 26.14 below apply.

ICTA 1988, s 396 (relief for Case VI corporation tax losses, see 47.24 LOSSES) does not apply to losses a company is treated as incurring under this provision, nor may Case VI losses be set against amounts a company is treated as receiving under this provision.

[*FA 1993, s 129*].

See also 46.3 LOAN RELATIONSHIPS.

Simon's Direct Tax Service. See **D2.941**.

26.14 **Charge and relief of non-trading gains and losses.** An amount which a company is treated as receiving under 26.13 above is brought into account as if it were a non-trading credit in respect of a loan relationship (see 46.3 LOAN RELATIONSHIPS). A loss is similarly treated as a non-trading debit. [*FA 1993, s 130*].

Simon's Direct Tax Service. See **D2.942, D2.943**.

26.15 **Alternative method of calculation.** Regulations (see *SI 1994 No 3227* as amended) provide for an alternative method of calculation of the amount of an initial exchange gain or loss in certain cases. In such cases 26.8–26.10 above do not apply as regards determination of those amounts, which are instead found by adding together the accrued amounts for each day in the accrual period. Subject to those regulations, the accrued amount for a day in an accrual period is found by dividing the amount determined under 26.8–26.10 above by the number of days in the accrual period. Where an accrual period does not begin at the beginning or end at the end of a day, such a day is for this purpose treated as a complete day. [*FA 1993, Sch 15 para 1*].

Exempt circumstances. Regulations (see *SI 1994 No 3227, regs 2, 12*) provide for the alternative method of calculation to apply where (apart from the regulations) an initial exchange gain or loss (other than a gain treated as a non-trading exchange gain under *FA 1993, s 140(9)*, see 26.18 below) accrues under 26.8–26.10 above in an accrual period as regards an asset, liability or contract which at any time in a day in the accrual period was held or owed in 'exempt circumstances'. The regulations also provide that, as regards any such day, the accrued amount is to be ascertained in accordance with prescribed rules, and are framed so that the accrued amount as regards a day depends on the extent to which the exempt circumstances apply. The regulations are, however, disapplied in relation to an exchange gain within *FA 1993, s 136(11)(d)* or *s 136A(9)(d)* (see 26.17 below).

'*Exempt circumstances*' are when an asset or contract is held, or a liability owed, either:

(*a*) for the purposes of long-term insurance business;

(*b*) for the purposes of mutual insurance business;

(*c*) for the purposes of the occupation of commercial woodlands;

(*d*) by an approved housing association; or

(*e*) by an approved self-build society.

[*FA 1993, Sch 15 paras 2, 6; SI 2001 No 3629, Article 80*].

Unremittable income. Regulations (see *SI 1994 No 3227, reg 3*) provide that, where prescribed conditions are fulfilled, and (apart from the regulations) an initial exchange gain or loss accrues under 26.8 or 26.10 above in an accrual period as regards an asset consisting of either a right to settlement under a qualifying debt or a unit of currency, and at any time on a day in the accrual period income represented by the asset was unremittable, the alternative method of calculation is to apply. The regulations also prescribe rules for ascertainment of the accrued amount as regards any such day, and are so framed that the accrued amount as regards a day depends on the extent to which the income it represents is unremittable.

Income is unremittable for this purpose if, in relation to the income, the appropriate claim under *ICTA 1988, s 584* (see 60.3 RESIDENCE) has been made, the conditions for the claim were satisfied, and those conditions have not ceased to be satisfied.

[*FA 1993, Sch 15 para 3*].

Matched liabilities. Regulations (see *SI 1994 No 3227, regs 4–12* as amended) provide that where, apart from the regulations, an initial exchange gain or loss accrues for an accrual period as regards a liability which consists of a duty to settle under a qualifying debt, and which is eligible to be matched on any day in the accrual period with an asset held by the company (and where other prescribed conditions are fulfilled), an election may be made to match the liability with the asset on any such day. The alternative method of calculation will then apply in determining the amount of the gain or loss. The regulations also prescribe rules for ascertainment of the accrued amount as regards any day for which an election has effect. The regulations are, however, disapplied in relation to an exchange gain within *FA 1993, s 136(11)(d)* or *s 136A(9)(d)* (see 26.17 below).

Eligibility of a liability to be matched with an asset is determined in accordance with rules which prescribe the descriptions of liabilities and assets which may be matched.

The regulations also provide broadly as follows.

(A) The conditions attaching to matching elections are set out. An election, which is irrevocable, must be made by the company owing the liability to be matched (except in the case of CONTROLLED FOREIGN COMPANIES (21), see (B) below). Partial matching is permitted, and an election for partial matching may be varied to increase the amount or percentage matched. An election may be treated as relating to another liability meeting the necessary conditions where the original liability ceases to match the asset concerned. Similarly, following a reorganisation within *TCGA 1992, s 126*, it may continue to have effect in relation to the new holding if the new holding meets the necessary conditions. In certain circumstances an election may have retrospective effect.

(B) Where the company owing the liability is a controlled foreign company, an election may be made by a UK resident company which has (or such companies which together have) a majority interest in the CFC (within *ICTA 1988, Sch 24 para 4(3)(4)*) in computing chargeable profits under *ICTA 1988, Sch 24* (see 21.10 CONTROLLED FOREIGN COMPANIES).

(C) Exchange differences are to be brought into account when an asset the subject of matching arrangements is disposed of (subject to deferral in the case of certain no gain, no loss disposals under *TCGA 1992*). There are special rules where a transfer to a non-resident company within *TCGA 1992, s 140* is involved.

(D) Gains and losses are computed and deferred where shares are replaced by a new holding within *TCGA 1992, s 127*, and that section or *TCGA 1992, s 116* applies.

HMRC's view of the application of certain of these regulations is set out in sections 2.22, 2.23 of the Explanatory Statement referred to at 26.5 above. See also Revenue Tax Bulletin August 1996 p 338.

[*FA 1993, Sch 15 paras 4, 6*].

For the availability of a matching election where a local currency election had been made in respect of a trade carried on through an overseas branch, see sections 2.20, 2.21 of the Explanatory Statement referred to at 26.5 above. For intra-group transactions to facilitate matching, see section 2.24 of that Statement.

Currency contracts: matching. Where:

(I) as regards a currency contract, an initial exchange gain or loss accrues (or would apart from the regulations accrue) to a company for an accrual period in relation to the second currency (see 26.9 above);

(II) the relevant duty (i.e. the company's duty under the contract as regards the second currency) is eligible to be matched on any day in the accrual period with an asset held by the company (and other prescribed conditions are fulfilled); and

(III) an election is made and has effect under the regulations to match the duty with the asset on any such day,

the alternative method of calculation will apply in determining the amount of the gain or loss. The regulations described above in relation to matched liabilities apply for these purposes with appropriate modification.

[*FA 1993, Sch 15 paras 4A, 6; SI 1994 No 3227, regs 4–12; SI 2000 No 3315*].

Combination of circumstances. Where regulations as above relating to exempt circumstances, to unremittable income and to matched liabilities (or to any two of these three) apply as regards the same liability and for the same accrual period, there is provision for further regulations which may instead provide for ascertainment of the accrued amount as regards any day falling within the period and identified in accordance with prescribed rules. [*FA 1993, Sch 15 para 5*]. Further regulations may similarly make such provision where regulations as above relating to exempt circumstances and matching of currency contracts apply as regards the same contract and for the same accrual period. [*FA 1993, Sch 15 para 5A*].

Local currency. Where regulations as above relate to exempt circumstances, to unremittable income, to matched liabilities, to matching of currency contracts or to combinations of circumstances, 26.24 below has effect as if references to 26.8–26.10 above included references to the alternative calculation schedule (*FA 1993, Sch 15*) and to the provisions of those regulations. [*FA 1993, Sch 15 para 7*].

General. Regulations (as above) are so framed that the accrued amount as regards a day is nil (so that an initial exchange gain or loss may be extinguished), and may make different provision about exchange gains and exchange losses. [*FA 1993, Sch 15 paras 8, 9*].

Simon's Direct Tax Service. See D2.930 *et seq.*

26.16 **Main benefit test.** *Loss relief restriction.* Where an exchange loss (whether trading or non-trading) would otherwise accrue to a company for an accrual period as regards an asset which is a right to settlement, or a liability which is a duty to settle, under a qualifying debt, that loss is not treated as so accruing if the nominal currency of the asset or liability is such that a main benefit expected to arise from holding the asset or owing the liability is the accrual of the loss. [*FA 1993, s 135*]. For the circumstances in which, where required, a direction will be made, see section 3.6 of the Explanatory Statement referred to at 26.5 above.

Use of non-sterling currency. Where a non-sterling currency would otherwise be used for the purposes of calculating the exchange gain or loss on a qualifying asset or liability (see 26.8-26.13 above and 26.24 below), then if:

(*a*) the main benefit that might be expected to accrue from use of that currency for those purposes is that no net initial exchange gain would accrue to the company; and

(*b*) a net initial exchange gain would accrue to the company if sterling were used for those purposes,

then sterling must be used to calculate the exchange gain on the asset or liability concerned. [*FA 1993, s 135A*].

Determination of adjustment. See 26.17 below as regards determinations of adjustments under these provisions which require the sanction of the Board.

Simon's Direct Tax Service. See D2.955.

26.17 **Arm's length test — loss relief restriction.** Where:

(*a*) a qualifying company acquires an asset consisting of a right to settlement, or incurs a liability consisting of a duty to settle, under a qualifying debt in a transaction which it would not have entered into, or whose terms would have been different, if the parties to the transaction had been dealing at arm's length; and

(*b*) an exchange loss (whether trading or non-trading) would otherwise accrue to the company for an accrual period as regards that asset or liability,

that loss is treated as not accruing to the company for that period. Where the accrual period is not the last to occur as regards the asset or liability while it is held or owed by the company, any loss so treated may be carried forward and set against exchange gains (of the same trade or part-trade or non-trading, as the case may be) for subsequent accrual periods as regards the same asset or liability (for earlier periods before later ones).

Where the only feature of the transaction which would have been different had it been at arm's length is that the amount of the debt would have been less (but not nil), the loss is not denied relief as above, but is treated as reduced to the amount it would have been had the amount of the debt been that which would have been incurred at arm's length. The amount by which the loss is so reduced may be carried forward as above.

Where:

(i) the asset concerned is a right arising under a loan made by the company;

(ii) the only feature of the transaction which would have been different had it been at arm's length is that interest would have been charged, or charged at a higher rate; and

(iii) for the accounting period which constitutes or includes the accrual period, the whole of the loan has been treated under *ICTA 1988, s 770* or, as the case may be, falls to be treated under *ICTA 1988, Sch 28AA* (see 67 TRANSFER PRICING) as if interest had been charged (or charged at a higher rate),

the loss is not denied relief as above. If part of the loan has been, or falls to be, treated as in (iii) above, a corresponding part only of the loss is not denied relief, and the balance may be carried forward as above.

[*FA 1993, s 136(1)–(10)*].

Where an inward loan has been, or falls to be, adjusted under *ICTA 1988, s 770* or *Sch 28AA*, the terms to be considered under *section 136* are the terms as so adjusted for tax purposes (see section 3.9 of the Explanatory Statement referred to at 26 5 above).

Groups of companies. None of the above restrictions apply where the companies concerned are members of the same group (under *TCGA 1992, s 170*, see 12.1 CAPITAL GAINS—GROUPS) when the transaction is entered into and throughout the accounting period which constitutes or includes the accrual period in which the loss accrues, provided that:

(A) the counterparty to the qualifying company incurring the loss concerned incurs a corresponding liability, or acquires a corresponding asset, under a qualifying debt as a result of the transaction, and an exchange gain in the same currency as the loss accrues to the counterparty as regards that liability or asset for an accrual period ending at the same time as that for which the loss accrues;

(B) throughout the accrual period concerned, each company holds or owes the asset or liability either for the purposes of one trade or for non-trading purposes; and

(C) 'amount X' and 'amount Y' are the same, where '*amount X*' is the amount of the loss concerned, and '*amount Y*' is the amount of the gain accruing to the counterparty as regards the corresponding liability or asset disregarding 26.18 below.

See 12.1 CAPITAL GAINS—GROUPS for the residence requirements for groups.

[*FA 1993, s 136(11)(12)*].

Initial exchange losses. Where the loss concerned represents the whole or part of an initial exchange loss in respect of a debt whose amount may vary (see 26.10 above), the reliefs from the non-arm's length prohibition on loss relief (other than carry-forward of the loss against future exchange gains on the same asset or liability) are disapplied. [*FA 1993, s 136(13)*]. Similar provisions, with appropriate modifications, are, however, applied to such losses by *FA 1993, s 136A*, introduced in *SI 1994 No 3232* by virtue of *FA 1993, s 136(14)*.

'Arm's length' considerations. In considering what transactions would have been entered into at arm's length, all factors are to be taken into account, including any interest or other sums that would have been payable, any currency that would have been involved, and the amount that any loan would have been. [*FA 1993, s 136(14)*].

Currency contracts. Where a qualifying company enters into a currency contract which would not have been entered into at all, or whose terms would have been different, if the parties thereto had been dealing at arm's length, and an exchange loss (whether trading or non-trading) would otherwise accrue to the company for an accrual period as regards that contract, that loss is treated as not accruing to the company for that period. Where the accrual period is not the last to occur as regards the contract while it is held by the company, any loss so treated may be carried forward and set against exchange gains (of the same trade or part-trade or non-trading, as the case may be) for subsequent accrual periods as regards the same contract (for earlier periods before later ones).

In considering for this purpose what transactions would have been entered into at arm's length, all factors are to be taken into account, including any currency and any amounts that would have been involved.

[*FA 1993, s 137*].

Determinations requiring the sanction of the Board. A determination of the amount of an adjustment under *FA 1993, s 136, s 136A* or s *137* (or under *FA 1993, s 135* or *s 135A*, see 26.16 above), in respect of the disregarding or reduction of any exchange loss, requires the Board's sanction, other than in certain cases where an agreement has been reached between the Board and the person concerned (see *FA 1998, s 110*(*5*)-(*7*)). Where such a determination is made for the purpose of giving a closure notice, giving a notice amending a partnership statement or return or making a discovery assessment, and the notice of the closure, amendment or discovery assessment is given to any person without the determination, so far as taken into account in the notice or assessment, having been approved by the Board, or without a copy of the Board's approval having been served on that person at or before the time the notice was given, the closure or amendment notice or discovery assessment is deemed to have been given or made (and in the case of an assessment notified) as if the determination had not been taken into account. The approval must apply specifically to the case in question and the amount determined, but may otherwise be given (either before or after the making of the determination) in any such form or manner as the Board may determine. An appeal relating to a determination approved by the Board may not question the Board's approval except to the extent that the grounds for questioning the approval are the same as the grounds for questioning the determination itself. [*FA 1998, s 110; FA 2001, Sch 29 para 38*].

Non-sterling trades. Where an exchange loss is carried forward for set-off against future exchange gains as above, and the loss and the gain are in different currencies, the loss is translated into the currency in which the gain is expressed for the purpose of the set-off. The translation is by reference to the London closing exchange rates for the first day of the accounting period coinciding with, or containing, the accrual period for which the set-off takes place. [*FA 1993, s 138*].

For the circumstances in which a direction will be given under the above provisions, see sections 3.7 to 3.16 of the Explanatory Statement referred to at 26.5 above.

Simon's Direct Tax Service. See D2.956, D2.957.

26.18 **Deferral of unrealised gains.** Where (apart from this provision) an 'unrealised' exchange gain (whether trading or non-trading) would accrue to a company as regards a 'long-term capital asset or liability' for an accrual period constituting or falling within an accounting period, the company may make a claim in relation to that gain (or part of it). Where such a claim is made as regards an asset or liability, the gain (or part) stipulated in the claim is treated as not accruing for the accrual period for which it would (apart from the claim) have accrued. For the next accrual period throughout which the asset is held or owed by the company, an exchange gain equal in amount to the gain deferred is treated as accruing to the company as regards the asset or liability. If the asset or liability is held or owed solely for the purposes of a trade (or part of a trade), the gain is an exchange gain of the trade (or part), and is within 26.11 above. If it is held or owed for non-trading purposes, it is a non-trading exchange gain, and is within 26.13 above. If it is held partly for trade and partly for non-trade purposes, the amount stipulated in the claim is apportioned on a just and reasonable basis, each apportioned part being dealt with accordingly as above. The application of this provision is subject to any further deferral claim as above.

Where an exchange gain of a trade (or part) is carried forward as above to a period in which the asset or liability in question is to any extent held or owed in 'exempt circumstances' (see 26.15 above), the gain is to that extent treated as a non-trading exchange gain to which 26.13 above applies. Any necessary apportionment is made on a just and reasonable basis.

For these purposes, a part of a trade is any part which is treated as a separate business for the purposes of *FA 1993, s 93* (use of non-sterling currency for corporation tax purposes, see 26.40 below) for the accounting period which constitutes or contains the accrual period to which the gain is deferred.

A claim as regards an accounting period may not be made or withdrawn more than two years after the end of the period if an assessment to corporation tax for the period has become final and conclusive, or more than six years after the end of the period in any other case, subject to any extension determined by the Board. It must stipulate the amount to be deferred and identify the asset or liability concerned. No claim may be made unless an amount is available for relief for the accounting period (see below), and the gains subject to the claim must not exceed that amount. Only one claim may be made as regards an accounting period, but a claim may be made in relation to more than one gain where two or more gains fall within the provisions. The amount to be deferred must correspond to, and be in the same currency as, the amount to be brought in in the following period.

An exchange gain or loss is '*unrealised*' for these purposes if the accrual period concerned is one which ends solely by virtue of an accounting period of the company coming to an end.

An asset or liability is a '*long-term capital asset or liability*' if it is a right to settlement or duty to settle under a qualifying debt and represents capital throughout the accounting period concerned, and the earliest time at which the creditor can require settlement of the debt, under the original terms, is not less than one year from its creation.

[*FA 1993, ss 139, 140, 143(1)(4)*].

Amount available for relief. An amount is available for relief for an accounting period as above if 'amount A' is exceeded by the lower of 'amount B' or 'amount C', and the amount available is the excess, where:

(*a*) '*Amount A*' is one-tenth of the company's profits for the accounting period on which corporation tax would fall finally to be borne (within *ICTA 1988, s 238(4)*) apart from any claim under this provision and any group relief claim;

(*b*) '*Amount B*' is the total unrealised exchange gains which accrue or would (apart from a claim under this provision) accrue to the company as regards long-term capital assets or liabilities (or both) in an accrual period or periods falling in or coinciding with the accounting period, less the total unrealised exchange losses which would so accrue as regards such assets or liabilities; and

(*c*) '*Amount C*' is the total exchange gains which accrue or would (apart from a claim under this provision) accrue to the company as regards 'relevant items' in an accrual period or periods falling in or coinciding with the accounting period, less the total exchange losses which would so accrue as regards such items.

[*FA 1993, s 141(1)–(5)*].

'*Relevant items*' are currency contracts and rights to settlement or duties to settle under a qualifying debt.

As regards Amounts B and C, exchange gains and losses may be of a trade or part-trade or non-trading.

[*FA 1993, s 141(6)(7)*].

Non-sterling trades. A gain or loss falling within the above deferral provisions which is expressed in a currency other than sterling is treated for these purposes as of an amount equal to the sterling equivalent.

The sterling equivalent is calculated by reference to the exchange rate applicable under *FA 1993, s 94* (conversion of non-sterling currency used for corporation tax purposes, see 26.41 below) in the case of the profits or losses for the accounting period concerned of the business (or part) to which the gain or loss relates (or would do so apart from a claim to deferral under these provisions). Where part of an exchange gain of a business (or part) is treated under *FA 1993, s 140(3)* (as above) as not accruing to a company for an accrual period, and the local currency of the business (or part) for the accounting period in which the accrual period falls (or with which it coincides) is a currency other than sterling (see 26.40 below), the amount the company is treated as receiving under 26.11 or 26.13 above in respect of the accounting period and by virtue of the gain (as reduced) is the amount computed and expressed in that currency.

Also for such accounting periods, where an exchange gain of a business (or part) is treated as above as accruing to a company for an accrual period, and the local currency of the business (or part) for the accounting period in which the accrual period falls (or with which it coincides) is a currency other than sterling, the amount of the gain is treated as the 'local currency equivalent' (see 26.8 above) expressed in sterling. The translation is made by reference to the London closing exchange rate for the last day of the accrual period.

[*FA 1993, s 142*].

General. Where an unrealised exchange gain representing the whole or part of an initial exchange gain accruing under 26.10 above would accrue as required for a deferral claim as above, and the whole or part of the unrealised exchange gain (apportioned on a just and reasonable basis) is attributable to any part by which the nominal amount of the debt has decreased, the company may not make a deferral claim as regards the part (or whole) so attributable. [*FA 1993, s 143*].

Regulations make special provision in certain cases, broadly as follows.

(i) Where a long-term capital debt is repaid and replaced by a similar debt within 30 days before or after the repayment, exchange gains and losses on the original debt are treated as unrealised, and gains may be deferred and treated as accruing on the replacement debt, subject to conditions as above.

(ii) The company's profits, for the purposes of calculating Amount A under (*a*) above, exclude overseas income and gains.

(iii) The calculation of the amount available for relief as above is modified where the claimant is a member of a group (and see sections 2.25 and 2.26 of the Explanatory Statement referred to at 26.5 above).

[*FA 1993, s 143(7); SI 1994 No 3228*].

Euroconversion. The conversion of long-term capital assets and liabilities from the currency of a State which has adopted the euro into euro (a 'euroconversion', see *SI 1998 No 3177, reg 3*) is in effect disregarded for these purposes. [*SI 1998 No 3177, reg 7*].

Simon's Direct Tax Service. See D2.945 *et seq.*

26.19 *Example*

On 1 October 2000, Tinkerbell plc, a UK trading company which prepares its accounts to 30 September, obtains a three year loan of NNL$750,000 from its Neverneverland parent, to buy plant. For the years ending 30 September 2001 and 30 September 2002, the following information relating to Tinkerbell plc is relevant.

	1 October 2000	30 September 2001	30 September 2002
Exchange rate NNL$/£	1.5	1.6	1.69
Loan from parent (in £)	500,000	468,750	443,787

	Y/e 30 September 2001	Y/e 30 September 2002
	£	£
Net exchange gains on qualifying advances, borrowings and currency contracts	36,000	18,000
Profits chargeable to corporation tax (inclusive of net exchange gains)	150,000	275,000

The exchange gains available for deferral for the years ending 30 September 2001 and 30 September 2002 are calculated as follows.

Y/e 30 September 2001

	£
Lower of unrealised exchange gains on long-term capital assets and liabilities (£500,000 – £468,750 =) £31,250 and net exchange gains £36,000	31,250
Less 10% of £150,000	15,000
Maximum deferral claim possible	£16,250
Profits chargeable to corporation tax if maximum deferral claim made (£150,000 – £16,250 =)	£133,750

Y/e 30 September 2002
(assuming maximum deferral claim is made for y/e 30 September 2001)

	£
Lower of unrealised exchange gains on long–term capital assets and liabilities (£468,750 – £443,787 + £16,250 =) £41,213 and net exchange gains (£18,000 + £16,250 =) £34,250	34,250
Less 10% of (£275,000 + £16,250 =) £291,250	29,125
Maximum deferral claim possible	£5,125
Profits chargeable to corporation tax if maximum deferral claim made (£275,000 + £16,250 – £5,125 =)	£286,125

26.20 **Irrecoverable debts.** Where:

(*a*) a qualifying company holds an asset or owes a liability consisting of a right to settlement, or duty to settle, under a qualifying debt; and

(*b*) as regards an accounting period of the company, all of the debt outstanding immediately before the end of the period could at that time reasonably have been regarded as irrecoverable, the company is treated as if at the end of that accounting period it ceased to be entitled to the asset or subject to the liability. Where these conditions are satisfied as regards part of the debt, the nominal amount of the debt is treated as correspondingly reduced immediately after the beginning of the next accounting period. [*FA 1993, s 144*].

Irrecoverable debts that become recoverable. Where:

(i) a debt has been treated as extinguished in an accounting period as above;

(ii) at a time falling after the end of the accounting period all or part of the debt is actually outstanding; and

(iii) at that time all or part of the debt actually then outstanding could reasonably have been regarded as recoverable,

then the company is treated as if, immediately after that time, the debt were reinstated in the amount so regarded as recoverable. Where a debt has been reduced rather than extinguished, or reinstated as above, further subsequent reinstatements may be made. [*FA 1993, s 145*].

Simon's Direct Tax Service. See D2.918.

26.21 **Early termination of currency contract.** Where a qualifying company ceases to be entitled to rights and subject to duties under a currency contract, and either:

(i) at the time it so ceases it has neither received nor made payments of any currency under the contract; or

(ii) it so ceases by virtue of the making or receiving of a net payment (in any currency) representing any difference in value between the reciprocal payments required under the contract,

the company is treated as follows:

(*a*) if it has a 'net contractual gain of a trade', it is treated as incurring a trading loss of the same amount in respect of the 'last relevant accounting period';

(*b*) if it has a 'net contractual loss of a trade', it is treated as receiving a trading gain of the same amount in respect of the 'last relevant accounting period';

(*c*) if it has a 'net contractual non-trading gain', it is treated as incurring under 26.13 above a loss equal in amount to that gain in the 'last relevant accounting period', and amount B is construed accordingly;

(*d*) if it has a 'net contractual non-trading loss', it is treated as receiving under 26.13 above an amount equal to that loss in the 'last relevant accounting period', and amount A is construed accordingly.

The '*last relevant accounting period*' is the accounting period in which the contract ceased.

The '*net contractual gain of the trade*' is the excess (if any) of the amounts the company is treated as receiving under 26.11 above over those it is treated as incurring under 26.11 above in respect of the trade (or part) and the contract and the last relevant accounting period and the company's earlier accounting periods (disregarding amounts brought in under this provision). The '*net contractual loss of the trade*' is the excess of those it so treated as incurring over those it is so treated as receiving. The '*net contractual non-trading gain or loss*' is similarly determined by reference to amounts the company is treated as receiving and incurring under 26.13 above. Where the amounts brought in under 26.11 above are in a currency other than the 'local currency of the trade' (see 26.18 above) for the last relevant accounting period, they are treated for these purposes as being in that local currency, calculated by reference to the London closing exchange rate for the day on which the contract ceased.

Where the company would otherwise have a net contractual gain or loss of a trade and either the trade ceased before the contract ceased or the company carries on 'exempt activities' immediately before that time, the company is treated for these purposes as not having that net contractual gain or loss, but as having a net contractual non-trading gain or loss of the same amount (converted, if necessary, to its sterling equivalent by reference to the London closing exchange rate for the day on which the contract ceased).

'*Exempt activities*' are defined in the same terms as 'exempt circumstances' under 26.15 above.

[*FA 1993, s 146*].

From 9 January 2001, where *SI 1994 No 3227, reg 5(2)(b)* (see 26.15 above) applies so as to reduce the amount of an initial exchange gain or loss which would otherwise accrue to a company as respects a liability, *FA 1993, s 146* (where it applies) has effect as if that reduction had not been made. [*SI 2000 No 3315, reg 11*].

Simon's Direct Tax Service. See **D2.926**.

26.22 **Reciprocal currency contracts.** Where a qualifying company enters into a currency contract which it closes out by entering into a second currency contract with reciprocal rights and duties, the company is treated as ceasing, at the time it enters into the second contract, to be entitled to rights and subject to duties under the first contract without having received or made any payment in pursuance of that contract, and the second contract is disregarded for the purposes of these provisions. [*FA 1993, s 147*].

See **Simon's Direct Tax Service D2.926**.

26.23 **Excess gains or losses.** Regulations prescribe conditions under which relief from tax is to be afforded in respect of an asset or liability, where:

(*a*) an unrelieved loss other than an exchange loss has accrued to a qualifying company as regards the asset or liability on the company's ceasing to be entitled or subject to it by virtue of an arm's length transaction; and

(*b*) exchange gains (whether trading or non-trading) have previously accrued to the company as regards the asset or liability in excess of any exchange losses which have so accrued.

On a claim being made by the company, an initial exchange loss (see 26.8 above) is treated as arising in respect of the asset or liability, equal in amount to the lesser of the amount in (*a*) (net of any non-taxable compensation, etc. received in respect of the loss) and the amount of the net exchange gains in (*b*). The claim must be made within two years of the end of the accounting period in which the non-exchange loss accrued.

Similar provisions apply to bring into charge an initial exchange gain where a non-chargeable gain accrues on the company's ceasing to be entitled to an asset or liability in respect of which net exchange losses have previously arisen.

Where a non-exchange loss for which relief has been obtained as above is subsequently recovered, there are provisions for cancellation of the relief.

A non-sterling exchange gain or loss is for these purposes converted into sterling at the London closing exchange rate for the last day of the accrual period for which the gain or loss accrues.

[*FA 1993, s 148; SI 1994 No 3229*].

Simon's Direct Tax Service. See **D2.965**.

26.24 **Local currency.** For the purposes of 26.8-26.10 above, the '*local currency*' is sterling, except where, at any time in the accrual period, an asset or contract was held, or a liability owed, by a qualifying company for the purposes of a business, or part of a business, and the currency in which the profits and gains of the business (or part) are computed for the accounting period in which the accrual period falls (or with which it coincides) is a non-sterling currency (see 26.40, 26.41 below). In these circumstances, that non-sterling currency is treated as the local currency. If, throughout the accrual period, only one local currency is involved, 26.8-26.13 above are applied by reference to that currency. If two or more are involved, they are applied separately by reference to each, and any exchange gain or loss of a business (or part) is ignored unless found in the currency which is the local currency of the business (or part) for the accounting period. In any other case, 26.8-26.13 above are applied by reference to sterling and are then applied separately by reference to each local currency involved (other than sterling), any exchange gains or loss of a business (or part) being ignored unless found in the local currency of that business (or part) for the accounting period (whether sterling or otherwise). For these purposes, a part of a business is any part of a business which is treated as a separate business for the accounting period for the purposes of *FA 1993, s 93* (see 26.40 below).

[*FA 1993, ss 149, 163*].

For the application of *FA 1993, s 149* where a local currency election (see 26.39 below) has been made in respect of a trade carried on through an overseas branch, see sections 2.17–2.19 of the Explanatory Statement referred to at 26.5 above.

Simon's Direct Tax Service. See D2.913.

26.25 **Exchange rate to be used.** *Translation times.* Provision is made for determination of the exchange rate to be used in finding the local currency equivalent at a translation time of the basic valuation of an asset or liability, the nominal amount of a debt outstanding, or an amount of currency.

(*a*) Where the translation time results solely from the ending of an accounting period:

- (i) any arm's length exchange rate used in the accounts as regards the asset etc. concerned for the last day of the accounting period for the two currencies concerned is used for that purpose;
- (ii) in the case of a currency contract (see 26.9 above), where, in conformity with generally accepted accounting practice (see 55.2 PROFIT COMPUTATIONS), an exchange rate for the two currencies concerned is *not* used in the accounts as regards the contract for the last day of the accounting period, any arm's length exchange rate implied in the contract is used for that purpose;
- (iii) where neither (i) nor (ii) applies, the London closing exchange rate for the two currencies concerned for the last day of the accounting period is used for that purpose.

(*b*) Where (*a*) does not apply:

- (i) where the exchange rate used in the accounts as regards the asset etc. concerned at the translation time represents the average of arm's length rates for all the days falling within a period, and there is no significant difference between the rates for any two consecutive such days, that is the exchange rate used for that purpose;
- (ii) where (i) does not apply but an arm's length exchange rate is used in the accounts at the translation time, that is the exchange rate used for that purpose;
- (iii) in the case of a currency contract (see 26.9 above), where, in conformity with generally accepted accounting practice (see 55.2 PROFIT COMPUTATIONS), an exchange rate for the two currencies concerned is *not* used in the accounts as regards the contract at the translation time, any arm's length exchange rate implied in the contract is used for that purpose;

(iv) where none of (i)–(iii) applies, but it is the company's normal practice to use an average exchange rate over a period, and the London closing exchange rate for the two currencies concerned for any day (other than the first) falling within the 'relevant period' does not differ significantly from that for the preceding day, then the exchange rate used for that purpose is the average of the London closing exchange rates for all the days falling within the relevant period;

(v) where none of (i)–(iv) applies, the exchange rate used for that purpose is the London closing exchange rate for the two currencies concerned for the day in which the translation time falls.

'*Relevant period*' in (*b*)(iv) above means the period beginning at the same time as the accounting period in which the translation time falls and ending at the end of the day in which the translation time falls.

[*FA 1993, s 150*].

Debts whose amounts vary. (*b*)(i)–(v) (other than (iii)) above apply in determining the exchange rate to be used in finding the local currency equivalent of any amount, at a time immediately after the nominal amount of a debt outstanding decreases or increases, with references to the translation time replaced by references to the time immediately after the increase or decrease. [*FA 1993, s 151*].

Simon's Direct Tax Service. See **D2.914**.

26.26 **Entitlement to, and identification of, an asset.** A company becomes entitled to an asset when its entitlement becomes unconditional, and in determining whether or not a company is unconditionally entitled to an asset, any transfer of the asset, or of any interest in or right over it, by way of security is ignored, except that:

(*a*) where it agrees (other than by way of a currency contract) to acquire an asset by transfer, it becomes entitled to it when the contract is made and not on a later transfer made pursuant to the contract;

(*b*) where it agrees to dispose of an asset by transfer, it ceases to be entitled to it when the contract is made and not on a later transfer made pursuant to the contract;

(*c*) if a contract is conditional, for the purposes of (*a*) and (*b*) above it is made when the condition is satisfied;

(*d*) if it ceases to be entitled to an asset and at a later time becomes entitled to the same asset, the asset is treated, with effect from the later time, as if it were a different asset.

The question whether a company becomes unconditionally entitled at a particular time to an asset falling within 26.8(*a*) above is determined without reference to whether or not there is a later time at or before which the whole or any part of the debt is required to be paid. This does not apply where the asset consists of a right to interest, in which case the company becomes unconditionally entitled to the asset at the time at or before which the interest is required to be paid.

Rights of the same kind to settlement under debts on securities, to which a company becomes entitled at different times, are treated as different assets, and the question of whether a transaction involves one or a number of such assets is determined according to the facts of the case concerned.

In deciding whether rights to settlement under debts on securities of a particular kind are held by a company, those acquired earlier are treated as disposed of before those acquired later (references to acquisition and disposal being to becoming and ceasing to be entitled). A similar identification rule applies in relation to shares held by a company. In either case, however, a different rule used in the company's accounts in accordance with generally accepted accounting practice (see 55.2 PROFIT COMPUTATIONS) is to be used for this purpose instead of the statutory identification rule.

Where a company would otherwise become or cease to be entitled to an asset at a particular time by virtue of the above provisions and, in drawing up its accounts in accordance with generally accepted accounting practice, it regards itself as becoming or ceasing to be entitled to the asset at a different time, the following further provisions apply.

(i) Where the asset falls within 26.8(*a*) above, and the time at which the company regards itself as becoming entitled to it is earlier than the time which would otherwise apply, the company is taken to become entitled to it at the earlier time. As regards any time beginning with the earlier time and ending immediately before the time which would otherwise have applied, the nominal amount of the debt is taken to be such amount as the company treats as the nominal amount in its accounts or, if different, that which it would so treat in accordance with generally accepted accounting practice.

(ii) Where the asset falls within 26.8(*a*) above and the debt concerned is a debt on a security, or where the asset is a share, and the time at which the company regards itself as becoming entitled to it is later than the time which would otherwise apply, the company is taken to become entitled to it at the later time.

(iii) Where the asset falls within 26.8(*a*) above and the debt concerned is a debt on a security, or where the asset is a share, and the time at which the company regards itself as ceasing to be entitled to it is later than the time which would otherwise apply, the company is taken to cease to be entitled to it at the later time.

A company is treated as becoming entitled to so much of any asset as consists in a right to receive interest brought into account under the LOAN RELATIONSHIPS (46) provisions at the following time (rather than that provided for under (i) above):

(A) where an accruals basis was used, the time the interest is treated as accruing;

(B) where a mark to market basis was used, the time the interest is treated as having become due and payable.

[*FA 1993, s 154*].

See also 26.28 below.

Simon's Direct Tax Service. See D2.915.

26.27 **Subjection to, and identification of, a liability.** A company becomes subject to a liability which is a qualifying liability consisting of a duty to settle under a qualifying debt when it becomes unconditionally subject to it, except that:

(*a*) where it agrees to acquire such a liability by transfer, it becomes subject to it when the contract is made and not on a later transfer made pursuant to the contract;

(*b*) where it agrees to dispose of a liability by transfer, it ceases to be subject to it when the contract is made and not on a later transfer made pursuant to the contract;

(*c*) if a contract is conditional, for the purposes of (*a*) and (*b*) above it is made when the condition is satisfied;

(*d*) if it ceases to be subject to such a liability and at a later time becomes subject to the same liability, the liability is treated, with effect from the later time, as if it were a different liability.

The question whether a company becomes unconditionally subject at a particular time to a qualifying liability consisting of a duty to settle under a qualifying debt (see 26.8 above) is determined without reference to whether or not there is a later time at or before which the whole or any part of the debt is required to be paid. This does not apply where the liability consists of a duty to pay interest, in which case the company becomes unconditionally subject to the liability at the time at or before which the interest is required to be paid.

Where a company would otherwise become subject to such a liability at a particular time by virtue of the above and, in drawing up its accounts in accordance with generally accepted accounting practice (see 55.2 PROFIT COMPUTATIONS), it regards itself as becoming subject to the liability at an earlier time, it is taken to have become subject to the liability at that earlier time. As regards any time beginning with that earlier time and ending immediately before the time which would otherwise have applied, the nominal amount of the debt is taken to be such amount as the company treats as the nominal amount in its accounts, or, if different, that which it would so treat in accordance with generally accepted accounting practice. A company is, however, treated as becoming subject to so much of any liability as consists in a liability to pay interest brought into account under the LOAN RELATIONSHIPS (46) provisions at the time the interest is treated as accruing (where an accruals basis was used) or having become due and payable (where a mark-to-market basis was used).

As regards a qualifying liability consisting of a provision by the company, the company becomes subject to such a liability at the time with effect from which it makes the provision, and ceases to be subject to such a liability at the time with effect from which it deletes the provision or (if different) the time with effect from which it would delete it under generally accepted accounting practice. Where it changes the amount of such a provision, it is treated with effect from the time the change becomes effective as deleting the earlier provision and as making a new provision in the revised amount.

As regards a qualifying liability within 26.8(A) or (B) above, a company ceases to be subject to such a liability, if this has not otherwise occurred earlier, when it becomes entitled to the right or share(s) concerned.

[*FA 1993, s 155*].

See also 26.28 below.

Simon's Direct Tax Service. See **D2.916**.

26.28 **Assets and liabilities — general.** The following questions are to be determined according to the facts of the case concerned.

(*a*) Whether a transaction (or series of transactions) involves the creation of one asset consisting of a right to settlement under a debt or a number of assets consisting of a number of such rights.

(*b*) Whether a transaction (or series of transactions) involves the creation of one liability consisting of a duty to settle under a debt or a number of liabilities consisting of a number of such duties.

(*c*) Whether a transaction (or series of transactions) involves the creation of both an asset (or assets) held and a liability (or liabilities) owed by the same company.

Where a company, in drawing up its accounts in accordance with generally accepted accounting practice (see 55.2 PROFIT COMPUTATIONS), regards itself as becoming entitled or subject to an asset or liability at a particular time, and as ceasing to be entitled or subject to the asset or liability at a later time, it is taken to become and cease to be so entitled or subject at those times provided that:

(i) at the earlier time it could reasonably be expected that it would become so entitled or subject; and

(ii) the asset or liability does not in fact come into existence before the later time but, if it did, would be a right to settlement, or duty to settle, under a qualifying debt.

In the period between the earlier and later times, the nominal amount of the debt is taken to be such amount as the company treats as the nominal amount in its accounts or, if different, that which it would so treat in accordance with generally accepted accounting practice.

[*FA 1993, s 156*].

Shares and rights to settlement of the same kind. Shares are of the same kind, and rights to settlement under debts on securities are of the same kind, if they are so treated by the practice of a recognised stock exchange, or would be so treated if dealt with on such an exchange. [*FA 1993, s 164(9)(10)*].

Security in the expression 'debt on a security' has the meaning given by *TCGA 1992, s 132*. [*FA 1993, s 164(11)*].

Simon's Direct Tax Service. See D2.915, D2.916.

26.29 **Chargeable gains.** The following provisions apply in relation to chargeable gains.

Currency. No chargeable gain or allowable loss accrues on the disposal (within *TCGA 1992*) by a qualifying company, on or after its 'commencement day' (see 26.32 below), of currency other than sterling, provided that immediately before the disposal the company did not hold the currency in '*exempt circumstances*' (defined in the same terms as under 26.15 above). [*FA 1993, Sch 17 paras 2, 3*].

Reconstructions, groups etc. This provision applies where there is a disposal or acquisition (within *TCGA 1992*) of:

(A) currency;

(B) a qualifying asset consisting of the right to settlement under a debt which is not a debt on a security;

(C) a qualifying asset consisting of the right to settlement under a debt on a security (within *TCGA 1992, s 132*); or

(D) an obligation which by virtue of *TCGA 1992, s 143* is regarded as an asset to the disposal of which that Act applies and which is a duty under a currency contract.

Where:

(I) the disposal or acquisition is by a qualifying company and is made on or after the company's commencement day, and immediately before the disposal or after the acquisition, as the case may be, the asset is held wholly for 'qualifying purposes'; and

(II) *TCGA 1992, s 139, s 171* would otherwise apply,

the *section* concerned does not apply as regards the disposal or acquisition and the corresponding acquisition or disposal. '*Qualifying purposes*' are purposes of long-term or mutual insurance business.

[*FA 1993, Sch 17 para 7*].

Simon's Direct Tax Service. See D2.969.

26.30 **Partnerships which include qualifying companies.** Revenue Statement of Practice, SP 4/98 deals with the application of foreign exchange, FINANCIAL INSTRUMENTS AND DERIVATIVE CONTRACTS (28) and LOAN RELATIONSHIPS (46) legislation to partnerships which include companies within those provisions. Where the current provisions are in point in relation to an accounting period of such a partnership, the approach of *FA 1994, s 172* as regards financial instruments (see 28.48 FINANCIAL INSTRUMENTS AND DERIVATIVE CONTRACTS) will be adopted. Thus where the partnership consists wholly of qualifying companies (within 26.6 above), the current provisions will be applied to the partnership as if it were a qualifying company.

For partnerships with one or more members which are not qualifying companies, the general rules, which require profits and losses to be computed as if the partnership were a company, ensure that corporation tax is applied to corporate members and income tax to individual members (see 52.2 PARTNERSHIPS). In such cases, partnership profits and losses will be computed both on the basis that the partnership is a qualifying company and on the basis that it is not, the appropriate computation being employed in relation to partners which are qualifying companies and those which are not (including in the latter case a separate corporation tax computation in the unusual case of a corporate partner which is not a qualifying company).

For these purposes, the partnership will be treated as itself entitled and subject to the assets and liabilities in question.

The main elements of the Statements of Practice are as follows.

Valuations of assets and liabilities (see 26.8 above) should be made in accordance with the accounting methods used by the partnership.

Anti-avoidance. The main benefit and arm's length rules at 26.16, 26.17 above will apply to the partnership (including any individual partners).

Capital gains tax. *TCGA 1992, s 59* (disposal of partnership assets) will continue to apply to the disposal of shares in partnership assets to which members who are not qualifying companies are entitled, regardless of the operation of the current (or the financial instruments or loan relationships) provisions.

Losses. A qualifying company's share of partnership trading exchange losses (or financial instrument losses or loan relationship deficits) will be relievable in the normal way. Its share of net partnership non-trading exchange gains or losses (and net non-trading gains or losses on financial instruments or loan relationship credits or debits) will in practice be merged with any other non-trading exchange gains or losses (or non-trading gains or losses on financial instruments or loan relationship credits or debits) accruing to it in its own right, for charge or relief in the normal way.

Differing accounting periods. Where partnership and company accounting periods differ, profits and losses will be allocated between the relevant company accounting periods, usually on a time basis.

Commencement day (see 26.32 below) where no partnership accounts are drawn up will be the first day of any period beginning after 22 March 1995 for which any financial statements are drawn up, or the earliest of the commencement days of qualifying company members.

Local currency elections. HMRC consider that an election may be made where at least one of the partners is a qualifying company, subject to the conditions of *SI 1994 No 3230* being applied to the partnership as if it were a company. All partners subject to corporation tax must sign the election, which will be irrevocable and will not cease to be valid on subsequent partnership changes. See 26.39 *et seq.* below for provisions replacing such elections, and in particular 26.42 below as regards partnerships involving companies.

Deferral of unrealised exchange gains (see 26.18 above). Claims may be made by partnerships which include qualifying companies. The whole of the profits, etc. of the partnership, as computed for corporation tax purposes, will be taken into account in computing the amount which may be deferred, but the deferral, and subsequent recovery, will be by reference to the proportion appropriate to qualifying company members. The special rules for groups of companies do not, however, apply to partnerships. Deferral claims in respect of any gains arising to a qualifying company other than through the partnership are dealt with separately.

Matching elections (see 26.15 above). HMRC previously considered that such elections were available to partnerships including qualifying companies only in relation to ships, aircraft and assets subject to capital gains tax held by a branch outside the UK. With effect for accounting periods ending after 31 March 1996, their revised view is that an election may be made for the full range of eligible assets. All partners subject to corporation tax must sign the election, and must also undertake to return any gain triggered by the disposal of a matched asset if they have left the partnership or reduced their asset share ratio. No election may be made to match a liability of a qualifying company which is not a share of a partnership liability with a partnership asset.

Anti-avoidance provisions (see 26.16 above) apply to the partnership (including any individual members) as if it were a qualifying company.

(Revenue Statement of Practice, SP 4/98).

See also 26.42 below.

Simon's Direct Tax Service. See D2.968.

26.31 **Miscellaneous.** *Anti-avoidance: change of accounting period.* Anti-avoidance provisions apply where a company changes the date on which an accounting period is to begin, and but for the change an exchange gain or gains would have accrued to the company or been bigger, or an exchange loss or losses would not have accrued to the company or would have been smaller (in each case whether trading or non-trading), and a purpose of the change was to secure those effects. In such a case the inspector (or on appeal the Commissioners) may arrive at the exchange gains and losses as if there had been no change of accounting date, and adjust the corporation tax liability for the accounting period as is just and reasonable. [*FA 1993, s 166*].

Controlled foreign companies. Where, for the purposes of the controlled foreign company legislation, a non-UK resident company accounting period begins by virtue of *ICTA 1988, s 751* (see 21.8 CONTROLLED FOREIGN COMPANIES), and an exchange gain or loss accrues for an accrual period constituting or falling within that accounting period, then if the company subsequently becomes UK resident, that exchange gain or loss is disregarded for any accounting period beginning on or after the date the company became UK resident. [*FA 1993, s 168A*].

Insurance companies. There are regulations (see *SI 1994 No 3231; SI 1996 No 673; SI 1996 No 1485; SI 1997 No 1155*) making special provision about the treatment for corporation tax purposes of exchange differences arising as regards assets and liabilities held or owed by insurance companies. [*FA 1993, s 168; FA 1995, s 52(2)*]. See Simon's Direct Tax Service D2.966.

Orders and regulations. The various requisite order- and regulation-making powers are provided. [*FA 1993, s 167*].

26.32 **Commencement and transitional provisions.** *Commencement of FA 1993 provisions.* Except in relation to chargeable gains (to which *FA 1993, Sch 17*, see 26.29 above, applied instead), the *FA 1993* provisions described above applied where a qualifying asset or liability was one to which the company became entitled or subject on or after its '*commencement day*', i.e. the first day of its first accounting period beginning on or after 23 March 1995, or the rights and duties under a currency contract were ones to which it became entitled and subject on or after that day. There were, however, transitional provisions (*SI 1994 No 3226*, introduced under the enabling provisions of *FA 1993, Sch 16*) dealing with qualifying assets and liabilities and currency contracts held or owed both immediately before and at the beginning of that day (for a summary of which see the 2001–02 and earlier editions of Tolley's Corporation Tax). To the limited extent that these are still required on the introduction of the new regime for accounting periods beginning on or after 1 October 2002, they are preserved by regulations under *FA 2002, s 81*, with appropriate modifications to ensure a smooth transition to the new regime. See *SI 2002 No 1969*.

Transition to new regime. Anti-avoidance provisions apply to prevent forestalling the effects of the new provisions for accounting periods beginning on or after 1 October 2002 by changing an accounting date to end an accounting period prematurely. The provision applies where an accounting period beginning on or after 1 October 2001 is ended before 30 September 2002 for the purpose of avoiding amounts being brought into account under the new regime that are greater (if credits) or smaller (if debits) than they would be under the *FA 1993* provisions. In such cases, the accounting period beginning before 1 October 2002 will be treated as if it were an accounting period beginning on or after 1 October 2002. [*FA 2002, Sch 23 para 24*].

A claim for deferral relief under *FA 1993, s 139* (see 26.18 above) may be made in respect of a gain accruing in the company's last accounting period beginning before 1 October 2002 notwithstanding the repeal of the *FA 1993* provisions, and any amount which, but for the repeal of *FA 1993, s 140*, would fall to be treated as an exchange gain in an accounting period beginning on or after 1 October 2002, is to be brought into account in that subsequent period as a loan relationship credit. Whether it is to be treated as of a trading or a non-trading nature is to be determined as it would have been under *section 140*. A company may elect, within two years after the end of its first accounting period beginning on or after 1 October 2002, to account for such a credit in six equal instalments over that and its following five accounting periods. Where such an election is made, any uncharged amounts must be brought into account immediately if the company ceases to be within the charge to corporation tax.

The Treasury has the power (under *FA 1996, s 84A* — see 46.6 LOAN RELATIONSHIPS) to provide for exchange gains and losses deferred under the matching rules in *FA 1993, Sch 15 para 4* (see 26.15 above) for accounting periods beginning before 1 October 2002 to be brought into account for an accounting period beginning on or after 1 October 2002 either as debits or credits within the loan relationship rules or as chargeable gains or allowable losses within *TCGA 1992*. See *SI 2002 No 1969* and *SI 2002 No 1970* (as amended by *SI 2004 No 3259* with effect for accounting periods beginning on or after 1 January 2005 to reflect the changes in the matching rules for foreign currency liabilities made by *FA 2004* for companies adopting international accounting standards).

[*FA 2002, Sch 23 para 25*].

26.33 CORPORATION TAX CURRENCY PROVISIONS

In tandem with the provisions dealt with at 26.5-26.32 above, corporation tax provisions of general application were introduced with effect for accounting periods beginning on or after 23 March 1995 (except in the case of *FA 1993, s 60*, see 26.34 below). Except as follows, the provisions relating to the use of non-sterling currencies were replaced by the *Finance Act 2000* provisions described at 26.39-26.42 below for accounting periods beginning on or after 1 January 2000 and ending on or after 21 March 2000. Where, however, for the accounting period immediately preceding the first accounting period to which the replacement provisions would otherwise apply, a company did *not* make a local currency election in respect of a trade (or part), the company could elect, by notice given to an officer of the Board before 1 September 2000, for the replacement provisions not to apply in relation to that trade (or part) until the first accounting period beginning on or after 1 July 2000. See generally HMRC Company Taxation Manual, CTM 76010 *et seq*.

For accounting periods beginning **on or after 1 October 2002**, these provisions are further modified by the *Finance Act 2002* as described at 26.39–26.42 below. The Treasury has the power to make further amendments by regulation to make different rules for different cases and to bring amounts into account in accounting periods beginning on or after 1 October 2002, as chargeable gains or allowable losses under *TCGA 1992*, or as credits or debits under the loan relationship rules.

For periods of account beginning on or after 1 January 2005, the provisions described at 26.39–26.41 below are replaced by the *FA 2004* provisions described at 26.35–26.38 below. [*FA 1993, s 95(6); FA 2000, s 105(4)(5); FA 2002, ss 80, 81, Sch 24; FA 2004, s 52, Sch 10 para 77; FA 2005, Sch 4 para 50*].

Simon's Direct Tax Service. See D2.17.

26.34 **Certain interest not allowed as a deduction.** For accounting periods beginning before 1 October 2002, where a qualifying company becomes subject to a qualifying debt (see 26.8 above) on or after its commencement day (see 26.32 above) and the interest payable exceeds a commercial return on the capital repayable (expressed in the 'settlement currency' (see 26.8 above)), then in computing the corporation tax chargeable for an accounting period, the excess interest paid in the period is disallowed as a deduction from total profits (if otherwise allowable). This provision is **repealed** for subsequent accounting periods following the assimilation of exchange gains and losses into the LOAN RELATIONSHIPS (46) rules. [*FA 1993, s 60; FA 2002, Sch 40 Pt 3(10)*].

26.35 **Post-FA 2004 rules The basic rule – sterling to be used.** For corporation tax purposes, a company's profits for an accounting period must be computed and expressed in sterling. [*FA 1993, s 92(1); FA 2004, Sch 10 para 77*].

26.36 **Operating and accounting currencies.** The application of the rule in 26.35 above to certain profits or losses falling to be computed in accordance with generally accepted accounting practice is subject to the following provisions.

(*a*) *Company operating in sterling and preparing accounts in another currency.* Where for a period of account a UK-resident company, in accordance with generally accepted accounting practice, prepares its accounts in a currency other than sterling (the '*accounts currency*') but identifies sterling as its 'functional currency' in those accounts, sterling must be used to compute its profits or losses for corporation tax purposes (falling to be computed in accordance with generally accepted accounting practice) as if the company prepared its accounts in sterling.

(*b*) *Company operating in currency other than sterling and preparing accounts in another currency.* Where for a period of account a UK-resident company, in accordance with generally accepted accounting practice, prepares its accounts in one currency (the '*accounts currency*') but identifies another currency other than sterling as its 'functional currency', sterling must be used to compute its profits or losses for corporation tax purposes (falling to be computed in accordance with generally accepted accounting practice) by:

(i) computing those profits or losses in the 'functional currency' as if the company prepared its accounts in that currency; and

(ii) taking the sterling equivalent of those profits or losses.

(*c*) *Company preparing accounts in currency other than sterling.* If, for a period of account a UK-resident company prepares its accounts in a currency other than sterling and neither (*a*) nor (*b*) above applies, sterling must be used to compute its profits or losses for corporation tax purposes (falling to be computed in accordance with generally accepted accounting practice) by:

(i) computing those profits or losses in the accounts currency; and

(ii) taking the sterling equivalent of those profits or losses.

This also applies to a non-UK resident company, if for a period of account the company prepares the accounts of its UK permanent establishment in a currency other than sterling.

'*Functional currency*' means the currency of the primary economic environment in which the company operates.

Where (*b*) and (*c*) above apply, it is assumed that any sterling amount mentioned in any other provision is its equivalent expressed in the currency used to prepare the company accounts.

[*FA 1993, ss 92(2), 92A–92C, 92E; FA 2004, Sch 10 para 77*].

26.37 **Rules for translating amounts into a different currency.** Where, for the purposes of computing the profits or losses of a company for an accounting period, an amount is required by 26.36 (*b*) or (*c*) above to be translated into its sterling equivalent, or into its equivalent expressed in the functional currency or accounts currency of the company, the translation must be made by reference to the average exchange rate for the current accounting period or an appropriate spot rate of exchange for the transaction in question. [*FA 1993, s 92D; FA 2004, Sch 10 para 77*].

26.38 **Transitional provision.** Any trading losses, losses from an overseas property business, management expenses or non-trading deficits on loan relationships carried forward to a company's first period of account beginning on or after 1 January 2005, are to be translated to sterling using the London closing exchange rate for the last day of the previous period of account. [*FA 2004, Sch 10 para 79; FA 2005, Sch 4 para 51*].

26.39 **Post-FA 2000 rules The basic corporation tax rule: sterling to be used.** Subject to 26.40, 26.41 below, a business's profits or losses, including management expenses and non-trading capital allowances and balancing charges, are computed and expressed in sterling. [*FA 1993, s 92; FA 2000, s 105(1); FA 2002, Sch 24 para 2*].

26.40 **Use of currency other than sterling.** *Accounts as a whole in foreign currency*. If in any accounting period, a company carries on a business and:

(*a*) the accounts of the company as a whole are prepared in a non-sterling currency in accordance with generally accepted accounting practice (see 55.2 PROFIT COMPUTATIONS); and

(*b*) if the company is non-UK resident, it makes a return of accounts for its UK permanent establishment (see 60.5 RESIDENCE — for accounting periods beginning before 1 January 2003, for its UK branch or agency) prepared in such a currency in accordance with such practice,

the profits or losses for the accounting period for corporation tax purposes (other than chargeable gains or losses under *TCGA 1992*) are determined as follows.

(i) Take the amount of all the profits and losses of the business computed and expressed in the '*relevant foreign currency*' (i.e. the non-sterling currency or, where two non-sterling currencies are involved, that in which the return of accounts is prepared).

(ii) Take account of any brought-forward management expenses, trading losses or non-trading loan relationship deficits so computed and expressed.

(iii) Take the sterling equivalent (see 26.41 below) of the amount found by applying (i) and (ii).

Accounts partly from statements in foreign currency. These provisions apply where, in any accounting period, a company carries on a business, and condition (1) below is fulfilled, or where, for accounting periods beginning on or after 1 October 2002, either of the conditions in (1) or (2) below is fulfilled.

(1) Either:

   (*a*) the accounts of the company as a whole are prepared in sterling but, so far as relating to part of the business, from financial statements and records prepared in a non-sterling currency using the closing rate/net investment method (as in Statement of Standard Accounting Practice SSAP 20); or

   (*b*) if the company is non-UK resident, it makes a return of accounts for its UK permanent establishment (see 60.5 RESIDENCE — for accounting periods beginning before 1 January 2003, for its UK branch or agency) prepared in sterling but, so far as relating to the business (or, for accounting periods beginning on or after 1 October 2002, part of the business, including any collection of assets and liabilities), prepared from financial statements and records prepared in a currency other than sterling using that method.

(2) Either:

(*a*) the accounts of the company as a whole are prepared in a non-sterling currency ('*the first currency*') in accordance with generally accepted accounting practice (see 55.2 PROFIT COMPUTATIONS) but, so far as relating to part of the business, from financial statements and records prepared in a different non-sterling currency ('*the second currency*') using the closing rate/net investment method; or

(*b*) if the company is non-UK resident, it makes a return of accounts for its UK permanent establishment (see 60.5 RESIDENCE — for accounting periods beginning before 1 January 2003, for its UK branch or agency) prepared in the first currency in accordance with such practice but, so far as relating to part of the business, prepared from financial statements and records prepared in the second currency using that method.

In these circumstances, the profits or losses of part of the business for corporation tax purposes (other than chargeable gains or allowable losses under *TCGA 1992*) for that accounting period are determined as follows.

(A) Take the amount of all the profits and losses of the part of the business computed and expressed in the '*relevant foreign currency*' (i.e. the non-sterling currency in which the financial statements and records are prepared).

(B) (For accounting periods beginning before 1 October 2002) take account of any brought-forward management expenses, trading losses or non-trading loan relationship deficits so computed and expressed.

(C) Either:

(*a*) where (1) above applies, take the sterling equivalent of the amount found by applying (A) (and, where relevant, (B)); or

(*b*) where, for accounting periods beginning on or after 1 October 2002, (2) above applies, take the first currency equivalent of the amount found by applying (A).

Where, for accounting periods beginning on or after 1 October 2002, (2) above applies, profits and losses are to be calculated using this method in preference to the method described at (i) to (iii) above for accounts as a whole in foreign currency. (Thus, where a company makes up its accounts as a whole in a non-sterling currency and has a permanent establishment (or branch) for which it uses the closing rate/net investment method in another non-sterling currency, the permanent establishment (or branch) accounts are to be translated into the reporting currency before being translated into sterling.)

General. For the purposes of either of the above (i.e. whether the accounts as a whole are in foreign currency or the accounts are partly from statements in foreign currency), sterling amounts in the capital allowances provisions are taken as the foreign currency equivalent (see 26.41 below), and different parts of a business carried on through different permanent establishments (or branches) which would be dealt with differently under the above rules are treated as separate businesses. 'Accounts' are the annual accounts required for *Companies Act 1985* purposes (or NI equivalent). If no such accounts are required, they are those the company is required to keep under the law of the country or territory in which it is incorporated or, if it is not required to keep any such accounts, those most closely corresponding to *Companies Act* accounts. 'Return of accounts' of a UK permanent establishment (or branch) means return of such accounts as HMRC may require under *FA 1998, Sch 18 para 3* (see 61.3 RETURNS).

[*FA 1993, ss 93, 93A; FA 2000, s 105(1); FA 2002, s 103(4), Sch 24 paras 3, 4; FA 2003, Sch 27 para 3*].

26.41 **Currency equivalents.** Translation into sterling of a receipt or expense or, for accounting periods beginning on or after 1 October 2002, the value of any asset, liability or derivative contract of a company for an accounting period is either:

(*a*) by reference to the rate used in the preparation of the company accounts as a whole for the period or, for accounting periods beginning on or after 1 October 2002, and with respect to derivative contracts, the exchange rate implied in a currency contract; or

(*b*) by reference to the London closing exchange rate for the 'relevant day'.

For accounting periods beginning on or after 1 October 2002, the '*relevant day*' means, where the exchange rate used in the accounts is the rate for a particular day, that day, and where an average rate for a number of days is used, each of those days. For earlier accounting periods, it is the day on which the company became entitled to the receipt or incurred (or is treated as having incurred) the expense.

(*a*) above applies only if the rate is either an arm's length exchange rate for the relevant day, or, for accounting periods beginning before 1 October 2002, an appropriate average of arm's length exchange rates for a period ending with that day (or a period not exceeding three months including that day) during which there was no significant day-to-day variation.

For accounting periods beginning on or after 1 October 2002, where the accounts as a whole are prepared in a foreign currency (see 26.40 above), the translation of any amounts into sterling is by reference to the arm's length rate for the '*appropriate day*', i.e. the day the rate for which would be used if the company's accounts were translated into sterling in accordance with generally accepted accounting practice (see 55.2 PROFIT COMPUTATIONS). Where the accounts as a whole are prepared in a foreign currency or are prepared partly from statements in a foreign currency (see 26.40 above), and an amount denominated in a foreign currency falls to be translated into another foreign currency, the translation into the relevant foreign currency is by reference to the arm's length exchange rate for the relevant day where that rate is used in the preparation of the accounts, or, in any other case, the London closing exchange rate for the relevant day.

For accounting periods beginning before 1 October 2002, the translations required by 26.40(iii) or (C) above are by reference to the London closing exchange rate for the last day of the accounting period in question, except that:

(1) where the accounts as a whole are prepared in a foreign currency, the company may elect, as regards the business (or part), by written notice to an officer of the Board, to use an appropriate average of arm's length exchange rates for the period instead. The election applies from the first day of the accounting period in which the notice is given. The election may similarly be withdrawn from the first day of the first accounting period beginning on or after the date of the notice of withdrawal, and no further election may then be made to have effect before the third anniversary of the day the withdrawal takes effect; and

(2) where the accounts are prepared partly from statements in a foreign currency and condition (1) in 26.40 above applies, and the company's accounts, so far as relating to the business (or part), are prepared by reference to an appropriate average of arm's length exchange rates for the accounting period, that exchange rate is to be used instead.

For accounting periods beginning before 1 October 2002, any receipt or expense taken into account in making a calculation under 26.40(i) or (ii) or (A) or (B) above which is denominated in a currency other than the non-sterling reporting currency is translated into that currency by reference to the London closing exchange rate for the relevant day. The translation into that currency of sterling amounts in the capital allowances provisions is similarly by reference to the London closing exchange rate for the day on which the capital expenditure is incurred.

These provisions do **not** affect the operation of the provisions dealt with at 26.5-26.32 above or the CONTROLLED FOREIGN COMPANIES (22) provisions. The provisions of *FA 1998, Sch 18 para 88* (see 7.5 ASSESSMENTS) do not affect the rate used to determine amounts which can no longer be altered.

[*FA 1993, ss 94, 94AA, 94AB; FA 2000, s 105(1); FA 2002, Sch 24 paras 5, 6*].

For the first accounting period to which these provisions apply to a company, the brought-forward amounts referred to at 26.40(ii) or (B) above are translated into the relevant currency by reference to the London closing exchange rate for the last day of the immediately preceding accounting period, and that rate is also applied to any balance of expenditure brought forward for machinery and plant capital allowance purposes. [*FA 2000, s 105(2)(3)*].

26.42 **Partnerships which include qualifying companies.** For accounting periods beginning before 1 October 2002, Revenue Statement of Practice, SP 2/01 deals with the application of the post-*FA 2000* provisions (as at 26.39-26.41 above) to partnerships which include 'qualifying companies' within the provisions described at 26.5 *et seq.* above. It supplements (and in one respect supersedes) Revenue Statement of Practice SP 4/98, which is described at 26.30 above. See 52.2 PARTNERSHIPS for the basic rules for computing profits of partnerships involving companies. For accounting periods beginning **on or after 1 October 2002**, provisions dealing with partnerships which include companies have been included within the rules on LOAN RELATIONSHIPS (46.27) and FINANCIAL INSTRUMENTS AND DERIVATIVE CONTRACTS (28.26), and SP 4/98 has accordingly been withdrawn.

The main elements of the Statement of Practice are as follows.

Election to defer application of the FA 2000 provisions (see 26.33 above). Where at least one of the partners in a partnership was a qualifying company, it was open to the partnership to elect for deferral of the *FA 2000* rules until its first accounting period beginning after 30 June 2000 (where the conditions for the election were met). The election had to be made before 1 September 2000 and to be signed by all the partners who at the time of the election were subject to corporation tax.

Computation of profits under FA 2000 rules. If:

(*a*) the partnership prepares its accounts as a whole in a non-sterling currency in accordance with generally accepted accounting practice (see 55.2 PROFIT COMPUTATIONS); or

(*b*) although partnership accounts as a whole are prepared in sterling, they are, so far as they relate to the business or part of the business, prepared using the closing rate/net investment method from financial statements prepared in a non-sterling currency,

then the *FA 2000* provisions will apply in determining the profits of UK-resident corporate members. This will also apply to non-resident members of a partnership where:

(i) the partnership accounts as a whole are prepared in a non-sterling currency and a non-sterling currency is used in the accounts of the UK part of the business; or

(ii) the partnership accounts as a whole are prepared in sterling but, so far as relates to part of its UK business, the accounts are prepared using the closing rate/net investment method from financial statements prepared in a non-sterling currency; or

(iii) the accounts supporting the partnership return under *TMA 1970, s 12AA* are in sterling but, so far as they relate to part of its UK business, they are prepared using the closing rate/net investment method from financial statements prepared in a non-sterling currency.

The profits or losses of the business or part business, as computed in the relevant foreign currency, should be allocated to corporate partnership members in accordance with their entitlement to share in partnership profits. This sum should then be adjusted to take account of the corporate partner's share of any brought-forward management expenses, trading losses or non-trading loan relationship deficits computed in the foreign currency (determined by reference to its partnership interest in the relevant accounting period). The sterling amount is then computed under *FA 1993, s 94* (see 26.41 above) to the extent necessary to find the company's corporation tax profits or losses for the period concerned.

Elections (and withdrawals) to use an average arm's length exchange rate under *FA 1993, s 94(5)* are only accepted where signed by all members who, at the time of the election, are subject to corporation tax. Once validly made, an election will not (unless validly withdrawn) cease to be effective on subsequent partnership changes. Elections take effect with reference to partnership accounting periods and not those of the corporate partners.

Where accounting periods of the partnership and a corporate member do not coincide, the company's shares in partnership sterling profits and losses are allocated between company accounting periods on a just and reasonable basis (usually by time apportionment). A company's share of losses computed in a foreign currency and not immediately utilised is carried forward in the foreign currency.

Non-partnership income. Where a company which is a member of a partnership also carries on its own business (or part) in a non-sterling currency, it is necessary to determine the sterling equivalent profits separately in respect of each such business (or part) under these rules, and to combine sterling amounts in arriving at the final corporation tax liability.

27 Exempt Organisations

Any income tax provision conferring an exemption from income tax also applies to corporation tax. [*ICTA 1988, s 9(4)*].

27.1 **Agricultural societies** established to promote 'the interests of agriculture, horticulture, livestock breeding or forestry' are exempt from tax on profits or gains 'from any exhibition or show held for the purposes of the society ... if applied solely to the purposes of the society'. [*ICTA 1988, s 510*]. See *Peterborough Royal Foxhound Show Society v CIR KB 1936, 20 TC 249; Glasgow Ornithological Association CS 1938, 21 TC 445*. An agricultural society may also qualify for relief as a charity.

27.2 **Non-resident central banks** as specified by Order in Council are exempt from tax on certain classes of income [*ICTA 1988, s 516*]; the issue departments of the Reserve Bank of India and the State Bank of Pakistan are exempt from corporation taxes. [*ICTA 1988, s 517; TCGA 1992, s 271(8); ITA 2007, Sch 1 para 104*]. See 8.5 BANKS.

27.3 **The British Museum** and **The Natural History Museum** are, on a claim, exempt from tax as CHARITIES (14). [*ICTA 1988, s 507; TCGA 1992, s 271(6); Museums and Galleries Act 1992, Sch 8 para 1(8)(9)*].

27.4 CHARITIES (14) are generally exempt.

27.5 **The Crown** is not within the taxing Acts; see *ICTA 1988, s 49(2)* and *s 829(2)*, *Bank voor Handel v Administrator of Hungarian Property HL 1954, 35 TC 311*, and *Boarland v Madras Electric Supply Corpn Ltd HL 1955, 35 TC 612*. But see *ITA 2007 s 978* (formerly *ICTA 1988, s 829(1)*) as to assessment, deduction and payment of tax by public offices and departments of the Crown.

27.6 **International organisations** (e.g. the United Nations (*SI 1974 No 1261*)) may be specified by Order in Council as exempt from certain taxes (*International Organisations Act 1968*), as may certain financial bodies under the *Bretton Woods Agreement Act 1945* (e.g. the International Monetary Fund (*SI 1946 No 36*)) and other bodies under the *European Communities Act 1972* (e.g. the North Atlantic Salmon Conservation Organisation (*SI 1985 No 1773*)). The International Development Association is exempt [*International Development Association Act 1960, s 3* and *SI 1960 No 1383*] as are the International Finance Corporation [*International Finance Corporation Act 1955, s 3* and *SI 1955 No 1954*] and the International Maritime Satellite Organisation. [*ICTA 1988, s 515; TCGA 1992, s 271(5)*]. The Treasury may also designate any of the international organisations of which the UK is a member (e.g. The European Bank for Reconstruction and Development (*SI 1991 No 1694*)) for the purpose of exemption from various requirements for the deduction of tax from payments made in the UK. [*ICTA 1988, s 582A*].

27.7 FRIENDLY SOCIETIES (31) within *ICTA 1988, ss 460–463* are generally exempt.

27.8 **The Historic Buildings and Monuments Commission for England** is exempt from tax, on a claim, as if it is a charity the whole of whose income is applied only for charitable purposes, and from tax on chargeable gains without claim. [*ICTA 1988, ss 339(9), 507(1), 577(9); TCGA 1992, s 271(7)*].

27.9 **Housing Associations and self-build societies** have certain exemptions. See 36 HOUSING ASSOCIATIONS ETC.

27.10 **Local authorities, local authority associations and health service bodies** (as defined by, respectively, *ICTA 1988, s 842A, s 519(3)* and *s 519A*). The income and gains of such bodies are exempt from corporation tax. The Treasury may by order disapply the exemption for a specified activity, or class of activity, of an NHS foundation trust. [*ICTA 1988, s 519; TCGA 1992, s 271(3); National Health Service and Community Care Act 1990, s 61(1); FA 2004, s 148; ITA 2007 Sch 1 para 235*]. HMRC guidance for NHS Foundation

Trusts on the tax treatment of non-core health care commercial activities is available on the HMRC website (at www.hmrc.gov.uk/specialist/ct-nhs.htm).

For payments of interest by local authorities, see 37.9 INCOME TAX IN RELATION TO A COMPANY.

27.11 The **National Heritage Memorial Fund** has the same exemptions as CHARITIES (14). A claim must be made, except in relation to chargeable gains. [*ICTA 1988, s 507(1); TCGA 1992, s 271(7)*].

27.12 A **scientific research association** is granted the same exemptions from tax as a charity (see 14 CHARITIES) and is exempted from corporation tax on capital gains if:

(*a*) the Association has as its object the undertaking of scientific research which may lead to or facilitate an extension of any class(es) of trade and is approved for these purposes by the Department of Trade and Industry (DTI); and

(*b*) it is prohibited by its Memorandum or similar instrument from distribution of its income or property, in any form, to its members (other than as reasonable payments for supplies, labour, power, services, interest and rent).

In relation to any accounting period of a scientific research association beginning on or after a day to be appointed by the Treasury by statutory instrument:

- the above requirement for approval by the DTI is to be dropped;
- the reference in (*a*) above to 'scientific research' is to be changed to 'research and development' (within the meaning given by *ICTA 1988, s 837A* — see 59.1 RESEARCH AND DEVELOPMENT EXPENDITURE — and subject to any *regulations* made under that *section*);
- it is clarified that the exemptions will relate to the accounting period for which the claim is made;
- the Treasury will be empowered to make *regulations* prescribing circumstances in which the conditions at (*a*) and (*b*) above are to be deemed not to be complied with, and to make *regulations* specifying (i) what is and is not an Association for these purposes, (ii) circumstances in which an association is to be deemed to have, or not to have, research and development as its object, (iii) circumstances in which research and development is to be deemed capable or incapable of achieving the objectives in (*a*) above or (iv) what is to be deemed to be, or not to be, a class of trade for these purposes.

[*ICTA 1988, s 508; TCGA 1992, s 271(6)(b); F(No 2)A 2005, s 13*].

The DTI issued guidance on 4 September 1998 on the criteria they will apply, with effect from that date, in making such determinations. By concession, tax exemptions will continue to be granted on the previous basis for accounting periods beginning before 1 September 1999, provided that exemption would have continued to apply under the previous practice and the association continues to satisfy (*b*) above. This applies also to bodies established before 4 September 1998 which would have obtained approval under the previous practice. (HMRC Extra-Statutory Concession, C31).

See also 59.9 RESEARCH AND DEVELOPMENT EXPENDITURE and 66.73 TRADING INCOME as regards relief for contributions to scientific research organisations.

Simon's Direct Tax Service. See **C4.535**.

27.13 Some STATUTORY BODIES (64) receive a measure of exemption.

27.14 **Registered schemes from 6 April 2006.** A new pension schemes tax regime, introduced by *FA 2004*, came into force on **6 April 2006**. It fully replaces the pre-existing rules for occupational pension schemes, personal (and stakeholder) pension schemes and retirement annuity schemes. The rules below remain valid for 2004/05 and 2005/06. A registered scheme will continue to be exempt from tax on its investment income and from chargeable gains on disposals of investments. [*TCGA 1992, s 271(1A); FA 2004, ss 186, 187(4); ITTOIA 2005, Sch 1 para 644*]. For the new regime, including charges made on scheme administrators and charges and surcharges for unauthorised payments, see Tolley's Income Tax under Pension Provision after 5 April 2006.

Approved occupational pension, retirement benefit and personal pension schemes, parliamentary pension schemes, National Insurance supplementary benefit schemes and certain overseas pension funds are exempt from tax on investment income and on chargeable gains arising on investments forming part of the fund. A contract entered into in the course of dealing in financial futures or traded options is regarded as an investment, and this treatment is extended to all futures and options contracts, and exemption applies to all income derived from transactions relating to such contracts (the fact that a contract may be capable of closure by payment of a sum rather than by delivery not being relevant for these purposes). [*ICTA 1988, s 592, ss 613–615, s 620(6); TCGA 1992, s 271(1); ITEPA 2003, ss 647–654; ITTOIA 2005, Sch 1 paras 253, 261, 445; SI 2004 No 2310, Article 30*].

Exemption of pension funds does not extend to repayment of tax credits attached to qualifying distributions made after 1 July 1997. [*F(No 2)A 1997, ss 19, 30, Sch 8 Pt II(9)*].

For the special provisions applicable to certain international pooled pension funds, see 43.12 INVESTMENT FUNDS.

Scheme surpluses. A 35% charge (40% for payments made before 11 May 2001) may arise on any payment made to an employer out of funds of an exempt scheme approved under *section 592(1)*. Although regulations provide for the charge to be treated as a charge to corporation tax for the purposes of assessment and collection, the payment is not treated as income of the employer, and the amount charged is not available for any exemption, relief or set-off. [*ICTA 1988, s 601; FA 2001, s 74; SI 1987 No 352*]. Where those provisions do not apply, any such repayment is taxable as a trading receipt, or under Schedule D, Case VI if the scheme did not relate to a trade. [*ICTA 1988, s 601(5); ITTOIA 2005, Sch 1 para 257*]. See Tolley's Income Tax under Retirement Schemes for details of these charges and of HMRC's powers to require scheme surpluses to be reduced under *ICTA 1988, Sch 22*. Under the latter provision, a proportion of the income and gains of an exempt approved scheme may cease to attract exemption as above if the requirements as to the reduction of a surplus are not met.

Approved superannuation funds which, immediately before 6 April 1980, enjoyed a similar exemption under *ICTA 1970, s 208* (repealed from that date by *FA 1971, Sch 3 para 1*) may claim exemption for chargeable gains arising from the disposal of investments held for the purposes of the fund, and for income derived from investments or deposits, underwriting commissions, and interest payable on certificates of deposit, in so far as such income, etc. is applied for those purposes. [*ICTA 1988, s 608; ITTOIA 2005, Sch 1 para 260*]. Annuities paid out of such a fund are taxable pension income, and PAYE applies accordingly. These provisions apply if the following conditions are satisfied:

(*a*) the fund has not been approved, and is not being considered for approval, under *FA 1970, Pt II, Ch II* or *ICTA 1988, Pt XIV, Ch I*;

(*b*) no contribution has been made to it since 5 April 1980.

Exemption may be claimed only if the terms on which benefits are payable from the fund have remained unaltered since 5 April 1980 (apart from certain minor rule amendments, see HMRC Extra-Statutory Concession, B43 as revised).

Pension Protection Fund. The Pension Protection Fund (PPF) (set up by *Pensions Act 2004* to assume responsibility for final salary occupational pension schemes (and other pension schemes with defined benefit elements) whose sponsoring employers have become insolvent, leaving insufficient assets in the scheme) is to be given broadly equivalent tax treatment to that of an HMRC-approved occupational pension scheme for 2005/06 (see Tolley's Income Tax under Retirement Schemes) and that of a registered pension scheme for 2006/07 onwards (see Tolley's Income Tax under Pension Provision after 5 April 2006).

Simon's Direct Tax Service. See **E7.1–E7.5**.

27.15 **Trade Unions.** Registered trade unions, provided that they are precluded from assuring more than £4,000 by way of gross sum or £825 p.a. by way of annuity (excluding annuities approved under *ICTA 1988, s 620(9)*) in respect of any one person, are exempt. The exemption is granted in respect of non-trading income and chargeable gains which are applicable and applied for the purpose of 'providing benefits', i.e. sickness, injury and superannuation payments, payments for loss of tools, etc. The limits may be increased by Treasury order. [*ICTA 1988, s 467*]. This includes legal expenses incurred in representing members at Industrial Tribunal hearings of cases alleging unfair dismissal, or in connection with a member's claim in respect of an accident or injury he has suffered, and general administrative expenses of providing such benefits. (HMRC Statement of Practice, SP 1/84). The exemption also applies to employers' associations registered as trade unions [*ICTA 1988, s 467(4)(b)*] and to the Police Federations for England and Wales, Scotland, and Northern Ireland, and other police organisations with similar functions. [*ICTA 1988, s 467(4)(c)*].

See **Simon's Direct Tax Service D4.636**.

27.16 Unit trusts (43.5 INVESTMENT FUNDS) and investment trusts (44.1 INVESTMENT TRUSTS) and VENTURE CAPITAL TRUSTS (69) are exempt from corporation tax on their capital gains. [*TCGA 1992, s 100(1)*].

27.17 The **United Kingdom Ecolabelling Board** may claim exemption as if it were a charity (see 14 CHARITIES). [*ICTA 1988, s 507(1)(e)*]. This exemption has been cancelled from 19 April 1999.

27.18 For the concessionary exemption of certain clubs and societies, see 70.8 VOLUNTARY ASSOCIATIONS, and for the principle that a person cannot derive a taxable profit from trading with itself, see 48 MUTUAL COMPANIES.

27.19 The **London Organising Committee of the Olympic Games Limited** (LOCOG), incorporated on 22 October 2004, is exempt from corporation tax with effect from that date. The provisions for the deduction of income tax at source in relation to annual payments (under *ICTA 1988, s 349(1)*) do not apply to payments to LOCOG and a claim may be made for the repayment of income tax. The Treasury may provide, by order, for the exemption to apply to a wholly owned subsidiary of LOCOG. They may also make further provision to restrict the application of the exemptions where it appears to the Treasury that LOCOG is acting in concert with a third party or is undertaking activities other than those in pursuance of the '*Host City Contract*' (under the *London Olympic Games and Paralympic Games Act 2006, s 1*). The Treasury may also repeal this provision by order. [*FA 2006, ss 65, 66*].

Similar exemptions may also be made, by order, in relation to the International Olympic Committee (IOC) and certain persons owned or controlled by it, and in relation to non-UK resident athletes and other non-resident persons temporarily in the UK to carry out Olympic-related business. [*FA 2006, ss 67, 68*].

27.20 The **National Endowment for Science, Technology and the Arts** from 2 July 1998.

28 Financial Instruments, Derivative Contracts and Securitisation Companies

Cross references. See 26 EXCHANGE GAINS AND LOSSES and 46 LOAN RELATIONSHIPS.

Simon's Direct Tax Service D2.10, D2.18.

Other sources. See also generally, HMRC Corporate Finance Manual.

The headings in this chapter are as follows.

28.1 INTRODUCTION

For accounting periods beginning on or after 1 October 2002, profits and losses arising to a company on its derivative contracts, including exchange gains and losses, are determined and charged or relieved under provisions contained in *FA 2002, s 83, Schs 26–28*. These provisions are subject to anti-avoidance rules, which are made retrospective to accounting periods beginning on or after 26 July 2001 unless the company ceased to be a party to the contract before that date (26 July 2001 being the date of the Revenue Consultation Document proposing the assimilation of EXCHANGE GAINS AND LOSSES (26) into the rules for LOAN RELATIONSHIPS (46) and financial instruments, and other related and anti-avoidance measures). The anti-avoidance rules are contained in *FA 1994, s 153* (forward premiums and discounts under currency contracts) and *s 168A* (qualifying contracts for unallowable purposes) as amended by *FA 2002, ss 69, 70*, and, for accounting periods beginning on or after 1 October 2002, by *FA 2002, Sch 26 paras 15, 23, 24*. These provisions (as further modified and extended by subsequent legislation and related regulations), referred to as the Derivative Contracts rules, are described at 28.2–28.28 below.

For earlier accounting periods, the tax treatment of profits and losses associated with financial instruments used by companies for managing interest rate and currency risk is determined by provisions contained in *FA 1994, ss 147–177, Sch 18*, repealed by *FA 2002, s 83* for accounting periods beginning on or after 1 October 2002. These provisions, referred to as the Financial Instruments rules, are described at 28.29–28.50 below. They are subject to the provisions of *FA 1996, ss 80–105, Schs 8–15* prior to their amendment by *FA 2002, Schs 23, 25* (see 46 LOAN RELATIONSHIPS). HMRC published an Explanatory Statement on Exchange Gains and Losses and Financial Instruments, containing guidance on these provisions and those relating to EXCHANGE GAINS AND LOSSES (26) under the *FA 1993* rules, to which reference is made in the text as appropriate.

The language of the legislation is substantially changed by *FA 2004, s 52, Sch 10* (as amended) for the revised UK financial reporting standards for financial instruments:

- FRS 25 based on the international accounting standard IAS 32 for which adoption is mandatory for all companies for accounting periods beginning on or after 1 January 2005; and
- FRS 26 based on the international accounting standard IAS 39 for which adoption is mandatory for listed companies for accounting periods beginning on or after 1 January 2005 and for unlisted companies using fair value accounting for accounting periods beginning on or after 1 January 2006.

Thus, the derivative contract provisions no longer rely on the concept of the application of 'authorised accounting methods' as set out in *FA 2002, Sch 26 para 17* (see 28.11 below) but instead, debits and credits are based on the profits of company accounts prepared in accordance with UK or international accounting standards. Accordingly, the term '*mark to market basis of accounting*' is no longer used and the legislation uses instead '*fair value basis of accounting*' (amounts being determined at arm's length prices). The new provisions thus have effect for periods of account beginning on or after 1 January 2005 and are referred to in this chapter as the 'post-2004 basis of computation'.

[*FA 2002, Sch 26 para 54; FA 2004, s 52, Sch 10 para 69; FA 2005, Sch 4 para 50*].

Numerous amendments to the provisions were made by *FA 2005* and *F(No 2)A 2005* and related regulations to take account of changes in accounting practice on the adoption of international accounting standards (see 28.10 below) and also to prevent certain avoidance schemes following disclosures made under the disclosure rules (see 5.26 ANTI-AVOIDANCE).

For accounting periods beginning before 23 March 1995 (and where the *FA 1994* provisions did not apply), the tax treatment of such instruments was determined on general principles, resulting in a high degree of uncertainty as to the correct treatment to be applied in many instances. Some assistance could be obtained, however, from the body of case law and practice relating to exchange gains and losses (prior to the enactment of the detailed provision in *FA 1993*), for which see 26.2–26.4 EXCHANGE GAINS AND LOSSES.

See Revenue Tax Bulletin December 1998 pp 617, 618 for an article giving preliminary guidance on HMRC approach to the taxation of global trading in the financial sector, in particular in relation to the means of rewarding capital provision and the assumption of risk within a highly integrated business. See also HMRC Statement of Practice 14/91, 21 November 1991 on the tax treatment of transactions in financial futures and options, which was replaced by HMRC Statement of Practice 3/02, 30 September 2002 to take into account the new rules for accounting periods beginning on or after 1 October 2002.

28.2 DERIVATIVE CONTRACTS RULES

For accounting periods beginning **on or after 1 October 2002**, the provisions in *FA 2002, s 83, Schs 26–28* (as amended) replace the financial instruments rules in *FA 1994, ss 147–177, Sch 18* (apart from consequential amendments in *section 176*) and the anti-avoidance provisions in *FA 2002, ss 69, 70*. The provisions are described in detail in 28.3–28.28 below. Their main effect is the assimilation of exchange gains and losses within the rules so that all profits and losses, including exchange gains and losses, arising to a company from its derivative contracts are taxable as income. They also extend the scope of the financial instruments regime to encompass all types of derivative contract (with certain exclusions), and the rules have been modified to align them more closely with those applicable to LOAN RELATIONSHIPS (46).

Except where otherwise indicated, the derivative contracts rules take priority over other legislation in respect of the tax treatment of derivative contracts to which the rules apply. This includes, e.g. priority over the capital gains rules in *TCGA 1992* and the provisions dealing with financial futures and commodities in *ICTA 1988, s 128*. However, derivative contracts do not include any contracts falling to be treated as loan relationships by virtue of *FA 1996, s 101* as amended by *FA 2002, Sch 27 para 19*.

[*FA 2002, s 83, Sch 26 para 1*].

For accounting periods beginning on or after 1 January 2005, and in some cases, for contracts entered into on or after 1 August 2004 in an accounting period ending on or after 17 September 2004, the derivative contracts regime is modified by *SI 2004 No 2201*. The changes provide for a comprehensive regime to deal with certain derivatives previously excluded from the regime including futures, options and similar contracts whose value derives essentially from property derivatives, the main object being to provide a simpler and more certain tax treatment for such derivatives. Non-trading profits, gains and losses on such derivative contracts are treated as capital gains and losses. The regulations also make changes concerning 'embedded derivatives' where the rights and liabilities under a host contract are split into those under a loan relationship and those under one or more derivative financial instruments (i.e. the '*embedded derivatives*') (see 28.27 below).

For periods of account beginning on or after 1 January 2005 and ending on or after 16 March 2005, further modification is made by *SI 2005 No 646* to stop avoidance using derivatives whose underlying subject matter is shares by including all such relevant contracts within the regime except those used to hedge assets which are shares on which chargeable gains arise.

For periods of account beginning on or after 1 January 2005 and ending variously on or after 16 March, 28 July and 17 August 2005, further modification is made by *SI 2005 No 2082* and, for accounting periods ending on or after 31 December 2005, *SI 2005 No 3440*. These regulations modify the provisions relating to 'embedded derivatives' (see 28.3 and 28.27 below) to reflect developments in accounting standards dealing with such derivatives, in particular to distinguish between contracts held at the time of a company's adoption of international accounting standards from contracts acquired at a later date. The regulations also clarify the tax treatment in relation to host contracts and embedded derivatives where the underlying subject matter is shares or rights of a unit holder in a unit trust, and they cover additional cases of contracts becoming derivative contracts for tax purposes as a result of the changes made by *SI 2005 No 646*.

For accounting periods ending on or after 30 December 2006 *SI 2006 No 3269* makes further modifications to the rules, in particular redefining terms relating to derivative contracts. The intention is also to provide for contracts which move into and out of the regime and to amend the treatment of certain credits as chargeable gains and to exclude from the regime certain contracts founded on shares.

[*FA 2002, Sch 26 paras 2–9, 11, 12, 45A–47; SI 2004 No 2201; SI 2005 No 646; SI 2005 No 2082; SI 2005 No 3440; SI 2006 No 3269*].

Simon's Direct Tax Service. See D2.19.

28.3 DERIVATIVE CONTRACTS

A company's '*derivative contracts*' are those of its 'relevant contracts' which are not prevented from being derivative contracts by virtue of their underlying subject matter (see 28.5 below) or by any other corporation tax provision and which meet the conditions in 28.4 below, subject to 28.6 to 28.8 below.

A '*relevant contract*' is:

(*a*) an 'option';

(*b*) a 'future'; or

(*c*) a 'contract for differences'.

Effectively, these definitions were intended to cover all types of derivative contract (which met certain accounting and other tests), broadly following the classification in the *Financial Services and Markets Act 2000* (*Regulated Activities*) *Order SI 2001 No 544* at *Articles 83–85*.

However, it has been found necessary to define further categories:

(*a*) 'plain vanilla contract';

(*b*) non-financial contract with embedded derivatives; and

(*c*) hybrid derivative.

A 'plain vanilla contract' is a contract which is a relevant contract, other than one which is treated as a relevant contract because it is a financial or non-financial contract with embedded derivatives or is a hybrid contract.

A 'non-financial contract with embedded derivatives' is a contract which is not a loan relationship where the company's transactions under the contract include embedded derivatives and other non-financial obligations.

A 'hybrid derivative' is a contract which either is not treated as a derivative financial instrument for accounting purposes solely because it does not fall within Financial Reporting Standard (FRS) 26 para 9(b), but is treated for accounting purposes as part of a financial asset or liability, or it is not already within the definition, but its subject matter is commodities or it is contract for differences and the underlying subject matter is:

(*a*) land;

(*b*) tangible moveable property, other than commodities which are tangible assets;

(*c*) intangible fixed assets;

(*d*) weather conditions;

(*e*) credit worthiness.

[*SI 2006 No 3269*].

A person becomes a party to a relevant contract which it enters into or acquires, and it acquires a relevant contract on becoming entitled to the rights, and subject to the liabilities, under the contract, whether by assignment or otherwise.

An '*option*' includes any instrument (a '*warrant*') which entitles the holder to subscribe for shares in a company or assets representing a loan relationship of a company, whether or not the shares or assets exist or are identifiable. A '*future*' is a contract for the sale of property under which delivery is to be made at a future date agreed when the contract is made, and at a price so agreed. A price is taken to be so agreed whether it is for a determined amount, or left to be determined by reference to a future market or exchange price, or so expressed as to allow for variations to take account of changes in quality and quantity on delivery. Excluded from the definitions of both 'option' and 'future', however, are contracts which are to be wholly settled by cash, or where, after the obligations to each party under the contract have been offset, the excess is to be settled by cash, and which do not provide for the delivery of any property, unless the underlying subject matter is currency.

A '*contract for differences*' is a contract which has the purpose or pretended purpose of securing a profit or avoiding a loss by reference to fluctuations in the value or price of property described in the contract or in an index or in other factors designated in the contract. Such an index or factor may be determined by reference to any matter, or to a numerical value attributed to any variation in a matter. A contract for differences does *not* include a future or option (as above), an insurance contract, a capital redemption policy effected in the course of a capital redemption business within the meaning of *ICTA 1988, s 458*, a contract of indemnity, a guarantee, a warranty or a loan relationship.

With effect for periods of account *beginning on or after 1 January 2005*, special provisions apply where a company is a party to a contract which is not a loan relationship but (in accordance with generally accepted accounting practice) the rights and liabilities under the contract are treated as divided between a debt component (the 'host contract') and a derivative component (the 'embedded derivative') (see 28.27–'embedded derivatives'). For derivative contracts purposes, the company is treated as party to a relevant contract whose rights and liabilities consist only of those of the embedded derivative. Where there is more than one embedded derivative, the company is treated as party to relevant contracts each of whose rights and liabilities consist only of those of one of the embedded derivatives. Each such relevant contract is to be treated as an option, a future or a contract for differences according to how the rights and liabilities of the embedded derivative would be treated if contained in a separate contract.

The Treasury has the power to amend, by order, the contracts falling within the definition of a derivative contract, and the exclusions therefrom, the intention being to ensure that account is taken of developments in markets and new types of derivatives. With effect for periods of account beginning on or after 1 January 2005, such regulations may be made to apply to periods of account before the regulations are made but not earlier than the beginning of the calendar year in which they are made.

[*FA 2002, Sch 26 paras 2, 12, 13, 53(1)(2); FA 2004, Sch 9 para 2; SI 2004 No 2201, Articles 3, 13; SI 2004 No 3270, Articles 1, 3; FA 2005, s 80, Sch 4 para 52*].

28.4 **Derivative contract requirements.** A relevant contract will be treated as a derivative contract in the following circumstances.

(*a*) *Contracts accounted for as derivative financial instruments.* The primary test of whether a contract is a derivative contract for this purpose is whether it is recognised as a derivative financial instrument under generally accepted accountancy principles. Thus, a relevant contract is a derivative contract for tax purposes in any accounting period if it is treated in the company's accounts of the accounting period as a derivative financial instrument for that accounting period in accordance with the relevant accounting standard used for that accounting period (or would be so treated if that standard applied to the company in respect of the relevant contract).

For accounting periods beginning on or after 1 January 2005, a relevant accounting standard is Financial Reporting Standard (FRS) 25, issued in December 2004. For accounting periods beginning before 1 January 2005, a relevant accounting standard is Financial Reporting Standard (FRS) 13, issued in September 1998 and having effect for accounting periods ending on or after 23 March 1999.

(*b*) *Contracts accounted for as, or forming part of, financial assets or liabilities.* For periods of account beginning on or after 1 January 2005 and ending on or after 17 August 2005, where a relevant contract does not fall within (*a*) above solely because it does not fall within the definition of a derivative financial instrument in FRS 26, paragraph 9(*b*), it is treated as a derivative contract for tax purposes if it is treated for accounting purposes as, or forming part of, a financial asset or liability. A relevant contract is treated as, or forming part of, a financial asset or liability for an accounting period if it is so treated in accordance with the relevant accounting standard used for that accounting period (or would be so treated if the company were a company which used a relevant standard for that accounting period in respect of the relevant contract). (See (*a*) above with respect to the meaning of a relevant standard in this case.)

(*c*) *Contracts not accounted for as derivative financial instruments.* For periods of account beginning before 1 January 2005 and ending before 16 March 2005, where contracts are not disclosed in the accounts as in (*a*) above (for example, contracts which behave more like debt assets which are accounted for as financial assets), they are nevertheless be treated as relevant contracts if they are certain contracts producing guaranteed returns, or guaranteed amounts payable on maturity, or providing insurance benefits (see 28.8 below). (The treatment of contracts providing insurance benefits as relevant contracts was added to *FA 2002, Sch 26 para 3*(*1*)(*b*) by *SI 2004 No 2201, Article 4*(*a*) because it was accidentally omitted when Sch 26 was enacted.) For accounting periods beginning before 1 January 2005, such a contract is only treated as a relevant contract if it is treated in the company's accounts of the accounting period as a financial asset for that accounting period in accordance with FRS 13 (see above) (or in accordance with any subsequent accounting standard which may replace FRS 13), or would be so treated if that standard applied to the company.

(*d*) *Contracts not falling within* (*a*) *to* (*c*) *above.* If a contract fails the tests set out in (*a*) to (*c*) above, it will nevertheless be treated as a derivative contract if its underlying subject matter is commodities, or it is a contract for differences whose underlying subject matter is:

(i) land (wherever situated) (for contracts entered into on or after 1 August 2004 in an accounting period ending on or after 17 September 2004);

(ii) tangible movable property, other than commodities which are tangible assets (for contracts entered into on or after 1 August 2004 in an accounting period ending on or after 17 September 2004);

(iii) intangible fixed assets (within *FA 2002, Sch 29 Pt 1* and excluding any assets within *Pt 10* of that *Schedule*);

(iv) weather conditions; or

(v) creditworthiness.

The Treasury has the power to amend, by order, the above requirements. With effect for periods of account beginning on or after 1 January 2005, such regulations may be made to apply to periods of account before the regulations are made but not earlier than the beginning of the calendar year in which they are made.

[*FA 2002, Sch 26 paras 3, 13; FA 2005, s 80, Sch 4 para 52; SI 2002 No 2201, Articles 1, 4; SI 2005 No 646; SI 2005 No 2082; SI 2006 No 3269*].

28.5 **Excluded contracts.** A relevant contract is not a derivative contract if its underlying subject matter consists wholly of, or is treated as consisting wholly of, any one or more of the following types of excluded property.

For periods of account beginning on or after 1 January 2005 and ending on or after 16 March 2005:

(i) in relation to futures or options, intangible fixed assets (within *FA 2002, Sch 29 Pt I* and excluding any assets within *Pt 10* of that *Schedule*) (thus futures and options will fall with the intangible assets regime under *FA 2002, Sch 29* – see 39 INTANGIBLE ASSETS);

(ii) in relation to relevant contracts satisfying the conditions set out below, shares in a company (other than shares treated as loan relationships under *FA 1996, ss 91A, 91B*) and rights of a unit holder under a unit trust scheme.

The conditions specified are that:

A the relevant contract is entered into by a life insurance business and the contract is an approved derivative under Rule 4.3.5 of the Integrated Prudential Sourcebook; or

B the relevant contract is entered into by a mutual trading company or by a company otherwise than for trading purposes to hedge an asset consisting of shares or rights of a unit holder under a unit trust scheme and the relevant contract is not deemed to be a contract to which the company is treated as party under *FA 1996, s 94A(2)(b)* (an embedded derivative); or

C the relevant contract is an option, quoted on a recognised stock exchange, to subscribe for shares in a company and is entered into by a mutual trading company or by a company otherwise than for trading purposes or by a company for the purpose of its life assurance business; or

D the relevant contract is held to hedge an asset representing a loan relationship with an embedded derivative and each relevant contract treated as an embedded derivative in the case of that loan relationship under *FA 1996, s 94A(2)(b)* is an embedded derivative within *FA 2002, Sch 26 paras 45D, 45F, 45FA, 45J* or *45K* (see 28.27 below).

For accounting periods ending on or after 31 December 2005, as regards (ii) above:

- a further exception from the exclusion for shares in a company is added (by *SI 2005 No 3440*) for shares in an open-ended investment company to which fair value accounting applies under *FA 1996, Sch 10 para 4*, and an exception from the exclusion for rights of a unit holder under a unit trust scheme is made for a scheme to which fair value accounting applies under *FA 1996, Sch 10 para 4*;
- condition (ii)B above is extended to include a hedging relationship between a relevant contract and any share capital of the company; and
- condition (ii)D is extended to cover a relevant contract held to hedge a liability (as well as an asset) representing a loan relationship with an embedded derivative.

Chargeable assets. As regards (ii) above, special provisions apply if the company was party to the relevant contract immediately before and at 3.00pm on 16 March 2005 and the contract became a derivative contract only from that time and immediately before that time, the contract was a chargeable asset (i.e. where a gain on the asset would be chargeable under *TCGA 1992*). In that case the company, on ceasing to be party to the contract, must bring into account the amount of any chargeable gain or allowable loss under *TCGA 1992* on the assumption that the asset had been disposed of immediately before 3.00pm on 16 March 2005 for a consideration equal to the contract value in the company accounts at the end of the accounting period immediately before its first new period. Further transitional provisions apply if the company was party to the relevant contract immediately before and on 28 July 2005 and the contract would have become a derivative contract from that date if an accounting period of the company had begun on that date, and immediately before that date, the contract was a chargeable asset. In that case the relevant contract is treated as a derivative contract entered into by the company on that date for a consideration equal to the fair value of the contract and, on ceasing to be party to the contract, the company must bring into account the amount of any chargeable gain or allowable loss on the assumption that the asset had been disposed of immediately before 28 July 2005 for a consideration equal to the fair value of the contract on that date. Where the company becomes party to a relevant contract which is a chargeable asset and not a derivative contract on or after 28 July 2005 but the contract would be a derivative contract on that date if an accounting period of the company began on that date, the relevant contract is to be treated as a derivative contract on and after the date the company becomes party to it.

For periods of account beginning before 1 January 2005 and ending before 16 March 2005:

(*a*) in relation to futures or options, intangible fixed assets (as per (i) above);

(*b*) shares in a company under which an entitlement to receive a distribution may arise or rights of a unit trust holder under a unit trust scheme;

(*c*) for accounting periods beginning before 1 January 2005, convertible or asset-linked securities representing loan relationships to which *FA 1996, s 92* or *s 93* applies (for accounting periods beginning on or after that date, *FA 1996, s 94A* replaces *s 92* and *s 93* – see 28.27 below on 'embedded derivatives');

(*d*) land, whether situated in the UK or elsewhere (not including crops, minerals, etc. in or on land) in respect of contracts entered into before 1 August 2004 or contracts entered into on or after that date in an accounting period ending before 17 September 2004 (from which time such contracts are treated as derivative contracts – see 28.4 above);

(*e*) tangible movable property, other than commodities which are tangible assets in respect of contracts entered into before 1 August 2004 or contracts entered into on or after that date in an accounting period ending before 17 September 2004 (from which time such contracts are treated as derivative contracts – see 28.4 above).

The above is subject to the qualifications in 28.7 below with respect to derivatives taxed on a chargeable gains basis and 28.8 below with respect to transitional provisions. See 28.6 below as regards whether underlying subject matter consists 'wholly' of excluded property.

Underlying subject matter. The underlying subject matter of a relevant contract is:

(1) in the case of an option, the property to be delivered on the exercise of the option;

(2) in the case of a future, the property which, if the future were to run to delivery, would fall to be delivered at the date and price agreed when the contract was made;

(3) in the case of a contract for differences, where the contract relates to fluctuations in the value or price of property described in the contract, it is the property so described, and where an index or factor is designated in the contract, it is the matter by reference to which the index or factor is determined. This may for example include interest rates, weather conditions or creditworthiness.

As regards (1) and (2) above, there is no requirement that the property actually be delivered, and if the property to be delivered is itself a derivative contract, the underlying subject matter is the underlying subject matter of that contract. As regards (3) above, interest rates are not the underlying subject matter of a contract where they are used merely in a formula to determine the amount of the payment where the date of payment may vary and the amount varies according to the date of payment.

For contracts entered into on or after 1 August 2004 in an accounting period ending on or after 17 September 2004, where the underlying subject matter of a relevant contract consists of or includes income from land, shares in a company or rights of unit trust holder or unit trust scheme (for example rent or dividends), the underlying subject matter is not to be treated as such by reason only of that income. (In other words, it is the land, not the rent that is a relevant underlying subject matter.)

The Treasury has the power to amend, by order, the above requirements. With effect for periods of account beginning on or after 1 January 2005, such regulations may be made to apply to periods of account before the regulations are made but not earlier than the beginning of the calendar year in which they are made.

[*FA 2002, Sch 26 paras 4–4C, 11–13; FA 2005, s 80, Sch 4 para 52; SI 2004 No 2201, Articles 1, 5, 12; SI 2005 No 646; SI 2005 No 2082; SI 2005 No 3440*].

28.6 **Mixed derivatives.** Special provisions apply where the underlying subject matter of a relevant contract consists of any one or more of the excluded types of property within 28.5 above in addition to property which is not so excluded, and which satisfies the accounting requirements noted in 28.4 above.

Non-excluded property subordinate or small. For contracts entered into before 1 August 2004 or contracts entered into on or after that date in an accounting period ending before 17 September 2004, if, when the contract is first entered into or acquired, the non-excluded property is either subordinate to the excluded property or of small value in comparison with the underlying subject matter of the contract as a whole, the non-excluded 'subordinate' or 'small' element of the underlying subject matter is to be disregarded. Where the excluded property element of the underlying subject matter of the relevant contract falls wholly within (*a*) or (*e*) and (*f*) of 28.5 above, the contract is treated as consisting wholly of excluded property within those categories. Similarly, where it falls wholly within (*b*) to (*d*), the contract is treated as consisting wholly of excluded property within those categories. (This provision is repealed by *SI 2004 No 2201, Article 11* because it is considered that the removal of property from the excluded contracts list in 28.5 will render this provision unnecessary.)

Split contracts. Where the non-excluded property is not 'subordinate' or 'small', then in the case of a derivative contract which is an option or a future, it is to be treated as two separate contracts using a just and reasonable apportionment, i.e. a relevant contract whose underlying subject matter consists of one or more of the excluded properties and a relevant contract whose underlying subject matter consists of the non-excluded property.

For contracts entered into before 1 August 2004 or contracts entered into on or after that date in an accounting period ending before 17 September 2004, where the underlying subject matter of a derivative contract which is an option or a future consists only of one of more of the types of excluded property falling within (*a*), (*e*) or (*f*) and one or more of the types falling within (*b*) to (*d*) of 28.5 above, it is to be treated as two separate contracts using a just and reasonable apportionment, i.e. a relevant contract whose underlying subject matter consists of one or more of the excluded properties within (*a*), (*e*) or (*f*) and a relevant contract whose underlying subject matter consists of one or more of the excluded properties within (*b*) to (*d*). This will not apply if, after disregarding any of the property as either 'subordinate' or 'small', the underlying subject matter of the contract consists only of items falling within (*a*), (*e*) or (*f*) or (*b*) to (*d*) but not within both categories. If this provision applies as a consequence of disregarding any underlying subject matter of a contract which is subordinate or of small value, so that the underlying subject matter consists wholly of one or more of any types of excluded property within (*a*) to (*f*), the disregarded property is to be apportioned between the two notional contracts on a just and reasonable basis. Where the underlying subject matter is disregarded as being subordinate to property falling within either (*a*), (*e*) or (*f*) or (*b*) to (*d*), it is to be apportioned to those two categories accordingly. (This provision is repealed by *SI 2004 No 2201, Article 17* because it is considered that the removal of property from the excluded contracts list in 28.5 will render this provision unnecessary.)

[*FA 2002, Sch 26 paras 9, 46, 47; SI 2004 No 2201, Articles 1, 11, 16, 17*].

28.7 **Qualifications to exclusions.** The following provisions are repealed for periods of account beginning on or after 1 January 2005 and ending on or after 16 March 2005.

Contracts held for the purposes of a trade. The exclusion of contracts whose underlying subject matter is shares, rights in a unit trust, or, for accounting periods beginning before 1 January 2005, convertible assets or asset-linked securities in 28.5(*b*) to (*d*) above, does not apply to contracts entered into or acquired for the purposes of a trade. This includes banking, share dealing and insurance trades.

Embedded derivatives. For accounting periods *beginning on or after 1 January 2005*, the exclusion of contracts whose underlying subject matter consists of or is treated as consisting wholly of shares in a company, does not apply where the contract of a company is a deemed relevant contract of which the rights and liabilities are treated as divided between a debt component (the 'host contract') and a derivative component (the 'embedded derivative') (see 28.27 –'embedded derivatives').

[*FA 2002, Sch 26 paras 5, 5A, 12; SI 2004 No 2201, Articles 1, 6, 7; SI 2004 No 3270, Articles 1, 4; SI 2005 No 646*].

28.8 **Contracts producing guaranteed returns, etc.** The following provisions are repealed for periods of account beginning after 31 December 2004 and ending after 15 March 2005.

The conditions for relevant contracts in 28.4 above, and for excluded contracts in 28.5 above, do not prevent contracts from being treated as relevant contracts if they are certain contracts producing guaranteed returns, or guaranteed amounts payable on maturity, or providing insurance benefits. Accordingly, contracts whose underlying subject matter is shares, rights in a unit trust, or, for accounting periods beginning before 1 January 2005, convertible assets or asset-linked securities, are treated as derivative contracts where they meet the conditions set out in (i) to (iii) below. In the case of mixed derivatives, where the underlying subject matter of a relevant contract consists of any one or more of the excluded types of property within 28.5(*b*) to (*d*) above, in addition to property which is not so excluded, the rules described in 28.6 above apply (for contracts entered into before 1 August 2004 or for contracts entered into after that date in an accounting period ending before 17 September 2004) to require the non-excluded property to be disregarded where it is either subordinate or small.

Transactions are for these purpose '*associated transactions*' if they are entered into or acquired in pursuance of the same scheme or arrangements, or of understandings of any kind, whether or not legally enforceable and whether or not the transactions are with different parties. This includes any case where it is reasonable to assume from the likely effect of the transactions, and/or the circumstances in which they were entered into, that they are not independent of each other.

(i) *Contracts producing guaranteed returns.* A contract will be treated as a derivative contract where it is designed to produce a 'guaranteed return', or where the contract and either or both of:

(*a*) one or more other relevant contracts, whose underlying subject matter consists wholly or partly of shares, rights in a unit trust, (or, for accounting periods beginning before 1 January 2005, convertible assets or asset-linked securities), which would be derivative contracts if the conditions in this provision were satisfied in relation to them, and

(*b*) one or more assets representing loan relationships to which *FA 1996, s 94A* applies but only to the extent that each of those assets represents the rights and liabilities of the host contract (see 28.27 – 'embedded derivatives'), or, for accounting periods beginning before 1 January 2005, one or more assets representing loan relationships to which *FA 1996, s 92* or *s 93* or *s 93A applies* (see 46.37 and 46.39 LOAN RELATIONSHIPS), are associated transactions designed to produce a 'guaranteed return', i.e. it would be reasonable to assume, from their likely effect and/or the circumstances in which they are entered into or acquired, that such result was a main purpose of the transaction(s).

A '*guaranteed return*' is produced when the risks from fluctuations in the underlying subject matter are reduced or eliminated so as to produce a return which is in substance a return of interest on an investment. This includes cases where the main reason for the choice of the underlying subject matter is that there is little or no risk of fluctuation (e.g. shares in a company, the assets of which comprise debt instruments with a fixed or predictable return). The return taken into account is the amount accruing from a contract or, in the case of a loan relationship, the amount payable to discharge the debt.

(ii) *Guaranteed amount payable on maturity*. A contract will be treated as a derivative contract where it is designed to secure that the 'relevant amount payable' does not fall below a 'guaranteed amount', or where the contract and one or more of the transactions referred to at (i)(*a*) and (*b*) above are associated transactions designed to produce such a result. The contract or transactions are so designed if it would be reasonable to assume, when considering the likely effect of the transaction(s) and/or the circumstances in which they are entered into or acquired, that such result was a main purpose of the transaction(s).

The '*guaranteed amount*' is 80% of the consideration paid or payable by the company for entering into or acquiring the contract or, where associated transactions are involved, by the company or a connected company (as determined by *FA 1996, ss 87(3)(4), 87A*, see 46.16 LOAN RELATIONSHIPS) for entering into or acquiring any one or more of the associated transactions. (This includes, for example, equity bonds providing returns linked to an index such as the FTSE 100 index but limiting the risk of exposure to a fall in the index.)

The '*relevant amount payable*' is the amount payable in money or money's worth to any person on the maturity of the contract or, where associated transactions are involved, on the maturity of any one or more of the associated transactions, i.e. the amount payable on the performance of the contract or the amount payable to discharge the money debt arising under a loan relationship.

Election to treat contract as two assets. Relevant contracts will not fall within this provision where an election is made to treat the contract as two separate contracts, one being a creditor loan relationship which is a 'relevant zero coupon bond' and the other an option over the underlying subject matter (usually shares) of the contract providing for a guaranteed amount payable on maturity. Any necessary apportionment is made on a just and reasonable basis. The option is not treated as a derivative contract to which these rules or (ii) above or (iv) below apply, the normal chargeable gains rules applying instead. A '*relevant zero coupon bond*' is a security issued when the consideration for entering into or acquiring the contract was payable, which is redeemable on the date (or latest date) on which the contract falls to be performed, which does not provide for any interest, and which has an issue price which is discounted at a market rate from the guaranteed amount payable on maturity. The zero coupon bond must be accounted for using fair value accounting (or, where the pre-FA 2004 basis of computation applies (see 28.1 above), an authorised mark to market basis of accounting) (see 46.30 LOAN RELATIONSHIPS). The election must be made within two years of the end of the first accounting period in which the company becomes a party to the relevant contract. It has effect for all subsequent accounting periods and is irrevocable. See also 28.28 below for the transitional rules relating to this election.

(iii) *Contracts to provide insurance benefits*. A contract will be treated as a derivative contract where it is held by a company carrying on long-term insurance business and where:

(*a*) the contract is or was entered into or acquired by the company to provide benefits under life insurance or capital redemption policies (effected in the course of a capital redemption business within the meaning of *ICTA 1988, s 458*);

(*b*) the terms of the policies permit a surrender of part of the benefits at intervals of one year or less; and

(*c*) the amount payable on such a partial surrender amounts in substance to a return of interest on an investment (e.g. the income paid on part surrender of a guaranteed income bond).

Basis of accounting. The debits and credits to be brought into account in respect of derivative contracts, which produce guaranteed returns, where guaranteed amounts are payable on maturity, or which provide insurance benefits, must be determined on the basis of fair value accounting. Where the pre-FA 2004 basis of computation applies (see 28.1 above), the debits and credits to be brought into account by a company in respect of its derivative contracts are those computed in accordance with an '*authorised mark to market basis of accounting*' (see 28.11 below).

[*FA 2002, Sch 26 paras 6–8, 10, 12, 21, 48; FA 2004, s 52, Sch 10 para 64; SI 2004 No 2201, Articles 1, 8–10, 13; SI 2005 No 646; SI 2005 No 2082, Article 9*].

28.9 TAXATION OF DERIVATIVE CONTRACTS

The credits or debits (computed as below) for an accounting period arising from a derivative contract are brought into account as follows.

(*a*) *Trading credits and debits.* Where the company enters into a derivative contract for trading purposes, credits or debits arising from the contract are treated as receipts or expenses of the trade for that period (in the case of expenses, overriding anything to the contrary in *ICTA 1988, s 74* (allowable deductions)).

(*b*) *Non-trading credits and debits.* Any credits or debits arising from derivative contracts *not* entered into for trading purposes are treated as if they were non-trading credits or debits arising under the loan relationships rules in *FA 1996, Pt 4 Ch 2*, and effectively aggregated with other non-trading loan relationship credits and debits, the net amount being chargeable under Schedule D, Case III or relievable as a non-trading deficit, as the case may be (see 46.3 LOAN RELATIONSHIPS).

Credits and debits to be brought into account comprise amounts which fairly represent all profits and losses arising to or incurred by the company from its derivative contracts and related transactions including exchange gains and losses (see below) arising from derivative contracts or related transactions (but see exception below) and all charges and expenses incurred by the company under or for the purposes of those contracts and transactions.

For accounting periods beginning before the pre-FA 2004 basis of computation (see 28.1 above), the debits and credits concerned are those recognised in accordance with an 'authorised accounting method' (see 28.11 below), excluding any amounts required to be transferred to a company's share premium account and including any adjustment made to the company's statutory accounts in respect of a change in the authorised accounting method used as respects a derivative contract. 'Profits and losses' in this case also include:

(i) those taken to or sustained by any reserves in accordance with generally accepted accounting practice (see 55.2 PROFIT COMPUTATIONS); and

(ii) forward premiums and discounts arising from a derivative contract whose underlying subject matter consists wholly or partly of currency and which are brought into account as profits and losses in accordance with generally accepted accounting practice. (See 28.33 below for the anti-avoidance provision relating to forward premiums and discounts arising in accounting periods beginning on or after 26 July 2001 and before 1 October 2002.)

'Charges and expenses' also include those incurred directly in bringing derivative contracts or related transactions into existence, entering into or giving effect to them, making payments under them or securing receipt of payments in accordance with them, including where they are incurred before the contract is entered into.

'*Related transactions*' include any acquisition or disposal (in whole or part) of rights or liabilities under the contract, including where such rights or liabilities are transferred or extinguished by a sale, gift, surrender or release, and where the contract is discharged by performance in accordance with its terms.

Exchange gains and losses. Profits and losses arising to a company from its derivative contracts and related transactions include exchange gains and losses arising from its derivative contracts. They do not, however, include an exchange gain or loss of a company to the extent that it:

(A) arises on a derivative contract whose underlying subject matter consists wholly or partly of currency; or

(B) results from the translation from one currency to another of the profit or loss of part of the company's business,

and, where the post-FA 2004 basis of computation applies (see 28.1 above), is recognised in the company's statement of total recognised gains and losses or statement of changes in equity. Nor do they include so much of an exchange gain or loss in relation to a derivative contract whose underlying subject matter consists wholly or partly of currency, as falls within a description prescribed for the purpose by Treasury order. Where the pre-FA 2004 basis of computation applies (see 28.1 above), profits and losses do not include so much of an exchange gain or loss as, in accordance with generally accepted accounting practice, is carried to or sustained by a reserve and set off by or against an amount representing any exchange gain or loss on a company asset which is similarly carried to or maintained by that reserve.

The Treasury has the power, by order, to include any exchange gains or losses from derivative contracts as credits or debits arising on derivative contracts and related transactions or as chargeable gains under *TCGA 1992*, or to make different provision for different cases. Regulations will allow for certain deferred exchange gains and losses on derivative contracts to be brought into account as chargeable gains or losses. Such deferred exchange gains and losses are either those taken to reserves and set off against amounts arising on assets in accounting periods beginning on or after 1 October 2002, or those deferred under the matching regulations for accounting periods beginning before 1 October 2002.

Regulations provide for the following.

(i) Transitional provisions in respect of the change of tax treatment of exchange gains and losses on the assimilation of the foreign exchange gains and losses rules into those for derivative contracts [*SI 2002 No 1969*]. These regulations amend and save *SI 1994 No 3227* which make provision for an alternative method of calculation to be used in certain circumstances for determining the amount to be treated as an exchange gain or loss under the old FA 1993 provisions.

(ii) The bringing into account of amounts, in relation to accounting periods beginning on or after 1 October 2002:

- relating to assets representing certain loan relationships and ships or aircraft;
- where the disposal is a no gain/no loss disposal under the *TCGA 1992*;

- where there is no *TCGA 1992* disposal of the asset by virtue of *TCGA 1992, s 116(10)* (reorganisations, conversions and reconstructions involving qualifying corporate bonds);
- where there is no *TCGA 1992* disposal of the asset by virtue of *TCGA 1992, s 127* (equation of original shares and new holding);
- where *TCGA 1992, s 127* applies, or would apply but for *TCGA 1992, s 116*, in relation to a transaction involving original shares which are or include certain assets; or
- where exchange gains or losses have fallen within *FA 1996, s 84A(4)* (where carried to or maintained in reserves in accordance with generally accepted accounting practice).

[*SI 2002 1970* (as amended by *SI 2004 No 3259* with effect for periods of account beginning on or after 1 January 2005 to reflect the changes in the matching rules for foreign currency liabilities made by *FA 2004* for companies adopting international accounting standards, and further amended with effect from 11 August 2005 by *SI 2005 No 2013*)].

(iii) For periods of account beginning on or after 1 January 2005, the calculations to determine the exchange gain or loss, and any residual profit or loss, arising from certain derivative contracts used to hedge exchange risks and accounted for using fair value accounting. Broadly, the exchange gain or loss is based on the company accounts to the extent the change in fair value is attributable to the spot rate of exchange between the base currency of the company and one or more currencies that form part of the underlying subject matter of the derivative contract or (if the currency or currencies do not form part of the underlying subject matter of the contract) the currency or currencies in which payments under the contract fall to be made. Where a fair value profit is not wholly attributable to an exchange gain or loss, the residual profit is the profit less the exchange gain or plus the exchange loss. Similarly, in the case of a fair value loss, the residual loss is the loss plus the exchange gain or less the exchange loss. [*SI 2005 No 3422*].

(iv) Exchange gains and losses arising from derivative contracts hedging shares etc. to be disregarded in certain cases where the contract is matched with shares, ships or aircraft. The regulations also provide specific rules in relation to matching. They have effect for periods of account beginning on or after 1 January 2005 (the amendments having effect for periods of account beginning on or after that date and ending after, in the case of *SI 2005 No 2012*, 11 August 2005, in the case of *SI 2005 No 3374*, 29 December 2005). [*SI 2004 No 3256, regs 4, 5* (the 'Disregard Regulations') (as amended by *SI 2005 No 2012, regs 5, 6* and *SI 2005 No 3374, regs 3, 5, 6*)].

(v) The disallowance of exchange losses where arrangements within a group are such that the group can choose whether or not to recognise an exchange gain or loss because of its ability to meet obligations under a derivative contract by settling in alternative currencies. (Such arrangements rely on exchange movements which can result in a loss but no corresponding gain.) The regulations have effect for accounting periods ending on or after 22 March 2006 unless the company ceased to be a party to the derivative contract before that date. [*SI 2006 No 843*].

(vi) The disallowance of an exchange loss arising on a derivative contract which is a synthetic hedge of currency risk. [*SI 2006 No 843* which has effect for accounting periods ending on or after 22 March 2006 unless the company ceased to be a party to the derivative contract before that date (as amended by *SI 2006 No 936* which has effect for accounting periods ending on or after that date except in the case of accounting periods beginning before 1 January 2006, in which case the amendment has effect for accounting periods ending on or after 29 March 2006, unless the company ceased to be a party to the derivative contract before that date)].

The above provisions under *FA 2002, Sch 26 para 16* will cease to have effect from a date to be appointed by Treasury order which may contain appropriate savings and transitional provisions. (This is largely due to conflicts with *SI 2004 No 3256* (the 'Disregard Regulations' – see above and 28.10 below) and thus the repeal of the provisions below and the laying of further secondary legislation is provided for by *F(No 2)A 2005, Sch 6 para 9*.)

An '*exchange gain or loss*' is defined as a profit, gain or loss arising as a result of comparing at different times the expression in one currency of the whole or some part of the valuation put by the company in another currency on an asset or liability representing a derivative contract of the company. The Treasury may provide by regulation the manner in which exchange gains or losses, or other profits, gains or losses, are computed where the company uses fair value accounting. Any such regulations may apply to periods of account beginning before the regulations are made but not earlier than the beginning of the calendar year in which they are made.

Where the disposal after 1 April 2002 of an asset does not give rise to a gain as a result of the substantial shareholding provisions under *TCGA 1992, Sch 7AC para 39* as inserted by *FA 2002, Sch 8* (see 13.25 CAPITAL GAINS—SUBSTANTIAL SHAREHOLDINGS), any corresponding gains or losses on derivative contracts previously matched with assets under the matching regulations, *SI 1994 No 3227*, will similarly, not be brought into account.

[*FA 2002, Sch 26 paras 12, 14–16, 54; FA 2004, s 52, Sch 10 paras 47, 48; FA 2005, s 80, Sch 4 para 37; F(No 2)A 2005, Sch 6 paras 4(5)(6), 9, 11; Sch 11 Pt 2(6); SI 2002 No 1969; SI 2002 No 1970; SI 2004 No 3256; SI 2004 No 3259; SI 2005 No 2012; SI 2005 No 2013; SI 2005 No 3374; SI 2005 No 3422; SI 2006 No 843; SI 2006 No 936; SI 2006 No 3236; SI 2007 No 948; SI 2007 No 950*].

28.10 **Computation in accordance with generally accepted accounting practice.** Where the post-FA 2004 basis of computation applies (broadly, following the adoption of international accounting standards, see 27.1 above), the derivative contract debits and credits to be brought into account for these purposes are those 'recognised in determining the company's profit or loss' for the period in accordance with generally accepted accounting practice. This is subject to any other provision of the derivative contract rules, in particular the computation of debits and credits in 27.9. For accounting periods ending on or after 6 March 2007, where a contract is a derivative contract treated for accounting purposes as a financial asset or liability, fair value accounting must be used to determine the amounts brought into account. [FA 2007, Sch 5 para 18]. If a company does not draw up its accounts in accordance with generally accepted accounting practice, or does not draw up accounts at all, the amounts to be brought into account are those that would be recognised had the company done so. This applies equally to amounts derived from earlier periods for which accounts were not drawn up in accordance with generally accepted accounting practice.

Amounts in this case that are '*recognised in determining the company's profit or loss*' are amounts recognised (including prior-year adjustments apart from corrections of fundamental errors) in the company's profit and loss account or income statement, in its statement of recognised gains and losses or statement of changes in equity, or in any other statement of items brought into account in determining the company's profits and losses for that period.

In the case of amounts recognised in the company's statement of recognised gains and losses or statement of changes in equity where the debit or credit represents a prior year adjustment, *SI 2004 No 3271* defers such debits and credits which (except for certain hedging contracts) are not to be brought into account in the first period of account beginning on or after 1 January 2005 but are instead to be brought into account in the first period of account *beginning on or after 1 January 2006*. (This is to bring the tax treatment in line with the mandatory adoption of FRS 26 and IAS 39 by companies using fair value accounting for accounting periods beginning on or after 1 January 2006.)

See *SI 2004 No 3256* ('the Disregard Regulations') (as amended by *SI 2005 No 2012, SI 2005 No 3374 and SI 2006 No 3236*) which provide for changes in fair value of certain derivative contracts (hedging contracts) to be disregarded for tax purposes when recognised in the accounts, and in some cases, to be brought back into account when the contract matures or is disposed of. The regulations have effect for periods of account beginning on or after 1 January 2005 to take account of the use of fair value accounting by companies on their adoption of international accounting standards. (The amendments have effect for periods of account beginning on or after that date and ending after, in the case of *SI 2005 No 2012* 11 August 2005, in the case of *SI 2005 No 3374*, 29 December 2005, in the case of *SI 2006 No 3236* 27 December 2006 and in the cases of *SI 2007 No 948* and *SI 2007 No 950*, 11 April 2007.) A company can elect out of the Disregard Regulations (thus not disregarding fair value movements) in relation to its currency, commodity, debt or interest rate contracts provided certain conditions are met if it wishes to follow the accounts and bring in the fair value adjustments. The time limit for such elections was initially set at before the start of a company's first accounting period beginning on or after 1 January 2005 or, if later, 31 March 2005. However, the deadline has been extended to before 1 October 2005 in the case of certain currency and commodity contracts and to before 31 March 2006 in the case of certain interest rate contracts (where the company can elect for an alternative tax treatment) or, if later, before the accounting period in which the company begins to use fair value accounting (i.e. if it does not adopt fair value accounting in relation to its derivative contracts in its first accounting period on or after 1 January 2005). The deadline has been further extended for elections for certain currency, commodity, debt or interest rate contracts to the later of 31 March 2007 and the last day before the start of an accounting period in which fair value accounting is adopted or the start of the company's first accounting period in which it has a contract to which the Regulations apply.

Change of accounting practice. Where a company prepares its accounts for one period (the '*earlier period*') in accordance with UK generally accepted accounting practice and for the next period (the '*later period*') in accordance with international accounting standards, or vice versa, then any difference between the closing 'accounting value' in the earlier period and the opening 'accounting value' in the later period is treated as a debit or credit (as the case may be) in the later period. This does not apply to the extent that such a credit or debit falls to be brought into account under any other provision.

In this case, *SI 2004 No 3271* (as amended by *SI 2005 No 3383*) defers specified debits and credits which are not to be brought into account in the first period of account beginning on or after 1 January 2005 but are instead brought into account over a ten-year period. Broadly, one-tenth of the applicable amount is brought into account for each of the ten years beginning with the later of the first accounting period of the company beginning on or after 1 January 2006 and the later period (but see below under deferment of transitional adjustments). This does not apply in the case of debits and credits in respect of dormant accounts of banks and building societies which instead are to be brought into account in the first accounting period beginning on or after 1 January 2007. Nor does it apply to specified debits and credits in relation to certain derivative contracts which are not brought into account for any accounting period. (This is to bring the tax treatment in line with the mandatory adoption of FRS 26 and IAS 39 by companies using fair value accounting for accounting periods beginning on or after 1 January 2006, the ten-year period for the deferral being chosen because of the uncertainty as to the size and direction of the transitional adjustments (see HMRC guidance, available on its website, on international accounting standards).)

'*Accounting value*' means the 'carrying value' of the assets or liabilities recognised for accounting purposes. The '*carrying value*' of a contract is to include amounts for accruals, amounts prepaid or received in advance and impairment losses including provisions for bad debts or doubtful debts. The provisions which apply to determine the credits and debits to be brought into account in respect of contracts with guaranteed returns, etc. (see 28.8 above), group transactions (see 28.18 below) or loan relationships with embedded derivatives (see 28.27 below), apply equally to determining the profits, gains and losses to be recognised in determining the carrying value. Where a company ceases to be a party to a derivative contract and debits or credits are brought into account in respect of profits or losses arising in the cessation period under *FA 2002, Sch 26 para 53(3)* (see 28.26 below), then any difference between the 'outstanding amount' in respect of the contract between the end of the earlier period and the beginning of the later period, is to be treated as a debit or credit falling within the above provisions (to be brought into account in the later period). The '*outstanding amount*' is the deferred income or loss recognised in the company's balance sheet (in accordance with generally accepted accounting practice) in respect of the profits, gains or losses arising in the cessation period and not already brought into account as credits or debits for derivative contracts purposes.

Deferment of transitional adjustments. The following provisions apply to arrangements entered into (other than in the ordinary course of business) on or after 14 December 2004 (other than in pursuance of legally binding arrangements entered into before that date) and defer relief for derivative contract debits where all the following circumstances apply.

(*a*) The company incurs a loss in respect of a derivative contract as a result of the transaction in respect of which a debit would (apart from this provision) be brought into account in a period of account beginning before 1 January 2005 and the sole or main purpose for entering into the transaction was to bring a debit into account in that period.

(*b*) Had the company continued to hold the asset or liability representing the derivative contract without entering into the transaction, a debit would have arisen in respect of the derivative contract in its first period of account beginning on or after 1 January 2005 which would have been deferred under *SI 2004 No 3271, reg 3* to be brought into account in the first period of account beginning on or after 1 January 2006 (see above). It is assumed for this purpose that the derivative contract has the same value at the beginning of the company's first period of account beginning on or after 1 January 2005 as it had at the time the transaction was entered into.

In this case, the debit in question is to be treated as arising under *SI 2004 No 3271* in the company's first period of account be

ginning on or after 1 January 2006. In determining the sole or main purpose of the transaction, regard shall be had to anything done by a connected company (within the meaning of *ICTA 1988, s 839*) and references to a company entering into a transaction include references to the company or its directors taking a decision about the derivative contract affecting its accounting treatment. [*FA 2005, s 82*].

Securitisation companies. In determining the profit or loss of a special purpose company used in securitisation transactions ('securitisation companies' – as defined in 28.51 below) for periods of account beginning on or after 1 January 2005 and ending before 1 January 2008 (subject to any regulations to extend the period beyond 1 January 2008), 'generally accepted accounting practice' ('GAAP') shall be taken to be UK generally accepted accounting practice as it applied to a period of account ending on 31 December 2004. The Treasury may make regulations to provide for special tax treatment for such companies. The regulations referred to may specify a period to apply to specified classes of securitisation company or different dates for different classes and they may also provide for such companies to elect either in or out of the regime [*FA 2005, ss 83, 84 as amended by FA 2006, s 101; FA 2007, s 59*].

Treasury powers. The Treasury has the power to vary these provisions by regulation (to meet the circumstances of particular cases and to make provisions subject to election or other prescribed conditions) to exclude amounts of a prescribed description recognised in determining the company's profit and loss account (as above), or requiring amounts of a prescribed description not so recognised to be brought into account in prescribed circumstances. Such regulations may prescribe the manner in which such amounts are to be brought into account and may also make provision in respect of amounts which derive from or relate to amounts brought into account in a previous period. With effect for periods of account beginning on or after 1 January 2005, such regulations may be made to apply to periods of account before the regulations are made but not earlier than the beginning of the calendar year in which they are made.

[*FA 2002, Sch 26 paras 17A–17C, 50A; FA 2004, s 52, Sch 10 paras 49–51, 67; FA 2005, ss 80, 82–84, Sch 4 paras 34, 52; FA 2006, Sch 6 para 21; SI 2004 No 3270, Article 12; SI 2004 No 3271; SI 2004 No 3347; SI 2005 No 3383; SI 2006 No 3236; SI 2006 No 3238; SI 2007 No 948; SI 2007 No 950*].

See HMRC's draft guidance on the basic tax rules for derivative contracts in accounting periods beginning on or after 1 January 2005. The guidance is to form part of HMRC's Corporate Finance Manual (CFM) 13250 to 13304.

28.11 **Authorised accounting methods.** Where the pre-FA 2004 basis of computation applies (see 28.1 above), except as below, the alternative accounting methods authorised for the purposes of the current provisions are a mark to market basis, under which a fair value (on the basis of a transfer at arm's length) is brought into account in each accounting period for each derivative contract to which it applies, and an accruals basis. Whichever method is used must:

(*a*) (subject to (*b*)–(*d*) below) conform with generally accepted accounting practice (see 55.2 PROFIT COMPUTATIONS);

(*b*) contain proper provision for allocating payments under a derivative contract or from a related transaction to accounting periods;

(*c*) contain proper provision for determining exchange gains and losses from a derivative contract for accounting periods; and

(*d*) in the case of an accruals basis, not contain any provision (other than provision for exchange losses or provision comprised in authorised bad debt arrangements, for which see 28.12 below) giving debits by reference to the valuation at different times of any derivative contract.

As regards (*b*), a mark to market basis must allocate payments to the accounting period in which they become due and payable. An accruals basis must:

(i) allocate payments to the period to which they relate, without regard to payment or receipt or their becoming due and payable;

(ii) apportion payments relating to two or more periods on a just and reasonable basis;

(iii) assume (subject to authorised bad debt arrangements, see 28.12 below) that every amount payable to the company under the contract will be paid in full when due;

(iv) secure the making of the adjustments required by authorised bad debt arrangements; and

(v) provide (subject to authorised bad debt arrangements), in respect of the release of liabilities owed by the company under a contract, for the appropriate amount to be credited to the company in the accounting period of the release.

Application of accounting methods. Different authorised accounting methods as described in (A) to (E) below, may be used as respects different derivative contracts, and for different accounting periods (or parts) as respects the same contract.

(A) *Accruals basis.* Where the method to be used is not determined by any of the methods in (B) to (E) below, an authorised accruals basis of accounting must be used.

(B) *Method used in accounts.* If an accounting basis which is, or which 'equates' with, an authorised accounting method is used as respects any derivative contract of a company in its 'statutory accounts' (see *FA 2002, Sch 26 para 52*), it, or the authorised method with which it equates, must similarly be used for periods covered by those accounts.

(C) *Election by non-resident company to use mark to market accounting basis.* A non-resident company can elect to use (with respect to a UK branch) a mark to market accounting basis for some or all of its derivative contracts if that method would be used as respects those contracts in drawing up its accounts if the company were a UK company following generally accepted accounting practice, but where that basis is not used for those contracts in its own statutory accounts. The election must be made within two years following the end of the company's first accounting period beginning on or after 1 October 2002 in which it is party to the derivative contract eligible for election. It is irrevocable and has effect for the accounting period in which it is made and all subsequent accounting periods. Where such an election is made, an equivalent election is also treated as made under *FA 1996, s 86(3A)*, having effect for the same accounting periods as respects any loan relationships to which the company is or may become a party, notwithstanding that the deemed election may fall outside of the prescribed time limits (see 46.31 LOAN RELATIONSHIPS).

(D) *Requirement for non-resident company to follow generally accepted accounting practice* where it does not make an election under (C) above. Where, if the company were a UK company following generally accepted accounting practice, it would use an authorised mark to market basis for an accounting period as respects some or all of its loan relationships and some or all of its derivative contracts, and it uses that basis in its statutory accounts as respects those loan relationships for that period but not as respects those derivative contracts for that period, it must use that basis for that accounting period in relation to every derivative contract for which it would be used under UK generally accepted accounting practice. Where such a company uses a basis of accounting other than an authorised mark to market basis in an accounting period (the 'preceding period') but must use an authorised mark to market basis for the succeeding accounting period (the 'first mark to market period') in accordance with this provision, it will be deemed to have disposed of the derivative contract immediately before the end of the preceding period for a fair value consideration and to have reacquired it immediately after the beginning of the first mark to market period for the same consideration.

(E) *Contracts producing guaranteed returns or amounts.* The authorised mark to market basis of accounting must be used for derivative contracts which produce guaranteed returns, where guaranteed amounts are payable on maturity, or which provide insurance benefits, under *FA 2002, Sch 26 paras 6–8* respectively (see 28.8 above).

A basis of accounting '*equates*':

(I) with an authorised accruals basis if (not being within (III)) it purports to allocate payments under a derivative contract to accounting periods according to when they are taken to accrue;

(II) with an authorised mark to market basis if it purports, in respect of a derivative contract, to produce credits or debits which relate to payments under the contract according to when they become due and payable, and which are computed by reference to the determination, as at different times in an accounting period, of a fair value (representing an arm's length valuation); and

(III) with an authorised mark to market basis if, otherwise being within (I), it purports to bring the derivative contract into account in each accounting period at fair value (representing an arm's length valuation) on the basis that any periodic payments to be made under the contract are to be disregarded to the extent they have already accrued, and the resulting credits and debits correspond, for all practical purposes, to those under an authorised mark to market basis.

For partnerships involving companies, see 28.26 below.

Where the post-FA 2004 basis of computation applies (see 28.1 above), the derivative contract debits and credits to be brought into account for these purposes are those 'recognised in determining the company's profit or loss' for the period in accordance with generally accepted accounting practice (see 28.10 above).

[*FA 2002, Sch 26 paras 17–21* as originally enacted; *FA 2004, s 52, Sch 10, paras 50, 51*].

28.12 **SPECIAL PROVISION FOR BAD DEBTS AND RELEASE OF LIABILITY**

Where the post-FA 2004 basis of computation applies (see 28.1 above) and a liability owed by the company to pay an amount under the contract is released, no credit is required to be brought into account in respect of the release if it is part of a statutory insolvency arrangement within the meaning given by ICTA 1988, s 834(1) or, for periods of account beginning before 1 January 2005, a relevant arrangement or compromise within the meaning given by *ICTA 1988, s 74(2)*.

Where the pre-FA 2004 basis of computation applies (see 28.1 above), except as detailed below, a departure is allowed from the normal accruals basis assumption that all amounts payable to a company in respect of its derivative contracts will be paid on time only for bad debts, for doubtful debts estimated to be bad and for debts released. The accounting arrangements allowing for the departure must also require adjustment by way of credit for any amount of a bad debt which is paid or which otherwise ceases to fulfil the conditions for relief. They must also require that the same treatment (for allowing the departure and bringing in any subsequent adjustment) is adopted in determining the credits and debits to be brought into account in respect of exchange gains and losses arising on the company's derivative contracts. Where a debt payable by a company under a derivative contract is released in an accounting period for which the debtor company uses the accruals basis as respects the contract in question, no credit is required to be brought in in respect of the release if it is part of a relevant arrangement or compromise (within the meaning given by *ICTA 1988, s 74(2)*).

[*FA 2002, Sch 26 para 22; FA 2004, s 52, Sch 10 paras 52, 53; FA 2005, s 80, Sch 4 paras 1, 8, 19*].

28.13 **SPECIAL COMPUTATIONAL PROVISIONS**

Unallowable purposes. Where, in any accounting period, a derivative contract of a company has an unallowable purpose, any '*exchange credits*' (i.e. credits attributable to exchange gains) and any debits in respect of the contract which, on a just and reasonable apportionment, are attributable to the unallowable purpose are not to be brought into account for that period, except as detailed below.

Where, in the case of a derivative contract, the debits relating to the unallowable purpose for an accounting period exceed the exchange credits relating to it in the same accounting period, the difference (the '*net loss*') may be brought into account as a debit to the extent that the 'accumulated net losses' for the period do not exceed the 'accumulated credits'. The '*accumulated net losses*' are the amount of any net loss arising from the derivative contract, either for that accounting period or for an earlier accounting period (beginning on or after 1 October 2002), less any amount already brought into account under this provision in an earlier accounting period. The '*accumulated credits*' are:

(A) the amount of any credits, other than exchange credits, arising from the derivative contract, either for that accounting period or for an earlier accounting period (beginning on or after 1 October 2002); less

(B) the amount of:

  (i) any debits arising on the derivative contract for that accounting period or any earlier accounting period ending on or after 17 March 2004, which are not referable to the unallowable purpose; and

  (ii) any net loss arising on the same derivative contract already brought into account under this provision in an earlier accounting period.

Amounts not brought into account by virtue of this provision are not to be brought into account in any other way for corporation tax purposes.

A purpose for which the company, at times during an accounting period, either is a party to a derivative contract or enters into any related transactions (see 28.9 above) is an '*unallowable purpose*' if it is not amongst the business or other commercial purposes of the company (which do not include the purposes of any part of its activities which are outside the charge to corporation tax). In this respect, a purpose which consists in the securing of a tax advantage (within *ICTA 1988, ss 703–709*, see 5.2 ANTI-AVOIDANCE) shall be treated as a business or other commercial purpose of the company only where it is not a main purpose for which the company is a party to the contract at the time or for which it entered into the transaction.

See also 28.46 for the corresponding anti-avoidance provisions applying under the earlier rules with effect from 26 July 2001.

[*FA 2002, Sch 26 paras 23, 24; FA 2004, Sch 9 para 4, Sch 10 para 55*].

28.14 **Capital expenditure.** Where any debit or credit for any accounting period in respect of a derivative contract is allowed by generally accepted accounting practice (see 55.2 PROFIT COMPUTATIONS) to be treated as an amount brought into account in determining the value of a fixed capital asset or project, it is to be treated as a derivative contract credit or debit to the extent it would be so treated if it were required by such practice to be brought into account in determining the company's profit or loss for that period. No amount can be brought into account as a derivative contract debit if it is taken into account as a debit arising from an intangible fixed asset under *FA 2002, Sch 29* (see INTANGIBLE ASSETS (39)). Where the post-FA 2004 basis of computation applies (see 28.1 above) and a debit is brought into account under this provision, no further debit will be allowed for the writing down of that debit attributable to the value of the fixed capital asset or project or for the amortisation or depreciation representing a writing off of the interest component of the asset. [*FA 2002, Sch 26 para 25; FA 2004, s 52, Sch 10 para 56*].

28.15 **Amounts recognised in equity or shareholders' funds.** For periods of account beginning on or after 1 January 2005, where debits or credits in respect of a derivative contract are, under generally accepted accounting practice, recognised in equity or shareholders' funds but not in any of the company's statements of items brought into account in computing profits or losses for the period, they are to be brought into account as if they were treated as profit and loss items. (Such items may, for example, be amounts taken to share premium account.) [*FA 2002, Sch 26 para 25A; FA 2005, s 80, Sch 4 para 35; F(No 2)A 2005, Sch 6 para 4(3)(6)*].

28.16 **Transfers of value to connected companies.** Where, on or after 6 March 2007, a company fails to exercise in full its rights under an option which was a derivative contract and there is a transfer of value by the company which held the option (the 'transferor') to a connected company (the 'transferee') which is not otherwise chargeable to corporation tax, a credit is brought into account by the transferor. The credit has to be brought into account in the accounting period in which the option expires, or would have expired had the rights under it been exercised. The amount of the credit is, where the option expired, the amount paid by the transferor for it and where any of the rights were exercised, an amount representing a just and reasonable proportion of the amount paid.

Before 6 March 2007, where a company fails to exercise it rights in full under an option which was a derivative contract, there is a transfer of value by the company which held the option (the 'transferor') to a 'connected' company (the 'transferee') which is not otherwise chargeable to corporation tax in respect of the contract, a credit is to be brought into account by the transferor in the accounting period in which the option expired, or would have expired had the rights under it been exercised. The credit to be brought into account is, where the option expired on or after 6 March 2007, the amount paid by the transferor for it and, where any of the rights were exercised, an amount representing a just and reasonable proportion of the amount paid. Where the option expired before 6 March 2007, the credit to be brought into account is the amount (if any) paid by the transferor to the transferee for the grant of the option by the transferee. In determining whether there is a transfer of value, it is assumed that, if the parties had not been connected, the option would not have expired and would have been exercised on the date it expired.

An option is within these provisions if it falls within the definition in 28.3 above, but without the exclusion of cases involving cash settlement.

Companies are '*connected*' for these purposes in an accounting period if, at any time in that period, there is a connection between the companies as determined by *FA 1996, ss 87(3)(4), 87A* (see 46.16 LOAN RELATIONSHIPS).

[*FA 2002, Sch 26 para 26; FA 2007, Sch 5 para 18*].

For transfers of value in general, see 67 TRANSFER PRICING.

28.17 **Exchange gains and losses where derivative contract not at arm's length.** Where, in an accounting period, a company is party to a derivative contract the provisions of which are not at arm's length, so that the transfer pricing provisions of *ICTA 1988, Sch 28AA* (see 67 TRANSFER PRICING) apply to treat the company as not being party to the contract, any exchange gains and losses arising in that accounting period as regards the derivative contract are to be disregarded in determining the related credits and debits. Where the transfer pricing provisions instead require profits and losses to be computed as if the contract had been on arm's length terms, any such exchange gain or loss is instead adjusted for those purposes to the amount which would have arisen if the contract had been on such terms. [*FA 2002, Sch 26 para 27*].

28.18 **Transactions within groups.** There are provisions requiring adjustments to ensure that intra-group transactions under the derivative contracts regime are tax neutral such provisions having been amended by *F(No 2)A 2005* to prevent the rules from being used to obtain a tax benefit. The provisions apply where, as a result of a related transaction (see 28.9 above) between two members of a group (both being within the charge to corporation tax in respect of the transaction), one of those companies (the 'transferee company') directly or indirectly replaces the other (the 'transferor company') as a party to a derivative contract, or becomes party to a contract equivalent to one to which the other company has ceased to be party. The provisions similarly apply where a series of transactions, having the same effect as a related transaction between two companies each of which has been a member of the same group at some time in the course of those transactions, results in such a replacement.

In determining the credits and debits to be brought the following provisions apply.

(*a*) Where the 'relevant transaction' **is on or after 16 March 2005**, the transferor company is treated as having entered into the transaction (or the first of a series of transactions, as the case may be) in the accounting period in which the transaction takes place for a consideration equal to the 'notional carrying value' of the derivative contract. The transferee is treated as having acquired the contract for a consideration equal to that amount for any accounting period in which it is party to the contract. (This means that where the transferee uses fair value accounting the movement in fair value in the accounting period of transfer will be the difference between the fair value at the end of that period and the carrying value to the transferor of the contract and where amortised cost is used, then the carrying value of the transferor will be used as the cost to the transferee.)

The '*notional carrying value*' is the amount that would have been the carrying value (see 28.10 above) of the contract in the transferor's accounts had a period of account ended immediately before the company ceased to be party to the contract. For that purpose, where the period of account begins before 1 January 2005, 'carrying value' is to be construed as if the period had begun on or after that date (the definition of 'carrying value' in 28.10 above having effect only for periods of account beginning on or after date).

In relation to 'relevant transactions' after 21 March 2006, where a discount arises (within the meaning of *FA 1996, s 100(3A)*, see 46.46(*d*) LOAN RELATIONSHIPS) in respect of the transaction (or series of transactions or transfer), the consideration treated as payable by the transferor company is to be increased by the amount of the discount.

(*b*) Where the 'relevant transaction' is before 16 March 2005, the credits and debits to be brought into account for the two companies are determined disregarding the transaction and treating the two companies as the same company. The transaction is not disregarded, however, for the purpose of identifying the company for which any other debit or credit is to be brought into account or, where the date of the transfer is after 8 April 2003, of determining the debits and credits to be brought into account in respect of exchange gains or losses and identifying the company which is to bring them into account.

A 'relevant transaction' is a related transaction (as in 46.5 above) or the first of a series of related transactions or a transfer by virtue of which these provisions apply or would apply but for the transferor company using fair value accounting (see below).

For accounting periods beginning on or after 1 April 2004 (subject to transitional provisions for accounting periods straddling that date), the transfer pricing provisions in *ICTA 1988, Sch 28AA* (see 67 TRANSFER PRICING) do not apply to debits or credits determined as above.

'Group' for these purposes is as under *TCGA 1992, s 170* (see 12.1 CAPITAL GAINS—GROUPS).

Similar provisions apply to certain transfers between insurance companies which result in one replacing the other as a party to a derivative contract (and the above provisions are correspondingly disapplied to certain such transfers).

Fair value accounting: These provisions do not apply where the transferor company uses fair value accounting (or, where the pre-FA 2004 basis of computation applies (see 28.1 above) an authorised mark to market basis of accounting) in respect of the derivative contract.

In this case, the amount to be brought into account by the transferor company (where the transferee company becomes party to the relationship after 8 April 2003) is the fair value (as defined by *FA 2002, Sch 26 para 54(1)* (amended by *FA 2006, Sch 6 para 24*)) of the contract as at the date of transfer to the transferee company. In relation to relevant transactions after 21 March 2006, where a discount arises (within the meaning of *FA 1996, s 100(3A)*, see 46.46(*d*) LOAN RELATIONSHIPS) in respect of the transaction (or series of transactions or transfer), the consideration treated as payable by the transferor company is to be increased by the amount of the discount.

The amount to be brought into account by the transferee company is:

(i) for relevant transactions after 21 March 2006, the same as the amount brought into account by the transferor company ignoring any discount required to be brought into account by that company;

(ii) for relevant transactions on or after 16 March 2005 and before 22 March 2006, the notional carrying value of the contract in the accounting period in which it becomes party to the contract or, for relevant transactions before that date, the same amount as brought into account by the transferor company.

[*FA 2002, Sch 26 paras 28–30; FA 2003, s 179; FA 2004, s 52, Sch 5 para 15(2), Sch 10 para 57; F(No 2)A 2005, Sch 7 paras 22, 23; FA 2006, Sch 6 paras 22, 23*].

28.19 **Degrouping charge.** A degrouping charge applies where after replacing the transferor company as party to a derivative contract as in 28.18 above, the transferee company ceases within the 'relevant six-year period' to be a member of the group on or after 16 March 2005. The '*relevant six-year period*' is the period of six years following a related transaction between two members of a group companies or following the last of a series of transactions between two companies each of which has been a member of the same group at some time in the course of those transactions.

In this case, the transferee company is treated (subject to the conditions below) as having assigned the rights and liabilities under the derivative contract immediately before the cessation for consideration equal to their fair value at that time and as having immediately reacquired them for the same amount. (Thus, any gain is brought into charge to tax under the derivative contract provisions immediately before the transferee leaves the group.)

Where a deemed disposal and reacquisition as above applies, the degrouping charge only applies if a credit would be brought into account by the transferee company on the assignment of the rights and liabilities under the derivative contract or, if that is not the case, a credit would be brought into account under the loan relationship rules (under *FA 1996, Sch 9 para 12A*, see 46.22 LOAN RELATIONSHIPS) in respect of a creditor loan relationship where the company has a hedging relationship (as defined by *FA 2002, Sch 26 para 12(14)*) between the derivative contract and the creditor relationship.

The degrouping charge does not apply where the transferee company ceases to be a member of the group by reason only of an exempt distribution within *ICTA 1988, s 213(2)*. However, if there is a chargeable payment (within the meaning of *ICTA 1988, s 214(2)*) within five years after making the exempt distribution, a degrouping charge arises as above but the transferee company is treated as having assigned the rights and liabilities under the derivative contract immediately before making the chargeable payment. As above, the degrouping charge only applies if a credit would be brought into account by the transferee company on the assignment of the rights and liabilities under the derivative contract or, if that is not the case, a credit would be brought into account under the loan relationship rules (under *FA 1996, Sch 9 para 12A*) in respect of a creditor loan relationship where the company has a hedging relationship (as defined by *FA 2002, Sch 26 para 12(14)*) between the derivative contract and the creditor relationship.

[*FA 2002, Sch 26 para 30A; F(No 2)A 2005, Sch 7 para 24*].

28.20 **Transfers on formation of a European Company.** The European Company Statute provides for the formation of a European Company or *Societas Europaea* ('SE') and applies to all member states with effect from 8 October 2004 (see 25.4 EUROPEAN COMMUNITY LEGISLATION). The *Statute* permits the formation of new SEs and also allows for the 'transformation' of existing companies into SEs and for the merger between two (or more) companies in different member states into an SE. Special UK tax provisions are required to deal with the formation of SEs by cross-border merger and those relating to derivative contracts are described below. The provisions are intended to be broadly tax-neutral. (Revenue Technical Note, 'Implementation of the European Company Statute', January 2005).

The provisions apply where an SE is formed on or after 1 April 2005 by the merger of two or more companies in accordance with *Council Regulation (EC) No 2157/2001, Arts 2(1), 17(2)* and each merging company is resident in a member state but not all of them are resident in the same member state.

A company is resident in a member state for this purpose if it is within a charge to tax under the law of the state as being resident for that purpose and it is not regarded, for the purposes of any DOUBLE TAX RELIEF (24) arrangements to which the state is a party, as resident in a territory not within a member state.

If, immediately after formation, the SE is within the charge to corporation tax (whether by virtue of residence in the UK or by trading in the UK through a UK permanent establishment), the transfer in the course of the merger of rights or liabilities under a derivative contract is disregarded and the transferor and transferee companies are treated as the same company, except for the purposes of identifying the company for which a debit or credit not relating to the transfer is to be brought into account and determining the debits and credits to be brought into account in respect of exchange gains or losses and identifying the company which is to bring them into account.

The above provisions do not apply unless the formation of the SE is effected for *bona fide* commercial reasons and is not part of a scheme or arrangements of which the main purpose or one of the main purposes is avoiding a liability to tax. Advance clearance can be obtained that this condition is met.

Where the transferor uses fair value accounting for the derivative contract the transfer is not to be disregarded as above but must be treated by both companies as being at fair value.

[*FA 2002, Sch 26 para 30B; F(No 2)A 2005, s 55*].

28.21 **Company ceasing to be UK-resident etc.** Where, on or after 17 March 2003, a company ceases to be UK-resident, it will be deemed to have assigned its rights and liabilities under its derivative contracts immediately before and to have reacquired them immediately after it ceased to be UK-resident, at their fair value, unless the rights and liabilities under the contract continue to be held or owed for the purposes of the company's UK permanent establishment (see 60.5 RESIDENCE). The provision similarly applies where rights or liabilities under a derivative contract cease to be held for the purposes of a UK permanent establishment of a non-UK resident company in any circumstances not involving a related transaction. (Thus, any profit or loss on the rights or liabilities will be brought into account as a derivative contract credit or debit.) [*FA 2002, Sch 26 para 22A; FA 2004, Sch 9 para 3, Sch 10 para 54*].

28.22 **Derivative contracts with non-residents.** Special provisions apply (except as below) where, as a result of any transaction entered into on or after 1 October 2002, either:

(*a*) a company and a non-resident both become party to a derivative contract; or

(*b*) a company becomes party to a derivative contract to which a non-resident is party or *vice versa*.

For each accounting period for any part of which the company and a non-resident are both parties to a derivative contract which makes provision for 'notional interest payments' (e.g. under an interest rate or currency swap), no 'relevant debits' arising to the company from the derivative contract may be brought into account by the company.

A '*relevant debit*' is the excess of the aggregate of 'notional interest payments' made by the company to the non-resident while they are both party to the contract over the aggregate of such payments made by the non-resident to the company. A '*notional interest payment*' is any payment of an amount determined (wholly or mainly) by applying a rate equal to a specified rate of interest to a specified notional principal amount for a specified period.

These special provisions do not apply:

(i) to a company which is a bank, a building society, a financial trader (see below) or a recognised clearing house (within *Financial Services and Markets Act 2000, s 285*) holding the derivative contract (otherwise than as agent or nominee) solely for the purposes of a UK trade (or part);

(ii) where the non-resident holds the derivative contract (otherwise than as agent or nominee) solely for the purposes of a UK trade (or part) carried on through a permanent establishment (or branch or agency – see 60.5 RESIDENCE); or

(iii) where arrangements made under *ICTA 1988, s 788* (see 24.3 DOUBLE TAX RELIEF) with the government of the territory in which the non-UK resident is resident (or, if the non-resident is party to the contract as agent or nominee of another person, with the government of the territory in which that other person is resident) make provision, whether for relief or otherwise, in relation to interest.

As regards (i) above, for the guidelines used by HMRC in deciding whether a company should be approved as a financial trader, see HMRC Statement of Practice SP 4/02, 30 September 2002.

[*FA 2002, Sch 26 para 31*].

28.23 **Provisions not at arm's length: amounts imputed.** For accounting periods beginning on or after 1 April 2004 (subject to transitional provisions for periods straddling that date), where, under the provisions *ICTA 1988, Sch 28AA* (see 67 TRANSFER PRICING), any amounts fall to be treated as profits or losses arising to, or charges or expenses incurred by, a company in respect of any of its derivative contracts or related transactions, those provisions will have effect so as to require credits or debits relating to the deemed amounts to be brought into account to the same extent as if they were actual amounts. This over-rides, for accounting periods beginning before 1 January 2005, any provisions of an authorised accounting method. [*FA 2002, Sch 26 para 31A; FA 2004, Sch 5 para 15(3), Sch 10 para 58*].

28.24 COLLECTIVE INVESTMENT SCHEMES

FA 2002, Sch 26 Pt 7 makes special provision in relation to such schemes. Broadly, these are as follows.

Authorised unit trusts and open-ended investment companies. 'Capital profits, gains or losses' arising to an authorised unit trust or an open-ended investment company on a derivative contract are to be disregarded under these provisions. '*Capital profits, gains or losses*' in this case are those which, in preparing accounts in accordance with UK generally accepted accounting practice, fall to be dealt with in the statement of total return (under the heading of 'net gains/losses on investments during the period' or 'other gains/losses') in accordance with the relevant Statement of Recommended Practice (SORP). Where the post-FA 2004 basis of computation applies (see 28.1 above) and the authorised unit trust or open-ended investment company prepares accounts in accordance with international accounting standards, the capital profits, gains or losses are those as defined by, for accounting periods beginning on or after 1 April 2006, *SI 2006 No 964, reg 12; SI 2006 No 3239* and *SI 2007 No 683*. The relevant SORP in the case of an authorised unit trust or an open-ended investment company is that relating to authorised investment funds issued by the Investment Management Association on 21 November 2003 (as modified, amended or revised) or any subsequent SORP replacing it). (See, generally, 43 INVESTMENT FUNDS). For a statement agreed between HMRC and the Investment Management Association confirming the tax treatment in these circumstances, see Revenue Tax Bulletin August 2002 pp 948–950.

Powers to make regulations replacing the above provisions to rationalise and modernise the regime for authorised unit trusts and open-ended investment companies are provided for by *F(No 2)A 2005, ss 17–19*.

Distributing offshore funds. In determining the UK equivalent profits of a distributing offshore fund, the corporation tax rules apply, as if the offshore fund were a UK Authorised Unit Trust, for the purposes of calculating profits or losses arising on derivative contracts. However, for accounting periods of an offshore fund ending before 22 July 2004, the profits or losses arising on a derivative contract are calculated on an income tax basis as if the offshore fund were an unauthorised unit trust and these rules will continue to apply after that date where the manager of the offshore fund so elects. (See 50 OFFSHORE FUNDS.)

Corporate holdings in unit trusts, open-ended investment companies and offshore funds. Special provisions apply where a company is party to a contract which is not a derivative contract and of which the underlying subject matter consists wholly or partly of rights in an authorised unit trust, shares in an open-ended investment company or a relevant interest in an offshore fund. Where in this case, the company or fund fails to satisfy the 'non-qualifying investments test' in *FA 1996, Sch 10 para 8*, the relevant contract will be treated as a derivative contract and fair value accounting (or, where the pre-FA 2004 basis of computation applies (see 28.1 above), an authorised mark to market basis) must be used to determine the derivative contract credits and debits. Broadly, the company will fail the test where its holding of interest-producing assets and similar contracts amount to over 60% of its total holdings.

Special provisions also apply where a contract becomes a contract subject to the above rule, whether by enactment of the provision or otherwise.

Investment trusts and venture capital trusts. With effect for accounting periods beginning on or after 1 October 2002, any capital profits, gains or losses arising to an investment trust or a venture capital trust from a derivative contract must not be brought into account in determining derivative contract credits or debits. Capital profits, gains or losses in this case are those which, in preparing accounts in accordance with UK generally accepted accounting practice, are carried to or sustained by a capital reserve in accordance with the relevant Statement of Recommended Practice (SORP) (or, in the case of a venture capital trust, would be so treated if the venture capital trust were an investment trust and were using the SORP). Where the post-FA 2004 basis of computation applies (see 28.1 above) and an investment trust or venture capital trust prepares accounts in accordance with international accounting standards, the capital profits, gains or losses are those as defined by *SI 2006 No 1182*. The relevant SORP is that relating to the Financial Statements of Investment Trust Companies issued by the Association of Investment Trust Companies in January 2003 and revised in December 2005 (as modified, amended or revised) or any subsequent SORP replacing it.

The excess of relevant credits over relevant debits from derivative contracts is to be treated as income from shares and securities for the purposes of determining whether or not a company may be approved as an investment trust or a venture capital trust under *ICTA 1988, s 842* or *s 842AA* respectively. (See generally 44.1 INVESTMENT TRUSTS and 69 VENTURE CAPITAL TRUSTS.)

Treasury powers. The Treasury may by order amend the above provisions so as to alter the definition of capital profits, gains or losses following the modification, amendment, revision or replacement of a SORP.

[*FA 2002, Sch 26 paras 32–40; FA 2004, s 145, Sch 10 paras 59–63, Sch 26 para 2, Sch 42 Pt 2(5); FA 2005, Sch 4 para 36; F(No 2)A 2005, ss 17–19; ITA 2007 Sch 1 para 605*].

28.25 INSURANCE AND MUTUAL TRADING COMPANIES

Special provisions in *FA 2002, Sch 26 Pt 8* apply to life assurance business (including annuity business) and to any other mutual trading or insurance or other mutual business. Otherwise, the provisions of *Schedule 26* apply to insurance and mutual trading companies as they do to other companies. [*FA 2002, Sch 26 paras 41–43; SI 2005 No 646*].

28.26 MISCELLANEOUS PROVISIONS

Derivative contracts ceasing to be held for trading purposes. A company is deemed to have disposed of and immediately reacquired a relevant contract at its fair value (representing an arm's length valuation) where:

(i) a company is party to a derivative contract, entered into or acquired for the purposes of its trade;

(ii) (for periods of account beginning on or after 1 January 2005 and ending on or after 17 August 2005) the underlying subject matter of the contract consists (or is treated as consisting) wholly of shares or rights of a unit holder in a unit trust (having regard to 28.6 above in relation to underlying subject matter which is subordinate or small);

(iii) at any time ('*the relevant time*') the company ceases to hold the contract for these purposes but continues to be a party to it; and

(iv) (for periods of account beginning on or after 1 January 2005 and ending on or after 17 August 2005) had the company entered into or acquired the contract immediately after the relevant time, it would not have been a derivative contract.

[*FA 2002, Sch 26 para 44; SI 2005 No 2082*].

Contracts becoming held for trading purposes. This provision only applies to relevant contracts whose underlying subject matter consists (or is treated as consisting) wholly of shares in a company, rights under a unit trust scheme or, for periods of account beginning before 1 January 2005 and ending before 16 March 2005, assets representing a loan relationship to which *FA 1996, s 92* or *s 93* applies (convertible or asset-linked securities), and in determining whether the underlying subject matter of a contract can be treated as consisting 'wholly' of such property, see 28.6 above. Where a company has such a contract which is a chargeable asset (under *TCGA 1992*) but which is not a derivative contract for the reason that it is not held for trading purposes, and it is appropriated by the company for trading purposes, a charge will arise at that time under *TCGA 1992, s 161(1)* on a deemed disposal at market value. The company cannot make an election under *TCGA 1992, s 161(3)* to convert the capital gain or loss into a revenue item. [*FA 2002, Sch 26 para 45; SI 2005 No 646*].

For accounting periods ending after 30 December 2006 these rules are repealed and instead sub-paragraph 43A applies where a company is party to a relevant contract which becomes a derivative contract and is a chargeable asset. When the company ceases to be a party to the relevant contract, it is treated as making a notional capital gains disposal immediately after the relevant contract becomes a derivative contract on or after 30 December 2006.

Amounts brought into account after company ceases to be party to a contract-. Where a company ceases to be party to a derivative contract in an accounting period and profits or losses arise to the company from the contract or a related transaction (see 28.9 above) in that period, then if the derivative contract credits or debits brought into account in that period do not represent the whole of those profits or losses, credits or debits in respect of the balance of profits or losses continue to be brought into account in any subsequent accounting periods as if the company had not ceased to be a party to the contract. [*FA 2002, Sch 26 para 53(3)–(5)*].

Embedded derivatives in connected party loans. For periods of account *beginning on or after 1 January 2005 and ending before 16 March 2005*, where a company is a party as creditor to a loan relationship with an embedded derivative (under *FA 1996, s 94A*, see 46.40 LOAN RELATIONSHIPS), and the loan relationship is with a connected party (under *FA 1996, s 87*), then no loss arising from any of the embedded derivative components of the contract will be treated as giving rise to a debit for derivative contracts purposes. This provision was repealed for accounting periods ending on or after 16 March 2005 so that embedded derivatives in connected party loans may be taxed on a chargeable gains basis (see 28.27 below). [*FA 2002, Sch 26 para 48A; SI 2004 No 3270, Art 11; SI 2005 No 2082*].

Partnerships involving companies. Where any of the partners in a partnership which carries on a trade, profession or business, and which is a party to a derivative contract, is a company, no account is taken of debits or credits in relation to the contract in calculating the profits of the partnership for corporation tax purposes. Each company partner is instead required to bring into account a share of the credits and debits in respect of the contract as follows. The credits and debits are determined separately for each company partner as if the contract was entered into or acquired by the company for trade purposes, and as if any transactions carried out by the firm in relation to the contract were carried out by the company. Where the post-FA 2004 basis of computation applies (see 28.1 above), to the extent that any exchange gains or losses are recognised in the firm's statement of recognised gains and losses or statement of changes in equity, they are treated as recognised in the corresponding statement of the company partner. (Where the pre-FA 2004 basis of computation applies, where any exchange gains or losses are taken to reserves and set off by or against another amount they are treated as having been taken to a reserve maintained by the company partner and set off by or against another amount.) The company is then required to bring into account a share of the credits and debits so determined corresponding to its share in partnership profits.

Where the company partner uses fair value accounting (or, where the pre-FA 2004 basis of computation applies, a mark to market basis of accounting) in relation to its interest in the firm the credits and debits determined as above must be determined on a fair value (or, where the pre-FA 2004 basis of computation applies, a mark to market) basis of accounting. Otherwise, where the pre-FA 2004 basis of computation applies, the accounting methods described at 28.11 above are to be applied as appropriate.

[*FA 2002, Sch 26 paras 49, 50; FA 2004, s 52, Sch 10 paras 65, 66*].

Prevention of deduction of tax. A company is not required to deduct income tax from any payment made under a derivative contract to which these provisions apply. [*FA 2002, Sch 26 para 51*].

Index-linked gilt-edged securities with embedded contracts for differences. Credits and debits arising on a derivative contract are not to be brought into account where, for accounting periods beginning on or after 1 January 2005:

(*a*) the rights and liabilities arising under a contract are split into two parts as set out in 28.27 below (under 'embedded derivatives'), with respect to a creditor relationship;

(*b*) the creditor relationship is an index-linked gilt-edged security giving rise to non-trading credits and debits in respect of the equivalent deemed loan relationship; and

(*c*) the 'embedded derivative' contract is a contract for differences.

[*FA 2002, Sch 26 para 45I; SI 2004 No 2201, Articles 1, 15*].

The Treasury Explanatory Notes to Finance Bill 2005 indicate that where the index is related to the economic environment of the currency of an indexed-linked gilt-edged security, *FA 1996, s 94* (see 46.41 LOAN RELATIONSHIPS) applies rather *than FA 1996, s 94A* (where the rights and liabilities arising under a contract are split into two parts as set out in 28.27 below – see 46.40 LOAN RELATIONSHIPS). But in other cases, for example, where the company holding gilts uses a currency other than sterling as its functional currency, they fall within *FA 1996, s 94A* and thus, the above provision applies. (In either case, the only debits or credits to be brought into account are those within the loan relationship regime ignoring the indexation element.)

28.27 DERIVATIVE CONTRACTS TAXED ON A CHARGEABLE GAINS BASIS

Regulations *SI 2004 No 2201, Article 15* and *SI 2004 No 3270, Articles 5–10* introduce provisions within *FA 2002, Sch 26* as set out below (for periods of account beginning on or after 1 January 2005 to cater for the adoption of international accounting standards) to ensure that certain non-trading increases and decreases in the value of derivatives fall within the capital gains regime rather than being treated as non-trading credits and debits under the derivative contract regime. In these cases, the amounts taxed or relieved as chargeable gains or allowable losses are determined by the derivative contracts *Schedule 26* provisions and, as is the case for contracts for futures and options within *TCGA 1992, s 143*, the chargeable gains are not reduced by indexation allowance. Amendments made by *SI 2005 No 2082* clarify the tax treatment in relation to host contracts and embedded derivatives where the underlying subject matter is shares or rights of a unit holder in a unit trust. Further amendments made by *SI 2005 No 3440* deal with issues not aniticipated prior to the adoption of international accounting standards. [*FA 2002, Sch 26 para 45A; SI 2004 No 2201, Article 15; SI 2004 No 3270, Articles 5–10*].

Derivative contracts relating to land etc. For contracts entered into *on or after 1 August 2004 in an accounting period ending on or after 17 September 2004*, non-trading increases and decreases in the value of derivative contracts are not treated as non-trading credits and debits under the derivative contracts regime but instead are treated as chargeable gains or allowable losses within the capital gains regime where:

(*a*) the underlying subject matter relates to land (wherever situated) or tangible movable property other than commodities which are tangible assets (*FA 2002, Sch 26 para 45C*); or

(*b*) the contract relates to 'property based total return swaps' (as set out in *FA 2002, Sch 26 para 45G*).

This treatment does not apply where the company is an authorised unit trust, an investment trust, an open-ended investment company or a venture capital trust. Nor does it apply in the case of a creditor relationship to an 'embedded derivative' (see below) which is an 'exactly tracking contract for differences' whose underlying subject matter is land or shares as set out in *FA 2002, Sch 26 para 45F* (see below), nor (for periods of account beginning on or after 1 January 2005 and ending on or after 16 March 2005) in such cases involving debtor relationships, as set out in *FA 2002, Sch 26 para 45K* (see below) (ignoring, for accounting periods ending on or after 31 December 2005, the provisions for existing assets in *paras 45F(2)(f)* and *45K(2)(e)* respectively). Where the underlying subject matter includes income, this is ignored where it is subordinate to the land or property in question, or small in value in comparison with the underlying subject matter of the derivative contract as a whole. The non-trading condition does not apply if the company is a mutual trading company or a party to the contract for the purpose of life assurance business.

There are also special provisions to carry back losses (see below).

[*FA 2002, Sch 26 paras 45A, 45C, 45G; SI 2004 No 2201, Articles 1, 15; SI 2004 No 3270, Articles 1, 8; SI 2005 No 2082; SI 2005 No 3440, Article 8*].

Embedded derivatives. For periods of account *beginning on or after 1 January 2005*, where international or UK GAAP permits or requires the rights and liabilities under a contract to be split into two parts, one representing the rights and liabilities under a loan relationship or debt security (the '*host contract*') and the other the rights and liabilities under one or more derivative financial instruments or equity instruments (including convertible securities of an issuing company) (the '*embedded derivative*'), the tax treatment of the two parts is similarly split. Thus, debits and credits arising from the loan relationship element fall within the loan relationship rules (see 46.40 LOAN RELATIONSHIPS) while the embedded derivative element falls within the derivatives tax regime. The embedded derivatives are treated as having the character (be it an option, a future or a contract for differences) which the rights and liabilities would have if contained in a separate contract.

This provision was introduced by *FA 2004, Sch 10 para 13* which replaced *FA 1996, ss 92* and *93* with *FA 1996, s 94A* (see 46.40 LOAN RELATIONSHIPS). With respect to transitional cases, HMRC have published a note (on 11 August 2005, available at www.hmrc.gov.uk/practitioners/hybrid-contract.pdf), 'Hybrid contracts and embedded derivatives—transitional rules', setting out the effect of changes to the taxation of financial assets and liabilities representing a loan relationship where the relevant contract is treated as containing one or more embedded derivatives, where it was made in a period beginning before 1 January 2005 and was in existence at the beginning of the first period to begin on or after that date. It also considers cases where the derivative is embedded in a financial asset or liability where the contract does not represent a loan relationship. It provides a number of examples in relation to convertible and asset-linked securities. The note has been published in advance of its inclusion in the HMRC Corporate Finance Manual, see generally, CFM 16100 *et seq*.

SIs 2004 No 2201 and *No 3270* introduce provisions within *FA 2002, Sch 26* to ensure that non-trading increases and decreases in the value of such derivatives fall within the capital gains regime (as with assets previously within *FA 1996, ss 92* and *93*) rather than being treated as non-trading credits and debits under the derivative contract regime. A chargeable gain or allowable loss will not arise where the substantial shareholdings exemptions under *TCGA 1992, Sch 7AC para 2* (see 13.5 CAPITAL GAINS – SUBSTANTIAL SHAREHOLDINGS) would apply to the gain arising on what would be a disposal of an option contained in a separate contract. *SIs 2005 No 2082* and *No 3440* introduce further provisions to clarify the tax treatment in relation to host contracts and embedded derivatives where the underlying subject matter is shares or rights of a unit holder in a unit trust and to deal with elections and issues not anticipated prior to the adoption of international accounting standards.

The regulations introduce provisions for the following types of contract subject to the capital gains regime, namely contracts with embedded derivatives which include the following.

(i) Options or deemed options relating to qualifying ordinary shares or mandatorily convertible preference shares under *FA 2002, Sch 26* within the following paragraphs.

- *Para 45D* – creditor relationships: embedded derivatives which are options. Provided the various conditions are met, the creditor relationship is not to be treated as a qualifying corporate bond (QCB) by virtue of *TCGA 1992, s 117(A1)* and so is not prevented from falling within the chargeable gains rules by virtue of the exemption for QCBs under *TCGA 1992, s 115 (1)(b)*. For periods of account beginning on or after 1 January 2005 and ending on or after 16 March 2005, this provision does not apply in relation to existing assets and *para 45FA* provides that where this provision would apply but for that exclusion, relevant debits and credits are not to be brought into account as non-trading debits or credits in respect of the loan relationship under *FA 2002, Sch 26 para 14(3)*. With effect for accounting periods ending after 30 December 2006, para 45FA is re-written to give details of the calculation of the disposal proceeds to be taken into account in the computation for capital gains purposes.

- *Para 45E* – exclusions from *para 45D*.

- *Para 45H* – treatment of net gains and losses on the terminal exercise of an option comprised in a derivative contract to which *para 45D* applies (with effect for periods of account beginning on or after 1 January 2005 and ending on or after 17 August 2005). Broadly, where an option to acquire shares is to any extent exercised or (for accounting periods ending on or after 31 December 2005) disposed of, debits and credits treated as allowable losses and chargeable gains under *TCGA 1992* are not also treated as such on the disposal of the asset representing the creditor relationship or on the disposal of the relevant shares. The share acquisition costs (allowable under *TCGA 1992, s 38(1)(a)*) are increased by chargeable gains, being the amount by which the sum of the initial carrying value of the derivative contract and amounts treated as relevant credits (under *FA 2002, Sch 26 para 45A(4)(a)(b)*) apportionable to the shares, exceeds amounts treated as relevant debits (under *FA 2002, Sch 26 para 45A(4)(b)*), in respect of debits and credits brought into account in the accounting period of the disposal in question, or in previous accounting periods. Conversely, the acquisition costs are reduced by allowable losses, these being an excess of relevant debits over the sum of relevant credits and the initial carrying value of the derivative contract. In the case where the allowable losses exceed the allowable costs, the excess over those costs is added to the disposal consideration.

- *Para 45HA* – treatment of credits and debits on terminal exercise of non-embedded option or running to delivery of future. This paragraph was inserted by *SI 2006 No 3269* with effect for accounting periods ending on or after 30 December 2006. It applies where a company is a party to a derivative which is a plain vanilla contract and an option or future and a right to acquire shares is exercised or delivery is taken in the accounting period.
- *Para 45J* – debtor relationships with embedded derivatives: deemed options (as amended with effect for periods of account beginning on or after 1 January 2005 and ending on or after 17 August 2005). Broadly, where the option is terminated (be it on its exercise, abandonment, or cashing-out) the profit or loss accruing to the issuer in relation to the embedded option is taxed under the capital gains regime.

(ii) Exactly tracking contracts for differences whose subject matter is land or qualifying ordinary shares under *FA 2002, Sch 26* under the following paragraphs.

- *Para 45F* – creditor relationships: embedded derivatives which are exactly tracking contracts for differences. Provided the various conditions are met, the creditor relationship is not to be treated as a qualifying corporate bond (QCB) by virtue of *TCGA 1992, s 117(A1)* and so is not prevented from falling within the chargeable gains rules by virtue of the exemption for QCBs under *TCGA 1992, s 115 (1)(b)*. For periods of account beginning on or after 1 January 2005 and ending on or after 16 March 2005, this provision does not apply in relation to existing assets and *para 45FA* provides that where this provision would apply but for that exclusion, relevant debits and credits are not to be brought into account as non-trading debits or credits in respect of the loan relationship under *FA 2002, Sch 26 para 14(3)*. With effect for accounting periods ending after 30 December 2006, para 45FA is re-written to give details of the calculation of the disposal proceeds to be taken into account in the computation for capital gains purposes and para 45HZA is added to give the treatment of net gains and losses on disposal of certain embedded derivatives.
- *Para 45K* – debtor relationships with embedded derivatives: deemed contracts for differences (as amended, with effect for periods of account beginning on or after 1 January 2005 and ending on or after 17 August 2005, to exclude existing liabilities owed by a company and as amended by *SI 2006 No 3269* for accounting periods ending on or after 31 December 2006).

(iii) Equity instruments under *FA 2002, Sch 26 para 45JA* with effect for periods of account beginning on or after 1 January 2005 and ending on or after 16 March 2005. This provides for the tax treatment of an issuer of convertible debt securities (other than in connection with a banking business) where the relevant contract is not treated as a derivative contract but is split between the rights and liabilities under the debtor relationship and rights and liabilities under an equity instrument. Broadly, no debits and credits are brought into account under *Schedule 26* in relation to the equity component. Instead, the excess of the amount paid by the issuer to the creditor in discharge of the obligations under the relationship (in relation to the equity component) over the carrying value of the relevant contract when the company became party to the debtor relationship is treated as an allowable loss for capital gains purposes.

The above provisions also apply to embedded derivatives within contracts which are not loan relationships but, with effect for periods of account beginning on or after 1 January 2005 and ending on or after 16 March 2005, an election can be made for this provision not to apply. However, for accounting periods ending on or after 31 December 2005, such an election cannot be made in the case of an embedded derivative contract whose underlying subject matter is commodities nor in the case of contracts of long-term insurance. Also for such accounting periods, where such an election (referred to as 'a disapplication election') is made by one group member, the election will deemed to have also been made by other group companies which are party to the contract. Certain definitions are altered with effect for accounting periods ending on or after 30 December 2006. [*FA 2002, Sch 26 paras 45L, 45LA; SI 2005 No 2082; SI 2005 No 3440, SI 2006 No 3269*].

See also 27.14 above for index-linked gilt-edged securities with embedded contracts for differences where the credits and debits arising on the derivative contract are not brought into account.

There are also special provisions to carry back losses (see below).

For periods of account beginning on or after 1 January 2005 and ending on or after 16 March 2005, see *FA 2002, Sch 26 para 45M* (as amended) for the tax treatment of host contracts and embedded derivatives whose underlying subject matter is shares or rights of a unit trust holder in a unit trust scheme.

[*FA 2002, Sch 26 paras 45A, 45D–45H, 45J–45M; SI 2004 No 2201, Articles 1, 15; SI 2004 No 3270, Articles 1, 6, 7, 9, 10; SI 2005 No 646; SI 2005 No 2082; SI 2005 No 3440, Articles 9, 11–14*].

Carry back of losses. Where there is a 'net loss' under the above provisions in an accounting period (the '*loss period*') and, in a previous accounting period falling wholly or partly within 24 months immediately preceding the start of the loss period, there is a 'net gain' under the above provisions, a claim can be made for the loss to be wholly or partly carried back and set against part or all of the gain (but not so as to reduce either the loss or the gain below nil). The claim must be made within two years of the end of the period in which the net loss arose. Losses must be set against gains of a later period before those of an earlier period. Where a gain period falls partly before the 24-month period mentioned above, the loss can only be offset against the proportion of the gain falling within the 24-month period (time-apportioned based on the number of days).

A '*net loss*' in this case is the sum of any allowable losses arising under the above provisions ('*paragraph 45A losses*') in a period less the sum of any chargeable gains arising under the above provisions ('*paragraph 45A gains*') in the same period, in both cases in respect of the company's derivative contracts. A '*net gain*' is the excess of paragraph 45A gains over paragraph 45A losses, further reduced by any non-paragraph 45A allowable losses. Any non-paragraph 45A allowable losses must be set against any non-paragraph 45A gains before the remainder is deducted from paragraph 45A gains.

[*FA 2002, Sch 26 para 45B; SI 2004 No 2201, Article 15*].

Equity options. For periods of account beginning on or after 1 January 2005 and ending on or after 17 August 2005, where:

- a company is party to a derivative contract which is not treated as an embedded derivative under *FA 1996, s 94A(2)(b)*;
- the derivative contract is an option to acquire shares and the rights under the derivative contract are exercised to any extent in the accounting period,

the following applies for the purpose of computing the chargeable gain on the disposal of the shares so acquired.

The share acquisition costs (allowable under *TCGA 1992, s 38(1)(a)*) are increased by an excess of amounts treated as credits over amounts treated as debits (under *FA 2002, Sch 26 para 14(3)*) brought into account in respect of the derivative contract arising in the accounting period of the disposal or in previous accounting periods. Similarly, the acquisition costs are reduced by an excess of debits over credits so arising. Where net debits exceed the allowable costs, the excess is added to the disposal consideration.

[*FA 2002, Sch 26 para 45HA; SI 2005 No 2082, Article 17; SI 2005 No 3440, Article 10*].

Contracts which cease to be derivative contracts. This provision applies where a company is a party to a relevant contract which is a derivative contract and the contract ceases to be a derivative. There is a deemed disposal for capital gains purposes at the time the contract ceased to be a derivative contract.

[*SI 2006 No 3269; FA 2002 Sch 26 paras 43A and B*].

28.28 TRANSITIONAL PROVISIONS

The company's '*commencement day*' is the first day of the company's first accounting period beginning on or after 1 October 2002. [*FA 2002, Sch 28 para 7*].

Change of accounting period. An anti-avoidance provision applies to prevent forestalling the effects of the new provisions by a change of accounting date. The provision applies where an accounting period beginning on or after 1 October 2001 is ended before 30 September 2002 for the purpose, or for purposes including the purpose, of securing, in the case of any subsequent accounting period beginning before 1 October 2002, that a smaller credit or larger debit falls to be brought into account under the old financial instruments rules than would have been the case under the new derivative contracts rules, or that a credit under the new rules is replaced by a nil amount under the old or a nil amount under the new rules replaced by a debit under the old. In this case, that accounting period will be treated as if it were an accounting period beginning on or after 1 October 2002. [*FA 2002, Sch 28 para 1*].

Provisions to prevent double counting, etc. A transitional provision applies where a company was party to a 'qualifying contract' (see 28.32 below) before its commencement day but had ceased to be a party to the contract before that day, and the contract would have been a derivative contract under the new rules had it still been held on that date. In this case, to the extent that any amounts have already been brought into account under the old rules, they are not required to be brought into account again under the new rules where they would otherwise fall to be so (e.g. profits and losses from the disposal of the contract which are permitted to be spread forward by an authorised accounting method).

A further transitional provision applies where a company is party to a qualifying contract immediately before and on its commencement day, and the contract becomes a derivative contract on that day. In this case, it is necessary to determine, as regards the contract, the difference between the amounts which would have been brought into account for earlier periods under the old exchange gains and losses and financial instruments rules (disregarding the anti-avoidance rules in 26.17 EXCHANGE GAINS AND LOSSES and 28.41–28.46 below) and those which would have been brought into account for such periods had the new derivative contracts rules applied (disregarding the anti-avoidance rules in 28.13, 28.14, 28.16, 28.17, 28.18 and 28.22 above). If a greater profit or smaller loss would have arisen under the old rules, a credit is brought into account in the first accounting period under the new rules. A debit is similarly brought in where a smaller profit or greater loss would have arisen under the old rules.

[*FA 2002, Sch 28 paras 2, 3, 7*].

Contracts becoming derivative contracts: chargeable assets. This provision applies where a company is party to a contract which, immediately before its commencement day, is not a qualifying contract (see 28.32 below) but which is a chargeable asset under the capital gains tax rules (i.e. where a gain on disposal would be chargeable under *TCGA 1992*, including any obligations and futures chargeable by virtue of *section 143* of that *Act*), and which becomes a derivative contract on that day. In this case, subject to the election noted below, when the company ceases to be a party to the contract, it must bring into account any chargeable gain or allowable loss which would have been treated as accruing to the company had it disposed of the contract immediately before its commencement day for a consideration equal to the value (if any) given to the contract in the company accounts at the end of the last accounting period beginning before its commencement day.

Alternatively, where the deemed disposal of the contract gives rise to an allowable loss, the company can elect, within two years after the end of the accounting period in which the company ceased to be a party to the contract, for the loss to be treated as a non-trading debit to be brought into account under *FA 1996, Pt 4 Ch 2* in respect of a loan relationship (see 46.3 LOAN RELATIONSHIPS).

[*FA 2002, Sch 28 para 4*].

Contracts where guaranteed amounts payable on maturity: election to treat as two assets. This transitional provision applies where:

(*a*) a company is a party to a contract immediately before and on its commencement day, which was not a qualifying contract under the financial instruments rules (see 28.32 below) but which was, immediately before its commencement day, a chargeable asset under the capital gains tax rules (i.e. where a gain on disposal would be chargeable under *TCGA 1992*, including any obligations and futures chargeable by virtue of *section 143* of that *Act*); and

(*b*) the contract would from that day, but for the election below, be a derivative contract designed to pay a guaranteed amount on maturity within 28.8 above.

In this case, the company may elect to treat the contract as two separate contracts, one being a creditor loan relationship which is a 'relevant zero coupon bond' (as under 28.8 above) and the other an option over the underlying subject matter (usually shares) of the contract providing for a guaranteed amount payable on maturity, with the same consequences as apply following the similar election under 28.8 above. The election must be made within two years after the end of the first accounting period beginning on or after 1 October 2002. It has effect for that and all subsequent accounting periods and is irrevocable.

Where such an election has been made by a company, then (subject to the election described below) when the company ceases to be a party to the contract, it must bring into account any chargeable gain or allowable loss which would have been treated as accruing to the company had it disposed of the contract immediately before its commencement day for a consideration equal to the value (if any) given to the contract in the company accounts at the end of the last accounting period beginning before its commencement day. Where the deemed disposal of the contract gives rise to an allowable loss, the company can instead elect, within two years after the end of the accounting period in which the company ceased to be a party to the contract, for the loss to be treated as a non-trading debit to be brought into account under *FA 1996, Pt 4 Ch 2* in respect of a loan relationship (see 46.3 LOAN RELATIONSHIPS).

[*FA 2002, Sch 28 para 5*].

Contracts becoming derivative contracts: futures and options producing guaranteed returns. This provision applies where a company is party to a contract which, immediately before the company's commencement day, was not a qualifying contract under the financial instruments rules (see 28.32 below) but to which *ICTA 1988, Sch 5AA* (guaranteed returns on transactions in futures and options, see 5.23 ANTI-AVOIDANCE) applied, and which becomes a derivative contract on that day. In this case, where an event occurs on or after the commencement day which, had *Schedule 5AA* continued to apply to the contract, would have given rise to chargeable profits under that *Schedule*, a credit representing those profits is to be brought into account under *FA 1996, Pt 4 Ch 2* (see 46.3

LOAN RELATIONSHIPS) as if it were a non-trading credit in respect of a loan relationship. The amount of the credit to be brought into account is the profits which would have been chargeable under *Schedule 5AA* plus any debits (and less any credits) arising in respect of the contract for accounting periods from the one beginning on its commencement day to that in which the event occurred. [*FA 2002, Sch 28 para 6*].

28.29 FINANCIAL INSTRUMENTS RULES

The provisions in *FA 1994, ss 147–177, Sch 18* apply to accounting periods beginning before 1 October 2002 and are repealed for accounting periods beginning on or after that date. The main elements of the provisions, which are described in detail in 28.30 *et seq.* below, are as follows.

(*a*) Profits and losses on qualifying instruments held by qualifying companies follow acceptable accounting treatment by reference to the qualifying payments they make and receive.

(*b*) Profits or losses are taxed as income.

(*c*) Profits or losses on contracts held for trade purposes are taken into account in measuring trading income in the normal way.

(*d*) Non-trading profits or losses are treated in the same way as non-trading exchange gains and losses (see 26.14 EXCHANGE GAINS AND LOSSES).

(*e*) Anti-avoidance provisions apply to protect the Exchequer.

(*f*) Special rules apply to particular classes of company.

(*g*) The provisions do not apply where an amount representing the same profit or loss is brought into account under the LOAN RELATIONSHIPS (46) provisions of *FA 1996, Ch II, Pt IV*.

28.30 **Accrual of profits and losses.** Where, as regards a 'qualifying contract' held by a 'qualifying company', 'amount A' exceeds 'amount B' for an accounting period, the excess is a profit on the contract accruing to the company for the period. Where 'amount B' exceeds 'amount A', a loss similarly accrues. Subject to the various adjustments referred to at 28.36, 28.38, 28.44 below (each of which is applied after any adjustments made under an earlier *section* or *sections*), those amounts are defined as follows, depending on whether the company's profit or loss on the contract for the accounting period falls to be computed on a mark to market basis incorporating a particular method of valuation, or on a particular accruals basis.

Mark to market basis. '*Amount A*' is the aggregate of the amount (or aggregate amount) of 'qualifying payment(s)' becoming due and payable to the company in the period and any increase for the period (or part for which contract held) in the value of the contract on the mark to market basis. '*Amount B*' is the aggregate of the amount (or aggregate amount) of 'qualifying payment(s)' becoming due and payable by the company in the period and any decrease for the period (or part for which contract held) in the value of the contract on the mark to market basis. See sections 6.20 and 6.21 of the Explanatory Statement referred to at 28.1 above for guidance on these calculations.

Particular accruals basis. '*Amount A*' is so much of the 'qualifying payment(s)' received (or falling to be received) by the company as is allocated to the period on the particular accruals basis, and '*Amount B*' is so much of such payment(s) made or falling to be made by the company as is so allocated.

Where a contract is a 'qualifying contract' as a result of a transfer or transfers of money's worth being disregarded under *FA 1994, s 152* (see 28.32 below), so much of any 'qualifying payment', and (where the mark to market basis applies) of any increase or reduction in the value of the contract, as relates to such transfer(s) is ignored in determining Amounts A and B.

Where the mark to market basis applies and a 'qualifying contract' becomes held by the company during an accounting period, it is assumed in determining Amounts A and B that the value of the contract is nil immediately after it becomes so held. Similarly where a 'qualifying contract' ceases to be held during an accounting period, the value is assumed to be nil immediately before it ceases to be so held, unless the contract is discharged by the making of payments none of which is a 'qualifying payment'.

[*FA 1994, s 155*].

Simon's Direct Tax Service. See D2.1020, D2.1022, D2.1023.

28.31 **Qualifying companies.** A '*qualifying company*' is any company within the charge to corporation tax. This does not, however, include the trustees of a unit trust scheme which is an authorised unit trust as respects an accounting period (who are deemed for other purposes to be a company by *ICTA 1988, s 468*(*1*), see 43.5 INVESTMENT FUNDS), or, in relation to 'currency contracts and options', an investment trust approved under *ICTA 1988, s 842* (see 44.1 INVESTMENT TRUSTS). [*FA 1994, s 154*].

Simon's Direct Tax Service. See D2.1004.

28.32 **Qualifying contracts.** A '*qualifying contract*' as regards a qualifying company is an 'interest rate contract or option', a 'currency contract or option' or a 'debt contract or option', to the rights or duties under which the company becomes entitled or subject on or after the company's 'commencement day'. [*FA 1994, ss 147*(*1*), *147A*(*1*)]. For interest rate and currency contracts and options, the '*commencement day*' is the first day of its first accounting period beginning on or after 23 March 1995. For debt contracts or option, it is 1 April 1996, subject to transitional provisions as below. [*FA 1994, ss 147*(*4*), *147A*(*1*), *177*(*1*)].

A company becomes entitled and subject to any such rights and duties when it becomes party to the contract or option. It holds the contract or option at any time at which it is entitled and subject to rights and duties under it, regardless of when the rights and duties fall to be exercised and performed. [*FA 1994, s 177*(*2*)].

As regards currency contracts or options held both immediately before and at the beginning of the commencement day, the company is treated as becoming entitled and subject to rights and duties thereunder at the latter time, and the same applies as regards interest rate contracts or options if the company's commencement day falls more than twelve months after the appointed day (see above). [*FA 1994, s 147*(*2*)(*3*)]. Where the company's commencement day falls within twelve months from the appointed day, the company may (except as below) elect for similar treatment to apply as regards interest rate contracts or options. If no election is made, then as regards interest rate contracts or options held six years after the commencement day, the company is treated as becoming entitled and subject to rights and duties thereunder on the first day of its first accounting period beginning after the end of that six years. [*FA 1994, s 148*(*1*)–(*3*)]. The election, which is irrevocable, must be made by notice served on the inspector within three months of the commencement day. No election may, however, be made by a company which is a member of a group of companies unless it is the principal company of the group, or it became a member of the group after the principal company's commencement day. An election by the principal company of a group has effect as regards companies whose commencement day falls within twelve months from the appointed day and which were members of the group on the principal company's commencement day. It continues to apply to companies leaving the group after that day, unless the election is made after the company leaves the group and it leaves the group before the expiry of the period during which the company could make an election (disregarding the group restriction) and before such an election has been made. The provisions of *TCGA 1992, s 170* (see 12.1 CAPITAL GAINS—GROUPS) apply as regards the meaning of 'group of companies' and 'principal company of a group'. [*FA 1994, s 148*(*4*)–(*9*)].

As regards debt contracts or options held both immediately before and on the commencement day, the company is treated as becoming entitled or subject to rights or duties thereunder on that date. See also 46.46 LOAN RELATIONSHIPS. [*FA 1994, s 147A(2)(3); FA 1996, Sch 15 para 25*].

An '*interest rate contract*' is a contract under which (whether or not subject to conditions) a company becomes entitled to a right to receive, or subject to a duty to make, a 'variable rate' payment at a specified time, and under which the only transfers of money or money's worth provided for are such payments, payments falling within *FA 1994, s 149(3)(4)* (see below) or payments falling within *FA 1994, s 151* (see below). [*FA 1994, s 149(1)(2)*]. The contract may include provision for a reciprocal 'fixed' or 'fixed rate' payment, and the contract terms may be satisfied by the making of a single net payment where two counter-payments fall to be made at the same time. [*FA 1994, s 149(3)(4)*]. A '*fixed*' payment is a payment of an amount specified in the contract. A '*fixed rate*' payment is a payment the amount of which falls to be determined (wholly or mainly) by applying to a notional principal amount specified in the contract, for a period so specified, a rate the value of which is at all times the same as that of a fixed rate of interest so specified, and a '*variable rate*' payment is similarly defined by reference to a variable rate of interest so specified. [*FA 1994, s 149(6)*]. For HMRC's view of the interpretation of these definitions, see section 6.12 of the Explanatory Statement referred to at 28.1 above. Where, as a result of the adoption of the euro by a State, a change in a variable rate of interest results in a change in the variable rate payment under a contract and hence to the rescission of the original contract and the making of a new contract, the new contract is in effect treated as if it were the original contract. [*SI 1998 No 3177, reg 8*].

An '*interest rate option*' is an option to enter into an interest rate contract (or an option to enter into such an option) if the only transfers of money or money's worth for which the option provides are payments falling within *FA 1994, s 151* (see below). [*FA 1994, s 149(5)*].

A '*currency contract*' is a contract under which the company becomes entitled to a right and subject to a duty to receive payment at a specified time of a specified amount of one currency (the '*first currency*') and to pay in exchange at the same time a specified amount of another currency (the '*second currency*'), and under which the only transfers of money or money's worth provided for are such payments, payments falling within *FA 1994, s 150(3)(4)* or *(9)* (see below) or payments falling within *FA 1994, s 151* (see below). [*FA 1994, s 150(1)(2)*]. For general guidance on the treatment of currency contracts, see section 7 of the Explanatory Statement referred to at 28.1 above, and Annexes 1 and 2 thereto.

The contract may include provision for the company to become entitled to receive, or to become subject to a duty to make, at a specified time, a payment the amount of which falls to be determined wholly or mainly by applying a specified rate of interest to a specified amount of the first currency (in relation to entitlements) or the second currency (in relation to duties). It may also include provision for the company to become entitled to a right and subject to a duty to receive payment at a specified time of a specified amount of the second currency and to pay in exchange at the same time a specified amount of the first currency. [*FA 1994, s 150(3)(4)*]. In both of these permissible additional provisions, the specified time must be earlier than that specified in the essential provision of the contract (as in the preceding paragraph) and a specified rate of interest must be a rate the value of which at any time is the same as that of the specified rate of interest. [*FA 1994, s 150(5)*]. Where, as a result of the adoption of the euro by a State, a change in the rate of interest specified in a currency contract results in the rescission of the original contract and the making of a new contract, the new contract is in effect treated as if it were the original contract. [*SI 1998 No 3177, reg 9*]. Similarly where the conversion of the amounts of one or both of the currencies in a currency contract results in the contract being rescinded and replaced by a new contract which, but for the adoption of the euro, would have been a currency contract, the new contract is in effect treated as if it were the original currency contract. [*SI 1998 No 3177, reg 10*].

A '*currency option*' is:

(*a*) an option to enter into a currency contract (or an option to enter into such an option), provided that the only transfers of money or money's worth for which the option provides are payments falling within *FA 1994, s 151* (see below); or

(*b*) an option the exercise of which at any time would result in the company becoming entitled to a right and subject to a duty to receive payment at that time of a specified amount of one currency and at the same time to pay in exchange a specified amount of another currency, provided that the only transfers of money or money's worth for which the option provides are such payments or payments falling within *FA 1994, s 151* (see below).

[*FA 1994, s 150(6)(7)*].

Where a contract is subject to a condition precedent the fulfilment of which at any time would result in the company becoming entitled and subject as under (*b*) above, the contract before fulfilment of the condition is treated as an option within (*b*) above, the fulfilment of the condition being treated as the exercise of that option, and the contract after fulfilment being treated as the contract resulting from that exercise. [*FA 1994, s 150(8)*].

It is immaterial that the rights and duties referred to above, in relation to payments of currency or (with appropriate modification) by reference to interest, may be satisfied by the making of a net payment of an amount determined by reference to the local currency equivalents at the relevant time of counter-payments required to be made at the same time, and a contract requiring a payment of such an amount at a specified time is treated as a currency contract. [*FA 1994, s 150(9)–(12)*].

A '*debt contract*' is a contract (other than an interest rate or currency contract or option), other than one to which *FA 1996, s 92* or *s 93* (convertible securities or securities indexed to chargeable assets, see 46.37 and 46.39 LOAN RELATIONSHIPS) applies, where either:

(i) (whether or not subject to conditions) a company is entitled, or subject to a duty, under the contract to become a party to a loan relationship (see 46.2 LOAN RELATIONSHIPS), and the only transfers of money or money's worth for which the contract provides (apart from those under the loan relationship) fall within the following:

  (*a*) a payment representing the price for becoming a party;

  (*b*) a payment determined by reference to the value at any time of the money debt by reference to which the loan relationship subsists;

  (*c*) a settlement payment determined by reference to the difference at specified times between the price for becoming a party and the value of the money debt by reference to which the relationship subsists (or would, if the relationship existed, subsist); and

  (*d*) payments falling within *FA 1994, s 151* (see below); or

(ii) (where (i) above does not apply, and whether or not subject to conditions) a company is entitled, or subject to a duty, under the contract to become treated as a person with rights and liabilities corresponding to those of a party to a loan relationship, and the only transfers of money or money's worth for which the contract provides are payments falling within *FA 1994, s 151* (see below) and settlement payments determined by reference to the difference at specified times between the price for becoming treated as a person with rights and liabilities corresponding to those of a party to a relationship and the value of the money debt by reference to which the relationship subsists (or would, if the relationship existed, subsist).

This applies equally where the entitlement or duty is to become a party to a relationship equivalent to a specified loan relationship, or relates to the making of payments within (i)(*a*), (*b*) or (*c*) above in relation to a specified loan relationship (and similarly in relation to an entitlement or duty to become treated as a person with rights and liabilities corresponding to those of a party to a loan relationship). The transfer of money's worth having a value of a particular amount is treated as a payment of that amount for these purposes.

Where a contract contains both provisions under which, whether or not subject to conditions, a company is entitled, or subject to a duty, to become a party to a loan relationship, and provisions having effect other than for the purposes of or in relation to such provisions, the first-mentioned provisions, together with the other contents of the contract attributable on a just and reasonable basis to those provisions, are treated as a separate contract. Where the contents of a contract are attributed between those two categories of provision, and the contract provides for a payment in money or money's worth which cannot be attributed only to one such category, the payment is apportioned between those categories on a just and reasonable basis.

Where, as a result of the adoption of the euro by a State, there is a euroconversion (see *SI 1998 No 3177, reg 3*) of a loan relationship, or of corresponding rights and liabilities, which results in the rescission of the original debt contract and the making of a new debt contract, the new contract is in effect treated as if it were the original contract. [*SI 1998 No 3177, reg 11*].

A '*debt option*' is an option to enter into a debt contract, or into an option for such an option, if the only transfers of money or money's worth for which the option provides are payments falling within *FA 1994, s 151* (see below).

[*FA 1994, s 150A*].

Provisions which may be included. A qualifying contract may include provision under which the company becomes entitled to a right to receive a payment in consideration of its entering into the contract or option, or becomes subject to a duty to make a payment in consideration of another person's entering into the contract or option. It may also include provision for all or any of the following payments in respect of the contract or option:

(i) a reasonable arrangement fee;

(ii) reasonable costs incurred;

(iii) a payment for securing, or in consequence of, its variation or termination;

(iv) a compensation payment for, or in consequence of, failure to comply with it.

[*FA 1994, s 151*].

Provisions which may be disregarded. Where:

(A) but for the inclusion in a contract or option of provisions for one or more transfers of money or money's worth, it would be a qualifying contract; and

(B) the present value of the transfer, or the aggregate of such values, is small (i.e. generally less than 5%, see Revenue Company Taxation Manual, CT 13494) compared with the aggregate of the present values of all 'relevant payments' as regards the later of the time the contract or option was entered into and the time the provisions were included in the contract or option,

the contract or option is treated for the purposes of *FA 1994, s 149* or *s 150* or *150A* (as appropriate) as if those provisions were not included in it.

'*Relevant payments*' are, in relation to a contract, 'qualifying payments' thereunder, or, in relation to an option, 'qualifying payments' thereunder and payments which, if it were exercised, would be 'qualifying payments' under the contract arising by virtue of its exercise.

[*FA 1994, s 152*].

A tax avoidance scheme creating debt contracts under which options were granted and premiums paid in relation to gilts so as to create a loss was held not to lead to a 'qualifying contract' within the meaning of *FA 1994, s 147A* in the case of *CIR v Scottish Provident Institution HL [2005] STC 15.*

Simon's Direct Tax Service. See D2.1010 *et seq.*

28.33 **Qualifying payments.** A '*qualifying payment*' is:

(*a*) in relation to a qualifying contract which is an interest rate contract, a payment falling within *FA 1994, s 149(2)–(4)* (see 28.32 above);

(*b*) in relation to a qualifying contract which is a currency contract, a payment falling within *FA 1994, s 150(3)* or *(9)* (see 28.32 above);

(*c*) in relation to a qualifying contract which is a currency option, a payment falling within *FA 1994, s 150(9)* (see 28.32 above);

(*d*) in relation to a qualifying contract which is a debt contract, a payment falling within *FA 1994, s 150A(5)(6)* (see 28.32 above);

(*e*) in relation to any qualifying contract, a payment falling within *FA 1994, s 151* (see 28.32 above).

The following are also '*qualifying payments*' in relation to a qualifying contract.

(i) A payment which, if it were a payment under the contract, would be within *FA 1994, s 151* (see 28.32 above), and a payment for securing the acquisition or disposal of the contract.

(ii) Where the qualifying contract is an interest rate or currency contract, and the company closes it out by entering into another contract with reciprocal obligations, any payment received by the company in consideration of its entering into the reciprocal contract, or paid by it in consideration of another person's entering into that contract. All other payments under the reciprocal contract, and all subsequent payments under the qualifying contract, are ignored for all tax purposes.

(iii) Subject as below, where the qualifying contract is a currency contract, and there is a difference between the local currency equivalents of the amounts of the first and second currencies (see 28.32 above) at the time immediately after the company becomes entitled to rights and subject to duties under the contract, the amount of the difference is (except for the purposes of certain transitional provisions, see 28.49 below) treated as a qualifying payment received (where the first currency equivalent exceeds the second currency equivalent) or made (where the second currency equivalent exceeds the first) by the company at the time specified in the contract for the purposes of *FA 1994, s 150(2)* (see 28.32 above).

As regards (iii) above, for accounting periods beginning **on or after 26 July 2001** (see 28.9 above for the corresponding provision under the new derivative contracts rules), unless the company had ceased to be a party to the contract before that date, this is replaced by a new rule requiring any forward discount or premium in relation to a currency contract to be treated as a qualifying payment received or made by the company.

Where the contract provides for a rate of exchange between the reporting currency and another currency:

(A) the amount of any forward discount is the excess of the acquisition 'spot price' over the acquisition 'contract price' or the excess of the sale 'contract price' over the sale 'spot price'; and

(B) the amount of any forward premium is the excess of the acquisition 'contract price' over the acquisition 'spot price' or the excess of the sale 'spot price' over the sale 'contract price'.

The '*contract price*' is the foreign currency to be acquired or disposed of under the contract using the exchange rate determined by the contract. The '*spot price*' is the amount of foreign currency to be acquired or disposed of under the contract using the exchange rate on the date on which the company becomes entitled to the rights and subject to the duties under the contract as used for the purposes of the company's accounts.

Where the currency contract provides for a rate of exchange between two currencies, neither of which is the reporting currency, the amounts to be treated as qualifying payments made or received are the amounts equivalent to any forward premiums and discounts brought into account in accordance with generally accepted accounting practice (see 55.2 PROFIT COMPUTATIONS).

Where, in conformity with generally accepted accounting practice, a qualifying company uses an authorised mark to market basis of accounting, or accounts for the contract at the forward rate or the rate implied in the contract, such that no forward premium or discount is shown in the accounts, no forward premiums or discounts are to be brought into account under these provisions.

[*FA 1994, s 153; FA 2002, s 70*].

Simon's Direct Tax Service. See **D2.1021**.

28.34 **Basis of accounting.** Where, for the purposes of the accounts (i.e. those required by the *Companies Act 1985* or equivalent) of a qualifying company for an accounting period, profits and losses on a qualifying contract held by the company are computed either on a mark to market basis, or on an accruals basis, satisfying the following requirements, the profits and losses for the period on the contract are computed on the same basis for the purposes of the charge under these provisions (see 28.37 below). In any other case, profits and losses on the contract are computed on a basis which does satisfy those requirements and which is specified in an agreement with the inspector or, failing such agreement, in a notice served on the company by the inspector.

Requirements: mark to market basis. As regards a qualifying contract held by the company:

(*a*) computing profits or losses on the contract on that basis must accord with generally accepted accounting practice (see 55.2 PROFIT COMPUTATIONS);

(*b*) all '*relevant payments*' (i.e. qualifying payments made or received, or falling to be made or received, by the company) must be allocated to the accounting period in which they become due and payable; and

(*c*) the method of valuation adopted must secure the contract is brought into account at a fair value (i.e. on an arm's length basis).

Requirements: accruals basis. As regards a qualifying contract held by the company:

(i) computing profits or losses on the contract on that basis must accord with generally accepted accounting practice (see 55.2 PROFIT COMPUTATIONS);

(ii) all 'relevant payments' (as above) must be allocated to the accounting periods to which they relate (disregarding those in which they are made or received or become due and payable); and

(iii) where necessary, such payments must be apportioned on a just and reasonable basis between two or more accounting periods to which they relate.

In determining whether this requirement is satisfied, regard is to be had to the corresponding treatment of any reciprocal payment(s) (i.e. payments being consideration (or part) for the relevant payment), but not to that of any other payment(s).

[*FA 1994, s 156*].

Simon's Direct Tax Service. See **D2.1020, D2.1022, D2.1023**.

28.35 **Basis of accounting: linked currency options.** The profit or loss on a qualifying contract which is a 'linked currency option' is computed on a mark to market basis of accounting. If the profit or loss would otherwise be computed on an accruals basis, the mark to market basis to be applied is such as satisfies the requirements of *FA 1994, s 156* (see 28.34 above), or would satisfy them but for the 'generally accepted accounting practice' requirement, and is specified in an agreement with the inspector or, failing such agreement, in a notice served on the company by the inspector.

A currency option is a '*linked currency option*' if the following conditions are fulfilled.

(*a*) If the option is exercisable by the company against the other party, another currency option is exercisable by that party against the company, or *vice versa*. Options exercisable by or against associated companies (within *ICTA 1988, s 416*, see 63.7 SMALL COMPANIES—REDUCED RATES) of either party are taken into account for this purpose. Where the currency option falls within *FA 1994, s 150(8)* (see 28.32 above), references to an option being exercisable are to be taken as referring to the contract being subject to fulfilment of a condition precedent resulting in a transfer of value (as defined).

(*b*) The terms of the two options in (*a*) must be such that they must be exercised (if at all) at the same (or substantially the same) time, and that the rights and duties under the contract which would arise if the one option were exercised are the same (or substantially the same) as those under the contract which would arise if the other option were exercised.

[*FA 1994, s 157*].

Simon's Direct Tax Service. See D2.1038.

28.36 **Basis of accounting: adjustments for changes.** The following apply where the profit or loss of a qualifying company for an accounting period is computed on a new accounting basis differing from that adopted for the immediately preceding accounting period.

(*a*) Amount A (see 28.30 above) is increased by any amount(s) not included in it for a preceding accounting period but which would have been so included had the new basis been adopted for that period, and a similar rule applies to Amount B (see 28.30 above).

(*b*) Amount A is decreased or, as the case may require, Amount B increased (see 28.50(*a*) below) by any amount(s) included in Amount A for a preceding accounting period but which would not have been so included had the new basis been adopted for that period, and a similar rule applies in relation to Amount B.

(*c*) (*a*) and (*b*) above also apply, with appropriate modification, where a contract or option becomes a qualifying contract by virtue of *FA 1994, s 147(2)* or *s 148(2)(3)* (see 28.32 above) at the start of an accounting period.

[*FA 1994, s 158*].

Simon's Direct Tax Service. See D2.1024.

28.37 **Treatment of profits and losses.** The treatment of a profit or loss accruing to a qualifying company as regards a qualifying contract for an accounting period (see 28.30 above) depends on whether the contract was at any time in the period held for trade purposes.

Trading profits and losses. Where throughout the period the contract was held solely for trade purposes, the whole of the profit or loss is treated as a trading profit or loss of the period (notwithstanding the provisions of *ICTA 1988, s 74*). Otherwise, the profit or loss is apportioned on a just and reasonable basis, so much as is attributable to trade purposes being so treated.

Non-trading profits or losses. Any part of the profit or loss not so treated as a trading profit or loss (or the whole of the profit or loss where appropriate) is treated as a non-trading profit or loss of the period. A non-trading profit is brought into account as if it were a non-trading credit in respect of a loan relationship (see 46.3 LOAN RELATIONSHIPS), and a non-trading loss is similarly treated as a non-trading debit.

[*FA 1994, ss 159, 160*].

Simon's Direct Tax Service. See **D2.1030, D2.1031**.

28.38 **Termination etc. of qualifying contract.** Where at any time in an accounting period a qualifying contract held by a qualifying company is terminated, or disposed of, or so varied as to cease to be a qualifying contract, and as regards the contract Amounts A and B fall to be determined for the period on a particular accruals basis under *FA 1994, s 155*(*5*) (see 28.30 above), Amounts A and/or B are adjusted in respect of so much of any qualifying payment as has previously been included in Amount A or Amount B but has not become due and payable to or by the company before the termination etc. of the contract. [*FA 1994, s 161*].

28.39 **Exchange gains and losses on currency contracts.** Where, as regards a currency contract, Amounts A and B fall to be determined for an accounting period on a mark to market basis under *FA 1994, s 155*(*4*) (see 28.30 above), Amounts A and/or B are adjusted for any 'exchange gain' or 'exchange loss' (see 26.11 EXCHANGE GAINS AND LOSSES) accruing to the company for the period as regards the contract. [*FA 1994, s 162*].

28.40 **Irrecoverable payments.** Where, on a claim within two years of the end of an accounting period, the whole or part of a qualifying payment to which a company is entitled at the end of the period could reasonably be regarded at that time as having become irrecoverable in the period, an appropriate adjustment, depending on whether the mark to market or a particular accruals basis has been adopted under *FA 1994, s 155* (see 28.30 above), is made to Amount A or, as the case may require, Amount B (see 28.50(*a*) below). A corresponding adjustment is made in any later accounting period in which an amount so treated as irrecoverable is in fact recovered. [*FA 1994, s 163*].

28.41 **Released payments.** Where, at any time in an accounting period, a company is released from a duty to make the whole or part of a qualifying payment, then as regards the qualifying contract and period, a corresponding adjustment is made to Amount B or, as the case may require, Amount A (see 28.50(*a*) below). [*FA 1994, s 164*].

28.42 **Anti-avoidance: transfers of value by qualifying companies.** Special provisions apply where, as a result of a qualifying company entering into a 'relevant transaction' on or after its commencement day (see 28.32 above), or as a result of the expiry on or after that day of an option held by it which, until its expiry, was a qualifying contract, there is a transfer of value by the company to an 'associated company' or an 'associated third party'. For the accounting period in which the transaction was entered into or the option expired, a corresponding adjustment is made to Amount B or, as the case may require, Amount A (see 28.50(*a*) below). There is such a transfer of value where the company's net assets are reduced, and those of the associated company or third party increased, as a result of the transaction or expiry, and the adjustment is equal to that reduction. Reasonable arrangement fees and costs within *FA 1994, s 151*(*2*)(*a*)(*b*) (see 28.32(i)(ii) above) are not taken into account for this purpose.

A '*relevant transaction*' is a transaction through which either the company becomes party to a qualifying contract, or the terms of a qualifying contract to which it is a party are varied. An '*associated company*' is as under *ICTA 1988, s 416* (see 63.7 SMALL COMPANIES—REDUCED RATES). A third party other than an associated company is an '*associated third party*' at the time when the relevant transaction is entered into or the option expires if the transaction is entered into, or the option allowed to expire, in pursuance of arrangements made with the third party, and, in pursuance of those arrangements, a transfer of value (as above) has been or will be made directly or indirectly to an associated company of the qualifying company by the third party or by a company which, when the arrangements were made, was an associated company of the third party. The inspector has appropriate information powers in relation to determination of the status of third parties.

[*FA 1994, s 165*].

See sections 6.27 and 6.28 of the Explanatory Statement referred to at 28.1 above as regards non-exercise of options and transfers of value through third parties.

Simon's Direct Tax Service. See D2.1035.

28.43 **Anti-avoidance: transfers of value to associated companies.** Special provisions apply where an adjustment is made under *FA 1994, s 165* (see 28.42 above), and either the transfer of value was to an associated company which was itself a qualifying company, or the transfer of value was to an associated third party and the related transfer of value is to an associated company which is itself a qualifying company and results from that company entering into a relevant transaction. An adjustment in the same amount is made for the 'corresponding accounting period or periods' of the associated company to Amount A or, as the case may require, Amount B (see 28.50(*a*) below).

The '*corresponding accounting period or periods*' means the accounting period or periods which comprise or together comprise the accounting period of the qualifying company in which the transaction was entered into or the option expired, with any necessary apportionment where there is more than one corresponding accounting period.

[*FA 1994, s 166*].

Simon's Direct Tax Service. See D2.1035.

28.44 **Anti-avoidance: transactions not at arm's length.** Special provisions apply where the parties to a 'relevant transaction' would not have entered into it had they been dealing at arm's length.

For each 'relevant accounting period' throughout which the other party is a qualifying company, a deduction is made from each of Amount A and Amount B to reduce it to nil.

For each 'relevant accounting period' for any part of which the other party is *not* a qualifying company, a deduction is made from Amount B so as to reduce it to nil, and the same amount is deducted from Amount A (but not so as to reduce Amount A to less than nil), and for each such 'relevant accounting period' other than the first, there is also deducted from Amount A or, as the case may require, added to Amount B such an amount as will secure that 'Amount C' does not exceed 'Amount D', where:

(*a*) '*Amount C*' is any amount by which the aggregate of Amounts A (adjusted as above) for the period and all previous relevant accounting periods exceeds such aggregate of Amounts B; and

(*b*) '*Amount D*' is any amount by which the aggregate of Amounts A (prior to adjustment as above) for the period and all previous relevant accounting periods exceeds such aggregate of Amounts B.

Similar adjustments are made where the parties would have entered into the transaction but on different terms, but by reference to the '*relevant proportion*' of the respective amounts, i.e. such proportion as may be just and reasonable having regard to the differences between the actual terms and those which would have applied at arm's length.

For all these purposes, any transfer of value the subject of an adjustment under *FA 1994, s 165* or *s 166* (see 28.42, 28.43 above) is disregarded. Otherwise, all factors are taken into account, including (in the case of an interest rate contract or option) any notional principal amounts and rates of interest that would have been involved, (in the case of a currency contract or option) any currencies and amounts that would have been involved, (in the case of a debt contract or option) the amount of the debt by reference to which any loan relationship that would have been involved would have subsisted, and any terms as to repayment, redemption or interest that, in the case of that debt or any asset representing it, would have been involved, and (in any such case) any transactions related to the relevant transaction.

A '*relevant transaction*' is a transaction entered into on or after the qualifying company's commencement day (see 28.32 above) as a result of which the company becomes party to a qualifying contract, or the terms of such a contract to which it is a party are varied. A '*relevant accounting period*' is the accounting period in which the transaction was entered into and each subsequent accounting period for all or part of which the company is party to the contract.

Determinations requiring the sanction of the Board. A determination of the amount of an adjustment under these provisions requires the Board's sanction, other than in certain cases where an agreement has been reached between the Board and the person concerned (see *FA 1998, s 110(5)-(7)*). Where such a determination is made for the purpose of giving a closure notice, giving a notice amending a partnership statement or return or making a discovery assessment, and the notice of the closure, amendment or discovery assessment is given to any person without the determination, so far as taken into account in the notice or assessment, having been approved by the Board, or without a copy of the Board's approval having been served on that person at or before the time the notice was given, the closure or amendment notice or discovery assessment is deemed to have been given or made (and in the case of an assessment notified) as if the determination had not been taken into account. The approval must apply specifically to the case in question and the amount determined, but may otherwise be given (either before or after the making of the determination) in any such form or manner as the Board may determine. An appeal relating to a determination approved by the Board may not question the Board's approval except to the extent that the grounds for questioning the approval are the same as the grounds for questioning the determination itself.

[*FA 1994, s 167; FA 1998, s 110; FA 2001, Sch 29 para 38*].

Simon's Direct Tax Service. See **D2.1036**.

28.45 **Anti-avoidance: qualifying contracts with non-residents.** Special provisions apply (except as below) where, as a result of any transaction entered into on or after its commencement day (see 28.32 above), either:

(*a*) a qualifying company and a non-resident both become party to a qualifying contract; or

(*b*) the company becomes party to a qualifying contract to which a non-resident is party; or

(*c*) a non-resident becomes party to a qualifying contract to which the company is party.

For each 'relevant accounting period' for any part of which the other party is not a qualifying company, a deduction is made from Amount B so as to reduce it to nil, and the same amount is deducted from Amount A (but not so as to reduce Amount A to less than nil), and for each such 'relevant accounting period' other than the first, there is also deducted from Amount A or, as the case may require, added to Amount B such an amount as will secure that 'Amount C' does not exceed 'Amount D', those Amounts being defined as under *FA 1994, s 167* (see 28.44 above).

A '*relevant accounting period*' is the accounting period in which the transaction was entered into and each subsequent accounting period for all or part of which the company and the non-resident are party to the contract.

These special provisions do not apply:

(i) to a qualifying company which is a bank, building society or financial trader (as defined, and see below) and which holds the contract (otherwise than as agent or nominee) solely for UK trade purposes;

(ii) where the non-resident holds the contract (otherwise than as agent or nominee) solely for the purposes of a UK trade (or part) carried on through a branch or agency; or

(iii) where arrangements made under *ICTA 1988, s 788* with the government of the territory in which the non-resident is resident (or, if the non-resident is party to the contract as agent or nominee of another person, with the government of the territory in which that other person is resident) make provision, whether for relief or otherwise, in relation to interest.

[*FA 1994, ss 168, 177(1); SI 2001 No 3629, Article 84*].

As regards (i) above, for the guidelines used by HMRC in deciding whether a company should be approved as a financial trader, see Revenue Statement of Practice, SP 3/95 (now superseded by SP 4/02).

Simon's Direct Tax Service. See D2.1037.

28.46 **Anti-avoidance: unallowable purposes.** For accounting periods ending **on or after 26 July 2001**, where a company is a party to a contract for an unallowable purpose and had not ceased to be a party to the contract before that date, any qualifying payments made under the contract that are, on a just and reasonable apportionment, referable to the unallowable purpose cannot be treated as Amount B payments under the contract. However, the amount to be disregarded cannot exceed the amount by which the whole of Amount B (including payments for both allowable and unallowable purposes) exceeds Amount A.

Where a company was party to the contract concerned on 26 July 2001, this provision will not apply to amounts attributable to that part of the accounting period falling before that date, and in determining the maximum disallowance, an apportionment is to be made, on a just and reasonable basis, between the parts of Amount A and Amount B attributable to the parts of the accounting period falling before and after that date.

An '*unallowable purpose*' is one which is not among the business or other commercial purposes of the company. Business or other commercial purposes do not include the purposes of any of the company's activities not within the charge to corporation tax. Nor do they include the purpose of securing a tax advantage (within *ICTA 1988, s 709*) for any person, where it is the main purpose, or one of the main purposes, for which the company is party to the contract concerned.

For the corresponding provisions under the new derivative contracts rules, see 28.13 above.

[*FA 1994, s 168A; FA 2002, s 69*].

28.47 **Anti-avoidance: currency contracts and currency options.** An anti-avoidance provision is introduced where, **on or after 30 September 2002**, a qualifying company (see 28.31 above) becomes party to a qualifying contract which is a currency contract or currency option (see 28.32 above), or where the terms of such a contract held by such a company are varied, and the following conditions are, or subsequently become, satisfied:

(*a*) in accordance with generally accepted accounting practice (see 55.2 PROFIT COMPUTATIONS), the company, in preparing its statutory accounts, uses the exchange rate implied by the contract (the 'accounting rate'); and

(*b*) there is a difference between the accounting rate and the 'final payment rate' of more than 1% of the 'final payment rate'.

The '*final payment rate*' is the exchange rate found by reference only to amounts which fall, or would apart from these provisions fall, to be regarded for the purposes of *FA 1994, s 150(2)* or *(7)* (see 28.32 above), as the case may be, as the amounts of the currency to be received, and the currency to be paid in exchange, under the contract.

Where this provision first applies in relation to the contract in an accounting period beginning before 1 October 2002, the relevant derivative contracts rules (see 28.2 *et seq.* above), and related transitional provisions (adapted as necessary), have effect in relation to the contract for that and any subsequent accounting periods.

Similarly where a qualifying contract is a currency contract which arises from the exercise of a currency option which is or was itself a qualifying contract (or a series of such options) and which (or any one of which) was entered into or varied on or after 30 September 2002, the relevant derivative contracts rules and transitional provisions have effect in relation to the currency option (or each of the series of options entered into or varied on or after that date) for the earliest accounting period in which the option (or any of the series of options) was so entered into or varied and any subsequent accounting periods.

These provisions do *not*, however, apply to any contract entered into or varied in an accounting period beginning after 30 September 2002 (i.e. one to which the derivative contracts rules already apply) unless the contract arises from the exercise of a currency option which was entered into or varied on or after that date and in an accounting period beginning on or before that date.

[*FA 2003, s 177*].

28.48 **Partnerships which include qualifying companies.** A partnership of which one or more members is a qualifying company (see 28.31 above) is treated as a qualifying company under the current provisions. Where one or more members of such a partnership is *not* a qualifying company, then for any accounting period for which profit or loss accrues to the partnership as regards one or more qualifying contracts, partnership profits and losses are computed both on the basis that the partnership is a qualifying company and on the basis that it is not, and the appropriate computation is employed in relation to partners which are qualifying companies and those which are not (in addition to any separate income tax computation which may be required). [*FA 1994, s 172*]. The partnership will accordingly be treated as itself entitled and subject to the assets and liabilities in question.

Revenue Statement of Practice, SP 4/98 deals with the application to such partnerships of the current provisions and those dealing with EXCHANGE GAINS AND LOSSES (26) and LOAN RELATIONSHIPS (46), in particular applying the approach of *FA 1994, s 172* (as above) to the former (see 26.30 EXCHANGE GAINS AND LOSSES). Further subjects are covered by the Statement of Practice as follows.

Valuations of assets and liabilities (see 28.34, 28.35 above) should be made in accordance with the accounting methods used by the partnership.

Anti-avoidance. The provisions at 28.42-28.45 above will apply to the partnership (including any individual partners).

Capital gains tax. *TCGA 1992, s 59* (disposal of partnership assets) will continue to apply to the disposal of shares in partnership assets to which members who are not qualifying companies are entitled, regardless of the operation of the current (or the exchange gains and losses or loan relationships) provisions.

Losses. A qualifying company's share of partnership trading losses on financial instruments (or trading exchange losses or loan relationship deficits) will be relievable in the normal way. Its share of net partnership non-trading gains or losses on financial instruments (and net non-trading exchange gains or losses and loan relationship credits or debits) will in practice be merged with any other non-trading gains or losses on financial instruments (or non-trading exchange gains or losses or loan relationship credits or debits) accruing to it in its own right, for charge or relief in the normal way.

Differing accounting periods. Where partnership and company accounting periods differ, profits and losses will be allocated between the relevant company accounting periods, usually on a time basis.

Commencement day (see 28.32 above) where no partnership accounts are drawn up will be the first day of any period beginning after 22 March 1995 for which any financial statements are drawn up, or the earliest of the commencement days of qualifying company members.

For accounting periods beginning **on or after 1 October 2002**, provisions dealing with partnerships which include companies have been included in the new rules on derivative contracts (see 28.29 above), and SP 4/98 has accordingly been withdrawn.

28.49 **Transitional provisions.** Where, at any time, a currency contract held by a qualifying company becomes a qualifying contract under *FA 1994, s 147(2)* (i.e. at the beginning of the company's commencement day, see 28.32 above), two transitional provisions apply.

(*a*) Where the contract is, at that time, held for the purposes of a trade (or part of a trade), in circumstances such that any profit or loss as regards the contract for an accounting period beginning before that time would be a profit or loss of that trade (or part), *FA 1994, s 153(4)* (definition of qualifying payment, see 28.33(iii) above) has effect as if *section 147(2)* did not apply (i.e. *section 153(4)* does not apply on the contract becoming a qualifying contract).

(*b*) Where the circumstances are such that any profit or loss as regards the contract for the accounting period beginning with that time would *not* be a profit or loss of a trade (or part of a trade) carried on by the company, *FA 1994, s 158(2)(4)* (adjustments for changes in basis of accounting, see 28.36(*a*) above) have effect in relation to the contract and the period as if *FA 1994, s 153(4)(5)* were omitted (i.e. as if 28.33(iii) above did not apply to extend the definition of a qualifying payment).

[*FA 1994, s 175*].

Simon's Direct Tax Service. See D2.1050 *et seq.*

28.50 **Miscellaneous**

(*a*) *Amounts to be deducted from Amount A or, as the case may require, Amount B and vice versa.* Any of the current provisions (other than *FA 1994, s 167*, see 28.44 above) which requires any amount to be deducted from Amount A or, as the case may require, added to Amount B requires the deduction to be made from Amount A unless it exceeds Amount A, in which case Amount A is to be reduced to nil and the excess added to Amount B. If Amount A is nil, the whole amount is added to Amount B. The same applies, with requisite modifications, to amounts to be deducted from Amount B or, as the case may require, added to Amount A. [*FA 1994, s 177(3)(4)*].

(*b*) *Insurance and mutual trading companies.* Special provisions in *FA 1994, Sch 18* apply to life assurance business (including annuity business) and to any other mutual trading or insurance or other mutual business. Otherwise, the provisions described at 28.30 to 28.49 above apply to insurance and mutual trading companies as they do to other qualifying companies. The Treasury has regulation-making powers. [*FA 1994, s 169*].

(*c*) *Investment trusts.* In applying the income retention test for approval of an investment trust under *ICTA 1988, s 842* (see 44.1(*g*) INVESTMENT TRUSTS), non-trading profits under *FA 1994, s 160* (see 28.37 above) for a period are treated as income derived from shares or securities. [*FA 1994, s 170*].

(*d*) *Prevention of deduction of tax.* A qualifying company is not required to deduct income tax from qualifying payments. [*FA 1994, s 174*].

(*e*) *Prevention of double charge.* Any amount charged on a qualifying company, or brought in in computing profits or losses of such a company, under the current provisions is not otherwise chargeable to corporation tax or brought in in computing profits or losses or chargeable gains. A corresponding restriction applies to any amount relieved or relievable under the current provisions. [*FA 1994, s 173*].

(*f*) *Amendments to other enactments.* (i) *ICTA 1988, s 434A(1)* is amended to exclude non-trading losses under these provisions. (ii) In determining UK equivalent profits under the offshore funds legislation in *ICTA 1988, Sch 27 para 5* (see 50.6 OFFSHORE FUNDS), the current provisions are ignored. [*FA 1994, s 176; FA 1996, Sch 14 para 23*].

28.51 **Securitisation companies.** Securitisation companies are special purpose vehicles which issue securities backed by assets to investors. There is an extended definition in the Regulations. The arrangement effectively channels income from the securitised assets to the investors in the form of interest. The companies are typically set up as companies or trusts independent of the enterprises from which their assets to be securitised are acquired. These companies have been affected by changes in accounting standards, effective from 1 January 2005. Had a temporary provision not been introduced in *FA 2005*, to extend UK GAAP for those companies, it is likely that the valuation of their assets using fair value accounting, with corresponding liabilities valued at amortised cost, would have generated a corporation tax liability they would have been unable to meet from their cash flow and would have placed them in danger of insolvency or at least adversely affected credit ratings. *FA 2006 s 101* extended the temporary regime to 1 January 2008. It is now proposed to bring in a permanent regime.

Five types of securitisation company are defined: a note-issuing company, an asset-holding company, an intermediate borrowing company, a warehouse company and a commercial paper funded company. A company must also have a retained profit, as defined, to qualify.

The Regulations do not apply to securitisation companies which do not satisfy a 'payments condition' or where they have 'an unallowable purpose' or to a company in existence on 1 January 2007 which is a securitisation company within *FA 2005 s 83* and satisfies certain conditions. However, in the latter case, the company may elect to come within the securitisation regime by making an irrevocable election within 18 months of the end of the first accounting period beginning on or after 1 January 2007.

The company's corporation tax profits under the Regulations is normally its retained profits (as adjusted for the difference between distributions received in the accounting period from other securitisation companies and the excess of dividends paid in all accounting periods less retained profits and dividends for the period and previous periods for the accounting period and previous periods). The Regulations provide for the company for modification of certain rules for calculating a company's profit for corporation tax.

For computation using GAAP see 28.10 above.

[*SI 2006 No 3296*].

See 4 ALTERNATIVE FINANCE ARRANGEMENTS for provisions relating to Sukuk, the Islamic equivalent of securitisation.

FA 2007 s 59 gives power to extend the period by which the legislation is delayed beyond 1 January 2008 by statutory instrument. Wide powers are also given to HMRC to amend the securitisation regime by statutory instrument.

[*FA 2007, s 59*].

29 Franked Investment Income

29.1 DEFINITION OF FRANKED INVESTMENT INCOME

Franked investment income ('FII') is the sum of the amount or value of dividends and other qualifying DISTRIBUTIONS (23) received by a UK resident company from another UK resident company and such proportion of each distribution as corresponds to:

(*a*) before 6 April 1999, the rate of ADVANCE CORPORATION TAX (3) ('ACT') in force when the distribution is made; or

(*b*) after 5 April 1999, the 'tax credit fraction' in force when the distribution is made.

[*ICTA 1988, ss 231(1), 238(1), 832(1); F(No 2)A 1997, s 30(2); FA 1998, Sch 3 paras 11, 39; ITTOIA 2005, Sch 1 para 113*].

The tax credit fraction is initially set at one-ninth from 6 April 1999. [*F(No 2)A 1997, s 30(3)*].

Dividends or interest, or (from 6 April 2005, subject to commencement provisions) payments of alternative finance return or profit share return under ALTERNATIVE FINANCE ARRANGEMENTS (4), received from BUILDING SOCIETIES (9) are not FII. [*ICTA 1988, s 476(3)(c), s 477A(3)(b); FA 2005, s 56, Sch 2 para 5* or *ITA 2007 Sch 1 para 602*].

See the 2004–05 or earlier editions of Tolley's Corporation Tax for the provisions relating to distributions before 6 April 1999.

Simon's Direct Tax Service. See A1.158, D1.303.

29.2 EFFECT WHEN A COMPANY RECEIVES FII

The recipient UK company can (subject to below) claim to have the tax credit paid to it only if it is wholly exempt from corporation tax (or exempt on all but trading income), or the distribution is expressly exempt under any provision of the *Tax Acts* (other than the general provision exempting distributions from corporation tax in *ICTA 1988, s 208*). [*ICTA 1988, s 231(2)*]. For distributions made after 1 July 1997, tax credit repayments may not be made, *inter alia*, to pension funds (as widely defined) or to insurance companies in respect of pension business income, although this does not apply to FRIENDLY SOCIETIES (31). From 6 April 1999, entitlement to tax credit repayments is generally abolished, except in relation to certain double taxation arrangements (see 24.3 DOUBLE TAX RELIEF). [*F(No 2)A 1997, ss 19, 23, 30, Sch 3, Sch 8 Pt II(9)*].

[*ICTA 1988, s 238(1); F(No 2)A 1997, Sch 4 para 8; FA 1998, Sch 3 para 11*].

29.3 SURPLUS FII

See Tolley's Corporation Tax 2004–05 or earlier editions for the tax treatment (for accounting periods beginning before 6 April 1999) where a company's FII exceeded its franked payments and (for accounting periods beginning before 2 July 1997) where a company could claim that any surplus FII be treated as profits chargeable to corporation tax and obtain tax credits relating to such surplus FII set off against the company's losses, including special provisions for financial concerns. [*ICTA 1988, ss 238, 241, 242, 243*].

29.4 DIVIDENDS FROM NON-RESIDENT COMPANIES

HMRC considered that a non-UK resident company could not claim repayment of tax credits under *section 242*, notwithstanding the existence of a non-discrimination clause in a double taxation convention between the UK and the country in which the company was resident. (HMRC Statement of Practice 2/95, now obsolete).

A number of UK companies applied to the Ch D for a declaration that the UK corporation tax rules, under which dividends from UK companies were not taxed but dividends from companies resident in other EC member states were subject to tax (*ICTA 1988, s 208*), contravened the EC Treaty. This is subject to a Franked Investment Income (Group Litigation Order) case involving the UK treatment of dividends received from non-resident companies and is currently awaiting a decision from the ECJ. In *Test Claimants in the FII Group Litigation v CIR (Case C-446/04)* the ECJ decided that, on the application of Articles 43 and 56 to the UK treatment of franked investment income:

- for companies holding 10% or more of the foreign subsidiary's share capital, the UK system was not, in principle, unacceptable, although some questions have been remitted to the UK courts for decision; and
- where there is less than a 10% holding, the UK rules which tax receipts without allowance for underlying tax are unacceptable.

The ECJ also held that payment of ACT on foreign dividends and the prohibition of surrender of ACT to overseas companies contravened the Treaty, while the restriction on offset of ACT against UK tax did not.

Decision on the FID regime and any claim for consequential loss has been left to the UK courts.

See also *Manninen v Finland, CJEC Case C-319/02; [2004] STC 1444* in which the CJEC held that the Finnish legislation, allowing for dividends from Finnish companies to attract a tax credit but not dividends from companies established outside Finland, contravened *Article 56EC* of the *EC Treaty*.

In the case of *UBS AG v HMRC [2006] EWHC 117 (Ch D)*, the court (in reversing the Special Commissioners' decision, allowed the claim made by a London branch of a Swiss bank for a payment of tax credits under *ICTA 1988, s 243* in respect of dividends received during 1993 to 1996. The court held that reference to a tax credit in this case included a tax credit under *ICTA 1988, s 231* as embraced by *ICTA 1988, s 788(3)(d)*. As such, it covered the payment of a tax credit to a foreign company.

See also 32.3 GROUPS OF COMPANIES in respect of the payment of ACT on dividends paid to non-resident companies.

30 Fraudulent or Negligent Conduct

Cross-references. See 7 ASSESSMENTS; 15 CLAIMS, 41 INTEREST ON UNPAID TAX; 53 PAYMENT OF TAX, 54 PENALTIES; 61.10 *et seq.* RETURNS for enquiries into company tax returns.

Simon's Direct Tax Service A3.15, A3.16.

30.1 INTRODUCTION

Where HMRC consider tax to have been lost by a company's fraudulent or negligent conduct (or, under earlier legislation, by its fraud, wilful default or neglect), they will seek to recover that tax, whether by formal assessment or by way of a contract settlement (see 30.8 below). In such cases, the normal time limits for assessment are extended (see 30.3 below), interest is chargeable on the understated tax (see 41 INTEREST ON UNPAID TAX) and PENALTIES (54) are incurred, which HMRC may mitigate in appropriate circumstances. In cases of serious fraud, HMRC may pursue a criminal prosecution. In most cases, the amount of tax lost will be established by the use of HMRC's enquiry powers, for which see 61.10 *et seq.* RETURNS, or the investigatory powers at 30.4–30.7 below. See also 7.2 ASSESSMENTS as regards HMRC's power to make 'discovery' assessments. For cases relating to fraudulent or negligent conduct, see Tolley's Tax Cases.

Revenue Codes of Practice 8 and 9, deals, respectively, with Special Compliance Office Investigations in cases other than suspected serious fraud and in cases of such fraud. Code 14, dealing with enquiries into company tax returns is issued at the start of every enquiry (except that in certain simple cases a short, single-page version is issued instead). The latest versions of these Codes are available on the HMRC website.

A new penalty regime is contained in *FA 2007, s 97, Sch 24*. See 54.3 PENALTIES.

For the validity of tax amnesties see *CIR v National Federation of Self-employed and Small Businesses Ltd HL 1981, 55 TC 133.*

30.2 CASE LAW ON FRAUDULENT OR NEGLIGENT CONDUCT

The following cases relate to old legislation for 'fraud, wilful default or neglect' assessments which has now been replaced by 'fraudulent or negligent conduct' assessments. The latter expression is not defined, and the cases may be of continued assistance in this respect.

The onus of proving fraud or wilful default is on the Crown (see e.g. *Hurley v Taylor CA 1998, 71 TC 268*), but the onus is on the taxpayer to prove the assessments are excessive (*Johnson v Scott CA 1978, 52 TC 383; Jonas v Bamford Ch D 1973, 51 TC 1; Nicholson v Morris CA 1977, 51 TC 95* and cf. *Barney v Pybus Ch D 1957, 37 TC 106* and *R v Spec Commrs (ex p Martin) CA 1971, 48 TC 1*). For the standard of proof required, see *Les Croupiers Casino Club v Pattinson CA 1987, 60 TC 196.*

Unexplained capital increases or admitted omissions may be held evidence of fraud or wilful default (*Amis v Colls Ch D 1960, 39 TC 148*; *Woodrow v Whalley Ch D 1964, 42 TC 249*; *Hudson v Humbles Ch D 1965, 42 TC 380*; *Hillenbrand CS 1966, 42 TC 617*; *Young v Duthie Ch D 1969, 45 TC 624*; *James v Pope Ch D 1972, 48 TC 142*; and cf. *Brimelow v Price Ch D 1965, 49 TC 41*). Wilful default may be by agent (*Clixby v Pountney Ch D 1967, 44 TC 515*; *Pleasants v Atkinson Ch D 1987, 60 TC 228*).

'*Neglect*' means negligence or a failure to give any notice, to make any return or to produce or furnish any document or other information required by or under the *Taxes Acts*. [*TMA 1970, s 118* as previously enacted]. Neglect may be by an agent (*Mankowitz v Special Commrs Ch D 1971, 46 TC 707*).

30.3 EXTENDED TIME LIMITS

Except where specifically provided, the normal time limit for assessments is six years after the end of the accounting period. [*FA 1998, Sch 18 para 46(1), Sch 19 para 17*]. In certain cases, however, as described below, extended limits apply to assessments for the purpose of making good a loss of tax.

An objection to the making of any assessment on the grounds that it is out of time can only be made on an appeal against the assessment. [*FA 1998, Sch 18 para 46(3*)].

Assessments made after 26 July 1989 relating to accounting periods ending after 31 March 1983. Where the loss of tax arises due to the *fraudulent or neglgent conduct* of a company (or of a person acting on behalf of the company), an assessment may be made at any time not later than 21 years after the end of the accounting period. If the company assessed so requires, the assessment may give effect to reliefs or allowances to which it would have been entitled had the necessary claims been made within the relevant time limits. [*FA 1998, Sch 18 paras 46(2), 65*].

For accounting periods ended before 1 July 1999, the equivalent time limit to those above was 20 years after the end of the accounting period.

An objection to the making of any assessment on the grounds that it is out of time can only be made on an appeal against the assessment. [*FA 1998, Sch 18 para 46(3)*].

Simon's Direct Tax Service. See **A3.221–A3.226.**

30.4 INVESTIGATORY POWERS

The self-assessment enquiry procedures are explained at 61.10–61.15 RETURNS; these operate in tandem with the provisions below and incorporate a separate power to call for documents.

HMRC powers to require documents and other particulars. For the following purposes, '*document*' has the same meaning as in *Civil Evidence Act 1968, Pt I* (or Scottish or Northern Ireland equivalent), but does not include personal records or journalistic material (within *Police and Criminal Evidence Act 1984, ss 12, 13*) (and those exclusions apply also to particulars contained in such records or material). The documents concerned are those in the possession or power of the person receiving the notice. Photographic, etc. facsimiles may be supplied provided the originals are produced if called for, and documents relating to any pending tax appeal need not be delivered. In practice, the latter also applies to documents relating to a pending referral of questions during an enquiry (see 61.13 RETURNS) (Hansard Standing Committee A, 8 May 2001, Cols 172–174). There are special provisions relating to computer records (see *FA 1988, s 127*). Documents in a person's 'possession or power' are those actually in existence at the time the notice is given, and not any which would have to be brought into existence in order to satisfy the notice.

Note that, before 18 April 2005, the functions of the Commissioners for HMRC referred to below were vested in the Board of Inland Revenue. Functions to be carried out by an officer of Revenue and Customs were to be carried out by an inspector (or, in certain cases, an officer of the Board).

(*a*) Where an officer of Revenue and Customs is of the reasonable opinion that documents contain, or may contain, information relevant to the tax liability of a person, he may (with the authority of the Commissioners for HMRC and the consent of a General or Special Commissioner) by notice in writing require that person to deliver such documents to him (but only after that person has been given reasonable opportunity to produce them).

The officer must give a written summary of his reasons for applying for consent to the giving of the notice. He is not required to identify any informant in the summary and no summary need be provided if the Special or General Commissioner giving consent so directs, and the Commissioner concerned must not so direct unless he is satisfied that the officer has reasonable grounds for believing that disclosure of the information in question would prejudice the assessment or collection of tax. The Commissioner concerned must not take part in, or be present, at any subsequent proceedings concerning an appeal made by the person if the Commissioner concerned has reason to believe that any of the documents which were the subject of the notice is likely to be adduced in evidence in those proceedings.

For an unsuccessful challenge to the validity of a notice, see *Kempton v Special Commrs & CIR Ch D 1992, 66 TC 249*. In *R v CIR (ex p Banque International à Luxembourg SA) QB 2000, 72 TC 597*, an application for judicial review based *inter alia* on the protections afforded by the European Convention on Human Rights was refused. In *R (oao Morgan Grenfell & Co Ltd) v Special Commr HL, [2002] STC 786*, the HL quashed a notice on the grounds that the Revenue were not entitled to require delivery of documents subject to legal professional privilege, a fundamental human right not expressly overridden by *TMA 1970, s 20(1)*.

(*b*) An officer of Revenue and Customs may similarly by notice in writing require a person to furnish him with such particulars as he may reasonably require as being relevant to any tax liability of that person.

The notice is subject to the same authority and giving of consent requirements as at (*a*) above, and the requirements there relating to the giving of a written summary and the obligation imposed on the Special or General Commissioner giving consent apply similarly in relation to particulars as they do there to documents.

(*c*) An officer of Revenue and Customs may similarly by notice in writing require any other person (including the Director of Savings) to deliver to him (or, if the person so elects, make available for inspection by a named officer of Revenue and Customs) documents relevant to any tax liability of a 'taxpayer'. A copy of the notice must be given to the taxpayer concerned unless, in a case involving suspected fraud, a General or Special Commissioner so directs. Production of documents originating more than six years before the notice cannot be required (unless the Commissioner who gave consent to the notice specifically allows it on being satisfied that there is reasonable ground for believing loss of tax through fraud).

'*Taxpayer*' includes an individual who has died (but any notice must be given no more than six years after the death) and a company which has ceased to exist.

The notice is subject to the same authority and giving of consent requirements as at (*a*) above, and the requirements there relating to the giving of a written summary and the obligation imposed on the Special or General Commissioner giving consent apply similarly, except that the summary must be given to, and the obligation imposed relates to an appeal brought by, the taxpayer rather than the person to whom the notice is given, and no summary need be given if the taxpayer is not, as above, given a copy of the notice.

For general limitations on these powers, see *R v O'Kane and Clarke (ex p Northern Bank Ltd) and related application QB 1996, 69 TC 187*, and for a review of the procedural and other requirements, see *R v CIR (ex p Ulster Bank Ltd) CA 1997, 69 TC 211*, in which *ex p Northern Bank Ltd* was in part disapproved.

A notice cannot require the production by a statutory auditor of his audit papers, nor by a tax adviser of communications with a client (or with any other tax adviser of his client) relating to advice about the client's tax affairs. This exemption does not, however, apply to explanatory documents concerning any other documents prepared with the client for, or for delivery to, HMRC, unless HMRC already has access to the information contained therein in some other document. Where the exemption is so disapplied, either the document must be delivered or made available to HMRC or a copy of the relevant parts must be supplied (which parts must be available if required for inspection).

HMRC's application of these provisions relating to papers of a statutory auditor or client communications of a tax adviser is set out in HMRC Statement of Practice 5/90. In particular, it is made clear that accountants' working papers will be called for only where voluntary access has not been obtained and it is considered absolutely necessary in order to determine whether a client's accounts or returns are complete and correct. Requests for access may on occasion extend to the whole or a particular part of the working papers, rather than just to information explaining specific entries, and HMRC will usually be prepared to visit the accountants' or clients' premises to examine the papers and to take copies or extracts. These restrictions on the use of its powers by HMRC do not apply in the circumstances described under (*d*) below. The restrictions also do not apply to 'link papers', i.e. those papers which show how the figures in a tax return are derived from the figures in the prime records (Revenue Tax Bulletin June 2003 pp 1031, 1032).

(*d*) An officer of Revenue and Customs may similarly, on an application authorised by the Commissioners for HMRC, give a notice in writing as under (*c*) above without naming the taxpayer concerned. Consent to the application must be obtained from a Special Commissioner, who must be satisfied that: it relates to a taxpayer or class of taxpayers whose identity(ies) is (are) not known; there are reasonable grounds to believe the taxpayer(s) to have failed to comply with the *Taxes Acts*, with the likelihood of serious prejudice to the assessment or collection of tax; and the information is not reasonably available from elsewhere. The recipient can object (with a right of appeal to the Special Commissioners), by notice in writing, within 30 days on the ground that it would be onerous for him to comply.

The requirements at (*a*) above relating to the giving of a written summary and the obligation imposed on the Special or General Commissioner giving consent do not apply. The exemption, and disapplication of the exemption, from the requirements of a notice under (*d*) above relating to the production of the papers of a statutory auditor or client communications of a tax adviser apply similarly, except that the exemption does not apply to any document giving the identity or address of any taxpayer to whom the notice relates or of any person who has acted on behalf of any such person, unless HMRC already has access to the information contained therein in some other document.

See *Re an Application by HMRC to Serve section 20 Notice (Sp C 517), [2006] SSCD 71* in which consent was granted to serve notice on a financial institution seeking information about UK credit card customers whose cards were associated with offshore bank accounts. For an unsuccessful application for judicial review of the issue of such a notice, see *R v CIR (ex p Ulster Bank Ltd) QB 2000, 73 TC 209.*

(*e*) An officer may similarly (with the authority of the Commissioners for HMRC and the consent of a Circuit judge in England and Wales, a sheriff in Scotland or a county court judge in Northern Ireland) by notice in writing require a '*tax accountant*' (i.e. a person who assists another in the preparation of returns, etc. for tax purposes) who has been convicted by or before any UK court of a tax offence or incurred a penalty under *TMA 1970, s 99* to deliver documents in his possession or power relevant to any tax liability of any of his clients. The notice must be issued within twelve months of the final determination of the conviction or penalty award.

Neither the requirements at (*a*) above relating to the giving of a written summary nor the exemption from the requirements of a notice under (*d*) above relating to the production of the papers of a statutory auditor or client communications of a tax adviser apply to the giving of a notice as above.

(*f*) The Commissioners for HMRC may require, by notice in writing, a person to deliver or furnish to a named officer of theirs documents or information as specified in (*a*) and (*b*) above relevant to the tax liability of that person.

The requirements at (*a*) above relating to the giving of consent and a written summary do not apply. However, notices cannot be given on or after 26 July 1990 under this power unless there are reasonable grounds for believing that that person may have failed, or may fail, to comply with any provision of the *Taxes Acts*, and that any such failure is likely to have led, or to lead, to serious prejudice to the proper assessment or collection of tax.

The notice must specify or describe the documents or particulars required, the time limit for production (generally not less than 30 days) and, except as above, the name of the taxpayer or client, as appropriate; and the person to whom they are delivered may take copies.

The penalty for failure to comply with a notice is given by *TMA 1970, s 98* (see 54.9 PENALTIES for this and the penalty for failure to allow access to computers). In addition there are severe penalties (in summary proceedings, a fine of the statutory maximum, and on indictment, imprisonment for two years and/or an unlimited fine) for the falsification, concealment, destruction or disposal of a document which is the subject of a notice, unless strict conditions and time limits are observed.

[*TMA 1970, s 20–20BB, s 20D; CRCA 2005, ss 5, 7*].

The person to whom notice is to be given is not entitled to attend or be legally represented at the meeting at which HMRC seek the consent of a Commissioner (*Applicant v Inspector of Taxes (Sp C 189), [1999] SSCD 128*).

Notices other than those under (*d*) and (*e*) above may relate to tax liabilities in EU member states other than the UK [*FA 1990, s 125*(*1*)(*2*)(*6*)] or in any other territory with which the UK has entered into a tax enforcement agreement or other arrangements providing for the obtaining of information. [*FA 2000, s 146*(*3*)(*4*); *FA 2006, s 174, Sch 26 Pt 8*(*2*)].

For an article setting out HMRC's view on the question of claims to legal or professional privilege in relation to requests for information under these provisions (other than where tax evasion or tax fraud is suspected), see Revenue Tax Bulletin April 2000 pp 743–746 (updated by Revenue Tax Bulletin December 2002 p 993 following the *Morgan Grenfell* case at (*a*) above) (and see 22.11 below).

From a date to be determined, powers under the *Police and Criminal Evidence Act 1984* are extended, in a limited way, to HMRC officers dealing with direct taxation. Primarily this gives HMRC officers, duly authorised for a specific or general purpose, the power to search a person, caution, arrest and bail. There is also the power to grant a search warrant on the application of an HMRC officer. [*FA 2007, ss 82, 84, 86*].

There are separate provisions for Scotland and Northern Ireland, to which *PACE 1984* does not apply, and to cover cross-border situations. [*FA 2007, ss 82–86*].

The search and seizure powers at 30.6 below will consequently no longer be needed and will be repealed from the date the Treasury order comes into force. The power to seek judicial authority to require the delivery of documents at 30.5 below will be restricted to circumstances where the equivalent police power cannot be used because the material concerned cannot be obtained using those powers.

30.5 **Order for delivery of documents in serious tax fraud cases.** The powers can only be used from a date to be fixed where the police powers referred to at 30.4 above cannot be used. An officer of HMRC may apply to the court for an order for delivery of, or access to, documents under *TMA 1970, s 20BA and Sch 1AA.* (See below.)

Authorised HMRC officers are also given powers of search, replacing those in *TMA 1970* (see 30.6 below).Under *TMA 1970, s 20BA, Sch 1AA* the Commissioners of HMRC may apply to the appropriate judicial authority (a circuit judge in England and Wales, a sheriff in Scotland or a County Court judge in NI) for an order requiring any person who appears to have in his possession or power documents specified or described in the order to deliver them to an officer of HMRC within ten working days after the day of service of the notice, or such longer or shorter period as may be specified in the order. The judicial authority must be satisfied, on information on oath given by an authorised officer of HMRC, that there is reasonable ground for suspecting that an offence involving serious tax fraud has been or is about to be committed, and that the documents may be required as evidence in proceedings in respect of the offence. In Scotland, a single sheriff may make orders in respect of persons anywhere in Scotland as long as one of the orders relates to a person residing or having a place of business at an address in the sheriff's own sheriffdom. Orders may not be made in relation to items subject to legal privilege (as defined) unless they are held with the intention of furthering a criminal purpose. Failure to comply with an order is treated as contempt of court, and there are severe penalties for falsification of documents.

Schedule 1AA lays down detailed requirements in relation to such applications, and these may be supplemented by regulations (see *SI 2000 No 2875*, as amended). In particular, a person is entitled to at least five days' notice of intention to apply for such an order, and to appear and be heard at the application, unless the judicial authority is satisfied that this would seriously prejudice investigation of the offence. Until the application has been dismissed or abandoned, or an order made and complied with, any person given such notice must not conceal, destroy, alter or dispose of any document to which the order sought relates, or disclose information etc. likely to prejudice the investigation, except with the leave of the judicial authority or the written permission of HMRC. Professional legal advisers may, however, disclose such information etc. in giving legal advice to a client or in connection with legal proceedings, provided that it is not disclosed with a view to furthering a criminal purpose. Failure to comply with these requirements is treated as failure to comply with an order under these provisions. The procedural rules where documents are delivered in accordance with an order are as under *TMA 1970, s 20CC(3)*-*(9)* (see 30.6 below).

See also HMRC Code of Practice COP 22.

[*TMA 1970, s 20BA, Sch 1AA; PACE 1984, ss 14B, 114, Sch 1; FA 2007, ss 82, 86*].

Simon's Direct Tax Service. See **A3.150** *et seq.*

30.6 **Search and seizure.** Until a date to be determined by Treasury Order (see 30.5 above), where there is reasonable suspicion of serious tax fraud, and there are reasonable grounds for believing that use of the procedure under *TMA 1970, s 20BA* (see 30.5 above) might seriously prejudice the investigation, the Commissioners of HMRC may apply to a Circuit judge etc. (as in 30.4(*d*) above) for a warrant to enter premises within 14 days to search and to seize any things which may be relevant as evidence. There are detailed procedural rules governing searches and the removal of documents etc.

The warrant need not specify the suspected fraud or the documents etc., searched for (*Rossminster Ltd HL 1979, 52 TC 160*). For the proper procedure in seeking and obtaining judicial review of a decision to grant such a warrant, and interim injunctions, see *R v CIR (ex p Kingston Smith (a firm)) QB 1996, 70 TC 264*. For the validity of warrants, see *R v CIR (ex p Tamosius & Partners) QB, [1999] STC 107*. If an HMRC officer executing a warrant has reasonable cause to believe that the data on a computer's hard drive might be required as evidence, he can seize and remove that computer even though it may also contain irrelevant material (*H (R oao) v CIR QB 2002, 75 TC 377*).

[*TMA 1970, ss 20C, 20CC, 20D; Criminal Justice and Police Act 2001, Sch 2 para 13; FA 2007, Sch 22 para 4*].

Simon's Direct Tax Service. See **A3.151, A3.1614C**.

30.7 **Barristers, advocates or solicitors.** A notice under 30.4(*a*), (*b*), (*c*) or (*d*) above to a barrister, advocate or solicitor can be issued only by the Commissioners of HMRC (although that power may be delegated, see *R v CIR (ex p Davis Frankel & Mead) QB 2000, 73 TC 185*) and he cannot (without his client's consent) be required to deliver under 30.4(*c*) and (*d*) above documents protected by professional privilege. [*TMA 1970, s 20B*(*3*)(*8*)]. As regards the search and seizure powers in 30.6 above, there is similarly an exclusion for documents protected by professional privilege or, from 28 July 2000, 'legal privilege' as more widely defined (but excluding items held with the intention of furthering a criminal purpose) [*TMA 1970, s 20C*(*4*)], and see also 30.5 above as regards similar protection in relation to an order under *TMA 1970, s 20BA* in cases involving serious tax fraud.

See *R v CIR (ex p Goldberg) QB 1988, 61 TC 403* as regards nature of documents subject to privilege, but note that the decision in that case was doubted in *Dubai Bank Ltd v Galadari CA, [1989] 3 WLR 1044*, a non-tax case. In relation to search and seizure under 30.6 above, it was held in *R v CIR (ex p Tamosius & Partners) QB, [1999] STC 1077* that the presence of independent counsel to determine the issue of privilege was 'to be encouraged', although it would not prevent action by the courts if counsel was wrong. The issue and execution of warrants to search a lawyer's offices was held not to be in breach of *Article 8* of the *European Convention on Human Rights* (*Tamosius v UK ECHR, [2002] STC 1307*).

For an article setting out HMRC's view on the question of claims to legal or professional privilege in relation to requests for information under these provisions (other than where tax evasion or tax fraud is suspected), see Revenue Tax Bulletin April 2000 pp 743–746 (updated by Revenue Tax Bulletin December 2002 p 993 following the *Morgan Grenfell* case at 30.4(*a*) above).

Simon's Direct Tax Service. See A3.1609, A3.1614A.

30.8 CONTRACT SETTLEMENTS

In cases of fraudulent or negligent conduct, the taxpayer may be invited to offer a sum in full settlement of liability for tax, interest and penalties (a 'contract settlement') and such offers are often accepted by HMRC without assessment of all the tax. A binding agreement so made cannot be repudiated afterwards by the taxpayer or his executors.

See *CIR v Nuttall CA 1989, 63 TC 148* for confirmation of power to enter into such agreements. Amounts due under such an agreement which are unpaid may be pursued by an action for a debt, but the Crown does not rank as a preferential creditor in respect of the sums due (*Nuttall* above; *CIR v Woollen CA 1992, 65 TC 229*).

See 54.13 PENALTIES for mitigation of penalties.

30.9 HMRC'S PRACTICE IN CASES OF SERIOUS TAX FRAUD

From 18 April 2005, criminal prosecutions for serious tax fraud in England and Wales are conducted by the Revenue and Customs Prosecutions Office, which is independent of HMRC. The Office has its own investigatory powers under *Serious Organised Crime and Police Act 2005, ss 60–62*. Before 18 April 2005, the Inland Revenue was itself a prosecuting authority and conducted its own prosecutions.

For new cases opened from 1 September 2005, the policy of the Commissioners of HMRC in cases of suspected serious tax fraud, as set out in Code of Practice COP 9 (2005), is as follows.

1. The Commissioners reserve complete discretion to pursue a criminal investigation with a view to prosecution where they consider it necessary and appropriate.
2. Where a criminal investigation is not considered necessary or appropriate the Commissioners may decide to investigate using the civil investigation of fraud procedure.
3. Where the Commissioners decide to investigate using the civil investigation of fraud procedure they will not seek a prosecution for the tax fraud which is the subject of

that investigation. The taxpayer will be given an opportunity to make a full and complete disclosure of all irregularities in their tax affairs.

4. However, where materially false statements are made or materially false documents are provided with intent to deceive, in the course of a civil investigation, the Commissioners may conduct a criminal investigation with a view to a prosecution of that conduct.

If the Commissioners decide to investigate using the civil investigation of fraud procedure the taxpayer will be given a copy of the above statement by an authorised officer.

Previously, the practice of the Board of Inland Revenue (and, after 18 April 2005, of HMRC) in cases of suspected serious tax fraud was set out in the so-called 'Hansard Statement' (last revised on 7 November 2002). This practice continues for investigations commenced before 1 September 2005. The practice was as follows.

(i) The Board reserve complete discretion to pursue prosecutions in the circumstances they consider appropriate.

(ii) Where serious tax fraud has been committed, they may accept a money settlement instead of pursuing a criminal prosecution.

(iii) They will accept a money settlement, and will not pursue a criminal prosecution, if the taxpayer, in response to being given a copy of the Hansard Statement by an authorised officer (meaning a current serving member of Inland Revenue Special Compliance Office), makes a full and complete confession of all tax irregularities.

(Revenue Internet Statement 8 November 2002; Revenue Tax Bulletin December 2002 pp 979–981). This replaced the previous Hansard Statement of 18 October 1990, which did not include the undertaking in (iii) above. Instead, the Board retained full discretion as to the course they would pursue. In considering this, it was the Board's practice to be *influenced* by the taxpayer having made a full confession and given full co-operation during the investigation, but they gave no explicit assurance that they would not prosecute in such cases.

See also Revenue Code of Practice COP 9 referred to at 30.1 above and reissued to cover the new Civil Investigations of Fraud procedure.

HMRC's policy is to use the civil investigation of fraud procedure wherever possible. Criminal investigation is reserved for cases where HMRC needs to send a strong deterrent message or where the conduct involved is such that only a criminal sanction is appropriate. Circumstances in which HMRC will usually consider commencing a criminal, rather than civil, investigation include:

- cases of organised or systematic fraud including conspiracy;
- where an individual holds a position of trust or responsibility;
- where materially false statements are made or materially false documents are provided in the course of a civil investigation;
- where deliberate concealment, deception, conspiracy or corruption is suspected;
- cases involving the use of false or forged documents;
- cases involving money laundering;
- where the perpetrator has committed previous offences or there is a repeated course of unlawful conduct or previous civil action;
- cases involving theft, or the misuse or unlawful destruction of HMRC documents;
- where there is evidence of assault on, threats to, or the impersonation of HMRC officials; and

- where there is a link to suspected wider criminality, whether domestic or international, involving offences not under the administration of HMRC.

When considering whether a case should be investigated under the civil investigation of fraud procedure or will be the subject of a criminal investigation, one factor considered by HMRC is whether the taxpayer has made a complete and unprompted disclosure of the offences committed.

(HMRC Internet Statement 20 December 2005, see www.hmrc.gov.uk/prosecutions/crim-inv-policy.htm).

See also 33.3 HMRC: ADMINISTRATION. Statements made or documents produced by or on behalf of a taxpayer are admissible as evidence in proceedings against him notwithstanding that reliance on the Board's practice above or on their policy for mitigating penalties (see 54.13 PENALTIES) may have induced him to make or produce them. [*TMA 1970, s 105; FA 2003, s 206(1)(2)(5)*].

Simon's Direct Tax Service. See A3.1647, A3.1648.

31 Friendly Societies

[*ICTA 1988, ss 459–466*]

Simon's Direct Tax Service D4.601 *et seq.*

31.1 **UNREGISTERED SOCIETIES**

On making a claim, those with incomes not exceeding £160 p.a. are wholly exempt from corporation tax (on both income and chargeable gains). [*ICTA 1988, s 459*].

31.2 **REGISTERED AND INCORPORATED SOCIETIES**

On making a claim, these are exempt from corporation tax (on both income and chargeable gains) on profits from 'life or endowment business' (see 31.4 below), subject to exceptions and conditions as below. [*ICTA 1988, ss 460(1), 461(1), 461B(1); ITA 2007 Sch 1 para 8*]. These exceptions and conditions do not, however, affect exemptions for profits arising under contracts made before 4 May 1966. [*ICTA 1988, s 462(2)*]. Treasury regulations (see *SI 1999 No 622* as amended) apply *ICTA 1988, Sch 19AB* (pension business — payments on account of tax credits and deducted tax) *mutatis mutandis* to tax exempt business of friendly societies, provided that not all the business of the society is tax-exempt. This is without prejudice to *ICTA 1988, s 463(1)*, see 31.7 below. [*FA 1993, s 121; FA 2001, Sch 33 Pt II(12)*]. The amendments to *Schedule 19AB* which prohibit the payment of tax credits to insurance companies in respect of pension business income do not apply to friendly societies until 6 April 1999. [*F(No 2)A 1997, Sch 3 para 12*]. Also, although tax credit payments are generally abolished from that date, they are temporarily reinstated in relation to distributions to friendly societies in respect of tax exempt business until 5 April 2004 [*FA 1998, s 90; FA 2001, Sch 33 Pt II(12); SI 1999 No 622*], and this applies similarly to non-exempt individual savings account business (see 31.7 below).

See 31.7 below for amendments to certain corporation tax provisions in their application to friendly societies' life and endowment business. In particular, relief for expenses attributable to exempt business against profits and gains from non-exempt business is prohibited, overturning the decision in *Homeowners Friendly Society Ltd v Barrett (Sp C 31), [1995] SSCD 90* with retrospective effect (except in certain cases where appeals were in progress at 21 April 1995).

Incorporated societies. The *Friendly Societies Act 1992* enables friendly societies to incorporate and take on new powers, and to provide a wider range of financial services through subsidiaries. *F(No 2)A 1992, s 56, Sch 9* introduced a large number of amendments and additional provisions to ensure that registered societies which incorporate, and societies newly established as incorporated societies, receive the same treatment as regards tax exemption as existing registered societies and that the incorporation of a registered society neither affects those exemptions nor results in any tax charges as a result of the incorporation, either on the society or on its members.

31.3 **Policy limits.** The exemption in 31.2 above does not apply to profits from pension or individual savings account business, or from other life or endowment business consisting of the granting of annuities exceeding £156 p.a., or of the assurance of gross sums under contracts under which the total premiums payable in any twelve-month period exceed a maximum figure as follows:

for contracts made after 30 April 1995	£270
for contracts made after 24 July 1991 and before 1 May 1995	£200
for contracts made after 31 August 1990 and before 25 July 1991	£150
for contracts made after 31 August 1987 and before 1 September 1990	£100

Where the premium under a contract made after 31 August 1987 and before 1 May 1995 was increased by a variation after 24 July 1991 and before 1 August 1992, or after 30 April

1995 and before 1 April 1996, the contract is treated for these purposes as having been made at the time of the variation. In determining these limits, no account is taken of any bonus or addition declared upon an assurance or accruing thereon by reference to an increase in the value of any investments, and, in relation to premium limits, so much of any premium as relates to exceptional risk of death or disability is disregarded, as is 10% of premiums payable more frequently than annually. [*ICTA 1988, s 460(2)–(12); FA 2003, s 172(5)(6)*].

31.4 **Policy conditions.** The exemption in 31.2 above of a society's 'life or endowment business' only applies to so much of that business as is attributable to policies which are 'qualifying policies', or which would be 'qualifying policies' but for members' holdings of policies with other societies causing them to exceed the limits on the contracts an individual may hold. [*ICTA 1988, s 462(1)*]. The following conditions must be satisfied in respect of all policies issued by a society under contracts made after 3 May 1966.

(*a*) The interval (the 'term' of the policy) between the making of the insurance (or, if the term started within the previous three months, the commencement of the term) and payment of the sum assured (or of the first instalment of the annuity) is at least ten years, with a saving for sums payable on the death or retirement due to ill health of the life insured or the person liable to pay the premiums. This requirement is reduced to five years from the beginning of the term if the payment is made to an infant and the premium payable in any year does not exceed £13, or if the payment is one of a series payable at intervals of five years or more, each of which (other than the final payment) does not exceed four-fifths of the premiums paid since the preceding payment.

(*b*) The premiums are of equal or rateable amounts, payable at intervals not exceeding one year over the whole term of the policy. For this purpose, the term of the policy excludes any period after the life insured or person liable to pay the premiums attains a specified age, provided that at least ten years of the term has then elapsed. A policy providing for commutation of future premiums after the expiration of ten years or of half the term (whichever occurs earlier), or when the person liable to pay the premiums becomes non-resident, is nevertheless deemed to satisfy these conditions. Premiums may also be paid by surrendering a sum which has become payable on the maturity of any other policy issued by the same society (or by a predecessor of it), in the course of its tax-exempt 'life or endowment business', to the person liable to pay the premiums or to his parent, and they may be waived by reason of disability.

(*c*) (Before 1 May 1995), the surrender value of the policy for the first ten years, or three-quarters of the term, whichever is the shorter, must not exceed the premiums paid or, if greater, the value (if any) prescribed by *Industrial Assurance Act 1923, s 24* or *Industrial Assurance and Friendly Societies Act 1929, s 3*.

[*ICTA 1988, Sch 15 para 3(2)–(4); FA 1995, Sch 10 para 4*].

The exemption in 31.2 above does not in any event apply in relation to profits attributable to contracts expressed at the outset not to be made in the course of tax-exempt 'life or endowment business', and either:

(i) made on or after 20 March 1991 for the assurance of gross sums; or

(ii) made before that date, where the society so elected.

A society could also elect for the exemption not to apply to profits attributable to contracts where, at the outset of the contract, it was assumed by the society not to be made in the course of tax-exempt life or endowment business (without being expressed either to be or not to be so), and the policy issued in pursuance of it was in the required form of a 'qualifying policy'.

[*ICTA 1988, s 460(2)(ca), s 462A*].

A friendly society includes all its branches. A society formed on the amalgamation of others is treated as being different from those others. However, if each of those others was within the exemption, and at least one was not a 'new society', the society resulting from the amalgamation is treated as having been registered before 4 May 1966. [*ICTA 1988, s 466*].

'*Life or endowment business*' means any business of effecting or carrying out contracts of insurance which fall within *SI 2001 No 544, Sch I Pt II, paras I, II or III* (before 1 December 2001, any business within *Friendly Societies Act 1992, Sch 2 Head A, Classes I–III*); any pension business; and the issue of, or undertaking of liability under, policies of insurance on human life and the granting of annuities on human life ('life assurance business'); but, for contracts made before 1 September 1996, excluding sickness benefit policies unless at least 60% of the premiums is attributable to the sickness provision and the policy also assures a gross sum, independent of sickness, on which no bonus or addition may be declared. Also excluded is the granting of annuities bought with the proceeds of maturity or surrender of any other policy issued by the same society in the course of its tax exempt life or endowment business. For contracts made before 1 September 1996, and those made on or after that date where the effecting and carrying out of the contract also constitutes business within *SI 2001 No 544, Sch I Pt II, paras I, II or III*, business within *Pt II para IV* is also included (and before 1 December 2001 a similar rule applied to business within *Friendly Societies Act 1992, Sch 2 Head A, Class IV*). [*ICTA 1988, s 466(1)(2); SI 2001 No 3629, Article 37*].

A policy issued by a friendly society is a '*qualifying policy*' only if it meets the conditions at (*a*), (*b*) and (*c*) above, and if in addition the minimum sum assured is at least 75% of the total premiums payable and (in relation to contracts with a 'new society' made before 25 July 1991) it is with a member over the age of 18 years. [*ICTA 1988, Sch 15 para 3(1)*]. A health insurance policy ceases to be a qualifying policy if the rights conferred by it are surrendered in whole or part. For the detailed application of the 75% test, see *ICTA 1988, Sch 15 para 3(5)–(11), para 4*. In the case of a society which is not a 'new society', a policy can be a qualifying policy even if it was made with a person under 18 years of age or the rights have been wholly or partly surrendered. Where a society which is not a 'new society' begins carrying on tax exempt life or endowment business, or carrying on such business on an enlarged scale or of a new character, HMRC may direct that it be treated, in respect of new business, as if it were a 'new society'. [*ICTA 1988, s 465*].

Policy includes an instrument evidencing a contract to pay an annuity on human life. [*ICTA 1988, s 466(2)*].

A '*new society*' is a society registered after 3 May 1966, or one registered in the previous three months which did not carry on any life or endowment business during that period, or an incorporated society, provided that it was not, before incorporation, excluded from being a new society. [*ICTA 1988, s 466(2)*].

Before 19 March 1985, broadly similar conditions applied, except for the requirement that policies be 'qualifying policies' (which was not necessary as all friendly society policies were qualifying policies) and absence of provision for a waiver of the requirement as to regular rateable premiums in cases of disability.

There are transitional provisions under which profits arising from certain policies issued in respect of insurances made after 31 May 1984 and before 19 March 1985, which either do not meet the 75% test under *ICTA 1988, Sch 15 para 3(5)–(11)* (see above) or fail to satisfy the conditions in *para 3(2)* (see above), are excluded from the exemption. The conditions in *section 460(1)* (see above) do not apply in respect of such policies. [*ICTA 1988, s 462(1)*].

Simon's Direct Tax Service. See **D4.604**.

31.5 **Conditions imposed on society's business.** Profits arising from 'life or endowment business' (see 31.4 above) are not within the exemption if the society was registered after 31 December 1957 and issued a single premium policy during the three months to 3 May 1966, or is an incorporated successor to such a society. [*ICTA 1988, s 460(2)(a)(aa)*].

For such business carried on before 1 June 1984, the exemption also did not apply if the society was one which was registered after 3 February 1966, did not carry on life or endowment business before 3 May 1966, and by its rules could carry on life or endowment business other than:

(i) industrial assurance business as defined in *Industrial Insurance Act 1923, s 1*(*2*);

(ii) certain sickness assurance; and

(iii) contracts exclusively for the assurance of a gross sum or annuity payable on death to or for the benefit of the deceased's widow (or widower, see Revenue Press Release 15 April 1981) or dependent child.

[*ICTA 1970, s 333*(*2*)].

If a society registered before 4 May 1966 commenced life or endowment business, or enlarged the scale or changed the character of such business, the Registrar had power to serve notice that it be treated as not being within the exemption. [*ICTA 1970, s 335*(*2*)–(*5*) *as amended*].

Where the rules are altered or there are amalgamations or acquisitions of societies, the exemption or non-exemption of previous contracts is unaffected. [*ICTA 1988, s 460*(*7*)–(*10*)].

As regards (iii) above, the Revenue were advised in 1984 that, contrary to what was generally believed, the promotion of contracts as investment or endowment contracts, on the basis of their surrender value after ten years:

(A) rendered their issue *ultra vires* and therefore the contracts not fully enforceable; and

(B) required that a lump sum intended to be payable on the surrender of an annuity be taken into account in the application of the monetary limits (see 31.3 above).

Under this revised interpretation of the law, many policies would have been *ultra vires* or in excess of the tax exempt limits. For contracts made before 1 June 1984, therefore, *Friendly Societies Act 1984, s 1* altered the law to what it was previously thought to be.

Advice was also given that, in the application of the monetary limits, any increase in the value of an investment-linked policy over the basic gross sum assured must be taken into account. *Friendly Societies Act 1984, s 2* therefore provided for such an increase to be ignored, irrespective of when the policy was made.

31.6 **Societies registered after 31 May 1973.** For societies registered after 31 May 1973, the exemption outlined in 31.2–31.5 above is, after 26 March 1974, restricted to life or endowment business, and a payment made to a member after that date otherwise than in the course of such business is treated as a qualifying distribution (see 23.17 DISTRIBUTIONS) in so far as it exceeds any sum paid or repaid by him to the society, less any payment made by the society to him after 26 March 1974. [*ICTA 1988, s 461*(*1*)(*3*)]. Similar provisions apply in relation to non-life or endowment business of incorporated successors to registered societies subject to the restriction, the denial of exemption being extended to include profits from subsidiaries. [*ICTA 1988, ss 461A, 461B*(*1*)–(*3*); *SI 2001 No 3629, Articles 34, 35*].

A society is outside the above provision if:

(*a*) its business is limited to the provision, in accordance with the rules of the society, of benefits for or in respect of employees of a particular employer or of a group of persons approved by the Registrar or (from 1 December 2001) HMRC; or

(*b*) it was registered before 27 March 1974 and its rules limit the aggregate amount payable in contributions and deposits to £1 per month, or such greater amount as may be authorised by the Registrar or HMRC. [*ICTA 1988, s 461*(*2*); *SI 2001 No 3629, Article 33*(*2*)].

If a society registered before 1 June 1973 begins life or endowment business (see 31.4 above), or enlarges the scale or changes the character of such business, the Registrar or HMRC may direct that it is to be treated as registered after 31 May 1973. [*ICTA 1988, s 461(6)–(10); SI 2001 No 3629, Article 33(4)–(6)*]. Incorporated societies may be the subject of directions with similar effect. [*ICTA 1988, s 461C; SI 2001 No 3629, Article 36*].

31.7 **Life and endowment business** which is **not exempt** is treated in the same way as mutual insurance business, or other long term business, carried on by insurance companies, subject to regulations made by the Treasury. Transfers (in whole or part) of the business of a friendly society to another society or to a company which is not a friendly society, and amalgamations of friendly societies and their conversion into companies which are not friendly societies, and transfers of long term business of insurance companies to friendly societies, are treated in the same ways as transfers of long term business between insurance companies, again subject to Treasury regulations. [*ICTA 1988, s 463*].

The Treasury regulations both for modifications of the Corporation Tax Acts and for transfers of business are consolidated, with effect for accounting periods beginning on or after 1 January 2005 in *SI 2005 No 2014* (*Friendly Societies* (*Modification of the Corporation Tax Acts*) *Regulations 2005*). For accounting periods beginning before 1 January 2005, the regulations were consolidated in *SI 1997 No 473* (as amended by *SI 1997 No 2877*, *SI 1998 No 1871, reg 25*, *SI 1999 No 2636*, *SI 2000 No 2710*, *SI 2001 No 3629, Articles 153–165*, *SI 2001 No 3975*, *SI 2002 No 1409*, *SI 2003 No 23*, *SI 2004 No 822* and *SI 2004 No 2310, Article 75*), with transitional amendment regulations in *SI 1997 Nos 471, 472*. See also *SI 1997 No 481* (amending *SI 1995 No 3237*).The 2005 Regulations modify the life assurance tax provisions to take into account changes made by *F(No 2)A 2005* and by the Financial Services Authority ('FSA') to their Handbook. See 48 MUTUAL COMPANIES.

31.8 **Societies ceasing to be registered.** Where a society ceases to be registered under *Friendly Societies Act 1992, s 91*, its existing tax exempt life and endowment business and any other exempt business, in so far in each case as it relates to contracts already entered into, continue to be exempt from corporation tax (on income or chargeable gains) on profits arising from it and each is treated as a separate business. In the latter case, the exemption is lost if the benefits are increased. [*ICTA 1988, s 460(11)(12), s 461(4), s 461B(5)–(7); SI 2001 No 3629, Article 33(3)*].

With effect on or after **19 July 2007**, when a friendly society's tax exempt business is transferred to an insurance company, the business transferred will be treated as a separate trade from the company's other insurance business and will remain exempt from corporation tax on income and chargeable gains. However, the favourable tax treatment is lost if premiums on policies transferred are increased above specified limits. HMRC are given wide powers to make regulations, which may affect periods before their date.

Where business, other than life assurance business, is transferred from a registered friendly society to an insurance company and the friendly society was exempt from corporation tax in respect of that business, the insurance company shall also have exemption on the contracts transferred. However, if the benefits are increased, the exemption will be lost for that accounting period and for future accounting periods. There is provision for modification of this legislation by statutory instrument.

Similar rules apply to incorporated friendly societies.

[*ICTA 1988 ss 460(11), (12); 461, 461B; SI 2001 No 3629, Article 33(3); FA 2007 Sch 12 paras 1, 4, 5, 6*].

32 Groups of Companies

Cross-references. See 12.1–12.40 CAPITAL GAINS—GROUPS; 21 CONTROLLED FOREIGN COMPANIES; 26.17, 26.29 EXCHANGE GAINS AND LOSSES; 45.1 LIQUIDATION ETC.; 53.2 PAYMENT OF TAX.

Simon's Direct Tax Service D2.6.

The headings in this chapter are as follows.

32.1 INTRODUCTION

Membership of a group may affect the tax treatment of dividends and charges paid between companies (see 32.2, 32.4 below). It may also enable certain losses etc. of one company to be relieved against the profits of another (32.6–32.8 below) and unused ACT (prior to its abolition) to be surrendered from one company to another (see 32.5 below). See also 47.21 LOSSES as regards restriction of losses where a fellow group member is the subject of a write-off of Government investment.

Note. For these reliefs, which may also apply to consortia (see 32.23 below), the definition of 'group' varies as indicated below. See also 12.1 CAPITAL GAINS—GROUPS.

32.2 INTRA-GROUP DIVIDENDS, CHARGES AND INTEREST

An election could be made jointly by the paying company and the receiving company, provided that each was resident in the UK and that the conditions set out in 32.4 below were satisfied, for *ICTA 1988, s 247* to apply to intra-group charges or (where they were paid before 6 April 1999) dividends, or to both. An election in relation to charges applied equally to interest payments in relation to which a debit fell to be brought into account on the paying company under the LOAN RELATIONSHIPS (46) provisions. The effect of such an election was:

(*a*) that income tax was not deductible from payments representing charges on the paying company's income or deductible interest (but see 32.4 below) and *ITA 2007, ss 449, 899, 901, 946, 962–964, 903* (formerly *ICTA 1988, ss 349, 350*) (see Tolley's Income Tax under Deduction of Tax at Source) did not apply; and

(*b*) that ACT was not payable in respect of dividends passing between them, which did not, therefore, constitute franked payments of one or FRANKED INVESTMENT INCOME (29) of the other, but were referred to as 'group income'.

These provisions **ceased to apply to dividends paid after 5 April 1999**, following the abolition of ACT, and are **abolished altogether for payments made after 11 May 2001** (and see now 37.3 and 37.4 INCOME TAX IN RELATION TO A COMPANY).

[*ICTA 1988, s 247(1)(2)(4)(4A); FA 1998, Sch 3 para 19; FA 2001, s 85(5)(6), Sch 33 Pt II(10)*].

An election had to be made by notice to the inspector, specifying the grounds of entitlement. The inspector could then accept the election, or reject it within three months, in which latter case the electors had the same rights of appeal as the paying company would have had against an assessment. See Tolley's Income Tax under Appeals. If accepted, the election was effective from the date of notification of acceptance (or three months from the giving of the notice, whichever was the earlier) in relation to dividends or charges paid after that date (subject to acceptance by HMRC of the election being made retrospectively). Either company could revoke an election from the date of giving notice in writing to that effect to the inspector. Where an election in respect of *dividends* was in force, the paying company could give written notice to the Collector that it was not to apply to such dividends (or parts of dividends) as were specified in the notice. Form CT61Z (return under *ICTA 1988, Sch 13*) contained a space for entry of such dividends; suitable completion of that form was accepted as satisfying the requirement for written notice. An election ceased to be in force on the companies' ceasing to fulfil the necessary conditions, and each company had at once to notify the inspector of such cessation. [*ICTA 1988, ss 247(3), 248; FA 1998, Sch 3 paras 19, 20*].

An election which referred only to charges was treated as extending to payments of interest in relation to which a debit fell to be brought into account under the LOAN RELATIONSHIPS (46) provisions. (Revenue Tax Bulletin April 1996 p 310).

Simon's Direct Tax Service. See **D2.605** *et seq.*

32.3 **Payments to non-UK resident companies.** Following the finding by the CJEC that the requirement that both parties to an election under *section 247* be UK-resident contravened EC law (*Metalgesellschaft Ltd & Others v CIR CJEC (Case C-397/98) and the joined case of Hoechst AG & Other v CIR CJEC (Case C-410/98), [2001] STC 452*), the High Court granted HMRC's application for a Group Litigation Order to enable claims pursuant to the CJEC decision to be managed.

On the entitlement to compensation, see *Pirelli Cable Holding NV and others v HMRC [2006] STC 548*. This case (in reversing the decision of the High Court) held that payments received from HMRC by European subsidiaries of two UK companies under the double taxation agreements (equal to 6.875% of the dividends paid to them) should be taken into account in calculating any compensation or restitution. The House of Lords also held that the parent companies would not have been entitled to tax credits in respect of dividends received under a group income election and that ACT was not a 'withholding tax' for the purposes of the EC Parent and Subsidiary Directive. The case was remitted to the High Court by the House of Lords, where Pirelli raised a further point that, had it made a group income election, the dividends paid to non-UK-resident subsidiaries would not have incurred ACT. The court considered whether this argument was well founded, and found that it was not (*Pirelli Cable Holding NV & Others v HMRC (No 2) [2007] EWHC 583(Ch)*).

In *Sempra Metals Ltd (formerly Metallgesallschaft Ltd) v CIR, CA [2005] STC 687* it was held that in providing for compensation, interest from the date on which ACT was paid until the date it was set off against mainstream corporation tax should be calculated on the basis of compound interest in order to provide for a 'full' remedy but that interest for the period from when the cause of action accrued until the date of judgment should be calculated on a simple basis (this being a matter for the national court).

It was held by the House of Lords in *Deutsche Morgan Grenfell Group plc v CIR House of Lords (and cross-appeal), HL [2006] UKHL 49L* that English law recognised a restitution claim for tax paid under a mistake of law and that the limitation period (under the *Limitation Act 1980*) ran from the date the mistake at law was discovered, which, in Deutsche Morgan Grenfell's case, was the date of the ECJ decision which made it clear that a mistake in law had occurred (8 March 2001). This confirmed the ruling by the High Court, following which provisions were introduced by *FA 2004, s 320* to prevent the *Limitation Act 1980, s 32(1)(c)* from applying in actions for restitution brought after 7 September 2003. (The Court of Appeal had found in favour of HMRC.)

FA 2007, s 107 provides that, unless judgment in favour of the taxpayer or his co-petitioners in a Group Litigation Action has been given by the House of Lords prior to 6 December 2006, the *Limitation Act 1980 s 32(1)(c)* does not apply in any action brought prior to 8 September 2003. Where judgment is given in favour of the taxpayer in a case heard between 6 December 2006 and **19 July 2007** the effect is reversed and any repayment made is repayable to HMRC with interest.

Following the High Court's decision, provisions were introduced by *FA 2004, s 320* to prevent the *Limitation Act 1980, s 32(1)(c)* from applying in actions for restitution brought after 7 September 2003 (see 15.10 CLAIMS).

Following the CJEC decision in *Metalgesellschaft*, the CJEC, in *Test Claimants in Class IV of the ACT Group Litigation (Pirelli UK plc, Essilor Ltd, Sony UK Ltd and BMW (GB) Ltd) v CIR, CJEC Case C-374/04; 12 December 2006, held that* EC Treaty Articles 43 and 56 did not preclude a member state from granting a tax credit to a company resident within it on dividends received from other resident companies, although no such credit was available on dividends from companies resident in other member states. Where the two states have a double taxation agreement in force between them and a third state does not, granting of a tax credit on a dividend paid by a company in the first state to one in the second state, but not to one in the third state, is not precluded.

See also the finding in *NEC Semi-Conductors Ltd (and other test claimants in FII group) v CIR HL [2007] UKHL 25* (involving ACT relating to dividends paid by a UK company to a non-EC resident company) that firstly, *ICTA 1988, s 247* did not discriminate against a UK company on the ground that the capital of the subsidiary was controlled by a non-resident company. The positions of the subsidiary and parent could not be de-coupled. Secondly, prevention of a group income election did not breach the double tax agreement. The taxpayer's appeal was dismissed.

In the ECJ case of *Denkavit International BV and Another v Ministre de l'Economie des Finances et de l'Industrie (Case-170/05)* it was held that EC Treaty Articles 43 and 48 did not permit a member state to impose a liability to tax on dividends paid to a non-resident parent company when a resident parent would not have suffered tax. This was the case even where a double taxation treaty allowed the parent to offset the tax in its country of residence.

See also 29.4 FRANKED INVESTMENT INCOME regarding the FII Group Litigation Order test case involving the UK treatment of dividends received from non-resident companies.

32.4 **Companies eligible.** The election was available only where the companies were resident in the UK and:

(*a*) the paying company was a '51% subsidiary' of the other, or of a company resident in the UK of which the recipient company was also a 51% subsidiary (but see (*c*) below); or (*b*) the paying company was a 'trading' or 'holding company' owned by a 'consortium' of which the recipient company was a member and not itself a '75% subsidiary' of any other company and not capable of becoming so by virtue of any existing 'arrangements' (see 32.19 below); or

(*c*) (in the case of payments other than dividends) the recipient company is a 51% subsidiary of the paying company.

[*ICTA 1988, s 247(1)(1A)(4); FA 1998, Sch 3 para 19*].

A '*51% (75%) subsidiary*' is a body corporate more than 50% (not less than 75%) of the 'ordinary share capital' of which is beneficially owned directly or indirectly by another. [*ICTA 1988, s 838*]. Share capital owned directly or indirectly in a non-resident body corporate, or owned indirectly through a company which holds it as trading stock, is disregarded in determining 51% subsidiary status, and a company is not treated as a 51% subsidiary unless the parent company would be beneficially entitled to more than 50% of any profits available for distribution to equity holders and of any assets so available on a winding-up (see 32.9 below). [*ICTA 1988, s 247(8)(8A)*].

'*Ordinary share capital*' means all the issued share capital of the company except non-participating shares carrying a fixed-rate dividend. [*ICTA 1988, s 832(1)*]. 'Issued share capital' does not include founder members' deposits in a company limited by guarantee (*South Shore Mutual Insurance Co Ltd v Blair (Sp C 215), [1999] SSCD 296*).

A '*holding company*' means a company the business of which consists wholly or mainly in holding shares or securities of trading companies which are its *90% subsidiaries* (i.e. in which it holds directly not less than 90% of the ordinary share capital). [*ICTA 1988, s 247(9)(a)*].

A '*trading company*' is a company the business of which consists wholly or mainly of the carrying on of a trade or trades. [*ICTA 1988, s 247(9)(b)*].

A company is owned by a '*consortium*' if three-quarters or more of its ordinary share capital is beneficially owned amongst them by companies resident in the UK, each owning at least one-twentieth and beneficially entitled to at least one-twentieth of any profits available for distribution to equity holders and of any assets so available on a winding-up (see 32.9 below). Such companies are the '*members of the consortium*'. [*ICTA 1988, s 247(9)(c)*].

32.5 SURRENDER OF ACT

The benefit of any ACT paid by, and not repaid to, a UK-resident company in respect of **dividends,** relating to accounting periods of that company beginning before 6 April 1999, could have been surrendered in whole or in part to any UK-resident 51% subsidiary of that company. [*ICTA 1988, s 240, Sch 13A; FA 1996, Sch 25; FA 1998, Sch 3 paras 13, 42, Sch 19 para 50*].

See Tolley's Corporation Tax 2005–06 or earlier editions for further details.

32.6 GROUP RELIEF

Relief from corporation tax for the items specified in 32.10 below may be surrendered (in whole or in part) by one 'member of a group of companies' (see 32.7 below) (the 'surrendering company') and claimed by another such member (the 'claimant company') against its own corporation tax liability by way of 'group relief'. The relief is also available to and from certain consortium companies, see 32.23 below.

Claims can be made:

(*a*) for trading losses and other amounts eligible for corporation tax relief (as set out in 32.10 below) where both the claimant and surrendering companies are resident in the UK or either resident in the UK or carrying on a UK trade through a permanent establishment (see 60.5 RESIDENCE — previously a branch or agency); or (*b*) **for accounting periods beginning on or after 1 April 2006,** for losses and other amounts not eligible for corporation tax relief (effectively for 'qualifying overseas losses' as set out in 32.16 below) arising to an 'EEA company'. An '*EEA company*' is a non-resident company within the charge to tax under the law of any European Economic Area (EEA) territory and which is either resident in any EEA territory or not so resident but carrying on a trade through a permanent establishment in any EEA territory. Accounting periods straddling 1 April 2006 are treated for this purpose as two separate periods. The amount of the claimant company's profits and the amount of the loss or other amount of the non-resident, surrendering company are apportioned to the two periods on a just and reasonable basis.

[*ICTA 1988, s 402*(*1*)-(*3B*)*; FA 2006, s 27, Sch 1 paras 1, 9*].

The change in legislation was in response to the case of *Marks and Spencer plc v Halsey (Case C-446/03), [2006] STC 237*, in which the company claimed group relief in respect of losses incurred by its European subsidiaries, the claims being rejected by HMRC and the Special Commissioners on the grounds that group relief was only available for losses recorded in the UK. The European Court of Justice ruled (on 13 December 2005) that although Articles 43 EC and 48 EC on the freedom of establishment and discrimination do not preclude the residence requirements, which prevent resident parent companies from deducting losses of non-resident subsidiaries, it is an infringement of those EC Treaty rights to deny group relief to a resident parent company where the non-resident subsidiary has exhausted all possibilities in its State of residence of utilising the losses in question. This followed the referral to the ECJ of the case by the High Court which stayed proceedings on the appeal of the company against the decision of the Special Commissioners (*Marks and Spencer plc v Halsey (Sp C 352), [2003] SSCD 70*). The High Court ruled (in *Marks and Spencer plc v Halsey Ch D [2006] STC 1235)* that, on the basis of the ECJ judgment, group relief was not available in the case of the French subsidiary. Claims in respect of the German and Belgian subsidiaries were remitted to the Special Commissioners to hear further evidence and submissions and to determine the appeals in light of this and the ECJ decision. Both parties appealed to the Court of Appeal, which rules that the UK group relief rules should not be struck out in their entirety, that what was meant by 'no possibility of use of losses locally' was 'a real possibility' rather than 'no real likelihood' and that that test can be met at or up to the time when the claimant company makes its claim for group (*Marks and Spencer plc v Halsey CA [2007] EWCA Civ 117*). The case will now return to the Special Commissioners to decide if Marks and Spencer fulfil the conditions for relief (subject to either or both parties appealing the Court of Appeal decision to the House of Lords.)

With effect for accounting periods beginning on or after 1 April 2006, it is specifically provided that group relief does not apply to authorised unit trusts or open-ended investment companies (see 43 INVESTMENT FUNDS) by *ICTA 1988, s 402*(*3AA*) treated as inserted by *SI 2006 No 964, reg 94*(*2*).

Simon's Direct Tax Service. See **D2.620** *et seq.*

32.7 **Group companies.** Companies are '*members of a group of companies*' if one is the '75% subsidiary' of the other or both are 75% subsidiaries of a third company. [*ICTA 1988, s 413*(*3*)(*a*)]. In the case of a claim within 32.6(*b*) above for relief for a qualifying overseas loss, either the surrendering, non-resident company must be a 75% subsidiary of the claimant company that is UK resident or both companies must be 75% subsidiaries of a third company that is UK resident. [*ICTA 1988, 402*(*2A*)(*2B*), *FA 2006, Sch 1 para 1*].

The residence of the companies constituting the group is not relevant although only UK-resident companies and companies carrying on a UK trade through a permanent establishment (or branch or agency) may claim group relief (see 32.6 above). See, however, 32.14 below as regards limitation of the application of the definition of 'group'. (For accounting periods ending before 1 April 2000, all the companies had to be UK-resident or resident elsewhere in the European Union or European Economic Area (following the ECJ decision in *ICI plc v Colmer [1996] STC 352*, see 32.23 below) [*FA 2000, Sch 27 paras 2, 6(1)*]. (See HMRC Company Taxation Manual, CTM 300–CTM 370 regarding international groups.)

'*75% subsidiary*' means a body corporate not less than 75% of the ordinary share capital (see 32.4 above) of which is beneficially owned directly or indirectly by another body corporate. [*ICTA 1988, s 838*]. Beneficial ownership is not affected by the existence of an option which may require disposal of shares at a future date (*J Sainsbury plc v O'Connor CA 1991, 64 TC 208*). For the purposes of group relief, however, a company is treated as not owning:

(*a*) any share capital held as trading stock; or

(*b*) any share capital which it owns indirectly and which is directly held by another body corporate as trading stock.

[*ICTA 1988, s 413(5)*].

Any share capital of registered INDUSTRIAL AND PROVIDENT SOCIETIES (38) is treated as ordinary share capital. [*ICTA 1988, s 413(4)*].

The company owning the shares must also be beneficially entitled to **at least 75%** of profits available for distribution to equity holders as such of the subsidiary **and** of assets similarly available in a winding-up. [*ICTA 1988, s 413(7)*].

With effect for accounting periods beginning on or after 1 April 2006, it is specifically provided that an open-ended investment company (see 43 INVESTMENT FUNDS) can not be treated as a member of a group by *ICTA 1988, s 413(3A)* treated as inserted by *SI 2006 No 964, reg 94(4)*.

Simon's Direct Tax Service. See **D2.621, D2.635** *et seq.*

32.8 An '**equity holder**' of a company is a holder of its 'ordinary shares' or a 'loan creditor' in respect of a loan other than a 'normal commercial loan'. [*ICTA 1988, Sch 18 para 1(1)*].

'*Ordinary shares*' means, for this purpose, all shares other than '*fixed-rate preference shares*', which are defined as shares:

(*a*) issued for consideration which is or includes new consideration (as defined in *ICTA 1988, s 254*, see 23.11 DISTRIBUTIONS); and

(*b*) carrying no rights to conversion into other shares or securities or acquisition of additional shares or securities; and

(*c*) on which any dividends are limited to a fixed amount, or to a fixed percentage of the nominal value, and represent no more than a reasonable commercial return on the new consideration received by the company for the issue of the shares; and

(*d*) on which any repayment right is limited to such consideration or is reasonably comparable with rights generally attached to listed fixed-dividend shares.

As regards (*b*) above, rights of conversion into shares or securities of the company's 'quoted parent company' are disregarded, as are rights of conversion into shares satisfying (*a*), (*c*) and (*d*) above, or securities satisfying (ii) and (iii) below, not themselves carrying conversion (other than into shares or securities in the 'quoted parent company') or acquisition rights.

[*ICTA 1988, Sch 18 para 1(2)(3)(5A)(5B)(8)*].

A company is another company's '*quoted parent company*' for these purposes if and only if:

(A) the other company is its 75% subsidiary (see 32.7 above), for which purpose it is assumed that the company *is* the 'quoted parent company' of the other;

(B) the parent is not itself a 75% subsidiary; and

(C) the parent's ordinary shares (or each class thereof) are listed on a recognised stock exchange or dealt in on the Unlisted Securities Market.

[*ICTA 1988, Sch 18 para 1(5C)(5D); ITA 2007, s 1005; FA 2007, Sch 26*].

'*Loan creditor*' is as defined in *ICTA 1988, s 417(7)* (see 16.3 CLOSE COMPANIES) except that banks are specifically included. [*ICTA 1988, Sch 18 para 1(4)*].

'*Normal commercial loan*' is one representing (in whole or in part) new consideration (as defined in *ICTA 1988, s 254*) and:

(i) which carries no right of conversion into other shares or securities or acquisition of additional shares or securities; and

(ii) the interest on which is dependent neither on the results of the company's business (or part thereof) nor on the value of its assets, and represents no more than a reasonable commercial return on the new consideration lent; and

(iii) on which any repayment right is limited to such consideration or is reasonably comparable with the amount generally repayable (in respect of an equal amount of new consideration) under the terms of issue of listed securities.

As regards (i) above, rights of conversion into shares or securities of the company's quoted parent company (as above) are disregarded, as are rights of conversion into shares satisfying (*a*), (*c*) and (*d*) above, or securities satisfying (ii) and (iii) above, not themselves carrying conversion (other than into shares or securities in the quoted parent company) or acquisition rights.

A loan is not within (ii) above by reason only of the fact that:

(I) the terms of the loan provide for a reduction in the rate of interest in the event of an improvement in that business (or part) or an increase in the value of any of those assets, or for an increase in the rate of interest in the event of a deterioration in the business (or part) or a diminution in the value of any of those assets; or

(II) where the loan was to be applied in the acquisition of land other than with a view to resale at a profit (or to incidental loan costs), and was secured only on that land, the terms of the loan are such that the only way the loan creditor can enforce payment is by exercising rights granted as security over that land.

A loan on which the amount of interest depends to an extent on the results of the company's business as above, covers a **limited recourse loan**. (HMRC Company Taxation Manual, CTM 81010).

[*ICTA 1988, Sch 18 para 1(5)(5A)(5B)(8)*].

Where any person has, directly or indirectly, provided new consideration for shares or securities in the company and that person (or any person connected with him, see 19 CONNECTED PERSONS) uses in his trade assets belonging to the company which have been the subject of certain capital allowances, that person and no other is treated as an equity holder in respect of those shares or securities and as beneficially entitled to any distribution of profits or assets attributable to those shares or securities. [*ICTA 1988, Sch 18 para 1(6)*].

Where this provision applies to a bank which has provided new consideration solely by way of a normal commercial loan in the normal course of its banking business, and the cost of the assets so used is less than such new consideration, the bank is treated as a loan creditor for an amount equal to that cost and therefore as an equity holder in respect of that amount. [*ICTA 1988, Sch 18 para 1(7)*].

32.9 **Profits available for distribution** represent the total profits of the subsidiary for the 'accounting period' or, if there is no such profit, £100 (the 'profit distribution'). All payments not otherwise treated as DISTRIBUTIONS (23) are included. In the case of a non-resident company trading through a UK permanent establishment (or branch or agency) (see 32.6 above), the total profits are determined as if it were UK-resident. [*ICTA 1988, Sch 18 para 2*]. 'Profits' for this purpose are the 'commercial' distributable profits (having regard to company law requirements), rather than those computed for tax purposes (see HMRC Company Taxation Manual, CTM 81035).

The **assets available for distribution in a winding-up** comprise any excess of assets over liabilities as shown in the subsidiary's balance sheet at the end of the accounting period, or (if there is no such excess or the balance sheet is prepared to a different date) £100. Any such asset received by the equity holder on a winding-up is treated as a distribution to him, notwithstanding that it would not otherwise be so treated.

Any new consideration provided by an equity holder for its shares which is then loaned to, or used to acquire shares in, that equity holder or any person connected with it (see 19 CONNECTED PERSONS) is to be deducted from the total distributable assets and from those distributable to that equity holder. [*ICTA 1988, Sch 18 para 3*].

The percentage of the profits or assets to which an equity-holding company is, or would be, beneficially entitled includes any indirect entitlement through another body corporate. [*ICTA 1988, Sch 18 para 6*].

'*Accounting period*' means any which is current at a time relevant to the group relief claim. [*ICTA 1988, Sch 18 para 7*].

There are detailed anti-avoidance provisions relating to the calculation of the relevant percentages in relation to equity holders of shares or securities with restricted or terminable rights. [*ICTA 1988, Sch 18 paras 4, 5*]. These also require comparisons to be made between the results of various bases of calculation, in particular in relation to option arrangements (the latter in effect reversing the decision in *J Sainsbury plc v O'Connor CA 1991, 64 TC 208*). [*ICTA 1988, Sch 18 paras 5A–5F; FA 2006, Sch 1 para 6*]. See 32.19 below for HMRC's interpretation of 'option arrangements'.

32.10 **Kinds of group relief.** Group relief is available on the amounts listed below in the manner specified.

(*a*) **Trading losses** computed as under *ICTA 1988, s 393(2)* or *s 393A(1)* (see 47.2 LOSSES) except losses:

(i) from trades falling within Schedule D, Case V; and

(ii) from trades not carried on on a commercial basis and with a view to the realisation of gain (with an exception for statutory functions)(see 47.9 LOSSES); and

(iii) which are denied relief by *ICTA 1988, s 397* (see 47.14 LOSSES).

The available losses include certain 'relievable amounts' in respect of exchange losses (see 26.14 EXCHANGE GAINS AND LOSSES) for accounting periods beginning before 1 October 2002, after which time they are included within loan relationship or derivative contract debits and credits. 'Non-trading deficits' on loan relationships are also in effect treated as trading losses for these purposes (see 46.3 LOAN RELATIONSHIPS), and for accounting periods beginning on or after 1 October 2002, these include non-trading debits on derivative contracts.

(*b*) **Capital allowances** deducted from or set against income from special leasing of plant and machinery may be surrendered in so far as they exceed such income for an accounting period (before deduction of losses or capital allowances brought forward) and the machinery or plant is not used by the lessee for a non-qualifying purpose (see Note (2) under 10.37 CAPITAL ALLOWANCES). See 47.2 LOSSES.

(*c*) **Management expenses** of companies with investment business (or, for accounting periods beginning before 1 April 2004, investment companies) (not brought forward from an earlier accounting period). See 42 INVESTMENT COMPANIES AND INVESTMENT BUSINESS. This relief does not apply to life insurance companies.

(*d*) **Charges on income.**

(*e*) **Schedule A losses**, excluding losses brought forward from earlier periods and losses incurred in a Schedule A business which was not carried on either on a commercial basis or in the exercise of statutory functions (see 56 PROPERTY INCOME).

(*f*) **Non-trading losses on intangible fixed assets** (from 1 April 2002) (see 39.6 INTANGIBLE ASSETS), excluding any brought forward from an earlier accounting period.

(*g*) **Qualifying overseas losses** of non-resident companies (from 1 April 2006) (see 32.16 below).

Amounts within (*a*) and (*b*) above are eligible for surrender regardless of whether the surrendering company has other profits of the same accounting period against which they could be set. Amounts within (*c*), (*d*), (*e*) and (*f*) above are available for surrender only to the extent that, in aggregate, they exceed the surrendering company's 'gross profits' of the accounting period, any excess being taken to consist first of charges on income, then of Schedule A losses, then of management expenses and finally of non-trading losses on intangible assets. '*Gross profits*' for this purpose are profits without any deduction in respect of amounts within (*a*)-(*f*) above or of 'any losses' etc. of other periods. The term '*any losses*' for this purpose does not include capital losses brought forward from a previous period and deducted as part of the computation of chargeable gains (see 11.3 CAPITAL GAINS). (*Taylor v MEPC Holdings Ltd HL 2003, [2004] STC 123*).

The availability of group relief as above is subject to restriction in the case of dual resident investing companies (see 32.27 below), certain ring-fenced activities (see 51.3 OIL COMPANIES), certain transactions in relation to the sale of lessor companies (see 5.17 ANTI-AVOIDANCE) and certain transactions by leasing partnerships (5.16 ANTI-AVOIDANCE).

[*ICTA 1988, ss 403-403ZE; CAA 1990, s 61(7); CAA 2001, s 260(7), Sch 2 para 36; FA 2002, Sch 25 para 45, Sch 30 para 2; FA 2006, ss 82, 83, Sch 10 para 43; SI 2004 No 2310, Articles 14, 15*].

Simon's Direct Tax Service. See D2.624 *et seq.*

32.11 A '*corresponding accounting period*' is any accounting period of the claimant company which falls wholly or partly within the accounting period of the surrendering company in which the amount for which group relief is claimed arose. [*ICTA 1988, s 413(2A); F(No 2)A 1997, Sch 7 para 7*]. See previous editions of Tolley's Corporation Tax in relation to accounting periods ending before the commencement of the provisions described at 32.12 below (which apply broadly for accounting periods ending after 1 July 1997).

Simon's Direct Tax Service. See D2.632.

32.12 **Limits on group relief.** The amount for which group relief may be claimed against total profits may not exceed the lesser of

(*a*) the 'unused part of the surrenderable amount for the overlapping period', and

(*b*) the 'unrelieved part of the claimant company's total profits for the overlapping period'.

The amount referred to in (*a*) above is so much of the total amount available for surrender for the accounting period of the surrendering company as is attributable (see below) to the 'overlapping period' and has not been the subject of any prior surrenders attributable to the 'overlapping period'.

The amount referred to in (*b*) above is so much of the total profits of the claimant company for the accounting period of the claim as is attributable (see below) to the 'overlapping period', reduced by any previously claimed group relief attributable to the 'overlapping period'.

The '*overlapping period*' is the period common to the accounting periods of both the claimant company and the surrendering company to which the claim relates, but excluding any part of the common period when:

- those companies are not both members of the same group and in the case of a non-UK resident company, carrying on a UK trade through a permanent establishment (or branch or agency); or
- (from 1 April 2006), in the case of a 'qualifying overseas loss' (see 32.16 below), the surrendering company is not a member of the same group as the claimant company (as defined for this purpose in 32.7 above) and is not resident or not carrying on a trade through a permanent establishment within an EEA territory.

The amount of prior surrenders attributed to the overlapping period is determined by attributing each earlier effective surrender in respect of the accounting period in question to the overlapping period in relation to that surrender, then further attributing a part (see below) of each such amount to any period common to the overlapping periods of the earlier surrender and the surrender in question and aggregating all the amounts so attributed. The amount of previously claimed group relief attributable to the overlapping period is similarly determined.

For the above purposes the group relief allowable on any claim is determined as at the time when it becomes final (i.e. when it can no longer be withdrawn) as if every claim which had previously become final were a prior claim and every claim which has not become final were a subsequent claim. Claims which would otherwise be treated as having been made at the same time are deemed to have been made in such order as the company or companies making them elect or jointly elect, or in the absence of such an election in such order as HMRC may direct. See the example at 32.13 below.

[*ICTA 1988, s 403A; FA 2006, Sch 1 paras 2, 9*].

Attribution to overlapping periods. Where an apportionment falls to be made under *section 403A* to determine how much of an amount for a period falls to be attributed to a part of the period, the apportionment is generally made on a time basis according to how much of the whole period coincides with the part. However, where as regards some or all of the apportionments to be made in any particular case this would lead to an unjust or unreasonable result in relation to any person, the apportionments are, to the extent necessary to avoid injustice and unreasonableness, made in such other manner as may be just and reasonable. [*ICTA 1988, s 403B*]. For 'just and reasonable' apportionment, see HMRC Company Taxation Manual, CTM 80260.

De-grouping charge. See 12.32 CAPITAL GAINS—GROUPS for the effect on *ICTA 1988, ss 403A, 403B* of the application of the de-grouping provisions of *TCGA 1992, s 179*.

Consortia. The above rules apply with appropriate modifications to consortium group relief claims (see 32.23 below). Additionally the following limitations apply.

(i) Where the claimant company is a member of a consortium, the amount which may be set off against its total profits for the overlapping period is the lowest in that period of the following percentages of the surrenderable amount:

  (A) the percentage (or average percentage) of the surrendering company's ordinary share capital which is beneficially owned by the claimant company;

  (B) the percentage (or average percentage) of any profits available for distribution to the surrendering company's equity holders to which the claimant company is beneficially entitled; and

(C) the percentage (or average percentage) of any assets of the surrendering company available for distribution to its equity holders on a winding-up to which the claimant company would be beneficially entitled.

(ii) Where the surrendering company is a member of a consortium, the amount which may be set off against the total profits of the claimant company for the overlapping period is the lowest in that period of the following percentages of those total profits:

(A) the percentage (or average percentage) of the claimant company's ordinary share capital which is beneficially owned by the surrendering company;

(B) the percentage (or average percentage) of any profits available for distribution to the claimant company's equity holders to which the surrendering company is beneficially entitled; and

(C) the percentage (or average percentage) of any assets of the claimant company available for distribution to its equity holders on a winding-up to which the surrendering company would be beneficially entitled.

(iii) Where the claimant (or surrendering) company is a subsidiary of a holding company owned by a consortium, (i) (or (ii)) above applies by reference to the holding company rather than the claimant (or surrendering) company.

Terms used in (i)–(iii) are defined as above and as in 32.7-32.9 above and 32.23 below.

In determining the average percentage of a member's interest in a consortium, a weighted average taking into account the length of time involved will be used. (HMRC Company Taxation Manual, CTM 80540).

[*ICTA 1988, s 403C*].

For provisions dealing with companies joining or leaving a group prior to the commencement of the above provisions (which apply broadly for accounting periods ending after 1 July 1997), see previous editions of Tolley's Corporation Tax.

32.13 *Example*

X Ltd incurs a trading loss in the year ending 31 December 2007 of £120,000. Throughout that period, it has two wholly-owned subsidiaries Y Ltd and Z Ltd. Y Ltd prepares accounts to 31 March, and has profits of £100,000 in the year ending 31 March 2007. Z Ltd prepares accounts to 30 September and has profits of £400,000 in the year ending 30 September 2007. No group relief claims or surrenders have been made other than those referred to below.

Y Ltd claims the maximum relief for the year ending 31 March 2007 by surrender from X Ltd.

Overlapping period three months to 31 March 2007

Maximum loss available for surrender

3/12 × £120,000 = £30,000

Maximum profits against which loss surrendered may be set

3/12 × £100,000 = £25,000

Thus X Ltd surrenders losses of £25,000 to Y Ltd.

Z Ltd then claims the maximum relief for the year ending 30 September 2007 by surrender from X Ltd.

Overlapping period nine months to 30 September 2007

Maximum loss available for surrender

	£
9/12 × £120,000 =	90,000
less amount previously surrendered (note (*a*))	25,000
	£65,000

Maximum profits against which loss surrendered may be set

9/12 × £400,000 = £300,000

Thus X Ltd surrenders losses of £65,000 to Z Ltd.

The balance of X Ltd's loss (£30,000) may be surrendered against losses of subsequent periods of Y Ltd and Z Ltd.

Note

(*a*) As the overlapping period in relation to the surrender to Y Ltd falls entirely within the overlapping period in relation to the surrender to Z Ltd, the whole of the loss surrendered in relation to the earlier period is deducted from that available for the later period.

32.14 **UK losses of non-resident companies.** In relation to group relief for UK losses of non-resident companies carrying on a UK trade through a permanent establishment (or branch or agency) (see 32.6 above), relief attributable to the UK permanent establishment is broadly restricted as follows. Amounts available for surrender under these provisions, in addition to any losses or other amounts available for surrender (from 1 April 2006) by non-resident companies, are as set out under 32.16 below.

Losses, etc. available for surrender by the non-resident company for an accounting period are those attributable to activities which:

(i) are not attributable to activities which are exempt under any double taxation relief arrangements (see 24.14 DOUBLE TAX RELIEF), disregarding any claim requirement; and

(ii) are attributable to activities the income or gains from which for that period are or (if there were any) would be brought into account in computing chargeable profits for corporation tax purposes.

There is also an exclusion for any amount corresponding to, or represented by, an amount which is allowable for foreign tax purposes against any 'non-UK profits', although this does not apply to amounts which are, or are an element in computing, profits exempted from that foreign tax. 'Foreign tax' for this purpose means any tax corresponding to income or corporation tax (including local and regional taxes), and any foreign tax provision by virtue of which the deductibility of an amount is dependent on whether or not it is deductible for UK tax purposes is disregarded. '*Non-UK profits*' are amounts (or elements in computing amounts) charged to foreign tax and not included in corporation tax total profits of any person for any accounting period.

Similarly the total profits for an accounting period against which relief may be claimed by a non-resident company are restricted to amounts comprised in the company's corporation tax chargeable profits for the period and not arising from activities exempt from corporation tax under any double taxation relief arrangements (and this restriction on the scope of total profits applies also for the purposes of the definition of 'non-UK profits' as above).

For these purposes, amounts are exempt under double tax relief arrangements if their effect is to cause any income or gains arising from the activities to be disregarded in computing chargeable profits.

[*ICTA 1988, s 403D; FA 2006, Sch 1 paras 3, 9*].

For an article on *section 403D*, giving examples of how it will apply in practice to companies resident in various foreign jurisdictions, see Revenue Tax Bulletin October 2000 pp 783–785.

For Revenue acquiescence in certain group relief claims involving UK branches of EEA-resident companies for periods prior to the enactment of *section 403D*, see Revenue Tax Bulletin August 2002 p 961.

32.15 **Overseas losses of UK-resident companies.** A loss, etc. of a UK-resident company is *not* available for surrender by way of group relief if it is 'attributable' to a permanent establishment (or branch or agency) through which the company carries on a trade outside the UK, and all or any part of it is, or represents, an amount allowable against 'non-UK profits' (as above) of any other person for the purposes of foreign tax under the law of the territory where the permanent establishment (or branch or agency) is situated. This restriction does *not* apply to amounts referable to life assurance business. 'Foreign tax' for this purpose means any tax corresponding to income or corporation tax (including local and regional taxes), and where, under a foreign tax provision, the deductibility of an amount is dependent on whether or not it is deductible for UK tax purposes, it is treated as deductible for the foreign tax purposes if, and only if, the UK-resident company is treated for the purposes of that tax as also resident in the territory in which the foreign tax is charged.

A loss, etc. is 'attributable' to a permanent establishment (or branch or agency) for this purpose if it would be available for surrender by way of group relief if it were computed only by reference to that permanent establishment and by the application of the same principles as apply to a permanent establishment through which a non-UK resident company carries on a trade in the UK (as above).

[*ICTA 1988, s 403E*].

For an article on *section 403E*, giving examples of how it will apply in practice to companies resident in various foreign jurisdictions, see Revenue Tax Bulletin October 2000 pp 783–785.

Simon's Direct Tax Service. See D2.633, D2.633A, D2.633B.

32.16 **Overseas losses of non-resident companies.** In relation to group relief for a 'qualifying overseas loss' of a company resident in an EEA territory or carrying on a trade in an EEA territory through a permanent establishment (see 32.6 above), relief attributable to the non-resident company is restricted as set out below and in 32.17 below. The relief applies to accounting periods beginning on or after 1 April 2006. Accounting periods straddling 1 April 2006 are treated for this purpose as two separate periods, the amount of the claimant company's profits and the amount of the loss or other amount of the non-resident, surrendering company being apportioned to the two periods on a just and reasonable basis.

A loss or other amount is treated as a '*qualifying overseas loss*' available for surrender as group relief by the non-resident company only where all the following conditions are met in relation to the EEA territory.

(*a*) *The equivalence condition.* The amount must correspond (in all material respects) to the amount that would be available for surrender as group relief under *ICTA 1988, s 403* (see 32.10 above) if the company were resident in the UK.

(*b*) *The EEA tax loss condition.* This condition is met if the loss or other amount eligible for relief from tax under the relevant territory is calculated in accordance with the applicable rules under the law of that territory and, in the case of a non-resident company resident in any EEA territory, the amount is not attributable to a permanent establishment through which the company carries on a trade in the UK. In the case of a non-resident company that is not resident but carries on a trade through a permanent establishment in any EEA territory, the amount must not be attributable to activities which are exempt from tax under any double taxation arrangements (which would have the effect, if a claim were made, that income and gains arising from those activities are ignored in calculating the company's taxable profits, income or gains under the relevant territory).

(*c*) *The qualifying loss condition*. In the case of a non-resident company that is resident, or not resident but carrying on a trade through a permanent establishment, in any EEA territory, a loss or other amount qualifies for group relief if it cannot be given relief in any EEA territory in any period and has not been given any other qualifying relief in any other territory outside the UK. The circumstances in which an amount qualifies for relief in any EEA territory, or qualified for relief in any other territory outside the UK, is widely defined and includes amounts which can be set off against chargeable profits, income or gains arising to persons other than the non-resident company and also amounts which can be relieved by the payment of a credit, elimination or reduction of a tax liability or 'by any other means of any kind'. Whether an amount can be relieved in a future period is to be determined immediately after the end of the current period. All possible steps must be taken by the company or any other person to obtain the relief so that, effectively, the amount will not qualify for group relief if there was a way in which relief could have been obtained.

(*d*) *The precedence condition*. In the case of a non-resident company ('the relevant company') that is resident, or not resident but carrying on a trade through a permanent establishment, in any EEA territory, a loss or other amount qualifies for group relief if it cannot be relieved in any other territory outside the UK which is a qualifying territory in relation to that company. A territory is a qualifying territory in relation to the relevant company if another company resident in that territory owns (directly or indirectly) any of its ordinary share capital or if a third company resident in the UK owns (directly or indirectly) any ordinary share capital of that other company. The relevant company in this case must be a 75% of the third company or a 75% subsidiary of a fourth company resident in the UK.

Where the above conditions are met so that a loss or other amount is available for surrender by way of group relief, the following provisions apply with respect to the calculation of the loss or other amount ('the EEA amount') arising to a non-resident company ('the EEA company') in any period ('the loss period'). The EEA amount must be recalculated in accordance with applicable UK tax rules, i.e. any applicable provision made by or under the Corporation Tax Acts. The EEA amount available for surrender by way of group relief is so much of the amount meeting the above conditions that does not exceed the relevant proportion of the amount given by that recalculation. (In other words, where only a proportion of the losses are available for surrender, because some of the losses are relievable elsewhere, that proportion of the UK recomputed amount will be available for surrender.) If the amount given by that recalculation is an amount of income or profits then none of the EEA amount will be available for surrender. The Treasury is given powers to modify such provisions, by regulation, for the purpose of recalculating the EEA amount.

In recalculating the EEA amount, it is to be assumed that:

(i) the EEA company is resident in the UK throughout the loss period (this not requiring any assumption of change in the place or places in which the EEA company activities are carried out), that it becomes so resident at the beginning of the loss period but does not necessarily cease to be so resident at the end of the loss period;

(ii) any trade carried on by the EEA company in the loss period wholly or partly in the EEA territory concerned, is carried on wholly or partly in the UK, and any estate, interests or rights in or over land held by the EEA company in the EEA territory concerned, are held in the UK (domestic concepts of law in relation to land in the EEA territory to be read so as to produce the result that most closely corresponds with that for property income purposes in relation to land in the UK);

(iii) an accounting period of the EEA company begins at the beginning of the loss period and ends on the earlier of the end of the loss period or the end of twelve months from the beginning of the loss period. In the latter case, it is to be assumed that a further accounting period begins when the previous one ends and ends on the earlier of the end of the loss period or the end of twelve months from the beginning of the further accounting period; and

(iv) if the EEA company incurred any capital expenditure on the provision of plant or machinery for the purposes of any activity before the beginning of the loss period, it is treated as incurred for a non-qualifying activity and then brought into use for a qualifying activity at the beginning of the loss period under *CAA 2001, s 13* (see 10.38(E)).

[*ICTA 1988, s 403F, Sch 18A; FA 2006, Sch 1 paras 4(1), 7, 9*].

See HMRC draft guidance, published on 12 April 2006 (at www.hmrc.gov.uk/ctsa/ext_group_relief.pdf), which refers to the ECJ decision in the *Marks & Spencer* case (see 32.6 above) and details how the extension to the group relief rules work.

32.17 **Unallowable overseas losses of non-resident companies.** In the case of a non-resident company that is resident, or not resident but carrying on a trade through a permanent establishment, in any EEA territory, where a loss or other amount (as set out in 32.16 above) arising to that company is not attributable for corporation tax purposes to any UK permanent establishment, it is not available for surrender by way of group relief if:

(*a*) it qualifies for group relief or arises to the non-resident company by reason only of 'relevant arrangements'; and

(*b*) the main purpose or one of the main purposes of the relevant arrangements was to secure that the amount would qualify for group relief.

'*Relevant arrangements*' are arrangements made on or after 20 February 2006 or arrangements made before that date where the amount arises or would (but for this provision) first qualify for group relief on or before that date. '*Arrangements*' includes any agreement, understanding, scheme, transaction or series of transactions (whether or not legally enforceable) made.

[*ICTA 1988, s 403G; FA 2006, Sch 1 para 4(2)*].

32.18 **Claims.** A claim for group relief under self-assessment must be included in the company tax return (or amended return) (see 61.3, 61.8 RETURNS) for the accounting period for which the claim is made. It must specify the amount claimed (which must be expressed in money at the time the claim is made) and the surrendering company. It must also state whether any of the following:

(*a*) the claimant company;

(*b*) the surrendering company; or

(*c*) any other company by reference to which either those companies are members of the same group or the conditions for consortium relief are satisfied,

was not UK resident in either or both of the surrendering company's accounting period to which the surrender relates or the corresponding accounting period of the claimant company.

The claim must be made (and may be withdrawn) at any time up to the latest of:

(i) the first anniversary of the filing date for the company tax return;

(ii) 30 days after closure of any enquiry into that return (unless the enquiry, being otherwise out of time, was limited (see 61.12 RETURNS) to matters to which a previous amendment making or withdrawing a group relief claim relates, or which are affected by the amendment);

(iii) 30 days after notice of any amendment of that return by HMRC following such an enquiry; and

(iv) 30 days after determination of any appeal against an amendment within (iii),

or at a later time if HMRC allow it (for which see 47.2 LOSSES).

These time limits override the normal time limits for amendment of a company tax return. Withdrawals of claims must be made by amending the return, and a claim can only be amended by withdrawal and replacement by another claim.

A claim may be made after the surrendering company has left the group (*A W Chapman Ltd v Hennessey Ch D 1981, 55 TC 516*).

A claim may be made for less than the full amount available for surrender at the time of the claim, but is ineffective if it is for more than that amount. The amount available for surrender at any time is the total amount available under *ICTA 1988, s 403* (see 32.10 above) on the basis of the surrendering company's tax return, disregarding any amendment whose effect is deferred pending completion of an enquiry (see 61.12 RETURNS), *less* all amounts for which notices of consent (see below) have been given and not withdrawn. Withdrawals are given effect before any claims made on the same day. Where claims are made on the same day for an aggregate amount in excess of the amount available for surrender, HMRC determines which of the claims is to be ineffective to prevent an excess arising. In practice, they will treat as ineffective the claim(s) in the lowest amount(s) consistent with achieving this objective (see HMRC Company Taxation Manual, CTM 97015, CTM 97070).

Claims may be made by more than one company in respect of the same surrendering company accounting period. [*ICTA 1988, s 402*(*5*)].

A claim requires the written consent of the surrendering company (and a consortium claim also that of each member of the consortium), which must be given to the officer of HMRC to whom the company makes its tax returns at or before the time the claim is made, and a copy of which must accompany the claim. The consent notice must give the names and tax district references of the surrendering company and the company to which relief is being surrendered, the amount of the relief, and the surrendering company accounting period to which the surrender relates. It may not be amended, but may be withdrawn (by notice to the officer to whom the consent was notified) and replaced within the normal time limits (as above). Notice of withdrawal must be accompanied by the written consent of the claimant company, unless the withdrawal is the result of a reduction in the amount available for surrender (for which see below), and the claimant company must, so far as it may do so, amend its return accordingly.

See, however, below as regards simplified claim and surrender procedures.

Where the surrendering company has already made its return for the period to which the surrender relates, it must, at the same time as giving its consent, amend its return to reflect that consent. Where the consent relates to a trading loss for which relief has already been obtained by carry-forward, the surrendering company must (notwithstanding any time limits otherwise applicable) amend its return(s) for the subsequent period(s) in which relief was given for the loss to reflect the consent (relief for such periods being treated as given for carry-forward losses of earlier accounting periods before later ones).

Where there is a reduction in the total amount available for surrender (as above) below the amount for which consent to surrender has already been given, the company must, within 30 days, withdraw its consent (and may issue new notices of consent) so as bring the total of amounts for which consent is given within the total amount available. Copies of the withdrawal notices and any new consents must be sent to the companies affected and to HMRC. If the company fails to take such corrective action, HMRC may by written notice to the company give directions as to which consents are to be treated as reduced or eliminated to the extent necessary to achieve that objective (subject to appeal in writing by the company within 30 days of the notice to the officer by whom it was given), and must copy the notice to any claimant company affected by those directions. A claimant company notified of any withdrawal or new consent or HMRC direction must, so far as it may do so, amend its return for the period in question accordingly.

Where a claimant company becomes liable to tax in consequence of receiving a notice of withdrawal or new consent or HMRC direction (as above), and any of the tax is unpaid six months after the company's 'time limit for claims' (see below), HMRC may, up to two years after that time limit, make an assessment in the name of the claimant company on any other company which has obtained group relief as a result of the surrender. The amount of the assessment is limited to the lesser of the amount of the unpaid tax and the amount of tax the other company saves by virtue of the surrender. The other company may recover the tax (and any interest thereon) from the claimant company. The company's 'time limit for claims' for this purpose is the latest of the dates in (i)–(iv) above on which the company could make or withdraw a group relief claim for the accounting period for which the claim in question was made.

An assessment may be made to recover group relief which in the opinion of HMRC is or has become excessive. This is without prejudice to the making of a discovery assessment (see 7.2 ASSESSMENTS) or to the making of adjustments by way of discharge or repayment of tax. As regards notices of assessment, time limits and appeals, the same conditions apply as in relation to discovery assessments. Where a claimant company fails, or is unable, to amend its return following receipt of a notice of withdrawal or new consent or HMRC direction (as above), an assessment may be made (if otherwise out of time) up to one year after the date of the notice (the date of the new notice if a new notice of consent follows a withdrawal notice).

Simplified arrangements. The *Corporation Tax (Simplified Arrangements for Group Relief) Regulations 1999 (SI 1999 No 2975)*(as amended) provide for a group of companies all, or substantially all, of whose tax returns are made to the same tax office to enter into special arrangements enabling an authorised company within the group to act for the group in relation to group relief claims. The authorised company may then, in a form provided or authorised by HMRC, provide a written statement containing the information necessary for the amendment of company tax returns of the companies covered by the arrangements for the purpose of making or withdrawing group relief claims and surrenders. Group companies are liable for any incorrect claim or return arising from the authorised company's statement. Consortium companies which can claim or surrender group relief may be included in the arrangements (and the authorised company may be a consortium company). For the detailed requirements as to the making of an application by an authorised company, and the consequences of entering into such arrangements, see *SI 1999 No 2975* (as amended) and HMRC Company Taxation Manual, CTM 97600 onwards. Note that it is not necessary for all the companies included in the arrangements to have identical accounting periods.

Overseas losses of non-resident companies. The above provisions apply to claims (from 1 April 2006) in respect of overseas losses of non-resident companies (see 32.6(*b*) and 32.16 above) with the following modifications. References to the relief being surrendered is to the EEA amount. References to the surrendering company's accounting period are to its deemed accounting period under 32.16(iii) above. Notice of consent of the surrendering company is to be given by the claimant company to the officer of HMRC to whom that company makes its returns and the requirement for the notice to contain details of tax district reference does not apply. Notice of withdrawal of consent is to be given by the claimant company and not the surrendering company. A notice of withdrawal and any new notice of consent under *FA 1998, Sch 18 para 75* (reduction in amount available for surrender) is to be sent to an officer of HMRC by the claimant rather than the surrendering company and any notice containing directions by an officer of HMRC is to be given to the claimant company. The claimant company rather than the surrendering company can appeal against such directions and the rest of *Sch 18* is to be similarly read with appropriate modifications.

Where a notice to produce documents is given to the claimant company for the purposes of an enquiry, the notice may require the claimant company to explain why the EEA amount meets the conditions for it to be treated as a qualifying loss and to provide details of the recalculation required (see 32.16 above). The claimant company may also be required to explain why the EEA amount is not prevented from being surrendered by virtue of the unallowable losses provision in 32.17 above.

[*FA 1998, Sch 18 paras 66–77A; FA 2006, Sch 1 para 8*].

A claim may be made after the surrendering company has left the group (*A W Chapman Ltd v Hennessey Ch D 1981, 55 TC 516*).

See 32.10 above as regards amounts available for relief.

Simon's Direct Tax Service. See **D2.630, D2.630A**.

32.19 **Arrangements for transfer of company to another group or consortium.** Relief is denied where two companies are members of a group and 'arrangements' are in existence by virtue of which one company could leave the group and join another group, or any person could gain control of one company but not the other, or a third company could succeed to the trade of one of the companies. Similar restrictions apply to consortium relief. [*ICTA 1988, s 410*]. (See Revenue Tax Bulletin December 1996 pp 372, 373 for application of the decision in *Steele v EVC International NV* (see 19.6 CONNECTED PERSONS) in relation to consortium 'arrangements', the effect of which was subsequently reversed by legislation.)

'*Arrangements*' for this purpose are those in existence during the relevant period irrespective of when they came into existence (*Pilkington Bros Ltd v CIR HL 1982, 55 TC 705*) and without regard to the extent of their implementation (*Irving v Tesco Stores (Holdings) Ltd Ch D 1982, 58 TC 1*). Arrangements which could not legally be carried out without variation of the underlying agreement were ineffective for these purposes (*Scottish and Universal Newspapers Ltd v Fisher (Sp C 87), [1996] SSCD 311*). The restriction of relief applies only to accounting periods or parts thereof during which the arrangements subsisted (*Shepherd v Law Land plc Ch D 1990, 63 TC 692*).

If the inspector 'has reason to believe' that 'arrangements' may exist or may have existed at any time material to the claim, he may require either company, in writing, to supply, within 30 days or such longer period as he may allow, a written declaration that such arrangements did not exist at any material time, and/or such information as he may reasonably require to satisfy himself whether such arrangements existed at any material time. [*FA 1973, s 32(1)(3)*].

'Arrangements' (and 'option arrangements', see 32.9 above) are the subject of HMRC practice and concession (see HMRC Statement of Practice, SP 3/93 and HMRC Extra-Statutory Concession C10 as revised). Under these, the special rules relating to 'arrangements' are not applied to the following.

(I) Certain types of agreement regulating the affairs of companies which hold shares or securities in a commercial joint venture company, under which those shares or securities could be transferred following certain triggering events, until such a triggering event occurs. Such agreements will be of a kind under which remaining members are allowed or required to acquire the holding of a departing company, or a departing company is allowed or required to transfer its holding to remaining members. For detailed guidance on the manner in which shares will be transferred under such an agreement, and of the triggering events which may apply, see HMRC Extra-Statutory Concession C10 as revised.

(II) The use of shares or securities as security for a loan, e.g. a mortgage. The mortgage etc. will not constitute 'arrangements' until an event occurs which allows the mortgagee to exercise his rights against the mortgagor, provided that, prior to the occurrence of such an event, the mortgagee possesses only such control over the shares etc.

as is required to protect his interest. If a default is remedied before the mortgagee exercises his rights, the default will not be regarded as having brought 'arrangements' into existence.

(III) Straightforward negotiations for the disposal of shares or securities in a company, before the point at which an offer is accepted subject to contract or on a similar conditional basis.

(IV) An offer to the public at large of shares in a business, unless there are exceptional features.

(V) Operations leading towards the disposal of shares or securities in a company, until any necessary approval by shareholders has been given, or the company's directors become aware that it will be given.

(VI) Where, following negotiations with a number of potential purchasers, the vendor concentrates on one, unless there were an understanding between them in the character of an option, e.g. if the offer, whether or not formally made, were allowed to remain open for an appreciable period, allowing the potential purchaser to choose the moment to create a bargain.

(VII) Company reconstructions requiring the approval of shareholders, until the necessary approval is given or the directors are aware that it will be given.

(I) and (II) above do not apply where the person standing to acquire shares, securities or control could (alone or with CONNECTED PERSONS (19)) dictate the terms or timing of the acquisition in advance of the triggering event. Membership of the joint venture company will not of itself result in members being 'connected'.

'Arrangements' (but not 'option arrangements') may exist even though not enforceable. If an agreement provides for the creation of specified option rights exerciseable at some future time, 'option arrangements' come into existence when the agreement is entered into.

(HMRC Statement of Practice, SP 3/93 and HMRC Extra-Statutory Concession C10 as revised). (SP 3/93 supersedes SP 5/80, published on 26 March 1980, but states that, although some features of SP 5/80 are omitted or revised, 'this does not indicate a more restrictive approach on the part of the Inland Revenue'.)

The power of a Minister to direct a statutory body as to the disposal of its (or any subsidiary's) assets is not an arrangement for this purpose. [*ICTA 1988, s 410*(*7*)].

See also HMRC Company Taxation Manual, CTM 80175–CTM 80205.

Simon's Direct Tax Service See D2.638.

32.20 **Payment for group relief.** If, in pursuance of an agreement between them, the claimant company reimburses the surrendering company by paying it an amount equal to, or less than, the relief surrendered by it as above, that payment is ignored in the corporation tax computations of both payer and payee and is not treated as a distribution or (for payments before 16 March 2005) a charge on income (see 55.4 PROFIT COMPUTATIONS). [*ICTA 1988, s 402*(*6*)*; F*(*No 2*)*A 2005, s 38, Sch 11 Pt 2*(*7*)].

32.21 **Other limitations on relief.** Relief may not be given more than once in respect of the same amount. [*ICTA 1988, s 411*(*1*)].

In the case where it is discovered that too much relief has been given, see 32.18 above.

See also 32.10 above.

32.22 **Relationship to other reliefs.** Group relief is deducted from the claimant company's total profits (see 32.10 above) before reduction by any 'relief derived from a subsequent accounting period', but as reduced by any other relief from tax (including relief in respect of charges on income under *ICTA 1988, s 338* or in respect of non-trading deficits on loan relationships (see 46.3 LOAN RELATIONSHIPS). Total profits for this purpose are calculated on the assumption that that company makes all relevant claims to set trading losses and capital allowances against total profits under *ICTA 1988, s 393A(1)* and *CAA 2001, s 260(3)* (or *CAA 1990, s 145(3)*) respectively. See 47.2 LOSSES and 10.2 CAPITAL ALLOWANCES.

'*Relief derived from a subsequent accounting period*' means trading losses carried back under *ICTA 1988, s 393A(1)(b)*, capital allowances carried back under *CAA 2001, s 260(3)* (or *CAA 1990, s 145(3)*), and non-trading deficits carried back under *FA 1996, s 83(2)* (see 46.3 LOAN RELATIONSHIPS). [*ICTA 1988, s 407; CAA 2001, Sch 2 para 37*].

Example

A Ltd (a group member) has the following, for the accounting periods shown.

	To 31 December 2006	To 31 December 2007
Case I (loss) brought forward	(£500)	—
Case I income/(loss)	£1,000	(£1,000)
Case III income	£500	£500
Charges paid	(£200)	(£200)

Group relief available to A Ltd will be subject to the following options and restrictions.

(*a*) *For the accounting period ended 31 December 2006*

(i) The loss brought forward and the charges paid must be relieved in priority to group relief. The maximum amount of group relief claimable will accordingly be the amount of profits on which corporation tax would otherwise be borne, i.e. £800.

(ii) If relief for this period is claimed under *section 393A(1)* for so much of the trading loss of the following period as cannot be relieved in that period, i.e. £500, such relief would be displaced by a group relief claim, and would then be available for carrying forward.

(*b*) *For the accounting period ending 31 December 2007*

Whether or not the company claims relief under *section 393A(1)*, no group relief is obtainable.

Simon's Direct Tax Service. See **D2.634.**

32.23 **Consortia.** Group relief is available where either the surrendering company or the claimant company is a member of a consortium and the other company is

(*a*) a 'trading company' which is 'owned by the consortium' and which is not a 75% subsidiary (see 32.7 above) of any company, or

(*b*) a trading company which

(i) is a '90% subsidiary' of a 'holding company' which is owned by the consortium, and

(ii) is not a 75% subsidiary of any other company, or

(*c*) a holding company which is owned by the consortium and which is not a 75% subsidiary of any company.

[*ICTA 1988, s 402(3)*].

No claim may be made where the shares in the other company (or its holding company) are held by the member of the consortium as trading stock. [*ICTA 1988, s 402(4)*]. The residence of the companies is not relevant in determining whether the consortium relationship requirement is satisfied (and see further below), although the claimant and surrendering companies must each either be resident in the UK or carry on a UK trade through a permanent establishment (or branch or agency). [*ICTA 1988, s 402(3A)(3B); FA 2000, Sch 27 paras 1, 2, 6(1); FA 2006, Sch 1 para 1(4)*]. (Before 1 April 2000, the companies had to be UK-resident or resident elsewhere in the European Union or European Economic Area (following the ECJ decision in *ICI plc v Colmer*, see below).)

Relief is restricted, where the claimant company is the consortium member, to the proportion of the surrendering company's losses, etc. corresponding to the consortium member's share in the consortium; and where the surrendering company is the consortium member, to the relief of the proportion of the claimant company's profits corresponding to the consortium member's share in the consortium. This provision ceases, however, to have effect following the introduction of the provisions described at 32.12 above. [*ICTA 1988, s 403(9)*].

Relief may also be restricted by reference to the surrendering company's losses, and the claimant company's profits, of the corresponding accounting period (see 32.11 above).

With effect for accounting periods beginning *on or after 1 October 2002*, relief may also be restricted where a company which is a consortium member claims consortium group relief and also claims bad debt relief in respect of a loan to the consortium company. In those circumstances, the combined relief is limited, on a cumulative group-wide basis, to the greater of the claims for bad debt relief and group relief respectively (see 46.11 LOAN RELATIONSHIPS). [*FA 1996, Sch 9 para 5A*; *FA 2002, Sch 25 para 23*].

See also 59.6 RESEARCH AND DEVELOPMENT EXPENDITURE for a restriction on surrendering losses by a small or medium-sized company which is owned by a consortium and is entitled to research and development relief.

A '*holding company*' is a company the business of which consists wholly or mainly in the holding of shares or securities in trading companies which are its 90% subsidiaries. [*ICTA 1988, s 413(3)*]. A single subsidiary will constitute its parent a holding company. (ICAEW Technical Release TAX 15/92, 23 October 1992, para 3). Prior to *FA 2000*, the group relief rules applied only to UK-resident companies. The House of Lords held in *ICI plc v Colmer HL, [1996] STC 352* that the UK legislation clearly required the subsidiaries to be considered to be UK-resident for this purpose, but on a reference to the European Court of Justice (*[1998] STC 874*) it was held that, in relation to EU subsidiaries, this requirement was incompatible with Community law. Following the ECJ decision, the House of Lords reconsidered and affirmed its decision in relation to companies resident outside the EU and EEA (*[1999] STC 1089*). (See HMRC Company Taxation Manual, CTM 80300–CTM 80370 regarding international groups and changes made by *FA 2000*.)

A '*trading company*' is a company the business of which consists wholly or mainly of the carrying on of a trade or trades. [*ICTA 1988, s 413(3)*].

A company is '*owned by a consortium*' if at least 75% of its 'ordinary share capital' is directly and beneficially owned amongst them by companies each owning at least one-twentieth, which are the 'members of the consortium'. [*ICTA 1988, s 413(6)*]. For this purpose, '*ordinary share capital*' means all the issued share capital of a company other than shares carrying a fixed rate of dividend with no further right to participate in profits. 'Issued share capital' does not include founder members' deposits in a company limited by guarantee (*South Shore Mutual Insurance Co Ltd v Blair (Sp C 215), 1999 STI 1681*).

A company is the '*90% subsidiary*' of another if not less than 90% of its ordinary share capital is **directly** owned by that other. [*ICTA 1988, s 838*]. The definition of 'ordinary share capital' given above applies. The parent company must also be beneficially entitled to at least 90% of profits available for distribution to the equity holders as such of the subsidiary and of assets similarly available in a winding-up. [*ICTA 1988, s 413(7)*]. See

32.8–32.9 above, and note that a holder of 'ordinary share capital' of a company may not qualify as an 'equity holder', for which a different definition of 'ordinary shares' applies. [*ICTA 1988, s 832(1), Sch 18*].

For the definition of a 75% subsidiary, see 32.7 above.

A claim for group relief requires the consent of all other members of the consortium. [*ICTA 1988, Sch 17A para 10(2); FA 1998, Sch 18 para 70(2)*].

Simon's Direct Tax Service. See **D2.622.**

32.24 *Examples*

(*A*) *Loss by company owned by consortium*

On 1 April 2007 the share capital of E Ltd was owned as follows.

	%
A Ltd	40
B Ltd	40
C Ltd	20
	100

All the companies were UK resident for tax purposes.

During the year ended 31 March 2008 the following events took place.

On 1.7.07 D Ltd bought 20% from A Ltd

On 1.10.07 C Ltd bought 10% from B Ltd

The companies had the following results for the year ended 31 March 2008.

		£
A Ltd	Profit	40,000
B Ltd	Profit	33,000
C Ltd	Profit	10,000
D Ltd	Profit	70,000
E Ltd	Loss	(100,000)

Consortium relief for the loss sustained by E Ltd would be available as follows.

	A Ltd	B Ltd	C Ltd	D Ltd
	£	£	£	£
Profits for the year ended 31.3.08	40,000	33,000	10,000	70,000
Deduct Loss surrendered by E Ltd	(25,000)	(33,000)	(10,000)	(15,000)
Chargeable profits	£15,000	—	—	£55,000

E Ltd

		Losses
	£	£
Loss for the year ended 31.3.08		100,000
Deduct Loss surrendered to A Ltd	(25,000)	
B Ltd	(33,000)	
C Ltd	(10,000)	
D Ltd	(15,000)	(83,000)
Not available for consortium relief		£17,000

Notes

(*a*) Loss relief for each member of the consortium is the lower of its share of the loss and its own profit for the overlapping period.

(*b*) The share of losses of E Ltd appropriate to each member is:

		%	£
A Ltd	40% × 3/12 + 20% × 9/12	25	25,000
B Ltd	40% × 6/12 + 30% × 6/12	35	35,000
C Ltd	20% × 6/12 + 30% × 6/12	25	25,000
D Ltd	20% × 9/12	15	15,000
		100	£100,000

(*B*) *Loss by consortium member*

A Ltd, B Ltd, C Ltd and D Ltd have for many years held 40%, 30%, 20% and 10% respectively of the ordinary share capital of E Ltd. All five companies are UK resident and have always previously had taxable profits. However, for the year ended 30 June 2006 D Ltd has a tax loss of £100,000, followed by taxable profits of £40,000 for the subsequent year. E Ltd's taxable profits are £80,000 and £140,000 for the two years ending 31 December 2006 and 31 December 2007 respectively.

With the consent of A Ltd, B Ltd and C Ltd, D Ltd can (if it wishes) surrender the following part of its loss of £100,000 to E Ltd.

	£
Common period 1.7.06 to 31.12.06	
E Ltd's profit 6/12 × £80,000 × 1/10	4,000
D Ltd's loss 6/12 × £100,000	(50,000)
Common period 1.1.07 to 30.6.07	
E Ltd's profit 6/12 × £140,000 × 1/10	7,000
D Ltd's loss 6/12 × £100,000	(50,000)

The lower common figures for the two periods are £4,000 and £7,000.

Therefore, E Ltd can claim £4,000 of D Ltd's loss against its own profits for the year ended 31.12.06 and £7,000 against its profits for the year ending 31.12.07.

32.25 **Group/consortium relief interaction.** Special provisions apply where both consortium group relief ('consortium relief') (see 32.23 above) and other group relief ('group relief') (see 32.6 *et seq.* above) may be claimed in respect of the same losses, etc., i.e. where either the member of a consortium or a company owned by a consortium is a member of a group, or both are members of separate groups. Restrictions apply to the consortium relief available as follows.

Company owned by consortium also a member of a group.

(i) Consortium relief is available to members of the consortium in respect of losses, etc. of the company owned by the consortium only after deduction of all possible group relief claims thereon (but taking into account any claims made by group companies in respect of other losses within the group).

(ii) The profits of the company owned by the consortium against which (or against a fraction of which) relief for losses, etc. of members of the consortium may be claimed are first reduced by any group relief claims it could make in respect of losses, etc. of other companies in the group (but taking into account any claims made by other group companies in respect of such losses).

Member of consortium also a member of a group (referred to as the 'link company').

(*a*) Any consortium relief claim the link company could make (disregarding any deficiency of profits) may be made by any other company in the group (provided that it is not itself a member of the consortium). The provisions at 32.12 above (which limit relief by reference to overlapping periods of the claimant and surrendering companies) apply as if any period during which the claimant company was not a group member were not comprised in the overlapping period and were a part of the claimant company's accounting period which did not coincide with any part of the surrendering company's accounting period. The total consortium relief of the link company and other companies in the same group may not exceed that claimable by the link company (but disregarding any deficiency of profits in the link company).

(*b*) Consortium relief may be claimed by a company owned by the consortium in respect of losses, etc. of members of the same group as the link company, which are not themselves members of the consortium, as if the surrendering company were a member of the consortium at all times at which the link company is a member. The fraction of the profits against which the losses, etc. may be claimed is determined by reference to the consortium member's share in the claimant company in the surrendering company's overlapping period of loss, etc. The provisions at 32.12 above (which limit relief by reference to overlapping periods of the claimant and surrendering companies) apply as if any period during which the surrendering company was not a group member were not comprised in the overlapping period and were a part of the claimant company's accounting period which did not coincide with any part of the surrendering company's accounting period. The total relief which may be claimed by the company owned by the consortium in an accounting period from the link company and other members of the same group may not exceed what it could have claimed from the link company if the link company's accounting period was the same as that of the company owned by the consortium.

Where a *company owned by a consortium* has trading losses and other profits against which the losses could be set under *ICTA 1988, s 393(2)* or *s 393A(1)* (see 47.2 LOSSES), the losses, etc. available for consortium relief are reduced by the amount of any such set-off which could be claimed. This operates in priority to (i) above where applicable.

Companies joining or leaving a consortium. See previous editions of Tolley's Corporation Tax for the provisions applying to companies joining or leaving a consortium prior to the introduction of the wider anti-avoidance provisions in *ICTA 1988, ss 403A–403C* by *F(No 2)A 1997, Sch 7* (for which see 32.12 above), which apply broadly to accounting periods ending after 1 July 1997.

[*ICTA 1988, s 403ZA(3)(4), s 405, s 406*].

Simon's Direct Tax Service. See D2.634.

32.26 *Example*

A Ltd owns 100% of the share capital of B Ltd

B Ltd owns 40% of the share capital of D Ltd

C Ltd owns 60% of the share capital of D Ltd

D Ltd owns 100% of the share capital of E Ltd

D Ltd owns 100% of the share capital of F Ltd

This can be shown as follows.

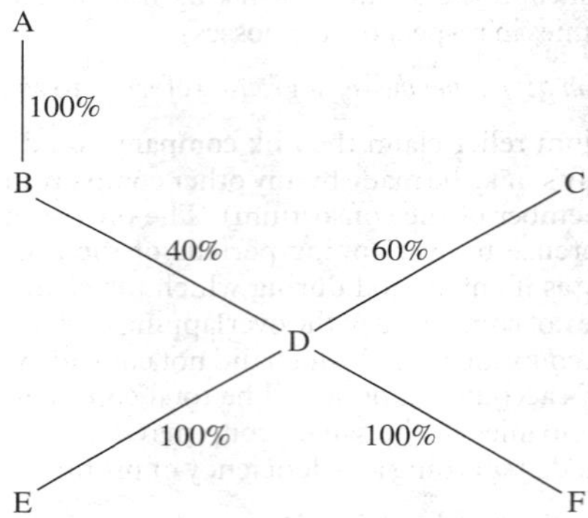

There are two groups, A and B, and D, E and F. D is owned by a consortium of B and C. This relationship has existed for a number of years with all companies having the same accounting periods. None of the companies has any losses brought forward.

The companies have the following results for year ended 31 July 2007.

A Ltd	£100,000	profit
B Ltd	£(30,000)	loss
C Ltd	£Nil	
D Ltd	£(20,000)	loss
E Ltd	£10,000	profit
F Ltd	£(3,000)	loss

E Ltd claims group relief as follows.

		£	£
Profit			10,000
Deduct Group relief: loss surrendered by F Ltd	note (*a*)	3,000	
Group relief: loss surrendered by D Ltd	note (*a*)	7,000	(10,000)
			—

A Ltd can claim group relief and consortium relief as follows.

		£	£
Profit			100,000
Deduct Group relief: loss surrendered by B Ltd	note (*b*)	30,000	
Consortium relief: loss surrendered by D Ltd	note (*c*)	5,200	(35,200)
Chargeable profit			£64,800

Notes

(*a*) Where a loss of a company owned by a consortium or of a company within its group may be used both as group relief and consortium relief, group relief claims take priority. In determining the consortium relief available, it is assumed that the maximum possible group relief is claimed after taking account of any other actual group relief claims within the consortium-owned company's group. As F Ltd has surrendered losses of £3,000 to E Ltd, D Ltd can only surrender £7,000 to E Ltd. Consortium relief is restricted to the balance of D Ltd's loss, i.e. £13,000. If E Ltd had not claimed £3,000 group relief for F Ltd's loss, D Ltd could have surrendered £10,000 to E Ltd by way of group relief and this would have reduced D Ltd's loss for consortium relief purposes to £10,000.

(*b*) Group relief available to A Ltd is the lower of £100,000 and £30,000.

(*c*) Consortium relief available to A Ltd is the lower of £70,000 (its profit as reduced by group relief) and £5,200 (40% of £13,000, see note (*a*) above). The relief available to A Ltd is the same as that which B Ltd could have claimed if it had had sufficient profits. A Ltd could also have claimed consortium relief in respect of F Ltd's loss if that had exceeded the £10,000 necessary to cover E Ltd's profit.

32.27 **Dual resident investing companies.** Group relief is not available for a loss, etc. of the company which would otherwise have been the surrendering company, if that company is a 'dual resident investing company'.

A UK resident company is a '*dual resident company*' if it is within the charge to tax under the laws of a territory outside the UK, whether it derives its company status under those laws, or because its place of management is in that territory, or because it is for any other reason regarded as resident in that territory, for the purposes of that charge. A dual resident company is a '*dual resident investing company*' in an accounting period if either:

(*a*) throughout that period it is not a '*trading company*', i.e. a company whose business consists wholly or mainly of the carrying on of a trade or trades; or

(*b*) although it is a trading company in that period, either:

(i) it carries on in that period a trade of which a main function is:

(A) acquiring and holding, directly or indirectly, investments of any kind, including interests in companies which are CONNECTED PERSONS (19) within *ICTA 1988, s 839*; or

(B) paying charges on income; or

(C) making payments similar to charges but which are deductible in computing its profits; or

(D) making payments in relation to which debits fall to be brought into account under the LOAN RELATIONSHIPS (46) provisions as regards loan relationships; or

(E) obtaining funds in connection with any activity within (A)–(D) above; or

(ii) although not within (i) above, it carries on any of the activities within (i)(A)–(E) above:

(A) to an extent which does not appear justified by any trade which it does carry on; or

(B) for a purpose which does not appear to be appropriate to any such trade.

[*ICTA 1988, s 404; SI 2004 No 2310, Article 16*].

Certain capital allowance restrictions apply to transactions between CONNECTED PERSONS (19) one of which is a dual resident investing company, as above. See also 10.38(C) CAPITAL ALLOWANCES, 12.2, 12.29 CAPITAL GAINS—GROUPS, and 47.10 LOSSES.

Simon's Direct Tax Service. See D4.133.

32.28 **ARRANGEMENTS FOR PAYMENT OF TAX**

HMRC may enter into arrangements with some or all of the members of a group of companies for one of those members to discharge the liabilities of each of those members to pay corporation tax for the accounting period(s) to which the arrangements relate. The arrangements may also cover interest and penalties and certain amounts treated as corporation tax liabilities. They do not affect the liability of any company to which the arrangements relate. A 'group' for this purpose is a company and all its 51% subsidiaries (i.e. companies more than 50% of whose ordinary share capital it beneficially owns, either directly or indirectly), together with 51% subsidiaries of those subsidiaries and so on. [*FA 1998, s 36*].

See 53.2 PAYMENT OF TAX for the detailed arrangements.

Simon's Direct Tax Service. See D2.821.

32.29 **SURRENDER OF TAX REFUND, ETC. WITHIN GROUP**

Where two companies within a group jointly give notice to the inspector, a 'tax refund relating to an accounting period' which falls to be made to one of them may be surrendered in whole or part to the other. The surrendering company is then treated as having received on the 'relevant date' a payment equal to the refund (or part), and the recipient company as having paid on that date corporation tax equal to the amount of the refund (or part) (except that in relation to tax-based penalties under *TMA 1970, s 94(6)* or *FA 1998, Sch 18 para 18* for excessive delay in rendering corporation tax returns (see 54.4 PENALTIES, 61.6 RETURNS) the corporation tax is treated as having been paid on the date of the notice referred to above). If the refund is of corporation tax and interest relating to that tax has been paid by the surrendering company, it is treated as having been paid by the recipient company. The notice referred to above must be given before the refund is made to the surrendering company.

Where the repayment to the surrendering company would have arisen from the carry-back of surplus ACT or losses or exchange losses, so that interest on tax repaid to the surrendering company would have been restricted (see 40.1 INTEREST ON OVERPAID TAX), a corresponding restriction applies in relation to the deemed payment by the claimant company.

The surrendering company accounting period to which the refund relates (the '*relevant accounting period*') must also be an accounting period of the recipient company. Both companies must be members of the group from the beginning of the relevant accounting period until the date of the notice referred to above.

A '*tax refund relating to an accounting period*' for these purposes means a repayment of corporation tax for the period, a repayment of income tax in respect of a payment received in the period, or a payment of the tax credit comprised in franked investment income received in the period. It also includes repayments of instalment payments (see 53.2 PAYMENT OF TAX).

The '*relevant date*' is the date on which corporation tax for the relevant accounting period became due and payable or, if later and if the refund is of corporation tax, the date on which the corporation tax was paid.

Any agreed payment by the recipient company to the surrendering company for a surrender as above (not exceeding the amount of the refund) is disregarded for tax purposes.

[*FA 1989, s 102*].

For the effect on these provisions of group payment arrangements (see 53.2 PAYMENT OF TAX), see Revenue Tax Bulletin April 2001 pp 834, 835 and also HMRC Company Taxation Manual, CTM 97400 *et seq.*

Simon's Direct Tax Service. See **D2.706A**.

32.30 *Example*

V Ltd has had, for some years, a 75% subsidiary, W Ltd, and both prepare accounts to 30 April. On 1 February 2007 (the due date), both companies make payments on account of their CT liabilities for the year ended 30 April 2006. V Ltd pays £250,000 and W Ltd pays £150,000. In January 2008, the liabilities are eventually agreed at £200,000 and £180,000 respectively. Before any tax repayment is made to V Ltd, the two companies jointly give notice that £30,000 of the £50,000 tax repayment due to V Ltd is to be surrendered to W Ltd. W Ltd makes a payment of £20,000 to V Ltd in consideration for the tax refund surrendered.

It is assumed for illustrative purposes that the rates of interest on overdue tax and overpaid tax are, respectively, 6.5% and 3% throughout.

If no surrender had been made, and all outstanding tax payments/repayments made on, say, 1 February 2008, the interest position would have been as follows.

		£
V Ltd		
Interest on CT repayment of £50,000 for the period 1.2.07 to 1.2.08	£50,000 × 3% =	1,500
W Ltd		
Interest on late paid CT of £30,000 for the period 1.2.07 to 1.2.08	£30,000 × 6.5% =	1,950
Net interest payable by the group		£450

The surrender has the following consequences.

(i) Only £20,000 of the repayment (the unsurrendered amount) is actually made, and is made to V Ltd together with interest of £600 (at 3% for one year).

(ii) V Ltd, the surrendering company, is treated as having received a CT repayment of £30,000 (the surrendered amount) on the 'relevant date' which in this case is the normal due date of 1.2.07, V Ltd having made its CT payment on time. V Ltd is thus not entitled to any interest on this amount.

(iii) W Ltd, the recipient company, is deemed to have paid CT of £30,000 on the 'relevant date', 1.2.07 as above. It thus incurs no interest charge.

(iv) The group has turned a net interest charge of £450 into a net interest receipt of £600, a saving of £1,050. This arises from the differential in the rates of interest charged on unpaid and overpaid tax. (The surrendered amount £30,000 × 3.5% (6.5 – 3) × 1 year = £1,050.)

(v) The payment of £20,000 by W Ltd to V Ltd, not being a payment in excess of the surrendered refund, has no tax effect on either company.

V Ltd could have given notice to surrender its full refund of £50,000 to W Ltd, instead of just £30,000. There would, in fact, have been no point in doing so, but if W Ltd had made its original CT payment later than the due date, so as to incur an interest charge on the £150,000 originally paid, a full surrender would have produced a saving as the amount surrendered would be treated as having been paid on the due date.

32.31 **DEMERGERS**

The provisions in *ICTA 1988, ss 213–218* are intended to facilitate the breaking-up of large companies and groups of companies by exempting certain distributions of assets from the normal tax treatment (see 23 DISTRIBUTIONS). General enquiries concerning the demerger legislation should be addressed to HMRC, Clearance and Counteraction Team, First Floor, 22 Kingsway, London WC2B 6NR. Market sensitive issues should be address to Eric Gardner and non-sensitive issues to Mohini Sawhney.

Simon's Direct Tax Service. See D1.5.

32.32 **Exempt distributions.** Subject to 32.35 below, the following are exempt distributions provided that they would otherwise have been distributions under the *Corporation Tax Acts* (see 23 DISTRIBUTIONS). (HMRC Statement of Practice, SP 13/80 as revised).

(*a*) The transfer to all or any of its 'members' by a company ('the distributing company') of 'shares' in a '75% subsidiary' which:

(i) are irredeemable; and

(ii) constitute the whole or 'substantially the whole' of the distributing company's holding of the subsidiary's 'ordinary share capital'; and

(iii) confer the whole or 'substantially the whole' of the distributing company's voting rights in the subsidiary.

(*b*) The transfer by the distributing company to another company or companies of:

(i) a 'trade' or trades (provided that no, or only a minor, interest in any such trade is retained); or

(ii) shares in one or more of its 75% subsidiaries. (In this case, the shares may be redeemable, but must otherwise meet the requirements set out in (*a*) above.)

To qualify for exemption, the transfer must be coupled with the issue by the transferee company (or companies) to all or any of the members of the distributing company of shares which:

(A) are irredeemable; and

(B) constitute the whole or 'substantially the whole' of the transferee company's issued ordinary share capital; and

(C) confer the whole or 'substantially the whole' of the voting rights in that company.

The carrying on of the transferred trade or trades or the holding of the transferred shares must constitute the only or main activity of each and every transferee company after the distribution. This is not construed as meaning 'for ever after', but an intention that the conditions should cease to be satisfied at some later time would require consideration under the anti-avoidance provisions (see below). (HMRC Statement of Practice, SP 13/80 as revised).

The distribution must be made wholly or mainly for the purpose of benefiting some or all of the 'trading activities' which before the distribution are carried on by a single company or 'group' and after the distribution will be carried on by two or more companies or groups. A distribution cannot be exempt if it forms part of a scheme or arrangements the main purpose or one of the main purposes of which is:

(1) the avoidance of tax (including stamp duty or stamp duty land tax); or

(2) the making of a 'chargeable payment' (see 32.35 below) (or what would be a chargeable payment if any of the companies were an unquoted company); or

(3) the acquisition (other than by members of the distributing company) of 'control' of that or of any other 'relevant company' or of any company in the same group as a relevant company; or

(4) the cessation of a trade; or

(5) the sale of a trade after the distribution.

[*ICTA 1988, s 213(1)–(11), s 218(1); FA 2003, Sch 18 para 3(3)*].

HMRC's interpretation of several of these requirements is contained in HMRC Statement of Practice, SP 13/80 as revised. In brief:

(i) the question of whether what is transferred constitutes a trade is considered from the transferee's point of view, and without regard to minor assets linked with trading assets. Whether only a part of the transferor's trade, or merely some of his assets, are transferred is not conclusive;

(ii) a 'minor interest in a trade' means around 10% or less, and does not include indirect involvement conferring no measure of control;

(iii) 'substantially the whole' means 90% or more;

(iv) the concurrent transfer of ordinary share capital to ordinary shareholders for consideration, or to preference shareholders, or of other shares or securities to ordinary shareholders, does not prevent relief being given under these provisions;

(v) 'after' in (5) means 'at any time after'.

For the treatment for income and capital gains tax purposes of trustees and beneficiaries where the trustees hold shares in a company which carries out an exempt distribution, see Revenue Tax Bulletin October 1994 pp 162–165 and HMRC Capital Gains Tax Manual, CG 33900 *et seq.*

Simon's Direct Tax Service. See **D1.502**.

32.33 *Definitions.* The '*distributing company*' must at the time of the distribution be a 'trading company' or a 'member of a trading group' and resident in the UK. After the distribution (again not meaning 'for ever after' — see 32.32 above), it must continue to be a trading company or the 'holding company' of a trading group except where the distributing company is itself the 75% subsidiary of another, when the following conditions must be satisfied instead.

(*a*) The group (or, if more than one, the largest group) to which it belongs at the time of the distribution must be a trading group.

(*b*) The distribution must be followed by other exempt distributions within 32.32(*a*) or (*b*)(ii) above, as a result of which members of the holding company of the 'group' (or the largest group) to which the distributing company belonged at the time of the distribution become members of:

(i) each and every transferee company to which a trade was transferred by the distributing company; or

(ii) each and every subsidiary shares in which were transferred by the distributing company; or

(iii) a company (other than that holding company) of which a company falling within (i) or (ii) above is a 75% subsidiary.

[*ICTA 1988, s 213*(*6*)(*b*)(*8*)(*e*)(*12*)].

See also 32.36 below.

A '*member*' of a company means a holder of ordinary share capital of that company. [*ICTA 1988, s 218*(*1*)].

'*Shares*' includes stock. [*ICTA 1988, s 218*(*1*)].

In determining whether a company the shares in which are transferred by the distributing company is a '75% subsidiary' of that company, shares therein owned indirectly by the distributing company are to be disregarded. The subsidiary must, at the time of transfer, be either a trading company or the holding company of a trading group.

For all the purposes of these provisions, the parent company is to be treated as not owning shares held as trading stock either directly, or indirectly through another body corporate. [*ICTA 1988, ss 213*(*5*), *218*(*2*)(*3*)].

'*Ordinary share capital*' is all the issued share capital of the company except that carrying a fixed dividend only. [*ICTA 1988, s 832*(*1*)]. 'Issued share capital' does not include founder members' deposits in a company limited by guarantee (*South Shore Mutual Insurance Co Ltd v Blair (Sp C 215), [1999] SSCD 296*).

'*Trade*' does not include dealing in shares, securities, land, trades or commodity futures, and '*trading activities*' are to be construed accordingly. [*ICTA 1988, s 218*(*1*)].

A '*group*', except for the purposes of 32.32(3) above, means a company and its 75% subsidiaries.

In 32.32(3) above, the term means a company and its 51% subsidiaries.

[*ICTA 1988, ss 213*(*11*), *218*(*1*)].

See also below regarding a 'trading company'.

'*Unquoted company*'. A company is unquoted if no class of shares or securities therein (disregarding debenture or loan stock or preferred shares) is listed in the Stock Exchange Official List and dealt in on the Stock Exchange. A company under the sole control of one or more companies which are not unquoted is outside this definition. [*ICTA 1988, s 218*(*1*)].

'*Control*' is as defined in *ICTA 1988, s 416*(*2*)–(*6*), see 16.2 CLOSE COMPANIES.

'*Relevant company*' comprises, in relation to any distribution, the distributing company, any 75% subsidiary the shares in which are transferred and, in relation to a distribution within 32.32(*b*) above, any transferee company. Each company must be resident in the UK at the time of the distribution. [*ICTA 1988, s 213*(*3*)(*4*)].

A '*trading company*' is one the business of which consists wholly or mainly in the carrying on of a trade or trades, and a '*trading group*' is a group the business of the members of which (taken together) consists wholly or mainly in the carrying on of a trade or trades. [*ICTA 1988, s 218*(*1*)].

A '*holding company*' means a company the business of which (disregarding any trade that it carries on) consists wholly or mainly in the holding of shares or securities of one or more companies which are its 75% subsidiaries. [*ICTA 1988, s 218*(*1*)].

32.34 **Relief from tax on capital gains.** Any exempt distribution within 32.32(*a*) above is not a capital distribution for the purposes of *TCGA 1992, s 122*, and will not, therefore, give rise to a deemed disposal. The distribution is treated as if it were a reorganisation of the distributing company's share capital for the purposes of *TCGA 1992, ss 126–130*. [*TCGA 1992, s 192*(*2*)]. See Tolley's Capital Gains Tax under Shares and Securities.

For distributions before 17 April 2002, an exempt distribution within 32.32(*b*)(ii) above was regarded as a scheme of reconstruction for the purpose of relief under *TCGA 1992, s 139* (see 11.9 CAPITAL GAINS), so that the transfer of assets to the transferee company was, in relation to corporation tax on capital gains, treated as giving rise to neither gain nor loss. (HMRC Statement of Practice, SP 5/85). See now 11.9 CAPITAL GAINS.

Where a company ceases to be a member of a group solely because of an exempt distribution (within 32.32(*a*) or (*b*) above), no charge arises under *TCGA 1992, s 179* (see 12.32 CAPITAL GAINS—GROUPS). This relief is withdrawn if a chargeable payment (see 32.35 below) is made within five years after the exempt distribution; the time limit for making assessments is extended (where necessary) to three years after the making of the chargeable payment. [*TCGA 1992, s 192*(*3*)(*4*)].

For the treatment of trustees and beneficiaries where the trustees hold shares in a company which carries out an exempt distribution, see HMRC Capital Gains Manual CG 33900.

32.35 **Chargeable payment connected with exempt distribution.** If within five years after an exempt distribution there is a 'chargeable payment', that payment is treated as:

(*a*) income chargeable to corporation tax under Schedule D, Case VI; and

(*b*) an annual sum payable otherwise than out of profits or gains chargeable to income tax for the purposes of *ITA 2007, ss 449, 901, 946, 962–964* (formerly *ICTA 1988, ss 349*(*1*), *350*) (requiring the payer to deduct and account for income tax at the basic rate) unless it is a transfer of *money's worth*; and

(*c*) a distribution for the purposes of *ICTA 1988, s 337A*(*1*) (previously *ICTA 1988, s 337*(*2*) and *s 338*(*2*)) (distributions may not be deducted as charges on income or in computing income).

In no case is the payment to be treated as a repayment of capital for the purposes of *ICTA 1988, s 210* or *s 211* (see 23.9, 23.10 DISTRIBUTIONS).

A '*chargeable payment*' is any 'payment' made by a 'company concerned in an exempt distribution':

(i) directly or indirectly to a member of that company or of any other such company; and

(ii) in connection with, or with any transaction affecting, the shares of that or any other such company; and

(iii) which is neither a distribution nor an exempt distribution nor made to a member of the same group as the paying company; and

(iv) which is not made for *bona fide* commercial reasons or forms part of a scheme or arrangements a main purpose of which is the avoidance of tax (including stamp duty and stamp duty land tax).

Where a company concerned in an exempt distribution is an 'unquoted company' (see 32.33 above), (i) above is extended to payments made by or to any other person in pursuance of a scheme or arrangements made with the unquoted company. If the unquoted company is:

(A) under the control of five or fewer persons; and

(B) not under the sole control of a company not within (A) above,

payments made in pursuance of a scheme or arrangements made with any of the persons referred to in (A) above are chargeable payments.

'*Payment*' includes a transfer of money's worth including the assumption of a liability.

A '*company concerned in an exempt distribution*' includes every relevant company and any company connected with a relevant company (or with any other company which is so connected) at any time between the exempt distribution and the chargeable payment. In establishing connection, *ICTA 1988, s 839* (see 19 CONNECTED PERSONS) applies.

[*ICTA 1988, ss 214, 218(1); FA 2002, Sch 30 para 1(3); FA 2003, Sch 18 para 3(4); ITTOIA 2005, Sch 5 para 111*].

See also 32.34 above.

Simon's Direct Tax Service. See D1.503.

32.36 **Winding-up etc.** The requirement for a distribution company to be a trading company or the holding company of a trading group after the distribution (see 32.33 above) is removed in the following circumstances.

(*a*) Distributions within 32.32(*a*) above

Where the transfer relates to two or more 75% subsidiaries of the distributing company which is then dissolved without there having been, after the exempt distribution, net assets of the company available for distribution in a winding-up or otherwise. A company will, concessionally, not be regarded as failing to meet these conditions merely because it retains, after the distribution, sufficient funds to meet the cost of liquidation and to repay a negligible amount (i.e. £5,000 or less) of share capital remaining. (HMRC Extra-Statutory Concession, C 11).

(*b*) Distributions within 32.32(*b*) above

Where there are two or more transferee companies, each of which receives a trade or shares in a separate 75% subsidiary of the distributing company, and the distributing company is dissolved without there having been, after the exempt distribution, net assets of the company available for distribution in a winding-up or otherwise.

[*ICTA 1988, s 213(7)(9)*].

32.37 **Returns.** Within 30 days after an exempt distribution, the distributing company must make a return to the inspector giving particulars of the distribution and the reasons why it is exempt. Where a clearance (see 32.39 below) has been given in respect of the distribution, the return need only refer to the clearance notification and confirm that the distribution is precisely that for which clearance application was made. (HMRC Statement of Practice, SP 13/80 as revised).

If a chargeable payment is made consisting of the transfer of money's worth, the payer must, within 30 days of the payment, make a return to the inspector giving particulars of:

(*a*) the transaction effecting the transfer; and

(*b*) the name and address of each and every recipient and the value of what is transferred to him; and

(*c*) any chargeable payment in money which accompanied the transfer.

In the case of a payment which is not a chargeable payment solely because it is made for *bona fide* commercial reasons and otherwise than for tax avoidance purposes (see 32.35 above), a return must be made within 30 days of the payment giving particulars of:

(i) in the case of a transfer of money's worth, the transaction by which it is effected; and

(ii) the name and address of each and every recipient and the value of the payment made to him; and

(iii) the circumstances by reason of which the payment is not a chargeable payment.

[*ICTA 1988, s 216*].

See, however, 32.39 below.

32.38 **Power to obtain information.** If the inspector has reason to believe that a distribution which is otherwise exempt may form part of a scheme or arrangements within *ICTA 1988, s 213*(*11*) (see 32.32(1)–(5) above) he may give written notice to any relevant company or any person controlling such a company to supply the following information within such time as may be specified in the notice (but not less than 30 days).

(*a*) A written declaration stating whether or not, according to information which the company or that person has or can reasonably obtain, any relevant scheme or arrangements exist or have existed.

(*b*) Such other information as the inspector may reasonably require for the purposes of *ICTA 1988, s 213*(*11*) and the company or that person has or can reasonably obtain.

Similar powers exist, *mutatis mutandis*, if the inspector has reason to believe that a payment which is not otherwise a chargeable payment has been made in pursuance of such a scheme or arrangements as are outlined in 32.35 above. In addition, the inspector may require from any recipient of such payment the name and address of anyone on whose behalf it was received. [*ICTA 1988, s 217*].

If the inspector has reason to believe that a person has not delivered an account or made a return in accordance with the provisions outlined above, he may give written notice to that person to supply such information as the inspector may reasonably require for the purposes of *ICTA 1988, s 214*(*1*)(*b*) or *s 216*(*2*)–(*4*). [*ICTA 1988, s 217*(*2*)].

32.39 **Clearance.** Application may be made for advance determination that a distribution is exempt or that a payment is not chargeable.

Applications for clearance should be addressed to Mohini Sawhney, Clearance and Counteraction Team, First Floor, 22 Kingsway, London WC2B 6NR (or, if market-sensitive information is included, to Eric Gardner at that address). Applications may be faxed to 020–7438 4409 or emailed to reconstructions@gtnet.gov.uk (after advising Eric Gardner (on 020–7438 6585) if market-sensitive information is included). Application may be made in a single letter to the same address for clearance under *ICTA 1988, s 215* and under any one or more of *ICTA 1988, s 225* (see 57.6 PURCHASE BY A COMPANY OF ITS OWN SHARES), *ICTA 1988, s 707* (transactions in securities, see 5.2 ANTI-AVOIDANCE), *TCGA 1992, s 138*(*1*) (share exchanges, see Tolley's Capital Gains Tax under Anti-Avoidance), *TCGA 1992, s 139*(*5*) (reconstructions involving the transfer of a business, see 11.9 CAPITAL GAINS), *TCGA 1992, s 140B* (transfer of a UK trade between EU member states, see 11.11 CAPITAL GAINS), *TCGA 1992, s 140D* (transfer of non-UK trade between EU member states, see 11.12 CAPITAL GAINS) and *FA 2002, Sch 29 para 88* (see 39.27 INTANGIBLE ASSETS).

The application must fully and accurately disclose all facts and circumstances material for the decision of HMRC, failing which any clearance granted is void. In general, it should include the following.

(i) The name of each relevant company (see 32.33 above), its tax district and reference, residence status, whether it is a distributing, subsidiary or transferee company (see 32.32 above) in relation to the proposed transactions, and whether it is a trading company or holding company (see 32.33 above) under the demerger provisions definitions, or some other type of company.

(ii) Details of the group structure where appropriate.

(iii) A statement of the reasons for the demerger, the trading activities to be divided, the anticipated trading benefits and any other benefits expected to accrue.

(iv) A detailed description of all the proposed transactions, including any prior transactions or rearrangements in preparation for the demerger, making it clear why it is considered that all the relevant conditions are satisfied.

(v) Confirmation, together with all relevant information, that the distribution is not excluded from relief as part of a scheme (see 32.32 above), and a statement of the circumstances (if any) in which it is envisaged that control of a relevant company might be acquired by someone other than a member of the distributing company, or that a trade carried on by one of those companies before or after the demerger might cease or be sold.

(vi) The latest available balance sheets and profit and loss accounts of the existing companies (as listed at (i) above), and, where appropriate, a consolidated group balance sheet and profit and loss account, with a note of any material relevant changes between balance sheet date and the proposed demerger.

Where, exceptionally, it is not possible to explain the purpose of a demerger adequately in writing, HMRC will invite the applicants to an interview.

(HMRC Statement of Practice, SP 13/80 as revised).

HMRC may call for further particulars within 30 days of the receipt of the application, or of particulars previously requested, and if these are not supplied within a further 30 days (or such longer period as HMRC may allow) HMRC need not proceed further on the application. Subject to this, HMRC must notify its decision to the applicant within 30 days of the receipt of the application or of the particulars last requested. If the decision is unfavourable, or not communicated to him within the time limit, the applicant may, within 30 days after the receipt of the decision or after the expiry of the time limit, require HMRC to place the matter before the Special Commissioners. The decision of the Special Commissioners is then treated as that of HMRC.

Where a clearance has been given in respect of a payment which would otherwise be a chargeable payment, there is no obligation to make a return under these provisions (see 32.37 above).

[*ICTA 1988, ss 215, 216*(*4*)].

A company which becomes or ceases to be connected (see 19 CONNECTED PERSONS and 32.35 above) with another company may seek clearance for any payment which may be made at any time after it became, or ceased to be, so connected (whether or not there is any present intention to make any payment). No payment to which a clearance relates is to be treated as chargeable merely by reason of the company's being, or having been, connected with the other company. [*ICTA 1988, s 215*].

Simon's Direct Tax Service. See D1.504.

32.40 **Consequences of demerger.** The types of demerger detailed at 32.32(*a*) and (*b*)(ii) above result in a change of ownership of the subsidiary company demerged. If this is accompanied by a major change in the nature or conduct of the trade (which may result from those management changes the legislation is designed to bring about), the provisions of *ICTA 1988, ss 768, 768A* (see 47.13 LOSSES), and *s 768D* (see 56 PROPERTY INCOME) may be triggered. Briefly, these act to prohibit the carry-forward of losses arising before the change of ownership to be used in periods after the change of ownership. Since such restrictions contradict the intention of the demerger legislation, HMRC will consider sympathetically the application of *ICTA 1988, s 768, s 768A, s 768D* and *s 245* where they apply as a result of an exempt distribution, and the underlying ownership of the trade is unchanged.

33 HMRC: Administration

Simons Direct Tax Service. See A2.3

33.1 STRUCTURE OF HMRC

From 18 April 2005, the collection and management of corporation tax is administered by the **Commissioners for Her Majesty's Revenue and Customs (HMRC)**. [*TMA 1970, s 1; Commissioners for Revenue and Customs Act 2005, Sch 4 para 12*]. Previously, this tax was administered by the Commissioners of Inland Revenue (normally referred to as 'the Board'). [*TMA 1970, s 1(1) as originally enacted*]. All the functions vested in the Board before that date (with the exception of prosecutions for tax offences — see below) are now vested in the Commissioners for HMRC. [*Commissioners for Revenue and Customs Act 2005, s 5; SI 2005 No 1126*].

Under the Commissioners for HMRC are officers of Revenue and Customs who are civil servants. Such officers may undertake the functions previously vested in either Inland Revenue officers or Customs and Excise officers, but not both at the same time. In relation to corporation tax, officers of Revenue and Customs have broadly taken over the functions previously vested in officers of the Board of Inland Revenue, inspectors of taxes and collectors of taxes. [*Commissioners for Revenue and Customs Act 2005, ss 6, 7, Sch 1*]. As such they are responsible for processing returns, making assessments, dealing with claims, allowances and appeals, carrying out enquiries and collection and recovery of tax.

Criminal prosecutions of tax offences in England and Wales are conducted by an independent Revenue and Customs Prosecutions Office, whose director is appointed by the Attorney General. [*Commissioners for Revenue and Customs Act 2005, ss 34–42, Sch 3*]. Before 18 April 2005, the Inland Revenue was itself a prosecuting authority in England and Wales (see 33.3 below) and conducted its own prosecutions.

In this publication, 'HMRC' means Her Majesty's Revenue and Customs, and any references to 'HMRC' are to both HMRC and the Inland Revenue.

HMRC maintains an internet website (www.hmrc.gov.uk/home.htm) which provides access to detailed information on many aspects of corporation tax.

Small businesses. Proposals to integrate and streamline services to small businesses were published in March 2005 as 'Working towards a new relationship: small business'.

33.2 **Appeal Commissioners.** Appeals against assessments or amendments of self-assessments are heard by:

(*a*) the General Commissioners (local persons appointed on a voluntary basis by the Lord Chancellor or, in Scotland, by the Secretary of State) [*TMA 1970, s 2*]; or

(*b*) the Special Commissioners (full-time civil servants, being barristers, advocates or solicitors etc. of at least ten years' standing, appointed for this purpose) [*TMA 1970, s 4; Courts and Legal Services Act 1990, Sch 10 para 30*].

The Lord Chancellor has powers, by regulation, to change the names by which the General and Special Commissioners are to be referred to. [*F(No 2)A 1992, s 75*].

With effect from 1 April 2001, provisions are introduced which:

(i) prohibit courts from ordering a General Commissioner to pay costs relating to any acts or omissions in the execution of his duties as such (except in relation to proceedings in which he is being tried for an offence or is appealing against a conviction), the court being able instead to order the 'relevant Minister' to make such payment; and

(ii) require the 'relevant Minister' to indemnify a General Commissioner or Clerk (or assistant) to the General Commissioners against certain costs or damages,

except in cases involving bad faith. The '*relevant Minister*' is the Lord Chancellor or, in Scotland, the Secretary of State.

[*TMA 1970, ss 2A, 3A; Access to Justice Act 1999, ss 102, 103; SI 2001 No 916*].

See 6.4, 6.7 APPEALS as regards jurisdiction of Commissioners and the conduct of appeals before them.

33.3 'CARE AND MANAGEMENT' POWERS

As noted at 33.1 above, the Commissioners for HMRC have responsibility for the 'collection and management' of taxes, including corporation tax. Before 18 April 2005, the Board of Inland Revenue had responsibility for the 'care and management' of direct taxes. The extent and limits of these care and management powers were considered before the courts on a number of occasions.

For the validity of amnesties by the Board, see *R v CIR (ex p National Federation of Self-employed and Small Businesses Ltd) HL 1981, 55 TC 133*. HMRC EXTRA-STATUTORY CONCESSIONS (33) have been the subject of frequent judicial criticism (see Lord Edmund-Davies' opinion in *Vestey v CIR (No 1) HL 1979, 54 TC 503* for a review of this), but their validity has never directly been challenged in the Courts. In *R v HMIT (ex p Fulford-Dobson) QB 1987, 60 TC 168*, a claim that the Revenue had acted unfairly in refusing a concession where tax avoidance was involved was rejected, but the taxpayer's right to seek judicial review of a Revenue decision to refuse the benefit of a concession was confirmed in *R v HMIT (ex p Brumfield and Others) QB 1988, 61 TC 589*. A decision by the Revenue to revoke its authorisation to pay a dividend gross was upheld in *R v CIR (ex p Camacq Corporation) CA 1989, 62 TC 651*. For a general discussion of the Board's care and management powers, and an example of a ruling by the Court that the Board had exercised a discretionary power reasonably, see *R v CIR (ex p Preston) HL 1985, 59 TC 1*. Where a discretionary power is given to the Revenue, it is an error in law to proceed on the footing that the power is mandatory (*R v HMIT and Others (ex p Lansing Bagnall Ltd) CA 1986, 61 TC 112*). See also *R v CIR (ex p J Rothschild Holdings plc) CA 1987, 61 TC 178*, where the Revenue were required to produce internal documents of a general character relating to their practice in applying a statutory provision.

The Inland Revenue policy of selective prosecution for criminal offences in connection with tax evasion did not render a decision in a particular case unlawful or *ultra vires*, provided that the case was considered on its merits fairly and dispassionately to see whether the criteria for prosecution were satisfied, and that the decision to prosecute was then taken in good faith for the purpose of collecting taxes and not for some ulterior, extraneous or improper purpose (*R v CIR (ex p Mead and Cook) QB 1992, 65 TC 1*).

The making of a 'forward tax agreement', by which the Inland Revenue renounced their right and duty to investigate the true financial and other circumstances of the other party during the period of the agreement in return for payments of money, was not a proper exercise of the Inland Revenue's care and management powers, and was accordingly *ultra vires* and illegal. As such, it was not unfair of the Revenue to end the agreement. (*Al Fayed & Others v Advocate-General for Scotland, [2004] STC 1703*).

33.4 HMRC RULINGS

For the extent to which taxpayers may rely on guidance given by HMRC, see the letter from the Deputy Chairman to the various professional bodies following the decision in *R v CIR (ex p Matrix-Securities Ltd) HL 1994, 66 TC 587*.

HMRC may provide a post-transaction ruling for a transaction after it has occurred but before the tax return is submitted. Rulings will only be given where the tax treatment of a transaction is in doubt, for example in relation to unusual transactions or transactions entered into in usual circumstances. See Code of Practice 10 (as revised April 1999) for the types of transactions on which a ruling can be given, the extent to which HMRC will be bound by the ruling, the effect of the ruling on interest and penalties and the procedures in obtaining such a ruling.

33.5 **TAXPAYER COMPLAINTS**

Taxpayer's Charter. The Board of Inland Revenue and HM Customs and Excise jointly produced a Taxpayer's Charter setting out the principles they try to meet in their dealings with taxpayers, the standards they believe the taxpayer has a right to expect, and what people can do if they wish to appeal or complain. Copies are available from local tax or collection offices and from local VAT offices.

HMRC publish a series of codes of practice setting out the standards of service people can expect in relation to specific aspects of the Revenue's work (see 34 HMRC EXPLANATORY PUBLICATIONS). Most of these are available on the HMRC website.

33.6 **HMRC error.** Code of Practice 1 (see 33.5 above), 'Putting things right when we make mistakes' (revised November 2003), outlines the complaints procedure and gives general advice on the circumstances in which payment may be claimed from HMRC as a consequence of Revenue mistake or unreasonable delay. These fall into three categories.

(*a*) *Claiming back costs.* Any reasonable costs paid as a direct result of Revenue error, such as postage, 'phone calls, travelling expenses, professional fees, financial charges, and interest on overpaid tax and national insurance, may be reclaimed. If the extra costs arose because of HMRC delay in dealing with the taxpayer's affairs, interest normally charged on overdue tax or national insurance owed by the taxpayer may be waived, or interest paid on money owed by HMRC, during the unreasonable delay.

(*b*) *Compensation for worry and distress.* If HMRC's actions have affected the taxpayer particularly badly, HMRC may pay compensation (usually in the range £25 to £500) to acknowledge and apologise for the way the taxpayer was treated.

(*c*) *Further mistakes or delays in dealing with complaint.* If HMRC handle a complaint badly, or take an unreasonable time to deal with it, compensation (usually in the range £25 to £500) may be paid, on top of any reasonable costs, to reflect this.

33.7 **Revenue Adjudicator.** A taxpayer who is not satisfied with HMRC's response to a complaint has the option of putting the case to an independent Adjudicator for the Inland Revenue (now part of HMRC). The adjudicator's office considers complaints about HMRC's handling of a taxpayer's affairs, e.g. excessive delays, errors, discourtesy or the exercise of Revenue discretion. Matters subject to existing rights of appeal are excluded.

Complaints normally go to the adjudicator only after they have been considered by the Controller of the relevant Revenue office, and where the taxpayer is still not satisfied with the response received. The alternatives of pursuing the complaint to HMRC's Head Office, to an MP, or (through an MP) to the Ombudsman continue to be available. The adjudicator reviews all the facts, considers whether the complaint is justified, and, if so, makes recommendations as to what should be done. HMRC will normally accept the recommendations 'unless there are very exceptional circumstances'.

The adjudicator also investigates complaints about Customs and Excise and the Valuation Office Agency (now part of HMRC).

The address is The Adjudicator's Office, Haymarket House, 28 Haymarket, London SW1Y 4SP (tel. 020–7930 2292, e-mail address: adjudicators@gtnet.gov.uk).

Complaints normally go to the Adjudicator only after they have been considered by, firstly, the Customer Relations or Complaints Manager and, secondly, the Director of the relevant Revenue office, and where the taxpayer is still not satisfied with the response received. The alternatives of pursuing the complaint to HMRC's Head Office, to an MP, or (through an MP) to the Parliamentary Ombudsman continue to be available. The Adjudicator reviews all the facts, considers whether the complaint is justified, and, if so, settles the complaint by mediation or makes recommendations as to what should be done. The Revenue normally accept the recommendations.

The Adjudicator publishes an annual report.

See also HMRC leaflet AO1 'The Adjudicator's Office'.

Leave to apply for judicial review of the rejection by the Adjudicator of a complaint concerning the use of information from unidentified informants was refused in *R v Revenue Adjudicator's Office (ex p Drummond) QB 1996, 70 TC 235*.

33.8 COMMUNICATIONS

Open Government. Information on HMRC policies and decisions is widely available. Most internal HMRC guidance manuals are available on the HRMC website (at www.hmrc.gov.uk/manuals/index.htm).

33.9 **Telephone Helplines.** An employers' telephone helpline on 0845 7143143 can be used for general enquiries about PAYE, national insurance and value added tax registration. The service is available from 0830 to 1700 on working days. Calls will be charged at local rates. See also 20.7 CONSTRUCTION INDUSTRY SCHEME.

There is also a helpline for **new employers** on 0845 607 0143 (0800 to 2000 weekdays, 1000 to 1600 weekends), where the employer may register for PAYE, order an information pack on the operation of payroll tax and national insurance, and obtain help and information on payroll queries. Arrangements may also be made for access to business support teams and workshops providing further assistance.

A range of other helplines for general and specific enquiries is available on the HMRC website (at www.hmrc.gov.uk/contactus/by-phone.htm).

33.10 **Use of electronic communications.** The Commissioners of Inland Revenue (and of Customs and Excise) have broad powers (which now vest in the Commissioners for HMRC) to make regulations, by statutory instrument, to facilitate two-way electronic communication in the delivery of information, e.g. tax returns (and see 61.28 RETURNS), and the making of tax payments. The regulations may allow or require the use of intermediaries such as internet service providers. They will have effect notwithstanding any existing legislation requiring delivery or payment in a manner which would preclude the use of electronic communications or intermediaries. [*FA 1999, ss 132, 133*]. The intention is to provide a range of electronic services which taxpayers can use as an alternative to paper if they so wish.

See *The Income and Corporation Taxes* (*Electronic Communications*) *Regulations 2003* (*SI 2003 No 282*) (which replace the *Income Tax* (*Electronic Communications*) *Regulations 2000* (*SI 2000 No 945*) as amended) and directions thereunder by the Commissioners, which make provision for electronic communications in relation to delivery of returns and other information under *TMA 1970, ss 8–9, 9A–9D, 12AA, 12AB, 12AC–12AE, 59DA, 59E* or *Sch 1A* or *FA 1998, ss 30–36* or *Sch 18* and payments or repayments in connection with the operation of those provisions. See also *SI 2002 No 680*. See also the directions issued under the *Income Tax* (*Employments*) *Regulations 1993* (*SI 1993 No 744*), *regs 42A*(*1*), *42A*(*2*)(*c*)(*ii*), *46ZC*(*1*)(*b*), *46ZD*(*4*)(*f*) and *46ZF*(*1*), specifying approved methods for mandatory electronic communications by employers to whom an e-filing notice was issued between 26 October and 31 December 2003, and the directions issued under the *Income Tax* (*Incentive Payments for Voluntary Electronic Communication of PAYE Returns*) *Regulations 2003* (*SI 2003 No 2495*), *reg 4*(*1*), specifying approved methods for voluntary electronic filing.

HMRC's Corporation Tax Online service allows company tax returns, including tax computations and accounts, to be filed over the Internet.

Mandatory e-filing. The Commissioners of Inland Revenue (now HMRC) have been given extremely wide powers to make regulations requiring the use of electronic communications for the delivery of information required or authorised to be delivered under tax legislation. The powers have been further extended by *FA 2007*. [*FA 2002, ss 135, 136; FA 2003, ss 204, 205; FA 2007, ss 93, 94*]. The *Income Tax (Employments) Regulations 1993* (*SI 1993 No 744*), as amended by *SI 2003 No 2494* to provide for mandatory electronic payroll e-filing, provide that, where an e-filing notice has been issued by 31 December following a 'specified date':

(*a*) employers with 250 or more employees ('large employers') are required to file electronically from 2004/05; and

(*b*) employers with 50 or more employees ('large or medium-sized employers') are required to file electronically from 2005/06.

The '*specified date*' is the date on which the employer is treated as a 'large employer' or a 'large or medium-sized employer'. The specified date is to be announced annually by means of a direction by the Board but is to be no later than 30 November of the year preceding that in which the relevant PAYE payments are made.

For small employers with less than 50 employees, see below for incentives for voluntary electronic payroll e-filing.

The regulations provide for a default surcharge for payments not received by the collector in accordance with the regulations by the applicable due date rising from 17% of the PAYE payable for the third default to 83% for the twelfth and subsequent defaults. Penalties are also chargeable where PAYE returns and accompanying information are not delivered electronically by the applicable due date. The penalties rise on a sliding scale from £900 for 'large employers' with 250 to 399 employees, and from £600 for 'large or medium-sized employers' with 50 to 249 employees, to £3,000 for 1,000 or more employees in both cases. Interest is payable on unpaid penalties under *TMA 1970, s 103A*. See 65.28 TIME LIMITS for the applicable due dates.

See also the Revenue Tax Bulletin February 2003 pp 995, 996 for an article summarising the e-filing requirements.

Incentives for electronic communications. Regulations may be made by statutory instrument by the Commissioners of Inland Revenue in relation to matters under their care and management (and by the Commissioners of Customs and Excise in relation to theirs) for the provision of incentives to use electronic communications. These may include discounts (or payments or repayments), or additional time for compliance or payment, or more convenient intervals for the delivery of information or the making of payments. Anything received by way of incentive is not regarded as income for corporation tax purposes. The regulations may make provision as to the conditions of entitlement to incentives and for their withdrawal (which may be authorised to be made by direction), and may provide for penalties up to £1,000 for failure to comply with any specified provision. They may make different provision for different cases, and may make such incidental, supplemental, consequential or transitional provision as the Commissioners think fit. [*FA 2000, s 143, Sch 38; ITTOIA 2005, Sch 1 para 518*]. See *SI 2001 No 56; SI 2001 No 1081, reg 22*.

The *Income Tax (Incentive Payments for Voluntary Electronic Communication of PAYE Returns) Regulations 2003* (*SI 2003 No 2495* as amended by *SI 2005 No 826*) provide for the payment of incentives to employers with less than 50 employees ('small employers') who file electronically, falling from £250 for 2004/05 to £75 for 2008/09.

See also 61.28 RETURNS for incentives for making certain returns over the Internet.

33.11 **HMRC disclosure of information.** A memorandum of understanding has been agreed between HMRC and the Financial Reporting Review Panel (FRRP) on the principles underlying the provision of information that may be disclosed by HMRC to the FRRP under the *Companies (Audit, Investigations and Community Enterprise) Act 2004*. (Revenue Statement 24 June 2005, SWTI (2005) 1197.)

33.12 INTERNATIONAL CO-OPERATION

With effect from 19 July 2006, *FA 2006, ss 173–175* provide for international agreements about mutual assistance in tax enforcement, covering exchange of information foreseeably relevant to the administration, enforcement or recovery of UK or foreign tax, the recovery of debts and the service of documents relating to UK or foreign tax. Any information that can be disclosed to another territory under this provision can be disclosed to HMRC by any other Government department and such information can be disclosed by HMRC to an authorised officer of any territory with whom arrangements have been made. Information may not, however, be disclosed under any such arrangements unless HMRC are satisfied that the counterparty is bound by, or has undertaken to observe, rules of confidentiality at least as strict as those applying in the UK. The power under *TMA 1970, s 20(1)-(8)(8C)-(9)* (see 30.4 FRAUDULENT OR NEGLIGENT CONDUCT) to call for information relevant to income tax, corporation tax or capital gains tax liabilities can accordingly be used to obtain information in respect foreign tax liabilities covered by the arrangements.

The above provisions replace and widen similar provisions under *ICTA 1988, s 815C* (as amended by *FA 2002, s 88* and *FA 2003, s 198*) and *ICTA 1988, s 788(2)*. Any provisions in existing Orders made prior to 19 July 2006 are to have effect from that date as if they were included (where they could have otherwise been so included) in an Order made under *FA 2006, s 173*. This also applies to arrangements covering UK or foreign taxes other than those in relation to which such Orders had effect.

The above provision similarly applies in relation to inheritance tax (replacing the provision in *IHTA 1984, s 220A*).

Co-operation between tax authorities of EU member states. The Mutual Assistance Directive (*Directive 77/799/EEC* as amended) provides for the exchange of information between tax authorities of EU member states to enable them to correctly assess liabilities to the taxes covered by the *Directive* (which include taxes on income and capital). The requirements of the *Directive* are transposed into UK domestic law by *FA 1978, s 77; FA 1990, s 125(5)(6); FA 2003, s 197(1)–(6), Sch 43 Pt 5(1)*. By virtue of amending *Directive 2004/56/EC*, the Mutual Assistance Directive now extends to the notification of instruments and decisions by the tax authority of a member state, to persons residing in that State, at the request of the tax authority of the member state from which the instrument or decision emanates. This requirement is transposed into UK domestic law by *F(No 2)A 2005, s 68* with effect in relation to requests received by HMRC (and its predecessors) on and after 1 January 2005.

Recovery of taxes etc. due in other EC member states. Provision is made for the recovery in the UK of amounts in respect of which a request for enforcement has been made in accordance with the Mutual Assistance Recovery Directive (*Directive 76/308/EEC* as amended by *Directive 2001/44/EC*) by an authority in another EU member state. Disclosure of information by a UK tax authority (i.e. the Commissioners of HMRC, the Commissioners of Inland Revenue, the Commissioners of Customs and Excise or, in relation to certain agricultural levies, the relevant Minister) for these purposes (or for the purposes of a request for enforcement by the UK) is not generally precluded by any obligation of secrecy.

Broadly, the UK tax authority has the same powers it would have for a corresponding claim in the UK, in particular in relation to penalties and interest. Treasury regulations may make provision as to what UK claim corresponds to a foreign claim, and for other procedural and supplementary matters (for which see *SI 2004 No 674* as amended by

SI 2005 No 1709). Regulations may also be made by the relevant UK tax authority for the application, non-application or adaptation of the law applicable to corresponding UK claims, without prejudice to its application when not dealt with by such regulations.

No proceedings may be taken against a person under these provisions if he shows that proceedings relevant to the liability in question are pending (i.e. still open to appeal), or about to be instituted, before a competent body in the member state in question. This does not apply if the foreign proceedings are not prosecuted or instituted with reasonable expedition, or if regulations made by the UK tax authority apply a UK enactment that permits proceedings in the case of a corresponding UK claim. If a final decision on the foreign claim (i.e. one against which no further appeal lies or would be in time), or a part of it, has been given in favour of the taxpayer by a competent body in the member state in question, no proceeding may be taken under these provisions in relation to the claim (or part).

The Treasury may amend, replace or repeal any of the above provisions by regulations for the purpose of giving effect to future amendments to the Directive.

[*FA 2002, s 134, Sch 39; SI 2004 No 674; SI 2005 No 1479; SI 2005 No 1709*].

33.13 **ASSETS RECOVERY AGENCY**

Under *Proceeds of Crime Act 2002, Pt 6*, the Director of the Assets Recovery Agency is empowered, after 23 February 2003, to carry out the functions vested in HMRC and its officers. It was announced on 11 January 2007 that the Agency is to be merged with the Serious Organised Crime Agency ('SOCA').

In order to carry out HMRC functions, the Director must have reasonable grounds to suspect that:

(*a*) income arising or a gain accruing to a person in respect of a chargeable period is chargeable to income tax or is a chargeable gain and arises or accrues as a result (whether wholly or partly, directly or indirectly) of the 'criminal conduct' of that person or another; or

(*b*) a company is chargeable to corporation tax on its profits arising in a chargeable period and the profits arise as a result (whether wholly or partly, directly or indirectly) of the criminal conduct of the company or another person,

and must serve a notice on HMRC specifying the person or company, the period or periods concerned, and the functions which he intends to carry out. The periods involved may include periods beginning before the *Act* was passed.

For the purpose of the exercise by the Director of any function so vested in him, it is immaterial that he cannot identify a source for any income. An assessment made by the Director under *TMA 1970, s 29* (discovery assessment) in respect of income charged to tax under *ITTOIA 2005, Pt 5 Ch 8* (income not otherwise charged — see Tolley's Income Tax under Miscellaneous Income), or, before 2005/06, under Schedule D, Case VI cannot be reduced or quashed only because it does not specify (to any extent) the source of the income.

The Director may cease carrying out the functions specified in the notice at any time (by notifying HMRC), but *must* so cease where the conditions allowing the notice to be made are no longer satisfied. Any assessment made by him under *TMA 1970, s 29* is subsequently invalid to the extent that it does not specify a source for income.

For the above purposes, '*criminal conduct*' is conduct which constitutes an offence anywhere in the UK or which would do so if it occurred there, but does not include conduct constituting an offence relating to a matter under the care and management of HMRC.

It should be noted that the vesting of a function in the Director under these provisions does not divest HMRC or its officers of the function (so that, for example, HMRC can continue to carry out routine work). Certain functions, as listed in *Proceeds of Crime Act 2002, s 323(3)*, cannot be carried out by the Director. If the Director serves notice in relation to a company and in respect of a chargeable period or periods, the general Revenue functions vested in the Director do not include functions relating to any requirement which is imposed on the company in its capacity as an employer and relates to a tax year which does not fall wholly within the chargeable period(s).

Appeals in respect of actions carried out by the Director in the exercise of Revenue functions are to the Special Commissioners. In hearing such appeals, the Special Commissioners may be assisted by one or more assessors selected for their special knowledge and experience of the matter to which the appeal relates from a panel appointed for the purpose by the Lord Chancellor.

[*Proceeds of Crime Act 2002, ss 317, 318(1)(2), 319, 320(1)–(3), 323(1)(3), 326(1)(2); SI 2003 No 120; ITTOIA 2005, Sch 1 para 582*].

A company whose tax affairs are being investigated by the Assets Recovery Agency should check the Assets Recovery Agency website (www.assetsrecovery.gov.uk) for guidance on how their cases will be dealt with.

33.14 CONFIDENTIALITY

For the confidential treatment of information supplied to HMRC see Tolley's Income Tax under HMRC: Confidentiality of Information.

33.15 REVIEW OF LINKS WITH LARGE BUSINESS

Sir David Varney's report on his Review of Links with Large Business was presented in November 2006. There were a number of recommendations highlighted:

- introducing an advance rulings process;
- extending the clearances process;
- using a risk-based approach to enquiries; and
- settling transfer pricing enquiries within 18 months.

See HMRC internet statements at http://www.hmrc.gov.uk/large-business/review-outcomes.htm and http://www.hmrc.gov.uk/large-business/review-2007.htm) for further details.

34 HMRC Extra-Statutory Concessions

Simon's Direct Tax Service Part H4.

The following is a summary of the concessions applicable to companies published in HMRC Pamphlet ESC (2004) (available on HMRC's website), or subsequently announced. It should be borne in mind that in a particular case there may be special circumstances which will require to be taken into account in considering the application of a concession. A concession will not be given in any case where an attempt is made to use it for tax avoidance.

See also 33.3 HMRC: ADMINISTRATION.

A37 **Tax treatment of directors' fees received by partnerships and other companies.** Under certain conditions, such fees may be included in computing partnership profits or in the corporation tax assessment of the other company. See Tolley's Income Tax under Employment Income.

B1 **Machinery or plant: changes from 'renewals' to the capital allowances basis.** Capital allowances may be claimed on expenditure which has been the subject of a renewals allowance, provided that all items of the same class are changed to the new basis. See 10.38 CAPITAL ALLOWANCES.

B4 **Maintenance and repairs of property obviated by alterations etc.: Schedule A assessments.** The estimated cost is allowed, provided that the alterations do not amount to reconstruction, and that there is no change of use rendering such maintenance and repairs unnecessary. Withdrawn from 1 April 2001. See 56.17 PROPERTY INCOME.

B5 **Maintenance expenses of owner-occupied farms not carried on on a commercial basis.** Where a loss claim against general income is precluded under *ICTA 1988, s 393A(3)* or *ICTA 1988, s 397* (see 47.9, 47.14 LOSSES), relief for the cost of maintenance, repairs and insurance of agricultural land and buildings is granted as under *ICTA 1988, s 33.* One third of the relevant expenditure on a farmhouse is regarded as agricultural and the rest as domestic. Withdrawn from 1 April 2001. See 66.50 TRADING INCOME.

B7 **Benevolent gifts by traders** may be allowable trading expenses. See 66.56, 66.76 TRADING INCOME.

B8 **Double taxation relief: income consisting of royalties and know-how payments.** Payments made by an overseas resident to a UK trader for the use of copyright etc. are treated as arising outside the UK except in so far as they represent consideration for services (other than merely incidental services) rendered in the UK by the recipient to the payer. See 24.4 DOUBLE TAX RELIEF.

B10 **Income of contemplative religious communities, or of their members,** which is paid into the common fund of such communities which are not charities, is regarded as income of each member up to the amount of the basic personal allowance for the year. Where the aggregate of 'allowable figures' exceeds income of the community, the excess may be set against chargeable gains of that year.

B11 **Compensation for the compulsory slaughter of farm animals.** Provided that no election for the Herd Basis (see 55.10 PROFIT COMPUTATIONS) is in force in respect of the animals, the profit attributable to the compensation (calculated as required in the Concession) may be spread over the three years following that in which the slaughter took place. See 66.50 TRADING INCOME.

B16 **Fire safety: capital expenditure incurred on certain trade premises (a) in Northern Ireland and (b) by lessors**

(*a*) Notwithstanding that *Fire Precautions Act 1971* (and, consequently, *CAA 2001, s 29*) does not apply to NI, relief is generally given on the same basis as in Great Britain. Where the expenditure qualifies for relief under *CAA 2001, s 271* (hotel buildings allowance), it may nevertheless be treated as above, provided that the claimant renounces his relief under *section 271*.

(*b*) Relief is allowed where the lessor incurs the expenditure himself, if similar expenditure by the tenant or licensee would have qualified for relief.

See 10.25 CAPITAL ALLOWANCES.

B17 Capital allowances: sale of invested patent to an associate. Obsolete. See 10.50 CAPITAL ALLOWANCES.

B20 **Capital allowances for buildings: sales by property developers of buildings which have been let.** Where an industrial building, qualifying hotel or commercial building in an enterprise zone is sold by a person whose trade consists of the construction for sale of buildings, and has in the meanwhile been occupied by a tenant, writing-down allowances are concessionally made to the purchaser on the amount of the purchase price (or the construction cost if less) as if the vendor's expenditure were on capital rather than revenue account. Now superseded by *CAA 1990, s 10*(*4*)(*5*). See 10.14 CAPITAL ALLOWANCES.

B29 **Treatment of income from caravan sites where there is both trading and associated letting income.** In such circumstances, letting income from caravans and caravan pitch sites may be treated as income of the trade. See 56.2 PROPERTY INCOME.

B30 **Income from property in Scotland: property managed as one estate.** Obsolete for accounting periods beginning on or after 1 April 2001.

B38 **Tax concessions on overseas debts.** Relief may be available where they form part of profits assessable under Schedule D, Case I or Case II. See 8.3 BANKS.

B40 **UK investment managers acting for non-resident clients.** The exemptions of *TMA 1970, ss 78*(*2*), *82* are extended in certain cases. Obsolete after 5 April 2005. See Tolley's Income Tax under Non-Residence.

B41 **Claims to repayment of tax.** Where an over-payment of tax has arisen because of official error, and there is no doubt or dispute as to the facts, claims to repayment of tax are accepted outside the statutory time limit (generally six years from the end of the year concerned). See Tolley's Income Tax under Claims.

B42 **'Free gifts' and insurance contracts.** Certain incentive gifts offered in connection with the issue of insurance policies are disregarded. See Tolley's Income Tax under Life Assurance Policies.

B46 **Automatic penalties for late company and employers' and contractors' end-of-year returns.** A short period of grace is allowed for submission of annual returns. See 54.4 PENALTIES, 61.6 RETURNS and Tolley's Income Tax under Penalties.

B47 **Furnished lettings of dwelling houses — wear and tear of furniture.** As an alternative to the renewals basis, an allowance of 10% of rent may be claimed. See 56.4 PROPERTY INCOME.

B49 **CAA 2001, s 532 — repaid grants.** Capital allowances will be given for repayments of grants which were deducted from expenditure qualifying for capital allowances. See 10.2 CAPITAL ALLOWANCES.

B50 **Capital allowances for caravans on holiday caravan sites.** An extended definition of 'caravan' applies for this purpose. Superseded by *CAA 2001, s 23*(*5*). See 10.26 CAPITAL ALLOWANCES.

B52 **Subcontractors in the construction industry: the multiple turnover tests.** Until 1 August 2001, the number of partners or directors taken into account in determining the three-year turnover threshold may be taken as the maximum number at any time in the last six months of the three-year period, rather than at any time in the whole period, where this is more favourable. Obsolete after August 2001. See 20.5 CONSTRUCTION INDUSTRY SCHEME.

B53 **Non-residents and gains on life insurance policies.** (i) The treatment, in the case of non-residents, of life assurance gains is brought more into line with that of other forms of income. (ii) The reporting requirements in relation to non-resident policy holders are relaxed. (iii) The transitional reliefs for holders of personal portfolio bonds issued before 17 March 1998 are extended. See Tolley's Income Tax under Life Assurance Policies. Updated and re-issued in August 2005 as C33, but B53 applies for gains arising on chargeable events which arose or are treated as having arose before 6 April 2002.

B54 **Tax relief for expenditure on films, tapes and discs confirmed.** Notwithstanding the changes made by *FA 2000, s 113(2)*, expenditure on the production of master audio tapes and discs will continue to be treated as of a revenue nature. Replaced by legislation under the FA 2006 regime. See 66.52 and 66.53 TRADING INCOME.

B55 **Farming losses.** *ICTA 1988, s 397* is disapplied for accounting periods ending in the years to 31 March 2001 and/or 2002 provided certain conditions as to profits in earlier years are satisfied. See 47.14 LOSSES.

B56 **Slaughter of immature animals intended to be replacements.** For the duration of the 2001 foot and mouth outbreak, certain animals slaughtered before giving birth may be treated as having been mature. See 55.10 PROFIT COMPUTATIONS.

C1 **Credit for underlying tax: dividends from trade investments in overseas companies.** Credit is given along a chain of shareholdings in certain circumstances. See 24.10 DOUBLE TAX RELIEF.

C2 **Loan and money societies,** in computing corporation tax liability, may deduct the grossed up amounts of certain payments to members. Withdrawn from April 2001. See 70.3 VOLUNTARY ASSOCIATIONS.

C3 **Holiday clubs and thrift funds** are, for certain purposes, regarded as being outside the scope of corporation tax. Withdrawn from April 2001. See 70.4 VOLUNTARY ASSOCIATIONS.

C4 **Trading activities for charitable purposes** are exempt subject to certain conditions. See 14.6(ii) CHARITIES.

C5 **Industrial and provident societies** carrying on trades may treat certain income as trading income for the purposes of loss relief under *ICTA 1988, s 393(8)* (see 47.4 LOSSES). See 38.5 INDUSTRIAL AND PROVIDENT SOCIETIES.

C8 **Close companies: loan creditors.** Certain money brokers are excluded from 'loan creditors' in establishing close company control. See 16.3 CLOSE COMPANIES.

C9 **Associated close and small companies.** The rights and powers of a person's relatives (other than spouse and children) are not attributed to him in certain circumstances, and various other concessions made as regards associated status. See 63.7 SMALL COMPANIES—REDUCED RATES.

C10 **Groups of companies: arrangements.** Certain agreements etc. will not constitute 'arrangements' for the various purposes of the legislation relating to groups of companies. See 32.19 GROUPS OF COMPANIES.

C11 **Demerger: ICTA 1988, s 213(7).** The conditions imposed following a distribution are relaxed. See 32.36 GROUPS OF COMPANIES.

C12 A **retail co-operative society** which prepares half-yearly or quarterly accounts can be treated as having yearly accounting periods ending on an agreed date. See generally 2.7 ACCOUNTING PERIODS.

C13 **'Second and third tier' agricultural co-operative associations** are treated as if members of the basic level associations were members of them. See generally 38.4 INDUSTRIAL AND PROVIDENT SOCIETIES.

C15 **Dissolution of unincorporated associations: distributions to members.** Small distributions by social or recreational associations which have not carried on a trade or business are not treated as distributions under *ICTA 1988, s 209*. See 23.15(*b*) DISTRIBUTIONS.

C16 **Dissolution of companies under Companies Act 1985, ss 652, 652A: distributions to shareholders.** Distributions of assets to members on such a dissolution will in most circumstances not be treated as distributions under *ICTA 1988, s 209*. See 23.15(*a*) DISTRIBUTIONS.

C28 **Loan relationships.** Certain connections between creditor and debtor companies will be disregarded for the purposes of granting bad debt reliefs. Withdrawn for accounting periods beginning on or after 1 October 2002. See 46.9 LOAN RELATIONSHIPS.

C30 **Authorised unit trusts and open-ended investment companies – waivers of distributions.** Distribution treatment is disapplied in the case of certain *de minimis* waivers of distributions (or accumulations). See 43.6 INVESTMENT FUNDS.

C31 **Scientific research associations.** Tax exemptions will temporarily continue under the previous practice following a change in the DTI guidance on the qualification requirements. See 27.12 EXEMPT ORGANISATIONS.

D10 **Unquoted shares acquired before 6 April 1965: disposal following reorganisation of share capital.** Where, in consequence of a reorganisation of share capital before 6 April 1965, a valuation at that date is required, or time apportionment is limited, under *TCGA 1992, Sch 2 para 19*, the gain chargeable to corporation tax on a disposal of the entire holding (whether in a single transaction or in separate transactions in the same accounting period) is limited to the actual gain realised. See Tolley's Capital Gains Tax under Assets held on 6 April 1965.

D15 **Relief for the replacement of business assets: unincorporated associations.** Relief is available in respect of assets owned by companies whose shares are wholly (or apart from a very small proportion) held by or on behalf of such an association or its members. See Tolley's Capital Gains Tax under Rollover Relief.

D16 **Relief for the replacement of business assets: repurchase of same asset** will give rise to relief where for purely commercial reasons. See Tolley's Capital Gains Tax under Rollover Relief.

D17 **Unit trusts for exempt unitholders: TCGA 1992, s 100(2).** Exemption is not lost through intermittent holding of units by the managers under ordinary arrangements. Replaced by *F(No 2) Act 2005, s 20*. See 43.13 INVESTMENT FUNDS.

D18 **Default on mortgage granted by vendor.** In such circumstances and where the vendor regains beneficial ownership of the asset and so elects, the chargeable gain is limited to the net proceeds obtained from the transactions and the loan treated as never having existed. See Tolley's Capital Gains Tax under Disposal.

D22 **Relief for the replacement of business assets: expenditure on improvements to existing assets** may attract relief provided that the existing assets are used only for trade purposes, or are so used on completion of the improvements. See Tolley's Capital Gains Tax under Rollover Relief.

D23 **Relief for the replacement of business assets: partition of land on the dissolution of a partnership.** Partitioned assets are treated as new assets provided that the partnership is immediately dissolved. See Tolley's Capital Gains Tax under Rollover Relief.

D24 **Relief for the replacement of business assets: asset not brought immediately into trading use** may attract relief provided that:

(*a*) it is proposed to incur expenditure on work for the purpose of enhancing its value;
(*b*) the work begins as soon as possible after acquisition, and is completed within a reasonable time;
(*c*) on completion of the work, the asset is taken into use for trade purposes only; and
(*d*) the asset is not let or used for non-trade purposes between acquisition and being taken into use for trade purposes.

See Tolley's Capital Gains Tax under Rollover Relief.

D25 **Relief for the replacement of business assets: expenditure on acquisition of an interest in an asset already used for the purposes of a trade** will attract relief as if the further interest acquired was a new asset taken into use for trade purposes. See Tolley's Capital Gains Tax under Rollover Relief.

D26 **Relief for exchange of joint interests** in land will apply to exchanges after 19 December 1984, on the lines of that available on compulsory purchase. After 29 October 1987, the relief is further extended to exchanges of joint interests in milk or potato quota in parallel with such exchanges of land. See Tolley's Capital Gains Tax under Land.

D33 **Capital gains tax on compensation and damages.** Damages derived from underlying assets will be treated as exempt where the asset is exempt, and where there is no underlying asset damages will be exempt. See Tolley's Capital Gains Tax under Assets.

D34 **Rebasing and indexation: shares held at 31 March 1982.** A single holding treatment will apply even if the shares were acquired before 7 April 1965. See Tolley's Capital Gains Tax under Assets held on 31 March 1982.

D38 **Capital gains tax: qualifying corporate bonds.** A further relief may apply to certain bonds which became qualifying corporate bonds through a change in definition, although not evidenced by a qualifying loan. See Tolley's Capital Gains Tax under Losses.

D39 **Extensions of leases.** Relief is given where a lessee surrenders an existing lease and is granted a new, longer lease at arm's length on the same property at a different rent, but otherwise on the same terms. See Tolley's Capital Gains Tax under Land.

D42 **Mergers of leases.** Indexation allowance may be given on the costs of acquisition of a lease by reference to the date on which it was acquired, even though it ceased to exist on the acquisition of a superior interest in the property, such as the freehold reversion. This replaces an earlier practice for disposals after 28 June 1992. See Tolley's Capital Gains Tax under Land.

D44 **Rebasing and indexation: shares derived from larger holdings held at 31 March 1982.** A more favourable basis of valuation at 31 March 1982 for rebasing and indexation purposes may be available in relation to shares and securities acquired intra-group. See Tolley's Capital Gains Tax under Assets held on 31 March 1982.

D47 **Temporary loss of charitable status due to reverter of school and other sites.** Liabilities which may arise in the period before charitable status is re-established will be discharged or repaid. See 14.1 CHARITIES.

D50 **Capital gains tax treatment of compensation.** Gains arising on compensation from foreign governments may in certain circumstances be exempt. See Tolley's Capital Gains Tax under Disposal.

D51 **Transfer from a close company at undervalue.** *TCGA 1992, s 125* is not applied in certain cases where the transfer gives rise to a charge under other provisions. See 11.21 CAPITAL GAINS.

D52 **Share exchanges, company reconstructions and amalgamations — incidental costs of acquisition and disposal and warranty payments** may be treated as consideration given for the new holding. See Tolley's Capital Gains Tax under Shares and Securities.

I 1 **Gas and oil allowance.** Gas may be excluded from oil won and saved for certain PRT and APRT oil allowances.

I 3 **OTA 1975, Sch 3 para 9.** Certain time limits are extended.

I 4 **OTA 1983, s 9(5): tariff receipts allowance in respect of foreign 'user' fields** may be backdated to the date on which tariffs were first received or receivable.

I 5 **PRT instalments** may be withheld where production ceases following catastrophic loss or damage.

The following concessions applicable to individuals are also relevant to companies.

A37 **Tax treatment of directors' fees received by partnerships and other companies.** Where a company has the right to appoint a director to the board of another company and the director is required to hand over to the first company any fees or emoluments received from the second company (and does so), and the first company agrees to accept liability to corporation tax on the fees, the director is not charged to tax on those fees. Where the first company is not chargeable to corporation tax but to income tax (e.g. a non-resident company not trading through a branch or agency in the UK) and agrees to accept liability, tax is deducted at the basic rate from the fees. This practice is extended to the case where the first company has no formal right to appoint the director to the board but the director is required to, and does, hand over his fees, provided the first company is (*a*) chargeable to corporation tax on its income and (*b*) not a company over which the director has 'control'. '*Control*' for this purpose means the power of a person by shareholding or voting power (whether directly or through another company), or under Articles of Association, to secure that the company's affairs are conducted according to his wishes. [*ICTA 1988, s 840*]. For this purpose, the rights and powers of his spouse, his children and their spouses, and his parents are taken into account.

A69 **Building societies: conversion to company status.** Certain declarations made to a building society are treated as having been made to the successor company following conversion to company status. See 8.9 BANKS, 9.6 BUILDING SOCIETIES.

35 HMRC Statements of Practice

Simon's Direct Tax Service Part H3.

The following is a summary of those Statements of Practice published in HMRC Pamphlet SOP (2004) (available on HMRC's website), or subsequently announced, which are referred to in this book.

Statements are divided into those originally published before 18 July 1978 (which are given a reference letter (according to the subject matter) and consecutive number, e.g. A34) and later Statements (which are numbered consecutively in each year, e.g. SP 6/94).

Certain Statements marked in SOP as obsolete continue to be referred to in the text (having been relevant within the last six years), and the original source is quoted in such cases, as it is where the Statement awaits inclusion in SOP.

As regards HMRC internal guidance manuals, see 33.8 HMRC: ADMINISTRATION.

B1 **Treatment of VAT.** Guidance on the general principles applied in dealing with VAT in the computation of corporation tax liabilities. See 68 VALUE ADDED TAX.

B6 **Goods sold subject to reservation of title.** Goods treated as purchases in the accounts of the buyer will be similarly treated for tax purposes. See 66.75 TRADING INCOME.

C1 **Lotteries and football pools.** Where part of the cost of a ticket is to be donated to a club, etc., that part is, in certain circumstances, not treated as a trading receipt. See 66.9 TRADING INCOME, 70.6 VOLUNTARY ASSOCIATIONS.

C10 **Valuation fees.** Costs related to *Companies Act 1985* compliance are regarded as allowable expenses. See 66.66 TRADING INCOME.

D21 **Capital gains tax: 6 April 1965 valuation time limit: company leaving group: TCGA 1992, ss 178, 179.** HMRC will exercise discretion to extend the time limit as appropriate. See 12.32 CAPITAL GAINS—GROUPS.

SP 8/79 **Compensation for acquisition of property under compulsory powers.** Guidance as to the treatment of compensation for temporary loss of profits and expenses. See 18.2 COMPENSATION, DAMAGES, ETC.

SP 4/80 **Industrial Buildings Allowance: industrial workshops constructed for separate letting to small businesses.** Claims for estates consisting of small industrial workshops can be made on a global rather than individual basis. See 10.21 CAPITAL ALLOWANCES.

SP 5/80 **Group relief: ICTA 1988, s 410.** Guidance is given on the application of this section. (Revenue Press Release 26 March 1980). (Superseded by SP 3/93 below.) See 32.19 GROUPS OF COMPANIES.

SP 13/80 **Demergers: ICTA 1988, ss 213–218.** Guidance on the application of the provisions and on clearance procedures. See 32.32 ET SEQ. GROUPS OF COMPANIES.

SP 5/81 **Expenditure on farm drainage.** Certain expenditure to restore drainage is permitted as revenue expenditure. See 66.50 TRADING INCOME.

SP 8/81 **Replacement of business assets: groups of companies.** Conditions for relief explained where assets are disposed of or acquired by group companies after cessation or before commencement of trading. See 12.29 CAPITAL GAINS—GROUPS.

SP 11/81 **Additional redundancy payments: ICTA 1988, s 90.** The provisions for allowance as a deduction of such payments extended to partial discontinuances. See 66.40 TRADING INCOME.

SP 12/81 **Construction industry tax scheme: carpet fitting** is considered to be outside the scope of the scheme. See 20.2 CONSTRUCTION INDUSTRY SCHEME.

SP 2/82 **Company purchasing own shares: ICTA 1988, ss 219–229.** The conditions for relief are clarified. See 57.4(2), 57.6 PURCHASE BY A COMPANY OF ITS OWN SHARES.

SP 1/84 **Trade unions: provident benefits: legal and administrative expenses.** See 27.15 EXEMPT ORGANISATIONS.

SP 6/84 **Non-resident lessors: ICTA 1988, s 830.** The factors governing liability to tax on profits or gains of such lessors of mobile drilling rigs etc. are outlined. See 60.10 RESIDENCE.

SP 5/85 **Capital gains; division of a company on a share for share basis.** It is made clear that the existing practice (see D14 above) extends to demergers within *ICTA 1988, ss 213–218*. Superseded by *FA 2002, s 45, Sch 9*. See 11.9 CAPITAL GAINS, 32.34 GROUPS OF COMPANIES.

SP 2/86 **Offshore Funds.** Various aspects of the legislation are clarified. See 50.4–50.6 OFFSHORE FUNDS.

SP 1/87 **Exchange rate fluctuations.** HMRC practice following the *Marine Midland* decision is explained. (Replaced by SP 2/02 below.) See 26.3, 26.4 EXCHANGE GAINS AND LOSSES.

SP 9/87 **Capital allowances: hotels.** HMRC's interpretation of the provision of breakfast and evening meals by a qualifying hotel. See 10.18 CAPITAL ALLOWANCES.

SP 6/88 **Double taxation relief: capital gains tax.** The conditions under which relief is available are clarified. See 24.5 DOUBLE TAX RELIEF.

SP 6/89 **Delay in rendering tax returns: interest on overdue tax: TMA 1970, s 88.** The circumstances in which interest will be sought are clarified. See 41.4 INTEREST ON UNPAID TAX.

SP 1/90 **Company residence.** HMRC's interpretation of the application of the case law on company residence is explained. See 60.1, 60.2 RESIDENCE.

SP 2/90 **Guidance notes for migrating companies: notice and arrangements for payment of tax.** See 60.8 RESIDENCE.

SP 3/90 **Stocks and long-term contracts.** Revenue practice as regards bases of valuation and changes therein. Obsolete. See 66.31 TRADING INCOME.

SP 1/91 **Small companies' rate of corporation tax and corporation tax starting rate.** The claims procedure is explained. See 63.1, 63.4 SMALL COMPANIES—REDUCED RATES.

SP 3/91 **Finance lease rental payments.** See 66.54 TRADING INCOME.

SP 7/91 **Double taxation: business profits: unilateral relief.** Revenue practice as regards admission of foreign taxes for relief is revised. See 24.2 DOUBLE TAX RELIEF.

SP 10/91 **Corporation tax: a major change in the nature or conduct of a trade.** HMRC's interpretation of that expression is explained. See 12.16 CAPITAL GAINS—GROUPS, 47.13 LOSSES.

SP 12/91 **Income tax: 'in the ordinary course' of banking business.** HMRC's interpretation of this expression is explained. (Superseded by SP 4/96 below.) See 8.2 BANKS.

SP 16/91 **Accountancy expenses arising out of accounts investigations.** Revenue practice on the allowance of such expenses. See 66.63 TRADING INCOME.

SP 2/92 **Transactions within ICTA 1988, s 765A: movements of capital between residents of EC member states.** Guidance as to when the relevant provisions apply and on procedural matters. See 5.10 ANTI-AVOIDANCE.

SP 4/92 **Capital gains re-basing elections.** Certain disposals are ignored in relation to the time limit for such elections. See 12.30 CAPITAL GAINS—GROUPS.

SP 3/93 **Groups of companies: arrangements.** Guidance on HMRC's interpretation of 'arrangements' for the various purposes of the group legislation. See 32.4, 32.9, 32.19, 32.23 GROUPS OF COMPANIES.

SP 5/93 **UK/Czechoslovakia double taxation Convention.** The Convention is regarded as applying to the Czech and Slovak Republics. See 24.14 DOUBLE TAX RELIEF.

SP 6/93 **UK/Yugoslavia double taxation Convention.** The Convention is regarded as applying to Croatia, Slovenia, Macedonia and the former Republic of Yugoslavia. Now replaced and superseded by SP 3/04 (see below). See 24.14 DOUBLE TAX RELIEF.

SP 12/93 **Double taxation — dividend income — tax credit relief** for dividends paid under a 'company tax deducted' arrangement may be restricted. See 24.10 DOUBLE TAX RELIEF.

SP 15/93 **Business tax computations rounded to nearest £1,000** will be accepted in certain cases. See 61.19 RETURNS.

SP 5/94 **Associated companies for small companies' relief and corporation tax starting rate — holding companies.** The circumstances in which a holding company is disregarded in calculating profits limits are explained. See 63.7 SMALL COMPANIES—REDUCED RATES.

SP 2/95 **Payment of tax credits to non-resident companies.** HMRC consider that a claim for repayment of tax credits under *ICTA 1988, s 242* may not be made by a non-resident company notwithstanding the existence of a non-discrimination clause in the relevant double tax treaty. See 24.3 DOUBLE TAX RELIEF.

SP 3/95 **Financial instruments: definition of financial trader for purposes of FA 1994, s 177(1).** The guidelines used by HMRC in deciding whether a company should be approved as a financial trader are explained. (Replaced by SP 4/02 below.) See 28.45 FINANCIAL INSTRUMENTS AND DERIVATIVE CONTRACTS.

SP 8/95 **Venture capital trusts — default terms in loan agreements.** Certain event of default clauses will not disqualify a loan from being a security for the purposes of approval. See 69.2 VENTURE CAPITAL TRUSTS.

SP 4/96 **Income tax — interest paid in the ordinary course of a bank's business.** HMRC's interpretation of this requirement is explained. See 8.2 BANKS.

SP 1/97 **The electronic lodgement service.** HMRC's operation and detailed requirements of the scheme are explained. See 61.28 RETURNS.

SP 2/97 **Authorised unit trusts, approved investment trusts, and open-ended investment companies — monthly savings schemes.** A simplified method of calculating the chargeable gain arising on a disposal may be used. (Superseded by SP 2/99 below.) See 43.5 INVESTMENT FUNDS.

SP 3/97 **Investment trusts investing in authorised unit trusts or open-ended investment companies.** The conditions under which such investments may be made are clarified. See 43 INVESTMENT FUNDS and 44.1 INVESTMENT TRUSTS.

SP 4/97 **Taxation of commission, cashbacks and discounts.** HMRC's views are outlined. See 66.25 TRADING INCOME.

SP 7/98 **Enterprise investment scheme, venture capital trusts and capital gains tax reinvestment relief — location of activity.** The requirement that trade(s) be carried on 'wholly or mainly in the UK' is clarified. (Superseded by SP 3/00 below.) See 69.3(*b*) VENTURE CAPITAL TRUSTS.

SP 3/99 **Advance pricing agreements (APAs).** The detailed administration of the scheme of APAs relating to transfer pricing issues is explained. See 67 TRANSFER PRICING.

SP 1/00 **Corporate venturing scheme — applications for advance clearance under FA 2000, Sch 15 Pt X.** The requirements for such applications are set out. See 22.9 CORPORATE VENTURING SCHEME.

SP 2/00 **Venture capital trusts, the enterprise investment scheme, the corporate venturing scheme and enterprise management incentives — value of 'gross assets'.** HMRC's general approach to the valuation of gross assets is explained. Replaced SP 5/98. See 22.6 CORPORATE VENTURING SCHEME, 69.3(E) VENTURE CAPITAL TRUSTS.

SP 3/00 **Enterprise investment scheme, venture capital trusts, corporate venturing scheme, enterprise management incentives and capital gains tax reinvestment relief — location of activity.** The requirement that trade(s) be carried on 'wholly or mainly in the UK' is clarified. Replaces SP 7/98 above. See 22.7 CORPORATE VENTURING SCHEME, 69.3(2)(b) VENTURE CAPITAL TRUSTS.

SP 4/00 **Tonnage tax.** Detailed administrative practice for the entire tonnage tax regime is set out. See 55.16 PROFIT COMPUTATIONS.

SP 1/01 **Treatment of investment managers and their overseas clients.** Guidance is given on the application of the *FA 1995* rules. See 60.5, 60.6 RESIDENCE

SP 2/01 **Improving the tax system for international companies: local currency statement of practice.** The treatment of partnerships which include 'qualifying companies' under the *FA 1993* rules is outlined. See 26.42 EXCHANGE GAINS AND LOSSES.

SP 3/01 **Relief for underlying tax.** The treatment of foreign dividends paid out of profits subject to variable rates of tax or where there are accumulated losses is clarified. (Revenue Press Release 27 November 2001; Annex D to Technical Note 'An Exemption for Substantial Shareholdings). See 24.10 DOUBLE TAX RELIEF.

SP 4/01 **Double taxation relief — status of the UK's double taxation conventions with the former USSR and with newly independent states.** The current position is clarified. See 24.14 DOUBLE TAX RELIEF.

SP 5/01 **Loss relief, capital allowances and group relief.** The conditions for acceptance of late claims for relief are set out. See 47.2 LOSSES.

SP 1/02 **Corporation tax self-assessment and chargeable gains valuations.** Certain enquiries remaining open solely because of an unagreed chargeable gains valuation will be limited to outstanding matters relating to the valuation. See 61.10 RETURNS.

SP 2/02 **Exchange rate fluctuations.** Revenue practice is explained. (Replaces SP 1/87 above, but does not apply to companies within the charge to corporation tax.) (Revenue Internet Statement 30 September 2002.) See 26.3, 26.4 EXCHANGE GAINS AND LOSSES.

SP 4/02 **Definition of financial trader for the purposes of FA 2002, Sch 26 para 31.** The guidelines used by HMRC in deciding whether a company should be approved as a financial trader are explained. (Replaces SP 3/95 above.) (Revenue Internet Statement 30 September 2002.) See 28.22, 28.45 FINANCIAL INSTRUMENTS AND DERIVATIVE CONTRACTS.

SP 5/02 **Exemptions for companies' gains on substantial shareholdings: sole or main benefit test: TCGA 1992, Sch 7AC para 5.** Revenue guidance is given on the application of the anti-avoidance rule. (Revenue Internet Statement 29 October 2002.) See 13.8 CAPITAL GAINS — SUBSTANTIAL SHAREHOLDINGS.

SP 3/04 **Double taxation relief: Status of the UK's double taxation conventions with the former Socialist Federal Republic of Yugoslavia.** This replaces and supersedes Statement of Practice 6/93. It confirms that the provisions of the UK/Yugoslavia Double Taxation Convention will be treated as remaining in force between the UK and respectively, Bosnia-Herzegovina, Croatia, Macedonia, Serbia and Montenegro and Slovenia. See 24.14 DOUBLE TAX RELIEF.

SP 1/06 **Self-Assessment: Finality and Discovery.** This clarifies how much information a taxpayer needs to provide in the tax return to remove the possibility of a discovery assessment. See 7.2 ASSESSMENTS.

36 Housing Associations etc.

Simon's Direct Tax Service D4.637 *et seq.*

36.1 EXEMPTIONS FOR APPROVED ASSOCIATIONS

Housing associations within the meaning of *Housing Associations Act 1985* (or the corresponding NI enactment) which are approved by the Secretary of State for the Environment, the Secretary of State for Scotland or Wales, or the Head of the Department of the Environment for NI (or under delegated authority) may claim that rent to which they are entitled from their members be disregarded for tax purposes.

Interest payable by a housing association is also disregarded (in relation to the association) unless it relates to any period not subject to a tenancy in which case the amount of interest attributable to that property is treated as so paid. The total yearly interest paid by an association is apportioned in the ratio that rents bear to the total rent roll, and for this purpose a notional rent is attributed to each unlet property at the rate payable when it was last let by the association.

[*ICTA 1988, s 488(1)(2)(6)(7A)*].

Example

A housing association pays yearly interest of £4,000 in 2007/08. It has three properties, two of which are occupied and one vacant. The last rent charged for this latter property was £400 p.a.

Rents	£
Property A	400
Property B	800
Property C (unoccupied)	400
Total rents	£1,600

Interest attributable to

Property A	$\frac{400}{1,600} \times £4,000$	£1,000
Property B	$\frac{800}{1,600} \times £4,000$	£2,000
Interest attributable to let properties treated as not paid		£3,000

The balance of £1,000 interest paid by the association is treated as so paid for tax purposes.

The Treasury may, by statutory instrument, make provision for the deduction of tax from certain interest payments by housing associations. See 37.6 INCOME TAX IN RELATION TO A COMPANY and Tolley's Income Tax under Deduction of Tax at Source.

[*ICTA 1988, s 488*].

36.2 APPROVED ASSOCIATIONS

A housing association may only be approved as in 36.1 above if certain conditions are satisfied.

(*a*) The association must be (or be deemed to be) duly registered under *Industrial and Provident Societies Act 1965* or its NI equivalent.

(*b*) Membership must be restricted to tenants or prospective tenants, and the grant or assignment of tenancies must be restricted to members.

(*c*) The association must satisfy such other requirements as may be laid down by the approving authority (under *ICTA 1988, s 488(8)*).

[*ICTA 1988, s 488(6)*].

36.3 CLAIMS

A claim must be made to the inspector within two years of the end of the accounting period to which it relates, in such form and containing such particulars as may be prescribed by HMRC, but it is understood that there is no prescribed standard form for such a claim. [*ICTA 1988, s 488(9); FA 1999, Sch 4 paras 15, 18*].

For a claim to be effective, the following requirements must substantially be complied with for the period to which the claim relates:

(*a*) none of its property was let otherwise than to a member;

(*b*) none of its property was occupied other than by a member (or, for a maximum period of six months after a member's death, by his personal representatives); and

(*c*) all covenants required to be included in grants of tenancies by the approving authority (under *section 488(8)*) have been observed.

If HMRC subsequently discover that these conditions (and those outlined in 36.1, 36.2 above) have not been fulfilled during the period to which the claim relates, acceptance of the claim may be withdrawn and the tax liability of all persons concerned adjusted accordingly. Similar adjustments are to be made, where necessary, on the acceptance of a claim. Such adjustments are made where, following an enquiry, the association's claim or company tax return is amended. [*ICTA 1988, s 488(4)(10)(11)(11A)*].

36.4 RELIEF BY GRANT

Housing associations as defined in *Housing Associations Act 1985*, which are not approved under *section 488* and do not trade for profit, may claim relief from corporation tax, by means of a grant. See *Haywards Heath Housing Society v Hewison Ch D 1966, 43 TC 321*. The claim must be made to the Secretary of State for the Environment or the Secretary of State for Scotland or Wales and the association must show that, throughout the period for which the claim is made, the association carried out the provision or maintenance of houses for letting or of hostels, and activities incidental thereto. The form of the claim and its supporting evidence are as may be required by the Minister, and HMRC are authorised to disclose information to him. The terms and conditions of the grant are within the Minister's discretion, save that no relief is available for tax attributable to activities other than those specified above. These provisions do not extend to NI. A housing association must be registered to be eligible for relief. [*Housing Act 1988, s 54*].

36.5 CHARGEABLE GAINS

An approved housing association within *section 488* may claim exemption from corporation tax on chargeable gains accruing on the sale of any property which is or has been occupied by a tenant of the association. [*ICTA 1988, s 488*(*5*)]. A claim is made as under 36.3 above. [*ICTA 1988, s 488*(*9*)–(*11*)]. Disposals of land and other assets by a housing association (as defined in *Housing Associations Act 1985*) to the Housing Corporation or Housing for Wales (or the Secretary of State) under a scheme within *Housing Act 1964, s 5* or *Housing Associations Act 1985, Sch 7 para 5,* and subsequent disposals of those assets by the Corporation, etc. to a single housing association, are treated as taking place on a no gain, no loss basis. The same applies to

(*a*) transfers of land between the Housing Corporation or Housing for Wales (or the Secretary of State) and *registered* housing associations,

(*b*) transfers of land between such associations, and

(*c*) transfers under a direction from the Corporation, etc. of property other than land between such associations.

Similar relief applies to NI housing associations from 6 April 1984.

[*TCGA 1992, ss 218–220; Housing Act 1988, Sch 17 para 93; Government of Wales Act 1998, Sch 16 paras 77-80*].

A disposal to a registered housing association of an estate or interest in land otherwise than at arm's length may, on a joint claim, be treated as at a 'no gain, no loss' consideration, the transferor's acquisition being treated as that of the association on a subsequent disposal. [*TCGA 1992, s 259*].

36.6 APPROVED SELF-BUILD SOCIETIES

A self-build society (within the meaning of *Housing Associations Act 1985*) which is registered (or deemed to be registered) under *Industrial and Provident Societies Act 1965* and which is approved by the Secretary of State (or under delegated authority) may claim relief from corporation tax on rent receivable from its members and on chargeable gains arising on the disposal of any land to a member, provided that none of its land is occupied by a non-member. The relief applies, with appropriate modification, to NI self-build societies. [*ICTA 1988, s 489; Housing Act 1996, Sch 3 para 8*]. Claims are made as outlined in 36.3 above.

Disposals of land by unregistered self-build societies to the Housing Corporation or Housing for Wales (or the Secretary of State) are treated as being for such consideration that no chargeable gain or allowable loss arises. [*TCGA 1992, s 219; Housing Act 1988, Sch 17 para 93; Government of Wales Act 1998, Sch 16 para 79*].

37 Income Tax in relation to a Company

Cross-reference. See 32 GROUPS OF COMPANIES.

37.1 INTRODUCTION

The corporation tax liability of a company is computed by reference to income tax principles, except as otherwise provided. [*ICTA 1988, s 9; ITTOIA 2005, Sch 1 para 7*]. See 55.3 PROFIT COMPUTATIONS.

37.2 *Income tax* is not charged on the income (other than income received in a fiduciary or representative capacity) of a company resident in the UK or, if the company is resident abroad, on any income which is chargeable to corporation tax (regarding which see 60 RESIDENCE). [*ICTA 1988, s 6(2)*].

37.3 PAYMENTS BY A COMPANY ETC.

(*a*) **Annual payments.** Income tax at the basic rate is deductible from annuities, annual payments and patent royalties (and this applies whether the payments are made by a company or any other person, but see below as regards inter-company payments). [*ICTA 1988, s 349(1); ITA 2007, s 449*]. But certain annual payments made for non-taxable consideration or, if made on or after 2 December 2004, for dividends, do not have tax deducted and (where made before 16 March 2005) are not a charge for corporation tax purposes. [*ICTA 1988, s 125; FA 2005, s 91; F(No 2)A 2005, s 38(3)(7)(13), Sch 11 Pt 2(7)*]. See further details in 5.20 ANTI-AVOIDANCE.

(*b*) **Interest.** Income tax at the lower rate is deductible from yearly interest of money chargeable to tax under *ITTOIA 2005, Pt 4 Ch 2* (or before 2005/06 Schedule D, Case III) (as it applies for income tax purposes, regarding which see Tolley's Income Tax, under Savings and Investment Income) if such interest is paid:

(i) *by* a company or local authority (otherwise than in a fiduciary or representative capacity), or

(ii) *by* or for a partnership of which a company is a member; or

(iii) *to* a person whose usual place of abode is outside the UK (subject to 37.4 below).

[*ICTA 1988, s 349(2); FA 2004, s 105(5); ITTOIA 2005, Sch 1 para 148(3); ITA 2007, s 449*].

See, however, below as regards certain payments by companies and local authorities.

For payments on or after 6 April 2005 by a company which is a financial institution, *ICTA 1988, s 349* has effect in relation to alternative finance return or profit share return (see 4 ALTERNATIVE FINANCE ARRANGEMENTS) as it has effect in relation to interest. This applies to alternative finance arrangements entered into on or after 6 April 2005 subject to commencement rules for arrangements entered into before that date where a profit share return is payable on or after that date. [*FA 2005, s 56, Sch 2 para 3; ITA 2007 Sch 1 para 452*].

Interest under the *Late Payment of Commercial Debts (Interest) Act 1998* (or under a contractual right but for which that *Act* would have applied) is *not* 'yearly interest'. (Revenue Tax Bulletin August 1999 pp 686, 687).

For advances made on or after 29 April 1996, interest payable on an advance from a bank (within *ICTA 1988, s 840A*, see 8.1 BANKS) is excluded where the person beneficially entitled to the interest is within the charge to corporation tax in respect of it, as is interest paid by such a bank in the ordinary course of its business. See 8.2

BANKS for earlier provisions and generally. See also 8.9 BANKS as regards certain payments of interest by banks and certain other borrowers. Interest paid to BUILDING SOCIETIES (9) is payable gross, including (for payments on or after 6 April 2005) alternative finance return and profit share return under ALTERNATIVE FINANCE ARRANGEMENTS (4) treated as interest. [*ICTA 1988, s 349(3)(3A), s 476(9), s 477A(7); FA 2005, Sch 2 para 5; ITA 2007, ss 449, 901*]. For other specific exclusions from the deduction requirement, see Tolley's Income Tax (under Deduction of Tax at Source).

'*UK public revenue dividends*' (i.e. any income from securities which is paid out of the UK or NI public revenue, but excluding interest on local authority stock (see (i) above)) are, from 1 April 2001, payable under deduction of tax, subject to any provision to the contrary in the *Taxes Acts* (and see in particular 37.8 below as regards gilt-edged securities). HMRC have wide powers to make regulations governing the accounting arrangements and modifying *ITA 2007, ss 449, 899, 901, 903, 946, 962–964* (formerly *ICTA 1988, ss 349, 350*) in their application to UK public revenue dividends. [*ICTA 1988, ss 349(3C)(4), 350A; FA 2000, s 112(2)-(5)*]. For the deduction of tax from UK public revenue dividends by paying agents before 1 April 2001, see *ICTA 1988, ss 118A-118K* and regulations thereunder.

Interest paid on '*quoted Eurobonds*' (i.e. listed securities issued by a company and carrying a right to interest) is excluded from the above provisions for deduction of tax from interest **from 1 April 2001**. For payments made before that date, the exclusion applies only where the security is in bearer form and:

(A) the payment is made by or through a person who is not in the UK; or

(B) where (A) above does not apply, either:

  (i) the bond is held in a 'recognised clearing system' (as designated by HMRC); or

  (ii) the beneficial owner of the bond is non-UK resident and is beneficially entitled to the interest.

HMRC have regulatory powers to disapply (B) above unless certain declarations confirming eligibility are received by the payer or HMRC have issued the appropriate notice. See *SI 1996 No 1779*. [*ICTA 1988, ss 124, 841A; FA 2000, s 111(2)(6), Sch 40 Pt II(17)*].

Broadly, designation by HMRC as a 'recognised clearing system' requires that the applicant for designation is a substantial and reputable organisation which is internationally accepted in the Eurobond market as a clearing system for holding and trading in internationally traded Eurobonds for the institutions which participate in that market. Cedel and Euroclear have been so designated.

(*c*) **Copyright and design royalties and public lending rights.** Subject to the special rules for inter-company payments (see below) and to the exemption for payments between associated companies in EU member states (see 37.4 below), income tax must be deducted at the basic rate from such payments to an owner whose usual place of abode is outside the UK as if they were annual payments. A paying agent must deduct his commission (if any) before the tax is computed. [*ICTA 1988, ss 536, 537, 537B*].

But see 32 GROUPS OF COMPANIES for elections to pay intra-group and intra-consortium dividends without accounting for ACT and to pay charges without deducting income tax.

Certain payments by companies and local authorities. The provisions listed at (i) to (iv) below (which require tax to be deducted on the making of certain payments) do not apply to payments made by a company **after 31 March 2001**, or by a local authority **after**

30 September 2002, where the company or local authority reasonably believes that, at the time the payment is made, one of the following conditions is satisfied. For payments made on or before 30 September 2002, either (*a*) or (*b*) must be satisfied, for payments made after that date any one of (*a*)–(*e*) may be satisfied.

(*a*) The person beneficially entitled to the income in respect of which the payment is made is a UK-resident company (or, for payments made before 1 October 2002, a partnership of which each member is such a company — see now (*e*) below).

(*b*) The person beneficially entitled to the income in respect of which the payment is made is a non-UK resident company which carries on a trade in the UK through a permanent establishment (see 60.5 RESIDENCE — previously a branch or agency) and in computing whose 'chargeable profits' (see 60.5, 60.6 RESIDENCE) the payment falls to be brought into account.

(*c*) The payment is made to (or, from 1 December 2002, to the nominee of) one of the following:

- (i) a local authority;
- (ii) a health service body within *ICTA 1988, s 519A(2)*;
- (iii) a public officer or department of the Crown within *ICTA 1988, s 829(1)*;
- (iv) a charity within *ICTA 1988, s 506(1)* (see 14.1 CHARITIES);
- (v) a body mentioned in *ICTA 1988, s 507(1)* (bodies afforded the same tax exemptions as charities, see 27.8, 27.11, 27.17 EXEMPT ORGANISATIONS);
- (vi) a scientific research organisation within *ICTA 1988, s 508*;
- (vii) the United Kingdom Atomic Energy Authority;
- (viii) the National Radiological Protection Board;
- (ix) the administrator of an approved pension scheme within *ICTA 1988, s 592(2)* or *s 608(2)* (see 27.14 EXEMPT ORGANISATIONS);
- (x) the trustees of a Parliamentary pension fund within *ICTA 1988, s 613(4)*;
- (xi) the persons entitled to receive the income of certain colonial, etc. pension funds within *ICTA 1988, s 614(3)*;
- (xii) the trustees or managers of a retirement annuity trust scheme within *ICTA 1988, s 620(6)*;
- (xiii) a person holding investments or deposits of an approved personal pension scheme within *ICTA 1988, s 643(2)*.

(*d*) The person to whom the payment is made is (or is the nominee of) the plan manager of an individual investment plan under *ITTOIA 2005, Pt 6 Ch 3* (before 2005/06 a personal equity plan or individual savings account under *ICTA 1988, s 333* or a TESSA account with *ICTA 1988, s 326A*), and receives the payment in respect of plan investments. For payments on or after 6 April 2005, it is no longer a condition, as it was for payments made before that date, that the payer must 'reasonably believe' the individual investor to be exempt from tax on the interest.

(*e*) The person beneficially entitled to the income in respect of which the payment is made is a partnership each member of which is either:

- (i) a body within (*c*) above; or
- (ii) a UK-resident company; or

(iii) a non-UK resident company which carries on a trade in the UK through a permanent establishment (or branch or agency) and in computing whose 'chargeable profits' (see 60.5, 60.6 RESIDENCE) the company's share of the payment falls to be brought into account' or

(iv) the European Investment Fund.

The Treasury has powers by order to amend the persons and bodies to whom (*c*) and (*f*)(ii)–(iv) above apply.

This applies equally to payments by a partnership of which a company or local authority is a member, but not where a company makes a payment acting as trustee or agent for another person.

The provisions concerned are:

(i) *ICTA 1988, s 349(1)* (certain annuities and other annual payments and royalties and other sums paid for the use of UK patents);

(ii) *ICTA 1988, s 349(2)(a)(b)* (UK interest);

(iii) *ICTA 1988, s 349(3A)* (dividends or interest on securities issued by building societies); and

(iv) *ICTA 1988, s 349ZA(2)* (before 6 April 2005 *ICTA 1988, s 524(3)(b)*) (proceeds of sale of UK patent rights).

(i)–(iii) above do not apply to those provisions as applied under *ICTA 1988, s 777(9)* (certain payments to non-residents) or *ICTA 1988, Sch 23A para 4(2)* (manufactured overseas dividends). See above and 5.9 ANTI-AVOIDANCE for the general application of these provisions.

Where HMRC have reasonable grounds for believing that none of the relevant conditions above will be satisfied in relation to any payment at the time the payment is made, they may give a direction to a company or local authority (or a partnership of which a company or local authority is a member) disapplying the above relief in relation to any such payment. The direction may refer to either a particular payment or a specified description of payment, but may not apply to payments made before the giving of the direction.

Where a company or local authority (or a partnership of which a company or local authority is a member) makes a payment without deduction of tax in the reasonable belief that one of the relevant conditions above applied, but none of the relevant conditions was in fact met, *ICTA 1988, s 350* and *Sch 16* (see 37.5 below) apply as if tax was deductible under *ITA 2007 ss 449, 899, 901, 903* (formerly *ICTA 1988, s 349*).

Penalties of up to £3,000 (and £600 per day for continuing failure) may be imposed under *TMA 1970, s 98* for failure to deduct and account for tax where the conditions for the relief described above are not satisfied.

[*ICTA 1988, ss 349A-349D; TMA 1970, s 98(4A)-(4C); FA 2001, s 85; FA 2002, s 94, Sch 40 Pt 3(14); SI 2002 No 2931; ITTOIA 2005, Sch 1 paras 133, 141, 150, 151; F(No 2)A 2005, s 22; Sch 11 Pt 2(3)*].

Deduction of tax from annual payments under *ICTA 1988, s 349(1)* does not apply to payments to the London Organising Committee of the Olympic Games Limited (see 27.19 EXEMPT ORGANISATIONS).

See Revenue Tax Bulletin August 2001 pp 867, 868 for a brief summary of the provisions and an indication of HMRC's approach to the 'reasonable belief' requirement.

Cross-border royalties. For payments made by companies **after 30 September 2002** of royalties within *ITA 2007, ss 449, 901* (formerly *ICTA 1988, s 349(1)*) in respect of which the company reasonably believes that, at the time the payment is made, the 'payee' (i.e. the person beneficially entitled to the income in respect of which the payment is made) is entitled to relief under any double tax arrangements, the company may, if it thinks fit, calculate the sum to be deducted from the payment under *section 349(1)* by reference to the rate of income tax appropriate to the payee under the arrangements (and, if appropriate, pay the interest gross). If the payee was not so entitled, the company must account for the tax as if the above rule had never applied, and HMRC have powers to direct the company that it is not to apply to a particular payment or payments. 'Royalty' for this purpose includes any payment received as consideration for the use of, or the right to use, any copyright, patent, trade mark, design, process or information, and any proceeds of sale of all or any part of any patent rights. Information about such payments may be required in a company's tax return (subject to a penalty of up to £3,000 under *FA 1998, Sch 18 para 20* (see 61.26 RETURNS) for failure). Penalties of up to £3,000 (and £600 per day for continuing failure) may be imposed under *TMA s 98* for failure to deduct and account for tax where the conditions for the relief described above are not satisfied. [*ICTA 1988, s 349E; TMA 1970, s 98(4D); FA 2002, s 96*]. See also 37.4 below.

Simon's Direct Tax Service. See **A3.402** *et seq.*

37.4 **INTEREST AND ROYALTIES: EXEMPTION FROM INCOME TAX**

The EU Directive 2003/49/EC of 3 June 2003 on a common system of taxation applicable to interest and royalty payments made between associated companies of EU member states is implemented in the UK for payments made **on or after 1 January 2004** unless indicated otherwise below. The Treasury may amend by order the provisions set out below for the purpose of implementing any amendment to or replacement of the Directive adopted after 8 April 2004. [*FA 2004, ss 97, 106; ITTOIA 2005, s 757, Sch 1 paras 631, 639*]. See *SI 2005 No 2899* dealing with the accession of new member states to the EU and various transitional arrangements.

Exemption from income tax. Except as below, payments of interest or royalties are not liable to income tax provided that at the time the payment is made:

(*a*) it is made by a UK company or a UK permanent establishment of an EU company (but not a UK company's permanent establishment in a territory other than the UK);

(*b*) the person beneficially entitled to the income is an EU company (but not such a company's UK or non-EU permanent establishment);

(*c*) the companies referred to in (*a*) and (*b*) above are 25% associates (see below); and

(*d*) if the payment is one of interest, HMRC has issued an exemption notice.

As regards (*a*) above, a payment is treated as made by a permanent establishment in a territory of a company resident in another territory (and not by the company) if and to the extent that it represents a tax-deductible expense for that permanent establishment. As regards (*b*) above, the person beneficially entitled to the income is an EU company's UK or non-EU permanent establishment (rather than the company) if and to the extent that the payment is directly connected to the permanent establishment's business and is subject to corporation tax (or foreign equivalent) in the State where the permanent establishment is situated. As regards (*c*) above, two companies are '*25% associates*' if one of them holds directly 25% or more of the capital or voting rights in the other or a third company holds directly 25% or more of the capital or voting rights in each of them. As regards (*d*) above, the procedures governing the issue of exemption notices are set out in the *Exemption from Tax for Certain Interest Payments Regulations 2004* (*SI 2004 No 2622*). The regulations also make provision for the cancellation of an exemption notice where the conditions are not satisfied and also for the recovery of tax. [*FA 2004, ss 98–100; ITTOIA 2005, ss 758–762, Sch 1 paras 632–634; SI 2004 No 2622; ITA 2007, s 758, Sch 1 paras 576, 577*].

Payment of royalties without deduction at source. For payments made of royalties within *ITA 2007 ss 449, 901* (formerly *ICTA 1988, s 349(1)*) in respect of which the company reasonably believes that, at the time the payment is made, the payment falls within the above exemption under *ITTOIA 2005,s 758* (or, before 6 April 2005, *FA 2004, s 98*), the company may, if it thinks fit, make the payment without deduction of tax. If the exemption did not in fact apply to the payment, the company must account for the tax as if the above rule had never applied, and HMRC have powers to direct the company that it is not to apply to a particular payment or payments (and such directions may be varied or revoked by subsequent directions). If, before the royalty payment is made, the company beneficially entitled to the payment believed the exemption would apply but has subsequently become aware that it would not, it must without delay notify HMRC and the company making the payment. Information about such payments may be required in a company's tax return (subject to a penalty of up to £3,000 under *FA 1998, Sch 18 para 20* (see 61.26 RETURNS) for an incorrect or uncorrected return). Penalties of up to £3,000 (and £600 per day for continuing failure) may be imposed under *TMA 1970, s 98* for failure to deduct and account for tax where the exemption does not apply and the company did not believe or could not reasonably have believed that it would apply. Where the exemption applies but a payment has been made subject to deduction of tax source, a claim for relief may be made to HMRC. [*TMA 1970, s 98(4DA); FA 2004, ss 101, 102, 105; ITTOIA 2005, Sch 1 paras 379, 635(2)–(4), 636*].

Special relationships. The above exemption does not apply to so much of any interest or royalties paid between parties in a 'special relationship' as exceeds the amount that would have been paid in the absence of such relationship (i.e. payments exceeding an arm's length amount (which may be nil)). '*Special relationship*' in this case is construed in the same way as under *ICTA 1988, ss 808A* (in the case of interest) and *808B* (in the case of royalties) as set out in 24.4 DOUBLE TAX RELIEF. This provision does not affect any claim for double taxation relief under *ICTA 1988, s 788* (see 24.3 DOUBLE TAX RELIEF). [*FA 2004, s 103; ITTOIA 2005, ss 763, 764, Sch 1 para 635(5), 637*].

Anti-avoidance. The above exemption does not apply to a payment of interest or royalties made **on or after 8 April 2004** where the main purpose or one of the main purposes for the creation or assignment of the debt-claim in the case of interest, or the right in respect of royalties, is to take advantage of the exemption. [*FA 2004, s 104; ITTOIA 2005, s 765, Sch 1 para 638*]. (This might apply for example where a loan from a non-EU resident company is routed through an EU-resident associate.)

Claims. Guidance notes on the implementation of the EU Directive and on how HMRC, Centre for Non-Residents deal with applications for relief from UK tax are available on HMRC's website (www.hmrc.gov.uk/cnr/form_crossborder.htm). The Centre for Non-Residents has published guidance notes, CNR DT 6 and 7, dealing with the above changes, the accession of 10 additional states to the European Union on 1 May 2004, and how this affects claims for relief.

37.5 INCOME TAX DEDUCTIONS FROM PAYMENTS

A UK-resident company must make a return to the Collector of Taxes of:

(i) payments from which it was liable to deduct income tax and the income tax for which it is accountable; and

(ii) credits that it claims for income tax deducted from payments received.

[*ICTA 1988, s 350(4), Sch 16 paras 3, 5; ITA 2007, ss 946, 962*].

Returns must be made for 'return periods' which end on 31 March, 30 June, 30 September, 31 December and at the end of an accounting period of the company. Such returns must be made within 14 days of the end of the return period. [*ICTA 1988, Sch 16 para 2*]. If a relevant payment is made outside an accounting period, a return must be made within 14 days of the payment. If a company becomes aware of an error in the return, it must submit an amended return for that period. [*ICTA 1988, Sch 16 paras 7A, 9*].

Credit can be claimed in a return for income tax deducted from payments received in the accounting period in which the return period falls. [*ICTA 1988, Sch 16 para 5*].

The company is liable to pay to HMRC the income tax it deducted (or was liable to deduct) from payments (against which it may claim credit for income tax deducted from payments received) at the time by which the return is to be made, i.e. 14 days after the end of the return period (or 14 days after a payment which is not made in an accounting period). An officer of HMRC has power to assess the company if he considers that a return is incorrect, or believes that a payment has not been returned. [*ICTA 1988, Sch 16 paras 4, 5*].

See 8.9 BANKS as regards returns of tax deducted from bank interest payments and 9.4 BUILDING SOCIETIES as regards building society interest.

See 41.7 INTEREST ON UNPAID TAX for the position if such income tax is not paid by the due date. The raising of an assessment on the company does not affect the due date of payment of the tax for interest purposes. [*ICTA 1988, Sch 16 para 4(2)*].

Return form CT61 is used for making returns required as above.

For the information which must be provided by the payer in relation to a distribution, see 23.17 DISTRIBUTIONS.

Non-UK resident companies (and non-corporates) are directly liable to assessment under *ICTA 1988, s 350*, as *ICTA 1988, Sch 16* does not apply. See 41.7 INTEREST ON UNPAID TAX as regards interest on late paid tax under such assessments.

Simon's Direct Tax Service. See **D1.610** *et seq.*

37.6 INCOME TAX SUFFERED BY A COMPANY

See 37.3 above which also indicates the extent to which income tax will be deducted from payments received by a company. Companies receive payments under deduction of tax much less frequently following changes made by *FA 2001* and *FA 2002* (see 37.3 above). See Tolley's Income Tax under Deduction of Tax at Source with regard to income tax deducted from payments by individuals.

See 37.5 above for the relief that a company may obtain by setting off such income tax against its accountability to HMRC for income tax deducted from payments by it in the same accounting period. For tax deducted from 'relevant loan interest', however, the company may claim repayment of the tax directly.

To the extent that relief is not obtained as above by a UK resident company (e.g. where income tax suffered on receipts exceeds income tax deducted from payments), such excess income tax suffered on receipts is set off against the corporation tax assessable on the company for the accounting period. If it exceeds the corporation tax payable, the company may claim a repayment. See 61.7 RETURNS. [*ICTA 1988, s 7(2)*].

No payment received *from* another company resident in the UK is to be treated as made out of profits or gains brought into charge to income tax, and the obligation to deduct income tax is not affected by the fact that the recipient company is not chargeable to income tax. [*ICTA 1988, s 7(4)*].

37.7 *Example*

S Ltd, a company with two associated companies, prepares accounts each year to 31 October. During the two years ending 31 October 2007 it makes several payments (not being interest) from which basic rate income tax is deducted and receives several sums under deduction of basic rate income tax.

The following items are shown net.

	Receipts	Payments
	£	£
21.12.05		7,800
4.1.06	3,900	
9.8.06	7,800	
24.10.06	11,700	
25.3.07		7,800
14.8.06		9,360

The adjusted profits (*before* taking account of the gross equivalents of the above amounts) were as follows.

	£
Year ended 31.10.06	630,000
Year ended 31.10.07	860,000

S Ltd will use the following figures in connection with the CT61 returns rendered to HMRC and will also be able to set off against its corporation tax liability the income tax suffered as shown.

Return period	Payments	Receipts	Cumulative payments less receipts	Income tax paid/ (repaid) with return
	£	£	£	£
Year ended 31.10.06				
1.11.05 to 31.12.05	7,800		7,800	2,200
1.1.06 to 31.3.06		3,900	3,900	(1,100)
1.4.06 to 30.6.06 (No return)			3,900	
1.7.06 to 30.9.06		7,800	(3,900)	(1,100)
1.10.06 to 31.10.06		11,700	(15,600)	
				—
Year ended 31.10.07				
1.11.06 to 31.12.06 (No return)				
1.1.07 to 31.3.07	7,800		7,800	2,200
1.4.07 to 30.6.07 (No return)			7,800	
1.7.07 to 30.9.07	9,360		17,160	2,640
1.10.07 to 31.10.07 (No return)			17,160	
				£4,840

Taxable profits

	Year ended 31.10.06	Year ended 31.10.07
	£	£
Adjusted profits as stated	630,000	860,000
Add Cumulative receipts £15,600 + net tax £4,400	20,000	
Deduct Cumulative payments £17,160 + tax of £4,840		22,000
Taxable profits	£650,000	£838,000

Tax payable

	Year ended 31.10.06	Year ended 31.10.07
	£	£
CT @ 30% on profits	195,000	251,400
Deduct Income tax suffered	4,400	
Net liability	£190,600	£251,400

37.8 GILT-EDGED SECURITIES

See Tolley's Income Tax under Savings and Investment Income for provisions of general application, and in particular for the general availability of gross payment of interest on gilt-edged securities. For the general corporation tax treatment of gilts, see 46 LOAN RELATIONSHIPS.

37.9 LOCAL AUTHORITY SECURITIES

A local authority (as defined in *ICTA 1988, s 842A*) must (except as below) deduct income tax from payments of yearly interest at the lower rate for the year in which the payment is made. [*ICTA 1988, s 349(2); ITA 2007 s 449*].

Local authority securities issued in foreign currency. Interest on such securities issued after 5 April 1982 is, if the Treasury so directs, paid without deduction of income tax and exempt from income tax (but not corporation tax) in the hands of a non-resident beneficial owner. Where for repayment of the principal amount due under a security there is an option between sterling and one or more foreign currencies, these provisions apply only if that option is exercisable solely by the holder of the security. Income from such securities is not exempt merely because it is deemed to be income of a non-resident. [*ICTA 1988, s 581(1)-(3)*]. For securities issued before 6 April 1982, similar provisions apply where the securities were issued in the currency of a country outside the scheduled territories at the time of issue. [*ICTA 1988, s 581(6); ITTOIA 2005, s 755(1), Sch 1 paras 241, 242*].

38 Industrial and Provident Societies

Cross-references. 36 HOUSING ASSOCIATIONS; 48.1 MUTUAL COMPANIES.

Simon's Direct Tax Service D4.625 *et seq.*

38.1 The legislation outlined below applies to industrial and provident societies registered or deemed to be registered under *Industrial and Provident Societies Act 1965* or its NI equivalent. [*ICTA 1988, s 486*(*12*)]. See 38.4 below.

38.2 SHARE OR LOAN INTEREST PAID

Share or loan interest paid by a society is not a distribution (see 23 DISTRIBUTIONS). [*ICTA 1988, s 486*(*1*)]. Such interest payable by a society is treated as interest under a loan relationship (see 46.2 LOAN RELATIONSHIPS), provided that the society makes a return to the inspector, within three months of the end of the relevant accounting period, showing the name and place of residence of every recipient of more than £15 and the amount paid to him. [*ICTA 1988, s 486*(*1*)(*6*)(*7*)]. See also 38.4 below.

Such interest is paid by a society without deduction of income tax (unless paid to a person whose usual place of abode is abroad, when income tax is deductible under *ITA 2007, ss 449, 899, 901, 903* (formerly *ICTA 1988, s 349*)). [*ICTA 1988, s 486*(*2*)(*3*)]. It is chargeable to corporation tax on the recipient under Schedule D, Case III. [*ICTA 1988, s 486*(*4*)].

38.3 AMALGAMATIONS AND TRANSFERS OF ENGAGEMENTS

Assets disposed of by one society to another on a union, amalgamation or transfer of engagements are treated as disposed of, for the purpose of capital gains computations, at such a consideration as would secure that no gain or loss accrues on the disposal. [*ICTA 1988, s 486*(*8*)]. See also 38.4 below.

38.4 CO-OPERATIVE ASSOCIATIONS

The provisions outlined in 38.2, 38.3 above apply to co-operative associations established and resident in the UK with the primary objective of assisting their members in the carrying on of agricultural or horticultural businesses on land occupied by them in the UK or of fishery businesses. A 'co-operative association' is a body of persons with a written constitution from which the Minister of Agriculture, Fisheries and Food (or the Secretary of State for Scotland, or the Minister of Agriculture for NI, as the case may be) is satisfied that the body is 'in substance' a co-operative association. [*ICTA 1988, s 486*(*9*)(*12*)]. See also HMRC Extra-Statutory Concessions, C12, C13.

38.5 TRADING LOSSES

Trading losses brought forward under *ICTA 1988, s 393*(*1*) (see 47.2 LOSSES) may, concessionally, be set off against:

(*a*) interest under Schedule D, Case III;

(*b*) annual interest received under deduction of tax; and

(*c*) amounts assessable under Schedule D, Case V.

(HMRC Extra-Statutory Concession, C5).

39 Intangible Assets

Simon's Direct Tax Service D2.16.

The headings in this chapter are as follows.

39.1 INTRODUCTION

A regime for the treatment of expenditure and receipts in respect of intangible assets was introduced by *FA 2002, s 84, Schs 29, 30*. It applies *only to companies* and only to assets acquired or created on or after 1 April 2002 (subject to transitional arrangements, see 39.37 below). The regime encompasses expenditure on the creation, acquisition and enhancement of intangibles (including abortive expenditure) as well as on their preservation and maintenance, and also applies to payments for the use of such assets, e.g. royalties. Profits on disposal of such assets are taxed as income. Losses on disposal and payments are relievable against income. The tax treatment of amortisation normally follows the accounts treatment. A form of rollover relief (similar to, but not to be confused with, capital gains tax rollover relief) is available where realisation proceeds of intangibles are reinvested in new intangibles.

See generally HMRC Corporate Intangibles Research and Development (CIRD) Manual, CIRD 10000 *et seq.*

39.2 INTANGIBLE FIXED ASSETS

Except as otherwise indicated, transactions involving gains or losses in respect of 'intangible fixed assets' are dealt with *for corporation tax purposes* as described in this chapter, no other charges or reliefs applying in respect of those transactions.

An '*intangible asset*' for this purpose has the meaning it has under 'generally accepted accounting practice'. In particular it includes 'intellectual property', other assets such as agricultural quota, franchises and telecommunication rights and, except as otherwise indicated, is extended to include 'goodwill' (as defined under 'generally accepted accounting practice' and excluding goodwill which appears only in consolidated accounts). Such an asset is an '*intangible fixed asset*' if it is acquired or created for use on a continuing basis in the course of the company's activities. This includes an option or other right either to acquire an intangible asset which, if acquired, would be a fixed asset, or to dispose of an intangible fixed asset. It is generally irrelevant whether or not the asset is capitalised in the company's accounts.

'*Intellectual property*' is:

(*a*) any patent, trade mark, registered design, copyright or design right, plant breeders' rights or rights under *Plant Varieties Act 1997, s 7*, or corresponding or similar right under foreign law;

(*b*) any economically valuable information or technique not protected by a right within (*a*); or

(*c*) any licence or other right in respect of anything within (*a*) or (*b*).

'*Generally accepted accounting practice*' is as defined by *FA 2004, s 50* (and, for periods of account beginning before 1 January 2005, *ICTA 1988, s 836A*) (see 55.2 PROFIT COMPUTATIONS). Accounts drawn up in accordance with generally accepted accounting practice are referred to in this chapter as 'correct'. Where incorrect accounts are drawn up, or accounts are not drawn up at all, these provisions are applied to amounts as they would have appeared had correct accounts been drawn up. This applies equally to amounts derived from earlier periods with incorrect accounts. In determining whether a company's accounts are correct, reference may be made to consolidated group accounts as regards the useful life or economic value of any asset. Resort cannot be made to such accounts if prepared under the law of a foreign jurisdiction on a basis that diverges substantially from generally accepted accounting practice in relation to the useful life or economic value of any assets. Nor, for periods of account beginning on or after 1 January 2005, can resort be made to the consolidated accounts if they are drawn up using a different accounting framework from that used for the company's individual accounts and as a result they are prepared on a basis that differs substantially from that of the individual accounts in relation to the useful life or economic value of any assets.

[*FA 2002, s 102(1)(2), Sch 29 paras 1–6; FA 2005, s 80, Sch 4 para 38*].

39.3 EXCLUDED ASSETS

Where (or to the extent that) an asset is excluded as follows, any option or other right to acquire or dispose of it is similarly excluded. Assets which are partly excluded are treated as two separate assets, one within the current provisions, the other subject to the normal corporation tax provisions, with any necessary apportionments being made on a just and reasonable basis.

The following assets are **excluded entirely** from the current provisions.

(*a*) An asset representing rights enjoyed by virtue of an estate, interest or right in or over land, or rights in relation to tangible movable property (see *FA 2002, Sch 29 para 73*).

(*b*) An asset treated in the company accounts as an intangible asset but which in a previous accounting period was treated as a tangible asset on which capital allowances (on plant and machinery) were claimed (see *FA 2002, Sch 29 para 73A*). This applies for periods of account **beginning on or after 1 January 2005**.

(*c*) Certain oil licences (see *FA 2002, Sch 29 para 74*).

(*d*) Financial assets (see *FA 2002, Sch 29 para 75 as amended by FA 2002, Sch 23 para 24, Sch 27 para 26*), subject to special provision in relation to finance leases under *FA 2002, Sch 29 para 104(2)(a)* (see 39.35 below).

(*e*) An asset representing:

(i) shares or other rights in relation to the profits, governance or winding up of a company;

(ii) rights under a trust (other than a right which falls, for accounting purposes, to be treated as representing an interest in trust property which is an intangible fixed asset within these provisions); or

(iii) the interest of a partner in a partnership (other than an interest which falls, for accounting purposes, to be treated as representing an interest in partnership property which is an intangible fixed asset within these provisions).

(*f*) An asset to the extent it is held either for a non-commercial purpose or for the purpose of activities in respect of which the company is not within the charge to corporation tax.

(*g*) An asset held by a film production company to the extent it represents production expenditure on a film under the FA 2006 regime (see 66.51 and 66.52 TRADING INCOME), the assets being treated as created when the film was completed.

The following assets are **excluded except as regards '*royalties*'**, i.e. any payment in respect of the enjoyment or exercise of rights that constitute an intangible fixed asset.

(i) An asset to the extent that it is held for the purposes of any mutual trade or business (other than life assurance business) or by an insurance company (but excluding computer software) for the purposes of its life assurance business within *ICTA 1988, Pt 12 Ch 1*.

(ii) An asset held by a company to the extent that it represents expenditure by the company on:

- the production of the original master version (as defined) of a film that commenced principal photography before 1 April 2006;
- the acquisition before 1 October 2007 of the original master version of a film that commenced principal photography before 1 April 2006; or
- the production or acquisition of a 'master version' (as defined) of a sound recording.

(iii) An asset held by a company to the extent that it represents expenditure by the company on computer software falling to be treated for accounting purposes as part of the costs of the related hardware.

The following assets are **excluded to the extent specified**.

(A) An asset held by a company to the extent that it represents expenditure by the company on research and development (within *ICTA 1988, s 838*, see 59 RESEARCH AND DEVELOPMENT) is excluded from the provisions as follows.

(i) The provisions at 39.4, 39.5 below for the computation of tax debits and credits do not apply, *except for* credits in respect of receipts recognised as they accrue and debits reversing such credits.

(ii) The provisions at 39.7 below for debits and credits on the realisation of intangible fixed assets apply as if the cost of the asset did not include any of the research and development expenditure.

(B) An asset held by a company to the extent that it represents capital expenditure (as determined for capital allowance purposes) by the company on computer software in respect of which the company has so elected is excluded from the provisions as follows.

(i) The provisions at 39.4, 39.5 below for the computation of tax debits and credits do not apply, *except for* credits in respect of receipts recognised as they accrue and debits reversing such credits.

(ii) The provisions at 39.7 below for debits and credits on the realisation of intangible fixed assets apply as if the cost of the asset did not include any expenditure in respect of which the election was made.

(iii) A credit is brought in under the current provisions only to the extent that the receipts to which the credit relates do not fall to be taken into account in computing disposal values for capital allowance purposes under *CAA 2001, s 72.*

Such an election must specify the expenditure to which it relates, must be made in writing to HMRC within two years after the end of the accounting period in which the expenditure was incurred, and is irrevocable.

The election is similarly available to insurance companies carrying on life assurance business in respect of so much of any capital expenditure on computer software as is not referable to its basic life assurance and general annuity business.

[*FA 2002, Sch 29 paras 72–83, 138, 139; FA 2004, s 52, Sch 10 para 71; FA 2005, Sch 4 para 50; FA 2006, ss 51, 77(4)(5)*].

39.4 **COMPUTATION OF TAX DEBITS**

Debits are brought into account for tax purposes in respect of three types of loss relating to intangible fixed assets which are 'recognised in determining the company's profit or loss'. Amounts in this case are '*recognised in determining the company's profit or loss*' for a period if they are recognised (including prior-year adjustments apart from corrections of fundamental errors) in the company's profit and loss account or income statement, in its statement of recognised gains and losses or statement of changes in equity, or in any other statement of items brought into account in determining the company's profits and losses for that period. This also includes amounts which would have been so recognised if the profit and loss or other such statement as mentioned above had been drawn up in accordance with generally accepted accounting practice (see 39.2 above). No such debit arises, however, in relation to amounts brought into account in connection with the realisation of an intangible fixed asset (see 39.7 below).

Expenditure written off as it is incurred. Where expenditure is recognised in determining the profit or loss (and does not relate to previously capitalised expenditure, see below), a corresponding debit is brought into account for tax purposes, equal in amount to the accounting debit except in so far as the further provisions described in this chapter otherwise require. This applies to expenditure for the purpose of acquiring or creating, or establishing title to, the asset, by way of royalty in respect of use of the asset, or on maintaining, preserving or enhancing, or defending title to, the asset, and includes abortive expenditure. However, capital expenditure on tangible assets is excluded in determining expenditure on intangible assets.

ICTA 1988, s 74(1)(m)(p), s 817(1)(b) (regarding annual payments and royalties) do not prevent relief being given for such debits.

Writing-down of capitalised cost. Where a loss is recognised in determining the profit or loss in respect of capitalised expenditure (by way of amortisation, or as a result of an impairment review (which does not, however, include the valuation of an asset to determine the initial amount to be capitalised)), a corresponding debit is brought into account for tax purposes, equal in amount to the accounting debit except in so far as the further provisions described in this chapter otherwise require, and subject to the election described below.

Where the amount of the expenditure on the asset (the 'accounting expenditure') is adjusted for tax purposes (the 'tax expenditure'), e.g. where the cost is reduced as a result of reinvestment relief (see 39.9 below), then for the period of account in which the expenditure is first capitalised the tax debit is the amount which bears the same relation to the accounting debit as the tax expenditure bears to the accounting expenditure. For subsequent periods, the accounting debit is adjusted in the ratio which the 'tax written-down value' immediately before the accounting write-down bears to the accounting value. The '*tax written-down value*' of an asset for this purpose is the expenditure as adjusted for tax purposes *less* the debits previously brought into account (as above) *plus* the credits previously brought into account (see 39.5 below) (taking account of any debits or credits brought into account on a change of accounting policy, see 39.36 below). On a part realisation of the asset, the previous written-down value is reduced to the proportion which the carrying values for accounting purposes immediately after the part realisation represent of those immediately before it, and subsequent allowances are based on this amount.

A company may, however, elect instead to write down the cost of an asset at a fixed rate for tax purposes (and this applies whether or not the asset is written down for accounting purposes). The election, which is irrevocable, must be made in writing within two years after the end of the accounting period in which the asset was acquired or created by the company, and has effect in relation to all capitalised expenditure on the asset. The debit is at an annual rate of 4% of the capitalised tax expenditure on the asset (see above), but limited to the balance of the 'tax written-down value' (which for this purpose is the tax expenditure as adjusted for tax purposes *less* the fixed rate allowances previously given, with an adjustment being made as above in the case of a part realisation and taking account of any debits or credits brought into account on a change of accounting policy, see 39.36 below). After a part realisation the allowance is given by reference to the accounting value of the part retained immediately after the part realisation plus that of any subsequent expenditure (subject to any adjustments required for tax purposes).

Reversal of earlier accounting credit. A loss may be recognised in determining the profit or loss which reverses (in whole or part) a gain previously recognised and in respect of which a credit was brought into account for tax purposes (see 39.5 below). In such a case, a corresponding debit is brought into account for tax purposes, the amount bearing the same relation to the accounting loss as the previous tax credit bore to the accounting gain (or part) reversed.

This does not apply to a loss recognised by way of amortisation, or as a result of an impairment review, of an asset previously revalued (see 39.5 below).

[*FA 2002, Sch 29 paras 7–12, 27–29, 133–136; FA 2004, Sch 10 para 76; FA 2005, Sch 4 paras 39, 40, 42, 43, 46*].

Example A

A company acquires an intangible fixed asset in year 1 at a capitalised cost of 2,000, amortised on a straight-line basis over 10 years. As a result of a reinvestment relief claim (see 39.8 below), the cost for tax purposes is reduced to 1,600. The charge in the accounts in each of years 1 to 10 (200) is thus reduced to a tax debit of (200 × 1,600/2,000 =) 160.

In year 2 further expenditure of 700 on the asset is capitalised. The revised book value of (2,000 – 200 + 700 =) 2,500 is amortised over a further 10 years at 250 a year. The tax written-down value is (1,440 + 700 =) 2,140, so that the charge in the accounts becomes (250 × 2,140/2,500 =) 214.

Example B

A company acquires an intangible fixed asset with an indefinite life for 1,000 in year 1. There is no amortisation charge in the accounts. It elects for the fixed-rate write-down for tax purposes. No adjustment is required to the cost for tax purposes, and the tax debit is thus 40 a year.

In year 10 the asset is partly realised for 700, 600 of the book value of the asset being set against the disposal in the accounts, giving a profit on disposal of 100 and a revised book value of 400.

The tax written-down value at the end of year 9 is (1,000 – (9 × 40) =) 640. The remaining tax expenditure set against the disposal proceeds is (600/1,000 × 640 =) 384, resulting in a taxable profit on sale of 316. The tax written-down value is reduced to (400/1,000 × 640 =) 256. The fixed rate deduction is reduced to 400 @ 4%, i.e. 16 over the following 16 years.

39.5 COMPUTATION OF TAX CREDITS

Credits are brought into account for tax purposes in respect of five types of accounting credit relating to intangible fixed assets as set out below. No such credit arises, however, in relation to amounts brought into account in connection with the realisation of an intangible fixed asset (see 39.7 below). Where the following provisions require an amount to be '*recognised in determining the company's profit or loss*' for a period, this is an amount recognised (including prior-year adjustments apart from corrections of fundamental errors) in the company's profit and loss account or income statement, in its statement of recognised gains and losses or statement of changes in equity, or in any other statement of items brought into account in determining the company's profits and losses for that period. It also includes an amount which would have been so recognised if the profit and loss or other such statement as mentioned above had been drawn up in accordance with generally accepted accounting practice (see 39.2 above).

Receipts recognised as they accrue. Where a gain representing a receipt in respect of an intangible asset is recognised in determining the profit or loss, a corresponding credit is brought into account for tax purposes, equal in amount to the accounting gain except in so far as the further provisions described in this chapter otherwise require.

Revaluations. Where the accounting carrying value of an intangible fixed asset is increased on a revaluation (including a valuation of an asset which has a balance sheet value but has not previously been valued, and the restoration of past losses), a credit is brought into account for tax purposes of the lesser of:

(*a*) an amount bearing the same relation to the increase in value as the tax written-down value immediately before the revaluation bears to the accounting book value by reference to which the revaluation is carried out; or

(*b*) the 'net aggregate amount of relevant tax debits' previously brought into account.

The '*net aggregate amount of relevant tax debits*' is the difference between the debits (in respect of the writing-down of capitalised cost, see 39.2 above) and credits (under the current revaluations provision) previously brought into account for tax purposes in respect of the asset concerned. Such debits and credits also take account of any adjustments on a change of accounting policy as described at 39.36 below).

The above does not apply to an asset in respect of which an election has been made for tax write-down at a fixed rate (see 39.4 above).

Negative goodwill. Where an accounting gain is recognised in determining the profit or loss in respect of negative goodwill arising on an acquisition of a business, a corresponding tax credit is brought into account, equal in amount to so much of the accounting gain as, on a just and reasonable apportionment, is attributable to intangible fixed assets.

Reversal of earlier accounting debit. A gain may be recognised in determining the profit or loss account which reverses (in whole or part) a loss previously recognised and in respect of which a debit was brought into account for tax purposes (see 39.4 above). In such a case, a corresponding credit is brought into account for tax purposes, the amount bearing the same relation to the accounting gain as the previous tax debit bore to the accounting loss (or part) reversed. This does not apply to a gain on a revaluation (as above).

Receipts in respect of royalties. For any accounting period beginning after 4 December 2005, a credit is to be brought into account for a receipt in respect of a royalty in so far as it does not give rise to a credit which (as above) is taken into account as a receipt recognised as it accrues (whether in the period of account in which it is received or a subsequent period of account). The credit is to equal so much of the amount as does not give rise to such a credit and is to be brought into account in the period the receipt is recognised in the accounts. This provision is deemed to have always had effect in relation to any credits so brought into account. Accounting periods straddling 5 December 2005 are treated as two separate accounting periods, one beginning on the date and the other ending immediately before it.

[*FA 2002, Sch 29 paras 13–17, 134, 135; FA 2004, Sch 10 para 74; FA 2005, Sch 4 paras 40, 41, 46; FA 2006, s 77(2)(3)(10(11)*].

39.6 GIVING EFFECT TO CREDITS AND DEBITS

Credits and debits under the current provisions are given effect according to the purpose for which the asset concerned is used, as follows, with any necessary apportionment where an asset is held for more than one of the following purposes being made on a just and reasonable basis

Assets held for trade purposes. Credits and debits are given effect as receipts and expenses of the trade in computing the profits of the trade.

Assets held for property business purposes. Credits and debits are given effect as receipts and expenses of the property business in computing business profits. A '*property business*' for this purpose is a 'Schedule A business' or an 'overseas property business' (see 56 PROPERTY INCOME). Commercial lettings of furnished holiday accommodation which are treated as a trade under *ICTA 1988, s 503* are similarly so treated for these purposes.

Assets held for mines, transport undertakings, etc. purposes. Credits and debits are given effect as receipts and expenses of the concern in computing profits under Schedule D, Case I. This applies to concerns listed in *ICTA 1988, s 55(2)*.

Assets held for other purposes. Credits and debits in respect of assets used for purposes other than the above (described as 'non-trading credits and debits') are aggregated, and the aggregate 'non-trading gain' or 'non-trading loss' given effect as follows.

A non-trading gain is chargeable under Schedule D, Case VI.

Relief for a non-trading loss may be claimed, in whole or part, by set-off against total profits. Such a claim must be made within two years after the end of the accounting period to which it relates, or within such further period as HMRC may allow. To the extent that the loss is neither so relieved nor surrendered by way of group relief, it is carried forward as a non-trading debit of the following accounting period. See 47.2 LOSSES and, as regards group relief claims generally, 32.10 GROUPS OF COMPANIES.

Similar provisions to those in *ICTA 1988, s 768B* or *768C* (see 42.8 INVESTMENT COMPANIES AND INVESTMENT BUSINESS) apply to restrict relief for non-trading losses under the current provisions on change of ownership of an investment company (see *ICTA 1988, s 768E; FA 2002, Sch 30 para 4*).

Insurance companies. There are special provisions dealing with the application of the current provisions to insurance companies (see *FA 2002, Sch 29 para 36*).

[*FA 2002, Sch 29 paras 30–36, Sch 30 paras 2, 4; SI 2004 No 2310, Article 67; FA 2007, Sch 8 para 27*].

39.7 REALISATION OF INTANGIBLE FIXED ASSETS

'*Realisation*' of an intangible fixed asset for this purpose means a transaction (including any event giving rise to an accounting gain) which results, in accordance with generally accepted accounting practice (see 39.2 above), in its ceasing to be recognised in the balance sheet or in its carrying value being reduced (the latter being referred to as a 'part realisation'). This applies to an asset that has no balance sheet value (or no longer has one) as if it had one.

Where there is a realisation of an intangible fixed asset in respect of which tax debits have been brought into account under *FA 2002, Sch 29 para 9* or *para 10* (writing-down of capitalised cost, see 39.4 above), or under *para 116A* (adjustment on change of accounting policy, see 39.36 below) a tax credit (or debit) is brought into account equal to the amount by which the 'proceeds of realisation' (if any) exceed (or are less than) the 'tax written-down value' of the asset (see 39.4 above) immediately before the realisation. If no tax debits have been brought into account in respect of the asset, the same applies by reference to the cost of the asset recognised for tax purposes, i.e. (subject to any adjustment for tax purposes) the amount of the capitalised expenditure for accounting purposes. Otherwise, a tax credit is brought into account equal to the full amount of the 'proceeds of realisation'. In the case of a part realisation, the tax written-down value (or cost) is for these purposes reduced in the same proportion as that by which the accounting carrying value is reduced as a result of the realisation. Thereafter, the cost of the asset (where no tax debits have been brought into account in respect of it) is that immediately after the part realisation plus any subsequent expenditure.

The '*proceeds of realisation*' are those recognised for accounting purposes reduced by amounts so recognised as incidental realisation costs, subject to any adjustment required for tax purposes.

The above provisions are subject to the reinvestment relief rules in 39.8 below.

Abortive realisation expenditure. A loss recognised in determining the profit or loss in respect of abortive expenditure on realisation of an intangible fixed asset gives rise to a corresponding tax debit which, subject to any adjustment required for tax purposes, is equal in amount to the accounting loss.

[*FA 2002, Sch 29 paras 18–26, 135, 136; FA 2004, Sch 10 para 75; FA 2005, Sch 4 para 40*].

Example

A company realises part of an intangible fixed asset with accounting book value of £5,000 and tax written-down value of £4,000 for £3,750, the book value of the part retained being £1,875. The amount to be set against the sale proceeds in arriving at the tax credit to be brought into account is (£4,000 × (£5,000 – £1,875)/£5,000 =) £2,500, so that the tax credit is (£3,750 – £2,500 =) £1,250.

39.8 RELIEF IN CASE OF REINVESTMENT

Where a company invests the proceeds of realisation of an intangible asset (the 'old asset') in other such assets, and the proceeds exceed the capitalised cost (if any) for accounting purposes (so far as recognised for tax purposes) of the old asset, it may claim relief as below. In the case of a part realisation, the cost for this purpose is reduced to the same proportion as the reduction in accounting value as a result of the part realisation bears to that value immediately before the part realisation (and so on for subsequent part realisations).

Full relief is available if the old asset was a 'chargeable intangible asset' of the company throughout the period of its ownership by the company, but if this condition was met for a substantial part, but not the whole, of that period (including the time of realisation), relief is available as if a corresponding part of the asset were a separate asset in respect of which the relief is available (any necessary apportionments being made on a just and reasonable basis). The other assets in which the proceeds are invested must also have been 'chargeable intangible assets' immediately after the expenditure on them was incurred, and the expenditure must have been incurred in the period beginning one year before, and ending three years after, the date of realisation of the old asset (which period may be extended as HMRC may by notice allow in any particular case), and must be capitalised by the company for accounting purposes. Expenditure is for this purpose treated as incurred when recognised for accounting purposes. Reacquisition of the old asset is treated as acquisition of a different asset for these purposes. Deemed realisations and reacquisitions are disregarded for these purposes (except as detailed in 39.18, 39.19 below).

An asset is a '*chargeable intangible asset*' in relation to a company at any time if, were it to be realised at that time, any gain on realisation would give rise to a credit within 39.7 above (disregarding the availability of relief under this provision or by virtue of the transfer being treated as 'tax-neutral'). References to a transfer being treated as '*tax-neutral*' mean that it is not regarded in relation to the current provisions as involving any realisation by the transferor or acquisition by the transferee, with anything done by the transferor in relation to the asset being treated as having been done by the transferee.

The relief is given by reducing both the proceeds of realisation of the old asset and the cost of the other assets acquired (so far as recognised for tax purposes) by the amount available for relief. The amount available for relief is the amount by which the lesser of the proceeds of realisation of the old asset and the cost of the other assets acquired exceeds the cost of the old asset (adjusted as referred to above in the case of part realisation). Other parties to the transactions are not affected by the relief claim.

Where, in periods of account beginning on or after 1 January 2005, there is a change in accounting policy which results in an intangible fixed asset that was treated as one asset ('*the original asset*') in the earlier period, being treated as two or more assets ('*the resulting assets*') in the later period (see 39.36 below), the cost of each of the resulting assets for the purposes of reinvestment relief is taken as a proportion of the cost of the original asset. The proportion is arrived at by multiplying the cost by the same fraction as is applied in arriving at the tax written down value of the asset on a disaggregation of assets on a change of accounting policy (the opening accounting value of the resulting asset in the later period over the aggregate opening accounting values of the resulting assets at that time).

The relief must be claimed in the company's return for the period (see 15.1 CLAIMS), and must specify the old asset(s) to which the claim relates, the expenditure on other assets by reference to which relief is claimed and the amount of relief claimed. Relief is given on a provisional basis where the company declares, in its return for a period in which it has realised an intangible fixed asset, that it proposes to reinvest the proceeds so as to give rise to relief of a specified amount. The provisional relief lapses four years after the end of the accounting period in which the realisation occurred if it has not already been superseded by an actual claim to relief or withdrawn, and on its ceasing to have effect all necessary adjustments are made, notwithstanding any time limits on assessments, etc.

[*FA 2002, Sch 29 paras 37–45, 137, 140; FA 2005, s 80, Sch 4 para 44*].

Example

An intangible fixed asset with cost (for accounting and tax purposes) of £1,000 is part realised for £900, its book value thereby being reduced from £500 to £400. The proceeds of realisation (£900) exceed the appropriate proportion of the cost (£1,000 × (£500 – £400)/£500 =) £200, so that full relief is available on reinvestment of £900 or more.

If a further part realisation for £600 reduces the book value from £300 to £150, the original cost of £1,000 is reduced by the part taken into account on the earlier part realisation (£200) to £800. Since the realisation proceeds (£600) exceed the appropriate proportion of the balance of the cost (£800 × (£300 – £150)/£300 =) £400, full relief is available on reinvestment of £600 or more.

If full reinvestment relief is claimed, then on a subsequent disposal of the asset, in arriving at the tax credit or debit to be taken into account, the original cost of £1,000 is reduced by £600, the cost taken into account on the earlier part realisations.

39.9 **GROUPS OF COMPANIES**

For the purposes of the current provisions, the capital gains tax definition of a group of companies is adopted (see 12.1 CAPITAL GAINS—GROUPS). [*FA 2002, Sch 29 paras 46–54; F(No 2)A 2005, s 63*]. The following modifications apply in the application of the current provisions to such groups.

39.10 **Transfers within a group.** The transfer intra-group of an intangible fixed asset is treated as 'tax-neutral' (see 39.8 above) provided the asset is a 'chargeable intangible asset' (see also 39.8 above) in relation to the transferor company before and the transferee company after the transfer. This does **not**, however, apply where either the transferor or the transferee is an incorporated friendly society within *ICTA 1988, s 461A* (see 31.2 FRIENDLY SOCIETIES) or the transferee is a dual-resident investing company within *ICTA 1988, s 404* (see 32.27 GROUPS OF COMPANIES). The provisions of *ICTA 1988, Sch 28AA* (see 67 TRANSFER PRICING) do not apply to such intra-group transfers treated as 'tax neutral'.

Interaction with treatment of company reconstructions or amalgamations. These rules take precedence over the company reconstruction and amalgamation rules at 39.22 below.

[*FA 2002, Sch 29 paras 55, 84(3); FA 2004, Sch 5 para 16(2)*].

39.11 **Roll-over relief on reinvestment.** *Application to group member.* For the purposes of the rules at 39.8 above, where the realisation of the old asset is by one company in a group and the reinvestment in other assets by another (not being a dual resident investing company (see 32.27 GROUPS OF COMPANIES)), then provided that the other assets are 'chargeable intangible assets' in relation to the latter company immediately after the expenditure is incurred, and are not acquired from another group member by a 'tax-neutral transfer' (see 39.10 above), the companies may jointly claim to be treated as the same person. [*FA 2002, Sch 29 para 56*].

39.12 *Acquisition of company becoming group member.* For the purposes of the rules at 39.8 above, expenditure by a company ('A') on the acquisition of a 'controlling interest' in a company ('B'), where company B (or one or more other companies not in the same group as company A before it acquired that interest but which become so immediately after (and as a result of) that acquisition) holds intangible fixed assets (the 'underlying assets'), is treated as equivalent to expenditure on acquiring the assets themselves. The 'chargeable intangible assets' requirement under 39.8 above has then to be met by reference to the company by which they are held immediately after that acquisition. Company A acquires a '*controlling interest*' in company B by acquiring shares in company B such that they become members of the same group immediately after the acquisition, having not been so immediately before the acquisition. The amount of expenditure treated as incurred by company A on the underlying assets is then the lesser of the 'tax written down value' (see 39.4 above) of the underlying assets immediately before the acquisition and the amount or value of the consideration for the acquisition of the controlling interest. In these circumstances, relief under 39.8 above must be claimed jointly by company A and the company or companies holding the underlying assets, and the tax written down value of the underlying assets in the hands of the company or companies holding the underlying assets is reduced by the amount available for relief (see 39.8 above). Any necessary allocation of the reduction between different underlying assets is made by the company which holds them (or, if there is more than one such company, as they agree between them). [*FA 2002, Sch 29 para 57*].

39.13 **Degrouping.** *Company ceasing to be group member.* Where

(i) a company which is a member of a group transfers to another company an intangible fixed asset (the 'relevant asset') which is a 'chargeable intangible asset' (see above) in relation to the former company before the transfer and the latter company after the transfer, and

(ii) the transferee company, having been a member of the group at the time of the transfer or having subsequently become so, ceases to be a member after the transfer but within six years after the date of the transfer at a time when it (or an 'associated company' (see 39.14 below) leaving the group at the same time) still holds the relevant asset,

then for the purposes of the current provisions, the transferee company is treated as if, immediately after the relevant asset was transferred to it, it had disposed of and reacquired it at its then market value. Any resulting adjustments to be made for tax purposes by the transferee company (or by a company to which the relevant asset has subsequently been transferred) in relation to the period between the transfer of the relevant asset to the transferee company and that company ceasing to be a group member is made by bringing in the aggregate net credit or debit as if it had arisen immediately before the transferee company left the group.

To determine how effect is to be given to debits and credits in these circumstances (see 39.6 above), it is the purposes for which the relevant asset was held by the transferee company immediately after the transfer which are considered, except that if it was then held by that company for the purposes of a trade, a property business or a mine or transport undertaking, etc. which ceased before it left the group, any debit or credit is instead treated as a non-trading debit or credit.

These provisions are subject to *FA 2002, Sch 29 paras 59–62* (see 39.14–39.17 below).

[*FA 2002, Sch 29 para 58*].

In these and the following degrouping provisions:

(*a*) companies are '*associated*' if, by themselves, they would form a group of companies (see 39.9 above);

(*b*) an asset acquired by a company is treated as the same as an asset owned at a later time by the company (or by an associated company) if the second asset derives its value in whole or part from the first; and

(*c*) references to a company leaving a group do not include cases where it does so in consequence of another group member ceasing to exist.

[*FA 2002, Sch 29 paras 63, 64*].

39.14 *Associated companies leaving group at same time.* The provisions in 39.13 above do not apply where the transferor and transferee companies are 'associated companies' and leave the group at the same time. Where, however, the transferee company subsequently leaves another group which has a 'connection' with the first (for which see the corresponding capital gains provisions of *TCGA 1992, s 179* at 12.32 CAPITAL GAINS—GROUPS), 39.13 above applies as if it was the second group of which both companies were members at the time of the transfer.

[*FA 2002, Sch 29 para 59*].

39.15 *Principal company becoming member of another group.* The provisions in 39.13 above do not apply where a company leaves a group by reason only of the fact that the 'principal company of the group' (see 12.1 CAPITAL GAINS—GROUPS) joins another group (the 'second group'). If, however, within six years after the transfer to it of the relevant asset, the transferee company at any time ceases to satisfy the condition that it is both a '75% subsidiary' and an 'effective 51% subsidiary' (for both of which again see 12.1 CAPITAL GAINS—GROUPS) of one or more members of the second group, and at that time the asset is held by either the transferee company or another company in the same group, the transferee company is treated for the purposes of the current provisions as if, immediately after the transfer to it of the asset, it had realised and immediately reacquired it at its market value at the time of the transfer. Any resulting adjustments to be made for tax purposes by the transferee company (or by a company to which the relevant asset has subsequently been transferred) in relation to the period between the transfer of the relevant asset to the transferee company and that company ceasing to satisfy the condition referred to above are made by bringing in the aggregate net credit or debit as if it had arisen immediately before the transferee company ceased to satisfy that condition.

To determine how effect is to be given to debits and credits in these circumstances (see 39.6 above), it is the purposes for which the relevant asset was held by the transferee company immediately after the transfer which are considered, except that if it was then held by that company for the purposes of a trade, a property business or a mine or transport undertaking, etc. which ceased before it ceased to satisfy the condition referred to above, any debit or credit is instead treated as a non-trading debit or credit.

These provisions are subject to 39.17 below.

[*FA 2002, Sch 29 para 60*].

39.16 *Company ceasing to be a member of a group by reason of exempt distribution.* 39.13 and 39.15 above do not apply where a company ceases to be a member of a group by reason only of an 'exempt distribution' within *ICTA 1988, s 213(2)* (see 32.32 GROUPS OF COMPANIES), unless there is a 'chargeable payment' within *ICTA 1988, s 214(2)* (see 32.35 GROUPS OF COMPANIES) within five years after the making of the exempt distribution (in which case all necessary adjustments for tax purposes may be made within the three years after the making of the chargeable payment). For the purposes of the '75% subsidiary' test in 32.33 GROUPS OF COMPANIES, a company is not treated as owning any share capital in a company if a profit on sale of the shares would be treated as a trading receipt, by the company itself if it owns them directly or, if it owns them indirectly, by the company which owns them directly.

[*FA 2002, Sch 29 para 61*].

39.17 *Merger carried out for bona fide commercial reasons.* The provisions in 39.13–39.16 above do not apply where the transferee company leaves the group as part of a 'merger' carried out for *bona fide* commercial reasons and not having avoidance of liability to tax as a main purpose. '*Merger*' is specially defined for this purpose in *FA 2002, Sch 29 para 62(2)–(5)*. [*FA 2002, Sch 29 para 62*].

39.18 *Application of relief on reinvestment in relation to degrouping charge.* The provisions described at 39.8 above apply with the following modifications where, under 39.13 or 39.15 above, the transferee company is treated as having realised (and immediately reacquired) an asset immediately after the transfer by the transferor company.

(*a*) The requirement for the old asset to be a chargeable intangible asset applies in relation to the transferor company.

(*b*) The period within which expenditure on the other assets must be incurred applies by reference to the date the transferee company ceased to be a group member (in 39.13 above) or ceased to satisfy the requisite condition (in 39.15 above) rather than the date of realisation of the asset.

(*c*) References to the proceeds of realisation of the old asset are read as referring to the amount (market value) for which the transferee is treated as having realised it.

Any reduction of the deemed realisation proceeds as a result of a claim to reinvestment relief does not, however, affect the deemed cost of reacquisition by the transferee company.

[*FA 2002, Sch 29 para 65*].

39.19 *Reallocation of degrouping charge within group*. Where, by virtue of the provisions in 39.13 or 39.15 above, a realisation gain giving rise to a charge under 39.7 above accrues to a company ('company X'), the gain (or any part of it) may be treated as accruing to any other company ('company Y') which, at the 'relevant time', is a member of the 'relevant group', if both companies jointly so elect, provided that, at the 'relevant time', company Y:

(*a*) is either UK-resident or carrying on a UK trade through a UK permanent establishment (see 60.5 RESIDENCE — previously a UK branch or agency) in respect of the profits or gains of which it is not exempt from corporation tax under double tax arrangements; and

(*b*) is not either an incorporated friendly society within *ICTA 1988, s 461A* (see 31.2 FRIENDLY SOCIETIES) or a dual-resident investing company within *ICTA 1988, s 404* (see 32.27 GROUPS OF COMPANIES).

The gain (or part) is then treated as a non-trading credit (see 39.6 above) accruing to company Y at the 'relevant time' (and as so accruing in respect of an asset held for the purposes of a UK permanent establishment (or branch or agency) where it is not UK-resident).

The '*relevant time*' is immediately before company X ceased to be a group member (in 39.13 above) or ceased to satisfy the requisite condition (in 39.15 above), and the '*relevant group*' is the group of which it ceased to be a member (in 39.13 above) or the second group (in 39.15 above).

The election must be made by written notice to HMRC within two years after the end of the accounting period (of company X) in which the relevant time falls.

Where such an election has been made, company Y may claim relief on reinvestment (see 39.8 above) as if the deemed realisation had been made by company Y and not company X, the conditions as regards the old asset being treated as met if they would have been had there been no election and had the claim had been made by company X. The proceeds of realisation and the cost of the old asset are similarly what they would have been on a claim by company X. Where the election relates to only part of the gain on the deemed realisation, relief may be claimed as if a corresponding part of the asset had been the subject a separate deemed realisation, with any necessary apportionments being made accordingly.

[*FA 2002, Sch 29 paras 66, 67*].

39.20 *Recovery of degrouping charge from another group company or controlling director*. Where a degrouping charge falls to be brought into account on a company for an accounting period under 39.13 or 39.15 above, or following an election under 39.19 above, and corporation tax assessed on the company for that period remains unpaid six months after the due date, provision is made for recovery from the following persons of the amount referable to the degrouping charge (or the outstanding tax if less).

(*a*) If the defaulting company was a member of a group at the 'relevant time', a company which was at that time the principal company of the group and any other company which at any time in the period of twelve months ending with the 'relevant time' was a member of that group and owned the asset in respect of which the degrouping charge arose (or any part of it).

(*b*) If at the 'relevant time' the defaulting company is non-UK resident but carries on a UK trade through a permanent establishment (see 60.5 RESIDENCE — previously a branch or agency), any person who is, or during the period of twelve months ending with the 'relevant time' was, a 'director' (as widely defined) having 'control' (within *ICTA 1988, s 416*) of the defaulting company or of a company that has, or within that period had, control of the defaulting company.

Somewhat wider definitions of 'group' and 'principal company' apply for these purposes (by reference to 51% subsidiaries rather than 75% subsidiaries). The '*relevant time*' is when the defaulting company ceased to be a group member (in 39.13 above) or ceased to satisfy the requisite condition (in 39.15 above), or whichever of those times would have applied had there been no election (in 39.19 above).

An HMRC notice requiring payment from another person as above (within 30 days from the date of the notice) has effect (as regards recovery, interest and appeals) as if it were a notice of assessment. It must be served within three years after the date of final determination (for which see *FA 2002, Sch 29 para 70(2)–(4)*) of the corporation tax liability of the defaulting company for the accounting period for which the degrouping charge fell to be brought into account. The company paying the tax may recover it from the defaulting company, but the payment is not an allowable deduction for tax purposes.

[*FA 2002, Sch 29 paras 68–70*].

39.21 **Intra-group payments in respect of reliefs.** A payment either for group rollover relief (see 39.11, 39.12 above) or for the reallocation of a degrouping charge (see 39.19 above) is not taken into account for corporation tax purposes as regards the payer or the payee provided that it does not exceed the amount of the relief.

A payment for group rollover relief means a payment made in connection with a claim for relief under 39.8 above by virtue of the provisions in 39.11 or 39.12 above, by the company whose proceeds of realisation are reduced as a result of that claim, to a company whose acquisition costs are thereby reduced (in 39.11 above), or the tax written-down value of whose assets is thereby reduced (in 39.12 above), under an agreement between the companies. The amount of the relief in such a case is the amount of the reduction as a result of the claim in the acquisition costs, or the tax written-down value of the assets, as the case may be, of the company to which the payment is made.

A payment for the reallocation of a degrouping charge means a payment made in connection with an election under the provisions in 39.19 above, by the company to which the chargeable realisation gain accrues to the company to which, as a result of the election, the whole or part of that gain is treated as accruing, under an agreement between the companies. The amount of the relief in such a case is the amount treated as a result of the election as accruing to the company to which the payment is made.

[*FA 2002, Sch 29 para 71*].

39.22 TRANSFER OF BUSINESS OR TRADE

Company reconstruction involving transfer of business. Where a scheme for the reconstruction of any company or companies within *TCGA 1992, s 136* involves the transfer of the whole or part of the business of one company to another, and the transferor company receives no part of the consideration for the transfer (otherwise than by the transferee company taking over liabilities of the business), the following provisions apply. This is, however, conditional on the reconstruction being effected for *bona fide* commercial reasons and not as part of a scheme or arrangements a main purpose of which is avoidance of liability to income tax, corporation tax or capital gains tax (although advance clearance may be obtained that this condition is met, see 39.27 below).

If the assets transferred include intangible fixed assets which are chargeable intangible assets (see 39.8 above) in relation to the transferor company immediately before the transfer and in relation to the transferee company immediately thereafter, the transfer of those assets is treated for the purposes of the current provisions as tax-neutral (see 39.8 above). This does not, however, apply where either company is an incorporated friendly society within *ICTA 1988, s 461A* (see 31.2 FRIENDLY SOCIETIES) or a dual-resident investing company within *ICTA 1988, s 404* (see 32.27 GROUPS OF COMPANIES).

See 39.10 above for the interaction between these provisions and those dealing with transfers within a group.

[*FA 2002, Sch 29 para 84*].

39.23 **Transfer of UK trade between companies resident in different EU member states.** Special provisions apply where an '*EU company*' (i.e. a body incorporated under the law of a member state) resident in one member state transfers the whole or part of a trade carried on in the UK to an EU company resident in another member state in exchange for securities (including shares) in the latter company, and both companies make a claim. This is, however, conditional on the reconstruction or amalgamation being effected for *bona fide* commercial reasons and not as part of a scheme or arrangements a main purpose of which is avoidance of liability to income tax, corporation tax or capital gains tax (although advance clearance may be obtained that this condition is met, see 39.27 below).

A company is regarded for these purposes as resident in a member state under the laws of which it is chargeable to tax because it is regarded as so resident (unless it is regarded under double tax arrangements entered into by the member state as resident in a territory not within any of the member states).

Where such a claim is made, if the transfer includes intangible fixed assets which are chargeable intangible assets (see 39.8 above) in relation to the transferor company immediately before the transfer and in relation to the transferee company immediately thereafter, the transfer of those assets is treated for the purposes of the current provisions as tax-neutral (see 39.8 above).

[*FA 2002, Sch 29 para 85*].

39.24 **Transfer of intangible assets on formation of European Company.** The European Company Statute provides for the formation of a European Company or *Societas Europaea* ('SE') and applies to all member states with effect from 8 October 2004 (see 25.4 EUROPEAN COMMUNITY LEGISLATION). The *Statute* permits the formation of new SEs and also allows for the 'transformation' of existing companies into SEs and for the merger between two (or more) companies in different member states into an SE. Special UK tax provisions are required to deal with the formation of SEs by cross-border merger and those relating to intangible assets are described below. The provisions are intended to be broadly tax-neutral. (Revenue Technical Note, 'Implementation of the European Company Statute', January 2005).

The provisions apply where an SE is formed on or after 1 April 2005 by the merger of two or more companies in accordance with *Council Regulation (EC) No 2157/2001, Arts 2(1), 17(2)* and each merging company is resident in a member state but not all of them are resident in the same member state.

A company is resident in a member state for this purpose if it is within a charge to tax under the law of the state as being resident for that purpose and it is not regarded, for the purposes of any DOUBLE TAX RELIEF (24) arrangements to which the state is a party, as resident in a territory not within a member state.

Transfer of intangible assets. Where intangible assets are transferred as part of the merger process and the provisions in 39.22 above (transfer of business or trade under FA 2002, Sch 29 para 84) do not apply to the assets, the transfer is treated as tax-neutral (see 39.8 above). The assets must be chargeable intangible assets (see 39.8 above) both in the hands of the transferor immediately before the transfer and in the hands of the transferee immediately afterwards.

These provisions do not apply unless the formation of the SE is for *bona fide* commercial reasons and is not part of a scheme or arrangements of which the main purpose or one of the main purposes is avoiding liability to tax. Advance clearance can be obtained that this condition is met (see 39.27 below).

[*FA 2002, Sch 29 para 85A; F(No 2)A 2005, s 52*].

Transfer of non-UK trade. Where:

(*a*) in the course of the merger a UK-resident company transfers to a company resident in another member state the whole or part of a trade carried on by the UK company immediately before the transfer through a permanent establishment in a member state other than the UK;

(*b*) the transfer includes all the transferor company's assets used in that trade or part;

(*c*) the transfer includes intangible fixed assets:

(i) which are chargeable intangible assets (see 39.8 above) in relation to the transferor company immediately before the transfer; and

(ii) in the case of one or more of which the proceeds of realisation exceed the cost recognised for tax purposes; and

(*d*) no claim is made under the provisions at 39.25 below in relation to those assets,

then, if tax would have been chargeable under the law of the other member state in respect of the transfer of those assets but for the Mergers Directive (*90/434/EEC*), double tax relief (whether unilateral or by agreement) is available as if the amount of tax which would have been so payable but for the Directive were payable.

These provisions do not apply unless the formation of the SE is for *bona fide* commercial reasons and is not part of a scheme or arrangements of which the main purpose or one of the main purposes is avoiding liability to tax. Advance clearance can be obtained that this condition is met (see 39.27 below).

[*FA 2002, Sch 29 para 87A; F(No 2)A 2005, s 53*].

39.25 **Postponement of charge on transfer of assets to non-resident company.** Special provisions apply where a UK-resident company carrying on a non-UK trade through a permanent establishment (see 60.5 RESIDENCE — previously a branch or agency) transfers the whole or part of that trade together with its assets, or its assets other than cash, to a non-UK resident company in exchange, wholly or partly, for shares (or shares and loan stock) in that company, so that thereafter it holds one-quarter or more of the transferee company's ordinary share capital. This is, however, conditional on the transfer being effected for *bona fide* commercial reasons and not as part of a scheme or arrangements a main purpose of which is avoidance of liability to income tax, corporation tax or capital gains tax (although advance clearance may be obtained that this condition is met, see 39.27 below).

If such a transfer includes intangible fixed assets which are chargeable intangible assets (see 39.8 above) in relation to the transferor company immediately before the transfer ('*relevant assets*'), that company may claim as follows.

(*a*) If the proceeds of realisation of a relevant asset exceed the cost recognised for tax purposes, they are treated as reduced by the excess or, if the securities are not the whole of the consideration for the transfer, by a proportion of the excess corresponding to the proportion that the market value of the securities at the time of the transfer bears to the market value of the whole of the consideration at that time.

(*b*) If at any time after the transfer the transferor company realises the whole of the securities held by it immediately before that time, it must bring into account for tax purposes a credit equal to the aggregate of the amounts by which proceeds of realisation were reduced under (*a*) above (so far as not already recovered under this provision or (*c*) below). If it realises part only of the securities, this applies to a proportion of that aggregate corresponding to the proportion that the market value of the part of the securities disposed of bears to the market value of the securities held immediately before the disposal. Disposals within *TCGA 1992, s 171* (no gain, no loss disposals, see 12.3 CAPITAL GAINS—GROUPS) are disregarded for this purpose, but the first subsequent disposal of the securities not so disregarded is then treated as a disposal by the transferor company.

(*c*) If at any time within six years after the transfer the transferee company realises all of the relevant assets held by it immediately before that time, the transferor company must bring into account for tax purposes a credit equal to the aggregate of the amounts by which proceeds of realisation were reduced under (*a*) above (so far as not already recovered under (*b*) above or under this provision). If only part of the relevant assets so held is disposed of at that time, the credit is reduced to the proportion applicable to the relevant assets disposed of. Intra-group disposals are disregarded for this purpose, but the first subsequent disposal of the relevant assets not so disregarded is then treated as a disposal by the transferee company.

No claim may be made under this provision where a claim is made under 39.26 below in relation to the transfer.

[*FA 2002, Sch 29 para 86*].

39.26 **Transfer of non-UK trade.** Where:

(*a*) a UK-resident '*EU company*' (i.e. a body incorporated under the law of a member state) transfers to an EU company resident in another member state the whole or part of a trade carried on by the UK company immediately before the transfer through a permanent establishment (or branch or agency) in a member state other than the UK;

(*b*) the transfer includes all the transferor company's assets used in that trade or part (with the possible exception of cash);

(*c*) the transfer is wholly or partly in exchange for securities (which includes shares) issued by the transferee company; and

(*d*) the transfer includes intangible fixed assets:

  (i) which are chargeable intangible assets (see 39.8 above) in relation to the transferor company immediately before the transfer; and

  (ii) in the case of one or more of which the proceeds of realisation exceed the cost recognised for tax purposes,

the transferor company may claim as follows, provided that the transfer is effected for *bona fide* commercial reasons and not as part of a scheme or arrangements a main purpose of which is avoidance of liability to income tax, corporation tax or capital gains tax (although advance clearance may be obtained that this condition is met, see 39.27 below).

Where tax would have been chargeable under the law of the other member state in respect of the transfer of those assets but for the Mergers Directive (*90/434/EEC*), double tax relief (whether unilateral or by agreement) is available as if the amount of tax which would have been so payable but for the Directive (assuming all possible reliefs had been claimed and losses arising on the transfer set off against gains so arising so far as permissible under that law) were payable.

A company is regarded for these purposes as resident in a member state under the laws of which it is chargeable to tax because it is regarded as so resident (unless it is regarded under double tax arrangements entered into by the member state as resident in a territory not within any of the member states).

No claim may be made under this provision where a claim is made under 39.25 above in relation to the transfer.

[*FA 2002, Sch 29 para 87*].

39.27 **Clearance.** Application may be made for clearance that the transactions in 39.22–39.26 above are *bona fide* commercial and not for tax avoidance purposes. The provisions are similar to those in *TCGA 1992, s 138* (see 11.10 CAPITAL GAINS and Tolley's Capital Gains Tax under Anti-Avoidance). [*FA 2002, Sch 29 para 88; F(No 2)A 2005, s 59(5)*].

Applications for clearance should be addressed to Mohini Sawhney, Clearance and Counteraction Team, Anti-Avoidance Group Intelligence, First Floor, 22 Kingsway, London WC2B 6NR (or, if market-sensitive information is included, to Eric Gardner at that address). Applications may be faxed to 020–7438 4409 or emailed to reconstructions@hmrc.gsi.gov.uk (after advising Eric Gardner (on 020–7438 6585) if market-sensitive information is included). Application may be made in a single letter to the same address for clearance under *FA 2002, Sch 29 para 88* and under any one or more of *ICTA 1988, s 215* (demergers, see 32.39 GROUPS OF COMPANIES), *ICTA 1988, s 225* (see 57.6 PURCHASE BY A COMPANY OF ITS OWN SHARES), *ICTA 1988, s 707* (transactions in securities, see 5.2 ANTI-AVOIDANCE), *TCGA 1992, s 138(1)* (share exchanges, see Tolley's Capital Gains Tax under Anti-Avoidance), *TCGA 1992, s 139(5)* (reconstructions involving the transfer of a business, see 11.9 CAPITAL GAINS), *TCGA 1992, s 140B* (transfer of a UK trade between EU member states, see 11.11 CAPITAL GAINS) and *TCGA 1992, s 140D* (transfer of non-UK trade between EU member states, see 11.12 CAPITAL GAINS).

39.28 **Transfer of life assurance business.** Where there is a transfer between two companies:

(*a*) under an 'insurance business transfer scheme' within *Financial Services and Markets Act 2000, s 105* (or an excluded scheme within *section 105(3), Case 2, 3 or 4*) of business consisting of the effecting or carrying out of 'contracts of long-term insurance' (within *SI 2001 No 544, Sch 1 Pt 2*); or

(*b*) which is a 'qualifying overseas transfer' within *ICTA 1988, Sch 19AC para 4A*,

and the assets transferred include intangible fixed assets which are chargeable intangible assets (see 39.8 above) in relation to the transferor company immediately before the transfer and in relation to the successor company immediately thereafter, the transfer of those assets is treated for the purposes of the current provisions as tax-neutral (see 39.8 above)

[*FA 2002, Sch 29 para 89*].

39.29 **Transfer of business of building society to company.** Provisions equivalent to those relating to capital gains in *TCGA 1992, s 216* (see 9.6 BUILDING SOCIETIES) apply in relation to the current provisions to treat the transfer of chargeable intangible assets as tax-neutral (see 39.8 above). [*FA 2002, Sch 29 para 90*].

39.30 **Amalgamation of, or transfer of engagements by, certain societies and associations.** Provisions equivalent to those relating to capital gains in *TCGA 1992, s 215* (see 9.3 BUILDING SOCIETIES) and *ICTA 1988, s 486(8)(9)* (see 38.3, 38.4 INDUSTRIAL AND PROVIDENT SOCIETIES) apply in relation to the current provisions to treat the transfer of chargeable intangible assets as tax-neutral (see 39.8 above) on the amalgamation of, or transfer of engagements by, building societies, industrial and provident societies and co-operative associations. [*FA 2002, Sch 29 para 91*].

39.31 TRANSACTIONS BETWEEN RELATED PARTIES

A person ('P') is a '*related party*' in relation to a company ('C') in the following circumstances.

(*a*) P is a company, and either P controls or has a major interest in C or *vice versa*.

(*b*) P is a company and P and C are both under the control of the same person (other than the Crown or certain governmental or international institutions).

(*c*) C is a close company (see 16 CLOSE COMPANIES) and P is a 'participator' (or an 'associate' of a 'participator') in C or, in relation to transfers or accounting periods beginning on or after 16 March 2005 (see below), a 'participator' in a company that controls, or has a major interest in, C (those terms being as under *ICTA 1988, s 417* (see 16.3, 16.5 CLOSE COMPANIES) but excluding from 'participator' certain loan creditors).

(*d*) P is a company and C is another company in the same group (see 39.9 above). This provision has effect for debits and credits brought into account for accounting periods beginning on or after 20 June 2003, and deductions are not available in such accounting periods in relation to debits and credits brought into account in earlier accounting periods. An accounting period straddling 20 June 2003 is to be treated as two separate accounting periods for this purpose, one ending on 19 June 2003 and the other beginning on 20 June 2003.

As regards (*c*) above, the extension of the related parties rule to a participator in a company that controls or has a major interest in a close company, applies for the purposes of 39.32 below, otherwise than for determining debits or credits to be brought into account, to transfers of assets on or after 16 March 2005. For all other purposes, it applies to debits or credits to be brought into account for accounting periods beginning on or after 16 March 2005 and is deemed to always have had effect in relation to the debits and credits brought into account in such periods. Where an accounting period straddles that date, it is treated for this purpose as two separate accounting periods, the first ending on 15 March 2005 and the second beginning on 16 March 2005.

For these purposes:

(i) '*control*' in relation to a company is the power of a person to secure that the company's affairs are conducted in accordance with their wishes, either through shareholding or voting power (in or in relation to any company) or through powers conferred by the articles of association or other regulatory document of any company;

(ii) a person has a '*major interest*' in a company if it and any other person together control the company, with each of them having at least 40% of the rights and powers by means of which they have such control.

'*Connected persons*' are specially defined in *FA 2002, Sch 29 para 101*, broadly as under *ICTA 1988, s 839* (see 19 CONNECTED PERSONS) but with the omission of the 'partners' and 'persons acting together' provisions at 19.3 and 19.6 respectively.

For the wide-ranging attribution of rights and powers of other persons for these purposes, see *FA 2002, Sch 29 paras 97–99*.

[*FA 2002, Sch 29 paras 95–101; FA 2003, s 184; ITTOIA 2005, Sch 1 para 580;* (*F*(*No 2*)*A 2005, s 41*(*3*)(*7*)–(*9*)].

39.32 **Transfer between company and related party.** Where an intangible asset is transferred by a company to a related party or *vice versa* and the asset is a chargeable intangible asset (see 39.8 above) in relation to the transferor immediately before the transfer or in relation to the transferee immediately thereafter, the transfer of those assets is treated for all tax purposes, as regards both transferor and transferee, as being at market value, *except* in any of the following circumstances.

(*a*) The transfer pricing provisions of *ICTA 1988, Sch 28AA* (see 67 TRANSFER PRICING) apply (whether or not the consideration for the transfer falls to be adjusted under that *Schedule*).

(*b*) The transfer is, under any of the current provisions, tax-neutral (see 39.8 above).

(*c*) In relation to transfers on or after 16 March 2005, an asset is transferred from the company to a related party at less than market value or to the company by the related party at more than its market value and:

- the related party is not a company, or is a company in relation to which the asset is not an intangible asset falling within these provisions; and
- the transfer results in an amount being taken into account (or to an amount which would be taken into account but for the market value rule) in computing any person's taxable income, profits or losses by virtue of *ICTA 1988, s 209* (see 23 DISTRIBUTIONS) or *ITEPA 2003, Pt 3* (see Tolley's Income Tax under Employment Income). In this case, the market value rule above does not apply for the purposes of those provisions.

(*d*) In relation to transfers on or after 16 March 2005, the asset is transferred to the company by a related party who makes a claim for hold-over relief on gifts for business assets under *TCGA 1992, s 165* (see Tolley's Capital Gains Tax under Hold-Over Reliefs). In this case, the transfer is treated as being at market value less the amount of the held-over gain and any necessary adjustments may be made to the company's tax position as a result of the claim.

As regards (*a*) above, the consideration falls within *Sch 28AA* without falling to be adjusted in a case where the conditions in *Sch 28AA para 1*(*1*) are met (see 67.3(*a*)(*b*) TRANSFER PRICING) but the actual and arm's length provisions do not differ, (and, for accounting periods beginning **before 1 April 2004**, had they differed so as to confer a potential advantage in relation to UK taxation within *Sch 28AA para 5*(*1*), *para 5*(*2*) would not have applied to eliminate the potential advantage (see 67.5 TRANSFER PRICING)).

As regards (*c*) above, an example is given by the Explanatory Notes to the Finance (No 3) Bill 2005 of a controlling shareholder transferring an intangible asset to the company for £10,000 when the asset is worth only £1,000 where the market value rule does not prevent the shareholder from being taxed on a distribution representing the consideration received for the asset in excess of its value.

[*FA 2002, Sch 29 para 92; FA 2004, s 37*(*2*), *Sch 5 para 16*(*3*)*;* (*F*(*No 2*)*A 2005, s 41*(*2*)(*6*)].

39.33 **Reinvestment relief in case of part realisation involving related party.** Reinvestment relief (see 39.8 above) does not apply in relation to the part realisation of an intangible fixed asset by a company if, as a result of or in connection with the part realisation, a related party acquires an interest of any description in the asset or in another asset deriving all or part of its value from that asset. [*FA 2002, Sch 29 para 93*].

39.34 **Delayed payment of royalty to related party.** Where a royalty (see 39.3 above) payable by a company to or for the benefit of a related party is not paid in full by twelve months after the end of the period of account in which a debit in respect of it is recognised by the company for accounting purposes (see 39.4 above), and credits representing the full amount of the royalty are not brought into account under the current provisions (see 39.5 above) in any accounting period by the person to whom it is payable, the royalty is brought into account under the current provisions only when it is paid. [*FA 2002, Sch 29 para 94*].

39.35 SUPPLEMENTARY PROVISIONS

Research and development. With effect for accounting periods beginning on or after 1 January 2005, where a deduction is allowed for revenue expenditure on research and development (see 59 RESEARCH AND DEVELOPMENT EXPENDITURE), which is brought into account in determining the value of an intangible asset, no deduction for tax purposes will be allowed in the amortisation of so much of the value of the intangible asset as is attributable to that expenditure. [*FA 2004, s 53; SI 2004 No 3268*].

Treatment of grants etc. Where a grant or other payment is intended by the payer to meet, directly or indirectly, a company's expenditure on an intangible fixed asset, any gain recognised in determining the company's profit or loss in respect of the grant etc. is treated as representing a receipt in respect of the asset (and hence as within 39.5 above). This does not, however, apply to grants under *Industrial Development Act 1982, Pt 2* or corresponding

NI grants (see 58.1 REGIONAL DEVELOPMENT GRANTS), any profit and loss account gain in respect of which is disregarded for the purposes of the current provisions. Where the bringing of such an exempt grant into account by a company results in a reduction in the amount of a loss recognised in determining the profit or loss, or in the amount of expenditure on an intangible fixed asset capitalised for accounting purposes, the amount of the reduction is added back for the purposes of the current provisions. [*FA 2002, Sch 29 paras 102, 103; FA 2005, Sch 4 para 40*].

Finance leasing etc. The Treasury has wide regulatory powers to make provision for the application of the current provisions in relation to a company which is a finance lessor of an intangible asset which is the subject of a finance lease. The term 'finance lease' has the meaning for this purpose that it has for accounting purposes, including hire-purchase, conditional sale and other like arrangements, and 'finance lessor' and 'finance lessee' have a corresponding meaning. [*FA 2002, Sch 29 para 104*]. For the initial regulations under this provision, see *SI 2002 No 1967*.

Assets acquired or realised together. Assets acquired of or disposed of in a single bargain are treated as acquired or disposed of together, notwithstanding any separate pricing or separate acquisitions or disposals. Where assets are acquired together, values allocated in accordance with generally accepted accounting practice (see 39.2 above) to particular assets are accepted for the purposes of the current provisions, and in the absence of such allocation a just and reasonable apportionment is made. Where assets are disposed of together, a just and reasonable apportionment of the disposal proceeds is made. [*FA 2002, Sch 29 para 105*].

Deemed market value acquisition: adjustment of amounts in case of nil accounting value. Where a company is treated under the current provisions as acquiring an asset at market value, but the accounting value of the asset transferred, in the hands of the transferee, is nil, then:

(*a*) the cost of the asset recognised for accounting purposes;

(*b*) the accounting value of the asset; and

(*c*) the amount of any loss recognised for accounting purposes in respect of capitalised expenditure on the asset,

are all taken to be such as would have been recognised had the asset been acquired at market value. Any revaluation of the asset (see 39.5 above) is disregarded. [*FA 2002, Sch 29 para 106*].

Fungible assets. Assets of a nature to be dealt in without identifying the particular assets involved, and which are of the same kind and held by the same person in the same capacity (e.g. milk quotas), are treated for the purposes of the current provisions as indistinguishable parts of a single asset which grows or diminishes as assets of the same kind are added or realised. [*FA 2002, Sch 29 para 107*]. See also 39.37 below for transitional rules.

Assets ceasing to be chargeable intangible assets. Where an asset ceases to be a chargeable intangible asset in relation to a company (see 39.8 above) either:

(*a*) on the company's ceasing to be UK-resident; or

(*b*) on the asset beginning to be held for the purposes of a mutual trade or business; or

(*c*) (in the case of a non-UK resident company) in any circumstances not involving the realisation of the asset by the company,

the current provisions have effect as if the company had, immediately before the triggering event, realised and immediately reacquired the asset at its market value at that time. An election may be made for a gain arising by virtue of (*a*) above to be postponed in certain cases where the asset concerned is held for the purposes of a non-UK trade carried on through a permanent establishment (see 60.5 RESIDENCE — previously a branch or agency). [*FA 2002, Sch 29 paras 108, 109*].

Asset becoming chargeable intangible asset. Where an asset becomes a chargeable intangible asset in relation to a company (see 39.8 above) either

(*a*) on the company's becoming UK-resident, or

(*b*) on the asset ceasing to be held for the purposes of a mutual trade or business, or

(*c*) (in the case of a non-UK resident company) on its beginning to be held for the purposes of a trade carried on in the UK through a permanent establishment (see 60.5 RESIDENCE — previously a branch or agency),

the current provisions have effect as if the company had, immediately after the triggering event, acquired the asset at its book value at that time. [*FA 2002, Sch 29 paras 110, 135*].

Tax avoidance. Arrangements (as widely defined) a main object of which are to enable a company to obtain a debit (or a greater debit) under 39.4 above or to avoid (or reduce) a credit under 39.7 above are disregarded in determining such debits and credits. [*FA 2002, Sch 29 para 111; FA 2003, s 184*].

Expenditure not generally tax-deductible. No debit may be brought in under the current provisions (see 39.4 above) in respect of expenditure which would not be an allowable trade deduction under:

(*a*) *ICTA 1988, s 577* (business entertainment or gifts);

(*b*) *ICTA 1988, s 577A* (crime-related expenditure);

(*c*) *ICTA 1988, s 578A* (expensive hired cars); or

(*d*) *FA 1989, s 76(1)–(3)* (certain retirement benefits).

[*FA 2002, Sch 29 para 112*].

Delayed payment of employees' remuneration. Where a debit in respect of employees' remuneration is recognised by a company for accounting purposes but the remuneration is not treated as received as employment income within nine months after the end of the period of account in which the debit is recognised, the remuneration is brought into account under the current provisions (see 39.4 above) only when it is paid. This applies equally to '*potential remuneration*', i.e. amounts reserved in the employer's accounts with a view to it becoming remuneration, which is regarded as received when it becomes remuneration so treated as above. Any necessary apportionment for these purposes is made on a just and reasonable basis. If a tax calculation has to be made before the nine months has expired and when remuneration (as above) has not been paid, it is to be assumed that it will not be paid before the end of the nine-month period. If it is subsequently paid before the end of that period, and a claim is made to HMRC within two years after the end of the period of account concerned, the calculation may be adjusted. Remuneration is treated as paid when it is treated as received by the employee under *ITEPA 2003*, or would be so treated if it were not exempt income.

A similar provision applies in relation to pension contributions not paid until after the end of the period of account in which the associated debit is recognised.

[*FA 2002, Sch 29 paras 113, 114; FA 2003, Sch 24 para 10(2); FA 2004, Sch 17 para 8*].

Bad debts etc. For the purposes of the current provisions, no debit may be brought into account in respect of a debt (monetary or otherwise) except by way of impairment loss or to the extent the debt is released as part of a statutory insolvency arrangement. (For periods of account beginning before 1 January 2005 (before the introduction of 'impairment loss' terminology), a debt is brought into account on the assumption that the amount payable will be paid in full when it becomes due except to the extent that the debt is bad, or estimated to be bad, or is released as part of a statutory insolvency arrangement.) Any gain brought into account for accounting purposes by the debtor in respect of a release as part of a statutory insolvency arrangement is disregarded. Otherwise, any gain relating to an unpaid debt in respect of an intangible fixed asset which is brought into account for accounting purposes by the debtor is treated as regards credits in respect of receipts recognised as they accrue (see 39.7 above) as a gain in respect of the asset. Any necessary apportionment for these purposes is made on a just and reasonable basis. [*FA 2002, Sch 29 para 115; FA 2005, s 80, Sch 4 para 20*].

Controlled foreign companies ('CFCs'). In computing the chargeable profits of a CFC (see 21.10 CONTROLLED FOREIGN COMPANIES), the following assumptions are made in applying the current provisions.

(*a*) Subject to the commencement rules for the current provisions (see 39.37 below), any intangible fixed asset acquired or created by the company before the first accounting period for which an apportionment has been made under the CFC provisions, or which is an ADP exempt period under those provisions, is assumed to have been acquired or created by the company at the beginning of that accounting period at a cost equal to its value for accounting purposes at that time.

(*b*) It is assumed that the company has not claimed any reinvestment relief or made any provisional declaration of entitlement to such relief (see 39.8 above), notwithstanding the general assumption referred to in 21.10(iv), although notice may be given as described in 21.10(iv) modifying or disapplying this assumption.

[*FA 2002, Sch 29 para 116*].

39.36 CHANGE OF ACCOUNTING POLICY

The following provisions apply for periods of account **beginning on or after 1 January 2005**. Where there is a change in accounting policy in preparing a company's accounts from one period of account to the next in accordance with the law and practice applicable in relation to those periods, then if there is any accounting difference between the closing accounting value of the assets concerned in the earlier period and their opening value in the later period, a corresponding debit or credit (as the case may be) is to be taken into account for tax purposes in the later period. This applies in particular where a company prepares its accounts for one period in accordance with UK generally accepted accounting practice and for the next period in accordance with international accounting standards, or vice versa.

Change of value. Where, as a result of the change of accounting policy, there is a difference between the closing accounting value of an intangible fixed asset in the earlier period and its opening accounting value in the later period, the amount of the debit or credit to be brought into account (subject to the cap as noted below) is the proportion of the accounting difference that the tax written down value of the asset at the end of the earlier period bears to the accounting value at that time. The tax written down value of the asset at the beginning of the later period is then taken to be the tax written down value at the end of the earlier period as reduced by the debit or increased by the credit (as the case may be). Subsequently, the cost of the asset for tax purposes is the tax written down value (as reduced or increased) together with the cost recognised for tax purposes of any subsequent expenditure that is capitalised for accounting purposes and the tax written down value is to be determined taking account only of subsequent debits and credits. This does not apply to an intangible fixed asset in respect of which an election for writing down at a fixed-rate has been made (see 39.4 above). Nor does it apply where, in respect of the accounting difference, a debit or credit is brought into account for tax purposes on the reversal of an earlier accounting credit or debit, or in respect of a revaluation gain (see 39.4 and 39.5 above).

Disaggregation. A change of accounting policy may result in an intangible fixed asset that was treated as one asset ('*the original asset*') in the earlier period, being treated as two or more assets ('*the resulting assets*') in the later period. In this case, where, as a result of the change of accounting policy, there is a difference between the closing accounting value of the original asset in the earlier period and the opening accounting value of the resulting assets in the later period, the amount of the debit or credit to be brought into account (subject to the cap noted below) is the proportion of the accounting difference that the tax written down value of the original asset at the end of the earlier period bears to the accounting value of that asset at that time.

The tax written down value of each resulting asset at the beginning of the later period is then taken to be the proportion of the tax written down value of the original asset at the end of the earlier period (as reduced by the debit or increased by the credit as the case may be) that the opening accounting value of that asset in the later period bears to the aggregate opening accounting values of the resulting assets at that time. Subsequently, the cost of each resulting asset for tax purposes is the tax written down value (as above) together with the cost recognised for tax purposes of any subsequent expenditure that is capitalised for accounting purposes and the tax written down value is to be determined taking account only of subsequent debits and credits.

This does not apply where an election for writing down at a fixed-rate has been or is subsequently made (see 39.4 above) in respect of the original or resulting assets (see below). Nor does it apply where, in respect of the accounting difference, a debit or credit is brought into account for tax purposes on the reversal of an earlier accounting credit or debit, or in respect of a revaluation gain (see 39.4 and 39.5 above).

Original asset subject to fixed-rate writing down. Where a change in accounting policy results in the disaggregation of assets (as above) and an election for writing down at a fixed-rate (see 39.4 above) has been or is subsequently made in respect of the original asset, the election applies to the original asset for periods up to and including the earlier period, and to the resulting assets for the later and subsequent periods. The tax written down value of each resulting asset at the beginning of the later period is then taken to be the proportion of the tax written down value of the original asset at the end of the earlier period that the opening accounting value of that asset in the later period bears to the aggregate opening accounting values of the resulting assets at that time. Subsequently, the cost of each resulting asset for tax purposes is the tax written down value (as above) together with the cost recognised for tax purposes of any subsequent expenditure that is capitalised for accounting purposes and the tax written down value is to be determined taking account only of subsequent debits and credits.

Resulting assets subject to fixed-rate writing down. Where a change in accounting policy results in the disaggregation of assets (as above) and no election for writing down at a fixed-rate (see 39.4 above) has been made in respect of the original asset, such an election may be made in respect of any of the resulting assets provided it is made within two years after the end of the accounting period in which the original asset was acquired or created. The effect of the election is that the original asset is treated as consisting of as many assets ('notional original assets') as there are resulting assets, each notional original asset being treated as the same asset as one of the resulting assets (its 'corresponding resulting asset'). An appropriate proportion of every amount falling to be taken into account in relation to the original asset is to be attributed to each notional original asset, the 'appropriate portion' being ascertained by reference to its corresponding resulting asset. The '*appropriate proportion*' in this case is the amount which the opening accounting value of that asset in the later period bears to the aggregate opening accounting values of all the resulting assets at that time. The provisions of this chapter apply to each of the notional original assets and its corresponding resulting asset accordingly.

Cap on credit to be brought into account. Where a change in accounting policy results in a difference between the closing accounting value of the asset (or, in the case of disaggregation, the original asset) in the earlier period and the opening accounting value of the asset (or the resulting assets) in the later period, the amount of any credit to be brought into account for tax purposes is limited to the net aggregate amount of relevant tax debits previously brought into account, this being the total debits previously brought into account in respect of the asset (or, in the case of disaggregation, the original asset at the end of the earlier period) less the total credits previously brought into account in respect of that asset.

Subsequent events. Where there is a further change in accounting policy affecting an asset to which these provisions have already applied, these provisions are to apply again. Where there is a subsequent part realisation affecting an asset to which these provisions have already applied, the provisions of *FA 2002, Sch 29 para 29* apply. In this case the tax written-down value of the intangible asset immediately after the subsequent part realisation is found by reducing its written-down value immediately before the subsequent part realisation by the fraction equal to its carrying value (for accounting purposes) immediately after the part realisation divided by that immediately before it. Subsequent allowances are based on that amount.

[*FA 2002, Sch 29 paras 116A–116H; FA 2004, s 52, Sch 10 para 72; FA 2005, s 80, Sch 4 para 45*].

39.37 COMMENCEMENT AND TRANSITIONAL PROVISIONS

The commencement date for the purposes of the current provisions is 1 April 2002. [*FA 2002, Sch 29 para 117*].

Assets created or acquired after commencement. Except as below, the current provisions apply only to intangible fixed assets of a company which are:

(*a*) created by the company after commencement; or

(*b*) acquired by the company after commencement other than from a related party (see 39.31 above); or

(*c*) acquired by the company after commencement from a related party (see 39.31 above) where either:

  (i) the asset is acquired from a company in relation to which the asset was a chargeable intangible asset (see 39.8 above) immediately before the acquisition; or

  (ii) the asset is acquired from an intermediary who acquired the asset after commencement from a third person. Neither the company and the third person nor the intermediary and the third person can be related parties (see 39.31 above) for this to apply; or

  (iii) the asset was created by any person after commencement.

For these purposes (except in the case of certain internally-generated assets, see below) an asset is regarded as acquired or created after commencement to the extent that expenditure on its acquisition or creation is so incurred, and acquisition expenditure is generally treated as incurred when it is recognised for accounting purposes. There are, however, two special cases.

(A) Acquisition expenditure which does not qualify for any form of tax relief against income under existing law, and which would be treated as incurred after commencement under the general rule, is treated as incurred before commencement if the asset is (or would be) treated as disposed of and acquired before commencement for chargeable gains purposes.

(B) Creation or acquisition expenditure which under existing law qualifies for any capital allowance is treated as incurred when an unconditional obligation to pay it comes into being (notwithstanding that all or any part of the expenditure may not be required to be paid until a later date).

If only part of the expenditure on an asset is incurred after commencement, the expenditure is treated as being on two separate assets, one within and one outside the current provisions, with any necessary apportionment being made on a just and reasonable basis.

Intangible fixed assets not within (*a*)–(*c*) above are referred to as '*existing assets*'. As regards application of certain of the current provisions to certain existing assets, see further below.

[*FA 2002, Sch 29 paras 118, 120, 123–125*].

Royalties. A '*royalty*' is defined as any payment in respect of the enjoyment or exercise of rights that are an intangible fixed asset. The current provisions apply to royalties only where they are recognised for accounting purposes after commencement, and royalties brought into account for tax purposes before commencement are not brought into account again after commencement. To the extent that royalties would have been brought in before commencement had the current provisions been in force, but were not, they are brought in immediately after commencement. A royalty is brought into account for these purposes if it would have been had the person concerned been within the charge to corporation tax. These rules are not affected by the above rules determining whether assets are within the current provisions.

In relation to debits and credits brought into account for any accounting period beginning after 4 December 2005, these rules cannot be interpreted as allowing or requiring an amount to be brought into account in connection with the realisation of an existing asset within 39.7 above. For this purpose, accounting periods straddling 5 December 2005 are treated as two separate accounting periods, one beginning on that date and the other ending immediately before it.

[*FA 2002, Sch 29 paras 118(6), 119, 139; FA 2006, s 77(6)(7)(10)(11)*].

Internally-generated assets. Internally-generated *goodwill* is regarded as created before (and not after) commencement of the current provisions if the business in question was carried on at any time before commencement by the company or a related party (see 39.31 above). Other internally-generated assets representing expenditure which under existing law does not qualify for any capital allowance ('*non-qualifying expenditure*') are regarded as created before (and not after) commencement if the asset in question was held at any time before commencement by the company or a related party (see 39.31 above). If only part of the expenditure on an asset is non-qualifying expenditure, the expenditure is correspondingly treated as being on two separate assets, with any necessary apportionment being made on a just and reasonable basis. [*FA 2002, Sch 29 paras 121, 122*].

Fungible assets. The commencement provisions apply to fungible assets (see 39.35 above) as if existing assets (see above) and other intangible fixed assets were assets of different kinds, the single asset consisting of existing assets itself being an existing asset and the single asset consisting of other intangible fixed assets being subject to the current provisions. Realisation of an intangible fixed asset which, apart from this special treatment, would form part of a single asset comprising both types of asset are regarded as diminishing the existing asset component in priority to the component consisting of assets subject to the current provisions. Intangible fixed assets acquired by a company which would not otherwise be existing assets are treated as such to the extent that, under the following rules, they are identified with existing assets realised by the company.

(1) Assets acquired are identified with existing assets of the same kind realised by the company within 30 days either side of the acquisition.

(2) Assets realised earlier are identified before assets realised later.

(3) Assets acquired earlier are identified before assets acquired later.

[*FA 2002, Sch 29 para 126*].

Assets acquired on transfer of business. Where an existing asset (see above) in the hands of a company is transferred to another company **after 27 June 2002**, and the transfer is one to which *TCGA 1992, s 139* (company reconstruction or amalgamation), *TCGA 1992, s 140A* (transfer of UK trade to company resident in another member state) or *TCGA 1992, s 140E* (transfer on formation of SE: assets left within UK tax charge) applies (see 11.9, 11.11, 11.13 CAPITAL GAINS), so that the transferor company is treated as disposing of the asset for a no gain, no loss consideration, the asset is treated as an existing asset in the hands of the transferee company. [*FA 2002, Sch 29 para 127; F(No 2)A 2005, s 59(6)*].

Assets treated as existing assets. The following provisions apply in relation to debits and credits brought into account for any accounting period beginning after 4 December 2005 and for this purpose, they are deemed to have always had effect in relation to any credits so brought into account. Accounting periods straddling 5 December 2005 are treated as two separate accounting periods: one beginning on that date and the other ending immediately before it.

Assets whose value derives from existing assets. (This anti-avoidance provision is aimed at the type of scheme which commonly involves the grant of a long-term licence over an intangible asset for a lump sum.) Where a company acquires an intangible fixed asset from a related party after the commencement of the intangible fixed assets regime and the asset is created after the commencement, it will be treated as an existing asset in the hands of the company (and so excluded from the regime) in so far as its value is derived in whole or in part from another asset which:

- has not at any time after 4 December 2005 been a chargeable intangible asset in the hands of the company or related transferor or another related party of the company or transferor; and
- has been an existing asset in the hands of the related transferor or in the hands of another related party of the company or transferor.

The value of an asset is derived from another asset where assets have been merged or divided or have changed their nature, or where rights or interests in or over assets have been created or extinguished. Where only part of the value of the acquired asset is derived from the existing asset, it is treated as a separate existing asset to the extent that its value is so derived, any necessary apportionment being made on a just and reasonable basis.

Assets acquired in connection with disposals of existing assets. Where a company acquires an intangible fixed asset it will be treated as an existing asset where the acquisition is made directly or indirectly in consequence of or otherwise in connection with a disposal of an existing asset by a person who at the time of the disposal is a related party in relation to the company. This provision applies where the asset acquired would otherwise be a chargeable intangible asset in the hands of the company at the time of the acquisition, and a disposal of an existing asset can include a part disposal or any other disposal of the asset (under the capital gain tax rules). It does not matter whether the asset disposed of is the same as the one acquired, whether the acquisition and disposal take place at the same time or whether the acquired asset is acquired by the merging of two or more assets or by any other way. This anti-avoidance provision applies to transactions such as where a company grants a licence out of an existing trademark and claims to have made a part-disposal of the trade mark to which the 'no loss, no gain' rule under *TCGA 1992, s 171* applies while the company to whom the licence was granted claims it is a newly created intangible fixed asset. (Explanatory notes to draft legislation published on 5 December 2005.)

[*FA 2002, Sch 29 paras 127A, 127B; FA 2006, s 77(8)(10)(11)*].

Application of relief on reinvestment in relation to existing assets. Where a company realises an existing asset after commencement, the rules for relief on reinvestment (see 39.8 above) apply with the necessary modifications. [*FA 2002, Sch 29 paras 130, 131*]. For the transitory interaction with capital gains roll-over relief, see *FA 2002, Sch 29 para 132* (as amended by *F(No 2)A 2005, s 41(4)(10)*).

Special provisions. See *FA 2002, Sch 29 paras 128, 129* for special provisions relating to *telecommunications rights* within *FA 2000, Sch 23* (as replaced by *ITTOIA 2005, Pt 2 Ch 10*, see 66.79 TRADING INCOME) and *Lloyd's syndicate capacity*.

40 Interest on Overpaid Tax

The headings in this chapter are as follows.

40.1 ACCOUNTING PERIODS ENDING ON OR AFTER 1 JULY 1999

For accounting periods ending on or after 1 July 1999, to which self-assessment applies, a repayment or payment carries interest from the 'material date' until the payment order is issued where the repayment or payment falls to be made in respect of any of the following:

(*a*) corporation tax for the period;

(*b*) surplus advance corporation tax in respect of distributions made in accounting periods beginning before 6 April 1999 under the foreign income dividend scheme (see Tolley's Corporation Tax 2004–05 or earlier editions);

(*c*) income tax in respect of a payment received in the period;

(*d*) a tax credit comprised in any franked investment income received in such a period falling to be wholly or partly paid to the company;

(*e*) research and development tax credits (see 59 RESEARCH AND DEVELOPMENT) for accounting periods ending after 31 March 2000 (or, in the case of vaccine research, in relation to expenditure incurred after 21 April 2003);

(*f*) land remediation tax credits (see 55.8 PROFIT COMPUTATIONS) or life assurance company tax credits for accounting periods ending after 31 March 2001;

(*g*) film tax credits payable under the FA 2006 regime (see 66.52 TRADING INCOME).

In the case of certain 'large' companies, which are required to make instalment payments in respect of their corporation tax liabilities (see 53.2 PAYMENT OF TAX), a special rate (see 40.5 below) applies to any excess instalment payments until nine months after the end of the accounting period concerned and a lower rate applies to repayments made after that time. The special higher rate also applies to corporation tax payments made by a company, which is *not* a large company, before the day following the expiry of nine months after the end of an accounting period. Interest is payable from the date of payment until that day although not for periods before the first instalment date which would apply if the company were a large company.

Details of the rates, including those for instalment payments by 'large companies', are as set out in 40.5 below.

Interest under these provisions is paid without deduction of tax. Where interest is payable under these provisions to a company within the charge to corporation tax, it is brought into account in computing profits or income under the loan relationship rules (see 46.46 LOAN RELATIONSHIPS).

The '*material date*' is:

(i) for corporation tax, the later of the date the corporation tax was paid and the date on which it became (or would have become) due and payable, i.e. nine months after the end of the accounting period (see 53.1 PAYMENT OF TAX);

(ii) for income tax repayments and payments of tax credit in relation to (*c*) or (*d*) above, the day after the end of the accounting period in which the payment was received by the company;

(iii) (in relation to accounting periods beginning before 6 April 1999) for repayments of surplus ACT, the date on which corporation tax for the period became (or would have become) due and payable, i.e. nine months after the end of the accounting period;

(iv) in the case of a tax repayment in respect of repayment, release or writing off of a close company loan under *ICTA 1988, s 419(4)*, the later of the date the entitlement to the tax repayment accrued (i.e. the date nine months after the end of the accounting period in which the loan etc. was made or, if the loan had not been repaid, released or written off at that date, the date nine months after the end of the accounting period in which it was repaid, released or written off) and the actual date of payment of the tax to be repaid. (For a loan made in an accounting period ending before 31 March 1996, it is the later of the date the loan (or part) was repaid and the actual date of payment of the tax);

(v) in the case of research and development, land remediation and film tax credits, the filing date (see 61.3 RETURNS) for the company tax return for the accounting period for which the credit is claimed (or if later the date of receipt by HMRC of the return (or amended return) containing the claim).

In relation to repayments within (iv) above, the repayment is treated as if it were a repayment of corporation tax for the accounting period in which the loan (or part) was repaid, released or written off.

Corporation tax repayments are as far as possible treated as repayments of tax paid on a later rather than an earlier date.

Interest is restricted where losses of an accounting period are carried back under *ICTA 1988, s 393A(1)* (see 47.6 LOSSES) to an accounting period not falling wholly within the twelve months preceding the period in which the loss was incurred. Interest on any repayment of corporation tax paid for the earlier period, or on any payment of income tax or tax credit in respect of payments received in that period, is only payable from nine months after the end of the accounting period in which the loss arose.

To the extent that a repayment of corporation tax, or of income tax in respect of a payment received, arose from surplus ACT carried back from a subsequent accounting period beginning before 6 April 1999, interest as above is only payable from nine months after the end of the accounting period in which the surplus ACT arose. Where, as a result of the loss being carried back, surplus ACT arises in the earlier period (beginning before 6 April 1999) which is itself carried back, the provisions described above in relation to interest in relation to the period in which the surplus ACT is applied are amended to prevent such interest being payable for any time before nine months after the end of the accounting period in which the loss arose (rather than the period in which the surplus ACT arose). (These provisions do not apply where the period to which the loss or surplus ACT is carried back ended before 1 October 1993, but the provisions of *ICTA 1988, s 825* (see 40.4 below) have similar effect.) See Revenue Tax Bulletin April 1996 pp 304, 305 for an example illustrating the point that *ICTA 1988, s 826* only applies to repayments of tax paid for accounting periods ending after 30 September 1993, regardless of whether a repayment for an earlier period may arise from surplus ACT carried back from such a period.

See also 24.6 DOUBLE TAX RELIEF as regards similar provisions relating to relief for excess unrelieved foreign tax.

Similar restrictions also apply where a non-trading deficit on a company's loan relationships is carried back on a claim under *FA 1996, s 83(2)* (see 46.3 LOAN RELATIONSHIPS).

For accounting periods ending on or after 1 July 1999, where, solely as a result of a change in a company's corporation tax liability, it appears to HMRC that any interest paid under these provisions ought not to have been paid, it is recoverable without assessment as if it were INTEREST ON UNPAID TAX (41).

[*ICTA 1988, ss 826, 826A; FA 1998, s 34, Sch 3 para 38, Sch 4 paras 1-3, 5; FA 1999, s 90; FA 2000, Sch 21 para 1, Sch 30 para 29; FA 2001, Sch 23 para 3; FA 2002, Sch 14 para 1; FA 2006, Sch 5 para 26; SI 1998 No 3175, reg 8*].

Simon's Direct Tax Service. See A3.1332–A3.1334.

Repayment supplement is not paid in respect of out of date claims, since the amount repaid is regarded as an *ex gratia* payment made without acceptance of any legal liability. (HMRC Repayment Claims Manual, RM 5104).

In the case of *Sempra Metals Ltd v CIR, Ch D [2004] STC 1178, (*following the finding by the CJEC that the requirement that both parties to an election under *section 247* be UK-resident contravened EC law), it was held that in providing for compensation, interest from the date on which ACT was paid until the date it was set off against mainstream corporation tax should be calculated on the basis of compound interest but that interest for the period from when the cause of action accrued until the date of judgment should be calculated on a simple basis.

40.2 **EXAMPLES**

(*A*) *Self-assessment*

X Ltd prepares accounts to 31 December. On 15 June 2007 it submits its tax return for the year ended 31 December 2006 showing a corporation tax liability for the period of £14,000, and accompanied by a payment of £7,000. On 1 October 2007 it makes a further payment of £7,000. It subsequently submits an amended return showing a reduced liability of £12,500, and £1,500 is repaid to the company on 1 December 2007.

It is assumed that interest rates for corporation tax repayments other than by instalment remain unchanged after 6 September 2006.

X Ltd will be entitled to interest on overpaid tax, calculated as follows.

		£
15.6.07 to 30.9.07	£7,000 × 5.25% × 108/365 =	108.74
1.10.07 to 30.11.07	£1,500 × 4% × 61/365 =	10.03
Total interest		£118.77

(*B*) *Instalment payments*

Z Ltd has no associated companies and had taxable profits in excess of £1,500,000 for the year ended 31 March 2006. For the year ended 31 March 2007, Z Ltd pays £143,000 for the first instalment on 30 September 2006, this being equivalent to a quarter of its estimated corporation tax liability of £572,000. The same amount is paid on the due dates for the second and third instalments and on 5 July 2007 for the fourth instalment. On 3 September 2008, the tax liability is agreed at £506,800 and £65,200 is repaid to the company on 22 September 2008.

The rates of interest are assumed for the purposes of this example to remain unchanged after 6 September 2006.

The interest on tax overpaid is calculated as follows.

Instalments due on quarter dates £506,800 × ¼ = £126,700

	£
14 October 2006 to 19 November 2006	
143,000 – 126,700 = £16,300 @ 4.25% × 37/365 =	74.35
20 November 2006 to 13 January 2007	
143,000 – 126,700 = £16,300 @ 4.75% × 55/365 =	116.67
14 January 2007 to 21 January 2007	
286,000 – 253,400 = £32,600 @ 4.75% × 90/365 =	33.94
22 January 2007 to 13 April 2007	
286,000 – 253,400 = £32,600 @ 5% × 82/365	366.19
14 April 2007 to 20 May 2007	
429,000 – 380,100 = £48,900 @ 5% × 37/365 =	247.85
21 May 2007 to 4 July 2007	
429,000 – 380,100 = £48,900 @ 5.25% × 45/365 =	316.51
5 July 2007 to 13 July 2007	
572,000 – 380,100 = £191,900 @ 5.25% × 9/365 =	248.42
14 July 2007 to 31 December 2007	
572,000 – 506,800 = £65,200 @ 5.25% × 171/365 =	1,603.65
1 January 2008 to 21 September 2008	
572,000 – 506,800 = £65,200 @ 4% × 264/365 =	1,886.33
Interest on overpaid tax	4,893.91

40.3 **ACCOUNTING PERIODS ENDING BEFORE 1 JULY 1999**

For accounting periods ending after 30 September but before 1 July 1999, the provisions described in 40.1 above in relation to self-assessment accounting periods similarly apply, but with a number of differences, namely:

- interest on overpaid tax is not chargeable to corporation tax;
- the special rates for instalment payments for certain 'large' companies in respect of payments of corporation tax does not apply to pre-self-assessment accounting periods;
- the 'material date' for income tax repayments and payments of tax credit is the due and payable date for corporation tax for the accounting period concerned, i.e. nine months after the end of that accounting period.

The interest rates are set out in 40.5 below.

[*ICTA 1988, ss 826, 826A*].

40.4 ACCOUNTING PERIODS ENDING ON OR BEFORE 30 SEPTEMBER 1993

Where a repayment falls to be made to a company for an accounting period ending on or before 30 September 1993, of either corporation tax (including ACT), income tax or the tax credit attached to franked investment income, and the repayment is made more than twelve months after the 'material date', the repayment carries interest (a '*repayment supplement*').

The rates of interest are as set out in 40.5 below.

Interest is disregarded for all tax purposes. In relation to repayments before 6 April 1993, the tax concerned had to amount to £100 or more for interest to be payable.

The interest runs to the end of the tax month (i.e. the month from the sixth day of one calendar month to the fifth day of the next) in which the order for repayment is issued, and commences on the date determined as follows.

		Interest commences
(a)	Corporation tax originally paid on or after the first anniversary of the 'material date'.	At the beginning of the tax month following the next anniversary of the 'material date' after the tax was paid.
(b)	In any other case (i.e. corporation tax paid before the first anniversary of the 'material date', income tax and tax credits relating to the relevant accounting period).	At the beginning of the tax month following the first anniversary of the 'material date'.

'*Material date*' means the earliest due date for payment of corporation tax for the accounting period in question (i.e. the date specified at 53.3 PAYMENT OF TAX).

Repayment supplement is not paid in respect of out of date claims, since the amount repaid is regarded as an *ex gratia* payment made without acceptance of any legal liability. (HMRC Repayment Claims Manual, RM 5104).

Corporation tax repayments are as far as possible treated as repayments of tax paid on a later rather than an earlier date.

[*ICTA 1988, s 825; FA 1989, ss 178, 179*].

Example

The earliest due date for payment of corporation tax by X Ltd is 9 months after the end of each accounting period. An estimated assessment for the accounting period 1 April 1992–31 March 1993 is raised on 23 April 1994, charging tax of £21,000. This is paid on 7 May 1994 and an appeal made against the assessment. The appeal is determined on 28 August 1995, following which the assessment is increased to charge a further £2,790.46. This further amount is paid on 1 October 1995. Subsequently, relief is claimed for part of a trading loss of the next following accounting period, and a corporation tax repayment of £6,726.64 is made on 15 November 1996.

The 'material date' is 9 months after the end of the accounting period, i.e. 1 January 1994.

Repayment supplement is calculated as follows.

(i) The tax of £2,790.46 falls within (*a*) above, and interest accordingly runs from the beginning of the income tax month following the first anniversary of the material date after the date of payment, i.e.

Date of payment	1 October 1995
Anniversary of material date	1 January 1996
Interest runs from	6 January 1996

Interest runs to the end of the income tax month in which the repayment is made (i.e. to 5 December 1996), a total of 11 months. For calculations, see below.

(ii) The balance of the repayment (£3,936.18) is attributable to the tax paid on 7 May 1994. This tax falls within (*b*) above, and interest accordingly runs *from* the beginning of the income tax month following 1 January 1995 (i.e. 6 January 1995). Interest runs *to* 5 December 1996, a total of 23 months.

Calculations

(i)	£2,790.46 @ 7.00% × 1⁄12 =	16.28
	£2,790.46 @ 6.25% × 10⁄12 =	145.34
(ii)	£3,936.18 @ 6.25% × 2⁄12 =	41.00
	£3,936.18 @ 7.00% × 11⁄12 =	252.57
	£3,936.18 @ 6.25% × 10⁄12 =	205.00
Total supplement		£660.19

Using the interest factor tables published by HMRC, the factors for the relevant months are:

January 1995	3.1532
January 1996	3.2219
December 1996	3.2799

The interest due is then calculated as:

£2,790.46 × (3.2799 – 3.2219) =	£161.85
+ £3,936.18 × (3.2799 – 3.1532) =	£498.71
Total supplement	£660.56

In order to qualify for the repayment supplement, the company must have been resident in the UK for the accounting period in connection with which the repayment of tax is made. Interest is paid for each **complete** tax month only.

In *R v CIR (ex p Commerzbank AG) QB 1991, 68 TC 252*, repayment supplement was held not to fall within the scope of double tax agreements, but on a reference to the European Court of Justice (see *68 TC 264*), the Court upheld the view that, in the case of EC member states, such discrimination against non-UK resident companies was prevented by the relevant Articles of the Treaty of Rome. HMRC invited claims to repayment supplement by companies resident within the EC for an accounting period for which a repayment was made without supplement, where the repayment was made more than twelve months after the end of the accounting period and in the six years before the date of the ECJ decision (13 July 1993).

Repayments relating to surplus ACT carried back to an earlier period claimed under *ICTA 1988, s 239(3)* and tax on repayment of loans to participators etc. claimed under *ICTA 1988, s 419(4)* (see 16.9–16.13 CLOSE COMPANIES) are treated as repayments of tax for the accounting period in which the surplus ACT arose or the loan repayment was made. Similarly, a repayment relating to the carry back of a loss to an earlier period under *ICTA 1988, s 393A(1)* is treated as a repayment of tax paid for the period in which the loss was incurred, unless the earlier period falls wholly within the twelve months preceding the accounting period of the loss. This applies also to the repayment of a tax credit arising from a claim under *ICTA 1988, s 242* relating to the relief of losses under *ICTA 1988, s 393A(1)*, and to the carry-back of relievable amounts in respect of exchange losses (see 26.14 EXCHANGE GAINS AND LOSSES). These provisions continue to apply where the accounting period in which the loss or surplus ACT etc. arose ended after 30 September 1993, provided that the period for which the tax was repaid ended on or before that date.

For a case in which a repayment for earlier years (by means of a revised postponement application) was sought and made in advance of formal determination of surplus ACT available, but was held to have resulted from a claim to carry back ACT, see *Savacentre Ltd v CIR CA 1995, 67 TC 381.*

The above provisions do not apply to amounts paid by order of a court having power to allow interest.

40.5 INTEREST RATES

The rate of interest is adjusted automatically by reference to the average of base lending rates of certain clearing banks, the formula being the rounded-down average base rate less 1%, the subtotal being reduced by the full rate of corporation tax and rounded down. [*FA 1989, ss 178, 179; SI 1989 No 1297* as amended].

It is understood that a denominator of 365 is used in calculations of repayment interest regardless of whether or not a leap year is involved.

Self-assessment. *Corporation tax repayments.* For corporation tax repayments for accounting periods ending on or after 1 July 1999, the following rate of interest applies, changes being announced in Revenue Press Releases.

4.00% p.a. from 6 September 2006

3.00% p.a. from 6 September 2005 to 5 September 2006

4.00% p.a. from 6 September 2004 to 5 September 2005

3.00% p.a. from 6 December 2003 to 5 September 2004

2.00% p.a. from 6 August 2003 to 5 December 2003

3.00% p.a. from 6 November 2001 to 5 August 2003

4.00% p.a. from 6 May 2001 to 5 November 2001

5.00% p.a. from 6 February 2000 to 5 May 2001

4.00% from 6 March 1999 to 5 February 2000

5.00% p.a. from 7 January 1999 to 5 March 1999

The rates listed below in relation to pre-self-assessment accounting periods ending before 1 July 1999 continue to apply in relation to other interest payments.

Instalment payments and other tax paid early. For accounting periods ending on or after 1 July 1999, a special rate of interest applies in the case of certain 'large' companies, which are required to make instalment payments in respect of their corporation tax liabilities (see 53.2 PAYMENT OF TAX). The special rate (which is generally from 0.25% to 1.25% higher than that referred to above) applies to any excess instalment payments until nine months after the end of the accounting period concerned. The lower rate referred to above applies to repayments made after that time.

The special rate also applies to corporation tax payments made early by a company, which is *not* a large company, early being before the day following the expiry of nine months after the end of an accounting period. Interest is payable from the date of payment until that day although not for periods before the first instalment date which would apply if the company were a large company.

The special rate changes more frequently than the normal rate, and changes are announced in Revenue Press Releases. Details are as follows.

5.25% p.a. from 21 May 2007

5.00% p.a. from 22 January 2007 to 20 May 2007

4.75% p.a. from 20 November 2006 to 21 January 2007

4.50% p.a. from 14 August 2006 to 19 November 2006

4.25% p.a. from 15 August 2005 to 13 August 2006

4.50% p.a. from 16 August 2004 to 14 August 2005

4.25% p.a. from 21 June 2004 to 15 August 2004

4.00% p.a. from 17 May 2004 to 20 June 2004

3.75% p.a. from 16 February 2004 to 16 May 2004

3.50% p.a. from 17 November to 15 February 2004

3.25% p.a. from 21 July 2003 to 16 November 2003

3.50% p.a. from 17 February 2003 to 20 July 2003

3.75% p.a. from 19 November 2001 to 16 February 2003

4.25% p.a. from 15 October 2001 to 18 November 2001

4.50% p.a. from 1 October 2001 to 14 October 2001

4.75% p.a. from 13 August 2001 to 30 September 2001

5.00% p.a. from 21 May 2001 to 12 August 2001

5.25% p.a. from 16 April 2001 to 20 May 2001

5.50% p.a. from 19 February 2001 to 15 April 2001

5.75% p.a. from 21 February 2000 to 18 February 2001

5.50% p.a. from 24 January 2000 to 20 February 2000

5.25% p.a. from 15 November 1999 to 23 January 2000

5.00% p.a. from 20 September 1999 to 14 November 1999

4.75% p.a. from 21 June 1999 to 19 September 1999

5.00% p.a. from 19 April 1999 to 20 June 1999

5.25% p.a. from 15 February 1999 to 18 April 1999

5.75% p.a. from 18 January 1999 to 14 February 1999

6.00% p.a. from 7 January 1999 to 17 January 1999

[*SI 1998 No 3175, reg 8; SI 1998 No 3176, regs 4, 7, 8*].

Pre-self-assessment rates. The following rates apply to corporation tax repayments for accounting periods ending before 1 July 1999 and to other interest payments. Changes are announced in Revenue Press Releases. Current and earlier rates are as follows.

2.75% p.a. from 6 September 2006

2.00% p.a. from 6 September 2005 to 6 September 2006

2.75% p.a. from 6 September 2004 to 5 September 2005

2.00% p.a. from 6 December 2003 to 5 September 2004

1.25% p.a. from 6 August 2003 to 5 December 2003

2.00% p.a. from 6 November 2001 to 5 August 2003

2.75% p.a. from 6 May 2001 to 5 November 2001

3.50% p.a. from 6 February 2000 to 5 May 2001

2.75% p.a. from 6 March 1999 to 5 February 2000

3.25% p.a. from 6 January 1999 to 5 March 1999

4.00% p.a. from 6 August 1997 to 5 January 1999

3.25% p.a. from 6 February 1996 to 5 August 1997

4.00% p.a. from 6 March 1995 to 5 February 1996

3.25% p.a. from 6 October 1994 to 5 March 1995

2.50% p.a. from 6 January 1994 to 5 October 1994

3.25% p.a. from 1 October 1993 to 5 January 1994

[*SI 1989 No 1297, regs 3BA, 3BB*].

Accounting periods ending on or before 30 September 1993. The following rates apply to corporation tax repayments for accounting periods ending on or before 30 September 1993 and to other interest payments. Changes are announced in Revenue Press Releases. Current and earlier rates are as follows.

5.75% p.a. from 6 September 2006

5.00% p.a. from 6 September 2005 to 5 September 2006

5.75% p.a. from 6 September 2004 to 5 September 2005

5.75% p.a. from 6 September 2004 to 5 September 2005

4.25% p.a. from 6 August to 5 December 2003

5.00% p.a. from 6 November 2001 to 5 August 2003

5.75% p.a. from 6 May 2001 to 5 November 2001

6.50% p.a. from 6 February 2000 to 5 May 2001

5.75% p.a. from 6 March 1999 to 5 February 2000

6.50% p.a. from 6 January 1999 to 5 March 1999

7.25% p.a. from 6 August 1997 to 5 January 1999

6.25% p.a. from 6 February 1996 to 5 August 1997

7.00% p.a. from 6 March 1995 to 5 February 1996

6.25% p.a. from 6 October 1994 to 5 March 1995

5.50% p.a. from 6 January 1994 to 5 October 1994

6.25% p.a. from 6 March 1993 to 5 January 1994

7.00% p.a. from 6 December 1992 to 5 March 1993

7.75% p.a. from 6 November 1992 to 5 December 1992

9.25% p.a. from 6 October 1991 to 5 November 1992

10.00% p.a. from 6 July 1991 to 5 October 1991

10.75% p.a. from 6 May 1991 to 5 July 1991

11.50% p.a. from 6 March 1991 to 5 May 1991

12.25% p.a. from 6 November 1990 to 5 March 1991

13.00% p.a. from 6 November 1989 to 5 November 1990

12.25% p.a. from 6 July 1989 to 5 November 1989

11.50% p.a. from 6 January 1989 to 5 July 1989

10.75% p.a. from 6 October 1988 to 5 January 1989

9.75% p.a. from 6 August 1988 to 5 October 1988

7.75% p.a. from 6 May 1988 to 5 August 1988

8.25% p.a. from 6 December 1987 to 5 May 1988

9.00% p.a. from 6 September 1987 to 5 December 1987

8.25% p.a. from 6 June 1987 to 5 September 1987

9.00% p.a. from 6 April 1987 to 5 June 1987

9.50% p.a. from 6 November 1986 to 5 April 1987

8.50% p.a. from 6 August 1986 to 5 November 1986

11.00% p.a. from 6 May 1985 to 5 August 1986

8.00% p.a. from 6 December 1982 to 5 May 1985

12.00% p.a. from 6 January 1980 to 5 December 1982

9.00% p.a. from 6 April 1974 to 5 January 1980

6.00% p.a. before 6 April 1974

Interest factor tables for use as ready reckoners in calculating interest on overpaid tax were published by HMRC and updated as rates changed up to 5 April 1999. (Revenue Press Release 11 March 1999).

[*SI 1989 No 1297* (*as amended*)].

40.6 HMRC ERROR

HMRC Code of Practice No 1 sets out the circumstances in which they will consider paying a repayment supplement on money owed to the taxpayer for any period during which there has been undue delay on the part of HMRC. See 33.6 HMRC: ADMINISTRATION.

40.7 UNAUTHORISED DEMANDS FOR TAX

There is a general right to interest under *Supreme Court Act 1981, s 35A* in a case where a taxpayer submits to such an unauthorised demand, provided that the payment was not made voluntarily to close a transaction. (*Woolwich Equitable Building Society v CIR HL 1992, 65 TC 265*).

40.8 VALUE ADDED TAX

Value added tax repayment supplements under *VATA 1994, s 79* are disregarded for corporation tax purposes. [*ICTA 1988, s 827*(*2*) ; *ITTOIA 2005, Sch 1 para 332*].

40.9 OVER-REPAYMENTS

See 53.10 PAYMENT OF TAX, 7.3 ASSESSMENTS as regards assessment of overpaid interest under these provisions.

41 Interest on Unpaid Tax

Cross-reference. See also 68.5 VALUE ADDED TAX.

The headings in this chapter are as follows.

41.1 ACCOUNTING PERIODS ENDING ON OR AFTER 1 JULY 1999

In relation to accounting periods ending on or after 1 July 1999 to which self-assessment applies, corporation tax carries interest from the due and payable date (nine months and one day after the end of the accounting period, see 53.1 PAYMENT OF TAX), even if it is a non-business day, until payment. In the case of certain 'large' companies which are required to make instalment payments in respect of their corporation tax liabilities (see 53.2 PAYMENT OF TAX), a special rate of interest (see 41.5 below) applies to unpaid instalments until nine months after the end of the accounting period.

See 41.7 below as regards ACT for accounting periods beginning before 6 April 1999. Where corporation tax assessed on a company may be assessed on other persons in certain circumstances, the due and payable date is that which refers to the company's liability. An assessment to recover excessive tax credit and interest thereon carries interest from the date of payment of the tax credit.

Details of interest rates are set out at 41.5 below.

Interest payable under these provisions is deductible in computing income, profits or losses under the loan relationship rules (see 46.46 LOAN RELATIONSHIPS). In the case of interest on tax assessable under *ICTA 1988, Sch 13* or *Sch 16*, this applies in relation to return periods in a self-assessment accounting period.

Interest is not calculated until a return is made or some other charge to tax arises. (HMRC Pamphlet 'A Guide to Corporation Tax Self Assessment' para 5.4.4). In the case of quarterly instalment payments, interest (and penalties) is only calculated after the company has filed its return (or HMRC have determined the liability in the absence of a return) *and* the normal due date has passed. (Revenue Tax Bulletin April 1999 p 647). See also Revenue Tax Bulletin April 2001 pp 833, 834.

Interest on tax subsequently discharged is adjusted or repaid so as to secure that the total is as it would have been had the tax discharged never been charged.

However, where losses of an accounting period are carried back under *ICTA 1988, s 393A(1)* (see 47.6 LOSSES) to an accounting period not falling wholly within the twelve months preceding the period in which the loss was incurred, and if the carry-back had not been claimed interest would have arisen on unpaid corporation tax for that earlier period, then such interest may only be relieved by virtue of the carried-back losses from nine months after the end of the accounting period in which the loss was incurred.

Similar restrictions also apply where a non-trading deficit on a company's loan relationships is carried back on a claim under *FA 1996, s 83(2)* (see 46.3 LOAN RELATIONSHIPS). Where relief is given by repayment, the amount repaid is, as far as possible, treated as if it were a discharge of the corporation tax charged for that period.

Similarly, where the discharge arises from the set-off (prior to its abolition) of surplus ACT of a later accounting period, calculation of any interest payable takes account of that set-off only from nine months after the end of the accounting period in which the surplus ACT arose. A claim for carry-back of any surplus ACT for the earlier period resulting from the loss relief claim is disregarded for this purpose, but the provisions described above in relation to interest for the period to which the surplus ACT is carried back are then amended so that interest continues to run until nine months after the end of the accounting period in which the loss was incurred (rather than that in which the surplus ACT arose).

Interest on tax charged on certain loans by close companies (see 16.9–16.13 CLOSE COMPANIES) is not, however, refunded when tax is repaid following repayment, release or writing off of the loan, and any relief from tax under *ICTA 1988, s 419* is, for the purposes of refund of interest under *TMA 1970, s 91*, set only against tax assessed under *section 419*. Interest ceases to run, however, from the date of the repayment, etc. and for this purpose any tax unpaid at that time is assumed, as far as possible, to be tax under *section 419* (see HMRC Pamphlet 'A Guide to Corporation Tax Self Assessment', para 5.4.2).

[*TMA 1970, ss 87A, 90, 91(1A)(1B)(2A), 109(3A)–(5); FA 1998, Sch 3 para 4, Sch 4 para 4; ITTOIA 2005, Sch 1 para 378; SI 1998 No 3175, reg 7*].

Simon's Direct Tax Service. See **A3.1323,A3.1324**.

Foot and mouth outbreak — relief from interest on unpaid tax. Where HMRC have agreed that payment of any tax be deferred because of the foot and mouth outbreak in 2001, no interest is chargeable on the amount so deferred for the period from 31 January 2001 (or, if HMRC so direct, any later date from which the deferral agreement has effect) to the date on which the deferral agreement ceases to have effect (subject to any agreed extension of the deferral period because of the continued outbreak). If the agreement is for payment by instalments, the deferral period in relation to each instalment ends on the date by which the instalment is to be paid. However, if an instalment is not paid by the agreed date (without HMRC agreement to a further deferral), the whole agreement ceases to have effect on that date. Provision is also made for a deferral agreement to be assumed to have been made, with the like consequences to an actual agreement, where it was not made but HMRC are satisfied that it could have been made. The terms of such a notional agreement are assumed to be such as HMRC are satisfied would have been agreed in the circumstances. This relief applies until ended by the Treasury order, such cessation not to affect its continued operation in relation to deferral agreements already in effect. A deferral agreement is effective whether made before or after the enactment of this provision or before or after the due date for the tax concerned. [*FA 2001, s 107*]. For the full range of measures relating to the foot and mouth outbreak, see Revenue Tax Bulletin Special Edition May 2001.

41.2 EXAMPLES

(*A*) *General*

S Ltd (which has no associated companies) prepares accounts to 31 December. On 31 May 2007, it makes a payment of £120,000 on account of its corporation tax liability for the year to 31 July 2006, the due date being 1 May 2007. On completing its corporation tax return, the company ascertains its total CT liability for that year to be £142,500 and makes a further payment of £22,500 on 16 July 2007. Following an enquiry by HMRC, various adjustments are made and the final CT liability is agreed at £145,500 on 25 November 2007. The company pays a further £3,000 on 5 January 2008.

It is assumed that interest rates remain unchanged after 6 September 2006.

Interest on overdue tax will be payable as follows.

		£
1.05.07 to 31.05.07	£120,000 × 7.5% × 30⁄366 =	737.70
1.05.07 to 16.07.07	£22,500 × 7.5% × 76⁄366 =	350.41
1.05.07 to 05.01.08	£3,000 × 7.5% × 248⁄366 =	153.07
Total interest charge		£1,241.18

(*B*) *Refund of interest charged*

On 1 November 2006, T Ltd pays CT of £100,000 for its year ended 31 December 2006. The due date for payment was 1 October 2007. The liability is finally agreed at £80,000 and a repayment of £20,000 is made to T Ltd on 1 March 2008.

Assuming that interest rates remain unchanged after 6 September 2006, the interest position will be as follows.

(i) T Ltd will be charged interest on £100,000 for the period 1.10.07 to 1.11.07 (31 days). The charge will be raised following payment of the £100,000 on 1.11.07.

£100,000 × 7.5% × 31⁄366 = £635.25

(ii) The company will be entitled to interest on overpaid tax of £20,000 for the period 1.11.07 (date of payment) to 1.3.08 (date of repayment) (120 days).

£20,000 × 4% × 120⁄366 = £265.21

(iii) T Ltd will also receive a refund of interest charged on £20,000 for the period 1.10.07 to 1.11.07.

£20,000 × 7.5% × 31⁄365 = £127.40

(*C*) *Instalment payments*

R Ltd has no associated companies and had taxable profits in excess of £1,500,000 for the year ended 31 March 2006. For the year ended 31 March 2007, R Ltd makes instalment payments of £110,000 (this being equivalent to a quarter of its estimated corporation tax liability of £440,000) on the first three due dates. The last instalment is not paid until 24 July 2007. On 3 September 2008, the tax liability is finally agreed at £524,800. R Ltd pays the balance due of £84,800 on 10 September 2008.

The rates of interest are assumed for the purposes of this example to remain unchanged after 21 May 2007.

The interest on tax unpaid is calculated as follows.

Instalments due on quarter dates £524,800 × ¼ = £131,200

	£
14 October 2006 to 19 November 2006	
131,200 – 110,000 = £21,200 @ 5.75% × 37/366	123.23
20 November 2006 to 13 January 2007	
131,200 – 110,000 = £21,200 @ 6% × 55/366 =	191.15
14 January 2007 to 13 April 2007	
262,400 – 220,000 = £42,400 @ 6% × 90/366 =	625.57
14 April 2007 to 20 May 2007	
393,600 – 330,000 = £63,600 @ 6.25% × 37/366 =	401.84
21 May 2007 to 13 July 2007	
393,600 – 330,000 = £63,600 @ 6.5% × 54/366 =	609.93
14 July 2007 to 23 July 2007	
524,800 – 330,000 = £194,800 @ 6.5% × 10/366=	345.96
24 July 2007 to 31 December 2007	
524,800 – 440,000 = £84,800 @ 6.5% × 161/366 =	2,424.68
1 January 2008 to 9 September 2008	
524,800 – 440,000 = £84,800 @ 7.5% × 252/366 =	4379.02
Interest on unpaid tax	£9,101.38

41.3 ACCOUNTING PERIODS ENDING BEFORE 1 JULY 1999

For liabilities in relation to accounting periods ending after 30 September 1993 and before 1 July 1999, the provisions described in 41.1 above in relation to self-assessment accounting periods similarly apply, but with a number of differences, namely:

- interest is paid without deduction of tax and is not deductible in computing income, profits or losses;
- the special rates for instalment payments for certain 'large' companies in respect of payments of corporation tax does not apply to pre-self-assessment accounting periods.

Interest rates are set out at 41.5 below.

[*TMA 1970, ss 87A, 90, 91(1A)(1B)(2A), 109(3A)–(5); FA 1998, Sch 3 para 4, Sch 4 para 4*].

41.4 ACCOUNTING PERIODS ENDING ON OR BEFORE 30 SEPTEMBER 1993

In relation to accounting periods ending on or before 30 September 1993, corporation tax carries interest from a 'reckonable date' (even if it is a non-business day) until payment. Interest of £30 or less arising in respect of any assessment may be remitted where the notice of assessment is issued before 19 April 1993. [*TMA 1970, s 86*]. See also 41.7 below as regards ACT.

Details of interest rates are set out at 41.5 below.

Interest is payable gross and is not deductible from profits or income. [*TMA 1970, s 90*].

Interest on tax subsequently discharged is adjusted or repaid so as to secure that the total is as it would have been had the tax discharged never been charged, except that where a trading loss of an accounting period ending after 31 March 1991 is carried back and set against profits of an accounting period starting more than twelve months before the start of the period in which the loss arose (see 47.6 LOSSES), interest which would otherwise have arisen in respect of corporation tax unpaid for the earlier period will continue to run until the due and payable date for corporation tax for the accounting period in which the loss arose. Tax repaid is as far as possible treated as if it were a discharge of tax charged for the period, but not of tax charged by assessments made after the repayment and not so as partially to relieve tax charged by more than one assessment. [*TMA 1970, s 91*].

Interest on tax charged on certain loans by close companies (see 16.9–16.13 CLOSE COMPANIES) is not refunded when tax is repaid following repayment of the loan, and any relief from tax under *ICTA 1988, s 419* is, for the purposes of refund of interest under *TMA 1970, s 91*, set only against tax assessed under *section 419*. [*TMA 1970, s 109(4)(5)*].

The '*reckonable date*' is normally the due and payable date. Where there is an appeal and postponement application, so that special rules apply for determining the due and payable date of non-postponed, postponed and additional tax (see 53.4 PAYMENT OF TAX), it is the due and payable date *unless* that date is later than the date given by the Table in *TMA 1970, s 86*. In that case, the reckonable date is the later of the date given by the Table and the date on which tax under the assessment would have been due and payable had there been no appeal against it.

In transitional cases, where a notice requiring a return of profits for an accounting period ended before 1 October 1993 is served after 31 December 1993, and the tax assessed for that accounting period does not become due and payable until after the date falling nine months after the end of the period, the reckonable date will be that date. HMRC are given power to mitigate any resulting interest, and have stated that interest will not be charged if an assessment is made bringing sufficient tax into charge by the normal due date (in line with the normal practice on charging interest under *TMA 1970, s 88* for delay in making a return which applied before the introduction of Pay and File, see below). Where such an assessment is not made, the interest charge will be reduced to ensure, as far as possible, that it does not exceed what it would have been under the pre-Pay and File provisions (see above). Also, where the accounting period in question runs to the normal company accounting date (or, if it is the first accounting period, to a date notified to the inspector within eight months of its ending), and either the company has notified its chargeability or a notice has been issued requiring a return and the return is made within the Pay and File time limit, interest will be charged only from the later of 60 days after issue of the notice and the normal due date. (Revenue Tax Bulletin August 1993 p 84).

The Table date referred to above is generally six months after the normal due and payable date in relation to an accounting period (i.e. in most cases 15 months after the end of the accounting period). In the case of tax charged on certain loans by close companies (see 16.9–16.13 CLOSE COMPANIES), however, it is the last day of the three months after the end of the financial year in which the loan was made. [*TMA 1970, ss 86, 109(2)*].

Tax lost through fault of taxpayer. Where an assessment for an accounting period ending on or before 30 September 1993 is raised to make good tax lost due to the taxpayer's fault, the tax is chargeable with interest under *TMA 1970, ss 88, 88A* (as amended) and not under *TMA 1970, s 86*, from the date on which the tax ought originally to have been paid. The rates of interest are as 41.1 above, except that it was chargeable at 3% prior to 19 April 1967, and at 6% from 19 April 1967 to 18 April 1969. This provision does not, however, apply in relation to ACT or income tax deducted from payments made by the company. [*TMA 1970, s 88(2)*]. For the extent to which regard should be had to events after the making of an assessment in determining whether *section 88* applies, see *Billingham v Myers CA 1996, 68 TC 512*. See also Tolley's Income Tax under Fraudulent or Negligent Conduct.

In the case of tax charged on certain loans by close companies (see 16.9–16.13 CLOSE COMPANIES), the date on which the tax ought to have been paid is, for the purposes of *section 88*, taken as the first day of the financial year following that in which the loan was made. [*TMA 1970, s 109(3)*].

Interest will not generally be charged as above where the late assessment results from delay in submission of a return unless that delay is 'substantial', i.e. if the relevant return has not been made by the later of 30 days after the date of issue of the return and 31 October following the end of the tax year in which the income or chargeable gain arose. It will similarly not be charged where it is not possible to lodge the return but, within that time limit, information sufficient for the raising of an adequate estimated assessment is provided. (HMRC Statement of Practice, SP 6/89). This Statement of Practice refers mainly to individual taxpayers, but, by analogy, a company which has not submitted accounts and computations within seven months after the end of an accounting period should, if no estimated assessment has been received (or if an inadequate estimated assessment has not been appealed against), provide the inspector with the necessary information to raise an adequate estimated assessment, in order to avoid an interest charge under *TMA 1970, s 88*. The 'reasonable excuse' provisions of *TMA 1970, s 118(2)* (see 54.10 PENALTIES) do not apply as regards *section 88* interest in relation to failures occurring after 26 July 1989.

Simon's Direct Tax Service. See A3.1320 *et seq.*

Example

A CT assessment was issued to R Ltd for its accounting year ended 31 August 1993. The relevant facts are as follows.

Corporation tax charged	£60,000	
Assessment issued		25.4.94
Company appealed and claimed to postpone £20,000 of the tax charged		20.5.94
Commissioners determined that only £15,000 of the tax charged could be postponed		27.6.94
Appeal determined, total tax payable £73,000		15.11.94
Amended assessment raised by Inspector		21.11.94
Normal due date		1.6.94
Table date		1.12.94
Tax payments made	£40,000	10.8.94
	£33,000	19.12.94

Interest on unpaid tax is calculated over the following periods.

£40,000	27.7.94 to 10.8.94
£5,000	27.7.94 to 19.12.94
£15,000	1.12.94 to 19.12.94
£13,000	1.12.94 to 19.12.94

Note

It is assumed that the notice requiring a return of profits was served before 1 January 1994.

41.5 **INTEREST RATES**

The rate of interest is adjusted automatically by reference to the rounded-down average of base lending rates of certain clearing banks, the formula being such average base rate plus

2.5%, the subtotal being reduced by the small companies rate of corporation tax (see 63 SMALL COMPANIES—REDUCED RATES) and rounded-down.

It is understood that a denominator of 366 is used in calculations of such interest regardless of whether or not a leap year is involved.

Self-assessment. *Overdue corporation tax payments.* For underpayments of corporation tax for accounting periods ending on or after 1 July 1999, the following rate of interest applies, changes being announced in Revenue Press Releases.

7.50% p.a. from 6 September 2006

6.50% p.a. from 6 September 2005 to 5 September 2006

7.50% p.a. from 6 September 2004 to 5 September 2005

6.50% p.a. from 6 December 2003 to 5 September 2004

5.50% p.a. from 6 August 2003 to 5 December 2003

6.50% p.a. from 6 November 2001 to 5 August 2003

7.50% p.a. from 6 May 2001 to 5 November 2001

8.50% p.a. from 6 February 2000 to 5 May 2001

7.50% p.a. from 6 March 1999 to 5 February 2000

8.50% p.a. from 7 January 1999 to 5 March 1999

Overdue instalment payments. For accounting periods ending on or after 1 July 1999, a special rate of interest applies in the case of certain 'large' companies, which are required to make instalment payments in respect of their corporation tax liabilities (see 53.2 PAYMENT OF TAX). The special rate of interest (which is generally from 1 to 1.75% lower than the normal interest rates above from 20 April 2000 onwards) applies to any unpaid instalments until nine months after the end of the accounting period (whereafter the normal interest rate (above) applies). The special rate changes more frequently than the normal rate, and changes are announced in Revenue Press Releases. Details are as follows.

6.50% p.a. from 21 May 2007

6.25% p.a. from 22 January 2007 to 20 May 2007

6.00% p.a. from 20 November 2006 to 21 January 2007

5.75% p.a. from 14 August 2006 to 19 November 2006

5.50% p.a. from 15 August 2005 to 13 August 2006

5.75% p.a. from 16 August 2004 to 14 August 2005

5.50% p.a. from 21 June 2004 to 15 August 2004

5.25% p.a. from 17 May 2004 to 20 June 2004

5.00% p.a. from 16 February 2004 to 16 May 2004

4.75% p.a. from 17 November to 15 February 2004

4.50% p.a. from 21 July 2003 to 16 November 2003

4.75% p.a. from 17 February 2003 to 20 July 2003

5.00% p.a. from 19 November 2001 to 16 February 2003

5.50% p.a. from 15 October 2001 to 18 November 2001

5.75% p.a. from 1 October 2001 to 14 October 2001

6.00% p.a. from 13 August 2001 to 30 September 2001

6.25% p.a. from 21 May 2001 to 12 August 2001

6.50% p.a. from 16 April 2001 to 20 May 2001

6.75% p.a. from 19 February 2001 to 15 April 2001

7.00% p.a. from 20 April 2000 to 18 February 2001

8.00% p.a. from 21 February 2000 to 19 April 2000

7.75% p.a. from 24 January 2000 to 20 February 2000

7.50% p.a. from 15 November 1999 to 23 January 2000

7.25% p.a. from 20 September 1999 to 14 November 1999

7.00% p.a. from 21 June 1999 to 19 September 1999

7.25% p.a. from 19 April 1999 to 20 June 1999

7.50% p.a. from 15 February 1999 to 18 April 1999

8.00% p.a. from 18 January 1999 to 14 February 1999

8.25% p.a. from 7 January 1999 to 17 January 1999

[*SI 1989 No 1297, regs 3ZA, 3ZB; SI 1998 No 3175, reg 7; SI 1998 No 3176, regs 4–6; SI 2000 No 893*].

Pre-self-assessment rates. The following rates apply to late payments of corporation tax and other interest payments for accounting periods ending before 1 July 1999. Changes are announced in Revenue Press Releases. Current and earlier rates are as follows.

6.00% p.a. from 6 September 2006

5.25% p.a. from 6 September 2005 to 5 September 2006

6.00% p.a. from 6 September 2004 to 5 September 2005

5.25%* p.a. from 6 December 2003 to 5 September 2004

4.25% p.a. from 6 August 2003 to 5 December 2003

5.00% p.a. from 6 November 2001 to 5 August 2003

6.00% p.a. from 6 May 2001 to 5 November 2001

6.75% p.a. from 6 February 2000 to 5 May 2001

5.75% p.a. from 6 March 1999 to 5 February 2000

6.50% p.a. from 6 January 1999 to 5 March 1999

7.50% p.a. from 6 August 1997 to 5 January 1999

6.25% p.a. from 6 February 1996 to 5 August 1997

7.00% p.a. from 6 March 1995 to 5 February 1996

6.25% p.a. from 6 October 1994 to 5 March 1995

5.50% p.a. from 6 January 1994 to 5 October 1994

6.25% p.a. from 1 October 1993 to 5 January 1994

* Note that the rate applying from 6 December 2003 to 5 September 2004 was originally stated as 5% but was restated as 5.25% in a correction announced by HMRC on 6 September 2005. HMRC have stated that no attempt will be made to recover any further interest due where interest was charged at the incorrect rate unless, exceptionally, the liability is reviewed. (HMRC News Release 27/05).

[*FA 1989, ss 178, 179; FA 1999, s 92(5); SI 1989 No 1297* (*as amended*)].

Accounting periods ending on or before 30 September 1993. The rate of interest is adjusted automatically by reference to the average of base lending rates of certain clearing banks, the formula being such average base rate plus 2.5%, the subtotal being reduced by the basic rate of income tax. [*FA 1989, ss 178, 179; SI 1989 No 1297*].

Changes are announced in Revenue Press Releases. Current and earlier rates are as follows.

5.75% p.a. from 6 September 2006

5.00% p.a. from 6 September 2005 to 5 September 2006

5.75% p.a. from 6 September 2004 to 5 September 2005

5.00% p.a. from 6 December 2003 to 5 September 2004

4.25% p.a. from 6 August 2003 to 5 December 2003

5.00% p.a. from 6 November 2001 to 5 August 2003

5.75% p.a. from 6 May 2001 to 5 November 2001

6.50% p.a. from 6 March 2001 to 5 May 2001

(see below as regards period 31 January 1997 to 5 March 2001)

6.25% p.a. from 6 February 1996 to 30 January 1997

7.00% p.a. from 6 March 1995 to 5 February 1996

6.25% p.a. from 6 October 1994 to 5 March 1995

5.50% p.a. from 6 January 1994 to 5 October 1994

6.25% p.a. from 6 March 1993 to 5 January 1994

7.00% p.a. from 6 December 1992 to 5 March 1993

7.75% p.a. from 6 November 1992 to 5 December 1992

9.25% p.a. from 6 October 1991 to 5 November 1992

10.00% p.a. from 6 July 1991 to 5 October 1991

10.75% p.a. from 6 May 1991 to 5 July 1991

11.50% p.a. from 6 March 1991 to 5 May 1991

12.25% p.a. from 6 November 1990 to 5 March 1991

13.00% p.a. from 6 November 1989 to 5 November 1990

12.25% p.a. from 6 July 1989 to 5 November 1989

11.50% p.a. from 6 January 1989 to 5 July 1989

10.75% p.a. from 6 October 1988 to 5 January 1989

9.75% p.a. from 6 August 1988 to 5 October 1988

7.75% p.a. from 6 May 1988 to 5 August 1988

8.25% p.a. from 6 December 1987 to 5 May 1988

9.00% p.a. from 6 September 1987 to 5 December 1987

8.25% p.a. from 6 June 1987 to 5 September 1987

9.00% p.a. from 6 April 1987 to 5 June 1987

9.50% p.a. from 6 November 1986 to 5 April 1987

8.50% p.a. from 6 August 1986 to 5 November 1986

11.00% p.a. from 1 May 1985 to 5 August 1986

8.00% p.a. from 1 December 1982 to 30 April 1985

12.00% p.a. from 1 January 1980 to 30 November 1982

9.00% p.a. from 1 July 1974 to 31 December 1979

6.00% p.a. from 19 April 1969 to 30 June 1974

Following the amendment by *SI 1996 No 3187* of the basis on which rates of interest are determined with effect from 31 January 1997, no rate was (due to an inadvertent omission) specified for the purposes of *TMA 1970, s 86* as it applied for the purposes of accounting periods ending on or before 30 September 1993, until the position was corrected by *SI 2001 No 204* with effect from 6 March 2001. No interest thus accrued from 31 January 1997 to 5 March 2001 on unpaid corporation tax relating to such accounting periods. It would appear that interest was incorrectly collected in relation to that period of accrual in some 7,000 cases, and HMRC has taken steps to identify all such cases. As soon as practicable, they repaid interest so wrongly charged (with the equivalent of repayment supplement on the amount overcharged), and took steps to ensure that interest was not incorrectly charged on any amounts currently stood over which were subsequently released for collection. (Revenue Tax Bulletin December 2000 p 812).

Interest factor tables for use as ready reckoners in calculating interest on overdue tax were published by HMRC and updated as rates changed up to 5 April 1999. (Revenue Press Release 11 March 1999).

41.6 DATE OF PAYMENT OF TAX

Effective dates of payment. HMRC take the date of payment in respect of each payment method to be as follows.

(1) *Cheques, cash, and postal orders* handed in at an HMRC office or received by post — the day of receipt by HMRC *unless* received by post following a day on which the office was closed for whatever reason, in which case it is the day on which the office was first closed. Under *FA 2007, s 95*, HMRC have the power to provide that payments made by cheque are 'made' for tax purposes at the date the cheque is cleared.

(2) *Electronic funds transfer* — payment by BACS (transfer over two days) or CHAPS (same day transfer) — one day prior to receipt by HMRC.

(3) *Bank giro or Girobank* — the date on which payment was made at the bank or post office.

(Revenue Special 'Working Together' Tax Bulletin July 2000 p 3).

For the purposes of *TMA 1970* and *ICTA 1988, ss 824, 825* and *826* (see 40 INTEREST ON OVERPAID TAX), where any payment to an officer of HMRC or HMRC itself is received by cheque and the cheque is paid on its first presentation to the bank on which it is drawn, the payment is treated as made on the date of receipt of the cheque by the officer or HMRC. [*TMA 1970, s 70A*].

41.7 ACT AND INCOME TAX DEDUCTED FROM PAYMENTS

As regards (i) (for accounting periods beginning before 6 April 1999) ACT and (ii) income tax payable by companies that they have deducted from yearly interest and other payments, interest arises if payment is made after the due date. The rates of interest for payments due on or after 14 October 1999 (i.e. under self-assessment) are as under 41.1(ii) above. For payments due before that date they are as under 41.4 above (but with rates from 31 January 1997 to 5 August 1997 6.25%, from 6 August 1997 to 5 January 1999 7.25%, from

6 January 1999 to 5 March 1999 6.50%, from 6 March 1999 to 5 February 2000 5.75% and from 6 February 2000 to 5 March 2001 6.50%). [*TMA 1970, s 87; FA 1989, s 178; FA 1998, Sch 3 para 3; SI 1989 No 1297, regs 3, 3AA, 3AC; SI 1999 No 2637, reg 4*].

For *UK-resident companies*, the due dates are 14 days after the expiry of the return periods (ending 31 March, 30 June, 30 September, 31 December and with the ending of an accounting period) in which the relevant dividends or other payments were made and interest will run from these dates even if they are non-business days. [*ICTA 1988, Schs 13, 16; FA 1998, Sch 3 para 41*]. Where ACT is assessed on a qualifying distribution which is not a payment, or on a payment of an uncertain nature, the due date is 14 days after the issue of the notice of assessment. [*ICTA 1988, Sch 13 para 10(2); FA 1998, Sch 3 para 41*].

If a payment is made by a company on a date not falling within an accounting period of the company, tax is due 14 days after the payment. [*ICTA 1988, Sch 13 para 9, Sch 16 para 9; FA 1998, Sch 3 para 41*].

Where ACT or income tax paid is repaid or discharged following the receipt in a later return period of FII or income suffering tax by deduction, interest will nevertheless be chargeable where the original payment was late. It will, however, cease to run 14 days after the end of the later return period, or, if the return for that period was made within those 14 days, from the date of the return. [*TMA 1970, s 87(2)(3); FA 1998, Sch 3 para 3*].

See 37.5 INCOME TAX IN RELATION TO A COMPANY.

For *non-UK resident companies* (and non-corporates), assessment is directly under ITA 2007, ss 946, 962–964 (formerly *ICTA 1988, s 350*) (see 37.5 INCOME TAX IN RELATION TO A COMPANY). Interest under *TMA 1970, s 86* runs from 31 January following the end of the year of assessment. See Revenue Tax Bulletin February 2001 p 827 for the application of these provisions (and for the omission in practice of any interest charge on assessments issued before 1 February 2001 or for 1998/99 or earlier years).

In the case of *Mellham Ltd v Burton (Collector of Taxes) HL [2006] STC 908*, interest was held not to be payable on overdue ACT to the extent that, if paid, it would have been repaid or set off against mainstream corporation tax.

Simon's Direct Tax Service. See **A3.1326**.

41.8 EXCHANGE RESTRICTIONS

Where corporation tax is payable in respect of income or chargeable gains arising abroad which cannot be remitted to the UK due to action of the foreign government, HMRC may allow the tax to remain uncollected. If so, interest ceases to run from the date on which HMRC were in possession of the information necessary to make their decision. No interest is payable if that date is within three months of the due and payable date.

Where a demand for payment is subsequently made by the Collector, interest begins to run again unless the tax is paid within three months. [*TMA 1970, s 92*]. See 60.3 RESIDENCE.

41.9 HMRC ERROR

HMRC Code of Practice No 1 sets out the circumstances in which they will consider waiving a charge to interest on unpaid tax where there has been undue delay on the part of HMRC. See 33.6 HMRC: ADMINISTRATION.

42 Investment Companies and Investment Business

Cross-references. See 16.18 CLOSE COMPANIES as regards close investment-holding companies.

Simon's Direct Tax Service D4.401 *et seq.*

42.1 INTRODUCTION

For accounting periods **beginning on or after 1 April 2004**, subject to provisions for accounting periods straddling that date (see 42.2 below), relief for management expenses is extended to companies with investment business whether or not they qualify as investment companies.

The Treasury has the power to make consequential amendments, by order, to any legislation as a result of the changes (set out below), and different provisions can be made in different cases whether incidental, consequential, supplemental, transitional or savings provisions. Where such an order is made on or before 31 December 2004, it may have effect for accounting periods ending before the date on which the order is made but not before 1 April 2004. [*FA 2004, s 46*].

HMRC have issued guidance in their Company Taxation Manual at CTM 08210–CTM 08260 on the capital expenditure and unallowable purposes rules (see 42.2 below).

Companies with investment business. A company with investment business is defined as 'any company whose business consists wholly or partly in the making of investments'. [*ICTA 1988, s 130; FA 2004, s 38(2)–(5)*]. (It will include, for example, a trading company with shares in subsidiary companies.) The term '*making of investments*' carries the same meaning in this context as in the context of the definition below of an investment company.

Investment companies. An investment company is defined as 'any company whose business consists wholly or mainly in the making of investments and the principal part of whose income is derived therefrom'. [*ICTA 1988, s 130*]. It accordingly will include unit trusts and open-ended investment companies (43 INVESTMENT FUNDS) and investment trusts (44.1 INVESTMENT TRUSTS). '*The making of investments*' does not require turning them over (*Tyre Investment Trust Ltd KB 1924, 12 TC 646*). For treatment of income from land as investment income, see *Webb v Conelee Properties Ltd Ch D 1982, 56 TC 149.*

It appears that a company's status as an 'investment company' is to be based on its activities over a representative period, see *FPH Finance Trust Ltd v CIR HL 1944, 26 TC 1311.*

A company formed to run a family estate was held not to be an investment company (under similar Irish legislation) in *Casey v Monteagle Estate Co HC(I) 1960, [1962] IR 106*. A similar decision was reached by the Special Commissioner in *Tintern Close Residents Society Ltd v Winter (Sp C 7), [1995] SSCD 57*, in which a company formed to 'acquire, hold, manage and deal with' common land and buildings on a residential estate was held not to be an investment company. See Revenue Tax Bulletin October 1995 pp 253, 254 for an appreciation of this decision and for HMRC's view of the scope of *section 130*, for which see also HMRC Company Taxation Manual, CTM 08050. In *Cook v Medway Housing Society Ltd Ch D 1996, 69 TC 319*, however, the business of a society formed to acquire and manage local authority housing stock was held to consist in the making of investments.

For accounting periods beginning before 1 April 2004, savings banks (other than trustee savings banks or successor companies) are considered to be investment companies. [*ICTA 1988, s 130; FA 2004, ss 38, 42*].

42.2 MANAGEMENT EXPENSES

Accounting periods beginning on or after 1 April 2004. For accounting periods beginning on or after 1 April 2004, subject to provisions for periods straddling that date (see below), any management expenses of a company's investment business are deductible in computing its total profits for corporation tax purposes for an accounting period where 'referable to that accounting period (see below). No such deduction is allowed for expenses deductible in computing profits under any other provision. Management expenses in this case are allowed to the extent that they relate to the management of the company's investment business, which consists of the making of investments, provided the company does not hold such investments for an unallowable purpose (see below) during the accounting period. Any apportionment of expenses necessary to meet the requirements of these provisions is to be made on a just and reasonable basis. However, for accounting periods beginning on or after 20 June 2007, no deduction is given for any management expenses if:

(*a*) any part of them is incurred directly or indirectly with the main purpose or one of the main purposes of obtaining a tax advantage; or

(*b*) they are paid as part of arrangements having as their main purpose or one of their main purposes of obtaining a tax advantage.

The tax advantage may be a deduction or an increased deduction for management expenses or any other tax advantage (within *ICTA 1988, s 840ZA*). This exclusion does not apply if tax relief is denied under the manufactured payments provisions. The term 'management expenses' includes all expenditure treated as a deduction under *ICTA 1988, s 75*. Where an accounting period straddles 20 June 2007, the accounting period is treated as split into two accounting periods and the deduction for management expenses is calculated by reference to the relative rules in force.

[*ICTA 1988, s 75(1)(2((2A)–(2C)(4)(10); FA 2004, ss 38(1), 42; FA 2007, s 28(2),(5),(6)*]. (Details of the changes are summarised in the Revenue Tax Bulletin August 2004, p 1145.)

Unallowable purpose. An '*unallowable purpose*' in this case is a purpose that is not a business or other commercial purpose of the company or one in respect of which the company is not within the charge to corporation tax. [*ICTA 1988, s 75(5); FA 2004, s 38(1)*]. See HMRC Company Taxation Manual CTM 08210–CTM 08230 for their guidance on management expenses and the unallowable purposes rules. The guidance indicates that the test would not be failed solely by virtue that the company's investments generate dividends exempt from tax under *ICTA 1988, s 208*, or capital gains covered by the substantial shareholdings exemption or exempt under *TCGA 1992, s 100(1)* (in the case of authorised unit trusts etc.), or that the investment is in a company which itself is not within the charge to corporation tax (for example, a non-UK resident subsidiary). If the investments are held directly or indirectly relating to arrangements the main purpose or one of the main purposes of which is to obtain a greater deduction for management expenses or any other tax advantage, they will be treated as not held for business or other commercial purpose. This applies for accounting periods commencing on or after 20 June 2007 but where an accounting period straddles 20 June 2007, the accounting period is treated as split into two accounting periods for the purposes of calculating any relief. [*ICTA 1988 s 75(5A)(11); FA 2007, s 28(3)–(6)*].

Reduction for income derived from non-taxable sources. Management expenses must be reduced by any income derived from non-taxable sources (other than FRANKED INVESTMENT INCOME (29)) held in the course of a company's investment business or, in the case of a non-UK resident company, non-taxable sources held in the course of its investment business carried on through a UK permanent establishment which is property or rights used by, or held by or for that establishment (see 60.5 RESIDENCE). [*ICTA 1988, s 75(6); FA 2004, s 38(1)*].

Capital expenditure. Expenses of a capital nature are not deductible as management expenses except to the extent they fall to be so treated as surplus capital allowances (see 42.5 below) or by virtue of any other provision. [*ICTA 1988, s 75(3); FA 2004, s 38(1)*]. For accounting periods beginning before 1 April 2004, capital expenditure was considered not to be excluded by the legislation then in force (see 42.4 below in respect of the *Camas* case). See HMRC Company Taxation Manual, CTM 08240–CTM 08260.

Carry forward of excess management expenses etc. Any management expenses unrelieved in an accounting period may be carried forward and treated as management expenses of the next succeeding accounting period and may continue to be so carried forward until relieved. Any charges on income paid in the accounting period, to the extent they are paid for the purpose of the company's investment business, or unused capital allowances relating to the company's investment business (see 42.5 below), may similarly be carried forward as management expenses. [*ICTA 1988, s 75(8), (9); FA 2004, s 38(1)*]. See also 42.5 below with regard to losses of a Schedule A business.

Accounting period to which management expenses are referable. Management expenses are referable to the accounting period that coincides with the period of account in which they are debited to the company accounts (be it charged in the profit or loss account or income statement, the statement of recognised gains or losses or statement of changes in equity, or other statement) in accordance with generally accepted accounting practice. Where the company's period of account does not coincide with an accounting period for corporation tax purposes (for example where the company's period of account exceeds twelve months), the expenses are to be apportioned between any accounting periods falling within the period of account on a time basis unless that would give an unjust or unreasonable result in which case a just and reasonable method is to be used.

Special provisions apply in the case where management expenses are not debited to a company's accounts in accordance with generally accepted accounting practice. In that case, they are referable to the accounting period to which they would have been referable had they been debited in accordance with the above provisions. Where management expenses are not otherwise referable to an accounting period by virtue of the above provisions, they are referable to the accounting period to which they would have been referable on the assumption that there is a period of account coinciding with that accounting period (where it does not otherwise coincide), and so much of the expenses are debited for any such deemed period of account as would fall to be debited in accordance with generally accepted accounting practice. These provisions do not take precedence over any other provision of the Corporation Taxes Acts which provides for amounts to be treated as management expenses referable to an accounting period.

[*ICTA 1988, s 75A; FA 2004, s 39; FA 2005, s 80, Sch 4 para 22*].

Credits reversing management expense deductions. Where a credit is brought into account by a company in a period of account ending on or after 1 April 2004 (the '*reversal period*') that reverses some or all of a debit made in respect of management expenses in an earlier period of account then, provided the period of account coincides with an accounting period beginning on or after 1 April 2004, the amount by which the earlier debit is reversed is to be:

(*a*) set against any management expenses (excluding and brought forward expenses) deductible for that accounting period; and

(*b*) any amount remaining after reducing those management expenses to nil is to be charged to tax under Schedule D Case VI for that period.

A credit for these purposes reverses a debit irrespective of whether it has been paid or unpaid, or paid and subsequently repaid. In considering the amount of the debit in the earlier accounting period, any unrelieved, excess management expenses carried forward from an earlier accounting period are to be disregarded. No account is to be taken of any amount of the credit that is taxable under other provisions whether in the relevant accounting period or any earlier accounting period. The '*relevant accounting period*' in this case is the latest accounting period of the company falling wholly or partly in the reversal period.

Where the reversal period does not coincide with an accounting period, the amount of the reversal is to be apportioned between any accounting periods falling within the reversal period and only that amount apportioned to an accounting period beginning on or after 1 April 2004 is to be dealt with for that period in accordance with (*a*) and (*b*) above. The apportionment is to be made on a time basis unless that would give an unjust or unreasonable result in which case a just and reasonable method is to be used. Where an accounting period does not coincide with, or fall within, any period of account of the company, a period of account is to be deemed to coincide with that accounting period.

The amounts to be taken into account under these provisions are the amounts which would have been credits if determined in accordance with generally accepted accounting practice.

[*ICTA 1988, s 75B; FA 2004, s 45*].

Accounting period straddling 1 April 2004. Where an accounting period begins before and ends on or after 1 April 2004, that accounting period is deemed to consist of two separate accounting periods, the first beginning with the straddling period and ending on 31 March 2004 and the second beginning on 1 April 2004 and ending with the straddling period. However, in the case of an investment company, this does not have effect in determining the amounts deductible in the straddling period of management expenses carried forward from accounting periods beginning before 1 April 2004, or sums treated as management expenses under any other provision. [*FA 2004, s 43*(*5*),(*6*)].

Transitional provisions: management expenses carried forward. Where management expenses have been disbursed in an accounting period beginning before 1 April 2004 and have been carried forward so that they would have been treated under the old rules (*ICTA 1988, s 75*(*3*) as originally enacted) as disbursed in the first accounting period beginning on or after 1 April 2004, they are to be treated as if they were management expenses deductible for that period under the new rules (*ICTA 1988, s 75*(*9*) introduced by *FA 2004, s 38*(*1*)). To the extent that the expenses are deductible by an investment company in an accounting period beginning before 1 April 2004 (excluding any unrelieved excess carried forward to a later accounting period), they may not be deducted in an accounting period beginning on or after 1 April 2004. Where management expenses incurred by an investment company in an accounting period beginning before 1 April 2004:

(*a*) were not deductible in that period (because they had not been disbursed) but

(*b*) would have been deductible had the new rules been in force for that accounting period (because they were properly charged to the company's accounts in that accounting period),

they are treated as deductible in the first accounting period beginning on or after 1 April 2004. [*FA 2004, s 43*(*1*)–(*4*)].

42.3 **Accounting periods beginning before 1 April 2004.** For accounting periods beginning before 1 April 2004, subject to provisions for accounting periods straddling that date (see 42.2 above), management expenses of a UK resident investment company are deductible in computing total profits for corporation tax purposes. They include commissions, but exclude expenses otherwise deductible in computing profits or in relation to which a debit falls to be brought into account in respect of a loan relationship (see 46.2 LOAN RELATIONSHIPS). But such expenses must be reduced by any income derived from sources not charged to tax such as share register amendment fees received. [*ICTA 1988, s 75*(*1*)(*1A*)(*2*); *F*(*No 2*)*A 1997, Sch 6 para 2; FA 1998, Sch 3 para 9; FA 2004, ss 38, 42, Sch 42 Pt 2*(*3*)].

Any unrelieved excess in an accounting period may be carried forward and treated as management expenses of the next succeeding accounting period (together with unused capital allowances plus charges on income paid in the accounting period wholly and exclusively for the purposes of the company's business), and may continue to be so carried forward until relieved. [*ICTA 1988, s 75*(*3*)–(*5*) (as originally enacted)]. See also 42.5 below with regard to losses of a Schedule A business.

42.4 **Amounts treated as management expenses.** *Levies and awards of costs* under the *Financial Services and Markets Act 2000* are treated as management expenses, and *repayments* under that *Act* are chargeable under Schedule D, Case VI. [*ICTA 1988, s 76B; Financial Services and Markets Act 2000, s 411(2); SI 2001 No 3629, Article 16(7)(8); FA 2004, Sch 6 para 1*].

Certain provisions are specifically extended to include management expenses. Thus secondary Class 1, Class 1A, and from 6 April 1999 Class 1B national insurance contributions [*ICTA 1988, s 617(3)(4)*], statutory redundancy payments [*ICTA 1988, s 579(3)*], payments in relation to certain employee trusts [*ICTA 1988, s 85A; FA 1989, s 67*] (see 66.45 TRADING INCOME), costs of establishing certain profit sharing and share option schemes [*ICTA 1988, s 84A*], payments to certain approved pension schemes [*ICTA 1988, s 592(4); FA 1993, s 112*] (but not to non-approved schemes [*FA 1989, s 76*]), additional payments to redundant employees (see 66.43 TRADING INCOME) [*ICTA 1988, s 90*], contributions to local enterprise agencies and companies, urban regeneration companies and training and enterprise councils [*ICTA 1988, ss 79–79B; FA 2003, s 180*] and certain training costs [*ICTA 1988, s 588*] are allowable management expenses. Conversely, *ICTA 1988, s 577* (and *CAA 2001, s 269*) apply to restrict allowance of entertainment expenditure, and *ICTA 1988, s 577A* to prohibit a deduction for certain illegal payments. The provisions of *ICTA 1988, s 781* (taxation as income of certain capital sums received by persons to whom tax relief is allowable in respect of payments under a lease of an asset other than land) similarly apply to investment businesses (and for accounting periods beginning before 1 April 2004, investment companies). (Consequential amendments were made to the above provisions by *SI 2004 No 2310* following the extension of the relief for management expenses to companies with investment business.)

Costs incurred on an acquisition by merger or takeover of another company were held to be allowable as management expenses in *Camas plc v Atkinson CA, [2004] STC 860* on the grounds that the activities on which the expenditure was incurred were part of the process of managerial decision-making and it was further held that capital expenditure was not excluded by the legislation in force at the time. (Note that the new *ICTA 1988, s 75(3)* introduced by *FA 2004, s 38(1)* specifically excludes expenditure of a capital nature from deduction as management expenses from 1 April 2004 (see 42.2 above). Management expenses do not include an exchange loss on the payment of interest (*Bennet v Underground Electric Railways Co of London Ltd KB 1923, 8 TC 475*); or brokerage and stamp duty on investment changes (*Capital and National Trust Ltd v Golder CA 1949, 31 TC 265*); or payments to the guarantor of loan stock capital by the investment company issuing the stock (*Hoechst Finance Ltd v Gumbrell CA 1983, 56 TC 594*). In *Holdings Ltd v CIR (Sp C 117), [1997] SSCD 144*, a Special Commissioner held that fees for professional advice concerning an investment company's potential liabilities under letters of assurance given to the bankers of a trading subsidiary were allowable. In *L G Berry Investments Ltd v Attwooll Ch D 1964, 41 TC 547*, the Special Commissioners' finding that part of the directors' remuneration was not allowable was upheld. For the interaction of management expenses and double tax relief, see *Jones v Shell Petroleum Co Ltd HL 1971, 47 TC 194.*

Contributions made to an approved profit sharing scheme within *ICTA 1988, s 186* (including, for example, sums paid to meet trustees' capital gains tax liability) are allowable as management expenses. (CCAB Memorandum TR 308, June 1978).

Where an investment company provides relocation packages for its employees who are obliged to relocate, reasonable costs may be allowed as management expenses. However, where the company acquires the beneficial interest in the employee's property, the purchase and subsequent sale of the property will normally fall to be dealt with under the CAPITAL GAINS (11) provisions. (Revenue Tax Bulletin May 1994 p 124).

Other items which generally qualify as management expenses include accounts, share register and annual general meeting costs; registered office expenses; stock exchange quotation cost; valuation costs; and Export Credit Guarantee Department payments.

See generally HMRC Company Taxation Manual, CTM 08150 *et seq.*

42.5 **Miscellaneous.** *Schedule A losses.* Where a company with investment business (or, for accounting periods beginning before 1 April 2004, an investment company) continues to carry on an investment business (or continues to be an investment company) but ceases to carry on a Schedule A business (see 56 PROPERTY INCOME), any unrelieved losses from that business may be carried forward and treated as management expenses of the following accounting period. [*ICTA 1988, s 392A(3); SI 2004 No 2310, Article 12*].

Capital allowances. CAPITAL ALLOWANCES (10) on machinery and plant are added to management expenses referable to any accounting period to the extent they cannot be deducted from the income of the business. Balancing charges are treated as income of the business. [*ICTA 1988, s 75(7)* (as introduced by *FA 2004, s 38(1)*; previously *ICTA 1988, s 75(4)*); *CAA 2001, ss 15(1)(g), 18, 253; CAA 1990, s 28; FA 2004, s 42*); *SI 2004 No 2310, Articles 52–54*].

Employee remuneration. A provision made in the accounts in respect of employees' remuneration, which is not paid within nine months of the end of the accounting period in which the provision is made, is not allowed as a deduction until the accounting period in which the remuneration is paid. [*FA 1989, s 44; ITEPA 2003, Sch 6 para 158; FA 2003, Sch 24 para 10; SI 2004 No 2310, Article 42*].

Appeals. Appeals on management expense matters in relation to investment companies for accounting periods beginning before 1 April 2004 are to the Special Commissioners. For accounting periods ending after that date, the general rules in *TMA 1970* apply (see 6.1 APPEALS) and the General Commissioners will be able to adjudicate subject to a company's right to opt for the appeal to be heard by the Special Commissioners. [*ICTA 1988, s 75(5); FA 2004, s 38*].

Claims. Claims may be made to set off unrelieved management expenses of an accounting period as GROUP RELIEF (32.10) under *ICTA 1988, s 403*.

Simon's Direct Tax Service. See **D4.403** *et seq.*

42.6 **Example** XYZ Ltd, an investment company, rents out rooms, halls and equipment to conference providers. It makes up accounts to 31 March.

The following details are relevant.

	31.3.03	31.3.04
	£	£
Rents received	38,000	107,000
Interest receivable accrued (gross)	10,000	5,000
Chargeable gains	18,000	48,000
Management expenses		
attributable to property	20,000	25,000
attributable to management	50,000	40,000
Capital allowances		
attributable to property	1,000	500
attributable to management	2,000	1,000
Business charges on income	35,000	35,000

The corporation tax computations are as follows.

Year ended 31.3.03

		£	£
Schedule A			
Rents			38,000
Deduct	Capital allowances	1,000	
	Management expenses	20,000	(21,000)
			17,000
Schedule D, Case III			10,000
Chargeable gains			18,000
			45,000
Deduct	Management expenses	50,000	
	Capital allowances	2,000	(52,000)
			(7,000)
Deduct	Business charges		(35,000)
Unrelieved balance carried forward			£(42,000)

Year ended 31.3.04

		£	£
Schedule A			
Rents			107,000
Deduct	Capital allowances	500	
	Management expenses	25,000	(25,500)
			81,500
Schedule D, Case III			5,000
Chargeable gains			48,000
			134,500
Deduct	Management expenses	40,000	
	Capital allowances	1,000	
	Unrelieved balance from previous accounting period	42,000	(83,000)
			51,500
Deduct	Business charges		(35,000)
Profit chargeable to corporation tax			£16,500

On 1 April 2004, XYZ Ltd diversified and began to provide conference services itself.

The following details are relevant for its accounting period ending 31 March 2007.

	31.3.07
	£
Income from conferences	65,000
Rents received	40,000
Interest receivable accrued (gross)	5,000
Conference costs	22,000
Management expenses	
attributable to property	20,000
attributable to management	73,000
Capital allowances	
attributable to conferences	2,000
attributable to property	400
attributable to management	800

The corporation tax computations are as follows.

Year ended 31.3.07

		£	£	£
Schedule D				
Trading income				65,000
Deduct	Conference costs		22,000	
	Capital allowances		2,000	
				(24,000)
				41,000
Schedule A				
Rents			40,000	
Deduct	Capital allowances	400		
	Management expenses	20,000	(20,400)	
				19,600
Schedule D, Case III				5,000
Deduct	Management expenses	73,000		
	Capital allowances	800		
				(73,800)
Unrelieved balance carried forward				£(8,200)

42.7 LOSSES ON UNQUOTED SHARES

As regards relief for losses on unquoted shares subscribed for in certain trading companies, see 47.19 LOSSES.

42.8 CHANGE IN OWNERSHIP

Deductions. Restrictions apply on the use of management expenses, charges and loan relationship deductions brought forward where there is a change in the ownership of a company with an investment business or, for accounting periods beginning before 1 April 2004 (subject to provisions for accounting periods straddling that date (see below)), an investment company. The restrictions mirror those for trading losses in *ICTA 1988, s 768* (see 47.13 LOSSES) and apply where either:

(*a*) after the change there is a 'significant increase' in the company's capital; or

(*b*) within the period from three years before to three years after the change there is a major change in the nature or conduct of the company's business. This includes a change in the nature of the company's investments, even if it is the result of a gradual process which began before that period; or

(*c*) the change occurs after the scale of business activities carried on by the investment company has become small or negligible and before any considerable revival.

There is a '*significant increase*' in the company's capital if 'amount B' is more than twice 'amount A' or exceeds it by at least £1 million, where:

- 'amount A' is the lower of (I) the amount of its capital immediately before the change and (II) the highest amount below which its capital did not fall during a 60-day period in the year immediately preceding the change; and
- 'amount B' is the highest amount below which its capital did not fall during a 60-day period in the three years beginning with the change.

For this purpose, the amount of the company's capital (expressed in sterling and rounded up to the nearest pound) is the aggregate of (I) its paid up share capital (including any share premium account), (II) any outstanding debts (including interest due) incurred by the company for any money borrowed or capital assets acquired by the company, for any right to receive income created in favour of the company, or for consideration the value of which to the company (at the time the debt was incurred) was substantially less than the amount of the debt (including any premium thereon), and (III) any outstanding redeemable loan capital.

As regards (II) above, loan capital or debt issued or incurred for money lent to the company in the ordinary course of a banking business is excluded. (ICAEW Technical Release TAX 22/95, 17 August 1995, para 172).

Where these provisions apply:

(i) the accounting period in which the change occurs is treated as two separate accounting periods, up to and after the change, the 'amounts in issue' being apportioned as specified below between those parts;

(ii) in computing the total profits of the company for an accounting period ending after the change, no deduction is made under *ICTA 1988, s 75* (see 42.2 above) by reference to the management expenses deductible (or, for accounting periods beginning before 1 April 2004, the sums disbursed) or allowances falling to be made for an accounting period beginning before the change, or for charges paid in such an accounting period; and

(iii) the debits and, where the change in ownership is after 9 February 2005, the non-trading deficits to be brought into account in respect of the company's loan relationships (see 46.3 LOAN RELATIONSHIPS), including, for accounting periods beginning on or after 1 October 2002, any debits relating to the company's derivative contracts (SEE 28.9 FINANCIAL INSTRUMENTS AND DERIVATIVE CONTRACTS), are restricted by *ICTA 1988, Sch 28A, Pt IV* (see below).

Where deductions have been restricted as above, in applying the *Capital Allowances Acts* provisions relating to balancing charges by reference to any event after the change, any allowance or deduction falling to be made for any period before the change is disregarded in so far as the profits or gains of that and any subsequent chargeable period before the change are insufficient to give effect to it (assuming that it is relieved in priority to any loss not attributable to such an allowance or deduction).

The '*amounts in issue*' within (i) above are:

(A) any amounts treated as management expenses referable to (or, for accounting periods beginning before 1 April 2004, management expenses (including commissions) disbursed for) the accounting period being divided, but excluding any which (apart from these provisions) would be deductible otherwise than under *ICTA 1988, s 75*;

(B) any charges paid in that period wholly and exclusively for the purposes of the company's business;

(C) any management expenses or charges brought forward to that period;

(D) any capital allowances which would (apart from these provisions) be added to the management expenses of that period;

(E)

  (i) the Schedule D, Case III profits and gains arising from the company's loan relationships, or non-trading deficit (if any) on those relationships, for that period, disregarding amounts within (ii)–(iv) below;

  (ii) any non-trading debit (not within (iv) below) falling to be brought into account for that period in respect of any debtor relationship;

  (iii) any non-trading deficit carried forward to that period under *FA 1996, s 83(3A)* (*section 83(3)* for accounting periods beginning before 1 October 2002); and

  (iv) any non-trading debit for that period under the transitional provisions of *FA 1996, Sch 15 para 13* in respect of any debtor relationship;

  (see 46.2, 46.3, 46.47 LOAN RELATIONSHIPS);

(F) from 1 April 2002:

  (i) any non-trading debits or credits in respect of intangible fixed assets falling to be brought into account for that period; and

  (ii) any non-trading loss on intangible fixed assets carried forward to that period;

  (see 39.6 INTANGIBLE ASSETS); and

(G) any other amounts by reference to which the profits or losses of that period would (apart from these provisions) be calculated.

The basis of apportionment of amounts within (A)–(G) above is as follows.

- Amounts within (A) above are apportioned in accordance with generally accepted accountancy principles as if accounts were drawn up for each part of the period (or for accounting periods beginning before 1 April 2004, by reference to the time payment is due).
- Amounts within (B) above are apportioned by reference to the time payment is due.
- Amounts within (C) and (E)(iii) above are apportioned to the pre-change part of the period in full.
- Amounts within (D), (E)(i) and (G) above are apportioned on a time basis.

- Amounts within (E)(ii) above, where an amortised cost basis (for accounting periods beginning before 1 January 2005, an accruals basis) applies, are apportioned by reference to the time of accrual of the amount to which the debit relates *except* in the case of certain late interest payments where interest is brought into account when paid, or where an adjustment is required under *FA 1996, Sch 9 para 17* or *para 18* (certain debits relating to discounted securities to be brought into account on redemption, see 46.26 LOAN RELATIONSHIPS), where the debit is apportioned to the pre-change part of the period in full.
- Amounts within (E)(iv) and F(ii) above are apportioned to the pre-change part of the period in full.
- Amounts within (F)(i) above are apportioned in accordance with generally accepted accountancy principles (see 39.2 INTANGIBLE ASSETS) as if accounts were drawn up for each part of the period.

If in any case such apportionment would work unreasonably or unjustly, a just and reasonable method of apportionment may be substituted.

Disallowed debits and non-trading deficits. A restriction applies under (iii) above by reference to non-trading debits to be brought into account on an amortised cost (for accounting periods beginning before 1 January 2005, an accruals) basis under the LOAN RELATIONSHIPS (46) provisions and, for accounting periods beginning on or after 1 October 2002, to non-trading debits arising on derivative contracts brought into account under the FINANCIAL INSTRUMENTS AND DERIVATIVE CONTRACTS (28) provisions and which are treated as non-trading debits arising on loan relationships. Where the change in ownership is after 9 February 2005, the restriction also applies to non-trading deficits (this provision having been omitted in error from earlier legislation). The restriction prevents non-trading debits, or as the case may be, non-trading deficits from being carried forward beyond the change of ownership date to the extent to which the aggregate of the debits noted above (including any amounts brought into account for any previous period ending after the change in ownership) exceed the profits chargeable to corporation tax for the accounting period ending with the change in ownership.

Assessment. Where these provisions are triggered by circumstances or events at any time in the three years after the change, an assessment to give effect to them may be made within six years of that time (or the latest such time).

Information. For the purposes of these provisions the inspector may, by notice in writing, require any person who is the registered owner of shares, stock or securities of a company to state whether he is the beneficial owner thereof and, if not, to supply the name and address of the person(s) on whose behalf he holds them.

[*ICTA 1988, s 768B, Sch 28A paras 1–12; FA 1998, s 82(3)(4); FA 2002, Sch 25 para 58(1)–(6), Sch 27 para 9, Sch 30 para 4(4)(5); FA 2004, ss 41, 42, Sch 6 para 3, Sch 10 para 45; SI 2004 No 2310, Articles 39, 66; F(No 2)A 2005, Sch 7 para 3(1)(5)(8)(9)*].

See 47.13 LOSSES as regards what constitutes a 'major change' in the nature or conduct of a trade or business, which may be relevant to (*b*) above.

Asset transferred within group. Where there is a change in ownership of a company with investment business or, for accounting periods beginning before 1 April 2004 (subject to provisions for accounting periods straddling that date (see below)), an investment company and none of (*a*)–(*c*) above applies, restrictions similarly apply where

(1) after the change the company acquires an asset from another company in the same group so that *TCGA 1992, s 171* applies (transaction treated as giving rise to neither gain nor loss, see 12.2 CAPITAL GAINS—GROUPS), and

(2) a chargeable gain (the 'relevant gain') arises to the company on disposal of the asset (or of an asset deriving its value wholly or partly from that asset — in particular where

the original asset was a leasehold, the lessee has acquired the reversion and the freehold is disposed of) within three years of the change.

The accounting period of the change is split as in (i) above, and if the total profits of the company for the accounting period in which the relevant gain accrues include, in accordance with *TCGA 1992, s 8(1)* and *Sch 7A* (see 11.3 CAPITAL GAINS, 12.8 CAPITAL GAINS—GROUPS), an amount in respect of chargeable gains, the deductions as in (ii) and (iii) or (iv) above may not be set against profits equal to the lesser of that amount and the amount of the relevant gain.

The '*amounts in issue*', in addition to those detailed in (A)–(G) above, include:

(H) the chargeable gains included, in accordance with *TCGA 1992, s 8(1)* and *Sch 7A*, in the total profits for the period being divided (as above).

The same basis of apportionment applies as is referred to in relation to (A)–(G) above, with the amount within (H) above being apportioned, in so far as it exceeds the relevant gain, to the pre-change part of the divided period, an amount equivalent to the relevant gain (or, if less, the amount within (H) above) being apportioned to the post-change part of the divided period.

The restriction which applies under *section 768B* (see above) to non-trading debits and non-trading deficits arising on loan relationships applies equally under these provisions.

The assessment and information powers under *section 768B* (see above) apply equally under these provisions.

From 1 April 2002 these provisions also apply with appropriate modifications where, following a change in ownership of an investment company or, for accounting periods beginning on or after 1 April 2004, a company with investment business, it acquires an intangible fixed asset within *FA 2002, Sch 29* intra-group on a tax-neutral basis (see 39.10 INTANGIBLE ASSETS), and a tax credit falls to be brought into account on the company (see 39.7 INTANGIBLE ASSETS) on realisation of the asset (or an asset deriving its value from that asset) within three years. The '*amounts in issue*' are correspondingly extended.

[*ICTA 1988, s 768C, Sch 28A paras 13–17; FA 2002, Sch 25 para 58(7)–(10), Sch 27 para 10, Sch 30 para 4(2)(6)(7); FA 2004, ss 41, 42, Sch 6 para 4; SI 2004 No 2310, Article 39; F(No 2)A 2005, Sch 7 para 3(2)(6)–(9)*].

Schedule A losses. Where, in relation to a company with investment business or, for accounting periods beginning before 1 April 2004 (subject to provisions for accounting periods straddling that date (see below)), an investment company carrying on a Schedule A business or an overseas property business (see 56 PROPERTY INCOME), either

(I) (*a*), (*b*) or (*c*) above applies (so that the provisions of *section 768B* apply, or would apply, in relation to management expenses and charges), or

(II) *Section 768C* (see above) applies in relation to an asset transferred within a group,

similar restrictions apply to prevent Schedule A losses (see 56 PROPERTY INCOME) incurred before the change being set against profits arising after the change. [*ICTA 1988, s 768D; FA 2004, ss 41, 42, Sch 6 para 5*].

Non-trading losses on intangible fixed assets. Where, in relation to a company with investment business or, for accounting periods beginning before 1 April 2004 (subject to provisions for accounting periods straddling that date (see below)), an investment company, either

(*aa*) (*a*), (*b*) or (*c*) above applies (so that the provisions of *section 768B* apply, or would apply, in relation to management expenses and charges), or

(*bb*) *section 768C* (see above) applies in relation to an asset transferred within a group, similar restrictions apply to prevent non-trading losses on intangible fixed assets (see 39.6 INTANGIBLE ASSETS) incurred before the change being set against profits arising after the change. [*ICTA 1988, s 768E; FA 2002, Sch 30 para 4(3); FA 2004, ss 41, 42, Sch 6 para 6*].

Accounting period straddling 1 April 2004. Where an accounting period straddles 1 April 2004 and there is a change of ownership during the straddling period, then for the purposes of ICTA 1988, *ss 768B, 768C* and *Sch 28A* (see above), the straddling period is treated as consisting of two periods before making any division required by *ICTA 1988, ss 768B(4), s 768C(3)*. The first period is treated as beginning with the straddling period and ending on 31 March 2004 and the second beginning on 1 April 2004 and ending with the straddling period. The treatment as two separate periods in this case has effect in determining the amounts deductible in respect of management expenses carried forward from accounting periods beginning before 1 April 2004, and in determining sums treated as management expenses under any other provision. [*FA 2004, s 43(7)*].

General. The provisions of *ICTA 1988, s 769* (rules for ascertaining change in ownership, see 47.13 LOSSES) apply with appropriate modification in relation to these provisions as they apply to *ICTA 1988, ss 768, 768A*.

Simon's Direct Tax Service. See **D4.413** *et seq*.

43 Investment Funds

Cross–references. See 11.9, 11.25 CAPITAL GAINS, 12.2, 12.28 CAPITAL GAINS—GROUPS, 28.24 FINANCIAL INSTRUMENTS AND DERIVATIVE CONTRACTS, 46.43 LOAN RELATIONSHIPS, 55.4 PROFIT COMPUTATIONS.

Simon's Direct Tax Service D4.1301 *et seq.*

The headings in this chapter are as follows.

43.1 AUTHORISED INVESTMENT FUNDS

The legislation applying to '*authorised investment funds*' ('AIFs'), which include open-ended investment companies ('OEICs') and authorised unit trusts ('AUTs') (see 43.2 and 43.3 below) is set out in *SI 2006 No 964* under powers in *F(No 2)A 2005, ss 17–19.*. The new regulations, which have effect for accounting periods beginning on or after 1 April 2006 (and for disposals and distributions made on or after that date), consolidate the separate sets of rules governing AUTs and OEICs into the one set of regulations, amend some provisions and make new ones to simplify and update the tax regime. With effect from that date, *ICTA 1988, ss 468H–468Q* in relation to AUTs and *SIs 1997 Nos 1154* and *1715, 2002 No 1973* and *2003 No 1831* in relation to OIECs are repealed. [*SI 2006 No 964, regs 1, 3; SI 2006 No 982; SI 2006 No 3239; SI 2007 No 683*].

Collective investment schemes. Unit trusts and open-ended investment companies are the most common forms of 'collective investment schemes'. A '*collective investment scheme*' is an arrangement with respect to property of any description, including money, the purpose or effect of which is to enable persons taking part in the arrangements (whether by becoming owners of all or part of the property or otherwise) to participate in or receive profits or income arising from the acquisition, holding, management or disposal of the property or sums paid out of such profits or income. [*Financial Services and Markets Act 2000, s 235; FA 2004, s 118(4); SI 2001 No 3629, Arts 62(2), 70; SI 2006 No 964, regs 6, 8*]. The object of such a scheme is to enable a large number of investors to pool their money by investing in a professionally managed fund of investments, thus spreading risk. A body corporate (other than an open-ended investment company) is not regarded as a collective investment scheme, so that INVESTMENT TRUSTS (44), VENTURE CAPITAL TRUSTS (69), INDUSTRIAL AND PROVIDENT SOCIETIES (38) and FRIENDLY SOCIETIES (31) are not collective investment schemes. Certain limited liability partnerships may however meet the criteria. (HMRC Company Taxation Manual CTM 48070).

Individual savings accounts (ISAs). The *Individual Savings Accounts Regulations 1998* (*SI 1998 No 1870* as amended) enable investments in authorised investment funds to be held in individual savings accounts (see Tolley's Income Tax under Exempt Income) and similar rules applied to personal equity plans (*SI 1997 No 1716* as amended).

43.2 **Open-ended investment companies.** OEICs are investment companies in which shares are continuously created or redeemed, according to investor demand. An OEIC is defined as a company incorporated in the UK to which the *Financial Services and Markets Act 2000, s 236* applies.

For accounting periods beginning on or after 1 April 2006 (and in relation to disposals and distributions made on or after that date), the taxation of OEICs and their shareholders are covered partly by primary legislation and mainly by *SI 2006 No 964* (the new regulations for authorised investment funds) set out in 43.4–43.10 below. Before that date they were provided for mainly by the *Open-ended Investment Companies (Tax) Regulations 1997 (SI 1997 No 1154)* (as amended). These regulations are repealed with effect from that date by virtue of *SI 2006 No 964, reg 111.*.

[*ICTA 1988, s 468A; FA 1995, s 152; F(No 2)A 2005, ss 16–19, Sch 11 Pt;2(3); SI 1997 No 1715; SI 2001 No 3629, Article 166; SI 2002 No 1973; SI 2003 No 1831; SI 2004 No 2310, Article 76; SI 2006 No 964, reg 4; SI 2006 No 982; ITA 2007 Sch 1 para 605*].

Regulations also deal with VAT (*Value Added Tax (Finance) Order 1997 (SI 1997 No 510)*) and stamp duty and stamp duty reserve tax (*Stamp Duty and Stamp Duty Reserve Tax (Open-ended Investment Companies) Regulations 1997 (SI 1997 No 1156), (Amendment) Regulations 1999 (SI 1999 No 1467)* and *(Amendment No 2) Regulations 1999 (SI 1999 No 3261)*) in relation to OEICs.

Simon's Direct Tax Service. See D4.1335, D4.1336.

43.3 **Authorised unit trusts.** An '*authorised unit trust*' is a 'unit trust scheme' which is the subject of an order under *Financial Services and Markets Act 2000, s 243* for the whole or part of an accounting period. A '*unit trust scheme*' is as defined under *Financial Services and Markets Act 2000*, but subject to certain exclusions by Treasury order (see *SI 1988 Nos 266, 267, 268 as amended; SI 1992 Nos 571, 3133; SI 1994 No 1479; SI 2000 Nos 2549, 2550, 2551*). [*ICTA 1988, ss 468(6), 469(7); TCGA 1992, s 99(2); Financial Services and Markets Act 2000, Sch 20 para 4(3)(4); SI 2006 No 964, reg 5*]. See also 43.12 below as regards court common investment funds.

For accounting periods beginning on or after 1 April 2006 (and in relation to disposals and distributions made on or after that date), the taxation of OEICs and their shareholders are covered partly by primary legislation and mainly by *SI 2006 No 964* (the new regulations for authorised investment funds) set out in 43.4–43.10 below. With effect from that date *ICTA 1988, ss 468H–468Q* are repealed by virtue of *F(No 2)A 2005, s 17(1)* and *SI 2006 No 982*.

43.4 **Umbrella company and umbrella schemes.** An '*umbrella company*' is an OEIC which provides for separate pooling of shareholder contributions and of the profits or income out of which payments are made to those shareholders and under which they may exchange rights in one pool for those of another. Each of the parts of an umbrella company is regarded for the purpose of these provisions as an OEIC unless expressly provided for elsewhere in any other tax provisions but the umbrella company as a whole is not be regarded as an OEIC nor as a company. [*ICTA 1988, s 468A; F(No 2)A 2005, s 16; SI 2006 No 964, reg 7*].

'*Umbrella schemes*' are authorised unit trust schemes which provide for separate pools of contributions and of the profits or income out of which payments are made to the participants and under which they may exchange rights in one pool for those of another. Each of the parts of an umbrella scheme is regarded for the purpose of these provisions as an authorised unit trust but the scheme as a whole is not be regarded as an authorised unit trust or an any other form of collective investment scheme. [*ICTA 1988, s 468(7)–(9); FA 1994, s 113; SI 2006 No 964, reg 7*].

43.5 TAX TREATMENT OF AUTHORISED INVESTMENT FUNDS

Corporation tax. The *Tax Acts* have effect as if the trustees of an AUT were a company resident in the UK, and the rights of unit holders were shares in the company. Expenses of management (including managers' remuneration) are allowed (for accounting periods beginning before 1 April 2004, as if the company were an investment company (see 42 INVESTMENT COMPANIES AND INVESTMENT BUSINESS)). [*ICTA 1988, ss 468(1)(4); SI 2004 No 2310, Article 20*].

A special rate of corporation tax applies to OEICs and to the trustees of an AUT, equal to the lower rate of income tax (currently 20%). In the case of unit trusts, it applies for the year of assessment beginning in the financial year. [*ICTA 1988, ss 468(1A), 468A; F(No 2)A 2005, s 16; SI 1997 No 1154, reg 5*].

SI 2006 No 964, reg 94(2)–(4) makes it clear that authorised investment funds cannot form part of any arrangements for group relief purposes.

Capital gains. For capital gains purposes, any unit trust scheme is treated as if the scheme were a company and the rights of the unit holders shares in the company, and, in the case of an authorised unit trust, as if the company were UK resident and ordinarily resident. [*TCGA 1992, s 99(1)*]. Capital gains, realised by OIECs or AUTs (including umbrella companies or umbrella schemes (see 43.4 above), for the benefit of investors, are not chargeable gains. [*TCGA 1992, s 100(1)*]. For company reorganisations involving authorised unit trusts, see 11.9 CAPITAL GAINS.

See Tolley's Capital Gain Tax under Unit Trusts and Other Investment Vehicles for the capital gains tax treatment of disposals, amalgamation with or conversion of an AUT to an OEIC, accumulation units and monthly savings schemes.

Loan relationships and derivative contracts. 'Capital profits, gains or losses' arising to an authorised investment fund from a derivative contract or (with effect for accounting periods beginning on or after 1 October 2002) from a creditor relationship are to be disregarded under these provisions. '*Capital profits, gains or losses*' in this case are those which, in preparing accounts in accordance with UK generally accepted accounting practice, fall to be dealt with in the statement of total return (under the heading of 'net gains/losses on investments during the period' or 'other gains/losses') in accordance with the relevant Statement of Recommended Practice (SORP). Interest distributions paid by an authorised investment fund are taxable under the loan relationship rules (see 46 LOAN RELATIONSHIPS) as if they were interest payable on a loan. A deficit on a loan relationship of an authorised investment fund cannot be carried back to set against profits of an earlier accounting period under *FA 1996, s 83(2)(c)*. [*SI 2006 No 964, regs 8, 10–14*; replacing *ICTA 1988, s 468L(5)–(7)* and *SI 1997 No 1154* (as amended) from 1 April 2006; *SI 2006 No 982*].

Futures and options. For accounting periods beginning before 1 October 2002, income derived from transactions relating to futures or options contracts is exempt from tax under Schedule D, Case I in the hands of the trustees of an AUT. A contract is not excluded from this exemption by the fact that any party is, or may be, entitled to receive and/or liable to make only a payment of a sum (rather than a transfer of assets other than money) in full settlement of all obligations. [*ICTA 1988, s 468AA; FA 2002, Sch 27 para 6*]. See now 28.24 FINANCIAL INSTRUMENTS AND DERIVATIVE CONTRACTS. For the underlying reasons for the repeal of *section 468AA*, see Revenue Tax Bulletin August 2002 p 949. See HMRC Tax Bulletin December 2005 p 1262 for HMRC's confirmation that new investment strategies allowed by the Financial Services Authority for authorised funds do not alter the presumption that authorised funds are investment vehicles and will not be conducting a trade. The tax treatment of profits and losses from derivative contracts will continue to follow the presentation in accounts prepared in accordance with the accounting SORP.

43.6 DISTRIBUTIONS MADE BY AUTHORISED INVESTMENT FUNDS

The total amount available for distribution to participants is to be shown in the distribution accounts as available for distribution either as dividends (a 'dividend distribution'), or as yearly interest (which may not include any amount chargeable to corporation tax under Schedule A or as income of an overseas property business) (an 'interest distribution').

These provisions do not apply to an authorised investment fund which is a registered pension scheme within the meaning of *FA 2004, Pt 4* or is treated as having become such a scheme under *FA 2004, Sch 36*. [*SI 2006 No 964, regs 16, 17* replacing *ICTA 1988, ss 468H(6), 468I* and *SI 1997 No 1154* (as amended) from 1 April 2006; *SI 2006 No 982*].

For these purposes, the making of a distribution includes the investment of an amount on behalf of the participant in respect of his accumulation units (this being subject to the treatment of de minimis amounts – see below). [*SI 2006 No 964, regs 15, 18(4)(b), 22(4)* replacing *ICTA 1988, s 468H(2)* and *SI 1997 No 1154* (as amended) from 1 April 2006].

Interest distributions. An '*interest distribution*' is treated as a payment of yearly interest made on the '*distribution date*' (i.e. the date specified under the fund or, if there is no such date, the last day of the distribution period), to the participants in proportion to their rights, including interest paid to a participant not liable to income tax. No amount may be shown as an interest distribution unless the authorised investment fund satisfies a 'qualifying investments test' throughout the distribution period. This requires that, at all times in the period, at least 60% of the market value of the fund's investments is represented by 'qualifying investments'.

'*Qualifying investments*' means the investment of funds within any of the following categories.

1 Money placed at interest.

2 Securities (excluding shares in a company).

3 Shares in a building society.

4 Qualifying units in another authorised investment fund (which itself satisfies the qualifying investments test in relation to 1–3 above and 5–8 below).

5 Derivative contracts (for accounting periods beginning on or after 1 October 2002) whose underlying subject matter consists wholly of any one or more of 1–4 above or (for accounting periods beginning on or after 1 April 2006) currency.

6 Contracts for differences (for accounting periods beginning on or after 1 October 2002) whose underlying matter consists wholly of any one or more of interest rates, creditworthiness or (for accounting periods beginning on or after 1 April 2006) currency.

7 Derivative contracts (for accounting periods beginning on or after 1 April 2006) not within 5 or 6 above where there is a hedging relationship (as defined) between the derivative contract and an asset within 1–4 above.

8 Alternative finance arrangements. (Funds invested in ALTERNATIVE FINANCE ARRANGEMENTS (4) are qualifying investments under *SI 2006 No 964, reg 20* from 1 April 2006. For interest distributions before that date and broadly on or after 6 April 2005, qualifying investments of money placed at interest includes money invested under alternative finance arrangements. [*FA 2005, s 56, Sch 2 para 4* as repealed by *SI 2006 No 964, reg 92*].)

[*SI 2006 No 964, regs 15, 18–21* replacing *ICTA 1988, s 468L* and *SI 1997 No 1154* (as amended) from 1 April 2006; *FA 2002, Sch 27 para 7; SI 2006 No 982*].

Dividend distributions. A '*dividend distribution*' is treated as a dividend on shares paid on the distribution date (as above), to the participants in proportion to their rights, including dividends paid to a participant not liable to corporation tax. [*SI 2006 No 964, regs 15, 22* replacing *ICTA 1988, s 468J* and *SI 1997 No 1154* (as amended) from 1 April 2006; *ITTOIA 2005, Sch 1 para 179; SI 2006 No 982*].

De minimis amounts. An authorised investment fund is not treated as making an interest or dividend distribution if:

- the fund has (in accordance with FSA rules) an agreed '*de minimis limit*' (an amount in respect of which a distribution of fund income is not required if the amount shown in the fund's distribution accounts as available for distribution does not exceed that limit);
- the fund has a de minimis amount shown in the distribution accounts as available for distribution to participants but waives distribution of that amount and carries it forward as an amount available for distribution in the next distribution period; and
- none of the fund's units in issue on the 'distribution date' (see below) are in bearer form.

[*SI 2006 No 964, reg 23*]. This provision, which comes into effect for accounting periods beginning on or after 1 April 2006, puts the existing practice in HMRC Extra-Statutory Concession, C30 onto a statutory footing.

43.7 TAX TREATMENT OF PARTICIPANTS

These provisions do not apply to an authorised investment fund which is a registered pension scheme within the meaning of *FA 2004, Pt 4* or is treated as having become such a scheme under *FA 2004, Sch 36*. [*SI 2006 No 964, reg 25* replacing *ICTA 1988, s 468H(6)* and *SI 1997 No 1154* (as amended) from 1 April 2006].

43.8 **Participants chargeable to income tax.** For interest distributions made **on or after 16 October 2002** to a participant chargeable to income tax, lower rate tax is deductible under *ITA 2007, s 449* (formerly *ICTA 1988, s 349(2)*) unless either:

(*a*) the participant is either a company or the trustees of a unit trust scheme; or

(*b*) either the 'residence condition', the 'reputable intermediary condition' or, for distributions after 5 April 2007, the 'non-liability condition' is met with respect to the participant on the distribution date.

However, if the participant is a company which is a trustee of the trust to which (or under which) the distribution is made (or received), the obligation to deduct tax is not excluded by virtue of the fact that the participant is a company and one of the other conditions would have to be satisfied for the exemption to apply. In the case of accumulation units, the obligation to deduct tax is an obligation to deduct a sum out of the amount being credited to scheme capital on the participant's behalf.

[*SI 2006 No 964, reg 26* replacing, from 1 April 2006, *ICTA 1988, ss 468L, 468M* (as amended by *FA 2003, s 203, Sch 43 Pt 5(3); ITTOIA 2005, Sch 1 para 180*), *SI 1997 No 1154* (as amended), *SI 2003 No 1830* and *SI 2003 No 1831*].

The '*residence condition*' requires broadly that a valid declaration is made to the legal owner of the authorised investment fund, in prescribed form, that either the participant is not ordinarily resident in the UK or, if the units are held by the participant as personal representative of a deceased holder, the deceased was not ordinarily resident in the UK at the time of his death. [*SI 2006 No 964, regs 30–33, 75* replacing, from 1 April 2006, *ICTA 1988, ss 468O, 468P* as amended by *FA 2003, s 203(4)–(8)* and *SI 1997 No 1154* (as amended)].

The '*reputable intermediary condition*' requires broadly that the interest distribution is paid on behalf of the participant to a company which is subject to certain money laundering controls, and that the legal owner has reasonable grounds for believing the participant to be non-UK ordinarily resident. If it subsequently transpires that the participant was in fact ordinarily resident, the tax which should have been deducted is payable by the legal owner under *ICTA 1988, s 350, Sch 16*. See *TMA 1970, s 98(4E)* for penalty provisions. [*SI 2006 No 964, regs 27–29* replacing, from 1 April 2006, *ICTA 1988, ss 468O(1A)–(1B), 468PA* as inserted by *FA 2003, s 203(6)(9)* and *SI 1997 No 1154* (as amended)].

The '*non-liability condition*' requires broadly, for distributions after 5 April 2007, that the person beneficially entitled to the interest is unlikely to be chargeable to income tax for the tax year in which the distribution is made and a 'qualifying certificate' (as defined) to that effect has been given to the legal owner. [*SI 2006 No 964, regs 1, 34–46*]. This effectively extends the circumstances in which distribution can be paid gross to fall into line with the treatment of bank interest.

See *SI 2006 No 964, regs 71–74* for requirements to notify HMRC where interest distributions are made without deduction of tax and the powers of HMRC in this respect.

For interest distributions made **before 16 October 2002**, lower rate tax was deductible unless the 'residence condition' was fulfilled with respect to the unit holder on the distribution date. That condition required a declaration as described above in relation to later distributions, except for company and trustee unit holders. In relation to company unit holders, the declaration had to be that the company was not UK resident. In the case of distributions made to or received under a trust, under *SI 1994 No 2318*, the requirement was for a valid declaration from the trustees both that they were non-UK resident and that each beneficiary known to them satisfied the individual or company residence conditions as appropriate (except that where the whole of the distribution was, or was treated as, income of a person other than the trustees, the residence conditions applied only to that person). If the gross income in the distribution accounts derived entirely from 'eligible income', payments to unit holders satisfying the appropriate residence condition could be made without deduction of tax. There was a formula for determining the amount which could be so paid where the gross income did not derive entirely from 'eligible income' (see *ICTA 1988, s 468N(4)–(6)*). *SI 1994 No 2318* also provided HMRC with the appropriate powers to determine whether interest distributions were properly paid gross. '*Eligible income*' was defined in *ICTA 1988, s 468M(4)(5)* (as amended) broadly as income which would not be subject to deduction if received directly by a non-UK resident.

Guidance notes are available on HMRC's website (at www.hmrc.gov.uk/specialist/auth-unit-trust-notes.htm) for managers and operators of AUTs and OEICs about the circumstances in which interest distributions of such funds can be paid without deduction of income tax. Various forms are also available including forms for individuals who are not ordinarily resident and companies (where they have joint holdings with individuals) which are non-resident, to make a declaration to obtain payment without deduction of income tax.

43.9 **Participants chargeable to corporation tax.** *Interest distributions.* Where, on the distribution date, the participant is within the charge to corporation tax, the obligation to deduct tax does not apply to interest distributions unless the participant is a company which is a trustee of the trust to which (or under which) the distribution is made (or received). In the case of accumulation units, the obligation to deduct tax is an obligation to deduct a sum out of the amount being invested on the participant's behalf. [*SI 2006 No 964, reg 47*]. See *SI 2006 No 964, regs 71–74* for requirements to notify HMRC where interest distributions are made without deduction of tax and the powers of HMRC in this respect.

Dividend distributions. Where, on the distribution date, the participant is within the charge to corporation tax, then (unless the participant is the manager of the authorised investment fund in the ordinary course of business) for the purpose of computing the unit holder's corporation tax liability, the 'unfranked' part of a dividend distribution is treated:

(i) as an annual payment and not as a dividend distribution or interest distribution; and

(ii) as having been received by the participant after deduction of income tax at the lower rate for the tax year in which the distribution date falls from a corresponding gross amount.

Where tax is deemed to have been deducted under (ii) above, repayment to the participant may not exceed the participant's portion (by reference to participants' rights in the fund in the distribution period in question) of the legal owner's net liability to corporation tax in respect of that gross income, as reduced by any double tax relief, whether under an agreement or by way of credit under *ICTA 1988, s 790(1)* (see 24.2, 24.3 DOUBLE TAX RELIEF). In determining the amount repayable tax treated as having been deducted by virtue of (ii) above is set off In priority to any other tax subject to deduction under *ICTA 1988, s 7, Sch 16*. The statement sent to the participant relating to the distribution must show the legal owner's net liability to corporation tax in respect of the gross income.

The '*unfranked*' part of the dividend distribution is found by the formula:

$$U = \frac{A \times C}{D}$$

where:

U is the unfranked part of the dividend distribution to the participant;

A is the amount of the dividend distribution;

C is such amount of the gross income of the fund as does not derive from franked investment income, as reduced by the amount of the legal owner's net liability to corporation tax in respect of that gross income less any double tax relief, whether under an agreement or by way of credit under *ICTA 1988, s 790(1)* (see 24.2, 24.3 DOUBLE TAX RELIEF)); and

D is the gross income of the fund as in C (and similarly reduced), but including any part deriving from franked investment income.

[*SI 2006 No 964, regs 48–52, 70* replacing, from 1 April 2006, *ICTA 1988, s 468Q* and *SI 1997 No 1154* (as amended); *SI 2006 No 981*].

43.10 QUALIFIED INVESTOR SCHEMES

A '*qualified investor scheme*' (QIS) is a fund, authorised by the Financial Services Authority, in which a statement that the fund is a qualified investor scheme is included in the instrument constituting the scheme. [*SI 2006 No 964, reg 53(3)*]. Only institutional and certain sophisticated investors are eligible to participate in such schemes, which can be set up from 2004.

A special tax regime applies to participants with a 'substantial holding' in a QIS with effect from 1 April 2006 (6 April 2006 for individuals). Broadly, the regime operates as follows. The participant is required to ascertain the market value the holding at specified measuring dates. The participant is charged to tax by reference to the difference in the market value of the holding between two specified measuring dates. The aggregate of those differences for an accounting period (or tax year) is taken. Where the aggregate is a positive amount, that amount is charged to tax under Schedule D, Case VI (or under *ITTOIA 2005, Pt 5 Ch 8*) (and a negative amount is an income loss). As increases in the value of a holding are taxed under the regime as income, no chargeable gain arises on disposals of all or part of the holding. A gain will arise at the time of the disposal, however, in respect of any increase in the value of the holding (or part) before entry into the regime. See Tolley's Capital Gain Tax under Unit Trusts and Other Investment Vehicles for full details.

The regime does not apply to participants which are charities, registered pension schemes, insurance companies (where the holding is held as an asset of its long-term insurance fund), friendly societies, persons in whose hands any profit on a sale of units in the QIS would be trading income, and other QISs.

For these purposes, a holding in a QIS is a '*substantial holding*' if the participant, either alone or together with associates (within *ICTA 1988, s 417*) or connected persons (within *ICTA 1988, s 839* — see 19 CONNECTED PERSONS), owns (otherwise than as a nominee or bare trustee) units which represent rights to 10% or more of the net asset value of the fund.

[*SI 2006 No 964, regs 53–69*].

43.11 **COURT COMMON INVESTMENT FUNDS**

Court common investment funds (CCIFs) are a form of unit trust set up by the Lord Chancellor under *Administration of Justice Act 1982, s 42(1)*. They are available only for individuals whose money is under control of certain courts, e.g. road accident victims and the mentally incapacitated. The Public Trustee as Accountant General of the Supreme Court holds all units in the fund on the investors' behalf. As regards any income arising to a CCIF and any distribution made, CCIFs are treated for tax purposes as authorised unit trusts. The investment manager is treated as the trustee, and the persons whose interests entitle them, as against the Accountant General (or other authorised person), to share in the fund's investments are treated as the unit holders.

With effect in relation to income arising on or after 6 April 2003, the categories of persons treated as the unit holders in such authorised unit trusts are extended to include certain other persons authorised by the Lord Chancellor to hold the shares, either on their own behalf or on behalf of others. This reflects a planned change in the rules under which such funds operate.

[*ICTA 1988, s 469A; FA 2003, s 183, Sch 43 Pt 3(17)*].

Simon's Direct Tax Service. See D4.1340.

43.12 **UNIT TRUSTS NOT TREATED AS AUTHORISED UNIT TRUSTS**

Special provisions apply to the income of a unit trust scheme not within 43.3 above unless the trustees are non-UK resident. Such a trust is outside the scope of *ICTA 1988, s 468* (see 43.3 above). Income arising to the trustees is treated as income of the trustees (rather than the unit holders), and is subject to basic rate tax. Capital allowances are available to the trustees (but, since the trustees are not treated as a company, there is no relief for management expenses). The unit holders are treated as receiving annual payments, under deduction of basic rate tax, equal to their respective entitlements to the grossed-up income available for distribution or investment. The date the payment is treated as having been made is the latest (or only) date for distribution under the terms of the trust or (if there is no such date or it is more than twelve months after the end of the distribution period) the last day of the distribution period. For the definition of 'distribution period', see *ICTA 1988, s 469(6)*.

No tax credit is attached to any qualifying distributions received by the trustees, who are not treated as having paid income tax thereon (and the latter applies also to non-qualifying distributions (see 23.7 DISTRIBUTIONS) received by the trustees).

The liability of the trustees to account for tax deducted from annual payments treated as made by them, so far as not covered by tax deducted from income received, is reduced where there is a cumulative uncredited surplus of income on which they are chargeable to tax over such annual payments.

[*ICTA 1988, s 469; F(No 2)A 1997, s 29, Sch 4 para 12; ITTOIA 2005, Sch 1 para 181*].

Pension fund pooling. Special provision is made by regulations to ensure that certain international pooled pension funds (registered as 'pension fund pooling vehicles') are transparent for UK tax purposes, by disapplying the tax rules for unauthorised unit trusts (as above). Participants in such schemes must be approved by HMRC, and are treated for income tax, capital allowances and capital gains tax purposes as though they themselves owned directly a share of each of the trust assets. There is also relief from stamp duty (or stamp duty reserve tax) on transfers of assets (other than land or buildings) by participants into the scheme. Participation in pension fund pooling vehicles is restricted to registered pension schemes, UK-based superannuation funds used primarily by companies employing British expatriates working overseas, and pension funds established outside the UK broadly equivalent to UK registered pension schemes. [*SI 1996 Nos 1583, 1585* as amended]. The position in the country in which any overseas participator is based will of course be crucial to the operation of such schemes.

Simon's Direct Tax Service. See D4.1325.

43.13 UNIT TRUSTS FOR EXEMPT UNIT HOLDERS

If, for any reason other than non-residence, none of the holders of units in a unit trust scheme would be liable to capital gains tax (or to corporation tax on chargeable gains) on a disposal of units, gains accruing to the trust itself are not chargeable gains. With effect for 2005–06 onwards, in determining whether this exemption applies, no account is taken of units which are disposed of by a unit holder and are held by the fund managers pending disposal. (For previous years, this provision was covered by Revenue Extra-Statutory Concession D17.) No account to be taken of the possibility of a corporation tax charge on income arising in respect of a gain accruing on a disposal by an insurance company or an incorporated or registered friendly society (see 31.2 FRIENDLY SOCIETIES). [*TCGA 1992, s 100(2–2B)*; *F(No 2)A 2005, s 20*].

This exemption applies whenever the gains accrued, but is of practical importance only in relation to unit trust schemes which have not been designated as authorised unit trusts (in 43.3 above).

44 Investment Trusts

Cross–references. See 11.9 CAPITAL GAINS, 12.1, 12.37 CAPITAL GAINS—GROUPS, 28.50 FINANCIAL INSTRUMENTS AND DERIVATIVE CONTRACTS, 42.2 INVESTMENT COMPANIES AND INVESTMENT BUSINESS, 46.43 LOAN RELATIONSHIPS.

The headings in this chapter are as follows.

44.1 INVESTMENT TRUSTS

An investment trust is a 'company' fulfilling the following conditions.

(*a*) It is not a close company.

(*b*) It is resident in the UK.

(*c*) It derives its income wholly or mainly (in practice, 70% or more) from 'shares' or securities or from certain investments in housing (see below).

(*d*) No 'holding' in any one company represents more than 15% of the value of its investments, unless that company is itself an investment trust or would be so but for being unquoted. This requirement is waived in respect of investments which, when acquired, represented no more than 15% of the value of the investments, and in respect of an investment held on 6 April 1965, provided that the holding represented not more than 25% of the overall value of the investments at that date. There is no waiver in either case where there has been an 'addition' to the holding.

(*e*) Its 'ordinary share capital' (and every class thereof, if there is more than one) is listed in the Official List of the Stock Exchange.

(*f*) Its Memorandum or Articles prohibit the distribution by way of dividend of gains arising from the sale of investments.

(*g*) It does not retain an amount greater than 15% of its income derived from shares and securities or from certain investments in housing (see below) in any accounting period.

(*h*) It is approved by HMRC.

From **19 July 2007**, 'income' in the above does not include offshore income gains.

As regards (*c*) above, in determining the amount of the company's income, no account is to be taken of the income chargeable to Schedule D, Case VI under *ICTA 1988, s 75B(7)(b)* (see 42.2 INVESTMENT COMPANIES AND INVESTMENT BUSINESS). For accounting periods beginning on or after 1 January 2008 (the date having been originally set at 1 January 2006), offshore income gains (computed under *ICTA 1988, s 761*), arising from disposals of material interests in offshore funds not qualifying for 'distributing fund' status (see 50 OFFSHORE FUNDS), will no longer qualify as eligible investment income. This is a change of interpretation by HMRC who now consider that the disposal of a material interest is a disposal of a capital asset (notwithstanding the treatment under *ICTA 1988, 761* as income) and that the deemed income cannot be said to derive from 'shares' or securities. (See HMRC Tax Bulletin, Issue 79, October 2005 pp 1242–1243 as amended by HMRC Internet Notice 23 November 2005.)

As regards (*c*) and (*g*) above, in determining the amount of the company's income or the amount of its income derived from shares and securities, the amount to be brought into account in respect of the company's LOAN RELATIONSHIPS (46) is to be determined without reference to any of its debtor relationships.

Also as regards (*c*) and (*g*) above, stock lending fees are not regarded as income from securities (see HMRC Capital Gains Manual, CG 41417). Also as regards (*c*) and (*g*) above, units in an authorised unit trust are treated as shares in a company, and where condition (*d*) above is then relevant, and in relation to open-ended investment companies ('OEICs', see 43 INVESTMENT FUNDS), that condition is regarded as being satisfied *provided that*, during any accounting period in which units in the unit trust or shares in the OEIC were held by the investment trust, the unit trust or OEIC itself satisfied the condition at (*c*) above. This will always be considered to be the case where the unit trust is a securities fund under the relevant regulations or the OEIC is a securities company under the corresponding OEIC regulations (and for certain similarly constituted sub-funds). (HMRC Statement of Practice SP 3/97). As regards (*g*), see also 28.50(*d*) FINANCIAL INSTRUMENTS AND DERIVATIVE CONTRACTS concerning treatment of certain profits as income derived from shares or securities.

(*g*) above does not apply if the amount the company would be required to distribute to meet the 15% requirement for a period is less than £10,000 (proportionately reduced for periods of less than twelve months), or if the company is required by law to retain income in excess of the 15% limit for the period. The latter exclusion only applies, however, if the aggregate of the excess of retentions over those required by law and any distribution for the period is less than £10,000 (proportionately reduced for periods of less than twelve months). As regards the measure of income retained under (*g*) above, see HMRC Capital Gains Manual, CG 41437 *et seq.*

'*Company*' includes any body corporate or unincorporated association, but not a partnership.

'*Shares*' includes stock.

'*Holding*' means the shares or securities of whatever class or classes held in any one company. Where, in connection with a 'scheme of reconstruction' (previously a 'scheme of reconstruction or amalgamation') (see 11.9 CAPITAL GAINS), a company issues shares or securities to persons holding shares or securities in another in respect of, and in proportion to (or as nearly as may be in proportion to) such holdings, without the recipients' becoming liable for any consideration, the old and the new holdings are treated as the same. If the investing company is a member of a group (i.e. a company and its 51% subsidiaries), money owed to it by another group member is treated as a security and, as such, as part of its holding in that other group member. Holdings in companies which are members of a group (whether or not including the investing company) are treated as holdings in a single company.

An '*addition*' is made to a holding whenever the investing company acquires further shares or securities in any company in which it already has a holding, otherwise than by being allotted them without liability for consideration (e.g. a bonus issue). The holding is deemed to have been acquired at the date of the latest addition.

[*ICTA 1988, s 842; TCGA 1992, s 288(1); FA 2002, Sch 9 para 4(7), Sch 25 para 56, Sch 40 Pt 3(2); FA 2004, s 45(4); FA 2007, s 57(3)*].

'*Ordinary share capital*' is as defined in *ICTA 1988, s 832(1)*. See 12.1 CAPITAL GAINS—GROUPS.

Investment trusts are exempt from tax on capital gains realised on disposals. [*TCGA 1992, s 100(1)*].

For the treatment of forward currency transactions as being of a capital or revenue nature, and their effect on the test in (*c*) above, see HMRC Capital Gains Manual, CG 41445. For loan relationships of investment trusts, see 46.43 LOAN RELATIONSHIPS.

For company reorganisations involving investment trusts, see 11.9 CAPITAL GAINS. For the transfer of assets within a group of companies to a company which subsequently becomes an investment trust, see 12.37 CAPITAL GAINS—GROUPS.

See, generally, HMRC Capital Gains Manual CG 41400 *et seq.*

44.2 **Investments in housing.** The following rules apply to accounting periods beginning before 19 July 2006 and are repealed following the introduction of the regime for real estate investment trusts commencing for accounting periods beginning on or after 1 January 2007 (see 44.3 *et seq.* below).

Investment in residential properties by investment trusts is permitted. A property must have first been acquired after 31 March 1996, have subsequently been let on an assured tenancy, and must satisfy certain other conditions. In particular:

(i) the trust's interest must be either freehold or under a long lease (i.e. with at least 21 years remaining) at low rent (i.e. not more than £250 p.a. (£1,000 p.a. in Greater London));

(ii) the cost of the property (including construction, renovation or conversion costs and certain costs of related interests) must not exceed £85,000 (£125,000 in Greater London) (both figures variable by Treasury order);

(iii) the property must have been let without a lease premium and without an option to purchase being granted to the tenant (or an associate); and

(iv) the interest acquired by the trust must not have been subject to any letting or statutory tenancy other than a shorthold tenancy, and the trust must not have made any arrangements for letting, at the time of acquisition of the interest. Prior arrangements by CONNECTED PERSONS (19) of the trust are similarly excluded, except for certain arrangements for continuation of a shorthold tenancy.

Where a connected person has previously acquired the interest in the property, or another interest which that person continues to hold when the trust acquires its interest, the time at which the interest was first acquired by the connected person is treated as being the time when the interest was first acquired by the company.

Rents and other receipts deriving from such properties are '*eligible rental income*'.

Provided that these conditions are met, in addition to the normal capital gains exemption, profits chargeable in respect of eligible rental income ('*housing investment profits*') are chargeable at the small companies rate and are excluded from 'basic profits' (see 63.1, 63.2 SMALL COMPANIES—REDUCED RATES).

The provisions apply *mutatis mutandis* to Scotland.

[*ICTA 1988, ss 508A, 508B, 842(1)(a)(1AA); FA 2006, ss 143, 145, Sch 26, Pt 4*].

Simon's Direct Tax Service. See D4.422.

44.3 **REAL ESTATE INVESTMENT TRUSTS**

With effect for **accounting periods beginning on or after 1 January 2007**, a new regime enables listed, UK-resident, property companies which carry on 'property rental business' to opt to become real estate investment trusts (REITs). REITs must distribute at least 90% of net taxable profits on rental income to investors, withholding tax at the basic rate. Provided a company meets the eligibility criteria for a REIT, the qualifying profits and gains from the 'property rental business' will not be subject to corporation tax but profits on any other business will be subject to corporation tax at the full companies rate (whether or not the REIT otherwise qualifies for the small companies rate). To the extent that dividends paid by the trust derive from the 'tax-exempt' profits and gains they are taxed in the hands of the recipient as property income rather than as distributions. Companies wishing to enter the regime must pay an entry charge. [*FA 2006, ss 106, 107, 112, 119, 121, 122, 145, Sch 16; ITA 2007, ss 973, 974*].

44.4 **Property rental business.** *A 'property rental business'* is a business forming part of a Schedule A business or overseas property business (see 56 PROPERTY INCOME). However, the following type of business is not a property rental business:

- incidental letting of property (wherever situated) held in connection with a property trade;
- letting of property used for administrative purposes but temporarily not required for those purposes where it is let for a term of not more than three years and the space let is comparatively small compared to that occupied for administrative purposes;
- letting of property by one member of a group to another member or to a company the shares in which are 'stapled' to the shares of a group member, where the property is treated as owner-occupied in accordance with generally accepted accounting practice. The shares of one company are treated as '*stapled*' to those of another where the rights attaching to the shares of the one company contain terms that make it beneficial or necessary for those shares to be sold or acquired with the shares of the other company;
- provision of services in connection with overseas property where the services would not fall within Schedule A if provided in connection with a UK property;
- entering into structured finance arrangements in connection with factoring of rent and other income receipts (see 5.13 ANTI-AVOIDANCE).

A business is not a property rental business in so far as it gives rise to the following type of income or profits:

- income in connection with a caravan site treated as trading receipts under *ITTOIA 2005, s 20(1)*;
- rent in respect of an electric-line wayleave;
- rent in respect of the siting of a gas or oil pipeline or of a wind turbine;
- rent in respect of the siting of a mast or similar structure for use in a mobile telephone network or other system of electronic communication;
- dividends from shares in a company within the REIT regime;
- income from an interest in a limited liability partnership on a winding-up under *ICTA 1988, s 118ZA(4)*.

HMRC may, by order, amend the above exclusions.

[*FA 2006, s 104, Sch 16*].

44.5 **Qualifying conditions.** In order to qualify for REIT status, a number of conditions must be met by both the company and by the business activities of the company.

44.6 *Conditions for company*. A company may elect by notice for REIT status if it meets the following two conditions:

(*a*) the company is resident in the UK and not in another place in accordance with the tax laws of that other place;

(*b*) the company is not an open-ended investment company (see 43.2 INVESTMENT FUNDS);

The company must also meet the following four conditions throughout an accounting period to remain within the scheme in that period.

(i) The company is not a close company (see 16 CLOSE COMPANIES) or is so only by virtue that a limited partnership, which is a collective investment scheme (see 43.1 INVESTMENT FUNDS), is a participator of the company. For this purpose, a company will be treated as a close company even if prevented from being close by virtue of *ICTA 1988, ss 414(5), 415(4)(a)*.

(ii) There must be no more than one class of ordinary shares issued by the company and issued shares must either form part of the company's ordinary share capital or be non-voting fixed-rate preference shares (as set out in 21.13(b) CONTROLLED FOREIGN COMPANIES).

(iii) In the case of any borrowings, the interest payable to the loan creditor must not exceed a reasonable commercial return nor be contingent upon the results of all or any part of the company's business or on the value of any of its assets. On repayment of the loan, the creditor must not be entitled to an amount exceeding the amount lent, or if repayment is made by way of listed securities, the amount must be reasonably comparable with the amount generally repayable. However, a loan is not treated as dependent on the company's results only due to the interest under the contract being reduced if the results improve or being increased should the results deteriorate.

(iv) The company's ordinary share capital is listed on a recognised stock exchange.

Where a company breaches (i) and (iv) as a result of its becoming a member of a group, or another group, the REIT provisions will continue to apply. Where (i) is breached as the result of the actions of someone other than the company, the REIT provisions will continue to apply to the company provided the breach is corrected before the end of the next accounting period. If there is no such correction, the REIT provisions will cease to apply at the end of the accounting period in which the breach took place. In the case of a breach of (*c*) or (i) in any other circumstances, the REIT provisions cease to have effect from the end of the accounting period prior to that in which the breach took place.

A breach of condition (ii) will be disregarded if it takes place at the same time as a breach of condition (i) for calculating the number of breaches of condition (ii) and the total number of breaches. However the same rule does not apply when condition (i) is breached due to and at the same time as a breach of condition (ii).

The following further rules apply. Where a breach lasts for more than one but not two accounting periods, it shall count as one breach. Where a breach lasts for three consecutive accounting periods, it shall not be a minor breach.

[*FA 2006, s 106; FA 2007, Sch 17 para 2; SI 2006, No 2864*].

44.7 *Conditions for business.* In order to qualify for REIT status the company must have a property rental business (whether or not it has any other business) throughout an accounting period which qualifies as a 'tax-exempt business'. A property rental business qualifies as such if the conditions (*a*) to (*b*) below are met and if at least 90% of the profits of the property rental business (see 44.10 below) arising in an accounting period are distributed by way of dividend on or before the filing date for the company's tax return for the accounting period. The distribution condition does not apply to the extent it would be unlawful by virtue of a UK law or the law of a non-UK jurisdiction as prescribed by HMRC regulations for this purpose. Where part of a distribution has been withheld to avoid or reduce a tax charge which may be imposed if the REIT makes a distribution to investors with a shareholding of 10% or more (see 44.14 below), it will nevertheless count as having been made. Where the 90% condition is not satisfied, the REIT regime shall continue to apply, provided that MCT will be charged on an amount calculated as follows as if it were Sch D Case VI income:

P – D

Where P = 90% of profits of the rental business in the accounting period; and

D = total profits of the rental business distributed before the filing date for that accounting period.

However, no tax will be due if the company pays an additional dividend within three months of the date the final profits from the rental business for the period are finalised and the additional dividend means the distribution condition is met. Such a dividend must be ignored for calculating whether the condition has been met in any other accounting period. No deduction is permitted from the taxable amount for this purpose.

[SI 2006 No 2864 para 6].

In addition, the following conditions must be met throughout the accounting period.

(*a*) The property rental business must involve at least three properties. A property is treated as a single property if it is rented or available for rent as a commercial or residential unit separate from any other such unit (for example, a shop within a shopping complex or a flat within an apartment block).

(*b*) No one property is to have a value of more than 40% of the total value of all the properties involved in the property rental business.

A property involved in a business includes any estate or interest in land which is exploited in earning income for that business.

Other non-tax exempt business. The following conditions must also be met in relation to the proportion of a company's tax-exempt business relative to its other business.

(i) The 'profits' arising from the company's tax-exempt business in the accounting period must amount to at least 75% of the aggregate of the profits arising from that business and from any other business in that period. '*Profits*' in this case are those before deduction of tax as calculated in accordance with international accounting standards, excluding realised and unrealised gains and losses on property disposals and, excluding changes in the fair value of hedging derivative contracts (as defined) and amounts out of the company's normal business over its history, however they are treated in the accounts.

(ii) The value of the assets involved in the tax-exempt business at the beginning of the accounting period must be at least 75% of the total value of assets held by the company.

As regards the valuation of assets in (*b*) and (ii) above, they must be valued in accordance with international accounting standards and where the valuation can be made on either a cost or fair value basis, a fair value basis must be used. Any liabilities secured against or relating to the assets are ignored for this purpose.

Where conditions (i) or (ii) are not satisfied, the REIT regime will continue to apply provided, in the case of (i), the profits from the exempt business are at least 50% of the total profits for the accounting period and in the case of a breach of (ii), the assets of the tax exempt business are at least 50% of the total assets. This relaxation does not apply if the breach takes place in three consecutive accounting periods, in which case the breach is not minor. There must be no more than two breaches under each of (i) and (ii). *SI 2006 No 2864 reg 7* in a period of ten years beginning with the date of breach.

[*FA 2006, ss 107, 108, 114, 142, 144; SI 2006 No 2864; FA 2007, Sch 17 paras 3, 4, 9(b)*].

44.8 *Information requirements regarding breaches.* As soon as a company becomes aware it is in breach, it must supply details of the date, the requirement that was breached and the nature of the breach and any steps the company has taken to avoid the breach.

[*SI 2006/2864 reg 9*].

44.9 **Entry into the regime.** *Notice of entry.* A company can enter into the REIT regime from the beginning of an accounting period specified by written notice to HMRC before the beginning of that period. The notice must be accompanied by a statement by the company that the conditions set out in 44.6 above are reasonably expected to be satisfied throughout the specified accounting period. There is a facility for a new company seeking to qualify. Where the applicant is a close company, condition (i) in 44.6 above is not expected to apply on the first day of a new REIT's accounting period, as its shares will not have been listed and dealt in during the previous year. However, it is expected to be listed and dealt in for the rest of the accounting period. The notice must include a statement by the company confirming that conditions (*a*), (*b*), (ii) and (iii) have been complied with. HMRC may prescribe, by order any other information or documents to be given in or with the notice. Once a company enters the regime, it will remain with the regime until it ceases to be within the regime as a result of a termination event set out in 44.18 below. [*FA 2006, ss 109, 110; FA 2007, Sch 17 para 5*].

Effects of entry. On entry into the regime, the company's property rental business is treated as ceasing to exist at the point of entry and for corporation tax purposes, one accounting period ends immediately before entry and another begins on entry for the new, tax-exempt business. The assets involved in that business are treated for corporation tax purposes as sold immediately before the entry and reacquired immediately after the entry at their market value and any gains arising as a result are not chargeable gains. On any subsequent disposal (apart from one following an early exit from the regime – see 44.18 below) of such an asset (whether actual or deemed), that deemed consideration at market value is to be used as its base cost. For capital allowances purposes, the new business is treated as acquiring the assets at their written-down value as though the pre-entry business had not ceased. [*FA 2006, ss 105, 111, 141*].

Entry charge. On entry into the regime, the company is charged under Schedule D Case VI on a notional amount of income which is treated as arising in respect of the company's non tax-exempt business. The notional income is 2% of the aggregate market value of the assets treated as transferred to the tax-exempt business divided by the rate of tax applicable to the company's non-tax exempt business. No loss, deficit, expense or allowance may be set off against the notional income or tax charge.

The company can elect to spread the notional income over four years. In this case, the first instalment is treated as arising on the date of entry and the other three on the first three anniversaries of that date and, for this purpose, the percentage referred to above is 0.5% for the first instalment, 0.53% for the second, 0.56% for the third and 0.6% for the fourth instalment. The election must be given to HMRC with the notice for entry and is irrevocable. If the company ceases to be a REIT before the third anniversary of entry, any remaining instalments become chargeable immediately. The specified percentage rates may be amended by Treasury order (but not retrospectively) to reflect a change in interest rates.

[*FA 2006, s 112*].

44.10 **Calculation of profits.** The profits arising from the tax-exempt business (as calculated above) are not chargeable to corporation tax. Those arising from non-tax-exempt business are chargeable to corporation tax at the full companies rate. The small companies rate does not apply to REITs. [*FA 2006, s 119*].

For the purposes of attributing distributions (in 44.11(3) below) or determining whether the REIT meets the 90% distribution test (in 44.7 above) or the debt financing ratio (in 44.15 below), profits are calculated as follows.

The profits of a property rental business are calculated using the Schedule A rules in *ICTA 1998, s 21A* (see 56 PROPERTY INCOME) whether the profits relate to UK or overseas business. However, the exclusion for Schedule A purposes relating to debits and credits arising from loan relationships and derivative contracts does not apply in respect of loan relationships, certain embedded derivative contracts and certain hedging relationships entered into for the purpose of the tax-exempt business. Income and expenditure relating partly to tax-exempt business and partly to non-tax exempt business is to be apportioned on a reasonable basis. Any capital allowances available will automatically be taken into account in the calculation of profits of the tax-exempt business without the requirement for a claim under *CAA 2001, s 3*.

[*FA 2006, s 120; FA 2007, Sch 17 para 9*].

Ring-fencing and offset of losses. The new business is effectively ring-fenced and treated as a separate business distinct from the pre-entry business, any non-tax exempt business and the business after cessation of the regime ('the post-cessation business') (see 44.18 below). A loss incurred by the tax-exempt business cannot be set off against profits of any non-tax exempt business and vice versa. A loss incurred by the pre-entry business cannot be set off against profits of the tax-exempt business and a loss incurred by the tax-exempt business cannot be set against the profits of any post-cessation business. Receipts accruing after entry relating to the pre-entry business cannot be treated as receipts of the tax-exempt business. ('*Loss*' in this case also includes a deficit, expense, charge or allowance.)

For the purpose of calculating the amount of profits, *ICTA 1988, s 392B* is disapplied so that losses arising from an overseas part of the tax-exempt property business can be set off against the UK part of the business. Also for this purpose, the exemption from the transfer pricing rules for small and medium-sized enterprises (see 67.7 TRANSFER PRICING) does not apply to the company's exempt or non-tax exempt business.

[*FA 2006, ss 105, 113*].

44.11 **Distributions.** *Treatment of shareholders' dividends from REITs.* Distributions made from the REITs tax-exempt profits (including gains) are taxable on the shareholder (whether or not UK resident) under Schedule A in the case of a company chargeable to corporation tax or as profits of a UK property business in the case of a person other than a company chargeable to income tax.

A non-resident shareholder is not subject to taxation as a non-resident landlord in respect of the distributions. In the case of certain traders where distributions would normally be taxable under Schedule D Case I, such as financial traders and members of Lloyd's, the REIT distribution will continue to be taxable under those rules. '*Property income dividends*' (distributions from tax-exempt income of REITs, commonly known as 'PIDs') do not fall to be treated as property income for double tax treaty purposes. They derive from shares, therefore they are dividends and the dividend article applies. However, where a REIT pays a dividend, not derived from property income and with a one-ninth tax credit attached, no tax credit repayment claim may be made (as a UK shareholder would not be entitled to claim a repayment).

The property income treatment applies in the case of companies which are members of a partnership. A tax credit does not apply to these distributions. Distributions from one or more REITs are treated, in the hands of the shareholder, as the profits of a single business separate from any other Schedule A or UK or overseas property business. This applies equally, in the case of a shareholder which is a partnership, to receipts by a partner of a share of any distribution. Property income treatment continues to apply to distributions deriving from the profits of a tax-exempt business after a company has left the REIT regime. [*FA 2006, s 121*].

Deduction of tax. Where a REIT makes a distribution from its tax-exempt profits (including gains), the rules for the assessment, collection and recovery of tax are to be prescribed by Treasury regulations. In particular, the regulations may require the company to deduct income tax at source at the basic rate and may specify classes of shareholder to whom distributions can be made gross. The regulations may also contain detailed provisions for the calculation and payment of tax, claims and appeals, payment of interest, notices and returns, etc. The regulations may also apply to distributions deriving from the profits of a tax-exempt business after a company has left the REIT regime. Where part of a distribution has been withheld to avoid or reduce a tax charge which may, by regulation, be imposed if the REIT makes a distribution to investors with 10% or more of the company's dividends, share capital or voting rights, it will nevertheless count as having been made. [*FA 2006, ss 114, 122, 144; (ITA 2007, ss 973, 974*].

Attribution of distributions. In identifying which distributions derive from the REIT's tax-exempt property business (and which, therefore, are liable to deduction of tax at source and treatment as property income in the hands of the recipient), the distributions are to be attributed in the following order:

(1) payments made to meet the 90% distribution requirement in 44.7 above;

(2) distributions deriving from activities chargeable to tax in relation to income (excluding gains on capital assets) to the extent that the company may determine;

(3) distributions of profits of the company's property rental business (up to the amount of such profits not yet identified as having been distributed);

(4) distributions of gains arising from the tax-exempt business which, by virtue of 44.12 below, are not chargeable gains;

(5) other distributions.

[*FA 2006, s 123*].

Example

In its first period as a REIT a company has the following profits.

	£000
Tax-exempt business	
Net rental income	5,500
Less: capital allowances	(500)
Tax-exempt income	5,000
Tax-exempt gains on disposal of rental property	250
Non-exempt business	
Investment income	200
Gain on sale of fixed asset	150

The REIT distributes £5,500,000 in respect of that year's profits. This can be attributed to profits in the following ways.

A: Attributing as much as possible to tax-exempt business

		£000
90% distribution requirement	((1) above)	4,500
Balance of tax-exempt income	((3) above)	500
Tax-exempt gain	((4) above)	250
Other activities	((5) above)	250
		5,500

B: Attributing as much as possible to non-tax exempt business

		£000
90% distribution requirement	((1) above)	4,500
Investment income	((2) above)	200
Other income*	((2) above)	500
Profits of tax-exempt income	((3) above)	300
		5,500

* £500,000 is the difference between the tax measure of tax-exempt business income (£5m) and the accounting measure (£5.5m) represented by capital allowances. (See Explanatory Notes to Clause 123 of Finance (No 2) Bill 2006.)

Where a REIT distributes to a person with more than the maximum holding and it has not taken reasonable steps to avoid so doing, the company is treated as receiving an amount of income equivalent to

$$\left(DO \times SO \times \frac{(BRT)}{(MCT)}\right) + \left(DP \times SP \times \frac{(BRT)}{(MCT)}\right)$$

Where

DO = the total amount of the company's tax exempt profits distributed in respect of ordinary shares.

SO = is the lesser of

excessive shareholder's percentage interest; and

percentage interest of recipient of distributions.

BRT =the basic rate of time at the time of the distribution.

DP = the REIT's total tax exempt profits distributed in respect of preference shares.

SP = the lesser of the percentage of rights:

in respect of preference shares by the holder of the excessive rights; and

held by the distribution recipient in respect of which the distribution was made

MCT =the UK corporation tax rate on residual profits.

The amount arrived at is charged to corporation tax at the full rate under Sch D Case VI as if it were income of the REIT for the accounting period in which the distribution was made. No deductions may be made from the amount chargeable.

There are regulations requiring a REIT which makes a distribution to a holder of excessive rights to provide information to HMRC.

[*SI 2006 No 2864 reg 10,11*].

44.12 **Capital gains.** A gain arising on the disposal of an asset used wholly and exclusively for the purpose of a tax-exempt business is not a capital gain. Nor is an asset chargeable if it has been used partly for a tax-exempt business and partly for a non-tax exempt business during one or more periods which in aggregate amount to less than one year. Where an asset has been used partly for a tax-exempt business and partly for a non-tax exempt business during one or more periods which in aggregate amount to at least one year, the gain is not chargeable to the extent that it can reasonably be attributed to the tax-exempt business on the basis of the length of time and extent to which the asset has been used in each business. Gains arising in respect of the non-tax exempt business are chargeable to corporation tax at the full rate and the small companies rate does not apply.

Movement of assets out of ring-fence. An asset used wholly and exclusively for the purpose of the tax-exempt business which begins to be used (otherwise than by being disposed of in the course of a trade) wholly and exclusively in a non-tax exempt business is treated as disposed of by the tax-exempt business and immediately re-acquired by the non-tax exempt business for a consideration equal to the market value of the asset. On any subsequent disposal (apart from one following an early exit from the regime – see 44.18 below) of such an asset (whether actual or deemed), the deemed consideration at that market value is to be used as its base cost. This treatment excludes assets disposed of in the course of a trade (see below). For capital allowances purposes, the assets are not treated as having been transferred, the non-tax exempt business being treated as standing in the shoes of the tax-exempt business.

Where an asset which has been used wholly and exclusively for the purpose of the tax-exempt business is disposed of in the course of a trade for the purposes of the non-tax exempt business, there is no deemed sale and re-acquisition but the asset is treated as disposed of in the course of the non-tax exempt business. This applies in particular where a company develops property, where the cost of development exceeds 30% of the fair value of the property at entry or acquisition, whichever is the later, and where the property is disposed of within three years from the completion of the development. Where an asset held by the tax-exempt business at entry is disposed of in the course of a trade, the company can claim repayment of a proportion of the entry charge (at 44.9 above) relating to that asset. The proportion is the market value of the asset at entry divided by the aggregate market value of assets treated as sold and re-acquired on entry, ignoring any assets of negative market value.

Movement of assets into ring-fence. An asset used wholly and exclusively for the purpose of the non-tax exempt business which begins to be used wholly and exclusively in a tax-exempt business, is treated as disposed of by the non-tax exempt business and immediately re-acquired by the tax-exempt business for a consideration equal to the market value of the asset. For capital allowances purposes, the assets are not treated as having been transferred, the tax-exempt business being treated as standing in the shoes of the non-tax exempt business.[*FA 2006, ss 124–127, 141*].

44.13 **Disposal proceeds awaiting re-investment.** Where a company disposes of an asset used wholly and exclusively for the purposes of the tax-exempt business and holds the proceeds in 'cash', the proceeds will count as an asset of the tax-exempt business for the purpose of the 75% rule in 44.7(i) above for the period of 24 months from the date of the disposal. Any income derived from those proceeds is treated as income from the non-tax exempt business. Where the proceeds are used to enter into a loan relationship (such as a bank deposit) any profits or losses arising from that relationship (such as bank interest) is not treated as part of the profits of the tax-exempt business but are taxable under the loan relationship rules as arising in the non-tax exempt business. '*Cash*' in this case includes any currency held on deposit or gilt stocks or bonds or other investments as specified by HMRC regulations. Where the asset disposed of was used partly for the tax-exempt business and partly for the non-tax exempt business this provision applies to the proportion of the disposal proceeds that may reasonably be attributed to the tax-exempt business on the basis of the length of time and extent to which the asset has been used in each business. [*FA 2006, ss 118, 144*].

44.14 **Maximum shareholding.** A charge may be imposed, by Treasury regulation, on a REIT if it makes a distribution to or in respect of a person who is beneficially entitled (directly or indirectly) to 10% or more of the company's share capital or dividends or controls more 10% or more of its voting rights. [*FA 2006, s 114*].

44.15 **Debt financing.** The Treasury may make regulations for a tax charge to be imposed on a REIT that does not meet a minimum financing cost ratio. The charge may be imposed where, for an accounting period, the aggregate of the profits (see 44.10 above) from the tax-exempt property business (before the offset of capital allowances and losses brought forward from a previous accounting period) plus the finance costs in respect of that business divided by those finance costs is less than 1.25. (In other words, the debt finance must not exceed four times the amount of the profits, computed as indicated above.) Finance costs in this case include:

- debtor relationship debits other than those in respect of exchange losses from such relationships;
- exchange gains or losses from a debtor relationship in relation to debt finance;
- debits or credits arising from derivative contracts in relation to debt finance;
- financing costs arising under finance leases; and
- any other costs that under generally accepted accounting practice are considered to arise from a financing transaction.

Where the ratio of the REIT's financing cost ratio exceeds 1.25, the company is charged to corporation tax (MCT) on the difference between the financing costs and what those would have been had the 1.25 ratio been complied with, as income under Sch D Case VI to MCT. No deductions or reliefs may be set against these chargeable profits.

[*FA 2006, ss 115, 144; FA 2007, Sch 17 para 6; SI 2006, No 2864*].

44.16 **Minor or inadvertent breach.** The Treasury may make regulations to deal with minor or inadvertent breaches of the conditions for the company in 44.6(*c*) and (i) above and of the conditions for the business in 44.7 above. A company which has given notice of entry into the regime (44.9 above) must notify HMRC as soon as reasonably practicable if those conditions cease to be satisfied. The regulations may provide for the company to be removed from the regime at a specified time (which may be before the breach) or for the company to remain within the regime but with specified modifications. They may also provide for a tax charge and make provision by reference to the extent of a failure to satisfy a requirement or by reference to the number of requirements not satisfied or make provision in relation to anything done by the company or regarding any sum arising or treated as arising either after the regulations take effect, or in the calendar year in which they are made. They may limit the frequency with which a company may rely on the 'minor breach' provisions and may include tax avoidance provisions. This is subject to a termination notice being given under 44.18 below. [*FA 2006, ss 116, 144; FA 2007 Sch 17 para 7*].

44.17 **Cancellation of tax advantage.** If HMRC consider that a company has tried to obtain a 'tax advantage' under these provisions for itself or another person, they may, by notice to the company, counteract the advantage and assess the company to an additional amount of corporation tax under Schedule D Case VI equivalent to the value of the tax advantage. The tax advantage may be counteracted by adjustment by way of an assessment, amendment of a tax return, cancellation of a right of repayment or a requirement for the return of a repayment already made. A 'tax advantage' has the meaning given under (from 6 April 2007 *ICTA 1988 s 840ZA* (formerly *ICTA 1988, s 709*) and includes in particular entering into arrangements to avoid or reduce the entry charge under 44.9 above. A tax advantage does not, however, include benefits arising from the REIT regime unless the sole or main purpose of joining the regime is to create or inflate a loss, deduction or expense or to have another effect which may be specified by Treasury regulation. An appeal against a notice to cancel a tax advantage may be made to the Special Commissioners by written notice to HMRC within 30 days from the date of the notice to the company. [The Special Commissioners may quash the notice, confirm it or vary it].

[*FA 2006, ss 117, 144; FA 2007, Sch 17 para 8*].

44.18 **Leaving the regime.** *Termination by notice.* A REIT can give notice in writing to HMRC specifying a date (to be later than that on which HMRC receives the notice) at the end of which the REIT regime is to cease to apply to the company. [*FA 2006, s 128*].

HMRC may give written notification to a REIT that the regime is to cease to apply to it if:

(*a*) the company has relied on the minor or inadvertent breach provisions (see 44.16 above) on a 'specified' number of occasions in a specified period ('specified' meaning specified by Treasury regulations);

(*b*) the company has been given a specified number of notices in relation to the cancellation of a tax advantage in a specified period (see 44.17 above); or

(*c*) HMRC consider that the breach of the company conditions (see 44.6 above) or tax-exempt business conditions (see 44.7 above) or an attempt by the company to obtain a tax advantage is so great that it no longer qualifies for REIT status.

Such a notice must state the reason for the termination. The regime will cease to apply (subject to the early exit provisions below) at the end of the accounting period before that in which the event occurs (or the last event occurs) which caused HMRC to give the notice. Appeal against such a notice may be made to the Special Commissioners by notice in writing to HMRC within 30 days from the date on which the notice is given to the company.

[*FA 2006, ss 129, 144*].

Automatic termination. If any of the company conditions (*a*), (*b*), (ii) or (iii) in 44.6 above are not satisfied in an accounting period, the REIT regime is treated as ceasing to apply to the company at the end of the previous accounting period. A company which gave notice of entry, as set out in 44.9 above, must notify HMRC as soon as is reasonably practicable if any of those conditions cease to be satisfied. [*FA 2006, s 130*].

Effects of cessation. On leaving the regime, the company's tax-exempt business is treated as ceasing to exist immediately before the cessation and for corporation tax purposes, an accounting period of the non-tax exempt business ends on cessation and a new accounting period of the company (in respect of the '*post-cessation*' business) begins. The assets involved in the tax-exempt business immediately before cessation are treated for corporation tax purposes as sold immediately before cessation by the tax-exempt business and reacquired immediately after cessation by the post-cessation business at their market value. On any subsequent disposal (apart from one following an early exit – see below) of such an asset (whether actual or deemed), the deemed consideration at that market value is to be used as its base cost. For capital allowances purposes, the post-cessation business is treated as acquiring the assets at their written-down value as though the tax-exempt business had not ceased. [*FA 2006, ss 105, 131, 141*].

Effects of early exit. The following rule applies if the company leaves the REIT regime by notice and has been within the regime for a continuous period of less than ten years immediately before the cessation. Where the company disposes of an asset that was part of the tax-exempt regime within a period of two years beginning with the date of cessation, any deemed disposals that applied to that asset on entry to the regime (under 44.9 above), on transfer out of the ring fence (under 44.12 above) or on exit from the regime (as above), are ignored in calculating the gain on the disposal.

The following rules apply if the company leaves the REIT regime as a result of an HMRC termination notice or an automatic termination and has been within the regime for a continuous period of less than ten years immediately before the cessation. HMRC may direct that:

(i) the effects of a regime provision are modified. In particular, they may alter the time the company is treated as leaving the REIT regime as a result of the termination notice or automatic termination and they may disapply or alter the effect of the provisions which exempt the profits and gains of the REIT's property rental business from corporation tax;

(ii) the effects of other corporation tax provisions are applied, disapplied or modified, in particular to prevent all or part of a loss, deficit or expense from being set off or otherwise used at all or in a specified manner.

Appeal against such a direction may be made to the Special Commissioners, who may quash HMRC's direction, confirm it or vary it.

[*FA 2006, ss 132, 133; FA 2007, Sch 17 para 13*].

44.19 **Non-residents.** Double taxation treaties contain a variety of ways for dealing with dividends. It is necessary to consider in each case how the treaty provisions affect Property Income Dividends (PIDs). Details of any relief available to a resident of another country who is paid a PID can be found at http://www.hmrc.gov.uk/cnr/dtdigest.pdf. A claim must be made in respect of each dividend, but any number of PIDs may be included in each claim.

The first claim must first be sent for certification to the tax authority in which the claimant is resident. It should then be sent to HMRC. Subsequent claims should be sent direct to HMRC, unless the country of residence is Switzerland, in which case all claims must first be sent to the tax authority there for certification. Some country-specific claim forms will be issued in due course.

44.20 **Groups.** A group of companies may elect for REIT status and for that purpose, the REIT provisions apply to a group of companies as they do to a single company subject to the modifications set out in 44.21–44.33 below.

For this purpose a group includes a company ('the principal company'), its '75% subsidiaries' (as defined in *ICTA 1988, s 838*) and their 75% subsidiaries and so on. It does not include companies which are not 'effective 51% subsidiaries' (as defined in *TCGA 1992, s 170*) of the principal company nor does it include insurance companies or their subsidiaries or open-ended investment companies. Subject to provisions for joint ventures (see 44.36 below), a company cannot be a member of more than one group and if it would otherwise be, the group of which it is a member is to be determined by *TCGA 1992, s 170(6)*.

The no gain/no loss provision in *TCGA 1992, s 171* does not apply to disposals by or to a company within the REIT regime.

In relation to the following group reliefs, the tax-exempt businesses of the group members are treated as a separate group distinct from the pre-entry businesses of those companies, the non-tax exempt businesses and the post-cessation businesses:

- actual or notional transfers within a group under *TCGA 1992, ss 171, 171A*;
- reallocation of rolled-over gains within a group under *TCGA 1992, ss 179A, 179B*;
- group relief under *ICTA 1988, ss 402–413*;
- loan relationships under *FA 1996, Sch 9*;
- derivative contracts under *FA 2002, Sch 26*; and
- intangible fixed assets under *FA 2002, Sch 29*.

[*FA 2006, ss 105, 134–136*].

44.21 **Modifications relating to groups.** Except where indicated below, references above to a company are to be read as references to a group. Groups within the REIT regime are referred to below as REIT groups. References to a UK resident company are to a company resident in the UK and not in another jurisdiction by virtue of the tax laws of that jurisdiction. Reference to the UK profits of a group is to the amount shown in the financial statements of the group's property rental business as profits of UK resident members and as profits of the UK business of non-resident members. References to a UK business are references to the business of UK resident members and the UK business of non-resident members. For the application of the provisions to the activities of non-resident members of the group, see *FA 2006, Sch 17 para 32*. [*FA 2006, Sch 17 paras 1, 3, 4, 32*].

44.22 **Conditions.** *Conditions for principal company.* The conditions to be met by a company at 44.6 above to qualify for REIT status are to be read as references to a principal company of a group and that company must in addition prepare and submit to HMRC financial statements for the accounting period for:

(*a*) all the group's tax-exempt property rental business;

(*b*) the group's tax-exempt UK property business; and

(*c*) the group's other, non-tax exempt business.

The statements for (*a*) and (*c*) above must specify for each member, in accordance with international accounting standards, the income, expenses, profits before tax excluding gains or losses on property (whether realised or not) and assets valued at the beginning of the accounting period using fair value (where there is a choice) and ignoring liabilities secured against or relating to those assets. The statement in relation to (*b*) above must specify, for each member, profits calculated in accordance with 44.10 above. Where a subsidiary company is not wholly owned, the income, expenses, gains, losses, assets and liabilities of that subsidiary are to be reduced by the proportion of the subsidiary owned by non-group members. Further provisions in relation to the financial statements are contained in *SI 2006 No 2865*.

[*FA 2006, Sch 17 paras 2, 5, 31; FA 2007, Sch 17 para 16; SI 2006, No 2865*].

Conditions for business. The property rental businesses of the group members are treated as a single business.

With respect to the 90% distribution condition at 44.7 above, at least 90% of the 'UK profits' of the property rental business arising in an accounting period must be distributed by the principal company by way of dividend on or before the filing date for the principal company's tax return for the accounting period. '*UK profits*' for this purpose are those in the financial statements of the tax-exempt property rental business of the group's UK resident members. Compliance with the distribution condition is treated as unlawful to the extent it applies to the profits attributable to a member's property rental business and compliance by the member would be unlawful by virtue of a UK law or the law of a non-UK jurisdiction as prescribed by HMRC regulations for this purpose. Where part of a distribution has been withheld to avoid or reduce a tax charge which may be imposed if the principal company makes a distribution to investors with a shareholding of 10% or more (see 44.28 below), it will nevertheless count as having been made.

With respect to 44.7(*c*) above, for the purpose of determining owner-occupation, the reference to a company is treated as a reference to a group member. The members of a group are treated as a single company and if the shares of one group member are stapled to those of another company, that other company and the members of the group are treated as a single company.

With regard to the conditions in relation to the proportion of a company's tax-exempt business relative to its other business in 44.7(i) and (ii) above, the income and assets tests are applied to determine the balance of business between the group's tax-exempt business, based on the financial statements for (*a*) above, and the group's non-tax exempt business, based on the financial statements for (*c*) above.

[*FA 2006, Sch 17 paras 2, 6, 7, 13, 31*].

44.23 **Entry into the regime.** *Notice of entry.* The notice to enter the regime under 44.9 above must be given by the principal company. With respect to the requirement for the accompanying statement that the relevant conditions are reasonably expected to be satisfied in relation to the company throughout the specified accounting period, the reference to the company is to be treated as reference to the principal company. [*FA 2006, Sch 17 para 8*].

Effects of entry. The reference in 44.9 above to the pre-entry business of the company is to be read as a reference to the pre-entry business of a UK resident member of the group. The deemed disposal and re-acquisition of assets has effect in relation to each UK resident member and references to the pre-entry or tax-exempt business of the company is to be read as a reference to the company as a group member. The cessation of an accounting period before and the beginning of a new accounting period on entry applies to each UK resident member.

If a UK resident company becomes a member of a REIT group the effects of entry at 44.9 above apply to the company at the time it joins the group. References to the pre-entry business of the company are to be read as references to its business before it joins the group and references to the tax-exempt business of the company as references to the company as a member of the group's property rental business.

Where a subsidiary company is not wholly owned, and a proportion of the assets of a group member's property rental business are excluded from a financial statement (see 44.22 above), the excluded amount is to be ignored for the purposes of these provisions.

[*FA 2006, Sch 17 paras 9, 10*].

Entry charge. In applying the entry charge at 44.9 above, the rules apply to each member of the group and the notional income is treated as arising to each member of the group's non-tax exempt business. In determining the market value of assets treated as sold and re-acquired, where a subsidiary company is not wholly owned, and a proportion of the assets of a group member's property rental business are excluded from a financial statement (see 44.22 above), the excluded amount is to be ignored for this purpose.

For non-UK resident members of the group, the effects of entry apply to the UK property rental business carried on by them. The references to corporation tax is to be read as a reference to income tax under Schedule D Case VI. Reference to the rate at which the company pays tax on the notional income is to be read as a reference to the non-resident company's marginal rate of UK tax.

Where a company joins a REIT group, the entry charge applies to a company on joining a group as if it were entering into the REIT regime. In this case, reference to the non-tax exempt business of a company is to be read as a reference to the non-tax exempt business of the company as a group member.

[*FA 2006, Sch 17 para 11*].

44.24 **Calculation of profits.** The exemption from tax (at 44.10 above) applies to the tax exempt property rental business of UK resident members of the group and the UK property rental business of non-UK resident members. Where a subsidiary company is not wholly owned, and a proportion of the profits of a group member's property rental business are excluded from a financial statement (see 44.22 above), the excluded amount is to be treated for corporation tax purposes as profits of the member to the extent it is a member of the group's non-tax exempt business. [*FA 2006, Sch 17 para 17*].

Ring-fencing and offset of losses. The ring-fencing provisions in 44.10 above apply to the various parts of a REIT group as they do to the various parts of a REIT company. The provisions also apply in relation to each UK resident group member and for this purpose, the group member's business, in so far as it is a member of the group's tax-exempt property rental business, is treated as a separate business distinct from the business of the group member:

- before the group entered into the REIT regime or before the company joined the REIT group;

- in so far as it is a member of the group's non-tax exempt business; and
- after the group has ceased to be part of the regime or after the company has left the REIT group (see 44.31 below).

Accordingly, the losses of the tax-exempt part of a group are not available for offset against the profits of the non-tax exempt parts and vice versa.

Where a subsidiary company is not wholly owned, and a proportion of the profits of a group member's property rental business are excluded from a financial statement (see 44.22 above), the excluded amount is to be treated for corporation tax purposes as profits of the member to the extent it is a member of the group's non-tax exempt business.

[*FA 2006, Sch 17 para 12*].

44.25 **Distributions.** *Tax liability of the shareholder.* The provisions relating to distributions received by shareholders at 44.11 above relate to distributions made by the principal company in respect of the tax-exempt rental profits and gains of the group's UK resident members. The rules apply to distributions out of tax-exempt profits made by the principal company after the group leaves the regime just as they do to distributions from such profits made by a company after it leaves the regime. [*FA 2006, Sch 17 para 18*].

Deduction of tax. The provisions relating to the deduction of income tax from distributions at 44.11 above relate to distributions made by the principal company in respect of the tax-exempt rental profits and gains of the group's UK resident members. [*FA 2006, Sch 17 para 19*].

Attribution of distributions. The provision at 44.11 above dealing with the attribution of distributions applies to the principal company of a group and in identifying the part of the distribution relating to tax-exempt business, reference to the company's tax-exempt business is to a member of the group's tax-exempt property rental business. [*FA 2006, Sch 17 para 20*].

44.26 **Capital gains.** The provisions in 44.12 above relating to exemption from corporation tax on chargeable gains apply to each UK resident group member. For that purpose, references to the tax-exempt or the non-tax exempt business of the company are to be read as references to the group member to the extent it is a member of the group's tax-exempt or non-tax exempt property rental business. Where a subsidiary company is not wholly owned, and a proportion of the profits of a group member's property rental business are excluded from a financial statement (see 44.22 above), the excluded amount is to be treated for corporation tax purposes as profits of the member to the extent it is a member of the group's non-tax exempt business. With respect to transfers out of the ring-fence in relation to property developed by the company and sold within three years of completion, such property being treated as if it were never part of the tax-exempt business, reference to the company is a reference to the group member. [*FA 2006, Sch 17 paras 21, 22*].

44.27 **Disposal proceeds awaiting reinvestment.** The provisions in 44.13 above, regarding the treatment of funds retained following the disposal of an asset used in the tax-exempt business, apply equally to a REIT group, the references to tax-exempt and non-tax exempt business of a company being treated as references to the tax exempt property rental business and the other non-tax exempt business of the group. [*FA 2006, Sch 17 para 16*].

44.28 **Maximum shareholding.** A charge may be imposed, by Treasury regulation, on the principal company of a REIT group if it makes a distribution to or in respect of a person who is beneficially entitled (directly or indirectly) to 10% or more of the principal company's share capital or dividends or controls more 10% or more of its voting rights. [*FA 2006, Sch 17 para 13*].

44.29 **Debt financing.** The Treasury may make regulations for a tax charge to be imposed on a REIT group that does not meet a minimum financing cost ratio. The charge may be imposed where, for an accounting period, the aggregate of:

- the UK profits of the group's property rental business (see 44.24 above) as set out in the financial statement for the group's tax-exempt UK property business in 44.22(*b*) above (before the offset of capital allowances); plus
- all the financing costs in respect of that business (as set out in that financial statement),

divided by the external financing costs (excluding intra-group funding costs) in respect of the group's tax-exempt UK business as set out in the financial statement for all the group's tax-exempt property rental business (in 44.22(*a*) above) is less than 1.25.

See 44.10 above for what is included in financing costs.

[*FA 2006, Sch 17 para 14*].

Where the ratio of the REIT group's financing cost ratio exceeds 1.25, the principal company in the group is charged to corporation tax as income under Sch D Case VI to MCT on the excess of the external financing costs which exceed what they would have been had the 1.25 ratio been complied with. No deductions or reliefs may be set against these chargeable profits.

[*SI 2006 No 2864 reg 13*].

44.30 **Cancellation of tax advantage.** The provisions in 44.17 above apply equally to a REIT group member as they do to a single company REIT. An appeal to the Special Commissioners under those provisions may be made by the group member on which the assessment is made. [*FA 2006, Sch 17 para 15*].

44.31 **Leaving the regime.** *Termination by notice.* Notices in 44.18 above must be made by or to the principal company of the group and an appeal under those provisions may be made by the principal company. [*FA 2006, Sch 17 paras 23, 24*].

Effects of cessation. The provisions relating to the effects of cessation in 44.18 above apply in relation to each UK resident group member and for this purpose:

- a reference to the company's tax-exempt business is a reference to that group member in so far as it is a member of the group's tax-exempt property rental business;
- a reference to the company's non- tax exempt business is a reference to that group member in so far as it is a member of the group's non-tax exempt business; and
- a reference to the company's post-cessation business is a reference to that group member as a member of the group's post-cessation business.

If a UK resident company leaves the REIT group:

- a reference to the company's tax-exempt business is a reference to that group member as a member of the group's tax-exempt property rental business;
- a reference to the company's non-tax exempt business is a reference to that group member as a member of the group's non-tax exempt business; and
- a reference to the company's post-cessation business is a reference to that group member after it ceases to be a member of the group.

Where a subsidiary company is not wholly owned, and a proportion of the profits of a group member's property rental business are excluded from a financial statement (see 44.22 above), the excluded amount is to be ignored for the purpose of these provisions.

[*FA 2006, Sch 17 paras 25, 26*].

Effect of early exit. The provisions in 44.18 above relating to the effects of a company leaving the regime within ten years of joining apply to disposals by individual group members of assets of the group's tax-exempt property rental business. The provisions apply where a UK resident company ceases to be a member of the REIT group and where the group had been within the regime, or where the company had been a member of that group, for a continuous period of less than ten years. Where a group member disposes of an asset that was part of the group's tax-exempt property rental business within a period of two years beginning with the date on which the company ceases to be a group member, the deemed disposal provisions (set out at 44.18 above) are ignored in calculating the gain on the disposal. An HMRC termination notice or an automatic termination may relate to the group as a whole or to one or more members and may, in particular, alter the effects of the provisions relating to groups. An appeal against such notice or automatic termination may be made by the principal company. [*FA 2006, Sch 17 paras 27–29*].

44.32 **Demergers.** Where a REIT leaves a group it may, if it satisfies the conditions immediately after it leaves the group, give notice under *FA 2006, s 109* to HMRC by the day it leaves. It must specify in the notice an accounting period commencing on the day it leaves the group. It will qualify as a REIT from that date even if it does not expect to satisfy the conditions in paragraphs (i) to (iv) at 44.6 above throughout the first accounting period. The company has six months to qualify, during which it will be treated as a REIT. If it fails to satisfy all the conditions by the time six months has expired, it will be treated as if it had not been a REIT from the date it left the group.

The REIT must also show that:

(*a*) the property rental business includes at least three properties; and

(*b*) no one property represents 40% or more of the total value of the properties forming the property rental business.

Where there is a demerger, involving a REIT transferring a tax exempt asset to a 75% subsidiary and a subsequent disposal of that subsidiary by the REIT, and the subsidiary subsequently gives a notice under *FA 2006, s 109* specifying an accounting period commencing within six months of the date of transfer, the REIT provisions apply from the beginning of that accounting period. The purchasing company may give notice under *FA 2006, s 110* (as modified by *FA 2007*) even if conditions (i) to (iv) in 44.6 are not complied with throughout the period stated in the notice.

[*FA 2006, s 126A*; *FA 2007, Sch 17 paras 11, 16*].

Where there is a demerger, *FA 2006, ss 111, 112, 125* (as amended by *FA 2007, Sch 17* (see 44.9, 44.18 above)) do not apply.

44.33 **Takeovers.** If a company within the REIT regime becomes a member of a REIT group or if a member of a REIT group becomes a member of another REIT group, the provisions that would apply on entry into the regime including the entry charge (under 44.9 as modified by 44.23 above) and on leaving the regime (under 44.18 as modified by 44.31 above) will not have effect. [*FA 2006, Sch 17 para 33*].

44.34 **Penalties.** Penalties under *TMA 1970, s 98* will apply for failure to comply with:

- the requirement to provide a notice of a minor or inadvertent breach or with any requirements imposed by regulations in relation to such breaches under 44.16 above;
- requirements imposed by regulations in connection with deduction of income tax from distributions under 44.11 above;
- the requirement to provide notice of a breach of company conditions in relation to automatic termination under 44.18 above; and
- the requirement to meet the company conditions and for the principal company to send in financial statements as part of those conditions under 44.6 and 44.22 above.

An initial penalty will apply of to £300 and if the failure continues after this penalty has been imposed, a further penalty of up to £60 per day can be imposed for each day the failure continues.

[*FA 2006, s 140*].

44.35 **Administration.** When a company makes a distribution from its tax exempt business it must deduct tax at the basic rate in force for the year of payment under which the conditions for gross payment are made.

[*SI 2006 No 2867 regs 2,* 3].

Where a company in a group makes a distribution from tax exempt income, it must make a return by the nineteenth of the month for each calendar quarter, plus a fifth return to the accounting date if that does not fall on a calendar quarter. A reconciliation of the payments for the year has also to be delivered within 14 days of the accounting date, with the distributions attributed as to source as laid out in *FA 2006 s 123*. The tax deducted from the distribution must be paid over to HMRC, without assessment, with the same deadlines as for returns. The company has to give the recipient a dividend counterfoil showing gross, tax deducted and net amount paid.

No tax is to be deducted if the payee is a company resident or trading in the UK, a local authority, NHS Trust, public office or department of the Crown, charity or similarly treated body, the EIF, scientific research organisation, various pension funds, ISAs, CTF, PEP funds which are to apply the payment for permitted purposes or a partnership otherwise qualifying.

[*SI 2006 No 2867 regs 2, 4, 6, 7*].

HMRC has power to assess where it believes that tax due has not been paid.

[*SI 2006 No 2867 reg 9*].

44.36 **Miscellaneous provisions.** *Manufactured dividends.* Special provisions apply to dividends that represent payments of distributions of the tax-exempt profits of a REIT or principal company of a REIT group. [*FA 2006, s 139, Sch 17 para 30; ITA 2007 s 918*].

Charities. For charitable companies and REITs see 14.16 CHARITIES.

Joint ventures. Regulations have been made by the Treasury to apply the regime to a joint venture in which a REIT is involved. *SI 2006 No 2866* takes effect from 1 January 2007 and deals with property companies involved in joint ventures. There is a joint venture for this purpose if the venturing company (ie that giving the notice) and another company carry on a joint venture or a member of a group has a joint venture interest.

Where a venturing company is in a joint venture, a joint venture look through notice may be given by that company, if the following conditions are satisfied:

(*a*) the venturing company is carrying a joint venture with another person;

(*b*) the joint venture is carried on by a company;

(*c*) the joint venture company is carrying on a property rental business;

(*d*) the venturing company is beneficially entitled to 40% or more of the profits available for distribution;

(*e*) the venturing company is beneficially entitled to 40% or more of the assets on a winding up;

(*f*) the joint venture's property rental business does not involve owner-occupied property;

(*g*) the joint venture company would satisfy *FA 2006 s 108* Conditions 1 and 2 if references to the tax exempt business referred to the joint venture company's property rental business and as if references to the company were to the joint venture company.

For the purposes of (*f*) and (*g*) owner-occupied property includes property owned by the joint venture company and occupied by the venturing company. [*SI 2006 No 2866*].

Once notice has been given by a venturing company, it will continue until that company ceases to fulfil conditions (*d*) or (*e*) above as to entitlement to profits or assets. The venturing company's accounts are prepared in accordance with *SI 2006 No 2865*, as amended for the joint venture situation.

[*SI 2006 No 2866, regs 1–6; SI 2006 No 2865*].

The REIT rules as regards entry into the scheme and the corporation tax regime apply to the joint venture company. Similar treatment applies to groups of companies entering a joint venture.

Regulations to apply the REIT regime to joint ventures may take effect retrospectively.

[*FA 2006, s 138; FA 2007, Sch 17 para 14*].

45 Liquidation etc.

Cross-reference. See 60.2 RESIDENCE.

Simon's Direct Tax Service. See **D2.532.**

45.1 **INTRODUCTION**

Effect on group relationship. The passing of a resolution, or the making of an order, or any other act, for the winding-up of a company does not mean that a company (or any of its 75% subsidiaries) ceases to be a member of a group for the purpose of the capital gains provisions in *TCGA 1992, ss 171–181*, regarding which see 12.1 CAPITAL GAINS—GROUPS. [*TCGA 1992, s 170(11)*]. For other group purposes, e.g. group relief, such acts bring about the end of the group relationship, although the making of an administration order would not of itself bring about such a change. (ICAEW Guidance Note TR 799, June 1990).

45.2 **Release of debts.** The release does not give rise to a taxable receipt in the debtor company in relation to debts released as part of a statutory insolvency arrangement within the meaning of *ICTA 1988, s 834(1)* (or, for periods of account beginning before 1 January 2005, a voluntary arrangement under *Insolvency Act 1986* or a compromise or arrangement under *Companies Act 1985, s 425* (or NI equivalent)). [*ICTA 1988, s 94; FA 2005, s 80, Sch 4 paras 4, 8*)]. The creditor will obtain relief for a debt so released, provided that it is released wholly and exclusively for trade purposes. [*ICTA 1988, s 74(1)(j)* (as originally enacted), *ICTA 1988, s 88D; FA 2005, Sch 4 para 2*)].

45.3 **Vesting of company's assets in liquidator.** The vesting of a company's assets in a liquidator is disregarded for capital gains purposes and all acts of the liquidator in relation to those assets are treated as acts of the company. [*TCGA 1992, s 8(6)*].

Expenses of winding-up. All expenses properly incurred in a voluntary winding-up, including the remuneration of the liquidator, are payable out of the company's assets in priority to all other claims. [*Insolvency Act 1986, s 115*]. *Insolvency Rules 1986, Rule 4.218(1)* provides that expenses of a liquidation are to be paid out of the assets in the order of priority therein specified, subject to a discretionary power of the court under *Insolvency Act 1986, s 156* to vary the order where assets are insufficient to satisfy liabilities. [*SI 1986 No 1925, Rules 4.218(1), 4.220*]. Included in the normal order of priority is the amount of any corporation tax on chargeable gains accruing on the realisation of any asset of the company. [*Rule 4.218(1)(p)*]. Notwithstanding the specific inclusion of corporation tax on chargeable gains, corporation tax chargeable on a company's post-liquidation profits is to be treated as a 'necessary disbursement' of the liquidator (within *Insolvency Rules 1986, Rule 4.218(1)(m)*), and thus as an expense requiring priority as above (*Re Toshoku Finance UK plc, Kahn and another v CIR HL, [2002] STC 368*). (See, however, 46.9 LOAN RELATIONSHIPS for the provisions in *FA 1996, Sch 9 para 6A* (introduced by *FA 2002, Sch 25 para 25*) which prevent liability arising in the particular circumstances of this case for accounting periods beginning on or after 1 October 2002.)

45.4 **Profits arising in winding-up.** A company is chargeable to corporation tax on the profits arising in the winding-up of the company. [*ICTA 1988, s 8(2)*].

45.5 **CHARGE TO CORPORATION TAX IN FINAL AND PENULTIMATE YEARS**

Liquidation. Corporation tax is charged on the profits of a company arising in the winding-up in the financial year (i.e. a year to 31 March — see 1 INTRODUCTION AND RATES OF TAX) in which the affairs of the company are completely wound up (the final year) at the rate of corporation tax fixed or proposed for the previous financial year (the penultimate year), except that if, before the affairs of the company are completely wound up, the rate of corporation tax for the final year has been fixed or 'proposed', then that rate shall apply. Where the winding-up commenced before the company's final year, the company's profits arising in the penultimate year are charged at the rates applicable to that year. [*ICTA 1988, s 342(1)–(3)(8)*].

For the above purposes, the rate of corporation tax means the full rate or, if applicable, the small companies rate, and chargeable gains are reduced by the appropriate fraction where this applies. '*Proposed*' means by a Budget resolution. [*ICTA 1988, s 342(7)*].

An assessment on a company's profits for an accounting period falling after the commencement of the winding-up is not invalid because made before the end of the accounting period. The liquidator may determine beforehand an assumed date when the winding-up will be completed for the purpose of making an assessment for a period intended to end with the completion of the winding-up. A date so assumed will not alter the company's final and penultimate year, and if it falls short of the actual completion date, a new accounting period will commence from the assumed date and *ICTA 1988, s 12(7)* (length of accounting period after commencement of winding-up, see 45.6 below) will apply as if that new accounting period began with the commencement of the winding-up. [*ICTA 1988, s 342(4)–(6)*].

In the company's final accounting period, any income consisting of INTEREST ON OVERPAID TAX (40) is excluded from charge provided that it does not exceed £2,000. [*ICTA 1988, s 342(3A)*].

Crown priority was abolished with effect from 29 December 1986, except for sums due at the 'relevant date':

(*a*) on account of net tax deductions the company was liable to make under PAYE from taxable earnings paid during the twelve months before that date; and

(*b*) in respect of deductions required to be made in the twelve months before that date under the CONSTRUCTION INDUSTRY SCHEME (20).

The '*relevant date*' is:

(i) if the company is being wound up by the court, then:

  (*a*) if the winding-up order immediately follows the discharge of an administration order, the date of the administration order; or

  (*b*) if (*a*) does not apply, and the company had not commenced voluntarily to be wound up before the making of the winding-up order, the date of first appointment of a provisional liquidator or, if no such appointment has been made, the date of the winding-up order;

(ii) if (i) does not apply, the date of passage of the winding-up resolution.

[*Insolvency Act 1986, s 175, Sch 6*].

This remaining Crown priority was **abolished** by *Enterprise Act 2002, s 251* from 15 September 2003. [*SI 2003 No 2093*].

Corporation tax on chargeable gains is a 'necessary expense' of a winding-up within the meaning of *Companies Act 1985, s 560* (*Re Mesco Properties Ltd CA 1979, 54 TC 238*).

The Crown may set off a debt due **from** one Government Department to the company against a debt due **to** another Department (or other Departments) under *Bankruptcy Act 1914, s 312*. See *Re Cushla Ltd Ch D, [1979] STC 615* which involved a VAT repayment and liabilities to HMRC and the DSS (now the Department for Work and Pensions).

Administration. Where a company enters administration on or after 15 September 2003 when the *Enterprise Act 2002, s 248* came into force, corporation tax is charged on the profits arising in the administration in the financial year (i.e. a year to 31 March — see 1 INTRODUCTION AND RATES OF TAX) in which the 'relevant event' occurs (the 'final year') at the rate of corporation tax fixed or proposed for the previous financial year (the 'penultimate year'). If, however, the rate of corporation tax for the final year has been fixed or proposed (by Budget Resolution) before the 'relevant event', then that rate shall apply. Where the company entered administration before its final year, the profits arising in the penultimate year are charged at the rate applicable to that year. The rate of corporation tax for these purposes means the full rate or, if applicable, the small companies rate. The '*relevant event*' is the sending by the administrator of a notice under *Insolvency Act 1986, Sch B1 para 84(1)* (company moving from administration to dissolution) or, if the company entered administration other than under that *Act*, anything else done for a like purpose.

An assessment on a company's profits for an accounting period in which the company is in administration is not invalid because made before the end of the accounting period. In making an assessment after the company enters administration and before the relevant event, the administrator may act on an assumption as to the date on which an accounting period will end by reason of the occurrence of the relevant event. A date so assumed will not alter the company's final and penultimate year, and if it falls short of the actual date, a new accounting period will commence from the assumed date, and *ICTA 1988, s 12(3)* (see 2.4 ACCOUNTING PERIODS) will apply as if the company entered administration at the start of that new accounting period.

In the accounting period ending with the relevant event, any INTEREST ON OVERPAID TAX (40) is excluded from charge provided that it does not exceed £2,000.

[*ICTA 1988, s 342A; FA 2003, Sch 41 paras 3, 5(1)*].

45.6 ACCOUNTING PERIODS

On the commencement of a winding-up (being the passing by the company of a resolution for winding-up, the presentation of a successful petition for winding-up etc.), an accounting period ends and a new one commences. Thereafter an accounting period only ends on the expiration of twelve months from its beginning or by completion of the winding-up (but see 45.5 above). [*ICTA 1988, s 12(7)*].

Where a company enters administration on or after 15 September 2003 when the *Enterprise Act 2002, s 248* came into force, an accounting period ends immediately before the administration commenced, and another begins immediately thereafter (and if the company was being wound up at that time, *section 12(7)* is disapplied thereafter). [*ICTA 1988, s 12(7ZA); FA 2003, Sch 41 paras 1, 5*]. Previously, neither the filing of an administration order petition nor the making of an administration order would bring about the end of an accounting period. (ICAEW Guidance Note TR 799, June 1990).

45.7 CANCELLATION OF TAX ADVANTAGES

See *ICTA 1988, ss 703–709*, as described at 5.2 ANTI-AVOIDANCE.

46 Loan Relationships

Cross-references. See 4 ALTERNATIVE FINANCE ARRANGEMENTS, 37.8 INCOME TAX IN RELATION TO A COMPANY.

Simon's Direct Tax Service. See **D2.11, D2.18**.

Other sources. See HMRC Company Taxation Manual, CTM 50000 *et seq.* and HMRC Corporate Finance Manual.

The headings in this chapter are as follows.

46.1 INTRODUCTION

The rules for the taxation of loan relationships were introduced by *FA 1996, ss 80–105, Schs 8–15* with effect from 1 April 1996 to treat all profits and losses made by companies on debtor or creditor relationships as income items. These rules were substantially amended by *FA 2002, s 82, Sch 25* with effect for accounting periods beginning **on or after 1 October 2002** to assimilate the special rules applying to exchange gains and losses. Thus interest payments and discounts and premiums, including exchange gains and losses arising in accounting periods beginning on or after 1 October 2002, are generally taxed or relieved as income on an accruals basis or, in the case of capital movements for lenders, on a mark to market basis. Subject to certain prohibitions, the rules are designed to align with the way in which companies draw up their statutory accounts.

Amendments were also made, by *FA 2002, Sch 25* in particular, to the rules relating to connected parties and bad debts (see 46.9 below), and new provisions were introduced by *FA 2002, ss 71–78* to counter avoidance schemes. These provisions are described at 46.28, 46.37, 46.38 and 46.39 below, and have been made retrospective to have effect either for accounting periods ending, or for amounts paid or accruing, **on or after 26 July 2001**, or for accounting periods ending **after 19 December 2001**.

The language of the legislation was substantially changed by *FA 2004, s 52, Sch 10* (as amended) for the revised UK financial reporting standards for financial instruments based on the international accounting standards (IAS), adoption of which was mandatory for listed companies for periods of account beginning on or after 1 January 2005 (see 28.1 FINANCIAL INSTRUMENTS AND DERIVATIVE CONTRACTS). Thus, the loan relationship provisions no longer rely on the concept of the application of 'authorised accounting methods' as set out in *FA 1996, s 86* (see 46.31 below) but instead, loan relationship debits and credits are based on the profits of company accounts prepared in accordance with UK generally accepted accounting practice or international accounting standards. Accordingly, the terms '*authorised accruals basis of accounting*' and '*mark to market basis of accounting*' are no longer used. The legislation uses instead the broadly equivalent terms of 'amortised cost basis of accounting' (the actual cost as adjusted for cumulative amortisation and any impairment, repayment or release) and 'fair value basis of accounting' (amounts being determined at arm's length prices). The new provisions have effect for periods of account **beginning on or after 1 January 2005** and are referred to in this chapter as the 'post-2004 basis of computation'. [*FA 1996, s 103(1); FA 2004, s 52, Sch 10 para 17; FA 2005, Sch 4 para 50*].

Numerous amendments to the provisions were made by *FA 2005, F(No 2)A 2005* and *FA 2006* to take account of changes in accounting practice (see 46.7 below) and also to prevent certain avoidance schemes following disclosures made under the disclosure rules (see 5.26 ANTI-AVOIDANCE).

Trading items continue to be dealt with under Schedule D, Case I, and non-trading items are brought within Schedule D, Case III.

The pre-*FA 1996* rules, which previously applied to both corporate borrowers and lenders and individual investors, continue (subject to substantial modification and simplification) to apply to individual investors. For the modified income tax rules on discounts from 6 April 1996, see Tolley's Income Tax under Savings and Investment Income.

For various transitional provisions, see 46.47 below.

See also 28 FINANCIAL INSTRUMENTS AND DERIVATIVE CONTRACTS, over which the current provisions generally take priority.

46.2 TAXATION OF LOAN RELATIONSHIPS

All profits or gains arising to a company from 'loan relationships' are chargeable to corporation tax as income. To the extent that the company is a party to the relationship for trade purposes, the income is trading income. Otherwise, it is brought into account under Schedule D, Case III. See 46.3 below. Where interest is charged to tax as a trading receipt, this does not affect the requirement for deduction of tax by the payer (see 37.3(*b*) INCOME TAX IN RELATION TO A COMPANY). See Revenue Tax Bulletin August 1999 pp 685, 686.

For the treatment of deficits on 'loan relationships', see 46.3 below.

Unless otherwise specified, a charge or relief under these provisions precludes any other charge to or relief from corporation tax in respect of the same matter.

[*FA 1996, s 80*].

A company has a '*loan relationship*' wherever it is a creditor or debtor as respects any 'money debt' which arises from a transaction for the lending of money, i.e. any debt which is, under general law, a loan. For this purpose a debt is not taken to arise from such a transaction to the extent that it arises from rights conferred by shares in a company under which an entitlement to receive distributions may arise, and, for accounting periods beginning before 1 October 2002, the same applies as regards permanent interest bearing shares ('PIBS') issued by building societies (although only in respect of gains (and losses), which are therefore brought within the charge to corporation tax on chargeable gains, interest on PIBS being within the loan relationship rules). For accounting periods beginning on or after 1 October 2002, the loan relationship rules were extended to include all building society shares, and thus to profits and losses on PIBS. Subject to this, a debt is taken to arise from such a transaction where an instrument is issued by any person for the purpose of representing security for, or the rights of a creditor in respect of, the debt. 'Loan relationship' thus includes gilt-edged securities, corporate bonds, overdrafts and other corporate debt, but not trade debts (although see 46.46 below as regards interest on such debts, and also as regards other specific exclusions) and profits or gains on certificates of deposit (HMRC Inspector's Manual, IM 4602). Certain types of interest or imputed interest which do not arise from a loan relationship are treated as if they did so as regards interest credits and debits (see 46.46 below). For the circumstances in which a capital grant may be considered a loan relationship, see HMRC Company Taxation Manual, CTM 51210.

A '*money debt*' is a debt falling to be settled by:

(*a*) payment of money;

(*b*) the transfer of a right to settlement under a debt falling to be so settled; or

(*c*) in relation to loan relationships to which a company is a party **after 21 March 2006**, the issue or transfer of any shares in any company (mandatory convertibles).

For accounting periods beginning after 30 September 2002, the settlement as above may be at the option of the debtor or creditor and any other option exercisable by either party is to be disregarded. This reverses the decision in *HSBC Life (UK) Ltd v Stubbs and related appeals (Sp C 295) 2001, [2002] SSCD 9* in which certain financial futures contracts entered into with derivatives dealers, involving both an option for cash settlement and one for settlement in a non-cash form, were held not to constitute loan relationships.

As regards (*c*), where, by virtue of this provision, a relationship becomes a loan relationship on or after 22 March 2006 and an asset representing the creditor relationship was, immediately before that date, a chargeable asset under the capital gains rules, the asset is treated as having been disposed of at its fair value immediately before that date. Any chargeable gain or allowable loss on the deemed disposal is treated as accruing to the company when it ceases to be a party to the loan relationship.

[*FA 1996, ss 81*(*1*)–(*4*)*, 103*(*1*)*; FA 2002, s 82, Sch 25 paras 2, 14; FA 2006, Sch 6 para 10*].

ALTERNATIVE FINANCE ARRANGEMENTS (4) entered into on or after 6 April 2005 are treated as loan relationships. This is subject to commencement rules for arrangements entered into before that date where a profit share return is payable on or after that date. [*FA 2005, s 50*(*3*)].

For these purposes, any payment or interest in pursuance of any of the rights or liabilities under a loan relationship, or under the agreement(s) by virtue of which the relationship exists (including a security representing the relationship), are treated as made or payable under that relationship. 'Money' is not restricted to sterling. [*FA 1996, s 81*(*5*)(*6*)].

See also 46.46 below regarding the treatment of the loan relationship as continuing where provisions continue to be made on an amortised cost basis (where the pre-FA 2004 basis of computation applies, on an accruals basis, see 46.1 above) after a company ceases to be a party to a loan relationship.

Simon's Direct Tax Service. See **D2.1102–D2.1104, D2.1801** *et seq.*

46.3 **Charge to, and relief from, tax.** The credits or debits for an accounting period in respect of any loan relationship (computed as described at 46.5 *et seq.* below) are brought into account as follows.

(*a*) Where the loan relationship is for trading purposes, they are treated as receipts or expenses of the trade for that period (in the case of expenses, notwithstanding *ICTA 1988, s 74* (allowable deductions)). (This does not affect the requirement for deduction of tax by the payer (see 37.3(*b*) INCOME TAX IN RELATION TO A COMPANY), see Revenue Tax Bulletin August 1999 pp 685, 686.)

(*b*) Where there are credits and/or debits in respect of a non-trading relationship, they are aggregated, and the net amount is chargeable under Schedule D, Case III or relievable as a non-trading deficit (see below) as the case may be.

[*FA 1996, s 82*].

For a creditor company, a loan relationship is taken to be for trade purposes only if it is a party to the relationship in the course of activities forming an integral part of that trade.

Non-trading deficits: accounting periods beginning before 1 October 2002

Relief for all or part of a non-trading deficit of an accounting period (the '*deficit period*') may be claimed either:

(i) by set-off against profits of the same period; or

(ii) by group relief under *ICTA 1988, s 403ZC* (see 32.6 *et seq.* GROUPS OF COMPANIES); or

(iii) by carry-back and set-off against profits of earlier accounting periods falling within the twelve months immediately preceding the deficit period, arising from non-trading loan relationships; or

(iv) by carry-forward and set-off against non-trading profits (i.e. profits exclusive of trading income) for the next accounting period.

Claims must be made within two years of the end of the deficit period (or, in the case of a claim under (iv) above, the next following accounting period), or within such further period as HMRC may allow.

See below for the detailed rules on such claims. Different claims may be made as respects different parts of a non-trading deficit, but not so as to give relief more than once.

Any part for which relief is not so claimed is carried forward and treated as a deficit of the next accounting period, in respect of which, however, relief may only be claimed for that period under (iv) above (and the deficit brought forward is disregarded for the purposes of any claim under (iv) above relating to a deficit arising in that next accounting period).

Where, however, the company is established for *charitable purposes* only, no relief may be claimed for a non-trading deficit under (i)–(iv) above.

A claim under (i) above is given effect after relief for brought forward trading losses, but before relief under *ICTA 1988, s 392A(1)* or *s 393A(1)* (losses relieved against profits of current or earlier accounting periods, see 47.2, 47.6 LOSSES, 56 PROPERTY INCOME) or under (iii) above. Relief against oil companies' ring-fenced profits is prohibited.

A claim under (iii) above must exclude any amounts claimed under (i) or (ii) above. Relief is given for later accounting periods before earlier ones. Profits of an accounting period straddling the start of the twelve month period immediately preceding the deficit period are apportioned for this purpose. Relief is given after any relief under (i) or (ii) above and after any relief for losses or deficits of accounting periods before the deficit period, for trade charges, for trading losses of the same or subsequent periods, or, for companies with investment business (or for accounting periods beginning before 1 April 2004, investment companies) (42 INVESTMENT COMPANIES AND INVESTMENT BUSINESS), for plant and machinery capital allowances, management expenses or business charges.

Non-trading deficits: accounting periods beginning on or after 1 October 2002

With effect for accounting periods beginning on or after 1 October 2002, separate claims are no longer required for group relief or to carry forward a deficit as noted below, and non-trading debits and credits on derivative contracts (see 28.9 FINANCIAL INSTRUMENTS AND DERIVATIVE CONTRACTS) are treated as non-trading debits and credits on loan relationships.

A non-trading deficit of an accounting period (the '*deficit period*') may be claimed, to the extent not already surrendered as group relief (under *ICTA 1988, s 403*, see 32.6 *et seq.* GROUPS OF COMPANIES), either:

(A) by set-off against profits of the deficit period; or

(B) by carry-back and set-off against profits of earlier accounting periods arising from non-trading loan relationships.

Any non-trading deficit for which relief is not claimed under (A) or (B) above, or surrendered as group relief, is carried forward and set against non-trading profits for succeeding accounting periods. The carried forward non-trading deficit is set against the non-trading profits of the accounting period immediately following the deficit period. This is subject to a claim for any amount of that deficit to be excepted from being set against non-trading profits of the accounting period immediately following the deficit period in which case it is treated as a non-trading deficit of that accounting period to be carried forward for offset against non-trading profits of succeeding accounting periods. (Such a claim may be made, for example, to allow for any double taxation relief to be used that would otherwise be wasted.)

Where a company is established for *charitable purposes* only, no relief is available or may be claimed for a non-trading deficit.

Claims under (A) and (B) above must be made within two years of the end of the deficit period or within such further period as HMRC may allow. A claim for a part or the whole of the deficit to be treated as a non-trading deficit of the immediately following accounting period, to be carried forward for offset against non-trading profits of succeeding accounting periods, must be made within two years of the end of that period.

A claim under (A) above is given effect after relief for brought forward trading losses, but before relief under *ICTA 1988, s 392A(1)* or *s 393A(1)* (losses relieved against profits of current or earlier accounting periods, see 47.2, 47.6 LOSSES, 56 PROPERTY INCOME) or under (B) above. Relief against oil companies' ring-fenced profits is prohibited. Different claims may be made as respects different parts of a non-trading deficit, but not so as to give relief more than once.

A claim under (B) above must exclude any amount claimed under (A) above or surrendered as group relief. Only profits for the accounting periods (or parts) falling within a twelve-month period immediately preceding the deficit period may be relieved and relief is given for later accounting periods before earlier ones. Profits of an accounting period straddling the start of the twelve-month period are apportioned for this purpose on a time basis unless this would produce an unjust or unreasonable result, in which case it is made on a just and reasonable basis. Relief is given after any group relief or relief under (A) above and after any relief for losses or deficits of accounting periods before the deficit period, for trade charges, for trading losses of the same or subsequent periods, or, for companies with investment business (or, for accounting periods beginning before 1 April 2004, investment companies) (42 INVESTMENT COMPANIES AND INVESTMENT BUSINESS), for plant and machinery capital allowances, management expenses or business charges.

Deficit brought forward from previous regime

Any amount of non-trading deficit carried forward under *FA 1996, s 83(3)* from an accounting period beginning before 30 September 2002 to an accounting period beginning on or after that date may not be set against anything other than non-trading profits.

[*FA 1996, ss 83, 103(2), Sch 8; FA 2002, Sch 25 paras 3, 17–19, 61A, Sch 26 para 14; FA 2003, Sch 37 para 6; SI 2004 No 2310, Article 50*].

Simon's Direct Tax Service. See **D2.1135, D2.1136, D2.1860** *et seq.*

46.4 *Examples*

(A) Loan relationship for trading purpose

A Ltd requires additional trade finance, and on 1 January 2007 enters into an agreement with Bank plc to borrow £100,000 for three years. Interest at 6% p.a. is payable at six-month intervals commencing 1 July 2007. Legal fees and other professional costs in relation to the loan amount to £2,800, paid in December 2006. The company's accounting reference date is 31 March, and it adopts an authorised accruals basis of accounting for all its loan relationships.

A Ltd's accounts for the year ended 31 March 2007 show the following:

	£	£
Turnover		1,400,000
Purchases and expenses (all allowable for tax purposes)	900,000	
Finance charges		
Bank plc interest to 31 March 2006	1,500	
Legal fees etc.	2,800	
Depreciation*	120,000	1,024,300
Net profit per accounts		£375,700

* Capital allowances for the year are £95,000.

A Ltd's corporation tax computation for the same period is as follows.

	£
Net profit per accounts	375,700
Add: Depreciation	120,000
Less: Capital allowances	(95,000)
Corporation tax adjusted profit	£400,700

The accrued interest on the bank loan taken for trading purposes will be treated for corporation tax purposes as a trade expense.

The profit and loss charge for each relevant accounting period will be as follows.

Year ended	31.3.07	31.3.08	31.3.09	31.3.10
	£	£	£	£
Expenses	2,800	—	—	—
Interest payable	1,500	6,000	6,000	4,500

This conforms to the authorised accruals basis of accounting (and the amortised cost basis), as interest will be allocated to the period to which it relates.

(B) Loan relationship for non-trading purpose

T Ltd, a trading company, bought £10,000 nominal of gilt-edged securities at £94 per £100 nominal stock as a speculative venture on 1 January 2006. The securities will be redeemed on 1 January 2009 at par. Interest at 5% is payable annually on 31 December. The company uses the authorised accruals basis of accounting for all its loan relationships. The accounting reference date is 31 March.

As the purchase does not relate to the company's trade, the income will be assessed under Schedule D, Case III. In addition to the interest, the company will be taxable on the discount, spread over three years.

Year ended	31.3.06	31.3.07	31.3.08	31.3.09
	£	£	£	£
Interest received	125	500	500	375
Discount	50	200	200	150
Schedule D, Case III	175	700	700	525

(C) Non-trading deficit on a loan relationship

C Ltd, which is not a member of a group, made a loan to X Ltd, outside its normal trading activities. X Ltd defaults on the loan on 1 October 2006, leaving a balance of £8,500 due to C Ltd. The accounting reference date is 31 March.

C Ltd's computations for relevant years are as follows.

Year ended	31.3.05	31.3.06	31.3.07	31.3.08
	£	£	£	£
Schedule D, Case I	10,000	11,000	800	12,000
Schedule D, Case III (non-trading loan relationships)	2,000	2,000	100	400

The £8,500 debit is set against the non-trading loan relationship credit of £100 in the year ending 31 March 2007, and the remaining deficit of £8,400 may be relieved in whole or in part in three different ways (group relief not being available), as follows.

	£
Non-trading deficit	8,400
(1) Set against total profits for year ended 31 March 2007	(800)
(2) Carry back against Schedule D, Case III profits from non-trading loan relationships of the preceding accounting period	(2,000)
(3) Carry forward and set against non-trading profits for year ended 31 March 2008	(400)
Net deficit to carry forward against subsequent non-trading profits	£5,200

46.5 **COMPUTATION OF DEBITS AND CREDITS**

The credits and debits to be brought into account by a company in respect of its loan relationships are sums which, when taken together, fairly represent, for the accounting period in question:

(*a*) all profits, gains and losses (capital or otherwise) which (disregarding interest and any charges or expenses) arise to the company from its loan relationships and 'related transactions'; and

(*b*) all interest under its loan relationships and all charges and expenses incurred under, or for the purposes of, those relationships and transactions.

Subject to *FA 1996, Sch 9 para 15* (see 46.25 below), a '*related transaction*' is any disposal or acquisition (in whole or part) of rights or liabilities under a relationship. This includes the transfer or extinguishment of any such rights or liabilities by any sale, gift, exchange, surrender, redemption or release. Certain transfers under *Proceeds of Crime Act 2002, Pt 5*, known as 'Pt 5 transfers' (by which property obtained through unlawful conduct is vested in an appointed trustee for civil recovery), which would otherwise be 'related transactions', are, however, disregarded for this purpose except for the purpose of identifying the person for whom debits or credits not related to the transfer are to be brought into account.

Charges and expenses within (*b*) above include only those incurred directly:

(i) in bringing any of the loan relationships into existence;

(ii) in entering into or giving effect to any of the related transactions;

(iii) in making payments under any of the relationships or in pursuance of any of the related transactions; or

(iv) in taking steps for ensuring the receipt of payments under any of the relationships or in pursuance of any of the related transactions.

They do, however, include charges and expenses connected with entering into, or giving effect to any obligation under, a prospective loan relationship or related transaction into which the company has not entered at the time they are incurred. See HMRC Corporate Finance Manual, CFM 5210 for examples of the expenses allowed.

[*FA 1996, s 84; FA 2002, Sch 25 para 4; FA 2004, Sch 10 para 1*].

Costs directly incurred in varying the terms of a loan relationship may be brought into account as a debit under *FA 1996, s 84*. Guarantee fees are excluded unless the loan would not have been advanced without the provision of a guarantee, but may be allowable as trading deductions where incurred wholly and exclusively for trade purposes and not in respect of capital. (HMRC Company Tax Manual CT 12369 and HMRC Corporate Finance Manual CFM 5210 onwards).

Simon's Direct Tax Service. See **D2.1115-D2.1117, D2.1820.**

46.6 **Exchange gains and losses.** With effect for accounting periods beginning *on or after 1 October 2002*, the reference to profits, gains and losses arising to a company from its loan relationships includes a reference to exchange gains and losses. However, exchange gains or losses will not be brought into account as credits or debits where the post-FA 2004 basis of computation applies (see 46.1 above), if they are recognised in the company's statement of recognised gains and losses or statement of changes in equity having arisen:

(*a*) on an asset or liability representing a loan relationship of the company; or

(*b*) as a result of the translation from one currency to another of the profit or loss of part of the company's business.

Where the pre-FA 2004 basis of computation applies (see 46.1 above), the legislation states that such exchange gains and losses are disregarded where they are carried to or sustained by a company reserve in accordance with generally accepted accounting practice.

The Treasury has the power to vary these provisions by regulation to meet the circumstances of particular cases and to determine whether exchange gains and losses should be disregarded or whether to bring back into account, either as debits or credits within the loan relationship rules or as chargeable gains or losses within *TCGA 1992*, amounts of any gains or losses which have been deferred by virtue of these provisions. Such regulations allow certain deferred exchange gains and losses to be brought into account, either where they are taken to reserves and set off against amounts arising on assets in accounting periods beginning on or after 1 October 2002 or where they were deferred under the matching regulations for accounting periods beginning before 1 October 2002.

Regulations provide for the following.

(i) Transitional provisions in respect of the change of tax treatment of exchange gains and losses on the assimilation of the foreign exchange gains and losses rules into those for loan relationships. [*SI 2002 No 1969*].

(ii) The bringing into account of amounts, in relation to accounting periods beginning on or after 1 October 2002:

- relating to assets representing certain loan relationships and ships or aircraft;
- where the disposal is a no gain/no loss disposal under *TCGA1992*;
- where there is no *TCGA 1992* disposal of the asset by virtue of *TCGA 1992, s 116(10)* (reorganisations, conversions and reconstructions involving qualifying corporate bonds);
- where there is no *TCGA 1992* disposal of the asset by virtue of *TCGA 1992, s 127* (equation of original shares and new holding);
- where *TCGA 1992, s 127* applies, or would apply but for *TCGA 1992, s 116*, in relation to a transaction involving original shares which are or include certain assets; or
- where exchange gains or losses have fallen within *FA 1996, s 84A(4)* (where carried to or maintained in reserves in accordance with generally accepted accounting practice).

[*SI 2002 No 1970* (as amended by *SI 2004 No 3259* with effect for periods of account beginning on or after 1 January 2005 to reflect the changes in the matching rules for foreign currency liabilities made by *FA 2004* for companies adopting international accounting standards, and further amended with effect from 11 August 2005 by *SI 2005 No 2013*)].

(iii) For periods of account beginning on or after 1 January 2005, the calculations to determine the exchange gain or loss, and any residual profit or loss, arising from certain loan relationship assets or liabilities used to hedge exchange risks and accounted for using fair value accounting. Broadly, the exchange gain or loss is based on the company accounts to the extent the change in fair value is attributable to the spot rate of exchange between the currency in which the asset or liability is denominated and the base currency of the company. Where a fair value profit is not wholly attributable to an exchange gain or loss, the residual profit is the profit less the exchange gain or plus the exchange loss. Similarly, in the case of a fair value loss, the residual loss is the loss plus the exchange gain or less the exchange loss. [*SI 2005 No 3422*].

(iv) Exchange gains or losses arising from liabilities or assets hedging shares etc. to be disregarded in certain cases where the contract is matched with shares, ships or aircraft. The regulations also provide specific rules in relation to matching. They have effect for periods of account beginning on or after 1 January 2005 (amendments having effect for periods of account beginning on or after that date and ending after, in the case of *SI 2005 No 2012*, 11 August 2005, in the case of *SI 2005 No 3374*, 29 December 2005). [*SI 2004 No 3256, regs 3, 5* (the 'Disregard Regulations') (as amended by *SI 2005 No 2012, regs 4, 6, SI 2005 No 3374, regs 3, 4, 6, SI 2007 No 948*)].

(v) The disallowance of exchange losses where arrangements within a group are such that the group can choose whether or not to recognise an exchange gain or loss because of its ability to meet obligations under a loan relationship by settling in alternative currencies. (Such arrangements rely on exchange movements which can result in a loss but no corresponding gain.) The regulations have effect for accounting periods ending on or after 22 March 2006 unless the company ceased to be a party to the loan relationship before that date. [*SI 2006 No 843*].

The above provisions under *FA 1996, s 84A* will cease to have effect from a date to be appointed by Treasury order which may contain appropriate savings and transitional provisions. (This is largely due to conflicts with *SI 2004 No 3256* (the 'Disregard Regulations') and thus the repeal of the provisions below and the laying of further secondary legislation is provided for by *F(No 2)A 2005, Sch 6 para 9.*)

An '*exchange gain or loss*' is defined as a profit, gain or loss arising as a result of comparing at different times the expression in one currency of the whole or some part of the valuation put by the company in another currency on an asset or liability representing a loan relationship of the company. The Treasury may provide by regulation the manner in which exchange gains or losses, or other profits, gains or losses, are computed where the company uses fair value accounting. Any such regulations may apply to periods of account beginning before the regulations are made but not earlier than the beginning of the calendar year in which they are made.

For accounting periods beginning *before 1 October 2002*, without prejudice to the special EXCHANGE GAINS AND LOSSES (26) provisions, any accounting requirement for currency translation or conversion, under which sums reflecting currency gains or losses are included in credits or debits, is disregarded.

[*FA 1996, ss 84A, 103(1A)(1AA)(1B), Sch 9 para 4; FA 2002, s 79, Sch 23 paras 3, 7; FA 2004, Sch 10 para 2; FA 2005, s 80, Sch 4 para 29; F(No 2)A 2005, Sch 6 paras 4(4)(6), 9, 10; Sch 11 Pt 2(6)*].

For special provisions (which apply until a date to be determined by statutory instrument for introduction of the new repo regime – see 5.5 ANTI-AVOIDANCE) for the bringing into account as loan relationship debits or credits of exchange gains and losses on a sale and repurchase of securities to which *ICTA 1988, s 730A* applies (see 5.6 ANTI-AVOIDANCE), which have effect where the agreement to sell the securities was made on or after 9 April 2003, see *ICTA 1988, s 730BB* (introduced by *FA 2003, Sch 38 paras 11, 12*) and the Revenue Tax Bulletin August 2003 pp 1052–1053.

46.7 **Generally accepted accounting practice.** Where the post-FA 2004 basis of computation applies (see 46.1 above), the loan relationship debits and credits to be brought into account for these purposes are those 'recognised in determining the company's profit or loss' for the period in accordance with generally accepted accounting practice. This is subject to the any other provision of the loan relationship rules, in particular the computation of debits and credits in 46.5 above. If a company does not draw up its accounts in accordance with generally accepted accounting practice, or does not draw up accounts at all, the amounts to be brought into account are those that would be recognised had the company done so. This applies equally to amounts derived from earlier periods for which accounts were not drawn up in accordance with generally accepted accounting practice.

Amounts in this case that are '*recognised in determining the company's profit or loss*' are amounts recognised (including prior-year adjustments apart from corrections of fundamental errors) in the company's profit and loss account or income statement, in its statement of recognised gains and losses or statement of changes in equity, or in any other statement of items brought into account in determining the company's profits and losses for that period. In the case of amounts recognised in the company's statement of recognised gains and losses or statement of changes in equity where the debit or credit represents a prior year adjustment, *SI 2004 No 3271* defers such debits and credits (see below under change of accounting practice).

See *SI 2004 No 3256* ('the Disregard Regulations') (as amended by *SI 2005 No 2012* and *SI 2005 No 3374*) which provide for certain profits and losses from loan relationships arising from changes in fair value of certain derivative contracts (hedging contracts, including embedded derivatives within host loan relationships) to be disregarded for tax purposes when recognised in the accounts, and in some cases, to be brought back into account when the contract matures or is disposed of. The regulations have effect for periods of account beginning on or after 1 January 2005 to take account of the use of fair value accounting by companies on their adoption of international accounting standards. (The amendments have effect for periods of account beginning on or after that date and ending after, in *SI 2005 No 2012*, 11 August 2005, in the case of *SI 2005 No 3374*, 29 December 2005.) A company can elect out of the Disregard Regulations (thus not disregarding fair value movements) if it wishes to follow the accounts. The time limit for such elections was initially set at before the start of a company's first accounting period beginning on or after 1 January 2005 or, if later, 31 March 2005. However, the deadline has been extended to before 1 October 2005 in the case of certain currency and commodity contracts and to before 31 March 2006 in the case of certain interest rate contracts (where the company can elect for an alternative tax treatment) or, if later, before the accounting period in which the company begins to use fair value accounting (i.e. if it does not adopt fair value accounting in relation to such contracts in its first accounting period beginning on or after 1 January 2005).

[*FA 1996, ss 85A, 85B; FA 2004, s 52, Sch 10 para 3; FA 2005, s 80, Sch 4 para 26; FA 2006, Sch 6 para 11*].

Amounts not fully recognised for accounting purposes. Special provisions apply where a company:

- is, or is treated as being, a party to a creditor loan relationship; and
- is, or is treated as being, a party to a debtor relationship or (for accounting periods beginning on or after 9 May 2007 or beginning before that date and the transaction in question falls after that date), has at any time made an amount, the 'relevant capital contribution', to a company which forms part of its share or other capital or, for accounting periods ending before 9 May 2007 or parts of accounting period falling before 9 May 2007, has at any time issued share capital, which for accounting purposes is treated as a liability; and

where, in accordance with generally accepted accounting practice, amounts are not fully recognised in the accounts (in determining the profit or loss in the period) in respect of the relationship or liability.

In relation to periods of account ending after 21 March 2006 (but see below), it is to be assumed that an amount in respect of the whole relationship is recognised in the company's profit or loss for the period when determining the debits or credits to be brought into account for tax purposes in respect of a debtor or creditor relationship. However, any debits brought into account for any period in respect of a debtor relationship must not exceed the amount of any credits brought into account in respect of a creditor relationship. Where, apart from this provision, any debits or credits are brought into account in respect of a relationship to which this provision applies (i.e. where only part of a loan relationship is not recognised in the accounts), then any other debits or credits to be brought into account as a result of this provision are to be determined in using the same basis of accounting. In any other case, they are to be determined using an amortised cost basis of accounting.

In relation to periods of account beginning before 22 March 2006 amounts are to be brought into account as a result of this provision only if they relate to any time on or after that date.

[*FA 1996, s 85C; FA 2006, Sch 6 para 12; FA 2007, Sch 5 para 11*].

Change of accounting practice. Where, in accordance with UK generally accepted accounting practice, a company prepares its accounts for one period (the '*earlier period*') using an amortised cost basis in respect of its assets and liabilities, and for the next period (the '*later period*') uses a fair value accounting basis, or vice versa, then the following provisions apply.

(*a*) Any difference between the closing 'accounting value' of an asset or liability representing a loan relationship in the earlier period and the opening 'accounting value' in the later period, is treated as a debit or credit (as the case may be) in the later period. In this case, *SI 2004 No 3271* (as amended by *SI 2005 No 3383*) defers any debits and credits so that they are not to be brought into account in the first period of account beginning on or after 1 January 2005 but are instead to be brought into account over a ten-year period. Broadly, one-tenth of the applicable amount is brought into account for each of the ten years beginning with the later of the first accounting period of the company beginning on or after 1 January 2006 and the later period (but see below under deferment of transitional adjustments). This does not apply in the case of debits and credits in respect of dormant accounts of banks and building societies that instead are to be brought into account in the first accounting period beginning on or after 1 January 2007. This excludes debits and credits in relation to loan relationship assets or liabilities falling to be fully discharged at the latest on a date within an accounting period beginning on or after 1 January 2005 and before 1 January 2006. (This is to bring the tax treatment in line with the mandatory adoption of FRS 26 and IAS 39 by companies using fair value accounting for accounting periods beginning on or after 1 January 2006, the ten-year period for the deferral being chosen because of the uncertainty as to the size and direction of the transitional adjustments (see HMRC guidance, available on its website, on international accounting standards).)

(*b*) Where the company ceases to be party to a loan relationship and *FA 1996, s 103(6)* provides for debits and credits to be accounted for as though the relationship had not ceased (see 46.46 below), then any difference between 'the amount outstanding' in respect of the loan relationship at the end of the earlier period and 'the amount outstanding' at the beginning of the later period is treated as a debit or credit (as the case may be) in the later period.

As regards (*a*) above, '*accounting value*' means the 'carrying value' of the assets or liabilities recognised for accounting purposes and for this purpose, '*carrying value*' includes accruals, prepayments and impairment losses (including provisions for bad and doubtful debts). In order to stop a number of avoidance schemes, *FA 1996, Sch 9 para 19A para 4B* (as introduced by *FA 2005, Sch 4 para 31* and amended by *F(No 2)A 2005, Sch 6 para 4(2)*) provides for other provisions in *FA 1996* to apply in determining the carrying value for this purpose (for example, the use of cost basis where parties are connected as required by *FA 1996, s 87(2)*) as they apply for the purpose of determining loan relationship debits and credits. In determining the value of a company asset at the end of the earlier period, no account is to be taken of any debit that has previously been disallowed for tax purposes in a period of account beginning before 1 January 2005 either because it was disallowed under *ICTA 1988, s 74(1)(j)* (being a general bad debt provision for a trade debt – see 66.21 TRADING INCOME) or because of the assumption required by *FA 1996, Sch 9 para 5(1)* (that all amounts due under a creditor relationship will be paid on time for bad debts, doubtful debts estimated to be bad and for debts released – see 46.8 below).

As regards (*b*) above, '*the amount outstanding*' means so much of the amount recognised in the company's balance sheet as deferred income or loss arising in the cessation period (within *FA 1996, s 103(6)*) as has not yet brought into account.

These provisions do not apply if the differences as detailed above (or debits or credits) are brought into account under any other loan relationship provisions.

[*FA 1996, Sch 9 para 19A; FA 2004, s 52, Sch 10 para 36; FA 2005, s 80, Sch 4 para 31; F(No 2)A 2005, Sch 6 para 4(2)(6); SI 2004 No 3271; SI 2004 No 3347*].

Deferment of transitional adjustments. The following provisions apply to arrangements entered into (other than in the ordinary course of business) on or after 14 December 2004 (other than in pursuance of legally binding arrangements entered into before that date) and defer relief for loan relationship debits where all the following circumstances apply.

(i) The company incurs a loss in respect of a loan relationship as a result of the transaction in respect of which a debit would otherwise be brought into account in a period of account beginning before 1 January 2005 and the sole or main purpose for entering into the transaction was to bring a debit into account in that period.

(ii) Had the company continued to hold the asset or liability representing the loan relationship without entering into the transaction, a debit would have arisen in respect of the loan relationship in its first period of account beginning on or after 1 January 2005 which would have been deferred under, *SI 2004 No 3271, reg 3* to be brought into account in the first period of account beginning on or after 1 January 2006 (see (*a*) above). It is assumed for this purpose that the loan relationship has the same value at the beginning of the company's first period of account beginning on or after 1 January 2005 as it had at the time the transaction was entered into.

In this case, the debit in question is to be treated as arising under *SI 2004 No 3271* in the company's first period of account beginning on or after 1 January 2006. In determining the sole or main purpose of the transaction, regard shall be had to anything done by a connected company (within the meaning of *ICTA 1988, s 839*) and references to a company entering into a transaction include references to the company or its directors taking a decision about the loan relationship affecting its accounting treatment.

[*FA 2005, s 82; SI 2004 No 3271; SI 2005 No 3383; SI 2006 No 3238; SI 2007 No 950*].

Securitisation companies. In determining the profit or loss of a special purpose company used in securitisation transactions ('securitisation companies' – as defined) for periods of account beginning on or after 1 January 2005 and ending before 1 January 2008, 'generally accepted accounting practice' shall be taken to be UK generally accepted accounting practice as it applied to a period of account ending on 31 December 2004. The Treasury may make regulations to provide for special tax treatment for such companies. [*FA 2005, ss 83, 84* as amended by *FA 2006, s 101*].

Treasury powers. The Treasury has the power to vary these provisions by regulation to meet the circumstances of particular cases, including regulations to deal with a change of accounting basis, to allow for amounts to be disregarded or to bring such amounts into or back into account, or into account to a prescribed extent or over a prescribed period, or to prevent amounts being taken into account to the extent they derive from or relate to amounts brought into account in a previous period. Where, in accordance with generally accepted accounting practice, assets or liabilities that were previously dealt with on an amortised cost basis are required to be dealt with for accounting purposes on the basis of fair value accounting, the Treasury may by regulation provide (as necessary to meet the circumstances of particular cases) that such amounts continue to be determined on an amortised cost basis of accounting. Such regulations may be made to apply to periods of account before the regulations are made but not earlier than the beginning of the calendar year in which they are made.

SI 2004 No 3271, reg 5 allows certain assets, which have been dealt with for accounting purposes on an amortised cost basis of accounting (treated as 'held-to-maturity' under IAS 32 and 39) and which have subsequently been required to be dealt with on a fair value basis of accounting (treated as 'available for sale' under IAS 32 and 39), to continue to be dealt with on an amortised basis of accounting for tax purposes, subject to an election for this provision not to apply.

[*FA 1996, ss 85B(3), 90A, Sch 9 para 19B; FA 2004, s 52, Sch 10 paras 3, 8, 36; FA 2005, s 80, Sch 4 para 52; SI 2004 No 3271; SI 2004 No 3347; SI 2005 No 3383*].

Pre-FA 2004 basis. Where the pre-FA 2004 basis of computation applies (see 46.1 above), the debits and credits to be brought into account by a company in respect of its loan relationships are those computed in accordance with an 'authorised accounting method' (see 46.30 below). Profits, gains and losses for this purpose exclude amounts required to be transferred to share premium account, but include those that are, in accordance with generally accepted accounting practice, carried to or sustained by any other reserve maintained by the company. For accounting periods beginning *on or after 1 October 2002*, where there is a change in the authorised accounting method used as respects a loan relationship either within an accounting period or for successive accounting periods, any amounts that are brought into account for the purpose of the statutory accounts in respect of that change are to be treated as loan relationship debits or credits even where they would not otherwise be treated as such. [*FA 1996, s 84; FA 2002, Sch 25 para 4; FA 2004, s 52, Sch 10 para 1*].

46.8 **DEBT RELEASES AND IMPAIRMENT LOSSES**

Amendments were introduced by *FA 2004, Sch 4* and *F(No A) 2005, Sch 6* to ensure that loan relationship computations take account of changes in standard accounting practice. The term 'impairment losses' has been introduced in place of references to 'bad' and 'doubtful debts' (with effect for periods of account beginning on or after 1 January 2005) to reflect the terminology used by international accounting standards. Thus, references below to an impairment loss can be read as references, in the old terminology, to a bad or doubtful debt. In the case where the post-FA 2004 basis of computation applies, the concept of impairment is a feature of the 'amortised cost basis of accounting' (see 46.1 above). Accordingly, there are no statutory rules (other than those below in 46.9 onwards) governing the treatment of bad debts where they fall to be dealt with on an amortised cost basis of accounting. Where the pre-FA 2004 basis of computation applies, the provisions allow for a departure from the normal accruals basis assumption that all amounts due under a creditor relationship will be paid on time for bad debts, for doubtful debts estimated to be bad and for debts released. The accounting arrangements allowing the departure must also require adjustment by way of credit for any debt ceasing to fulfil the conditions for relief. For accounting periods beginning *on or after 1 October 2002*, there is an additional condition for such a departure to be allowed, that, in relation to exchange gains and losses, the arrangements allowing the departure must require a debt to be left out of account to the extent that the departure is allowed, and to be brought back into account when the departure ceases to be allowed.

[*FA 1996, Sch 9 para 5(1)–(2A); FA 2002, Sch 23 para 8; FA 2004, s 52, Sch 10 para 20*].

Cases where credit need not be brought into account. Where a liability under a debtor relationship is released in an accounting period for which the debtor company uses an amortised cost basis of accounting (or, where the pre-FA 2004 basis of computation applies, an accruals basis (see 46.1 above)) as respects the relationship in question, no credit is required to be brought into account in any of the following circumstances.

(i) The release is part of a statutory insolvency arrangement (or for periods of account beginning before 1 January 2005, a relevant arrangement or compromise) (see 45.2 LIQUIDATION ETC.).

(ii) The relationship is such that *FA 1996, s 87* (parties to relationship having connection) imposes an amortised cost basis of accounting (or, where the pre-FA 2004 basis of computation applies (see 46.1 above), an authorised accruals basis) (for which see 46.9 and 46.16 below). However, this does not apply in the case where a credit is required to be brought into account in periods of account beginning on or after 1 January 2005 on a deemed release of impaired debt becoming held by a connected company (see above).

(iii) For releases made *on or after 10 December 2003*, where either of the parties is in one of the forms of insolvency procedure noted at 46.9(i) below and where:

- in the case where the creditor is insolvent, the relationship between the parties immediately before but not immediately after the company enters into the insolvency procedure, is such that *FA 1996, s 87* imposes an amortised cost basis of accounting (or where the pre-FA 2004 basis of computation applies (see 46.1 above), an authorised accruals basis);
- in the case where the debtor is insolvent, the relationship between the parties is not one where *FA 1996, s 87* applies (for which see 46.9 below).

(iv) For periods of account beginning *on or after 1 January 2005*, where the release is in consideration of shares (or an entitlement to shares) forming part of the ordinary share capital of the debtor company.

[*FA 1996, Sch 9 para 5(3)–(8); FA 2002, Sch 23 para 8; FA 2004, s 52, Sch 8 para 3, Sch 10 para 20; FA 2005, s 80, Sch 4 para 11*].

Release of liability under creditor relationship: restriction of relief. The restrictions for relief for impairment losses detailed in 46.9 and 46.11 below apply equally in relation to a debit in respect of a release of a liability of a creditor company as they apply in relation to an impairment loss with effect for periods of account beginning on or after 1 January 2005. [*FA 1996, Sch 9 para 5ZA; FA 2005, s 80, Sch 4 para 12*].

46.9 **Impairment losses and connected parties.** Where *FA 1996, s 87* (parties to relationship having connection, see 46.16 below) requires an amortised cost basis of accounting (or, where the pre-FA 2004 basis of computation applies an authorised accruals basis, see 46.1 above) to be applied for an accounting period as regards a creditor relationship of a company, an 'impairment loss' (bad debt) may be brought into account (or, where the pre-FA 2004 basis of computation applies (see 46.1 above), a departure from the assumption that every amount due under the relationship will be paid in full is allowed (see 46.8 above)) only in the following circumstances:

(*a*) as provided in 46.11 below in relation to consortium relief;

(*b*) as detailed in (i) to (iii) below in relation to insolvency procedure and companies becoming connected; and

(*c*) where the company treats the liability as discharged in consideration of shares (or an entitlement to shares) forming part of the ordinary share capital of the debtor company, and *section 87* would not have applied before the shares (or entitlement) were acquired.

An '*impairment loss*' is a debit relating to an uncollectable amount of the loan or financial asset (i.e. a bad debt). In the case, where the post-FA 2004 basis of computation applies (see 46.1 above), an impairment loss is not allowed, no credit is to be brought into account for the reversal of the loss.

With effect for transactions taking place on or after 2 December 2004, where in any period a related transaction (see 46.5 above) takes place in relation to a loan relationship, the debits in respect of the relationship for that period shall be no more, and the credits no less, than they would have been had the transaction not taken place (disregarding any amounts which would have accrued after the transaction took place). Before that date, where in any period a company ceases to be a party to the relationship, the debits in respect of the relationship for that period shall be no more, and the credits no less, than they would have been had the relationship not ceased (disregarding any amounts which would have accrued after the relationship ceased). (The new rules thus cover all related transactions including part as well as full disposals.)

These provisions do not affect the debits and credits to be brought into account for accounting periods beginning on or after 1 October 2002 in respect of exchange gains and losses arising from the debt. See below for concessional disregard of a connection within *section 87* in certain cases for these purposes for accounting periods beginning before 1 October 2002.

For accounting periods beginning on or after 1 October 2002, impairment losses are allowed (or, where the pre-FA 2004 basis of computation applies (see 46.1 above), departures are allowed from the assumption that every amount due under a loan relationship will be paid in full) in the following circumstances.

(i) *Creditor company insolvent.* Where a creditor company is in insolvent liquidation or administration or, in relation to accounting periods *ending on or after 10 December 2003*, insolvent administrative receivership, under the *Insolvency Act 1986* or NI equivalent, or a provisional liquidator has been appointed under that *Act* or NI equivalent, or corresponding processes under foreign law are in place, the loss (or, where the post-FA 2004 basis of computation applies (see 46.1 above), departure) is allowed at a time in the course of the winding up or administration, or when the appointment of the administrative receivership or provisional liquidator is in force, or at a corresponding time under the foreign process. The creditor company will not, in those circumstances, be required to recognise interest or discounts arising on loan relationships to the extent that the debts cannot be paid in full. (Where a company ceased to be in insolvent liquidation or administration before 9 April 2003, the provision as originally enacted applies, to broadly similar effect.) This reverses the decision in *Re Toshoku Finance UK plc*, where a credit had to be brought into account for the tax due on the interest accruing during the period of liquidation on a connected party loan relationship although the debtor was not in a position to repay the debt, see 45.3 LIQUIDATION, ETC.)

(ii) *Companies in loan relationship becoming connected.* Where, in relation to related transactions taking place before 2 December 2004, a creditor company becomes connected with the debtor company in an accounting period beginning on or after 1 October 2002, but was not so connected in a previous accounting period, and an impairment loss (or, where the pre-FA 2004 basis of computation applies (see 46.1 above), a departure) was allowed in that previous accounting period, it will continue to be allowed for periods in which the parties are connected, to the extent that the debits do not in total exceed the value of the debt shown in the creditor company's accounts at the end of the accounting period immediately preceding that in which the connection arose.

(iii) *Creditor acquiring impaired debt becoming connected.* Where, in relation to related transactions taking place before 2 December 2004, a creditor company acquired its rights under the loan relationship in an arm's length transaction in an accounting period in which there was no connection between the creditor company and the person from whom the rights were acquired, and there had been no such connection between the creditor company and the debtor company at any time during the period beginning four years before the date on which the rights to the loan relationship were acquired and ending twelve months before that date, the impairment loss (or, where the pre-FA 2004 basis of computation applies (see 46.1 above), a departure) will be allowed to the extent that the total of debits brought into account by the creditor company in respect of the loan relationship do not exceed the amount paid by that company to acquire those rights. (For transitional provisions, see 46.47 below under *Other chargeable asset etc. adjustments*.)

As regards (ii) and (iii) above, there is a connection between a company and another person for an accounting period if, at any time during that period, the other person is a company and either one company controls the other or both companies are under the control of the same person. 'Control' for this purpose is as defined by *FA 1996, s 87A*, see 46.16 below).

Cessation of connection. For accounting periods beginning on or after 1 October 2002, where relief for impairment losses has been denied in an accounting period due to a connection between the parties under *FA 1996, s 87*, and the connection ceases in a subsequent accounting period, no debits (and for periods of account beginning before 1 January 2005, no credits) are to be brought into account in respect of any recovery or deterioration of those debts in that or any later accounting period to the extent that they correspond to debits or credits which were disallowed because of the connection.

[*FA 1996, Sch 9 paras 6–6C; FA 2002, Sch 23 para 9, Sch 25 paras 24–27; FA 2003, Sch 41 paras 4, 5(2); FA 2004, s 52, Sch 8 para 4, Sch 10 paras 22–25; FA 2005, s 80, Sch 4 paras 13–15*].

46.10 **Deemed release of liability on impaired debt becoming held by connected party.** There is deemed to be a release by a creditor company of its rights under a loan relationship in the following two cases where the deemed release occurs *on or after 16 March 2005*.

(*a*) The first case is where, subject to the exception below, a company ('the new creditor') acquires rights under a loan relationship from an unconnected party ('the old creditor') and immediately after doing so is connected with the debtor company. (This may be because the new creditor was already connected with the debtor company, or because it acquired shares in the debtor company at the same time as the debt.) The new creditor must not be 'connected' with the old creditor in the period of account in which it acquires the rights under the loan relationship.

Where the 'carrying value' of the liability exceeds the amount or value of any consideration given by the new creditor company for the rights to that liability, the release (treated as a taxable credit of the debtor) is deemed to be the amount of the excess and to take place when the new creditor acquires the debt. The '*carrying value*' in this case is the amount that would have been the carrying value of the liability in the debtor's accounts if a period of account had ended immediately before the new creditor became party to the loan relationship. In determining the carrying value of a liability or debt asset no account is to be taken of accruals, prepayments or impairment losses.

(*b*) The second case is where parties to a loan relationship are unconnected but later become connected (for example, if the creditor acquires a majority shareholding in the debtor) and the creditor company would have adjusted the carrying value of the debt asset in its accounts for impairment had a period of account ended immediately before the companies became connected. The provisions relating to carrying value in (*a*) above apply equally in this case. The release (treated as a taxable credit in the debtor's accounts) in this case is deemed to be the amount of the impairment adjustment and to take place when the companies become connected.

Exception. As regards (*a*) above, there is no deemed release where the new creditor acquires the rights under the loan relationship from the unconnected old creditor under an arm's length transaction and there was no connection between the new creditor and the debtor company at any time in the period beginning four years before, and ending twelve months before, the date on which the new creditor company acquired the rights.

Companies are '*connected*' for this purpose if, at any time in a period of account, one has control over the other or both are under the control of the same person (other than the Crown or a government department). 'Control' in this case is as defined by *FA 1996, s 87A* for the purposes of *FA 1996, s 87*. *FA 1996, s 88* (see 46.16 below) applies in this case (so that companies dealing in securities are not treated as being connected where connected party debt is acquired in the course of a trade).

[*FA 1996, Sch 9 para 4A; FA 2005, Sch 4 para 10; F(No 2)A 2005, Sch 6 para 5*].

See also HMRC Corporate Finance Manual CFM 5560 to CFM 5566.

46.11 **Impairment losses and consortium relief.** With effect for accounting periods beginning on or after 1 October 2002, this provision applies to restrict relief where impairment losses (or where the pre-FA 2004 basis of computation applies (see 46.1 above), debits for bad and doubtful debts) have been brought into account in respect of a loan made by a company which is a member of a consortium (the '*member company*'), or by any fellow group member (not being a member of the consortium), to a company owned by the consortium (the '*consortium company*') or, where it is a holding company, to a consortium company which is its subsidiary. Membership of a group is determined for these purposes as under *ICTA 1988, Pt 10 Ch 4* (see 32.7 GROUPS OF COMPANIES) and ownership of the consortium company as under *ICTA 1988, s 413(7)* (see 32.23 GROUPS OF COMPANIES). (Note that this provision does not affect ordinary group relief, since bad debt relief is restricted where the parties to the loan relationship are connected under *FA 1996, s 86* as detailed in 46.9 above.)

The restriction of relief (which effectively allows for relief to be given to the higher of the bad debt provision or the group relief claim) works as follows.

(*a*) *Restriction of bad debt debits.* The 'relevant net debit' is reduced (but not below nil) by the amount of any group relief which may be surrendered by the consortium company and which is claimed in the same 'group accounting period' by the member company or by any fellow group member. Where a reduction is to be made to more than one debit (where bad debt relief is claimed by more than one company), it is to be apportioned between the debits in proportion to their respective amounts.

The '*relevant net debit*' is the excess of the total impairment losses (or where the pre-FA 2004 basis of computation applies (see 46.1 above), debits for bad or doubtful debts) brought into account for that accounting period by the member company or by any fellow group member over the total of any credits so brought into account in that period in respect of debt recoveries.

A '*group accounting period*' means any accounting period beginning on or after 1 October 2002 of the member company or any accounting period of a fellow group member beginning on or after that date and 'corresponding' to such a member company accounting period. Such periods are regarded as the same accounting period for the purposes of this provision. An accounting period of a group member '*corresponds*' to an accounting period of a member company if:

(i) the two accounting periods coincide;

(ii) the accounting period of the member company includes more than half of the accounting period of the group member; or

(iii) the accounting period of the member company includes part of the accounting period of the group member, but the remainder of that period does not fall within any accounting period of the member company.

(*b*) *Subsequent recovery of bad debt.* Where, in any group accounting period, there is a 'surplus of related debt recovery credits', each of the related debt recovery credits is to be reduced (but not below nil) by a corresponding proportion of the cumulative reduction made in earlier group accounting periods to the debits in (*a*) above (so far as not previously so apportioned). There is a '*surplus of related debt recovery credits*' if the total bad debt recovery credits brought into account by the member company and any fellow group member exceed the total impairment losses (or, where the pre-FA 2004 basis of computation applies (see 46.1 above), bad debt debits) brought into account by those companies for that period on the relevant loans. Where a recovery is to be made in respect of more than one credit (where a bad debt is recovered by more than one member company), it is to be apportioned between the credits in proportion to their respective amounts.

(*c*) *Restriction of group relief based on earlier bad debt relief.* Any claim for group relief for a group accounting period by the member company or a fellow group member, in respect of amounts available for surrender by the consortium company, is to be reduced (but not below nil) by the cumulative net amount of the relevant net debits for earlier group accounting periods (as reduced under (*a*) above) in respect of the relevant loans (i.e. the claim for group relief is to be reduced by the actual amount of debt relief claimed). The restriction applies only to that amount of the group relief claim that exceeds the bad debt debits of the same accounting period (the 'top slice'). If there is more than one such group relief claim, the reduction is to be apportioned between them in proportion to their respective amounts.

(*d*) *Group relief claim to restrict future impairment loss.* Where there is a claim for group relief as in (*c*) above, but there are no relevant net debits in the same group accounting period in respect of the relevant loan, the amount of the claim is taken into account when considering restrictions under (*a*) above in subsequent accounting periods. Thus, the claim for group relief is treated as carried forward for the purposes of this provision to the next accounting period, and, in addition to any actual claim for that period, is used to restrict impairment losses (or, where the pre-FA 2004 basis of computation applies (see 46.1 above), bad debt debits) as under (*a*) above.

[*FA 1996, Sch 9 para 5A; FA 2002, Sch 25 para 23; FA 2004, s 52, Sch 10 para 21*].

See also HMRC Corporate Finance Manual, CFM 5560 to CFM 5566.

46.12 *Example*

CC Ltd is a consortium company owned equally by three member companies, X Ltd, Y Ltd and Z Ltd. In the year to 31.12.05 X Ltd writes off £100,000 of a loan it has made to CC Ltd. In the same year, CC Ltd surrenders losses of £20,000 to X Ltd, to W Ltd (a subsidiary of X Ltd) and Y Ltd. In the year to 31.12.06 X Ltd considers that £50,000 of the bad debt in respect of the loan to CC Ltd is recoverable. Also in that year, Z Ltd writes off £30,000 of a loan it had made to CC Ltd of £50,000. In the year to 31.12.07 X Ltd writes off a further bad debt on another loan to CC Ltd of £15,000 and CC Ltd surrenders losses of £20,000 to X Ltd and Y Ltd and £40,000 to Z Ltd. In the year to 31.12.08 Z Ltd writes off the balance of the loan it had made to CC Ltd. In the same year, CC Ltd surrenders losses of £5,000 to each of the member companies.

There are no bad debt write-offs or recoveries or group relief claims other than those mentioned above.

	X Ltd	Y Ltd	Z Ltd
	£	£	£
Year to 31/12/05			
Impairment loss	100,000		
Group relief	40,000		
Net relevant debit as restricted under (*a*)	60,000		
Group relief	40,000	20,000	
Net relevant debit c/fwd	*60,000*		

	X Ltd	Y Ltd	Z Ltd
	£	£	£
Year to 31/12/06			
Credit to reverse Impairment loss	(50,000)		30,000
Restriction to impairment loss in year to 31/12/05	40,000		
Net relevant credit under (*b*) above	(10,000)		
Cumulative net relevant debit c/fwd	*50,000*		*30,000*
Year to 31/12/07			
Impairment loss	15,000		
Group relief claim	20,000		
Net relevant debit as restricted under (*a*)	Nil		
Group relief claim	20,000	20,000	40,000
Less restriction under (*c*) above	5,000		30,000
Group relief allowed under (*c*) above	15,000	20,000	10,000
Cumulative net relevant debit c/fwd	*45,000*		—
Year to 31/12/08			
Impairment loss			20,000
Group relief claim in year to 31/12/07			10,000
Group relief claim in year	5,000	5,000	5,000
Net relevant debit as restricted under (*d*)			5,000
Group relief claim	5,000	5,000	5,000
Restriction under (*c*) above	5,000		
Group relief allowed	—	5,000	5,000
Cumulative net relevant debit c/fwd	*40,000*		*5,000*

Where any credit is brought into account by the consortium company in respect of the release of a debt owed to the member company, the released amount is not to be treated as a debit by the member company for the purposes of this provision.

When determining the amount of group relief which can be claimed, *ICTA 1988, s 403C* has priority over this provision. See generally 32.23 et seq. GROUPS OF COMPANIES for consortium and group relief claims.

46.13 **Revaluation of debts.** With effect for periods of account beginning on or after 1 January 2005, where a creditor company uses an amortised cost basis of accounting and revalues an asset representing a loan relationship:

(*a*) no debits can be brought into account for loan relationship purposes except an impairment loss or releases of any liability under the relationship; and

(*b*) no credits can be brought into account in respect of a reversal of any debits disallowed either under (*a*) above or, for periods of account beginning before 1 January 2005, by virtue of the assumption in *FA 1996, Sch 9 para 5(1)* (that debts will be fully paid on time except for write-offs, specific provisions and releases – see 46.8 above), or because the exceptions in *ICTA 1988, s 74(1)(j)* (for write-offs and provisions in the case of insolvency, etc.) did not apply.

A '*revaluation*' of an asset for these purposes includes any provision or allowance made by the company reducing the carrying value of the asset (or group of assets including the asset in question).

This provision does not affect debits to be brought into account in respect of exchange gains and losses.

[*FA 1996, Sch 9 para 6D; FA 2005, s 80, Sch 4 para 16*].

46.14 **Writing off of government investment and overseas sovereign debt.** No credit is required to be brought into account in respect of the release of a liability by which a government investment is written off (for which see generally 47.21 LOSSES).

For periods of account beginning before 1 January 2005, there are special provisions restricting relief in respect of sovereign debt, i.e. debt owed or guaranteed by an overseas State authority or estimated to be impaired because of restrictions imposed by an overseas State or State authority. These rules are repealed for periods of account beginning on or after that date and there are transitional provisions to provide relief on provisions not already allowed for tax and losses on loans disposed of before the provisions were repealed.

[*FA 1996, Sch 9 paras 7–9; FA 2004, Sch 10 paras 26, 27; FA 2005, s 80, Sch 4 para 17*].

Simon's Direct Tax Service. See **D2.1120, D2.1835**.

46.15 **Concessional bad debt relief.** By concession, for accounting periods beginning before 1 October 2002, where a connection within *FA 1996, s 87* would otherwise prevent a creditor company obtaining bad debt relief (as described above), the company may (for this purpose only) choose (in respect of all its loan relationships potentially falling within the concession) that (*a*)–(*c*) below apply in determining whether there is a connection within *section 87*. The company must notify the office dealing with its tax affairs that it wishes to take advantage of the concession, and must then within twelve months of the end of any accounting period notify that office of the relief it wishes to claim under the concession for the period.

(*a*) The rights and powers of 'associates' to be attributed to a person in applying *ICTA 1988, s 416* (definition of 'control') exclude those attributed to a participator by virtue only of the holder being a partner of the participator. This will, for example, prevent a company which is a general partner in a venture capital partnership automatically being treated as connected with a company in which the partnership is investing.

(*b*) Rights attributable to a company as loan creditor in respect of a loan made in the ordinary course of its business of providing finance are disregarded in determining whether it has control (within *ICTA 1988, s 416*) of the debtor company by virtue of entitlement to the greater part of its assets available for distribution among the participators on a winding-up, etc. This mirrors the statutory provision which already applies in the case of loans made by banks (see 46.16 below).

(*c*) A company's possession, or entitlement to possession, of fixed rate preference shares (within *ICTA 1988, s 95*) which do not carry voting rights is disregarded in determining control within *ICTA 1988, s 416*, provided that:

(i) the creditor company is not a close company within *ICTA 1988, s 414* (see 16.1 CLOSE COMPANIES);

(ii) the creditor company entered into the loan relationship in the ordinary course of its business of providing finance, and it (or any other company in the same group) similarly subscribed for the preference shares in the ordinary course of such a business;

(iii) where the creditor company (or a member of the same group) acquired the preference shares through the exchange of loan for shares, it did so in the ordinary course of its business of providing finance, and the face value of the debt was significantly more than the market value of the shares for which it was exchanged; and

(iv) the debtor company is within the charge to corporation tax in respect of any loan relationship exchanged for shares and any continuing loan relationship with the creditor company.

Where a company takes advantage of the concession, it must also accept any subsequent charges arising in respect of recoveries, decreases in provisions or profits on disposals of debts for which relief has been given under the concession. Where a loan relationship previously within the concession subsequently falls outside its terms, the connection will be treated as having started at that time. Relief previously given will not be withdrawn (except where there is a recovery, etc.). Relief is allowed under the concession in certain circumstances for loans in existence at 1 April 1996 where the creditor and debtor are connected as a result of an earlier exchange of shares.

The concession also deals with certain other ancillary matters, in particular its application to debt equity swaps and the effects of subsequent connection outside the concession.

(HMRC Extra-Statutory Concession, C28).

This concession is withdrawn for accounting periods beginning *on or after 1 October 2002* in consequence of the widening of the connected party rules under *FA 1996, s 87* and *87A*. See 46.16 below.

Simon's Direct Tax Service. See D2.1122.

46.16 SPECIAL COMPUTATIONAL PROVISIONS

Connected parties. In the case of a loan relationship of a company where there is a 'connection' between the company and the other party to the relationship (including any person standing indirectly in that position by reference to a series of loan relationships, or money debts which would be loan relationships were the company a debtor or creditor), the debits and credits brought into account must be determined on an amortised cost basis of accounting (or, where the pre-FA 2004 basis of computation applies (see 46.1 above), an authorised accruals basis).

Where the post-FA 2004 basis of computation applies (see 46.1 above) and there is a change of accounting basis (from a fair value basis of accounting to an amortised cost basis or vice versa) between one accounting period and the next, resulting in a difference between the amount recorded in the accounts at the end of one period and the amount recorded at the beginning of the next period, such difference is to be brought into account in the next period. This provision applies where the requirement to use an amortised cost basis of accounting, by virtue of a 'connection' between the parties to the loan relationship, begins or ceases to apply.

Where the post-FA 2004 basis of computation applies (see 46.1 above) and, in accordance with generally accepted accounting practice, assets or liabilities that were previously dealt with on an amortised cost basis are required to be dealt with for accounting purposes on the basis of fair value accounting, the Treasury may by regulation provide (as necessary to meet the circumstances of particular cases) that such amounts continue to be determined on an amortised cost basis of accounting.

For this purpose there is a '*connection*' between a company and another person for an accounting period if at any time in the period (subject to *FA 1996, s 88*, see below) (or, for accounting periods beginning before 1 October 2002, in the two years before the beginning of the period):

(*a*) where the other person is a company, one company controls the other or both are under the control of the same person (other than the Crown, a Minister of the Crown, a government or NI department, a foreign sovereign power or an organisation of which two or more sovereign powers, or their governments, are members); or

(*b*) in any case, for accounting periods beginning before 1 October 2002, the other person is a participator (or an 'associate' (within *ICTA 1988, s 417*, see 16.5 CLOSE COMPANIES) of a participator) in the company, it being a close company. 'Participator' is as under *ICTA 1988, s 417* (see 16.3 CLOSE COMPANIES) but disregarding loan creditors as such.

See *Conlon Construction Ltd v Jarman [2004] SSCD 6* for the interpretation of *FA 1996, s 87* where a creditor was treated as a participator of a close company by reason of it being both a member of the company and a loan creditor but where it would not have been considered to be connected with the debtor in an accounting period beginning after 30 September 2002.

Where a partnership which carries on a trade, profession or a business has a loan relationship with a company, any connection between companies, and the effect of any such connection, is to be determined as though each of the partners (excluding the general partner of a limited partnership which is a collective investment scheme within *Financial Services and Markets Act 2000, s 235* – see 46.43 below) holds a separate loan relationship with the company equivalent to that partner's share of the partnership's loan relationship. The partner's share is that corresponding to the its share in partnership profits.

[*FA 1996, ss 87, 90A; FA 2002, Sch 25 para 7; FA 2004, s 52, Sch 10 paras 4, 8*].

Meaning of 'control'. For accounting periods beginning before 1 October 2002, '*control*' is based on *ICTA 1988, s 416(2)–(6)* (see 16.2 CLOSE COMPANIES). For accounting periods beginning on or after that date, in relation to a company it means the power of a person to secure:

(i) by means of the holding of shares or possession of voting power in, or in relation to, the company or any other company, or

(ii) by virtue of any powers conferred by the articles of association or other document regulating the company or any other company,

that the affairs of the company are conducted in accordance with his wishes.

'*Shares*' for this purpose do not include those held by companies where a profit on sale would be a trading receipt (e.g. banks or financial traders), and powers arising from such shares are similarly excluded. This does not apply where such shares are assets of an insurance company's long-term insurance fund within *ICTA 1988, s 431(2)*.

Where a partnership has shares or powers in a company, these are attributed to company partners in proportion to their share in the partnership profits. This excludes a general partner of a limited partnership which is a collective investment scheme within *Financial Services and Markets Act 2000, s 235* (see 46.43 below) (so that it cannot be regarded as controlling the partnership for the purposes of this provision).

[*FA 1996, s 87A; FA 2002, Sch 25 para 8*].

Where the *only* link between two parties is the loan relationship in question, the two parties will not be connected, even where the size of the loan would entitle the loan creditor to the greatest part of the assets in a winding up. The exclusion of loan creditors applies only in determining whether a particular loan creditor is connected with the debtor company — the rights of all loan creditors will be taken into account in applying the control tests to other parties. (HMRC Corporate Finance Manual CFM 5420, CFM 5404, CFM 5410 onwards).

As regards (*b*), connection through participation is not mutual, i.e. 'connection' has to be considered separately in relation to the debtor in a loan relationship and the creditor in the relationship. (HMRC Company Taxation Manual, CTM 53850).

Exemption. Where a company is party to a creditor relationship in an accounting period in 'exempt circumstances', any 'connection' otherwise within *FA 1996, s 87* (see above) with a person who (directly or indirectly) stands in the position of the debtor is disregarded for the purposes of that *section*. Where the debtor is also a company, this does not apply in relation to that company. A company is party to a relationship in an accounting period in '*exempt circumstances*' if:

(A) in the course of carrying on activities forming an integral part of a trade carried on in that period it disposes of or acquires assets representing creditor relationships;

(B) for that period, where the pre-FA 2004 basis of computation applies (see 46.1 above), the company uses an authorised mark to market basis of accounting as respects all creditor relationships represented by assets acquired in the course of those activities;

(C) the asset representing the creditor relationship in question was acquired in the course of those activities and is either listed on a recognised stock exchange at the end of that period or a security which must be redeemed within twelve months of issue;

(D) at some time in that period assets of the same kind as the asset representing the creditor relationship in question are in the beneficial ownership of persons other than the company; and

(E) in not more than three months (in aggregate) in that period is the equivalent of 30% or more of the assets of that kind in the beneficial ownership of connected persons (and a connected person is taken as having beneficial ownership of an asset wherever there is (apart from the current exemption) a connection within *FA 1996, s 87* between the person having beneficial ownership of the asset and a person who (directly or indirectly) stands in the position of debtor as respects the debt by reference to which any loan relationship represented by that asset subsists).

As regards (D) above, assets are taken to be of the same kind where they are so treated by the practice of any recognised stock exchange (or would be if dealt with on such an exchange).

The definition of 'exempt circumstances' is modified in the case of an insurance company carrying on basic life and general annuity business.

[*FA 1996, s 88; FA 2004, s 52, Sch 10 para 5*].

Simon's Direct Tax Service. See **D2.1118, D2.1836.**

46.17 **Late interest.** Where debits are brought into account in respect of a debtor loan relationship (in the accounts of the borrower) under *FA 1996, s 87* (parties to relationship having connection, see 46.16 above – using an amortised cost basis of accounting (or, where a pre-FA 2004 basis of computation applies, an authorised accruals basis, see 46.1 above)), then if:

(*a*) interest payable under the relationship is not paid within twelve months of the end of the accounting period in which it would otherwise be treated as accruing; and

(*b*) credits representing the full amount of the interest are not brought into account for any accounting period in respect of the corresponding creditor relationship,

debits relating to interest payable under the relationship are not brought into account until the interest is paid.

For accounting periods beginning *on or after 1 October 2002*, restriction of debits for late paid interest due to connected creditors applies in any of the following circumstances where the debtors and creditors are treated as being connected to each other.

(i) There is, for the '*relevant accounting period*' (i.e. the accounting period referred to in (*a*) above), a connection with the meaning of *FA 1996, s 87* (see 46.16 above) between the debtor company and the creditor.

(ii) At any time in the relevant accounting period, the debtor company is a 'close company' and the creditor is either:

- a 'participator' in the debtor company or, for accounting periods beginning on or after 4 March 2005 (but see transitional rules below), a person who controls a company which is such a participator (a 'participator company');
- an 'associate' of a person who is a participator in the debtor company at that time or, for accounting periods beginning on or after 4 March 2005 (but see transitional rules below), an associate of a person who controls a participator company at that time;
- a company controlled by a participator in the debtor company or for accounting periods beginning on or after 4 March 2005 (but see transitional rules below), a person who controls a participator company; or
- a company in which the participator in the debtor company has a 'major interest'.

However, the restriction does not apply where:

- for accounting periods beginning on or after 4 March 2005 (but see transitional rules below), either:
  - the debtor company is a 'CIS-based close company' and a 'small or medium-sized enterprise' (as defined by *ICTA 1988, Sch 28AA para 5D*), and the creditor is not 'resident' (as defined by *ICTA 1988, Sch 28AA para 5B(6)*) in a 'non-qualifying territory' (as defined by *ICTA 1988, Sch 28AA para 5E*); or
  - the debt is owed to (or to persons acting for) a 'CIS limited partnership' no member of which is resident in a non-qualifying territory (this to be confirmed in writing by the partnership to the debtor company) and the debtor company is a small or medium-sized enterprise;
- for accounting periods beginning before 4 March 2005 (see transitional rules below), the creditor is not, and is not acting for, a 'CIS limited partnership' (or, for accounting periods ending before 10 December 2003, a limited

partnership which is a collective investment scheme within the meaning of the *Financial Services and Markets Act 2000, s 235* – see 46.43 below) (but see below).

(iii) The creditor is a company in which the debtor company has a 'major interest' at any time in the relevant accounting period or *vice versa*.

(iv) The loan is made by the trustees of a retirement benefits scheme (within *ICTA 1988, s 611*) and, at any time in the relevant accounting period, the debtor company is the employer operating the scheme, or is connected with the employer under *FA 1996, s 87* (see 46.16 above), or the employer is a company in which the debtor company has a 'major interest' or which itself has a major interest in the debtor company.

This provision also applies to indirect creditor loan relationships where there is a series of loan relationships, or money debts which would be loan relationships if a company directly stood in the position of creditor or debtor. In this case, the reference to the corresponding creditor relationship in (*b*) above includes a person who indirectly stands in the position of a creditor.

A '*CIS-based close company*' is a company that would not be close apart from the attribution under *ICTA 1988, s 416*(*6*) of the rights and powers of a partner in a 'CIS limited partnership' to other partners by virtue of *ICTA 1988, s 417*(*3*)(*a*). A '*CIS limited partnership*' is a limited partnership which is a collective investment scheme or would be a collective investment scheme if not a body corporate, within the meaning of the *Financial Services and Markets Act 2000, s 235* (see 46.43 below).

With regard to the addition to the list of creditors in (ii) above which are treated as connected with the debtors for accounting periods beginning on or after 4 March 2005, accounting periods straddling 4 March 2005 are treated, for these purposes only, as two separate periods, the first ending with the day before that date and the second beginning on that date. Profits and losses are computed accordingly for the two periods and then aggregated (so that the above rules cannot affect profits arising before the relevant date). As regards the exclusion from the restriction for CIS-based companies etc. in (ii) above for accounting periods beginning on or after 4 March 2005, where the debt finance is provided to a person under a contract entered into before 4 March 2005, its application in such a case is delayed until accounting periods beginning on or after 1 April 2007 or, if the contract is varied before that date, the date of the variation. The provision above for straddling periods applies equally in this case whether the relevant date is 4 March 2005, 1 April 2007 or the date of the variation. An advance made on or after 4 March 2005 in accordance with terms agreed before that date or a change in the applied interest rate in accordance with terms agreed before that date are not regarded as variations to the contract for these purposes (see the HMRC website (at www.hmrc.gov.uk/international/transferpricing.pdf)).

For these purposes, a '*close company*' is as defined in *ICTA 1988, s 414* (see 16.1 CLOSE COMPANIES) but includes non-resident companies. An '*associate*' is as defined in *ICTA 1988, s 417*(*3*),(*4*) (see 16.5 CLOSE COMPANIES). '*Control*' is as defined in *FA 1996, s 87A* (see 46.16 above). A '*participator*' in relation to a company is a person who, by virtue of *ICTA 1988, s 417* (see 16.3 CLOSE COMPANIES), is treated as such for the purposes of the close company legislation other than by reason only of being a loan creditor. In relation to interest which would, apart from these provisions, be treated as accruing on or after 9 April 2003, a person who is thus a participator in a company which controls another company is treated as also being a participator in that other company.

For a discussion of when interest can be treated as paid (under (*a*) above), see HMRC Corporate Finance Manual, CFM 5610. See also CFM 5616 for HMRC's view of when credits (under (*b*) above) should be treated as being 'brought into account' by the creditor.

Major interest. A company ('company A') has a '*major interest*' in another company ('company B') if company A and one other person ('P') together control (within *FA 1996, s 87A*, see 46.16 above) company B, and each of P and company A have at least 40% of the total interests, rights and powers subsisting in company B giving that control. Connected companies' interests, rights and powers are attributed to company A and (if it is a company) P for this purpose (companies being connected if one controls the other or they are under common control). This is, however, subject, for accounting periods **beginning before 17 March 2004,** to company A (or a connected company) and P (or, if P is a company, a connected company) either both being a creditor of company B or both being a debtor of company B in respect of a loan relationship. Certain shares and powers are disregarded for these purposes. Where interests, rights or powers are held in partnership, these are apportioned to company partners in proportion to their share in partnership profits. Where a partnership which carries on a trade, profession or a business has a loan relationship with a company, each company partner is for the purposes of this test treated as holding a separate loan relationship with the company corresponding to their share in partnership profits. A general partner of a limited partnership which is a collective investment scheme within the meaning of the *Financial Services and Markets Act 2000, s 235* (see 46.43 below) is disregarded for these purposes.

[*FA 1996, Sch 9 paras 2, 20; FA 2002, Sch 25 paras 22, 36; FA 2003, Sch 37 para 2; FA 2004, s 52, Sch 8 paras 2, 7; Sch 42 Pt 2(4); F(No 2)A 2005, Sch 8 paras 2, 4*].

46.18 *Example*

On 1 October 2005, Subco Ltd, a UK trading company preparing accounts to 30 September, obtains a three-year loan of US $850,000 from its parent company to finance the purchase of plant. Interest on the loan is payable at 5% p.a. at the end of every six months. The first interest payment is made on the due date on 31 March 2005 and the interest due is accrued thereafter but no further payments are made, due to Subco's financial difficulties, until 31 March 2008. Also on 1 October 2005, Subco bought a forward currency contract of $850,000 for delivery on 30 September 2008 in order to repay the loan.

Assume that the exchange rates and sterling amounts at the relevant dates are:

Date	$ to £	£ equivalent of loan	Interest paid – £	Interest accrued – £
1.10.05	1.85	459,459		
31.3.06	1.90		11,184	
30.9.06	1.70	500,000		12,500 (*a*)
30.9.07	1.85	459,459		22,973 (*a*)
31.3.08	1.90		44,737	
30.9.08	1.85	459,459	11,486	

The cost of the forward currency contract gives rise to allowable debits of £15,000 per year, calculated on an amortised cost basis of accounting.

The company incurs the following loan relationship credits and debits.

Year ending	30.9.06	30.9.07	30.9.08
	£	£	£
Non-trading debits:			
Interest (notes (*a*) and (*b*))	11,184	22,973	33,854
Non-trading derivative contract debits	15,000	15,000	15,000
Total loan relationship debits	(26,184)	(37,973)	(48,854)
Exchange gain (losses) on loan	(40,541)	40,541	—
Exchange gain on interest (note (*c*))			605
Non-trading loan relationship profit		2,568	
Non-trading loan relationship deficit	(66,725)		(48,249)

Notes

(*a*) Interest payable on 30 September 2006 of $21,250 is not paid by 30 September 2007 and so the debit cannot be accounted for until the accounting period in which it is paid, the year ending 30 September 2008. The interest which would under the amortised cost basis be accounted for in the year ending 30 September 2007 is paid within twelve months of that date and accordingly, is deductible in that period.

(*b*) In the year ending 30 September 2008, the interest accounted for is the amount paid on 31 March 2008 (not already accounted for in the year ending 30 September 2007) of £22,368 ($42,500/1.90) and the amount paid on 30 September 2008 of £11,486.

(*c*) The exchange gain represents the difference between the amount of the interest accounted for in the period which was paid on 31 March 2008 of £22,368 ($42,500/1.90) and the amount at which that interest was accrued on 30 September 2007 of £22,973 ($42,500/1.85).

46.19 **Imported losses etc.** Special rules apply for an accounting period (the '*loss period*') of a company (the '*chargeable company*') where:

(*a*) there is a loss arising in connection with a loan relationship of the company which would fall to be brought into account under these provisions; and

(*b*) that loss is wholly or partly referable to a time when the chargeable company (or any predecessor in the same position as respects the loan relationship at that time) would not have been liable to UK tax on any profits or gains arising from the relationship.

In those circumstances, the amounts brought into account in that period in respect of that relationship are adjusted to ensure that no part of the loss referable to such a time is treated for the purposes of the current provisions as arising in any accounting period of the chargeable company or as otherwise available to be brought into account for corporation tax purposes.

This provision does not apply where a fair value basis of accounting is used (but, where the pre-FA 2004 basis of computation applies (see 46.1 above), it only applies where an authorised accruals basis is used) as respects the loan relationship.

[*FA 1996, Sch 9 para 10; FA 2002, Sch 25 para 28; FA 2004, s 52, Sch 10 para 28*].

Simon's Direct Tax Service. See **D2.1123, D4.1874**.

46.20 **Transactions not at arm's length.** Where debits or credits falling to be brought into account in respect of a loan relationship relate to amounts arising from a non-arm's length 'related transaction' (as in 46.5 above) (or are incurred for the purposes of such a transaction), they are determined on the assumption that the transaction was entered into on the same terms it would have been if at arm's length between independent persons. This does not, however, apply to:

- debits arising from the acquisition of rights under a loan relationship for less than market value; or
- any related transaction on or after 16 March 2005 where the transaction is one, or part of a series of transactions, to which 46.21 (continuity of treatment to provide for tax neutral intra-group transactions) below applies or would apply but for the fact that the transferor uses fair value accounting; or
- any related transaction before 16 March 2005 between two members of a group of companies (see 12.1 CAPITAL GAINS—GROUPS) or to any of a series of transactions by a member of a group which together have the same effect as a related transaction between members of a group; or
- (for accounting periods beginning on or after 1 October 2002) exchange gains or losses (and see further below); or
- (for accounting periods beginning on or after 1 April 2004 subject to transitional rules for periods straddling that date) amounts falling within *ICTA 1988, Sch 28AA* (see 67 TRANSFER PRICING) whether or not the amounts fall to be adjusted. (The amount falls within *Sch 28AA* without falling to be adjusted in a case where the conditions in *Sch 28AA para 1(1)* are met (see 67.3(*a*)(*b*) TRANSFER PRICING) but the actual provision does not differ from the arm's length provision.)

The exclusion applies only if both group members are within the charge to corporation tax in respect of the transaction. See 12.1 CAPITAL GAINS—GROUPS with regard to the residence requirements for groups of companies.

Exchange gains and losses. For accounting periods beginning *on or after 1 October 2002*, similar treatment applies to exchange gains and losses as follows.

(*a*) Where a company has a debtor relationship in an accounting period, and either:

  (i) the whole or part of any interest or other distribution paid in respect of securities of the company representing that relationship falls to be regarded as a distribution under *ICTA 1988, s 209(2)(e)(vii)* (or, for accounting periods beginning before 1 April 2004 (subject to transitional rules for periods straddling that date), *s 209(2)(da)* – the thin capitalisation rules being subsumed within the transfer pricing rules from that date) (see 23.5, 23.6 DISTRIBUTIONS); or

  (ii) the profits and losses of the company fall by virtue of *ICTA 1988, Sch 28AA* (for accounting periods beginning on or after 1 April 2004 (subject to transitional rules for periods straddling that date), *Sch 28AA para 1*) (not made at arm's length) to be computed as if the loan had not, or had not in part, been made,

  the whole, or a proportionate part, of any exchange gains or losses arising in respect of a liability representing the debtor relationship are to be ignored in determining the loan relationship debits and credits.

(*b*) Where a company has a creditor relationship in an accounting period, and, had the parties been dealing at arm's length, either the transaction giving rise to the loan would not have been entered into at all or the loan would have been smaller, any exchange gains or losses arising in respect of an asset representing the relationship, or in the case of a reduced arm's length loan the non-arm's length element thereof, are to be ignored in determining the loan relationship debits and credits. This does not, however, apply to the extent that the same amount of exchange gains or losses is brought into account (or would be brought into account apart from *FA 1996, s 84A(2)–(10)*, see under Exchange gains and losses in 46.6 above) by a person having a corresponding debtor relationship.

However, for accounting periods ending on or after 6 December 2006, further provisions apply (but where a loan relationship takes place in an accounting period straddling 6 December 2006, and the relationship was terminated before that date, the new provisions do not apply to it). These provisions apply where there is a debtor (or guarantor) company which would be treated as having a loan relationship, if a claim were made under *ICTA 1988, Sch 28AA para 6D(2)* (see 67.8 TRANSFER PRICING) and that company is 'connected' with the corresponding company (see 28.16 FINANCIAL INSTRUMENTS AND DERIVATIVE CONTRACTS). It must be assumed, for determining the exchange gains and losses to be brought into account, that a claim has been made. Where more than one company is treated as having a debtor relationship in respect of the same transactions, the total debtor exchange gains must not exceed the total creditor exchange losses and the total debtor exchange losses must not exceed the total creditor exchange gains.

Imputed interest and other amounts. Where, under *ICTA 1988, Sch 28AA* (see 67 TRANSFER PRICING), any amount falls to be treated as interest payable under a loan relationship of a company, those provisions have effect as if the amounts were actual interest. For accounting periods beginning on or after 1 April 2004 (subject to transitional rules for periods straddling that date), where, any amounts fall under those provisions to be treated as profits, gains or losses (of a revenue or capital nature) arising to, or charges or expenses incurred by, a company in respect of any of its loan relationships or related transactions, those provisions will similarly have effect so as to require credits or debits relating to the deemed amounts to be brought into account to the same extent as if they were actual amounts.

[*FA 1996, Sch 9 paras 11, 11A, 16; FA 2002, Sch 23 paras 10, 11; FA 2004, ss 34(4), 37, Sch 5 paras 6, 8, Sch 10 paras 30, 34; F(No 2)A 2005, Sch 7 para 16; FA 2007, Sch 5 para 14*].

Simon's Direct Tax Service. See **D2.1150, D2.1869, D2.1870.**

46.21 **Continuity of treatment: groups etc.** There are provisions requiring adjustments to ensure that intra-group transactions under the loan relationships regime are tax neutral such provisions having been amended by *F(No 2)A 2005* to prevent the rules from being used to obtain a tax benefit. The provisions apply where, as a result of a 'related transaction' (as in 46.5 above) between two members of a group (both being within the charge to corporation tax in respect of the transaction), one of those companies (the 'transferee company') directly or indirectly replaces the other (the 'transferor company') as a party to a loan relationship or becomes party to a loan relationship which is 'equivalent' (for which see *FA 1996, Sch 9 para 12(7A)*) to a loan relationship to which the other company has ceased to be a party. The provisions similarly apply where a series of transactions, having the same effect as a related transaction between two companies each of which has been a member of the same group at some time in the course of those transactions, results in such a replacement.

The following provisions apply in determining the credits and debits to be brought into account.

(*a*) Where the 'relevant transaction' is on or after 16 March 2005, the transferor company is treated as having entered into the transaction (or the first of a series of transactions, as the case may be) in the accounting period in which the transaction takes place for a consideration equal to the 'notional carrying value' of the loan relationship asset or liability. The transferee is treated as having acquired the loan relationship asset or liability for a consideration equal to that amount for any accounting period in which it is party to the relationship, (This means that where the transferee uses fair value accounting the movement in fair value in the accounting period of transfer will be the difference between the fair value at the end of that period and the carrying value to the transferor of the asset or liability and where amortised cost is used, then the carrying value of the transferor will be used as the cost to the transferee.)

The '*notional carrying value*' is the amount that would have been the carrying value (see 46.7 above) of the asset or liability in the transferor's accounts had a period of account ended immediately before the company ceased to be party to the loan relationship. For that purpose, where the period of account begins before 1 January 2005, 'carrying value' is to be construed as if the period had begun on or after that date (the definition of 'carrying value' in 46.7 above having effect only for periods of account beginning on or after date).

In relation to relevant transactions after 21 March 2006, where a discount arises (within the meaning of *FA 1996, s 100(3A)*, see 46.46(*d*) below) in respect of the transaction (or series of transactions or transfer), the consideration treated as payable by the transferor company is to be increased by the amount of the discount.

(*b*) Where the 'relevant transaction' is before 16 March 2005, the credits and debits to be brought into account for the two companies are determined disregarding the transaction(s) and treating the two companies as the same company. The transaction is not disregarded, however, for the purpose of identifying the company for which any other debit or credit is to be brought into account or, where the transferee company becomes party to the relationship after 8 April 2003, of determining the debits and credits to be brought into account in respect of exchange gains or losses and identifying the company which is to bring them into account.

A '*relevant transaction*' is a related transaction (as in 46.5 above) or the first of a series of related transactions or a transfer by virtue of which these provisions apply or would apply but for the transferor company using fair value accounting (see below).

The transfer pricing provisions of *ICTA 1988, Sch 28AA* (see 67 TRANSFER PRICING) do not apply to amounts so determined in (*a*) or (*b*) above for accounting periods beginning on or after 1 April 2004 (subject to transitional rules for periods straddling that date).

'Group' for these purposes is as under *TCGA 1992, s 170* (see 12.1 CAPITAL GAINS—GROUPS).

The provisions apply equally where one company becomes a party to a loan relationship with rights equivalent to those of the other company under a loan relationship to which the other company previously ceased to be a party. Rights are 'equivalent' for this purpose if they give entitlement to the same rights against the same persons as to capital, interest and dividends and to the same enforcement remedies, notwithstanding differences in nominal value, in the form held or in the manner of transfer.

Similar provisions apply to certain transfers between insurance companies which result in one replacing the other as a party to a loan relationship (and the above provisions are correspondingly disapplied to certain such transfers).

The above provisions apply only to transactions in respect of which both group members are within the charge to corporation tax. See 12.1 CAPITAL GAINS—GROUPS with respect to the residence requirements for groups of companies.

Fair value accounting: accounting periods beginning on or after 1 October 2002. These provisions do not apply where the transferor company uses, or (for relevant transactions after 21 March 2006) is regarded as using, fair value accounting (or, for accounting periods beginning before 1 January 2005 (see 46.1 above), an authorised mark to market basis of accounting) in respect of the loan relationship.

In this case, the amount to be brought into account by the transferor company (where the transferee company becomes party to the relationship after 8 April 2003) is the 'fair value' (as defined by *FA 1996, s 103(1)* (amended by *FA 2006, Sch 6 para 18*)) of the asset (or rights under or interest in the asset) or liability as at the date on which the transferee becomes a party to the loan relationship. In relation to relevant transactions after 21 March 2006, where a discount arises (within the meaning of *FA 1996, s 100(3A)*, see 46.46(*d*) below) in respect of the transaction (or series of transactions or transfer), the consideration treated as payable by the transferor company is to be increased by the amount of the discount.

The amount to be brought into account by the transferee company is:

(i) in the case of relevant transactions after 21 March 2006, the same as the amount brought into account by the transferor company ignoring any discount required to be brought into account by that company;

(ii) in the case of transactions before 22 March 2006, the notional carrying value of the asset or liability in the accounting period in which it becomes party to the relationship or, where the relevant transaction is before 16 March 2005 and:

- the transferee company becomes party to the relationship after 8 April 2003, the same amount as brought into account by the transferor company;
- the transferee company becomes party to the relationship before 8 April 2003, the fair value of the asset, or of the rights under or interest in the asset, as at the date on which that company becomes party to the loan relationship.

For this purpose, in relation to relevant transactions after 21 March 2006, the transferor company is regarded as using fair value accounting as respects the loan relationship only if the debits and credits brought into account in respect of the relationship are determined on a fair value basis, whether or not it uses fair value accounting as respects the relationship.

Where for accounting periods beginning before 1 January 2005, the transferee company uses an accruals basis of accounting, it must make an adjustment under *FA 1996, s 90* (see 46.33 below).

[*FA 1996, Sch 9 para 12; FA 2002, Sch 25 para 29; FA 2003, Sch 37 para 3; FA 2004, Sch 5 para 7, Sch 10 para 31; F(No 2)A 2005, Sch 7 para 17; FA 2006, Sch 6 para 19*].

In the case of *Greene King No 1 Ltd v Adie Sp C, [2005] SSCD 398 (SP C 465)* the debt liabilities of the taxpayer company were assumed by is parent company by novation at fair value which was greater than the book value of the debt in the taxpayer company. The claim for the difference as a non-trading loan relationship deficit under *FA 1996, s 83(2)(a)* was allowed on the basis that (before the *FA 2002* amendments above for accounting periods beginning after 30 September 2002) *FA 1996, Sch 9 para 12* did not apply to a novation of liabilities.

46.22 **Degrouping charge.** A degrouping charge applies where after replacing the transferor company as party to a loan relationship as in 46.21 above, the transferee company ceases within the 'relevant six-year period' to be a member of the group on or after 16 March 2005. The '*relevant six-year period*' is the period of six years following a related transaction between two members of a group companies or following the last of a series of transactions between two companies each of which has been a member of the same group at some time in the course of those transactions.

In this case, the transferee company is treated (subject to the conditions below) as having assigned the loan relationship asset or liability immediately before the cessation for consideration equal to its fair value at that time and as having immediately reacquired it for the same amount. (Thus, any gain is brought into charge to tax under the loan relationship provisions immediately before the transferee leaves the group.)

Where a deemed disposal and reacquisition as above applies, the degrouping charge only applies if a credit would be brought into account by the transferee company on the assignment of the asset or liability or, if that is not the case, a credit would be brought into account under the derivative contract rules (under *FA 2002, Sch 26 para 30A*, see 28.19 FINANCIAL INSTRUMENTS AND DERIVATIVE CONTRACTS) where the loan relationship is a creditor relationship and the company has a hedging relationship (as defined by *FA 2002, Sch 26 para 12(14)*) between a derivative contract and the creditor relationship.

The degrouping charge does not apply where the transferee company ceases to be a member of the group by reason only of an exempt distribution within *ICTA 1988, s 213(2)*. However, if there is a chargeable payment (within the meaning of *ICTA 1988, s 214(2)*) within five years after making the exempt distribution, a degrouping charge arises as above but the transferee company is treated as having assigned the loan relationship asset or liability immediately before making the chargeable payment. As above, the degrouping charge only applies if a credit would be brought into account by the transferee company on the assignment of the asset or liability or, if that is not the case, a credit would be brought into account under the derivative contract rules (under *FA 2002, Sch 26 para 30A*) where the loan relationship is a creditor relationship and the company has a hedging relationship between a derivative contract and the creditor relationship.

[*FA 1996, Sch 9 para 12A; F(No 2)A 2005, Sch 7 para 18*].

46.23 **Transfers on formation of a European Company.** The European Company Statute provides for the formation of a European Company or *Societas Europaea* ('SE') and applies to all member states with effect from 8 October 2004 (see 25.4 EUROPEAN COMMUNITY LEGISLATION). The *Statute* permits the formation of new SEs and also allows for the 'transformation' of existing companies into SEs and for the merger between two (or more) companies in different member states into an SE. Special UK tax provisions are required to deal with the formation of SEs by cross-border merger and those relating to loan relationships are described below. The provisions are intended to be broadly tax-neutral. (Revenue Technical Note, 'Implementation of the European Company Statute', January 2005).

The provisions apply where an SE is formed on or after 1 April 2005 by the merger of two or more companies in accordance with *Council Regulation (EC) No 2157/2001, Arts 2(1), 17(2)* and each merging company is resident in a member state but not all of them are resident in the same member state.

A company is resident in a member state for this purpose if it is within a charge to tax under the law of the State as being resident for that purpose and it is not regarded, for the purposes of any DOUBLE TAX RELIEF (24) arrangements to which the State is a party, as resident in a territory not within a member state.

If, immediately after formation, the SE is within the charge to corporation tax (whether by virtue of residence in the UK or by trading in the UK through a UK permanent establishment), the transfer in the course of the merger of an asset or liability representing a loan relationship is disregarded and the transferor and transferee companies are treated as the same company, except for the purposes of identifying the company for which a debit or credit not relating to the transfer (such as interest) is to be brought into account and determining the debits and credits to be brought into account in respect of exchange gains or losses and identifying the company which is to bring them into account.

The above provisions do not apply unless the formation of the SE is effected for *bona fide* commercial reasons and is not part of a scheme or arrangements of which the main purpose or one of the main purposes is avoiding a liability to tax. Advance clearance can be obtained that this condition is met.

Where the transferor uses fair value accounting for the loan relationship the transfer is not to be disregarded as above but must be treated by both companies as being at fair value.

[*FA 1996, Sch 9 para 12B; F(No 2)A 2005, s 54*].

46.24 **Loan relationships for unallowable purposes.** Any debits which, on a just and reasonable apportionment, are attributable to an 'unallowable purpose' of a loan relationship in an accounting period are not to be brought into account for that period as loan relationship debits or for any other corporation tax purposes. For accounting periods beginning *on or after 1 October 2002*, this also applies to both debits and credits in respect of exchange gains and losses. A purpose for which the company, at times during an accounting period, either is a party to a loan relationship or enters into a 'related transaction' (as in 46.5 above) is an '*unallowable purpose*' if it is not amongst the business or other commercial purposes of the company (which do not include the purposes of any part of its activities which are outside the charge to corporation tax). In this respect a purpose which consists in the securing of a tax advantage (as defined by *ICTA 1988, s 840ZA* from 6 April 2007, formerly within *ICTA 1988, ss 703–709*), see 5.2 ANTI-AVOIDANCE) for any person is a business or other commercial purpose only where it is not a main purpose for which the company is a party to the relationship or entered into the transaction. [*FA 1996, Sch 9 para 13; FA 2002, Sch 23 para 13, Sch 25 para 30; FA 2004, Sch 10 para 32*]. For guidance on the application of the unallowable purposes rule in *FA 1996, Sch 9 para 13*, see HMRC Company Taxation Manual, CTM 56700 *et seq.* and HMRC Corporate Finance Manual, CFM 6216 *et seq.* See also Revenue Tax Bulletin February 2003 pp 1001, 1002 for a specific application of the rule. Details of transactions can be submitted to HMRC in advance for advice on whether the provisions would be applied (see HMRC Corporate Finance Manual, CFM 6228).

Simon's Direct Tax Service. See **D2.1151, D2.1871**.

46.25 **Repo transactions and stock-lending.** From a date to be determined by statutory instrument, *FA 1996, Sch 9 para 15* is replaced. The new version (introduced by *FA 2007, Sch 14 para 18*) applies if a company stops being a party to any loan relationship in any period but under generally accepted accounting practice amounts representing the loan relationships appear in the company's accounts covering the date the relationship ceases or some later period. In such a case, the company has to bring into account the amounts in respect of the loan relationship, even though it has ceased. Any question about the company's loan relationship is determined by reference to the circumstances immediately before the relationship ceased. Where a transaction is within the 'repo' provisions (see 5.5 ANTI-AVOIDANCE) the provisions in *Sch 9 para 15* do not apply to it.

Until a date to be determined by statutory instrument, a 'related transaction' (as in 46.5 above) does not include a disposal or acquisition of rights or liabilities under a loan relationship made in pursuance of any 'repo or stock-lending arrangements'. In consequence, the transferor ('A') does not cease to be a party to the loan relationship, but the above provision does not prevent the transferee ('B') from being treated, for transfers from A to B on or after 2 December 2004 (whenever the arrangements in question were entered into), as a party to the loan relationship as a result of the transfer.

For transfers before 2 December 2004, the transferee is not treated as becoming a party to the loan relationship, although these provisions do not prevent interest from being brought into account as a loan relationship credit on the transferee.(Thus, the new provisions allow for any profits arising under the loan relationship, rather than just the interest, to be taxed.)

'*Repo or stock-lending arrangements*' were arrangements consisting in or involving an agreement or series of agreements under which provision is made:

(*a*) for the transfer from A to B of any rights under that relationship;

(*b*) for A (the transferor) subsequently to be entitled, or to become entitled, or to be required, to have the same or equivalent (as above in relation to *FA 1996, Sch 9 para 12*) rights transferred back to him, or to have rights in respect of benefits accruing in respect of that relationship on redemption.

As regards the transfer back to A in (*b*) above, the transfer had to be made by B so that the two parties to the agreement to buy and sell the rights are the same two parties to the agreement to resell and repurchase the rights. This applies to transfers back to A under arrangements consisting in or involving an agreement made after 26 June 2006 for the transfer of rights by A to B, or an agreement made after that date providing for a transfer to give effect to the entitlement or requirement in (*b*) above otherwise than by B. (This provision reverses the Special Commissioners' decision, confirmed by the High Court in *HMRC v Bank of Ireland Britain Holdings Ltd [2007] EWHC 941 (Ch)* (see 5.9 ANTI-AVOIDANCE).)

For transfers from A to B on or after 2 December 2004 and before a date to be determined by statutory instrument (whenever the arrangements in question were entered into) it is clarified that it is only the transfer from A to B and the transfer back to A that are not treated as related transactions.

In relation to agreements to sell securities made before 9 April 2003, the transferor includes a connected person within *ICTA 1988, s 839* (see 19 CONNECTED PERSONS).

In relation to agreements to sell securities made on or after 9 April 2003, arrangements excluded from *ICTA 1988, s 730A* (as amended by *FA 2002, Sch 25 para 52*) (deemed payments of loan interest in the case of the sale and repurchase of securities, see 5.6 ANTI-AVOIDANCE), by virtue of *subsection* (*8*) of that *section*, are *not* 'repo or stock-lending arrangements'.

The exclusion does not apply to any redemption or discharge of rights or liabilities under a loan relationship to which any repo or stock-lending arrangements relate. The substitution of any securities on or after 2 December 2004 in any case involving a repo arrangement is to be treated for this purpose as if it were an initial transfer from A to B.

The exclusion does not affect the availability or otherwise of double tax relief under *ICTA 1988, s 807A*(*2A*) (see 24.4 DOUBLE TAX RELIEF).

[*FA 1996, Sch 9 para 15; FA 2002, Sch 25 para 32; FA 2003, Sch 38 paras 18, 19; F(No 2)A 2005, Sch 7 para 19; FA 2006, Sch 6 para 20; FA 2007, Sch 14 para 10*].

See also *SI 1998 No 3177, reg 19* as regards certain rights accruing on the conversion of a loan relationship from the currency of a state which has adopted the euro into euro.

Simon's Direct Tax Service. See D2.1117, D2.1844.

46.26 **Deeply discounted securities where companies have a connection and where issued by a close company.** These provisions deal with the situation where, for any accounting period (the 'relevant period'):

(*a*) a debtor relationship is represented by a 'deeply discounted security' issued by a company (or before amendments made by ITTOIA 2005, a 'relevant discounted security');

(*b*) at any time in that period:

  (i) for accounting periods beginning on or after 1 October 2002, another company stands in the position of creditor in respect of that security; or

  (ii) for accounting periods beginning before that date, the security, or any entitlement to rights attached to it, is beneficially owned by the company, or the company is indirectly entitled, by reference to a series of loan transactions, to the benefit of any rights attached to the security);

(*c*) the issuing company was 'connected' with the other company for that period; and

(*d*) the credits representing the full amount of the discount referable to that period are not brought into account for any accounting period in respect of the corresponding creditor relationship.

As regards (*b*)(i) above, this applies to a company which indirectly stands in the position of the creditor as it does to the creditor as respects a deeply discounted security, including where it does so by reference to a series of loan relationships or money debts which would be loan relationships if a company directly stood in the position of creditor or debtor. For accounting periods beginning before 9 April 2003, this applied only where the indirect connection was through a series of deeply discounted securities (and provision is made for proportionate application of the new provision where such an accounting period ends on or after that date).

Where these provisions apply, the debits to be brought into account in respect of the relationship are adjusted so that every debit which relates to the amount of the discount and which is referable to the relevant period is brought into account instead for the accounting period of redemption. The amount of the discount referable to the relevant period for this purpose is the amount which would otherwise be brought into account for the relevant period relating to the difference between the issue price and the amount payable on redemption. That difference is determined on the basis that 'redemption' does not include any redemption which may be made before maturity otherwise than at the option of the holder, and refers to the earliest occasion on which the holder may require redemption, and that the amount payable on redemption excludes any interest.

Companies are '*connected*' for these purposes for the relevant period if, at any time in that period (or, for accounting periods beginning before 1 October 2002, in the two years before the beginning of that period), one controls, or, for accounting periods beginning on or after 1 October 2002, has a 'major interest' (see 46.17 above) in, the other, or both are under the control of the same person (other than the Crown, a Minister of the Crown, a government or NI department, a foreign sovereign power or an organisation of which two or more sovereign powers, or their governments, are members).

For accounting periods beginning before 1 October 2002, the test of control is based on *ICTA 1988, s 416(2)–(6)* (see 16.2 CLOSE COMPANIES). For accounting periods beginning on or after 1 October 2002, control in relation to a company has the same meaning as in *FA 1996, s 87A* (see 46.16 above). Where, as a consequence of this amendment, an issuing company becomes connected with the holder of the discounted security, these rules do not apply if the security was held on the first day of the issuer's first accounting period beginning on or after 1 October 2002.

FA 1996, s 88 (see 46.16 above) applies with appropriate modifications to exempt certain cases from this provision as it would apply to exempt the corresponding creditor relationship.

A '*deeply discounted security*' for these purposes is as defined for the purposes of the income tax rules under *ITTOIA 2005, s 430* and prior to *ITTOIA 2005*, the term previously used of '*relevant discounted security*' was as defined for the purposes of the income tax rules under *FA 1996, Sch 13 para 3* (and see Tolley's Income Tax under Savings and Investment Income for the full definition). It means, broadly, any security which is such that, as at the time of issue, the amount payable on maturity or any other possible occasion of redemption exceeds (or may exceed) the issue price by more than 0.5% of that amount payable on maturity etc. for each year in the 'redemption period' up to a maximum of 30 years.

Exclusions include:

(A) shares in a company;

(B) gilt-edged securities which are not strips;

(C) excluded indexed securities (broadly, where the amount payable on redemption is linked to the value of capital gains tax chargeable assets);

(D) life assurance policies and capital redemption policies (see 46.29 below).

Close companies. A similar restriction applies where:

(I) a debtor relationship of a close company is represented by a deeply discounted security issued by the company;

(II) at any time in (or, for accounting periods beginning before 1 October 2002, before) the accounting period in question (the '*relevant period*') the creditor as respects that security (or, for accounting periods beginning before 1 October 2002, the beneficial owner of the security) was either:

(i) a 'participator' in the debtor company(within *ICTA 1988, s 417*, see 16.3 CLOSE COMPANIES) or, for accounting periods beginning on or after 4 March 2005 (but see transitional rules below), a person who controls a company which is such a participator (a 'participator company'); or

(ii) an 'associate' (within *ICTA 1988, s 417(3)(4)*, see 16.5 CLOSE COMPANIES) of a participator in the debtor company or, for accounting periods beginning on or after 4 March 2005 (but see transitional rules below), an associate of a person who controls a participator company; or

(iii) a company 'controlled' by a participator in the debtor company (within *ICTA 1988, s 416(2)–(6)*, see 16.2 CLOSE COMPANIES) or, for accounting periods beginning on or after 4 March 2005 (but see transitional rules below), by a person who controls a participator company.

However, the restriction does not apply in relation to the debtor relationship in the case of the following exceptions.

- For accounting periods beginning on or after 1 October 2002, the discounted security is held by the creditor where that creditor is a company and brings into account credits representing the full amount of the discount referable to the period in respect of the corresponding creditor relationship.
- For accounting periods ending on or after 10 December 2003, the issuing company is a 'CIS-based close company' and, for accounting periods beginning on or after 4 March 2005 (but see transitional rules below), is a small or medium-sized enterprise (as defined by *ICTA 1988, Sch 28AA para 5D*), and the creditor is not 'resident' (as defined by *ICTA 1988, Sch 28AA para 5B(6)*) in a 'non-qualifying territory' (as defined by *ICTA 1988, Sch 28AA para 5E*).
- For accounting periods beginning on or after 4 March 2005 (but see transitional rules below), the debt is owed to (or to persons acting for) a 'CIS limited partnership' no member of which is resident in a non-qualifying territory at any time in the period where the creditor is connected with the debtor (this to be confirmed in writing by the partnership to the debtor company) and the issuing company is a small or medium-sized enterprise.

A '*CIS-based close company*' is a company that would not be close apart from the attribution under *ICTA 1988, s 416(6)* of the rights and powers of a partner in a 'CIS limited partnership' to other partners by virtue of *ICTA 1988, s 417(3)(a)*. A '*CIS limited partnership*' is a partnership which is a collective investment scheme (see 46.43 below) or would be if not a body corporate.

'Participator' excludes a person who is such by reason only of being a loan creditor of the company (for accounting periods beginning before 1 October 2002, by virtue only of his holding a relevant discounted security issued by the company), and in the case of a banking business, securities acquired in the ordinary course of the business are disregarded. For accounting periods beginning on or after 9 April 2003 (and with proportionate application for accounting periods which straddle that date), a participator in a company which controls another company is treated for this purpose as a participator in that other company.

With regard to the addition to the list of creditors in (II) above which are treated as connected with the debtors for accounting periods beginning on or after 4 March 2005, the accounting periods straddling 4 March 2005 are treated, for these purposes only, as two separate periods, the first ending with the day before that date and the second beginning on that date. Profits and losses are computed accordingly for the two periods and then aggregated (so that the above rules cannot affect profits arising before the relevant date). As regards the exclusion from the restriction for CIS-based companies etc. in (II) above for accounting periods beginning on or after 4 March 2005, where the debt finance is provided to a person under a contract entered into before 4 March 2005, its application in such a case is delayed until accounting periods beginning on or after 1 April 2007 or, if the contract is varied before that date, the date of the variation. The provision above for straddling periods applies equally in this case whether the relevant date is 4 March 2005, 1 April 2007 or the date of the variation. An advance made on or after 4 March 2005 in accordance with terms agreed before that date or a change in the applied interest rate in accordance with terms agreed before that date are not regarded as variations to the contract for these purposes (see the HMRC website (at www.hmrc.gov.uk/international/transferpricing.pdf)).

The debits brought into account in respect of the loan relationship are adjusted so that every debit relating to the amount of the discount referable to the relevant period is brought into account in the accounting period in which the security is redeemed instead of the relevant period (unless the security is redeemed in the relevant period). Where a debit is not brought into account in an accounting period beginning before 1 October 2002, and the deeply discounted security has not been redeemed before the first day of the company's first accounting period beginning on or after that date, these provisions will have effect to bring the debits into account in the accounting period in which the security is redeemed.

Where a discounted security is held for only part of an accounting period, the restriction of the debit in respect of the discounted security is to be time apportioned. This provision applies to a company which indirectly stands in the position of the creditor as it does to the creditor as respects a deeply discounted security, including where it does so by reference to a series of loan relationships or money debts which would be loan relationships if a company directly stood in the position of creditor or debtor. For accounting periods beginning before 9 April 2003, this applied only where the indirect connection was through a series of relevant discounted securities (and provision is made for proportionate application of the new provision where such an accounting period ends on or after that date).

[*FA 1996, Sch 9 paras 17, 18; FA 2002, Sch 25 paras 33, 34, 61–63; FA 2003, Sch 37 paras 2, 4, 5; FA 2004, Sch 8 para 6; ITTOIA 2005, Sch 1 para 489; F(No 2)A 2005, Sch 8 paras 3, 4*].

Simon's Direct Tax Service. See D2.1119, D2.1826.

46.27 **Partnerships involving companies.** Where any of the partners in a partnership which carries on a trade, profession or business is a company, and a money debt is owed to or by the partnership, no account is taken of debits or credits in relation to the money debt, or any loan relationship arising from it, in calculating the profits of the partnership for corporation tax purposes. Each company partner is instead required to bring into account a share of those debits and credits as follows. The credits and debits are determined separately for each company partner as if the money debt were owed to or by the company for trade purposes, and as if anything done by or in relation to the firm in connection with the money debt were done by or in relation to the company. The company must then bring into account a share of those debits and credits corresponding to its share in partnership profits.

Where the company's accounting date or functional currency differs from that of the partnership, HMRC consider that the company is not required to substitute its own accounting date or functional currency for that of the partnership in computing the company partner's credits and debits. (Revenue Tax Bulletin December 2002 pp 987–989).

Where the pre-2004 basis of computation applies (see 46.1 above), an authorised accruals basis of accounting must be used by the company partners to determine the debits and credits to be brought into account. However, where a company partner uses an authorised mark to market basis for its interest in the partnership, it must similarly use an authorised mark to market basis in determining those debits and credits, unless any provisions within the loan relationship rules require an authorised accruals basis to be used. Similarly, where the post-2004 basis of computation applies (see 46.1 above), and where a company partner uses fair value accounting for its interest in the partnership, it must use fair value accounting in determining those debits and credits.

Credits and debits relating to exchange gains or losses are generally included in the determination of credits and debits (as in 46.6 above) but may be excluded to the extent that they are recognised in the firm's statement of recognised gains or losses or statement of changes in equity (or, where the pre-2004 basis of computation applies (see 46.1 above), to the extent they are carried to and sustained by partnership reserves).

Where the partnership holds a deeply discounted security (within the meaning of *FA 1996, Sch 9 para 17* — see 46.26 above) each partner is treated as beneficially entitled to a separate share of the security corresponding to their share in partnership profits.

Where a company partner is a debtor or creditor in relation to money lent by or to the partnership, and the company controls the partnership by virtue of *ICTA 1988, s 840*, the connection rules in *FA 1996, s 87(3)(a)* (see 46.9 above) relating to impairment losses (or, where the pre-2004 basis of computation applies (see 46.1 above), relief for bad debts) apply for the accounting period in question in determining the credits and debits of each of the company partners. Control of the partnership may for this purpose be by the company alone or by the company together with other company partners which it controls or is controlled by or which are under common control ('control' for this purpose being as under *FA 1996, s 87A* (see 46.16 above)). (This provision does not affect the treatment of a loans made by partners to the partnership which are treated as partners' equity.)

[*FA 1996, Sch 9 para 19; FA 2002, Sch 25 para 35; FA 2004, s 52, Sch 10 para 35*].

As a result of the above legislation applying for accounting periods beginning on or after 1 October 2002, HMRC Statement of Practice, SP 4/98 (see 46.45 below) has been withdrawn.

46.28 **Rate of interest reset.** This provision applies from the 'relevant day' where the object, or one of the main objects, of a company entering into or becoming a party to a creditor loan relationship was to secure a tax advantage (within the meaning of *ICTA 1988, s 709*, see 5.2 ANTI-AVOIDANCE), whether for itself or another person, and the difference between the issue price of the asset representing the relationship and its fair value after a change in either:

(i) the rate of interest;

(ii) the amount payable to discharge the debt; or

(iii) the time at which any payments relating to the asset (whether interest or otherwise) fall due,

is at least 5% of the issue price. With effect from the day on which those conditions are satisfied, a basis of fair value accounting (or, where the pre-FA 2004 basis of computation applies (see 46.1 above), an authorised mark to market basis of accounting) must be used by any company as respects a creditor relationship represented by the asset.

The '*relevant day*' is 19 December 2001 in the case where a change in the interest payable brings the provisions into effect, or 24 April 2002 in any other case.

Where the pre-FA 2004 basis of computation applies (see 46.1 above) and the use of the mark to market basis results in a change of accounting method (see below), no debit is to be brought into account under *FA 1996, s 90(2)(c), (3)(b)* (debits brought into account in the accounting period in which the change of method takes effect). Where this provision applies in a case where a mark to market basis of accounting was not used before the relevant day in respect of an asset representing a creditor relationship, the asset is treated as having been acquired by the company on that day at its fair value. See 46.17 above as respect a change of accounting basis in the case of connected parties where the post-FA 2004 basis of computation applies (see 46.1 above).

The fair value of an asset for these purposes is to be determined on the assumption that all amounts payable by the debtor will be paid in full as they fall due.

[*FA 1996, s 88A; FA 2002, s 71; FA 2004, s 52, Sch 10 para 6*].

46.29 **Miscellaneous provisions.** *Options etc.* Where the amortised cost basis of accounting (or, where the pre-2004 basis of computation applies (see 46.1 above), the accruals basis) applies for an accounting period, and the question of an amount becoming due under a loan relationship after the end of the period (or of its amount or timing) depends on the exercise of an option by a party to the relationship, it is assumed that the option will be exercised in the manner which, as at the end of the period, appears most advantageous to that party (disregarding taxation). This applies equally where the option is exercisable by an associate of a party to the relationship (within *ICTA 1988, s 417(3)(4)*, see 16.5 CLOSE COMPANIES), and where a similar power is exercisable other than under an option. [*FA 1996, Sch 9 para 3; FA 2004, s 52, Sch 10 para 19*].

Distributions. Credits and debits relating to any amounts treated as DISTRIBUTIONS (23) are excluded from these provisions, but this does not prevent them from being brought into charge to corporation tax for other purposes. [*FA 1996, Sch 9 para 1; FA 2002, Sch 25 para 20*].

Interest etc. relating to capital expenditure. Debits or credits in respect of a loan relationship which, under generally accepted accounting practice, are allowed to be treated as amounts brought into account in determining the value of a fixed capital asset or project are to be brought into account as if they were treated as profit and loss items. However, no debit may be brought into account under these rules if it has been taken into account in determining a debit arising from any INTANGIBLE ASSETS (39) under *FA 2002, Sch 29*. Where the pre-2004 basis of computation applies (see 46.1 above) and a debit is brought into account under this provision, no further debit will be allowed for the writing down of that debit attributable to the value of the fixed capital assets or project or for the amortisation or depreciation representing a writing off of the interest component of the asset. [*FA 1996, Sch 9 para 14; FA 2002, Sch 25 para 31; FA 2004, s 52, Sch 10 para 33*]. See Simon's Direct Tax Service D2.1124.

Interest etc. recognised in equity or shareholders' funds. For periods of account beginning on or after 1 January 2005, where debits or credits in respect of a loan relationship are, under generally accepted accounting practice, recognised in equity or shareholders' funds but not in any of the company's statements of items brought into account in computing profits or losses for the period, they are to be brought into account as if they were treated as profit and loss items. (Such items may, for example, be amounts taken to share premium account or interest treated for accounting purposes as a dividend on equity.) [*FA 1996, Sch 9 para 14A; FA 2005, s 80, Sch 4 para 30*].

Company ceasing to be UK-resident etc. Where, on or after 17 March 2003, a company ceases to be UK-resident, it will be deemed to have assigned the assets and liabilities representing its loan relationships immediately before and to have reacquired them immediately after it ceased to be UK-resident, at their fair value, unless the assets or liabilities continue to be held or owed for the purposes of the company's UK permanent establishment (see 60.5 RESIDENCE). The provision similarly applies where an asset or liability ceases to be held for the purposes of a UK permanent establishment of a non-UK resident company in any circumstances not involving a related transaction. (Thus, any profit or loss on an asset or liability will be brought into account as a loan relationship credit or debit.) This does not apply, however, if, on or after 16 March 2005, the provisions in 46.22 above apply (application of degrouping charge where a transferee company leaves the group within six years) and the company leaves the group under those provisions at the same time as it ceases to be UK-resident. (the provisions in 46.27 above having priority over this provision). [*FA 1996, Sch 9 para 10A; FA 2004, Sch 8 para 5, Sch 10 para 29; F(No 2)A 2005, Sch 7 para 15*].

Life assurance policies and capital redemption contracts. For accounting periods beginning on or after 1 October 2002, debits and credits relating to a life assurance policy (within the meaning of *ICTA 1988, Pt 13 Ch 2*) are excluded from these provisions, but this does not prevent their being brought into charge to corporation tax for other purposes.

This provision similarly applies from the same date to capital redemption policies but the exclusion ceases to have effect on or after 10 February 2005 (whenever the policy was effected) so that the loan relationship rules apply (which puts beyond doubt that a capital redemption bond cannot give rise to an allowable capital loss – see the Explanatory Notes to Finance Bill (No 3) 2005). Where a capital redemption policy is held by a company immediately before 10 February 2005 and on or after that date is a creditor relationship of the company, the company is treated as having assigned all the rights in the policy immediately before 10 February 2005 and to have acquired the creditor relationship for money or money's worth of an amount equal to what the carrying value in the company's accounts would have been had an accounting period of the company on that date. (See 46.7 above as regards 'carrying value'.) However, the gain which would have fallen to be brought into account on the deemed assignment under *ICTA 1988, s 547(1)(b)* is to be brought into account for the accounting period in which the company ceases to be party to the creditor relationship if that period does not coincide with the accounting period in which the assignment is deemed to have happened.

[*FA 1996, Sch 9 para 1A; FA 2002, Sch 25 para 21; F(No 2)A 2005, Sch 7 para 14*].

46.30 PRE-2004 BASIS COMPUTATIONAL PROVISIONS

Authorised accounting methods. Where the pre-FA 2004 basis of computation applies (see 46.1 above), except as below, the alternative accounting methods authorised for the purposes of the current provisions are an accruals basis and a mark to market basis under which a fair value (on the basis of a transfer at arm's length) is brought into account in each accounting period for each loan relationship to which it applies. Whichever method is used must:

(*a*) conform (subject to (*b*)–(*d*) below) to generally accepted accounting practice (see 55.2 PROFIT COMPUTATIONS);

(*b*) contain proper provision for allocating payments under a loan relationship or, for accounting periods beginning *on or after 1 October 2002*, as a result of a 'related transaction' (see 46.5 above) to accounting periods;

(*c*) (for accounting periods beginning *on or after 1 October 2002*) contain proper provision for determining exchange gains and losses from loan relationships for accounting periods; and

(*d*) in the case of an accruals basis, not contain any provision (other than authorised bad debt arrangements, for which see 46.9 above, or, for accounting periods beginning *on or after 1 October 2002*, provision for exchange losses) giving debits by reference to the valuation at different times of any asset representing a loan relationship.

As regards (*b*), a mark to market basis must allocate payments to the accounting period in which they become due and payable. An accruals basis must:

(i) allocate payments to the period to which they relate, without regard to payment or receipt or their becoming due and payable;

(ii) apportion payments relating to two or more periods to those periods on a just and reasonable basis;

(iii) assume (subject to authorised bad debt arrangements, see 46.9 above), in relation to a creditor company, that every amount payable under the relationship will be paid in full when due;

(iv) secure the making of the adjustments required by authorised bad debt arrangements; and

(v) provide (subject to authorised arrangements for bad debt and for writing off government investments, see 46.9 and 46.14 above), in respect of debts released, for the appropriate amount to be credited to the debtor in the accounting period of the release.

Where a purchased loan is repayable on demand, (i) above does not always require that the loan is brought in on acquisition at full value (thus producing an immediate credit of the difference between that value and acquisition cost). If generally accepted accounting practice would not recognise the discount in the accounting period of the acquisition (whether or not the debt was doubtful), immediate recognition of the profit for tax purposes may also be inappropriate. However, in the case of a loan relationship between connected parties (see below), the assumption must still be made that all amounts will be paid in full without relief for bad or doubtful debts (see 46.9 above), so that the discount must be recognised on a time-scale which would be realistic for a loan repayable on demand and neither bad nor doubtful. (Revenue Tax Bulletin June 1997 pp 441, 442).

[*FA 1996, s 85; FA 2002, Sch 23 para 4, Sch 25 para 5; FA 2004, s 52, Sch 10 para 3*].

46.31 **Application of accounting methods.** *Where the pre-FA 2004 basis of computation applies* (see 46.1 above), different authorised accounting methods may be used as respects different loan relationships, and for different accounting periods (or parts) as respects the same relationship. If an accounting basis which is, or which 'equates' with, an authorised accounting method is used as respects any loan relationship in a company's 'statutory accounts' (see *FA 1996, s 86(8)(9)*), it, or the authorised method with which it equates, must similarly be used for periods covered by those accounts. Where the method to be used is not thereby determined or, in the case of UK branches of overseas companies, is not determined as set out below, an authorised accruals basis must be used.

A basis of accounting '*equates*':

(*a*) with an authorised accruals basis, if (not being within (*b*)) it purports to allocate payments under a loan relationship to accounting periods according to when they are taken to accrue;

(*b*) with an authorised mark to market basis if, otherwise being within (*a*), it purports to bring the loan relationship into account in each accounting period at a value representing an arm's length valuation on the basis that interest already accrued under the relationship was to be disregarded, and the resulting credits and debits correspond, for all practical purposes, to those under an authorised mark to market basis; and

(*c*) with an authorised mark to market basis, if (not being within (*a*)) it purports, in respect of a loan relationship, to produce credits or debits which relate to payments under the relationship according to when they become due and payable, and which are computed by reference to the determination, as at different times in an accounting period, of a fair value (on the basis of a transfer at arm's length).

UK branches of overseas companies. For accounting periods beginning *on or after 1 October 2002*, a non-resident company can elect to use (with respect to a UK branch) a mark to market accounting basis for those of its loan relationships for which it would use that method if its accounts were drawn up in accordance with generally accepted accounting practice for UK companies but for which that basis is not used in its own statutory accounts. Where such an election is made, an equivalent election is also treated as made under *FA 2002, Sch 26 para 19*, with effect for the same accounting periods, as respects any derivative contracts to which the company is or may become a party in any of those accounting periods, notwithstanding that the deemed election may fall outside the prescribed time limits for a *paragraph 19* election (see 28.11(C) FINANCIAL INSTRUMENTS AND DERIVATIVE CONTRACTS). The election must be made within two years after the end of the company's first accounting period beginning on or after 1 October 2002 in which it becomes a party to a loan relationship eligible for the election. It has effect for the accounting period in which it is made and all subsequent accounting periods, and is irrevocable.

If a non-resident company does not make such an election, and the correct basis under generally accepted UK company accounting practice for some or all of both its loan relationships and its derivative contracts would be an authorised mark to market basis, then if it uses that basis for an accounting period in its statutory accounts for those derivative contracts but not for those loan relationships, it must, for the purposes of these provisions, use that basis for that accounting period for all those of its loan relationships for which it would be used under generally accepted UK company accounting practice.

[*FA 1996, s 86; FA 2002, Sch 25 para 6; FA 2004, s 52, Sch 10 para 3*].

46.32 **Inconsistent application.** For accounting periods beginning before 1 October 2002, where there is any inconsistency or other material difference between the way in which an authorised accounting method is applied as respects the same loan relationship in successive accounting periods, a balancing debit or credit must be brought into account in the later of those periods (the '*second period*'). The amount to be debited or credited (as appropriate) is the aggregate (treating debits or net debits as negative) of:

(*a*) a debit (or, if the result is negative, a credit) equal to the amount by which the aggregate credits actually brought into account for all previous periods (i.e. periods before the second period) in which the accounting method was used exceeds the aggregate which would have been brought in had the method been applied in those periods in the same way as it was in the second period; and

(*b*) a credit (or, if the result is negative, a debit) equal to the amount by which the aggregate debits actually brought into account for all previous periods in which the accounting method was used exceeds the aggregate which would have been brought in had the method been applied in those periods in the same way as it was in the second period.

For accounting periods beginning on or after 1 October 2002, this provision is rendered unnecessary, since a similar adjustment will be made in the company's profit and loss account in accordance with generally accepted accounting practice and debits and credits brought into account accordingly by virtue of *FA 1996, s 84* (see 46.5 above).

[*FA 1996, s 89; FA 2002, Sch 25 para 9*].

46.33 **Change of accounting basis.** For accounting periods beginning on or after 1 October 2002 and where the pre-FA 2004 basis of computation applies (see 46.1 above), where there is a change in accounting method, the debits or credits will be brought into account by *FA 1996, s 84* where profits and losses are accounted for in accordance with generally accepted accounting practice (see 46.5 above). As a result, the following provisions only apply where the change of method is by reason of the application of the loan relationship rules but will not apply where such a change is mirrored in the company's statutory accounts. See 46.16 above as regards a change in accounting basis in the case of connected companies where the post-FA 2004 basis of computation applies (see 46.1 above).

Where, for accounting periods beginning before 1 October 2002 (after which see below), the use of one authorised accounting method is superseded by another during an accounting period as respects the same loan relationship, it is to be assumed that:

(*a*) the party ceased to be a party to the relationship immediately before the change, and again became a party to it immediately after the change;

(*b*) the relationship before the change is separate and distinct from the relationship after the change;

(*c*) the amount payable under each of the transactions comprised in the assumptions in (*a*) above was equal to the fair value (on the basis of a transfer at arm's length) of the relationship;

(*d*) so far as relevant, the amount in (*c*) above is deemed to have become due at the time of the change.

Each method is then applied on those assumptions as respects the part of the period for which it is used, the associated debits and credits being taken into account for the period. Where the change takes place at the beginning of an accounting period, the aggregate net credit or debit which would have arisen by the application of the methods actually used for that period and for the previous period without the making of those assumptions is subtracted from the aggregate which would have arisen on those assumptions, and the resulting net credit or debit is brought into account for the period as from the beginning of which the change takes effect.

Where a mark to market basis is superseded by an accruals basis of accounting, the relationship in question is one to which the company is still a party at the end of the accounting period (or part) for which the accruals basis is used, and the amount which would have accrued in that period (or part) falls to be determined in accordance with the above assumptions, that amount is computed using the closing value at the end of that period (or part) *without* making those assumptions. Previously, this provision applied whether or not the company was still a party to the loan relationship in question at the end of the period (or part) for which the accruals basis was used, and the amount falling to be determined as above was taken to be (B – A), where:

A is the amount which on those assumptions is given as an opening value for the period (or part); and

B would have been taken to be the closing value applicable as at the end of that period (or part) if such an accounting basis had always been used.

[*FA 1996, s 90; FA 1997, s 83; FA 2002, Sch 25 para 10; FA 2004, s 52, Sch 10 para 7*].

Simon's Direct Tax Service. See **D2.1110, D2.1113, D2.1815.**

46.34 DEDUCTION OF TAX

This provision deals with the situation where a company receives a payment under deduction of income tax, and a credit relating to that interest has been brought into account on the company under the current provisions for an accounting period ending more than two years before receipt of the payment. On a claim, the income tax deducted may be set against the corporation tax liability for the accounting period in which the payment is received.

In determining for which accounting period a credit was brought in in respect of a subsequent interest payment, interest payments are identified with the earliest possible outstanding liability for interest under the relationship in question, according to the accounting method most recently used. Thus where an accruals basis is used, the earliest outstanding liability is determined by reference to the time the interest accrued, whilst if a mark to market basis is used, it is determined by reference to the time the interest became due and payable.

A claim must be made to an officer of HMRC by the end of two years after the accounting period in which the payment is received or, if later, by the end of six years after the accounting period in which the credit in respect of the interest was brought into account.

Where a claim would be out of time in respect of a payment of interest, no claim may be made under *ICTA 1988, Sch 16 para 5* (see 37.5 INCOME TAX IN RELATION TO A COMPANY) for set-off of that payment.

This provision is repealed by *FA 2002, Sch 25 para 11* following the effective abolition, with effect from 1 April 2001, of withholding tax on payments to persons subject to corporation tax (see 37.3 INCOME TAX IN RELATION TO A COMPANY).

[*FA 1996, s 91; FA 2002, Sch 25 para 11*].

Simon's Direct Tax Service. See **D2.1138**.

46.35 **SPECIAL CASES**

Shares treated as loan relationships. A share in one company (the '*issuing company*') held on or after 16 March 2005 by another company (the '*investing company*') is treated for an accounting period of the investing company as if it were rights under a creditor relationship of that company. Such treatment applies to that part of an accounting period during which it is 'subject to outstanding third party obligations' and an 'interest-like investment'. Where this provision applies, distributions in respect of the share are treated as if they were not distributions within *ICTA 1988, s 209(2)(a)(b)* (see 23.1, 23.2 DISTRIBUTIONS), and the debits and credits to be brought into account under the loan relationship rules must be determined on the basis of fair value accounting. For accounting periods ending before 22 March 2006, this treatment applies to an accounting period if the above conditions are met at any time in that period.

For this purpose, a share is '*subject to outstanding third party obligations*' if it is subject to undischarged obligations ('*third party obligations*') to meet unpaid calls on it or to make a contribution to the capital of the issuing company that could affect the share's value and those obligations are obligations of a person other than the investing company. A share is an '*interest-like investment*' if its nature is such that its fair value is likely to increase at a rate which represents a return on an investment of money at a commercial rate of interest (as defined) and is unlikely (ignoring fluctuations resulting from exchange rate changes) to deviate to a substantial extent from that rate of increase. It is assumed for this purpose that any third party obligations will be met in the amounts and at the time at which they are due and that no transaction (or series of transactions) intended to cause the share not to be an interest-like investment will be entered into. In determining debits and credits for the purpose of these transactions, amounts are left out of account which would cause those assumptions not to be met.

In relation to shares held by the company on or after 22 March 2006, a share is also '*subject to outstanding third party obligations*' if it is, or will, or might under any 'relevant arrangements' be, subject to third party obligations (as defined above) and those obligations can include obligations of the investing company which, under any 'relevant arrangements' will, or might be, discharged directly or indirectly by a person other than the investing company. '*Arrangements*' include any agreement or understanding (whether or not legally enforceable) and they are '*relevant*' if entered into at any time on or before the share was issued. In relation to an accounting period beginning before 22 March 2006, debits and credits are to be brought into account under the loan relationship rules as a result of these changes only in respect of amounts relating to any time on or after that date. In relation to shares held on or after 6 March 2007, 'shares' do not include shares in a building society. For straddling accounting periods, such shares are to be left out of account only if they relate to a time on or after that date.

A share is treated as continuing to be held by a company notwithstanding that it has been transferred to another person under a repo or stock lending arrangement or under a transaction treated as not involving a disposal by *TCGA 1992, s 26* (transfer of asset by way of security).

[*FA 1996, s 91A; F(No 2)A 2005, Sch 7 paras 10(2)(7), 13; FA 2006, Sch 6 para 13; FA 2007, Sch 5 para 12*].

Non-qualifying shares. A share is also treated as rights under a creditor relationship for that part of an accounting period of an investing company during which the above provisions do not apply and the share is a 'non-qualifying share' and is not in any event treated as such rights under *FA 1996, Sch 10 para 4* (holdings in unit trusts and offshore funds — see 46.43 below). Where this provision applies, distributions in respect of the share are treated, during those times, as if they were not distributions within *ICTA 1988, s 209(2)(a)(b)* (see 23.1, 23.2 DISTRIBUTIONS), and the debits and credits to be brought into account under the loan relationship rules must be determined on the basis of fair value accounting. For accounting periods ending before 22 March 2006, this treatment applies to an accounting period if the above conditions are met at any time in that period and if the conditions relating to outstanding third party obligations under *FA 1996, s 91A* (above) do not apply throughout that period in relation to the share. For an accounting period beginning before that date, debits and credits are to be brought into account under the loan relationship rules as a result of these changes only in respect of amounts relating to any time on or after that date.

A share is a 'non-qualifying share' if *ICTA 1988, s 95* (taxation of dealers in respect of distributions — see 57.7 PURCHASE OF A COMPANY OF ITS OWN SHARES) does not apply to distributions in respect of it and if one or more of the conditions listed below is satisfied. Broadly, and subject to further conditions and exclusions, those conditions are as follows.

1. The assets of the issuing company are of such a nature that the fair value of the share is likely to increase at a rate which represents a return on an investment of money at a commercial rate of interest and is unlikely (ignoring fluctuations resulting from exchange rate changes) to deviate to a substantial extent from that rate of increase. This condition is not satisfied if the whole or substantially the whole by fair value of the assets of the issuing company are 'income producing' (as defined). It is assumed that no transaction (or series of transactions) intended to cause this condition not to be satisfied will be entered into by the investing company and where the condition is satisfied, no debits are to be brought into account in relation to any such transactions that would (apart from that assumption) cause the condition not to be satisfied.

2. The share is 'redeemable' (as defined), is designed to produce a return which equates, in substance, to the return on an investment of money at a commercial rate of interest and is not an 'excepted share' (as defined). (Note that the definition of 'redeemable' shares is amended by *FA 2006, Sch 6 para 15* for shares held on or after 12 May 2006 and the definition of 'excepted shares' is amended for shares held on or after 22 March 2006.)

3. There is a scheme or arrangement under which the share and one or more 'associated transactions' (as defined) are together designed to produce a return which equates, in substance, to the return on an investment of money at a commercial rate of interest. This condition is not satisfied if the share by itself is within either of the above conditions, or would be but for falling within the income producing assets or excepted share exemptions from those conditions. Where this condition is satisfied debits and credits in relation to any such associated transaction is to be brought into account on a fair value basis by the investing company under the derivative contracts rules (see 28 DERIVATIVE CONTRACTS AND FINANCIAL INSTRUMENTS) as if it were, or were a transaction in respect of, a derivative contract (if that is not in fact the case).The Treasury has the power to add, vary or remove conditions by regulations.

[*FA 1996, ss 91B–91F; F(No 2)A 2005, Sch 7 paras 10(3)–(5)(7), 13; FA 2006, Sch 6 paras 13–15; FA 2007, Sch 5 para 13*].

Where, at any time on or after 16 March 2005, either *FA 1996, s 91A* or *s 91B* above begins to apply in the case of any shares, the investing company is deemed for chargeable gains purposes to have disposed of the share immediately before that time, and to have immediately reacquired it, at its fair value. This does not apply in the case of a share held by a company at the end of 15 March 2005 and at the beginning of 16 March 2005 if either of the provisions applies at the beginning of 16 March 2005. In the latter case, *TCGA 1992, s 116* (reorganisations involving qualifying corporate bonds (see Tolley's Capital Gains Tax) applies on the assumption that the share became an asset representing a creditor relationship of the company, and therefore a qualifying corporate bond, as a result of a 'relevant transaction' on 16 March 2005 in relation to which the share immediately before 16 March 2005 was the 'old asset' and the asset representing the creditor relationship immediately after the beginning of that day was the 'new asset'. (See Tolley's Capital Gains Tax under Qualifying Corporate Bonds for the meaning of these expressions.)

Where at any time, either *FA 1996, s 91A* or *s 91B* above cease to apply to a share, the investing company is deemed for chargeable gains purposes to have disposed of the share immediately before that time, and to have immediately reacquired it, at its fair value. If the deemed disposal occurs before 1 January 2006 in respect of a share to which *TCGA 1992, s 116* applied in the circumstances indicated above, the disposal is not regarded as a disposal for the purposes of *TCGA 1992, s 116(10)(b)(c)* (gain or loss on old asset deemed to accrue on disposal of new asset) and the share continues to be treated as the new asset for the purposes of that section.

[*FA 1996, s 91G; F(No 2)A 2005, Sch 7 para 10(6)*].

See HMRC guidance on 'Shares as Debt Rules' to be published in the HMRC Corporate Finance Manual, CFM6322–CFM6388, for the background on the avoidance schemes giving rise to this legislation, an overview and HMRC's interpretation of the legislation, transitional rules and the interaction with the arbitration rules (see 5.27 ANTI-AVOIDANCE).

46.36 **Benefits derived by connected persons.** In the case of a creditor relationship to which a company is a party after 21 March 2006, the creditor company must use fair value accounting for any credits brought into account where:

- the return to the creditor company from the relationship is less than a '*commercial return*' (a return on an investment of money at a commercial rate of interest);
- another company connected with the creditor (see 19 CONNECTED PERSONS) derives any benefit (including value in any form) as a result of any arrangements made in consequence of, or otherwise in connection with, the relationship, and
- the benefit derived by the connected company is designed to make up for part or all of the amount lost to the creditor company as a result of the return being less than a commercial return.

'*Arrangements*' includes any agreement or understanding (whether or not legally enforceable). In determining the return to the creditor company from the relationship any benefit, which it derives directly or indirectly from the above benefit derived by the connected company, is to be disregarded. Amounts are to be brought into account as a result of this provision only to the extent that they relate to any time after 21 March 2006.

[*FA 1996, s 93C; FA 2006, Sch 6 para 16*].

46.37 **Convertible securities etc.: creditor relationships.** The following provisions apply (subject to the transitional rules below) *where the pre-FA 2004 basis of computation applies* (see 46.1 above). Where a loan relationship is a convertible security as set out in (*a*) to (*h*) below, the amounts falling to be brought into account under the current provisions in respect of the relationship are confined to those relating to interest and, (for accounting periods beginning on or after 1 October 2002) exchange gains and losses, and must be ascertained using an authorised accruals basis of accounting. The normal chargeable gains provisions apply to the asset representing the relationship as if it did not represent a loan relationship, with the appropriate adjustment for interest accrued but not received. This provision does not, however, apply to a loan relationship the disposal of which would fall to be treated as in the course of activities forming an integral part of a trade carried on by the company.

For accounting periods beginning on or after 1 October 2002, an adjustment is also to be made for exchange gains and losses in an accounting period where this provision applies, or for a just and reasonable fraction of the exchange gains or losses where an asset does not fall within this provision for the whole of the accounting period. The consideration for disposal of the asset is to be increased to include any net exchange losses and decreased to exclude any net exchange gains brought into account as loan relationship debits or credits. Where the exclusion of net exchange gains would reduce the consideration to below nil, the excess gain is to be treated as part of the incidental costs incurred on disposal of the asset (under *TCGA 1992, s 38(1)(c)*).

For the treatment of such securities where the post-FA 2004 basis of computation applies, see the embedded derivative provisions at 46.40 below and at 28.27 DERIVATIVE CONTRACTS AND FINANCIAL INSTRUMENTS.

The above provisions apply to an asset if:

(*a*) it represents a creditor relationship of a company;

(*b*) the rights attached to it include provision by virtue of which the company is, or may become, entitled to acquire any shares in a company (subject to (*c*) below);

(*c*) for accounting periods ending on or after 26 July 2001, the only shares which may be acquired under (*b*) above are 'qualifying ordinary shares' or 'mandatorily convertible preference shares';

(*d*) the extent to which shares may be acquired under (*b*) is not determined using a cash value specified in the provision or ascertainable by reference to its terms;

(*e*) it is neither a 'deeply discounted security' (within *ITTOIA 2005, s 430*) (or before the application of *ITTOIA 2005*, a 'relevant discounted security' (within *FA 1996, Sch 13 para 13*)) (see 46.26 above) nor, for accounting periods ending on or after 26 July 2001, an 'excluded indexed security' (within *ITTOIA 2005, s 433* or, before the application of *ITTOIA 2005*, within *FA 1996, Sch 13 para 13*);

(*f*) for accounting periods ending on or after 26 July 2001, the company holding the asset does not have the right to require any person other than the issuing company to acquire it for an amount involving a 'deep gain' on redemption (see 46.26 above);

(*g*) when it came into existence, there was more than a negligible likelihood that the rights to acquire shares (as in (*b*) above) would in due course be exercised to a significant extent; and

(*h*) for accounting periods ending on or after 26 July 2001, the rights to acquire shares (as in (*b*) above), when fully exercised, would result in the replacement of the entire asset by shares (plus any cash in respect of a fractional share entitlement, which must not exceed 5% of the value of the shares), and the ending of the creditor relationship.

As regards (*c*) above, '*mandatorily convertible preference shares*' are shares (other than 'qualifying ordinary shares') which must, within 24 hours of acquisition, be converted into or exchanged for 'qualifying ordinary shares'. '*Qualifying ordinary shares*' are shares which are either listed on a recognised stock exchange or shares in a holding or trading company (within *TCGA 1992, Sch A1 para 22(1)*), and which are not shares carrying no right to payment of a dividend or other profit share in the company or a right only to a dividend at a fixed rate. In either case these conditions must have been met when the asset in question came into existence and at all times since.

If an asset continuing to represent a creditor relationship ceases after that date to be a convertible security within these provisions (which would be the case if it becomes a relevant discounted security), there is deemed to be a disposal and reacquisition by the company at current value (adjusted for accrued interest and any exchange gains and losses as above) under the appropriate accounting method, with the resulting gain or loss deferred under *FA 1996, s 92(8)* concerning share reorganisations etc. involving the issue of a qualifying corporate bond (see Tolley's Capital Gains Tax under Qualifying Corporate Bonds). The 'current value' is not simply the market value at that time (see HMRC Corporate Finance Manual, CFM 6161). For disposals after 1 April 2002, the gain held over may be exempt under *TCGA 1992, Sch 7AC* (see 13 CAPITAL GAINS—SUBSTANTIAL SHAREHOLDINGS).

Those of the above provisions which apply to accounting periods ending on or after 26 July 2001 do not apply to determine, in relation to any part of an accounting period falling before that date, whether or not an asset falls within *section 92*. Nor do they apply, for accounting periods straddling that date, to any assets representing a loan relationship to which the company ceased be a party before that date. An asset held on 26 July 2001 to which *section 92* ceases to apply by virtue only of the changes applicable from that date will be treated for capital gains purposes as disposed of and reacquired immediately before that date.

Issuing company not to be connected company. The above provisions do not apply for accounting periods ending on or after 19 December 2001 to assets held on or after that date where there is a 'connection' between the issuer and the holder. They cease to apply where such a connection arises after the issue of the security, in which case a deemed disposal will arise for chargeable gains purposes (as above). However, they continue to apply where either:

(i) the parties were not so connected in an accounting period ending before 19 December 2001 when the creditor company held the asset; or

(ii) immediately before 19 December 2001, one of the companies was not a '100% subsidiary' of the other company and they were not both 100% subsidiaries of a third company.

'*Connection*' for these purposes is as defined by *FA 1996, s 87(3)* (see 46.16 above). '*Subsidiary*' is as defined by *ICTA 1988, s 838* (substituting 100% for 75% in the definition of '75% subsidiary').

This provision does not apply to determine, in relation to any part of an accounting period falling before 19 December 2001, whether or not an asset falls within *FA 1996 s 92*. Nor does it apply to any assets representing the loan relationship which the company ceased to hold before that date even though held in that accounting period. An asset held on 19 December 2001 to which *section 92* ceases to apply by virtue only of the changes applicable from that date will be treated for capital gains purposes as disposed of and reacquired immediately before that date.

Transitional rules. Where a company holds an asset to which the above provisions apply at the end of the last accounting period beginning before the post-2004 basis of computation applies (see 46.1 above), the asset will be deemed for capital gains purposes to have been disposed of immediately before and reacquired immediately after that time by virtue of *FA 1996, s 92(7)* (as if the asset had ceased to be a *section 92* asset without ceasing to represent a creditor relationship of the company). The resulting gain or loss is deferred under *FA 1996, s 92(8)* concerning share reorganisations etc. involving the issue of a qualifying corporate bond (see Tolley's Capital Gains Tax under Qualifying Corporate Bonds).

[*FA 1996, s 92; FA 1999, s 65(7)(9); FA 2002, ss 72, 73, Sch 23 para 5; FA 2004, s 52, Sch 10 para 9; ITTOIA 2005, Sch 1 paras 486, 507*].

Simons Direct Tax Service. See D21841.

46.38 **Convertible securities etc: debtor relationships.** *This provision applies where the pre-FA 2004 basis of computation applies* (see 46.1 above) to amounts falling to be paid *on or after 26 July 2001*, and to related expenses accruing on or after that date, with respect to a liability if:

(*a*) the liability represents a debtor loan relationship (i.e. it applies to the issuer of the securities); and

(*b*) the rights attached to the asset representing the corresponding creditor relationship include provision by virtue of which a company is or may become entitled to acquire (by conversion, exchange or otherwise) any shares in the debtor or another company. In these circumstances, amounts are not to be treated as loan relationship debits of the debtor company where they are:

(i) amounts payable in connection with rights to acquire any shares in another company except where the debtor has entered into the loan relationship in the ordinary course of a banking or securities dealing business (securities being defined as under *ICTA 1988, s 473*); or

(ii) charges or expenses (within *FA 1996, s 84(3)*(*b*)–(*d*), see 46.5(ii)–(iv) above) incurred by the debtor company in connection with the acquisition of shares by another person in the debtor or other company as under (*b*) above.

An authorised accruals basis of accounting must be used to ascertain any amounts which are treated as loan relationship debits for this purpose except where the debtor company entered into the loan relationship in the ordinary course of a banking or securities dealing business.

For the treatment of such securities where the post-FA 2004 basis of computation applies, see 46.40 below and at 28.27 DERIVATIVE CONTRACTS AND FINANCIAL INSTRUMENTS..

[*FA 1996, s 92A; FA 2002, s 74; FA 2004, s 52, Sch 10 para 10, Sch 42 Pt 2*(*6*)].

46.39 **Asset-linked loan relationships.** The following provisions apply (subject to the transitional rules below) *where the pre-FA 2004 basis of computation applies* (see 46.1 above). Where a loan relationship is 'linked' to the value of chargeable assets, the amounts falling to be brought into account under the current provisions in respect of the relationship are confined to those relating to interest, and must be ascertained using an authorised accruals basis of accounting. The normal chargeable gains provisions apply to the asset representing the relationship as if it did not represent a loan relationship, with the appropriate adjustment for interest accrued but not received.

This provision does not, however, apply to a loan relationship the disposal of which would fall to be treated as in the course of activities forming an integral part of a trade carried on by the company. For accounting periods ending on or after 26 July 2001, this exclusion is extended to refer to assets the disposal of which would fall to be treated as in the course of activities forming an integral part of such a trade, to liabilities entered into in the course of such activities, and to loan relationships within *FA 1996, s 93A* (guaranteed return, see below).

A loan relationship is '*linked*' to the value of chargeable assets if, in pursuance of any provision having effect for the purposes of the relationship, the discharge payment is determined by applying to the amount of the original loan a percentage change over the 'relevant period' in the value of chargeable assets of any particular description (or, for accounting periods ending before 26 July 2001, in an index of the value of such assets — neither the retail prices index nor any similar foreign general prices index is such an index). If, however, there is such a provision which is made subject to any other provision applying to the determination of the amount of the discharge payment, whose only effect is to place a lower limit on the discharge payment of a specified percentage (which must not be more than 10%) of the original loan, then that other provision is disregarded for this purpose.

An asset is for these purposes a chargeable asset if, for accounting periods ending before 26 July 2001, any disposal gain would be a chargeable gain (assuming the asset to belong to the company and not to be one the disposal of which would fall to be treated as in the course of activities forming an integral part of a trade carried on by the company, and disregarding gains rolled over into the asset on a capital reorganisation, etc.). For accounting periods ending *on or after 26 July 2001*, an asset is only a chargeable asset for these purposes where the loan relationship is linked to an estate or interest in land or 'qualifying ordinary shares' listed on a recognised stock exchange. '*Qualifying ordinary shares*' are shares other than shares carrying no right to payment of a dividend or other profit share in the company or carrying a right only to a dividend at a fixed rate.

The new provisions for accounting periods ending on or after 26 July 2001 do not apply where the company ceased to be a party to the loan relationship concerned before that date, even though it may have been a party to the loan relationship in the accounting period. They also do not apply to determine, in relation to a part of an accounting period falling before that date, whether a loan relationship is within *section 93*.

The '*relevant period*' is the period between the time of the original loan and the discharge of the debt, or any other period in which almost all of that period is comprised and which differs from it exclusively for valuation purposes.

Asset-linked loan relationships involving guaranteed returns. As noted above, with effect for accounting periods ending on or after 26 July 2001 (and where the company had not ceased to be a party to the loan relationship in question before that date), *FA 1996, s 93* (which provides for chargeable gains treatment for asset-linked loan relationships) does not apply to loan relationships within *FA 1996, s 93A*. This applies to any creditor loan relationship where that loan relationship and one or more other transactions (consisting of the disposal of futures or options) are 'associated transactions' designed to produce a guaranteed return comprising the repayment of the loan relationship and the disposal of the futures or options.

The loan relationship and other transactions are for this purpose designed to produce a guaranteed return where it is reasonable to assume when considering the likely effect of the transactions, and/or the circumstances in which they are entered into, that such result was the main purpose (or one of the main purposes) of the transactions. A 'guaranteed return' is produced when the risks from fluctuations in the underlying subject matter are reduced or eliminated so as to produce a return which in substance equates to a return of interest on an investment. This includes cases where the main reason for the choice of the underlying subject matter is that there is little or no risk of fluctuation (e.g. shares in a company the assets of which comprise debt instruments with a fixed or predictable return). References to the underlying subject matter are, in the case of loan relationships, references to the value of chargeable assets to which the loan relationship is linked. In the case of a disposal of futures or options, such references are to, or to the value of, the commodities, shares, stocks or securities, interest rates, indices or other matters to which, or to the value of which, the futures or options are referable.

For these purposes, for accounting periods beginning before 1 October 2002, references to returns from or disposals of futures or options and to 'associated transactions' are to be construed in accordance with *ICTA 1988, Sch 5AA paras 4–6* (as amended by *FA 2002, s 78*) (guaranteed returns on transactions in futures and options, see 5.23 ANTI-AVOIDANCE). Where profits and losses arising from such futures or options fall within *ICTA 1988, Sch 5AA*, the return is to be treated as income in accordance with that *Schedule*. *Schedule 5AA* no longer applies for corporation tax purposes with effect for accounting periods beginning on or after 1 October 2002, after which time *FA 1996, s 93A* has effect for loan relationships and *FA 2002, Sch 26 para 6* has effect in relation to derivative contracts (see 28.8 FINANCIAL INSTRUMENTS AND DERIVATIVE CONTRACTS), and for such accounting periods references above to disposals of futures or options and to their underlying subject matter are references to derivative contracts and to their underlying subject matter.

Loan relationships ceasing to be asset-linked. With effect for accounting periods ending on or after 26 July 2001 (and provided that the company had not ceased to be a party to the loan relationship in question before that date), where, after 25 July 2001, a loan relationship ceases to be linked to the value of assets (within *FA 1996, s 93*, as detailed above) but the company continues to be a party to that loan relationship, there is a deemed disposal and reacquisition by the company of the asset representing the loan relationship immediately before it ceased to be within *section 93*. The amount to be used for the deemed disposal and reacquisition of the asset, is the current value (adjusted for any accrued interest) under the appropriate accounting method, with the resulting gain or loss deferred under *FA 1996, s 93B(3)* concerning share reorganisations etc. involving the issue of a qualifying corporate bond (see Tolley's Capital Gains Tax under Qualifying Corporate Bonds). The 'current value' is not simply the market value at that time (see HMRC Corporate Finance Manual, CFM 5931).

Transitional rules. Where a company holds an asset to which the above provisions apply at the end of the last accounting period beginning before the post-FA 2004 basis of computation applies (see 46.1 above), the asset will be deemed for capital gains purposes to have been disposed of immediately before and reacquired immediately after that time by virtue of *FA 1996, s 93B* (as if the asset had ceased to be a *section 93* asset without ceasing to represent a creditor relationship of the company). The resulting gain or loss is deferred under *FA 1996, s 93B(3)* as above.

For the treatment of such securities where the post-FA 2004 basis of computation applies, see the embedded derivative provisions at 46.40 below and at 28.27 DERIVATIVE CONTRACTS AND FINANCIAL INSTRUMENTS.

[*FA 1996, ss 93, 93A, 93B; FA 2002, ss 75–78, Sch 27 paras 17–21, 25; FA 2004, s 52, Sch 10 para 11*].

Simons Direct Tax Service. See **D2.1845**.

46.40 **Loan relationships with embedded derivatives.** Special provisions apply *where the post-FA 2004 basis of computation applies* (see 46.1 above) to loan relationships with 'embedded derivatives'. This is where a company, in accordance with generally accepted accounting practice, splits the rights and liabilities under the loan relationship into those under the loan relationship (the 'host contract') and '*embedded derivatives*' which are those under one or more derivative financial instruments or equity instruments (including convertible securities of an issuing company – see 46.38 above). In this case, the host contract will fall, for corporation tax purposes, within the loan relationship rules of *FA 1996, Chapter 2 Part 4* and the embedded derivatives within the derivative contracts rules under *FA 2002, Sch 26* (see 28 FINANCIAL INSTRUMENTS AND DERIVATIVE CONTRACTS). The embedded derivatives are treated as having the character (be it an option, a future or a contract for differences) which the rights and liabilities would have if contained in a separate contract.

Election. Where a company, in a period of account beginning on or after 1 January 2005, is not permitted to adopt split treatment for its loan relationships containing embedded derivatives ('*relevant assets*') because it still uses 'old UK GAAP', but it would have been able to adopt such treatment had it been subject to international accounting standards or 'new UK GAAP', it can elect for the embedded derivative provisions to apply in relation to those assets. '*Old UK GAAP*' and '*new UK GAAP*' mean generally accepted accounting practice as it applied respectively to periods of account beginning before 1 January 2005, and periods beginning on or after that date.

The election is irrevocable and has effect in relation to all relevant assets held by the company including those subsequently acquired. It must be made in writing to an HMRC officer by 31 December 2005 or after that date if:

(*a*) the company does not hold relevant assets at the beginning of its first period of account beginning or after 1 January 2005, but subsequently acquires such assets, in which case it must elect within 90 days of acquiring its first relevant asset; or

(*b*) the company does not have a period of account beginning in 2005 but holds relevant assets at the beginning of its first period of account beginning after the end of that year, in which case it must elect within 90 days after the beginning of that period of account.

If made on or before 31 December 2005, an election has effect from the first day of a company's first period of account beginning on or after 1 January 2005. If made after 31 December 2005 in accordance with (*a*) above (because of a first-time acquisition of relevant assets), the election has effect from the beginning of the period of account in which the first relevant asset is acquired. If made after 31 December 2005 in accordance with (*b*) above (because it does not have a period of account beginning in 2005), the election has effect from the beginning of the company's first period of account beginning on or after 1 January 2005.

Where such an election is made, *FA 1996, Sch 9 para 19A* (see 42.7 above under change of accounting policy) and the equivalent derivative contracts provision in *FA 2002, Sch 26 para 50A* (see 28.10 FINANCIAL INSTRUMENTS AND DERIVATIVE CONTRACTS) apply from the date the election has effect. The effect is that, where the tax treatment of a relevant asset changes as a result of an election, any changes in value of a company's loan relationships or derivative contracts is taken into account as a debit or credit even though there has been no actual change in accounting policy.

The above election provisions are introduced by *F(No 2)A 2005, Sch 6 para 7* to replace similar provisions in *FA 2005, Sch 4 para 28(3)(4)* and similar treatment applies in relation to transactions occurring before 20 July 2005, any election made under the *FA 2005* provisions being treated as made under the above provisions.

[*FA 1996, s 94A; FA 2004, s 52, Sch 10 para 13; FA 2005, Sch 4 para 28; F(No 2)A 2005, Sch 6 para 7*].

Convertible securities. Where a convertible security that is a qualifying corporate bond is converted into shares, *TCGA 1992, s 116(8A)* provides that, for loan relationship purposes, the event is treated as a disposal at market value. But where the security is treated under *FA 1996, s 94A(1)* as both a loan relationship and a derivative contract, that provision is disapplied with effect for conversions taking place after 26 May 2005. [*TCGA 1992, s 116(8B); F(No 2)A 2005, Sch 6 para 8*]. See Tolley's Capital Gains Tax under Qualifying Corporate Bonds.

46.41 **Gilt-edged securities.** *Index-linked*. Where, for periods of account beginning on or after 1 January 2005, a loan relationship is represented by an index-linked gilt-edged security, the debits and credits brought into account for this purpose must be determined using fair value accounting and an adjustment is to be made wherever the fair value of the security is to be found at two different times and there is a change in the retail price index between those times. The carrying value of the security is to be increased or decreased, as the case may be, at the earlier time by the same percentage as the percentage increase or reduction in the retail price index between the earlier and later time. (Thus, any increase or reduction in value attributable to a change in the retail prices index is left out of account in computing the loan relationship debit or credit.)

For periods of account beginning before 1 January 2005, there is no requirement for the debits and credits brought into account to be determined using fair value accounting and the provisions require the adjustment to be made to any non-trading debits and credits (see 46.3 above) to be brought into account in respect of the relationship. Wherever the authorised accounting method gives credits or debits by reference to the value of the gilt at two different times, and there is a change in the retail prices index (RPI) between the months in which those times fall, the value at the earlier time is adjusted for the RPI change. Where an authorised accruals basis of accounting is used, the value at the earlier time is to be taken as the amount accrued (disregarding any interest) before that time.(Thus, as above, any increase or reduction in value attributable to a change in the retail prices index is left out of account in computing the loan relationship debit or credit.)

The Treasury may by order disapply this provision, or specify a different basis of adjustment, in relation to any description of index-linked gilt (but not with retrospective effect).

See generally HMRC Company Taxation Manual, CTM 57600 *et seq*.

(Note the above indexed-linked gilt-edged securities provisions of *FA 1996, s 94*, and *FA 2002, Sch 25 para 12*, which amended those provisions, were repealed by *FA 2004, Sch 10 para 12* and *Sch 42 Pt 2(6)*. These provisions are deemed by *FA 2005, Sch 4 para 27* not to have been repealed.)

Strips. Where a gilt is exchanged for strips of the same security, it is treated as redeemed at market value and the strips as acquired at that value in total, apportioned by reference to their own market values. Similarly where strips are consolidated into a gilt, each strip is treated as redeemed at market value and the gilt as acquired at the sum of those values The Treasury may make regulations for determining market value for these purposes.

Special rules for 3.5% Funding Stock 1999/2004 and 5.5% Treasury Stock 2008/2012. Where a loan relationship represented by these gilts is held otherwise than in the course of activities forming an integral part of a trade carried on by the company, debits and credits falling to be brought into account under the current provisions in respect of the relationship are confined to those relating to interest, and where the pre-FA 2004 basis of computation applies (see 46.1 above), must be ascertained using an authorised accruals basis of accounting.

[*FA 1996, ss 94–96; FA 2002, Sch 25 para 12; FA 2004, s 52, Sch 10 paras 12, 14, 15; FA 2005, s 80, Sch 4 para 27*].

Simon's Direct Tax Service. See **D2.1129, D2.1843**.

46.42 **Manufactured interest.** This provision applies where an amount is payable under any contract or arrangements relating to the transfer of an asset representing a loan relationship, and that amount ('*manufactured interest*') is, or falls to be treated as, representative of interest ('*the real interest*') under the relationship. For the purposes of the current provisions, the manufactured interest is treated as interest under a loan relationship, and as regards the company to whom the manufactured interest is payable, as if that relationship were the one under which the real interest is payable.

For accounting periods beginning *on or after 1 October 2002*, the only debits or credits to be taken into account are those relating to that interest. This limitation to the tax charge is removed with effect for related transactions on or after 16 March 2005 (a '*related transaction*' being defined (see 46.5 above) as any disposal or acquisition of rights or liabilities under a relationship). With effect for related transactions on or after that date in respect of a right to receive manufactured interest (i.e. if a company disposes of the rights without disposing of the associated asset), the company is treated as continuing to have a relationship for the purpose of bringing a credit into account even though the manufactured interest is not payable to the company.

See 46.3 above for the determination of the trading or non-trading nature of the associated debits and credits.

Until a date to be determined by statutory instrument for introduction of the new repo regime (see 5.5 ANTI-AVOIDANCE), the above applies equally to deemed manufactured interest payments under *ICTA 1988, s 736B(2)* or *s 737A(5)* (deemed manufactured payments in the case of stock lending arrangements and sale and repurchase of securities) (or from a date to be determined under *ICTA 1988, s 736B(2)* only). For the manufactured interest provisions generally, see 5.9 ANTI-AVOIDANCE.

[*FA 1996, s 97; FA 2002, Sch 25 para 13; F(No 2)A 2005, Sch 7 para 11, FA 2007, Sch 14 para 16*].

Simon's Direct Tax Service. See **D2.1128, D2.1829**.

46.43 **Collective investment schemes.** *FA 1996, s 98, Sch 10* make special provision in relation to such schemes. Broadly, these are as follows.

Investment trusts and venture capital trusts. With effect for accounting periods beginning on or after 1 October 2002, any capital profits, gains or losses arising to an investment trust or a venture capital trust from a creditor relationship must not be brought into account in determining loan relationship credits or debits. Capital profits, gains or losses in this case are those which, in preparing accounts in accordance with UK generally accepted accounting practice, are carried to or sustained by a capital reserve in accordance with the relevant Statement of Recommended Practice (SORP) (or, in the case of a venture capital trust, would be so treated if the venture capital trust were an investment trust and were using the SORP). Where the post-FA 2004 basis of computation applies (see 46.1 above) and where an investment trust or venture capital trust prepares accounts in accordance with international accounting standards, the capital profits, gains or losses are those as defined by *SI 2006 No 1182*. The relevant SORP is that relating to the Financial Statements of Investment Trust Companies issued by the Association of Investment Trust Companies in January 2003 and revised in December 2005 (as modified, amended or revised) or any subsequent SORP replacing it.

For accounting periods beginning before 1 October 2002, the Treasury may by order require the adoption of a modified accounting method for creditor relationships of investment trusts and venture capital trusts. See *SI 2001 No 391* as regards investment trusts.

[*FA 1996, Sch 10 paras 1–1B; FA 2002, Sch 25 para 37; FA 2004, s 52, Sch 10 para 38*]. See generally 44.1 INVESTMENT TRUSTS and 69 VENTURE CAPITAL TRUSTS.

Authorised unit trusts and open-ended investment companies. With effect for accounting periods beginning on or after 1 October 2002, 'capital profits, gains or losses' arising to an authorised unit trust or an open-ended investment company on a creditor relationship must not be brought into account as loan relationship debits or credits. '*Capital profits, gains or losses*' in this case are those which, in preparing accounts in accordance with UK generally accepted accounting practice, fall to be dealt with in the statement of total return (under the heading of 'net gains/losses on investments during the period' or 'other gains/losses') in accordance with the relevant Statement of Recommended Practice (SORP). Where the post-FA 2004 basis of computation applies (see 46.1 above) and where the authorised unit trust or open-ended investment company prepares accounts in accordance with international accounting standards, the capital profits, gains or losses are those as defined, for accounting periods beginning on or after 1 April 2006, by *SI 2006 No 964, reg 12*. The relevant SORP in the case of an authorised unit trust or an open-ended investment company, is that relating to authorised investment funds, issued by the Investment Management Association on 21 November 2003 (as modified, amended or revised) or any subsequent SORP replacing it.

For accounting periods beginning before 1 October 2002, the loan relationship provisions as far as they relate to creditor relationships do not apply in computing the profits or losses of authorised unit trusts. Instead, the income tax provisions applicable to unauthorised unit trusts apply.

Transitional rules deal with the tax treatment of interest receivable, amounts deductible under the accrued interest scheme and accruals in respect of relevant discounted securities (or, where the rules apply after 5 April 2005, 'deeply discounted securities') where they are affected by the 1 October 2002 change, to ensure that the relevant amounts are brought into charge as loan relationship debits or credits.

[*FA 1996, Sch 10 paras 2–2B; FA 2002, Sch 25 paras 38, 64; FA 2004, s 52, Sch 10 paras 39, 40; F(No 2)A 2005, ss 17–19; ITTOIA 2005, Sch 1 para 579*]. See generally 43 INVESTMENT FUNDS. For a statement agreed between HMRC and the Investment Management Association confirming the tax treatment in these circumstances, see Revenue Tax Bulletin August 2002 pp 948–950.

Distributing offshore funds. In determining the UK equivalent profits of an offshore fund, the corporation tax rules apply, as if the offshore fund were a UK Authorised Unit Trust, for the purposes of calculating profits or losses arising on a creditor relationship. However, for accounting periods of an offshore fund ending before 22 July 2004, and with effect for accounting periods beginning on or after 1 October 2002, in determining the UK equivalent profit of a distributing offshore fund, the profits or losses arising on a creditor relationship are calculated on an income tax basis as if the offshore fund were an unauthorised unit trust and these rules will continue to apply for accounting periods ending on or after 22 July 2004 where the manager of the offshore fund so elects. *FA 1996, Sch 10 para 2* (see above) applies to the fund in determining total profits as it applies to authorised unit trusts. [*ICTA 1988, Sch 27 para 5(3)(d); FA 1996, Sch 10 para 3; FA 2002, Sch 25 para 39; FA 2004, s 145, Sch 26 para 1*]. See generally 50 OFFSHORE FUNDS.

In determining the UK equivalent profit of a distributing offshore fund, the corporation tax rules apply, as if the offshore fund were a UK Authorised Unit Trust. for the purposes of calculating profits or losses arising on derivative contracts. the profits or losses arising on a derivative contract are calculated on an income tax basis as if the offshore fund were an unauthorised unit trust

Corporate holdings in authorised unit trusts, (*with effect for accounting periods beginning on or after 1 April 2006*) *open-ended insurance companies, and offshore funds.* Holdings of rights under a unit trust scheme, open-ended investment company or any relevant interests in an offshore fund which fail to satisfy the 'non-qualifying investments test' in *FA 1996, Sch 10 para 8* (as amended by *SI 2006 No 981*), are treated for the purposes of the current provisions as rights under creditor relationships, in relation to which a fair value basis of accounting (or, where the pre-FA 2004 basis of computation applies (see 46.1 above), an authorised mark to market basis) must be used. Debits or credits are to be left out of account for these purposes if any investment or liability was incurred with a '*relevant avoidance intention*' (being the intention to eliminate or reduce the credits or creating or increasing the debits brought into account under these provisions). This latter change applies to accounting periods ending on or after 6 March 2007 in the case of investments and in the case of liabilities to accounting periods ending on or after 9 May 2007. However, where the accounting period straddles those dates, only transactions on or after those dates are taken into account. Credits relating to distributions of an authorised unit trust or to distributions after 1 April 2006 of an open-ended investment company, other than 'interest distributions' (as defined in *SI 2006 No 964, reg 18(3)*) are excluded. There are special rules dealing with cases where a holding comes within, or ceases to be within, these provisions. The '*non-qualifying investments test*' requires that not more than 60% of the market value of scheme or fund investments is represented by 'qualifying investments' (see 43.6 INVESTMENT FUNDS). A '*relevant interest in an offshore fund*' is an interest which is a 'material interest in an offshore fund' within *ICTA 1988, s 759*, or would be but for the requirement that unit trust schemes and other arrangements constitute collective investment schemes. [*FA 1996, Sch 10 paras 4–8; FA 2004, s 52, Sch 10 para 41; FA 2007, Sch 5 para 16; SI 1997 No 213; SI 2006 No 964, regs 90, 95; SI 2006 No 981*].

Simon's Direct Tax Service. See D2.1140, D2.1142, D2.1152, D2.1850, D2.1851.

46.44 **Insurance companies.** There are special provisions dealing with the application of the current provisions to loan relationships of insurers. In particular, the provisions do not apply to premiums, trust fund assets and liabilities of corporate members of Lloyd's. [*FA 1996, s 99, Sch 11; FA 2002, Sch 23 paras 14, 15, Sch 25 para 40; FA 2003, Sch 33 paras 3(2), 8(3); FA 2004, s 52, Sch 10 para 42; F(No 2)A 2005, Sch 7 para 20; SI 1998 No 1200; SI 1999 No 1643; SI 2005 No 3465*].

Simon's Direct Tax Service. See **D4.526**.

46.45 **Partnerships which include companies.** For accounting periods beginning before 1 October 2002, HMRC Statement of Practice, SP 4/98 deals with the application of the loan relationships, EXCHANGE GAINS AND LOSSES (26) and FINANCIAL INSTRUMENTS AND DERIVATIVE CONTRACTS (28) legislation to partnerships which include companies within those provisions. Where the old provisions are in point in relation to an accounting period of such a partnership, the approach of *FA 1994, s 172* as regards financial instruments (see 28.48 FINANCIAL INSTRUMENTS AND DERIVATIVE CONTRACTS) will be adopted. Thus where the partnership consists wholly of companies within the current provisions, they will be treated as applying to the partnership.

For partnerships with one or more members which are not companies within the current provisions, the general rules, which require profits and losses to be computed as if the partnership were a company, ensure that corporation tax is applied to corporate members and income tax to individual members (see 52.2 PARTNERSHIPS). In such cases, partnership profits and losses will be computed both on the basis that the partnership is within the current provisions and on the basis that it is not, the appropriate computation being employed in relation to partners which are within the provisions and those which are not (including in the latter case a separate corporation tax computation in the unusual case of a corporate partner which is not within the provisions).

For these purposes, the partnership will be treated as itself a party to the loan relationship(s) in question.

For accounting periods beginning on or after 1 October 2002, SP4/98 is withdrawn, since the derivative contracts rules dealing with partnerships involving companies cover these provisions (see 46.27 above). For accounting periods beginning before 1 October 2002, the main elements of the Statement of Practice are as follows.

The *authorised accounting method* used should be that used in the partnership accounts (assuming it uses an authorised accounting method).

Continuity of treatment: groups etc. The provisions of *FA 1996, Sch 9 para 12* (see 46.21 above) concerning continuity of treatment in intra-group transfers will not apply where a loan relationship is transferred to or by a partnership.

A change in *partnership profit-sharing ratios*, including a case where a company joins or leaves a partnership, does not of itself give rise to a related transaction in a loan relationship to which the partnership is a party.

Capital gains tax. TCGA 1992, s 59 (disposal of partnership assets) will continue to apply to the disposal of shares in partnership assets to which members who are not subject to corporation tax are entitled, regardless of the operation of the current (or the exchange gains and losses or financial instruments) provisions.

Connected persons and FA 1996, s 87. A partnership treated as a company (as above) is *not* so treated for the purposes of the connected persons rules in *FA 1996, s 87* (see 46.16 above).

Interest paid or received under deduction of tax. Yearly interest paid by or on behalf of the partnership should be paid under deduction of tax. Tax deducted from interest received by the partnership will be apportioned amongst the company partners in the same proportion as the interest under the loan relationship is apportioned.

Losses. A qualifying company's share of partnership trading loan relationship deficits (or exchange or financial instrument losses) will be relievable in the normal way. Its share of net partnership non-trading loan relationship credits or debits (and net non-trading exchange or financial instrument gains or losses) will in practice be merged with any other non-trading loan relationship credits or debits (or non-trading exchange or financial instrument gains or losses) accruing to it in its own right, for charge or relief in the normal way.

Differing accounting periods. Where partnership and company accounting periods differ, profits and losses will be allocated between the relevant company accounting periods, usually on a time basis.

Anti-avoidance provisions under the current provisions apply to the partnership (including any individual members) as if it were a qualifying company.

46.46 **MISCELLANEOUS PROVISIONS**

Money debts etc. not arising from the lending of money. Certain money debts which do not arise from a loan relationship are nevertheless treated as payable under a loan relationship. Such a money debt could, for instance, be a trade debt, unpaid or overpaid tax or a compensation award. This applies where the money debt is one of the following.

(*a*) Interest payable by or to a company, or

(*b*) (For accounting periods beginning *on or after 1 October 2002*) exchange gains or losses arising to a company; or

(*c*) (For periods of account beginning on or after 1 January 2005) an impairment loss (or credit in respect of a reversal of an impairment loss) arising in relation to a trading receipt or a receipt of a Schedule A or overseas property business; or

(*d*) Discounts (of an income or capital nature) arising to a creditor company in respect of a money debt to which the company is party on or after 16 March 2005 (subject to the transitional provisions below) where

- the money debt would not be treated as a trading receipt if it is consideration (or part-consideration) for the disposal a disposal of property,
- the money debt does not arise from the disposal of property which is a loan relationship or a derivative contract the disposal of which (after 21 March 2006) is a 'relevant disposal', and
- the discounts would be accounted for as an alternative finance return (see 4 ALTERNATIVE FINANCE ARRANGEMENTS).

A discount will arise, in particular, where the company disposes of a property for consideration which is wholly or partly deferred, the amount of the total consideration is greater than that which the purchaser would have paid if payment was required in full at the time of the disposal and some or all of the excess can reasonably be regarded as being a return on an investment of money at interest (and, thus, as being a discount arising from the money debt).

In relation to the disposal of property (after 21 March 2006) which is a loan relationship or a derivative contract, a '*relevant disposal*' is one as respects which the whole consideration is brought into account under the derivative contract rules or it is one to which the group provisions at 46.21 above, or at 28.18 FINANCIAL INSTRUMENTS AND DERIVATIVE CONTRACTS, apply or would apply but for the use of fair value accounting.

Interest payable on a money debt includes payments which fall under *ICTA 1988, Sch 28AA* (see 67 TRANSFER PRICING) to be treated as interest on a money debt or an amount treated as a money debt.

Where a company has a relationship to which these provisions apply, the matters in (*a*) to (*c*) above are treated as matters arising under or in relation to a loan relationship but the only debits or credits to be brought into account under these provisions in respect of the relationship are those relating to those matters and any references in other provisions to loan relationships is taken to include a relationship to which these provisions apply. With effect for money debts which are assets on or after 16 March 2005, this also applies in the case of:

(A) a money debt falling within (*a*) above, to the profits (but not losses) arising to the company from any 'related transaction' in respect of the right to receive interest (i.e. if it disposes of the rights without disposing of the associated asset) and the company is treated as continuing to have a relationship even though the interest is not payable to the company (a '*related transaction*' is defined in 46.5 above as any disposal or acquisition of rights or liabilities under a relationship);

(B) a money debt falling within (*d*) above, to discounts arising to the from the money debt, any impairment or reversal of impairment in respect of the discount (credits to be determined using an amortised basis of accounting) and profits (but not losses) arising to the company from any related transaction.

Where a company has a relationship to which these provisions apply by virtue of (*a*) above but enters into a related transaction in respect of the right to receive interest, the company will continue to be treated as having a relationship under these provisions for the purposes of bringing debits and credits into account under (A) above even though the interest is not payable to the company.

Where a company is party to a money debt on or after 16 March 2005 but in a period of account beginning before 1 January 2005, then in applying these provisions for that period, (*a*) to (*c*) above include any discount arising to the company from the money debt and any profits, impairment or reversal of impairment of discount and the only debits or credits to be brought into account are those relating to (*a*) or (*b*) above. To the extent that the discount arising from a money debt accrued before 16 March 2005, no credits are to be brought into account in respect of the discount and equally no debits or credits are to be brought into account as respect an impairment or reversal of impairment. Where a related transaction took place before 16 March 2005 no credits are to be brought into account in respect of the profits arising as noted above.

These provisions do not apply to profits, gains or losses arising on money debts, which fall within the derivative contracts regime or the intangible assets regime.

See 46.3 above with respect to the determination of the trading or non-trading nature of the associated debits and.

Any debits or credits which relate to INTEREST ON OVERPAID TAX (40) or INTEREST ON UNPAID TAX (41) are treated as non-trading debits or credits. Where the debits or credits are treated as trading items, the company is treated as being a party to the loan relationship for trading purposes.

Exchange gains and losses arising on money debts are not to be taken into account under this provision where they relate to:

(i) UK tax; or

(ii) foreign tax (unless deductible under *ICTA 1988, s 811*);

(iii) amounts which would, but for any statutory provision (other than *ICTA 1988, s 74(1)(f)* or (*g*), which relate to capital expenditure) prohibiting such deduction, be deductible in computing Schedule D, Case I profits, or as a management expense; or

(iv) for accounting periods beginning on or after 1 April 2004, expenses of insurance companies within Step 1 of *ICTA 1988, s 76(7)*.

The money debts owed *to* a company on which exchange gains and losses arising are taken into account by virtue of this provision include any currency held by the company and certain deferred acquisition costs of an insurance company. The money debts owed *by* a company to which this applies include any provision for future liabilities in the company's statutory accounts which would be incurred and fall to be taken into account in computing the profits or losses of a trade, a Schedule A business or an overseas property business (within the meaning of *ICTA 1988, s 70A*) and, in the case of an insurance company, certain provisions for unearned premiums and unexpired risks.

These provisions do not apply to exchange gains and losses in relation to a money debt arising from an obligation to repurchase securities under *ICTA 1988, s 730A(1)(b)* (see 5.6 ANTI-AVOIDANCE) where the company stands, or has stood, in the position of a creditor or debtor as respects that debt. (Special provision is made in relation to such exchange gains and losses under *ICTA 1988, s 730BB*, see 46.6 above.)

[*FA 1996, s 100; FA 1998, s 108(4)(5), Sch 4 para 7; FA 2002, Sch 23 para 6; FA 2003, Sch 38 para 14; FA 2005, s 80, Sch 4 para 9; F(No 2)A 2005, Sch 7 para 12; FA 2006, Sch 6 para 17; SI 2004 No 2310, Article 49*].

Simon's Direct Tax Service. See **D2.1104**, **D2.1864**.

Financial instruments. *FA 2002, Sch* 26 (derivative contracts) (or, for accounting periods beginning before 1 October 2002, *FA 1994, Pt IV, Ch II* (financial instruments) do not apply to any profit or loss accruing to a company on a derivative contract (or, for accounting periods beginning before 1 October 2002, on a 'qualifying contract') (see 28.3, 28.32 FINANCIAL INSTRUMENTS AND DERIVATIVE CONTRACTS), by virtue of which the company is a party to a loan relationship, for any accounting period for which an amount representing that profit or loss, or the profit or loss accruing on that contract, is brought into account under those provisions. This does not apply, however, where the post-FA 2004 basis of computation applies (see 46.1 above), to the treatment of embedded derivatives. [*FA 1996, s 101(1)(1A); FA 2002, Sch 27 para 19; FA 2004, s 52, Sch 10 para 16*].

Simon's Direct Tax Service. See **D2.1106**.

Restriction of relief. A debit in respect of interest will not be a loan relationship debit (whether a payment or not) if at any time, a scheme has been effected or arrangements made whereby the sole or main benefit which might be expected to accrue to the payer was a reduction in a tax liability. Any question as to whether a benefit might be expected to accrue from a transaction, where group relief is claimed under *ICTA 1988, s 403* for trading or non-trading debits, is to be determined by reference to the claimant company and the surrendering company taken together. The restriction of relief has effect in relation to payments on or after 6 April 2005 of alternative finance return or profit share return under ALTERNATIVE FINANCE ARRANGEMENTS (4) as it has effect in relation to payments of interest. This applies to alternative finance arrangements entered into on or after 6 April 2005 subject to commencement rules for arrangements entered into before that date where a profit share return is payable on or after that date. [*ICTA 1988, s 787; FA 2002, Sch 25 para 53; FA 2005, s 56, Sch 2 para 8*].

Provisions made on accruals basis after company ceases to be a party. For accounting periods beginning on or after 1 October 2002, where a company has ceased to be a party to a loan relationship in an accounting period and the whole of the profits or losses arising in that period have not been accounted for as loan relationship credits or debits in that period, then any amounts not yet brought into account shall continue to be brought into account as credits or debits in any subsequent accounting periods as if the company had not ceased to be a party to that loan relationship, by reference to the circumstances in the period in which the company ceased to be a party to the relationship. [*FA 1996, s 103(6); FA 2002, Sch 25 para 16*].

Funding bonds issued in respect of interest on certain debts. The loan relationship rules do not affect the provisions of *ICTA 1988, s 582* with respect to funding bonds issued in respect of interest on certain debts, or, from 6 April 2005, subject to commencement provisions, the payment of alternative finance return or profit share return under ALTERNATIVE FINANCE ARRANGEMENTS (4). [*FA 2002, Sch 25 para 50; FA 2005, s 56, Sch 2 para 7*].

Funding Bonds etc. issued in respect of interest by any Government, public authority or institution, or company are treated as income equal to bonds' value when issued; but their eventual redemption is not treated as a payment of the interest. 'Bonds' includes 'stocks, shares, securities or certificates of indebtedness'. Companies by or through which the bonds are issued and which, if the amount treated as income had been an actual payment of interest, would have been required to deduct tax therefrom, must retain a proportionate amount of these bonds equal to tax at the savings rate on their value, and are accountable to HMRC accordingly, with the right to tender the bonds in payment. Where retention is impracticable they may be relieved of liability on their furnishing a list of recipients, who are then assessed direct under Schedule D, Case VI for corporation tax purposes or *ITTOIA 2005, Pt 4 Ch 2* for income tax purposes. [*ICTA 1988, s 582; FA 1996, s 134, Sch 6 para 14, Sch 20 para 32; FA 2002, Sch 25 para 50; ITTOIA 2005, Sch 1 para 243*].

In *Finance Ltd v Inspector of Taxes Sp C, [2005] SSCD 407 (Sp C 466)*, it was held that the foreign exchange legislation in *FA 1993, ss 125–170* applied to funding bonds issued in respect of interest obligations (prior to the repeal of that legislation) and that *ICTA 1988, s 582* did not prevent the application of that legislation.

46.47 TRANSITIONAL PROVISIONS

For transitional rules (other than those with continuing consequences, as referred to below) for accounting periods straddling 1 April 1996 as respects continuing loan relationships following the introduction of the loan relationship rules for accounting periods ending after 31 March 1996, see Tolley's Corporation Tax 2001/02 or earlier edition.

Change of accounting period. With effect for accounting periods beginning *on or after 1 October 2002*, anti-avoidance provisions apply to prevent forestalling the effects of the new provisions by changing an accounting date to end an accounting period prematurely. The provision applies where an accounting period beginning on or after 1 October 2001 is ended before 30 September 2002 for the purpose, or for purposes including the purpose, of securing, in the case of any subsequent accounting period beginning before 1 October 2002, that a smaller credit or larger debit falls to be brought into account under the revised than would have been the case under the earlier rules, or that a credit under the revised provisions is replaced by a nil amount under the earlier ones or a nil amount under the revised provisions replaced by a debit under the earlier ones. In this case, that accounting period will be treated as if it were an accounting period beginning on or after 1 October 2002. [*FA 2002, Sch 23 para 25*].

Deferred foreign exchange gains. Where a claim for deferral relief was made under *FA 1993, s 139* (see 26.18 EXCHANGE GAINS AND LOSSES) in respect of a gain accruing in the company's last accounting period beginning before 1 October 2002, any amount which, but for the repeal of *FA 1993, s 140*, would fall to be treated as an exchange gain in an accounting period beginning on or after 1 October 2002, is to be brought into account in that subsequent period as a loan relationship credit. Whether it is to be treated as a trading or non-trading credit is to be determined in accordance with *section 140* as though that legislation had continued in force. A company may elect within two years following the end of its first accounting period beginning on or after 1 October 2002 to account for the gain in six equal instalments over the first six accounting periods beginning on or after 1 October 2002. Where such an election is made, any uncharged amounts must be brought into account immediately if the company ceases to be within the charge to corporation tax.

The Treasury has the power (under *FA 1996, s 84A* – see 46.6 above) to provide for exchange gains and losses deferred under the matching regulations in *FA 1993, Sch 15 para 4* (see 26.15 EXCHANGE GAINS AND LOSSES) for accounting periods beginning before 1 October 2002 to be brought into account for an accounting period beginning on or after 1 October 2002, either as debits or credits within the loan relationship rules or as chargeable gains or losses within *TCGA 1992*. See *SI 2002 No 1969 and SI 2002 No 1970* (as amended by *SI 2004 No 3259*).

[*FA 2002, Sch 23 para 26*].

Pre-31 March 1996 trading relationships. Adjustments are required for any amounts which would have been brought into account as respects a loan relationship in computing profits or losses for trade purposes if the company had ceased to be a party to the relationship on 31 March 1996 and an accounting period had ended on that date. Any difference between the 'notional closing value' and the 'adjusted closing value' of the relationship as at 31 March 1996 is brought into account (see below).

The '*notional closing value*' at 31 March 1996 is the amount which at that date fell to be brought into account in computing trading profits or losses, as representing the value of the company's rights or liabilities under the relationship, or which would have fallen to be so brought into account had an accounting period ended on that date. If no amount is given by this definition, the notional closing value is the amount which would have been deductible for trade purposes as representing the cost of becoming a party to the relationship had the company ceased to be a party to it on 31 March 1996. In the case of creditor relationships continuing after 13 November 1996 (and certain replacement relationships), the cost of acquiring any right to accrued interest is excluded (except in certain cases where interest accruing before the company became a party to the relationship but paid to the company after it became a party to the relationship has been brought into account for corporation tax purposes). The '*adjusted closing value*' at 31 March 1996 is the opening value as at 1 April 1996 under the current provisions of the rights and liabilities under the relationship (and see further below as regards 'opening value' in certain cases). In the case of both the notional and the adjusted closing value, a different value is taken where the asset or liabilities representing a loan relationship is or are a 'relevant qualifying asset' or 'relevant liabilities'. The notional closing value is then the value given by *FA 1996, Sch 15 para 12* (see below under 'Other chargeable asset etc. adjustments') as at 31 March 1996 of that asset or those liabilities, and the adjusted closing value is the opening value of the asset or liabilities as at 1 April 1996 under the current provisions (and see further below as regards 'opening value' in certain cases). A '*relevant qualifying asset*' is a 'qualifying asset' within *FA 1993, Pt II, Ch II* the value of which has been determined on the first day of the company's first accounting period to begin after 22 March 1995 for the purpose of calculating any attributed amount (see 26.8 EXCHANGE GAINS AND LOSSES). A '*relevant liability*' is a liability the value of which has been so determined as at that day.

Where an accruals basis of accounting is used as respects a loan relationship for the first accounting period ending after 31 March 1996, the opening value as at 1 April 1996 of the rights and liabilities under the relationship is the value (disregarding interest) treated under *FA 1996, Sch 15 para 4* as having accrued before that date.

Any adjustment required as above is made by bringing the difference between the notional and adjusted closing values into account in the accounting period in which the company ceases to be a party to the relationship. If the notional exceeds the adjusted closing value, and the relationship is a debtor relationship, the difference is brought in as a credit. Similarly if the adjusted exceeds the notional closing value and the relationship is a creditor relationship, the difference is brought in as a credit. Otherwise, it is brought in as a debit.

[*FA 1996, Sch 15 paras 5, 6; FA 1997, Sch 13 paras 4, 7*].

Chargeable assets continuing to be held after 31 March 1996. This provision applies where, on 31 March 1996, a company held any asset representing (in whole or part) a loan relationship to which it was a party, and the company did not dispose of that asset on that date, and is not otherwise deemed to have done so. It does not apply where the asset is:

(*a*) an asset to which *FA 1996, s 92* (convertible securities etc., see 46.37 above) or *FA 1996, Sch 15 para 15* (see below under 'Unit trusts etc.') applies; or

(*b*) an asset representing a loan relationship to which *FA 1996, s 93* (relationships linked to the value of chargeable assets, see 46.39 above) applies; or

(*c*) a 'relevant qualifying asset' (see above under *Pre-31 March 1996 trading relationships*).

Where a 'relevant event' occurs in relation to such an asset, any chargeable gain or allowable loss which would have accrued to the company if the asset had been disposed of on 31 March 1996 for a market value consideration is (subject to the election referred to below) brought into account in the accounting period in which the relevant event occurs. The gain or loss is reduced by any amount already brought into account on an accruals or mark to market basis in relation to the asset as respects times before 1 April 1996. A '*relevant event*' occurs on the first occasion after 31 March 1996 when any company falls to be treated as making a disposal (other than a no gain, no loss disposal) of the asset or of any asset falling to be treated as the same as that asset. Where the disposal is by a company other than the one holding the asset on 31 March 1996, the chargeable gain or allowable loss is brought into account on that company. Special rules apply to ensure that a gain or loss deemed to accrue under *TCGA 1992, s 116*(*10*)(*b*) (crystallisation of gain or loss on shares exchanged for qualifying corporate bonds on reorganisation, etc., see Tolley's Capital Gains Tax under Qualifying Corporate Bonds) which is included in the deemed gain or loss under these provisions does not give rise to further charge or allowance. Where the relevant event had not occurred before 14 November 1996, the deemed gain or loss under these provisions is computed without reference to *TCGA 1992, s 119*(*6*)(*7*) (transfer of securities with or without accrued interest, see Tolley's Capital Gains Tax under Shares and Securities).

Where the company was non-UK resident at any time before 1 April 1996 when it held the asset other than through a UK branch or agency, the company is treated for these purposes as having acquired the asset at market value on the first day on which a gain on the asset could have been included in the company's profits chargeable to corporation tax. This applies through any chain of no gain, no loss disposals.

For these purposes, a company ceasing to be within the charge to corporation tax at any time is treated as disposing of all its assets at market value immediately before that time.

Where this provision results in an amount being brought into account for an accounting period as an allowable loss, the company may instead elect for that amount to be treated as a debit under the current provisions for that period. The debit is a trading or non-trading debit (see 46.3 above) according to the treatment which would apply to any other debits as respects the same loan relationship for that period. The election must be made within two years after the relevant event. An election may not be made in respect of a loss on an asset which, as at 1 April 1996, fell under *TCGA 1992, s 127* or *214*(*9*) to be treated as the same as an asset not representing a loan relationship, or would have done so but for *TCGA 1992, s 116*(*5*).

[*FA 1996, Sch 15 paras 8, 9; FA 1997, Sch 13 para 5; FA 2000, Sch 29 para 45*].

Other chargeable asset etc. adjustments. An adjustment may be required where an authorised accruals basis of accounting is applied for the first accounting period ending after 31 March 1996 to a loan relationship represented by a 'relevant asset' or under which any liability is a 'relevant liability'. Where, had the company ceased to be a party to the relationship on 31 March 1996, no amount would have fallen to be brought into account in computing trading profits or losses for any accounting period ending on or after that date, the accounting method is taken to require a 'notional closing value' as at 31 March 1996 to be given to that asset or liability.

In the case of loan relationships continuing after 13 November 1996 (and certain replacement relationships), an adjustment is required where there is a difference between (*a*) the 'notional closing value' at 31 March 1996 and (*b*) the amount which, in a computation on an authorised accruals basis and assuming such a basis had always been used as respects the relationship, would be taken as representing the accrued value of the relationship on 1 April 1996. That difference is brought into account under the current provisions for the accounting period in which the company ceases to be a party to the relationship, as a credit where (*b*) exceeds (*a*), otherwise as a debit. Where a credit accordingly arises for an accounting period beginning on or after 1 October 2002, it is treated as reduced (but not below nil) by the amount of any deemed allowable loss which would have been brought into account as respects the same loan relationship on a disposal of the asset on 31 March 1996 but for the application of the connected party rules in *TCGA 1992, s 251*(*4*) (no allowable loss on disposal of debt acquired from a connected person).

The debit or credit is a non-trading debit or credit (see 46.3 above).

Where the company ceases to be within the charge to corporation tax at any time, it is treated for these purposes as ceasing to be a party to the relationship immediately before that time.

With effect for accounting periods beginning *on or after 1 October 2002*, where a creditor company acquired its rights under the loan relationship

(i) in an arm's length transaction on or before 31 March 1996,

(ii) in an accounting period in which there was no connection between the creditor company and the person from whom the company acquired the asset but there was a connection between the creditor company and the debtor company, and

(iii) there was no such connection between the creditor and the debtor company at any time during the period beginning four years before the date on which the rights to the loan relationship were acquired and ending twelve months before that date,

the amount (*b*) referred to above which is to be deducted from the notional 31 March 1996 closing value is the greater of the fair value of the rights on 1 April 1996 and their value at the time the company ceases to be a party to the loan relationship. There is for this purpose a 'connection' between the company and another person for an accounting period at any time during which the other person is a company and one company controls the other or both companies are under the control of the same person ('control' being within *ICTA 1988, s 416(2)–(6)*, see 16.2 CLOSE COMPANIES). Where the company is a close company, there is such a 'connection' where the other person is a 'participator' (or an 'associate' of a participator) in that company (those terms being as in *ICTA 1988, s 417*, see 16.3, 16.5 CLOSE COMPANIES, except that a person is not for this purpose regarded as a participator by reason only of being a loan creditor of the company).

A '*relevant asset*' is a chargeable asset (as defined, and generally excluding qualifying corporate bonds) or a 'relevant qualifying asset'. For the meaning of 'relevant qualifying asset' and 'relevant liability', see above under *Pre-31 March 1996 trading relationships*.

The '*notional closing value*' of an asset or liability as at 31 March 1996 is its market value or, if it is a relevant qualifying asset or a relevant liability, the value given to it on the first day of the company's first accounting period beginning after 22 March 1995 for the purpose of computing any attributed amount. An election could, however, be made in relation to all the company's relevant qualifying assets to which a notional closing value would otherwise be given as above and which would be chargeable assets but for the EXCHANGE GAINS AND LOSSES (26) provisions. The effect of the election is that the notional closing value as at 31 March 1996 is the market value as at 1 April 1996. The election had to be made in writing to an officer of the Board before 1 October 1996.

[*FA 1996, Sch 15 paras 11, 11A, 12; FA 1997, Sch 13 paras 6, 7; FA 2002, Sch 25 paras 41, 42*].

47 Losses

Cross-references. See 32.6–32.22 GROUPS OF COMPANIES.

Simon's Direct Tax Service. See **D2.4**.

47.1 See 11.3 CAPITAL GAINS for the treatment of capital losses and 51 OIL COMPANIES for losses of such companies.

The headings in this chapter are as follows.

47.2 **SET-OFF OF TRADING LOSSES**

A company which 'carries on a trade' within Schedule D, Case I may claim that losses incurred in that trade be set off against other profits (including chargeable gains) of the same accounting period. [*ICTA 1988, s 393A(1)(a)*]. Claims must be made within two years of the end of the accounting period in which the loss is made or within such further period as HMRC may allow. [*ICTA 1988, s 393A(10)*]. HMRC's approach in practice to admittance of late claims is as follows.

(*a*) In general, late claims will only be admitted where they could not have been made timeously for reasons beyond the company's control, e.g. where, at the date of expiry of the time limit, the company or its agents were unaware of profits against which relief for losses could be claimed, or the amount of such profits or losses was under discussion with HMRC (and the delay was not substantially the company's (or agents') fault).

(*b*) In such cases claims (or the withdrawal of claims and submission of fresh claims) will be admitted up to the amount of the profit or loss in question.

(*c*) Other reasons would be 'beyond the company's control' where all of the following applied:

- (i) an officer of the company was ill or otherwise absent for a good reason;
- (ii) the absence or illness arose at a critical time and prevented the making of the claim in question;
- (iii) there was good reason why the claim was not made before the absence or illness arose; and
- (iv) there was no other person who could have made the claim timeously.

(*d*) The following would **not** be regarded as reasons 'beyond the company's control':

- (i) oversight or negligence on the part of the company or its agent;

(ii) failure, without good reason, to compute the necessary figure;

(iii) the wish to avoid commitment pending clarification of the effects of making the claim;

(iv) illness or absence of an agent or adviser to the company.

(*e*) There may be other cases where, in all the circumstances, it would be unreasonable for HMRC to refuse a late claim. The following criteria may be relevant:

(i) the reason why a claim is late. Even if not within the above criteria, it will still be taken into account in assessing the circumstances as a whole;

(ii) the extent to which it is late;

(iii) the consequences for the company of refusal of the claim;

(iv) any particularly unusual features.

(*f*) In all cases, if the late claim forms part of a tax avoidance scheme, that will be taken into account.

(*g*) Delay in making the claim after the circumstances which caused it to be late have ceased to apply may result in the claim being rejected.

(HMRC Statement of Practice, SP 5/01).

For other provisions to which this Statement of Practice applies, see 10.2 CAPITAL ALLOWANCES, 32.18 GROUPS OF COMPANIES, 47.6, 47.8 below and 15.3 CLAIMS. See also generally HMRC Company Taxation Manual, CTM 04590.

A trading loss is computed in the same way as trading income. [*ICTA 1988, s 393(7), s 393A(9)(a)(b)*]. For accounting periods ending before 1 April 2001, a claim could require that unrelieved capital allowances which fell to be given by discharge or repayment of tax for an accounting period (i.e. they were not deducted as trading expenses) should augment or create a loss for that period. Allowances brought forward from an earlier period could not be included in such a claim. There are, however, no allowances for traders which are now given in this way. [*CAA 1990, s 145(3); ICTA 1988, s 393A(5)(6); CAA 2001, Sch 2 para 32(2)*].

A company '*carries on a trade*' if it is within the charge to corporation tax in respect of that trade. [*ICTA 1988, s 393(10), s 393A(9)(c)*].

Note that *capital losses* cannot generally be set off against trading profits (but see 47.19 below regarding certain losses of investment companies on unquoted shares).

See 26.14 EXCHANGE GAINS AND LOSSES as regards relief of certain 'relievable amounts' in respect of exchange losses.

See also 47.9, 47.15, 47.18–47.21 below.

Simon's Direct Tax Service. See **D2.404.**

47.3 *Example*

A Ltd is a trading company with investment business (see 42.8 INVESTMENT COMPANIES AND INVESTMENT BUSINESS). Its results for the year ended 31 March 2008 show:

	£
Trading loss	(100,000)
Schedule A	30,000
Schedule D, Case III	40,000
Chargeable gains	72,000
Management expenses	(20,000)
Qualifying charitable donations	(10,000)

The loss may be relieved as follows.

	£
Schedule A	30,000
Schedule D, Case III	40,000
Chargeable gains	72,000
	142,000
Deduct Management expenses	(20,000)
	122,000
Deduct Trading loss	(100,000)
	22,000
Deduct Qualifying charitable donations	(10,000)
Profits chargeable to CT	£12,000

47.4 CARRY-FORWARD OF TRADING LOSSES

Where a company which carries on a trade (see 47.2 above) suffers losses in that trade in an accounting period, those losses may be carried forward and set off against any 'trading income' from 'the same trade' in succeeding accounting periods. So long as the company carries on that trade, its trading income therefrom is treated as reduced by the losses so carried forward (or the balance of such losses not relieved in an earlier accounting period). [*ICTA 1988, s 393(1)*].

For the purpose of computing losses under these provisions, the excess of charges on income over the profits against which they are deductible is treated as a trading expense in so far as they were incurred wholly and exclusively for the purposes of the trade. [*ICTA 1988, s 393(9)*]. See 66.18 TRADING INCOME as regards the meaning of 'wholly and exclusively' and, for a case on the application of *section 393(9)*, *Commercial Union Assurance Co plc v Shaw CA 1999, 72 TC 101*. Otherwise a loss is computed in the same way as trading income. [*ICTA 1988, s 393(7)*]. See 47.9 below as regards determination of losses, and 32.10 GROUPS OF COMPANIES for group relief interaction.

'*Trading income*' means the income which is, or would be, included in respect of a particular trade in the total profits of the company. But where a loss incurred under Schedule D, Case I or V is carried forward to a later accounting period the trading income for which is insufficient to absorb it, interest and dividends which would be trading receipts but for having been otherwise subjected to tax (as in the case of banks, share dealers, and other companies carrying on financial business) are to be included in trading income. [*ICTA 1988, s 393(8)*]. In *Bank Line Ltd v CIR CS 1974, 49 TC 307*, it was held that, to constitute trading receipts for this purpose, the interest etc. must arise from capital actively employed in the trade and in a real and practical sense at risk in the ordinary course of current trading. Interest etc. received on reserve funds was thus excluded. Similarly in *Nuclear Electric plc v Bradley HL 1996, 68 TC 670*, the crucial test was considered to be whether the investments were employed in the business (of producing and selling electricity) in the year in question. The Court of Appeal, whose judgment was approved, considered decisive the facts that the liabilities against which the investments were provided were liabilities to third parties rather than customers, and that, in view of the long-term nature of the liabilities, the business could be carried on for a long period without maintaining a fund of investments at all. HMRC have confirmed that dividend income normally ranks as a trade receipt only where it is an integral part of the business operations to employ capital to produce such income, for example in the case of banks and other financial concerns. (HMRC Business Income Manual, BIM 40801, 40805). For the general inclusion of trade interest in trading income, see 46 LOAN RELATIONSHIPS.

As to what constitutes '*the same trade*' for these purposes, see *Morning Post Ltd v George KB 1940, 23 TC 514* and *Robroyston Brickworks Ltd v CIR CS 1976, 51 TC 230* (change of ownership of trade — but see now 47.10 below); *Gordon & Blair Ltd v CIR CS 1962, 40 TC 358* (cessation of manufacturing, retention of retailing); *Seaman v Tucketts Ltd Ch D 1963, 41 TC 422* (cessation of manufacturing and retailing, commencement of intra-group servicing); *Bispham v Eardiston Farming Co [1919] Ltd Ch D 1962, 40 TC 322* (transfer of trade from one farm to another); *Rolls-Royce Motors Ltd v Bamford Ch D 1976, 51 TC 319* (transfer of part of existing trade); *Kawthar Consulting Ltd v HMRC [2005] SSCD 524 (Sp C 477)* (change of trade from providing computer software and hardware to IT consultancy). See also 47.9–47.17, 47.21 below.

Simon's Direct Tax Service. See **D2.406.**

47.5 *Example*

B Ltd has carried on the same trade for many years. The results for the years ended 31 January 2006, 2007 and 2008 are shown below.

	2006	2007	2008
	£	£	£
Trading profit/(loss)	(200,000)	100,000	50,000
Schedule A	15,000	10,000	20,000
Schedule D, Case III	5,000	20,000	30,000
Chargeable gains	56,000	47,000	40,000
Management expenses	—	(90,000)	—

B Ltd may claim to set off the trading loss against other profits of the same accounting period. Assuming the claim is made (and that no claim is made to carry back the balance of the loss), the loss will be set off as follows.

47.5 Losses

	£	Loss memorandum £
Year ended 31 January 2006		
Trading loss		(200,000)
Schedule A	15,000	
Schedule D, Case III	5,000	
Chargeable gains	56,000	
	76,000	
Deduct Trading loss	(76,000)	76,000
	—	
		(124,000)
Year ended 31 January 2007		
Schedule D, Case I	100,000	
Deduct Loss brought forward	(100,000)	100,000
	—	(24,000)
Schedule A	10,000	
Schedule D, Case III	20,000	
Chargeable gains	47,000	
	77,000	
Deduct Management charges (restricted)	(77,000)	
Profits chargeable to CT	—	
		(24,000)

Management expenses carried forward £13,000

	£	Loss memorandum £
Year ended 31 January 2008		
Schedule D, Case I	50,000	
Deduct Loss brought forward	(24,000)	24,000
	26,000	
Schedule A	20,000	
Schedule D, Case III	30,000	
Chargeable gains	40,000	
	116,000	
Deduct: management expenses	(13,000)	
Profits chargeable to CT	£103,000	

47.6 **CARRY-BACK OF TRADING LOSSES**

Where a company incurs a trading loss in an accounting period and makes a claim to set the loss against other profits of that accounting period (see 47.2 above), it may additionally claim that the balance of the loss not so relieved be carried back. It is then set against the profits (including chargeable gains) of preceding accounting periods (at some time during which it was carrying on the same trade) falling wholly or partly within the period of twelve months immediately preceding the accounting period in which the loss is incurred. Profits of an accounting period beginning before, and ending within, that period are apportioned on a time basis. No relief is available for accounting periods ending earlier. The profits of each accounting period are treated as reduced by losses so carried back (or the balance of such losses not relieved in a later accounting period). Partial relief claims are not allowed, i.e. if carry-back of a loss is claimed, any part of the loss not relieved in the immediately preceding accounting period must be carried back to the period before that and so on, and losses of earlier accounting periods are relieved in priority to those of later periods.

A three year carry-back period applies to terminal losses (see 47.8 below) and to certain losses arising from the special allowances for North Sea oil and gas installation decommissioning costs. A three year carry-back period also applied for losses incurred in an accounting period ending on or before or straddling 1 July 1997 (see Tolley's Corporation Tax 2003/04 or earlier edition).

[*ICTA 1988, s 393A(1)(b)(2)–(2C)*].

A trading loss is computed in the same way as trading income. [*ICTA 1988, s 393(7), s 393A(9)(a)(b)*]. A claim could require that unrelieved capital allowances which fell to be given by discharge or repayment of tax for an accounting period (i.e. they were not deducted as trading expenses) should augment or create a loss for that period. Allowances brought forward from an earlier period could not be included in such a claim. There are, however, no longer any allowances for traders which are given in this way. [*CAA 1990, s 145(3)(4); ICTA 1988, s 393A(5)(6); CAA 2001, Sch 2 para 32(2)*].

Excess charges are excluded from losses available to be carried back (see 55.4 PROFIT COMPUTATIONS). Losses may not be carried back so as to interfere with relief given in earlier periods for trade charges. [*ICTA 1988, s 393A(8)*].

Claims must be made within two years of the end of the accounting period in which the loss is made or within such further period as HMRC may allow (for which see 47.2 above). [*ICTA 1988, s 393A*(*10*)].

See also 47.9 and 47.14 below.

Simon's Direct Tax Service. See **D2.405**.

Foot and mouth outbreak. For the full range of measures, including early claims to loss relief, in relation to the 2001 foot and mouth disease outbreak, see Revenue Tax Bulletin Special Edition May 2001.

47.7 *Examples*

(*A*) *General*

For the years ending 31 March 2007 and 31 March 2008, X Ltd has the following results.

	2007	2008
	£	£
Trading profit/(loss)	60,000	(200,000)
Schedule A	25,000	30,000
Schedule D, Case III	15,000	10,000
Chargeable gains	15,000	45,000
Management expenses	(40,000)	—

The loss can be relieved as follows.

			Loss memorandum
	£	£	£
Year ended 31 March 2008			
Trading loss			(200,000)
Schedule A		30,000	
Schedule D, Case III		10,000	
Chargeable gains		45,000	
		85,000	
Deduct Management expenses		(40,000)	
		45,000	
Deduct Trading loss		(45,000)	45,000
Profits chargeable to CT		—	
			(155,000)

	£	£	Loss memorandum £
Year ended 31 December 2007			
Schedule D, Case I		60,000	
Schedule A		25,000	
Schedule D, Case III		15,000	
Chargeable gains		15,000	
		115,000	
Deduct Management expenses		(40,000)	
		75,000	
Deduct Loss carried back		(75,000)	75,000
Profits chargeable to CT		—	
Loss carried forward			£80,000

(*B*) *Accounting periods of different lengths*

Y Ltd, which previously made up accounts to 31 December, changes its accounting date after the year ended 31 December 2005 to 30 September. Its results for the accounting periods to 31 December 2005, 30 September 2006 and 30 September 2007 are as follows.

	12 months 31.12.05	9 months 30.9.06	12 months 30.9.07
	£	£	£
Trading profit/(loss)	255,000	(90,000)	(420,000)
Schedule D, Case III	25,000	30,000	—
Chargeable gains	40,000	—	20,000

Y Ltd makes all available loss relief claims so as to obtain relief against the earliest possible profits.

The computations are summarised as follows.

	12 months 31.12.05	9 months 30.9.06	12 months 30.9.07
	£	£	£
Schedule D, Case I	255,000	—	—
Schedule D, Case III	25,000	30,000	—
Chargeable gains	40,000	—	20,000
	320,000	30,000	20,000
Loss relief			
ICTA 1988, s 393A(1)(a)		(30,000)	(20,000)
ICTA 1988, s 393A(1)(b)	(140,000)		
Profits chargeable to CT	£180,000	—	—

Loss memoranda

	9 months 30.9.06	12 months 30.9.07	Total
	£	£	£
Trading loss	90,000	420,000	510,000
Relieved against current year profits	(30,000)	(20,000)	(50,000)
Relieved by carry-back to y/e 31.12.05	(60,000)	(80,000)	(140,000)
Carried forward	Nil	£320,000	£320,000

Note. The 'specified period' for carry-back of the loss of the year ended 30 September 2007 is the twelve months from 1 October 2005 to 30 September 2006. Thus only one-quarter (£80,000) of the profits of the year ended 31 December 2005 are available for offset against the loss of the year ended 30 September 2007.

47.8 CARRY-BACK OF TERMINAL LOSSES

The relief described at 47.6 above (which permits the carry back of trading losses) also applies where a loss is incurred in the accounting period in which the trade ceases, except that losses incurred in the twelve months prior to cessation may be carried back three years (with losses of any accounting period falling partly within and partly outside that twelve-month period being apportioned on a time basis).

In determining terminal losses for relief as above, charges on income paid wholly and exclusively for trade purposes are treated as trading expenses to the extent that total charges exceed any profits from which they may be deducted. The part of a loss as in (*b*) above which is apportioned to the part of the accounting period falling outside the twelve-month period is reduced by a similarly apportioned part of the charges treated as trading expenses (with no corresponding increase in the loss apportioned to the part of the accounting period falling within the twelve-month period).

Claims to relief must be made within two years of the end of the accounting period in which the loss is incurred, or within such further period as HMRC may allow (for which see 47.2 above).

[*ICTA 1988, s 393A*].

In *Electronics Ltd v HM Inspector of Taxes [2005] SSCD 512 (Sp C 476)*, a claim for terminal loss relief on the closure of two of the company's six divisions was denied on the basis that the trade of all six divisions was a single trade. The Special Commissioners considered the trade of all divisions to be too similar to be broken down into discrete categories and that the place of operational management was not decisive in determining whether there was more than one trade.

For the circumstances in which an inspector may allow a claim for carry-back of losses from the final period of account of a company which has collapsed despite no formal accounts having been prepared for the period, see HMRC Company Taxation Manual, CTM 04570.

Simon's Direct Tax Service. See **D2.405.**

47.9 LOSSES ELIGIBLE FOR RELIEF

A loss is not available for relief under 47.2 or 47.6 above unless

(*a*) the trade is carried on in the exercise of functions conferred by or under any enactment, or

(*b*) for the accounting period in question, the trade was carried on **on a commercial basis and with a view to the realisation of gain** either in the trade itself or in any larger undertaking of which it formed part.

A trade carried on so as to afford a 'reasonable expectation of gain' is treated as carried on with a view to the realisation of gain, but if there is a change in the manner of carrying on the trade in an accounting period, it is treated as having throughout that period been carried on in the same manner as at the end of that period. [*ICTA 1988, s 393A*(*3*)(*4*)].

These provisions are without prejudice to those in 47.14 below.

For the determination of the amount of losses see 61.7 RETURNS.

Simon's Direct Tax Service. See **D2.408, D2.720.**

47.10 COMPANY RECONSTRUCTIONS

The following provisions apply where, on a company ('the predecessor') ceasing to carry on a trade, another company ('the successor') begins to carry it on, and:

(*a*) on, or within two years after, the cessation, the trade is 'owned' as to at least three-quarters by the same persons as owned a similar interest within a year before the cessation; and

(*b*) throughout the periods referred to above, the trade is carried on by a company which is within the charge to tax in respect of it.

References to 'the trade' include any other trade comprising the activities of the original trade.

[*ICTA 1988, s 343*(*1*)].

'*Ownership*'. A trade carried on by two or more persons is treated as owned by them in the shares in which they are entitled to the profits thereof.

A trade or an interest therein belonging to trustees (other than for charitable or public purposes) is treated as owned by the persons entitled to the trust's income for the time being.

A trade or an interest therein belonging to a company shall (if necessary to bring the provisions of *section 343* into effect) be treated as owned by:

(i) the beneficial owners of the 'ordinary share capital' of the company in proportion to their holdings; or

(ii) the company's 'parent company'; or

(iii) the beneficial owners of the 'ordinary share capital' of the parent company in proportion to their holdings; or

(iv) the person or body of persons controlling a corporate shareholder within (i)–(iii) above.

'*Ordinary share capital*' is as defined in *ICTA 1988, s 832(1)*. See 32.4 GROUPS OF COMPANIES.

A '*parent company*' is one owning, directly or indirectly, three-quarters of the ordinary share capital of the company (determined in accordance with *ICTA 1988, s 838(5)–(10)*) and which is not also a subsidiary of a third company.

In determining for the purposes of (*a*) and (*b*) above to what extent a trade belongs to the same persons, persons who are 'relatives' and the persons from time to time entitled to the income under a trust are respectively treated as a single person.

'*Relative*' means spouse or (from 5 December 2005) civil partner, ancestor, lineal descendant, brother or sister.

[*ICTA 1988, s 344; SI 2005 No 3229, reg 66*].

Terminal losses. The special reliefs for terminal losses (see 47.8 above) are not available to the predecessor. [*ICTA 1988, s 343(4A)*].

Trading losses may be carried forward (see 47.4 above) against income arising from the same trade to the successor, as if there had been no succession.

Where the amount of the 'relevant liabilities' immediately before a transfer exceeds the open market value of 'relevant assets' at that time, the losses which may be carried forward are reduced or extinguished by the amount of that excess. Where there are repeated successions (see below), the restriction applies only to transfers after 18 March 1986, and does not affect any earlier transfers on or before that date.

'*Relevant assets*' are assets which were vested in the predecessor immediately before the transfer, and which were not transferred to the successor, together with consideration given to the predecessor by the successor in respect of the change of company carrying on the trade (but the assumption by the successor of any liabilities of the predecessor is not treated as consideration for this purpose).

'*Relevant liabilities*' are liabilities outstanding and vested in the predecessor immediately before the transfer, and not transferred to the successor, but excluding any liability representing share capital, share premium account, reserves or 'relevant loan stock' of the predecessor unless such liability arose on a conversion of a liability not representing any such item within one year before the transfer. Where a liability was transferred to the successor, but the creditor agreed to accept part payment in settlement of the whole, the balance of the liability is treated as not having been transferred to the successor.

Any assets or liabilities apportioned to a successor on a previous application of these provisions (see below) are excluded.

'*Relevant loan stock*' is any loan stock or similar security, secured or unsecured, but excluding any in respect of which, at the time the liability giving rise to it was incurred, the creditor was carrying on a trade of lending money. The amount of a liability representing relevant loan stock which is not a relevant liability, but which is secured on a relevant asset, is deducted from the value of the asset for the purposes of this provision.

[*ICTA 1988, s 343(3)(4), s 344(5)–(12)*].

Capital allowances are given to, and balancing charges made on, the successor as if there had been no succession (and losses are calculated accordingly unless the successor is a 'dual resident investing company' (see 32.27 GROUPS OF COMPANIES) and begins to carry on the trade after 31 March 1987. [*ICTA 1988, s 343(2)*]. Where the trade is transferred during the currency of accounting periods of the companies concerned:

(i) writing-down allowances are calculated on the 'pool' at the end of the transferee's accounting period, and apportioned on a time basis between the periods in which each company carried on the trade;

(ii) first-year allowances are given to the company incurring the expenditure; and

(iii) balancing adjustments are made on the company carrying on the trade at the relevant time.

(CCAB Guidance Notes TR 500, 10 March 1983). See also HMRC Capital Allowances Manual, CA 15400.

An anti-avoidance measure has been introduced, with effect for cessations on or after 22 November 2006, to counter the use of reconstructions of companies carrying on a 'business of leasing plant and machinery' (see 5.17 ANTI-AVOIDANCE) to avoid tax. Where the predecessor and successor companies carry on the business otherwise than in partnership, for capital allowances purposes, they are not treated as the same person under *ICTA 1988 s 343(2)* unless the principal company of the group is the same before and after the change, or, from 21 March 2007, in the case of a consortium, the percentage of the successor held by the principal company is the same before and after the reconstruction. Where the parties are carrying on the leasing business in partnership, the predecessor has to stop trading on the date of transfer for *s 343(2)* to apply. The effect of this is to ensure that the companies share the same principal company for the purposes of *FA 2006, Sch 10* (sale of lessor company carrying on business of leasing plant or machinery – see 5.17 ANTI-AVOIDANCE).

If *s 343(2)* does not apply to a transfer, for capital allowances purposes there is deemed to be a disposal by the predecessor of the leasing assets at market value and an acquisition by the successor at that value on the date of cessation of the trade.

[*ICTA 1988, s 343A*; *FA 2007 Sch 6, para 1*].

Securities within ICTA 1988, s 731 held as trading stock are treated as having been sold by the predecessor and acquired by the successor at market value at the time of the succession. See 5.7 ANTI-AVOIDANCE. [*ICTA 1988, s 343(5)*].

Repeated successions are each treated in accordance with the above provisions, provided that the conditions in (*a*) and (*b*) above are satisfied on each occasion.

Where the successor takes over **part only** of the predecessor's trade, or where the activities to which it succeeds are carried on as part only of the successor's existing trade, the transferred activities are treated as a separate trade and receipts, expenses, etc. are apportioned as may be just. See *Falmer Jeans Ltd v Rodin Ch D, 1990, 63 TC 55* for a case in which this provision was held to apply. If more than one company's liability is affected, the matter is determined by:

(A) the General Commissioners having jurisdiction over both companies (if any); or

(B) in default of (A), such body of General Commissioners, having jurisdiction over one of the companies, as HMRC may direct; or

(C) if the companies agree, or in any other case, the Special Commissioners.

Each company is entitled to appear before, and be heard by, the Commissioners, or to make written representations. [*ICTA 1988, s 343(8)–(10)*].

See also 47.12 and 47.13 below.

47.11 Losses

Simon's Direct Tax Service. See D2.515.

47.11 *Example*

A Ltd and B Ltd are two wholly-owned subsidiaries of X Ltd. All are within the charge to corporation tax, although A Ltd has accumulated trading losses brought forward and unrelieved of £200,000 and has not paid tax for several years. As part of a group reorganisation, A Ltd's trade is transferred to B Ltd on 31 October 2007.

A Ltd's balance sheet immediately before the transfer is as follows.

	£		£
Share capital	100,000	Property	90,000
Debenture secured on property	50,000	Plant	20,000
Group loan	10,000	Stock	130,000
Trade creditors	300,000	Trade debtors	120,000
Bank overdraft	60,000		
	520,000		
Deficit on reserves	(160,000)		
	£360,000		£360,000

Book values represent the approximate open market values of assets. B Ltd takes over the stock and plant to continue the trade, paying £150,000 to A Ltd and taking over £15,000 of trade creditors relating to stock. A Ltd is to collect outstanding debts and pay remaining creditors.

A Ltd's 'relevant assets' are:

	£
Freehold property (£90,000 – £50,000)	40,000
Trade debtors	120,000
Consideration from B Ltd	150,000
	£310,000

A Ltd's 'relevant liabilities' are:

	£
Bank overdraft	60,000
Group loan	10,000
Trade creditors (£300,000 – £15,000)	285,000
	£355,000

Tax losses transferable with trade:
£200,000 – £(355,000 – 310,000) = £155,000

47.12 **PRIVATISATION**

British Telecommunications plc ('British Telecom') is treated for all purposes of corporation tax as being the same person as British Telecommunications, to whose business it succeeded on privatisation, except that it is not regarded by virtue of the above provision alone as a nationalised undertaking within *TCGA 1992, s 170(12)*. Additionally, there is a bar on the carry forward to the successor company of losses arising in the Post Office non-telecommunications business prior to their separation. [*British Telecommunications Act 1981, s 82; Telecommunications Act 1984, s 72*]. Similar provisions apply in relation to the successor companies to the British Airways Board and the National Freight Corporation [*ICTA 1988, s 513*], the British Airports Authority [*British Airports Act 1986, s 77*], the British Gas Corporation [*Gas Act 1986, s 60*], the British Steel Corporation [*British Steel Act 1988, s 11*], the General Practice Finance Corporation [*Health and Medicines Act 1988, s 6*], statutory port undertakings [*Ports Act 1991, s 35*], the National Research Development Council and National Enterprise Board [*British Technology Group Act 1991, s 12*], milk marketing boards [*Agriculture Act 1993, Sch 2 Pt I; FA 1996, s 203*], Northern Ireland Airports Ltd [*FA 1994, s 253, Sch 25*] and the Atomic Energy Authority [*Atomic Energy Authority Act 1995, Sch 3*]. See also *Water Act 1989, s 95*, *Electricity Act 1989, s 90, Sch 11*, *Environmental Protection Act 1990, ss 6–9*, *Coal Industry Act 1994, Sch 4*, *Broadcasting Act 1996, Sch 7*, *Transport Act 2000, Sch 26* and *Scottish Water* (*Transfer of Functions, etc.*)(*Tax Provisions*) *Order 2002* (*SI 2002 No 653*), and, as regards the *Railways Act 1993*, *FA 1994, s 252, Sch 24*.

Surplus ACT arising to the successor company on privatisation may not be carried back to a period before the transfer (*CIR v Aberdeen Milk Co Ltd CS, 73 TC 563*).

47.13 **CHANGE IN OWNERSHIP OF A COMPANY**

For changes in ownership of companies with investment business or, for accounting periods beginning before 1 April 2004, investment companies, see 42.8 INVESTMENT COMPANIES AND INVESTMENT BUSINESS.

The provisions outlined below apply if:

(*a*) within any period of three years there is a 'change in the ownership of a company' preceded or followed by, or coinciding with, a 'major change in the nature or conduct of a trade' carried on by the company; or

(*b*) at any time after the scale of activities in a trade carried on by a company has become small or negligible, and before any considerable revival in the trade, there is a change in the ownership of the company.

[*ICTA 1988, s 768(1)*].

There is a '*change in the ownership of a company*' if:

(i) a single person acquires as beneficial owner more than half the ordinary share capital (see *ICTA 1988, s 832(1)* or 32.4 GROUPS OF COMPANIES) of the company; or

(ii) two or more persons each acquire as beneficial owner a holding of at least 5% (or an addition to the holding sufficient to raise it to 5%) of the company's ordinary share capital, and the combined holdings exceed half that capital. Acquisitions by, and holdings of, CONNECTED PERSONS (19) are treated as a single acquisition or holding.

See, however, 32.40 GROUPS OF COMPANIES for the interaction of these provisions and the demerger provisions of *ICTA 1988, ss 213–218*.

In comparing a person's holdings at any two dates, he is to be treated at the later date as having acquired whatever he did not hold at the earlier date, irrespective of intervening acquisitions and disposals. Comparisons are made in percentage terms throughout.

Acquisitions of shares on death are left out of account as is any gift which was unsolicited and made without regard to these provisions.

The date of any acquisition corresponds with the date of the contract of sale, or with the assignment of the benefit of that contract, or with the acquisition of the option to acquire, as the case may be.

Where the existence of extraordinary rights or powers renders ownership of the ordinary share capital an inappropriate test of change of ownership, holdings of all kinds, or of any particular kind, of share capital, voting power or any other special kind of power may be taken into account instead.

A change in the direct ownership of a company is ignored if, before and after the change, it continues to be a '75% subsidiary' of the same company. Where there is a change in the ownership of a company under *ICTA 1988, s 769*, then the person(s) whose holding(s) is (are) taken into account under (i) or (ii) above is (are) deemed to acquire at the time of the change the 'appropriate proportion' of the ordinary share capital (or other rights or powers, see above) of any other company owned by the company whose ownership has changed. The '*appropriate proportion*' is the whole where only one person's holding is taken into account, in any other case the proportion of the aggregate holdings taken into account acquired by each person whose holding is taken into account.

'*75% subsidiary*' is defined by reference to direct or indirect ownership of at least 75% of ordinary share capital, with an additional requirement that the parent company would be beneficially entitled to at least 75% of any profits available for distribution to equity holders and of any assets so available on a winding-up (see 32.9 GROUPS OF COMPANIES).

No event or situation preceding a change of ownership to which these provisions have applied is to be taken into account in ascertaining whether a subsequent change has taken place.

[*ICTA 1988, s 769*].

'*Major change in the nature or conduct of a trade*' includes a major change in the type of property dealt in, or the services or facilities provided, in the trade, or in customers, outlets or markets, even if that change is the result of a gradual process which began outside the three-year period. A '*change*' for these purposes is to be decided by a qualitative test but in determining whether a change is '*major*' the change should not be viewed in isolation but a quantitative test of fact and degree should be applied (*Willis v Peeters Picture Frames Ltd CA (NI) 1982, 56 TC 436*). [*ICTA 1988, s 768(4)*]. The cessation of a trade is unlikely to be regarded as a major change in the nature or conduct of the trade, although the events leading up to it may be so; the interposition of a holding company between a company and its shareholders usually represents a change in ownership, but does not represent a major change in the nature or conduct of a trade carried on by the company. (ICAEW Technical Memorandum TR 854, 2 December 1991).

HMRC Statement of Practice, SP 10/91 (as revised) sets out other factors to which HMRC will have regard in considering whether there has been a major change in the nature or conduct of a trade or business. This applies for the purposes of the instant provisions and for the purposes of *ICTA 1988, s 767A* (company purchase schemes, see 53.5 PAYMENT OF TAX), *ICTA 1988, s 768B* (change in ownership of investment companies, see 42.8 INVESTMENT COMPANIES AND INVESTMENT BUSINESS), *TCGA 1992, Sch 7A* (restriction on pre-entry losses, see 12.16 CAPITAL GAINS—GROUPS) and *SI 1999 No 358* (carry forward of shadow ACT, see 3.8 ADVANCE CORPORATION TAX—SHADOW ACT). These would include changes in factors such as location of the business premises, identity of suppliers, management or staff, methods of manufacture, or pricing or purchasing policies, in so far as they are indicative of a major change. It will not be regarded as a major change in the nature or conduct of a trade where all that has happened is that changes have been made to increase efficiency, or to keep pace with developing technology in the industry concerned or with developing management techniques, or to rationalise the product range by withdrawing unprofitable items and, possibly, replacing them with new items of a related kind. Although it is acknowledged that every case rests on its own facts, examples are cited where a change would *not* be regarded as major. These include removal from several obsolescent factories to one new factory without a change of product, the replacement of mechanical manufacturing components by electronic ones, and a switch by a dealership of brands dealt in where the same market is satisfied before and after the switch. Examples cited where a major change *would* be regarded as occurring include a saloon car dealership switching to tractors, a switch from owning a public house to operating a discotheque from the same (converted) premises, and a switch from fattening pigs for their owners to buying pigs for fattening and resale. Other examples relevant to changes in ownership of investment companies (see 42.8 INVESTMENT COMPANIES AND INVESTMENT BUSINESS) are also given.

Where these provisions have to be considered in relation to the transfer of part of a trade which is to be treated as the transfer of a separate trade under *ICTA 1988, s 343(8)* (see 47.10 above), SP 10/91 indicates that the transfer of the part-trade will not of itself be regarded as a major change in the nature or conduct of either the part-trade transferred or that retained. Instead, each of the trades (or the relevant part of a combined trade) after the transfer will be compared with the equivalent part of the combined trade before the transfer. In cases where the transfer occurs *after* the relevant change of ownership, however, it may be necessary to consider whether it involves a major change in the nature or conduct of the undivided trade as it subsisted at the date of the change in ownership, and in such cases it may be appropriate to regard the transfer as constituting a major change, depending on the surrounding circumstances. HMRC will not, however, take this point if there was no other major change in either the original trade, or the parts into which it was divided, in the relevant period.

Where these provisions apply, no relief may be claimed under *ICTA 1988, s 393* against the income or other profits of an accounting period ending after the change of ownership for losses incurred in an accounting period beginning before the change. Relief may similarly not be claimed under *ICTA 1988, s 393A(1)* for a loss incurred in an accounting period ending after the change to be set against profits of an accounting period beginning before the change. For these purposes only, the accounting period in which the change takes place is treated as two separate accounting periods, ending with the date of the change and beginning with the following date respectively. The profits or losses of the whole period are apportioned to each on a time basis, or by such other method as is just and reasonable. [*ICTA 1988, s 768(1)–(3), s 768A*].

If the carry-forward of loss relief is restricted as above, in applying the provisions of the *Capital Allowances Acts* relating to balancing charges arising by reference to any event after the change of ownership, any allowance or deduction falling to be made in taxing the company's trade for any chargeable period before the change is to be disregarded in so far as the profits or gains of that and any subsequent chargeable period before the change are insufficient to give effect to it (assuming such effect to be given before any loss relief not attributable to any such allowance or deduction). [*ICTA 1988, s 768(6)(7)*].

Company reconstructions. Where the change in ownership takes place after a company reconstruction under *ICTA 1988, s 343* (see 47.10 above), for the purposes of the restriction on carry-forward of relief under *ICTA 1988, s 768*, references to the trade at (*a*) and (*b*) above *include* the trade as carried on by the predecessor, and relief for losses incurred before the company reconstruction are restricted in the same way as losses incurred after the company reconstruction. [*ICTA 1988, s 768(5)*].

Assessment. An assessment may be made within six years after the circumstances or events (after the change but within the three-year period) which bring these provisions into operation, in order to give effect to these provisions. [*ICTA 1988, s 768(8)*].

Powers to obtain information. The inspector may, by notice in writing, require any person who is the registered owner of shares, stock or securities of a company, to state whether he is the beneficial owner thereof, and, if not, to supply the name and address of the person or persons on whose behalf he holds them. [*ICTA 1988, s 768(9)*].

Schedule A losses. Where either (*a*) or (*b*) above applies in relation to a company carrying on a Schedule A business or an overseas property business (see 56 PROPERTY INCOME), so that the provisions described apply, or would apply, in relation to trading losses, a similar restriction applies to prevent Schedule A losses (see 56 PROPERTY INCOME) incurred before the change being set against profits arising after the change. [*ICTA 1988, ss 768D, 769*].

General. These provisions are intended to prevent the purchase of companies with accumulated trading or property losses, in order to claim relief against the purchaser's trading profits and vice versa.

See also 3.8 ADVANCE CORPORATION TAX—SHADOW ACT, 42.8 INVESTMENT COMPANIES AND INVESTMENT BUSINESS and 53.5 PAYMENT OF TAX.

Simon's Direct Tax Service. See D2.410.

47.14 FARMING AND MARKET GARDENING

A loss incurred in any accounting period in carrying on a trade of farming or market gardening cannot be relieved against other income or gains or carried back if a loss, ignoring capital allowances, has been incurred in that period and in each of the five years up to the beginning of that accounting period. [*ICTA 1988, s 397; CAA 2001, Sch 2 para 34; ITTOIA 2005; Sch 1 para 169; ITA 2007, Sch 1 para 74*].

ICTA 1988, s 397 does **not** deny relief where:

(i) the farming, etc. is part of, and ancillary to, a larger trading undertaking; or

(ii) the farming, etc. activities in the year are carried on in a way which might reasonably be expected to produce profits in the future and the activities in the preceding five years could not reasonably have been expected to become profitable until after the year under review. [*ICTA 1988, s 397(3)(4)*].

There is also a **temporary concessional relief** from the application of *section 397* for an accounting period ending in either the year to 31 March 2001 or the year to 31 March 2002 (or to both such years) where the former is the sixth, or the latter the sixth or seventh, consecutive year of losses, provided that the six or seven year period of losses was immediately preceded by a year of profit, and that in the three years immediately preceding that year of profit there was at least one other year of profit. (HMRC Extra-Statutory Concession, B55).

Simon's Direct Tax Service. See B3.531.

47.15 LEASING

Where a company incurs capital expenditure on machinery or plant which it lets to another person under a leasing contract, and that company would otherwise be entitled to relief under *ICTA 1988, s 393(1)(2)* or *s 393A(1)* (see 47.2–47.6 above) for losses *incurred on that contract*, the relief is denied if, in the accounting period for which a 'first-year allowance' (where available) in respect of the expenditure is made, arrangements exist for a 'successor company' to take over all or part of the first company's obligations under the leasing contract. [*ICTA 1988, s 395(1)*].

'*Losses incurred on a leasing contract*' (and profits arising) are computed, and are treated for relief purposes, as if the leasing contract constituted a separate trade, begun at the time of the letting. [*ICTA 1988, s 395(3)(4)*]. Loss relief is thus restricted to future profits on the leasing contract.

'*First-year allowance*' is as defined in *CAA 2001, Pt II* (or *CAA 1990, Pt II*). [*ICTA 1988, s 395(1)*]. See 10.27 CAPITAL ALLOWANCES.

'*Successor company*' is as defined in *section 343* (see 47.10 above) **or** a company connected with the first company. [*ICTA 1988, s 395(2)*]. See 19 CONNECTED PERSONS.

Sale of lessors. For restriction of relief for losses in the case where there is a change in the ownership of a company carrying on a business of leasing plant or machinery, see 5.17 ANTI-AVOIDANCE.

Leasing partnerships. For restriction of relief for losses in the case where there is a change in the interest of a company in a business, carried on in partnership, of leasing plant or machinery, see 5.16 and 5.17 ANTI-AVOIDANCE. For restrictions on the set-off against an individual's total income of certain losses arising from first-year allowances incurred by the individual in partnership with a company, see Tolley's Income Tax under Losses.

Simon's Direct Tax Service. See **D2.409.**

47.16 COMPANIES IN PARTNERSHIP

There is a restriction on loss relief where a company ('the partner company') is a member of a trading partnership and arrangements exist whereby another partner (or a person connected with him, see 19 CONNECTED PERSONS) receives any payment or enjoys any benefit in money's worth in respect of the partner company's 'share in the profits or losses' of the partnership or whereby the partner company (or a person connected with it) receives any payment or enjoys any such benefit in respect of its share of losses (other than by way of a payment for group relief, see 32.6–32.22 GROUPS OF COMPANIES).

If the above conditions are satisfied for any accounting period, the company's share of partnership losses and charges on income (see *ICTA 1988, s 338*) may be set off only against its share of profits from the partnership's trade, and no other loss incurred by the company in that period may be set against such profits.

[*ICTA 1988, s 116; FA 1998, Sch 3 para 10*].

The company's '*share in the profits or losses*' of the partnership is determined under *ICTA 1988, s 114(2)* (see 52 PARTNERSHIPS), but with appropriate deductions and additions for capital allowances and balancing charges.

See also 47.15 above and 47.21 below and 52.8 PARTNERSHIPS.

47.17 OIL COMPANIES

See 51.10 OIL COMPANIES.

47.18 DEALINGS IN COMMODITY FUTURES

For accounting periods beginning **on or after 1 October 2002**, if, apart from *ICTA 1988, s 128* and *TCGA 1992, s 143(1)*, gains arising in the course of dealing in financial futures or qualifying options would constitute profits or gains chargeable to corporation tax under Schedule D, Case V or VI other than as profits of a trade, any loss arising in the course of that dealing is not allowable against profits or gains so chargeable. For earlier periods, for both income tax and corporation tax purposes, similar provisions applied, but with the exclusion of losses arising from transactions to which *ICTA 1988, Sch 5AA* applied.

If a company carries on the trade of dealing in commodity futures in partnership, and a scheme has been effected or arrangements have been made whereby the sole or main benefit that might be expected to accrue to the company from its partnership interest is the making of a loss to be set off against general income under *ICTA 1988, s 393(2)* or *s 393A(1)* (see 47.2 and 47.6 above), such relief is denied. Any relief already given is recouped by an assessment under Schedule D, Case VI.

[*ICTA 1988, s 399; FA 2002, Sch 27 para 4; ITTOIA 2005, Sch 1 para 171*].

47.19 LOSSES ON UNLISTED SHARES

Investment companies (as defined by *ICTA 1988, s 130* – see 42.1 INVESTMENT COMPANIES AND INVESTMENT BUSINESS – but excluding the holding company of a 'trading group') may claim relief against income for losses arising on the disposal of unlisted shares for which it subscribed and which are ordinary share capital of 'qualifying trading companies'. The vendor must have been an investment company throughout the six years prior to the sale (or for a shorter such period before which it had not been a 'qualifying trading company' or an 'excluded company') and must not have been 'associated' with, or a member of the same group as, the qualifying trading company during its ownership of the shares. [*ICTA 1988, s 573(1)*].

The shares must have been issued in consideration of money (or money's worth). [*ICTA 1988, s 573(6)*].

A claim is available only if

- the disposal is at arm's length for full consideration, or
- the disposal is by way of a distribution in a winding-up, or
- the value of the shares has become negligible and a claim to that effect made under *TCGA 1992, s 24(2)* or
- the disposal consists of the entire loss, destruction, dissipation or extinction of an asset (within *TCGA 1992, s 24(1)*).

[*ICTA 1988, s 575(1)*].

A 'holding' for this purpose means the shares in a company held in a pool of the same class of shares owned by one person in one capacity. [*ICTA 1988, s 576(1D); ITA 2007, Sch 1 para 120*].

The allowable loss is as calculated for the purposes of corporation tax on chargeable gains. [*ICTA 1988, s 573(1)*]. The normal rules for the substitution of market value for consideration apply [*TCGA 1992, s 17*], so that the allowable loss may not exceed the actual loss incurred.

Companies are '*associated*' where one controls the other or both are under common control, control being as defined in *ICTA 1988, s 416* (see 16.2 CLOSE COMPANIES). [*ICTA 1988, s 573(5)*].

As regards shares issued after **5 April 1998**, a '*qualifying trading company*' is a company which:

(*a*) either (i) on the date of disposal meets the trading, control and independence, qualifying subsidiaries and (for shares issued on or after 17 March 2004) the property managing subsidiaries requirements below, or (ii) has ceased to meet any of those requirements within three years before that date and has not since that cessation been an 'excluded company', an '*investment company*' (within *ICTA 1988, s 130*, but excluding the holding company of a 'trading group') or a '*trading company*' (i.e. a company, other than an excluded company, whose business consists wholly or mainly of the carrying on of a trade or trades, or which is the holding company of a trading group); and

(*b*) either (i) has met each of the requirements in (*a*)(i) above for a continuous period of at least six years prior to the disposal (or prior to the cessation in (*a*)(ii) above, as the case may be), or (ii) has met each of those requirements for a shorter continuous period ending with the disposal or cessation and has not previously been an excluded company, an investment company or a trading company; and

(*c*) met the gross assets requirement below both immediately before and immediately after the issue of the shares and (for shares issued after 6 March 2001) met the unquoted status requirement below at the 'relevant time'; and (*d*) has carried on its business wholly or mainly in the UK throughout the period ending with the date of disposal of the shares and beginning with the incorporation of the company, or, if later, one year before the date on which the shares were issued.

For shares issued before 7 March 2001, it was also a condition that the company be an 'unquoted' company (as defined for the purposes of the unquoted status requirement below) throughout that part of the period mentioned in (*d*) above that falls before 7 March 2001.

As regards shares issued **before 6 April 1998**, a '*qualifying trading company*' is a company none of whose shares have been listed on a recognised stock exchange at any time in the period ending with the date of disposal of the shares and beginning with the incorporation of the company, or, if later, one year before the date on which the shares were subscribed for, and which:

(*aa*) either (i) is a trading company on the date of the disposal, or (ii) has ceased to be a trading company within the previous three years and has not since that time been an investment company or an 'excluded company'; and

(*bb*) either (i) has been a trading company for a continuous period of six years ending on the date of disposal of the shares or the time it ceased to be a trading company, or (ii) if shorter, a continuous period ending on that date or that time and had not before the beginning of that period been an excluded company or an investment company; and

(*cc*) has been resident in the UK since incorporation until the date of disposal.

Securities on the Alternative Investment Market ('AIM') are treated as unlisted for these purposes. (Revenue Press Release 20 February 1995).

An '*excluded company*' is a company which has a trade consisting mainly of dealing in land, in commodities or futures or in shares, securities or other financial instruments (as regards shares issued before 6 April 1998 — dealing in shares, securities, land, trades or commodity futures) or which is not carried on a commercial basis with a reasonable expectation of profit, or a company which is the holding company of a group other than a trading group, or which is a building society (see 9 BUILDING SOCIETIES) or a registered industrial and provident society (as defined).

A '*trading group*' is a 'group' (i.e. a company and its 51% subsidiaries) the business of the members of which, taken together, consists wholly or mainly in the carrying on of a trade or trades (disregarding any trade carried on by a subsidiary which is an excluded company or, as regards shares issued before 6 April 1998, which is non-UK resident).

The six requirements referred to at (*a*) to (*c*) above are as follows.

The trading requirement. The company must either:

(i) exist wholly for the purpose of carrying on one or more 'qualifying trades' (see 22.7 CORPORATE VENTURING SCHEME) (disregarding purposes having no significant effect on the extent of its activities); or

(ii) be a '*parent company*' (i.e. a company that has one or more 'qualifying subsidiaries' (as defined)) and the business of the '*group*' (i.e. the company and its qualifying subsidiaries) must not consist wholly or as to a substantial part in the carrying on of 'non-qualifying activities'.

Where the company intends that one or more other companies should become its qualifying subsidiaries with a view to their carrying on one or more qualifying trades, then, until any time after which the intention is abandoned, the company is treated as a parent company and those other companies are included in the group for the purposes of (ii) above.

For the purpose of (ii) above, the business of the group means what would be the business of the group if the activities of the group companies taken together were regarded as one business. Activities are for this purpose disregarded to the extent that they consist in:

- holding shares in or securities of any of the company's subsidiaries;
- making loans to another group company;
- holding and managing property used by a group company for the purposes of a qualifying trade or trades carried on by any group company; or
- holding and managing property used by a group company for the purposes of research and development from which it is intended either that a qualifying trade to be carried on by a 'group company' will be derived or, for shares issued after 5 April 2007, a qualifying trade carried on or to be carried on by a group company will benefit. '*Group company*' includes, for this purpose, any existing or future company which will be a group company at any future time.

Activities are similarly disregarded to the extent that they consist, in the case of a subsidiary whose main purpose is the carrying on of qualifying trade(s) and whose other purposes have no significant effect on the extent of its activities (other than in relation to incidental matters), in activities not in pursuance of its main purpose.

'*Non-qualifying activities*' are:

- excluded activities within 22.7 CORPORATE VENTURING SCHEME; and
- non-trading activities (other than research and development (as defined)).

References in the definition of 'qualifying trade' and 'excluded activities' at 22.7 CORPORATE VENTURING SCHEME to 'period B' are to be taken for the above purposes to refer to the continuous period mentioned in (*b*) above.

For the ascertainment of the purposes for which a company exists, see HMRC Venture Capital Schemes Manual VCM 15070.

A company ceases to meet the trading requirement if, before the time that is relevant for the purposes of (*a*) above, a resolution is passed or an order is made for the winding-up of the company or if the company is dissolved without winding-up. This does not, however, apply if the winding-up is for genuine commercial reasons and not part of a scheme a main purpose of which is tax avoidance and the company continues, during the winding-up, to be a trading company. (Note that the continuation of trading condition now applies in relation to shares issued after 5 April 2001 but did originally apply up to and including 20 March 2000, after which a drafting error inadvertently altered the law.) For shares issued after 20 March 2000, a company does not cease to meet the trading requirement by reason of anything done as a consequence of its being in administration or receivership (both as defined by *ITA 2007, s 252*), provided everything so done and the entry into administration or receivership are for genuine commercial (and not tax avoidance) reasons. For shares issued after 16 March 2004, these provisions are extended to refer also to the winding-up, dissolution, administration or receivership of any of the company's subsidiaries.

The control and independence requirement. The issuing company must not:

(I) control another company other than a qualifying subsidiary (as defined) or, for shares issued before 21 March 2000, have a 51% subsidiary other than a qualifying subsidiary, 'control' being construed in accordance with *ICTA 1988, s 416(2)–(6)* and being considered with or without connected persons within *ITA 2007, s 993*;

(II) be a 51% subsidiary of another company or otherwise under the control of another company, 'control' being construed in accordance with *ITA 2007. s 995* (previously, after 20 March 2000, *ICTA 1988, s 840* and before that in accordance with *ICTA 1988, s 416(2)–(6)*) and again being considered with or without connected persons; or

(III) be capable of falling within (I) or (II) by virtue of any arrangements (as very broadly defined).

The qualifying subsidiaries requirement. The company must not have any subsidiaries other than qualifying subsidiaries (as defined).

The property managing subsidiaries requirement. For shares issued on or after 17 March 2004, any 'property managing subsidiary' (as defined) that the company has must be a 'qualifying 90% subsidiary' (as defined).

The gross assets requirement. The value of the company's gross assets must not exceed £7 million immediately before the issue of the shares in respect of which relief is claimed and must not exceed £8 million immediately afterwards. In relation to shares issued before 6 April 2006, these limits were £15 million and £16 million respectively; the higher limits continue to apply in relation to shares issued after 5 April 2006 to a person who subscribed for them before 22 March 2006. If the issuing company is a parent company, the gross assets test applies by reference to the aggregate gross assets of the company and all its qualifying subsidiaries (disregarding certain assets held by any such company which correspond to liabilities of another).

The general approach of HMRC to the gross assets requirement is that the value of a company's gross assets is the sum of the value of all of the balance sheet assets. Where accounts are actually drawn up to a date immediately before or after the issue, the balance sheet values are taken provided that they reflect usual accounting standards and the company's normal accounting practice, consistently applied. Where accounts are not drawn up to such a date, such values will be taken from the most recent balance sheet, updated as precisely as is practicable on the basis of all the relevant information available to the company. Values so arrived at may need to be reviewed in the light of information contained in the accounts for the period in which the issue was made, and, if they were not available at the time of the issue, those for the preceding period, when they become available. The company's assets immediately before the issue do not include any advance payment received in respect of the issue. Where shares are issued partly paid, the right to the balance is an asset, and, notwithstanding the above, will be taken into account in valuing the assets immediately after the issue regardless of whether it is shown in the balance sheet. (HMRC SP 2/00).

The unquoted status requirement. For shares issued on or after 7 March 2001, the company must be 'unquoted' at the time (the '*relevant time*') at which the shares are issued and no arrangements must then exist for it to cease to be unquoted. If, at the time of issue, arrangements exist for the company to become a wholly-owned subsidiary of a new holding company by means of a share exchange within the provisions below, no arrangements must exist for the new company to cease to be unquoted. A company is '*unquoted*' if none of its shares etc. are listed on a recognised stock exchange or on a foreign exchange designated for the purpose, or dealt in on the Unlisted Securities Market (now closed) or outside the UK by such means as may be designated for the purpose. Securities on the Alternative Investment Market ('AIM') are treated as unquoted for these purposes. (Revenue Press Release 20 February 1995). If the company is unquoted at the time of the share issue, it does not cease to be unquoted in relation to those shares solely because they are listed on an exchange which becomes a recognised stock exchange or is designated by an order made after the date of the issue (see HMRC Venture Capital Schemes Manual VCM 15020).

Treasury power to amend requirements. The Treasury may amend the above requirements by order.

[*ICTA 1988, ss 293, 298, 486, 576(4)(4A); FA 1998, s 80; FA 2001, Sch 15 para 38, Sch 33 Pt II(3); FA 2007, Sch 16 para 11, Sch 26 para 12(2)*].

[*ICTA 1988, s 576(4)(4A)(4B)(5); FA 2001, Sch 15 para 38, Sch 33 Pt II(3); FA 2007, Sch 16 para 11, Sch 26 para 12(2)*].

Claims. Relief must be claimed within two years of the end of the accounting period in which the loss was incurred. [*ICTA 1988, s 573*(*2*)].

Relief is given against income of the accounting period in which the loss was incurred and, if the company was then an investment company and the claim so requires, any balance of loss may be set against the proportion of income of preceding accounting periods arising in the twelve months before the start of the accounting period in which the loss was incurred. It must be claimed before any deduction for charges on income, management expenses or other expenditure available against profits generally. An earlier loss is relieved in priority to a later one. [*ICTA 1988, s 573*(*2*)(*3*)(*4*)*; FA 2000, Sch 16 para 3*(*2*)]. Where relief for a loss on disposal of shares is claimed under *FA 2000, Sch 15 Pt VII* (see 22.20 CORPORATE VENTURING SCHEME), it must be claimed in priority to relief under *ICTA 1988, s 573*. [*ICTA 1988, s 573*(*4A*)*; FA 2000, Sch 15 para 70*].

Identification. Where a company holds shares of the same class, only some of which qualify for the above relief because they were subscribed for, then disposals are identified with acquisitions on a 'last in, first out' basis, and relief is limited to the cost of the qualifying shares.

There is an exception to the above rule where the holding includes any of the following:

(i) shares in respect of which business expansion scheme relief was given and not withdrawn;

(ii) shares to which enterprise investment scheme income tax relief is attributable; or

(iii) shares to which enterprise investment scheme capital gains deferral relief is attributable.

See Tolley's Income Tax and Tolley's Capital Gains Tax under Enterprise Investment Scheme. In such cases, disposals are identified in accordance with the identification rules generally applicable to such shares (broadly, a 'first in, first out' basis).

A similar exception applies where the holding includes shares to which corporate venturing scheme investment relief is attributable, and which were held continuously from issue to disposal (see 22.2, 22.20(*a*) CORPORATE VENTURING SCHEME). The identification rules under that scheme (see 22.17 CORPORATE VENTURING SCHEME) apply instead.

Loss relief under these provisions on the disposal of qualifying shares which form part of a share pool (see Tolley's Capital Gains Tax under Shares and Securities — Identification Rules) is restricted to the sums which would be allowed as deductions in computing the loss if the qualifying shares had been acquired and disposed of as a separate holding.

[*ICTA 1988, s 576*(*1*)-(*1C*)].

Anti-avoidance. Any claim to relief will bring in the provisions of *TCGA 1992, s 30* (value-shifting to give a tax-free benefit) so that the relief may be adjusted for any benefit conferred whether tax-free or not. [*ICTA 1988, s 576*(*2*)].

Company reconstructions. Where, following a reorganisation or reduction of share capital, the shares disposed of represent a new holding identifiable under *TCGA 1992, s 127* with 'old shares', relief is not available unless it could have been given, on the disposal of the old shares for full consideration, at the reorganisation, etc. had this legislation then been in force and had the reorganisation, etc. been a chargeable occasion producing a loss. Where these conditions are not fulfilled, but 'new consideration' was given for the new holding, relief is limited to the allowable part of the new consideration. Where, under *TCGA 1992, s 137*, shares are deemed to have been disposed of on a reorganisation, etc., no relief is available under the above provisions. [*ICTA 1988, s 575*(*2*)(*3*)].

'*New consideration*' is money or money's worth excluding any surrender or alteration to the original shares (or rights attached thereto), and excluding the application of assets of the company or of distributions declared but not made out of those assets. [*ICTA 1988, s 576*(*5*)].

Where relief is claimed under these provisions, no relief may be claimed against chargeable gains in respect of the loss so relieved, and all necessary adjustments to corporation tax in respect of chargeable gains may be made. [*ICTA 1988, ss 573(4), 576(3)*].

Simon's Direct Tax Service. See **D2.416.**

47.20 *Example*

Z Ltd has been an investment company since its incorporation in 1972. It is not part of a trading group and has no associated companies. It makes up accounts to 31 December. On 6 February 2007, Z Ltd disposed of part of its holding of shares in T Ltd for full market value. Z Ltd makes no global re-basing election under *TCGA 1992, s 35(5)*.
Details of disposal

Contract date	6.2.07
Shares sold	2,000 Ord
Proceeds (after expenses)	£4,500

Z acquired its shares in T Ltd as follows.

				£
6.4.80 subscribed for	1,000	shares	cost (with expenses)	5,000
6.4.90 acquired	1,500	shares	cost (with expenses)	4,000
	2,500			£9,000

T Ltd shares were valued at £3 per share at 31 March 1982. T Ltd has been a UK resident trading company since 1980. Its shares are not quoted on a recognised stock exchange.

Z Ltd may claim that part of the loss incurred be set off against its income as follows.

Identification on last in, first out basis.
(i) Shares acquired 6.4.90 (not subscribed for)

	£
Proceeds of 1,500 shares	
$\frac{1,500}{2,000} \times £4,500$	3,375
Cost of 1,500 shares	(4,000)
Capital loss *not* available for set-off against income	£(625)

(ii) Shares acquired 6.4.80 (subscribed for)	Cost basis	31.3.82 value basis
	£	£
Proceeds of 500 shares $\frac{500}{2,000} \times £4,500$	1,125	1,125
Cost of 500 shares	(2,500)	
31.3.82 value		(1,500)
	£(1,375)	£(375)
Capital loss available for set-off against income		£(375)

The loss of £375 is available primarily against income of the year ended 31 December 2007, with any balance being available against, broadly speaking, income of the 12 months ended 31 December 2006 (see 47.19 above).

47.21 **WRITE-OFF OF GOVERNMENT INVESTMENT**

Where any amount of Government investment in a company is written-off, an equal amount is set against the company's 'tax losses' as at the end of the accounting period before that in which the investment was written-off, and against such losses of subsequent accounting periods until the amount written-off is extinguished. [*ICTA 1988, s 400(1)*].

'*Tax losses*' at the end of an accounting period are any trading losses, losses from a Schedule A or overseas property business, management expenses, capital allowances or allowable capital losses available for carry-forward at the end of the period, and any unused charges on income of the period. [*ICTA 1988, s 400(2); SI 2004 No 2310, Article 13*]. The set-off is made against allowable capital losses of a period only after all other tax losses of the period have been exhausted. [*ICTA 1988, s 400(3)*].

In determining the tax losses at the end of the accounting period before that of the write-off, valid claims for group relief, or for relief of trading losses or capital allowances against profits generally and/or of earlier accounting periods, are effective provided that they are made before the write-off date. Such claims made on or after that date are ineffective until the amount written-off has been set off in full. [*ICTA 1988, s 400(4)*].

Where the company concerned is a member of a group (see 32.4 GROUPS OF COMPANIES), the set-off for an accounting period may be made against tax losses of any other company which is a group member at the end of the accounting period, any allocation between group companies being on a 'reasonable and just' basis. [*ICTA 1988, s 400(5)*].

An amount of Government investment in a company is treated as written off if:

(*a*) its liability to repay money lent out of public funds by a Minister of the Crown or Northern Ireland department is extinguished; or

(*b*) any of its shares subscribed for out of public funds by a Minister etc. are cancelled; or

(*c*) any 'commencing capital debt' (i.e. any debt to a Minister etc. assumed as such under an enactment) is reduced otherwise than by being paid off; or

(*d*) any 'public dividend capital' (i.e. any amount paid by a Minister etc. under an enactment which so describes it or which corresponds with enactments relating to similar payments so described) is reduced otherwise than by being repaid.

The amount and date of the write-off are determined accordingly. No restriction is, however, made under these provisions if, and to the extent that, the amount written-off is replaced in some other form by money provided out of public funds by a Minister etc. [*ICTA 1988, s 400(7)–(10)*].

Where a government investment is written off by the extinguishment, in whole or part, of a liability under a loan relationship, these provisions apply notwithstanding *FA 1996, s 80(5)* (matters to be brought into account in the case of loan relationships only under *FA 1996, Pt IV, Ch II*, see 46.2 LOAN RELATIONSHIPS). [*ICTA 1988, s 400(9A)*].

Simon's Direct Tax Service. See D2.411.

47.22 SCHEDULE A

Losses arising from a Schedule A business in an accounting period are set against total profits of that period. Any balance of unrelieved loss may be carried forward and treated as a Schedule A loss of the following and succeeding accounting periods, for so long as the company continues to carry on the Schedule A business. Relief is, however, denied for non-commercial losses in the same circumstances as apply in the case of trading losses under *ICTA 1988, s 393A(3)(4)* (see 47.9 above). [*ICTA 1988, s 392A*]. See generally 56 PROPERTY INCOME.

For losses from overseas property businesses, see 47.23 below.

See also 42.5 INVESTMENT COMPANIES AND INVESTMENT BUSINESS for the conversion of Schedule A losses to management expenses where an investment company ceases to carry on a Schedule A business, and also 42.8 for restrictions applying to Schedule A losses on the change of ownership of an investment company or a company with investment business.

47.23 SCHEDULE D, CASE V

Losses from overseas trades and from overseas property businesses (see 56 PROPERTY INCOME), both of which are within Schedule D, Case V, are available for carry forward against future profits from the same trade or business (subject, in the case of overseas property businesses, to the same commerciality test as applies to Schedule A business losses, see 47.22 above). [*ICTA 1988, ss 392B, 393*]. Otherwise, there is no statutory relief for Schedule D, Case V losses.

47.24 SCHEDULE D, CASE VI

Losses on transactions in respect of which a company is within the charge to corporation tax under this Case may be set off against income from such transactions in the same or any subsequent accounting period. Such income is then treated as reduced by so much of the loss as has not been relieved in an earlier accounting period. [*ICTA 1988, s 396*].

These provisions do not apply to losses within *ICTA 1988, ss 34–36* (premiums, leases at an undervalue, etc.) (see 56.8 to 56.10 PROPERTY INCOME), nor to certain amounts in respect of exchange losses (see 26.14 EXCHANGE GAINS AND LOSSES) nor, for disposals on or after 1 April 2007, to Case VI profits of non-distributing offshore funds. [*FA 2007, s 57*].

Companies in partnership (see 47.6 above). Where tax in respect of any of the profits of a partnership of which a company is a member (and to which arrangements as outlined in 47.16 above apply) is chargeable under Schedule D, Case VI, so much of such profits or losses as forms the company's share is treated (for the purposes of *ICTA 1988, s 116*) as arising from a trade carried on by the partnership and any allowance under *CAA 2001, s 19* or *CAA 1990, s 61(1)* as made in taxing that trade. [*ICTA 1988, s 116; CAA 2001, Sch 2 para 21*].

47.25 **DOUBLE TAXATION**

Interest, dividends or royalties accruing to a non-resident company carrying on a business in the UK which have been treated as tax-exempt under double taxation arrangements are not to be excluded from trading income or profits of the business so as to give rise to losses to be set off against income or profits. [*ICTA 1988, s 808*].

48 Mutual Companies

Cross-references. See 9 BUILDING SOCIETIES; 56.17(*b*) PROPERTY INCOME; 70 VOLUNTARY ASSOCIATIONS.

Simon's Direct Tax Service B3.237 *et seq.*

48.1 INTRODUCTION

A person cannot derive a taxable profit from trading with himself except in certain cases of self-supply by a trader of trading stock, see *Sharkey v Wernher HL 1955, 36 TC 275*. This principle is extended to a group of persons engaged in mutual activities of a trading nature, if there is an identifiable 'fund' for the common purpose with complete identity between contributors to, and participators in, the fund (the 'mutuality principle'). A body not liable as regards transactions with members may nevertheless be liable under Schedule D, Case I on transactions with non-members and is liable in the ordinary way on any investment etc. income. Whether the mutuality principle applies depends on the facts. For mutual insurance see *Styles v New York Life Insce Co HL 1889, 2 TC 460* (an early leading case on the mutuality principle but there are now special provisions for life insurance companies). See also *Liverpool Corn Trade Association Ltd v Monks KB 1926, 10 TC 442* (trade association providing corn exchange etc. held to be trading and not 'mutual' — but see 66.76 TRADING INCOME for special arrangements available for trade associations); *English & Scottish Joint CWS Ltd v Assam Agricultural IT Commr PC 1948, 27 ATC 332* (wholesale co-operative with two members held to be trading and not mutual — there was no 'common fund'). A members' club does not trade and is not liable on its surplus from the provision of facilities for members (*Eccentric Club Ltd CA 1923, 12 TC 657*), but it is liable on the surplus attributable to non-members (*Carlisle & Silloth Golf Club v Smith CA 1913, 6 TC 48*). For further cases, see Tolley's Income Tax under Mutual Trading.

48.2 PAYMENTS ON LIQUIDATION ETC.

If at any time a payment made to a body corporate for the purpose of its mutual business has been allowed as a deduction in computing the profits of a trade for corporation tax purposes, any money or money's worth received in respect of the liquidation or dissolution of that body not representing loan or other capital subscribed or income charged to corporation tax in its hands is:

(*a*) chargeable as a trading receipt of that trade if the recipient company is a person, or one of the persons, carrying it on (notional discontinuances under *ICTA 1988, s 337(1)* being ignored); or

(*b*) chargeable on the recipient company under Schedule D, Case VI for the accounting period in which it is received if, though the company is not then carrying on the trade, it was the person or one of the persons carrying it on at the time the original payment was made.

In the latter case, if the trade has been permanently discontinued before the sum is received deduction is made therefrom of expenses or losses (other than those arising from the discontinuance) which would have been allowed to the company carrying on the trade if it had not ceased, and any unused balance of CAPITAL ALLOWANCES (10) down to the date of discontinuance. These provisions do not apply where the original payment was made to a registered industrial and provident society.

[*ICTA 1988, s 491; ITTOIA 2005, Sch 1 paras 94, 189*].

These provisions apply only to *companies* and *incorporated societies* carrying on a trade. Professional societies, trade protection societies etc. do not usually engage in trading and so will normally be exempt on surpluses from members.

48.3 CREDIT UNIONS

In making loans to its members or placing its surplus funds on deposit, a credit union (within *Industrial and Provident Societies Act 1965* or *Credit Unions (Northern Ireland) Order 1985*) is not regarded as trading and interest received on the former is not chargeable to tax. Other income is liable to corporation tax. Share or loan interest etc. paid by a credit union is disregarded for corporation tax purposes. For accounting periods ending after 31 March 1996, references to interest received or paid are replaced by references to credits or debits brought into account in respect of loan relationships, to similar effect. [*ICTA 1988, s 487*].

48.4 MUTUAL LIFE ASSURANCE COMPANIES

Payments made to persons participating in the mutual activities of a company carrying on mutual life assurance business are not treated as DISTRIBUTIONS (23). [*ICTA 1988, s 490(2)*].

49 Non-Corporate Distribution Rate

Cross-reference. See 1 INTRODUCTION AND RATES OF TAX, 63 SMALL COMPANIES—REDUCED RATES.

Simons Direct Tax Service. See **D2.113–D2.119**.

49.1 CORPORATION TAX ON DISTRIBUTIONS TO NON-CORPORATES

With effect for distributions made **after 31 March 2004 and before 1 April 2006**, a special rate, the '*non-corporate distribution rate*', applies where a company, which has an underlying rate of corporation tax of less than that rate, makes (or is treated as making) one or more 'non-corporate distributions' in any accounting period. The rate is 19% (the small companies' rate) for the financial years 2004 and 2005, the special rate no longer applying for the financial year 2006 onwards.

Where an accounting period straddles 1 April 2004 it is treated for this purpose as two separate accounting periods, one ending on 31 March 2004 and one beginning on 1 April 2004, and the profits are apportioned between the two periods pro rata on a time basis unless that method produces an unjust or unreasonable result in which case the profits are to be apportioned using a just and reasonable method. Equally, where an accounting period straddles 1 April 2006, it is treated as two separate accounting periods, one ending on 31 March 2006 and one beginning on 1 April 2006, and the profits are apportioned between the two periods.

A '*non-corporate distribution*' (NCD) is a distribution to a person, beneficially entitled to it, who is not a company. Distributions to a partnership are treated as made to the partners irrespective of whether the partnership is treated as a legal person or body corporate in the jurisdiction under which it is formed.

The company's '*underlying rate of tax*' is the corporation tax charged (apart from this provision) as a percentage of its basic profits (on which corporation tax is actually borne) for the accounting period using the general rate of tax fixed for companies taking into account the reliefs relevant to the starting or small companies' rates. No account is taken of any other relief reducing the amount or rate of tax payable (such as double tax relief). If profits are later reduced by a loss carried back from a later accounting period (or by a loss carried forward from an earlier accounting period), the calculation has to be reworked. (HMRC Company Taxation Manual, CTM 14125.)

The special (19%) rate is applied to the amount of the company's basic profits of an accounting period that matches the NCDs made (or treated as made) and the company's underlying rate of tax is applied to the remainder.

Where the distributions made (or treated as made) in an accounting period do not exceed the company's basic profits the 19% rate is effectively applied to the amount of the NCDs made, the company's underlying tax rate applying to the remainder.

Where the distributions made (or treated as made) exceed the company's basic profits the 19% rate is applied to that proportion of basic profits that the NCDs bear to total distributions, the company's underlying tax rate applying to the remainder.

Where an NCD is not made in an accounting period of a company, it is treated as made in the next accounting period of the company. For distributions 'treated as made' see 49.2 below.

[*ICTA 1988, s 13AB, Sch A2 paras 2–5, 16, 18; FA 2004, s 28, Sch 3; FA 2005; s 13; FA 2006, s 26(2)(8)–(11)*].

See generally HMRC Company Taxation Manual, CTM 14105–CTM 14310.

See HMRC Tax Bulletin Issue 76, April 2005 p 1199 for HMRC's view that, in the majority of cases, where goodwill is transferred by a sole trader (or partnership) to a company on the incorporation of a business, before the company has commenced trading, at a value higher than its market value, the excess is to be treated as a distribution for the purposes of *ICTA 1988,s 209(2)(b)* or *209(4)* (see 23.2 and 23.8 DISTRIBUTIONS). Where the transfer takes place on or after 1 April 2004, the distribution is to be taken into account in computing the corporation tax liability at the NCD rate. If it is clear that there was no intention to transfer the goodwill at excess value and that reasonable efforts were made to carry out the transfer at market value by using a professional valuation, the distribution can be 'unwound'.

Examples

(*A*) *Basic profits matching non-corporate distributions*

In its accounting period ending 31 March 2006, A Ltd makes a profit chargeable to corporation tax of £9,500 and distributes the same amount in that accounting period to the sole shareholder, Mr X. The company's basic profits are taxable at the corporation tax starting rate of 0% and thus, the underlying rate is 0%. However, the basic profits match the non-corporate distribution of £9,500 and an amount equal to the NCDs is therefore taxed at the non-corporate distribution rate of 19% resulting in corporation tax due of £1,805.

Note that in practice if a company wanted to distribute the full amount of taxable profits for an accounting period in that accounting period, then in the absence of reserves brought forward, only the net profits after tax (as calculated for accounts purposes) would be available for distribution.

(*B*) *Basic profits exceeding non-corporate distributions*

AB Ltd is owned 80% by Mr X and 20% by Z Ltd and has no associated companies. In its accounting period ending 31 March 2006, AB Ltd makes a profit chargeable to corporation tax of £45,000. In the same period, the company pays dividends of £20,000 to Mr X and £5,000 to Z Ltd. AB Ltd's corporation tax is computed as follows.

		£
Profits chargeable to corporation tax		45,000
Corporation tax @ 19%		8,550.00
Less: marginal relief:	(£50,000 – £45,000) × 19/400	237.50
Underlying corporation tax		8,312.50
Underlying rate of tax	(£8,312.50/£45,000) × 100	18.47%

The underlying rate of 18.47% is less than 19% so the tax payable is calculated as follows.

		£
Non-corporate distribution	£20,000 @ 19%	3,800.00
Remaining profits at underlying rate	£25,000 @ 18.47%	4,617.50
Corporation tax payable		£8,417.50

Note: In this case, the company distributions did not exceed the amount of its basic profits so the non-corporate distribution rate applies to the full amount of NCDs and the effective underlying rate to the corporate distribution and the remaining profits.

(C) *Non-corporate distributions exceeding basic profits*

AC Ltd is wholly owned by Mr Y and has no associated companies. In its accounting period ending 31 March 2006, AC Ltd has basic profits of £25,000. It has reserves brought forward from previous years of £30,000. In the same period, the company pays dividends of £45,000 to Mr Y.

In this case, the company distributions exceed the amount of its basic profits and therefore all of its profits of £25,000 are chargeable to corporation tax at the NCD rate of 19%. If half of the distribution had been made to a corporate shareholder, only half of the profits would be chargeable to corporation tax at the NCD rate of 19% and half would be charged at the underlying rate. See 49.2 below as to the carry forward of excess NCDs.

49.2 ALLOCATIONS TO OTHER COMPANIES AND CARRY FORWARD

Group companies. The amount by which NCDs exceed the amount of matching basic profits for a period (as set out in 49.1 above) (referred to as '*excess NCDs*') must, in certain circumstances, be allocated to another company (the '*recipient company*') in which case the recipient company is treated as if it had made the NCD in the period to which it is allocated. If the distributing company is a member of a group at the end of the distribution period, any excess NCDs must be allocated, so far as possible, to other group companies as set out in 49.3 below. Any excess NCDs not so allocated to another group company are to be carried forward by the distributing company and treated as having been made (in addition to any distributions actually made) in its next accounting period.

Singleton or group companies. Excess NCD's are carried forward and are treated as all or part of the NCDs of the next accounting period. To the extent that they cannot be matched with profits of that period, excess NCDs brought forward continue to be carried forward to the next period and to subsequent accounting periods until fully utilised. (HMRC Company Taxation Manual, CTM 14165).

A '*group*' in this case is taken to mean a company and all its 51% subsidiaries and their 51% subsidiaries and so on determined in accordance with *ICTA 1988, s 838*. A company is treated as a 51% subsidiary of another company providing that other company has a right to, or in fact receives more than 50% of distributions of the subsidiary. The parent company is to be treated as not owning any share capital held as trading stock, or any share capital which it owns indirectly, and which is directly held by another body corporate as trading stock.

A holding company (a company with one or more 51% subsidiaries from which it has received one or more distributions) that is not carrying on a business is deemed to be carrying on a business and to be within the charge to corporation tax for the purposes of these provisions.

[*ICTA 1988, s 13AB, Sch A2 paras 6, 7, 13, 14, 17, 18; FA 2004, s 28, Sch 3; FA 2006, Sch 26 Pt 3(1)*].

Example

ABC Ltd is owned 80% by Mr P and 20% by Q Ltd and has no associated companies. In its accounting period ending 30 September 2005, ABC Ltd makes a profit chargeable to corporation tax of £20,000. On 30 September 2005, the company pays dividends of £20,000 to Mr P and £5,000 to Q Ltd. ABC Ltd's corporation tax is computed as follows.

		£
Profits chargeable to corporation tax		20,000
Corporation tax @ 19%		3,800
Less: marginal relief:	(£50,000 – £20,000) × 19/400	1,425
Underlying corporation tax		2,375
Underlying rate of tax	(£2,375/£20,000) × 100	11.875%

The underlying rate of tax is less than 19% so the tax payable is calculated as follows.

		£
Non-corporate distributions	£16,000 @ 19% (*see note below*)	3,040
Remaining profits at underlying rate	£4,000 @ 11.875%	475
Corporation tax payable		£3,515

Note: The total distributions of £25,000 exceed the basic profits so only 80% (NCDs £20,000 / total distributions £25,000 = 80%) of the profits, i.e. £16,000 (80% x £20,000) are matched with the NCDs. Since the excess NCDs of £4,000 cannot be allocated to another company, they are carried forward to the next accounting period and are treated as NCDs made (in addition to any distributions actually made) in ABC Ltd's next accounting period.

49.3 **ALLOCATION TO GROUP COMPANIES**

Available profits. NCDs can only be allocated to other group companies to the extent they have 'available profits', i.e. their basic profits for an accounting period exceed the NCDs they have made (or are already treated as having made) in that period. The maximum amount of NCDs which can be so allocated is that proportion of the recipient company's available profits that the distributing company's NCDs bear to its total distributions.

In determining the amount of the recipient company's available profits at any time, account is only to be taken of the excess NCDs previously allocated to it and still remaining with it. Thus, as stated in HMRC Company Taxation Manual, CTM 14250, 'excess NCDs that are the subject of the allocation are not taken into account where arriving at the recipients company's available profits for the purpose of that allocation.'

Where excess NCDs are to be allocated to the same recipient company by more than one company within the group, the profits are to be calculated separately for each allocation. For the first allocation, the amount of available profits is calculated in taking into account the recipients company's own NCDs only. For the calculation of available profits for the second allocation, the excess NCDs from the first allocation are treated as part of the recipient company's own NCDs and are therefore taken into account. Similarly, for any subsequent allocation, any excess NCDs from previous allocations are taken into account unless they have been withdrawn in which case the available profits are adjusted accordingly. (HMRC Company Taxation Manual, CTM 14250.)

[*ICTA 1988, s 13AB, Sch A2 para 7; FA 2004, Sch 3; FA 2006, Sch 26 Pt 3*(*1*)].

Example

J Ltd is owned 80% by Mr T and 20% by Z Ltd. During its accounting period ending 31 December 2005, it receives no income other than a distribution of £15,000 from its 75%

subsidiary, K Ltd. J Ltd distributes £12,000 to Mr T and £3,000 to Z Ltd on 31 December 2005. K Ltd has chargeable profits of £15,000 for its accounting period ending on the same date and distributes £20,000 on that date of which £5,000 is made to Ms V who owns the remaining 25% of the company. There are no other associated companies involved. The corporation tax for the two companies is computed as follows.

J Ltd

J Ltd has no chargeable profits in the period and therefore, it has excess NCDs (in respect of the distribution of £12,000 to Mr T) which must be allocated as far as possible within the group or otherwise carried forward (see 49.2 above).

The profits available for allocated NCDs are K Ltd's profits of £15,000 less its NCDs of £5,000, i.e. £10,000. The maximum NCDs which can be allocated by J Ltd is 80% of that amount (the proportion that J Ltd's NCDs bear to its total distributions), i.e. £8,000. Accordingly, NCDs of £8,000 are allocated to K Ltd and £4,000 are carried forward.

K Ltd

		£
Non-corporate distributions		5,000
Matched to basic profits (*see note 1 below*)	£15,000 × 25%	3,750
K Ltd excess NCDs carried forward		1,250
Profits chargeable to corporation tax	£15,000 @ 19%	2,850
Less: marginal relief (*see note 2 below*)	(£25,000 – £15,000) × 19/400	475
Underlying corporation tax		2,375
Underlying rate of tax	(£2,375/£15,000) × 100	15.83%
K Ltd's own NCD		3,750
NCDs allocated by J Ltd		8,000
Total NCDs (*see note 3 below*)		11,750
Total distributions (*see note 3 below*)		28,000
Corporation tax chargeable:		
On NCDs (11,750/28,000 × 15,000)	£6,295 @ 19%	1,196.05
Remaining profits at underlying rate	(£15,000 – £6,295) @ 15.83%	1,378.00
Corporation tax payable		£2,574.05

Notes:

1 The total distributions made by K Ltd of £20,000 exceed its basic profits of £15,000 so only 25% (NCDs £5,000 / total distributions £20,000 = 25%) of the profits, i.e.

£3,750 (25% x £15,000) are matched with the NCDs. Since the excess NCDs of £1,250 cannot be allocated to another company, they are carried forward to the next accounting period.

2 There are two associated companies so the starting companies' upper limit for marginal relief is halved to £25,000.

3 Once NCDs of £8,000 are allocated to K Ltd, that company is treated as having made them in the period in which they are allocated in addition to its own NCD of £3,750. The total distributions are therefore treated as being £28,000. The NCD rate is then applied as calculated in the example at 49.2 above after the allocation has been made (HMRC Company Taxation Manual, CTM 14225).

49.4 **Corresponding accounting periods.** Excess NCDs must be allocated to the recipient company for a corresponding accounting period. The recipient company's first corresponding accounting period is its accounting period in which the last day of the distributing company's accounting period in which the distribution is made (the '*distributing period*') falls. This will be the recipient company's only corresponding accounting period unless that period is shorter than the distributing period, in which case excess NCDs can be allocated to any subsequent accounting period which begins before the end of a period of the same length as the distributing period and beginning on the same day as the recipient company's first corresponding accounting period. Where there is more than one corresponding accounting period, excess NCDs must be allocated as fully as possible to the first before any allocation is made to the second and so on. [*ICTA 1988, s 13AB, Sch A2 para 8; FA 2004, Sch 3; FA 2006, Sch 26 Pt 3*(*1*)].

Examples

(*A*)

Sub Ltd is wholly owned by Holding Ltd which is wholly owned by individual shareholders. Holding Ltd has no source income other than dividends paid by Sub Ltd which it then passes on to its shareholders.

- Holding Ltd has a 12-month accounting period ending on 31 March 2005; and
- Sub Ltd has a 12-month accounting period ending on 30 June 2005.

The last day of Holding Ltd's distributing period is 31 March 2005 which falls within Sub Ltd's (the recipient company) accounting period to 30 June 2005, which is therefore a corresponding accounting period. Both accounting periods are the same length so Sub Ltd's accounting period ending 30 June 2005 is its only corresponding accounting period and any excess NCDs are allocated to it in that period.

(*B*)

The facts are as in (A) above except that Sub Ltd has a 9-month accounting period beginning on 1 January 2005 and ending on 30 September 2005. Its next accounting period is for the 12 months to 30 September 2006.

The last day of Holding Ltd's distributing period is 31 March 2005 which falls within Sub Ltd's (the recipient company) accounting period to 30 September 2005, which is therefore a corresponding accounting period. However, Sub Ltd's accounting period is shorter than the distributing period. Sub Ltd has a subsequent accounting period which begins (1 October 2005) before the end of the 12-month period beginning on the same day as its first corresponding accounting period (i.e. before 31 December 2005). Therefore, Sub Ltd has two corresponding accounting periods

Excess NCDs are allocated first to Sub Ltd's 9-month accounting period ending 30 September 2005 and any surplus NCDs remaining are then allocated to its subsequent accounting period (which under transitional rules is the period treated as ending on

31 March 2006).

49.5 **Degrouping.** Special provisions cover degrouping whereby a company ('company A') ceases to be in the same group as another company ('company B') but both companies remain under the control (as defined in *ICTA 1988, s 416* – see 16.2 CLOSE COMPANIES) of the same person or persons. The provisions apply where, at the end of an accounting period of company A (the '*relevant time*'), which ends on or after but no more than two years after the degrouping:

(*a*) company A has excess NCDs that (apart from this provision) cannot be allocated to other group companies;

(*b*) the business activities of company A and any other companies in the A group are negligible; and

(*c*) the business activities of company B and any other companies in the B group are not negligible.

In this case, company B and companies in its group are treated as members of the same group as company A at the relevant time for the purposes of allocating the excess NCDs. Any excess NCDs are firstly allocated under the rules outlined above in 49.3 and 49.4. Any remaining excess NCDs must be allocated (ignoring the restrictions in 49.3 above) to company B or, if different, to the company in the B group that at the relevant time has the greatest number of non-corporate members, to the accounting period of that company that includes the relevant time. If there is more than one company meeting this criterion in the B group, the excess NCDs must be apportioned between them based on their basic profits in the accounting period to which the NCDs are to be allocated.

For the purposes of carrying forward excess NCDs (under 49.2 above), the company to which the allocation is made is treated as having made the distribution in the accounting period in which the allocation is made.

[*ICTA 1988, s 13AB, Sch A2 paras 9, 13; FA 2004, Sch 3; FA 2006, Sch 26 Pt 3(1)*].

See 49.8 below regarding the treatment for the purpose of these provisions of an accounting period in which a company ceases to be a member of a group as two accounting periods.

49.6 **Procedure.** The allocation of excess NCDs must be made by the distributing company with the agreement of the recipient company. If excess NCDs are not allocated within nine months of the end of the distribution period (see 49.4 above) or within nine months of the relevant time (see 49.5 above), they may be so allocated by an officer of HMRC. In either case, the allocation may be varied (or reduced to nil) by agreement between the relevant companies. If further excess NCDs have to be allocated and no variation is agreed within one year after it becoming apparent that a variation is required, the allocation may be varied (or reduced to nil) by an officer of HMRC. Such variation may in turn be varied by agreement between the relevant companies and if no further variation is agreed within one year after such requirement becoming apparent, the variation may be further varied by an officer of HMRC.

No allocation, or variation of an allocation, of excess NCDs may be made after more than one year following the final determination (within the meaning of *FA 1998, Sch 18 para 88*) of the tax affairs of:

(*a*) the distributing company in relation to the distributing period;

(*b*) in the case of allocation to group companies (49.3 above) or in the case of degrouping (49.5 above), all recipient or potential recipient companies in relation to accounting periods to which an allocation may be made,

whichever is the later. In the case where the tax affairs are reopened, an allocation, or variation of an allocation, may (and shall if necessary) be made at any time within one year from the date on which the tax affairs are finally determined.

[*ICTA 1988, s 13AB, Sch A2 para 10; FA 2004, Sch 3; FA 2006, Sch 26 Pt 3*(*1*)].

Allocations made by officers of HMRC should not be made (unless it is necessary to do so in exceptional cases) at the earliest opportunity but that companies should be given an opportunity to make the allocation themselves. Where an allocation is made by an officer of HMRC, it should be so made on a just and reasonable basis (based on the information to hand) in the same way as the company itself would have made the allocation. (HMRC Company Taxation Manual, CTM 14230).

49.7 **Amounts over-allocated.** If an amount of excess NCDs allocated to another company later proves to be excessive, the excess reverts to the distributing company. Where two or more companies are involved the amounts revert in the opposite order to that in which they were made, or if they were made at the same time, in proportion to the original allocations. [*ICTA 1988, s 13AB, Sch A2 para 11; FA 2004, Sch 3; FA 2006, Sch 26 Pt 3*(*1*)].

49.8 **Company ceasing to be a member of a group.** An accounting period in which a company ceases to be a member of a group is treated for the purpose of these provisions as two accounting periods, one ending immediately before the company ceases to be a member of the group and the other consisting of the remainder of the period. A company ceases to be in a group where it and another company cease to be in the same group. [*ICTA 1988, s 13AB, Sch A2 para 15; FA 2004, Sch 3; FA 2006, Sch 26 Pt 3*(*1*)].

49.9 **Allocations to non-resident companies.** The provisions as to the allocation of excess NCDs to other companies apply equally, with any necessary modifications, to non-UK resident companies and references to basic profits and accounting periods are to be read as references to what would have been the case had the companies been UK resident at all material times (see 60 RESIDENCE). [*ICTA 1988, s 13AB, Sch A2 para 12; FA 2004, Sch 3; FA 2006, Sch 26 Pt 3*(*1*)].

50 Offshore Funds

Simon's Direct Tax Service B7.4.

50.1 INTRODUCTION

After 31 December 1983 'offshore income gains' arising on disposals of certain interests in offshore funds which are considered not to distribute sufficient income are charged to corporation tax under Schedule D, Case VI rather than to capital gains tax. Broadly, the capital gains tax regime applies to any part of such a gain accruing before 1 January 1984 but the whole of the gain arising thereafter (without indexation) is taxed as income. Special provisions apply to funds operating equalisation arrangements.

See generally HMRC Inspector's Manual IM 4075–4121 and the HMRC Offshore Funds Guide Manual. For a review of the offshore funds legislation with particular reference to changes made by *FA 2004* (as referred to in this chapter where appropriate), see Revenue Tax Bulletin Issue 73, October 2004 pp 1152–1155 (as amended – see HMRC Tax Bulletin Issue, October 2005 p 1246).

50.2 DISPOSAL OF MATERIAL INTERESTS IN NON-QUALIFYING OFFSHORE FUNDS

The offshore fund rules apply to a disposal by any person of an asset:

(*a*) if, at the time of the disposal, the asset constitutes a **'material interest'** in an **'offshore fund'** (see 50.4 below) which is or has at any 'material time' been a **'non-qualifying offshore fund'** (see 50.5 below); or

(*b*) if:

(i) at the time of the disposal, the asset constitutes an interest in a UK resident company or in a unit trust scheme within *ICTA 1988, s 469(7)* which has UK resident trustees; and

(ii) at a 'material time' after 31 December 1984 the interest was a material interest in a 'non-qualifying offshore fund'. (For account periods (see 50.5 below) ending before 22 July 2004, this condition was that the company or unit trust was a 'non-qualifying offshore fund' and the asset constituted a 'material interest' in that fund.) For this purpose the provisions of *TCGA 1992, s 127*, equating original shares with a new holding on reorganisation, apply.

[*ICTA 1988, s 757(1); FA 1984, s 92(1); FA 2004, s 145, Sch 26 para 4(2)*].

A '*material time*' is any time after 31 December 1983 or, if later, the earliest date on which any 'relevant consideration' was given for the acquisition of the asset. '*Relevant consideration*' is that given by or on behalf of the person making the disposal or a predecessor in title which would be taken into account in determining any gain or loss on disposal under *TCGA 1992*. [*ICTA 1988, s 757(7)*].

With some modifications, a disposal occurs for offshore fund purposes if there would be a disposal under *TCGA 1992*. Death is an occasion of charge as the deceased is deemed to have made a disposal at market value, immediately before his death, of any asset which was or had at any time been a 'material interest' in a 'non-qualifying offshore fund'. In addition, neither *TCGA 1992, s 135* nor *s 136* will apply, and there will therefore be a disposal at market value, if an exchange or arrangement is effected in such a way that an interest in a 'non-qualifying offshore fund', is exchanged for an interest in a distributing fund. The same principle applies to exchanges of different classes of interest where they form separate funds in their own right (see 50.4 below). [*ICTA 1988, s 757(2)–(6), s 762A; FA 2002, Sch 9 para 4(5); FA 2004, s 145, Sch 26 para 4(3)(4), para 15(1)*].

A *Pt 5* transfer under *Proceeds of Crime Act 2002* (as in 10.2(xi) CAPITAL ALLOWANCES) of an asset within (*a*) or (*b*) above is not treated as a disposal for offshore fund purposes where no compensating payment is made to the transferor. [*Proceeds of Crime Act 2002, Sch 10 paras 7, 10*].

50.3 OFFSHORE FUNDS OPERATING EQUALISATION ARRANGEMENTS.

There are specific provisions to enable funds operating 'equalisation arrangements' to satisfy the 'distribution test' (see 50.6 below) which the nature of such funds might otherwise preclude. As a corollary, provision is also made to ensure that the 'accrued income' paid to outgoing investors as part of their capital payments is treated as income for tax purposes when the fund qualifies as a distributor.

Definition. For these purposes, an offshore fund operates '*equalisation arrangements*' where the first distribution paid to a person acquiring a 'material interest' by way of 'initial purchase' includes a payment which is a return of capital (debited to the fund's 'equalisation account') determined by reference to the income which had accrued to the fund in the period before that person's acquisition. An acquisition is by way of '*initial purchase*' if it is by way of direct purchase from the fund's managers in their capacity as such.

Where a sub-fund or class of interest is treated as a fund in its own right (see 50.4 below), this definition applies with appropriate modifications.

'Accrued income' chargeable to income tax — application of offshore fund rules. A disposal is one to which the offshore fund provisions apply, subject to exception below, if it is a disposal by any person of a 'material interest' in an 'offshore fund' operating equalisation arrangements where:

(i) the disposal proceeds are not a trading receipt; and

(ii) the fund *is not*, and *has not been*, at any material time (see above) a 'non-qualifying offshore fund' (see 50.5 below)

(i.e. the provisions apply also to *distributing* funds (see 50.6 below) with equalisation arrangements).

Capital gains tax rules for disposals apply as they do for other offshore fund disposals (see 50.1 above) with some variations. Death is not treated as a disposal in this context. In addition, *TCGA 1992, s 127* (reorganisations etc.) (including that section as applied by certain other *TCGA 1992* provisions) does not apply and there is a disposal at market value in such circumstances.

Exception. The offshore fund legislation does *not* apply as indicated above to a disposal where the fund's income for the period preceding the disposal is of such a nature that the part relating to the interest in question is in any event chargeable as mentioned at 50.7(*b*) below on the person disposing of the interest (or would be so chargeable if residence/domicile/situation of assets requirements were met).

[*ICTA 1988, s 757(2)(3), s 758; FA 2002, Sch 9 para 4(6); FA 2004, s 145, Sch 26 para 5; SI 2004 No 2572, reg 3*].

50.4 MATERIAL INTERESTS IN OFFSHORE FUNDS

An **'offshore fund'** is a 'collective investment scheme' constituted by:

(*a*) a company resident outside the UK; or

(*b*) a unit trust scheme within *ICTA 1988, s 469(7)* which has non-UK resident trustees; or

(*c*) any other arrangements taking effect under overseas law which create rights in the nature of co-ownership under that law.

'Collective investment scheme' means, before 1 January 2007, as defined by *Financial Services and Markets Act 2000, s 235* and on or after 1 January 2007, any arrangements which are a collective investment scheme for the purposes of the *Financial Services and Markets Act 2000, Pt 17*, or would be if the words 'within a period appearing to him to be reasonable' were omitted from s *236*(*3*)(*a*) of that Act.For account periods (see 50.5 below) ending on or after 22 July 2004, sub-funds of a main fund (the umbrella fund) and different classes of interest in a main fund constitute separate offshore funds. This allows the test for distributing status (see 50.6 below) to be applied to them independently. The offshore funds legislation is appropriately modified in its application to such sub-funds and classes of interest (see *SI 2004 No 2572*).

[*ICTA 1988, ss 756A–756C, s 759*(*1*)(*1A*)*; SI 2001 No 3629, Article 45; FA 2004, s 145, Sch 26 paras 3, 6*(*2*)*; FA 2007, s 57*(*2*)].

A **'material interest'** is one which, when acquired, could reasonably be expected to be realisable (by any means, either in money or in asset form) within seven years for an amount reasonably approximate to its proportionate share of the market value of the fund's assets. For these purposes, an interest in an offshore fund which at any time is worth substantially more than its proportionate share of the fund's underlying assets is not to be regarded as so realisable. [*ICTA 1988, s 759*(*2*)*–*(*4*)]. If shares in a quoted overseas company have habitually been traded at or near net asset value, and an investor in these shares had a reasonable expectation, on acquisition, of a future sale at or near such value, those shares are likely to represent a 'material interest'. (HMRC Statement of Practice, SP 2/86).

Exceptions. The following are not material interests:

(i) interests in respect of loans etc. made in the ordinary course of banking business;

(ii) rights under insurance policies;

(iii) shares in a company resident outside the UK where:

  (*a*) the shares are held by a company and the holding is necessary or desirable for the maintenance and development of a trade carried on by the company, or by an associated company within *ICTA 1988, s 416*; and

  (*b*) the shares confer at least 10% of the voting rights and, on winding-up, a right to at least 10% of the assets after discharging all prior liabilities; and

  (*c*) the shares are held by not more than ten persons and all confer both voting rights and a right to assets on winding-up; and

  (*d*) at the time of acquisition of the shares the company could reasonably expect to realise its interest for market value within seven years only by virtue of (I) an arrangement requiring the company's fellow participators to purchase its shares and/or (II) provisions of either the overseas company's constitution or an agreement between the participators regarding that company's winding-up.

(iv) interests in companies resident outside the UK at any time when the holder is entitled to have the company wound up and to receive in that event in the same capacity more than 50% of the assets after discharging all prior liabilities.

[*ICTA 1988, s 759*(*5*)*–*(*8*)].

HMRC have also indicated that normal commercial loans or other debt instruments entitling the lender to no more than a fixed return of principal on redemption, and which are not geared to the underlying asset value of the borrower's business, are not regarded as 'material interests'. (HMRC Statement of Practice, SP 2/86).

'Market value' for the purposes of the offshore funds legislation is determined according to capital gains tax rules with necessary modifications of *TCGA 1992, s 272*(*5*) (market value in relation to rights in unit trust schemes) where appropriate. [*ICTA 1988, s 759*(*9*)].

50.5 NON-QUALIFYING OFFSHORE FUNDS

An offshore fund is **'non-qualifying'** except during an 'account period' in respect of which it is certified by HMRC as a distributing fund pursuing a 'full distribution policy' (see 50.6 below). For these purposes, the first '*account period*' begins when the fund begins to carry on its activities or, if later, on 1 January 1984. An '*account period*' ends on the fund's accounting date or, if earlier, twelve months from the beginning of the period or on the fund's ceasing to carry on its activities. In addition, if the fund is a non-UK resident company, an '*account period*' ends when it becomes UK resident, and if the fund is a unit trust with non-UK resident trustees, it ends when those trustees become UK resident. Where a sub-fund or class of interest is treated as a fund in its own right (see 50.4 above), references to '*account period*' are to the account period of the main fund. [*ICTA 1988, s 760(1)(2)(8)–(10A); FA 1984, s 95(8); FA 2004, s 145, Sch 26 para 7(3)*].

Conditions for certification. The investment conditions for certification are significantly relaxed in relation to account periods ending on or after 22 July 2004. For earlier account periods, and subject to the modifications of conditions for certification in certain cases noted below, an offshore fund is not to be certified as a 'distributing fund' for any account period if, at any time in that period:

(*a*) more than 5% by value of the fund's assets consists of interests in other offshore funds (but see below); or

(*b*) more than 10% by value of the fund's assets consists of interests in a single company. For this purpose:

- (i) the value of an interest in a single company is determined as at the most recent occasion (in that account period or earlier) on which the fund acquired an interest in that company for money or money's worth. However an occasion is disregarded if it is one on which *TCGA 1992, s 127* (equation of original shares and new holding) applied, including that *section* as applied by later provisions of *TCGA 1992* (reorganisations, conversion of securities etc.), and on which no consideration is given for the interest other than the interest in the original holding;
- (ii) an interest is disregarded, except for determining the total value of the fund's assets, if it consists of a current or deposit account provided in the normal course of its banking business by a company whose business it is to provide such account facilities in any currency for members of the public and bodies corporate; and
- (iii) Government-owned national or supra-national bodies whose activities are directed not with a view to commercial profits, but to the exercise of a wider social or economic function, are not regarded as companies for this purpose (HMRC Statement of Practice, SP 2/86); or

(*c*) the fund's assets include more than 10% of the issued share capital, or any class of it, in any company; or

(*d*) there is more than one class of material interests (see 50.4 above) in the fund and, were each class and the assets represented by it in a separate offshore fund, each such separate fund does not pursue a 'full distribution policy'. For this purpose, interests held solely by persons involved in the management of the fund's assets are disregarded if they carry no right or expectation to participate in profits and no right to anything other than the return of the price paid on winding-up or redemption.

For account periods ending on or after 22 July 2004, all of the above conditions are removed apart from (*a*). It follows that the commentary below on inadvertent failures and modifications of conditions apply, in relation to such account periods, only to condition (*a*). As a transitional measure, sub-funds that constitute an offshore fund in their own right as a result of *FA 2004* (see 50.4 above) may have regard to the investments of the main fund (the umbrella fund) in applying the test at (*a*) above for account periods ending between 22 July 2004 and 31 December 2005 inclusive.

Where HMRC are satisfied that an apparent failure to comply with any of (*a*)–(*c*) above occurred inadvertently and was remedied without unreasonable delay, that failure may be disregarded.

[*ICTA 1988, s 760(3)–(7), Sch 27 para 14; FA 2004, Sch 26 paras 13, 14(7) 17*].

Modifications of conditions for certification. The conditions for certification in (*a*)–(*d*) above are modified in certain cases.

(A) **Investments in second tier funds.** If offshore funds ('primary funds') would fail to meet the conditions in (*a*) to (*c*) above because of investments in other offshore funds (referred to below as 'second tier funds') which could themselves be certified as qualifying distributing funds (without any modification of the (*a*) to (*c*) conditions), then the primary funds' interests in the second tier funds are left out of account, except for determining the total value of the primary funds' assets, in establishing whether the primary funds are prevented by (*a*) to (*c*) above from being certified as distributing funds. In addition, where the above applies, if at any time in a primary fund's account period that fund's assets include an interest in another offshore fund or in any company and the qualifying second tier fund's assets also include an interest in that other fund or company, then the primary fund's interest is aggregated with its proportionate share of the second tier fund's interest in determining whether the primary fund is within the limits in (*a*) to (*c*) above. Its share of the second tier fund's interest is the proportion which the average value during its account period of its own holding of interests in the second tier fund bears to the average value during the period of all interests in the second tier fund. [*ICTA 1988, s 760(3), Sch 27 paras 6, 7, 9; FA 2004, Sch 26 para 14(2)(3)*].

(B) **Investments in trading companies.** Where the assets of an offshore fund include an interest in a company whose business is wholly the carrying on of trade(s) the limit of 10% of a fund's assets invested in a single company in (*b*) above is increased to 20% and the 10% limit on the proportion of a class of share in any company in (*c*) above is increased to allow holdings of less than 50%. For these purposes companies are excluded if their business consists to any extent of banking or moneylending or of dealing, including dealing by way of futures contracts and traded options, in commodities, currency, securities, debts or other assets of a financial nature. [*ICTA 1988, s 760(3), Sch 27 paras 4(2), 10; FA 2004, Sch 26 para 14(4)*]. Dealing in commodities, currency and financial assets incidental to the business of a company will be disregarded in determining whether the company is trading. (HMRC Statement of Practice, SP 2/86).

(C) **Wholly-owned subsidiaries.** Where an offshore fund has a wholly-owned subsidiary company, the receipts, expenditure, assets and liabilities of the fund and the subsidiary are aggregated so that the fund and the subsidiary are treated as one for the purposes of determining whether the fund is within the limits in (*a*) to (*d*) above. In the same way, the interest of the fund in the subsidiary and any distributions or other payments between the fund and the subsidiary are left out of account. A wholly-owned subsidiary is one owned either directly and beneficially by the fund, or directly by the trustees of the fund for the benefit of the fund, or, in the case of a fund within 50.4(*c*) above, in some other equivalent manner. Where the subsidiary has only one class of issued share capital, ownership of at least 95% of that capital by the offshore fund constitutes the subsidiary a wholly-owned subsidiary for this purpose, and only a corresponding proportion of the subsidiary's receipts, expenditure, assets and liabilities are then aggregated with those of the offshore fund. [*ICTA 1988, s 760(3), Sch 27 para 11; FA 2004, Sch 26 para 14(5); SI 2004 No 2572, reg 4(1)(6)*].

(D) **Subsidiary dealing and management companies.** The investment restriction in (*c*) above does not apply to so much of an offshore fund's assets as consists of share capital of a company which is either:

(1) a wholly-owned subsidiary of the fund (as defined in (C) above) whose sole function is dealing in material interests in the offshore fund for management and administrative purposes and which is not entitled to any distribution from the fund; or

(2) a subsidiary management company of the fund whose sole function is to provide the fund, or other funds with an interest in the company, with advisory services or administrative, management and related property holding services on arm's length commercial terms. For the purposes of determining whether a company is a subsidiary management company of a fund, that company and any wholly-owned subsidiary companies it may itself have are regarded as a single entity. [*ICTA 1988, s 760(3), Sch 27 para 12; FA 2004, Sch 26 para 14(6)*].

(E) **Disregard of certain investments.** Certain holdings which would otherwise fall within the restriction at (*c*) above are not taken into account for the purposes of that restriction. This applies where no more than 5% of the value of the offshore fund's assets consists of such holdings and of interests in other non-qualifying offshore funds. [*ICTA 1988, s 760(3), Sch 27 para 13; FA 2004, Sch 26 para 14(6)*].

50.6 **THE DISTRIBUTION TEST**

An offshore fund pursues a **'full distribution policy'** with respect to an account period if:

(*a*) a distribution is made for that account period or for some other period falling wholly or partly within that period; and

(*b*) subject to modifications below, the distribution represents at least 85% of the fund's income and not less than 85% of its 'UK equivalent profits' for that period; and

(*c*) the distribution is made during or within six months after the end of the account period (the six-month limit may be extended at HMRC's discretion); and

(*d*) the form of the distribution is such that if any part of it were received in the UK by a company or an individual resident there and did not form part of the profits of a trade, profession or vocation, it would be chargeable to:

- corporation tax under Schedule D Case III in respect of income arising from securities or possessions out of the UK or under Schedule D Case V; or

- to income tax under any of the provisions listed at *ITTOIA 2005, s 830(2)* (relevant foreign income — see Tolley's Income Tax under Foreign Income) (or, before 2005/06, under Schedule D, Case IV or V).

These conditions may equally be satisfied by any two or more distributions taken together. [*ICTA 1988, Sch 27 para 1(1); ITTOIA 2005, Sch 1 para 350(2); F(No 2)A 2005, s 23(2)*].

The basic conditions in (*a*) to (*d*) above are modified in certain cases (see 50.7 below).

A fund is treated as pursuing a full distribution policy for any account period in which there is no income and no 'UK equivalent profits', or for account periods ending after 28 November 1994 for which gross fund income does not exceed 1% of the average value of fund assets during the period, but it will not be so treated for any account period for which no accounts are prepared. [*ICTA 1988, Sch 27 para 1(2)(2A)(3)(3A); FA 1995, s 134(4)(9); SI 2004 No 2572, reg 4(1)(2)*].

Non-UK legal restrictions. Where in an account period an offshore fund is subject to non-UK legal restrictions on making distributions by reason of an excess of losses over profits as computed according to the law in question, a deduction is allowed from the fund's income of any amount which cannot be distributed but which would otherwise form part of the fund's income for that account period. [*ICTA 1988, Sch 27 para 1*(*6*)(*7*); *SI 2004 No 2572, reg 4*(*1*)(*2*)].

Apportionment of income and distributions between account periods. Where a period for which accounts are made up or for which a distribution is made covers the whole or part of two or more account periods of the fund, the income or distribution is apportioned on a time basis according to the number of days in each period. A distribution made out of specified income but not for a specified period is attributed to the account period in which the income arose. Where no period or income is specified, a distribution is treated as made for the last account period ending before the distribution. If the distribution made, or treated as made, for an account period exceeds the income of that period the excess is reallocated to previous periods, to later periods before earlier ones, until exhausted, unless the distribution was apportioned on a time basis as mentioned above in which case the excess is first reapportioned on a just and reasonable basis to the other account period(s). [*ICTA 1988, Sch 27 para 1*(*4*)(*5*)].

'UK equivalent profits' of an offshore fund are the total profits, excluding chargeable gains, on which, after allowing for any deductions available, corporation tax would be chargeable, assuming that:

- (i) the offshore fund is a UK resident company in the account period in question, but in no other; and
- (ii) the account period is an accounting period of that company; and
- (iii) any dividends or distributions from a UK resident company are included.

The rules for LOAN RELATIONSHIPS (46) and derivative contracts (see 26 FINANCIAL INSTRUMENTS AND DERIVATIVE CONTRACTS) used to be disregarded for this purpose, and it was assumed that income tax, rather than corporation tax, rules applied, as they did for unauthorised unit trusts. However, for account periods ending on or after 22 July 2004, the corporation tax rules relating to creditor loan relationships and profits/losses from derivative contracts apply as if the fund were an authorised unit trust. This change in treatment does not apply to funds in existence on or before 22 July 2004 unless they elect for it to apply. Such an election, once made, is irrevocable. Where, in a case where no election has been made, a new sub-fund or class of interest is established *after* 22 July 2004 and is regarded as a separate offshore fund by virtue of 50.4 above, the change in treatment does not apply to the sub-fund or class either, so that they always take the same treatment as the 'parent' fund.

Any UK government securities or securities of foreign states which are exempt from tax (see 37.8 INCOME TAX IN RELATION TO A COMPANY) must be brought into account in determining the fund's total profits.

Whether a fund is trading will turn on the particular facts, but in general a fund would not normally be regarded as trading in respect of relatively infrequent transactions, or where the intention was merely to hedge specific investments which were not associated with trading activities. (HMRC Statement of Practice, SP 2/86).

The deductions referred to above include a deduction equal to that allowed against a fund's income where non-UK legal restrictions prevent distribution (see above) and a deduction equal to any foreign capital tax allowed as a deduction in determining the fund's income for the account period in question.

Interest paid to a non-UK resident is deductible in the same way as if it were paid to a UK resident. UK income tax (whether suffered by deduction or by assessment) is available as a deduction. (HMRC Statement of Practice, SP 2/86).

[*ICTA 1988, Sch 27 para 5; FA 1996, Sch 10 para 3; FA 2002, Sch 26 para 35; FA 2004, s 145, Sch 26 paras 1, 2; SI 2004 No 2572, regs 4(1)(5), 6, 7); ITTOIA 2005, Sch 1 para 350(4)*].

50.7 MODIFICATIONS OF DISTRIBUTION TEST

The basic rules of the distribution test in 50.6(*a*) to (*d*) above are modified in various circumstances.

(*a*) **Funds operating equalisation arrangements.** Where an offshore fund operates such arrangements (see 50.3 above) throughout an account period (see 50.5 above), an amount equal to any 'accrued income' which is part of the consideration for certain disposals in that period is treated as a distribution for the purposes of the distribution test. This applies to a disposal:

(i) which is a disposal of a material interest in the fund to either the fund or the fund managers in their capacity as such; and

(ii) which is one to which the offshore fund rules apply (whether or not by virtue of their application to disposals from distributing funds with equalisation arrangements — see 50.3 above), or which is one to which the rules would apply if the provisions regarding the non-application of *TCGA 1992, ss 127, 135* applied generally and not only for the purpose of determining whether a disposal from a distributing fund with equalisation arrangements is brought within the rules (see 50.3 above); and

(iii) which is not a disposal within the *exception* at 50.3 above (where the income of the fund is, or would be, chargeable to tax under Schedule D, Case IV or V in any event).

The '*accrued income*' referred to above is that part of the consideration which would be credited to the fund's equalisation account if the interest were resold to another person by way of 'initial purchase' (see 50.3 above) on the same day. However, there are provisions to ensure that this accrued income figure is reduced where the interest disposed of was acquired by way of initial purchase (by any person) after the beginning of the account period by reference to which the accrued income is calculated. In addition, where an offshore commodity dealing fund (see also (*c*) below) operates equalisation and there is a disposal within (i) to (iii) above, one half of the accrued income representing commodity profits is left out of account in determining what part of the disposal consideration represents accrued income.

For the purposes of the distribution test, the distribution which the fund is treated as making on a disposal is treated as being paid to the person disposing of his interest, in the income form required by 50.6(*d*) above, out of the income of the fund for the account period of disposal. Where a distribution is made to the managers (in their capacity as such) of a fund operating equalisation arrangements it is disregarded for the purposes of the distribution test except to the extent that it relates to that part of the period for which the distribution is made during which the managers (in that capacity) held that interest.

[*ICTA 1988, Sch 27 paras 2, 4(4); SI 2004 No 2572, reg 4(1)(3)*].

(*b*) **Funds with income taxable on investors.** Where sums forming part of the income of an offshore fund within 50.4(*b*) or (*c*) above:

(i) are chargeable to corporation tax under Schedule D Case III in respect of income arising from securities or possessions out of the UK or under Schedule D Case V in the hands of the company (or would be so chargeable if the assets from which the income is derived were situated outside the UK where this is not, in fact, the case); or

(ii) are chargeable to income tax under any of the provisions listed at *ITTOIA 2005, s 830(2)* (relevant foreign income — see Tolley's Income Tax under Foreign Income) (or, before 2005/06, under Schedule D, Case IV or V) in the hands of an individual (with the same proviso as in (i) above); or

(iii) would be so chargeable if the company or individual were UK resident or if the individual were domiciled in the UK and both resident and ordinarily resident there,

any such sums which are not actually part of a distribution complying with the part of the distribution test in 50.6(*c*) and (*d*) above are treated as distributions which do so comply made out of the income of which they are part and paid to the holders of the interests in question. [*ICTA 1988, Sch 27 para 3; ITTOIA 2005, Sch 1 para 350(3); F(No 2)A 2005, s 23(3)(4)*].

(*c*) **Funds with commodity dealing income.** Where an offshore fund's income includes commodity dealing profits, half of those profits are left out of account in determining the fund's income and UK equivalent profits for the purposes of the distribution test in 50.6(*b*) above. '*Commodities*' are defined as tangible assets dealt with on a commodity exchange, excluding currency, securities, debts or other financial assets. '*Dealing*' includes dealing by way of futures contracts and traded options. Where the fund's income includes both commodity dealing profits and other income, its expenditure is apportioned on a just and reasonable basis and the non-commodity dealing business is treated as carried on by a separate company when determining what expenditure, if any, is deductible under *ICTA 1988, s 75* (management expenses, see 42 INVESTMENT COMPANIES AND COMPANIES WITH INVESTMENT BUSINESS). See also (*a*) above for position where a commodity dealing fund operates equalisation arrangements. [*ICTA 1988, Sch 27 para 4; SI 2004 No 2572, reg 4(1)(4)*].

(*d*) **Wholly-owned commodity dealing subsidiaries.** In a situation within 49.4(C) above, the fund and the subsidiary dealing company are similarly treated as a single entity for the purposes of the distribution test. [*ICTA 1988, Sch 27 para 11; SI 2004 No 2572, reg 4(1)(6)*].

(*e*) **Investments in second tier funds.** In a situation within 50.5(A) above, the UK equivalent profits of the primary fund for the period are increased by its 'share' of the 'excess income' (if any) of the second tier fund in determining whether not less than 85% of the primary fund's UK equivalent profits are distributed. The '*excess income*' of the second tier fund is the amount by which its UK equivalent profits exceeds its distributions. There are provisions for apportioning excess income between periods on a time basis when the account periods of the primary and second tier funds do not coincide. The primary fund's '*share*' of the excess income is the proportion which the average value during its account period of its own holding of interests in the second tier fund bears to the average value of all interests in that fund. [*ICTA 1988, Sch 27 paras 6, 8, 9*].

50.8 CERTIFICATION PROCEDURE

Fund requesting certification. Application for certification as a distributing fund for an account period must be made within six months of the end of that period and should be sent to the HMRC Offshore Funds Centre, 1st Floor, Concept House, 5 Young Street, Sheffield S1 4LB. The application must be accompanied by a copy of the fund's accounts covering or including the account period for which certification is sought and provision of the required information in relation to the account period in question will assist HMRC in its consideration of the application. For details of the information required see HMRC Offshore Funds Guide Manual at OSFG 01050.

Where HMRC is satisfied that the necessary conditions are met it must certify the fund as a distribution fund for the period in respect of which application was made. HMRC must give written notice if, after application, it determines that no certificate should be issued. It must also give notice where it appears that the accounts or other information provided do not make full and accurate disclosure of all relevant matters, in which case any notice of certification previously given is void. The fund may appeal to the Special Commissioners against HMRC decisions within ninety days. The Special Commissioners have jurisdiction to review any decision of HMRC relevant to a ground of the appeal. [*ICTA 1988, Sch 27 paras 15, 16; SI 2004 No 2572, reg 4*(*1*)(*7*)].

A list of offshore funds which have been granted UK distributor status is available on HMRC's website.

Investor requesting certification. No appeal may be brought against a tax assessment (see 50.9 below) on the grounds that a fund should have been certified as a distributing fund in respect of an account period. However, where a fund does not apply for certification, an investor, who is assessed to tax for which he would not be liable if the fund were certified, may by notice in writing require HMRC to take action with a view to determining whether the fund should be so certified.

If more than one request from an investor is received, HMRC is taken to have complied with each if it complies with one.

Broadly, the procedure is as follows.

(i) HMRC invites the fund to apply for certification. The time limit for application (see above) is then extended, if necessary, to 90 days from the date of HMRC's invitation.

(ii) If the fund does not then apply for certification HMRC must determine the question as if such application had been made having regard to any accounts or information provided by the investor.

(iii) If, after HMRC has determined that the fund should not be certified, other accounts or information are provided which were not previously available, they must reconsider their determination.

(iv) HMRC must notify the investor who requested them to take action of their decision.

(v) HMRC has wide powers enabling it to disclose to interested parties information regarding HMRC or Special Commissioner decisions or details of any notice given to a fund regarding a lack of full and accurate disclosure of information (see above).

[*ICTA 1988, Sch 27 paras 17, 18, 20*].

Postponement of tax. There are provisions to enable an investor to apply for tax assessed to be postponed pending HMRC's determination of the question of certification. [*ICTA 1988, Sch 27 para 19*].

50.9 CHARGE TO CORPORATION TAX OF OFFSHORE GAIN

Where a disposal to which the offshore fund rules apply (including a disposal of a holding in a distributing fund operating equalisation arrangements — see 50.3 above) gives rise to an 'offshore income gain', then subject to below, that gain is treated for all purposes as income arising to the investor at the time of disposal and is chargeable to corporation tax under Schedule D, Case VI in the accounting period in which the disposal is made.

For HMRC practice as regards identification of part disposals out of mixed holdings where a non-qualifying offshore fund has subsequently obtained distributor status, see HMRC Inspector's Manual IM 4120, 4121.

The following provisions have effect in relation to corporation tax on offshore income gains as they have in relation to corporation tax on chargeable gains.

(*a*) *TCGA 1992, s 2* (persons chargeable).

(*b*) *TCGA 1992, s 10* (gains accruing to non-residents carrying on a trade in the UK through a branch or agency) except that assets need not be situated in the UK.

(*c*) *TCGA 1992, s 12* (foreign assets of UK resident or ordinarily resident persons with foreign domicile chargeable on remittance basis).

Charitable exemption applies similarly to that for capital gains (see 14.7 CHARITIES).

Where a disposal to which the offshore fund rules apply is one of settled property, any offshore income gain will escape the Schedule D, Case VI charge provided that the general administration of the trust is ordinarily carried on outside the UK and a majority of the trustees are not resident or not ordinarily resident in the UK.

[*ICTA 1988, s 761; ITTOIA 2005, Sch 1 para 308; F(No 2)A 2005, s 23(1)*].

HMRC do not regard an offshore income gain as qualifying as eligible investment income for the purposes of *ICTA 1988 s 842*. This view was stated in HMRC Tax Bulletin October 2005 page 1242. The date from which it is effective has been postponed to 1 January 2008. (See HMRC internet statement dated 15 December 2006.)

50.10 COMPUTATION OF OFFSHORE INCOME GAIN

The computation of the gain depends upon whether the disposal is of an interest in a non-qualifying fund (see 50.11 below) or of an interest involving an equalisation element (see 50.12 below).

50.11 **Disposals of interests in non-qualifying funds.** A '*material disposal*' (one to which the offshore fund rules apply otherwise than by virtue of the provisions regarding distributing funds operating equalisation arrangements — see 50.3 above and 50.12 below) gives rise to an '*offshore income gain*' equal to the 'unindexed gain' or, if less, the 'post-1983 gain'.

Subject to the modifications to the CGT rules mentioned in 50.1 above and to exceptions below, the '*unindexed gain*' is the gain calculated under CGT rules without indexation allowance and without regard to any corporation tax charge arising under the offshore fund rules. The exceptions are as follows.

(*a*) Where there has been indexation on an earlier disposal on a no gain/no loss basis within *TCGA 1992, s 56(2)*, the unindexed gain on the material disposal is computed as if indexation had not been available on the earlier disposal and, subject to that, as if the earlier disposal had produced neither gain nor loss.

(*b*) If the material disposal forms part of a transfer to which *TCGA 1992, s 162* applies (rollover relief on transfer of business), the unindexed gain is computed without any deduction falling to be made under that section in computing a chargeable gain.

(*c*) Any claim for relief under *FA 1980, s 79* (relief for gifts) does not affect the computation of the unindexed gain on the disposal. (See now *TCGA 1992, s 67*.)

(*d*) In the case of an insurance company carrying on life assurance business, where a profit from overseas life assurance business, attributable to a material disposal, is taken into account in the computation under *ICTA 1988, s 441*, the unindexed gain, if any, accruing on disposal is computed as if *TCGA 1992, s 37(1)* did not apply. For accounting periods beginning before 1 January 1992, this applies equally where a profit arising from general annuity business attributable to a material disposal is taken into account (or would be but for the provisions relating to offshore income gains of insurance companies (see 50.13 below)) in the computation under *ICTA 1988, s 436*.

(*e*) Where the computation of the unindexed gain would otherwise produce a loss, the unindexed gain is treated as nil so that no loss can arise on a material disposal.

[*ICTA 1988, Sch 28 paras 1–3, 5; FA 1990, Sch 7 para 7; FA 1991, Sch 7 para 10*].

'Post-1983 gains'. A person making a material disposal who acquired, or is treated as having acquired, the interest in question in the offshore fund before 1 January 1984, is treated as having disposed of and immediately reacquired his interest at market value on that date. The offshore income gain from 1 January 1984 to the date of disposal is then calculated in the ordinary way. If the person making the material disposal acquired the interest in question by way of a deemed no gain/no loss disposal (other than those arising by virtue of the indexation provisions of *FA 1982, s 86(5), Sch 13*) any previous owner's acquisition of the interest is treated as his acquisition of it. [*ICTA 1988, Sch 28 para 4*].

50.12 **Disposals involving an equalisation element.** A disposal is a '*disposal involving an equalisation element*' if it is a disposal to which the offshore fund rules apply by virtue of the provisions relating to distributing funds operating equalisation arrangements (see 50.3 above). Such a disposal gives rise to an '*offshore income gain*' of an amount equal, subject to below, to the 'equalisation element' relevant to the asset disposed of. [*ICTA 1988, Sch 28 para 6(1)(3); SI 2004 No 2572, reg 5*].

The 'equalisation element' is the amount which would be credited to the fund's equalisation account in respect of accrued income if, on the date of the disposal, the asset disposed of were acquired by another person by way of 'initial purchase' (see 50.3 above). However, where the person making the disposal acquired the asset in question after the beginning of the account period by reference to which the accrued income is calculated, or at or before the beginning of that period where that period began before and ended after 1 January 1984, there are provisions to ensure that the equalisation element is reduced to exclude any part which accrued prior to either 1 January 1984 or to the investor's period of ownership. Where any of the accrued income represents commodity dealing profits (within 50.7(*c*) above) half of that income is left out of account in determining the equalisation element. [*ICTA 1988, Sch 28 para 6(2)(4)–(6); SI 2004 No 2572, reg 5*].

'Part I gains'. Where the offshore income gain as computed above would exceed the 'Part I gain', the offshore income gain is reduced to the lower figure. If there is no 'Part I gain' there can be no offshore income gain. The '*Part I gain*' is, broadly, the amount which would be the offshore income gain on the disposal if the disposal were a 'material disposal' within 50.11 above (i.e. within *ICTA 1988, Sch 28 Part I*) as modified by certain consequential amendments. [*ICTA 1988, Sch 28 paras 7, 8*].

50.13 MISCELLANEOUS

Offshore income gains accruing to persons resident or domiciled abroad. There are consequential provisions made in connection with gains accruing to certain non-resident investors in offshore funds which modify, for the purposes of the offshore fund legislation, provisions relating to:

(*a*) chargeable gains accruing to certain non-resident companies under *TCGA 1992, s 13*;

(*b*) gains of non-resident settlements under *TCGA 1992, ss 80–98*;

(*c*) avoidance of tax by the transfer of assets abroad under *ITA 2007, ss 716–735* (formerly *ICTA 1988, ss 739, 740*).

To the extent that an offshore income gain is treated by virtue of (*a*) or (*b*) above as having accrued to any person resident or ordinarily resident in the UK, that gain is not deemed to be the income of any individual under *ITA 2007, ss 716–735* (formerly *ICTA 1988, s 739* or *s 740*) or any provision of *ITTOIA 2005, Pt 5 Ch 5*, previously *ICTA 1988, Pt XV* (settlements). [*ICTA 1988, s 762); ITTOIA 2005, Sch 1 para 309*].

Capital gains tax. There are provisions to prevent a double charge to tax when a disposal gives rise to both an offshore income gain and a chargeable gain for capital gains tax purposes.

Where an offshore income gain arises on a 'material disposal' within 50.11 above, that gain is deducted from the sum which would otherwise constitute the amount or value of the consideration in the calculation of the capital gain arising under *TCGA 1992* (on 'the 1992 Act disposal'), although the offshore gain is not to be taken into account in calculating the fraction under *TCGA 1992, s 42(2)* (part disposal).

Where the 1992 Act disposal forms part of a transfer within *TCGA 1992, s 162* (rollover relief on transfer of business wholly or partly for shares) then, in determining the amount of the deduction from the gain on the old assets, the offshore income gain is deducted from the value of the consideration received in exchange for the business.

Where an exchange of shares or securities constitutes a disposal of an interest in an offshore fund (see 50.1 and 50.3 above), the amount of any offshore income gain to which the disposal gives rise is treated as consideration for the new holding.

Where the offshore fund provisions apply to a disposal of an interest in a fund operating equalisation arrangements (see 50.3 above) and the disposal

(*a*) is not to the fund or to its managers in their capacity as such, and

(*b*) gives rise to an offshore income gain in accordance with 50.12 above, and

(*c*) is followed subsequently by a distribution to either the person who made the disposal or to a person connected with him (within *ICTA 1988, s 839*, see 19 CONNECTED PERSONS) and that distribution is referable to the asset disposed of,

then the subsequent distribution (or distributions) is (are) reduced by the amount of the offshore income gain.

[*ICTA 1988, s 763; FA 2004, s 145, Sch 26 para 15(2)*].

For disposals on or after 6 March 1998, exemption from capital gains tax under *TCGA 1992, s 76(1)* is disapplied where the disposal is of an interest in a trust which has at any time been an offshore trust, or where the interest disposed of originated in a trust which has at any time been an offshore trust. [*TCGA 1992, s 76(1A)(1B)(3); FA 1998, s 128*]. See Tolley's Capital Gains Tax under Offshore Settlements.

50.14 *Example*

R Ltd, is a UK-resident company which draws up accounts to 31 March. It invests in non-qualifying offshore funds as follows.

			£
(i)	**ABC fund**		
	30.11.82	1,000 shares purchased at £10 per share	10,000
	1.1.84	Market value per share = £20	20,000
	1.4.08	On amalgamation with XYZ fund (an offshore fund which is not and has not been non-qualifying) the 1,000 original shares are exchanged for 2,000 new shares in XYZ which have a value of £15 per share	30,000
(ii)	**DEF fund**		£
	1.8.83	500 units purchased at £25 per unit	12,500
	1.1.84	Market value per unit = £20	10,000
	1.2.08	500 units sold for £40 per unit	20,000

R Ltd has offshore income gains and capital gains/losses in its accounting period ending 31 March 2008 as follows.

Offshore income gains

Disposal on 1.2.08 of 500 DEF units

	Post-1983 gain	Unindexed gain
	£	£
Disposal proceeds	20,000	20,000
Market value at 1.1.84	10,000	
Cost		12,500
	£10,000	£7,500

As the unindexed gain is less than the post-1983 gain, the offshore income gain chargeable under Schedule D, Case VI is £7,500.

Disposal on 1.4.08 of 1,000 ABC shares

	Post-1983 gain	Unindexed gain
	£	£
Disposal consideration	30,000	30,000
Market value at 1.1.84	20,000	
Cost		10,000
	£10,000	£20,000

The offshore income gain chargeable under Schedule D, Case VI is the £10,000 post-1983 gain as this is less than the unindexed gain.

Capital gains computation

Disposal on 1.2.08 of 500 DEF units

	£
Disposal proceeds	20,000
Offshore income gain	7,500
	12,500
Cost	12,500
Chargeable gain/allowable loss	Nil

Disposal on 1.4.08 of 1,000 ABC shares

There is no liability to corporation tax on capital gains as the share exchange is not treated as a disposal under *TCGA 1992, s 135* (exchange of securities for those in another company). See Tolley's Capital Gains Tax.

Note

(*a*) The £10,000 offshore income gain arising on the exchange of ABC shares for XYZ shares will be treated as part of the acquisition cost for capital gains purposes on a subsequent disposal of XYZ shares (see 50.13 above).

51 Oil Companies

Simon's Direct Tax Service D4.10.

51.1 The general provisions of the Taxes Acts apply to oil companies with modifications by the *Oil Taxation Acts 1975* and *1983*; *Petroleum Revenue Tax Act 1980*; *Advance Petroleum Revenue Tax Act 1986*; and annual *Finance Acts.*

See *Oil Taxation Act 1975, s 2, Sch 3* in relation to the valuation and pricing of North Sea oil as amended by *FA 2006, ss 146–148, Schs 18, 26* to ensure that tax is paid on the full value of oil with effect broadly for deliveries and appropriations on or after 1 July 2006. See *FA 1987, s 61, Sch 10* for the valuation for tax purposes of disposals of oil as amended by *FA 2006, ss 149, 150* broadly with effect from that date.

51.2 PETROLEUM REVENUE TAX

Petroleum revenue tax (PRT) is imposed on profits (based on total receipts (subject to seasonal supply adjustments) less specified deductions) from winning oil (including gas sold to British Gas) in the UK, the territorial seas and the continental shelf (see 60.10 RESIDENCE).

The tax is charged on the computed profits of half-yearly periods ending 30 June and 31 December and commencing with the first of those periods in which specified initial production is attained. Tax is payable six months after the end of each period, or 30 days after the issue of the notice of assessment, if later. For timing of assessments to PRT, see *Amoco (UK) Exploration Co v CIR Ch D 1983, 57 TC 147*. A payment on account of tax is due without assessment at the time for submission of a return, two months after the end of the period. Certain reliefs apply to help marginal fields.

The rate of tax is 50%. [*OTA 1975, s 1*(*2*)].

Transfer of a share of oil won out of an oil field from one 'participator' oil company to another will generally be disregarded where the obligations connected with the oil field, as regards that share, remain with the transferor company. Companies involved in certain agreements with the British National Oil Corporation will thus be liable to PRT on their profits from oil passed to BNOC. [*OTA 1975, Pt I*].

PRT is abolished for oil and gas fields given development consent after 15 March 1993. On or after 1 July 2007, fields are not liable to PRT where they have been decommissioned, and subsequently redeveloped. [*FA 1993, s 185*; *FA 2007, s 102*].

PRT liability is removed where the infrastructure of pre-16 March 1993 fields on the UK continental shelf is used to transport, process or provide services to other fields in relation to tariffs received in a chargeable period ending on or after 30 June 2004 under a contract entered into after 8 April 2003 from oil or gas fields given development consent after that date. The contract can also relate to an existing field if it has not made use of certain PRT liable assets in the UK or on its shelf in the six years ending on 8 April 2003. [*Oil Taxation Act 1983, ss 6A, 6B, Sch 2; FA 2004, s 285, Sch 37*].

51.3 SPECIAL CORPORATION TAX PROVISIONS

Provisions apply to treat the activities of each 'field' as a separate trade and a 'ring fence' excludes the set-off of external losses, etc. except the net final loss of another field. [*ICTA 1988, s 492*].

The reduction in the main rate of corporation tax from 30% to 28% for the financial year 2008 does not apply to ring fence profits. See 1 INTRODUCTION AND RATES OF TAX.

The increased small companies rate of corporation tax to 20% for financial year 2007 does not apply to ring fence profits. See 63 SMALL COMPANIES—REDUCED RATES.

Special provisions impose market valuation of oil disposed of or appropriated in certain circumstances. [*ICTA 1988, s 493; FA 2006, s 151, Sch 18 para 12*].

Losses from the oil activities may, however, be carried forward and set against trading income of subsequent accounting periods from activities which, apart from the 'ring fence' provisions, would form part of the same trade. [*ICTA 1988, s 492(4)*].

Similarly, where a company's non-oil activities give rise to an excess of charges on income over profits, the charges available for surrender by group relief may be calculated ignoring the oil activities. If, however, there is an excess of charges over profits for the oil activities, the normal rules apply to allow the overall excess of charges to be surrendered. The gross profits of the surrendering company against which charges (and certain other items) must first be set do not include certain ring fence profits. Non-ring fence loan relationship debits are treated as non-trading debits (see 46.3 LOAN RELATIONSHIPS). [*ICTA 1988, ss 494, 494A; FA 2002, Sch 25 para 17; F(No 2)A 2005, Sch 11 Pt 2(7)*].

There are also provisions restricting the set-off of lease payments under sale and leaseback transactions. In the case of finance leases where the sale takes place after 8 March 1999, the finance charge element of such payments can be set against ring fence profits only to the extent that the finance raised is used for oil extraction activities or in purchasing certain oil rights. This is extended in the case of a 'long funding operating lease' (as defined in *CAA 2001, s 70YI(1)*, see 10.34 CAPITAL ALLOWANCES) in relation to expenditure incurred on or after 1 April 2006 which is deductible against the lessee's profits (after appropriate deductions). [*ICTA 1988, s 494AA; FA 2006, Sch 9 para 1*].

The aggregate gains and losses on certain disposals are also brought within the ring fence, as is any charge under *TCGA 1992, s 178(3)* in respect of an asset acquired on such a disposal. An aggregate loss on such disposals may, however, on election be treated as a non-ring fence loss. [*ICTA 1988, ss 492, 494, 502(1); FA 2002, Sch 23 para 17*]. The ring fence rules also apply to prevent rollover of gains on certain disposals other than into assets used only for the ring fence trade (which assets are conclusively presumed to be depreciating assets for this purpose). [*TCGA 1992, s 198; ITTOIA 2005, Sch 1 para 440*].

There are special provisions relating to disposals of oil licences relating to undeveloped areas [*TCGA 1992, ss 194–196; FA 1996, s 181*] and preventing double allowances being given for research and development expenditure in relation to disposals of oil licences. [*CAA 2001, s 555, Sch 3 para 91; CAA 1990, ss 138A, 138B; FA 1996, s 180*].

Intangible costs of drilling the second and subsequent production wells in an area are not allowable where they were incurred after 25 November 1996 (unless incurred before 26 November 1997 under a contract entered into before 26 November 1996 and not varied on or after that date to increase such costs). Such costs will attract mineral extraction capital allowances ('MEAs', see 10.39 CAPITAL ALLOWANCES). Similarly, in relation to claims made after 25 November 1996, MEAs are denied in cases where oil licences are transferred, and the purchaser would otherwise obtain allowances for expenditure which had already been allowed in full to the seller. [*ICTA 1988, s 91C; CAA 2001, s 407(4), Sch 3 para 85; CAA 1990, s 115(2A); FA 1997, s 66*].

For ownership for capital allowance purposes of certain assets transferred under oil production sharing contracts to the government or representative of the production territory, see *CAA 2001, ss 167-170* (previously *CAA 1990, s 64A*).

PRT is deductible in computing profits for corporation tax purposes. [*ICTA 1988, s 500*]. An agreed amount is repayable whether or not the relevant corporation tax assessment has been made (or loss agreed) (*Elliss v ICI Petroleum Ltd Ch D 1983, 57 TC 176*).

51.4 **Abandonment expenditure.** A provision by a company for anticipated future expenditure on the completion of North Sea exploitation, in dismantling installations used and (as required under its licence) in 'cleaning up' the sea bed, was disallowed as capital when incurred in *RTZ Oil & Gas Ltd v Elliss Ch D 1987, 61 TC 132*. Companies may, however, elect for 100% capital allowances in respect of net expenditure incurred on demolition of offshore machinery and plant as part of the closing down of a field under an abandonment programme within *Petroleum Act 1987, Pt I*. Such expenditure incurred after cessation of the ring fence trade but within three years may be allowed in the final accounting period of that trade. Where a charge to corporation tax arises as a result of a PRT repayment attributable to the carry-back of losses, the repayment will be treated as chargeable for the accounting period in which ends the PRT period in which the loss accrued, rather than (as previously) for the accounting period for which the deduction was originally given. There is, however, a cap on the PRT repayment interest which may arise where losses are carried back to earlier periods.

For expenditure incurred after 6 August 2000 (or certain earlier expenditure in connection with activities after that date) these provisions are extended to abandonment costs of preparation for reuse and of removing and mothballing installations pending their reuse or demolition. Normal writing-down allowances (available for demolition costs under the general provision in *CAA 1990, s 62* or *CAA 2001, s 26*) are also available for such expenditure *not* connected with abandonment. [*CAA 1990, ss 62AA–62B; CAA 2001, ss 161A–165; FA 2001, Sch 20*].

See *FA 1980, Sch 17 para 15* (as substituted by *FA 2004, s 288*) in respect of terminal losses.

Relief for expenditure on abandonment guarantees, and for certain other abandonment expenditure, is allowed as a deduction in computing ring fence income. [*FA 1991, ss 62–65*].

51.5 **Supplementary charge.** For accounting periods beginning **on or after 1 January 2006** a sum equal to **20%** of adjusted profits of a company's ring fence trade is chargeable as if it were corporation tax (for accounting periods beginning before that date and after 16 April 2002, the charge was **10%**). Accounting periods straddling 1 January 2006 are treated as two separate accounting periods, the profits apportioned to those periods in proportion to the number of days in each period and the charge for the straddling period being the sum of the charges in the two periods. Transitional rules apply in relation to the application of the Instalment Payments Regulations. The adjustment required to those profits is to eliminate 'debt finance costs' (as defined) from the computation. [*ICTA 1988, s 501A; FA 2002, s 91, Sch 23 para 18, Sch 27 para 8; FA 2006, s 152, Sch 9 para 2*]. See also *ICTA 1988, ss 501B, 501C* (introduced by *FA 2002, ss 92, 93*) for assessment, recovery and postponement of the supplementary charge and transitional provisions.

51.6 **First-year allowances.** For expenditure incurred **on or after 17 April 2002,** two types of first-year allowance are made available for expenditure on assets provided wholly for use in a ring fence trade.

For such expenditure on *plant and machinery*, the rate of allowance is **100%** (except in the case of long-life asset expenditure, for which it is **24%**), and the allowance is subject to the usual exclusions from first-year allowances and to clawback where the plant or machinery in question is used for less than five years in the ring fence trade. [*CAA 2001, ss 45F, 45G, 46(1), 52(3); FA 2002, s 63, Sch 21 Pt I*].

For such expenditure on assets giving entitlement to *mineral extraction allowances*, the rate is **100%**. Expenditure on acquisition of mineral assets is excluded, as is expenditure incurred on acquiring assets representing expenditure incurred by a connected person within *ICTA 1988, s 839* (see 19 CONNECTED PERSONS). Artificially inflated claims are excluded. [*CAA 2001, ss 416A–416E, 418(4), 419(1)(3)–(5); FA 2002, s 63, Sch 21 Pt II*]. (See 10.39 CAPITAL ALLOWANCES.)

Although not strictly first-year allowances, allowances at **100%** are available for qualifying expenditure on research and development under *CA 2001, Pt 6* for the purpose of a ring trade (see 10.52 CAPITAL ALLOWANCES).

Deferral of first-year allowances. In relation to claims for first-year allowances, capital expenditure as above which is incurred in the year ended 31 December 2005 can, by election, be treated as being incurred on the first day of the company's first accounting period beginning on or after 1 January 2006. (This enables such allowances to be offset against ring fence profits which are charged at the higher rate of the supplementary charge from 1 January 2006; see 51.5 above.) The election must be made by notice to HMRC by 31 December 2007. [*FA 2006, s 153*].

See 10 CAPITAL ALLOWANCES for details of the above and for application of capital allowance provisions generally.

51.7 **Ring fence exploration supplement.** For accounting periods **beginning on or after 1 January 2006** (subject to the transitional rules below), a company carrying on a ring fence trade or engaged in activities with a view to carrying on a ring fence trade, can claim a Ring Fence Expenditure Supplement (RFES). The RFES replaces and extends the Exploration Expenditure Supplement (EES) below and is introduced to provide additional relief for expenditure by North Sea oil companies which are exploring for oil or gas or are in the development phase and which do not yet have any taxable income against which to offset their exploration, appraisal and development costs and capital allowances. The supplement is initially set at 6% (but variable by Treasury order) and can be claimed in respect of:

(*a*) qualifying pre-commencement expenditure incurred in the course of oil extraction activities before the trade is set up and commenced;

(*b*) losses incurred in the trade; and

(*c*) some or all of the supplement allowed in earlier periods.

The supplement increases the value of unused expenditure carried forward from one period to another by a compound 6% per annum and applies to all unrelieved expenditure incurred on or after 1 January 2006. The expenditure can be carried forward until it can be used against income and the supplement can be claimed for a maximum of six accounting periods which need not be consecutive.

As regards (*a*) above, the expenditure, which must be incurred in the course of oil extraction activities, must be subsequently allowable as a deduction in calculating the profits of the ring fence trade or must be relevant R&D expenditure incurred by an SME (for which an R&D tax credit is not claimed). The supplement is effectively added to the pool of pre-commencement expenditure (subject to transitional rules) and is treated as incurred by the company when the trade commences and there are rules to treat each accounting period separately. As regards (*b*) above, the supplement is effectively added to the post-trading expenditure pool and can be carried forward as a trading loss (subject to transitional rules for accounting periods straddling 1 January 2006). In either case, the pooled expenditure must be reduced by any disposal receipts and by any losses set off under *ICTA 1988, ss 393, 393A* or against unrelieved group ring fence profits. Claims must be made as claims for the commencement period with the same time limit as for group relief claims under *FA 1998, Sch 18 para 74*.

Exploration supplement. For an accounting period ending on or after 1 January 2004 but before 1 January 2006, a company carrying on a ring fence trade, or engaged in oil and gas exploration and appraisal with a view to carrying on a ring fence trade, can claim a supplement initially set at 6% (but variable by Treasury order) in respect of:

(i) qualifying capital expenditure incurred before the trade is set up and commenced;

(ii) losses incurred in respect of qualifying capital expenditure on research and development; and

(iii) some or all of the supplement allowed in earlier periods.

The supplement thus increases the value of unused allowances carried forward from one period to the next by a compound 6% per annum (the purpose being to help maintain allowances for new industry entrants unable to make immediate use of them). As regards

(i) above, the supplement is effectively added to the pool of expenditure allowing for additional capital allowances to be claimed when the trade commences. As regards (ii) above, the supplement increases the loss. To qualify for the supplement, the expenditure on oil and gas exploration must be incurred on or after 1 January 2004 but before 1 January 2006 and subject to a claim for capital allowances. The supplement can be claimed for a maximum of six accounting periods which need not be consecutive.

Transitional provisions. Transitional provisions deal with accounting periods straddling 1 January 2006, preserve the benefits of the EES into the new rules and deal with ring fence losses incurred in deemed accounting periods ending before 1 January 2006.

[*ICTA 1988, ss 496A, 496B, Schs 19B, 19C; FA 2004, s 286, Sch 38; FA 2006, s 154, Sch 19; ITA 2007, s 1003*].

51.8 **Payment of tax.** For accounting periods ending on or after 1 July 2005, corporation tax and supplementary charge on ring fence profits are excluded from the calculation of 'mainstream' corporation tax instalment payments (see 53.2 PAYMENT OF TAX) and such profits are subject instead to a separate set of rules under *SI 1998 No 3175, reg 5A*. Large companies are required to pay ring fence profits in no more than three instalments. This does not affect any amounts treated as becoming due and payable before 1 July 2005. [*SI 1998 No 3175, reg 5A*; *SI 2005 No 889*].

51.9 **Anti-avoidance.** The provisions of *ICTA 1988, s 770* (trading transactions at other than market price) are modified in regard to 'transfer-pricing'. [*ICTA 1988, s 771*].

51.10 **Losses.** Special provisions apply to losses incurred before 31 December 1972. In general, such losses

(*a*) **may not** be carried forward against income from the activities treated as a separate trade under *ICTA 1988, s 492* unless they were incurred in such activities,

(*b*) **may** be carried forward against income of the same trade (other than a trade falling within (*a*) above) to the extent of

(i) such trading income arising between 1 January 1973 and 11 July 1974 and

(ii) £50 million,

whichever is the greater.

[*F(No 2)A 1975, s 43*].

52 Partnerships

Cross-reference. See also 26.30 EXCHANGE GAINS AND LOSSES, 28.48 FINANCIAL INSTRUMENTS AND DERIVATIVE CONTRACTS, 46.27, 46.45 LOAN RELATIONSHIPS, 47.16, 47.24 LOSSES.

Simon's Direct Tax Service. See **D4.8**.

52.1 A partnership cannot be a company (see *ICTA 1988, s 832(1)*), but a company can be a member of a partnership, in which case the tax effects are as set out below.

52.2 ASSESSMENTS

Where one of the persons carrying on a trade, profession or business in partnership is a company, the partnership profits excluding chargeable gains are computed as for corporation tax purposes and by reference to ACCOUNTING PERIODS (2), but ignoring distributions, charges on income, capital allowances, balancing charges, losses brought forward or carried back and pre-trading expenditure. The company is chargeable to corporation tax as if its apportioned share of profits, and of each of the items specified above, arose from a trade, etc. it carried on alone in the accounting period or periods comprising the partnership accounting period (with any necessary apportionment between such periods). All computations are to be made without regard to any change in the partners. Individual partners are charged to tax in respect of their profit shares and given relief for losses in the same way as if all the partners were individuals. [*ICTA 1988, ss 111, 114, 115*].

Where the control and management of the partnership business is situated abroad, any UK resident company partner is assessable as if the partnership were resident in the UK. [*ICTA 1988, ss 114(1), 115(4)*]. Where a UK-resident company is a member of a partnership which is resident abroad or which carries on any trade etc. the control and management of which is outside the UK, any arrangements under a double treaty which relieve partnership income or capital gains from UK tax are not to affect any UK tax liability in respect of the UK-resident company partner's share of such income or gains. If the resident partner's share of income consists of or includes a share in a qualifying distribution made by a UK-resident company, the partner is, despite the arrangements, entitled to the share of the tax credit in respect of the distribution corresponding to the partner's share of the distribution. [*ICTA 1988, s 115(5)–(5B)* (*ICTA 1988, ss 112(4)(5), 115(5)* as originally enacted)*; ITTOIA 2005, Sch 1 para 95*].

The company tax return of a company in a partnership is required to include details from the partnership return (for which see Tolley's Income Tax under Returns).

Simon's Direct Tax Service. See **D4.802** *et seq.*

52.3 *Example*

X Ltd and Mr Brown have been in partnership for many years and share profits in the ratio 2:1. The partnership's trading results for the year ended 30 September 2007 are as follows.

	Trading profits	Capital allowances
	£	£
Year ended 30 September 2007	72,000	33,000

X Ltd's chargeable profits in respect of the partnership are as follows.

		£
Year ended 30.9.07		
Trading profits		48,000
Deduct Capital allowances		22,000
Schedule D, Case I		£26,000

Mr Brown's trading income for tax purposes is as follows.

2007/08 Profits	y/e 30.9.07	£13,000

Note

Capital allowances are a deduction in arriving at profits for both income and corporation taxes.

52.4 INTEREST PAID

Yearly interest of money chargeable to tax under ITTOIA 2005, Pt 4 Ch 2 (or before 2005/06 Schedule D, Case III as it applies for income tax purposes) and paid by a partnership of which a company is a member must be paid under deduction of income tax at the lower rate in force for the year in which the payment is made. [*ICTA 1988, s 349(2); ITTOIA 2005, Sch 1 para 148(3); ITA 2007, s 449*]. See, however, 37.3 INCOME TAX IN RELATION TO A COMPANY for relief from deduction of certain payments after 31 March 2001 to companies within the charge to corporation tax and 37.4 INCOME TAX IN RELATION TO A COMPANY for relief on certain payments made on or after 1 January 2004 between associated companies of different EU member states.

52.5 CHANGES IN PARTNERSHIP

On changes in corporate partnerships, the trade is treated as transferred from a company ceasing to be a partner to a company then becoming a partner. [*ICTA 1988, s 114(1)(c)*].

52.6 PARTNERSHIP LIABILITIES

Partnership liabilities include the whole of the income tax liability of the individual partners, notwithstanding that a company partner's profit share is liable only to corporation tax. Furthermore, individual partners are not obliged to give credit for personal allowances etc., provided that HMRC issues the partnership assessment on that basis. (*Barber v Eppell, QB 24 February 1981.*)

52.7 ANTI-AVOIDANCE

Realisation of capital. Anti-avoidance provisions apply where a company realises capital from a partnership on or after 17 March 2004 either by way of directly or indirectly receiving back any capital from the partnership or by disposing of all or part of it's partnership interest on or after that date. The provisions apply where:

(*a*) the capital realised exceeds the company's contribution to the partnership (including any amount paid by the company to acquire an interest in the partnership but excluding any amount originally contributed by a person from whom the company acquired the partnership interest and any contributions made after the capital realisation);

(*b*) that excess results wholly or partly from an arrangement under which the profits of the partnership for any period (but excluding any profits derived from income arising before 17 March 2004 (such profits to be derived on a just and reasonable basis)) were not, or not fully, allocated to the company in accordance with its capital share; and

(*c*) had such profits been allocated to the company in accordance with its due share, some or all of them would have been chargeable to corporation tax.

In this case, the company is chargeable to tax under Schedule D Case VI on so much of the amount of:

(i) the excess of the realised capital over contributions (as in (*a*) above), that does not exceed

(ii) the amount by which the company's due share of allocated profits exceed the amount allocated to it.

In computing the amount in (ii) above, any amounts that would not be regarded as income, or taken into account in computing income in a computation of chargeable profits, are to be excluded.

In computing the due share of profits which should have been allocated to the company in accordance with its capital share, the company's capital share is to be determined as an average for the chargeable period in which the profits arose (based on the number of days in that period). The capital in this case is taken to include any amount originally contributed by a person from whom the company acquired a partnership interest and amounts provided by way of a loan which carries interest below an arm's length rate.

Where this provision applies to the same company and partnership more than once (whether because there are two or more receipts of consideration relating to the same disposal or for any other reason), the charge on each subsequent occasion is computed as above and then reduced (but not below nil) by any amount already brought into charge.

'Capital' in this case includes anything accounted for as partners' capital or equity in the partnership accounts drawn up in accordance with generally accepted accounting practice or in the absence of such accounts, anything which would be so accounted for had such accounts been drawn up. Where a partnership is dissolved by reason of one of the partners acquiring the interests of the others, the remaining partner is deemed at that point to realise all its capital for this purpose.

Where there is a change in partnership membership, the partnership is to be treated as the same where a company is a member before and remains a member after the change.

[*FA 2004, ss 131, 132*].

Interaction with chargeable gains. The provisions ensure that where a company is chargeable to corporation tax as above on a receipt on or after 17 March 2004 from the disposal of all or part of it's partnership interest on or after that date (a '*section 131 disposal*') the amount subject to the *section 131 charge* will be taken into account in computing gains under the chargeable gains legislation (see 11.1 CAPITAL GAINS) so as to avoid double taxation. Specifically, where a chargeable gain arises on a 'relevant disposal' or where the total chargeable gains on such disposals exceed any allowable losses on such disposals:

(A) any chargeable gain accruing to a company on a 'relevant disposal' must be excluded from the computation of chargeable gains under *TCGA 1992, s 8*(*1*) accruing to the company in the same accounting period;

(B) any allowable loss accruing to a company on a 'relevant disposal' must be excluded from the amount of allowable losses, under *TCGA 1992, s 8*(*1*); and

(C) instead, the 'net relevant gain' is to be included in the computation of chargeable gains accruing to the company in the same accounting period accounting period as the one in which the receipt from the *section 131* disposal arose.

A '*relevant disposal*' is any disposal of an asset (in accordance with *TCGA 1992*) that alone or together with other disposals of assets constitutes a *section 131* disposal. A '*net relevant gain*' is the excess of chargeable gains accruing to the company on relevant disposals over any allowable losses on such disposals as reduced (but not below nil) by the amount chargeable under *FA 2004, s 131* (above).

Where *FA 2004, s 131* and these provisions apply more than once as a result of two or more receipts of consideration in relation to the same *section 131* disposal, the net relevant gain is to be included in the chargeable gains computation in relation only to the first such receipt. However, the chargeable amount under *FA 2004, s 131* to be deducted in computing the net relevant gain in relation to the first receipt, is the total of the chargeable amounts found in relation to all the receipts.

Where an allowable loss arising other than on a relevant disposal cannot be deducted from a chargeable gain arising from a relevant disposal by virtue of (*a*) to (*c*) above, it can be deducted from the total chargeable gains accruing to the company in the same accounting period as the one in which the receipt from the *section 131* disposal arose to the extent it has not been deducted from any other chargeable gain. However such a loss, or one or more of such losses, cannot be so deducted to the extent that it exceeds the net relevant gain in the case where (*a*) to (*c*) above applies, if it arises from a transaction or transactions between CONNECTED PERSONS (19) to which *TCGA 1992, s 18(3)* applies.

For these purposes, *TCGA 1992, ss 37(1) and 39(2)* (exclusions from consideration and allowable deductions) are ignored in computing the chargeable gain or allowable loss on a relevant disposal.

[*FA 2004, s 133*].

Leasing partnerships. For restriction of relief for losses in the case where there is a change in the interest of a company in a business, carried on in partnership, of leasing plant or machinery, see 5.16 and 5.17 ANTI-AVOIDANCE.

52.8 LIMITED PARTNERSHIPS

Where a company which is a 'limited partner' in a partnership sustains a loss or incurs capital expenditure in the partnership trade, or pays a charge in connection with it, relief may be restricted.

A '*limited partner*' is a partner carrying on a trade:

(*a*) as a limited partner in a limited partnership registered under the *Limited Partnerships Act 1907*; or

(*b*) as a general partner in a partnership, but who is not entitled to take part in the management of the trade, and who is entitled to have his liabilities for debts or obligations incurred for the trade discharged or reimbursed by some other person, in whole or beyond a certain limit; or

(*c*) who, under the law of any territory outside the UK, is not entitled to take part in the management of the trade, and is not liable beyond a certain limit for debts or obligations incurred for the trade.

The restriction applies to any excess of the loss, etc. in respect of the trade during an accounting period of the partner company over the company's 'contribution' to the trade at the end of that accounting period (or at the time the company ceased to carry on the trade if it did so during that accounting period). That excess may not be relieved under:

(i) *ICTA 1988, s 393(2)* or *s 393A(1)* (see 47.2 LOSSES);

(ii) *CAA 1990, s 145* (see 10.37 CAPITAL ALLOWANCES);

(iii) *ICTA 1988, s 338* (see 55.4 PROFIT COMPUTATIONS); or

(iv) *ICTA 1988, s 403* (see 32.10 GROUPS OF COMPANIES),

other than against profits arising from the trade. ((ii) above is no longer of any application.)

A further restriction applies where relief has previously been given under any of the provisions at (i)–(iv) above to the company (or to any other company) for a loss, etc. of the partner company in the partnership trade in any accounting period at any time during which the partner company carried on the trade as a limited company. Relief for the loss, etc. for the accounting period in question is restricted by the excess of the sum of the loss, etc. for that accounting period and the earlier amounts so relieved, over the 'contribution'.

The company's '*contribution*' to the trade at any time is the aggregate of:

(A) capital contributed and not directly or indirectly withdrawn (excluding any the company is or may be entitled to withdraw at any time it carries on the trade as a limited partner, or which it is or may be entitled to require another person to reimburse to it); and

(B) any profits of the trade to which the company is entitled but which it has not received in money or money's worth.

[*ICTA 1988, ss 117, 118; CAA 2001, Sch 2 paras 22, 23*].

52.9 **LIMITED LIABILITY PARTNERSHIPS**

From 6 April 2001, where a trade, profession or other business is carried on by a limited liability partnership (an 'LLP') within *Limited Liability Partnerships Act 2000, s 1* with a view to profit, all the activities of the LLP (i.e. anything it does) are treated as carried on in partnership by its members and not by the LLP as such. Anything done by, to or in relation to the LLP for the purposes of, or in connection with, any such activities is treated as done by, to or in relation to the members as partners, and property of the LLP is treated as held by the members as partnership property. In the *Corporation Tax Acts* references to a partnership or to members of a partnership include an LLP to which the above applies and members of such an LLP, and references to a company or to members of a company do not include an LLP or members of an LLP.

Where an LLP no longer carries on any trade, profession or other business with a view to profit, the above provisions continue to apply if the cessation is only temporary or during a winding up following a permanent cessation (provided, in the latter case, that the winding up is not for reasons connected in whole or part with tax avoidance and is not unreasonably prolonged). They cease to apply on the appointment of a liquidator or (if earlier) on the making of a winding-up order by the court, or on the occurrence of any corresponding event under the law of a country or territory outside the UK.

Similar provisions apply for capital gains tax purposes (see *TCGA 1992, s 59A* inserted by *Limited Liability Partnerships Act 2000, s 10(3)* and amended by *FA 2001, s 75(2)*, *TCGA 1992, s 156A* inserted by *Limited Liability Partnerships Act 2000, s 10(4)* and *TCGA 1992, s 169A* inserted (with effect from 3 May 2001) by *FA 2001, s 75(3)*). See Tolley's Capital Gains Tax under Partnerships and Hold-Over Reliefs.

For HMRC's views on how the members of a limited liability partnership carrying on a trade or profession are to be taxed, see Revenue Tax Bulletin December 2000 pp 801–805.

ICTA 1988, s 118 (see 52.8 above) applies to company members of LLPs as it does to company members of limited partnerships, except as follows.

(1) A member's contribution to a trade at any time (a 'relevant time') is the greater of the 'amount subscribed' by the member and the amount of its liability on a winding up (see below). The '*amount subscribed*' by a member is the amount contributed to the LLP as capital, less so much of that amount (if any) as:

(*a*) it has previously, directly or indirectly, drawn out or received back; or (*b*) it so draws out or receives back during the five years beginning with the relevant time; or

(*c*) it is or may be entitled so to draw out or receive back at any time when it is a member of the LLP; or

(*d*) it is or may be entitled to require another person to reimburse to it.

The amount of the liability of a member on a winding up is the amount which it is liable to contribute to the assets of the LLP in the event of its being wound up, and which it remains liable so to contribute for at least the period of five years beginning with the relevant time (or until the partnership is wound up if that happens before the end of that period).

(2) Amounts relating to a trade carried on by a member of an LLP which, apart from this provision, are prevented from being given or allowed by *section 118* are referred to as the member's '*total unrelieved loss*'. In each subsequent year of assessment in which the member continues to carry on the trade and any of the total unrelieved loss remains outstanding (see below), the balance of the total unrelieved loss is treated for the purposes of *ICTA 1988, ss 393A(1), 403* (see 47.2 LOSSES, 32.10 GROUPS OF COMPANIES) and *section 118* as it applies in relation to those *sections*, as increasing any loss incurred in the trade in that year of assessment or, if no such loss is incurred, as consisting of such a loss. The amount of the total unrelieved loss remaining outstanding in a year of assessment is the total amount less any part of it for which relief has been given in that or any earlier year of assessment *other than* by virtue of this provision and any part for which relief has been given for an earlier year of assessment *under* this provision (or would have been so given had a claim been made).

[*ICTA 1988, ss 118ZA–118ZD; Limited Liability Partnerships Act 2000, s 10(1); FA 2001, s 75; ITTOIA 2005, Sch 1 para 97*].

Investment LLPs and property investment LLPs. A number of tax exemptions for income and gains are disapplied where they are received by a member of a 'property investment LLP' as such, and interest relief under *ICTA 1988, s 362* (see Tolley's Income Tax under Interest Payable) is denied where the partnership is an 'investment LLP'.

An '*investment LLP*' is an LLP whose business consists wholly or mainly in the making of investments and the principal part of whose income is derived therefrom, and a '*property investment LLP*' is similarly defined by reference to investments in land. The status of an LLP in this respect is determined for each period for which partnership accounts are drawn up. [*ICTA 1988, s 842B*].

Exemptions are *disapplied* in the case of property investment LLPs as follows.

(*a*) *Pension funds, etc.* (i) Exemptions under *ICTA 1988, ss 592(2), 608(2)(a), 613(4), 614(3)–(5), 620(6), 643(2)* (see 27.14 EXEMPT ORGANISATIONS and Tolley's Income Tax under Personal Pension Schemes), including exemptions for related stock lending fees and income from related futures and options. [*ICTA 1988, s 659D*]. (ii) Corresponding exemption from the trusts rate of income tax under *ICTA 1988, s 686* (accumulation and discretionary trusts, see Tolley's Income Tax under Settlements). [*ICTA 1988, s 686(6A)*]. (iii) Corresponding exemptions under *TCGA 1992, s 271(1)* (see 27.14 EXEMPT ORGANISATIONS). [*TCGA 1992, s 271(12*].

(*b*) *Insurance companies.* The policyholders' share (as specially determined) of certain income and gains is treated as referable to basic life assurance and general annuity business, rather than pension business, and double tax credit relief and capital allowances are attributed to different categories of business accordingly. [*ICTA 1988, ss 438B, 438C, 804B(2)(4); CAA 2001, s 545(3)*].

(*c*) *Friendly societies.* Exemption under *ICTA 1988, s 460* of profits from life and endowment business, or under *ICTA 1988, s 461* or *s 461B* of profits from other business of registered or incorporated societies. [*ICTA 1988, ss 460(2)(cb), 461(3A), 461B(2A)*]. See 31.2, 31.6 FRIENDLY SOCIETIES.

[*FA 2001, s 76, Sch 25*].

53 Payment of Tax

Cross-references. See 3 ADVANCE CORPORATION TAX; 37 INCOME TAX IN RELATION TO A COMPANY; 41 INTEREST ON UNPAID TAX; 51 OIL COMPANIES; 60.5, 60.6 RESIDENCE.

The headings in this chapter are as follows.

53.1 DUE DATES FOR PAYMENT

Subject to the instalment provisions described at 53.2 below, corporation tax is due and payable on the day following the expiry of nine months from the end of the accounting period, on the basis of the amount computed in the company tax return for the period (see 61.7 RETURNS). Any excess over the tax payable of 'relevant amounts' stated in the company tax return is repaid. '*Relevant amounts*' are corporation tax paid and not repaid, corporation tax refunds surrendered to the company intra-group (see 32.29 GROUPS OF COMPANIES), certain income tax suffered and CONSTRUCTION INDUSTRY SCHEME (20) deductions. [*TMA 1970, s 59D; FA 2002, s 40*(*3*)].

A company may claim repayment of corporation tax paid for an accounting period where the company's circumstances change so that it has grounds for believing that the amount paid exceeds its probable (although not yet finally established) liability. No claim may be made before the 'material date' in relation to the tax (see 40.1 INTEREST ON OVERPAID TAX). If the tax is the subject of an outstanding appeal, the company may apply to the Commissioners for a determination of the amount to be repaid (and the application may be combined with a postponement application under *TMA 1970, s 55*, see 53.4 below). If the company tax return (see 61.3 RETURNS) has not been made, CONSTRUCTION INDUSTRY SCHEME (20) deductions are ignored for these purposes. [*TMA 1970, s 59DA*]. 'Large' companies to which instalment payments apply are precluded from making a claim under *section 59DA* where a claim for repayment of instalment payments is made (see 53.2 below). [*SI 1998 No 3175, reg 6*(*8*)].

As regards due dates for payment of tax for **accounting periods ending before 1 July 1999**, i.e. before the introduction of self-assessment, see the 2005–06 and earlier editions of Tolley's Corporation Tax.

53.2 INSTALMENT PAYMENTS

A system of quarterly accounting for corporation tax was phased in for 'large companies' from accounting periods ending on or after 1 July 1999 to accounting periods ending before 1 July 2002 (see transitional provisions below), the provisions described below operating for accounting periods ending on or after that date. [*TMA 1970, s 59E; SI 1998 No 3175*]. Corporation tax for this purpose includes any liability under *ICTA 1988, s 419* (loans to participators, see 16.9 CLOSE COMPANIES) or *s 747*(*4*)(*a*) (amounts apportioned in respect of controlled foreign companies, see 21.8 CONTROLLED FOREIGN COMPANIES).

The self-assessment company tax return (see 61.3 RETURNS) requires the company to state whether it is liable to make instalment payments on account of its corporation tax liabilities. Although HMRC will at some stage check the position, initial payment applications, interest calculations, etc. will be based on the company's statement of its position.

(HMRC Company Taxation Manual CTM 92690). For entries required on form CT600, see Revenue Tax Bulletin April 2001 pp 831–833.

Large companies. A '*large company*', subject to the exclusions described below, is a company whose profits in any accounting period exceed the small companies rate upper relief limit (the 'upper relevant maximum amount') in force at the end of the accounting period (see 63.2 SMALL COMPANIES—REDUCED RATES). This is currently £1,500,000 divided by one plus the number of 'associated companies' (if any) at any time in the period (see 63.7 SMALL COMPANIES—REDUCED RATES), proportionately reduced for periods of less than twelve months. Certain adjustments made in the case of insurance companies are, however, disregarded. A company is *not* large as respects an accounting period for which:

(*a*) its total corporation tax liability, reduced by any deductions under the CONSTRUCTION INDUSTRY SCHEME (20) from payments in the period, does not exceed £10,000 (£5,000 in relation to accounting periods ending before 1 July 2000), proportionately reduced for accounting periods of less than twelve months; or

(*b*) its profits do not exceed £10,000,000, provided that it was not a large company (disregarding the £10,000,000 exclusion) in the twelve months preceding the period.

As regards (*b*) above, the £10,000,000 limit is reduced in the same proportion as the upper relevant maximum amount for short accounting periods or where there are associated companies (see 63.2, 63.7 SMALL COMPANIES—REDUCED RATES), except that the number of associated companies required to be taken into account is determined as at the end of the immediately preceding accounting period, or at the commencement of the accounting period concerned if there was no immediately preceding accounting period or there was a gap between the two accounting periods. Also as regards (*b*) above, a company is treated as not having been large in the twelve months preceding the period in question where either:

(i) during any part of the twelve months it did not exist or did not have an accounting period; or

(ii) an accounting period during which it was not a large company (other than by virtue of (*b*) above) either falls within or ends in the twelve months.

'Profits' of an accounting period for these purposes are the assessable profits on which corporation tax finally falls to be charged for the period plus FRANKED INVESTMENT INCOME (29) ('FII') of the period other than any FII received from fellow group members (and distributions are treated as coming from within the group if, but only if, dividends so received are group income or would be if the companies so elected (see 32.2, 32.4 GROUPS OF COMPANIES)).

[*SI 1998 No 3175, regs 2(2)(3), 3; SI 2000 No 892*].

Instalments. Subject to the transitional provisions described below, amounts in respect of a large company's total corporation tax liability for an accounting period (as reduced by any deductions under the CONSTRUCTION INDUSTRY SCHEME (20) from payments in the period) become due and payable in up to four instalments as follows.

(1) The first instalment is due six months and thirteen days from the start of the accounting period, and the last instalment is due three months and fourteen days from the end of the accounting period, except that if the latter date precedes the former (i.e. where the accounting period is less than three months), a single instalment equal to the total corporation tax liability is due and payable on the latter date.

(2) Where there is a gap of more than three months between the two dates referred to in (1) above (i.e. where the accounting period is longer than six months), a second instalment is due and payable three months after the first, and if the gap exceeds six months, a third instalment is due and payable three months after the second. Thus for

the year ending 31 December 2004, instalments will be due on 14 July 2004, 14 October 2004, 14 January 2005 and 14 April 2005.

(3) The amount of the first instalment (other than in the case of the single instalment referred to in (1) above) is the total corporation tax liability divided by the number of months in the accounting period (including a decimal equivalent to two places of any days in excess of a whole number of months) and multiplied by three.

(4) The amount of any second or third instalment (other than the final instalment) is the smaller of the amount calculated as in (3) above and the balance remaining of the total corporation tax liability. (The latter can apply only where the estimated amount of that liability has been substantially reduced (see below) since the previous instalment.)

(5) The amount of the final instalment is the balance remaining of the total corporation tax liability.

Thus in the case of the year ending 31 December 2004 instanced at (2) above, the four instalments are each of one-quarter of the final corporation tax liability. For an accounting period of eight months ending 31 August 2004, instalments are due on 14 July 2004, 14 October 2004 and 14 December 2004, the first two being of three-eighths of the total corporation tax liability and the final one of the balance of one-quarter.

Where the company's estimate of the amount of its total corporation tax liability for the period is revised, subsequent instalment payments are recalculated accordingly, and top-up payments may be made at any time. The due and payable amount of each instalment for the purposes of interest on over- or under-payments (see below) is that based on the total corporation tax liability as returned by the company (or as determined by the inspector where the normal due date has passed).

[*SI 1998 No 3175, reg 5*].

As regards estimation of quarterly payments, see HMRC guidance published on their website (at www.hmrc.gov.uk/ctsa/quarterly_payments.htm).

Although HMRC will send a reminder and payslip (Form CT608) to those companies which it appears likely will be required to make instalment payments, it is in any event the company's responsibility to make such payments if they are due. Since payments are processed automatically, it is important to ensure that the correct payslip is used or the correct reference quoted to prevent misallocation. (HMRC Company Taxation Manual CTM 92550 and Revenue Tax Bulletins April 1999 p 646 and April 2001 p 833).

A *repayment* may be claimed where the company has grounds for believing that changed circumstances since an instalment or instalments were paid has rendered its earlier calculation of its total corporation tax liability excessive, so that the aggregate amount of the instalments paid exceeds what would have been payable by the date of the claim based on the new figure for that liability. Repayment of that excess may be claimed, and the claim must state the amount to be repaid and the grounds for the company's belief that its earlier calculation was excessive. If an appeal against an assessment, or an amendment of a self-assessment, in respect of the total liability for the accounting period concerned is outstanding, the company may apply to the Commissioners for a determination of the amount to be repaid pending determination of the appeal. Such claims and applications are treated in the same way as appeals, and an application for determination of a repayment may be combined with an application for postponement of payment of tax under *TMA 1970, s 55* (see 53.4 below).

Alternatively, the provisions of *FA 1989, s 102* (surrender of tax refund within group, see 32.29 GROUPS OF COMPANIES) are applied to allow the surrender of excess instalment payments intra-group.

[*SI 1998 No 3175, regs 6, 9; SI 1999 No 1929*].

Transitional provisions. For accounting periods ending before 1 July 2002, only a proportion of the total corporation tax liability is subject to instalment payment as above, the balance being payable on the normal due date nine months and one day after the end of the accounting period. The proportion subject to instalment payment is as follows.

(A) For accounting periods ending after 30 June 1999 and before 1 July 2000, **60%**.

(B) For accounting periods ending after 30 June 2000 and before 1 July 2001, **72%**.

(C) For accounting periods ending after 30 June 2001 and before 1 July 2002, **88%**.

See example below.

[*SI 1998 No 3175, reg 4*].

Interest on unpaid instalments. Unpaid instalment payments carry interest at a special rate from the due date to the date of payment during the period until nine months after the end of the accounting period concerned (whereafter the normal interest rate provisions apply). The special rate was set initially at 8.25% p.a., whereas the rate applicable under self-assessment from the normal corporation tax due date was initially set at 8.5% (and the differential will generally vary between 1 and 1.75% from 20 April 2000). See 41.1 INTEREST ON UNPAID TAX for the rates. [*TMA 1970, s 87A*].

Interest on overpaid instalments. Excess payments in respect of instalments carry interest at a special rate (which also applies to early payments by companies not liable to pay by instalments) from the date the excess arises (but not earlier than the due date of the first instalment) until it is extinguished (but not later than nine months after the end of the accounting period concerned, from when the normal interest rate provisions apply). The special rate was initially set at 6% p.a., whereas the rate applicable under self-assessment from the normal corporation tax due date was initially set at 5% p.a. (and the differential will vary between 0.25% and 1.25%). See 40.1 INTEREST ON OVERPAID TAX for the rates. [*ICTA 1988, s 826*].

Information, etc. powers. HMRC have powers to require the production of a wide range of information and records relating to instalment payments once the filing date for the return for the accounting period (normally twelve months after the end of the period, see 61.8 RETURNS) has passed. [*SI 1998 No 3175, regs 10-12; SI 1999 No 1929*]. HMRC will seek to make use of these powers only where there are indications that a company may have deliberately or recklessly failed to comply with its instalment payment obligations, or fraudulently or negligently made a repayment claim (see HMRC Company Taxation Manual CTM 92770 and HMRC Enquiry Manual, EM 8320).

Penalties. Where interest is charged on unpaid instalments as above, and the company, or a person acting on its behalf, either:

(I) deliberately or recklessly failed to make an instalment payment; or

(II) fraudulently or negligently made a claim for repayment of an excess amount of instalment payments,

the company is liable to a penalty of up to twice the amount of the interest. [*SI 1998 No 3175, reg 13*]. HMRC will seek a penalty under these provisions only in the most serious cases involving flagrant abuse of the regulations (see HMRC Enquiry Manual EM 8330, Revenue Tax Bulletin August 1999 pp 683, 684, and further guidance published on HMRC's website (at www.hmrc.gov.uk/ctsa/penpowers.htm).

Generally, penalties under *TMA 1970, s 98* apply for any failure to provide information, produce documents, etc. as required under these provisions.

Anti-avoidance. A special anti-avoidance provision may apply where, in the period from 25 November 1997 to 29 June 2002, a company either:

(*aa*) changes the dates of any of its accounting periods which would otherwise have been consecutive and of twelve months duration and have ended in that period; and/or

(*bb*) enters into arrangements or transactions which have the effect of transferring taxable profits intra-group.

If the result is that, on various assumptions about what would have happened if the company had not done so, corporation tax on profits of any accounting period beginning after 1 July 1998 and ending before 1 July 2002 becomes payable on a later date (whether under the instalment arrangements or under the normal corporation tax payment arrangements), then an amount corresponding to interest by reference to the overall deferral of payments may become chargeable on the company. There are various exclusions depending on the timing and circumstances of the decision by the company to take the action in question.

For an example of the application of this provision, see HMRC Company Taxation Manual CTM 92810.

[*SI 1998 No 3175, reg 14*].

Group payment arrangements. Any group of companies with instalment payment liabilities which wishes to do so may make arrangements (under *FA 1998, s 36*) with HMRC to account for corporation tax relating to accounting periods ending on or after 31 December 1999 on a group basis rather than company by company (see 32.28 GROUPS OF COMPANIES). This will enable profit forecasts to be made at group level and mitigate the interest differential on over- and under-paid tax. Groups wishing to take part in such arrangements should contact the Group Payment Team at the appropriate Accounts Office (Shipley tel. 01274 539561 or Cumbernauld tel. 01236 783488).(HMRC Company Taxation Manual CTM 97410.)

Broadly, a nominated company may contract with HMRC to make instalment payments on behalf of group companies covered by the arrangements ('participating companies') on the due dates on the basis of the most recent forecast of group profits. Once all the participating companies have either filed their returns or had their corporation tax liabilities determined by HMRC (the 'closing date', which cannot be earlier than the normal due date nine months after the end of the accounting period), the nominated company will be issued with a notice showing what it has paid and the liability at the closing date. It will then be invited to make good any shortfall, or allocate it to any company whose liability it has reason to believe will decrease after the closing date, and to apportion payments to the participating companies. It may allocate any surplus to participating companies or require its repayment.

The arrangements need not apply to all group members, and separate arrangements may be entered into for different sub-sets within a group. Not all companies covered by the arrangements need be UK-resident, although the nominated company must be. All companies must have filed returns and paid the due tax in respect of their last but one accounting period. They must have a common accounting period (subject to special arrangements for companies joining the group and aligning their accounting date). There is provision for either the nominated company or HMRC to remove a company from the arrangements in specified circumstances where the rules regarding eligibility to enter the arrangements would no longer be met. Any group wishing to take part in the arrangements must normally deliver its signed contract to the appropriate Accounts Office (as above) at least two months prior to the first instalment payment due date. All payments must be made by electronic funds transfer.

For detailed requirements, see HMRC Company Taxation Manual CTM 97400 *et seq* which also includes the group payment arrangement contract and the administrative and guidance notes. Guidance is also provided in Revenue Tax Bulletins April 1999 pp 647–650 and April 2001 pp 831–836. These include the entries required on return form CT600, the effect of arrangements on tax repayments and group surrenders thereof, the allocation of payments under an arrangement, the departure from a group of a participating company and the treatment of long periods of account.

Insurance companies and friendly societies. Special provision is made for the interest consequences of the set-off of a provisional repayment under *ICTA 1988, Sch 19AB* (see 31.2 FRIENDLY SOCIETIES) against an instalment payment under the current provisions. [*SI 1998 No 3175, reg 15*].

Oil and gas companies. For accounting periods ending on or after 1 July 2005, corporation tax and supplementary charge on ring fence profits (from oil and gas extraction or oil rights within the UK or UK Continental Shelf, see 51 OIL COMPANIES) are excluded from the calculation of 'mainstream' corporation tax instalment payments and such profits are subject instead to a separate set of rules. Large companies will be required to pay ring fence profits in no more than three instalments. This does not affect any amounts treated as becoming due and payable before 1 July 2005. [*SI 1998 No 3175, reg 5A*; *SI 2005 No 889*].

HMRC guidance. See generally HMRC Company Taxation Manual CTM 92500 *et seq.* See also Revenue Tax Bulletins April 1999 pp 645–650, February 2000 pp 723–726 and April 2001 pp 831–836 and HMRC publication CTSA/BK3 'A Modern System for Corporation Tax Payments.

Example A Ltd has the following corporation tax liabilities.

Year ended 31 December	1999	2000	2001	2002
	£'000	£'000	£'000	£'000
	2,565	2,250	1,280	1,575

The due dates and corporation tax payable are as follows.

	£
y/e 31 December 1999	
14 July 1999, 14 October 1999, 14 January 2000 and 14 April 2000	384,750
1 October 2000	1,026,000
y/e 31 December 2000	
14 July 2000, 14 October 2000, 14 January 2001 and 14 April 2001	405,000
1 October 2001	630,000
y/e 31 December 2001	
14 July 2001, 14 October 2001, 14 January 2002 and 14 April 2002	281,600
1 October 2002	153,600
y/e 31 December 2002	
14 July 2002, 14 October 2002, 14 January 2003 and 14 April 2003	393,750

Simon's Direct Tax Service. See D2.705 *et seq.*, **D2.841** *et seq.*

53.3 PAYMENT: SPECIAL CASES

Tax payments may be made in euro through automated banking systems, from euro accounts or (at certain locations) in euro bank notes (but not coins). Costs incurred in respect of a euro payment drawn on an overseas bank account will be borne by the taxpayer, but other administrative costs will not be passed on. The exchange rate used is the one in force when the payment is presented by the clearing bank. If the conversion rate used leaves a shortfall, the difference will have to be paid. If it results in an overpayment, any repayment arising will be made in sterling.

For payment by cheque see 41.6 INTEREST ON UNPAID TAX and for payment electronically see 33.10 HMRC: ADMINISTRATION.

53.4 PAYMENT OF TAX PENDING APPEAL

Where there is an appeal against an amendment of a self-assessment, an assessment to corporation tax other than a self-assessment or an assessment to income tax on company payments (but excluding income tax accountable by quarterly etc. returns, see 41.7 INTEREST ON UNPAID TAX), the full amount charged will be due and payable unless the appellant applies for payment of part of the tax assessed to be postponed. The application must in the first instance be made in writing to HMRC within 30 days after the date of the issue of the notice of assessment, stating the amount of tax believed to be overcharged (and payment of which is to be postponed), and the grounds for that belief. Application may be made outside the normal 30-day time limit if there is a change in circumstances giving grounds for belief that the appellant is overcharged. In HMRC's view, this condition requires a change in the circumstances in which the original decision not to apply for postponement was made, not just a change of mind, e.g. further accounts work indicating a substantially excessive assessment, or further reliefs becoming due. (Notes of CCAB meeting with Revenue on the 1982 Finance Bill TR 477, 22 June 1982). The appellant and a Revenue officer may agree the amount of tax to be postponed and written confirmation of such agreement shall be treated as if the Commissioners had determined it. Failing such agreement the appeal Commissioners determine the amount, in the same way as an appeal. Any tax which is the subject of such an application and which is not postponed by agreement or by the Commissioners shall be due and payable as if charged by an assessment issued on the date of the Commissioners' determination (or of written confirmation of the agreement with HMRC's officer) and against which no appeal is pending. If circumstances change, a further application may be made by either the appellant or HMRC's officer giving notice to the other to vary the amount postponed. On determination of the appeal, any tax overpaid is repaid and any postponed tax then becoming collectable or not previously charged becomes due and payable as if charged under an assessment issued when the inspector issues to the appellant notice of the total amount payable. [*TMA 1970, s 55; FA 1994, Sch 19 para 18; FA 1998, Sch 19 para 28; SI 1998 No 3173*].

See also 61.7 RETURNS.

Simon's Direct Tax Service. See **A3.1308, D2.833**.

53.5 RECOVERY OF TAX FROM THIRD PARTIES

Change in ownership of company: corporation tax. Where it appears to HMRC that:

(*a*) there has been a change in ownership of a company;

(*b*) any corporation tax assessed on the company for an accounting period beginning before the date of the change remains unpaid at any time after the '*relevant date*' (i.e. the date six months after the date of the corporation tax assessment); and

(*c*) any of the three conditions referred to below is fulfilled,

any of the following persons may be assessed and charged in the name of the company to an amount of corporation tax as below:

(i) any person who at any time during the '*relevant period*' (i.e. the period of three years before the change in ownership, but not so as to include any period before a previous change in ownership) had 'control' of the company; and

(ii) any company of which a person within (i) has at any time in the three years before the change in ownership had 'control'.

'*Control*' is as under *ICTA 1988, s 416* (see 16.2 CLOSE COMPANIES), except that 50% only (rather than 'the greater part') of the share capital, issued share capital or voting power is sufficient to give control, and where two or more persons together satisfy any of the conditions for control, control will only be imputed to each of them where they have acted together to put themselves in a position where they will in fact satisfy the condition in question.

The three alternative conditions referred to at (*c*) above are as follows.

(A) At any time during the three years before the change in ownership the activities of a trade or business of the company cease or the scale of those activities become small or negligible, and there is no significant revival of those activities before the change occurs.

(B) At any time after the change in ownership, but under arrangements made before that change, the activities of a trade or business of the company cease or the scale of those activities become small or negligible.

(C)

(*a*) At any time during the six years beginning three years before the change in ownership, there is a major change in the nature or conduct of a trade or business of the company, and also any such change achieved gradually as the result of a series of transfers — see 47.13 LOSSES generally);

(*b*) assets of the company are transferred (including any disposal, letting or hiring of an asset, and any grant or transfer of any right, interest or licence in or over it, or the giving of any business facilities with respect to it) to a person within (i) above (or to a person connected with such a person within *ICTA 1988, s 839*), or under arrangements which enable any of those assets (or assets representing those assets) to be transferred to such a person, during the three years before the change in ownership (or after the change but under arrangements made before the change); and

(*c*) the major change in the nature or conduct of the trade or business of the company is attributable to the transfer(s) of the company's assets.

The tax charged in an assessment under these provisions must not exceed the amount of the tax which, at the time of the assessment, remains unpaid by the company, and the assessment is not out of time if made within three years of the final determination of the liability of the company for the accounting period concerned. *TMA 1970, s 87A* (see 41.1 INTEREST ON UNPAID TAX) apply in relation to tax so assessed by reference to the company's due and payable (or reckonable) date. The tax paid is not an allowable deduction for any tax purposes, but the payer is entitled to recover an amount equal to the tax (and any interest thereon under *TMA 1970, s 87A*) from the company. An amount so recovered (or received under an indemnity in this respect) is not chargeable to tax on the recipient. (Revenue Tax Bulletin April 1995 p 208).

Power to obtain information. The inspector may, by notice in writing, require any person who is the registered owner of shares, stock or securities of a company to state whether he is the beneficial owner thereof and, if not, to supply the name and address of the person(s) on whose behalf he holds them.

Rules for ascertaining change in ownership. The provisions of *ICTA 1988, s 769* (see 47.13 LOSSES) apply with appropriate modification in relation to these provisions as they apply to *ICTA 1988, ss 768, 768A*.

[*ICTA 1988, ss 767A, 767B*].

See also 11.8, 11.9 CAPITAL GAINS, 12.31, 12.32 CAPITAL GAINS—GROUPS and 60.7 RESIDENCE.

Change in ownership of company: postponed corporation tax. Provisions supplementing the above deal with cases where a corporation tax liability has been postponed to a period commencing after a change in ownership. *ICTA 1988, s 769* (see 47.13 LOSSES), modified as for *ICTA 1988, s 767A* (see above), applies for determining whether there is a change in ownership of a company.

Where it appears to HMRC that there has been a change in the ownership of a company (the 'transferred company'), and that any corporation tax relating to an accounting period ending on or after the change which has been assessed on that company or an 'associated' company remains unpaid at any time more than six months after it was assessed, then (subject to the further condition referred to below) any one of the persons listed below may be assessed and charged (in the name of the company in default) to an amount of corporation tax not exceeding the amount remaining unpaid. Such an assessment is not out of time if made within three years of the date of final determination of the liability of the company in default for the accounting period for which the tax was assessed. INTEREST ON UNPAID TAX (41) then runs by reference to the date of the original liability of the transferred (or 'associated') company.

A company is '*associated*' with another for these purposes if, at the time of the assessment (or at an earlier time before the change in ownership), it has control of or is controlled by the other or they are under common control. 'Control' is defined as for *ICTA 1988, s 767A* (above).

The further condition referred to above is that it would be reasonable (apart from these provisions) to infer, from either or both of the terms of any transactions entered into in connection with the change (for which see below) and the other circumstances of the change and of any such transactions, that at least one of those transactions was entered into by one or more of the parties to it on the assumption that a 'potential tax liability' would be unlikely to be met, or met in full, were it to arise.

A '*potential tax liability*' is a corporation tax liability which, in circumstances reasonably foreseeable at the time of change in ownership (or in circumstances the occurrence of which is something of which there was at that time a reasonably foreseeable risk), would or might arise from an assessment made, after the change in ownership, on the transferred company or an associated company (see above), whether or not a particular associated company.

A transaction is for these purposes entered into in connection with a change in ownership if the change is effected by the transaction (with or without other transactions) or by other transactions forming part of the same series of transactions or scheme (by whomsoever entered into). A 'scheme' is any scheme, arrangements or understanding, whether or not legally enforceable, involving one or more transactions, and the cases in which transactions form part of a scheme or series include cases in which it would be reasonable to assume that one or more of them would not have been entered into independently of the other(s), or that if entered into independently it would not have taken the same form or been on the same terms.

The persons who may be assessed and charged are any person who at any time during the 'relevant period' had control of the transferred company, and any company of which such a person has at any time had control within the period of three years before the change in ownership. The '*relevant period*' is the period of three years before the change in ownership, or if, during that three years, there was an earlier change in ownership of the transferred company, the period between those changes.

Tax paid under these provisions is not an allowable deduction for tax purposes, but the payer is entitled to recover an amount equal to the tax (and any interest thereon) from the transferred (or associated) company.

HMRC has wide powers to require any person (subject to certain exclusions) to supply (within not less than 30 days) specified documents and other particulars relating to liabilities which may arise under these provisions (but excluding documents etc. relating to the conduct of any pending tax appeal).

[*ICTA 1988, ss 767AA, 767B, 767C*].

Simon's Direct Tax Service. See D2.517.

Recovery of tax payable by non-resident company. Where corporation tax assessed on a non-UK resident company (i.e. in respect of UK branch profits) remains in whole or part unpaid six months after the due date, the following companies may be served notice by HMRC requiring them to pay the tax.

(1) Any company which was, at any time in the 'relevant period', a 51% subsidiary (by reference to ordinary share capital) of the non-resident company, or of which the non-resident company was a 51% subsidiary, or where both were 51% subsidiaries of a third company.

(2) Any company which was, at any time during the 'relevant period', a member of a consortium which owned (see 32.23 GROUPS OF COMPANIES) the non-resident company at that time.

(3) Any company which was, at any time during the 'relevant period', a member of the same group (as for group relief purposes, see 32.7 GROUPS OF COMPANIES) as a company which was at that time a member of a consortium which owned (see 32.23 GROUPS OF COMPANIES) the non-resident company.

The '*relevant period*' is the period beginning twelve months before the start of the accounting period in question and ending when the unpaid tax first became payable.

The notice may require payment, within 30 days of service, of the unpaid tax or (in the case of a company within either or both of (2) and (3) above but not within (1) above) of an appropriate proportion thereof (see *FA 2000, Sch 28 para 5*). A payment made in pursuance of a notice is not an allowable deduction in computing profits, but the paying company may recover the amount from the non-resident company. The notice must state the amount of the unpaid tax, the date it first became payable and the amount required to be paid by the recipient. For recovery and appeals purposes, it has effect as if it were a notice of assessment of an amount of tax due from the recipient. INTEREST ON UNPAID TAX (41) runs from the original due date.

HMRC have three years from the date on which the liability of the non-resident company is finally determined (including a determination under *FA 1998, Sch 18 para 36* or *37* in the absence of a full return, see 61.18 RETURNS) in which to serve notice under these provisions. In the case of a self-assessed liability, including one superseding a determination, the date of determination of the liability is taken as the last date on which notice of an enquiry into the return may be given (see 61.10 RETURNS), or, if such notice is given, 30 days after the action which concludes the enquiry process (see 61.15 RETURNS). In the case of a discovery assessment (see 7.2 ASSESSMENTS), it is the due and payable date or (if there is an appeal against the assessment) the date the appeal is finally determined.

[*FA 2000, s 98, Sch 28*].

Simon's Direct Tax Service. See D2.642.

53.6 RECOVERY OF TAX FROM OFFICERS

Tax which has fallen due may be recovered from the treasurer or acting treasurer (the 'proper officer') of a company which is not a body corporate or not incorporated under a UK enactment or by charter. That officer then has a right of reimbursement out of moneys coming into his hands on behalf of that company, and to be indemnified by the company for any balance. [*TMA 1970, s 108(2)(3)*].

53.7 PARTNERSHIP LIABILITIES

See 52.6 PARTNERSHIPS.

53.8 **DATE OF PAYMENT**

As to the date on which tax is treated as having been paid, see 41.6 INTEREST ON UNPAID TAX.

53.9 **PAYMENT ELECTRONICALLY**

HMRC have been given the power to require tax to be paid electronically.

[*FA 2007, s 94*].

53.10 **OVER-REPAYMENTS**

Corporation tax over-repaid and not assessable under *FA 1998, Sch 18 para 41* may be assessed under Schedule D, Case VI as if it were unpaid tax. Any associated excess INTEREST ON OVERPAID TAX (40) may be included in the assessment. The time limit for such assessments is extended to the end of the accounting period following that of the repayment if it would otherwise be out of time, subject to the usual fraudulent or negligent conduct provisions.

Similar provisions apply to enable excess set-offs or payments of tax credit to be recovered, including any INTEREST ON OVERPAID TAX (40) in respect of tax credits.

Where the assessment is to recover a repayment of tax paid for an accounting period, or a repayment of tax on a payment received in an accounting period, the assessment is treated as being for that accounting period, and the sum assessed carries interest under *TMA 1970, s 87A* (see 41.1 INTEREST ON UNPAID TAX) from the date the repayment being recovered was made until payment.

These provisions also apply the discovery assessment rules of *FA 1998, Sch 18 paras 41–48* to recovery assessments, and extend the period during which assessments may be made to the completion of enquiries in certain cases. See 61.17 RETURNS.

[*ICTA 1988, s 252; FA 1998, Sch 3 para 21, Sch 18 paras 52, 53*].

Simon's Direct Tax Service. See **D2.826**.

53.11 **CERTIFICATES OF TAX DEPOSIT**

Companies may make deposits, evidenced by Certificates of Tax Deposit, with HMRC for the subsequent payment of tax, and any liability met by the tendering of such a deposit (and accrued interest) is treated as paid on the normal due date, or on the date of the deposit if later. Petroleum royalties may also be paid in this way. The minimum initial deposit is £500 with minimum additions of £250 subject to a continuing minimum of £500. Certificates are obtainable from the office of any Collector of Taxes. Deposits of £100,000 or over must be made by direct remittance to the Bank of England.

Series 7 Certificates may, however, not be purchased for use against corporation tax liabilities, income tax liabilities under PAYE or the construction industry tax deduction scheme, or VAT liabilities.

Interest, which is payable gross but taxable, will accrue for a maximum of six years from the date of deposit to the date of payment of tax (or, if earlier, the normal due date for payment of tax, i.e. disregarding the fact that the payment date may be later due to late issue of the assessment in question or to an appeal having been made against the assessment). A deposit may be withdrawn for cash at any time but will then receive a reduced rate of interest. Where a certificate is used in settlement of a tax liability, interest at the higher rate up to the normal due date may be less than interest at the encashment rate up to the reckonable date. In such circumstances the taxpayer may instruct the Collector to calculate interest on the latter basis. (ICAEW Technical Release TAX 13/93, 30 June 1993). The rates of interest, published by the Treasury, and calculated by reference to the rate on comparable investment with the Government, vary with the size and period of the deposit, and the rate payable on a deposit is adjusted to the current rate on each anniversary of the deposit.

Deposits are not transferable except in settlement of tax payable by the depositor's holding company, subsidiary company, or fellow-subsidiary.

Profits or gains on certificates of deposit issued after 31 March 1996 are chargeable to tax within the loan relationship provisions (see 46.46 LOAN RELATIONSHIPS). See HMRC Inspector's Manual, IM 4602.

For rates of interest, see Tolley's Income Tax under Certificates of Deposit. Information on current rates may be obtained from any Revenue Collection Office or from Inland Revenue Finance (CTD) on Worthing 01903 700222 ext 2064 or 2066 or from HMRC's website (www.hmrc.gov.uk/howtopay/ctd_interest_rates.pdf). See also HMRC's website (at www.hmrc.gov.uk/howtopay/cert_tax_deposit.htm).

Simon's Direct Tax Service. See A3.1335.

54 Penalties

Cross-reference. See also 60.7 RESIDENCE and 68.5 VALUE ADDED TAX.

Simon's Direct Tax Service A3.8, D2.846.

54.1 NOTIFICATION OF COMING WITHIN CHARGE TO CORPORATION TAX.

With effect for accounting periods beginning on or after 22 July 2004, a company (but not an unincorporated association or partnership) must give notice to HMRC of when its first accounting period begins (e.g. when the company starts its business) and of when any subsequent accounting period begins that does not follow on immediately from the end of a previous accounting period (see 61.1 RETURNS). Failure to do so renders the company liable to penalties under *TMA 1970, s 98* of up to £300 for the initial failure and up to £60 per day for continuing failure thereafter or, for fraudulently or negligently giving an incorrect notice, up to £3,000 (see 54.9 below). See 54.10 below as regards 'reasonable excuse' for failure. [*FA 2004, s 55*].

54.2 NOTIFICATION OF CHARGEABILITY

A company chargeable to corporation tax which has not already made a company tax return for an accounting period, and has not received a notice requiring such a return (see 61.3 RETURNS), must give notice of its chargeability to the inspector within twelve months from the end of the period.

Failure to do so under SELF-ASSESSMENT (62) renders the company liable to a penalty not exceeding so much of the tax payable for the period as remains unpaid twelve months after the end of the period, any relief deferred under *ICTA 1988, s 419(4A)* in respect of the repayment, etc. of a loan to a participator (see 16.12 CLOSE COMPANIES) being disregarded.

[*FA 1998, Sch 18 para 2*].

See 54.10 below as regards reasonable excuse for failure.

Simon's Direct Tax Service. See A3.816, D2.802.

54.3 PENALTIES FOR INACCURACIES IN DOCUMENTS FILED WITH HMRC

From a date to be fixed (expected to be 1 April 2008), a new regime is introduced for penalties in respect of errors in company tax returns claims for allowances, deductions or reliefs, other documents submitted to HMRC and in accounts forming the basis of a return. Any such regime will apply where an inaccuracy in the document provided leads to an underpayment of tax, over-repayment of tax or overstated statement of loss and where such an error was careless or deliberate.

The new regime will also apply where there is an understated assessment issued by HMRC and the taxpayer has not taken reasonable steps to notify them of the understatement within 30 days of the date of the under-assessment. In deciding whether or not reasonable steps were taken, HMRC will take into account what steps it would regard as reasonable, and whether the taxpayer knew or should have known about the understatement.

The amount of penalties (related to the degree of culpability in terms of percentage of 'potential lost revenue') is as follows:

- careless – i.e. the taxpayer has not taken reasonable care – 30%;
- deliberate but not concealed – i.e. no steps taken to conceal – 70%; and
- deliberate and concealed – 100%.

An inaccuracy in a document given to HMRC by the company which is neither careless or deliberate when it is given, is to be treated as careless if the company discovered the inaccuracy later and fails to take reasonable steps to inform HMRC.

The definition of '*potential lost revenue*' is the amount of tax due or payable as a result of correcting the error. The calculation differs depending on whether there was a single error or there were multiple errors. In a straightforward case, the calculation follows from the definition. Group relief is ignored in calculating potential lost revenue (although an inaccurate claim for relief may give rise to a penalty). Relief under *ICTA 1988, s 419(4)* where a loan to a participator is repaid or written off is also ignored. For multiple errors, careless inaccuracies are taken as corrected before deliberate inaccuracies and any over-statements relating to the same period are taken into account. Such overstatements are set off firstly against understatements not liable to a penalty, then careless understatements, then deliberate but not concealed understatements and finally against deliberate and concealed understatements. Possible overpayments to be repaid to another person are not taken into account. Where the error is in the quantum of a loss, and not all the loss has been set off in calculating a tax liability, the potential lost revenue is calculated as the total of the tax relating to the loss set off, plus 10% of the loss which was not so used. However, where there is no reasonable likelihood of the taxpayer using the loss, the potential lost revenue in respect of it is treated as nil. If the error has resulted in delaying a tax liability, the potential revenue lost is equivalent to 5% of the delayed tax for each year of delay.

Deductions from penalties are given for disclosure to HMRC. Disclosure must include telling HMRC about the inaccuracy, giving them reasonable help to quantify the tax lost and giving HMRC access to records. A 30% penalty may be reduced, or eliminated, where the taxpayer makes an unprompted disclosure and may be reduced to between 15% and 30% where he makes a prompted disclosure.

For a 70% penalty, an unprompted disclosure may allow HMRC to reduce the penalty to between 20% and 70% while for a prompted disclosure the penalty may be reduced to between 35% and 70%. For a 100% penalty, the reduction is from 30% to 100% and from 50% and 100% respectively for unprompted and prompted disclosures. In every case, HMRC decides on the reduction by considering the 'quality' of the disclosure (including timing, nature and extent). A disclosure is '*unprompted*' if it is made when the person making it has no reason to believe that HMRC has discovered or are about to discover the inaccuracy or under-assessment.

HMRC have the power to mitigate a penalty for special circumstances. Such special circumstances do not include ability to pay or the fact that the taxpayer's liability is compensated for by another taxpayer's overpayment. HMRC may suspend all or part of a penalty by giving the company notice in writing. The notice must state the part of the penalty to be suspended, the period of suspension (not more than two years) and the conditions with which the taxpayer company must comply. The penalty may only be suspended if the conditions would help the company to avoid further penalties for careless inaccuracies. The notice may state the action the company has to take and the timescale for this action. If, at the end of the period, the company can show that the conditions were complied with, the specified part or all the penalty may be cancelled, otherwise, the suspended part or all the penalty is payable. While a penalty is suspended, if the company becomes liable for another penalty, the suspended penalty becomes payable.

A penalty will be assessed, and the assessment will be treated like any other corporation tax assessment. Where there was an error in the return, the assessment must be issued within twelve months of the end of the appeal period for a return in respect of which the penalty was incurred or, if there is no such assessment, the date the error was corrected. Where there was an error in an assessment issued by HMRC, the assessment must be made within twelve months of the end of the appeal period for the amended assessment which corrected the understatement.

HMRC have the power to suspend all or part of a penalty for careless inaccuracy.

The taxpayer has a right of appeal to the General Commissioners.

Where HMRC think that a director or secretary of the taxpayer company was responsible for a deliberate error, that officer will be liable for the penalty along with the company.

No penalty is due in respect of any error where the taxpayer has been convicted of an offence in respect of it.

A company is liable for a careless inaccuracy in a document where the inaccuracy was caused by a third party acting on the taxpayer company's behalf (e.g. a professional agent). However, where the taxpayer company satisfies HMRC that it took reasonable care to avoid the inaccuracy or unreasonable failure, the company is not liable. In looking at the degree of culpability (see above) a reference to the taxpayer company includes a reference to a third party acting on its behalf. Where the taxpayer company is a member of a partnership, a co-partner may be liable to a penalty if the inaccuracy also affects the partner's tax liability. Potential lost revenue is to be calculated separately for each partner, the suspension rules will apply jointly to the company and its partner's penalty and a reference to the taxpayer company is to include a reference to the partner. The company has a right of appeal against the partner's penalty, in addition to its own rights of appeal.

These provisions will come into force at a date or dates to be determined by statutory instrument.

[*FA 2007, a 97; Sch 24*].

54.4 FAILURE TO RENDER RETURN

A company which fails to make a return for any period, when required to do so by notice (see 61.6 RETURNS), is liable to a penalty of £200 (£100 if the return is delivered within three months of the final day for delivery). If the return period is one for which accounts are required under *Companies Act 1985* (or NI equivalent), penalties do not apply provided that the return is delivered by the last day for delivery of those accounts. The penalties are increased to £1,000 and £500 respectively for failure in relation to a return for an accounting period where a penalty under these provisions was incurred for each of the two immediately preceding accounting periods, and the company was within the charge to corporation tax for the whole of the three accounting periods. (See *Lessex Ltd v Spence Sp C [2004] SSCD 79* where three successive defaults straddled the introduction of the self-assessment system applying to accounting periods ending on or after 1 July 1999 and a drafting error in *FA 1998, Sch 18 para 17(3)* was not considered to prevent the higher penalty from applying.) An additional penalty is imposed, where the return is still outstanding at the later of the end of the final day for delivery of the return and 18 months after the end of the return period. The additional penalty is 10% of the tax unpaid at the time the penalty arises if the return is delivered within two years after the end of the return period, otherwise 20%. The tax taken into account for this purpose under SELF-ASSESSMENT (62) is the tax payable for the return period, disregarding any relief deferred under *ICTA 1988, s 419(4A)* in respect of the repayment, etc. of a loan to a participator, see 16.12 CLOSE COMPANIES.

[*FA 1998, Sch 18 paras 17, 18, 19*].

By concession, automatic penalties are not charged provided that the return is received on or before the last business day within seven days following the filing date. (HMRC Extra-Statutory Concession, B46).

If, exceptionally, the company is unable to produce final figures for the return by the due date, it should make estimates to the best of its ability and alert the inspector to the basis on which the estimates are made. When the company can replace the estimates with accurate figures, or becomes aware that an estimate is no longer the best estimate, the inspector should be so informed without unreasonable delay. Provided these guidelines are followed, no late filing penalty (see above) or incorrect return penalty (see 54.5 below) should be imposed, provided in the latter case that neither fraud nor negligence was involved. The inclusion in a return of unreasonable estimates, while not invalidating the return, may render the company liable to incorrect return penalties. Any extension of the time limit for making a return under *TMA 1970, s 118(2)* (see 54.10 below) must be agreed with the inspector in advance. (HMRC Company Tax Manual, CT 10413).

See 54.10 below as regards reasonable excuse for failure.

See Revenue Tax Bulletin October 2003 p 1064 regarding the automation of late filing penalties.

Simon's Direct Tax Service. See A3.817, D2.821.

54.5 **NEGLIGENCE OR FRAUD**

The following provisions are repealed with effect from the introduction of the penalty provisions in 54.3 above.

The maximum penalty for negligently or fraudulently delivering, making, or submitting an incorrect return or claim for allowance or relief etc., or incorrect accounts, in addition to any tax actually chargeable, is the amount of tax underpaid, by reason of the incorrectness, for the accounting period(s) to which the return etc. relates.

See also 61.26 RETURNS.

Accounts are deemed to have been submitted on behalf of a company unless it is shown that they were submitted without the company's consent or connivance.

[*FA 1998, Sch 18 paras 20, 89*].

Simon's Direct Tax Service. See A3.810.

54.6 For the position if an agent is negligent or fraudulent, see *Mankowitz v Special Commrs Ch D 1971, 46 TC 707* and cf. *Clixby v Pountney Ch D 1967, 44 TC 515*. Assisting in, or inducing, the preparation or delivery of any information, return, accounts or other document known to be incorrect and to be, or to be likely to be, used for any tax purpose carries a maximum penalty of £3,000. [*TMA 1970, s 99; FA 1989, s 166*]. See also 54.15 below.

54.7 **FAILURE TO DISCLOSE TAX AVOIDANCE SCHEMES**

Failure to notify HMRC of the notifiable proposals or notifiable arrangements, or failure to notify the client of the relevant scheme reference number under the provisions of *FA 2004, ss 308(1)(3), 309(1), 310, s 312(1), s 313A, s 313B* (see 5.26 ANTI-AVOIDANCE) will render the scheme promoter etc. liable to a penalty of up to £5,000. A further penalty or penalties will be imposed of up to £600 for each day on which the failure continues after the above penalty is imposed.

A penalty of the 'prescribed sum' is provided for failure to comply with *FA 2004, ss 313A, 313B* (pre-disclosure enquiry). The 'prescribed sum' is to be determined by regulation.

Parties to notifiable arrangements who fail to notify HMRC of the scheme reference number etc. under *FA 2004, s 313(1)* will be liable to a penalty of £100 in respect of each scheme to which the failure relates. The penalty will be increased for a second failure, occurring within three years from the date on which the first failure began, to £500 in respect of each scheme to which the failure relates (whether or not the same as the scheme to which the first failure relates). Any further such failures occurring within three years from the date on which the previous failure began, will result in a penalty of £1,000 in respect of each scheme to which the failure relates (whether or not the same as the schemes to which any of the previous failures relates).

[*TMA 1970, s 98C; FA 2004, s 315(1); FA 2007, s 108 para 9*].

Simon's Direct Tax Service. See **A3.1935, A3.1936**

54.8 INTEREST ON PENALTIES

Penalties imposed under FA 1998, Sch 18 in connection with the company tax return, carry interest calculated from the due date (broadly, 30 days after issue of a notice of determination by an officer of HMRC or immediately upon determination by Appeal Commissioners or judgment of the High Court — see 53.10 below) to the date of payment. [TMA 1970, s 103A]. Rates of interest on penalties are synonymous with those on unpaid tax — see 41.1 INTEREST ON UNPAID TAX.

54.9 OTHER RETURNS ETC.

Failure to render any return, certificate, statement or other document required under the provisions listed in the Table in *TMA 1970, s 98* carries a maximum penalty of £300, plus £60 for each day the failure continues after that penalty is imposed (but not for any day for which such a daily penalty has already been imposed).

The maximum penalty for fraudulently or negligently making an incorrect return, etc. under any of these provisions is £3,000.

Penalties for failure to render information etc. required by notice cannot be imposed after the failure is rectified, and daily penalties can similarly not be imposed where the information etc. was required other than by notice. [*TMA 1970, s 98; FA 1989, s 164*].

Special penalties are imposed by regulation in relation to failure to make a return in accordance with provisions under the PAYE and CONSTRUCTION INDUSTRY SCHEME (20) regulations and under the mandatory PAYE e-filing regulations (see 33.10 HMRC: ADMINISTRATION). [*TMA 1970, s 98A; FA 1989, s 165; SI 1993 No 744* (*as amended by SI 2003 No 2494*)].

See 55.9 PROFIT COMPUTATIONS as regards penalties under *TMA 1970, s 98B* in relation to European Economic Interest Groupings.

Failure to allow access to computer records renders a person liable to a £500 penalty. [*FA 1988, s 127*].

For unlawfully possessing or disposing of an exemption certificate relating to a sub-contractor in the construction industry, or making false statements relating thereto, the maximum penalty is £3,000 (a maximum fine of £5,000 applying before 1 August 1999). [*ICTA 1988, s 561(10)(11); FA 1995, Sch 27 para 3*].

See 54.10 below as regards reasonable excuse for failure.

Penalties for failure to keep records as required under *FA 1998, Sch 18 para 21* (see 61.9 RETURNS) apply of up to £3,000. [*FA 1998, Sch 18 para 23*]. A penalty also applies of £50, plus a daily fine of up to £150 for continuing failure, for failure to provide documents as required under *FA 1998, Sch 18 para 27* (see 61.11 RETURNS).[*FA 1998, Sch 18 para 29*].

54.10 REASONABLE EXCUSE FOR FAILURE

It is generally provided that a person is deemed not to have failed to do anything required to be done where there was a reasonable excuse for the failure and, if the reasonable excuse ceased, provided that the failure was remedied without unreasonable delay after the excuse had ceased. Similarly, a person is deemed not to have failed to do anything required to be done within a limited time if he did it within such further time as HMRC, or the Commissioners or Revenue officer concerned, may have allowed. [*TMA 1970, s 118(2)*]. In *Creedplan Ltd v Winter (Sp C 54), [1995] SSCD 352*, the Special Commissioner, in confirming a penalty under *TMA 1970, s 94(1)(a)* (before its repeal on the introduction of self-assessment), considered that 'there is no reasonable excuse ... for sending in a return which was less than was required' (but cf. *Akarimsons Ltd v Chapman (Sp C 116), [1997]*

SSCD 140 in which a penalty under *section 94(1)(b)* was quashed). See also *Steeden v Carver (Sp C 212), [1999] SSCD 283*, in which reliance on HMRC's advice as to the practical extension of a deadline, unequivocally given, was held to be 'as reasonable an excuse as could be found'.

See HMRC Company Taxation Manual, CTM 94140 for HMRC approach to 'reasonable excuse'.

54.11 COMMISSIONERS' PRECEPTS

Summary penalties in accordance with *TMA 1970, s 98* (see 54.9 above) may be determined by Commissioners against an appellant who fails to comply with a precept, order for inspection, or other request for evidence. [*TMA 1970, ss 51, 53*]. If a person refuses or neglects to obey a witness summons; appears but refuses to be sworn; or refuses to answer any lawful question concerning the matters under consideration, the maximum penalty is £50 (with no provision for a continuing penalty). A person who is confidentially employed in the taxpayer's affairs (e.g. his servant or agent) has the right to refuse to be sworn or to answer any question to which he objects. [*TMA 1970, s 52*]. For appeals against summary penalties, see *QT Discount Foodstores Ltd v Warley Commrs Ch D 1981, 57 TC 268.*

54.12 PROCEDURE

The following does not apply to the penalties dealt with at 54.3 above.

Except in the case of:

(*a*) penalty proceedings instituted before the courts in cases of suspected fraud (see below);

(*b*) penalties imposed for failure to comply with Commissioners' precepts (see 54.11 above);

(*c*) penalties under:

- (i) *TMA 1970, s 93(1)(a)*,
- (ii) *TMA 1970, s 98(1)(i)* (see 54.9 above),
- (iii) *TMA 1970, s 98A(2)(a)(i)* (see 54.9 above), or
- (iv) *TMA 1970, s 98B(2)(a)* (see 54.9 above),

(for which see further below),

an authorised officer of HMRC may make a determination imposing a penalty of an amount which he considers correct or appropriate.

The notice of determination must state the date of issue and the time within which an appeal can be made. It cannot be altered unless:

(i) there is an appeal (see below); or

(ii) an authorised officer discovers that the penalty is or has become insufficient (in which case he may make a further determination); or

(iii) the penalty arises under *FA 1998, Sch 18 para 18(2)*, and an authorised officer subsequently discovers that the amount of tax is or has become excessive (in which case it is to be revised accordingly).

A penalty under these provisions is due 30 days after the date of issue of the notice of determination, and is treated as tax charged under an assessment and due and payable. [*TMA 1970, ss 100, 100A;*].

Appeals. The general appeals provisions (see APPEALS (6)) apply to an appeal against a determination as if it were an appeal against an assessment to tax, and the Commissioners are given broad specific powers to confirm, set aside or amend determinations.

Without prejudice to the general procedural rules in *TMA 1970, s 56*, an appeal against a determination lies to the High Court (in Scotland, the Court of Session). [*TMA 1970, s 100B*].

Proceedings before Commissioners. For a penalty within (*c*) above, an authorised officer may commence proceedings before the General or Special Commissioners. The proceedings are by way of information in writing to the Commissioners, and upon summons issued by them to the defendant (or defender), and are heard and decided in a summary way. An appeal lies to the High Court (or Court of Session) on a question of law or, by the defendant (defender), against the amount. The court can confirm, set aside or vary the determination as seems appropriate. The penalty is treated as tax charged in an assessment and due and payable. [*TMA 1970, s 100C*].

Proceedings before court. If HMRC consider that liability arises from fraud by any person, proceedings can be brought in the High Court (or Court of Session). If the Court does not find fraud proved, it can nevertheless impose a penalty to which it considers the person liable. [*TMA 1970, s 100D*].

General matters. Non-receipt of notice of the hearing at which the Commissioners awarded penalties is not a ground of appeal to the courts. A mere denial of liability to penalties implies an intention by the taxpayer to set up a case in refutation, and details must be supplied.

Statements made or documents produced by or on behalf of a company are admissible evidence in proceedings against it, notwithstanding that reliance on HMRC's practice in cases of full disclosure may have induced it to make or produce them. For statements made, or documents produced, on or after 10 July 2003, the detailed provision is amended to reflect changes to the 'Hansard' procedure (for which see Tolley's Income Tax under Fraudulent or Negligent Conduct: Offers by taxpayer). [*TMA 1970, s 105; FA 2003, s 206*].

The imposition of penalties calculated as a percentage of unpaid tax was held to be in the nature of 'criminal' (rather than 'civil') proceedings for the purposes of the European Convention on Human Rights in *King v United Kingdom (Nos 1 & 2), ECHR Case 13881/02, [2004] STC 911*.

For relevant cases, see Tolley's Income Tax and/or Tolley's Tax Cases.

Simon's Direct Tax Service. See **A3.820** *et seq*.

54.13 MITIGATION OR LIMITATION OF PENALTIES

The following mitigation rules do not apply to penalties under *FA 2007, Sch 24*. For the separate rules applicable to those penalties see 54.3 above.

HMRC may mitigate penalties before or after judgment [*TMA 1970, s 102*]. See Tolley's Tax Cases generally.

Where two or more tax-geared penalties relate to the same liability, the aggregate amount of the penalties is limited to the greater or greatest penalty applicable. [*TMA 1970, s 97A; FA 1998, Sch 18 para 90*].

Negotiated settlements. In the case of tax-based penalties where a maximum penalty of 100% is in strict law exigible, the inspector will start with the figure of 100% and then take the following factors into account in arriving at the penalty element which he will expect to be included in any offer in settlement of liabilities.

(*a*) Disclosure. A reduction of up to 20% (or 30% where there has been full voluntary disclosure), depending on how much information was provided, how soon, and how that contributed to settling the investigation.

(*b*) Co-operation. A reduction of up to 40%, depending upon a comparison of the extent of co-operation given in the investigation with the co-operation which the inspector believes would have been possible.

(*c*) Gravity. A reduction of up to 40%, depending upon the nature of the offence, how long it continued and the amounts involved.

(HMRC Pamphlet IR 160).

Simon's Direct Tax Service. See A3.826.

54.14 **TIME LIMITS**

The time within which a penalty can be determined, or proceedings commenced, depends on the penalty, as follows.

(*a*) If the penalty is ascertainable by reference to tax payable, the time is the later of six years after the penalty was incurred and three years after the determination of the amount of the tax.

(*b*) If the penalty arises under *TMA 1970, s 99* (see 54.6 above), the time is 20 years after the date when it was incurred.

(*c*) If the penalty is payable under *FA 2007, Sch 24 para 1*, the assessment must be made within twelve months from the end of the appeal period for the decision correcting the inaccuracy. If there was no assessment, the twelve-month period runs from the date on which the inaccuracy was corrected.

(*d*) If the penalty is payable under *FA 2007, Sch 24 para 2*, the time is twelve months from the end of the appeal period for the amended assessment which corrected the understatement.

(*e*) In any other case, the time is six years from the time when the penalty was, or began to be, incurred.

[*TMA 1970, s 103*].

Final determination of tax. Provisional agreement of the amount due subject to the inspector's being satisfied with statements of assets, etc. is not final determination for these purposes (*Carco Accessories Ltd v CIR CS 1985, 59 TC 45*).

Simon's Direct Tax Service. See A3.823.

54.15 **FAILURE TO STATE TAX CREDIT ETC.**

Failure to provide the required written statement of the amount of dividend or interest paid and the amount of the related tax credit etc. (see 23.17 DISTRIBUTIONS) carries a penalty of £60 for each offence with a maximum of £600 in respect of any one distribution etc. [*ICTA 1988, ss 234(4), 234A(9)*].

54.16 **LIABILITY UNDER CRIMINAL LAW**

'False statements to the prejudice of the Crown and public revenue' are criminal offences. (*R v Hudson CCA 1956, 36 TC 561*).

Apart from the above, false statements in income tax returns, or for obtaining any allowance, reduction or repayment may involve liability to imprisonment for up to two years, under the *Perjury Act 1911, s 5*, for 'knowingly and wilfully' making materially false statements or returns for tax purposes. Also, in Scotland, summary proceedings may be taken under *TMA 1970, s 107*.

The Crown Prosecution Service ('CPS') is not precluded from instituting criminal proceedings in circumstances where HMRC has accepted a monetary settlement. (*R v W and another CA, [1998] STC 550*). The Attorney-General made it clear, however, in a

Parliamentary Written Answer, that proceedings brought by the CPS will ordinarily encompass charges relating to tax evasion only in circumstances where that is incidental to allegations of non-fiscal criminal conduct. A 'Convention between Prosecuting Authorities to provide arrangements for ensuring effective co-ordination of decision making and handling in related cases which are the responsibility of different authorities' was established on 11 February 1998 (for which see the Attorney General's Press Release of that date). See Hansard Vol 310, No 155 at Cols 230, 231 and Revenue Tax Bulletin June 1998 pp 544, 545.

See HMRC Prosection Policy Statement (available on their website at www.hmrc.gov.uk/prosecutions/prosecution-policy.htm) and the HMRC Investigation Policy (at that address) which replaces HMRC Statement of Practice, SP 2/88 on its Prosecutions and Criminal Policy.

54.17 The penalties referred to at 54.2–54.16 above may also, where appropriate, apply to individuals. See Tolley's Income Tax (under Penalties) for these and also for procedure and other relevant cases.

55 Profit Computations

Cross reference. See subjects dealt separately under 1.2 INTRODUCTION AND RATES OF TAX, 5 ANTI-AVOIDANCE, 10 CAPITAL ALLOWANCES, 11 CAPITAL GAINS, 21 CONTROLLED FOREIGN COMPANIES, 24 DOUBLE TAX RELIEF, 26 FOREIGN EXCHANGE GAINS AND LOSSES, 28 FINANCIAL INSTRUMENTS AND DERIVATIVE CONTRACTS, 32 GROUPS OF COMPANIES, 37 INCOME TAX IN RELATION TO A COMPANY, 39 INTANGIBLE ASSETS, 42 INVESTMENT COMPANIES AND INVESTMENT BUSINESS, 46 LOAN RELATIONSHIPS, 47 LOSSES, 56 PROPERTY INCOME, 59 RESEARCH AND DEVELOPMENT EXPENDITURE, 60.3 RESIDENCE, 66 TRADING INCOME, 67 TRANSFER PRICING.

Simon's Direct Tax Service D2.2.

The headings in this chapter are as follows.

55.1 PROFITS TO BE INCLUDED

'Profits' are defined as 'income and chargeable gains' [*ICTA 1988, s 6*(*4*)(*a*)] and include:

(*a*) overseas profits of a UK resident company, whether remitted to the UK or not [*ICTA 1988, s 70*(*1*)];

(*b*) profits arising in the winding-up of a company [*ICTA 1988, s 8*(*2*)] (see 45 LIQUIDATION ETC.);

(*c*) profits accruing to the company's benefit under any trust, or arising from a PARTNERSHIP (52), which would be chargeable if they accrued to the company directly [*ICTA 1988, s 8*(*2*)]; and

(*d*) dividends or interest from BUILDING SOCIETIES (9).

Profits do not include dividends and any other DISTRIBUTIONS (23) from UK resident companies [*ICTA 1988, s 208*], nor profits accruing to the company in a fiduciary or representative capacity and in which it has no beneficial interest. [*ICTA 1988, s 8*(*2*)].

As regards certain directors' fees paid to other companies, see HMRC Extra Statutory Concession, A 37.

For treatment of profits arising from underwriting business of a corporate member of Lloyd's, see *FA 1994, ss 219–230, Sch 21* (as amended).

Periods of account. A '*period of account*' in relation to a trade or profession or other business means a period for which accounts are drawn up. [*ICTA 1988, s 832*(*1*); *FA 2002, s 103*(*1*)].

55.2 **Generally accepted accounting practice.** *FA 1998, s 42* provided that the profits of a trade, profession or vocation must generally be computed for tax purposes on an accounting basis giving a true and fair view, subject to any adjustment required or authorised by law. This imposes a general requirement to apply an earnings basis (see below) for tax purposes, whilst at the same time importing the accountancy concept of 'materiality', allowing a practical view to be taken of the time at which immaterial amounts are recognised. The 'true and fair view' rule requires neither the auditing of accounts, nor additional disclosure, nor the preparation of a true and fair view balance sheet. Neither does it require accounts to be drawn up on any particular basis (provided the necessary adjustments are made in the tax computation). See Revenue Press Release 17 March 1998. For HMRC's view of what is meant by 'true and fair view', see Revenue Tax Bulletin December 1998 pp 606–615. See HMRC Business Income Manual BIM 31045–31047 as regards the concept of materiality.

With effect from 24 July 2002, the above was replaced by a broadly similar requirement for trading profits to be computed in accordance with '*generally accepted accounting practice*' (GAAP) The term 'generally accepted accounting practice' is increasingly used throughout the *Taxes Acts*. The definition of '*generally accepted accounting practice*' is defined by *FA 2004, s 50* and, for periods of account beginning before 1 January 2005, by *ICTA 1988, s 836A*. Under the old rules, it is defined as meaning such practice as it applies for accounts of companies incorporated or formed under the law of any part of the UK drawn up on a true and fair view basis, and has the same meaning in relation to individuals, non-UK companies and entities other than companies. The requirement continues to be subject to any adjustment required or authorised by law; see, for example, the prohibition at 66.18 TRADING INCOME on deducting capital expenditure. With effect for periods of account beginning on or after 1 January 2005, the definition is extended to cover such practice as it applies for accounts of companies prepared in accordance with international accounting standards ('IAS accounts'), including the standards not yet adopted by the European Commission. [*ICTA 1988, s 836A; FA 2002, s 103(1)(2); FA 2004, s 50; FA 2005, s 80, Sch 4 paras 25, 49, 50*].

Where one company within a group of companies (as defined in *TCGA 1992, s 170(3)–(6)* – broadly, a a parent and its 75% subsidiaries) prepares accounts in accordance with international accounting standards and another company in the same group prepares accounts in accordance with UK generally accepted accounting practice and, as a result, a tax advantage is gained in relation to a transaction or a series of transactions, the profits will be computed for tax purposes as though both companies prepared accounts in accordance with UK generally accepted accounting practice. '*Tax advantage*' is as defined in *ICTA 1988, s 709* (see 5.2 ANTI-AVOIDANCE) and '*series of transactions*' is as defined by *ICTA 1988, Sch 28AA* – see 67.3 TRANSFER PRICING. [*FA 2004, s 51; FA 2005, Sch 4 para 50*].

For HMRC's view on the relationship between accounting profits and taxable profits, see HMRC Business Income Manual BIM 31000–31120 and Revenue Tax Bulletin December 1997 pp 485, 486, February 1999 pp 623–625, April 1999 pp 636–641, December 1999 pp 707–709, June 2001 pp 859, 860. For generally accepted accounting practice and accounting standards, see BIM 31020–31070.

See 66.5 TRADING INCOME generally for the application of accounting principles and 66.6 TRADING INCOME for the tax treatment where there is, from one period of account of a trade etc. to the next, a 'change of basis' in computing Schedule D, Case I or II profits. [*FA 2002, s 64, Sch 22; FA 2005, s 81*].

55.3 CORPORATION TAX COMPUTATIONS

Profits are computed *separately for each source* within the charge to corporation tax (see 1.2 INTRODUCTION and 60.3 RESIDENCE) under the income tax provisions applicable to income from that source as if the accounting period were a year of assessment, and in accordance with income tax law and practice (excluding provisions applicable solely to individuals, and subject to any special corporation tax provision, see below and 66 TRADING INCOME) for the year of assessment in which the accounting period ends, but on the basis *of the actual income arising in the accounting period.*

From the mid-1990s the move has been towards a separate computational regime for corporation tax, with special rules on, for example, interest (see 46 LOAN RELATIONSHIPS), INTANGIBLE ASSETS (39) and RESEARCH AND DEVELOPMENT (59). The law relating to the taxation of 'trading income' (previously within Schedules A, D and F and the cases of Schedule D) was consolidated in *Income Tax (Trading and Other Income) Act 2005* (*ITTOIA 2005*) as part of the Tax Law Rewrite programme, and has effect for income tax purposes for 2005/06 and subsequent years and, for corporation tax purposes where relevant, for accounting periods ending after 5 April 2005. [*ITTOIA 2005, s 883(1)*]. For corporation tax purposes, income continues to be computed and assessments made under Schedules A and D and the Cases of Schedule D, as if they were still part of income tax law, and not under *ITTOIA 2005*. Accordingly, it can no longer be assumed that the coverage in Tolley's Income Tax of any particular type of trading receipt or deduction etc. applies equally for corporation tax purposes and so all such matters are now dealt within this work – see in particular 66 TRADING INCOME.

Where a change in the law effected by *ITTOIA 2005* alters the tax consequences for an accounting period straddling 5 April 2005 of a transaction or event occurring before 6 April 2005, the company may elect for that change not to have effect as regards that period. For corporation tax purposes, the election must be made no later then two years after the end of the straddling accounting period. [*ITTOIA 2005, s 878(1), Sch 2 para 11*].

Save as otherwise provided, any provision of the Income Tax Acts (other than *ITTOIA 2005*) conferring an exemption from income tax also applies to corporation tax.

[*ICTA 1988, ss 9, 836B; ITTOIA 2005, Sch 1 paras 7; 340*].

Schedule D, Case III as it applies for corporation tax purposes encompasses tax in respect of non-trading profits or gains from loan relationships (see 46.3 LOAN RELATIONSHIPS), tax in respect of any annuity or other annual payment (not chargeable under Schedule A) payable in respect of anything other than a loan relationship (wherever, and at whatever intervals, payable), and (where it does not fall within the loan relationship rules, see 46.46 LOAN RELATIONSHIPS) any discount arising otherwise than in respect of a loan relationship. Schedule D, Case IV, and Case V in so far as it applies to profits or gains from loan relationships previously within Case III, are accordingly disapplied for corporation tax purposes. [*ICTA 1988, s 18(3A); F(No 2)A 2005, Sch 7 para 12(9); Sch 11 Pt 2(8)*].

Income of a trade assessable under Schedule D, Case V is to be computed in accordance with the rules of Schedule D, Case I. [*ICTA 1988, s 70(2)*]. Income from an overseas property business assessable under Schedule D, Case V (see 56 PROPERTY INCOME) is to be computed in accordance with the rules of Schedule A. [*ICTA 1988, s 70A*].

Corporation tax is charged under Schedule D, Case VI in respect of any annual profits or gains not falling under any other case of Schedule D and not charged by virtue of any other Schedule. [*ICTA 1988, s 18(3)*]. See 66.3 TRADING INCOME for post-cessation receipts chargeable to tax under Schedule D Case VI.

Under the Tax Law Rewrite programme, the provisions relating to income from employment, previously within Schedule E, are rewritten as part of the *Income Tax (Earnings and Pensions) Act 2003* ('*ITEPA 2003*'), which has effect for income tax purposes for 2003/04 and subsequent years and for corporation tax purposes for accounting periods ending after 5 April 2003. For accounting periods which straddle that date, the company may elect (by notice to HMRC within two years of the end of the accounting period) for the provisions as they applied prior to the rewriting to continue in force for that period. Otherwise, the transitional provisions in *ITEPA 2003* apply to the straddling period as if references to the tax year 2003/04 were references to the straddling period and as if references to 6 April 2003 were to the first day of the straddling period. Certain provisions relating to employee share schemes do not have effect for any part of an accounting period which falls before 6 April 2003. [*ITEPA 2003, s 723, Sch 7 paras 90–92*].

See 26.39 *et seq.* EXCHANGE GAINS AND LOSSES as regards use of currencies other than sterling.

Subject to any express authorising provision, no deduction may be made in computing profits in respect of any dividends or other DISTRIBUTIONS (23), nor in computing income from any source in respect of any charges on income (see 55.4 below). No deduction may be made in computing income from any source for corporation tax purposes in respect of interest (except under the LOAN RELATIONSHIPS (46) provisions) or (from 1 April 2002) losses from 'intangible fixed assets' (except under the INTANGIBLE ASSETS (39) provisions). [*ICTA 1988, s 337A* (*as amended by FA 2002, Sch 30 para 1*)*; previously ICTA 1988, ss 337(2), 337A; ICTA 1988, s 817; ITTOIA 2005, Sch 1 para 327*].

See, however, 55.4–55.6 below regarding allowance of 'charges on income'. See also 55.8 *et seq.* below and 66 TRADING INCOME as regards special corporation tax computational provisions.

Total profits for the accounting period are arrived at by aggregating the amounts shown by these separate computations.

See also 10 CAPITAL ALLOWANCES as to the means of making such allowances, and generally 55.18 *et seq.* below.

See 61.19 RETURNS as regards rounding of tax computations.

Simon's Direct Tax Service. See **D2.202** *et seq.*

55.4 ALLOWANCE FOR 'CHARGES ON INCOME'

Charges on income. Before *FA 1996* removed yearly interest from *ICTA 1988, s 338* and instead brought it within the loan relationship regime, the list of 'charges on income' that could be offset against profits for corporation tax purposes was extensive. The following items, so far as they are not dividends or other distributions and are not deductible in computing income (see below), are what remain (in considering the past six years) within the classification of 'charges on income'.

(*a*) For payments made before 16 March 2005 (subject to the transitional provisions below), any annuity or other annual payment (not being in respect of LOAN RELATIONSHIPS (46) (e.g. interest) or royalties within *FA 2002, Sch 29* (see INTANGIBLE ASSETS (39)).

(*b*) Before 1 April 2002, any royalty or other sum in respect of the user of a patent.

(*c*) Qualifying donations to charities (see 14.11 CHARITIES) notwithstanding the restrictions referred to below, and certain gifts of shares and securities to charities (see 14.14 CHARITIES).

As regards (*a*) above, payments made on or after 16 March 2005 are deductible as management expenses (see 42 INVESTMENT COMPANIES AND COMPANIES WITH INVESTMENT BUSINESS) (or expenses of an insurance company where they meet the requirements for such expenses and the following transitional rules apply.

- Where an accounting period straddles 16 March 2005, to the extent that an annuity or other annual payment made before 16 March 2005 is deductible as a charge on income, it is not deductible as a management expense or as an expense of an insurance company in that or any subsequent accounting period.
- Where an annuity or other annual payment is made on or after 16 March 2005 which would not have been deductible as a management expense or as an expense of an insurance company by reason only of it being treated as a charge on income, it is deductible as a management expense or as an expense of an insurance company for the accounting period in which the payment is made.

As part of the reform of corporation tax (see 1.1 INTRODUCTION AND RATES OF TAX) it is proposed that the concept of 'charges on income' be abandoned. In advance of the reform, annuities and other annual payments (in (*a*) above) have been removed by *F(No 2)A 2005* from the classification of charges on income as an anti-avoidance measure (see Explanatory Notes to Finance Bill 2005) so all that now remains as a charge on income are donations and gifts to charity under (*c*) above.

Specifically excluded from charges on income is:

(i) any payment *to* a non-resident *unless* the paying company is UK resident, and either the company deducts, and accounts under *ICTA 1988, Sch 16* (see 37.3 INCOME TAX IN RELATION TO A COMPANY) for, income tax under *ITA 2007, ss 449, 901, 903* (formerly *ICTA 1988, s 349*), or the payment is payable out of income chargeable under Schedule D, Case V, or (for payments made after 31 March 2001) the person beneficially entitled to the interest is a company which carries on a trade in the UK through a permanent establishment (see 60.5 RESIDENCE — previously a branch or agency) and in computing whose 'chargeable profits' (see 60.5, 60.6 RESIDENCE) the payment falls to be brought into account; and

(ii) any payment *by* a non-resident company *unless* it is incurred wholly and exclusively for the purposes of a trade carried on (or to be carried on) in the UK through a permanent establishment (see 60.5 RESIDENCE — previously a branch or agency); and

(iii) any payment which is charged to capital (see 55.6 below), or is not ultimately borne by the company; and

(iv) any payment not made under a liability incurred for valuable and sufficient consideration (in relation to which an expected business advantage is not sufficient, see *Ball v National and Grindlays Bank Ltd CA 1971, 47 TC 287*); and

(v) any annual payment for non-taxable consideration or, if made on or after 2 December 2004, for dividends within *ICTA 1988, s 125* (see 5.20 ANTI-AVOIDANCE).

As regards (i) above, a company is regarded as having deducted the full amount of income tax in cases where it deducts at a reduced rate, or makes no deduction, in accordance with a direction from HMRC International (see *SI 1970 No 488, reg 6*).

[*ICTA 1988, ss 125(1), 338–338B* (*ICTA 1988, s 338(2)–(7)* as originally enacted)*; FA 2001, s 85(3)(4); FA 2002, Sch 30 para 1(2); FA 2005, s 91; F(No 2)A 2005, s 38(8)–(13); Sch 11 Pt 2(7)*].

A sum is deductible in computing income when it is so deductible under the ordinary principles of commercial trading, whether or not it is actually so deducted (*Wilcock v Frigate Investments Ltd Ch D 1981, 55 TC 530*). For a case in which relief for interest paid under a circular arrangement was allowed, see *MacNiven v Westmoreland Investments Ltd HL 2001, 73 TC 1*.

Relief. Charges on income are deductible in the accounting period in which they are paid from company profits as reduced by all other reliefs except group relief (see 32.6 GROUPS OF COMPANIES). [*ICTA 1988, s 338* (*s 338(1)* as originally enacted); *FA 2002, Sch 30 para 1(2)*].

Annuities to former partners. Where a partnership business is incorporated, or a company takes over a partnership, and the agreement in either case refers to the company assuming responsibility for payment of an annuity to a former partner, then provided that the annuity is commercial in amount, the payment will not be prevented by (iii) above from being a charge on income. *ICTA 1988, s 125* (annual payments for non-taxable consideration, see 37.3(*a*) INCOME TAX IN RELATION TO A COMPANY) is not in practice considered to apply to such payments in respect of a *bona fide* commercial transaction. (HMRC Company Taxation Manual, CTM 09090).

Excess charges. Charges on income (provided that they are incurred wholly and exclusively for the purposes of a trade) are taken into account in computing losses to be carried forward and terminal losses, but not losses to be carried back. See 47.4–47.8 LOSSES.

Simon's Direct Tax Service. See **D2.210** *et seq*.

55.5 *Example*

X Ltd, a UK resident company, made a Schedule D, Case I profit of £30,000 in the year to 31 October 2005 and had Schedule A income of £25,000. It paid the following charges (shown gross).

	Situation (i)	Situation (ii)
	£	£
Annual payments (other than interest)		
paid 31 January 2005	25,000	2,500
paid 31 July 2005	25,000	2,500
Donations to charity	15,000	60,000

The corporation tax position is as follows.

	£	£
Schedule D, Case I	30,000	30,000
Schedule A	25,000	25,000
	55,000	55,000
Deduct: management expenses	(25,000)	(2,500)
	30,000	52,500
Charges on income £40,000/£62,500, restricted to	30,000	52,500
Chargeable profits	Nil	Nil
Excess charges carried forward	£10,000	£2,500
Unrelieved charitable donations		£7,500

55.6 **Charged to capital.** In a number of pre-corporation tax cases it was established that if in its commercial accounts a company elects to capitalise interest, e.g. interest on money borrowed to finance a capital scheme, thereby increasing the fund available for distribution to its shareholders, that interest cannot be said to have been paid out of its profits charged to income tax, with the consequence that it must account for the income tax deducted from the interest (under legislation similar to *section 349*). The leading case here is *Chancery Lane Safe Deposit & Offices Co Ltd v CIR HL 1965, 43 TC 83*, in which interest on moneys used to finance the reconstruction of the company's premises was capitalised. This decision was followed in *Fitzleet Estates Ltd v Cherry HL 1977, 51 TC 708*. See also *Central London Railway Co v CIR HL 1936, 20 TC 102* and *B W Nobes & Co Ltd v CIR HL 1965, 43 TC 133*.

55.7 **PARTICULAR COMPUTATIONAL MATTERS**

The following paragraphs refer to matters (in alphabetical order) relating to corporation tax, or of relevance to companies and not dealt with in the other chapters. See 66 TRADING INCOME for the computation of trading profits. See also 10 CAPITAL ALLOWANCES, 26 FOREIGN EXCHANGE GAINS AND LOSSES, 28 DERIVATIVE CONTRACTS AND FINANCIAL

INSTRUMENTS, 39 INTANGIBLE ASSETS, 46 LOAN RELATIONSHIPS, 56 PROPERTY INCOME and 59 RESEARCH AND DEVELOPMENT.

55.8 CONTAMINATED LAND REMEDIATION EXPENDITURE

Capital expenditure. Relief is available for capital expenditure incurred **on or after 1 April 2001** which is 'qualifying land remediation expenditure' incurred by a company in respect of 'land' in the UK acquired by the company for the purposes of a trade or Schedule A business carried on by it. '*Land*' is defined as 'any estate, interest or rights in or over land' and for these purposes, 'land' includes buildings (see HMRC Corporate Intangibles, Research & Development Manual, CIRD 60130 and *Interpretation Act 1978, Sch 1*).

This applies where, at the time of the acquisition, all or part of the land was in a contaminated state *other than* wholly or partly as a result of the company's own actions or inaction (or the actions or inaction of a person with a 'relevant connection' to the company). Such expenditure is, if the company so elects by written notice, allowed as a deduction in computing the profits of the trade or business for the accounting period in which the expenditure was incurred (and may also attract the enhanced deduction described below). If it was incurred before the trade or business was commenced, it is treated as having been incurred on the first day of trading. The election must specify the accounting period in respect of which it is made and must be made within two years after the end of that period. The relief does **not** apply to so much of the 'qualifying land remediation expenditure' as represents expenditure which has been allowed as a deduction for an earlier accounting period or in respect of which any CAPITAL ALLOWANCES (10) have been, or may be, given. [*FA 2001, s 70, Sch 22 para 1, Sch 23 para 1*].

See generally the HMRC Corporate Intangibles Research and Development Manual, CIRD 60000 *et seq.*

'*Qualifying land remediation expenditure*' is expenditure meeting the following five conditions.

(*a*) It must be on land all or part of which is in a '*contaminated state*', i.e. it is in such a condition, by reason of substances in, on or under it, that 'harm' is being caused (or there is a possibility of harm being caused) or 'pollution of controlled waters' (i.e. the entry into 'controlled waters' of any poisonous, noxious or polluting matter or any solid waste matter) is being, or is likely to be, caused. A 'nuclear site' (as defined) is excluded. '*Harm*' in this context means:

   (i) harm to the health of living organisms;

   (ii) interference with the ecological systems of which any living organisms form part;

   (iii) offence to the senses of human beings; or

   (iv) damage to property.

   '*Controlled waters*' are as under *Water Resources Act 1991, Pt III* or comparable Scottish or NI legislation.

(*b*) It must be on 'relevant land remediation' undertaken directly by the company or on its behalf. '*Relevant land remediation*' is the doing of any works, the carrying out of any operations or the taking of any steps in relation to the land (or adjoining or adjacent land), or any controlled waters affected by the state of that land, for the purpose of preventing or minimising, or remedying or mitigating the effects of, any harm, or any pollution of controlled waters, by reason of which the land is in a contaminated state, or restoring the land or waters to their former state. Preparatory activities are included provided that they are for the purpose of assessing the condition of the land or waters concerned and are connected to the remediation activities undertaken by the company or on its behalf.

(*c*) It must be incurred on employee costs (see below) or on materials employed directly in the remediation or be 'qualifying expenditure on sub-contracted land remediation'.

(*d*) It must be expenditure which would not have been incurred had the land not been in a contaminated state. Any increase in expenditure by reason only of the land being in a contaminated state is treated as satisfying this condition, as is expenditure on works done, operations carried out or steps taken mainly for the purposes described in (*b*) above.

(*e*) No grant or subsidy may be received in respect of the expenditure, nor may it be met directly or indirectly by any person other than the company (any unallocated payment being allocated for this purpose in a just and reasonable manner).

As regards (*c*) above, employee costs include all employment income (other than benefits in kind), employer NICs and pension contributions paid to, or in respect of, directors or employees directly and actively engaged in the relevant land remediation in (*b*) above. If between 20% and 80% of a director's or employee's time is spent directly and actively so engaged, an appropriate proportion of costs related to him or her qualify. If less than 20% is so spent, none of the costs qualify, and if more than 80%, all of the costs qualify. Staff providing support services (e.g. secretarial or administrative services) are not thereby treated as engaged in the activities they support. '*Qualifying expenditure on sub-contracted land remediation*' is expenditure consisting of payments made for sub-contracted remediation work. Except where the company and the sub-contractor are connected persons (within *ICTA 1988, s 839*), such payments qualify in full. Where the company and the sub-contractor are connected persons, then provided that, in accordance with generally accepted accounting practice (see 55.2 above), the whole of the sub-contractor payment and all of the sub-contractor's 'relevant expenditure' has been brought into account in determining the sub-contractor's profit or loss for a 'relevant period', the whole of the sub-contractor payment (up to the amount of the sub-contractor's 'relevant expenditure') qualifies. '*Relevant expenditure*' is expenditure on employee costs or materials (as under (*c*) above), not of a capital nature, which is incurred by the sub-contractor in carrying on, on behalf of the company, the activities to which the sub-contractor payment relates, and which satisfies (*e*) above. A '*relevant period*' is a period for which the sub-contractor draws up accounts and which ends not more than twelve months after the end of the period of account of the company in which, in accordance with generally accepted accounting practice (see 55.2 above), the sub-contractor payment is brought into account in determining the company's profit or loss. Any necessary apportionment of expenditure for these purposes is made on a just and reasonable basis.

A person has a '*relevant connection*' to a company if he is or was a 'connected person' within *ICTA 1988, s 839* either when the action (or inaction) in question occurred, or when the land in question was acquired by the company, or at any time when the remediation work was undertaken.

[*FA 2001, s 70, Sch 22 paras 2-11, 31; ITEPA 2003, Sch 6 para 258; FA 2004, Sch 17 para 7*].

Land remediation relief. Where 'qualifying land remediation expenditure' (as above) is incurred by a company **on or after 1 April 2001** in respect of land in the UK acquired by the company for the purposes of a trade or Schedule A business carried on by it, '*land remediation relief*' is available for the accounting period in which that expenditure is allowed as a deduction in computing profits of the trade or business. This applies where, at the time of the acquisition, all or part of the land was in a contaminated state *other than* wholly or partly as a result of the company's own actions or inaction (or the actions or inaction of a person with a relevant connection to the company, as above). [*FA 2001, s 70, Sch 22 para 12*]. The relief takes two forms.

(*a*) For any accounting period for which land remediation relief is available and in which the company is carrying on a trade or Schedule A business in computing profits from which qualifying land remediation expenditure is deductible (including capital expenditure allowed as a trade deduction as above), the company may claim relief for an additional 50% of that expenditure, i.e. for **150%** of that expenditure in total. [*FA 2001, s 70, Sch 22 para 13*].

(*b*) For an accounting period in which the company has a 'qualifying land remediation loss', it may claim a '*land remediation tax credit*' equal to 16% of the amount of that loss. The 16% figure is subject to revision by the Treasury by order. A '*qualifying land remediation loss*' arises for an accounting period in which the company is entitled to relief under (*a*) above and incurs a loss in the trade or Schedule A business concerned. The amount of the qualifying land remediation loss is so much of the trading or Schedule A business loss as is 'unrelieved' or, if less, 150% of the related qualifying land remediation expenditure. A trading or Schedule A business loss is '*unrelieved*' for this purpose to the extent that the loss has not and could not have been relieved by a claim under *ICTA 1988, s 393A*(*1*)(*a*) or *s 392A*(*1*) (against profits of the same period, see 47.2, 47.22 LOSSES), and has not otherwise been relieved (including under *ICTA 1988, s 393A*(*1*)(*b*) against profits of earlier periods, see 47.6 LOSSES), and has not been surrendered under *ICTA 1988, s 403*(*1*) (group or consortium relief, see 32.6 *et seq*. GROUPS OF COMPANIES). Losses carried back or brought forward to the accounting period in question are disregarded for this purpose. Special rules apply to Schedule A business losses treated under *ICTA 1988, s 432AB*(*3*) as expenses of an insurance company. [*FA 2001, s 70, Sch 22 paras 14, 15; SI 2004 No 2310, Article 58*].

See below as regards claims for land remediation tax credits. On such a claim, HMRC will pay to the company the amount of the tax credit, and the amount of the company's trading or Schedule A business losses available to be carried forward from the period will accordingly be reduced by the amount of the qualifying land remediation loss for the period (or by a corresponding proportion thereof where the amount of the tax credit claimed was less than 16% of the qualifying land remediation loss). Special rules apply to restrict the carry forward of Schedule A business losses treated under *ICTA 1988, s 432AB*(*3*) as expenses of an insurance company. Where a tax credit has been claimed in respect of a qualifying land remediation loss, the related qualifying land remediation expenditure is treated as non-allowable expenditure for capital gains tax purposes under *TCGA 1992, s 39*. [*FA 2001, s 70, Sch 22 paras 16*(*1*), *17, 19; SI 2004 No 2310, Article 59*].

The tax credit payment is not treated as income for any tax purposes, and (together with any interest paid with it, see below) may be applied to any corporation tax liability of the company. Where there is an enquiry into the company's tax return for the period (see 61.10 RETURNS), payment need not be made until the enquiry is completed (although HMRC has discretion to make a payment on a provisional basis if they think fit). Similarly payment need not be made until all PAYE and NICs payments for payment periods (i.e. periods ending on the fifth day of each month for which liability to account for PAYE and NICs arises) ending in the accounting period have been made. [*FA 2001, s 70, Sch 22 paras 16*(*2*)–(*5*)].

Claims and overpayments. As regards (*b*) above, a claim for payment of a land remediation tax credit must be made in a company tax return (or amended return) (see 61.3 RETURNS) for the accounting period for which the credit is claimed, within one year of the filing date for that return (see 61.8 RETURNS) or by such later time as HMRC may allow. It can similarly only be amended or withdrawn by amendment of the company tax return within the same time limit. It must specify the quantum of the amount claimed. Penalties not exceeding the excess credit claimed apply for fraudulent or negligent claims, and for failure to remedy other incorrect claims without unreasonable delay. [*FA 1998, Sch 18 paras 10*(*2A*), *83G–83L; FA 2001, Sch 23 paras 4, 6*]. For recovery of overpayments of land remediation tax credit, see 61.17 RETURNS.

INTEREST ON OVERPAID TAX (40) applies to land remediation tax credit payments from the filing date (see 61.3 RETURNS) for the company tax return for the accounting period for which the credit is claimed (or if later the date of receipt by HMRC of the return (or amended return) containing the claim) until payment. Such interest is recovered (as if it were INTEREST ON UNPAID TAX (41)) where there is a change in the tax credit payable resulting in an assessment (or amendment) to recover an amount of the credit (unless the change in the available credit results in a change in the company's corporation tax liability – see 40.1(vi) INTEREST ON OVERPAID TAX – or is in whole or part to correct an HMRC error). [*ICTA 1988, s 826(1)(e)(3B)(8A)(8BA); FA 2001, Sch 23 para 3*].

Anti-avoidance. Any transaction attributable to arrangements (including any scheme, agreement or understanding, whether or not legally enforceable) whose sole or main object is to enable a company to obtain a relief or payment under any of the above provisions to which it would not otherwise be entitled, or a greater relief or payment than that to which it would otherwise be entitled, is disregarded in determining the amount of any such relief or payment. [*FA 2001, Sch 22 para 29*].

Life assurance business. Where profits arising to an insurance company from life assurance business are computed as under Schedule D, Case I, the reliefs referred to above do not apply. [*FA 2001, Sch 22, para 20*]. For the special provisions where life assurance business profits are not so computed, see *FA 2001, Sch 22 paras 21-28* as amended by *SI 2004 No 2310, Articles 60–63*.

55.9 EUROPEAN ECONOMIC INTEREST GROUPINGS

A European Economic Interest Grouping ('EEIG') within *Directive No. 2137/85/EEC* (which applies to all EEIGs established within the European Economic Area), wherever it is registered, is regarded as acting as the agent of its members. Its activities are regarded as those of its members acting jointly, each member being regarded as having a share of EEIG property, rights and liabilities. With effect for accounting periods beginning *on or after 1 October 2002*, however, the loan relationship rules have effect in relation to a grouping as if it were a partnership (in particular in the application of *FA 1996 s 87A, Sch 9 paras 19, 20*, see 46.16, 46.17, 46.27 LOAN RELATIONSHIPS). A person is regarded as acquiring or disposing of a share of the EEIG assets not only where there is an acquisition or disposal by the EEIG while he is a member but also where he becomes or ceases to be a member or there is a change in his share of EEIG property.

A member's share in EEIG property, rights or liabilities is that determined under the contract establishing the EEIG or, if there is no provision determining such shares, it will correspond to the profit share to which he is entitled under the provisions of the contract. If the contract makes no such provision, members are regarded as having equal shares.

Where the EEIG carries on a trade or profession, the members are regarded for the purposes of tax on income and gains as carrying on that trade or profession in partnership.

[*ICTA 1988, s 510A; FA 2002, Sch 25 para 49*].

Contributions to an EEIG from its members are not assessable on the EEIG, and the members are not assessable on distributions from the EEIG. (HMRC EEIGs Manual, EEIG 34).

For the purposes of making assessments to income tax, corporation tax or capital gains tax on members of EEIGs (or of securing that members are so assessed), an inspector may, in the case of an EEIG which is registered, or has an establishment registered, in Great Britain or Northern Ireland, by notice require the EEIG to make a return containing such information as the notice may require, accompanied by such accounts and statements as the notice may require, within a specified time. In any other case, he may issue a similar notice to any UK resident member(s) of the EEIG (or if none is so resident, to any member(s)). Notices may differ from one period to another and by reference to the person on whom they are served or the description of EEIG to which they refer. Where a notice is given to an EEIG registered in Great Britain or Northern Ireland (or having an establishment registered there), the EEIG must act through a manager, except that if there is no manager who is an individual, the EEIG must act through an individual designated as a representative of the manager under the *Directive.* The return must in all cases include a declaration that, to the best of the maker's knowledge, it is correct and complete, and where the contract establishing the EEIG requires two or more managers to act jointly for the EEIG to be validly bound, the declaration must be given by the appropriate number of managers. [*TMA 1970, s 12A*].

A penalty not exceeding £300 (and £60 per day for continued failure) may be imposed in the case of failure to comply with a notice under the above provisions. The penalties are multiplied by the number of members of the EEIG at the time of the failure or at the end of the day for which a continuing penalty is imposed. No penalty may be imposed after the failure has been remedied, and if it is proved that there was no income or chargeable gain to be included in the return, the maximum penalty is £100. Fraudulent or negligent delivery of an incorrect return, etc. or of an incorrect declaration may result in a penalty not exceeding £3,000 for each member of the EEIG at the time of delivery, and the act or omission giving rise to the penalty is treated as the act or omission of each member of the EEIG for the purposes of fraud or negligence assessments and consequential claims. [*TMA 1970, ss 36(4), 98B; FA 1998, Sch 18 para 91*].

Simon's Direct Tax Service. See D4.901–D4.903.

55.10 HERD BASIS

See generally HMRC Business Income Manual BIM 55501–55640.

Animals kept for the purposes of a trade. Animals and other living creatures kept for the purposes of farming or similar trades (e.g. animal or fish breeding) are generally treated as trading stock (see 66.75 TRADING INCOME) unless:

- they are part of a herd in relation to which an election is made under *ICTA 1988, s 97, Sch 5* for the 'herd basis' to apply; or
- the animals etc. are kept wholly or mainly for the work they do in connection with the trade or for public exhibition or racing or other competitive purposes.

[*ICTA 1988, s 97, Sch 5 paras 1, 7, 9(1)(2)(5) ITTOIA 2005, Sch 1 para 343*].

Animals etc. are exempt from capital gains tax as wasting assets within *TCGA 1992, s 45*.

Herd basis — definitions. For the purposes of the herd basis rules, an '*animal*' means any living creature, a '*herd*' includes a flock and any other collection of animals, and a '*production herd*' means a herd of animals of the same species, irrespective of breed, kept by a farmer or other trader wholly or mainly for the saleable produce obtainable from the living animal, which includes the young of the animal and any other product obtainable from it without slaughtering it. The herd basis provisions apply equally to animals kept singly and to shares in animals.

Immature animals kept in a production herd are generally not regarded as part of the herd for these purposes, but if:

- the nature of the land on which the herd is kept is such that replacement animals have to be bred and reared on that land (e.g. acclimatised hill sheep);
- the immature animals in question are bred and maintained in the herd for the purpose of replacing animals in the herd;
- it is necessary to maintain the immature animals for that purpose,

the immature animals are regarded as part of the herd in so far as they are required to prevent a fall in numbers.

An immature animal which is not regarded as part of the herd is regarded as added to the herd when it reaches maturity. Female animals are treated as becoming mature when they produce their first young or, in the case of laying birds, when they first lay (but see below as regards temporary concession during the 2001 foot and mouth outbreak).

[*ICTA 1988, Sch 5 para 8(1)–(5), para 9(2)–(4); ITTOIA 2005, Sch 1 para 343*].

Herd basis elections. An election for the herd basis to have effect must specify the class of production herd to which it relates and must be made not later than two years after the end of the first accounting period during the whole or part of which a production herd of the class specified was first kept by the company. The election is irrevocable, and has effect in relation to all the production herds of the class to which it relates, including any which the farmer has ceased to keep before making the election or starts to keep after making the election. The election cannot relate to more than one class of production herd, but separate elections can be made for different classes. Two or more production herds are of the same class if the animals kept in those herds are of the same species (irrespective of breed) and the saleable produce for which the herds are wholly or mainly kept is of the same kind. An election has effect for every accounting period in which the farmer carries on the trade and keeps a production herd of the relevant class. [*ICTA 1988, Sch 5 paras 2, 8(6); ITTOIA 2005, Sch 1 para 343*].

See below as regards a further opportunity to make an election in a case of compulsory slaughter.

Further assessments may be made for any accounting period as necessary, and repayments may be made (on a claim), to give effect to a herd basis election. [*ICTA 1988, Sch 5 para 11); ITTOIA 2005, Sch 1 para 343*].

Five-year gap between keeping herds. If a farmer has kept a production herd of a particular class and then ceases to keep herds of that class for at least five years, the farmer is thereafter treated as if he had never previously kept a herd of that class. In HMRC practice (in HMRC Business Income Manual BIM 55630), any herd basis election previously made in relation to herds of that class is automatically allowed to lapse. (This is given statutory effect for income tax purposes for 2005/06 onwards (see Change 36 listed in Annex 1 to the Explanatory Notes to the Income Tax (Trading and Other Income) Bill).) [*ICTA 1988, Sch 5 para 4; ITTOIA 2005, Sch 1 para 343*].

Consequences of herd basis election. Where a herd basis election is in force, the animals in the herd are in effect treated as capital assets instead of as trading stock. The initial cost of the herd is not deductible in computing trading profits, and its value is not brought into account. No deduction is allowed for additions to the herd (as opposed to replacement animals — see below). If the additional animal was previously part of trading stock, a receipt must be brought into account equal to the cost of breeding it, or acquiring it, and rearing it to maturity. If it is not possible to ascertain actual costs of breeding and rearing, an alternative deemed cost method may be used (HMRC Business Income Manual BIM 55410, 55530). [*ICTA 1988, Sch 5 para 3(2)(3); ITTOIA 2005, Sch 1 para 343*].

Replacement animals. The replacement of an animal dying or ceasing to be a member of a herd gives rise to a trading receipt equal to the disposal proceeds (if any) of the animal replaced, and a trading deduction equal to the cost of the replacement animal (so far as not otherwise allowable) but limited to the cost of an animal of similar quality to that replaced (for which see Revenue Tax Bulletin October 2001 pp 890, 891). See below for meaning of disposal proceeds. Where the animal replaced was compulsorily slaughtered, and the replacement animal is of inferior quality, the trading receipt is restricted to the amount allowable as a deduction in respect of the new animal. [*ICTA 1988, Sch 5 para 3(4)–(6), (12); ITTOIA 2005, Sch 1 para 343*].

Whether a particular animal brought into the herd replaces an animal disposed of is a question of fact, requiring a direct connection between the disposal and the later addition rather than a simple restoration of numbers. As a practical matter, HMRC will accept that replacement treatment is appropriate where animals are brought into the herd within twelve months of the corresponding disposal. Where disposal and replacement are in different accounting periods, the overall profit or loss may either be brought in in the first period and any necessary adjustment made in the second, or the profit or loss arising in the first period may be held over to the second period. Where the interval is more than twelve months, there is unlikely to be sufficient evidence to support the necessary connection where the new animal is bought in. Where animals are home bred, however, a longer interval may be reasonable where e.g. there is insufficient young stock to replace unexpected disposals. (See HMRC Business Income Manual, BIM 55520 and Revenue Tax Bulletin February 1997 p 396).

Where the whole herd is replaced, this is treated as the replacement of a number of animals, being the smaller of the number in the old herd and in the new. [*ICTA 1988, Sch 5 para 3(7)*]. Where the new herd is the larger, the net increase will be treated as additions to the herd. Where the new herd is the smaller, but not substantially so (i.e. the provisions described below in relation to a substantial reduction do not apply), the net reduction in the number of animals is treated as giving rise to a corresponding sale without replacement (see below). [*ICTA 1988, Sch 5 para 3(11)*].

Disposal of animals from the herd. Where an animal is disposed of from the herd, any profit is brought into account as a trading receipt and any loss is deductible as an expense. This does not apply if the animal is replaced (for which see above) or on a disposal of the whole or a substantial part of the herd within a 12-month period (for which see below). The profit or loss is computed by reference to disposal proceeds and the cost of breeding the animal, or acquiring it, and rearing it to maturity. Market value is substituted for acquisition cost if the animal was acquired other than for valuable consideration. [*ICTA 1988, Sch 5 para 3(10); ITTOIA 2005, Sch 1 para 343*]. For HMRC's interpretation of this provision, including a change of view on how the profit on such disposals is to be computed, see Revenue Tax Bulletin April 2003 pp 1024, 1025.

For the purposes of the herd basis rules, the disposal of an animal includes its death or destruction as well as its sale, and disposal proceeds include sale proceeds and, in the case of death or destruction, insurance or compensation money received and proceeds of carcass sales. [*ICTA 1988, Sch 5 para 3(12); ITTOIA 2005, Sch 1 para 343*].

On the disposal of the whole or a substantial part of the herd, either all at once or over a period of 12 months or less, any profit is not brought into account as a receipt and any loss is not deductible as an expense. (A 'substantial' part of the herd is regarded as 20% or more of it (but this does not prevent a smaller percentage from being regarded as 'substantial' in any particular case). This reflects HMRC practice — see HMRC Business Income Manual BIM 55525, but has statutory effect for income tax purposes for 2005/06 onwards.) If, however, the farmer acquires, or starts to acquire, a new production herd of the same class within five years of the disposal, the replacement rules above apply and the disposal proceeds of any animal are brought into account when the 'replacement' animal is acquired.

Where the disposal of all or a substantial part of a herd is for reasons wholly outside the trader's control and a 'replacement' animal is of inferior quality to the old, the replacement rules above apply as they do when animals are slaughtered under a compulsory slaughter order (whether or not that is indeed the case).

[*ICTA 1988, Sch 5 para 3(7)–(9); ITTOIA 2005, Sch 1 para 343*].

Elections following compulsory slaughter. Where compensation is receivable in respect of the whole, or a substantial part (normally 20% or more), of a production herd slaughtered by order under animal diseases laws, the farmer may, notwithstanding the time limits above, elect for the herd basis to apply. The election must be made not later than two years after the end of the qualifying accounting period, i.e. the first accounting period in which the compensation falls (or would otherwise fall) to be taken into account as a trading receipt. The election has effect for that accounting period and each subsequent accounting period of account in which the farmer carries on the trade and keeps a production herd of that class. [*ICTA 1988, Sch 5 para 6; ITTOIA 2005, Sch 1 para 343*].

Compensation paid under the BSE Suspects Scheme and the BSE Selective Cull (where the animal was born after 14 October 1990) is for compulsory slaughter, and for these purposes includes Selective Cull 'top-up' payments. Payments under the Calf Processing Scheme, the Over Thirty Month Scheme and the BSE Selective Cull where the animal was born before 15 October 1990 are *not* for compulsory slaughter. See Revenue Tax Bulletin February 1997 pp 396, 397 for this and for the application of these provisions to BSE compensation generally. For compulsory slaughter in cases where the herd basis does not and could not apply, see 66.50(*a*) TRADING INCOME.

Anti-avoidance. There are provisions for the prevention of avoidance of tax in the case of a non-arm's length transfer of all or part of a production herd where either transferor and transferee are bodies of persons under common control or the sole or main benefit of the transfer relates to its effect on a herd basis election. [*ICTA 1988, Sch 5 para 5*].

Information etc. Where an election has effect, HMRC may by notice require the farmer to make returns of information as to the animals kept and their produce. [*ICTA 1988, Sch 5 para 10*].

Foot and mouth outbreak 2001. For the full range of measures, including acceptance of herd basis elections, in relation to the 2001 foot and mouth disease outbreak, see Revenue Tax Bulletin Special Edition May 2001 and Revenue Tax Bulletin October 2001 pp 890, 891. In particular, by concession, certain replacement animals slaughtered before giving birth may be regarded as having been mature notwithstanding *ICTA 1988, Sch 5 para 8(4)* (see above), and hence treated as having been part of the herd rather than trading stock (HMRC Extra Statutory Concession B56).

Simon's Direct Tax Service. See **B3.515** *et seq.*

Example

A farming company acquires a dairy herd and elects for the herd basis to apply. The movements in the herd and the tax treatment are as follows.

Year 1	*No*	*Value*
		£
Mature		
Bought @ £150	70	10,500
Bought in calves @ £180		
(Market value of calves £35)	5	900
Immature		
Bought @ £75	15	1,125

55.10 Profit Computations

Year 1	No	Value
		£
Herd Account		
Friesians	70	10,500
Friesians in calf (5 × £(180 – 35))	5	725
Closing balance	75	£11,225
Trading Account		£
Calves (5 × £35)	5	175
Immature Friesians	15	1,125
Debit to profit and loss account		£1,300

Year 2	No	Value
		£
Mature		
Bought @ £185	15	2,775
Sold @ £200	10	2,000
Died	3	—
Immature		
Born	52	—
Matured @ 60% of market value of £200 (note (*a*))	12	1,440

Herd Account	No	No	£	£
Opening balance		75		11,225
Increase in herd				
Purchases	15		2,775	
Transferred from trading stock	12		1,440	
	27			
			4,215	
Replacement cost £4,215 × 13⁄27	(13)		2,029	
Non-replacement animals cost		14		2,186
Closing balance		89		£13,411

Year 2

	No	Value £
Trading Account		£
Sale of 10 mature cows replaced		(2,000)
Transfer to herd — 14 animals		(2,186)
Cost of 13 mature cows purchased to replace those sold/deceased (13/15 × £2,775)		2,405
Net credit to profit and loss account (note (*b*))		£(1,781)

Year 3

	No	Value £
Mature		
Jerseys bought @ £250	70	17,500
Friesians slaughtered @ £175 (market value £185)	52	9,100
Immature		
Friesians born	20	—
Matured		
Friesians @ 60% of market value of £190 (note (*a*))	15	1,710

Herd Account	No	£	£
Opening balance	89		13,411
Increase in herd			
Jerseys	18		4,500
52 Improvement Jerseys @		250	
less Market value of Friesians		185	
52 @		65	3,380
Transfer from trading stock			
Friesians	15		1,710
Closing balance	122		£23,001

Trading Account	£
Compensation	(9,100)
Transfer to herd	(1,710)
Purchase of replacements (note (*c*)) (52 × £185)	9,620
Net credit to profit and loss account	£(1,190)

Year 4

The farmer ceases dairy farming and sells the whole herd.

		No	Value
			£
Mature			
Jerseys sold @ £320		70	22,400
Friesians sold @ £200		52	10,400
Immature			
Friesians sold @ £100		65	6,500

Herd Account			£
Opening balance		122	23,001
Friesians	52		
Jerseys	70		
Sales		(122)	(32,800)
Profit on sale (note (*d*))			£(9,799)

Trading Account	£
Sale of 65 immature Friesians	(6,500)
Credit to profit and loss account	£(6,500)

Notes

(*a*) The use of 60% of market value was originally by agreement between the National Farmers' Union and HMRC (see HMRC Business Economic Note 19: Farming — Stock Valuation for Income Tax purposes, at paragraph 7.2). Alternatively, the actual cost of breeding or purchase and rearing could be used.

(*b*) As the cost of rearing the 12 cows to maturity will already have been debited to the profit and loss account, no additional entry is required to reflect that cost. Due to the fact that the animals were in opening stock at valuation and will not be in closing stock, the trading account will in effect be debited with that valuation.

(*c*) The cost of the replacements is restricted to the cost of replacing like with like.

(*d*) Provided these animals are not replaced by a herd of the same class within five years the proceeds will be tax-free.

55.11 INTELLECTUAL PROPERTY

For corporation tax purposes, expenditure and receipts in respect of intellectual property created or acquired from an unrelated party **on or after 1 April 2002** generally falls within the intangible assets regime. See in particular the commencement and transitional rules for that regime at 39.37 INTANGIBLE ASSETS. The provisions below apply (subject to the transitional provisions) to expenditure on such assets not falling within that regime.

See 10.23 and 10.50 CAPITAL ALLOWANCES for allowances on capital expenditure in acquiring know-how and patent rights; 37.3 and 37.4 INCOME TAX IN RELATION TO A COMPANY for patent royalties and other royalties paid to non-residents; 24.4 DOUBLE TAX RELIEF for DTR treatment of royalties from abroad; 27.12 EXEMPT ORGANISATIONS as regards research institution spin-out companies; 66.30, 66.62, 66.66, 66.67 and 66.73 TRADING INCOME for trading receipts and expenses with regard to intellectual property.

Simon's Direct Tax Service. See **B3.8.**

Income from intellectual property. Where not treated as trading etc. receipts, royalties, patent income and other income from 'intellectual property' is chargeable, on general principles (see 55.3 above), under Schedule D, Case VI if from a UK source, or Case V if from a non-UK source. [*ICTA 1988, s 18*].See also below for the spreading of patent royalties etc. over several tax years.

For income tax purposes for 2005/06 onwards, 'intellectual property' is specially chargeable to income tax under *ITTOIA 2005, Pt 5 Ch 2*. For these purposes, '*intellectual property*' is defined in *ITTOIA 2005, s 579* as:

(*a*) any patent, trade mark, registered design, copyright, design right or performer's or plant breeder's right;

(*b*) any rights under the law of any part of the UK which are similar to such rights;

(*c*) any rights under the law of any territory outside the UK which correspond or are similar to such rights; and

(*d*) any idea, information or technique not protected by a right within (*a*)–(*c*) above

Intellectual property is similarly defined for corporation tax purposes under *FA 2000, Sch 20 para 7* in relation to RESEARCH AND DEVELOPMENT EXPENDITURE (59.2(3)) but otherwise definitions are provided only for:

- '*patent rights*', which means the right to do or authorise the doing of anything which would, but for the right, be an infringement of a patent. [*ICTA 1988, s 533(1)*]; and
- '*know-how*', which means any industrial information or techniques likely to assist in manufacturing or processing goods or materials, in working a mine, oil-well or other source of mineral deposits (including searching for, discovery or testing of deposits or winning access thereto), or in carrying out any agricultural, forestry or fishing operations. [*ICTA 1988, s 533(7)*]. HMRC consider that it does not include information about marketing, packaging or distribution Revenue Tax Bulletin, August 1993 p 86).

Patent royalties may be subject to deduction of tax at source (see 37.3 and 37.4 INCOME TAX IN RELATION TO A COMPANY), as are other royalties paid to non-UK residents

Patent income and expenses. '*Patent income*' means any royalty or other sum paid in respect of the use of a patent or any amount on which corporation tax is payable in relation to (i) the sale of patent rights under *ICTA 1988, ss 524, 525* (see below) or (ii) balancing charges under the capital allowances code for patent rights (see 10.50 CAPITAL ALLOWANCES).

Relief can be claimed for expenses incurred by a company, otherwise than for the purposes of a trade, in connection with the grant, maintenance or extension of the term of a patent or in connection with a rejected or abandoned patent application, provided that, if the expenses had been incurred for the purposes of a trade, they would have been allowable in calculating the profits of that trade.

Where a claim is made, the expenses are deducted or set off against the company's 'patent income' for the accounting period in which they are incurred with any unallowed balance being carried forward indefinitely against patent income without further claim. For this purpose, '*patent income*' has the same meaning as above, but any CAPITAL ALLOWANCES (10.50) must be deducted before relief is given for the expenses.

[*ICTA 1988, ss 526, 528, 533(1); CAA 2001, Sch 2 para 46; ITTOIA 2005, Sch 1 paras 203, 205*].

Spreading of patent royalties. Where royalties are received, less tax, for user of a patent which comprises two or more complete years, the corporation tax liabilities are reducible, on application, to the total that would have been payable if the royalties had been paid by equal instalments (corresponding to the number of complete years concerned, but not exceeding six years) made at yearly intervals ending with the date of actual receipt. [*ICTA 1988, s 527; ITTOIA 2005, Sch 1 para 204*].

Sales of patent rights. Profits from sales of the whole or part of any patent rights (including receipts for rights for which a patent has not yet been granted), which consist wholly or partly of a capital sum, are chargeable to tax under Schedule D Case VI. The company is charged to tax if a UK resident or, if not UK resident, where the patent is a UK patent. If the company is non-UK resident, the charge does not apply if it is within the charge to corporation tax in respect of the sale proceeds.

In the case of a sale by a non-UK resident, the purchaser may have to deduct tax at source under *ITA 2007 s 901* (formerly *ICTA 1988, s 349(1)*) (see 37.3 INCOME TAX IN RELATION TO A COMPANY) although this may be modified by double tax agreements.

References above to the sale of patent rights include the exchange of patent rights, and in the case of such an exchange, references above and below to the proceeds of sale and the price include the consideration for the exchange, and references to capital sums included in the proceeds include references to so much of the consideration for the exchange as would have been a capital sum if it had been a money payment. Where patent rights are acquired or disposed of together with other property, the acquisition costs or proceeds, as appropriate, must be apportioned on a just and reasonable basis.

Spreading provisions. In the case of a UK-resident company, the chargeable profits are spread equally over a period of six tax years, starting with the accounting period in which the proceeds are received. If the proceeds are received in instalments, each instalment is likewise spread over six tax years. The company may elect, by notice to an officer of HMRC, to disapply spreading, so that the profits (or instalments) are taxed in the accounting period in which they were received. The election must be made within two years after the end of the accounting period in which the profits or instalment were received.

Where a body corporate commences winding-up during the period over which the charge is spread in that period, no such election can be made and any charge arising under the spreading provisions becomes immediately chargeable in the accounting period in which winding-up commences.

The making of an election for spreading does not affect the amount of income tax to be deducted by the purchaser in the case of a sale by a non-UK resident, and any adjustment required as a result of such an election is made by repayment of tax on a year by year basis.

Licences. The acquisition of a licence in respect of a patent is treated for the purposes of the above provisions as a purchase of patent rights, and the grant of a licence is treated as a sale of part of such rights. Where, however, the licence is a licence to exercise the rights to the exclusion of all other persons (including the grantor) for the whole of the period until the rights come to an end, the grant is treated as a sale of the whole of the rights. The use in certain circumstances of an invention, which is the subject of a patent, by the Crown or a foreign government is treated as use under a licence.

[*ICTA 1988, ss 524, 525, 533(1)–(6); ITTOIA 2005, Sch 1 paras 201, 202, 209*].

Disposal of know-how. Subject to the exceptions below, profits arising where consideration is received for the disposal of 'know-how' are chargeable to corporation tax under

Schedule D Case VI. Also included within the charge are profits arising where consideration is received for giving, or wholly or partly fulfilling, an undertaking (whether or not legally enforceable) which is given in connection with a disposal of know-how and which restricts or is designed to restrict any person's activities in any way.

The profits chargeable to tax are the amount of the consideration less any expenditure incurred by the recipient wholly and exclusively in the acquisition or disposal of the know-how. Expenditure can only be taken into account for tax purposes once (whether under this provision or otherwise). See also 10.2(vi) CAPITAL ALLOWANCES for contributions to expenditure by public bodies, etc. which applies for these purposes.

The charge does not apply if:

- the consideration is brought into account as a revenue receipt under general principles (see above under Income from intellectual property);
- the consideration is brought into account as a disposal value under the capital allowances know-how code (see 10.23 CAPITAL ALLOWANCES);
- the consideration is treated as a trading receipt (see 66.62 TRADING INCOME);
- the consideration is received as part of the disposal of all or part of a trade and is treated as a capital receipt for goodwill under these provisions) (see 66.62 TRADING INCOME); or
- the disposal is by way of a sale and the buyer is a body of persons (including a firm) over which the seller or buyer has control or the buyer and seller are both bodies of persons and another person has control over them both.

[*ICTA 1988, ss 531(4)–(8), 532; ITTOIA 2005, Sch 1 paras 207, 208*].

55.12 LIFE POLICIES ETC. HELD BY COMPANIES

A gain arising under a policy, etc. held by or for a company is generally brought into charge to corporation tax under Schedule D, Case VI (with a right of recovery against trustees where the policy, etc. was held in trust), but policies, etc. issued before 14 March 1989 are excluded. [*ICTA 1988, s 546C(7)(b), s 547(1)(b)(1A)(4)(8), s 551A; FA 2001, Sch 28 paras 10, 11, 16; ITTOIA 2005, Sch 1 para 216*]. Certain events which are excluded from the charge on individual policy holders are treated as chargeable events where, immediately before the event, the rights conferred by the policy were in the beneficial ownership of a company, or were held on trusts created, or as security for debt owed, by a company. [*ICTA 1988, s 540(5A)*]. *ICTA 1988, s 548* (which treats certain loans as giving rise to a partial surrender of rights under a policy) is also applied to policies issued after that date and held by or for companies. [*ICTA 1988, s 548(1)(3); ITTOIA 2005, Sch 1 para 218*]. Special provisions apply in relation to chargeable events in respect of 'qualifying endowment policies' (within *ICTA 1988, Sch 15 para 2*) held as security for a debt owed by the company. [*ICTA 1988, s 541(4A)–(5)*].

For these purposes, a policy made before 14 March 1989 is to be treated as made on or after that date if it is varied on or after that date so as to increase the benefits secured or to extend the term of the policy, and any exercise of rights conferred by the policy is to be regarded for this purpose as a variation. [*ICTA 1988, s 539(9)*].

For policies issued, varied or with a right exercised on or after 21 March 2007, an anti-avoidance provision countering the use of life assurance policies to shelter investment income is introduced. In calculating the gain on a chargeable event, the total of premiums paid is reduced by the total commission on the policy 'rebated' (as defined) or 'reinvested' (as defined). Policies to which the provisions apply must involve payment of commission (which includes any passing of value to or for the benefit of an intermediary or a person connected with him) that has, at any time, been rebated or re-reinvested.

The anti-avoidance provision applies if one of two conditions apply. The first is that the total amount paid under the policy (including lump sum payments, in the case of an annuity contract) paid in a 'relevant period' exceeded £100,000. The second is that the premiums on all policies exceed the threshold of £100,000 at some time when the taxable person held the policy.

The '*relevant period*' is either that beginning at the start of the tax year in which the chargeable event occurred and ending with that event or any of the three preceding tax years.

The threshold and the definition of 'the relevant period' may be amended by statutory instrument.

[*ICTA 1988, s 548A, 548B*; *FA 2007, s 29*].

See generally Tolley's Income Tax under Life Assurance Policies.

55.13 PERSONAL SERVICE COMPANIES AND MANAGED SERVICE COMPANIES

For 2000/01 and subsequent tax years, provisions have been introduced to remove opportunities for the avoidance of tax and Class 1 national insurance contributions by the use of intermediaries such as personal service companies. The rules (commonly known as IR35 after the Revenue Budget Press Release in 1999) apply where the worker would otherwise be an employee of the client or the income would be income from an office held by the worker.

As this is essentially an income tax and national insurance measure, the main coverage is in Tolley's Income Tax at Chapter 60.

A personal service company which is within IR35 will have to make an adjustment in its corporation tax computation. The deemed employment payment, and associated national insurance contributions, are treated as an allowable expense in computing the business profits (or losses) of the intermediary for the period of account in which the payment is made (but for no other period of account).

ITTOIA 2005, s 163; FA 2000, Sch 12 para 17; ITEPA 2003, Sch 6 para 244(2).

Legislation is included in *FA 2007* to remove the tax saving opportunities offered by managed service companies (also known as composite companies). IR35 was not effective with these companies, therefore the legislation removes them from the IR35 regime entirely.

Instead, PAYE and Class 1 NICs will have to be deducted from the full amount of all payments or benefits provided to the workers. There is also provision to ensure that those workers are not more favourably treated than ordinary employees so far as travel and subsistence are concerned. To ensure companies do not close down and avoid the liabilities, powers are given to HMRC to recover the tax from all or any parties involved.

The provisions apply from 6 April 2007 for income tax and from a date later in 2007 for national insurance.

[*FA 2007, s 25 Sch 3*].

As these are essentially an income tax and national insurance measure, the main coverage of which is in Tolley's Income Tax PERSONAL SERVICE COMPANIES ETC.

55.14 SETTLEMENTS

Discretionary payments by trustees treated as income of the payee are taken as being net after tax at the rate applicable to trusts. [ICTA 1988, *s* 687]. Where *s 687* applies to a payment made after 1 July 1997 to a company within the charge to corporation tax, other than a charity (within *ICTA 1988, s 506(1)*) or a body treated as a charity under *ICTA 1988, s 507, s 508*, the payment is disregarded for corporation tax purposes, and no credit is given, or repayment made, of the tax deducted. In the case of non-UK resident companies, this applies to so much (if any) of the payment as is comprised in the company's profits for corporation tax purposes [*F(No 2)A 1997, s 27*].

55.15 MINERAL ROYALTIES

Where a company resident in the UK which in any accounting period is entitled to receive 'mineral royalties' under a lease, licence or agreement conferring a right to win and work minerals in the UK or under a sale or conveyance of such minerals, only one-half of any such royalties receivable in any accounting period is treated as income for corporation tax purposes.

Management expenses available for set-off against those royalties, whether under the general rules for computing PROPERTY INCOME (56) or under the special rules (in 56.17 PROPERTY INCOME) for taxing a 'UK section 12(4) concern' (mines, quarries etc.), are similarly reduced by one-half.

For these purposes, '*mineral royalties*' means so much of any rents, tolls, royalties or periodical payments as relates to the winning and working of 'minerals'. '*Minerals*' means all minerals or substances in or under land which are ordinarily worked for removal, by either underground or surface working, but does not include water, peat, top-soil or vegetation. A '*mineral lease or agreement*' means a lease, profit à prendre, licence or other agreement conferring a right to win and work minerals in the UK; a contract for the sale or conveyance of minerals in or under land in the UK; or a grant of a right (other than an ancillary right) under *Mines (Working Facilities and Support) Act 1966, s 1*.

Where Betterment Levy (which was abolished after July 1970) was not chargeable on the grant of the lease, or any subsequent renewal, extension or variation of it, the other half of the royalties receivable is treated as a chargeable gain for purposes of corporation tax on chargeable gains.

Where, on the last disposition (before 23 July 1970) affecting the lease, Betterment Levy was chargeable under Case B (as defined by *Land Commission Act 1967, Pt III*) the chargeable gain, as above, is limited to a fraction (base value of that disposition/ consideration received) of one-half of the royalties received. After 5 April 1988, this limitation applies only if it applied to a chargeable period ending on or before that date. But if such a lease is renewed, extended or varied after 22 July 1970, one-half of any subsequent royalty receipt is treated as a chargeable gain.

Where payments under a mineral lease etc. relate both to the winning and working of minerals and to other matters, the part to be treated as mineral royalties for these purposes will be calculated under regulations made by HMRC. See *SI 1971 No 1035*.

These chargeable gains are assessable in full, without any deduction on account of expenditure incurred.

Terminal Losses. If the mineral lease comes to an end while the person entitled to receive the royalties still has an interest in the land, and an allowable loss would then arise to that person if the interest was sold for a price equal to its market value, the person may claim to be treated for corporation tax on capital gains purposes as if the interest had been sold, and immediately reacquired, at that price, the resultant loss being allowed, on election, either (*a*) against corporation tax on capital gains for the accounting period in which the lease expires, or (*b*) against chargeable gains, in respect of mineral royalties under the lease, in accounting periods falling within the previous 15 years.

[*ICTA 1988, ss 121, 122; TCGA 1992, ss 201–203; ITTOIA 2005, Sch 1 paras 105, 106*].

Simon's Direct Tax Service. See **B3.460, C2.1111**.

55.16 TONNAGE TAX

'Qualifying companies', or groups of companies of which at least one member is a 'qualifying company', may elect for their corporation tax profits from the activities of 'qualifying ships' to be calculated by reference to the net tonnage of each of those ships, and for losses to be left out of account for corporation tax purposes. All 'qualifying companies' within a group must be taxed on the same basis. The regime was amended by FA 2005 to implement the recommendations of the 'Post Implementation Review of Tonnage Tax', issued by the Revenue and Department of Transport in December 2004, and to ensure compliance with European Community guidelines on state aid to the maritime transport industry.

A '*qualifying company*' is a company within the charge to corporation tax which operates 'qualifying ships' which are strategically and commercially managed in the UK (for which see Revenue Tax Bulletin October 2000 p 787). Certain temporary cessations from operating any 'qualifying ships' may be disregarded.

'*Qualifying ships*' are broadly ships carrying on certain activities which are of at least 100 tons gross tonnage, but excluding fishing and factory support vessels, pleasure craft, harbour and river ferries, offshore installations (within *ICTA 1988, s 837C* or, for accounting periods ending before 1 April 2004, offshore installations such as fixed and floating oil rigs and platforms, floating production, storage and offtake vessels), existing dedicated shuttle tankers subject to the petroleum revenue tax regime, dredgers (other than, from 1 July 2005, certain 'qualifying dredgers' as defined), and any vessel whose main purpose is the provision of goods or services normally provided on land. Other types of vessel may be added to or removed from the excluded categories by Treasury order. The activities in which they must be engaged are transportation by sea, the provision of marine assistance or the provision of transport for services necessarily provided at sea. They may also, to a limited extent, include certain secondary and incidental activities (see *SI 2000 No 2303, reg 3*). From 1 July 2005, new flagging rules apply (subject to transitional provisions) for qualifying dredgers and tugs which must be registered in a member state to qualify for tonnage tax (or other state aids). Other ships may be registered under any flag but where the relevant conditions are met, operators bringing 'new' ships within tonnage tax will have to do so under a member state registration. Otherwise, ships can still qualify if they are re-registered to a Community flag within three months of first operation. A '*new*' ship for these purposes is, broadly, one which is brought within tonnage tax (in a financial year which is not excepted by Treasury Order) after the later of 1 July 2005 or the end of the first accounting period in which the company (or group) became a tonnage tax company but the financial year 2005 is excepted by *SI 2005 No 1480* and the financial year 2006 is excepted by *SI 2006 No 333*.

Foreign dividends from non-UK resident shipping companies are (subject to conditions) also included in the profits covered by an election, as is any loan relationship credit (see 46.5 LOAN RELATIONSHIPS), any derivative contract credit (or, for accounting periods beginning before 1 October 2002, any profit on an interest rate or currency contract (see 28.3–28.8, 28.32 FINANCIAL INSTRUMENTS AND DERIVATIVE CONTRACTS) or, for accounting periods beginning before 1 October 2002, any exchange gain (see 26.7 EXCHANGE GAINS AND LOSSES) which would otherwise be treated as trading income. Otherwise, investment income is excluded.

Profits within the tonnage tax regime are 'ring-fenced', with appropriate anti-avoidance measures to prevent exploitation of the regime, and there are similarly capital allowance 'ring-fencing' provisions (as amended by *FA 2005*) (see also *SI 2000 No 2303, regs 4–8* as regards machinery and plant written-down values on exit from the regime or on transfer to use for offshore activities). No chargeable gains will arise during the currency of the election in relation to assets used for the qualifying activities, and balancing charges (on the disposal of assets for which capital allowances had previously been given) will be phased out using a sliding scale.

Capital allowances to lessors leasing to companies within the tonnage tax regime are similarly 'ring-fenced' and restricted.

Special provisions apply to the chartering in of qualifying ships and joint charters and to the chartering out of short-term over-capacity. There are also special rules for offshore activities in the UK sector of the continental shelf, and for group mergers and demergers.

Companies participating in the tonnage tax regime must also meet a minimum training obligation (for which see also *SI 2000 No 2129* as amended).

For existing qualifying companies, the *election* initially had to be made within twelve months from 28 July 2000. If the company was not a qualifying company on that date, it may have been made up to twelve months after its first becoming a qualifying company. In the case of a group no member of which was a qualifying company on 28 July 2000, it may have been made within twelve months of a group company first becoming a qualifying company, provided that the group is not substantially the same as a group which at any earlier time had a member which was a qualifying company. The election generally had effect from the beginning of the accounting period in which it was made (or, where that accounting period began before 1 January 2000, from the beginning of the following accounting period), subject to earlier or later effect in certain cases with HMRC agreement.

The Treasury has, however, provided a further opportunity for an election into tonnage tax by *SI 2005 No 1449* which allows for an election to be made at any time during the period beginning on 1 July 2005 and ending on 31 December 2006. The election in relation to this further period generally has effect from the beginning of the accounting period in which it was made (or, where that accounting period began before 1 January 2005, from the beginning of the following accounting period), subject to earlier or later effect in certain cases with HMRC agreement.

Special provisions apply in relation to mergers and demergers.

The election normally remains in effect for ten years for so long as the company (or group) qualifies and is not excluded, and (subject to the training requirements having been met) may at any time be renewed (such renewal being treated in effect as a valid new election).

The election ceases to have effect where a withdrawal notice is given by the company (or group) during a period beginning on 7 April 2005 and ending on 31 March 2006 provided the election in respect of which the withdrawal notice is given was in force for the whole of the three-year period ending on 7 April 2005. The withdrawal notice has effect at the end of the accounting period preceding the first accounting period of the company to begin after 1 July 2005 and is subject to transitional provisions. The Treasury may provide further opportunities for the withdrawal of elections by statutory instrument.

There is provision for exit charges on a company leaving the tonnage tax regime, and a bar on re-entry to the regime within ten years.

The Treasury may make provision by regulations for the application of the above provisions to activities carried on by a company in partnership. See now *SI 2000 No 2303, regs 8–13*.

[*FA 2000, s 82, Sch 22; CAA 2001, Sch 2 para 108; FA 2002, Sch 23 para 23, Sch 27 para 23; FA 2003, s 169, Sch 32; FA 2004, Sch 27 para 7, Sch 42 Pt 2(18); FA 2005, s 93, Sch 7; FA 2006, Sch 9 paras 8–10; SI 2005 No 1449; SI 2005 No 1480*].

A very lengthy and detailed Statement of Practice, setting out administrative practice for the operation of the entire regime and structured in the same order as the legislation, is contained in HMRC Statement of Practice, SP 4/00.

55.17 CORPORATION TAX RETURN

See 61.29 RETURNS for the self-assessment return form (Form CT600).

55.18 **EXAMPLES**

The following examples illustrate various aspects of corporation tax computations, including computational profit adjustments, loss relief and group considerations.

55.19 A Ltd, incorporated on 1 June 2000, commences business on 1 January 2007. The accounts for the year ended 31 December 2007 show the following.

	£		£
Wages and salaries	178,400	Gross trading profit	2,274,760
Directors' remuneration	82,200	Income from property	8,000
Rent, rates and insurance	49,200	Government securities	340
Motor expenses	38,000	UK company dividends	1,500
Bad debts	8,200	Profit on sale of shares	64,000
Research and development	36,000		
General expenses	94,000		
Legal and professional costs	16,000		
Overdraft interest	6,000		
Debenture finance charges	3,500		
Audit and accountancy	16,000		
Depreciation of fixed assets	82,000		
Loss on sale of fixed assets	6,000		
Net profit	1,733,100		
	£2,348,600		£2,348,600

The following further information is available.

(*a*) Capital allowances for the year are:

	£
Plant and machinery (including advertising sign)	48,000
Industrial buildings allowance (re premises let)	24,000
Research and development	24,000

(*b*) Bad debts consist of:

		£
Trade debts written off		6,100
Reserve created	— general	1,800
	— specific	300
		£8,200

(*c*) General expenses include:

		£
Advertising — erection of permanent sign (see (*a*) above)		1,050
Defalcations by junior staff		1,280
Entertaining	— small promotional gifts	1,400
	— customers	4,100
	— staff Christmas party	450
Gifts, donations	— wines, etc. on exhibition stand	800
	— trade protection society	250
	— Oxfam (within *ICTA 1988, s 339*)	500
	— political party	500
Inducement to planning official		750
Interest on unpaid tax		500
New premises — rehabilitation costs		3,000
Share sale — commission and fees		1,500
VAT — penalty for late return		400

(*d*) The company qualifies as a small and medium-sized enterprise for the purpose of research and development expenditure. The £36,000 qualifies as 'relevant' expenditure (see 59 RESEARCH AND DEVELOPMENT) of which £24,000 relates to the cost of a dedicated research employee and £8,000 to consumable items.

(*e*) Legal and professional costs consist of:

Company secretarial services	6,150
Debenture issue (see (*f*) below)	1,800
Debt collection	2,100
Industrial tribunal representation	750
Lease variation	1,000
Patent infringement claim work	3,400
Preparation of staff service agreements	800
	£16,000

(*f*) Debenture finance charges relate to £50,000 nominal stock issued on 1 January 2001 for trade finance at £96 per £100, carrying interest at 6.6% payable annually in arrears, for redemption 31 December 2010. The charge to profit and loss comprises interest of £3,300 and redemption reserve costs of £200 on a straight line basis. As these are arrived at under an amortised cost basis of accounting, the charges are allowable for tax purposes. The issue costs included in legal and professional costs (see (*e*) above) are also allowable.

The overdraft interest charge is similarly on an amortised cost basis and allowable.

The £340 Government securities credit relates to £9,000 4% Treasury Stock acquired in March 2006 at £9,080 with four years to redemption. It represents gross interest £360 less £20 premium amortisation charge on a straight line basis. It is thus properly chargeable under Schedule D, Case III as a non-trade credit. The interest was received on 7 March and 7 September.

(*g*) Chargeable gain on share sale 30 September 2007 £51,100.

(*h*) 26-year lease on new premises, at annual rent £22,500, purchased on 1 January 2001 at a premium of £200,000.

Cost of rehabilitation of premises to make suitable for trade use, between 1 January 2006 and 31 March 2007, £18,000.

Rates, etc. incurred before 1 January 2007, £20,000.

The computation for *year ended 31 December 2007* is as follows.

		£	£
Net profit			1,733,100
Add: Bad debts — general reserve		1,800	
Advertising — sign erection		1,050	
Entertaining		4,100	
Gifts, donations	— wines, etc.	800	
	— Oxfam	500	
	— political party	500	
Inducement		750	
Interest on unpaid tax		500	
New premises — rehabilitation costs		3,000	
Share sale commission and fees		1,500	
VAT penalty		400	
Lease variation expenses		1,000	
Depreciation		82,000	
Loss on sale of fixed assets		6,000	103,900
			1,837,000
Less: Income from property		8,000	
Government securities		340	
Dividends received		1,500	
Profit on share sale		64,000	73,840
			1,763,160
Less: Plant and machinery allowances		48,000	
Research and development allowances		24,000	
Research and development relief		18,000	
Lease premium allowance 200,000 (1 – 25/50) ÷ 26		3,846	
Pre-trading expenditure in seven years before 1 January 2007 (rent and rates)		110,000	203,846
			£1,559,314

	£	£
Schedule D, Case I trading profit		1,559,314
Income from property	8,000	
Less: Industrial buildings allowance	8,000	
		—
Chargeable gain		51,100
Total profits		1,610,414
Less: Non-trading loan relationship debit (interest on unpaid tax £500 *less* interest on securities £340)		160
		1,610,254
Less: Industrial buildings allowance in excess of property income (Schedule A loss, see 56 PROPERTY INCOME)		16,000
		1,594,254
Less: Charges paid — qualifying donation		500
Profits chargeable to corporation tax		£1,593,754
Tax chargeable:		
FY 2006 @ 30% on ¼ × 1,593,754 = 398,438		119,531.40
FY 2006 @ 30% on ¾ × 1,593,754 = 1,195,316		358,594.80
		£ 478,126.20

55.20 D Ltd and E Ltd are wholly-owned subsidiaries of C Ltd, no other company being associated with any of them. Results for each for the year ended 31 December 2007 are as follows.

	£
C Ltd	
Trading profit (after capital allowances)	452,000
Chargeable gain on disposal	65,000
D Ltd	
Trading loss (after capital allowances)	87,000
Income chargeable Schedule D, Case III	2,000
E Ltd	
Trading profit (after capital allowances)	118,000
Income from property	2,000

Ignoring group relief, the computation for each company is as follows.

C Ltd

Total profits	£517,000

The upper limit for profits to be taxable at the small companies rate is £300,000 *divided by* 1 + the number of associated companies, i.e. £100,000. The limits for marginal relief are similarly reduced to profits between £100,000 and £500,000. C Ltd's profits are thus taxable in full at 30%.

Corporation tax liability:	
FY 2006 @ 30% on ¼ × 517,000 = 129,250	38,775
FY 2007 @ 30% on ¾ × 517,000 = 387,750	116,325
Corporation tax payable	£155,100

D Ltd

Total profits	2,000
Less: Trading loss set against profits [*ICTA 1988, s 393A(1)*]	2,000
Corporation tax liability	—
Trading loss unrelieved	85,000
Loss available for group relief	£85,000

E Ltd

Total profits	£120,000

Since this is between the upper and lower limits for marginal small companies relief (see under C Ltd above), such relief is available.

Corporation tax liability:		
FY 2006 @ 30% on ¼ × 120,000 = 30,000	9,000	
Less: 11/400 × (125,000 – 30,000)	2,612	
		6,388
FY 2007 @ 30% on ¾ × 120,000 = 90,000	27,000	
Less: 1/40 × (375,000 – 90,000) =	7,125	
		19,875
Corporation tax payable		£26,263

If D Ltd surrenders its losses by group relief, £65,000 to C Ltd, £20,000 to E Ltd, the computations are as follows.

C Ltd

Total profits		517,000
Less: Group relief		65,000
Profits chargeable to corporation tax		£452,000
Corporation tax liability:		
FY 2006 @ 30% on ¼ × 452,000 = 113,000	33,900	
Less: 1¹⁄₄₀₀ × (125,000 – 113,000)	330	
		33,570
FY 2007 @ 30% on ¾ × 452,000 = 339,000	101,700	
Less: ¹⁄₄₀ × (375,000 – 339,000) =	900	
		100,800
Corporation tax payable		£134,370

D Ltd

Losses available for group relief	85,000
Less: Losses surrendered	85,000

E Ltd

Total profits	120,000
Less: Group relief	20,000
Profits chargeable to corporation tax	£100,000
Corporation tax liability:	
FY 2006 @ 19% on ¼ × 100,000 = 25,000	4,750
FY 2007 @ 20% on ¾ × 100,000 = 75,000	15,000
Corporation tax payable	£19,750

This gives the optimum group tax position, as any switch of group relief from C Ltd to E Ltd saves tax on E Ltd at 19%, whereas C Ltd's marginal tax rate is 32.5%. A switch of relief from E Ltd to C Ltd has no effect on the overall liability, as E Ltd would also be taxable at a marginal rate of 32.5% on its additional profits coming into charge.

56 Property Income

Cross references. See 10.9 CAPITAL ALLOWANCES for flat conversion allowances and 10.10 *et seq.* CAPITAL ALLOWANCES for allowances available in respect of leased industrial buildings.

Simon's Direct Tax Service. See A4.1–A4.5.

Headings in this chapter are as follows.

56.1 INTRODUCTION

Assessments of property income is made under Schedule A. The current regime, incorporating the concept of a 'Schedule A business' and *including furnished lettings* (previously chargeable under Schedule D, Case VI), was introduced by *FA 1995* for income tax purposes only and, with effect from 1 April 1998, the *Finance Act 1998* it was extended to corporation tax with the necessary amendments and modifications. [*FA 1998, s 38, Sch 5*]. For periods before that date see Tolley's Corporation Tax 2003/04 or earlier editions.

The law relating to the taxation of 'trading income' and 'property income' (previously within Schedules A, D and F and the cases of Schedule D) was consolidated in *Income Tax (Trading and Other Income) Act 2005* (*ITTOIA 2005*) as part of the Tax Law Rewrite programme and has effect for income tax purposes for 2005/06 and subsequent years and, for corporation tax purposes where relevant, for accounting periods ending after 5 April 2005. [*ITTOIA 2005, s 883(1)*]. For corporation tax purposes, property income continues to be computed and assessments made under Schedule A as if it were still part of income tax law, and not under *ITTOIA 2005* (see 55.3 profit computations). Accordingly, it can no longer be assumed that the coverage in Tolley's Income Tax of any particular type of receipt or deduction etc. relating to a 'property business' applies equally for corporation tax purposes and so all such matters are now dealt with in this chapter.

Corporation tax is charged on rents etc. (see 56.2 below) less deductible expenses (see 56.3 below). Certain lease premiums etc. are also taxable (see 56.16 below).

Where this work refers simply to a '*property business*', then unless the context clearly suggests otherwise, it means either a UK property business or an overseas property business (see in both cases 56.2 below). In this chapter, '*lease*' includes an agreement for a lease (in so far as the context permits) and any tenancy. '*Premises*' includes land. [*ICTA 1988, s 24(1)*]. '*Land*' includes an estate or interest in land.

56.2 CHARGE TO TAX

Schedule A applies to the annual profits arising from a business carried on for the exploitation, as a source of rents or other receipts, of any estate, interest or rights in or over land in the United Kingdom. This includes:

(*a*) payments in respect of a licence to occupy, or otherwise to use, land, or the exercise of any other right over land; and (*b*) rent-charges, ground annuals, feu duties and other annual payments reserved in respect of, or charged on or issuing out of, the land.

It includes receipts from furnished lettings in most cases, unless the lettings fall within Schedule D, Case I; amounts paid for the use of furniture in connection with furnished lettings (with a corresponding allowance of expenses in connection with its provision), again unless the profits are within Schedule D, Case I; and casual lettings. It also includes lettings from caravans and house boats which are at a fixed location. However, if a company carries on material activities connected with the operation of a caravan site and those activities themselves constitute a trade or a part of a trade, the income and expenses of letting the caravans and/or pitches can be included in computing the profits of that trade instead of being treated as those of a property business within Schedule A (see HMRC Extra Statutory Concession B29). See (C) below as regards furnished holiday lettings.

The following items are excluded from the computation for corporation tax purposes:

(i) interest payable, and other amounts falling within the loan relationships legislation in *FA 1996, Pt IV, Ch II* (see 46 LOAN RELATIONSHIPS);

(ii) profits and losses on derivative contracts falling within *FA 2002, Sch 26* (or, for accounting periods beginning before 1 October 2002, financial instruments falling within the legislation in *FA 1994, Pt IV, Ch II*) (see 28 FINANCIAL INSTRUMENTS AND DERIVATIVE CONTRACTS); and

(iii) foreign exchange gains and losses falling within (i) or (ii) above (or, for accounting periods beginning before 1 October 2002, within the legislation in *FA 1993, Pt II, Ch II* (see 26 EXCHANGE GAINS AND LOSSES)).

Schedule A does not include:

- profits from occupying land (e.g. from woodlands);
- profits chargeable to corporation tax under Schedule D, Case I from farming and market gardening [*ICTA 1988, s 53(1); ITTOIA 2005, Sch 1 para 32*];
- profits chargeable to corporation tax under Schedule D, Case I from mining, quarrying and other such concerns [*ICTA 1988, s 55; ITTOIA 2005, Sch 1 para 33*];
- trading receipts and expenses from tied premises [*ICTA 1988, s 98, ITTOIA 2005, Sch 1 para 77*];
- rent charged to corporation tax under Schedule D in connection with mines, quarries, etc. [*ICTA 1988, s 119; ITTOIA 2005, Sch 1 para 103*]; or
- rent charged to corporation tax under Schedule D in connection with electric line wayleaves (see 56.17 below). [*ICTA 1988, s 120(1); ITTOIA 2005, Sch 1 para 104*].

The letting of all property in the UK by the same person is to be treated as a single business, except in the case of the following. (See 56.17(a) below for rental income from land outside the UK.)

(A) *Companies not resident in the UK.* In the case of a non-resident company trading in the UK through a permanent establishment (see 60.5 RESIDENCE — previously a branch or agency), a Schedule A business within the charge to corporation tax is treated as a separate business from any UK property business chargeable to income tax. [*ICTA 1988, s 15(1A); ITTOIA 2005, Sch 1 para 8*]. See 60.4 *et seq.* RESIDENCE.

(B) *Insurance companies.* There are special rules dealing with the profits of Schedule A businesses and overseas property businesses in the case of insurance companies. [*ICTA 1988, ss 432AA, 432AB, 434E, 441B;CAA 2001, s 544, Sch 2 para 39*]. The single business concept does not apply to insurance companies as the computation of profits is based on the component business parts, which have different tax treatments.

(C) *Furnished holiday lettings*. Income from the commercial letting of furnished holiday accommodation which does not amount to the carrying on of a trade falls within Schedule A, having previously generally been within Schedule D, Case VI. For various purposes it is treated as income from a separate trade and all such lettings are treated as one trade, separate from any other trade or the trade forming the remainder of the company's Schedule A business. [*ICTA 1988, s 503*]. See 56.5 below.

[ICTA 1988, s 15; FA 2002, Sch 27 para 2].

Flat management companies. Residential service charges received by an occupier-controlled flat management company are normally received as capital by the landlord in his capacity as trustee. See 61.4 RETURNS with regard to the concessional exemption from the requirement to deliver returns. See HMRC Property Income Manual, PIM 1070. For a general article on the trust implications of flat management companies, service charge funds and sinking funds, see Revenue Tax Bulletin August 2000 pp 770–774.

Miscellaneous. Receipts from sales of turf have been held to be within Schedule A although they may alternatively be taxed as trading income (*Lowe v J W Ashmore Ltd Ch D 1970, 46 TC 597*); but receipts from sale of colliery dross bings were held to be capital (*Roberts v Lord Belhaven's Exors CS 1925, 9 TC 501*). Sums received for licence to tip soil on land were held to be capital (*McClure v Petre Ch D 1988, 61 TC 226*). Note that these cases were decided under the pre-1 April 1998 regime, which differed in a number of material respects from the current rules.

56.3 COMPUTATION OF AMOUNT CHARGEABLE

Schedule A profits are to be computed in accordance with the principles applicable to the computation of trading profits for the purposes of Schedule D, Case I (see 66 TRADING INCOME). These include the fundamental rules that profits or losses be computed in accordance with generally accepted accounting practice (GAAP), that capital receipts and expenditure be excluded and that, subject to any specific rule to the contrary, expenditure is not deductible unless incurred wholly and exclusively for the purposes of the business. Profits are calculated on an accruals basis rather than a cash basis [*FA 1998, ss 42, 46(1)(2); ITTOIA 2005, Sch 1 paras 500, 502*] and the following rules apply:

(*a*) the rules of apportionment (see below) [*ICTA 1988, s 72*];

(*b*) business entertaining expenses [*ICTA 1988, s 577; CAA 2001, s 269*];

(*c*) expenditure involving crime [*ICTA 1988, s 577A*];

(*d*) redundancy payments [*ICTA 1988, ss 579 and 580*];

(*e*) training courses and counselling for employees [*ICTA 1988, ss 588, 589A* and (prior to *ITEPA 2003, Sch 6 para 7*) *ss 589, 589B*];

(*f*) consideration for restrictive undertakings [*FA 1988, s 73(2)*];

(*g*) deductions in respect of certain employees' remuneration [*FA 1989, s 43* as amended by *ITEPA 2003, Sch 6 para 157; FA 2003, Sch 24 para 10(1)*]; and

(*h*) expenses relating to non-approved retirement benefit schemes [*FA 1989, s 76.*

The following further provisions apply for Schedule A purposes:

(i) the computational provisions relating to the Schedule D charge within *ICTA 1988, Pt IV, Ch V* (*ICTA 1988, ss 74–99*) (see 66 TRADING INCOME) apply generally to the computation of Schedule A profits as if the Schedule A business were a trade, except in the case of the treatment of premiums taxed as rent under *ICTA 1988, s 87* (see 56.12 below) and the treatment of receipts and expenses relating to tied premises as those of a trade under *ICTA 1988, s 98* (see 66.22 TRADING INCOME);

(ii) the provisions relating to post-cessation receipts and expenses, etc.(see below) [*ICTA 1988, ss 103–106, 110*];

(iii) the provisions for the treatment of a company commencing or ceasing to carry on a trade [*ICTA 1988, s 337(1)*];

(iv) relief for pre-trading expenditure (see 66.69 TRADING INCOME) [*ICTA 1988, s 401(1); ITTOIA 2005, Sch 1 para 172*]; and

(v) change of accounting basis (see 66.6 TRADING INCOME) [*FA 2002, s 64, Sch 22*].

In the case of *Kato Kagaku Co Ltd v HMRC SpC 598* a deduction from property income was claimed for an indemnity payment paid in respect of a swap contract entered into in connection with obtaining finance for the purpose of purchasing the rented property. The appeal was allowed in part: the indemnity payment was a capital payment, but a deduction was available as the payment was an incidental cost of finance but not in respect of that part of the payment which arose due to exchange rate fluctuations. The indemnity was not a premium.

ICTA 1988, ss 34 et seq. continue to provide for the treatment of premiums on the grant of leases or subleases of less than 50 years.

[ICTA 1988, ss 21A, 21B; FA 2001, Sch 23 para 1; ITTOIA 2005, Sch 1 paras 12, 13; FA 2006, s 102(3)].

For a general article on what constitutes an allowable repair for Schedule A, see Revenue Tax Bulletin June 2002, pp 935, 936.

See also 55.8 PROFIT COMPUTATIONS as regards reliefs for certain expenditure on remediation of contaminated land.

See generally the HMRC Property Income Manual.

In practice, a cash basis may be used instead of a full earnings basis (as required by GAAP) where gross annual receipts do not exceed £15,000, provided that it is used consistently and gives a reasonable overall result not substantially different from that produced on an earnings basis (see HMRC Property Income Manual, PIM 1101).

Profits or losses on contracts taken out to hedge interest payments deductible in computing profits or losses of the property business will normally be taxed or relieved as receipts or deductions of that business. Such profits or losses would generally be computed on an accruals basis in accordance with normal accountancy practice. Similarly deposits paid to landlords by tenants or licensees will ordinarily be receipts of the business, to be recognised in accordance with generally accepted accountancy practice, normally by being deferred and matched with the related costs. Excess deposits which are refunded should be excluded from the business receipts. (See HMRC Property Income Manual, PIM 1051 and PIM 2105). As regards allowable legal and professional and other costs, see HMRC Property Income Manual, PIM 2200.

Apportionment of profits. Where a period of account of a property business does not coincide with an accounting period, profits must be apportioned to accounting periods. This must normally be done by reference to the number of days in the periods concerned [*ICTA 1988, ss 21A(2), 72; ITTOIA 2005, Sch 1 para 44*]. In practice, the company may choose any other method, e.g. months and part-months, if it is reasonable to do so and so long as the chosen method is applied consistently. This choice is given statutory effect for 2005/06 onwards for income tax purposes by *ITTOIA 2005, s 275*.

Commencement and discontinuance. Where a company starts or ceases to carry on a UK property business or to be within the charge to corporation tax in respect of a UK property business, it is treated as starting or ceasing to carry on the business at that time. [*ICTA 1988, ss 110, 337(2); FA 2002, Sch 30 para 1; ITTOIA 2005, Sch 1 paras 90, 145*].

Post-cessation receipts. Corporation tax is charged on any 'post-cessation receipts' of a UK property business under Schedule D, Case VI by adopting the rules applicable to trades under *ICTA 1988, ss 103–106, 110* (see 66.3 TRADING INCOME) in suitably modified form. A '*post-cessation receipt*' is a sum which is received after a company permanently ceases to carry on a UK property business and which arises from the carrying on of the business before cessation. The charge for any accounting period is on the full amount of post-cessation receipts for that period. The charge does not apply in relation to an overseas property business. [*ICTA 1988, s 21B; ITTOIA 2005, Sch 1, para 13*].

Deduction for energy-saving expenditure. From a date to be fixed by statutory instrument, a deduction is available for expenditure on energy-saving items for a dwelling-house. The expenditure on equipment installed in the building, rather than in the individual dwelling-house, may be claimed, although it must be for a dwelling-house's benefit. The conditions for relief are:

(i) the company carries on a Schedule A business;

(ii) the property in question is used in the course of that business;

(iii) the expenditure is incurred before 1 April 2015;

(iv) a deduction is not prohibited on the grounds that the expenditure is not incurred wholly, exclusively and necessarily for the purposes of the Schedule A business;

(v) the expenditure is capital in nature;

(vi) the expenditure is not incurred while the property is in the course of construction;

(vii) the company has an interest at the time the item is installed; and

(viii) it does not qualify for capital allowances.

Expenditure may be apportioned so as to give an amount qualifying for deduction and an ineligible amount. The definition of an 'energy-saving item' will be set out in Regulations.

No deduction is granted if the property in question is used for a furnished holiday lettings business in the accounting period in which the expenditure is incurred. Expenditure on energy-saving items for a property will not qualify for relief to the extent it is not for the benefit of a dwelling-house i.e. if it benefits the property generally but not individual dwelling-houses. Pre-trading expenditure deemed to be incurred on the first day the company carries on the Schedule A business under *ICTA 1988 s 401* does not qualify for a deduction unless it was incurred within the six months prior to commencement of the trade.

Wide powers are provided for determining the details of the relief by regulation.

[*ICTA 1988 ss 31ZA–ZC; FA 2007 s 17; SI 2007 No 945*].

56.4 FURNISHED LETTINGS

Furnished lettings are taxable as, or as part of, a property business (and the computational rules at 56.3 above thus apply). See 56.5 below for special rules for furnished holiday lettings.

A furnished letting is a lease or other arrangement under which a sum is payable for the use of premises (which expression includes a caravan or houseboat) and the person entitled to the use of the premises is also entitled to the use of furniture. Any consideration receivable for the use of furniture is chargeable as property income in the same way as rent (and expenditure incurred in providing furniture is treated accordingly). This does not apply to any amount taken into account in computing profits of a trade involving the making available of furniture for use in premises. [*ICTA 1988, s 15(1)*].

Dependent on the nature of the lettings, including their frequency and the extent to which the landlord provides services, e.g. cleaning, laundry and meals, the letting may amount to a trade of providing serviced accommodation and be within Schedule D, Case I rather than Schedule A. Alternatively, the provision of services may amount to a trade separate to the letting (cf. *Salisbury House Estate Ltd v Fry HL1930, 15 TC 266*). In *Gittos v Barclay Ch D 1982, 55 TC 633*, the letting of two villas in a holiday village was held not to amount to trading. A similar decision was reached in *Griffiths v Jackson; Griffiths v Pearman Ch D 1982, 56 TC 583* in relation to the extensive letting of furnished rooms to students. Note that all the decisions cited were made before 1 April 1998 when non-trading furnished lettings were within Schedule D, Case VI rather than Schedule A.

Capital allowances are not due on plant or machinery let for use in a dwelling-house (see 10.8 CAPITAL ALLOWANCES) (but see 56.5 below as regards furnished holiday lettings). Furniture and furnishing may be dealt with on the renewals basis but an alternative HMRC concession is to allow as depreciation 10% of the rents received as reduced by any council tax and water rates or material payments for services borne by landlord but normally a tenant's burden. Where the 10% deduction is allowed, no further deduction is given for the cost of renewing furniture or furnishings, nor for fixtures such as cookers, dishwashers or washing machines which, in unfurnished accommodation, the tenant would normally provide for himself. However, the cost of renewing fixtures which are an integral part of the building (e.g. baths, toilets, washbasins) may be claimed in addition, provided that they are revenue repairs to the fabric. Any different basis in use for a particular case prior to 1975/76 will not normally be disturbed (HMRC Extra Statutory Concession B47). See *Abidoye v Hennessey Ch D 1978, [1979] STC 212.*

56.5 **Furnished holiday lettings.** In so far as a UK property business consists in the 'commercial letting' of 'furnished holiday accommodation' (a 'furnished holiday lettings business') for an accounting period, it is treated as a trade chargeable under Schedule D Case I for the purposes of relief for losses under *ICTA 1988, ss 392A–396* (see 47 LOSSES).

In addition, a furnished holiday lettings business is a qualifying activity for the purposes of capital allowances on plant and machinery (see 10.24 CAPITAL ALLOWANCES). In contrast to furnished lettings generally, plant or machinery provided for use in a dwelling-house is not precluded, but the 10% wear and tear allowance in 56.4 above cannot be claimed as an alternative.

All commercial lettings of furnished holiday accommodation by a particular company (or partnership) are treated as a single trade or, for capital allowances purposes, as a single qualifying activity, separate from any genuine trade or other qualifying activity carried on by that company.

Where there is a letting of accommodation only part of which is holiday accommodation, such apportionments are to be made as are just and reasonable.

A loss may not be relieved both under this provision and under any other relief provision.

'*Commercial letting*' is letting (whether or not under a lease) on a commercial basis and with a view to the realisation of profits, and accommodation is let '*furnished*' if the tenant is entitled to use of the furniture. For a case in which the 'commercial letting' test was satisfied despite a significant excess of interest over letting income, see *Walls v Livesey (Sp C 4), [1995] SSCD 12*, but see also *Brown v Richardson (Sp C 129), [1997] SSCD 233* in which the opposite conclusion was reached. See Revenue Tax Bulletin October 1997 pp 472, 473 for HMRC's view of the requirements in this respect.

'*Holiday accommodation*' is accommodation which:

(*a*) is available for commercial letting to the public generally as holiday accommodation for at least 140 days in the twelve-month period referred to below; and

(*b*) is so let for at least 70 such days.

It must, however, not normally be in the same occupation for more than 31 consecutive days at any time during a period comprising seven months, not necessarily continuous but including any months in which it was let as in (*b*) above, within the twelve-month period. (This requirement is relaxed for income tax purposes by *ITTOIA 2005, s 325* — see Change 76 listed in Annex 1 to the Explanatory Notes to the Income Tax (Trading and Other Income) Bill).) The words 'in the same occupation' refer to tenants and do not prevent relief being due where the owner himself occupies the property outside the holiday season (HMRC Property Income Manual PIM 4110).

The twelve-month period referred to above is the accounting period in question, unless:

(1) the accommodation was not let by the company as furnished accommodation in the preceding accounting period, in which case the twelve-month period runs from the date such letting commenced in the accounting period in question; or

(2) the accommodation was let by the company as furnished accommodation in the preceding accounting period but is not so let in the succeeding accounting period, in which case the twelve-month period is the twelve months ending with the date such letting ceased in the accounting period in question.

In satisfying the 70-day test in (*b*) above, averaging may be applied to the number of let days of any or all of the accommodation let by the company which either is 'holiday accommodation' or would be 'holiday accommodation' if it satisfied the 70-day test on its own. An election for averaging must be made within two years following the end of the accounting period in which the accommodation was let. It must specify the accommodation to be included in the averaging calculation; 'holiday accommodation' cannot be included in more than one averaging election for an accounting period. See below for an example of how averaging works. (Averaging is, strictly speaking, by reference to the number of let days in the accounting period rather than in the twelve-month period referred to above; this is illogical and *ITTOIA 2005, ss 324, 326* remove the anomaly for income tax purposes — see Change 77 listed in Annex 1 to the Explanatory Notes to the Income Tax (Trading and Other Income) Bill).

[*ICTA 1988, ss 503, 504; CAA 2001, ss 15–17; CAA 1990, s 29; ITTOIA 2005, Sch 1 paras 195, 196, 526–528*].

Furnished holiday accommodation may include caravans (Revenue Press Release 17 May 1984).

See Tolley's Income Tax under Property Income for the letting of furnished holiday accommodation treated as a trade for certain income tax purposes [*ICTA 1988, s 504A; ITTOIA 2005, Sch 1 para 197*]. See Tolley's Capital Gains Tax as regards relief from capital gains tax in respect of furnished holiday lettings.

See 56.17 below in relation to the foot and mouth outbreak.

Simon's Direct Tax Service. See **A4.108A**.

Example

X Ltd owns and lets out furnished holiday cottages. None is ever let to the same person for more than 31 consecutive days. Three cottages have been owned for many years but Rose Cottage was acquired on 1 June 2007 (and first let on that day) while Ivy Cottage was sold on 30 June 2007 (and last let on that day).

In B Ltd's accounting period ending 31 March 2008, days available for letting and days let are as follows.

	Days available	Days let
Honeysuckle Cottage	180	160
Primrose Cottage	130	100
Bluebell Cottage	150	60
Rose Cottage	150	60
Ivy Cottage	30	5

Additional information

Rose Cottage was let for 30 days between 1 April and 31 May 2008.

Ivy Cottage was let for 50 days in the period 1 July 2006 to 31 March 2007 but was available for letting for 110 days in that period.

Qualification as 'furnished holiday accommodation'

Honeysuckle Cottage qualifies as it meets both the 140-day availability test and the 70-day letting test.

Primrose Cottage does *not* qualify although it is let for more than 70 days as it fails to satisfy the 140-day test. Averaging (see below) is only possible where it is the 70-day test which is not satisfied.

Bluebell Cottage does not qualify by itself as it fails the 70-day test. However it may be included in an averaging election.

Rose Cottage qualifies as furnished holiday accommodation. It was acquired on 1 June 2007 so qualification in the accounting period ending 31 March 2008 is determined by reference to the period of twelve months beginning on the day it was first let, in which it was let for a total of 90 days.

Ivy Cottage was sold on 30 June 2007 so qualification is determined by reference to the period from 1 July 2006 to 30 June 2007 (the last day of letting). It does not qualify by itself as it was let for only 55 days in this period but it may be included in an averaging election.

Averaging election for accounting period ending 31 March 2008

	Days let
Honeysuckle Cottage	160
Bluebell Cottage	60
Rose Cottage	90
Ivy Cottage	55

$$\frac{160 + 60 + 90 + 55}{4} = 91.25\text{days}$$

All four cottages included in the averaging election now qualify as furnished holiday accommodation as each is deemed to have been let for 91.25 days in the accounting period ending 31 March 2008. If the average had been less than 70, the two cottages which qualify in any case could have been included in an averaging election together with one of the non-qualifying cottages (leaving the other as non-qualifying). If averaging three cottages still did not improve the position, an average of just two could be tried.

56.6 DISTRIBUTIONS FROM REAL ESTATE INVESTMENT TRUSTS (REITS)

A distribution received from a Real Estate Investment Trust (REIT) (see below) by a shareholder within the charge to corporation tax is treated in the shareholder's hands as profits of a Schedule A business to the extent that it is paid out of the tax-exempt profits (including tax-exempt chargeable gains) of the REIT. Basic rate tax is deducted at source by the REIT; the shareholder remains liable for any excess liability, i.e. excess of the higher rate of tax over the basic rate. The distribution does not carry a tax credit. A distribution made by a company that has ceased to be an REIT is subject to the special treatment to the extent that it is paid out of tax-exempt profits made while the company was an REIT.

Distributions within the special treatment are treated in the shareholder's hands as profits of a single business, regardless of the fact that they may come from different REITs or be received by the shareholder in different capacities. The single business is separate from any Schedule A or overseas property business carried on by the shareholder. These rules apply to a corporate partner's share of any such distributions received by a partnership as if it were received by it as a direct shareholder.

If the shareholder is non-UK resident, a distribution out of tax-exempt profits is again treated as profits of a Schedule A business, but this does not preclude its being dealt with under the relevant dividend article of a double tax agreement (Treasury Explanatory Notes to Finance Bill 2006). Such distributions are outside the non-resident landlords regime at 56.16 below.

The special treatment does not apply to distributions falling to be taken into account in computing the recipient's trading profits (see 66.74 TRADING INCOME under Dealers in securities) or on shares held in a Lloyd's underwriter's premium trust fund or ancillary trust fund (see Tolley's Income Tax under Underwriters at Lloyd's).

The requirements concerning deduction of basic rate tax at source are to be set out in regulations made by statutory instrument. These may specify classes of shareholder to whom distributions out of tax-exempt profits can be made without deduction of tax, require REITs to provide shareholders with certificates containing specified information and provide in certain cases for repayment to the shareholder of the tax deducted (presumably in cases where the tax deducted exceeds the shareholder's overall corporation tax liability).

There are rules to determine the extent to which a distribution of an REIT is made out of its tax-exempt profits. It is one of the conditions of tax-exempt status that at least 90% of the profits of an REIT's property rental business is paid out as dividends within a specified time (see 44.11 INVESTMENT TRUSTS for how the distributions are attributed firstly to the tax-exempt profits and then to other profits).

[*FA 2006, ss 121–123*].

Regulations may be made by Treasury order to impose a tax charge on an REIT if it makes a distribution to a shareholder with a 10% interest or more in the company or its dividends. A distribution that is withheld in order to prevent or reduce such a charge is nevertheless treated as having been made for the purposes of the regulations dealing with deduction of basic rate tax at source. [*FA 2006, ss 107(9)(b), 114, 122(4)*].See generally 44.3 *et seq.* INVESTMENT TRUSTS.

56.7 TREATMENT OF LOSSES

Schedule A losses. A Schedule A loss may be set off against the company's total profits for the same accounting period. Any unrelieved part of the loss may be treated as a Schedule A loss of succeeding periods, for set-off against total profits of such periods, provided that the company continues to carry on the Schedule A business in the period concerned. Where the company is a company with investment business (or for accounting periods beginning before 1 April 2004, an investment company) (see 42.5 INVESTMENT COMPANIES AND INVESTMENT BUSINESS), and the Schedule A business ceases, unrelieved losses can be treated as excess management expenses, provided that the company continues to be a company with investment business (or an investment company). These reliefs are available only where the Schedule A business is carried on on a commercial basis or in the exercise of statutory functions (see 47.9 LOSSES). [*ICTA 1988, s 392A; SI 2004 No 2310, Article 12*]. Where a claim is made to set off a non-trade loan relationship deficit against the gross profits for the deficit period, that deficit is set off before relief for Schedule A losses. [*FA 1996, Sch 8 para 1*]. See 46.3 LOAN RELATIONSHIPS.

Group relief. Group relief is available for Schedule A losses excluding losses brought forward from earlier periods and losses incurred in a Schedule A business which was not carried on either on a commercial basis or in the exercise of statutory functions. [*ICTA 1988, s 403*]. See 32.10 GROUPS OF COMPANIES.

Change of ownership of company. The carry forward of Schedule A losses is restricted on the change of ownership of a company in a similar manner as applies to trading losses and excess management expenses. [*ICTA 1988, ss 768D, 769*]. See 42.8 INVESTMENT COMPANIES AND INVESTMENT BUSINESS, 47.13 LOSSES.

56.8 LEASE PREMIUMS ETC.

If a premium is payable under a '*short-term lease*' (i.e. a lease whose effective duration, see below, is 50 years or less), or under the terms on which such a lease is granted, the company to which it is due (whether or not the landlord) is treated as entering into a transaction for the purpose of generating income from land. An amount must be brought into account as a receipt in computing the profits of the property business which consists of or includes that transaction (see 66.4 above) for the tax year in which the lease is granted. The amount to be brought into account is

$$P \times \frac{50 - Y}{50}$$

where

P = the amount of the premium, and

Y = the number of *complete* periods of twelve months (*other than the first*) comprised in the effective duration of the lease.

Example

A Ltd grants a 14-year lease of premises for a premium of £50,000 in its accounting period ended 30 June 2007. The amount to be included as a receipt in computing the profits of its property business for that period is as follows.

$$£50{,}000 \times \frac{50 - 13}{50} = £\,37{,}000$$

Note that these provisions refer to leases granted and not to leases assigned. *ICTA 1988, s 38* contains rules for ascertaining the effective duration of a lease, which is not necessarily the same as its contractual duration; in particular, any rights the tenant has to extend the lease, or any entitlement of the tenant to a further lease of the same premises, may possibly be taken into account. In this connection, HMRC have the power to demand any information relevant to the duration of the lease.

If the terms on which a lease is granted oblige the tenant to carry out work on the premises (other than work such as normal repairs or maintenance which, if incurred by the landlord, would be deductible expenditure in computing the profits of his property business), the lease is treated as requiring the payment of a premium (or additional premium) to the landlord of the amount by which the value of the landlord's interest increases as a result of the obligation.

If the terms on which a lease is granted require the tenant to pay a sum in lieu of rent for a period (and that period is less than 50 years) the company to whom the sum is due (whether or not the landlord) is treated as if it were entitled to a premium equal to that sum. *ITTOIA 2005* makes it explicit that this applies irrespective of the duration of the lease itself, and in particular whether or not it is a short-term lease, though HMRC have always taken that view in any case (see Change 68 listed in Annex 1 to the Income Tax (Trading and Other Income) Bill). The charge to corporation tax is made for the accounting period in which the sum becomes payable. The value of Y in the above formula is the number of complete periods of twelve months (other than the first) comprised in the period in relation to which the sum is payable (but excluding any part of the period other than that in relation to which the sum is payable.

See generally HMRC Property Income Manual PIM 1200–1214.

Payment by instalments. Where any premium etc. is payable by instalments, the tax thereon may itself be paid by such instalments as HMRC may allow in the particular case; the tax instalment period cannot exceed eight years or, if less, the period during which the premium instalments are payable. See HMRC Property Income Manual PIM 1220.

[*ICTA 1988, ss 24, 34, 38, 39(1); ITTOIA 2005, Sch 1 paras 17, 22*].

Capital gains tax. See Tolley's Capital Gains Tax for the treatment of chargeable gains arising from disposal by way of a lease. Note particularly that the part of the premium chargeable to income tax is omitted from the computation of the chargeable gain.

Surrender under the terms of a lease. If, under the terms on which a short-term lease is granted, a sum becomes payable by the tenant as consideration for the surrender of the lease, consequences ensue as above as if that sum were a premium. See HMRC Property Income Manual PIM 1214. [*ICTA 1988, ss 34(1)(4)(6)(7A), 39(1); ITTOIA 2005, Sch 1 para 17*].

Variation or waiver of term of lease. If a sum becomes payable by a tenant otherwise than by way of rent as consideration for the variation or waiver of the terms of a lease, and the sum is due to the landlord or to a company connected with the landlord (within 19 CONNECTED PERSONS) (and the period for which the variation or waiver has effect is 50 years or less) consequences ensue as above as if that sum were a premium. The charge to corporation tax is made for the accounting period in which the contract for the variation or waiver is entered into. The value of Y in the above formula is the number of complete periods of twelve months (other than the first) comprised in the period for which the variation or waiver has effect (but excluding any part of that period preceding the time at which the variation or waiver takes effect or falling after the time at which it ceases to have effect). [*ICTA 1988, s 34(1)(5)(6)(7)(7A); ITTOIA 2005, Sch 1 para 17*].

ITTOIA 2005 makes it explicit that this applies irrespective of the duration of the lease itself, and in particular whether or not it is a short-term lease, though HMRC have always taken that view in any case (see Change 68 listed in Annex 1 to the Income Tax (Trading and Other Income) Bill). See HMRC Property Income Manual PIM 1216.

Simon's Direct Tax Service. See A4.2.

56.9 **Leases granted at undervalue.** If a short-term lease (as in 56.8 above) was granted at an undervalue and is assigned at a profit, similar consequences ensue as in 56.8 above as regards the assignor as if the assignor had received a premium (except that the opportunity to pay the tax by instalments is not available). The charge to corporation tax is made for the accounting period in which the consideration for the assignment becomes payable. The value of P in the formula in 56.8 above is the lesser of the profit on the assignment and the amount of the undervalue (adjusted to take account of any profits on earlier assignments of the same lease). This does not apply in relation to a lease granted before 6 April 1963 or pursuant to a contract entered into before that date. [*ICTA 1988, ss 35, 39(1); ITTOIA 2005, Sch 1 para 18*].

56.10 **Sale of land with right to reconveyance.** If land is sold subject to terms requiring it to be reconveyed on a future date to the vendor or a person connected with the vendor (within 19 CONNECTED PERSONS) for a price lower than the sale price, similar consequences ensue as in 56.8 above as regards the vendor as if the vendor had received a premium. *ITTOIA*

2005 makes it explicit that this applies only if the period beginning with the sale and ending with the earliest date on which, under the said terms, the land could fall to be reconveyed is 50 years or less (see Change 72 listed in Annex 1 to the Income Tax (Trading and Other Income) Bill). The charge to corporation tax is made for the accounting period in which the sale occurs. The value of P in the formula in 56.8 above is the excess of the sale price over the price at which the land is to be reconveyed. The value of Y is the number of complete periods of twelve months (other than the first) comprised in the period of 50 years or less referred to above.

Similar provisions apply (with appropriate modifications) if, instead of being reconveyed, the land is to be leased back to the vendor or to a person connected with the vendor. (They do not, however, apply if the lease is granted and begins to run within one month after the sale.) In this case, the sale price is compared to the total of (i) any premium payable for the lease and (ii) the value on the date of sale of the right to lease back the land.

If the date for the reconveyance (or leaseback) is not fixed under the terms of the sale and the reconveyance price (or the total of (i) and (ii) above) varies dependent upon that date, the price (or total) is taken to be the lowest possible under the terms of the sale. There is provision for any overpaid tax to be repaid if the actual date of reconveyance (or of the grant of the lease) turns out to be different to the date by reference to which the tax charge was calculated; a claim for repayment must be made within six years after the reconveyance (or the grant of the lease).

[*ICTA 1988, s 36; ITTOIA 2005, Sch 1 para 19*].

See HMRC Property Income Manual PIM 1222, 1224, 1226. For the so-called 'treasury arrangement' to avoid a charge under these provisions where there is a genuine commercial reason for the owner of mineral-bearing land to sell with a right to repurchase, see HMRC Property Income Manual PIM 1228. See 5.15 ANTI-AVOIDANCE for other provisions concerning the sale and leaseback of land.

56.11 **Sub-leases etc.** Relief is due if any of the charges at 56.8 above apply, or the charge on assignment at 56.9 above applies, and the grant of the lease in question is out of a 'taxed lease' (or a head lease) or, as the case may be, the assignment in question is of a 'taxed lease' (or a head lease). A '*taxed lease*' is one in respect of which there has already been such a charge (or there would have been a charge but for the availability of this relief). Thus, in broad terms, the relief applies where the taxable company is itself a tenant and its own landlord has received a premium or other taxable sum in respect of the same property.

The amount given by the formula in 56.8 above is reduced by the proportion of amount previously charged which the duration of the sub-lease bears to the duration of the head lease. The amount of the reduction can be found by the formula:

$$\frac{PC \times LRP}{TRP}$$

where:

PC = the amount given by the formula in 56.8 above in respect of the previous charge;

LRP = the length of the 'receipt period' of the receipt under calculation; and

TRP = the total 'receipt period' of the receipt by reference to which the previous charge was made.

The '*receipt period*' is:

- in the case of a premium (or similar sum) or a sum payable for the surrender of a lease, the effective duration of the lease (see 56.8 above);
- in the case of a sum payable in lieu of rent, the period for which it is payable,

- in the case of a sum payable for variation or waiver, the period for which the variation or waiver has effect; and
- in the case of an assignment, the effective duration of the lease remaining at the date of the assignment.

If the current charge is under 56.8 above and the sub-lease relates to only part of the premises subject to the head-lease, the relief is reduced proportionately on a just and reasonable basis.

Example

A Ltd grants a 14-year lease of premises to B Ltd for a premium of £50,000 in June 2007. The amount to be included as a receipt in computing the profits of A Ltd's property business in its accounting period ending 31 December 2007 is £37,000 as computed in the *Example* in 56.8 above.

After 4 years, i.e. in June 2011, B Ltd grants a 10-year sub-lease for which it receives a premium of £60,000. The amount to be included as a receipt in computing the profits of B Ltd's property business for its accounting period ending 31 December 2011 is as follows.

		£
Normal calculation	$£60{,}000 \times \dfrac{50-9}{50}$	49,200
Less relief as above	$\dfrac{£37{,}000 \times 10}{14}$	26,429
		£22,771

The relief is restricted to the 'unrelieved balance' of the value of PC in the above formula. The '*unrelieved balance*' is found by deducting the following from the value of PC:

- any relief previously given under these provisions;
- any deductions allowed under 56.12 below; and
- any deductions allowed under *ICTA 1988, s 87* (deductions allowed where the land is used for the purposes of a trade etc. — see 66.71 TRADING INCOME),

so far as attributable to the charge to which PC relates.

If there is more than one previous charge in relation to which there is an unrelieved balance, an amount of relief is computed separately for each previous charge and then aggregated, but the total relief cannot exceed the total of the unrelieved balances.

For these purposes, in a case where the previous charge resulted from the tenant's obligation to carry out work on the premises (see 56.8 above), the value of PC in the above formula is recomputed as if that obligation had not included the carrying out of any work that results in expenditure qualifying for CAPITAL ALLOWANCES (10).

If the relief would otherwise exceed the amount from which it is deductible, it is restricted to that amount.

[*ICTA 1988, s 37(1)–(3), (7)–(9), Sch 30 paras 2, 3; ITTOIA 2005, Sch 1 para 20*].

The above provisions applied equally for the purposes of income tax before 2005/06 and corporation tax before the financial year 2005. For 2005/06 onwards, the income tax rules are in *ITTOIA 2005, ss 287–290* (the above narrative being largely based on these provisions) but the equivalent corporation tax rules remain in ICTA 1988, s 37 (as amended by *ITTOIA 2005, Sch 1 para 20* from 1 April 2005). *ITTOIA 2005, ss 296–298* and *ICTA 1988, s 37(2)* seek to ensure that the two sets of rules interact, for example where the landlord is an individual and the tenant is a company. The tenant remains entitled to the above relief even though the previous charge, i.e. the charge on the landlord etc., is a charge to income tax rather than corporation tax.

See generally HMRC Property Income Manual PIM 2300–2340.

56.12 **Other deductions available to tenant.** A tenant is allowed a deduction, in computing the profits of the tenant's property business, by reference to a premium etc. charged on the landlord. The deduction is available to a tenant under a 'taxed lease' (or head lease). A '*taxed lease*' is a lease by reference to which any of the charges at 56.8 have arisen, or the charge on assignment at 56.9 above has arisen (or would have done so but for the availability of the relief at 56.11 above). The deduction is available for any 'qualifying day' on which the whole or part of the premises subject to the taxed lease is either occupied by the tenant for the purposes of carrying on a property business or sub-let. It is given by treating an amount calculated as below as a revenue expense of the tenant's property business, but *not* so as to override any statutory rule governing deductible expenditure generally (see 56.3 above). A '*qualifying day*' is a day that falls within the 'receipt period' (as defined in 56.11 above) of the receipt charged under 56.8 or 56.9 above).

The amount of the expense for *each* qualifying day is the amount given by the formula in 56.8 above in respect of the charge under 56.8 or 56.9 above divided by the number of days in its receipt period.

Examples

(A)

A Ltd grants a 14-year lease of premises to B Ltd for a premium of £50,000 on 1 June 2007. The amount to be included as a receipt in computing the profits of A Ltd's property business for its accounting period ending 31 December 2007 is £37,000 as computed in the *Example* in 56.8 above. B Ltd immediately sub-lets the premises but does not receive any premium.

The number of days in the 14-year receipt period is 5,113. The deduction due to B Ltd in calculating the profits of its property business for any one qualifying day is £37,000 divided by 5,113 = £7.24. For the accounting period ending 31 December 2007, the available deduction is £7.24 x 214 (1.6.05 to 31.12.05) = £1,549.

If, however, the tenant is also entitled to relief under 56.11 above, the tenant is treated as incurring a revenue expense for a qualifying day only to the extent (if any) that the daily amount computed as above exceeds the daily amount of the relief under 56.11.

(B)

The sub-letting in *Example* (A) above ceases in the accounting period ending 31 December 2010. On 1 January 2011, B Ltd again grants a sub-lease of the premises but this time for a period of 11 years at a premium of £70,000. The amount to be included as a receipt in computing the profits of B Ltd's property business for the year ending 31 December 2011 is as follows.

		£
Normal calculation as in 56.8	$£70{,}000 \times \frac{50-10}{50}$	56,000
Less relief as 56.11	$\frac{£37{,}000 \times 11}{14}$	29,071
		£26,929

The number of days in the 11-year receipt period of the sub-lease is 4,018. The daily amount of the relief given is therefore £29,071 divided by 4,018 = £7.24. This equals the daily expense computed in Example (A); as there is no excess, B Ltd is not entitled to any deduction for a revenue expense under these provisions for any of the 4,018 qualifying days covered by the sub-lease.

Supposing B Ltd had been able to obtain a premium of only £30,000 for the 11-year sub-lease. The amount to be included as a receipt in computing the profits of B Ltd's property business for the year ending 31 December 2011 would then be as follows.

		£
Normal calculation as in 56.8	$£30{,}000 \times \frac{50-10}{50}$	24,000
Less $\frac{£37{,}000 \times 11}{14}$ = £29,071 but restricted to		24,000
		Nil

The daily amount of the relief given is now £24,000 divided by 4,018 = £5.97. This is less than the daily expense of £7.24 computed in Example (A), the deficit being £1.27. B Ltd would be entitled to a deduction of £1.27 as a revenue expense for each of the 4,018 qualifying days covered by the sub-lease.

If a sub-lease relates to only part of the premises covered by the main lease, the above rules are applied separately to the different parts of the premises, the premium under the main lease being apportioned between those parts on a just and reasonable basis.

If the premises subject to the taxed lease (or head lease) are used for the purposes of a trade, profession or vocation instead of for those of a property business, very similar rules apply under *ICTA 1988, s 87*, with the deduction being given as an expense in computing the profits of the trade etc. See 66.71 TRADING INCOME.

The total of the deductions allowed under these provisions, any deductions allowed under *ICTA 1988, s 87* referred to above and any relief given under 56.11 above cannot exceed the amount charged under 56.8 or, where appropriate, 56.9 above.

[*ICTA 1988, ss 37(4)–(6), (9), 37A, 39(1); ITTOIA 2005, Sch 1 paras 20, 21*].

The above provisions applied equally for the purposes of income tax before 2005/06 and corporation tax before the financial year 2005. For 2005/06 onwards, the income tax rules are in *ITTOIA 2005, ss 292–295* (the above narrative being based on these provisions) but the equivalent corporation tax rules are in *ICTA 1988, s 37(4)–(6), (9)* (as amended by *ITTOIA 2005, Sch 1 para 20*) and in *ICTA 1988, s 37A* (as introduced by *ITTOIA 2005, Sch 1 para 21*). *ITTOIA 2005, ss 296–298* and *ICTA 1988, ss 37(9)* and *37A* seek to ensure that the two sets of rules interact, for example where the tenant is a company and the landlord is an individual. The tenant remains entitled to the above deduction even though the lease premium is charged to income tax rather than corporation tax.

See generally HMRC Property Income Manual PIM 2300–2340.

Simon's Direct Tax Service. See **A4.221** *et seq.*

56.13 **Information re leases.** Information, including consideration for their grant or assignment etc., may be required, subject to penalty for non-compliance, from present or former lessees or occupiers, or from agents managing property or receiving rents etc. [*TMA 1970, ss 19, 98; ITTOIA 1988, Sch 1 para 367*].

56.14 RENT FACTORING

The following provisions apply to transactions entered into after 20 March 2000 and before 6 June 2006 and are repealed by *FA 2006, Sch 6 para 1* as a consequence of the introduction of the wider provisions described at 5.13 ANTI-AVOIDANCE.

For the following purposes a transaction entered into after 20 March 2000 and before 6 June 2006 is a '*finance agreement*' if, in accordance with generally accepted accounting practice, the accounts of a company receiving money under the transaction would record a financial obligation in relation thereto, and any amount so received is a '*finance amount*'. In the case of a member of a group of companies, this applies also to the consolidated group accounts. A company is treated for this purpose as receiving any money which falls to be taken into account as a receipt in calculating the company's corporation tax liability (or would do so were the company UK-resident).

If a finance agreement transfers a right to receive rent (including any sum chargeable under Schedule A or in the course of a UK property business) in respect of UK land (other than by means of the grant of a lease of UK land), any person receiving a finance amount is treated as receiving it as rent in the chargeable period in which the agreement is made in the course of a Schedule A or UK property business, and the finance amount is taken into account in computing profits of that business for that period. 'Transfer of a right to receive rent' includes any arrangement under which rent ceases to form part of the receipts taken into account in computing a company's liability to income tax or corporation tax.

This provision does *not* apply where either:

(*a*) (in relation to finance agreements entered into before 16 March 2005) the term over which the financial obligation is to be reduced exceeds 15 years (no account being taken of any period beginning after the financial obligation has been substantially reduced and during which the arrangements for reduction differ from the arrangements applicable in a previous period otherwise than as the result of a provision for periodic review, on commercial terms, of rent under a lease); or

(*b*) the arrangements for reduction of the financial obligation substantially depend on the entitlement to a capital allowance of a person not connected (within *ICTA 1988, s 839*) with the person from whom the right to receive rent was transferred; or

(*c*) *ICTA 1988, s 36(1)* or *ITTOIA 2005, s 284* (sale with right to reconveyance, see 56.10 above) applies (disregarding, in the former case, the extension under *section 36(3)* to cases where land is leased back to the vendor within one month after the sale), or would apply if the price at which an estate or interest is sold were to exceed the price at which it is to be reconveyed; or (*d*) *ICTA 1988, s 780* (sale and leaseback) applies (see 5.15 ANTI-AVOIDANCE); or

(*e*) the finance amount is brought into account in computing Schedule D, Case I profits other than by virtue of *FA 1989, s 83* (life assurance receipts).

Where the provision *does* apply, *ITTOIA 2005, s 285* does not apply and *ICTA 1988, s 36*(*1*) does *not* apply if it would do so only by virtue of *section 36*(*3*).

See also 5.16 ANTI-AVOIDANCE with respect to rent factoring of leases of plant or machinery.

Interposed leases. Where, under a finance agreement, a lease under which a premium is payable is granted in respect of UK land, and it is in respect of the receipt of the premium that the financial obligation would be recorded (i.e. the premium is effectively a loan in return for the right to receive future rental income), the person to whom the premium is payable is treated as receiving it as rent in the chargeable period in which the agreement is made in the course of a Schedule A or UK property business, and the premium is taken into account in computing profits of that business for that period. This provision does *not* apply if:

(i) (in relation to finance agreements entered into before 16 March 2005, subject to the qualifications below) the term over which the financial obligation is to be reduced exceeds 15 years (and see the qualification under (*a*) above); or

(ii) (in relation to finance agreements entered into before 16 March 2005, subject to the qualifications below) the length of the lease (calculated as under *ICTA 1988, s 38*, see 56.8 above) either does not exceed 15 years or is not significantly different from the term over which the financial obligation is to be reduced; or

(iii) the arrangements for reduction of the financial obligation substantially depend on the entitlement to a capital allowance of a person not connected (within *ICTA 1988, s 839*) with the person who granted the lease in respect of which the premium is payable; or

(iv) all or part of the premium is brought into account in computing Schedule D, Case I profits other than by virtue of *FA 1989, s 83* (life assurance receipts), or in computing the profits of a trade carried on wholly or partly in the UK under *ITTOIA 2005*.

As regards (i) and (ii) above, where a finance agreement was entered into between 20 March 2000 and 15 March 2005 (inclusive) and the interposed lease provisions would apply but for (i) and (ii) above, no deduction is allowed, in any accounting period ending on or after 16 March 2005, for the rental payments (falling within those provisions) made on or after date, as a trading expense under Schedule D Case I, a management expense or expense of an insurance company if they would otherwise be so deductible. Where the payment is made on or after 16 March 2005 in respect of a rental period straddling that date, the disallowance applies only to the amount relating to that part of the period falling on or after that date.

Where the provision *does* apply, *ICTA 1988, s 34* and *ITTOIA 2005, ss 277–281* (treatment of premiums as rent, see 56.8 above) do *not* apply.

Insurance business. As regards companies carrying on insurance business, the above provisions do not require any amount to be brought in in any life assurance business profits computation made on Schedule D, Case I principles. *ICTA 1988, s 432A* (apportionment of income and gains between different classes of business) has effect in relation to any sum which is or would be treated as received by virtue of the above provisions.

Definitions. A 'lease' for the above purposes includes an underlease, sublease, tenancy or licence and an agreement for any of those things, but does not include a mortgage or heritable security. 'Premium' includes any like sum, whether payable to the immediate or a superior landlord or to a person connected (within *ICTA 1988, s 839*) with either (and in

Scotland it includes a grassum payable to any landlord or intermediate landlord on the creation of a sub-lease), and also certain payments deemed to be premiums under *ICTA 1988, s 34(4)(5)*.

[*ICTA 1988, ss 43A–43G; FA 2000, s 110; FA 2002, Sch 40 Pt 3(16); SI 2001 No 3629, Article 15; ITTOIA 2005, Sch 1 paras 26–30; FA 2005, Sch 4 para 21; F(No 2)A 2005, s 39, Sch 7 para 1; FA 2006, Sch 6 para 1*].

56.15 CAPITAL GAINS

Any Schedule A (or UK property) business consisting of the letting of furnished holiday accommodation is treated as a trade for the purposes of replacement of business assets relief, relief for loans to traders, retirement relief and substantial shareholdings exemption. See 13 CAPITAL GAINS—SUBSTANTIAL SHAREHOLDINGS and Tolley's Capital Gains Tax under Furnished Holiday Accommodation, Losses and Rollover Relief. [*TGCA 1992, s 241; FA 2002, Sch 8 para 3; ITTOIA 2005, Sch 1 para 441*].

56.16 NON-RESIDENT LANDLORDS—COLLECTION FROM AGENTS OR TENANTS

Where a landlord is non-UK resident, tax is to be deducted at source by the agent for the property or, where there is no agent, the tenant, with a final settling up with the non-resident landlord. The regulations giving effect to these requirements provide broadly as follows.

(i) Letting agents who receive or have control over UK property income of a non-resident must operate the scheme.

(ii) Where there is no letting agent acting, tenants of a non-resident must operate the scheme.

(iii) Tenants who pay less than £100 per week do not have to operate the scheme unless asked to do so by HMRC.

(iv) Letting agents and tenants who have to operate the scheme must pay tax at the basic rate each quarter on the non-resident's UK property income less certain allowable expenses and deductions, and must give the non-resident an annual certificate showing details of tax deducted.

(v) Non-residents whose property income is subject to deduction of tax may set the tax deducted against their UK tax liability through their self-assessment.

(vi) Non-residents may apply to HMRC for approval to receive their UK property income without deduction of tax provided that:

   (*a*) their UK tax affairs are up to date;

   (*b*) they have never had any obligations in relation to UK tax; or

   (*c*) they do not expect to be liable to UK income tax,

   and that they undertake to comply with all their UK tax obligations in the future. An appeal may be made against refusal or withdrawal of approval

The regulations also make provision for interest on unpaid tax and for payments on account under self-assessment, and set out details of the annual information requirements on those operating the scheme, and of other information to be supplied on request. Penalties apply under *TMA 1970, s 98* for non-compliance with these return and information provisions.

[*ICTA 1988, s 42A(4)–(7); SI 1995 No 2902; ITTOIA 2005, Sch 1 para 25*].

HMRC publish detailed guidance notes for those required to operate the scheme (see www.hmrc.gov.uk/cnr/nrl_guide_notes.pdf and www.hmrc.gov.uk/cnr/nr_landlords.htm).

Simon's Direct Tax Service. See A4.503.

56.17 **MISCELLANEOUS PROVISIONS**

Capital allowances on plant and machinery. A property business is a qualifying activity for the purposes of such allowances under *CAA 2001, Pt 2* (see 10.24 CAPITAL ALLOWANCES). Capital allowances were similarly available under *CAA 1990, Pt II* on plant or machinery as if the property business were a separate trade for which the item was provided (subject to further separation where there are furnished holiday lettings — see 56.5 above). Allowances are thus given as expenses, and charges treated as receipts, of the business. Plant or machinery provided for use in a dwelling-house is excluded (with a just and reasonable apportionment of expenditure where such use is partial). [*CAA 2001, ss 15, 16, 35; CAA 1990, s 28A; ITTOIA 2005, Sch 1 paras 526, 527, 533*].

Overseas property business. Rental income from land situated outside the UK is chargeable under Schedule D Case V. The letting is treated as a separate business and the same computational rules (including the lease premium rules) apply in determining the receipts and expenses to be included in the Schedule A computation as if the property were situated in the UK. [*ICTA 1988, s 70A*]. The special rules governing the tax treatment of furnished holiday lettings do not apply to an overseas property business. [*ICTA 1988, s 70A*(*6*)]. Case V losses may be carried forward and set off against Case V profits from the same business in subsequent accounting periods, provided that the business is carried on on a commercial basis or in the exercise of statutory functions. [*ICTA 1988, s 392B*].

Non-resident companies are within the charge to income tax (not corporation tax) in certain circumstances (see 60 RESIDENCE). Where a company starts or ceases an overseas property business or to be within the charge to corporation tax in respect of an overseas property business, it is treated as starting or ceasing to carry on the business at that time. [*ICTA 1988, s 337*(*2*)*; FA 2002, Sch 30 para 1; ITTOIA 2005, Sch 1 para 145*].

Mutual businesses. The normal exemption for mutual companies (48) does not extend to property businesses, the transactions and relationships involved in mutual business being instead treated as if they were between persons between whom no relationship of mutuality existed. Any surplus is chargeable on the company to which the profits arise or which is entitled to the profits. (This does not affect the treatment of Co-operative Housing Associations — see 36 HOUSING ASSOCIATIONS).[*ICTA 1988, s 21C; ITTOIA 2005, Sch 1 para 14*].

Land managed as one estate. The election relating to land in one ownership and managed as one estate under *ICTA 1988, s 26* (whereby the cost of maintenance can be set against a notional Schedule A rental income called the 'annual value') is abolished for accounting periods beginning on or after 1 April 2001. [*FA 1998, s 39*].

Items apportioned on sale of land. Where on the sale of a property, any receipts or outgoings due to be received or paid by the vendor is apportioned to the purchaser, it is treated as having been received or paid by the purchaser immediately after completion. Similarly, where part of a receipt or payment due to be received or paid by the purchaser is apportioned to the vendor that part is treated as if the vendor had received or paid it in the period immediately before completion. Where such receipts and outgoings are apportioned to the vendor, then, in computing the profits of the vendor's property business, the part apportioned to the vendor is treated as being of the same nature, i.e. revenue or capital, as the receipt or outgoing itself. [*ICTA 1988, s 40; ITTOIA 2005, Sch 1 para 23*]. So, for example, if rent is receivable in arrears and the sale price includes an accrual for rent receivable up to date of sale, the amount of that accrual is income in the hands of the vendor and not capital.

Sea walls. For allowances for expenditure on making sea walls, see *ICTA 1988, s 30*; *ITTOIA 2005, Sch 1 para 15* and *Hesketh v Bray CA 1888, 2 TC 380*.

Maintenance and repairs of property. Under HMRC Extra Statutory Concession B4, withdrawn from 1 April 2001, the estimated cost of any maintenance and repairs obviated by alterations etc., was allowed provided the alterations were not so extensive as to amount to reconstruction, and there had been no such change in the use of the property as would have rendered the repairs etc., unnecessary.

Electric-line wayleaves. Where rent is receivable for a UK electric-line wayleave, it is chargeable to corporation tax under Schedule D. If, however, a company carries on a UK property business in relation to some or all of the land to which the wayleave relates and the business has other receipts for the accounting period in question, the rent receivable for the wayleave is brought into account under Schedule A instead of Schedule D.

Rent is receivable for a UK electric-line wayleave if it is receivable in respect of an easement enjoyed in the UK, which includes any right, privilege or benefit in, over or derived from land in connection with any electric, telegraph or telephone wire or cable, including supporting poles or pylons and related apparatus. All references above to 'rent' include any other receipt in the nature of rent and, in particular, the 'other receipts' referred to in 56.3 above.

[*ICTA 1988, s 120; ITTOIA 2005, Sch 1 para 104*].

Easements falling outside *ICTA 1988, s 120* are charged to corporation tax under Schedule D Case VI [*ICTA 1988, s 18(3)*]. Where the receipts fall to assessed under Schedule D, the non-statutory practice is for the receipts to fall within Schedule D Case I where they can be regarded as trading income or otherwise under Schedule D Case VI. Single lump sum payments are treated as capital receipts. (See HMRC Property Income Manual, PIM 1114.) For income tax purposes, *ITTOIA 2005, ss 22, 344* provide for rents received to be treated as property income but where all the rents relate to land associated with a trade, for them to be treated as trade income at the taxpayer's choice. (See Change 5 listed in Annex 1 to the Income Tax (Trading and Other Income) Bill.)

Mines, quarries etc. Profits of mines, quarries, gravel pits, sand pits, brickfields, ironworks, gas works, canals, railways, rights of fishing, rights of markets, fairs and tolls and like concerns (as specified in *ICTA 1988, s 55*) are computed and charged to corporation tax under Schedule D (see 66.65 TRADING INCOME). [*ICTA 1988, s 119*].

Foot and mouth outbreak. For the full range of measures, in particular in relation to rent waivers and including easing of restrictions on relief for furnished holiday lettings losses, in relation to the 2001 foot and mouth disease outbreak, see Revenue Tax Bulletin Special Edition May 2001.

57 Purchase by a Company of its Own Shares

Simon's Direct Tax Service. See **D1.134, D2.504** *et seq.*

57.1 INTRODUCTION

Companies Act 1985, s 162 et seq. permit a company to purchase its own shares, subject to various conditions. Such a purchase would normally be classified for tax purposes as a DISTRIBUTION (23), but in order to increase the attractions to entrepreneurs and investors of equity capital, *FA 1982* introduced a measure of relief for certain companies, generally small and family ones. See 57.2 *et seq.* below.

Under *The Companies (Acquisition of Own Shares)(Treasury Shares) Regulations 2003* (*SI 2003 No 1116*), companies will, from 1 December 2003, be able to purchase *and hold* their own shares (such shares generally being referred to as 'treasury shares'). The tax consequences of the acquisition by a company with share capital of its own shares are accordingly set out as detailed below, similarly from 1 December 2003. This will not make any difference to the tax treatment of own shares purchased and immediately cancelled, but enables the position to be determined where it is not clear at the time of the purchase whether any of the shares are subsequently to be cancelled.

(*a*) The acquisition by a company of its own shares is not treated as the acquisition of an asset.

(*b*) A company is not treated as a member of itself by reason of the acquisition or holding of its own shares.

(*c*) (Subject to (*f*) below) the company's issued share capital is treated as reduced by the nominal value of the shares acquired.

(*d*) (Subject to (*f*) below) such of those shares as are not cancelled on acquisition are treated as if they had been so cancelled.

(*e*) Any subsequent cancellation of the shares by the company is disregarded (and so is not treated as a disposal of an asset and does not give rise to an allowable capital loss).

(*f*) Where the shares are issued to the company as bonus shares, i.e. as paid up otherwise than by the receipt of 'new consideration' (within *ICTA 1988, s 254*, see 23.11 DISTRIBUTIONS), (*c*) and (*d*) above do not apply, and the shares are treated as not having been issued.

(*g*) Where, disregarding (*a*)–(*f*) above, a company holds any of its own shares and issues bonus shares in respect of any of those shares, these provisions do not prevent the existing shares from being the company's holding for the purposes of *TCGA 1992, s 126* (company reorganisations etc., see Tolley's Capital Gains Tax under Shares and Securities), although this does not apply where *section 126* is applied in a modified form by virtue of any other enactment.

(*h*) Where a company disposes of its own shares and, but for (*a*)–(*f*) above, would be regarded as holding the shares immediately before the disposal, (d), (e) and (*f*) above cease to apply in relation to the shares disposed of (the '*relevant shares*'), and:

- (i) the relevant shares are treated as having been issued by the company as new shares to the acquirer at the time of the disposal (and not as having been disposed of by the company at that time);
- (ii) the acquirer is treated as having subscribed for the shares an amount equal to the amount or value of the consideration (if any) payable for the disposal;
- (iii) if the amount or value of that consideration does not exceed the nominal value of the shares, the share capital of those shares is to be treated for the

purposes of *ICTA 1988, Part 6* (company distributions, etc.) as if it were an amount equal to the amount or value of the consideration; and

(iv) if the amount or value of that consideration exceeds their nominal value, the shares are treated as if they had been issued at a premium representing that excess.

(*i*) Where a company purchases its own shares and the price payable is a Schedule D, Case I or II expense (i.e. the company is a share dealer), (*a*)–(*g*) above do not apply, and (*h*) above does not apply to the disposal by the company of any of the shares.

[*FA 2003, s 195; SI 2003 No 3077*].

For consequential changes relating to stamp duties and venture capital trust investments, see *FA 2003, Sch 40*.

57.2 SPECIAL RELIEFS

Treatment as a DISTRIBUTION (23) does not apply to certain payments (and other items normally treated as distributions) made by a company for the purchase, redemption or repayment of its own shares. Such payments etc.,in the hands of the vendor, are brought into account for capital gains purposes only (but see 57.7 below as regards dealers in securities).

See, however, 23.9 DISTRIBUTIONS as regards certain subsequent bonus issues.

Where the purchase, etc. *is* treated as a distribution, see also 23.16 DISTRIBUTIONS as regards capital gains consequences.

The conditions for non-distribution treatment of such payments are set out at 57.3, 57.4 below. Revenue Tax Bulletin February 1996 pp 280–282 contains a short article dealing with various matters which in HMRC's experience are sometimes overlooked or misunderstood, although these are all covered in this chapter.

Simon's Direct Tax Service. See **D1.134, D2.504.**

57.3 CONDITIONS TO BE SATISFIED BY COMPANY

For the special relief in 57.2 above to apply, the following conditions must be satisfied.

(i) The company must be an 'unquoted company', i.e. neither the company, nor any company of which it is a '*51% subsidiary*', must have any class of shares listed in the official list of a stock exchange. (Shares dealt in on the Stock Exchange Unlisted Securities Market were not treated as quoted, see HMRC Share Valuation Manual, SVM 09060.)

Securities on the Alternative Investment Market ('AIM') are similarly treated as unquoted for these purposes. (HMRC Share Valuation Manual, SVM 09070).

A company is a '*51% subsidiary*' of another if more than 50% of its ordinary share capital is beneficially owned directly or indirectly by the other company. [*ICTA 1988, s 838*].

(ii) The company must be either a 'trading company' or the 'holding company of a trading group' (for definitions, see 32.33 GROUPS OF COMPANIES). For this purpose, 'trade' does not include dealing in shares, securities, land or futures.

[*ICTA 1988, ss 219(1), 229(1)*].

Simon's Direct Tax Service. See **D2.504.**

57.4 CONDITIONS TO BE SATISFIED IN RESPECT OF PURCHASE ETC.

There are two different sets of conditions, one of which must be met to enable the payment etc. to qualify for the treatment as in 57.2 above. In addition, as a general condition, the consideration must be in money and must be paid immediately, i.e. instalment payment is not possible. (Revenue Tax Bulletin February 1996 p 281).

(1) Substantially the whole of the payment etc. (apart from any sum applied in paying capital gains tax on the disposal) must be used to meet the payee's inheritance tax liability on a death, within two years of that death, being a liability he could not have met without undue hardship other than through the purchase etc. of the shares or the purchase etc. of its own shares by another company within 57.3 above. [*ICTA 1988, s 219*(*1*)(*b*)].

(2) The purchase etc. of the shares must be made wholly or mainly to benefit a trade carried on by the company or by any '75% subsidiary'; it must not form part of a scheme or arrangement the main, or one such, purpose of which is either the obtaining by the vendor of a share in the company's profits without receiving a dividend, or the avoidance of tax; and the further conditions (i) to (viii) below must be satisfied in relation to the vendor. [*ICTA 1988, s 219*(*1*)(*a*)]. As regards whether a purchase etc. is for the benefit of the trade, HMRC have given their interpretation in HMRC Statement of Practice, SP 2/82. This emphasises that the purpose must be the benefit of a trade and not, for example, the benefit of the vending shareholder (although he will usually also benefit), or of some wider commercial purpose to which the payment etc. may be put, or of a non-trading activity of the trading company. Generally, the condition will be satisfied where (after taking into account any associate's interests) the vending shareholder is genuinely giving up his entire interest of all kinds in the company. Four examples are cited.

(*a*) The withdrawal of his investment by an outside shareholder providing equity finance.

(*b*) The retirement of the proprietor of a company to make way for new management.

(*c*) The death of a shareholder, on which his personal representatives or the beneficiaries do not wish to keep the shares.

(*d*) A disagreement over the management of the company.

In the last example, however, the condition would only be satisfied if the disagreement would, as will usually be the case, have an adverse effect on the running of the trade. It would not be satisfied if the disagreement were, for example, over whether the company should discontinue trading and become an investment company, and the vending shareholder advocated the continuance of trading.

It may happen that the company wants, but cannot afford, to buy out a shareholder completely. In these circumstances, it is acceptable for the repurchase to proceed and for the shareholder to lend part of the consideration back to the company immediately after the purchase. Where the shares are of high market value and the issued capital is relatively small, this could result in the shareholder continuing to be 'connected with' the company (see condition (vii) below). To prevent this, it is acceptable for the company to make a bonus issue to increase its issued capital before the repurchase. (Revenue Tax Bulletin February 1996 p 281).

Where a shareholder is only 'substantially reducing' his interest (see (iii) below), the only situations in which HMRC envisage the condition being satisfied are where a complete disinvestment is to be achieved in a number of transactions, or where a small shareholding (not exceeding 5% of issued share capital) is retained for sentimental reasons.

A company is a '*75% subsidiary*' of another if not less than 75% of its ordinary share capital is beneficially owned directly or indirectly by the other company. [*ICTA 1988, s 838*].

The further conditions which must be satisfied (as above) are as follows.

(i) The vendor (and any nominee holder) must be **resident** and (except for companies) **ordinarily resident** in the UK in the year of assessment of the purchase etc. The residence and ordinary residence of trustees is determined as under *TCGA 1992, s 69* (see Tolley's Capital Gains Tax under Settlements), and that of personal representatives follows that of the deceased immediately before his death.

(ii) The vendor must have held the shares for the **five years** before the purchase etc. If he acquired them under a will or intestacy, or as a personal representative, ownership by the deceased person (and, in the former case, by his personal representative) counts as ownership by the vendor, and the qualifying period is reduced to three years. Similarly, where the shares were transferred to the vendor by his spouse or (from 5 December 2005) civil partner living with him at the time of transfer, the spouse's or partner's ownership counts as ownership by the vendor *provided that* the transferor either is still his spouse or partner living with him or is deceased at the time of the purchase etc. Where identification of different holdings of shares of the same class is necessary, earlier acquisitions are taken into account before later ones, and previous disposals identified with later acquisitions before earlier ones, for this purpose.

Except in the case of certain shares allotted as stock dividends and falling within *ICTA 1988, s 249* (see Tolley's Income Tax under Savings and Investment Income), the time of acquisition of shares acquired through a reorganisation of share capital or conversion of securities etc. is that determined under *TCGA 1992, Pt IV, Ch II* (i.e. generally the date of acquisition of the original shares) (see Tolley's Capital Gains Tax under Shares and Securities).

(iii) The vendor's shareholding must be **substantially reduced** or eliminated by the purchase etc.

A shareholding is '*substantially reduced*' if and only if the proportion of the company's issued share capital held by him immediately after the purchase etc. does not exceed 75% of that immediately before the purchase. It is **not** regarded as so reduced if the share of profits to which the vendor would be entitled (beneficially except in the case of trustees or personal representatives) on a *distribution of available profits* by the company immediately after the purchase etc. exceeds 75% of the corresponding share immediately before the purchase etc.

Profits available for distribution by a company are as defined in *Companies Act 1985, s 263* (broadly, accumulated realised profits not distributed or capitalised *less* accumulated realised losses not written off) *plus* £100 *plus*, where any person is entitled to periodic distributions calculated by reference to fixed rates or amounts, the amount required to make the maximum distribution to which he would be entitled for a year. The division of profits available for distribution also assumes that the full amount of any such fixed entitlement for a year is attributed to the person entitled to it. Where the total of the payments etc. made at one time for the purchase etc. of the company's own shares exceeds the profits available for distribution, those profits are increased by the amount of the excess for the purposes of these provisions.

(iv) **Associated persons.** If, immediately after the purchase etc, any shares in the company are owned by an *associate* of the vendor, the combined interests of the vendor and his associate(s) must satisfy (iii) above.

'*Associate*' includes spouse or (from 5 December 2005) civil partner and minor children, and a broad range of relationships whereby an individual or company may be able to influence the actions of another, or to benefit from the co-ordination of their actions. See *ICTA 1988, s 227* as regards trustees and certain employees.

(v) If the company making the purchase etc. is, immediately before that purchase etc., a member of a 'group of companies', and, immediately after the purchase etc., either:

(*a*) the vendor owns shares in other group member(s); or

(*b*) he still owns shares in the company making the purchase etc. *and* had immediately before the purchase etc. owned shares in other group member(s),

then (iii) above must be satisfied in relation to his interest in the group as a whole, taken as the average of his proportionate holdings of the issued share capital of the company purchasing (etc.) the shares and of all other group members in which he holds shares immediately before or after the purchase etc. (including, for averaging purposes, companies in which he held shares immediately before or after the purchase etc. but in which he holds no shares when the average is to be determined).

A '*group of companies*' for this purpose is a company (not a 51% subsidiary (see 57.3(i) above) of any other company) and its 51% subsidiaries, *except that* a company which ceased to be a 51% subsidiary of another before the time of purchase etc. of the shares is treated as continuing to be such a subsidiary if at that time there were arrangements in existence under which it could again become such a subsidiary. Also, where the whole or a significant part of the business first carried on within three years before the purchase etc. by an unquoted company (see 57.3(i) above), the 'successor company', was previously carried on by the company purchasing (etc.) the shares (or by a member of the same group), the successor company and any company of which it is a 51% subsidiary are treated as being members of the same group as the company purchasing (etc.) the shares.

(vi) Where an associate (see (iv) above) of the vendor owns shares in any company in the same group (see (v) above) as the company purchasing (etc.) the shares immediately before the purchase etc., the combined interests of vendor and associate(s) must satisfy (v) above.

(vii) The vendor must not, immediately after the purchase etc., be 'connected with' the company purchasing (etc.) the shares or any company in the same group (see (v) above).

He is so '*connected with*' a company if, together with his associates (see (iv) above), he directly or indirectly possesses or is (or will be) entitled to acquire:

(*a*) more than 30% of its voting power, its issued ordinary share capital, or its issued share capital and loan capital (i.e. any debt incurred by the company for money borrowed, for capital assets acquired, for any right to income created in its favour or for insufficient consideration); or

(*b*) rights enabling him to more than 30% of its assets *available for distribution to the company's equity holders* (see 32.8, 32.9 GROUPS OF COMPANIES), or if he has 'control' of it. '*Control*' for this purpose means the power of a person by shareholding or voting power (whether directly or through another company), or under Articles of Association, to secure that the company's affairs are conducted according to his wishes. [*ICTA 1988, s 840*]. An interest in loan capital acquired in the normal course of a money-lending business is disregarded provided the lender takes no part in the management or conduct of the company.

(viii) The purchase etc. must not be part of a scheme or arrangement the likely result of which is the acquiring by the vendor of rights such that, had he had them immediately after the purchase etc., any of (iii) to (vii) above could not have been satisfied. Any transaction within one year of the purchase etc. is deemed to be part of a scheme of which the purchase etc. is also a part.

Where any of (iii) to (viii) above are not satisfied, they will nevertheless be treated as satisfied where the vendor proposed or agreed to the purchase etc. in order that the conditions in (iv) or (vi) above regarding the substantial reduction of combined interests of a vendor and his associate(s) could be satisfied in respect of a purchase etc. of shares owned by such an associate, to the extent that that result is produced by virtue of the purchase etc.

[*ICTA 1988, s 219(1)(a), ss 220–229; SI 2005 No 3229, regs 49, 50*].

For a case where the above conditions, in particular condition (iii) above, were not met, see the case of *Preston Meats Ltd v Hammond [2005] SSCD 90.*

Simon's Direct Tax Service. See **D2.507.**

57.5 HMRC INFORMATION POWERS

Within 60 days of making a payment etc. treated by the company as not being a distribution under the provisions at 57.2 to 57.4 above, the company must notify the inspector of the particulars of the payment etc., and why it is regarded as falling within those provisions. If within 57.4(2) above, any person connected with the company (see 57.4(2)(vii) above) who knows of any scheme or arrangement within 57.4(2)(viii) above must give details thereof to the inspector within 60 days of his coming to know of both the payment etc. and the scheme etc.

If the inspector has reason to believe that a payment etc. treated by the company as being within the above provisions may form part of a scheme etc. within 57.4(2) or 57.4(2)(viii) above, he may require the company or any person connected with it (see 57.4(2)(vii) above) to furnish him, within not less than 60 days, with a written declaration as to whether, according to information reasonably obtainable, any such scheme, etc. exists or has existed, and with such other information reasonably required by him as the company or person can reasonably obtain.

Any person receiving a payment etc. treated as falling within the above provisions, or on whose behalf such a payment etc. is received, may be required to notify the inspector as to whether he received the payment etc. on his own or another's behalf and, in the latter case, to supply the other person's name and address.

The penalty provisions of *TMA 1970, s 98* (see Tolley's Income Tax under Penalties) apply to returns required as above.

[*ICTA 1988, s 226*].

57.6 CLEARANCE PROCEDURE

A company may apply in writing for clearance from HMRC that a proposed transaction falls or, as the case may be, does not fall within the provisions at 57.2 to 57.4 above. HMRC must notify its decision within 30 days of receiving the application or, if further particulars are requested, within 30 days of the furnishing of the last such particulars. Such particulars must be requested within 30 days of the application (or of the furnishing of particulars previously requested), and must be supplied by the company within 30 days (or such longer period as HMRC may allow). Failure to supply full and accurate information voids any clearance. [*ICTA 1988, s 225*].

Applications for clearance should be addressed to Mohini Sawhney, Clearance and Counteraction Team, Anti-Avoidance Group Intelligence, First Floor, 22 Kingsway, London WC2B 6NR (or, if market-sensitive information is included, to Eric Gardner at that address). Applications may be faxed to 020–7438 4409 or emailed to reconstructions@hmrc.gsi.gov.uk (after advising Eric Gardner (on 020–7438 6585) if market-sensitive information is included). Application may be made in a single letter to the same address for clearance under *ICTA 1988, s 225* and under any one or more of *ICTA 1988, s 215* (demergers, see 32.39 GROUPS OF COMPANIES), *ICTA 1988, s 707* (transactions in securities, see 5.2 ANTI-AVOIDANCE), *TCGA 1992, s 138(1)* (share exchanges, see Tolley's Capital Gains Tax under Anti-Avoidance), *TCGA 1992, s 139(5)* (reconstructions involving the transfer of a business, see 11.9 CAPITAL GAINS), *TCGA 1992, s 140B* (transfer of a UK trade between EU member states, see 11.11 CAPITAL GAINS), *TCGA 1992, s 140D* (transfer of non-UK trade between EU member states, see 11.12 CAPITAL GAINS) and *FA 2002, Sch 29 para 88* (see 39.27 INTANGIBLE ASSETS).

The application should state whether the purchase, etc. is regarded as falling within *ICTA 1988, s 219(1)(a)* or *s 219(1)(b)* (see 57.4(2) or (1) above respectively), and give details of any earlier clearance applications (by the company or by a fellow group member). If the purchase etc. is regarded as within *ICTA 1988, s 219(1)(a)*, the application should include:

(i) the name, tax district and reference number, and status (e.g. whether a trading company, etc.) of the purchasing (etc.) company, and confirmation that it is unquoted;

(ii) full details of any group of which it is a member, and of company and (if appropriate) group shareholdings;

(iii) details of the proposed share purchase and of any other transactions between the company and vendor at or about the same time, and confirmation that the purchase is permitted by the company's Articles;

(iv) full details of any prior transactions and of the reasons for, and the benefits expected from, the purchase, etc.;

(v) confirmation, with any necessary calculations, etc., that the other conditions outlined in 57.4(2) above are satisfied; and

(vi) the company's latest available balance sheet and profit and loss account (and, in the case of a member of a group, those of any fellow group members and, if appropriate, of the group as a whole) together with a note of any later relevant and material changes.

If the purchase, etc. is regarded as within *ICTA 1988, s 219(1)(b)*, the application should include the information as at (i) to (iv) and (vi) above, together with full details of the inheritance tax liability concerned and of the circumstances in which 'undue hardship' would arise.

An application for clearance that a proposed purchase, etc. does **not** fall within the provisions at 57.2 TO 57.4 above should give full details of the purchasing (etc.) company and of the proposed purchase, etc., and be accompanied by a statement of the grounds on which clearance is sought.

(HMRC Statement of Practice, SP 2/82).

Simon's Direct Tax Service. See D2.509.

57.7 DEALERS IN SECURITIES

Any distribution by UK-resident companies (and payments representative thereof) received by a dealer in securities, and any payment representative of such a distribution (or payment) made by such a dealer, must be taken into account in the dealer's Schedule D, Case I or II computation. This is subject from 1 July 2004 to *ICTA 1988, Sch 23A para 7A* in relation to manufactured payments under arrangements having an unallowable purpose (see 5.9 ANTI-AVOIDANCE). See 66.74 TRADING INCOME.

Accordingly, where a dealer receives such a distribution, the normal exemption from corporation tax of UK company distributions (see 23.16 DISTRIBUTIONS) does not apply.

A person is for these purposes a dealer in relation to any distribution if, on a sale of the shares in respect of which the distribution is made, the price would be taken into account in computing Schedule D, Case I or II profits (assuming that it would not fall to be treated as a qualifying distribution) other than insurance business profits.

[*ICTA 1988, s 95; FA 2003, Sch 43 Pt 3(6); FA 2004, 137(2); ITTOIA 2005, Sch 1 para 74*].

The requirement for certain profits from insurance business to be calculated on Schedule D, Case I principles does not bring them within *section 95* (see *Oakes v The Equitable Life Assurance Society; Bibby v The Prudential Assurance Co Ltd Ch D 2000, 73 TC 235*).

58 Regional Development Grants

Simon's Direct Tax Service B3.929.

58.1 **TREATMENT FOR TAX PURPOSES**

Capital expenditure. Regional development grants, under *Industry Act 1972, Part I*, were payable on expenditure on certain buildings and certain new plant, machinery and mining works in special development areas, development areas, intermediate areas and derelict land clearance areas (which altogether covered a large part of UK except S.E. England).

The amount of a grant does **not** operate to reduce capital expenditure on which CAPITAL ALLOWANCES (10) are claimable, except where the grant results in a reduction in the expenditure allowable for PRT purposes (see 51 OIL COMPANIES). [*CAA 2001, s 534(1), Sch 3 para 106; CAA 1990, s 153(1); FA 1982, ss 137, 138*]. The same provisions apply to corresponding grants in NI.

Revenue expenditure. Any such grant paid to a trader under *Industry Act 1972, s 7* or *8* or the corresponding NI legislation (and certain other NI payments) and not designated as paid for specified capital expenditure or as compensation for the loss of capital assets is treated as a trading receipt (or, in the case of companies with investment business (or for accounting periods beginning before 1 April 2004, investment companies), as a Case VI receipt) in so far as it would not otherwise be so treated. [*ICTA 1988, s 93; SI 2004 No 2310, Article 11*]. An 'interest relief grant' under that *section* was held to be a trading receipt in *Burman v Thorn Domestic Appliances (Electrical) Ltd Ch D 1981, 55 TC 493*, as was an indeterminate grant under that *section* in *Ryan v Crabtree Denims Ltd Ch D 1987, 60 TC 183*.

Grants treated as exempt. Grants under *Industrial Development Act 1982, Part II* to traders, etc. or to investment companies are exempt from corporation tax. [*ICTA 1988, s 92*].

59 Research and Development Expenditure

Simon's Direct Tax Service D2.12

The headings in this chapter are as follows.

59.1 INTRODUCTION

Relief for expenditure of a revenue nature on 'research and development' applies for expenditure incurred **on or after 1 April 2000** in the case of 'small or medium-sized enterprises' and for expenditure incurred **on or after 1 April 2002** in the case of 'large companies'. [*FA 2000, Sch 20 para 26(1); FA 2002, Sch 12 para 20(1)*]. For reliefs for research and development expenditure of a capital nature (previously 'scientific research allowances'), see 10.52 CAPITAL ALLOWANCES.

Additional reliefs are available along similar lines for expenditure incurred on or after 22 April 2003 on research and development relating to certain vaccines or medicines. [*FA 2002, s 54, Schs 13, 14; SI 2003 No 1472*].

See 59.2, 59.9 and 59.18 below respectively for details of each of these reliefs.

From 1 November 2006, six specialist R&D units, located in Cambridge, Croydon, Leicester, Maidstone, Manchester and Southampton, will deal with all R&D tax credit claims from companies apart from those dealt with by the Large Business Service. From that date companies and agents should, with specific exceptions, send corporation tax returns with R&D tax credit claims to the specialist unit dealing with the postcode for the location of the main R&D activity of the company. See HMRC Tax Bulletin, October 2006 pp 1316–1319 for further details. The aim of these specialist units is to improve the handling of claims, to provide greater consistency from HMRC in dealing with claims and to raise awareness of the scheme. Their creation follows the Government's evaluation of the scheme published on 2 December 2005 and proposed improvements to the scheme as a result of the Cox Review of 'Creativity in Business'. This also follows the case of *BE Studios Ltd v Smith & Williamson Ltd Ch D [2006] STC 358* in which it was held that HMRC allowed the company's tax credit claims in error and that its activities did not qualify for the relief.

HMRC guidance. See Revenue Tax Bulletin December 2002 Special Edition for a general description, with a number of examples, of all three reliefs. See HMRC's 'Guide to research and development tax relief for small and medium-sized companies and their advisers', available on their website (at www.hmrc.gov.uk/randd/intro.htm), on how the scheme works, on making claims and whether a company is qualified to make a claim, and on common errors. (See also the Revenue Working Together Issue 20, February 2005 for a summary of recent changes, practical issues and common errors found in claims.) See generally HMRC Corporate Intangibles Research and Development (CIRD) Manual.

'*Research and development*' ('*R & D*') means activities treated as such under generally accepted accounting practice (see 55.2 PROFIT COMPUTATIONS), subject to Treasury regulations (see further below) excluding any activities from, or adding them to, the definition. It does not include oil and gas exploration and appraisal (within *ICTA 1988, s 837B*). Any dispute as to what constitutes research and development is subject to the normal appeal procedures. [*ICTA 1988, s 837A; FA 2000, Sch 19 para 1, Sch 20 para 25*(*1*); *FA 2002, Sch 12 para 19*(*1*), *Sch 40 Pt 3*(*16*)]. *SI 2004 No 712* imports the 'Guidelines on the meaning of research and development (R & D) for tax purposes' issued by the Secretary of State for the Department of Trade and Industry on 5 March 2004 for prescribing activities which are or are not to be treated as research and development. These replace, from 1 April 2004, earlier guidelines in *SI 2000 No 2081* issued on 28 July 2000 but the new definition can be used for periods prior to April 2004 (see HMRC Corporate Intangibles Research and Development Manual, CIRD 81900).

'Small or medium-sized enterprise'. From a day to be appointed by statutory instrument (but which will not be earlier than 1 April 2007), the definition of an SME (see below) is changed for the purpose of relief on research and development expenditure. The limits are raised to 500 employees, €100m turnover and €86m net assets.

For accounting periods ending on or after 1 January 2005 and up to a date to be determined, a 'small or medium-sized enterprise' ('SME') means, subject to the qualifications set out below, a 'micro, small or medium-sized enterprise' as defined in *Commission Recommendation 2003/361/EC* of 6 May 2003 (although the Treasury may substitute another definition by order). This requires that the company has less than 250 employees and either or both of annual turnover not exceeding €50 million and annual balance sheet total not exceeding €43 million. In determining whether a company qualifies as a SME, its employee and financial figures must be aggregated with 100% of the figures for any 'linked enterprise' and with the amount of the figures for any 'partner enterprise' situated immediately 'upstream' or 'downstream' from it, proportionate to the percentage interest in the capital or voting rights (whichever is greater).

A '*linked enterprise*' is widely defined by the *Recommendation* but broadly covers enterprises where one has a majority of the voting rights in the other, has the right to appoint or remove the majority of the management of the other and has the right to exercise a dominant influence over the other. '*Partner enterprises*' are enterprises, other than linked enterprises, one of which (the '*upstream enterprise*') holds (solely or jointly with one or more linked enterprises) at least 25% of the capital or voting rights of the other (the '*downsteam enterprise*').

A company will not qualify as a SME if at least 25% of its capital or voting rights are controlled by one or more public bodies. A company will still qualify as a SME if the 25% threshold is reached or exceeded by enterprises which are public investment corporations, venture capital companies, institutional investors (including regional development funds), universities or non-profit research centres, autonomous local authorities with an annual budget of less than €10 million and fewer than 5,000 inhabitants, or groups of individuals with regular venture capital investment activity who invest equity capital in unquoted businesses ('business angels'), provided the total investment of those investors in the same enterprise is less than €1,250,000.

A company is not a SME until it has satisfied these criteria over two consecutive accounting periods, and similarly does not cease to be one until it has ceased to fulfil the criteria over two accounting periods. However, this condition is disregarded in determining whether a company qualifies as a SME in an accounting period in which the limits for the employee or financial figures are exceeded where the company on its own does not exceed the limits but would do so if its figures were added to those of a partner or linked enterprise and the partner or linked enterprise would on its own exceed the limits. In determining whether a company qualifies as a SME in its first accounting period ending on or after 1 January 2005, the above provisions are treated as applying to the immediately preceding accounting period.

[*FA 2000, Sch 20 para 2*; *SI 2004 No 3267; SI 2005 No 3376*].

For accounting periods ending before 1 January 2005, a '*small or medium-sized enterprise*' is as defined in *Commission Recommendation 96/280/EC* of 3 April 1996 (although the Treasury may substitute another definition by order). [*FA 2000, Sch 20 para 2*, as originally enacted]. This requires that the company, together with any other company in which it holds more than 25% of the capital or voting rights, has less than 250 employees and either or both of annual turnover not exceeding €40 million and annual balance sheet total not exceeding €27 million. A company the capital or voting rights in which are owned as to more than 25% by enterprises not themselves small or medium-sized enterprises is excluded *unless* either those enterprises are public investment corporations, venture capital companies or institutional investors not exercising individual or joint control over the company in question, or the company's capital is spread in such a way that it is not possible to determine by whom it is held, and the company declares that it can legitimately presume that it is not owned as to 25% or more by an enterprise or enterprises which are not small or medium-sized. A company is not a small or medium-sized enterprise until it has satisfied these criteria over two consecutive financial years, and similarly does not cease to be one until it has ceased to fulfil the criteria over two financial years.

'Large Company'. A '*large company*' is a company which does not qualify as a small or medium-sized enterprise (as above). [*FA 2002, Sch 12 para 2; SI 2005 No 3376*].

59.2 SMALL OR MEDIUM-SIZED ENTERPRISES ('SMES')

Conditions for relief. An SME (see 59.1 above) is entitled to R & D tax relief as described below for an accounting period in which it has 'qualifying R & D expenditure' of not less than £10,000 for accounting periods beginning on or after 27 September 2003 (proportionately reduced for accounting periods of less than 12 months) which is allowable as a trade deduction for that period (disregarding the pre-trading expenditure provisions of *ICTA 1988, s 401*, see 59.3 below) or which would be so allowable if, at the time of the expenditure, the company had been carrying on a trade consisting of the activities in respect of which it was incurred. For accounting periods beginning before 27 September 2003 the limit was £25,000. For accounting periods ending on or after 1 April 2002, the limit applies by reference to the aggregate of the SME's 'qualifying R & D expenditure' and its 'qualifying sub-contracted R & D expenditure' within *FA 2002, Sch 12 para 8* (see 59.9 below) so allowable. The relief does not apply to expenditure incurred before 1 April 2000 (or, in relation to 'qualifying sub-contracted R & D expenditure', 1 April 2002), again disregarding *ICTA 1988, s 401*, and for accounting periods straddling 1 April 2000 or 1 April 2002, only so much of the period as falls on or after that date is considered for this purpose. For accounting periods beginning on or after 9 April 2003, a new class of expenditure ('qualifying additional SME expenditure') within *FA 2002, Sch 12 para 10B* (see 59.11 below) is also included and the limit for such expenditure is £10,000.

'*Qualifying R & D expenditure*' is expenditure (other than capital expenditure) meeting the following conditions.

(1) It must be attributable to 'relevant R & D' undertaken directly by the company or on its behalf. '*Relevant R & D*' in relation to a company is R & D which is either related to a trade carried on by the company or from which it is intended that such a trade will be derived, and includes R & D which may lead to or facilitate an extension of that trade, or which is of a medical nature and has a special relation to the welfare of workers employed in that trade.

(2) It must be incurred on:

- staffing costs; or
- (from 27 September 2003) externally provided workers; or
- (from 1 April 2004) software or consumable items (before that date, consumable stores); or
- (from a day to be appointed by the Treasury, but not earlier than 1 April 2006) relevant payments to subjects of a clinical trial; or
- sub-contracted R & D.

Staffing costs include all employment earnings (other than benefits in kind), employer NICs and pension contributions, and such costs are within (1) if paid to, or in respect of, directors or employees directly and actively engaged in R & D within (1). . For expenditure incurred before 27 September 2003, the appropriate proportion of the staffing cost is allowable where the director or employee is only partly directly and actively involved in relevant R&D. For expenditure incurred before that date, if between 20% and 80% of a director's or employee's time is spent directly and actively so engaged, an appropriate proportion of the related staffing costs qualify. If less than 20% is so spent, none qualify, and if more than 80% the whole of the costs qualify. Staff providing support services (e.g. secretarial or administrative services) are not thereby treated as engaged in the activities they support, although ancillary staff employed in a dedicated R & D facility (e.g. technicians, maintenance, clerical and security staff) may qualify. *FA 2004* clarifies (for expenditure on or after 1 April 2004) that benefits in kind are not to be included in staff costs (their being included in the definition of earnings for expenditure incurred in accounting periods ending on or after 6 April 2003 by virtue of ITEPA 2003).

'*Consumable items*' are defined as consumable or transformable materials including water, fuel and power. An appropriate portion of the costs are allowed if the software or consumable items are only partly employed directly in R & D. Software or consumable items employed in the provision of secretarial, administration or other support services, in the support of other activities, are not to be treated as directly employed in those activities. Expenditure incurred before 1 April 2004 is incurred on consumable stores if so treated in accordance with generally accepted accounting practice (see 55.2 PROFIT COMPUTATIONS), and it falls within (1) if the stores are directly employed in R & D.

For HMRC's view as to what constitutes permissible staffing costs and consumable stores for this purpose, see Revenue Tax Bulletin December 2002 Special Edition pp 13, 14. This considers in particular the 'directly and actively engaged' staffing costs requirement and its application to clerical and administrative staff, supervisors and managers. As regards consumable stores, the full cost of recyclable products may be claimed. As regards the meaning of consumable or transformable materials, see HMRC CIRD Manual at 82400.

'*Relevant payments*' to subjects in a '*clinical trial*' are payments to those participating in an investigation in human subjects undertaken in connection with the development of a health care treatment or procedure.

A company incurs expenditure on sub-contracted R & D if it makes a payment to a sub-contractor in respect of R & D within (1) contracted out by the company to that person. Except where the company and the sub-contractor are, or elect to be treated as if they were, connected persons (as to which see further below), 65% of such payments qualifies.

A company incurs expenditure on externally provided workers if it makes a payment (a '*staff provision payment*') to another person (the '*staff provider*') in respect of the supply to the company, by or through the staff provider, of the services of externally provided workers. A person is an '*externally provided worker*' in relation to the company if:

(*a*) he is an individual;

(*b*) he is not a director or employee of the company;

(*c*) he personally provides, or is under an obligation personally to provide, services to the company under the terms of a contract between him and the staff provider by or through whom the services are supplied;

(*d*) he is subject to (or to the right of) supervision, direction or control by the company as to the manner in which those services are provided;

(*e*) the provision of the services to the company does not constitute the carrying on of activities contracted out by the company.

Such expenditure is 'attributable to relevant R & D' to the extent that the externally provided workers are directly and actively engaged in such R & D. Services supplied in support of such activities carried on by others (e.g. secretarial or administrative services) are excluded. Except where the company and the staff provider are, or elect to be treated as if they were, connected persons (as to which see further below), 65% of such staff provision payments qualifies.

(3) Any intellectual property created as a result of the R & D is or will be vested in the company (either alone or with others). 'Intellectual property' for this purpose means:

(*a*) any industrial information or techniques likely to assist in the manufacture or processing of goods or materials, the working of, or winning access to, mines, oil wells or other mineral deposits, or the carrying out of any agricultural, forestry or fishing operations; and

(*b*) any patent, trade mark, registered design, copyright, design right or plant breeders' right, and any corresponding or similar rights under the law of a country outside the UK.

(4) The expenditure must not have been incurred in carrying on activities contracted out to the company by any other person. (See HMRC CIRD Manual at 84250 for what is considered to be subcontracting.)

(5) The expenditure must not be subsidised. This excludes expenditure in respect of all or part of which State aid notified to and approved by the European Commission is or has been obtained (or where such aid is or has been obtained for any other expenditure attributable to the same R & D project). To the extent that some other grant or subsidy is obtained in respect of expenditure, or it is otherwise met directly or indirectly by any person other than the company, it is similarly excluded. Aid, grants, etc. not allocated to particular expenditure are for this purpose allocated in a just and reasonable manner. Reliefs under the current provisions, the provisions of *FA 2002, Sch 12* (see 59.9 below) and the provisions of *FA 2002, Sch 13* (vaccine research etc., see 59.18 below) are not State aid for this purpose.

As regards (2) above in so far as it relates to sub-contractor payments, special provision is made where the company and the sub-contractor are connected persons within *ICTA 1988, s 839*. Provided that, in accordance with generally accepted accounting practice (see 55.2 PROFIT COMPUTATIONS), the whole of the sub-contractor payment and all of the sub-contractor's 'relevant expenditure' has been brought into account in determining the sub-contractor's profit or loss for a 'relevant period', the whole of the sub-contractor payment (up to the amount of the sub-contractor's 'relevant expenditure') qualifies. Any necessary apportionment of expenditure for these purposes is made on a just and reasonable basis. Similar connected persons provisions apply, and an election is similarly available, in relation to expenditure on externally provided workers.

'*Relevant expenditure*' is expenditure on staffing costs, or software or consumable items (or, before 1 April 2004, consumable stores), or (from a day appointed by the Treasury but not earlier than 1 April 2006) payments to subjects of a clinical trial, or (from 27 September 2003) externally provided workers (as under (2) above), not of a capital nature, which is incurred by the sub-contractor in carrying on, on behalf of the company, the activities to which the sub-contractor payment relates, and which satisfies (5) above.

A '*relevant period*' is a period of account ending not more than twelve months after the end of the period of account of the company in which, in accordance with generally accepted accounting practice, the sub-contractor payment is brought into account in determining the company's profit or loss.

The company and the sub-contractor may in any case jointly and irrevocably elect to be treated as connected for these purposes in relation to all sub-contractor payments paid under the same contract or other arrangement, such election to be made by written notice to HMRC within two years after the end of the company accounting period in which the contract or arrangement is entered into.

[*FA 2000, Sch 20 paras 1-12, 26; FA 2002, Sch 15; ITEPA 2003, Sch 6 para 245; FA 2003, s 168(3)(a), Sch 31 paras 2–7; SI 2003 No 2497; FA 2004, s 141, Sch 17 para 7; SI 2005 No 123; FA 2006, s 28, Sch 2 para 1*].

59.3 **Reliefs.** The following reliefs are available where a company is entitled to R & D tax relief (as above) for an accounting period.

(*a*) If, in that period, it is carrying on a trade in computing the profits of which a deduction may be claimed for qualifying R & D expenditure (as above), the company may claim relief for an additional 50% of that expenditure, i.e. for **150%** of that expenditure in total.

(*b*) If, in that period, it has incurred qualifying R & D expenditure which is *not* allowable as under (*a*), but which would have been so allowable had it then been carrying on a trade consisting of the activities in respect of which the expenditure was incurred (i.e. pre-trading expenditure), the company may elect to be treated as having incurred a trading loss in the accounting period equal to **150%** of the amount of the expenditure, for which relief may be claimed in the usual ways (see 47 LOSSES). The pre-trading expenditure rules of *ICTA 1988, s 401* (see 66.69 TRADING INCOME) do not then apply to treat the expenditure as incurred on the first day of trading. Such an election must be made in writing to HMRC, specifying the accounting period to which it relates, within two years after the end of that period.

The trading loss may not be carried back to an earlier accounting period under *ICTA 1988, s 393A(1)(b)* (see 47.6 LOSSES) unless the company is entitled to R & D tax relief for the earlier period. If and when the company begins, in the same or any subsequent accounting period, to carry on a trade derived from the R & D in relation to which the relief was obtained, the loss (to the extent not otherwise relieved or surrendered) is treated as if it were a trading loss brought forward to that period under *ICTA 1988, s 393* (see 47.4 LOSSES).

(*c*) For an accounting period in which the company has a 'surrenderable loss', the company may instead claim an 'R & D tax credit' equal to the lesser of:

(i) 16% of the amount of the 'surrenderable loss'; and

(ii) the company's total PAYE and Class 1 NICs liability for payment periods (i.e. periods ending on the fifth day of each month for which liability to account for PAYE and NICs arises) ending in the accounting period.

The 16% figure is subject to revision by the Treasury by order. PAYE and Class 1 NICs liabilities are determined for this purpose disregarding any deduction in respect of working families' tax credits or disabled person's tax credits, and for Class 1 NICs, deductions in respect of statutory sick pay and statutory maternity pay are also disregarded.

A '*surrenderable loss*' arises for an accounting period where either (*a*) above applies and the company incurs a trading loss in the accounting period in the trade concerned, or (*b*) above applies and the company is thereby treated as incurring a trading loss. The amount of the surrenderable loss is so much of that trading loss as is 'unrelieved' or, if less, 150% of the related qualifying R & D expenditure. A trading loss is '*unrelieved*' for this purpose to the extent that the loss has not and could not have been relieved by a claim under *ICTA 1988, s 393A(1)(a)* (against profits of the same period, see 47.2 LOSSES), and has not otherwise been relieved (including under *ICTA 1988, s 393A(1)(b)* against profits of earlier periods, see 47.6 LOSSES), and has not been surrendered under *ICTA 1988, s 403(1)* (group or consortium relief, see 32.6 *et seq.* GROUPS OF COMPANIES). Losses carried back or brought forward to the accounting period in question are disregarded for this purpose.

See 59.4 below as regards claims for R & D tax credits. On such a claim, HMRC will pay to the company the amount of the tax credit, and the amount of the company's trading losses available to be carried forward from the period is accordingly reduced by the surrenderable loss for the period (or by a corresponding proportion thereof where the amount of the credit was less than 16% of the surrenderable loss). The payment is not treated as income for any tax purposes, and (together with any interest paid with it, see below) may be applied by HMRC to any outstanding corporation tax liability of the company. Where there is an enquiry into the company's tax return for the period (see 61.10 RETURNS), payment need not be made until the enquiry is completed (although HMRC have discretion to make a payment on a provisional basis if they think fit). Similarly payment need not be made until all the relevant PAYE and NICs payments (as above) have been made.

[*FA 2000, Sch 20 paras 13-20, 23*].

59.4 **Claims and overpayments.** For accounting periods ending on or after 31 March 2006, a claim for R&D tax relief must be made in a company tax return (or amended return) (see 61.3 RETURNS) for the accounting period for which the claim is made, within one year of the filing date for that return (see 61.8 RETURNS) or by such later time as HMRC may allow. It can similarly only be amended or withdrawn by amendment of the company tax return within the same time limit. It must specify the quantum of the amount claimed. For accounting periods ending before 31 March 2006, a claim for payment of an R & D tax credit (under (*c*) above) must be made (amended or withdrawn) in a company tax return (or amended return) for the accounting period for which the credit is claimed within the same time limits. Claims for enhanced deductions could be made under the normal rules within six years from the end of the accounting period to which they related (see 15.1 CLAIMS). Under transitional provisions, claims for enhanced deductions relating to accounting periods ending after 31 March 2002 and before 31 March 2006 must be made, amended or withdrawn at any time up to 31 March 2008 or by such later time as HMRC may allow. Penalties not exceeding the excess credit claimed apply for fraudulent or negligent claims, and for failure to remedy other incorrect claims without unreasonable delay. [*FA 1998, Sch 18 paras 10(2), 83A-83F; FA 2000, Sch 21 paras 2, 4; FA 2006, Sch 3 paras 2–5, 10, 11*].

From 1 November 2006 all R&D tax credit claims will be dealt with by one of seven specialist units (based in Croydon, Cambridge, Leicester, Maidstone, Manchester, Southampton and Cardiff – covering Wales, Scotland and Northern Ireland), to which claimant companies should send their corporation tax returns. There are four exceptions to this: companies dealt with by the Large Business Centre; by the speciality pharmaceutical units;

by small company enterprise centres (in Cardiff or Maidstone); or charities dealt with at Bootle. All these enterprises should continue sending their returns to the same office as before. See HMRC internet statement 1 November and 18 December 2006 and http://www.hmrc.gov.uk/randd/practice-note.pdf.

Late claims should be dealt with in accordance with Statement of Practice 5/01 (HMRC CIRD Manual 81800). For recovery of overpayments of R & D tax credit, see 7.3 ASSESSMENTS.

59.5 **Anti-avoidance.** Any transaction attributable to arrangements (including any scheme, agreement or understanding, whether or not legally enforceable) whose sole or main object is to enable a company to obtain a relief or payment under (*a*), (*b*) or (*c*) above to which it would not otherwise be entitled, or a greater relief or payment than that to which it would otherwise be entitled, is disregarded in determining the amount of any such relief or payment. [*FA 2000, Sch 20 para 21*].

59.6 **Consortium relief.** Where a company claims relief under (*a*) or (*b*) above for an accounting period at any time during which it is owned by a consortium whose members include at least one company which is *not* an SME (as above), no amount may be surrendered (see 32.23 GROUPS OF COMPANIES) in respect of that period to any member which is not an SME. [*FA 2000, Sch 20 para 22*].

59.7 **Expenditure on intangible assets.** With effect for accounting periods beginning on or after 1 January 2005, revenue expenditure on research and development is deductible under these provisions where it is brought into account by the company in determining the value of an intangible asset (see 39 INTANGIBLE ASSETS). In this case, no deduction for tax purposes will be allowed in the amortisation of so much of the value of the intangible asset as is attributable to that expenditure. Nor will a deduction be allowed to the extent that a deduction has been made, or a relief obtained, for tax purposes in respect of the same expenditure in a previous accounting period. [*FA 2004, s 53; SI 2004 No 3268*].

59.8 **Miscellaneous.** A *company not within the charge to corporation tax* which incurs qualifying R & D expenditure is treated as having accounting periods as if it were carrying on a trade consisting of the activities in respect of which that expenditure is incurred which commenced when it started to carry on the R & D. [*FA 2000, Sch 20 para 25(3)*].

INTEREST ON OVERPAID TAX (40) applies to R & D tax credit payments from the filing date (see 61.3 RETURNS) for the company tax return for the accounting period for which the credit is claimed (or if later the date of receipt by HMRC of the return (or amended return) containing the claim) until payment. Such interest is recovered (as if it were INTEREST ON UNPAID TAX (41)) where there is a change in the tax credit payable resulting in an assessment (or amendment) to recover an amount of the credit (unless the change in the available credit results in a change in the company's corporation tax liability – see 40.1(vi) INTEREST ON OVERPAID TAX – or is in whole or part to correct an HMRC error). [*ICTA 1988, s 826(1)(d)(3A)(8A)(8BA); FA 2000, Sch 21 para 1*].

See also 59.10 below as regards relief for R &D expenditure on work subcontracted *to* SMEs.

59.9 LARGE COMPANIES, WORK SUB-CONTRACTED TO SMES AND ADDITIONAL RELIEF FOR SMES

Large companies. A company is entitled to R & D tax relief as described below for an accounting period throughout which it is a large company (i.e. it is not an SME, see 59.1 above) and for which its 'qualifying R & D expenditure' is not less than the prescribed limit (proportionately reduced for accounting periods of less than 12 months) and is allowable as a trade deduction for that period (including pre-trading expenditure so deductible by virtue of *ICTA 1988, s 401*, see 66.69 TRADING INCOME). The prescribed limit for accounting periods beginning on or after 9 April 2003, is reduced from £25,000 to £10,000. See, also, further below as regards extension of the relief to SMEs in respect of sub-contract work and for entitlement of SMEs to certain additional relief available to large companies. The relief does not apply to expenditure incurred before 1 April 2002 (disregarding *ICTA 1988, s 401*), and an accounting period straddling 1 April 2002 is treated for these purposes as if the part starting on that date were a separate accounting period.

Where a company may choose to defer expenditure by including it in the balance sheet, it qualifies for relief for the period in which it is carried to profit and loss (provided all the other conditions are satisfied in that period). (Revenue Tax Bulletin Special Edition December 2002 p 3).

Claims. See HMRC CIRD Manual at 85100 for the LBO Practice Note 14 (IB 92/03) on its general approach to claims to R&D tax relief (for which see 59.12 above). Although it is not applicable to non-LBO cases, it may provide a basis for discussion of the best approach to agreeing claims with inspectors dealing with large companies outside the LBO.

'*Qualifying R & D expenditure*' is expenditure in one of the following three categories.

(A) *Expenditure on direct R & D.* This must meet the following conditions:

  (i) it must be incurred on R & D directly undertaken by the company;

  (ii) it must be incurred on staffing costs, or software or consumable items (or, before 1 April 2004, consumable stores), or (from 1 April 2006) relevant payments to subjects of a clinical trial; or (from 9 April 2003) externally provided workers (for which see 59.2(2) above, except that the abolition of the 20% and 80% limits on part-qualifying remuneration applies from 9 April 2003 rather than 27 September 2003). See 59.2 above for explanations of what this expenditure includes;

  (iii) it must be attributable to 'relevant R & D' in relation to the company (for which see 59.2(1) above);

  (iv) it must not be capital expenditure; and

  (v) if it is incurred in carrying on activities contracted out *to* the company, they must be contracted out *by* either another large company or any person otherwise than in the course of a trade, profession or vocation, the profits of which are chargeable under Schedule D, Case I or II or as trading profits under *ITTOIA 2005*.

(B) *Expenditure on sub-contracted R & D.* This must meet the following conditions:

  (i) it must be incurred in making payments to a 'qualifying body', an individual or a partnership of individuals in respect of '*sub-contracted R & D*', i.e. R & D contracted out *by* the company to the body, individual or partnership concerned;

  (ii) the sub-contracted R & D must be directly undertaken on behalf of the company by the body, individual or partnership concerned;

  (iii) the expenditure must be attributable to 'relevant R & D' in relation to the company (for which see 59.2(1) above);

  (iv) it must not be of a capital nature; and

  (v) if the sub-contracted R & D is itself contracted out *to* the company, it must be contracted out *by* either another large company or any person otherwise than in the course of a trade, profession or vocation, the profits of which are chargeable under Schedule D, Case I or II or as trading profits under *ITTOIA 2005*.

(C) *Expenditure on contributions to independent R & D.* This must meet the following conditions:

(i) it must be incurred in making payments to a 'qualifying body', an individual or a partnership of individuals for the purpose of funding '*funded R & D*', i.e. R & D carried on by the body, individual or partnership concerned;

(ii) the funded R & D must be 'relevant R & D' in relation to the company (for which see 59.2(1) above);

(iii) the funded R & D must not be contracted out *to* the body, individual or partnership concerned by any other person; and

(iv) if the payment is made to an individual, the company must not, at the time of the payment, be connected with the individual within *ICTA 1988, s 838* (see 19 CONNECTED PERSONS), and if it is made to a partnership (other than a 'qualifying body'), it must not at that time be so connected with any member of the partnership.

A '*qualifying body*' for the above purposes is:

- a charity within *ICTA 1988, s 506(1)* (see 14.1 CHARITIES);
- an 'institute of higher education' within *Further and Higher Education Act 1992* (or Scottish or NI equivalent);
- a scientific research organisation within *ICTA 1988, s 508* (see 27.12 EXEMPT ORGANISATIONS);
- a health service body within *ICTA 1988, s 519A* (see 27.10 EXEMPT ORGANISATIONS); or
- any other body prescribed, or of a description prescribed, for the purpose by Treasury regulation.

[*FA 2002, Sch 12 paras 1–6, 17–20; FA 2003, s 168(3)(b), (4)(b)(c), Sch 31 paras 9, 10, 19; FA 2004, s 141; FA 2006, s 28, Sch 2 para 2; SI 2006 No 959*].

59.10 **Work subcontracted to SMEs.** An SME (see 59.1 above), in addition to any R & D tax relief under the provisions of *FA 2000, Sch 20* (see 59.2 above), is entitled to R & D tax relief under the current provisions for 'qualifying sub-contracted R & D expenditure' for an accounting period in which its 'aggregate R & D expenditure' is not less than the prescribed limit (proportionately reduced for accounting periods of less than 12 months) and is allowable as a trade deduction for that period (including pre-trading expenditure so deductible by virtue of *ICTA 1988, s 401*, see 66.69 TRADING INCOME). The prescribed limit for accounting periods beginning on or after 9 April 2003, is £10,000 (reduced from £25,000 for earlier accounting periods). '*Aggregate R & D expenditure*' is the aggregate of 'qualifying sub-contracted R & D expenditure', qualifying R & D expenditure under the earlier provisions of *FA 2000, Sch 20* (see 59.2 above) and, for accounting periods beginning on or after 9 April 2003, 'qualifying additional SME expenditure' (see 59.11 below).

'*Qualifying sub-contracted R & D expenditure*' is non-capital expenditure incurred by the SME on R & D that is contracted out *to* it either by a large company or by any person otherwise than in the course of a trade, profession or vocation (the profits of which are chargeable under Schedule D, Case I or II or as trading profits under *ITTOIA 2005*), and which is in one of the following two categories.

(i) *Expenditure on R & D directly undertaken by the SME.* This must meet the following additional conditions:

(*a*) it must be incurred on staffing costs, or software or consumable items (or, before 1 April 2004, consumable stores) or (from 1 April 2006) relevant payments to subjects of a clinical trial; or (from 9 April 2003) externally provided workers (for which see 59.2(2) above, except that the abolition of the 20% and 80% limits on part-qualifying remuneration applies from 9 April 2003 rather than 27 September 2003); and

(*b*) it must be attributable to 'relevant R & D' in relation to the SME (for which see 59.2(1) above).

(ii) *Expenditure on R & D directly undertaken on the SME's behalf.* This must meet the following additional conditions:

(*a*) it must be incurred in making payments to a 'qualifying body' (as above), an individual or a partnership of individuals in respect of R & D contracted out *by* the SME to the body, individual or partnership concerned;

(*b*) it must be attributable to 'relevant R & D' in relation to the SME (for which see 59.2(1) above); and

(*c*) the R & D must be directly undertaken on behalf of the SME by the body, individual or partnership concerned.

Where these conditions are met, the SME is entitled to relief under these provisions for the qualifying sub-contracted R & D expenditure.

[*FA 2002, Sch 12 paras 7–10, 17–20; FA 2003, s 168*(*3*)(*b*), (*4*)(*b*), *Sch 31 paras 12–14, 19; FA 2004, s 141; FA 2006, s 28, Sch 2 para 2; SI 2006 No 959*].

59.11 **SME entitlement to relief available to large companies.** For accounting periods beginning on or after 9 April 2003, an SME (see 59.1 above), in addition to any R & D tax relief under the provisions of *FA 2000, Sch 20* (see 59.2 above) or *FA 2002, Sch 12 para 7* (work subcontracted to SMEs, see above), is entitled to R & D tax relief under the current provisions for 'qualifying additional SME expenditure' for an accounting period for which its 'aggregate R & D expenditure' (as above) is at least £10,000 (proportionately reduced for accounting periods of less than twelve months), i.e. it fulfils the same conditions as for the relief for work subcontracted to SMEs described above. '*Qualifying additional SME expenditure*' is expenditure which:

(*a*) had the SME been a large company throughout the accounting period would have been qualifying R & D expenditure of that company (as above);

(*b*) is not qualifying R & D expenditure in the case of the SME for the purposes of *FA 2000, Sch 20* (see 59.2 above) by reason only that it is subsidised expenditure (see 59.2(5) above); and

(*c*) is not qualifying subcontracted R & D expenditure (see above) in the case of the SME.

[*FA 2002, Sch 12 paras 10A, 10B; FA 2003, Sch 31 para 15*].

59.12 **Relief and clawback of relief.** If a company (whether large or SME) is entitled to R & D tax relief under the current provisions for an accounting period, then in so far as it is carrying on a trade in computing the profits of which a deduction may be claimed for the qualifying R & D expenditure (as above), the company may claim relief for an additional 25% of that expenditure, i.e. for **125%** of that expenditure in total. [*FA 2002, Sch 12 para 11; FA 2003, Sch 31 para 17*]. Where a company receives a refund of the whole or part of any qualifying expenditure within (B), (C) or (ii) above, or of any qualifying additional SME expenditure as above, for which it has obtained such enhanced relief, an additional **25%** of the payment is treated as income chargeable under Schedule D, Case I for the accounting period in which the payment is made. [*FA 2002, Sch 12 para 15; FA 2003, Sch 31 para 18*].

59.13 **Claims.** For accounting periods ending on or after 31 March 2006, a claim for R & D tax relief must be made in a company tax return (or amended return) (see 61.3 RETURNS) for the accounting period for which the claim is made, within one year of the filing date for that return (see 61.8 RETURNS) or by such later time as HMRC may allow. It can similarly only be amended or withdrawn by amendment of the company tax return within the same time limit. It must specify the quantum of the amount claimed. For accounting periods ending before 31 March 2006, a claim for enhanced deductions could be made under the normal rules within six years from the end of the accounting period to which they related (see 15.1 CLAIMS). Under transitional provisions, claims for enhanced deductions relating to accounting periods ending after 31 March 2002 and before 31 March 2006 must be made, amended or withdrawn at any time up to 31 March 2008 or by such later time as HMRC may allow. [*FA 1998, Sch 18 paras 10(2B), 83LA–83LE; FA 2006, Sch 3 paras 2, 6, 10, 11*].

From 1 November 2006 all R&D tax credit claims will be dealt with by one of seven specialist units, to which claimant companies should send their corporation tax returns (see 59.4 above for details). There are four exceptions to this: companies dealt with by the Large Business Centre; by the speciality pharmaceutical units; by small company enterprise centres (in Cardiff or Maidstone); or charities dealt with at Bootle. All these enterprises should continue sending their returns to the same office as before. See HMRC internet statement 1 November 2006 and http://www.hmrc.gov.uk/randd/practice-note.pdf.

Late claims should be dealt with in accordance with Statement of Practice 5/01 (HMRC CIRD Manual 81800).

59.14 **Anti-avoidance.** Any transaction attributable to arrangements (including any scheme, agreement or understanding, whether or not legally enforceable) whose sole or main object is to enable a company to obtain a relief under the current provisions to which it would not otherwise be entitled, or a greater relief than that to which it would otherwise be entitled, is disregarded in determining the amount of any such relief. [*FA 2002, Sch 12 para 16*].

59.15 **Expenditure on intangible assets.** With effect for accounting periods beginning on or after 1 January 2005, revenue expenditure on research and development is deductible under these provisions where it is brought into account by the company in determining the value of an intangible asset (see 39 INTANGIBLE ASSETS). In this case, no deduction for tax purposes will be allowed in the amortisation of so much of the value of the intangible asset as is attributable to that expenditure. Nor will a deduction be allowed to the extent that a deduction has been made, or a relief obtained, for tax purposes in respect of the same expenditure in a previous accounting period. [*FA 2004, s 53; SI 2004 No 3268; FA 2007, Sch 8 para 26*].

59.16 **Insurance companies.** An insurance company (within *ICTA 1988, Pt 12 Ch 1*) carrying on life assurance or annuity business and which would otherwise qualify as an SME (as above) is instead treated as a 'large company' for the purposes of the current provisions. There are special provisions for relief under the current provisions, and corresponding arrangements for the clawback of relief, in such cases. [*FA 2002, Sch 12 paras 12, 13, 15, 19(1)*].

59.17 **Groups of companies.** Where a company ('A') makes a payment to another company ('B') which, at the time of the payment, is a member of the same group (for group relief purposes, see 32.7 GROUPS OF COMPANIES) in respect of activities contracted out by A to B, and the expenditure incurred on the payment is R & D expenditure (as above) of A, then:

- any of the contracted-out activities directly undertaken by B are treated (so far as it would not otherwise be the case) as R & D directly undertaken by B; and
- where B contracts any of those activities out to a third party ('C') which directly undertakes them, a payment by B to C in respect of those contracted-out activities, they are treated (so far as it would not otherwise be the case) as R & D contracted out by B to C.

[*FA 2002, Sch 12 para 14*].

59.18 VACCINE RESEARCH ETC.

Conditions for relief. A company is entitled to tax relief as described below for an accounting period for which its 'qualifying expenditure' is not less than £10,000 (proportionately reduced for accounting periods of less than 12 months). For accounting periods beginning before 27 September 2003, the limit was £25,000. See below in relation to each category of 'qualifying expenditure' as regards determination of whether it is 'for an accounting period'. The relief does not apply to expenditure incurred before 22 April 2003 for this purpose (pre-trading expenditure treated as deductible on or after that date by virtue of *ICTA 1988, s 401* being disregarded (see 59.19(*b*) below)), and an accounting period straddling 22 April 2003 is treated for these purposes as if the part starting on that date were a separate accounting period. The additional reliefs provided by *FA 2003, Sch 31 paras 21–24* are subject to EU approval.

R & D is for these purposes '*qualifying R & D activity*' if it relates to:

- vaccines or medicines for the prevention or treatment of tuberculosis or malaria;
- vaccines for the prevention of infection by human immunodeficiency virus; or
- vaccines or medicines for the prevention of the onset, or treatment, of acquired immune deficiency syndrome resulting from infection by human immunodeficiency virus in clades A, C, D or E (or such other clade(s) as may be prescribed by Treasury order).

The Treasury may also make provision by regulations further defining the permissible areas of research. The vaccines or medicines must be for use in humans.

R & D is for these purposes '*relevant R & D*' in relation to a company if either it is related to a trade carried on by the company (or may lead to or facilitate an extension of that trade) or it is R & D from which it is intended that such a trade will be derived.

'*Qualifying expenditure*' is expenditure in one of the following three categories.

(A) *Expenditure on direct R & D.* This must meet the following conditions:

(i) it must be incurred on 'qualifying R & D activity' (as above) directly undertaken by the company;

(ii) the qualifying R & D activity on which it is incurred must be 'relevant R & D' (as above) in relation to the company;

(iii) it must not be capital expenditure;

(iv) it must be incurred on staffing costs, or software or consumable items (or, before 1 April 2004, consumable stores), or (from a day appointed by the Treasury but not earlier than 1 April 2006) relevant payments to subjects of a clinical trial; or (from 27 September 2003) externally provided workers (for which see 59.2(2) above); and

(v) it must not be incurred in carrying on activities the carrying on of which is contracted out *to* the company by any person; and

(vi) it must not be subsidised (for which see 59.2(5) above).

Such expenditure is incurred 'for an accounting period' if:

(I) in the case of an SME, it is allowable as a trade deduction for that period (disregarding the pre-trading expenditure provisions of *ICTA 1988, s 401*, see 66.69 TRADING INCOME) or would be so allowable if, at the time of the expenditure, the company had been carrying on a trade consisting of the activities in respect of which it was incurred; or

(II) in the case of a company which is not an SME, it is allowable as a trade deduction for that period (including pre-trading expenditure so deductible by virtue of *ICTA 1988, s 401*, see 66.69 TRADING INCOME).

(B) *Expenditure on sub-contracted R & D.* This must meet the following conditions:

(i) it must be on R & D directly undertaken on behalf of the company by the sub-contractor;

(ii) it must be on 'qualifying R & D activity' (as above);

(iii) the qualifying R & D activity in respect of which it is incurred must be 'relevant R & D' (as above) in relation to the company;

(iv) it must not be capital expenditure; and

(v) it must not be subsidised (for which see 59.2(5) above).

As regards whether such expenditure is incurred 'for an accounting period', the provisions in (A)(I) and (II) above apply. See also further below as regards determination of the amount of the expenditure qualifying under this category.

(C) *Expenditure on contributions to independent R & D.* This must meet the following conditions:

(i) it must be incurred on payments made to a charity within *ICTA 1988, s 506(1)* (see 14.1 CHARITIES), a scientific research organisation within *ICTA 1988, s 508* (see 27.12 EXEMPT ORGANISATIONS) or a university, for the purpose of funding '*qualifying R & D activity*' carried on by the body concerned;

(ii) that activity must relate to a trade carried on by the company.

Such expenditure is incurred 'for an accounting period' if it is on contributions paid in that period.

As regards (B) above, where the sub-contractor is a charity within *ICTA 1988, s 506(1)* (see 14.1 CHARITIES), a scientific research organisation within *ICTA 1988, s 508* (see 27.12 EXEMPT ORGANISATIONS) or a university, all expenditure satisfying the conditions in (B)(i)–(v) above is qualifying expenditure. Otherwise, the following provisions apply for determining the amount of the qualifying expenditure. For these purposes, a company ('the principal') incurs expenditure within this category if it makes a payment (a 'sub-contractor payment') to another person (the 'sub-contractor') in respect of R & D contracted out by the company to that person.

(1) Where the principal and the sub-contractor are connected persons within *ICTA 1988, s 839* (see 19 CONNECTED PERSONS), and, in accordance with generally accepted accounting practice (see 55.2 PROFIT COMPUTATIONS), the whole of the sub-contractor payment, and all of the sub-contractor's 'relevant expenditure, has been brought into account in determining the sub-contractor's profit or loss for a 'relevant period', the whole of the payment (up to the amount of that 'relevant expenditure') is qualifying expenditure (subject to (B)(i)–(v) above). Any necessary apportionment of expenditure is made on a just and reasonable basis.

A '*relevant period*' is a period for which accounts are drawn up by the sub-contractor and which ends no more than twelve months after the end of the principal's period of account in which the sub-contractor payment is, in accordance with generally accepted accounting practice, brought into account in determining the principal's profit or loss.

'*Relevant expenditure*' is expenditure incurred by the sub-contractor in carrying on, on behalf of the principal, the activities to which the sub-contractor payment relates and which satisfies three other conditions:

(*a*) it must not be of a capital nature as regards the sub-contractor;

(*b*) it must be incurred on staffing costs, software or consumable items (or, before 1 April 2004, consumable stores), or (from a day appointed by the Treasury but not earlier than 1 April 2006) relevant payments to subjects of a clinical trial; or (from 27 September 2003) externally provided workers (for which see 59.2(2) above); and

(*c*) it must not be subsidised (for which see 59.2(5) above).

The principal and the sub-contractor may in any case jointly and irrevocably elect for these 'connected person' provisions to apply to sub-contractor payments made by the principal to the sub-contractor. Such an election must be made in writing to HMRC within two years after the end of the accounting period of the company in which the contract or other arrangement is entered into, and must relate to all sub-contractor payments under the same contract or other arrangement.

(2) Where (1) above does not apply (and no election is made for it to apply), 65% of any sub-contractor payment is treated as qualifying expenditure (subject to (B)(i)–(v) above).

[*FA 2002, Sch 13 paras 1–12, 27(1)(2), 28; FA 2003, Sch 31 paras 21–24; FA 2004, s 141; FA 2006, s 28, Sch 2 para 3; SI 2003 No 1472; SI 2005 No 123*].

59.19 **Reliefs: SMEs.** For expenditure incurred on or after 1 April 2007 when the SME is carrying on a trade, the company may, without prejudice to any other deduction in respect of that expenditure, claim a deduction of 50% of the expenditure in computing profits of the trade for that period. For expenditure incurred prior to 1 April 2007, a 50% deduction is allowed for expenditure qualifying for relief under *FA 2000, Sch 20* (see 59.2 above) and 150% of so much of the expenditure as does not do so.

From 1 April 2007, a loss available for surrender is the lower of:

(*a*) when the company is trading and the loss arises in that trade, so much of the loss as is unrelieved; and

(*b*) where the expenditure is deductible in computing the profits of a trade, the total of the deduction under *FA 2002, Sch 13 para 14* and any non-Schedule 20 expenditure, or, where the expenditure is pre-trading expenditure and a deemed trading loss is claimed, the total deemed trading loss so claimed under *FA 2002, Sch 13 para 15*.

However, from a date to be appointed, but not earlier than 1 April 2007, where the claimant company is a 'larger SME', i.e. it qualifies under the wider limits (see 59.1), the deduction is 50% of the qualifying expenditure which is non-Schedule 20 expenditure and the 50% deduction mentioned in (*a*) above does not apply. In addition, (ii) above does not apply. It is replaced by 150% of that part of the trading or pre-trading expenditure which qualifies as non-Schedule 20 expenditure. In considering expenditure on or after the appointed day, the amendments to the rules for determining an SME are to be treated as always having had effect.

[*FA 2002, Sch 13 para 15A; FA 2007, ss 49, 50*].

The following reliefs are available where an SME is entitled to tax relief for qualifying expenditure (as above) for an accounting period.

(*a*) If, in that period, the SME is carrying on a trade, it may, without prejudice to any other deduction in respect of that expenditure, claim a deduction in computing profits of the trade for that period of **50%** of so much of the expenditure as also gives rise to relief under *FA 2000, Sch 20* (see 59.2 above) and **150%** of so much of the expenditure as does not do so.

(*b*) If, in that period, the SME is not carrying on a trade, it may elect to be treated as having incurred a trading loss in the accounting period, for which relief may be claimed in the usual ways (see 47 LOSSES), equal to **50%** of so much of the expenditure as also gives rise to relief under *FA 2000, Sch 20* (see 59.2 above) and **150%** of so much of the expenditure as does not do so. The pre-trading expenditure rules of *ICTA 1988, s 401* (see 66.69 TRADING INCOME) do not then apply to treat the expenditure as incurred on the first day of trading. Such an election must be made in writing to HMRC, specifying the accounting period to which it relates, within two years after the end of that period.

The trading loss may not be carried back to an earlier accounting period under *ICTA 1988, s 393A(1)(b)* (see 47.6 LOSSES) unless the company is entitled to relief under this provision for the earlier period. If and when the company begins, in the same or any subsequent accounting period, to carry on a trade derived from the R & D in relation to which the relief was obtained, the loss (to the extent not otherwise relieved or surrendered) is treated as if it were a trading loss brought forward to that period under *ICTA 1988, s 393* (see 47.4 LOSSES).

(*c*) For an accounting period in which the company has a 'surrenderable loss', the company may instead claim a tax credit equal to 16% of the amount of the 'surrenderable loss'. There is, however, a limit on the total of the tax credits under this provision and under *FA 2000, Sch 20* (see 59.3(*c*) above), which must not exceed the company's total PAYE and Class 1 NICs liability for payment periods (i.e. periods ending on the fifth day of each month for which liability to account for PAYE and NICs arises) ending in the accounting period.

The 16% figure is subject to revision by the Treasury by order. PAYE and Class 1 NICs liabilities are determined for this purpose disregarding any deduction in respect of working families' tax credits or disabled person's tax credits, and for Class 1 NICs, deductions in respect of statutory sick pay and statutory maternity pay are also disregarded.

A '*surrenderable loss*' arises for an accounting period where either (*a*) above applies and the company incurs a trading loss in the accounting period in the trade concerned, or (*b*) above applies and the company is thereby treated as incurring a trading loss. The amount of the surrenderable loss is the lower of so much of that trading loss as is 'unrelieved' and the total amount deductible under (*a*) or (*b*) above, as the case may be. A trading loss is '*unrelieved*' for this purpose to the extent that the loss has not and could not have been relieved by a claim under *ICTA 1988, s 393A(1)(a)* (against profits of the same period, see 47.2 LOSSES), and has not otherwise been relieved (including under *ICTA 1988, s 393A(1)(b)* against profits of earlier periods, see 47.6 LOSSES), has not been surrendered under *ICTA 1988, s 403(1)* (group or consortium relief, see 32.6 et seq. GROUPS OF COMPANIES), and has not been surrendered under *FA 2000, Sch 20 para 15* (for R & D tax credit under *Sch 20*, see 59.3 above). Losses carried back or brought forward to the accounting period in question are disregarded for this purpose.

See below as regards claims for such tax credits. On such a claim, HMRC will pay to the company the amount of the tax credit, and the amount of the company's trading losses available to be carried forward from the period is accordingly reduced by the surrenderable loss for the period (or by a corresponding proportion thereof where the amount of the credit was less than 16% of the surrenderable loss). The payment is not treated as income for any tax purposes, and (together with any interest paid with it, see below) may be applied to any corporation tax liability of the company.

Where there is an enquiry into the company's tax return for the period (see 61.10 RETURNS), payment need not be made until the enquiry is completed (although HMRC have discretion to make a payment on a provisional basis if they think fit). Similarly payment need not be made until all the relevant PAYE and NICs payments (as above) have been made.

[FA 2002, Sch 13 paras 13–20].

59.20 **Reliefs: large companies.** Without prejudice to any other deduction in respect of qualifying expenditure, where a company which is not an SME is entitled to tax relief for qualifying expenditure (as above) for an accounting period, then in so far as it is carrying on a trade in computing the profits of which a deduction may be claimed for the qualifying expenditure, the company may claim relief for an additional **50%** of that expenditure, i.e. for **150%** of that expenditure in total. If the qualifying expenditure is not so deductible, the company may claim to treat **150%** of the expenditure as if it were so deductible.[*FA 2002, Sch 13 para 21*].

59.21 **Claims and overpayments.** For accounting periods ending on or after 31 March 2006, a claim for R & D tax relief must be made in a company tax return (or amended return) (see 61.3 RETURNS) for the accounting period for which the claim is made, within one year of the filing date for that return (see 61.8 RETURNS) or by such later time as HMRC may allow. It can similarly only be amended or withdrawn by amendment of the company tax return within the same time limit. It must specify the quantum of the amount claimed. For accounting periods ending before 31 March 2006, a claim for payment of an R & D tax credit (under (*c*) above) must be made (amended or withdrawn) in a company tax return (or amended return) for the accounting period for which the credit is claimed within the same time limits. Claims for enhanced deductions could be made under the normal rules within six years from the end of the accounting period to which they related (see 15.1 CLAIMS). Under transitional provisions, claims for enhanced deductions relating to accounting periods ending after 31 March 2002 and before 31 March 2006 must be made, amended or withdrawn at any time up to 31 March 2008 or by such later time as HMRC may allow. Penalties not exceeding the excess credit claimed apply for fraudulent or negligent claims, and for failure to remedy incorrect claims without unreasonable delay. [*FA 1998, Sch 18 paras 10(3), 83M–83R; FA 2002, Sch 14 paras 2, 4; FA 2006, Sch 3 paras 2, 7–11*]. For recovery of overpayments of the tax credit, see 7.3 ASSESSMENTS.

From 1 November 2006 all R&D tax credit claims will be dealt with by one of seven specialist units, to which claimant companies should send their corporation tax returns (see 59.4 above for details). There are four exceptions to this: companies dealt with by the Large Business Centre; by the speciality pharmaceutical units; by small company enterprise centres (in Cardiff or Maidstone); or charities dealt with at Bootle. All these enterprises should continue sending their returns to the same office as before. See HMRC internet statement 1 November 2006 and http://www.hmrc.gov.uk/randd/practice-note.pdf.

59.22 **Refunds of contributions.** Where a company receives a payment refunding the whole or part of any qualifying expenditure, either within (B) above where the sub-contractor is a charity, a scientific research organisation or a university or within (C) above, for which it has obtained relief under the current provisions, a proportion of the payment (**50%** or **150%**, depending on the level of relief obtained for the qualifying expenditure) is additionally treated as income chargeable under Schedule D, Case I for the accounting period in which the payment is made. [*FA 2002, Sch 13 para 25*].

59.23 **Anti-avoidance.** Any transaction attributable to arrangements (including any scheme, agreement or understanding, whether or not legally enforceable) whose sole or main object is to enable a company to obtain a relief or tax credit under the current provisions to which it would not otherwise be entitled, or a greater relief or tax credit than that to which it would otherwise be entitled, is disregarded in determining the amount of any such relief or tax credit. [*FA 2002, Sch 13 para 24*].

59.24 **Expenditure on intangible assets.** With effect for accounting periods beginning on or after 1 January 2005, revenue expenditure on research and development is deductible under these provisions where it is brought into account by the company in determining the value of an intangible asset (see 39 INTANGIBLE ASSETS). In this case, no deduction for tax purposes will be allowed in the amortisation of so much of the value of the intangible asset as is attributable to that expenditure. Nor will a deduction be allowed to the extent that a deduction has been made, or a relief obtained, for tax purposes in respect of the same expenditure in a previous accounting period. [*FA 2004, s 53; SI 2004 No 3268*].

59.25 **Insurance companies.** An insurance company (within *ICTA 1988, Pt 12 Ch 1*) carrying on life assurance or annuity business and which would otherwise qualify as an SME (as above) is treated as not being an SME for the purposes of the current provisions. There are special provisions for reliefs and tax credits under the current provisions, and corresponding arrangements for clawback of relief, in such cases. [*FA 2002, Sch 13 paras 22, 23, 25, 27*(*1*)].

59.26 **Miscellaneous.** *Companies not within the charge to corporation tax* which incur qualifying expenditure are treated as having accounting periods as if the qualifying R & D activity on which the expenditure is incurred were a trade carried on by the company, starting when it started to carry on that activity. [*FA 2002, Sch 13 para 27*(*3*)].

INTEREST ON OVERPAID TAX (40) applies to tax credit payments under these provisions from the filing date (see 61.3 RETURNS) for the company tax return for the accounting period for which the credit is claimed (or if later the date of receipt by HMRC of the return (or amended return) containing the claim) until payment. Such interest is recovered (as if it were INTEREST ON UNPAID TAX (41)) where there is a change in the tax credit payable resulting in an assessment (or amendment) to recover an amount of the credit (unless the change in the available credit results in a change in the company's corporation tax liability – see 40.1(vi) INTEREST ON OVERPAID TAX – or is in whole or part to correct an HMRC error). [*ICTA 1988, s 826*(*1*)(*da*)(*3AA*)(*8A*)(*8BA*)*; FA 2002, Sch 14 para 1*].

60 Residence

Cross-references. See 2.3 ACCOUNTING PERIODS; 5.10, 5.11 ANTI-AVOIDANCE; 8.5 BANKS; 11.10, 11.23 CAPITAL GAINS; 21 CONTROLLED FOREIGN COMPANIES; 23.5 DISTRIBUTIONS; 24 DOUBLE TAX RELIEF; 26 EXCHANGE GAINS AND LOSSES; 32.27 GROUPS OF COMPANIES; 37.2 INCOME TAX IN RELATION TO A COMPANY; 67 TRANSFER PRICING. For special rules concerning disposals of certain interests in offshore funds, see 50 OFFSHORE FUNDS.

Simon's Direct Tax Service D4.1.

60.1 RESIDENCE

After 14 March 1988, a company incorporated in the UK is regarded for the purposes of the *Taxes Acts* as resident there, irrespective of any rule of law giving a different place of residence.

This 'incorporation test' does not, however, apply in the following circumstances.

(*a*) Where, immediately before 15 March 1988, a company was carrying on business and was not UK resident, having ceased to be so resident in pursuance of a Treasury consent given under *ICTA 1988, s 765* (or any predecessor legislation), and, where the consent was a general consent, the company was liable, by reason of domicile, residence or place of management, to tax on income in a territory outside the UK. If, after 14 March 1988, the company ceases to carry on business or, where the consent was a general consent, ceases to be taxable in a territory outside the UK, the incorporation test applies after that time (or after 14 March 1993 if later).

(*b*) Where a company which carried on business at any time before 15 March 1988 ceased to be UK resident after 14 March 1988 in pursuance of a Treasury consent, and immediately thereafter carried on business. If, after ceasing to be UK resident, the company at any time ceases to carry on business, the incorporation test applies after that time (or after 14 March 1993 if later).

(*c*) Where a company not within (*a*) above carried on business at any time before 15 March 1988, and was not UK resident immediately before that date, the incorporation test applies only after 14 March 1993.

(*d*) Where a company not within (*b*) above carried on business at any time before 15 March 1988, and ceases to be UK resident on or after that date in pursuance of a Treasury consent, the incorporation test applies only after 14 March 1993.

If a company within (*a*)–(*d*) above becomes UK resident at a time after 14 March 1988, the incorporation test applies to it after that time.

Residence for the purposes of (*a*)–(*d*) above is determined without reference to the incorporation test.

A company which is no longer carrying on any business, or is being wound up outside the UK, is treated as continuing to be resident in the UK if it was regarded as so resident immediately before it ceased business or any of its activities came under the control of the liquidator (or foreign equivalent). [*FA 1988, s 66, Sch 7*].

HMRC International Manual INTM 120140 clarifies HMRC's interpretation of three points in relation to the above rule.

(i) As regards whether a company is 'carrying on business' at a particular time, 'business' has a wider meaning than 'trade', and can include, for instance, the purchase of stock prior to trading, or the holding of investments (which could include the holding of shares in a subsidiary company, or a holding consisting of a single non-income producing investment). A company (e.g. a 'shelf' company) whose transactions have been limited to those formalities necessary to maintain its registration is not regarded as having carried on business. Where, in terms of the application of general case law to the question of residence (see 60.2 below), a company can demonstrate that it is or was resident outside the UK by reference to the place 'where its real business is carried on', it will have carried on business for the above purposes.

(ii) As regards the requirement under (*a*) that a company be taxable in a territory outside the UK, the liability must be to tax on income, so that liability to a flat rate fee or lump sum duty does not fulfil the test. It is, however, satisfied where the company is within the charge to tax, even though it may pay no tax because, for example, it makes losses or claims double taxation relief.

(iii) The exceptions granted to companies who have ceased to be resident in pursuance of a Treasury consent do not apply to companies who ceased to be resident without Treasury consent but who were subsequently informed by letter that no action would be taken against them.

Companies becoming resident under the above provisions are under an obligation to notify chargeability (see 54.2 PENALTIES) where appropriate, whether or not notice has been served requiring a return (see 61.3 RETURNS).

A company which would otherwise be regarded as UK-resident (whether under *FA 1988, s 66(1)*, *s 66A* or by virtue of some other rule of law), and which is regarded for the purposes of any double taxation arrangements under *ICTA 1988, s 788* as resident in a territory outside the UK and as not UK-resident, is treated as resident outside the UK and as not UK-resident. (See Revenue Tax Bulletin December 1994 p 179 for a list of double tax agreements to which this is applicable.) It is assumed for this purpose that the company has made a claim for relief under the arrangements, in consequence of which a decision falls to be made as to its residence status thereunder.

[*FA 1994, s 249; F(No 2)A 2005, s 60(2)*].

See generally Revenue Tax Bulletin December 1994 pp 179–181 for the application in practice of *FA 1994, s 249*.

European Companies (SEs). An SE (a European Company — see 25.4 EUROPEAN COMMUNITY LEGISLATION) which transfers its registered office to the UK on or after 1 April 2005 in accordance with *Council Regulation (EC) 2157/2001, Art 8* is regarded upon registration in the UK as resident in the UK for tax purposes. If a different place of residence is given by any rule of law, that place is not taken into account for tax purposes. Where this rule applies, the SE is not treated as ceasing to be UK-resident by reason only of the subsequent transfer from the UK of its registered office. [*FA 1988, s 66A; F(No 2)A 2005, s 60(1)(3)*]. This provision is subject to *FA 1994, s 249* above.

Note. For DOUBLE TAX RELIEF (24) purposes, the definition of residence will often be affected by the terms of the relevant agreement. For the circumstances in which HMRC will certify that a company is UK resident for the purposes of double tax agreements, see Revenue Tax Bulletin December 2002 pp 989–991.

Simon's Direct Tax Service. See D4.105 *et seq.*

60.2 **Central management and control.** There is no general statutory definition of residence, and before the enactment of the deeming provisions described in 60.1 above the courts had determined that a company resides where its real business is carried on, i.e. *where its central management and control actually abide*. This criterion continues to apply for companies incorporated outside the UK and for companies covered by the transitional provisions. In the following cases, the company was held to be managed and controlled from, and hence resident in, the UK: *Calcutta Jute Mills Co Ltd v Nicholson Ex D 1876, 1 TC 83* (UK company operating abroad but directors and shareholders meeting in UK); *De Beers Consolidated Mines Ltd v Howe HL 1906, 5 TC 198* (South African company operating there but important affairs controlled from UK where majority of directors resided); *New Zealand Shipping Co Ltd v Thew HL 1922, 8 TC 208* (New Zealand company with New Zealand directors, but overall control lay with separate London board); *American Thread Co v Joyce HL 1913, 6 TC 163* (UK company operating in USA with US directors in charge of current business, but overall control in London); *John Hood & Co Ltd v Magee KB (I) 1918, 7 TC 327* (company registered in both UK and USA, with the only director resident in USA, but general meetings and material trading activities in UK). But in *A-G v Alexander Ex D, (1874) LR 10 Ex 20*, a foreign state bank with a UK branch was held resident abroad, notwithstanding that shareholders' meetings were held in London.

See *Untelrab Ltd v McGregor; Unigate Guernsey Ltd v McGregor (Sp C 55), [1996] SSCD 1*, in which subsidiaries of a UK-resident parent were held to be resident where their boards met and their business was transacted, as they did 'function in giving effect to [the] parent's wishes', notwithstanding that they were 'complaisant to do [the parent company's] will'. The Special Commissioners also held that the burden of proving residence on an appeal lies on the Crown.

See also *Wood and another v Holden CA [2006] STC 443*, in which a married couple who were resident in the UK entered into a sophisticated scheme involving non-UK resident companies, with the aim of avoiding CGT on a share disposal by taking advantage of *TCGA 1992, s 171*. The Revenue issued assessments on the basis that *TCGA 1992, s 171* did not apply because the 'central management and control' of the Dutch company to which the shares were transferred was exercised in the UK, by or on behalf of the husband. The Court of Appeal held that the company in question was resident in Netherlands as contended by the taxpayers. It argued that, in determining where central management and control was exercised, a distinction had to be made 'between cases where control of the company is exercised through its own constitutional organs (the board of directors or the general meeting) and cases where the functions of those constitutional organs are "usurped" – in the sense that management and control is exercised independently of, or without regard to, those constitutional organs.' In the former case, it was important to recognise whether outside advisors dictated or merely influenced the decisions to be taken. The fact that the board may not have taken due care and consideration in making their decisions was not considered relevant in establishing the place of management and control. It was further held that, in appealing against an adjustment to a self-assessment, although the statutory burden of proof falls on the taxpayer, if the taxpayer produces evidence which suggests the assessment is wrong, 'the evidential basis must pass to the Revenue'.

HMRC's approach to applying the basic test is firstly to ascertain whether the directors in fact themselves exercise central management and control; if so, to determine where that central management and control is exercised (not necessarily where they meet); if not, to establish where and by whom it is exercised. The concept of the place of central management and control is directed at the highest level of control of the company's business, rather than the place where the main business operations are to be found. This must always be a question of fact in any particular case, but the place of directors' meetings will usually be of significance if they are the medium through which central management and control is exercised. If, however, central management and control is in reality exercised by, for example, a single individual, the company's residence will be where that individual exercises his powers. With regard to the particular problem of residence of a subsidiary, HMRC would not normally seek to impute to the subsidiary the residence of its parent unless the parent in effect usurps the functions of the Board of the subsidiary. Matters taken into account would include the extent to which the directors of the subsidiary take decisions on their own authority as to investment, production, marketing and procurement without reference to the parent (and see below).

In all cases, HMRC will seek to determine whether a major objective of the existence of any particular factors bearing on residence is the obtaining of tax benefits from residence or non-residence, and to establish the reality of the central management and control. (HMRC Statement of Practice, SP 1/90).

See 60.1 above as regards deemed residence of companies incorporated in the UK. However, under the general law, incorporation in the UK and compliance with the requirements of the *Companies Acts* do not in themselves render a company resident here. See *Todd v Egyptian Delta Land and Investment Co Ltd HL 1928, 14 TC 119* and cf. *Eccott v Aramayo Francke Mines Ltd HL 1925, 9 TC 445*. A company may be resident in more than one country. See *Swedish Central Railway Co Ltd v Thompson HL 1925, 9 TC 342*, and for an authoritative discussion of dual residence, *Union Corporation Ltd v CIR HL 1953, 34 TC 207*.

As regards companies in liquidation, the appointment of a UK liquidator of a non-UK resident company may result in the company's becoming UK resident. The exercise of central management and control remains, however, a question of fact, and if it is exercised overseas by the liquidator, or if the liquidator acts in accordance with the wishes of non-resident shareholders so that it is not in fact exercised in the UK, the company will not become UK resident. (ICAEW Guidance Note TR 799, June 1990).

A company may have a domicile (see *Gasque v CIR KB 1940, 23 TC 210*), but it would seem from the *Union Corporation* case above that, for a company, ordinary residence and residence are synonymous. Similar rules apply for ascertaining the residence of PARTNERSHIPS (52).

Note. For DOUBLE TAX RELIEF (24) purposes, the definition of residence will often be affected by the terms of the relevant agreement. For the circumstances in which HMRC will certify that a company is UK resident for the purposes of double tax agreements, see Revenue Tax Bulletin December 2002 pp 989–991.

See 32.27 GROUPS OF COMPANIES as regards certain 'dual resident investing companies'.

Simon's Direct Tax Service. See **D4.104**.

60.3 OVERSEAS INCOME AND CHARGEABLE GAINS

A UK resident company is chargeable to corporation tax on its overseas profits, and income, whether remitted to the UK or not. [*ICTA 1988, s 70(1)*].

Where control of a UK resident company's trade rests abroad, the trade is a foreign possession, income from which is within Case V of Schedule D (*Egyptian Hotels Ltd v Mitchell HL 1915, 6 TC 152, 542*).

Where overseas income cannot, despite reasonable endeavour, be remitted to the UK, by reason of the laws or executive action of, or the impossibility of obtaining foreign currency in, the territory concerned, and where the income has not been realised outside that territory for sterling or an unblocked currency, then that income may be disregarded if the company so claims before any assessment by reference to that income becomes final. The claim must be made within two years of the end of the accounting period in which the income arises.

When the above conditions are no longer satisfied, the income becomes chargeable (on its value at that date taking into account foreign taxes chargeable on it in the territory concerned). Disputes are to be settled by the Special Commissioners.

[*ICTA 1988, s 584; ITTOIA 2005, Sch 1 para 245*].

Where tax on overseas income or chargeable gains has been assessed, HMRC may allow that tax to remain uncollected, without payment of interest, if they are satisfied that the income etc. cannot be remitted due to government action in the country of origin and that it is otherwise reasonable to do so. Interest then ceases to run from the date on which HMRC were first in possession of information necessary to enable them to agree to deferment. If that date is three months or less from the due and payable date, no interest is payable. But where a demand is later made for payment of the deferred tax, interest is exigible if the tax is not paid within three months of that demand. [*TMA 1970, s 92*]. HMRC may defer collection indefinitely.

60.4 **NON-RESIDENT COMPANIES**

See 60.5, 60.6 below for the profits in respect of which non-resident companies are liable to tax and for the liability of 'UK representatives'.

Non-resident companies are assessable under Case III or Case V of Schedule D, as appropriate, on income which would fall within those cases if the company were resident in the UK (but excluding income specifically exempt in the hands of non-residents). [*ICTA 1988, s 70(3)*]. In general, reduced rates of corporation tax for small companies (see 63 SMALL COMPANIES—REDUCED RATES) will be available (governed by world-wide company profits) as if the overseas company were UK resident, provided that there is a non-discrimination clause in the relevant double tax treaty. Associated companies are taken into account wherever resident. (CCAB Guidance Notes TR 500, 10 March 1983).

See Revenue Tax Bulletin August 1995 pp 237–239 as regards application of the arm's length principle in measuring the profits chargeable on a non-resident in respect of UK trading. See generally, HMRC International Manual, INTM 260000 *et seq*.

Income tax borne by a non-resident company on income on which it is liable to corporation tax is set off against the corporation tax chargeable. If income tax suffered on such income exceeds the corporation tax liability for the relevant accounting period, repayment of the excess may be claimed. [*ICTA 1988, ss 7(5), 11(3); FA 1998, Sch 18 para 10*].

A non-resident company is not liable to UK income tax on its UK income chargeable to corporation tax as above. [*ICTA 1988, s 6(2)(b)*]. It is liable to UK income tax on income from other sources in the UK (excluding income specifically exempt in the hands of a non-resident).

Where a non-resident company is within the charge to corporation tax in respect of one source and is assessable to income tax on that from another source, capital allowances related to each source are given against income from that source according to the rules of the tax involved. [*CAA 2001, s 566; CAA 1990, s 149*].

Where a company becomes UK resident during a year of assessment, it is liable to capital gains tax on gains arising in the year prior to its becoming resident. Similarly, on a company's ceasing to be UK resident during a year of assessment, it is liable to capital gains tax on gains arising in the year after it ceases to be resident.

Non-payment of tax. There are special arrangements for collection of corporation tax unpaid within six months of the due date where any part of the tax relates to a chargeable gain accruing to the company on a disposal **before 1 April 2000**. HMRC may seek to recover that tax (or part) within three years of its determination from any person who is, or in the twelve months before the disposal was, a controlling director of the company (or of a company controlling it) or a member of the same 51% group. [*TCGA 1992, s 191; FA 2000, Sch 29 para 9(1)(3)*]. See now 12.31 CAPITAL GAINS—GROUPS.

See 21 CONTROLLED FOREIGN COMPANIES as regards special rules applying to those with an interest in such companies. See 32.27 GROUPS OF COMPANIES as regards certain 'dual resident investing companies'.

Simon's Direct Tax Service. See **D4.122** *et seq*.

60.5 **Accounting periods beginning on or after 1 January 2003.** A company not resident in the UK is liable to corporation tax only if it is carrying on a trade in the UK through a 'permanent establishment' there. If it does so, its '*chargeable profits*' are all profits attributable to that establishment, wherever arising, which consist of:

(*a*) trading income arising directly or indirectly through or from that establishment;

(*b*) income from property or rights used by, or held by or for, that establishment; or (*c*) chargeable gains within *TCGA 1992, s 10B* from assets used for the permanent establishment or for the trade carried on by the company through it (see Tolley's Capital Gains Tax under Overseas Matters).

For the purpose of determining the amounts of such profits, there are attributed to the permanent establishment the profits it would have made if it were a distinct and separate enterprise, engaged in the same or similar activities under the same or similar conditions, dealing wholly independently with the non-resident company. It is assumed for this purpose that the establishment has the same credit rating as the non-resident company and has such equity and loan capital as it could reasonably be expected to have in the above circumstances. No deduction may be made for tax purposes for costs in excess of those that would have been incurred on those assumptions. Transactions between the establishment and any other part of the non-resident company are treated as taking place on arm's length terms. Expenses, including executive and general administrative expenses, incurred for the purposes of the establishment, whether in the UK or elsewhere and whether or not incurred or reimbursed by the establishment, are deductible, at the actual cost to the non-resident company, if they would have been allowed to a UK-resident company.

There are prohibitions on deductions for certain payments in respect of intangible assets, and for certain interest and other financing costs, where the other party is any other part of the non-resident company. Special provision is made in relation to goods or services provided by the non-resident company to the establishment. *Part 3* of the new *ICTA 1988, Sch A1* makes special provision applicable only to non-resident banks. (See also HMRC Banking Manual at BAM32000 *et seq.*). HMRC may make special provision (by regulations) in relation to insurance companies (for which see *SI 2003 No 2714* in respect of the application of *ICTA 1988, s 11A*(*2*)).

A company has a '*permanent establishment*' in a territory only if it has a 'fixed place of business' there through which its business is wholly or partly carried on, or its agent has and habitually exercises there authority to do business on its behalf. A '*fixed place of business*' includes a place of management; a branch; an office, factory or workshop; an installation or structure for the exploration of natural resources; a mine or quarry, oil or gas well or any other place of extraction of natural resources; and a building site or construction or installation project.

A company is *not* regarded as having a permanent establishment in a territory by reason of the fact that:

(i) it carries on business there through an agent of independent status acting in the ordinary course of his business; or

(ii) a fixed place of business is maintained there for the purpose of carrying on company activities, or such activities are carried on there for or on behalf of the company by an agent, and those activities are, in relation to the company's business as a whole, only of a 'preparatory or auxiliary character'. Activities of such a character include:

- the use of facilities for the purpose of storage, display or delivery of goods or merchandise belonging to the company;
- the maintenance of a stock of goods or merchandise belonging to the company for that purpose or for the purpose of processing by another person; and
- purchasing goods or merchandise, or collecting information, for the company.

The following are treated, in relation to a transaction carried out on behalf of the company, as within the exclusion under (i) above, subject to the further conditions referred to below:

(A) a broker;

(B) an investment manager (i.e. a person providing investment management services) acting in an independent capacity in relation to an investment transaction, provided that the requirements of the '20% rule' (see below) are met;

(C) a Lloyd's member's agent or syndicate managing agent for the company, in relation to a transaction carried out in the course of the company's underwriting business (the company being a corporate member of Lloyd's).

A transaction is for this purpose carried out by one person 'on behalf of' another where he undertakes the transaction himself (whether on behalf of or to the account of the other) or gives instructions for it to be carried out. A person is regarded as acting in an independent capacity on behalf of a company only if their relationship is, having regard to its legal, financial and commercial characteristics, a relationship between persons carrying on independent businesses and dealing with each other at arm's length.

As regards (A) and (B) above, the transactions must be carried out in the ordinary course of a broking or investment management business, which may be part of a larger business, and for the customary consideration, but the broker or investment manager must not fall to be treated as a permanent establishment of the company in relation to any other transaction carried out in the same accounting period.

As regards (B) above, an '*investment transaction*' is a transaction in shares or stock, in futures or options contracts (not relating to land), including those which may be settled by payment rather than by delivery, or in any other securities, or consisting in the buying or selling of foreign currency or the placing of money at interest, or such other transaction as may be designated by Treasury order. The following further transactions have been designated with effect from 12 April 2007, where conditions (i) to (iii) are met:

(i) the transaction is in Community tradable emissions allowances or transferable units under the Kyoto protocol;

(ii) a chargeable gain does not arise as a result of the transaction, nor is the gain taken into the profits attributable to a permanent establishment;

(iii) the transaction is not already an investment transaction.

[*SI 2007 No 964*].

The requirements of the '*20% rule*' are broadly that the interests of the investment manager and CONNECTED PERSONS (19) in the profits of the non-resident company's investment transactions do not, or are not intended to, amount to 20% or more, with special provisions applying in relation to the non-resident company's participation in collective investment schemes (see *FA 2003, Sch 26 paras 4, 5*). If all the conditions other than the 20% rule are satisfied in relation to a particular transaction, the requirements of that rule are treated as met in relation to so much of the company's chargeable profits deriving from the transaction as does not represent profits in which the manager (or connected persons) do have an interest.

Where a non-resident company is party to ALTERNATIVE FINANCE ARRANGEMENTS (4) in relation to an arrangement giving rise to an alternative finance return under *FA 2005, s 47* or *FA 2005, s 49A*, the company is not treated as having a UK permanent establishment by virtue of anything done in relation to the arrangement.

[*ICTA 1988, ss 11, 11AA, Sch A1; FA 2003, ss 148, 149, 152, Schs 25–27; FA 2005, s 48(2); FA 2006, s 95(9)*].

Assessment, collection and recovery of corporation tax. Obligations and liabilities in relation to corporation tax which are imposed on a non-resident company are also imposed on its 'UK representative'. This applies to the assessment, collection and recovery of tax, or of interest on tax. A UK 'permanent establishment' (see above) through which the non-resident company carries on a trade is the company's '*UK representative*' in relation to the 'chargeable profits' attributable to that establishment (see above), and continues to be so even after it ceases to be a permanent establishment through which the company carries on a trade. It is treated as a person separate and distinct from the company for these purposes.

Either the company itself or its UK representative may satisfy any such obligation or liability, and the company is bound by the acts or omissions of its UK representative. Formal notices, demands, etc. must, where relevant, be given or notified to, or served on, the UK representative for these provisions to apply to it. The company is not bound by a mistake in information provided by its UK representative in pursuance of such an obligation unless it resulted from an act or omission of the company, or from one to which the company consented or in which it connived. Similarly the UK representative is not by virtue of these provisions liable to be proceeded against for a criminal offence in relation to any of the above unless it committed the offence itself or consented to, or connived in, its commission.

[*FA 2003, s 150*].

Assessment, collection and recovery of income tax. Obligations and liabilities in relation to income tax which are imposed on a non-resident company *as a trustee* are also imposed on a branch or agency which is the company's 'UK representative' in relation to the amounts giving rise to the tax. This applies to the assessment, collection and recovery of tax, or of interest on tax. Either the company itself or its 'UK representative' may satisfy such obligations and liabilities, and the company is bound by the acts or omissions of its 'UK representative'. A person is, however, guilty of a criminal offence in relation to any of the above only where he committed the offence himself or consented to, or connived in, its commission. Formal notices, etc., where relevant, must be notified to the 'UK representative' for these provisions to apply. The 'UK representative' is treated as a person separate and distinct from the company for these purposes.

The branch or agency through which a non-resident company carries on any trade, profession or vocation in the UK is the company's '*UK representative*' in relation to income referable to the branch or agency, even after cessation of the branch or agency. Where the trade, etc. is carried on in partnership, the partnership is the '*UK representative*'. The following are, however, excluded:

(1) an agent acting other than in the course of carrying on a regular agency for the company;

(2) a broker;

(3) an investment manager acting in an independent capacity through whom certain investment transactions (see *FA 1995, s 127(3)–(12)*) are carried out;

(4) a Lloyd's member's agent or syndicate managing agent for the company;

(5) any party to, or person acting for a non-resident person who is party to, ALTERNATIVE FINANCE ARRANGEMENTS (4) within *FA 2005, s 47* (entered into on or after 6 April 2005) or within *FA 2005, s 49A* (entered into on or after 1 April 2006).

As regards (2) and (3) above, the transactions must be carried out in the ordinary course of a broking or investment management business, which may be part of a larger business, and for the customary consideration, but the broker or investment manager must not otherwise be the '*UK representative*' of the company.

As regards (3) above, HMRC Statement of Practice 1/01 clarifies the requirements for the exclusion to apply. In particular, a person is not regarded as acting in an independent capacity on behalf of the non-resident unless, having regard to its legal, financial and commercial characteristics, their relationship is on an arm's length basis as between independent businesses. The test will be regarded as satisfied where any of the following applies (although this list is not exhaustive).

(*aa*) The provision of services to the non-resident (and persons connected with the non-resident) is not a substantial part (i.e. it must be less than 70%) of the investment management business (or that condition is satisfied within 18 months from the start of a new investment management business).

(*bb*) An intention to satisfy (*aa*) above was not met for reasons outside the manager's control, despite reasonable steps being taken to fulfil that intention.

(*cc*) Investment management services are provided to a collective fund, the interests in which are quoted or otherwise freely marketed, e.g. as unit trust units.

(*dd*) Investment management services are provided to a widely held collective fund. (This will apply mostly to non-transparent overseas funds, and will be regarded as satisfied if either no majority interest in the fund was held by five or fewer persons (and persons connected with them), or no interest of more than 20% was held by a single person (and persons connected with that person).)

A subsidiary may be considered independently of its parent for these purposes. The Statement of Practice clarifies certain other aspects of the conditions for exclusion, and their interaction with the independence test outlined above.

(HMRC Statement of Practice, SP 1/01).

An '*independent agent*' is a person who is a non-resident company's UK representative in respect of any agency in which he acts on the company's behalf in an independent capacity, i.e. their relationship is at arm's length between independent businesses. Such an agent is entitled to be indemnified in respect of any of the company's liabilities discharged by him, and to retain out of sums received on behalf of, or due to, the company amounts sufficient to meet any such liabilities. Information requirements imposed on an independent agent only require that, so far as practicable, he acts to the best of his knowledge and belief after taking all reasonable steps to obtain the necessary information. This does not, however, relieve the company itself from its obligations in this respect, nor bind the company by any error or mistake (unless resulting from the company's own acts or omissions, or from acts or omissions to which it consented or in which it connived). Similarly, such an agent is not liable to any civil penalty or surcharge resulting from the acts or omissions of others (to or in which he neither consented nor connived), provided that he can show that he is unable to recover the amount thereof out of moneys retained (as above).

[*FA 1995, ss 126, 127, Sch 23; FA 2003, Sch 27 paras 4, 5; ITTOIA 2005, Sch 1 para 479; FA 2005, s 48*(*3*)*; FA 2006, s 95*(*10*)].

Limit on income tax chargeable. A limit is imposed on the amount of income tax chargeable on a non-resident company, broadly to the sum of the tax otherwise chargeable, disregarding certain excluded income, and any tax deducted at source from the excluded income. [*FA 1995, ss 128, 129; FA 2003, s 151, Sch 27 paras 6, 7; ITTOIA 2005, Sch 1 paras 480, 622; ITA 2007 Sch 1 para 452*].

Simon's Direct Tax Service. See B3.125, B3.125A.

60.6 **Accounting periods beginning before 1 January 2003.** A company not resident in the UK but carrying on a trade in the UK through a branch or agency is liable to corporation tax on its '*chargeable profits*', i.e.

(*a*) trading income arising through or from the branch or agency, and

(*b*) income from property or rights used by, or held by or for, the branch or agency (excluding DISTRIBUTIONS (23) from UK resident companies), and

(*c*) chargeable gains from assets used for the branch or agency (see Tolley's Capital Gains Tax under Overseas Matters).

[*ICTA 1988, ss 6, 11; TCGA 1992, s 10*(*3*)].

Assessment, collection and recovery of tax. Obligations and liabilities in relation to income tax or corporation tax which are imposed on non-resident companies are also imposed on a branch or agency which is the company's 'UK representative' in relation to the amounts giving rise to the tax. This applies to the assessment, collection and recovery of tax, or of interest on tax. Either the company itself or its 'UK representative' may satisfy such obligations and liabilities, and the company is bound by the acts or omissions of its 'UK representative'. A person is, however, guilty of a criminal offence in relation to any of the above only where he committed the offence himself or consented to, or connived in, its commission. Formal notices, etc., where relevant, must be notified to the 'UK representative' for these provisions to apply. The 'UK representative' is treated as a person separate and distinct from the company for these purposes.

The branch or agency through which a non-resident company carries on any trade, profession or vocation in the UK is the company's '*UK representative*' in relation to income and gains referable to the branch or agency, even after cessation of the branch or agency. Where the trade, etc. is carried on in partnership, the partnership is the '*UK representative*'. The following are, however, excluded:

(A) an agent acting other than in the course of carrying on a regular agency for the company;

(B) a broker;

(C) an investment manager acting in an independent capacity through whom certain investment transactions (see *FA 1995, s 127*(*3*)–(*12*)) are carried out;

(D) a Lloyd's member's agent or syndicate managing agent for the company.

As regards (B) and (C) above, the transactions must be carried out in the ordinary course of a broking or investment management business, which may be part of a larger business, and for the customary consideration, but the broker or investment manager must not otherwise be the '*UK representative*' of the company.

As regards (C) above, HMRC Statement of Practice SP 1/01 (for which see 60.5 above) clarifies the requirements for the exclusion to apply.

An '*independent agent*' is a person who is a non-resident company's UK representative in respect of any agency in which he acts on the company's behalf in an independent capacity, i.e. their relationship is at arm's length between independent businesses. Such an agent is entitled to be indemnified in respect of any of the company's liabilities discharged by him, and to retain out of sums received on behalf of, or due to, the company amounts sufficient to meet any such liabilities. Information requirements imposed on an independent agent only require that, so far as practicable, he acts to the best of his knowledge and belief after taking all reasonable steps to obtain the necessary information. This does not, however, relieve the company itself from its obligations in this respect, nor bind the company by any error or mistake (unless resulting from the company's own acts or omissions, or from acts or omissions to which it consented or in which it connived). Similarly, such an agent is not liable to any civil penalty or surcharge resulting from the acts or omissions of others (to or in which he neither consented nor connived), provided that he can show that he is unable to recover the amount thereof out of moneys retained (as above).

[*FA 1995, ss 126, 127, Sch 23*].

Limits on income chargeable. Limits are imposed on the amount of income tax or corporation tax chargeable on a non-resident company, broadly to the sum of the tax otherwise chargeable, disregarding certain excluded income, and any tax deducted at source from the excluded income. [*FA 1995, ss 128, 129*].

Simon's Direct Tax Service. See B3.125, B3.125A.

60.7 COMPANY BECOMING NON-RESIDENT

If, at any time (the '*relevant time*'), a company ceases to be resident in the UK, and does not cease to exist, then (*a*) it is deemed to dispose of, and immediately re-acquire, all its assets at their market value at that time, and

(*b*) rollover relief under *TCGA 1992, s 152* is not subsequently available by reference to disposals of old assets made before that time.

If at any later time the company carries on a trade in the UK through a permanent establishment (see 60.5 above — previously a branch or agency), (*a*) above does not apply to any assets which, immediately after the relevant time, are situated in the UK and are used in or for a trade, or are used or held for the permanent establishment. Similarly (*b*) above does not apply to new assets acquired after the relevant time which are so situated and used or held. For this purpose assets situated in the UK include various assets and rights relating to exploration or exploitation activities in the UK or designated areas of the sea within *TCGA 1992, s 276*.

[*TCGA 1992, s 185*].

If the deemed disposal in (*a*) above includes any '*foreign assets*' (i.e. assets situated, and used in or for a trade carried on, outside the UK), postponement of tax will be available, as described below, if:

(i) immediately after the relevant time the company was a 75% subsidiary of a company (the '*principal company*') which was resident in the UK (i.e. not less than 75% of its ordinary share capital was owned directly by the principal company); and

(ii) both companies so elect in writing within two years after that time.

Any excess of gains over losses arising on the foreign assets included in the deemed disposal is treated as a single chargeable gain not accruing to the company on that disposal. An equal amount (the '*postponed gain*') is instead treated as follows.

If, within six years after the relevant time, the company disposes of any assets (the '*relevant assets*') chargeable gains on which were taken into account in arriving at the postponed gain, a chargeable gain equal to the whole, or the 'appropriate proportion', of the postponed gain, so far as this has not already been treated as a chargeable gain under these provisions, is deemed to accrue to the principal company. The '*appropriate proportion*' is the proportion which the chargeable gain taken into account in arriving at the postponed gain in respect of the part of the relevant assets disposed of bears to the aggregate of the chargeable gains so taken into account in respect of the relevant assets held immediately before the time of the disposal.

If at any time:

(*a*) the company ceases to be a 75% subsidiary of the principal company on a disposal by the principal company of ordinary shares in it; or

(*b*) after the company otherwise ceases to be a 75% subsidiary, the principal company disposes of ordinary shares in it; or

(*c*) the principal company ceases to be resident in the UK,

a chargeable gain equal to so much of the postponed gain as has not previously been charged under these provisions is deemed to arise to the principal company.

If any part of the postponed gain becomes chargeable on the principal company, and the subsidiary has unrelieved capital losses, the companies may jointly elect, in writing within two years, for part or all of the losses to be set against the amount so chargeable.

[*TCGA 1992, s 187*].

Simon's Direct Tax Service. See **D4.131.**

60.8 **Notification and arrangements to pay tax.** A company must, before ceasing to be resident in the UK, give to HMRC:

(*a*) notice of its intention to cease to be UK resident, specifying the time when it intends so to cease;

(*b*) a statement of the amount of tax which it considers payable for periods beginning before that time; and

(*c*) particulars of the arrangements which it proposes to make to secure payment of that tax.

It must also make arrangements to secure the payment of that tax, and the arrangements must be approved by HMRC. Guidance notes regarding the giving of notice and the making of arrangements have been published by HMRC. (HMRC Statement of Practice, SP 2/90 as revised). In particular, notice under (*a*) above should be sent to Hazel Ford, CT & VAT (International CT), 100 Parliament Street, London SW1A 2BQ.

Any reference to tax payable includes the following (and tax under corresponding earlier legislation):

(i) tax under PAYE regulations;

(ii) income tax payable under *ITA 2007, ss 946, 962* (formerly *ICTA 1988, s 350*(*4*)(*a*)) (company payments which are not distributions, see 37.3 INCOME TAX IN RELATION TO A COMPANY);

(iii) income tax payable under *ICTA 1988, s 555* – or, from 6 April 2007, *ITA 2007 ss 965–970* (entertainers and sportsmen) or regulations under *ICTA 1988, s 476*(*1*) (see 9.3 BUILDING SOCIETIES);

(iv) any amount payable under *ICTA 1988, s 559*(*4*) (see 20.2 CONSTRUCTION INDUSTRY SCHEME);

(v) any amount payable under *FA 1973, Sch 15 para 4* (territorial extension of charge to tax, see 60.10 below);

(vi) interest on tax within (i)–(v) (whether or not the tax is paid).

Any question as to the amount of tax payable is to be determined by the Special Commissioners. If any information provided by the company does not fully and accurately disclose all the material facts and considerations, any resulting approval is void. [*FA 1988, s 130*].

A person who is, or who is deemed to be, involved in a failure to comply with the foregoing provisions is liable to a penalty not exceeding the amount of unpaid tax for periods beginning before the failure occurred. [*FA 1988, s 131*].

Any tax not paid within six months of becoming payable can, within the three years following determination of the amount, be recovered from a person who is, or who was so in the year before residence ceased, a member of the same group or a controlling director. See 12.1 CAPITAL GAINS—GROUPS with regard to the definition of a group which applies also in the twelve-month period before residence ceases. [*FA 1988, s 132*].

Simon's Direct Tax Service. See D4.131.

60.9 BANKS, INSURANCE COMPANIES AND DEALERS IN SECURITIES

Banks, insurance companies and dealers in securities which are non-resident but carrying on business in the UK are not exempt on income from overseas securities, stocks and shares by reason of non-residence. Income previously covered by *ICTA 1988, s 48* (foreign state securities) or *ICTA 1988, s 123*(*4*) (foreign dividends and interest on quoted Eurobonds) had, notwithstanding the exemption otherwise conferred by those provisions, to be included in computing profits and losses. [*ICTA 1988, s 474*(*1*)]. See *Owen v Sassoon Ch D 1950, 32 TC 101* in which funds deposited against default by a Lloyd's underwriter were held to be within *ICTA 1988, s 474*.

In the case of insurance companies, the above provisions apply to insurance business of any category. [*ICTA 1988, s 474(1)(b)*].

See Tolley's Income Tax under Life Assurance Policies for special treatment of policies issued by non-UK resident companies outside the scope of UK tax.

60.10 **UNITED KINGDOM**

The United Kingdom for tax purposes comprises England, Scotland, Wales and Northern Ireland. The Channel Islands (Jersey, Guernsey, Alderney, Sark, Herm and Jethou) and the Isle of Man are not included. Great Britain comprises England, Scotland and Wales only.

Territorial extension of tax area. The territorial sea of the UK is regarded as part of the UK for tax purposes. Earnings, profits and gains from exploration or exploitation activities in a designated area (under *Continental Shelf Act 1964, s 1(7)*) (and unlisted shares deriving most of their value from assets used for such activities) are treated as arising in the UK. Transfers of exploration or exploitation rights by a company not resident in the UK to a company which is so resident or which is resident in the same territory, are brought within the provisions relating to intra-group transfers. See 12.1–12.32 CAPITAL GAINS—GROUPS. A resident licence-holder under *Petroleum (Production) Act 1934* may be held accountable for the liability of a non-resident and may be required by the inspector to provide information concerning transactions with other persons and emoluments or other payments made. [*ICTA 1988, s 830; FA 1973, s 38, Sch 15; TCGA 1992, s 276; ITEPA 2003, s 41; ITTOIA 2005, Sch 1 paras 335, 387, 388*].

For the liability of a non-resident company engaged in exploration and exploitation activities to apply PAYE to its employees subject to tax on employment income, see *Clark v Oceanic Contractors Incorporated HL 1982, 56 TC 183*. For the liability to tax on profits or gains of non-resident lessors of mobile drilling rigs, vessels or equipment used in connection with exploration or exploitation activities, see HMRC Statement of Practice, SP 6/84.

Simon's Direct Tax Service. See **A1.153.**

61 Returns

Simon's Direct Tax Service. See D2.7, D2.8.

The headings in this chapter are as follows.

61.1 **RETURNS OF PROFITS ETC.**

The company tax return must include a self-assessment by the company of its corporation tax liability on the basis of the information contained in the return, and taking account of reliefs or allowances claimed in the return. See 61.3 *et seq.* below.**Notification of coming within charge to corporation tax.** With effect for accounting periods beginning on or after 22 July 2004, a company (but not an unincorporated association or partnership) must give notice to HMRC of when its first accounting period begins (e.g. when the company starts its business) and of when any subsequent accounting period begins that does not follow on immediately from the end of a previous accounting period (e.g. when the company restarts its business after a period of dormancy). The notice stating when the accounting period began must be given to any HMRC officer within three months after the beginning of the accounting period in question. It must be in writing and contain other information as prescribed by regulation. The information required by *SI 2004 No 2502* includes the name, address of the registered office and registered number of the company, the nature and principal place of business, the accounting date, details of the directors, details of any former business taken over, details of the parent company if part of a group, and the date on which there was an obligation (if any) to operate PAYE. The penalty provisions of *TMA 1970, s 98* apply for failure to give such notice (up to £300 for the initial failure and up to £60 per day for continuing failure thereafter) or for fraudulently or negligently giving an incorrect notice (up to £3,000) (see 54.1 PENALTIES). See 54.10 PENALTIES as regards 'reasonable excuse' for failure. [*FA 2004, s 55; SI 2004 No 2502*].

61.2 **Notification of chargeability.** A company chargeable to corporation tax which has not already made a company tax return for an accounting period, and has not received a notice requiring such a return (see 61.3 below), must give notice of its chargeability to the inspector within twelve months from the end of the period. Failure to do so renders the company liable to a penalty not exceeding so much of the corporation tax chargeable on its profits for the period as remains unpaid twelve months after the end of the period (disregarding any relief deferred under *ICTA 1988, s 419(4A)* in respect of the repayment, etc. of a loan to a participator, see 16.12 CLOSE COMPANIES). [*FA 1998, Sch 18 para 2*]. See 54.10 PENALTIES as regards 'reasonable excuse' for failure. See Simon's Direct Tax Service D2.802.

61.3 **SELF-ASSESSMENT RETURNS**

The Revenue published a detailed 'Guide to Corporation Tax Self Assessment', a free copy of which was sent to tax agents in May 1999. It has been largely superseded by guidance material included in the HMRC manuals but it is still available on the HRMC website (at www.hmrc.gov.uk/ctsa/ctsaguide.pdf) because it provides a useful summary of the CTSA legislation in *FA 1998, Sch 18*. Reference is made to it below where relevant.

See generally HMRC Company Taxation Manual, CTM 90000 *et seq.*

If so required by notice (Form CT603), a company must make a 'company tax return' on a prescribed form (or an approved substitute) of such information, relevant to its corporation tax liabilities, as is reasonably required under the notice. Supporting accounts, statements and reports may similarly be required. A completed return form unaccompanied by the related accounts and computations does not satisfy the filing obligation (see HMRC Company Taxation Manual, CTM 93090). Details of assets acquired on which chargeable gains or allowable losses may arise may also be required.

Most company tax returns will be by companies resident in the UK throughout the return period, and required to prepare accounts under *Companies Act 1985* (or NI equivalent) for a period consisting of, or including, the return period, and in such cases the accounts required are only those it is required to prepare under the *Companies Acts*, and any attachments required under the *Companies Acts* must also accompany the company tax return. In *Slater Ltd and others v Beacontree General Commrs Ch D 2001, 74 TC 471* (and also the subsequent case of *Slater Ltd & Others v Beacontree Commrs (No 2), Ch D [2004] STC 1342*), it was, however, held that that restriction on the accounts which may be required did not restrict the information which may be required in support of those accounts. In the case of a non-resident company trading through a UK permanent establishment (or branch or agency), the accounts required are (English language) trading and profit and loss accounts of both the company and the UK permanent establishment together with the balance sheet of the company and (if prepared) of the UK permanent establishment. Other companies are required to deliver the accounts they are required to prepare by law or under their constitution. (HMRC Company Taxation Manual, CTM 93180). HMRC point out in Working Together issue 27 – June 2007 that it is the full accounts which must accompany the CTSA return, not abbreviated accounts.

Forms CT603 are usually issued to all active companies between three and seven weeks after the end of the period specified in them, which is usually a period thought to be an accounting period of the company. In a continuing case this will be based on the company's history. In the case of a new, or newly active, company, it will be based on information provided by the company in Form CT41G, which is issued to all such companies. If the company does not reply to such enquiries, it is assumed that the first accounting period runs for twelve months from the date of incorporation (see 61.1 above on the duty to give notice on coming within charge to corporation tax). (Revenue Guide to Self-Assessment, paras 2.2, 2.3.1). As regards dormant companies, Forms CT204 are sent at intervals of not more than five years to check whether the company has traded or carried on any other activity, received any income or disposed of any assets in the review period, and to enquire about its future intentions. (Revenue Guide to Self-Assessment, para 2.4). See below as regards discretionary treatment as dormant of certain members' clubs etc.

The company tax return form prescribed by HMRC under *TMA 1970, s 113(1)* is Form CT600, which, with the accompanying guidance notes, also explains the requirements as to accompanying accounts, statements and reports. See 61.29 below as regards layout of the return. Guidance on HMRC's main requirements for substitute forms is available from HMRC's Business Services. Form CT600 and guidance notes are normally issued with the notice requiring a return, except where an agent acts for the company or the company is recorded as using an approved substitute version of the return form (see HMRC Company Taxation Manual, CTM 93140).

The return must include a declaration to the effect that, to the best of the knowledge of the person making it, it is correct and complete, and must be delivered (together with all the supplementary information, etc. required) by the 'filing date', i.e. the later of:

(*a*) twelve months after the end of the period to which it relates;

(*b*) twelve months after the end of the period of account in which falls the last day of the accounting period to which it relates (except that periods of account in excess of 18 months are treated as ending after 18 months for this purpose); and

(*c*) three months after service of the notice requiring the return,

(and see HMRC Company Taxation Manual, CTM 93040 for detailed application of these dates).

[*FA 1998, Sch 18 paras 3, 4, 11, 13, 14; ITA 2007, Sch 1 para 385*].

Before making their returns, companies may ask their Tax Office (on Form CG34) to check their valuations used for capital gains purposes in completing their returns. (HMRC Share Valuation Manual, SVM 24041).

A return is not 'delivered' to the inspector until it is received in the inspector's office. As regards (*c*) above, the date of service of the notice is the fourth working day after the date of posting unless the company proves otherwise. (HMRC Company Taxation Manual, CTM 93040, CTM 93080). HMRC usually issue an acknowledgement of receipt of every company tax return (HMRC Company Taxation Manual, CTM 93270).

The notice requiring the return specifies the period to which it relates. A return is required for any accounting period which ends during or at the end of that period (separate returns being required if there is more than one such accounting period). If no accounting period ends during or at the end of the specified period, but there is an accounting period which commences during that period, then a return is required for the part of the specified period which falls before the start of that accounting period. If the company was outside the corporation tax charge throughout the specified period a return is required for the whole of the period. If none of the above applies, no return is required in response to the notice. [*FA 1998, Sch 18 para 5*].

Where the company carries on a trade, profession or business in partnership, the return must include its share of any income, loss, consideration, tax, credit or charge stated in the partnership return under *TMA 1970, s 12AB* for any period including, or including any part of, the company tax return period. [*FA 1998, Sch 18 para 12*].

See 25.4 EUROPEAN COMMUNITY LEGISLATION regarding the application of the corporation tax provisions where a company ceases to be UK-resident in the course of the formation of an SE or where an SE becomes non-UK resident.

Simon's Direct Tax Service. See D2.805 *et seq.*, D2.821.

61.4 **Concessional exemption from requirement to deliver return.** Members' clubs and similar organisations that exist primarily for recreational and other non-commercial purposes may, at the inspector's discretion, be treated as dormant even though they receive small amounts of investment income. HMRC will write to the company proposing this treatment, and if a company has not had such a letter the treatment does not apply. If a concern to which the concessional treatment applies is sent a notice to file, it will still have to make a return, and it will be expected to give notice of chargeability (see 61.2 above) if there are changes to the types and level of its income, to its rules or constitution, or to the way its financial affairs are controlled, or if chargeable assets are likely to be disposed of.

The treatment applies where the annual corporation tax liability is not expected to exceed £100 and the club is run exclusively for the benefit of its own members. The dormant status will be subject to review at least every five years. The concessional treatment is not extended to:

(i) a privately owned club run by its members as a commercial enterprise for personal profit;

(ii) a housing association or registered social landlord (under *Housing Associations Act 1986*);

(iii) a trade association;

(iv) a thrift fund;

(v) a holiday club;

(vi) a friendly society; or

(vii) a company that is a subsidiary of, or wholly owned by, a charity.

For each year of dormancy, the body must have no anticipated allowable trading losses, no chargeable assets likely to be disposed of and no anticipated payments subject to deduction of tax at source.

The concessional treatment is also extended to non-profit-making flat management companies which pay no dividends and make no other distributions of profit, *which nevertheless remain liable to income tax* if they receive investment income on sinking funds, etc. held in designated accounts. Generally, where the annual income is below £1,000 and is taxed at source, a return will not be required every year.

(HMRC Internet Statement 25 August 2006 (available at www.hmrc.gov.uk/ctsa/small-tax-liabilities.htm).)

61.5 **Estimates.** Where, despite the company's best efforts, a figure cannot be finalised by the filing date, the company may make its best estimate of the figure, tell the inspector that the figure is estimated and say when a final figure is expected. Provided that the company has taken all reasonable steps, a return so completed is not incomplete. If the company subsequently becomes aware that the estimate is no longer a 'best estimate', or that it can be replaced by an accurate figure, this information should be sent to the inspector without unreasonable delay. If estimates are submitted which prove not to be reasonable, the return is not thereby rendered incomplete, although penalties may arise if the return was completed fraudulently or negligently (see 61.16 below). (HMRC Company Taxation Manual, CTM 93280).

61.6 **Failure to render return.** A company which fails to make a return for any period, when required to do so, is liable to a penalty of £200 (£100 if the return is delivered within three months of the final day for delivery). If the return period is one for which accounts are required under *Companies Act 1985* or NI equivalent (see above), penalties do not apply provided that the return is delivered by the last day for delivery of those accounts. Extensions granted by the Secretary of State for the delivery of *Companies Act* accounts are taken into account in this context, and in practice the disapplication of penalties also applies where the return period overlaps the *Companies Act* accounts period (see HMRC Company Taxation Manual, CTM 93070 and CTM 94100). The penalties are increased to £1,000 and £500 respectively for failure in relation to a return for an accounting period where a penalty under these (or preceding) provisions was incurred for each of the two immediately preceding accounting periods, and the company was within the charge to corporation tax for the whole of the three accounting periods. An additional penalty is imposed where the return is still outstanding at the later of the end of the filing date and 18 months after the end of the return period. The additional penalty is 10% of the tax unpaid at the time the penalty arises if the return is delivered within two years after the end of the return period, otherwise 20%. The tax taken into account for this purpose is the unpaid tax for the return period (disregarding any relief deferred under *ICTA 1988, s 419(4A)* in respect of the repayment, etc. of a loan to a participator, see 16.12 CLOSE COMPANIES). [*FA 1998, Sch 18 paras 17, 18, 19*]. By concession, automatic penalties are not charged provided that the return is received on or before the last business day within seven days following the filing date. (HMRC Extra-Statutory Concession, B46).

61.7 **Self-assessment and payment of tax.** The company tax return must include a self-assessment by the company of its corporation tax liability on the basis of the information contained in the return, and taking account of reliefs or allowances claimed in the return. For this purpose a return is regarded as a return for an accounting period if the period is so treated in the return and is not longer than twelve months, whether or not it is in fact an accounting period. The self-assessment is required even if no tax is payable or a repayment due.

The calculation proceeds in four steps.

Step 1 The corporation tax chargeable on the company's profits (including its share(s) of any partnership profits) is calculated by applying the applicable rate or rates of corporation tax to those profits.

Step 2 Effect is given to any available set-offs or reliefs under:

(i) *ICTA 1988, s 13(2)* or (for financial years 2000 to 2005) *s 13AA(2)* (marginal small companies' reliefs, see 63.2, 63.5 SMALL COMPANIES—REDUCED RATES);

(ii) *FA 2000, Sch 15 Pt V* (CORPORATE VENTURING SCHEME (22));

(iii) *FA 2002, Sch 16 Pt 5* (COMMUNITY INVESTMENT TAX RELIEF (17));

(iv) *ICTA 1988, s 788* or *s 790* (double taxation relief, see 24.2, 24.3 DOUBLE TAX RELIEF); or

(v) *SI 1999 No 358* (surplus ACT under the shadow ACT system, see 3.5 ADVANCE CORPORATION TAX—SHADOW ACT).

Step 3 Amounts assessable or chargeable as if they were corporation tax under *ICTA 1988, s 419(1)* (loans to close company participators, see 16.9 CLOSE COMPANIES) or *ICTA 1988, s 747(4)(a)* (see 21.8 CONTROLLED FOREIGN COMPANIES) are added, as reduced by any reliefs specific to those amounts.

Step 4 Amounts to be set off against the overall corporation tax liability under *ICTA 1988, s 7(2)* or *s 11(3)* (income tax borne by deduction, see 37.6 INCOME TAX IN RELATION TO A COMPANY, 60.4 RESIDENCE) are deducted.

[*FA 1998, Sch 18 paras 7, 8; FA 2002, Sch 17 para 5; FA 2006, s 26(7)–(11)*].

Subject to the instalment provisions applicable to 'large' companies (see below and 53.2 PAYMENT OF TAX), corporation tax is due and payable on the day following the expiry of nine months from the end of the accounting period, on the basis of the amount computed (as above) in the company tax return for the period. Any excess over the tax payable of 'relevant amounts' stated in the company tax return is repaid. '*Relevant amounts*' are corporation tax paid and not repaid, corporation tax refunds surrendered to the company intra-group (see 32.29 GROUPS OF COMPANIES), income tax as described in *Step 4* above (so far as not set off under that calculation) and CONSTRUCTION INDUSTRY SCHEME (20) deductions. [*TMA 1970, s 59D; FA 2002, s 40(3)*]. Payment applications and reconciliations by HMRC relate to a single accounting period (without the issue of 'taxpayer statements' covering more than one chargeable period as under income tax self-assessment). (HMRC Company Taxation Manual, CTM 97160).

A company may claim repayment of corporation tax paid for an accounting period where the company's circumstances change so that it has grounds for believing that the amount paid exceeds its probable (although not yet finally established) liability. The claim must state the amount the company considers has been overpaid and the grounds for believing the payment to have become excessive. No claim may be made before the 'material date' in relation to the tax (see 40.1 INTEREST ON OVERPAID TAX). If the tax is the subject of an outstanding appeal, the company may apply to the Commissioners for a determination of the amount to be repaid (and the application may be combined with a postponement application under *TMA 1970, s 55*, see 53.4 PAYMENT OF TAX). If the company tax return has not been made, CONSTRUCTION INDUSTRY SCHEME (20) deductions are ignored for these purposes. [*TMA 1970, s 59DA*]. 'Large' companies to which instalment payments apply are precluded from making a claim under *section 59DA* where a claim for repayment of instalment payments is made (see 53.2 PAYMENT OF TAX). [*SI 1998 No 3175, reg 6(8)*].

See generally 40.1 INTEREST ON OVERPAID TAX, 41.1 INTEREST ON UNPAID TAX.

The company tax return requires the company to state whether it is liable to make instalment payments on account of its corporation tax liabilities (see 53.2 PAYMENT OF TAX). Although HMRC will at some stage check the position, initial payment applications, interest calculations, etc. will be based on the company's statement of its position. (HMRC Company Taxation Manual, CTM 92550, CTM 92690).

Losses, etc. It should be noted that losses and other negative amounts also have to be included in the return and become final in the same way as the assessment itself, and are similarly subject to enquiry, although this would not apply to e.g. a loss in a self-assessment return brought forward from a pre-self-assessment period. The same figure must be used for a negative amount which becomes final in any other return affected by it. (HMRC Company Taxation Manual, CTM 95440, CTM 95430). The use of the figure in another return does not give HMRC an opportunity to enquire into the figure by means of an enquiry into that return (although this does not prevent an enquiry into the use of the negative amount in that return). (HMRC Company Taxation Manual, CTM 04150).

Simon's Direct Tax Service. See **D2.808, D2.841** *et seq.*

61.8 **Amendments to returns.** The company may, by notice to HMRC within twelve months of the filing date (see above), amend its own return. A return made for the wrong period must be amended within twelve months of what would have been the final date for delivery of a return for the period if it had been an accounting period. HMRC may, by notice to the company, amend the return to correct obvious errors or mistakes (including arithmetical errors and errors of principle, but *not* where any judgment as to the accuracy of figures in the return is involved) up to nine months after the date of delivery of the return (or after the date of the amendment if the correction relates to a company amendment). An HMRC correction is, however, of no effect if the company amends the return so as to reject the correction or, if the time limit for an amendment has passed, gives written notice rejecting it to the officer of HMRC by whom the notice of correction was issued within three months of the date of issue. [*FA 1998, Sch 18 paras 15(1)(4), 16*].

Amendments to returns must be in such form, and accompanied by such information, etc., as HMRC may require. [*FA 1998, Sch 18 para 15(2)(3)*]. No official form is prescribed for this purpose, and amendments may be made using an unofficial form or by correspondence. (HMRC Company Taxation Manual, CTM 93300).

61.9 RECORD KEEPING

A company which may be required to deliver a company tax return (see 61.3 above) for any period must preserve for at least six years after the end of that period the records required to enable it to make a complete and correct return for the period. This includes records and supporting documents (e.g. accounts, books, deeds, contracts, vouchers and receipts) of all receipts and expenses, and the matters in respect of which they arise, and, in the case of a trade involving dealing in goods, of all trade sales and purchases. If the company is required by notice to deliver a return for the period, the records must be preserved until the later of the end of the six years and either:

(*a*) the date on which any enquiry into the return is completed (see 61.8 above); or

(*b*) if there is no enquiry, the date on which HMRC no longer have power to enquire into the return (see 61.10 below).

If the notice requiring the return is given after the expiry of the six years, the records which must be preserved are any which the company still has in its possession at the time the notice is given.

The duty to preserve records may generally be satisfied by the preservation of the information contained in them (e.g. in electronic form), and a copy of any document forming part of the records is admissible in evidence before the Commissioners to the same extent as the records themselves. This does not, however, apply to vouchers, certificates etc. which show tax credits or deductions at source of UK or foreign tax, e.g. dividend vouchers, interest vouchers (including those issued by banks and building societies), or to evidence of tax deducted from payments to sub-contractors under the CONSTRUCTION INDUSTRY SCHEME (20), which must be preserved in their original form.

The maximum penalty for failure to preserve records as above is £3,000 in relation to any one accounting period. No penalty is incurred where the records not preserved are such as might have been needed only for the purposes of claims, elections or notices not included in the return, or where they are vouchers, certificates, etc. showing UK tax credits or deductions at source (e.g. dividend vouchers and interest certificates) and HMRC are satisfied that other documentary evidence supplied to them proves any facts they reasonably require to be proved and which the voucher, etc. would have proved. In practice, HMRC will seek such penalties only in the more serious cases where, for example, records have been destroyed deliberately to obstruct an enquiry or there has been a history of serious record-keeping failures (see HMRC Enquiry Manual, EM 4650).

[*FA 1998, Sch 18 paras 21-23*].

See generally, HMRC Enquiry Manual, EM 1001 *et seq*. See Revenue Tax Bulletin October 1998, at pp 587–589 for an article on the general application in practice of the record-keeping requirement (and April 2002 pp 925, 926 for clarification of that article), and at pp 579, 580 on its application to transfer pricing matters. Both these extracts are reproduced in Appendix 2 to HMRC's Guide to Self-Assessment.

Simon's Direct Tax Service. See D2.811.

61.10 ENQUIRIES INTO RETURNS

For accounting periods ending after 31 March 2008, an enquiry must be opened within twelve months after the date the return was filed with HMRC unless the return was filed late, when the rules are unchanged (see below). However, where the company is a member of a group (other than a small group), the enquiry window continues to run until twelve months from the filing date. A group is defined as 'a parent undertaking and its subsidiary undertaking' and a group broadly qualifies as 'small' for a year if two or more of the qualifying conditions are met in that year and the preceding financial year. The qualifying conditions are met by a group in a year in which it satisfies two or more of the following requirements—

1 Aggregate turnover	Not more than £5.6 million net (or £6.72 million gross)
2 Aggregate balance sheet total	Not more than £2.8 million net (or £3.36 million gross)
3 Aggregate number of employees	Not more than 50

'Net' means after any set-offs and other adjustments made to eliminate group transactions and 'gross' means without those set-offs and other adjustments. A company may satisfy any relevant requirement on the basis of either the net or the gross figure.

For accounting periods ending on or before 31 March 2008, HMRC may enquire into a company tax return if they give notice of their intention to do so within twelve months after the filing date (see 61.3 above) or, if the return was delivered after that date, by the quarter day (31 January, 30 April, 31 July or 31 October) next following the first anniversary of the day on which the return was delivered. HMRC consider that notice is 'given' when the notice is issued, which, in the case of notice by post, means the date of posting (see HMRC Enquiry Manual, EM 1506, EM 1510, EM 1525), but in a Special Commissioner's decision on the similar provisions for individual self-assessment, it was held that service of the notice is treated as effected at the time at which the letter would be delivered in the ordinary course of post, i.e. on the second working day after posting for first class mail or on the fourth working day after posting for second class mail (*Wing Hung Lai v Bale (Sp C 203) [1999] SSCD 238*). It was held in the case of *R (oao Spring Salmon and Seafood Ltd) v CIR, CS [2004] STC 444* that a notice of enquiry made under *FA 1998, Sch 18 para 24* was not required to be made in writing.

An enquiry following an amendment to a return must be notified by the quarter day next following the first anniversary of the making of the amendment, and if it is given at a time when notice of an enquiry could no longer have been given had the return not been amended, is limited to matters to which the amendment relates or which are affected by it. (In practice, except where an amendment relates to or affects matters fundamental to the whole return, HMRC enquiries will normally be limited to the area of the return that was amended, regardless of whether a full enquiry would still be in time (see HMRC Enquiry Manual, EM 1520)).

Only one notice of enquiry may be given in respect of a return, except one given in consequence of an amendment (or further amendment(s)) by the company of the return.

HMRC does not have to justify an enquiry, by stating dissatisfaction with the return or identifying particular aspects giving cause for concern, and will not give reasons (although they may identify particular areas on which the enquiry will focus). Enquiries will range from questioning simple errors not identified during initial processing of the return through to full in-depth reviews of companies' affairs, including the underlying records. Business documents and records will commonly be requested. Although random selection will play a part, most enquiry cases will continue to be selected on the basis of a judgment, informed by all the information in HMRC's possession, of the risk of tax loss. (HMRC Enquiry Manual, EM 1050–EM 1070, EM 1503, EM 1550–EM 1581).

Conduct of enquiry. Code of Practice No 14 (updated in April 2003) covers all aspects of enquiries under self-assessment. It is given to companies concerned at the start of every enquiry (except that where a simple enquiry is expected to be settled by a brief exchange of correspondence and not to involve penalties, a single-page version of the Code is issued instead).

When the time limit for opening an enquiry into a return has passed, HMRC can still ask questions about the return, but further action can only be taken in cases of fraudulent or negligent conduct or failure to disclose all relevant information (see 7.2 ASSESSMENTS and 30 FRAUDULENT OR NEGLIGENT CONDUCT). (HMRC Enquiry Manual, EM 1053, EM 3250 *et seq.*).

Subject to the limitation referred to above in the case of enquiries into amendments to returns, an enquiry extends to anything contained (or required to be contained) in the return, including any claim or election and any amount that affects or may affect the tax liability of another accounting period or another company. If it appears to HMRC that the return is, or may be, for the wrong period, or has become for the wrong period as a result of a direction from HMRC under *ICTA 1988, s 12(5A)* (see 2.4 ACCOUNTING PERIODS), the enquiry may extend to the period for which the return should have been made. A return is for this purpose made for the wrong period if either it is made for a period treated as, but not in fact, an accounting period, or it is made on the basis that there is no accounting period ending in or at the end of the period specified in the notice requiring the return but there is in fact such an accounting period. The time limits for notice of enquiry into a return for the wrong period are by reference to the date by which the return would have been required to be delivered had the period for which the return was made not been the wrong period.

For accounting periods beginning on or after 1 April 2004, an enquiry may also extend to consideration of whether to give a company, which is a medium-sized enterprise, a transfer pricing notice under *ICTA 1988, Sch 28AA para 5C* (see 67.7 TRANSFER PRICING). An enquiry may also extend to a notice under *ICTA 1988, s 804ZA* in respect of schemes and arrangements designed to increase double taxation relief (as introduced, for payments of foreign tax on or after 16 March 2005, by *FA 2005, s 87* – see 5.19 ANTI-AVOIDANCE) or to a notice under *F(No 2)A 2005, s 24* or *s 26* in respect of tax arbitrage (see 5.27 ANTI-AVOIDANCE) or *TCGA 1992, s 184G* or *s 184H* (avoidance utilising losses — see 11.4 CAPITAL GAINS).

These provisions are amended to provide for extended time limits in the cases of non-annual accounting of general insurance business and of insurance companies and friendly societies with non-annual actuarial investigations.

[*FA 1998, Sch 18 paras 24-26, 85-87; FA 2004, s 37*(2), *Sch 5 para 10; FA 2005, s 88*(3)(5); *F(No 2)A 2005, s 29*(1); *Companies Act 2006, s 474*(1); *FA 2006, s 71*(2); *FA 2007, s 96*].

Where an enquiry remains open after expiry of the period within which a notice of enquiry may be issued solely because of an unagreed valuation for the purpose of computing chargeable gains of a company or other body within the charge to corporation tax, HMRC will not raise further enquiries into unrelated matters unless, had the enquiry already been completed, a discovery could have been made (see 7.2 ASSESSMENTS). This does not inhibit HMRC from enquiring into matters relating to the valuation which were not raised on first reference. (HMRC Statement of Practice, SP 1/02).

In March 2002, the Revenue published a framework within which income tax self-assessment enquiries will be worked and to which professional advisers are encouraged to adhere. Particular topics covered are the opening enquiry letter, requests for and conduct of interviews and meetings, and requests for non-business bank and building society accounts (plus credit/charge/store card details). (Revenue 'Working Together' Bulletin No 8, March 2002). A similar framework, suitably adapted, applies to corporation tax self-assessment enquiries. See Revenue 'Working Together' Bulletin No 12, March 2003.

Simon's Direct Tax Service. See D2.815 *et seq.*

61.11 **Power to call for documents.** After (or at the same time as) giving notice of an enquiry, HMRC may by notice require the company to produce such documents (including computer records) in the company's possession or power, and such information in such form, as they may reasonably require for the purposes of the enquiry. The notice is not restricted to documents, etc. the company is obliged to keep (see 61.9 above), but may require other information such as a profit and loss account, a balance sheet or a detailed factual account of how an entry in a return is made up, so long as they are relevant to the purposes of the enquiry and are in the company's possession or power. (HMRC Enquiry Manual, EM 1555, EM 1560, EM 2200 *et seq.*). (In *Slater Ltd and others v Beacontree General Commrs Ch D 2001, 74 TC 471* (and also the subsequent case of *Slater Ltd & others v Beacontree Commrs (No 2), Ch D [2004] STC 1342*), it was held that the exemptions conferred on companies by the *Companies Act 1985* on the accounts which may be required did not restrict the information which may be required in support of those accounts.)

The notice must specify a period of not less than 30 days (from the date of receipt of the notice — see *Self-assessed v Inspector of Taxes (Sp C 207), [1999] SSCD 253*) within which the documents, etc. are to be produced, although if the company has genuine difficulty in meeting the deadline, HMRC may be prepared to agree a revised time scale (HMRC Enquiry Manual, EM 1580, EM 2217, EM 2250).

Documents, etc. relating to the conduct of any pending appeal or referral (see below) of questions to the Special Commissioners by the company (i.e. those brought into existence as part of the preparation for presentation of the appeal or referral, see HMRC Enquiry Manual, EM 2218) are excluded.

For a case on the scope of such a notice, see *Mother v Inspector of Taxes (Sp C 211), [1999] SSCD 279* (concerning the similar powers in *TMA 1970, s 19A* relating to individual self-assessment enquiries).

Photographic or other facsimile copies of documents may be produced, but HMRC may by notice require production for inspection of the originals within a specified time of not less than 30 days. HMRC may take copies of, or make extracts from, any document produced to them.

The company may appeal in writing against any such notice within 30 days of the notice being given. The appeal is heard and determined in the same way as an appeal against an assessment, and the Appeal Commissioners are required to confirm the notice only in so far as the documents or information appear to them to be reasonably required for the purposes of the enquiry, and to set it aside in so far as that condition is not met, their decision being final and conclusive. To the extent that a notice is confirmed on appeal, it must be complied with within 30 days after determination of the appeal.

The penalty for failure to comply with a notice is £50 and, for each day on which the failure continues after imposition of such a penalty, a further penalty not exceeding £30 if the penalty is determined by an officer of HMRC under *TMA 1970, s 100* or £150 if it is determined by the Commissioners under *TMA 1970, s 100C* (see 54.12 PENALTIES), subject to the normal right of appeal. No penalty may be imposed after the failure has been remedied.

No penalty can be imposed where it is genuinely impossible to comply with a notice, e.g. where the documents, etc. concerned do not exist. If such documents, etc. were required to be kept, a penalty, as under 61.9 above, may arise, but no penalty for failure to produce can arise. (Revenue Guide to Self-Assessment, paras 6.10.7, 6.10.8).

[*FA 1988, s 127; FA 1998, Sch 18 paras 27–29; FA 2001, Sch 29 para 38*(*4*)].

For powers to obtain information from third parties under *TMA 1970, s 20 et seq.*, see 30.4 FRAUDULENT OR NEGLIGENT CONDUCT.

61.12 **Amendments during enquiry.** If during the course of an enquiry HMRC form the opinion that the company's self-assessed tax is insufficient and that unless the assessment is immediately amended there is likely to be a loss of tax, they may by notice to the company amend its self-assessment to make good the deficiency. An appeal in writing may be made against such an amendment within 30 days of the notice, but will not be heard and determined before completion of the enquiry (although application for postponement may be made under *TMA 1970, s 55*, see 53.4 PAYMENT OF TAX). If the enquiry is limited to matters arising from an earlier amendment by the company of its self-assessment (as above), the notice may only apply to a deficiency attributable to that amendment. In practice, HMRC normally ask the company to make an additional payment on account to cover any deficiency identified during an enquiry, and only make an amendment as above where the company refuses to make such a payment and they believe that tax is at risk, e.g. where the company might dispose of its assets or go into liquidation (see HMRC Enquiry Manual, EM 1936, EM 1951).

If a company amends its return during an enquiry, the amendment does not restrict the scope of the enquiry, but may be taken into account in the enquiry. So far as the amendment affects the self-assessed tax, or any amount that affects or may affect the tax payable for another accounting period or by another company, it does not take effect until after the enquiry is completed (without prejudice to any claim for repayment of tax under *TMA 1970, s 59DA*, see 61.7 above). On completion of the enquiry, if the conclusions in the closure notice (see below) state either that the amendment was not taken into account or that no amendment is required arising from the enquiry, the deferred amendment takes effect immediately. Otherwise, it is taken into account by the company in amending its return in accordance with the closure notice.

In practice, if the closure notice states that no amendment of the return is required, HMRC will give effect to the company amendment, and if it states that the return should be amended in consequence of the enquiry, the suggested amendments will normally take account of the company amendment. Where it says that the amendment has not been taken into account, the company may, if it so wishes, include its own amendment with those it makes in accordance with the closure notice, although this gives HMRC the opportunity (as above) to make further enquiries into matters relating to or affected by that amendment. (See HMRC COTAX Manual under Enquiries/CTSA Enquiries/Taxpayer Amendments; Revenue Guide to Self-Assessment, para 6.12.6).

[*FA 1998, Sch 18 paras 30, 31*].

61.13 **Referral of questions to Special Commissioners.** For enquiries commencing on or after (or in progress on) 11 May 2001, any question arising in connection with the subject matter of the enquiry while it is in progress may be referred to the Special Commissioners for their determination. Written notice of referral must be given to the Commissioners jointly by HMRC and the company, specifying the question(s) being referred, and more than one such referral may be made during the course of an enquiry. Either side may withdraw the notice at any time up to the first hearing by the Commissioners by written notice to the other party and to the Commissioners. While proceedings on such a referral are in progress, no closure notice may be given nor any application made for a closure direction (see below). Proceedings are for this purpose treated as still in progress until the question(s) is (are) determined by the Commissioners and there is no further possibility of the determination(s) being varied or set aside (other than by virtue of an out-of-time appeal for which permission could be granted). The Commissioners' determination is binding on the parties as if it were a decision on a preliminary issue on an appeal (and similar rights of appeal against the determination apply), and must be taken into account by HMRC in reaching their conclusions on the enquiry. [*FA 1998, Sch 18 paras 31A–31D; FA 2001, Sch 29 para 7; SI 2001 No 4024*].

61.14 **Completion of enquiry.** An enquiry into a return is completed when a closure notice is issued by HMRC to the company stating their conclusions. If the return was for the wrong period, the notice must designate the accounting period for which a return should have been made. If there is more than one accounting period ending in or at the end of the period specified in the notice requiring a return, the closure notice may only designate the first of those accounting periods for which no return has been delivered. If there is then another period for which a return should have been made under the original notice, and which no other return by the company can be amended to refer to, the original notice is taken to require the company to deliver a return in respect of the outstanding period. The filing date for the return for that period is the later of the original filing date and the thirtieth day after it is finally determined that the outstanding return is required.

The company may apply to the Commissioners for a direction that HMRC give a closure notice within a specified period. Any such application is heard and determined as if it were an appeal. The Commissioners must give a direction unless they are satisfied that HMRC have reasonable grounds for not giving a closure notice within a specified period. Such a direction does not require HMRC to confirm that the company's return and self-assessment are correct, and the closure notice will include HMRC's conclusions based on the information available at the time of completion and representing what they believe to be the correct amounts to be included in the return on the basis of that information (see

HMRC Enquiry Manual, EM 5620, Revenue Guide to Self-Assessment para 6.14.6). See *Jade Palace Ltd v HMRC [2006] SSCD 419 (Sp C 540)* in which such a direction was given.

[*FA 1998, Sch 18 paras 32, 33, 35*].

61.15 **Amendment of return following completion.** The company has 30 days following completion of an enquiry into a return to amend the return in accordance with the conclusions in the closure notice and, if the return was for the wrong period, to make it a return for the period designated in the notice, and to make such amendments of its other returns as may be required to give effect to those conclusions. Any time limit constraints are lifted for this purpose. If after the 30 days has elapsed HMRC are not satisfied that the return is correct and complete and for the appropriate period, and that amendments required to other returns have been made, they have a further 30 days to make such amendments as they consider necessary. An appeal may be made in writing within 30 days of notification to the company of any such amendment(s). [*FA 1998, Sch 18 para 34*].

61.16 **Penalties.** The maximum penalty for:

(*a*) negligently or fraudulently delivering, or failing within a reasonable time to remedy, an incorrect return; or

(*b*) making any incorrect return, statement or declaration in connection with a claim for any allowance, deduction or relief or

(*c*) submitting incorrect accounts,

in addition to any tax actually chargeable, is the amount of tax underpaid, by reason of the incorrectness, for the accounting period(s) to which the return etc. relates (disregarding any relief deferred under *ICTA 1988, s 419(4A)* in respect of the repayment, etc. of a loan to a participator, see 16.12 CLOSE COMPANIES). Accounts are deemed to have been submitted on behalf of a company unless it is shown that they were submitted without the company's consent or connivance.

Where more than one tax-geared penalty is incurred in relation to an accounting period, each penalty after the first is reduced so that the total penalties in relation to any particular part of the tax do not exceed the amount of the greatest penalty imposed in relation thereto. For an example, see HMRC Company Taxation Manual, CTM 94240.

[*FA 1998, Sch 18 paras 20, 89, 90; ITA 2007, Sch 1 para 385*].

Contract settlements (see 30.8 FRAUDULENT OR NEGLIGENT CONDUCT) for all outstanding liabilities will continue to be available in appropriate cases, in particular where penalties are involved. (HMRC Enquiry Manual, EM 6001).

61.17 **Choice between cases of Schedule D.** There are provisions concerning enquiries into a return which includes amounts which may be taxed on more than one basis, i.e. under Case I or Case III or V of Schedule D, or (in relation to life assurance business) under Case I of Schedule D or on the 'I minus E' basis. HMRC have the right to determine (finally and conclusively) which method is to be used (the 'Crown option'). The powers to require production of documents, etc. under *FA 1998, Sch 18 paras 27-29* (see 61.11 above) apply equally for this purpose. [*FA 1998, Sch 18 para 84*].

61.18 DETERMINATIONS WHERE NO RETURN DELIVERED

If no return is delivered, in response to a notice requiring one, on or before the filing date for the return required by the notice (see 61.3 above) (or, if no such date can be ascertained, by the later of 18 months from the end of the period specified in the notice and three months from the date of service of the notice (which is assumed to be four working days after its issue), (see HMRC Company Taxation Manual, CTM 95350)), HMRC have power to determine, to the best of their information and belief, the tax payable by the company for the accounting period or periods ending in or at the end of the period specified in the notice. They may also determine what those accounting periods are if they have insufficient information to identify the company's accounting periods.

Notice of a determination under these provisions must be served on the company, stating the date of issue, but no determination may be made more than five years after the first day on which the power of determination could have been exercised. The determination is of no effect if the company shows that it has no accounting period ending in or at the end of the period specified in the notice requiring the return, or that it has delivered the return(s) for that accounting period or each of those accounting periods, or that no return is yet due for any such period. An effective determination is superseded where, before the expiry of five years from the day on which the power of determination first became exercisable (or, if later, the expiry of twelve months from the date of the determination), the company delivers a return for an accounting period ending in or at the end of the period specified in the notice requiring a return. If there is more than one determination in relation to the notice concerned, the determination superseded is that for the period which is, or most closely approximates to, the period for which the return is made.

In practice HMRC normally review cases for determination 18 months after the end of what is assumed or believed to be the company's accounting period. If the filing date is believed to be later than that, they will wait until after the presumed filing date before making a determination. Where, for example, they believe there would be a risk of loss of tax if no immediate action was taken, or the absence of a return prevents a proper review of other companies in the same group, an earlier review may be made of the need for a determination. (HMRC Company Taxation Manual, CTM 95340).

If a return is delivered, in response to a notice requiring one, for an accounting period ending in or at the end of the period specified in the notice, but it appears to HMRC that there is another ('outstanding') period so ending which is or may be an accounting period, they have power to determine, to the best of their information and belief, the corporation tax payable by the company for the outstanding period. The power becomes exercisable once the filing date for the outstanding period has passed without a return being delivered, or, if no such filing date can be ascertained, once the later of 30 months from the end of the period specified in the notice and three months from the date of service of the notice has passed without a return for the outstanding period being delivered.

Notice of a determination under these provisions must be served on the company, stating the date of issue, but no determination may be made more than five years after the first day on which the power of determination could have been exercised. The determination is of no effect if the company shows that the outstanding period is not an accounting period or that it has delivered a return for that period. An effective determination is superseded where, before the expiry of five years from the day on which the power of determination first became exercisable (or, if later, the expiry of twelve months from the date of the determination), the company delivers a further return for an accounting period ending in or at the end of the period specified in the notice requiring a return.

The power to make a determination in the circumstances described above includes power to determine any of the constituent amounts required to calculate the amount of tax payable. The notice of determination may be accompanied by a notice of any determination by HMRC of the due and payable dates under *TMA 1970, s 59D* or *s 59E* (see 53.1 PAYMENT OF TAX). For enforcement purposes (i.e. payment, collection and recovery, interest, penalties, etc.) the determination has effect as if it were a self-assessment, and is treated as made for an accounting period where HMRC had insufficient information to determine whether a period was an accounting period (see above). Where any proceedings have been begun for the recovery of tax charged by a determination, and before the proceedings are concluded the determination is superseded (as above), the proceedings may be continued as if they were for the recovery of so much of the tax charged by the self-assessment as is due and payable but unpaid.

[*FA 1998, Sch 18 paras 36–40; FA 2001, Sch 29 para 17*].

Simon's Direct Tax Service. See **D2.821, D2.822**.

61.19 ROUNDING OF TAX COMPUTATIONS

To reduce the compliance burden on large companies whose statutory accounts are produced in round thousands, HMRC are generally prepared to accept profit computations for tax purposes in figures rounded to the nearest £1,000 from single companies with an annual turnover of at least £5 million (including investment and estate income) in the accounts in question or in the preceding year, where rounding at least to that extent has been used in preparing the accounts. (Turnover of groups of companies is not aggregated for this purpose.) Such computations must be accompanied by a certificate by the person preparing the computations stating the basis of rounding, and confirming that it is unbiased, has been applied consistently and produces a fair result for tax purposes (and stating the program or software used where relevant), or, if there have been no changes from the previous year in these respects, confirming the unchanged basis. The rounding may not extend to the tax payable or other relevant figures of tax. Rounding is not acceptable where it would impede the application of the legislation, or where recourse to the underlying records would normally be necessary to do the computation. Thus it is not acceptable e.g. in computations of chargeable gains (except in relation to the incidental costs of acquisition and disposal), in accrued income scheme computations, in computations of tax credit relief, in relation to the CFC exemption limit (see 21.12(iv) CONTROLLED FOREIGN COMPANIES) or in certain capital allowance computations. The inspector may exceptionally insist that roundings are not used in other circumstances. (HMRC Statement of Practice, SP 15/93).

See generally Simon's Direct Tax Service B3.903 as regards the form of accounts.

61.20 EXAMPLES OF RETURN PERIODS

(*A*)

Aquarius Ltd has always prepared its accounts to 31 October. In 2007, it changes its accounting date, preparing accounts for the nine months to 31 July 2007. On 31 January 2007, HMRC issue a notice specifying a return period of 1 November 2005 to 31 October 2006. On 31 January 2008, they issue a notice specifying a return period of 1 November 2006 to 31 October 2007.

In respect of the first-mentioned notice, Aquarius Ltd is required to make a return for the period 1.11.05 to 31.10.06.

In respect of the second of the above-mentioned notices, the company is required to make a return for the period 1.11.06 to 31.7.07.

(*B*)

Pisces Ltd has always prepared its accounts to 31 December. In 2007, it changes its accounting date, preparing accounts for the nine months to 30 September 2007. On 15 December 2007, HMRC issue a notice specifying a return period of 1 October 2006 to 30 September 2007.

Pisces Ltd is required to make returns both for the period 1.1.06 to 31.12.06 and for the period 1.1.07 to 30.9.07.

(*C*)

Aries Ltd has always prepared accounts to 31 October. After 2006, it changes its accounting date, preparing accounts for the fifteen months to 31 January 2008. On 21 August 2007, HMRC issue a notice specifying a return period of 1 November 2005 to 31 October 2006. On 31 January 2008, they issue a notice specifying a return period of 1 November 2006 to 31 October 2007.

In respect of the first-mentioned notice, Aries Ltd is required to make a return for the period 1.11.05 to 31.10.06 accompanied by accounts and tax computations for that period.

In respect of the second of the above-mentioned notices, the company is required to make a return for the accounting period 1.11.06 to 31.10.07 accompanied by accounts and tax computations for the period of account 1.11.06 to 31.1.08.

(D)

Taurus Ltd has always prepared accounts to 31 October. After 2006, it changes its accounting date, preparing accounts for the fifteen months to 31 January 2008. On 31 January 2007, HMRC issue a notice specifying a return period of 1 November 2005 to 31 October 2006. On 1 April 2007, they issue a notice specifying a return period of 1 November 2006 to 31 January 2007.

In respect of the first-mentioned notice, the position is as in (C) above.

In respect of the second of the above-mentioned notices, Taurus Ltd is not required to make a return, but should notify HMRC of the correct accounting dates and periods.

(E)

Gemini Ltd was incorporated on 1 July 2004 but remained dormant until 1 April 2006 when it began to trade. The first trading accounts were prepared for the year to 31 March 2007 and the company retains that accounting date. On 1 May 2008, HMRC issue notices specifying return periods of 1 July 2004 to 30 June 2005, 1 July 2005 to 30 June 2006, 1 July 2006 to 30 June 2007 and 1 July 2007 to 31 March 2008.

In respect of the notice for the period 1.7.04 to 30.6.05, Gemini Ltd is required to make a return for that period.

In respect of the notice for the period 1.7.05 to 30.6.06, the company is required to make a return for the period 1.7.05 to 31.3.06.

In respect of the notice for the period 1.7.06 to 30.6.07, the company is required to make a return for the period 1.4.06 to 31.3.07 accompanied by accounts and tax computations for that period.

In respect of the notice for the period 1.7.07 to 31.3.08, the company is required to make a return for the period 1.4.07 to 31.3.08 accompanied by accounts and tax computations for that period.

(F)

The final dates for the filing with HMRC of the returns in (A)–(E) above, and for the payment of corporation tax (assuming none of the companies concerned fall within the definition of a 'large company', see 53.2 PAYMENT OF TAX), are as follows.

Return period	*Filing date*	*Payment date*
(A) above		
1.11.05 – 31.10.06	31.10.07	1.8.07
1.11.06 – 31.7.07	31.7.08	1.5.08
(B) above		
1.1.06 – 31.12.06	15.3.08	1.10.07
1.1.07 – 30.9.07	30.9.08	1.7.08

(C) above		
1.11.05 – 31.10.06	21.11.07	1.8.07
1.11.06 – 31.10.07	31.1.09	1.8.08
(D) above		
1.11.05 – 31.10.06	31.10.07	1.8.07
(E) above		
1.7.04 – 30.6.05	1.8.08	—
1.7.05 – 31.3.06	1.8.08	—
1.4.06 – 31.3.07	1.8.08	1.1.08
1.4.07 – 31.3.08	31.3.09	1.1.09

Notes

(*a*) The time allowed for filing returns is effectively extended to the time allowed under the *Companies Act 1985* if this would give a later filing date. This will not be so in the majority of cases.

(*b*) HMRC may grant an extension, on an application by the company, if satisfied that the company has a 'reasonable excuse' (see 54.10 PENALTIES) for not being able to meet the filing date as above.

61.21 RETURNS OF INCOME TAX DEDUCTED FROM PAYMENTS MADE BY A COMPANY

Returns must be made by reference to 'return periods'. A '*return period*' ends on 31 March, 30 June, 30 September and 31 December and at the end of a company's accounting period. [*ICTA 1988, Sch 13 para 1; FA 1998, Sch 3 para 41*].

[*ICTA 1988, Sch 16*]. For details, see 37.5 INCOME TAX IN RELATION TO A COMPANY.

61.22 RETURNS OF NON-QUALIFYING DISTRIBUTIONS

Where a company makes a *non-qualifying distribution* (see 23.17 DISTRIBUTIONS) it must make a return to the inspector (*a*) within 14 days of the end of the accounting period in which the distribution is made or (*b*) if the distribution is not made in any accounting period, within 14 days of when it is made. The return must show particulars of the transaction, the name and address of the person(s) receiving the distribution and the amount or value received by each. [*ICTA 1988, s 234(5)–(9)*].

Simon's Direct Tax Service. See **D1.606.**

61.23 RETURNS OF STOCK DIVIDENDS ISSUED

Where a company issues stock dividends (see 23.15(*g*) DISTRIBUTIONS), it must make a return to the inspector within 30 days of the end of the return period as specified in 61.21 above. The return must show the first date on which the company was required to issue the shares, particulars of terms of issue and the cash equivalent of the share capital (for 2005/06 onwards) in accordance with *ITTOIA 2005, s 412*. See Tolley's Income Tax under Savings and Investment Income. [*ICTA 1988, s 250; ITTOIA 2005, Sch 1 para 120*].

Simon's Direct Tax Service. See **D1.607.**

61.24 RETURNS OF INTEREST BY BANKERS ETC.

On receipt of notice from an inspector, any person (including the National Savings Bank and a building society) paying or crediting interest, on money received or retained in the

UK in the ordinary course of his business, must make a return for any specified year of assessment (ending not more than three years before the date of service of the notice). The return must show the name and address of the recipient, the gross amount of interest paid or credited and the amount (if any) of tax deducted. The payer may exclude from that return interest paid to a person who has so requested and has given written notice that the person beneficially entitled to the interest is a non-UK resident company. Similarly, where a declaration of non-ordinary residence has been given to the payer to enable interest to be paid gross (see 8.9 BANKS, 9.4 BUILDING SOCIETIES), and the person who made that declaration has so requested, the payer is not required to include interest paid, credited or received before 6 April 2001 in the return under this provision. Notices may be issued concerning different parts or branches of a business. HMRC have powers by statutory instrument to make regulations requiring further prescribed information with the return, or providing that prescribed information is *not* required, or requiring information and returns to be in prescribed form, or providing for inspection of books, documents, records, etc. [*TMA 1970, s 17;FA 2000, s 145; SI 1990 No 2231; SI 2001 Nos 404, 405*].

Returns may similarly be required from any other person paying interest or receiving it on behalf of others. [*TMA 1970, s 18; FA 2000, s 145; SI 2001 No 405*].

With effect for interest payments on or after 6 April 2001, *SI 2001 No 405* excludes a wide range of payments from the application of *TMA 1970, ss 17* and *18*. In particular, the automatic reporting of payments to non-residents applies only to interest paid to individuals. For guidance on the making of information returns under *TMA 1970, s 17* and *s 18*, see HMRC's website (at www.hmrc.gov.uk/s17-s18guidance/index.htm). HMRC have issued revised specifications for returns for the reporting year beginning 6 April 2004.

With effect for payments on or after 6 April 2005, references to interest paid without deduction of income tax in *TMA 1970, ss 17* and *18* include references to alternative finance return or profit share return under ALTERNATIVE FINANCE ARRANGEMENTS (4). This applies to alternative finance arrangements entered into on or after 6 April 2005 subject to commencement rules for arrangements entered into before that date where a profit share return is payable on or after that date. [*FA 2005, s 56, Sch 2 para 2*].

61.25 **EC Directive on the Taxation of Savings.** *The Reporting of Savings Income Information Regulations 2003* (*SI 2003 No 3297* as amended) implement into UK law the EC Directive on the Taxation of Savings (*Directive 2003/48/EC*, 3 June 2003), designed to counter cross-border tax evasion by individuals on their savings income. The Directive, referred to as the Savings Directive or the Savings Tax Directive, came into effect on 1 July 2005. Under the Directive, prescribed UK paying agents, e.g. businesses and public bodies that pay savings income to, or collect savings income for, individuals resident elsewhere in the EC will have to report details of the income and the payee to HMRC, who will then pass on the information to the corresponding tax authority in the payee's country of residence. Similar information regarding UK-resident payees will flow in the opposite direction. (Austria, Belgium and Luxembourg are expected to impose, for a transitional period, a withholding tax as an alternative to exchanging information.)

The regulations prescribe the types of paying agent and payee within the scheme, the information required, the time limits for compliance and the penalties for non-compliance, and it provides for inspection of paying agents' records. For these purposes, '*savings income*' means interest (including premium bond winnings but not interest unrelated to a money debt or penalty charges for late payments), interest accrued or capitalised at the sale, refund or redemption of a money debt, and certain income distributed by or realised upon the sale, refund or redemption of shares or units in a collective investment fund (see 43.1 INVESTMENT FUNDS). Treasury regulations may also implement any similar arrangements made with non-EC countries (see further below). For HMRC guidance on savings income reporting and other related items, see www.hmrc.gov.uk/esd-guidance/index.htm. See also Treasury Explanatory Notes to Finance Bill 2003, European Commission Press Release 4 June 2003, Revenue Press Releases 30 June 2003, 22 September 2003 and Revenue Internet Statement 19 December 2003.

The Savings Directive applies to all 24 (as at 1 July 2005) EC member states. The EC has concluded similar savings taxation agreements with Andorra, Liechtenstein, San Marino, Monaco and Switzerland. These territories will apply a withholding tax and will exchange information at the request of tax authorities of EC member states in all criminal or civil cases of tax fraud etc. on a reciprocal basis. Similar agreements have been concluded by individual EC member states with ten dependent and associated territories of the UK and the Netherlands (Anguilla, Aruba (*SI 2005 No 1458*), the British Virgin Islands (*SI 2005 No 1457*), the Cayman Islands, Gibraltar (*SI 2006 No 1453*), Guernsey (*SI 2005 No 1262*), the Isle of Man (*SI 2005 No 1263*), Jersey (*SI 2005 No 1261*), Montserrat (*SI 2005 No 1459*), the Netherlands Antilles (*SI 2005 No 1460*) and the Turks & Caicos Islands). The British Virgin Islands, Guernsey, the Isle of Man, Jersey, the Netherlands Antilles and the Turks and Caicos Islands will apply a withholding tax during the same transitional period as applies to Austria, Belgium and Luxembourg. The agreements with Anguilla, Aruba, the Cayman Islands and Montserrat provide for exchange of information. The agreements with Anguilla, Cayman Islands and Turks and Caicos Islands do not, for the time being, have a reciprocal effect, as the residents of those territories are not taxable on their savings income. As the UK and Gibraltar are not separate member states, the Directive does not apply between them (HMRC Internet Statement 5 July 2005), but a bilateral agreement was signed on 19 December 2005 between the UK and Gibraltar under which those territories will exchange information with each other and by virtue of which Gibraltar will operate a withholding tax during the above-mentioned transitional period.

Where, under the Savings Directive or equivalent arrangements made with non-EC member states, a withholding tax is levied as an alternative to exchanging information, relief is available for such withholding tax against UK income tax and capital gains tax liabilities or, to the extent that set-off is not possible, by repayment. As an alternative, application may be made to HMRC for a certificate which can be presented to a paying agent to enable savings income to be paid to the applicant without deduction of such withholding tax.

Simon's Direct Tax Service. See **A3.120** and **F1.119**.

61.26 RETURNS OF INCOME FROM UK SECURITIES

A person receiving income on behalf of, or by or through whom income is paid to, another person resident in the UK must, within 28 days (or such longer time as may be specified in the necessary notice) make a return giving details similar to those in 61.24 above. [*TMA 1970, s 24*].

61.27 OTHER RETURNS

For returns by employers, hoteliers, stockbrokers, partnerships etc. and in respect of fees, commissions and copyrights, see Tolley's Income Tax under Returns. For returns by companies purchasing own shares, see 57.3 PURCHASE BY A COMPANY OF ITS OWN SHARES. For returns of Eurobond interest payments, see 37.3(*b*) INCOME TAX IN RELATION TO A COMPANY.

61.28 ELECTRONIC FILING OF TAX RETURNS ETC.

After 4 March 2003, companies, organisations paying corporation tax and their agents can use the HMRC corporation tax online service to send the Company Tax Return (CT600), supplementary pages A to J, and accounts and computations over the Internet. The returns can be submitted using the HMRC's free Online Tax Return – CT or an authorised third party software package. Details of software available are listed on the HMRC website. There are otherwise no facilities for electronic submission of company self-assessment tax returns. An online filing facility is similarly available for PAYE and certain other returns and until 31 March 2006, an electronic lodgement facility was also available for such returns as set out below.

Electronic lodgement. The electronic lodgement service was withdrawn with effect from 31 March 2006. (HMRC News Release 29 September 2005). Before that date it operated as set out below.

Certain other returns required to be made to HMRC or to an officer of HMRC may, subject to the conditions detailed below, be lodged electronically. The provision under which the return is required must be specified for this purpose by Treasury order, which will also appoint a commencement day. Any supporting documentation (including accounts, statements or reports) required to be delivered with a return may similarly be lodged electronically if the return is so lodged (or may instead be delivered by the last day for submission of the return).

The normal powers and rights applicable in relation to returns, etc. delivered by post are applied to information transmitted electronically. A properly made and authenticated hard copy (see (*c*) below) is treated in any proceedings as if it were the return or other document in question, but if no such copy is shown to have been made, a hard copy certified by an officer of HMRC to be a true copy of the information transmitted is so treated instead.

There are four conditions for electronic lodgement.

(*a*) The transmission must be made by a person approved for the purpose by HMRC. A person seeking approval must be given notice of the grant or refusal of approval, which may be granted for the transmission of information on the person's own behalf or on behalf of another person or persons. Approval may be withdrawn by notice from a given date, and any notice refusing or withdrawing approval must state the grounds. An appeal against refusal or withdrawal must be made within 30 days of such notice having been given, and lies to the Special Commissioners, who may grant approval from a specified date if they consider the refusal or withdrawal to have been unreasonable in all the circumstances.

(*b*) The transmission must comply with any requirements notified by HMRC to the person making it, including in particular any relating to the hardware or software to be used.

(*c*) The transmission must signify, in an approved manner, that a hard copy was made under arrangements designed to ensure that the information contained in it is the information in fact transmitted.

(*d*) The information transmitted must be accepted under a procedure selected by HMRC for this purpose, which may in particular consist of or include the use of specifically designed software.

As regards (*c*) above, the hard copy must have been authenticated by the person required to make the return:

(i) in the case of a return required by notice, by endorsement with a declaration that it is to the best of his knowledge correct and complete; or

(ii) otherwise by signature.

[*TMA 1970, s 115A, Sch 3A*].

Agents may pre-register for the electronic lodgement service. Copies of an information pack and registration form are available from the Agent Educator in all local tax offices. HMRC Statement of Practice SP 1/97, 16 January 1997, describes how they will operate electronic lodgement and the detailed requirements.

Simon's Direct Tax Service. See A3.166.

Mandatory e-filing. Electronic filing for PAYE returns will be mandatory from 2004/05 for employers with 250 or more employees ('large employers') and from 2005/06 for employers with 50 or more employees ('large or medium-sized employers'). See 33.10 HMRC: ADMINISTRATION.

Incentives for electronic communications. Regulations may be made by statutory instrument by the Commissioners of HMRC in relation to matters under their care and management for the provision of incentives to use electronic communications. These may include discounts (or payments or repayments), or additional time for compliance or payment, or more convenient intervals for the delivery of information or the making of payments. Anything received by way of incentive is not regarded as income for corporation tax purposes. The regulations may make provision as to the conditions of entitlement to incentives and for their withdrawal (which may be authorised to be made by direction), and may provide for penalties up to £1,000 for failure to comply with any specified provision. They may make different provision for different cases, and may make such incidental, supplemental, consequential or transitional provision as the Commissioners think fit. [*FA 2000, s 143, Sch 38; ITTOIA 2005, Sch 1 para 518*].

Voluntary e-filing. The *Income Tax (Incentive Payments for Voluntary Electronic Communication of PAYE Returns) Regulations 2003* (*SI 2003 No 2495* as amended by *SI 2005 No 826*) provide for the payment of incentives to employers with less than 50 employees ('small employers') who file electronically, of £250 for 2004/05 falling to £75 for 2008/09.

Internet filing discount. From April 2001 VAT returns and/or their PAYE end-of-year returns could be filed via the internet and for the 2000/01, small businesses filing their returns and paying any tax due electronically were entitled to a discount of £50, or £100 for both VAT and PAYE filing, and a further £50 where there were one or more working families' or disabled person's tax credit cases. (Revenue Press Releases 16 February 2000, 21 March 2000(BN1D)). See *SI 2001 No 56; SI 2001 No 1081, reg 22.*

61.29 CORPORATION TAX RETURN

The form of company tax return (see 61.3 above) specified by HMRC is Form CT600 (2006) Version 2, which will be issued (together with the CT600 Guide (2006) Version 2) with Form CT603, the notice requiring a return. Additional or replacement copies may be obtained from HMRC's website (at www.hmrc.gov.uk/ctsa/returns.htm) or from the CTSA Orderline (tel. 0845–300 6555). The following supplementary pages can also be obtained online or supplied on request to the Orderline.

CT600A *Loans to participators by close companies.* This must be completed if the company is a close company and made loans to an individual participator, or associate of a participator, that remained outstanding at the end of the period. See 16.9 *et seq.* CLOSE COMPANIES.

CT600B *Controlled foreign companies.* This must be completed if the company had an interest of 25% or more in the period in a foreign company which was controlled from the UK. See 21 CONTROLLED FOREIGN COMPANIES. See also HMRC International Manual, INTM 214010–214040 as regards completion of these supplementary pages.

CT600C *Group and consortium companies.* This must be completed if the company is claiming or surrendering any amounts under the group or consortium relief provisions or any eligible unrelieved foreign tax for the period. See 32.6 *et seq.* GROUPS OF COMPANIES, 24.11 DOUBLE TAX RELIEF.

CT600D *Insurance companies and friendly societies.* This must be completed if, in the period, the company either made claims under *ICTA 1988, Sch 19AB* to provisional payments (including notional repayments in respect of tax on gilt interest), or entered into business which it treats as overseas life assurance business.

CT600E *Charities and community amateur sports clubs.* This must be completed if the company is, in the period, a charity or community amateur sports club claiming exemption or partial exemption from tax. See 14 CHARITIES, 70.8 VOLUNTARY ASSOCIATIONS.

CT600F *Tonnage tax.* This must be completed where an election has been made for the alternative tonnage tax regime (see 55.16 PROFIT COMPUTATIONS).

CT600G *Corporate venturing scheme*. This must be completed if the company is claiming relief under the CORPORATE VENTURING SCHEME (22).

CT600H *Cross-border royalties*. This must be completed if the company made cross-border royalty payments after 1 October 2002 without deduction of tax or under deduction of tax at a treaty-specified rate (see 37.3 INCOME TAX IN RELATION TO A COMPANY).

CT600I *Supplementary charge in respect of ring fence trades*. This must be completed if the company carried on a ring fence trade in a period beginning (or deemed to have begun) after 16 April 2002. See 51.5 OIL COMPANIES.

CT600J *Disclosure of tax avoidance schemes*. This must be completed for notifiable arrangements on or after 18 March 2004 (see 5.26 ANTI AVOIDANCE).

Form CT600 (2006) consists of an opening page requiring company information, a summary of the return information and information on completion of the return. There are then a number of sections as follows:

- Turnover.
- Income – this includes profits from loan relationships, overseas income, property business, intangible fixed assets, tonnage tax and other profits not included in turnover.
- Chargeable gains.
- Losses brought forward against certain investment income.
- Non-trading deficits brought forward on loan relationships or derivative contracts.
- Deductions and reliefs – this includes corporate venturing scheme losses, losses on unquoted shares, management expenses, certain interest distributions, property business losses, non-trading losses from loan relationships and intangible fixed assets, capital allowances, trading losses carried back from subsequent periods, charges and group relief.
- The figure of profits chargeable to corporation tax.
- Tax calculation, arriving at the figure of corporation tax chargeable.
- Tax reliefs and deductions including Corporate Venturing Scheme investment relief, Community investment relief, double tax relief and ACT.
- Calculation of tax outstanding or overpaid, arriving at the figure of tax payable.
- Tax reconciliation – including tax credits payable or receivable, ring fence corporation tax and supplementary charge in respect of ring fence trades, tax already paid or outstanding, tax overpaid or tax refunds surrendered to the company.
- Indicators, including whether the company falls within the quarterly instalment payments regime, is within a group payment arrangement, has written down or sold intangible assets or has made cross-border royalty payments.
- Research and development expenditure and land remediation enhanced expenditure.
- Information about capital allowances and balancing charges.
- Losses, deficits and excess amounts – the various types must be listed and group companies must show the maximum amounts available for surrender by group or consortium relief.
- Overpayments and repayments – this must be completed if a repayment claim is made.

The final section is a declaration by the signatory.

A four-page, shorter version of the return, CT600 (Short) (2006) Version 2 may be used by companies with simpler tax affairs and where the only supplementary pages required are CT600A, CT600E and CT600J.

62 Self-Assessment

Simon's Direct Tax Service D2.8.

62.1 ACCOUNTING PERIODS ENDING ON OR AFTER 1 JULY 1999

For accounting periods ending on or after 1 July 1999, the self-assessment regime was extended to the pre-existing 'Pay and File' regime which had been introduced for accounting periods ending after 30 September 1993. [*FA 1994, s 199(2)(b); SI 1998 No 3173*]. Corporation tax for this purpose includes amounts chargeable under *ICTA 1988, s 419* (loans to participators, see 16.9 *et seq.* CLOSE COMPANIES) and *ICTA 1988, s 747* (CONTROLLED FOREIGN COMPANIES (21)). [*FA 1998, Sch 18 para 1*]. The return and self-assessment provisions are brought together in *FA 1998, Sch 18.*

For the revisions to the controlled foreign company and transfer pricing régimes to bring them within self-assessment, see 21.1 CONTROLLED FOREIGN COMPANIES and 67 TRANSFER PRICING respectively.

The essence of the self-assessment system is that returns are processed on receipt, by transfer to HMRC's computer system, without checking (save in so far as amendments are required to enable the return to be processed, e.g. to correct arithmetical errors), with any enquiries being carried out later (within the statutory time limits, see 61.10 RETURNS).

The relevant provisions are set out at 6 APPEALS, 7 ASSESSMENTS, 15 CLAIMS, 53 PAYMENT OF TAX and 61 RETURNS. See also 30 FRAUDULENT OR NEGLIGENT CONDUCT.

63 Small Companies—Reduced Rates

Cross-reference. See 16.18 CLOSE COMPANIES, 49 NON-CORPORATE DISTRIBUTIONS RATE, 60.4 RESIDENCE, 43.5 INVESTMENT FUNDS and 44.1 INVESTMENT TRUSTS.

Simon's Direct Tax Service D2.109–D2.113.

63.1 SMALL COMPANIES RATE

As mentioned in 1.2 INTRODUCTION AND RATES OF TAX, a special reduced rate of corporation tax, known as the 'small companies rate', applies to the 'basic profits' of a UK resident company the 'profits' of which do not exceed £300,000 (£250,000 for financial years 1991, 1992 and 1993, lower for earlier financial years) (the 'lower limit') for a 12-month accounting period, with marginal relief as in 63.2 below (but in both cases see 63.7 below where there are associated companies). See, however, 16.18 CLOSE COMPANIES as regards close investment-holding companies to which the reduced rate does not apply. See also 63.4 below as regards the lower 'starting rate' introduced from financial year 2000.

The rate for the financial year 2007 (other than on 'ring fence profits' where the rate remains at 19%) is 20%, for the financial years 2002 to 2006 it is **19%**, and that for financial years 1999 to 2001 inclusive is 20%. [*ICTA 1988, s 13; FA 2001, s 55; FA 2002, s 31; FA 2003, s 134; FA 2004, s 26; FA 2005, s 11; FA 2006, 25; FA 2007, s 3(1)*]. The rates for financial years 2008 and 2009 are 21% and 22% respectively. Where a company's accounting period straddles the end of a financial year (31 March), and the lower limits for the two financial years contained in the accounting period differ, then the periods before 1 April and after 31 March are treated as separate accounting periods for this purpose. [*FA 1989, s 35(3); FA 1991, s 25(3); FA 1994, s 86(3)*].

'*Profits*' (but not the 'basic profits') are the profits on which corporation tax falls finally to be borne plus FRANKED INVESTMENT INCOME (29). There is, however, an exclusion for franked investment income received:

(*a*) in relation to distributions from a '51% subsidiary' or from a fellow 51% subsidiary of a parent company (which, for accounting periods ending before 1 April 2001, must in either case be UK-resident);

(*b*) in relation to distributions from a 'trading' or 'holding company' owned by a 'consortium' of which the recipient company is a member and which is not itself a '75% subsidiary' of any other company or capable of becoming so by virtue of any existing arrangements (which similarly, for accounting periods ending before 1 April 2001, must be UK-resident); or

(*c*) in relation to distributions before 6 April 1999, from companies within the same group (for which purpose distributions are treated as coming from within the group if dividends so received are group income or would be if the companies so elected, see 32.2, 32.4 GROUPS OF COMPANIES).

(*a*) and (*b*) above apply equally to franked investment income received by another person on behalf of or in trust for the company, but not to any received by the company on behalf of or in trust for another person.

A '*51% (75%) subsidiary*' is a body corporate more than 50% (not less than 75%) of the 'ordinary share capital' of which is beneficially owned directly or indirectly by another. Share capital owned directly or indirectly in a body corporate (for accounting periods ending before 1 April 2001, in a non-resident body corporate), or owned indirectly through a company which holds it as trading stock, is disregarded in determining 51% subsidiary status, and a company is not treated as a 51% subsidiary unless the parent company would be beneficially entitled to more than 50% of any profits available for distribution to equity holders and of any assets so available on a winding-up (see 32.9 GROUPS OF COMPANIES).

'*Ordinary share capital*' means all the issued share capital of the company except non-participating shares carrying a fixed-rate dividend, but 'issued share capital' does not include founder members' deposits in a company limited by guarantee (*South Shore Mutual Insurance Co Ltd v Blair (Sp C 215), [1999] SSCD 296*).

A '*holding company*' means a company the business of which consists wholly or mainly in holding shares or securities of trading companies which are its '*90% subsidiaries*' (i.e. in which it holds directly not less than 90% of the ordinary share capital). A '*trading company*' is a company the business of which consists wholly or mainly of the carrying on of a trade or trades. A company is owned by a '*consortium*' if at least 75% of its ordinary share capital is beneficially owned amongst them by companies (for accounting periods ending before 1 April 2001, UK-resident companies), each owning at least 5% and beneficially entitled to at least 5% of any profits available for distribution to equity holders and of any assets so available on a winding-up (see 32.9 GROUPS OF COMPANIES). Such companies are the '*members of the consortium*'.

'*Basic profits*' are the profits on which corporation tax falls finally to be borne. See 44.2 INVESTMENT TRUSTS for the exclusion from basic profits *for small companies rate purposes only* of certain housing investment profits (prior to the introduction of real estate investment trusts (see 44.3 *et seq.* INVESTMENT TRUSTS) for accounting periods beginning on or after 1 January 2007).

[*ICTA 1988, s 13(7)–(8AB), s 13ZA, s 247(1A)(8)–(9A), s 832(1), s 838(1); FA 1998, Sch 3 para 7; FA 2001, s 86*].

Claims. The small companies rate (or marginal relief, see 63.2 below) must be claimed. In practice, a clear indication in the company's return, computation or accompanying correspondence that profits of the accounting period should be charged at the small companies rate (or attract marginal relief) is accepted as a valid claim. The claim should, however, include a statement of the number (or absence) of associated companies in the period (see 63.7 below). (HMRC Company Tax Manual 03670).

For an accounting period of less than twelve months, or one overlapping the end of a financial year, see 63.2 below.

'*Ring fence profits*': ring fence profits are defined as any income from oil extraction activities or oil rights and capital gains on disposal of an interest in an oil field or an asset used in oil extraction. [*ICTA 1988, s 502; TCGA 1992, s 197; FA 2007, s 3*].

Simon's Direct Tax Service. See D2.109.

63.2 **Marginal relief.** Where the 'profits' of a UK resident company for a 12-month accounting period exceed a lower limit (the 'lower relevant maximum amount') but do not exceed an upper limit (the 'upper relevant maximum amount'), the corporation tax otherwise chargeable on the 'basic profits' is reduced by the following amount (unless there are associated companies, see 63.7 below).

$$\text{Small companies rate marginal fraction} \times (\text{Upper relevant maximum amount} - \text{Profits}) \times \frac{\text{Basic profits}}{\text{Profits}}$$

'*Profits*' and '*basic profits*' are as defined in 63.1 above.

The small companies rate marginal fraction for the financial year 2007 is 1/40, that for the financial years 2002 to 2006 is 11/400, that for financial years 1997 to 2001 inclusive is 1/40, that for financial year 1996 is 9/400, that for financial years 1994 and 1995 is 1/50, and the upper and lower limits for those years are set at £1,500,000 and £300,000 respectively. Where the profits consist of basic profits only, the effective marginal rate is 32.5% for the financial year 2007, 32.75% for financial years 2002 to 2006, 32.5% for financial years 1999 to 2001 inclusive, 33.5% for financial years 1997 and 1998, 35.25% for financial year 1996, 35% for financial years 1994 and 1995. For 2007, the marginal relief fraction for ring fence profits remains at 11/400.

Marginal relief for earlier years is granted by reference to the following fractions and figures.

	Upper limit	Lower limit	Relief fraction	Marginal rate
1991–1993	£1,250,000	£250,000	1/50	35%
1990	£1,000,000	£200,000	9/400	36.25%
1989	£750,000	£150,000	1/40	37.5%
1988	£500,000	£100,000	1/40	37.5%

[ICTA 1988, s 13(2)(3); FA 2001, s 55(b); FA 2002, s 31(b); FA 2003, s 134(b); FA 2004, s 26(b); FA 2005, s 11(b); FA 2006, s 25(b); *FA 2007, s 3(2)*].

Where a company has both ring fence and other profits, there are special rules for apportioning profits between the ring fence and non-ring fence profits for marginal relief purposes.

Where a company's accounting period straddles the end of a financial year (31 March), and the upper or lower limits for the two financial years contained in the accounting period differ, then the periods before 1 April and after 31 March are treated as separate accounting periods for the purposes of small companies relief. [*FA 1989, s 35(3); FA 1991, s 25(3); FA 1994, s 86(3)*].

Where an accounting period is less than twelve months, the upper and lower limits are proportionately reduced. [*ICTA 1988, s 13(6)*].

The chargeable profits of an accounting period which overlaps the end of a financial year are, if necessary, apportioned between the two years. [*ICTA 1988, s 8(3)*].

See 63.1 above as regards claims for relief.

63.3 *Examples*

(A)

In its accounting period 1 April 2007 to 31 March 2008, X Ltd, a trading company, has chargeable profits of £300,000, including chargeable gains of £40,000, and also has franked investment income of £75,000 (representing net distributions received of £67,500). X Ltd has no associated companies.

Corporation tax payable is calculated as follows.

	£
Corporation tax at full rate of 30% on £300,000	90,000
$\frac{1}{40} \times £(1{,}500{,}000 - 375{,}000) \times \frac{300{,}000}{375{,}000}$	22,500
Corporation tax payable	£67,500

(B)

In its accounting period 1 April 2007 to 31 March 2008, Y Ltd, a trading company, has chargeable profits of £375,000 including chargeable gains of £40,000, but has no franked investment income. Y Ltd has no associated companies.

Corporation tax payable is calculated as follows.

	£
Corporation tax at full rate of 30% on £375,000	112,500
$\frac{1}{40}$ × £(1,500,000 – 375,000)	28,125
Corporation tax payable	£84,375

An alternative method of calculation, where there is no franked investment income, is to apply small companies rate up to the small companies rate limit and marginal rate (32.5% for FY 2007) to the balance of profits. Thus:

		£
£300,000	at 20%	60,000
75,000	at 32.5%	24,375
£375,000		£84,375

(*C*)

In its accounting period 1 January 2007 to 31 December 2007, Z Ltd had chargeable profits of £540,000 and franked investment income of £60,000. Z Ltd had no associated companies during that period.

Corporation tax payable is calculated as follows.

			£	£
Part of the accounting period falling in financial year 2006				
Profits $\frac{3}{12}$ × £600,000	=	£150,000		
Basic profits $\frac{3}{12}$ × £540,000	=	£135,000		
Lower relevant maximum	=	£75,000		
Corporation tax at full rate				
£135,000 at 30%			40,500	
Less marginal relief				
$\frac{11}{400}$ × £(375,000 – 150,000) ×		$\frac{135,000}{150,000}$	5,569	
				34,931

Part of the accounting period falling in financial year 2007

Profits 9/12 × £600,000	=	£450,000		
Basic profits 9/12 × £540,000	=	£405,000		
Lower relevant maximum	=	£225,000		
Corporation tax at full rate				
£405,000 at 30%			121,500	
Less marginal relief				
1/40 × £(1,125,000 – 450,000) ×		$\frac{405,000}{450,000}$	15,188	
				106,312
Corporation tax payable				£141,243

63.4 **STARTING RATE**

For financial years 2000–2005 a special 'corporation tax starting rate' applies to the 'basic profits' of a UK resident company the 'profits' of which do not exceed a specified amount (the '*first relevant amount*'), with marginal relief as in 63.5 below (but in both cases see 63.7 below where there are associated companies). The starting rate does not, however, apply to close investment-holding companies (see 16.18 CLOSE COMPANIES) or to investment trusts in receipt of eligible rental income (see 44.2 INVESTMENT TRUSTS). The starting rate is abolished for financial year 2006 onwards.

'*Basic profits*' and '*profits*' are defined as for small companies rate purposes (see 63.1 above).

The starting rate is **0%** for financial years 2002 to 2005 having been initially set at **10%** (for financial years 2000 and 2001). The first relevant amount for all years is **£10,000** for a twelve-month accounting period, being proportionately reduced for shorter accounting periods. An accounting period straddling 31 March 2000 is for these purpose treated as two separate accounting periods ending on and beginning immediately after that date.

[*ICTA 1988, s 13AA(1)(4)(6)-(8); FA 1999, ss 28(1)(7), 29; FA 2001, s 56; FA 2002, s 32; FA 2003, s 135; FA 2004, s 27; FA 2005, s 12; FA 2006, s 26(1)*].

The chargeable profits of an accounting period which overlaps the end of a financial year are, if necessary, apportioned between the two years. Accounting periods straddling 1 April 2006 are treated as two separate accounting periods, one ending on 31 March 2006 and other beginning on 1 April 2006, the profits and basic profits to be apportioned between the two periods. [*ICTA 1988, s 8(3); FA 2006, s 26(8)–(11)*].

Claims. The starting rate (or marginal relief, see 63.5 below) must be claimed. In practice, a clear indication in the company's return, computation or accompanying correspondence that profits of the accounting period should be charged at the starting rate (or attract marginal relief) is accepted as a valid claim. The claim should, however, except in the case of an unincorporated association or other members' club or society, include a statement of the number (or absence) of associated companies in the period (see 63.7 below). (HMRC Statement of Practice, SP 1/91 as revised).

Simon's Direct Tax Service. See **D2.112**.

63.5 **Marginal relief.** Where the profits for a twelve-month accounting period of a company otherwise entitled to claim application of the corporation tax starting rate exceed the first relevant amount but do not exceed an upper limit (the '*second relevant amount*'), the company may claim that the corporation tax chargeable on its basic profits be calculated as if the rate of corporation tax were the small companies rate (see 63.1 above) and then reduced by the following amount (unless there are associated companies, see 63.7 below).

$$\text{Starting rate marginal fraction} \times (\text{Second relevant amount} - \text{Profits}) \times \frac{\text{Basic profits}}{\text{Profits}}$$

'*Profits*' and '*basic profits*' are as defined in 63.1 above.

The first and second relevant amounts for the financial years 2000 to 2005 are **£10,000** and **£50,000** respectively. The starting rate marginal fraction for financial years 2002 to 2005 is 19/400, that for financial years 2000 and 2001 is 1/40.

Where a company's accounting period is less than twelve months, the first and second relevant amounts are proportionately reduced.

An accounting period straddling 31 March 2000 is for these purpose treated as two separate accounting periods ending on and beginning immediately after that date.

[*ICTA 1988, s 13AA(2)-(7); FA 1999, ss 28(1)(7), 29; FA 2001, s 56(b); FA 2002, s 32(b); FA 2003, s 135(b); FA 2004, 27(b); FA 2005, s 12(b); FA 2006, s 26(1)*].

See 63.4 above as regards accounting periods overlapping the end of a financial year or straddling 1 April 2006 and as regards claims for relief.

63.6 *Examples*

(*A*)

In its accounting period 1 April 2005 to 31 March 2006, X Ltd, a trading company, has chargeable profits of £10,000, including chargeable gains of £400, and also has franked investment income of £2,500 (representing net distributions received of £2,250). X Ltd has no associated companies.

Corporation tax payable is calculated as follows.

	£
Corporation tax at small companies rate of 19% on £10,000	1,900
$\frac{19}{400} \times £(50,000 - 12,500) \times \frac{10,000}{12,500}$	1,425
Corporation tax payable	£75

(*B*)

In its accounting period 1 April 2005 to 31 March 2006, Y Ltd, a trading company, has chargeable profits of £12,500 including chargeable gains of £400, but has no franked investment income. Y Ltd has no associated companies.

Corporation tax payable is calculated as follows.

	£
Corporation tax at small companies rate of 19% on £12,500	2,375
19/400 × £(50,000 – 12,500)	1,781
Corporation tax payable	£594

An alternative method of calculation, where there is no franked investment income, is to apply the starting rate up to the starting rate limit and the marginal rate (23.75% for FY 2005) to the balance of profits. Thus:

		£
£10,000	at 0%	—
2,500	at 23.75%	594
£12,500		£594

(*C*)

In its accounting period 1 January 2002 to 31 December 2002, Z Ltd had chargeable profits of £18,000 and franked investment income of £2,000. Z Ltd had no associated companies during that period.

Corporation tax payable is calculated as follows.

Part of the accounting period falling in financial year 2001

Profits 3/12 × £20,000	=	£5,000
Basic profits 3/12 × £18,000	=	£4,500
First relevant amount	=	£2,500
Second relevant amount	=	£12,500

	£	£
Corporation tax at small companies rate		
£4,500 at 20%	900	
Less marginal relief		
$1/40 \times £(12,500 - 5,000) \times \frac{4,500}{5,000}$	169	
		731

Part of the accounting period falling in financial year 2002

Profits $\frac{9}{12}$ × £20,000	=	£15,000
Basic profits $\frac{9}{12}$ × £18,000	=	£13,500
First relevant amount	=	£7,500
Second relevant amount	=	£37,500

Corporation tax at small companies rate		
£13,500 at 19%	2,565	
Less marginal relief		
$\frac{19}{400} \times £(37{,}500 - 15{,}000) \times \frac{13{,}500}{15{,}000}$	962	
		1,603
Corporation tax payable		£2,334

63.7 **ASSOCIATED COMPANIES**

The upper and lower relevant maximum amounts mentioned in 63.1 and 63.2 above, and for financial years 2000–2005 the first and second relevant amounts mentioned in 63.4 and 63.5 above, in each case (as reduced where an accounting period is less than twelve months), are divided by one plus the number of 'associated companies' which the company has in the accounting period. [*ICTA 1988, s 13(3)b), s 13AA(4)(b); FA 1999, s 28(1); FA 2006, Sch 26 Pt 3(1)*].

A company is an '*associated company*' of another for this purpose if one of the two has 'control' of the other or both are under the control of the same person or persons. This may include non-UK resident companies. '*Control*' is as defined in *ICTA 1988, s 416*, see 16.2 CLOSE COMPANIES. In applying the definition, however, HMRC will not seek to attribute to any person the rights and powers of relatives, other than those of his or her spouse and minor children, except where there is substantial commercial interdependence between the companies. (Note that from 5 December 2005 references to spouses was extended by the *Tax and Civil Partnership Regulations 2005* (*SI 2005 No 3229*) to cover civil partners.) Similarly, two companies will not be treated as associated where they may be treated as under common control, or one may be treated as controlled by the other, only by taking into account fixed rate preference shares held as a business investment by a non-close company taking no part in management etc., or where that control is by an otherwise unconnected commercial loan creditor (not being a close company) or trustee. (HMRC Extra-Statutory Concession, C9). See HMRC Company Taxation Manual, CTM 60250 for HMRC's view of control where companies are under the control of more than one person or group of persons. For two companies to be under the control of the same persons, an irreducible group of persons having control of one must be identical with an irreducible group of persons having control of the other (i.e. in neither case could any definition of control be satisfied if any one of them were excluded).

An associated company is counted even if it was associated for part of the accounting period only and two or more are counted even if they were associated for different parts of the accounting period. However, an associated company which has not carried on any trade or business at any time in that accounting period (or the part thereof when it was associated) is disregarded.

[*ICTA 1988, s 13(4)(5), s 13AA(5); FA 1999, s 28(1)*].

In *Gascoines Group Ltd v Inspector of Taxes and related appeals Ch D, [2004] STC 844*, a company controlled by trustees of a trust was considered to be associated with other companies controlled by the settlor of that trust. The trustees were associates of the settlor by virtue of *ICTA 1988, s 417(3)(b)* and therefore, the rights of the trustees were to be attributed to the settlor who was to be taken to have control over the company controlled by the trustees (by virtue of *ICTA 1988, s 416(6)*).

In *HMRC v Salaried Persons Postal Loans Ltd Ch D [2006] STC 1315*, the High Court upheld the decision of the Special Commissioners that the company, whose sole activity was the continuation of the letting of former trading premises after it ceased to trade, was not carrying on a business. For a case in which a company whose sole activity was the receipt of bank deposit interest was held not to be carrying on any business, see *Jowett v O'Neill and Brennan Construction Ltd Ch D 1998, 70 TC 566*. Similarly a company set up for the sole purpose of owning a holiday home used exclusively by its sole shareholder and his family was held not to be carrying on any business (*John M Harris (Design Partnership) Ltd v Lee (Sp C 130), [1997] SSCD 240*). See, however, *Land Management Ltd v Fox (Sp C 306), 2002 STI 403*, in which an associated company whose principal activity was as an investment company with income derived from a tenanted residential freehold property was held to be carrying on a business (and this applied also to three subsidiary financial activities). HMRC in practice disregard a non-trading holding company if it has no assets (other than shares in 51% subsidiaries (see 63.1 above)), no income or gains (other than dividends distributed in full to its shareholders and which are (or could be) group income under *ICTA 1988, s 247(1)* (where applicable, see 32.2 GROUPS OF COMPANIES) and no entitlement to a deduction, as charges or management expenses, in respect of any outgoings. (HMRC Company Tax Manual 03590).

For a case on the inclusion of non-UK resident members of a group in determining the number of associated companies for the purpose of calculating the upper and lower relevant maximum amounts mentioned in 63.1 and 63.2 above, see *Jansen Nielsen Pilkes Ltd v Tomlinson (Inspector of Taxes) (Sp C 405) [2004] SSCD 226*.

Where a company's accounting period straddles the end of a financial year (31 March), and the marginal relief limits for the two financial years contained in the accounting period differ, then the periods before 1 April and after 31 March are treated as separate accounting periods for these purposes. [*FA 1989, s 35(3); FA 1991, s 25(3); FA 1994, s 86(3)*].

Simon's Direct Tax Service. See **D2.110**.

63.8 *Examples*

(*A*)

Y Ltd has profits, consisting wholly of income, of £320,000 for the 12-month accounting period ended 31 December 1994. It had no associated company until 1 November 1994, when its shares were acquired by a company with three wholly-owned subsidiaries, of which one was dormant throughout the 12-month period.

Y Ltd is to be treated as having no associated company in the notional accounting period from 1 January to 31 March 1994, but as having three associated companies (i.e. its new parent and that company's existing active subsidiaries) throughout the notional accounting period from 1 April to 31 December 1994. (This difference arises because of the change of marginal relief limits from 1 April 1994 — see above.)

Y Ltd's profits for the notional accounting period (see 63.2 above) from 1 January to 31 March 1994 are:

$$£320,000 \times \frac{3}{12} = £80,000$$

The upper limit of profit for marginal relief for that notional period is

$$£1,250,000 \times \frac{3}{12} = £312,500$$

The relief for the notional accounting period is thus

$$\frac{1}{50} \times (312,500 - 80,000) = £4,650$$

Y Ltd's profits for the notional accounting period from 1 April to 31 December 1994 are

$$£320,000 \times \frac{9}{12} = £240,000$$

The upper limit of profit for marginal relief for that notional period is

$$\left(£1,500,000 \times \frac{9}{12}\right) \div 4 = £281,250$$

The relief for the notional accounting period is thus

$$\frac{1}{50} \times (281,250 - 240,000) = £825$$

and (subject to any loss or group relief being available) the corporation tax charge for the accounting period on Y Ltd will be:

Financial year 1993	£80,000 @ 33%	26,400
Financial year 1994	£240,000 @ 33%	79,200
		105,600
Less marginal small companies' relief (4,650 + 825)		5,475
		£100,125

(*B*)

The figures and other information are exactly as in (A) above for the year ended 31 December 1997. Y Ltd is, however, treated as having three associated companies throughout the accounting period. There is no change in the marginal relief limits and hence no split into two notional accounting periods. (The change in the corporation tax rate and in the marginal relief fraction require only that the profits be apportioned to the relevant financial years, see 1.2 INTRODUCTION AND RATES OF TAX.)

Y Ltd's corporation tax liability for the year ended 31 December 1997 is therefore calculated as follows.

FY 1996

	£
£80,000 at 33%	26,400
Less 9/400 × (93,750 – 80,000) =	309
	26,091

FY 1997

	£
£240,000 at 31%	74,400
Less 1/40 × (281,250 – 240,000) =	1,031
	73,369

	£
Total liability: FY 1996	26,091
FY 1997	73,369
	£99,460

(*C*)

The figures and other information are exactly as in (B) above but for the year ended 31 December 1999. There is no change in the marginal relief limits nor in the marginal relief fraction. Hence the change in the corporation tax rate only requires the profits to be apportioned to the relevant financial years (see 1.2 INTRODUCTION AND RATES OF TAX).

Y Ltd's corporation tax liability for the year ended 31 December 1999 is therefore calculated as follows.

		£
Financial year 1998	£80,000 @ 31%	24,800
Financial year 1999	£240,000 @ 30%	72,000
		96,800
Less 1/40 × (375,000 – 320,000) =		1,375
Corporation tax liability		£95,425

(*D*)

The figures and other information are exactly as in (B) above but for the year ended 31 December 2002. There is no change in the marginal relief limits nor in corporation tax rate. Hence the change in the marginal relief fraction only requires the profits to be apportioned to the relevant financial years (see 1.2 INTRODUCTION AND RATES OF TAX).

Y Ltd's corporation tax liability for the year ended 31 December 2002 is therefore calculated as follows.

FY 2001

	£
£80,000 at 30%	24,000
Less 1/40 × (93,750 – 80,000) =	344
	23,656

FY 2002

	£
£240,000 at 30%	72,000
Less 11/400 × (281,250 – 240,000) =	1,134
	70,866

	£
Total liability: FY 2001	23,656
FY 2002	70,866
	£94,522

63.9 CORPORATION TAX ON DISTRIBUTIONS TO NON-CORPORATES

With effect for distributions made **after 31 March 2004 and before 1 April 2006**, a special rate, the '*non-corporate distribution rate*', applies where a company, which has an underlying rate of corporation tax of less than that rate (19% for the financial years 2004 and 2005 – the small companies' rate), makes (or is treated as making) one or more '*non-corporate distributions*' in any accounting period. [*ICTA 1988, s 13AB, Sch A2; FA 2004, s 28, Sch 3; FA 2005, s 13; FA 2006, s 26*(*2*)]. See 49 NON-CORPORATE DISTRIBUTION RATE for further details.

Simon's Direct Tax Service. See D2.113.

64 Statutory Bodies

Simons Direct Tax Service. See **D4.3**

64.1 **Marketing Boards.** Agricultural marketing boards etc. which are obliged to pay any trading surplus into a reserve fund (with restricted rights of repayment etc.) may deduct such payments from the profits of the trade carried on by them. Any withdrawal from the fund which is not required to be passed on to a Minister or government department, producers, or persons paying levies or duties, is treated as a trading receipt. [*ICTA 1988, s 509*].

64.2 The **Atomic Energy Authority** and the **National Radiological Protection Board** are exempt from corporation tax under:

- Schedule A (or under ITTOIA 2005, Pt 3 so far as it relates to the profits of a UK property business); or
- Schedule D (or trading income under *ITTOIA 2005*) in respect of yearly interest or other annual payments received or in respect of public revenue dividends (or income within ITTOIA 2005, Pt 4 Ch 10 (distributions from authorises unit trusts)) received; or
- ITTOIA 2005, Pt 4 Ch 3 (or before 2004–05, Schedule F) in respect of distributions received.

Income and chargeable gains from investments or deposits held for the purposes of a pension scheme operated by the former are also exempt.

[*ICTA 1988, s 512; TCGA 1992, s 271(7); ITTOIA 2005, Sch 1 para 199*].

64.3 **Harbour reorganisation schemes.** Where, under such a scheme, the trade of a body corporate (other than a limited liability company) is transferred to a harbour authority, the trade is not treated as discontinued; loss relief is given and capital allowances and corporation tax on chargeable gains apply as if there had been no change. If only part of the body corporate's trade is transferred, it is treated as a separate trade. [*ICTA 1988, s 518*].

64.4 **Local authorities, local authority associations and health service bodies** are exempt from tax. [*ICTA 1988, ss 519, 519A, 842A; TCGA 1992, ss 271(3), 288(1); ITA 2007, Sch 1 para 340*]. See 27.10 EXEMPT ORGANISATIONS.

64.5 The **Nuclear Decommissioning Authority** (NDA) is granted exemption on trading income arising or accruing to it or to an 'NDA company' from the carrying on of exempt activities. An '*NDA company*' is defined as a 'relevant site licensee' (as defined) or a company of which the ordinary share capital is owned directly or indirectly by the NDA. Exempt activities are specified by regulation (for which see *SI 2005 No 644* which also provides further conditions to be satisfied by a site licensee for it to qualify as an NDA company). [*Energy Act 2004, ss 27–30, 47, Sch 4; FA 2006, ss 99, 100*].

64.6 Subject to the special provisions above and, where appropriate, to the Crown exemption (see 27.5 EXEMPT ORGANISATIONS), statutory bodies are liable in the ordinary way to corporation tax on their income and capital gains. Whether their activities amount to trading depends on the facts. See *Mersey Docks and Harbour Board v Lucas HL 1883, 2 TC 25* (trading surplus held chargeable notwithstanding that it had to be applied in reducing debt), *Port of London Authority v CIR CA 1920, 12 TC 122*, and *Forth Conservancy Board cases, HL 1928, 14 TC 709*, and *HL 1931, 16 TC 103* (liable under Case VI on surplus from shipping dues) and *British Broadcasting Corporation v Johns CA 1964, 41 TC 471* (liable under Case I on profits from publications etc. but not on rest of surplus; not entitled to Crown exemption). For further cases, see Tolley's Tax Cases.

64.7 **Statutory corporation borrowing in foreign currency.** Interest on securities issued after 5 April 1982 by, or on a loan to, a statutory corporation (as defined) in a currency other than sterling shall, if the Treasury directs, be paid without deduction of income tax and be exempt from income tax (but not corporation tax) in the hands of a non-resident beneficial owner of such securities or, in the case of a loan, in the hands of the person for the time being entitled to repayment or eventual repayment of the loan. Securities issued before 6 April 1982 in the currency of a country outside the scheduled territories at the time of issue were similarly treated. [*ICTA 1988, s 581(4); ITTOIA 2005, s 755(1), Sch 1 paras 241, 242*].

65 Time Limits

Except where other time limits are prescribed, claims, elections etc. must be made within six years of the end of the accounting period to which they relate. [*TMA 1970, s 43(1); FA 1998, Sch 18 para 55*]. See also Tolley's Income Tax.

It should be noted that a number of time limits (particularly in relation to procedural matters) were revised following the introduction of self-assessment for accounting periods ending **on or after 1 July 1999**.

Simon's Direct Tax Service A3.620, D2.711, D2.809, D2.831 *et seq.*

65.1 ACCOUNTING PRINCIPLES

(*a*) *On a change of basis from realisation basis to mark to market basis*, election to spread the adjustment income equally over six periods of account beginning with the first period to which the new basis applies. Election to be made within twelve months after the end of the first accounting period to which the new basis applies. [*FA 2002, Sch 22 para 9*]. See 66.6 TRADING INCOME.

(*b*) *On a change of accounting approach in calculating profits in compliance with UK GAAP (or international accounting standards if applicable)*, election to treat the 'UITF 40' adjustment as arising and charged in an accounting period rather than spreading it over three to six years. Election to be made within one year of the filing date of the company's tax return for the accounting period for which the election is made. [*FA 2006, Sch 15 para 13*]. See 66.6 TRADING INCOME.

65.2 ADVANCE CORPORATION TAX

Claims for ACT to be surrendered must be made within **six years** of the end of the accounting period to which it relates. See 32.5 GROUPS OF COMPANIES.

ACT is **abolished** after 5 April 1999 (see 3.1 ADVANCE CORPORATION TAX).

65.3 APPEALS

(*a*) Formal notice of appeal against an amendment to a corporation tax return following an enquiry or against an assessment which is not a self-assessment, must be lodged within **30 days** after the date of issue of the notice of amendment or assessment. See 6.1 APPEALS.

(*b*) For appeals to the High Court from the General Commissioners, written requests for a stated case must be made to the Clerk for the Commissioners within **30 days** of the determination. See 6.19 APPEALS.

(*c*) Appeals on a question of residence or domicile must be lodged within **three months** of receipt of written notice of HMRC's decision. See 15.8 CLAIMS.

(*d*) Except as indicated above, appeals against amendments to claims etc. must be made within **30 days** of the receipt of the decision on a claim or of an amendment of a claim, as the case may be. See 15.8 CLAIMS.

65.4 CAPITAL ALLOWANCES

(*a*) Claims for machinery or plant allowances to be set off against income other than that against which they are primarily given must be made within **two years** of the end of the accounting period for which the allowances are made. [*CAA 2001, s 260(6); CAA 1990, s 145(5)*].

(*b*) A notice that machinery or plant on which allowances have been given has ceased, during the 'requisite period', to be used for a 'qualifying purpose' must be given within **three months** of the end of the accounting period in which the non-qualifying use takes place, or within **30 days** of the cessation's coming to the notice of the lessor, whichever is the later. [*CAA 2001, ss 119, 120; CAA 1990, s 23(2)(3), s 48(3)(6), s 49(2)(3)*].

(*c*) Election for a change in the law effected by *CAA 2001* not to have effect for an accounting period ending on 1 April 2001 or straddling that date must be made within two years after the end of the accounting period. See 10.1 CAPITAL ALLOWANCES.

See generally 10 CAPITAL ALLOWANCES.

65.5 CAPITAL GAINS

(*a*) **Assets held on 6 April 1965.** An election for such assets to be valued at 6 April 1965 must be made within **two years** after the end of the accounting period in which the relevant disposal was made. [*TCGA 1992, Sch 2 para 17*]. For certain concessional treatment on a company's leaving a group see 12.32 CAPITAL GAINS—GROUPS.

(*b*) **Assets held on 31 March 1982.** An irrevocable election for assets to be valued at 31 March 1982 must be made within two years of the end of the accounting period in which the first relevant disposal occurs (or such longer time as HMRC may allow).

(*c*) **Assets of negligible value.** A claim must be made within **two years** after the end of the accounting period in which the relevant date falls. See Tolley's Capital Gains Tax.

(*d*) **Groups of companies.** A company leaving a group remains liable for unpaid corporation tax on chargeable gains arising from the disposal of any asset formerly owned by that company while it was a member of the group where the disposal occurs within **twelve months** following its departure from the group. [*TCGA 1992, s 190*].

(*e*) **Know-how.** Joint election for so much of the consideration for the sale of a trade (or part of a trade) **not** to be treated as a payment for goodwill must be made within **two years** of the disposal. [*ICTA 1988, s 531(3)*]. See 66.62 TRADING INCOME.

(*f*) **Residence.** An election for any part of the 'postponed gain' on cessation of residence which becomes chargeable to be offset by capital losses of the subsidiary concerned must be made within **two years** of the cessation of residence. See 60.7 RESIDENCE.

(*g*) **Rollover relief** is only available if the acquisition of the new assets is made within **three years** after the disposal of the old or within **twelve months** before. See 12.29 CAPITAL GAINS—GROUPS.

For further details of the above and other time limits, see Tolley's Capital Gains Tax under the appropriate heading.

65.6 CHARGEABILITY TO TAX

A company chargeable to corporation tax for any accounting period which has not received notice requiring a return for that period must notify the inspector that it is so chargeable within **one year** of the end of that period. See 59.3 SELF-ASSESSMENT. [*TMA 1970, s 10; FA 1988, s 121; FA 1998, Sch 18 para 2, Sch 19 para 1*].

65.7 COMING WITHIN CHARGE TO CORPORATION TAX

With effect for accounting periods beginning on or after 22 July 2004 a company must give notice to HMRC of when its first accounting period begins and of when any subsequent accounting period begins that does not follow on immediately from the end of a previous accounting period. The notice must be given within three months after the beginning of the accounting period in question. See 61.1 RETURNS. [*FA 2004, s 55*].

65.8 **CONSTRUCTION INDUSTRY: TAX DEDUCTION SCHEME**

The requirements are equivalent to those in 65.28(*a*) and (*b*) below (except that the relevant form is SC 35). [*SI 1993 No 743*].

65.9 **CONTAMINATED LAND REMEDIATION EXPENDITURE**

(*a*) Election for 'qualifying land remediation expenditure' of a capital nature to be allowed as a deduction from trade or Schedule A business profits must be made within **two years** after the end of the accounting period in respect of which it is made. [*FA 2001, Sch 22 para 1*(*8*)].

(*b*) Claims for 'land remediation tax credit' (and 'life assurance company tax credit') must be included in the company tax return (or amended return) and must be made within **one year** of the filing date for that return or by such later time as HMRC may allow. [*TMA 1970, ss 83G–83L; FA 2001, Sch 23 paras 4, 6*].

65.10 **CONTROLLED FOREIGN COMPANIES**

Claims under *ICTA 1988, Sch 24 para 9*, for losses of certain periods to be taken into account in computing chargeable profits, are to be made within **20 months** after the end of the accounting period. The same applies to claims under *para 4* for certain deemed claims and elections to be disregarded in computing chargeable profits. [*ICTA 1988, ss 747–756, Schs 24–26; FA 1998, Sch 17*]. See 21.10 CONTROLLED FOREIGN COMPANIES.

65.11 **CORPORATE VENTURING SCHEME**

(*a*) The compliance statement to the effect that shares qualify for the relief must be made by the issuing company within **two years** after the end of the accounting period in which the shares were issued (or, if later, by two years after the minimum trading period condition is satisfied). [*FA 2000, Sch 15 para 42*(*4*)]. See 22.4 CORPORATE VENTURING SCHEME.

(*b*) Claims for set-off of allowable losses against income must be made within **two years** after the end of the accounting period in which the loss was incurred. [*FA 2000, Sch 15 para 68*]. See 22.20 CORPORATE VENTURING SCHEME.

65.12 **DIRECTORS' REMUNERATION**

A claim for the computation for a period of account to be adjusted for directors' remuneration paid after the computation has been made, but within nine months after the end of the period, must be made within **two years** of the end of the period of account. [*FA 1989, s 43*(*5*)*; ITEPA 2003, Sch 6 para 157*]. See 66.43 TRADING INCOME. (See also Tolley's Income Tax under Trading Income for 2005/06 onwards where such matters are dealt with by way of amendment to the self-assessment tax return and the two-year limit no longer applies.)

65.13 **DOUBLE TAXATION**

Relief by way of credit for foreign tax in respect of any income must be claimed within **six years** after the end of the accounting period for which the income is chargeable or, if later, within one year after the end of the accounting period in which the foreign tax is paid. [*ICTA 1988, s 806*(*1*)(*b*)]. A similar time limit applies to claims to utilise unrelieved foreign tax. [*ICTA 1988, s 806G, 806M*(*7*)*; FA 2000, Sch 30 paras 21, 23*].

See 24.5 DOUBLE TAX RELIEF.

65.14 **EMPLOYEE SHARE OWNERSHIP TRUSTS**

Claims for relief for contributions to qualifying trusts must be made within **two years** of the end of the period of account for which the sum is charged as an expense of the company. The relief is **abolished** for accounting periods beginning **on or after 1 January 2003**. [*FA 1989, s 67(6); FA 2003, s 142(1)*]. See 66.45 TRADING INCOME.

65.15 ERROR OR MISTAKE

Relief for an error or mistake in the corporation tax return must be claimed within **six years** after the relevant accounting period. [*TMA 1970, s 33; FA 1998, Sch 18 para 51, Sch 19 para 15*]. See 15.9 CLAIMS. See also 15.10 CLAIMS.

65.16 EXCHANGE GAINS AND LOSSES

(*a*) With respect to a gain which was deferred under *FA 1993, s 139* and brought into account in the first accounting period beginning on or after 1 October 2002 as a loan relationship credit, an election to account for the gain in six equal instalments over the first six accounting periods beginning on or after that date must be made within **two years** following the end of the first accounting period beginning on or after 1 October 2002. [*FA 2002, Sch 23 para 25*]. See 26.32 EXCHANGE GAINS AND LOSSES.

(*b*) For accounting periods beginning before 1 October 2002, a claim for deferral of unrealised gains on long-term capital assets or liabilities must be made within **two years** of the end of the accounting period for which the exchange gain accrued if an assessment for the period has become final and conclusive (otherwise **six years** or such longer period as HMRC may determine). [*FA 1993, s 139(6)–(8)*]. See 26.18 EXCHANGE GAINS AND LOSSES.

(*c*) For accounting periods beginning before 1 October 2002, a claim for relief of non-exchange losses in respect of assets or liabilities in respect of which exchange gains have previously arisen must be made within **two years** of the end of the accounting period in which the non-exchange losses accrued. [*SI 1994 No 3229, reg 2(7)*]. See 26.23 EXCHANGE GAINS AND LOSSES.

65.17 FILM TAX RELIEF

A claim for film tax relief must be made in a company tax return (or amended return) for the accounting period for which the claim is made, within one year of the filing date for that return or by such later time as HMRC may allow. It can similarly only be amended or withdrawn by amendment of the company tax return within the same time limit. See 66.52 TRADING INCOME. [*FA 1998, Sch 18 para 83W; FA 2006, Sch 5 para 29*].

65.18 FINANCIAL INSTRUMENTS AND DERIVATIVE CONTRACTS

(*a*) An election with respect to certain contracts held immediately before and on the first day of the first accounting period beginning on or after 1 October 2002, to treat a derivative contract as two separate contracts, must be made within **two years** of the end of the first accounting period beginning on or after that date. [*FA 2002, Sch 28 para 5(5)(6)*]. See 28.28 FINANCIAL INSTRUMENTS AND DERIVATIVE CONTRACTS.

(*b*) Where an election under (*a*) above is made and the disposal of the contract gives rise to an allowable loss, an election for the loss to be treated as a non-trading loan relationship debit (see 46.3 LOAN RELATIONSHIPS) must be made within **two years** following the end of the accounting period in which the company ceased to be a party to the contract. [*FA 2002, Sch 28 para 5(9) (10)*]. See 28.28 FINANCIAL INSTRUMENTS AND DERIVATIVE CONTRACTS.

(*c*) Where the pre-FA 2004 basis of computation applies, an election by a non-resident company to use (with respect to a UK branch) a mark to market accounting basis for some or all of its derivative contracts (such election being treated as also extended to the company's loan relationships under *FA 1996, s 86(3A)*) must be made within **two years** following the end of the first accounting period beginning on or after 1 October

2002 in which the company is party to the derivative contract eligible for election. [*FA 2002, Sch 26 para 19*]. See 28.11 FINANCIAL INSTRUMENTS AND DERIVATIVE CONTRACTS.

(*d*) For accounting periods beginning before 1 October 2002, a claim for certain qualifying payments to be treated as having become irrecoverable in an accounting period must be made within **two years** of the end of the accounting period. See 28.40 FINANCIAL INSTRUMENTS AND DERIVATIVE CONTRACTS.

65.19 GROUP RELIEF

For the position under self-assessment, see 15.2 CLAIMS.

65.20 HERD BASIS

An election by a farming company for the herd basis must be made within **two years** of the end of the first accounting period during which a production herd of the class concerned was kept or in which compensation is received for compulsory slaughter. [*ICTA 1988, Sch 5 paras 2, 6*]. See 55.10 HERD BASIS.

65.21 HOUSING ASSOCIATIONS

Exemption from corporation tax on rents and chargeable gains must be claimed within **two years** of the end of the relevant accounting period. The same applies to self-build societies. See 36 HOUSING ASSOCIATIONS ETC.

65.22 INCOME TAX

(*a*) Elections for charges on income to be paid within groups of companies without deduction of income tax become effective **three months** after they are made, or on the inspector's notifying his satisfaction therewith. See 32.2 GROUPS OF COMPANIES.

(*b*) Returns of income tax deducted from payments made by a company are due within **14 days** of the end of the return period. See 37 INCOME TAX IN RELATION TO A COMPANY.

65.23 INTANGIBLE ASSETS

(*a*) An election to replace accounts depreciation with a fixed writing-down allowance must be made within **two years** after the end of the accounting period in which the asset was created or acquired. [*FA 2002, Sch 29 para 10*]. See 39.4 INTANGIBLE ASSETS.

(*b*) An election to exclude from the intangible assets provisions certain expenditure on computer software must be made within **two years** after the end of the accounting period in which the expenditure was incurred. [*FA 2002, Sch 29 para 83*]. See 39.3 INTANGIBLE ASSETS.

65.24 LOAN RELATIONSHIPS

(*a*) Relief for a non-trading deficit of an accounting period beginning on or after 1 October 2002, may be claimed by set-off against other profits of the period or by carry back within **two years** of the end of the accounting period (or within such longer time as HMRC may allow). A claim for part or all of the deficit to be excepted from being set against non-trading profits of the accounting period immediately following the deficit period and treated as a non-trading deficit of that period to be carried forward for offset against non-trading profits of succeeding accounting periods, must be made within **two years** of the end of that period. [*FA 1996, s 83, Sch 8 para 4; FA 2002, Sch 25 paras 3, 19*]. See 46.3 LOAN RELATIONSHIPS.

(*b*) *Relief for a non-trading deficit* of an accounting period beginning before 1 October 2002 may be claimed by set-off against other profits of the period, by group relief or by carry back within **two years** of the end of the accounting period (or within such longer time as HMRC may allow). Carry-forward to the following period must be claimed within **two years** of the end of that period (or within such longer time as HMRC may allow). [*FA 1996, s 83(6)(7)*]. See 46.3 LOAN RELATIONSHIPS.

(*c*) Where the pre-FA 2004 basis of computation applies, an election by non-resident company to use (with respect to a UK branch) a mark to market accounting basis for some or all of its loan relationships (such election being treated as also extended to the company's derivative contracts under *FA 2002, Sch 26 para 19*) must be made within **two years** following the end of the first accounting period beginning on or after 1 October 2002 in which the company is party to a loan relationship eligible for election. [*FA 1996, s 86 (3A)(3B); FA 2002, Sch 25 para 6*]. See 46.31 LOAN RELATIONSHIPS.

(*d*) *Income tax deducted from certain payments giving rise to a loan relationship credit may be set against corporation tax liability* on a claim within **two years** of the end of the accounting period in which the payment from which tax was deducted was received or, if later, by the end of the period of **six years** after the end of the accounting period in which the loan relationship credit was brought into account. [*FA 1996, s 91(6)*]. See 46.34 LOAN RELATIONSHIPS.

65.25 LOANS TO PARTICIPATORS

The time limit for claiming repayment of tax paid on a loan by a close company to certain participators is **six years** after the end of the **financial year** in which the loan is repaid. See 16.12 CLOSE COMPANIES.

65.26 OVER-REPAID TAX

Assessments to recover tax over-repaid may, if otherwise out of time, be made up to the end of the accounting period following that of the repayment or, if later, within **three months** of the closure of an HMRC enquiry into a self-assessment return. [*FA 1998, Sch 18 para 53, Sch 19 para 13*].

65.27 PATENTS

(*a*) Where a company resident in the UK sells patent rights wholly or partly for a capital sum, and does not wish that sum to be spread over six years, an election to have the entire sum charged to tax for the accounting period in which it was received must be made within **two years** of the end of that period.

(*b*) A non-resident company selling UK patent rights wholly or partly for a capital sum may claim to have that sum spread over six years (and not treated as a single lump sum) within **two years** of the end of the accounting period in which it was received.

[*ICTA 1988, ss 524, 525*].

See 55.11 INTELLECTUAL PROPERTY.

65.28 PAYE

(*a*) Remittances must be made to the Collector within **14 days** after the end of the tax month (ending on the fifth of the calendar month) or in certain cases the tax quarter (ending on 5 July etc.). Where the payment is made by an approved method of electronic communication in respect of PAYE payments made after 5 April 2004, the time limit is extended to **17 days** in both cases. (See 33.10 HMRC: ADMINISTRATION.) [*SI 1993 No 744, regs 40, 41 (as amended by SI 2003 No 2494)*].

(*b*) End-of-year returns, deduction cards and Form P35 are due within **44 days** after the end of the tax year. [*SI 1993 No 744, reg 43*].

(*c*) Supplementary end-of-year returns are due within **61 days** after the end of the tax year. [*SI 1993 No 744, reg 46*].

65.29 PAYMENT OF TAX

Corporation tax is generally payable **nine months** after the end of the accounting period (subject to any requirement for instalment payment). See 53 PAYMENT OF TAX.

65.30 PRE-TRADING EXPENDITURE

An election for a pre-trading debit on a loan relationship to be deferred to the period in which the trade commences must be made within **two years** of the end of the accounting period in which the debit arose. [*ICTA 1988, s 401*(*1AB*)].

65.31 RESEARCH AND DEVELOPMENT EXPENDITURE

(*a*) A claim for R & D tax relief for an accounting period must be made, amended or withdrawn in the company tax return (or amended return) for which the claim is made, within one year of the filing date for that return (see 61.8 RETURNS) or by such later time as HMRC may allow. For accounting periods ending before 31 March 2006, this applied only in the case of a claim for payment of an R & D tax credit (claims for enhanced deductions could be made under the normal six-year rule). See 59 4, 59.13 and 59.21 RESEARCH AND DEVELOPMENT EXPENDITURE for transitional provisions. [*FA 1998, Sch 18 paras, 83A-83F, 83LA–83LE, 83M–83R; FA 2000, Sch 21 paras 2, 4; FA 2002, Sch 14 para 4; FA 2006, Sch 3*].

(*b*) An election for 'connected persons treatment' to be applied to all sub-contractor payments made under the same contract or arrangement must be made within **two years** after the end of the accounting period in which the contract or arrangement is entered into. [*FA 2000, Sch 20 para 11; FA 2002, Sch 13 para 10*]. The similar election in relation to staff provision payments must be made within a similar time limit. [*FA 2000, Sch 20 para 8D*(*4*)*; FA 2003, Sch 31 para 6*].

(*c*) An election for the alternative treatment of pre-trading expenditure in an accounting period must be made within **two years** after the end of the accounting period to which the election relates. [*FA 2000, Sch 20 para 14*(*6*)*; FA 2002, Sch 13 para 15*(*4*)].

See 59 RESEARCH AND DEVELOPMENT.

65.32 RETURNS

(*a*) Company tax returns must be made within **one year** of the end of the accounting period (or of the period of account in which falls the last day of the accounting period) or, if later, within **three months** of the date of the notice requiring the return. [*FA 1998, Sch 18 para 14*]. See 61.3 RETURNS.

(*b*) *Non-qualifying distributions* must be returned within **14 days** of the end of the accounting period in which they were made or within **14 days** of their having been made (if they were not made in an accounting period).

(*c*) *Stock dividends* must be returned within **30 days** of the end of the return period.

See 61.21 *et seq.* RETURNS and 65.1 and 65.22 above.

65.33 TRADING LOSSES

A claim for trading losses to be set off against profits of the same or an earlier accounting period must be made within **two years** of the end of the accounting period in which the losses were incurred, or within such further period as HMRC may allow. [*ICTA 1988, s 393A*(*10*)]. See 47 LOSSES.

65.34 TRADING STOCK

On the discontinuance of a profession, an election for work in progress to be taken at cost may be made up to **two years** after the end of the accounting period in which the discontinuance occurs. [*ICTA 1988, s 101*(*2A*); *ITTOIA 2005, Sch 1 para 80*]. See 66.75 TRADING INCOME.

65.35 UNLISTED SHARES

Claims for relief of losses on such shares by investment companies must be made within **two years** of the end of the accounting period in which the loss was incurred. [*ICTA 1988, s 573*]. See 47.19 LOSSES.

65.36 UNREMITTABLE INCOME

A claim for unremittable income to be left out of account must be made within **two years** after the end of the accounting period in which the income arose. [*ICTA 1988, s 584*(6)]. See 60.3 RESIDENCE.

66 Trading Income

Cross-references. See 5 ANTI-AVOIDANCE, 21 CONTROLLED FOREIGN COMPANIES, 24 DOUBLE TAX RELIEF, 32 GROUPS OF COMPANIES, 39 INTANGIBLE ASSETS, 42 INVESTMENT COMPANIES AND INVESTMENT BUSINESS, 47 LOSSES, 55 PROFIT COMPUTATIONS, 59 RESEARCH AND DEVELOPMENT EXPENDITURE, 60.3 RESIDENCE, 67 TRANSFER PRICING.

The law relating to the taxation of 'trading income' (previously within Schedules A, D and F and the cases of Schedule D) was consolidated in *Income Tax (Trading and Other Income) Act 2005* (*ITTOIA 2005*) as part of the Tax Law Rewrite programme,and has effect for income tax purposes for 2005/06 and subsequent years and, for corporation tax purposes where relevant, for accounting periods ending after 5 April 2005. [*ITTOIA 2005, s 883(1)*]. For corporation tax purposes, trading income continues to be computed under Schedule D Cases I and II as if it were still part of income tax law, and not under *ITTOIA 2005* (see 55.3 profit computations). Accordingly, it can no longer be assumed that the coverage in Tolley's Income Tax of any particular type of trading receipt or deduction etc. applies equally for corporation tax purposes and so all such matters are now dealt with in this work.

The headings in this chapter are as follows.

66.1 CHARGE TO TAX

Tax is charged under Schedule D, Case I on the profits or gains of trades and under Schedule D Case II for professions on wholly or partly in the UK by UK resident companies. [*ICTA 1988, s 18; ITTOIA, Sch 1 para 9*]. Businesses carried on wholly abroad are 'possessions' within Schedule D, Case V but a business controlled from the UK is within Cases I and II even though the day-to-day trading activities are carried on wholly abroad (see 60 RESIDENCE).

Trade 'includes every trade, manufacture, adventure or concern in the nature of trade' [*ICTA 1988, s 832(1)*]. For what is a trade, see generally 66.8–66.16 below and in particular, in relation to isolated or speculative transactions, 66.12 below. For a discussion on the *scope* of a trade, see HMRC Business Income Manual BIM 21000–21040. There are certain provisions applicable only to trades and others applicable only to professions but the distinction between the two is of limited practical importance. In a Hong Kong case it was held that stockbrokers were carrying on a trade, not a profession or business (*Kowloon Stock Exchange Ltd v Commr of Inland Revenue PC, [1984] STC 602*). There are a number of cases turning on whether a business was an exempt profession as specially defined for the purposes of (now defunct) excess profits duty and similar taxes. For these see Tolley's Tax Cases. For professions or vocations (e.g. actor) which necessarily involve carrying out numerous engagements see Tolley's Income Tax under Artistes in the chapter on Trading Income.

In the rest of this chapter, 'trade' includes 'profession' unless otherwise stated (or the context indicates otherwise) and similarly (where relevant) Case I includes Case II.

Income from land. Rents and other income derived from the exploitation of proprietary interests in land are within Schedule A (see 56 PROPERTY INCOME) and not treated as income derived from a trade. [*ICTA 1988, s 18(3); ITTOIA, Sch 1 para 9*]. The leading case is *Salisbury House Estate Ltd v Fry HL 1930, 15 TC 266*, and see also *Sywell Aerodrome Ltd v Croft CA 1941, 24 TC 126*; *Webb v Conelee Properties Ltd Ch D 1982, 56 TC 149*. For relaxations to this rule, see 66.22 below (tied premises), 66.61 below (surplus business accommodation), 56.2 PROPERTY INCOME (caravan sites) and 56.17 PROPERTY INCOME (electric-line wayleaves). The commercial *occupation* of UK land with a view to realisation of profits is treated as the carrying on of a trade (though this does not apply to woodlands). [*ICTA 1988, s 53(3)(4); ITTOIA, Sch 1 para 32*]. See 66.50 below as regards farming and market gardening.

Mines, quarries etc. Profits of mines, quarries, gravel pits, sand pits, brickfields, ironworks, gas works, canals, railways, rights of fishing, rights of markets, fairs and tolls and like concerns are computed and charged to corporation tax under Schedule D Case I. [*ICTA 1988, s 55; ITTOIA, Sch 1 para 33*]. This includes rent received in connection with such concerns (see 56.17 PROPERTY INCOME).

Oil-related activities. The carrying on of oil-related activities (i.e. oil extraction activities within *ICTA 1988, s 502(1)* and any activities consisting of the acquisition, enjoyment or exploitation of oil rights) as part of a trade is treated for corporation tax purposes as a separate trade in itself. [*ICTA 1988, s 492(1); ITTOIA 2005, Sch 1 para 190*].

Periods of account. A '*period of account*' in relation to a trade or profession or other business means a period for which accounts are drawn up. [*ICTA 1988, s 832(1); FA 2002, s103(1)*].

See 55.1 PROFIT COMPUTATIONS and 66.5 below for the application of generally accepted accounting practice.

66.2 COMMENCEMENT OR CESSATION

Where a company starts or ceases an a trade or to be within the charge to corporation tax in respect of a trade, it is treated as starting or permanently ceasing to carry on the trade at that time. [*ICTA 1988, s 337(1); FA 2002, Sch 30 para 1; ITTOIA 2005, Sch 1 paras 90, 145*].

For a short article on the distinction between succession to a trade, extension of an existing trade and commencement of a new trade, see Revenue Tax Bulletin February 1996 pp 285, 286. For an in-depth discussion, see HMRC Business Income Manual BIM 70500–70690.

Simon's Direct Tax Service. See B3.3.

66.3 **Post-cessation receipts.** Corporation tax is charged under Schedule D, Case VI on 'post-cessation receipts' arising from a trade or profession, carried on partly or wholly in the UK, to the extent that they have not been brought into account in computing trading profits for any period and that they are not otherwise chargeable to tax. The charge is made on the full amount of post-cessation receipts received in the accounting period subject to the allowable deductions set out below. A post-cessation receipt is not chargeable if it represents income arising outside the UK and accruing to a non-UK resident.

For these purposes, a '*post-cessation receipt*' is a sum which a company receives after permanently discontinuing a trade (including on a change of ownership which, under *ICTA 1988, s 337(1)* (company beginning or ceasing to carry on a trade, see above), is treated as a permanent discontinuance) but which arises from the carrying on of the trade before cessation. Certain sums as below are specifically treated as being, or as not being (as the case may be), post-cessation receipts.

Receipts within the legislation will include, *inter alia*, royalties and similar amounts which under decisions such as *Carson v Cheyney's Exor HL 1958, 38 TC 240*, prior to the original legislation being enacted, had been held not to be taxable.

Debts. To the extent that a deduction has been made, in computing the profits of the trade, for an impaired loss or a release of liability (see 66.21 below), any amount received after cessation in settlement of that debt is a post-cessation receipt. If an amount owed *by* the trader is released, in whole or in part, after cessation, the amount released is a post-cessation receipt; this applies only if a trading deduction was allowed for the expense giving rise to the debt and does not apply if the release of the debt is part of a statutory insolvency arrangement (as defined in 66.21 below).

Transfers of rights. If the right to receive a post-cessation receipt is transferred for value to another person (other than one who succeeds to the trade), the transferor is treated as receiving at that point a post-cessation receipt equal to the consideration for the transfer or, if the transfer is not at arm's length, the value of the rights transferred. The post-cessation receipts themselves are not then charged when received by the transferee.

If, however, the right to receive any sums arising from the transferor's trade are transferred to a company which does succeed to the trade, then, to the extent (if any) that they were not brought into account in computing the transferor's profits for any pre-cessation period, those sums are treated as trading receipts of the transferee as and when received. They are not post-cessation receipts.

Allowable deductions. A deduction from post-cessation receipts is allowed for any loss, expense or debit or capital allowance that would have been deductible if the trade had not ceased, has not been relieved in any other way and which does not arise directly or indirectly from the cessation itself. In the case of a loss, relief is given against the first available post-cessation receipts, i.e. receipts for an earlier accounting period in priority to those for a later one, but not so as give relief for a loss against receipts charged for an accounting period before that in which the loss is made.

[*ICTA 1988, ss103, 104–106, 110; ITTOIA 2005, Sch 1 paras 82–90; FA 2005, Sch 4 para 5*].

Simon's Direct Tax Service. See **B4.213** *et seq.*

66.4 **Case law.** Whether or not a company has commenced/ceased trading and, if so, the date, are questions of fact.

- Preliminary activities in setting up a business do not amount to trading (*Birmingham & District Cattle By-Products Co Ltd v CIR KB 1919, 12 TC 92*). Carrying on negotiations to enter into contracts which, when formed, constitute operational activity, does not amount to trading (*Mansell v HMRC [2006] SSCD 605 (Sp C 551)*). For pre-trading expenditure, see 66.69 below.

- For whether the sale of a business can be effective for tax purposes before the vending agreement, see *Todd v Jones Bros Ltd KB 1930, 15 TC 396* and contrast *Angel v Hollingworth & Co Ch D 1958, 37 TC 714*.

- 'Permanent discontinuance' does not mean a discontinuance which is everlasting (see *Ingram v Callaghan CA 1968, 45 TC 151*) but a trade may continue notwithstanding a lengthy break in active trading (*Kirk & Randall Ltd v Dunn KB 1924, 8 TC 663* but contrast *Goff v Osborne & Co (Sheffield) Ltd Ch D 1953, 34 TC 441*).

- The trade was held to have been continuous when the owner of a drifter continued to manage it after its war-time requisition (*Sutherland v CIR CS 1918, 12 TC 63*); when a flour miller and baker gave up a mill (*Bolands Ltd v Davis KB(IFS) 1925, 4 ATC 532*); when a barrister took silk (*Seldon v Croom-Johnson KB 1932, 16 TC 740*); when a building partnership transferred construction activities to a company but retained building land and continued to sell land with houses built thereon by the company (*Watts v Hart Ch D 1984, 58 TC 209*).

- A new trade was held to have commenced when the vendor of a business retained the benefit of outstanding hire-purchase agreements (*Parker v Batty KB 1941, 23 TC 739*) and when the vendor of a business got commission on open contracts completed by the purchaser (*Southern v Cohen's Exors KB 1940, 23 TC 566*).

It is similarly a question of fact whether a trader expanding by taking over an existing business and operating it as a branch has succeeded to the trade. See e.g. *Bell v National Provincial Bank of England Ltd CA 1903, 5 TC 1* (bank succeeded to trade of single-branch bank taken over); *Laycock v Freeman Hardy & Willis Ltd CA 1938, 22 TC 288* (shoe retailer did not succeed to trade of manufacturing subsidiaries taken over); *Briton Ferry Steel Co Ltd v Barry CA 1939, 23 TC 414* (steel manufacturer succeeded to trade of tinplate manufacturing subsidiaries taken over); and *Maidment v Kibby Ch D 1993, 66 TC 137* (fish and chip shop proprietor did not succeed to trade of existing business taken over). See also *H & G Kinemas Ltd KB 1933, 18 TC 116* (cinema company disposed of existing cinemas and opened new one, held to commence new trade).

Whether or not there has been a commencement etc. has arisen in a number of cases where the activities of a company have altered on e.g. a change of shareholdings or a group reconstruction or on its absorption of another trade or part-trade. See e.g. *Robroyston Brickworks Ltd c CIR CS 1976, 51 TC 205* (trade of a brick-manufacturing company treated as continuous despite closure of works and their re-opening five months later, following the acquisition of its shares by another company, at different premises and with different staff); *Howden Boiler & Armaments Co Ltd v Stewart CS 1924, 9 TC 205* (shell-making considered an extension of the existing business as boilermakers); *Gordon & Blair Ltd v CIR CS 1962, 40 TC 358* (brewing company treated as ceasing the trade of brewing and beginning a new trade of beer selling when it ceased brewing but continued to sell beer supplied to its specification by another company); *Cannon Industries Ltd v Edwards Ch D 1965, 42 TC 625* (assembly of electric food mixers for retail sale treated as extension of existing trade of manufacture of gas cookers).

66.5 APPLICATION OF ACCOUNTANCY PRINCIPLES

See 55.2 PROFIT COMPUTATIONS as regards the requirement that generally accepted accounting practice (GAAP) be adhered to in the computation of taxable profits. Even prior to this, it had always been the case that, since the starting figure in computing profits was that brought out by the accounts of the business, accountancy principles were of the greatest importance. They could not, however, override established income tax principles (*Heather v P-E Consulting Group Ltd CA 1972, 48 TC 293*; *Willingale v International Commercial Bank Ltd HL 1977, 52 TC 242*; but see *Threlfall v Jones CA 1993, 66 TC 77*; *Johnston v Britannia Airways Ltd Ch D 1994, 67 TC 99*). See also *RTZ Oil & Gas Ltd v Elliss Ch D 1987, 61 TC 132*. A 'provision for a future operating loss', whose inclusion could not be said to have 'violated existing accounting principles', was disallowed in *Meat Traders Ltd v Cushing (Sp C 131), [1997] SSCD 245*). See *Robertson v CIR (Sp C 137), [1997] SSCD 282* as regards timing of inclusion of insurance agents' advance commission. See also *Herbert Smith v Honour Ch D 1999, 72 TC 130* for the timing of deductions in respect of future rents under leases of premises ceasing to be used for business purposes, and Revenue Press Release 20 July 1999 for Revenue practice following that decision.

Per Sir Thomas Bingham MR in *Threlfall v Jones*: '... I find it hard to understand how any judge-made rule could override the application of a generally accepted rule of commercial accountancy which (a) applied to the situation in question, (b) was not one of two or more rules applicable to the situation in question and (c) was not shown to be inconsistent with the true facts or otherwise inapt to determine the true profits or losses of the business'. FRS 18 now requires companies to choose accounting policies that are most appropriate to their particular circumstances (see Revenue Tax Bulletin April 2002 p 923 to 924).

If an entity has correctly followed an International Accounting Standard or USA standard, which does not conflict with UK GAAP, including the requirements of FRS 18 (accounting policies), and this accurately reflects the facts, the accountancy treatment will comply with the requirement of *FA 1998, s 42* above (HMRC Business Income Manual BIM 31027). This pre-dates the widening of the term 'generally accepted accounting practice' to include international accounting standards where appropriate (see 55.2 PROFIT COMPUTATIONS).

For HMRC's view on the relationship between accounting profits and taxable profits, see HMRC Business Income Manual BIM 31000–31120 and BIM 42215. For generally accepted accounting practice and accounting standards, see BIM 31020–31070. For the timing of deductions where an expense is taken to the balance sheet rather than charged immediately against profits, i.e. *deferred revenue expenditure*, see HMRC Business Income Manual BIM 42215, 42220. For *provisions*, see HMRC Business Income Manual BIM 46500 *et seq.* and Revenue Press Release 20 July 1999, HMRC Business Income Manual BIM 31000 onwards.

66.6 **Adjustments on change of basis.** Except as detailed below, these provisions apply to changes of accounting basis taking effect in periods of account ending on or after 1 August 2001, and replace the similar earlier provisions of *FA 1998, s 44, Sch 6* (for which see Tolley's Income Tax under Cash Basis), which, however, dealt only with changes of accounting basis. The tax adjustment described below is required where there is, from one period of account of a trade etc. to the next, a 'change of basis' in computing Schedule D, Case I or II profits, and the bases adopted before and after the change accorded with the law or accepted practice applicable in relation to the respective periods of account.

A '*change of basis*' for this purpose is:

(*a*) a change of accounting principle or practice which, in accordance with 'generally accepted accounting practice' (see above), gives rise to a prior period adjustment;

(*b*) a change in the statutory tax adjustments applied (including a change resulting from a change of view as to application of the statute but excluding a change made to comply with an amendment to the statute which was not applicable to the earlier period of account); or

(*c*) with effect for periods of account beginning on or after 1 January 2005, a change from using UK generally accepted accounting practice to using generally accepted accounting practice with respect to accounts based on international accounting standards.

Subject to the special cases referred to below, the adjustment required is calculated as follows.

(i) Taxable receipts and allowable expenses of the trade etc. for periods of account before the change are determined on the old and new bases, and the net understatement of profits (or overstatement of losses) on the old basis compared with the new basis determined (a negative figure indicating a net overstatement of profits (or under-statement of losses)).

(ii) That figure is then adjusted for any difference between the closing stock or work in progress for the last period of account before the change and the opening stock or work in progress for the first period of account after the change, also taking account of any change in the basis of calculating those amounts.

(iii) Finally an adjustment is made for depreciation to the extent that it was not the subject of an adjustment for corporation tax purposes in the last period of account before the change but would be the subject of such an adjustment on the new basis.

A *positive* adjustment is treated as a trade etc. receipt arising on the last day of the first period of account after the change, or for periods of account beginning on or after 1 January 2005, the first day of the first period of account after the change. A *negative* adjustment is treated as an expense of the trade etc. arising on that day. No further deduction is allowed for amounts taken into account in calculating the adjustment.

Special rules modify (i)–(iii) above in a number of cases.

(A) *Expenses spread over more than one period of account after the change* on the new basis which were brought into account before the change on the old basis are excluded from the calculation at (i) above, but may not be deducted for any period of account after the change.

(B) *Adjustment not required until asset realised or written off*. Where the change of basis results from a tax adjustment affecting the calculation of amounts within (ii) or (iii) above, the adjustment required by (ii) or (iii) is brought into account only when the asset concerned is realised or written off.

(C) *Change from realisation basis to mark to market*, i.e. from recognition of a profit or loss on an asset only when it is realised to bringing assets into account in each period of account at fair value. Any adjustment required by (i) above for an understatement of profit (or overstatement of loss) in relation to an asset that is trading stock within *ICTA 1988, s 100* is not given effect until the period of account in which the value of the asset is realised. An election may, however, be made for the adjustment charge to be spread over six periods of account beginning with the first period after the change. The election must be made in writing to an officer of HMRC within twelve months after the end of the first accounting period to which the new basis applies. If the trade etc. is permanently discontinued before the whole of the adjustment charge has been brought into charge, the uncharged balance is charged as if it arose immediately before the discontinuance. Special provision is made for the application of this rule in the case of insurance business transfers.

The current provisions apply to a change taking effect in a period of account ending before 1 August 2001 if the relevant tax return for the period of the change (or for a later period ending before that date) is delivered or voluntarily amended by the taxpayer on or after that date. Any resulting adjustment is given effect for the first period of account ending on or after that date if it would otherwise be given effect in an earlier period.

Spreading of UITF 40 adjustment. A positive adjustment can be spread over three to six years (as set out below) where it arises from a change in accounting approach, in the first period of account ending on or after 22 June 2005, in calculating profits in compliance with UK GAAP (or international accounting standards if applicable), in particular SSAP 9 and Application Note G to FRS 5 as interpreted by Urgent Issue Task Force Abstract 40 ('UITF 40' issued by the Accounting Standards Board on 10 March 2005).

SSAP (Statement of Standard Accounting Practice) 9 relates to the accounting rules for 'Stocks and Long-Term Work in Progress' and Application Note G of FRS (Financial Reporting Standard) 5 (on 'Reporting the Substance of Transactions) relates to 'Revenue Recognition'. UITF 40 concerns the interaction between the Application Note and SSAP 9 and clarifies the principles governing the recognition of revenue in the accounts for work in progress in relation to contracts for services. Broadly, it indicates that revenue arising from services provided on an ongoing basis should be accounted for as it arises. Where contracts for a single service are accounted for as a long-term contract (lasting more than one year or more than one accounting period) and the obligations under the contract are performed gradually over a period of time, revenue is to be recognised as the activity progresses based on the appropriate proportion of the fair value of the contract. If the consideration for services is contingent upon some future event, revenue is not to be recognised until that even occurs. This is in contrast to previous practice where the revenue was recognised when billed and it is thought this will give rise to large adjustments in some cases.

Where a positive adjustment arises as a result of the above change in accounting policy, the amount chargeable to tax in the first three accounting periods beginning with that in which the whole of the adjustment would otherwise arise, is to be equal to the lower of one-third of the original adjustment (as calculated above) and one-sixth of the 'business profits' for that period. If the whole of the original adjustment is not charged to tax in those three years, an amount is to be charged to tax in the fourth and fifth accounting periods equal to the lower of the amount remaining untaxed, one-third of the original adjustment and one-sixth of the 'business profits' for that period. Any amount still remaining untaxed is treated as arising, and is charged to tax in, the sixth accounting period. '*Business profits*' for this purpose are profits as calculated for corporation tax purposes excluding any adjustment for a change in accounting policy as above and any capital allowances or balancing charges.

Special rules apply in the case where an accounting period is less than one year in length as a result of a change in accounting date, the company entering into administration (under *ICTA 1988, s 12(7ZA)* or an insurance business transfer scheme (under *ICTA 1988, s 12(7A)(7B)*). In this case, the one-third of the original adjustment is proportionally reduced for the short period. Where any of the accounting periods falling within six years following the change in accounting policy is a short period, the rules relating the fourth and fifth accounting periods apply to all accounting periods after the third period and before that in which the sixth anniversary of the change falls, and the rule above relating to the sixth accounting period applies to the accounting period in which that anniversary falls. If any amount remains untaxed and an accounting period comes to an end because the company ceases to be within the charge to corporation tax or winding-up proceedings (under *ICTA 1988, s 12(7)*) are commenced, the rule for the sixth accounting period applies in relation to that final period. If the company permanently ceases to carry on the business for any other reason, the charge is spread as above ignoring the alternative limit for one-sixth of the business profits for the period.

A company can elect for an amount up to the whole of the amount of the adjustment not previously charged to be treated as arising and charged in an accounting period rather than spreading it as above. The election must be made within one year of the filing date of the company's tax return for the accounting period for which the election is made. If such an election is made, any spreading calculations in subsequent periods are to be made as though the original adjustment is reduced by the amount in respect of which the election is made.

Partnerships. In the case of trades, professions or vocations carried on by a company in partnership, the adjustment (as above) is calculated as if the partnership were a company resident in the UK. Each partner's share is determined according to the profit-sharing arrangements for the twelve months immediately before the first day of the first period of account for which the new basis was adopted, and an election for spreading of an adjustment under (C) above, or under the rules for spreading the UITF 40 adjustment, must be made jointly by all persons who were partners in that twelve-month period.

If the partnership ceases to carry on a business on the date of the change in policy the UITF 40 adjustment is to be divided among the members according to the profit-sharing arrangements in the twelve-month period immediately preceding the cessation. If the cessation occurs on or after the date of the change in policy but before the first anniversary of that date, the adjustment is to be divided according to the profit-sharing arrangements for the period between that date and the date of cessation. If the cessation occurs after the first anniversary of the date of the change in policy, the adjustment is to be divided according to the profit-sharing arrangements for the period between the immediately preceding anniversary of that date and the date of cessation. If a UITF 40 election is made after cessation, it must be made by each former partner separately.

The UITF spreading adjustments do not affect the loan relationship or derivative contracts rules applying to partnerships.

[*FA 2002, s 64, Sch 22; ITTOIA 2005, Sch 1 paras 576, 578; FA 2005, s 81; F(No 2)A 2005, Sch 6 para 1; FA 2006, Sch 15 paras 9–15*].

See HMRC Business Income Manual BIM 34000–34135, 74200–74275 and HMRC Helpsheet IR238 available on the HMRC website (at www.hmrc.gov.uk/sa/uitf-40.htm).

66.7 WHETHER A TRADE CARRIED ON

See generally 66.1 above. The following covers the consideration of whether an activity amounts to trading by a company but see Tolley's Income Tax under Trading Income in relation to trading by individuals or partnerships. See also 48 MUTUAL COMPANIES and 64 STATUTORY BODIES. Special types of activity are dealt with below in alphabetical order.

Simon's Direct Tax Service. See **B3.2**.

66.8 **Avoidance schemes.** A line is drawn between transactions of a trading nature which remain trading even though entered into to secure tax advantages and transactions so remote from ordinary trading as to be explicable only as fiscal devices and hence not trading.

In *Ransom v Higgs and Kilmorie (Aldridge) Ltd v Dickinson etc. HL 1974, 50 TC 1* the taxpayers entered into complex arrangements to siphon development profits into the hands of trustees. They succeeded, the Crown failing to establish that, looked at as a whole, the arrangements constituted trading. In *Johnson v Jewitt CA 1961, 40 TC 231* an elaborate and artificial device to manufacture trading losses was held not to amount to trading, but see *Ensign Tankers (Leasing) Ltd v Stokes HL 1992, 64 TC 617*, where the company's investment in two film production partnerships was entered into with a view to obtaining first-year capital allowances. See also *Black Nominees Ltd v Nicol Ch D 1975, 50 TC 229* and *Newstead v Frost HL 1980, 53 TC 525.* See generally ANTI-AVOIDANCE (3).

66.9 **Betting.** Betting by professional bookmakers is assessable (*Partridge v Mallandaine QB 1886, 2 TC 179*) even if carried on in an unlawful way (*Southern v A B KB 1933, 18 TC 59*)). Also exempt from CGT. [*TCGA 1992, s 51(1)*]. Receipts from newspaper articles based on betting system held assessable in *Graham v Arnott KB 1941, 24 TC 157.*

Lotteries and football pools promotion constitutes trading, but where a pool or small lottery is run by a supporters club or other society on terms that a specified part of the cost of the ticket is to be donated to a club or body within the purposes in *Lotteries and Amusements Act 1976, s 5(1)*, the donation element is not treated as a trading receipt (HMRC Statement of Practice, SP/C1). For further detail, see HMRC Business Income Manual BIM 61600–61615. See 14.6(iii) CHARITIES as regards charitable lotteries.

66.10 **Horse racing etc.** Racing and selling the progeny of a brood mare was held to constitute trading in *Dawson v Counsell CA 1938, 22 TC 149.* In *Norman v Evans Ch D 1964, 42 TC 188* the share of prize monies for letting racehorses was held to be within Schedule D, Case VI. Profits from stallion fees are assessable and assessments under both Schedule D, Case I and Case VI have been upheld (*Malcolm v Lockhart HL 1919, 7 TC 99*; *McLaughlin v Bailey CA (I) 1920, 7 TC 508*; *Jersey's Exors v Bassom KB 1926, 10 TC 357*; *Wernher v CIR KB 1942, 29 TC 20*; *Benson v Counsell KB 1942, 24 TC 178*) but wear and tear allowances (the forerunner of modern capital allowances on plant etc.) for stallions was refused in *Derby v Aylmer KB 1915, 6 TC 665.* Profits from greyhound breeding were held to be trading in *Hawes v Gardiner Ch D 1957, 37 TC 671.* 'Private' horse racing and training is not normally trading (cf. *Sharkey v Wernher HL 1955, 36 TC 275*).

66.11 **Illegal trading.** Crime, e.g. burglary, is not trading but the profits of a commercial business are assessable notwithstanding the business may be carried on in an unlawful way, e.g. 'bootlegging' (*Canadian Minister of Finance v Smith PC 1926, 5 ATC 621* and cf. *Lindsay Woodward & Hiscox v CIR CS 1932, 18 TC 43*), operating 'fruit machines' illegal at the time (*Mann v Nash KB 1932, 16 TC 523*), street bookmaking illegal at the time (*Southern v A B KB 1933, 18 TC 59*) and prostitution (*CIR v Aken CA 1990, 63 TC 395*). But penalties for trading contrary to war-time regulations held not deductible (*CIR v E C Warnes & Co KB 1919, 12 TC 227*; *CIR v Alexander von Glehn & Co CA 1920, 12 TC 232*). See also 66.9 above. See 66.59 below as regards prohibition on deduction of expenditure involving crime.

Simon's Direct Tax Service. See **B3.220**.

66.12 **Isolated or speculative transactions.** For property transactions and share dealing see66.15 and 66.16 respectively.

Whether the surplus on the purchase and resale of assets, otherwise than in the course of an established commercial enterprise, is derived from an 'adventure or concern in the nature of trade' (see 66.1 above) depends on the facts. Para 116 of the Final Report of the Royal Commission on the Taxation of Profits and Income (1955 HMSO Cmd. 9474) lists six 'badges of trade': (i) the subject matter of the realisation; (ii) length of period of ownership; (iii) frequency or number of similar transactions; (iv) supplementary work on assets sold; (v) reason for sale; (vi) motive. Other relevant factors may be the degree of organisation, whether the taxpayer is or has been associated with a recognised business dealing in similar assets and how the purchases were financed. For a recent review of the factors to be considered, see *Marson v Morton Ch D 1986, 59 TC 381*.

Although in disputed cases HMRC may make alternative Case I and Case VI assessments, it would seem from *Pearn v Miller KB 1927, 11 TC 610* and *Leeming v Jones HL 1930, 15 TC 333* (see 66.15 below) that as regards isolated transactions the liability, if any, will be under Case I.

Case I assessments were upheld on a purchase and resale of war surplus linen (*Martin v Lowry HL 1926, 11 TC 297* — a leading case); a purchase, conversion and resale of a ship (*CIR v Livingston CS 1926, 11 TC 538*); transactions in brandy (*Cape Brandy Syndicate v CIR CA 1921, 12 TC 358*), whisky (*Lindsay Woodward* at 66.11 above), whisky in bond (*P J McCall decd v CIR KB(IFS) 1923, 4 ATC 522*; *CIR v Fraser CS 1942, 24 TC 498*); 'turning over' cotton mills (*Pickford v Quirke CA 1927, 13 TC 251*); purchase and resale of cotton spinning plant (*Edwards v Bairstow & Harrison HL 1955, 36 TC 207*); and purchase and resale of toilet rolls (*Rutledge v CIR CS 1929, 14 TC 490*). But in *Jenkinson v Freedland CA 1961, 39 TC 636* the Commissioners' finding that a profit on the purchase, repair and sale (to associated companies) of stills was not assessable, was upheld, and in *Kirkham v Williams CA 1991, 64 TC 253*, the Commissioners' decision that the sale of a dwelling house built on land partly acquired for storage etc. was an adventure in the nature of trade was reversed in the CA.

Simon's Direct Tax Service. See **B3.211** *et seq.*

66.13 **Liquidators or receivers.** Whether a liquidator or receiver is continuing the company's trade or merely realising its assets as best he can, is a question of fact. For liquidators or receivers see *Armitage v Moore QB 1900, 4 TC 199*; *CIR v 'Old Bushmills' Distillery KB(NI) 1927, 12 TC 1148*; *CIR v Thompson KB 1936, 20 TC 422*; *Wilson Box v Brice CA 1936, 20 TC 736*; *Baker v Cook KB 1937, 21 TC 337*.

66.14 **Miscellaneous.** Assessments under Case I were upheld on a committee operating golf links owned by a Town Council (*Carnoustie Golf Course Committee v CIR CS 1929, 14 TC 498*); trustees under a private Act managing a recreation ground (*CIR v Stonehaven Recreation Ground Trustees CS 1929, 15 TC 419*); temporary joint coal merchanting (*Gardner and Bowring Hardy & Co v CIR CS 1930, 15 TC 602*); promotion of mining companies to exploit mines (*Murphy v Australian Machinery etc. Co Ltd CA 1948, 30 TC 244* and cf. *Rhodesia Metals v Commr of Taxes PC 1940, 19 ATC 472*); purchase and resale of amusement equipment (*Crole v Lloyd HC 1950, 31 TC 338*).

A company which made loans to another company to finance a trading venture was held not to be trading itself (*Stone & Temple Ltd v Waters*; *Astrawall (UK) Ltd v Waters Ch D 1995, 67 TC 145*).

The activities of the British Olympic Association (which included the raising of funds through commercial sponsorship and the exploitation of its logo, but many of which were non-commercial) were held as a whole to be uncommercial and not to constitute a trade (*British Olympic Association v Winter (Sp C 28), [1995] SSCD 85*).

For whether *ostrich farming* (i.e. the ownership of ostriches which are looked after on the owner's behalf by others) amounts to trading, and for the consequences of such trading, see Revenue Tax Bulletin June 1996 pp 318, 319.

See also *J Bolson & Son Ltd v Farrelly CA 1953, 34 TC 161* (deals in vessels by company operating boat services held a separate adventure) and *Torbell Investments Ltd v Williams Ch D 1986, 59 TC 357* (dormant company revived for purpose of acquiring certain loans held to have acquired them as trading stock). But a company formed to administer a holidays with pay scheme for the building etc. industry was held not trading (*Building & Civil Engineering etc. Ltd v Clark Ch D 1960, 39 TC 12*). Assessments on profits from promoting a series of driving schools were upheld in *Leach v Pogson Ch D 1962, 40 TC 585*; in concluding that the profit from *first* sale was assessable, Commissioners were entitled to take into account the subsequent transactions.

66.15 **Property transactions.** This paragraph relates to transactions in land and buildings otherwise than in the course of an established business of property development, building etc. For HMRC's view, see HMRC Business Income Manual BIM 60000–60165. For other sales of property see 66.70 below.

A line is drawn between realisations of property held as an investment or as a residence and transactions amounting to an adventure or concern in the nature of trade. The principles at 66.12 above apply suitably adapted.

In *Leeming v Jones HL 1930, 15 TC 333* an assessment on the acquisitions and disposal of options over rubber estates was confirmed by Commissioners. The Crown had defended the assessment under both Schedule D, Case I (trading income) and Schedule D, Case VI (miscellaneous income). In a Supplementary Case the Commissioners found there had been no concern in the nature of the trade. The Court held there was no liability. Per Lawrence LJ 'in the case of an isolated transaction … there is really no middle course open. It is either an adventure in the nature of trade, or else it is simply a case of sale and resale of property.' See also *Pearn v Miller KB 1927, 11 TC 610* and *Williams v Davies* below.

Property transactions were held to be trading in *Californian Copper Syndicate v Harris CES 1904, 5 TC 159* (purchase of copper bearing land shortly afterwards resold); *Thew v South West Africa Co CA 1924, 9 TC 141* (numerous sales of land acquired by concession for exploitation); *Cayzer, Irvine & Co v CIR CS 1942, 24 TC 491* (exploitation of landed estate acquired by shipping company); *Emro Investments v Aller* and *Lance Webb Estates v Aller Ch D 1954, 35 TC 305* (profits carried to capital reserve on numerous purchases and sales); *Orchard Parks v Pogson Ch D 1964, 42 TC 442* (land compulsorily purchased after development plan dropped); *Parkstone Estates v Blair Ch D 1966, 43 TC 246* (industrial estate developed—land disposed of by sub-leases for premiums); *Eames v Stepnell Properties Ltd CA 1966, 43 TC 678* (sale of land acquired from associated company while resale being negotiated). See also *Bath & West Counties Property Trust Ltd v Thomas Ch D 1977, 52 TC 20*. Realisations were held to be capital in *Hudson's Bay v Stevens CA 1909, 5 TC 424* (numerous sales of land acquired under Royal Charter — contrast *South West Africa Co* above); *Tebrau (Johore) Rubber Syndicate v Farmer CES 1910, 5 TC 658* (purchase and resale of rubber estates — contrast *Californian Copper* above).

In *Rand v Alberni Land Co Ltd KB 1920, 7 TC 629* sales of land held in trust were held not trading but contrast *Alabama Coal Iron Land v Mylam KB 1926, 11 TC 232*; *Balgownie Land Trust v CIR CS 1929, 14 TC 684*; *St Aubyn Estates v Strick KB 1932, 17 TC 412*; *Tempest Estates v Walmsley Ch D 1975, 51 TC 305*. Sales of property after a period of letting held realisations of investments or not trading in *CIR v Hyndland Investment Co Ltd CS 1929, 14 TC 694*; *Glasgow Heritable Trust v CIR CS 1954, 35 TC 196*; *Lucy & Sunderland Ltd v Hunt Ch D 1961, 40 TC 132* but held trading in *Rellim Ltd v Vise CA 1951, 32 TC 254* (notwithstanding that company previously admitted as investment company); *CIR v Toll Property Co CS 1952, 34 TC 13*; *Forest Side Properties (Chingford) v Pearce CA 1961, 39 TC 665*. But sales by liquidator of property owned by companies following abandonment of plan for their public flotation held not trading in *Simmons v CIR HL 1980, 53 TC 461* (reversing Commissioners' decision). In *Rosemoor Investments v Inspector of Taxes (Sp*

C 320), [2002] SSCD 325, it was not open to the Commissioners to recharacterise as trading a complex transaction routed via an investment company subsidiary and structured to produce capital.

Simon's Direct Tax Service. See **B3.6**.

66.16 **Share dealing.** Share dealing with the public is strictly controlled by the *Financial Services and Markets Act 2000*. This paragraph is concerned with share transactions entered into (generally through the Stock Exchange) by persons not authorised to deal under that Act and the question arises whether they amount to an adventure or concern in the nature of trade. The principles of 66.12 above apply suitably adapted. The prudent management of an investment portfolio may necessitate changes in the holdings but this is not normally trading. Stock Exchange speculation, particularly by individuals, may be quasi-gambling and not trading — see Pennycuick J in *Lewis Emanuel & Son Ltd v White Ch D 1965, 42 TC 369* in which, reversing the Commissioners' finding, he held that the Stock Exchange losses of a fruit etc. merchanting company were from a separate trade of share dealing but observed that gambling by the company would have been *ultra vires*. Subsequent *Companies Act* changes have, however, removed any such restriction on the activities of most companies (see HMRC Inspector' Manual IM 129a). In *Cooper v C & J Clark Ltd Ch D 1982, 54 TC 670*, the losses of a manufacturing company on its sale of gilts, in which it had invested temporarily surplus cash, were allowed as a set-off against its general trading profits. An individual speculating in stocks and shares and commodity futures was held to be trading in *Wannell v Rothwell Ch D 1996, 68 TC 719* (although loss relief was refused on the grounds that the trading was 'uncommercial', see 47.8(*a*) LOSSES), but the opposite conclusion was reached in *Salt v Chamberlain Ch D 1979, 53 TC 143*.

For share dealing by investment companies see *Scottish Investment Trust Co v Forbes CES 1893, 3 TC 231* and *Halefield Securities Ltd v Thorpe Ch D 1967, 44 TC 154*. For trading in secured loans, see *Torbell Investments Ltd v Williams Ch D 1986, 59 TC 357*.

For share sales connected with an existing business see 66.74 below.

66.17 CHARGEABLE INCOME AND ALLOWABLE DEDUCTIONS

The following paragraphs refer to matters of relevance to companies in computing trading profits. See 55 PROFIT COMPUTATIONS for the general principles in computing profits chargeable to corporation tax. See also 10 CAPITAL ALLOWANCES, 26 FOREIGN EXCHANGE GAINS AND LOSSES, 28 DERIVATIVE CONTRACTS AND FINANCIAL INSTRUMENTS, 39 INTANGIBLE ASSETS, 46 LOAN RELATIONSHIPS, 56 PROPERTY INCOME and 59 RESEARCH AND DEVELOPMENT. Headings are in alphabetical order.

See HMRC Business Income Manual BIM 50000 *et seq.* for HMRC guidance on measuring the profits of a wide range of particular trades.

66.18 GENERAL

See 55.2 PROFIT COMPUTATIONS re the requirement to adhere to generally accepted accounting practice (GAAP), 66.5 above re the application of accountancy principles generally and 66.6 above re adjustments required on a change of basis.

The provisions for computing business profits are in *ICTA 1988, ss 74–99*. The general rules for expenses are in *ICTA 1988, s 74*. These are few and simple and little changed since

Napoleonic times. There are no corresponding rules for receipts. Hence practice is largely based on principles evolved over the years and endorsed by the Courts. It has, however, been clarified that, wherever they appear in income tax legislation in the context of computing trading profits, the words 'receipts' and 'expenses' refer generally to items brought into account as credits or debits in computing those profits, and contain no implication that an amount has actually been received or paid. [*FA 1998, s 46(1)*].

For income tax purposes, *ITTOIA 2005, s 31* introduces a new rule for 2005/06 onwards which is intended to resolve any conflict between statutory rules prohibiting a deduction in computing trading profits and statutory rules permitting such a deduction. It does so by giving priority, with specified exceptions, to the rule permitting the deduction. In practice, such conflict will rarely occur. See Change 6 listed in Annex 1 to the Explanatory Notes to the Income Tax (Trading and Other Income) Bill).

The two rules next described below have for countless years been among the most fundamental rules as to the calculation of taxable business profits.

Capital expenditure and receipts. In computing trading profits, no deduction is allowed for items of a capital nature unless it is specifically provided otherwise. This principle is derived, as regards expenses, from *ICTA 1988, s 74(1)(f)(g)* and generally because the charge to tax is on *income*. See also *ICTA 1988, s 817(2)*. By the same token, capital receipts are not brought into account; this is made explicit for income tax purposes for 2005/06 onwards but was already a long-established principle. [*ITTOIA 2005, s 96*].

As to the distinction between capital and revenue expenditure and between capital and income receipts, 'no part of our law of taxation presents such almost insoluble conundrums as the decision whether a receipt or outgoing is capital or income for tax purposes' (Lord Upjohn in *Strick v Regent Oil Co Ltd HL 1965, 43 TC 1* q.v. for a comprehensive review of the law). A widely used test is the 'enduring benefit' one given by Viscount Cave in *Atherton v British Insulated & Helsby Cables Ltd HL 1925, 10 TC 155*. For recent reviews of the cases, see *Lawson v Johnson Matthey plc HL 1992, 65 TC 39* and *Halifax plc v Davidson (Sp C 239), [2000] SSCD 251*. In the latter case, costs incurred by a building society on conversion to a public limited company were disallowed as capital expenditure to the extent that they related to payment of statutory cash bonuses to non-voting members of the society, but otherwise allowed. In *Dass v Special Commissioner and others [2006] All ER (D) 152*, the High Court held that an examination fee under consideration was incurred 'with a view to bringing into existence an asset or advantage for the enduring benefit of a trade' and was attributable to capital.

It is by virtue of *ICTA 1988, s 74(1)(f)* that depreciation of fixed assets is not allowable in computing profits (see 10.1 CAPITAL ALLOWANCES) (*In re Robert Addie & Sons CES 1875, 1 TC 1*). Where the depreciation charge in the accounts was reduced by capitalising part of it and including that part in the balance sheet value of stock (i.e. as an overhead cost), it was held by the House of Lords that net depreciation (i.e. the amount after deduction of depreciation included in stock) had to be added back in arriving at taxable profits on the basis that if the profit or loss was arrived at by deducting the net figure, the gross figure could not be adjusted for in the tax computation. Accounting principles stated that the profit or loss for a period of account had to take into account only revenue and expenditure relating to that year. (*HMRC v William Grant & Sons Distillers Ltd; Small (Inspector of Taxes) v Mars UK Ltd [2007] UKHL 15)*.

A gain or loss on the sale of a capital asset not included in trading profits is dealt with according to the provisions relating to capital gains tax. A sale of a fixed asset on which capital allowances have been claimed may result in a balancing charge or allowance, see 10 CAPITAL ALLOWANCES.

The revenue or capital nature of a payment is fixed at the time of its receipt (*Tapemaze Ltd v Melluish Ch D 2000, 73 TC 167*, following *Morley v Tattersall CA 1938, 40 TC 671*).

For a brief note on HMRC's approach to challenging schemes or arrangements designed to turn income into capital (or capital expenditure into a revenue deduction), see Revenue Tax Bulletin June 1997 p 438.

For HMRC's own guidance on capital *v* income, see HMRC Business Income Manual BIM 35000–35910.

The 'wholly and exclusively' rule. For an expense to be deductible, it must, *inter alia*, have been incurred 'wholly and exclusively for the purposes of the trade'. (For income tax purposes for 2005/06 onwards, it is specifically provided that if an expense is incurred for a *dual purpose*, this rule does not prohibit a deduction for any *identifiable* part or *identifiable* proportion of the expense which is incurred wholly and exclusively for the purposes of the trade; but this simply reflects a long-established principle (see below). [*ITTOIA 2005, s 34*].) [*ICTA 1988, s 74*(*1*)(*a*)].

For a review of the leading cases on the 'wholly and exclusively' rule, see *Harrods (Buenos Aires) Ltd v Taylor-Gooby CA 1964, 41 TC 450* and for a frequently quoted analysis of the words see *Bentleys, Stokes & Lowless v Beeson CA 1952, 33 TC 491*. Following that case the dual purpose rule (now in *ITTOIA 2005, s 34*) has figured prominently in Court decisions. 'Dual expenditure is expenditure that is incurred for more than one reason. If one of the reasons is not for business purposes, the expenditure fails the statutory test and there is no provision that allows a "business" proportion' (HMRC Business Income Manual BIM 37007). *However*, in practice, where an identifiable part or proportion of an expense has been laid out wholly and exclusively for the purposes of the trade, HMRC do not disallow that part or proportion on the grounds that the expense is not *as a whole* laid out wholly and exclusively for the purposes of the trade (BIM 37007). See Tolley's Income Tax under Trading Income.

A purely incidental consequence of a business expense does not, however, preclude its being wholly and exclusively for business purposes (HMRC Business Income Manual BIM 37007, 37400). See, for example, *Robinson v Scott Bader Ltd*, 66.43 below.

It should be borne in mind that the trade for whose purposes the expenditure is incurred must be that in which the expense arose. For a successful appeal against a decision in favour of HMRC on this point, see *Vodafone Cellular Ltd v Shaw CA 1997, 69 TC 376*.

For HMRC's own guidance on the 'wholly and exclusively' rule, see HMRC Business Income Manual BIM 37000–38600.

Private Finance Initiative ('PFI') projects. For a series of articles on the tax aspects of PFI projects (dealing with the introduction by the public sector body of surplus land, or cash derived therefrom, with stamp duty considerations, with income arising from leases of fully serviced accommodation and with the scope of a PFI operator's trade), see Revenue Tax Bulletin April 1999 pp 642–645, October 1999 pp 694–697, August 2002 p 950. See also HMRC Business Income Manual BIM 64000–64405.

Simon's Direct Tax Service. See **B3.9, B3.12**.

66.19 ADVERTISING

Expenditure generally is allowable (but not capital outlay such as fixed signs (but see *Leeds Permanent Building Society v Proctor Ch D 1982, 56 TC 293*), nor initial costs etc. of new business). Contribution to campaign for Sunday opening held allowable (*Rhymney Breweries Ch D 1965, 42 TC 509*). As to political campaign see *Tate & Lyle HL 1954, 35 TC 367*, contrasted with *Boarland v Kramat Pulai Ch D 1953, 35 TC 1*. See HMRC Business Income Manual BIM 42550–42555.

66.20 APPLICATION OF PROFITS

A requirement that a trading surplus is to be applied in a particular way does not remove the trade from Case I (*Mersey Docks and Harbour Board v Lucas HL 1883, 2 TC 25*) and applications of the profits under the requirement are not allowable deductions (*City of Dublin Steam Packet Co v O'Brien KB(I) 1912, 6 TC 101*; *Hutchinson & Co v Turner HC 1950, 31 TC 495*; *Young v Racecourse Betting Control Board HL 1959, 38 TC 426* and cf.

Pondicherry Rly Co PC 1931, 10 ATC 365; *Tata Hydro-Electric Agencies PC 1937, 16 ATC 54*; *India Radio & Cable Communication Co PC 1937, 16 ATC 333*).

For circumstances in which the profits of a trade may not accrue to the proprietor, see *Alongi v CIR CS 1991, 64 TC 304*.

66.21 BAD DEBTS — IMPAIRMENT LOSSES

The term 'impairment losses' has been introduced by *FA 2005, Sch 4* in place of references to 'bad' and 'doubtful debts' (with effect for periods of account beginning on or after 1 January 2005) to reflect the terminology used by international accounting standards. Thus, references below to an impairment loss can be read as references, in the old terminology, to a bad or doubtful debt. At the same time, the provisions in *ICTA 1988, s 74(1)(j)* allowing a deduction for bad debts, etc. are replaced with provisions in *ICTA 1988, s 88D* as below, which have the same effect and do not represent a change of law.

For the purposes of these provisions, 'debt' includes an obligation or liability which may be met otherwise than by the payment of money.

In the case of debts not falling with the regimes for LOAN RELATIONSHIPS (46), DERIVATIVE CONTRACTS (28) or INTANGIBLE FIXED ASSETS (39), a deduction is allowed in respect of a debt owed to the company for:

(a) an impairment loss; or

(b) a debt release to the extent the debt is released wholly and exclusively for the purposes of that trade as part of a 'statutory insolvency arrangement'.

A '*statutory insolvency arrangement*' is defined in *ICTA 1988, s 834* as a voluntary arrangement under, or by virtue of, *Insolvency Act 1986* (or Scottish or NI equivalents) or a compromise or arrangement under *Companies Act 1985, s 425* (or NI equivalent) or any corresponding arrangement or compromise under, or by virtue of, the law of a non-UK jurisdiction. This definition, introduced by *FA 2005*, replaces the definition in *ICTA 1988, s 74(2)* of a 'relevant arrangement or compromise' in order to cover insolvencies under non-UK jurisdictions for periods of account beginning on or after 1 January 2005.

For income tax purposes, *ICTA 1988, s 74(1)(j),(2)* is replaced by *ITTOIA 2005, s 35* from 2005/6 onwards.

[*ICTA 1988, ss 74(1)(j), 88D; ITTOIA 2005, Sch 1 para 45; FA 2005, s 80, Sch 4 paras 1, 2, 8*].

Where a trade is treated as notionally discontinued (see 66.2 above), the allowance extends to debts taken over by the successor company to the extent that amounts proving irrecoverable after the debts have been taken over exceed any deduction previously allowed for impairment losses. Similar treatment applies to recoveries. [*ICTA 1988, ss 89, 106(2); ITTOIA 2005, Sch 1 paras 65, 85; FA 2005, Sch 4 para 3*].

If a debt owed to a company by a trader is released (otherwise than as part of a statutory insolvency arrangement — see above), and the expense giving rise to the debt has been allowed as a deduction for corporation tax purposes, the amount released is treated as a trading receipt arising on the date of release. [*ICTA 1988, s 94; ITTOIA 2005, Sch 1 para 73; FA 2005, Sch 4 para 4*]. For accounting periods starting before 1 January 2002, the Revenue interpreted the decision in *British Mexican Petroleum Co Ltd v Jackson HL, 16 TC 570* as meaning that trade debts *not* released but nevertheless written back were not taxable; they now take the view that the 'true and fair view' requirement (see 66.5 above) requires such write-backs to be taxed, subject only to the exception provided for releases under statutory insolvency arrangements (Revenue Tax Bulletin December 2001 pp 901, 902 and see now HMRC Business Income Manual BIM 40265). See generally Business Income Manual BIM 40201 *et seq*.

For debt recoveries and releases after the cessation of a trade, see 66.3 above. Bad debt allowances are not applicable where the business is assessed on a cash basis (see Tolley's Income tax under Cash Basis. For VAT on bad debts, see 68.2 VALUE ADDED TAX.

The provision for a bad or doubtful debt for a period of account may reflect events after the balance sheet date in so far as they furnish additional evidence of conditions that existed at the balance sheet date. See Revenue Tax Bulletin August 1994 p 154, which also outlines the evidence which inspectors may require in support of the allowance of a provision. It is not possible to employ hindsight to revisit a past computation of taxable profit so as to provide for a debt in a period of account in which there was no evidence that it would eventually prove to be bad (*Thompson v CIR (Sp C 458), [2005[SSCD 320*).

Where an asset accepted in satisfaction of a trading debt is of market value (as at the date of acceptance) less than the outstanding debt, the deficit may be allowed as a deduction, provided the trader agrees that, on a disposal of the asset, any excess of disposal proceeds over that value (up to the amount by which the debt exceeds that value) will be brought in as a trading receipt (such receipt being excluded from any chargeable gain computation on the disposal) (HMRC Business Income Manual BIM 42735).

An allowance agreed under conditions of full disclosure cannot be withdrawn because of a subsequent change in the circumstances (*Anderton & Halstead Ltd v Birrell KB 1931, 16 TC 200*) but an allowance for year 1 may be revised, upwards or downwards, in the year 2 computation by reference to the circumstances for year 2 and similarly for later years. The amount of the allowance depends on the likelihood of recovery. This is a question of fact but the fact that the debtor is still in business is not itself a reason for refusing an allowance (*Dinshaw v Bombay IT Commr PC 1934, 13 ATC 284*). See also *Lock v Jones KB 1941, 23 TC 749.*

General bad debt provisions, i.e. not relating to specific debts, are not deductible. However where there are a large number of comparatively small debts, making the 'valuation' of individual debts impracticable, HMRC will normally agree to an allowance in accordance with a formula based on the bad debt experience of the business. Typical businesses are mail-order firms and firms with a large proportion of hire-purchase sales. Where hire-purchase is involved the formula may also cover the spread of the profit on hire-purchase sales. But no provision for the estimated cost of collecting future debt instalments is permissible (*Monthly Salaries Loan Co Ltd v Furlong Ch D 1962, 40 TC 313*).

Where a builder sold houses leaving part of the sale proceeds with Building Societies as collateral security for mortgages by the purchasers, it was held the amounts should be brought in at valuation when the houses were sold and if practicable and otherwise when released by the Building Society (*John Cronk & Sons Ltd v Harrison HL 1936, 20 TC 612* and cf. *Chibbett v Harold Brookfield & Son Ltd CA 1952, 33 TC 467*). A similar decision was reached in *Absalom v Talbot HL 1944, 26 TC 166* where amounts were left on loan to the purchasers. See also *Lock v Jones* above. The HL judgments in *Absalom v Talbot* are an important review of the treatment of trading debts.

The normal debt considered for allowance is a debt for goods or services supplied or a debt in a business, such as banking or money-lending, which consists of advancing money (see e.g. *AB Bank v Inspector of Taxes (Sp C 237), [2000] SSCD 229*). Losses on advances by a brewery company to its customers were allowed as on the evidence it habitually acted as banker for them in the course of its brewing business (*Reid's Brewery v Male QB 1891, 3 TC 279*). But losses on advances to clients by solicitors were refused as there was no evidence that they were money-lenders (*CIR v Hagart & Burn-Murdoch HL 1929, 14 TC 433*; *Rutherford v CIR CS 1939, 23 TC 8*. See also *Bury & Walkers v Phillips HC 1951, 32 TC 198* and contrast *Jennings v Barfield Ch D 1962, 40 TC 365*). An allowance was refused for an irrecoverable balance due from the managing director of a company as outside the company's trade (*Curtis v J & G Oldfield Ltd KB 1925, 9 TC 319*). See also *Roebank Printing Co Ltd v CIR CS 1928, 13 TC 864.*

Advances to finance or recoup the losses of subsidiary or associated companies are capital. Allowances were refused in *English Crown Spelter v Baker KB 1908, 5 TC 327* and *Charles Marsden & Sons v CIR KB 1919, 12 TC 217* for losses on advances to facilitate the supply of materials for the trade of the lender as were losses on an advance to a company under the same control (*Baker v Mabie Todd & Co Ltd KB 1927, 13 TC 235*), amounts written off in respect of the losses of a subsidiary (*Odhams Press Ltd v Cook HL 1940, 23 TC 233*) and payments to meet the operating losses of a subsidiary (*Marshall Richards Machine Co Ltd v Jewitt Ch D 1956, 36 TC 511*). See also *CIR v Huntley & Palmers Ltd KB 1928, 12 TC 1209*; *Henderson v Meade-King Robinson & Co Ltd KB 1938, 22 TC 97*; and *Stone & Temple Ltd v Waters; Astrawall (UK) Ltd v Waters Ch D 1995, 67 TC 145*. (N.B. The loss of a subsidiary may be eligible for group relief — see 32.10 GROUPS OF COMPANIES.)

Losses relating to trade debts with a subsidiary were, however, held allowable in *Sycamore plc and Maple Ltd v Fir (Sp C 104), [1997] SSCD 1.*

Payments by the purchaser to discharge the unpaid liabilities of the vendor to preserve goodwill etc. allowed in *Cooke v Quick Shoe Repair Service KB 1949, 30 TC 460.*

See 66.83 below for relief for certain unremittable overseas debts of trades carried on at least partly in the UK.

Note. Loans made to a trader for the setting up or purposes of his trade and irrecoverable are in certain circumstances allowable as a loss for capital gains tax — see Tolley's Capital Gains Tax.

For losses under guarantees see 66.57 below.

See generally HMRC Business Income Manual BIM 42700–42750.

Simon's Direct Tax Service. See **B3.1315** *et seq.*

66.22 BREWERIES, DISTILLERIES, LICENSED PREMISES

Tied premises. Receipts and expenses in respect of 'tied premises' which would otherwise be brought into account under Schedule A (see 56.2 PROPERTY INCOME) are instead brought into account as trading receipts or expenses. Premises outside the UK are for this purpose treated as if they were in the UK. Any necessary apportionment (e.g. where rents etc. relate only in part to the tied premises or where only part of the premises qualifies) is on a just and reasonable basis. '*Tied premises*' are premises through which goods supplied by a trader are sold or used by another person, where the trader has an estate or interest in the premises which he treats as property employed for trade purposes. [*ICTA 1988, s 98; ITTOIA 2005, Sch 1 para 77*]. (*Note.* These rules are of general application, although of most common application in the licensed trade.)

Case law. Repairs, rates, insurance premiums paid on behalf of tied tenants allowable (*Usher's Wiltshire Brewery v Bruce HL 1914, 6 TC 399*) but not extra expenditure incurred to keep licensed houses open while undergoing rehabilitation (*Mann Crossman & Paulin Ltd v Compton KB 1947, 28 TC 410*) or compensation to a tenant displaced on a licence transfer (*Morse v Stedeford KB 1934, 18 TC 457*). For compensation paid on the termination of tenancies of tied houses, see *Watneys (London) Ltd v Pike Ch D 1982, 57 TC 372.* Losses on advances to 'customers and connections' held allowable (*Reid's Brewery v Male QB 1891, 3 TC 279*).

The expenses of an unsuccessful application for licences were held not allowable (*Southwell v Savill Bros KB 1901, 4 TC 430* — it was conceded that expenses of successful applications are capital) nor expenses of applying for licence transfers (*Morse v Stedeford* above; *Pendleton v Mitchells & Butlers Ch D 1968, 45 TC 341*). Contributions by a brewer to a trade association to promote Sunday opening in Wales allowed in *Cooper v Rhymney Breweries Ch D 1965, 42 TC 509.* Compensation Fund levies deductible (*Smith v Lion Brewery HL 1910, 5 TC 568*) but not monopoly value payments (*Kneeshaw v Albertolli KB 1940, 23 TC 462*; *Henriksen v Grafton Hotels Ltd CA 1942, 24 TC 453*).

Damages paid to hotel guest injured by falling chimney held not allowable — see *Strong & Co v Woodifield* at 66.26 below. For accrued whisky storage rents see *Dailuaine-Talisker Distilleries v CIR CS 1930, 15 TC 613*; *CIR v Oban Distillery Co CS 1932, 18 TC 33* and *CIR v Arthur Bell & Sons CS 1932, 22 TC 315.*

Where a brewery company ceased brewing but continued to sell beer brewed for it by another company it was held to have discontinued its old trade and commenced a new one (*Gordon & Blair Ltd v CIR CS 1962, 40 TC 358*).

Simon's Direct Tax Service. See **B3.410–B3.413**.

66.23 CAR OR MOTOR CYCLE HIRE

Where a 'car or motor cycle' of which the retail price when new (i.e. unused and not second-hand) exceeds £12,000 is hired for the purposes of a trade, the hire charge is reduced for tax purposes by multiplying it by the fraction

$(12{,}000 + RP) \div 2RP$

where RP is the retail price when new. If the price paid for the car by the lessor when new is known, it can be used as the retail price when new, but otherwise the manufacturer's list price, net of any discount generally available but inclusive of extras and VAT, should be used (HMRC Business Income Manual BIM 47717).

For this purpose, a '*car or motor cycle*' is a mechanically propelled road vehicle which is neither (1) of a construction primarily suited for the conveyance of goods or burden of any description nor (2) of a type not commonly used as a private vehicle and unsuitable for such use. As regards (2), see the case law referred to at 10.27(ii) CAPITAL ALLOWANCES.

The restriction does *not* apply to cars or motor cycles used wholly or mainly for a trade of hire to, or carriage of, members of the public and satisfying the same conditions as apply for the similar exception at 10.27(A) CAPITAL ALLOWANCES. As regards hire-purchase agreements (as defined) under which there is an option to purchase for a sum not more than 1% of the retail price when new, the finance charge element, which strictly falls within the definition of a hire charge, is also excluded from the restriction. (For income tax purposes for 2005/06 onwards, this exclusion is extended to hire-purchase agreements under which there is no option to purchase, and it seems that this was previously applied by HMRC in practice (see Change 11 listed in Annex 1 to the Explanatory Notes to the Income Tax (Trading and Other Income) Bill).)

Also *excluded* from the restriction is expenditure incurred after 16 April 2002 on hiring cars (but *not* motorcycles) first registered after that date which are 'electrically-propelled' or have 'low carbon dioxide emissions' (for which see 10.27 CAPITAL ALLOWANCES) for a period of hire beginning before 1 April 2008 under a contract entered into before that date.

'Hire charges' for these purposes were held to include payments under a finance lease providing a revolving facility for the purchase of vehicles for use in a contract hire operation (*Lloyds UDT Finance Ltd and Another v Britax International GmBH and Another CA 2002, 74 TC 662*).

Where the above restriction has applied, any subsequent rental rebate (or debt release other than as part of a statutory insolvency arrangement — see 66.21 above) is reduced for tax purposes in the same proportion as the hire charge restriction. (For income tax purposes for 2005/06 onwards, this treatment extends to amounts brought in as post-cessation receipts (see 66.3 above) after the trade has ceased.)

[*ICTA 1988, ss 578A, 578B; CAA 1990, s 35(2)–(4); FA 1991, s 61; F(No 2)A 1992, s 71; CAA 2001, Sch 2 para 52, Sch 3 para 113; FA 2001, Sch 12 Pt II para 11; FA 2002, s 60; ITTOIA 2005, Sch 1 para 238*].

See HMRC Business Income Manual BIM 47715–47720.

See 10.30(A) CAPITAL ALLOWANCES for the restriction of writing-down allowances in respect of *capital* expenditure on the acquisition of a car costing over £12,000.

66.24 CEMETERIES AND CREMATORIA

In computing profits of a trade consisting of, or including, the carrying on of a cemetery or the carrying on of a crematorium (and, in connection therewith, the maintenance of memorial garden plots), a deduction as a trading expense for any period of account is allowed for:

- the capital cost of purchasing and preparing land (including cost of levelling, draining or otherwise making suitable) sold for interments or memorial garden plots *in that period*; and

- a *proportion* (based on the ratio of number of grave-spaces/garden plots sold in the period to that number plus those still available — see *Example* below) of 'residual capital expenditure'.

'*Residual capital expenditure*' is the total 'ancillary capital expenditure' incurred before the end of the period of account in question after subtracting (i) amounts previously deducted under these provisions, and (ii) any sale, insurance or compensation receipts for assets representing ancillary capital expenditure and sold or destroyed. '*Ancillary capital expenditure*' is capital expenditure incurred on any building or structure (other than a dwelling-house), or on the purchase or preparation of other land not suitable or adaptable for interments or garden plots, which is in the cemetery or memorial garden and is likely to have little or no value when the cemetery or garden is full; it also includes capital expenditure on the purchase or preparation of land taken up by said buildings and structures.

For these purposes, sales of land in a cemetery include sales of interment rights, and sales of land in a memorial garden include appropriations of part of the garden in return for dedication fees etc. Expenditure met by subsidies cannot be deducted as above (the detailed rules being similar to those at 10.2(vi) CAPITAL ALLOWANCES).

Any change in the persons carrying on the trade is ignored; allowances continue as they would to the original trader, disregarding any purchase price paid in connection with the change itself.

[*ICTA 1988, s 91; CAA 2001, Sch 2 para 19; ITTOIA 2005, Sch 1 para 67*].

For the treatment of lump sums for grave maintenance etc., see HMRC Business Income Manual BIM 52505, 52510. For the treatment of expenditure and receipts in connection with the provision of niches and memorials, see BIM 52520, 52525.

As regards crematoria, see also *Bourne v Norwich Crematorium Ch D 1967, 44 TC 164*.

Simon's Direct Tax Service. See **B3.420, B3.1322**.

Example

GE Ltd, which operates a funeral service, owns a cemetery for which accounts to 31 December are prepared. The accounts to 31.12.07 reveal the following.

(i)	Cost of land representing 110 grave spaces sold in period	£3,400
(ii)	Number of grave spaces remaining	275
(iii)	Residual capital expenditure on buildings and other land unsuitable for interments	£18,250

The allowances available are		£
(*a*)	Item (i)	3,400
(*b*)	$\frac{110}{110+275} \times £18,250$	5,214
		£8,614

Note

(*a*) £8,614 will be allowed as a deduction in computing GE Ltd's trading profits for the period of account ending on 31 December 2007.

66.25 **COMMISSION, CASHBACKS AND DISCOUNTS**

HMRC Statement of Practice SP 4/97 sets out HMRC's views on the tax treatment of commissions, cashbacks and discounts. The types of payment with which the Statement is concerned are as follows.

Commissions. Sums paid by the providers of goods, investments or services to agents or intermediaries as reward for the introduction of business, or in some cases paid directly by the provider to the customer. Sums paid to an agent or intermediary may be passed on to the customer or to some other person.

Cashbacks. Lump sums received by a customer as an inducement for entering into a transaction for the purchase of goods, investments or services and received as a direct consequence of having entered into that transaction. The payer may be either the provider or another party with an interest in ensuring that the transaction takes place.

Discounts, i.e. where the purchaser's obligation to pay for goods, investments or services is less than the full purchase price, other than as a result of commissions or cashbacks.

The Statement also deals with commissions or cashbacks which are netted off, or invested or otherwise applied for the benefit of the purchaser, or where extra value is added to the goods, investments or services supplied (e.g. the allocation of bonus units in an investment) (although in the case of the addition of value to investments this may represent a return on the investment, which is outside the scope of the Statement).

The Statement provides detailed guidance on the circumstances in which Schedule D liability may arise under either Case I or II as trading income or Case VI as miscellaneous income, on receipts of commission etc. It also considers deductibility of commission etc. passed on to customers.

Generally, ordinary retail arm's length customers will not be liable to income tax or capital gains tax. The Statement outlines the circumstances in which receipts are treated as tax-free, or payments qualify for tax relief, and contains an element of concession for those who, in the ordinary course of their business, earn commission relating to their own transactions. It contains a warning that the principles outlined may not be followed where tax avoidance schemes are involved, or where the arrangements for the commission etc. include an increase in the purchase price of the goods etc. involved. The tax treatment of the payer and the recipient are in all cases considered independently of one another.

For an article explaining the legal basis of this approach, see HMRC Business Income Manual BIM 40655–40710.

66.26 COMPENSATION, DAMAGES ETC. — PAYMENTS

For compensation and redundancy payments to directors or employees see 66.43 below. An important case is *Anglo-Persian Oil Co Ltd v Dale CA 1931, 16 TC 253* in which a substantial payment by a company for the cancellation of its principal agency, with ten years to run, was held to be allowable. It was not for a capital asset nor to get rid of an onerous contract (cf. *Mallett v Staveley Coal CA 1928, 13 TC 772*) but to enable it to rationalise its working arrangements. The decision was applied in *Croydon Hotel & Leisure Co Ltd v Bowen (Sp C 101), [1996] SSCD 466*, in which a payment for the termination of a hotel management agreement was held to be allowable. See also *Vodafone Cellular Ltd v Shaw CA 1997, 69 TC 376* (payment for release from onerous agreement), in which the principle underlying the decision in *Van den Berghs Ltd v Clark* (see 66.27(*b*) below) was applied, but cf. *Tucker v Granada Motorway Services Ltd HL 1979, 53 TC 92*, where a payment to modify the method of calculating the rent was held to be capital, and *Whitehead v Tubbs (Elastics) Ltd CA 1983, 57 TC 472*, where a payment to alter the terms of a capital loan by removing borrowing restrictions on the borrower was held to be capital.

A payment by a shipping company for cancelling an order it had placed for a ship was held capital (*'Countess Warwick' SS Co Ltd v Ogg KB 1924, 8 TC 652* and contrast *Devon Mutual Steamship Insce v Ogg KB 1927, 13 TC 184*). A payment to an associated company in return for its temporarily ceasing production held allowable (*Commr of Taxes v Nchanga Consolidated Copper Mines PC 1964, 43 ATC 20*) as were statutory levies on a brewery for a Compensation Fund where a licence is not renewed (*Smith v Lion Brewery Co Ltd HL 1910, 5 TC 568*) and a payment to secure the closure of a rival concern (*Walker v The Joint Credit Card Co Ltd Ch D 1982, 55 TC 617*). Payments by a steel company to secure the closure of railway steel works were held capital (*United Steels v Cullington (No 1) CA 1939, 23 TC 71*) as were payments to safeguard against subsidence on a factory site (*Bradbury v United Glass Bottle Mfrs CA 1959, 38 TC 369*; compare *Glenboig Union Fireclay* at 66.27(*c*) below) and a payment for cancelling electricity agreement on closure of a quarry (*CIR v Wm Sharp & Son CS 1959, 38 TC 341*). For compensation paid on the termination of tied houses of breweries, see *Watneys (London) Ltd v Pike Ch D 1982, 57 TC 372*.

Where damages awarded by a Court against a solicitor were later compounded, the compounded amount (accepted as allowable) was held to be an expense of the year in which the Court award was made (*Simpson v Jones Ch D 1968, 44 TC 599*). See also *CIR v Hugh T Barrie Ltd CA(NI) 1928, 12 TC 1223*.

Damages paid by a brewery to a hotel guest injured by a falling chimney were held to have been incurred by it *qua* property owner and not *qua* trader and not deductible (*Strong & Co of Romsey Ltd v Woodifield HL 1906, 5 TC 215*). Penalties for breach of war-time regulations and defence costs not allowed (*CIR v Warnes & Co KB 1919, 12 TC 227*; *CIR v Alexander von Glehn & Co Ltd CA 1920, 12 TC 232*), nor fines imposed by professional regulatory body (*McKnight v Sheppard Ch D 1996, 71 TC 419*), nor damages for breach of American 'anti-trust' law (*Cattermole v Borax & Chemicals Ltd KB 1949, 31 TC 202*). See also *G Scammell & Nephew v Rowles CA 1939, 22 TC 479*; *Fairrie v Hall KB 1947, 28 TC 200*; *Golder v Great Boulder Proprietary HC 1952, 33 TC 75*; *Knight v Parry Ch D 1972, 48 TC 580*; *Hammond Engineering v CIR Ch D 1975, 50 TC 313*.

Simon's Direct Tax Service. See **B3.1329**.

66.27 COMPENSATION, DAMAGES ETC. — RECEIPTS

(*a*) **Capital sums** (i.e. sums not taken into account in computing income) received as compensation for damage, injury, destruction or depreciation of assets are subject to corporation tax on capital gains [*TCGA 1992, s 22(1)*] (but this does not apply to compensation or damages to an individual for wrong or injury to his person or in his profession or vocation). [*TCGA 1992, s 51(2)*]. See Tolley's Capital Gains Tax.

(*b*) **Cancellation or variation of trading contracts and arrangements.** An important case is *Van den Berghs Ltd v Clark HL 1935, 19 TC 390* in which a receipt on the termination of a profit-sharing arrangement was held to be capital. The arrangement related to the whole structure of the recipient's trade, forming the fixed framework within which its circulating capital operated. Compensation etc. receipts were also held to be capital in *Sabine v Lookers Ltd CA 1958, 38 TC 120* (varying car distributor's agreement); *British-Borneo Petroleum v Cropper Ch D 1968, 45 TC 201* (cancelling a royalty agreement); *Barr Crombie & Co Ltd v CIR CS 1945, 26 TC 406* (terminating agreement as ship-managers); but the opposite conclusion was reached in *Consultant v Inspector of Taxes (Sp C 180), [1999] SSCD 63* (termination of profit participation agreement). A payment by the liquidator of a shipping company to its managers as authorised by the shareholders held not assessable (*Chibbett v Robinson & Sons KB 1924, 9 TC 48*).

Compensation etc. receipts on the cancellation of contracts receipts from which, if completed, would have been trading receipts are normally themselves trading receipts, to be credited in the computations for the period in which cancelled. See *Short Bros Ltd v CIR* and *Sunderland Shipbuilding Co Ltd v CIR CA 1927, 12 TC 955* (cancellation of order for ships); *CIR v Northfleet Coal Co KB 1927, 12 TC 1102*; *Jesse Robinson & Sons v CIR KB 1929, 12 TC 1241* (cancellation of contracts for sale of goods etc.); *Greyhound Racing Assn v Cooper KB 1936, 20 TC 373* (cancellation of agreement to hire greyhound track); *Shove v Dura Mfg Co Ltd KB 1941, 23 TC 779* (cancellation of commission agreement). Similarly compensation to a merchanting company on cancellation of a contract to supply goods to it was held a trading receipt (*Bush, Beach & Gent Ltd v Road KB 1939, 22 TC 519*). See also *United Steel v Cullington (No 1) CA 1939, 23 TC 71*; *Shadbolt v Salmon Estates KB 1943, 25 TC 52*; *Sommerfelds Ltd v Freeman Ch D 1966, 44 TC 43*; *Creed v H & M Levinson Ltd Ch D 1981, 54 TC 477*.

Compensation received on the termination of agencies is a trading receipt unless the agency, by reason of its relative size etc., is part of the 'fixed framework' (see *Van den Berghs* above) of the agent's business. See *Kelsall Parsons CS 1938, 21 TC 608*; *CIR v Fleming & Co CS 1951, 33 TC 57*; *CIR v David MacDonald & Co CS 1955, 36 TC 388*; *Wiseburgh v Domville CA 1956, 36 TC 527*; *Fleming v Bellow Machine Co Ch D 1965, 42 TC 308*; *Elson v James G Johnston Ltd Ch D 1965, 42 TC 545* (in all of which the compensation etc. was held to be a trading receipt). See also *Anglo-French Exploration Co Ltd v Clayson CA 1956, 36 TC 545*.

For payments received on termination of building society agencies, see HMRC Capital Gains Tax Manual CG 13050 *et seq.*

(*c*) **Compensation etc. relating to capital assets.** Compensation to a company making fireclay goods for refraining from working a fireclay bed under a railway line was held to be capital (*Glenboig Union Fireclay Co Ltd v CIR HL 1922, 12 TC 427* and cf. *Thomas McGhie & Sons v BTC QB 1962, 41 ATC 144* and *Bradbury v United Glass Bottle CA 1959, 38 TC 369*), but compensation to a colliery from the Government for requisition of part of its mining area was held to be a trading receipt (*Waterloo Main Colliery v CIR (No 1) KB 1947, 29 TC 235*). Compensation to a shipping company for delay in the overhaul of a ship was held to be a trading receipt (*Burmah Steam Ship Co v CIR CS 1930, 16 TC 67*) as was compensation to a jetty owner for loss of its use after damage by a ship (*London & Thames Haven v Attwooll CA 1966, 43 TC 491*) and compensation for the detention of a ship (*Ensign Shipping Co v CIR CA 1928, 12 TC 1169* but contrast *CIR v Francis West CS 1950, 31 TC 402*).

For insurance recoveries see 66.60 below.

(*d*) **Compensation on compulsory acquisition etc.** Where compensation is paid for the acquisition of business property by an authority possessing powers of compulsory acquisition, any amounts included as compensation for temporary loss of profits or losses on trading stock or to reimburse revenue expenditure, such as removal expenses and interest, are treated as trading receipts. (See HMRC Statement of Practice, SP 8/79 and HMRC Business Income Bulletin BIM 40115. This Statement of Practice was originally issued as consequence of *Stoke-on-Trent City Council v Wood Mitchell & Co Ltd CA 1978, [1979] STC 197*.)

(*e*) **Other compensation etc. receipts.** Voluntary payments to an insurance broker on the loss of an important client company (made by its parent company) were held, approving *Chibbett v Robinson* and *Carnaby Harrower* (see (*b*) above), not to be assessable (*Simpson v John Reynolds & Co CA 1975, 49 TC 693*) and similarly for voluntary payments from a brewer to a firm of caterers for the surrender of the leases of tied premises (*Murray v Goodhews CA 1977, 52 TC 86*) but *ex gratia* payments to an estate agent who had not been given an agency he expected were held, on the facts, to be additional remuneration for work already done and assessable. (*McGowan v Brown & Cousins (Stuart Edwards) Ch D 1977, 52 TC 8*). A payment to a diamond broker under informal and non-binding arbitration as damages for the loss of a prospective client was held assessable (*Rolfe v Nagel CA 1981, 55 TC 585*). Compensation for 'loss of profits' following the destruction of the premises of a business not recommenced was held to be of a revenue nature in *Lang v Rice CA (NI) 1983, 57 TC 80*. For compensation receipts relating to the terms on which business premises are tenanted, see 66.71 below.

For the treatment of compensation received by businesses as customers of e.g. utility companies for interruptions and other service deficiencies, see HMRC Business Income Manual BIM 40101.

Damages awarded to a theatrical company for breach of a licence it had, were held to be assessable (*Vaughan v Parnell & Zeitlin KB 1940, 23 TC 505*) as was compensation received by a development company under legislation for restricting development (*Johnson v W S Try Ltd CA 1946, 27 TC 167*). A retrospective award for a war-time requisition of trading stock was held to be a trading receipt of the year of requisition (*CIR v Newcastle Breweries Ltd HL 1927, 12 TC 927*).

66.28 CONTINGENT AND FUTURE LIABILITIES

For forward contracts see 66.29 below.

Where a company is required under overseas legislation to make leaving payments to its employees, a provision in its accounts for its prospective liability is permissible if capable of sufficiently accurate calculation (*Owen v Southern Railway of Peru HL 1956, 36 TC 602*). The allowance each year is the actual payments as adjusted for any variation between the opening and closing provisions but the deductible provision for the year in which the legislation was enacted may include an amount in respect of previous services of the employees (*CIR v Titaghur Jute Factory Ltd CS 1978, 53 TC 675*).

No deduction is normally permissible for future repairs or renewals (*Clayton v Newcastle-under-Lyme Corpn QB 1888, 2 TC 416*; *Naval Colliery Co Ltd v CIR HL 1928, 12 TC 1017*; *Peter Merchant Ltd v Stedeford CA 1948, 30 TC 496*). However, this rule is now subject to Financial Reporting Standard FRS 12 (see 66.72(*b*) below). No deduction is permissible for the future cost of collecting debts (*Monthly Salaries Loan Co v Furlong Ch D 1962, 40 TC 313*) or for future payments of damages in respect of accidents to employees unless liability has been admitted or established (*James Spencer & Co v CIR CS 1950, 32 TC 111*). See also *Albion Rovers Football Club v CIR HL 1952, 33 TC 331* (wages deductible when paid). A provision for regular major overhaul work accrued due on aircraft engines was allowed in *Johnston v Britannia Airways Ltd Ch D 1994, 67 TC 99* (but see now Revenue Tax Bulletin February 1999 p 624 and further below as regards changes in accounting practice superseding this decision).

For provisions by insurance companies for unexpired risks etc., see *Sun Insurance Office v Clark HL 1912, 6 TC 59.* For the liability of cemetery companies in receipt of lump sums for the future maintenance of graves, see *Paisley Cemetery Co v Reith CES 1898, 4 TC 1* and *London Cemetery Co v Barnes KB 1917, 7 TC 92.*

A provision by a company engaged in the exploitation of a North Sea oil field, for anticipated future expenditure on the completion of the exploitation, in dismantling installations used and (as required under its licence) in 'cleaning up' the sea bed, was disallowed as capital when incurred in *RTZ Oil & Gas Ltd v Elliss Ch D 1987, 61 TC 132.*

See generally HMRC Business Income Manual BIM 42201, 46500–46565. See also Revenue Press Release 20 July 1999, and FRS 12 and articles in the Revenue Tax Bulletin April 1999 pp 636–639 and December 1999 pp 707–709 commenting on its implications for the treatment of provisions in tax computations.

Simon's Direct Tax Service. See B3.916, B3.1211 *et seq.*

66.29 **CONTRACTS**

For compensation etc. on the cancellation or variation of contracts see 66.26 and 66.27 above. For work in progress under contracts see 66.75 below.

Where a taxpayer took over a coal merchanting business on the death of his father, an amount paid for the benefit of contracts between his father and suppliers was held capital (*John Smith & Son v Moore HL 1921, 12 TC 266* and see *City of London Contract Corpn v Styles CA 1887, 2 TC 239*). The completion of outstanding contracts following a partnership dissolution (*Hillerns & Fowler v Murray CA 1932, 17 TC 77*) and on a company going into liquidation (*Baker v Cook KB 1937, 21 TC 337*) held to be trading.

Where under a long-term contract goods were invoiced as delivered, the sale proceeds are receipts of the year of delivery (*J P Hall & Co Ltd v CIR CA 1921, 12 TC 382*). If contract prices are varied retrospectively the resultant further sums are assessable or deductible for the years applicable to the sums at the original prices (*Frodingham Ironstone Mines Ltd v Stewart KB 1932, 16 TC 728*; *New Conveyor Co Ltd v Dodd KB 1945, 27 TC 11*). Compare *English Dairies Ltd v Phillips KB 1927, 11 TC 597*; *Isaac Holden & Sons Ltd v CIR KB 1924, 12 TC 768* and contrast *Rownson Drew & Clydesdale Ltd v CIR KB 1931, 16 TC 595.*

Losses because of a fall in prices fixed under forward contracts etc. cannot be anticipated (*Edward Collins & Sons Ltd v CIR CS 1924, 12 TC 773*; *Whimster & Co v CIR CS 1925, 12 TC 813*) and cf. *Wright Sutcliffe Ltd v CIR KB 1929, 8 ATC 168*; *J H Young & Co v CIR CS 1924, 12 TC 817*; *CIR v Hugh T Barrie Ltd CA(NI) 1928, 12 TC 1223.*

66.30 **DEDUCTION OF TAX AT SOURCE—AMOUNTS PAID UNDER**

The combined effect of *ICTA 1988, s 74(1)(m)(p)* is to prohibit the deduction in computing profits of annuities, annual payments (other than interest), patent royalties etc. payable under deduction of tax at source (see 37.3 INCOME TAX IN RELATION TO A COMPANY). For interest see 46.34 LOAN RELATIONSHIPS. See 55.4 PROFIT COMPUTATIONS for the treatment of 'charges on income'. For the treatment for corporation tax purposes of expenditure and receipts falling with the intangible assets regime, see 39 INTANGIBLE ASSETS, in particular the commencement and transitional rules for that regime at 39.37.

ICTA 1988, s 74(1)(m) applies only to amounts 'payable out of the profits'. Payments made before the profits can be ascertained are not payable 'out of the profits' and therefore were not within the *section 74(1)(m)* prohibition. For this see *Gresham Life Assce v Styles HL 1890, 3 TC 185* and *Paterson Engineering Co Ltd v Duff KB 1943, 25 TC 43.* See also *Ogden v Medway Cinemas Ltd KB 1934, 18 TC 691* and *Moss Empires Ltd v CIR HL 1937, 21 TC*

264. (For this reason, *section 74*(*1*)(*m*) is not rewritten in *ITTOIA 2005* and no longer applies for income tax purposes, though no change in the law is intended.) Patent royalties continue to be non-deductible in computing profits (see 66.67 below).

66.31 **EMBEZZLEMENT ETC.**

Losses allowed as deductions, but not misappropriation by partner or director. See *Bamford v ATA Advertising Ch D 1972, 48 TC 359* and cf. *Curtis v J & G Oldfield Ltd KB 1925, 9 TC 319*. Where defalcations were made good by the auditor who admitted negligence, a refund held to be a trading receipt for the year in which made (*Gray v Penrhyn KB 1937, 21 TC 252*).

See 66.59 below as regards prohibition on deduction of expenditure involving crime.

66.32 **EMPLOYEES (AND DIRECTORS): BENEFITS**

See 66.44 below as regards timing of benefits.

66.33 **Counselling services etc.** Expenditure on counselling and other outplacement services which falls within the earnings exemption of *ITEPA 2003, s 310* (see Tolley's Income Tax under Employment Income) is deductible in computing the profits of the employer's trade. [*ICTA 1988, ss 589A, 589B; ITEPA 2003, Sch 6 paras 69, 70; ITTOIA 2005, Sch 1 para 251*].

66.34 **Council tax.** An employer who pays the council tax for an employee will normally be able to claim a deduction for it. If such payments are also made on behalf of members of the employee's family, they too are deductible if they are part of the employee's remuneration package (which would normally mean they were paid under the contract of employment). (HMRC Business Income Manual BIM 46820).

66.35 **Employees seconded to charities or educational bodies.** If an employer seconds an employee temporarily to a charity (as defined in *ICTA 1988, s 506*) — see 14.1 CHARITIES), any expenditure of the employer which is attributable to the employment is deductible in computing the employer's profits to the extent to which it would have been deductible if the employee's services had continued to be available to the employer. This relief is extended to secondments to educational establishments (as defined and including education authorities, educational institutions maintained by such authorities, and certain other educational bodies). (For income tax purposes for 2005/06 onwards, the expenditure is deductible whether or not it would have been deductible if the employee's services had continued to be available to the employer; this restriction apparently not being applied in practice (see Change 16 listed in Annex 1 to the Explanatory Notes to the Income Tax (Trading and Other Income) Bill). [*ICTA 1988, s 86; ITTOIA 2005, Sch 1 para 60*].

66.36 **Interest on director's property loan.** Where interest is paid by a company on a loan (other than an overdraft) taken out by a director to purchase land (including buildings etc.) occupied rent-free by the company and used for business purposes, it is considered that the company can obtain relief as a trading expense for the interest in the normal way (under *ICTA 1988, s 74*(*1*)(*a*)), and that the payments would not normally constitute either remuneration or a benefit of the director. (See HMRC Business Income Manual BIM 45755–45765.)

66.37 **Key employee insurance.** Premiums on policies in favour of the employer insuring against death or critical illness of key employees are generally allowable, and the proceeds of any such policies are treated as trading receipts. However, in *Beauty Consultants Ltd v Inspector of Taxes (Sp C 321), [2002] SSCD 352*, premiums on a policy insuring a company against the death of either of its controlling shareholder-directors were disallowed, in that the premiums benefited the shareholders personally by improving the value of their shares. In *Greycon Ltd v Klaentschi (Sp C 372), [2003] SSCD 370*, it was held that the company's sole purpose in taking out key man policies was to meet a requirement of an agreement under which funding and other benefits were obtained from another company, that the policies had a capital purpose and that, consequently, the proceeds of those policies were not trading receipts. See generally HMRC Business Income Manual BIM 45525, 45530.

66.38 **National insurance contributions ('NICs').** Secondary (i.e. employers') Class 1 NICs are deductible in computing profits. Relief is similarly available for Class 1A NICs (payable by an employer where benefits-in-kind are provided to employees) and for Class 1B NICs (payable in respect of PAYE settlement agreements — see Tolley's Income Tax under Pay As You Earn). [*ICTA 1988, s 617(3)–(5); ITEPA 2003, Sch 6 para 87(3); ITTOIA 2005, Sch 1 para 262*].

66.39 **Payments for restrictive undertakings.** Payments to employees for restrictive undertakings, falling to be treated as earnings of the employee under *ITEPA 2003, s 225* (or, before 2003/04, *ICTA 1988, s 313*), are deductible in computing profits. [*FA 1988, s 73(2)–(4); ITEPA 2003, Sch 6 para 155; ITTOIA 2005, Sch 1 para 402*].

66.40 **Redundancy payments.** Redundancy payments, or other employer's payments, under *Employment Rights Act 1996* (or NI equivalent) are allowable. Rebates recoverable are trading receipts. [*ICTA 1988, ss 579, 580; ITEPA 2003, s 309, Sch 6 paras 63, 64; ITTOIA 2005, Sch 1 para 239*].

Non-statutory redundancy and similar payments are normally deductible unless made on the cessation of trading (but now see following paragraphs) (*CIR v Anglo-Brewing Co Ltd KB 1925, 12 TC 803*; *Godden v Wilson's Stores CA 1962, 40 TC 161*; *Geo Peters & Co v Smith Ch D 1963, 41 TC 264*) or as part of the bargain for the sale of shares of the company carrying on the business (*Bassett Enterprise Ltd v Petty KB 1938, 21 TC 730*; *James Snook & Co Ltd v Blasdale CA 1952, 33 TC 244*). See also *Overy v Ashford Dunn & Co KB 1933, 17 TC 497* and contrast *CIR v Patrick Thomson Ltd CS 1956, 37 TC 145*. A payment to secure the resignation of a life-director who had fallen out with his co-directors was allowed in *Mitchell v B W Noble Ltd CA 1927, 11 TC 372*. See also *O'Keeffe v Southport Printers Ltd Ch D 1984, 58 TC 88*. For provisions for future leaving payments see 66.28 above.

Payments made, to employees taken on for trade purposes, under a pre-existing contractual or statutory obligation which was a consequence of their being so taken on are not disallowed by virtue of the 'wholly and exclusively' rule at 66.18 above merely because it is the cessation of the trade that crystallises the liability to pay (Revenue Tax Bulletin February 1999 pp 630, 631).

Payments in addition to the statutory payment made on cessation of trading are allowable deductions if they would have been allowable had there been no cessation. Allowance is up to three times the statutory payment. Cessation of trade in this case includes a deemed discontinuance under *ICTA 1988, s 337(1)*. [*ICTA 1988, s 90; ITTOIA 2005, Sch 1 para 66*]. In practice, allowance is similarly given for such payments made on cessation of *part* of a trade. (HMRC Statement of Practice, SP 11/81). (For income purposes this is given statutory authority in *ITTOIA 2005, s 79* for 2005/06 onwards, see Change 18 in Annex 1 to the Explanatory Notes to the Income Tax (Trading and Other Income) Bill.)

A gratuitous payment made on partial cessation of a company's trade to a managing director who nevertheless continued thereafter to be a director was held non-deductible in *Relkobrook Ltd v Mapstone (Sp C 452), 2005 STI 158*.

Relief under *ICTA 1988, s 579 or s 90* (*as above*) is given for the period of account in which the payment is made (or, if paid after cessation, for the period of account in which falls the last day on which the trade is carried on). Where, instead, relief is due under general principles, a provision for future payments may be allowed as a deduction for a period of account provided that:

(*a*) it appears in the commercial accounts in accordance with generally accepted accounting principles;

(*b*) it was accurately calculated (normally requiring the identification of the individual employees affected) using the degree of hindsight permitted by SSAP 17;

(*c*) a definite decision to proceed with the redundancies was taken during the period; and

(*d*) payment was made within nine months of the end of the period.

(HMRC Business Income Manual BIM 46615).

See generally HMRC Business Income Manual BIM 46600–46615.

66.41 **Retirement and benevolent provisions.** See Tolley's Income Tax under Retirement Schemes and, for 2006/07 onwards, under Pension Provision after 5 April 2006 for the tax treatment of such schemes generally. The deductibility of payments by the employer under such schemes is set out below.

Pension provisions after 5 April 2006. For accounting periods ending after 5 April 2006 in relation to contributions to registered pension schemes, contributions made by an employer are deductible in computing profits for the period of account in which they are made (subject to the spreading provisions below). The contributions must meet the normal conditions for expenditure deductible in computing trading profits, in particular the 'wholly and exclusively' rule (see 66.18 above), but it is specifically provided that they are not treated as capital expenditure even if they would fall to be so treated under general principles.

Certain payments an employer may make to discharge his statutory obligations in relation to an under-funded defined benefits scheme are treated as contributions to the scheme for the above purposes and, if made after cessation of the employer's business, are treated as if made immediately before cessation. Otherwise, no sums other than contributions are deductible in connection with the cost of providing benefits under the employer pension scheme; this overrides any contrary rule that might apply under generally accepted accounting practice.

HMRC are empowered to make regulations (see *SI 2005 No 3458*) restricting the deductibility of contributions to a registered scheme in respect of an individual if the individual's benefits from the scheme are dependent on the non-payment of benefits from an employer pension scheme which is not a registered scheme or if the transfer value of the individual's rights under the registered scheme is reduced by virtue of benefits being payable out of the non-registered scheme.

Where the contributions paid by an employer in a period of account exceed 210% of the contributions paid in the previous period of account, relief for the excess contributions may fall to be spread over more than one period of account as follows. Firstly, identify the amount of current period contributions that exceeds 110% of previous period contributions (the '*relevant excess contributions*'). If this amount is less than £500,000, spreading does not apply. Otherwise, relief for the relevant excess contributions is spread over the current and following periods of account as follows.

Amount of relevant excess contributions	*Spread equally over*
£500,000 to £999,999 inclusive	2 periods of account
£1,000,000 to £1,999,999 inclusive	3 periods of account
£2,000,000 or more	4 periods of account

This has been HMRC practice but was given statutory effect by *FA 2004,s 197*. If the current and previous periods of account are unequal in length, the amount of the previous period contributions is adjusted proportionately in order to determine the excess (if any). Any contributions paid in the current period to fund cost of living increases in current pensions are disregarded in determining any excess, as are any contributions to fund a future service liability for employees joining the scheme in the current period. If the employer ceases business, such that some of the excess contributions would otherwise remain unrelieved, the otherwise unrelieved amount is relieved in the period of account which ends with the date of cessation or, at the employer's option, is apportioned on a daily basis over the whole of the spreading period up to the date of cessation.

[*FA 2004, ss 196–200; FA 2005, Sch 10 para 39; ITTOIA 2005, Sch 1 paras 646–649*].

See HMRC draft guidance on employers' contributions to registered pension schemes (available on their website at www.hmrc.gov.uk/practitioners/registered-contributions.htm) to be published in the HMRC Business Income Manual at BIM 46000 *et seq*.

Simon's Direct Tax Service. See E7.506.

Pension provision before 6 April 2006. Ordinary annual contributions to an exempt approved pension scheme are deductible in computing profits for the period of account in which they are made. It is specifically provided that they are not treated as capital expenditure even if they would fall to be so treated under general principles. In like manner, such contributions are deductible under *ICTA 1988, s 75* as management expenses of a company with investment business. A payment by the employer to the scheme discharging the employer's liability under *Social Security Pensions Act 1975, s 58B* or *Pension Schemes Act 1993, s 144* (or NI equivalent) is treated as a contribution to the scheme, and if the trade etc. has ceased before the payment is made, is deductible as if paid on the last day on which the trade etc. was carried on. Contributions other than ordinary annual contributions are also deductible, but HMRC may require the deduction to be spread over more than one year. Tax relief is given only for contributions actually paid, and not, for example, for any provision for such contributions. [*ICTA 1988, s 592(4)–(6A); SI 2004 No 2310, Sch para 30; SI 2004 No 3269*].

See HMRC Publication IR 12 para 5.7 *et seq*. and Pensions Update No 16, 30 May 1996 for practice on spreading of contributions (broadly over up to four years where special contributions amount to £500,000 or more in a chargeable period). A Revenue decision on spreading is not subject to review on appeal (*Kelsall v Investment Chartwork Ltd Ch D 1993, 65 TC 750*).

Where an employer's business changes hands see *Clarke v Musker Ch D 1956, 37 TC 1*. Legal and other expenses of establishing a scheme and running expenses of a revenue nature will be allowed. (HMRC Publication IR 12 paras 5.9, 5.10).

For repayments out of overfunded schemes, see Tolley's Income Tax under Retirement Schemes for Employees.

Expenses incurred in, or with a view to, providing benefits pursuant to a non-approved scheme, are not allowed as a deduction in computing trading income (nor, in the case of a company with investment business, as management expenses) unless the benefits are within the charge to income tax on receipt or payments made are treated as income when paid, and those exceptions do not apply unless the sums concerned have actually been expended. These restrictions do not, however, apply to contributions to overseas superannuation funds within *ICTA 1988, s 615(6)* or to certain retirement benefits schemes established outside the UK. [*FA 1989, s 76; FA 1996, Sch 39 para 2; ITEPA 2003, Sch 6 para 161; FA 2004, Sch 17 para 10(4); ITTOIA 2005, Sch 1 para 409; SI 2004 No 2310, Sch para 43*].

In cases not involving approved funds, a company's initial lump sum to cover past service on the setting up of a contributory pension scheme was disallowed as capital (*Atherton v British Insulated & Helsby Cables Ltd HL 1925, 10 TC 155*) as was a lump sum contribution to an employees' benevolent fund (*Rowntree & Co Ltd v Curtis CA 1924, 8 TC 678*). However, a series of payments to trustees to build up an indeterminate fund for the benefit of employees for whom pension arrangements might prove inadequate was allowable (*Jeffs v Ringtons Ltd Ch D 1985, 58 TC 680*). The cost of an annuity to replace a pension was allowed (*Hancock v General Reversionary & Investment Co Ltd KB 1918, 7 TC 358*) but not the cost of a policy for payment to a company of annuities equal to (allowable) pensions it paid (*Morgan Crucible Co Ltd v CIR KB 1932, 17 TC 311*). A gratuity on retirement was allowed (*Smith v Incorporated Council of Law Reporting KB 1914, 6 TC 477*) as was a lump sum in commutation of (allowable) premiums under a staff assurance scheme (*Green v Cravens Railway Wagon Co Ch D 1951, 32 TC 359*) but not premiums paid by a 'family company' to secure pensions for its directors (*Samuel Dracup & Sons Ltd v Dakin Ch D 1957, 37 TC 377*) nor payments to commute voluntary pensions on the cessation of trading (*Anglo Brewing Co Ltd KB 1925, 12 TC 803*).

A sum transferred from an unapproved fund on reconstruction to an approved was allowed (*Lowe v Peter Walker & R Cain CA 1935, 20 TC 25*).

Payments directly or indirectly for the benefit of employees are generally allowed as deductions, including donations to hospitals and charities, unless capital or abnormal (*Rowntree & Co v Curtis CA 1924, 8 TC 678*; *Bourne & Hollingsworth v Ogden KB 1929, 14 TC 349*). See also *Hutchinson & Co v Turner HC 1950, 31 TC 495*. Subscriptions to BUPA and similar group schemes for employees are deductible.

Simon's Direct Tax Service. See **E7.231, E7.257**.

66.42 **Training costs.** Costs incurred by an employer in respect of employee training are generally allowable as a trading expense. For a Revenue view of the circumstances in which such relief may be prohibited by the 'wholly and exclusively' rule at 66.18 above, see HMRC Business Income Manual BIM 35660.

Retraining course expenses paid or reimbursed by an employer and satisfying the conditions of the earnings exemption in *ITEPA 2003, s 311* (see Tolley's Income Tax under Employment Income) are deductible in computing the profits of the employer's trade (or as a management expense). Similar provisions relating to recovery of tax, information and penalties as apply in relation to the earnings exemption apply in relation to this deduction. (For income tax purposes for 2005/06 onwards, the entitlement to deduction is no longer dependent, in part, on the employee's exemption (see Change 17 listed in Annex 1 to the Explanatory Notes to the Income Tax (Trading and Other Income) Bill).) [*ICTA 1988, s 588; ITEPA 2003, Sch 6 para 67; ITTOIA 2005, Sch 1 para 250*]. See 66.81 below as regards contributions to training and enterprise councils.

66.43 EMPLOYEES (AND DIRECTORS): REMUNERATION

Bona fide remuneration is deductible including bonuses, commissions, tax deducted under PAYE and the cost of board, lodging, uniforms and benefits provided. The deduction is for the remuneration etc. payable; future payments cannot be anticipated (*Albion Rovers Football Club v CIR HL 1952, 33 TC 331*). The remuneration etc. must be shown to be wholly and exclusively for the purposes of the trade. In *Stott & Ingham v Trehearne KB 1924, 9 TC 69* an increase in the rate of commission payable to the trader's sons was disallowed as not on a commercial footing. See also *Johnson Bros & Co v CIR KB 1919, 12 TC 147*, *Copeman v Wm Flood & Sons Ltd KB 1940, 24 TC 53* and *Earlspring Properties Ltd v Guest CA 1995, 67 TC 259*. Payments by a farming couple to their young children for help on the farm were disallowed in *Dollar v Lyon Ch D 1981, 54 TC 459*. For excessive payments to 'service company' see *Payne, Stone Fraser* at 66.66 below. For wife's wages see *Thompson v Bruce KB 1927, 11 TC 607*; *Moschi v Kelly CA 1952, 33 TC 442*. The salary etc. of an employee for service in an overseas subsidiary was allowed in computing the profits of the parent in *Robinson v Scott Bader & Co Ltd CA 1981, 54 TC 757*. The secondment was wholly and exclusively for the purposes of the parent's business, notwithstanding the benefit to the subsidiary's business.

Any excess of the market value over the par value of shares issued to employees at par is not deductible (*Lowry v Consolidated African Selection Trust Ltd HL 1940, 23 TC 259*). For payments to trustees to acquire shares for the benefit of employees, see *Heather v P-E Consulting Group CA 1972, 48 TC 293*, *Jeffs v Ringtons Ltd Ch D 1985, 58 TC 680* and *E*

Bott Ltd v Price Ch D 1985, 59 TC 437, and contrast *Rutter v Charles Sharpe & Co Ltd Ch D 1979, 53 TC 163* and *Mawsley Machinery Ltd v Robinson (Sp C 170), [1998] SSCD 236*. See also 66.45 below.

Simon's Direct Tax Service. See B3.1336.

66.44 **Timing of deductions.** In calculating trading profits for a period of account, no deduction is allowed for an amount charged in the accounts in respect of employees' remuneration unless it is paid no later than nine months after the end of the period of account. Remuneration paid at a later time (and otherwise deductible) is deductible for the period of account *in which* it is paid. For these purposes, 'remuneration' includes any amount which is, or falls to be treated as, earnings for income tax purposes, and includes remuneration of office holders as well as other employees. Remuneration is treated as paid when it falls to be treated for tax purposes as received by the employee (see Tolley's Income Tax under Employment Income). These provisions apply whether the amount charged is in respect of particular employments or employments generally and apply equally to remuneration for which provision is made in the accounts (or, for periods ended before 27 November 2002 and see below under Employee benefit contributions, which is held by an intermediary) with a view to its becoming employees' remuneration. Computations prepared before the end of the said nine-month period must be prepared on the basis that any still unpaid remuneration will not be paid before the expiry of that nine-month period and thus will not be deductible for the period of account in question. If, in fact, such remuneration *is* paid by the end of the nine-month period, the computation may be adjusted accordingly on a claim being made to HMRC no later than two years after the end of the period of account in question. (For income tax purposes for 2005/06 onwards the matter may be dealt with by way of amendment to the self-assessment tax return (see Change 8 listed in Annex 1 to the Explanatory Notes to the Income Tax (Trading and Other Income) Bill).)

These provisions apply to non-trade businesses as they do to trades, professions and vocations. For accounting periods ending after 5 April 2003 but before 6 April 2004, due to a drafting error in *ITEPA 2003*, they did not apply to professions or vocations.

[*ITTOIA 2005, ss 36, 37, 865, Sch 2 para 12; FA 1989, s 43; ITEPA 2003, Sch 6 para 157; FA 2003, Sch 24 paras 10(1), 11; FA 2004, Sch 17 para 4*].

Similar provisions apply in relation to companies with investment business (for accounting periods beginning before 1 April 2004, to investment companies) and insurance companies. [*FA 1989, s 44; ITEPA 2003, Sch 6 para 158; FA 2003, Sch 24 para 10(1); SI 2004 No 2310, Sch para 42*].

Payments to an employee benefit trust were held to fall within these restrictions in *Dextra Accessories Ltd and Others v Macdonald HL, [2005] UKHL 47* (and see now below under Employee benefit contributions).

Employee benefit contributions. Legislation was introduced in *FA 2003* to 'counter the avoidance of tax and national insurance contributions (NICs) through the abuse of employee benefit trusts' (Pre-Budget Report Press Release REV/C&E 1, 27 November 2002). It provides rules for the timing of deductions for 'employee benefit contributions'. To this extent, these rules replace the timing rules described above. They apply in relation to deductions otherwise allowable in computing profits for periods ending after 26 November 2002 in respect of contributions made after that date. For these purposes, an '*employee benefit contribution*' is a payment of money, or the transfer of an asset, by the employer to a scheme manager (third party before 21 March 2007) (e.g. the trustees of an employee benefit trust) who is entitled or required, under the terms of an employee benefit scheme, to hold or use the money or asset to provide benefits to employees. A deduction is allowed only to the extent that, during the period in question or within nine months after the end of it, 'qualifying benefits' are provided, or 'qualifying expenses' are paid, out of the contributions. (If the employer's contribution is itself a qualifying benefit, it is sufficient that the contribution be made during the period or within those ensuing nine months.) Any amount thus disallowed remains available for deduction in any subsequent period during which it is used to provide qualifying benefits. For these purposes, qualifying benefits are treated as provided, and expenses are treated as paid, as far as possible out of employee benefit contributions, with no account being taken of any other receipts or expenses of the scheme manager (third party before 21 March 2007).

A '*qualifying benefit*' is a payment of money or transfer of assets (other than by way of loan) that gives rise to *both* a charge to tax on employment income and a charge to NICs (or would do so but for available exemptions for duties performed outside the UK) or is made in connection with termination of employment or (for 2006/07 onwards) is made under an employer-financed retirement benefits scheme. Money benefits are treated for these purposes as provided at the time the money is treated as received (See Tolley's Income Tax under Employment Income for the rules). '*Qualifying expenses*' are those expenses (if any) of the scheme manager (third party before to 21 March 2007) in operating the scheme that would have been deductible in computing profits if incurred by the employer. Where a qualifying benefit takes the form of the transfer of an asset, the amount provided is the aggregate of the amount that would otherwise be deductible by the employer (in a case where the scheme manager (or third party) acquired the asset from the employer) and the amount expended on the asset by the scheme manager (or third party). If, however, the amount charged to tax under *ITEPA 2003* (or which would be so charged if the duties of employment were performed in the UK) is lower than that aggregate, any amount deductible under these provisions at any time is limited to that lower amount; this rule is aimed at a situation where the asset falls in value after its acquisition by the third party but before its transfer to the employee (Treasury Explanatory Notes to Finance Bill 2003).

These restrictions do not apply to disallow deductions for consideration given for goods or services provided in the course of a trade or profession, contributions to a retirement benefits scheme, approved personal pension scheme, registered pension scheme, qualifying overseas pension scheme (if the employee is a relevant migrant member — see Tolley's Income Tax under Pension Provision after 5 April 2006) or accident benefit scheme (as defined).

Computations prepared before the end of the said nine-month period must be prepared by reference to the facts at the time of computation. If any contributions are used for qualifying purposes after that time, but within the nine months, the computation may be adjusted accordingly (subject to the normal time limits for amending self-assessment tax returns).

[*FA 2003, s 143, Sch 24; SI 2004 No 2310, Sch para 71; FA 2007, s 34(1)–(6), 13*].

For the receipts basis generally, see Tolley's Income Tax under Employment Income.

66.45 EMPLOYEE SHARE SCHEMES

For accounting periods beginning on or after 1 January 2003 (subject to transitional provisions, see below), corporation tax relief is available for a company (the 'employing company') where, by reason of an employment with that company (whether it is his or another person's employment), a person either acquires shares (an 'award of shares'), or obtains an option to acquire shares in pursuance of which he acquires shares (the 'grant of an option'). 'Employment' for this purpose includes former or prospective employment, the holding of an office, and being a member of a company whose affairs are managed by the members. 'Shares' includes stock and an interest in shares or stock.

There are special provisions (for which see below) where the shares acquired are 'restricted shares' or 'convertible shares'.

The person acquiring the shares or obtaining the option is referred to below as the 'recipient', and the employee by reference to whose employment the shares are acquired or the option granted as the 'employee'.

The relief is dependent on the following requirements being met.

(*a*) The business for the purposes of which the award or grant is made must be carried on by the employing company and be within the charge to corporation tax (which it is if, or to the extent that, it is carried on by a company within the charge to corporation tax in respect of profits of the business).

(*b*) The shares acquired must be irredeemable, ordinary, fully paid-up shares and either:

(i) of a class listed on a recognised stock exchange (see 16.6 CLOSE COMPANIES); or

(ii) in a company not under the control (within *ICTA 1988, s 840*) of another company; or

(iii) in a company under the control of a company (not being a close company (see 16 CLOSE COMPANIES) or a company which would be a close company if UK-resident) whose shares are listed on a recognised stock exchange.

(*c*) The company whose shares are acquired must be:

(i) the employing company; or

(ii) a company of which (at the time of the award or grant) the employing company is a 51% subsidiary; or

(iii) a company which (at the time of the award or grant) is a member of a consortium which owns a company within (i) or (ii); or

(iv) a company which (at the time of the award or grant) is a member of a consortium of which a company within (i) or (ii) is also a member at that time, and is also a member of the same 'commercial association of companies' as another company owned by the consortium; or

(v) a company which has a 51% subsidiary within (iv); or

(vi) (in relation to the grant of an option but *not* an award of shares), a 'qualifying successor company' (see below).

(*d*) The employee must, in the case of an award of shares, be subject to an income tax charge under *ITEPA 2003* in respect of the award, or would be so chargeable if, at all material times, the employee was UK-resident and ordinarily resident and the duties of the employment were performed in the UK. (See, however, below for the special rules applying in the case of awards of restricted shares.) In the case of the grant of an option, the requirement is that the acquisition of shares pursuant to the option is a chargeable event within *ITEPA 2003, s 476* in relation to the employee (whether or not any employment income thereby arises), or would be such a chargeable event if the employee was UK-resident and ordinarily resident and the duties of the employment were performed in the UK. If the shares are acquired pursuant to the option after the death of the employee, this condition is treated as met if it would have been were the employee still alive.

As regards (*c*)(iii) and (iv) above, a company is a member of a consortium owning another company if it is one of five or fewer companies which between them beneficially own at least 75% of that company's ordinary share capital, with each of them so owning at least 10%. As regards (*c*)(iv), a '*commercial association of companies*' means a company together with such of its associated companies (within *ICTA 1988, s 416*) as carry on businesses which are of such a nature that the businesses of the company and those associated companies, taken together, may reasonably be considered to make up a single composite undertaking.

Award of shares. Subject to the special rules for 'restricted' or 'convertible' shares (see below), the amount of relief is equal to the difference between the market value of the shares at the time of the award and the total amount or value of any consideration given in respect of the shares, by whomsoever given, with just and reasonable apportionment of any consideration given only partly in respect of the shares. Excluded from such consideration, however, is the performance of duties of, or in connection with, the employee's employment with the employing company. Just and reasonable apportionment also applies to the amount of the relief if the award was made only partly for the purposes of a business within (*a*) above.

Grant of option. Subject to the special rules for 'restricted' or 'convertible' shares (see below), the amount of relief is equal to the difference between the market value of the shares at the time they are acquired pursuant to the option and the total amount or value of any consideration given in respect of the grant of the option or the acquisition of the shares, by whomsoever given, with just and reasonable apportionment of any consideration given only partly in respect of the grant or acquisition. Excluded from such consideration, however, are the performance of duties of, or in connection with, the employee's employment with the employing company, and certain employer national insurance contributions which the employee has elected to pay. Just and reasonable apportionment also applies to the amount of the relief if the option was granted only partly for the purposes of a business within (*a*) above. Where shares are acquired pursuant to an option after the death of the employee, (*d*) above is treated as met if it would have been were the employee still alive. Similarly where the shares are acquired after the death of the option holder, the current provisions apply as if he were still alive and the shares were acquired by him.

Where another company obtains control (within *ICTA 1988, s 840*) of a company whose shares are the subject of an option within these provisions, and the option holder and the acquiring company agree to roll over the rights into a new option relating to shares in a 'qualifying company' (the '*qualifying successor company*' in (*c*)(vi) above), the new option stands in the shoes of the old as far as the application of the current provisions is concerned. A '*qualifying company*' is a company meeting conditions (*c*)(i)–(v) above as they apply to an employing company.

How relief is given. Subject to the special rules for restricted and convertible shares (see below), for both awards and option grants, the amount of the relief is allowable as a deduction for corporation tax purposes (as a management expense in the case of a company with investment business (or, for accounting periods beginning before 1 April 2004, an investment company), or as an expense of an insurance company carrying on life assurance business) for the accounting period in which the recipient acquires a beneficial interest in the shares, rather than that in which they are conveyed or transferred (if different). A just and reasonable apportionment is made where the award or grant was made for the purposes of more than one business within the charge to corporation tax.

Transfer of business within a group. There is special provision for relief under the current provisions to be given to a successor company (or companies) where, between the award of the shares, or the grant of the option, and the occurrence of the event which determines for which accounting period the relief is available, the whole, or substantially the whole, of the business for the purposes of which the award or grant was made is transferred intra-group to the successor company (or companies). Companies are for this purpose members of the same group if one is a 51% subsidiary of the other or both are 51% subsidiaries of a third company.

Relationship with other deductions. A deduction under *ICTA 1988, Sch 4AA, para 2, 3, 9* or *10(3)* (in relation to a share incentive plan) is given in priority to relief under the current provisions, and no relief is available under the current provisions in respect of shares in relation to which a deduction is allowable, or has been made, under any of those provisions. Where relief under the current provisions *is* available, no other corporation tax deduction is allowed to any company in respect of expenses directly related to the provision of the shares, including any amount paid or payable by the employing company in respect of the employee's participation in an employee share scheme. This does *not* exclude relief for the expenses of establishing the employee share scheme under which the shares are acquired, or of meeting or contributing to its administration costs, or of borrowing for the purposes of the scheme, or for fees, commission, stamp duty or similar incidental expenses of acquiring the shares.

[*FA 2003, Sch 22 paras 59–67, 70–73, Sch 23 paras 1–17, 23–32; SI 2004 No 2310, Sch paras 69, 70*].

Restricted shares. Special rules apply to awards of 'restricted shares' or their acquisition pursuant to the grant of an option. Shares are '*restricted shares*' if they are restricted securities (or a restricted interest in securities) within *ITEPA 2003, ss 423, 424* (as amended by *FA 2003, Sch 22 para 3*). The requirement at (*d*) above (as regards the income tax position of the employee) is replaced in the case of awards of restricted shares by a requirement that the employee must either be subject to an income tax charge under *ITEPA 2003, Pt 3 Ch 1* in respect of the award or, not being subject to such a charge, will be subject to a charge by virtue of *ITEPA 2003, s 426* (or would be but for the death of the employee) on the occurrence of a chargeable event under that section in relation to the shares (or in either case would be so chargeable if the residence and place of performance conditions in (*d*) above were met).

The relief is available on the award of the shares or their acquisition pursuant to the option, or on any chargeable event within *ITEPA 2003, s 426* in relation to the shares, or on the death of the employee. Determination of the amount and timing of the relief in each of those situations is set out in *FA 2003, Sch 23 paras 21(3)–(11), 22* as inserted by *FA 2003, Sch 22 para 68* and amended by *FA 2006, s 93(2)* in relation to shares beneficially acquired after 31 August 2003.

[*FA 2003, Sch 22 para 68, Sch 23 paras 18–22; FA 2004, Sch 16 para 5; FA 2006, s 93*].

Convertible shares. Special rules apply to awards of 'convertible shares' or their acquisition pursuant to the grant of an option. Shares are '*convertible shares*' if they are convertible securities (or an interest in convertible securities) within *ITEPA 2003, s 436* (as amended by *FA 2003, Sch 22 para 4*), and for certain purposes convertible securities which are *not* shares are taken to be convertible shares.

The relief is available on the award of the shares or their acquisition pursuant to the option, or on any chargeable event in relation to the shares, or on the death of the employee. Determination of the amount and timing of the relief in each of those situations is set out in *FA 2003, Sch 23 paras 22C(3)–(11), 22D* as inserted by *FA 2003, Sch 22 para 69* and amended by *FA 2006, s 93(3)* in relation to shares beneficially acquired after 31 October 2003.

[*FA 2003, Sch 22 para 69, Sch 23 paras 22A–22D; FA 2004, Sch 16 para 5; FA 2006, s 93*].

Transitional provisions. Relief is not available under the current provisions to the extent that a deduction is available or has been made to any company in respect of expenses referable, directly or indirectly, to the provision of the same shares for an accounting period beginning before 1 January 2003. Provision is also made for the application of the predecessor provisions to those in *ITEPA 2003* to apply where relevant. [*FA 2003, Sch 23 para 33*].

The changes to the employee securities and options provisions brought in by *FA 2003, Sch 22* required significant consequential changes to the current provisions to ensure that the relief is not adversely affected. These generally apply from the day appointed by the Treasury for the purpose, and have been incorporated in the above coverage. For the current provisions as they applied before those changes, see *FA 2003, Sch 23* disregarding the amendments to it by *FA 2003, Sch 22*. The application of the relief is broadly unaffected.

Transfer pricing. For an article on the interaction of the new provisions with the transfer pricing rules (see 67 TRANSFER PRICING), see Revenue Tax Bulletin February 2003 pp 1002–1007.

66.46 **Share incentive plans.** Subject to the exceptions below, the following are allowable deductions in computing company trading profits (or as management expenses in the case of companies with investment business or as expenses of an insurance company) in connection with an approved share incentive plan within *ITEPA 2003, Sch 2* (see Tolley's Income Tax under Share-Related Employment Income and Exemptions):

(*a*) the market value (at time of acquisition by the plan trustees, and see below) of free and matching shares awarded to employees under the plan (the deduction being given *to the employer company* for the period of account in which the shares are awarded);

(*b*) any excess of the market value (at time of acquisition by the plan trustees, and determined as for capital gains tax purposes) of partnership shares over the amounts paid by participating employees to acquire them (the deduction being given *to the employer company* for the period of account in which the shares are acquired on participants' behalf);

(*c*) expenditure incurred by a company in establishing a plan (the deduction being given for the period of account in which the expenditure is incurred, unless HMRC approve the plan more than nine months after the end of that period, in which case the deduction is given for the period of account in which approval is given);

(*d*) contributions by a company to the expenses of plan trustees in operating a plan, *excluding* expenses in acquiring shares (other than incidental costs such as fees, commission, stamp duty etc.) but *including* interest on money borrowed to acquire shares.

Once a deduction is made under (*a*) or (*b*) above, no other deduction (other than any within (*c*) or (*d*) above) may be made by the employer company or any associated company (as defined) in respect of the provision of the shares, and no deduction within (*a*) or (*b*) above may then be made by any other company in that respect. Once a deduction is made under (*c*) above, no other deduction may be made in respect of the costs of setting up the plan.

For the purposes of (*a*) above, market value is determined as for capital gains tax purposes, and, for the purposes of that determination (and also for those of (iii) below), shares acquired by the trustees on different days are deemed to be awarded under the plan on a first in/first out basis. In the case of a group plan (i.e. a plan established by a parent company and extending to one or more companies under its control), the total market value of the shares awarded is apportioned between the relevant employer companies by reference to the number of shares awarded to the employees of each company.

No deduction is allowed under (*a*) or (*b*) above:

(i) in respect of shares awarded to an individual whose earnings from the eligible employment are not, at the time of the award, taxable earnings (whether or not subject to the remittance basis as regards overseas earnings);

(ii) in respect of shares that are liable to depreciate substantially in value for reasons that do not apply generally to shares in the company;

(iii) if a deduction has been made (on whatever basis), by the company, or an associated company (as defined) in respect of providing the same shares for the plan trust or for another trust (whatever its nature or purpose); or

(iv) in respect of the subsequent award of shares previously forfeited by participants (such shares being treated as acquired by the trustees at time of forfeit for no consideration).

No deduction is allowed under (*c*) above if any employee acquires rights under the plan, or the trustees acquire any shares, before the plan receives Revenue approval. Subject to (*d*) above, no deduction is allowed for expenses in providing dividend shares.

On withdrawal of HMRC approval to a plan, HMRC may, by notice, direct that any deductions made under (*a*) or (*b*) above be withdrawn also, in which case the aggregate deductions made are treated as a trading receipt of the company concerned for the period of account in which HMRC notify withdrawal of approval (or, in the case of an investment company, as income chargeable under Schedule D, Case VI arising at the time of notice of withdrawal). See Tolley's Income Tax under Share-Related Employment Income and Exemptions for right of appeal.

A payment made after 5 April 2003 by the employer company to the trustees sufficient to enable them to acquire (other than from a company) a significant block of shares (at least 10% of the employer company's ordinary share capital) attracts a deduction (in computing trading profits etc.) which, in contrast to the above, is not deferred until the shares are awarded to employees. The deduction falls to be given for the period of account in which falls the first anniversary of the date of acquisition, provided the 10% requirement is then met. The deduction will, however, be clawed back unless at least 30% of those shares are awarded within five years of acquisition by the trustees and all of the shares are awarded within ten years; if all the shares are subsequently awarded, the deduction is reinstated at that later time. An appropriate proportion of the original deduction is also subject to clawback if the plan terminates before all the shares have been awarded or if shares are awarded to an individual within (i) above. In the event of HMRC withdrawing their approval to the plan, the same provisions apply as above as regards potential withdrawal of deductions.

[*ICTA 1988, s 85B, Sch 4AA; FA 2000, Sch 8 paras 2(1), 3(1), 105–114, 121(10)(11), 125, 126; ITEPA 2003, Sch 2 paras 92, 94, Sch 6 paras 12, 109; SI 2004 No 2310, Sch para 35*].

66.47 **Employee share ownership trusts.** A UK resident company may obtain relief under Schedule D as a trading expense (or as a management expense) in respect of contributions in an accounting period beginning **before 1 January 2003** to the trustees of a trust which is a 'qualifying ESOP trust', provided that at least some of the company's employees (or those of a company it controls (within *ICTA 1988, s 840*)) are eligible to benefit from the trust. The relief must be claimed within two years of the end of the period of account, and is given only if the payment is used by the trustees, within nine months of the end of the period of account (or such longer time as HMRC may allow), for any of the following purposes:

(*a*) the acquisition of shares in the company which established the trust;

(*b*) the repayment of borrowings;

(*c*) the payment of interest on borrowings;

(*d*) the payment of sums to beneficiaries;

(*e*) the meeting of expenses (including payment of income tax or capital gains tax — see HMRC Business Income Manual BIM 44025).

Contributions received are deemed to be used first to meet expenditure for qualifying purposes, expenditure for non-qualifying purposes being treated as far as possible as met out of other income (e.g. dividends or interest) (HMRC Business Income Manual BIM 44030).

In view of the new statutory deduction for the cost of providing shares for employee share schemes (see above), this relief is repealed in respect of contributions made in company accounting periods beginning on or after 1 January 2003.

[*FA 1989, s 67; FA 2003, s 142(1)*].

A charge to tax to be made, in certain circumstances, on the trustees, but recoverable also from the company if not paid within six months of becoming final and conclusive, where the above relief has previously been given. [*FA 1989, s 68; ITTOIA 2005, Sch 1 para 407*].

Expenditure on establishing a QUEST is deductible in computing the company's trading profits (or, in the case of a company with investment business, is deductible as a management expense). If the deed establishing the trust is executed more than nine months after the end of the period of account in which the expenditure is incurred, it is treated as incurred in the period in which the deed is executed. [*ICTA 1988, s 85A; SI 2004 No 2310, Sch para 6*].

See Tolley's Income Tax under Qualifying Employee Share Ownership Trusts for the definition of a QUEST), for the charge on trustees and for certain information requirements relating to trustees. See Tolley's Capital Gains Tax under Shares and Securities for details of a limited rollover relief on sale of shares to the trustees of such a trust in *TCGA 1992, ss 227–235*.

Non-qualifying employee share ownership trusts. For the treatment of contributions to employee share ownership trusts not within the above provisions which are not capital expenditure on general principles but which are required under UITF 13 to be treated as giving rise to an asset in the employer's accounts, see Revenue Tax Bulletin February 1997 pp 399, 400. Broadly, relief for the contributions is deferred until the rights in the shares are transferred to employees, although this would not prevent a deduction for a properly calculated provision reflecting employees' accruing entitlement to such benefits.

66.48 **Profit sharing and share option schemes.** Expenditure on establishing an approved profit sharing scheme, SAYE option scheme or CSOP scheme (see Tolley's Income Tax under Share-Related Employment Income and Exemptions) is deductible in computing the company's trading profits (or, in the case of a company with investment business, is deductible as a management expense) provided that:

(*a*) in the case of a profit sharing scheme, the trustees acquire no shares under the scheme before it is approved; or

(*b*) in the case of a SAYE or CSOP scheme, no employee or director obtains rights under the scheme before it is approved.

If the scheme is approved more than nine months after the end of the period of account in which the expenditure is incurred, it is for these purposes treated as incurred in the period in which the approval is given. (Note that, under the provisions for phasing out approved profit sharing schemes, HMRC will not approve a scheme unless the application was received by them before 6 April).

[*ICTA 1988, s 84A; ITEPA 2003, Sch 6 para 11; SI 2004 No 2310, Sch para 4*].

In the case of an approved profit sharing scheme, a similar deduction is available for payments made to the scheme trustees which are either (i) necessary to meet their reasonable administration expenses or (ii) applied by them, within nine months after the end of the period of account in which the expense is charged (or such longer time as HMRC may allow), in acquiring shares for appropriation to participants. As a consequence of the phasing out of approved profit sharing schemes, no deduction is available under (i) above for any payment made more than three years after the last appropriation made in accordance with the scheme before 1 January 2003. Similarly, no deduction is available under (ii) above for (1) any payment made after 5 April 2002 or (2) any payment made after 20 March 2000 and before 6 April 2002 unless the shares thus acquired are appropriated no later than nine months after the end of the period of account in which the payment was made and before 1 January 2003. [*ICTA 1988, s 85; FA 2000, s 50; SI 2004 No 2310, Sch para 5*].

66.49 ENTERTAINMENT AND GIFTS

Subject to the exceptions below, no deduction is allowed in computing profits for expenses incurred in providing entertainment (including hospitality oif any kind) or gifts. This includes sums paid to or on behalf of an employee (including a director), or put at the employee's disposal, *exclusively* for meeting expenses incurred, or to be incurred, by the employee in providing the entertainment or gift. (See Tolley's Income Tax under Employment Income for the employee position.) It also includes expenses incidental to providing entertainment or gifts.

Entertainment expenditure is not within the above prohibition if:

- the entertainment is of a kind which it is the trader's trade to provide and it is provided in the ordinary course of that trade either for payment or free of charge for advertising purposes; or
- the entertainment is provided for the trader's employees (except where such entertainment is incidental to the entertainment of non-employees).

Gifts are not within the above prohibition if:

- they are of an item which it is the trader's trade to provide and are made for advertising purposes; or
- they incorporate a conspicuous advertisement for the trader *and* do not consist of food, drink, tobacco or a token or voucher exchangeable for goods *and* the cost to the trader of all such gifts to the same person in the same basis period does not exceed £50 (£10 for 2000/01 and earlier years); or
- they are provided for the trader's employees (except where such gifts are incidental to the providing of gifts for non-employees); or
- they are made to a charity or to either of the similar organisations specified in *ICTA 1988, s 577(9)*.

[*ICTA 1988, s 577; CAA 2001, Sch 2 para 51; FA 2001, s 73; ITEPA 2003, Sch 6 para 62; SI 2004 No 2310, Sch para 23; ITTOIA 2005, Sch 1 para 235*].

Deductions were allowed for items provided in the ordinary course of a trade of providing entertainment (see *Fleming v Associated Newspapers Ltd HL 1972, 48 TC 382*) or provided gratuitously for advertising to the public generally. [*ICTA 1988, s 577(10)*]. See also the VAT cases of *C & E Commissioners v Shaklee International and Another CA, [1981] STC 776* and *Celtic Football and Athletic Co Ltd v C & E Commissioners CS, [1983] STC 470*. There is also a restriction on capital allowances where plant or machinery is used to provide entertainment, with similar exceptions as above where relevant (see 10.24 CAPITAL ALLOWANCES).

For an article on the scope and application of these rules, see Revenue Tax Bulletin August 1999 pp 679–682 as supplemented by Revenue Tax Bulletin February 2000 p 729. For further comprehensive guidance on business entertainment, see HMRC Business Income Manual BIM 45000–45090.

Simon's Direct Tax Service. See **B3.1437, B3.1370**.

66.50 FARMING AND MARKET GARDENING

Farming or market gardening in the UK is treated for corporation tax purposes as trading. All the UK farming carried on by a particular person (other than as part of a different trade) is treated as a single trade. Farming carried on by a partnership of which a company is partner is, however, separate from any farming carried on by individual partners. This does not apply to the woodlands or to land being prepared for forestry use. [*ICTA 1988, ss 53(1)(2), 832(1); ITTOIA 2005, Sch 1 para 32*]. See *Bispham v Eardiston Farming Co Ch D 1962, 40 TC 322* and *Sargent v Eayrs Ch D 1972, 48 TC 573*. The matters listed below are of particular application to farming or (where relevant) market gardening.

(*a*) **Compensation for compulsory slaughter.** Where compensation is received for compulsory slaughter of animals to which the herd basis (see 55.10 PROFIT COMPUTATIONS) does not and could not apply, any excess of the amount received over the book value or cost of those animals may, by concession, be excluded from the year of receipt and treated, by equal instalments, as profits of the next three years. (HMRC Extra Statutory Concession, B11). (In practice, the profit on an animal born in the year of slaughter is deemed to be 25% of the compensation received.) For a worked example of this spreading relief, see HMRC Business Income Manual BIM 55185; see also Revenue Tax Bulletin October 2001 p 890 as regards certain aspects of the concession, in particular with regard to its application during the 2001 foot and mouth outbreak.

Compensation paid under the BSE Suspects Scheme and the BSE Selective Cull (where the animal was born after 14 October 1990) is for compulsory slaughter, and for these purposes includes Selective Cull 'top-up' payments. Payments under the Calf Processing Scheme, the Over Thirty Month Scheme and the BSE Selective Cull where the animal was born before 15 October 1990 are *not* for compulsory slaughter. (Revenue Tax Bulletin February 1997 pp 396, 397).

(*b*) **Drainage.** Where land is made re-available for cultivation by the restoration of drainage or by re-draining, the net expenditure incurred (after crediting any grants receivable) will be allowed as revenue expenditure in farm accounts provided it excludes (i) any substantial element of improvement (e.g. the substitution of tile drainage for mole drainage) and (ii) the capital element in cases in which the present owner is known to have acquired the land at a depressed price because of its swampy condition (HMRC Statement of Practice, SP 5/81).

(*c*) **Farmhouses.** The apportionment of the running costs of a farmhouse between business and private use should be based on the facts of the case for the year of account in question (HMRC Business Income Manual BIM 55250).

Maintenance expenses of owner-occupied farms not carried on on a commercial basis. Where a loss claim was precluded by *ICTA 1988, ss 393A(3), 397* (see 47.9, 47.14 LOSSES), relief for maintenance etc. of land, houses etc. could be claimed under *ICTA 1988, s 33*. Despite the repeal of *section 33* for corporation tax purposes from 1 April 1998, HMRC still allowed relief to be claimed, by virtue of this concession, for expenditure which would have qualified under *section 33* had it still been in force. The concession was withdrawn after 31 March 2001. (HMRC Business Income Manual BIM 75610).

(*d*) **Foot and mouth outbreak.** For the special measures for the 2001 outbreak, see Revenue Tax Bulletin Special Edition May 2001 and Revenue Tax Bulletin October 2001 pp 890, 891. For 2007 outbreak, see HMRC news release 8 August 2007.

(*e*) **Grants and subsidies.** See generally 66.77 below. As regards the time at which a receipt should be brought in for tax purposes, a distinction should be drawn between grants to meet particular costs and those subsidising the sale proceeds of a specific crop. The former should reduce the costs in question (and if those costs are included in the closing stock valuation, the net cost should be used), whereas the latter should be recognised as income of the year in which the crop is sold. (Revenue Tax Bulletin February 1993 p 53). A grant subsidising trading income generally is a trading receipt of the period when the entitlement to the grant was established, provided that it can be quantified with reasonable accuracy. As regards instalments of grant, the tax treatment should follow accounting practice, which provides that information available before accounts are completed and signed should be taken into account as regards those to which entitlement arose in the period of account. (Revenue Tax Bulletin February 1994 p 108).

As regards animal grants and subsidies, these are generally recognised either at the end of the retention period or on receipt. Either of these bases will be accepted for tax purposes provided that it is consistently applied, as will any other basis which reflects generally accepted accounting practice provided that it does not conflict with tax law. A change of basis should be made only where the need for change outweighs the requirement for accounts to be prepared on a consistent basis, and will be dealt with in accordance with HMRC Statement of Practice SP 3/90 (see 66.75 below). (Revenue Tax Bulletin December 1994 p 182).

The following relate to specific types of farm support payment.

(i) *Advances under British Sugar Industry (Assistance) Act 1931*, linked with sugar production and prices, were held to be assessable as trading receipts (*Smart v Lincolnshire Sugar Co Ltd HL 1937, 20 TC 643*).

(ii) *Arable area payments*. Payments under the 1992 scheme for land set aside may be treated as sales subsidies, and hence recognised when the crops are sold. Valuations based on 75% of market value (see (*i*) below) should include the same proportion of the related arable area payments. (Revenue Tax Bulletin February 1994 p 109). See (*f*)(v) below for specific comment on oilseed support payments.

(iii) *Dairy herd conversion scheme*. Grants for changing from dairying to meat production were held to be assessable as trading receipts (*White v G & M Davis Ch D 1979, 52 TC 597*; *CIR v Biggar CS 1982, 56 TC 254*).

(iv) *Flood rehabilitation grants* in excess of rehabilitation costs (admitted to be capital) were held to be capital receipts (*Watson v Samson Bros Ch D 1959, 38 TC 346*).

(v) *Oilseed support scheme*. Payments of aid under the 1992 scheme are a subsidy towards the selling price, and as such should be recognised as income at the time of sale. If the final amount is not known when the accounts are prepared, but it is reasonably certain that a further payment will be received, the tax computations should be kept open to admit the final figure. If a reasonable estimate is included in the accounts and the difference when the final amount is known has only a small effect on the overall tax liability, the inspector may agree to recognise the difference in arriving at profits of the following year. (Revenue Tax Bulletin February 1993 p 53).

(vi) *Ploughing subsidies* were held to be assessable as trading receipts (*Higgs v Wrightson KB 1944, 26 TC 73*).

(*f*) **Milk.** *Superlevy*. HMRC's view is that superlevy is an allowable trading deduction, but that the purchase of additional quota to avoid superlevy does not give rise to a deduction for either the superlevy thus avoided or the sum which would have been paid to lease rather than purchase the additional quota. (HMRC Business Income Manual BIM 55340 and BIM 55315).

Residuary Milk Marketing Board receipts. B Reserve Fund distributions and sums repaid to producers under the Rolling Fund arrangements on the flotation of Dairy Crest (in the latter case whether taken in cash or in shares) are income receipts of the trade. Any element of a B Reserve Fund payment described as interest may also be treated as a trade receipt. Post-cessation treatment (see 66.3 above) will apply where appropriate. (Revenue Tax Bulletin August 1997 p 461).

Milk Marque Ltd shares. Bonus preference shares (or loan stock) issued in October 1998 to dairy farmers supplying the company form part of the trading receipts of the farmer, the appropriate measure of the income (and of the capital gains tax base cost) being the nominal value of the shares (Revenue Tax Bulletin August 1999 p 685).

For capital gains tax considerations generally, see Tolley's Capital Gains Tax under Assets and Rollover Relief.

(*g*) **Share farming.** HMRC consider that both parties to a share farming agreement based on the Country Landowners Association model may be considered to be carrying on a farming trade for tax purposes. In the case of the landowner, he must take an active part in the share farming venture, at least to the extent of concerning himself with details of farming policy and exercising his right to enter onto his land for some material purpose, even if only for the purposes of inspection and policy-making. (Country Landowners Association Press Release 19 December 1991).

(*h*) **Short rotation coppice.** The cultivation of 'short rotation coppice' (i.e. a perennial crop of tree species planted at high density, the stems of which are harvested above ground level at intervals of less than ten years) is treated for tax purposes as farming and not as forestry, so that UK land under such cultivation is farm or agricultural land and not woodlands. [*FA 1995, s 154; ITTOIA 2005, Sch 1 para 481*]. For HMRC's view of the taxation implications of short rotation coppice, see HMRC Business Income Manual BIM 55120.

(*i*) **Stock valuations.** See 55.10 PROFIT COMPUTATIONS for the herd basis, and, for trading stock generally, 66.75 below. In general, livestock is treated as trading stock unless the herd basis applies, and home-bred animals may be valued, if there is no adequate record of cost, at 75% for sheep and pigs (60% for cattle) of open market value. Dead stock may be taken at 75% of market value.

Where an animal grant or subsidy for which application has been made has not been taken into account for a particular period but has been applied for, and that application materially affects the value of the animal, the grant or subsidy should be taken into account as a supplement to the market value when deemed cost is computed. Grants or subsidies applied for but not recognised as income in the period concerned should also be taken into account in arriving at net realisable value for stock valuation purposes. (Revenue Tax Bulletin December 1994 p 182).

(*j*) **Subscriptions** to the **National Farmers Union** are allowable in full.

(*k*) **Sugar beet outgoers scheme.** Receipts and payments derived from the disposal of contract tonneage entitlement under contracts between farmers and British Sugar are to be dealt with on revenue and not capital account, i.e. as taxable receipts and allowable deductions in computing profits. Payments for entitlement which are amortised in the accounts over the period for which the entitlement may reasonably be expected to be of value to the business are similarly allowed for tax purposes. (Revenue Tax Bulletin October 2001 pp 891, 892).

(*l*) **Trading profits.** Proceeds from the sale of trees (mostly willows planted by the taxpayer) were held to be farming receipts (*Elmes v Trembath KB 1934, 19 TC 72*), but no part of the cost of an orchard with nearly ripe fruit purchased by a fruit grower was an allowable deduction in computing his profits, which included receipts from the sale of the fruit (*CIR v Pilcher CA 1949, 31 TC 314*). Proceeds from sales of turf were held to be trading receipts from farming (*Lowe v J W Ashmore Ltd Ch D 1970, 46 TC 597*).

(*m*) **Woodlands grants.** The Forestry Commission's Woodland Grant Scheme (WGS) provides grants for the establishment and maintenance of woodlands. These grants are not taxable. Where the woodland concerned is being established on agricultural land, WGS participants can also apply to join the Farm Woodland Premium Scheme (FWPS). This is administered by the Department for Environment, Food and Rural Affairs (Defra) and provides annual payments of up to £300 per hectare for up to 15 years to the farmer to compensate for lost farming income as a result of converting the land to woodland. Because the annual payments are made in lieu of farming income, they must be included in trading profits and are chargeable to income tax. (Sources: Defra and HMRC Business Income Manual BIM 55165).

For these and other aspects of farming taxation, see HMRC Business Income Manual BIM 55000–55730, 73000–73190 and 75600–75650.

Simon's Direct Tax Service. See **B3.5**.

66.51 FILMS AND SOUND RECORDINGS

A new regime (the 'FA 2006 regime') for film production companies applies in relation to films that commence principal photography on or after 1 January 2007, or expenditure incurred on or after 31 March 2008 (whenever the film is made).

The *FA 2006* regime is as set out at 66.52 below. The previous provisions (the 'pre-*FA 2006* regime', described at 66.53 below) for corporation tax relief no longer apply to production expenditure on films commencing principal photography after 31 December 2006. Relief under the old rules is available for acquisition expenditure on films commencing principal photography before 1 January 2007 where expenditure is incurred before **1 October 2007**, thereafter, relief being available under the rules for INTANGIBLE ASSETS (39). Relief for preliminary expenditure under the old rules no longer applies to expenditure incurred after 19 July 2006. Further regulations are expected and the dates may be deferred by these.

[*FA 2006, ss 46, 47, 53; SI 2006 No 3265; SI 2006 No 3399*].

The Treasury have powers to make provision, by order (approved by a resolution of the House of Commons), regarding the tax treatment of films which have commenced principal photography before 1 January 2007 but are not completed by a date to be specified. [*FA 2006, s 52*].

For background information see the consultation document 'The Reform of Film Tax Incentives: Promoting the Sustainable Production of Culturally British Films', published on 29 July 2005, available on the Treasury website (at www.hm-treasury.gov.uk). A summary of the new regime and partial draft guidance is set out on the HMRC website (at www.hmrc.gov.uk/films). For detailed coverage, with examples, of how the old rules are applied in practice, see HMRC Business Income Manual BIM 56000–56530. This replaced, with effect from 15 April 2003, Statement of Practice SP 1/98.

66.52 FA 2006 regime.

Film tax relief. Under the FA 2006 regime (see 66.51 above for commencement provisions) corporation tax relief is available for expenditure on a 'film' that qualifies for relief. A '*film*' includes any record, however made, of a sequence of visual images that is capable of being used as a means of showing that sequence as a moving picture. [*SI 2006/3399*].

A film qualifies for relief if all the following conditions are met.

(A) The film must be 'intended' for '*theatrical release*' (i.e. release to the paying public at the commercial cinema with the intention of obtaining the significant proportion of earnings from the release). A film is '*intended*' for theatrical release throughout an accounting period if it is intended for release at the end of that period. If it is not intended for release at the end of an accounting period, the condition is treated as not being met throughout that accounting period or in any subsequent accounting period but this does not affect any earlier accounting period where the condition was met.

(B) The film must be a '*British*' film, i.e. certified by the Secretary of State under the *Films Act 1985, Sch 1A*. (See *FA 2006, Sch 5 paras 15–25; SI 2007 No 1050, para 10*).

(C) At least 25% of the 'core expenditure' on the film incurred by the 'film production company' (or in the case of a 'qualifying co-production', by the 'co-producers') must be on '*UK expenditure*' (goods or services used or consumed in the UK) any apportionment between UK and non-UK expenditure to be made on a fair and reasonable basis. '*Core expenditure*' is the 'production expenditure' on pre-production, principal photography and post production. '*Production expenditure*' is expenditure on the film-making activities which are the activities involved in the development, pre-production, principal photography and post production of the film. The term 'principal photography' can include the generation of computer images in the film.

There can be only one 'film production company' in relation to the film. A 'film production company' is widely defined for this purpose to ensure the company has an active involvement in the film production and that its participation is not restricted to the provision or arrangement of finance. A '*film production company*' in relation to a film is the company that (otherwise than in partnership):

- is responsible for the pre-production, principal photography and the post-production of the film and is actively engaged in planning and decision-making during these stages;
- is responsible for delivery of the completed film;
- directly negotiates, contracts and pays for rights, goods and services in relation to the film.

A company may elect out of the regime, i.e. not to be treated as a film production company. The election must be made in the company's corporation tax return (either in the original return or by amendment to the original return). Similarly, the return may be withdrawn only in the original or amended return for the period. The election applies to films commencing principal photography in the accounting period in respect of which the return containing the election was made and subsequent accounting periods.

In the case of a '*qualifying co-production*' (a film treated as a national film in the UK by virtue of an agreement between the UK government and any other government, international organisation or authority) the film production company is a company that (otherwise than in partnership) is a co-producer and makes an effective creative, technical and artistic contribution to the film. A '*co-producer*' is a person who is a co-producer for the purposes of the qualifying co-production agreement. If there is more than one company that fits the description of a film production company in relation to a film, the company most directly engaged in the activities referred to is the film production company.

[*FA 1998 Sch 18 para 10*; *FA 2006, ss 31–36, 38–41; SI 2006 No 3265; SI 2006 No 3399; FA 2007 s 58*].

Computation of profits and gains. In relation to films certified by the Secretary of State, under the *Films Act 1985 Sch 1*, as British films for the purpose of film tax relief and intended for theatrical release at the time principal photography commences, the production activities of the film production company in relation to the film are treated as a trade separate from any of its other activities. Such trade is treated as commencing when pre-production of the film begins or, if earlier, when any income from the film is received by the company. Development expenditure incurred in relation to the film before the company begins to trade may be treated as expenditure of that trade incurred immediately after the company begins to carry it on. If such expenditure has already been taken into account for other tax purposes, the company tax return must be amended accordingly (notwithstanding any limitation on the time within which an amendment may normally be made).

Expenditure incurred by the company on film-making activities in connection with the film or on activities with a view to exploiting the film ('*costs of the film*') is deductible as revenue expenditure subject to the normal restrictions under the Corporation Taxes Acts. Expenditure is treated as revenue if it would otherwise be regarded as capital by reason only of being incurred on the creation of the film. Similarly, 'income from the film' which would otherwise be regarded as capital in nature is taxable as revenue. '*Income from the film*' includes receipts from the sale of the film or rights in it, royalties or other payments for use of the film or aspects of it, payments for rights to produce games or other merchandise, and receipts by way of a profit share agreement.

In determining the profit or loss for the first period of account, the costs of the film incurred in that period are brought into account as a debit and the proportion of estimated total income from the film treated as earned in the period is brought into account as a credit. For any subsequent period of account, the difference between the costs of the film incurred to date and the corresponding amount for the previous period is brought into account as a debit. Similarly, the difference between the proportion of estimated total income from the film treated as earned at the end of that period and the corresponding amount for the previous period is brought into account as a credit.

The proportion of estimated total income from the film treated as earned at the end of any period of account is determined by the formula C/T × I where C is the total costs incurred to date, T is the estimated total cost of the film and I is the estimated total income from the film. Estimates are to be made as at the balance sheet date for each period of account, on a fair and reasonable basis and considering all relevant circumstances.

Costs are treated as incurred when they are represented in the state of completion of the work in progress. Accordingly, payments in advance are to be ignored until work has been completed and deferred payments recognised to the extent the work is represented in the state of completion. Unpaid amounts are included in costs only if there is an unconditional obligation to pay them but if the obligation is linked to income being earned from the film, the costs can be included only when the appropriate amount of income is or has been taken into account.

No relief is available for expenditure for which relief has been given under the pre-FA 2006 regime (which covers income tax as well as corporation tax) (see 66.53 below).

[*FA 2006, s 37, Sch 4; SI 2006 No 3265; SI 2006 No 3399; SI 2007 No 1050 para 9*].

Enhanced relief. Film tax relief is available for expenditure on a film that commences principal photography on or after 1 January 2007 and qualifies for film tax relief (as above). The film production company can claim an enhanced deduction in respect of '*qualifying expenditure*' on the film, such expenditure being defined as 'core expenditure' (see above). The rate of enhancement is:

- 100% for a '*limited-budget film*' (one on which the core expenditure is £20 million or less (the expenditure being deemed equal to an arm's length amount in the case of transactions between CONNECTED PERSONS (19)); and
- 80% for any other film.

For the first period of account during which the trade is carried on, the additional deduction is the relevant enhancement rate above multiplied by the lower of:

- the amount of the qualifying UK expenditure; or
- 80% of the total amount of qualifying expenditure.

For any subsequent period of account the additional deduction is:

- the relevant enhancement rate above multiplied by the lower of the amount of the qualifying UK expenditure incurred to date or 80% of the total amount of qualifying expenditure incurred to date;
- less the amount of the additional deduction (or aggregate amount of additional deductions) given in the previous period (or periods).

Film tax credits. A film production company may claim a film tax credit for an accounting period in which it has a '*surrenderable loss*' which is equal to the lower of the amount of the trading loss for that period and the 'available qualifying expenditure'. The credit is not treated as income for tax purposes. A credit can be claimed for the whole or part of a surrenderable loss surrendered in a period at the rate of:

- 25% for a limited-budget film (as defined above); and
- 20% for any other film.

The trading loss is accordingly reduced for any amount so surrendered.

For the first period of account during which the trade is carried on, the '*available qualifying expenditure*' is the lower of:

- the amount of the qualifying UK expenditure; or
- 80% of the total amount of qualifying expenditure.

For any subsequent period of account the '*available qualifying expenditure*' is:

- the lower of the amount of the qualifying UK expenditure incurred to date or 80% of the total amount of qualifying expenditure incurred to date;
- less the amount of the loss surrendered (or aggregate amounts surrendered) in the previous period (or periods).

In determining the amount of the available qualifying expenditure for tax credit purposes, no account is taken of costs still unpaid four months after the end of the period of account in question.

Where a company is entitled to a film tax credit and makes a claim, the credit will be paid by HMRC but any amount payable in respect of the credit or interest thereon may be applied in discharging the company's liability to corporation tax. HMRC need not pay the credits (or may pay as much as they think fit) until the completion of enquiries into the company's tax return. Nor need they pay the credits before the company has settled its liabilities in an accounting period for PAYE, Class 1 National Insurance contributions or tax for foreign entertainers under *ICTA 1988, s 555*. Relief is denied to the extent it arises from artificially inflated claims (as defined).

[*FA 2006, s 34, Sch 5 paras 1–14; SI 2006 No 3265; SI 2006 No 3399*].

Claims and overpayments. A claim for film tax relief must be made in a company tax return (or amended return) (see 61.3, 61.8 RETURNS) for the accounting period for which the claim is made, within one year of the filing date for that return or by such later time as HMRC may allow. It can similarly only be amended or withdrawn by amendment of the company tax return within the same time limit. It must specify the quantum of the amount claimed. Penalties not exceeding the excess credit claimed apply for fraudulent or negligent claims, and for failure to remedy an incorrect claim without unreasonable delay. [*FA 1998, Sch 18 paras 10(4), 83S–83X; FA 2006, Sch 5 paras 27–29*].

Late claims should be dealt with in accordance with Statement of Practice 5/01 (HMRC CIRD Manual 81800). For recovery of overpayments of film tax credit, see 7.3 ASSESSMENTS.

Entitlement to relief. Entitlement to the above relief is further conditional on the film continuing to meet the requirements for certification as a 'British film', the minimum percentage on UK expenditure and status (where a claim is made on that basis) as a limited-budget film.

In the company's '*final accounting period*', in which the film is completed or abandoned, the company tax return for that period must state that the film has been completed or abandoned and be accompanied by:

(*a*) a final certificate (from the Secretary of State under the *Films Act 1985, Sch 1*) (such a certificate also having effect for previous periods). Without the certificate, or if the certificate is revoked, entitlement to relief is withdrawn for any period and the company tax return must be amended for any period for which relief was claimed, If the film is abandoned, the return may be accompanied by an interim certificate in which case the company would still be entitled to relief in that or any previous period;

(*b*) a final statement of the amount of core expenditure that is UK expenditure. If the condition for UK expenditure is not met, entitlement to relief is withdrawn for any period and the company tax return must be amended for any period for which relief was claimed; and

(*c*) in the case where relief is claimed on the basis that the film is a limited-budget film, a final statement of core expenditure on the film. If the return shows the film is not a limited-budget film (or, if the film is abandoned, it would not have been such a film if it were completed, having regard to the proportion of work completed), entitlement to the limited-budget film relief is withdrawn for any period and the company tax return must be amended for any period for which such relief was claimed.

In any earlier accounting period of the company the company tax return must:

(i) be accompanied by an interim certificate (similarly from the Secretary of State under the *Films Act 1985, Sch 1*). If an interim certificate ceases to be in force or is revoked then, unless a final certificate is provided as above, entitlement to relief is withdrawn for any period for which relief depended on the certificate and the company tax return for any such period must be amended accordingly;

(ii) state the amount of planned core expenditure that is UK expenditure and that the UK expenditure condition will be met on completion of the film. If it subsequently appears that the UK expenditure condition will not be met, relief is withdrawn for any period for which its entitlement depended on such a statement and the company tax return for any such period must be amended accordingly; and

(iii) in the case where relief is claimed on the basis that the film is a limited-budget film, state the amount of planned core expenditure on the film and that the conditions for such expenditure will be met on completion of the film. If it subsequently appears that the condition will not be met, limited-budget relief is withdrawn for any period and the company tax return for any such period for which such relief has been claimed must be amended accordingly.

The normal time limits for amendments or assessments do not apply in this case.

[*FA 2006, Sch 5 paras 30–34*].

Losses. In the accounting periods of the film production company before that in which the film is completed or abandoned, relief for a trading loss is available only to the extent that it can be carried forward under *ICTA 1988, s 393(1)* to be set against profits of the same trade in a later period. Any such loss as is not attributable to film tax relief is treated as a loss incurred in the period to which it is carried forward.

To the extent they are not attributable to film tax relief, losses in later periods may be set against the profits of the same or earlier period under *ICTA 1988, s 393A* or surrendered as group relief under *ICTA 1988, s 403*. The amount of a trading loss attributable to film tax relief is the total loss less the amount of the loss there would have been had there been no additional deduction for enhanced relief in that or in any earlier period. This does not apply to a loss to the extent it is carried forward or surrendered as a terminal loss (as below).

If a film production company ceases to carry on the trade, it can elect to surrender part or all of any remaining losses (which could otherwise be carried forward as above) to another of its trades in relation to a qualifying film. The loss would be treated as a loss brought forward by that other trade in the accounting period following that at the end of which the cessation takes place. Part or all of such a loss can also be surrendered to a trade in relation to a qualifying film of another company in the same group (for group relief purposes).

That company may elect for the surrendered loss to be treated as a loss brought forward by it in its accounting period following that in which or at the end of which the cessation of the surrendering company takes place.

[*FA 2006, ss 43–45*].

Regulations have been issued (*SI 2007 No 678*) which provide for the treatment of a terminal loss arising from film relief. A loss claim by a claimant company in respect of a terminal loss incurred by another group company must be included in the claimant company's corporation tax return for the accounting period of the claim, either when the return is filed or by amending the self assessment within the required time limit. The claim must state the surrendering company's name and the amount of relief, which must be quantifiable at the time the claim is made.

The claim must also give details of any group company not resident in the UK for tax purposes either in the surrendering company's accounting period of claim or the claimant's corresponding accounting period.

The amount available for surrender is calculated by taking the surrendering company's loss under *FA 2006 s 45* and deducting all amounts for which that company has given, and not withdrawn, notices of consent. There are rules to determine which claims and withdrawals are to be matched. (*SI 2007 No 678 para 7(4)* and *(5)*). The surrendering company's written consent ('notice of consent') is required to the claim, which must state:

A the surrending company's name, tax reference and its accounting period to which the claim relates;

B the claimant company's name, tax reference and its accounting period to which the claim relates; and

C the amount of the terminal loss being surrendered.

A notice may not be amended, but can be withdrawn (by notice to the officer who had received the original notice of consent) and replaced. The notice of withdrawal must contain the consent of the surrendering company, unless the reason for the withdrawal is that the loss available for relief has been reduced. The surrendering company must also submit an amended corporation tax return or returns, if the return or returns for the periods in question have already been filed. If it does not do so, the notice is not effective.

A claim may be withdrawn until the latest of:

(*a*) a year from the claimant company's filing date for the accounting period of claim;

(*b*) where an enquiry has been opened, 30 days after the enquiry is closed;

(*c*) where a return is amended following an enquiry, 30 days after the amendment is issued; and

(*d*) where an amendment is appealed, 30 days after the appeal is settled,

but HMRC may agree to a later time limit.

There are provisions requiring the surrendering company to withdraw the notice or notices of consent where the amount available for surrender is reduced. (*SI 2007 No 678 para 13*).

HMRC are given power to assess any other company which benefited from a loss relief claim where the tax due by the claimant company after a notice has been withdrawn remains unpaid six months after the surrendering companies time limit for claims, provided that the assessment must not be made more than two years after the time limit expires. The company so assessed has a right of recovery against the claimant company. (*SI 2007 No 678 para 14*). There is also a power to assess where the relief given is found to be excessive. (*SI 2007 No 678 para 15*).

[*SI 2007 No 678*].

Sound recordings. Expenditure on the production or acquisition of the 'original master version' of a sound recording (including any rights held or acquired in it) is treated as expenditure of a revenue nature. An '*original master version*' is a master tape or master audio disc and the term 'sound recording' does not include a film soundtrack. Receipts from disposal of the original master version of the sound recording are similarly treated as revenue receipts in the period of account (or if no accounts are made up, accounting period) in which they are received. Such receipts can include amounts received from the disposal of any interest or rights in or over the original master version (including those created by the disposal), and insurance or compensation or similar money derived from the original master version.

Where the company's trade consists of, or includes, the exploitation of original master versions of sound recordings which are not trading stock of that trade, the above expenditure and any revenue expenditure (whether incurred as above or otherwise) is allocated to periods of account (or if no accounts are made up, to accounting periods) using an 'income matching' rule. So much of the expenditure as is just and reasonable is allocated to the relevant period having regard to:

- the amount of the expenditure that remains unallocated at the beginning of the period;
- the proportion which the estimated value of the original master version realised in the period (by way of income or otherwise) bears to the sum of the value so realised and the estimated remaining value at the end of the period; and
- the need to bring the whole expenditure into account over the time during which the original master version is expected to be realised.

Additional amounts can be allocated to a period provided the amount so allocated does not exceed the value of the original master version realised in that period (by way of income or otherwise).

[*FA 2006, ss 48–50*].

The above provisions put HMRC Extra Statutory Concession B54 on a statutory footing.

Treasury powers. The Treasury have powers to make provision, by order (approved by a resolution of the House of Commons) to make various amendments. They may provide that certain activities are not film-making activities, amend the definition or vary the minimum percentage of UK expenditure, provide that particular sorts of expenditure are not qualifying expenditure or amend the percentage of qualifying expenditure used to calculate the enhanced deduction. They may also, by order, vary the way in which surrenders and claims of losses are made. [*FA 2006, ss 33, 35, 41, 45, Sch 5 paras 3, 4*].

66.53 **The pre-FA 2006 regime** See 66.51 above regarding the withdrawal from 1 January 2007 of the provisions set out below.

Treatment of expenditure as revenue. 'Production expenditure' or 'acquisition expenditure' (see (*a*) and (*b*) below) incurred for the purposes of a trade is treated as revenue expenditure. See below, however, as regards an available election for this rule *not* to apply to expenditure on certain 'certified master versions' (see (*f*) below) of films. Where expenditure is treated as revenue, any receipts from the disposal of any interest or right in or over the 'original master version' and any insurance, compensation etc. derived from it are treated as revenue receipts.

Position before FA 2000, s 113. For expenditure on the *acquisition* of a film, tape or disc incurred before 6 April 2000, the above rule applied only to expenditure which would otherwise have constituted expenditure on plant or machinery for capital allowances purposes, and the definition of 'original master version' was different in various respects to that given at (*c*) below (though see also the reference below to HMRC Extra Statutory

Concession, B54). This was also the case as regards expenditure on the *production* of a film where principal photography commenced before 21 March 2000. If, however, principal photography commenced before that date but the film was 'completed' (see (*d*) below) on or after that date, the person incurring the expenditure could elect (irrevocably) for the revised rule and definition to apply.

[*F(No 2)A 1992, s 40A; CAA 1990, s 68; FA 2000, s 113; CAA 2001, Sch 2 para 82, Sch 3 para 116; ITTOIA 2005, Sch 1 para 453; FA 2005, Sch 3 paras 18, 31; FA 2006, ss 46, 53, Sch 26 Pt 3(4)*].

Definitions for the purposes of the provisions both above and below.

(*a*) '*Production expenditure*' is expenditure incurred on the production of the 'original master version' of a film or sound recording. It does not, under HMRC and film industry practice, include interest or incidental costs of obtaining finance (the normal rules for deducting such expenditure applying instead); and for income tax purposes this exclusion has statutory effect for 2005/06 onwards (see Change 39 listed in Annex 1 to the Explanatory Notes to the Income Tax (Trading and Other Income) Bill).

(*b*) '*Acquisition expenditure*' is expenditure incurred on the acquisition of the 'original master version' of a film or sound recording. (Again. it does not include interest or incidental costs of obtaining finance (see (*a*) above)).

(*c*) The '*original master version*' means, in relation to a film, the original master negative, tape or disc or, in relation to a sound recording, the original master audio tape or disc. The expression includes any rights in the original master version of the film or sound recording that are held or acquired with it. The original master version of a film also includes the original master version of its soundtrack (if any).

(*d*) A film is '*completed*' when it is first in a form in which it can reasonably be regarded as ready for copies to be made and distributed for public exhibition.

(*e*) '*Preliminary expenditure*' (see below) means, in relation to a film, non-refundable expenditure incurred with a view to deciding whether to make the film and payable before the first day of principal photography. It is generally known in the industry as development expenditure or pre-production expenditure.

(*f*) '*Certified master version*' (see below) means, in relation to a film, an original master negative, tape or disc which is certified by the Secretary of State (in practice, the Department for Culture, Media and Sport (DCMS)) as a qualifying film, tape or disc. Certification is under *Films Act 1985, Sch 1 para 3* which applies certain criteria as to the British, EU or Commonwealth nature of the film; for more details, see the DCMS website (at www.culture.gov.uk/creative_industries/film).

The references in (*a*)–(*c*) above to sound recordings had statutory authority before *FA 2000, s 113* referred to above. They continue to apply thereafter, but only by concession (HMRC Extra Statutory Concession, B54). For income tax purposes, for 2005/06 onwards, they again have statutory authority (see Change 38 listed in Annex 1 to the Explanatory Notes to the Income Tax (Trading and Other Income) Bill).

Each part of a series of films is treated as a separate film unless the DCMS give a direction to the contrary.

[*F(No 2)A 1992, s 40A(1)(5), s 41(2), s 42(2), s 43; CAA 1990, s 68; FA 2000, s 113; CAA 2001, Sch 2 para 82; ITTOIA 2005, Sch 1 paras 453, 457–459; FA 2005, Sch 3 paras 18, 23, 24, 31; FA 2006, Sch 26 Pt 3(4)*].

Allocation of expenditure to periods of account. In a trade consisting of or including the exploitation of the original master versions (see (*c*) above) of films and sound recordings, production or acquisition expenditure (see (*a*) and (*b*) above) otherwise deductible is allocated to periods of account on a just and reasonable basis. In so allocating expenditure to any period of account, regard must be had to the expenditure unallocated at the beginning of the period, the expenditure incurred in the period, the proportion which the estimated value of the original master version realised in the period (whether by way of income or otherwise) bears to the sum of the value so realised and the estimated remaining value at the end of the period, and the need to bring the whole expenditure into account over the time during which the value of the original master version is expected to be realised (known as the 'income matching' method of allocation). The amount thus allocated to the period can then be increased up to an amount equal to the value of the original master version realised in the period (whether by way of income or otherwise) (known as the 'cost recovery' method if a claim is made for that purpose within two years after the end of the period in question. (The requirement for a claim to be made is dropped for income tax purposes for 2005/06 onwards (see Change 40 listed in Annex 1 to the Explanatory Notes to the Income Tax (Trading and Other Income) Bill).)

These provisions do not apply if the original master version in question constitutes trading stock under *ICTA 1988, s 100*(*2*)) (see 66.75 below).

Expenditure cannot be allocated to a period of account under the above rules if it is allocated to any period under *F*(*No 2*)*A 1992, s 42* and in that case, no other production or acquisition expenditure in respect of that original master version can be allocated to that period under the above rules.

See below as regards an available election for these rules *not* to apply to expenditure on certain certified films.

[*F*(*No 2*)*A 1992, ss 40B, 40C, 41*(*7*), *42*(*8*); *CAA 1990, s 68; FA 1996, Sch 21 para 32*(*2*)(*3*); *CAA 2001, Sch 2 para 82, Sch 3 para 116; ITTOIA 2005, Sch 1 paras 454, 455, 457; FA 2005, Sch 3 paras 19, 20, 31; FA 2006, Sch 26 Pt 3*(*4*)].

If, exceptionally, no accounts are drawn up, any reference above and in the special rules below to a period of account is to be taken as a reference to the company's accounting period. [*F*(*No 2*)*A 1992, s 40B*(*3*), *s 40D*(*5*), *s 43*(*1*); *CAA 2001, Sch 2 para 82; ITTOIA 2005, Sch 1 paras 454, 456; FA 2005, Sch 3 paras 24, 31; FA 2006, Sch 26 Pt 3*(*4*)].

Certified films. Each of the special rules below applies where

- the trade consists of or includes the exploitation of films,
- the films do not constitute trading stock under *ICTA 1988, s 100*(*2*)) (see 66.75 below),
- the expenditure in question is of a revenue nature,
- the original master version (see (*c*) above) of the film in question is a '*certified master version*' (see (*f*) above),
- (with effect from, broadly, 17 April 2002) the theatrical release condition below is met, and
- no election has been made as below to disapply these rules in relation to the expenditure.

[*F*(*No 2*)*A 1992, s 41*(*1*), *s 42*(*1*)–(*3*)(*8*); *ITTOIA 2005, Sch 1 paras 457, 458; FA 2005, Sch 3 paras 22, 23, 31; FA 2006, Sch 26 Pt 3*(*4*)].

Theatrical release condition. Unless an application for certification (as below) was received before 17 April 2002, the special rules below are restricted, for films completed after 16 April 2002, or completed before 1 January 2002 but not certified before 17 April 2002, to films genuinely intended for theatrical release, i.e. for exhibition to the paying public at the commercial cinema. The relevant intention for this purpose is the intention, at the time the film is completed (see (*d*) above), of the person then entitled to determine how the film is to be exploited. A film is not regarded as genuinely intended for theatrical release unless it is intended that a significant proportion of the film's earnings should be obtained by such exhibition.

A film commissioned before 18 April 2002 and on which the principal photography commenced before 1 July 2002 is *not* so excluded from the reliefs *provided that* it is a drama with an average production expenditure greater than £500,000 per hour of running time of the completed film. 'Production expenditure' for this purpose includes all expenditure on production of the film, whenever and by whomsoever incurred, other than any which, at the time of completion, has not been paid and is not the subject of an unconditional obligation to pay within four months after that time. It is increased to an arm's length amount in the case of certain connected person transactions. 'Drama' does not include anything in the nature of an advertisement or promotional film, a training film, a discussion programme, news or current affairs programme, quiz show, panel show, variety show or similar entertainment, or a film of a live event, or of a theatrical or artistic performance given otherwise than for the purpose of being filmed, but does include a documentary involving the dramatic reconstruction of events if the dramatic content forms 50% or more of the running time.

[*FA 2002, s 99*].

Preliminary expenditure (see (*e*) above) (incurred before 19 July 2006, see 66.51 above). A deduction may be claimed for a period for any expenditure payable in the period (or in an earlier period) which can reasonably be said to have been incurred in deciding whether or not to make a film (as defined in *Films Act 1985, Sch 1 para 1*), and which is not payable under a contract etc. whereby it may be repaid if the film is not made. If the decision taken is to make the film, this applies to expenditure incurred before commencement of principal photography, up to a maximum of 20% of the budgeted expenditure as at the first day of principal photography. It must be reasonably likely that if the film had been completed, where this is not actually the case, the original master version of it would have been a certified master version. No relief may be claimed where a deduction has previously been made for the expenditure, or an election made in respect of it under *F(No 2)A 1992, s 40D* (see above).

A claim must be made within two years after the end of the period of account in which the expenditure becomes payable. (For income tax purposes from 2005/06 onwards, there is no requirement for a claim to be made (see Change 40 listed in Annex 1 to the Explanatory Notes to the Income Tax (Trading and Other Income) Bill).)

[*F(No 2)A 1992, ss 41, 43; CAA 2001, Sch 2 paras 83, 85; ITTOIA 2005, Sch 1 para 457; FA 2005, Sch 3 paras 22, 31; FA 2006, ss 46, 53, Sch 26 Pt 3(4)*].

Production or acquisition expenditure (see (*a*) and (*b*) above and see 66.51 above for withdrawal of reliefs). As an alternative to the general allocation rules above, up to **one-third** of the total deductible production or acquisition expenditure in respect of a certified master version of a film can be claimed for allocation to a period of account (no earlier than that in which the film is completed — see (*d*) above). Before making the one-third calculation, the expenditure must be reduced by any preliminary expenditure already allocated as above and any expenditure allocated under the accelerated deductions below for limited budget films. For a period of account of less than 12 months, the one-third fraction is reduced proportionately. The expenditure allocated to any period cannot exceed the total production or acquisition expenditure not already allocated to that period or any other period. If any production or acquisition expenditure in respect of the original master version is allocated to a period of account under the general allocation rules above, no other production or acquisition expenditure in respect of the original master version can be allocated to that period under the above rules.

A claim is irrevocable and must be made within two years after the end of the period to which it relates. (For income tax purposes from 2005/06 onwards, there is no requirement for a claim to be made (see Change 40 listed in Annex 1 to the Explanatory Notes to the Income Tax (Trading and Other Income) Bill).)

The following changes are made by *FA 2005*.

(i) For expenditure incurred on or after 2 December 2004 (excluding any 'pre-announcement expenditure' — see (ii) below), other than in relation to a film in production on that date, these allocation rules apply only if, in relation to production expenditure, the original master version (see (*c*) above) was owned by the company carrying on the trade at the time the film was completed (see (*d*) above) or, in relation to acquisition expenditure, the original master version (see (*c*) above) has not previously been acquired by the company carrying on the trade.

(ii) Also with effect from 2 December 2004 and in relation to both production and acquisition expenditure (but not in relation to a film in production on that date), these allocation rules apply only if there has not been a previous deduction in relation to the film, taking into account deductions made to other persons and deductions made under the rules for limited-budget films below as well as those made under the instant rules. The intention is that relief should be given only once on any film, either for production or acquisition expenditure, but not both, and that the relief is given for the deduction first made. In the case of simultaneous deductions, HMRC are given power to decide which one is to be treated as made first. But double deductions are not prevented if both deductions relate *entirely* to 'pre-announcement expenditure'. '*Pre-announcement expenditure*' is expenditure incurred before 2 December 2004. However, expenditure incurred on or after that date in pursuance of an unconditional obligation is treated as if incurred before that date and is thus included in pre-announcement expenditure; the question of whether an obligation was unconditional is decided on the facts immediately before 2 December 2004, and certain possible conditions are disregarded for this purpose (see *FA 2005, Sch 3 para 32*(2)).

(iii) For films *in production* on 2 December 2004, there are transitional rules to prevent a deduction for acquisition expenditure if the acquisition is not the first acquisition of the original master version of the film by the acquirer or if there has been a previous deduction for another acquisition of the film.

(iv) In relation to expenditure on films whose first day of principal photography is on or after 2 December 2004 (but not where any of the expenditure being allocated is 'pre-announcement expenditure' — see (ii) above), these allocation rules cannot be used if the film is within the rules for limited-budget films below.

(v) In relation to expenditure on films whose first day of principal photography is on or after 2 December 2004 (but not 'pre-announcement expenditure' — see (ii) above), any expenditure which remains unpaid when the film is completed (see (*d*) above), and which is not at that time the subject of an unconditional obligation to pay within four months after completion, is excluded from production expenditure for the purposes of these allocation rules. (A similar prohibition already applied for limited-budget films under the rules below). The rules as to *when* expenditure is incurred for these purposes follow those for capital allowances (see 10.2(iv) CAPITAL ALLOWANCES).

(vii) In relation to expenditure on films whose first day of principal photography is on or after 2 December 2004 (but not where any of the expenditure being allocated is 'pre-announcement expenditure' — see (ii) above), the total amount of acquisition expenditure to be allocated under these rules is restricted to the 'total production expenditure in respect of the original master version'. (A similar prohibition already applied for limited-budget films under the rules below). Where the acquisition expenditure includes pre-announcement expenditure in excess of the total production expenditure, the restriction is to the total pre-announcement expenditure instead of the total production expenditure. Subject to the exclusion in (v) above, *'total production expenditure in respect of the original master version'* includes all the production expenditure (see (*a*) above) in respect of the original master version (see (*c*) above), whenever incurred and whether or not incurred by the trader in question.

[*F(No 2)A 1992, s 42; FA 2000, s 113(3)(4)(6); CAA 2001, Sch 2 para 84; ITTOIA 2005, Sch 1 para 458; FA 2005, Sch 3 paras 1, 7, 9, 23, 31–33; FA 2006, ss 46, 53, Sch 26 Pt 3(4)*].

Accelerated deductions for limited-budget certified films. These may be claimed for expenditure incurred after 1 July 1997 on a film completed after 1 July 1997 **and before 1 January 2007** with a 'total production expenditure in respect of the original master version' of **£15 million** or less and on which the first day of principal photography falls before 1 April 2006. As regards acquisition expenditure only, it is an additional condition that the expenditure be incurred before 1 October 2007. Any of the 2006 and 2007 dates quoted above may be deferred by Treasury order. (As regards deductions made under these provisions before 2 July 2005, the expenditure, be it production or acquisition expenditure, has to have been incurred before that date, but the later dates quoted above are of no relevance.) The rules as to *when* expenditure is incurred for these purposes follow those for capital allowances (see 10.2(iv) CAPITAL ALLOWANCES).

'Total production expenditure in respect of the original master version' includes all the production expenditure (see (*a*) above) in respect of the original master version (see (*c*) above), whenever incurred and whether or not incurred by the trader in question. But any expenditure which remains unpaid when the film is completed (see (*d*) above), and which is not at that time the subject of an unconditional obligation to pay within four months after completion, is ignored. Where any of the expenditure relates to transactions between CONNECTED PERSONS (19), the equivalent arm's length amount is substituted if greater; for films whose first day of principal photography is on or after 2 December 2004, this rule has effect only for the purpose of applying the £15 million rule and for no other purpose.

Where these conditions are satisfied, up to **100%** of the total deductible production expenditure or acquisition expenditure (see (*b*) above) in respect of a certified master version of a film can be allocated to any period of account (no earlier than that in which the film is completed — see (*d*) above). In the case of production expenditure, any unpaid expenditure falling to be ignored as above cannot be so allocated.

In the case of acquisition expenditure, the total amount that can be allocated under these provisions is restricted to the total production expenditure in respect of the original master version. Where the first day of principal photography was on or after 2 December 2004, any of the expenditure being allocated is 'pre-announcement expenditure' (see (ii) above) and the total production expenditure would have been greater if it were not for the disapplication for these purposes of the connected persons rule above, the restriction is to the lower of the pre-announcement expenditure and what would otherwise have been the total production expenditure.

If any production or acquisition expenditure in respect of the original master version is allocated to a period of account under the general allocation rules above, no other production or acquisition expenditure in respect of the original master version can be allocated to that period under the above rules.

Expenditure can only be allocated as above if a claim is made for that purpose (under *F(No 2)A 1992, 42*) within two years following the end of the period of account to which the claim relates. (For income tax purposes from 2005/06 onwards, there is no requirement for a claim to be made (see Change 40 listed in Annex 1 to the Explanatory Notes to the Income Tax (Trading and Other Income) Bill).)

Similar changes are made by *FA 2005* as are outlined at (i) and (ii) above. Previously (for expenditure incurred on or after 30 June 2002), the 100% allocation was not available for acquisition expenditure unless the acquisition was by, or directly from, the producer (i.e. the person who commissions the making of the film and is entitled to control its exploitation) and was the first such acquisition.

[*F(No 2)A 1992, s 42(4); F(No 2)A 1997, s 48; CAA 2001, Sch 2 para 99; FA 2001, s 72; FA 2002, ss 100, 101; ITTOIA 2005, Sch 1 paras 458; 498; FA 2005, s 58(1)(4)(5), Sch 3 paras 1, 2, 23, 26, 31–33; FA 2006, Sch 26 Pt 3(4)*].

After the current system of accelerated allowances terminates (see above for end dates), the Government intend to replace it with a new relief, available only to companies, for certified films with a total production expenditure of not more than £20 million. HMRC provides further details on their website (at www.hmrc.gov.uk/ctsa/tax-relief-films.pdf).

Election to disapply the above rules in the case of certified films. A company carrying on a trade consisting of, or including, the exploitation of original master versions of films may elect for the above provisions of *F(No 2)A 1992, ss 40A, 40B not* to apply in relation to expenditure incurred on the production or acquisition of an original master version (see (*c*) above) of a film, where:

- the original master version is a certified master version (see (*f*) above);
- its value is expected to be realisable over a period of not less than two years; and
- (with effect from, broadly, 17 April 2002) the theatrical release condition, described above under Certified films, is met.

The election, which is irrevocable, must relate to the whole of the expenditure incurred, or to be incurred, on the production or acquisition of the original master version in question. It must be made no later than two years following the end of the period of account in which the original master version is completed. For this purpose, the master version of a film is completed when the film is first in a form in which it can reasonably be regarded as ready for copies to be made and distributed for public exhibition or, in relation to acquisition expenditure, at the time of acquisition if later. The principal effect of the election is to treat production or acquisition expenditure as capital expenditure, except to the extent (if any) that it would qualify as revenue expenditure under general principles. No election is available in relation to expenditure on the production or acquisition of the original master version of a film if any of that expenditure has been subject to a claim under *F(No 2)A 1992, ss 41, 42* above.

[*F(No 2)A 1992, ss 40D; CAA 1990, s 68; CAA 2001, Sch 2 para 82, Sch 3 paras 116, 117; ITTOIA 2005, Sch 1 para 456; FA 2005, Sch 3 paras 21, 31; FA 2006, Sch 26 Pt 3(4)*].

Anti-avoidance: deferred income agreements. The following provisions are designed to counter tax avoidance by companies which have benefited from film tax reliefs and defer income from the film for more than 15 years; they have effect where any deferred income agreements are entered into **on or after 2 December 2004**. There are two sets of provisions, depending on whether the deferred income agreement was already in existence when the relief was given or was entered into after that time.

For these purposes, a company is not to be regarded as entering into an agreement on or after 2 December 2004 if it did so in pursuance of its obligation which immediately before that date was an unconditional obligation; and an obligation is not to be regarded as conditional if it depended on a condition the fulfillment of which was outside that company's control.

The first set of provisions applies where a claim for a deduction is made by a company ('C') under *F(No)A 1992, s 42* above (relief for production or acquisition) for expenditure relating to a film and there are in existence at that time one or more 'deferred income agreements' in respect of the film, being agreements to which C is or has been a party and which it entered into on or after 2 December 2004. An amount of excess relief, computed as below, is brought into account as a receipt in computing C's trading profits for the period of account for which the deduction was made. If, however, immediately after the end of the '15-year period', C is still carrying on the trade, it is treated as incurring at that time production or acquisition expenditure of an amount equal to the excess relief, but this notional expenditure can be allocated to periods of account only under the normal allocation rules of *F(No)A 1992, s 40B* above and not under the special rules for certified films. The excess relief for these purposes is:

$$D \times \left(1 - \frac{T1}{T2}\right)$$

where:

D = the deduction made;

T1 = the number of days in the '15-year period; and

T2 = the number of days from the 'operative date' to the 'final deferral date' inclusive.

The '*15-year period*' is the 15 years beginning with the 'operative date'. The '*operative date*' is the date of acquisition where the expenditure deducted is acquisition expenditure; in any other case, it is the date the film is completed (see (*d*) above). The '*final deferral date*' is the 'last date of deferral' in relation to the deferred income agreement or, where there is more than one such agreement, the latest of those dates. The '*last date of deferral*' is the last date on which an amount of guaranteed income will or may arise under the 'deferred income agreement.

A '*deferred income agreement*' is an agreement which:

- (whether or not it supplements or varies another agreement) guarantees an amount of income arising from exploitation of the film and has the effect that the 'last date of deferral' (as above) falls after the end of the 15-year period referred to above; or
- supplements or varies an earlier agreement which guarantees an amount of income arising from exploitation of the film and has the effect that the 'last date of deferral' (as above) falls after the end of the 15-year period and after the last date of deferral (if any) in relation to the earlier agreement.

The fact that any earlier agreement may have existed before 2 December 2004 does not prevent the deferred income agreement in question from falling within these provisions if it is entered into on or after that date, and 'agreement' includes a series of agreements. An agreement guarantees income for these purposes if it sets out to achieve the receipt of at least that amount.

The second set of provisions is similar, but applies where the deduction had already been made before the deferred income agreement is entered into. This time, the excess relief is brought into account as a receipt in computing C's trading profits for the period of account in which it enters into the agreement and is reduced by any amounts already recovered under these provisions, including any amounts recovered by virtue of C's entering into any previous deferred income agreements in respect of the film concerned after the deduction or claim was made.

[*FA 2005, ss 60–63; FA 2006, Sch 26 Pt 3*(*4*)].

Anti-avoidance: exit charges. The following provisions are designed to counter tax avoidance by groups of companies which have benefited from film tax reliefs and defer income from the film permanently; they apply to 'exit events' occurring **on or after 2 December 2004**. An '*exit event*' occurs to a company ('C') in any of the following three cases: when:

(A) it ceases to be a 75% subsidiary of the principle company of a group of companies (as defined); or

(B) it ceases to be within the charge to corporation tax; or

(C) it makes a 'relevant disposal at an undervalue' within the meaning given below.

When an exit event occurs, it gives rise to a chargeable event and in each of the above cases, C is treated as receiving an amount of trading income equal to the 'chargeable amount' immediately before the exit event occurs. A chargeable event occurs if:

- C was a 'film rights company' immediately before the time of the exit event; and
- C, or another company, claimed a deduction for expenditure relating to the film under *F(No 2)A 1992, s 42* (relief for production or acquisition expenditure) either before that time or for the first time after that time (whether before, on or after 2 December 2004).

C is a '*film rights company*' if it is party to an agreement which provides for a minimum guaranteed amount of income from the exploitation of a film, it carries on a '*relevant trade*' (a trade or business involving the exploitation of films or receipt of income derived therefrom) and is a 75% subsidiary of the principal company of a group of companies.

C leaves group or ceases to be within charge to corporation tax.

In the case of (A) above where C leaves the group, the amount equal to the chargeable event amount is treated as a trading loss brought forward under *ICTA 1988, s 393* to the accounting period of C in which the exit event occurs. The loss can only be set off against the minimum guaranteed income arising after C leaves the group (thus preventing a double charge to tax) and not against any other income or gains and, in particular, not against the deemed chargeable amount treated as arising immediately before the exit event.

In the case of (A) or (B) above, the '*chargeable amount*' is equal to the value of the rights to guaranteed income immediately before the exit event. This is calculated by adding together the net present value of each payment which is found by the formula:

$$\frac{RI}{(1+T)^i}$$

where:

RI = the amount of each payment that C is designed to receive under the guaranteed income agreement;

T = the 'temporal discount rate'; and

^{i} = the number of days from the day on which the exit event occurs to the day the guaranteed income payment is to be received, inclusive, divided by 365.

The '*temporal discount rate*' is 3.5% or such rate as may be specified by Treasury regulations.

C makes relevant disposal at an undervalue.

Where C makes a 'relevant disposal at an undervalue' (as in (C) above), a '*relevant disposal*' is a disposal by C to a third party, directly or indirectly, of rights to guaranteed income under the guaranteed income agreement. The disposal is '*at an undervalue*' when the amount of the disposal consideration ('V1') is less than the 'value of the disposed rights' immediately before the disposal ('V2') whether the rights are disposed of alone or as part of a larger disposal. (Where the disposed rights are part of a larger disposal, the amount of the consideration for the larger disposal which is attributable to the relevant disposal is to be determined on a just and reasonable basis.) The '*chargeable amount*' in this case is the difference between V1 and V2.

Where the third party is within the charge to corporation tax, the amount equal to the chargeable amount is treated as a trading loss brought forward under *ICTA 1988, s 393* to the accounting period in which the third party acquires the disposed rights. The loss can only be set off against income derived directly from the disposed rights and not against any other income or gains. (Where the third party is within the charge to income tax, the chargeable amount is similarly treated as a trading loss brought forward under *ICTA 1988, s 385* to the year of assessment in which the third party acquires the disposed rights.)

The '*value of the disposed rights*' immediately before the disposal is calculated by adding together the net present value of each payment which is found by the formula:

$$\frac{DI}{(1+T)^i}$$

where:

DI = the amount of each payment that C is designed to receive under the guaranteed income agreement by virtue of the disposed rights but which C has not brought into account for tax purposes immediately before the disposal;

T = the 'temporal discount rate' (see above); and

i = the number of days from the day on which the relevant disposal occurs to the day the guaranteed income payment is to be received, inclusive, divided by 365.

[*FA 2005, ss 66–71; FA 2006, Sch 26 Pt 3(4)*].

Leasing. See 66.54 below as regards restrictions on relief under the above provisions where finance leasing arrangements are involved.

Simon's Direct Tax Service. See **B3.1360** *et seq.*

66.54 FINANCE LEASE RENTALS

Long funding leases of plant or machinery. The rules on leasing of *plant or machinery* are reformed by *FA 2006, s 81, Sch 8* with effect from, broadly, **1 April 2006** (see 10.34 CAPITAL ALLOWANCES for the detailed commencement and transitional provisions). For long funding leases (within 10.34), the new regime grants entitlement to capital allowances to the lessee rather than to the lessor as previously. See also 66.64 below. It follows that the Statement of Practice described below can have no application to a long-funding lease of plant or machinery. The *FA 1997* anti-avoidance provisions summarised below are specifically disapplied in relation to such leases.

Statement of Practice. In relation to finance leases entered into after 11 April 1991, HMRC practice described below applies to rentals payable by a lessee under a finance lease, i.e. a lease which transfers substantially all the risks and rewards of ownership of an asset to the lessee while maintaining the lessor's legal ownership of the asset. The treatment of such rentals depends upon whether or not SSAP 21 has been applied. This practice has no implications for the tax treatment of rentals receivable by the lessor, nor for the availability of capital allowances to the lessor. (HMRC Statement of Practice, SP 3/91 and Revenue Press Release 11 April 1991).

Finance lease rentals are revenue payments for the use of the asset, and, both under normal accounting principles and for tax purposes, should be allocated to the periods of account for which the asset is leased in accordance with the accruals concept. Where there is an option for the lessee to continue to lease the asset after expiry of the primary period under the lease, regard should be had, in allocating rentals to periods of account, to the economic life of the asset and its likely period of use by the lessee, as well as to the primary period.

Under SSAP 21, the lessee is required to treat a finance lease as the acquisition of an asset subject to a loan, to be depreciated over its useful life, with rentals apportioned between a finance charge and a capital repayment element. This treatment does not, however, affect the tax treatment, which remains as described above.

Where SSAP 21 has not been applied, the lessee's accounting treatment of rental payments is normally accepted for tax purposes, provided that it is consistent with the principles described above. If not, computational adjustments are made to secure the proper spreading of the rental payments.

Where SSAP 21 has been applied, the finance charge element of the rental payments for a period of account is normally accepted as a revenue deduction for that period. In determining the appropriate proportion of the capital repayment element to be deducted for tax purposes, a properly computed commercial depreciation charge to profit and loss account will normally be accepted. Where, however, the depreciation charge is not so computed, the appropriate proportion for tax purposes will be determined in accordance with the principles described above.

For comment on the principles set out in SP 3/91, and on their application to particular arrangements, see Revenue Tax Bulletin February 1995 pp 189–193. This considers in particular: sums paid before the asset comes into use; depreciation of leased assets (and the interaction with SSAP 21); long-life assets; termination adjustments; fixtures leases; and the interaction of SP 3/91 with statutory restrictions on relief for rental payments.

See generally HMRC Business Income Manual BIM 61000–61075 (leasing: general) and BIM 61100–61195 (finance leasing).

See also above under Long funding leases of plant or machinery.

Anti-avoidance — return in capital form. *FA 1997, Sch 12 Pt I* applies from 26 November 1996 in relation to asset leasing arrangements which are dealt with by generally accepted accounting practice (see 66.5 above) as finance leases or loans, and whose effect is that some or all of the investment return is or may be in non-rental form and would not, apart from these provisions, be wholly taxed as lease rental. The principal purposes of the provisions are to charge any person entitled to the lessor's interest to tax by reference to the income return for accounting purposes (taking into account the substance of the matter as a whole, e.g. as regards connected persons or groups of companies); and to recover reliefs etc. for capital and other expenditure as appropriate by reference to sums received which fall within the provisions. The provisions are described below.

FA 1997, Sch 12 Pt I applies where an asset lease (as widely defined) is or has at any time been granted in the case of which the following conditions are or have been satisfied at some time (the '*relevant time*') in a period of account of the current lessor. Where the conditions have been satisfied at a relevant time, they are treated as continuing to be satisfied unless and until the asset ceases to be leased under the lease or the lessor's interest is assigned to a person not 'connected' with the assignor or certain other prior or subsequent lessors. Persons who are CONNECTED PERSONS (19) (within *ICTA 1988, s 839*) at any time in the period from the earliest time at which any of the leasing arrangements were made to the time when the current lessor finally ceases to have an interest in the asset or any arrangements relating to it are for these purposes treated as so connected throughout that period.

FA 1997, Sch 12 Pt I does *not* apply if (or to the extent that), as regards the current lessor, the lease falls to be regarded as a long funding lease (within 10.34 CAPITAL ALLOWANCES) of plant or machinery.

[*FA 1997, Sch 12 paras 1, 2, 23, 25, 30; FA 2006, Sch 9 para 7(1)(2)(4)*].

The conditions referred to above are as follows.

(*a*) At the relevant time, and under generally accepted accounting practice, the leasing arrangements fall to be treated as a finance lease or loan in relation to which either:

  (i) the lessor (or a connected person) is the finance lessor; or

  (ii) the lessor is a member of a group of companies for the purposes of whose consolidated accounts the finance lease or loan is treated as subsisting.

(*b*) A sum (a '*major lump sum*') is or may be payable to the lessor (or a connected person) under the leasing arrangements which is not rent but which falls to be treated, under generally accepted accounting practice, partly as repayment of some or all of the investment in respect of the finance lease or loan and partly as a return on that investment.

(*c*) Not all of the part of the major lump sum which is treated as a return on the investment (as in (*b*) above) would, apart from these provisions, be brought into account for tax purposes, as 'normal rent' from the lease for periods of account of the lessor, in chargeable periods of the lessor ending with the 'relevant chargeable period'. The '*relevant chargeable period*' is the chargeable or basis period (or latest such period) consisting of or including all or part of the period of account in which that sum is or may be payable under the arrangements. A '*normal rent*' for a period of account is the amount which (apart from the current provisions) the lessor would bring in for tax purposes in the period as rent arising from the lease.

(*d*) The period of account of the lessor in which the relevant time falls (or an earlier period during which he was the lessor) is one for which the 'accountancy rental earnings' in respect of the lease exceed the normal rent. The '*accountancy rental earnings*' for a period are the greatest of the '*rental earnings*' for the period in respect of the lease (i.e. the amount treated under generally accepted accounting practice as the gross return on investment for the period):

(i) of the lessor;

(ii) of any person connected with the lessor; and

(iii) for the purposes of consolidated group accounts of a group of which the lessor is a member.

Where (ii) or (iii) applies and the lessor's period of account does not coincide with that of the connected person or the consolidated group accounts, amounts in the periods of account of the latter are apportioned as necessary by reference to the number of days in the common periods.

The normal rent for a period of account for these purposes is determined by treating rent as accruing and falling due evenly over the period to which it relates (unless a payment falls due more than twelve months after any of the rent to which it relates is so treated as accruing).

(*e*) At the relevant time, either:

(i) arrangements exist under which the lessee (or a connected person) may directly or indirectly acquire the leased asset (or an asset representing it — see *FA 1997, Sch 12 para 26*) from the lessor (or a connected person), and in connection with that acquisition the lessor (or a connected person) may directly or indirectly receive a '*qualifying lump sum*' from the lessee (or a connected person) (i.e. a non-rental sum part at least of which would be treated under generally accepted accounting practice as a return on investment in respect of a finance lease or loan); or

(ii) in the absence of such arrangements, it is in any event more likely that the acquisition and receipt described in (i) above will take place than that, before any such acquisition, the leased asset (or the asset representing it) will have been acquired in an open market sale other than by the lessor or lessee (or persons connected with either of them).

[*FA 1997 Sch 12 paras 3, 4, 20–24, 30; FA 2002, Sch 40 Pt 3(16); FA 2005, s 80, Sch 4 para 32*].

Where *Part I* applies to a lease for a period of account of the current lessor, the consequences are as follows.

Current lessor to be taxed by reference to accountancy rental earnings. Where the accountancy rental earnings in respect of the lease for a period of account exceed the normal rent for that period, the accountancy rental earnings are substituted for the normal rent for tax purposes. The substituted amount is treated as having accrued evenly over the period of account (disregarding periods for which the asset was not leased).

Where the reverse applies (i.e. the normal rent exceeds the accountancy rental earnings), and there is a 'cumulative accountancy rental excess', the rent otherwise taxable for the period (the '*taxable rent*') is reduced (although not below the accountancy rental earnings) by setting it against that excess. An '*accountancy rental excess*' for a period to which these provisions apply is the excess (if any) of the accountancy rental earnings over the normal rent for the period, and the '*cumulative accountancy rental excess*' is so much of the aggregate of accountancy rental excesses of previous periods (after allowing for certain bad debts, see below) as has not been set against taxable rents for previous periods or against certain chargeable gains disposal consideration (see below). '*Normal rental excess*' and '*cumulative normal rental excess*' (see below) are correspondingly defined, except that the normal rental excess for a period for which the taxable rent is reduced as above is the excess (if any) of the normal rent (reduced by a similar amount) over the accountancy rental earnings.

If there is a cumulative normal rent excess (as above) for a period of account for which the taxable rent is increased in amount to the accountancy rental earnings, the taxable rent for the period (as so increased) is reduced (but not below the normal rent) by set-off against that excess, and the accountancy rental excess for the period (as above) is the excess (if any) of the taxable rent as so determined over the normal rent.

On an assignment of the current lessor's interest under the lease treated under *TCGA 1992, s 35(3)(d)* as at neither gain nor loss (see Tolley's Capital Gains Tax under Assets Held on 31 March 1982), a period of account of the assignor is treated as ending, and of the assignee as beginning, with the assignment. Any unused cumulative accountancy rental excess or cumulative normal rental excess at the time of the assignment is transferred to the assignee.

Where accountancy rental earnings for a period of account are substituted for normal rent for tax purposes (as above), and a bad debt deduction in excess of the accountancy rental earnings falls to be made for the period, any cumulative accountancy rental excess for the period is reduced (but not below nil) by that excess. If the accountancy rental earnings do not exceed the normal rent, any bad debt deduction acts to reduce the amount of the normal rent against which a cumulative accountancy rental excess may be set, and the cumulative accountancy rental excess is reduced (but not below nil) by any excess of the bad debt deduction over the normal rent. There is provision for such reductions in the cumulative accountancy rental excess to be reversed in the event of subsequent bad debt recoveries or reinstatements.

There are corresponding provisions relating to the effect of bad debt deductions on cumulative normal rental excesses.

In determining the *chargeable gain on a disposal* by the current lessor (or a connected person) of his interest under the lease (or of the leased asset or an asset representing it), the disposal consideration is reduced (but not below nil) by setting against it any cumulative accountancy rental excess (as above) for the period of account of the disposal. This does not preclude the exclusion from the disposal consideration under *TCGA 1992, s 37* of any amount chargeable to tax on income, except to the extent (if any) that it is represented by any cumulative accountancy rental excess set off under this provision (on the current disposal or previously). On a part disposal, the cumulative accountancy rental excess is apportioned in the same manner as the associated acquisition costs, and any further apportionment is on a just and reasonable basis where there is more than one simultaneous disposal. For all purposes of *FA 1997, Sch 12*, the period of account of the current lessor is treated as ending, and a new period as beginning, immediately before such a disposal (or simultaneous such disposals).

If these provisions come to apply to a lease to which the provisions of *FA 1997, Sch 12 Pt II* (see below) already apply, the cumulative accountancy rental excess or cumulative normal rent excess are determined as if these provisions had applied throughout the period for which *Part II* in fact applied.

[*FA 1997, Sch 12 paras 5–10, 12, 14, 30; ITTOIA 2005, Sch 1 para 494(3)*].

Capital allowances. Where an occasion occurs on which a major lump sum (as in (*b*) above) falls to be paid, there are provisions for the withdrawal of earlier reliefs etc. for expenditure incurred by the current lessor in respect of the leased asset. This applies to reliefs etc. for capital expenditure under *CAA 2001* or under 66.24 above (cemeteries and crematoria) or 66.84 below (waste disposal). Deductions allowed under *F(No 2)A 1992, ss 40B, 42* or *F(No 2)97, s 48* (films and sound recordings — see 66.53 above) are similarly withdrawn. The earlier reliefs etc. are withdrawn either by the bringing in of a disposal value or by the imposition of a balancing charge or, in the case of cemetery etc., waste disposal or film etc. expenditure allowed as a deduction, by the bringing in of a countervailing receipt. These provisions apply equally to capital allowances for contributors to capital expenditure under *CAA 2001, ss 537–542*. [*FA 1997, Sch 12 para 11; CAA 2001, Sch 2 para 98; ITTOIA 2005, Sch 1 para 494(2); FA 2005, Sch 3 paras 25, 31*].

Existing schemes for which (a)–(e) above become satisfied after 26 November 1996. Where a lease of an asset forms part of an 'existing scheme' (as below) for which conditions (*a*)–(*e*) above only become satisfied after 26 November 1996, *FA 1997, Sch 12* applies as if a period of account of the current lessor ended and another began both immediately before and immediately after those conditions came to be satisfied, i.e. as if there was a brief separate period of account during which they became satisfied. Any cumulative accountancy rental excess which would have arisen for that period, had the conditions been satisfied at all times on or after 26 November 1996, is treated as so arising, and the current lessor is treated as if, at the end of the immediately preceding period, there had accrued an additional amount of rent equal to that excess (which rent is, however, left out of account in determining normal rent for comparison with accountancy rental earnings, as above). Similarly a cumulative normal rent excess which would have arisen on those assumptions is treated as having arisen in the period in which the conditions came to be satisfied.

A lease of an asset forms part of an '*existing scheme*' if a contract in writing for the lease was made before 26 November 1996 and either:

(i) no terms of the contract remained to be agreed on or after that date, and any conditions were satisfied before that date; or

(ii) the requirements in (i) are satisfied before the end of the period ending with the later of 31 January 1997 and the expiry of six months after the making of the contract, or within such further time as HMRC may allow in any particular case, and in its final form the contract does not differ materially from how it stood when originally made. [*FA 1997, Sch 12 paras 13, 27*].

For HMRC's views on various points of interpretation regarding these provisions, see HMRC Finance Leasing Manual 21.01 onwards.

Finance leases not within above anti-avoidance provisions. *FA 1997, Sch 12 Pt II* applies from 26 November 1996 to arrangements, not within *Part I* (above), which involve the lease of an asset and are of a kind which would be treated under generally accepted accounting practice as finance leases or loans. The main purpose of the provisions is to charge tax on amounts equal to the income return on investment under generally accepted accounting practice (taking into account the substance of the matter as a whole, e.g. as regards connected persons or groups of companies). *Part II* accordingly applies where a lease of an asset forming part of a new scheme is granted on or after 26 November 1996, and condition (*a*) above is satisfied at some time on or after that date in a period of account of the current lessor, but the anti-avoidance provisions of *Part I* described above do not apply because not all of conditions (*b*)–(*e*) above are or have been satisfied at such a time. Where condition (*a*) was satisfied at some time on or after 26 November 1996, it is treated as continuing to be satisfied until either the asset ceases to be leased under the lease or the lessor's interest is assigned to (i) a person not connected with the assignor, (ii) any other person who was the lessor before the assignment, or (iii) any person who becomes the lessor after the assignment under arrangements made by a person who was the lessor (or a person connected with the lessor) at some time before the assignment. A lease which ceases to be within *Part II* following assignment will come within the provisions again if the conditions are again satisfied.

FA 1997, Sch 12 Pt II does *not* apply if (or to the extent that), as regards the current lessor, the lease falls to be regarded as a long funding lease (within 10.34 CAPITAL ALLOWANCES) of plant or machinery.

[*FA 1997, Sch 12 paras 15, 16; FA 2002, Sch 40 Pt 3(16); FA 2006, Sch 9 para 7(1)(3)(4)*].

Where *Part II* applies, the provisions of *FA 1997, Sch 12 paras 5–10, 12* for the taxation of the current lessor by reference to accountancy rental earnings (see above) apply to the lease. [*FA 1997, Sch 12 para 17*].

For HMRC's views on various points of interpretation regarding these provisions, see HMRC Finance Leasing Manual 21.01–21.27.

Finance leasing generally. See 10.28, 10.38(A)(C) CAPITAL ALLOWANCES for other finance lease capital allowance restrictions. It was held in *Caledonian Paper plc v CIR (Sp C 159), [1998] SSCD 129* that annual or semi-annual payments of commitment fees, guarantee fees and agency fees relating to guarantees required in relation to finance leasing arrangements were deductible in computing profits, but that a one-off management fee was not.

Simon's Direct Tax Service. See B3.1310.

66.55 FRANCHISING

For companies acquiring and selling franchises after 31 March 2002, the intangible assets regime (see 39 INTANGIBLE ASSETS) is likely to apply and takes precedence over the below.

Under a business system franchising agreement (i.e. an agreement under which the franchisor grants to the franchisee the right to distribute products or perform services using that system), there is generally an initial fee (payable in one sum or in instalments) and continuing, usually annual, fees.

The capital or revenue treatment of the initial fee depends on what it is for. To the extent that it is paid wholly or mainly for substantial rights of an enduring nature, to initiate or substantially extend a business, it is a capital payment (as are any related professional fees). (See 66.18 above for general principles.) It is immaterial that the expenditure may prove abortive, and the treatment of the payment in the hands of the franchisor is irrelevant. However, where goods or services of a revenue nature are supplied at the outset (e.g. trading stock or staff training), HMRC will accept that an appropriate part of the initial fee is a revenue payment, provided that the sum claimed fairly represents such items, and that it is clear that the items are not separately charged for in the continuing fees. The costs of the franchisee's own initial training are not normally allowable.

The continuing fee payable by the franchisee is generally a revenue expense.

(HMRC Business Income Manual BIM 57620).

See generally HMRC Business Income Manual BIM 57600–57620.

66.56 GIFTS AND DONATIONS ETC.

See also 66.49 above (entertainment and gifts).

The fact that a receipt is gratuitous is not in itself a reason for its not being a trading receipt. See *Severne v Dadswell Ch D 1954, 35 TC 649* (payments under war-time arrangements held trading receipts although *ex gratia*); *CIR v Falkirk Ice Rink CS 1975, 51 TC 42* (donation to ice rink from associated curling club held taxable); *Wing v O'Connell Supreme Court (IFS) 1926, [1927] IR 84* (gift to professional jockey on winning race taxable).

In relation to *ex gratia* payments on the termination of long-standing business arrangements, a distinction is drawn between parting gifts as personal testimonials (not taxable as business receipts) and payments which, on the facts, can be seen as additional rewards for services already rendered or compensation for a loss of future profits (taxable). For cases see 66.27(*e*) above.

Cremation fees (often known as 'ash cash') assigned in advance, and paid directly, to a medical charity may escape liability to tax on miscellaneous income where the doctor entitled to them is not chargeable to tax on trading income, but liability to tax on trading income is not affected by such assignment. See HMRC Business Income Manual BIM 54015.

Gifts to charities and educational establishments. A relief is available for certain gifts by traders to charities and similar bodies (see 14.13 CHARITIES), to 'designated educational establishment' or a registered community amateur sports club (see 70.8 VOLUNTARY ASSOCIATIONS).

Where the gift is of an article manufactured by the company, or of a type sold by the company, in its trade, it is not required to bring in any amount as a trading receipt in respect of the disposal of the article.

Expenditure incurred in making a gift to a charity is not subject to the restrictions on business entertainment expenditure (see 66.49 above) but must be 'wholly and exclusively' incurred for the purposes of the trade if it is to be deductible against profits. [*ICTA 1988, s 577*(*8*)(*9*)]. Costs incurred in respect of an employee temporarily seconded to a charity or educational establishment continue to be deductible either from the trading profits under Case I or as a management expense, as appropriate, as if wholly and exclusively incurred for business purposes. [*ICTA 1988, s 86; ITTOIA 2005, Sch 1 para 60*].

For gifts to educational establishments only:

- the article must classified as plant or machinery if the establishment had incurred expenditure on it for the purposes of a trade carried on by it; and
- for the relief to apply, a claim must be made within two years beginning at the end of the accounting period in which the gift is made and it must specify both the article and the educational establishment concerned.

For income tax purposes for 2005/06 onwards the requirement that a gift to an educational establishment should qualify as plant and machinery in its hands is removed s well as the need to make a claim for the relief to apply. Also for gifts *other than* to educational establishments, the wording is slightly less restrictive so that gifts can be made 'for the purpose' rather than *to* the charity etc. (see Changes 29–31 listed in Annex 1 to the Explanatory Notes to the Income Tax (Trading and Other Income) Bill). Where the gift is of an item of plant or machinery used in the course of the company's trade, its disposal value for capital allowances purposes (see 10.29 CAPITAL ALLOWANCES) is nil. (Before *CAA 2001* had effect, see 10.1 CAPITAL ALLOWANCES, this rule operated slightly differently in that no disposal value was required to be brought into account.)

The value of any benefit received by the company or by a person connected with the company (see 19 CONNECTED PERSONS), which is in any way attributable to the making of a gift for which relief has been given as above, must be brought into account as a trading receipt in the accounting period in which the benefit arises or, if the company is not chargeable to tax under Schedule D, Case I or II, under Schedule D, Case VI.. (For income tax purposes for 2005/06 onwards, the value of the benefit is treated as arising on the date of receipt of the benefit or; if the trade had ceased by then, the benefit is treated as a post-cessation receipt for tax purposes.(see Changes 21 and 22 listed in Annex 1 to the Explanatory Notes to the Income Tax (Trading and Other Income) Bill).)

'*Designated educational establishment*' means any educational establishment designated (or of a category designated) in regulations, broadly all UK universities, public or private schools and further and higher educational institutions (see *SI 1992 No 42* as amended by *SI 1993 No 561*).

[*ICTA 1988, ss 83A, 84; CAA 2001, s 63(2)–(4), Sch 2 paras 16, 17; ITTOIA 2005, Sch 1 paras 57, 58, 535;*].

By concession, other gifts are allowed as deductions provided that they are (i) wholly and exclusively for the purposes of the business, (ii) made for the benefit of a body or association established for educational, cultural, religious, recreational or benevolent purposes which is local to the donor's business activities and not restricted to persons connected with the donor and (iii) reasonably small in relation to the scale of the donor's business (HMRC Extra Statutory Concession, B7). In *Bourne & Hollingsworth v Ogden KB 1929, 14 TC 349* an abnormally large donation was disallowed. For donations of part of cost of ticket in football pools and lotteries, see 66.9 above.

Simon's Direct Tax Service. See **B3.1323, B3.1324**.

66.57 GUARANTEES

Losses under guarantees of the indebtedness of another are analogous to impairment losses (see 66.21 above) and similar principles apply. Losses were allowed as a deduction to a solicitor under the guarantee of a client's overdraft (*Jennings v Barfield Ch D 1962, 40 TC 365*) and to a film-writer under guarantee of loans to a film company with which he was associated (*Lunt v Wellesley KB 1945, 27 TC 78*) but refused to a company under a guarantee of loans to an associated company with which it had close trading connections (*Milnes v J Beam Group Ltd Ch D 1975, 50 TC 675*) and a guarantee of loans to a subsidiary (*Redkite Ltd v Inspector of Taxes [1996] SSCD 501*). See also *Bolton v Halpern & Woolf CA 1980, 53 TC 445* and *Garforth v Tankard Carpets Ltd Ch D 1980, 53 TC 342*.

A loss by an asphalt contractor under a guarantee to an exhibition (for which he hoped but, in the event, failed to work) allowed (*Morley v Lawford & Co CA 1928, 14 TC 229*).

Payments under guarantees made to a trader for the setting up or the purposes of the trade and irrecoverable are in certain circumstances allowable as a loss for capital gains tax. [*TCGA 1992, s 253*]. See Tolley's Capital Gains Tax.

66.58 HIRE-PURCHASE

Where assets are purchased under hire-purchase agreements, the charges (the excess of the hire-purchase price over the cash price, sometimes called interest but not true interest) are, appropriately spread, allowable deductions (*Darngavil Coal Co Ltd v Francis CS 1913, 7 TC 1*). See 66.21 above for the bad debt etc. provisions of hire-purchase traders. For relief on capital element, see 10.38(A) CAPITAL ALLOWANCES.

For whether goods sold under hire-purchase are trading stock, see *Lions Ltd v Gosford Furnishing Co Ltd & CIR CS 1961, 40 TC 256* and cf. *Drages Ltd v CIR KB 1927, 46 TC 389*.

See generally HMRC Business Income Manual BIM 40550–40555 (hire-purchase receipts) and BIM 45350–45365 (hire-purchase payments).

Simon's Direct Tax Service. See **B3.1310.**

66.59 ILLEGAL PAYMENTS ETC.

In computing profits chargeable under Schedule D, no deduction may be made in respect of expenditure (including incidental costs) incurred (*a*) in making a payment the making of which constitutes a criminal offence, or (*b*) (after 31 March 2002) in making a payment outside the UK where the making of a corresponding payment in any part of the UK would constitute a criminal offence there. A deduction is similarly denied for any payment induced by a demand constituting blackmail or extortion. Relief as a management expense is similarly denied. [*ICTA 1988, s 577A; FA 2002, s 68; SI 2004 No 2310, Sch para 24; ITTOIA 2005, Sch 1 para 236*].

For a discussion of the circumstances in which the above may apply, see HMRC Business Income Manual BIM 43100–43185.

Simon's Direct Tax Service. See **B3.1332.**

66.60 INSURANCE

Premiums for business purposes are normally allowable including insurance of assets, insurance against accidents to employees, insurance against loss of profits and premiums under mutual insurance schemes (cf. *Thomas v Richard Evans & Co HL 1927, 11 TC 790*; for trade associations, see 66.76 below). For war risk premiums, see *ICTA 1988, s 586*.

Any corresponding recoveries are trading receipts (or set off against trading expenses or capital, according to the nature of the policy. Where a deduction was allowed for a loss or expense and the trader recovers a capital sum under an insurance policy or contract of indemnity in respect of that loss or expense, the deduction must be disallowed up to the amount of the recovery. [*ICTA 1988, s 74(1)(l)*]. For income tax purposes for 2005/06 onwards, *ITTOIA 2005, s 106* uses different wording, specifying that the sum recovered must be brought into account, up to the amount of the deduction, as a trading receipt. This is said to reflect previous practice based on accountancy treatment (see Change 28 listed in Annex 1 to the Explanatory Notes to the Income Tax (Trading and Other Income) Bill). Otherwise, if capital, the recovery may be taken into account, where appropriate, for the purposes of CAPITAL ALLOWANCES (10) or CAPITAL GAINS (11).

The whole of a recovery in respect of the destruction of trading stock was held to be a trading receipt of the year of destruction, notwithstanding that it exceeded the market value of the stock lost or not all the stock was replaced (*Green v J Gliksten & Son Ltd HL 1929, 14 TC 364*; *Rownson Drew & Clydesdale Ltd v CIR KB 1931, 16 TC 595*). The total recovery under a loss of profits was held a trading receipt although in excess of the loss suffered (*R v British Columbia Fir & Cedar PC 1932, 15 ATC 624*). See also *Mallandain Investments Ltd v Shadbolt KB 1940, 23 TC 367.* For recoveries under accidents to employees see *Gray & Co v Murphy KB 1940, 23 TC 225*; *Keir & Cawder Ltd v CIR CS 1958, 38 TC 23.* Where a shipping company insured against late delivery of ships being built for it, both premiums and recoveries held capital (*Crabb v Blue Star Line Ltd Ch D 1961, 39 TC 482*).

Premiums on policies in favour of the employer insuring against death or critical illness of key employees are generally allowable, and the proceeds of any such policies trading receipts. However, in *Beauty Consultants Ltd v Inspector of Taxes (Sp C 321), [2002] SSCD 352*, premiums on a policy insuring a company against the death of either of its controlling shareholder-directors were not allowed as deductions; the 'dual purpose rule' at 66.18 above applied, in that the premiums benefited the shareholders personally by improving the value of their shares. In *Greycon Ltd v Klaentschi (Sp C 372), [2003] SSCD 370*, it was held that the company's sole purpose in taking out key man policies was to meet a requirement of an agreement under which funding and other benefits were obtained from another company, that the policies had a capital purpose and that, consequently, the proceeds were not trading receipts.

Commissions. HMRC Statement of Practice SP 4/97 (see 66.25 above) deals widely with commissions, cashbacks and discounts.

See also *Robertson v CIR (Sp C 137), [1997] SSCD 282* as regards timing of inclusion of insurance agents' advance commission.

66.61 **INVESTMENT INCOME (INCLUDING LETTING INCOME)**

Investment income may be treated as a trading receipt where it is the fruit derived from a fund employed and risked in the business (see *Liverpool and London and Globe Insurance Co v Bennett HL 1913, 6 TC 327*). This treatment is not confined to financial trades, but the making and holding of investments at interest must be an integral part of the trade. See *Nuclear Electric plc v Bradley HL 1996, 68 TC 670*, in which (in refusing the company's claim) the crucial test was considered to be whether the investments were employed in the business (of producing electricity) in the accounting period in question. The Court of Appeal, whose judgment was approved, considered decisive the facts that the liabilities against which the investments were provided were liabilities to third parties, not to customers, and that, in view of the long-term nature of the liabilities, the business could be carried on for a long period without maintaining any fund of investments at all. See also *Bank Line Ltd v CIR* (below).

See 47.19 LOSSES as regards relief available to investment companies for losses on shares subscribed for in certain unlisted trading companies,

Payments received in lieu of dividends in contango operations were held to be trading receipts in *Multipar Syndicate Ltd v Devitt KB 1945, 26 TC 359*; also co-operative society 'dividends' on trading purchases (*Pope v Beaumont KB 1941, 24 TC 78*). For interest received by underwriters on securities deposited with Lloyd's see *Owen v Sassoon HC 1950, 32 TC 101* and for discount receivable on bills see *Willingale v International Commercial Bank Ltd HL 1978, 52 TC 242*.

In certain cases income received under deduction of tax was unable to be included in a Schedule D, Case I or II assessment (cf. *F S Securities Ltd v CIR HL 1964, 41 TC 666*; *Bucks v Bowers Ch D 1969, 46 TC 267*; *Bank Line Ltd v CIR CS 1974, 49 TC 307*), and nor, subject to the Crown option between Cases could income received gross from sources within Schedule D, Cases III, IV or V (cf. *Northend v White & Leonard & Corbin Greener Ch D 1975, 50 TC 121*) and also from sources *explicitly* within Schedule D, Case VI.

Rents receivable and other letting income are within the charge to tax on property income as opposed to trading income (see 66.1 above).

If, however, a company lets **surplus business accommodation** and the conditions below are satisfied, it may choose to include the receipts and expenses of the letting in computing its trading profits instead of treating them as receipts and expenses of a property business. The conditions are that the let accommodation must be 'temporarily surplus to requirements', it must not be part of trading stock, it must be part of a building of which another part is used to carry on the trade, and the letting receipts must be relatively small. For these purposes, 'letting' includes a licence to occupy. Once the receipts and expenses of a letting are included in trading profits, all subsequent receipts and expenses of the letting must similarly be so included. This relaxation of the main rule above is applied by HMRC in practice (see Revenue Tax Bulletin February 1994 p 115) but for income tax purposes it applies by statute for 2005/06 onwards under *ITTOIA 2005, s 21*. The statute additionally contains rules for determining whether or not accommodation is '*temporarily surplus to requirements*'. It must have been used for trading within the last three years or acquired within that period; the trader must intend to use it for trading in future; and the letting itself must be for a term of no more than three years. The position is judged as at the beginning of a period of account. (See Change 4 listed in Annex 1 to the Explanatory Notes to the Income Tax (Trading and Other Income) Bill).

See 56.2 PROPERTY INCOME for a further relaxation of the main rule above, this time in relation to caravan site operators.

66.62 KNOW-HOW

For corporation tax purposes, 'know-how' created or acquired from an unrelated party **on or after 1 April 2002** generally falls within the intangible assets regime. See in particular the commencement and transitional rules for that regime at 39.37 INTANGIBLE ASSETS. The following applies where know-how does not fall within that regime.

'*Know-how*' is any industrial information and techniques likely to assist in (*a*) manufacturing or processing goods or materials, (*b*) working, or searching for etc., mineral deposits, or (*c*) agricultural, forestry or fishing operations. For capital allowances on purchases of know-how, see 10.23 CAPITAL ALLOWANCES.

Where know-how used in the vendor's trade is disposed of, with the trade thereafter continuing, the consideration received is treated as a trading receipt, except to the extent that it is brought into account as a disposal value for capital allowances purposes (see 10.23 CAPITAL ALLOWANCES). This does not apply to a sale between bodies of persons (which includes partnerships) under the same control.

If the know-how is disposed of as part of the disposal of all or part of the trade, both vendor and purchaser are treated for corporation tax purposes as if the consideration for the know-how were a payment for goodwill. They may, however, jointly elect to disapply this treatment (within two years of the disposal, and provided they are not bodies under common control), and it is disapplied in any event in relation to the purchaser if, prior to his acquiring it, the trade was carried on wholly outside the UK. In either case, the purchaser may then claim capital allowances on the expenditure (see 10.23(iii) CAPITAL ALLOWANCES).

Any consideration received for a restrictive covenant in connection with a disposal of know-how is treated as consideration received for the disposal of the know-how. An exchange of know-how is treated as a sale of know-how.

[*ICTA 1988, ss 531, 533(7); CAA 2001, Sch 2 para 48; ITTOIA 2005, Sch 1 paras 207, 209*].

In *Delage v Nugget Polish Co Ltd KB 1905, 21 TLR 454*, payments for the use of a secret process, payable for 40 years and based on receipts, were held to be annual payments subject to deduction of tax at source. See also *Paterson Engineering v Duff KB 1943, 25 TC 43*.

For patents, see 66.67 below.

Simon's Direct Tax Service. See **B3.861** *et seq.*

66.63 LEGAL AND PROFESSIONAL EXPENSES

The costs of forming a company are capital but in so far as they relate to loan capital may qualify for relief by virtue of *ICTA 1988, s 401* (pre-trading expenditure, see 66.69 below).

The expenses of a company incorporated by charter in obtaining a variation of its charter etc. were allowed (*CIR v Carron Co HL 1968, 45 TC 18*). See also *McGarry v Limerick Gas HC(IFS) [1932] IR 125* and contrast *A & G Moore & Co v Hare CS 1914, 6 TC 572*. In general, the costs of maintaining existing trading rights and assets are revenue expenses (*Southern v Borax Consolidated KB 1940, 23 TC 597*; *Bihar etc. IT Commr v Maharaja of Dharbanga PC 1941, 20 ATC 337* and compare *Morgan v Tate & Lyle Ltd HL 1954, 35 TC 367*). But the incidental costs of acquiring new assets etc. are part of their capital cost. The expenses of obtaining or renewing a lease of business premises are strictly capital but, in practice, the expenses of renewing leases under 50 years are generally deductible (although a proportionate disallowance may apply where a lease premium is involved — see HMRC Business Income Manual BIM 46420). The cost of an unsuccessful application to vary a carrier's licence was disallowed (*Pyrah v Annis & Co CA 1956, 37 TC 163*) as was the cost of an unsuccessful application for planning permission (*ECC Quarries Ltd v Watkis Ch D 1975, 51 TC 153*. For excise licences, see 66.22 above.

Legal expenses in defending charges brought by a professional regulatory body were allowed as deductions on the grounds that they were incurred to prevent suspension or expulsion and thus to protect the taxpayer's business (applying *Tate & Lyle Ltd* (above)), although the fines imposed were disallowed (see 66.26 above) (*McKnight v Sheppard HL 1999, 71 TC 419*).

Costs incurred by a partner in connection with the dissolution of the partnership were disallowed in *C Connelly & Co v Wilbey Ch D 1992, 65 TC 208*.

The cost of tax appeals even though successful is not deductible (*Allen v Farquharson Bros & Co KB 1932, 17 TC 59*; *Smith's Potato Estates v Bolland HL 1948, 30 TC 267*; *Rushden Heel Co v Keene HL 1948, 30 TC 298*). Where an accountant etc. agrees the tax liabilities based on the accounts he prepares, normal annual fees are allowed as a deduction but not fees for a special review of settled years (*Worsley Brewery Co v CIR CA 1932, 17 TC 349*).

Additional accountancy expenses incurred as a result of an 'in-depth' examination by HMRC of a particular year's accounts will normally be allowed as a deduction if the investigation does not result in an adjustment to the profits of any earlier year or in the imposition of interest or interest and penalties in relation to the current year. Where the investigation reveals discrepancies and additional liabilities for earlier years, or results in a settlement for the current year including interest (with or without penalties), the expenses will be disallowed. (HMRC Statement of Practice, SP 16/91). In its application to self-assessment enquiries, the Statement of Practice is reworded to make it clear that the prohibition on allowance of accountancy expenses applies only where the enquiry reveals negligent or fraudulent conduct (see Revenue Interpretation RI 192 and see Revenue Tax Bulletin October 1998 p 596).

It is HMRC's view that premiums for a fee protection insurance policy, which entitles the policy holder to claim for the cost of accountancy fees incurred in negotiating additional tax liabilities resulting from negligent or fraudulent conduct, are not allowable. Even if the policy covers other risks as well, the premiums cannot be apportioned between allowable and non-allowable elements. (Revenue Tax Bulletin June 2003 p 1036).

Simon's Direct Tax Service. See **B3.1387**.

66.64 LONG FUNDING LEASES OF PLANT OR MACHINERY

The rules on leasing of plant and machinery are reformed by *FA 2006, s 81, Sch 8* with effect from, broadly, **1 April 2006**. For 'long funding leases', the new regime grants entitlement to capital allowances to the lessee rather than to the lessor as previously (see 10.34 CAPITAL ALLOWANCES). There are corresponding changes to the tax treatment of lease rentals, to ensure that the lessor is no longer taxed on, and the lessee does not obtain a deduction for, the capital element of rentals (see below). The new regime applies only to leases which are essentially financing transactions, known as '*funding leases*', comprising mainly finance leases but also some operating leases. Leases of less than five years' duration are excluded from the regime, as are pre-1 April 2006 leases. There are transitional rules to enable leases finalised on or after 1 April 2006 to remain within the pre-existing regime in appropriate circumstances. See 10.34 under Commencement/transitional provisions. The coverage below considers firstly the lessor's position and then the lessee's. The provisions differ in each case according to whether the lease is a long funding operating lease or a long funding finance lease.

As regards finance leases that fall outside the definition of a long funding lease or preceded its introduction, see 66.54 above.

Lessors. *Long funding operating leases.* For any period of account for the whole or any part of which the company is the lessor of plant or machinery under a 'long funding operating lease' (see 10.34(3) CAPITAL ALLOWANCES), it is entitled to a deduction as follows in computing its profits (so as to compensate it for non-entitlement to capital allowances). Firstly, determine the 'relevant value' in accordance with *ICTA 1988, s 502(4)(5)*. This varies depending on whether or not there has been any previous use of the plant or machinery by the lessor and on the nature of any such previous use. In the most straightforward case where the sole use has been leasing under the long funding operating lease, the relevant value is equal to cost. Secondly, deduct from the relevant value the amount that is expected (at the commencement of the term of the lease — see *CAA 2001, s 70YI(1)*) to be the 'residual value' of the plant or machinery (i.e. its estimated market value assuming a disposal at the end of the term of the lease, less the estimated costs of that disposal). This gives the expected gross reduction in value over the term of the lease. Next, time-apportion that figure between all periods of account that coincide wholly or partly with the term of the lease. The resulting figure for each period of account is the amount deductible for that period.

Where the lessor (as above) incurs additional capital expenditure on the plant or machinery that is not reflected in its market value at the commencement of the term of the lease, an additional deduction is due as follows. Determine the amount which, at the time the additional expenditure is incurred, is expected to be the residual value of the plant or machinery. Deduct the amount previously expected to be the residual value. If this produces a positive amount, determine how much of that amount is attributable to the additional expenditure. Next, deduct the attributable amount from the amount of the additional expenditure. This gives the expected reduction in value of the additional expenditure over the remainder of the term of the lease. Time-apportion that figure between all periods of account that coincide wholly or partly with the term of the lease and which end after the additional expenditure is incurred. The resulting figure for each such period of account is the additional amount deductible for that period.

In the period of account in which a long funding operating lease *terminates*, any profit arising to the lessor from the termination must be brought into account as trading income and any loss so arising must be brought into account as a revenue expense. The profit or loss is computed as follows.

(1) Determine the 'termination amount' (for which see 10.34 CAPITAL ALLOWANCES under Lessors) and subtract from it any sums paid to the lessee that are calculated by reference to the 'termination value' (as defined by *CAA 2001, s 70YH*), e.g. lease rental refunds.

(2) Determine the 'relevant value' as above and subtract from it all deductions (other than additional deductions) allowable as above to that same lessor up to the date of termination.

(3) If any additional capital expenditure has been incurred as above, determine the total amount thereof and subtract from it all additional deductions allowable as above to that same lessor up to the date of termination.

(4) If the total in (1) above exceeds the aggregate of the totals in (2) and (3), a profit arises equal to the excess.

(5) If the total in (1) above falls short of the aggregate of the totals in (2) and (3), a loss arises equal to the deficit.

In computing the lessor's profits for the period of account in which termination occurs, no trading deduction is allowed for any sums paid to the lessee that are calculated by reference to the 'termination value' (as these are brought into account in (1) above).

[*ICTA 1988, ss 502E–502G, 502L(2)(4); FA 2006, Sch 8 para 11*].

Long funding finance leases. For any period of account in which the company is the lessor of plant or machinery under a 'long funding finance lease' (see 10.34(4) CAPITAL ALLOWANCES), the amount to be brought into account as his taxable income from the lease is the amount of the 'rental earnings' in respect of the lease. The '*rental earnings*' for any period is the amount that, in accordance with generally accepted accounting practice (GAAP), falls to be treated as the gross return on investment for that period in respect of the lease. If, in accordance with GAAP, the lease falls to be treated as a loan in the accounts in question, so much of the lease rentals as fall to be treated as interest are treated for these purposes as rental earnings. There is also provision for exceptional profits or losses (including capital items) arising from the lease to be brought into account for tax purposes, as trading income or as revenue expenditure, if they fall to be brought into account under GAAP in the period of account in question but otherwise than as part of the profits calculation.

Where the lease *terminates* and any sum calculated by reference to 'termination value' (as defined by *CAA 2001, s 70YH*) is paid to the lessee, e.g. lease rental refunds, no deduction is allowed for that sum in computing the lessor's trading profits, except to the extent (if any) that it is brought into account in determining rental earnings.

[*ICTA 1988, ss 502B–502D, 502L(4); FA 2006, Sch 8 para 11*].

Insurance companies. Special provisions apply to lessor companies carrying on life assurance business. The provisions ensure that the general apportionment rules in *ICTA 1988, s 432A* apply to net amounts of profits or losses arising from long funding leases and that, in taking receipts into account in a Schedule D Case I computation the above provisions are ignored. [*ICTA 1988, s 502H; FA 2006, Sch 8 para 11*].

Lessees. *Long funding operating leases.* In computing the profits of a company for any period of account in which it is the lessee of plant or machinery under a 'long funding operating lease' (see 10.34(3) CAPITAL ALLOWANCES), the otherwise allowable deductions in respect of amounts payable under the lease must be reduced as follows.

Firstly, determine the 'relevant value' in accordance with *ICTA 1988, s 502K(4)(5)*. In the straightforward case where the sole use of the plant or machinery has been in a qualifying activity (within 10.24 CAPITAL ALLOWANCES) carried on by the lessee, the relevant value is equal to the market value of the plant or machinery at the commencement (see *CAA 2001, s 70YI(1)*) of the term of the lease. Secondly, deduct from the relevant value the amount that is expected (at the commencement of the term of the lease) to be the market value of the plant or machinery at the end of the term of the lease. This gives the expected gross reduction over the term of the lease. Next, time-apportion that figure between all periods of account that coincide wholly or partly with the term of the lease. The resulting figure for each period of account is the amount of the reduction for that period.

[*ICTA 1988, ss 502K, 502L; FA 2006, Sch 8 para 11*].

Long funding finance leases. In computing the profits of a company for any period of account in which it is the lessee of plant or machinery under a 'long funding finance lease' (see 10.34(4) CAPITAL ALLOWANCES), the amount deducted in respect of amounts payable under the lease must not exceed the amount that, in accordance with GAAP, falls to be shown in the lessee's accounts as finance charges in respect of the lease. If, in accordance with GAAP, the lease falls to be accounted for as a loan, it is for this purpose treated as if it fell to be accounted for as a finance lease.

Where the lease *terminates* and a sum calculated by reference to 'termination value' (as defined by *CAA 2001, s 70YH*) is paid to the lessee, e.g. lease rental refunds, that sum is not brought into account in computing the lessee's trading profits for any period. (It is, however, brought into account in calculating the disposal value of the plant or machinery for capital allowances purposes — see 10.34 CAPITAL ALLOWANCES under Lessees: Disposal events and values).

[*ICTA 1988, ss 502I, 502J, 502L(4); FA 2006, Sch 8 para 11*].

66.65 **MINES, QUARRIES ETC.**

See 10.39 *et seq.* CAPITAL ALLOWANCES for mining etc. expenditure so allowable. The relevant legislation which applied before 1 April 1986 originated from 1945 and may therefore affect any pre-1945 decisions below. See also 55.15 PROFIT COMPUTATIONS in respect of 'mineral royalties' under a lease, licence or agreement conferring a right to win and work minerals in the UK or under a sale or conveyance of such minerals.

The cost of sinking (*Coltness Iron Co v Black HL 1881, 1 TC 287*), deepening (*Bonner v Basset Mines KB 1912, 6 TC 146*) or 'de-watering' (*United Collieries v CIR CS 1929, 12 TC 1248*) a pit is capital.

A lump sum paid at the end of a mining lease for surface damage was held capital (*Robert Addie & Sons v CIR CS 1924, 8 TC 671*) but not periodic payments during the currency of the lease based on acreage worked (*O'Grady v Bullcroft Main Collieries KB 1932, 17 TC 93*). *Bullcroft* was decided before the enactment of what is now *ICTA 1988 s 119* and rents and tonnage payments for the right to withdraw surface support are easements within *section 119* (*CIR v New Sharlston Collieries CA 1936, 21 TC 116*). For shortworkings, see *Broughton & Plas Power v Kirkpatrick QB 1884, 2 TC 69*; *CIR v Cranford Ironstone KB 1942, 29 TC 113*. Provision for the future costs of abandoning an oil field and of restoring hired equipment used therein to its original state held capital (*RTZ Oil and Gas Ltd v Elliss Ch D 1987, 61 TC 132*).

For HMRC's view of the treatment of payments by mining concerns to landowners for restoration for surface damage, see HMRC Business Income Manual BIM 62025. In particular, a payment of compensation for ascertained past damage is allowable, as is a provision for such expenditure where made in accordance with generally accepted accounting practice and accurately quantified.

Purchase of unworked deposits by sand and gravel merchant held capital (*Stow Bardolph Gravel Co Ltd v Poole CA 1954, 35 TC 459*) as was purchase of land with nitrate deposits by chemical manufacturer (*Alianza Co v Bell HL 1905, 5 TC 172*) and payment by oil company for unwon oil in wells it took over (*Hughes v British Burmah Petroleum KB 1932, 17 TC 286*). See also *Golden Horse Shoe v Thurgood CA 1933, 18 TC 280* (purchase of tailings for gold extraction, allowable) and *CIR v Broomhouse Brick CS 1952, 34 TC 1* (purchase of blaes for brick manufacture, allowable).

See generally HMRC Business Income Manual BIM 62000–62085.

Production wells etc. The costs of drilling the second and subsequent production wells in an area are not generally allowable. [*ICTA 1988, s 91C; ITTOIA 2005, Sch 1 para 71*]. Although not specifically stated in the statute, this prohibition applies particularly to intangible drilling costs. For a discussion of this, see HMRC Oil Taxation Manual OT 26237. Such costs may attract mineral extraction capital allowances (see 10.39 *et seq.* CAPITAL ALLOWANCES).

66.66 **MISCELLANEOUS EXPENSES AND RECEIPTS**

Card winnings of club proprietor, trading receipts (*Burdge v Pyne Ch D 1968, 45 TC 320*). For lotteries and football pools, see 66.9 above.

Computer software. Subject to the application of the INTANGIBLE ASSETS (39) regime, HMRC's views on the treatment of expenditure on computer software are summarised as follows.

Software acquired under licence. Regular payments akin to a rental are allowable revenue expenditure, the timing of deductions being governed by correct accountancy practice (see 66.5 above). A lump sum payment is capital if the licence is of a sufficiently enduring nature to be considered a capital asset in the context of the licencee's trade (see 66.18 above), e.g. where it may be expected to function as a tool of the trade for several years. Equally the benefit may be transitory (and the expenditure revenue) even though the licence is for an indefinite period. Inspectors will in any event accept that expenditure is revenue expenditure where the software has a useful economic life of less than two years. Timing of the deduction in these circumstances will again depend on correct accountancy practice.

Where the licence is a capital asset, capital allowances are available (see 10.25 CAPITAL ALLOWANCES).

Expenditure on a package containing both hardware and a licence to use software must be apportioned before the above principles are applied.

Software owned outright. The treatment of expenditure on such software (including any in-house costs) follows the same principles as are described above in relation to licensed software.

(HMRC Business Income Manual 35800).

For the treatment of expenditure on systems modification work relating to the Year 2000 problem and to EMU conversion, see Revenue Tax Bulletin April 1998 p 531. Broadly, such work will always be a revenue matter unless it is carried out as part of a major new project instituting changes on such a scale as to be of a capital nature in relation to the business.

See HMRC Business Income Manual BIM 35800–35865 for a detailed analysis of HMRC's views generally. See also Simon's Direct Tax Service B3.1518.

Export Credits Guarantee Department. A deduction is allowed for amounts paid by a company to that Department under an agreement entered into by virtue of arrangements made under *Export and Investment Guarantees Act 1991, s 2* or with a view to entering into such an agreement. [*ICTA 1988, s 88; ITTOIA 2005, Sch 1 para 64*].

Mutual concerns, distribution of assets from. If a deduction has been allowed (in computing trading profits) for a payment to a corporate mutual concern for the purposes of its mutual business and the company receives a distribution in money or money's worth upon the winding-up or dissolution of the mutual concern, the amount or value received is a trading receipt. This applies only if the assets being distributed represent profits of the mutual concern. Under HMRC practice, this does not apply to distributions of chargeable gains. (This has statutory authority for income tax purposes for 2005/06 onwards; see Change 27 listed in Annex 1 to the Explanatory Notes to the Income Tax (Trading and Other Income) Bill). If the trade has ceased by the time of the distribution, the amount or value received is chargeable under Schedule D, Case VI. (For income tax purposes from 2005/06, it is treated as a post-cessation receipt; see Change 22 listed in Annex 1 to the Explanatory Notes to the Income Tax (Trading and Other Income) Bill). [*ICTA 1988, s 491; ITTOIA 2005, Sch 1 para 189*]. See 48 MUTUAL COMPANIES.

Overpayments received, due to errors by customers or their banks which the taxpayer neither caused nor facilitated, held not to be trading receipts (*Anise Ltd and Others v Hammond (Sp C 364), [2003] SSCD 258*).

Purchases/sales of assets. See *T Beynon & Co v Ogg KB 1918, 7 TC 125* (profits of colliery agent from deals in wagons held trading receipts); *Gloucester Railway Carriage v CIR HL 1925, 12 TC 720* (sale by wagon manufacturer of wagons previously let, held trading receipts); *Bonner v Frood KB 1934, 18 TC 488* (sale of rounds by credit trader, held trading receipts).

Reimbursements of capital expenditure spread over 30 years held capital as regards both payer and recipient (*Boyce v Whitwick Colliery CA 1934, 18 TC 655*). For allowances from railway in respect of traffic on sidings paid for by trader see *Westcombe v Hadnock Quarries KB 1931, 16 TC 137*; *Legge v Flettons Ltd KB 1939, 22 TC 455*.

Excessive payments to **service company** of professional firm held not deductible (*Stephenson v Payne, Stone Fraser & Co Ch D 1967, 44 TC 507*).

Timber purchases and sales. For purchases and sales of standing timber by timber merchants see *Murray v CIR CS 1951, 32 TC 238*; *McLellan, Rawson & Co v Newall Ch D 1955, 36 TC 117*; *Hood Barrs v CIR (No 2) HL 1957, 37 TC 188*; *Hopwood v C N Spencer Ltd Ch D 1964, 42 TC 169*; *Russell v Hird and Mercer Ch D 1983, 57 TC 127*. For sales of trees by farmer see *Elmes v Trembath KB 1934, 19 TC 72*.

Trade marks or designs. Expenses are deductible if incurred in obtaining, for the purposes of a trade, the registration of a trade mark or design, the renewal of registration of a trade mark or the extension of the period for which the right in a registered design subsists. [*ICTA 1988, s 83; Copyright, Designs and Patents Act 1988, Sch 7 para 36(1)(2); Trade Marks Act 1994, s 106(2), Sch 5; ITTOIA 2005, Sch 1 para 56*]. For corporation tax purposes expenditure and receipts in respect of intellectual property acquired or created **on or after 1 April 2002** falls within the intangible assets regime. See in particular the commencement and transitional rules for that regime at 39.37 INTANGIBLE ASSETS.

Transfer fees. The accounting treatment of transfer fees paid by football or other sports clubs may be affected by either FRS 10 issued by the Accounting Standards Board on 4 September 1997 or the FRS for Smaller Entities issued by the Board on 10 December 1998. Where a transfer fee is paid under a contract entered into before the beginning of the first accounting period for which either of those standards has effect, then unless the club elects to the contrary (within two years after the end of that accounting period), the tax treatment of the payment is not affected by anything in the standard. Any necessary adjustments to give effect to this provision may be made, notwithstanding any relevant time limits. [*FA 1999, s 63; ITTOIA 2005, Sch 1 para 506*].

Valuation fees. Property valuation fees incurred in order to comply with *Companies Act 1985, Sch 7 para 1* are allowable as trading or management expenses. (HMRC Statement of Practice, C10). It is understood that regular property valuation fees (other than in connection with property acquisitions or sales) are similarly allowable.

Video tape rental. Relief for the cost of acquiring video tapes for hire may be obtained by way of either:

(i) capital allowances (provided the useful economic life is at least two years);

(ii) valuation basis (where the useful economic life is two years or less); or

(iii) renewals basis.

See Revenue Tax Bulletin October 1995 pp 254, 255 for a discussion of each of these methods in this context. See also HMRC Business Income Manual BIM 67200–67220.

Websites. The cost of setting up a website is likely to be capital expenditure; the regular update costs are likely to be revenue expenses (see HMRC Business Income Manual BIM 35870).

General. See also *Thompson v Magnesium Elektron CA 1943, 26 TC 1* (payments based on purchases, held trading receipts); *British Commonwealth International Newsfilm v Mahany HL 1962, 40 TC 550* (payments to meet operating expenses, trading receipts); *CIR v Pattison CS 1959, 38 TC 617* (weekly instalments for business, capital).

66.67 PATENTS

For corporation tax purposes, expenditure and receipts in respect of intellectual property acquired or created **on or after 1 April 2002** falls within the intangible assets regime. See in particular the commencement and transitional rules for that regime at 39.37 INTANGIBLE ASSETS.

Expenses (agent's charges, patent office fees etc.) are deductible if incurred in obtaining, for the purposes of a trade, the grant of a patent or the extension of its term. Expenses are also deductible in connection with a rejected or abandoned application for a patent made for the purposes of the trade. [*ICTA 1988, s 83; ITTOIA 2005, Sch 1 para 56*].

For capital expenditure on the purchase of patent rights see 10.50 CAPITAL ALLOWANCES.

Sums received on the sale of patent rights may, dependent on the facts, be trading receipts (*Rees Roturbo Development v Ducker HL 1928, 13 TC 366*; *Brandwood v Banker KB 1928, 14 TC 44*; *CIR v Rustproof Metal Window CA 1947, 29 TC 243* and cf. *Harry Ferguson (Motors) v CIR CA(NI) 1951, 33 TC 15*). Other sums are taxable under *ICTA 1988, s 524*, see 55.11 PROFIT COMPUTATIONS.

Where a company held a patent for renovating car tyres, lump sums received by it under arrangements for giving the payer a *de facto* franchise in his area, were held to be capital receipts (*Margerison v Tyresoles Ltd KB 1942, 25 TC 59*).

Royalties and other sums paid for the use of patents are not deductible in computing trading profits. [*ICTA 1988, s 74(1)(p)*]. For spreading of patent royalties received, see 55.11 PROFIT COMPUTATIONS.

For know-how and trade marks, see 66.62 and 66.66 respectively.

Simon's Direct Tax Service. See **B3.841** *et seq.*, **B3.13102**.

66.68 POOLING OF PROFITS

Where traders pool profits or act together in consortia but so as not to form PARTNERSHIPS (56) or trade jointly (cf. *Gardner and Bowring Hardy v CIR CS 1930, 15 TC 602*; *Geo Hall & Son v Platt Ch D 1954, 35 TC 440*) each trader's share of the pooled profits will normally be treated as a receipt of his main trade and any payment under the arrangement by one trader to another will be deductible in computing his profits (*Moore v Stewarts & Lloyds Ltd CS 1905, 6 TC 501* and cf. *United Steel v Cullington (No 1) CA 1939, 23 TC 71)*. In *Utol Ltd v CIR KB 1943, 25 TC 517* payments by one company to another under a profit sharing arrangement were held to be dividends payable less tax under the law then in force. For compensation received on the termination of a profit sharing arrangement see *Van den Berghs* at 66.27(*b*) above.

66.69 PRE-TRADING EXPENDITURE

The general rule is that trading expenditure is deductible when incurred and hence is not allowable if incurred before trading commenced (cf. *Birmingham & District Cattle By-Products Ltd v CIR KB 1919, 12 TC 92*). The rule is modified for certain pre-trading capital expenditure, including scientific research expenditure and abortive exploration expenditure by mining concerns (see 10 CAPITAL ALLOWANCES).

Expenditure incurred for the purposes of a trade not more than seven years before the commencement of that trade, which would be allowable in computing the profits of that trade if incurred after such commencement, is treated as having been incurred on the first day of trading. The expenditure must have been incurred by the company who carries on the trade on commencement. Expenditure otherwise deductible, e.g. pre-trading purchases of stock or advance payments of rent, is not within this special relief.

There is a special relief for non-trading debits arising under the loan relationship provisions (see 46.3 LOAN RELATIONSHIPS). The provisions for relief of allowable pre-trading expenditure do not apply to expenditure in relation to which such debits arise. The company may, however, elect for a non-trading debit not to be brought into account in the period in which it arises, within two years of the end of that period. If the company then begins to carry on a trade within seven years after the end of that period, and the debit would have been a trading debit if it had been given in the accounting period in which the trade commenced, it is brought into account as a trading debit in that period.

[*ICTA 1988, s 401; ITTOIA 2005, Sch 1 para 172*].

The above provisions apply equally to a Schedule A business carried on by a company (see 56 PROPERTY INCOME).

Simon's Direct Tax Service. See **B3.1204**.

66.70 **PROPERTY SALES AND OTHER PROPERTY RECEIPTS**

As to whether a trade of property dealing is carried on, see 66.15 above; for rents receivable, see 66.61 above. For builders and property developers generally, see HMRC Business Income Manual BIM 51500–51665.

Sales of property by builders in special circumstances have been considered in a number of cases. Profits held trading receipts in *Spiers & Son v Ogden KB 1932, 17 TC 117* (building activities extended); *Sharpless v Rees KB 1940, 23 TC 361* (sale of land acquired for hobby abandoned for health reasons); *Shadford v H Fairweather & Co Ch D 1966, 43 TC 291* (sale of site after development plan dropped); *Snell v Rosser, Thomas & Co Ch D 1967, 44 TC 343* (sale of land surplus to requirements); *Bowie v Reg Dunn (Builders) Ch D 1974, 49 TC 469* (sale of land acquired with business); *Smart v Lowndes Ch D 1978, 52 TC 436* (sale of land in wife's name). Sales of property built but let meanwhile held trading in *J & C Oliver v Farnsworth Ch D 1956, 37 TC 51*; *James Hobson & Sons v Newall Ch D 1957, 37 TC 609*; *W M Robb Ltd v Page Ch D 1971, 47 TC 465* and this notwithstanding active building given up (*Speck v Morton Ch D 1972, 48 TC 476*; *Granville Building Co v Oxby Ch D 1954, 35 TC 245*). But in *Harvey v Caulcott HC 1952, 33 TC 159* the sales were held realisations of investments and in *West v Phillips Ch D 1958, 38 TC 203* some houses were treated as investments and others as trading stock. See also *Andrew v Taylor CA 1965, 42 TC 557*. Sales of houses retained after business *transferred* held sales of investments in *Bradshaw v Blunden (No 1) Ch D 1956, 36 TC 397*; *Seaward v Varty CA 1962, 40 TC 523*. See also *Hesketh Estates v Craddock KB 1942, 25 TC 1* (profit on sale of brine baths held trading receipt of mixed business including land development).

For house sales subject to ground rents etc., see *CIR v John Emery & Sons HL 1936, 20 TC 213*; *B G Utting & Co Ltd v Hughes HL 1940, 23 TC 174*; *McMillan v CIR CS 1942, 24 TC 417*; *Heather v Redfern & Sons KB 1944, 26 TC 119*. For ground rents (England) and feu duties (Scotland) there should be credited the lower of their market value and cost, the cost being taken as the proportion of the cost of the land and building in the ratio of the market value to the sum of the market value and the sale price. For ground annuals (Scotland) which are perpetual the realisable value is brought in. The right to receive the rent then becomes part of the fixed capital of the trade, whose subsequent sale is not taken into account for corporation tax purposes. Any premiums on the grant of leases are part of the sale proceeds.

Turf sales by a farmer were held to be farming receipts in *Lowe v J W Ashmore Ltd Ch D 1970, 46 TC 597*. For timber sales see 66.66 above.

A lump sum received by a property investment company in return for the assignment for a five-year term of a stream of rental income was held to be a capital receipt for part disposal of the company's interest (*CIR v John Lewis Properties plc CA, [2003] STC 117*), but see now 56.14 PROPERTY INCOME as regards special rent factoring provisions.

Any excess of allowable deductions over rent received by a builder from property held as trading stock may be allowed as a trading expense (HMRC Business Income Manual BIM 51555).

Annuities under *Agriculture Act 1967* for giving up (after attaining age of 55) uncommercial agricultural land are treated as earned income and receipts of grants under the same *Act* for the same reason are exempt from capital gains tax. [*TCGA 1992, s 249*].

Where sales of land etc., are capital, the profits on assets disposed of are liable to capital gains tax. But see also 5.14 ANTI-AVOIDANCE for provisions affecting land or land development. [*ICTA 1988, s 776*].

For transactions not at market value see 66.75 below.

Simon's Direct Tax Service. See **B3.6**.

66.71 RENTS ETC. FOR BUSINESS PREMISES

Rents paid for business premises are deductible in computing profits. For repairs see 66.72 below. As regards rents receivable, see 66.61 above.

Where premises partly used privately (e.g. shop with residential accommodation above), *ICTA 1988, s 74(1)(c)* provides, for the allowance of not more than two-thirds of the rent unless the circumstances justify a higher proportion. In practice, the allowance is normally two-thirds for retail businesses and, although not provided for in the legislation, rates and 'common' repairs may be similarly apportioned. For this see *Wildbore v Luker HC 1951, 33 TC 46*. For allowance for use of home for business, see *Thomas v Ingram Ch D 1979, 52 TC 428*. See also *Mason v Tyson Ch D 1980, 53 TC 333* (expenses of flat used occasionally to enable professional man to work late not allowed as a deduction). (For income tax purposes for 2005/06 onwards, *ICTA 1988, s 74(1)(c)* is replaced by the specific power to apportion dual purpose expenditure given by *ITTOIA 2005, s 34*; see 66.18 above under the 'wholly and exclusively' rule and see the note on clause 34 in the Explanatory Notes to the Income Tax (Trading and Other Income) Bill).

Where premises became redundant or were closed down, continuing rents (less sub-letting receipts) were allowed as a deduction (*CIR v Falkirk Iron CS 1933, 17 TC 625*; *Hyett v Lennard KB 1940, 23 TC 346*) but not payments to secure the cancellation of leases no longer required (*Mallett v Staveley Coal & Iron CA 1928, 13 TC 772* (the leading case here); *Cowcher v Richard Mills & Co KB 1927, 13 TC 216*; *Union Cold Storage v Ellerker KB 1939, 22 TC 547*; *Dain v Auto Speedways Ch D 1959, 38 TC 525*; *Bullrun Inc v Inspector of Taxes (Sp C 248), [2000] SSCD 384*). See also *West African Drug Co v Lilley KB 1947, 28 TC 140*. Where the rent of a motorway service station was calculated by reference to takings, a lump sum payment for the exclusion of tobacco duty from takings was held capital (*Tucker v Granada Motorway Services HL 1979, 53 TC 92*), but, distinguishing *Granada Motorways*, an amount received by a company in respect of its agent's negligent failure to serve its landlord with counter-notice of a notice of an increase in its rent, was held to be a trading receipt in *Donald Fisher (Ealing) Ltd v Spencer CA 1989, 63 TC 168*. Rent for a building not required for occupation for business purposes but to control access to the lessee's works was held deductible (less sub-let rents) in *Allied Newspapers v Hindsley CA 1937, 21 TC 422*.

For allowance of a provision in respect of future rents under leases of premises ceasing to be used for business purposes, see *Herbert Smith v Honour Ch D 1999, 72 TC 130*. Following that decision, HMRC now accept that there is no longer a tax rule which denies provisions for anticipated loses or expenses (see Revenue Press Release 20 July 1999). See the article in the Revenue Tax Bulletin December 1999 pp 707–709 summarising HMRC's current view, in particular in relation to error or mistake relief claims (see 19.7 CLAIMS) arising from the change of view.

Additional rent liability incurred to obtain the freehold reversion to premises already rented held capital (*Littlewoods Mail Order v McGregor CA 1969, 45 TC 519* following *CIR v Land Securities HL 1969, 45 TC 495*), as were periodical payments to reimburse capital expenditure incurred by landlord (*Ainley v Edens KB 1935, 19 TC 303*) and payments based on production for grant of sisal estates (*Ralli Estates v East Africa IT Commr PC 1961, 40 ATC 9*). But payments for the use of a totalisator calculated by reference to its cost were allowed (*Racecourse Betting Control Board v Wild KB 1938, 22 TC 182*) as were rents subject to abatement dependent on profits (*Union Cold Storage v Adamson HL 1931, 16 TC 293*). For Scottish duplicands see *Dow v Merchiston Castle School CS 1921, 8 TC 149*. Rent paid by partnership to partner owning business premises allowed (*Heastie v Veitch & Co CA 1933, 18 TC 305*). For excessive payments to professional 'service company' see *Payne, Stone Fraser* at 66.66 above.

Rates and council tax. Business rates are deductible in the same way as rent. Council tax may similarly be deducted where it is attributable to premises (or part) used for trade purposes. (Revenue Press Release 16 March 1993).

Premiums. Certain lease premiums etc. in relation to leases not exceeding 50 years are chargeable on the landlord to an extent which varies with the length of the lease (see 56.8 PROPERTY INCOME). For any part of the 'relevant period' (as defined in *ICTA 1988, s 87(9)* — generally the duration of the lease) during which the company occupies the premises for the purposes of a trade or (with certain limitations) deals with its interest therein as property employed for the purposes of a trade, the company is treated as paying *additional rent* for the. This is deductible in computing the company's trading profits, subject to any rule that might prohibit such deduction in a particular case (e.g. the 'wholly and exclusively' rule). For each day of the relevant period on which the above conditions are satisfied, the amount of additional rent treated as incurred is the amount which falls to be included in computing the landlord's property income divided by the total number of days in the relevant period. If only part of the leased land is used for trading purposes, the amount is proportionately reduced. The amount is also proportionately reduced to the extent, if any, to which the company is entitled to an allowance under *CAA 2001, s 403* (mineral asset expenditure — see 10.40(*b*) CAPITAL ALLOWANCES).

If the company itself grants a sublease out of the leased property at a taxable premium, it is treated as paying additional rent only to the extent, if any, that the daily amount computed above exceeds the daily reduction in its own taxable premium. For more detail of how this rule operates, see 56.11 PROPERTY INCOME. If the sublease relates to only part of the premises covered by the main lease, the above rules are applied separately to the different parts of the premises, the premium under the main lease being apportioned between those parts on a just and reasonable basis.

The above rules apply whether the premium is chargeable to income tax or corporation tax in the hands of the landlord. (For income tax purposes for 2005/06 onwards, they also apply in relation to leases of property *outside* the UK where the landlord's property business is an overseas property business; see Change 13 listed in Annex 1 to the Explanatory Notes to the Income Tax (Trading and Other Income) Bill).

[*ICTA 1988, ss 87, 87A; CAA 2001, Sch 2 para 18; ITTOIA 2005, Sch 1 paras 62, 63*].

Otherwise, lease premiums are not deductible in computing trading profits (cf. *MacTaggart v Strump CS 1925, 10 TC 17*).

Reverse premiums. In *New Zealand Commissioner of Inland Revenue v Wattie and another PC 1998, 72 TC 639*, the decision in which has persuasive authority in the UK, it was held that a lump sum paid by a landlord to a prospective tenant as an inducement to enter into a lease at an above-market rental (generally known as a reverse premium) was a receipt of a capital nature. Legislation was introduced to counter this decision, and it applies in relation to any 'reverse premium' received on or after 9 March 1999 except where, disregarding any arrangements made on or after that date, the recipient was entitled to the premium immediately before that date. For these purposes, a '*reverse premium*' is a payment or other benefit received by way of inducement in connection with a transaction (the '*property transaction*') entered into by the company or a person 'connected' with the company (see below), where:

(*a*) the property transaction is one under which the company or connected person becomes entitled to an estate or interest in, or a right in or over, land; and

(*b*) the payment (or other benefit) is made (or provided) by:

  (i) the person (the '*grantor*') by whom that estate, interest or right is granted, or was granted at an earlier time; or

  (ii) a person 'connected' with the grantor; or

  (iii) a nominee of (or a person acting on the directions of) the grantor or a person connected with the grantor.

As regards (*b*)(i) above, the use of the word 'grantor' means that the provisions do not apply when a freehold is conveyed. The most common occasion on which the provisions will apply will be a payment by a landlord as an inducement to a tenant to take a new lease, but they may apply where an existing tenant pays a new tenant an inducement to take over the remaining term of a lease if (and only if) (*b*)(ii) or (iii) applies to the existing tenant (Revenue Tax Bulletin December 1999 pp 711–713).

For the purposes of these provisions, persons are '*connected*' with each other if they are connected within *ICTA 1988, s 839* (see 19 CONNECTED PERSONS) at any time during the period when the 'property arrangements' are entered into. The '*property arrangements*' comprise the property transaction and any arrangements entered into in connection with it (whether earlier, simultaneously or later).

A reverse premium is treated as a receipt of a revenue nature. Where the property transaction is entered into by the recipient of the reverse premium for the purposes of a trade carried on (or to be carried on), the reverse premium must be taken into account in computing the trading profits. In any other case, the reverse premium is to be treated as a receipt of a UK property business, or (as the case may be) an overseas property business (see 56 PROPERTY INCOME), carried on by the recipient.

It is understood that accountancy principles require the receipt to be brought into account by spreading over the period of the lease or, if shorter, to the first rent review. This treatment must normally be followed for tax purposes (see 66.5 above) but, as an anti-avoidance measure, is overridden where:

(A) two or more parties to the property arrangements (see above) are connected persons (see above); and

(B) the terms of the those arrangements differ significantly from those which, at that time and under prevailing market conditions, would be regarded as reasonable and normal between persons dealing at arm's length in the open market.

In such case, the full amount or value of the reverse premium must be brought into account in the period of account in which the property transaction (see above) is entered into or, where applicable, the first period of account of the trade which the recipient subsequently begins to carry on.

None of these provisions apply to the extent that the payment or benefit is consideration for the first leg of a sale and leaseback arrangement within *ICTA 1988, s 779* or *s 780(1)* (see 5.15 ANTI-AVOIDANCE) or is taken into account under *CAA 2001, s 532* (contributions to expenditure) to reduce the recipient's expenditure qualifying for capital allowances (see 10.2(vi) CAPITAL ALLOWANCES).

[*FA 1999, s 54, Sch 6; CAA 2001, Sch 2 para 104; SI 2004 No 2310, Sch para 51; ITTOIA 2005, Sch 1 para 509*].

It will be seen that a reverse premium within the above provisions is not confined to a lump sum payment and that 'other benefit' may include, for example, a contribution to the tenant's costs or an assumption of the recipient's liabilities under an existing lease. 'Other benefit' must, however, represent money or something capable of being turned into money. It does not include a sum foregone or deferred by the provider, rather than actually expended, such as a rent free period. See the article in the Revenue Tax Bulletin December 1999 pp 711–713, in particular in relation to the meeting of the tenant's costs.

Payment of reverse premium. The payment of a reverse premium by a company to achieve the assignment of a lease which had become disadvantageous (due to the company's failure to meet its obligations under a repairing covenant) was held to be on capital account (*Southern Counties Agricultural Trading Society Ltd v Blackler (Sp C 198), [1999] SSCD 200*). HMRC take the view that where a reverse premium is paid by a developer trading in property, it is deductible in computing his trading profits (Revenue Press Release 9 March 1999).

For HMRC approach to these rules, see HMRC Business Income Manual BIM41050–BIM41145.

Simon's Direct Tax Service. See **A4.235**.

General. See 5.15 ANTI-AVOIDANCE [*ICTA 1988, s 779*] regarding restrictions where there is a lease-back at a non-commercial rent and [*ICTA 1988, s 780*] for taxation of capital sums received on certain lease-backs.

Simon's Direct Tax Service. See **B3.13130**.

66.72 REPAIRS AND RENEWALS

(*a*) **General.** Expenditure held to be capital as described at (*b*) and (*c*) below may qualify for CAPITAL ALLOWANCES (10). Any allowable expenditure is deductible in the period when incurred and not when the repairs etc. accrued (*Naval Colliery Co Ltd v CIR HL 1928, 12 TC 1017*). Provisions for future repairs and renewals were held not allowable in *Clayton v Newcastle-under-Lyme Corpn QB 1888, 2 TC 416* and *Peter Merchant Ltd v Stedeford CA 1948, 30 TC 496*, but see now 66.5 above, and HMRC Business Income Manual BIM 46515, 46901, for the wider current acceptance of the application of normal accountancy principles in this context. Hence a provision for regular major overhaul work accrued due on aircraft engines was allowed as a deduction in *Johnston v Britannia Airways Ltd Ch D 1994, 67 TC 99* (but see now Revenue Tax Bulletin February 1999 p 624 as regards changes in accounting practice superseding this decision).

(*b*) **Business premises.** The general rule is that expenditure on additions, alterations, expansions or improvements is capital but the cost of repairs, i.e. restoring a building to its original condition, is allowable. However, the use of modern materials in repairing an old building does not make the expenditure capital (*Conn v Robins Bros Ltd Ch D 1966, 43 TC 266*), and HMRC now consider that this applies to the replacement of single-glazed windows by double-glazed equivalents (see Revenue Tax Bulletin June 2002 p 936). If the expenditure is capital, the estimated cost of 'notional repairs' obviated by the work is not allowable (see *Wm P Lawrie* and *Thomas Wilson (Keighley)* below).

As regards provisions for such expenditure, *ICTA 1988, s 74(1)(d)* prohibits any deduction 'beyond the sum actually expended' for repairs of premises, and HMRC previously considered that this debarred any allowance for such provisions (see HMRC Business Income Manual BIM 46901). A Revenue contention to this effect was rejected by the Special Commissioners in *Jenners Princes Street Edinburgh Ltd v CIR (Sp C 166), [1998] SSCD 196*. HMRC now accept that provisions properly made under Financial Reporting Standard 12 are tax deductible except where there is an express rule to the contrary (e.g. provisions for capital expenditure). (Revenue Press Release 20 July 1999). FRS 12 imposes a requirement for accounting periods ending after 22 March 1999 that for a provision to be allowable it must be a present obligation (either legal or constructive) as a result of a past event; it must be probable that a transfer of economic benefits will be required to settle the obligation; and it must be possible to make a reliable estimate of the amount of that obligation. See Revenue Tax Bulletin April 1999 pp 636–639. See also the article in the Revenue Tax Bulletin December 1999 pp 707–709 summarising HMRC's current view, in particular in relation to error or mistake relief claims (see 15.9 CLAIMS) arising from the change of view. It should be noted that HMRC's view is that *Jenners* would have been decided differently if FRS 12 had been in operation at the time (see HMRC Business Income Manual BIM 46550). (Following the *Jenners* decision, the phrase 'beyond the sum actually expended' serves no real purpose and is not repeated in *ITTOIA 2005*.)

A renewal of a building, i.e. a complete re-construction, is capital (*Fitzgerald v CIR Supreme Court (IFS) 1925, 5 ATC 414*; *Wm P Lawrie v CIR CS 1952, 34 TC 20*). The cost of rebuilding a factory chimney was held capital in *O'Grady v Bullcroft Main Collieries KB 1932, 17 TC 93* but allowed in *Samuel Jones & Co v CIR CS 1951, 32 TC 513* where the chimney was an integral part of the building. For roof replacements see *Wm P Lawrie* (above) and *Thos Wilson (Keighley) v Emmerson Ch D 1960, 39 TC 360*. The replacement of the ring in a cattle auction mart and of a stand in a football ground were held not to be repairs in *Wynne-Jones v Bedale Auction Ltd Ch D 1976, 51 TC 426* and *Brown v Burnley Football Co Ltd Ch D 1980, 53 TC 357* respectively in which the problem is reviewed.

Cost of barrier against coastal erosion held capital (*Avon Beach & Cafe v Stewart HC 1950, 31 TC 487*); also replacing a canal embankment (*Phillips v Whieldon Sanitary Potteries HC 1952, 33 TC 213*) and building new access road (*Pitt v Castle Hill Warehousing Ch D 1974, 49 TC 638*).

For a modern case (involving the insertion of plastic pipes within dilapidated metal ones over substantial lengths of a gas pipe network, held to be capital), see *Auckland Gas Co Ltd v CIR PC, [2000] STC 527*. *Auckland Gas* was considered but distinguished in *Transco plc v Dyall (Sp C 310), [2002] SSCD 199*, in which the insertion of plastic pipes in cast iron ones was on a selective basis and had not changed the character of the pipeline system as a whole.

Where on taking a lease of dilapidated property the dilapidations were made good under a covenant in the lease, the cost was held disallowable as attributable to the previous use of the premises (*Jackson v Laskers Home Furnishers Ch D 1956, 37 TC 69*) but when cinemas were acquired in a state of disrepair (but still fit for public showings) because of war-time restrictions on building work, the cost of the repairs was allowed (*Odeon Associated Theatres Ltd v Jones CA 1971, 48 TC 257*). See also (*c*) below. In practice, expenditure on repairing and redecorating newly acquired premises is allowed unless abnormal (and likely to be reflected in the purchase price or rent payable). See generally HMRC Business Income Manual BIM 46906.

Dilapidations of a repair nature on the termination of a lease are generally deductible.

For repairs to tied premises see 66.22 above.

From 1 October 2004, *Disability Discrimination Act 1995* requires service providers to make 'reasonable adjustments' to their premises to tackle any physical features that prevent disabled people from using their services. Whilst this does not give rise to any substantive changes to pre-existing tax treatment, HMRC have published online some related guidance covering such matters as ramps, toilets and washing facilities, signs, hand rails, lighting, doors, lifts, steps and stairs, alterations to walls and floors, car parks and paths. See www.hmrc.gov.uk/specialist/disability-act-guidance.htm

(*c*) **Plant and other business assets etc.** The general rules at (*b*) above apply to plant with the important modification that expenditure on the renewal of plant is allowed as a deduction as an alternative to capital allowances. For this see 10.38(H) CAPITAL ALLOWANCES. Replacements and alterations of trade tools (meaning any implement, utensil or article) are allowable deductions notwithstanding the fact that the expenditure would otherwise be capital. [*ICTA 1988, s 74(1)(d)*]. The cost of initial and additional tools is capital and not deductible but may well attract plant and machinery capital allowances (see 10.25 CAPITAL ALLOWANCES).

For repairs soon after the acquisition of an asset see *Law Shipping v CIR CS 1923, 12 TC 621* and *CIR v Granite City SS Co CS 1927, 13 TC 1* in which the cost of repairs to ships attributable to their use before acquisition, was held capital. But see

Odeon Associated Theatres at (*b*) above in which *Law Shipping* was distinguished. See also *Bidwell v Gardiner Ch D 1960, 39 TC 31* in which the replacement of the furnishings of a newly acquired hotel was held capital.

Expenditure on renewal of railway tracks was allowed in *Rhodesia Railways v Bechuanaland Collector PC 1933, 12 ATC 223*, distinguishing *Highland Railway v Balderston CES 1889, 2 TC 485* in which held capital. Abnormal expenditure on dredging a channel to a shipyard was held capital in *Ounsworth v Vickers Ltd KB 1915, 6 TC 671* but the cost to a Harbour Board of removing a wreck (*Whelan v Dover Harbour Board CA 1934, 18 TC 555*) and of renewing moorings (*In re King's Lynn Harbour CES 1875, 1 TC 23*) was allowed. For shop fittings see *Eastmans Ltd v Shaw HL 1928, 14 TC 218*; *Hyam v CIR CS 1929, 14 TC 479*. See also *Lothian Chemical v Rogers CS 1926, 11 TC 508*.

(*d*) **Assets held under an operating lease.** A deduction may be allowed for a provision to cover future repairs of assets held under an operating lease which contains a repairing obligation (for example, tenants' repairing leases of property). The obligation, required under FRS 12 (see (*b*) above), subsists from the signing of the lease. (HMRC Business Income Manual BIM 46535). It is unlikely HMRC would have accepted such a deduction prior to the decision in *Jenners* at (*b*) above.

See generally HMRC Business Income Manual BIM 46900–46970.

Simon's Direct Tax Service. See **B3.13131, B3.13132.**

66.73 RESEARCH AND DEVELOPMENT

For enhanced tax reliefs for research and development expenditure incurred from 1 April 2000, see 59 RESEARCH AND DEVELOPMENT EXPENDITURE.

Revenue expenditure incurred by a company on 'research and development' related to its trade, whether undertaken directly or on its behalf, is allowable as a deduction in computing profits. Expenditure incurred in the acquisition of rights in, or arising out of, the research and development is excluded, but the allowable expenditure otherwise includes all expenditure incurred in, or providing facilities for, carrying it out. Research and development 'related' to a trade includes any which may lead to or facilitate an extension of the trade, or which is of a medical nature and has a special relation to the welfare of workers employed in the trade. These provisions apply equally to expenditure on oil and gas exploration and appraisal (within *ICTA 1988, s 837B*).

For accounting periods beginning after 31 December 2004, HMRC expenditure by a company on research and development is not precluded from deduction under these provisions by reason only of the fact that it is brought into account in determining the value of an intangible asset, but there are rules to prevent double relief in respect of the same expenditure.

Scientific research associations. Relief is similarly given allowed for any sum paid to an approved scientific research association having as its object 'scientific research' related (with the extended meaning referred togiven above) to the class of trade concerned, or to any and for any sum paid to an approved university, college research institute etc. to be used for such research. The association or university etc. must be approved for the purpose by the Secretary of State. '*Scientific research*' means any activities in the fields of natural or applied science for the extension of knowledge. Any question as to what constitutes scientific research is to be referred by HMRC to the Secretary of State, whose decision is final.

In relation to sums paid to a scientific research association in an accounting period of the association beginning on or after the day appointed under *F(No 2)A 2005, s 13*(6), these provisions, in so far as they apply to sums paid to such associations, are amended in line with the amendments made by *F(No 2)A 2005, s 13* at 27.12 EXEMPT ORGANISATIONS.

The scientific research association to which the sum is paid no longer has to be approved, but it does have to be within the exemptions at 27.12 and must have as its object the undertaking of 'research and development' which may lead to or facilitate an extension of the class of trade to which the payer's trade belongs.

[*ICTA 1988, ss 82A, 82B; CAA 1990, ss 136, 139(1)(3); FA 2000, Sch 19 para 5; FA 2004, s 53; SI 2004 No 3268; ITTOIA 2005, Sch 1 paras 54, 55; F(No 2)A 2005, s 15*].

For *capital expenditure* on research and development, see 10.52 CAPITAL ALLOWANCES.

For the definition of 'research and development', see 59.1 RESEARCH AND DEVELOPMENT EXPENDITURE.

66.74 **SHARES AND SECURITIES**

For whether a trade of 'share dealing' carried on see 66.16 above. For transactions not at market value see 66.75 below.

Profits and losses on realisations of investments by a bank in the course of its business enter into its Case I profits (*Punjab Co-operative Bank v Lahore IT Commr PC 1940, 19 ATC 533* and see *Frasers (Glasgow) Bank v CIR HL 1963, 40 TC 698*) and similarly for insurance companies (*Northern Assce Co v Russell CES 1889, 2 TC 551*; *General Reinsurance Co v Tomlinson Ch D 1970, 48 TC 81* and contrast *CIR v Scottish Automobile CS 1931, 16 TC 381*). Profits/losses held capital in *Stott v Hoddinott KB 1916, 7 TC 85* (investments acquired by architect to secure contracts); *Jacobs Young & Co v Harris KB 1926, 11 TC 221* (shares held by merchanting company in subsidiary wound up); *Alliance & Dublin Consumers' Gas Co v Davis HC(IFS) 1926, 5 ATC 717* (investments of gas company earmarked for reserve fund). A profit by a property dealing company on the sale of shares acquired in connection with a property transaction was held a trading receipt (*Associated London Properties v Henriksen CA 1944, 26 TC 46*) but contrast *Fundfarms Developments v Parsons Ch D 1969, 45 TC 707* and see now 5 ANTI-AVOIDANCE.

Shares allotted for mining concessions granted by company dealing in concessions held trading receipts at market value (*Gold Coast Selection Trust v Humphrey HL 1948, 30 TC 209*). See also *Murphy v Australian Machinery & Investment Co CA 1948, 30 TC 244* and *Scottish & Canadian Investment Co v Easson CS 1922, 8 TC 265*.

For options, see *Varty v British South Africa Co HL 1965, 42 TC 406* (no profits or loss until shares sold). See also *Walker v Cater Securities Ch D 1974, 49 TC 625*.

Conversion etc. of shares and securities held as circulating capital. Where a new holding of shares or securities (as defined) is issued in exchange for an original holding a profit on sale of which would fall to be treated as part of trading profits, the transaction is treated as not involving any disposal of the original holding, the new holding being treated as the same asset as the original holding. This applies only to transactions which result in the new holding being equated with the original holding under *TCGA 1992, ss 132–136* (capital gains rollover in cases of conversion etc.) or *TCGA 1992, s 134* (compensation stock). This rule applies only if the original holding is beneficially owned by a bank, insurance company or share dealer holding such securities as trading stock. For income tax purposes for 2005/06 onwards the requirement that the shares must be beneficially held by the trader has been dropped (see Change 42 listed in Annex 1 to the Explanatory Notes to the Income Tax (Trading and Other Income) Bill).

For periods of account ending on or after 1 August 2001, the above rule does not apply to shares or securities for which unrealised profits or losses (computed on a mark to market basis by reference to fair value) are brought into account in the period of account in which the transaction takes place. Where consideration is receivable in addition to the new holding, the above rule applies only to a proportion of the original holding, computed by reference to the market value of the new holding and the other consideration received.

[*ICTA 1988, s 473; FA 2002, s 67; ITTOIA 2005, Sch 1 para 183*].

Stock lending fees. Such fees relating to investments eligible for relief under *ICTA 1988, s 592(2), s 608(2)(a), s 613(4), s 614(3), s 620(6)* or *s 643(2)* (pension scheme funds etc., see Tolley's Income Tax under Retirement Schemes, Retirement Annuities and Personal Pension Schemes) are themselves eligible for relief under those *sections*. [*ICTA 1988, s 129B*].

Dealers in securities. Any distribution by a UK-resident company (or payment representative of such a distribution) *received by* a dealer in securities is taken into account (exclusive of any tax credit) in computing the dealer's trading profits. Accordingly the normal exemption from corporation tax of UK company distributions under *ICTA 1988, s 208* does not apply.

Any payment *made by* a dealer which is representative of a UK company distribution is similarly brought into the computation of trading profits.

A person is for these purposes a dealer in relation to a distribution if, on a sale of the shares or stock in respect of which the distribution is made, the price would be taken into account in computing trading profits (assuming that it would not fall to be treated as a distribution) other than insurance business profits.

See 5.21 ANTI-AVOIDANCE as regards arrangements to pass on the value of dividend tax credits.

[*ICTA 1988, s 95; FA 2003, Sch 43 Pt 3(6); FA 2004, s 137(2)(6); ITTOIA 2005, Sch 1 para 74*].

Extra return on new issues of securities. Where:

(*a*) securities of a particular kind are issued (being the original issue of securities of that kind);

(*b*) new securities of the same kind are issued subsequently;

(*c*) a sum (the 'extra return') is payable by the issuer in respect of the new securities, to reflect the fact that interest is accruing on the old securities and calculated accordingly; and

(*d*) the issue price of the new securities includes an element (separately identified or not) representing payment for the extra return,

the extra return is treated for all tax purposes (except corporation tax) as a payment of interest, but the issuer is not entitled to tax relief, either as a deduction in computing profits or otherwise as a deduction or set-off, for the payment. [*ICTA 1988, s 587A*].

Euroconversion of shares. Costs incurred in respect of the conversion of a trading company's shares or other securities from the currency of a State which has adopted the euro into euro (a 'euroconversion', see *SI 1998 No 3177, reg 3*) which is effected solely by the issue of replacement shares and other securities are allowable as a Schedule D, Case I deduction. In the case of an investment company or, for accounting periods beginning on or after 1 April 2004, a company with investment business (or, subject to special provisions, a company carrying on life assurance business), such costs are treated as management expenses (see 42.4 INVESTMENT COMPANIES AND INVESTMENT BUSINESS). [*SI 1998 No 3177, Pt II; SI 2004 No 2310, Article 77*].

General. See also 5 ANTI-AVOIDANCE, including transactions in securities to obtain tax advantage [*ICTA 1988, s 703*] and dividend-stripping [*ICTA 1988, s 736*].

For share transactions entered into to secure tax advantages see 66.8 above and for transactions in dividend-stripping before the enactment of existing legislation see Tolley's Tax Cases.

66.75 **STOCK IN TRADE AND WORK IN PROGRESS**

See generally HMRC Business Income Manual BIM 33000–33630. Following the adoption for tax purposes of the 'true and fair view' accounting basis (subject to any statutory adjustment) for periods of account beginning after 6 April 1999 (see 66.5 above), HMRC Statement of Practice SP 3/90 (to which references are made below) is generally superseded and is accordingly withdrawn. However, the principles drawn from that Statement continue to be relevant for subsequent accounting periods (except as referred to below).

Basis of valuation. The general rule has long been that stock is to be valued at the lower of cost and market value. Leading cases are *Minister of National Revenue v Anaconda American Brass Co PC 1955, 34 ATC 330* and *BSC Footwear v Ridgway HL 1971, 47 TC 495*. Market value held to be replacement price for a merchant (*Brigg Neumann & Co v CIR KB 1928, 12 TC 1191*) and retail price for a retailer in *BSC Footwear* above (Revenue prepared to take price net of any selling commission). Stock may be valued partly at cost and partly at market value where lower (*CIR v Cock Russell & Co KB 1949, 29 TC 387*). The base stock method is not permissible (*Patrick v Broadstone Mills CA 1953, 35 TC 44*) nor is 'LIFO' (*Anaconda American Brass* above). See also *Ryan v Asia Mill HL 1951, 32 TC 275*. The cost should include as a minimum the cost of materials and direct labour but the accounts treatment of overheads is normally accepted (*Duple Motor Bodies v Ostime HL 1961, 39 TC 537*).

However, HMRC now take the view that any valuation of stock included in financial statements prepared in accordance with generally accepted accounting practice (see 66.5 above) should be accepted provided that:

- it reflects the correct application of the principles of normal accountancy;
- the method pays sufficient regard to the facts; and
- the basis does not violate the taxing statutes as interpreted by the courts.

(HMRC Business Income Manual BIM 33115).

A mark to market basis of valuation, used mainly by financial institutions and commodity dealers and under which stock is valued at market value, may also be acceptable (HMRC Business Income Manual BIM 33160).

The principal accounting standard governing stock is SSAP 9.

For the use of formulae in computing stock provisions and write-downs, see Revenue Tax Bulletin December 1994 p 184. Broadly, inspectors will accept formulae which reflect a realistic appraisal of future income from the particular category of stock and which result in the stock being included at a reasonable estimate of net realisable value. Where computations are accepted without enquiry, it is on the assumption that profits are arrived at in accordance with such principles. (Revenue Tax Bulletin December 1994 p 184).

For the treatment of depreciation taken into account in arriving at stock valuations, see Revenue Tax Bulletin June 2002 pp 936, 937. See also the *Mars UK Ltd* and *William Grant & Sons Ltd* cases in 66.18 above.

For motor dealer stock valuations, see Revenue Tax Bulletin August 1994 p 156.

As regards valuation of professional work in progress, it is understood that the following principles are, in broad terms, currently accepted by HMRC:

(i) nothing should be included for partners' time;

(ii) direct employment costs of fee-earners and direct overheads applicable, such as secretarial salaries, stationery, telephone costs etc. should be included;

(iii) general production overheads for general office areas, conference rooms etc. should be excluded, whilst those for individual office areas directly applicable should be discounted by, say, 30% for non-productive time; and

(iv) contingent fees should be included.

(Taxation Vol 141, No 3654 p 126, 30 April 1998). For further guidance on valuation of professional work in progress, see the detailed note agreed between the Revenue and the ICAEW in Revenue Tax Bulletin December 1998 pp 607–615.

Changes in basis of valuation. Where the stock was found to be grossly undervalued it was held that an assessment to rectify the closing undervaluation must be reduced by the opening undervaluation to bring out the true profits (*Bombay IT Commr v Ahmedabad New Cotton Mills Co PC 1929, 9 ATC 574*). But where a company altered its method of dealing with accrued profits on long-term contracts and the closing work in progress in the year 1 accounts on the old basis was substantially below the opening figure in the year 2 accounts on the new basis, held, distinguishing *Ahmedabad*, the difference must be included in the year 2 profits (*Pearce v Woodall-Duckham Ltd CA 1978, 51 TC 271*). See also HMRC Statement of Practice, SP 3/90.

Where there is a change in the basis of valuation, the following practice is applied for tax purposes. If the bases of valuation both before and after the change are valid bases, the opening figure for the period of change must be the same as the closing figure for the preceding period. If the change is from an invalid basis to a valid one, the opening figure for the period of change must be arrived at on the same basis as the closing figure for that period, and liabilities for earlier years will be reviewed where it is possible to do so. (HMRC Statement of Practice, SP 3/90 and see now HMRC Business Income Manual BIM 33199). See, however, *Woodall-Duckham Ltd* (above) as regards long-term contracts.

See 66.6 above for spreading of the tax charge in relation to adjustments on a change of accounting basis arising from the interpretation of UITF 40.

Long-term contracts. HMRC accept that accurate provisions for foreseen losses on long-term contracts (e.g. in the construction industry) made in accordance with correct accounting practice are tax deductible. (Revenue Press Release 20 July 1999 and see now HMRC Business Income Manual BIM 33025).

In *Symons v Weeks and Others Ch D 1982, 56 TC 630*, it was held that progress payments under the long-term contracts of a firm of architects did not fall to be brought into account for tax before the relevant contract was completed, notwithstanding that they exceeded the figure brought in for work in progress, calculated on the correct principles of commercial accounting.

See above for changes of basis.

Goods sold subject to reservation of title. Where the supplier of goods reserves the title in them until payment is made (as a protection should the buyer become insolvent) and meanwhile the goods are treated by both parties for accountancy purposes as having been sold/purchased, HMRC will follow the accounts treatment (HMRC Statement of Practice, B6). See Note A of Financial Reporting Standard No 5 and HMRC Business Income Manual BIM 33375.

Goods on consignment stock are normally treated as stock in the hands of the supplier until disposed of by the consignee (e.g. sale or return) (HMRC Statement of Practice, B6).

For **forward contracts**, see 66.29 above.

Insurance recoveries. See 66.60 above.

Transactions not at market value. Where trading stock is disposed of otherwise than by way of trade, the realisable value is to be credited for tax purposes. This was established by *Sharkey v Wernher HL 1955, 36 TC 275* approving *Watson Bros v Hornby KB 1942, 24 TC 506*. It applies, *inter alia*, to goods taken out of stock by a retailer for his own use (see below). It was applied in *Petrotim Securities Ltd v Ayres CA 1963, 41 TC 389* to a disposal of shares at gross under-value as part of a tax avoidance scheme, but in *Ridge Securities Ltd v*

CIR Ch D 1963, 44 TC 373, dealing with the other end of the same scheme, it was held that the same principle applied to acquisitions of trading stock otherwise than by way of trade, market price being substituted for the actual purchase price. But the principle is not applicable to sales or purchases by way of trade notwithstanding not at arm's length. Hence when a share dealing company acquired shares at substantial overvalue from an associated company, the claim by the Revenue for market value failed (*Craddock v Zevo Finance Co HL 1946, 27 TC 267*), and when a property dealing company acquired property from its controlling shareholder at substantial undervalue, its claim to substitute market value failed (*Jacgilden (Weston Hall) v Castle Ch D 1969, 45 TC 685*). See also *Skinner v Berry Head Lands Ch D 1970, 46 TC 377* and *Kilmorie (Aldridge) v Dickinson HL 1974, 50 TC 1*.

Appropriations to trading stock of assets held in another capacity are generally treated as a disposal and reacquisition at market value. Where a chargeable gain or allowable loss would otherwise arise for capital gains tax purposes under *TCGA 1992, s 161(1)*, the company may elect for the market value to be reduced for these purposes by the amount of the chargeable gain (or increased by the amount of the allowable loss), the trading profits being computed accordingly and the appropriation being disregarded for capital gains tax purposes. The election must be made within two years after the end of the accounting period in which the asset is appropriated. [*TCGA 1992, s 161(3)(3A)*].

What constitutes stock. Greyhounds kept by greyhound racing company not trading stock (*Abbot v Albion Greyhounds (Salford) KB 1945, 26 TC 390*). Payments by cigarette manufacturer for cropping trees (not owned by it) for leaves used in manufacture, held to be for materials (*Mohanlal Hargovind of Jubbulpore v IT Commr PC 1949, 28 ATC 287*). For payments for unworked minerals, sand and gravel etc., (including tailings etc.) by mines, quarries etc. see 66.65 above. For payments for oil by oil companies, see *Hughes v British Burmah Petroleum KB 1932, 17 TC 286*; *New Zealand Commr v Europa Oil (NZ) PC 1970, 49 ATC 282*; *Europa Oil (NZ) v New Zealand Commr PC, [1976] STC 37*. For timber see 66.66 above and *Coates v Holker Estates Co Ch D 1961, 40 TC 75*.

Valuation on cessation of trade. Under *ICTA 1988, s 100* where a trade is discontinued (or so treated for tax purposes by *ICTA 1988, s 337(1)*), the following provisions apply. Any 'trading stock' at cessation must be valued as set out in (1) and (2) below in computing taxable profits. '*Trading stock*' is widely defined for these purposes by *ICTA 1988, s 100(2)* and includes any work in progress of a trade (though not of a profession, for which see below).

(1) If the trading stock at cessation is sold to a person carrying on (or intending to carry on) a trade in the UK who can deduct the cost as an expense for corporation tax purposes, the stock is valued at the amount realised on the sale. If, however, the two parties to the sale are connected persons (defined more broadly than by *ICTA 1988, s 839*), arm's length value is to be taken instead. (Neither rule applies to a transfer of farm animals where the anti-avoidance rules for the herd basis (at 55.10 PROFIT COMPUTATIONS) apply.) If, on or after 24 July 2002, the stock is sold with other assets, the amount realised is arrived at on a just and reasonable apportionment; previously no provision was made for any apportionment. For the purposes of these rules, a 'sale' includes a transfer for valuable consideration, with related expressions then being defined accordingly.

    Where arm's length value exceeds both (i) actual sale price and (ii) acquisition value (broadly, the amount that would have been deductible in respect of the stock had it been sold in the course of trade immediately before cessation), connected persons may jointly elect to substitute the greater of (i) and (ii) for the arm's length value. The election must be made within two years after the end of the accounting period in which cessation occurred.

    The cost of the trading stock to the buyer is taken to be the value determined under the above rules (or the corresponding corporation tax rules) in relation to the seller.

Any question as to the application of these rules is to be determined by the General or Special Commissioners in the same way as an appeal. If both trades are within the jurisdiction of the same body of General Commissioners, any such question must be determined by them, unless all parties agree that it should be determined by the Special Commissioners instead. In any other case, the question is determined by the Special Commissioners. See *Bradshaw v Blunden (No 2) Ch D 1960, 39 TC 73*; *CIR v Barr (No 2) CS 1955, 36 TC 455*.

These rules are not applicable to woodlands managed on a commercial basis (*Coates v Holker Estates* above). For their application to 'hire-purchase debts' see *Lions Ltd v Gosford Furnishing Co Ltd & CIR CS 1961, 40 TC 256*. A contention by the Revenue that the rules did not apply to a transfer of closing stock simultaneous to a cessation was rejected in *Moore v Mackenzie Ch D 1971, 48 TC 196*.

(2) In all cases not within (1) above, trading stock is to be valued at the price it would have realised if sold in the open market at the time of the cessation.

For accounting periods beginning on or after 1 April 2004 (subject to transitional provisions), the above provisions are disapplied in relation to any trading stock if a transfer pricing adjustment (see 67 TRANSFER PRICING) falls to be made in connection with any provision made or imposed in relation to that stock and having effect in connection with the cessation.

Similar rules as above apply in relation to '*work in progress*' (as defined by *ICTA 1988, s 101(3)*) on cessation of a profession, except that there is no special rule for a transfer of work in progress to a connected person. Additionally, an election is available to the effect that, in computing profits to the date of cessation, closing work in progress is valued at cost and any realised excess over cost is then treated as a post-cessation receipt (see 66.3 above); the election must be made no later than two years after the end of the accounting period in which the cessation occurred.

[*ICTA 1988, ss 100–102; FA 2002, ss 105(1), 106; FA 2004, s 30(9), s 37(1)(2), Sch 5 para 2; ITTOIA 2005, Sch 1 paras 79–81*].

See ICAEW Technical Release TAX 7/95, 15 February 1995, for a guidance note on the taxation implications of various treatments of transfers of work in progress and debtors on incorporation of a professional partnership.

Recovery of assets under *Proceeds of Crime Act 2002, Pt 5*. Where the transfer of trading stock is a *Pt 5* transfer under *Proceeds of Crime Act 2002* (as in 10.2(xi) CAPITAL ALLOWANCES) and the stock is to be treated, as a result of the transfer, as if sold in the course of the trade, it is treated, for the purpose of computing taxable profits and notwithstanding *ICTA 1988, s 100* above (if applicable), as sold at cost price. [*Proceeds of Crime Act 2002, Sch 10 para 11; ITTOIA 2005, Sch 1 para 583(6)*].

Simon's Direct Tax Service. See **B3.10**.

66.76 SUBSCRIPTIONS AND CONTRIBUTIONS

Trade and professional associations. Ordinary annual subscriptions to local associations, including Chambers of Commerce, are normally allowed as deductions in computing profits. Subscriptions to larger associations are deductible, and receipts therefrom chargeable, if the association has entered into an arrangement with HMRC under which it is assessed on any surplus of receipts over allowable expenditure (the association should be asked). Most associations enter into the arrangement but if not the deduction is restricted to the proportion applied by the association for purposes such that it would have been deductible if so applied by the subscriber (*Lochgelly Iron & Coal Co Ltd v Crawford CS 1913, 6 TC 267*). For other cases see Tolley's Tax Cases. Subscriptions to the Economic League are not deductible (*Joseph L Thompson & Sons Ltd v Chamberlain Ch D 1962, 40 TC 657*).

By concession, the payment of an ordinary annual subscription to a local trade association by a non-member is not regarded as a gift, and is thus normally allowed as a deduction notwithstanding 66.56 above, provided it satisfies the 'wholly and exclusively' rule at 66.18 above (HMRC Extra Statutory Concession, B7).

Contributions to mutual insurance associations are deductible even though used to create a reserve fund (*Thomas v Richard Evans & Co Ltd HL 1927, 11 TC 790*). See also 48 MUTUAL COMPANIES.

Local enterprise agencies. Expenditure incurred in making any contribution (whether in cash or kind) to an 'approved local enterprise agency' is specifically allowed as deduction in computing profits if it would not otherwise be deductible. If, however, in connection with the making of the contribution, the company or a person connected with the company (see 19 CONNECTED PERSONS) receives (or is entitled to receive) any related benefit, whether or not from the organisation itself, the value of the benefit is recovered by a charge under Schedule D, Cases I or II or VI.

'*Approved local enterprise agency*' is any body approved by the Secretary of State who is satisfied (i) its sole objective is the promotion or encouragement of industrial and commercial activity or enterprise in a particular area of the UK and with particular reference to small businesses, or (ii) one of its principal objectives is as in (i) *and* it maintains a separate fund for that objective. The agency must be precluded from making dividends, gifts etc. to its members or managers. Approval may be conditional and may be withdrawn retrospectively.

[*ICTA 1988, s 79, ITTOIA 2005, Sch 1 para 48*].

Training and enterprise councils, local enterprise companies and business link organisations. Identical provisions to those described above in relation to local enterprise agencies apply to a contribution to a training and enterprise council which has an agreement with the Secretary of State to act as such, or to a local enterprise company which has an agreement with Scottish Enterprise or Highlands and Islands Enterprise to act as such, or to a business link organisation authorised by the Secretary of State to use a service mark designated for these purposes. [*ICTA 1988, s 79A; SI 2004 No 2310, Sch para 3; ITTOIA 2005, Sch 1 para 49*].

Urban regeneration companies. Identical provisions to those described above in relation to local enterprise organisations apply to a contribution made after 31 March 2003 to an urban regeneration company designated as such by Treasury order. A body may be so designated only if its sole or main function is to co-ordinate the regeneration of a specific urban area in the UK in association with public and local authorities. Designation orders may be backdated by up to three months or, in the case of the first such order, to 1 April 2003. [*ICTA 1988, s 79B; FA 2003, s 180; SI 2004 No 2310, Sch para 3; ITTOIA 2005, Sch 1 para 50*]. The first designations are made by *SI 2004 No 439*.

66.77 SUBSIDIES, GRANTS ETC.

For payments under the **Business Start-up scheme**, see Tolley's Income Tax under Trading Income (Subsidies, grants etc.).[*ICTA 1988, s 127*; *ITTOIA 2005, Sch 1 para 108*]. Where the business is run through a company, the payments are made to the individual as agent of the company and are treated as Case VI income of the company. (HMRC Business Income Manual BIM 40400, 40405).

Farming support payments. See 66.50 above.

Fishing grants. For the tax treatment of decommissioning grants, laying-up grants, exploratory voyage grants and joint venture grants under *SI 1983 No 1883*, see HMRC Business Income Manual BIM 57001.

Football pools promoters. Certain contributions to the Football Trust 1990 by pools promoters for football ground improvements are allowable as deductions in the pools promoter's trade, as are certain payments by them to other trustees established mainly for the support of athletic sports or games (but with power to support the arts). [*FA 1990, s 126; FA 1991, s 121; ITTOIA 2005, Sch 1 paras 416, 418*]. See also 10.2(vi) CAPITAL ALLOWANCES.

Industrial development grants. Grants to a company under *Industrial Development Act 1982, s 7 or s 8* (or corresponding NI legislation) are trading receipts, unless the grant is designated as made towards the cost of specified capital expenditure or as compensation for loss of capital assets or, exceptionally, is made towards the meeting of a corporation tax liability. [*ICTA 1988, s 93; ITTOIA 2005, Sch 1 para 72*].

An earlier interest relief grant under *Industry Act 1972* was held to be assessable in *Burman v Thorn Domestic Appliances (Electrical) Ltd Ch D 1981, 55 TC 493*, as was a similar grant undifferentiated between revenue and capital in *Ryan v Crabtree Denims Ltd Ch D 1987, 60 TC 183*, applying *Gayjon Processes Ltd* (below) and distinguishing *Seaham Harbour* (below). Regional development grants under *Industrial Development Act 1982, Part II* to traders etc. or investment companies are not to be treated as trading income or management expenses. [*ICTA 1988, s 92*].

Research grant by trading company to medical practitioner held assessable (*Duff v Williamson Ch D 1973, 49 TC 1*). For research grants and fellowships generally, see HMRC Business Income Manual BIM 65151.

Temporary employment subsidy was paid under *Employment and Training Act 1973, s 5* (as amended by *Employment Protection Act 1975, Sch 14 para 2*) as a flat-rate weekly payment or (in the textile, clothing and footwear industries) by way of reimbursement of payments made to workers on short time.

Such payments were held to be taxable as trading receipts in *Poulter v Gayjon Processes Ltd Ch D 1985, 58 TC 350*, distinguishing the grants made by the Unemployment Grants Committee in *Seaham Harbour* (below).

Unemployment grants. Subsidy to dock company (from Unemployment Grants Committee) for extension work to keep men in employment held, although grant made in terms of interest, not a 'trade receipt' for tax purposes (*Seaham Harbour v Crook HL 1931, 16 TC 333*).

See 10.2(vi) CAPITAL ALLOWANCES for effect of grants and subsidies on capital allowances.

Simon's Direct Tax Service. See **B3.929**.

66.78 TAXATION

Income tax and corporation tax are not deductible in computing profits (cf. *Allen v Farquharson Bros & Co KB 1932, 17 TC 59*). Overseas taxes may be subject to DOUBLE TAX RELIEF (24) but any such tax not relieved by credit on overseas income included in the profits may generally be deducted [*ICTA 1988, s 811*] but not on UK income, e.g. profits of UK branches (*CIR v Dowdall O'Mahoney & Co Ltd HL 1952, 33 TC 259*).

In *Harrods (Buenos Aires) v Taylor-Gooby CA 1964, 41 TC 450* an annual capital tax imposed by the Argentine on foreign companies trading there was not a tax on the profits and was allowable.

As regards relief for national insurance contributions by employers in respect of employees, see 66.38 above.

For taxation appeals see 66.63 above. For VAT, see 68 VALUE ADDED TAX.

Simon's Direct Tax Service. See **B3.13145**.

66.79 TELECOMMUNICATIONS RIGHTS

See *FA 2002, Sch 29 paras 127, 128* for application, in relation to telecommunications rights, of the special provisions for the taxation of INTANGIBLE FIXED ASSETS (39) which apply to assets acquired or created on or after 1 April 2002. (See in particular the commencement and transitional rules for that regime at 39.37).The provisions below apply to rights acquired before that date.

Special rules applied in relation to licences granted under *Wireless Telegraphy Act 1949, s 1* as a result of bidding for such licences under *Wireless Telegraphy Act 1998, s 3* regulations, and to rights derived directly or indirectly therefrom. They also applied to indefeasible rights to use a telecommunications cable system ('IRUs') acquired after 20 March 2000, unless they were acquired from an 'associate' (within *ICTA 1988, s 417(3)(4)*, see 16.5 CLOSE COMPANIES) or an 'associated company' (within *ICTA 1988, s 416(1)* (see 16.11 CLOSE COMPANIES) or, in relation to an individual, being a company of which that individual has control under *ICTA 1988, s 416(2)-(6)* (see 16.2 CLOSE COMPANIES)) which acquired them on or before that date, and to derived rights.

Acquisition costs and disposal proceeds in respect of such rights which, in accordance with generally accepted accounting practice (see 66.5 above), may be taken into account in determining accounting profit or loss, and which are so taken into account in any relevant statutory accounts required under *Companies Act 1985, s 226* (or NI or foreign equivalent), are treated as being of a revenue nature in computing profits chargeable to corporation tax. This applies equally to costs of extension of attached rights or of cancellation or restriction of rights attached to derivative rights, and to receipts from cancellation or restriction of attached rights or from granting derivative rights or extensions of rights attached to derivative rights.

Similar treatment applies to amounts in respect of the revaluation of such rights provided that, in accordance with generally accepted accounting practice (see 66.5 above), they fall to be taken into account for accounting purposes, whether or not they may be so taken into account in determining profit or loss or are so taken into account in any relevant statutory accounts. The period of account for which such an amount is taken into account for tax purposes is that in which it is recognised for accounting purposes in accordance with generally accepted accounting practice.

Where the taxpayer company is a member of a group of companies (within *Companies Act 1985, s 262(1)* or NI or foreign equivalent) which is required to produce consolidated group accounts (within *Companies Act 1985, s 227* or NI or foreign equivalent), the company's accounting policies, and method of applying those policies, in respect of rights within these provisions must not be more cautious than that adopted in the group accounts. This applies in relation to each group of which the company is a member, if there is more than one.

[*FA 2000, s 87, Sch 23; ITTOIA 2005, Sch 1 paras 517, 523*].

See generally HMRC Corporate Intangibles Research and Development Manual, CIRD 70000 *et seq*. For an article giving HMRC's view on the interpretation of *FA 2000, Sch 23* (as replaced by *ITTOIA 2005, Pt 2 Ch 10*), see Revenue Tax Bulletin December 2000 pp 815–817.

66.80 TIED PETROL STATIONS ETC.

For tied licensed premises see 66.22 above.

'Exclusivity payments' by petrol company to retailers undertaking to sell only its goods were allowed in computing its profits in *Bolam v Regent Oil Co Ltd Ch D 1956, 37 TC 56* (payments for repairs carried out by retailer), *BP Australia Ltd PC 1965, 44 ATC 312* (lump sums paid for sales promotion) and *Mobil Oil Australia Ltd PC 1965, 44 ATC 323*, but held capital in *Strick v Regent Oil HL 1965, 43 TC 1* where the payment took the form of a premium to the retailer for a lease of his premises (immediately sub-let to him).

In the hands of the retailer, exclusivity payments were held capital when for capital expenditure incurred by him (*CIR v Coia CS 1959, 38 TC 334*; *McLaren v Needham Ch D 1960, 39 TC 37*; *Walter W Saunders Ltd v Dixon Ch D 1962, 40 TC 329*; *McClymont and Another v Jarman (Sp C 387) 2003, [2004] SSCD 54*) but revenue when for repairs etc. (*McLaren v Needham* above) or sales promotion (*Evans v Wheatley Ch D 1958, 38 TC 216*) or where petrol sales were a relatively small part (some 30%) of the company's turnover (*Tanfield Ltd v Carr (Sp C 200), [1999] SSCD 213*).

For a summary of HMRC's view of such arrangements, see HMRC Business Income Manual BIM 40300.

66.81 TRAINING

Costs incurred by an employer in respect of employee training are generally allowable as a trade expense. See 66.42 above for this and as regards certain other allowable employee training costs, and 66.76 above as regards contributions to training and enterprise councils.

66.82 UNCLAIMED BALANCES

Unclaimed balances for which a firm was liable to account were held not assessable despite their being distributed to partners (*Morley v Tattersall CA 1938, 22 TC 51*). Such balances held by a pawnbroker are, however, assessable when claimants' rights expire (*Jay's, the Jewellers v CIR KB 1947, 29 TC 274*), and deposits on garments not collected were held trade receipts assessable when received (*Elson v Prices Tailors Ch D 1962, 40 TC 671*). The fact that trading receipts were subsequently, and correctly, treated for accountancy purposes as an element in a sale of fixed assets did not alter their nature for tax purposes (*Tapemaze Ltd v Melluish Ch D 2000, 73 TC 167*). See 66.21 above for releases of debts owing.

66.83 UNREMITTABLE AMOUNTS

Where a trade is carried on partly in the UK and partly overseas, so that liability to UK corporation tax arises on trading profits, amounts received or receivable overseas (e.g. from export sales) which cannot be brought to the UK because of foreign exchange restrictions would nevertheless fall to be included in computing profits, with no relief being available under *ICTA 1988, s 584* (unremittable overseas income — see 60.3 RESIDENCE), i.e. because the overall profits of the trade do not arise outside the UK, or under *ICTA 1988, s 88D* in respect of impairment losses (for periods of account beginning before 1 January 2005, *ICTA 1988, s 74(1)(j)* in respect of bad and doubtful debts) (see 66.21 above), i.e. because a debt is not impaired or bad merely because it is unremittable.

Relief is provided in such circumstances by concession (HMRC Extra Statutory Concession B38. Where amounts cannot be remitted solely as a result of local foreign exchange control restrictions, for at least twelve months after the end of the accounting period in which the amount concerned was received or the debt arose, relief may be claimed, provided that:

(*a*) the assessment in question is not final and conclusive;

(*b*) all reasonable endeavours have been made to secure payment and remittance to the UK of funds;

(*c*) receipts or debts have not been used to finance expenditure or investment outside the UK;

(*d*) (in the case of debts) the debt cannot be discharged in the UK; and (*e*) the taxpayer agrees to the withdrawal of relief by an addition to profits for the period in which the concessional relief ceases to be available (see below).

As regards (*c*) above, debts are regarded as having been used to finance expenditure outside the UK where they are used, or might have been used, to meet expenditure or guarantee a liability incurred in the same territory by the trader or by a person with whom the trader has a special relationship, or where they remain unpaid by reason of such a relationship.

Relief for debts is available only to the extent that they are not insured. Relief is given by a deduction from trading profits for the accounting period in which the receipt or debt is recognised as unremittable. Any excess may be carried forward against trading profits of subsequent periods.

Relief is withdrawn where the restrictions or (*c*) above cease to apply, or the receipt or debt is otherwise applied outside the UK or exchanged for or discharged in a remittable currency.

This concession also applies to unremittable bank interest in appropriate circumstances (see 8.3 BANKS).

(HMRC Extra Statutory Concession, B38).

The above relief became statutory for income tax purposes for 2005/06 onwards under *ITTOIA 2005, ss 187–191* with two principal differences. The relief is allowed as a deduction in calculating trading profits without the need for a claim for that purpose and relief for a debt is denied only to the extent that an insurance recovery has been received in respect of the debt rather than to the extent it is insured. (See Change 50 listed in Annex 1 to the Explanatory Notes to the Income Tax (Trading and Other Income) Bill.)

66.84 WASTE DISPOSAL

Expenditure on purchase and reclamation of tipping sites by a company carrying on a waste disposal business was held to be capital in *Rolfe v Wimpey Waste Management Ltd CA 1989, 62 TC 399*, as were instalment payments for the right to deposit waste material in *CIR v Adam CS 1928, 14 TC 34*. See also *McClure v Petre Ch D 1988, 61 TC 226*, where the receipt of sum for licence to tip soil was also held to be capital.

Site restoration expenditure. A company making a 'site restoration payment', in the course of carrying on a trade, may deduct the payment in computing profits for the period of account (i.e. a period for which an account is drawn up) in which the payment is made. A payment will not qualify for relief to the extent that it represents either expenditure allowed as a trading deduction for prior periods or capital expenditure qualifying for capital allowances.

A '*site restoration payment*' is a payment made:

(*a*) in connection with the restoration of a site (or part thereof); and

(*b*) in order to comply with any condition of a 'relevant licence', or any condition imposed on the grant of planning permission to use the site for the carrying out of 'waste disposal activities', or any term of a 'relevant agreement'.

'*Waste disposal activities*' are the collection, treatment, conversion and final depositing of waste materials, or any of those activities.

A '*relevant licence*' is a disposal licence under the *Control of Pollution Act 1974, Pt I* (or NI equivalent), a waste management licence under the *Environmental Protection Act 1990, Pt II* (or NI equivalent), a permit under regulations under *Pollution Prevention and Control Act 1999, s 2* or an authorisation for the disposal of radioactive waste or a nuclear site licence.

A '*relevant agreement*' is an agreement under *Town and Country Planning Act 1971, s 52, Town and Country Planning (Scotland) Act 1972, s 50* or *Town and Country Planning Act 1990, s 106* (or NI equivalent) regulating the development or use of land.

[*ICTA 1988, s 91A; SI 2000 No 1973; ITTOIA 2005, Sch 1 para 68*].

For restoration expenditure generally (including provisions for such expenditure), see HMRC Business Income Manual BIM 67440.

Site preparation expenditure. A deduction is allowed as below in computing profits where a company incurs, in the course of a trade, 'site preparation expenditure' in relation to a 'waste disposal site', and, at the time when the company first deposits waste materials on the site in question, it holds a current 'waste disposal licence'. Expenditure incurred for trade purposes by a company about to carry on the trade is for this purpose treated as incurred on the first day of trading. The deduction is not available where the company incurring the expenditure recharges it to another person who holds the licence when first depositing waste (see HMRC Business Income Manual, BIM 67440). A claim for the deduction must be made in the prescribed manner and HMRC may also require plans and other documents to verify it. (For income tax purposes for 2005/06 onwards, no such claim is required (see Change 48 listed in Annex 1 to the Explanatory Notes to the Income Tax (Trading and Other Income) Bill.)

A '*waste disposal site*' is a site used (or to be used) for the disposal of waste materials by their deposit on the site, and in relation to such a site, '*site preparation expenditure*' is expenditure on preparing the site for the deposit of waste materials (and may include expenditure on earthworks). This includes expenditure incurred before the relevant licence is granted, and in particular expenses associated with obtaining the licence itself (HMRC Business Income Manual, BIM 67440 and BIM 67445).

In relation to the period of account in question, the '*allowable amount*' of the expenditure is:

$$(A - B) \times \frac{C}{C+D}$$

where:

A is the site preparation expenditure incurred by the company at any time before the beginning of, or during, the period in question in relation to the site in question and in the course of carrying on the trade. It does not include any expenditure which either has been allowed as a trading deduction for a prior period or is capital expenditure qualifying for capital allowances;

B is the amount (or aggregate of amounts) allowed as a trading deduction under this provision in prior periods and as regards expenditure incurred in relation to the site in question;

C is the volume of waste materials deposited on the site in question during the period in question, excluding any deposited before 6 April 1989;

D is the capacity of the site in question not used up for the deposit of waste materials as at the end of the period in question.

In addition, where any expenditure which would otherwise be included in A was incurred before 6 April 1989, A is reduced by an amount determined by:

$$E \times \frac{F}{F+G}$$

where:

E is so much of the initial expenditure (that is, the expenditure which would otherwise be included in A) as was incurred before 6 April 1989;

F is the volume of waste materials deposited on the site in question before 6 April 1989;

G is the capacity (expressed in volume) of the site in question not used up for the deposit of waste materials immediately before 6 April 1989.

Where a company (the 'predecessor') which has incurred site preparation expenditure as above in the course of a trade ceases to carry on the trade, or to carry it on so far as it relates to that site, and another company (the 'successor') begins to carry it on, or to carry on in the course of a trade the activities formerly carried on by the predecessor in relation to that site, then provided that:

(i) the whole of the site is transferred to the successor (although not necessarily the same estate or interest in the site); and

(ii) the successor holds a relevant licence in relation to the site which is in force when it first deposits waste material on the site,

the successor's trade is treated for these purposes as the same as that carried on by the predecessor, and the successor stands in the predecessor's shoes as regards allowances in relation to the site. [*ICTA 1988, ss 91B, 91BA; SI 2000 No 1973; ITTOIA 2005, Sch 1 paras 69, 70*].

See generally HMRC Business Income Manual BIM 67405–67520.

Leasing. See 66.54 above as regards restrictions on relief under the above provisions where finance leasing arrangements are involved.

Simon's Direct Tax Service. See **B3.13164**.

Landfill tax. HMRC's views on the deductibility of landfill tax in computing trading income are as follows.

Site operators. Treatment of landfill tax charged on to customers will follow the generally accepted accounting practice. As regards self-generated waste, landfill tax (net of any credit following a contribution to an environmental trust) will be allowed as a deduction so long as the other costs incurred in disposing of the waste are deductible.

Customers of site operators. The landfill tax element of the global charge does not need to be separately invoiced, and deductibility of the landfill tax element will follow that of the non-landfill tax element of the charge.

Environmental trust contributions. Site operators may obtain relief from landfill tax by making such contributions, the deductibility of which is to be determined in the circumstances of each particular case under the normal test of whether the expenditure is incurred wholly and exclusively for trade purposes. In the case of an unconnected trust engaged in projects of possible use to the operator, the payment would *prima facie* be deductible. If the operator has some degree of control over the trust, or the income of the trust is ultimately received by a person connected with the operator, it might be less clear that the payment was for the purposes of the operator's own trade. Similarly if the trust's objects were insufficiently related to the operator's trade, it might be considered that contributions were for a general philanthropic, and hence non-trade, purpose.

(HMRC Business Income Manual, BIM 67525 and BIM 67530).

67 Transfer Pricing

Cross Reference. See 23.5 DISTRIBUTIONS, 33.10 HMRC ADMINISTRATION, 54.5–54.9 PENALTIES.

Simon's Direct Tax Service B3.927, D2.20.

Other sources. Global Transfer Pricing: Principles and Practice, Transfer Pricing: A UK Perspective. See also the HMRC International Manual at 430,000 *et seq.*

The headings in this chapter are as follows.

67.1 ACCOUNTING PERIODS BEGINNING AFTER 31 MARCH 2004

For accounting periods beginning **on or after 1 April 2004** (and see below for accounting periods straddling that date), the scope of the transfer pricing requirements set out at 67.2–67.13 are extended so that they apply to both UK and cross-border transactions. The thin capitalisation rules (see 23.5 DISTRIBUTIONS) are repealed and subsumed within the transfer pricing rules (see 67.4 below) and new rules apply to companies giving guarantees for third party loans (see 67.4 and 67.8 below). Dormant companies (see 67.6 below) and small and medium-sized enterprises (see 67.7 below) will, in most circumstances, be exempt from applying the transfer pricing and thin capitalisation rules. Where an adjustment is required by the provisions to increase the profits of one party, the corresponding adjustments provisions (see 67.8 below) are extended so that the connected UK party can make a compensating reduction in their taxable profits, and new provisions allow for a 'balancing payment' to be made tax-free up to the amount of the compensating adjustment (see 67.9 below).

Where an accounting period of a company straddles 1 April 2004, it is treated, for the purposes of calculating the company's profits and losses, as two separate accounting periods, the first ending on 31 March 2004 and the second, to which the new rules apply, beginning on 1 April 2004.

[*ICTA 1988, Sch 28AA; FA 2004, ss 30–37, Sch 5*].

The legislation in FA 2004 follows the Revenue's Technical Note on 'Corporation tax reform: the next steps' published on 10 December 2003 for consultation. See generally HMRC International Manual at 430,000 *et seq.* on a number of transfer pricing issues and at 560,000 *et seq.* on thin capitalisation. HMRC guidance on the provision of documentation stresses that a business would not be expected to carry out extensive research or incur significant costs in producing documentation where the amounts at stake would not generally be significant and where both parties to a transaction were subject to similar levels of taxation. Similarly, HMRC would only put resources into making transfer pricing enquiries where the amounts of tax at stake appeared to be large.

The European Commission has adopted a Code of Conduct on transfer pricing documentation to standardise the documentation that multinational companies of different member states must provide to their respective tax authorities on their pricing of cross-border intra-group transactions. (See the European Commission Press Release IP/06/850 of 28 June 2006, available on the Europa website (at www.consilium.europa.eu).)

Penalties. For a transitional period covering accounting periods **beginning on or after 1 January 2004 and ending on or before 31 March 2006**, penalties will be waived where the only reason for imposing the penalty is that the business had kept insufficient records required by *FA 1998, Sch 18 para 23* to demonstrate that results are 'arm's length' results. Equally, the penalties imposed by *FA 1998, Sch 18 para 20* or *ITA 2007 Sch 1 para 385* for negligently preparing an incorrect return and by *TMA 1970, s 99* for an agent who knowingly assists in the preparation of an incorrect return etc, will be waived where the only evidence for the penalty is the lack of records needed to demonstrate the use of arm's length prices. (See 54.5–54.9 PENALTIES.) [*FA 2004, s 33*].

67.2 **ACCOUNTING PERIODS ENDING ON OR AFTER 1 JULY 1999**

For accounting periods ending **on or after 1 July 1999**, for which corporate self-assessment applies, and subject to transitional arrangements (see 67.14 below), *ICTA 1988, s 770A* and *Sch 28AA* replaces *ICTA 1988, ss 770–773* (see 67.15 below). [*FA 1998, s 108(1)(2)(5), Sch 16; SI 1998 No 3173*]. Schedule 28AA is further amended for accounting periods beginning on or after 1 April 2004 by *FA 2004, ss 30–32, 34–36* as set out at 67.1 above. *Schedule 28AA* is to be construed so as best to secure consistency between the effect given to the basic rules of the *Schedule* (under *paragraph 1*, see below) and the principles of the OECD model tax convention and transfer pricing guidelines. [*ICTA 1988, Sch 28AA para 2*]. The guidelines are currently published by the OECD as 'Transfer Pricing Guidelines for Multinational Enterprises and Taxation Administrations', and can be purchased from HMSO outlets. HMRC International Manual sets out HMRC's views on those guidelines and on the principles and operation of the legislation on transfer pricing at INTM 430000 *et seq.* and provides practical guidance on enquiries and the operation of the mutual agreement procedure contained in UK double taxation conventions at INTM 460000 *et seq.*

67.3 **Basic rule.** *Schedule 28AA* applies where provision (the '*actual provision*') has been made or imposed as between two persons (the '*affected persons*') by means of a transaction or series of transactions, and at the time the provision was made or imposed either:

(*a*) one of the affected persons was directly or indirectly participating in the management, control or capital of the other; or

(*b*) there was a person or persons who was or were directly or indirectly participating in the management, control or capital of each of the affected persons.

Except as below, if the actual provision differs from the provision which would have been made at arm's length as between independent enterprises (or if no provision would have been so made) and confers a 'potential advantage' (see 67.5 below) in relation to UK taxation on one of the affected persons or (whether or not the same advantage) on each of them, the profits and losses (and certain items treated as losses) of the potentially advantaged person, or of each of them, are computed for tax purposes as if the arm's length provision had been made or imposed (or, as the case may be, no provision made) instead of the actual provision. See also HMRC International Manual, INTM 432040.

'Transactions' etc. A 'transaction' for these purposes includes schemes or arrangements of any kind, understandings and mutual practices (whether or not legally enforceable), and a 'series' of transactions includes a number of transactions entered into in pursuance of, or in relation to, the same scheme or arrangement. A series of transactions is not prevented from being regarded as the means by which provision has been made or imposed between two persons by reason only that there is no transaction in the series to which both those persons are parties, or one or more transactions to which neither of them is a party, or that the parties to any scheme or arrangement in pursuance of which the transactions are entered

into do not include one or both of them. The broad scope of the legislation means that some arrangements involving third parties which were not transfer pricing transactions under *ICTA 1988, s 770* (see 67.13 below) are now within the scope of *ICTA 1988, Sch 28AA* (see HMRC International Manual, INTM 432050).

'Participation in management' etc. A person is for these purposes treated as directly participating in the management, control or capital of another person at a particular time if and only if (but subject to the provisions below on persons acting together in relation to financing arrangements), at that time, the other person is a body corporate or partnership which that person controls (within *ICTA 1988, s 840*, see 57.4(2)(vii) PURCHASE BY A COMPANY OF ITS OWN SHARES). Similarly indirect participation requires that the person (the '*potential participant*') either would be taken to be participating directly if certain rights and powers (see *ICTA 1988, Sch 28AA para 4(3)-(6)(10)-(12)*), including future rights and powers, were attributed to him, or is one of a number of 'major participants' in the other person's enterprise. A person is a '*major participant*' in another person's enterprise when the other person is a body corporate or partnership, and he is one of two persons who control (as above) the other person, each of whom has at least 40% of the holdings, etc. giving that control (again after attribution of certain rights and powers as above).

Persons acting together in relation to financing arrangements. For accounting periods beginning on or after 4 March 2005 (subject to transitional provisions, see below), the meaning of 'indirectly participating' above is extended by *ICTA 1988, Sch 28AA para 4A* to include circumstances where a number of parties act together in relation to the 'financing arrangements' of a business and could collectively control the business.

(i) For the purposes of (*a*) above (determining whether one of the affected persons was participating in the management, etc. of another), a person ('X') is treated as indirectly participating in the management etc. of another ('Y') if:

- the actual provision relates, to any extent, to financing arrangements for Y (where Y is a body corporate or partnership);
- X and other persons acted together in relation to the arrangements; and
- X would be taken to have control of Y if, at any 'relevant time', there were attributed to X the rights and powers of each of those other persons (taking into account any additional rights or powers that would be attributed to any person if *ICTA 1988, Sch 28AA para 4* (see under '*Participation in management etc.*' above) applied in that person's case).

(ii) For the purposes of (*b*) above (determining whether there was a person (or persons) participating in the management, etc. of each of the affected persons), the rule in (i) above applies where the financing arrangements are for one of the affected persons and X would be taken to have control of each of the affected persons.

It is immaterial whether the persons acting together did so at the time the actual provision is made or imposed or did so at some earlier time.

'*Financing arrangements*' are arrangements made for providing or guaranteeing, or otherwise in connection with, any debt, capital or other form of finance. A '*relevant time*' is any time when the persons were so acting together and also any time in the six months after they ceased to do so. Where the conditions in (*a*) or (*b*) above are satisfied by virtue only of the above rule, a transfer pricing adjustment can be required only to the extent that the actual provision relates to the financing arrangements in question.

ICTA 1988, Sch 28AA para 4A above applies in relation to accounting periods beginning on or after 4 March 2005. However, by way of transitional protection for debt finance provided to a person under a contract entered into before 4 March 2005, its application in such a case is delayed until accounting periods beginning on or after 1 April 2007 or, if the contract is varied before that date, the date of the variation. Accounting periods straddling 4 March 2005, 1 April 2007 or the date of a variation (as the case may be) are treated, for these purposes only, as two separate periods, the first ending with the day before whichever of those dates is relevant and the second beginning on that date. Profits and losses are computed accordingly for the two periods and then aggregated (so that the above rules cannot affect profits arising before the relevant date). An advance made on or after 4 March 2005 in accordance with terms agreed before that date or a change in the applied interest rate in accordance with terms agreed before that date are not regarded as variations to the contract for these purposes (see the HMRC website (at www.hmrc.gov.uk/international/transferpricing.pdf)).

By virtue of *ICTA 1988, Sch 28AA para 4B*, to the extent that the actual provision relates to financing arrangements, the conditions at (*a*) and (*b*) above are to be judged not only at the time the provision is made or imposed but at all times within the following six months; so to this extent transfer pricing adjustments may be triggered by events occurring up to six months before the necessary relationship exists between the parties. This applies in relation to accounting periods beginning on or after 4 March 2005 in all cases but, by virtue of the rule for straddling periods above which applies equally here, does not affect the calculation of profits arising before that date.

For more detail on the financing arrangements rules, see the HMRC website (at www.hmrc.gov.uk/international/transferpricing.pdf).

[*ICTA 1988, Sch 28AA paras 1, 3, 4, 4A, 4B, 14; F(No 2)A 2005, Sch 8 paras 1(1)–(4), 4*].

67.4 **Thin capitalisation.** *FA 2004* has repealed the rules in *ICTA 1988, s 209(2)(da), (8A)–(8F)*, whereby excessive payments of interest by companies which are thinly capitalised are treated as distributions (see 23.5 DISTRIBUTIONS). Instead, interest attributable to the excessive part of debt finance between connected companies is disallowed under the transfer pricing legislation. The main features of the old regime otherwise remain (see below) and the general transfer pricing provisions apply. In particular the provisions for compensating adjustments apply, including for guarantors of third party loans, and exemption from deduction at source under *ICTA 1988, s 349* can be claimed (see 67.8 below). There is a new provision relating to securitisation financing arrangements (see 67.9 below). The new regime applies to accounting periods **beginning on or after 1 April 2004** (and see 67.1 above for periods straddling that date).

Provision in relation to securities. The transfer pricing rules apply to a provision which differs from an arm's length provision in relation to a 'security' issued by a company ('*the issuing company*') to another company ('*the lending company*'). In considering whether the provision is at arm's length, account is to be taken of all factors including whether, in the absence of a 'special relationship' (and whether or not it is the business of the lending company to make loans generally):

(*a*) the loan would have been provided at all;

(*b*) the amount would have been advanced; and

(*c*) the rate of interest or other terms of the loan would have been agreed.

A '*security*' can include a loan or advance of money, whether secured or not. A '*special relationship*' in this case means any relationship where the issuing company and lending company are connected under the circumstances set out at 67.3 (*a*) and (*b*) above.

In considering whether the provision is made at arm's length, no account is to be taken of any 'guarantee' (or inference drawn from a 'guarantee') provided by a company with which the issuing company has a 'participatory relationship', when determining:

(i) the appropriate level or extent of the issuing company's overall indebtedness;

(ii) whether the issuing company would have issued the security or whether the lending company would have advanced the loan or the particular amount of the loan; and

(iii) the rate of interest and other terms expected in such a transaction.

A company has a '*participatory relationship*' with another in this case where one of them is directly or indirectly participating in the management, control or capital of the other, or the same person or persons is or are directly or indirectly participating in the management, control or capital of each of them.

A '*guarantee*' in this case includes any surety, relationship, arrangement, connection or understanding (whether formal or informal), such that the lending company has a reasonable expectation that the loan will be repaid by the guarantor (or guarantors) in the event of default by the issuing company.

Clarification is provided by HMRC on the new thin capitalisation rules in HMRC International Manual at 560,000 *et seq.* Under the heading of 'separate entity', it is explained that actual assets or liabilities such as shares in subsidiaries and intra group loans are not to be disregarded when assessing the borrowing capacity of a company but that they should be taken into account to the same extent that they would be by an unconnected lender. This effectively means that all assets and liabilities in direct or indirect subsidiaries should be taken into account. It goes on to explain that the repeal of the UK grouping rule in calculating an individual company's debt capacity does not in practice affect the UK sub-group as a whole because of the provisions for loan guarantees and in particular the compensating adjustment for guarantors (see 67.8 below).

HMRC have issued a guidance note (26 April 2007) and draft statement of practice giving details of changes to clearance procedures for financial transactions and thin capitalisation agreements. See http://www.hmrc.gov.uk/cnr/clearance-processes.htm.

Guarantees etc. Similar provisions apply where the actual provision is made or imposed by means of a series of transactions which include the issue of a 'security' (see above) by one of the affected persons and the provision of a 'guarantee' (see above) by the other affected person (see 67.3 above) (whether or not the issuing company and lending company are so connected). The effect of the provisions is that the interest attributable to the excessive part of such a loan is disallowed as if the loan was received from a connected party. In considering whether the provision is at arm's length, account is to be taken of all factors including whether, in the absence of a 'special relationship' (see above) (and whether or not it is the business of the guarantor to make guarantees generally):

(A) the guarantee would have been provided at all;

(B) the particular amount would have been guaranteed; and

(C) the consideration for the guarantee or other terms would have been agreed.

No account is to be taken of any guarantee (or inference drawn from a guarantee) provided by a company with which the issuing company has a 'participatory relationship', when determining any of (i) to (iii) above.

[*ICTA 1988, Sch 28AA paras 1A, 1B; FA 2004, ss 34, 37*].

67.5 **Potential advantage.** The actual provision confers a '*potential advantage*' on a person in relation to UK taxation where its effect, compared to that of the corresponding arm's length provision, would be a reduction in chargeable profits or increase in losses (or conversion of profits into losses) of that person for any chargeable period. In determining the chargeable profits or allowable losses for this purpose in the case of a non-UK resident company, no account is to be taken of any income on which the income tax charge is limited under *FA 2003, s 151* (see 60.5 RESIDENCE).

Where, however, for accounting periods beginning before 1 April 2004 (and see 67.1 above for periods straddling that date), the following conditions are satisfied in relation to each of the persons as between whom an actual provision was made, no such potential advantage is conferred on either of them (except in the case of 'ring-fenced trades', see below):

(i) they are within the charge to income or corporation tax in respect of profits arising from the activities in relation to which the actual provision was made or imposed (and not exempt in respect of all or any part of the income or profits from those activities), and where it is an income tax charge which applies, they are UK-resident for all chargeable periods for which it so applies;

(ii) they neither have an entitlement to a foreign tax credit in any chargeable period in relation to profits from such activities, nor would have any such entitlement if there were any such profits or if they exceeded a certain amount;

(iii) the amounts taken into account in computing profits or losses from such activities for any chargeable period in relation to which (i) above is satisfied do not include any income from which a deduction is made for foreign tax (where no credit is allowable); and

(iv) (in the case of a person who is an insurance company within *ICTA 1988, s 431*) the profits from such activities in respect of which the company is within the charge to corporation tax do not include any in the computation of which acquisition expenses have been brought into account under *FA 1989, s 86* or in relation to which a lower rate of tax is fixed by *FA 1989, s 88* or *s 88A*.

For accounting periods **beginning on or after 1 April 2004** (and see 67.1 above for periods straddling that date), the above rules cease to have effect and the transfer pricing provisions apply to transactions between UK-resident taxpayers as they do to cross-border transactions.

[*ICTA 1988, Sch 28AA paras5, 14; FA 2004, ss 30(2), 37*].

67.6 **Exemption for dormant companies.** For accounting periods **beginning on or after 1 April 2004** (and see 67.1 above for periods straddling that date), the transfer pricing provisions do not apply, when calculating the profits or losses for any chargeable period, to companies which:

(*a*) are dormant throughout the accounting period ending on 31 March 2004, or if there is no such accounting period, the three-month period ending on that date; and

(*b*) have continued to be dormant at all times since the end of that period apart from any transfer pricing adjustments.

For these purposes, '*dormant*' has the same meaning as in *Companies Act 1985, s 249AA(4)–(7)*.

[*ICTA 1988, Sch 28AA para 5A; FA 2004, ss 31(3), 37*].

67.7 **Exemption for small and medium-sized enterprises.** For accounting periods **beginning on or after 1 April 2004** (and see 67.1 above for periods straddling that date), the transfer pricing provisions do not apply, when calculating the profits or losses for any chargeable period, to a company which is a small or medium-sized enterprise. Such companies are as defined in the Annex to the Commission Recommendation *2003/361/EC* of 6 May 2003 with the modifications set out in *ICTA 1988, Sch 28AA para 5D* (as inserted by *FA 2004, s 31*). Broadly, a small enterprise is defined as a business with less than 50 employees and either turnover or assets of less than €10 million and a small or medium-sized enterprise as a business with less than 250 employees and either turnover of less than €50 million or assets of less than €43 million. Associated enterprises are taken into account in determining whether a company is a small or medium-sized enterprise.

Exceptions. The exemption will not apply where:

(*a*) a small or medium-sized enterprise elects for the exemption not to apply, such election being irrevocable;

(*b*) at the time the actual provision was made or imposed, the other affected person or a 'party to the relevant transaction' is resident and liable to tax in a 'non-qualifying territory' (whether or not also resident in a 'qualifying territory');

(*c*) as respects any provision made or imposed, HMRC gives notice (a '*transfer pricing notice*') to a medium-sized enterprise, which is the advantaged party, requiring that company to increase profits or reduce losses of that chargeable period on an arm's length basis.

As regards (*b*) above, where the actual provision is or was imposed by means of a series of transactions, a '*party to a relevant transaction*' is or was a party to one or more of those transactions. A company is not considered liable to tax in a non-qualifying territory if the liability relates only to income sourced from that territory or capital situated there. A '*non-qualifying territory*' is a territory which is not a qualifying territory. A '*qualifying territory*' is defined as:

(i) the UK; or

(ii) a territory with which the UK has a double tax treaty (under *ICTA 1988, s 788*) containing a non-discrimination article (see *ICTA 1988, Sch 28AA para 5E*) unless that territory has been designated as non-qualifying in regulations made by the Treasury; or

(iii) a territory with which the UK has a double tax treaty (under *ICTA 1988, s 788*) and which is designated as qualifying in regulations made by the Treasury.

Transfer pricing notices issued to medium-sized companies. As regards (*c*) above, a transfer pricing notice, which may only be given following a notice of enquiry, may specify that an arm's length adjustment is to be made in respect of a certain, or certain type of, provision or in respect of all provisions which would fall within the transfer pricing rules but for the above exemption. The recipient of a notice may appeal in writing to the officer of HMRC identified for the purpose in the transfer notice, within 30 days from the date the notice is given (see 6.1 APPEALS) but only on the grounds that the company is a small rather than a medium-sized enterprise. The company receiving the notice may amend the company tax return to which the notice relates at any time within 90 days of the date the notice was given, or if an appeal is made, the day on which the appeal is finally determined or abandoned. HMRC may issue a closure notice once the 90 days have elapsed, or if earlier, once the tax return has been amended for the purpose of complying with the notice.

Where a medium-sized company is not excepted from exemption under (*a*) or (*b*) above, there is no need for the company's tax return to take account of the transfer pricing rules. However, this does not prevent the company's tax return from becoming incorrect if a transfer pricing notice is issued and the return is not amended within the period of 90 days as noted above when it should have been amended.

[*ICTA 1988, Sch 28AA paras 5B–5E; FA 2004, ss 31(4), 37*].

67.8 **Elimination of double counting.** Where a potential advantage is conferred (as above) on only one of the affected persons (the '*advantaged person*'), and the other person (the '*disadvantaged person*') is:

(*a*) for accounting periods **beginning on or after 1 April 2004** (and see 67.1 above for periods straddling that date), within the charge to corporation tax (or income tax) in respect of profits arising from the relevant activities; or

(*b*) for accounting periods **beginning before 1 April 2004** (and see 67.1 above for periods straddling that date), within 67.5(i) above (or would be if any exemption from tax were disregarded),

then (except as below) the disadvantaged person may claim application of the arm's length provision rather than the actual provision (over-riding any applicable time limits for the necessary adjustments). Such a claim may only be made if the arm's length provision has similarly been applied in the case of the advantaged person (in his return or following a determination, see 67.11 below), and the computations in the case of each of them on that basis must be consistent.

Where the conditions at 67.3 (*a*) and (*b*) above are satisfied only by virtue of *ICTA 1988, Sch 28AA para 4A* (financing arrangements — see 67.3 above), no claim by the disadvantaged person can be made where the actual provision is provision in relation to a security issued by one of the affected persons and the security is guaranteed by a person with whom the issuer of the security has a 'participatory relationship'. Appropriately modified versions of 67.3 (*a*) and (*b*) above, as extended by *para 4A*, apply to determine the existence or otherwise of a '*participatory relationship*'. See 67.3 above for the commencement date of this provision.

Claims: time limits. The claim must be made within two years of the making of the return or the giving of the notice taking account of the determination, as the case may be, and a claim based on a return which is subsequently the subject of such a notice may be amended within two years of the giving of the notice. (These time limits may be extended in certain cases where HMRC fails to give proper notice to disadvantaged persons under *FA 1998, s 111(3)*.)

[*ICTA 1988, Sch 28AA para 6; FA 2001, Sch 29 para 35; FA 2004, ss 30(3)–(5), 35, 37; F(No 2)A 2005, Sch 8 paras 1(5), 4*].

Transfers of trading stock etc. For accounting periods **beginning on or after 1 April 2004** (and see 67.1 above for periods straddling that date), a special provision applies where trading stock (as defined in *ICTA 1988, s 100(2)*) or work in progress in a trade is transferred between associated parties at other than an arm's length price, and a transfer pricing adjustment is applied in the case of the advantaged person. In that case, a compensating adjustment may be claimed (as above) in respect of closing trading stock or work in progress by the disadvantaged person in the accounting period ending on or after the last day of that of the advantaged person in which the stock transfer occurred. [*ICTA 1988, Sch 29AA para 6A; FA 2004, s 32(2), 37*].

Controlled foreign companies. For accounting periods **beginning on or after 1 April 2004** (and see 67.1 above for periods straddling that date), a special provision applies where a transfer pricing adjustment has been applied to the profits or losses of a controlled foreign company the profits of which fall to be wholly apportioned to, and taxable in, the UK by virtue of *ICTA 1988, s 747(3)(4)* (see 21 CONTROLLED FOREIGN COMPANIES). In this case, the controlled foreign company is treated as an advantaged person such that a compensating adjustment may be claimed (as above) by the disadvantaged party or parties (and references above to an advantaged person include a reference to a controlled foreign company). [*ICTA 1988, Sch 28AA para 6B; FA 2004, s 32*].

Thin capitalisation. Where the thin capitalisation provisions in 67.4 above apply in accounting periods beginning on or after 1 April 2004 (and see 67.1 above for periods straddling that date), a compensating adjustment may be claimed (and the claim may be amended) by the disadvantaged person or by the advantaged person on behalf of the disadvantaged person. Such a claim (a paragraph 6C claim) may be made before or after the arm's length provision has been applied in the case of the advantaged person (in his return or following a determination – see 67.11 below) but the claim must be consistent with that computation. If the claim is not consistent with the computation, it is treated as if it were amended to make it consistent, allowing for any required adjustments to be made (whether by discharge or repayment of tax, the making of assessments or otherwise). (In making a paragraph 6C claim before the transfer pricing provision is applied, the lending company is not treated as chargeable under Schedule D Case III on so much of the interest subject to the transfer pricing adjustment (see '*Reciprocal treatment*' below) and thus, the condition for deducting tax at source under *ITA 2007 s 449* (formerly *ICTA 1988, s 349(2)*) is not met The borrowing company may thus pay interest to a non-resident lender without deduction of tax at source.) Claims must be made or amended before the expiry of the time limits noted above and the provisions of *TMA 1970, Sch 1A* (claims made outside a return) apply for this purpose. [*ICTA 1988, Sch 28AA para 6C; FA 2004, s 35(3)*]

Thin capitalisation: guarantees. Where a transfer pricing adjustment to disallow interest follows from the provision of a guarantee (see 67.4 above), the guarantor company can claim a compensating adjustment as if it was the borrower (the 'issuing company') and had paid the interest subject to the disallowance. Amounts are brought into account in computing the guarantor company's profits and losses accordingly. Where there is more than one guarantor, the total amount claimed by way of a compensating adjustment must not exceed the amount of interest disallowed. A claim can also be made by the issuing company on behalf of the guarantor company or companies. Where a claim is made by a guarantor and the lending company subsequently makes a claim for a compensating adjustment in respect of the same loan, the claim made by the lending company must be reduced to the extent of the claim made by the guarantor company. A claim made by the guarantor company will not be allowed where the lending company has earlier made a compensating adjustment claim for the full amount of the interest disallowance. The provisions above relating to claims and time limits apply equally to claims made by a guarantor company or by the issuing company on behalf of the guarantor company. [*ICTA 1988, Sch 28AA para 6D; FA 2004, s 35(3)*]

Reciprocal treatment. Where a transfer pricing adjustment applies to disallow interest and the lending company claims a compensating adjustment under either *ICTA 1988, Sch 28AA para 6* or *6C*, the interest disallowed as a deduction for the borrower is correspondingly not treated as Schedule D Case III income for the lending company. (The condition for deduction at source in *ICTA 1988, s 349(2)* is therefore not met so that where a paragraph 6C claim is made (see above) the borrowing company can pay interest to a not-resident lender without deduction of tax at source.) [*ICTA 1988, Sch 28AA para 6E; FA 2004, s 35(4)*].

Foreign taxation. Where a claim for a compensating adjustment is made, it is assumed, as respects any foreign tax credit which has been or may be given to the disadvantaged person, that that foreign tax does not include tax which would not be or have become payable if the arm's length provision had also been substituted for the purposes of that tax, and that the profits from the activities in relation to which the actual provision was made or imposed and in respect of which the tax credit relief arises are reduced to the same extent as they are treated as reduced by virtue of the claim.

Where the application of the arm's length provision in a computation following such a claim involves a reduction in the amount of any income, and that income also falls to be treated as reduced under *ICTA 1988, s 811(1)* by an amount of foreign tax (where credit relief is not available), the former reduction is treated as made before the latter, and the deductible foreign tax excludes that paid on so much of the income as is represented by the amount of the former reduction.

Any adjustment to double tax reliefs as above may be given effect by set-off against any relief or repayment arising from the claim, and may be made without regard to any time limit on assessments or amendments.

[*ICTA 1988, Sch 28AA para 7*].

67.9 **Balancing payments.** For accounting periods **beginning on or after 1 April 2004** (and see 67.1 above for periods straddling that date), where a transfer pricing adjustment applies in the case of the advantaged company and a claim for a compensating adjustment can be made by the disadvantaged company (see 67.8 above), the disadvantaged company may make a balancing payment to the advantaged company by reason of the transfer pricing adjustment. Provided such balancing payments do not in aggregate exceed the amount of the available compensating adjustment, the payments shall not be taken into account when computing profits or losses for tax purposes or be regarded as distributions or (for payments before 16 March) charges on income (see 55.4 PROFIT COMPUTATIONS). The '*available compensating adjustment*' is the difference between the profits and losses of the disadvantaged company computed on the basis of the actual provision and computed for the purposes of making the compensating adjustment under 67.8 above (taking profits as positive amounts and losses as negative amounts). [*ICTA 1988, Sch 28AA para 7A; FA 2004, s 30(6); F(No 2)A 2005, Sch 11 Pt 2(7)*].

Balancing payments made by guarantors: thin capitalisation. Where a transfer pricing adjustment applies in the case of the advantaged company and a claim for a compensating adjustment can be made by a guarantor company (see 67.8 above), the guarantor company may make balancing payments to the issuing company (i.e. the borrower) by reason of the transfer pricing adjustment. Provided such balancing payments do not in aggregate exceed the amount of the compensating adjustment, the payments shall not be taken into account for corporation tax purposes when computing profits or losses of the guarantor company (or companies) or of the issuing company, or be regarded as distributions or (for payments before 16 March 2005) charges on income (see 55.4 PROFIT COMPUTATIONS). The compensating adjustment in this case is the total reductions in interest or other amounts payable under the security subject to the guarantee (and thus treated as paid by the guarantor). [*ICTA 1988, Sch 28AA para 7C; FA 2004, s 36(3); F(No 2)A 2005, Sch 11 Pt 2(7)*].

Election to pay tax instead of balancing payment: thin capitalisation. Special provisions apply where the actual provision subject to a claim for a compensating adjustment under 67.8 above, is a provision in relation to a security (the 'relevant security') (see 67.4 above on thin capitalisation). In that case, instead of making a balancing payment as above, the disadvantaged company may elect to assume responsibility for the additional tax liability in relation to an accounting period of the advantaged company where the additional liability results from the transfer pricing adjustment in relation to the relevant security (i.e. a disallowance of interest or other amounts). The tax liability in this case would not be treated as a liability of and recoverable from the advantaged company but would be treated as a corporation tax liability of the disadvantaged company. The disadvantaged company may only make such an election where:

(*a*) the actual provision relating to the security forms part of a capital market arrangement involving the issue of a capital market investment (as defined in the *Insolvency Act 1986, s 72B(1), Sch 2A paras 1–3*) of a total value of at least £50 million; and

(*b*) the securities representing the capital market investment are issued wholly or mainly to independent persons (not the disadvantaged company and not persons having a participatory relationship (as defined in 67.4 above) with any of the affected companies).

The election, which is irrevocable, must be made in the disadvantaged company's tax return (whether by amendment or otherwise) for the chargeable period in which the relevant security is issued and has effect for that period and all subsequent chargeable periods (i.e. the lifetime of the loan). For this purpose, securities issued in a chargeable period beginning before 1 April 2004 are treated as though issued in a chargeable period beginning on that date. HMRC may refuse to accept such an election but only after a notice of enquiry has been issued to the disadvantaged company in respect of the tax return containing the election.

The above provisions relating to an election to pay tax instead of a balancing payment apply equally, with necessary modifications, in cases where a transfer pricing is made in respect of third party loans subject to a guarantee provided by a connected company (see 67.4 above).

[*ICTA 1988, Sch 28AA paras 7B, 7D; FA 2004, s 36(2)(4)*].

67.10 **Capital allowances and capital gains.** These provisions do not affect the computation of capital allowances or balancing charges under the *Capital Allowances Acts*, or of capital gains or allowable losses under *TCGA 1992*, and do not require any income or losses to be treated as on capital rather than revenue account. However, for accounting periods **beginning on or after 1 April 2004** (and see 67.1 above for periods straddling that date), a compensating adjustment (see 67.10 above) may affect the computation of such allowances, charges, gains or losses. [*ICTA 1988, Sch 28AA para 13; CAA 2001, Sch 2 para 68; FA 2004, ss 32(4), 37*].

67.11 **Determinations requiring the sanction of HMRC.** A determination of an amount falling to be brought into account under these provisions, other than in certain cases where an agreement has been reached between HMRC and the person concerned (see *FA 1998, s 110(5)-(7)*), requires HMRC's sanction. Where such a determination is made for the purpose of giving a closure notice, giving a notice amending a partnership statement or return or making a discovery assessment, and the notice of the closure, amendment or discovery assessment is given to any person without the determination, so far as taken into account in the notice or assessment, having been approved by HMRC, or without a copy of HMRC's approval having been served on that person at or before the time the notice was given, the closure or amendment notice or discovery assessment is deemed to have been given or made (and in the case of an assessment notified) as if the determination had not been taken into account. The approval must apply specifically to the case in question and the amount determined, but may otherwise be given (either before or after the making of the determination) in any such form or manner as HMRC may determine. An appeal relating to a determination approved by HMRC may not question HMRC's approval except to the extent that the grounds for questioning the approval are the same as the grounds for questioning the determination itself. [*FA 1998, s 110; FA 2001, Sch 29 para 38*]. For the requirement that HMRC give notice of determinations to persons who it appears to them may be 'disadvantaged persons' (as above) by reference to the subject-matter of the determination, see *FA 1998, s 111* (as amended).

See also HMRC International Manual, INTM 434010–434080.

67.12 **Appeals.** An appeal against an amendment of a return, the refusal of a claim or a discovery assessment or determination involving the application of *Schedule 28AA* lies to the Special Commissioners. Where the appeal relates to any provision as between two persons each of whom falls:

(*a*) for accounting periods **beginning on or after 1 April 2004** (and see 67.1 above for periods straddling that date), within the charge to income or corporation tax in respect of profits arising from relevant activities; or

(*b*) for accounting periods **beginning before 1 April 2004** (and see 67.1 above for periods straddling that date), within 67.5(i) above,

each person is entitled to appear before and be heard by the Special Commissioners, or to make written representations to them, and the Commissioners must determine that aspect of the appeal separately from any other, that separate determination being treated as made in an appeal to which each of those persons was a party. [*ICTA 1988, Sch 28AA para 12; FA 2004, s 30(8)*].

67.13 **Miscellaneous.** For accounting periods beginning on or after 1 October 2002, amounts brought into account in respect of exchange gains and losses relating to LOAN RELATIONSHIPS (46) or in respect of derivative contracts (see 28.2 FINANCIAL INSTRUMENTS AND DERIVATIVE CONTRACTS) are not subject to application of an arm's length provision as above, but this does not affect the application of *Schedule 28AA* for the purposes of *FA 1996, Sch 9 para 11A* (as amended by *FA 2007 Sch 5 para 14*) (see 46.20 LOAN RELATIONSHIPS) or *FA 2002, Sch 26 para 27* (see 28.17 FINANCIAL INSTRUMENTS AND DERIVATIVE CONTRACTS) in the case of contracts not entered into at arm's length. For earlier accounting periods, amounts brought into account in respect of EXCHANGE GAINS AND LOSSES (26) and financial instruments (see 28 FINANCIAL INSTRUMENTS AND DERIVATIVE CONTRACTS) adjustments are not subject to application of an arm's length provision as above, but this does not affect the application of *Schedule 28AA* for the purposes of *FA 1993, ss 136, 136A* in the case of certain loan interest (see 26.17 EXCHANGE GAINS AND LOSSES). [*ICTA 1988, Sch 28AA para 8; FA 2002, Sch 23 para 21, Sch 27 para 15*].

There are also special provisions relating to transactions involving oil and gas [*ICTA 1988, Sch 28AA paras 9, 10*] and to 'ring-fenced' oil and gas exploration activities amended for accounting periods beginning on or after 1 April 2004 (and see 67.1 above for periods straddling that date) (see 51.3 OIL COMPANIES). [*ICTA 1988, Sch 28AA para 11; FA 2004, s 30(7); ITTOIA 2005, Sch 1 para 351*].

The provisions apply to unit trust schemes (see 43.5 INVESTMENT FUNDS) as if they were bodies corporate, with appropriate modification. [*ICTA 1988, Sch 28AA para 14(5)*].

67.14 **Transitional provisions.** *Schedule 28AA* does not apply in the case of any potentially disadvantaged person as respects the consequences, at any time before 17 March 2001, of the difference between an actual and an arm's length provision if:

(*a*) the actual provision is made or imposed under contractual arrangements entered into by that person before 17 March 1998;

(*b*) the control requirement in 67.3(*a*) or (*b*) above (as the case may be) is satisfied in the case of the actual provision and that person only by his indirect participation as a major participant in the other person's enterprise (see above);

(*c*) that person's rights and obligations under the actual provision have not been varied or continued by a transaction entered into after 17 March 1998 and before that time; and

(*d*) that person is not, and has not been, a party to any transaction by virtue of which he could, in the period between 17 March 1998 and that time, have secured the variation or termination of those rights and obligations.

[*FA 1998, s 108(6)*].

67.15 ACCOUNTING PERIODS ENDING BEFORE 1 JULY 1999

Where either the buyer or the seller (each being a 'body of persons' or a partnership) is controlled by the other party to the contract, or both are controlled by the same person(s), any sale (including letting and hiring of property, grant or transfer of rights or licences, or giving of business facilities (for which see *Waterloo plc v CIR (Sp C 301), [2002] SSCD 95*)) at a price other than market price at the time of completion (or, if earlier, of giving possession) may (if HMRC so directs) be adjusted by HMRC as follows:

(*a*) if the price is **below** market price, the latter is substituted in computing the *seller's* profits unless the buyer, being a UK resident trader, is entitled to deduct the price paid in computing his own profits;

(*b*) if the price is **above** market price, the latter is substituted in computing the *buyer's* profits unless the seller, being a UK resident trader, would have to bring in, as a trade receipt, the price received.

The extension of these provisions to the 'giving of business facilities' is capable of bringing the making of interest-free loans within their scope (*Ametalco UK v CIR; Ametalco Ltd v CIR (Sp C 94), [1996] SSCD 399*).

'*Control*', for this purpose, means the power of a person by shareholding or voting power (whether direct or through another company) or under Articles of Association, to secure that the company's affairs are conducted according to that person's wishes. For this purpose, there may be attributed to a person the powers of:

(i) his nominees;

(ii) his spouse;

(iii) the brother, sister, ancestor or lineal descendant of himself or of his spouse;

(iv) the spouse of a person within (iii);

(v) any person with whom he is in partnership;

(vi) the spouse, brother, sister, ancestor or lineal descendant of any person within (v);

(vii) the nominees of any person within (ii) to (vi).

If the person is the trustee of a settlement, he is deemed to have the powers of any settlor, and of any individual or body corporate connected with that settlor. See 19 CONNECTED PERSONS. As to trustee holdings, see *Lithgows CS 1960, 39 TC 270*.

In the case of partnerships, 'control' includes the right to a share of more than one-half of the firm's assets or profits. [*ICTA 1988, s 773, s 839(1)–(4)(8), s 840*].

HMRC may, by notice in writing given to any body corporate, require it to supply, within such time (not being less than 30 days) as may be specified in the notice, such particulars as may be so specified of any 'related transaction' which appears to HMRC:

(A) to be, or to be connected with, a transaction which might fall within the section;

(B) to be relevant in determining whether a direction under the section could or should be given;

(C) to be relevant in determining the market price of any property sold.

A '*related transaction*' is one to which the body corporate to which notice is given (or a body corporate 'associated' with it) was a party. Bodies corporate are '*associated*' if one is controlled by the other or both are controlled by the same person or persons.

Where HMRC feels that a direction might be given in respect of a transaction each party to which is a 51% subsidiary of the same UK parent, one being non-resident, notice may be served on the parent requiring access to the books, accounts etc. of the parent or of its subsidiaries which relate to that transaction. The parent has a right of appeal first to HMRC and then, within 30 days of HMRC's rejection, to the Special Commissioners.

An HMRC officer may in certain circumstances and with the authority of the Commissioners of HMRC enter premises to examine books, etc. [*ICTA 1988, s 772(1)–(7)*].

Where a direction is given, all necessary adjustments are made, by assessment, repayment or otherwise, to give effect to it. [*ICTA 1988, s 770(3)*]. This applies equally to adjustment of open assessments (*Glaxo Group Ltd and others v CIR CA 1995, 68 TC 166*). Appeals involving questions arising from directions are to that extent to be referred to and determined by the Special Commissioners. [*ICTA 1988, s 772(8)*].

Nothing in *section 770* is to affect the operation of any provision of *CAA 1990*. [*ICTA 1988, s 773(1)*].

For an article on the application of the transfer pricing rules to employee share scheme costs, in particular in relation to the decision in *Waterloo plc v CIR (Sp C 301), [2002] SSCD 95* referred to above, see Revenue Tax Bulletin February 2003 pp 1002–1007.

In 1995 and 1996, the OECD published its report 'Transfer Pricing Guidelines for Multinational Enterprises and Tax Administrations' and supplementary material, containing guidelines on the general principles to be applied in determining transfer prices for tax purposes. These can be purchased from HMSO outlets. An article in the Revenue Tax Bulletin October 1996 pp 345–349 sets out HMRC's position on those guidelines and also provides some practical guidance on the operation of the Mutual Agreement Procedure contained in UK double taxation conventions.

See 26.17 EXCHANGE GAINS AND LOSSES as regards interaction with these provisions.

See generally HMRC International Manual, INTM 436010–436120 for guidance on transfer pricing prior to corporation tax self-assessment.

67.16 **PRACTICAL ISSUES**

Employee share schemes. For an article on the application of the transfer pricing rules to employee share scheme costs, in particular in relation to the decision in *Waterloo plc v CIR (Sp C 301), [2002] SSCD 95* referred to at 67.15 above in relation to pre-1 July 1999 periods, see Revenue Tax Bulletin February 2003 pp 1002–1007. See also 'Draft Guidance: Implications of Transfer Pricing for Employee Share Schemes Operated by UK Groups' available on HMRC's website (www.hmrc.gov.uk/international/shareschemes.pdf).

Pre-transaction guidance. Revenue Policy International, 100 Parliament Street, London SW1A 2BQ may be approached for pre-transaction guidance on the likely tax treatment in particular cases when financial arrangements are in the process of being put in place. See Revenue Tax Bulletin October 1998 pp 579–582, 587, 588 for general guidance on the record-keeping required for self-assessment under the above provisions and on the application of the provisions to financial transactions and arrangements; December 1998 pp 603–605 for guidance on penalties under those provisions; April 2000 pp 740–742 for the practical implications of the new regime for non-UK resident landlords; and August 2002 pp 943–947 for guidance on the nature of the risk assessment carried out by HMRC before undertaking a transfer pricing enquiry and a suggested timetabling framework for such enquiries. See also HMRC International Manual, INTM 433020–433070 for guidance on record-keeping; INTM 460000 *et seq.* for internal HMRC guidance on transfer pricing enquiries.

67.17 **ADVANCE PRICING AGREEMENTS**

Applications received by HMRC after 21 March 2007 will, in accordance with an internet statement dated 26 April 2007, be dealt with under a new system, based broadly on self-assessment criteria (process now, check later). (See: http://www.hmrc.gov.uk/cnr/clearance-processes.htm and draft statement of practice.) A clearance will be issued in response to every application where the criteria are met (these differ from treaty to treaty). Where they are not met, correspondence will be entered into by HMRC with the applicant. The detail of the application will be considered along with the risk assessment of the applicant's self-assessment return, and an enquiry opened at that time, if appropriate.

The taxpayer will still have the option of entering into a thin capitalisation agreement, but it is important it is made clear at the outset that the company is seeking such an agreement.

A taxpayer may apply to HMRC for an agreement, on a prospective basis, on the resolution of complex transfer pricing issues relating to any one or more of the following matters which fall, or might fall, to be determined.

(*a*) The attribution of income to a permanent establishment or branch or agency (see 60.5 RESIDENCE) through which the taxpayer has been carrying on, or is proposing to carry on, a trade in the UK.

(*b*) The attribution of income to any permanent establishment of the taxpayer (wherever situated) through which he has been carrying on, or is proposing to carry on, any business.

(*c*) The extent to which income which has arisen or which may arise to the taxpayer is to be taken for any purpose to be income arising outside the UK.

(*d*) The treatment for tax purposes of any provision operating between the taxpayer and any 'associate' of his. Persons are '*associates*' for this purpose if (as in 67.3(*a*) and (*b*) above in relation to *Schedule 28AA*) one directly or indirectly participates, at the time of the making or imposition of the provision, in the management, control or capital of the other, or the same person or persons so participate in the management, control or capital of each of them (with further special provision in relation to sales of oil).

(*e*) The treatment for tax purposes of any provision operating between a 'ring fence trade' carried on by the taxpayer and any other activities the taxpayer carries on. A '*ring fence trade*' for this purpose is a trade which is treated as a separate trade under *ICTA 1988, s 492(1)* (oil extraction activities, see 51.3 OIL COMPANIES), or would be so treated if a different trade were also carried on.

The application must set out the taxpayer's understanding of what would, in his case, be the effect, in the absence of any agreement, of the provisions in relation to which clarification is sought, and in what respects clarification is required. He must also propose how the clarification might be effected in a manner consistent with that understanding.

Where HMRC and the taxpayer have entered into such an agreement (an 'advance pricing agreement' or 'APA') in relation to a chargeable period, then (except as below) any questions relating to those matters are, to the extent provided for in the APA, to be determined in accordance with the APA rather than by reference to the legislative provisions which would otherwise have applied. However, where the relevant matter falls within (*d*) or (*e*) above and not within (*a*), (*b*) or (*c*) above, the only legislative provisions which can be displaced are those contained in *Schedule 28AA* (as above). Where an APA relating to a chargeable period beginning or ending before the date of the APA provides for the manner in which consequent adjustments are to be made, those adjustments are to be made in the manner provided for in the APA.

An APA does not, however, have effect in relation to the determination of any question which relates to:

(i) a time after that from which an officer of HMRC has revoked the APA in accordance with its terms; or

(ii) a time after or in relation to which any provision of the APA has not been complied with, where the APA was conditional upon compliance with that provision; or

(iii) any matter as respects which any other essential conditions have not been, or are no longer, satisfied.

The APA must contain a declaration that it is made for the purposes of *FA 1999, s 85*. It may be made on or after 27 July 1999 and may apply in relation to any chargeable period ending on or after that date (and this may include periods ending before the date of the APA). It is for HMRC to ensure that the APA is modified so as to be consistent with any double taxation arrangements.

Where the APA makes provision for its modification or revocation by HMRC, this may take effect from such time (including a time before the modification or revocation) as HMRC may determine.

Any party to an APA must provide HMRC with all such reports and other information as he may be required to provide under the APA or by virtue of any request made by an officer of HMRC in accordance with its terms.

An APA is deemed never to have been made where, before it was made, the taxpayer fraudulently or negligently provided HMRC with false or misleading information in relation to the application for the APA or in connection with its preparation, and HMRC notifies the taxpayer that the APA is nullified by reason of the misrepresentation. A penalty not exceeding £10,000 may apply for so giving such false or misleading information.

[*FA 1999, ss 85, 86; ITTOIA 2005, Sch 1 para 508*].

Effect of APA on third parties. Where an APA has effect in relation to any provision between the taxpayer and another person, then in applying the 'double counting' rules (see above) of *Schedule 28AA* to the other person, the arrangements set out in the APA similarly apply in determining any question as to:

(A) whether the taxpayer is a person on whom a potential advantage in relation to UK taxation is conferred by the actual provision; or

(B) what constitutes the arm's length provision in relation to the actual provision.

This is subject to any APA made between HMRC and the other person. The notice requirements of *FA 1998, s 111* are correspondingly amended.

[*FA 1999, s 87*].

For a detailed explanation of how APAs are administered, see HMRC Statement of Practice, SP 3/99 (as revised) and HMRC International Manual, INTM 469000 *et seq.* The contact address for APA applications and other information is Ian Wood, CT & VAT (International CT), 100 Parliament Street, London SW1A 2BQ or, where oil taxation is involved, Nic Perks or Malcolm Phelps, Revenue Policy, International, Oil Taxation Office (APAs), Melbourne House, Aldwych, London WC2B 4LL. See also Revenue Tax Bulletin October 1999 pp 697, 698 for a note on the scope of agreements, and for procedural guidance relating to bilateral agreements in the light of HMRC's experiences and observations in concluding agreements with treaty partners under double tax treaty mutual agreement procedures.

67.18 ARBITRATION CONVENTION

The Convention (*90/463/EEC*) on the elimination of double taxation in connection with the adjustment of profits of associated enterprises required member states to adopt certain procedures and to follow the opinion of an advisory commission in certain cases of dispute relating to transfer pricing adjustments (although it appears that no such commission was ever appointed). In its original form, the Arbitration Convention came into force for five years from 1 January 1995, and was extended to 31 December 2004 through the Extension Protocol published in 2000. The last of the 15 'old' EU states finally ratified the Extension Protocol in July 2004, meaning that the Convention has only been legally in force between these 15 states since that date. It will now automatically be extended every five years for a further five years, unless the signatory states decide otherwise (see Revenue Tax Bulletin August 1998 pp 575, 576).

ICTA 1988, s 815B makes provision for domestic legislation and agreements to be over-ridden where necessary under the Convention, and *ICTA 1988, s 816(2A)* and *FA 1989, s 182A* provide the necessary information powers and confidentiality requirements in relation to disclosures of information to an advisory commission. [*F(No 2)A 1992, s 51*].

Code of Conduct. The European Commission has presented a proposal for a Code of Conduct to ensure a more effective and uniform application of the Convention by EU member states. The Code would determine procedural rules covering time limits for dealing with complaints, arrangements concerning the advisory commission that must be established to deal with disputes concerning the elimination of double taxation following transfer-pricing adjustments, and the suspension of tax collection during the dispute resolution period. See the European Commission Press Release of 27 April 2004 (IP/04/542) (SWTI [2004] 1125).

67.19 EXAMPLES

(*A*)

A Ltd provides management and administrative services to a number of its wholly-owned subsidiaries. All companies in the group have accounting periods ending on 31 March and do not qualify as small or medium-sized enterprises for transfer pricing purposes. For the accounting period ending 31 March 2007, A Ltd makes a charge for its management and administrative services to B Ltd of £450,000. Following an enquiry into A Ltd's return for that period, it is agreed that the arm's length value of the services to A Ltd was £600,000. An adjustment is accordingly made of £150,000 to increase A Ltd's taxable profits by that amount.

B Ltd can claim (within the required time limit, see 67.8 above) to apply a corresponding adjustment to reduce its taxable profits for the same period by £150,000 (increasing its deductible expenses to £600,000). B Ltd may also make a balancing payment to A Ltd of up to £150,000 without it being treated as a distribution or charge on income or otherwise taken into account for tax purposes.

(*B*)

On 1 July 2006, B Ltd is granted a loan of £5,000,000 at 6% interest p.a. from an unassociated bank. The loan is guaranteed by B Ltd's parent company, G plc. Both companies draw up accounts for the year ended 30 June and neither company qualifies as a small or medium-sized enterprise for transfer pricing purposes. Following an enquiry into B Ltd's return for the accounting period ending 30 June 2007, HMRC successfully maintain that, in the absence of the guarantee from G plc, the bank would not have advanced more than £1,000,000 to B Ltd. Accordingly, an adjustment is made to increase B Ltd's profits for the period by £240,000 in disallowing the interest on £4,000,000 of the loan.

G plc could make a claim (or B Ltd could claim on its behalf) for a corresponding adjustment before or after the transfer pricing adjustment is made in B Ltd's return, or following the determination (but within the required time limit, see 67.8 above), so that it is treated as having paid the interest subject to the disallowance. Accordingly, provided the interest in G plc's case would not be subject to a transfer pricing adjustment, G plc could claim a deduction for £240,000 in respect of the interest paid by B Ltd.

G plc can make a balancing payment of up to £240,000 to B Ltd without it being treated as a distribution or charge on income or otherwise taken into account for tax purposes. Alternatively, where the conditions (*a*) and (*b*) in 67.9 above are met, G plc can elect to pay the tax liability in respect of the interest disallowed, of £72,000 (at 30%). In that case, B Ltd would not have to pay the tax liability arising in respect of the transfer pricing adjustment.

68 Value Added Tax

See HMRC Business Income Manual BIM 31500–31625 and, generally, Tolley's Value Added Tax.

68.1 NON-TAXABLE PERSONS

VAT which is related to expenditure deductible for corporation tax purposes is also deductible. Capital allowances on any such expenditure are based on the VAT-inclusive cost. See HMRC Statement of Practice, B1.

68.2 TAXABLE PERSONS

Income and expenditure are taken into account *exclusive* of VAT, and capital allowances are determined accordingly. However, capital allowances on motor cars are computed on the VAT-inclusive cost and entertainment expenses *disallowed* for corporation tax purposes include VAT. The full amount of a bad debt (i.e. including irrecoverable VAT) is allowable as a trading expense. See HMRC Statement of Practice, B1.

68.3 PARTLY-EXEMPT PERSONS

Entertainment expenses and expenditure on motor cars are treated as under 68.2 above. Input VAT on items of expenditure which constitute exempt output must be allocated to the categories of such expenditure, and will be treated for corporation tax purposes as part of that expenditure. Inspectors are prepared to consider any 'reasonable arrangements' for allocation.

VAT unreclaimed due to the excessive cost of keeping the necessary records may be treated as part of the expenditure to which it relates for corporation tax purposes. See HMRC Statement of Practice, B1.

68.4 PRE-INCORPORATION EXPENDITURE

Regulations may be made to allow deduction as input tax of VAT paid on goods acquired before incorporation and for services supplied before that time for its benefit or in connection with its incorporation. [*VATA 1994, s 24* (*6*)(*c*)].

68.5 INTEREST, PENALTIES, SURCHARGE AND REPAYMENT SUPPLEMENT

No deduction is allowed for corporation tax purposes in respect of any payment by way of VAT

(*a*) penalty under *VATA 1994, ss 60–70* or *FA 2003, s 25* or *s 26,*

(*b*) interest under *VATA 1994, s 74,* or

(*c*) surcharge under *VATA 1994, s 59.*

Similarly any VAT repayment supplement under *VATA 1994, s 79* is disregarded for corporation tax purposes. [*ICTA 1988, s 827; FA 2003, s 40; ITTOIA 2005, Sch 1 para 332*].

See 70.8 VOLUNTARY ASSOCIATIONS as regards certain repayments to sports clubs.

68.6 FLAT RATE SCHEME

An optional VAT flat rate scheme was introduced as *VATA 1994, s 26B* by *FA 2002, s 23.* The scheme is available to all businesses with a VAT-exclusive annual taxable turnover of up to £150,000 in the year of entry to the scheme, and with a VAT-exclusive turnover, including the value of exempt supplies and other non-taxable income, of up to £187,500 (the amounts were £100,000 and £125,000 respectively from 25 April 2002 to 9 April 2003).

Where the company uses the flat-rate scheme, receipts and expenses to be taken into account will generally be *inclusive* of normal output and input VAT (assuming the small business to be a non-taxable person), but the flat-rate VAT itself can either be deducted from turnover or treated as a separate expense and in either case is an allowable deduction for tax purposes. Any irrecoverable VAT on capital items will form part of their cost for the purposes of CAPITAL ALLOWANCES (10).

For HMRC's view as to how profits chargeable under Schedule D, Case I or II are to be computed by businesses adopting the scheme, see HMRC Business Income Manual BIM 31585.

69 Venture Capital Trusts

Cross-references. See 28.24 FINANCIAL INSTRUMENTS AND DERIVATIVE CONTRACTS, 46.43 LOAN RELATIONSHIPS.

Simon's Direct Tax Service. See **C3.11, D4.1350** *et seq*, **E3.6**.

69.1 INTRODUCTION

The venture capital trust scheme described at 69.2 *et seq.* below was introduced in 1995 to encourage individuals to invest in unquoted trading companies through such trusts by providing reliefs for income tax and capital gains tax (see 69.5 and 69.6 below).

The Treasury has wide powers to make regulations governing all aspects of the reliefs applicable to venture capital trust investments, and for the requirements as regards returns, records and provision of information by the trust. [*ITA 2007, ss 272, 284; FA 1995, s 73; FA 2002, s 109, Sch 33 paras 14–16; ITTOIA 2005, Sch 1 para 477; FA 2007, Sch 16 para 21*]. [See *SI 1995 No 1979; SI 1999 No 819*].

See generally HMRC Venture Capital Schemes Manual, VCM 10000–17320, VCM 60000 *et seq* and the guidance at www.hmrc.gov.uk/guidance/vct.htm.

For company reorganisations involving venture capital trusts, see 11.9 CAPITAL GAINS. For the transfer of assets within a group of companies to a company which subsequently becomes a venture capital trust, see 12.38 CAPITAL GAINS—GROUPS.

From 25 September 2000, a centralised service became operational for companies newly raising money under the venture capital trust scheme. All enquiries about whether a company meets the requirements should be made to Small Company Enterprise Centre, Ty Glas, Llanishen, Cardiff, CF14 5ZG (Tel. 029 2032 7400; fax 029 2032 7398; e-mail: enterprise.centre@ir.gsi.gov.uk). This initial point of contact is supported by specialist Revenue units that deal with the corporation tax affairs, and the monitoring, of such companies as well as companies raising money under other types of venture capital scheme or granting options under enterprise management incentives. (Revenue Press Release 25 September 2000). The approval of venture capital trusts themselves is dealt with by HMRC (CTTG) (see 69.2 below).

69.2 CONDITIONS FOR APPROVAL

A '*venture capital trust*' ('VCT') is a company approved for this purpose by HMRC. CLOSE COMPANIES (16) are excluded. The time from which an approval takes effect is specified in the approval, and may not be earlier than the time the application for approval was made. [*ITA 2007, ss 259, 283; ICTA 1988, s 842AA(1); FA 2002, Sch 33 paras 7, 17*].

Except as detailed further below, approval may not be given unless HMRC are satisfied that the following six conditions are met in relation to the most recent complete accounting period of the company and will be met in relation to the accounting period current at the time of the application for approval.

The listing condition. The company's ordinary shares (or each class thereof) must be listed in the official UK list (within *Financial Services and Markets Act 2000, Pt 6*) throughout those accounting periods. (Before **19 July 2007**, this requirement operated by reference to the Official List of the Stock Exchange.)

The nature of income condition. The company's income (as defined) must be derived wholly or mainly from shares or 'securities'.

'*Securities*' for these purposes are deemed to include liabilities in respect of certain loans not repayable within five years, and any stocks or securities relating to which are not re-purchasable or redeemable within five years of issue. Provided that the loan is made on normal commercial terms, HMRC will not regard a standard event of default clause in the loan agreement as disqualifying a loan from being a security for this purpose. If, however, the clause entitled the lender (or a third party) to exercise any action which would cause the borrower to default, the clause would not be regarded as 'standard'. (HMRC SP 8/95).

The income retention condition. An amount greater than 15% of its income (as defined) from shares and securities must not be retained by the company.

This condition does not apply for an accounting period if the amount the company would be required to distribute is less than £10,000 (proportionately reduced for periods of less than twelve months), or if the company is required by law to retain income in excess of the 15% limit. The latter exclusion only applies, however, if the aggregate of the excess of retentions over those required by law and any distribution is less than £10,000 (proportionately reduced for periods of less then twelve months).

The 15% holding limit condition. No 'holding' in any company other than a VCT (or a company which could be a VCT but for the listing condition above) may represent more than 15% of the value of the company's investments at any time in those periods.

For this purpose, and that of the 70% qualifying holdings condition below, the meaning of 'the company's investments' is extended after 5 April 2007 to include (if it would not otherwise include) money in the company's possession and any sum owed to the company over which the company has 'account-holder's rights', i.e. the right to require payment either to the company or at its direction. Anything to which the company is not beneficially entitled is excluded (though, for this purpose, a company *is* beneficially entitled to sums subscribed for shares issued by it and anything representing such sums).

If this condition was met when a holding in a company was acquired, it is treated as continuing to be met until any more shares or securities of the company are acquired (otherwise than for no consideration).

'*Holding*' means the shares or securities of whatever class or classes held in any one company. Where, in connection with a 'scheme of reconstruction' (within *TCGA 1992, s 136*; previously a 'scheme of reconstruction or amalgamation'), a company issues shares or securities to persons holding shares or securities in another in respect of, and in proportion to (or as nearly as may be in proportion to) such holdings, without the recipients' becoming liable for any consideration, the old and the new holdings are treated as the same. Holdings in companies which are members of a group (i.e. a company and its 51% subsidiaries), whether or not including the company whose holdings they are ('company A'), are treated as holdings in a single company if they are not excluded from the 15% holding limit condition. If company A is a member of a group, money owed to it by another group member is treated as a security and, as such, as part of its holding in that other group member.

See below for the value of the company's investments.

The 70% qualifying holdings condition. Throughout the accounting periods at least 70% by value of the company's investments must be represented by shares or securities in 'qualifying holdings'.

This condition is relaxed where, on or after 6 April 2007, a VCT makes a disposal of a holding of shares or securities which was part of its qualifying holdings throughout the preceding six months provided that the consideration for the disposal is not wholly '*new qualifying holdings*' (i.e. shares or securities which, on transfer to the VCT, form part of its qualifying holdings). In such a case, the company is treated for the purposes of determining whether this condition is, has been, or will be met:

- as continuing to hold the holding or, where the consideration consists partly of new qualifying holdings, part of the holding (see further below) for six months; and
- as if the value of its investments in that period were reduced (but not below the value of its qualifying holdings) by any monetary consideration for the disposal.

The value of the holding or part in the six months following disposal is treated as being equal to its value immediately before the disposal. For this purpose, the part of the holding that the VCT is treated as continuing to hold is the proportion of the holding equal to:

$$\frac{TC - NQH}{TC}$$

where

TC = the market value of the total consideration for the disposal, and

NQH = the market value of the new qualifying holdings.

This relaxation of the condition does not apply at any time in respect of shares or securities acquired with money raised on a second or subsequent issue of VCT shares, the use of which is at that time ignored under the provisions below. The relaxation also does not apply to disposals between two companies during a merger within 1. or 2. below.

Where this condition is breached inadvertently, and the position is corrected without delay after discovery, approval will in practice not be withdrawn on this account. Full details of any such inadvertent breach should be disclosed to HMRC as soon as it is discovered. (Revenue Press Release 14 September 1995). It is not clear whether this practice continues after 6 April 2007. See also below under 'Withdrawal of approval' as regards the Treasury power to make regulations

On a second and subsequent issue of shares by an approved VCT, this condition and the 30% eligible shares condition below do not have to be met, in relation to the money raised by the further issue, in the accounting period of the further issue or any later accounting period ending no more than three years after the making of the further issue. In relation to shares issued after 5 April 2004, *SI 2004 No 2199, reg 14* limits the operation of this rule by stipulating that the money raised by the further issue must be for the purposes of acquiring additional investments which do fulfil the conditions. Where any of that money (or assets derived therefrom) is used for another purpose, then from a time immediately before that use, the whole of the money raised by the issue is deemed to be included in the company's investments in applying the percentage tests in the two conditions. If any of the money is used by the VCT to buy back its own shares, this stipulation is treated, in particular, as not fulfilled if HMRC regard the purchase as not insignificant in relation to the issued ordinary share capital of the VCT or if it is made as a result of a general offer to members. If the money is raised by a successor VCT (in a merger) and used to buy shares in the merging companies, the stipulation is treated, in particular, as not fulfilled if the money so used exceeds the least of three specified limits.

See the 15% holding limit condition above for the meaning of 'the company's investments' and see below for the value of investments.

The 30% eligible shares condition. At least 30% of the company's qualifying holdings (by value) must be represented throughout the accounting periods by holdings of '*eligible shares*', i.e. ordinary shares carrying no present or future preferential right to dividends or to assets on a winding up and no present or future right to redemption.

See the 70% qualifying holdings condition above where a VCT makes a second or subsequent issue of shares and see below for the value of investments.

[*ITA 2007, ss 274, 276, 277, 280, 280A, 285, Sch 2 paras 64, 66, 67; ICTA 1988, ss 842(1A)(1AB)(2)–(3), 842AA(2)(5A)(5B)(11); FA 2002, Sch 9 para 4(7), Sch 25 paras 56, 57, Sch 33 paras 11, 16; FA 2006, Sch 14 para 8; FA 2007, Sch 16 para 20, Sch 26 para 12(6)*].

Value of investments. The value of any investment for the purposes of the 15% holding limit condition, the 70% qualifying holdings condition and the 30% eligible shares condition above is the value when the investment was acquired, except that where it is added to by a further holding of an investment of the same description (otherwise than for no consideration), or a payment is made in discharge of any obligation attached to it which increases its value, and then it is the value immediately after the most recent such addition or payment.

For this purpose, where, in connection with a 'scheme of reconstruction' (within *TCGA 1992, s 136*; previously a 'scheme of reconstruction or amalgamation'), a company issues shares or securities to persons holding shares or securities in another in respect of, and in proportion to (or as nearly as may be in proportion to) such holdings, without the recipients' becoming liable for any consideration, the old and the new holdings are treated as the same.

Where

(i) shares or securities in a company are exchanged for corresponding shares and securities in a new holding company; or

(ii) a VCT exercises conversion rights in respect of certain convertible shares and securities,

then, subject to detailed conditions (see *ITA 2007, ss 326–329*), the value of the new shares is taken to be the same as the value of the old shares when they were last valued for these purposes.

Where, under a company reorganisation or other arrangement,

- a VCT exchanges a qualifying holding for other shares or securities (with or without other consideration), and
- the exchange is for genuine commercial reasons and not part of a tax avoidance scheme or arrangements,

regulations provide a formula which values the new shares or securities by reference to the proportion of the value of the old shares or securities that the market value of the new shares or securities bears to the total consideration receivable. If no other consideration is receivable, the value of the new is identical to that of the old. The provisions extend to new shares or securities received in pursuance of an earn-out right conferred in exchange for a qualifying holding, in which case an election is available (under *reg 10*) to modify the formula by effectively disregarding the earn-out right itself.

[*ITA 2007, ss 278, 279, Sch 2 para 65; ICTA 1988, ss 842(3), 842AA(5)–(5AE)(11); FA 2000, Sch 18 para 8(2); FA 2002, Sch 9 para 4(7); SI 2002 No 2661*].

Alternative conditions. Where any of the above conditions are not met, approval may nevertheless be given where HMRC are satisfied as to the meeting of those conditions (and in some cases other conditions imposed by regulations) in certain future accounting periods. [*ITA 2007, s 275; ICTA 1988, s 842AA(4)*].

Withdrawal of approval. Approval may be withdrawn where there are reasonable grounds for believing that either:

(A) the conditions for approval were not satisfied at the time the approval was given; or

(B) a condition that HMRC were satisfied (as above) would be met has not been or will not be met; or

(C) in either the most recent complete accounting period or the current one, one of the six conditions above has failed or will fail to be met (unless the failure was allowed for as above); or

(D) where, in relation to a second or further issue by an approved VCT, the 70% qualifying holdings condition and the 30% eligible shares condition above do not have to be met in the period of issue or certain following accounting periods (see above), one of the six conditions above will fail to be met in the first period for which those two conditions must be met; or

(E) any other conditions prescribed by regulations have not been met in relation to, or to part of, an accounting period for which the 70% qualifying holdings condition and the 30% eligible shares condition above do not have to be met.

The withdrawal is effective from the time the company is notified of it, except that:

(1) where approval is given on HMRC's being satisfied as to the meeting of the relevant conditions in future accounting periods, and is withdrawn before all six of the conditions above have been satisfied in relation to either a complete twelve-month accounting period or successive complete accounting periods constituting a continuous period of twelve months or more, the approval is deemed never to have been given; and

(2) for the purposes of relief for capital gains accruing to a VCT under *TCGA 1992, s 100* withdrawal may be effective from an earlier date, but not before the start of the accounting period in which the failure occurred (or is expected to occur).

An assessment consequent on the withdrawal of approval may, where otherwise out of time, be made within three years from the time notice of the withdrawal was given.

For the detailed requirements as regards granting and refusal (and withdrawal) of approval, and appeals procedures, see *SI 1995 No 1979, Pt II*.

Applications for approval should be made to HMRC (CTTG), Sapphire House, 550 Streetsbrook Road, Solihull, B91 1QU.

[*ITA 2007, ss 281, 282; ICTA 1988, s 842AA(6)–(10); FA 2002, s 109, Sch 33 para 12*].

FA 2007 introduced provisions for the making of Treasury regulations to enable a VCT to apply to HMRC for a determination that they will not exercise, for a certain period, their power to withdraw approval by reason of a specified breach, including a future breach, of the above conditions (see *ITA 2007, s 284(1)(aa)(2)(3)*).

Mergers. For mergers of two or more VCTs which take place on or after 17 April 2002, regulations enable the merging VCTs to retain VCT status and provide for investors in the merged VCTs who continue as investors in the 'successor company' not to lose their tax reliefs. This treatment applies to two types of merger:

1 where shares in one of the merging companies (company A) are issued to members of the other merging company or companies in exchange for their shares in that other company or by way of consideration for a transfer to company A of the whole or part of the business of that other company;

2 where shares in a company (company B) which is not one of the merging companies are issued to members of the merging companies in exchange for their shares in those companies or as consideration for a transfer to company B of the whole or part of the businesses of those companies.

Company A or, as appropriate, company B is the '*successor company*'.

For the regulations to apply, a merging company or the successor company must apply to HMRC for approval, and approval must be granted before the merger takes place. For the procedure for obtaining approval see *SI 2004 No 2199, reg 10*. HMRC will not approve the merger unless they are satisfied that strict conditions are met, including that the merger is for *bona fide* commercial reasons and is not part of a scheme or arrangements with a tax avoidance purpose. For the detailed conditions, see *SI 2004 No 2199, reg 9(3)*. Where approval is obtained, the following apply:

- income tax investment relief within 69.5 below cannot be obtained in respect of any shares issued to effect the merger by the successor company, and such shares are ignored in determining whether the 'permitted maximum' has been exceeded;
- the nature of income, income retention, 70% qualifying holdings, 30% eligible shares and 15% holding limit conditions, and the provisions at 69.3 below apply to the successor company:
  - (i) as if the property of the merging companies were vested in the successor company (so that transfers between a merging company and the successor company are disregarded);
  - (ii) disregarding, in the hands of the successor company, any assets consisting in rights against, or shares or securities of, another company which is a merging company; and
  - (iii) disregarding, in the hands of the successor company, the use of any money which, in the hands of another company which is a merging company, would have been disregarded under *ITA 2007, s 280(2)* (use of money raised by further issue of shares to be ignored for certain periods for the purposes of the 70% qualifying holdings and 30% eligible shares conditions — see above), for the same periods as are mentioned in that provision;
- a disposal by a merging company to the successor company after the merger of an asset held by the merging company immediately before, or in the period during which, the merger takes place is not prevented by *TCGA 1992, s 171(2)(cc)* (see 12.2 CAPITAL GAINS—GROUPS) from being treated as at no gain/no loss,
- for the purposes of the income tax reliefs at 69.5 below and capital gains tax deferral relief at 69.6 below (see Tolley's Capital Gains Tax under Venture Capital Trusts):
  - (i) any share for share exchange or share for business transfer is not treated as a disposal of the 'old shares' (i.e. the shares for which the shares issued to effect the merger (the '*new shares*') were issued or, in the case of a share for business transfer, the shares in respect of which the new shares were issued) or as a chargeable event for the purposes of deferral relief;
  - (ii) any other act (including the giving of relief) carried out, of failure to act, in relation to the old shares is treated as carried out, or omitted, in relation to the corresponding new shares; and
  - (iii) references to the company in which the old shares were held are to be read as references to the successor company;
- for the purposes of capital gains tax relief on disposal (see Tolley's Capital Gains Tax under Venture Capital Trusts), if the successor company is not otherwise a VCT at the time the shares issued to effect the merger are acquired but is a VCT at the time of a subsequent disposal of the shares, it is treated as a VCT at and from the time of acquisition;
- where any of the qualifying holding requirements at 69.3 below (other than the qualifying subsidiaries requirement) were satisfied to any extent or for any period in relation to an investment held by a merging company immediately before the merger, they are treated as satisfied to the same extent or for the same period when held by the successor company, as if the two companies were the same company;
- for the purposes of the 15% test at (*d*) above and the qualifying subsidiaries requirement at 69.3 below, the period in which the merger takes place is disregarded and if as a result of the merger that test or requirement is no longer met, it is treated as met for a period of one year;

- for the purposes of the 70% qualifying holdings, 30% eligible shares and 15% holiding limit conditions above and the proportion of eligible shares requirement at 69.3 below, the value of investments in the hands of the successor company immediately after the merger is taken to be their value when last valued before the merger in accordance with the rules governing those conditions and that requirement, unless there has been a transaction other than the merger as a result of which the investments would fall to be revalued; and
- where provisional approval of a merging company other than the successor company is withdrawn following the merger, the withdrawal takes effect from the time the company is notified of it (and the approval is not deemed never to have been given).

[*ITA 2007, ss 321–325, FA 2002, s 109, Sch 33 paras 8–10; SI 2004 No 2199, regs 1, 9–13*].

Winding-up. Regulations enable a VCT commencing winding-up on or after 17 April 2002 to retain its VCT status during a 'prescribed winding-up period', thereby enabling investors' reliefs to continue for that period.

A VCT-in-liquidation can obtain this treatment:

- if it has been approved as a VCT continuously for at least three years ending with the commencement of the winding-up (five years where the VCT, having previously obtained approval, issues ordinary share capital between 6 April 2004 and 5 April 2006, without having done so before 6 April 2004); or
- where the winding-up is by court order, it is approved as a VCT immediately before the commencement.

The winding-up must be for *bona fide* commercial reasons and not part of tax avoidance arrangements and the VCT-in-liquidation must notify HMRC of the commencement. A VCT-in-liquidation which has been at any time a merger company (see above) other than a successor company does not qualify. The '*prescribed winding-up period*' for these purposes is the three years beginning with the commencement of the winding-up, but if the winding-up ends, the company ceases to be wound up or is dissolved, the period comes to an end on the earliest of those events.

Where the VCT-in-liquidation fulfils the above requirements, the following apply.

(I) For the purposes of the income tax relief on investments (see 69.5 below), the commencement of the winding-up does not affect the status of the VCT-in-liquidation as a VCT (i.e. the commencement itself is not treated as an event leading to the withdrawal of approval and the provisions for withdrawal of relief are not triggered by it).

(II) Gains accruing to the VCT-in-liquidation during the prescribed winding-up period on disposal of assets acquired before the commencement of the winding-up are not chargeable gains (and losses are not allowable losses).

(III) Capital gains tax relief on disposal of VCT shares (see 69.6 below) is available (provided that the other conditions for that relief are met) for disposals in the prescribed winding-up period as if the VCT-in-liquidation were a VCT. If, at the end of that period the VCT-in-liquidation still exists and the conditions for approval as a VCT (see above) are not then fulfilled, approval is treated, for the purposes of that relief, as withdrawn at that time.

(IV) For the purposes of capital gains tax deferral relief on reinvestment in VCT shares (see 69.6 below), the VCT-in-liquidation is treated throughout the prescribed winding-up period as a VCT and no chargeable event can occur during that time by reason of withdrawal of approval. If the VCT-in-liquidation still exists at the end of the period, a chargeable event is deemed to occur immediately after that time.

[*FA 2002, s 109, Sch 33 paras 1–8; SI 2004 No 2199, regs 1–7*].

Simon's Direct Tax Service. See D4.1351, E3.602.

69.3 QUALIFYING HOLDINGS

A VCT's holding of shares or securities in a company is comprised in its '*qualifying holdings*' at any time if the shares or securities were first issued to the VCT, and have been held by it ever since, and the following 14 requirements are satisfied at that time.

Where any of the maximum qualifying investment, use of money raised or relevant company to carry on the relevant qualifying activity requirements would be met as to only part of the money raised by the issue, and the holding is not otherwise capable of being treated as separate holdings, it is treated as two separate holdings: one from which that part of the money was raised, the other from which the rest was raised, with the value being apportioned accordingly to each holding. In the case of the use of money raised requirement, this does not require an insignificant amount applied for non-trade purposes to be treated as a separate holding.

[*ITA 2007, ss 286, 293(7); ICTA 1988, Sch 28B paras 1, 6(3)*].

The maximum qualifying investment requirement. The holding in question must not, when it was issued, have represented an investment in excess of the 'maximum qualifying investment' for the period from six months before the issue in question (or, if earlier, the beginning of the tax year of the issue) to the time of the issue. For this purpose, the maximum qualifying investment for a period is exceeded so far as the aggregate amount of money raised in that period by the issue to the VCT during that period of shares or securities of the company exceeds £1 million. Where this limit is exceeded, the shares or securities which represent the excess are treated as not being part of the holding concerned (so that £1 million can be included as a qualifying holding) and the money raised by those shares or securities is ignored for the purpose of any subsequent application of this requirement. Disposals are treated as far as possible as eliminating any such excess. The £1 million limit is proportionately reduced where, at the time of the issue, the qualifying trade is carried on, or is to be carried on, in partnership or as a joint venture, and one or more of the other parties is a company. [*ITA 2007, s 287; Sch 2 para 68; ICTA 1988, Sch 28B para 7*].

The no guaranteed loan requirement. The holding in question must not include any securities (as defined in 69.2 above) relating to a guaranteed loan. A security relates to a guaranteed loan if there are arrangements entitling the VCT to receive anything (directly or indirectly) from a 'third party' in the event of a failure by any person to comply with the terms of the security or the loan to which it relates. It is immaterial whether or not the arrangements apply in all such cases. '*Third party*' means any person other than the investee company itself and, if it is a parent company that meets the trading requirement below, its subsidiaries. This condition applies for accounting periods (of the VCT) ending after 1 July 1997, but does not apply in the case of shares or securities acquired by the VCT by means of investing money raised by the issue by it before 2 July 1997 of shares or securities (or money derived from the investment of any such money raised). [*ITA 2007, s 288, Sch 2 para 69; ICTA 1988, Sch 28B para 10A*].

The proportion of eligible shares requirement. At least 10% (by value) of the VCT's *total* holding of shares in and securities of the company must consist of 'eligible shares' (as defined for the purposes of the 15% eligible shares condition at 69.2 above — broadly, ordinary, non-preferential, shares). For this purpose, the value of shares etc. at any time is taken to be their value immediately after the most recent of the events listed below, except that it cannot thereby be taken to be less than the amount of consideration given by the VCT for the shares etc. The said events are as follows.

- The acquisition of the shares etc. by the VCT.
- The acquisition by the VCT (other than for no consideration) of any other shares etc. in the same company which are of the same description as those already held.

- The making of any payment in discharge (or part discharge) of any obligation attached to the shares etc. in a case where such discharge increases the value of the shares etc.

This requirement applies for accounting periods (of the VCT) ending after 1 July 1997, but, if necessary in order to satisfy the requirement, one may disregard shares and securities acquired by the VCT by means of investing money raised by the issue by it before 2 July 1997 of shares or securities (or money derived from the investment of any such money raised).

[*ITA 2007, s 289, Sch 2 para 70; ICTA 1988, Sch 28B para 10B*].

The trading requirement. The company must either:

(*a*) exist wholly for the purpose of carrying on one or more 'qualifying trades' (disregarding any purpose having no significant effect on the extent of its activities); or

(*b*) be a '*parent company*' (i.e. a company that has one or more 'qualifying subsidiaries' — see the qualifying subsidiaries requirement below) and the business of the '*group*' (i.e. the company and its qualifying subsidiaries) must not consist wholly or as to a substantial part (i.e. broadly 20% — see HMRC Venture Capital Schemes Manual VCM 17040) in the carrying on of 'non-qualifying activities'.

Where the company intends that one or more other companies should become its qualifying subsidiaries with a view to their carrying on one or more qualifying trades, then, until any time after which the intention is abandoned, the company is treated as a parent company and those other companies are included in the group for the purposes of (*b*) above. (This provision is made explicit in *ITA 2007* but reflects previous practice (see Change 61 listed in Annex 1 to the Explanatory Notes to *ITA 2007*).)

For the purpose of (*b*) above, the business of the group means what would be the business of the group if the activities of the group companies taken together were regarded as one business. Activities are for this purpose disregarded to the extent that they consist in:

(i) holding shares in or securities of any of the company's subsidiaries;

(ii) making loans to another group company;

(iii) holding and managing property used by a group company for the purposes of a qualifying trade or trades carried on by any group company; or

(iv) holding and managing property used by a group company for the purposes of research and development from which it is intended either that a qualifying trade to be carried on by a group company will be derived or, for shares issued after 5 April 2007, a qualifying trade carried on or to be carried on by a group company will benefit.

References in (iv) above to a group company include references to any existing or future company which will be a group company at any future time.

Activities are similarly disregarded to the extent that they consist, in the case of a subsidiary whose main purpose is the carrying on of qualifying trade(s) and whose other purposes have no significant effect on the extent of its activities (other than in relation to incidental matters), in activities not in pursuance of its main purpose.

'*Non-qualifying activities*' are:

(I) activities within (*a*)-(*c*)(*e*)-(*m*) Tolley's Capital Gains Tax under Chapter 21 Enterprise Investment Scheme (other than those within (*e*) which do not result in a trade being excluded from being a qualifying trade); and

(II) non-trading activities.

[*ITA 2007, ss 290, 332, Sch 2 para 71; ICTA 1988, Sch 28B paras 3, 10; FA 2001, Sch 16 para 1*].

A company does not cease to meet this requirement by reason only of anything done as a consequence of its being in administration or receivership (both as defined — see *ITA 2007, s 331*), provided everything so done and the making of the relevant order are for genuine commercial (and not tax avoidance) reasons. [*ITA 2007, s 292, Sch 2 para 73; ICTA 1988, Sch 28B para 11A; FA 2000, Sch 18 para 7(1); FA 2004, Sch 19 para 15*].

Qualifying trade. A trade is a 'qualifying trade' if it is conducted on a commercial basis with a view to the realisation of profits and it does not, at any time in period B (see below), consist to a substantial extent in the carrying on of 'excluded activities'. For these purposes, 'trade' (except in relation to the trade mentioned in (*m*) below) does not include a venture in the nature of trade. '*Excluded activities*' are:

(*a*) dealing in land, commodities or futures, or in shares, securities or other financial instruments; or

(*b*) dealing in goods otherwise than in an ordinary trade of wholesale or retail distribution (see below); or

(*c*) banking, insurance or any other financial activities; or

(*d*) (before 7 March 2001) oil extraction activities (but without prejudice to relief in respect of oil exploration (see 22.6(*b*) above) for which the activities would otherwise qualify); or

(*e*) leasing or letting or receiving royalties or licence fees; or

(*f*) providing legal or accountancy services; or

(*g*) 'property development';

(*h*) farming or market gardening;

(*j*) holding, managing or occupying woodlands, any other forestry activities or timber production;

(*k*) operating or managing hotels or comparable establishments (i.e. guest houses, hostels and other establishments whose main purpose is to offer overnight accommodation with or without catering) or property used as such;

(*l*) operating or managing nursing homes or residential care homes (both as defined) or property used as such;

(*m*) providing services or facilities for any trade, profession or vocation concerned in (*a*) to (*l*) and carried on by another person (other than a parent company), where one person has a 'controlling interest' in both trades,

without the exclusion (before 7 March 2001) of oil extraction activities, and taking references to 'period B' in relation to that scheme as references to the period since issue of the shares to the VCT. The exclusions at (*g*)–(*l*) (and the reference to those in exclusion (*m*)) have effect for the purpose of determining whether any shares or securities are, as at any time after 16 March 1998, to be regarded as comprised in the qualifying holdings of a VCT. However, those exclusions do not apply in relation to shares and securities acquired by the VCT by means of the investment of:

- money raised by the issue before 17 March 1998 of shares in or securities of the VCT; or
- money derived from the investment by the VCT of money so raised.

As regards (*f*) above, the provision of the services of accountancy personnel is the provision of accountancy services (*Castleton Management Services Ltd v Kirkwood (Sp C 276), [2001] SSCD 95*).

Exclusions (*k*) and (*l*) apply only if the person carrying on the activity in question has an estate or interest (e.g. a lease) in the property concerned or occupies that property.

HMRC regard as 'substantial' for the above purposes a part of a trade which consists of 20% or more of total activities, judged by any reasonable measure (normally turnover or capital employed). (HMRC Venture Capital Schemes Manual VCM 17040). As regards (*a*) above, dealing in land includes cases where steps are taken, before selling the land, to make it more attractive to a purchaser; such steps might include the refurbishment of existing buildings. (HMRC Venture Capital Schemes Manual VCM 17050).

As regards (*b*) above, a trade of wholesale distribution is a trade consisting of the offer of goods for sale either to persons for resale (or processing and resale) (which resale must be to members of the general public for their use or consumption) by them. A trade of retail distribution is a trade in which goods are offered or exposed for sale and sold to members of the general public for their use or consumption. A trade is not an ordinary wholesale or retail trade if it consists to a substantial extent of dealing in goods collected or held as an investment (or of that and any other activity within (*a*)–(*m*) above), and a substantial proportion of such goods is held for a significantly longer period than would reasonably be expected for a vendor trying to dispose of them at market value. Whether such trades are 'ordinary' is to be judged having regard to the following features: those under (A) supporting the categorisation as 'ordinary'; those under (B) being indicative to the contrary.

(A)

- (i) The breaking of bulk.
- (ii) The purchase and sale of goods in different markets.
- (iii) The employment of staff and incurring of trade expenses other than the cost of goods or of remuneration of persons connected (within *ITA 2007, s 993*) with a company carrying on such a trade.

(B)

- (i) The purchase or sale of goods from or to persons connected (within *ITA 2007, s 993*) with the trader.
- (ii) The matching of purchases with sales.
- (iii) The holding of goods for longer than would normally be expected.
- (iv) The carrying on of the trade at a place not commonly used for wholesale or retail trading.
- (v) The absence of physical possession of the goods by the trader.

As regards the application of (*e*) above in relation to shares issued after 5 April 2000, a trade is not excluded from being a qualifying trade solely because at some time in period B it consists to a substantial extent in the receiving of royalties or licence fees substantially attributable (in terms of value) to the exploitation of 'relevant intangible assets'.

A '*relevant intangible asset*' is an 'intangible asset' the whole or greater part of which (by value) has been created by the issuing company or by a company which was a qualifying subsidiary of the issuing company throughout the period during which it created the whole or greater part (by value) of the asset. For this purpose only, '*issuing company*' includes a company all of whose shares were acquired by the issuing company at a time when the only shares issued in the issuing company were subscriber shares and the consideration for the acquisition consisted wholly in the issue of shares in the issuing company. Before 6 April 2007, the whole or greater part of the asset had to be created by the company carrying on the trade or by a company which throughout the creation of the asset was the 'holding company' of that company or a qualifying subsidiary of that holding company. In relation to shares issued before 6 April 2007, an activity is not treated as an excluded activity if it would otherwise have become such an activity on or after that date by reason only of the change in this definition.

A '*holding company*' is for these purposes a company with one or more 51% subsidiaries which is not itself a 51% subsidiary. Where the asset is 'intellectual property', it is treated as created by a company only if the right to exploit it vests in that company (alone or with others). The term '*intellectual property*' incorporates patents, trade marks, copyrights, design rights etc. and foreign equivalents. An '*intangible asset*' is an asset falling to be treated as such under generally accepted accounting practice, including all intellectual property and also industrial information and techniques (see HMRC Venture Capital Schemes Manual VCM 17310).

As regards the application of (*e*) above in relation to shares issued before 6 April 2000, a company engaged throughout the period B in the production of original master films, tapes or discs is not excluded from the scheme by reason only of its receipt by way of trade of royalties or licence fees, provided that all royalties and licence fees received by it in the relevant period are in respect of films etc. produced by it in that period or in respect of by-products arising therefrom. The company may also be engaged in the distribution of films produced by it in period B. Similarly, royalties and licence fees attributable to research and development which a company carrying on a trade has engaged in throughout the period B do not prevent the trade being a qualifying trade.

Also as regards (*e*) above, a trade will not be excluded by reason only of its consisting of letting ships, other than offshore installations (previously oil rigs) or pleasure craft (as defined), on charter, provided that

(i) the company beneficially owns all the ships it so lets,

(ii) every ship beneficially owned by the company is UK-registered,

(iii) throughout period B, the company is solely responsible for arranging the marketing of the services of its ships, and

(iv) in relation to every letting on charter, certain conditions as to length and terms of charter, and the arm's length character of the transaction, are fulfilled,

and if any of (i)–(iv) above is not fulfilled in relation to certain lettings, the trade is not thereby excluded if those lettings and any other excluded activities taken together do not amount to a substantial part of the trade.

For HMRC's views on the scope of the exclusions in relation to (*e*) above, see Revenue Tax Bulletin August 2001 pp 877, 878.

'*Property development*', in (*g*) above, means the development of land by a company, which has (or has had at any time) an 'interest in the land' (as defined), with the sole or main object of realising a gain from the disposal of an interest in the developed land.

As regards (*m*) above, a person has a '*controlling interest*' in a trade etc. carried on by a company if he controls (within *ICTA 1988, s 416*) the company; or if the company is close and he or an 'associate' is a director of the company and the owner of, or able to control, more than 30% of its ordinary share capital; or if at least half of its ordinary share capital is directly or indirectly owned by him. In any other case it is obtained by his being entitled to at least half of the assets used for, or income arising from, the trade etc. In either case, the rights and powers of a person's 'associates' are attributed to him. An '*associate*' of any person is: any 'relative' (i.e. spouse, civil partner, ancestor or linear descendant) of that person, the trustee(s) of any settlement in relation to which that person or any relative (living or dead) is or was a settler; and, where that person has an interest in any shares or obligations of a company which are subject to any trust or are part of a deceased estate, the trustee(s) of the settlement or the personal representatives of the deceased; and, if that person is a company, any other company which has an interest in those shares or obligations. For this purpose, 'settlor' is defined as in *ITA 2007, ss 467–473*.

[*ITA 2007, ss 189, 192–199, 253, 257(3), Sch 1 para 483; ICTA 1988, ss 297, 298; FA 2000, Sch 17 para 13; FA 2001, Sch 15 paras 5, 40; FA 2004, Sch 27 para 4; FA 2007, Sch 16 paras 11(1)(7), 13, 14*].

The Treasury may, by statutory instrument, amend any of the above provisions. [*ITA 2007, s 200; ICTA 1988, s 298(4)*].

The changes in the rules concerning receipt of royalties and licence fees which apply in relation to EIS shares issued after 5 April 2000 also have effect for the purpose of determining whether shares or securities issued after that date are to be regarded as comprised in a VCT's qualifying holdings.

The definition of 'controlling interest' in relation to the above-mentioned conditions is also revised to permit holdings of non-voting fixed-rate preference shares, and rights as a loan creditor, to be disregarded.

'Research and development' from which it is intended that a qualifying trade carried on 'wholly or mainly in the UK' will either be derived or, for shares issued to the VCT after 5 April 2007, benefit is treated as the carrying on of a qualifying trade. Preparing to carry on such research and development does not, however, count as preparing to carry on a trade. '*Research and development*' has the meaning given by *ITA 2007, s 1006*.

[*ITA 2007, ss 300, 303–310, 313(5)–(7), Sch 2 paras 78, 81–85; ICTA 1988, Sch 28B paras 4, 5, 10, 13; FA 2000, Sch 18 para 5; FA 2004, Sch 27 para 5; FA 2007, Sch 16 para 12*].

In considering whether a trade is carried on '*wholly or mainly in the UK*', the totality of the trade activities is taken into account. Regard will be had, for example, to where capital assets are held, where any purchasing, processing, manufacturing and selling is done, and where the company employees and other agents are engaged in its trading operations. For trades involving the provision of services, both the location of the activities giving rise to the services and the location where they are delivered will be relevant. No one factor is itself likely to be decisive in any particular case. A company may carry on some such activities outside the UK and yet satisfy the requirement, provided that the major part of them, that is over one-half of the aggregate of these activities, takes place within the UK. Thus relief is not excluded solely because a company's products or services are exported, or because its raw materials are imported, or because its raw materials or products are stored abroad. Similar principles apply in considering the trade(s) carried on by a company and its qualifying subsidiaries.

In the particular case of a ship chartering trade, the test is satisfied if all charters are entered into in the UK and the provision of crews and management of the ships while under charter take place mainly in the UK. If these conditions are not met, the test may still be satisfied depending on all the relevant facts and circumstances.

(HMRC SP 3/00).

The carrying on of a qualifying activity requirement. In relation to shares or securities issued to the VCT after 16 March 2004, a 'qualifying company' (whether or not the same such company at all times) must, when the shares were issued to the VCT and at all times since, have been carrying on one of the following two '*qualifying activities*':

(A) carrying on a 'qualifying trade' (see the trading requirement above) 'wholly or mainly in the UK' (see the trading requirement above); or

(B) preparing to carry on a qualifying trade which, at the time the shares were issued, was intended to be carried on wholly or mainly in the UK.

The second of these conditions is, however, relevant only for a period of two years after the issue of the shares, by which time the intended trade must have been commenced by a 'qualifying company', and ceases to be relevant at any time within those two years after the intention is abandoned.

For these purposes, '*qualifying company*' means the issuing company itself or any 'qualifying 90% subsidiary' of that company. (In determining the time at which a qualifying trade begins to be carried on by a 'qualifying 90% subsidiary', any carrying on of the trade by it before it became such a subsidiary is disregarded.) For the purposes of (B) above only, a qualifying 90% subsidiary includes any existing or future company which will be a qualifying 90% subsidiary at any future time.

A company (the subsidiary) is a '*qualifying 90% subsidiary*' of the issuing company at any time when:

- the issuing company possesses at least 90% of both the issued share capital of, and the voting power in, the subsidiary;
- the issuing company would be beneficially entitled to at least 90% of the assets of the subsidiary available for distribution to equity holders on a winding-up or in any other circumstances;
- the issuing company is beneficially entitled to at least 90% of any profits of the subsidiary available for distribution to equity holders;
- no person other than the issuing company has control (within *ITA 2007, s 995* — see 19 CONNECTED PERSONS) of the subsidiary; and
- no arrangements exist by virtue of which any of the above conditions would cease to be met.

For the above purposes, *ICTA 1988, Sch 18 paras 1, 3* apply, with appropriate modifications, to determine the persons who are equity holders and the percentage of assets available to them. A subsidiary does not cease to be a qualifying 90% subsidiary by reason only of it or any other company having commenced winding up or by reason only of anything done as a consequence of any such company being in administration or receivership, provided the winding-up, entry into administration or receivership (both as defined) or anything done as a consequence of its being in administration or receivership is for genuine commercial reasons and is not part of a tax avoidance scheme or arrangements. Also, the listed conditions are not regarded as ceasing to be satisfied by reason only of arrangements being in existence for the disposal of the issuing company's interest in the subsidiary if the disposal is to be for genuine commercial reasons and is not to be part of a tax avoidance scheme or arrangements.

On or after 6 April 2007, a company (company A) is also a qualifying 90% subsidiary of the issuing company if:

- company A would be a qualifying 90% subsidiary of another company (company B) if that company were the issuing company and company B is a 'qualifying 100% subsidiary' of the issuing company; or
- company A is a qualifying 100% subsidiary of company B and company B is a qualifying 90% subsidiary of the issuing company.

No account is taken for this purpose of any control the issuing company may have of company A. The definition of a qualifying 90% subsidiary is used to define a '*qualifying 100% subsidiary*', replacing the references in that definition to 'at least 90%' with references to '100%'.

In relation to shares or securities issued to the VCT **on or before 16 March 2004**, the issuing company or a 'relevant qualifying subsidiary' must, when the shares were issued to the VCT and at all times since, have been either

- carrying on a qualifying trade wholly or mainly in the UK, or
- preparing to carry on a qualifying trade which, at the time the shares were issued, it intended to carry on wholly or mainly in the UK,

but the second of these conditions is relevant only for a period of two years after the issue of the shares, by which time the trade must have commenced as intended, and ceases to be relevant at any time within those two years after the intention is abandoned. For this purpose, a '*relevant qualifying subsidiary*' is, broadly, a company which is 90% owned by the issuing company (or by a subsidiary of the issuing company) and which otherwise satisfies the conditions of *ICTA 1988, Sch 28B para 10* (as amended prior to *FA 2004*).

[*ITA 2007, ss 291, 301, Sch 2 paras 72, 79; ICTA 1988, Sch 28B paras 3, 5A; FA 2004, Sch 19 paras 9, 10, 16; FA 2007, Sch 16 paras 17, 18*].

A company does not cease to meet this requirement by reason only of anything done as a consequence of its being in administration or receivership (both as defined), provided everything so done and the making of the relevant order are for genuine commercial (and not tax avoidance) reasons. [*ITA 2007, s 292, Sch 2 para 73; ICTA 1988, Sch 28B para 11A; FA 2000, Sch 18 para 7(1); FA 2004, Sch 19 para 15*].

The maximum amount raised annually through risk capital schemes requirement. Subject to the commencement provisions below, the total amount of 'relevant investments' in the issuing company and its subsidiaries in the year ending with the date of issue of the holding in question must not exceed £2 million. Investments in subsidiaries count towards the limit if the company concerned was a subsidiary of the issuing company at any time in the year, whether or not it was a subsidiary at the time of the investment.

A '*relevant investment*' in a company is made if:

(*aa*) an investment of any kind in the company is made by a VCT; or

(*bb*) the company issues shares (money having been subscribed for them) and provides HMRC with an ENTERPRISE INVESTMENT SCHEME compliance statement under *ITA 2007, s 205* or a CORPORATE VENTURING SCHEME (22) compliance statement under *FA 2000, Sch 15 para 42* in respect of the shares.

Investments within (*bb*) above are treated as made when the shares concerned are issued.

Where this requirement is not met as a consequence of the provision of an EIS or CVS compliance statement, it is treated as met throughout the period from the time of issue of the holding to the time the compliance statement was provided.

This requirement does not have to be satisfied in relation to an investment by the VCT of money raised by the issue of its shares or securities before 6 April 2007 or of money derived from the investment of such money.

An investment made by a VCT is not a relevant investment within (*aa*) above if it is made before 6 April 2007 or if it is an investment of money raised by the issue of shares or securities of the VCT before that date or of money derived from the investment of such money. An issue of shares before 19 July 2007 or to the 'managers of an approved fund' which closed before that date is not a relevant investment within (*bb*) above.

[*ITA 2007, s 292A; FA 2007, Sch 16 paras 6, 8*].

The use of the money raised requirement. The money raised by the issue of shares to the VCT must be employed *wholly* (disregarding insignificant amounts) for the purposes of the 'relevant qualifying activity'. At any time within 12 months after the issue (or after the date of commencement of the qualifying trade where this is later than the date of issue) this condition is treated as satisfied if at least 80% of that money has been, or is intended to be, so employed. At any time within the following 12 months, the condition is treated as satisfied if at least 80% of that money *has been* so employed. For this purpose, a qualifying activity is a '*relevant qualifying activity*' if it was a qualifying activity at the time the shares were issued, or if it is a qualifying trade and preparing to carry it on was a qualifying activity at that time. The above rules apply for the purpose of determining whether any shares or securities are, as at any time after 6 March 2001, to be regarded as comprised in the qualifying holdings of the VCT. Previously, the requirement was treated as satisfied at any time within the first twelve-month period if *all* the money was intended to be so employed, and no special treatment applied in the following twelve months. [*ITA 2007, s 293, Sch 2 para 74; ICTA 1988, Sch 28B para 6; FA 2001, Sch 16 para 2; FA 2004, Sch 19 para 11*].

Money whose retention can reasonably be regarded as necessary or advisable for financing current business requirements is regarded as employed for trade purposes (HMRC Venture Capital Schemes Manual VCM 12080, 62150–62153).

In relation to buy-outs (and in particular management buy-outs), HMRC will usually accept that where a company is formed to acquire a trade, and the funds raised from the VCT are applied to that purchase, the requirement that the funds be employed for the purposes of the trade is satisfied. Where the company is formed to acquire another company and its trade, or a holding company and its trading subsidiaries, this represents an investment rather than employment for the purposes of the trade. However, HMRC will usually accept that the requirement is satisfied if the trade of the company, or all the activities of the holding company and its subsidiaries, are hived up to the acquiring company as soon as possible after the acquisition. In the case of a holding company and its subsidiaries, to the extent that the trades are not hived up, the holding cannot be a qualifying holding. (Revenue Tax Bulletin August 1995 pp 243, 244).

The relevant company to carry on the relevant qualifying activity requirement. In relation to shares or securities issued to the VCT **after 16 March 2004**, at all times after the issue of the holding the relevant qualifying activity by reference to which the use of money raised requirement is satisfied must not be carried on by any person other than the issuing company or a 'qualifying 90% subsidiary' (see the carrying on of a qualifying activity requirement above) of that company.

This requirement is not treated as not met merely because the trade in question is carried on by a person other than the issuing company or a qualifying subsidiary at any time after the issue of the shares and before the issuing company or a qualifying 90% subsidiary carries on the trade. The carrying on of the trade by a partnership of which the issuing company or a qualifying 90% subsidiary is a member, or by a joint venture to which any such company is a party, is permitted.

The requirement is also not regarded as failing to be met if, by reason only of a company being wound up or dissolved or being in administration or receivership (both as defined), the qualifying trade ceases to be carried on by the issuing company' or a qualifying 90% subsidiary and is subsequently carried on by a person who has not been connected (within *ITA 2007, s 993* — see 19 CONNECTED PERSONS — but with the modifications to the meaning of 'control' that apply for the purposes of the control and independence requirement below) with the issuing company at any time in the period beginning one year before the shares were issued. This let-out applies only if the winding-up, dissolution or entry into administration or receivership (and everything done as a consequence of the company being in administration or receivership) is for genuine commercial reasons and not part of a tax avoidance scheme or arrangements.

In relation to shares or securities issued to the VCT **on or before 16 March 2004**, where the company is a 'parent company' within (*b*) above, the '*trader company*' (i.e. the company carrying on (or preparing to carry on) the required qualifying trade) must either:

- satisfy the requirements in (*a*) above; or
- be a company in relation to which those requirements would be satisfied if activities within (i) to (iv) above, or consisting of a subsidiary making loans to its parent, were disregarded; or
- be a 'relevant qualifying subsidiary' which either:
  (1) exists wholly for the purpose of carrying on activities within (iii) or (iv) above (disregarding purposes capable of having no significant effect (other than in relation to incidental matters) on the extent of its activities); or

(2) has no corporation tax profits and no part of its business consists in the making of investments.

A '*relevant qualifying subsidiary*' is, broadly, a company which is 90% owned by the investee company (or by a subsidiary of that company) and which otherwise satisfies the conditions of *ICTA 1988, Sch 28B para 10* (as amended prior to *FA 2004*).

[*ITA 2007, s 294, Sch 2 para 75; ICTA 1988, Sch 28B para 6(AB)–(AG); FA 2004, Sch 19 paras 11, 16*].

The unquoted status requirement. The issuing company must be an '*unquoted company*' (whether or not UK resident), i.e. none of its shares, stocks, debentures or other securities must be:

- listed on a recognised stock exchange, or a designated exchange outside the UK; or
- dealt in on the Unlisted Securities Market, or outside the UK by such means as may be designated for the purpose by order.

Securities on the Alternative Investment Market ('AIM') are treated as unquoted for these purposes. (Revenue Press Release 20 February 1995).

If the company ceases to be an unquoted company at a time when its shares are comprised in the qualifying holdings of the VCT, this requirement is treated as continuing to be met, in relation to shares or securities acquired before that time, for the following five years.

[*ITA 2007, s 295; ICTA 1988, Sch 28B para 2; FA 2007, Sch 26 para 12(7)*].

The control and independence requirement. The company must not 'control' (with or without 'connected persons') any company other than a 'qualifying subsidiary' (see the qualifying subsidiaries requirement below), nor must another company (or another company and a person connected with it) control it. Neither must arrangements be in existence by virtue of which such control could arise. For these purposes, '*control*' is as under *ICTA 1988, s 416*, except that possession of, or entitlement to acquire, fixed-rate preference shares (as defined) of the company which do not, for the time being, carry voting rights is disregarded, as is possession of, or entitlement to acquire, rights as a loan creditor of the company. '*Connected persons*' are as under *ITA 2007, s 993* (see 19 CONNECTED PERSONS) except that the definition of 'control' therein is similarly modified. [*ITA 2007, ss 296, 313(4)–(7); ICTA 1988, Sch 28B paras 9, 13*].

For the application of the control and independence requirement to co-investors in a company, and in particular the question of whether co-investors are connected by virtue of their acting together to secure or exercise control of the company, see Revenue Tax Bulletin October 1997 pp 471, 472.

The gross assets requirement. The value of the company's gross assets or, where the company is a parent company, the value of the 'group assets', must not have exceeded £7 million immediately before the issue or £8 million immediately thereafter. In relation to shares and securities issued by investee companies after 5 April 1998 and before 6 April 2006, these limits were £15 million and £16 million respectively. For the purpose of determining whether shares or securities acquired by the VCT are to be regarded as comprised in its qualifying holdings, the higher limits continue to apply in relation to shares or securities issued by investee companies on or after 6 April 2006 but acquired with money raised by the issue of shares in the VCT before that date or money derived from the investment by the VCT of any such money.

'*Group assets*' are the gross assets of each of the members of the group, disregarding assets consisting in rights against, or shares in or securities of, another member of the group.

[*ITA 2007, s 297, Sch 2 para 76; ICTA 1988, Sch 28B para 8; FA 2006, Sch 14 para 2*].

The general approach of HMRC is that the value of a company's gross assets is the sum of the value of all the balance sheet assets. Where accounts are actually drawn up to a date immediately before or after the issue, the balance sheet values are taken provided that they reflect usual accounting standards and the company's normal accounting practice, consistently applied. Where accounts are not drawn up to such a date, such values will be taken from the most recent balance sheet, updated as precisely as practicable on the basis of all the relevant information available to the company. Values so arrived at may need to be reviewed in the light of information contained in the accounts for the period in which the issue was made, and, if they were not available at the time of the issue, those for the preceding period, when they become available. The company's assets immediately before the issue do not include any advance payment received in respect of the issue. Where shares are issued partly paid, the right to the balance is an asset, and, notwithstanding the above, will be taken into account in valuing the assets immediately after the issue regardless of whether it is stated in the balance sheet. (HMRC SP 2/00).

The number of employees requirement. The 'full-time equivalent employee number' for the issuing company must be less than 50 at the time the holding is issued. If the company is a parent company, the sum of the full-time equivalent employee numbers for it and each of its qualifying subsidiaries must be less than 50 at that time.

This requirement must be satisfied only in relation to holdings issued on or after 6 April 2007. It does not, however, have to be satisfied in relation to such holdings if they are acquired by the investment of money raised by the issue before 6 April 2007 of shares in or securities of the VCT or of money derived from the investment of such money.

A company's '*full-time equivalent employee number*' is the number of its full-time employees plus, for each employee who is not full-time, a just and reasonable fraction. Directors count as employees for this purpose, but employees on maternity or paternity leave and students on vocational training are excluded.

[*ITA 2007, s 297A; FA 2007, Sch 16 para 3*(*3*)(*5*)–(*7*)].

The qualifying subsidiaries requirement. Any subsidiary that the issuing company has must be a 'qualifying subsidiary'.

A subsidiary is a '*qualifying subsidiary*' of the issuing company if the following conditions are satisfied in relation to that subsidiary and every other subsidiary of the issuing company.

In relation to shares or securities issued to the VCT **after 16 March 2004**, the subsidiary must be a **51%** subsidiary (see *ICTA 1988, s 838*) of the issuing company and no person other than the issuing company or another of its subsidiaries may have control (within *ICTA 1988, s 840* — see 19 CONNECTED PERSONS) of the subsidiary. Furthermore, no arrangements may exist by virtue of which either of these conditions would cease to be satisfied. The conditions are not regarded as ceasing to be satisfied by reason only of the subsidiary or any other company in the process of being wound up or by reason only of anything done as a consequence of its being in administration or receivership, provided the winding-up, entry into administration or receivership or anything done as a consequence of its being in administration or receivership is for genuine commercial reasons and is not part of a tax avoidance scheme or arrangements.

In relation to shares or securities issued to the VCT **on or before 16 March 2004**, the issuing company, or another of its subsidiaries, must possess at least **75%** of the issued share capital of, and the voting power in, the subsidiary, and be beneficially entitled to at least **75%** of the assets available for distribution to equity holders on a winding-up etc. (see *ICTA 1988, Sch 18 paras 1, 3*) and of the profits available for distribution to equity holders. No other person may have control (within *ITA 2007, s 995* — see 19 CONNECTED PERSONS) of the subsidiary. Furthermore, no arrangements may exist by virtue of which any of these conditions could cease to be satisfied. A subsidiary does not fail these conditions by reason only of the fact that it is being wound up, provided that the winding-up is for *bona fide* commercial reasons and is not part of a tax avoidance scheme or arrangements.

The conditions above are not regarded as ceasing to be satisfied by reason only of arrangements being in existence for the disposal of the interest in the subsidiary held by the issuing company (or, as the case may be, by another of its subsidiaries) if the disposal is to be for genuine commercial reasons and is not to be part of a tax avoidance scheme or arrangements.

[*ITA 2007, ss 298, 302, 989, Sch 2 para 80; ICTA 1988, Sch 28B paras 3*(*6*)*, 10; FA 2004, Sch 19 para 12*].

The property managing subsidiaries requirement. In relation to shares or securities issued to the VCT **after 16 March 2004,** the company must not have a 'property managing subsidiary', which is not a 'qualifying 90% subsidiary' (see the carrying on of a qualifying activity requirement above) of the company. A '*property managing subsidiary*' is a subsidiary whose business consists wholly or mainly in the holding or managing of 'land' or any 'property deriving its value from land' (as defined). [*ITA 2007, s 299, Sch 2 para 77; ICTA 1988, Sch 28B para 10ZA; FA 2004, Sch 19 para 13*].

Withdrawal of approval. Approval may be **withdrawn** where there are reasonable grounds for believing that either:

(A) the conditions for approval were not satisfied at the time the approval was given; or

(B) a condition that HMRC were satisfied (as above) would be met has not been or will not be met; or

(C) where (ii) above applies, any other conditions prescribed by regulation in relation to the three-year period have not been met; or

(D) in either the most recent complete accounting period or the current one, one of conditions (*a*)–(*d*) above has failed or will fail to be met (unless the failure was allowed for under (i)–(iii) above); or

(E) where, in relation to a second or further issue by an approved VCT, (*b*) above does not have to be met in the period of issue or certain following accounting periods (see above), either:

 (i) one of conditions (*a*)–(*d*) above will fail to be met in the first period for which (*b*) above must be met; or

 (ii) any other conditions prescribed by regulations have not been met in relation to, or to part of, an accounting period for which (*b*) above does not have to be met.

The withdrawal is effective from the time the company is notified of it, except that:

(1) where approval is given under (i)–(iii) above, and is withdrawn before all the conditions (*a*)–(*d*) above have been satisfied in relation to either a complete twelve-month accounting period or successive complete accounting periods constituting a continuous period of twelve months or more, the approval is deemed never to have been given; and

(2) for the purposes of relief for capital gains accruing to a VCT under *TCGA 1992, s 100*, withdrawal may be effective from an earlier date, but not before the start of the accounting period in which the failure occurred (or is expected to occur).

An assessment consequent on the withdrawal of approval may, where otherwise out of time, be made within three years from the time notice of the withdrawal was given.

[*ICTA 1988, s 842AA*(*6*)*–*(*10*)].

69.4 **Supplementary provisions.** *Winding up of the issuing company.* Where the company is being wound up, none of the requirements listed at 69.2 above are regarded on that account as not being satisfied provided that they would be met apart from the winding up, and that the winding up is for genuine commercial reasons and is not part of a scheme or arrangement a main purpose of which is the avoidance of tax. [*ITA 2007, s 312, Sch 2 para 86; ICTA 1988, Sch 28B para 11; FA 2004, Sch 19 para 14*].

Power to amend requirements. The Treasury have power by order to modify the trading requirement, the carrying on of a qualifying activity requirement and the qualifying subsidiaries requirement as they consider expedient, and to alter the cash limits referred to in the maximum qualifying investment requirement and the gross assets requirement above. [*ITA 2007, s 311; ICTA 1988, Sch 28B para 12*].

Restructuring. Where shares or securities in a company are exchanged for corresponding shares and securities in a new holding company, then subject to detailed conditions, including HMRC approval, to the extent that any of the requirements listed below was satisfied in relation to the old shares, it will generally be taken to be satisfied in relation to the new shares. The consideration for the old shares must consist wholly of the issue of shares in the new company. Certain deemed securities (see 66.2 above) which are not thus acquired by the new company may be disregarded where these provisions would otherwise be prevented from applying.

The requirements to which the above provision applies are:

- the maximum qualifying investment requirement;
- the proportion of eligible shares requirement;
- the trading requirement;
- the carrying on of a qualifying activity requirement;
- the use of money raised requirement;
- the relevant company to carry on the relevant qualifying activity requirement;
- the gross assets requirement; and
- the number of employees requirement.

[*ITA 2007, ss 326–328, Sch 2 para 87; ICTA 1988, Sch 28B para 10C; FA 2007, Sch 16 para 3(4)*].

Conversion of shares. Where a VCT exercises conversion rights in respect of certain convertible shares and securities, then subject to detailed conditions, for the purposes of the requirements listed below, the conversion is treated as an exchange of new shares for old shares to which the restructuring provisions above apply. The requirements are:

- the maximum qualifying investment requirement;
- the proportion of eligible shares requirement;
- the carrying on of a qualifying activity requirement;
- the use of money raised requirement;
- the relevant company to carry on the relevant qualifying activity requirement; and
- the gross assets requirement.

[*ITA 2007, s 329, Sch 2 para 87; ICTA 1988, Sch 28B para 10D*].

Reorganisations etc. Where, under a company reorganisation or other arrangement,

- a VCT exchanges a qualifying holding for other shares or securities (with or without other consideration), and

- the exchange is for genuine commercial reasons and not part of a tax avoidance scheme or arrangements,

the new shares or securities may be treated as being qualifying holdings for a specified period even if some or all of the requirements at 66.3 above are not otherwise satisfied. Regulations specify the circumstances in which, and conditions subject to which, they apply and which requirements are to be treated as met. Where the new shares or securities are those of a different company than before and they do not meet any one or more of the above requirements (disregarding the maximum qualifying investment requirement and the use of the money raised requirement), those requirements are treated as met for, broadly, three years in the case of shares, or five years in the case of securities, reduced in either case to, broadly, two years where the company is not, or ceases to be, an unquoted company as in the unquoted status requirement above. A formula is provided for valuing the new shares or securities for the purposes of the proportion of eligible shares requirement above. The provisions extend to new shares or securities received in pursuance of an earn-out right conferred in exchange for a qualifying holding, in which case an election is available (under *reg 10*) to modify the said valuation formula by effectively disregarding the earn-out right itself. [*ITA 2007, s 330, Sch 2 para 88; ICTA 1988, Sch 28B para 11B; FA 2000, Sch 18 para 8(1); SI 2002 No 2661*].

[*ITA 2007, ss 300, 303–311; ICTA 1988, Sch 28B paras 4, 5, 13(2)–(5); FA 2000, s 65, Sch 18 paras 4–6; FA 2002, s 103(4); FA 2004, Sch 27 para 5(3)–(6)*].

Simon's Direct Tax Service. See **D4.1363, E3.602**.

69.5 INCOME TAX RELIEFS

Relief from income tax is granted in respect of both investments in VCT share issues (up to £200,000 for 2004–05 onwards, previously £100,000, in a year of assessment) and distributions from such trusts (in respect of shares acquired up to a 'permitted maximum' in any year of assessment). The rate of relief for investments (given by deduction from the individual's income tax liability) is 30% in relation to shares issued on or after 6 April 2006 (40% for shares issued on or after 6 April 2004 and 20% for shares issued before that date). [*ICTA 1988, s 332A, Sch 15B; FA 1999, s 70; FA 2000, Sch 18 paras 1, 3; FA 2001, Sch 16 para 3; FA 2002, Sch 17 para 3; FA 2003, Sch 40 para 1; FA 2004, s 94(1), Sch 19 paras 1–3; ITTOIA 2005, Pt 6 Ch 5, Sch 1 paras 140, 346; FA 2006, Sch 14 paras 4, 7, Sch 26 Pt 3(17)*].

See 69.2 above as regards mergers and winding-up of VCTs. For the detailed conditions for both reliefs, and for the circumstances in which investment relief is withdrawn, see Tolley's Income Tax under Venture Capital Trusts.

Simon's Direct Tax Service. See **E3.640** *et seq*.

69.6 CAPITAL GAINS TAX RELIEFS

The capital gains of a VCT are not chargeable gains. [*TCGA 1992, s 100(1)*]. In addition, individual investors in VCTs are entitled to two reliefs:

(*a*) on disposal of VCT shares (up to a 'permitted maximum' acquired in any year of assessment); and

(*b*) for shares issued before 6 April 2004, by deferral of chargeable gains on re-investment in VCT share issues (up to the income tax relief limit, see 69.5 above).

[*TCGA 1992, ss 151A, 151B, Sch 5C; FA 2000, Sch 18 paras 2, 3; FA 2002, Sch 9 para 5(9); FA 2004, Sch 19 paras 4–7; ITTOIA 2005, Sch 1 para 437*].

See 69.2 above as regards mergers and winding-up of VCTs. For the detailed conditions for these reliefs, and for relief on withdrawal of approval, see Tolley's Capital Gains Tax under Venture Capital Trusts. See also Simon's Direct Tax Service C3.1103 *et seq*.

70 Voluntary Associations

See 61.4 RETURNS as regards tax returns by members' clubs and similar organisations.

Simons Direct Tax Service. See **D4.3**.

See generally HMRC Pamphlet IR 46.

70.1 INTRODUCTION

A club or society, being either an incorporated body or an unincorporated association, is liable to corporation tax on its income and capital gains, which includes interest received and profits from non-members (see 70.2 below). See 61.4 RETURNS with regard to the concessional exemption from the requirement to deliver returns where the annual corporation tax liability is not expected to exceed £100. For the special treatment of certain societies, see 9 BUILDING SOCIETIES, 14 CHARITIES, 27 EXEMPT ORGANISATIONS, 31 FRIENDLY SOCIETIES, 36 HOUSING ASSOCIATIONS, 38 INDUSTRIAL AND PROVIDENT SOCIETIES and 48 MUTUAL COMPANIES. Generally, see HMRC explanatory pamphlet IR 46 'Clubs, Societies and Associations'. See *CIR v Worthing Rugby Football Club Trustees CA 1987, 60 TC 482* and *Blackpool Marton Rotary Club v Martin Ch D 1988, 62 TC 686*. See also Revenue Tax Bulletin October 1998 p 600 for HMRC's approach to such bodies with trivial liabilities.

70.2 MUTUAL TRADING

A members' club does not carry on a trade and is not liable on its surplus from the provision of facilities for members, even though the membership fluctuates. Any surplus arising from the supply of goods or services to non-members is taxable. See 48.1 MUTUAL COMPANIES. See also 70.8 below as regards members' sports clubs.

70.3 LOAN AND MONEY SOCIETIES

Dividends and interest paid to members are subject to deduction of income tax at an average rate based on the reduced rates which would be applicable to members. The grossed-up amounts are then deductible in computing the societies' corporation tax liability. (HMRC Extra-Statutory Concession, C2). The concession is withdrawn from April 2001. See Revenue Press Release 3 March 2000.

70.4 HOLIDAY CLUBS AND THRIFT FUNDS

Such funds and clubs formed annually for the purpose of saving for holidays are regarded as being outside the scope of corporation tax. Where income not subjected to composite rate tax is received, liability in respect of such income paid to members or expended for their benefit is restricted to the total amount which would have been charged had the members received the income directly. (HMRC Extra-Statutory Concession, C3). The concession is withdrawn from April 2001. See Revenue Press Release 3 March 2000.

70.5 INVESTMENT CLUBS

Chargeable gains and allowable losses made by investment clubs are apportioned among the members, each individual being assessed to capital gains tax on his share of the whole. If the club has not more than 20 members with an *average* investment of not more than £5,000, then if the annual subscription to the club does not exceed £1,000, and its total annual gains are less than £5,000, the secretary may apply (on Form 185–1) for the gains and losses to be agreed by the inspector of the district in which he lives. Each member's share can then be accepted by his own local inspector without further argument. Otherwise, the total gains and the member's share must be separately agreed.

70.6 LOTTERIES ETC.

Where a football pool or small lottery is to be run by a supporters' club or other society on the basis that a stated percentage or fraction of the cost of each ticket will be given to a club or body conducted and established wholly or mainly for one or more of the purposes specified in *Lotteries and Amusements Act 1976*, the donation element as stated in the cost of each ticket may be excluded in computing for tax purposes the profits of the trade of promoting the pool or lottery. (HMRC Statement of Practice, C1).

70.7 DISSOLUTION

An unincorporated association which sells its only fixed asset and closes down is liable to corporation tax on any chargeable gain arising by virtue of *ICTA 1988, s 832(1)*.

70.8 MEMBERS' SPORTS CLUBS

For HMRC's views on the circumstances in which a members' sports club's commercial activities can give rise to taxable trading profits (or to allowable trading losses), see Revenue Tax Bulletin December 1997 pp 488–490.

VAT repayments. Repayments under *SI 1994 No 687* which are returned to members *pro rata* to the VAT originally paid by them do not give rise to a distribution for tax purposes. Interest on the repayments is chargeable to corporation tax, but other supplemental payments are not chargeable. See Revenue Tax Bulletin April 1995 p 209.

Community amateur sports clubs. From 1 April 2002, an amateur club which, as required by its constitution, is open to all, without discrimination and at reasonable cost, and has as its main purpose a '*qualifying purpose*' (i.e. the provision of facilities for, and promotion of participation in, a sport or sports designated for the purpose by Treasury order) may apply to HMRC for registration, and if HMRC registers the club, will be entitled to certain tax exemptions. For the detailed requirements, see *FA 2002, Sch 18 Pt I*. *SI 2002 No 1966* designates the eligible sports for these purposes as those appearing on the list of activities recognised by the various National Sports Councils (which is available on the Sport England website at www.sportengland.org/recognition_of_activities.htm). A list of registered clubs is published on HMRC's website (at www.hmrc.gov.uk/casc/registered-clubs.pdf).

For any accounting period ending on or after 1 April 2002 throughout which it is registered, and for which its Schedule D, Case I income (before deduction of expenses) does not exceed an annual limit (proportionately reduced for accounting periods of less than 12 months) and is wholly applied for qualifying purposes, the club may claim exemption from corporation tax on that income. The limit is £30,000 for accounting periods ending on or after 1 April 2004, increased from £15,000 for accounting periods ending before that date. A part of an accounting period during which a club is registered may be treated as a separate accounting period for this purpose (with appropriate apportionment). Similarly, an exemption may be claimed in relation to Schedule A income provided it does not exceed an annual limit. The limit is £20,000 for accounting periods ending on or after 1 April 2004, increased from £10,000 for accounting periods ending before that date. Where an accounting period straddles 1 April 2004, for the purpose of determining whether the applicable limits are exceeded, the parts of the accounting period falling before and after that date are treated as two separate accounting periods and a relevant proportion of trading income is apportioned to each period. Similar exemptions apply to Schedule D, Case III interest income, Gift Aid income (see further below) and chargeable gains. Any such exemption is, however, correspondingly reduced where the club incurs expenditure for non-qualifying purposes (and in certain circumstances this may also require cancellation of exemption in earlier accounting periods).

Provision is also made for a deemed market value disposal for chargeable gains purposes of property held by a club when it either ceases to be registered or ceases to hold the property for qualifying purposes, any gain being outside the exemption. To the extent (if any) that the property represents consideration for the disposal of assets by the club, the exemption on any such disposal is similarly withdrawn. The chargeable gain on such a deemed disposal can be assessed up to three years after the end of the accounting period to which the deemed disposal relates.

Reliefs for donors. A number of charitable reliefs are extended to registered clubs for gifts made on or after 6 April 2002. These are *ITA 2007, ss 59, 413–430* (formerly *FA 1990, s 25*) (individual Gift Aid donations), *ITA 2007 Sch 1 para 420*; *ICTA 1988, s 83A* and *CAA 2001, s 63(2)* (gifts in kind, see 14.13 CHARITIES), *TCGA 1992, s 257* (chargeable gains relief for gifts to charities) and *IHTA 1984, s 23* (inheritance tax relief for gifts to charities).

General. Provision is made for registration (and termination thereof) by HMRC, and for appeals, information requirements, etc.

[*FA 2002, s 58, Sch 18; FA 2004, s 56*].

71 Finance Act Summaries: Corporation Tax Provisions

FINANCE ACT 2007

(Royal Assent 19 July 2007)

s 2	**Charge and main rate for financial year 2008.** The full rate is set at 28% for profits other than ring fenced profits and 30% for ring fenced profits. See 1.3(a) INTRODUCTION AND RATES OF TAX.
s 3	**Small companies' rate and fraction for financial year 2007.** The small companies' rate is set at 20% and the marginal relief fraction accordingly at 1/40 for other than ring fenced profits and 19% and 11/400 for ring fenced profits. See 1.3(a) INTRODUCTION AND RATES OF TAX; 63.1, 63.2 SMALL COMPANIES—REDUCED RATES.
s 17	**Corporation tax deduction for expenditure on energy-saving items.** A deduction is available for expenditure incurred between a date to be appointed and 31 March 2015 by a company on installing an energy-saving item in a dwelling-house used by the company in a Schedule A business. The expenditure must not be a prohibited deduction under the 'wholly and exclusively' rule and must not otherwise qualify for capital allowances. See 56.5 PROPERTY INCOME.
s 25	**Managed service companies (MSCs).** These are defined in the legislation and mainly comprise companies operating in a composite format. Such companies are exempted from the IR35 legislation for personal service companies. All income paid by the MSC to a director or associate of an MSC is to be subject to income tax (PAYE) and NIC. There are powers for HMRC to recover the tax from third parties should the MSC fail to pay. See 55.13 PROFIT COMPUTATIONS.
s 27	**Restrictions on allowable capital losses.** This is an anti-avoidance measure to restrict relief for a capital loss to situations where another person has realised a capital gain. See 11.3 CAPITAL GAINS.
s 28	**Anti-avoidance – management expenses claims.** No deduction is to be allowed for management expenses where any part of the expenditure is incurred to obtain a tax advantage. See 42 INVESTMENT COMPANIES AND INVESTMENT BUSINESS.
s 29	**Life policies etc.: effect of rebated or reinvested commission.** An anti-avoidance provision to prevent the use of life assurance policies to shelter tax due on investment income. See 55.12 PROFIT COMPUTATIONS.
s 30, Sch 5	**Avoidance involving financial instruments.** Several anti-avoidance measures are introduced to counter avoidance schemes (disclosed under DOTAS) using financial instruments. See 5 ANTI-AVOIDANCE; 12.2 CAPITAL GAINS—GROUPS; 46 LOAN RELATIONSHIPS.
s 31, Sch 6	**Companies carrying on the business of leasing plant or machinery.** This extends the scope of the anti-avoidance provisions applying to companies carrying on a trade of leasing plant and machinery on their own or in partnership to cover changes in ownership and reconstructions of companies with leasing trades See 5.17 ANTI-AVOIDANCE.

s 32	**Restrictions on buying losses or gains: tax avoidance schemes.** Following the measures introduced in *FA 2006*, further provisions are introduced to restrict set off of losses on pre-change assets against gains on disposal of pre-change assets. See 12.6 CAPITAL GAINS—GROUPS.
s 34	**Employee benefit contributions.** Relief for employee benefit contributions is further restricted. A deduction against taxable profits will be given only to the extent the amount has been paid to an employee within nine months of the year end in a form subject to income tax and national insurance. See 56.44 TRADING INCOME.
s 35	**Schemes designed to increase double taxation relief.** For any payments of foreign tax on or after 6 December 2006, income received on or after that date, or any act or omission on or after that date, 'foreign tax' includes UK tax treated as foreign tax by *ICTA 1988, s 801*. See 5.19 ANTI-AVOIDANCE.
s 36	**Industrial and agricultural buildings allowances.** Balancing adjustments are being discontinued for industrial buildings allowances, agricultural allowances and hotels allowances as the first stage of phasing out these allowances altogether. See 10.3, 10.15, 10.18 CAPITAL ALLOWANCES.
s 37	**Capital allowances.** The rate for first-year allowances for small enterprises remains at 50% for a further year for qualifying expenditure incurred between 1 April 2007 to 31 March 2008. See 10.27 CAPITAL ALLOWANCES.
s 44, Sch 12	**Transfers of business from friendly societies to insurance companies.** Where a friendly society's tax exempt life insurance business is transferred to an insurance company, the exemption will be preserved provided that the benefits are not increased after the transfer. See 31 FRIENDLY SOCIETIES.
s 45	**Tax exempt business of friendly societies.** Policies will remain exempt from tax where a policy is assigned by an individual other than for money or money's worth. See 31 FRIENDLY SOCIETIES.
s 47	**Sale and re-purchase of securities (repos).** A new regime is introduced for repos – which are divided into four categories: debtor repo, debtor quasi-repo, creditor repo and creditor quasi-repo. The regime will come into force after consultation. See 5.5 ANTI-AVOIDANCE.
s 48	**Controlled foreign companies.** This measure is intended to amend the CFC rules in the light of the ECJ's judgment in *Marks & Spencer* so that a UK parent may fall outside the CFC regime by demonstrating genuine economic activity in the state with the lower tax regime. See 21 CONTROLLED FOREIGN COMPANIES.
s 49	**Vaccine research relief: amount of deduction for SMEs.** Restricts vaccine research relief available to SMEs to 50% on top of the normal R&D relief. See 59.18 RESEARCH AND DEVELOPMENT EXPENDITURE.
s 50	**Research and development tax relief: definition of SME.** The definition of an SME is to be widened to include enterprises with up to 500 employees, turnover of up to 100 million euros and profits of up to 80 million euros. See 59.2 RESEARCH AND DEVELOPMENT EXPENDITURE.

s 51, Sch 16	**Venture capital schemes.** These provisions make changes to the VCT and Corporate Venturing schemes. There is a new definition of 'qualifying trade'. There is a restriction of the number of employees a company or group may have at the time of the issue and on the amount which can be raised in any twelve-month period. Certain of the provisions are aligned between the VCT, enterprise management incentive and corporate venturing schemes. See 23 CORPORATE VENTURING SCHEME; 69 VENTURE CAPITAL TRUSTS.
s 52, Sch 17	**Real estate investment trusts.** The provisions for REITs are revised. The revisions take effect from 1 January 2007, the date the new regime commenced. See 44.6–44.10 INVESTMENT TRUSTS.
s 53	**Alternative finance investment bond.** The provisions are extended to cover Shari'a compliant bonds (known as Sukuk) which are similar to collective investment bonds. They are brought within the loan relationship rules. See 4.6 ALTERNATIVE FINANCE ARRANGEMENTS.
s 57	**Offshore investment funds.** Changes are made to the qualifying conditions for a distributing fund, plus other small amendments to the offshore funds rules. See 50.4 OFFSHORE FUNDS.
s 58	**Election out of special rules for film production companies.** An election to remain outside the film corporation tax relief scheme is now provided for. The election must be made in the company's tax return, or as an amendment to that return. See 66.52 TRADING INCOME.
s 59	**Securitisation companies.** The regime for securitisation companies is due to take effect on 1 January 2008. This section allows implementation to be delayed beyond 1 January 2008 and also gives wide powers for amendment of the regime by statutory instrument. See 28.51 FINANCIAL INSTRUMENTS, DERIVATIVE CONTRACTS AND SECURITISATION COMPANIES.
s 60	**Gift aid: limits.** The percentage of the monetary value of benefits which may be received without denying gift aid is increased. See 14.11 CHARITIES.
s 82, s 84, s 87 Sch 22	**Criminal investigations: powers of HMRC.** The powers of former Revenue officers are extended in line with those of former Customs officers. See 30.4 FRAUDULENT OR NEGLIGENT CONDUCT.
s 83	**Northern Ireland criminal investigations.** Increased powers per s 81 above extended to Northern Ireland. See 30.4 FRAUDULENT OR NEGLIGENT CONDUCT.
s 85, Sch 23	**Criminal investigations: Scotland.** Increased powers per s 81 above extended to Scotland. See 30.4 FRAUDULENT OR NEGLIGENT CONDUCT.
s 86	**Search warrants.** Revised powers of search, replacing existing powers, are extended to officers of HMRC in specified circumstances. See 30.4 FRAUDULENT OR NEGLIGENT CONDUCT.
s 93	**Mandatory electronic filing of returns.** HMRC is given the power to provide for any return to be filed electronically. See 33.10 HMRC: ADMINISTRATION.
s 94	**Mandatory electronic payment.** HMRC is given the power to provide for any payment of tax to be made electronically. See 53.9 PAYMENT OF TAX.

s 95	**Payment by cheque.** HMRC is given the power to treat a payment as made when a cheque is cleared. See 41.6 INTEREST ON UNPAID TAX.
s 96	**Enquiry into returns.** For a company not a member of a group, in respect of accounting periods ending on or after 1 April 2008 where the return is filed on time, the enquiry window will run to twelve months after the date the return is filed. See 61.10 RETURNS.
s 96, Sch 24	**Penalties for errors.** A new regime is introduced. Errors are classified as careless, deliberate but not concealed and deliberate and concealed. The penalty in any case, in terms of the percentage of lost revenue (as defined) is laid down in the legislation. This inhibits taxpayers' ability to negotiate a penalty downwards. See 54.3 PENALTIES.
s 102	**Abolition of PRT for fields recommissioned after earlier decommissioning.** Abolition of PRT in these cases to take effect on or after 1 July 2007 See 51.3 OIL COMPANIES.
s 107	**Limitation period in old actions for mistake of law relating to direct tax.** The limitation period for recovery of tax paid under a mistake at law under an action brought before 8 September 2003 is restricted to six years, the same period during which HMRC have the right to recover tax. (There is already legislation in place to deal with actions brought after that date.) The measure does not apply to an action which has been decided in its favour (or under a group litigation order or to which it is a party) by the House of Lords before **19 July 2007**. See 15.10 CLAIMS.
s 108	**Disclosure of tax avoidance schemes.** This provision gives HMRC power to act where it is suspected that an avoidance scheme used has not been disclosed to them. See 5.26 ANTI-AVOIDANCE.
s 109 Sch 26	**Meaning of 'recognised stock exchange' etc.** These provisions lay down a new definition of 'recognised stock exchange' for the purpose of corporation tax and tax on capital gains and for the valuation of holdings for tax on such gains. See 14.9 CAPITAL GAINS.
s 110	**Mergers Directive: regulations.** The Treasury is given wide powers to make regulations concerning certain mergers. See 11.12 CAPITAL GAINS.

72 Table of Cases

Note: Citation where appropriate is of the Official Reports of Tax Cases, Simon's Tax Cases, one set of the official series (i.e. either the Law Reports or the Weekly Law Reports), and the All England Law Reports. Only in default of these are other series referred to. For abbreviations, see page ix.

A

Clayson, Anglo-French Exploration Co Ltd *v* — 18.4, 66.27
CA 1956: 35 TC 545; [1956] 1 WLR 325; [1956] 1 All ER 762.

Cleary *v* CIR — 5.2
HL 1967: 44 TC 399; [1967] 2 All ER 48; [1967] 2 WLR 1271.

Clixby *v* Pountney — 30.2, 54.6
Ch D 1967: 44 TC 515; [1968] Ch 719; [1968] 1 All ER 802.

Close Bros Ltd, Blackburn *v* — 18.4
Ch D 1960: 39 TC 164.

Coates *v* Arndale Properties Ltd — 12.4
HL 1984: 59 TC 516; [1984] STC 637; [1984] 1 WLR 1328; [1985] 1 All ER 15.

Cohen's Executors, Southern *v* — 66.4
KB 1940: 23 TC 566; [1940] 3 All ER 439.

Cole Bros Ltd *v* Phillips — 10.25
HL 1982: 55 TC 188; [1982] STC 307; [1982] 1 WLR 1450; [1982] 2 All ER 247.

Collins *v* Addies — 16.13
CA 1992: 65 TC 190; [1992] STC 746.

Colmer, ICI plc *v* — 32.23
HL 1996: 72 TC 1; [1996] STC 352; [1996] 1 WLR 469; [1996] 2 All ER 23; [1999] STC 1089.

Colmer (Case C–264/96), ICI plc *v* — 32.7, 32.23
ECJ 1998: [1998] STC 874; [1999] 1 WLR 108.

Coltness Iron Co *v* Black — 66.65
HL 1881: 1 TC 287; (1881) 6 App Cas 315.

Coman, Rotunda Hospital Dublin (Governors of) *v* — 14.2
HL 1920: 7 TC 517.

Commercial Union Assurance Co plc *v* Shaw — 24.7, 47.4
CA 1998: 72 TC 101; [1999] STC 109.

Commerzbank AG, CIR *v* — 24.15
Ch D 1990: 63 TC 218; [1990] STC 285.

Commerzbank AG, ex p., R *v* CIR — 24.3, 40.4
QB 1991: 68 TC 252; [1991] STC 271.

Commerzbank AG, ex p., R *v* CIR — 24.3, 40.4
CJEC 1993: 68 TC 264; [1993] STC 605; [1994] 2 WLR 128; [1993] 4 All ER 37.

Commissioner of Taxes *v* Nchanga Consolidated Copper Mines Ltd — 18.8, 66.26
PC 1964: [1964] AC 948; [1964] 1 All ER 208.

Conelee Properties Ltd, Webb *v* — 42.1, 66.1
Ch D 1982: 56 TC 149; [1982] STC 913.

Conlon Construction Ltd *v* Jarman — 46.16
Sp C 2003: [2004] SSCD 6.

Conservative and Unionist Central Office *v* Burrell — 1.2
CA 1981: 55 TC 671; [1982] STC 317; [1982] 1 WLR 522; [1982] 2 All ER 1.

Consolidated African Selection Trust Ltd, Lowry *v* — 66.43
HL 1940: 23 TC 259; [1940] AC 648; [1940] 2 All ER 545.

Consolidated Goldfields plc *v* CIR — 6.20, 6.22
Ch D 1990: 63 TC 333; [1990] STC 357.

Cook, H & G Kinemas Ltd *v* — 66.4
KB 1933: 18 TC 116.

Cook *v* Medway Housing Society Ltd — 42.1
Ch D 1996: 69 TC 319; [1997] STC 90.

Cook, Odhams Press Ltd *v* — 66.21
HL 1940: 23 TC 233; [1940] 3 All ER 15.

Cooke *v* Beach Stations Caravans Ltd — 10.25
Ch D 1974 49 TC 514; [1974] STC 402; [1974] 1 WLR 1398; [1974] 3 All ER 159.

D

Fitton *v* Gilders & Heaton 10.2
Ch D 1955: 36 TC 233.
Fitzleet Estates Ltd *v* Cherry 6.22, 55.6
HL 1977: 51 TC 708; [1977] STC 397; [1977] 1 WLR 1345; [1977] 3 All ER 996.
Fitzwilliam (Countess) *v* CIR 5.1
HL 1993: [1993] STC 502; [1993] 1 WLR 1189; [1993] 3 All ER 184.
Fleming *v* Bellow Machine Co Ltd 18.4, 66.27
Ch D 1965: 42 TC 308; [1965] 1 WLR 873; [1965] 2 All ER 513.
Fletcher, Yuill *v* 5.14
CA 1984: 58 TC 145; [1984] STC 401.
Fletcher & Fletcher *v* Harvey 6.10
CA 1990: 63 TC 539; [1990] STC 711.
Flood, Mistletoe Ltd *v* 8.2
Sp C 2003: [2003] SSCD 66.
Flood (Wm) & Sons Ltd, Copeman *v* 66.43
KB 1940: 24 TC 53; [1941] 1 KB 202.
Floor *v* Davis 19.6
HL 1979: 52 TC 609; [1979] STC 379; [1979] 2 WLR 830; [1979] 2 All ER 677.
Forbes, Scottish Investment Trust Co *v* 66.16
CES 1893: 3 TC 231.
Forest Side Properties (Chingford) Ltd *v* Pearce 6.10
CA 1961: 39 TC 665; [1961] TR 143.
Fortes Autogrill Ltd, Hampton *v* 10.25
Ch D 1979: 53 TC 691; [1980] STC 80.
Forth Conservancy Board, CIR *v*, (No 1) 64.6
HL 1928: 14 TC 709; [1929] AC 213.
Forth Conservancy Board, CIR *v*, (No 2) 64.6
HL 1931: 16 TC 103; [1931] AC 540.
Forth Investments Ltd *v* CIR 6.10
Ch D 1976: 50 TC 617; [1976] STC 399; [1976] TR 161.
Foulsham, Pickles *v* 7.1
HL 1925: 9 TC 261; [1925] AC 458; [1925] All E R 706; 4 ATC 133.
Fox, Land Management Ltd *v* 63.7
Sp C 2002: [2002] SSCD 152.
Fox *v* Rothwell 6.5
(Sp C 50), [1995] SSCD 336.
Francis, J C Decaux (UK) Ltd v 10.33
SP C 1996: [1996] SSCD 281 (SP C 84).
Franks, Venn *v* 6.8
CA 1958: 38 TC 175.
Freeman, Sommerfelds Ltd *v* 18.3, 66.27
Ch D 1966: 44 TC 43; [1967] 1 WLR 489; [1967] 2 All ER 143.
Freeman Hardy & Willis Ltd, Laycock *v* 66.4
CA 1938: 22 TC 288; [1938] 4 All ER 609.
Frigate Investments Ltd, Wilcock *v* 55.4
Ch D 1981: 55 TC 530; [1982] STC 198.
Frost, Carvill *v* 6.17
Sp C: (Sp C 447), [2005] SSCD 208.
Fry, Salisbury House Estate Ltd *v* 56.4, 66.1
HL 1930: 15 TC 266; [1930] AC 432.
Fulford-Dobson, ex p, R *v* HMIT 33.3
QB 1987: 60 TC 168; [1987] STC 344; [1987] 3 WLR 277.
Furlong, Munby *v* 10.25
CA 1977: 50 TC 491; [1976] 1 WLR 410; [1976] 1 All ER 753.

H

Case	Paragraph
H (R oao) *v* CIR QB 2002: 75 TC 377; [2002] STC 1354.	30.6
H & G Kinemas Ltd *v* Cook KB 1933: 18 TC 116.	66.4
Hafton Properties Ltd *v* McHugh Ch D 1986: 59 TC 420; [1987] STC 16.	8.2, 16.3
Hagans Caravans (Manufacturing) Ltd, McKinney *v* CA(NI) 1997: 69 TC 526; [1997] STC 1023.	10.2, 6.21
Hagart & Burn-Murdoch, CIR *v* HL 1929: 14 TC 433; [1929] AC 286.	66.21
Halefield Securities Ltd *v* Thorpe Ch D 1967: 44 TC 154.	66.16
Halifax plc *v* Davidson Sp C 2000: [2000] SSCD 251 (Sp C 239).	9.6, 66.18
Hall, Fairrie *v* KB 1947: 28 TC 200; [1947] 2 All ER 141.	18.8, 66.26
Hallamshire Industrial Finance Trust Ltd *v* CIR Ch D 1978: 53 TC 631; [1979] STC 237; [1979] 1 WLR 620; [1979] 2 All E R 433.	7.1
Halsey, Marks and Spencer plc *v* Sp C 2003: [2003] SSCD 70.	32.6
Halsey, Marks and Spencer plc *v* CJEC 2003: (Case C-446/03); [2006] STC 237.	32.6, 32.16
Halsey, Marks and Spencer plc *v* Ch D 2006: [2006] STC 1235; [2006] EWHC 811.	32.6
Hammond (Insp of Taxes), Preston Meats Ltd *v* Sp C 2004: [2005] SSCD 90.	57.4
Hampton *v* Fortes Autogrill Ltd Ch D 1979: 53 TC 691; [1980] STC 80.	10.25
Hancock *v* General Reversionary & Investment Co Ltd KB 1918: 7 TC 358; [1919] 1 KB 25.	66.41
Harris, Californian Copper Syndicate Ltd *v* Ex (S) 1904: 5 TC 159.	66.15
Harris (John M) (Design Partnership) Ltd *v* Lee Sp C 1997: [1997] SSCD 240.	63.7
Harrods (Buenos Aires) Ltd *v* Taylor-Gooby CA 1964: 41 TC 450.	66.18, 66.78
Hart, Pepper *v* HL 1992: 65 TC 421; [1992] STC 898; [1992] 3 WLR 1032; [1993] 1 All E R 42.	6.22
Hart, Watts *v* Ch D 1981: 58 TC 209; [1982] STC 99.	66.4
Harton Coal Co Ltd, CIR *v* Ch D 1960: 39 TC 174; [1960] Ch 563; [1960] 3 All ER 48.	16.2
Harvey, Fletcher & Fletcher *v* CA 1990: 63 TC 539; [1990] STC 711.	6.10
Hatton *v* CIR Ch D 1992: [1992] STC 140.	5.1
Hawes *v* Gardiner Ch D 1957: 37 TC 671.	66.10
Haywards Heath Housing Society Ltd *v* Hewison Ch D 1966: 43 TC 341.	36.4
Heather *v* P-E Consulting Group Ltd CA 1972: 48 TC 293; [1973] 1 All ER 8.	66.5, 66.43

Ramsay (WT) Ltd *v* CIR 5.1, 5.20
HL 1981; 54 TC 101; [1981] STC 174; [1981] 2 WLR 449; [1981] 1 All ER 865.
Rank Xerox Ltd *v* Lane 6.19
HL 1979: 53 TC 185; [1979] STC 740; [1981] AC 269; [1979] 3 WLR 594; [1979] 3 All E R 657.
Ransom *v* Higgs 66.8
HL 1974: 50 TC 1; [1974] STC 539; [1974] 1 WLR 1594; [1974] 3 All ER 949.
Rawling, Eilbeck *v* 5.1
HL 1981: 54 TC 101; [1981] STC 174; [1981] 2 WLR 449; [1981] 1 All ER 865.
Re an Application by HMRC to Serve section 20 Notice 30.4
Sp C 2006: (Sp C 517) [2006 SSCD 71.
Redden, Owton Fens Properties Ltd *v* 6.1
Ch D 1984: 58 TC 218; [1984] STC 618.
Reed *v* Nova Securities Ltd 12.4
HL 1985: 59 TC 516; [1985] STC 124; [1985] 1 WLR 193; [1985] 1 All ER 686.
Regent Oil Co Ltd, Strick *v* 66.18, 66.80
HL 1965: 43 TC 1; [1966] AC 295; [1965] 3 All ER 174.
Reid's Brewery Co Ltd *v* Male 66.21, 66.22
QB 1891: 3 TC 279; [1891] 2 QB 1.
Revenue Adjudicator's Office, R *v* (ex p. Drummond) 33.7
QB 1996: 70 TC 235; [1996] STC 1312.
Rewe Zentralfinanz eG *v* Finanzamt Köln-Mitte 13.17A
CJEC Case C-347/04; 29 March 2007 unreported
Reynolds & Broomhead, Thomas *v* 10.25
Ch D 1987: 59 TC 502; [1987] TC 135.
Reynolds (John) (Insurances) Ltd, Simpson *v* 18.5, 66.27
CA 1975: 49 TC 693; [1975] STC 271; [1975] 1 WLR 617; [1975] 2 All ER 88.
Richards, Gurney *v* 10.27
Ch D 1989: 62 TC 287; [1989] STC 682; [1989] 1 WLR 1180.
Richardson, Brown *v* 56.5
Sp C 1997: [1997] SSCD 233 (Sp C 129).
Richardson, Valleybright Ltd (in voluntary liquidation) *v* 6.21
Ch D 1984: 58 TC 290; [1985] STC 70.
Richardson & Bottoms Ltd, Slater *v* 6.10
Ch D 1979: 53 TC 155; [1979] STC 630; [1980] 1 WLR 563; [1979] 3 All E R 439.
Ridgway, BSC Footwear Ltd *v* 66.75
HL 1971: 47 TC 495; [1972] AC 544; [1971] 2 All ER 534.
Road, Bush, Beach & Gent Ltd *v* 18.3, 66.27
KB 1939: 22 TC 519; [1939] 1 KB 524; [1939] 3 All ER 302.
Roberts *v* Granada TV Rental Ltd 10.27
Ch D 1970: 46 TC 295; [1970] 1 WLR 889; [1970] 2 All ER 764.
Roberts *v* Belhaven's (Lord) Exors 56.2
CS 1925: 9 TC 501.
Robertson *v* CIR 66.5, 66.60
Sp C 1997: [1997] SSCD 282 (Sp C 137).
Robertson *v* CIR (No 2) 6.17
Sp C: (Sp C 313) [2002] SSCD 242.
Robinson *v* Scott Bader & Co Ltd 66.18, 66.43
CA 1981: 54 TC 757; [1981] STC 436; [1981] 1 WLR 1135; [1981] 2 All ER 1116.
Robinson (J) & Sons, Chibbett *v* 18.5, 66.27
KB 1924: 9 TC 48.
Robinson (J) & Sons *v* CIR 18.3
KB 1929: 12 TC 1241.

S

U

W

73 Table of Statutes

74 Statutory Instruments

1946 No 36 Bretton Woods Agreement Order in Council SR&O 1946 27.6
1955 No 1954 International Finance Corporation Order 1955 27.6
1960 No 1383 International Development Association Order 1960 27.6
1970 No 488 DTR (Taxes on Income) (General) Regulations 1970 24.13; 55.4
1971 No 1035 Mineral Royalties (Tax) Regulations 1971 55.15
1974 No 1261 United Nations and International Court of Justice (Immunities and Privileges) Order 1974 27.6
1985 No 1773 European Communities (Immunities and Privileges of the North Atlantic Salmon Conservation Organisation) Order 1985 27.6
1987 No 352 Pension Scheme Surpluses (Administration) Regulations 1987 27.14
1988 No 266 Capital Gains Tax (Definition of Unit Trust Scheme) Regulations 1988 43.3
No 267 Income Tax (Definition of Unit Trust Scheme) Regulations 1988 10.19; 14.8; 43.3
No 1153 Building Societies (Transfer of Business) Regulations 1988 9.6
1989 No 473 Finance Act 1988 (Commencement) Order 1989 33.2
No 1297 The Taxes (Interest Rate) Regulations 1989 40.5; 41.5
No 1339 Limitation (Northern Ireland) Order 1989 15.10; 32.3
1990 No 1671 Movements of Capital (Required Information) Regulations 1990 5.10
No 2231 Income Tax (Building Societies) (Dividends and Interest) Regulations 1990 9.1; 9.4; 61.24
No 2232 Income Tax (Deposit-takers) (Interest Payments) Regulations 1990 8.9
1991 No 512 Income Tax (Building Societies) (Annual Payments) Regulations 1991 9.3
No 702 Building Societies (Designated Capital Resources) (Permanent Interest Bearing Shares) Order 1991 9.7
No 1694 International Organisations (Miscellaneous Exemptions) Order 1991 27.6
No 2874 The Disability Living Allowance and Disability Working Allowance (Northern Ireland Consequential Amendments) Order 1991 10.27; 10.30; 10.35
1992 No 10 Income Tax (Building Societies) (Audit Powers) Regulations 1992 9.4
No 12 Income Tax (Deposit-takers) (Audit Powers) Regulations 1992 8.9
No 13 Income Tax (Deposit-takers) (Interest Payments) (Amendment) Regulations 1992 8.9
No 14 Income Tax (Deposit-takers) (Non-residents) Regulations 1992 8.9
No 15 Income Tax (Interest Payments) (Information Powers) Regulations 1992 8.9
No 42 Taxes (Relief for Gifts) (Designated Educational Establishments) Regulations 1992 66.56
No 571 Income Tax (Definition of Unit Trust Scheme) (Amendment) Regulations 1992 10.19; 43.3
No 3133 Income Tax (Definition of Unit Trust Scheme) (Amendment No 2) Regulations 1992 43.3
No 3218 Banking Coordination (Second Council Directive) Regulations 1992 8.1
No 3234 Income Tax (Prescribed Deposit-takers) Order 1992 8.9
1993 No 561 Taxes (Relief for Gifts) (Designated Educational Establishments) (Amendment) Regulations 1993 66.56
No 743 Income Tax (Sub-Contractors in the Construction Industry) Regulations 1993 6.10; 20; 65.8
No 744 Income Tax (Employments) Regulations 1993 33.10; 54.9; 65.28
No 1957 Double Taxation Relief (Taxes on Income) (General) (Manufactured Overseas Dividends) Regulations 1993 5.9
No 2004 Income Tax (Manufactured Overseas Dividends) Regulations 1993 5.9
1994 No 687 VAT (Sport, Physical Education and Fund-Raising Events) Order 1994 70.8
No 1479 Income Tax (Definition of Unit Trust Scheme) (Amendment) Regulations 1994 14.8; 43.3
No 1811 Special Commissioners (Jurisdiction and Procedure) Regulations 1994 6.7; 6.15–6.17; 6.23

2001 No 56 Income Tax (Electronic Communications) (Incentive Payments) Regulations 2001 33.10; 61.28
No 204 The Taxes (Interest Rate) (Amendment No. 1) Regulations 2001 41.5
No 391 Investment Trusts (Approval of Accounting Methods for Creditor Relationships) Order 2001 46.43
No 404 Income Tax (Building Societies) (Dividends and Interest) (Amendment) Regulations 2001 9.4; 61.24
No 405 Income Tax (Interest Payments) (Information Powers) (Amendment) Regulations 2001 61.24
No 406 Income Tax (Deposit-takers) (Interest Payments) (Amendment) Regulations 2001 8.9
No 544 Financial Services and Markets Act 2001 (Regulated Activities) Order 2001 28.3; 31.4; 39.28
No 810 The Capital Allowances (Corresponding Northern Ireland Grants) Order 2001 10.2
No 916 The Access to Justice Act 1999 (Commencement No. 7, Transitional Provisions and Savings) Order 2001 6.13; 33.2
No 1156 Double Taxation Relief (Taxes on Income) (Underlying Tax on Dividends and Dual Resident Companies) Regulations 2001 24.11
No 1163 Double Taxation Relief (Surrender of Relievable Tax Within a Group) Regulations 2001 24.11
No 1531 Income Tax (Sub-contractors in the Construction Industry) (Amendment) Regulations 2001 20.14
No 2541 The Capital Allowances (Energy-saving Plant and Machinery) Order 2001 10.27; 10.33
No 3629 Financial Services and Markets Act 2000 (Consequential Amendments) (Taxes) Order 2001 8.1; 8.9; 26.15; 28.45; 31.4; 31.6–31.8; 42.4; 43.1; 43.2; 50.4; 56.14
No 3873 Double Taxation Relief (Surrender of Relievable Tax Within a Group) (Amendment)
Regulations 2001 24.11
No 3975 Friendly Societies (Modification of the Corporation Tax Acts) (Amendment) Regulations 2001 31.7
No 4024 Referrals to the Special Commissioners Regulations 2001 61.13

2002 No 653 Scottish Water (Transfer of Functions, etc.) (Tax Provisions) Order 2002 11.24; 47.12
No 680 Income Tax (Employments and Electronic Communication) (Miscellaneous Provisions) Regulations 2002 33.10
No 1409 Financial Services and Markets Act 2000 (Consequential Amendments) (Taxes) Order 2002 8.1; 31.7
No 1818 The Capital Allowances (Energy-saving Plant and Machinery) (Amendment) Order 2002 10.27
No 1966 Relief for Community Amateur Sports Clubs (Designation) Order 2002 70.8
No 1967 Corporation Tax (Finance Leasing of Intangible Assets) Regulations 2002 39.35
No 1968 Income Tax (Prescribed Deposit-takers) Order 2002 8.9
No 1969 Exchange Gains and Losses (Transitional Provisions and Savings) Regulations 2002 26.5; 26.32; 28.9; 46.6; 46.47
No 1970 Exchange Gains and Losses (Bringing into Account Gains or Losses) Regulations 2002 26.32; 28.9; 46.6; 46.47
No 1973 Open-ended Investment Companies (Tax) (Amendment) Regulations 2002 43.1; 43.2
No 2225 Income Tax (Sub-contractors in the Construction Industry) (Amendment) Regulations 2002 20.13; 20.17
No 2406 Controlled Foreign Companies (Excluded Countries) (Amendment No 2) Regulations 2002 21.12
No 2661 Venture Capital Trust (Exchange of Shares and Securities) Regulations 2002 69.2; 69.3; 69.4
No 2931 ICTA 1988, s 349B(3) Order 2002 37.3
No 2976 The General Commissioners and Special Commissioners (Jurisdiction and Procedure) (Amendment)Regulations 2002 6.10; 6.17

2003 No 23 Friendly Societies (Modification of the Corporation Tax Acts) (Amendment) Regulations 2003 31.7
No 88 FA 2002, s 57(3), (4)(a) (Appointed Day) Order 2003 17.1
No 96 Community Investment Tax Relief (Accreditation of Community Development Finance Institutions) Regulations 2003 17.1
No 120 The Proceeds of Crime Act 2002 (Commencement No 4, Transitional Provisions and Savings) Order 2003 33.13
No 282 Income and Corporation Taxes (Electronic Communications) Regulations 2003 33.10
No 536 Income Tax (Sub-contractors in the Construction Industry and Employments) (Amendment) Regulations 2003 20.17
No 1116 Companies (Acquisition of Own Shares) (Treasury Shares) Regulations 2003 57.1
No 1472 The Finance Act 2002, Schedule 13 (Appointed Day) Order 2003 59.1; 59.18
No 1744 The Capital Allowances (Energy-saving Plant and Machinery) (Amendment) Order 2003 10.27
No 1829 The Double Taxation Relief (Surrender of Relievable Tax Within a Group) (Amendment) Regulations 2003 24.11
No 1830 The Income Tax (Authorised Unit Trusts) (Interest Distributions) Regulations 2003 43.8
No 1831 The Open-ended Investment Companies (Tax) (Amendment) Regulations 2003 43.1; 43.2; 43.8
No 1861 The Corporation Tax (Treatment of Unrelieved Surplus Advance Corporation Tax) (Amendment) Regulations 2003 3.9
No 2076 The Capital Allowances (Environmentally Beneficial Plant and Machinery) Order 2003 10.27
No 2093 The Enterprise Act 2002 (Commencement No. 4 and Transitional Provisions and Savings) Order 2003 6.10; 45.5
No 2494 The Income Tax (Employments) (Amendment) Regulations 2003 33.10; 65.28
No 2495 The Income Tax (Incentive Payments for Voluntary Electronic Communication of PAYE Returns) Regulations 2003 33.10; 61.28
No 2497 The Finance Act 2003, Section 168 (Appointed Day) Order 2003 59.2
No 2582 The Income Tax (Manufactured Overseas Dividends) (Amendment) Regulations 2003 5.9
No 2714 The Non-resident Insurance Companies Regulations 2003 60.5
No 3077 The Finance Act 2003, Section 195 and Schedule 40 (Appointed Day) Order 2003 57.1
No 3297 The Reporting of Savings Income Information Regulations 2003 61.25

2004 No 16 The Companies Act 1985 (Accounts of Small and Medium-Sized Enterprises and Audit Exemption) (Amendment) Regulations 2004 10.27
No 439 The Urban Regeneration Companies (Tax) (Designation) Order 2004 66.76
No 674 The Recovery of Duties and Taxes Etc. Due in Other Member States (Corresponding UK Claims, Procedure and Supplementary) Regulations 2004 33.12
No 712 The Research and Development (Prescribed Activities) Regulations 2004 59.1
No 1274 The Double Taxation Relief (Taxes on Income) (New Zealand) Order 2004 24.14
No 1863 Tax Avoidance Schemes (Prescribed Description of Arrangements) Regulations 2004 5.26
No 1864 Tax Avoidance Schemes (Information) Regulations 2004 5.26
No 1865 Tax Avoidance Schemes (Promoters and Prescribed Circumstances) Regulations 2004 5.26
No 2093 The Capital Allowances (Energy-saving Plant and Machinery) (Amendment) Order 2004 10.27
No 2094 The Capital Allowances (Environmentally Beneficial Plant and Machinery) (Amendment) Order 2004 10.27
No 2199 The Venture Capital Trust (Winding up and Mergers) (Tax) Regulations 2004 69.2; 69.4
No 2201 The Finance Act 2002, Schedule 26, Parts 2 and 9 (Amendment) Order 2004 28.2; 28.4–28.8; 28.26; 28.27

No 2865 Real Estate Investment Trusts (Financial Statements of Group Real Estate Investment Trusts) Regulations 2006 44.22
No 2866 Real Estate Investment Trusts (Joint Ventures) Regulations 2006 44.36
No 2867 Real Estate Investment Trusts (Assessments and Recovery of Tax) Regulations 2006 44.35
No 3239 Authorised Investment Funds (Tax) (Amendment) Regulations 2006 28.24; 43.1
No 3265 The Finance Act 2006, Section 53(2) (Films and Sound Recordings: Power to Alter Dates) Order 2006 66.51
No 3269 The Finance Act 2002, Schedule 26, (Parts 2 and 9) (Amendment) Order 2006 28.2; 28.3; 28.26; 28.27
No 3281 Films (Certification) Regulations 2006 66.52
No 3291 The Capital Gains Tax (Definition of Permanent Interest Bearing Share) Regulations 2006 9.7
No 3296 The Taxation of Securitisation Companies Regulations 2006 28.51
No 3399 The Finance Act 2006 Section 53(1) (Films and Sound Recordings)(Appointed Day) Order 2006 66.51

2007 No 46 The Finance Act 2004 (Section 61(2), (Relevant Percentage) Order 2007 20.3
No 303 The Capital Allowances (Leases of Background Plant or Machinery for a Building) Order 2007 10.34
No 304 The Long Funding Leases (Elections) Regulations 2007 10.34
No 672 The Income Tax (Construction Industry Scheme) (Amendment) Regulations 2007 20.9
No 678 The Corporation Tax (Surrender of Terminal Losses on Films and Claims for Relief) Regulations 2007 66.52
No 683 The Authorised Investment Funds (Tax) (Amendment) Regulations 2007 28.24; 43.1
No 831 Income Tax: The Energy-Saving Items Regulations 2007 56.3
No 945 The Business Premises Renovation Allowances Regulations 2007 10.5
No 948 The Loan Relationships and Derivative Contracts (Disregard and Bringing into Account of Profits and Losses) (Amendment) Regulations 2007 28.9
No 949 The Finance Act 2005, Section 92 and Schedule 6, (Appointed Day) Order 2007 10.5
No 950 The Loan Relationships and Derivative Contracts (Change of Accounting Practice) (Amendment) Regulations 2007 28.9; 46.7
No 964 Finance Act 2003 Paragraph 3(3) of Schedule 26, (Designated Transactions) Regulations 2007 60.5
No 1050 The Corporation Tax (Taxation of Films) (Transitional Provisions) Regulations 2007 66.52

75 Index

This index is referenced to the chapter and paragraph number. The entries printed in bold capitals are main subject headings in the text. For the meaning of words and phrases, see under Definitions.

75 Index

75 Index

75 Index

75 Index

75 Index

H

P

Q

R

W